Merriam-Webster's
ENCYCLOPEDIA
of WORLD
RELIGIONS

Merriam-Webster's
ENCYCLOPEDIA
of WORLD
RELIGIONS

Wendy Doniger, Consulting Editor

Merriam-Webster, Incorporated
Springfield, Massachusetts

A GENUINE MERRIAM-WEBSTER

The name *Webster* alone is no guarantee of excellence. It is used by a number of publishers and may serve mainly to mislead an unwary buyer.

Merriam-Webster™ is the name you should look for when you consider the purchase of dictionaries or other fine reference books. It carries the reputation of a company that has been publishing since 1831 and is your assurance of quality and authority.

Library of Congress Cataloging-in-Publication Data

Merriam-Webster's encyclopedia of world religions.
     p.   cm.
    Includes bibliographical references.
    ISBN 0-87779-044-2
    1. Religion Encyclopedias. I. Merriam-Webster, Inc. II. Title: Encyclopedia of world religions.
BL31.M47 1999
200´.3—dc21
                                      99-33147
                                          CIP

Made in the United States of America

2345RRD02010099

ADVISORS AND AUTHORS

Consulting Editor
Wendy Doniger
Mircea Eliade Distinguished
Service Professor of the History
of Religions
University of Chicago

Primary Contributors

Buddhism
Frank Reynolds
Professor of the History
of Religions
University of Chicago

**Comparative Religion
and Religious Studies**
Hans H. Penner
Preston H. Kelsey Professor
of Religion
Dartmouth College

Christianity
Jaroslav Pelikan
Sterling Professor of History
(Emeritus)
Yale University

Islam
Juan E. Campo
Professor of Religious Studies
University of California
at Santa Barbara

Judaism
Jacob Neusner
Distinguished Research Professor
of Religious Studies
University of South Florida

Religions of Ancient Peoples
Morten Warmind
Adjunct Professor
Copenhagen University

Religions of East Asia
Norman Girardot
Professor of Religion Studies
Lehigh University

Religions of India
John Stratton Hawley
Professor of Religion
Barnard College
Columbia University

Religions of Indigenous Peoples
Davíd L. Carrasco
Professor of Religion
Princeton University

Additional Contributors

African Religions
Laura Grillo
College of Wooster

Buddhism
Jeff Shirkey
University of Chicago

Christianity
James O'Donnell
("St. Augustine")
University of Pennsylvania

Gnosticism
Karen King
Harvard University

Hinduism
Paul Arney
Columbia University

Jeffery Kripal ("Śāktism")
Westminster College

James Locktefeld
Carthage College

Christian Novetzke
Columbia University

Brian K. Smith
New York University

Rupa Visnawath
Columbia University

Susan Wadley
("Ḍholā")
Syracuse University

Islam
Kevin Reinhart
("Ṭahāra")
Dartmouth College

Jainism
John Cort
Denison University

Martha Ann Selby
Southern Methodist University

Judaism
Alan J. Avery-Peck
College of the Holy Cross

Philip R. Davies
("Dead Sea Scrolls")
University of Sheffield

Ithamar Gruenwald
("Qabbalah and Jewish
Mysticism")
Tel Aviv University

Steven Katz
("The Holocaust")
Boston University

Sara Mandell
University of South Florida

Steve Mason
("Flavius Josephus")
York University

Jacob Staub
Reconstructionist
Rabbinical College

James R. Strange
University of South Florida

Millennialism
Richard Landes
Boston University

Native American Religions
Christopher Jocks
Dartmouth College

Lawrence E. Sullivan
Harvard University

New Religious Movements
Murray Rubinstein
Baruch College

Brian K. Smith
New York University

Sikhism
Gurinder Singh-Mann
Columbia University

CONTENTS

Major Articles ▶

16 African Religions

48 Anatolian Religions

250 Confucianism

316 Egyptian Religion

370 Germanic Religion

584 Judaism

714 Mesopotamian Religions

726 Millennialism

868 Pre-Columbian Meso-
American Religions

876 Pre-Columbian South
American Religions

920 Religious Experience

reating a one-volume encyclopedia of the world's religions is an exercise in self-restraint. Religion is a vast and only vaguely defined topic, one which can easily expand to encompass the entire range of a culture's self-expressions: customs, institutions, art, and literature. Add to that assignment the necessity that one cover as many religions as possible, past and present, and one is quickly confronted with a daunting challenge: how most meaningfully to address the subject in the space of a single volume and 3,500 articles?

While it may not be possible to cover the subject exhaustively between two covers, we have brought a million words to bear on the problem. Our task has been to provide an overview of the subject, to provide significant detail concerning important figures, movements, historical periods, and religious themes. By binding these themes together with an intricate system of cross-references, we seek to convey an appreciation of how these themes are interconnected across distances equally temporal, geographical, and cultural. We also include a rich set of maps and illustrations, including 32 color plates, to document and celebrate the nontextual dimensions of religious experience. And finally, by means of a carefully researched and updated scholarly bibliography, we hope to equip the reader to set off on a fruitful course of further discovery. Our aim was to tell the story of the world's religions in such a way as to tempt the reader beyond the present volume; for religion is not contained within a book, but lies out in the world, and it is there that it will most fully be known.

We feel that we have produced a work that is useful, accessible to a wide range of readers, and unique in many of its strengths. The broad scope of *Encyclopædia Britannica* has here been melded with the lexical resources of Merriam-Webster to produce a work that is notable both for the rigor of its scholarship and the exacting detail of its pronunciations and etymologies.

The efforts of a large number of people at both organizations were critical to the success of this effort. The *Encyclopedia of World Religions* was initially planned by John Morse, Mark Stevens, and Michael Shally-Jensen at Merriam-Webster, with advice from Robert McHenry of Encyclopædia Britannica. Mark Stevens coordinated the project at Merriam-Webster, while Anita Wolff directly administered the project at Britannica. Christine Sullivan contributed significantly to all phases of the publishing process and played a leading role in the editing and management of the encyclopedia.

Pronunciations were provided by Sharon Goldstein, with help from James Rader and Brian Sietsema; assistance in specific languages was rendered by William Baker, Tej Bhatia, Wallace Chafe, Tommy Choe, Sándor Csúcs, Gyula Decsy, Joanne Despres, Wendy Doniger, Thomas Dousa, Dewi Evans, Francesca Forrest, Erika Gilson, Norman Girardot, Charles Hallisey, Jeffrey Harlig, John Hartmann, Kenneth Hill, Michael Hillmann, Nicholas Hopkins, Kathryn Josserand, David Justice, Satish and Sudhir Kamatkar, Dennis King, Daniel Long, Samuel Martin, Gregory McMahon, Jacob Neusner, Pekka Sammallahti, Mark Southern, George Thompson, Shantha Uddin, James Weiner, and May Kyi Win. The review and composition of etymological text was performed by James Rader. Kara Noble, Maria Sansalone, and Donna Rickerby oversaw electronic implementation and trafficking of documents at Merriam-Webster. Encyclopædia Britannica staff members who were important to the success of the project include Dale Hoiberg, Xia Zhihou, Stephen Ostrander, and Elizabeth Dunn in Editorial; John Judge, Steven Kapusta, Jon Hensley, and John Draves in the Art Department; Mimi Srodon and Marilyn Barton in Production Control; Sylvia Wallace, Dennis Skord, Pat Bauer, Letricia A. Dixon, Beth Edwards, Andrea R. Field, Jordan Finkin, Amy Huberman, Glenn Jenne, Sandra Langeneckert, Wendy O'Donnell, and Locke Peterseim in the Copy Department; Mary Voss, Vincent Star, Steven Bosco, Bruce Walters, and Ray Goldberger of the Publishing Technology Group; Melvin Stagner, Carol Gaines, and Danette Wetterer in Composition; and John Nelson, David Wiggins, Jason Kowalczyk, and Amelia Gintautas in Cartography. Anne-Marie Bogdan compiled the bibliography. Photo research was done by Laurie Platt Winfrey, Van Bucher, Christopher Deegan, and Robin Sand at Carousel Research, Inc.

MARK DILLER, EDITOR

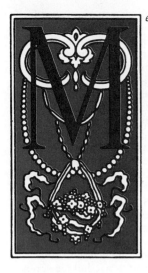

erriam-Webster's Encyclopedia of World Religions seeks to respond in a systematic way to the growing importance of religion in the contemporary world. We enter the new millennium in the middle of a conversation that has been building to a crisis throughout the 20th century, between people who live religion and people who study it, sometimes to justify it but more often to challenge it. Religious faith is an explicitly contested issue in politics—locally (prayers in school), nationally (the influence of Christian values upon legislative and judicial policy), and internationally (the Serbian-Kosovar conflict being one among many)—but many participants in these encounters are genuinely trying to understand one another's positions. This book is intended both for people who believe in religion and for people who do not, in the hopes of establishing a sound body of knowledge about religion to be used in formulating a common ground for both of them to stand on in their ongoing conversation. Just as the *Guinness Book of Records* was invented (as the name Guinness suggests) to supply bartenders with data with which to head off heated arguments before they came to blows and the destruction of pub property, perhaps a good encyclopedia of religion could forestall brawls about religion on a far, far more devastating global scale.

Religion has always been a matter of life and death, not only in terms of its own functions (baptism and burial) but as a rallying point for deciding the life, more often the death, of large groups of people labeled infidels. Generally speaking, however, in the past it was deemed sufficient just to know one's own religion in order to go to war to defend it against the infidels; now we have begun to understand that we need a broader—dare we say encyclopedic?—understanding of other peoples' religions if we want *not* to go to war, and not to be the infidels ourselves.

The growing prominence of newspaper and television coverage of religious factors embedded in world-shaking events taking place both at home and abroad has unfortunately not been matched by an equally deepening, or even broadening, understanding of those issues. The pressures on politicians and journalists to make judgments about religion quickly, often on the basis of ludicrously inadequate knowledge, has eroded rather than nurtured the public availability of reliable information. This is precisely the moment to assemble a body of knowledge that is as objective and authoritative as possible, and the critical need for such knowledge explains why so many encyclopedias of religion have appeared in recent years. We need to know, for instance, not only how many Muslims there are in the world (in the United States they are more numerous than Episcopalians), but how many different ways there are to be a Muslim, and what the different groups among them believe and do.

It might be argued, however, that religion is not a fitting subject for an encyclopedia, that religion—so formless, so subjective, such a moving target—cannot be pinned down within a genre that promises organized, comprehensive factual data. The very phrase "from A to Z," or, to use the religious phrase, "alpha to omega," promises a totality that we cannot deliver. The present volume answers that challenge with the extreme test case, as Americans have long regarded Merriam-Webster's reference library and the *Encyclopædia Britannica* as the two ultimate sources of dispassionate, objective, authoritative knowledge, and many will transfer to this volume the same expectations. (Consider a parallel authority that existed in the Middle Ages, when disputes were often settled by resorting to what was called the *Sortes Virgilianes*, or "Virgil's Lottery," a kind of premodern Ouija board. Faced with an important decision, one would close one's eyes, open a volume of Virgil at random, and place one's finger upon the page, to a line which was then read out to give the advice that was sought.) For many Americans, Merriam-Webster's functions as the *Oxford English Dictionary* functions in England, not merely to describe, to document what was, what words meant, but to proscribe and to dictate what should be, what words ought to be. Periodic reports about the inclusion of *ain't* in the dictionary bring to wide public attention the tension between the descriptive and proscriptive, without resolving it; yet people still insist that if a word is in *Webster's*, it exists, and if it isn't, it doesn't. As for the *Britannica*, I grew up in a home where the dinner table was often hastily cleared, in mid-course, to make way for a volume of the *Britannica* thrown down, sometimes with considerable force, and opened to a passage which was then read forth to silence an opponent: "There, you see? I told you so."

Webster and the *Britannica* came to represent the apotheosis of the approach to knowledge made famous by Jack Webb(ster?) on the old television series *Dragnet*: "Just the facts, ma'am, nothing but the facts." But it behooves us to make a distinction between facts, objectivity, and authority. The scales have fallen from our postmodern eyes and we have become aware of our epistemological nakedness, as we have been told that there is no such thing as objective knowledge, no such thing as "just" a fact. But even the philosopher-historian R.G. Collingwood, a champion of this view, admitted that, though you can indeed tell the story of Caesar's assassination in various ways, there are ways in which you can't tell it: you can't say that Caesar killed Brutus. In dismissing the argument that, as complete objectivity is impossible in these matters, one might as well let one's sentiments run loose, the economist Robert Solow likened it to saying that, as a perfectly aseptic environment is impossible, one might as well conduct surgery in a sewer. Within this sort of commonsense limit, there are facts, and an encyclopedia tries to gather them and to check them; the better the encyclopedia, the more likely the facts are to accord with other conventions of evidence.

But the selectivity of that gathering and of those conventions is what is at stake in the game of objectivity, for a different sort of objectivity is needed for science and for religion. Scholars of religion have often opposed the truth claims of people who believe in religion, only to fall into the arms of superrationalists who oppose the sympathetic study of religion and would allow it to be studied only within the sterile confines of an objectivity that is in any case impossible and is probably not even desirable. Such attempts to play the game of objectivity with the Big Boys on the playing fields of the harder sciences often tend to play down the more subtle but equally genuine sort of objectivity that both scholars of religion and religious believers can bring to their conversations, a critical judgment that makes them aware of their own faith claims. This is the spirit in which the present volume has been prepared.

For we cannot simply rely upon even good encyclopedias from the recent past. Time erodes old subjectivities and creates new criteria of objectivity. Every attempt to include religion within an encyclopedia, from Diderot to the *Britannica*, was inevitably tarred with the prejudices and skewed by the polluted agendas of the age in which it was written; it is this shift in perspective, even more than the accumulation of new "factual" knowledge, that has necessitated constant updating. As our knowledge and attitudes change in time, we look back on each previous attempt as "subjective" and strive to do better; we never reach the ever-receding horizon of objectivity, but we get closer with each new attempt.

In an age of postmodernism, we need Jack Webb(ster) more than ever. Precisely because we have come to understand the limits of objectivity even in science, let alone in religion, the present volume's dogged and often successful attempts to provide authoritative, if not objective, knowledge is particularly valuable. Neither facts nor objectivity, but authoritative writing is what an encyclopedia strives for, and to be not merely a fact-checking service but a learned and responsible guide over the shifting sands of factual evidence. The scholars whom we have assembled in this volume are leaders in their fields, whose opinions have the status of something like facts, who know enough about what they are writing about to select what is most likely to be true and most likely to be important, and who are challenged by the prestige of the Merriam-Webster/Britannica reputation for solid knowledge and the hope of applying those standards to the ever-elusive field of religion. We have tried to extricate ourselves from the massive force-field of Western, Christian ways of viewing the world and to include classes of people other than white, male elites. We have tried to be inclusive of various approaches as well as a broad variety of topics, to codify information in a way that makes it accessible to various interpretations, and to acknowledge the subjectivity of the selection of the facts that we have included even while making every effort to ascertain that they are, in fact, facts.

WENDY DONIGER, CONSULTING EDITOR

EXPLANATORY NOTES

his book contains entries for historical and legendary figures, religious movements, divinities and supernatural characters, ritual implements, place-names, theological concepts, and other ideas connected in some way with religion. For the most part the presentation of information in these entries requires little explanation, but the following notes will assist the reader.

Entry names

In most cases, vernacular usage has governed spelling. For languages not written in the Roman alphabet, the following conventions have been adopted:

Russian and other nonromanized languages have been transcribed using the systems followed in the *Encyclopædia Britannica*. The languages of modern and classical India are transcribed in accordance with accepted scholarly usage, though some terms that are widely used in English-speaking countries (such as SHIVA and KRISHNA) follow the conventional spelling.

Chinese names are romanized under the Wade-Giles system, with the alternate Pinyin romanization also given. In Japanese and Korean names, with few exceptions, the distinction between family and personal names is observed. (In those languages normal name order places the family name first; hence in this work no comma usually appears between family and personal name as it does in an inverted English name—as, for example, Yamazaki Ansai. Entries on individuals from modern times, however, may appear with the family name followed by a comma—*i.e.*, MOON, SUN MYUNG.)

Alphabetization

Alphabetization is letter-by-letter, not word-by-word. Thus ACTA SANCTORA falls between ACTAEON and ACTS OF THE APOSTLES. The order of entries is determined by ordinary rules of alphabetization applied to the entry names and by the following additional rules:

Diacritical marks, marks of punctuation, hyphenation, and spaces within titles are ignored, as are Roman numerals.

Names beginning with M', Mac, or Mc are alphabetized according to their spelling.

Cross-references

Cross-references are indicated by SMALL CAPITALS. Cross-references have been used extensively in an attempt to demonstrate the interconnections between various ideas. Only the first occurrence of a word within a given article will be designated as a cross-reference. In some instances, the cross-reference is not exactly identical with the entry title, but the reference should be apparent to the reader. Personal names are not inverted in these cross-references in running text—MARTIN LUTHER directs the reader to the entry LUTHER, MARTIN.

Dates in text

In general, dates following the titles of works indicate the date of first publication. The date following mention of a foreign-language title is the year in which the book was first published in the original language. For ancient works, the "publication date" is problematic. Dates of composition are given in these cases.

We have chosen to use the abbreviations BCE/CE ("Before the Common Era"/ "Common Era"), rather than the more traditional BC/AD, in recognition of the presuppositions which lie behind the latter terms. The article MILLENNIALISM, by contrast, does occasionally list dates AD, as such a designation is intrinsic to the material that article is discussing.

Translations in text

For non-English-language works, the date of publication is usually followed by a translation in roman type. Italicized titles within parentheses indicate that the work has been published in English. For example, in the MARTIN BUBER entry, an untranslated work is treated in this manner: *Chassidischen Bücher* ("Hasidic Books," 1927). Another work that was translated into English is treated in this manner: *Ich und Du* (1923; *I and Thou*). In this example, 1923 indicates the date of publication of the original German text and *I and Thou* is the title of the English translation. Of course, the English-language version will not always be a literal rendering of the original title.

Etymologies

Etymologies in this book are meant to provide historical and philological background for the study of religion. The book provides etymologies for some common nouns, but for most proper nouns, such as personal or geographical names, etymologies have not been given. Etymologies for the names of gods are given only where the etymology is reasonably certain. Ordinarily, etymologies are enclosed in parentheses and placed after the pronunciation and before the body of the entry. In some entries the origin of the word is discussed in the text, and there a parenthetical etymology will be lacking unless it provides additional data.

Pronunciation

This book provides pronunciation respellings for most entry words. All personal names are given phonetic transcriptions. The only entry words without respellings are familiar words and place-names, such as the first two words in SEVEN AGAINST THEBES, the last word in CH'ENG-CHU SCHOOL, and all the words in KINGS OF ROME. Connectives are replaced by ellipses in transcriptions: HARUT AND MARUT \ha-ˈrüt . . . ma-ˈrüt\. The pronunciation for all words without respellings may be found in *Merriam-Webster's Collegiate Dictionary, Tenth Edition*. Pronunciation respellings are also included for most alternative spellings and other variant forms. Original names and the full patronymic forms of Arabic names are not usually transcribed:

IBN SĪNĀ \ˌi-bən-ˈsē-nä\, *also called* Avicenna \ˌa-və-ˈse-nə\, *Arabic in full* Abū ʿAlī al-Ḥusayn ibn ʿAbd Allāh ibn Sīnā

Foreign-language names are generally respelled to approximate their native pronunciation, unless an anglicized pronunciation is in widespread use. A variant, sometimes preceded by the label *Angl*, is added for names with familiar anglicizations and for names and terms that are likely to be anglicized because of the difficulty they present. Additional notes on pronunciation are found in the following Guide to Pronunciation.

The following paragraphs set out the value of the pronunciation symbols in English and other languages. Symbols which are not letters of the English alphabet are listed first. Sounds discussed are also rendered in symbols from the International Phonetic Alphabet (IPA) where appropriate.

\ \

Pronunciation respellings are printed between reversed virgules. Pronunciation symbols are printed in roman type, and language labels and other descriptors are printed in italics.

\'͵\

A high-set stress mark precedes a syllable with primary (strongest) stress; a low-set mark precedes a syllable with secondary (medium) stress. Stress in English words is manifested especially as a change in intonation; in other languages stress may be realized as a marked jump in pitch (up or down), increased energy, or lengthening of syllables. Some languages, such as French, show few distinctions between stressed and unstressed syllables except in phrases. Chinese and Vietnamese distinguish words by differing pitches of syllables. Japanese words are spoken with intonational contours that are very unlike English stress. These various prosodic features are approximated by renderings in terms of English stress.

\-\

Hyphens are used in respellings to separate syllables. The placement of these hyphens is based on phonetic and orthographic criteria and may not match the phonological syllabication of a given language.

\, ;\

Pronunciation variants are separated by commas; groups of related variants are separated by semicolons.

\ə\

is a neutral vowel found in unstressed syllables in English as in anoint, collide, data (IPA [ə]).

\'ə, ͵ə\

as in cut, conundrum (IPA [ʌ]).

\ə̇\

is a high, unrounded, centralized vowel as in Russian *bylo* 'was (neut.)', Turkish *kız* 'girl', Chinese *shih* 'lion,' and Japanese *netsuke* 'netsuke' (IPA [ɨ, ɪ, ɯ]). This is not a distinctive vowel of English, but it may be heard as a variant of the unstressed vowels \i\ and \ə\, as in the last syllables of *biologist* and *matches*. In anglicized pronunciations \ə̇\ may be replaced in Turkish names by \i\, in Russian names by \i\ or \ē\, and in Chinese names by \ər\ or \ir\; the vowel may be dropped entirely in anglicizations of Japanese names.

\əi\

as in Welsh *lleuad* 'moon' (IPA [əɨ]) or in Welsh *eira* 'snow' (IPA [əi]). Neither of these diphthongs occur in English. The first is produced as a sequence of \ə\ and \ə̇\ and the second as a sequence of \ə\ and \ē\ or \i\. Both sounds may be anglicized as \ā\.

\'ər, ər\

further, merger, bird (IPA [ɜ, ɚ]). In names from India the vowel, which appears in English spelling as *a*, is much the same as the vowel of cut (IPA [ʌ]).

\a\

as in rap, cat, sand, lamb (IPA [æ]). This vowel may be reduced to \ə\ in unstressed syllables.

\ā\

as in way, paid, late, eight. In English pronunciation this symbol stands for a diphthong (IPA [ei, eɪ]). In most other languages this symbol should be understood as a short or long monophthong of the front mid-high vowel (IPA [e, e:]). In anglicized pronunciations the English diphthong may be substituted.

\ä\

as in opt, cod, mach (IPA [ɑ]). The low, back, unrounded vowel of American English is often pronounced with some lip-rounding in British English when the vowel is spelled with the letter o (IPA [ɒ]). This may be reduced to \ə\ in unstressed syllables.

\ȧ\

as in French *chat* 'cat,' *table* 'table' (IPA [a]). This sound is also found in some Eastern dialects of American English, as in the pronunciation of *car* in the speech of some Bostonians; it is also the initial element of the diphthong \ī\ in words like *wide* or *tribe*. The sound \ȧ\ can be characterized as a vowel produced with the tongue in a position midway between that of \a\ and \ä\, or as the vowel \ə\ produced with the jaws somewhat further apart. In Arabic the vowel \ȧ\ may be fronted somewhat to \a\ or even \e\ when it occurs as a short vowel in closed syllables. In anglicized pronunciations \ȧ\ may be replaced by \ä\ or \a\.

\ar\

as in air, care, laird (IPA [ær]). In many American dialects this may also be pronounced as \er\ (IPA [ɛr]).

\au̇\

as in out, loud, tout, cow (IPA [aʊ, au]).

\b\

as in bat, able, rib (IPA [b]). This symbol is also used to transcribe a sound in names from India which appears in English spelling as *bh* and which in the original language is a voiced aspirate (IPA [bʰ]).

\b̲\

as in the "soft" *b* or *v* of Spanish *hablar* 'speak' or *Avila* 'Avila' (IPA [β]). This sound is a voiced bilabial fricative, formed by setting the mouth in the position for \b\ but separating the lips just enough to allow the passage of breath as with \v\. The sound \b̲\ may be anglicized as \v\.

\ch\

as in **ch**air, rea**ch**, ca**tch**er (IPA [tʃ]).

\d\

as in **d**ay, re**d**, la**dd**er (IPA [d]). This symbol is also used to transcribe two other sounds in names from India. One appears in English spelling as *dh* and in the original language is a voiced aspirate (IPA [dʰ]). The other appears in transliteration as *ḍ* and in the original language is a retroflex sound, produced with the tip of the tongue curled back toward the hard palate (IPA [ɖ, ɖ]). (See also the section on \t\ below.)

\e\

as in **e**gg, b**e**d, b**e**t (IPA [ε]). This symbol is also used sometimes to transcribe the short monophthongal front mid-high vowel found in some languages (IPA [e]). This vowel may be reduced to \ə\ or \i\ in unstressed syllables.

\ꞌē, ̩ē\

as in **e**at, r**ee**d, fl**ee**t, p**ea** (IPA [i, i:]). This sound may be diphthongized in some dialects of English, but it is a monophthong in most other languages.

\ē\

as in penn**y**, geni**e** (IPA [i, ɪ]). In some English dialects the unstressed \ē\ is pronounced as a vowel similar to \i\.

\f\

as in **f**ine, cha**ff**, o**ff**ice (IPA [f]).

\g\

as in **g**ate, ra**g**, ea**g**le (IPA [g]). This symbol is also used to transcribe a sound in names from India which appears in English spelling as *gh* and which in the original language is a voiced aspirate (IPA [gʰ]).

\ḡ\

as in Spanish *lago* 'lake' (IPA [ɣ]). This sound is a voiced velar fricative, produced by setting the mouth in the position for \g\ but separating the tongue from the hard palate just enough to allow the passage of breath as with the sound \k̲\. The sound \ḡ\ may be anglicized as \g\.

\h\

as in **h**ot, a**h**oy (IPA [h]). This sound appears only at the beginning of syllables in English; in languages such as Arabic and Persian this sound may also be found at the end of a syllable.

\hl\

as in Welsh *llaw* 'hand' or Icelandic **hl**aup 'slide' (IPA [ɬ]). This sound is a voiceless \l\: it can be approximated by producing \h\ while holding the mouth in the position for \l\. The sound \hl\ may be anglicized as \l\.

\hr\

as in Welsh **rh**ad 'free' or Icelandic **hr**aun 'lava' (IPA [r̥]). This sound is a voiceless consonantal \r\: it can be approximated by producing \h\ while holding the mouth in the position for \r\. The sound \hr\ may be anglicized as \r\.

\hw\

as in **wh**eat, **wh**en (IPA [ʍ]). In some dialects of English this sound is replaced by \w\.

\i\

as in **i**ll, h**i**p, b**i**d (IPA [ɪ]). This vowel may be reduced to \ə\ in unstressed syllables.

\ī\

as in **ai**sle, fr**y**, wh**i**te, w**i**de (IPA [ai, aɪ, ɑi, ɑɪ]).

\ir\

as in **h**ear, infer**ior**, m**irr**or, p**ier**ce (IPA [ɪr]). In some American dialects this may be pronounced as \ēr\ (IPA [ir, i:r]) in many words. The pronunciation \ēr\ also occurs in words and names from India spelled with the combination *īr*.

\j\

as in **j**ump, fu**dg**e, bu**dg**et (IPA [dʒ]).

\k\

as in **k**ick, ba**k**er, **sc**am, as**k** (IPA [k]). This symbol is used also to respell the voiceless uvular stop of Arabic and Persian (IPA [q]), which appears in English spellings as the letter *q*. For the latter sound the tongue is brought in contact with the soft palate rather than the hard palate.

\k̲\

as in lo**ch**, Ba**ch**, German *Bu**ch*** (IPA [x]), and German *i**ch*** 'I' (IPA [ç]). This sound is a voiceless velar or palatal fricative, which is produced by setting the mouth in the position for \k\ but separating the tongue from the hard palate just enough to allow the passage of breath. The symbol \k̲\ is used also to respell the voiceless pharyngeal fricative of Arabic and Persian (IPA [ħ]), which appears in English spellings as *ḥ*. In European names \k̲\ may be anglicized as \k\; in Arabic, Persian, and Hebrew names it may be anglicized as \h\.

\l\

as in **l**ap, pa**l**, a**ll**ey (IPA [l, ɫ]). In some contexts this sound may be heard as a syllabic consonant (IPA [l̩]), which in this book is respelled as \-əl\, as at **Babel, Tower of** \'bā-bəl, 'ba-\.

\m\
as in **m**ake, ja**m**, ha**mm**er (IPA [m]).

\n\
as in **n**ow, wi**n**, ba**nn**er (IPA [n]). In some contexts this sound may be heard as a syllabic consonant (IPA [n̩]), which in this book is respelled as \-ən\, as at **Armageddon** \ˌär-mə-'ge-dən\. In Japanese names this symbol used at the end of syllables represents the uvular nasal sound in that language. The symbol \n\ is also used to transcribe a sound in names from India which appears in transliteration as *n̩* and which in the original language is pronounced as a retroflex sound (IPA [n̩, ɳ]).

\ⁿ\
is used to show nasalization of the preceding vowel, as in French *en* \äⁿ\ 'in'.

\ŋ\
as in ri**ng**, si**ng**er, go**ng** (IPA [ŋ]). In English this sound appears only at the end of a syllable, but in non-European languages it may occur at the beginning of a syllable followed either by a vowel or another consonant. In these contexts \ŋ\ may be anglicized as \əŋg\.

\ō\
as in **oa**k, b**oa**t, t**oe**, g**o** (IPA [o, o:, ou]). This sound is a diphthong in most dialects of English, but it is a monophthong in most other languages. In the Received Pronunciation of British English the diphthong is \əu̇\ (IPA [əʊ]), where the initial element is a central mid vowel.

\ȯ\
as in h**aw**k, b**aw**l, c**au**ght, **ou**ght, Utah (IPA [ɔ]). In some dialects of American English this sound is replaced by \ä\. The vowel \ȯ\ may be reduced to \ə\ in unstressed syllables.

\œ\
as in French n**eu**f 'new' and German K**ö**pfe 'heads' (IPA [œ]). This vowel can be approximated by producing the vowel \e\ while rounding the lips as if pronouncing the vowel \ȯ\. The sound \œ\ may be anglicized as \ər\ with a very light \r\ sound.

\æ\
as in French d**eu**x 'two' and German L**ö**hne 'wages' (IPA [ø]). This vowel can be approximated by producing the vowel \ā\ while rounding the lips as if pronouncing the vowel \ō\. The sound \æ\ may be anglicized as \u̇r\ or \ər\ with a very light \r\ sound.

\ȯi\
as in **oy**ster, t**oy**, f**oi**l (IPA [ɔɪ, ɔi]).

\ȯr\
as in c**or**e, b**or**n, **oar** (IPA [ɔr]). In some American dialects this may also be pronounced as \ōr\ (IPA [or]) in many words.

\p\
as in **p**et, ti**p**, u**pp**er (IPA [p]).

\r\
as in **r**ut, ta**r**, e**rr**or, ca**r**t. What is transcribed here as \r\ in reality represents several distinct sounds. As an English consonant \r\ is produced with the tongue tip slightly behind the teethridge (IPA [ɹ]). As a semi-vowel in words like *cart* and *fore* \r\ appears as retroflexion of the tongue tip in some dialects and as a transitional vowel like \ə\ in the so-called "R-dropping" dialects of American and British English.

In other languages \r\ represents a stronger consonant, such as a trill or tap of the tongue tip against the teethridge (IPA [r, ɾ]) or a trill of the back of the tongue against the soft palate (IPA [ʀ]). These \r\ sounds may all be anglicized with the \r\ of English.

\s\
as in **s**ink, ba**ss**, la**ss**o, **c**ity (IPA [s]).

\sh\
as in **sh**in, la**sh**, pre**ss**ure (IPA [ʃ]).

\t\
as in **t**op, pa**t**, la**t**er (IPA [t]). In some contexts, as when a vowel or \r\ precedes and an unstressed vowel follows, the sound represented in English spelling by *t* or *tt* is pronounced in most American speech as a voiced flap produced by tapping the tongue tip against the teethridge (IPA [ɾ]). In similar contexts the sound represented by *d* or *dd* has the same pronunciation. The symbol \t\ is also used to transcribe a sound in names from India which appears in transliteration as *t̩* and which in the original language is pronounced as a retroflex sound (IPA [t̩, ʈ]).

\th\
as in **th**ird, ba**th**, Ka**th**y (IPA [θ]).

\t̲h̲\
as in **th**is, o**th**er, ba**th**e (IPA [ð]).

\ü\
as in **oo**ze, bl**ue**, n**oo**n (IPA [u, u:, uʊ]). This sound is a diphthong in most dialects of English, but it is a monophthong in most other languages.

\u̇\
as in w**oo**l, t**oo**k, sh**ou**ld, p**u**t (IPA [ʊ]).

\ᵫ\
as in German B**ü**nde 'unions,' f**ü**llen 'to fill' (IPA [ʏ]). This vowel can be approximated by producing the

vowel \i\ while rounding the lips as if pronouncing the vowel \u̇\. The sound \œ\ may be anglicized as \yu̇\ or \u̇\.

\œ̄\
as in German *kühl* 'cool' and French *vue* 'view' (IPA [y]). This vowel can be approximated by producing the vowel \ē\ while rounding the lips as if pronouncing the vowel \ü\. The sound \œ̄\ may be anglicized as \yü\ or \ü\.

\v\
as in **v**eer, ro**v**e, e**v**er (IPA [v]).

\w\
as in **w**ell, a**w**ash (IPA [w]).

\y\
as in **y**outh, **y**et, law**y**er (IPA [j]). In some languages the consonant \y\ may occur after a vowel in the same syllable, as in French *famille* \fà-'mēy\ 'family.' The pronunciation of \y\ in these contexts is the same as at the beginning of a syllable in English.

\ʸ\
is used to show palatalization of a preceding consonant, as in French *campagne* \käⁿ-'pàn^y\ 'country' and Russian *perestroika* \pʸi-rʸi-'strȯi-kə\ 'restructuring' (IPA [ʲ]). A palatalized consonant is produced with the body of the tongue raised as if in the position to pronounce \y\. In anglicized pronunciations \ʸ\ may be sounded as the consonantal \y\ of English when it falls in the middle of a syllable or as \-yə\ at the end of French words. In anglicizations of Russian and other Slavic names it may be omitted entirely.

\z\
as in **z**oo, ha**z**e, ra**z**or (IPA [z]).

\zh\
as in plea**s**ure, deci**s**ion (IPA [ʒ]).

ə	in anoint, collide, data	m	make, jam, hammer
'ə, ˌə	cut, conundrum	n	now, win, banner
ə̇	biologist, matches	ⁿ	shows that a preceding vowel is nasalized, as in French *en* \äⁿ\
əi	Welsh *lleuad*, *eira*	ŋ	ring, singer, gong
'ər, ər	further, merger, bird	ō	oak, boat, toe, go
a	rap, cat, sand, lamb	ȯ	hawk, bawl, caught, ought, Utah
ā	way, paid, late, eight	œ	French *neuf*, German *Köpfe*
ä	opt, cod, mach	œ̄	French *deux*, German *Löhne*
à	French *chat*, *table*	ȯi	oyster, toy, foil
ar	air, care, laird	ȯr	core, born, oar
aù	out, loud, tout, cow	p	pet, tip, upper
b	bat, able, rib	r	rut, tar, error, cart
b̲	Spanish *hablar*, *Avila*	s	sink, bass, lasso, city
ch	chair, reach, catcher	sh	shin, lash, pressure
d	day, red, ladder	t	top, pat, later
e	egg, bed, bet	th	third, bath, Kathy
'ē, ˌē	eat, reed, fleet, pea	t̲h̲	this, other, bathe
ē	penny, genie	ü	ooze, blue, noon
f	fine, chaff, office	u̇	wool, took, should, put
g	gate, rag, eagle	ue	German *Bünde*, *füllen*
g̲	Spanish *lago*	ūe	German *kühl*, French *vue*
h	hot, ahoy	v	veer, rove, ever
hl	Welsh *llaw*, Icelandic *hlaup*	w	well, awash
hr	Welsh *rhad*, Icelandic *hraun*	y	youth, yet, lawyer
hw	wheat, when	ʸ	shows palatalization of a preceding consonant, as in French *campagne* \käⁿ-'pånʸ\
i	ill, hip, bid	z	zoo, haze, razor
ī	aisle, fry, white, wide	zh	pleasure, decision
ir	hear, inferior, mirror, pierce	\ \	reversed virgules used to mark the beginning and end of a phonetic respelling
j	jump, fudge, budget	'	mark preceding a syllable with primary stress: boa \'bō-ə\
k	kick, baker, scam, ask	ˌ	mark preceding a syllable with secondary stress: bee-line \'bē-ˌlīn\
k̲	loch, Bach, German *Buch*, *ich*	-	mark indicating syllable divisions
l	lap, pal, alley		

For more information *see* Guide to Pronunciation.

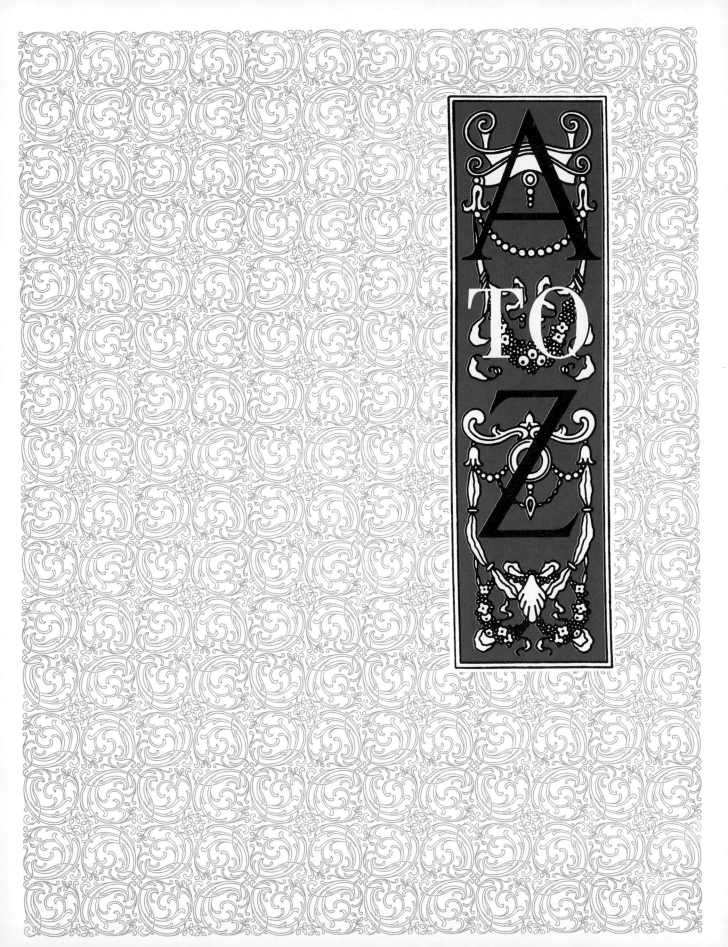

AARON \'ar-ən, 'er-\ (fl. *c.* 14th century BCE), the founder and head of the Jewish PRIESTHOOD, who, with his brother MOSES and sister Miriam, led the Israelites out of Egypt. The figure of Aaron as found in the PENTATEUCH is built up from several different sources of religious tradition. He has appeared in varying roles in the thought and traditions of Christianity.

Aaron is described in the OLD TESTAMENT book of EXODUS as a son of Amram and Jochebed (Exodus 6:20; Numbers 26:59) of the tribe of Levi (Exodus 4:14), three years older than his brother Moses. He acted together with his brother in the desperate situation of the Israelites in Egypt (Exodus 5; 6:26; 7–12) and took an active part in the Exodus (Exodus 16; 17:10; 19:24). Although Moses was the actual leader, Aaron acted as his "mouth" (Exodus 4:16). The two brothers went to the pharaoh together, and it was Aaron who told him to let the people of Israel go, using his magic rod in order to show the might of YAHWEH. When the pharaoh finally decided to release the people, Yahweh gave the important ordinance of the PASSOVER, the annual remembrance of the Exodus, to Aaron and Moses (Exodus 12). But Moses alone went up on MOUNT SINAI (Exodus 19:20), and he alone was allowed to come near to Yahweh. Moses later was ordered to "bring near" Aaron and his sons, and they were anointed and consecrated to be priests by a perpetual statute (Exodus 27:21). Aaron's sons were to take over the priestly garments after him. Aaron is not represented as an entirely holy and blameless person, however. It was he who, when Moses was delayed on Mount Sinai, made the GOLDEN CALF that was idolatrously worshiped by the people (Exodus 32).

Once a year, on YOM KIPPUR (the Day of Atonement), Aaron was allowed to come into the HOLY OF HOLIES, the most sacred part

of the TABERNACLE, or SANCTUARY, in which the Hebrew tribes worshiped, bringing his offering (Leviticus 16). Together with his sister Miriam, Aaron spoke against Moses because he had married a foreigner (a Cushite woman, Numbers 12:1); but, in the rebellion of Korah the LEVITE, Aaron stood firmly at the side of Moses (Numbers 16). According to Numbers 20, Aaron died on the top of Mount Hor at the age of 123; in Deuteronomy 10, which represents another tradition, he is said to have died in Moserah and was buried there.

Aaron in Jewish and Christian thought. Aaron is a central figure in the traditions about the Exodus, though his role varies in importance. At the beginning he seems to be coequal with Moses, but after the march out of Egypt he is only a shadow at Moses' side. Moses is obviously the leading figure in the tradition, but it is also clear that he is pictured as delegating his authority in all priestly and cultic matters to Aaron and "his sons."

Aaron continued to live as a symbol in Jewish religion and traditions. In the QUMRĀN sect, a Jewish community that flourished just before and contemporary with the birth of CHRISTIANITY, Aaron was a symbol for a strong priesthood.

At the end of time, men of the community should be set apart, as a select group in the service of Aaron. Only the sons of Aaron should "administer judgment and wealth," and, according to the MANUAL OF DISCIPLINE, two MESSIAHS were expected, a priestly one of Aaron, and one of Israel. According to a fragment found near Qumrān, the priest would have the first seat in the banquets in the last days and bless the bread before the messiah of Israel; here "the sons of Aaron" have the highest position.

In the TALMUD and MIDRASH (Jewish commentative writings), Aaron is seen less as a symbol than as the leading personality at the side of Moses. The relationship between the two brothers is painted as prototypical in the Haggadah (the nonlegal parts of the Talmud and Midrash; *see* HALAKHAH AND HAGGADAH). In the Mishnaic treatise Avot (Avot 1:12) Rabbi HILLEL praised Aaron as a man of goodwill who wanted to teach his fellowmen the Law.

Many attempts have been made to explain Aaron's participation in the episode of the golden calf (SIFRA to Deuteronomy 307). According to some exegetes, Aaron had to make the calf in order to avoid being killed. In the 11th century, the French commentator RASHI contended that the calf was a symbol of the leader, Moses, who was at that time on the mountain. The relationship between Moses and Aaron is also discussed in the Talmud. Some traditionists have wondered why Aaron, and not Moses, was appointed HIGH PRIEST. The answer has been found in an indication that Moses was rejected because of his original unwillingness when he was called by Yahweh. It also seems to have been hard for some traditionists to accept that Aaron was described as older than Moses.

The first Christian communities accepted Aaron, "the sons of Aaron," or "the order of Aaron" as symbols of the highest priesthood. But in the Letter to the Hebrews, Christ is described as a high priest according to the order of MELCHIZEDEK, which was set against "the order of Aaron" (Hebrews 5:2–5; 7:11–12). Of the CHURCH FATHERS, Cyril of Alexandria says that Aaron was divinely called to a priesthood and that he was a type of Christ. Gregory the Great translates the name Aaron as "mountain of strength" and sees in him a redeemer who mediated between God and man.

AARONIC PRIESTHOOD \a-'rä-nik, e-\, in JUDAISM, hereditary priesthood descended from AARON. *See* KOHEN.

AARONIC PRIESTHOOD, Church of Jesus Christ of Latter-day Saints (MORMON) priests whose primary concern is church finances and administration.

ABBESS, the superior of certain communities of nuns. The first historical record of the title is on a Roman inscription dated *c.* 514.

Current CANON LAW stipulates that to be elected, an abbess must be at least 40 years old and a professed nun for at

Aaron's rod (in the form of a serpent) swallows up the serpents of Pharoah's sages and sorcerers, Nuremberg Bible *(1483)*
By courtesy of The Bridgeman Art Library

least 10 years. She is solemnly blessed by the diocesan bishop in a rite similar to that of the blessing of ABBOTS. Her blessing gives her the right to certain pontifical insignia: the ring and sometimes the CROSIER. In medieval times abbesses occasionally ruled double monasteries of monks and nuns and enjoyed various privileges and honors.

ABBOT, *Late Latin and Greek* abbas, the superior of a monastic community of certain orders—*e.g.,* BENEDICTINES, CISTERCIANS, and TRAPPISTS. The word derives from the Aramaic *ab* ("father"), or *aba* ("my father"), which in the SEPTUAGINT (the Greek translation of the OLD TESTAMENT) and in NEW TESTAMENT Greek was written *abbas.* Early Christian Egyptian monks renowned for age and sanctity were called *abbas* by their disciples, but, when MONASTICISM became more organized, superiors were called *proestos* ("he who rules") or *hēgoumenos* in the East and the Latin equivalent, *praepositus,* in the West. ST. BENEDICT OF NURSIA (*c.* 480–*c.* 547) restored the word *abbas* in his rule, and to this early concept of spiritual fatherhood through teaching he added authority over temporal matters as well.

An abbot is elected by the chapter of the monastery by secret ballot. He must be at least 30 years old, professed at least 10 years, and an ordained priest. He is elected for life except in the English congregation, where he is elected for a term of 8–12 years. The election must be confirmed by the Holy See or by some other designated authority. The bishop of the DIOCESE in which the monastery is situated confers the abbatial blessing, assisted by two abbots. Chief among the privileges of an abbot are the rights to celebrate the liturgy, to give many blessings normally reserved to a bishop, and to use the pontifical insignia.

In Eastern monasticism, self-governing monasteries are ruled by several elder monks, whose leader is called abbot.

'ABD AL-GHANĪ \'äb-dùl-ḡà-'nē\, *in full* 'Abd al-Ghanī ibn Ismā'īl al-Nābulusī (b. March 19, 1641, Damascus—d. March 5, 1731), Syrian mystic writer.

Orphaned at an early age, 'Abd al-Ghanī joined the Islamic mystical orders of the QĀDIRĪYA and the NAQSHBANDĪYA. He

then spent seven years in isolation, studying mystic expressions of divine experiences. His written works include discourses on SUFISM, travel accounts, poetry, eulogies, correspondence, PROPHECY, and dream interpretation. A key element in his Sufi writing is the concept of *waḥdat al-wujūd* ("divine existential unity" of God and the universe and, hence, of man). His travel accounts are considered by many to be the most important of his writings; the descriptions of his journeys in Syria, Egypt, and the Hijaz in Arabia, provide vital information on the customs, beliefs, and practices of the peoples and places he visited.

'ABD ALLĀH IBN AL-'ABBĀS \,äb-dùl-'lä-,i-bən-əl-,äb-'bas\, *also called* Ibn 'Abbās (b. *c.* 619—d. 687/688, aṭ-Ṭā'if, Arabia), a Companion of the Prophet MUHAMMAD, one of the greatest Islamic scholars and the first exegete of the QUR'AN.

Ibn 'Abbas is renowned for his knowledge of both sacred and profane tradition and for his critical interpretations of the Qur'an. From his youth he gathered information concerning the words and deeds of Muhammad from other Companions and gave classes on the interpretation of the Qur'an. His commentaries on the Qur'an were later collected into a book (TAFSĪR) and incorporated into the commentaries of AL-BUKHĀRĪ and AL-TABARĪ.

'ABD AL-QĀDIR AL-JĪLĀNĪ \,äb-dùl-'kä-dir-əl-jē-'lä-nē\ (b. 1077/78, Nif, Persia—d. 1166, Baghdad), traditional founder of the QĀDIRĪYA order of SUFISM, a mystical branch of ISLAM.

Al-Jīlānī studied Islamic law in Baghdad and first appeared as a preacher in 1127. His reputation as a teacher attracted numerous disciples, and he is said to have converted many Jews and Christians. He reconciled the mystical nature of the Sufi calling with the sober demands of Islamic law. His concept of Sufism was as of a JIHAD waged against egotism and worldliness in order to submit to God's will. He retains a popular following from Senegal to India and Indonesia among those who consider him a divine mediator and miracle worker. His tomb in Baghdad is visited by Muslims from many lands.

'ABDUH, MUHAMMAD \'äb-,dü, -,dù\ (b. 1849, Egypt—d. July 11, 1905, near Alexandria), religious scholar, jurist, and liberal reformer who led the late 19th-century movement in Egypt and other Muslim countries to revitalize Islamic teachings and institutions.

'Abduh attended the mosque school in Ṭanṭā and subsequently AL-AZHAR UNIVERSITY in Cairo, receiving the degree of *'ālim* (scholar) in 1877. In 1872 he fell under the influence of Jamāl ad-Dīn al-Afghānī, the revolutionary pan-Islamic Persian preacher, who stimulated 'Abduh's interest in theology, philosophy, and politics. Afghānī was expelled for political reasons from Egypt in 1879 and 'Abduh was exiled to his village, but the next year he became editor of the government's official gazette, which he used to preach resistance to Anglo-French political encroachment and the need for social and religious reform. He was implicated in 'Urābī Pasha's rebellion against foreign control in 1882 and was again exiled. Rejoining Afghānī in Paris for several months in 1884, 'Abduh helped publish the revolutionary journal *Al-'Urwa al-wuthqā* ("The Firmest Bond"). He then taught for three years in an Islamic college in Beirut.

In 1888 'Abduh was permitted to return to Egypt, where he was appointed a judge in the National Courts of First Instance; in 1891 he became a judge at the Court of Appeal. In 1899, with British help, he became MUFTI of Egypt. He effected reforms in the administration of Islamic law (*see* SHARĪ'A) and of religious endowments and issued advisory opinions on such controversial matters as the permissibility of eating meat slaughtered by Christian and Jewish butchers and of accepting interest paid on loans. 'Abduh also lectured at al-Azhar and, against conservative opposition, induced reforms in the administration and curriculum there. He established a benevolent society that operated schools for poor children. On the Legislative Council he supported political cooperation with Britain and legal and educational reform in Egypt; these views earned him the approval of the British, but the hostility of the *khedive* (ruling prince) 'Abbās Ḥilmī and of the nationalist leader Muṣṭafā Kāmil.

In addition to his articles in the official gazette and *Al-'Urwa al-wuthqā*, 'Abduh's most important writings included *Risālat al-tawḥīd* ("Treatise on the Oneness of God"); a polemic on the superiority of Islam to Christianity in Islam's greater receptivity to science and civilization; and a commentary on the Qur'an, completed after his death by a disciple. In theology 'Abduh sought to establish the harmony of reason and revelation, the freedom of the will, and the primacy of the ethical implications of religious faith over ritual and dogma. He asserted that a return to the pristine faith of the earliest age of Islam would both restore the Muslims' spiritual vitality and provide an enlightened criterion for the assimilation of modern scientific culture.

In matters of Islamic law regarding family relationships, ritual duties, and personal conduct, 'Abduh promoted considerations of equity, welfare, and common sense, even when this meant disregarding the literal texts of the Qur'an. 'Abduh has been widely revered as the chief architect of the modern reformation of Islam.

ABEL \'ā-bəl\, second son of ADAM AND EVE, who was slain by his older brother, CAIN (GENESIS 4:1–16). Abel, a shepherd, offered the Lord the firstborn of his flock. God respected Abel's sacrifice but did not respect that offered by Cain. In a rage, Cain murdered Abel, then became a fugitive because of the curse placed upon the ground (a curse of infertility) onto which Abel's blood had spilled.

Genesis makes the point that divine authority backs self-control and brotherhood but punishes jealousy and violence. In the NEW TESTAMENT the blood of Abel is cited as an example of the vengeance of violated innocence (Matthew 23:35; Luke 11:51).

ABELARD, PETER \à-bā-'lår, *Angl* 'a-bə-‚lärd\ (b. 1079, Le Pallet, Brittany [now in France]—d. April 21, 1142, Priory of Saint-Marcel, Burgundy [now in France]), French theologian and philosopher.

The outline of Abelard's career is described in his famous *Historia calamitatum* ("History of My Troubles"). He was born the son of a knight and sacrificed his inheritance in order to study philosophy in France. Abelard provoked quarrels with two of his masters, Roscelin of Compiègne and Guillaume de Champeaux. Roscelin was a nominalist who asserted that universals (terms such as "red," or

"beauty," by which objects can be grouped) are nothing more than mere words; Guillaume upheld a form of Platonic Realism according to which universals exist independently of the objects they describe. Abelard brilliantly elaborated a philosophy of language that, while showing how words could be used significantly, stressed that language itself is not able to demonstrate the truth of things (RES) that lie in the domain of physics.

Abelard traveled as one of the exponents of Aristotelian logic who were called the Peripatetics. While teaching in Paris he was tutoring the young Héloïse, niece of Canon Fulbert. Abelard and Héloïse began having an affair and had a son whom they called Astrolabe. They then married secretly. To escape her uncle's wrath Héloïse withdrew into the convent of Argenteuil outside Paris. Abelard suffered castration at Fulbert's instigation. He then embraced the monastic life at the royal abbey of Saint-Denis near Paris and forced the unwilling Héloïse to become a nun at a convent in Argenteuil.

At Saint-Denis Abelard extended his reading in theology. His reading of the BIBLE and of the writings of the CHURCH FATHERS led him to make a collection of quotations that seemed to represent inconsistencies of teaching by the church. He arranged his findings in a compilation entitled *Sic et non* ("Yes and No"); and in it he formulated basic rules with which students might reconcile apparent contradictions of meaning and distinguish the various senses in which words had been used over the course of centuries. He also wrote the first version of his book called *Theologia*, which was formally condemned as heretical and burned by a council held at Soissons in 1121. Abelard's dialectical analysis of the mystery of God and the TRINITY was held to be erroneous, and he was placed in the abbey of Saint-Médard under house arrest. He returned to Saint-Denis but a dispute with that monastic community caused Abelard to

Abelard, with Héloïse, miniature portrait by Jean de Meun, 14th century

By courtesy of the Musée Condé, Chantilly, France; photograph, Giraudon—Art Resource

flee. In 1125 he accepted election as ABBOT of the remote Breton monastery of Saint-Gildas-de-Rhuys. There, too, his relations with the community deteriorated, and, after attempts had been made upon his life, he returned to France.

About 1135 Abelard went to the Mont-Sainte-Geneviève outside Paris to teach and write. He produced further drafts of his *Theologia* in which he analyzed the sources of belief in the Trinity. He also wrote a book called *Ethica*, or *Scito te ipsum* ("Know Thyself"), a short masterpiece in which he analyzed the notion of SIN and reached the drastic conclusion that human actions are in themselves neither good nor bad. What counts with God is a man's intention; sin is not something done; it is uniquely the consent of a human mind to what it knows to be wrong. He also wrote *Dialogus inter philosophum, Judaeum et Christianum* ("Dialogue Between a Philosopher, a Jew, and a Christian") and a commentary on St. Paul's letter to the Romans, the *Expositio in Epistolam ad Romanos*, in which he outlined an explanation of the purpose of Christ's life and death, which was to inspire men to love him by example alone.

On the Mont-Sainte-Geneviève Abelard drew crowds of pupils; he also, however, aroused deep hostility and was resoundingly condemned at a council held at Sens in 1140, a judgment confirmed by Pope Innocent II. He withdrew to the great monastery of Cluny in Burgundy. There, under the skillful mediation of the abbot, Peter the Venerable, he made peace with his opponents and retired from teaching.

ABHIDHAMMA PIṬAKA \'ə-bē-'də-mə-'pi-tə-kə\ (Pāli: "Basket of Special Doctrine," or "Further Doctrine"), *Sanskrit* Abhidharma Piṭaka \'ə-bē-'dər-mə, -'där-\, the third—and historically the latest—of the three "baskets," or collections of texts, that together comprise the Pāli canon of THERAVĀDA Buddhism. The other two collections are the SUTTA PIṬAKA and the VINAYA PIṬAKA. Unlike those, however, the seven *Abhidhamma* works are not generally claimed to represent the words of the BUDDHA GOTAMA; nevertheless, they are highly venerated.

This work of doctrinal material represents a development in a rationalistic direction of summaries or numerical lists that had come to be used as a basis for meditation—lists that, among the more mystically inclined, contributed to the PRAJÑĀPĀRAMITĀ literature of MAHĀYĀNA Buddhism.

The *Abhidhamma* corpus has had a checkered history. It was not accepted as canonical by the MAHĀSAṄGHIKA school, the forerunners of Mahāyāna. Various Mahāyāna texts have been classified as *Abhidhamma*, including the *Prajñāpāramitā-sūtra*s in Tibet and, in China, the *Diamond Sutra* (see DIAMOND CUTTER SUTRA).

The Pāli *Abhidhamma Piṭaka* encompasses the following texts, or *pakaraṇas*: (1) *Dhammasaṅgaṇi* ("Summary of Dharma"), a psychologically oriented manual of ethics; (2) *Vibhaṅga* ("Division," or "Classification"), a kind of supplement to the *Dhammasaṅgaṇi*; (3) *Dhātukathā* ("Discussion of Elements"), another supplementary work; (4) *Puggalapaññatti* ("Designation of Person"), largely a collection of excerpts from the *Sutta Piṭaka*, classifying human characteristics in relation to stages on the Buddhist path; (5) *Kathāvatthu* ("Points of Controversy"), attributed to Moggaliputta, president of the third Buddhist Council (3rd century BCE), the only work in the Pāli canon assigned to a particular author; historically one of the most important of the seven, the *Kathāvatthu* is a series of questions from a non-Theravāda point of view, with their implications refuted in the answers; (6) *Yamaka* ("Pairs"), a series of questions on psychological phenomena, each dealt with in two

opposite ways; (7) *Paṭṭhāna* ("Activations," or "Causes"), a complex and voluminous treatment of causality.

ABHIDHAMMATTHA-SAṄGAHA \'ə-bē-də-'mət-tə-'səŋ-gə-hə\ (Pāli: "Summary of the Meaning of *Abhidhamma*"), one of the most important THERAVĀDA Buddhist manuals of psychology and ethics. A digest of the *Abhidhamma* corpus of the Theravāda tradition, it was composed in India or in Burma (Myanmar), the chief center for *Abhidhamma* studies. Written in Pāli by the monk Anuruddha, it dates from no earlier than the 8th century CE and probably from the 11th or 12th.

A handbook rather than an expository work, it deals in less than 50 pages with the entire seven texts of the ABHIDHAMMA PIṬAKA and has been the subject of an extensive exegetical literature in the centuries since its composition. The subject matter of the *Abhidhammattha-saṅgaha* includes enumerations of the classes of consciousness, the qualities of matter, the varieties of rebirth, and a number of meditation exercises. Its purpose is to elicit a realization of the impermanence of all things, leading to enlightenment.

ABHIDHARMAKOŚA \'ə-bē-,dər-mə-'kō-shə, -,där-\, *also called* Abhidharmakośa-Śāstra \-'shäs-trə\ (Sanskrit: "Treasury of Higher Law"), *Chinese* A-P'i-Ta-Mo Chü-She Lun, *Japanese* Abidatsuma-Kusha-Ron, an introduction to the seven *Abhidharma* (Pāli: *Abhidhamma*) treatises in the SARVĀSTIVĀDA canon and a systematic digest of their contents, dealing with a wide range of philosophical, cosmological, ethical, and salvational doctrine.

Its author, VASUBANDHU, who lived in the 4th or 5th century CE in the northwestern part of India, wrote the work while he was still a monk of the Sarvāstivāda order, before he embraced MAHĀYĀNA, on whose texts he was later to write a number of commentaries. As a Sarvāstivāda work the *Abhidharmakośa* is one of few surviving treatments of scholasticism not written in Pāli and not produced by Theravādins. The product of both great erudition and considerable independence of thought, the *Abhidharmakośa* authoritatively completed the systematization of Sarvāstivāda doctrine and at the same time incorporated Mahāyānist tendencies. It provides much information on doctrinal differences between ancient Buddhist schools.

Translated into Chinese within a century or two after it was written, the *Abhidharmakośa* has been used in China, Japan, and Tibet as an authoritative reference on matters of doctrine. In China it provided the basis for the Abhidharma (Chinese Chü-She; Japanese Kusha) sect.

ABHINAVAGUPTA \,ə-bi-nə-və-'gùp-tə\ (*c.* 10th–11th century, Kashmir, India), philosopher, ascetic, and outstanding representative of the "recognition" (*pratyabhijñā*) school of Kashmir Śaivite (see ŚAIVISM) monism. This school conceived of the god SHIVA (who is ultimate reality), the individual self, and the universe as essentially one. Abhinavagupta was a prolific writer on philosophy and aesthetics. Among Abhinavagupta's most notable philosophic works are the *Īśvara-pratyabhijñā-vimarśinī* and the more detailed *Īśvara-pratyabhijñā-vivṛti-vimarśinī*, both commentaries on works by an earlier philosopher, Utpala.

He is also well known for his *Tantrāloka* ("Light on the *Tantra*s"). His enduring contributions to Hindu thought include his conception of Shiva as self-veiling and simultaneously self-manifesting, a process of play that creates the possibility for the religious practitioner to recognize Shiva through heightened self-consciousness. Through his interpretation of RASA (aesthetic sentiment), Abhinavagupta was a key figure in elaborating resonances between aesthetics and the theory of religious experience.

ABLUTION, a prescribed washing of the body or items such as clothing or ceremonial objects, with the intent of purification or dedication. Water, sometimes mixed with salt or other ingredients, is most commonly used, but washing with blood is not uncommon, and cow urine has been used in India.

The follower of SHINTŌ rinses hands and mouth with water before approaching a shrine. Monks of the THERAVĀDA Buddhist tradition wash themselves in the monastery pool before meditation. The upper-caste Hindu bathes in water before performing morning worship (*pūjā*) in the home. Jewish law requires washing of the hands after rising in the morning and before meals that include bread—as well as ritual immersion of the entire body for new converts to JUDAISM, for women prior to marriage and after each menses, and for men at the beginning of the Sabbath. (*See also* TOHORAH *and* MIKVEH.) Roman Catholic and some Eastern Orthodox priests prepare themselves for the EUCHARIST by ritual washing of the hands. Among some Brethren sects in the United States, ceremonial foot washing is performed on certain occasions. Muslim piety requires that the devout wash their hands, feet, and face before each of the five daily prayers; the use of sand is permitted where water is unavailable. (*See also* TAHARA.)

Abraham Guarding His Sacrifice, *painting by James Tissot*
By courtesy of the Jewish Museum, New York City; photograph, Joseph Parnell

Ablution may carry a wide range of meanings. The stain of ritual uncleanness may be felt to be physically real; the act of cleansing may be only symbolic of desired purity of soul; or the two attitudes may be combined.

ABRAHAM \ˈā-brə-ˌham\, *Arabic* Ibrahim \i-brä-ˈhēm\ (fl. early 2nd millennium BCE), first of the Hebrew PATRIARCHS and a figure revered by JUDAISM, CHRISTIANITY, and ISLAM. According to the book of GENESIS, God called Abraham to found a new nation in CANAAN.

The most that can be done to compile a biography of Abraham is to apply the interpretation of modern historical

findings to biblical materials so as to arrive at a probable judgment as to the background of events in his life.

According to the biblical account, Abram ("The Father [or God] Is Exalted"), who is later named Abraham ("The Father of Many Nations"), a native of Ur in Mesopotamia, is called by God (YAHWEH) to leave his own country and people and journey to an undesignated land, where he will become the founder of a new nation. He obeys the call and (at 75 years of age) proceeds with his barren wife, Sarai, later named SARAH ("Princess"), his nephew Lot, and other companions to Canaan (located between Syria and Egypt).

There he receives promises and a COVENANT from God that his "seed" will inherit the land and become a numerous nation. He has a son, Ishmael, by his wife's maidservant HAGAR and a legitimate son by Sarah, ISAAC, who is to be the heir of the promise. Yet Abraham is ready to obey God's command to sacrifice Isaac as a test of his faith, which he is not required to consummate in the end because God substitutes a ram for Isaac.

Geographically, the saga of Abraham unfolds between two landmarks, "Ur of the Chaldeans" (Ur Kasdim) of the family, or clan, of Terah and the cave of Machpelah. For the most part, scholars agree that Ur Kasdim was the Sumerian city of Ur, today Tall al-Muqayyar (or Mughair), about 200 miles southeast of Baghdad.

At Sarah's death, Genesis relates that Abraham purchased the cave of Machpelah near Hebron, together with the adjoining ground, as a family burial place. It is the first clear ownership of a piece of the promised land by Abraham and his posterity. Toward the end of his life, he sees to it that his son Isaac marries a girl from his own people back in Mesopotamia rather than a Canaanite woman. In the story of Genesis, Abraham dies at the age of 175 and is buried next to Sarah in the cave of Machpelah.

Abraham is pictured in Genesis with various characteristics: a righteous man, with wholehearted commitment to God; a man of peace (in settling a boundary dispute with his nephew Lot), compassionate (he argues and bargains with God to spare the people of SODOM AND GOMORRAH), and hospitable (he welcomes three visiting ANGELS); a quick-acting warrior (he rescues Lot and his family from a raiding party); and an unscrupulous liar (to save himself he passes off Sarah as his sister and lets her be picked by the Egyptian pharaoh for his harem). He appears as both a man of great spiritual depth and strength and a person with common human weaknesses and needs. Still, it was Abraham who received messages from God—not in dreams or visions, but in ordinary speech.

In Judaism, Abraham is taken as the model of virtue for his having observed all the commandments though they had not yet been revealed by God. Abraham was the first to acknowledge the one true God; this he did by process of reason, as portrayed by Rabbi Isaac in connection with the Genesis verse 12:1, "Now the Lord said to Abraham, 'Go [from your country and your kindred and your father's house to the land that I will show you']." In GENESIS RABBAH (c. 450 CE) Rabbi Isaac compared Abraham to the case of someone who was traveling from one place to another when he saw a great house on fire. He said, "Is it possible to say that such a great house has no one in charge? The owner of the house then looked out and said to him, 'I am the one in charge of the house.' Thus, since Abraham our father [took the initiative and] said, 'Is it possible for the world to endure without someone in charge?' the Holy One, blessed be He, [responded and] looked out and said to him, 'I am the one in charge of the house, the Lord of all the world.'" Therefore, within Judaism, not only is Abraham the first man to recognize the true God, on some level his very righteousness causes God to begin the process of revelation.

It was also from Abraham that ISRAEL received the divine power to communicate with God. It is he who is credited with founding the morning prayer (the daily service involving recitation of the SHEMA and the Eighteen Benedictions; see AMIDAH) and originating the commandments involving show-fringes on garments and phylacteries. Abraham is also the founder of the rite of CIRCUMCISION for the Jews— "entry into the covenant of Abraham our father" refers to circumcision. See also AKEDAH.

For Christianity, Abraham has always stood as the father of all believers (Romans 4:11). His faith, his willingness to trust in God, has been the model of all the saints of subsequent periods (Hebrews 11), and "it was reckoned to him for righteousness" (Romans 4:3) as the ground of his justification before God, whether by faith without works (Romans 3) or by faith and works (James 2). The obedience expressed in his willingness to sacrifice Isaac made Abraham, in the words of SØREN KIERKEGAARD, "the knight of infinite resignation," and was read as the typological prophecy of "He [God] who did not spare his own Son but gave him up for us all" (Romans 8:32). "Abraham's bosom" (Luke 16:22) was, for the Gospels as it had already been for Judaism, a name for eternal life in heaven, and the declaration attributed to Jesus, "Before Abraham was, I am" (John 8:58), is one of the strongest affirmations anywhere in the NEW TESTAMENT of his eternal identity with the God of Israel as the great "I AM WHO I AM" (EXODUS 3:14).

The figure of Abraham in Islam was formulated from biblical and rabbinic narratives current in Arabia, Syria, Iraq, and Egypt during the 7th to 8th centuries CE. The QUR'AN, which mentions the name of Abraham more than 60 times (compared to around 130 times for MOSES, some 20 times for JESUS CHRIST, and less than 10 times for MUHAMMAD), depicts him as the prototypical prophet—the intimate of God, who endured opposition from his own people to promote true religion (e.g., Qur'an 3:65–68, 4:125, 6:74–83). The Qur'an also credits him with building God's "house" in MECCA (the KA'BA) with the assistance of his son Ishmael (Ismā'īl), and

instituting the HAJJ (Qur'an 2:125–28). Indeed, Islamic tradition generally ascribes the foundation of the hajj rites to Abraham and his family, including the stoning of the three pillars at Mina and the celebration of the sacrificial feast that marks the end of the hajj.

Islamic hagiographies included Abraham in the lineages of Muhammad and other major prophets. He was also one of the extraordinary beings encountered by Muhammad during his ascension (MI'RĀJ). Sufis later saw in Abraham a model for generosity because of his willingness to sacrifice his own son; and for perseverance because of his enduring the fires of affliction out of love for God.

ABRAHAMS, ISRAEL \'ā-brə-ˌhamz\ (b. Nov. 26, 1858, London, Eng.—d. Oct. 6, 1925, Cambridge), one of the most distinguished Jewish scholars of his time, the author of *Jewish Life in the Middle Ages* (1896).

In 1902, after teaching at Jews' College, London, Abrahams was appointed reader in Talmudics (rabbinic literature) at the University of Cambridge. From 1888 to 1908 he was editor, jointly with Claude G. Montefiore, of the *Jewish Quarterly Review*. Although of strict Orthodox upbringing, Abrahams was among the founders of the Liberal movement, an Anglo-Jewish group that stressed the universality of Jewish ethics, minimized ritual and custom, and originally eschewed ZIONISM.

In *Jewish Life in the Middle Ages*, Abrahams concluded that Christian medievalism had a lasting effect on the Jews, particularly in deepening the process of Jewish isolation from the rest of society. *Studies in Pharisaism and the Gospels*, 2 vol. (1917–24), includes a series of essays based on an examination of the NEW TESTAMENT treatment of JUDAISM. Abraham's work *Chapters on Jewish Literature* (1899) surveyed the period from the fall of Jerusalem in 70 CE to the death of the Jewish philosopher MOSES MENDELSSOHN in 1786.

ABRAXAS \ə-'brak-səs\, *also spelled* abrasax \'a-brə-ˌsaks\, sequence of Greek letters considered as a word and inscribed on charms, AMULETS, and gems in the belief that it possessed magical qualities. Second-century GNOSTICISM, and other dualistic sects, as well, personified Abraxas and initiated a cult sometimes related to worship of the sun god. BASILIDES of Egypt, an early 2nd-century Gnostic teacher, viewed Abraxas as the supreme deity and the source of divine emanations, the ruler of all the 365 heavens, or circles of creation—one for each day of the solar year, 365 being the numerical value of the Greek letters in "abraxas."

Abraxas stone
By courtesy of the trustees of the British Museum

ABSALOM \'ab-sə-ləm\ (fl. c. 1020 BCE, Palestine), third and favorite son of DAVID, king of ISRAEL and JUDAH.

In 2 Samuel 13–19 Absalom was attractive, insolent, lawless, and doomed to a tragic fate. He is first mentioned as murdering his half brother Amnon, David's eldest son, in revenge for the rape of his sister Tamar. For this he was banished for a time. Later Absalom organized a revolt against David, and enjoyed initial success. When David fled with a few of his followers to Jordan, the usurper pursued them with his forces but was completely defeated in "the forest of Ephraim" (apparently west of Jordan). JOAB, Absalom's cousin, found Absalom entangled by the hair in an oak tree, and killed him. To David, the loss of his son, worthless and treacherous as he was, brought grief that outweighed his own safety and restoration.

ABSOLUTION, in CHRISTIANITY, the pronouncement of remission (forgiveness) of SINS to the penitent. In ROMAN CATHOLICISM and EASTERN ORTHODOXY, penance is a SACRAMENT and the power to absolve lies with the priest, who can grant release from the guilt of sin. In the NEW TESTAMENT the GRACE of forgiveness is seen as originating in JESUS CHRIST and being subsequently extended to sinners by members of the Christian PRIESTHOOD. In the early Christian church, the priest publicly absolved repentant sinners after they had confessed and performed their penance in public. During the Middle Ages, however, private CONFESSION became the usual procedure, and thus absolution followed in private. The priest absolved the penitent sinner using the formula, "I absolve thee from thy sins in the name of the Father and of the Son and of the HOLY SPIRIT." The Eastern Orthodox churches generally employ a formula such as "May God, through me, a sinner, forgive thee . . ."

In Protestant churches, absolution is usually a public rather than a private declaration. In general, Protestant churches have tended to confine absolution to prayers for forgiveness and the announcement of God's willingness to forgive all those who truly repent of their sins. In these denominations, absolution is neither a judicial act nor a means by which the forgiveness of sins is conferred but is, instead, a statement of divine judgment and divine forgiveness. Nevertheless, a formula for the public confession of sins and the public pronouncement of forgiveness is included in most Christian liturgies.

ĀBU, MOUNT \\'ä-bü\\, city, southwestern Rājasthān state, northwestern India, situated on the slopes of a mountain of the Ārāvalī Range for which it is named. It is an important PILGRIMAGE site in JAINISM and is regarded as one of the several *tīrtha-kṣetras* ("crossing grounds"), where liberated ARHATS (saints who are not considered to be *tīrthaṅkaras*) are said to have reached MOKṢA, or final emancipation. The medieval Jain temples at nearby Dilwara, built of white marble, are known for their exceptional beauty, especially the Tejpal temple, built about 1200 CE, which is known for the delicacy and richness of its carving.

ABŪ ḤANĪFA \\ə-ˌbü-ha-'nē-fä\\, *in full* Abū Ḥanīfa al-Nu'mān ibn Thābit (b. 699, Kufa, Iraq—d. 767, Baghdad), Muslim jurist and theologian whose systematization of Islamic legal doctrine (*see* SHARĪ'A) was acknowledged as one of the four canonical schools of Islamic law. The school of Abū Ḥanīfa acquired such prestige that its doctrines were applied by a majority of Muslim dynasties and are widely followed today in India, Pakistan, Turkey, Central Asia, and Arab countries.

Abū Ḥanīfa's native city was an intellectual center of Iraq, and he belonged to the *mawālī*, the non-Arab Muslims, who stimulated intellectual activity in Islamic lands. In early youth he was attracted to theological debates, but later, disenchanted with theology, he turned to law and for about 18 years was a disciple of Ḥammād (d. 738), then the most noted Iraqi jurist. After Ḥammād's death, Abū Ḥanīfa became his successor. He also learned from the Meccan traditionist 'Aṭā' (d. *c.* 732) and the founder of the SHI'ITE law, Ja'far al-Ṣādiq (d. 765).

By Abū Ḥanīfa's time a vast body of legal doctrine had accumulated from attempts to apply Islamic norms to legal problems, but a uniform code was lacking. Abū Ḥanīfa discussed each legal problem with his students before formulating any doctrine, attempting not only to address actual problems but to solve problems that might arise in the future. Because of his somewhat rationalist orientation and his reserve about traditions that were not well authenticated, his school was sometimes denounced as the school of *ra'y* (independent opinion), as opposed to that of HADITH (authoritative tradition).

As a speculative jurist, Abū Ḥanīfa imposed systematic consistency on legal doctrine. His decisions emphasize systematic over material considerations, disregarding established practices and judicial and administrative convenience in favor of systematic and technical legal considerations. Compared with those of his contemporaries, the Kufan ibn Abī Laylā (d. 765), the Syrian Awzā'ī (d. 774), and the Medinese Mālik (d. 795), his doctrines are more carefully formulated and consistent and his technical legal thought more highly developed and refined.

ABYDOS \\ə-'bī-dəs\\, *Egyptian* Abdu, *Coptic* Ebot, *modern* al-'Arabat al-Madfuna, prominent sacred city and one of the most important archaeological sites of ancient Egypt. The site, located in the low desert west of the Nile near al-Balyanā, was a royal NECROPOLIS of the first two dynasties and later a PILGRIMAGE center for the worship of OSIRIS.

Excavations at Abydos at the end of the 19th century by Emile-Clément Amélineau and Sir Flinders Petrie uncovered a series of pit tombs, apparently belonging to the kings of the first two dynasties of Egypt. Doubt has subsequently been raised as to whether these tombs actually held the pharaohs whose names they bore. Some of the 2nd-dynasty pharaohs, however, may in fact have been buried at Abydos, where imposing brick funerary enclosures were built at the northwestern end of the necropolis area.

The tutelary deity of the necropolis was the jackal god, called Khenti-amentiu in the Old Kingdom; in the 5th dynasty, his cult was gradually absorbed by that of Osiris, and the city soon became the focal point of the cult of Osiris. Abydos became a place of pilgrimage for pious Egyptians, who desired above all else to be buried as close as possible to the recognized tomb of Osiris, which was located at Abydos. For those who could not afford to be buried there, stelae were set up, inscribed with the dead man's name and titles and a prayer to the god. Thousands of these stelae have been found in the city's cemeteries.

The pharaohs, though now buried near their city of residence rather than at Abydos, encouraged the cult of the deified king at Abydos, and they took special care to embellish and enlarge the temple of Osiris there. Some pharaohs had a cenotaph or a MORTUARY TEMPLE at Abydos. The temple of Seti I, one of the most beautiful of all such temples, included seven sanctuaries, approached through two broad hypostyle halls. In a long gallery leading to other rooms is a relief showing Seti and his son Ramses making offerings to the cartouches of 76 of their dead predecessors beginning with Menes. Behind the temple of Seti I is a structure known as the Osireion; it is an underground hall containing a central platform with 10 monolithic pillars surrounded by a channel of water.

Around and between the various temples of Abydos is a vast complex of cemeteries used in every period of early Egyptian history, from the prehistoric age to Roman times.

ACESTES \ə-'ses-tēz\, in Greek mythology, legendary king of Segesta (*Greek* Egesta) in Sicily. His mother, Egesta, had been sent from Troy by her parents to save her from being devoured by a sea serpent. Going to Sicily she met the river god Crimisus, by whom she became the mother of Acestes.

Acestes appears notably in the Aeneid, offering hospitality to AENEAS when he lands in Sicily. Acestes' function is to emphasize the mythological connection of Sicily with Troy; in Greek legend Aeneas, whose descendants founded Rome, traveled no farther than Sicily. In the Aeneid Acestes brings the funeral games of ANCHISES, Aeneas' father, to a climax by shooting into the air an arrow that becomes a comet, a sign of Anchises' eternal life.

ACHILLES \ə-'ki-lēz\, in Greek mythology, son of the mortal PELEUS, king of the MYRMIDONS, and the NEREID, or sea NYMPH, THETIS. He was the greatest Greek warrior in the Trojan War. A non-Homeric tale relates that Thetis dipped the infant Achilles in the waters of the River STYX, making him invulnerable but for the part of his heel by which she held him—the proverbial "Achilles' heel."

As a youth Achilles, who was fated to die in battle, was sent to Scyros, where he was dressed as a girl and hidden among the king's daughters (one of whom, Deïdamia, bore him a son, NEOPTOLEMUS). The Greeks discovered him when Achilles could not resist examining a display of weapons.

In the 10th year of the war at Troy a quarrel with AGAMEMNON occurred when Achilles insisted that Agamemnon restore Chryseis, his prize of war, to her father, a priest of APOLLO, in order to stop a god-sent plague. Agamemnon retaliated by claiming Achilles' favorite slave girl, Briseis.

Achilles refused further service, and the Greeks were lost without him until Patroclus, Achilles' favorite companion, entered the fighting in Achilles' armor. The Trojan hero HECTOR slew Patroclus, and Achilles obtained new armor from the god HEPHAESTUS and slew Hector. After dragging Hector's body behind his chariot, Achilles eventually returned it to Hector's father, PRIAM. The *Iliad* makes no mention of the death of Achilles, though the *Odyssey* mentions his funeral. Later traditions stated that Achilles was slain by Priam's son PARIS, whose arrow was guided by Apollo.

ACIS \'ā-sis\, in Greek mythology, the son of Pan (FAUNUS) and the NYMPH Symaethis. He was a beautiful shepherd of

Achilles killing Penthesilea during the Trojan War, interior of an Attic cup, c. 460 BCE; in the Antikensammlungen, Munich
The Mansell Collection

Sicily, the lover of the NEREID Galatea. His rival, POLYPHEMUS the CYCLOPS, surprised them together and crushed him with a rock. His blood, gushing forth from beneath, was metamorphosed by Galatea into a river bearing his name, Acis or Acinius (the modern Jaci) at the base of Mount Etna. The story is in no other extant source but Ovid.

ACOLYTE (from Greek: *akolouthos*, "server," "companion," or "follower"), in ROMAN CATHOLICISM, a person permitted to assist in liturgical celebrations, especially the eucharistic liturgy. The first probable reference to the office is c. 189–199, and it was mentioned frequently in Roman documents after the 4th century. Acolytes also existed in North Africa but were unknown outside Rome and North Africa until the 10th century, when they were introduced throughout the Western church. The COUNCIL OF TRENT (1545–63) defined the order and hoped to reactivate it on the pastoral level, but it became only a step leading to the PRIESTHOOD. A directive of Pope Paul VI decreed that the office of acolyte should no longer be called a minor order but a ministry and that it should be open to laymen.

In the Eastern church, the order was not accepted. In Anglican and Lutheran churches, acolytes are generally laypersons who light the candles at church services.

ACONTIUS \ə-'kän-shē-əs, -shəs\, in Greek legend, a youth who, in love with the daughter of a noble family, wrote "I swear to wed Acontius" on an apple and threw it at her feet. She picked the apple up and read the words aloud, thus binding herself by an OATH that caused her to fall ill whenever she attempted to marry another. In response to an oracle she finally married Acontius.

ACOSMISM \ā-'käz-,mi-zəm\, in philosophy, the view that God is the sole and ultimate reality and that finite objects and events have no independent existence. Acosmism has been equated with PANTHEISM, the belief that everything is God. G.W.F. Hegel coined the word to defend Benedict de Spinoza, who was accused of ATHEISM for rejecting the traditional view of a created world existing outside God. Hegel argued that Spinoza could not be an atheist because pantheists hold that everything is God, whereas atheists make a godless world the sole reality.

Acosmism has also been used to describe the philosophies of Hindu VEDĀNTA, BUDDHISM (although Buddhism is not, in fact, an acosmic religion), and Arthur Schopenhauer.

ACOSTA, URIEL \ä-'kȯs-tə\, *original name* Gabriel Da Costa (b. c. 1585, Oporto, Port.—d. April 1640, Amsterdam,

Neth.), rationalist who became an example for Jews as a martyr to intolerance in his own religious community.

The son of an aristocratic family of Marranos (Spanish and Portuguese Jews forcibly converted to ROMAN CATHOLICISM), Acosta studied CANON LAW. Convinced that there was no salvation through the Roman Catholic church, he turned to JUDAISM. After converting his mother and brothers to his beliefs, they fled to Amsterdam. After CIRCUMCISION, he took Uriel as his given name.

Acosta soon decided that the prevailing form of Judaism was not biblical but rather an elaborate structure based on rabbinic legislation. He formulated 11 theses (1616) attacking RABBINIC JUDAISM as nonbiblical, for which he was excommunicated. Acosta then prepared a larger work condemning rabbinic Judaism and denying the immortality of the soul (1623–24). Acosta found it impossible to bear the isolation of EXCOMMUNICATION, though, and he recanted. Excommunicated again after he was accused of dissuading Christians from converting to Judaism, he made a public recantation in 1640 after enduring years of ostracism. After writing a short autobiography, *Exemplar Humanae Vitae* (1687; "Example of a Human Life"), he shot himself. *Exemplar* depicted revealed religion as disruptive of natural law and a source of hatred and superstition. In contrast, he advocated a faith based on natural law and reason.

ACTAEON \ak-'tē-ən\, in Greek mythology, a Boeotian hero and hunter. According to Ovid's *Metamorphoses*, Actaeon accidentally saw the virgin goddess ARTEMIS naked while she was bathing on Mount Cithaeron; she changed him into a stag and he was pursued and killed by his own hounds. In another version, he offended Artemis by boasting that his skill as a hunter surpassed hers.

The story was well known in antiquity, and several of the tragic poets presented it on the stage (*e.g.,* Aeschylus' lost *Toxotides*, "The Archeresses").

ACTA SANCTORUM \'ak-tə-saŋk-'tō-rəm\ (Latin: "Acts of the Saints"), vast collection of biographies and legends of the Christian saints.

The idea was conceived by Heribert Rosweyde, who intended to publish, from early manuscripts, 18 volumes of lives of the saints with notes attached. In 1629, with the death of Rosweyde, Jean Bolland was chosen to continue the work. Bolland and his associate Henschenius (Godefroid Henskens) modified and extended the original plan of the *Acta;* he arranged the saints according to the date of the observance of their deaths, included doubtful cases (but with notes), and added indexes, chronologies, and histories to each chapter. The parts completed during Bolland's life were *January* (2 vol., 1643) and *February* (3 vol., 1658), containing the biographies and legends of the saints whose feast days fell in those two months.

In his researches Bolland corresponded and traveled widely, investigating previously unexamined sources in Italian libraries. His work was continued by Henschenius and Papebroch (Daniel van Papenbroeck). From this core of hagiographers would develop the Bollandists, a small group of Belgian JESUITS who still edit and publish the *Acta Sanctorum.* In addition to the extensive amounts of biographical material that is of importance for both ecclesiastical and general history, this work is distinguished for its use of the principles of historical criticism.

ACTS OF THE APOSTLES, THE, *abbreviated as* Acts, fifth book of the NEW TESTAMENT, an invaluable history of the early Christian church that also throws light on the epistles of PAUL THE APOSTLE.

Acts was written in Greek, presumably by the Evangelist LUKE, whose gospel concludes where Acts begins, namely, with Christ's ASCENSION into heaven. Therefore, New Testament scholarship has come to view "Luke-Acts" as one book in two volumes. Acts was apparently written in Rome, perhaps between 70 and 90 CE. After an introductory account of the descent of the HOLY SPIRIT on the Apostles at PENTECOST (interpreted as the birth of the church), Luke pursues as a central theme the spread of CHRISTIANITY to the GENTILE world under the guiding inspiration of the Holy Spirit. He also describes the church's gradual drawing away from Jewish traditions. The missionary journeys of St. Paul are given a prominent place because this close associate of Luke was the preeminent apostle to the Gentiles.

'ĀDA \'ä-də\ (Arabic: "custom"), in Islamic law, a local custom that is given a particular consideration by judicial authorities even when it conflicts with some principle of Islamic law (SHARĪ'A). Muslim communities developed their *'āda*s before accepting ISLAM and did not abandon them entirely afterward. Thus among the Minangkabau in Indonesia, where many Muslims still retain traditions of other religions, a matriarchate is recognized, contrary to the Sharī'a; in parts of India, Muslims adopt children, forbidden by canon law, and then again circumvent the Sharī'a by providing them with an inheritance. Such *'āda*s are accepted by religious courts as legitimate local laws that must be respected in order to foster harmony in the community.

ADAB \'a-,dab, 'ä-,däb, 'ä-däb\, Islamic concept and literary genre distinguished by its broad humanist concerns; it developed during the height of 'Abbāsid culture in the 9th century and continued through the Muslim Middle Ages.

The original sense of the word was "norm of conduct," or "custom," derived in ancient Arabia from ancestors revered as models, but the term later acquired a connotation of good breeding, courtesy, and urbanity. *Adab* became the knowledge of poetry, oratory, tribal history, rhetoric, grammar, and philology that qualified a man to be called wellbred, or *adīb.* Such men produced an erudite *adab* literature of humanity and human achievements. They included such writers as the 9th-century essayist al-Jāḥiẓ of Basra and his 11th-century follower Abū Ḥayyān al-Tawḥīdī; the 9th-century Kūfan critic, philologist, and theologian Ibn Qutayba; and the 11th-century poet al-Ma'arrī.

As the golden age of the 'Abbāsids declined, however, the boundaries of *adab* narrowed into belles lettres: poetry, elegant prose, anecdotal writing (*maqāmāt*). In the modern Arab world *adab* merely signifies literature.

ADAD \'ā-,dad, 'ä-,däd\, weather god of the Babylonian and Assyrian pantheon. The name may have been brought into Mesopotamia by Amorites. His Sumerian equivalent was ISHKUR and the West Semitic was HADAD.

Adad's rains caused the land to bear grain, wine, and food; hence his title Lord of Abundance. His storms and hurricanes, evidences of his anger, brought darkness, want, and death. The bull and the lion were sacred to him. Adad's father was the heaven god ANU, but he is also designated as the son of BEL, Lord of All Lands and god of the atmosphere. His consort was Shalash, which may be a Hurrian name. The symbol of Adad was the cypress, and six was his sacred number. In Babylonia, Assyria, and Aleppo in Syria, he was also the god of oracles and DIVINATION.

Detail of an illustration of Adam and Eve by Giulio Clovio, from the Book of Hours *of Cardinal Alessandro Farnese, completed 1546*
By courtesy of the Pierpont Morgan Library, New York City

ADAM AND EVE \'a-dəm . . . 'ēv\, in the Judeo-Christian and Islamic traditions, the parents of the human race.

In the BIBLE there are two accounts of their creation. According to the PRIESTLY CODE (P) of the 5th or 6th century BCE (GENESIS 1:1–2:4a), God, or ELOHIM, on the sixth day of Creation created all the living creatures and, "in his own image," man both "male and female." God then blessed the couple, told them to be "fruitful and multiply," and gave them dominion over all other living things. According to the YAHWIST SOURCE (J) of the 10th century BCE (Genesis 2:4b–7, 2:15–4:1, 4:25), God, or YAHWEH, created Adam when the earth was still void, forming him from dust of the ground (*ha-ʾadamah*) and breathing "into his nostrils the breath of life." God then gave Adam the primeval GARDEN OF EDEN to tend but, on penalty of death, commanded him not to eat of the fruit of the "tree of knowledge of good and evil." Subsequently God created other animals but, finding these insufficient, put Adam to sleep, and from his rib fashioned Eve. The two were innocent until Eve yielded to the temptations of the serpent and Adam joined her in eating the forbidden fruit, whereupon they both recognized their nakedness and donned fig leaves as garments. God recognized their transgression and proclaimed their punishments—for the woman, pain in childbirth and subordina-

tion to man, and, for the man, the need to work the ground in toil and sweat for his subsistence.

Their first children were CAIN and ABEL. Abel, the keeper of sheep, was highly regarded by God and was killed by Cain out of envy. Another son, SETH, was born to replace Abel, and the two human stems, the Cainites and the Sethites, descended from them. Adam and Eve had "other sons and daughters," and death is said to have come to Adam at the age of 930.

Important works within JUDAISM that treat the Genesis story include GENESIS RABBAH. That work states that through Adam's SIN the perfection of Adam and all creation was lost (Genesis Rabbah 11:2; 12:6). Originally, Adam and Eve were created upright like the ANGELS (Genesis Rabbah 8:11), as fully developed adults (Genesis Rabbah 14:7), and were created last so as to have dominion over all earlier creation (Genesis Rabbah 19:4). At the time of Adam's creation some angels anticipated Adam's love and mercy, others the falsehood and strife he would bring. The philosopher PHILO JUDAEUS (d. 45–50 CE) said that the two creation narratives told of two distinct Adams, a heavenly Adam created in God's image, and another formed from the dust of the earth. This second Adam, though his mind was in the image of God, succumbed to physical passions by eating the fruit, and subsequently his intellectual capacity degraded.

In the Christian NEW TESTAMENT, Paul sees Adam as a forerunner to Christ, "a type of the one who was to come" (Romans 5:12). As Adam initiated the life of humans upon earth, so Christ initiates the new human life. Because of the sin of Adam, death came upon all men; because of the righteousness of Christ, life is given to all men. Thus it was Adam's sin and not failure to observe the Law that made the GENTILES sinners; therefore, all people stand in need of the GRACE of Christ. In later Christian theology, this view developed into the concept of ORIGINAL SIN.

In the QUR'AN (especially *sūra*s 2, 7, 15, 17, and 20), Allāh created Adam from clay but exalted him with such knowledge that the angels were commanded to prostrate themselves before him. All did but the angel IBLĪS (SATAN), who subsequently in the Garden tempted both Adam and his "wife" to eat of the forbidden fruit. Allāh then sent them down on earth, where their progeny were doomed to live as enemies, but offered Adam and his progeny eternal guidance if they would follow only him. According to Qurʾanic teachings, Adam's sin was his alone and did not make all people sinners. Later Islamic traditions have Adam descending from paradise to Ceylon (Sarandīb) and Eve descending to Jidda in Arabia; after a separation of 200 years, they met near Mount ʿArafāt and began conceiving children. The first two sons, Qābīl and Hābīl, each had a twin sister, and each son married his brother's sister. Qābīl subsequently killed Hābīl. Later, Shīth was born without a sister and became Adam's favorite and his spiritual heir (*wasī*). Eve eventually bore 20 sets of twins, and Adam had 40,000 offspring before he died.

ADAPA \'ä-dä-ˌpä\, in Mesopotamian mythology, legendary sage and citizen of Eridu. Adapa was endowed with vast intelligence by EA (Sumerian: Enki), the god of wisdom. One day while he was fishing, the south wind blew so violently that Adapa was thrown into the sea. In his rage he broke the wings of the south wind, which then ceased to blow. ANU (Sumerian: An), the sky god, summoned him to receive punishment, but the god Ea, who was jealous of Adapa, cautioned him not to touch the bread and water that would be offered. When Adapa came before Anu, the two heavenly doorkeepers TAMMUZ and NING-ISHZIDA interceded for him and explained that as Adapa had been endowed with omniscience he needed only immortality to become a god. Anu then offered Adapa the bread and water of eternal life, but he refused it, and mankind became mortal.

ADHĀN \a-'than\, Muslim call to Friday public worship and to the five daily times of prayer proclaimed by the MUEZZIN as he stands at the door or side of a small mosque or in the MINARET of a large one. Modern calls to prayer are commonly taped for broadcast over public address systems, radio, and television.

The *adhān* was originally a simple "Come to prayer," but, according to tradition, MUHAMMAD consulted his followers with a view to investing the call with greater dignity. The matter was settled when 'Abd Allāh ibn Zayd dreamed that the faithful should be summoned by a crier. The standard Sunnite (*see* SUNNI) *ad-hān* can be translated as: "God is

Sikh priest with the Ādi Granth
Foto Features

most great. I testify that there is no god but God. I testify that Muhammad is the Prophet of God. Come to prayer. Come to salvation. God is most great. There is no god but God." The first phrase is proclaimed four times, the final phrase once, and the others twice, the worshipers making a set response to each phrase. SHI'ITES add, "I testify that 'Ali is close to God (*walī Allāh*)" after testifying that Muhammad is the Prophet, and they say, "Come to the best of actions" after the call to salvation. These phrases are each repeated twice.

ĀDI-BUDDHA \'ä-dē-,bùd-də, -,bü-də, -,bú-də\, among some sects of MAHĀYĀNA BUDDHISM, the first, or self-existing, Buddha, from whom are said to have evolved the five DHYĀNI-BUDDHAS. Though the concept of an Ādi-Buddha was never generally popular, a few groups, particularly in Nepal, Tibet, and Java, elevated VAIROCANA to the position of Ādi-Buddha or named a new deity, such as Vajradhara or Vajrasattva, as the supreme lord. The Ādi-Buddha is represented in painting and sculpture as a crowned Buddha, dressed in princely garments and wearing the traditional ornaments of a BODHISATTVA.

ĀDI GRANTH \'ä-dē-'grənt, -'grən-tə\ (Punjabi: "Original Book"), the primary scripture of SIKHISM. The core of the *Ādi Granth* consists of hymns composed by NĀNAK (1469–1539), a Sikh GURŪ and the founder of the tradition. By the late 17th century, when the text reached its canonical form, the *Ādi Granth* included over 6,000 hymns and poems, of which over 4,500 were written by six Sikh Gurūs. The rest are attributed to bards associated with the 16th-century Sikh court and 15 non-Sikh saint-poets known in Sikh tradition as Bhagats ("devotees"). The language of these hymns might be called "sant bhāṣā," the lingua franca of medieval poets of northern India.

The text of the *Ādi Granth* is divided into three parts. It opens with a liturgical section comprising three daily prayers, to be recited at sunrise, sunset, and at the end of the day. The second section constitutes the main body of the text, and is divided into 31 separate subsections organized according to the musical mode (*rāga*) assigned for their singing. The final section includes hymns that are intended to be recited but are not set to music.

Gurū GOBIND SINGH (1666–1708, Gurū 1675–1708), the 10th Gurū of the Sikhs, is believed to have elevated the *Ādi Granth* to a unique position at the time of his death. He discontinued the lineage of living Gurūs and substituted for it the teaching authority of the *Ādi Granth*. Sikhs therefore customarily call the *Ādi Granth* the Śrī Gurū Granth Sāhib ("Honorable Gurū in book form"). Since Gurū Gobind Singh's time, the *Ādi Granth* has played the commanding role in Sikh devotional and ceremonial life. It is the Gurū to which reference is made when Sikh places of worship are called GURDWĀRAs ("houses of the Gurū"), occupying the central place both in the physical space itself and in every liturgy celebrated there. With few exceptions, Sikh homes contain the complete text of the *Ādi Granth* or a smaller version of it (*guṭkā*). The printed edition of the *Ādi Granth*, in its standard pagination, contains 1,430 pages.

ADITI \'ə-di-tē, 'ä-\ (Sanskrit: "the Boundless"), in the Vedic phase of Hindu mythology, the personification of the infinite. She is referred to as the mother of many gods, especially her sons, the Ādityas, who are a class of celestial deities. She supports the sky, sustains all existence, and nourishes the earth and thus is often represented as a cow.

The Ādityas vary in number from 6 to 12. VARUNA is their chief, and they are called like him "upholders of ṛta ('divine order')." In post-Vedic texts they include VISHNU in his AVA-TAR as the dwarf Vāmana and Vivasvat as the sun.

ADMETUS \ad-'mē-təs\, in Greek legend, son of Pheres, king of Pherae. Desiring the hand of Alcestis, the daughter of PELIAS, king of Iolcos, Admetus was required to harness a lion and a boar to a chariot. APOLLO yoked them, and Admetus obtained Alcestis. Finding that Admetus was soon to die, Apollo persuaded the Fates to prolong his life, on the condition that someone could be found to die in his place. Alcestis consented, but she was rescued by HERACLES, who successfully wrestled with Death at the grave.

ADONIS \ə-'dä-nis, -'dō-\, in Greek mythology, a youth of remarkable beauty, the favorite of the goddess APHRODITE. Traditionally, he was the product of an incestuous union between Smyrna/Myrrha and her father, the Syrian king Theias. Charmed by his beauty, Aphrodite put the newborn infant Adonis in a box and handed him over to the care of PERSEPHONE, the queen of the Underworld, who afterward refused to give him up. An appeal was made to ZEUS, who decided that Adonis should spend a third of the year with Persephone and a third with Aphrodite, the remaining third being at his own disposal. Adonis became an enthusiastic hunter and was killed by a wild boar. Aphrodite pleaded for his life with Zeus, who allowed Adonis to spend half of each year with her and half in the underworld.

Annual festivals called Adonia were held at Byblos and elsewhere in honor of Adonis. The name Adonis is believed to be of Phoenician origin (from *'adōn*, "lord").

ADOPTIONISM \ə-'däp-shə-,ni-zəm\, either of two Christian heresies: one, developed in the 2nd and 3rd centuries, is also known as Dynamic MONARCHIANISM and came to be called Adoptionism only in modern times; the other began in the 8th century in Spain and was concerned with the teaching of Elipandus, archbishop of Toledo. Wishing to distinguish in JESUS CHRIST the operations of each of his natures, human and divine, Elipandus referred to Christ in his humanity as "adopted son" in contradistinction to Christ in his divinity, who is the Son of God by nature. The son of MARY, assumed by the Word, thus was not the Son of God by nature but only by adoption.

In 798 Pope Leo III held a council in Rome that condemned the Adoptionism of Felix, bishop of Urgel (whose support Elipandus had gained), and anathematized him. Felix was forced to recant in 799 and was placed under surveillance. Elipandus remained unrepentant, however, and continued as archbishop of Toledo, but the Adoptionist view was almost universally abandoned after his death. A version of Adoptionism was temporarily revived in the 12th century in the teachings of PETER ABELARD.

ADRET, SOLOMON BEN ABRAHAM \ä-'dret\, *Hebrew* Rabbi Shlomo Ben Abraham Adret, *acronym* Rashba \räsh-'bä\ (b. 1235, Barcelona, Spain—d. 1310, Barcelona), spiritual leader of the Spanish Jewish community (known as El Rab de España ["the Rabbi of Spain"]); he is remembered partly for his controversial decree of 1305 threatening to excommunicate all Jews less than 25 years old (except medical students) who studied philosophy or science.

As a leading scholar of the TALMUD, Adret received inquiries on Jewish law from all over Europe, and his replies (more than 3,000 of which remain) strongly influenced the later development of codes of Jewish law. Adret's other writings include commentaries on the Talmud and polemics defending it against attacks by non-Jews.

Late in life, Adret became embroiled in a quarrel between the followers of the medieval Jewish philosopher MAI- MONIDES and the members of a conservative, antirationalist movement led by ASTRUC OF LUNEL, who believed that the followers of Maimonides were undermining the Jewish faith through their use of allegory in interpreting the BIBLE. Although Adret's ban against the study of philosophy and science did not bring about an end to such studies, it precipitated a bitter controversy among Jews in Spain and southern France that continued during his last years.

ADVAITA \əd-'vī-tə\ (Sanskrit: "Nondualism"), most influential of the schools of VEDĀNTA, a central philosophy of India. It has its historical beginning with the 7th-century thinker Gauḍapāda, author of the *Māṇḍūkya-kārikā*, a commentary in verse form on the *Māṇḍūkya Upaniṣad.*

Gauḍapāda, responding to the MAHĀYĀNA Buddhist philosophy of *śūnyavāda* ("emptiness"), argued that there is no duality; the mind, awake or dreaming, moves through MĀYĀ (illusion); and only nonduality *(advaita)* is the final truth. This truth is concealed by the ignorance of illusion. There is no becoming, either of a thing by itself or of a thing out of some other thing. There is ultimately no individual self or soul (JĪVA), only ĀTMAN (the ultimate self).

The philosopher Śaṅkara (c. 700–750) built further on Gauḍapāda's foundation, principally in his commentary on the *Vedānta Sūtra*s, the *Śārīraka-mīmāṃsā-bhāṣya* ("Commentary on the Study of the Embodied Self"). Śaṅkara argued that the *Upaniṣad*s teach the nature of BRAHMAN (the absolute). Fundamental for Śaṅkara is the tenet that only the nondual Brahman is ultimately real. The experience of selfhood is our primary means of access to this truth: self is not different from Brahman. To perceive this identity is to be released from the illusory thrall *(māyā)* of reality at its penultimate levels, filled with distinctions and dualities.

Śaṅkara points to scriptural texts, either stating identity ("You are that") or denying difference ("There is no duality here"), as declaring the true meaning of a Brahman without qualities (NIRGUṆA). Other texts that ascribe qualities (SAGUṆA) to Brahman refer not to the ultimate nature of Brahman but to its personality as God (ĪŚVARA).

Human perception of Brahman as differentiated and plural stems from a certain beginningless ignorance *(ajñāna, avidyā)* that follows almost necessarily from the conditions of existence. Yet the empirical world is not totally unreal, for it is a misapprehension of the real Brahman.

Śaṅkara had many followers who continued and elaborated his work, notably the 9th-century philosopher Vācaspati Miśra. The Advaita literature is extremely extensive, playing a major role in Hindu thought.

ADVENT (from Latin: *adventus*, "coming"), the Christian church's period of preparation for the celebration of the birth of JESUS CHRIST at CHRISTMAS and also of preparation for the SECOND COMING of Christ. It begins on the Sunday nearest to November 30 (St. Andrew's Day) and is the beginning of the church year. It is uncertain when the season was first observed; the Council of Tours (567) mentioned an Advent season.

Although a penitential season, Advent is no longer kept with the strictness of LENT, and fasts are no longer required. In many countries it is marked by a variety of popular observances, such as the lighting of Advent candles.

ADVENTIST \əd-'ven-tist, ad-; 'ad-,ven-\, member of any of a group of Protestant Christian churches arising in the United States in the 19th century and distinguished by their doctrinal belief that the SECOND COMING of JESUS CHRIST is close at hand. Adventism is rooted in Hebrew and Christian prophetism, messianism, and millennial expectations recorded in the BIBLE (see MILLENNIUM; MILLENNIALISM). Adventists believe that at Christ's Second Coming he will separate the saints from the wicked and inaugurate his millennial (1,000-year) kingdom.

History. It was in an atmosphere of millennialist revival in the United States that WILLIAM MILLER (1782–1849) began to preach. After a period of skepticism, he had a religious conversion and began to study the books of Daniel and REVELATION TO JOHN and to preach as a BAPTIST. He concluded that Christ would come, in conjunction with a fiery conflagration, sometime between March 21, 1843, and March 21, 1844, and was encouraged in his views by a number of clergymen and numerous followers.

When Christ did not return on the first appointed date, Miller and his followers set a second date, Oct. 22, 1844. The quiet passing of this day led to what is called the "Great Disappointment" among Adventists and the convening of a Mutual Conference of Adventists in 1845. Those who met, however, found it difficult to shape a confession and form a permanent organization.

Among those who persisted after the failure of Miller's PROPHECY were Joseph Bates, James White, and his wife, Ellen Harmon White. These Adventists, called Millerites in the press, believed that Miller had set the right date, but that they had interpreted what had happened incorrectly. Reading Daniel, chapters 8 and 9, they concluded that God had begun the "cleansing of the heavenly sanctuary"—i.e., an investigative judgment that would be followed by the pronouncing and then the execution of the sentence of judgment. What actually began in 1844, then, in their view, was an examination of all of the names in the Book of Life. Only after this was completed would Christ appear and begin his millennial reign. Though they did not set a new date, they insisted that Christ's Advent was imminent. They also believed that observance of the seventh day, Saturday, rather than Sunday, would help to bring about the Second Coming. These Millerites founded an official denomination, the SEVENTH-DAY ADVENTISTS, in 1863.

Other Adventist bodies emerged in the 19th century as a direct or indirect result of the prophecy of William Miller. These include the Evangelical Adventists (1845), Life and Advent Union (1862), Church of God (Seventh Day; 1866), Church of God General Conference (Abrahamic Faith; 1888), and the Advent Christian Church. These Advent Christians reject the teachings of the Seventh-day Adventists about SABBATH observance and dietary laws. They are congregational in polity and coordinate work in the United States and throughout the world through the Advent Christian General Conference of America. In 1964 the Advent Christian Church united with the Life and Advent Union.

Beliefs and practices. Seventh-day Adventists accept the authority of both the OLD TESTAMENT and NEW TESTAMENT. In their interpretation of Christ's ATONEMENT they follow a doctrine of ARMINIANISM, which emphasizes human choice and God's election, rather than a doctrine emphasizing God's sovereignty as in CALVINISM. They also argue that Christ's death was "provisionally and potentially for all men," yet efficacious only for those who avail themselves of its benefits.

In addition to the emphasis upon the Second Advent of Christ, two other matters set them apart from other Christians. First, they observe Saturday, rather than Sunday, as the Sabbath. This day, according to the Bible, was institut-ed by God since the Creation, and the commandment concerning Sabbath rest is a part of God's eternal law. Second, they avoid eating meat and taking narcotics and stimulants, which they consider to be harmful. Though they appeal to the Bible for the justification of these dietary practices, they maintain that these are based upon the broad theological consideration that the body is the temple of the HOLY SPIRIT and should be protected.

Institutions. Adventists stress tithing and therefore have a high annual giving per capita that allows them to carry on worldwide missionary and welfare programs. Sending out its first missionary, John Nevins Andrews, in 1874, Seventh-day Adventism eventually expanded into a worldwide movement, with churches in nearly every country by the late 20th century. By that time the church had more than 5,500,000 members.

The Advent Christian General Conference of America, the church's main governing body, has its headquarters in Takoma Park, Washington, D.C., and meets quadrennially. Local conferences provide pastoral oversight for the local congregations, which are governed by elected lay elders and deacons. The General Conference supervises evangelism in more than 500 languages, a large parochial school system, and numerous medical institutions called sanitariums. Publishing houses are operated in many countries, and Adventist literature is distributed door-to-door by volunteers.

AEACUS \'ē-ə-kəs\, in Greek mythology, son of ZEUS and Aegina, the daughter of the river god Asopus. Aeacus was celebrated for justice and in Attic tradition became a judge of the dead. His successful prayer to Zeus for rain during a drought was commemorated by a temple at Aegina, where a festival, the Aiakeia, was held in his honor.

AEDON \ā-'ē-dän\, in Greek mythology, a daughter of Pandareus of Ephesus. She was the wife of the king of Thebes. Envious of her sister-in-law, NIOBE, who had many children, she planned to murder Niobe's son, but by mistake killed her own son, Itylus. Turned by ZEUS into a nightingale, her song is a lament for her dead son.

AEGIS, also spelled egis, plural aegises, or egises, in ancient Greece, supernatural item, possibly a leather cloak or breastplate, generally associated with ZEUS, the king of the gods. Zeus's daughter ATHENA was most prominently associated with it, but occasionally another god used it—e.g., APOLLO in the Iliad. As early as Homer the aegis was decorated with golden tassels.

AENEAS \ē-'nē-əs, i-\, mythical hero of Troy and Rome, son of the goddess APHRODITE and ANCHISES. Aeneas was a member of the royal line at Troy and cousin of HECTOR. Homer implies that Aeneas did not like his position of subordinate to Hector, and from that suggestion arose a later tradition that Aeneas helped to betray Troy to the Greeks. The more common version, however, made Aeneas the leader of the Trojan survivors after Troy was taken by the Greeks. In any case, Aeneas survived the war.

As Rome expanded over Italy and the Mediterranean, its patriotic writers began to construct a mythical tradition that would at once dignify their land with antiquity and satisfy a latent dislike of Greek cultural superiority. The fact that Aeneas, as a Trojan, represented an enemy of the Greeks and that tradition left him free after the war made him peculiarly fit for the part assigned him, i.e., the founding of Roman greatness.

It was Virgil who gave the various strands of legend related to Aeneas the form they have possessed ever since. The family of Julius Caesar, and consequently of Virgil's patron Augustus, claimed descent from Aeneas, whose son ASCANIUS was also called Iulus. Virgil created his masterpiece, the *Aeneid* (written *c.* 29–19 BCE), portraying the journeying of Aeneas from Troy westward to Sicily, Carthage, and finally to the mouth of the Tiber in Italy.

When Troy fell, Virgil recounts, Aeneas was commanded by Hector in a vision to flee and to found a great city overseas. Aeneas gathered his family and followers and took the household gods (small images) of Troy, but, in the confusion of leaving the burning city, his wife disappeared. Her ghost informed him that he was to go to a western land where the Tiber River flowed. He then embarked upon his long voyage, touching at Thrace, Crete, and Sicily and meeting with numerous adventures that culminated in shipwreck on the coast of Africa near Carthage. There he was received by DIDO, the widowed queen. They fell in love, and he lingered there until he was sharply reminded by MERCURY that Rome was his goal. Guilty and wretched, he immediately abandoned Dido, who committed suicide, and Aeneas sailed on until he finally reached the mouth of the Tiber. There he was well received by LATINUS, the king of the region, but other Italians, notably Latinus' wife and TURNUS, leader of the Rutuli, resented the arrival of the Trojans and the projected marriage alliance between Aeneas and Lavinia, Latinus' daughter. War broke out, but the Trojans were successful and Turnus was killed. Aeneas then married Lavinia and founded Lavinium.

AEOLUS \'ē-ə-ləs\, in Greek mythology, controller of the winds and ruler of the floating island of Aeolia. In the *Odyssey* he gave ODYSSEUS a favorable wind and a bag in which the unfavorable winds were confined. Odysseus' companions opened the bag; the winds escaped and drove them back to the island.

AEON \'ē-ən, 'ē-,än\, *also spelled* eon (Greek: "age," or "lifetime"), in GNOSTICISM and MANICHAEISM, one of the orders of spirits, or spheres of being, that emanated from the Godhead and were attributes of the nature of the absolute.

The first aeon emanated directly from the unmanifest divinity and was charged with a divine force. As successive emanations of aeons became more remote from divinity they increased in number while they were charged with successively diminished force. At a certain level of remoteness, the possibility of error invaded the activity of aeons; in most systems, such error was responsible for the creation of the material universe. For many, JESUS CHRIST was the most perfect aeon who redeemed the error embodied in the material universe; the HOLY SPIRIT was usually a subordinate aeon. In certain systems, aeons were regarded positively as embodiments of the divine; in others, they were viewed negatively as vast media of time, space, and experience through which the human soul must painfully pass to reach its divine origin.

Aeon is also an important and frequently used term in the canonical books of the NEW TESTAMENT, where, with cognates, it occurs more than 100 times. In this usage, its original meaning was "age," it is, however, also translated in certain instances as "world."

AESIR \'ā-zir, 'a-, -sir\, *Old Norse* Æsir, *singular* Áss, in GERMANIC RELIGIONS, one of two main groups of deities. The other was called VANIR. Four of the Aesir were common to the Germanic nations: ODIN, god of war and poetry, magician, and chief of the Aesir; FRIGG or Frea, Odin's wife; TYR, god of war; and THOR, whose name was the Germanic word for thunder. Some of the other important Aesir were BALDER, Bragi, and possibly HEIMDALL.

AETHRA \'ēth-rə\, in Greek mythology, daughter of King Pittheus of Troezen and wife of Aegeus, king of Athens. She became mother of THESEUS by either Aegeus or POSEIDON. Later she guarded HELEN after she had been stolen from Sparta by Theseus; in retribution Aethra was made Helen's slave and followed her to Troy. Freed after the war, Aethra killed herself in grief for her son.

AFRICAN GREEK ORTHODOX CHURCH, religious movement in East Africa that represents a prolonged search for a more African-oriented form of CHRISTIANITY. It began when an Anglican in Uganda, Reuben Spartas, heard of the independent, all-black African Orthodox Church in the United States and founded his own African Orthodox Church in 1929. In 1932 he secured ORDINATION by the U.S. church's archbishop from South Africa, whose episcopal orders traced to the ancient Syrian Jacobite (MONOPHYSITE) Church of India. However, after concluding that the U.S. body was heterodox, the African Church added the term Greek and from 1933 developed an affiliation with the Alexandrian patriarchate of the Greek Orthodox church (*see* EASTERN ORTHODOXY).

In 1966 tensions arising from missionary paternalism, inadequate material assistance, and young Greek-trained priests who were not particularly African-oriented led Spartas and his followers into secession. The churches belonging to this new group, the African Orthodox Autonomous Church South of the Sahara, have asserted their African autonomy and accommodated to African customs (including polygamy and CLITORIDECTOMY [ritual circumcision of females]). At the same time, their vernacular versions of the Liturgy of St. John Chrysostom and use of vestments and ICONS represent a search for the connection with the primitive church.

AFRICAN METHODIST EPISCOPAL CHURCH, African-American Methodist denomination in the United States, formally organized in 1816. It developed from a congregation formed of African-Americans who withdrew in 1787 from St. George's Methodist Episcopal church in Philadelphia because of racial discrimination. They built Bethel African Methodist Church in Philadelphia, and in 1799 Richard Allen was ordained its minister by Bishop Francis Asbury of the Methodist Episcopal Church.

In 1816 Allen convoked African-American leaders of Methodist churches from several Middle Atlantic states to consider the future form of church organization among American Methodists of African origin. The outcome was the creation of the African Methodist Episcopal Church, and the selection and consecration of Allen as its first bishop. The new denomination soon established itself in other states, chiefly in the North, and then after the American Civil War also in the South. It also assumed a mandate to spread the gospel to the African continent, as well as to communities with African roots such as Haiti, where its first missionary was sent in 1827. As part of its mission, the African Methodist Episcopal Church founded colleges and seminaries, the best known of which is Wilberforce University in Wilberforce, Ohio (1856). Its more than 6,000 churches have a total membership of over two million.

AFRICAN RELIGIONS

Any attempt to generalize about the nature of "African religions" risks implying that there is homogeneity among all African cultures. In fact, Africa is a vast continent encompassing both geographic variation and tremendous cultural diversity.

Each of the more than 50 modern nations that occupy the continent has its own particular history and each in turn comprises numerous ethnic groups with different languages and unique customs and beliefs. African religions are as diverse as the continent is varied. Nevertheless, long cultural contact, in degrees ranging from trade to conquest, has forged some fundamental commonalities among religions within subregions, allowing for some generalizations to be made about the distinguishing features of indigenous religions. (Religions such as ISLAM or CHRISTIANITY that were introduced to Africa are not covered in this article.)

Although they often have been described as fixed and unchanging, in fact African indigenous traditions, like all religions, exhibit both continuity with the past and innovation. In the face of recent social, economic, and political upheavals, African religions have adapted to the changing needs of their communities.

WORLDVIEW AND DIVINITY

No single body of orthodox RELIGIOUS BELIEFS and practices can properly be identified as African. However, it is possible to identify similarities in worldviews and ritual processes across geographic and ethnic boundaries. Generally speaking, African religions hold that there is one creator God, maker of a dynamic universe. Myths commonly relate that after setting the world in motion, the Supreme Being withdrew and remains remote from the concerns of human life. The Dinka of The Sudan recount a myth, reiterated in many traditions across the continent, that explains that when the first woman lifted her pestle to pound millet, she struck the sky, causing God to withdraw. The story explains that although this withdrawal introduced toil, sickness, and death, it also freed humans from the constraints of God's immediate control. In fact, cults to the "high God" are notably absent from many African religions. Instead, prayers of petition or sacrificial offerings are directed toward secondary divinities, who are messengers and intermediaries between the human and sacred realms.

Fulani villagers of northern Nigeria celebrate the initiation of adolescent boys into adulthood
Peter Buckley—Photo Researchers

In West Africa, among the Ashanti of Ghana, elders regularly pour LIBATIONS and offer prayers to Nyame, the Creator, giving thanks and seeking blessing. But it is the veneration of matrilineal ancestors that is most significant in Ashanti ritual life, since they are considered the guardians of the moral order. According to the mythology of the Dogon of Mali, the Creator, Amma, brought the world into existence by mixing the primordial elements with the vibration of his spoken word. However, the principal cult is not to Amma but to the Nommo, primordial beings and first ancestors. In Nigeria the Yoruba hold that the Almighty Creator, Olorun, oversees a pantheon of secondary divinities, the *orisha*. Devotion to the *orisha* is active and widespread, but Olorun has neither priests nor cult group. Similarly, in the great lakes region of East Africa, the Supreme Being, Mulungu, is thought to be omnipresent but is sought in prayer of last resort; clan divinities are appealed to for intervention in most human affairs.

RITUAL AND RELIGIOUS SPECIALISTS

African religiousness is not a matter of adherence to a doctrine. Its focus is pragmatic, concerned with supporting fecundity and sustaining the community. African religions therefore emphasize maintaining a harmonious relationship with the divine powers within the cosmos, and their rituals attempt to harness cosmic powers and channel them for the good. Ritual is the means by which a person negotiates a responsible relationship within the community and with the ancestors, the spiritual forces within nature, and the gods.

The cults of the divinities are visible in the many shrines and altars consecrated in their honor. Shrines and altars are generally not imposing or even permanent structures. They can be as insubstantial as a small marker in a private courtyard. Right relations with the divinities are maintained through prayers, offerings, and sacrifices. The shedding of blood in ritual sacrifice releases the vital force that sustains life, and it precedes most ceremonies in which the ancestors or divinities are called upon for blessing. Blood sacrifice expresses the reciprocal bond between divinity and devotee.

Ancestors also serve as mediators by providing access to spiritual guidance and power. Death is not a sufficient condition for becoming an ancestor. Only those who lived a full measure of life, cultivated moral values, and achieved social distinction may attain this status. Ancestors are thought to reprimand those who neglect or breach the moral order by troubling the errant descendants with sickness or misfortune until restitution is made. When serious illness strikes, then, it is assumed that the cause is to be traced to interpersonal and social conflict. It is a moral dilemma as much as a biological crisis.

Ritual often marks a transition between physiological stages of life (such as puberty or death) coupled with a change in social status (as from child to adult). Such RITES OF PASSAGE are natural occasions for initiation, a process of socialization and education that enables the novice to assume the new social role. Initiation also involves the gradual cultivation of knowledge about the nature and use of sacred power. The Sande secret society of the Mande-speaking peoples is an important example, because its religious vision and political power extend across Liberia, Sierra Leone, Côte d'Ivoire, and Guinea. Sande initiates girls by teaching them domestic skills and sexual etiquette, as well as the religious significance of womanhood and female power. The society's sacred mask of the spirit Sowo reveals in iconographic form the association of women with water spirits and attests to the creative power of both. Among the mask's most striking features are the coils of flesh at the neck, representing concentric rings of water from which women, initially water spirits themselves, first emerged. The neck coils function like the HALO in Western art, signifying the wearer as human in form but divine in essence.

CIRCUMCISION and CLITORIDECTOMY are common and widespread rites of initiation. Although the surgical removal of the clitoris and parts of the labia minora is more radical and more dangerous than male circumcision, both forms of genital mutilation are understood to be important means by which gender is culturally defined. Within some cultures there exists the belief that genital surgery removes all vestiges of ANDROGYNY, as the anatomical parts correlating with the opposite sex are cut away. Cosmogonic myths justify the surgery as reiterating primordial acts that promoted fecundity. In this way religions define the sacred status of sex and fertility.

Possession trance is the most dramatic and intimate contact that occurs between devotee and divinity. In most cases possession is actively sought, induced through the ritual preparation of the participant. Techniques that facilitate this altered state of consciousness range from inhaling vapors of medicinal preparations to rhythmic chanting, drumming, and dancing. Although this practice may in some cases be reserved for religious specialists or priests, among the devotees of the *vodun* ("divinities") in Benin, any initiate may become a receptacle of the gods. The possessed are referred to as "horsemen," because they are "mounted" by the spirits and submit to their control. Once embodied, the presiding god engages the congregation in dialogue and delivers messages.

Contact with the divinities is not always so direct; mediators between the human and divine realms are often necessary. Specialists range from simple officiants at family altars to prophets, sacred kings, and diviners. Certain priests are invested with powers that identify them more fully with the gods. Thus, for the Dogon the *hogon* is not just a simple officiant but a sacred persona. His saliva is the source of the life-giving humidity, and his foot must not touch the earth directly or the ground would dry up. Such persons must submit to a number of ritual interdictions, because their ritual purity guarantees the sustained order of the world.

The power of a king is often derived from the association of kingship with the forces of nature. In Swaziland the king is both a political and a ritual leader; the ritual renewal of his office is performed in conjunction with the summer solstice, when the celestial bodies are at their most powerful. The king is purified and washed, and the water running off his body is thought to bring the first rains of the new season. Among the Yoruba a succession of kings became deified, and

The faces of Arusha boys from Tanzania are painted in preparation for the coming of age circumcision ceremony
George Holton—Photo Researchers

their histories were infused with myths about a royal pantheon of secondary divinities. Such is the case of Shango, once the king of Oyo, who now is an *orisha* associated with thunder.

Diviners are ritual specialists who have mastered a learned technique for reading signs that communicate the will of the divinities. Typically, diviners possess a gift of clairvoyance and are therefore considered to share in the power of insight that is usually reserved to the spirits. Divinatory ritual is the centerpiece of African religions, because it opens to all a channel of mediation with the gods. According to the Yoruba, 401 *orisha* "line the road to heaven." Diviners identify the personal *orisha* to which an individual should appeal for guidance, protection, and blessing.

Witches are also humans with intermediating power; however, theirs is ambiguous and therefore dangerous and must be controlled. The Gelede ritual masquerades of the Yoruba are lavish spectacles designed to represent and honor the "Great Mothers," elderly women considered to possess the secret knowledge of life itself, and the power of transformation. While considered "witches," the Great Mothers are not, however, the personification of evil. They can be beneficent, bringing wealth and fertility, or they can invoke disaster in the form of disease, famine, or barrenness. Because their power to intercede surpasses that of the ancestors or the divinities, they are called the "owners of the world." Gelede is therefore executed to appease the witches, in order to marshal their secret powers for the benefit of society. However, throughout Africa much misfortune is ultimately explained as the work of WITCHCRAFT, and diviners are sought to provide protective medicines and AMULETS.

MYTHOLOGY

In African oral cultures it is myths that embody philosophical reflections, express ultimate values, and identify moral standards. Unlike Western mythology, African myths are not recounted as a single narrative story, nor is there any established corpus of myth. Instead, myths are embedded and transmitted in ritual practice.

African mythology commonly depicts the cosmos anthropomorphically (*see* ANTHROPOMORPHISM).The human body is a microcosm and incorporates the same primordial elements and essential forces that make up the universe. Because the human body is conceived as the twin of the cosmic body, twinship is a predominant theme in much West African myth and ritual. According to COSMOGONY shared by the Dogon, Bambara, and Malinke peoples of Mali, the primordial beings were twins. Twins therefore represent the ideal. Every individual shares in the structure of twinship, in that the placenta is believed to be the locus of one's destiny and the soul's twin. Following a birth, the placenta is buried in the family compound and watered for the first week of the child's life. Among the Ashanti of Ghana, twins are permanently assigned a special status akin to that of living shrines, because as a sign of abundant fertility they are repositories of sacredness. For the Ndembu of the Democratic Republic of the Congo, by contrast, twins represent an excess of fertility more characteristic of the animal world than the human, and rituals are undertaken to protect the community from this anomalous condition.

The trickster is a prevalent type of mythic character in African mythology. Tricksters overturn convention and are notorious for pursuing their insatiable appetites and shameless lusts, even at the price of disaster. Yet even as the trickster introduces disorder and confusion into the divine plan, he paves the way for a new, more dynamic order. To the Fon of Benin, Legba is such a trickster. He is a troublemaker who disrupts harmony and sows turmoil. However, Legba is not viewed as evil but rather as a revered transformer. Like other such trickster figures, Legba presides over DIVINATION. Called the "linguist," he translates for humans the otherwise cryptic messages of Mawu, the Supreme Being. Through divination, he also allows for new possibility. Tricksters thus communicate an important paradox: The cosmos, although grounded in a divinely ordained order, is characterized by constant change.

NEW RELIGIONS, INDEPENDENT CHURCHES, AND PROPHETIC MOVEMENTS

New religious movements have proliferated in sub-Saharan Africa in the wake of European colonialism as one response of Africans to the loss of cultural, economic, and political control. Independent, or indigenous, churches have arisen largely in reaction against European Christian MISSIONS. The independent churches established in the 20th century have played a significant role in the postcolonial struggle for national independence. Religious vision and fervor, combined with the will for political self-determination, have inspired new movements throughout Africa. Today, independent churches constitute more than 15% of the total Christian population in sub-Saharan Africa.

The Harrist church was one of the first to receive the sanction and support of the state. Its founder, William Wadé Harris, was a prophet-healer who claimed that the angel GABRIEL visited him while he was in prison for participating in a political revolt in his native Liberia. After his release Harris moved to neighboring Côte d'Ivoire (where the European Christian missions had not been very successful) in order to lead his own vigorous evangelical campaign. (*See* HARRIS MOVEMENT.)

In contrast with indigenous religious systems, which are generated and sustained by the community, Christian prophetic movements are organized around an individual. However, these movements are like indigenous religions in that they are preoccupied with healing. Prophets are considered charged by God with the task of purifying the people and struggling against witchcraft. Public CONFESSIONS, EXORCISMS, and purifying BAPTISMS are dominant features. In the Democratic Republic of the Congo Simon Kimbangu inaugurated a healing revival in 1921 that drew thousands of converts to Christianity. Kimbangu's powerful ministry was viewed as a threat by Belgian colonial authorities, who arrested him. His imprisonment only stirred the nationalist fervor of his followers. The KIMBANGUIST CHURCH survived and was eventually recognized by the state. In 1969 the church, which now has more than 4 million adherents, was admitted to the WORLD COUNCIL OF CHURCHES.

In contrast, neotraditional movements retain elements of indigenous African belief and ritual within the context of Christian liturgy. These syncretic cults incorporate important aspects of African religious expression, such as the practice of secrecy characteristic of the Sande societies in West Africa, and fundamental beliefs, such as the reliance upon the intervention of ancestral spirits. An example is the Bwiti cult originating with the Fang of Gabon, which fused traditional ancestral cults with Christian symbolism and theology and messianic prophetic leadership. Such new African churches have tried to sustain a sense of community and continuity, even amidst rapid and dramatic social change.

Some scholars regard the new African religions as manifestations of social or religious protest—by-products of the struggle for political self-determination and the establishment of independent nation-states. However, the persistence and proliferation of indigenous religions suggest that they possess the necessary openness to experimentation and renewal to enable Africans to accommodate the changing character and needs of their communities.

Yoruba staff from southwestern Nigeria carried in ceremonial dances by devotees of the orisha *Shango*
Werner Forman Archive—
Art Resource

AFRICAN RELIGIONS, ART OF, artistic expression that alludes to RELIGIOUS BELIEFS and supports rituals of indigenous African faiths. Both African religion and African art have been subject to problematic interpretations based on evolutionary theories that were borrowed from biology and inappropriately applied to the social sciences and humanities. As a result, they have been characterized as "primitive." Additionally, in being perceived as "traditional" expressions, they have been deemed static and timeless. Assuming African art to be produced by anonymous, untrained artisans, Western museums have typically treated it as "artifact," housing it in museums of natural history rather than fine arts. In fact, although both African religion and African art do draw on indigenous legacies, they also allow for innovation and for the imaginative appropriation of new forms.

Generalizations about African aesthetics, without specific reference to peoples or their compositions, are perilous. However, one consistent aesthetic criterion is the achievement of balance between total abstraction and naturalistic representation. Realistic portraiture is avoided; instead, through stylized representation the African artist aims at achieving vividness and equilibrium. African sculptures successfully convey spiritual power precisely because they are not bound by resemblance.

Much African art aims at actualizing spiritual forces, not merely representing them. Moreover, objects do not embody power in their own right. They must be activated by an act of consecration or through repeated ritual. Statuettes called "FETISHES" give substance to invisible spiritual intermediaries. The Lobi of Burkina Faso carve such figures, which they call *bateba*. Once activated, the *bateba* can be invoked for aid but will die if neglected.

Masks and masquerading bring the plastic arts of sculpture and textiles into dynamic conjunction with the performing arts of music and dance. Whereas Westerners associate masks with disguise and pretense and tend to assume that masks represent spirits of the dead, this interpretation does not do justice to the complexity of masking traditions. In fact, the majority of figures depicted are not "spirits" but ancestors, CULTURE HEROES, and gods; significant events in which these mythic beings figure are sometimes reenacted in performances. Some masks are not anthropomorphic figures at all but complex superstructures representing cosmic dynamics or the cosmic order. Their forms are predicated on cosmological ideas as much as on formal, aesthetic qualities.

Another important intersection of art and religion is the sculptural representation of deities. In Nigeria, Shango, the Yoruba thunder god, is known for his unpredictable anger, likened to thunderbolts. His two-headed ax expresses his vital force and the ambiguity of power. Priests of Shango (both male and female) who experience possession trance carry staffs representing their dramatic access to Shango's power. The staff depicts a woman kneeling in supplication, while the symbolic two-headed ax extends from her head. The dark color of the staff represents the trance itself, the hidden quality of spiritual knowledge.

Nonfigurative art objects also mediate spiritual power. The stools of the Ashanti of Ghana provide earthly homes for departed kings and other ancestors. Made of wood from trees believed to be the abode of spirits, the stools are ceremonially blackened with a mixture of kitchen soot, spiders' webs, and eggs. The elements respectively represent wisdom, subjugation of enemies, and peace, honoring the function of the immortal guardians of social order.

Thus, African art objects belong to a broader realm of ritual experience and lose meaning when displayed as emblems of aesthetic judgment alone. On the other hand, preoccupation with context to the detriment of appreciation of style fails to do justice to the power of the form through which meaning is expressed.

ĀGAMA \ˈä-gə-mə\ (Sanskrit: "tradition, received teachings"), post-Vedic SCRIPTURES conveying ritual knowledge that are considered to have been revealed by a personal divinity. Śaivite scriptures, dating probably to the 8th century, are particularly so designated, in contrast to the Vaiṣṇava Saṃhitās and Śākta TANTRAS (*see* ŚAIVISM, VAIṢṆAVISM, *and* ŚĀKTISM). The texts are grouped according to the sects that follow a particular āgamic tradition—*e.g.*, the Śaiva-siddhānta or, on the Vaiṣṇava side, PĀÑCARĀTRA. The *āgama*s provide vital information on the earliest codes of temple building, image making, and religious procedure.

AGAMEMNON \ˌa-gə-ˈmem-ˌnän\, in Greek legend, king of Mycenae in Argos. He was the son (or grandson) of ATREUS and the brother of MENELAUS. After the murder of Atreus by a nephew, Aegisthus, Agamemnon and Menelaus took refuge with Tyndareus, king of Sparta, whose daughters, Clytemnestra and HELEN, they respectively married. By Clytemnestra, Agamemnon had a son, ORESTES, and three daughters, IPHIGENEIA (Iphianassa), ELECTRA (Laodice), and Chrysothemis. Menelaus succeeded Tyndareus, while Agamemnon recovered his father's kingdom.

After PARIS (Alexandros) carried off Helen, Agamemnon called on the chieftains of Greece to unite in war against the Trojans. He himself furnished 100 ships and was chosen commander of the combined forces. The fleet assembled at the port of Aulis in Boeotia but was prevented from sailing by calms or contrary winds that were sent by the goddess ARTEMIS because Agamemnon had in some way offended her. To appease the wrath of Artemis, Agamemnon sacrificed his own daughter Iphigeneia—although, in some versions of the myth an animal was substituted and Iphigeneia survived.

After the capture of Troy, Agamemnon returned with CASSANDRA, the daughter of PRIAM, as his war-prize, but upon arrival he was murdered by Clytemnestra and her lover Aegisthus. When his son Orestes had grown to manhood he returned and avenged his father by killing Clytemnestra and Aegisthus.

AGAPE \ə-ˈgä-pā, ä-, -pē; ˈä-gə-ˌpā, *chiefly Brit* ˈa-gə-pē\, *Greek* agapē, in the NEW TESTAMENT, the fatherly love of God for mankind, and mankind's reciprocal love for God. The term necessarily extends to the love of one's fellow man. The CHURCH FATHERS used agape to designate both a rite (using bread and wine) and a meal of fellowship to which the poor were invited. The historical relationship between the agape, the Lord's Supper, and the EUCHARIST is uncertain. Some scholars believe the agape was a form of the Lord's Supper and the Eucharist the sacramental aspect of that celebration. Others interpret agape as a fellowship meal held in imitation of gatherings attended by Jesus and his disciples; the Eucharist is believed to have been joined to this meal later but eventually to have become totally separated from it. The possibility that Jesus may have given a new significance to Jewish ritual gatherings of his day has complicated the problem of interpretation.

AGDISTIS: *see* GREAT MOTHER OF THE GODS.

AGGADAH \\,ä-gä-'dä, ə-'gä-də\: *see* HALA-KHAH AND HAGGADAH.

AGLAUROS \ə-'glȯr-əs\, in Greek mythology, eldest daughter of the Athenian king CE-CROPS. Aglauros died with her sisters by leaping from the Acropolis after seeing the infant Erechthonius, a human with a serpent's tail. Aglauros had a SANCTUARY on the Acropolis in which young men of military age swore an OATH to her as well as to ZEUS and to other deities. The honor, however, may have stemmed from another legend—that Aglauros had sacrificed herself for the city during a protracted war.

AGNI \'əg-nē\ (Sanskrit: "Fire"), in HIN-DUISM, a fire god second only to INDRA in the VEDIC mythology of ancient India. He is equally the fire of the sun, of lightning, and of the hearth—hence, of all three levels in the Vedic COSMOLOGY. As the fire of sacrifice, he is the mouth of the gods, the carrier of the oblation, and the mes-

Agni with characteristic symbol of the ram; in the Guimet Museum, Paris
Giraudon—Art Resource

senger between human and divine. Agni is ruddy-hued and has two faces—one beneficent and one malignant. In the RG VEDA he is sometimes identified with RUDRA, the forerunner of the later god SHIVA. Though Agni has no independent sect in modern Hinduism, he is invoked in many ceremonies, and where Vedic rites persist, as in weddings, his presence is central.

AGNOSTICISM (from Greek: *agnōstos*, "unknowable"), the doctrine that humans cannot know the existence of anything beyond the phenomena of their experience. The term has come to be equated in popular parlance with skepticism about religious questions.

Agnosticism both as a term and as a philosophical position gained currency through its espousal by Thomas Huxley (1825–95), who is thought to have coined the word agnostic (as opposed to "gnostic") in 1869 to designate one who repudiated traditional Judeo-Christian THEISM and yet disclaimed doctrinaire ATHEISM, in order to leave such questions as the existence of God in abeyance.

There are thus two related but nevertheless distinct viewpoints suggested by the term. It may mean no more than the suspension of judgment on religious questions about God's existence for lack of critical evidence. But Huxley's own elaboration on the term makes clear that the suspension of judgment on questions about God's existence was thought to invalidate Christian beliefs about "things hoped for" and "things not seen." Huxley's role in the struggle over the teachings of Charles Darwin helped to establish this connotation as the primary one in the definition of agnosticism. When such prominent defenders of the Darwinian hypothesis as Clarence Darrow likewise labeled themselves as agnostics, the writers of popular apologetic pamphlets found it easy to equate agnosticism with hostility to conventional Christian tenets.

AGNUS DEI \'äg-,nüs-'dä-ē, 'än-,yüs-; 'ag-nəs-'dā, -'dē-,ī\ (Latin), *English* Lamb of God, designation of JESUS CHRIST in Christian liturgical usage. It is based on the saying of JOHN THE BAPTIST: "Behold, the Lamb of God, who takes away the sin of the world!" (John 1:29). In the liturgy of ROMAN CATHOLICISM the Agnus Dei is employed in the following text: "Lamb of God, who takest away the sins of the world, have mercy upon us! Lamb of God, who takest away the sins of the world, have mercy upon us! Lamb of God, who takest away the sins of the world, grant us peace!" It comes between the LORD'S PRAYER and the EUCHARIST and unites the sacrifice of the liturgy to the sacrifice of Christ on the Cross as the Lamb of God, calling to mind the sacrifice of the lamb in the cultus of the OLD TESTAMENT. The churches of the ANGLICAN COMMUNION and of LUTHERANISM have both retained the Agnus Dei in their eucharistic rites.

The name is also applied to figures of Christ as the Lamb of God, especially to waxen disks impressed with this figure and blessed by the pope.

AGRIONIA \,a-grē-'ō-nē-ə\ (from Greek: *agrios*, "wild," or "savage"), in ancient GREEK RELIGION, a festival celebrated annually in Boeotia and elsewhere in honor of DIONYSUS. Myth states that the daughters of Minyas, king of Orchomenus, having ignored the rites of the god, were driven mad by Dionysus and ate the flesh of one of their children; as punishment they were turned into bats or birds.

AHAB \'ā-,hab\, *also spelled* Achab (fl. 9th century BCE), seventh king of the northern kingdom of Israel (reigned *c.* 874–*c.* 853 BCE), according to the OLD TESTAMENT (1 Kings 16:29–22:40), and son of King Omri (1 Kings 16:29–30). External to the BIBLE, the reign of Ahab is mentioned in the monolith inscription of King Shalmaneser III of Assyria and in the Moabite Stone, although the latter does not specifically name Ahab.

Omri left to Ahab an empire that comprised not only territory east of the Jordan River, in Gilead and probably Bashan, but also the land of Moab, whose king was tributary (according to the Moabite Stone). The southern kingdom of JUDAH, if not actually subject to Omri, was certainly a subordinate ally. Ahab's marriage to JEZEBEL, daughter of Ethbaal of Sidon, revived an alliance with the Phoenicians that had been in abeyance since the time of SOLOMON.

Throughout Ahab's reign, however, a fierce border war was waged with Syria (1 Kings 20ff.) in which Israel, in spite of occasional victories, proved the weaker, and in the meantime Mesha, king of Moab, successfully revolted and occupied the southern portions of the territory of GAD. The forces of Israel retained enough strength to contribute the second-largest contingent of soldiers to the combined armies that checked the westward movement of Shalmaneser III at Karkar. After the Assyrians were repulsed, however, the alliance broke up, and Ahab met his death fighting the Syrians in a vain attempt to recover Ramoth-Gilead (1 Kings 22:34–37; 2 Chronicles 18).

Jezebel attempted to set up the worship of the Canaanite god BAAL in the capital city of Samaria and to maintain the Oriental principle of the absolute power and authority of the sovereign (1 Kings 16:31–33). This roused the hostility of a conservative party which held to traditional Hebrew democratic conceptions of society and adhered to the worship of the national god, YAHWEH. As representative of this party, the prophet ELIJAH protested against both the establishment of the Baal priests and Ahab's judicial murder of Naboth (1 Kings 18; 21:17–29). To the reign of Ahab may be traced the beginning of that sapping of the national life which led to the condemnations of the 8th-century prophets and to the downfall of Samaria.

AHAZ \'ā-,haz\, *also spelled* Achaz \'ā-,kaz\, *Assyrian* Jehoahaz \ji-'hō-ə-,haz\ (fl. 8th century BCE), king of JUDAH (*c.* 735–720 BCE) who became an Assyrian vassal (2 Kings 16; 2 Chronicles 28; Isaiah 7–8).

Ahaz's kingdom was invaded by Pekah, king of ISRAEL, and Rezin, king of Syria, in an effort to force him into an alliance with them against Assyria. Acting against the counsel of the prophet ISAIAH, Ahaz appealed for aid to Tiglath-pileser III, king of Assyria. Assyria defeated Syria and Israel, and Ahaz presented himself as a vassal to the Assyrian king. Soon Assyria exacted a heavy tribute and the Assyrian gods were introduced into the TEMPLE OF JERUSALEM.

AHIṂSĀ \ə-'him-,sä, -'hiⁿ-\ (Sanskrit: "noninjury"), the fundamental ethical virtue of the Jains of India, highly respected in HINDUISM and BUDDHISM as well. In modern times, MAHATMA GANDHI developed his theory of passive political resistance on the principle of *ahiṃsā*.

In JAINISM, *ahiṃsā* is the standard by which all actions are judged. For householders observing the small vows (*anuvrata*), the practice of *ahiṃsā* requires that they not kill any animal life, but for ascetics observing the great vows (*mahāvrata*), *ahiṃsā* requires that no knowing or unknowing injury be inflicted on any living substance. Living matter (*jīva*) includes humans, animals, insects, plants, and atoms, and the same law governs the entire cosmos. The interruption of another *jīva*'s spiritual progress increases one's own karmic load and delays one's liberation from the cycle of rebirths. Many Jain practices, such as not eating or drinking after dark or the wearing of cloth mouth-covers (*mukhavastrikā*) by monks, are based on this principle.

AHĪR \ə-'hir\, cattle-tending CASTE widespread in northern and central India. Their name connects them to the Ābhīras of Sanskrit literature, who are mentioned in the epic MAHĀBHĀRATA. Certain scholars have contended that these cattlemen, once concentrated in southern Rajasthan and Sind, played an important role in the early development of the god KRISHNA as the cowherd; others dispute the notion. However one resolves the historical issue, residents of the Braja (Vraja) region in Uttar Pradesh, where Krishna is regarded as having spent his pastoral boyhood, often identify him as an Ahīr.

AHITHOPHEL \ə-'hi-thə-,fel\, in the OLD TESTAMENT, one of King DAVID'S most trusted advisers who took a leading part in the revolt of David's son ABSALOM. Ahithophel's defection was a severe blow to David. Having consulted Ahithophel

about his plans to proceed against David, Absalom then sought advice from Hushai, another of David's counselors. Hushai betrayed Absalom's cause by deliberately proposing an inferior scheme, which Absalom accepted. Ahithophel, recognizing that Hushai had outwitted him, foresaw the disastrous defeat of Absalom's forces and took his own life (2 Samuel 15:31–37; 16:20–17:23).

AH KIN \'äh-'kēn\ (Mayan: "He of the Sun"), regular clergy of the Yucatec Maya in PRE-COLUMBIAN MESO-AMERICAN RELIGIONS. The Yucatec title Ah Kin (from *ah*, "the holder of a certain position" and *kin*, "sun, day, feast day") might be loosely translated "the day-priest," or "the calendar-priest." The Ah Kin are known historically for their performance in the ritual sacrifice of victims, whose hearts were offered to the Mayan gods. The chief priest (Ah Kin Mai) served in the various capacities of administrator, teacher, healer, astronomer, adviser to the chief, and diviner. The office of Ah Kin was hereditary, passing from priests to their sons, but training was also extended to the sons of the nobility who showed inclinations toward the PRIESTHOOD.

AHL AL-BAYT \,ä-həl-äl-'bīt, ,äl-äl-\ (Arabic: "People of the House"), designation in ISLAM for the holy family of the Prophet MUHAMMAD, particularly his daughter FĀṬIMA, her husband ʿALĪ (who was also Muhammad's cousin), and their descendants.

SHIʿITES closely identify this family with the IMAMS, whom they regard as the legitimate holders of authority in the

Exercising the Jain principle ahiṃsā, *a Satish Jain feeds grain to crows in a New Delhi marketplace as a service to God*
Reuters—Kamal Kishore/Archive Photos

Muslim community, the infallible bearers of sacred knowledge, and the source of messianic deliverance in the end time. Since the 12th and 13th centuries most SUFI orders have included members of the Prophet's family in their elaborate spiritual lineages (silsilas), which they trace back to the Prophet through 'Alī

Aside from MECCA, shrines containing the remains of members of the Prophet's family and their heirs are the most popular Muslim PILGRIMAGE centers. These include the shrines of 'Alī in NAJAF (Iraq), HUSAYN in KARBALĀ' (Iraq) and Cairo (Egypt), 'ALĪ AL-RIDĀ in MASHHAD (Iran), and Mu'īn al-Dīn Chistī in Ajmer (western India). In many Muslim societies people known as SHARĪFS and SAYYIDS hold privileged status by descent from the holy family. Among those claiming such status in the 20th century were King Ḥasan II of Morocco (b. 1929), King Hussein of Jordan (1935–99), Ṣaddam Hussein of Iraq (b. 1937), and ABŪ'L-'ALĀ' MAWDŪDĪ of India/Pakistan (1903–79). *See also* TARIQA; ZIYARA.

AHL AL-KITĀB \,ä-həl-ål-kē-'tab, ,äl-ål-\ (Arabic: "People of the Book"), in Islamic thought, those who are possessors of divine books (*i.e.*, the TORAH, the GOSPEL, and the AVESTA of ZOROASTRIANISM), as distinguished from those whose religions are not based on divine revelations.

The Prophet MUHAMMAD gave many privileges to *Ahl al-kitāb* that are not to be extended to others, including freedom of worship; thus, during the early Muslim conquests, Jews and Christians were not forced to convert to ISLAM. Muslim authorities are responsible for the protection of *Ahl al-kitāb*, for, "he who wrongs a Jew or a Christian will have myself [the Prophet] as his indicter on the day of judgment." After Muhammad's death, his successors sent instructions to their generals and provincial governors not to interfere with *Ahl al-kitāb* in their worship and to treat them with full respect.

Muslim men may marry women from *Ahl al-kitāb* even if the latter choose to remain in their religion; Muslim women, however, are not allowed to marry men from *Ahl al-kitāb* unless they convert to Islam. The children resulting from such mixed marriages must be raised as Muslims, according to the SHARĪ'A.

AHL-E ḤAQQ \,ä-hə-le-'häk, ,ä-le-\ (Arabic: "People of Truth," or "People of God"), *also mistakenly called* 'Alī Ilāhīs, *or* 'Aliyu'llāhīs ("Adherents to the Divinity of 'Alī"), secret, loosely organized, syncretistic religion appearing in the 15th century. Their beliefs were derived largely from IS-LAM. The religion is centered in western Iran and Iraq and is especially prevalent among the Kurds and Turkmens. They retain the 12 IMAMS of ITHNĀ 'ASHARĪYAH Shi'ism and certain aspects of Islamic MYSTICISM. Influenced by extremist SHĪ'ITE groups (GHULĀT), they preach seven successive manifestations of God and the transmigration of souls, which pass through 1,001 incarnations and in the process receive the proper reward for their actions. The ultimate purification (becoming "luminous") is limited to those who in the initial creation were destined to be good and were created of yellow, rather than black, clay. On the Day of Judgment the good will enter Paradise and the wicked will be annihilated. Their rites include animal sacrifice.

The chief source of information about the sect are the *Furqān al-akhbār* and the *Shāhnāma-ye ḥaqīqāt*, written in the late 19th or early 20th century by Hājj Ni'matallāh.

AHMAD BĀBĀ \'äk-məd-'bä-bä\, *in full* Abū al-'Abbās Aḥmad ibn Aḥmad al-Takrūrī al-Massūfī (b. Oct. 26, 1556, Arawān, near Timbuktu, Songhai Empire—d. April 22, 1627, Timbuktu), jurist, writer, and a cultural leader of the western Sudan.

A descendant of a line of jurists, Aḥmad Bābā was educated in Islamic culture, including jurisprudence. His *fatwās* (legal opinions) are noted for their clarity of thought and clear exposition of Islamic judicial principles (*see* SHARĪ'A). He also compiled *Nail al-ibtihāj*, a biographical dictionary of the famous MĀLIKĪ LEGAL SCHOOL (one of the four schools of Islamic law) jurists; this work is still an important source of information concerning the lives of Mālikī jurists and Moroccan religious personalities.

AHMADĪYA \,äh-má-'dē-ə\, a modern Islamic sect and the generic name for various SUFI (Muslim mystic) orders. The sect was founded in Qādiān, the Punjab, India, in 1889 by MĪRZĀ GHULĀM AHMAD (c. 1839–1908), who claimed to be the *mahdī* (*see* MAHDI), the Christian MESSIAH, an incarnation of the Hindu god KRISHNA, and a reappearance (*burūz*) of MU-HAMMAD. The sect preaches, among other tenets, that JESUS feigned death and RESURRECTION but in actuality escaped to India, where he died at the age of 120, and that JIHAD represents a battle against unbelievers to be waged by peaceful methods rather than by violent military means.

On the death of the founder, Mawlawī Nūr-al-Dīn was elected by the community as *khalīfa* ("successor"). In 1914, when he died, the Aḥmadīya split. The original, Qādiānī, group recognized Ghulām Aḥmad as prophet (*nabīā*) and his son Hadrat Mīrzā Bashīr al-Dīn Maḥmūd Aḥmad as the second CALIPH. The new Lahore society, however, accepted Ghulām Aḥmad only as a reformer (*mujaddid*).

The Qādiānīs relocated to Rabwah, Pakistan, in 1947; there are also communities in India and West Africa as well as in Great Britain, Europe, and the United States. They are a highly organized community with a considerable financial base. They are zealous missionaries, preaching Aḥmadī beliefs as the one true ISLAM, with Muhammad and Mīrzā Ghulām Aḥmad as prophets.

Members of the Lahore group are also proselytizers, though more concerned in gaining converts to Islam than to their particular sect. Led from its inception by Mawlānā Muhammad 'Alī until his death in 1951, the sect has been active in English- and Urdu-language publishing and in liberalizing Islam.

Aḥmadīya also designates several Sufi orders, the most important of which is that of Egypt named after Aḥmad al-Badawī, one of the greatest saints of Islam (d. 1276). Al-Badawī achieved great fame for his knowledge of Islamic sciences, but he eventually abandoned speculative theology and devoted himself to contemplation in seclusion. Soon he became known as a miracle-working saint and had thousands of followers. He arrived in Ṭanṭā (north of Cairo, Egypt) in 1236. His followers were also called Sutūhīya from *ashāb al-saṭh* (the people of the roof); according to one anecdote, when al-Badawī arrived at Ṭanṭā, he climbed upon the roof of a private house and stood motionless looking into the sun until his eyes became red and sore. This action was then imitated by some of his followers. After al-Badawī's death, the Aḥmadīya was headed by 'Abd al-'Āl, a close disciple who ruled the order until his death in 1332. Before his death, 'Abd al-'Āl ordered a shrine built on al-Badawī's tomb, which was later replaced by a large mosque.

The Aḥmadīya order, which is representative of certain types of dervishes, faced great opposition from Muslim legalists, who, in general, opposed all Sufism, and from political figures who felt threatened by the order's tremendous popular influence. The Aḥmadīya is one of the most popular orders in Egypt, and the three yearly festivals in honor of al-Badawī are major celebrations. Numerous minor orders are considered branches of the Aḥmadīya and are spread all over the Islamic world. Among these are the Shinnāwīya, the Kannāsīya, the Bayyūmīya, the Sallāmīya, the Ḥalabīya, and the Bundārīya.

AḤMAD KHAN, SAYYID \'a-mad-'k̲ä̲n\, *also called* Sir Sayyid (b. Oct. 17, 1817, Delhi—d. March 27, 1898, Alīgarh, India), Muslim educator, jurist, and author, founder of the Anglo-Mohammedan Oriental College at Alīgarh, Uttar Pradesh, India (now called ALĪGARH MUSLIM UNIVERSITY), and the principal motivating force behind the revival of Indian ISLAM in the late 19th century. In 1888 he was made a Knight Commander of the Star of India.

After a limited education Aḥmad Khan became a clerk with the East India Company in 1838. He qualified three years later as a subjudge and served in the judicial department at various places.

His career as an author (in Urdu) started at the age of 23 with religious tracts. In 1847 he brought out a noteworthy book, *Āthār al-ṣanādīd* ("Monuments of the Great"), on the antiquities of Delhi. Even more important was his pamphlet, "The Causes of the Indian Revolt." During the Indian Mutiny of 1857 he had taken the side of the British, but in this booklet he laid bare the weaknesses and errors of the British administration that had led to countrywide dissatisfaction and eventual rebellion. The booklet had considerable influence on British policy. Meanwhile, he began a sympathetic interpretation of the BIBLE, wrote *Essays on the Life of Mohammed* (1870), and wrote several volumes of a modernist commentary on the QUR'AN. In these works he sought to harmonize the Islamic faith with the scientific and politically progressive ideas of his time.

In 1867 he was transferred to Benares (now VARANASI), a city with great religious significance for the Hindus. About the same time a movement started at Benares to replace Urdu, the language cultivated by the Muslims, with Hindi. This movement and the attempts to substitute Hindi for Urdu in the publications of the Scientific Society convinced Aḥmad Khan that the paths of the Hindus and the Muslims must diverge. Thus, during a visit to England (1869–70) he prepared plans for a great educational institution, described as "a Muslim Cambridge." On his return he set up a committee for the purpose and also started an influential journal, *Tahdhīb al-akhlāq* ("Moral Reform"), for the "uplift and reform of the Muslim"; out of these efforts grew Alīgarh Muslim University. In 1886 he organized the All-India Muhammadan Educational Conference, which met annually at different places to promote education and to provide the Muslims with a common platform. Until the founding of the Muslim League in 1906, it was the principal national center of Indian Islam.

Aḥmad Khan advised the Muslims against joining active politics. He argued that, in a country where communal divisions were all-important and education and political organization were confined to a few classes, parliamentary democracy would work only inequitably. Muslims, generally, followed his advice and abstained from politics until several years later when they had established their own political organization.

AḤMED YESEVĪ \äk-'met-ˌye-se-'vē\, *also spelled* Aḥmad Yasawī \äk-'med-ˌyä-sä-'vē\ (b. second half of the 11th century, Sayrām [now in Kazakhstan]—d. 1166, Yasī, Turkistan [now Turkmenistan]), poet and Sufi (*see* SUFISM) mystic who exerted a powerful influence on the development of mystical orders throughout the Turkish-speaking world.

Legends indicate that his father died when the boy was young and his family moved to Yasī, where he began his mystical teaching, hence his name. He is said to have gone to Bukhara to study with the great Sufi leader Yūsuf Hamadānī and other famous mystics. Finally he returned to Yasī. The extant work attributed to the poet is the *Dīvān-i Ḥikmet* ("Book of Wisdom"), containing poems on mystical themes. Scholars believe that they are probably not his though they are probably similar in style and sentiment to what he wrote. Legends about his life were spread throughout the Turkish Islamic world, and he developed a tremendous following. The conqueror Timur erected a magnificent mausoleum over his grave in 1397/98, which attracted pilgrims who revered him as a saint.

Aḥmed Yesevī wrote poetry for the people, and his mystical order was a popular Islamic brotherhood that also preserved ancient Turco-Mongol practices and customs in their ritual. His poetry deeply influenced Turkish literature, paving the way for the development of mystical folk literature.

AHRIMAN \ah-ˌrē-'man; 'är-i-mən, -ˌmän\, *Avestan* Angra Mainyu ("Destructive Spirit") \aŋ-'ra-mīn-'yü\, the evil spirit in the dualistic doctrine of ZOROASTRIANISM. His essential nature is expressed in his principal epithet—Druj, "the Lie." The Lie expresses itself as greed, wrath, and envy. To aid him in attacking the light, the good creation of AHURA MAZDĀ, Ahriman created DEMONS embodying envy and similar qualities. Believers expect Ahriman to be defeated in the end of time by Ahura Mazdā. PARSIS tend to see Ahriman as an ALLEGORY of human evil.

AḤSĀ'Ī, AḤMAD AL- \ˌäl-äk̲-'sä-ē, -'sī\, *in full* Shaykh Aḥmad ibn Zayn al-Dīn Ibrāhīm al-Aḥsā'ī (b. 1753, Al-Ḥasa, Arabia [now in Saudi Arabia]—d. 1826, near Medina), visionary and founder of the SHI'ITE Muslim Shaykhī sect of Iran and Iraq.

After nearly 50 years of study and travel in eastern Arabia and Iraq, al-Aḥsā'ī taught religion in Yazd and Kirmanshah, Persia. His interpretation of Shi'ism attracted many followers, including the Qajar rulers, but also aroused controversy. He claimed knowledge directly from visions of MUHAMMAD and the IMAMS, and he was influenced by the thought of MULLĀ ṢADRĀ (d. 1640), the leading Shi'ite gnostic at the school of Isfahan. Al-Aḥsā'ī argued for the existence of an archetypal level of reality (*Hūrqalyā*) in the cosmos between the divine realm and the earth. Some *Uṣūlī* (rationalist) Shi'ite authorities objected to his opinions on Muhammad's heavenly ascent (MI'RĀJ), the concealment of the Imam MAHDĪ, and human resurrection; he maintained that each involved individual spirit bodies existing in the intermediate world, rather than physical ones. Al-Aḥsā'ī challenged scholarly Shi'ite doctrines on God and the imams by contending that the imams were originally beings of divine light who participated in the creation of the world. Moreover, he refuted the authority of *Uṣūlī* jurists, who regarded themselves as spiritual caretakers of the Shi'ite community during the Imam Mahdī's absence.

Al-Aḥsā'ī's final breach with Shi'ite authorities occurred between 1822 and 1824, when a group of authorities residing in Iran and the holy cities in Iraq formally denounced him as an infidel. Following his excommunication, the shaykh left KARBALĀ' and died during a pilgrimage to MECCA.

When he died, however, he was still widely regarded as a leading religious authority. His successor as the leader of the Shaykhīs was Sayyid Kāẓim Rashtī (d. 1843).

AHURA MAZDĀ

\ə-'hûr-ə-'maz-də, -'mäz- \ (Avestan: "Wise Lord"), *also spelled* Ormizd \'ȯr-,mizd\, *or* Ormazd \'ȯr-,mazd\, supreme god in ancient Iranian religion, especially in the religious system of the Iranian prophet ZOROASTER (7th century–6th century BCE). Ahura Mazdā was worshiped by the Persian king Darius I (reigned 522 BCE–486 BCE) and his successors as the greatest of all gods and protector of the just king.

Ahura Mazdā, from a doorway of the main hall of the Council Hall, Persepolis, Persia
By courtesy of the Oriental Institute, the University of Chicago

According to Zoroaster, Ahura Mazdā created the universe and the cosmic order that he maintains. He created the twin spirits SPENTA MAINYU and Angra Mainyu (AHRIMAN)—the former beneficent, choosing truth, light, and life, the latter destructive, choosing deceit, darkness, and death. The struggle of the spirits against each other makes up the history of the world.

In ZOROASTRIANISM, as is reflected in a collection of texts called the AVESTA, Ahura Mazdā is identified with the beneficent spirit and directly opposed to the destructive one. The beneficent and evil spirits are conceived as mutually limiting, coeternal beings, the one above and the other beneath, with the world in between as their battleground. In late sources (3rd century CE onward), Zurvān ("Time") is made the father of the twins Ormazd and Ahriman (Angra Mainyu) who, in orthodox Mazdaism, reign alternately over the world until Ormazd's ultimate victory.

Something of this conception is reflected in MANICHAEISM, in which God is sometimes called Zurvān, while Ormazd is his first emanation, Primal Man, who is vanquished by the destructive spirit of darkness but rescued by God's second emanation, the Living Spirit.

'Ā'ISHA

\'ä-ē-shə\, *in full* 'Ā'isha bint Abī Bakr, *byname* Umm al-Mu'minīn ("Mother of the Faithful") (b. 614, Mecca, Arabia [now in Saudi Arabia]—d. July 678, Medina), the third and most favored wife of the Prophet MUHAMMAD.

All Muhammad's marriages had political motivations, and in this case the intention seems to have been to cement ties with 'Ā'isha's father, Abū Bakr, who was one of Muhammad's most important supporters. 'Ā'isha's personal charm secured her a place in his affections that was not lessened by his subsequent marriages. It is said that in 627 she accompanied the Prophet on an expedition but became separated from the group. When she was later escorted back to MEDINA by a man who had found her in the desert, Muhammad's enemies claimed that she had been unfaithful.

Muhammad, who trusted her, had a revelation asserting her innocence and publicly humiliated her accusers.

When Muhammad died in 632, 'Ā'isha remained politically inactive until the time of 'Uthmān (644–656; the third CALIPH), during whose reign she played an important role in fomenting opposition that led to his murder in 656. She led an army against his successor, 'ALĪ, but was defeated in the Battle of the Camel. (The engagement derived its name from the fierce fighting that centered around the camel upon which 'Ā'isha was mounted.) She was captured by her opponents but was allowed to live quietly in Medina. She is credited with having transmitted up to 1,210 HADITH and having possession of an early codex of the QUR'AN.

AJANTA CAVES

\ə-'jən-tə \, Buddhist rock-cut cave temples and monasteries, near Ajanta village, north-central Mahārāshtra state, western India, celebrated for their wall paintings. The temples are hollowed out of granite cliffs on the inner side of a 70-foot ravine in a river valley. The group of some 30 caves was excavated between the 1st century BCE and the 7th century CE and consists of two types, *caitya*s ("sanctuaries") and VIHARAS ("monasteries"). The fresco-type paintings depict Buddhist legends and divinities with a beautiful exuberance and vitality that is unsurpassed in Indian art.

AJAX THE GREATER,

Greek Aias, in Greek legend, son of Telamon, king of Salamis, described in the *Iliad* as being of great stature and colossal frame, second only to ACHILLES in strength and bravery. He engaged HECTOR (the chief Trojan warrior) in single combat and, with the aid of the goddess ATHENA, rescued the body of Achilles from the hands of the Trojans. He competed with the Greek hero ODYSSEUS for the armor of Achilles but lost, which so enraged him that it caused his death. Ajax was the tutelary hero of the island of Salamis, where he had a temple and an image and where a festival called Aianteia was celebrated in his honor.

AJAX THE LESSER,

Greek Aias, in Greek legend, son of Oileus, king of Locris. In spite of his small stature, he held his own among the other heroes before Troy; but he was also boastful, arrogant, and quarrelsome. For his crime of dragging King PRIAM's daughter CASSANDRA from the statue of ATHENA and violating her, he barely escaped being stoned to death by his Greek allies. Voyaging homeward, his ship was wrecked, but he was saved. For boasting of his escape, he was cast by POSEIDON into the sea and drowned. Ajax was worshiped as a hero by the Opuntian Locrians (who lived on the Malian Gulf in central Greece), who always left a vacant place for him in their battle line.

AKALAṄKA \,ə-kə-'läŋ-kə\ (fl. 8th century), an important DIGAMBARA logician within JAINISM. Accounts of his life, composed several centuries after he lived, claim that he and his brother secretly studied in a Buddhist monastery in order to learn Buddhist doctrine. They were discovered to be Jains, and his brother was killed by the Buddhists. Akalaṅka fled to the court of the king of Kaliṅga. There by a combination of magic and logic he defeated a prominent Buddhist monk in public debate and so established the superiority of Jainism.

Akalaṅka is credited with laying the foundation for the developed form of Jain logic. He provided Jain logic with an effective doctrine of PRAMĀṆAS, or proofs, that served as a bridge between earlier Jain logic and non-Jain schools of logic. This allowed Akalaṅka to debate non-Jains on logical grounds that were acceptable to both sides. In particular, he used these tools to counter the influence of the Buddhist logician DHARMAKĪRTI. Later Jain philosophers adopted and built upon the system developed by Akalaṅka.

AKĀLĪ DAL \ə-'kä-lē-'dəl\, *also called* Shiromani Akālī Dal (Punjabi: "Followers of the Timeless One" [God]), Sikh political party in British and independent India (*see also* SIKHISM). The title Akālī refers to 18th-century Sikh soldiers made famous by the courage they displayed when they gathered to fight against the Mughals and later the Afghans. The modern Akālī Dal came into existence in 1920 as Sikh volunteers took up the responsibility of reforming the administration of Sikh GURDWĀRAS (temples). When the SHIROMAṆĪ GURDWĀRĀ PRABANDHAK COMMITTEE (SGPC) was established in 1925 as the authoritative Sikh body for specifically religious matters, the Akālī Dal came to see itself in a parallel way as the sole protector of the political interests of the Sikh community. It was given the task of representing Sikh interests—unsuccessfully, many felt—in the negotiations that preceded the partition of the Punjab in 1947.

The Akālī Dal has historically found itself in conflict with the central government of India in Delhi. Its sustained efforts led to the founding in 1966 of the present-day state of Punjab, where Sikhs are in the majority and Punjabi is the official language. The Akālī Dal was the only political party that offered stiff resistance to Prime Minister Indira Gandhi's effort to stifle democratic institutions in the Punjab in the mid-1970s. Drawing its support principally from the Sikh peasantry, it is the oldest regional political party on the Indian political scene. It has been in and out of power at the state level from the late 1960s onward.

AKĀL TAKHAT \ə-'kāl-'tə-kət\, Takhat *also spelled* Takht \'tək-tə\ (Punjabi: "Throne of the Timeless One [God]"), shrine facing the GOLDEN TEMPLE in AMRITSAR, the most sacred religious site of SIKHISM. The origin of the Akāl Takhat is traditionally associated with Guru HARGOBIND (1595–1644, Guru 1606–44), the sixth Sikh GURŪ. He is believed to have held court at this spot, executing his responsibilities as the temporal leader of the Sikh community. During the 18th century the Akāl Takhat served as the place for Sikh leaders to gather and discuss issues confronting the community.

With the Punjab Gurdwara Act of 1925, the management of historic Sikh GURDWARAS (temples) came under the newly created SHIROMANI GURDWARA PRABANDHAK COMMITTEE

(SGPC). Since then the Akāl Takhat has functioned as the primary place from which to announce decisions of the SGPC. A *hukamnāmā* ("order") issued from the Akāl Takhat is considered mandatory for all Sikhs. In the 1980s, under the leadership of the charismatic SANT JARNAIL SINGH BHINDRANWALE, Sikh militants working for the creation of KHALISTAN, an independent Sikh state, made the Akāl Takhat their base. Sant Bhindranwale was killed in a battle between his followers and Indian army troops in 1984. In this confrontation, the Akāl Takhat was irreparably damaged; it was demolished and a new one was constructed in its place. Some within the Sikh community have felt that the Akāl Takhat should be taken from the control of the SGPC, so that the moral authority of the Akāl Takhat would be uncompromised by any sectarian or political agenda.

AKBAR \'ak-bər, -,bär\, *in full* Abū-al-Fatḥ Jalāl-al-Dīn Muhammad Akbar (b. Oct. 15, 1542, Umarkot, Sind, India—d. 1605, Āgra), greatest of the Mughal emperors of India (reigned 1556–1605), who extended Mughal power over most of the Indian subcontinent. Akbar is also noted as the founder of the DĪN-I ILĀHĪ (Persian: "Divine Faith"), an elite eclectic religious movement, which never numbered more than 19 adherents.

Akbar was the son of the emperor Humāyūn and at the age of 13 was made governor of the Punjab. When Humāyūn died in 1556 the succession was in doubt until Hemu, a rebellious Hindu minister, was defeated by a Mughal force at Panipat.

At Akbar's accession his rule extended over little more than the Punjab and the area around Delhi, but he gradually consolidated and extended his rule over Mālwa and the Hindu Rājput states. One of the notable features of Akbar's government was the extent of Hindu, and particularly Rājput, participation. Rājput princes attained the highest ranks, as generals and as provincial governors, in the Mughal service. Discrimination against non-Muslims was reduced by abolishing the taxation of pilgrims and the tax payable by non-Muslims in lieu of military service.

In 1573 Akbar conquered Gujarāt, and he then annexed Bengal in 1576. Toward the end of his reign, Akbar embarked on a fresh round of conquests. Kashmir was subjugated in 1586, Sind in 1591, and Qandahār in 1595. Mughal troops now moved south of the Vindhya Mountains into the Deccan in peninsular India. By 1601 Khāndesh, Berār, and part of Ahmadnagar were added to Akbar's empire.

Akbar possessed a powerful and original mind and encouraged free intellectual debate within his court. His inquiries into Christian doctrines misled the JESUIT missionaries he invited to his court into thinking that he was on the point of conversion. He persuaded the Muslim jurists at his court to accept him as arbiter on points of Islamic law in dispute among them. He encouraged religious discussions between Muslims, Hindus, PARSIS, and Christians that were continued by a small group of courtiers who shared with Akbar a taste for MYSTICISM, and who developed a set of doctrines and ceremonies known as the Divine Faith (Dīn-i Ilāhī). The Dīn-i Ilāhī was essentially an ethical system, prohibiting such SINS as lust, sensuality, slander, and pride and enjoining the virtues of piety, prudence, abstinence, and kindness. The soul was encouraged to purify itself through yearning for God, CELIBACY was condoned, and the slaughter of animals was forbidden. There were no sacred SCRIPTURES or a priestly hierarchy. In its ritual, it borrowed heavily from ZOROASTRIANISM, making light (Sun and fire) an object of divine worship and reciting, as in HINDUISM, the 1,000 Sanskrit names of the Sun.

In practice, however, the Dīn-i Ilāhī functioned as a personality cult contrived by Akbar around his own person. Members of the religion were handpicked by Akbar according to their devotion to him. Because the emperor styled himself a reformer of ISLAM, there was some suggestion that he wished to be acknowledged as a prophet also. The ambiguous use of formula prayers (common in SUFISM) such as *Allāhu akbar*, "God is most great," or perhaps "God is Akbar," hinted at a divine association as well.

Akbar's religion was generally regarded by his contemporaries as a Muslim innovation or a heretical doctrine; two sources from his own time—both hostile—accuse him of trying to found a new religion. The influence and appeal of the Din-i Illahi were limited, though it survived in the religious thinking of Akbar's great-grandson Dārā Shikōh (1615–59), who wrote Persian translations of sacred Hindu scriptures. The ideas of both men triggered a strong conservative reaction in Indian Islam, particularly during the reign of Aurangzeb (ruled 1658–1707), who put his brother Dārā Shikōh to death.

AKEDAH \ˌä-kā-ˈdä\ (Hebrew: "Binding"), referring to the binding of ISAAC as related in GENESIS 22. ABRAHAM bound his son Isaac on an altar at Moriah, as he had been instructed by God. An ANGEL stopped Abraham when he was about to slay his son and replaced Isaac with a ram; this is the last of the 10 trials to which God subjected Abraham. Abraham here exemplifies obedience and Isaac embodies the martyr in JUDAISM. Because 2 Chronicles 3:1 refers to Moriah as the mountain on which the Temple is built, the story further explains the site of the TEMPLE OF JERUSALEM. Building the Temple there invokes the binding of Isaac as source of merit: God is asked to remember Abraham's faithfulness and thereby to show mercy to his children. The sounding of the ram's horn, or SHOFAR, is also meant to elicit remembrance in the New Year (ROSH HASHANAH) rite. On fast days, SYNAGOGUE prayer includes, "Remem-ber for us the covenant and loving kindness and oath that you swore to Abraham our father on Mount Moriah, consider the binding with which Abraham our father bound his son Isaac on the altar, suppressing his compasion so as to do your will, so may your compassion outweigh your anger against us."

CHRISTIANITY found in the binding of Isaac an archetype for the sacrifice of Jesus (TERTULLIAN, *Adversus Marcionem* 3:18). ISLAM (QUR'AN 37:97–111) points to the Akedah as the embodiment of submission—in that version, however, it was Ishmael and not Isaac (who was not yet born) that was the proposed victim.

AKH \ˈäk\, in EGYPTIAN RELIGION, the spirit of a deceased person and, with the KA and BA, a principal aspect of the soul. By enabling the soul to assume temporarily any form it desired, for the purpose of revisiting the earth or for its own enjoyment, the *akh* characterized the soul of a deceased person as an effective entity in the next world. The *akh*-soul was generally represented as a bird and could appear to the living as a ghost.

AKIBA BEN JOSEPH \ə-ˈkē-və-ben-ˈjō-səf, ə-ˈkē-bə-, -ˈjō-zəf\ (b. *c.* 40 CE—d. *c.* 135, Caesarea, Palestine [now in Israel]), one of the most important early rabbinic authorities in both legal and exegetical matters. In the MISHNAH and TOSEFTA far more legal statements are ascribed to him than to any other authority of any generation. Additionally, he is

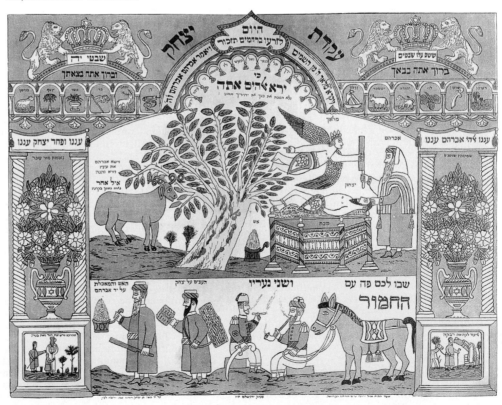

The binding of Isaac (Akedah), from a handmade Midrash (1888)
The Jewish Museum—Art Resource

depicted as having a unique approach to interpreting SCRIP-TURE, owing to his belief that as the BIBLE is derived from God, it therefore contains no redundancies. Accordingly, he is said to have ascribed significance and purpose to every element of the text, including spelling and orthography. Thus, he found meaning in seemingly redundant words, odd spellings, and even single letters occurring in the Bible.

Rabbinic sources depict Akiba as central in the early organization of Tannaitic law and refer to his "Great Mishnah compilation." The idea that Akiba organized a collection of Tannaitic laws is reflected in and developed by the Talmud BAVLI Sanhedrin 86a, which asserts that all anonymous rules in the Mishnah, Tosefta, and SIFRA reflect Akiba's legal perspective. While this clearly is not in any way literally true—frequently Akiba is cited in dispute with anonymous statements—it highlights later rabbinic masters' perception of Akiba's importance.

While early rabbinic sources cite Akiba's legal pronouncements, later texts develop a detailed story of his life: the stories relate his birth into a humble family, that in his youth he was unlearned and an enemy of scholars, and that he worked as a shepherd for Kalba Savua, the wealthiest man in Jerusalem, and became interested in study of TORAH when, against her father's wishes, Kalba Savua's daughter Rachel agreed to marry him if he would devote himself to study. According to Talmudic legend, Akiba fulfilled Rachel's request by leaving her for 24 years, eventually returning, the Talmud claims, with 24,000 of his own students. Ultimately, Akiba headed an academy in Benei Berak.

Akiba is said to have enthusiastically welcomed the BAR KOKHBA revolt and to have seen in Bar Kokhba the long-awaited MESSIAH, a belief that distinguished him from his rabbinic colleagues. During the revolt, for continuing publicly to teach Torah, Akiba was imprisoned by the Romans and finally tortured to death. His death is recorded as follows (Babylonian Talmud Berakhot 61b):

> The hour at which they brought Akiba out to be put to death was the time for reciting the Shema prayer [which proclaims the unity of God]. They were combing his flesh with iron combs while he was accepting upon himself the yoke of the Kingdom of Heaven. His disciples said to him, "Our master, to such an extent?" He said to them, "For my whole life I have been troubled by this verse [Deuteronomy 6:5, 'and you shall love the Lord your God with all your heart, and] with all your soul,' [meaning] even though he takes your soul. I wondered when I shall have the privilege of carrying out this commandment. Now that it has come to hand, should I not carry it out?" He held on to the word "One" [in the statement "the Lord is One"] until his soul expired. An echo came forth and said, "Happy are you, Rabbi Akiba, that your soul expired with the word 'one.'" . . . An echo went forth and proclaimed, "Happy are you, Rabbi Akiba, for you are selected for the life of the world to come."

AKṢOBHYA \ək-'shō-byə\, in MAHĀYĀNA and VAJRAYĀNA BUDDHISM, one of the five "self-born" Buddhas. *See* DHYĀNI-BUDDHA.

ĀLAYA-VIJÑĀNA \'ä-lə-yə-vig-'nyä-nə\ (Sanskrit: "Store of Consciousness"), in BUDDHISM, key concept of the Vijñānavāda (YOGĀCĀRA) school. The school maintains that

Albertus Magnus, detail of a fresco by Tommaso da Modena, c. 1352; in the Church of San Nicolo, Treviso
Alinari—Art Resource

no external reality exists but that knowledge, and therefore a knowable, exists; thus, knowledge itself is the object of consciousness. The Vijñānavādans postulate a higher consciousness with a universe that consists of an infinite number of possible ideas that lie inactive. This latent consciousness projects an interrupted sequence of thoughts, while it itself is in restless flux until the KARMA, or accumulated consequences of past deeds, is destroyed. This consciousness creates the illusive force (MAYA) that determines the world of difference and produces the erroneous notions of an I and a non-I in humans. That duality is conquered only by enlightenment (BODHI), which transforms a person into a BUDDHA.

ALBERTUS MAGNUS, SAINT \al-'bər-təs-'mag-nəs\, *English* Saint Albert the Great \'al-bərt\, *byname* Albert of Cologne \kə-'lōn\ (b. *c.* 1200, Lauingen an der Donau, Swabia [Germany]—d. Nov. 15, 1280, Cologne; canonized Dec. 16, 1931; feast day November 15), DOMINICAN bishop and philosopher best known as a teacher of ST. THOMAS AQUINAS and as a proponent of Aristotelianism. He was the most prolific writer of his century and established the study of nature as a legitimate science within the Christian tradition. By papal decree in 1941, he was declared the patron saint of all who cultivate the natural sciences.

Albertus, the eldest son of a German lord, attended the University of Padua and joined the Dominican order there in 1223. He continued his studies at Padua and Bologna and in Germany and then taught theology. Sometime before 1245 he was sent to the convent of Saint-Jacques at the University of Paris, where he came into contact with the works of Aristotle, newly translated from Greek and Arabic, with commentaries (by IBN RUSHD [Averroës]).

It was probably at Paris that Albertus began working on a monumental presentation of the entire body of knowledge of his time. He wrote commentaries on the BIBLE and on all the known works of Aristotle, both genuine and spurious, paraphrasing the originals but frequently adding "digressions" in which he expressed his own observations, "experiments," and speculations. The term experiment for Albertus indicates a careful process of observing, describing, and classifying. Apparently in response to a request that he explain Aristotle's *Physics*, Albertus undertook—as he states at the beginning of his *Physica*—"to make . . . intelligible to the Latins" all the branches of natural science, logic, rhetoric, mathematics, astronomy, ethics, economics, politics, and metaphysics. While he was working on this project, which took about 20 years to complete, he probably had among his disciples Thomas Aquinas.

Albertus distinguished the way to knowledge by revelation and faith from the way of philosophy and of science; the latter follows the authorities of the past according to their competence, but it also makes use of observation and proceeds by means of reason and intellect to the highest degrees of abstraction. For Albertus these two ways are not opposed. All that is really true is joined in harmony. Although there are mysteries accessible only to faith, other points of Christian doctrine are recognizable both by faith and by reason—*e.g.*, the doctrine of the immortality of the individual soul. He defended this doctrine in several works against the teaching of the Latin followers of Ibn Rushd, who held that only one intellect, which is common to all human beings, remains after the death of man and who were accused of teaching a doctrine of double truth.

Albertus' works represent the entire body of European knowledge of his time not only in theology but also in philosophy and the natural sciences. His importance for medieval science essentially consists in his bringing Aristotelianism to the fore against reactionary tendencies in contemporary theology. (On the other hand, without feeling any discrepancy in it, he also gave the widest latitude to Neoplatonic speculation.) He is accorded a preeminent place in the history of science because of this achievement.

ALBIGENSES \,al-bə-'jen-,sēz\, *also called* Albigensians \,al-bə-'jen-sē-ənz\, the heretics—especially the CATHARI—of 12th–13th-century southern France. The name, apparently given to them at the end of the 12th century, is hardly exact, for the movement centered at Toulouse and in nearby districts rather than at Albi (ancient Albiga). The HERESY, which had penetrated into these regions probably by trade routes, came originally from eastern Europe. *See also* BOGOMILS; PAULICIANS.

It is exceedingly difficult to form any very precise idea of the Albigensian doctrines because present knowledge of them is derived from their opponents and from the very rare and uninformative Albigensian texts which have come down to us. What is certain is that, above all, they formed an anti-sacerdotal party in permanent opposition to the ROMAN CATHOLIC church and raised a continued protest against the corruption of the clergy of their time.

The first Catharist heretics appeared in Limousin between 1012 and 1020. Protected by William IX, duke of Aquitaine, and soon by a great part of the southern nobility, the movement gained ground in the south, and in 1119 the Council of Toulouse in vain ordered the secular powers to assist the ecclesiastical authority in quelling the heresy. The movement maintained vigorous activity for another 100 years, until Pope INNOCENT III, having tried pacific con-

version, in 1209 ordered the CISTERCIANS to preach the crusade against the Albigenses. This Albigensian Crusade, which threw the whole of the nobility of the north of France against that of the south and destroyed the Provençal civilization, ended, politically, in the Treaty of Paris (1229), which destroyed the independence of the princes of the south but did not extinguish the heresy, in spite of the wholesale massacres of heretics. The INQUISITION, however, operating unremittingly in the south at Toulouse, Albi, and other towns during the 13th and 14th centuries, succeeded in crushing it.

ALBO, JOSEPH \'äl-bō\ (b. *c.* 1380, Monreal?, Aragon [Spain]—d. *c.* 1444), Jewish philosopher and theologian of Spain who is noted for his classic work of Jewish dogmatics, *Sefer ha-'iqqarim* (1485; "Book of Principles").

Albo participated in the Disputation of Tortosa (1413–14), a definitive confrontation between Spanish Jews and Christians, in which he distinguished himself by his ability to explain Jewish SCRIPTURES. The *Sefer ha-'iqqarim*, completed in Castile about 1425 (although not published for some 60 years), was probably intended as a work of Jewish APOLOGETICS in the face of Christian criticism. In this work Albo sought to enumerate those fundamental dogmas or articles of faith of JUDAISM that are essentially derived from the divine law and can thus be eternally valid for other religions as well. *Sefer Ha-ikkarim* (1929–30), edited and translated by Isaac Husik, was the first translation into English.

ALCINOUS \al-'si-nō-əs\, in Greek mythology, king of the Phaeacians (on the legendary island of Scheria), son of Nausithoüs, and grandson of the god POSEIDON. In Homer's *Odyssey* he entertained ODYSSEUS, who had been cast by a storm on the island. Scheria was identified with Corcyra, where Alcinous was revered as a hero. In the Argonautic legend, Alcinous lived on the island of Drepane, where he received JASON and MEDEA in their flight from Colchis.

ALCITHOË \al-'si-thō-ē\, in Greek legend, the daughter of Minyas of Orchomenus, in Boeotia. She and her sisters once refused to participate in Dionysiac festivities. Later Dionysiac music clanged about them, the house was filled with fire and smoke, and the sisters were metamorphosed into bats and birds. According to Plutarch, the sisters, driven mad for their impiety, cast lots to determine which one of their children they would eat. According to legend, their female descendants were pursued at the AGRIONIA by a priest of DIONYSUS who would kill the one he caught.

ALCMAEON \alk-'mē-ən\, *also spelled* Alcmeon, in Greek myth, the son of the seer Amphiaraus and his wife Eriphyle. When Amphiaraus set out with the expedition of the SEVEN AGAINST THEBES, which he knew would be fatal to him, he commanded his sons to avenge his death by slaying Eriphyle (who had been bribed by Polyneices with the necklace of HARMONIA to persuade her husband to fight) and by undertaking a second expedition against Thebes. After leading the Epigoni (the sons of the Seven) in the destruction of Thebes, Alcmaeon carried out his father's injunctions by killing his mother, but as a punishment he was driven mad and pursued by the ERINYES (goddesses of vengeance) from place to place.

On his arrival at Psophis in Arcadia, he was purified by its king, Phegeus, whose daughter Arsinoë (or Alphesiboea) he married, making her a present of the fatal necklace and the robe of Harmonia, which brought misfortune to all who possessed them. The land was cursed with barrenness, and an oracle declared that Alcmaeon would not find rest until he reached a spot on which the sun had never shone at the time he slew his mother. Such a spot he found at the mouth of the Achelous River, where an island had recently been formed. There he settled and, forgetting his wife, married Callirrhoë, the daughter of the river god. Phegeus and his sons, however, pursued and killed Alcmaeon. On his death, Callirrhoë prayed that her two young sons might grow to manhood at once and avenge their father. Her prayer was granted, and her sons, Amphoterus and Acarnan, slew Phegeus. After his death Alcmaeon was worshiped at Thebes; his tomb was at Psophis.

'ALENU \ä-'lā-nü\ (Hebrew: "it is our duty"), the opening word of an ancient Jewish prayer recited at the end of the three periods of daily prayer since the Middle Ages. The first section is a prayer of thanks for having set Israel apart for the service of God; the second section, omitted by those who follow the rite of the SEPHARDI, expresses a hope for the coming of the messianic age, when GENTILES will accept the one God. The 'alenu ends with the phrase: "And the Lord will become king over all the Earth; on that day the Lord will be one and his name one" (Zechariah 14:9).

Though tradition ascribes the 'alenu to JOSHUA, it is often credited to Abba Arika, also known as Rav (3rd century CE), the head of a Jewish academy at Sura in Babylonia. The 'alenu was originally part of the additional (musaf) service for ROSH HASHANAH (New Year) and was later added to the YOM KIPPUR (Day of Atonement) liturgy. On the High Holy Days it is included in the AMIDAH, the main section of the daily prayers, and is repeated in full by the CANTOR. The version used in the ASHKENAZI (German) ritual was censored by Christian church authorities, who interpreted a sentence as a slighting reference to Jesus and so ordered its deletion. REFORM JUDAISM may use a modified form of the 'alenu that is called Adoration in the ritual.

ALEXANDRIA, SCHOOL OF \,a-lig-'zan-drē-ə\, first Christian institution of higher learning, founded in the mid-2nd century CE in Alexandria, Egypt. Under its earliest known leaders (Pantaenus, CLEMENT OF ALEXANDRIA, and ORIGEN), it became a center of the allegorical method of biblical interpretation (see ALLEGORY), espoused a rapprochement between Greek culture and Christian faith, and asserted orthodox Christian teachings against heterodox views in an era of doctrinal flux.

ALEXANDRIA, SYNOD OF (362 CE), the most important of the meetings of Christian bishops held in Alexandria, Egypt. It was summoned by the bishop of Alexandria, ATHANASIUS. It allowed clergy that were readmitted to communion after making common cause with Arians to return to their former ecclesiastical status, provided they had not themselves subscribed to ARIANISM. The SYNOD stated explicitly that the HOLY SPIRIT, not a created being, is of the same substance (homoousios) as the Father and the Son (see HOMOOUSIAN), and it clearly defined the Christological terms "person" and "substance."

ALFASI, ISAAC BEN JACOB \äl-'fä-sē\, Alfasi also spelled Al-Phasi, also called Rabbi Isaac Fasi, or (by acronym) RIF (b. 1013, near Fès, Morocco—d. 1103, Lucena, Spain), Talmudic scholar who wrote a codification of the TALMUD known as Sefer ha-Halakhot ("Book of Laws"), which ranks with the great codes of MOSES MAIMONIDES and KARO.

Alfasi lived most of his life in Fès (from which his surname was derived), where he wrote his digest of the Talmud, the rabbinical compendium of law, lore, and commentary. In 1088, in fear of the local government, he fled to Spain, where, in Lucena, he became head of the Jewish community and established a noted Talmudic academy. Alfasi provoked a rebirth of Talmudic study in Spain, and his influence was instrumental in moving the center of such studies from the Eastern to the Western world.

His codification deals with the Talmud's legal aspects, or HALAKHAH (Hebrew Law), including civil, criminal, and religious law. It omits all homiletical passages as well as portions relating to religious duties practicable only in Palestine and is unusual for its focus on the actual text. His commentaries summarize the thought of the geonim who presided over the two great Jewish academies in Babylonia between the middle of the 7th and the end of the 13th century. In addition, his work played a major role in establishing the primacy of the BAVLI (the Babylonian Talmud), as edited and revised by three generations of ancient sages, over the YERUSHALMI (the Palestinian Talmud), the final compilation of which had been interrupted by external pressures. Alfasi's Sefer ha-Halakhot is still important in YESHIVA studies.

ĀLHĀ \'äl-,hä\, major oral epic of North India whose principal characters are sometimes claimed to be REINCARNATIONS of the heroes of the MAHĀBHĀRATA in the Kalī age (the fourth age in Hindu beliefs; see YUGA).

'ALĪ \'ä-lē, 'ä-; ä-'lē\, in full 'Alī ibn Abī Ṭālib (b. c. 600, Mecca—d. January 661, Kūfa, Iraq), cousin and son-in-law of MUHAMMAD, and fourth CALIPH (successor to Muhammad), reigning from 656 to 661. The question of his right to the caliphate resulted in the split in ISLAM into SUNNI and SHI'ITE branches. He is revered by the Shi'ites as the first IMAM, the true successor to the Prophet.

'Alī was the son of Abū Ṭālib, chief of a clan of the QURAYSH. When his father became impoverished, 'Alī was taken under the care of his cousin Muhammad, then still a businessman in MECCA, who himself had been cared for by 'Alī's father as a child. When Muhammad began his career as a prophet, 'Alī, though only 10 years old, became one of the first converts to Islam. Later, he married Muhammad's daughter FĀṬIMA, who bore him two sons, ḤASAN and ḤUSAYN.

'Alī is said to have been a courageous fighter in the expeditions Muhammad conducted to consolidate Islam. He was also one of Muhammad's scribes and led several important missions. When the inhabitants of Mecca finally accepted Islam without a battle, it was 'Alī who smashed their idols in the KA'BA (holy shrine).

Muhammad died on June 8, 632. Some say he had nominated 'Alī as his successor while he was returning from his "farewell pilgrimage" to Mecca. Others maintain that Muhammad died without naming a successor. 'Alī, while attending the last rites of the Prophet, was confronted by the fact that Abū Bakr, Muhammad's closest friend and the father of 'Ā'ISHA, one of the Prophet's wives, had been chosen as caliph. 'Alī did not submit to Abū Bakr's authority for some time, but neither did he actively assert his own rights, possibly in order to prevent bloody tribal strife. He retired and led a quiet life in which religious works became his chief occupation. The first chronologically arranged version of the QUR'AN is attributed to him, and his knowledge of HADITH aided the caliphs in various legal problems.

Depiction of Muhammad (left) declaring ʿAlī his successor, according with the Shiʿite tradition
The Granger Collection

ʿAlī became caliph following the murder of ʿUthmān, the third caliph. His brief reign was beset by difficulties due mostly to the corrupt state of affairs he inherited. He based his rule on the Islamic ideals of social justice and equality, but his policy was a blow to the interests of the Quraysh aristocracy of Mecca who had grown rich in the Muslim conquests. In order to embarrass ʿAlī they demanded that he bring the murderers of ʿUthmān to trial; when he refused, a rebellion against him was instigated in which two prominent Meccans along with ʿĀʾisha took a leading part. This rebellion, known as the Battle of the Camel (the camel ridden by ʿĀʾisha), was quelled. A second rebellion was on the point of being crushed when its leader, Muʿāwiya, a kinsman of ʿUthmān and the governor of Syria, proposed arbitration. ʿAlī was forced by his army to accept adjudication, greatly weakening his position. Soon he had to fight some of the very people who had earlier forced him to accept arbitration but now denounced it. Known as Khawārij (Seceders), they were defeated by ʿAlī in the Battle of Nahrawān. Meanwhile, Muʿāwiya followed an aggressive policy, and by the end of 660 ʿAlī had lost control of Egypt and of the Hijaz. While praying in a mosque at Kūfa in Iraq a Khārijite, intent on avenging the men slain at Nahrawān, struck ʿAlī with a poisoned sword. Two days later ʿAlī died and was buried at Nujaf, near Kūfa. His mausoleum became one of the principal Shiʿite pilgrimage centers. *See* GHULĀT.

ʿAlī's political discourses, sermons, letters, and sayings, collected by ash-Sharīf ar-Raḍī (d. 1015) in a book entitled *Nahj al-balāghah* ("The Road of Eloquence") with commentary by Ibn Abī al-Ḥadīd (d. 1258), are well known in Arabic literature. Muslims consider him to be an embodiment of the virtues of justice, learning, and mystical insight. In popular piety he is regarded as an intercessor with God, and certain quasi-gnostic groups maintain that he is the Perfect Man. Some, like the ʿAlawī of Syria, even hold that he is a human incarnation of God.

ʿALĪ AL-RIḌĀ \ä-ʾlē-ȧl-rē-ʾdä\, *in full* Abū al-Ḥasan ibn Mūsā ibn Jaʿfar ʿAlī al-Riḍā (b. 765/768/770, Medina, Arabia [now in Saudi Arabia]—d. 818, Ṭūs, Iran), eighth IMAM of the Twelver SHIʿITES, noted for his piety and learning until 817, when the CALIPH al-Maʾmūn, in an attempt to heal the division between the majority SUNNIS and the Shiʿites, appointed him his successor. The appointment aroused varying reactions—few of them, even among the Shiʿites, wholly favorable—and Iraq rose up in rebellion. Al-Maʾmūn gradually changed his policy. The court party set out from Merv for Baghdad, and on the way ʿAlī al-Riḍā died, after a brief illness, at Ṭūs. Shiʿite historians attribute his death to poison, possibly administered by the caliph himself. His shrine (MASHHAD) at Ṭūs became a PILGRIMAGE place and gave its name to the city (Mashhad, or Meshed, in Iran). Many miracles are attributed to ʿAlī al-Riḍā by the Shiʿites.

ALĪGARH MUSLIM UNIVERSITY \ˌä-lē-ʾgər, ˈä-lē-ˌgär\, *also known as* Anglo-Mohammedan Oriental College, *or* Anglo-Muhammadan Oriental College, the first center of Islamic and Western higher education in India. Located in Alīgarh, southeast of Delhi, it was founded as a school in May 1875 by the Muslim educator, jurist, and author AḤMAD KHAN out of his desire to found "a Muslim Cambridge." After his retirement in 1876, Aḥmad Khan devoted himself to enlarging it into a college. Raised to university status in 1920, partly through the efforts of Aga Khan III, the university became the intellectual cradle of the Muslim League and the Muslim state of Pakistan. A separate women's college was added in 1926. Alīgarh's curriculum encompasses modern humanities and sciences as well as traditional Islamic learning.

ALKA \ˈäl-kə\ (Lithuanian: "sacred precinct"), *also called* alkas, in ancient BALTIC RELIGION, an open-air religious site—forest, hill, river—that was sacred. Trees could not be cut in such forests, sacred fields could not be plowed, and fishing was not allowed in the holy waters. The rituals of various religious cults, involving animal sacrifice and human CREMATION, took place at the *alka*s. The sense of the ancient alka is preserved in the modern Lithuanian word *alkvietė,* meaning any holy place or site of worship.

ALKALAI, JUDAH BEN SOLOMON HAI \ˌal-kə-ʾlī\ (b. 1798, Sarajevo, Bosnia, Ottoman Empire [now Bosnia and Herzegovina]—d. 1878, Jerusalem, Palestine), Sephardic RABBI and an advocate of Jewish colonization of Palestine.

Alkalai was taken to Jerusalem at an early age, and there he was reared and educated for the rabbinate. At 25 he became rabbi of a congregation of SEPHARDI in Semlin (now Zemun, Yugos.), a border town of the Austrian Empire across the Sava River from Belgrade. There he wrote a book arguing that a physical "return to Israel" (*i.e.,* to Eretz Yisraʾel, the Holy Land in Palestine) was a precondition for redemption (salvation), instead of the symbolic "return to Israel" by means of repentance and resuming the ways of God. This doctrine was unacceptable in ORTHODOX JUDAISM and generated much controversy. His second book was a reply to heated attacks on his proto-Zionist views.

After the Damascus Affair, an anti-Semitic outburst of 1840, Alkalai took to admonishing Jews that the event was part of a divine design to awaken Jews to the reality of their condition in exile. Believing that Jews should migrate nowhere but to Palestine, he traveled in England and about Europe seeking support, but his efforts came to naught. Finally in 1871 he left his congregation at Semlin and went to Palestine, where he created a society for settlement. It too failed. But Alkalai's writings did have some effect, particularly one book, *Goral Ladonai* (1857; "A Lot for the Lord"). These and his personal migration helped pave the way for the ZIONISM of THEODOR HERZL and others.

ALLĀH \'ä-lə, 'a-, -,lä; ä-'lä\ (Arabic: "God"), the one and only God in ISLAM. Etymologically, the name Allāh is probably a contraction of the Arabic *al-Ilāh*, "the God." *Allāh* is the standard Arabic word for "God" and is used by Arabic-speaking Christians as well as by Muslims.

Allāh is the pivot of the Muslim faith. The QUR'AN constantly preaches Allāh's reality, his inaccessible mystery, his "beautiful" names, and his actions on behalf of his creatures. Three themes preponderate: (1) Allāh is creator, judge, and rewarder; (2) he is unique (*wāḥid*) and inherently one (*aḥad*); and (3) he is omnipotent and all-merciful. God is the "Lord of the Worlds," the most high, "nothing is like unto him," and this in itself is to the believer a request to adore Allāh as protector and to glorify his powers. God, moreover, is most compassionate, the originator of what is good and beautiful in the world; he "loves those who do good" (Qur'an 2:195), and is "closer than the jugular vein" (Qur'an 50:16). In SUFISM, he is the beloved with whom the mystic seeks union.

Muslim piety has collected, in the Qur'an and in the HADITH, the 99 "most beautiful names" (*al-asmā' al-ḥusnā*) of God, and these names have become objects of devoted recitation and meditation. Among the names of Allāh are the One and Only, the Living One, the Subsisting (*al-Ḥayy al-Qayyūm*), the Real Truth (*al-Ḥaqq*), the Sublime (*al-'Aẓīm*), the Wise (*al-Ḥakīm*), the Omnipotent (*al-'Azīz*), the Hearer (*al-Samī'*), the Seer (*al-Baṣīr*), the Omniscient (*al-'Alīm*), the Witness (*al-Shāhid*), the Protector (*al-Wakīl*), the Benefactor (*al-Raḥmān*), the Merciful (*al-Raḥīm*), and the Constant Forgiver (*Ghafūr, Ghaffār*).

The profession of faith (SHAHĀDA) by which a person is introduced into the Muslim community consists of the affirmation that there is no god but Allāh and that MUHAMMAD is his prophet. For pious Muslims, every action is opened by an invocation of the divine name (*basmala*). The formula *in shā'a Allāh*, "if God wills," appears frequently in daily speech. This formula is the reminder of an ever-present divine intervention in the order of the world and the actions of human beings. Muslims believe that nothing happens and nothing is performed unless it is by the will or commandment of Allāh. The personal attitude of a Muslim believer, therefore, is a complete submission to God, "whom one does not question" but whom one knows according to his (Qur'anic) word to be a fair judge, at once formidable and benevolent, and the supreme help. In essence, the surrender to God (*islām*) is the religion itself.

ALLEGORY, a work of written, oral, or artistic expression that uses symbolic fictional figures and actions to convey truths or generalizations about human conduct or experience. Like metaphor, an allegory expresses spiritual, psychological, or abstract intellectual concepts in terms of material and concrete objects. Fable and PARABLE are short, simple forms of allegory.

Allegory is a method of interpretation that encourages the discovery of meaning below the surface of a text; it was, consequently, particularly attractive to those authors who combined belief in the oracular truth of the BIBLE with a degree of discomfort at the contents of certain biblical books. Law, history, PROPHECY, poetry, and even JESUS' parables yielded new meanings when allegorized. The Song of Songs was read, not as a poem celebrating the love of a man and a woman, but as an allegory of the love of God for his people. The battles in the Book of Joshua were understood as pointing to the warfare of Christians "against the spiritual hosts of wickedness in the heavenly places" (Ephesians 6:12). In the Gospel parables, meanwhile, in the story of the good SAMARITAN (Luke 10:30–37) an allegorical meaning was sought for the thieves, the Samaritan's beast, the inn, the innkeeper, and the two pence.

Closely allied to allegorical interpretation, if not indeed a species of it, is typological interpretation, in which certain persons, objects, or events in the OLD TESTAMENT are seen to set forth at a deeper level persons, objects, or events in the NEW TESTAMENT. ADAM, for example (regarded as a historical person), was thought to prefigure Christ in his human aspect, JOSHUA to prefigure the victorious militant Christ. NOAH's ark (GENESIS 6:14–22) was interpreted to typify the church, outside which there is no salvation; ISAAC carrying the wood for the sacrifice (Genesis 22:6) typifies Jesus carrying the cross; Rahab's scarlet cord in the window (Joshua 2:18–21) prefigures the blood of Christ; and so on. These are not merely sermon illustrations but rather aspects of a hermeneutical theory that maintains that this further significance was designed (by God) from the beginning.

Allegorical thinking is most fully reflected in the period of its greatest vogue, the High Middle Ages. The early CHURCH FATHERS sometimes used a threefold method of interpreting texts, encompassing literal, moral, and spiritual meanings. This was refined and commonly believed to have achieved its final form in the medieval allegorist's "fourfold theory of interpretation." This method also began every reading with a search for the literal sense of the passage. It moved up to a level of ideal interpretation in general, which was the allegorical level proper. Still higher, the reader came to the tropological level, which told him where his moral duty lay. Finally, since Christian thought was apocalyptic and visionary, the method reached its apogee at the anagogic level, at which the reader was led to meditate on the final cosmic destiny of all Christians and of himself as a Christian hoping for eternal salvation.

ALL SAINTS' DAY, the day commemorating all the saints of the Christian church, both known and unknown, celebrated on November 1 in the Western churches and on the first Sunday after PENTECOST in the Eastern churches. Its origin cannot be traced with certainty, and it has been observed on various days in different places. The first evidence for the November 1 date of celebration and of the broadening of the festival to include all saints as well as all martyrs occurred during the reign of Pope Gregory III (731–741), who dedicated a chapel in St. Peter's, Rome, on November 1 in honor of all saints. In 800, All Saints' Day was kept by Alcuin on November 1, and it also appeared in a 9th-century English calendar on that day. In 837 Pope Gregory IV ordered its general observance. In medieval England, the festival was known as All Hallows, and its eve is

All Souls' Day, which Peruvians celebrate as the Day of the Dead, feasting the dead in a cemetery
Photo by Victor Englebert—Photo Researchers

still known as HALLOWEEN, which has become a secular holiday in its own right in the United States.

ALL SOULS' DAY, in ROMAN CATHOLICISM, church day for commemorating baptized Christians who are believed to be in PURGATORY because they have died with the guilt of lesser SINS on their souls. It is celebrated on November 2. Roman Catholic doctrine holds that the prayers of the faithful on earth will help cleanse these souls in order to fit them for the vision of God in heaven.

From antiquity certain days were devoted to intercession for particular groups of the dead. The institution of a day for a general intercession on November 2 is due to Odilo, Abbot of Cluny (d. 1048). The date, which became practically universal before the end of the 13th century, was chosen to follow ALL SAINTS' DAY. Having celebrated the feast of all the members of the church who are believed to be in heaven, the church on earth turns, on the next day, to commemorate those souls believed to be suffering in purgatory.

Latin American countries celebrate All Souls' Day, calling it the Day of the Dead (El Dia de los Muertos). The day combines indigenous pre-Christian celebrations honoring the dead with Roman Catholic beliefs. On this day Latin Americans visit grave sites of deceased family members, picnic there, and hold other festivities. There is a rich tradi-

tion of associated folk art, including food, sculpture, and graphic arts representing skeletons, skulls, and the spirits of the dead.

ALMOHADS \'al-mǝ-ˌhadz\, *Arabic* al-Muwaḥḥidūn ("Those Who Affirm the Unity of God"), Berber confederation that created an Islamic empire in North Africa and Spain (1130–1269), founded on the religious teachings of IBN TŪMART (d. 1130).

A Berber state arose in Tinmel in the Atlas Mountains of Morocco *c.* 1120, inspired by Ibn Tūmart and his demands for puritanical moral reform and a strict concept of the unity of God (TAWḤĪD). In 1121 Ibn Tūmart proclaimed himself the MAHDĪ, and, as spiritual and military leader, began the wars against the ALMORAVIDS. Under his successor, 'Abd al-Mu'min, the Almohads brought down the Almoravid state in 1147, subjugating the Maghrib, and captured Marrakech, which became the Almohad capital. Almoravid domains in Andalusia, however, were left virtually intact until the CALIPH Abū Ya'qūb Yūsuf (reigned 1163–84) forced the surrender of Seville in 1172; the extension of Almohad rule over the rest of Islamic Spain followed. During the reign of Abū Yūsuf Ya'qūb al-Manṣūr (1184–99), serious Arab rebellions devastated the eastern provinces of the empire, while in Spain the Christian threat remained constant, despite al-Manṣūr's victory at Alarcos (1195). Then, at the battle of Las Navas de Tolosa (1212), the Almohads were dealt a shattering defeat by a Christian coalition from Leon, Castile, Navarre, and Aragon. They retreated to their North African provinces, where soon afterward the Ḥafṣids seized power at Tunis (1236), the 'Abd al-Wādids took Tilimsān (Tlemcen) (1239), and, finally, Marrakech fell to the Marīnids (1269).

The original puritanical outlook of Ibn Tūmart was soon lost. The building of richly ornamented Andalusian monuments in the manner of the Almoravids began with Ibn Tūmart's successor 'Abd al-Mu'min. Neither did the movement for a return to traditionalist ISLAM survive; both the mystical Sufis (*see* SUFISM) and the philosophical schools represented by IBN ṬUFAYL and IBN RUSHD (Averroës) flourished under the Almohad kings.

ALMORAVIDS \al-'mōr-ǝ-ˌvidz\, *Arabic* al-Murābiṭūn ("Those Dwelling in Fortified Convents," or "Warrior-Monks"), confederation of Berber tribes—Lamtūnah, Gudālah, Massūfah—of the Ṣanhājah clan, whose religious zeal and military enterprise built an empire in northwestern Africa and Muslim Spain in the 11th and 12th centuries. These Saharan Berbers were inspired to improve their knowledge of Islamic doctrine by their leader Yaḥyā ibn Ibrāhīm and the Moroccan theologian 'Abd Allāh ibn Yasīn. Under Abū Bakr al-Lamtūnī and later Yūsuf ibn Tāshufīn, the Almoravids merged their religious reform fervor with the conquest of Morocco and western Algeria as far as Algiers between 1054 and 1092. They established their capital at Marrakech in 1062. Yūsuf assumed the title of *amīr al-muslimīn* ("commander of the Muslims") but still paid homage to the 'Abbāsid CALIPH in Baghdad. He moved into Spain in 1085, as the old caliphal territories of Córdoba were falling before the Christians and Toledo was being taken by Alfonso VI of Castile and Leon. At the Battle of al-Zallāqah, near Badajoz, in 1086 Yūsuf halted an advance by the Castilians but did not regain Toledo.

The whole of Muslim Spain, however, except Valencia, eventually came under Almoravid rule. In the reign (1106–42) of 'Ali ibn Yūsuf the union between Spain and Africa was consolidated, but the Almoravids were a Berber minority at the head of the Spanish-Arab empire, and while they tried to hold Spain with Berber troops and the Maghrib with a strong Christian guard, they could not restrain the Christian reconquest that began with the fall of Saragossa in 1118. In 1125 the ALMOHADS began a rebellion in the Atlas Mountains and after 22 years of fighting emerged victorious. Marrakech fell in 1147. Almoravid leaders survived only for a time in Spain and the Balearic Isles.

ALOAD \ə-'lō-ˌad\, *Greek* Aloada, *or* Aloeida, in Greek myth, name for either Otus or Ephialtes, the gigantic twin sons of Iphimedeia by the god POSEIDON. The Aloads fought against the Olympian gods and endeavored to storm Olympus, but APOLLO destroyed them before they reached manhood. In a later myth they sought ARTEMIS (goddess of wild animals, vegetation, and childbirth) and HERA (wife of ZEUS) in marriage, whereupon Artemis appeared between them in the shape of a stag, which they attempted to kill but instead slew each other.

ALPHA AND OMEGA, first and last letters of the Greek alphabet, which, within CHRISTIANITY, have come to signify the comprehensiveness of God, implying that God includes all that can be. In the NEW TESTAMENT book REVELATION TO JOHN, the term is used as the self-designation of God and of Christ. The reference in Revelation likely had a Jewish origin, based on such OLD TESTAMENT passages as Isaiah 44:6 ("I am the first and the last"). In rabbinic literature, the word *emet* ("truth"), composed of the first and last letters of the Hebrew alphabet, is "the seal of God" and carries somewhat the same connotation as Alpha and Omega.

ALTAR, raised structure or place that is used for sacrifice, worship, or prayer.

Altars probably originated when certain localities (a tree, a spring, a rock) came to be regarded as holy or as inhabited by spirits or gods, whose intervention could be solicited by the worshiper. The worshiper's gifts to propitiate or please the gods were placed on an altar nearby. In some religions a stone or heap of stones or a mound of earth probably sufficed for this purpose. With the institution of sacrifice in sanctuaries and temples, elaborate altars were built of stone or brick on which the victim was killed and its blood channeled off or its flesh burned. The altars used in ancient Israel consisted of a rectangular stone with a basin hollowed out on its top. The four corners of the basin terminated in projections; these "horns" came to be regarded as the altar's holiest part, so that anyone clinging to them was immune from molestation. The altars used elsewhere in the Middle East ranged from small upright stands for burning incense to the great rectangular stone altars built in Egyptian temples during the period of the New Kingdom.

The ancient Greeks built altars at the entrances and in the courtyards of their houses, in marketplaces and public buildings, and in sacred groves in the countryside. There were city altars, on which fire continually burned, and temple altars, which were built in front of the temple rather than within it. The great altar of ZEUS at Pergamum (now in the Berlin State Museum) has fine examples of the relief sculptures with which the Greeks decorated their altars. Lofty, imposing altars were used for powerful gods such as Zeus or ATHENA, while lower altars were thought more suitable for such domestic deities as HECATE.

When the Christians began to build churches, a wooden altar table was placed in the choir or in the apse. These al-

tars gradually came to be built of stone, and the remains of martyrs were customarily reburied beneath them. In Western churches from as early as the 4th century, the altar was covered by a canopy-like structure, the baldachin, which rested on columns placed around the altar. The altar was further ornamented by an altarpiece, a screen or wall behind it covered with paintings or sculptures. During the Middle Ages side altars were built in the larger Western churches so that multiple masses could be celebrated, sometimes simultaneously.

ALTIS \'al-tis\, in GREEK RELIGION, a sacred grove or precinct in OLYMPIA, Greece. It was an irregular, walled, quadrangular area measuring more than 200 yards on each side. In it were the temples of ZEUS and of HERA; the principal altars and votive offerings; the small treasuries built by various Dorian states; and the administration buildings for the Olympic Games, which were held nearby. Outside the sacred place were the stadium, hippodrome, baths, and other accommodations for visitors.

ĀLVĀR \'äl-ˌvär, 'al-\, any of a group of South Indian mystics who in the 6th to 9th centuries wandered from temple to temple singing ecstatic hymns in adoration of the god VISHNU. The tradition is that there were 12 Ālvārs. The songs of the Ālvārs rank among the world's greatest devotional literature. Among the followers of SHIVA, the counterparts of the Ālvārs were the Nāyanārs.

The name Ālvār means, in the Tamil language in which they sang, "one who is immersed—drowned—in Vishnu." Their BHAKTI (religious devotion) was intensely passionate. The Ālvārs are sometimes described as falling unconscious in rapture before images of Vishnu enshrined in local temples, and the locative elements in their poetry are notable.

The most famous of the Ālvārs is NAMMĀLVĀR who lived from 880–930 CE and composed four works. The best known of these works, and indeed one of the best-known works of *bhakti* in South India of any period or language, is the *Tiruvāymoli*, a 1,102 verse poem to Vishnu. The hymns of the Ālvārs were gathered in the 10th century by Nāthamuni, a leader of the ŚRĪ VAISNAVA sect. The collection is called *Nālāyira Prabandham* ("Collection of 4,000 Songs").

AMALEKITE \'a-mə-ˌle-ˌkīt, ə-'ma-lə-\, member of an ancient nomadic tribe or tribes, described in the OLD TESTAMENT as relentless enemies of Israel (EXODUS 17:8–13; Numbers 14:44–45; Judges 3:12–14; 6:3–5; 1 Samuel 15:2–5; 27:8–9; 30:1–2, 11–20; 2 Samuel 1:1–10; 8:12), even though they were closely related to EPHRAIM, one of the TWELVE TRIBES OF ISRAEL. Their district was south of JUDAH and probably extended into northern Arabia (1 Samuel 15:7). The Amalekites harassed the Hebrews during their Exodus from Egypt and attacked them at Rephidim near MOUNT SINAI, where they were defeated (Exodus 17:8–13). They were among the nomadic raiders defeated by GIDEON (Judges 6:1–8:32) and were condemned to annihilation by Samuel (1 Samuel 15:2–3). Their final defeat occurred in the time of HEZEKIAH (1 Chronicles 4:43).

AMALTHAEA \ˌa-mal-'thē-ə\, in Greek (originally Cretan) mythology, the foster mother of ZEUS. She is represented as the goat that suckled the infant god in a cave in Crete or as a NYMPH who fed him the milk. Amalthaea filled one of the goat's horns with flowers and fruits and presented it to Zeus, who placed it, together with the goat, among the stars. The horn, commonly known as the CORNUCOPIA, was a symbol of inexhaustible plenty and became the attribute of various divinities and of rivers as fertilizers of the land.

AMARĀVATI \,ə-mə-'rä-və-tē, ,ä-\, *also spelled* Amaravathi, town, east-central Andhra Pradesh state, southern India. Situated on the Krishna River, it was an ancient Buddhist center. Its monasteries and university attracted students from throughout India and the Far East. The Buddhist STUPA at Amarāvati was one of the largest in India, though only traces of it now remain. Amarāvati is known for the relief sculptures that were a part of its great Buddhist shrine, although most of these are now in museums.

AMAR CHITRA KATHĀ \ə-'mər-'chi-trə-'kə-,tä, ə-'mär-\, extremely popular contemporary Indian comic book series (in English and some vernacular languages) depicting episodes from the epics RĀMĀYAṆA and MAHĀBHĀRATA, and the lives and exploits of deities, sages, prophets, saints, and mortal religious leaders from all of India's major religious traditions. The series also includes biographies of India's most celebrated political leaders and freedom fighters.

AMAR DĀS \ə-'mər-däs, -'mär-\ (b. 1479, Khadur?, India—d. 1574, Goindwāl), in SIKHISM, the third GURŪ (1552–74). Amar Dās was responsible for a major phase of consolidation and expansion of the early Sikh community. He founded the town of Goindwāl (originally, Govindvāl ["town of God"]), on the main route from Lahore to Delhi, as the center of Sikh authority. He strengthened the existing institutions of Sikh SCRIPTURE, liturgy, and *langar* ("community kitchen"), and introduced a religio-administrative structure of 22 *manjīs* (literally, "cots," in function "seats"), which created the possibility of effective governance for the entire, increasingly far-flung Sikh community. Persons appointed to occupy these seats in distant areas were to provide doctrinal guidance for their constituents, encourage the entry of others into the Sikh community, and serve as links between the local congregations and the center at Goindwāl. In order to enhance the cohesion between distant congregations and Goindwāl, Gurū Amar Dās created patterns of PILGRIMAGE calibrated to a newly formed Sikh calendar. By incorporating two preexisting festivals, Vaisākhī (at the time of the spring harvest) and DĪVĀLĪ (at the fall harvest), and changing their orientation, he established two major occasions when all Sikhs were encouraged to come to Goindwāl and participate in communal celebrations.

AMATERASU \,ä-mä-tā-'rä-,sü\, *in full* Amaterasu Ōmikami (Japanese: "Heaven-illuminating Great Divinity"), celestial sun goddess from whom the Japanese imperial family claims descent, and an important SHINTŌ deity. She was born from the left eye of her father, IZANAGI, who bestowed upon her a necklace of jewels and placed her in charge of *Takamagahara* ("High Celestial Plain"), the abode of all the KAMI (objects of worship in Shintō and other indigenous religions of Japan). One of her brothers, the storm god SUSANOO, was sent to rule the sea plain. Before going, Susanoo went to take leave of his sister. As an act of good faith, they produced children together, she by chewing and spitting out pieces of the sword he gave her, and he by doing the same with her jewels. Susanoo then began to behave very rudely—he broke down the divisions in the rice fields, defiled his sister's dwelling place, and finally threw a flayed horse into her weaving hall. Amaterasu withdrew in protest into a cave, and darkness fell upon the world.

The other 800 myriads of gods conferred on how to lure the sun goddess out. They collected cocks, whose crowing precedes the dawn, and hung a mirror and jewels in a *sakaki* tree in front of the cave. The goddess Amenouzume began a dance on an upturned tub, partially disrobing herself, which so delighted the assembled gods that they roared with laughter. Amaterasu became curious how the gods could make merry while the world was plunged into darkness and was told that outside the cave there was a deity more illustrious than she. She peeped out, saw her reflec-

Amaterasu, Shintō goddess of the sun,
by Utagawa Kunisada (1785–1864)
Victoria and Albert Museum, London—Art Resource

tion in the mirror, heard the cocks crow, and was thus drawn out from the cave. The *kami* then quickly threw a *shimenawa,* or sacred rope of rice straw, before the entrance to prevent her return to it. This episode is the model for the later Shintō renewal ritual (*see* MATSURI).

Amaterasu's chief place of worship is the GRAND SHRINE OF ISE, the foremost Shintō shrine in Japan. She is manifested there in a mirror that is one of the three Imperial Treasures of Japan (the others being a jeweled necklace and a sword).

AMAZON, in Greek mythology, member of a race of women warriors. The story of the Amazons probably originated as a variant of a tale recurrent in many cultures, that of a distant land organized oppositely from one's own. The ascribed habitat of the Amazons necessarily became more remote as Greek geographic knowledge developed. Traditionally, one of the labors required of the Greek hero HERACLES was leading an expedition to obtain the girdle of the Amazons' queen (Hippolyte).

Subsidiary tales grew up to explain why, if the whole nation consisted of women, it did not die out in a generation. The most common explanation was that the Amazons mated with men of another people, kept the resulting female children, and sent the male children away to their fathers. In another tale, THESEUS attacked the Amazons either with Heracles or independently. The Amazons in turn invaded Attica but were finally defeated, and at some point Theseus married one of them, ANTIOPE.

Ancient Greek works of art often depicted combats between Amazons and Greeks; that between Theseus and the Amazons was a particular favorite. As portrayed in these works, the Amazons were similar in model to the goddess ATHENA, and their arms were the bow, spear, light double ax, a half shield, and, in early art, a helmet. In later art they were more like the goddess ARTEMIS and wore a thin dress, girded high for speed.

Amazon of the type known as "Mattei," Roman copy after an original attributed to the Athenian sculptor Phidias, c. 440 BCE; in the Vatican Museum
Alinari—Art Resource

According to some accounts, the Amazon River was renamed by the 16th-century Spanish explorer Francisco de Orellana for the fighting women he claimed to have encountered on what was then the Marañon River.

AMBEDKAR, BHIMRAO RAMJI \əm-ˈbäd-kər\ (b. April 14, 1891, Mhow, India—d. Dec. 6, 1956, New Delhi), most in-

fluential leader of the DALIT ("Oppressed") groups, also identified as the Harijans ("Children of God"), UNTOUCHABLES, or scheduled-caste or low-caste Indians.

Born of an untouchable MAHAR family of western India, he was as a boy humiliated by his high-caste schoolfellows. Awarded a scholarship by the Gaekwar (the ruler) of Baroda, he studied at Columbia University (Ph.D.) and the University of London (D.Sci.), passing the bar from Gray's Inn. He entered the Baroda Public Service at the Gaekwar's request, but, again ill-treated by colleagues, he turned to legal practice and teaching. He soon established his leadership among the scheduled CASTES, founded several journals on their behalf, instituted depressed-classes conferences, and succeeded in obtaining special representation for them in the legislative councils of the government.

In 1947 Ambedkar became the law minister of the government of India. He took a leading part in the framing of the Indian constitution, outlawing discrimination against untouchables. He resigned in 1951, disappointed at his lack of influence in the government. In October 1956, in despair because of the perpetuation of untouchability in Hindu practice, Ambedkar honored a vow he had made two decades earlier and renounced HINDUISM to become a Buddhist. Some 200,000 fellow untouchables joined him at a ceremony in Nagpur. This began a revitalization of BUDDHISM in India that has been called "engaged Buddhism." Pictures and statues of Ambedkar are familiar features of the Indian public landscape. In many circles his status as a secular saint rivals that of GANDHI.

AMBROSE, SAINT \ˈam-ˌbrōs, -ˌbrōz\, *Latin* Ambrosius \am-ˈbrō-zhəs, -zē-əs\ (b. *c.* 339 CE, Augusta Treverorum, Belgica, Gaul [Trier, Ger.]—d. 397, Milan; feast day December 7), bishop of Milan, biblical critic, and initiator of ideas that gave a model for conceptions of church-state relations.

Ambrose was reared in Rome by his widowed mother and his elder sister Marcellina, a nun. Duly promoted to the governorship of Aemilia-Liguria in *c.* 370, he lived at Milan and was unexpectedly acclaimed as bishop by the people of the city in 374. Ambrose was chosen as a compromise candidate to avoid a disputed election, and thus changed from an unbaptized layman to a bishop in eight days.

An imperial court frequently sat in Milan. In confrontations with this court, Ambrose showed a directness that combined the republican ideal of the prerogatives of a Roman senator with a vein of demagoguery. In 384 he secured the rejection of an appeal for tolerance by non-Christian members of the Roman senate, whose spokesman, Quintus Aurelius Symmachus, was his relative. In 388 he rebuked the emperor Theodosius for having punished a bishop who had burnt a Jewish SYNAGOGUE. On the other hand, he served as a loyal and resourceful diplomat. In his letters and in his funeral orations on the emperors Valentinian II and Theodosius, Ambrose established the medieval concept of a Christian emperor as a dutiful son of the church "serving under orders from Christ," and so subject to the advice and strictures of his bishop.

Ambrose's relations with the emperors formed only part of his commanding position among the lay governing class of Italy. He absorbed Greek learning, Christian and non-Christian alike—notably the works of PHILO JUDAEUS, ORIGEN, ST. BASIL THE GREAT of Caesarea, and Plotinus (see NEOPLATONISM). This learning he used in sermons expounding the BIBLE and, especially, in defending the "spiritual" meaning of the OLD TESTAMENT. He also composed important treatises, including *On the Holy Spirit*, *On the Duties of Ministers*, and *On the Mysteries*. Sermons, the dating of which unfortunately remains uncertain, were Ambrose's main literary output and remain an important source on the transmission of Greek philosophy and theology in the West. By such sermons Ambrose gained his most notable convert, AUGUSTINE, afterward bishop of Hippo in North Africa.

Ambrose introduced new Eastern melodies to the West with his HYMNS—e.g., "Aeterne rerum Conditor" ("Framer of the Earth and Sky") and "Deus Creator omnium" ("Maker of All Things, God Most High"). He advocated the most austere ASCETICISM: noble families were reluctant to let their marriageable daughters attend the sermons in which he urged upon them the crowning virtue of virginity.

Although Ambrose may have imposed his will on emperors, he never considered himself as a precursor of a polity in which the church dominated the state: for he acted from a fear that CHRISTIANITY might yet be eclipsed by a non-Christian nobility. In a near-contemporary mosaic in the chapel of S. Satiro in the church of S. Ambrogio, Milan, Ambrose appears as he wished to be seen: a simple Christian bishop clasping the book of Gospels. For Augustine, he was the model bishop: a biography was written in 412 by Paulinus, deacon of Milan, at Augustine's instigation.

AMEN \ˌä-'men, ˌā-\, expression of agreement, confirmation, or desire used in worship by Jews, Christians, and Muslims. The meaning of the Semitic root from which it is derived is "firm," "fixed," or "sure," and the related Hebrew verb means "to be reliable" and "to be trusted." The Greek OLD TESTAMENT usually translates amen as "so be it"; in the English BIBLE it is often rendered as "verily," or "truly."

In its earliest use in the Bible, the amen occurred initially and referred back to the words of another speaker with whom there was agreement. It usually introduced an affirmative statement. The use of the initial amen, single or double in form, to introduce solemn statements of Jesus in the Gospels (77 times in the Gospels) had no parallel in Jewish practice. Such amens expressed the certainty and truthfulness of the statement that followed.

Use of the amen in Jewish temple liturgy as a response by the people at the close of a DOXOLOGY or other prayer uttered by a priest seems to have been common as early as the time of the 4th century BCE. This Jewish liturgical use of amen was adopted by the Christians. JUSTIN MARTYR (2nd century CE) indicated that amen was used in the liturgy of the EUCHARIST and was later introduced into the baptismal service.

A final amen, added by a speaker who offered thanksgiving or prayers, public or private, to sum up and confirm what he himself had said, is found in the Psalms and is common in the NEW TESTAMENT. Jews used amen to conclude prayers in ancient times, and Christians closed every prayer with it. As HYMNS became more popular, the use of the final amen was extended.

Although Muslims make little use of amen, it is stated after every recital of the first SŪRA.

AMERICAN FRIENDS SERVICE COMMITTEE (AFSC), organization to promote peace and reconciliation through programs of social service and public information, founded by American and Canadian Friends (Quakers; *see* FRIENDS, SOCIETY OF) in 1917. In World War I, the AFSC helped conscientious objectors to find alternative-service possibilities, and this was continued during World War II. In peacetime the AFSC continued such national and international programs as community development, racial reconciliation, aid to migrant workers, relief to civilians in war-torn areas, and refugee work. Its program of Voluntary International Service Assignments (VISA) served as a model for the U.S. Peace Corps. In 1947 the AFSC was awarded the Nobel Prize for Peace jointly with the Friends Service Council, its British counterpart. AFSC headquarters are in Philadelphia.

AMERICAN HEBREW CONGREGATIONS, UNION OF, oldest American federation of Jewish congregations (founded 1873, Cincinnati, Ohio).

The union was organized by Rabbi ISAAC MAYER WISE for the immediate purpose of establishing and supporting a seminary for the training of American-born RABBIS. Two years later the union established Hebrew Union College, the first successful rabbinic seminary in the United States. In 1950 this college merged with the Jewish Institute of Religion of New York, founded in 1922 by Rabbi Stephen S. Wise. Both institutions were long-time centers of REFORM JUDAISM and are still supported by the union.

The union organized five auxiliary groups: the National Federation of Temple Sisterhoods (1913), of Temple Brotherhoods (1923), of Temple Youth (1939), and of Temple Secretaries (1943) and the National Association of Temple Educators (1955). Each group operates independently within the union and promotes those activities that best suit it. The union has sponsored or cosponsored religious schools, teacher seminars, a correspondence school, student study groups, and leadership training courses, often in cooperation with other groups.

The union, now numbering nearly 900 Reform congregations (including several in Canada), is affiliated with the World Union for Progressive (Reform) JUDAISM and maintains headquarters in New York City.

AMESHA SPENTA \'ä-me-shə-'spen-tə\ (Avestan: "beneficent immortal"), *Pahlavi* amshaspend, in ZOROASTRIANISM, any of the six divine beings or ARCHANGELS created by AHURA MAZDĀ, the Wise Lord, to help govern creation. Three are male, three female. Ministers of his power against the evil spirit, AHRIMAN, they are depicted clustered about Ahura Mazdā on golden thrones attended by ANGELS. They are the everlasting bestowers of good. They are worshiped separately and each has a special month, festival, and flower and presides over an element in the world order. In later Zoroastrianism each is opposed by a specific archfiend.

Of the six, Asha Vahishta (Avestan: Excellent Order, or Truth) and VOHU MANAH are by far the most important. Asha Vahishta is the lawful order of the cosmos according to which all things happen. He presides over fire, sacred to the Zoroastrians as the inner nature of reality. To the devotee he holds out the path of justice and spiritual knowledge. Vohu Manah (Avestan: Good Mind) is the spirit of divine wisdom, illumination, and love. He guided ZOROASTER'S soul before the throne of heaven. He welcomes the souls of the blessed in paradise. Believers are enjoined to "bring down Vohu Manah in your lives on earth" through profound love in marriage and toward one's fellowman. He presides over domestic animals. Khshathra Vairya (Desirable Dominion), who presides over metal, is the power of Ahura Mazdā's kingdom. The believer can realize this power in action guided by Excellent Order and Good Mind. Spenta Armaiti (Beneficent Devotion), the spirit of devotion and faith, guides and protects the believer. She presides over earth. Haurvatāt (Wholeness or Perfection) and Ameretāt (Immortality), often mentioned together as sisters, preside over water and plants and may come to the believer in reward for participation in the natures of the other *amesha spenta*s.

AMIDAH \,ä-mē-'dä, ä-'mē-dä\, *plural* Amidoth \,ä-mē-'dōt\, or Amidot, *Hebrew* 'Amida ("Standing"), in JUDAISM, the main section of morning, afternoon, and evening prayers, recited while standing up. On weekdays the Amidah consists of 19 BENEDICTIONS: 3 paragraphs of praise, 13 of petition, and another 3 of thanksgiving. Some call this section of the daily prayer by the ancient name, *shemone 'esre* (Hebrew: "eighteen"), although the 19th benediction was added around 100 CE.

On SABBATHS and festivals and at NEW MOON services, the Amidah consists of the first 3 praises and the last 3 thanksgivings, but a special paragraph for the appropriate day replaces the usual 13 benedictions in the middle. Thus the Amidah at these services has only seven sections and is known as *bircath sheva*.

During the worship service, the Amidah is first recited by each individual as a silent prayer, giving any sinner a chance to atone without embarrassment. The prayer is then repeated aloud by the reader. All Jewish services include an Amidah.

◆ 1. "Blessed be Thou, O Lord, our God and God of our fathers, God of Abraham, God of Isaac, and God of Jacob, the great, the mighty, and the fearful God—God Most High—who bestowest goodly kindnesses, and art the Creator ["Koneh," which signifies primarily "Creator" and then "Owner"] of all, and rememberest the love of [or for] the Fathers and bringest a redeemer for their children's children for the sake of [His] Thy name in love. King, Helper, Savior, and Shield; blessed be Thou, Shield of Abraham."

2. "Thou art mighty forever, O Lord ["Adonai," not the Tetragrammaton]: Thou resurrectest the dead; art great to save. Sustaining the living in loving-kindness, resurrecting the dead in abundant mercies, Thou supportest the falling, and healest the sick, and settest free the captives, and keepest [fulfillest] Thy [His] faith to them

that sleep in the dust. Who is like Thee, master of mighty deeds [=owner of the powers over life and death], and who may be compared unto Thee? King sending death and reviving again and causing salvation to sprout forth, Thou art surely believed to resurrect the dead. Blessed be Thou, O Lord, who revivest the dead."

3. "Thou art holy and Thy name is holy, and the holy ones praise Thee every day. Selah. Blessed be Thou, O Lord, the holy God."

4. "Thou graciously vouchsafest knowledge to man and teachest mortals understanding: vouchsafe unto us from Thee knowledge, understanding, and intelligence. Blessed be Thou, O Lord, who vouchsafest knowledge."

5. "Lead us back, our Father, to Thy Torah; bring us near, our King, to Thy service, and cause us to return in perfect repentance before Thee. Blessed be Thou, O Lord, who acceptest repentance."

6. "Forgive us, our Father, for we have sinned; pardon us, our King, for we have transgressed: for Thou pardonest and forgivest. Blessed be Thou, O Gracious One, who multipliest forgiveness."

7. "Look but upon our affliction and fight our fight and redeem us speedily for the sake of Thy name: for Thou art a strong redeemer. Blessed art Thou, O Lord, the Redeemer of Israel."

8. "Heal us and we shall be healed; help us and we shall be helped: for Thou art our joy. Cause Thou to rise up full healings for all our wounds: for Thou, God King, art a true and merciful physician: blessed be Thou, O Lord, who healest the sick of His people Israel."

9. "Bless for us, O Lord our God, this year and all kinds of its yield for [our] good; and shower down [in winter, "dew and rain for"] a blessing upon the face of the earth: fulfil us of Thy bounty and bless this our year that it be as the good years. Blessed be Thou, O Lord, who blessest the years."

10. "Blow the great trumpet for our liberation, and lift a banner to gather our exiles, and gather us into one body from the four corners of the earth; blessed be Thou, O Lord, who gatherest the dispersed of Thy [His] people Israel."

11. "Restore our judges as of yore, and our counselors as in the beginning, and remove from us grief and sighing. Reign Thou over us, O Lord, alone in loving-kindness and mercy, and establish our innocence by the judgment. Blessed be Thou, O Lord the King, who lovest righteousness and justice."

12. "May no hope be left to the slanderers; but may wickedness perish as in a moment; may all Thine enemies be soon cut off, and do Thou speedily uproot the haughty and shatter and humble them speedily in our days. Blessed be Thou, O Lord, who strikest down enemies and humblest the haughty."

13. "May Thy mercies, O Lord our God, be stirred over the righteous and over the pious and over the elders of Thy people, the House of Israel, and over the remnant of their scribes, and over the righteous proselytes, and over us, and

bestow a goodly reward upon them who truly confide in Thy name; and assign us our portion with them forever; and may we not come to shame for that we have trusted in Thee. Blessed be Thou, O Lord, support and reliance for the righteous."

14.   "To Jerusalem Thy city return Thou in mercy and dwell in her midst as Thou hast spoken, and build her speedily in our days as an everlasting structure and soon establish there the throne of David. Blessed be Thou, O Lord, the builder of Jerusalem."

15.   "The sprout of David Thy servant speedily cause Thou to sprout up; and his horn do Thou uplift through Thy victorious salvation; for Thy salvation we are hoping every day. Blessed be Thou, O Lord, who causest the horn of salvation to sprout forth."

16.   "Hear our voice, O Lord our God, spare and have mercy on us, and accept in mercy and favor our prayer. For a God that heareth prayers and supplications art Thou. From before Thee, O our King, do not turn us away empty-handed. For Thou hearest the prayer of Thy people Israel in mercy. Blessed be Thou, O Lord, who hearest prayer."

17.   "Be pleased, O Lord our God, with Thy people Israel and their prayer, and return [*i.e.*, reestablish] the sacrificial service to the altar of Thy House, and the fire-offerings of Israel and their prayer [offered] in love accept Thou with favor, and may the sacrificial service of Israel Thy people be ever acceptable to Thee. And may our eyes behold Thy merciful return to Zion. Blessed be Thou who restorest Thy [His] Shekinah to Zion."

18.   "We acknowledge to Thee, O Lord, that Thou art our God as Thou wast the God of our fathers, forever and ever. Rock of our life, Shield of our help, Thou art immutable from age to age. We thank Thee and utter Thy praise, for our lives that are [delivered over] into Thy hands and for our souls that are entrusted to Thee; and for Thy miracles that are [wrought] with us every day and for Thy marvelously [marvels and] kind deeds that are of every time; evening and morning and noontide. Thou art [the] good, for Thy mercies are endless: Thou art [the] merciful, for Thy kindnesses never are complete: from everlasting we have hoped in Thee. And for all these things may Thy name be blessed and exalted always and forevermore. And all the living will give thanks unto Thee and praise Thy great name in truth, God, our salvation and help. Selah. Blessed be Thou, O Lord, Thy name is good, and to Thee it is meet to give thanks."

19.   "Bestow peace, happiness, and blessing, grace, loving-kindness, and mercy upon us and upon all Israel Thy people: bless us, our Father, even all of us, by the light of Thy countenance, for by this light of Thy countenance Thou gavest us, O Lord our God, the law of life, loving-kindness, and righteousness, and blessing and mercy, life and peace. May it be good in Thine eyes to bless Thy people Israel in every time and at every hour with Thy peace. Blessed be Thou,

O Lord, who blessest Thy [His] people Israel with peace."

Sabbath.   "Our God and God of our fathers! be pleased with our rest; sanctify us by Thy commandments, give us a share in Thy law, satiate us of Thy bounty, and gladden us in Thy salvation; and cleanse our hearts to serve Thee in truth: let us inherit, O Lord our God, in love and favor, Thy holy Sabbath, and may Israel, who hallows [loves] Thy name, rest thereon. Blessed be Thou, O Lord, who sanctifiest the Sabbath." ◆

(As translated in "Shemoneh 'Esreh," *The Jewish Encyclopedia* [1907], vol. 11, pgs. 270–272.)

There are numerous variations on the special benedictions that apply to festivals.

AMISH \'ä-mish, 'a-, 'ā-\, *also called* Amish Mennonite, member of a conservative Christian group in North America, primarily members of the Old Order Amish Mennonite Church. They originated in Europe as followers of Jakob Ammann, a 17th-century MENNONITE elder whose teachings caused controversy and SCHISM during the years 1693–97 among the Mennonites in Switzerland, Alsace, and south Germany. Ammann insisted that any Mennonite who had been excommunicated should be shunned or avoided by all other Mennonites and that anyone who told a falsehood should be excommunicated. He introduced washing of feet into the worship service and taught that church members should dress in a uniform manner, that beards should not be trimmed, and that it was wrong to attend services in a state church. Although he subsequently sought reconciliation with those who disagreed with him, the attempts failed. Amish settlements and congregations sprang up in Switzerland, Alsace, Germany, Russia, and Holland, but migration to North America in the 19th and 20th centuries and assimilation with Mennonite groups gradually eliminated the Amish in Europe.

The Amish began migrating to North America early in the 18th century and first settled in eastern Pennsylvania, where a large settlement is still found. Schisms and disruptions occurred after 1850 because of tensions between the "old order," or traditional Amish, and those who wished to adopt "new order" or progressive methods and organizations. During the next 50 years about two-thirds of the Amish either formed separate, small churches of their own or joined either the Mennonite Church or the General Conference Mennonite Church.

Those who continued the characteristic lifestyle of the Amish are primarily members of the Old Order Amish Mennonite Church. In the late 20th century there were about 50 Old Order Amish settlements in the United States and Canada, the largest in Pennsylvania, Ohio, Indiana, Iowa, Illinois, and Kansas. Their settlements are divided into autonomous congregations of about 75 baptized members. If the district becomes much larger it is again divided because the members meet in each other's homes. There are no church buildings. Each district has a bishop, two to four preachers, and an elder. The Amish differ little from the Mennonites in formal doctrine. Holy Communion is celebrated twice each year, and washing of feet is practiced by both groups. Adults are baptized and admitted to formal membership in the church at about age 17 to 20. Services are conducted in Palatine German, commonly known as

Pennsylvania Dutch, with some English, as well.

The Amish are known for their plain clothing and their plain way of life. They tend to live on largely self-sufficient family farms. The men wear broad-brimmed black hats, beards, and homemade plain clothes fastened with hooks and eyes instead of buttons. The women wear bonnets and long full dresses. No jewelry is worn. The Amish also shun telephones and electric lights and drive horses and buggies rather than automobiles.

AMITĀBHA \ˌə-mē-'tä-bə\ (Sanskrit: "Infinite Light"), *Japanese* Amida \'ä-mē-dä\, *Chinese* O-mi-t'o \'ə-'mē-'twȯ, 'ō-'mē-'tō\, in BUDDHISM, the great savior deity worshiped today principally by followers of PURE LAND BUDDHISM in Japan. As related in the SUKHĀVATĪ VYŪHA SŪTRA (the Indian text that was the fundamental SCRIPTURE of the Pure Land sects), it was many ages ago that a monk named Dharmākara made a number of vows, the 18th of which promised that, on his attaining buddhahood, all who believed in him and who called upon his name would be born into his paradise and would reside there in bliss until such time as they had obtained NIRVANA. Having accomplished his vows, the monk reigned as the Buddha Amitābha in the Western Paradise, called Sukhāvatī, the Pure Land.

Great bronze Amida (Daibutsu) at Kamakura, Japan, 1252
Asuka-en

The cult of Amitābha, which emphasizes faith above all else, came to the forefront in China about 650 CE and from there spread to Japan, where it led in the 12th and 13th centuries to the formation of the Pure Land school and the True Pure Land school, both of which continue to have large followings today. Amitābha as a savior figure was never as popular in Tibet and Nepal as he was in East Asia, but he is highly regarded in those countries as one of the five "self-born" buddhas who have existed eternally (*see* DHYĀNI-BUDDHA). According to this concept Amitābha manifested himself as the earthly BUDDHA GOTAMA and as AVALOKITEŚVARA (who is a BODHISATTVA). Some of the attributes given to Amitābha include: his color is red, his posture one of meditation (*dhyāna-mudrā*), his symbol the begging bowl, his mount the peacock, his consort Pāṇḍarā, his family Rāga, his element water, his sacred syllable "ba," or "āh," his SKANDHA (element of existence) *saṇjñā* (perceptions of sense objects), his direction the west, his sense perception taste, and his location in the human body the mouth.

As a bestower of longevity, Amitābha is called Amitāyus (Sanskrit: "Infinite Life"). In China and Japan the two names are often used interchangeably, but in Tibet the two forms are never confounded, and Amitāyus is worshiped in a special ceremony in Tibetan Buddhism for obtaining long life. He is depicted wearing ornaments and a crown and holding the ambrosia vase from which spill the jewels of eternal life.

AMITĀYURBUDDHADHYĀNA SŪTRA \ˌə-mē-'tä-yùr-ˌbùd-də-'dyä-nə-'sü-trə\ (Sanskrit: "Discourse Concerning Meditation on Amitāyus"), basic text of PURE LAND BUDDHISM, along with the larger and smaller SUKHĀVATĪ VYŪHA SŪTRAS (Sanskrit: "Description of the Western Paradise Sutras"). The sutra presents 16 forms of meditation as means of reaching the Pure Land and concludes that even the most wicked can attain this paradise by invoking the name of Amitāyus (AMITĀBHA).

The sutra was translated into Chinese under the title *Kuan-wu liang-shou ching* in 424 CE and has inspired many

Chinese commentaries. The Japanese version is entitled *Kammuryōju-kyō*. The Sanskrit original has been lost.

AMMONITE \'a-mə-ˌnīt\, any member of an ancient Semitic people whose principal city was Rabbath Ammon, in Palestine. The book of GENESIS traces the origin of the tribe through Ammon (Ben-Ammi), the son of Lot by an incestuous union with one of his daughters (Genesis 19:36–38). The "sons of Ammon" were in a long-standing, though sporadic, conflict with the Israelites (Deuteronomy 2:16–37; Judges 11:4, 12–33). Archaeological data indicate that the city of Rabbath Ammon was a powerful city-state as early as the 18th century BCE.

With difficulty, the Ammonites' fortress capital was captured by ISRAEL'S King DAVID. An Ammonite woman, one of many foreigners taken into King SOLOMON'S harem, was responsible for inducing the king to worship the Ammonite god Milcom (1 Kings 11:1).

During the reign of JEHOIAKIM (6th century BCE), the Ammonites allied themselves with the Chaldeans, Syrians, and others in an attack on JUDAH (2 Kings 24:2) and also harassed the Israelites when they attempted to rebuild the TEMPLE OF JERUSALEM after the BABYLONIAN EXILE. In the 2nd century BCE they were defeated by Judas Maccabeus (*see also* MACCABEES).

AMOGHAVAJRA \ə-ˌmō-gə-'vəj-rə\, 8th-century Indian Buddhist monk and missionary to China, a disciple of VAJRABODHI. In addition to the translations of Buddhist texts he made with his master, Amoghavajra is credited with introducing to China the important aspects of Esoteric

Amon, bronze statue,
c. 750–550 BCE
By courtesy of the Brooklyn Museum

BUDDHISM (*see* VAJRAYĀNA), including the ceremony of Ullambana, or All Souls' Day.

AMON \'ä-mən\, *also spelled* Amun, Amen, *or* Ammon, Egyptian deity who was revered as king of the gods. Amon may have been originally a local deity at Khmun (Hermopolis) in Middle Egypt; his cult reached Thebes, where he became the patron of the pharaohs by the reign of Mentuhotep I (2008–1957 BCE). At that date he was already identified with the sun god RE of HELIOPOLIS and, as Amon-Re, was received as a national god. Represented in human form, sometimes with a ram's head, or as a ram, Amon-Re was worshiped as part of the Theban triad including a goddess, MUT, and a youthful god, KHONS.

Amon's name meant The Hidden One, and his image was painted blue to denote invisibility. This attribute of invisibility led to a popular belief during the New Kingdom (1539–c. 1075 BCE) in the knowledge and impartiality of Amon, making him a god for those who felt oppressed.

Amon's influence was closely linked to the political well-being of Egypt. During the Hyksos domination (c. 1630–c. 1523 BCE), the princes of Thebes sustained his worship. Following the Theban victory over the Hyksos, Amon's stature and the wealth of his temples grew. In the late 18th dynasty Akhenaton (Amenhotep IV) directed his religious reform against the traditional cult of Amon, but he was unable to turn people from their belief in Amon and the other gods; and, under Tutankhamen, Ay, and Horemheb (1332–1292 BCE), Amon was gradually restored as the god of the empire and patron of the pharaoh.

In the New Kingdom, religious speculation among Amon's priests led to the concept of Amon as part of a triad (with PTAH and Re) or as a single god of whom all the other gods, even Ptah and Re, were manifestations. Under the sacerdotal state ruled by the priests of Amon at Thebes (c. 1075–c. 950 BCE), Amon evolved into a universal god who intervened through oracles in many affairs of state.

The succeeding 22nd and 23rd dynasties, the invasion of Egypt by Assyria (671–c. 663 BCE), and the sack of Thebes (c. 663 BCE) did not reduce the stature of the cult, which had acquired a second main center at Tanis in the Nile River delta. Moreover, the worship of Amon had become established among the Cushites of the Sudan, who were accepted by Egyptian worshipers of Amon when they invaded Egypt and ruled as the 25th dynasty (715–664 BCE). From this period onward, resistance to foreign occupation of Egypt was strongest in Thebes. Amon's cult spread to the oases, especially Siwa in Egypt's western desert, where Amon was linked with JUPITER. Alexander the Great won acceptance as pharaoh by consulting the oracle at Siwa, and he also rebuilt the SANCTUARY of Amon's temple at Luxor. The early Ptolemaic rulers contained Egyptian nationalism by supporting the temples, but, starting with Ptolemy IV Philopator in 207 BCE, nationalistic rebellions in Upper Egypt erupted. During the revolt of 88–85 BCE, Ptolemy IX Soter II sacked Thebes, dealing Amon's cult a severe blow. In 27 BCE a strong earthquake devastated the Theban temples, while in the Greco-Roman world the cult of ISIS and OSIRIS gradually displaced Amon.

AMOR \'ä-ˌmōr, 'ä-\: *see* CUPID.

AMORA \ə-'mōr-ə\ (Hebrew and Aramaic: "interpreter," or "reciter"), *plural* amoraim \ˌä-mō-'rä-im\, from the 3rd century CE, a Jewish scholar attached to one of several academies in Palestine (Tiberias, Sepphoris, Caesarea) or in Babylonia (Nehardea, Sura, Pumbedita). The *amoraim* collaborated in writing the GEMARA, collected interpretations of and commentaries on the MISHNAH, TOSEFTA, and Baraitot (*see* BARAITA). Writing in various Aramaic dialects interspersed with Hebrew, the two groups of *amoraim* began work about 200 CE on the Gemara (or Mishnah commentary) section of the TALMUD. Because the Babylonian *amoraim* worked about a century longer than their counterparts in Palestine, completing their work about 600 CE, the Talmud BAVLI ("Babylonian Talmud") was more comprehensive and, consequently, more authoritative than the Talmud YERUSHALMI ("Palestinian Talmud"), which lacks the Babylonian interpretations. In Palestine an ordained *amora* was called a RABBI; in Babylonia, a *rav*, or *mar*. *See also* TANNA.

AMOS \'ā-məs\ (fl. 8th century BCE), the first Hebrew prophet to have a biblical book named for him. He foretold the destruction of the northern kingdom of ISRAEL (although he did not specify Assyria as the cause) and, as a prophet of doom, anticipated later OLD TESTAMENT prophets.

The little that is known about Amos' life has been gleaned from his book, which was partly or wholly compiled by other hands. A shepherd by occupation and native of Tekoa (Amos 1:1; 7:14–15), 12 miles south of Jerusalem, Amos flourished during the reigns of King UZZIAH (c. 783–742 BCE) of JUDAH (the southern kingdom) and King Jeroboam II (c. 786–746 BCE) of Israel (Amos 1:1; 2 Kings 14:23–29). He actually preached for only a short time.

Under the influence of visions of divine destruction of the Hebrews by such natural disasters as locusts and fire (Amos 7:1–6), Amos traveled from Judah to the richer, more powerful kingdom of Israel, where he began to preach. The time is uncertain, but the Book of Amos puts the date as two years before an earthquake that may have occurred in 750 BCE. Amos castigated corruption and social injustice among Israel, its neighbors, and Judah; he asserted God's absolute sovereignty; and he predicted the imminent destruction of Israel and Judah. After preaching at BETHEL, a famous shrine under the special protection of Jeroboam II, Amos was ordered to leave the country by Jeroboam's priest Amaziah (Amos 7:12–13). Thereafter his fate is unknown.

Amos believed that God's absolute sovereignty over humanity compelled social justice for all people, rich and poor alike (Amos 2:6–7a; 4:1; 5:11–12). Not even God's chosen people were exempt from this fiat, and even they had to pay the penalty for breaking it (Amos 2:4–8, 12–16; 3:1–9:10); hence, Amos also believed in a moral order transcending nationalistic interests. So distinctive is his style of expression that the reader often can distinguish those portions genuinely by Amos from parts probably invented by others, such as the concluding optimistic section foretelling the restoration of the Davidic kingdom (Amos 9:11–15).

AMPHICTYONY \am-'fik-tē-ə-nē\, *also spelled* amphictiony (from Greek *amphiktyones*, "dwellers around, neighbors"), in ancient Greece, association of neighboring states formed around a religious center. The most important was the Amphictyonic League (Delphic Amphictyony). Originally composed of 12 peoples dwelling around Thermopylae, the league was centered first on the shrine of DEMETER and later became associated with the Temple of APOLLO at DELPHI. Member states sent two kinds of deputies (*pylagorai* and *hieromnēmones*) to a council (*pylaia*) that met twice a year and administered the temporal affairs of the shrines and their properties, supervised the treasury, and conducted the

PYTHIAN GAMES. In the 4th century BCE the league rebuilt the Delphic temple. Although primarily religious, the league exercised a political influence through its membership OATH, forbidding destruction of member cities or the cutting off of water supplies; the *hieromnēmones* could punish offenders and even proclaim a sacred war against them. Other important amphictyonies were the Delian and, in the Archaic period, the Calaurian (composed of states around the Saronic Gulf).

AMPHION AND ZETHUS \'am-fē-ən . . . 'zē-thəs\, in Greek mythology, the twin sons of ZEUS by ANTIOPE. When children, they were left to die on Mount Cithaeron but were found and brought up by a shepherd. Amphion became a great singer and musician, Zethus a hunter and herdsman. As adults, they built and fortified Thebes, blocks of stone forming themselves into walls at the sound of Amphion's lyre. Amphion married NIOBE and killed himself after the loss of his family.

AMPHITRITE \,am-fə-'trī-tē\, in Greek mythology, the goddess of the sea, wife of the god POSEIDON. Poseidon chose Amphitrite from among her sisters as the NEREIDS performed a dance on the isle of Naxos. Refusing his offer of marriage, she fled to ATLAS, from whom she was retrieved by a dolphin sent by Poseidon. Amphitrite then became Poseidon's wife; he rewarded the dolphin by making it a constellation. In art Amphitrite was represented either enthroned beside Poseidon or driving with him in a chariot drawn by sea horses or other sea creatures.

AMPHITRYON \am-'fi-trē-,än, -ən\, in Greek mythology, son of Alcaeus, king of Tiryns. Having accidentally killed his uncle Electryon, king of Mycenae, Amphitryon fled with Alcmene, Electryon's daughter, to Thebes, where he was cleansed of guilt by King Creon, his maternal uncle. Alcmene refused to marry Amphitryon until he had avenged the death of her brothers, all of whom except one had fallen in battle against the Taphians. Creon offered his help if Amphitryon would rid him of the uncatchable Cadmeian vixen. Amphitryon borrowed CEPHALUS' invincible hound Laelaps, and ZEUS changed both Laelaps and the vixen to stone. The Taphians, however, remained invincible until Comaetho, the king's daughter, out of love for Amphitryon, cut off her father's golden hair, the possession of which rendered him immortal. On Amphitryon's return to Thebes he married Alcmene.

When Amphitryon was once absent at war, Alcmene became pregnant by Zeus, who slept with her in the guise of her husband; she became pregnant again by her real husband upon his return. Thus she bore twin boys: Iphicles the son of Amphitryon, and HERACLES the son of Zeus.

AMRITSAR \,əm-'rit-sər\ (Punjabi: "Pool of Nectar"), seat of Sikhism, and one of the largest cities in east Punjab.

Established as a new settlement in the late 1570s, the town was originally named Rāmdāspur, taking its name from its founder, Gurū RĀMDĀS (GURŪ 1574–81), the fourth Gurū of the Sikhs. At the center of the town is the *amritsar*. This square tank serves as a reflecting pool for the GOLDEN TEMPLE (Darbār Sāhib), Sikhism's most sacred structure. In the early 1630s, under pressure from the Mughal administration at Lahore, the religio-administrative center of Sikh life was shifted to the remote Shivālik hills, just south of the HIMALAYAS, but with the waning of Mughal power in the first quarter of the 18th century, Amritsar once again became the axis of Sikh life. At the direction of Mahārājā Ranjīt Singh (1780–1839), the copper domes of the Darbār Sāhib were covered with gold-plated sheets. The city became a major center of trade, and after the arrival of the British it continued to develop, becoming one of the largest grain markets in northern India.

Its pivotal role in Sikh history is secured by the fact that it houses not only the Darbār Sāhib but also the AKĀL TAKHAT and the SHIROMANĪ GURD-WĀRĀ PRABANDHAK COM-MITTEE, and that it served as the center of inspiration and organization for SANT JARNAIL SINGH BHIN-DRANWALE'S efforts to create the independent nation of KHALISTAN in the early 1980s.

AMULET, *also called* talisman, an object, either natural or man-made, believed to be endowed with special powers to protect or bring good fortune. Amulets are carried on the person or kept in the desired sphere of influence.

Natural amulets are of many kinds: precious stones, metals, teeth and claws of animals, bones, plants, and so on. Man-made amulets, equally varied, include religious medallions and small figurines. Among believers amulets are thought to derive power from their connection with natural forces, from religious associations, or from being made in a ritual manner at a favorable time.

The MacGregor papyrus of ancient Egypt lists 75 amulets. One of the commonest was the SCARAB beetle, worn by the living and dead alike. The scarab symbolized life—perhaps because it pushed a ball of dung that was identified with the sun and was believed to contain the beetle's eggs, or perhaps because its hieroglyph was the same as that for the verb "to become"—and was thought to restore the dead person's heart in the next world. In Egypt the magic formulas originally recited over amulets to give them their power were eventually inscribed and worn themselves.

In the Middle Ages Christian amulets included relics of saints and letters said to have been sent from heaven. Among Jews the preparation of amulets became a rabbinic function. Muslims often carry verses from the QUR'AN, the names of God, or associated sacred numbers within small satchels. Christians may wear crosses or crucifixes, and statuettes of the MADONNA are found in some Roman Cath-

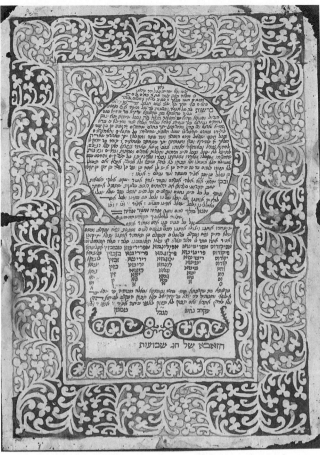

Moroccan amulet for Shavuot, the Jewish harvest festival
Erich Lessing—Art Resource

olic households. A popular type of amulet is the "good luck charm" such as the birthstone or rabbit's foot.

ANABAPTIST \,a-nə-'bap-tist\, *also called* Rebaptizer, member of a radical movement of the 16th-century Protestant REFORMATION. Its most distinctive tenet was adult BAPTISM. In the first generation of the movement, converts submitted to a second baptism, which was a crime punishable by death under the legal codes of the time. The Anabaptists denied that they were rebaptizers, for they repudiated their own infant baptism as a blasphemous formality. They considered the public CONFESSION of SIN and FAITH, sealed by adult baptism, as the only proper baptism. Following the Swiss Reformer HULDRYCH ZWINGLI, Anabaptists held that infants were not punishable for sin until an awareness of GOOD AND EVIL emerged within them, and that then they could exercise their own FREE WILL, repent, and accept baptism.

The Anabaptists also believed that the church was the community of the redeemed and should be separated from the state, which existed only for the punishment of sinners. Most Anabaptists opposed the use of the sword by Christians in the maintenance of social order and in the conduct of a just war. They also refused to swear civil oaths. For their beliefs thousands were put to death.

The Anabaptists did not aim to reform the medieval church. They were determined instead to restore the institutions and the spirit of the primitive church and were quite confident that they were living at the end of all ages. They readily recognized in their leaders divinely summoned prophets and apostles, and all converts stood ready to give a full account of their faith before the magistrates.

The Anabaptist movement originated in Zürich among a group of young intellectuals who rebelled against Zwingli's apparent subservience to the magistrates and his reluctance to proceed swiftly with a complete reform of the church. One of their leaders was Konrad Grebel, a highly educated humanist from a patrician family. The first adult baptisms took place at Zollikon, outside Zürich, at the beginning of 1525, and soon a mass movement was in progress.

The vehemence of the Anabaptist leaders and the revolutionary implications of their teaching led to their expulsion from one city after another. This simply increased the momentum of an essentially missionary movement. Soon civil magistrates took sterner measures, and most of the early Anabaptist leaders died in prison or were executed.

THOMAS MÜNTZER was among those (sometimes called "spirituals") who emphasized that the Anabaptists were living at the end of all ages. He was executed after leading Thuringian peasants in the revolt of 1525. His disciple Hans Hut (died in prison in Augsburg in 1527) was the principal radical Reformer in southern Germany.

Balthasar Hubmaier (executed in Vienna in 1528) was a leader in Nicholsburg, Moravia. Also in Moravia, where the ruling lords desired colonists and where many Anabaptists settled, a type of Anabaptism developed that stressed the community of goods modeled on the primitive church in Jerusalem. Under the leadership of Jakob Hutter the growing communes assumed his name. HUTTERITE groups survived and are now primarily located in the western United States and Canada.

Melchior Hofmann was the Anabaptist apostle in the Netherlands, where he developed a very large following. He taught that the world would soon end and that the new age would begin in Strasbourg, where he was imprisoned in 1533 and died *c.* 1543. Some of Hofmann's followers came under the influence of the Dutchman Jan Mathijs (died 1534) and of John of Leiden (Jan Beuckelson; died 1535). The two leaders and many refugees settled in 1534 in Münster, Westphalia, where they gained control of the city, established a communistic theocracy, and practiced polygamy. The city was captured in 1535 by an army raised by German princes, and the leaders were tortured and killed.

Modern historians have come to see the episode at Münster as an aberration of the Anabaptist movement. In the years following the episode, however, classical Protestants and Catholics increased the persecution of Anabaptists throughout Europe

without discrimination between the belligerent minority and the pacifist majority. The pacifist Anabaptists in the Netherlands and north Germany rallied under the leadership of the former priest Menno Simons and his lieutenant, Dirk Philips. Their followers survived and were eventually accepted as the MENNONITE religious group.

ANĀHITI \ə-'nä-hē-tē\, *also called* Anāhitā \ə-'nä-hē-,tä, -tə\, ancient Iranian goddess of fertility, royalty, and war. Possibly of Mesopotamian origin, her cult was made prominent by Artaxerxes II (reigned 404–359 BCE), and statues and temples were set up in her honor throughout the Persian empire. A common cult of the various peoples of the empire at that time, it persisted in Asia Minor long afterward. In the AVESTA she is called Ardvī Sūrā Anāhitā ("Damp, Strong, Untainted"); this seems to be an amalgam of two originally

Cylinder seal dating from the Achaemenid period, 6th–4th century BCE (above) and an imprint from that cylinder. The imprint shows a scene before either the queen or the goddess Anāhiti; in the Louvre, Paris
Erich Lessing—Art Resource

separate deities. In Greece Anāhiti was identified with ATHENA and ARTEMIS.

ANAN BEN DAVID \ä-'nän-,ben-dä-'vēd\ (fl. second half of the 8th century), Persian Jew, founder of the Ananites, an antirabbinical order from which the still-existing Karaite sect developed (*see* KARAISM).

Anan became prominent in the 760s, when he competed with his younger brother for the office of exilarch, head of the Jews of the BABYLONIAN EXILE. The office was hereditary, needing the confirmation of the ruling CALIPH, which Anan failed to obtain. He therefore declared himself antiexilarch and was jailed by the civil authorities. At his trial Anan pleaded that he had founded a new religion, one with similarities to ISLAM, and as a result was released and given government protection.

In 770 Anan wrote the definitive code of his order, the *Sefer ha-mitzwot* ("Book of Precepts"). Its unifying principle is its rejection of much of the TALMUD and of the rabbinate, which based its authority on the Talmud. Only the BIBLE is held to be valid, but it is interpreted with a mixture of freedom and literalism.

After Anan's death, his followers settled in Jerusalem. Eventually his sect developed into the order known as Karaism, which also was ascetically oriented and rejected Talmudic authority. When the State of ISRAEL was founded in 1948, several thousand Karaites settled there.

ĀNANDA \'ä-nən-də\ (Sanskrit: "joy," or "bliss"), in Indian philosophy of the UPANISHADS and the school of VEDĀNTA, an important attribute of the supreme being BRAHMAN. *Ānanda* is characteristically used in the *Taittirīya Upaniṣad* (*c.* 6th century BCE) to describe the nature of Brahman and, simultaneously, the highest state of the individual self. Such joy is identified with the joy that is brought to the self by its release from the usual entanglements of waking and bodily consciousness. In this sense *ānanda* continues to play an important role in various schools of Hindu philosophy, although its nature is differently interpreted.

ĀNANDA (fl. 6th century BCE, India), according to tradition, the first cousin of the BUDDHA GOTAMA, known as his "beloved disciple."

Ānanda was a monk and served as Gotama's personal attendant. According to the VINAYA PIṬAKA texts, it was he who persuaded the Buddha to allow women to become nuns. According to Buddhist tradition Ānanda was the only one of the Buddha's intimate disciples who had not attained enlightenment when the Buddha died. The tradition goes on to recount that he attained that goal just before the first council, at which he recited from his memory of the Buddha's teaching the SUTTA PIṬAKA (the "canonical" collection that contains the Buddha's sermons). A collection of verses ascribed to Ānanda himself is preserved in the *Theragāthā* segment of the *Sutta Piṭaka*.

ANANKE \ə-'naŋ-kē\, in Greek literature, necessity or FATE personified. In Homer the personification has not yet occurred, although even the gods admit they are limited in their freedom of action. Ananke becomes rather prominent in post-Homeric literature, particularly in the mystic cult of Orphism, but is definitely known to emerge into a cult only at Corinth, where she was worshiped with Bia ("Might," or "Force"). Because of her unalterable nature it was pointless to render to her offerings or sacrifice—"Nothing is stronger than dread Necessity" was a Greek byword.

In literature she is associated with the NYMPH Adrasteia, the Moirai (or Fates, of whom she was the mother, according to Plato in *The Republic*), and similar deities. In Italy she does not appear to have been worshiped at all; the description of Necessitas (Ananke) in Horace's CARMINA is purely literary.

ANATH \ä-'nät\, *also spelled* Anat, chief West Semitic goddess of love and war, the sister of the god BAAL.

Considered a beautiful young girl, she was often designated "the Virgin" in ancient texts. Probably one of the best known of the Canaanite deities, she was famous for her youthful vigor and ferocity in battle, and consequently was adopted as a favorite by the Egyptian king Ramses II (reigned 1279–13 BCE). Although Anath was often associated with the god RESHEPH in ritual texts, she was primarily known for her role in the myth of Baal's death and resurrection, in which she mourned and searched for him and finally helped to retrieve him from the netherworld.

Egyptian representations of Anath show a nude goddess, often standing on a lion and holding flowers. During the Hellenistic Age, the goddesses Anath and ASTARTE were blended into one deity, called ATARGATIS.

ANĀTHAPIṆḌIKA \ə-,nä-tə-'pin-di-kə\, in Buddhist tradition, a banker of Sāvatthi (modern Śrāvāsti) and early follower of the BUDDHA GOTAMA. Tradition states that Anāthapiṇḍika met the Buddha at Rājagaha and became deeply devoted to him. He invited the Buddha to his city, where he built for him a famous monastery at Jetavana, where the Buddha spent most of his time and delivered most of his sermons. He is depicted as an ideal layman within the Buddhist tradition.

ANATHEMA \ə-'na-thə-mə\ (Greek: "something set up or dedicated," in the Septuagint a translation of Hebrew *ḥērem* "thing dedicated [to consecration or destruction]"), in the OLD TESTAMENT, a creature or object set apart for sacrificial offering. Its return to profane use was strictly banned, and such objects, destined for destruction, thus became effectively accursed as well as consecrated (Leviticus 27:21, 28–29; Judges 1:17). Old Testament descriptions of religious wars call both the enemy and their besieged city anathema inasmuch as they were destined for destruction (Joshua 6:17–21; 1 Samuel 15:1–3).

In NEW TESTAMENT usage a different meaning developed. ST. PAUL used the word anathema to signify a curse and the forced expulsion of one from the community of Christians (Romans 9:3; 1 Corinthians 12:3; Galatians 1:8–9). In 431 CE ST. CYRIL OF ALEXANDRIA pronounced his 12 anathemas against the heretic NESTORIUS. In the 6th century anathema came to mean the severest form of EXCOMMUNICATION that formally separated a heretic completely from the Christian church and condemned his doctrines.

ANĀTMAN \ə-'nät-mən\ (Sanskrit: "non-self"), *Pāli* anatta, in BUDDHISM, the doctrine that there is in humans no permanent, underlying substance that can be called the soul. Instead, the individual is compounded of five factors of consciousness, known as SKANDHA, that are constantly changing. *Anātman* is a departure from the Hindu belief in ĀTMAN ("self"). In Buddhism, the absence of a self, ANITYA ("the impermanence of all being"), and DUKKHA ("suffering") are the three characteristics of all existence; recognition of these characteristics constitutes "right understanding," a component in the Path that leads to Enlightenment.

ANATOLIAN
RELIGIONS

The religions of Anatolia comprise the beliefs and practices of the ancient peoples and civilizations of Turkey and Armenia, including the Hittites, Hattians, Luwians, Hurrians, Assyrian colonists, Urartians, and Phrygians. This area, Asia Minor, shows a remarkable continuity in its worship. Beginning in the Neolithic Period (c. 7000–6000 BCE) and continuing for some 6,000 years, the population venerated a divine pair, mother goddess and weather god, the former in association with the lion, the latter with the bull; a divine son, associated with the panther; and a god of hunting whose symbolic animal was the stag. To the ancients, for whom the essence of a thing lay in its name, this continuity was less obvious than it is today. The many names under which the deities were known at different times and places now appear of less religious significance than the constancy of the types.

PREHISTORIC PERIODS

The earliest evidence of religious beliefs has come to light at the mound of Çatal Hüyük, to the south of modern Konya in central Turkey. Here archaeologists have discovered remains of a Neolithic village of mud-brick houses, many of which can be identified as shrines. They date to about 6500–5800 BCE. Huge figures of goddesses in the posture of giving birth, leopards, and the heads of bulls and rams are modeled on some of the walls. Other walls contain frescoes showing hunt scenes or vultures devouring headless human corpses. A painting from the site also shows images of the dead being stripped of flesh by vultures in a mortuary outside the village before being buried under platforms in the houses. Stone and terra-cotta statuettes found in these shrines represent a female figure, sometimes accompanied by leopards, and a male either bearded and seated on a bull or youthful and riding a leopard. Based on a carved plaque found at this site, it appears that the main deity was a goddess, a mistress of animals, with whom were associated a son and a consort.

At Kültepe, Turkey, statuettes have been recovered; the majority are abstract, disk-shaped idols without limbs, and many of them have two, three, or even four heads—perhaps a representation of a divine family, a mother goddess with consort and child or children. Molds for a pair of male and female figures—the female

Marble two-headed idol from Kültepe, Turkey, Bronze Age, c. 2000 BCE; in the Archaeological Museum, Ankara, Turkey
Giraudon—Art Resource

in most instances holds a baby—have been found at several sites at a somewhat later level.

Old Assyrian seal impressions contain an elaborate ICONOGRAPHY featuring a whole pantheon of deities, some recognizably Mesopotamian, others native Anatolian, distinguished by such features as dress, attendant animals, weapons, actions, and attitudes. Among them are several weather gods, all associated with a bull. A bull alone, carrying a PYRAMID upon its back, sometimes surmounted by a bird, is a particularly common motif. Other deities are a war god holding various weapons, a hunting god holding a bird or hare, a god in a horse-drawn chariot, another in a wagon drawn by boars, a goddess enthroned and surrounded by animals, a nude goddess, and several composite beings.

RELIGIONS OF THE HITTITES, HATTIANS, AND HURRIANS

Gods and myths. From 1700 to 1200 BCE the history of Asia Minor is well documented. The Hittites in the center, the Luwians in the south and west, and the Palaians in the north were speakers of related Indo-European languages. In the southeast were the Hurrians, comparatively late arrivals from the region of Lake Urmia. The Hattians, whose language appears to have become extinct, were most probably the earliest inhabitants of the kingdom of Hatti itself.

Each of these nations had its own pantheon, and individual cult centers had their own names for deities. It seems that the deity of each city was regarded as a distinct personality. There were also specialized weather gods, governing lightning, the clouds, rain, the palace, the royal person, the sceptre, and the the army. In the iconography, however, there was a well-defined and limited number of divine types.

The most widely worshiped Hittite deity was the weather god, and under the title "weather god of Hatti" he became the chief deity of the official pantheon, a great figure who bestowed kingship and brought victory in war. His name in Luwian, and probably also in Hittite, was TARHUN (Tarhund); in Hattic he was called Taru, and in Hurrian, TESHUB. As Tarhun's spouse, the great goddess of the city of Arinna (which has not been located) was exalted as patroness of the state. Her name in Hattic was Wurusemu, but the Hittites worshiped her under the epithet ARINNITTI. She is a sun goddess, but she may originally have had CHTHONIC (underworld) characteristics. The king and queen were her HIGH PRIEST and priestess.

The weather god of another city, Nerik, was regarded as the son of this supreme pair, and they had daughters named Mezzulla and Hulla and a granddaughter, Zintuhi. Telipinu was another son of the weather god and had similar attributes. He was a central figure in the Hittite myths.

There was also a male sun god, a special form of whom was the "sun god in the water," probably the sun as reflected in the waters of a lake. His name in Hittite was Istanu, borrowed from the Hattic Estan (Luwian Tiwat, Hurrian Shimegi). There was also a moon god (Hittite and Luwian Arma, Hurrian KUSHUKH), but he plays little part in the texts. According to official theology there also existed a sun god or goddess of the underworld. In this place resided the Sun on its journey from west to east during the night.

The god of hunting, denoted in text by the logogram KAL, appears frequently on Hittite monuments; he holds a bird and a hare, and he stands on a stag, his sacred animal. The war god also appears; his Hattic name was Wurunkatti ("King of the Land"), his Hurrian counterpart Hesui.

The Hittite goddess of love and war was called Shaushka in Hurrian. As a warrior goddess she was represented as a winged figure standing on a lion accompanied by doves and two female attendants.

Among the lesser deities, there was a mother goddess, Hannahanna "the grandmother," closely associated with birth, creation, and destiny, plus many mountains, rivers, springs, and spirits of past kings and queens who had "become gods" at death.

In general, the gods were imagined to have their own lives, though also needing the service of their worshipers, who in turn were dependent on the gods for their well-being. The gods lived in their temples, where they had to be fed, clothed,

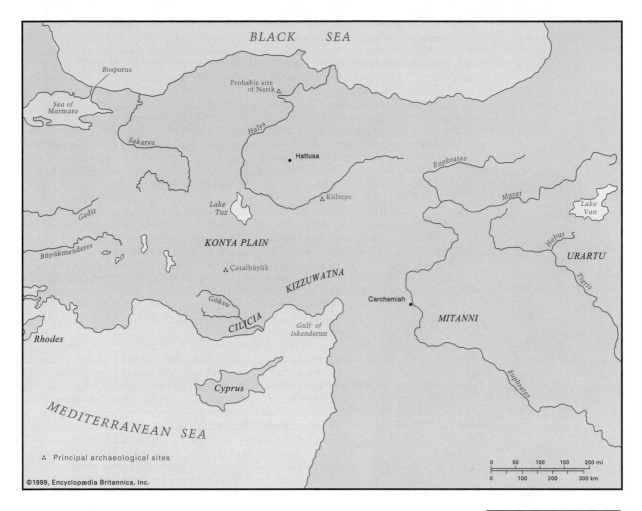

Principal religious centers of ancient Anatolia

washed, and entertained; without this service from humans the gods might withdraw in anger and so cause life on earth to wither and die. One of the most characteristic rituals of the Hittites was the invocation by which a god who had absented himself was induced to return and attend to his duties.

A particularly well-attested type of Anatolian myth occurs in connection with the invocation of an absent god and tells how the god once disappeared and caused a blight on earth, how he was sought and found, and eventually returned to restore life and vigor. In one such myth the weather god withdraws in anger and the search is conducted by the sun god (whose messenger is an eagle), the father of the weather god, his grandfather, and his grandmother Hannahanna. In another version, the weather god goes down to the netherworld through a hole in the ground, apparently the hole from which the river Marassantiya (modern Kızıl Irmak, in Turkey) gushed forth, which suggests that this weather god may really have been a god of the underground waters.

Another myth, "The Slaying of the Dragon," connected with the Hattian city Nerik, was apparently recited at a great annual spring festival called Purulli. It tells how the weather god fought the dragon and was at first defeated but subsequently, by means of a ruse, succeeded in getting the better of him and then killing him.

Both an elaborate epic of the struggle against Ullikummi and a *Theogony*, though written in Hittite, are Hurrian in origin and refer to Hurrian and even Mesopotamian deities. The *Theogony* tells of the struggle for kingship among the

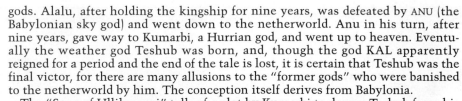

Basalt stele of Tarhun, god of thunderstorms, with a lightning flash in one hand and an axe in the other, from Til Barsip, Syria, c. 900 BCE; in the Louvre, Paris
Erich Lessing—Art Resource

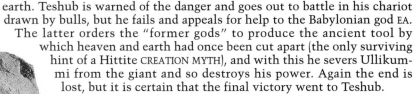

gods. Alalu, after holding the kingship for nine years, was defeated by ANU (the Babylonian sky god) and went down to the netherworld. Anu in his turn, after nine years, gave way to Kumarbi, a Hurrian god, and went up to heaven. Eventually the weather god Teshub was born, and, though the god KAL apparently reigned for a period and the end of the tale is lost, it is certain that Teshub was the final victor, for there are many allusions to the "former gods" who were banished to the netherworld by him. The conception itself derives from Babylonia.

The "Song of Ullikummi" tells of a plot by Kumarbi to depose Teshub from his supremacy by begetting a monstrous stone as champion. Ullikummi, the stone monster, grows in the sea, which reaches his waist, while his head touches the sky; he stands on the shoulder of Upelluri, a GIANT who carries heaven and earth. Teshub is warned of the danger and goes out to battle in his chariot drawn by bulls, but he fails and appeals for help to the Babylonian god EA. The latter orders the "former gods" to produce the ancient tool by which heaven and earth had once been cut apart (the only surviving hint of a Hittite CREATION MYTH), and with this he severs Ullikummi from the giant and so destroys his power. Again the end is lost, but it is certain that the final victory went to Teshub.

Rites and ceremonies. Hittite records give abundant evidence for a state religious cult. The king himself and all important state matters, including royal decrees and treaties, were placed under the protection of national deities. Confession and expiation formed the main themes of the extant royal prayers.

Many extant texts consist of descriptions of festivals in which the king or queen is the chief officiant. These festivals were numerous, but their names are largely unintelligible. Many of them were seasonal. The preliminary details, such as the robing of the king and his entry into the temple, accompanied by various dignitaries and by musicians playing their instruments, differed little from one festival to another. The festivals invariably culminated in LIBATIONS and frequently in a cultic meal. One such festival lasted 38 days and involved celebrations in a dozen different cities.

From tablets we know that the Hittites practiced a burial ritual for a king or queen that lasted 13 days; the body was cremated and the fire extinguished with potable liquids. The bones were then dipped in oil or fat and wrapped in cloth. A feast followed their placement on a stool in a stone chamber. Although CREMATIONS were practiced, burial of the body in an earthen grave was not uncommon. One site contains 72 burials, 50 of which were cremations. The other site contained only cremations, and the presence of some precious objects among them suggests that these might be burials of privileged persons.

RELIGIONS OF SUCCESSOR STATES

When Hattusa fell, about 1180 BCE, the Luwians moved eastward and southward into Cappadocia, Cilicia, and North Syria. Here they formed a number of small successor kingdoms. Shortly afterward the Phrygians crossed the Bosporus from Thrace and occupied the center of the Anatolian plateau, cutting off in the extreme southwest a remnant of the Luwian people, who became known as the Lycians and maintained their reverence for the Luwian gods Tarhun, Runda, Arma, and Santa into classical times.

The East Luwians, whose rulers used the Hittite hieroglyphic script to record their deeds, worshiped these same deities; but their chief goddess was KUBABA, who only appears in the archives of Hattusa except as the local goddess of Carchemish in Syria. Her prominence was due to political factors, for Carchemish was then the leading Hittite city.

In the east, the Hurrians formed a new kingdom, Urartu, which rose to power from about 900 to 600 BCE. Their national god was HALDI, and he is associated with a weather god, Tesheba, a sun goddess, Shiwini, and a goddess, Bagbartu (or Bagmashtu). Haldi is represented standing on a lion, Tesheba on a bull, Shiwini holding a winged sun disk above her head. The cult was practiced not only in temples but also in front of rock-hewn niches in the form of gates through which the deity was probably believed to manifest himself.

The Phrygian Mother goddess was Cybele, or Cybebe, a goddess of the mountains, out of which she was believed to manifest herself to her devotees. In Anatolia, Cybele's cult is marked by carved rock facades with niches or by rock-hewn thrones, on which the statue would be set; in front of these, the rites were celebrated in the open air. The high priest of Cybele was given the name of ATTIS, and—at least in later times—she was attended by a band of devotees called GALLI, whose orgiastic dancing, at the climax of which they castrated themselves, was notorious.

Bronze votive plaque of an armed god mounted on a lion, from Urartu, Turkey, 8th–7th century BCE; in the Louvre, Paris
Erich Lessing—Art Resource

The cult myth of these rites told how Cybele (known at Pessinus as AGDISTIS, from Mount Agdos [or Mount Agdistis] in the vicinity) loved a beautiful youth named Attis. According to the earliest version, Attis was killed by a boar. All later versions, however, refer to wild revelry and castration, while in one version Attis is afterwards turned into a pine tree. The "Phrygian rites" introduced into Rome under the Emperor Claudius (reigned 41–54 CE) included the ceremonious felling of a pine tree to represent the dead youth and its transport in procession to the temple. Still later, the sacrifice of a bull or a ram and the belief in the resurrection of Attis were added to the cult.

Among other deities, the goddess Ma of COMANA, despite her name (Mother), was distinct from Cybele and was identified with the war goddess BELLONA. The god Men, who appears on numerous monuments of the Hellenistic period, was an equestrian moon god, later identified with Attis.

ANCAEUS \an-'sē-əs\, in Greek mythology, the son of ZEUS or POSEIDON and king of the Leleges of Samos. In the Argonautic expedition, after the death of Tiphys, the helmsman of the *Argo*, Ancaeus took his place. While planting a vineyard, Ancaeus was told by a seer that he would never drink of its wine. When the grapes were ripe, he squeezed the juice into a cup and, raising it to his lips, mocked the seer, who retorted with the words "There is many a slip between cup and the lip." At that moment it was announced that a wild boar was ravaging the land. Ancaeus set down the cup, leaving the wine untasted, hurried out, and was killed by the boar.

ANCESTOR WORSHIP, any of a variety of religious beliefs and practices concerned with the spirits of dead persons regarded as relatives, some of whom may be mythical.

The core of ancestor worship is the belief in the continuing existence of the dead and in a close relation between the living and the dead, who continue to influence the affairs of the living. The spirits of the dead are often thought to help the living, but they often are thought to do harm if not propitiated. Veneration is shown those persons who in their lifetimes held positions of importance, such as heads of families, lineages, clans, tribes, kingdoms, and other social groups. In some societies only the spirits of the recently deceased are given attention; in others, all ancestors, near and remote in time, are included. In still other societies, one ancestor may be the focus of attention, and he or she is often regarded as a hero. In most societies, ancestor worship was only one element of a complex of SUPERNATURALISM, and seldom a dominant feature.

The presence or absence of ancestor worship relates in a general way to the importance of KINSHIP in the societies concerned. Where continuity of kinship and inheritance of property are very important, elders are characteristically regarded with respect, and the persistence of bonds of affinity with ancestors is favored. In modern China and Japan, where the importance of kinship and the size of kin groups have declined, traditional practices of ancestor worship have correspondingly declined.

All of the behavior and practices that are customary with regard to other kinds of supernatural beings are found in rites of ancestral worship—veneration and propitiation in the forms of prayers, offerings, sacrifices, the maintenance of moral standards, and festivals of honor that may include pageantry, music, dance, and other forms of art. Perhaps the only truly distinctive ritual acts of ancestor worship are commemorative ceremonies, held annually or at other fixed intervals, and tendance of graves, monuments, or other symbols commemorating them. Acts of piety toward ancestors reflect the idea that the spirits continue in some measure to be kin and are active participants in the life of the community. Whether ancestral spirits are themselves gods with powers or are intermediaries with higher powers, communion with them is a form of transcendence of ordinary states of existence, which may be a conscious or unconscious goal of the acts of devotion.

Ancestor worship in various forms was practiced among the ancient civilization of the Mediterranean, where cults of the dead sometimes also existed, and among later European peoples. Ancient EGYPTIAN RELIGION featured a cult of the dead but gave little attention to ancestral spirits except to those of royalty, which were venerated by the people and especially honored in rites observed by their royal descendants. In ancient GREEK RELIGION, ancestor worship overlapped with hero worship. Some ritual attention was given to spirits of household heads and political leaders, and the spirits of men whose deeds were heroic were sometimes elevated to immortality and made the objects of rites of reverence. Ancient Celts, Teutons, Vikings, and Slavic groups also conducted rites of propitiation and sacrifice.

Among nonliterate societies, well-developed ancestor cults are limited principally to peoples of sub-Saharan Africa, Melanesia, and some tribal groups of India and adjacent parts of Asia. The greatest development was in AFRICAN RELIGIONS, where ancestral spirits are commonly an important part of the roster of supernatural beings. Among the civilizations of Asia, the classic examples of ancestor worship have been China and Japan. In both societies, however, reverence for, rather than worship of, ancestors is a more nearly accurate description of the beliefs and practices. The spread of modern European culture weakened, displaced, or otherwise put an end to ancestor worship as an overt practice in most nonliterate societies, and technological, social, and ideological changes discouraged its continuation in more modern societies. Yet its remnants continue to be periodically significant in a number of Latin American, African, and Asian cultures.

The 19th-century sociologist Herbert Spencer regarded fear and consequent propitiation of the souls of ancestors as the earliest form of religion, an interpretation that later scholars set aside as unverifiable. Modern scholarship has followed the trend of the social sciences in considering ancestor cults in relation to other elements of religious complexes, the social order, and the whole of culture. Through their symbolic representations of kinship and of the social hierarchy of kin groups, the beliefs and acts of ancestor worship may be seen as establishing and reinforcing ideas of social roles and identities, thereby contributing to psychological well-being and social harmony. But ideas about ancestors may also be seen sometimes to instill as well as to allay anxiety. In this connection ancestor worship may have an important moral significance by encouraging social conformity.

ANCHISES \an-'kī-sēz, aŋ-\, in Greek mythology, member of the royal family of Troy; he was king of DARDANUS on Mount Ida. The goddess APHRODITE met him and bore him AENEAS. For revealing the name of the child's mother, Anchises was killed or struck blind by lightning. In later legend and in Virgil's *Aeneid*, he was conveyed out of Troy on the shoulders of his son Aeneas.

ANDANIA MYSTERIES \an-'dā-nē-ə\, ancient Greek mystery cult, held in honor of the goddess DEMETER and her daughter Kore (PERSEPHONE) at the town of Andania in Messenia. An inscription of 92 BCE gives directions for the conduct of the rites, although it relates no details of the initiation ceremonies. The ritual was performed by certain "holy ones" of both sexes, who were chosen from the various tribes.

Initiation seems to have been open to men, women, and children, bonded and free, and all costumes were to be severely plain and of inexpensive material. An exception was made for those who were to be "costumed into the likeness of deities," possibly indicating that a pageant or drama was performed. There was a procession, precedence in which was strictly regulated, and the main ceremonial was preceded by sacrifices to a number of deities.

ANDREW, SAINT \'an-,drü\ (d. traditionally 60/70 CE, Patras, Achaia [Greece]; feast day November 30), one of the

Twelve APOSTLES and brother of ST. PETER. He is the patron saint of Scotland and of Russia.

In the SYNOPTIC GOSPELS (Matthew, Mark, and Luke), Peter and Andrew were called from their fishing by Jesus to follow him, promising that he would make them fishers of men. In John's Gospel he is the first apostle named, and he was a disciple of ST. JOHN THE BAPTIST before Jesus' call.

Early Byzantine tradition (dependent on John 1:40) calls Andrew *protokletos*, "first called." Legends recount his missionary activity in the area about the Black Sea. Apocryphal writings centered on him include the Acts of Andrew, Acts of Andrew and Matthias, and Acts of Peter and Andrew. A 4th-century account reports his death by CRUCIFIXION, and late medieval accretions describe the cross as X-shaped. He is iconographically represented with an X-shaped cross.

ST. JEROME records that Andrew's relics were taken from Patras (modern Pátrai) to Constantinople (modern Istanbul) by command of the Roman emperor Constantius II in 357. From there the body was taken to Amalfi, Italy (Church of Sant' Andrea), in 1208, and in the 15th century the head was taken to Rome (St. Peter's, Vatican City). In September 1964 Pope Paul VI returned Andrew's head to Pátrai as a gesture of goodwill toward the Christians of Greece.

ANDROGYNY, in mythology, the state of having the characteristics of both male and female. Androgyny, as the union of male and female, can represent totality, completeness, or perfection; hence in some mythical traditions, a primal mythic being (*i.e.*, a creator or first human) is androgynous and thereby expresses in his or her person a union of disparate features or opposites. This does not express a chaotic hybrid but rather a creative totality (the "coincidence of opposites"). In other systems human procreation is explained in terms of a division of a complete, originally androgynous being (as in Plato's *Symposium* and in the Gnostic Gospel of Philip).

ANDROMACHE \an-'drä-mə-kē\, in Greek myth, the daughter of Eëtion (prince of Thebe in Mysia) and wife of HECTOR. All her relations perished in or shortly after the taking of Troy. When the captives were allotted, Andromache fell to NEOPTOLEMUS, the son of ACHILLES, whom she accompanied to Epirus and to whom she bore three sons. At Neoptolemus' death, HELENUS, the brother of Hector, inherited both Andromache and the kingdom. After the death of Helenus, Andromache returned to Asia Minor with her youngest son, Pergamus, who there founded a town named after himself.

Andromeda and the sea monster
Culver Pictures

ANDROMEDA \an-'drä-mə-də\, in Greek myth, daughter of King Cepheus and Queen Cassiope of Joppa in Palestine (called Ethiopia) and wife of PERSEUS. Cassiope offended the NEREIDS by boasting that Andromeda was more beautiful than they, so in revenge POSEIDON sent a sea monster to devastate Cepheus' kingdom. Since only Andromeda's sacrifice would appease the gods, she was chained to a rock and left to be devoured by the monster. Perseus flew by on PEGASUS, saw Andromeda, and asked Cepheus for her hand. Cepheus agreed, and Perseus slew the monster. At their marriage, however, her uncle Phineus tried to claim her as his betrothed. Perseus turned him to stone with MEDUSA'S head. Andromeda bore Perseus six sons and a daughter.

ANEKĀNTAVĀDA \ˌə-nā-ˌkän-tə-'vä-də, -'kän-tə-ˌvä-\, literally the "doctrine of non-onesidedness," a basic Jain (*see* JAINISM) ontological assumption that recognizes that any entity is at once enduring, but also undergoes change that is both constant and inevitable. This doctrine states that all entities have three aspects: substance (*dravya*), quality (*guṇa*), and mode (*paryāya*). The substance serves as a substratum for multiple qualities which must be understood as constantly undergoing modification. Thus, any entity has an abiding, continuous nature, but its qualities are in a state of constant flux.

AṄGAD \'əŋ-ˌgəd\, *also called* Lehna \lāh-'nä\, *or* Lahina \lə-hē-'nä\ (b. 1504, Matte di Sarai, India—d. 1552, Khadur), second GURŪ of the Sikhs (1539–52). Aṅgad was a *śakta* ("worshiper of the goddess," *see* ŚAKTI) before coming to the fold of Gurū NĀNAK, the founder of the Sikh community. He is known in the Sikh tradition for his loyalty to Gurū Nānak. Aṅgad was appointed Gurū in 1539 and was able to sustain the community after the death of Gurū Nānak and prepare it for later phases of expansion. In Sikh lore, Gurū Aṅgad is credited with having established a set of crucial institutions; he is also said to have originated the Punjabi script, Gurmukhi, in which the ĀDI GRANTH is written, and to have promoted the practice of community meals (*langar*) that broke down CASTE barriers. However, no historically credible documents support these attributions.

ANGEL (Greek: *angelos*, "messenger"), primarily in Western religions (*i.e.*, ZOROASTRIANISM, JUDAISM, CHRISTIANITY, and ISLAM), any of numerous spiritual beings, powers, or principles that mediate between the realm of the sacred and the profane realm of time and space.

Functioning as messengers or servants of the deity or as guardians of individuals or nations, angels have been classified into ranks or into hierarchies by theologians or philosophical thinkers, by sects that have become religions in their own right (for example, the DRUZE religion), and by syncretistic movements (for example, the dualistic sect GNOSTICISM).

The number of such celestial beings in the rankings—often 4, 7, or 12—was generally based on the theory of planetary spheres in Hellenistic or Iranian ASTROLOGY or on the hierarchy derived from Oriental monarchical government.

The archangel Jibrīl (Gabriel), Arabic miniature, 14th century
The Granger Collection

In Zoroastrianism, the AMESHA SPENTAS, or bounteous immortals, of AHURA MAZDĀ, the Good Lord, are arranged in a hierarchy of seven: SPENTA MAINYU (the Holy Spirit), VOHU MANAH (Good Mind), Asha (Truth), Ārmaiti (Right Mindedness), Khshathra Vairya (Kingdom), Haurvatāt (Wholeness), and Ameretāt (Immortality).

In Judaism, the hierarchy of angels—often called in the OLD TESTAMENT the "hosts of heaven" or the "company of divine beings"—is not strictly defined. In postbiblical Judaism—especially in apocalyptic literature, which describes God's dramatic intervention in history—seven angels, sometimes called ARCHANGELS, lead the heavenly hosts that in the TALMUD are viewed as countless. These seven, noted in the noncanonical *First Book of Enoch* (chapter 20), are: Uriel (leader of the heavenly hosts and guardian of *sheol*, the Underworld); Raphael (guardian of human spirits); Raguel (avenger of God against the world of lights); Michael (guardian of ISRAEL); Sariel (avenger of the spirits, "who SIN in the spirit"); GABRIEL (ruler of paradise, the seraphim, and the cherubim); and Remiel, also called Jeremiel (guardian of the souls in *sheol*). Of these, two (Michael and Gabriel) are mentioned in the Old Testament and two others (Raphael and Uriel) in the APOCRYPHA, a collection of noncanonical works.

In rabbinic literature, angels are classified into two basic groupings, higher and lower. Included among the higher group are the cherubim and seraphim, winged guardians of God's throne or chariot, and the *ofannim* (Hebrew: "wheels"), all of which are noted in the Old Testament. Among the sects associated with the DEAD SEA SCROLLS, the higher angels include the angels of light, darkness, destruction, and holiness.

Christianity developed a hierarchy of angels based on the Judaic tradition. In addition to angels, archangels, seraphim, and cherubim, five other spiritual angelic groups—named in the letters of Paul in the New Testament—were accepted in the church by the 4th century: virtues, powers, principalities, dominions, and thrones. Together they made up a hierarchy or choir of angels. As objects of devotion, special attention has been given to the archangels Michael, Gabriel, and Raphael in ROMAN CATHOLICISM and EASTERN ORTHODOXY.

Belief in angels (Arabic *malā'ika*) is a fundamental component of *imān* (faith) in Islam, often listed after belief in God (QUR'AN 2:285). Employing concepts of angelology familiar to Jews and Christians, the Qur'an speaks of winged angelic hosts gathered at God's throne, praising him, blessing the Prophet MUHAMMAD, assisting the faithful in battle, greeting the righteous in paradise, and torturing the damned in hell. At Adam's creation they voiced the fear that humans would "do evil and shed blood on earth" (Qur'an 2:30), but Adam, instructed by God, bested them in a naming contest. The Qur'an thus signals that humans rank above the angels and all other creatures in God's eyes, an idea echoed later in SUFISM.

Angels with specific traits and names, such as the Spirit (*rūḥ*), usually identified with Gabriel (Arabic JIBRĪL), the angel of death ('IZRĀ'ĪL), and the keeper of hell (Mālik) are mentioned in the Qur'an and Hadith. By the 11th century, Muslim theologians and visionaries had constructed elaborate hierarchies of angels, described as luminous creatures responsible for carrying out God's commands throughout the universe. Gabriel, perhaps the most esteemed archangel in the Islamic tradition, acts as intermediary between God and man and as bearer of revelation to the prophets, most notably to Muhammad. Muhammad could not at first identify the spirit that revealed itself to him, but once he accepted his calling, he recognized Gabriel as his constant helper. It was Gabriel who accompanied Muhammad on his night journey and ascension (MI'RĀJ). He is described variously as a black-haired man in white clothing, or as an awesome being with 600 wings, each pair so enormous that they crowd the space between East and West.

Many Muslims also believe in personal angels who record their good and evil deeds; they salute them at the conclusion of their prescribed daily prayers. The angels Munkar and Nakīr (not mentioned in the Qur'an) interrogate the dead in their graves, providing them a preview of the bliss or suffering they will experience after the final judgment. IBLĪS (SATAN), who refused to bow to Adam with the angels (Qur'an 2:34), is sometimes regarded as a fallen angel. Among Twelver SHI'ITES it is believed that the IMAMS receive divine guidance through angelic intermediaries, and are protected by them. Angels' names are also invoked in talismans and AMULETS designed to protect the wearer from illness or evil, a practice that has roots among the pre-Islamic religions of Africa and Asia. *See also* HĀRŪT AND MĀRŪT; JINN.

ANGLICAN COMMUNION, religious body of national, independent, and autonomous churches throughout the world that evolved from the Church of England. The Anglican Communion is united by loyalty to the archbishop of Canterbury in England as its senior bishop and titular leader and by agreement with the doctrines and practices defined in the BOOK OF COMMON PRAYER.

From the time of the REFORMATION, the Church of England followed explorers, traders, colonists, and missionaries into the far reaches of the known world. The colonial churches generally exercised administrative autonomy. It was probably not until the first meeting of the Lambeth Conference in 1867 that there emerged among the various churches and councils a consciousness of an Anglican Communion. Since its inception, the Lambeth Conference has been the principal cohesive factor in Anglicanism.

The DIOCESE, under the administration of a bishop, is the basic administrative unit throughout the Anglican Communion. The diocese is made up of parishes, or local church communities, each under the care of a pastor (rector). In many national churches, dioceses are grouped into provinces. In some, parishes may be grouped also below the diocesan level into rural deaneries and archdeaconries.

In the 20th century the Anglican Communion has played a prominent role in the ecumenical movement. A milestone in Anglican–Roman Catholic relations was reached in 1982 when Pope JOHN PAUL II met with Robert Runcie, the archbishop of Canterbury, at Canterbury to discuss prospects for reconciliation between the two churches.

ANICCA \ə-'ni-chə\, Buddhist doctrine of impermanence. *See also* ANITYA.

ANICONISM \ˌan-'ī-kə-ˌni-zəm\, opposition to the use of ICONS or visual images to depict living creatures or religious figures. Such opposition is particularly relevant to the Jewish, Islamic, and Byzantine artistic traditions.

The biblical Second Commandment (part of the First Commandment to Roman Catholics and Lutherans), "You shall not make yourself a graven image, or any likeness of anything," which had been intended as a protection against idol worship, came to have a restricting effect on Jewish art, though this effect varied in strength in different periods and was strongest on sculpture. Figural representations were absolutely prohibited in the early period of ISLAM and under the Berber dynasties of Africa and the Mamlūks of Egypt and Syria, though under the 'Abbāsids and most of the SHI'ITE and Turkish dynasties, it was excluded only from public buildings. In the Byzantine Empire, during the ICONOCLASTIC CONTROVERSY (725–843), a ban was imposed on the representations of saintly or divine personages.

ANIMALS, MASTER OF THE, supernatural figure regarded as the protector of game in the traditions of early hunting peoples. The name was actually devised by Western schol-

ars who have studied such hunting societies. In some traditions, the master of the animals is believed to be the ruler of the forest and guardian of all animals; in others, he is the ruler of only one species, usually a large animal of economic or social importance to the community. In some traditions he is pictured in human form, at times having animal attributes or riding an animal; in other traditions he is a giant animal or can assume animal form at will.

The master controls the game animals (or fish) or their spirits (in many myths, by penning them). He releases a certain number to the hunter as food. Only the allotted number may be killed, and the slain animal must be treated with respect. The master of the animals, if properly invoked, will also guide the hunter to the kill. The souls of the slain animals return to the master's pens and report their treatment. If this system is violated, the master will avenge an animal improperly slain, usually by withholding game. A ceremony then must be held to remove the offense or a SHAMAN sent to placate the master.

ANIMAL WORSHIP, veneration of an animal, usually because of its connection with a particular deity. The term was used by Western religionists in a pejorative manner and by ancient Greek and Roman polemicists against theriomorphic religions—those religions whose gods are represented in animal form. Most examples given for animal worship in early religions, however, are not instances of worship of an animal itself. Instead, the sacred power of a deity was believed to be manifested in an appropriate animal regarded as an EPIPHANY or incarnation of the deity.

The universal practice among hunting peoples of respect for and ceremonial behavior toward animals stems from the religious customs attendant on the conducting of the hunt and not from worship of the animal itself. Another phenomenon that has been confused with animal worship is TOTEMISM, in which animal or plant categories fulfill a social classificatory system.

In contemporary scholarship, the term animal worship seldom occurs, because it has been rejected as a misleading interpretive category. Indeed, apparent evidence for the practice is often misleading. Religious ICONOGRAPHY and ALLEGORY has sometimes used animal symbolism to draw on popular associations of certain qualities with certain animal species (*e.g.*, the association of wisdom with the owl lay behind ancient Greek depictions of ATHENA, the goddess of wisdom, with the owl).

ANIMISM \'a-nə-ˌmi-zəm\, belief in spiritual beings that are capable of helping or harming human interests. In *Primitive Culture* (1871), SIR EDWARD BURNETT TYLOR proposed the term and the view that animism is the first stage in the development of religion.

To the intellectuals of the 19th century, profoundly affected by Darwin's new biology, animism seemed a key to the so-called primitive mind—human intellect at the earliest knowable stage of cultural evolution. At present this view is considered to be rooted in a profoundly mistaken premise, as all contemporary cultures and religions reflect a fully evolved human intelligence.

In order to undertake a systematic study of the evolution of religion, Tylor required a "minimum definition of religion" and found it in "the Belief in Spiritual Beings." If it could be shown that no people was devoid of such minimal belief, then it would be known that all of humanity already had passed the threshold into "the religious state of culture." He assembled ethnographic cases and arranged them

The Annunciation, *detail from the* Maestà *altarpiece, 1311, by Duccio di Buoninsegna; in the Museo dell' Opera del Duomo, Siena, Italy*
Art Resource

in series from what seemed to him the simplest or earliest to the most complex or recent. In this way he argued that religion had evolved from a "doctrine of souls" arising from reflection upon death, dreams, and apparitions to a wider "doctrine of spirits," which eventually expanded to embrace powerful DEMONS and gods. Tylor asserted that humans everywhere would be impressed by the vividness of dream images and would reason that dreams of dead kin or of distant friends were proof of the existence of souls. The simple belief in these spiritual beings independent of natural bodies would, he thought, expand to include more elaborate religious doctrines, accompanied by rites designed to influence powerful spirits. Tylor showed that animistic beliefs exhibit great variety and often are uniquely suited to the cultures and natural settings in which they are found.

The term animism covers a range of spirits, from sojourning ghosts and mortal witches to perennial beings, whose natures and dispositions to humanity are attributed by categories. Spirits represent particular powers and must be handled accordingly. When trouble is encountered, the responsible witch, demon, or disgruntled spirit must be identified by the diviner. The cure may rely upon ritual cleansing, propitiation, or even the overpowering of the malevolent force through supernatural counteragency.

ANITYA \ə-'ni-tyə\ (Sanskrit), *Pāli* anicca \ə-'ni-chə\, in BUDDHISM, the doctrine of impermanence, one of the basic char-

acteristics of all existence. *Anitya*, ANĀTMAN ("non-self"), and DUKKHA ("suffering") together make up the *ti-lakkhaṇa*, or three characteristics of all phenomenal existence. One's recognition of this impermanence is one of the crucial components in a Buddhist's spiritual progress toward Enlightenment.

ANIUS \'a-nē-əs\, in Greek myth, the son of the god APOLLO and of Rhoeo, a descendant of the god DIONYSUS. Rhoeo, when pregnant, had been placed in a chest and cast into the sea by her father; floating to the island of Delos, she gave birth to Anius, who became a seer and a priest of Apollo. Anius' three daughters, Oeno, Spermo, and Elais—that is, Wine, Seed, and Oil—were granted by Dionysus the gift of bringing these three crops to fruition. They supplied both the Greek expedition on its way to Troy and AENEAS in his flight from Troy to Italy.

ANKH \'äŋk, 'aŋk\, ancient Egyptian hieroglyph signifying "life," a cross surmounted by a loop. It is found in ancient tomb inscriptions, and gods and pharaohs are often depicted holding it. The ankh forms part of hieroglyphs for such concepts as health and happiness. The form of the symbol suggests perhaps a sandal strap as its original meaning, though it has been seen as representing a magical knot. As a cross, it has been extensively used in the symbolism of the COPTIC ORTHODOX CHURCH.

ANNUNCIATION, in CHRISTIANITY, the announcement by the angel GABRIEL to the Virgin MARY that by the power of the HOLY SPIRIT she would conceive a son to be called Jesus (Luke 1:26–38).

The Feast of the Annunciation is celebrated on March 25 (Lady Day). The feast is first mentioned in texts dating to the 7th century. The Annunciation had a particularly important place in the arts and church decoration of the early Christian and medieval periods and in the devotional art of the Renaissance and Baroque. Moreover, because the event coincides with the INCARNATION OF JESUS CHRIST, it also represents a prelude to the redemption of the world.

ANSAR \\'an-,sär, an-'sär\\, *also called* al-Anṣār (Arabic: "Helpers"), term originally applied to some of the COMPANIONS OF THE PROPHET Muhammad. As a result of MUHAMMAD and his followers leaving MECCA for MEDINA (the HIJRA), the Ansar came into being; these were Medinese who aided Muhammad and his followers (the Muhajirun, meaning "emigrants"). The Ansar were members of the two major Medinese tribes, the feuding al-Khazraj and al-Aws, whom Muhammad had been asked to reconcile when he was still a rising figure in Mecca. They came to be his devoted supporters, constituting three-fourths of the Muslim army at the BATTLE OF BADR (624). When no one of their number was chosen to the caliphate to succeed Muhammad, they declined in influence as a group and eventually merged with other Muslims who had settled in Medina.

The term Ansar was then revived in the 19th century for the followers of AL-MAHDĪ (Muhammad Ahmad ibn as-Sayyid 'Abd Allāh) or for his successor or descendants. The Mahdī of Sudan deemed himself the divinely appointed restorer of ISLAM. The Ansar rose to prominence during the successful Sudanese wars and theocratic regime commanded by al-Mahdī from 1881 until his death in 1885. His disciple 'Abd Allāh succeeded to the temporal rule. But, following initial victories, his forces were gradually hunted down by Anglo-Egyptian armies and almost entirely destroyed in the Battle of Omdurman (Sept. 2, 1898); he himself was killed in the final Battle of Umm Dibaykarat (Nov. 24, 1899). Leadership of the movement then passed to the Mahdī's son 'Abd al-Raḥmān (d. 1959), who sought to make the Ansar into a religious and political force. He was succeeded as IMAM of the Ansar by his son Siddiq (d. 1961), who in turn was succeeded by a member of another branch of the family, Hadi ibn 'Abd al-Raḥmān. When the latter was killed fighting the leftist revolutionary government of The Sudan in 1970, most members of the Mahdī family fled into exile.

ANSELM OF CANTERBURY, SAINT \\'an-,selm\\ (b. 1033/34, Aosta, Lombardy—d. April 21, 1109, possibly at Canterbury, Kent, Eng., feast day April 21), founder of SCHOLASTICISM, a philosophical school of thought that dominated the Middle Ages.

Anselm received a classical education and was considered one of the better Latinists of his day. In 1057 he entered the BENEDICTINE monastery at Bec and in 1060 or 1061 took his monastic vows. His reputation for intellect and pi-

ety led to his election as prior of the monastery in 1063. In 1078 he became ABBOT of Bec.

In 1077 Anselm had written the *Monologium* ("Monologue"), an attempt to demonstrate the existence and attributes of God by reason alone rather than by the customary appeal to authorities. Moving from an analysis of the inequalities of various aspects of perfection, such as justice, wisdom, and power, Anselm argued for an absolute norm that is everywhere at all times, above both time and space, a norm that can be comprehended by the mind of man. Anselm asserted that that norm is God, the absolute, ultimate, and integrating standard of perfection.

Under Anselm, Bec became a center of monastic learning. He continued his efforts to answer questions concerning the nature and existence of God. His *Proslogium* ("Address," or "Allocution") established the ontological argument for the existence of God. In it he argued that even a fool has an idea of a being greater than which no other being can be conceived to exist; and that such a being must really exist, for the very idea of such a being implies its existence. (Anselm's argument was challenged by a contemporary monk, Gaunilo of Marmoutier, in the *Liber pro insipiente*, or "Book in Behalf of the Fool Who Says in His Heart There Is No God.")

During a visit to England, William II Rufus, the son and successor of Bec's benefactor, William the Conqueror, named Anselm archbishop of Canterbury (March 1093). Anselm accepted the position with an intention of reforming the English Church. He refused to be consecrated as archbishop until William acknowledged Urban II as the rightful pope against the ANTIPOPE Clement III. In fear of death from an illness, William agreed, and Anselm was consecrated Dec. 4, 1093. When William recovered, however, he demanded from the new archbishop a sum of money, which Anselm refused to pay lest it look like SIMONY (payment for an ecclesiastical position). This began an INVESTITURE CONTROVERSY—*i.e.*, a controversy over the question as to whether a secular ruler or the pope had the primary right to invest an ecclesiastical authority, such as a bishop, with the symbols of his office—which continued for years. Anselm attended the Council of Bari (Italy) in 1098 and presented his grievances against the king to Urban II. Not until the Synod of Westminster (1107), was the investiture dispute settled, allowing Anselm to spend the last two years of his life in relative peace.

After the Council of Bari, he withdrew to the village of Liberi and completed the manuscript of *Cur Deus homo?* ("Why Did God Become Man?") in 1099. This work became the classic treatment of the satisfaction theory of redemption, according to which sinful but finite man could never make satisfaction to the infinite God and could thus expect only eternal death. The instrument for bringing man back into a right relationship with God is the God-man (Christ), by whose infinite merits man is purified in an act of cooperative re-creation.

ANSHAR AND KISHAR \\'än-,shär . . . 'kē-,shär\\, in Mesopotamian mythology, the male and female principles, the twin horizons of sky and earth. Their parents were either Apsu and TIAMAT or LAHMU AND LAHAMU, the first set of twins born to Apsu and Tiamat. Anshar and Kishar, in turn, were the parents of ANU (An), the supreme heaven god.

ANTAEUS \\an-'tē-əs\\, in Greek myth, a GIANT of Libya, the son of POSEIDON and GAEA. He compelled all strangers who were passing through the country to wrestle with him.

Whenever Antaeus touched the earth (his mother), his strength was renewed, so that even if thrown to the ground, he was invincible. HERACLES, in combat with him, lifted him off the ground and crushed him to death.

ĀṆṬĀḶ \'än-ˌtäl\, *also spelled* Andal (fl. 9th century?), best known of the ĀḶVĀRS and the only female member of that select Vaiṣṇava (*see* VAIṢṆAVISM) family of poets. Her *Tiruppāvai*, a poem of loving adoration addressed to KRISHNA, is one of the most popular devotional works of Tamil poetry, and is performed annually in ŚRĪ VAIṢṆAVA temples. She herself represents a sort of "bridal MYSTICISM" directed toward VISHNU, and is one of the primary Hindu saints of South India.

ANTHESTERIA \ˌan-thə-'stir-ē-ə\, an Athenian festival in honor of DIONYSUS, held annually for three days in the month of Anthesterion (February–March) to celebrate the beginning of spring and the maturing of the wine stored at the previous vintage. On the first day LIBATIONS were offered to Dionysus from the newly opened casks. The second day was a time of popular merrymaking, but the state performed a secret ceremony in a SANCTUARY of Dionysus in the Lenaeum, in which the wife of the king Archon went through a ceremony of marriage to Dionysus. It may have been believed that the souls of the dead emerged from the Underworld on these days; people chewed leaves of whitethorn and smeared their doors with tar to protect themselves from evil. The third day was given over to CHTHONIC (Underworld) rites.

ANTHONY OF EGYPT, SAINT \'an-thə-nē, 'an-tə-\ (b. *c.* 251, Koma, near al-Minyā, Heptanomis [Middle Egypt], Egypt—d. Jan. 17?, 356, Dayr Mārī Antonios hermitage, near the Red Sea; feast day January 17), religious HERMIT and one of the earliest monks, considered the founder and father of organized Christian MONASTICISM.

A disciple of Paul of Thebes, Anthony began to practice an ascetic life at the age of 20 and after 15 years withdrew to Mount Pispir, where he lived from about 286 to 305. During the course of this retreat, he began his mythic combat against the Devil, withstanding a series of temptations famous in Christian theology and ICONOGRAPHY. (The temptations of Anthony have often been used as a subject in both literature and art, notably in the paintings of Hiëronymus Bosch, Matthias Grünewald, and Max Ernst.) About 305 he emerged from his retreat to instruct and organize the monastic life of the hermits who had established themselves nearby. When Christian persecution ended after the EDICT OF MILAN (313), he moved to a mountain in the Eastern Desert, between the Nile and the Red Sea, where the monastery Dayr Mārī Antonios still stands.

The monastic rule that bears Anthony's name was compiled from writings and discourses attributed to him in the *Life of St. Antony* (by Athanasius) and the *Apophthegmata patrum* and was still observed in the 20th century by a number of Coptic and Armenian monks. Anthony's popu-

St. Anthony of Egypt, by Albrecht Dürer, 1519
Culver Pictures

larity as a saint reached its height in the Middle Ages. The Order of Hospitallers of St. Anthony was founded near Grenoble, France (*c.* 1100), and this institution became a PILGRIMAGE center for persons suffering from the disease known as St. Anthony's fire (or ergotism). The black-robed Hospitallers, ringing small bells as they collected alms—as well as their pigs, allowed by special privilege to run free in medieval streets—became part of the later iconography associated with St. Anthony.

ANTHROPOMORPHISM \,an-thrə-pə-'mȯr-,fi-zəm\ (from Greek: *anthrōpos,* "human being," and *morphē,* "form"), the attribution of human form or other human characteristics to any nonhuman object. In religion, the term is applied to any statement that depicts what is sacred as having a bodily form resembling that of human beings, or as possessing qualities of thought, will, or emotion that are continuous with those experienced by humans. Any reference to the divine as having a human body or a part of a human body is an anthropomorphism—*e.g.,* the hand, the eye, or the mouth of God. References to the mental aspects of humans are also regarded as anthropomorphisms—*e.g.,* the will, the mind, the compassion, and the love of God.

Good examples of anthropomorphisms in religion are those of the ancient Greeks and Romans, whose gods resembled humans in almost everything except their immortality, their places of residence, and their magical powers over nature. Xenophanes (6th–5th century BCE) attacked the anthropomorphism of Homer and Hesiod in ascribing "to the gods all deeds that are a shame and a disgrace among men: thieving, adultery, fraud." Similarly, Plato repudiated the anthropomorphism of traditional Homeric mythology and instead asserted the idea, in accord with Xenophanes, that the divine is one, and beyond human powers of comprehension.

The classical Hebrew prophets, such as AMOS and ISAIAH, were vigorous critics of the anthropomorphism of their day, reminding their listeners, for example, that the moral judgments of God were not based upon the tribal preferences that influence human judgment. The prophets did not entirely abandon anthropomorphism, however, but freely employed refined anthropomorphic symbols as indispensable to their concept of God as personal. The author of the Book of Ecclesiastes carried the critique of anthropomorphism further, approaching the idea of an impersonal cosmic force in place of the Hebraic personal God.

The many gods of the Hindu tradition also often are conceived in anthropomorphic terms. It is a well established doctrine in HINDUISM that a god, out of his grace and as a boon to his devotees, willingly takes on human form in order to make himself more accessible to them. The god VISHNU, for example, incarnates periodically as one or another of his AVATARS. In the BHAGAVAD GĪTĀ, one of these avatars, KRISHNA, declares, "though myself unborn, undying, the lord of creatures . . . whenever sacred duty decays and chaos prevails, then I create myself." Furthermore, deities of all sorts are thought also to be present in the form of the images and ICONS worshiped in the temple and at home, many of which are human in form.

While many thinkers have believed it possible to purge THEISM (belief in the existence of God) of all traces of anthropomorphism, others have regarded the latter as essential to theistic knowledge and language, since these areas are necessarily conditioned by human self-experience; the human subject invariably interprets nonhuman reality after analogies drawn from human experience. This problem raises philosophical questions about the validity of theism, idealism, or any other form of knowledge.

ANTHROPOSOPHY \,an-thrə-'pä-sə-fē\, philosophy based on the premise that the human intellect has the ability to contact spiritual worlds. It was formulated by RUDOLF STEINER, an Austrian philosopher, scientist, and artist, who postulated the existence of a spiritual world comprehensible to pure thought but fully accessible only to the highest faculties latent in all humans. The term, based on Greek *anthrōpos,* "human being," and *sophia,* "wisdom," suggests roots in both THEOSOPHY and philosophy. Steiner regarded human beings as having originally participated in the spiritual processes of the world through a dreamlike consciousness. Claiming that an enhanced consciousness can again perceive spiritual worlds, he attempted to develop a faculty for spiritual perception independent of the senses. He founded the Anthroposophical Society in 1912. The society, now based in Dornach, Switz., has branches and schools around the world.

ANTICHRIST, the chief enemy of JESUS CHRIST. The earliest mention of the name Antichrist—which was probably coined in Christian eschatological literature (that is, literature concerned with the end of time)—is in the letters of St. John (1 John 2: 18, 22; 2 John 7), although the figure does appear in the earlier 2 Thessalonians as "the lawless one." The idea of a mighty ruler who will appear at the end of time and whose essence is enmity of God is older and was taken from JUDAISM.

Jewish ESCHATOLOGY had been influenced by Iranian and Babylonian myths of the battle of God and the Devil at the end of time. The OLD TESTAMENT conception of the struggle is found in the Prophecy of Daniel, written at the beginning of the Maccabean period (*c.* 167–164 BCE). The historical figure who served as a model for the Antichrist was Antiochus IV Epiphanes, the persecutor of the Jews, and he left a lasting impression upon the conception. Since then, ever-recurring characterizations of this figure are that he would appear as a mighty ruler at the head of gigantic armies, destroy three rulers (the three horns, Daniel 7:8, 24), persecute the saints (7:25), and devastate the Temple of God.

A Christian view of the Antichrist is given in 2 Thessalonians 2. Here the Antichrist appears as a tempter who works by signs and wonders and seeks to obtain divine honors; it is further signified that this "man of lawlessness" will obtain credence, especially among the Jews because they have not accepted the truth. This version of the figure of the Antichrist, who may now really for the first time be described by this name, appears to have been at once widely accepted in Christendom. The idea that Jews would believe in the Antichrist as punishment for not having believed in the true Christ seems to be expressed by the author of the Fourth Gospel (John 5:43). The conception of the Antichrist as a perverter of men led naturally to his connection with false doctrine (1 John 2:18, 22, 4:3; 2 John 7). In REVELATION TO JOHN the Antichrist is seen as a worker of wonders and a seducer.

In the Middle Ages the idea of the Antichrist developed into a powerful historical and political factor, especially in times of crisis. It became common for opponents, including popes and emperors, to call each other the Antichrist. Immense interest was focused on the person and date of the coming of the Antichrist and "the signs of the times" preceding it: upheavals in nature, wars, pestilence, famine, and other disasters. Preachers spread warnings of his coming in order to call the people to repentance throughout the 14th and 15th centuries.

During the REFORMATION, the Reformers, especially MARTIN LUTHER, did not attack individual popes but the PAPACY itself as the Antichrist. This idea that evil was embodied in the head of the church itself, with the clergy as the "body of the Antichrist," became the most powerful weapon to discredit and denigrate the papacy.

After the Reformation, emphasis on the Antichrist figure gradually diminished. Among some modern Protestant theologians the Antichrist can be interpreted as whatever denies the lordship of Christ and tends to deify a political power—within either the church or the state. In premillennial theology the expectation of a personal Antichrist at the end of time remains strong. (*See also* MILLENNIALISM.)

ANTIGONE, in Greek mythology, the daughter born of the incestuous union of OEDIPUS and his mother, Jocasta. After her father blinded himself upon discovering that he had killed his father and married his mother, Antigone and her sister Ismene served as Oedipus' guides, following him from Thebes into exile until his death near Athens. Returning to Thebes, they attempted to reconcile their quarreling brothers—Eteocles, who was defending his position as king, and Polyneices, who was attacking Thebes. Both brothers were killed, and their uncle Creon became king. After giving Eteocles a state funeral, he condemned the corpse of the traitor Polyneices to lie unburied. Antigone, though, buried Polyneices secretly. For that she was ordered by Creon to be executed and was immured in a cave, where she hanged herself. Her beloved, Haemon, son of Creon, committed suicide. (This is according to Sophocles' *Antigone*, but according to Euripides, Antigone escaped and lived happily with Haemon.)

ANTILOCHUS \an-'ti-lə-kəs\, in Greek legend, son of NESTOR, king of Pylos. One of the suitors of HELEN, he accompanied his father to the Trojan War and distinguished himself as acting commander of the Pylians. When Nestor was attacked by MEMNON (king of the Ethiopians), Antilochus saved his father's life at the sacrifice of his own, thus fulfilling the oracle that had bidden him "beware of an Ethiopian." According to two different traditions, Antilochus was either slain by HECTOR or, alternately, by PARIS in the temple of the Thymbraean APOLLO together with his friend ACHILLES.

ANTINOMIANISM \,an-ti-'nō-mē-ə-,ni-zəm\ (Greek: *anti*, "against"; *nomos*, "law"), doctrine according to which Christians are freed by GRACE from the necessity of obeying the Mosaic Law. The antinomians rejected the very notion of obedience as legalistic; to them the good life flowed from the inner working of the HOLY SPIRIT.

The ideas of antinomianism had been present in the early church, and some gnostic heretics believed that freedom from law meant license. The doctrine of antinomianism, however, grew out of the Protestant controversies on the law and the gospel and was first attributed to MARTIN LUTHER'S collaborator, Johann Agricola, whom Luther opposed on this issue. It also appeared in the Reformed branch of PROTESTANTISM. The left-wing ANABAPTISTS were accused of antinomianism, both for theological reasons and also because they opposed the cooperation of CHURCH AND STATE, which was considered necessary for law and order. For similar reasons, in the 17th century, Separatists, FAMILISTS, Ranters, and Independents in England were called antino-

mians by the established churches. The Evangelical movement at the end of the 18th century produced its own antinomians who claimed an inner experience and a "new life," which they considered the true source of good works.

ANTIOPE \an-'tī-ō-pē\, in Greek legend, the mother, by ZEUS, of the twins AMPHION AND ZETHUS. According to one account, her beauty attracted Zeus, who, assuming the form of a satyr, raped her. Pregnant and afraid of her father, she ran away and married Epopeus, king of Sicyon; she was later brought back and imprisoned by her uncle Lycus. On the way back from Sicyon, or after escaping from prison, Antiope bore Amphion and Zethus, who were brought up by herdsmen. Later she joined her sons, whereupon they killed Lycus and Dirce, his wife. Because of Dirce's murder, DIONYSUS, to whose worship she had been devoted, caused Antiope to go mad. She wandered over all of Greece until she was cured and married by PHOCUS of Tithorea, on Mt. Parnassus.

Antiope was also the name of a daughter of ARES, the god of war, and a queen of the AMAZONS. The Greek hero THESEUS stole her for his wife.

ANTIPOPE, in ROMAN CATHOLICISM, one who opposes the legitimately elected bishop of Rome, endeavors to secure the papal throne, and to some degree succeeds materially in the attempt. This abstract definition is necessarily broad and does not reckon with the complexity of individual cases. The elections of several antipopes are greatly obscured by incomplete or biased records, and at times even their contemporaries could not decide who was the true pope. It is impossible, therefore, to establish an absolutely definitive list of antipopes. Historically, antipopes have arisen as a result of a variety of causes; the following are some examples:

1. Doctrinal disagreement.

2. Deportation of the pope. (The emperor Constantius II, a follower of the heretical doctrine ARIANISM, exiled Pope Liberius for his orthodoxy [355] and imposed the archdeacon Felix on the Roman clergy as Pope Felix II. Eventually, Liberius was allowed to return.)

3. Double elections arbitrated by the secular authority. (In 418 the archdeacon Eulalius was elected by a faction. The rest of the clergy, however, chose the priest Boniface I, who was eventually recognized by the emperor.)

4. Double elections and subsequent recourse to a third candidate.

5. Change in the manner of choosing the pope.

A great number of antipopes date to the moving of the official residence of the PAPACY from Rome to Avignon, France, in the 14th century. This led to a SCHISM (the Great Western Schism) beginning in 1378 that resulted in a papacy in Rome (regarded as canonical), a papacy in Avignon (regarded as antipapal), and eventually a third papacy established by the Council of Pisa (also regarded as antipapal). Unity was finally achieved by the election of Martin V on Nov. 11, 1417.

ANTI-SEMITISM, hostility toward or discrimination against Jews as a religious or racial group. The terms "anti-Semitic" and "anti-Semitism" are translations of German *antisemitisch* and *Antisemitismus*, which first appeared in Germany in the autumn of 1879 to designate the anti-Jewish campaigns then underway in central Europe; their coinage is often attributed to the agitator Wilhelm Marr, though Marr did not use the words in print before 1880.

Anti-Semitism has existed to some degree wherever Jews

A World War II era poster from Nazi-occupied France produced by an anti-Semitic group known as the Collaborationist Institute for the Study of Jewish Questions. The poster reads "Jews Kill in the Shadows/Mark Them to Recognize Them," c. 1942
The Granger Collection

have settled outside of Palestine. By the 4th century CE, Christians had come generally to regard Jews as the crucifiers of Christ who, because of their repudiation of Christ and his church, had lost their homeland and were condemned to perpetual migration. When the Christian church became dominant in the Roman Empire, its leaders inspired many laws segregating Jews from Christians and curtailing Jews' religious rights.

In much of Europe during the Middle Ages, Jews were denied citizenship, barred from holding government and military posts, and excluded from membership in guilds and the professions. The claim that Jews sacrificed Christian children at PASSOVER was first made in the 12th century and, by the 1930s, had become part of Nazi propaganda, as did another instrument of 12th-century anti-Semitism—the compulsory yellow badge, which identified the wearer as a Jew. The segregation of Jewish urban populations into ghettos also dates from the Middle Ages and lasted until the 19th and early 20th centuries in much of Europe.

As some Jews became prominent in trade, banking, and moneylending, their success aroused the envy of the populace. This resentment prompted the expulsion of Jews from several countries or regions, including England (1290), France (14th century), Germany (1350s), Portugal (1496), Provence (1512), and the Papal States (1569). Persecutions

by the INQUISITION in Spain culminated in 1492 in the forced expulsion of that country's Jewish population. As a result the centers of Jewish life shifted from western Europe to Turkey, Poland, and Russia.

With the Enlightenment and the French Revolution Jews began to gain civil rights in western European countries. When Jewish economic and cultural successes once again aroused resentment and hostility and mixed with the reassertion of European nationalism, anti-Semitism acquired a racial character, as ethnically homogeneous peoples decried the existence in their midst of "alien" Jewish elements. Pseudoscientific theories asserting that the Jews were inferior to the so-called ARYAN races gave anti-Semitism new respectability and popular support, especially in countries where existing social or political grievances could be ostensibly blamed on Jews. In Germany and Austria in the late 19th century, anti-Semitism became an organized movement with its own political parties.

The Russian Empire had restricted Jews to western regions known as the PALE of Settlement ever since the 1790s. The empire's May Laws of 1882, enacted after widespread anti-Jewish riots had broken out in the Russian Pale the previous year, stripped Jews of their rural landholdings and restricted them to the towns and cities within the Pale. These measures spurred the emigration of several million Jews to the United States in the next four decades, plus a somewhat smaller emigration into western Europe.

In France the Dreyfus affair became a focal point for anti-Semitism. In 1894 Alfred Dreyfus, a highly placed Jewish army officer, was falsely accused of treason. His vindication was hampered by the French military and the bitterly anti-Semitic French press, and the controversy that ensued damaged the cohesion of French political life.

During the first decade of the 20th century, serious pogroms occurred in Kishinyov (now Chişinău, Moldova) in 1903 and 1905, and the Russian secret police published a forgery entitled *Protocols of the Learned Elders of Zion* that, as the supposed blueprint for a Jewish plot to achieve world domination, furnished propaganda for subsequent generations of anti-Semitic agitators. The widespread economic and political dislocations caused by World War I intensified anti-Semitism in Europe. In addition, the many Jewish Bolshevik leaders in the Russian Revolution of November 1917 gave anti-Semites a new focus for their prejudices in the threat of "Jewish Bolshevism." German anti-Semites joined forces with revanchist nationalists in attempting to blame Jews for that country's defeat.

The storm of anti-Semitic violence in Nazi Germany under the leadership of Adolf Hitler in 1933–45 also inspired anti-Jewish movements elsewhere. Anti-Semitism was promulgated in France by the Cagoulards (French: "Hooded Men"), in Hungary by the Arrow Cross, in England by the British Union of Fascists, and in the United States by the German-American Bund and the Silver Shirts.

The novelty of the Nazi brand of anti-Semitism was that it crossed class barriers. The idea of Aryan racial superiority appealed both to the masses and to economic and hereditary elites. In Germany anti-Semitism became official government policy—taught in the schools and elaborated in "scientific" journals and by a huge propaganda organization. In 1941 the liquidation of European Jewry became official party policy. An estimated 5,700,000 Jews were exterminated in such death camps as Auschwitz, Chełmno, Bełżec, Majdanek, and Treblinka during World War II.

After the Nazi defeat in 1945, anti-Semitism lost ground in western Europe and the United States, but developments in the Soviet Union and the Middle East gave it new significance in those areas. Anti-Semitic discrimination remained a feature of Soviet society from Stalinist times.

The immigration of large numbers of Jews to Palestine in the 20th century and the creation of the State of Israel (1948) aroused new currents of hostility within the Arab world that had previously tolerated the Jewish communities, resulting in the adoption of many anti-Jewish measures throughout the Muslim countries of the Middle East. In response, most of those countries' Jews immigrated to Israel in the decades after the latter's founding.

ANTYEŞTI \ənt-'yāsh-tē\, funeral rites of HINDUISM, varying according to the CASTE and religious sect of the deceased but generally involving CREMATION followed by disposal of the ashes in a sacred river.

At the approach of death, relatives and BRAHMINS are summoned, MANTRAS and sacred texts are recited, and ceremonial gifts are prepared. After death the body is removed to the cremation grounds, which are usually located on the bank of a river. The eldest son of the deceased and the officiating priest perform the final cremation rites. For 10 days the mourners are considered impure and are subject to certain TABOOS. During this period they perform rites intended to provide the soul of the deceased with a new spiritual body with which it may pass on to the next life. Ceremonies include the setting out of milk and water and the offering of rice balls. At a prescribed date the bones are collected and disposed of by burial or by immersion in a river. Rites honoring the dead, called *śrāddha*, continue to be performed by the survivors at specified times.

ANU \'ä-ˌnü\ (Akkadian), *Sumerian* An, in MESOPOTAMIAN RELIGION, the sky god. Anu, although theoretically the highest god, played only a small role in the mythology, hymns, and cults of Mesopotamia. He was the father not only of all the gods but also of evil spirits and DEMONS; Anu was also the god of kings and of the calendar. He was typically depicted in a headdress with horns, a sign of strength.

His Sumerian counterpart, An, dates from the oldest Sumerian period, at least 3000 BCE. Originally he seems to have been envisaged as a great bull, a form later envisioned as a separate mythological entity, the Bull of Heaven, which was owned by An. His holy city was Erech, in the southern herding region, and he may originally have belonged to the herders' pantheon. In Akkadian myth Anu was assigned a consort, Antum (Antu), but she seems often to have been confused with ISHTAR (Inanna).

ANUBIS \ə-'nü-bis\, *also called* Anpu \'än-ˌpü\, ancient Egyptian god of the dead, represented by a jackal or a jackal-headed man. In the Early Dynastic period and the Old Kingdom, he enjoyed a preeminent (though not exclusive) position as lord of the dead but was later overshadowed by OSIRIS. Said to be the inventor of EMBALMING, his particular concern was with the funerary cult and the care of the dead; he first employed this art on the corpse of Osiris. In his later role as the "conductor of souls," he was sometimes identified by the Greco-Roman world with the Greek HERMES in the composite deity Hermanubis.

AN YU \'än-'yü\, *also known as* An Hyang (b. 1243 CE—d. 1306), Korean scholar and educator of the Koryoc period (918–1392 CE) who helped to reconstitute the National Academy and establish a state treasury for national education. He is especially famed for his advancement of public

education based on CONFUCIANISM and NEO-CONFUCIANISM. In 1287 he accompanied King Chungnyol to the Mongol court in Peking where he encountered the texts of CHU HSI. Returning to Korea, An Yu privately studied these texts and promoted Korean national education based on the Neo-Confucian thought of these works. Eventually he became the director of the MUNMYO, the Korean national shrine to culture. Known as an opponent of Ch'an (ZEN) BUDDHISM in Korea, An Yu was the most famous Confucian scholar of his era.

APATURIA \ˌa-pə-'tùr-ē-ə, -'tyùr-\, Greek annual religious festival. At Athens it took place in the month of Pyanopsion (October–November) and lasted three days, on which occasion the various phratries (clans) of Attica met to discuss their affairs. The name probably means the festival of "common relationship." The most important day was probably the third, Koureotis, when children born since the last festival were presented by their fathers or guardians; after an OATH had been taken as to their legitimacy, their names were inscribed in the register.

APAUSHA \ə-'paù-shə\, in ancient Iranian religion, a demonic star who in an important myth does battle with TISHTRYA over rainfall.

APHRAATES \a-'frä-ə-ˌtēz\, *Syriac* Afrahat \ä-'frä-ät\ (fl. 4th century), Syrian ascetic and the earliest known Christian writer of the Syriac church in Persia.

Aphraates became a convert to CHRISTIANITY during the reign of the anti-Christian Persian king Shāpūr II (309–379), after which he led a monastic life, possibly at the Monastery of St. Matthew near Mosul, Iraq. Termed "the Persian Sage," Aphraates between the years 336 and 345 composed Syriac biblical commentaries, 23 of which have been preserved. They survey the Christian faith and are at times marked by a sharp polemical nature. Nine treatises against Jews, who were numerous in Mesopotamia and had established outstanding schools, are particularly acrimonious; they treat subjects such as EASTER, CIRCUMCISION, dietary laws, the supplanting of ISRAEL by GENTILES as the new chosen people, and Jesus' divine sonship.

Aphraates' writings are distinguished by their primitive biblical-theological tradition, unaffected by doctrinal controversies and linguistic complexity. Insulated from the intellectual currents of the Greco-Roman ecclesiastical world, Aphraates "Homilies," as they are known, manifest a teaching indigenous to early Syrian Christianity.

APHRODITE \ˌa-frə-'dī-tē\, in GREEK RELIGION, the goddess of sexual love and beauty. Because the Greek word *aphros* means "foam," the legend arose that Aphrodite was born from the white foam produced by the severed genitals of OURANUS, after his son CRONUS threw them into the sea, and Aphrodite was, in fact, widely worshiped as a goddess of the sea and of seafaring. She was also honored as a goddess of war, especially at Sparta, Thebes, Cyprus, and other places. Aphrodite was, however, primarily a goddess of love and fertility and even occasionally presided over marriage. Although prostitutes considered Aphrodite their patron, her public cult was generally solemn and even austere.

Aphrodite's worship came to Greece from the East, and many of her characteristics must be considered Semitic. Although Homer called her "Cyprian" after the island chiefly famed for her worship, she was already Hellenized by this time, and in Homeric mythology she was the daughter of

ZEUS and DIONE. In the *Odyssey*, Aphrodite was married to HEPHAESTUS, the lame smith god, though she played the field with the god of war, ARES (by whom she became the mother of HARMONIA).

Of Aphrodite's mortal lovers, the most important were the Trojan shepherd ANCHISES, by whom she became the mother of AENEAS, and the handsome youth ADONIS (in origin a Semitic deity and the consort of Ishtar-Astarte), who was killed by a boar while hunting and was lamented by women at the festival of Adonia. The cult of Adonis had Underworld features, and Aphrodite was also connected with the dead at DELPHI.

Aphrodite's main centers of worship were at Paphos and Amathus on Cyprus and on the island of Cythera, a Minoan colony, where her cult probably originated in prehistoric times. On the Greek mainland Corinth was the chief center of her worship. Her close association with EROS, the GRACES (Charites), and the Seasons (Horae) emphasized her role as a promoter of fertility. She was honored as Genetrix, the creative element in the world. Of her epithets, OURANIA (Heavenly Dweller) was honorific and applied to certain Oriental deities, and Pandemos (Of All the People) referred to her standing within the city-state. Among her symbols were the dove, pomegranate, swan, and myrtle.

APIS \ˈā-pis\ (Greek), *Egyptian* Hap, Hep, or Hapi, in ancient EGYPTIAN RELIGION, sacred bull deity worshiped at Memphis. The cult of Apis originated at least as early as the 1st dynasty (*c.* 2925–*c.* 2775 BCE). As Apis-Atum he was associated with the solar cult and was often represented with the sun-disk between his horns.

Apis was black and white and distinguished by special markings. Some sources said that he was begotten by a ray of light from heaven, and others that he was sired by an Apis bull. When a sacred bull died, the calf that was to be his successor was sought and installed in the Apieion at Memphis. His priests drew OMENS from his behavior, and his oracle had a wide reputation. When an Apis bull died, it was buried with great pomp at Ṣaqqārah, in underground galleries known as the SARAPEUM. It was probably in Memphis that the worship of SARAPIS (after the Greek form Osorapis, a combination of OSIRIS and Apis in the image of an eastern Greek god) arose under Ptolemy I Soter (305–282 BCE). From Alexandria, it spread to become one of the most widespread oriental cults in the Roman Empire.

Apis, painted on the bottom of a wooden coffin, c. *700* BCE; *in the Römer and Pelizaeus Museum, Hildesheim, Ger.*
Bavaria Verlag

APOCALYPSE, in many religious traditions of the West, the period of catastrophic upheaval that is to precede the ending of time and the coming of God to sit in judgment upon mankind. The term also refers to the literature containing prophecies about that time. (*See also* MILLENNIALISM.)

APOCALYPSE, FOUR HORSEMEN OF THE, in CHRISTIANITY, the figures who, according to the book of REVELATION TO JOHN (6:1–8), appear with the opening of the seven seals that bring forth the cataclysm of the APOCALYPSE. The first horseman rides a white horse, which scholars sometimes interpret to symbolize Christ; the second horseman rides a red horse and symbolizes war and bloodshed; the third rides a black horse and symbolizes famine; and the fourth horseman rides a pale horse and represents pestilence and death.

APOCALYPTICISM \ə-ˌpä-kə-ˈlip-tə-ˌsi-zəm\, eschatological views and movements that focus on revelations about a sudden and cataclysmic intervention of God in history; universal judgment; the salvation of the faithful ELECT; and the eventual rule of the elect with God in a renewed heaven and earth. Arising in ZOROASTRIANISM, Apocalypticism was developed more fully in the ESCHATOLOGY of JUDAISM, CHRISTIANITY, and ISLAM.

APOCRYPHA, in biblical literature, works outside an accepted canon of SCRIPTURE. The history of the term's usage indicates that it referred to a body of esoteric writings that were at first prized, later tolerated, and finally excluded. In its broadest sense *apocrypha* has come to mean any writings of dubious authority.

In modern usage the Apocrypha is the term for ancient Jewish books that are called deuterocanonical works in ROMAN CATHOLICISM—*i.e.*, those that are canonical for Catholics but are not a part of the Hebrew BIBLE. (These works are also regarded as canonical within EASTERN ORTHODOXY.) When the Protestant churches returned to the Jewish canon (Hebrew OLD TESTAMENT) during the REFORMATION period (16th century), the Catholic deuterocanonical works became for the Protestants "apocryphal"—*i.e.*, noncanonical. In 19th-century biblical scholarship a new term was coined for those ancient Jewish works that were not accepted as canonical by either the Catholic or Protestant churches; such books are now commonly called PSEUDEPIGRAPHA ("Falsely Inscribed")—*i.e.*, books that were wrongly ascribed to a biblical author.

At the time when Greek was the common spoken language in the Mediterranean region, the Old Testament—the Hebrew Bible—was incomprehensible to most of the population. For this reason, Jewish scholars produced the SEPTUAGINT, a translation of the Old Testament books from various Hebrew texts, along with fragments in Aramaic, into Greek. That version incorporated a number of works that later, non-Hellenistic Jewish scholarship at the Council of Jamnia (90 CE) identified as being outside the authentic Hebrew canon. The TALMUD separates these works as *Sefarim Hizonim* (Extraneous Books).

The Septuagint was an important basis for JEROME'S translation of the Old Testament into Latin for the VULGATE Bible; and, although he had doubts about the authenticity of some of the works that it contained —he was the first to employ the Greek word *apokryphos*, "hidden," "secret," in the sense "noncanonical"—he was overruled, and most of them were included in the Vulgate. On April 8, 1546, the COUNCIL OF TRENT declared the canonicity of nearly the entire Vulgate, excluding only the Third and Fourth Books of Maccabees, the Prayer of Manasseh, Psalm 151, and the First and Second Books of Esdras. Eastern Christendom, meanwhile, had accepted the Old Testament apocrypha as deuterocanonical—Tobit; Judith; the Wisdom of Solomon; and Ecclesiasticus (Wisdom of Jesus the Son of Sirach); Third Book of Esdras; First, Second, and Third Books of Maccabees; the Book of Baruch; and the Letter of Jeremiah.

Old Testament pseudepigrapha are extremely numerous and are attributed to various biblical personages from Adam to Zechariah. Some of the most significant of these works are the Ascension of Isaiah, the Assumption of Moses, the Life of Adam and Eve, the First and Second Books of Enoch, the Book of Jubilees, the Letter of Aristeas, and the Testaments of the Twelve Patriarchs.

All the NEW TESTAMENT apocrypha are pseudepigraphal, and most of them are acts, gospels, and epistles, though there are a number of apocalypses and some can be characterized as wisdom books. Some works relate encounters and events in mystical language and describe arcane rituals. Most of these works arose from sects that had been or would be declared heretical, such as, importantly, the Gnostics (*see* GNOSTICISM). In the early decades of CHRISTIANITY no orthodoxy had been established, and various parties or factions were vying for ascendancy and regularity in the young church. In this setting virtually all works that were advocating beliefs that later became heretical were destined to denunciation and destruction.

In addition to apocryphal works per se, the New Testament includes a number of works and fragments that are described by a second meaning of the term deuterocanonical: "added later." The Letter to the Hebrews attributed to Paul, who died before it was written, is one of these; others are the letters of James, Peter (2), John (2 and 3), and Jude, and the REVELATION TO JOHN. Fragments include Mark 16:9–20, Luke 22:43–44, and John 7:53 and 8:1–11. All are included in the Roman canon and are accepted by the Eastern Church and most Protestant churches.

APOLLO \ə-'pä-lō\, *byname* Phoebus, in GREEK RELIGION, the most widely revered and influential of all the gods. Though his original nature is obscure, from the time of Homer he was the god who sent or threatened from afar, made humans aware of their guilt and purified them of it, presided

Apollo Belvedere, *Roman copy of the Greek original attributed to Leochares, 4th century BCE; in the Vatican Museum, Rome*
Alinari—Art Resource

over religious law and the constitutions of cities, and communicated through prophets and oracles his knowledge of the future and the will of his father, ZEUS. Even the gods feared him, and only his father and his mother, LETO, could endure his presence. Distance, death, terror, and awe were summed up in his symbolic bow; his other attribute, the lyre, proclaimed the joy of communion with Olympus through music, poetry, and dance. He was also a god of crops and herds, primarily as a divine bulwark against wild animals and disease, as his epithet Alexikakos (Averter of Evil) indicates. His forename Phoebus means "bright" or "pure," and the view became current that he was connected with the sun.

Among Apollo's epithets was Nomios (Herdsman), and he is said to have served King ADMETUS of Pherae in the capacities of groom and herdsman as penance for slaying Zeus's armorers, the Cyclopes. He was also called Lyceius, presumably because he protected the flocks from wolves (*lykoi*); because herdsmen and shepherds passed the time with music, this may have been Apollo's original role.

Apollo apparently was of foreign origin, coming either from somewhere north of Greece or from Asia. Traditionally, he and his twin, ARTEMIS, were born on the isle of Delos. From there, according to the myths, Apollo went to Pytho (DELPHI), where he slew PYTHON, the serpent that guarded the area. He established his oracle by taking on the guise of a dolphin, leaping aboard a Cretan ship, and forcing the crew to serve him. Thus Pytho was renamed Delphi after the dolphin (*delphis*), and, by legend, the cult of Apollo Delphinius superseded that previously established there by GAEA. During the Archaic period (8th–6th century BCE), the fame of the Delphic oracle achieved pan-Hellenic status. The god's medium was the Pythia, a local woman over 50 years old, who, under his inspiration, delivered oracles in the main temple of Apollo. Other oracles of Apollo existed on the Greek mainland, Delos, and in Anatolia, but none rivaled Delphi in importance.

Although Apollo had many love affairs, they were mostly unfortunate: DAPHNE, in her efforts to escape him, was changed into a laurel, his sacred tree; Coronis (mother of ASCLEPIUS) was shot by Apollo's twin, Artemis, when Coronis proved unfaithful; and CASSANDRA (daughter of King PRIAM of Troy) rejected his advances and was punished by being made to utter true prophecies that no one believed.

APOLOGETICS, in CHRISTIANITY, intellectual defense of the truth of the Christian religion, usually considered a branch of theology. In Protestant usage, apologetics can be distinguished from polemics, in which the beliefs of a particular Christian sect are defended. In ROMAN CATHOLICISM, however, the term is used to mean the defense of Catholic teaching in its entirety.

Apologetics has traditionally been positive in its direct argument for Christianity and negative in its criticism of opposing beliefs. Its function is both to fortify the believer against his personal doubts and to remove the intellectual stumbling blocks that inhibit the conversion of unbelievers. Apologetics has steered a difficult course between dogmatism, which fails to take seriously the objections of non-Christians, and the temptation to undermine the strength of defense by granting too much to the skeptic. Apologetics has rarely been taken as providing a conclusive proof of Christianity and some theologians have been skeptical about the value of apologetics to a religion based on faith.

In the NEW TESTAMENT, the thrust of apologetics was defense of Christianity as the culmination of the Jewish religion and its prophecies concerning a MESSIAH. In the early church, the APOLOGISTS, such as JUSTIN MARTYR and TERTULLIAN, defended the moral superiority of Christianity over pre-Christian religions and pointed out Christianity's fulfillment of OLD TESTAMENT prophecies. In the later Middle Ages, apologists focused on Christianity's superiority over the rival religions of JUDAISM and ISLAM. In the 13th century, however, THOMAS AQUINAS developed a still-influential defense of belief in God based on Aristotelian theories of a first cause of the universe.

During the Protestant REFORMATION apologetics was substantially replaced by polemics, in which many sects sought to defend their particular beliefs rather than Christianity as a whole. The "NATURAL THEOLOGY" of both JOHN CALVIN and PHILIPP MELANCHTHON, however, does represent a strain of genuine Reformation apologetics. (Natural theology is generally characterized as the project of establishing religious truths by rational argument and without reliance upon revelations, its two traditional topics being the existence of God and the immortality of the soul.)

In the 18th century, Joseph Butler, an English bishop, met the rising challenge of DEISM in the wake of advancing science by arguing that a supernatural Christianity was at least as reasonable and probable as any scientific doctrine could be. A later Englishman, William Paley, argued that a universe exhibiting design must have a designer, much as a watch implies a watchmaker.

In the 19th century the historical reliability of the Gospels came under attack, and apologists stressed the difficulty of accounting for the RESURRECTION of JESUS CHRIST and the rapid spread of Christianity if SUPERNATURALISM were denied. Moral arguments for Christianity based on the philosophy of Immanuel Kant also gained prominence as attacks on historical and metaphysical apologetics increased. Further objections to Christianity based on the theory of evolution, the views of the German philosopher Friedrich Nietzsche, Marxism, and psychoanalysis have been met by apologists either by attempts to refute the fundamentals on which they are based, or by turning aspects of the criticisms into new arguments favorable to Christianity.

In the 20th century such Protestant theologians as the Germans RUDOLF BULTMANN and PAUL TILLICH abandoned the attempt to preserve the literal historical truth of the Gospels and focused on presenting Christianity as the best answer to the existential needs and questions of man. Other Protestants stress the need to make the ancient stories and symbols of Christianity meaningful to modern man in a "post-Christian" era dominated by materialistic ideologies. The German scholar KARL BARTH, however, expressed skepticism about the whole task of the apologetical system, insisting that Christianity must be rooted exclusively in faith. The Roman Catholic apologetical system of Thomas Aquinas and his intellectual successors has been profoundly influenced in the 20th century by the SECOND VATICAN COUNCIL. Contemporary apologetics in the Roman communion focuses principally on the community of believers, whose faith is under constant challenge by numerous competing views and value systems.

APOLOGIST, any of the Christian writers, primarily in the 2nd century, who attempted to provide a defense of CHRISTIANITY and criticisms of Greco-Roman culture. Many of their writings were addressed to Roman emperors, and it is probable that the writings were actually sent to government secretaries who were empowered to accept or reject them. Thus, some of the apologies assumed the form of briefs written to defend Christian practices and beliefs.

The Apologists usually tried to prove the antiquity of their religion by emphasizing it as the fulfillment of the prophecy of the OLD TESTAMENT; they argued that their opponents were really godless because they worshiped the false gods of mythology; and they insisted on the philosophical nature of their own faith as well as its high ethical teaching, claiming to follow in the best tradition of classical philosophers, especially of Socrates. Their works did not present a complete picture of Christianity because they were arguing primarily in response to charges proffered by their opponents.

The few manuscripts of the early Apologists that have survived owe their existence primarily to Byzantine scholars. In 914 Arethas, bishop of Caesarea Cappadociae, had a collection of early apologies copied for his library. Many of the later manuscripts were copied in the 16th century, when the COUNCIL OF TRENT was discussing the nature of tradition. The genuine writings of the Apologists were virtually unknown, however, until the 16th century.

APOPIS \ə-'pō-pis\, *also called* Apep, Apepi, *or* Rerek, ancient Egyptian DEMON of chaos, who had the form of a serpent and was the foe of the sun god, RE. Each night Apopis encountered Re at a particular hour in the sun god's ritual journey through the Underworld in his divine bark. SETH, who rode as guardian, attacked him with a spear and slew him, but the next night Apopis, who could not be finally killed, was there again to attack Re. The Egyptians believed that they could help maintain the order of the world and assist Re by performing rituals against Apopis.

APOSTASY (from Greek *apostasia*, "defection," "revolt"), the total rejection of CHRISTIANITY by a baptized person who, having at one time professed the faith, publicly rejects it. It is distinguished from HERESY, which is limited to the rejection of one or more Christian doctrines by one who maintains an overall adherence to JESUS CHRIST.

A celebrated controversy in the early church concerned sanctions against those who had committed apostasy during persecution and had then returned to the church when Christians were no longer being persecuted. Some early Christian emperors added civil sanctions to ecclesiastical laws regarding apostates. In the 20th century, the Roman Catholic Code of CANON LAW still imposed the sanction of EXCOMMUNICATION for those whose rejection of the faith fitted the technical definition of apostasy. But the absence of civil sanctions and an increasing tolerance of divergent viewpoints have tended to mitigate the reaction of believers to those who reject Christianity.

The term apostasy has also been used to refer to those who have abandoned the monastic and clerical states without permission. Additionally, apostasy may also refer to the rejection or renunciation of any faith; ISLAM and JUDAISM are non-Christian faiths in which the term is used.

APOSTLE (from Greek *apostolos*, "person sent"), any of the 12 disciples chosen by JESUS CHRIST; the term is also applied to others, especially PAUL, who was converted to CHRISTIANITY a few years after Jesus' death. In Luke 6:13 it is stated that Jesus chose 12 from his disciples "whom he named apostles," and in Mark 6:30 the Twelve are called Apostles. The full list of the Twelve is given with some variation in Mark 3, Matthew 10, and Luke 6 as: PETER; JAMES and JOHN, the sons of Zebedee; ANDREW; Philip; Bartholomew; MATTHEW; THOMAS; James, the son of Alphaeus; Thaddaeus, or Judas, the son of James; Simon the Cananaean, or the Zealot; and JUDAS ISCARIOT.

The privileges of the Twelve were to be in continual attendance on their master and to be the recipients of his special teaching and training. Three of them, Peter, James, and John, formed an inner circle who alone were permitted to witness such events as the raising of Jairus' daughter (Mark 5:37; Luke 8:51), the TRANSFIGURATION (Mark 9; Matthew 17; Luke 9), and the agony of Jesus in the Garden of GETHSEMANE (Mark 14:33; Matthew 26:37).

Special importance seems to have been attached to the number 12, which some scholars interpret as a reference to the 12 tribes of Israel. When a gap was left by the defection and death of the traitor Judas Iscariot, immediate steps were taken to fill it by the election of Matthias (Acts 1).

Paul himself received the title of Apostle, apparently on the ground that he had seen the Lord and received a commission directly from him. This appears to be in agreement with the condition in Acts that a newly appointed Apostle should be capable of giving eyewitness testimony to the RESURRECTION. According to some early Christian writers, however, some were called apostles after the period covered by the NEW TESTAMENT. The word also has been used to designate a high administrative or ecclesiastical officer.

APOSTLES' CREED, *also called* Apostolicum, a statement of faith used in the Roman Catholic, Anglican, and many Protestant churches. It is not officially recognized in the Eastern Orthodox churches. According to tradition, it was composed by the Twelve Apostles, but it actually developed from early interrogations of CATECHUMENS (persons receiving instructions in order to be baptized) by the bishop. An example of such interrogations used in Rome about 200 has been preserved in the *Apostolic Tradition* of Hippolytus. The bishop would ask, "Dost thou believe in God the Father almighty?" and so forth through the major Christian beliefs. Stated affirmatively, these statements became a creed; such creeds were known as baptismal creeds.

The present text of the Apostles' Creed is similar to the baptismal creed used in the church in Rome in the 3rd and 4th centuries. It reached its final form in southwestern France in the late 6th or early 7th century. Gradually it replaced other baptismal creeds and was acknowledged as the official statement of faith of the entire Catholic church in the West by the time of Pope INNOCENT III (1198–1216).

A modern English version of this creed (as used in the Roman Catholic church) is the following:

◆ **I believe in God, the Father almighty, creator of heaven and earth.**
I believe in Jesus Christ, his only Son, our Lord.
He was conceived by the power of the Holy Spirit and born of the Virgin Mary.
He suffered under Pontius Pilate, was crucified, died, and was buried.
He descended to the dead.
On the third day he rose again.
He ascended into heaven, and is seated at the right hand of the Father.
He will come again to judge the living and the dead.
I believe in the Holy Spirit,
the holy Catholic Church,
the communion of saints,
the forgiveness of sins,
the resurrection of the body,
and the life everlasting. Amen. ◆

APOSTOLIC CONSTITUTIONS, *formally* Ordinances of the Holy Apostles Through Clement, largest collection of ecclesiastical law that has survived from early CHRISTIANITY. The full title suggests that these regulations were drawn up by the Apostles and transmitted to the church by CLEMENT of Rome at the end of the 1st century. In modern times it is generally accepted that the constitutions were actually written in Syria about 380 CE and that they were the work of one compiler, probably an Arian (one who believes that Christ, the Son of God, is not fully divine but rather a created being).

The work consists of eight books. The first six are an adaptation of the *Didascalia Apostolorum*, written in Syria about 250 CE. They deal with Christian ethics, the duties of the clergy, the eucharistic liturgy, and various church problems and rituals. Book 7 contains a paraphrase and enlargement of the DIDACHE (*Teaching of the Twelve Apostles*) and a Jewish collection of prayers and liturgical material. In book 8, the first two chapters seem to be based on a lost work of Hippolytus of Rome, *Concerning Spiritual Gifts.* Chapters 3–22 apparently are based on Hippolytus' *Apostolic Tradition* and contain an elaborate description of the Antiochene liturgy, including the so-called Clementine liturgy. This is a valuable source for the history of the MASS. Chapters 28–46 of book 8 contain a series of canons, and chapter 47 comprises the so-called *Apostolic Canons*, a collection of 85 canons derived in part from the preceding constitutions and in part from the canons of the councils of Antioch (341) and Laodicaea (*c.* 360).

APOSTOLIC SUCCESSION, in

CHRISTIANITY, the doctrine that bishops represent an uninterrupted line of descent from the APOSTLES of JESUS CHRIST. According to this doctrine, bishops possess special powers handed down to them from the Apostles; these consist primarily of the right to ordain priests, to consecrate other bishops, and to rule over the clergy and church members in their DIOCESE. In ROMAN CATHOLICISM bishops also have the right to confirm church members.

The origins of the doctrine are obscure, and the NEW TESTAMENT records are variously interpreted. Those who accept apostolic succession as necessary for a valid ministry argue that it was necessary for Christ to establish a ministry to carry out his work and that he commissioned his Apostles to do this (Matthew 28:19–20). The Apostles in turn consecrated others to assist them and to carry on the work. Supporters of the doctrine also argue that evidence indicates that the doctrine was accepted in the very early church. About 95 CE CLEMENT, bishop of Rome, in his letter to the church in Corinth (FIRST LETTER OF CLEMENT), expressed the view that bishops succeeded the Apostles.

A number of Protestant Christian churches believe that the apostolic succession and church government based on bishops are unnecessary for a valid ministry. They argue that the New Testament gives no clear direction concerning the ministry, that various types of ministers existed in the early church, that the apostolic succession cannot be established historically, and that true succession is spiritual and doctrinal rather than ritualistic or juridical.

Roman Catholic, Eastern Orthodox, Old Catholic, and some other Christian churches accept the doctrine and believe that the only valid ministry is based on bishops whose office has descended from the Apostles. This does not mean, however, that each of these groups necessarily accepts the ministries of the other groups as valid.

APOTHEOSIS \ə-ˌpä-thē-ˈō-sis, ˌa-pə-ˈthē-ə-sis\, elevation to the status of a god. The term (from Greek *apotheoun*, "to make a god," "to deify") recognizes that some individuals

Faience bowl decoration with an Egyptian apotropaic eye, from Lachish, 15th–13th century BCE; in the Israel Museum, Jerusalem
Erich Lessing—Art Resource

may cross the dividing line between divine and human.

Ancient GREEK RELIGION was especially disposed to belief in heroes and DEMIGODS. Worship after death of historical persons or worship of the living as true deities occurred sporadically even before the conquests of Alexander the Great brought Greek life into contact with Oriental traditions. Ancient monarchies often enlisted the support of divine or semidivine individuals.

The corresponding Latin term is *consecratio.* The Romans, up to the end of the republic, had accepted only one official apotheosis, the god QUIRINUS having been identified with Romulus. The emperor Augustus, however, broke with this tradition and had Julius Caesar recognized as a god; Julius Caesar thus became the first representative of a new class of deities proper. The practice was steadily followed and was extended to some women of the imperial family and even to imperial favorites. The public practice of worshiping an emperor during his lifetime, except as the worship of his GENIUS, was in general confined to the provinces. The most significant part of the ceremonies attendant on an imperial apotheosis was the liberation of an eagle, which was supposed to bear the emperor's soul to heaven.

APOTROPAIC EYE \ˌa-pə-trō-ˈpā-ik\, a painting of an eye or eyes used as a symbol to ward off evil. It is seen in many cultures, for instance, the symbol commonly appears on Greek black-figured drinking vessels called kylikes ("eye cups"), from the 6th century BCE. The exaggeratedly large eye on these cups may have been thought to prevent dangerous spirits from entering the mouth with the wine. The apotropaic eye is also seen in Turkish and Egyptian art.

AQHAT EPIC \ˈäk-ˌhät\, ancient West Semitic legend probably concerned with the cause of the annual summer drought. The Aqhat Epic is known only in fragmentary form from three tablets in Ugaritic dating to *c.* 14th century BCE that were excavated from the tell of Ras Shamra in northern Syria. The epic records that Danel, a sage and king of the Haranamites, had no son until the god EL finally granted him a child, whom Danel named Aqhat. Some time later Danel offered hospitality to the divine craftsman KOTHAR, who in return gave Aqhat one of his marvelous bows. That bow, however, had been intended for the goddess ANATH, who became outraged that it had been given to a mortal. Anath made Aqhat a variety of tempting offers, including herself, in exchange for the bow, but Aqhat rejected all of them. Anath then lured Aqhat to a hunting party where she, disguised as a falcon, carried her henchman,

Yatpan, in a sack and dropped him on Aqhat. Yatpan killed Aqhat and snatched the bow, which he later carelessly dropped into the sea. Because of the blood shed in violence, a famine came over the land, leading Aqhat's sister and father to discover the crime and to set about avenging it. The conclusion is not known, however, because the text breaks off at that point.

AQSA MOSQUE, AL- \äl-'äk-sä\, mosque regarded by most Muslims since the 12th century as the third holiest (after those of MECCA and MEDINA), located on the edge of the Old City in Jerusalem. It is part of "the noble SANCTUARY" (al-haram al-sharif), which covers the site where the TEMPLE OF JERUSALEM once stood (the area is also known as the Temple Mount). Its name was derived from a passage in the QUR'AN (17:1) that speaks of MUHAMMAD's miraculous Night Journey (ISRĀ') from the Sacred Mosque (in Mecca) to the blessed "most distant Mosque" (al-masjid al aqsa), which became identified as the mosque in Jerusalem. According to some Islamic traditions Muhammad led other prophets in prayer there prior to his ascension (MIʿRĀJ).

The al-Aqsa Mosque was built by the Umayyad ruler al-Walid (d. 715), who also built the great mosque at Damascus. The plans of al-Aqsa Mosque can be reconstructed with a fair degree of certainty despite subsequent alterations and repairs. The mosque consisted of an undetermined number of naves (possibly as many as 15) parallel to each other in a north-south direction. It has a large internal space with a multiplicity of internal supports and an axial nave (a wider aisle on the axis of the building), which served both as a formal axis for compositional purposes and as a ceremonial one for the prince's retinue. The building was heavily decorated with marble, mosaics, and woodwork. There was no courtyard because the esplanade of the former Jewish temple served as the open space in front of the building.

In the 20th century al-Aqsa Mosque, together with the DOME OF THE ROCK, served as the symbolic focal point for the Palestinian nationalist movement. Palestinian leaders are interred nearby. After Israel gained control of east Jerusalem in June 1967, in accordance with the Israel Law for the Protection of the Holy Places, administration of the ḤARAM area remained in the hands of the Muslim authorities. The site is still maintained by the Jordanian ministry for religious endowments.

ARABIAN RELIGIONS, the religions practiced by the Arab tribes before the time of the Prophet MUHAMMAD and the embracing of ISLAM (7th century CE). These religions were polytheistic, and while some deities were held in common among various tribes and even with non-Arab peoples, and certain religious practices were likewise shared, there was also much local particularity. Knowledge of these religions remains incomplete. The principal sources are incised rock drawings (the oldest of which, dating back several millennia, suggest cults of the bull and of the ostrich), rock inscriptions in several Arabic dialects, monuments, and lesser archaeological remains, including written documents. Contemporary Jewish, Greek, and other writers make mention of Arabic gods and practices, and the QUR'AN and other Islamic writings and practices also preserve elements of the pre-Islamic religions.

Most of the gods of the Arab tribes were sky gods, often associated with heavenly bodies (chiefly the Sun and the Moon), and to them were ascribed powers of fecundity, protection, or revenge against enemies. At the head of the South Arabian pantheon was ʿAthtar, associated with VENUS and corresponding to the Mesopotamian ISHTAR.

ʿAthtar had superseded the ancient supreme Semitic god Il or EL, whose name survives nearly exclusively in theophoric names (names derived from or compounded with the name of a god; for example, Herodotos, meaning "given by Hera"). ʿAthtar was a god of the thunderstorm, dispensing natural irrigation in the form of rain. When qualified as Sharīqān, "the Eastern One" (possibly a reference to Venus as the Morning Star), he was invoked as an avenger against enemies.

Next to ʿAthtar, who was worshiped throughout South Arabia, each kingdom had its own national god, of whom the nation called itself the "progeny" (wld). In Saba' the national god was Almaqah (or Ilmuqah), a protector of artificial irrigation, lord of the temple of the Sabaean federation of tribes. The symbols of the bull's head and the vine motif that are associated with him are indicative of a sun god, a male consort of the sun goddess. In Maʿīn the national god Wadd ("Love") originated from North Arabia and probably was a moon god: the magic formula Wdᵓb, "Wadd is [my?] father," written on AMULETS and buildings, is often accompanied by a crescent moon with the small disk of Venus. In Ḥaḍramawt the national god Syn was also a sun god. The sun goddess Shams was the national deity of the kingdom of Ḥimyar. Other aspects of Shams are certainly concealed in some of the many and still obscure South Arabian female divine epithets.

As to the various lesser or local deities, the nature and even the gender of many remain unknown. In Qatabān, Anbay and Ḥawkam are invoked together as (the gods) "of command and decision[?]." The name Anbay is related to that of the Babylonian god NABU, while Ḥawkam derives from the root meaning "to be wise." They probably represent twin aspects of Babylonian Nabu-Mercury, the god of fate and science and the spokesman of the gods. In Ḥaḍramawt, Ḥawl was probably a moon god. In Maʿīn, Nikraḥ was a healer patron; his shrine, located on a hillock in the middle of a large enclave marked by pillars, was an asylum for dying people and women in childbirth.

North Arabian gods are named for the first time in the annals of the 7th-century BCE Assyrian king Esarhaddon, in which he reports having returned to the oasis of Adumatu (Dūmat al-Jandal) the idols previously confiscated as war booty by his father, Sennacherib. Among the gods named by Esarhaddon are ʿAtarsamāin, ʿAtarqurumā, Nukhay, and Ruldayu. Herodotus wrote that the Arabs worshiped as sole deities Alilat, whom he identifies with both OURANIA and APHRODITE, and Orotalt, identified with DIONYSUS. Ruldayu and Orotalt are phonetic transcriptions of the same name, Rudā, a sun god. In the Nabataean kingdom the counterpart of Dionysus was the great god nicknamed dū-Sharā (Dusares), "the one of Sharā" from the name of the mountain overlooking Petra. He was a rival to Shayʿ al-Qawm, "the Shepherd of the People," he "who drinks no wine, who builds no home," the patron of the nomads and also worshiped by the Liḥyānites. Nukhay, perhaps a solar god, was worshiped by the Thamūdaeans and Ṣafaites.

Al-Ilāt, or Allāt ("the Goddess"), was known to all pantheons. She is a daughter or a consort, depending on the region, of al-Lāh or ALLĀH ("the God"), Lord of the KAʿBA in MECCA. Al-Ilāt formed a trio with the goddesses al-ʿUzzā ("the Powerful") and Manāt (or Manawat, "Destiny"). Among the Nabataeans al-ʿUzzā was assimilated to Venus and Aphrodite and was the consort of Kutbāʾ or al-Aktab ("the Scribe"; MERCURY); among the Thamudaeans, however, she was assimilated to 'Attarsamay (or 'Attarsam). Manāt was depicted as NEMESIS in the Nabataean ICONOGRAPHY. The three goddesses were called the "Daughters of Allāh" in pre-Islamic Mecca, and they are mentioned in the Qur'an (53:19–22).

The sanctuaries, sometimes carved in the rock on high places, consisted of a ḤARAM, a sacred open-air enclosure, accessible only to unarmed and ritually clean people in ritual clothes. There the baetyl, a "raised stone," or a statue of the god, was worshiped. The Nabataeans originally represented their gods as baetyls on a podium, but later they gave them a human appearance.

The stone-built temples of the Nabataeans and South Arabians were more elaborate structures, consisting of a rectangular walled enclosure, near one end of which was a stone canopy or a closed cella or both, which contained the altar for sacrifices or the idol of the god. The Ka'ba in Mecca, which became the sacred shrine of the Muslims, has a similar structure: it is a closed cella (which was full of idols in pre-Islamic times) in a walled enclosure, with a well. A baetyl, the Black Stone, is inserted in the wall of the Ka'ba; it is veiled by a cloth cover (the *kiswah*).

To the gods were offered, on appropriate altars, sacrifices of slaughtered animals, LIBATIONS and fumigations of aromatics, votive objects, or persons dedicated to serve in the temple. A ritual slaughter of enemies in gratitude for a military victory is mentioned at the rock SANCTUARY of the sun goddess of Ḥimyar.

In addition to the northwestern Arabian *Kāhin*, "soothsayer," several kinds of priests and temple officials appear in Lihyānite, Nabataean, and South Arabian inscriptions, but their respective functions are not clear. North Arabian queens and ancient Qatabānian rulers bore priestly titles. In Saba', some priests (*rshw*) of 'Athtar, recruited on a hereditary basis from three clans, took office in turn for seven years as *kabir* (Semitic for "Great," or "Mighty"), in charge of the collection of the tithe and of the rites aimed at obtaining rain.

The priests interpreted the oracles, which, throughout Arabia, were mostly obtained by cleromancy (*istiqsām*): the answer (positive, negative, expectative, and so on) to a question asked of the god was obtained by drawing lots from a batch of marked arrows or sticks. Among the many other forms of DIVINATION known from pre-Islamic Arabia, only oneiromancy, or divination by means of dreams (possibly after incubation in the temple), is well attested in Sabaean texts.

Throughout pre-Islamic Arabia, "truces of God" allowed people to attend in security the yearly PILGRIMAGES to important shrines. The rites included purification and the wearing of ritual clothing, sexual abstinence, abstention from shedding blood, and circuits performed (*ṭawāf, dawār*) around the sacred object; they were concluded by the slaughter of animals, which were eaten in collective feasts. Today such practices still form the core of the Islamic pilgrimage to Mecca.

The sovereigns of Saba' performed a rite called "hunting the game of 'Athtar and the game of Kurūm." This rite was aimed at obtaining rain, and that is also the aim of a formal tribal ibex hunt still performed today in Ḥaḍramawt (an ancient South Arabian kingdom that occupied what are now southern and southeastern Yemen and the present-day Sultanate of Oman [Muscat and Oman]). *Istisqā'*, a collective rogation for rain with magical rites, in times of acute drought, is mentioned by the Muslim tradition and in two Sabaean texts. The rite is still part of the Islamic ritual.

South Arabian texts confessing offenses against ritual cleanliness, along with data from classical sources and the Muslim tradition on pre-Islamic customs, contribute to outline an ancient Arabian code of ritual cleanliness similar to that of the Leviticus and of Muslim jurisprudence.

ARACHNE \ə-'rak-nē\ (Greek: "Spider"), in Greek mythology, the daughter of Idmon of Colophon in Lydia. Arachne was a skillful weaver who challenged ATHENA. The goddess wove a tapestry depicting the gods in majesty, while that of Arachne showed their amorous adventures. Enraged at the perfection of her rival's work, Athena tore it to pieces, and in despair Arachne hanged herself. But the goddess out of pity loosened the rope, which became a cobweb; Arachne herself was changed into a spider.

ARAHANT \'ə-rə-ˌhənt\ (Pāli), *Sanskrit* arhat \'ər-ˌhət, 'är-\ ("one who is worthy"), in BUDDHISM, a perfected person, one who has gained insight into the true nature of existence and has achieved NIRVANA (spiritual enlightenment). The *arahant*, having freed himself from the bonds of desire, will not be reborn again.

The state of an *arahant* is considered in the THERAVĀDA tradition to be the proper goal of a Buddhist. Four stages of attainment are described in Pāli texts: (1) the state of the "stream-enterer"—*i.e.*, a convert (*sotāpanna*)—achieved by overcoming false beliefs; (2) the "once-returner" (*sakadāgāmin*), who will be reborn only once again, a state attained by diminishing lust, hatred, and illusion; (3) the "never-returner" (*anāgāmin*), who, after death, will be reborn in a higher heaven, where he will become an *arahant*, a state attained by overcoming sensuous desire and ill will, in addition to the attainments of the first two stages; and (4) the *arahant*. Except under extraordinary circumstances, a man or woman can become an *arahant* only while living in a monastery. Those who become *arahant*s serve as especially efficacious "fields of merit" for those who have not yet attained the final goal.

MAHĀYĀNA Buddhists criticize the *arahant* ideal on the grounds that the BODHISATTVA is a higher goal of perfection, for the bodhisattva vows to remain within the cycle of rebirths in order to work for the good of others. This divergence of opinion is one of the fundamental differences between the Theravāda and Mahāyāna traditions.

In China, as well as in Korea, Japan, and Tibet, *arahant*s (Chinese: *lohan*; Japanese: *rakan*) were often depicted on the walls of temples in groups of 16. They represent 16 close disciples of the BUDDHA GOTAMA who were entrusted by him to remain in the world in order to provide people with objects of worship.

ĀRAṆYAKAS \ä-'rən-yə-kəz\ (Sanskrit: "Books of the Forest"), a later development of the BRĀHMAṆAS, or expositions of the VEDAS, which were composed in India in about 700 BCE. The *Āraṇyaka*s are attached only to the ṚG VEDA and the *Yajur Veda*. Traditionally the *Āraṇyaka*s have been distinguished from the *Brāhmaṇa*s through the characterization that they contain information on secret rites to be carried out only by certain persons, especially those who had withdrawn into the forest at the onset of the third stage of life recognized in the classical Hindu system of ASHRAMS. While it is true that the *Āraṇyaka*s are given over to explanations of the symbolic and allegorical meanings of Vedic ritual, this does not markedly separate them either from the earlier *Brāhmaṇa*s or from the UPANISHADS, many of which were composed later.

Ara Pacis, Rome
Alinari—Art Resource

ARA PACIS \'ä-rǝ-'pä-sis; 'ä-rǝ-'pä-chis, -kis\, *also called* Ara Pacis Augustae (Latin: "Altar of the Augustan Peace"), shrine consisting of an altar in a walled enclosure erected in Rome by the emperor Augustus and dedicated on Jan. 30, 9 BCE. The sculptures on the walls and the altar representing the shrine's dedication ceremonies, scenes from Roman legend, and floral motifs are among the finest examples of Roman art.

ĀRATĪ \'är-ä-tē\: *see* PŪJĀ.

ARBAʿ KANFOT \är-'bä-kän-'fōt\, *also spelled* arbaʿ kanfoth (Hebrew: "four corners"), *also called* ṭallit qaṭan \tä-'lēt-kä-'tän\, *or* tallith katan ("small shawl"), Jewish religious garment that apparently came into use during times of persecution as a substitute for the larger and more conspicuous prayer shawl (ṬALLIT). Both garments have fringes (*tzitzit*) on the four corners. The *ṭallit*, however, generally falls across the head, neck, and shoulders, while the *arbaʿ kanfot* has an opening for the head so that it can be worn beneath the upper garments. Orthodox male Jews, including children, wear the *arbaʿ kanfot* during the day to fulfill the requirement of wearing fringes (Numbers 15:37–41) as reminders of God's commandments.

ARCHANGEL, any of several rulers or princes of ANGELS in the hierarchy of angels of the major Western religions, especially JUDAISM, CHRISTIANITY, and ISLAM, and of certain syncretic religions, such as GNOSTICISM. They include GABRIEL, Michael, Raphael, and Uriel in Judeo-Christian tradition.

ARCHBISHOP, in the Christian church, a bishop who, in addition to his ordinary episcopal authority in his own DIOCESE, usually has jurisdiction (but no superiority of order) over the other bishops of a province. It seems to have been introduced in the Eastern church in the 4th century as an honorary title of certain bishops. In the Western church it was little known before the 7th century, and it did not become common until the Carolingian emperors revived the right of METROPOLITANS (bishops presiding over a number of dioceses) to summon provincial SYNODS. The metropolitans then commonly assumed the title of archbishop to mark their preeminence over the other bishops. The COUNCIL OF TRENT (1545–63) reduced the powers of the archbishop, which had been quite extensive in the Middle Ages.

In the Orthodox and other churches of the East, the title of archbishop is far more common than in the West, and it is less consistently associated with metropolitan functions. In EASTERN ORTHODOXY there are also autocephalous archbishops who rank between bishops and metropolitans.

In the Protestant churches of continental Europe, the title of archbishop is rarely used. It has been retained by the LUTHERAN bishop of UPPSALA, who is metropolitan of Sweden, and by the Lutheran bishop of Turku in Finland.

In the Church of England (*see* ANGLICAN COMMUNION) the ecclesiastical government is divided between two archbishops: the archbishop of Canterbury, who is called the "primate of all England" and metropolitan of the province of Canterbury, and the archbishop of York, who is called the "primate of England" and metropolitan of York.

ARCHITECTURE AND RELIGION: *see* SACRED ARCHITECTURE.

ARCHON \\'är-ˌkän, -kən\\ (Greek: "Ruler," "Leader"), in GNOSTICISM, any of a number of world-governing powers that were created with the material world by a subordinate deity called the DEMIURGE (Creator).

Because the Gnostics regarded the material world as evil or as the product of error, Archons were viewed as maleficent forces. They numbered 7 or 12 and were identified with the seven planets of antiquity or with the signs of the zodiac. Sometimes the Demiurge and the Archons were identified with the God, the ANGELS, and the law of the OLD TESTAMENT and hence received Hebrew names. The recurring image of Archons is that of jailers imprisoning the divine spark in human souls held captive in material creation. The gnosis sent from the realms of divine light beyond the universe through the divine emanation (AEON) JESUS enabled Gnostic initiates to pass through the spheres of the Archons into the realms of light.

ARDHANĀRĪŚVARA \\ˌär-də-nä-'rēsh-və-rə\\ (Sanskrit: "Lord Who Is Half Woman"), composite male-female figure of the Hindu god SHIVA, together with his consort PĀRVATĪ. The right (male) half of the figure is adorned with the traditional ornaments of Shiva. Half of the hair is piled in matted locks, half of a third eye is visible on the forehead, a tiger skin covers the loins, and serpents are used as ornaments. The left (female) half shows hair well combed and knotted, half of a TILAK (a round dot) on the forehead, one breast, a silk garment caught with girdles, and the foot tinted red with henna.

According to most authorities the figure signifies that the male and female principles are inseparable. A popular explanation, as given in the *Śiva Purāṇa*, is that BRAHMĀ created male beings and instructed them to create others, but they were unable to do so. Brahmā realized his omission and created females. Another legend states that the sage (*ṛṣi*) Bhṛṅgi had vowed to worship only one deity and so failed to circumambulate and to prostrate himself before Pārvatī. Pārvatī tried to force him to do so by asking to be united with her lord, but the sage assumed the form of a beetle and continued to circle only the male half, whereupon Pārvatī became reconciled and blessed Bhṛṅgi.

ARES \\'ā-rēz, 'ar-ēz\\, in GREEK RELIGION, god of war or, more properly, the spirit of battle. Unlike his Roman counterpart, MARS, his worship was not extensive. From at least the time of Homer, who established him as the son of ZEUS and HERA, Ares was one of the Olympian deities; his fellow gods and even his parents, however, were not fond of him (*Iliad* v, 889 ff.). Nonetheless, he was accompanied in battle by his sister ERIS (Strife) and his sons (by APHRODITE) Phobos and Deimos (Panic and Rout). Also associated with him were two lesser war deities: Enyalius, who is virtually identical with Ares himself, and Enyo, a female counterpart.

Ares' worship was largely in the northern areas of Greece, and his cult had many interesting local features. At Sparta a nocturnal offering of dogs—an unusual sacrificial victim, which might indicate a CHTHONIC (Underworld) deity—was made to him as Enyalius. During his festival at Geronthrae in Laconia, no women were allowed in the sacred grove, but at Tegea he was honored in a special sacrifice by only women as Gynaikothoinas ("Entertainer of Women"). At Athens he had a temple at the foot of the Areopagus ("Ares' Hill").

The mythology surrounding the figure of Ares is not extensive. He was associated with Aphrodite from earliest times; in fact, Aphrodite was known locally (*e.g.*, at Sparta) as a war goddess, apparently an early facet of her character. Occasionally, Aphrodite was Ares' legitimate wife, and by her he fathered Deimos, Phobos, and HARMONIA. By AGLAUROS, the daughter of CECROPS, he was the father of Alcippe. He was the father of at least two of HERACLES' adversaries: Cycnus and Diomedes of Thrace.

ARETHUSA \\ˌar-i-'thü-sə\\, in Greek mythology, a NYMPH who gave her name to a spring in Elis and to another on the island of Ortygia, near Syracuse.

Arethusa on a silver coin, c. 413 BCE; in the National Archaeological Museum, Syracuse, Sicily
Konrad Helbig

The river god Alpheus fell in love with Arethusa, who was in the retinue of ARTEMIS. Arethusa fled to Ortygia, where she was changed into a spring. Alpheus, however, made his way beneath the sea and united his waters with those of the spring. In an earlier form of the legend, it was Arethusa, not Arethusa, who was the object of the river god's affections and who escaped by smearing her face with mire, so that he failed to recognize her. The story probably originated from the fact that Artemis Alpheiaia was worshiped in both Elis and Ortygia and also that the Alpheus in its upper part runs underground.

ARGONAUT, in Greek legend, any of a band of 50 heroes who went with JASON in the ship *Argo* to fetch the Golden Fleece.

Jason's uncle ATHAMAS had two children, Phrixus and Helle, by his first wife, the goddess Nephele. Ino, his second wife, hated the children and persuaded Athamas to sacrifice Phrixus as the only means of alleviating a famine. But before the sacrifice, Nephele appeared to Phrixus, bringing a ram with a golden fleece on which he and his sister Helle tried to escape over the sea. Helle fell off and was drowned in the strait that after her was called the Hellespont. Phrixus safely reached the other side, and, proceeding to Colchis on the farther shore of the Euxine (Black) Sea, he sacrificed the ram and hung up its fleece in the grove of ARES, where it was guarded by a sleepless serpent.

Jason's uncle PELIAS had usurped the throne of Iolcus in Thessaly, which rightfully belonged to Jason's father, Aeson. Pelias promised to surrender his kingship if Jason would retrieve the Golden Fleece. Jason called upon the noblest heroes of Greece to take part in the expedition. According to the original story, the crew consisted of the chief members of the Minyans; later, other and better-known heroes, such as Castor and Polydeuces, were added.

The Argonauts underwent various trials on their voyage to Colchis. At the entrance to the Euxine Sea the Argonauts met Phineus, the blind and aged king whose food was constantly polluted by the Harpies. After being freed by the winged sons of BOREAS, Phineus told them the course to

Colchis and how to pass through the Symplegades—two cliffs that clashed constantly together. Jason sent ahead a dove that was damaged between the rocks, but the *Argo* slipped through while the rocks were rebounding. From then the rocks became fixed and never closed again.

When the Argonauts finally reached Colchis, they found that the king, Aeëtes, would not give up the fleece until Jason yoked the king's fire-snorting bulls and plowed the field of Ares. That accomplished, the field was to be sown with dragon's teeth from which armed men were to spring. Aeëtes' daughter, MEDEA, who had fallen in love with Jason, gave him a salve that protected him from the bulls' fire and advised him to cast a stone at the newborn warriors to cause them to fight to the death among themselves. After these tasks were accomplished, Aeëtes still refused to give over the fleece. Medea, however, put the serpent to sleep, and Jason was able to abscond with the fleece and Medea. Aeëtes' pursuit was foiled when Medea killed her brother and tossed his body parts into the sea for her father to gather. Eventually the *Argo* reached Iolcos and was placed in a grove sacred to POSEIDON in the Isthmus of Corinth.

ARGUS PANOPTES \'är-gəs-pan-'äp-tēz\ (Greek: "All Seeing"), figure in Greek myth described as the son of Inachus, Agenor, or Arestor or as an aboriginal hero (autochthon). His surname derives from the hundred eyes in his head or all over his body. Argus was appointed by the goddess HERA to watch the cow into which IO had been transformed, but he was slain by HERMES. His eyes were transferred by Hera to the tail of the peacock.

ARHAT, in BUDDHISM, a perfected person, one who has gained insight into the true nature of existence and has achieved NIRVANA (spiritual enlightenment). *See* ARAHANT.

ARIADNE \,ar-ē-'ad-nē\, in Greek mythology, daughter of Pasiphaë and the Cretan king MINOS. She fell in love with THESEUS and gave to him either a clew (a ball of thread) or glittering jewels with which to retrace his passage through the Labyrinth. Here versions of the tale diverge: she was abandoned by Theseus and hanged herself; Theseus carried her to Naxos and left her there to die or to marry the god DIONYSUS; or she died in childbirth on Cyprus.

ARIANISM \'ar-ē-ə-,ni-zəm\, Christian HERESY first proposed early in the 4th century by the Alexandrian presbyter ARIUS. It affirmed that JESUS CHRIST is not truly divine but a created being. Arius' basic premise was that God alone is self-existent and immutable. Thus, the Son, who is a created being (not self-existent) and a being who grew and changed (not immutable) cannot be God. The Son must, therefore, be deemed a creature who has been called into existence out of nothing and has had a beginning. Moreover, the Son can have no direct knowledge of the Father since the Son is finite and of a different order of existence.

According to its opponents, especially the bishop ATHANASIUS, Arius' teaching reduced the Son to a DEMIGOD, reintroduced POLYTHEISM (since worship of the Son was not abandoned), and undermined the Christian concept of redemption since only he who was truly God could be deemed to have reconciled man to the Godhead.

The controversy seemed to have been brought to an end by the COUNCIL OF NICAEA (325 CE), which condemned Arius and his teaching and issued a creed to safeguard orthodox Christian belief. This creed states that the Son is *homoousion tō Patri* ("of one substance with the Father"), thus de-

claring him to be all that the Father is: He is completely divine. In fact, however, this was only the beginning of a long-protracted dispute (*see* HOMOOUSIAN).

From 325 to 337 the Arian leaders, exiled after the Council of Nicaea, tried, with some success, to return to their churches and sees and to banish their enemies. From 337 to 350 Constans, sympathetic to the orthodox Christians, was emperor in the West, and Constantius II, sympathetic to the Arians, was emperor in the East. At a church council held at Antioch (341), an affirmation of faith that omitted the *homoousion* clause was issued.

In 350 Constantius became sole ruler of the empire, and under his leadership the Nicene party (orthodox Christians) was largely crushed. The extreme Arians then declared that the Son was "unlike" (*anomoios*) the Father. These anomoeans succeeded in having their views endorsed at Sirmium in 357, but their extremism stimulated the moderates, who asserted that the Son was "of similar substance" (*homoiousios*) with the Father. Constantius supported this view, which was approved in 360 at Constantinople; all previous creeds were rejected.

After Constantius' death (361), the orthodox Christian majority in the West consolidated its position. The homoiousian majority in the East began to realize its fundamental agreement with the Nicene party. When the emperors Gratian (367–383) and Theodosius I (379–395) took up the defense of orthodoxy, Arianism collapsed. In 381 the second ecumenical council met at Constantinople. Arianism was proscribed, and a statement of faith which came to be known as the NICENE CREED was approved.

Although this ended the heresy in the empire, Arianism continued among some of the Germanic tribes to the end of the 7th century. In modern times some Unitarians (*see* UNITARIANISM) are virtually Arians in that they are unwilling either to reduce Christ to a mere human being or to attribute to him a divine nature identical with that of the Father. The JEHOVAH'S WITNESSES regard Arius as a forerunner of CHARLES TAZE RUSSELL, the founder of their movement.

ARINNITTI \,ä-ri-'ni-tē\, *Hattian* Wurusemu, Hittite sun goddess, the principal deity and patron of the Hittite empire and monarchy. Her consort was the weather god Taru. Arinnitti's precursor seems to have been a mother-goddess of Anatolia, symbolic of earth and fertility. Arinnitti's attributes were righteous judgment, mercy, and royal authority. The powerful Hittite queen Puduhepa adopted Arinnitti as her protectress; the queen's seal showed her in the goddess' embrace. *See* ANATOLIAN RELIGIONS.

ARION \ə-'rī-ən\, semilegendary Greek poet and musician of Methymna in Lesbos. He is said to have invented the dithyramb (choral poem or chant performed at the festival of DIONYSUS). His father's name, Cycleus, indicates the connection of the son with the cyclic or circular chorus of the dithyramb. None of his works survives, and only one story about his life is known.

After a successful performing tour of Sicily and Magna Graecia, Arion sailed for home. The sailors resolved to kill him and seize the wealth he had collected. Arion begged permission to sing a song and sang a dirge accompanied by his lyre. He then threw himself overboard; but he was miraculously carried to shore by a dolphin. Thus he proceeded to Corinth, arriving before the ship. There Arion's friend Periander, tyrant of Corinth, summoned the sailors and demanded what had become of the poet. Upon testifying that he had remained behind, they were suddenly confronted by

Arion himself. The sailors confessed and were punished, and Arion's lyre and the dolphin became the constellations Lyra and Delphinus.

ARISTAEUS \,ar-i-'stē-əs\, in GREEK RELIGION, a divinity whose worship was widespread but whose character in myth is somewhat obscure. The name is derived from the Greek *aristos*, "best." Aristaeus—son of APOLLO and CYRENE, a nymph—was born in Libya but later went to Thebes, where he received instruction from the MUSES in the arts of healing and PROPHECY and became the son-in-law of CADMUS and the father of ACTAEON. After much travel, he reached Thrace, where he finally disappeared near Mt. Haemus.

Aristaeus is said to have introduced the cultivation of bees, the vine, and the olive and was the protector of herdsmen and hunters. He was often identified with ZEUS, Apollo, and DIONYSUS. He was represented as a young man dressed like a shepherd and sometimes carrying a sheep.

ARIUS \'ar-ē-əs\ (b. *c.* 250, Libya—d. 336, Constantinople [now Istanbul, Turkey]), Christian priest of Alexandria, Egypt, whose teachings gave rise to a theological doctrine known as ARIANISM, which, for affirming the created, finite nature of Christ, was denounced by the early church as a major HERESY.

An ascetical leader of a Christian community in the area of Alexandria, Arius attracted a large following with a message integrating NEOPLATONISM, which accented the absolute oneness of the divinity as the highest perfection, with a literal, rationalist approach to the NEW TESTAMENT. This view was publicized about 323 through the poetic verse of his major work, *Thalia* ("Banquet"), and was widely spread by popular songs written for laborers and travelers.

The COUNCIL OF NICAEA, in May 325, declared Arius a heretic after he refused to sign the formula of faith stating that Christ was of the same divine nature as God. Influential support from colleagues in Asia Minor succeeded in effecting Arius' return from exile and his readmission into the church after consenting to a compromise formula. Shortly before he was to be reconciled, however, Arius died.

ARIYA-PUGGALA \'ə-rē-ə-'pủg-gə-lə\ (Pāli: "noble being"), *Sanskrit* arya-pudgala \'ə-rē-ə-'pủd-gə-lə\, in THERAVĀDA BUDDHISM, a person who has attained one of the four levels of holiness. A first type of holy person, called a *sotapannapuggala* ("stream-enterer"), is one who will attain NIRVANA after no more than seven rebirths. Another type of holy person is termed a *sakadagamin* ("once-returner"), or one who is destined to be reborn in the human world only once more before reaching nirvana. A third type of *ariya-puggala* is the *anagamin* ("never-returner"), or one who will not be reborn in the human realm and will enter the realm of the gods at the time of death. The never-returner, however, is still not considered to have reached nirvana.

According to Theravāda Buddhism the highest level of holiness is reached by the ARAHANT, one who has reached final and absolute emancipation from all rebirths in any human or superhuman realm. The *arahant*—a model person for Theravāda Buddhists—is to be distinguished from the personal ideal of the MAHĀYĀNA schools, the BODHISATTVA. The latter is a holy person who has reached enlightenment but refuses to enter nirvana, choosing rather to teach his insights until all creatures have similarly been liberated.

ARJAN \'ər-jən, 'är-\ (b. 1563, Goindwāl, Punjab, India—d. May 30, 1606, Lahore, Punjab, Mughal Empire [now in Pa-

kistan]), fifth GURŪ of the Sikhs (1581–1606). Gurū Arjan took over the leadership of the community from his father, Gurū RĀMDĀS, in 1581 and successfully expanded it. He updated the text of Sikh SCRIPTURE and prepared the *Kartārpur Pothī*, the volume upon which the canonical ĀDI GRANTH is largely based. He also completed the construction of the GOLDEN TEMPLE (also called the Darbār Sāhib) and was instrumental in founding four important Sikh towns in central Punjab. He was a prolific poet and created hymns of great lyrical quality. SIKHISM grew considerably during his tenure, posing a threat to the local Mughal administration. This caused the provincial Mughal ruler to summon him to Lahore, where he died in official custody, the first martyr of the tradition.

ARJUNA \'ər-jủ-nə, '-är\, one of the five Pāṇḍava brothers, heroes of the Indian epic, the MAHĀBHĀRATA. Arjuna's hesitation before a massive battle that would cause him to kill

The hermitage by the Gaṅgā, detail of a granite relief depicting the penance of Arjuna, from Mahābalipuram, Tamil Nadu, early 7th century CE
Photograph, P. Chandra

his kinsmen and would also cause unthinkable destruction on the race, became the occasion for his friend and charioteer, the god KRISHNA, to deliver a discourse on duty, or the right course of human action. These verses are collectively known as the BHAGAVAD GĪTĀ, one of the most celebrated religious texts of India. Arjuna's stature as an exemplar of skill, duty, and compassion, as well as a seeker of true knowledge, makes him a central figure in Hindu myth and theology.

ARK, *also called* Ark of the Law, *Hebrew* Aron, *or* Aron ha-Qodesh ("Holy Ark"), in Jewish SYNAGOGUES, an ornate cabinet that enshrines the sacred TORAH scrolls used for public worship. Because it symbolizes the HOLY OF HOLIES of the ancient TEMPLE OF JERUSALEM, it is the holiest place in the synagogue and the focal point of prayer. The ark is reached by steps and is commonly placed so that the worshiper facing it also faces Jerusalem. When the scrolls are removed for religious services, the congregation stands, and a solemn ceremony accompanies the opening and closing of the ark doors.

ASHKENAZI (German-rite) Jews cover the doors of the ark with a richly embroidered cloth (*parocheth*), while SEPHARDIC (Spanish-rite) Jews place the cloth inside. Before or near the cabinet hangs the eternal light (*ner tamid*), and generally an inscription of the TEN COMMANDMENTS (often in abbreviated form) or some other relevant sacred text is placed above the doors.

ARK OF THE COVENANT, *Hebrew* Aron Ha-Berit, in JUDAISM and CHRISTIANITY, the chest that in biblical times housed the two tablets of the Mosaic Law (EXODUS 25:16; 40:20; 1 Kings 8:9). The ARK rested in the HOLY OF HOLIES inside the TABERNACLE of the ancient TEMPLE OF JERUSALEM and was seen only by the HIGH PRIEST of the Israelites on YOM KIPPUR, the Day of Atonement (Exodus 30:10; Leviticus 16).

The LEVITES carried the Ark with them during the Hebrews' wanderings in the wilderness (Numbers 10:33). Following the conquest of CANAAN, the Ark resided at SHILOH (1 Samuel 3–6), but from time to time it was carried into battle by the Israelites (Numbers 10:35–36; 1 Samuel 4:3–9). Taken to Jerusalem by King DAVID (2 Samuel 6), it was eventually placed in the Temple by King SOLOMON (1 Kings 8:6). The final fate of the Ark is unknown.

ARKONA \är-'kō-nə\, West Slavic citadel-temple of the god SVANTOVIT, dating from the 9th–10th century CE and destroyed in 1168/69 by Christian Danes when they stormed the island of Rügen in the southwestern Baltic. Saxo Grammaticus, the 12th-century Danish historian, wrote that the Arkona was a log-built temple topped by a red roof and surrounded by a wooden fence, splendidly carved and bearing various painted symbols; the inner temple chamber had partitions of heavy tapestry. In this inner sanctum loomed the statue of Svantovit, which had four heads and throats joined together facing in opposite directions. Saxo mentions that not only the Wends but also Scandinavian neighbors paid tribute to Svantovit. When the statue was cut and removed, the Danes carried away seven boxes of treasures (gifts to the god). Excavations in 1921 proved the actual existence of the temple. Repeated excavations in 1969–70 revealed an earlier layer of the SANCTUARY dated to the 10th and possibly 9th century CE. *See also* SLAVIC RELIGION.

ARMAGEDDON \ˌär-mə-'ge-dən\, in the NEW TESTAMENT, place where the kings of the earth under demonic leadership will wage war on the forces of God at the end of world history. The word Armageddon occurs in the BIBLE only once, in the REVELATION TO JOHN (16:16: "the place which is called in Hebrew Armageddon"). No such Hebrew word is known, however, and the name has been variously interpreted, perhaps most plausibly as "Mountain of Megiddo." The Palestinian city of Megiddo was probably used as a symbol for such a battle because of its strategic importance. Megiddo was the scene of many battles, and Revelation seems to imply that the "hill" on which the city fortress stood, or the "mountain" heights behind it, had become a symbol of the final battlefield where God's heavenly armies will defeat the demon-led forces of evil. Other biblical references suggest Jerusalem as the site of this battle.

ARMENIAN RITE, the system of liturgical practices and discipline observed by both

The triumph of the Ark of the Covenant over paganism, mural painting from the synagogue at Doura-Europus, Syria, 3rd century CE
By courtesy of the Bollingen Foundation, photograph, Fred Anderegg

the Armenian Apostolic (Eastern Orthodox) Church and the Armenian Catholics. The Armenians were converted to CHRISTIANITY by St. Gregory the Illuminator about 300 CE. The liturgy used by churches of the Armenian rite—the Liturgy of St. Gregory Illuminator—is usually divided into five parts: (1) the prayers of preparation in the sacristy, (2) the prayers of preparation in the SANCTUARY, (3) the preparation and consecration of the gifts, (4) the liturgy of the CATECHUMENS, and (5) the liturgy of the faithful, culminating in Communion.

Churches of the Armenian rite, unlike Byzantine churches, are generally devoid of ICONS and, in place of an ICONOSTASIS (screen), have a curtain that conceals the priest and the altar during parts of the liturgy. The Communion itself is given in two species (bread and wine), as in other Orthodox churches. For its worship services the Armenian rite is dependent upon such books as the *Donatzuitz*, the order of service; the *Badarakamaduitz*, the book containing all the prayers used by the priest; the *Giashotz*, the book of midday, containing the Epistle and Gospel readings for each day; and the *Z'amagirq*, the book of hours, containing the prayers and psalms of the seven daily offices, primarily matins, prime, and vespers.

ARMILUS \'är-mə-ləs\, in Jewish mythology, an enemy who will conquer Jerusalem and persecute Jews until his final defeat at the hands of God or the true MESSIAH. His destruction symbolizes the ultimate victory of good over evil in the messianic era. Some sources depict Armilus as partially deaf and partially maimed, the frightful offspring of SATAN or evil creatures. Parallel legends exist in the figures of the ANTICHRIST and of AHRIMAN, the Persian god of evil.

ARMINIANISM \är-'mi-nē-ə-,ni-zəm\, a theological movement in CHRISTIANITY that represents a reaction to the Calvinist doctrine of PREDESTINATION (*see also* CALVINISM). The movement, named for JACOBUS ARMINIUS, who became involved in a highly publicized debate with his colleague Franciscus Gomarus, a rigid Calvinist, began early in the 17th century and asserted that God's sovereignty and man's FREE WILL are compatible. For Arminius, God's will as unceasing love was the determinative initiator and arbiter of human destiny. The movement that became known as Arminianism, however, tended to be more liberal than was Arminius himself.

Dutch Arminianism was originally articulated in the Remonstrance (1610), a theological statement signed by 45 ministers and submitted to the Dutch states general. The SYNOD OF DORT (1618–19) was called by the states general to pass upon the Remonstrance. The five points of the Remonstrance asserted that: (1) election (and condemnation on the day of judgment) was conditioned by the rational faith or nonfaith of man, (2) the ATONEMENT, while qualitatively adequate for all men, was efficacious only for the man of faith, (3) unaided by the HOLY SPIRIT, no person is able to respond to God's will, (4) GRACE is not irresistible, and (5) believers are able to resist SIN but are not beyond the possibility of falling from grace. The crux of REMONSTRANT Arminianism lay in the assertion that human dignity requires an unimpaired freedom of the will.

The Dutch Remonstrants were condemned by the Synod of Dort and suffered political persecution for a time, but by 1630 they were legally tolerated. They have continued to exert liberalizing tendencies in Dutch Protestant theology.

In the 18th century, JOHN WESLEY was influenced by Arminianism. Arminianism was an important influence in METHODISM, which developed out of the Wesleyan movement. A still more liberal version of Arminianism went into the making of American UNITARIANISM.

ARMINIUS, JACOBUS \är-'mi-nē-əs\ (b. Oct. 10, 1560, Oudewater, Neth.—d. Oct. 19, 1609, Leiden), theologian and minister of the Dutch REFORMED CHURCH who opposed the strict Calvinist teaching on PREDESTINATION and who developed a system of belief known later as ARMINIANISM.

Arminius attended school at Utrecht and continued his education at the universities of Leiden (1576–82), Basel, and Geneva (1582–86). After brief stays at the University of Padua, in Rome, and in Geneva, he returned to Amsterdam. He was ordained there in 1588. In 1603 Arminius was called to a theological professorship at Leiden, which he held until his death. These last six years of his life were dominated by theological controversy, in particular by his disputes with his colleague Franciscus Gomarus.

Arminius was forced into controversy against his own choice. He had earlier affirmed the Calvinist view of predestination, which held that those elected for salvation were chosen prior to Adam's fall, but gradually predestination came to seem too harsh a position because it did not allow human decision a role in the achieving of salvation. Hence Arminius came to assert a conditional election, according to which God elects to life those who will respond in faith to the divine offer of salvation. In so doing, he meant to place greater emphasis on God's mercy.

After his death some of his followers gave support to his views by signing the Remonstrance, a theological dictum that was debated in 1618–19 at the SYNOD OF DORT, at which all the delegates were supporters of Gomarus. REMONSTRANT Arminianism was condemned by the synod, the Arminians present were expelled, and many others suffered persecution. In 1629, however, the works of Arminius (*Opera theologica*) were published for the first time in Leiden, and by 1630 the Remonstrant Brotherhood had achieved legal toleration. It was finally recognized officially in the Netherlands in 1795. In its emphasis on the GRACE of God, Arminianism influenced the development of METHODISM in England and the United States.

ART AND RELIGION, one of the best tools with which to examine and discover the similarities and differences of WORLD RELIGIONS. By making concrete some of the cognitive dimensions of a religion, art also allows for the study of the tradition's structure. But the significance of religious art is not merely tied to the religious ideas contained in such art—the extent of artistic representations in a specific tradition also allows for the understanding of the significance of political, economic, and craft constraints on a religion in a particular historical period.

Art obviously expresses, "rationalizes," the central conceptions of a religion. It encompasses the structure of a religion from its cosmological myths to representations of doctrine and ritual practice. But religious art does not always act in concert with theology. It must be remembered that cathedrals, Hindu temples, and the Taj Mahal were not built in a day and presuppose a vast network of interrelated political, economic, and social relations that must all be taken into account in any understanding of a particular artistic tradition.

Scholars have often focused on a specific symbol or element in religious art, reading the work as if it were a code in which a particular representation always and invariably has the same specific meaning, regardless of the period or context. It is often stated, for example, that a Hindu temple always faces East, and the direction East is then interpreted as a reference to the rising sun and the powers of nature. This focus, however, usually distorts the meaning of both the work of art and the religious tradition in which it was executed; the meaning of the symbol as well as of the work itself is constituted by a web of relations between various symbols, *i.e.*, the symbol's meaning is constituted by its position with respect to other symbols in the same cultural system. Symbols in themselves lack meaning. In the above example, the geographic representation East bears cosmological significance in that it is the abode of the gods in HINDUISM. Its opposite is the West, the domain of the anti-gods and darkness. Moreover, East/West is opposite North/South, which is the domain of human beings and the ancestors. The Hindu temple facing East is thus a complex microcosm framed by the four huge temple gates found in most South Indian temples.

For a general discussion of principles of artistic representation, *see* ICONOGRAPHY; SYMBOL. For surveys of traditional categories of art, *see* SACRED ARCHITECTURE and MUSIC AND RELIGION. The art of particular religious traditions is treated in the following articles: AFRICAN RELIGIONS, ART OF; JUDAISM, ART OF; CHRISTIANITY, ART OF; BUDDHISM, ART OF.

ARTEMIS \'är-tə-mis\, in GREEK RELIGION, the goddess of wild animals, the hunt, vegetation, and of chastity and childbirth. Artemis was the daughter of ZEUS and LETO and the twin sister of APOLLO. Her character and function varied greatly from place to place, but, apparently, behind all forms lay the goddess of wild nature, who danced, usually accompanied by NYMPHS, in mountains, forests, and marshes. Besides killing game she also was believed to protect it, especially the young; hence her title Mistress of Animals.

Artemis may originally have developed out of ISHTAR (INANNA) in the East. Many of her local cults, such as that of Artemis Orthia at Sparta, preserved traces of other deities, often with Greek names.

While the mythological roles of other prominent Olympians evolved in the works of the poets, the lore of Artemis developed primarily from cult. Dances of maidens representing tree nymphs (dryads) were especially common in Artemis' worship as goddess of vegetation, a role especially popular in the Peloponnese. Throughout the Peloponnese, bearing such epithets as Limnaea and Limnatis (Lady of the Lake), Artemis supervised waters and lush wild growth, attended by nymphs of wells and springs (NAIADS). In parts of the peninsula her dances were wild and lascivious.

Outside the Peloponnese, Artemis' most familiar form was as Mistress of Animals. Poets and artists usually pictured her with the stag or hunting dog, but the cults showed considerable variety. For instance, the Tauropolia festival at Halae Araphenides in Attica honored Artemis Tauropolos (Bull Goddess), who received a few drops of blood drawn by sword from a man's neck.

The frequent stories of the love affairs of Artemis' nymphs may have originally been told of the goddess herself. The poets after Homer, however, stressed Artemis' chastity. The wrath of Artemis was proverbial. Yet Greek sculpture avoided Artemis' unpitying anger as a motif; in fact, the goddess herself did not become popular as a sculptural subject until the 4th century BCE.

ARTHA \'är-tə\ (Sanskrit: "purpose," "meaning," "wealth," or "property"), in HINDUISM, the pursuit of material advantage, one of the four traditional aims in life. The sanction

for *artha* rests on the assumption that—setting aside the exceptional few who can proceed directly to the final aim of MOKṢA—material well-being is a basic necessity and is an appropriate pursuit for a householder (the second of the four life stages). Furthermore, *artha* is closely tied to the activities of statecraft, which maintains the general social order and prevents anarchy. Still, *artha* must always be regulated by the superior aim of DHARMA, or righteousness.

ARVAL BROTHERS \'är-vəl\, *Latin* Fratres Arvales \'frä-trēz-är-'vā-lēz\, in ancient Rome, college or PRIESTHOOD whose chief original duty was to offer annual public sacrifice for the fertility of the fields. The brotherhood was almost forgotten in republican times but was revived by Augustus and probably lasted until the time of Theodosius I (reigned 379–395). It consisted of 12 members, elected for life from the highest ranks, including the emperor during the principate. Literary allusions to them are scarce, but 96

Artemis as a huntress; in the Louvre, Paris
Alinari—Art Resource

of the *acta*, or minutes, of their proceedings, inscribed on stone, were found in the grove of the Dea Dia near Rome.

ARYAN \\'ar-ē-ən, 'er-, 'är-\\ (from Sanskrit: *ārya*, "noble"), prehistoric people who, scholars once assumed, invaded and settled in Iran and northern India. It was postulated that from their language, also called Aryan, the Indo-European languages of South Asia descended. In the 19th century the term was used as a synonym for "Indo-European" and also, more restrictively, to refer to the Indo-Iranian languages. In the 20th century, however, the entire notion that there was an "Aryan invasion" of the Indian subcontinent has been disputed by Hindu nationalists and by a large number of scholars as a fallacy of colonial Orientalism. While the idea that there was an Aryan invasion enjoys less popularity than it once did, the exact status of Indo-Aryan languages in relation to other ancient language groups in the Indian subcontinent has remained a subject of continuing debate, as has the closely related question of cultural diffusion and interaction. Such questions gain special significance from the fact that the VEDAS and their attached literature belong to the Indo-Aryan language family. At issue is their intrinsic relation to India and the fact that in Vedic literature the term *ārya* is used to distinguish privileged members of society from others.

During the 19th century there arose a notion—propagated most assiduously by the Comte de Gobineau and later by his disciple Houston Stewart Chamberlain—of an "Aryan race," those who spoke Indo-European languages, who were considered to be responsible for all human progress, and who were also morally superior to "Semites," "yellows," and "blacks." The Nordic, or Germanic, peoples came to be regarded as the purest "Aryans." This notion, which had been repudiated by anthropologists by the second quarter of the 20th century, was seized upon by Adolf Hitler and the Nazis and made the basis of the German government policy of exterminating Jews, Gypsies, and other "non-Aryans."

ARYA-PUDGALA: *see* ARIYA-PUGGALA.

ARYA SAMAJ \\'är-yə-sə-'mäj\\, *Sanskrit* Ārya Samāja ("Society of Noble Ones"), vigorous reform sect of modern HINDUISM, founded in 1875 by DAYANANDA SARASVATI, whose aim was to reestablish a regard for the VEDAS as revealed truth. He rejected all later accretions to the Vedas as degenerate but, in his own interpretation, included much post-Vedic thought, such as the doctrines of KARMA and of rebirth.

The Arya Samaj has always had its largest following in West and North India. It is organized in local *samājas* ("societies") that send representatives to provincial *samājas* and to an all-India *samāja*. Each local *samāja* elects its own officers in a democratic manner.

The Arya Samaj opposes IDOLATRY, animal sacrifice, ANCESTOR WORSHIP, a CASTE system based on birth rather than on merit, untouchability, child marriage, PILGRIMAGES, priestly craft, and temple offerings. It upholds the infallibility of the Vedas, the doctrines of karma and rebirth, the SANCTITY OF THE COW, the importance of the individual SACRAMENTS (SAMSKĀRAS), the efficacy of Vedic oblations to the fire, and programs of social reform. It has worked to further the education of girls and women and to encourage inter-caste marriages; has built missions, orphanages, and homes for widows; and has undertaken famine relief and medical work. It has also established a network of schools and colleges. From its beginning it was an important factor in the growth of nationalism. It has been criticized, however, as overly dogmatic and militant and as having exhibited hostility toward both CHRISTIANITY and ISLAM.

ASAHARA, SHOKO \\ä-sä-'hä-rä-'shō-ˌkȯ\\, *original name* Chizuo Matsumoto (b. March 2, 1955, Kumamoto prefecture, Japan), founder of AUM SHINRIKYO ("Supreme Truth"), a radically millenarian new religious movement in Japan (*see* MILLENNIALISM; NEW RELIGIOUS MOVEMENTS).

Asahara was born partially blind and was sent to a school for the blind. After graduating in 1975 and failing to gain admission to medical school, he studied acupuncture and pharmacology. He opened his own pharmacy in Chiba, specializing in Chinese medicaments. In 1982 he was arrested for selling fake remedies, and after his conviction for fraud his business went bankrupt.

During this period Asahara had become a member of a small new religion, Agonshu, a movement with strong Hindu and Buddhist elements. After his trial and a period of spiritual soul-searching he established his own new religion, Aum Shinsen-no-kai, later known as Aum Shinrikyo, in 1984. Asahara began handing out leaflets, preaching on street corners, and teaching YOGA and healing through the use of herbal medicines.

By 1989, when the Tokyo metropolitan government granted Aum Shinrikyo legal status as a religious organization, Asahara had begun calling himself the "Holy Pope," "Savior of the Country," and "Tokyo's Christ." The sect claimed to have 30,000 followers in Japan and abroad. In 1990 Asahara fielded a list of 25 candidates for the Diet (the Japanese parliament) with the idea that their victory would give him the prime ministership. Aum's candidates, however, were rejected by the electorate.

This failure led to an inward shift of Aum theology and strategies. Aum's belief system was based on the millenarian conviction that the modern period is a prelude to the end of humanity and the beginning of a cosmic cycle. Asahara predicted a series of disasters that would foreshadow the end of the world. Accordingly, Aum members had been gathering arms and supplies of the nerve gas sarin. In 1995 they released the gas in the Tokyo subway system, an attack that killed 12 and injured 5,000. Asahara and members of his sect were arrested and the sect's sites were taken over. Investigations revealed that the movement had been developing biological weapons and had acquired over one billion dollars (U.S.) in assets, which it used to influence the government, various segments of the economic establishment, and criminal organizations.

ASALLUHE \\ä-säl-'lü-ˌkä\\, in MESOPOTAMIAN RELIGION, Sumerian deity, city god of Ku'ar, near Eridu in the southeastern marshland region. Asalluhe was active with the god Enki (Akkadian: EA) in rituals of LUSTRATION (purification) magic and was considered his son. He may originally have been a god of thundershowers, as his name, "Man-Drenching Asal," suggests; he would thus have corresponded to the other Sumerian gods ISHKUR and NINURTA. In incantations Asalluhe was usually the god who first called Enki's attention to existing evils. He was later identified with MARDUK of Babylon.

ĀSANA \\'ä-sə-nə\\ (Sanskrit: "sitting posture"), in the YOGA system of Indian philosophy, an immobile posture that a person assumes in an attempt to isolate the mind by freeing it from attention to bodily functions. It is the third of the eight prescribed stages intended to lead the aspirant to *samādhi,* the trancelike state of perfect concentration. As many as 32 or more different *āsana*s have been enumerated, perhaps the most common being the *padmāsana* ("lotus posture"). In the visual arts of India, *āsana* refers to the posture of seated figures or to the seats on which they sit.

ASANGA \'ä-səŋ-gə\ (fl. 4th–5th century CE, b. Puruṣapura, India), an influential Buddhist philosopher who is often recognized as the founder of the YOGĀCĀRA school of idealism.

Asanga was the eldest of three brothers, the sons of a BRAHMIN court priest at Puruṣapura, all of whom became monks in the SARVĀSTIVĀDA order. Dissatisfied with the Sarvāstivāda doctrinal concepts of *śūnyatā* ("EMPTINESS") and *pudgala* ("person"), he turned to the MAHĀYĀNA tradition for which he developed a new interpretation. Asanga and the Yogācāra school that he initiated held that the external world exists only as mental images that have no real permanence. A "storehouse" of consciousness (the *ālaya-vijñāna*) contains the trace impressions of the past and the potentialities of future actions. Asanga's great contribution was his analysis of the *ālaya-vijñāna* and setting forth of the stages (*bhūmi*) leading to Buddhahood. Among his important works is the *Mahāyāna-saṃgraha* ("Compendium of the Mahāyāna").

ASCANIUS \a-'skā-nē-əs\, in Roman legend, son of the hero AENEAS and founder of Alba Longa, near Rome. In different versions, Ascanius is placed variously in time. Those set earlier cite the Trojan Creusa as his mother. After the fall of Troy, Ascanius and Aeneas escaped to Italy, where Aeneas founded Lavinium, the parent city of Alba Longa and Rome. Ascanius became king of Lavinium after his father's death. Thirty years after Lavinium was built, Ascanius founded Alba Longa and ruled it until he died. In the Roman historian Livy's account, however, Ascanius was born to Aeneas and Lavinia after the founding of Lavinium. Ascanius was also called Iulus, and the gens Julia (including the family of Julius Caesar) traced its descent from him.

ASCENSION, in Christian belief, the ascent of JESUS CHRIST into heaven on the 40th day after his RESURRECTION. In the first chapter of THE ACTS OF THE APOSTLES, after appearing to the Apostles on various occasions during a period of 40 days, Jesus was taken up in their presence and was then hidden from them by a cloud, a frequent biblical image signifying the presence of God. Although the Ascension is alluded to in other books of the NEW TESTAMENT, the emphasis and the imagery differ. In The Gospel According to John, the glorification described by the Ascension story seems to have taken place immediately after the Resurrection.

The meaning of the Ascension for Christians is derived from their belief in the glorification and exaltation of Jesus following his death and Resurrection. The Ascension indicates a new relationship between Jesus and his Father and between him and his followers, rather than a simple physical relocation from earth to heaven. The Ascension of Jesus is mentioned both in the Apostles' Creed, a Western profession of faith used for BAPTISM in the early church, and in the NICENE CREED. The feast of the Ascension ranks with CHRISTMAS, EASTER, and PENTECOST in the universality of its observance among Christians. The feast has been celebrated 40 days after Easter in both Eastern and Western CHRISTIANITY since the 4th century.

A distinctive feature of the feast's liturgy in the Western churches is the extinguishing of the Paschal candle after the Gospel has been read, as a symbol of Christ's leaving the earth. Despite the suggestion of separation indicated in this act, the whole liturgy of Ascensiontide, through the 10 days to Pentecost, is marked by joy in the final triumph of the risen Lord. One of the central themes of the feast is the kingship of Christ, and the implication that the Ascension was the final redemptive act conferring participation in the divine life on all who are members of Christ.

In the Middle Ages various ritual practices that came to be associated with the feast included a PROCESSION, in imitation of Christ's journey with his Apostles to the Mount of Olives, as well as the raising of a crucifix or a statue of the risen Christ through an opening in the church roof.

The view of the Ascension presented by Christian art has varied. In a 5th-century painting, Christ is seen climbing a hill and grasping the hand of God, that is, God is pulling Christ into heaven. A version of the Ascension developed in Syria in the 6th century emphasizes Christ's divinity, showing him frontally, standing immobile in a mandorla, or almond-shaped aureole, elevated above the earth and supported by ANGELS. He holds a scroll and makes a gesture of BENEDICTION. This type of Ascension, which follows the Roman tradition of representing the APOTHEOSIS of an emperor, often figured prominently in the monumental decoration of Byzantine churches. By the 11th century, the West had also adopted a frontal representation. In the Western version, however, the humanity of Christ is emphasized: he extends his hands on either side, showing his wounds. He is usually in a mandorla but is not always supported or even surrounded by angels; thus, he ascends to heaven by his own power. The Ascension remained important as a devotional subject in the art of the Renaissance and Baroque periods, both of which retained the ICONOGRAPHY of Christ displaying his wounds.

ASCETICISM, the practice of the denial of physical or psychological desires in order to attain a spiritual ideal or goal.

Originally a concept referring to physical proficiency, Greek *askēsis* (literally, "exercise," "training," from the verb *askeō,* "I prepare, fashion, practise, exercise") and its derivatives came to be applied to mental, moral, and spiritual abilities. Among the Greeks the notion of intellectual training was applied to the realm of ethics in the ideal of the sage who is able to act freely to choose or refuse a desired object or an act of physical pleasure. This kind of *askēsis,* involving training the will against a life of sensual pleasure, was exemplified by the Stoics (ancient Greek philosophers who advocated the control of the emotions by reason). The view that one ought to deny one's lower desires—understood to be the sensuous, or bodily desires—in contrast with one's spiritual desires that were considered to be virtuous aspirations, became a central principle in ethical thought, particularly evident in the work of Plato and the Neoplatonic philosophers.

The value of asceticism in strengthening an individual's mental and physical discipline has been a part of many religions and philosophies throughout history. Many factors were operative in the rise and cultivation of religious asceticism: the fear of hostile influences from DEMONS; the view that one must be in a state of ritual purity in order to enter into communion with the divine; the desire to invite the attention of sacred beings to the self-denial being practiced by their suppliants; the idea of earning pity, compassion, and salvation by merit using self-inflicted acts of ascetical practices; the sense of guilt and SIN that prompts the need for ATONEMENT; the view that asceticism is a means to gain access to supernatural powers; and the power of dualistic concepts that have been at the source of efforts to free the spiritual part of humanity from the defilement of the body. Among HINDUISM, BUDDHISM, and CHRISTIANITY, there is a further conceptualization of earthly life as transitory, which prompts a desire to anchor one's hope in liberation from the suffering of such life.

Abstinence and fasting are by far the most common of all ascetic practices, though CELIBACY has been regarded as the first commandment in all strictly ascetic movements. Other common practices include abdication of worldly goods, neglect of personal hygiene, the reduction of movement, and the deliberate inducement of pain. Pain-producing asceticism has appeared in many forms, including exhausting or painful exercises, self-laceration, particularly castration, and FLAGELLATION, which developed into a mass movement in Italy and Germany during the Middle Ages and is still practiced by some local Christian and Islamic sects.

Asceticism in the form

In the Philippines, ritual ascetism is practiced by flagellants during Good Friday observances
Archive Photos

of seclusion, physical discipline, and the quality and quantity of food prescribed has played an important role in connection with the puberty rites and rituals of admission to the tribal community. Isolation was and is practiced by young men about to achieve the status of manhood in the Blackfoot and other Native American tribes of the northwestern United States. On important occasions, such as funerals and war, TABOOS involving abstinence from certain food and cohabitation were imposed. For the priests and chiefs these taboos were much stricter.

In India, in the late Vedic period (c. 1500 BCE–c. 200 BCE), the ascetic use of TAPAS ("heat," or austerity) became associated with meditation and YOGA, inspired by the idea that *tapas* brings enlightenment. This view of *tapas* gained in importance among the Yogas and the Jainas. According to JAINISM, liberation becomes possible only when all passions have been exterminated. In Jainism and Buddhism a monastic system evolved, with monks and nuns devoted to rigorous asceticism in the quest of perfection and in the pursuit of chastity and truthfulness. Complete detachment from all possessions and connections in Jainism made paramount the MENDICANT life of meditation and spiritual exercises dependent upon the fulfillment of vows of poverty.

In Christianity all of the types of asceticism have found realization. Abstinence, fasts, and vigils were common in

the lives of the early Christians, but some ramifications of developing Christianity became radically ascetic. During the first centuries ascetics stayed in their communities, assumed their role in the life of the church, and centered their asceticism on martyrdom and celibacy. Though asceticism was rejected by the leaders of the Protestant REFORMATION, certain forms of asceticism did emerge in CALVINISM, PURITANISM, PIETISM, early METHODISM, and the OXFORD MOVEMENT. Related to asceticism is the Protestant work ethic, which consists of a radical requirement of accomplishment symbolized in achievement in one's profession and, at the same time, demanding strict renunciation of the enjoyment of material gains acquired legitimately.

The adherents of early ISLAM knew only fasting, which was obligatory in the month of RAMAḌĀN. MONASTICISM is rejected in the QUR'AN. Nonetheless, ascetic forces among Christians in Syria and Mesopotamia were assimilated by Islam in the ascetic movement known as ZUHD (self-denial) and later in that of SUFISM, which incorporated ascetic ideals and methods.

ASCLEPIUS \a-'sklē-pē-əs\, *Greek* Asklepios, *Latin* Aesculapius \,es-kyù-'lā-pē-əs, ,ēs-\, Greco-Roman god of medicine, son of APOLLO and the NYMPH Coronis. CHIRON the CENTAUR taught him the art of healing. At length ZEUS, afraid that Asclepius might render all men immortal, slew him with a thunderbolt. Homer, in the *Iliad*, mentions him only as a skillful physician; in later times, however, he was honored as a hero and eventually worshiped as a god. Because it was supposed that Asclepius effected cures of the sick in dreams, the practice of sleeping in his temples became common.

Asclepius' usual attribute was a staff with a serpent coiled around it. A similar but unrelated emblem, the CADUCEUS, with its winged staff and intertwined serpents, is frequently used as a medical emblem but represents the staff of HERMES.

ASERET YEME TESHUVA \ä-'ser-et-ye-'mā-tə-shü-'vä\, *English* Ten Days of Penitence, the first 10 days of the Jewish religious year, *i.e.*, the 1st through the 10th of the month of Tishré.

ASGARD \'az-ˌgärd, 'as-\, *Old Norse* Ásgardr, in Norse MYTHOLOGY, the dwelling place of the gods. Legend divided Asgard into 12 or more realms, including VALHALLA, the home of ODIN and the abode of heroes slain in earthly battle; Thrudheim, the realm of THOR; and Breidablik, the home of BALDER. Each important god had his own palace in Asgard, and many Germanic peoples believed that these mansions were similar in design to those of their own nobility. Asgard could be reached from earth only by the bridge Bifrost (the rainbow). *See also* GERMANIC RELIGION.

ASHʿARĪ, ABŪ AL-ḤASAN AL- \al-'ä-shä-rē\ (b. 873/874, Basra, Iraq—d. *c.* 935/936, Baghdad), Arab Muslim theologian noted for having integrated the rationalist methodology of the speculative theologians into the framework of orthodox ISLAM. He founded a theological school that later claimed as members such celebrated authors as AL-GHAZĀLĪ and IBN KHALDŪN.

It is generally agreed that al-Ashʿarī belonged to the family of the celebrated COMPANION OF THE PROPHET Abū Mūsā al-Ashʿarī (d. 662/663), though some theologians opposed to his ideas contest the claim. Since this would have made him by birth a member of the Arab-Muslim aristocracy of the period, he must have received a careful education. Basra was at that time one of the centers of intellectual ferment in Iraq, which, in turn, was the center of the Muslim world.

His works, especially the first part of *Maqālāt al-Islāmīyīn* ("Teachings of the Islamists"), and the accounts of later historians record that al-Ashʿarī very early joined the school of the great theologians of that time, the Muʿtazilites. He became the favorite disciple of Abū ʿalī al-Jubbāʾī, head of the Muʿtazilites of Basra in the late 9th and early 10th centuries, and remained a Muʿtazilite until his 40th year. During that period of his life, he undertook the composition of a work in which he gathered the opinions of the diverse schools on the principal points of Muslim theology. This work, the first volume of the current edition of the *Maqālāt*, is valuable for what it records of Muʿtazilite doctrines. It remains one of the most important sources for retracing the history of the beginnings of Muslim theology.

At the age of 40, by which time he had become a specialist in theology and was well known for his oral controversies and his written works, al-Ashʿarī quit his master, al-Jubbāʾī, abandoned Muʿtazilite doctrine, and was converted to a more traditional, or orthodox, Islamic theology. It had become apparent to him that, in his former disputations, the reality of God as well as that of man had become so sterilized and desiccated that it had become little more than matter for rational manipulation.

Al-Ashʿarī proclaimed his new faith publicly and started combating his former colleagues. He even attacked his old master, al-Jubbāʾī, refuting his arguments in speech and writing. It was then, perhaps, that he took up again his first work, the *Maqālāt*, to add to the objective exposition rectifications more conformable to his new beliefs. In this same period, he composed the work that marks clearly his break with the Muʿtazilite school: the *Kitāb al-Lumaʿ* ("The Luminous Book").

It was not until his former master died in 915 that al-Ashʿarī decided to establish himself in Baghdad. He soon became aware of the importance assumed by a group of faithful of the SUNNA, the disciples of AḤMAD IBN ḤANBAL. Soon after, he composed, or perhaps put the last touches to, one of his most famous treatises, the *Ibānah ʿan uṣūl al-diyānah* ("Statement on the Principles of Religion"), which contains passages venerating the memory of Ibn Ḥanbal.

In the years that followed, al-Ashʿarī focused his theological reflection on certain positions of the mystic AL-MUḤĀSIBĪ and of two theologians, Ibn Kullāb and Qalanisī, laying the bases for a new school of theology. After he died, his disciples slowly disentangled the main lines of doctrine that eventually became the stamp of the Ashʿarite school.

ASHER \'a-shər\, one of the TWELVE TRIBES OF ISRAEL that in biblical times constituted the people of ISRAEL who later became the Jewish people. The tribe was named after the younger of two sons born to JACOB (also called Israel) and Zilpah, the maidservant of Jacob's first wife, LEAH (GENESIS 30:12). After the Israelites took possession of the Promised Land, JOSHUA assigned territory to each of the tribes (Joshua 13–19). The tribe of Asher apparently settled among the Phoenicians in the upper region of Palestine, beyond the tribe of ZEBULUN and west of the tribe of NAPHTALI.

Following the death of King SOLOMON (922 BCE), the Israelites separated into the northern Kingdom of Israel (representing 10 tribes) and the southern Kingdom of JUDAH (1 Kings 11:26ff.; 2 Chronicles 10). When the northern kingdom was conquered by the Assyrians in 721 BCE, the 10 tribes, including Asher, were partially dispersed (2 Kings 17:5–6; 18:9–12). In time they were assimilated by other peoples and thus disappeared as distinctive units. Jewish legends refer to them as the TEN LOST TRIBES OF ISRAEL.

ASHERAH \ə-'shē-rə\, ancient West Semitic goddess. Her full name was probably "She Who Walks in the Sea," but she was also called "Holiness," and, occasionally, Elath, "the Goddess." In Ugaritic tradition, Asherah's consort was EL, and by him she was the mother of 70 gods. As MOTHER GODDESS she was widely worshiped throughout Syria and Palestine, although she was frequently paired with BAAL, who often took the place of El in practical cult; as Baal's consort, Asherah was usually given the name BAALAT.

The word *asherah* in the OLD TESTAMENT was used in reference to the goddess and to a wooden cult object associated with her worship.

ASHI \ä-'shē\ (b. *c.* 352 CE—d. *c.* 427), preeminent Babylonian AMORA, or interpreter of the MISHNAH.

Ashi was head of the Jewish Academy at Sura, Babylonia, and was one of two chief editors who fixed the canon of the Babylonian TALMUD. Under Ashi's leadership the academy, which had been closed since 309, was revived, and the gigantic task of collating scattered notes, sayings, legislative opinions, and homiletic lore was conducted for more than 30 years. Ashi headed the Sura Academy for more than 50 years, and he also established the nearby city of Mata Mehasya as the focus of amoraic learning. One of his sons, Tabyomi, succeeded him at the Sura Academy. After an interruption of several decades, Ashi's work was completed by a staff of scholars from the academy.

ASHKENAZI \ˌäsh-kə-'nä-zē, ˌash-kə-'na-\ (from the Hebrew *Ashkenaz*, meaning "Germany"), *plural* Ashkenazim \-zim, -zēm\, any of the Jews who lived in the Rhineland valley and in neighboring France before their migration eastward to Poland, Lithuania, and Russia after the Crusades (11th–13th century). After the 17th-century persecutions in eastern Europe, large numbers of these Jews resettled in western Europe, where they assimilated with other Jewish communities. In time, all Jews who had adopted the "German rite" SYNAGOGUE ritual were referred to as Ashkenazim to distinguish them from Sephardic (Spanish rite) Jews. Ashkenazi differ from SEPHARDI in their pronunciation of Hebrew, in cultural traditions, in synagogue cantillation (chanting), in their widespread use of Yiddish (until the 20th century), and especially in synagogue liturgy.

Today Ashkenazim constitute more than 80 percent of all the Jews in the world, numbering more than 11,000,000 in the late 20th century. In Israel the numbers of Ashkenazim and Sephardim are roughly equal, and the chief rabbinate has both an Ashkenazic and a Sephardic chief RABBI on equal footing.

ASHRAM \\'äsh-rəm, -,räm\\, *also spelled* ashrama, *Sanskrit* āśrama ("ascetic's dwelling," "place or mode of life associated with religious exertion"), in HINDU-ISM, any of the four stages of life through which the "twice-born" Hindu ideally will pass. The stages are those of (1) the student (*brahmacārī*), who is devoted and obedient to the teacher; (2) the householder (*gṛhastha*), who works to sustain the family and to help support priests, while also fulfilling duties toward gods and ances-

Asherah, detail from an ivory box from Minat al-Baydạ̄' near Ras Shamra, Syria, c. 1300 BCE; in the Louvre, Paris
Giraudon—Art Resource

tors; (3) the HERMIT (*vanaprastha*), who withdraws from concern with material things and pursues ascetic and yogic practices; and (4) the homeless MENDICANT (SANNYĀSĪ), who renounces all possessions to wander and beg for food, concerned only with the eternal. In the classical system, the vigorous pursuit of MOKṢA (spiritual liberation) is reserved for those persons who are in the last two stages of life. In practice, however, many *sannyasī*s have never married, a fact which shows that even as an ideal the four-ashram system has been questioned.

It developed as a theological construct in the 1st millennium CE—an upper-caste, male ideal only rarely achieved in personal or social reality.

In a second meaning, the term *āśrama*, familiarly spelled ashram in English, denotes a place of refuge, especially one removed from urban life, where spiritual and/or yogic disciplines are pursued. Often these ashrams are associated with the presence of a central teaching figure, a GURU, who is the object of common adoration on the part of other ashram residents. The guru may or may not belong to a formally constituted order or spiritual community.

ASHUR \\'ä-,shur\\, in MESOPOTAMIAN RELIGION, city god of Ashur and national god of Assyria. In the beginning he was perhaps only a local deity of the city that shared his name. From about 1800 BCE, however, he was identified with the Sumerian ENLIL (Akkadian: BEL), while under the Assyrian king Sargon II (reigned 721–705 BCE), he was brought into association with Anshar, the father of An (Akkadian: ANU) in the CREATION MYTH. Under Sargon's successor Sennacherib, attempts were made to transfer to Ashur the primeval

achievements of MARDUK, as well as the whole ritual of the NEW YEAR FESTIVAL of Babylon, no doubt as part of the political struggle between Babylonia and Assyria. The Assyrians believed that he granted rule over Assyria and supported Assyrian arms against enemies; detailed written reports from the Assyrian kings about their campaigns were even submitted to him. He appears a mere personification of the interests of Assyria as a political entity, with little character of his own.

'ĀSHŪRĀ' \\ə-'shur-ə\\, Muslim holy day observed on the 10th of Muḥarram, the first month of the Islamic year (Gregorian date variable). 'Āshūrā' was originally designated in 622 by MUHAMMAD, soon after the HIJRA, as a day of fasting from sunset to sunset, probably patterned after the Jewish Day of Atonement, YOM KIPPUR. When relations between Jews and Muslims became strained, however, Muhammad made RAMADĀN the Muslim month of fasting, leaving the 'Āshūrā' fast a voluntary observance, as it has remained among the Sunnites (*see* SUNNI).

Among the SHI'ITES, 'Āshūrā' is a major festival, the tazia (*ta'ziyah*), commemorating the martyrdom of ḤUSAYN, son of 'ALĪ and grandson of Muhammad, on the 10th of Muḥarram, AH 61 (Oct. 10, 680), in KARBALĀ' (present-day Iraq). It is a period of expressions of grief and of PILGRIMAGE to Karbalā'; passion plays are also presented, commemorating the death of Ḥusayn, in Iran. Shi'ites in the Middle East, South Asia, and even the Americas observe this holiday with processions and assemblies, inspired by the slogan, "Every day is 'Āshūrā', every place is Karbalā'." Such observances played a pivotal role in toppling the regime of Muhammad-Reẓā Shāh during the Iranian Revolution (1978–79).

ASH WEDNESDAY, in the Western Christian church, the first day of LENT, occurring 6½ weeks before EASTER—between February 4 and March 11, depending on the date of Easter. In the early church, the length of the Lenten celebration varied. In the 7th century, 4 days were added before the first Sunday in Lent in order to establish 40 fasting days, in imitation of JESUS' fast in the desert.

In Rome penitents began their period of public penance on the first day of Lent. They were sprinkled with ashes, dressed in sackcloth, and obliged to remain apart until they were reconciled with the Christian community on MAUNDY THURSDAY, the Thursday before Easter. When these practices fell into disuse (8th–10th century), they were symbolized by placing ashes on the heads of the entire congregation. This practice continues in ROMAN CATHOLICISM, using ashes obtained by burning the palms used on the previous PALM SUNDAY. Worship services are also held on Ash Wednesday in the churches of the ANGLICAN COMMUNION, in LUTHERAN-

ISM, and in some other Protestant churches. In EASTERN OR-
THODOXY, churches begin Lent on a Monday and therefore
do not observe Ash Wednesday.

ASIA MINOR, RELIGIONS OF: *see* ANATOLIAN RELIGIONS.

ASKR AND EMBLA \'äs-kər . . . 'em-blä\, in Norse mythology, the first man and first woman, respectively, parents of
the human race. They were created from tree trunks found
on the seashore by three gods—ODIN, Hoenir, and Lodur.
Odin gave them breath, or life, Hoenir gave them understanding, and Lodur gave them their senses and outward
appearance. Whereas Odin is a well-known god, almost
nothing is known of his companions.

ASMODEUS \,az-mə-'dē-əs, ,as-\, *Hebrew* Ashmedai \,äsh-
mə-'dī\, in Jewish mythology, the king of DEMONS. According to the apocryphal book of Tobit, Asmodeus, smitten for
Sarah, the daughter of Raguel, killed her seven successive
husbands on their wedding nights. Following instructions
given to him by the ANGEL Raphael, Tobias overcame Asmodeus and married Sarah.

The TALMUD (Pesahim 110a; Gittin 68a–b) relates that SO-
LOMON captured the demon and pressed him into slave la-
bor during the construction of the First TEMPLE OF JERUSALEM.
Other haggadic (*see* HALAKAH AND HAGGADAH) legends (*e.g.*,
Numbers Rabbah 11:3) depict Asmodeus as a more benefi-
cent figure.

AŚOKA \ə-'shō-kə, -'sō-\, *also spelled* Ashoka (d. 238? BCE,
India), last major emperor in the Mauryan dynasty of India.
His vigorous patronage of BUDDHISM during his reign (c. 265–
238 BCE) furthered the expansion of that religion throughout India. Following his successful but bloody conquest of
the Kaliṅga country on the east coast, Aśoka renounced
armed conquest and adopted a policy that he called "conquest by DHARMA (principles of right life)."

In order to gain wide publicity for his teachings and his
work, Aśoka made them known by means of oral announcements and also engraved them on rocks and pillars
at suitable sites. These inscriptions—the ROCK EDICTS and
Pillar Edicts (*e.g.*, the lion capital of the pillar found at Sarnath, which has become India's national emblem)—provide
information on his life and acts. Aśoka visited Buddhist
holy sites, commended particular Buddhist teachings, and
sought to ensure proper order in the Buddhist monastic
community. He sent "dharma ministers" and Buddhist emissaries to various areas within his realm and beyond.

In the centuries following Aśoka's death, the Buddhist
community generated many legends about him that played
an important role in their understanding and evaluation of
political authority. His support for Buddhism was vividly
dramatized, for example, in the legendary accounts that describe his construction of 84,000 STUPAS (funerary monuments) throughout his realm and the festival of the great
gift, at which he gave all of his wealth to the Buddhist
SANGHA. In some contexts, particularly in the THERAVĀDA
tradition of Sri Lanka and mainland Southeast Asia, Aśoka
has been depicted as an ideal king who could serve as a positive model for Buddhist rulers. In other Buddhist contexts
he became a figure whose role as an ideal was modified by a
recognition of the ambiguities inherent in the exercise of
secular power. But throughout Buddhist history all across
Asia he has been remembered as an embodiment of Buddhist secular virtues and an example of a ruler who supported and guided the Buddhist community.

ĀSRAVA \'äs-rə-və, 'äsh-\, in Buddhist philosophy, the illusion stemming from the mind and the senses. *See* KILESA.

ASSEMBLIES OF GOD, Pentecostal denomination of the
Protestant church, considered the largest such denomination in the United States. It was formed by a union of several small Pentecostal groups at Hot Springs, Ark., in 1914.
The council of some 120 clergy who effected this union
adopted a polity blending Congregational (*see* CONGREGA-
TIONALISM) and PRESBYTERIAN elements. The council elected
an Executive Presbytery to serve as the central administrative group.

Except for pronouncing that "the Holy inspired SCRIP-
TURES are the all-sufficient rule for faith and practice . . . and
we shall not add to or take from them," that first General
Council postponed action on the matter of a definitive doctrinal statement. Subsequently, however, a *Statement of
Fundamental Truths* was adopted. The document demonstrated that the Assemblies of God are Trinitarian (believing in God as Father, Son, and HOLY SPIRIT) and Arminian
(accepting the doctrines of both GRACE and FREE WILL; *see*
ARMINIANISM).

They also subscribed to two ordinances (BAPTISM by total
immersion in water and the Lord's Supper), held a view of
sanctification (becoming holy) that may be described as
"progressive," or gradual, rather than "instantaneous" in
regard to moral purity, and, finally, were strongly premillennial (believing in the doctrine of Christ's Second Advent
before the 1,000-year reign of Christ and his saints).

In addition to extensive foreign missions, the denomination conducts home missions among foreign-language
groups in America's urban centers, on Native American
reservations, in prisons, and among the deaf and the blind.
They also operate the Gospel Publishing House at the
church headquarters in Springfield, Mo., two colleges of
arts and science—Southern California College (Costa Me-
sa) and Evangel College (Springfield, Mo.)—and regional Bible institutes.

ASSUMPTION (Late Latin: *assumptio*, "act of taking up"),
in the theology of ROMAN CATHOLICISM and EASTERN ORTHO-
DOXY, doctrine that MARY, the mother of JESUS CHRIST, was
taken (assumed) into heaven, body and soul, following the
end of her life on earth. There is no explicit mention of the
Assumption in the NEW TESTAMENT.

The development of this doctrine is closely related to a
feast that passed from a general celebration in Mary's honor
to one celebrated on August 15 commemorating her dormition, or falling asleep. The feast, which originated in the
Byzantine Empire, was brought to the West, where the
term Assumption replaced Dormition to reflect increased
emphasis on the glorification of Mary's body as well as her
soul. Although the Dormition had been a frequent iconographic theme in the East, there was an initial unwillingness to accept apocryphal accounts of the Assumption. By
the end of the Middle Ages, however, there was a general
acceptance in both the East and the West.

The doctrine was declared dogma for Roman Catholics
by Pope PIUS XII in the *Munificentissimus Deus* on Nov. 1,
1950. The Assumption is not considered a revealed doctrine among the Eastern Orthodox and is considered an obstacle to ecumenical dialogue by many Protestants.

The Assumption as a theme in Christian art originated in
western Europe during the late Middle Ages, and since the
13th century the Assumption has been widely represented
in church decoration. Characteristic representations of the

Assumption show the Virgin, in an attitude of prayer and supported by ANGELS, ascending above her open tomb, around which the Apostles stand in amazement. Through the 15th century she was shown surrounded by an almond-shaped aureole; in the 16th century this was replaced by a cluster of clouds.

AṢṬACHĀP \ˌəsh-tä-'chäp\ (Hindi: "Eight Seals"), group of 16th-century Hindi poets, four of whom are claimed to have been disciples of VALLABHA, and four of his son and successor, Viṭṭhalnāth. The greatest of the group was SŪRDĀS, who is remembered as a blind singer and whose descriptions of the exploits of the child-god KRISHNA are particularly well known. Other members of the Aṣṭachāp group were Paramānanddās, Nanddās, Kṛṣṇadās, Govindsvāmī, Kumbhandās, Chītasvāmī, and Caturbhujdās. Unlike Sūrdās, whose association with the Vallabhite community may well have been invented by Vallabhites after the fact, many of the other Aṣṭachāp poets do betray a clear sectarian affiliation. Poems written by the Aṣṭachāp form the core group of hymns sung to Krishna in Vallabhite temples.

ASTARTE \ə-'stär-tē\, *also spelled* Ashtart \'ash-ˌtärt\, great goddess of the ancient Near East, chief deity of Tyre, Sidon, and Elath. She was worshiped as Astarte in Egypt and UGARIT and among the Hittites, as well as in CANAAN. Her Akkadian counterpart was ISHTAR. Later she became assimilated with the Egyptian deities ISIS and HATHOR, and in the Greco-Roman world with APHRODITE, ARTEMIS, and JUNO. Astarte, goddess of love and war, shared so many qualities with her sister, ANATH, that they may originally have been seen as a single deity. Hebrew scholars now feel that the goddess Ashtoreth mentioned so often in the BIBLE is a deliberate compilation of the Greek name Astarte and the Hebrew word *boshet*, "shame," indicating contempt for her cult. Ashtaroth, the plural form of the goddess's name in Hebrew, became a term denoting goddesses and paganism.

SOLOMON, married to foreign wives, "went after Ashtoreth the goddess of the Sidonians" (1 Kings 11:5). Later the cult places dedicated to Ashtoreth were destroyed by JOSIAH. Astarte/Ashtoreth is the Queen of Heaven to whom the Canaanites had burned incense and poured LIBATIONS (Jeremiah 44).

ĀSTIKA \'äs-ti-kə\, in Indian philosophy, any orthodox school of thought, defined as one that accepts the authority of the VEDAS. The six orthodox philosophic systems are those of Sāṃkhya and YOGA, NYĀYA and Vaiśeṣika, and Mīmāṃsā and VEDĀNTA.

The term *āstika* comes from the Sanskrit *asti*, which means "there is." Contrasted to the *āstika* systems are the *nāstika* (Sanskrit: from *na asti*, "there is not"), the individuals and schools that do not accept the reality (that is, the "there is-ness") of an underlying ground of being such as the BRAHMAN concept in HINDUISM. Included among the *nāstika* schools are the Buddhists, Jains, the ascetic Ājīvikas, and the materialistic Cārvākas.

ASTROLOGY, type of DIVINATION that consists in interpreting the influence of planets and stars on earthly affairs in order to predict or affect the destinies of individuals, groups, or nations.

Astrology originated in Mesopotamia, perhaps in the 3rd millennium BCE, but attained its full development in the Western world much later, within the orbit of Greek civilization of the Hellenistic period. It spread to India in its old-

The Twelve Signs of the Zodiac and the Sun, Ermengol de Beziers, Breviare d'Amour, Provencal codex (13th century); in the Biblioteca Real, El Escorial, Madrid, Spain
Giraudon—Art Resource

er Mesopotamian form. Islamic culture absorbed it as part of the Greek heritage, and passed it on to European culture in the Middle Ages, when western Europe was strongly affected by Islamic science.

The Egyptians also contributed, though less directly, to the rise of astrology. In order that the starry sky might serve them as a clock, the Egyptians selected a succession of 36 bright stars whose risings were separated from each other by intervals of 10 days. Each of these stars, called *decans* by Latin writers, was conceived of as a spirit with power over the period of time for which it served; they later entered the zodiac as subdivisions of its 12 signs.

Once established in the classical world, the astrological conception of causation invaded all the sciences, particularly medicine and its allied disciplines. The Stoics, espousing the doctrine of a universal "sympathy" linking the human microcosm with the macrocosm of nature, found in astrology a virtual map of such a universe.

Throughout classical antiquity the words astronomy and astrology were synonymous. In the first Christian centuries the modern distinction between astronomy, the science of stars, and astrology, the art of divination by the stars, began to appear. As against the omnipotence of the stars, CHRISTIANITY taught the omnipotence of their Creator. To the determinism of astrology Christianity opposed the freedom of the will. But within these limits the astrological worldview was accepted. To reject it would have been to reject the whole heritage of classical culture, which had assumed an astrological complexion. Even at the center of Christian history, Persian MAGI were reported to have followed a celestial OMEN to the scene of the Nativity.

Although various Christian councils condemned astrology, the belief in the worldview it implies was not seriously shaken. In the late Middle Ages, a number of universities, among them Paris, Padua, Bologna, and Florence, had chairs of astrology. The revival of ancient studies by the humanists only encouraged this interest, which persisted into the Renaissance and even into the REFORMATION.

In pre-Imperial China, the belief in an intelligible cosmic order had found expression in charts that juxtaposed natural phenomena with human activities and fate. When Western astronomy and astrology became known in China through Arabic influences in Mongol times, their data were integrated into the Chinese astrological corpus. In the later centuries of Imperial China it was standard practice to have a HOROSCOPE cast for each newborn child and at all decisive junctures in life.

In the West, it was the Copernican revolution of the 16th century that dealt the geocentric worldview of astrology its shattering blow. As a popular pastime, however, astrology has continued into modern times.

ASTRUC OF LUNEL \ås-'trūk . . . lū-'nel\, *original name* Abba Mari ben Moses ben Joseph, *also called* Don Astruc, *or* ha-Yareaḥ ("The Moon") (b. 1250?, Lunel, near Montpellier, France—d. after 1306), anti-rationalist Jewish zealot who incited Rabbi SOLOMON BEN ABRAHAM ADRET of Barcelona, the most powerful rabbi of his time, to restrict the study of science and philosophy, thereby nearly creating a schism in the Jewish community of Europe.

Although Astruc revered MAIMONIDES, who had attempted to reconcile Aristotle's philosophy with JUDAISM, he deplored what he considered the excesses of Maimonides' followers, who, he believed, undermined the Jewish faith by interpreting the BIBLE via ALLEGORY. In a series of letters, Astruc persuaded Rabbi Adret to issue a ban in 1305 forbidding, on pain of EXCOMMUNICATION, the study or teaching of science and philosophy by those under the age of 25. This ban provoked a counterban by other Jewish leaders against those who followed Adret's proscription. A threatened schism among the Jewish communities of France and Spain was averted only in 1306, when Philip IV expelled the Jews from France. Astruc then settled in Perpignan, the mainland capital of the kingdom of Majorca, and vanished from view. But he published his correspondence with Rabbi Adret, which primarily covered the restrictions on studies. *Minḥat qenaot* ("Meal Offering of Jealousy"), as the collected correspondence is entitled, reveals much of the religious and philosophical conflicts of Judaism in that era. The epithet ha-Yareaḥ is derived from his polemical work *Sefer ha-yareaḥ* ("The Book of the Moon"), the title of which refers to the town of Lunel (French *lune*, meaning "moon").

ASTYANAX \ə-'stī-ə-ˌnaks\, in Greek myth, son of HECTOR and ANDROMACHE; he was also known as Scamandrius, after the River Scamander. After the fall of Troy he was hurled from the battlements of the city by NEOPTOLEMUS. According to medieval legend, however, he survived the war and founded the line that led to Charlemagne.

ASURA \'ə-sù-rə\, *Avestan* ahura (Sanskrit: "lord"), in Hindu mythology, class of beings defined by their opposition to the DEVAS, or *sura*s (gods). In its oldest Vedic usage,

asura refers to a human or divine leader. Increasingly its plural form predominated, designating a class of beings opposed either to the Vedic gods or to those who opposed them. Later these *asura*s came to be understood as DEMONS. This pattern was reversed in Iran, where *ahura* came to mean the supreme god and the *daeva*s became demons. In Hindu mythology, when the *asura*s and the *deva*s together were CHURNING THE MILK-OCEAN in order to extract from it the *amṛta* (elixir of immortality), strife arose over the possession of the *amṛta*. This conflict is never ending.

AŚVAGHOṢA \ˌäsh-və-'gō-shə, -sə\, *also spelled* Ashvaghosa (b. 80? CE, Ayodhyā, India—d. 150?, Peshāwar), philosopher and poet who is considered India's greatest poet, before Kālidāsa, and the father of Sanskrit drama.

Aśvaghoṣa was born a BRAHMIN. It is known that he was an outspoken opponent of BUDDHISM until, after a heated debate with a noted Buddhist scholar on the relative merits of the Hindu religion and Buddhism, he accepted Buddhism and became a disciple of his erstwhile opponent.

A brilliant orator, Aśvaghoṣa is said to have spoken at length on MAHĀYĀNA Buddhist doctrine at the fourth Buddhist council, which he reportedly helped organize. His fame lay largely in his ability to explain the intricate concepts of Mahāyāna Buddhism. Among the works attributed to him are the BUDDHACARITA ("The Life of Buddha") in verse, the *Mahālaṅkara* ("Book of Glory"), and—though his authorship of this text is far less likely—the *Mahāyāna-śraddhotpāda-śāstra* ("The Awakening of Faith in the Mahāyāna").

AŚVAMEDHA \ˌäsh-və-'mā-də, ˌäsh-wə-\, *also spelled* ashvamedha, or ashwamedha (Sanskrit: "horse sacrifice"), grandest of the Vedic religious rites of ancient India, performed by a king to celebrate his preeminence. The ceremony is described in detail in various Vedic writings, particularly the *Śatapatha Brāhmaṇa*. A hand-picked stallion was allowed to roam freely for a year under the protection of a royal guard. If the horse entered a foreign country, its ruler had either to fight or to submit. If the horse was not captured during the year, it was brought back to the capital accompanied by the rulers of the lands it entered, and then sacrificed at a great public ceremony. The wandering horse was said to symbolize the sun in its journey over the world and, consequently, the power of the king over the whole earth. On successfully carrying out a horse sacrifice, the king could assume the title of *cakravartin* ("universal monarch"). The rite ensured the prosperity and fertility of the entire kingdom.

In historical times the practice was condemned by the Buddha and seems to have suffered a decline, but it was revived by Puṣyamitra Śuṅga (reigned 187–151 BCE). Samudra Gupta (c. 330–c. 380 CE) issued coins in commemoration of his successful completion of an *aśvamedha*. It may have continued as late as the 11th century, when it is said to have taken place in the Cōḷa Empire.

ATALANTA \ˌa-tə-'lan-tə\, in Greek mythology, a renowned and swift-footed huntress, probably a parallel and less important form of the goddess ARTEMIS. Traditionally, she was the daughter of Schoeneus of Boeotia or of Iasus and Clymene of Arcadia. She was left to die at birth but was suckled by a she-bear; later she took part in the Calydonian boar hunt and, more famously, offered to marry anyone who could outrun her—but those whom she overtook she speared.

In one race Hippomenes (or Milanion) was given three of the golden apples of the HESPERIDES by APHRODITE; when he dropped them, Atalanta stopped to pick them up and so lost the race. Their son was Parthenopaeus, who later fought as one of the SEVEN AGAINST THEBES after the death of King OEDIPUS. Atalanta and her husband, proving ungrateful to Aphrodite, copulated in a shrine of the goddess Cybele (or of ZEUS), for which they were turned into lions.

ATARGATIS \ə-'tär-gə-tis\, great goddess of northern Syria; her chief SANCTUARY was at Hierapolis (modern Manbij), northeast of Aleppo, where she was worshiped with her consort, HADAD. Her ancient temple there was rebuilt about 300 BCE by Queen Stratonice, and her cult spread to various parts of the Greek world, where the goddess was generally regarded as a form of APHRODITE.

In nature she resembled her Phoenician counterpart, ASTARTE; she also showed some kinship with the Anatolian Cybele. Primarily she was a goddess of fertility, but as the *baalat* ("mistress") of her city and people, she was also responsible for their protection and well-being. Hence she was commonly portrayed wearing the mural crown and holding a sheaf of grain, while the lions who supported her throne suggest her strength and power over nature.

ATE \'ā-tē, 'ä-\, Greek semidivine figure who induced ruinous actions. She made ZEUS take a hasty OATH that resulted in the hero HERACLES becoming subject to Eurystheus, ruler of Mycenae. Zeus then cast Ate out of Olympus; she remained on earth, working evil and mischief. She was followed by the Litai ("Prayers"—personifications of the supplications offered up to the gods), the old and crippled daughters of Zeus, who repaired the harm done by her.

ATHALIAH \ˌa-thə-'lī-ə\, *also spelled* Athalia, in the OLD TESTAMENT, the daughter of AHAB and JEZEBEL and wife of Jeham, king of JUDAH. After the death of Ahaziah, her son, Athaliah usurped the throne and reigned for seven years. She massacred all the members of the royal house of Judah (2 Kings 11:1–3), except Joash. A successful revolution was organized in favor of Joash, and she was killed.

ATHAMAS \'a-thə-məs\, in Greek mythology, king of the prehistoric Minyans in the ancient Boeotian city of Orchomenus. His first wife was the goddess Nephele. But later Athamas became enamored of Ino, the daughter of CADMUS, and neglected Nephele, who disappeared in anger. Athamas and Ino incurred the wrath of the goddess HERA because Ino had nursed DIONYSUS. Athamas went mad and slew one of his sons, Learchus; Ino, to escape, threw herself into the sea with her other son, Melicertes. Both were afterward worshiped as marine divinities—Ino as LEUCOTHEA, Melicertes as Palaemon. Athamas fled from Boeotia and finally settled at Phthiotis in Thessaly.

Atalanta, Greek marble statue; in the Louvre, Paris
Giraudon—Art Resource

ATHANASIAN CREED \ˌa-thə-'nā-zhən, -shən\, *also called* Quicumque Vult \kwī-'kəm-kwē-'vəlt\ (from the opening words in Latin), a Christian profession of faith in about 40 verses. It is regarded as authoritative in ROMAN CATHOLICISM and in some Protestant churches. It has two sections, one dealing with the TRINITY and the other with the INCARNATION, and it begins and ends with warnings that unswerving adherence to such truths is indispensable to salvation. The virulence of these damnatory clauses has led some critics, especially in the Anglican churches, to secure restriction or abandonment of the use of the creed.

A Latin document composed in the Western church, the creed was unknown to the Eastern church until the 12th century. Since the 17th century, scholars have generally agreed that it was not written by ATHANASIUS (died 373) but was probably composed in southern France during the 5th century. In 1940 the lost *Excerpta* of Vincent of Lérins (flourished 440) was discovered to contain much of the language of the creed. Thus, either Vincent or an admirer of his has been considered the possible author. The earliest known copy of the creed was included as a prefix to a collection of homilies by Caesarius of Arles (died 542).

ATHANASIUS, SAINT \ˌa-thə-'nā-zhəs, -shəs\ (b. *c.* 293 CE, Alexandria—d. May 2, 373, Alexandria; feast day May 2], theologian, ecclesiastical statesman, and Egyptian national leader; he was the chief defender of Christian orthodoxy in the 4th-century battle against ARIANISM, which promulgated that the Son of God was a creature of like, but not of the same, substance as God the Father.

ATHARVA VEDA \ə-ˌtär-və-'vā-də\, collection of hymns and incantations that forms the fourth and final collection (Saṃhitā) of Vedic utterances.

ATHEISM, the critique and denial of belief in God. As such, it is the opposite of THEISM, which affirms the reality of God and seeks to demonstrate His existence. Atheism is to be distinguished from AGNOSTICISM, which leaves open the question whether there is a God or not; for the atheist, the nonexistence of God is a certainty.

Atheism has emerged recurrently in Western thought. Plato argued against it in the *Laws*, while Democritus and Epicurus argued for it in the context of their materialism. Niccolò Machiavelli in the 16th century contributed to atheism in the political sphere by affirming the independence of politics from morals and religion. The 18th century witnessed the emergence of atheism among the French Encyclopedists, who combined British EMPIRICISM with René

Descartes's mechanistic conception of the universe. David Hume, in his *Dialogues Concerning Natural Religion* (1779), argued against the traditional proofs for the existence of God, as did Immanuel Kant. Neither Hume nor Kant were atheists, but their restriction of human reason to sense experience undercut NATURAL THEOLOGY and left the existence of God a matter of pure faith. In the 19th century, atheism was couched in the materialism of Karl Marx and others and pitted against the metaphysical position of SPIRITU-ALISM. Modern atheism takes many different forms other than that of materialism. In short, atheism has been rooted in a vast array of philosophical systems.

One of the most important 19th-century atheists was LUD-WIG FEUERBACH (1804–72), who put forward the argument that God is a projection of man's ideals. Feuerbach associated his denial of God with the affirmation of man's freedom: the disclosure that God is mere projection liberates man for self-realization. Marx drew on Feuerbach's thesis that the religious can be resolved into the human, though he also held that religion reflects socio-economic order and alienates man from his labor product and, hence, from his true self. Charles Darwin (1809–82) developed a scientific theory of natural history that challenged the Judeo-Christian concept of God. Later, SIGMUND FREUD (1856–1939) drew on Darwinian themes when he discussed the historical development of the religious mindset. According to Freud, belief in God represents a childlike psychological state in which the image of a father-figure is projected upon the forces of nature.

A third strain in modern atheism is the existentialist. Friedrich Nietzsche (1844–1900) proclaimed the "death of God" and the consequent loss of all traditional values. The only tenable human response, he argued, is that of nihilism—without God, there is no answer to the question of purpose and meaning in life. In Nietzsche's view, the death of God freed humanity to fulfill itself and find its own essence. In the 20th century Jean-Paul Sartre, Albert Camus, and others continued the theme. Human freedom, according to Sartre, entails the denial of God, for God's existence would threaten our freedom to create our own values through free ethical choice.

ATHENA \ə-'thē-nə\, *also spelled* Athene \ə-'thē-nē\, in ancient GREEK RELIGION, protectress of Athens, goddess of war,

handicraft, and practical reason. She was probably a pre-Hellenic goddess taken over by the Greeks.

In the myths Athena was the daughter of ZEUS and Metis, whom Zeus had swallowed while she was pregnant so that Athena would be born from the father only. Athena sprang in full battle armor from Zeus' forehead, in some versions after HEPHAESTUS had split open Zeus' head with an ax. She was thought to have had neither husband nor offspring. She may not have been described as a virgin originally, but virginity was attributed to her very early and was the basis for the interpretation of her epithets Pallas and Parthenos.

Athena was the goddess of crafts and skilled pursuits in general, especially known as the patroness of spinning and weaving. That she ultimately became allegorized to personify wisdom and righteousness was a natural development of her patronage of skill. In Homer's *Iliad*, Athena was presented in particular as the goddess of martial skill, and in numerous scenes she inspired and fought alongside the Greek heroes. Athena's moral and military superiority to the other warlike divinity of Greece, ARES, derived in part from the fact that she represented the intellectual and civilized side of war and the virtues of justice and skill, whereas Ares largely represented mere blood lust. In the *Iliad*, Athena was the divine form of the heroic, martial ideal: she personified excellence in close combat, victory, and glory, and wore upon her shield the AEGIS of Zeus which inspired irresistible fear in her opponents. Athena appears in the *Odyssey* as the tutelary deity of ODYSSEUS, and myths from later sources portray her similarly as helper of PERSEUS and HERACLES (Hercules). As the guardian of the welfare of kings, Athena equally represented the qualities of good counsel, prudent restraint, and practical insight.

Roman marble copy (c. 130 CE) of the statue of Athena Parthenos by Phidias (438 BCE); in the National Archaeological Museum, Athens
Alinari—Art Resource

In post-Mycenaean times the city, especially its citadel, replaced the palace as Athena's domain. She was widely worshiped but had special importance at Athens, to which she gave her name. Her emergence there as city goddess, Athena Polias ("Athena of the City"), accompanied the ancient city-state's transition from monarchy to democracy. She was associated with birds, particularly the owl, and with the snake. Her birth and her contest with POSEIDON, the sea god, for the suzerainty of the city were depicted on the pediments of the PARTHENON. Athena's birthday festival, the

PANATHENAEA, concerned the growth of vegetation. The similarly purposed Procharisteria celebrated the goddess's rising from the ground with the coming of spring.

Two Athenians, the sculptor Phidias and the playwright Aeschylus, contributed significantly to the cultural dissemination of Athena's image. She inspired three of Phidias' sculptural masterpieces, including the colossal gold and ivory statue of Athena Parthenos which was housed in the Parthenon until the 5th century CE. Copies of this statue are still extant.

ATĪŚA \ə-'tē-shə\, *also called* Dīpaṅkara \dē-'pəŋ-kə-rə\ (b. 982—d. 1054, Nyethang, Tibet [now Nyetang, China]), Indian Buddhist reformer whose teachings formed the basis of the Tibetan Bka'-gdams-pa ("Those Bound by Command") sect, founded by his disciple 'Brom-ston.

Atīśa left India for Tibet around 1040. He established monasteries there and wrote treatises emphasizing the three schools of BUDDHISM: the THERAVĀDA, the MAHĀYĀNA, and the VAJRAYĀNA. He taught that the three schools follow in this succession and must be practiced in this order.

ATLANTIS \ət-'lan-tis\, *also spelled* Atalantis \,a-tə-'lan-tis\, *or* Atlantica \ət-'lan-ti-kə\, legendary island of unknown location. The principal sources for the legend are two of Plato's dialogues, *Timaeus* and *Critias*. Plato described Atlantis as an island larger than Asia Minor and Libya combined, situated just beyond the Pillars of HERACLES (the Straits of Gibraltar). It was the home of an advanced civilization, but the island was eventually swallowed up by the sea as a result of earthquakes. Atlantis is probably merely a legend, invented by Plato to make a point, but the idea has seized the imagination of innumerable authors since then, who have variously located it in the Black Sea or the waters off of South America.

ATLAS \'at-ləs\, in Greek mythology, son of the TITAN Iapetus and the NYMPH Clymene (or Asia) and brother of PROMETHEUS (creator of mankind). Atlas was said to support the weight of the heavens on his shoulders. Later the name of Atlas was transferred to a range of mountains in northwestern Africa, and Atlas was subsequently represented as the king of that district, turned into a rocky mountain by the hero PERSEUS, who showed him the GORGON's head. According to the Greek poet Hesiod, Atlas was one of the Titans who took part in their war against ZEUS, for which he was condemned to his heavenly burden.

ĀTMAN \'ät-mən\ (Sanskrit: "breath, self"), one of the basic concepts in Hindu philosophy, describing that eternal core of the personality that survives death and transmigrates to a new life or is released from the bonds of existence. Although in the early Vedic texts it occurred mostly as a reflexive pronoun (oneself), in the later UPANISHADS it develops into a philosophic topic: *ātman* is that which makes the other organs and faculties function and for which they function; *ātman* underlies all the activities of a person, as BRAHMAN (the absolute) underlies the workings of the universe. So fundamental is the sense of unchanging identity signified by *ātman* that it is familiarly identified with Brahman itself, especially by adherents of ADVAITA VEDĀNTA.

ĀTMĀRĀMJĪ \,ät-mä-'räm-jē\ (b. 1837, Lahera, Punjab—d. 1896, Gujranwala, Punjab), important Jain reformer and revivalist monk. He was born a Hindu but as a child came under the influence of Sthānakavāsī Jain monks and was initiated as a Sthānakavāsī monk in 1854. He was renowned for his prodigious memory and intellectual skills. He pursued an independent study of Jain texts, in particular the Sanskrit commentaries on the Jain canon, commentaries which at that time Sthānakavāsī monks were discouraged from studying. As a result of his studies he became convinced that the Mūrtipūjak position on the worship of images of the Jinas (also called TĪRTHAṄKARAS, considered in JAINISM to be godlike saviors who have succeeded in crossing over life's stream of rebirths and have made a path for others to follow) was correct, and the iconoclastic position taken by the Sthānakavāsī was wrong. In 1876, along with 18 monk followers, he was reinitiated as a Mūrtipūjak monk in the Tapā Gacch in Ahmedabad, the major city of Gujarat, and given the new name Muni Ānandavijay. He was made *ācārya* (monastic leader) in a public ceremony in 1887 in Palitana—a center of Mūrtipūjak PILGRIMAGE in Gujarat—and he was given the name Ācārya Vijayānandasūri. Ātmārāmjī came into contact with European scholars of Jainism, and as a result he was invited to the 1893 World's Parliament of Religions in Chicago—an invitation he declined, as any mode of travel besides walking barefooted would have violated monastic rules.

Ātmārāmjī was a prolific author and tireless reformer. He defended the Mūrtipūjak position on image-worship against the Sthānakavāsīs; defended the position of fullfledged *saṃvegī* monks against the house-holding monks known as *yatis* who owned monasteries, traveled in vehicles, handled money, and followed many other practices perceived as lax by orthoprax Jains; and he argued in favor of the Tapā Gacch against other Mūrtipūjak *gacch*s (lineages) on a variety of details of monastic practices. The movement he helped spearhead led to a predominance of the Mūrtipūjak Tapā Gacch among Gujarati Jains. Monks in his direct disciplic lineage now number well over 500.

ATON \'ä-tən, 'a-\, *also spelled* Aten, *also called* Yati, in ancient EGYPTIAN RELIGION, a sun god, depicted as the solar disk emitting rays terminating in human hands, whose worship briefly was the state religion. The pharaoh Akhenaton (reigned 1353–36 BCE) introduced the radical innovation that Aton was the only god. In opposition to the Amon-Re PRIESTHOOD of Thebes, Akhenaton built the city Akhetaton (now Tell el-Amarna) as the center for Aton's worship.

The most important surviving document of the new religion is the Aton Hymn, which focuses on the world of nature and the god's beneficent provision for it. The hymn opens with the rising of the sun: "Men had slept like the dead; now they lift their arms in praise, birds fly, fish leap, plants bloom, and work begins. Aton creates the son in the mother's womb, the seed in men, and has generated all life. He has distinguished the races, their natures, tongues, and skins, and fulfills the needs of all. Aton made the Nile in Egypt and rain, like a heavenly Nile, in foreign countries. He has a million forms according to the time of day and from where he is seen; yet he is always the same." The only person who knows and comprehends the god fully is said to be Akhenaton, together with his wife, Nefertiti. The hymn to the Aton has been compared in imagery to Psalm 104 ("Bless the Lord, O my soul").

The religion of the Aton is not completely understood. Akhenaton and Nefertiti worshiped only this sun god. For them he was "the sole god." Akhenaton had dropped his older name Amenhotep, and the name "Amon" was also hacked out of the inscriptions throughout Egypt. The funerary religion dropped Osiris, and Akhenaton became the source of blessings for the people after death. The figure of Nefertiti replaced the figures of protecting goddesses at the corners of a stone sarcophagus. But the new religion was rejected by the Egyptian elite after Akhenaton's death, and the populace had probably never adopted it in the first place. After Akhenaton's death, the old gods were reestablished and the new city abandoned.

ATONEMENT, process by which a person removes obstacles to his reconciliation with God. It is a recurring theme in religion and theology. Rituals of expiation and satisfaction appear in most religions as the means by which the religious person reestablishes or strengthens his or her relation to the holy or divine. Atonement is often attached to sacrifice, and both often connect ritual cleanness with moral purity and religious acceptability.

The term *atonement* developed in the English language in the 16th century from the phrase "at onement," meaning "being set at one," or "reconciliation." It was used in the various English translations of the BIBLE, including the KING JAMES VERSION (1611), to convey the idea of reconciliation and expiation, and it has been a favorite way for Christians to speak about the saving significance of the death of JESUS CHRIST. Various theories of the Atonement of Christ have arisen: satisfaction for the SINS of the world; redemption from the Devil or from the wrath of God; a saving example of true, suffering love; the prime illustration of divine mercy; a divine victory over the forces of evil. In Christian orthodoxy there is no remission of sin without "the shedding of [Christ's] blood" (Hebrews 9:26).

In JUDAISM vicarious atonement has little importance. For a traditional Jew, atonement is expiation for one's own sin in order to attain God's forgiveness. This may be achieved in various ways, including repentance, payment for a wrong action, good works, suffering, and prayer. Repentance and changed conduct are usually stressed as the most important aspects of atonement. The 10 "days of awe," culminating in the Day of Atonement (YOM KIPPUR), are centered on repentance.

ATREUS \'ā-ˌtrüs, 'ā-trē-əs\, in Greek myth, the son of PELOPS and his wife, Hippodamia. Atreus was the elder brother of Thyestes and was the king of Mycenae.

A curse, said to have been pronounced by Myrtilus, a rival who died by Pelops' hand, plagued the descendants of Pelops. His sons Alcathous, Atreus, and Thyestes set upon a bloody course with the murder of their stepbrother Chrysippus, the son of Pelops' union with a NYMPH. After the crime the three brothers fled their native city of Pisa; Alcathous went to Megara, and Atreus and Thyestes stopped at Mycenae, where Atreus became king. But Thyestes either contested Atreus' right to rule or seduced Atreus' wife, Aërope, and thus was driven from Mycenae. To avenge himself, Thyestes sent Pleisthenes (Atreus' son, whom Thyestes had brought up as his own) to kill Atreus, but the boy was himself slain, unrecognized by his father.

When Atreus learned the identity of the slain boy, he recalled Thyestes to Mycenae in apparent reconciliation. At a banquet Atreus served Thyestes the flesh of Thyestes' own son (or sons), whom Atreus had slain in vengeance. Thyestes fled in horror to Sicyon; there he impregnated his own daughter Pelopia in the hope of raising one more son to avenge himself against his brother. Atreus subsequently married Pelopia and she bore Aegisthus, who was actually the son of Thyestes, her father.

Later, AGAMEMNON and MENELAUS—sons of Atreus and Aërope—found Thyestes and imprisoned him at Mycenae. Aegisthus was sent to murder Thyestes, but each recognized the other because of the sword that Pelopia had taken from her father and given to her son. Father and son slew Atreus, seized the throne, and drove Agamemnon and Menelaus out of the country.

ATTIS \'a-tis\, *also spelled* Atys, mythical consort of the GREAT MOTHER OF THE GODS (classical CYBELE, or Agdistis); he was worshiped in Phrygia, Asia Minor, and later throughout the Roman Empire, where he was made a SOLAR DEITY in the 2nd century CE. The worship of Attis and the Great Mother included the annual celebration of mysteries on the return of the spring season. Attis, like the Great Mother, was probably indigenous to Asia Minor, adopted by the invading Phrygians and blended by them with a mythical character of their own. According to the Phrygian tale, Attis was a beautiful youth born of Nana, the daughter of the river Sangarius, and the hermaphroditic Agdistis. Having become enamored of Attis, Agdistis struck him with frenzy as he was about to be married, with the result that Attis castrated himself and died. Agdistis in repentance prevailed upon ZEUS to grant that the body of the youth should never decay or waste. Attis has often been interpreted as a vegetation god, his myth expressing the rhythm of the seasons. *See also* ANATOLIAN RELIGIONS.

ATUM \'ä-təm\, *also called* Tem \'tem\, *or* Tum \'təm\, in ancient EGYPTIAN RELIGION, one of the manifestations of the sun and creator god, perhaps originally a local deity of HELIOPOLIS. Atum's myth merged with that of the great sun god RE, giving rise to the deity Re-Atum. When distinguished from Re, Atum was the creator's original form, living inside the Nun, the primordial waters of chaos. At creation he emerged to engender himself and the gods. He was identified with the setting sun and was shown as an aged figure who had to be regenerated during the night, to appear as KHEPRI at dawn and as Re at the sun's zenith. Atum was often identified with snakes and eels.

AUGEAS \'o̅-jē-əs, o̅-'jē-əs\, *also spelled* Augeias, *or* Augias, in Greek mythology, king of the Epeians in Elis, a son of the sun god HELIOS. He possessed immense herds, and King Eurystheus imposed upon HERACLES the task of clearing out all of Augeas' stables unaided in one day. Heracles did so by redirecting the Alpheus River through them. Although Augeas had promised Heracles a tenth of the herd, he later refused, alleging that Heracles had acted only in the service of Eurystheus. Heracles thereupon led an army against him and slew Augeas and his sons.

AUGSBURG CONFESSION \'ȯgz-ˌbərg\, *Latin* Confessio Augustana, the 28 articles that constitute the basic confession of LUTHERANISM, presented June 25, 1530, at the Diet of Augsburg to the emperor Charles V. The principal author was the Reformer PHILIPP MELANCHTHON, who drew on earlier Lutheran statements of faith. The purpose was to defend the Lutherans against misrepresentations and to provide a statement of their theology that would be acceptable to ROMAN CATHOLICS. The Catholic theologians replied with the so-called Confutation, which condemned 13 articles of the Confession, accepted 9 without qualifications, and approved 6 with qualifications. The emperor refused to receive a Lutheran counter-reply, but Melanchthon used it as the basis for his Apology of the Augsburg Confession

(1531). The unaltered 1530 version of the Confession has always been authoritative for Lutherans, but proponents of the eucharistic doctrine of HULDRYCH ZWINGLI and JOHN CALVIN received a modified edition prepared by Melanchthon (the *Variata* of 1540).

The first 21 articles of the Unaltered Augsburg Confession set forth the Lutherans' overall doctrine. The remaining seven articles discuss abuses that had crept into the Western church in the centuries before the REFORMATION: Communion under one kind (the people received the bread only), enforced priestly CELIBACY, the MASS as an expiatory sacrifice, compulsory CONFESSION, human institutions designed to merit GRACE, abuses in connection with MONASTICISM, and the expanded authority claimed by the bishops.

The Confession, originally written in German and Latin, was translated into English in 1536 and was a definite influence on both the THIRTY-NINE ARTICLES of the ANGLICAN COMMUNION and the Twenty-five Articles of Religion of METHODISM.

AUGURY, prophetic divining of the future by observation of natural phenomena—particularly the behavior of birds and animals and the examination of their entrails and other parts, but also by scrutiny of man-made objects and situations. The term derives from the official Roman augurs, whose constitutional function was to discover whether or not the gods approved of a proposed course of action, especially political or military. Two types of divinatory sign, or OMEN, were recognized: the most important was that deliberately watched for, such as lightning, thunder, flights and cries of birds, or the pecking behavior of sacred chickens; of lesser importance was that which occurred casually, such as the unexpected appearance of animals sacred to the gods, or such other mundane signs as the accidental spilling of salt, sneezing, stumbling, or the creaking of furniture.

Cicero's *De divinatione* (*Concerning Divination*), dated probably 44 BCE, provides the best source on ancient divinatory practices. Both he and Plato distinguish between augury that can be taught and augury that is divinely inspired in ecstatic trance. The Chinese I CHING ("Book of Changes") interprets the hexagram created by the tossing of yarrow stalks. Among the vast number of sources of augury, each with its own specialist jargon and ritual, were atmospheric phenomena (aeromancy), cards (cartomancy), dice or lots (cleromancy), dots and other marks on paper (geomancy), fire and smoke (pyromancy), the shoulder blades of animals (scapulimancy), entrails of sacrificed animals (haruspicy), or their livers, which were considered to be the seat of life (hepatoscopy).

AUGUSTINE, SAINT \ˈȯ-gə-ˌstēn, ȯ-ˈgəs-tin\, *also called* Saint Augustine of Hippo (b. Nov. 13, 354 CE, Tagaste, Numidia—d. Aug. 28, 430, Hippo Regius), Roman Catholic bishop and theologian who left a profound impression on Christian thought. He was born to modestly prosperous parents in a small farming community in Roman north Africa. He benefited from the best education available and became a teacher. For some years he was a member of a Manichean church in Carthage. After traveling to Rome and then Milan, where he gained a teaching position in the university and fell under the influence of Bishop Ambrose and of Neoplatonic philosophy, he underwent a conversion experience and in 387 was baptized. He returned to Africa and in 396 was consecrated bishop of Hippo, a post he held until he died in 430, while the city was under siege by a Vandal army.

St. Augustine of Hippo, fresco by Sandro Botticelli, 1480; in the Church of Ognissanti, Florence
Alinari—Art Resource

Augustine was a memorable and persuasive preacher and a deft guardian and promoter of his church in difficult political times. He wrote incessantly: five million words of his books, letters, and sermons survive to this day. His best-known books, the *Confessions* (a meditation on God's GRACE as seen in Augustine's early life and priestly mission), *The City of God* (on the place of CHRISTIANITY in history), *On Christian Doctrine* (a manual for the preparation of preachers and the study of SCRIPTURE), and *On the Trinity* (on the fundamental Christian doctrines of God), are often translated and still read with profit. His 400 or more surviving sermons are perhaps his least-known works today, but they are in many ways the most distinctive, developing characteristic themes for a wide audience in brief compass, often full of verbal drama and beauty.

In one of his earliest surviving works, Augustine set out a pair of themes that remained remarkably consistent through his life. "What is it you seek to know?" is the question he posed to himself in an interior dialogue. "Just two things: God and the soul" is the reply. These themes proved inexhaustible for Augustine.

For Augustine, God is spirit and power, majesty and absent presence. God is invisible but ubiquitous; he allows humankind to stray and is inexorable in exacting justice but also boundless in mercy. The sum of qualities predicated of God by Augustine rarely adds up to a simple description, and the paradoxical complexity of that description leads to some of his most characteristic doctrines and their characteristic difficulties.

The human soul is scarcely less problematic: divine and animal, free and constrained, powerful and helpless. There has been much debate among scholars about Augustine's views on the origin of the soul, a topic he was careful to leave undecided. But soul for him is undeniably important, as it was for many of his Christian contemporaries, who strove to describe the nature and qualities of something they had never seen. How divine is soul? Does it descend from some other world into this one? Augustine seemed to think so. But how then does SIN come into the soul?

Augustine's biblical commentaries and sermons pursue these themes in various ways. The most austere works of his later years address what would later reemerge as the Calvinist doctrine of "double PREDESTINATION" (*i.e.*, God elects those who will be saved and selects at the same time those who will be damned). The doctrine is, however, hedged about with conciliatory gestures meant to soften the harshness of a judgmental God who could condemn people for a sin they inherited but did not themselves commit. The history of Christian theology in the West is marked by outbreaks of controversy around just this issue, with Augustine himself cited by all sides engaged in such quarrels.

But Augustine was not the most severe of moral judges. His Christianity has ample place for those who struggle imperfectly to better themselves, who fall and rise again. He opposed sects (notably MANICHAEISM, DONATISM, and PELAGIANISM) that held a perfectionist view of human life. Augustine has a reputation, not unjustified, for a gloomy and restrictive view of sexuality, but among his contemporaries he numbered among the moderates.

Undoubtedly, the *Confessions* are Augustine's greatest literary work and the vehicle by which he has reached modern minds most effectively. The work is neither autobiography nor confession in a modern sense, but it contains elements of both. The deeds of his youth are rehearsed, very selectively, in order to relate a moral tale of fall into sin and rise to salvation. The conversion scenes offer a complex tableau of the forms of redemption of mind, body, and spirit that Augustine had experienced. The last books offer meditation on Scripture and in so doing bring together the life of the individual with the story of GENESIS and implicitly the history of Christianity. In the end, for Augustine, there is only one story in the world (creation, fall, redemption) and only two players (God and humankind).

In his lifetime, many quarreled with Augustine, and a few scorned him. But in the main, he won respect even among his enemies. No charge of unorthodoxy ever stuck for long, and even those who abandoned his doctrines of predestination in the Middle Ages and after generally did so respectfully and cautiously. For the Latin Middle Ages, he was the most authoritative Christian writer after PAUL. Once the REFORMATION sundered Christianity on the issue of freedom and predestination, the less rhetorical, more cautious THOMAS AQUINAS edged to the fore of official Catholic teaching, but Augustine remained and remains the more astonishing and the more enticing of the two.

AUGUSTINE OF CANTERBURY, SAINT, *also called* Austin (b. Rome?–d. May 26, 604/605, Canterbury, Kent, Eng.; feast day, England and Wales, May 26; elsewhere May

28), first archbishop of Canterbury and the apostle of England; he was the founder of the Christian church in southern England.

Augustine was prior of the BENEDICTINE monastery of St. Andrew, Rome, when Pope GREGORY I chose him to lead an unprecedented MISSION of about 40 monks to England, most of which was not yet Christian. They left in June 596, but, arriving in southern Gaul, they were warned of the perils awaiting them and sent Augustine back to Rome. There Gregory encouraged him with letters of commendation, and he set out once more. The entourage landed in the spring of 597 on the Isle of Thanet, off the southeast coast of England, and was well received by King Aethelberht. With his support, their work led to many conversions, including that of the king. The next autumn Augustine was consecrated bishop of the English by St. Virgilius at Arles.

Thousands of Aethelberht's subjects were reportedly baptized by Augustine on CHRISTMAS Day 597, and he subsequently dispatched two of his monks to Rome with a report of this extraordinary event and a request for further help and advice. They returned in 601 with the pallium (*i.e.*, symbol of METROPOLITAN jurisdiction) from Gregory for Augustine and with more missionaries, including the celebrated SS. Mellitus, Justus, and Paulinus.

Augustine founded Christ Church, Canterbury, as his cathedral and the monastery of SS. Peter and Paul (known after his death as St. Augustine's, where the early archbishops were buried), which came to rank as the second Benedictine house in all Europe. In 604 he established the episcopal sees of London (for the East Saxons), consecrating Mellitus as its bishop, and of Rochester, consecrating Justus as its bishop.

AUGUSTINIAN \ˌȯ-gə-ˈsti-nē-ən\, *also called* Austin, in the ROMAN CATHOLIC church, member of any of the religious orders and congregations of men and women whose constitutions are based on the Rule of ST. AUGUSTINE, which was widely disseminated after his death, 430 CE. More specifically, the name designates members of two main branches of Augustinians, the Augustinian Canons and the Augustinian Hermits. Modern emphasis of the Augustinians has been on MISSION, educational, and hospital work.

The Augustinian Canons were, in the 11th century, the first religious order of men in the Roman Catholic church to combine clerical status with a full common life. The order flourished until the Protestant REFORMATION, during which many of its foundations perished. The French Revolution also put an end to a number of its houses.

The Augustinian Hermits were one of the four great MENDICANT orders of the Middle Ages. After being dispersed by the Vandal invasion of northern Africa (*c.* 428), a number of congregations of hermits who had been following the Rule of St. Augustine founded monasteries in central and northern Italy. These monasteries remained independent until the 13th century, when Pope Innocent IV in 1244 established them as one order and when Alexander IV in 1256 called them from their seclusion as hermits to an active lay apostolate in the cities. The order spread rapidly throughout Europe and took a prominent part in both university life and ecclesiastical affairs; perhaps its most famous member was the Protestant Reformer MARTIN LUTHER in the 16th century.

An offshoot of the Augustinian Hermits are the Augustinian Recollects, formed in the 16th century by FRIARS who desired a rule of stricter observance and a return to the eremetic ideals of solitude and contemplation.

AUM SHINRIKYO \'ōm-'shēn-rē-ˌkyō, *Angl* 'aùm-shēn-'rē-\, ("Supreme Truth"), radical religious movement founded by SHOKO ASAHARA, combining elements taken from HINDUISM and folk BUDDHISM. The movement honors SHIVA, the Hindu god of destruction and regeneration and was founded in the millenarian expectation of a series of disasters that would bring an end to this world and inaugurate a new cosmic cycle. *See also* MILLENNIALISM; NEW RELIGIOUS MOVEMENTS.

Asahara had been a member of Agonshu, a small new religion that incorporated elements of Hinduism and Buddhism, but after an economic and spiritual crisis he founded his own new religion Aum Shinsen-no-kai (later known as Aum Shinrikyo), which he incorporated in 1984. Asahara spent the next few years building his movement through preaching, teaching YOGA, and publishing books that predicted the coming of ARMAGEDDON as early as 1997. The sect's recruiting methods aroused suspicion, and it allegedly used sleep deprivation, isolation, and mind-altering drugs as a means of keeping followers in line. The movement was also suspected of having used kidnappings, beatings, and even murder to stifle opponents and prevent government investigation. By 1989, however, Aum was recognized as an official religion and claimed 10,000 followers in Japan and 20,000 abroad, mostly in Russia, with regional offices in the U.S., Germany, and Sri Lanka. Asahara's successes prompted him to field a group of candidates for the Diet (the Japanese parliament), with the hopes that he would be able to become prime minister. Aum's candidates were decisively defeated, however, and this failure channeled the movement's energies in a new direction.

Many folk Buddhist millenarian sects saw the modern period as a prelude to the end of humanity and beginning of a cosmic cycle; to this Asaraha added Hindu elements and set himself at the center as agent of the divine will. He predicted a series of disasters, such as war between Japan and the United States, that would foreshadow the final battle, Armageddon, and the end of the world in this corrupt age. Aum was to be an agent in hastening the end of this period. To that end, Aum members gathered weapons and supplies of the nerve gas sarin, which they released into the Tokyo subway system in 1995. Asahara and members of his sect were arrested and the sect's sites were taken over.

AUNG SAN SUU KYI \'aùŋ-'sän-'sü-'chē\ (b. June 19, 1945, Rangoon, Burma [now Yangôn, Myanmar]), Buddhist-oriented political leader of the democratic opposition to the military government in Myanmar and winner of the 1991 Nobel Prize for Peace.

Aung San Suu Kyi was the daughter of Aung San (a martyred national hero of independent Burma). After attending university and settling in England for several years, she returned to Burma (the name for her country that she preferred to use) and became the leader of the newly formed National League for Democracy. Her party won 80

Aung San Suu Kyi
Reuters—Apichart Weerawong—Archive Photos

percent of the parliamentary seats in a 1990 election that was immediately abrogated by the military regime. During much of the 1990s Suu Kyi was kept under house arrest but continued to advocate nonviolent resistance and to call for the observance of human rights. She rebuffed government efforts that encouraged her to leave Burma and continued to be a major symbol of hope for those who opposed military rule in that country. During this time she also formulated a sociopolitical orientation grounded in Buddhist thought that was opposed to the brand of Buddhist traditionalism sponsored by the ruling generals.

AURGELMIR \'aùr-gəl-ˌmir\: *see* YMIR.

AUROBINDO, ŚRĪ \ˌôr-ə-'bin-dō\, *original name* Aurobindo Ghose, Aurobindo *also spelled* Aravinda (b. Aug. 15, 1872, Calcutta, India—d. Dec. 5, 1950, Pondicherry), seer, poet, and Indian nationalist who originated the philosophy of cosmic salvation through spiritual evolution.

Aurobindo entered a Christian convent school in Darjeeling and then, still a boy, he was sent to England for further schooling. At the University of Cambridge he became proficient in two classical and three modern European languages. After returning to India in 1892, he took various administrative and professorial posts in Baroda and Calcutta, and then turned to the study of YOGA and Indian languages, including classical Sanskrit.

From 1902 to 1910, Aurobindo embarked on a course of action to free India from British rule. As a result of his political activities and revolutionary literary efforts, he was imprisoned in 1908. Two years later he fled to the French colony of Pondichéry (modern Pondicherry) in southeastern India, where he devoted himself for the rest of his life solely to the development of his philosophy. There he founded an ASHRAM (retreat) as an international cultural center for spiritual development.

According to Aurobindo's theory of cosmic salvation, the paths to union with BRAHMAN are two-way streets, or channels: Enlightenment comes from above (thesis), while the spiritual mind (supermind) strives through yogic illumination to reach upward from below (antithesis). When these two forces blend, a gnostic individual is created (synthesis). This yogic illumination transcends both reason and intuition and eventually leads to the freeing of the individual from the bonds of individuality, and, by extension, all humankind will eventually achieve MOKṢA (liberation).

Aurobindo's voluminous, complex, and sometimes chaotic literary output includes philosophical pondering, poetry, plays, and other works. Among his works are *The Life Divine* (1940), *The Human Cycle* (1949), *The Ideal of Human Unity* (1949), *On the Veda* (1956), *Collected Poems and Plays* (1942), *Essays on the Gita* (1928), *The Synthesis of Yoga* (1948), and *Savitri: A Legend and a Symbol* (1950).

AUSEKLIS \'aù-se-klis\ (Latvian), *Lithuanian* Aušrinė \aù-'shrʸi-nʸā\, in BALTIC RELIGION, the morning star and deity of the dawn. The Latvian Auseklis was a male god, the Lithuanian Aušrinė a female.

Related in name to the Vedic Uṣas and the Greek EOS, goddesses of dawn, Auseklis is associated in Latvian mythology with MĒNESS (Moon) and SAULE (Sun), being subordinate to the former and along with him a suitor of Saule's daughter, Saules meita. According to Lithuanian traditions Aušrinė had an adulterous relationship with the moon god, Mėnuo, for which Mėnuo was punished by the god Perkūnas (Latvian: PĒRKONS).

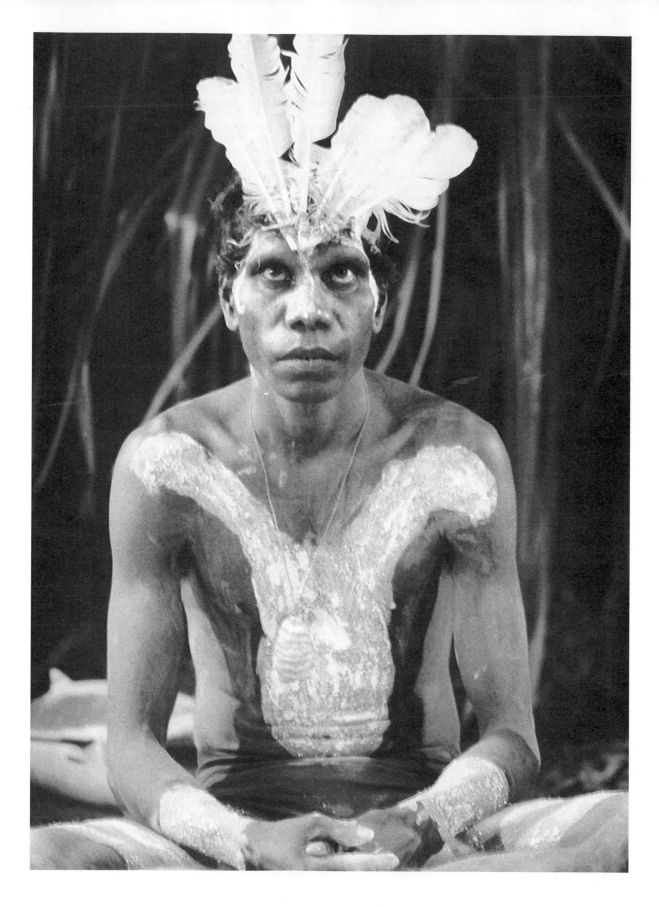

AUSTRALIAN ABORIGINAL RELIGION

Themes the beliefs and ritual practices of the indigenous population of Australia, who are known as Aboriginals, show a unique contrast between the complexity of their social organization and religious life and the relative simplicity of their material technologies.

HISTORICAL AND CULTURAL CONTEXT

Aboriginals came originally from somewhere in Asia and have been in Australia for at least 40,000 years. The first settlement occurred during an era of lowered sea levels, when there was an almost continuous land bridge between Asia and Australia. By 30,000 years ago most of the continent was sparsely occupied.

By the time of European settlement in 1788, population densities ranged from about 1 to 8 square miles per person in fertile riverine and coastal areas to more than 35 square miles per person in the vast interior deserts. More than 200 different languages were spoken, and most Aboriginals were bilingual or multilingual. The largest entities recognized by the people were grouped around speakers of the same language, sometimes referred to by Europeans as "tribes." There may have been as many as 500 such groups. There was no consciousness of a shared national identity. However, the Aboriginal worldview tended to be expansive, with a perception of "society" as a community of common understandings and behaviors shared well beyond the confines of the local group.

The Aboriginals were hunter-gatherers who grew no crops and did not domesticate animals (apart from the dingo, a type of wild dog). The need to balance population with resources meant that most of the time people were dispersed into small food-gathering groups. But when food resources permitted, large gatherings would be organized, and much of the social and religious business of the society would be transacted over a two- to three-week period of intense activity.

RITUAL AND PRACTICE

The dreaming and totemic beliefs. The Aboriginal worldview centered on the "DREAMING," or "Dreamtime," a complex and comprehensive concept embodying the past, present, and future, as well as virtually every aspect of life. It includes the creative era at the dawn of time, when mythic beings shaped the land and

An Australian Aboriginal wearing body paint, feathers, and shell ornaments
Carlos Sanudo—Monkmeyer

Rock painting of a kangaroo; from Ubirr (Obiri Rock), Kakadu National Park, Australia
Mimi Forsyth—Monkmeyer

populated it with flora, fauna, and human beings and left behind the rules for social life. After their physical death and transformation into heavenly or earthly bodies, the creative beings withdrew into the spiritual realm.

The Aboriginals saw their way of life as ordained by the creative acts of the Dreaming beings; everything that existed was fixed for all time in the mythic past, and all that humans were asked to do was obey the law of the Dreaming and perform correctly the rituals upon which life depended. Aboriginals were constantly surrounded by the signs of existence and power of spiritual forces, as features of the landscape provided tangible proofs of the reality and powers of the Dreaming beings. Through dreams and other states of altered consciousness, the living could come into contact with the spiritual realm and gain strength from it, and a rich complex of myths, dances, and rituals bound the human, spiritual, and physical realms tightly together into a single cosmic order. Spirit beings acted as messengers to communicate with the living and to introduce new knowledge into human society.

Through Aboriginal systems of totemic belief, individuals and groups were linked to both the things of nature and the beings of the spiritual realm. TOTEMISM is a symbol system that connects individuals and groups to particular places and events and provides them with a unique account of their coming into being. It thus underpins individual identity while at the same time linking a person to many others who share similar associations. Many of the mythic beings in Australia were "totemic" in the sense of exemplifying in their own persons, in their outward form, the common life-force pervading particular species. Others, originating in human or near-human form, entered some physiographic feature or were metamorphosed as hills or rocks or turned into various creatures or plants.

Initiation. A child's spirit was held to come from the Dreaming in order to animate a fetus. In some cases, this was believed to occur through an action of a mythic being who might or might not be reincarnated in the child. Even when Aboriginals acknowledged a physical bond between parents and child, the most important issue for them was the spiritual heritage.

In general, puberty among girls was not ritually celebrated. In those areas in which it was celebrated, however, it was usually marked by either total or partial seclusion and by food TABOOS. Ritual defloration and hymen cutting were also practiced in a few areas. For a boy, his formal instruction as a potential adult began with the rite of initiation. All boys were initiated, the age at the first rite varying from 6 to 16, depending on the locale. Generally, once he had reached puberty and facial hair had begun to show, he was ready for the initial rituals.

Initiation was a symbolic reenactment of death and rebirth in order to achieve new life as an adult. The symbolism of death appeared as the novice left his camp, the women would wail and other noises would be made, symbolizing the voice of a mythic being who was said to swallow the novice and later vomit him forth into a new life. Initiation in Aboriginal Australia was a prelude to the religious activity in which all men participated. It meant, also, learning a wide range of things directly concerned with the practical aspects of social living, and the rites included songs and rituals having an educational purpose.

CIRCUMCISION was an important rite over the greater part of Australia. Subincision (the slitting of the underside of the penis) was especially significant in its association with secret-sacred ritual. Other rites included piercing of the nasal septum, tooth pulling, and the blood rite, the blood being used for anointing or sipping (red ochre was sometimes used as a substitute for blood). Hair removal, scarring, and playing with fire were also fairly widespread practices.

SACRED ART

Each cultural area had its own distinctive style of art. TJURUNGA (sacred object) art, consisting of incised patterns on flat stones or wooden boards, though, was fairly common throughout Australia. In central Australia, body decoration and elaborate headdresses on ritual occasions, using feather down, blood, and ochres, were especially striking. Everywhere, sacred ritual provided the incentive for making a large variety of objects, and the act of making them was itself one of the appropriate rites. Shaped and decorated receptacles for bones were common in eastern Arnhem Land. Also common were carved wooden figures of mythic beings and of contemporary persons for ritual use or as memorial posts for the dead.

Paintings in ochre on sheets of bark were used mostly for the instruction of novices. In western Arnhem Land, naturalistic patterns showing figures against an open background were the norm; there was also a unique kind of "X-ray" art that depicted the internal organs. Also widespread were cave and rock paintings or engravings, and SAND PAINTINGS associated with desert rituals.

Geographic distribution of Aboriginals

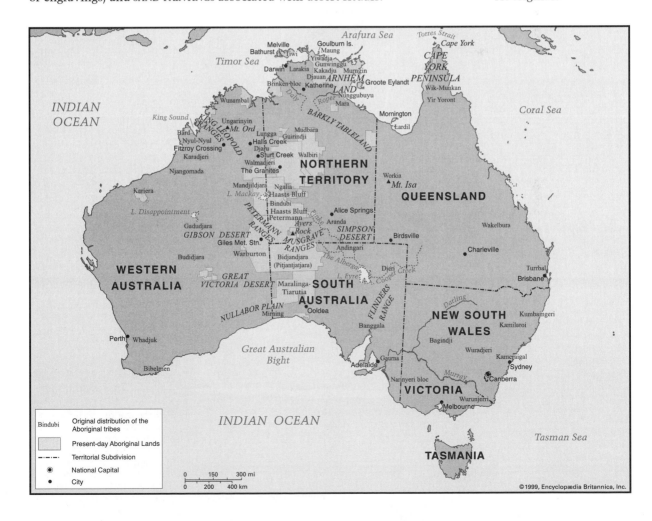

AUTOCEPHALOUS CHURCH \ˌȯ-tō-'se-fə-ləs\, in the modern usage of the CANON LAW of EASTERN ORTHODOXY, a church that enjoys total canonical and administrative independence and elects its own PRIMATES and bishops. The term was used in medieval Byzantine law in its literal sense of "self-headed" (Greek: *autokephalos*), or independent, and was applied to individual DIOCESES that did not depend upon the authority of a provincial METROPOLITAN. Today the Orthodox archbishopric of Mount Sinai, with the historic monastery of St. Catherine, still enjoys this privilege.

Most modern Orthodox autocephalies are national churches, but some are limited only geographically and include the territories of several states. The autocephalous churches maintain canonical relations with each other and enjoy communion in faith and SACRAMENTS. There is between them a traditional order of precedence, with the ecumenical patriarchate of Constantinople (modern Istanbul) enjoying the first place.

The heads of individual autocephalous churches bear different titles: PATRIARCH (in Constantinople, Alexandria, Antioch, Jerusalem, Moscow, Georgia, Serbia, Romania, and Bulgaria), ARCHBISHOP (in Athens and Cyprus), or metropolitan (in Poland and America).

AUTOLYCUS \ȯ-'tä-lə-kəs\, in Greek mythology, the father of Anticleia, who was the mother of the hero ODYSSEUS. Later ancient authors made Autolycus the son of the god HERMES. He was believed to live at the foot of Mount Parnassus and was famous as a thief and swindler. One version of the story states that SISYPHUS, during a visit to Autolycus, recognized his stolen cattle; on that occasion Sisyphus seduced Autolycus' daughter Anticleia and hence Odysseus was really the son of Sisyphus, not of Laertes, whom Anticleia afterward married. The story sought to establish a close connection between Hermes, the god of theft and of cunning, and three persons—*i.e.*, Sisyphus, Odysseus, and Autolycus—who were seen as the incarnate representations of that practice and quality.

AVADĀNA \ˌə-və-'dä-nə\, legendary material centering on the BUDDHA's explanations of events by a person's worthy deeds in a previous life. In the THERAVĀDA tradition the Pāli cognate (*Apadāna*) is the title of a "canonical" collection of such stories. *Avadāna*s include the *Divyāvadāna* ("Divine Avadāna"), consisting of 38 legends, including some about the great Buddhist emperor AŚOKA, and the *Avadāna Śataka*, which contains 100 *Avadāna* stories.

Avalokiteśvara, bronze figure from Kurkihār, Bihār, 9th century
By courtesy of Patna Museum, Patna (Bihār); photograph, Royal Academy of Arts, London

AVALOKITEŚVARA \ˌə-və-ˌlō-ki-'tāsh-və-rə\ (Sanskrit: *avalokita*, "looking on"; *īśvara*, "lord"), *Chinese* Kuan-yin \'gwän-'yin, 'kwän-\, *Japanese* Kannon \'kän-'nȯn\, the BODHISATTVA of infinite compassion and mercy, possibly the most popular of all Buddhist deities, beloved throughout many areas of the Buddhist world. He supremely exemplifies the bodhisattva's resolve to postpone his own buddhahood until he has helped every being on earth achieve emancipation. His name has been variously interpreted as "the lord who looks in every direction" and "the lord of what we see" (that is, the actual, created world).

Avalokiteśvara is the earthly manifestation of the self-born, eternal Buddha, AMITĀBHA, whose figure is represented in his headdress, and he guards the world in the interval between the departure of the historical BUDDHA, Gotama, and the appearance of the future Buddha, MAITREYA. Avalokiteśvara protects against shipwreck, fire, assassins, robbers, and wild beasts. He is the creator of the fourth world, the universe in which we live.

According to legend, his head once split with grief at realizing the number of wicked beings in the world yet to be saved. Amitābha Buddha caused each of the pieces to become a whole head and placed them on his son in 3 tiers of 3, then the 10th, and topped them all with his own image. Sometimes the 11-headed Avalokiteśvara is represented with thousands of arms, which rise like the outspread tail of a peacock around him. In painting he is usually shown white in color (in Nepal, red). His female consort is the goddess TĀRĀ. His traditional residence is the mountain Potala, and his images are frequently placed on hilltops.

The height of the veneration of Avalokiteśvara in northern India occurred in the 3rd–7th century. In China (where he became known as KUAN-YIN) he was recognized as early as the 1st century CE and had become very popular by the 6th century. Representations of the bodhisattva in China prior to the Sung dynasty (960–1126) are unmistakably masculine in appearance. Later images display attributes of both genders. One interpretation of this development contends that the bodhisattva is neither male nor female but has transcended sexual distinctions, as he has all other dualities in the sphere of SAMSĀRA (the temporal world). According to this opinion, the flowing drapery and soft contours of the body seen in statues and paintings have been intentionally combined with a visible moustache to emphasize the absence of sexual identity. Furthermore, the LO-

TUS SUTRA relates that Avalokiteśvara has the ability of assuming whatever form is required to relieve suffering and also has the power to grant children. Another point of view, while accepting the validity of this philosophical doctrine, holds that from at least the 12th century the popular devotional cult of Kuan-yin has superimposed onto the bodhisattva qualities of an indigenous Chinese goddess.

Among the followers of the PURE LAND sect, who look to rebirth in the Western Paradise of the Buddha Amitābha, Kuan-yin forms part of a ruling triad, along with Amitābha and the bodhisattva Mahasthāmaprāpta. Images of the three are often placed together in temples, and Kuan-yin is shown in paintings welcoming the dead to the Western Paradise. This cult of Kuan-yin is based on SCRIPTURES of the Pure Land school that were translated into Chinese between the 3rd and 5th centuries.

The bodhisattva was introduced into Tibet—where he is called Spyan-ras gzigs ("With a Pitying Look")—in the 7th century, where he quickly became the most popular figure in the pantheon. Ultimately many Tibetans came to believe that he was, and still is, successively reincarnated in each DALAI LAMA. He is credited with introducing the prayer formula *om maṇi padmehūṃ!* (frequently translated "the jewel is in the lotus") to the people of Tibet.

The cult of Avalokiteśvara/Kuan-yin probably reached Japan (where he is called KANNON) by way of Korea soon after BUDDHISM was first introduced into the country; the earliest known images at the Hōryū-ji (*ji*, "temple") in Nara date from the mid-7th century. The worship of the bodhisattva was never confined to any one sect and continues to be widespread throughout Japan.

As in China, some ambivalence exists about Kannon's gender. In Japan Kannon's ability to assume innumerable forms has led to seven major representations: (1) Shō Kannon, the simplest form, usually shown as a seated or standing figure with two hands; (2) Jū-ichi-men Kannon, a two-or four-handed figure with 11 heads; (3) Senju Kannon, the bodhisattva with 1,000 arms; (4) Jun-tei Kannon, one of the least common forms, represented as a seated figure with 18 arms, sometimes related to the Indian goddess Cuntī (mother of 700,000 buddhas); (5) Fukū-kenjaku Kannon, a form popular with the Tendai (T'IEN-T'AI) sect, whose special emblem is the lasso; (6) Ba-tō Kannon, shown with a fierce face and a horse's head in the headdress, probably related to the Tibetan protector of horses, Hayagrīva; (7) Nyo-i-rin Kannon, shown seated, with six arms, holding the wish-fulfilling jewel.

The virtues and miracles of Avalokiteśvara are accounted in many Buddhist *sūtra*s. The *Avalokiteśvara Sūtra* was incorporated into the widely popular *Lotus Sutra* in the 3rd century CE, though it continues to circulate as an independent work in China and is the main scripture of his cult worship there.

AVATAMSAKA SŪTRA \ˌə-və-ˈtəm-sə-kə-ˈsü-trə\, *in full* Mahavaipulya-Buddha Āvataṃsaka-sūtra (Sanskrit: "The Great and Vast Buddha Garland Sutra"), *also called* Garland Sutra, MAHĀYĀNA Buddhist text that speaks of the deeds of the BUDDHA and of their resulting merits that blossom like a garland of flowers. The discourse begins with the Buddha's Enlightenment, attended by a chorus of BODHISATTVAS (those destined to become enlightened) and divine beings. There follows a great assembly in the palace of the god INDRA, where the Buddha teaches that all beings have the BUDDHA NATURE, that all phenomena are mutually originating and interdependent, and that, finally, all is Buddha.

Scholars value the text for showing the evolution of thought from early Buddhism to fully developed Mahāyāna. Several versions of the text seem to have existed, one reputedly containing as many as 100,000 verses. A translation entitled *Hua-yen ching* first appeared in China around 400 CE and gave rise to the HUA-YEN (Kegon) sect.

AVATAR \ˈa-və-ˌtär\, *Sanskrit* avatāra \ˌə-və-ˈtär-ə\, *Hindi* avatār ("descent"), in HINDUISM, the appearance of a deity in human or animal form to counteract some particular evil in the world. The term usually refers to 10 "descents" of VISHNU, whose evolutionary sequence is unmistakable: Matsya (fish), Kūrma (tortoise), VARĀHA (boar), NARASIMHA (half man, half lion), VĀMANA (dwarf), PARAŚURĀMA (RĀMA with the ax), Rāma (hero of the RĀMĀYAṆA epic), KRISHNA (the divine cowherd), the BUDDHA GOTAMA, and KALKĪ (the incarnation yet to come). The number of Vishnu's avatars can vary, and their identity alter, with individual texts and ICONS. Thus Krishna's half-brother BALARĀMA sometimes replaces him in the 10-member sequence as the third Rāma; Krishna then sometimes replaces the Buddha. Equally important, there may be a resistance to understanding Krishna as in any way subordinate to Vishnu. In the BHAGAVAD GĪTĀ Krishna himself plays the supernal role normally associated with Vishnu. He tells ARJUNA: "Whenever there is a decline of righteousness and rise of unrighteousness then I send forth Myself. For the protection of the good, for the destruction of the wicked, and for the establishment of righteousness, I come into being from age to age."

AVEMPACE: *see* IBN BĀJJAH.

AVERROËS: *see* IBN RUSHD.

AVESTA \ə-ˈves-tə\, *also called* Zend-Avesta \ˌzend-ə-ˈves-tə\, the primary scriptural collection of ZOROASTRIANISM, containing largely hymns, prayers, liturgical formulas, and appeals to righteousness ascribed to the prophet ZOROASTER (Zarathushtra). The extant Avesta is all that remains of a much larger body of SCRIPTURE, said to have been destroyed when Alexander the Great conquered Persia. The present Avesta was assembled from remnants and standardized under the Sasanian kings (3rd–7th century CE).

The Avesta is in five parts. Its religious core is a collection of ancient songs or hymns, the *Gāthā*s, thought to be close to the words of Zoroaster himself. They form a middle section of the chief liturgical part of the canon, the *Yasna*, which contains the rite of the preparation and sacrifice of HAOMA. The *Visp rat* is a lesser liturgical scripture, containing homages to a number of Zoroastrian spiritual leaders. The *Vendidad*, or *Vidēvdāt*, is the main source for Zoroastrian law, both ritual and civil. It also gives an account of creation and the first man, YIMA. The *Yasht*s are 21 mythic hymns to various YAZATAS (ANGELS) and ancient heroes. The *Khūrda Avesta* (or Little Avesta) is a group of minor texts, hymns, and prayers for specific occasions.

AVICENNA: *see* IBN SĪNĀ.

AVIGNON PAPACY \ˌȧ-vē-ˈnyōⁿ\, Roman Catholic PAPACY during the period 1309–77, when the popes took up residence at Avignon (now in France) instead of at Rome, primarily because of the current political conditions.

Distressed by factionalism in Rome and pressed to come to France by Philip IV, Pope Clement V moved the papal capital to Avignon, which at that time belonged to vassals of the pope. In 1348 it became direct papal property. Although the Avignon papacy was overwhelmingly French in complexion (all seven of the popes during the period were French, as were 111 of the 134 CARDINALS created), it was not so responsive to French pressure as contemporaries assumed or as later critics insisted. During this time the Sacred College of Cardinals began to gain a stronger role in the government of the church; a vast reorganization and centralization of administrative offices and other agencies was effected; reform measures for the clergy were initiated; expanded missionary enterprises, which reached as far as China, were stimulated; university education was promoted; and numerous attempts were made by the popes to settle royal rivalries and to establish peace. Nevertheless, antagonism, especially in England and Germany, to the residency at Avignon damaged the prestige of the papacy.

After Gregory XI reestablished the papal capital in Rome, cardinals of the Sacred College selected a second pope, who assumed the vacant Avignon seat. This marked the onset of the Great SCHISM. A succession of such "ANTIPOPES" were selected, and the Great Schism was not healed until 1417. The increased power and ambitions of the cardinals led, no doubt, to the Great Schism and to the subsequent emergence of CONCILIARISM, a theory that a general council of the church has greater authority than the pope and may, if necessary, depose him. Thus, the Avignon papacy also contributed to the religious, intellectual, and political climate which would foment the Protestant REFORMATION.

AYODHYA \ə-'yōd-yä\ (Sanskrit), *Hindi* Ayodhyā, city in south-central Uttar Pradesh state, northern India, on the Ghāghara (Gogra) River. An ancient city dating to roughly the 6th century BCE, Ayodhya is often regarded as one of the seven holiest places of HINDUISM, revered because of its association, in the great Indian epic poem RĀMĀYAṆA, with the birth and rule of RĀMA and with the rule of his father, Daśaratha.

Not until about the 14th century is there evidence that a firm association had been made between the physical place called Ayodhya and its mythic namesake in the *Rāmāyaṇa.* Rather, virtually all early writers, most of them Buddhist or Jain, refer to it as Sāketa and report that it was visited by the founders of both faiths. Its importance as a Buddhist center can be gauged from the statement of the Chinese Buddhist monk FA-HSIEN in the 5th century CE that there were 100 monasteries there. In that same century a Gupta emperor calling himself a *parama bhāgavata* (great devotee of VISHNU) moved his capital there from Pāṭaliputra, identifying the former Sāketa as Rāma's city, Ayodhya. The capital moved soon again, but subsequent centuries witnessed at least intermittent Vaiṣṇava patronage (*see* VAIṢṆAVISM), along with a significant presence of JAINISM and BUDDHISM. In 1226 Ayodhya became the capital of the province of Avadh under the Delhi sultanate, and it was not until the 18th century (under the Muslim nawabs of Avadh, who ruled from nearby Faizabad) that major Hindu construction resumed, although the city remained an important destination for Hindu PILGRIMAGE in the meantime.

In 1528, a lieutenant of the Mughal emperor Babur built the structure that has come to be called Bābri Masjid ("Babur's Mosque") on a site traditionally identified as Rāma's birthplace. Whether he destroyed a preexisting Hindu temple to do so has been the subject of deep dispute, both public and scholarly. That dispute is one of many focused on the site, especially since India's independence. In 1949, for example, an image of Rāma was said to have manifested itself inside the mosque, causing a protracted legal struggle. (Many decades later, several Rāmānandī ascetics claimed responsibility for the act.) In 1990 riots in northern India followed the storming of the mosque by zealous Hindus intent on erecting a temple on the site; the ensuing crisis brought down the Indian government. Two years later, on Dec. 6, 1992, the mosque was demolished in a few hours by a crowd of Hindu militants organized by the VISHVA HINDU PARISHAD with support from the Rashtriya Swayamsevak Sangh and the BHARATIYA JANATA PARTY. It is estimated that more than 1,000 people—mostly Muslims—died in the rioting that swept through India following the mosque's destruction.

ĀYURVEDA \'ä-yər-ˌvā-də\, in India, well-organized and highly articulated system of traditional medicine. Āyurveda is attributed to Dhanvantari, the physician of the pantheon of HINDUISM, who received it from BRAHMĀ. It is understood as one of the "limbs of the VEDA" (*vedāṅga*).

Indian medicine has a long history. Its earliest concepts are set out in the Vedas, especially in the metrical passages of the ATHARVA VEDA, which may possibly date as far back as the 2nd millennium BCE. The Vedas do make reference to magical practices for the treatment of diseases, but Āyurvedic practioners take as their seminal texts the *Caraka Saṃhitā* and *Suśruta Saṃhitā*, compiled roughly 1st–4th century CE. These texts analyze the human body in terms of earth, water, fire, air, and ether—which in turn yield the three bodily humors (*doṣas*): wind, bile, and phlegm. These then correspond to the three qualities or temperaments (*guṇas*) that pervade the universe. Thus, Āyurveda participates in a broader organization of knowledge that makes its appearence in a range of Hindu (and also BUDDHIST) religious texts. The early development of Āyurveda as a system owes a significant debt to traveling ascetics who also served as healers.

Āyurvedic medicine is still a favored form of health care in India, where a large percentage of the population use this system exclusively or combined with Western medicine, and Āyurvedic medicine has an increasingly important profile in the West. The Indian Medical Council was set up in 1971 by the Indian government to establish maintenance of standards for undergraduate and postgraduate education. It establishes suitable qualifications in Indian medicine and recognizes various forms of traditional practice, including the Āyurvedic system. India has roughly 100 colleges at which Āyurvedic medicine is taught.

Āyurvedic medicine has both preventive and curative aspects. The preventive component emphasizes the need for a strict code of personal and social hygiene, the details of which depend upon individual, climatic, and environmental needs. Bodily exercises, the use of herbal preparations, dietary controls, and YOGA form a part of the remedial measures. The curative aspect of Āyurvedic medicine involves the use of herbal medicines, external preparations, physiotherapy, and diet. It is a principle of Āyurvedic medicine that the preventive and therapeutic measures be adapted to the personal requirements of each patient.

AYYAPPAN \'ä-yə-pən\, *also called* Sartavu, *or* Śāsta, in HINDUISM, a deity who is always and at all times celibate, generally depicted in a yogic posture, wearing a bell around his neck. His most prominent shrine is at Sabarimalai in the southern Indian state of Kerala, and he enjoys popularity mostly in Kerala, though the neighboring states of Tamil Nadu and Karnataka also house many Ayyappan temples. Ayyappan may bear a historical relationship to the tutelary deity Aiyanar of Tamil Nadu. The most public aspect of the worship of Ayyappan is the annual PILGRIMAGE to Śabarimalai in which only men, pre-adolescent girls, and post-menopausal women are allowed to participate. Prior to the journey, pilgrims, who annually number around one million, are required to observe strict vows of CELIBACY and abstain from meat and intoxicants for a period of, traditionally, 41 days. Pilgrims climb barefoot to the hilltop where the shrine is located, and during the pilgrimage unity and brotherhood are emphasized, while linguistic and economic differences among participants are minimized, leading some to speculate that BUDDHISM influenced the worship of Ayyappan. A late Sanskrit text describes Ayyappan as the son of SHIVA and VISHNU (with the latter in his form as the enchantress Mohini). Abandoned by his parents with but a bell around his neck, he was adopted by a Pantalam king of Kerala, and, soon after, his divinity was recognized and a shrine erected to him. Other tales and songs in Malayalam and Kodagu describe his adoption by a local king. They focus on his later life, in which he grew to be a renowned warrior who first set out to defeat and was subsequently worshiped by the Muslim chieftain Vavar (to whom there is a shrine en route to Śabarimalai).

AZALĪ \a-za-'lē\, any member of the BĀBĪ movement (followers of a 19th-century Iranian prophet, the BĀB) who chose to remain faithful to the Bāb's teachings and to his chosen successor, Mirza Yaḥya, who was given the religious title Ṣobḥ-e Azal, after a split in the movement occurred in 1863. For about 13 years after the Bāb's execution, followers recognized Ṣobḥ-e Azal as their leader. In 1863, when Ṣobḥ-e Azal's half-brother BAHĀ' ULLĀH privately declared that he was "him whom God shall manifest"—a new prophet foretold by the Bāb—the community split. The Azalīs rejected the claims of Bahā' Ullāh as premature, arguing that the world must first accept Bābī laws in order to be ready for the new prophet. Most Bābīs, however, favored Bahā' Ullāh and in 1867 a new religion, the BAHĀ'Ī FAITH, developed.

The Azalīs, located now almost exclusively in Iran, have retained the original teachings of the Bāb's *Bayān* ("Revelation") and supplemented them with the instructions of Ṣobḥ-e Azal. The group has remained considerably smaller than the Bahā'īs and may number no more than a few thousand members.

AZAZEL \ə-'zā-zəl, 'a-zə-,zel\, in Jewish myth, a DEMON or evil spirit to whom, in the ancient rite of YOM KIPPUR (Day of Atonement), a SCAPEGOAT was sent bearing the SINS of the Jewish people. The ritual was carried out by the HIGH PRIEST in the Second Temple and is described in the MISHNAH. Two male goats were chosen for the ritual, one designated by lots "for the Lord," the other "for Azazel" (Leviticus 16:8). After the priest symbolically transferred all the sins of the Jewish people to the scapegoat, the goat destined "for Azazel" was driven into the wilderness and cast over a precipice to its death. Azazel was the personification of uncleanness and later was sometimes described as a fallen ANGEL.

AZHAR UNIVERSITY, AL- \ȧl-'ȧz-hȧr\, chief center of SUNNI Islamic learning in the world, centered on the mosque of that name in the medieval quarter of Cairo, Egypt. It was founded by the Fāṭimids in 970 CE and was formally organized by 988. The basic program of studies

Al-Azhar Mosque (domed building on the right), with adjoining buildings of al-Azhar University
Robert Frerck—Odyssey Productions

was, and still is, Qur'anic EXEGESIS, Islamic law, theology, and the Arabic language. Nineteenth- and twentieth-century efforts at modernization have resulted in the addition of medicine, science, engineering, agriculture, philosophy, and social sciences to the curriculum, now taught at its new supplementary campus at Naṣr City.

Al-Azhar attracts students from as far as China, Indonesia, Morocco, and Somalia. Women have been admitted since 1962 to a separate college in the university. Azharī SHAYKHS comprise the voice of "official ISLAM" in Egypt today through their publications, sermons, and broadcasts on radio and television.

AZTEC RELIGIONS: *see* PRE-COLUMBIAN MESO-AMERICAN RELIGIONS.

BA \\'bä\\, in ancient EGYPTIAN RELIGION, with KA and AKH, a principal aspect of the soul; it appears in bird form, expressing the mobility of the soul after death. Originally written with the sign of the jabiru bird, and thought to be an attribute of only the god-king, the *ba* was later represented by a man-headed hawk, often depicted hovering over the mummies of king and populace alike. Graves frequently had narrow passages for visitation by the *ba*.

BAAL \\'bāl, 'bäl\\, god worshiped in many ancient Middle Eastern communities, especially among the Canaanites, who apparently considered him a fertility deity and one of the most important gods in the pantheon. As a Semitic common noun *baal* (Hebrew *ba'al*) meant "owner" or "lord." Thus, "Baal" designated the universal god of fertility, and in that capacity his title was Prince, Lord of the Earth. He was also called the Lord of Rain and Dew, the two forms of moisture that were indispensable for fertile soil in CANAAN. In Ugaritic and OLD TESTAMENT Hebrew, Baal's epithet as the storm god was He Who Rides on the Clouds. In Phoenicia he was called Baal Shamen, Lord of the Heavens.

Knowledge of Baal's characteristics and functions derives chiefly from a number of tablets uncovered from 1929 onward at UGARIT (modern Ras Shamra), in northern Syria, and dating to the middle of the 2nd millennium BCE. In the mythology of Canaan, Baal, the god of life and fertility, was locked in mortal combat with MOT, the god of death and sterility. If Baal triumphed, a seven-year cycle of fertility would ensue; but, if he were vanquished by Mot, seven years of drought and famine would ensue. Ugaritic texts tell of other fertility aspects of Baal, such as his relations with ANATH, his consort and sister, and also his siring a divine bull calf from a heifer.

But Baal was not exclusively a fertility god. He was also king of the gods, having seized the divine kingship from YAMM, the sea god.

The myths also tell of Baal's struggle to obtain a palace comparable in grandeur to those of other gods. Baal persuaded ASHERAH to intercede with her husband EL, the head of the pantheon, to authorize the construction of a palace. The god of arts and crafts, KOTHAR, then built for Baal the most beautiful of palaces, spread over an area of 10,000 acres. The myth may refer in part to the construction of Baal's own temple in the city of Ugarit. Near Baal's temple was that of Dagon, given in the tablets as Baal's father.

The worship of Baal was popular in Egypt from the later New Kingdom in about 1400 BCE to its end (1075 BCE). Through the influence of the Aramaeans, who borrowed the Babylonian pronunciation BEL, the god ultimately became known as the Greek Belos, identified with ZEUS.

Baal was also worshiped by various communities as a local god. The Old Testament speaks frequently of the Baal of a given place or refers to Baalim in the plural, suggesting local deities, or "lords," of various locales. It is not known to

what extent the Canaanites considered those various Baalim identical, but the Baal of Ugarit does not seem to have confined his activities to one city, and doubtless other communities agreed in giving him cosmic scope.

For the early Hebrews, "Baal" designated the Lord of Israel, just as "Baal" farther north designated the Lord of Lebanon or of Ugarit. What later made the very name Baal anathema to the Israelites was the program of JEZEBEL, in the 9th century BCE, to introduce into Israel her Phoenician cult of Baal in opposition to the official worship of YAHWEH (1 Kings 18). By the time of the prophet HOSEA (mid-8th century BCE) the antagonism to Baalism was so strong that the use of the term Baal was often replaced by the contemptuous *boshet* ("shame"); in compound proper names, for example, ISHBOSHETH replaced the earlier Ishbaal.

BAALAT \\'bā-ə-,lat\\, *also spelled* Ba'alat, *or* Ba'alath (from West Semitic: *ba'alat*, "lady"), common synonym for the special goddess of a region; also, the chief deity of Byblos. Very little is known of Baalat, "the Lady [of Byblos]," but because of the close ties between Byblos and Egypt, she was often represented with a typically Egyptian hairstyle, headdress, and costume, and by the 12th dynasty (1991–1786 BCE) she was equated with the Egyptian goddess HATHOR. To the Greeks Baalat was a form of the goddess ASTARTE.

BA'AL SHEM \\'bäl-'shem\\, *also spelled* baalshem (Hebrew: "master of the name"), *plural* ba'ale shem, in JUDAISM, title bestowed upon men who reputedly worked wonders and effected cures through secret knowledge of the ineffable names of God. During the 17th and 18th centuries, there appears to have been a proliferation of wonder-workers, *ba'ale shem*, in eastern Europe. Traveling the countryside, these men were said to perform cures by means of herbs, folk remedies, and the TETRAGRAMMATON (four Hebrew letters signifying the ineffable name of God). They also inscribed AMULETS with the names of God to assist in their cures and were reported to be especially efficacious in exorcising DEMONS. Because the *ba'ale shem* combined FAITH HEALING with practical QABBALAH (use of sacred formulas and amulets), they frequently clashed with physicians and were constantly ridiculed both by rabbinic authorities and by followers of the Jewish Enlightenment (HASKALAH).

Preeminent among the *ba'ale shem* was Israel ben Eliezer (d. 1760), commonly called BA'AL SHEM ṬOV (or simply the Besht), founder of the social and religious movement known as HASIDISM.

BA'AL SHEM ṬOV \\'bäl-'shem-'tōv\\ (Hebrew: "Master of the Good Name"), *byname of* Israel ben Eliezer, *acronym* Beshṭ \\'besht\\ (b. *c.* 1700, probably Tluste, Podolia, Pol.—d. 1760, Medzhibozh), in JUDAISM, charismatic founder (*c.* 1750) of HASIDISM. He was responsible for divesting QABBAL-

Ba above a dead man, from the Egyptian Book of the Dead

AH of the rigid ASCETICISM imposed on it by ISAAC BEN SO-LOMON LURIA in the 16th century.

As a young orphan the Besht held various semi-menial posts connected with SYNAGOGUES and Hebrew elementary religious schools. Later he retired to the Carpathian Mountains to engage in mystical speculation, meanwhile eking out his living as a lime digger. His reputation as a healer, or BA'AL SHEM, who worked wonders by means of herbs, talismans, and AMULETS inscribed with the divine name, began to spread. He later became an innkeeper and a ritual slaughterer and, about 1736, settled in the village of Medzhibozh, in Podolia (Poland). From this time until his death, he devoted himself almost entirely to spiritual pursuits.

The Besht made a deep impression on his fellow Jews by going to the marketplace to converse with simple people and by dressing like them. Such conduct by a holy man was fiercely condemned in some quarters but enthusiastically applauded in others. The Besht placed great value on this type of spiritual ministration.

While still a young man, the Besht had become acquainted with such figures as Rabbi Naḥman of Gorodënka and Rabbi Naḥman of Kosov, already spoken of as creators of a new life, and with them he regularly celebrated the ritual of the three SABBATH meals. In time it became customary for them to deliver pious homilies and discourses after the third meal, and the Besht took his turn along with the others. Many of these discourses were later recorded and have been preserved as the core of Hasidic literature. When the Besht's spiritual powers were put to a test by other members of the group, he reportedly recognized a mezuzah (a small parchment inscribed with scriptural verses) as ritually "unfit" by means of his clairvoyant powers.

The Besht gradually renounced the strict asceticism of his companions, hoping instead to "prevail upon men to live by the light of these three things: love of God, love of Israel, and love of TORAH." His teaching centered on three main points: communion with God; service in ordinary bodily existence, proclaiming that every human deed done "for the sake of heaven" (even stitching shoes and eating) was equal in value to observing formal commandments; and rescue of the "sparks" of divinity that, according to the Qabbalah, were trapped in the material world.

A letter attributed to, but not signed by, the Besht affirms that the author made "the ascent of the soul," met the MESSIAH in heaven, and asked him when he would come. The answer he received was: "When your well-springs shall overflow far and wide"—meaning that the Besht had first to spread the teaching of Hasidism. According to one view, the story indicates that the advent was central in the Besht's belief; according to another, it effectively removes messianic redemption from central concern in the life that must be lived here and now.

During his lifetime, the Besht brought about a great social and religious upheaval. In an atmosphere marked by new rituals and religious ECSTASY, he created a new spiritual climate in small houses of prayer outside the synagogues. The changes were further emphasized by the wearing of distinctive garb and the telling of stories. Though the Besht never visited Israel and left no writings, by the time he died, he had given to Judaism a new religious dimension in Hasidism that continues to flourish.

BĀB, THE \'bȧb\, *byname* of Mīrzā 'Alī Muhammad of Shiraz \mēr-'zȧ-a-'lē-mō-'ham-ˌmad . . . shē-'rȧz\ (b. Oct. 20, 1819, or Oct. 9, 1820, Shiraz, Iran—d. July 9, 1850, Tabriz), merchant's son whose claim to be the Bāb (Arabic: "Gateway") to the hidden IMAM (the perfect embodiment of Islamic faith) gave rise to BĀBISM and made him one of the central figures of the BAHĀ'Ī FAITH.

At an early age 'Alī Muhammad became familiar with the Shaykhī school of the SHI'ITE branch of ISLAM and with its leader, Sayyid Kāzim Rashtī, whom he met on a PILGRIMAGE. 'Alī Muhammad borrowed heavily from the Shaykhīs' teaching in formulating his own doctrine, and they, especially Sayyid Kāzim's disciple Mullā Ḥusayn, seem to have encouraged his proclamation of himself as the Bāb. Traditionally, the Bāb had been considered to be a spokesman for the 12th and last imam, or leader of Shi'ite Islam, believed to be in hiding since the 9th century; since that time,

Statuette of Baalat

others had assumed the title of Bāb. Such a proclamation fit in well with the Shaykhīs' interest in the coming of the MAHDĪ, or messianic deliverer.

On May 23, 1844, 'Alī Muhammad wrote and simultaneously intoned a commentary, the *Qayyūm al-asmā'*, on the SŪRA ("chapter") of Joseph from the QUR'AN. This event prompted 'Alī Muhammad, supported by Mullā Ḥusayn, to declare himself the Bāb. The same year he assembled 18 disciples, who along with him added up to the sacred Bābī number 19, and were called *ḥurūf al-ḥayy* ("letters of the living"). They became apostles of the new faith in the various Persian provinces.

Late in his active period, 'Alī Muhammad abandoned the title Bāb and considered himself no longer merely the "gateway" to the expected 12th imam (*imām mahdī*), but the imam himself, or the *qā'im*. Later he declared himself the *nuqṭah* ("point") and finally an actual divine manifestation. Among his followers, Bābīs and later AZALĪS, he is known as *noqṭey-e ūlā* ("primal point"), *ḥazrat-e a'lā* ("supreme presence"), *jamāl-e mobārak* ("blessed perfection"), and even *ḥaqq ta'ālā* ("truth almighty"). The Bahā'īs acknowledge him as a forerunner of Bahā' Ullāh—the founder of the Bahā'ī faith—but they do not use any of his titles except Bāb.

The six-year career of the Bāb was marked by a struggle for official recognition and by a series of imprisonments. He was suspected of fomenting insurrection, and some of his followers engaged in bloody uprisings. He had to do battle with the *mujtahid*s and mullahs, who were unreceptive to the idea of a Bāb who would supersede their authority and provide another avenue to the Truth. His missionaries were arrested and expelled from Shiraz, and the Bāb was arrested near Tehran and imprisoned in the fortress of Māhkū (1847) and later in the castle of Chehrīq (1848), where he remained until his execution. Assembling at the convention of Badasht in 1848, the Bāb's followers declared a formal break with Islam.

A committee of *mujtahid*s decided he was dangerous to the existing order and demanded his execution. On the first volley from the firing squad he escaped injury; only the ropes binding him were severed, a circumstance that was interpreted as a divine sign. On the second volley he was killed and his body disposed of in a ditch. Several years later it was buried by the Bahā'īs in a mausoleum on Mt. Carmel, in Palestine.

The Bāb wrote much, not only in his native Persian but also in Arabic. Among the most important are the Arabic and the longer Persian versions of his *Bayān*. Although these are the holy books of Bābī revelation, all the writings of the Bāb and his successors are considered divinely inspired and equally binding. *See also* AHSĀ'Ī, AḤMAD AL-.

BABA-YAGA \ˌbä-bä-ˈyä-gä\, *also called* Baba-Jaga, in Russian FOLKLORE, an ogress who steals, cooks, and eats her victims, usually children. A guardian of the fountains of the water of life, she lives with two or three sisters (all known as Baba-Yaga) in a forest hut which spins continually on birds' legs; her fence is topped with human skulls. Baba-Yaga can fly—in an iron kettle or in a mortar that she drives with a pestle—creating tempests as she goes. She often accompanies Death on his travels, devouring newly released souls.

BABEL, TOWER OF \ˈbā-bəl, ˈba-\, in biblical literature, structure built in the land of Shinar (Babylonia) some time after the Flood. The story of its construction, given in GENESIS 11:1–9, appears to be an attempt to explain the existence of diverse human languages. According to Genesis, the Babylonians wanted to build a mighty city and a tower "with its top in the heavens." God disrupted the work by so confusing the language of the workers that they could no longer understand one another. The city was never completed, and the people were dispersed over the face of the earth. The myth may have been inspired by the Babylonian tower temple north of the MARDUK temple, which in Babylonian was called Bab-ilu ("Gate of God"), Hebrew form Babel, or Bavel. The similarity in pronunciation of Babel and *balal* ("to confuse") led to the play on words in Genesis 11:9: "Therefore its name was called Babel, because there the Lord confused the language of all the earth."

The Tower of Babel, *oil painting by Pieter Bruegel the Elder, 1563*
By courtesy of the Kunsthistorisches Museum, Vienna

BĀBISM \ˈbä-ˌbi-zəm\, religion that developed in Iran around Mīrzā 'Alī Muhammad, who claimed to be a *bāb* (Arabic: "gateway"), or divine intermediary, in 1844.

Its beliefs are set forth in the *Bayān* ("Exposition"), a holy book written by the BĀB that promotes a universal law in place of all existing religious legal codes. Babīs, followers of the Bāb, prefer to call themselves *ahl al-Bayān* ("People of the *Bayān*"). Although some of Bābism's provisions were milder than the SHARĪʿA, particularly in regard to the status of women, it permitted both offensive and defensive JIHAD as a means for propagating itself. It originated as a messianic movement in Twelver Shiʿism (*see* ITHNĀ ʿASHARĪYA), and after violent suppression by Iranian ʿULAMĀʾ and forces of the state in the 1840s, it gave way to the BAHĀʾĪ FAITH, which holds ʿAlī Muhammad to be the "Gateway" to BAHĀʾ ULLĀH. *See also* MESSIANISM.

BABYLONIAN EXILE, *also called* Babylonian Captivity, the forced detention of Jews in Babylonia following the latter's conquest of the kingdom of JUDAH in 598/7 and 587/6 BCE. Not all the Jews were forced to leave Palestine; Jews left Babylonia to return to Palestine at various times; and some Jews chose to remain in Babylonia—this latter group constituting the first of numerous Jewish communities living permanently in the Diaspora.

The first deportation may have been in 597 BCE, when King JEHOIACHIN was deposed and apparently sent into exile with his family, his court, and thousands of workers, or it may have followed the destruction of Jerusalem by Nebuchadrezzar II in 586; if so, the Jews were held in Babylonian captivity for 48 years. The exile formally ended in 538 BCE, when the Persian conqueror of Babylonia, Cyrus the Great, gave the Jews permission to return to Palestine. Among those who accept a tradition (Jeremiah 29:10) that the exile lasted 70 years, some choose the dates 608 to 538, others 586 to about 516 (the year when the rebuilt Temple was dedicated in Jerusalem). *See* JERUSALEM, TEMPLE OF.

Although the Jews suffered greatly and faced powerful cultural pressures in a foreign land, they maintained their national spirit and religious identity. Elders supervised the Jewish communities, and EZEKIEL was one of several prophets who kept alive the hope of one day returning home. This was possibly also the period when SYNAGOGUES were first established, for the Jews observed the SABBATH and religious holidays, practiced CIRCUMCISION, and substituted prayers for former ritual sacrifices in the Temple.

BABYLONIAN TALMUD \täl-ʾmüd; ʾtäl-ˌmu̇d, ʾtal-məd\: *see* BAVLI.

BACAB \bä-ʾkäb\, in Mayan mythology, any of four divine brothers (or four manifestations of a single deity), who supported the multilayered sky from their assigned positions at the four cardinal points of the compass. They were probably the offspring of ITZAMNÁ (the supreme deity) and IXCHEL (the goddess of weaving, medicine, and childbirth). Each Bacab presided over one year of the four-year cycle. The four directions and their corresponding colors (east, red; north, white; west, black; south, yellow) played an important part in the Mayan religious and calendrical systems. *See also* PRE-COLUMBIAN MESO-AMERICAN RELIGIONS.

BACCHANALIA \ˌba-kə-ʾnāl-yə, ˌbä-\, *also called* Dionysia \ˌdī-ə-ʾni-zhē-ə, -ʾnē-, -shē-\, in Greco-Roman religion, any of the several festivals of Bacchus (DIONYSUS). The most famous of the Greek Dionysia were in Attica and included the Lesser Dionysia, characterized by simple rites; the Lenaea, which included a festal procession and dramatic performances; the ANTHESTERIA, which was essentially a drinking feast; the Greater Dionysia, accompanied by dramatic performances in the theater of Dionysus, which was the most famous of all; and the Oschophoria ("Carrying of the Grape Clusters").

The public Greek festivals were probably also celebrated in the Hellenic areas of lower Italy. A private, secret form of the Bacchanalia was introduced into Rome. According to the historian Livy the Bacchanalia were at first held in secret, attended by women only, on three days of the year. Later, admission was extended to men, and celebrations took place as often as five times a month. The reputation of these festivals as orgies led in 186 BCE to a decree of the Roman Senate that prohibited the Bacchanalia throughout Italy, except in certain special cases.

BACCHUS: *see* DIONYSUS.

BADB \ʾbīv, ʾbä̱thv\, Irish war goddess. *See* MACHA.

BADR, BATTLE OF \ʾbä-dər\ (624), first military victory of MUHAMMAD. It seriously damaged Meccan prestige, while strengthening the political position of Muslims in MEDINA and establishing ISLAM as a force to be reckoned with in the Arabian Peninsula.

Since their emigration from MECCA (622), the Muslims in Medina had depended on constant raids on Meccan caravans for economic survival. When word of a particularly wealthy caravan escorted by Abū Sufyān, head of the Umayyad clan, reached Muhammad, a raiding party of about 300 Muslims, to be led by Muhammad himself, was organized. By filling the wells on the caravan route near Medina with sand, the Muslims lured Abū Sufyān's army to battle at Badr, near Medina, in March 624. Despite the superior numbers of the Meccan forces (about 1,000 men), the Muslims scored a complete victory. The success at Badr was recorded in the QURʾAN as a divine sanction of the new religion: "It was not you who slew them, it was God . . . in order that He might test the Believers by a gracious trial from Himself" (8:17). Those Muslims who fought at Badr became known as the *badrīyūn* and make up one group of the COMPANIONS OF THE PROPHET.

BAECK, LEO \ʾbek\ (b. May 23, 1873, Lissa, Posen, Prussia [now Leszno, Pol.]—d. Nov. 2, 1956, London), RABBI in REFORM JUDAISM, theologian, the spiritual leader of German Jewry during the Nazi period, and the leading liberal Jewish religious thinker of his time.

Baeck studied for the rabbinate in Breslau and Berlin, received his Ph.D. in philosophy at the University of Berlin in 1895, and was ordained in 1897 by the progressive Hochschule in Berlin. He was one of the two rabbis within the German Rabbinical Association who refused to condemn the Zionist (*see* ZIONISM) leader THEODOR HERZL (1860–1904) and the First Zionist Congress then meeting in Basel. Baeck first served as rabbi in Oppeln, Silesia (1897–1907), then in Düsseldorf (1907–12), and finally Berlin (1912–42).

The Essence of Judaism (1905) established Baeck as the leading liberal Jewish theologian. Baeck stressed the dynamic nature of religion, the ongoing development that is man's response to the categorical "Ought," the Divine Imperative. The influence of the German-Jewish philosopher Hermann Cohen (1842–1918) and of Neo-Kantianism is visible, but behind it stands the ethical rigorism of traditional rabbinic thought. The next edition of this work (1922), greatly expanded, articulated his "religion of polarity" with its dialectical movement between the "mystery" of the divine presence in life and the "commandment" of the ethical imperative that comes in the encounter with God. Judaism was seen as the supreme expression of morality, a universal message expressed through the particular existence of Israel.

Traditional Jews disliked Baeck's early (1901) claim that JESUS was a profoundly Jewish figure and his view in *The Gospel as a Document of Jewish Religious History* (1938) that the Gospels belonged with the contemporary works of rabbinical literature. Christians, on the other hand, felt challenged by his definition of Judaism as the "classic" rational faith confronting a "romantic" CHRISTIANITY of emotion, in his essay "Romantic Religion" (1922). Baeck's final work, written in part while in a Nazi concentration camp, *This People Israel: The Meaning of Jewish Existence* (1955), moves from the essence of an "ism" to the concrete existence of a people and creates an approach to Jewish life that must be set alongside the thought of the great 20th-century Jewish religious philosophers MARTIN BUBER (1878–1965) and FRANZ ROSENZWEIG (1886–1929).

In 1933 the German Jewry organized into the Reichsvertretung der Juden in Deutschland (National Agency of Jews in Germany) under Baeck and Otto Hirsch (1885–1941). Millions of dollars were spent annually on emigration, economic help, charity, education, and culture. Meanwhile, at the conference table with the Nazis, Baeck and the others battled for time so that lives could be saved. The group expected that Jews would survive Hitler behind ghetto and prison walls—a tragic error of judgment, but extermination camps were as yet inconceivable. In both public and private, Baeck's life was a pattern of moral resistance that, after five arrests, brought him to the Theresienstadt (Terezín) concentration camp. Baeck set up classes inside the camp, lecturing on Plato and Kant in a small barracks. This, too, was a way of resistance. There were also Christian inmates to whom Baeck served as pastor.

On May 8, 1945, the day before Baeck was to be executed, the Russians liberated Theresienstadt, and Baeck stopped the inmates from killing the guards. He settled in England and taught and lectured in Britain and the United States, including a term at Hebrew Union College in Cincinnati, Ohio. His final writings, notably *Individuum Ineffabile* (1948) and *This People Israel*, continued to express hope in humanity and the human situation as the area of the revelation.

BAETYLUS \'bē-tə-ləs, -tyə-\, *also spelled* baetulus, in GREEK RELIGION, a sacred stone or pillar. Numerous holy stones existed in antiquity, generally attached to the cult of some particular god and looked upon as his abiding place or symbol. The most famous example is the holy stone at DELPHI, the Omphalos ("navel"), that reposed in the Temple of APOLLO there and supposedly marked the exact center of the earth. A second stone at Delphi was said to have been the

An example of a baetylus, the Omphalos at Delphi, ancient marble copy of an original now lost; in the Archaeological Museum, Delphi, Greece
Alinari—Art Resource

one that CRONUS, the TITAN, swallowed; it was thought to be ZEUS himself in his symbolic, or baetylic, form.

Sometimes the stones were formed into pillars or into groups of three pillars. Such columns were sometimes placed before a shrine; others were used as mileposts and often shaped into human form. The baetylus became the parent form for altars and iconic statuary.

BAHĀ'Ī FAITH \bä-'hī, bə-\, religion founded in Iran in the mid-19th century by Mīrzā Ḥoseyn 'Alī Nūrī, who is known as BAHĀ' ULLĀH (Arabic: "Glory of God"). The cornerstone of Bahā'ī belief is the conviction that Bahā' Ullāh and his forerunner, who was known as the BĀB, were manifestations of God, who in his essence is unknowable. Bahā'īs believe that all the founders of the world's great religions have been manifestations of God and agents of a progressive divine plan for the education of the human race. Bahā' Ullāh's peculiar function was to overcome the disunity of religions and establish a universal faith. Bahā'īs believe in the oneness of humanity and devote themselves to the abolition of racial, class, and religious prejudices. Bahā'ī teaching is chiefly concerned with social ethics; the religion has no PRIESTHOOD and observes no formal SACRAMENTS in its worship.

The Bahā'ī religion originally grew out of BĀBISM, which was founded in 1844 by Mīrzā 'Alī Muhammad of Shīrāz in Iran. He predicted the appearance of a new prophet or messenger of God who would overturn old beliefs and customs and usher in a new era; these beliefs originated within the SHI'ITE sect of ISLAM, which believed in the forthcoming return of the 12th IMAM (successor of MUHAMMAD), who would renew religion and guide the faithful. Mīrzā 'Alī Muhammad assumed the title of the Bāb (Arabic: "Gateway"), and soon his teachings spread throughout Iran, provoking strong opposition from both the Shi'ite authorities and the government. The Bāb was arrested, incarcerated, and executed in 1850. Large-scale persecutions of his adherents, the Bābīs, followed and ultimately cost 20,000 lives.

One of the Bāb's earliest disciples and strongest exponents was Mīrzā Ḥoseyn 'Alī Nūrī, who had assumed the name of Bahā' Ullāh. Bahā' Ullāh was arrested in 1852 and jailed in Tehrān, Iran. He was released in 1853 and exiled to Baghdad, where his leadership revived the Bābī community. In 1863, shortly before being moved by the Ottoman government to Constantinople, Bahā' Ullāh declared that he was the messenger of God foretold by the Bāb. An overwhelming majority of Bābīs acknowledged his claim and thenceforth became known as Bahā'īs. Bahā' Ullāh was subsequently confined by the Ottomans in Adrianople (now Edirne, Turkey) and then in Acre in Palestine (now 'Akko, Israel). Before Bahā' Ullāh died in 1892, he appointed his eldest son, 'Abd ol-Bahā (1844–1921), to be the leader of the Bahā'ī community and the authorized interpreter of his teachings. 'Abd ol-Bahā actively administered the movement's affairs and spread Bahā'ism to North America, Europe, and other continents. He appointed his eldest grandson, SHOGHI EFFENDI RABBĀNĪ (1897–1957), as his successor. The Bahā'ī faith underwent a rapid expansion beginning in the 1960s, and by the late 20th century it had a worldwide representation comprised of more than 150 national spiritual assemblies (national governing bodies) and about 20,000 local spiritual assemblies. After an Islamic revolutionary government came to power in Iran in 1979, the 300,000 Iranian Bahā'īs there again fell victim to state-sanctioned persecution.

The writings and spoken words of the Bāb, Bahā' Ullāh, and 'Abd ol-Bahā form the SCRIPTURES of the Bahā'ī faith. Membership in the Bahā'ī community is open to all who profess faith in Bahā' Ullāh and accept his teachings. Every Bahā'ī is under the obligation to pray daily; to abstain from narcotics, alcohol, or any substances that affect the mind; to practice monogamy; to obtain the consent of parents to marriage; and to attend the Nineteen Day Feast on the first day of each month of the Bahā'ī calendar. If capable, those between the ages of 15 and 70 are required to fast from sunrise to sunset for 19 days each year. The Nineteen Day Feast, originally instituted by the Bāb, brings together the Bahā'īs of a given locality for prayer and the reading of scriptures. The feasts are designed to ensure universal participation in the affairs of the community and the cultivation of the spirit of brotherhood and fellowship. In Bahā'ī temples there is no preaching; services consist of recitation of the scriptures of all religions.

The Bahā'īs use a calendar established by the Bāb and confirmed by Bahā' Ullāh, in which the year is divided into 19 months of 19 days each, with the addition of 4 intercalary days (5 in leap years). The year begins on the first day of spring, March 21, which is one of several holy days in the Bahā'ī calendar.

The governance of the Bahā'ī community begins on the local level with the election of a local SPIRITUAL ASSEMBLY. The local assembly has jurisdiction over all affairs of the Bahā'ī community. Each year Bahā'īs elect delegates to a national convention that elects a national spiritual assembly with jurisdiction over Bahā'īs throughout an entire country. Periodically an international convention of national spiritual assemblies elects a supreme governing body known as the Universal House of Justice, which was established in 1963. This body applies the laws promulgated by Bahā' Ullāh and legislates on matters not covered in the sacred texts. The seat of the Universal House of Justice is in Haifa, Israel, in the immediate vicinity of the shrines of the Bāb and 'Abd ol-Bahā, and near the shrine of Bahā' Ullāh at Bahjī near 'Akko.

There are also appointive institutions, such as the continental counselors and, at one time, the Hands of the Cause of God. The original members of the Hands of the Cause of God were appointed by Bahā' Ullāh and then by Shoghi Effendi. In 1973 the functions of the Hands of the Cause were taken over by the International Teaching Center. This group and the continental counselors are both appointed by the Universal House of Justice.

BAHĀ' ULLĀH \bə-'hä-ùl-'lä\, *also spelled* Bahā' Allāh \bə-'hä-al-'lä\ (Arabic: "Splendor of God"), *original name (Persian)* Mīrzā Ḥoseyn 'Alī Nūrī, (b. Nov. 12, 1817, Tehran, Iran—d. May 29, 1892, Acre, Palestine [now 'Akko, Israel]), founder of the BAHĀ'Ī FAITH; he claimed to be the manifestation of the unknowable God.

Mīrzā Ḥoseyn was a member of the SHIʿITE branch of ISLAM. He subsequently allied himself with Mīrzā 'Alī Mu-

hammad of Shīrāz, who was known as the BĀB (Arabic: "Gateway") and was the head of the Bābīs, a Muslim sect professing a privileged access to final truth. After the Bāb's execution by the Iranian government for treason (1850), Mīrzā Ḥoseyn joined Mīrzā Yaḥyā (also called Ṣobḥ-e Azal), his own half brother and the Bāb's spiritual heir, in directing the Bābī movement. Mīrzā Yaḥyā later was discredited, and Mīrzā Ḥoseyn was exiled by orthodox SUNNI Muslims successively to Baghdad, Kurdistan, and Constantinople (Istanbul). There, in 1867, he publicly declared himself to be the divinely chosen *imām* MAHDĪ ("rightly guided leader"), whom the Bāb had foretold. The resulting factional violence caused the Ottoman government to banish Mīrzā Ḥoseyn to Acre.

At Acre, Bahā' Ullāh, as he was by then called, developed the formerly provincial Bahā'ī doctrine into a comprehensive teaching that advocated the unity of all religions and the universal brotherhood of man. Emphasizing social ethics, he eschewed ritual worship and devoted himself to the abolition of racial, class, and religious prejudices. His place of confinement in Acre became a center of pilgrimage for Bahā'ī believers from Iran and the United States.

BAHINĀBĀĪ, BAHINI \bə-'hi-nä-'bä-ē\ (b. 1628 CE, Devago, in the Indian state of Maharashtra—d. 1700, Bahinābāī), poet-saint (*sant*), remembered as a composer of devotional songs (*abhangas*) in Marathi to the Hindu deity Viṭṭhal. Her work is preserved through oral performance (KĪRTAN), old handwritten manuscripts, and modern printed collections. Bahinābāī, in her autobiographical songs, describes herself as a devotee of another Marathi saint, TUKĀRĀM (1608–1649 CE), whom she met when her maternal family and her husband, a Brahmin astrologer, lived near Tukārām's village of Dehu. Bahinābāī (whose given name means "sister") records that her husband violently opposed her association with Tukārām because of Tukārām's low caste (ŚŪDRA). Her songs from this period describe her feeling of abandonment by her God and her struggle to perpetuate her faith; she also criticizes Brahmins who have lost their faith and, in a series of songs, defines a "Brahmin" as a person of good works and sincere devotion, regardless of caste. Though Bahinābāī's husband partially relented later, her contact with Tukārām occurred only in dreams, visions, and brief observances of his religious performances. Bahinābāī's verses both attack and defend a wife's duties (*strī-dharma*) in her community, exploring the struggle between those duties and her desire to follow Tukārām's spiritual example. Bahinābāī's songs suggest that she was very familiar with the BHAGAVAD GĪTĀ and UPANISHADS, as well as VEDĀNTA and SAMKHYĀ schools of thought, though she was most likely unable to read or to write. The transcription of her verses into old handwritten manuscripts is said to have begun with her son, Viṭhobā, who wrote them down from memory after her death.

BAHYA BEN JOSEPH IBN PAKUDA \'bà-yä-ben-'jō-səf-,i-bən-pà-'kü-dä, -'jō-zəf-\ (fl. second half of the 11th century), *dayyan*—i.e., judge of a rabbinical court—in Muslim Spain and author of a highly influential work of ethical guidance.

Via the Islamic mystics (*see* SUFISM), Bahya was influenced by NEOPLATONISM as to the nature of God and the soul's quest for him. From the Islamic system of dialectical theology called KALAM he borrowed proofs for the existence of God. About 1080 Bahya wrote *Al-Hidāyah ilā-farā' id al-qulūb* ("Duties of the Heart"). Critical of his predecessors who had emphasized the "duties of the body," or obligatory outward actions such as religious ritual and ethical practice, Bahya looked to the "duties of the heart," the attitudes and intentions that determine the state of a person's soul and alone give value to one's acts. In an inaccurate 12th-century translation into Hebrew by JUDAH BEN SAUL IBN TIBBON, Ḥovot ha-levavot, it became a classic of Jewish philosophic and devotional literature. An English translation, *Duties of the Heart* (1925–47; reprinted 1962), was completed by Moses Hyamson.

BALAAM \'bā-ləm\, non-Israelite prophet described in the OLD TESTAMENT (Numbers 22–24) as a diviner who is urged by Balak, the king of Moab, to place a curse on the people of ISRAEL. Balaam states that he will utter only what his god YAHWEH inspires, but he is willing to accompany the MOABITE messengers to Balak. He is met en route by an ANGEL of Yahweh, who is recognized only by Balaam's ass, which refuses to continue. Then Balaam's eyes are opened, and the angel permits him to go to Balak but commands him not to curse but to bless Israel. Despite pressure from Balak, Balaam remains faithful to Yahweh and blesses the people of Israel. In later literature (the Second Letter of Peter 2:15), however, Balaam is held up as an example of one who apostasized for the sake of material gain. In RABBINIC JUDAISM, some RABBIS venerate Balaam as a prophet comparable to MOSES (Numbers Rabbah 20:1, Tanha, Balak 1; SIFRE TO DEUTERONOMY), while others remember him as evil, haughty, and proud (Avot 5:19) and cite him as the reason the HOLY SPIRIT departed from the GENTILES. There is conjecture that Balaam represents JESUS in Haggadic (*see* HALAKHAH AND HAGGADAH) literature.

BALARĀMA \,bə-lə-'rä-mə\, in Hindu mythology, elder half-brother of KRISHNA. Sometimes Balarāma is considered one of the 10 AVATARS (incarnations) of the god VISHNU, one of the "three RĀMAS" alongside Paraśurāma (Rāma with an axe) and Rāmacandra (hero of the RĀMĀYAṆA epic). Other legends identify him as the incarnation in human form of the serpent Śeṣa, and he may originally have been an agricultural deity. As early as the 2nd–1st century BCE he is depicted holding a plowshare and a pestle with a snake canopy above his head. In this early period he seems to appear in sculpture at least as frequently as Krishna himself. In paintings Balarāma is always shown with fair skin, in contrast to Krishna's blue complexion. The stories associated with him emphasize his love of wine and his enormous strength.

BALDER \'bȯl-dər, 'bäl-\, *Old Norse* Baldr, in Norse mythology (*see* GERMANIC RELIGION), the son of ODIN and FRIGG. Beautiful and just, he was the favorite of the gods. The Icelandic scholar Snorri (*c.* 1220) relates in his EDDA how the gods amused themselves by throwing objects at him, knowing that he was immune from harm. However, the blind god Höd, deceived by the evil LOKI, killed Balder by hurling mistletoe, the only thing that could hurt him. The giantess Thökk, probably Loki in disguise, refused to weep the tears that would release Balder from Hell.

Some scholars believe that the passive, suffering figure of Balder was influenced by that of Christ. The Danish historian Saxo Grammaticus (*c.* 1200), however, depicts him as a warrior engaged in a feud over the hand of a woman.

BALL GAME, in PRE-COLUMBIAN MESO-AMERICAN cultures, ceremonial contest, not unlike modern soccer. The object of the game was to propel a gutta-percha ball through the air without touching it with the hands; if it went through a

Mayan ball court from c. 775 CE, *in Copán, Honduras*
Imgard Groth

small hole in the carved stone disk, or hit that circular goal, the game was won. Tremendous exchanges of personal property resulted from such a victory—indeed, often life itself was forfeit in important contests. *See* TLACHTLI.

BALOR \'bȧ-lər\, in Celtic mythology, chief of the chaotic race of FOMOIRE—the demonic race that threatened the Irish people until they were subdued in the second great battle of MAG TUIRED (Moytura). When Balor was a boy, he looked into a potion being brewed by his father's DRUIDS, and the fumes caused him to grow a huge, poisonous eye. The eye had to be opened by attendants, and it killed anything on which it gazed. Balor was eventually killed by his grandson, the god LUGUS (Lugh), in the climactic battle between the TUATHA DÉ DANANN, or race of gods, and the Fomoire.

BALTIC RELIGION, beliefs and practices of the Balts, ancient inhabitants of the Baltic region of eastern Europe.

The study of Baltic religion has developed as an offshoot of the study of Baltic languages, in some respects the most conservative modern Indo-European language family. Just as these languages—Old Prussian, Latvian, and Lithuanian—correlate closely with the ancient Indian language Sanskrit, so does Baltic religion exhibit many features that conform to Vedic (ancient Indian) and Iranian ideas. Thus Baltic religious concepts help in the understanding of the formation and structure of the oldest phases of Indo-European religion.

The most important divinities in Baltic religion were the sky gods—DIEVS (the personified sky), PĒRKONS (the Thunderer), SAULE (the sun [female]), and MĒNESS (the moon [male]). A forest divinity, common to all Baltic peoples, is called in Latvian Meža māte and in Lithuanian Medeinė ("Mother of the Forest"). She again has been further differentiated into other divinities, or rather she was also given metaphorical appellations with no mythological significance, such as Krūmu māte ("Mother of the Bushes"), Lazdu māte ("Mother of the Hazels"), Lapu māte ("Mother of the Leaves"), Ziedu māte ("Mother of the Blossoms"), and even Sēṇu māte ("Mother of the Mushrooms"). Forest animals are ruled by the Lithuanian Žvėrinė opposed to the Latvian Meža māte. The safety and welfare of buildings is cared for by the Latvian Mājas gars ("Spirit of the House"; Lithuanian Kaukas), the Latvian Pirts māte ("Mother of the Bathhouse"), and additionally Rijas māte ("Mother of the Threshing House").

There are a large number of beautifully described lesser mythological beings whose functions are either very limited or completely denoted by their names. Water deities are Latvian Jūras māte ("Mother of the Sea"), Ūdens māte ("Mother of the Waters"), Upes māte ("Mother of the Rivers"), and Bangu māte ("Mother of the Waves"; Lithuanian Bangpūtys), while atmospheric deities are Latvian Vēja māte ("Mother of the Wind"), Lithuanian Vėjopatis ("Master of the Wind"), Latvian Lietus māte ("Mother of the Rain"), Miglas māte ("Mother of the Fog"), and Sniega māte ("Mother of the Snow"). Even greater is the number of beings related to human activities, whose names only are still to be found, for example Miega māte ("Mother of Sleep") and Tirgus māte ("Mother of the Market").

Also important was the goddess of destiny or luck, LAIMA. The real ruler of human fate, she is mentioned frequently together with Dievs in connection with the process of creation. Although Laima determines a man's unchangeable destiny at the moment of his birth, he can still lead his life well or badly within the limits prescribed by her. She also determines the moment of a person's death.

The Devil, VELNS (Lithuanian Velnias), has a well-defined role. He is commonly represented as stupid, and Baltic FOLKLORE often represents the Devil as a German landlord. Another evil being is the Latvian Vilkacis, Lithuanian Vilkatas, who corresponds to the werewolf in the traditions of other peoples. The belief that the dead do not leave this world completely is the basis for both good and evil spirits. As good spirits the dead return to the living as invisible beings (Latvian velis, Lithuanian vėlė), but as evil ones they return as persecutors and misleaders (Latvian vadātājs, Lithuanian vaidilas).

The primary themes of Baltic mythology as it survives in folklore are the structure of the world and the enmity between Saule and Mēness. The four-line folk songs called dainas, which resemble Vedic verses, portray the world in dualistic terms, mentioning šī saule (literally "this sun"; metaphorically ordinary everyday human life) and viņa saule (literally "the other sun"; metaphorically the invisible world where the sun goes at night, which is also the abode of the dead). The notion of a sun tree, or WORLD TREE, is one of the most important cosmic concepts. This tree grows at the edge of the path of Saule, who in setting hangs her belt on the tree in preparation for rest. It is usually considered to be an oak but is also described as a linden or other kind of tree. The tree is said to be located in the middle of the world ocean or generally to the west.

Excavations have revealed circular wooden temples, approximately 15 feet in diameter, and a statue of a god may have been erected in the center. The existence of open-air holy places or sites of worship among the Balts is confirmed by both the earliest historical documents and folklore. Such places were holy groves, called ALKA in Lithuanian. Later the word came to mean any holy place or site of worship (Lithuanian alkvietė). The usual sites were little hills, where the populace gathered and sacrificed during holy festivals. Another important ritual site was the bathhouse, in which birth ceremonies and funerals were performed. Various places in the home were considered to be abodes of spirits, and each work site had its GUARDIAN SPIRIT, to whom sacrifices were offered.

Special rites evolved for the festivals of the summer solstice and the harvest and for beginning various kinds of spring work. Such spring work included sending farm animals to pasture or horses to forage for the first time, plowing the first furrow, and starting the first spring planting. The birth of a child was especially noted. Laima was responsible for both mother and child. One birth rite, called pirtīžas, was a special sacral meal in which only women took part. Marriage rites were quite extensive and corresponded closely to similar Old Indian ceremonies. Fire and bread had special importance and were taken along to the house of the newly married couple.

BANARAS: *see* VARANASI.

BANĀRSĪDĀS \bə-ˌnär-sē-ˈdäs\ (b. 1586—d. 1643), Jain mystic and poet (*see* JAINISM) who is credited with writing one of the first autobiographies in India, his *Ardhakathānaka*, or "Half a Tale." It is invaluable for information on daily life in urban north India during Mughal times.

Banārsīdās was born into a family of ŚVETĀMBARA Jain merchants in Agra. As a youth he was a libertine and an author of erotic Hindi verses. At age 19 he underwent a change, eventually becoming a wealthy merchant who followed all the forms of ritual and personal conduct expected of a pious, upright Jain. At age 35 he underwent another change, this time rebelling against all outward ritual forms, which he came to see as empty of any spiritual meaning. He was drawn toward a group of laymen, of a generally DIGAMBARA leaning, known as Adhyātma ("Innermost Soul"), who engaged in study and discussion of spiritual matters. This group also rejected the authority of all monks. In this context he was introduced by a Digambara lay scholar to the 9th-century *Gommaṭasāra* of Nemicandra, which explained the 14-rung (GUṆASTHĀNA) path to liberation. This allowed Banārsīdās to re-accept image worship and other outward forms of ritual as lower stages on the spiritual ladder. He also encountered the *Samayasāra* of the 2nd–3rd century Digambara mystic KUNḌAKUNḌA, which explains a two-truth vision of reality as perceived from the worldly (*vyavahāra*) and absolute (*niścaya*) perspectives. Banārsīdās wrote a Hindi version of it. He became a leader of the Adhyātma movement. While the movement itself died out within a century of Banārsīdās, its principles live on in the Digambara Terāpantha, which is still an influential sect in north India.

BANDĀ SINGH BAHĀDUR \bən-ˈdä-ˈsiṅ-gə-ˈbə-hä-dər, -ˈsiṅ-bə-ˈhä-dùr\ (b. 1670, Pūnch, India—d. June 1716, Delhi), in SIKHISM, first military leader to wage an offensive war against the Mughal rulers of India, thereby temporarily extending Sikh territory. Information about Bandā Singh's early life is scant. In his early life, he became a Vaiṣṇava ascetic. In 1708, GURŪ GOBIND SINGH met him in Nānded, a town on the banks of the Godāvarī River in southern India, baptized him as a KHĀLSĀ Sikh, and named him Bandā Singh. The Gurū sent Bandā Singh to the Punjab with the specific directive that he organize the Sikhs. It was under his command that they captured Sirhind, the most powerful Mughal garrison between Delhi and Lahore, in 1710.

Bandā Singh established his capital in nearby Mukhlispur ("city of the purified"), created an official seal, and struck new coins. The inscriptions on the seal and the coins indicate that Bandā Singh regarded ultimate authority as being vested with God and the Gurūs. Some years later Mughal forces ousted Bandā Singh from the Sirhind area, chased his army into the Shivālik hills, and eventually captured him in the Gurdāspur area. Along with several hundred men, Bandā Singh was taken to Delhi, where he was executed.

His military achievements earned him the epithet Bahādur ("brave"), and emblazoned on the Sikh imagination that it was the prerogative of the Khālsā Sikh to rule the Punjab.

BANNĀ', ḤASAN AL- \'hȧ-sȧn-ȧl-bȧ-'na\ (b. 1906, Maḥmudīya, Egypt—d. February 1949, Cairo), Egyptian political and religious leader who established a new religious society, the MUSLIM BROTHERHOOD, and played a central role in Egyptian political and social affairs.

After attending the teaching school at Damanhūr, Ḥasan al-Bannā' enrolled at the Dār al-'Ulūm, a teacher-training school in Cairo, which also maintained a traditional religious and social outlook. He completed his training and in 1927 was assigned to teach Arabic in a primary school in the city of Ismailia (Al-Ismā'īlīya), near the Suez Canal, which was a focal point for the foreign economic and military occupation of Egypt. In March 1928, with six workers from a British camp labor force, he created the Society of Muslim Brothers (Arabic: al-Ikhwān al-Muslimūn), which aimed at a rejuvenation of ISLAM, the moral reform of Egyptian society, and the expulsion of the British from Egypt. By the advent of World War II the Muslim Brotherhood had become a potent element on the Egyptian scene, attracting significant numbers of students, civil servants, and urban laborers.

Many of the members came to view the Egyptian government as having betrayed the interests of Egyptian nationalism. Ḥasan al-Bannā' tried to maintain a tactical alliance with the government, but in the turmoil of the postwar years many elements of the society passed beyond his authority, and members were implicated in a number of assassinations, notably that of Prime Minister an-Nuqrāshī in December 1948. With the connivance of the government, Ḥasan al-Bannā' himself was assassinated in the following year.

BAPTISM, in CHRISTIANITY, the SACRAMENT of regeneration and initiation into the Christian church; the word derives from the Greek verb *baptō*, "I dip, immerse." According to a theme of ST. PAUL THE APOSTLE, probably influenced by Jewish belief in the CIRCUMCISION of adult proselytes, baptism is death to a former life and the emergence of a new person, signified by the conferring of a new name; it is the total annulment of the SINS of one's past, from which one emerges a totally innocent person. At baptism, one becomes a member of the church and is incorporated into the body of JESUS CHRIST. The forms and rituals of the various churches vary, but baptism almost invariably involves the use of water and the Trinitarian invocation, "I baptize you: In the name of the Father, and of the Son, and of the HOLY SPIRIT." The candidate may be wholly or partly immersed in water, the water may be poured over the head of the one baptized, or a

Baptism in the Cathedral of Oaxaca, Mexico
Kathy Sloane—Photo Researchers

few drops may be sprinkled or placed on the head.

Ritual immersion has traditionally played an important part in JUDAISM, as a symbol of purification (in the MIKVAH, a RITUAL BATH) or as a symbol of consecration (in rituals of conversion, accompanied by special prayers). It was particularly significant in the rites of the ESSENES. According to the Gospels, ST. JOHN THE BAPTIST baptized Jesus Christ. Although there is no actual account of the institution of baptism by Jesus, the Gospel According to Matthew portrays the risen Christ issuing the "Great Commission" to his followers: "Go therefore and make disciples of all nations, baptizing them in the name of the Father and of the Son and of the Holy Spirit, teaching them to observe all that I have commanded you." Elsewhere in the NEW TESTAMENT, however, this formula is not used. Some scholars thus suggest that the quotation in Matthew reflects a tradition formed by a merging of the idea of spiritual baptism (as in Acts 1:5), early baptismal rites (as in Acts 8:16), and reports of PENTECOSTALISM after such rites (as in Acts 19:5–6).

Baptism occupied a place of great importance in the Christian community of the 1st century, but scholars disagree over whether it was to be regarded as essential to the new birth and to membership in the KINGDOM OF GOD or only as an external sign or symbol of inner regeneration. By the 2nd century, the irreducible minimum for a valid baptism appears to have been the use of water and the invocation of the TRINITY. Usually the candidate was immersed three times, but there are references to pouring as well. Most of those baptized in the early church were converts from Greco-Roman religions and therefore were adults.

In Catholicism, baptism is normally conferred by a priest, but the church accepts the baptism conferred by anyone having the use of reason "with the intention of doing what the church does." As the sacrament of rebirth it cannot be repeated. (In ROMAN CATHOLICISM, baptism is conducted conditionally in case of doubt of the fact of baptism or the use of the proper rite.)

Two points of controversy still exist in modern times. One is baptism by pouring rather than immersion, even though immersion was probably the biblical and early Christian rite. The second is the baptism of infants. There is no certain evidence of this earlier than the 3rd century, and the ancient baptismal liturgies are all intended for adults. The liturgy and the instructions clearly assume an adult who accepts the rite; without this decision the sacrament cannot be received. The Roman Catholic church accepts this principle by introducing adults (GODPARENTS), who make the decision for the infant at the commission of the parents. It is expected that the children will accept the decision made for them and will thus supply the adult decision that was presumed.

During the REFORMATION the Lutherans, Reformed, and Anglicans accepted the Catholic attitude toward infant baptism. Baptism was, however, one of the most dramatic points differentiating radical reformers (such as the ANABAPTISTS) from the rest of PROTESTANTISM. Michael Sattler (c. 1500–27), MENNO SIMONS, and Balthasar Hubmaier (1485–1528) led the opposition to infant baptism.

In modern times the largest Christian groups that practice adult rather than infant baptism are the BAPTISTS and the Christian Church (DISCIPLES OF CHRIST).

BAPTIST, member of a group of Protestant Christians who share most of the basic beliefs of PROTESTANTISM but who hold as an article of faith that only believers should be baptized and that it must be done by immersion. The Baptists do not constitute a single church or denominational structure, but most of them adhere to a congregational form of church government.

Two groups of Baptists emerged in England during the PURITAN reform movement of the 17th century. While sharing the view that only believers should be baptized, the two groups differed with respect to the nature of the ATONEMENT of JESUS. Those who regarded the atonement as general (i.e., for all persons) came to be called General Baptists. Those who interpreted it as applying only to the particular body of the ELECT acquired the name Particular Baptists.

The General Baptists trace their beginnings to the Baptist church founded in London c. 1611 by THOMAS HELWYS and his followers. They had returned from Amsterdam, where they had gone because of religious persecution. While in Amsterdam, they adopted the beliefs of their original leader JOHN SMYTH, who, by studying the NEW TESTAMENT, decided that only believers should be baptized. Through the work of the original London congregation, other General Baptist congregations were formed and the movement spread. In doctrine they followed ARMINIANISM. In the late 17th and 18th centuries, the General Baptists declined in numbers and influence. Churches closed and many members gravitated toward UNITARIANISM. The General Baptists were continued by a new group organized in 1770, the New Connection General Baptists, who had been influenced by the Methodist revival led by JOHN WESLEY (see METHODISM).

Particular Baptists originated with a Baptist church established in 1638 by two groups who left an Independent church (i.e., churches not in communion with the Church of England) in London. Members of the new church believed that only believers (not infants) should be baptized. Doctrinally, they followed CALVINISM, which holds to the doctrine of a particular atonement, i.e., that Christ died only for the elect (see PREDESTINATION).

The Particular Baptists grew more rapidly than the General Baptists, but growth subsequently slowed as the Particular Baptists emphasized their doctrine of salvation only for the elect and did not work to gain new members. After 1750, however, they were influenced by the Methodist movement, and new interests in evangelism and MISSIONS brought about renewed growth. Through the leadership of William Carey, the English Baptist Missionary Society was organized in 1792, and Carey went to India as the society's first missionary. Baptists were influential in the religious and political life of Great Britain in the 19th century, but membership and influence declined after World War I.

Baptist origins in the United States can be traced to ROGER WILLIAMS, who established a Baptist church in Providence in 1639 after being banished by the Puritans from Massachusetts Bay. Williams soon left and leadership passed to John Clarke. Though Rhode Island remained a Baptist stronghold, the center of Baptist life in colonial America was Philadelphia.

Baptist growth was spurred by the GREAT AWAKENING of the mid-18th century. Increases were especially dramatic in the Southern colonies, where Shubael Stearns established a church at Sandy Creek, N.C., in 1755. From this center revivalistic preachers fanned out across the southern frontier, establishing a Baptist dominance in the region that persists to the present. The membership of revivalistic Baptists continued to grow rapidly in the 19th century, assisted by lay preachers and a congregational church government well adapted to frontier settings.

Baptists in the United States were not united in a national body until 1814, when an increasing interest in foreign missions necessitated a more centralized organization. The General Convention was soon torn apart, however, by dissension over slavery. A formal split occurred in 1845 when the Southern Baptist Convention was organized in Augusta, Ga., and was confirmed when the Northern Baptist Convention was organized in 1907. Southern Baptists and Northern Baptists (later American Baptists) developed distinct regional characteristics following the Civil War and still exhibit different tendencies in theology, ecumenical involvement, missionary activity, and worship.

African Baptist churches, now grouped primarily in two large conventions, constitute another major segment of Baptists in the United States. Organized by freed slaves after the Civil War, these churches have often served as the social and spiritual center of the African-American community. African-American Baptist churches and ministers, led by Martin Luther King, Jr., played a significant role in the Civil Rights movement of the 1960s. These churches and ministers continued as vital elements of organization through the 1980s, as was evident in the presidential candidacies (1984, 1988) of Jesse Jackson.

Baptists maintain that authority in matters of faith and practice rests, under Christ, with the local congregation of baptized believers. These local congregations are linked voluntarily into state, regional, and national organizations for cooperative endeavors such as missions, education, and philanthropy. The larger organizations, however, have no control over the local churches. The separation of CHURCH AND STATE has historically been a major tenet of Baptist doctrine. Baptist worship is centered around the exposition of the SCRIPTURES in a sermon. Extemporaneous prayer and hymn-singing are also characteristic.

Baptists in the 20th century have provided leadership for diverse theological movements, notably WALTER RAUSCHENBUSCH in the SOCIAL GOSPEL movement, Harry Emerson Fosdick and Shailer Mathews in American MODERNISM, and BILLY GRAHAM in contemporary Evangelicalism.

BARAITA \bə-'rī-tə\ (Hebrew: "Outside Teaching"), *plural* Baraitot \bə-,rī-'tōt\, any of the ancient ORAL TRADITIONS of Jewish religious law that were not included in the MISHNAH attributed to Tannaite authorities. The Baraitot, dispersed singly throughout the YERUSHALMI (Palestinian) and BAVLI (Babylonian) talmuds, are often recognizable by such introductory words as "it was taught" or "the RABBI taught." Since the Mishnah was selective and concisely phrased, Baraitot preserved oral traditions of Jewish law that might otherwise have been lost.

BARCLAY, ROBERT \'bär-klē, -klā\ (b. Dec. 23, 1648, Gordonstoun, Moray, Scot.—d. Oct. 3, 1690, Ury, Aberdeen), leader of the SOCIETY OF FRIENDS (Quakers) whose *Apology for the True Christian Divinity* (1678) became a standard statement of Quaker doctrines.

After returning to Scotland from his education in Paris, Barclay joined the Society of Friends in 1666. For a public debate at Aberdeen in 1675, he published *Theses Theologicae*, a set of 15 propositions of the Quaker faith. To amplify them further, he published the *Apology* three years later. This early and enduring exposition of Quaker beliefs defined Quakerism as a religion of the "inner light"—that light being the HOLY SPIRIT within the believer.

In 1677 Barclay and other Quaker leaders, including William Penn (1644–1718), visited Holland and northern Germany to promote the Quaker movement. Repeatedly imprisoned and persecuted at home, Barclay and Penn found a friend in James II, then duke of York. Their influence with him helped secure a patent for themselves and 10 other society members to settle in that area of present-day New Jersey, then called East Jersey. The group emigrated to America in 1682. After serving from 1682 to 1688 as nominal governor of East Jersey, Barclay returned to Scotland and died at his estate at Ury.

BARDESANES \,bär-də-'sā-nēz\, *also called* Bardaisan, *or* Bar Daiṣān \,bär-dī-'sän\ (b. July 11, 154, Edessa, Syria [now Urfa, Turkey]—d. c. 222, Edessa), a leading representative of Syrian GNOSTICISM. Bardesanes was a Christian missionary in Syria after his conversion in 179.

His chief writing, *The Dialogue of Destiny, or The Book of the Laws of the Countries*, recorded by a disciple, Philip, is the oldest known original composition in Syriac literature. Bardesanes attacked the fatalism of the Greek philosophers after Aristotle (4th century BCE), particularly regarding the influence of the stars on human destiny. Mingling Christian influence with Gnostic teaching, he denied the creation of the world, of SATAN, and of evil by the supreme God, attributing them to a hierarchy of deities.

Aided by his son Harmonius, Bardesanes wrote many of the first Syriac hymns to popularize his teachings. Their literary value earned for him renown in the history of Syriac poetry and music.

BAR KOKHBA \,bär-'kȯk-bä\, *original name* Simeon bar Kosba, Kosba *also spelled* Koseba, Kosiba, *or* Kochba (d. 135 CE), Jewish leader who led an unsuccessful revolt (132–135 CE) against Roman dominion in Palestine.

In 131 the Roman emperor Hadrian decided upon a policy of Hellenization to integrate the Jews into the empire. CIRCUMCISION was proscribed, a Roman colony (Aelia) was founded in Jerusalem, and a temple to JUPITER Capitolinus

was erected over the ruins of the TEMPLE OF JERUSALEM. The Jews rebelled in 132, Simeon bar Kosba at their head. He was reputedly of Davidic descent, and a 4th-century story alleges that he was hailed as the MESSIAH by the greatest RABBI of the time, AKIBA BEN JOSEPH, who gave him the title Bar Kokhba ("Son of the Star"), a messianic allusion. Bar Kokhba took the title *nasi* ("prince") and struck his own coins, with the legend "Year 1 of the liberty of Jerusalem."

The Jews took Aelia by storm and badly mauled the Romans' Egyptian Legion, XXII Deiotariana. In the summer of 134 Hadrian himself visited the battlefield and summoned the governor of Britain, Gaius Julius Severus, to his aid with 35,000 men of the Xth Legion. Jerusalem was retaken, and Severus gradually wore down and constricted the rebels' area of operation, until in 135 Bar Kokhba was himself killed at Betar, his stronghold in southwest Jerusalem. The remnant of the Jewish army was soon crushed; Jewish war casualties are recorded as numbering 580,000, not including those who died of hunger and disease. Judaea was desolated, the remnant of the Jewish population annihilated or exiled, and Jerusalem barred to Jews thereafter.

In 1952 and 1960–61 a number of Bar Kokhba's letters to his lieutenants were discovered in the Judaean desert.

BARMEN, SYNOD OF \'bär-mən\, meeting of German Protestant leaders at Barmen in the Ruhr, in May 1934, to organize Protestant resistance to National Socialism (Nazism). The SYNOD was of decisive importance in the development of the German CONFESSING CHURCH. Representatives came from Lutheran, Reformed, and United churches, although some of the church governments had already been captured by men loyal to Adolf Hitler, and others had decided to limit their activities to passive resistance. The Pastors' Emergency League, headed by Martin Niemöller, was the backbone of the active resistance.

At Barmen the representatives adopted six articles, called the Theological Declaration of Barmen, or the Barmen Declaration, that defined the Christian opposition to National Socialist ideology and practice. The major theological influence was that of KARL BARTH. The declaration was cast in the classical form of the great confessions of faith, affirming major biblical teachings and condemning the important heresies of those who were attempting to accommodate CHRISTIANITY to National Socialism.

BAR MITZVAH \bär-'mits-və, ,bär-mēts-'vä\ (Hebrew: "One who is subject to the commandment"), *plural* Bar Mitzvot \,bär-mēts-'vōt\, Jewish religious ritual and family celebration commemorating a boy's 13th birthday—this being the age that bestows on a Jewish male responsibility to keep the commandments and allows entry into the community of JUDAISM. The boy may henceforth don PHYLACTERIES (religious symbols worn on the forehead and left arm) during the weekday-morning prayers and may be counted an adult whenever 10 male adults are needed to form a quorum (*minyan*) for public prayers.

In a public act of acknowledging religious majority, the boy is called up during the religious service to read from the TORAH. This event may take place on any occasion following the 13th birthday at which the Torah is read but generally occurs on the SABBATH.

Most elements of the Bar Mitzvah celebration did not appear until the Middle Ages. REFORM JUDAISM replaced Bar Mitzvah, after 1810, with the confirmation of boys and girls together, generally on the feast of SHAVUOT. In the 20th century, however, many Reform congregations restored the

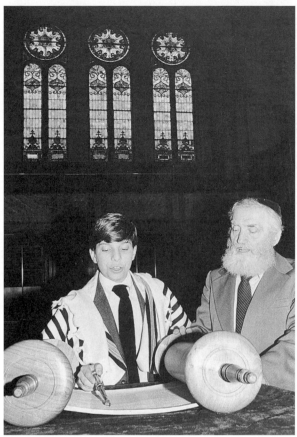

Bar Mitzvah ceremony at the Temple of Kehilath Jeshurun, New York City
Van Bucher—Photo Researchers

Bar Mitzvah rite. A separate ceremony has been instituted within Reform and CONSERVATIVE JUDAISM, and especially in RECONSTRUCIONIST synagogues, to mark the adulthood of girls, called Bat Mitzvah.

BARROW: *see* BURIAL MOUND.

BARTH, KARL \'bärt\ (b. May 10, 1886, Basel, Switz.—d. Dec. 9/10, 1968, Basel), Swiss theologian, among the most influential of the 20th century, who initiated a radical change in Protestant thought, stressing the "wholly otherness of God" over the anthropocentrism of 19th-century liberal theology.

Barth was born in Basel, the son of Fritz Barth, a professor of NEW TESTAMENT and early church history at Bern. He studied at the universities of Bern, Berlin, Tübingen, and Marburg. After serving as a pastor in Geneva from 1909 to 1911, he was appointed to the working-class PARISH of Safenwil, in Aargau canton.

The 10 years Barth spent as a minister were the formative period of his life. Deeply shocked by the disaster that had overtaken Europe in World War I and disillusioned by the collapse of the ethic of religious idealism, he questioned the liberal theology of his German teachers and its roots in the rationalist, historicist, and dualist thought arising from the Enlightenment. Through study of the teaching of St. Paul in the Epistle to the Romans, he struggled to clarify the relation between JUSTIFICATION and social righteousness, which governed all he had to say in later life about the relation of the Gospel to the power of the state and the oppression of the poor.

His first major work, *Der Römerbrief* (1919; *The Epistle to the Romans*), established his position as a notable theologian with a new message about the sheer Godness of God and the unlimited range of his GRACE. The critical and explosive nature of his theology came to be known as "dialectical theology," or "the theology of crisis"; it initiated a trend toward neoorthodoxy in Protestant theology. On the basis of this publication, Barth in 1921 was appointed professor of theology at the University of Göttingen; he was later appointed to chairs at Münster (1925) and Bonn (1930).

In 1934 he published *Nein! Antwort an Emil Brunner* (Eng. trans., "No!" in *Natural Theology* [1946]), a response to Brunner's essay "Nature and Grace." In his response, Barth traced the adoption of Germanic pre-Christian elements and ANTI-SEMITISM by the German Christian movement and its perversion of historic CHRISTIANITY. With the accession of Adolf Hitler to power in 1933, Barth became deeply involved in the church struggle. He was one of the founders of the so-called CONFESSING CHURCH, which reacted vigorously against Nazi nationalist ideology and the attempt to set up a German Christian church. The famous Barmen Declaration of 1934, largely based on a draft that Barth had prepared, expressed his conviction that the only way to offer effective resistance to the secularizing and paganizing of the church in Nazi Germany was to hold fast to true Christian doctrine. Barth's refusal to take the oath of unconditional allegiance to the Führer cost him his chair in Bonn in 1935. He was quickly offered the chair of theology in his native Basel, however. From that date until the end of the war, he continued to champion the cause of the Confessing Church, of the Jews, and of oppressed people generally. After the war and the collapse of the Third Reich, Barth was much concerned about the future of Germany, declaring that, although responsible for the disasters to themselves and to the world, the Germans now needed friends to help them become a free people.

Barth was concerned to establish the truth that God can be known only in accordance with his nature and to reject the 19th-century view that saw an identity between the Spirit of God and religious self-consciousness. Drawing on the CHURCH FATHERS and the Reformers, Barth demanded a return to the prophetic teaching of the BIBLE (in Jeremiah and the writings of ST. PAUL THE APOSTLE), of which he believed the Reformers were authentic exponents. The essence of the Christian message for Barth was the overwhelming love of the absolutely supreme, transcendent God, who comes in infinite condescension to give himself to mankind in unconditional freedom and grace.

After the war Barth continued to interest himself

Karl Barth, 1965
Horst Tappe

keenly in current theological discussion, participating in controversies regarding BAPTISM, HERMENEUTICS, "demythologizing," and others. His authority and prestige made a profound impression when he spoke at the opening meeting of the Conference of the WORLD COUNCIL OF CHURCHES in Amsterdam in 1948. Another notable event in his later years was a visit to Rome following the SECOND VATICAN COUNCIL (1962–65), of which he wrote in *Ad limina apostolorum.*

BARZAKH, AL- \ȧl-'bär-zȧk\, in Islamic belief, the period between the burial of the dead and their final judgment.

It is a widespread Muslim belief that when someone dies the ANGEL of Death (*malāk al-mawt*) arrives, sits at the head of the deceased, and addresses the soul according to its known status. According to the *Kitāb al-rūh*—("Book of the Soul") written in the 14th century by the Hanbali theologian Muhammad ibn Abi-Bakr ibn Qayyim al-Jawziyah— wicked souls are instructed "to depart to the wrath of God." Fearing what awaits them, they seek refuge throughout the body and have to be extracted by the angels, who then place the soul in a hair cloth. A full record is made, and the soul is then returned to the body in the grave. "Good and contented souls" are instructed "to depart to the mercy of God." They leave the body, are wrapped by angels in a perfumed shroud, and are taken to the "seventh heaven," where the record is kept. These souls, too, are then returned to their bodies.

Two angels colored blue and black, known as Munkar and Nakīr, then question the deceased about basic doctrinal tenets. In a sense this trial at the grave (*fitnat al-qabr*) is a show trial, the verdict having already been decided. Believers hear it proclaimed by a herald, and in anticipation of the comforts of *al-janna* (the Garden, or "paradise") their graves expand "as far as the eye can reach." Unbelievers fail the test. The herald proclaims that they are to be tormented in the grave; a door opens in their tomb to let in heat and smoke from *jihannam* ("hell"), and the tomb itself contracts. The period between burial and the final judgment is known as *al-barzakh.* At the final judgment (*yaum al-ḥisāb*), unbelievers and the god-fearing are alike resurrected. Both are endowed with physical bodies, with which to suffer or enjoy whatever lies in store for them.

BASAVA \'bə-sə-,vä, 'bəs-vä\, *also spelled* Basavanna (fl. mid-12th century, Karnataka region, South India), Hindu religious reformer, teacher, theologian, and administrator of the royal treasury of the Cālukya king. Basava is the subject of the *Basava Purāṇa,* one of the sacred texts of the Hindu Vīraśaiva (LIṄGĀYAT) sect. According to tradition, he was the founder of the Vīraśaivas, but study of Cālukya inscriptions indicates that he in fact revived an existing sect.

Basava helped to spread the Vīraśaiva sect by teaching and by dispersing funds to Vīraśaiva guilds. His uncle, a prime minister, arranged his appointment as chief of the treasury, and for several years he and his faction enjoyed a great deal of popularity. But other factions at court were apparently resentful of his power and the flourishing of Vīraśaiva MENDICANTS under his patronage. As a result of their accusations, he fled the kingdom, dying soon thereafter. His poetry to SHIVA as "Lord of the meeting rivers" has earned him a place at the front rank of Kannada literature and the literature of Hindu devotion (BHAKTI) generally.

BASILICA \bə-'si-li-kə, -'zi-\, in ROMAN CATHOLICISM and EASTERN ORTHODOXY, canonical title of honor given to church buildings that are distinguished either by their an-

tiquity or by their role as international centers of worship because of their association with a major saint, an important historical event, or, in the Orthodox Church, a national PATRIARCH. The title gives the church certain privileges, principally the right to reserve its high altar for the POPE, a CARDINAL, or a patriarch.

In architecture, "basilica" in its earliest usage designated any number of large, roofed public buildings in ancient Rome and pre-Christian Italy. Gradually, however, the word became limited to buildings with rectangular walled structures and an open hall extending from end to end, usually flanked by side aisles set off by colonnades (in large buildings often running entirely around the central area), and with a raised platform at one or both ends. One type of smaller secular basilica had side aisles extending the length of the sides only and an apse at one end. It was this type that the early Christians adopted for their churches. A later feature, the transept, a lateral aisle crossing the nave just before the apse, created the cross-shaped plan that became standard for churches in western Europe throughout the Middle Ages.

In the typical Early Christian basilica the nave rose considerably higher than the side aisles, the wall that supported the nave roof stood above the level of the side aisle roofs and could thus be pierced at the top with windows to light the center of the church. This high nave wall is called the clerestory. The apse opened from the nave by a great arch known as the triumphal arch. After the 10th century a round or square campanile, or bell tower, was added. The exterior of such a building was simple and was rarely decorated. The simplicity of the interior, however, provided surfaces suitable for elaborate ornamentation.

The basilica plan, with its nave, aisles, and apse, remained the basis for church building in the Western church. It gradually passed out of use in the Eastern church, however, eclipsed by the radial plan on which the EMPEROR JUSTINIAN I constructed the domed cathedral of HAGIA SOPHIA at Constantinople (now Istanbul).

BASILIDES \,ba-sə-'lī-dēz, -zə-\ (fl. 2nd century CE, Alexandria), scholar and teacher, who founded a school of GNOSTICISM known as the Basilidians. He probably was a pupil of Menander in Antioch, and he was teaching in Alexandria at the time of the emperors Hadrian and Antoninus Pius.

In the 3rd century CLEMENT OF ALEXANDRIA wrote that Basilides claimed to have received a secret tradition—on which he apparently based his gnosis, or esoteric knowledge—from Glaucias, an interpreter of the ST. PETER THE APOSTLE. In addition to psalms and odes, Basilides wrote commentaries on the GOSPELS and also compiled a "gospel" for his own sect; only fragments of these writings have been preserved. Contradictory accounts of Basilides' theology have been provided by Clement, as well as by the theologians Hippolytus of Rome and SAINT IRENAEUS, though his system of belief appears to have included elements of NEOPLATONISM, the NEW TESTAMENT, and other Gnostic systems.

Basilides was succeeded by his son, Isidore, and the Basilidian school still existed in Egypt in the 4th century. Its followers were the first to keep the day of the BAPTISM of JESUS on January 6 or 10, celebrating it with an all-night vigil.

BASIL THE GREAT, SAINT \'bā-zəl, 'ba-, -səl\, *Latin* Basilius \bə-'si-lē-əs, -'zi-\ (b. *c.* 329 CE, Caesarea Mazaca, Cappadocia—d. Jan. 1, 379, Caesarea; Western feast day January 2; Eastern feast day January 1), early CHURCH FATHER who defended Christian orthodoxy against ARIANISM.

Basil was born of a distinguished Christian family of Caesarea. He studied at Caesarea and Constantinople and (c. 351–356) at Athens, where he formed a friendship with Gregory of Nazianzus. On returning home he began a secular career, but the influence of his pious sister Macrina, later a NUN and ABBESS, confirmed his earlier inclination to the ascetic life. With a group of friends, he established a monastic settlement on the family estate at Annesi in Pontus.

In 357 he made an extensive tour of the monasteries of Egypt, and in 360 he assisted the Cappadocian bishops at a SYNOD at Constantinople. He had been distressed by the general acceptance of the Arian Creed of the Council of Ariminum the previous year and especially by the fact that his own bishop, Dianius of Caesarea, had supported it. Shortly before the death of Dianius (362), Basil was reconciled to him and later was ordained PRESBYTER (priest) to assist Dianius' successor, the new convert EUSEBIUS. Tensions between the men led Basil to withdraw to Annesi. In 365 Basil was called back to Caesarea, when the church was threatened by the Arian emperor Valens. His theological and ecclesiastical policy thereafter aimed to unite against Arianism the former semi-Arians and the supporters of Nicaea under the formula "three persons (*hypostases*) in one substance (*ousia*)," thus preserving both unity and the necessary distinctions in the theological concept of the godhead. On Eusebius' death in 370, Basil became his successor, although he was opposed by some of the other bishops in the province.

As bishop of Caesarea, Basil was METROPOLITAN (ecclesiastical PRIMATE of a province) of Cappadocia. He founded charitable institutions to aid the poor, the ill, and travelers. When Valens passed through Caesarea in 371, Basil defied his demand for submission. In 372 Valens divided the province, and Basil considered this a personal attack, since Anthimus of Tyana thus became metropolitan for the cities of western Cappadocia. Basil countered by installing supporters in some of the border towns—GREGORY OF NAZIANZUS at Sasima and his own brother GREGORY OF NYSSA. This tactic was only partially successful, but Basil escaped the attacks that Valens launched on orthodox bishops elsewhere.

Basil's numerous and influential writings stemmed from his practical concerns as monk, pastor, and church leader. The *Longer Rules* and *Shorter Rules* (for monasteries) and other ascetic writings distill the experience that began at Annesi: they were to exert strong influence on the monastic life of Eastern Christianity (*see* EASTERN ORTHODOXY). Basil's preserved sermons deal mainly with ethical and social problems. The "Address to Young Men," defends the study of classical literature by Christians (Basil himself made considerable critical use of Greek philosophical thought). "Against Eunomius" defends the deity of the Son against an extreme Arian thinker, and "On the Holy Spirit" expounds the deity of the spirit implied in the church's tradition, though not previously formally defined. Basil is most characteristically revealed in his letters, of which more than 300 are preserved. Many deal with daily activities; others are, in effect, short treatises on theology

or ethics; several of his Canonical Epistles, decisions on points of discipline, have become part of the CANON LAW of the Eastern Orthodox church. The extent of Basil's actual contribution to the magnificent series of eucharistic prayers known as the Liturgy of St. Basil is uncertain. But at least the central prayer of consecration (setting apart the bread and wine) reflects his spirit and was probably in use at Caesarea in his own lifetime.

Basil's health was poor. He died soon after Valens' death in the Battle of Adrianople had opened the way for the victory of Basil's cause.

BASMALAH \\'bàs-mà-là\\, *also called* tasmiya, in ISLAM, the formula-prayer: *bi'sm Allāh al-raḥmān al-raḥīm*, "in the name of God, the Merciful, the Compassionate." This invocation, which was first introduced by the QUR'ĀN, appears at the beginning of every Qur'anic SŪRA (chapter) except the ninth and is frequently recited by Muslims to elicit God's blessings on their actions. The *basmalah* also introduces all formal documents and transactions and must always preface actions that are legally required or recommended. An abbreviated version precedes certain daily rituals, such as meals. Magicians often use the *basmalah* in AMULETS, claiming that the prayer was inscribed in ADAM's side, GABRIEL'S wing, SOLOMON'S seal, and JESUS CHRIST'S tongue.

BASTET \\'bäs-,tet, 'bas-\\, *also called* Bast, *or* Ubasti, in EGYPTIAN RELIGION, goddess worshiped in the form of a lioness, and later a cat. Bastet's nature changed after the domestication of the cat around 1500 BCE. She was native to Bubastis in the Nile River delta but also had an important cult at Memphis. In the Late and Ptolemaic periods large cemeteries of mummified cats were created at both sites, and thousands of bronze statuettes of the goddess were deposited as votive offerings. Small figures of cats were also worn as AMULETS; this too was probably related to the cult of Bastet.

Bastet is represented as a lioness or as a woman with a cat's head: she carries an ancient percussion instrument, the sistrum, in her right hand; a breastplate (in Bastet's case, surmounted with the head of a lioness), in her left hand; and a small bag over her left arm. She wears an elaborately ornamented dress. Her cult was carried to Italy by the Romans, and traces have been found in Rome, Ostia, Nemi, and Pompeii.

BATHSHEBA \\bath-'shē-bə\\, in the OLD TESTAMENT (2 Samuel 11, 12; 1 Kings 1, 2), the beautiful daughter of Eliam and wife of Uriah the Hittite. She was seduced by DAVID and became pregnant. David then had Uriah killed and married her. Their first child died, but Bathsheba later gave birth to SOLOMON. When David was dying, Bathsheba successfully conspired with the prophet Nathan to block Adonijah's succession to the throne and to win it for Solomon, after which she occupied an influential position as the queen mother.

BĀṬINĪYA \\,bä-tē-'nē-ə\\, in ISLAM, sects—the ISMĀ'ĪLĪS, in particular—that interpreted religious texts exclusively on the basis of their hidden, or inner,

Statuette of Bastet, 22nd–25th dynasty, c. 950–664 BCE

115

meanings (Arabic: *bāṭin*). This type of interpretation gained currency about the 8th century among certain esoteric SHIʿITE sects, especially the schismatic Ismāʿīlīs, who believed that beneath every obvious or literal meaning of a sacred text lay a secret, hidden meaning, which could be arrived at through *taʾwīl* (interpretations by ALLEGORY). They further stated that MUHAMMAD was only the transmitter of the literal word of God, the QURʾAN, but it was the IMAM (divinely inspired leader) who was empowered to interpret, through *taʾwīl*, its true, hidden meaning.

Speculative philosophy and theology eventually influenced the Bāṭinīya, though they remained always on the side of esoteric knowledge; some Sufis were also placed among the Bāṭinīya for their insistence on an esoteric body of doctrine known only to the initiate (*see* SUFISM). Although the Ismāʿīlīs had always acknowledged the validity of both *bāṭin* and *ẓāhir*, about the 12th century the Nusairis (Nuṣayrīya) and the DRUZE came to accept only the hidden meanings and exalted the imam to extraordinary heights.

SUNNI Muslim scholars condemned the Bāṭinīya for interpretations that rejected the literal meaning and accused them of producing confusion and controversy through a multiplicity of readings, thereby allowing ignorant or mischievous persons to claim possession of religious truths. The Bāṭinīya were further labeled as enemies of Islam, bent upon destroying the Sunnis' conception of the faith.

BAU \\ˈbaù\\ (Sumerian), *also called* Nininsina, *Akkadian* Gula, *or* Ninkarrak, in MESOPOTAMIAN RELIGIONS, city goddess of Urukug in the Lagash region and, as Nininsina, the Queen of Isin, city goddess of Isin, south of Nippur.

Bau seems originally to have been goddess of the dog; as Nininsina she was long represented with a dog's head, and the dog was her emblem, though later she became a goddess of healing. She was a daughter of An, king of the gods, and the wife of Pabilsag, a rain god who was also called NINURTA, or Ningirsu.

BĀUL \\ˈbä-ùl\\ (Bengali: "Madman"), member of an order of religious singers of Bengal known for their unconventional behavior and for the spontaneity of their mystical verse. There is little detailed information about the development of the order, as their songs began to be collected and written down only in the 20th century, but it is known to have existed since the 17th century and probably has deeper roots. The membership consists of both Hindus and Muslims, and the tenor of worship is syncretic (*see* SYNCRETISM, RELIGIOUS). According to Bāul doctrine, the Supreme is manifest in active form in menstrual blood and in passive form in semen. To unite these two aspects of divinity and reverse the process of creation leading to death and rebirth, Bāuls practice a sexual and yogic regimen. Their songs frequently speak of this discipline, but do so in symbolic language intended to obscure aspects of its meaning from the uninitiated. A major theme is the love between the human personality and the indwelling, personal divinity. Many Bengali authors have acknowledged an indebtedness of inspiration to Bāul verse.

BAVLI \\ˈbäv-lē\\, *also called* Talmud Bavli, *or* the Babylonian Talmud, *or* the Talmud, second and more authoritative of the two TALMUDS (the other Talmud being the YERUSHALMI) produced by RABBINIC JUDAISM. Completed about 600 CE, the Bavli served as the constitution and bylaws of Rabbinic JUDAISM.

Several attributes of the Bavli distinguish it from the Talmud Yerushalmi (Palestinian Talmud) and must be considered in accounting for its great intellectual influence. First, the Bavli shows how practical reason can work to make diverse issues and actions conform to a single principle. Second, it shows how applied logic discerns the regular and the orderly in the confusion and disorder of everyday conflict.

The Bavli in its 37 tractates is entirely uniform, stylistic preferences exhibited on any given page characterize every other page of the document, and diverse topics produce only slight differentiation in modes of analysis. The task of interpretation in the Talmudic writing was to uncover the integrity of the truth that God manifested in the one and unique revelation, the TORAH (both oral and written). By integrity was meant a truth that was unified and beyond all division. The message of the first document of the oral Torah, the MISHNAH, was the hierarchical unity of all being in the One on high. Since the Bavli's authorship undertook precisely the same inquiry, the way that the Mishnah and the Bavli deal with the problem of showing the integrity of truth illuminates for the reader how the two dominant documents of Judaism set matters forth.

The Mishnah's version of the integrity of truth focuses upon the unity of all being within a hierarchy. The Mishnah's overriding proposition is that all classes of things stand in a hierarchical relationship to one another, and, in that encompassing hierarchy, there is place for everything. The theological proposition that is implicit but never spelled out, of course, is that one God occupies the pinnacle of the hierarchy of all being—to that one God all things turn upward, from complexity to simplicity; from that one God all things flow downward, from singularity to multiplicity. To state with emphasis the one large argument—the metaproposition—that the Mishnah's authorship sets forth in countless small ways: the very artifacts that appear multiple in fact form classes of things, and, moreover, these classes themselves are subject to a reasoned ordering by appeal to this-worldly characteristics signified by properties and indicative traits.

The Bavli's version of the integrity of truth matches the Mishnah's theme of the hierarchical unity of all being with the Bavli's insistence that many principles express a single one—many laws embody one governing law, which is the law behind the laws. However, the difference in the documents may be seen, in how, for instance, the Mishnah establishes a world in stasis: lists of like things, subject to like rules. In contrast, the Bavli portrays a world in motion: lists of like things form series, but series also conform to rules. The Bavli's paramount intellectual trait is its quest through abstraction for the unity of the law and the integrity of truth. That same quest insists on the fair and balanced representation of conflicting principles behind discrete laws—not to serve the cause of academic harmony but to set forth how, at their foundations, the complicated and diverse laws may be explained by appeal to simple and few principles. The conflict of principles then is less consequential than the demonstration that diverse cases may be reduced to only a few principles.

Both Talmuds, the Yerushalmi and the Bavli, treat the same issues of the Mishnah, yet the second Talmud radically differs from the first, and the two Talmuds rarely intersect other than at a given Mishnah paragraph or TOSEFTA selection. This is not so surprising, for, despite the fact that the Yerushalmi is 200 years older than the Bavli, scholars do not believe the framers of the Bavli to have had access to the Yerushalmi during the Bavli's redaction. (Though some sayings known to the editors of the Yerushalmi also circulated among those of the Bavli.) Therefore, each Talmud pursues its own interests when reading a passage shared with the other. No substantial, shared exegetical protocol or tradition, whether in fully spelled-out statements in so many words, or in the gist of ideas, or in topical conventions, or in intellectual characteristics, governed the two Talmuds' reading of the same Mishnah paragraph. The Bavli presents an utterly autonomous statement, speaking in its own behalf and in its own way about its own interests.

If we compare the way in which the two Talmuds read the same Mishnah, we discern consistent differences between them. The principal difference between the Talmuds is the same difference that distinguishes jurisprudence from philosophy. The Yerushalmi talks in details, the Bavli in large truths; the Yerushalmi tells us what the Mishnah says, the Bavli, what it means. How do the two Talmuds compare?

> 1. The Yerushalmi analyzes evidence, the Bavli investigates premises;
> 2. The Yerushalmi remains wholly within the limits of its case, the Bavli vastly transcends the bounds of the case altogether;
> 3. The Yerushalmi wants to know the rule, the Bavli asks about the principle and its implications for other cases.

The Yerushalmi provides an EXEGESIS and amplification of the Mishnah; the Bavli, a theoretical study of the law in all its magnificent abstraction, transforming the Mishnah into testimony to a deeper reality altogether: to the law behind the laws.

BAYON, THE \'bä-ˌyōn\, Cambodian Buddhist PYRAMID temple constructed *c.* 1200 at the behest of Jayavarman VII (1181–*c.* 1220), who had broken with Khmer tradition and adopted MAHĀYĀNA Buddhism.

In order to conform with traditional MYTHOLOGY, the Khmer kings built themselves a series of artificial moun-

The Bayon at the Angkor Thom complex, Angkor, Cambodia
George Holton—Photo Researchers

tains on the Cambodian plain at the royal city of Angkor, each crowned by shrines containing images of gods and of themselves, their families, and their ancestors. Most of the temple mountains are oriented east to west, the main gates facing east. Originally the Bayon was designed to serve as the primary locus of the royal cult and to serve as Jayavarman's personal mausoleum; it stood at the center of Angkor Thom, the new capital that Jayavarman built. The four-sided central tower is carved with faces, some of which seem to represent Jayavarman in the guise of AVALOKITEŚVARA, the great BODHISATTVA. Each side of the tower is oriented to a cardinal direction. The central tower is surrounded by an additional 12 towers; each side of these towers has a carved face of Avalokiteśvara as well. In total, there are 54 towers at the Bayon site, all with carved bas-relief visages. The bas-reliefs depict Jayavarman's military victories as well as scenes of ordinary life, providing a picture of 13th-century Cambodians at work, rest, and play.

BEATIFICATION, in ROMAN CATHOLICISM, second stage in the process of CANONIZATION.

BEATITUDE, any of the blessings said by JESUS CHRIST in the SERMON ON THE MOUNT as told in the NEW TESTAMENT in MATTHEW 5:3–12 and in the Sermon on the Plain in LUKE 6:20–23. They are named from the initial words (*beati sunt*, "blessed are") of those sayings in the Latin VULGATE Bible. Beatitudes are found in other places in the New Testament (*e.g.,* Matthew 11:6, Luke 7:23, and John 20:29) and appear to be adapted from similar opening words contained in some of the Psalms (*e.g.,* Psalms 32:1).

In the Revised Standard Version, the nine Beatitudes of Matthew 5:3–12 read as follows:

◆   Blessed are the poor in spirit, for theirs is the kingdom of heaven.
  Blessed are those who mourn, for they shall be comforted.
  Blessed are the meek, for they shall inherit the earth.
  Blessed are those who hunger and thirst for righteousness, for they shall be satisfied.
  Blessed are the merciful, for they shall obtain mercy.
  Blessed are the pure in heart, for they shall see God.
  Blessed are the peacemakers, for they shall be called sons of God.
  Blessed are those who are persecuted for righteousness' sake, for theirs is the kingdom of heaven.
  Blessed are you when men revile you and persecute you and utter all kinds of evil against you falsely on my account. Rejoice and be glad, for your reward is great in heaven, for so men persecuted the prophets who were before you. ◆

BECKET, SAINT THOMAS \'be-kit\, *also called* Thomas à Becket, *or* Thomas of London (b. *c.* 1118, Cheapside, London—d. Dec. 29, 1170, Canterbury, Kent, Eng.; canonized 1173; feast day December 29), chancellor of England (1155–62) and archbishop of Canterbury (1162–70) during the reign of King Henry II.

Thomas was born to Norman parents of the merchant class. He was educated first at Merton priory, then in a City of London school, and finally at Paris. He was introduced by his father to Archbishop Theobald, a former ABBOT of Bec. Thomas won Theobald's confidence, acted as his agent, and was sent by him to study civil and CANON LAW.

In 1154 Theobald, as a reward of his services, appointed Thomas archdeacon of Canterbury, an important and lucrative post, and less than three months later recommended him to Henry as chancellor. Here Thomas showed to the full his brilliant abilities, razing castles, repairing the Tower of London, conducting embassies, and raising and leading troops in war. He was trusted completely by the king.

The movement known as the GREGORIAN REFORM had spread from Italy and had begun to influence English churchmen. Leading points in its program were free elections to clerical posts, inviolability of church property, freedom of appeal to Rome, and clerical immunity from lay tribunals. Under Henry I and Stephen, the archbishops had stood out for these reforms, sometimes with partial success. Henry II, however, undoubtedly aimed for strict control over the church, and Becket had aided him. With the death of Theobald in 1161, Henry hoped to appoint Becket as archbishop and thus complete his program.

For almost a year after the death of Theobald the see of Canterbury was vacant. Thomas was aware of the king's intention and tried to dissuade him by warnings of what would happen. Henry persisted and Thomas was elected. Once consecrated, Thomas changed both his outlook and his way of life. He became devout and austere and embraced the PAPACY and its canon law. Greatly to Henry's displeasure, he took up the matter of "criminous clerks." In western Europe, accused clerics for long had enjoyed the privilege of standing trial before the bishop rather than secular courts and usually received milder punishments than lay courts would assess. The position of Thomas, that a guilty cleric could be degraded and punished by the bishop but should not be punished again by lay authority—"not twice for the same fault"—was canonically a plausible argument which ultimately prevailed. The crisis came at Clarendon (Wiltshire, January 1164), when the king demanded in the Constitutions of Clarendon his right to punish criminal clerics, forbade EXCOMMUNICATION of royal officials and appeals to Rome, and gave to the Crown the revenues of vacant sees and the power to influence episcopal elections. Thomas, after verbally accepting the constitutions, revoked his assent and appealed to the pope.

Good relations between Thomas and Henry were now at an end; the archbishop was summoned to trial by the king on a point of feudal obligation. At the Council of Northampton (Oct. 6–13, 1164), it was clear that Henry intended to ruin and imprison or to force the resignation of the archbishop. Thomas fled in disguise and took refuge

Murder of Thomas Becket; illustration from an English psalter,   1200
By courtesy of the trustees of the British Library

with Louis VII of France. Pope Alexander III received Becket with honor but hesitated to act decisively in his favor in fear that he might throw Henry into the arms of the Holy Roman emperor Frederick I and his ANTIPOPE, Paschal III.

Thomas' exile lasted for six years (Nov. 2, 1164–Dec. 2, 1170). Henry meanwhile had seized the properties of the archbishop and his supporters and had exiled all Thomas' close relatives. Several abortive attempts were made at reconciliation, but new acts of hostility by the king and declarations of excommunication hurled by Thomas at his opponents embittered the struggles.

Finally, in 1170, Henry had his eldest son crowned as coking by the archbishop of York, Becket's old rival. This was a flagrant breach of papal prohibition and of the immemorial right of Canterbury to crown the king. Thomas, followed by the pope, excommunicated all responsible. Henry, fearing an interdict for England, met Thomas at Fréteval (July 22), and it was agreed that Thomas should return to Canterbury and receive back all the possessions of his see. Neither party withdrew from his position regarding the Constitutions of Clarendon, which on this occasion were not mentioned. Thomas returned to Canterbury (December 2) and was received with enthusiasm, but further excommunications of the hostile royal servants, as well as his ready acceptance of tumultuous acclaim by the crowds, infuriated Henry in Normandy.

Some violent words of Henry were taken literally by four leading knights of the court, who proceeded swiftly to Canterbury (December 29), forced themselves into the archbishop's presence, and followed him into the cathedral. There, at twilight, after further altercation, they cut him down with their swords. His last words were an acceptance of death in defense of the church of Christ.

Within a few days after Thomas' death, his tomb became a goal of PILGRIMAGE, and he was canonized by Alexander III in 1173. In 1174 Henry did penance at Canterbury and was absolved.

BEDE THE VENERABLE, SAINT
\'bēd\ (b. 672/673, traditionally Monkton in Jarrow, Northumbria—d. May 25, 735, Jarrow; canonized 1899; feast day May 25), Anglo-Saxon theologian, historian, and chronologist, best known today for his *Historia ecclesiastica gentis Anglorum* ("Ecclesiastical History of the English People"), a source vital to the history of the conversion to Christianity of the Anglo-Saxon tribes. During his lifetime and throughout the Middle Ages Bede's reputation was based mainly on his scriptural commentaries, copies of which found their way to many of the monastic libraries of western Europe. His method of dating events from the time of the incarnation, or JESUS CHRIST'S birth—*i.e.*, BC and AD—came into general use through the popularity of the *Historia ecclesiastica* and two works on chronology.

Reared from the age of seven by Abbot St. Benedict Biscop, Bede was ordained deacon when 19 years old and priest when 30.

Bede's works fall into three groups: grammatical and "scientific," scriptural commentary, and historical and biographical. His earliest works include treatises on spelling, HYMNS, figures of speech, verse, and epigrams. His first treatise on chronology, *De temporibus* ("On Times"), with a brief chronicle attached, was written in 703. In 725 he completed a greatly amplified version, *De temporum ratione* ("On the Reckoning of Time"), with a much longer chronicle. Both these books were mainly concerned with the reckoning of EASTER. Bede's method of dating events from the time of Christ's birth came into general use via these works.

In 731/732 Bede completed his *Historia ecclesiastica*. Divided into five books, it recorded events in Britain from the raids by Julius Caesar (55–54 BCE) to the arrival in Kent (597 CE) of St. Augustine. For his sources he claimed the authority of ancient letters, the "traditions of our forefathers," and his own knowledge of contemporary events. Although overloaded with the miraculous, it is the work of a scholar anxious to assess the accuracy of his sources and to record only what he regarded as trustworthy evidence. It remains an indispensable source for some of the facts and much of the feel of early Anglo-Saxon history.

BEECHER, HENRY WARD \'bē-chər\ (b. June 24, 1813, Litchfield, Conn., U.S.—d. March 8, 1887, Brooklyn, N.Y.), U.S. Congregational minister (*see* CONGREGATIONALISM) whose oratorical skill and social concern made him one of the most influential Protestant spokesmen of his time.

The son of a minister, Beecher spent three postgraduate years in Cincinnati, Ohio, at Lane Theological Seminary, of which his father became president in 1832. In 1837 Beecher became minister to a small PRESBYTERIAN congregation at Lawrenceburg, Ind. He gradually became a highly successful preacher and lecturer. Beecher furthered his reputation through *Seven Lectures to Young Men* (1844), vivid exhortations on the vices and dangers in a frontier community.

In 1847 he accepted a call to Plymouth Church (Congregational), Brooklyn, N.Y., where he drew weekly crowds of 2,500 by the early 1850s. He gradually became more emphatic in opposing slavery, and his lectures of 1863 in England won over audiences initially hostile to him and to the Northern point of view. Increasingly outspoken after the Civil War, he supported a moderate Reconstruction policy for the South and advocated women's suffrage, evolutionary theory, and scientific BIBLICAL CRITICISM. His outlets for these issues, in addition to Plymouth Church, were the *Independent*, a Congregational journal he edited in the early 1860s, and the nondenominational *Christian Union* (later *Outlook*), which he founded in 1870.

BEECHER, LYMAN (b. Oct. 12, 1775, New Haven, Conn. [U.S.]—d. Jan. 10, 1863, Brooklyn, N.Y.), U.S. PRESBYTERIAN clergyman in the revivalist tradition.

A graduate of Yale in 1797, he held pastorates at Litchfield, Connecticut, and at Boston, Massachusetts. After turning his attention to evangelizing the West, he became president of the newly founded Lane Theological Seminary in Cincinnati, Ohio (1832–50), and also assumed a new pastorate there (1832–42). His CALVINISM, however, considered strict by Bostonian standards, proved so mild for western Presbyterians that Beecher was tried for HERESY, but his SYNOD acquitted him.

Beecher was called by a contemporary "the father of more brains than any other man in America." Among the 13 children of his three marriages, HENRY WARD BEECHER and Harriet Beecher Stowe achieved fame. Five others well known in their day were Catharine (1800–78), a leader in the women's education movement; Edward (1803–95), a minister, college president, and anti-slavery writer; Charles (1815–1900), Florida's superintendent of public instruction; Isabella (1822–1907), a champion of legal rights for women; and Thomas (1824–1900), an early advocate of adapting church life to modern urban conditions.

BEELZEBUB \bē-'el-zi-,bəb, 'bēl-, 'bel-\, in the BIBLE, the prince of the DEVILS. In the OLD TESTAMENT (in the form Baalzebub), it is the name given to the god of the Philistine city of Ekron (2 Kings 1:1–18). Neither name is found elsewhere in the Old Testament, and there is only one reference to it in other Jewish literature. Reference to Beelzebub is made in the NEW TESTAMENT (Matthew 10:25; 12:27). *See also* SATAN; LUCIFER.

BEGUINES \'be-,gēn, bā-'gēn\, women in the cities of northern Europe who, from the Middle Ages, led lives of religious devotion without joining an established religious order.

So-called "holy women" first appeared in Liège toward the end of the 12th century. The use of the Old French word *beguine* to designate such women was established by the 1230s. Its etymology is uncertain; it seems to have originated as a pejorative term.

The movement began among upper-class women and spread to the middle class. In addition to addressing the spiritual needs of its adherents, it responded to problems caused by a surplus of unattached women in urban areas. Most Beguines lived together in communities called beguinages. In Germany groups of up to 60 or 70 women lived together in houses; in the Low Countries they usually lived in individual houses within walled enclosures. Most supported themselves, often by nursing or cloth- or lace-making, and they spent time in religious contemplation. Beguines promised to preserve chastity while they remained in the community, but they were free to leave it and marry.

Some communities and individuals cultivated intense forms of MYSTICISM. These circumstances led many people to suspect them of heretical tendencies. Throughout the 13th century they were the object of prejudice and of restrictive legislation. Official policy varied until the 15th century, when a consistent policy of toleration was established. Meanwhile, however, the beguinal movement had declined; many of its members joined formal religious orders. Some communities still exist, mainly in Belgium; most operate charitable institutions.

One of the most remarkable Beguines was Marguerite Porete, who was burned for HERESY in Paris in 1310. Her mystical work *Miroir des simples âmes* (c. 1300; *The Mirror of Simple Souls*) is thought to be the greatest religious tract written in Old French.

The male counterparts of Beguines were known as Beghards. They never achieved the same prominence, and the few communities that survived in Belgium were suppressed during the French Revolution.

BEHEMOTH \bi-'hē-məth\, in the OLD TESTAMENT, a powerful, grass-eating animal whose "bones are tubes of bronze, his limbs like bars of iron" (Job 40:18). Jewish mythology relates that the righteous will witness a spectacular battle between Behemoth and Leviathan in the messianic era and later feast upon their flesh. Some sources identify Behemoth, who dwells in the marsh and is not frightened by the turbulent river Jordan, as a hippopotamus and Leviathan as a crocodile, whale, or snake.

BEKTASHĪ \bek-'tä-shē\ *Turkish* Bektaşi \ˌbek-tä-'shē\, in IS-LAM, any member of an order of mystics traditionally founded by Ḥājjī Bektāsh Walī of Khorāsān, Iran. The order acquired definitive form in the 16th century in Anatolia and spread to the Ottoman Balkans, particularly Albania.

Originally one of many Sufi orders (*see* SUFISM) within orthodox SUNNI Islam, the Bektashi order in the 16th century adopted tenets of the SHĪʿITES, including a veneration of ʿALĪ, the fourth successor of the prophet MUHAMMAD, as a member of a trinity with ALLĀH and the Prophet himself. The Bektashis were lax in observing daily Muslim laws and allowed women to take part in ritual wine drinking and dancing during devotional ceremonies. The Bektashis in the Balkans adapted such Christian practices as the ritual sharing of bread and the CONFESSION of sins. Their mystical writings made a rich contribution to Sufi poetry. After 1925, when all Sufi orders were dissolved in Turkey, the Bektashī leadership shifted to Albania. With the banning of religion in Albania in 1967, Bektashī devotions were carried on by communities in Turkey, Albanian regions of the Balkans, and the United States.

BEL \'bel\, the Akkadian counterpart of the Sumerian deity ENLIL. Bel is derived from the Semitic word BAAL, or "lord." Bel had all the attributes of Enlil, and his status and cult were much the same. Bel, however, gradually came to be thought of as the god of order and destiny. In Greek writings references to Bel indicate this Babylonian deity and not the Syrian god of Palmyra of the same name.

BELENUS \'be-lə-nəs\ (Gaulish: possibly, "Bright One"), an ancient and widely worshiped deity in CELTIC RELIGION; he was associated with healing. The festival of BELTANE (or Beltine) held on May 1 in Gaelic-speaking lands was possibly originally connected with his cult. On that day the cattle were purified and protected by fire before being put out to the open pastures for the summer.

There is evidence of the cult of Belenus in northern Italy, Noricum in the eastern Alps, and southern Gaul. Belenus is often identified with APOLLO and probably also combined solar and curative elements.

BELIEF, RELIGIOUS, belief in the objects and assertions of a religion. While such a definition may initially seem clear, it is inherently problematic: if "religion" is thought of as a set of beliefs and practices, then the definition is circular. The problem of defining what makes a belief distinctively "religious" can therefore be difficult to solve. A religious belief can be said to be something that the believer holds to be deeply true; but again the question of what relation "religious truth" has to other types of truth, such as scientific truth, must first be answered before a definition is to be based on this premise.

Most modern authors, rather than defining religious belief per se, instead attempt to delineate its general characteristics. So, for instance, religious beliefs can often be distinguished from other beliefs in a cultural system by stressing the importance that superhuman beings hold within religious beliefs. The great gods and goddesses of religions are usually thought of as such beings, but the great personages of religion—be it the prophets or founders such as MOSES, JESUS, MUHAMMAD, and the BUDDHA GOTAMA—are also good examples. Religious beliefs almost always involve such beings, all within a complex web of other beliefs and attitudes such as hopes, fears, and desires. Belief in superhuman beings is not to be confused, however, with the notion of the supernatural or a transcendental realm, since there are many religions in which such concepts are either lacking or denied.

Religious beliefs also tend to function as explanations regarding the world and events in the world, including the human experience of suffering, the existence of evil, and similar existential issues. It is this function of religious beliefs that has caused the most controversy in the STUDY OF RELIGION, particularly with regard to the debate on the relation between SCIENCE AND RELIGION.

There are three general positions on the question of how religious truth-claims are to be evaluated in light of modern science. The first position asserts that all religious beliefs are false: they attempt to explain perceived phenomena in a way that is often contrary to scientific principles, and in any case religious beliefs cannot be empirically verified. Most scholars who take this position are quick to point out that holding a false belief does not entail irrationality, no more than it was irrational for people to hold that certain diseases were caused by "bad air" prior to the discoveries of pathogens such as bacteria.

The second position states that religious beliefs are neither true nor false, since their meaning does not depend on truth conditions. Rather, these scholars hold, religious beliefs refer to emotional states or systems of morality, and thus are different in kind from the sort of claims which science makes. From this vantage point, religion and science talk about entirely different things.

The third position holds that the truth conditions of religious beliefs are simply beyond verification, since they refer to those things that are not, and perhaps cannot, be known: the beginning of all things, the meaning of life, and what happens after death. The scholars who hold this view also tend to hold a theory of "two truths," one scientific and one symbolic (or religious). The debate is not settled.

BELIT \'bā-lit\ (Akkadian), *Sumerian* Ninlil, in MESOPOTAMIAN RELIGION, a goddess, the consort of the god BEL (Sumerian: ENLIL) and a deity of destiny. She was worshiped especially at Nippur and Shuruppak and was the mother of the moon god, SIN (Sumerian: Nanna). In Assyrian documents Belit is sometimes identified with ISHTAR (Sumerian: Inanna) of Nineveh and is sometimes the wife of either ASHUR, the national god of Assyria, or of Enlil, god of the atmosphere.

The Sumerian Ninlil was a grain goddess, known as the Varicolored Ear (of barley). She was the daughter of Haia, god of the stores, and Ninshebargunu (or Nidaba). One myth recounted the rape of Ninlil by her consort, Enlil. He saw Ninlil bathing in a canal and raped and impregnated her. For his crime he was banished to the Underworld, but Ninlil followed. In the course of their journey Enlil assumed three different guises, each one ravishing and impregnating Ninlil. The myth seems to represent the process of wind-pollination, ripening, and the eventual withering of the crops and their subsequent return to the earth (corresponding to Ninlil's sojourn in the Underworld).

BELLEROPHON \bə-'ler-ə-ˌfän\, *also called* Bellerophontes \bə-ˌler-ə-'fän-ˌtēz\, hero in Greek legend. In the *Iliad* he was the son of GLAUCUS, who was the son of SISYPHUS. Anteia (or Stheneboea), wife of Proetus, the king of Argos, made sexual overtures to Bellerophon, which were rejected; she therefore falsely accused him to her husband. Proetus then sent Bellerophon to the king of Lycia with a message that he was to be killed. The king, repeatedly unsuccessful in his assassination attempts, finally recognized Bellerophon as more than human and married him to his daughter. Bellerophon lived in prosperity until he fell out of favor with the gods, lost two of his children, and wandered grief-stricken over the Aleian Plain.

Later authors added that, while still at Corinth, Bellerophon tamed the winged horse PEGASUS with a bridle given to him by ATHENA and that he used Pegasus to fight the CHIMERA and afterward to punish Anteia. He supposedly earned the wrath of the gods by trying to fly up to Olympus and was thrown from Pegasus and crippled.

BELLONA \bə-'lō-nə\, *original name* Duellona, in ROMAN RELIGION, goddess of war, identified with the Greek Enyo. Sometimes known as the sister or wife of MARS, she has also been identified with his female cult partner Nerio. Her temple at Rome stood in the Campus Martius, outside the city's gates. There the Senate met to discuss generals' claims to triumphs and to receive foreign ambassadors. In front of it was the *columna bellica*, where the ceremony of declaring war by the *fetiales* (a group of priestly officials) took place.

Bellerophon with Pegasus, stone bas-relief; in the Palazzo Spada, Rome
Alinari—Art Resource

BELTANE \'bel-ˌtān, -tin\, *also spelled* Beltine, *Irish* Beltaine *or* Belltaine, *also known as* Cétsamain, in CELTIC RELIGION, a festival held on the first day of May, celebrating the beginning of summer and open pasturing. Beltane is first mentioned in a glossary attributed to Cormac, bishop of Cashel and king of Munster, who was killed in 908. Cormac describes how cattle were driven between two bonfires on Beltane as a magical means of protecting them from disease before they were led into summer pastures—a custom still observed in Ireland in the 19th century.

In early Irish lore a number of significant events took place on Beltane, which long remained the focus of folk traditions and tales in Ireland, Scotland, and the Isle of Man. As did other Celtic peoples, the Irish divided the year into two main seasons. Winter and the beginning of the year fell on November 1 (SAMHAIN) and midyear and summer on May 1 (Irish: Beltaine). These two junctures were thought to be critical periods when the bounds between the human and supernatural worlds were temporarily erased; on May Eve, witches and fairies roamed freely, and measures had to be taken against their enchantments.

Cormac derives the word *Beltaine* from the name of a god Bel, or Bil, and the Old Irish word *tene*, "fire." Despite linguistic difficulties, some 20th-century scholars have maintained modified versions of this etymology, linking the first element of the word with the Gaulish god BELENUS.

BENDIS \'ben-dis\, Thracian goddess of the moon; the Greeks usually identified her with the goddess ARTEMIS. She is often represented holding two spears.

Apart from areas adjacent to Thrace, the cult of Bendis gained prominence only in Athens. At the outbreak of the Peloponnesian War, the Athenians allowed the founding of a SANCTUARY for the goddess and shortly afterward created a state festival, the Bendideia, for her. The first celebration was held on the 19th of Thargelion (May–June), 429 BCE, at the Piraeus, the seaport of Athens, and included two processions, a torch race on horseback, and a vigil.

BENEDICT OF NURSIA, SAINT \'be-nə-ˌdikt . . . 'nər-shē-ə, -shə; 'nûr-sē-ə\ (b. *c.* 480, Nursia, Kingdom of the Lombards [now in Italy]—d. *c.* 547; feast day July 11, formerly March 21), founder of the BENEDICTINE monastery at Monte Cassino and the father of Western monasticism; the rule that he established became the norm for monastic living throughout Europe.

The only recognized authority for the facts of Benedict's life is Book 2 of the Dialogues of ST. GREGORY THE GREAT, who said that he had obtained his information from Benedict's disciples. He gives no dates, however. Benedict's life spanned the decades in which the decayed imperial city became the Rome of the medieval PAPACY.

As a young man Benedict retreated from Rome to the country and lived alone for three years, furnished with food and monastic garb by a monk of one of the monasteries nearby. He was persuaded to become ABBOT of one of these monasteries. His reforming zeal was resisted, however, and an attempt was made to poison him. He returned to his cave retreat; but again disciples flocked to him, and he founded 12 monasteries, each with 12 monks, with himself in control of all. Later, he left the area, while the 12 monasteries continued in existence. A few disciples followed him south, where he settled near Cassino. The district was still largely non-Christian, but the people were converted by his preaching. His sister Scholastica, who came to live nearby as the head of a nunnery, died shortly before her brother.

Benedict had begun his monastic life as a HERMIT, but he had come to see the difficulties and spiritual dangers of a solitary life. As a layman, his Rule is concerned with a life spent wholly in a community of laymen, and among his contributions to the practices of the monastic life none is more important than his establishment of a full year's probation, followed by a solemn vow of obedience to the Rule as mediated by the abbot of the monastery to which the monk vowed a lifelong residence.

On the constitutional level, Benedict's supreme achievement was to provide a succinct and complete directory for the government and the spiritual and material well-being of a monastery. The abbot, elected for life by his monks, is bound only by the law of God and the Rule, but he is continually advised that he must answer for his monks, as well as for himself, at the judgment seat of God. He appoints his own officials—prior, cellarer (steward), and the rest—and controls all the activities of individuals and the organizations of the common life. Ownership, even of the smallest thing, is forbidden. The ordering of the offices for the canonical hours (daily services) is laid down with precision.

The working day is divided into three roughly equal portions: five to six hours of liturgical and other prayer; five hours of manual work, whether domestic work, craft work, garden work, or field work; and four hours reading of the SCRIPTURES and spiritual writings. This balance of prayer, work, and study is another of Benedict's legacies. All work was directed to making the monastery self-sufficient and self-contained.

Until 1938 the Rule had been considered as a personal achievement of St. Benedict. In that year, however, it was suggested that an anonymous document, the "Rule of the Master" *(Regula magistri)*—previously assumed to have plagiarized part of the Rule—was in fact one of the sources drawn on by St. Benedict. Though absolute certainty has not yet been reached, most competent scholars favor the earlier composition of the "Rule of the Master." If this is accepted, about one-third of Benedict's Rule is derived from the Master—this includes the writings on humility, obedience, and the abbot, which are among the most familiar and admired sections of the Rule. Even so, the Rule that imposed itself all over Europe was the

St. Benedict of Nursia, detail of a polyptych by Segna di Buonaventura, early 14th century
By courtesy of the Metropolitan Museum of Art, New York City, Gift of Reinhardt and Co., 1924

Rule of St. Benedict, derived from disparate sources, but providing a directory at once practical and spiritual for the monastic way of life, that continued for 1,500 years.

BENEDICTINE \‚be-nə-'dik-‚tēn\, member of the Order of Saint Benedict (O.S.B.), the confederated congregations of monks and lay brothers who follow the rule of life of ST. BENEDICT OF NURSIA. The Benedictines, strictly speaking, do not constitute a single religious order because each monastery is autonomous.

Benedict wrote his rule with his own abbey in mind; the rule spread slowly in Italy and Gaul, and by the 7th century it had been applied to women, as nuns, whose patroness was deemed Scholastica, sister of Benedict.

By the time of Charlemagne at the beginning of the 9th century, the Benedictine Rule had supplanted most other observances in northern and western Europe. During the five centuries following the death of Benedict, the monasteries multiplied both in size and in wealth. They were the chief repositories of learning and literature in western Europe and were also the principal educators.

The great age of Benedictine predominance ended about the middle of the 12th century, and the history of the main line of Benedictine MONASTICISM for the next three centuries was to be one of decline and decadence.

The 15th century saw the rise of a new Benedictine institution, the congregation. In 1424 the congregation of Santa Giustina of Padua instituted reforms that breathed new life into Benedictine monasticism. Superiors were elected for three years, and the monks no longer took vows to a particular house but to the congregation. This radical reform spread to all the Benedictines. In the turmoil of the Protestant REFORMATION in the 16th century the monasteries and nunneries disappeared almost entirely from northern Europe, and, for almost a century, they suffered greatly in France and central Europe. Benedictinism revived in France and Germany during the 17th century, and though the 18th century witnessed a new decline, from the middle of the 19th century Benedictine monasteries and nunneries again began to flourish. Foundations, including Solesmes in France and Maria Laach in Germany, arose throughout Europe; monks and nuns returned to England; congregations were established in North and South America; and monasteries scattered all over the world.

BENEDICTION, a verbal blessing of persons or things, commonly applied to invocations pronounced in God's name by a priest or minister, usually at the conclusion of a religious service. The Aaronic benediction, which reads, "The Lord bless you and keep you: The Lord make his face to shine upon you, and be gracious unto you: The Lord lift up his countenance upon you, and give you peace" (Numbers 6:24–26) was incorporated by MARTIN LUTHER into his German MASS. It is also used in the Mozarabic liturgy of Spain before the reception of the Host. Some Christian churches, however, prefer the benediction of ST. PAUL THE APOSTLE (2 Corinthians 13:14).

In ROMAN CATHOLICISM, benediction commonly means a blessing of persons (*e.g.,* the sick) or objects (*e.g.,* religious articles).

BENE-ISRAEL \bə-‚nā-'iz-rē-əl, -rā-\ (Hebrew: "Sons of Israel"), Jews of India who for centuries lived in Bombay and adjacent regions isolated from other Jewish influences.

According to two equally unverifiable traditions, they arrived in India as a result of a shipwreck or are a remnant of the TEN LOST TRIBES OF ISRAEL. When the existence of a Jewish community in India first attracted public attention in the 18th century, the group still adhered to such Jewish practices as CIRCUMCISION, observance of the SABBATH, certain dietary laws, and the celebration of several major festivals. David Ezekiel Rahabi (1694–1772) and Samuel Ezekiel Divekar (1730–97), both of Cochin, were instrumental in revivifying JUDAISM among the Bene-Israel; contact with Arabic-speaking Jews of Baghdad also facilitated this renewal. The first of numerous Bene-Israel SYNAGOGUES, all following the liturgy of the SEFARDI, was built in Bombay in 1796.

Though the Bene-Israel speak Marathi and differ little from their Hindi neighbors in appearance, they claim pure Jewish blood. This contention created problems when a majority of the Bene-Israel migrated to the State of Israel after 1948, for the chief rabbinate objected to their marriage with other Jews on the grounds that the Bene-Israel could not have properly observed rabbinic laws governing marriage and divorce. A compromise was reached in 1964: The Bene-Israel as a group were declared full-fledged Jews, but the chief rabbinate reserved to itself the right to decide the legitimacy of individual marriages.

BENJAMIN \'ben-jə-mən\, one of the 12 tribes that in biblical times constituted the people of ISRAEL, and one of the two tribes (along with JUDAH) that later became the Jewish people. The tribe was named after the younger of two children born to JACOB (also called Israel) and his second wife, Rachel (GENESIS 35:16–18).

After the death of MOSES, JOSHUA led the Israelites into the Promised Land and, dividing the territory among the 12 tribes, assigned south-central Palestine to the tribe of Benjamin (Joshua 18:11ff.). Members of the tribe were separated when two distinct kingdoms were established after the death of King SOLOMON (922 BCE) and the territory of Benjamin was divided between them (1 Chronicles 9:3). Jews belonging to the 10 tribes of the northern kingdom of Israel disappeared after the Assyrian conquest of 721 BCE and are known in legend as the TEN LOST TRIBES OF ISRAEL (2 Kings 17:5–6; 18:9–12). Benjaminites in the southern kingdom of Judah were assimilated by the more powerful tribe of Judah and gradually lost their identity. Modern Jews thus consider themselves to be descendants of the tribes of Judah and Benjamin. SAUL, the first of Israel's kings, and ST. PAUL THE APOSTLE were both of the tribe of Benjamin.

BEOWULF \'bā-ə-ˌwulf\, heroic poem, the highest achievement of Old English literature and the earliest European vernacular epic. Preserved in a single manuscript (Cotton Vitellius A XV) from c. 1000, it deals with events of the early 6th century and is believed to have been composed between 700 and 750. It did not appear in print until 1815. Although originally untitled, it was later named after the Scandinavian hero Beowulf, whose exploits and character provide its connecting theme. There is no evidence of a historical Beowulf, but some characters, sites, and events in the poem can be historically verified.

The poem falls into two parts. It opens in Denmark, where King Hrothgar's splendid mead hall, Heorot, has been ravaged for 12 years by nightly visits from an evil monster, Grendel, who carries off Hrothgar's warriors and devours them. Unexpectedly, young Beowulf, a prince of the Geats of southern Sweden, arrives with a small band of retainers and offers to cleanse Heorot of its monster. The king is astonished at the little-known hero's daring but welcomes him, and, after an evening of feasting, the King

retires, leaving Beowulf in charge. During the night Grendel comes from the moors, tears open the heavy doors, and devours one of the sleeping Geats. He then grapples with Beowulf, whose powerful grip he cannot escape. He wrenches himself free, tearing off his arm, and leaves, mortally wounded.

The next day is one of rejoicing in Heorot. But at night as the warriors sleep, Grendel's mother comes to avenge her son, killing one of Hrothgar's men. In the morning Beowulf seeks her out in her cave at the bottom of a mere and kills her. He cuts the head from Grendel's corpse and returns to Heorot. The Danes rejoice once more. Hrothgar makes a farewell speech about the character of the true hero, as Beowulf, enriched with honors and princely gifts, returns home to King Hygelac of the Geats.

The second part passes rapidly over King Hygelac's subsequent death in a battle (of historical record), the death of his son, and Beowulf's succession to the kingship and his peaceful rule of 50 years. But now a fire-breathing dragon ravages his land and the doughty but aging Beowulf engages it. The fight is long and terrible and a painful contrast to the battles of his youth. Painful, too, is the desertion of his retainers except for his young kinsman Wiglaf. Beowulf kills the dragon but is mortally wounded. The poem ends with his funeral rites and a lament.

Beowulf belongs metrically, stylistically, and thematically to the inherited Germanic heroic tradition. Many incidents, such as Beowulf's tearing off the monster's arm and his descent into the mere, are familiar motifs from FOLKLORE. The ethical values are manifestly the Germanic code of loyalty to chief and tribe and vengeance to enemies. Yet the poem is so infused with a Christian spirit that it lacks the grim fatality of many of the lays of the EDDAS or of the Icelandic sagas. Beowulf himself seems more altruistic than other Germanic heroes or the heroes of the Iliad. It is significant that his three battles are not against men, which would entail the retaliation of the blood feud, but against evil monsters, enemies of the whole community and of civilization itself. Many critics have seen the poem as a Christian ALLEGORY, with Beowulf the champion of goodness and light against the forces of evil and darkness. His sacrificial death is not seen as tragic but as the fitting end of a hero.

BERAKHAH \bə-rä-'ka\ (Hebrew: "blessing"), *plural* berakhot \-'kōt\, in JUDAISM, a BENEDICTION that is recited at specific points of the SYNAGOGUE liturgy, during private prayer, or on other occasions (*e.g.*, before performing a commandment). Most berakhot begin with the words *Barukh Attah Adonai Eloheinu Melekh ha-Olam* ("Blessed art Thou, O Lord our God, King of the Universe").

Berakhot for food and wine are customarily recited in many Jewish homes as a grace before meals—*e.g.*, "Blessed art Thou, O Lord our God, King of the Universe, who hast created the fruit of the vine." Many of the berakhot also thank God for sanctifying ISRAEL through the holidays.

BERLIN, ISAIAH BEN JUDAH LOEB \bər-'lin\, *also called* Isaiah Pick (b. October 1725, Eisenstadt, Hungary [now in Austria]—d. May 13, 1799, Breslau, Silesia, Prussia [now Wrocław, Pol.]), Jewish scholar noted for his textual commentaries on the TALMUD and other writings.

The son of a well-known Talmudic scholar, he moved to Berlin as a youth. He became a member of the rabbinate late in life (1787), and in 1793 he was elected RABBI of Breslau. Berlin's writings are distinguished for their critical and historical insight. Among his works are commentaries, notes, and glosses on many early works of Jewish scholarship. His commentary on the Talmud, *Masoret ha-Shas* ("Talmud Tradition"), supplements an earlier work by a Frankfort rabbi and is the best known of his collated texts (noting variant readings and parallel passages).

BERNADETTE OF LOURDES, SAINT \‚ber-nȧ-'det . . . 'lürd, *Angl* ‚bər-nə-'det . . . 'lürdz\, *original name* Marie-Bernarde Soubirous (b. Jan. 7, 1844, LOURDES, France—d. April 16, 1879, Nevers; canonized Dec. 8, 1933; feast day April 16, but sometimes February 18 in France), miller's daughter whose visions led to the founding of the shrine of Lourdes.

Bernadette was from a poverty-stricken family. She contracted cholera in the epidemic of 1854 and suffered from other ailments through-out her life. Between February 11 and July 16, 1858, at the age of 14, she is said to have had a series of visions of the Virgin MARY, who revealed her identity with the words "I am the IMMACULATE CONCEPTION." Bernadette steadfastly defended the genuineness of these visions, despite strong opposition from her parents, the local clergy, and civil authorities, as she relayed messages she said were given her by the Virgin. To escape public attention she became a boarder in the local school run by the Sisters of Charity of Nevers. In 1866 she was granted admission into the novitiate in the mother

St. Bernadette
BBC Hulton Picture Library

house at Nevers. There she completed her religious instruction and passed her remaining years in prayer and seclusion. The chapel of the St. Gildard Convent, Nevers, contains her body.

BERNARD OF CLAIRVAUX, SAINT \ber-'nȧr...kler-'vȯ... *Angl* bər-'närd\ (b. 1090, probably Fontaine-les-Dijon, near Dijon, Burgundy—d. Aug. 20, 1153, Clairvaux, Champagne; canonized Jan. 18, 1174; feast day August 20), CISTERCIAN monk and mystic, the founder of the abbey of Clairvaux and one of the most influential churchmen of his time.

Born of landowning aristocracy, Bernard turned away from his literary education, begun at the school at Châtillon-sur-Seine, and from ecclesiastical advancement toward a life of renunciation and solitude. Bernard sought the counsel of the abbot of Cîteaux, Stephen Harding, and decided to enter this struggling new community that had been established to restore Benedictinism to a more primitive and austere pattern of life. He entered the Cîteaux community in 1112, and from then until 1115 he cultivated his spiritual and theological studies.

In 1115 Stephen Harding appointed him to lead a small group of monks to establish a monastery at Clairvaux, on the border of Burgundy and Champagne. Bernard and his companions endured extreme deprivations for well over a decade before Clairvaux was self-sufficient. Meanwhile, as Bernard's health worsened, his spirituality deepened. Under pressure from his ecclesiastical superiors and his friends, he

retired to a hut near the monastery and to the discipline of a quack physician. It was here that his first writings evolved. They are characterized by references to the CHURCH FATHERS and by the use of analogues, etymologies, alliterations, and biblical symbols. He also produced a small but complete treatise on MARIOLOGY, "Praises of the Virgin Mother." Bernard was to become a major champion of a moderate cult of the Virgin, though he opposed the notion of the IMMACULATE CONCEPTION.

The mature and most active phase of Bernard's career occurred between 1130 and 1145. In these years both Clairvaux and Rome focused upon Bernard. Mediator and counselor for several civil and ecclesiastical councils and for theological debates during seven years of papal disunity, and the confidant of five popes, Bernard considered it his role to assist in healing the church of wounds inflicted by the ANTIPOPES and to oppose the rationalistic influence of the greatest and most popular dialectician of the age, PETER ABELARD. Bernard finally claimed a victory over Abelard, not because of skill or cogency in argument but because of his homiletical denunciation and his favored position with the bishops and the PAPACY.

His greatest literary endeavor, "Sermons on the Canticle of Canticles," was written during this active time. It was a love song supreme: "The Father is never fully known if He is not loved perfectly." Add to this one of Bernard's favorite prayers, "Whence arises the love of God? From God. And what is the measure of this love? To love without measure," and one has a key to his doctrine.

BERTINORO, OBADIAH (BEN ABRAHAM YARE) OF \‚ō-bə-'dī-ə . . . ‚ber-tē-'nōr-ō\ (b. *c.* 1450, Bertinoro, Papal States—d. before 1516), Italian rabbinic author whose commentary on the MISHNAH, incorporating literal explanations from the medieval commentator RASHI and citing rulings from the philosopher MOSES MAIMONIDES, is a standard work of Jewish literature and since its first printing in 1548 has been published in almost every edition of the Mishnah.

Bertinoro is also remembered as the author of three celebrated letters describing his three-year journey (1486–88) to Jerusalem and containing invaluable descriptions of the people and customs of the Jewish communities he visited on the way. The letters, written to Bertinoro's father and brother during the period 1488–90, have been published under the titles *Darkhei Ẓiyyon* and *HaMassa le-Ereẓ Yisrael* and translated into several languages. He lived in Jerusalem almost continuously after 1488, acting as spiritual head of the Jewish community there.

BES \'bes\, in ancient EGYPTIAN RELIGION, a minor god represented as a dwarf with large head, goggle eyes, protruding tongue, bowlegs, bushy tail, and usually a crown of feathers. The name Bes is now used to designate a group of deities of similar appearance with a wide variety of ancient names. The god's figure was intended to inspire joy or drive away pain and sorrow, his hideousness being perhaps supposed to scare away evil spirits. Contrary to the usual rule of representation, Bes was commonly shown full-faced rather than in profile. He was portrayed on mirrors, ointment vases, and other personal articles. He was associated with music and with childbirth and was represented in the "birth houses" devoted to the cult of the child god.

BETHEL \'be-thəl, be-'thel\, ancient city of Palestine, located just north of Jerusalem. Originally called Luz (GENESIS 28:19; Judges 1:23), and in modern times Baytin, Bethel was

important in OLD TESTAMENT times and was frequently associated with ABRAHAM and JACOB (Genesis 12:8; 13:3; 28:10–22; 35:1ff.). Excavations suggest that Bethel may have been the actual scene of the events described in the Old Testament as having taken place at Ai during the Israelite conquest of CANAAN (Joshua 8ff.)

After the division of ISRAEL, Jeroboam I (10th century BCE) made Bethel the chief SANCTUARY of the northern kingdom (Israel; 1 Kings 12:28–30), and the city was later the center for the prophetic ministry of AMOS (Amos 7:10–13). The city apparently escaped destruction by the Assyrians at the time of the fall of Samaria (721 BCE), but it was occupied by JOSIAH of JUDAH (reigned c. 640–c. 609 BCE; 2 Kings 23:4,15f.; 2 Chronicles 34:1–7).

BETHLEHEM, STAR OF, celestial phenomenon mentioned in the Gospel According to Matthew as leading "wise men from the East" to the birthplace of JESUS CHRIST. While the fact that the year of Jesus' birth is unknown prevents certain identification, natural events that might well have been considered important OMENS and described as stars include exploding stars (novae and supernovae), comets (Halley's Comet was visible in 12 and 11 BCE), meteors, and planetary conjunctions—i.e., apparent close approaches of two or more planets to each other.

Chinese annals record novae in 5 BCE and 4 BCE. Several striking planetary conjunctions also took place within 10 years of the chronological point now taken as the beginning of the Christian era. A triple conjunction in early 6 BCE, in which Mars, Jupiter, and Saturn stood at the points of a triangle, has often been mentioned as a possible explanation of the star. Prior to that, in 7 BCE, Jupiter and Saturn were for eight months within three degrees of each other and three times within that period passed within one degree. Several years later, on June 17, 2 BCE, the bright planets VENUS and Jupiter would have appeared to observers in Babylon to have merged just before setting in the general direction of Bethlehem to the west.

BEZA, THEODORE \'bē-zə\, *French* Théodore de Bèze \də-'bez\ (b. June 24, 1519, Vézelay, France—d. Oct. 13, 1605, Geneva), author, translator, educator, and theologian who assisted and later succeeded JOHN CALVIN as a leader of the Protestant REFORMATION centered at Geneva.

After studying law at Orléans, France (1535–39), Beza established a practice in Paris, where he published *Juvenilia* (1548), a volume of amorous verse that earned him a reputation as a leading Latin poet. On recovering from a serious illness, he underwent a conversion experience and in 1548 traveled to Geneva to join Calvin. A year later Beza became a professor of Greek at Lausanne, where he wrote in defense of the burning of the anti-Trinitarian heretic MICHAEL SERVETUS (d. 1553). For several years Beza traveled throughout Europe defending the Protestant cause. He returned to Geneva in 1558.

There, in 1559, with Calvin, he founded the new Geneva academy, destined to become a training ground for promotion of Calvinist doctrines. As its first rector, Beza was the logical successor to Calvin upon the reformer's death in 1564. Beza remained the chief pastor of the Geneva church for the rest of his life, contributing numerous works that influenced the development of Reformed theology.

Beza's sermons and commentaries were widely read in his time; his Greek editions and Latin translations of the NEW TESTAMENT were basic sources for the Geneva BIBLE and the KING JAMES VERSION (1611). His *De jure magistratum*

(1574), defending the right of revolt against tyranny, grew out of the St. Bartholomew's Day Massacre (1572), from which many surviving French Protestants were welcomed by Beza in Geneva. Beza's book overthrew the earlier Calvinist doctrine of obedience to all civil authority and became a major political manifesto of CALVINISM. His other works include anti-Catholic tracts, a biography of Calvin, and the *Histoire ecclésiastique des Églises réformées au royaume de France* (1580; "Ecclesiastical History of the Reformed Church in the Kingdom of France"). Both as a theologian and as an administrator, despite occasional charges of intolerance made against him, Beza is considered not only Calvin's successor but also his equal in securing the establishment of Calvinism in Europe.

BHADRABĀHU I \,bə-drə-'bä-hü\, Jain leader and philosopher who, after a serious 12-year-long famine, is held to have led an exodus from the Jain stronghold in northeastern India to Sravana-Belgola, near Mysore, southwestern India, about 300 BCE.

The DIGAMBARA sect of JAINISM, whose monks wear no clothing, recognizes Bhadrabāhu as their founder, claiming that he left the Mauryan capital Pāṭaliputra in the company of the first king of the dynasty, who had embraced the life of Jain mendicancy. Many inscriptions in the Mysore area lend credibility to an early southward migration, though not necessarily captained by Bhadrabāhu or Candra Gupta (Chandragupta Maurya). According to Digambara sources, monks in Bhadrabāhu's following returned to Pāṭaliputra after his death but were unable to accept doctrinal and practical changes that had been instigated in their absence by the faction that came to be called ŚVETĀMBARA. Śvetāmbara sources represent this history differently. Bhadrabāhu is believed to have been the author of three of the Jain sacred books as well as of *Niryukti*s, short commentaries on 10 of the 12 original sacred books. He is reputed to have died by realizing the Jain ideal of starving to death.

BHAGAVAD GĪTĀ \'bə-gə-,vəd-'gē-,tä\ (Sanskrit: "Song of God"), one of the greatest of the Hindu SCRIPTURES. It forms part of Book VI of the MAHĀBHĀRATA and is written in the form of a dialogue between the warrior Prince ARJUNA and his friend and charioteer, KRISHNA (often considered an earthly incarnation of the god VISHNU, but in the conception of the text itself he is the supreme divinity). The *Bhagavad Gītā*, consisting of 700 Sanskrit verses divided into 18 chapters, is of a later date than many parts of the *Mahābhārata* and was most probably written in the 1st or 2nd century CE.

The setting is a battlefield, just prior to the war between the PĀṆḌAVAS and the Kauravas (the cousins of the Pāṇḍavas). The two armies stand opposing each other, and, on seeing many of his friends and kinsmen among those lined up on the other side, Prince Arjuna hesitates. He considers whether it would not be better to allow himself to be slain by the enemy rather than to engage in a cruel albeit just war. He is recalled to his sense of duty as a warrior by Krishna, who points out to him that the higher way is the dispassionate discharge of his duty, performed sacrificially, with faith in Krishna, and without concern for personal triumph or gain.

The *Bhagavad Gītā* considers broadly the nature of ultimate reality. As a predominantly theistic work, it often describes that reality as a personal god, Krishna, but it also refers to the supreme as a seemingly impersonal transcendent absolute, and equally as the state of one's own awakened spirit. The *Bhagavad Gītā* elaborates and correlates three disciplines (YOGAS) creating the possibility for transcending the limitations of this world: JÑĀNA (knowledge or wisdom), KARMA (dispassionate action), and BHAKTI (love of God).

The earliest commentary on the *Bhagavad Gītā* is that of the great philosopher ŚAMKARA. Outstanding modern commentaries are those of B.G. Tilak, ŚRĪ AUROBINDO, MAHATMA GANDHI, and Sarvepalli Radhakrishnan. GITA PRESS was founded in the 1930s with the purpose of making the *Bhagavad Gītā* accessible to every Hindu, and the claim that it is the most widely revered Hindu scripture has gained plausibility throughout the 20th century.

BHĀGAVATA \'bä-gə-və-tə\ (Sanskrit: "One Belonging to the Glorious One [Vishnu]"), member of the earliest recorded Hindu sect, representing the beginnings of theistic, devotional worship and of modern VAIṢṆAVISM.

The Bhāgavata sect apparently originated among the Yādava people of the Mathura area in the centuries preceding the beginning of the Common Era. Inscriptional evidence locates it in surrounding North India in the 2nd century BCE. It was introduced into South India at an early date, quite possibly as early as the 3rd or 2nd century BCE, and continued to be prominent within Vaiṣṇavism until at least the 11th century. Some have argued that part of its success derived from royal patronage made possible by its relatively lenient approach to accepting initiates from nonbrahmanical communities.

The Bhāgavata system centered upon a personal god variously called VISHNU, VĀSUDEVA, KRISHNA, Hari, or Nārāyaṇa, and was known as *ekāntika dharma* ("religion with one object"—*i.e.*, MONOTHEISM). The religious poem the BHAGAVAD GĪTĀ (1st–2nd century CE) is the earliest extant exposition

of the Bhāgavata system, but the magisterial text is the BHĀGAVATA PURĀṆA, whose lengthy and influential 10th book focuses on Krishna. By the time of the *Gītā*, Vāsudeva (Krishna), the hero-deity of the Yādava clan, was identified with the Vedic Lord Vishnu. Bhāgavata religion, unlike Vedic practice (*see* VEDIC RELIGION), is associated with worship through images, and a case has been made that some of India's earliest extant temples, such as the impressive 8th-century temple of Vishnu as Vaikuṇṭha Perumāḷ in Kāñchīpuram, owe their design to Bhāgavata inspiration. It is also argued that the *Bhāgavata Purāṇa* should be understood as the great Bhāgavata SCRIPTURE, even from a relatively early date.

BHĀGAVATA PURĀṆA \'bä-gə-və-tə-pu̇-'rä-nə\ (Sanskrit: "Ancient Accounts of the Glorious One [VISHNU]"), the most celebrated text of a variety of Hindu sacred literature in Sanskrit that is known as the PURĀṆAS, and the specific text that is held sacred by the BHĀGAVATA sect. The *Bhāgavata Purāṇa* was probably composed about the 10th century, somewhere in the Tamil country of South India; its expression of BHAKTI owes a debt to that of the South Indian devotional poets, the ĀḶVĀRS. The *Purāṇa* is made up of some 18,000 stanzas divided into 12 books; but it is book 10, which deals with KRISHNA'S childhood and his years spent among the cowherds of Vṛndāvana, that accounts for its immense popularity with Vaiṣṇavas throughout India (*see* VAIṢṆAVISM). The attempts on Krishna's life made by his wicked uncle Kaṃsa, the childhood pranks he played on his foster mother Yaśodā, his love for the *gopīs* (cowherd wives and daughters) and their passionate abandonment to him are treated with endearing charm and grace, even while transfused with deep religious significance. In theology, the *Bhāgavata Purāṇa* attempts to build a synthesis between *bhakti* devotionalism and the abstract philosophy of ADVAITA VEDĀNTA.

The child Krishna stealing butter, painting from the Bhāgavata Purāṇa, *Kāṅgra school, 1790–1800*
The F.F. Wadia Collection, Pune, India

BHAIṢAJYAGURU \bī-'shəj-yə-'gu̇r-ü\ (Sanskrit), *Tibetan* Sman-Bla-Rgyal-Po \'man-lä-'gʸel-bō\, *Chinese* Yao-Shih-Fo \'yau̇-'shə-'fō, -'shər-\, *Japanese* Yakushi Nyorai \'yä-ku̇-shē-'nē-yō-rī\, the healing Buddha, widely worshiped in Tibet, China, and Japan. According to popular belief, some illnesses are effectively cured by merely touching Bhaiṣajyaguru's image or by calling out his name. More serious illnesses, however, require the performance of complex rituals, which are described in the *Bhaiṣajyaguru Sūtra*. He is associated with the "self-born," eternal Buddha, AKṢOBHYA (and by some Japanese sects with another eternal Buddha, *i.e.*, VAIROCANA), and rules over the Eastern Paradise.

In Japan, Bhaiṣajyaguru is especially venerated by the

Tendai (T'IEN-T'AI), SHINGON, and ZEN sects. In Japan he is often represented in the garb of a blue-skinned Buddha with his medicine bowl in one hand. In Tibet he often holds the medicinal myrobalan fruit. He has in his retinue 12 divine *yakṣa*, or nature spirits, generals who protect true believers. Chinese Buddhists, in a later phase, connected these generals with the 12 hours of the day and the 12 years of the Chinese calendar's cycle.

BHAJAN \ˈbə-jən\: *see* KĪRTAN or BHAKTI.

BHAKTI \ˈbək-tē\, in various South Asian religions, particularly HINDUISM, the devotional sentiment widely understood to be a predominant aspect of religious practice and expression. Derived from the Sanskrit verbal root *bhaj*, originally meaning "to share, to apportion," *bhakti* came to mean "love, sharing, worship, devotion." In BUDDHISM and JAINISM, *bhakti* was an infrequent technical term implying veneration and awe of the BUDDHA GOTAMA or MAHĀVĪRA, one factor among others, such as knowledge of SCRIPTURE or ASCETICISM, necessary for spiritual practice. In South Asian ISLAM, the rudiments of *bhakti* appeared in works of SUFISM, particularly during the reign of AKBAR (1556–1605), and in the veneration of a *pīr*, or charismatic Sufi figure. SIKHISM, emerging in the 16th century, incorporated many practices associated with *bhakti*, such as an emphasis on the name (NĀM) of God in worship. However, *bhakti* is most prevalent in Hinduism, where loosely interdependent religious communities arose with *bhakti* as a guiding theological and social principle. Proponents of *bhakti*—often called collectively "the *bhakti* movement"—challenged the dominance of sacrificial VEDIC RELIGION, CASTE boundaries, gender inequity, and the use of Sanskrit as the exclusive language of religion. *Bhakti* integrates aspects of personal RELIGIOUS EXPERIENCE, social protest, and a variety of ritual modes around a notion of intimacy with one's deity that colors all aspects of human existence.

Precursors to *bhakti* existed as early as the ṚG VEDA (c. 1200 BCE), where devotees extolled the virtues of certain deities, entreating the goddess SARASVATĪ, for example, to show benevolence. The word's earliest datable occurrence is in the work of the preeminent Sanskrit grammarian Pāṇini, who uses *bhakti* to mean "devotion." It also appears in the early Buddhist text, the THERAGĀTHĀ. Several early factors opened the way for *bhakti*'s appearance as a religious, social, and philosophical ideology. Jainism, Buddhism, and Upanishadic thought presented challenges to VEDIC RELIGION through their radical models of religious expression that emphasized communal support for individual effort toward spiritual evolution, rather than a reliance on priestly authority and sacrificial rituals. Concurrently, the Indian epics RĀMĀYAṆA and MAHĀBHĀRATA and the PURĀṆA literature about the lives of deities, depicted gods and goddesses in direct relationship with humans, joining together in war, love, and friendship. The most famous example of this is the intense relationship between KRISHNA and ARJUNA in the BHAGAVAD GĪTĀ (c. 1st century CE), where Krishna explicitly propounds *bhakti* in the context of Arjuna's loyalty and challenge.

By the early centuries of the Common Era, *bhakti* was apparent in various forms of religious expression, particularly during the "Golden Age" of the Gupta Empire (320–647 CE) and the reign of the Pallavas and the Pāṇḍyas in South India (4th–10th centuries CE). Temple construction became important as an act of *bhakti*. There, as in private homes, sacred icons were the objects of visual *bhakti*, a

process today known familiarly as DARŚAN, or "seeing," whereby a devotee sees and is seen by God. Another typical aspect of Hindu worship came to light in this ambiance: PŪJĀ, whereby the deities in image form are welcomed with flowers, fruits, and sweets as if they were honored guests in the devotee's home.

Temple construction and personal worship began to reflect sectarian preference for VISHNU, SHIVA, or manifestations of the Goddess (DEVĪ, ŚAKTI, DURGĀ). The first written records of songs voiced in a vernacular language rather than in Sanskrit appeared in Tamil in the 6th century in South India. In the course of the next several centuries, massive collections of Tamil hymns to Shiva and Vishnu emerged, soon to be accompanied by a separate literature describing the lives of the poets who produced them. The Śaiva poets are called collectively NĀYAṈĀRS, the Vaiṣṇava poets ĀḶVĀRS. Today *bhakti* poetry continues to be composed and sung in every South Asian language. *See also* ŚAIVISM and VAIṢṆAVISM.

Bhakti saint-poets have expressed their love of God through song in two general modes. In the first, SAGUṆA ("with traits"), the poets evoke the image of the deity, portrayed in human and tangible ways, with color, personality, and definition. Sometimes they take their inspiration from specific temple icons and sculpture, rich with physical detail, as well as from pilgrimages that bring *saguṇa* devotees to these holy sites. *Saguṇa bhakti* songs also explore various relationships between the deity and the devotee by conceiving of them in familiar human terms—*e.g.*, a child trusting in a parent, a servant humbled before his master, or a lover yearning for her beloved. Two good examples of saints "in love" with their God are the female poets MAHĀDEVĪ (12th century), who sings to her lord Shiva, "white as jasmine," and MĪRĀBĀĪ (16th century), who seeks shelter in Krishna, her beloved "mountain lifter." But female poets are not the only ones to suffer by being separated from a God portrayed as male; from the 1st millennium onward, male poets have assumed female personae to express the same longing.

A second *bhakti* mode, NIRGUṆA ("without traits"), conceives of divinity as singular and ineffable, beyond the realm of human perception. *Nirguṇa* saint-poets often challenge sensory religious practices such as *pūjā* and *darśan*, and question the efficacy of pilgrimages to temples and holy sites, as BASAVA (12th century) did in South India and KABĪR (15th century) in the North. They are apt to prefer a focus on the simple recitation of God's name. *Nirguṇa* saint-poets like Kabīr, RAVIDĀS, and NĀNAK (15–16th centuries) often articulated *bhakti*'s intensity in ways that elude comparison to the "natural" forms of relationship favored by *saguṇa* poets. Yet in the communities that formed around them, the teacher-student relationship loomed large, and in their own poetry as well we find the figure of the transcendent True Teacher (*satguru*)—either as an internal voice of authority or as an external guide or both. Finally, *nirguṇa* and *saguṇa* modes are sometimes indistinguishable, as with the 14th-century Marathi saint-poet NĀMDEV, who sings to his deity, "You are unfathomable . . . I see you wherever I go."

Bhakti has an explicitly theological dimension. Systematic theologians such as RĀMĀNUJA (11th–12th century) and VALLABHA (16th century) sought to achieve a rapprochement between the personalist convictions of *bhakti* and the abstract philosophical rigor of various schools of VEDĀNTA. Each proposed ways in which the universe could be understood as both displaying the divine, of which it is an embodiment, and obscuring it. Such theologies, like those that developed by and around BASAVA (from Karnataka), CAITANYA (from Bengal), NĀNAK (from the Punjab), and KABĪR (from the Gangetic valley), helped give distinctive regional forms to *bhakti*. Sometimes they also echoed sectarian styles that can be seen in poetry, social protest, ritual performance, and even cuisine.

BHAKTIVEDANTA, A(BHAY) C(HARANARAVINDA)

\ˌbək-ti-vā-'dän-tə, -'vā-dän-tə\, *also called* Swami Prabhupāda \'swä-mē-ˌprə-bù-'pä-də, -'prə-bù-ˌpäd\ (b. Sept. 1, 1896, Calcutta, India—d. Nov. 14, 1977, Vrindāvan, Uttar Pradesh), Indian religious leader who in 1965 founded the International Society for Krishna Consciousness (ISKCON), commonly known as the Hare Krishna movement.

In 1922 Bhaktivedanta, a pharmacist by trade, was urged by his GURU, a spiritual leader of one of the Vaiṣṇava sects of HINDUISM (*see* VAIṢṆAVISM), to preach the teachings of KRISHNA throughout the Western world. Thereafter Bhaktivedanta devoted much time as lecturer, writer, editor, and translator for the Vaiṣṇava sect to which he belonged. In 1933 he was formally initiated as a disciple at Allahābād, Uttar Pradesh.

Because his family did not share his religious interests, Bhaktivedanta turned over his business to a son and renounced all family ties in 1954 to devote his full time to religious work. He received the title of swami in 1959 and in 1965 moved to Boston and then New York City, where he established the headquarters of the Hare Krishna movement. The movement, which he claimed could affect the consciousness of a world afflicted with rampant materialism, became especially popular among young people, and many of the swami's books began to be studied on college and university campuses. Despite his failing health, by the time of his death Bhaktivedanta had written and published more than 50 books on ancient Vedic culture and had opened more than 100 centers throughout the world.

BHĀRATA NĀṬYA

\'bär-ə-tə-'nä-tyə\ (Sanskrit: "Bharata's dancing"), *also called* dasī āṭṭam; the principal of the classical dance styles of India (the others being *kuchipuḍi*, *kathak*, *kathakaḷi*, *manipuri*, and *orissi*). It is indigenous to Tamil Nadu but has become well known throughout India and abroad. *Bhārata nāṭya* serves the expression of Hindu religious themes and devotions, and its techniques and terminology have been traced back to ancient treatises such as the *Nāṭya-śāstra*, by the BRAHMIN sage and priest Bharata. It was originally performed exclusively by female temple dancers and was not brought to the stage for public performance until about 1930.

A program of *bhārata nāṭya* usually lasts two hours without interruption and includes a specific list of procedures, all performed by one dancer, who does not leave the stage or change costume. The accompanying orchestra—composed of drums, drone, and singer—occupies the back of the stage, led by the GURU, or teacher, of the dancer.

The dancer's feet beat out complicated counter rhythms; the legs are bent in a characteristic low squat; arms, neck, and shoulders are part of the movement. In the pantomime sections, the hands tell the story through conventional gestural language, while the face expresses the story. In the pure dance the hands are restricted to 11 hand poses.

Bhārata nāṭya has survived to the present through the DEVADĀSĪS, temple dancing girls who devoted their lives to their gods through this medium. In colonial times the institution of *devadāsī* fell into disrepute, and temple dancing

girls became synonymous with prostitutes. In the latter half of the 19th century in Tanjore, Chinnaiah, Ponnaiah, Vadivelu, and Shivanandam, four talented dancers who were brothers, revived the original purity of *dāsi āṭṭam* by studying and following the ancient texts and temple friezes, with missing links supplied by the socially spurned *devadāsī*s. Their popularized form of *dāsi āṭṭam* was called *bhārata nāṭya*.

BHARATIYA JANATA PARTY

\ˌbär-ə-'tē-yə-ˌjə-nə-'tä\ (Indian People's Party), *also called* BJP, political party of post-independence India that includes a strong Hindu nationalist component and that succeeded in forming a coalition government at the national level in 1998. Standing in the lineage of the earlier Jan Sangh Party, the BJP forms a triad with the Rashtriya Swayamsevak Sangh (RSS) and VISHVA HINDU PARISHAD (VHP). This triad is commonly called the Sangh Parivar ("Sangh" family [of organizations]), after the RSS, considered the parent group providing leadership for all three.

While a certain proportion of the BJP's success at the polls has followed from its attempt to represent itself as being opposed to the "corruption as usual" practices of the Congress Party and others, it has also attempted to mobilize sentiment in favor of a majority Hindu polity. Some of the key ideological planks in this program were laid out by V.D. Savarkar in 1923 under the banner HINDUTVA ("Hinduness"), a concept insisting that Hindus give true definition to Indian national identity because they embrace their "fatherland" (*pitṛbhūmi*) as "sacred land" (*puṇyabhūmi*). Such ideas have had the effect of estranging Muslims, Christians, and many low-caste Hindus from membership in the BJP. In the 1990s the BJP made efforts to include these groups, but its legacy as the party that supported the drive to de-

Bhārata nāṭya dance drama
Mohan Khokar

stroy the Babri Mosque in AYODHYA in 1992 has continued to brand it an ineradicably Hindu nationalist party in the minds of many, as does its ongoing alliance with avowedly anti-Muslim groups such as the Shiv Sena, a regional party in Maharashtra. The BJP's importation of explicit Hindu forms into political action and discourse—*e.g.*, its use of the vocabulary of Hindu pilgrimage or the language of sacrifice (YAJÑA)—cause it to be regarded with fear and deep suspicion by many committed to political secularism in contemporary India.

BHARTṚHARI \'bər-tri-,hə-rē, 'bär-\ (d. 650, Ujjain, India), Hindu philosopher, poet, and grammarian, author of the *Vākyapadīya* ("Words in a Sentence"), regarded as one of the most significant works on the philosophy of language in the *śabdādvaita* school of Indian thought.

Three collections of poetry are also attributed to him, attesting to his status as a legendary authority on life's multiple attractions. All are called *śataka* ("century"), owing to the fact that they each contain one hundred verses: the *Śṛngāra-* (love) *śataka*, *Nīti-* (ethical and polity) *śataka*, and *Vairāgya-* (dispassion) *śataka*. Legends of Bhartṛhari's life echo this range but are not entirely consistent with one another. One version says that he was attached to the court of the Maitraka king of Valabhi (modern Vala, Gujarat), where he cultivated the pleasures of this life; but he felt so torn by the needs of the soul that he withdrew to the monastic life on seven separate occasions, each time to reemerge. The 7th-century Buddhist traveler I-ching evidently heard a version of this narrative and believed Bhartṛhari's ASCETICISM to have been derived from BUDDHISM. A strong sense of personal irony enlivens the *śatakas*, as well as a consciousness of the strains and insults associated with being a poet in royal service. In keeping with the breadth of Bhartṛhari's persona, another work is sometimes also attributed to him: the *Bhaṭṭi kāvya* ("Poem of Bhaṭṭi"), in which the poet performs linguistic gymnastics to demonstrate the subtleties of Sanskrit.

BHĀVAVIVEKA \'bä-və-vi-'vā-kə\, 8th-century Indian Buddhist philosopher who was an interpreter of NĀGĀRJUNA, the founder of MĀDHYAMIKA school of philosophy. The disciples of Nāgārjuna who continued to limit the use of logic to a negative and indirect method, known as *prasaṅga*, are called the *prāsaṅgikas*: of these, Aryadeva, Buddhapalita, and CANDRAKĪRTI are the most important. Bhāvaviveka, however, followed the method of direct reasoning and thus founded what is called the Svātantrika (*svatantra*; "independent") school of Mādhyamika philosophy. With him Buddhist logic comes to its own. Bhāvaviveka developed a notion of two truths in which, at the level of conventional (as distinguished from ultimate) truth, reason could be used to support positive teachings and practices. The Svātantrika tradition played a very important role in the development of Buddhist philosophy in Tibet.

BHEDĀBHEDA \'bā-dä-'bā-də\ (Sanskrit: "difference and nondifference," or "identity in difference"), an important branch of VEDĀNTA. Its principal author was Bhāskara, probably a younger contemporary of the great thinker ŚAṂKARA. Against Śaṃkara's view that ultimately all distinctions are unreal and therefore any particular path of action is irrelevant for a liberated person (SANNYĀSĪ), Bhāskara upheld the doctrine of the "cumulative effect of acts and knowledge" (*jñāna-karma-samuccaya*) and declared that a person should only withdraw from active life once he has fulfilled its obligations. On the important issue of the relationship between BRAHMAN (the absolute) and the world, Bhāskara taught that Brahman is the substantial cause of the world, which becomes manifold through power or transformation akin to a spider weaving its web. The self is naturally one with Brahman, but is also different by virtue of conditions (UPĀDHIS) that are imposed on Brahman.

Although Bhāskara's doctrine never became as widely accepted as that of Śaṃkara, his work is important for its documentation of the typical BRAHMIN (priestly class) concern not just with MOKṢA (release) but with the implementation of DHARMA—caste and individual obligations that keep the world in balance and produce the good society.

BHIKṢU \'bik-shü\ (Sanskrit), *feminine* bhikṣuṇī \'bik-shù-,nē\, *Pāli* bhikku \'bik-kü\, *or (feminine)* bhikkunī \'bik-kù-,nē\, in BUDDHISM, one who has renounced worldly life and joined the mendicant and CONTEMPLATIVE community. While individuals may enter the monastic life at an early age—some renunciate communities include children in their preteens—a candidate for ordination must be 21 years of age and have parental permission.

The term bhiksu comes from a verbal root meaning "to beg." Thus, a Buddhist monk or nun is marked primarily by his or her practice of poverty and nonattachment to the material world. Originally, bhiksus were the mendicant followers of the BUDDHA GOTAMA who had left their families and worldly pursuits in order to meditate and to apply the Buddha's teachings to their everyday life. Bhiksus tended to live as a group in forest retreats near villages and towns; in exchange for food, the monks taught the townspeople Buddhist ways. Buddhist texts indicate that in the beginning the Buddha allowed only a male monastic community (the SANGHA) but later permitted women to establish a female order as well. (This *bhikṣuṇī* order has been maintained in some MAHĀYĀNA traditions but has not been maintained in the THERAVĀDA context.)

A *bhikṣu* is expected to follow the rules that were established by the Buddha and preserved in a text called the *Vinayā*. There are some 227 to 250 rules regulating the conduct of the *bhikṣu*s and an even greater number for *bhikṣuṇī*. Violations must be confessed in twice-monthly meetings (the *uposatha*). Four monastic rules, if broken, result in lifelong expulsion from the order: (1) having sexual relations, (2) taking or ordering the taking of life, (3) taking something as one's own that has not been freely given, and (4) making claims regarding one's spiritual attainments, powers, or degree of enlightenment.

The *bhikṣu*'s head and face are kept shaven. He wears three garments—an upper and lower robe and a stole—originally made of cast-off rags dyed with saffron, now more likely the gift of a layperson. He is allowed to retain only a minimum of possessions—his robes and stole, a girdle, an alms bowl, a razor, a needle and thread for mending, and a strainer to prevent his harming the small insects that might otherwise enter his drinking water.

The *bhikṣu* begs daily for his food; the donation of food by the laity is viewed as meritorious. The *bhikṣu* may eat no solid food between noon and the following morning. Except on holy days, which are vegetarian, meat may be eaten but only if it has not been cooked especially for a monk.

In the Theravāda countries of Southeast Asia, the monk commonly is prohibited from handling money and from doing physical labor. This is not the case in China and Japan, where Ch'an (ZEN) Buddhism early established the rule, "A day without work, a day without food."

BHINDRANWALE, SANT JARNAIL SINGH \,bin-də-rən-'vä-lā\ (b. 1947, Rhode, Punjab—d. June 6, 1984, Amritsar), SIKH religious leader and political revolutionary. Born into a Sikh peasant family, Jarnail Singh attended a residential Sikh seminary (*taksāl*) where students were trained to become *granthīs* (custodians of the GURDWĀRĀS), preachers, and *rāgīs* (singers of Sikh sacred hymns) at a nearby village, Bhindran. The chief of the Bhindran *taksāl*, Sant Gurbachan Singh, was widely revered. After his death in 1969, one of his followers, Sant Kartar Singh, moved to Mehta, 30 miles from AMRITSAR, and established a new *taksāl* there. Jarnail Singh accompanied him and succeeded him as head of the Mehta *taksāl* after his death in 1977.

Known for his charisma as well as his knowledge of the SCRIPTURE, history, and mythology of SIKHISM, Sant Jarnail Singh was asked by the Congress Party under Giani Zail Singh, who later became the president of India, to align with them in their effort to break the hold of the AKĀLĪ DAL on rank-and-file Sikhs. Sant Jarnail Singh obliged, but in the process he became increasingly aware of the role he might play in Sikh history. By setting himself as an example, Sant Jarnail Singh hoped to pull the Sikh community back to its traditions of bravery and martyrdom. He argued against the Akālī Party's policy of negotiating their demands peacefully with the central government in Delhi, insisting that political power in the Punjab was a Sikh right, not a gift of the Delhi regime. Sant Jarnail Singh succeeded in convincing a large number of rural Sikhs that the politics of the Akālī Dal were humiliating for them.

In July 1982, he moved to the GOLDEN TEMPLE (Darbār Sāhib) in Amritsar and began preaching that Sikhs should initiate a battle for creation of a separate state of KHALISTAN. He gathered a considerable following of like-minded militants and stockpiled weapons. In 1984 Prime Minister Indira Gandhi ordered Indian troops to attack the Darbār Sāhib complex, and in the confrontation that followed, hundreds of people were killed, including Sant Jarnail Singh. For many Sikhs, he died the death of a martyr. Especially in the Sikh diaspora, the hope of Khalistan remained a central feature of Sikh life.

BHŪT \'büt\, in the MYTHOLOGY of HINDUISM, a restless ghost. *Bhūt*s are believed to be malignant if they have died a violent death or have been denied funeral rites; they are particularly feared by women, children, and the newly married.

*Bhūt*s haunt trees, deserts, abandoned houses, the hearths and roofs of homes, crossroads, and boundaries but never rest on the ground. Rudimentary shrines are sometimes established for *bhūt*s, and when in fear of them a believer will invoke SHIVA, as he is considered to be their lord.

Sant Jarnail Singh Bhindranwale addressing his followers at Amritsar
AP—Wide World

BIBLE, the sacred SCRIPTURES of JUDAISM and CHRISTIANITY. The Christian Bible consists of the OLD TESTAMENT and the NEW TESTAMENT; in ROMAN CATHOLICISM and EASTERN ORTHODOXY, the Old Testament is slightly larger because of their acceptance of certain books and parts of books considered apocryphal in PROTESTANTISM. The Jewish Bible includes only the books known to Christians as the Old Testament. The arrangements of the Jewish and Christian canons differ considerably. However, the Protestant and Roman Catholic arrangements more nearly match one another.

Traditionally the Jews have divided their scriptures into three parts: the TORAH (the "Law"), or PENTATEUCH; the NEBI'IM (the "Prophets"); and the KETUBIM (the "Writings"), or Hagiographa. The Pentateuch, together with the book of Joshua, can be seen as the account of how ISRAEL became a nation and of how it possessed the Promised Land. The division designated as the "Prophets" continues the story, describing the establishment and development of the monarchy and presentation of the messages of the prophets to the people. The "Writings" include speculation on the place of evil and death in the scheme of things (Job and Ecclesiastes), the poetical works, and other historical books.

In the APOCRYPHA of the Old Testament, the purpose seems to have been to fill in some of the gaps left by the indisputably canonical books and to carry the history of Israel to the 2nd century BCE.

Like the Old Testament, the New Testament is a collection of books, including a variety of early Christian literature. The four GOSPELS deal with the life, the person, and the teachings of JESUS CHRIST, as he was remembered by the Christian community. THE ACTS OF THE APOSTLES carries the story of Christianity from the RESURRECTION of Jesus to the end of the career of PAUL. The Letters, or Epistles, are correspondence by various leaders of the early Christian church applying the message of the church to the sundry needs and problems of early Christian congregations. The REVELATION TO JOHN is the only canonical representative of a large genre of apocalyptic literature that appeared in the early Christian movement.

BIBLICAL CRITICISM, discipline that studies textual, compositional, and historical questions surrounding both the OLD TESTAMENT and the NEW TESTAMENT. Biblical criticism lays the groundwork for the meaningful interpretation of the BIBLE.

The major types of biblical criticism are (1) textual criticism, which is concerned with establishing the original or most authoritative text, (2) philological criticism, which is the study of the biblical languages for an accurate knowledge of vocabulary, grammar, and style of the period, (3) literary criticism, which focuses on the various literary genres embedded in the text in order to uncover evidence concerning date of composition, authorship, and original function of the various types of writing that constitute the Bible, (4) tradition criticism, which attempts to trace the development of the ORAL TRADITIONS that preceded written texts, and (5) form criticism, which classifies the written material according to the preliterary forms, such as PARABLE or hymn.

Other schools of biblical criticism that are more exegetical in intent—that is, concerned with recovering original meanings of texts—include redaction criticism, which studies how the documents were assembled by their final authors and editors, and historical criticism, which seeks to interpret biblical writings in the context of their historical settings.

The application of the scientific principles on which modern criticism is based depend in part upon viewing the Bible as a suitable object for literary study, rather than as an exclusively sacred text.

BIBLICAL INSPIRATION, the claim that the writers of sacred books acted under special divine guidance. It is in many ways an extension of the claim of divine revelation and of the belief that seers, visionaries, and prophets received not only the content of their message, but its form and even its very words, from a divine source. Thus, in ancient Greece, the Delphic ORACLE (and other oracles, as well) were the voice of the divine. In the Hebrew SCRIPTURE, the God of ISRAEL not only put words into the mouths of the prophets and other appointed messengers but often commanded them to write these words down exactly as given. The Christian NEW TESTAMENT affirmed this inspired quality about Hebrew scripture, and eventually the Christian APOSTLES and Evangelists were also seen as having been inspired directly by the HOLY SPIRIT. The highest doctrine of any of the "monotheisms of the Book" is that of ISLAM, where God is the only author of the QUR'AN and MUHAMMAD is merely his scribe.

The rise, within both JUDAISM (by such philosophers as Benedict de Spinoza) and CHRISTIANITY, of the historical-critical method of studying the Bible brought about conflict between the doctrine of biblical inspiration and scholarly study, and with it some of the most bitter theological controversies of the 19th and 20th centuries.

BIBLICAL SOURCE, any of the original oral or written materials that, in compilation, came to constitute the BIBLE of JUDAISM and CHRISTIANITY. Most of the writings in the OLD TESTAMENT are of anonymous authorship, and in many cases it is not known whether they were compiled by individuals or by groups. Nevertheless, by careful evaluation of internal evidence and with the aid of various schools of BIBLICAL CRITICISM, scholars have been able to identify certain sources and to arrange them chronologically.

The means by which the basic sources of the PENTATEUCH were distinguished and their chronology established provided the first clear picture of ISRAEL'S literary and religious development. The names by which these sources are now known, in chronological order, are: the YAHWIST, or J, source, so called because it employed as the Lord's name a Hebrew word transliterated into English as YHWH (called J from the German: JHVH) and spoken as "Yahweh"; the ELOHIST, or E, source, distinguished by its reference to the Lord as Elohim; the DEUTERONOMIST, or D, source, marked by distinctive vocabulary and style; and the PRIESTLY CODE, or P, source, which contains detailed ritual instructions.

Numerous other sources for the Old Testament have since been identified, including two of the earliest books of Hebrew literature, not now extant, parts of which are embedded in the early narratives. These, the "Book of the Wars of Yahweh" and the "Book of Yashar" (the Upright), were probably poetic in form.

The NEW TESTAMENT sources consist of the original writings that constitute the Christian SCRIPTURES, together with the ORAL TRADITION that preceded them. The first three Gospels are referred to as synoptic; i.e., they have a common source. Contemporary opinion holds that Mark served as a source for Matthew and Luke and that the latter two also share another common source, called Q (after the German word *Quelle,* "source"), consisting mainly of Jesus' sayings. The Gospel of John apparently represents an independent line of transmission.

Whereas most of the Old Testament authors are anonymous, the major New Testament sources are known, and the essential task in their study is to restore the texts as closely as possible to the original autographs. The main sources of evidence are manuscripts of the New Testament in Greek dating from the 2nd to the 15th century (some 5,000 of these manuscripts are known) and early versions in other languages, such as Syriac, Coptic, Latin, Armenian, and Georgian.

These sources are collectively referred to as "witnesses." Authoritative Bibles in contemporary translation are usually based on an eclectic text in which the witnesses show variant readings. In such cases, the reading that best suits the context and the author's known style is preferred.

Attempts to go beyond the original writings to reconstruct the oral tradition behind them are the province of the form of biblical criticism known as tradition criticism. Recent scholars have attempted with this method to recover the actual words of Jesus by removing the accretions attached to them in the course of transmission.

BIBLICAL TRANSLATION, the art and practice of rendering the BIBLE into languages other than those in which it was originally written. Both the OLD TESTAMENT and NEW TESTAMENT have a long history of translation.

The Old Testament was originally written almost entirely in Hebrew, with a few short elements in Aramaic. When the Persian empire gained control of the eastern Mediterranean basin, Aramaic became the dominant language of the area, and it became desirable to have the PENTATEUCH (the books of GENESIS, EXODUS, Leviticus, Numbers, and Deuteronomy) translated into the common language from Hebrew. The resulting TARGUMS (from Aramaic *meturgeman,* "translator") survived after original Hebrew scrolls had been lost.

By the mid-3rd century BCE Greek was the dominant language, and Jewish scholars began translating the Hebrew canon into that language. Because tradition held that each of the 12 tribes of Israel contributed six scholars to the project, the Greek version of the Jewish Bible came to be known later (in Latin) as the SEPTUAGINT (from *septuaginta,* meaning "70").

The Hebrew SCRIPTURES were the only Bible the early Christian church knew, and, as the young religion spread out through the Greek-speaking world, Christians adopted the Septuagint. In the meantime, many of the books of the Christian Bible, the New Testament, were first written or recorded in Greek, while others perhaps were recorded in Aramaic.

The spread of CHRISTIANITY necessitated further translations of both the Old and New Testaments into Coptic, Ethiopian, Gothic, and, most important, Latin. In 405 ST. JEROME finished translating a Latin version that was based firstly on the Septuagint and then on the original Hebrew, and this version, the VULGATE, despite corruption introduced by copyists, became the standard of Western Christianity for a thousand years or more.

Hebrew scholars at Talmudic schools in Palestine and

Babylonia about the 6th century CE began trying to retrieve and codify the Hebrew scriptures, restoring them authoritatively and in the Hebrew language. Over centuries they worked on the traditional text, known as the MASORETIC TEXT, which since its completion in the 10th century has come to be universally accepted.

Jerome's Latin Vulgate served as the basis for translations of both the Old Testament and the New Testament into Syriac, Arabic, Spanish, and many other languages, including English. The Vulgate provided the basis for the Douai-Reims Version (New Testament, 1582; Old Testament, 1609–10), which remained ROMAN CATHOLICISM's only authorized Bible in English until the 20th century.

The new learning in the 15th and 16th centuries revived the study of ancient Greek and led to new translations, among them one by the Dutch humanist DESIDERIUS ERASMUS, who in 1516 published an edition of the New Testament containing the Greek text together with his own translation into Latin. Meanwhile, in Germany, MARTIN LUTHER produced the first complete translation from the original Greek and Hebrew into a modern European language. His German-language translation of the New Testament was published in 1522 and that of the complete Bible in 1534.

The first complete English-language version of the Bible dates from 1382 and was credited to JOHN WYCLIFFE and his followers. But it was the work of the scholar WILLIAM TYNDALE, who from 1525 to 1535 translated the New Testament and part of the Old Testament, that became the model for a series of subsequent English translations. All previous English translations culminated in the KING JAMES VERSION (1611; known in England as the Authorized Version), which was prepared by 54 scholars appointed by King James I.

About the time of the invention of printing in 1450, there were only 33 different translations of the Bible. By about 1800 the number had risen to 71; by the late 20th century the entire Bible had been translated into nearly 325 languages, and portions of the Bible had been published in more than 1,800 of the world's languages.

BID'A \'bi-dä\, in ISLAM, any innovation that has no roots in the traditional practice (SUNNA) of the Muslim community. The ḤANBALĪ LEGAL SCHOOL, the most conservative legal school in Islam (and its modern survivor, the WAHHĀBĪS of Saudi Arabia), rejected *bid'a* completely, arguing that the duty of a Muslim is to follow the example set by MUHAMMAD and not try to improve on it.

Most Muslims, however, agreed that it was impossible to adapt to changing conditions without introducing some types of innovations. As a safeguard against any excesses, *bid'a*s were classified as either good (*ḥasan*) or praiseworthy (*maḥmūdah*), or bad (*sayy'a*) or blameworthy (*madhmūma*). They were then further grouped under five categories of Muslim law: (1) those that are required of the Muslim community (*farḍ kifāyah*): the study of Arabic grammar and philology as tools for the proper understanding of the QUR'AN, evaluation of HADITH to determine their validity, the refutation of heretics, and the codification of law; (2) those that undermine the principles of orthodoxy and thus constitute unbelief (KUFR); (3) those that are recommended (*mandūb*): the founding of schools and religious houses; (4) those that are disapproved (*makrūh*): the ornamentation of mosques and the decoration of the Qur'an; and finally (5) those that are indifferent (*mubāḥa*): fine clothing and good food.

BIDDLE, JOHN \'bi-dəl\ (b. 1615, Wotton-under-Edge, Gloucestershire, Eng.—d. Sept. 22, 1662, London), controversial lay theologian who was repeatedly imprisoned for his anti-Trinitarian views and who became known as the father of English UNITARIANISM.

Biddle was educated at Magdalen Hall, Oxford, and was subsequently appointed to the mastership of the free school in Gloucester. His reputation as a heretic in Anglican eyes originated with his manuscript of about 1644, *Twelve Arguments Drawn out of Scripture, Wherein the Commonly Received Opinion Touching the Deity of the Holy Spirit Is Clearly and Fully Refuted*, which was given to magistrates by a treacherous friend.

In 1645 Biddle was committed to prison. He was released on bail in 1647, but upon the publication of his manuscript the same year Biddle was once again taken into custody, and his *Twelve Arguments* was seized and burned. Two additional tracts were subsequently suppressed for attacking the doctrine that the three Persons of the Trinity—Father, Son, and Holy Ghost—were coequal. In 1648 Parliament made this HERESY a cause for the death penalty, but influential friends made it possible for Biddle to live under surveillance until 1652, when he was again imprisoned.

Freed in the same year under the protectorate of Oliver Cromwell, Biddle and his adherents, called Unitarians (*see* UNITARIANISM), began to meet regularly for Sunday worship. Soon after publication of his *Two-Fold Catechism* (1654), Biddle was again imprisoned. When Parliament was dissolved the next month, Biddle was free briefly but was then rearrested and tried for his heresy. Reluctant to see him executed, Cromwell rescued Biddle and sent him to one of the Scilly Isles in October 1655. In 1658 some of Biddle's friends sought and obtained his release, and he retired to the country to teach. On his return to London as a preacher in 1662 he was again arrested and fined £100. Unable to pay, he was immediately confined to prison, where he died.

BISHAMON \'bē-shä-ˌmȯn\, *also called* Bishamonten \ˌbē-shä-'mȯn-ten\, in Japanese mythology, one of the Shichifuku-jin ("Seven Gods of Luck"), a group of popular deities, all of whom are associated with good fortune and happiness. Bishamon is identified with the Buddhist guardian of the north, known as KUBERA, or Vaiśravaṇa. He is depicted as dressed in full armor, carrying a spear and a miniature PAGODA. He is the protector of the righteous and is the Buddhist patron of warriors.

The temple city of Shigi near Ōji (west-central Honshu) is dedicated to him. It was founded, according to tradition, by Shōtoku Taishi (573–621 CE), who attributed a victory over an enemy of BUDDHISM to Bishamon's assistance.

BISHOP, in some Christian churches, the chief pastor and overseer of a DIOCESE, an area containing several congregations. It is likely that the episcopacy, or threefold ministry of bishops, priests, and deacons, was well established in the Christian church by the 2nd century CE. ROMAN CATHOLICISM, EASTERN ORTHODOXY, and some other churches have maintained the view that bishops are the successors of the APOSTLES, a doctrine known as APOSTOLIC SUCCESSION. Until Feb. 11, 1989, when the Reverend Barbara Harris was ordained bishop in the Protestant Episcopal church, the apostolic-succession churches had reserved the office for men.

Until the Protestant REFORMATION in the 16th century, the bishop was the chief pastor, priest, administrator, and ruler of his Christian community. In the course of the Reformation, some of the new Protestant churches repudiated the office of the bishop, partly because they believed the office to have acquired such broad powers during the Middle Ages as to endanger its spiritual purity, and partly because they saw no basis for the institution in the NEW TESTAMENT. Thus, of the post-Reformation Christian communions, only the Roman Catholics, the Eastern Orthodox, Old Catholics, Anglicans, and a few others have maintained both the bishop's office and the belief that bishops have continued the apostolic succession. Some Lutheran churches (primarily in Scandinavia and Germany) have bishops, but, except for those in Sweden, they have not maintained the doctrine of apostolic succession. Most other Protestant churches do not have bishops.

Popes, CARDINALS, archbishops, PATRIARCHS, and METROPOLITANS are different gradations of bishops. A bishop is often assisted in the administration of his diocese by other, lesser bishops. Bishops alone have the right to confirm and ordain members of the clergy, and their main duty is to supervise the clergy within their diocese. In the Roman Catholic church, the bishop is selected by the pope, who is himself the bishop of Rome. In the ANGLICAN COMMUNION and other churches, a bishop is chosen by the dean and chapter of the cathedral of a diocese. Among the insignia traditional to a bishop are a miter, CROSIER (pastoral staff), pectoral cross, ring, and *caligae* (*i.e.,* stockings and sandals).

BITON: *see* CLEOBIS AND BITON.

BLACK MASS, in ROMAN CATHOLICISM, a requiem MASS during which the celebrant wears black vestments. The term is more commonly used, however, for a usually obscene burlesque of the true mass allegedly performed by satanic cults, in which the back of a naked woman serves as an altar and a validly consecrated host is used. The rite commonly incorporates other magical elements such as philtres or abortifacients.

Charges of SATANISM and celebration of the black mass have been made against persons accused of HERESY and WITCHCRAFT since early Christian times. Allegations were made against the Knights TEMPLAR in the 14th century and against the Freemasons in the 19th. Joris-Karl Huysmans' novel *Là-bas* (1891; *Down There*) describes a black mass celebrated in late 19th-century France.

BLACK STONE OF MECCA: *see* KA'BA.

BLASPHEMY, irreverence toward a deity or deities and, by extension, the use of profanity.

In CHRISTIANITY, blasphemy has points in common with HERESY but is differentiated from it in that heresy consists of holding a belief contrary to the orthodox one. Thus, it is not blasphemous to deny the existence of God or to question the established tenets of the faith unless this is done in a mocking and derisive spirit. In the Christian religion, blasphemy has been regarded as a SIN by moral theologians; ST. THOMAS AQUINAS described it as a sin against faith.

In ISLAM, insults or verbal attacks against God, the QU'RAN, and MUHAMMAD were the principle grounds for charges of blasphemy, which was understood as a form of disbelief (KUFR), APOSTASY (*ridda*), or heresy (*zandaqa*). The Qu'ran and HADITH, containing numerous condemnations of those opposed to Muhammad and his message, provided Muslim jurists with scriptural precedents. Muslims and non-Muslims alike could be charged with blasphemy, which, if legally substantiated, could incur any of several penalties, including censure, disinheritance, mandatory divorce, and even death. Historically, however, implementation of such measures rarely occurred, and when it did, it was at times of social or religious turmoil, under threat of foreign invasion. AL-ḤALLĀJ (d. 922) and other Sufis were accused of blasphemy for statements made in a state of mystical ECSTASY (*see* SUFISM). The most famous blasphemy case of the 20th century was that of the Anglo-Indian writer Salman Rushdie (b. 1947), who was condemned to death in a controversial ruling issued by AYATOLLAH RUHALLAH KHOMEINI (d. 1989) for allegedly having insulted the Prophet in his novel *The Satanic Verses* (1988).

In many other societies blasphemy in some form or another has been an offense punishable by law. The Mosaic Law decreed death by stoning as the penalty for the blasphemer. Under the Byzantine emperor JUSTINIAN I (reigned 527–565) the death penalty was decreed for blasphemy. In Scotland until the 18th century it was punishable by death, and in England it is both a statutory and a common-law offense, probably on the basis that an attack on religion is necessarily an attack on the state.

BLAVATSKY, HELENA PETROVNA \blə-'vat-skē\, *also called* Madame Blavatsky (b. Aug. 12 [July 31, Old Style], 1831, Yekaterinoslav, Ukraine, Russian Empire—d. May 8, 1891, London), Russian spiritualist, author, and cofounder of the Theosophical Society (*see* THEOSOPHY).

After a short-lived marriage, Blavatsky became interested in OCCULTISM and SPIRITUALISM and traveled extensively throughout Asia, Europe, and the United States; she also claimed to have spent several years in India and Tibet studying under Hindu gurus. In 1873 she went to New York City, where she became a close companion of H.S. Olcott, and in 1875 they and several other prominent persons founded the Theosophical Society.

In 1877 she published her first major work, *Isis Unveiled*, which criticized both science and religion and asserted that mystical experience and doctrine were the means to attain true spiritual insight and authority. Although *Isis Unveiled* attracted attention, the society dwindled. In 1879 Blavatsky and Olcott went to India; three years later they established a Theosophical headquarters at Adyar, near Madras, and began publication of the society's journal, *The Theosophist*, which Blavatsky edited from 1879 to 1888. The society soon developed a very strong following in India.

Blavatsky claimed extraordinary psychic powers. She was accused by the Indian press late in 1884 of concocting fictitious spiritualist phenomena. Protesting her innocence while on a tour of Germany, she returned to India in 1884 and met with an enthusiastic reception. The "Hodgson Report," the findings of an investigation in 1885 by the London Society for Psychical Research, declared her a fraud. Soon thereafter she left India in failing health. She lived quietly in Germany, Belgium, and finally in London, working on her small, meditative classic *The Voice of Silence* (1889) and her most important work, *The Secret Doctrine* (1888), which was an overview of Theosophical teachings. It was followed in 1889 by her *Key to Theosophy*.

At least 14 volumes of Blavatsky's *Complete Writings* were published by the early 1980s.

BLESSING WAY, central ritual of a complex system of ceremonies performed by the Navajo to restore equilibrium to the cosmos.

Of the many rituals classified by the Navajo according to their purpose, the largest group is the Chant Ways, which are concerned with curing and are divided into three groups. The first group are the Holy Way chants—including the Blessing Way, parts of which are found throughout most of the rituals, and the Wind Ways—all of which are used to cure diseases that can be traced to some violation of the supernatural provinces of the Holy People, or supernatural beings. These rituals are further classified into Peaceful Ways, which invoke the beneficence of the Holy People, and Injury Ways, which are primarily exorcistic.

The Blessing Way is a comparatively short ritual, taking only two days to perform. Performed for the general well-being of the community, rather than for specific curative purposes, it contains none of the typical features of curing rituals (*e.g.*, SAND PAINTINGS, prayer sticks, medicine songs, and herbs). To invoke good fortune—such as during childbirth, in blessing a new hogan (house), and in a girl's puberty ceremony—the Navajo family would have the Blessing Way sung at least twice a year. Parts of the Blessing Way are incorporated into almost all other Chant Ways.

The story of the Blessing Way contains details of the mythical events that occurred after the legendary emergence of the Navajo from the earth at creation. These events provide the prototypes for the organization of the cosmos, important Navajo ceremonials, and their central cultural institutions. (*See also* NATIVE AMERICAN RELIGIONS.)

BLODEUEDD \blō-'dəi-e<u>th</u>\, *also called* Blodeuwedd \blō-'dəi-we<u>th</u>\ (Welsh: "Flower-Form"), in the Welsh collection of stories called the MABINOGION, a beautiful girl fashioned from flowers as a wife for Lleu Llaw Gyffes (*see* LUGUS). Lleu's mother had put a curse on him that he would have no wife, and Blodeuedd was created to subvert the curse; she was unfaithful, however, and conspired with a lover to kill Lleu. The attempt failed and she was changed into an owl as a punishment.

BOANN \'bō-ən\, *also called* Boyne \'bóin\, in Irish MYTHOLOGY, sacred river personified as a MOTHER GODDESS. With DAGDA (or Daghda), chief god of the Irish, she was the mother of Mac ind Óg ("Young Son" or "Young Lad"), known also as Oenghus; mother, father, and son together formed one version of the divine triad familiar from Celtic mythology.

BODH GAYĀ \'bōd-'gī-ä\, *also spelled* Buddh Gayā \'bùd-'gī-ä\, village in central Bihār state, northeastern India, one of the holiest sites of BUDDHISM. Bodh Gayā has also been important for other Indian religious groups.

According to Buddhist tradition it was there, under the great BODHI TREE, that the BUDDHA GOTAMA was enlightened. A simple shrine was built by the emperor AŚOKA (3rd century BCE) to mark the spot. In the Kushān period

Painted clay bodhisattva, 11th century; in the lower Hua-yen Temple, Ta-t'ung, China
Gao Lishuang—ChinaStock Photo Library

(2nd century CE) this shrine was replaced by the present Mahābodhi temple, which was refurbished in the Pāla-Sena period (750–1200).

In the 16th century, after the collapse of Buddhism in India, the Mahābodhi temple was taken over by a Hindu (Śaivite, *see* ŚAIVISM) lineage and maintained as a temple devoted to the god VISHNU. During the period of British rule (specifically the late 19th century) the Mahābodhi temple was restored, and about the same time Buddhists outside India began to mount a campaign to return the temple to Buddhist control. In 1949 the Bihār government passed the Bodh Gayā Temple Act, and in 1953—in accordance with that act—a Management Committee was established that included four Śaiva members and four Buddhist members. Today Bodh Gayā has once again emerged as a major destination for Buddhist pilgrims.

BODHI \'bō-dē\ (Sanskrit and Pāli: "awakening," "enlightenment"), in BUDDHISM, the final enlightenment, which puts an end to the cycle of transmigration and leads to NIRVANA; it is comparable to the SATORI of ZEN Buddhism. The accomplishment of this "awakening" transformed Siddhārtha Gotama into a BUDDHA.

The final enlightenment remains the ultimate ideal of all Buddhists, to be attained by ridding oneself of false beliefs and the hindrance of passions. This is achieved by following the course of spiritual discipline known as the EIGHTFOLD PATH. MAHĀYĀNA Buddhism, while embracing this ideal, places a high value on the compassion of the BODHISATTVA, who postpones his own entrance into nirvana to work for the salvation of all sentient beings.

BODHIDHARMA \ˌbō-di-'dər-mə, -'där-\, *Chinese (Wade-Giles romanization)* Ta-Mo \'dä-'mō\, *Japanese* Daruma \'dä-rü-mä\ (fl. 6th century CE), legendary Indian monk who is credited with the establishment of the Ch'an (ZEN) school of BUDDHISM that flourished in East Asia. Considered the 28th Indian successor in a direct line from the BUDDHA GOTAMA, Bodhidharma is recognized by the Chinese Ch'an schools as their first patriarch.

According to the East Asian tradition Bodhidharma was a native of Conjeeveram near Madras; in 520 he traveled to Kuang (modern Canton). It is said that he was granted an interview with the emperor Wu-ti, who was famous for his good works. To the emperor's dismay, Bodhidharma stated that merit applying to salvation could not be accumulated through good deeds. For Bodhidharma meditation was the practice necessary to progress along the path to enlightenment.

BODHISATTVA \ˌbō-di-'sət-və, -wə\ (Sanskrit), *Pāli* bodhisatta \-'sət-tə\ ("one whose essence is *bodhi* [enlightenment]"), in BUDDHISM, the historical BUDDHA GOTAMA in his previous lives as a bodhisattva and in his final life prior to his enlightenment; also, other individuals who have taken a vow to become a buddha in this or in another life.

In MAHĀYĀNA Buddhism the decision of the bodhisattva to postpone his own final entrance into NIRVANA in order to alleviate the suffering of others is given special valuation. The ideal supplants the earlier, THERAVĀDA goal of the ARAHANT who perfects himself by following the Buddha's teachings and of the self-enlightened buddha, both of whom are criticized by Mahāyāna as concerned solely with their own personal salvation. The bodhisattva concept emphasizes that the virtue of compassion (*karuṇā*) is equal to the virtue of wisdom (*prajna*).

Once the bodhisattva declares his intention, he enters the first of 10 spiritual stages (*bhūmi*) and henceforward is reborn only in the world of men or of gods. In most cases the aspirant bodhisattva is a male but need not be a monk.

The celestial bodhisattvas, who are in some contexts considered to be manifestations of buddhas, are, however, great savior figures who—particularly in East Asia—often eclipse the historical Buddha in the personal devotion they inspire. Foremost is the compassionate and merciful AVALOKITEŚVARA, who is associated with the buddha AMITĀBHA. In China the most widely worshiped bodhisattvas are MAÑJUŚRĪ (representing wisdom), KṢITIGARBHA (the savior of the dead), Samantabhadra (representing happiness), and Avalokiteśvara (known in China as KUAN-YIN and often depicted as androgynous or feminine). In Tibet, Avalokiteśvara, Mañjuśrī, and VAJRAPĀṆI (who holds the thunderbolt) form a popular TRINITY.

BODHI TREE, *also called* bo tree \\'bō\\, according to Buddhist tradition, the pipal (*Ficus religiosa*) under which the BUDDHA GOTAMA sat when he attained enlightenment (BODHI) at BODH GAYĀ (near Gayā, India). The bodhi tree in Gayā, and other bodhi trees associated with it, have played an important role in Buddhist art and cultic life.

BODY MODIFICATIONS AND MUTILATIONS, the intentional permanent or semipermanent modifications of the living human body for religious, aesthetic, or social reasons. The methods of modification and mutilation used are incision, perforation, complete or partial removal, cautery, abrasion, adhesion, insertion of foreign bodies or materials, compression, distention, diversion, enlargement, and also staining.

Ritualistic motives for modification include ascetic mortification, magical protection, mourning, the indication of status or rank or group membership, bravado, and punishment. Ritual mutilation is generally used to modify the social position of an individual in a manner visible to and recognized by other members of the society. Mutilation may be performed as a part of initiation, marriage, or mourning rites, or it may be inflicted as a means of punishment, either for serious crimes or for social transgressions.

Mutilation and modification of the head include alterations of the skull, lips, teeth, tongue, nose, eyes, or ears. Deformation of the skull is the best-documented form, largely because archaeological skeletal remains clearly show its presence. Tabular deformations are produced by constant pressure of small boards or other flattened surfaces against the infant's head. Cranial deformation is known from all continents (except Australia) and from Oceania. It is rather rare in Africa south of the Sahara and apparently absent from south India.

Dental mutilations take the form of removal, usually of one or more incisors (ancient Peru, most Australian Aboriginals, some groups in Africa, Melanesia, and elsewhere); pointing in various patterns by chipping (Africa) or filing (ancient Mexico and Central America); filing of the surface, sometimes into relief designs (Indonesia); incrustation with precious stones or metal (Southeast Asia, India, ancient Mexico, and Ecuador); insertion of a peg between the teeth (India); and blackening (south India, hill peoples in Myanmar [Burma], some Malaysian groups).

Karamoja girl exhibiting scarification, Uganda
George Holton—Photo Researchers

Ancient Aztec and Maya Indians drew a cord of thorns through the tongue as a form of sacrifice; some Australian tribes draw blood from gashes under the tongue at initiation rites.

The best-known and most widespread genital modification is CIRCUMCISION. Subincision (opening the urethra along the inferior surface of the penis for a varying distance between the urinary meatus and the scrotum) is a common practice at puberty initiations among Australian Aboriginals and is recorded as a therapeutic measure among Fijians, Tongans, and Amazonian Indians. Customary unilateral castration (monorchy) is known in central Algeria, among the Beja (Egypt), Sidamo (Ethiopia), San and Khoikhoin (southern Africa), and some Australian Aboriginals, and on Ponape Island (Micronesia).

Female modifications include excision (of part or all of the clitoris—CLITORIDECTOMY, female circumcision—and sometimes also of the labia, mons, or both), in much of Africa, ancient Egypt, India, Malaysia, and Australia, and among the Skoptsy (a Russian Christian sect); incision (of the external genitalia, without removal of any part) among the Totonac (Mexico) and tropical South American Indians; infibulation (induced adhesion of the labia minora, leaving only a small orifice, to prevent sexual intercourse until the orifice is reopened by incision) in the Horn of Africa and among some Arabs; dilatation (of the vaginal orifice, often with incision) among some Australian Aboriginals; elongation of the labia (*tablier*), recorded for southern Africa and the Caroline Islands; and artificial defloration (among Australian Aboriginals and elsewhere).

Amputation of a phalanx or whole finger, usually as a form of sacrifice or in demonstration of mourning, was common among North American Indians, Australian Aboriginals, San and Khoikhoin, Nicobarese, Tongans, Fijians, and some groups in New Guinea, South America, and elsewhere. Amputation of the toes is less common but occurred in Fijian mourning.

Modification of the skin is accomplished primarily by tattooing and cicatrization, or scarification. In the former, color is introduced under the skin; in the latter, raised scars (keloids) are produced by incision or burning, usually in decorative patterns. Scarification occurs primarily among darker-skinned peoples (whose skin more readily forms keloids) in much of Africa, among Australian and Tasmanian aboriginals, and in many Melanesian and New Guinean groups; it is practiced both for aesthetic effect and to indicate status or lineage. Another form of skin modification is the introduction of objects under the skin: *e.g.*, magical protective AMULETS inserted under the skin by some peoples of Myanmar.

BOETHUSIAN \,bō-ē-'thü-zhən, -zē-ən\, member of a Jewish sect that flourished for a century or so before the destruction of Jerusalem in 70 CE. Their subsequent history is obscure, as is also the identity of Boethus, their founder. The Boethusians had certain similarities to the SADDUCEES, of whom they may have been a branch. Both parties associated with the aristocracy and denied the immortality of the soul and the resurrection of the body, because neither of these doctrines was contained in the written TORAH, or PENTATEUCH. The Boethusians testified to their disbelief in the "world to come" by living lives of luxury and by ridiculing the piety and ASCETICISM of the PHARISEES. The TALMUD speaks of the Boethusians in derisive tones.

BOGOMIL \'bä-gə-,mil, ,bə-gə-'mēl \, member of a dualist religious sect that flourished in the Balkans between the 10th and 15th centuries. It arose in Bulgaria in the mid-10th century from a fusion of neo-Manichaean doctrines and a local Slavonic movement aimed at reforming, in the name of an evangelical CHRISTIANITY, the recently established Bulgarian Orthodox Church. The Bogomils were so called after their alleged founder, the priest Bogomil.

The Bogomils' central teaching, based on a dualistic COSMOLOGY, was that the visible, material world was created by the devil. Thus, they denied the doctrine of the INCARNATION and rejected the Christian conception of matter as a vehicle of GRACE. They rejected BAPTISM, the EUCHARIST, and the whole organization of EASTERN ORTHODOXY. The moral teaching of the Bogomils was as consistently dualistic. They condemned those functions of man that bring him into close contact with matter, especially marriage, the eating of meat, and the drinking of wine.

During the 11th and 12th centuries Bogomilism spread over many European and Asian provinces of the Byzantine Empire. Its growth in Constantinople resulted, about 1100, in the trial and imprisonment of prominent Bogomils and in the public burning of their leader, Basil. In the second half of the 12th century, the Serbian ruler Stefan Nemanja was obliged to summon a general assembly to check it. By the early 13th century the dualistic communities of southern Europe—comprising the PAULICIANS and Bogomils in the east and the CATHARI in the west—formed a network stretching from the Black Sea to the Atlantic.

In the country of its birth Bogomilism remained a powerful force until the late 14th century. The Bulgarian authorities convened several church councils to condemn its teachings. With the Ottoman conquest of southeastern Europe in the 15th century, obscurity descended upon the sect. Traces of a dualistic tradition in the FOLKLORE of the South Slavs are all that remain today.

BÖHME, JAKOB \'bœ̄-mə, *Angl* 'bər-mə\ (b. 1575, Altseidenberg, near Görlitz, Saxony [Germany]—d. Nov. 21, 1624, Görlitz), German philosophical mystic and author who had a profound influence on such later movements as idealism and ROMANTICISM.

Böhme was born at the end of the Protestant REFORMATION period. He had little education and worked as a cobbler. In 1594 or 1595 he went to Görlitz, a town where Reformation controversies seethed. Martin Möller, the Lutheran pastor of Görlitz, was "awakening" many in the conventicles that he had established. In 1600, Böhme, probably stimulated by Möller, had a religious experience wherein he gained an insight that helped him to resolve the tensions of his age. The strain between medieval and Renaissance cosmologies (dealing with the order of the universe), the perennial PROBLEM OF EVIL, the collapse of feudal hierarchies, and the political and religious struggles of the time found resolution in Böhme's rediscovery, as he said, of the dialectical principle that "in Yes and No all things consist." This principle became known for Böhme as *Realdialektik* ("real dialectic").

Germinating for several years, the insight led him to write *Aurora, oder Morgenröthe im Aufgang* (1612)—an amalgam of theology, philosophy, and what then passed for ASTROLOGY, all bound together by a common devotional theme. A copy of *Aurora* fell into the hands of Gregory Richter, successor to Martin Möller as pastor, who condemned Böhme's pretensions to theology. Richter brought the matter up with the Görlitz town council, which forbade further writing on Böhme's part.

A period of silence ensued during which Böhme's ideas matured. He read the "high masters" as well as other unnamed books that were lent to him by the circle of neighbors and friends who were awed by the book-writing intellectual cobbler. These friends introduced Böhme to the writings of the Swiss physician Paracelsus. The alchemical and mystical views of Paracelsus further inspired Böhme's interest in nature MYSTICISM.

Although he never worked in a laboratory himself, Böhme did use its alchemical terms to describe both his nature mysticism and his subjective experiences, which he sought to integrate into a common framework. During this period Böhme wrote at least six tracts that were circulated guardedly among his friends. This second period of writing activity began in 1619, as the Thirty Years' War (1618–48) was beginning to gain momentum. The various strident controversies of the age forced Böhme into a period of religious APOLOGETICS wherein he had to protest his orthodoxy. He wrote a series of devotional tracts dealing with penitence, resignation, regeneration—traditional themes of German mysticism. In 1622 his friends had several of these devotional tracts printed in Görlitz under the title *Der Weg zu Christo* (*The Way to Christ*), a small work joining nature mysticism with devotional fervor. Publication of this tract brought about the intense displeasure of Richter, who incited the populace against Böhme.

In 1623 he wrote two major works: *The Great Mystery* and *On the Election of Grace*. The former explained the creation of the universe as told in GENESIS in terms of the Paracelsian three principles (including the mystical elements "salt," "sulfur," and "mercury"), thus joining Renaissance nature mysticism with biblical religion. The latter gave exposition in terms of dialectical insight to the problem of freedom that Calvinist PREDESTINATION (the view that man's destiny is determined by God) was then making acute. This theme later was taken up by the idealist philosopher Friedrich Schelling and by a German theologian, Franz von Baader, whose commentary for *On the Election of Grace* is still held in high regard by scholars.

In 1619 Böhme defiantly renewed his writing, and before he died he produced at least 30 works. His defiance of the town council of Görlitz brought him further difficulty, and he was banished. He fled to one of the neighboring castles where he clearly was the central figure in some kind of secretive group. There he fell sick, and, sensing that his end was near, he was taken back home to Görlitz. He was examined by ecclesiastical authorities and found orthodox enough to be given the sacrament, and then died.

BOJO GUKSA \\'pō-'jō-'kük-₁sä\\, *secular name* Chi-Nui \\'shē-'nŭ-ē\\ (b. 1158, Korea—d. 1210, Korea), Buddhist priest who founded the CHOGYE-CHONG (Chogye Sect), now one of the largest Buddhist sects in Korea. It is derived from ZEN Buddhism.

Bojo became a Buddhist follower at the age of eight and entered the priesthood at 25. He was greatly influenced by the doctrine of sudden enlightenment taught by the Chinese Zen Buddhist master HUI-NENG (638–713). In 1190 Bojo set up a new organization to counter the elaborate ritualistic practices that had crept into Korean BUDDHISM. In 1200 he moved to the Songkwang-sa (Songkwang Temple) in Mount Chiri, where he established the Chogye-chong, which stressed the importance of studying the AVATAMSAKA SŪTRA (*Garland Sutra*). In his last and most famous writing, "A Commentary on the Fa-chi-pieh-hang-lu," Bojo taught that the ultimate goal of Buddhism is to acquire the essential calmness of mind, free from external influence.

BON \\'pœⁿ\\, indigenous religion of Tibet that gave TIBETAN BUDDHISM much of its distinctive character.

The original features of Bon seem to have been largely concerned with the propitiation of demonic forces and included the practice of blood sacrifices. Later, there is evidence of a cult of divine kingship, the kings being regarded as manifestations of the sky divinity (reformulated in BUDDHISM as the REINCARNATION of LAMAS); oracular priests (their counterpart, the Buddhist soothsayers); and a cult of the gods of the atmosphere, the earth, and subterranean regions (now lesser deities in the Buddhist pantheon).

In the 8th and 9th centuries struggles took place between the ruling house of Tibet, whose members sided with Buddhism, and the powerful noble families, who sided with Bon. Challenged by the Buddhist use of written works, Bon developed into a systematized religion with specific doctrine and a sacred literature. Although any serious Bon claims to religious supremacy were ended by the late 8th-century persecution by King Khrisong Detsen, it was never completely destroyed and survives both in the aspects of Tibetan Buddhism that are mentioned above and as a living religion on the northern and eastern frontiers of Tibet.

BONA DEA \\'bō-nə-'dē-ə, -'dā-\\ (Latin: "Good Goddess"), in ROMAN RELIGION, deity of fruitfulness, both in the earth and in women. She was identified with various goddesses who had similar functions. The dedication day of her temple on the Aventine was May 1. Her temple was cared for and attended by women only, and the same was the case at a second celebration, at the beginning of December, in the house of a sovereign magistrate. Myrtle—a symbol of sexuality to the Romans—was forbidden. A sow was sacrificed and wine was drunk under the ritual name "milk." Inscriptions show that there was a public side to the worship of Bona Dea, where men could participate.

BONAVENTURE, SAINT \\₁bä-nə-'ven-chər, 'bä-nə-₁\\ (b. c. 1217, Bagnoregio, Papal States—d. July 15, 1274, Lyon; canonized April 14, 1482; feast day July 15), leading medieval

theologian, minister general of the FRANCISCAN order, and CARDINAL bishop of Albano.

He was a son of Giovanni of Fidanza, a physician. He fell ill while a boy and, by his own report, was saved from death by the intercession of ST. FRANCIS OF ASSISI. Entering the University of Paris in 1235, he received the master of arts degree in 1243 and then joined the Franciscan order, which named him Bonaventure in 1244. He studied theology in the Franciscan school at Paris from 1243 to 1248.

In 1248 he began to teach the Bible; from 1251 to 1253 he lectured on the *Sentences*, a medieval theology textbook, and he became a master of theology in 1254, when he assumed control of the Franciscan school in Paris. He taught there until 1257, producing many works, notably commentaries on the BIBLE and the *Sentences* and the *Breviloquium* ("Summary"), a summary of his theology. These works showed his deep understanding of SCRIPTURE and the Fathers of the early church—principally ST. AUGUSTINE—and of the philosophers, particularly Aristotle.

Bonaventure was particularly noted in his day for the rare ability to reconcile diverse traditions in theology and philosophy. He united different doctrines in a synthesis containing his personal conception of truth as a road to the love of God. In 1256 he defended the Franciscan ideal of the Christian life against William of Saint-Amour, a university teacher who accused the MENDICANTS (FRIARS who wandered about and begged for a living) of defaming the GOSPEL by their practice of poverty. Bonaventure's defense of the Franciscans and his personal probity led to his election as minister general of the Franciscans on Feb. 2, 1257.

The Franciscan order was at the time undergoing internal discord. One group, the Spirituals, took a rigorous view of poverty; another, the Relaxati, displayed a disturbing laxity of life. Bonaventure used his authority so prudently that, placating the first group and reproving the second, he preserved the unity of the order and reformed it in the spirit of St. Francis. Bonaventure based the revival of the order on his conception of the spiritual life, which he expounded in mystical treatises manifesting his Franciscan experience of contemplation as a perfection of the Christian life. Revered by his order, Bonaventure recodified its constitutions (1260), wrote for it a new *Life of St. Francis of Assisi* (1263), and protected it (1269) from an assault by Gerard of Abbeville, a teacher of theology at Paris, who renewed the charge of William of Saint-Amour.

Bonaventure's wisdom and tact moved Pope Gregory X to name him cardinal bishop of Albano, Italy, in May 1273. At the second Council of Lyon he was the leading figure in the reform of the church, reconciling the secular (parish) clergy with the mendicant orders. He also had a part in attempting to restore the Greek church to union with Rome. His death, at the council, was viewed as the loss of a wise and holy man. He was buried the same day in a Franciscan church with the pope in attendance.

BONHOEFFER, DIETRICH \\'bän-₁hȯ-fər, *German* 'bȯn-₁hœ-fər\\ (b. Feb. 4, 1906, Breslau, Prussia, Ger.—d. April 9, 1945, Flossenbürg, Bavaria), German Protestant theologian, important for his support of ECUMENISM and his view of CHRISTIANITY'S role in a secular world—he was a leading spokesman for the CONFESSING CHURCH, the center of German Protestant resistance to the Nazi regime. His involvement in a plot to overthrow Adolf Hitler led to his imprisonment and execution. His *Prisoner of God: Letters and Papers from Prison*, published posthumously in 1951, is perhaps the most profound document of his convictions.

Bonhoeffer grew up amid the academic circles of the University of Berlin. From 1923 to 1927 he studied theology at the universities of Tübingen and Berlin. At Berlin he was strongly attracted by the new "theology of revelation" being propounded elsewhere by KARL BARTH. After serving in 1928–29 as assistant pastor of a German-speaking congregation in Barcelona, he spent a year as an exchange student at Union Theological Seminary in New York City. On his return to Germany in 1931 he took up an appointment at the University of Berlin.

From the first days of the Nazi accession to power in 1933 he was involved in protests against the regime, especially its ANTI-SEMITISM, and, despite an absence when he served as a pastor in London (1933–35), Bonhoeffer became a leader in the CONFESSING CHURCH, which developed among German Protestants to resist Nazi control. In 1935 he was appointed to head a new seminary for the Confessing Church at Finkenwald (Pomerania), which continued in disguised form until 1940, despite its proscription by the political authorities in 1937. From this period dates *Nachfolge* (1937; *The Cost of Discipleship*), a study of the SERMON ON THE MOUNT in which he attacked the "cheap grace" being marketed in Protestant churches—*i.e.*, an unlimited offer of forgiveness, which in fact served as a cover for ethical laxity. It was in this rigorous and even ascetic guise (to which his later theme of "Christian worldliness" provides a contrast if not a contradiction) that Bonhoeffer first became widely known.

Bonhoeffer's involvement in the church's struggle took an increasingly political character after 1938, when his brother-in-law, the jurist Hans von Dohnanyi, introduced him to the group seeking Hitler's overthrow. Bonhoeffer was able to continue his work for the resistance movement under cover of employment in the Military Intelligence Department, which in fact was a center of the resistance. In May 1942 he flew to Sweden to convey to the British government the conspirators' proposals for a negotiated peace; these hopes were thwarted, however, by the Allies' "unconditional surrender" policy. Bonhoeffer was arrested on April 5, 1943, and imprisoned in Berlin. Following the failure of the attempt on Hitler's life on July 20, 1944, the discovery of documents linking Bonhoeffer directly with the conspiracy led to his execution.

In his work entitled *Ethik* (1949; *Ethics*) Bonhoeffer abjured all "thinking in terms of two spheres,"—*i.e.*, any dualistic separation of the church and the world, nature and GRACE, the sacred and the profane. He called for a unitive, concrete ethic founded on Christology, an ethic in which labor, marriage, and government are to be viewed as divinely imposed tasks or functions ("mandates") rather than orders of creation. Bonhoeffer urged a recovery of the concept of "the natural" in Protestant thought. In the prison writings, published in 1951 (*Widerstand und Ergebung*; *Letters and Papers from Prison*), Bonhoeffer asked whether man's increasing ability to cope

Bonhoeffer, 1939
By courtesy of Eberhard Bethge

with his problems without the hypothesis of God may not indicate the obsolescence of the "religious premise" upon which Christianity has hitherto been based. The stripping off of "religion," in the sense of otherworldliness and preoccupation with personal salvation, Bonhoeffer suggested, will in fact free Christianity for its authentic this-worldliness in accordance with its Judaic roots. The church should give up its inherited privileges in order to free Christians to "share in God's sufferings in the world" in imitation of JESUS CHRIST, "the man for others."

BONIFACE, SAINT \'bä-nə-fəs, -ˌfās\, *Latin* Bonifatius (b. *c.* 675, Wessex, England—d. June 5, 754, Dokkum, Frisia; feast day June 5), English missionary and reformer, often called the Apostle of Germany for his role in the Christianization of that country.

Boniface was educated by the BENEDICTINES and became a Benedictine monk, being ordained priest about the age of 30. From 716 to 722 he made two attempts to evangelize the Frisian Saxons but was balked by their king, Radbod. In 718 he accompanied a group of Anglo-Saxon pilgrims to Rome, where Pope Gregory II entrusted him with a mission to the PAGANS east of the Rhine; Gregory gave him at this time the name Boniface (his name was Wynfrid). Radbod died in 719, and Boniface returned to Frisia. In 722 he went to Hesse, where he established the first of many Benedictine monasteries.

So great was his success that he was called to Rome, where Gregory consecrated him a missionary bishop. The pope also provided him with a collection of canons (ecclesiastical regulations) and letters of recommendation to such important personages as Charles Martel, master of the Frankish kingdom, whose protection was essential to Boniface's success. It was the pagan awe of Martel's name that allowed Boniface to destroy the sacred oak of the Germanic god THOR at Geismar.

For 10 years (725–735) Boniface was active in Thuringia, where he met opposition, he said, "from ambitious and free-living clerics" whom he pursued relentlessly. Pope Zachary was forced to moderate the zeal of Boniface, who requested not only EXCOMMUNICATION but also solitary confinement for two "heretical" missionaries, Adalbert and Clement the Irishman—sentences that the pope avoided imposing by deliberate delay. Boniface's handling of missionaries whose methods he deplored seems at times to have been excessively severe.

Ordered by Pope Gregory III (731–741) to organize the church in Bavaria, Boniface initially established four bishoprics there. His work had far-reaching political repercussions, for his Christianization of Bavaria paved the way for the ultimate incorporation of the country into the Carolingian Empire. Boniface undertook the reform of the Frankish clergy and, wherever possible, of Irish missionaries. Between 740 and 745, five SYNODS were convened for this purpose. In 747 a reforming council was held for the entire Frankish kingdom with the wholehearted collaboration of Carloman and Pepin, the sons and heirs of Charles Martel.

Boniface's life ended in martyrdom at the hands of a band of Frisians, who killed him as he was reading the SCRIPTURES to Christian neophytes on PENTECOST Sunday. Boniface is buried at the monastery Fulda in a magnificent baroque SARCOPHAGUS.

BONIFACE VIII, *Latin* Bonifatius, or Bonifacius (b. *c.* 1235–40, Anagni, Papal States—d. Oct. 11, 1303, Rome), pope from 1294 to 1303, the extent of whose authority was vigorously challenged by the emergent powerful monarchies of western Europe, especially France.

Benedict Caetani was born of an old and influential Roman family. He studied law in Bologna and then for many years held increasingly important functions in the papal government. Martin IV made him cardinal-deacon in 1281, and it was Cardinal Benedict Caetani who confirmed the unhappy pope Celestine V in his wish to resign. After he had succeeded him as Boniface VIII, he found it advisable to intern the old man, who died soon after. Although Celestine died of natural causes, the death was open to suspicion and incriminating aspersions by Boniface's enemies.

Boniface's attempt to stop hostilities between Edward I of England and Philip IV of France became enmeshed with the tendency of these warring monarchs to tax the clergy without obtaining papal consent. Boniface refused to look on inactively while the struggle, which he was trying to terminate, was being financed at the cost of the church and the PAPACY. In 1296 he issued the bull *Clericis Laicos*, which forbade any imposition of taxes on the clergy without express license by the pope.

Philip IV forestalled the publication of *Clericis Laicos* with an order forbidding all export of money and valuables from France and with the expulsion of foreign merchants—a serious threat to papal revenues. The necessity of Boniface coming to terms with Philip, however, was primarily the result of an insurrection against Boniface by the Colonna family. A year of military action against the Colonnas followed, which ended with their unconditional surrender. They were absolved from EXCOMMUNICATION but were not reinstated in their offices and possessions; they therefore rebelled again and fled; some of them went to Philip.

A second conflict broke out in 1301 around the trumped-up charges against a French bishop and his summary trial and imprisonment. This was a threat to one of the gains that the papacy had made and maintained in the last two centuries: papal, rather than secular, control of the clergy. The pope could not compromise here, and in the bull *Ausculta Fili* ("Listen, Son") he sharply rebuked Philip.

Boniface hoped for a favorable termination of this conflict; the German king and prospective emperor, Albert I of Habsburg, was ready to give up his French alliance if the pope would recognize the legitimacy of his rule. This recognition was granted early in 1303. The Holy Roman Empire now was said by the Pope to possess an overlordship over all other kingdoms, including France. In November 1302 Boniface had issued an even more fundamental declaration concerning the position of the papacy in the Christian world, the bull *Unam Sanctam* ("One Holy"), a powerful but not novel invocation of the supremacy of the spiritual over the temporal power.

Meanwhile, Philip IV's councillor Guillaume de Nogaret pursued an actively anti-papal policy. Many unjustified accusations against Boniface, ranging from unlawful entry into the papal office to heresy, were raised at a secret meeting of the king and his advisers in the Louvre at Paris. Shortly after the Louvre meeting, at which Nogaret had demanded the condemnation of the pope by a general council of the church, Nogaret went to Italy.

When he learned that Boniface was about to excommunicate Philip, Nogaret, with the assistance of Sciarra Colonna, decided to capture the pope at Anagni. After two days the local people of Anagni rescued the pope and thus frustrated whatever further plans Nogaret may have had. During these two days Boniface was probably physically ill-treated. He returned to Rome and died soon after.

BOOK OF THE DEAD, ancient Egyptian collection of mortuary texts made up of SPELLS or magic formulas, placed in tombs to protect and aid the deceased in the hereafter. Probably compiled and re-edited during the 16th century BCE, the collection included COFFIN TEXTS dating from *c.* 2000 BCE, PYRAMID TEXTS dating from *c.* 2400 BCE, and other writings. Later compilations included hymns to RE, the sun god. Numerous authors, compilers, and sources contributed to the work. Scribes copied the texts on rolls of papyrus, often colorfully illustrated, and sold them to individuals for burial use. Many copies of the book have been found in Egyptian tombs, but none contains all of the approximately 200 known chapters. The collection, literally titled "The Chapters of Coming-Forth-by-Day," received its present name from Karl Richard Lepsius, the German Egyptologist who published the first collection of the texts in 1842.

BOOK OF THE DEAD, TIBETAN, *or* Bardo Thödrol \'bär-dœ̄-'tœ-dœl\, Tibetan Buddhist text which describes in detail the religious opportunities and the frightening apparitions that the deceased encounters day after day while in the 49-day interval between death and rebirth. In Tibet, Nepal, and Mongolia a LAMA will sometimes recite the Book of the Dead to the recently deceased in order to assist in the rebirth process.

BOREAS \'bōr-ē-əs\, in Greek mythology, the personification of the north wind. He carried off the beautiful Oreithyia, a daughter of ERECHTHEUS, king of Athens, to be his queen in Thrace; they had two sons, CALAIS AND ZETES. To show his friendliness for the Athenians, Boreas wrecked the fleet of the Persian king Xerxes off the promontory of Sepias in Thessaly; in return the Athenians built him a SANCTUARY or altar near the Ilissus and held a festival (Boreasmos) in his honor. In art Boreas was represented as winged.

BOROBUDUR \,bō-rō-bü-'dür\, *also spelled* Barabudur, Buddhist monument in central Java, Indonesia, 42 miles northwest of Yogyakarta. It was constructed between about 778 and 850 CE, under the Sailendra dynasty. The Borobudur monument combines the symbolic forms of the STUPA (originally a relic mound commemorating the BUDDHA GOTAMA), the temple mountain, and the MANDALA (a mystic Buddhist symbol of the universe, combining the square as earth and the circle as heaven). The style of Borobudur is

The stupa complex at Borobudur, Java
Robert Harding Picture Library—Photobank BKK

influenced by Indian Gupta and post-Gupta art. Within a few centuries of its construction the area suffered a volcanic eruption, and Borobuḍur was virtually buried in volcanic dust. It was then abandoned and overgrown by vegetation from about 1000 CE until its restoration by Dutch archaeologists in 1907–11 (a second UNESCO-supported restoration was completed in the early 1980s). Many consider Borobuḍur to be the most impressive of all Buddhist monuments.

Borobuḍur is a massive monument built over a natural hill. The base and the four successively higher galleries that constitute the lower segment of the monument are square. Each of these galleries extends all around the four sides of the monument and has walls on both sides, each of them covered by marvelously carved bas reliefs. The galleries, though they have no roof, are relatively enclosed. In contrast, the three upper levels are circular, open terraces on which 72 latticed stupas are situated. At the very top is a large central stupa 103 feet above the base.

A series of reliefs on the base and the galleries represent the ascending stages along the path to enlightenment. The reliefs on the base illustrate the effect of good and bad deeds in this life. Those on the walls of the first gallery depict events in the life of the historical Buddha and scenes from the JĀTAKAS (stories of his previous lives). The reliefs on the walls of the second, third, and fourth galleries contain scenes from the *Gandavyaha*, a famous MAHĀYĀNA *sūtra* that depicts a pilgrim's travels, including visits to Mahāyāna figures who teach and inspire. The most prominent figure is MAITREYA, the future buddha who presently resides in the Tuṣita heaven. The specific symbolism of the upper segment of the monument is obscure, but it is clear that the circular terraces and latticed stupas represent celestial realms and Buddhas who are accessible to those who have attained the highest levels of the path. The central stupa at the top is clearly the "sacred center," which may have contained an especially sacred relic or image. The monument provided a Mahāyāna-style PILGRIMAGE path for ordinary Buddhists and probably was the arena for special royal rituals as well.

BRAHMĀ \ˈbrä-mə, -mä\, from about 500 BCE to 500 CE in India, one of the major gods of HINDUISM, but gradually eclipsed by VISHNU, SHIVA, and the great Goddess (in her multiple aspects). Brahmā—associated with the Vedic creator god PRAJĀPATI, whose identity he came to assume—was born from a golden egg and created the earth and all things on it. Later sectarian myths describe him as having come forth from a lotus that issued from Vishnu's navel.

By the middle of the 1st millennium CE an attempt to synthesize the diverging sectarian traditions is evident in the doctrine of TRIMŪRTI, which considers Vishnu, Shiva, and Brahmā as three forms of the supreme, unmanifested deity. By the 7th century, when the Smārtas initiated their worship of five deities, omitting Brahmā, he had largely lost his claim as a supreme deity, although the *trimūrti* continued to figure importantly in both text and sculpture. Today there is no cult or sect that exclusively worships Brahmā, and few temples are dedicated to him. Nevertheless, all temples dedicated to Shiva or to Vishnu must contain an image of Brahmā.

Brahmā is usually depicted in art as having four faces, symbolic of a wide-ranging four-square capacity, as expressed in the four VEDAS (revealed SCRIPTURES), the four YUGAS ("ages"), the four VARṆAS (social classes), the four directions, the four stages of orthoprax life (*āśrama*s, see

ASHRAM), and so forth. He is usually shown with four arms, holding sacrificial instruments, PRAYER BEADS, and a book. He may be seated or standing on a lotus throne or on his mount, the *haṃsa* (ruddy goose). SĀVITRĪ and SARASVATĪ, respectively exemplars of faithfulness and of music and learning, frequently accompany him.

BRAHMA KUMĀRĪ \ˈbrä-mə-kù-ˈmär-ē\, *also spelled* Brahmakumari, Hindu spiritual association founded by a wealthy Sindhi merchant named Dada Lekhraj who, in 1936, began having visions, most notably of imminent large-scale destruction and chaos. These visions led him, his family, and others to believe that he served as the medium for SHIVA (whom the Brahma kumārīs call Shiv Baba), the Supreme Father. Lekhraj's first followers took to chanting the syllable "Om" along with him, and thus were called the OM Mandlis. By 1938, Lekhraj had appointed a group of women to lead his followers and donated all of his considerable wealth to them. His predominantly female following aroused considerable suspicion and hostility, especially since one of Lekhraj's most important teachings was CELIBACY, while many of the women were married or soon to be wed. Lekhraj and his followers retreated to Karachi (in modern day Pakistan), returning to India only in 1950, when they settled in Mount Abu, Rajasthan. They took to calling themselves the Brahma kumārīs, meaning "princesses (or daughters) of BRAHMĀ." The organization's upper echelons are still composed almost exclusively of women. The group holds that only those who remain celibate and free from vice will survive the upheavals Lekhraj foresaw and enjoy rebirth in the ensuing Golden Age, in which the sexes will be equal and reproduction will not require sexual intercourse. To attain spiritual purity, adherents must recognize themselves as souls, not bodies, whose true home is in the realm of Shiv Baba. This is effected through the practice they term *rāja* YOGA, a form of meditation wherein one focuses on the eyes of one's teacher in a darkened room, the teacher often being illuminated from behind by a light said to represent Shiv Baba. Lay members far outnumber celibates, who reside in the movement's centers in the major cities of India, the United States, Britain, and Hong Kong.

BRAHMAN, in the UPANISHADS, the supreme existence or absolute, the font of all things. The etymology of the Sanskrit is uncertain, but many scholars associate it with *brahman*, sacred utterance in a ritual context. In the Upanishads, Brahman is the eternal, conscious, irreducible, infinite, omnipresent, spiritual source of the universe.

Marked differences in interpretation characterize the various subschools of VEDĀNTA philosophy. According to the ADVAITA school, Brahman is categorically different from anything phenomenal, and human perceptions of differentiation are illusively projected on this reality. The BHEDĀBHEDA school maintains that Brahman is nondifferent from the world, which is its product, but different in that phenomenality imposes certain adventitious conditions (*upādhi*s) on Brahman. The VIŚIṢṬĀDVAITA school maintains that a relation between Brahman and the world of soul and matter exists that is comparable to the relation between soul and body and that phenomenality is a glorious manifestation of Brahman. The DVAITA school refuses to accept the identity of Brahman with either soul or matter, maintaining their ontological separation and the dependence of soul and matter on Brahman.

In early Hindu mythology, Brahman is sometimes personified as the creator god BRAHMĀ and placed in a triad of divine functions—Brahmā the creator, VISHNU the preserver, and SHIVA the destroyer—although these functions significantly overlap.

BRĀHMAṆA \\'brä-mə-nə\\, a number of prose discourses expounding on the VEDAS, the most ancient Hindu sacred literature, explaining the significance of the Vedas in ritual sacrifices and the symbolic import of the priests' actions. The word *brāhmaṇa* may mean either the utterance of a BRAHMIN or an exposition on the meaning of the sacred word. The *Brāhmaṇa*s belong to the period 900–600 BCE. They present a digest of accumulated teachings, illustrated by myth and legend, on various matters of ritual and on hidden meanings of the sacred texts. Their principal concern is with sacrifice, and they are the oldest extant sources for the history of Indian ritual. Their most distinctive contribution is to elaborate a series of correspondences tying Vedic sacrificial actions to all aspects of the cosmos; by no means do these homologies always agree. The ĀRAṆYAKAS and UPANISHADS are appended to the *Brāhmaṇa*s.

Of the *Brāhmaṇa*s handed down by the followers of the ṚG VEDA, two have been preserved, the *Aitareya Brāhmaṇa* and the *Kauṣītaki* (or *Śāṅkhayāna*) *Brāhmaṇa*. Discussed in these two works are "the going of the cows" (*gavāmayana*), the 12 days' rites (*dvādaśāha*), the daily morning and evening sacrifices (*agnihotra*), the setting up of the sacrificial fire (*agnyādhāna*), the new- and full-moon rites, and the rites for the installation of kings.

Properly speaking, the *Brāhmaṇa*s of the Sāma Veda are the *Pañcaviṃśa* (25 books), *Sadviṃśa* (26th), and the *Jaiminiya Brāhmaṇa*. They show almost complete accordance in their exposition of the "going of the cows" ceremony, the various SOMA ceremonies, and the different rites lasting from 1 to 12 days. Also described are the atonements required when mistakes or evil portents have occurred during sacrifices.

The *Brāhmaṇa*s of the Yajur Veda were at first inserted at various points in the texts alongside the material on which they commented. This was at variance with the practice followed by the teachers of the Ṛg Veda and the Sāma Veda. The Yajur Veda fell into two separate groups, the later White (Śukla) Yajur Veda, which separated out the *Brāhmaṇa*s from the Saṃhitās (collections of vedas), and the Black (KRISHNA) Yajur Veda, which did not. The *Śatapatha Brāhmaṇa* (or 100 "paths"), consisting of 100 lessons, belongs to the White Yajur Veda. Ranking next to the Ṛg Veda in importance, this *Brāhmaṇa* survives in two slightly differing versions. Elements closely connected with domestic ritual are introduced here.

Finally, to the Atharva Veda belongs the comparatively late *Gopatha Brāhmaṇa*. Relating only secondarily to the Saṃhitās and *Brāhmaṇa*s, it is in part concerned with the role played by the priest who supervised the sacrifice.

BRAHMAVIHĀRA \\'brä-mə-vi-'här-ə\\ (Sanskrit: "Brahmanic state or condition," "state of being in Brahman [heaven]"), in Buddhist philosophy, the four noble practices that, when followed, allow the practitioner to obtain subsequent rebirth into the BRAHMAN heaven. These four practices are the perfect virtues of (1) sympathy, which gives happiness to living beings (Sanskrit: *maitrī*); (2) compassion, which removes pain from living beings (*karuṇā*); (3) joy, the enjoyment of the sight of others who have attained happiness (*muditā*); and (4) equanimity, being free from attachment and being indifferent to living beings (*upekṣa*). These are also called the four *apramāṇa*s.

Brahmin priest reading a sacred text at a Vedic sacrifice
C.M. Natu

BRAHMIN \\'brä-mən\\, *also spelled* Brahman, *Sanskrit* brāhmaṇa \\'brä-mə-nə\\ (literally, "one possessing brahman [sacred utterance]"), usually considered the highest ranking of the four VARṆAS, or social classes, in Hindu India. Texts of the late Vedic period already contained the idea that society is functionally divided between Brahmins, or priests, warriors (of the KṢATRIYA class), traders (of the VAIŚYA class), and laborers (of the ŚŪDRA class). The basis of the age-old veneration of Brahmins is the belief that they are inherently of greater ritual purity than members of other CASTES and that they alone are capable of performing certain vital religious tasks, including the preservation of the four collections (Saṃhitās) of Vedic hymns and the development of the commentary associated with them. The study and recitation of these sacred SCRIPTURES was open to males of the first three *varṇa*s, but for centuries the great preponderance of Indian scholarship was in Brahmin hands.

Because of their high prestige and tradition of education, Brahmins have long exerted an important influence on secular affairs. Although political power lay normally with members of the warrior caste, Brahmins often acted as advisers and ministers of ruling chiefs, including the British. Many heads of state in independent India, including the Nehru dynasty, have Brahmin blood. During the 20th century in southern India and elsewhere, anti-Brahmin movements gathered considerable strength, though this did not largely affect their traditional position as priests, ministering both in temples and at domestic rites. The Brahmin family priest (*purohita*) still officiates at most Hindu life-cycle rituals.

The ritual purity of the Brahmins is maintained through a more or less complex regimen of dietary and religious observances. Most Brahmin castes are strictly vegetarian, and their members must abstain from certain occupations. They may not handle any impure material, such as leather or hides, or plow, but they may farm and do such agricultural work as does not violate these specific restrictions. A number have long been traders and businessmen. They may also accept employment as domestic servants; many well-to-do Hindus have Brahmin cooks, who are valued because custom permits members of all castes to eat the food they prepare.

The Brahmins are divided into 10 main territorial divisions, 5 of which are associated with the north and 5 with the south. The northern group consists of Sarasvatī, Gauḍa, Kannauj, Maithil, and Utkal Brahmins, and the southern group comprises Mahārāshtra, Āndhra, Drāviḍa, Karṇāṭa, and Malabār Brahmins.

BRAHMO SAMAJ \'brä-mō-sə-'mäj\, *Brahmo also spelled* Brahma, *Hindi* Brāhma Samāj ("Society of Brahman"), a quasi-Unitarian, monotheistic movement within HINDUISM, founded in Calcutta in 1828 by RAM MOHUN ROY. The Brahmo Samaj rejected the authority of the VEDAS and the doctrine of AVATARS (incarnations) and did not insist on belief in KARMA (causal effects of past deeds) or rebirth. It discarded Hindu rituals and adopted some Christian practices in its worship. Influenced by ISLAM and CHRISTIANITY, it denounced POLYTHEISM, idol worship, and the CASTE system. It had considerable success with its programs of social reform but remained largely an elite group without a significant popular following.

Portrait of Ram Mohun Roy, founder of Brahmo Samaj
Victoria & Albert Museum, London—Art Resource

Whereas Ram Mohun Roy wanted to reform Hinduism from within, his successor, DEBENDRANATH TAGORE, broke away in 1850 by repudiating Vedic authority. He tried, however, to retain some of the traditional Hindu customs, and a radical group led by KESHAB CHUNDER SEN seceded and organized the Brahmo Samaj of India in 1866 (the older group became known as the Adi—*i.e.*, original—Brahmo Samaj). The new branch was most influential in the struggle for social reform. It encouraged the education of women and campaigned for the remarriage of widows and for legislation to prevent child marriages. When Keshab arranged for his daughter to marry the prince of Cooch Behar, however, both parties were well under age. He was thus violating his own reformist principles, and many of his followers became angry and rebelled, forming a third *samāj*, or "association," the Sadharan (*i.e.*, common) Brahmo Samaj, in 1878. The Sadharan Samaj gradually reverted to the teaching of the UPANISHADS and carried on the work of social reform. Although the Brahmo movement lost force in the 20th century, its fundamental challenges to Hindu caste conventions have been encoded in the constitution of independent India.

BRÂN \'bran\ (Celtic: "Raven"), in CELTIC RELIGION, a gigantic deity who figured in the MABINOGION (a collection of medieval Welsh tales) as "crowned king over this Island"—that is, as king of Britain. Because of his stature, he and his court had to live in a tent, as no house had ever been built large enough to contain him. The most important aspect of Brân's myth concerned his wondrous severed head. The ancient Celts believed the human head to be the seat of the soul, and they believed it to be capable of independent life after the death of the body. They thought that it possessed powers of PROPHECY and was symbolic of fertility. They also believed that one of its functions was to provide entertainment in the otherworld.

According to the myth, Brân had been mortally wounded and requested his companions to cut off his head. He instructed them to take the head with them on their wanderings, telling them that it would not only provide them with entertainment and companionship but would also remain uncorrupted as long as they refrained from opening a certain door. If that door were opened, they would find themselves back in the real world and would remember all their sorrows. Eventually, they were to take the head and bury it on the White Mount in London. All happened as Brân had prophesied, and his companions passed 80 delightful years. The head was buried in London, where it kept away all invaders from Britain until it was finally unearthed. Brân is also the hero of *The Voyage of Brân*.

BRIAREUS \brī-'ar-ē-əs, -'er-\, *also called* Aegaeon, in Greek mythology, one of three 100-armed, 50-headed Hecatoncheires (from the Greek words for "hundred" and "arms"), the sons of the deities OURANUS and GAEA. According to one legend, Briareus and his brothers successfully aided ZEUS against the attack by the TITANS. Another account made Briareus an opponent of Zeus and one of the assailants of Olympus, who, after his defeat, was buried under Mount Etna. Yet another tradition made him a GIANT of the sea, an enemy of POSEIDON, and the inventor of warships.

BRICRIU'S FEAST \'bri-krüz-'fēst\, *Irish Gaelic* Fled Bricrenn, in early Irish literature, a comic, rowdy account of rivalry among Ulster warriors. One of the longest hero tales of the ULSTER CYCLE, it dates from the 8th century and is preserved in *The Book of the Dun Cow* (*c.* 1100). Bricriu, the trickster, promises the hero's portion of his feast to three different champions, Lóegaire, CONALL CERNACH, and CÚ CHULAINN. A violent dispute over precedence ensues, which leads to a series of contests. One night a GIANT carrying an ax challenges the knights to behead him in exchange for a chance to behead them in turn. On successive nights, Conall and Lóegaire behead the giant, who each time replaces his head and leaves but comes back to take his turn, only to find that the warriors have gone. At last Cú Chulainn beheads the giant and, when the giant returns, places his own head on the block, true to his bargain. The giant, really the wizard Cú Roi in disguise, proclaims Cú Chulainn the first hero of Ulster. This is considered the source for the beheading game used in *Sir Gawayne and the Grene Knight*.

BRIDGET OF SWEDEN, SAINT \'bri-jət\, *also spelled* Birgit, *or* Brigid, *Swedish* Sankta Birgitta av Sverige (b. *c.* 1303, Sweden—d. July 23, 1373, Rome [Italy]; canonized Oct. 8, 1391; feast day July 23, formerly October 8), patron saint of Sweden, founder of the BRIDGETTINE Order, and a mystic whose revelations were influential during the Middle Ages.

From an early age Bridget had remarkable religious visions. In 1316 she married; she bore eight children, including St. Catherine of Sweden. On the death of her husband in 1344, Bridget retired to the CISTERCIAN monastery of Alvastra on Lake Vetter. To the prior, Peter Olafsson, she dictated the revelations that came to her. One was a command to found a new religious order, for which she received papal permission in 1370. She went to Rome in 1350 and, except for several PILGRIMAGES, remained there for the rest of her life, constantly accompanied by Catherine. She worked among rich and poor, sheltering the homeless and sinners, and she worked untiringly for the return of the pope from Avignon to Rome (*see* AVIGNON PAPACY).

BRIDGETTINE \'bri-jə-tin, -,tīn, -,tēn\, *also spelled* Brigittine, member of the Order of the Most Holy Savior (O.SS.S.), a religious order of cloistered nuns founded by ST. BRIDGET OF SWEDEN in 1344 and approved by Pope Urban V in 1370. Bridget believed that she was called by JESUS CHRIST to found a strictly disciplined religious order that would contribute to the reform of monastic life. Her foundation contributed greatly to the culture of Scandinavia and Germany. At the time of the Protestant REFORMATION, the order was nearly destroyed. The modern Sisters of the Most Holy Savior of St. Bridget, founded at Rome in 1911 by Mother Elisabeth Hasselblad, were recognized by the Holy See in 1942 as an offshoot of the ancient order. Its members are CONTEMPLATIVES whose prayer life is directed to the reunion of all Christians and, in particular, to the return of Scandinavia to ROMAN CATHOLICISM.

BRIGIT \'bri-git\, *also called* Brigantia (Celtic: "High One"), in CELTIC RELIGION, ancient goddess of the poetic arts, crafts, PROPHECY, and DIVINATION; she was considered the equivalent of the Roman goddess MINERVA (Greek ATHENA). In Ireland this Brigit was one of three goddesses of the same name, daughters of the DAGDA, the great god of that country. Her two sisters were connected with healing and with the craft of the smith. Brigit was worshiped by the semisacred poetic class, the *filid*, who also had certain priestly functions.

Brigit was taken over into CHRISTIANITY as St. Brigit, but she retained her strong pastoral associations. Her feast day was February 1, which was also the date of the pre-Christian festival of IMBOLC, the season when the ewes came into milk. St. Brigit had a great establishment at Kildare in Ireland that was probably founded on a pre-Christian SANCTUARY. Her sacred fire there burned continually; it was tended by a series of 19 nuns and by the saint herself every 20th day. Brigit still plays an important role in modern Scottish folk tradition, where she figures as the midwife of the Virgin MARY. Numerous holy wells in the British Isles are dedicated to her.

Brigantia, patron goddess of the Brigantes of northern Britain, is substantially the same goddess as Brigit. Her connection with water is shown by her invocation in Roman times as "the NYMPH goddess"; several rivers in Britain and Ireland are named after her.

BRITOMARTIS \,bri-tə-'mär-tis\, Cretan goddess sometimes identified with the Greek ARTEMIS. Her name (in early inscriptions "Britomarpis") is perhaps of Minoan origin and was said to mean "sweet virgin" by the Roman geographer Solinus. According to myth, Britomartis was a daughter of ZEUS and lived in Crete; she was a huntress and a virgin. MINOS, king of Crete, fell in love with her and pursued her for

nine months until she, in desperation, leapt from a high cliff into the sea. She was caught in fishermen's nets and hauled to safety. For her chastity she was rewarded by Artemis with immortality. The Greeks also identified her with Aphaea, a primitive local goddess of Aegina.

BROWNE, ROBERT \'braůn\ (b. *c.* 1550—d. October 1633, Northampton, Northamptonshire, Eng.), Puritan Congregationalist church leader, one of the original proponents of the Separatist movement among NONCONFORMISTS that demanded separation from the Church of England. (*See also* CONGREGATIONALISM).

Educated at the University of Cambridge and ordained, he, with Robert Harrison, gathered a Separatist Church at Norwich in 1580. As a consequence of this and similar activities, he was imprisoned 32 times and in 1582 was exiled. He subsequently returned to England, however, and conformed to the ESTABLISHED CHURCH.

BUBER, MARTIN \'bü-bər\ (b. Feb. 8, 1878, Vienna—d. June 13, 1965, Jerusalem), German-Jewish religious philosopher, biblical translator and interpreter. Buber's philosophy was centered on the encounter, or dialogue, of man with other beings, particularly the relation with God.

Buber was brought up by his grandparents in Lemberg (now Lviv, Ukraine). Though taught Hebrew by his grandfather, during his adolescence his active participation in Jewish religious observances ceased altogether. In his university days in Vienna, Berlin, Leipzig, and Zürich, he was greatly influenced by Friedrich Nietzsche's proclamation of heroic nihilism and his criticism of modern culture. The Nietzschean influence was reflected in Buber's turn to ZIONISM and its call for a return to roots and a more wholesome culture. In 1916 Buber founded the influential monthly *Der Jude* ("The Jew"), which he edited until 1924 and which became the central forum for German-reading Jewish intellectuals. In it he advocated the highly unpopular cause of Jewish-Arab cooperation in the formation of a binational state in Palestine.

Buber
By courtesy of Israel Information Services

Buber's *Chassidischen Bücher* ("Hasidic Books," 1927) made the legacy of HASIDISM, the popular 18th-century eastern European Jewish pietistic movement, a part of Western literature. In Hasidism Buber saw a healing power for the malaise of JUDAISM and mankind in an age of alienation that had shaken relationships between man and God, man and man, and man and nature.

After the Nazis forbade Buber's lectures and teaching, in 1938 he immigrated to Palestine where he was appointed professor of social philosophy at Hebrew University in Jerusalem, a post he held until 1951. He was the first president of the Israeli Academy of Sciences and Arts, initiated the founding of the Teachers Training College for Adult Education in Jerusalem, and became its head in 1949.

After an early period of MYSTICISM, Buber abandoned the notion of a mystical union between man and God and embraced instead the notion of their encounter, which presupposes and preserves their separate existence. This basic view underlies Buber's mature thinking; it was expressed in his famous work *Ich und Du* (1923; *I and Thou*). According to this view, God, the great Thou, enables human I–Thou relations between man and other beings. A true relationship with God, as experienced from the human side, must be an I–Thou relationship, in which God is truly met and addressed, not merely thought of and expressed.

Toward God, any type of I–It relationship should be avoided, be it theoretical by making him an object of dogmas, juridical by turning him into a legislator of fixed rules or prayers, or organizational by confining him to CHURCHES, MOSQUES, or SYNAGOGUES. Buber saw the BIBLE as originating in the ever-renewed encounter between God and his people, and he ascribed most of the legal prescriptions of the TALMUD to what he called the spurious tradition removed from the Thou relation with God.

BUCER, MARTIN \\'büt-sər\, *also spelled* Butzer \\'bůt-sər\ (b. Nov. 11, 1491, Schlettstadt, Alsace—d. Feb. 28, 1551, England), Protestant Reformer, mediator, and liturgical scholar best known for his ceaseless attempts to make peace between conflicting reform groups.

Bucer entered the DOMINICAN order in 1506. He became acquainted with the works of the great humanist scholar ERASMUS and of MARTIN LUTHER. In 1521 Bucer withdrew from the Dominicans and in the following year he became pastor of Landstuhl, where he married a former nun. Excommunicated in 1523, he made his way to Strasbourg.

Strasbourg lay between the area influenced by the most important Swiss Reformer, HULDRYCH ZWINGLI—southern Germany and Switzerland—and the area influenced by Luther—northern Germany. After 1524 Luther and Zwingli clashed over the meaning of the words, "This is my body," a central phrase in the liturgy of the Lord's Supper. In 1529 the two leading Reformers and other Reformers engaged in a colloquy to settle the dispute. Luther held to the traditional view that Christ was really present in the SACRAMENT of the Lord's Supper (*see* TRANSUBSTANTIATION); Zwingli espoused a spiritual interpretation that was common among the humanists; Bucer, however, believed that the two opposing views could be reconciled. But when, at the end of the colloquy, Zwingli and Bucer proffered their hands in fellowship to Luther, he refused.

Bucer participated in nearly every conference on religious questions held in Germany and Switzerland between 1524 and 1548. In the various colloquies between PROTESTANTS and ROMAN CATHOLICS or between German Lutheran and Swiss Reform churchmen, Bucer often advocated the use of ambiguity—believing that the essential goal was the reform of the people and the doctrinal issues could be worked out later. At Wittenberg in 1536 Bucer took part in a conference between Lutheran and Reformed theologians, also attended by PHILIPP MELANCHTHON. It appeared for a time as though Bucer and Melanchthon were about to end the dispute over the Lord's Supper. Luther, in satisfaction over the apparent agreement, declared, "We are one, and we acknowledge and receive you as our dear brethren in the Lord." Melanchthon subsequently drew up the Wittenberg Concord incorporating the agreement, but it failed to effect a lasting union.

Bucer was sometimes charged as having no conviction except that the end justifies the means. In his defense he claimed that compromises were only a temporary measure. Bucer's policy of agreement by compromise was seen in a better light when it was applied to the problem of religious toleration. Under Bucer's policies there was less persecution of ANABAPTISTS and other minority groups in Strasbourg than in most of Europe.

Apart from promoting intra-Protestant union, Bucer had long dreamed of healing the Protestant-Catholic rift. The Holy Roman emperor Charles V, for political reasons, pursued similar aims. He accordingly called for a colloquy between Catholics and Protestants at Regensburg in 1541. Charles selected three Catholic and three Protestant theologians (including Bucer) to discuss the anonymous Regensburg Book, which proposed steps toward Catholic-Protestant union. Both Catholics and Protestants rejected the Regensburg Book. Charles settled the matter for a time by subduing the Protestant powers and by enforcing his own compromise scheme, the Augsburg Interim of 1548.

Bucer vigorously opposed acceptance of the Augsburg Interim by Strasbourg. The armies of Charles, however, prevailed, and Strasbourg discharged Bucer and several other Protestant ministers, all of whom were invited to England by the archbishop of Canterbury, Thomas Cranmer. There Bucer supported the official, cautious reform program of Cranmer and the scholarly Nicholas Ridley. He died in England in 1551.

BUCHIS \\'bü-<u>k</u>is\, in ancient EGYPTIAN RELIGION, white bull with black markings, worshiped as a favorite incarnation of the war god MONT. He was represented with the solar disk and two tall plumes between his horns. According to Macrobius, his hair grew in the opposite direction from that of ordinary animals and changed color every hour. At HERMONTHIS (modern Armant) in Upper Egypt, a special center of Mont's worship, a particular bull was chosen to receive a cult as Buchis. Upon its death, it was mummified and buried in a SARCOPHAGUS with divine honors. The mothers of these Buchis bulls received a similar burial.

BUDDHACARITA \\'bůd-də-'chə-ri-tə\, *in full* Buddhacarita-Kāvya-Sūtra (Sanskrit: "Poetic Discourse on the Acts of the Buddha"), poetic narrative of the life of the BUDDHA GOTAMA by the poet AŚVAGHOṢA (1st–2nd century CE). This sophisticated work is one of the earliest "biographies" extant of the Buddha. It is a rendition of his life that reflects a tremendous knowledge of Indian mythology and of pre-Buddhist philosophies, plus a court poet's interest in love, battle, and statecraft. Only the first half of the *Buddhacarita* remains intact in Sanskrit, but all 28 chapters are preserved in Chinese (5th century) and Tibetan translations.

BUDDHAGHOSA \\'bůd-də-'gō-sə, -shə\ (fl. early 5th century CE), in BUDDHISM, a THERAVĀDA scholar who was probably a native of northern India. Buddhaghosa traveled to Sri Lanka, where he discovered many Sinhalese Buddhist commentaries, which he translated into Pāli. He is also the author of the *Visuddhi-magga* ("Path to Purification"), which remains to the present day an authoritative compendium of Theravāda teaching.

BUDDHA GOTAMA \\'bůd-də-'go-tə-mə; *Angl* 'bü-də-'gō-tə-mə, 'bů-\, *clan name* Gotama, *also called* Siddhārtha \sid-'där-tə\ (fl. *c.* 6th–4th century BCE; b. Lumbini, near Kapilavastu, Śākya republic, Kosala kingdom [India]—d. Kusinārā, Malla republic, Magdha kingdom [India]), founder of BUDDHISM. The term buddha, literally meaning "awakened

Seated Buddha with attendants, carved ivory sculpture from Kashmir, c. 8th century CE; in the Prince of Wales Museum of Western India, Bombay
P. Chandra

one" or "enlightened one," is not a proper name but rather a title, and Buddhists traditionally believe that there will be innumerable buddhas in the future as there have been in the past, and that there are other buddhas in other presently existing cosmos as well. The Buddha who belongs to the present era of the cosmos in which we are living is often referred to as Gotama. When the term the Buddha is used, it is generally assumed that it refers to the Buddha Gotama.

According to virtually all Buddhist traditions, the Buddha lived many lives before his birth as Gotama; these previous lives are described in JĀTAKAS (birth stories) that play an important role in Buddhist art and education. Most Buddhists also affirm that the Buddha's life was continued in his teachings and his relics. The Pāli Tipitaka (*see* TRIPIṬAKA), which is recognized by scholars as the earliest extant record of the Buddha's discourses, and the later Pāli commentaries are the basis of the following account in which history and legend are inextricably intertwined.

The Buddha was born in the 6th or 5th century BCE in the kingdom of the Śākyas, on the borders of present-day Nepal and India. Gotama is said to have been born of the king and queen of the Śākyas, Suddhodna and MAHĀMĀYĀ. The Buddha's legend, however, begins with an account of a dream that his mother Mahāmāyā had one night before he was born: a beautiful elephant, white as silver, entered her womb through her side. BRAHMINS (Vedic priests) were asked to interpret the dream, and they foretold the birth of a son

who would become either a universal monarch or a buddha. The purported site of his birth, now called Rummindei, lies within the territory of Nepal. (A pillar placed there in commemoration of the event by AŚOKA, a 3rd-century-BCE Buddhist emperor of India, still stands.) The child was given the name Siddhattha (Sanskrit: Siddhārtha), which means "one whose aim is accomplished."

Gotama is said to have led a sheltered life of great luxury, which was interrupted when, on three excursions outside of the palace, he encountered an old man, an ill man, and a corpse. Each time he asked a servant to explain the phenomenon and was told that all men are subject to such conditions. Gotama then met up with a wandering ascetic and decided that he must discover the reason for such a display of serenity in the midst of such misery. Renouncing his princely life, he went in search of teachers who could instruct him in the way of truth. He took up the practice of various austerities and extreme self-mortifications, including severe fasting. These experiences eventually led Gotama to the conviction that such mortifications could not lead him to what he sought.

Buddhist mythology states that the Buddha went to meditate beneath a pipal tree (*Ficus religiosa*), now known as the BODHI tree. There he was tempted by MARA (the Buddhist "Lord of the Senses"), but Gotama remained unmoved. Later that night the Buddha was to realize the FOUR NOBLE TRUTHS, achieving enlightenment during the night of the full-moon day of the month of May (Vesakha) at a place now called BODH GAYA.

After this enlightenment, the story continues that the Buddha sought out five companions and delivered to them his first sermon, the *Dhammacakkappavattana Sutta* ("Sermon on Setting in Motion the Wheel of Truth"), at Sarnath. An ancient STUPA marks the spot where this event is said to have occurred. The Buddha taught that those in search of enlightenment should not follow the two extremes of self-indulgence and self-mortification. Avoiding these two extremes, the TATHAGATA ("He Who Has Thus Attained") discovers the middle path leading to vision, to knowledge, to calmness, to awakening, and to NIRVANA.

This middle path is known as the Noble EIGHTFOLD PATH, and consists of right view, right thought, right speech, right action, right living, right endeavor, right mindfulness, and right concentration. The First Noble Truth is that sentient existence is DUKKHA, always tainted with conflict, dissatisfaction, sorrow, and suffering. The Second Noble Truth is that all this is caused by selfish desire—*i.e.*, craving or *tanha*, "thirst." The Third Noble Truth is that there is nirvana—emancipation, liberation, and freedom for human beings from all this. The Fourth Noble Truth, the Noble Eightfold Path, is the way to this liberation.

After this sermon the five ascetics became the Buddha's first disciples, were admitted by him as monks (BHIKKHUS), and became the first members of the SANGHA ("community," or "order"). After the Buddha had trained followers, his mission was fulfilled. At Kusinara (the modern Kasia) on the full-moon day of the month of Vesakha (May), the Buddha Gotama entered *parinirvāṇa*—an end to the cycle of being reborn. His body was cremated by the Mallas in Kusinara, but a dispute over the relics of the Buddha arose between the Mallas and the delegates of rulers of several kingdoms. It was settled by a venerable Brahmin on the basis that they should not quarrel over the relics of one who preached peace. Stupas were then built over these relics.

BUDDHA NATURE: *see* TATHAGATA.

BUDDHISM

Apan-
Asian religion and philosophy, Buddhism was founded by
Siddhārtha Gotama in northeast India about the 5th century
BCE. Buddhism has played a central role in the Eastern world
and during the 20th century has spread to the West.

THE BUDDHA'S MESSAGE

The teaching attributed to the BUDDHA GOTAMA was transmitted orally by his
disciples, prefaced by the phrase "Evaṃ me sutaṃ" ("Thus have I heard"); therefore, it is difficult to say whether his discourses were related as they were spoken.
They usually allude, however, to the place, time, and community where he
preached; and there is concordance between various versions. An attempt was
made by Buddhist councils in the first centuries after the Buddha's death to establish his true and original teachings.

It may be said that the Buddha based his entire teaching on the fact of human
suffering. Existence is painful. The conditions that make an individual are precisely those that also give rise to suffering. Individuality implies limitation; limitation gives rise to desire; and, inevitably, desire causes suffering, since what is
desired is transitory, changing, and perishing. It is the impermanence of the object
of craving that causes disappointment and sorrow. By following the "path" taught
by the Buddha, the individual can dispel the "ignorance" that perpetuates this
suffering. The Buddha's doctrine was not one of despair. Living amid the impermanence of everything and being themselves impermanent, humans search for
the way of deliverance, for that which shines beyond the transitoriness of human
existence—in short, for enlightenment.

According to the Buddha, reality, whether of external things or the psychophysical totality of human individuals, consists in a succession and concatenation of
microseconds called *dhamma*s (these "components" of reality are not to be confused with another sense of *dhamma*, "law" or "teaching"). The Buddha departed from the main lines of traditional Indian thought in not asserting an essential
or ultimate reality in things.

Moreover, the Buddha did not want to assume the existence of the soul as a
metaphysical substance, but he admitted the existence of the self as the subject of

*Buddhist novice monk
praying in his monas-
tery cell*
Stephanie Dinkins—Photo
Researchers

BUDDHISM

action in a practical and moral sense. Life is a stream of becoming, a series of manifestations and extinctions. The concept of the individual ego is a popular delusion; the objects with which people identify themselves—fortune, social position, family, body, and even mind—are not their true selves. There is nothing permanent, and, if only the permanent deserves to be called the self, or ĀTMAN, then nothing is self. There can be no individuality without a putting together of components. This is becoming different, and there can be no way of becoming different without a dissolution, a passing away.

To make clear the concept of no-self (ANĀTMAN), Buddhists set forth the theory of the five aggregates or constituents (*khandha*s, or SKANDHAS) of human existence: (1) corporeality or physical forms (*rūpa*), (2) feelings or sensations (*vedanā*), (3) ideations (*saññā*), (4) mental formations or dispositions (*sankhāra*s, or SAMSKĀRAS), and (5) consciousness (*viññāna*). Human existence is only a composite of the five aggregates, none of which is the self or soul. A person is in a process of continuous change, with no fixed underlying entity.

The belief in rebirth, or SAMSĀRA, as a potentially endless series of worldly existences in which every being is caught up was already associated with the doctrine of KARMA (literally "act," or "deed") in pre-Buddhist India, and it was generally accepted by both the THERAVĀDA and the MAHĀYĀNA traditions (the two main traditions in Buddhism). According to the doctrine of karma, good conduct brings a pleasant and happy result and creates a tendency toward similar good acts, while bad conduct brings an evil result and creates a tendency toward repeated evil actions. This furnishes the basic context for the moral life of the individual.

The acceptance by Buddhists of the belief in karma and rebirth while holding to the doctrine of no-self gave rise to a difficult problem: how can rebirth take place without a permanent subject to be reborn? The relation between existences in rebirth has been explained by the analogy of fire, which maintains itself unchanged in appearance and yet is different in every moment—what may be called the continuity of an ever-changing identity.

Conviction that the above are fundamental realities led the Buddha to formulate the FOUR NOBLE TRUTHS: the truth of misery, the truth that misery originates within us from the craving for pleasure and for being or nonbeing, the truth that this craving can be eliminated, and the truth that this elimination is the result of a methodical way or path that must be followed. Thus, there must be an understanding of the mechanism by which a human being's psychophysical being evolves; otherwise, human beings would remain indefinitely in *samsāra*, in the continual flow of transitory existence.

Hence, the Buddha formulated the law of dependent origination (*paticca-samuppāda*, or PRATĪTYA-SAMUTPĀDA), whereby one condition arises out of another, which in turn arises out of prior conditions. Every mode of being presupposes another immediately preceding mode from which the subsequent mode derives, in a chain of causes. According to the classical rendering, the 12 links in the chain are ignorance (*avijjā*), karmic predispositions (*sankhāra*s), consciousness (*viññāna*), form and body (*nāma-rūpa*), the five sense organs and the mind (*salāyatana*), contact (*phassa*), feeling-response (*vedanā*), craving (*tanhā*), grasping for an object (*upādāna*), action toward life (*bhava*), birth (JĀTI), and old age and death (*jarāmarana*). Thus, the misery that is bound up with all sensate existence is accounted for by a methodical chain of causation.

The law of dependent origination of the various aspects of becoming remains fundamental in all schools of Buddhism. There are, however, diverse interpretations. Given this law, the question arises as to how one may escape the continually renewed cycle of birth, suffering, and death. Here ethical conduct enters in. It is not enough to know that misery pervades all existence and to know the way in which life evolves; there must also be a purification that leads to the overcoming of this process. Such a liberating purification is effected by following the Noble EIGHTFOLD PATH constituted by right views, right aspirations, right speech, right conduct, right livelihood, right effort, right mindfulness, and right meditational attainment.

The aim of religious practice is to be rid of the delusion of ego, thus freeing oneself from the fetters of this mundane world. One who is successful in doing so is said to have overcome the round of rebirths and to have achieved enlightenment. This is the final goal—not a paradise or a heavenly world.

The living process is likened to a fire burning. Its remedy is the extinction of the fire of illusion, passions, and cravings. The Buddha, the Enlightened One, is one who is no longer kindled or enflamed. Many terms are used to describe the state of the enlightened human being; the one that has become famous in the West is NIRVANA, translated as "dying out"—that is, the dying out in the heart of lust, anger, and delusion. But nirvana is not extinction, and indeed the craving for annihilation or nonexistence was expressly repudiated by the Buddha. Buddhists search not for mere cessation but for salvation. Though nirvana is often presented negatively as "release from suffering," it is more accurate to describe it in a more positive fashion: as an ultimate goal to be sought and cherished.

The Buddha left indeterminate questions regarding the destiny of persons who have reached this ultimate goal. He even refused to speculate as to whether such purified saints, after death, continued to exist or ceased to exist. Such questions, he maintained, were not relevant to the practice of the path and could not in any event be answered from within the confines of ordinary human existence. Still, he often affirmed the reality of the religious goal. For example, he is reported to have said: "There is an unborn, an unoriginated, an unmade, an uncompounded; were there not, there would be no escape from the world of the born, the originated, the made, and the compounded."

In his teaching, the Buddha strongly asserted that the ontological status (that is, whether it possesses existence) and character of the unconditioned nirvana cannot be delineated in a way that does not distort or misrepresent it. But what is more important is that he asserted with even more insistence that nirvana can be experienced—and experienced in this present existence—by those who, knowing the Buddhist truth, practice the Buddhist path.

SANGHA, SOCIETY, AND STATE

Monastic institutions.   The SANGHA is the assembly of Buddhist monks that has, from the origins of Buddhism, authoritatively studied, taught, and preserved the teachings of the Buddha. In their communities monks have served the laity through example and, as directed by the Buddha, through the teachings of morality (Pāli: *sīla*; Sanskrit: *śīla*). In exchange for their service the monks have received support from the laity, who thereby earn merit. Besides serving as the center of Buddhist propaganda and learning, the monastery offers the monk an opportunity to live apart from worldly concerns, a situation that has usually been believed necessary or at least advisable in order to follow strictly the path that leads most directly to release.

Origin and development of the sangha.   According to scholars of early Buddhism, at the time of the Buddha in northeastern India there existed numerous religious MENDICANTS or almsmen who wandered and begged individually or in groups. These men had forsaken the life of a householder and the involvement with worldly affairs that this entails in order to seek a doctrine and form of practice which would meaningfully explain life and offer salvation. When such a seeker met someone who seemed to offer such a salvatory message, he would accept him as a teacher (GURU) and wander with him. The situation of these mendicants is summed up in the greeting with which they met other religious wanderers. This greeting asked, "Under whose guidance have you accepted religious mendicancy? Who is your master (*sattha*)? Whose *dhamma* is agreeable to you?"

Buddhist monk in Thailand begging for his day's food. The laity gain merit by providing food to the monks
Van Bucher—Photo Researchers

The groups of mendicants that had formed around a teacher broke their wanderings during the rainy season (VASSA) from July through August. At this time they gathered at various rain retreats (*vassavāsa*), usually situated near villages. Here they would beg daily for their few needs and continue their spiritual quest. The Buddha and his followers may well have been the first group to found such a yearly rain retreat.

After the Buddha's death his followers did not separate but continued to wander and enjoy the rain retreat together. In their retreats the followers of the Buddha's teachings probably built their own huts and lived separately, but their sense of community with other Buddhists led them to gather biweekly at the time of the full and new moons to recite the PĀTIMOKKHA, or declaration of their steadfastness in observing the monastic discipline. This ceremony, in which the laity also participated, was called the *uposatha.*

Within the first several centuries after the Buddha's death, the *sangha* came to include two different groups of monks. One retained the wandering mode of existence; this group has been a very creative force in Buddhist history and continues to play a role in contemporary Buddhism, particularly in Sri Lanka and Southeast Asia. The other, much larger group gave up the forest life and settled in permanent monastic settlements (VIHARAS). There appear to be two major reasons for this change in the mode of living. First, the followers of the Buddha were able, through their confession of a common faith, to build up a certain coherent organization. Second, the laity gave meritorious gifts of land and raised buildings in which the followers of the Buddha might live permanently, assured of a supply of the staples of life and also fulfilling the Buddha's directive to minister to the laity. In this manner small *vihara*s were raised in northeastern India and adjoining areas into which Buddhism spread. With the reign of King AŚOKA, further developments occurred. Aśoka took a protective interest in the unity and well-being of the Buddhist monastic community, and, as a result of his support and influence, Buddhism developed a more universal orientation.

In the post-Aśokan period, Buddhist monasteries grew in size and acquired a great deal of wealth. By about the 5th century CE there developed MAHĀVIHĀRAS, or monastic centers, such as Nālandā in India. These were centers of Buddhist learning and propaganda, drawing monks from China and Tibet and sending forth missionaries to these lands. The institutions were open to the outside influence of a resurgent HINDUISM, however, which weakened Buddhism prior to its disappearance from India in the 13th century.

In all Buddhist countries, monasteries continued to serve as centers of missions and learning and as retreats. Different types of monastic establishments developed in particular areas and in particular contexts. In several regions there were at least two types of institutions. There were a few large public monasteries that usually functioned in greater or lesser accord with classical Buddhist norms. In addition, there were many smaller monasteries, often located in rural areas, that were much more loosely regulated. Often these were hereditary institutions in which the rights and privileges of the abbot were passed on to an adopted disciple. In areas where clerical marriage was practiced—for example, in medieval Sri Lanka and in post-Heian Japan—a tradition of blood inheritance developed.

Internal organization of the sangha. It appears that the earliest organization within Indian monasteries was democratic in nature. This democratic nature arose from two important historical factors. First, the Buddha did not, as was the custom among the teachers of his time, designate a human successor. Instead, the Buddha taught that each monk should strive to follow the path that he had preached. Thus there could be no absolute authority vested in one person, for the authority was the *dhamma* that the Buddha had taught. Second, the region in which Buddhism arose was noted for a system of tribal democracy, or republicanism, which was adopted by the early *sangha.*

When an issue arose, all the monks of the monastery assembled. The issue was put before the body of monks and discussed. If any solution was forthcoming, it had to be read three times, with silence signifying acceptance. If there was debate, a vote might be taken or the issue referred to committee or the arbitration of the elders of a neighboring monastery. As the *sangha* developed, a certain division of labor and hierarchical administration was adopted. The abbot became the head of this administrative hierarchy and was vested with almost unlimited powers over monastic affairs. The anti-authoritarian character of Buddhism, however, continued to assert itself. In China and Southeast Asian countries there has traditionally been a popular distaste for hierarchy, making rules difficult to enforce in the numerous almost independent monastic units.

As the Buddhist *sangha* developed, specific rules and rites were enacted that differ very little in all Buddhist monasteries even today. The rules by which the monks are judged and the punishments that should be assessed are found in the *vinaya* texts (*vinaya* literally means "that which leads"). The VINAYA PITAKA of the Theravāda canon contains precepts that were supposedly given by the Buddha as he judged a particular situation. While in the majority of cases the Buddha's authorship can be doubted, the attempt is made to refer all authority to the Buddha and not to one of his disciples. The heart of the *vinaya* texts is the *Pātimokkha*, which, in the course of the *sangha*'s development, became a list of monastic rules. The rules are recited by the assembled monks every two weeks, with a pause after each one so that any monk who has transgressed this rule may confess and receive his punishment. While the number of rules in the *Pātimokkha* differs in the various schools, with 227, 250, and 253, respectively in the Pāli, Chinese, and Tibetan canons, the rules are essentially the same. The first part of the *Pātimokkha* deals with the four gravest SINS, which necessarily lead to expulsion from the monastery. They are sexual intercourse, theft, murder, and exaggeration of one's miraculous powers. The other rules, in seven sections, deal with transgressions of a lesser nature, such as drinking or lying.

In the Theravāda countries—Sri Lanka, Myanmar (Burma), Thailand, Cambodia, and Laos—the Buddhist monastic community is composed primarily of male monks and novices (the order of nuns died out in the Theravāda world more than a millennium ago, and contemporary efforts to reestablish it have met with only minimal success), white-robed ascetics (including various types of male and female practitioners who remain outside the *sangha* but follow a more or less renunciatory mode of life), and laymen and laywomen. In some Theravāda countries, notably in mainland Southeast Asia, boys or young men were traditionally expected to join the monastery for a period of instruction and meditation. Thus,

World distribution of Buddhism

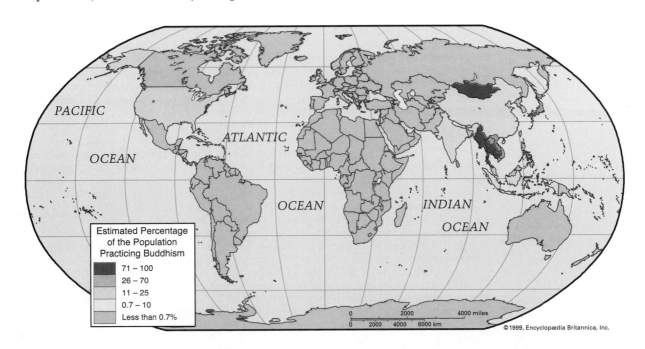

Estimated Percentage of the Population Practicing Buddhism

- 71 – 100
- 26 – 70
- 11 – 25
- 0.7 – 10
- Less than 0.7%

©1999, Encyclopædia Britannica, Inc.

the majority of men in these areas were involved with the monastic ethos. This practice has fostered a high degree of lay participation in monastic affairs.

In the Mahāyāna and VAJRAYĀNA countries of China and Tibet there was traditionally a stage of one year before the aspirant could become a novice. This was a year of probation when the aspirant did not receive TONSURE and remained subject to governmental taxation and service, while receiving instructions and performing menial tasks within the monastery. At the end of this one-year probationary period, the aspirant had to pass a test, including the recitation of part of a well-known *sūtra*—the length depending upon whether the applicant was male or female—and a discussion on various doctrinal questions. In China, one usually did not progress beyond the novice stage unless he or she was of exceptional character or was affiliated with the government.

According to *vinaya* rules, entry into the *sangha* is an individual affair, dependent upon the wishes of the individual and his family. In some Buddhist countries, however, ordination was often under the control of the state, and the state conducted the examinations to determine entry or advancement in the *sangha*. In certain situations ordination could be obtained not only through such examinations but also by the favor of high officials or through the purchase of an ordination certificate from the government. This selling of ordination certificates was at times abused by the government in order to fill its treasury.

The life of a Buddhist monk was originally one of wandering, poverty, begging, and strict sexual abstinence. The monks were supposed to live only on alms, to wear clothes made from cloth taken from rubbish heaps, and to possess only three robes, one girdle, an alms bowl, a razor, a needle, and a water strainer used to filter insects from the drinking water (so as not to kill or imbibe them). Most Buddhist schools still stress CELIBACY, although some groups, particularly in Tibet and Japan, have relaxed the monastic discipline, and some Vajrayāna schools have allowed sexual activity as an esoteric ritual that contributes to the attainment of release. Begging, however, has tended in all schools to become merely a symbolic gesture used to teach humility or compassion or to raise funds for special purposes. Also, the growth of large monasteries has often led to compromises on the rule of poverty. While the monk might technically give up his property before entering the monastery—although even this rule is sometimes relaxed—the community of monks might inherit wealth and receive lavish gifts of land. This acquisition of wealth has led at times not only to a certain neglect of the Buddhist monastic ideal but also to the attainment of temporal power. This factor, in addition to the self-governing nature of Buddhist monasteries and the early Buddhist connection with Indian kingship, has influenced the interaction of the *sangha* and the state.

Society and state. Though Buddhism is sometimes described as a purely monastic, otherworldly religion, this is not accurate. In the earliest phases of the tradition the Buddha was pictured as a teacher who addressed not only renouncers but lay householders as well. Moreover, although he is not depicted in the early texts as a social reformer, he does address issues of social order and responsibility.

Throughout Buddhist history, Buddhists have put forth varying forms of social ethics based on notions of karmic justice (the "law" that good deeds will be rewarded with happy results while evil deeds will entail suffering for the one who does them); the cultivation of virtues such as self-giving, compassion, and even-handedness; and the fulfillment of responsibilities to parents, teachers, rulers, and so on. Moreover, Buddhists have formulated various notions of COSMOGONY and COSMOLOGY that have provided legitimacy for the social hierarchies and political orders with which they have been associated. For the most part, Buddhism has played a conservative, moderating role in the generally hierarchical social and political organization of various Asian societies, but the tradition has on occasion given rise to more radical and revolutionary movements as well.

Over the course of Buddhism's long history, the relationship between the Buddhist community and state authority has taken many forms. The early Buddhist *sangha* in India appears to have been treated by Indian rulers as a self-governing unit not subject to their power unless it proved subversive or was threatened by internal or external disruption. Aśoka, the Buddhist king whose personal support and prestige helped Buddhism grow from a regional to a universal religion, appears to have been applying this policy of protection from disruption when he intervened in Buddhist monastic affairs to expel schismatics. He came to be remembered, however, as the Dharmarāja, the great king who protected and propagated the teachings of the Buddha.

In Theravāda countries Aśoka's image as a supporter and sponsor of the faith has traditionally been used to judge political authority. In general, Buddhism in Theravāda countries has been either heavily favored or officially recognized by the government, so that the golden age in which there is a creative interaction between the government and the monks has been viewed as an obtainable goal. The *sangha*'s role in this interaction has traditionally been to preserve the *dhamma* and to act as the spiritual guide and model, revealing to the secular power the need for furthering the welfare of the people. While the *sangha* and the government appear as two separate structures, there has been some intertwining; for monks (often of royal heritage) have commonly acted as temporal advisers, and the kings—at least in Thailand—occasionally have spent some time in the monastery. It should also be pointed out that Buddhist monastic institutions have served as a link between the rural peoples and the urban elites, helping to unify the various Theravāda countries.

In China the relationship between the *sangha* and the state has fluctuated. At times Buddhism has been seen as a foreign religion, as a potential competitor with the state, or as a drain on national resources of men and wealth. These perceptions have led to sharp purges of Buddhism and to rules curbing its influence. Some of the rules were an attempt to limit the number of monks and to guarantee governmental influence in ordination through state examinations and the granting of ordination certificates. Conversely, at other times, such as during the early centuries of the T'ang dynasty (618–845), Buddhism was almost considered the state religion. The government created a commissioner of religion to earn merit for the state by erecting temples, monasteries, and images in honor of the Buddha.

In Japan, Buddhism has experienced similar fluctuations. During the period from the 10th to the 13th century, monasteries gained great landed wealth and temporal power. They formed large armies of monks and mercenaries that took part in wars with rival religious groups as well as in temporal struggles. By the 14th century, however, their power began to wane, and, under the Tokugawa regime that took control in the 17th century, Buddhist institutions became, to a considerable degree, instruments of state power and administration.

Only in Tibet did Buddhists establish a theocratic polity that lasted for an extended period of time. Beginning in the 12th century, Tibetan monastic groups developed relationships with the powerful Mongol khans that often gave them control of governmental affairs in Tibet. In the 17th century the DGE-LUGS-PA school established a monastic regime that was able to maintain more or less continual control until the Chinese occupation in the 1950s.

During the immediate premodern period, each of the various Buddhist communities in Asia developed some kind of working relationship with the sociopolitical system in its area. Within the sweep of Western colonialism and especially after the establishment of new political ideologies and systems during the 19th and 20th centuries, these older patterns of accommodation between Buddhism and state authority were seriously challenged. In many cases bitter conflicts resulted—for example, between Buddhists and colonial regimes in Sri Lanka and Myanmar, between Buddhists and the Meiji reformers in Japan, and between Buddhists and many different communist regimes. In some cases, as, for instance, in Japan, these conflicts have been resolved and new modes of accommodation have been established. In other cases, such as that of Tibet, there has been no resolution.

Standing Buddha with his hands in the mudrā *(symbolic gesture) symbolizing "do not fight"; in Bangkok, Thailand*
Mimi Forsyth—Monkmeyer

BUDDHISM

Standing Buddha with his hands in the mudrā *symbolizing fearlessness, 2nd–4th century CE; from northern Pakistan*

Philadelphia Museum of Art—photograph, A.J. Wyatt, staff photographer

HISTORICAL DEVELOPMENT

The early councils. The early BUDDHIST COUNCILS (*sangīti*s, or "recitals") were concerned largely with the purity of the faith and practice of the monastic community. Unfortunately, legend and myth have so colored these accounts that scholars cannot be sure when and where they took place or even who took part in them. Though many scholars deny its very existence, all Buddhist traditions maintain that a council was called at Rājagaha (modern Rājgīr) immediately after the Buddha's death (the date of which is unknown). According to legend, this council (comprising 500 ARAHANTS, or accomplished monks) was responsible for the composition of the *vinaya* (code of monastic discipline), under the monk Upāli, and the *dhamma* (*i.e.*, the *sūtra*s, or Buddhist SCRIPTURES), under the monk ĀNANDA, even though the latter was supposedly brought to trial at the same council. Though there were memorizers of *sūtra*s and the *vinaya*, as well as authorized commentators, during the period of the first three Buddhist councils, the scriptures as such existed only in an inchoate oral form.

More scholars are prone to accept the historicity of the second council that was held at Vesālī (Sanskrit: Vaiśālī) a little more than a century after the Buddha's death. According to the tradition, a controversy arose between a certain Yasa and the monks of Vajji. The 10 points of discipline observed by the Vajjian monks and opposed by Yasa permitted storing salt in a horn, eating in the afternoon, and drinking buttermilk after meals. These and other rules were condemned by the council as being too lax. Many scholars believe the second council to have been closely associated with the controversy that led to the open division between two segments of the early community—the MAHĀSAṄGHIKA school, which displayed more liberal attitudes, and the Sthaviravāda (Theravāda) school, which took a more conservative stance.

According to Theravāda accounts, a third council was called by King Aśoka at Pāṭaliputta (Patna) about 250 BCE. Moggaliputta Tissa, president of the council, is said to have completed his *Abhidharma* (scholastic) treatise, the *Kathāvatthu* ("Points of Controversy"), during this council. It is also said that a controversy arose between two sects, the Sarvāstivādins and the Vibhajyavādins (usually identified with the early Theravādins), over the reality of past and future states of consciousness (*citta*s). After the Sarvāstivādin view that such states actually exist was condemned, the sect supposedly withdrew from the lower GAṄGĀ (Ganges) valley to Mathurā in the northwest. There it appears to have continued to develop as a transitional school between the older, more conservative schools and the nascent Mahāyāna ("Greater Vehicle") movement.

According to northern Buddhist traditions, a fourth council was held under King KANIṢKA, probably in the 1st century CE, at Jalandhar or in Kashmir. This council seems to have been limited to the composition of commentaries. Because it appears that the Sarvāstivādin viewpoint was the only one represented, scholars generally conclude that this was a sectarian synod rather than an actual ecumenical Buddhist council. At any rate, the fourth council has never been recognized by southern Buddhists.

Developments within India. *Expansion of Buddhism.* The Buddha was a charismatic leader who discovered and proclaimed a religious message and founded a distinctive religious community. Some of the members of that community were, like the Buddha himself, wandering ascetics. Others were laypersons who venerated the Buddha, followed those aspects of his teachings that were relevant to them, and provided the wandering ascetics with the material support that they required.

During the first several centuries after the Buddha's death, the story of his life was remembered and embellished, his teachings were preserved and developed, and the community that he had established became a significant religious force. Many of the followers of the Buddha who were wandering ascetics began to settle in permanent monastic establishments and to develop the procedures needed to maintain large monastic institutions. At the same time, the Buddhist laity came to include important members of the economic and political elite.

During the first century of its existence Buddhism spread from its place of origin in Magadha and Kosala throughout much of northern India, including the areas of Mathurā and Ujjayanī in the west. According to tradition, invitations to the Council of Vesālī, held just over a century after the Buddha's death, were sent to monks living in many distant places throughout northern and central India. By the middle of the 3rd century BCE, Buddhism had gained the favor of a Mauryan king who had established an empire that extended from the HIMALAYAS in the north almost as far south as Sri Lanka.

To the rulers of the kingdoms and republics arising in northeastern India, the patronage of sects with practices differing from orthodox Hinduism was one way of counterbalancing the enormous political power enjoyed by high-caste Hindus (BRAHMINS) in the affairs of state. The first Mauryan emperor, Candra Gupta (c. 321–c. 297 BCE), patronized JAINISM and finally became a Jain monk. His grandson, Aśoka, who ruled over the greater part of the subcontinent from about 270 to 230 BCE, became the archetypal Buddhist king. Aśoka attempted to establish in his realm a "true *dhamma*" based on the virtues of self-control, impartiality, cheerfulness, truthfulness, and goodness. Though he did not found a state church, he did attempt to forge a Buddhist-oriented culture that would include Hindu, Jain, Ājīvika (Ājīvaka), and Buddhist alike. Though Aśoka created a new ideal of kingship that would have powerful repercussions throughout the later Buddhist world, the various problems posed by a state of vast dimensions proved greater than he could solve. Soon after Aśoka's death, the Mauryan empire began to crumble.

Although Buddhists seem to have suffered some persecutions during the subsequent Śuṅga–Kāṇva period (185–28 BCE), Buddhism succeeded in maintaining and even expanding its influence. Buddhist monastic centers and magnificent Buddhist monuments such as the great STUPAS at Bhārhut and Sāñchi were established throughout the subcontinent, and these institutions often received royal patronage. In the early centuries of the Common Era, Buddhism was especially flourishing in northwestern India, and from there it spread rapidly into Central Asia and China.

Buddhism under the Guptas and Pālas. By the time of the Gupta dynasty (c. 320–c. 600 CE), Buddhism in India was being affected by the revival of Brahmanic religion and the rising tide of BHAKTI (Hindu devotionalism). During this period, for example, some Hindus were practicing devotion to the Buddha, whom they regarded as an AVATAR (incarnation) of the Hindu deity VISHNU.

During the Gupta period some monasteries joined together to form monastic centers (MAHĀVIHĀRAS) that functioned as universities. The most famous of these, located at NĀLANDA, had a curriculum that went far beyond the bounds of traditional Buddhism. Nālanda soon became the leading center for the study of Mahāyāna, which was rapidly becoming the dominant Buddhist tradition in India.

Though Buddhist institutions seemed to be faring well under the Guptas, various Chinese pilgrims visiting India between 400 and 700 CE could discern an internal decline in the Buddhist community and the beginning of the reabsorption of Indian Buddhism by Hinduism. Among these pilgrims were FA-HSIEN, Sung Yün, Hui-sheng, I-ching, and the 7th-century monk HSÜAN-TSANG, who found "millions of monasteries" in northwestern India reduced to ruins by the Huns, a nomadic Central Asian people. Many of the remaining Buddhists were developing their own form of Tantrism (*see* TANTRA).

Buddhism survived the Huns' destruction of the monasteries, especially in the northeast, and flourished for a time under the Buddhist Pāla kings (8th–12th century CE). These kings continued to protect the great monastic establishments, building such new centers as Odantapurī, near Nālanda, and establishing a system of supervision for all such *mahāvihāra*s. Under the Pālas, Tantric Buddhism (*i.e.*, Vajrayāna) became the dominant sect. Adepts of this sect, called SIDDHAS,

Reclining Buddha, 12th century CE; in the Galvihara shrine, Polonnaruwa, Sri Lanka
George Holton—Photo Researchers

identified nirvana with the passions, maintaining that one could "touch the deathless element with his body." During this period, the university of Nālanda became a center for the study of Tantric Buddhism and the practice of Tantric magic and rituals. Under the Pāla kings, contacts with China decreased as Indians began to turn their attention to Tibet and Southeast Asia.

The decline of Buddhism in India. With the collapse of the Pāla dynasty in the 12th century, Buddhism suffered another defeat, and this time it did not recover. Though some pockets of Buddhist influence remained, the Buddhist presence in India became so negligible that it could hardly be noticed. To some extent, Buddhism was so tolerant of other faiths that it was simply reabsorbed by a revitalized Hindu tradition. Likewise, Buddhism in India, having become mainly a monastic movement, probably paid little heed to the laity and, after the Muslim invaders sacked the Indian monasteries in the 12th century CE, Buddhists had little basis for recovery. After the destruction of the monasteries, the Buddhist laity showed little interest in restoring the "Way."

Contemporary revival. At the beginning of the 20th century Buddhism was virtually extinct in India. Since the early 1900s, however, a significant Buddhist presence has been reestablished. The incorporation of Sikkim in 1975 into the Republic of India has brought into the modern Indian nation a small Himalayan society that has a strong Buddhist tradition related to the Vajrayāna Buddhism of Tibet. Following the Chinese conquest of Tibet in the late 1950s, there was an influx of Tibetan Buddhists who established a highly visible Buddhist community in northern India. More importantly, though, a number of Buddhist societies were organized in the early decades of the 20th century by Indian intellectuals who found in Buddhism an alternative to a Hindu tradition that they could no longer accept. The mass conversion of large numbers of people from the so-called scheduled CASTES (formerly called UNTOUCHABLES), a movement originally led by BHIMRAO RAMJI AMBEDKAR, began in the 1950s. In October 1956 Ambedkar and several hundred thousand of his followers converted to Buddhism, and—although accurate figures are difficult to determine—the group has continued to grow. Some estimates indicate that the number of converts is as high as four million.

Sri Lanka and Southeast Asia. The first clear evidence of the spread of Buddhism outside India dates from the reign of King Aśoka (3rd century BCE). According to his inscriptions, Aśoka sent Buddhist emissaries not only to many different regions of the subcontinent but also into certain border areas as well. It is certain that Aśokan emissaries were sent to Sri Lanka and to an area called Suvarṇabhūmi that many modern scholars have identified with the Mon country in southern Myanmar and central Thailand.

Sri Lanka. According to the Sinhalese tradition, Buddhism took root in Sri Lanka with the arrival of Aśoka's son Mahinda and his six companions. Sent as missionaries by the Mauryan emperor, these travelers converted King Devānampiya Tissa and many of the nobility. Under King Tissa, the Mahāvihāra monastery was built, an institution that was to become the center of Sinhalese orthodoxy. After Tissa's death (c. 207 BCE) Sri Lanka fell into the hands of the South Indians until the time of Duṭṭhagāmaṇī (101–77 BCE), a descendant of Tissa, who overthrew King Eḷāra. During this time, as a reaction to the threat posed by the South Indians, Buddhism and Sri Lankan political formations became closely intertwined. Again, it was probably because of this danger that the Pāli canon was first written down under King Vaṭṭagāmaṇī Abhaya in the 1st century BCE. This king also built the Abhayagiri monastery, the main center of the various Mahāyāna movements in Sri Lanka. These developments were openly supported by King Mahāsena (276–303 CE). Under Mahāsena's son, Śrī Meghavaṇṇa, the "Tooth of the Buddha" was brought to Abhayagiri and made the national symbol.

During the 1st millennium CE in Sri Lanka, the ancient Theravāda tradition coexisted with various forms of Hinduism, Mahāyāna Buddhism, and Tantric Buddhism. Beginning in the 10th century, as Buddhism was declining in India, Sri Lanka became a major locus of a Theravāda Buddhist revival. As a result of this revival, Sri Lanka became a Theravāda kingdom, with a *sangha* that was unified under Theravāda auspices and a monarch who legitimated his rule in Theravāda terms. The new Theravāda tradition that was established spread from Sri Lanka into Southeast Asia, where it exerted a powerful influence.

In modern times Sri Lanka fell prey to the Western colonial powers (to the Portuguese in 1505–1658, the Dutch in 1658–1796, and finally the British in 1796–1947). Under King Kittisiri Rājasiha (1747–81) the ordination lineage was once again renewed, this time by monks recruited from Thailand.

The monastic community in Sri Lanka is now divided into three major bodies: (1) the Siam Nikaya, founded in the 18th century, a conservative and wealthy sect that admits only members of the Goyigama, the highest Sinhalese caste, (2) the Amarapura sect, founded in the 19th century, which has opened its ranks to members of lower castes, and (3) the reformed splinter group from the Siam Nikaya called the Ramanya sect. Among the laity several reform groups have been established. Among these the SARVODAYA community that is headed by A.T. Ariyaratne is especially important. This group has established religious, economic, and social development programs that have had a significant impact on Sinhalese village life.

Southeast Asia. In Southeast Asia the Buddhist impact has been made in very different ways in three different regions. In two of these (the region of Malaysia-Indonesia and the region on the mainland extending from Myanmar to southern Vietnam), the main connections have been trade routes with India and Sri Lanka. In Vietnam the main connections have been with China. It is certain that Buddhism reached these areas by the beginning centuries of the 1st millennium CE.

With the help of Indian missionaries such as the monk Guṇavarman, Buddhism had gained a firm foothold on Java well before the 5th century CE. Buddhism was also introduced at about this time in Sumatra, and, by the 7th century, the king of Śrīvijaya on the island of Sumatra was a Buddhist. When the Chinese traveler I-ching visited this kingdom in the 7th century, he noted that HĪNAYĀNA Buddhism was dominant in the area but that there were in addition a few Mahāyānists. It was also in the 7th century that the great scholar Dharmapāla from Nālanda visited Indonesia.

The Śailendra dynasty, which ruled over the Malay Peninsula and a large section of Indonesia from the 7th to the 9th century, promoted the Mahāyāna and Tantric forms of Buddhism. During this period major Buddhist monuments were

*Buddhist monk pauses
while cleaning
vegetation from a stupa
at Angkor Wat,
Cambodia*
John Spragens, Jr.—Photo
Researchers

erected in Java, among them the marvelous BOROBUDUR, which is perhaps the most magnificent of all Buddhist stupas (burial monuments). From the 7th century onward, Vajrayāna Buddhism spread rapidly throughout the area. King Kertanagara of Java (reigned 1268–92) was especially devoted to Tantric practice.

In the Malay Peninsula and Indonesia, as in India, Buddhism gradually lost its hold during the first half of the 2nd millennium CE. In many areas Buddhism was assimilated to Hinduism, forming a Hindu-oriented amalgam that in some places (for example, in Bali) has persisted to the present. In most of Malaysia and Indonesia, however, both Hinduism and Buddhism were replaced by ISLAM, which remains the dominant religion in the area. (In Indonesia and Malaysia, Buddhism exists as a living religion only among the Chinese minority, but there is a growing community of converts, with its greatest strength in the vicinity of Borobudur.)

A second pattern of Buddhist expansion in Southeast Asia developed in the mainland area that extends from Myanmar in the north and west to the Mekong delta in the south and east. According to the local Mon and Burman traditions, this is the area of Suvarṇabhūmi that was visited by missionaries from the Aśokan court. It is known that, by the early centuries of the 1st millennium CE, Buddhist kingdoms were beginning to appear in this region. In Myanmar and Thailand—despite the presence of Hindu, Mahāyāna, and Vajrayāna elements—the more conservative Hīnayāna forms of Buddhism were especially prominent throughout the 1st millennium CE. Farther to the east and south, in what is now Cambodia and southern Vietnam, various combinations of Hinduism, Mahāyāna Buddhism, and Vajrayāna Buddhism became dominant. Throughout much of the history of Angkor, the great imperial center that dominated Cambodia and much of the surrounding areas for many centuries, Hinduism seems to have been the preferred tradition, at least among the elite. In the late 12th and early 13th centuries, however, the Buddhist King Jayavarman VII built a new capital called Angkor Thom, with a temple complex that was dominated by Mahāyāna and Vajrayāna monuments; these monuments represent one of the high points of Buddhist architectural achievement.

In mainland Southeast Asia, as in Sri Lanka, a Theravāda reform movement began to develop in the 11th century. Drawing heavily on the Theravāda heritage that had been preserved among the Mon in southern Myanmar, as well as on the new reform tradition that was developing in Sri Lanka, this revival soon established the Theravāda tradition as the most dynamic tradition in Myanmar, where the Burmans had conquered the Mon. By the late 13th century the reform movement had spread to Thailand, where the Thai were gradually displacing the Mon as the dominant population. Within another two centuries the Theravāda reformers had spread their tradition to Cambodia and Laos.

The Theravāda preeminence that was thus established remained basically intact throughout the area during the remainder of the premodern period. The arrival of the Western powers in the 19th century, however, brought important changes. In Thailand, which retained its independence, a process of gradual reform and modernization took place. During the 19th century leadership in the reform and modernization process was taken by a new Buddhist sect, the Thammayut Nikāya, which was established and supported by the reigning Chakri dynasty. More recently, the reform and modernization process has become more diversified and has affected virtually all segments of the Thai Buddhist community.

In the other Theravāda countries in Southeast Asia, Buddhism has had a much more difficult time. In Myanmar, which endured an extended period of British rule, the *sangha* and the structures of Buddhist society have been seriously disrupted. Under the military regime of General Ne Win, established in 1962, reform and modernization were limited in all areas of national life, including religion. In Laos and Cambodia, both of which suffered an extended period of French rule followed by the devastation of the Vietnam War and the violent imposition of communist rule, the Buddhist community has been severely crippled. During the late 20th century, however, many signs of a Buddhist revival have begun to appear.

Funeral cortege in Saigon (now Ho Chi Minh City) of Buddhist monk Thich Quang Duo, who immolated himself to uphold claims of Buddhists in Vietnam during the Vietnam War
AFP—Archive Photos

There are some indications that Vietnam was involved in the early sea trade between India, Southeast Asia, and China and that Buddhism reached the country around the beginning of the 1st millennium CE, brought by missionaries traveling between India and the Chinese empire. The northern part of what is now Vietnam had been conquered by the Chinese empire in 111 BCE; it remained under Chinese rule until 939 CE. In the south there were two Indianized states, Funan (founded during the 1st century CE) and Champa (founded 192 CE). In these areas both Hīnayāna and Mahāyāna traditions were represented. The traditions that most affected the long-term development of Buddhism in Vietnam, however, were ZEN and PURE LAND traditions introduced from China into the northern and central sections of the country beginning in the 6th century CE.

The first *dhyāna* (Zen; Vietnamese: *thiên*), or "meditation," school was introduced by Vinītaruci, an Indian monk who had come to Vietnam from China in the 6th century. In the 9th century a school of "wall meditation" was introduced by the Chinese monk Vo Ngon Thong. A third major Zen school was established in the 11th century by the Chinese monk Thao Durong. From 1414 to 1428 Buddhism in Vietnam was persecuted by the Chinese, who had again conquered the country. Tantrism, TAOISM, and CONFUCIANISM were also filtering into Vietnam at this time. Even after the Chinese had been driven back, a Chinese-like bureaucracy closely supervised the Vietnamese monasteries. The clergy was divided between the highborn and Sinicized (Chinese-influenced), on the one hand, and those in the lower ranks, who often were active in peasant uprisings.

During the modern period these Mahāyāna traditions centered in northern and central Vietnam have coexisted with Theravāda traditions that have spilled over from Cambodia in the south. Rather loosely joined together, the Vietnamese Buddhists managed to preserve their traditions through the period of French colonial rule in the 19th and 20th centuries. During the struggle between North and South Vietnam in the 1960s and early '70s, many Buddhists worked to achieve peace and reconciliation, but they met with little success. Under the communist regime that completed its victory in Vietnam in the early 1970s, conditions have been difficult, but Buddhism has persisted. Reports in the late 1980s and early '90s indicated that new signs of vitality were beginning to appear.

Central Asia and China. *Central Asia.* By the beginning of the Common Era, Buddhism had probably been introduced into eastern Turkistan. According to tradition, a son of Aśoka founded the kingdom of Khotan around 240 BCE. The grandson of this king supposedly introduced Buddhism to Khotan, where it became the state religion. On more secure historical grounds, it is clear that the support given by the Indo-Scythian king Kaniṣka of the Kushān (Kuṣāṇa) dynasty, which ruled in northern India, Afghanistan, and parts of Central Asia in the 1st to 2nd century CE, encouraged the spread of Buddhism into Central Asia. Kaniṣka purportedly called an important Buddhist council; he patronized the Gandhāra school of Buddhist art, which introduced Greek and Persian elements into Buddhist iconography; and he supported Buddhist expansion within a vast region that extended far into the Central Asian heartland. In the northern part of Chinese Turkistan, Buddhism spread from Kucha (K'u-ch'e) to the kingdoms of Agnideśa (Karashahr), Kao-ch'ang (Turfan), and Bharuka (Aksu). According to Chinese travelers who visited Central Asia, the Hīnayānists (at least at the time of their visits) were strongest in Turfan, Shanshan, Kashgar, and Kucha, while Mahāyāna strongholds were located in Yarkand and Khotan.

In Central Asia there was a confusing welter of languages, religions, and cultures, and, as Buddhism interacted with these various traditions, it changed and developed. SHAMANISM, ZOROASTRIANISM, NESTORIAN CHRISTIANITY, and Islam all penetrated these lands and coexisted with Buddhism. For example, some of the Mahāyāna BODHISATTVAS, such as AMITĀBHA, may have been inspired in part by Zoroastrian influence. There is also evidence of some degree of syncretism between Buddhism and MANICHAEISM, an Iranian dualistic religion that was founded in the 3rd century CE.

Buddhism continued to flourish in parts of Central Asia until the 11th century, particularly under the patronage of the Uighur Turks. With the increasingly successful incursions of Islam (beginning in the 7th century CE) and the decline of the T'ang dynasty (618–907) in China, however, Central Asia ceased to be the important crossroads of Indian and Chinese culture that it once had been. Buddhism in the area gradually became a thing of the past.

China.   Although there are reports of Buddhists in China as early as the 3rd century BCE, Buddhism was not actively propagated in that country until the early centuries of the Common Era. Tradition has it that Buddhism was introduced after the Han emperor Ming Ti (reigned 57/58–75/76 CE) had a dream of a flying golden deity that was interpreted as a vision of the Buddha. Accordingly, the emperor dispatched emissaries to India, who subsequently returned to China with the *Sutra in Forty-two Sections,* which was deposited in a temple outside the capital of Lo-yang. In actuality, Buddhism entered China gradually, first primarily through Central Asia and, later, by way of the trade routes around and through Southeast Asia.

The Buddhism that first became popular in China during the Han dynasty was deeply colored with magical practices, making it compatible with popular Chinese Taoism. Instead of the doctrine of no-self, early Chinese Buddhists taught the indestructibility of the soul. Nirvana became a kind of immortality. They also taught the theory of karma, the values of charity and compassion, and the need to suppress the passions. Until the end of the Han dynasty, there was a virtual symbiosis between Taoism and Buddhism and a common propagation of the means for attaining immortality through various ascetic practices. It was widely believed that LAO-TZU, the founder of Taoism, had been reborn in India as the Buddha. Many Chinese emperors worshiped Lao-tzu and the Buddha on the same altar. The first translations of Buddhist *sūtra*s into Chinese—namely those dealing with such topics as breath control and mystical concentration—utilized a Taoist vocabulary to make the Buddhist faith intelligible to the Chinese.

After the Han period, in the north of China, Buddhist monks were often used by non-Chinese emperors for their political-military counsel as well as for their skill in magic. At the same time, in the south, Buddhism began to penetrate the philosophical and literary circles of the gentry. An important contribution to the growth of Buddhism in China during this period was the work of translation. The most important early translator was the learned monk KUMĀRAJĪVA, who, before he was brought to the Chinese court in 401 CE, had studied the Hindu VEDAS, the occult sciences, and astronomy, as well as the Hinayāna and Mahāyāna *sūtra*s.

During the 5th and 6th centuries CE Buddhist schools from India became established, and new, specifically Chinese schools began to form. Buddhism was becoming a powerful intellectual force in China, monastic establishments were proliferating, and Buddhism was becoming well-established among the peasantry. Thus, it is not surprising that, when the Sui dynasty (581–618) established its rule over a reunified China, Buddhism flourished as a state religion.

The golden age of Buddhism in China occurred during the T'ang dynasty. Though the T'ang emperors were usually Taoists themselves, they tended to favor Buddhism, which had become extremely popular. Under the T'ang the government extended its control over the monasteries and the ordination and legal status of monks. From this time forward, the Chinese monk styled himself simply *ch'en*, or "subject."

During this period several Chinese schools developed their own distinctive approaches. Some of them produced comprehensive systematizations of the vast body of Buddhist texts and teachings. There was a great expansion in the number of Buddhist monasteries and the amount of land they owned. It was also during this period that many scholars made PILGRIMAGES to India, heroic journeys that greatly enriched Buddhism in China, both by the texts that were acquired and by the intellectual and spiritual inspiration that was brought from India. Buddhism was never able to replace its Taoist and Confucian rivals, however, and in 845 the emperor Wu-tsung began a major persecution. According to records, 4,600 Buddhist temples and 40,000 shrines were destroyed, and 260,500 monks and nuns were forced to return to lay life.

Buddhism in China never recovered completely from the great persecution of 845. It did maintain much of its heritage, however, and continued to play a significant role in the religious life of China. On the one hand, Buddhism retained its identity as Buddhism and generated new forms through which it was expressed. These included texts such as the *yü lu*, or "recorded sayings," of famous teachers that were oriented primarily toward monks, as well as more literary creations such as the *Journey to the West* (written in the 16th century) and *The Dream of the Red Chamber* (18th century). On the other hand, Buddhism coalesced with the Confucian–Neo-Confucian and Taoist traditions to form a complex multireligious ethos within which all three traditions were more or less comfortably encompassed.

Among the various schools the two that retained the greatest vitality were the Ch'an school (better known in the West by its Japanese name, Zen) which was noted for its emphasis on meditation, and the Pure Land (Ching-t'u) tradition, which emphasized Buddhist devotion. The former school exerted the greatest influence among the cultured elite. It did so through various media, including the arts. Ch'an artists during the Sung dynasty (960–1279) used images of flowers, rivers, and trees, executed with sudden, deft strokes, to evoke an insight into the flux and EMPTINESS of all reality. The Pure Land tradition exerted a greater influence on the population as a whole and was sometimes associated with SECRET SOCIETIES and peasant uprisings. But the two seemingly disparate traditions were often very closely linked. In addition, they were mixed with other Buddhist elements such as the so-called "masses for the dead" that had originally been popularized by the practitioners of Esoteric (Vajrayāna) Buddhism.

During the early decades of the 20th century, China experienced a Buddhist reform movement aimed at revitalizing the Chinese Buddhist tradition and adapting Buddhist teachings and institutions to modern conditions. However, the disruptions caused by the Sino-

Representation of Vaiśravaṇa, the lokapāla *(one of the four guardians of the cardinal directions) of the north, 672–675 CE; in the Feng-Hsien Ssu (shrine) in the Lungmen caves, China*
Paolo Koch—Photo Researchers

Japanese War and the subsequent establishment of a communist government have not been helpful to the Buddhist cause. The Buddhist community was the victim of severe repression during the Cultural Revolution (1966–69).

Korea and Japan. *Korea.* Buddhism was first introduced into the Korean region when it was divided into the three kingdoms of Paekche, Koguryŏ, and Silla. After Buddhism was brought to the northern kingdom of Koguryŏ from China in the 4th century, it gradually spread throughout the other Korean kingdoms. As often happened, the new faith was first accepted by the court and then extended to the people. After the unification of the country by the kingdom of Silla in the 660s, Buddhism began to flourish throughout Korea. The monk WŎNHYO (617–686) was one of the most impressive scholars and reformers of his day. He was married and taught an "ecumenical" version of Buddhism that included all branches and sects. He tried to use music, literature, and dance to express the meaning of Buddhism. Another scholar of the Silla era was Ŭi-sang (625–702), who went to China and returned to spread the Hwaŏm (Chinese HUA-YEN) sect in Korea. The Chinese Ch'an sect (Zen) was introduced in the 8th century and, by absorbing the Korean versions of Hua-yen, T'IEN-T'AI (Tendai; a rationalist school), and Pure Land, gradually became the dominant school of Buddhism in Korea, as it did in Vietnam.

Early Korean Buddhism was characterized by a this-worldly attitude. It emphasized the pragmatic, nationalistic, and aristocratic aspects of the faith. Still, an indigenous tradition of shamanism influenced the development of popular Buddhism throughout the centuries. Buddhist monks danced, sang, and performed the rituals of shamans.

During the Koryŏ period (935–1392), Korean Buddhism reached its zenith. During the first part of this period the Korean Buddhist community was active in the publication of the *Tripitaka Koreana,* one of the most inclusive editions of the Buddhist sutras up to that time. After 25 years of research, a monk by the name of Ŭich'ŏn (1055–1101; *see* DAIGAK GUKSA) published an outstanding three-volume bibliography of Buddhist literature. Ŭich'ŏn also sponsored the growth of the T'ien-t'ai sect in Korea. He emphasized the need for cooperation between Ch'an and the other "Teaching" schools of Korean Buddhism.

Toward the end of the Koryŏ period, Buddhism began to suffer from internal corruption and external persecution, especially that promoted by the Neo-Confucians. The government began to put limits on the privileges of the monks, and Confucianism replaced Buddhism as the religion of the state. The Yi dynasty (1392–1910) continued these restrictions, and, since the end of World War II, Buddhism in Korea has been hampered by communist rule in North Korea and by the great vitality of Christianity in South Korea. Despite these challenges, Buddhists, particularly in South Korea, have both preserved the old traditions and initiated new movements.

Japan. The Buddhism that was initially introduced into Japan in the 6th century from Korea was regarded as a talisman (charm) for the protection of the country. The new religion was accepted by the powerful Soga clan but was rejected by others, thus causing controversies that resembled the divisions caused by the introduction of Buddhism in Tibet. In both countries, some believed that the introduction of Buddhist statues had been an insult to the native deities, resulting in plagues and natural disasters. Only gradually were such feelings overcome. Though the Buddhism of the Soga clan was largely magical, under the influence of Prince Shōtoku, who became regent of the nation in 593, other aspects of Buddhism were emphasized. Shōtoku lectured on various scriptures that emphasized the ideals of the layman and monarch, and he composed a "Seventeen-Article Constitution" in which Buddhism was adroitly mixed with Confucianism as the spiritual foundation of the state. In later times he was widely regarded as an incarnation of the bodhisattva AVALOKITEŚVARA.

During the Nara period (710–784), Buddhism became the state religion of Japan. Emperor Shōmu actively propagated the faith, making the imperial capital, Nara—with its "Great Buddha" statue (Daibutsu)—the national cult center. Buddhist schools imported from China became established in Nara, and state-subsidized provincial temples (*kokubunji*) made the system effective at the local level.

After the capital was moved to Heian-kyō (modern Kyōto) in 794, Buddhism continued to prosper. Chinese influence continued to play an important role, particularly through the introduction of new Chinese schools that became dominant at the royal court. MOUNT HIEI and MOUNT KŌYA became the centers for the new Tendai and Esoteric (SHINGON) schools of Buddhism, which were characterized by highly sophisticated philosophies and complex and refined liturgies. Moreover, Buddhism interacted with SHINTŌ and local traditions, and various distinctively Japanese patterns of Buddhist-oriented folk religion became very popular.

New schools of the Kamakura period. There was a turning point in the 12th and 13th centuries in Japanese history and in the history of Japanese Buddhism in particular. Late in the 12th century the imperial regime with its center at Heian collapsed, and a new feudal government, or shogunate, established its headquarters at Kamakura. As a part of the same process, a number of new Buddhist leaders emerged and established schools of Japanese Buddhism. These reformers included proponents of the Zen traditions such as EISAI and DŌGEN; Pure Land advocates such as HŌNEN, SHINRAN, and Ippen; and NICHIREN, the founder of a new school that gained considerable popularity. The distinctively Japanese traditions these creative reformers and founders established became—along with many very diverse synthetic expressions of Buddhist-Shintō piety—integral components of a Buddhist-oriented ethos that structured Japanese religious life into the 19th century. Also during this period many Buddhist groups allowed their clergy to marry, with the result that temples often fell under the control of particular families.

Zen Buddhist monk ringing the temple bell of the Eihei Temple monastery in Japan
Paolo Koch—Photo Researchers

Under the Tokugawa shogunate (1603–1867), Buddhism became an arm of the government. Temples were used for registering the populace; this was one way of preventing the spread of Christianity, which the feudal government regarded as a political menace. However, this association with the Tokugawa regime made Buddhism quite unpopular at the beginning of the Meiji period (1868–1912), at least among the elite. At that time, in order to set up Shintō as the new state religion, it was necessary for Japan's new ruling oligarchy to separate Shintō from Buddhism. This led to the confiscation of temple lands and the defrocking of many Buddhist priests.

During the period of ultranationalism (c. 1930–45), Buddhist thinkers called for uniting the East in one great "Buddhaland" under the tutelage of Japan. After the war, however, Buddhist groups, new and old alike, began to emphasize Buddhism as a religion of peace and brotherhood. During the postwar period the greatest visible activity among Buddhists has been among the new religions such as SŌKA-GAKKAI ("Value Creation Society") and RISSHŌ-KŌSEI-KAI ("Society for Establishing Righteousness and Friendly Relations").

Tibet, Mongolia, and the Himalayan Kingdoms. *Tibet.* Buddhism, according to the Tibetan tradition, was first given recognition in Tibet during the reign of Srong-brtsan-sgam-po (c. 627–c. 650). This king had two queens who were early patrons of the religion and were later regarded in popular tradition as incarnations of the Buddhist savioress TĀRĀ. The religion received active encouragement from Khri-srong-lde-btsan, during whose reign (c. 755–797) the first Buddhist monastery in Tibet was built at Bsam-yas (Samye), the first seven monks were ordained, and the celebrated Indian Tantric master PADMASAMBHAVA was invited to Tibet. Padmasambhava is credited with subduing the spirits and DEMONS associated with BON, the indigenous religion of Tibet, and with subjugating them to the service of Buddhism. At the time, influences from Chinese Buddhism were strong, but it is recorded that at the Council of Bsam-yas (792–794) it was decided that the Indian tradition should prevail.

Following a period of suppression that lasted almost two centuries (from the early 800s to the early 1000s), Buddhism in Tibet enjoyed a revival. During the 11th and 12th centuries many Tibetans traveled to India to acquire and translate Buddhist texts and to receive training in Buddhist doctrine and practice. With the assistance of the renowned Indian master ATĪŚA, who arrived in Tibet in 1042, Buddhism became established as the dominant religion. From this point forward Buddhism was the primary culture of the elite, was a powerful force in the affairs of state, and penetrated deeply into all aspects of Tibetan life.

One of the great achievements of the Buddhist community in Tibet was the translation into Tibetan of a vast corpus of Buddhist literature, including the *Bka'-'gyur* ("Translation of the Buddha Word") and *Bstan-'gyur* ("Translation of Teachings") collections.

A major development occurred in the late 14th or early 15th century when a great Buddhist reformer named TSONG-KHA-PA established the DGE-LUGS-PA school, known more popularly as the Yellow Hats. In 1578, representatives of this school succeeded in converting the Mongol Altan Khan, and, under the khan's sponsorship, their leader (the so-called third DALAI LAMA) gained considerable monastic power. In the middle of the 17th century the Mongol overlords established the fifth Dalai Lama as the theocratic ruler of Tibet.

The fifth Dalai Lama instituted the high office of Panchen Lama for the abbot of the Tashilhunpo monastery, located to the west of Lhasa. The Panchen lamas were regarded as successive incarnations of AMITĀBHA. The Manchus in the 18th

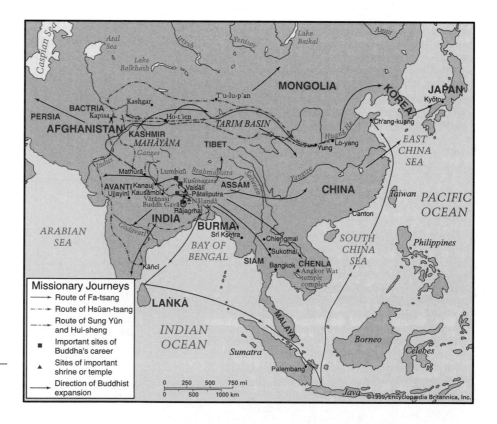

Important sites and routes of expansion of early Buddhism

century and subsequently the British, the Nationalist Chinese, and the Chinese communists have all tried to exploit the division of power between the Panchen and the Dalai lamas for their own ends. In 1950 Chinese forces occupied Tibet, and in 1959 the Dalai Lama fled to India after an unsuccessful revolt. The Chinese communists then took over his temporal powers. The Dalai Lama's followers are now based in Dharmsala, India, and in 1995 the Dalai Lama and the Chinese government each identified a different boy as the 11th Panchen Lama.

Mongolia.   The distinctive form of Buddhism that developed in Tibet has exerted a strong influence on neighboring areas and peoples. Most important was the conversion of the Mongol tribes to the north and east of Tibet. There are some indications that Buddhism was present among the Mongols as early as the 4th century, and during the 13th century close relationships developed between the Mongol court in China and some of the leaders of TIBETAN BUDDHISM. Kublai Khan himself became a supporter of the Tibetan form of Buddhism. Kublai Khan's Tibetan advisers helped to develop a block script for the Mongolian language, and many Buddhist texts were translated from Tibetan into Mongolian. In general, however, the religion failed to gain widespread popular support during this period.

In 1578 a new situation developed when the Altan Khan accepted the Dge-lugs-pa version of the Tibetan tradition and supported its spread among his followers at all levels of Mongol society. Over the centuries Mongolian scholars translated a large corpus of texts from Tibetan, and they produced their own sophisticated original texts. The Mongols based their Buddhist doctrine, practice, and communal organization on Tibetan models, but they developed and adapted them in a distinctive way.

Between 1280 and 1368 China was part of the Mongol empire, and the Mongols established their variant of Tibetan Buddhism in China. When they no longer held power in China, they continued to maintain the traditions they had developed in their homeland in the Central Asian steppes. During the 20th century, however, Mongolian Buddhism was undermined by the communist regimes that ruled in the Mongol areas of the former Soviet Union, Mongolia, and China.

Buddhism in the West.   During the long course of Buddhist history, Buddhist influences have from time to time reached the Western world, and there are occasional references to what seem to be Buddhist traditions in the writings of the Christian CHURCH FATHERS. Not until the modern period, however, is there evidence for a serious Buddhist presence in the Western world. Beginning in the mid-19th century, Buddhism was introduced into the United States and other Western countries by large numbers of immigrants, first from China and Japan but more recently from other countries, especially countries of Southeast Asia. Buddhism gained a foothold among a significant number of Western intellectuals and—particularly during the 1960s and early '70s—among young people seeking new forms of RELIGIOUS EXPERIENCE and expression. The interest of Westerners in Buddhism has been increased by the work of Buddhist missionaries such as the Japanese scholar D.T. SUZUKI (1870–1966) as well as by a number of Tibetan Buddhist teachers who came to the West after the Chinese conquest of their homeland in the late 1950s.

BUDDHISM IN THE CONTEMPORARY WORLD

Modern trends.   During the 19th and 20th centuries Buddhism has been forced to respond to new challenges and opportunities that cut across the regional religious and cultural patterns that characterized the Buddhist world in the premodern period. A number of Buddhist countries were subjected to Western rule, and even those that were not actually conquered felt the heavy pressure of Western religious, political, economic, and cultural influence. Modern rationalistic and scientific modes of thinking, modern notions of liberal democracy and socialism, and modern patterns of economic organization were introduced and became important elements in the thought and life of Buddhists and non-Buddhists in these countries. In this situation the Buddhists' response was twofold. They came to associate Buddhism with the religious and cultural identity that they sought to preserve and reassert in the face of Western domination. In addition, they sought to

(Top): Young Buddhist nuns in Namhsan, Myanmar; (bottom): Members of the Korean Buddhist temple at the annual Korean–American parade in New York City
(Top): Archive Newsphotos; (bottom): Katrina Thomas— Photo Researchers

initiate reforms that would make Buddhism a more appealing and effective force in the modern world.

The Buddhist concern to challenge Western domination manifested itself both in the specifically religious and in the religiopolitical sphere. In the former, Buddhists used a variety of measures to meet the challenge posed by the presence of Western Christian missionaries, often adopting modern Christian practices such as the establishment of Sunday schools, the distribution of tracts, and the like. They also attempted to strengthen the Buddhist cause through the initiation of Buddhist missions, including missions to the West, and through ecumenical cooperation among various Buddhist groups. Organizations such as the WORLD FELLOWSHIP OF BUDDHISTS (founded in 1950) and the World Buddhist Sangha Council (founded in 1966) were established to promote cooperation among Buddhists from all countries and denominations.

In the religiopolitical sphere, many Buddhist leaders—including many politically active monks—sought to associate Buddhism with various nationalist movements that were struggling to achieve political, economic, and cultural independence. Of course, the success of this strategy was tied to the success of the nationalist movements.

Three emphases have been especially important in the various reform movements. First, many Buddhist leaders have put forward a highly rationalized, Protestant-type interpretation of Buddhism that deemphasizes the supernormal and ritualized aspects of the tradition and focuses on the supposed continuity between Buddhism and modern science and on the centrality of ethics and morality. This interpretation, according to its proponents, represents a recovery of the true Buddhism of the Buddha.

A second, closely related emphasis that has been prominent among modern Buddhist reformers represents Buddhism as a form of religious teaching and practice that provides a basis for social, political, and economic life in the modern world. In some cases the focus has been on Buddhist ideas that supposedly provide a religious grounding for an international order supporting world peace. Other reformers have presented Buddhism as a basis for a modern democratic order or have advocated a Buddhist form of socialism.

Finally, Buddhist reformers have initiated and supported movements that give the Buddhist laity (and in some cases Buddhist women) a much stronger role than they have had in the past. In the Theravāda world, lay societies have been formed and lay-oriented meditation movements have enjoyed great success. In East Asia an anticlerical, lay-oriented trend that was evident even before the modern period has culminated in the formation and rapid expansion of new, thoroughly laicized Buddhist movements, particularly in Japan.

Challenges and opportunities. The status of contemporary Buddhist communities and the kinds of challenges those communities face differ radically from area to area. Five different kinds of situations can be identified.

First, there are a number of countries where previously well-established Buddhist communities have suffered severe setbacks that have curtailed their influence and seriously sapped their vitality. This kind of situation prevails primarily in countries ruled by communist governments where Buddhism has, for many decades, been subjected to intense pressures that have undercut its institutional power and weakened its influence on large segments of the population. This has happened in the Mongol areas of Central Asia, in China (outside of Tibet), in North Korea, and, to a lesser extent, in Vietnam.

Second, there are places where well-established Buddhist communities have suffered similar setbacks but have retained the loyalty of large segments of the population. Perhaps the most vivid example is Tibet, where the Chinese communists have implemented anti-Buddhist policies that, despite their brutality, have failed to break the bond between Buddhism and the Tibetan sense of identity. In Cambodia and Laos, similarly, communist rule (including even the reign of terror imposed by the Pol Pot regime that controlled Kampuchea from 1975 to 1979) does not seem to have broken the people's loyalty to Buddhism.

Third, there are situations in which the Buddhist community has retained a more or less accepted position as the leading religious force and has continued to exert a strong influence on political, economic, and social life. This is the case in Sri Lanka and Myanmar, where Buddhism is the dominant religion among the Sinhalese and Burman majorities, and in Thailand, where more than 90 percent of the population is counted as Buddhist. In Sri Lanka and Myanmar, ethnic conflict and (especially in Myanmar) authoritarian rule and economic stagnation have resulted in political instability that has had a disruptive effect on the local Buddhist communities. In Thailand, however, Buddhism has a firm position within a relatively stable and rapidly modernizing society.

The fourth type of situation is one in which well-developed Buddhist traditions are operating with a considerable degree of freedom and effectiveness in societies where Buddhism plays a more circumscribed role. This situation prevails in several of the Pacific Rim countries, including South Korea, Taiwan, and Singapore, and to a lesser extent in Southeast Asian countries such as Malaysia and Indonesia, where Buddhism is practiced by significant numbers of overseas Chinese. The primary example, however, is Japan, where Buddhism has continued to play an important role. In the highly modernized society that has developed in Japan, many deeply rooted Buddhist traditions, such as Shingon, Tendai, the Pure Land schools, Zen and the Nichiren school have persisted and have been adapted to changing conditions. At the same time, new Buddhist sects such as Rissho-Kosei-Kai and Soka-gakkai have gained millions of converts not only in Japan but also throughout the world.

Finally, new Buddhist communities have developed in areas where Buddhism disappeared long ago or never existed at all. Thus in India, where Buddhism had been virtually extinct since at least the 15th century, new Buddhist societies have been formed by Indian intellectuals, new Buddhist settlements have been established by Tibetan refugees, and a significant Buddhist community has been founded by converts from the so-called scheduled castes. In the West (particularly but not exclusively in the United States), important Buddhist communities have been established by immigrants from East and Southeast Asia. Buddhist influences have penetrated into many aspects of Western culture, and communities of Buddhist converts are active.

For more than two millennia Buddhism has been a powerful religious, political, and social force, first in India, its original homeland, and then in many other lands. It remains a powerful religious, political, and cultural force in many parts of the world today.

BUDDHISM, ART OF

BUDDHISM, ART OF, pictorial and representational works which developed out of a Buddhist context. Much of Buddhist art has been concerned with stories from the Buddha's life or other elements of Buddhist mythology. The introduction of BUDDHISM to East Asian cultures in the mid-6th century had a profound effect on local artistic traditions. Especially within Japanese and Korean sculpture, Buddhist subjects were almost always dominant.

The subject of Buddhist art is a vast and complex topic, and this article will merely attempt to sketch out a few of its dimensions. Treatments of related topic may be found in other articles, including BUDDHISM; STUPA; SACRED ARCHITECTURE; MANDALA; and EMERALD BUDDHA.

Early Buddhist artwork in India often drew on the mythology that surrounded the BUDDHA GOTAMA, illustrating key events in his "historical" life as well as scenes from the JĀTAKAS, the stories that told of his previous incarnations. In the earliest period of Buddhist-inspired carved stonework (2nd–1st centuries BCE), the Buddha was portrayed by a collection of symbols: a tree indicating his enlightenment (which is said to have occurred beneath the pipal, or BODHI TREE); a wheel portraying his first preaching (the wheel being both the symbol of the universal monarch [CHAKRAVARTIN] and of the Buddha as universal guide and teacher); and a miniature STUPA portraying his release, or NIRVANA (the stupa being the focus of the cult surrounding the Buddha's material remains).

From the 1st century BCE onward the Buddha Gotoma began to be figured in northwestern Indian sculpture; common types of Buddha images are those that represent his calling the earth to witness against MĀRA by touching it with the fingertips of the right hand, the meditating Buddha protected by a cobra's hood, and the Buddha lying on his right side as he enters final nirvana. These stereotyped presentations of him soon became the model for future use throughout Asia. The traditions of imagery relating to the Buddha Gotama thrive to this day chiefly in Sri Lanka and the Southeast Asian countries where THERAVĀDA Buddhism prevails.

From northwestern India, Buddhist architecture, ICONOGRAPHY, and painting passed into China and from there into the rest of East Asia. The spread of Buddhism into Asia served to introduce the complex mythology of MAHĀYĀNA Buddhism, with its various buddhas, BODHISATTVAS, and quasi-buddhas, to the local artistic traditions. Certain figures were more popular in representational art than others; especially popular in China, and hence in Japan and Korea,

Head of a bodhisattva, in terra-cotta; Central Asian, 6th–7th century
The Granger Collection

were AMITĀBHA, VAIROCANA, MAITREYA, MAÑJUŚRĪ, KṢITIGARBHA, and AVALOKITEŚVARA (as the goddess KUAN-YIN). Among Chinese works, of particular importance are the paintings of buddhas and bodhisattvas in the caves of TUN-HUANG (4th–10th century CE), particularly the so-called Cave of the Thousand Buddhas (Ch'ien-fo-tung, or Mokao-k'u). These temples have been well preserved in the Gobi desert, and the quality and quantity of their fresco paintings and texts has remained unmatched.

In Japan, Buddhist artwork had a tendency to ground spiritual experiences in the easily approachable guise of everyday life. Thus when ZEN Buddhists used monochrome painting as a form of participatory spiritual exercise, they often depicted subjects not obviously religious in theme. Bird-and-flower paintings were created and queried for insights into spiritual meaning, and landscape painting offered access to a symbolic meaning which referred to internal, spiritual journeys.

Esoteric (Tantric, or VAJRAYĀNA) Buddhism relies heavily on visualization in its ritual procedures. Thus the creation of an environment of worship was essential. The use of MANDALAS, expressed both in two dimensions as paintings and in three dimensions as ensembles of sculpture, invited the believer into a diagrammatic rendering of a spiritual cosmos. The deities or spiritual entities portrayed in these paired paintings represent both the realm of the transcendent, clear enlightenment and the humane, compassionate as-

Siddhārtha goes to school; Pakistan, 2nd–4th century CE
Victoria & Albert Museum, London—Art Resource

pects of the Buddha. It was the repetitive meditative practice of journey through and visceral assimilation of this symbolic, schematic cosmos that could lead the believer to an enlightenment of unity.

The main repository of Indian Mahāyāna and Vajrayāna iconographic traditions is Tibet, where Buddhism was introduced from the 8th to the 13th centuries. The introduction of Buddhism led to the arrival in Tibet of Buddhist craftsmen from Central Asia and later from Nepal and northwest India, all of which were then Buddhist lands. After the 10th century Tibet's cultural focus turned to internal forces, but until the communist takeover of 1959 the Tibetans preserved Indian (Pāla) styles of iconography, along with ancient techniques and styles of Indian Buddhist painting that were modified and enriched in some schools by much later influence from China. Tibetan metalworkers have excelled in producing fine things for ritual use: ritual lamps, vases, bowls, bells, PRAYER WHEELS, and decorated temple trumpets and horns. Among sculptural works, images of vast size, rising up through two or three stories, are quite often seen in Tibetan temples, and their construction and dedication is considered a work of vast religious merit.

BUDDHIST COUNCILS, *Pali* sangīti, in most Buddhist traditions, two early councils on Buddhist doctrine and practice. The first, which most modern scholars do not accept as historical, was supposedly held at Rājagṛha (modern Rājgīr, Bihār state, India) during the first rainy season after the BUDDHA GOTAMA'S death. According to the received accounts, the council involved the compilation of the remembered words of the Buddha, including the SUTRAS that he had preached and the monastic rules and procedures that he had prescribed. The second council, which most modern scholars do accept as historical, was held at Vaiśālī (Bihār state) a little more than a century later. It seems that the matters in dispute concerned the monastic rules and that the result was a split in the early SANGHA.

The THERAVĀDA tradition contains an account of a third council sponsored by King AŚOKA that was held in Pāṭaliputra (modern Patna) about 247 CE. The Theravādins contend that this council settled disputed matters in their favor, and that the *Kathāvatthu*, the fifth book of their ABHIDHAMMA PITAKA, contains an account of the examination and refutation of the views that were rejected. Different groups of Theravādins have recognized other councils (*sangīti*) that continued the process of extending and purifying the tradition. The Sinhalese have recognized as many as three such occasions including one at which the TRIPITAKA (the "three baskets" of the HĪNAYĀNA "canon") was supposedly committed to writing for the first time. The Burmese have officially recognized three such occasions, including the so-called fifth council called in Burma by King Mindon in 1871, and the so-called sixth council held in Yangôn in the 1950s. The Thai have recognized a total of nine *sangīti*, including a council held in Chiang Mai (Chiengmai) in the late 15th century and one held in Bangkok in the late 18th century.

Important Buddhist councils remembered by other Buddhist traditions include one sponsored by King KANIṢKA (*c.* 100 CE) in northwestern India that was attended by Hīnayāna monks of the SARVĀSTIVĀDIN school, and one, the Council of Lhasa, that was held in Tibet in the late 8th century. The Council of Lhasa featured a debate between a Chinese and an Indian monk that resulted—according to the Tibetan account—in a clear victory for the latter.

BUKHĀRĪ, AL- \ˌal-bu̇-ˈka̱-rē\, *in full* Abū ʿAbd Allāh Muhammad ibn Ismāʿīl al-Bukhārī (b. July 19, 810, Bukhara, Central Asia [now in Uzbekistan]—d. Aug. 31, 870, Khartank, near Samarkand), one of the greatest Muslim compilers and scholars of HADITH. His chief work is accepted by SUNNĪ Muslims—*i.e.*, those following the majority tradition—as second only to the QURʾAN as both a source of religious law and a sacred work.

Al-Bukhārī began learning the utterances and actions of the Prophet MUHAMMAD by heart while still a child. His travels in search of more information about them began with a PILGRIMAGE TO MECCA when he was 16. He then went to Egypt, and for 16 years he sought out informants from Cairo to Merv in Central Asia. Al-Bukhārī was an extremely scrupulous compiler, showing great critical discrimination and editorial skill in his selection of authentic traditions. From the approximately 600,000 traditions he gathered, he selected only about 7,275 that he deemed completely reliable and thus meriting inclusion in his *Kitāb al-Jāmiʿ al-ṣaḥīḥ*.

As a preliminary to his *Ṣaḥīḥ*, al-Bukhārī wrote *Kitāb al-Tārīkh al-kabīr* ("The Great History"), which contains biographies of the persons forming the chain of oral transmission and recollection of traditions back to the Prophet. Toward the end of his life, he was involved in a theological dispute in Nīshāpūr and left that city for Bukhara, but, following his refusal to give special classes for Bukhara's governor and his children, he was forced into exile.

BULGAKOV, SERGEY NIKOLAYEVICH \bül-ˈgȧ-kəf\ (b. June 16, 1871, Livny, Russia—d. July 12, 1944, Paris, France), economist and Russian EASTERN ORTHODOX theologian who most fully developed the philosophical system called sophiology, which centered on problems of the creation of the world and stressed the unity of all things.

Bulgakov began his clerical training at the seminary of Oryol, Russia, but he was influenced by Marxism to break with the church and become a student of political economics. After studying in Moscow, Berlin, Paris, and London, he taught at the universities of Kiev (1901–06) and Moscow (1906–18). During this period he wrote *Capitalism and Agriculture* (1901) and *Philosophy and Economics* (1912).

Bulgakov became disillusioned with Marxism, however, and returned to the church with a group of several former Marxists that included the philosopher Nikolay Berdyayev. Bulgakov's conversion is described in his own book *The Undying Light* (1917). Ordained a priest in 1918, he was prevented by the Bolshevik government from resuming his teaching and in 1923 was expelled from the Soviet Union. After two years in Prague he was made professor of theology and dean of the Russian Orthodox Theological Institute of Paris, where he taught until his death.

Bulgakov spent the last 20 years of his life developing sophiology, a philosophical-theological system built around the concept of *sophia* (Greek: "wisdom"). This concept, frequently found in the works of medieval mystics, is used by Bulgakov to signify the link connecting God and the created world. His doctrines of divine wisdom, however, were strongly opposed by several Orthodox theologians. Bulgakov's own bishop, Metropolitan Eulogius of Paris, and his colleagues at the institute supported him and protected his freedom to teach and to write.

BULL, in ROMAN CATHOLICISM, an official papal letter or document. The name is derived from the lead seal (Latin: *bulla*) traditionally affixed to such documents. Since the 12th century it has designated a letter from the pope carrying a *bulla* that shows the heads of the apostles PETER and PAUL. With the introduction of papal briefs in the 15th century for less significant communications, bulls were reserved for more important matters—*e.g.*, the CANONIZATION of saints and dogmatic pronouncements.

BULL CULT, prehistoric religious practice originating in the eastern Aegean and extending from the Indus Valley of Pakistan to the Danube in eastern Europe. The bull god's symbol was the phallus, and in the east the bull often was depicted as the partner of the great goddess of fertility. Numerous representations of the bull have been uncovered, many designed to be worn as a charm or AMULET. The cult continued into historic times and was particularly important in the INDUS VALLEY and on Crete—in both places the bull's "horns of consecration" were an important religious symbol.

BULL-ROARER, commonly a flat piece of wood, a few inches to a foot in length, fastened at one end to a string. When swung around in the air, it produces a whirring or howling sound likened to those of animals or spirits.

Among many ancient or indigenous peoples it had great mythic and religious significance. It has been observed in Australia, North and South America, and other areas where indigenous societies survive. It may symbolize totemic ancestors (*see* TOTEMISM), or it may be believed to cause or drive away sickness, warn women and children to stay away from men's sacred ceremonies, control the weather, and promote fertility of game animals and crops.

BULTMANN, RUDOLF (KARL) \'bùlt-,män\ (b. Aug. 20, 1884, Wiefelstede, Ger.—d. July 30, 1976, Marburg, W.Ger.), leading 20th-century NEW TESTAMENT scholar known for his program to "demythologize" the New Testament; *i.e.,* to interpret, according to the concepts of Existentialist philosophy, the essential message of the New Testament that was expressed in mythical terms.

At 19 Bultmann began his theological studies at the University of Tübingen. In 1921 he was appointed professor of New Testament at Marburg, where he remained until his retirement in 1951.

In 1921 Bultmann published his *Geschichte der synoptischen Tradition* (*History of the Synoptic Tradition*), an analysis of the traditional material used by the Evangelists MATTHEW, MARK, and LUKE and an attempt to trace its history in the tradition of the church prior to their use of it. This

established Bultmann's reputation as a scholar. At Marburg he was influenced by the Existentialist philosopher Martin Heidegger, who, Bultmann felt, was developing an analysis of human existence that was strikingly parallel to the understanding of human existence implied by the theologies of PAUL and JOHN, as Bultmann interpreted them.

It was during discussion with Heidegger that Bultmann developed his own theological position; namely, that Christian faith is, and should be, comparatively uninterested in the historical JESUS CHRIST and centered instead on the transcendent Christ. Christian faith, he asserted, is faith in the *kērygma* ("proclamation," *see* KERYGMA AND CATECHESIS) of the church, into which Jesus may be said to be risen (Bultmann's understanding of the RESURRECTION), and not faith in the historical Jesus. This position remained constant for Bultmann, and all his subsequent work, including his demythologizing proposal made in 1941, developed out of it.

During the Hitler years in Germany, Bultmann refused to modify his teaching in any way to suit Nazi ideology, and he supported the CONFESSING CHURCH. But, in his own words, he "never directly and actively participated in political affairs"; *i.e.,* he did not directly oppose the Nazi regime. With the resumption of contacts between the German universities and the rest of the world after World War II, Bultmann became a major international academic figure. He gave an extremely influential series of lectures in Britain in 1955 (*History and Eschatology: The Presence of Eternity*) and in the United States in 1958 (*Jesus Christ and Mythology*), and his demythologizing program became the subject of a multivolume series with the title *Kerygma und Mythos* (*Kerygma and Myth*).

BUNDAHISHN \,bùn-də-'hē-shən\ (Pahlavi: "Original Creation"), ZOROASTRIAN scripture giving an account of the creation, history, and duration of the world, the origin of man, and the nature of the universe. Written in Pahlavi, it dates from the 9th century CE but is based on ancient material from a lost part of the original AVESTA and preserves some pre-Zoroastrian elements.

BUNDLES, *also called* medicine bundles, in NATIVE AMERICAN RELIGIONS, in the tribes of the Great Plains, collections of magical objects of ritual importance. The bundles were often felt to offer protection against disease and general misfortune. Some bundles were personal, the contents of which had been suggested to the individual by a supernatural sponsor, while others were tribal property originating in the mythological past. They were handled reverently and opened according to definite rules. The opening of the Cheyenne sacred arrow bundle, for instance, was the focus of an elaborate tribal rite extending over four days. Among the Crow, the owner of a bundle was permitted to sell part of his power to other men who had not received visions and to create replica bundles for them.

BURĀQ \bù-'räk\, in Islamic tradition, a creature said to have transported the Prophet MUHAMMAD to heaven. Described as "a white animal, half-mule, half-donkey, with wings on its sides," the Burāq was originally introduced into the story of Muhammad's night journey (ISRĀ') from MECCA to Jerusalem and back, thus explaining how the journey could have been completed in a single night. In some traditions he became a steed with the head of a woman and the tail of a peacock. As the tale of the night journey became connected with that of Muhammad's ascension to heaven (MIʿRĀJ), the Burāq replaced the ladder as Muham-

Carved wood bull-roarer from New Guinea
By courtesy of the Metropolitan Museum of Art, New York City, gift of Mrs. John Crosby, 1909

Muhammad mounted upon the Burāq
By courtesy of Edinburgh University Library

mad's means of access into heaven. The Burāq was depicted in illuminated *mi'rāj* manuscripts; it still occurs in Afghan truck decorations, where it is intended, in part, to bring the truck under God's protection, and in Egyptian HAJJ murals where, although it is depicted alongside modern modes of transport that carry pilgrims to Mecca and MEDINA, it still contains the idea of a divine blessing.

Burāq is also the name Muslims give to the Western Wall on the Temple Mount in Jerusalem, where they say the creature was tethered during Muhammad's ascension.

BURIAL, funerary ritual in which human remains are deposited in the earth, a grave, or a tomb; consigned to the water; or exposed to the elements or carrion animals. Geography, religion, and the social system all influence burial practices. Climate and topography influence whether the body is buried under the ground, placed in water, burned, or exposed to the air. Religious and social attitudes help determine how elaborate the burial should be.

Inhumation. Burial in the ground by hollowing out a trench in the earth for the body or covering it with rocks or dirt dates back at least to Middle Paleolithic times. Grave burial, or inhumation, may be simple or elaborate. The old Norse people built BARROWS that sometimes reached enormous heights; in North America, large BURIAL MOUNDS were characteristic of eastern Native American cultures from 1000 BCE to 700 CE.

Graves may be mere shallow pits, or they may be intricate and beautifully fashioned subterranean palaces spacious enough to accommodate vast numbers of persons. The Paraca burial chambers in Peru, hewn out of solid rock 18 feet below the surface, were large enough to accommodate 400 corpses with all of the belongings that it was thought they would need in the afterworld. Customarily, however, graves have been for the burial of individuals.

Caves have also been used for the dead. The ancient Hebrews used natural single-chamber caves and hewed oblong recesses lengthwise into the walls to accommodate the dead, a custom that led to the building of mausoleums. There are thousands of rock temples in western India and in Sri Lanka, some of which received elaborate architectural and sculptural treatment. Both caves and earth graves en-

couraged the development of COFFINS and rich grave-clothes and burial goods.

Customarily the body is placed in an extended position, as if in sleep. Bodies of Muslims are laid on their right side and facing Mecca; those of Buddhists are laid with the head to the north. Native Americans often buried their dead in a fetal position, sometimes in a basket or clay urn, with knees under the chin and the body neatly tied into a death bundle. Upright burial has been favored by other people, particularly for warriors.

Water burial. The bodies of chiefs and heroes have often been set adrift on rivers and oceans in death ships. Among the Norse, even those who were interred were sometimes given such a bier—a custom that was widespread from Iceland to England during the 7th and 8th centuries CE. At Sutton Hoo in Suffolk, England, archaeologists found the remains of a wooden boat, 85 feet long, that had been dragged from the river and lowered into the ground.

Water burials have been common in other cultures. In the South Pacific it was customary to place the dead in a canoe and launch that on the water. In the Solomon Islands, bodies are simply laid on a reef to be eaten by sharks; in other places they are wrapped and weighted with stones. Scattering ashes on water is widely practiced, especially in Asia. In India, within a year after death, the remains are taken to the GAṄGĀ RIVER and thrown into the sacred water; if it is not possible to do that, they are thrown into another river or stream with the hope that they will eventually make their way to the Gaṅgā.

Exposure. Placing the body where it may be eaten by scavenging birds and animals or weathered to its essential elements has been held by many groups to be the most desirable form of disposal for spiritual as well as material reasons. ZOROASTRIANISM has been perhaps the most widely known for this type of burial, which developed out of the belief that the corpse is so unclean that to inter or to cremate it would contaminate the "pure elements" of earth, fire, and water. Since the 6th century BCE it has been their custom to leave bodies on mountains or hills at a distance from the community. In Bombay the PARSIS maintain "towers of silence," high circular structures. The dead are carried to them, and funeral servants place them on stone beds surrounding a central pit. After vultures have stripped the flesh from the bones—usually within a few hours—the bones are gathered and dropped into the central pit.

A number of people who expose the dead use trees and platforms (tree burial). Among them are the Balinese, the Nāga tribes of India, the tribes of central Australia, and various Native American groups. Commonly, the Sioux robed the dead in their best clothing, sewed them into a deerskin or buffalo shroud, and carried them to a platform about eight feet high. Possessions and gifts were placed on the scaffold, and the body was allowed to remain there for a year, when it was taken down and given an earth burial.

Second burial. Among many people, particularly in indigenous cultures, a period of waiting occurs between the first and a second burial that often coincides with the duration of decomposition. The origin of this practice is considered to be the different concept of death held by these peoples. In most modern societies, death is regarded as instantaneous; it is not so in other societies, where it is held to involve a slow change, a passage from the visible society of the living to the invisible one of the dead. These beliefs may lead to two burials—the interval between the two marking the time it takes for the spirit to pass over into the next world. A second burial of the remains then occurs (or, the remains may be disposed of in a communal area). In areas in which death is believed to be a slow change, customs other than two burials may take place—*e.g.*, during the period of decomposition the corpse is sometimes treated as if it were alive, provided with food and drink, and surrounded by company.

BURIAL MOUND, artificial hill of earth and stones built over the remains of the dead.

Burial mounds known as BARROWS were a type of burial place constructed in England from Neolithic (*c.* 4000 BCE) until late pre-Christian (*c.* 600 CE) times. Barrows of the Neolithic Period were long and contained the various members of a family or clan, while those of the Early Bronze Age (*c.* 1900 BCE) were round and were used to bury a single important individual. The bodies were placed in stone or wooden vaults, over which large mounds of soil were heaped. Both types of barrows continued to be used in England until the advent of Christianity.

Burial mounds were a peculiarly prominent feature of the protohistoric period in Japan (3rd–6th century CE), which is known as the tumulus period. The mounds, some of which are spectacularly large and impressive, consist of earthen

keyhole-shaped mounds surrounded by moats. They were used to bury royalty and prominent members of the aristocracy. One of the largest, the burial site of the 4th-century emperor Nintoku, on the outskirts of the city of Sakai, near Osaka, measures 1,594 feet in length and is 115 feet high.

Burial mounds were characteristic of the Indian cultures of east-central North America from about 1000 BCE to 700 CE. The most numerous ones, found in the Ohio and Mississippi river valleys, were large conical or elliptical mounds surrounded by extensive earthworks, and are assigned to the Hopewell and Adena cultures. Along the upper Mississippi River and the Great Lakes, some of the later Indian mounds are in the shape of animals and other forms.

BUSHIDŌ \\'bü-shē-ˌdō\\ (Japanese: "Way of the Warrior"), the code of conduct of the samurai class of Japan. In the mid-19th century Bushidō became the basis for the ethical training given to all of Japanese society, with the emperor replacing the feudal lord, or *daimyo*, as the object of loyalty and sacrifice.

Though the name Bushidō was not used until the 16th century, the idea of the code developed during the Kamakura period (1192–1333). Its precise content varied historically under the influence of ZEN Buddhist and Confucian thought, but its one unchanging ideal was martial spirit, including athletic and military skills as well as fearlessness toward the enemy in battle. Frugal living, kindness, honesty, and FILIAL PIETY were also highly regarded. But the supreme obligation of the samurai was to his lord, even if this might cause suffering to his parents.

Stone tumulus, or burial mound, from Pitten, Austria, 1500–1200 BCE
Erich Lessing—Art Resource

During the Tokugawa period (1603–1867) Bushidō thought was infused with Confucian ethics and made into a comprehensive system that stressed obligation or duty. The samurai was equated with the Confucian "perfect gentleman" and was taught that his essential function was to exemplify virtue to the lower classes. Obedience to authority was stressed, but duty came first even if it entailed violation of statute law. (*See* CONFUCIANISM.)

BUSHNELL, HORACE \\'bùsh-nəl\ (b. April 14, 1802, Bantam, Conn., U.S.—d. Feb. 17, 1876, Hartford, Conn.), Congregational minister and controversial theologian, sometimes called "the father of American religious liberalism."

Bushnell joined the Congregational Church (*see* CONGREGATIONALISM) in 1821, and in 1823 entered Yale to become a minister. Not until 1831, after qualifying for the bar, did his religious doubts diminish sufficiently for him to begin his theological education. He entered Yale Divinity School and in 1833 was ordained minister of the North Congregational Church in Hartford, where he served for more than 20 years until ill health forced his resignation.

A major figure in U.S. intellectual history, Bushnell stood between the orthodox tradition of Puritan New England and the new romantic impulses represented by Ralph Waldo Emerson, Samuel Taylor Coleridge, and especially FRIEDRICH SCHLEIERMACHER. His first significant publication, *Christian Nurture* (1847), was a thorough critique of the prevailing emphasis placed on the conversion experience by revivalists. In *God in Christ* (1849), published in the year of his mystical experience that illumined the Gospel for him, Bushnell challenged the traditional, substitutionary view of the ATONEMENT (*i.e.*, that the death of Christ was the substitute for man's punishment for SIN) and considered problems of language, emphasizing the social, symbolic, and evocative nature of language as related to religious faith and the mysteries of God. *Christ in Theology* (1851) defended his attitude toward theological language, giving special attention to metaphoric language and to an instrumental view of the TRINITY. In *Nature and the Supernatural* (1858) he viewed the twin elements of the title as constituting the one "system of God" and sought to defend from skeptical attack the Christian position on sin, miracles, INCARNATION, revelation, and Christ's divinity.

Bushnell's views were bitterly attacked, and in 1852 North Church withdrew from the local "consociation" in order to preclude an ecclesiastical HERESY trial. Despite such opposition, however, his ability to assemble and present coherent arguments guaranteed the impact and influence of his interpretation of CHRISTIANITY.

BUSIRIS \byù-'sī-rəs\, in Greek mythology, Egyptian king, son of POSEIDON and Lyssianassa (daughter of Epaphus, a legendary king of Egypt). After Egypt had been afflicted for nine years with famine, Phrasius, a seer of Cyprus, arrived in Egypt and announced that the famine would not end until an annual sacrifice of a foreigner to ZEUS was instituted. Later HERACLES, who had arrived in Egypt from Libya, was seized and brought to the altar, but he burst his bonds and slew Busiris and his son Amphidamas.

Some Greek writers made Busiris an Egyptian king and successor of Menes (traditionally the first king of a united Egypt), though others rejected him altogether. The name Busiris is most likely an earlier and less accurate hellenization of the name of the Egyptian god known later to the Greeks as OSIRIS; it derives from an Egyptian compound word meaning literally "temple of Osiris."

BU-STON \ˌpü-'dœⁿ, *Angl* ˌbü-'tōn\ (b. 1290—d. 1364), Tibetan Buddhist scholar who was a member of the Saskya-pa sect and for many years served as the head of the Zwa-lu monastery. Bu-ston formulated a notion of the "Three Turnings of the Buddhist Law" (HĪNAYĀNA, MĀHAYĀNA, and VAJRAYĀNA) which he employed in the organization of his important *History of Buddhism* and in his highly influential classification of texts considered to be "canonical" in the Tibetan tradition. He also generated what became the standard classification of Tantric texts into four groups: the Korya (Sanskrit: Kriyā) TANTRAS, the Carya (Sanskrit: Caryā) Tantras, the YOGA Tantras, and the Asvattavayoga (Sanskrit: Anuttarayoga) Tantras.

Bu-ston was active as a translater and interpreter for many Vajrayāna texts and was recognized as master of Vajrayāna/Tantric ritual practice. In addition, he was a student of Buddhist architecture who both wrote about Buddhist STUPAS and oversaw the construction of an important stupa in the Zwa-lu area.

BUTO \'byü-ˌtō, 'bü-\, *also called* Uto, Edjo, Wadjet, *or* Wadjit, the cobra goddess of ancient Egypt. Depicted as a cobra twined around a papyrus stem, Buto was the tutelary goddess of Lower Egypt. Buto and NEKHBET, the vulture-goddess of Upper Egypt, were the protective goddesses of the king and were sometimes represented together on the king's diadem as the symbol of his sovereignty over all of Egypt. The form of the rearing cobra of Buto on a crown is termed the uraeus. In mythology, Buto was nurse to the infant god HORUS and helped ISIS, his mother, protect him from his uncle, SETH, when she took refuge in the Delta swamps. The similarity of this myth to the Greek myth of LETO and APOLLO most probably led to a later identification of Buto with Leto.

Buto is also the Greek form of the ancient Egyptian Per Wadjit (Coptic Pouto: "House of Wadjit"), the name of the capital of the 6th Lower Egyptian nome (province), modern Tall al-Farā'īn. Buto was the goddess who was the local deity of this area.

BYZANTINE RITE, the system of liturgical practices and discipline observed by the Eastern Orthodox church and by the majority of Eastern-rite churches which are in communion with Rome. *See* EASTERN ORTHODOXY.

The Byzantine rite originated in the Greek city of Antioch (in modern Turkey); but it was developed and perfected in Byzantium, or Constantinople (modern Istanbul). The rite was associated primarily with the Great Church of Constantinople and used the Greek language. As Constantinople extended its influence, however, the rite was translated into the vernacular of the peoples who adopted it.

Several AUTOCEPHALOUS Eastern Orthodox churches follow canonical rites derived from the original Byzantine rite. The number of these churches has varied in history but has included the Church of Constantinople, the Church of Alexandria (Egypt), and the Church of Antioch (with headquarters in Damascus, Syria).

In the early Christian church, liturgies developed gradually and were essentially formed by the 6th century. Of the three liturgies in use by Byzantine-rite churches, the Liturgy of ST. JOHN CHRYSOSTOM is celebrated most frequently and is the normal church service. The Liturgy of ST. BASIL THE GREAT is longer and is used on 10 special occasions each year. The Liturgy of the Presanctified (of ST. GREGORY I the Great) is celebrated on Wednesdays and Fridays during LENT and from Monday to Wednesday of HOLY WEEK.

CABEIRI \kə-'bī-rē, -ˌrī\, *also spelled* Cabiri, important group of deities, probably of Phrygian origin, worshiped over much of Asia Minor, on the islands nearby, and in Macedonia and northern and central Greece. They were promoters of fertility and protectors of seafarers. Perhaps originally indefinite in number, in classical times there appear to have been two male deities, Axiocersus and his son and attendant Cadmilus, or Casmilus, and a less important female pair, Axierus and Axiocersa. The cult included fertility rites, rites of purification, and initiation. The two male Cabeiri were often confused with the DIOSCURI.

The Cabeiri are often identified with the Great Gods of Samothrace. In the period after the death of Alexander the Great (323 BCE), their cult reached its height.

CABRINI, SAINT FRANCES XAVIER \kə-'brē-nē\, *byname* Mother Cabrini (b. July 15, 1850, Sant' Angelo Lodigiano, Lombardy, Italy—d. Dec. 22, 1917, Chicago; canonized 1946; feast day December 22), founder of the Missionary Sisters of the Sacred Heart and first United States citizen canonized.

From childhood, she desired to become a missionary. In 1877 she took her vows, and soon after that she became known as Mother Cabrini. She founded (1880) the Missionary Sisters of the Sacred Heart. She planned to found a convent in China, but Pope LEO XIII directed her to "go west, not east," and she sailed with a small group of sisters for the United States in 1889. Their work in the United States was to be concentrated among the neglected Italian immigrants. She became a naturalized citizen of the United States in 1909. Although frequently in ill health, Mother Cabrini established 67 houses in such cities as Buenos Aires, Argentina (1896), Paris (1898), and Madrid (1899).

CACUS AND CACA \'kā-kəs . . . 'kā-kə\, in ROMAN RELIGION, brother and sister, respectively, originally fire deities of the early Roman settlement on the Palatine Hill, where "Cacus' stairs" were later situated. The Roman poet Virgil described Cacus as the son of the god VULCAN and as a monstrous fire-breathing brigand who terrorized the countryside. He stole some of the giant Geryon's cattle from the hero HERACLES and hid them in his lair on the Aventine Hill; but a lowing cow betrayed Cacus, and Heracles killed him. There are various versions of this story, which is traditionally connected with the establishment of Heracles' oldest Roman place of worship, the Ara Maxima, in the Forum Boarium (Cattle Market), whose name is believed to commemorate these events.

CADMUS \'kad-məs\, in Greek mythology, the son of PHOENIX or Agenor (king of Phoenicia) and brother of EUROPA. Europa was carried off by ZEUS, king of the gods, and Cadmus was sent out to find her. Unsuccessful, he consulted the Delphic ORACLE, which ordered him to give up his quest, follow a cow, and build a town on the spot where she lay down. The cow guided him to Boeotia (Cow Land), where

he founded the city of Thebes. Later, Cadmus sowed in the ground the teeth of a dragon he had killed. From these sprang a race of fierce, armed men, called Sparti (meaning Sown). Five of them assisted him to build the Cadmea, or citadel, of Thebes and became the founders of the noblest families of that city. Cadmus took as his wife HARMONIA, daughter of the divinities ARES and APHRODITE, by whom he had a son, Polydorus, and four daughters, Ino, Autonoë, Agave, and SEMELE. Cadmus and Harmonia finally retired to Illyria. But when the Illyrians later angered the gods and were punished, Cadmus and Harmonia were saved, being changed into black serpents and sent by Zeus to the Islands of the Blessed. According to tradition it was Cadmus who brought the alphabet to Greece.

CADUCEUS \kə-'dü-sē-əs, -'dyü-, -shəs\, Greek kērykeion, staff carried by HERMES as a symbol of peace. Among the ancient Greeks and Romans it became the badge of heralds and ambassadors, signifying their inviolability. Originally the caduceus was a rod or olive branch ending in two shoots and decorated with garlands or ribbons. Later the garlands were interpreted as two snakes entwined in opposite directions with their heads facing; and a pair of wings, in token of Hermes' speed, was attached to the staff above the snakes. Its similarity to the staff of ASCLEPIUS the healer (a staff branched at the top and entwined by a single serpent) resulted in modern times in the adoption of the caduceus as a symbol of the physician and as the emblem of the U.S. Army Medical Corps.

CAENEUS \'sē-ˌnüs\, in Greek mythology, the son of Elatus, a Lapith. At the marriage of PIRITHOUS, king of the Lapiths, the CENTAURS, who were guests, attacked the bride and other women, a scene that is frequently found depicted in Greek art. Caeneus joined in the ensuing battle and, because of his invulnerable body, was able to kill five Centaurs. In desperation the other Centaurs combined against him, beating him with huge pine trees until he was forced underground, never to appear again. A later story explained that Caeneus was originally a girl, Caenis, who was raped by the sea god POSEIDON and received as compensation the male sex and invulnerability.

CAESAROPAPISM \ˌsē-zə-rō-'pā-ˌpi-zəm\, political system in which the head of the state is also the head of the church and supreme judge in religious matters. The term is most frequently associated with the late Roman, or Byzantine, Empire. Most modern historians recognize that the legal Byzantine texts speak of interdependence between the imperial and ecclesiastical structures rather than of a unilateral dependence of the latter. ST. JOHN CHRYSOSTOM and most other authoritative Byzantine theologians denied imperial power over the church.

It was normal practice, however, for the Eastern Roman emperor to act as the protector of the universal church and as the manager of its administrative affairs. EUSEBIUS OF CAESAREA called CONSTANTINE "the overseer [*i.e.*, bishop] of external" (as opposed to spiritual) church problems (*episkopos tōn ektos*). Emperors presided over councils and their will was decisive in the appointment of PATRIARCHS.

Caesaropapism was more a reality in Russia, where the abuses of Ivan IV the Terrible went practically unopposed and where Peter the Great finally transformed the church into a department of the state (1721), although neither claimed to possess special doctrinal authority.

The concept of caesaropapism has also been applied in Western Christendom—for example, to the reign of Henry VIII in England, as well as to the principle *cujus regio, ejus religio* ("religion follows the sovereign"), which prevailed in Germany after the REFORMATION.

CAIN \'kān\, in the Biblical story of creation, first-born son of ADAM AND EVE, who murdered his brother ABEL (GENESIS 4:1–16). Cain, a farmer, became enraged when God accepted the offering of his brother Abel, a shepherd, in preference to his own. He murdered Abel and was banished from the settled country. Cain feared that in his exile he could be killed, so God gave him a sign for his protection (the mark of Cain) and a promise that if he were killed, he would be avenged sevenfold.

According to some early Christian writers, a Gnostic sect called CAINITES existed in the 2nd century CE.

CAINITE \'kā-ˌnīt\, member of a Gnostic sect (*see* GNOSTICISM) mentioned by IRENAEUS and other early Christian writers as flourishing in the 2nd century CE, probably in the eastern area of the Roman Empire. The Christian theologian ORIGEN declared that the Cainites had "entirely abandoned JESUS." They held that YAHWEH (the God of the Jews) was not merely an inferior DEMIURGE, as many Gnostics believed, but that he was positively evil because his creation of the world was perversely designed to prevent the reunion of the divine element in man with the unknown perfect God. The Cainites also reversed biblical values by revering such rejected figures as CAIN (whence their name), ESAU, and the Sodomites, all of whom were considered to be bearers of an esoteric, saving knowledge (gnosis). These biblical persons were said to have been punished by a jealous, irrational creator called Hystera (Womb).

The Cainites believed that perfection, and hence salvation, comes only by breaking all the laws of the OLD TESTAMENT. The violation of biblical prescriptions was, therefore, a religious duty. Because it was difficult to violate all biblical laws in a lifetime, the Cainites did not look for salvation in the created world but rather escape from it.

CAIRD, JOHN \'kerd\ (b. Dec. 15, 1820, Greenock, Renfrew, Scot.—d. July 30, 1898, Greenock), British theologian and preacher, and an exponent of THEISM in Hegelian terms.

Ordained a PRESBYTERIAN minister on graduating from Glasgow University (1845), Caird was appointed professor of theology at Glasgow in 1862 and principal of the university in 1873. In *An Introduction to the Philosophy of Religion* (1880) and in *The Fundamental Ideas of Christianity*, 2 vol. (1899; the Gifford lectures for 1892–93 and 1894–96), both of which follow Hegelian teaching closely, Caird argues that universal thought is the reality of all things and that the existence of this Infinite Thought, namely God, is demonstrated by the limitations of finite thought. Collected editions of Caird's writings include *Sermons* (1858) and *University Addresses* (1898).

Bas-relief panel depicting the murder of Abel by his brother Cain, by Jacopo della Quercia, 1425–38; in Bologna, Italy
Alinari—Art Resource

CAIRN \'kern\, a pile of stones used as a boundary marker, a memorial, or a burial site. Cairns are usually conical in shape and were often erected on high ground. BURIAL MOUND cairns date primarily from the Neolithic Period and the Early Bronze Age, though cairns are still used in some parts of the world as burial places. The term cairn is sometimes used interchangeably with BARROW.

CAITANYA \chī-'tən-yə\, *in full* Śrī Krṣṇa Caitanya (Krishna consciousness), *also called* Gaurāṅga \gaù-'räṅ-gə\, *original name* Viśvambhara Miśra (b. 1485, Nabadvīp, Bengal, India—d. 1533, Puri, Orissa), Hindu mystic whose worship of the god KRISHNA (Krṣṇa) with ecstatic song and dance had a profound effect on VAIṢṆAVISM in Bengal.

The son of a BRAHMIN, he grew up in an atmosphere of piety and affection. He received a thorough education in the Sanskrit SCRIPTURES and, after the death of his father, set up a school of his own. At the age of 22 he made a PILGRIMAGE to Gayā to perform his father's ŚRĀDDHA (death anniversary ceremony). While there he underwent a profound RELIGIOUS EXPERIENCE that transformed his outlook and personality. He returned to his home in Nabadvīp entirely indifferent to all worldly concerns.

A group of devotees soon gathered around Caitanya and joined him in the congregational worship called KĪRTAN, which consists in the choral singing of the name and deeds of God, often accompanied by dance movements and culminating in states of trance. In 1510 he received formal initiation as an ascetic and took the name Śrī Krṣṇa Caitanya.

Although Caitanya himself wrote no works on theology or religious practices, his selection of and charges to core disciples gave birth to a major Vaiṣṇava sect in his own life-time, called familiarly the Caitanya or Gauḍīya SAM-PRADĀYA. Caitanya's own frequent and prolonged experienc-es of religious rapture took their toll on his health; he himself diagnosed some of his seizures as epileptic. The ex-act date and circumstances of his death are unknown, but Caitanyaite tradition remembers him as having left his body by walking into the ocean at Puri while lost in a devo-tional trance.

CAITANYA MOVEMENT, *also called* Gauḍīya Vaiṣṇa-vism, emotional form of HINDUISM that has flourished from the 16th century, mainly in Bengal (Gauḍ), eastern Orissa, and Braj. It takes its name from the medieval saint CAITAN-YA (1485–1533), who inspired the movement. For Caitanya the legends of KRISHNA and his youthful beloved, RĀDHĀ, were symbolic and the highest expressions of the mutual love between God and the human soul. BHAKTI (devotion) superseded all other forms of religious practice and was conceived as complete self-surrender to the divine will.

The Caitanya movement had its beginnings in Nabadvīp (Bengal), Caitanya's birthplace. From the first, a favorite and characteristic form of worship was KIRTAN; *i.e.*, singing of simple hymns with the repetition of God's name, accom-panied by a drum and cymbals. This worship continued for several hours and usually resulted in states of religious ex-altation. Caitanya left the organization of his followers to his close companions, Nityānanda and Advaita. These three are called the three masters (*prabhu*), and their imag-es are established in temples of the sect.

A theology for the movement was worked out by a group of Caitanya's disciples who came to be known as the six *gosvāmī*s (religious teachers; literally, "lords of cows" or "masters of the senses"). The six *gosvāmī*s turned out a vo-luminous religious and devotional literature in Sanskrit, defining the tenets of the movement and its ritual practic-es. Although Caitanya appears to have been worshiped as an AVATAR of Krishna even during his lifetime, the theory of his dual incarnation, as Krishna and Rādhā in one body, was developed only by the later Bengali hymnists.

The present leaders of the sect, also called *gosvāmī*s, are (with some exceptions) the lineal descendants of Caitanya's early disciples and companions. The ascetics are known as VAIRĀGĪS (the "dispassionate"). A.C. BHAKTIVEDANTA Swami, founder of the International Society for Krishna Conscious-ness (ISKCON, commonly known as the Hare Krishna move-ment), was such a *vairāgī* when he established this most re-cent expression of Caitanya VAIṢṆAVISM.

CALAIS AND ZETES \'ka-lā-is . . . 'zē-tēz\, in Greek my-thology, the winged twin sons of BOREAS and Oreithyia. On their arrival with the ARGONAUTS at Salmydessus in Thrace, they liberated their sister Cleopatra, who had been thrown into prison by her husband, Phineus, the king of the coun-try. According to another story, they delivered Phineus from the Harpies. They were slain by HERACLES near the is-land of Tenos, possibly as a result of a quarrel with Tiphys, the pilot of the Argonauts. Tradition tells that Calais founded Cales in Campania.

CALCHAS \'kal-kəs\, in Greek mythology, the son of Thestor (a priest of APOLLO) and the most famous soothsayer among the Greeks at the time of the Trojan War. He fore-told the duration of the siege of Troy, demanded the sacri-fice of IPHIGENEIA, daughter of AGAMEMNON, and advised the construction of the wooden horse with which the Greeks

finally took Troy. It had been predicted that he would die when he met his superior in divination; the PROPHECY was fulfilled when Calchas met Mopsus after the war, at CLAROS or at Siris in Italy. Beaten in a trial of soothsaying, Calchas died of chagrin or committed suicide.

CALENDAR: *see* HINDU CALENDAR; JEWISH CALENDAR; MUSLIM CALENDAR.

CALIPH, *also spelled* calif, *Arabic* khalīfa ("successor"), ruler of the community in ISLAM. When MUHAMMAD died (June 8, 632), Abū Bakr succeeded to his political and ad-ministrative functions as *khalīfat rasūl Allāh*, or "succes-sor of the Messenger of God," but it was probably under 'Umar ibn al-Khaṭṭāb, the second caliph, that the term ca-liph came into use as a title of the civil and religious head of the Muslim state. In the same sense, the term was em-ployed in the QUR'AN in reference both to ADAM and to DAVID as the vice-regents of God.

The urgent need for a successor to Muhammad as politi-cal leader of the Muslim community was met by a group of Muslim elders in MEDINA who designated Abū Bakr, the Prophet's father-in-law, as caliph. Several precedents were set in the selection of Abū Bakr, including that of choosing as caliph a member of the QURAYSH tribe. The first four ca-liphs—Abū Bakr, 'Umar I, 'UTHMĀN, and 'ALĪ—largely estab-lished the administrative and judicial organization of the Muslim community and forwarded the policy begun by Muhammad of expanding the Islamic religion into new ter-ritories, including Syria, Jordan, Palestine, Iraq, Egypt, and portions of North Africa, Armenia, and Persia.

The assassination of 'Uthmān and the troubled caliphate of 'Alī that followed sparked the first sectarian split in the Muslim community. By the time of 'Alī's death in 661, Mu'āwiya I, a member of 'Uthmān's Umayyad clan, had wrested away the caliphate, and his rule established the Umayyad caliphate that lasted until 750. Despite the large-ly successful reign of Mu'āwiya, tribal and sectarian dis-putes erupted after his death. There were three caliphs be-tween 680 and 685, and only by nearly 20 years of military campaigning did the next one, 'Abd al-Malik, succeed in re-establishing the authority of the Umayyad capital of Dam-ascus. Under his son al-Walīd (705–715), Muslim forces took permanent possession of North Africa, converted the native Berbers to Islam, and overran most of the Iberian Peninsula as the Visigothic kingdom there collapsed. Progress was also made in the east with settlement in the Indus River valley. Umayyad power had never been firmly seated, however, and the caliphate disintegrated rapidly af-ter the long reign of Hishām (724–743). A serious rebellion broke out against the Umayyads in 747, and in 750 the last Umayyad caliph, Marwān II, was defeated in the Battle of Great Zab by the followers of the 'Abbāsid family.

The 'Abbāsids, descendants of an uncle of Muhammad, owed the success of their revolt in large part to their appeal to the aid of the SHI'ITE Muslims. According to the Shi'ites no caliph is legitimate unless he is a lineal descendant of the prophet Muhammad. The SUNNIS insist that the office belongs to the tribe of Quraysh, to which Muhammad him-self belonged, but this condition would have vitiated the claim of the Turkish SULTANS, who held the office after the last 'Abbāsid caliph of Cairo transferred it to Selim I. The first 'Abbāsid caliph, as-Saffāḥ (749–754), ordered the elimi-nation of the entire Umayyad clan; the only Umayyad of note who escaped was 'Abd al-Raḥman, who made his way to Spain and established an Umayyad dynasty that lasted until 1031. Thus, the ʿAbbāsids took the caliphate for themselves, leaving the Shiʿites to evolve into an alternative branch of Islam that was opposed to the Sunni consensus concerning legitimate authority.

Abū Bakr and his three immediate successors are known as the "perfect" or "rightly guided" caliphs (al-khulafāʾ al-rāshidūn). After them the title was borne by the 14 Umayyad caliphs of Damascus and subsequently by the 38 ʿAbbāsid caliphs of Baghdad, whose dynasty fell before the Mongols in 1258. There were titular caliphs of ʿAbbāsid descent in Cairo under the Mamlūks from 1258 until 1517, when the last caliph was captured by the Ottoman sultan Selim I. The Ottoman sultans then claimed the title and used it until it was abolished by the Turkish Republic on March 3, 1924.

After the fall of the Umayyad dynasty at Damascus (750), the title of caliph was also assumed by the Fāṭimid rulers of Egypt (909–1171), who claimed to descend from FĀṬIMA (daughter of Muhammad) and her husband, ʿAlī.

CALLIOPE \kə-ˈlī-ə-pē\, *also spelled* Kalliope, in Greek mythology, foremost of the nine MUSES, patron of epic poetry. At the behest of ZEUS, she judged the dispute between the goddesses APHRODITE and PERSEPHONE over ADONIS. In most accounts she and King Oeagrus of Thrace were the parents of ORPHEUS. She was also loved by the god APOLLO, by whom she had two sons, HYMEN and Ialemus. Other versions present her as the mother of Rhesus, king of Thrace and a victim of the Trojan War; or as the mother of LINUS the musician, who was inventor of melody and rhythm.

CALLISTO \kə-ˈlis-tō\, in Greek mythology, a NYMPH (although in some myths she is said to be a daughter of either LYCAON of Arcadia or of Nycteus or Ceteus). Callisto was one of the goddess ARTEMIS' hunting companions and swore to remain unwed. But she was seduced by ZEUS and, in several variations of the legend, was turned into a she-bear either by Zeus (to conceal his deed from HERA) or by Artemis or Hera (who were enraged at her unchastity). Callisto was then killed during the chase by Artemis, who, owing to the machinations of the jealous Hera, mistook Callisto for a real bear. Zeus then gave Arcas, his child with Callisto, to the Titaness Maia to raise. He then placed Callisto among the stars as the constellation Ursa Major (Great Bear). An alternative legend has it that Arcas was transformed into the constellation Arctophylax just as he was about to kill his mother during a hunt.

CALVIN, JOHN \ˈkal-vən\, *French* Jean Calvin, *or* Cauvin (b. July 10, 1509, Noyon, Picardy, France—d. May 27, 1564, Geneva), the leading French Protestant Reformer and the most important figure in the second generation of the Protestant REFORMATION. Calvin's interpretation of CHRISTIANITY, advanced above all in his *Institutio Christianae religionis* (1536, but elaborated in later editions; *Institutes of the Christian Religion*) is held to have had a major impact on the formation of the modern world.

Calvin was sent to the University of Paris in 1523 to be educated for the priesthood, but his family later decided

that he should be a lawyer; from 1528 to 1531, therefore, Calvin studied in the law schools of Orléans and Bourges and then returned to Paris.

During these years he was exposed to Renaissance humanism, influenced by ERASMUS and Jacques Lefêvre d'Étaples, which constituted the radical student movement of the time. This movement, which antedates the Reformation, aimed to reform church and society on the model of both classical and Christian antiquity, to be established by a return to the BIBLE studied in its original languages. Under its influence Calvin studied Greek and Hebrew as well as Latin, in preparation for serious study of the SCRIPTURES. It also intensified his interest in the classics. But the movement, above all, emphasized salvation of individuals by GRACE rather than good works and ceremonies.

Because the government became less tolerant of this reform movement, Calvin found it prudent to leave Paris in 1533. Eventually he made his way to Basel, Switz., then Protestant but tolerant of religious variety. Up to that point there is little evidence of Calvin's conversion to PROTESTANTISM, which was probably gradual. His beliefs underwent a change when he began to study theology intensively in Basel. Probably in part to clarify his own beliefs, he began to write. He began with a preface to a French translation of the Bible by his cousin Pierre Olivètan and then undertook what became the first edition of the *Institutes*, his masterwork, which, in its successive revisions, became the single most important statement of Protestant belief. The final versions appeared in 1559 and 1560.

Calvin, oil painting by an anonymous artist, c. 1550
By courtesy of the Boymans-van Beuningen Museum, Rotterdam

The *Institutes* had given Calvin some reputation among Protestant leaders. The Reformer and preacher Guillaume Farel, then struggling to plant Protestantism in Geneva, persuaded Calvin to help in this work. Protestantism had been imposed on Geneva chiefly as the price of military aid from Protestant Bern. The limited enthusiasm of Geneva for Protestantism, reflected by a resistance to religious and moral reform, continued almost until Calvin's death. The resistance was all the more serious because the town council exercised ultimate control over the church and the ministers, all French refugees. The main issue was the right of EXCOMMUNICATION, which the ministers regarded as essential to their authority but which the council refused to concede. The uncompromising attitudes of Calvin and Farel led to their expulsion from Geneva in May 1538.

Calvin found refuge for the next three years in the German Protestant city of Strasbourg, where he was pastor of a church for French-speaking refugees and also lectured on the Bible; there he published his commentary on the Letter of Paul to the Romans. During his Strasbourg years Calvin also learned much about the administration of an urban church from MARTIN BUCER, its chief pastor.

In September 1541 Calvin was invited back to Geneva, where the Protestant revolution had become increasingly insecure. The town council in November enacted his Ecclesiastical Ordinances, which instituted Calvin's conception of church order. It also established four groups of church officers: pastors and teachers to preach and explain the Scriptures, elders representing the congregation to administer the church, and deacons to attend to its charitable responsibilities. It undertook a wide range of disciplinary actions covering everything from the abolition of Roman Catholic "superstition" to the enforcement of sexual morality. A significant element of the population resented these measures, and the arrival of increasing numbers of French religious refugees in Geneva was a further cause of discontent. These tensions, as well as the persecution of Calvin's followers in France, help to explain the trial and burning of MICHAEL SERVETUS, a Spanish theologian preaching and publishing unorthodox beliefs about the TRINITY. Calvin was responsible for Servetus' arrest and conviction, though he had preferred a less brutal form of execution.

The struggle over control of Geneva lasted until May 1555, when Calvin finally prevailed. He had constantly to watch the international scene and to keep his Protestant allies in a common front. Toward this end he engaged in a massive correspondence with political and religious leaders throughout Protestant Europe. He continued his commentaries on Scripture, working through the whole NEW TESTAMENT (except the Book of Revelation) and most of the OLD TESTAMENT. During this period Calvin also established the Genevan Academy to train students in humanist learning in preparation for the ministry and positions of secular leadership. He also performed a wide range of pastoral duties, preaching regularly and often, performing numerous weddings and BAPTISMS, and giving spiritual advice.

CALVINISM \\'kal-və-ˌni-zəm\\, in PROTESTANTISM, the theology developed and advanced by JOHN CALVIN. The term also is used to identify the development of some of Calvin's doctrines by his followers, and also doctrines and practices derived from the works of Calvin and his followers that became the distinguishing characteristics of the REFORMED and PRESBYTERIAN CHURCHES.

In his theology, Calvin sought to hold in balance the full range of biblical teaching, arranged in a coherent pattern but not with absolute logical precision. He often refused to make conclusions that his followers were willing to make. Calvinism in its second form began to develop after Calvin's death in 1564. Certain developments, never postulated by him, tended to produce a more legalistic pattern in doctrine and discipline. Calvin's successor at Geneva, THEODORE BEZA, placed far more importance on the doctrine of double PREDESTINATION (the doctrine that some persons are elected to be saved and others to be damned) than had Calvin. Beza also emphasized literalism in the inspiration of the BIBLE, which led him to believe that the church must be presbyterian in government—*i.e.*, a form of governance that believes the church is a community in which Christ is head and all members are equal under him, and thus the ministry is given to the entire church and is distributed among many elected officers—and not episcopal (based on a hierarchical structure of bishops and priests). Beza and his followers in England (Thomas Cartwright) and Scotland (Andrew Melville) emphasized church discipline exercised by presbyterian organization as being fundamental to the church's existence. The Five Articles of the SYNOD OF DORT (1618–19) represented a powerful definition of this post-Calvin "Calvinism" and included the proposition that Christ died only for the ELECT (chosen), a statement that Calvin himself did not formally propose.

The deterministic element in Beza's Calvinism was modified by the introduction of COVENANT THEOLOGY, which emphasized the successive COVENANTS made by God with man (from ADAM through MOSES to JESUS CHRIST) in which man is to respond in obedience in daily life to God's commandments in the moral law, through the covenant of GRACE in Christ. The WESTMINSTER CONFESSION (1646), long the standard creed of English-speaking Presbyterians, was influenced by covenant theology. Another modification of Calvin's theology was the pietistic and pragmatic concern for personal salvation that developed in English PURITANISM.

Calvinism also refers to the theological emphasis and forms of church organization, worship, and discipline that became widespread in the 16th century. This emphasis is reflected in the various CONFESSIONS, CATECHISMS, and statements of faith of the Reformed and Presbyterian churches.

CALYPSO \\kə-'lip-sō\\, in Greek mythology, the daughter of ATLAS the TITAN (or OCEANUS or NEREUS). Calypso was a NYMPH of the mythical island of Ogygia. She entertained the Greek hero ODYSSEUS for seven years but could not overcome his longing for home even by a promise of immortality. At last the god HERMES was sent by ZEUS to ask her to release Odysseus. According to later stories she bore Odysseus a son Auson, or LATINUS, and twins, Nausithous and Nausinous.

CAMĀR \\chə-'mär\\, widespread CASTE in northern India whose hereditary occupation is tanning leather; the name is derived from the Sanskrit word *carmakāra*, or "skin worker." The more than 150 subcastes are characterized by well-organized panchayats (governing councils). Because their hereditary work obliged them to handle dead animals, the Camārs have suffered from the stigma of being considered UNTOUCHABLE (*see also* DALIT). Their settlements have often been outside higher caste Hindu villages. Each settlement has its own headman (*pradhān*), and larger towns have more than one such community headed by a *pradhān*. They allow widow remarriage, with either the husband's younger brother or a widower of the same subcaste. A segment of the caste follows the teaching of the saint Śiva Nārāyaṇa (*see* SATNĀMĪ SECT) and aims at "purifying" their customs in order to raise their social prestige. Other Camārs revere RAVIDĀS (Raidās), an influential 16th-century poet-saint of Banaras (VARANASI) who challenged the idea of pollution and its ritual manifestations. Still others have adopted BUDDHISM, following the lead of B.R. AMBEDKAR. While many still practice their traditional craft, tanning, many more are part of the broader agricultural and urban labor force.

CAMILLA \\kə-'mi-lə\\, in Roman mythology, legendary Volscian maiden who became a warrior and was a favorite of the goddess DIANA. According to the poet Virgil, her father, Metabus, was fleeing from his enemies with the infant Camilla when he reached the Amisenus (Amaseno) River. He fastened the child to a javelin, dedicated her to Diana, and hurled her across the river. He then swam to the opposite bank, where he rejoined Camilla.

Living among shepherds and in the woods, Camilla became a skilled hunter and warrior through her father's tutelage. She became the leader of a band of warriors that included a number of women, and fought in a battle against the Roman hero Aeneas; but she was killed by Arruns, an Etruscan, as she was chasing a retreating soldier.

CAMPBELL, ALEXANDER \\'kam-bəl *also* 'ka-məl\\ (b. Sept. 12, 1788, near Ballymena, County Antrim, Ire.—d. March 4, 1866, Bethany, W.Va., U.S.), American clergyman, writer, and founder of the DISCIPLES OF CHRIST.

He was the son of a PRES-BYTERIAN minister who emigrated in 1807 to the United States, where he promoted his program for Christian unity. Campbell espoused his father's program and emerged as the leader of a movement for religious reform. He began preaching in 1810 and soon settled in what is now Bethany, W.Va. He and his followers accepted BAPTISM by immersion in 1812 and joined the BAPTISTS the next year, but tension on other issues led to their dissociation from the Baptists in 1830.

In 1832 his followers, known as Disciples of Christ, or Christians (nicknamed Campbellites), joined Kentucky "Christians," followers of Barton W. Stone, to form the Disciples of Christ (Christian Church). Campbell presented a rationalistic and deliberative CHRISTIANITY that was based on the NEW TESTAMENT and was opposed to speculative theology and emotional REVIVALISM.

Campbell founded (1823) and edited the *Christian Baptist* (later the *Millennial Harbinger*). In 1840 he founded Bethany College and was its president until his death.

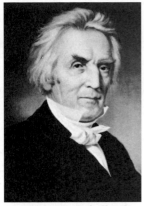

Alexander Campbell, oil painting by James Bogle; in the Campbell Homestead, Bethany, W.Va.
By courtesy of the T.W. Phillips Memorial Library, Bethany College, W.Va.

CANAAN \\'kā-nən\\, area variously defined in historical and biblical literature, but always centered on Palestine. Its original pre-Israelite inhabitants were called Canaanites. The names Canaan and Canaanite occur in cuneiform, Egyptian, and Phoenician writings from about the 15th century BCE as well as in the BIBLE. Canaan refers sometimes to an area encompassing all of Palestine and Syria, sometimes to the entire land west of the Jordan River, and sometimes to a strip of coastal land from Acre ('Akko) northward. The Israelites occupied and conquered Palestine, or Canaan, beginning in the late 2nd millennium BCE, or perhaps earlier; and the Bible justifies such occupation by identifying Canaan with the Promised Land, the land promised to the Israelites by God.

The civilization of coastal Canaan can be traced to Paleolithic and Mesolithic times; settlement in fixed towns and villages, however, appears not to have occurred until the Neolithic Period (c. 7000–c. 4000 BCE). The Semites first appear during the Early Bronze Age (c. 3000–2000 BCE). With the Middle Bronze Age (c. 2000–c. 1550 BCE) the recorded history of the area began. The Semitic Amorites, who penetrated Canaan from the northeast, became the dominant element of the population. Other invaders included the Egyptians, the Hyksos, and the Hurrians (the Horites of the OLD TESTAMENT). The Late Bronze Age (c. 1550–c. 1200 BCE) was mainly one of Egyptian control, although their power was contested by the Hittites of Anatolia (*see* ANATOLIAN RELIGIONS). The period was also marked by incursions of marauders called Hapiru or Apiru, a multiethnic group identified by many scholars with the original Hebrews, of whom the later Israelites were only one branch or confederation. By the end of the 13th century BCE, however, Egypt's domination over southern Canaan had waned, and the Hittites collapsed under the assault of enemies from the north.

During the transition from the Late Bronze to the Early Iron Age—probably c. 1250 BCE—the Israelites entered Canaan, settling at first in the hill country and in the south. In the following century, Canaan suffered further invasion at the hands of the Philistines, who appear to have come from Crete. They eventually established a coalition of five city-states on the southern coast of Canaan. Under the leadership of King DAVID (10th century BCE), the Israelites were finally able to break the Philistine power and vanquish the native Canaanites. Thereafter Canaan became, for all practical purposes, the Land of ISRAEL.

Most of what is known about Canaanite religion is derived from a series of tablets discovered at Ras Shamra, site of ancient UGARIT, on the north coast of Syria. The principal god was EL, but the jurisdiction over rainfall and fertility was delegated to BAAL, or HADAD. Other important deities included RESHEPH, lord of plague and the netherworld; KOTHAR, the divine craftsman; ASHERAH, consort of El; and ASTARTE, goddess of fertility.

The language of the Canaanites perhaps may be best described as an archaic form of Hebrew. The Canaanites were the first people, as far as is known, to use an alphabet.

CANDĪ \\'chən-dē\\, *also called* Caṇḍikā, in HINDUISM, the demon-destroying form of the goddess ŚAKTI, particularly popular in eastern India. She is known by various names, such as Mahāmāyā, or Abhayā (Sanskrit: "She Who Is Without Fear"). In her representation she is shown with either 8 or 10 arms and seated on a lion vehicle. Hundreds of folktales and songs tell of her exploits. She is the central figure of an extensive Middle Bengali literature known as *Caṇḍī-maṅgal*, the most famous of which is that of Mukundarāma Cakravartī (c. 16th century).

CANDLEMAS \\'kan-dəl-məs\\, in the Christian church, festival on February 2, commemorating the occasion when the Virgin MARY, in obedience to Jewish law, went to the Temple in Jerusalem both to be purified 40 days after the birth of her son and to present Jesus to God as her firstborn (Luke 2:22–38). The festival was formerly known in the Roman Catholic church as the Purification of the Blessed Virgin Mary and is now known as the Presentation of the Lord. In the Anglican church it is called the Presentation of Christ in the Temple. In the Greek church it is called Hypapante (Meeting), in reference to Jesus' meeting in the Temple with the aged SIMEON.

The earliest reference to the festival is from the late 4th century. By the middle of the 5th century the custom of observing the festival with lighted candles had been introduced, whence the name Candlemas.

CANDOMBLÉ \\,kän-,dōm-'blä\\, local name in Bahia state, Brazil, for the Brazilian MACUMBA tradition.

CANDRAKĪRTI \\'chən-drə-'kir-tē\\ (fl. c. 600–650 CE), principal representative of the Prāsaṅgika branch of the MĀDHYAMIKA school of MAHĀYĀNA Buddhist philosophy. One of Candrakīrti's most famous works is the *Prasannapadā*, a commentary on a basic text by NĀGĀRJUNA, the founder of the Mādhyamika school.

CANISIUS, SAINT PETER \\kə-'ni-shē-əs, -shəs\\, *Dutch* Sint Petrus Canisius, *or* Kanis (b. May 8, 1521, Nijmegen [now in The Netherlands]—d. Dec. 21, 1597, Fribourg,

CANNIBALISM

Switz.; canonized 1925; feast day December 21), doctor of the church, JESUIT scholar, and opponent of PROTESTANTISM.

Educated at the University of Cologne, Canisius became a Jesuit (1543) and taught at the universities of Cologne, Ingolstadt, and Vienna. He founded colleges at Munich (1559), Innsbruck (1562), Dillingen (1563), Würzburg (1567), Augsburg, and Vienna.

Perhaps more than any of his contemporaries, Canisius delayed the advance of Protestantism by his participation in the religious discussions at Worms (1557) and at the COUNCIL OF TRENT (1545–63) and the Diet of Augsburg (1559). He sought to renew the Roman Catholic church in Germany by means of his zealous preaching in various German towns, by the extension of the Jesuit order, and especially by his desire to provide worthy and scholarly priests. In 1580 he settled in Fribourg and founded a Jesuit college (now the University of Fribourg).

His major work was the Triple Catechism (1555–58), containing a lucid exposition of Roman Catholic dogma. It became the most famous catechism of the COUNTER-REFORMATION, going through 400 editions in 150 years.

CANNIBALISM, *also called* anthropophagy \‚an-thrə-'pä-fə-jē\, eating of human flesh. Although there are cases of people eating human flesh to avoid starvation, cannibalism has also been undertaken for ritual or religious. Even in cultures in which actual cannibalism has never been practiced, religious rituals may symbolically refer to cannibalism. Also, accusations of cannibalism have political force, whether or not the accused do in fact eat human flesh.

Until about a hundred years ago knowledge of cannibalism rested on travelers' accounts, colonial records, and missionary reports. The accuracy and objectivity of these sources has been called into serious question; travelers' tales often contained fanciful or exaggerated assertions, and European colonizers often used accusations of cannibalism to label indigenous people as savage and, hence, in need of domination. Indigenous people sometimes accused one another of cannibalism. Among the Sherbro of Sierra Leone in the late 1800s and early 1900s, political contenders went to colonial authorities to accuse rivals of cannibalism, in the hope that those rivals would be removed from power. Europeans also sometimes accused one another of cannibalism, as in the blood libel myth alleging that Jews sacrificed Christian children at Passover to obtain blood with which to make unleavened bread. This myth appeared in Europe in the 12th century but has surfaced sporadically through modern times. In general, stories of cannibalism told by one group about another have served as a way to assert that the other group is less than human. Some groups also have myths about their own past cannibalism; in this case cannibalism acts as a marker of a mythic "precultural" state rather than as an actual historical description.

Although many accusations of cannibalism were politically inspired fictions, 20th-century anthropological studies have nonetheless documented instances of cannibalism, recorded its symbolic meaning, and illuminated its cultural context. These studies show that HUMAN SACRIFICE and cannibalism were not necessarily related and that those whose flesh was eaten were not necessarily killed—or if they were killed, it may have been for reasons unrelated to cannibalism. It is clear, too, that cannibalism has a symbolic dimension, even when it is real. Although cannibalism was practiced in some places well into the 19th century—as, for instance, in Polynesia and New Guinea—colonial officials actively suppressed it, and it rarely occurs today.

In some cultures (notably the Aztec) cannibalism was a means of incorporating the divine. When the victim was offered as food to the gods, he or she took on the nature of a god. Thus, when the flesh of the victim was consumed by other humans, it transmitted this divinity to the eater. Cannibalism was also sometimes used to symbolize or create political superiority. In 19th-century Fiji, chiefs were the only ones allowed to distribute two of the three "great things"—whales' teeth and human flesh. (The chiefs themselves were the third "great thing.") Human flesh had such great ritual power to the Fijians that it had to be consumed with a special "cannibal fork" that prevented the eater from having to touch the meat.

Cannibalism has also played a role in rituals that create group or gender identities. The Bimin Kuskusmin of Papua New Guinea, for example, defined themselves as "true men" because they used appropriate ritual forms when engaging in anthropophagy, while saying that their neighbors, the Miyanmin, were barbaric because they treated human flesh as ordinary food. The Gimi, also of Papua New Guinea, incorporated cannibalism into rituals surrounding gender identity: women ate human flesh to become more fertile, but men who ate it were made as "weak as women." Symbols of cannibalism may be veiled references to gender and sexuality and hence may be used to create distinctions between the sexes.

In other cultures cannibalism was an important part of social cohesion. Among the Fore people of New Guinea, for instance, social bonds include a fictive KINSHIP created through exchange, and a man generally has the right to demand gifts—including pork—from his maternal kin. During the time the Fore practiced cannibalism they believed that when a man died, he had to repay the gift to his real and fictive maternal kin by yielding his flesh for them to eat. This practice came to light during epidemiological studies of kuru, a degenerative neurological disease that is transmitted by handling and ingesting the infected brain matter of human corpses.

In an instance of cannibalism in a modern context, in 1972 the surviving members of an Uruguayan rugby team whose plane crashed in the Andes ate their dead companions in order to avoid starvation. Some members of the team later asserted that their cannibalism brought them closer to the divine because it was a literal version of Holy Communion. They based their claim on the Roman Catholic doctrine of TRANSUBSTANTIATION, which posits that the bread and wine of the EUCHARIST are transformed into the real flesh and blood of JESUS CHRIST by their consecration during the MASS. The Catholic church absolved them from SIN but rejected any claims of greater significance.

CANONIZATION, official act of a Christian church declaring one of its deceased members worthy of public veneration and entering his or her name in the canon, or authorized list, of recognized saints. In the early church there was no formal canonization, but the cult of local martyrs was widespread. The translation of the martyr's remains from the place of burial to a church was equivalent to canonization. Gradually, ecclesiastical authorities intervened more directly; by the 10th century appeals were made to the pope. The first saint known to have been canonized by a pope was Ulrich, bishop of Augsburg (d. 973), who was canonized in 993 by Pope John XV (985–996). Pope Alexander III (1159–81) began to reserve the cases of canonization to the Holy See, and this became general law under Gregory IX (1227–41).

Pope Sixtus V (1585–90) assigned to the Congregation of Rites, one of the offices of the ROMAN CURIA, the duty of conducting the processes of BEATIFICATION (*i.e.,* a step toward canonization, whereby limited public veneration is permitted) and canonization. In the following century Pope Urban VIII forbade the public cult of any person not as yet beatified or canonized by the church, excepting those who were in possession of a public cult for at least 100 years.

Two types of beatification and canonization are distinguished: formal, or ordinary; and extraordinary, or equivalent. Formal beatification has entailed four steps: an informative process, introduction of the cause, the apostolic process, and four definite judgments.

The investigation of the candidate involves the gathering together of all material pertaining to the candidate's reputation for sanctity, the writings of the candidate, and information about miracles performed by the candidate either during his life or after death. The bishop appoints a person, called postulator of the cause, to promote the cause and also a promoter of the faith, commonly known as the "devil's advocate," to see that the entire truth is made known about the candidate. After the process is completed, if the pope orders the beatification, it is in the form of a solemn proclamation with a solemn MASS. Veneration then may be carried on in specified localities.

The canonization process is essentially the same, but at least two authentic miracles that were obtained through invocation must occur after the candidate's beatification—only then may the cause for canonization be introduced. Extraordinary, or equivalent, canonization is simply a papal confirmation that a person is a saint. It is applied only to persons whose veneration was immemorial at the time of Pope Urban VIII (1634).

Canonization in the Eastern Orthodox church is a solemn proclamation rather than a process. Spontaneous devotion toward an individual by the faithful establishes the usual basis for sainthood. The bishop accepts the petition, examines it, and delivers it to a commission that will render a final decision.

In the Anglican church, a commission was appointed in 1950 that discussed in subsequent years (especially at the 1958 Lambeth Conference) the question of canonization for members of its own communion. Feast days of certain saints, such as Saints Swithun and Cyprian, are recognized by the Anglican Communion. The observance of these days is optional for Anglicans.

CANON LAW, *Latin* jus canonicum, the body of laws made within certain Christian churches (in ROMAN CATHOLICISM, EASTERN ORTHODOXY, independent churches of Eastern Christianity, and the ANGLICAN COMMUNION) by lawful ecclesiastical authority for the government of the whole church or of some part thereof.

The word *canon* is derived from the Greek *kanōn,* which has the literal meaning of "measuring line," or "rule." The canon law concerns the constitution of the church, the relations between the church and other bodies, and matters of internal discipline. It is not per se a formulation of dogma; nonetheless, statements of the divine positive and natural law that are contained in the canons may be doctrinal in nature.

The Roman Catholic church. At no time during the first centuries of Christianity was there any attempt to enact uniform legislation for the whole church. Each community was ruled by its own customs and traditions, with, however, a certain uniformity indicating a common origin.

Such compilations of canon law as exist contain occasional decisions given by councils or by certain bishops.

These compilations began in the East, the first appearing in the province of Pontus. This contained 20 canons of Nicaea (325), together with others from the Councils of Ancyra (314) and Neocaesarea (early 4th century). The collection later grew to more than 150 canons, so well known that they were referred to by number at the COUNCIL OF CHALCEDON (451). It was further augmented by placing the so-called Apostolic Canons at the head of the collection. This was the Greek collection as first translated and introduced into the West. During the 6th century other documents were added. The Council in Trullo (692) enacted 102 canons and officially accepted the Greek collection above mentioned. The collection thus formed, together with 22 canons of the COUNCIL OF NICAEA (787), became the official canon law of the Greek and later of the Russian church.

In the West, even local collections are not mentioned until the 5th century, and not until the 8th and 9th centuries are there found traces of unification as a result of exchange of these collections among various regions. The most ancient and homogeneous of these is the African collection deriving from the almost annual plenary meetings of the African episcopate. This survives only in the collection called the *Hispana* and in that of Dionysius Exiguus.

It was against this background that John Gratian, a Camaldolese monk, published, sometime between 1139 and

A depiction of the first Council of Nicaea, which codified numerous points of canon law
Church of St. Menas, Heraklion, Crete

about 1150, his monumental treatise, known as the *Decretum Gratiani*, or *Decretum*. He drew his materials from the existing collections and included the canons of recent councils up to and including the LATERAN COUNCIL (1139). When necessary, he had recourse to the Roman law and made extensive use of the Fathers and ecclesiastical writers.

The *Decretum* served as the definitive collection of canon law for several centuries. To it were added new compilations of papal laws and decisions, and in 1500 the enlarged collection, known as the *Corpus Juris Canonici* ("Corpus of Canon Law"), was published in Paris.

On March 19, 1904, Pope Pius X issued a *motu proprio* decreeing the revision and codification of the canon law of the Latin church. A commission of CARDINALS was appointed for this purpose. After years of concerted labor, the new *Codex Juris Canonici* ("Code of Canon Law") was officially promulgated on May 27, 1917. Revision of the *Codex Juris Canonici* was undertaken, at the direction of POPE JOHN XXIII, to reflect the decrees and decisions of the SECOND VATICAN COUNCIL (1962–65). The second *Codex Juris Canonici* was signed by Pope John Paul II on Jan. 25, 1983.

The Eastern Orthodox church. Canon law of the Eastern and Western churches was much the same in form until these two groups separated in the SCHISM of 1054. In Eastern Christianity, however, because of doctrinal and nationalistic disputes during the 5th to 7th centuries, several church groups separated themselves from the nominal head of Eastern Christianity, the PATRIARCH of Constantinople, and developed their own bodies of canon law.

The Eastern churches. The churches of Eastern Christianity that separated from the patriarchal see of Constantinople developed bodies of canon law that reflected their isolated and—after the Arab conquests in the 7th century—secondary social position. Among these churches are the Syrian Orthodox Patriarchate of Antioch (in Syria), the Ancient Church of the East (the Assyrians), the Armenian Apostolic Church, and the COPTIC ORTHODOX CHURCH (in Egypt). Another independent church is the ETHIOPIAN ORTHODOX CHURCH.

Though these churches developed an extensive body of canon law throughout their histories, Western knowledge of their canon law has been very scant. In the 20th century, however, more than 300 manuscripts dealing with canon law were found in various isolated monasteries and ecclesiastical libraries of the Middle East. These manuscripts cover the period from the 3rd to the 14th century and deal with ecclesiastic regulations of the Syrian churches.

Anglican canon law. The British Parliament recognizes the British monarch as supreme head of the Church of England. The development of church law in the Anglican

Set of canopic jars with heads of (top) a human, (left) a baboon, (right) a falcon, and (bottom) a jackal
By courtesy of the Walters Art Gallery, Baltimore

Communion is held by some to be not canon law but, instead, the ecclesiastical law of the state. Proposals relating to any matter concerning the Church of England—other than dogma—are made by a Church Assembly (established in 1919) and are presented for approval to the ecclesiastical committee of Parliament. Upon the approval of both houses of Parliament, followed by royal approval, the proposal becomes law.

CANOPIC JAR \kə-'nō-pik, -'nä-\, in ancient Egyptian funerary ritual, a covered vessel of wood, stone, pottery, or faience in which was buried the embalmed viscera removed from a body during the process of mummification (*see* EMBALMING). The earliest canopic jars, which came into use during the Old Kingdom (c. 2575–c. 2130 BCE), had plain lids; but during the Middle Kingdom (c. 1938–c. 1600? BCE) the jars were decorated with sculpted human heads, probably representations of the deceased; from the 19th dynasty until the end of the New Kingdom (1539–1075 BCE), the heads represented the four sons of the god HORUS (*i.e.*, jackal-headed Duamutef, falcon-headed Qebehsenuf, human-headed Imset, and baboon-headed Hapy). The art of making canopic jars declined with the 20th dynasty (1190–1075 BCE), when the practice began of returning the viscera to the body.

CANTOR (Latin: "singer"), *Hebrew* ḥazzan ("overseer"), in JUDAISM and CHRISTIANITY, an ecclesiastical official in charge of music or chants.

In Judaism the cantor, or *ḥazzan*, directs liturgical prayer in the SYNAGOGUE and leads the chanting. He may be engaged by a congregation to serve for an entire year or merely to assist at the ceremonies of ROSH HASHANAH and YOM KIPPUR. In former times the duties of the *ḥazzan* included care of the synagogue, announcement of the beginning and the end of the SABBATH, removal of the TORAH scrolls from the Ark of the Law and their replacement after the service, care for the sick and the needy, and the religious education of children. His knowledge of music and Hebrew gradually transformed his role of assistant to the reader into that of director of the chanting during liturgical services.

In medieval Christianity the cantor was an official in charge of music at a cathedral. His duty, later undertaken by the organist, was to supervise the choir's singing, particularly the singing of the psalms and the canticles. The term was also used for the head of a college of church music—*e.g.*, the Roman *schola cantorum* of the early Middle Ages and the singing schools founded by Charlemagne.

CAO DAI \'kaù-'dī\, *Sino-Vietnamese* Cao-Đài ("High Tower," a Taoist epithet for the supreme god), syncretist modern Vietnamese religious movement with a strongly nationalist political character. Cao Dai draws upon ethical

Cao Dai temple at Tay Ninh, near Ho Chi Minh City (Saigon), Vietnam
Harrison Forman

precepts from CONFUCIANISM, occult practices from TAOISM, theories of KARMA and rebirth from BUDDHISM, and a hierarchical organization from ROMAN CATHOLICISM. Its pantheon of saints includes such diverse figures as the BUDDHA GOTAMA, CONFUCIUS, JESUS CHRIST, MUHAMMAD, Pericles, Julius Caesar, JOAN OF ARC, Victor Hugo, and Sun Yat-sen. God is represented as an eye in a triangle, a symbol that appears on the facades of the sect's temples. The religion's organization is patterned after that of Roman Catholicism, with a pope, cardinals, and archbishops. Worship involves elaborate rituals and festivals.

In 1919 NGO VAN CHIEU, an administrator for the French in Indochina, received a communication from the supreme deity during a SÉANCE. Chieu became the prophet of the new religion, which was formally established in 1926. A Cao Dai army was established in 1943 during the Japanese occupation of Indochina. After the war the Cao Dai was an effective force in national politics. In 1955–56 the government disbanded the Cao Dai army and forced the sect's pope, Pham Cong Tac, into exile. After the communist takeover in 1975 Cao Dai was reportedly repressed by the government. Centers of worship were established in Vietnamese refugee communities abroad, however, and by the early 1990s Cao Dai was reported to have some two million adherents in Vietnam, Cambodia, France, and the United States. Headquarters of the religion are at Tay Ninh, near Ho Chi Minh City (formerly Saigon).

CĀRAṆ \\'chär-ən\\, Hindu CASTE of hereditary genealogists, bards, and storytellers located in Gujarat state in western India. They claim origin from the Rājput castes of Rajasthan and may be of mixed BRAHMIN (priestly) and Rājput extraction. The Cāraṇ compose their ballad poetry, which features such themes as warriors and kings, in a special western Rajasthan dialect, called Diṅgal, that is not used for any other purpose.

CARDINAL, a member of the Sacred College of Cardinals, whose duties include electing the pope, acting as his principal counselors, and aiding in the government of the ROMAN CATHOLIC church. Cardinals serve as chief officials of the ROMAN CURIA (the papal bureaucracy), as bishops of major DIOCESES, and often as papal envoys.

The Latin word *cardinalis*, "chief," "principal" (from *cardo*, "hinge," "pivot"), began to be used around the beginning of the 6th century as an epithet of bishops, priests, or deacons whose attachment to a particular church was permanent. In Rome the first persons to be called cardinals were the deacons of the seven regions of the city. The name was also given to the senior priest in each of the "title" churches (the PARISH churches) of Rome and to the bishops of the seven sees surrounding the city. By the 8th century the Roman cardinals constituted a privileged class among the Roman clergy. They took part in the administration of the church of Rome and in the papal liturgy. By decree of a SYNOD of 769 only a cardinal was eligible to become pope. In 1059, during the pontificate of Nicholas II, cardinals were given the right to elect the pope.

In cities other than Rome the name began to be applied to certain ecclesiastics as a mark of honor. This usage of the word spread rapidly, and from the 9th century various episcopal cities had a special class among the clergy known as cardinals. The use of the title was reserved for the cardinals of Rome in 1567 by Pius V.

The College of Cardinals, with its structure of three orders (bishops, priests, and deacons), had its origin in the reform of Urban II (1088–99). These ranks within the College of Cardinals do not necessarily correspond to a cardinal's rank of ordination; *e.g.*, the bishop of a diocese such as New York City or Paris may be a cardinal priest.

The cardinal bishops are successors of the bishops of the sees just outside Rome. Prior to 1962 each of the cardinal bishops had full jurisdiction in his own see; since then, however, they preserve only the title without any of the functions, which passed to a bishop actually resident in the see. In 1965 Paul VI created cardinals from among the Eastern Catholic PATRIARCHS and arranged that they should become cardinal bishops on the title of their patriarchal sees.

The second and largest order in the Sacred College is that of the cardinal priests. Since the 11th century this order has been more conspicuously international than the orders of cardinal bishops and deacons, including the bishops of important sees from throughout the world.

The cardinal deacons are successors of the seven regional deacons. Originally, the order was limited to those who had advanced no further than the deaconate. Later legislation prescribed that a cardinal deacon be at least a priest.

The total number of cardinals was fixed at 70 by Sixtus V in 1586; John XXIII eliminated the restriction of 70, and since then the number has reached more than 100.

New cardinals are appointed only by the pope. He calls a secret consistory (meeting) of the cardinals and announces to them the names of the new cardinals. The newly named cardinals then receive the red biretta and the ring symbolic of the office in a public consistory.

CARGO CULT, any of the religious movements chiefly in Melanesia that exhibited belief in the imminence of a new age of blessing, to be initiated by the arrival of a special "cargo" of goods from supernatural sources—based on the observation by local residents of the delivery of supplies to colonial officials. Foreigners were sometimes accused of having intercepted material goods intended for the native peoples. If the cargo was expected by ship or plane, symbolic wharves or landing strips and warehouses were sometimes built in preparation, and traditional material resources were abandoned and foodstocks destroyed. New social organizations, sometimes imitative of the colonial police or armed forces, may be initiated.

The radically new age was thought to be inaugurated by cataclysmic events that will destroy the old order and bring a paradisal plenty, together with freedom and justice that may involve the reversal of the positions of white foreigners and indigenous peoples. The political implications and economic losses connected with these mass movements led colonial authorities to suppress them. They may, however, be understood as the expression of traditional millennial ideas (*see* MILLENNIALISM), often revived by the eschatological teaching of Christian MISSIONS.

Cargo cults led by prophets claiming a new revelation appeared in the late 19th century, caught public attention in the Papuan "Vailala Madness" in 1919, and proliferated by the score from the 1930s, especially in marginal and underdeveloped areas. In growing towns, cargo cults gave way to more secular movements.

CARMELITE \ˈkär-mə-ˌlīt\, member of one of the four great MENDICANT orders of the Middle Ages. The origin of the order can be traced to Mt. Carmel in Palestine, where a number of devout men established themselves near the traditional fountain of ELIJAH, an OLD TESTAMENT prophet, about 1155. Their rule was written between 1206 and 1214 by St. Albert, Latin PATRIARCH of Jerusalem, and approved in 1226 by Pope Honorius III. The monks hoped to continue on Mt. Carmel the way of life of the prophet Elijah, whom early Christian writers depict as the founder of MONASTICISM.

The early Carmelites were HERMITS: They lived in separate cells or huts and observed vows of silence, seclusion, abstinence, and austerity. Soon, however, the losses of the crusading armies in Palestine made Mt. Carmel unsafe for the Western hermits, and they set out, about 1240, for Cyprus, Sicily, France, and England. The first general chapter (legislative meeting) of the Carmelites was held in England in 1247 under St. Simon Stock, and the order was adapted to the conditions of the Western lands to which it had been transplanted: the order transformed itself from one of hermits into one of mendicant FRIARS. The first institution of Carmelite nuns was founded in 1452.

Of all the movements in the Carmelite order, by far the most important and far-reaching in its results was the reform initiated by ST. TERESA OF ÁVILA. After nearly 30 years in a Carmelite CONVENT, she founded (1562) in Ávila, Spain, a small convent wherein a stricter way of life was to be observed; it became the order of Discalced Carmelite Nuns (O.D.C.). St. Teresa succeeded in establishing not only nunneries but also, with the cooperation of Juan de Yepes (later ST. JOHN OF THE CROSS), a number of friaries of this stricter observance. Because Reformed Carmelites wore sandals in place of shoes and stockings, they came to be called the Discalced, or barefooted, Carmelites, to distinguish them from the older branch of the order.

Both orders suffered severely from the French Revolution and from suppression both by Napoleon and the liberal governments of the 19th century, but they have since been restored in most countries of western Europe, in the Middle East, Latin America, and the United States. The original order (Order of Brothers of the Blessed Virgin Mary of Mt. Carmel; White Friars; O.Carm.) is engaged primarily in preaching and teaching. The Discalced Carmelite Fathers (Order of Discalced Brothers of the Blessed Virgin Mary of Mt. Carmel; O.C.D.) is active in parishes and in foreign MISSIONS as a primarily pastoral and devotional order.

CARNEIA \kär-ˈnē-ə\, important religious festival among ancient Dorian-speaking Greeks, held in the month of Karneios (roughly August). The name is connected with Karnos, or Karneios (probably meaning "ram"), said to have been a favorite of the god APOLLO, killed by the descendants of HERACLES and commemorated to appease the god's anger; he may have been an old god displaced by Apollo. Five young men called Karneatai were chosen out of each tribe; one youth, decked with garlands, ran away, and the rest followed him; if he was overtaken, it was a good OMEN.

CARNIVAL, the festivity that takes place in many ROMAN CATHOLIC countries in the last days and hours of the pre-Lenten season. The word *carnival*, from *carnevale* in the Italian dialect of Rome and its environs, descends ultimately from Latin *carn-*, "meat," and *levare*, "to raise," "remove"; originally the word alluded to the commencement

A carnival celebration at Mardi Gras in New Orleans, La.
Sylvain Grandadam—Photo Researchers

of the 40-day Lenten fast (during which Roman Catholics formerly abstained from eating meat), though early in its history its reference shifted to the festive period preceding LENT. The historical origin of carnival is obscure; in its long history, however, the carnival played a significant role in the development of the popular theater, vernacular song, and folk dances.

The first day of the carnival season varies with both national and local traditions. Thus in Munich, Ger., and in Bavaria the carnival—known as Fastnacht in Munich and FASCHING in Bavaria—begins on the feast of EPIPHANY (January 6), while in Cologne, Ger., or the Rhineland it begins on November 11 at 11:11 AM. In France the celebration is restricted to Tuesday before ASH WEDNESDAY (Shrove Tuesday) and to *mi-carême*, that is, the Thursday of the third week of Lent.

In the United States the principal carnival celebration is in New Orleans, La., where the carnival season opens on Twelfth Night (January 6) and climaxes with the MARDI GRAS season commencing 10 days before Shrove Tuesday. The French name *Mardi Gras* means Fat Tuesday, from the custom of using all the fats in the home before Lent. The most famous modern carnival, however, is perhaps that of Rio de Janeiro. Masked balls, elaborate costumes, parades, and various other festivities mark such celebrations. In most cases, the modern celebration of carnival has taken on a strongly secular quality distinct from its roots in Christian and pre-Christian religion.

CARPOCRATIAN \,kär-pə-'krā-shən\, follower of Carpocrates, a 2nd-century Christian GNOSTIC. The sect flourished in Alexandria. Carpocratians revered JESUS as an ordinary man whose uniqueness flowed from the fact that his soul had not forgotten that its origin and true home was within the sphere of the unknown perfect God. Carpocratians completely rejected the created world by identifying themselves with spiritual reality. They claimed to communicate with demonic spirits and presented this as proof of their power over, and superiority to, the material world. The subversion of Jewish biblical law was considered a serious responsibility because they claimed the law came from evil ANGELS who created the world.

The Carpocratians have been called libertine Gnostics because they contended that the attainment of transcendent freedom depended on having every possible experience. Such an array of experiences normally required more than one lifetime, so the Carpocratians espoused the doctrine of the transmigration of souls, perhaps inspired by Indian or Pythagorean beliefs.

The Carpocratians made brightly colored ICONS with images of Plato, Pythagoras, Aristotle, Jesus, and others. Indeed, they were the first sect known to have used pictures of Christ. They also practiced magic for such purposes as the making of love potions.

CARTHUSIAN \kär-'thü-zhən, -'thyü-\, member of the Order of Carthusians (O.Cart.), an order of monks founded by St. Bruno of Cologne in 1084 in the valley of Chartreuse (Latin: Cartusia) in southeastern France. The Carthusians, who played an important role in the monastic-reform movement of the 11th and 12th centuries, combine the solitary life of HERMITS with a common life within the walls of a monastery. The monks live in individual cells, where they pray, study, eat, and sleep, gathering in the church only for the night office, morning MASS, and afternoon vespers. They eat together on Sundays and at great feasts, when they also have a period of conversation; and once a week they take a long walk together. At the Grande Chartreuse, as the motherhouse is known, the lay brothers distill the liqueur that bears the name of the motherhouse and of which the profits benefit religious causes and charities. Carthusian nuns, with a few monasteries in France and Italy, are also strictly cloistered and CONTEMPLATIVE.

CASSANDRA \kə-'san-drə, -'sän-\, in Greek mythology, the daughter of PRIAM, the last king of Troy, and his wife HECUBA. Cassandra was desired by the god APOLLO, who promised her the power of PROPHECY if she would grant his desires. Cassandra accepted the proposal, received the gift, and then refused the god her favors. Apollo revenged himself by ordaining that her prophecies should never be believed. She predicted such events as the fall of Troy and the death of AGAMEMNON, but her warnings went unheeded. In the distribution of the spoils after the capture of Troy, Cassandra fell to Agamemnon and was later murdered with him. She was worshiped, as Alexandra, with Apollo.

CASSIAN, SAINT JOHN \'ka-sē-ən, -shē-\, *also called* Johannes Eremita, *or* Johannes Massiliensis (b. 360, the Dobruja, Scythia—d. 435, Marseille; Eastern feast day February 29; feast day in Marseille July 23), ascetic, monk, theologian, and founder and first ABBOT of the famous abbey of Saint-Victor at Marseille.

Probably of Roman birth, Cassian became a monk at Bethlehem and later visited and was trained by the HERMITS and monks of Egypt. About 399 he went to Constantinople (now Istanbul), where he was ordained deacon by the patriarch, ST. JOHN CHRYSOSTOM. A few years later, after John had been illegally deposed, Cassian went to Rome to plead John's cause with the Pope and while there was ordained priest (405). Nothing is then known of his life until 415, when he founded a nunnery at Marseille, and also the abbey of Saint-Victor, of which he remained abbot until his death. He was a leading exponent, in its early phase, of SEMI-PELAGIANISM, a HERESY that flourished in southern France during the 5th century.

Cassian's most influential work is his *Institutes of the Monastic Life* (420–429); this, and his *Collations of the Fathers* (or *Conferences of the Egyptian Monks*), written as dialogues of the Desert Fathers, were influential in the further development of Western MONASTICISM.

CASSOCK, long garment worn by ROMAN CATHOLIC and other clergy both as ordinary dress and under liturgical garments. The cassock, with button closure, has long sleeves and fits the body closely. In the Roman Catholic church the color and trim vary with the ecclesiastical rank of the wearer: the pope wears white; cardinals scarlet, or black with scarlet trim, except in penitential seasons when they wear purple; archbishops and bishops black with red trim; and lesser clergy plain black.

The cassock was originally the out-of-doors and domestic dress of European laity as well as clergy, and its survival among the latter is merely the outcome of ecclesiastical conservatism. In cold weather it was worn under the tabard (a tunic with or without short sleeves) or chimere (a loose, sleeveless gown); sometimes in the Middle Ages the name chimere was given to it as well as to the sleeveless upper robe. In winter the cassock was often lined with furs. Its color varied with ecclesiastical or academic status.

In the Church of England the cassock, which with the gown is prescribed by a canon of 1604 as the canonical dress of the clergy, has been worn by the clergy since the REFORMATION. It has long ceased, however, to be the everyday walking dress of either Catholic or Anglican clergy and is now usually worn only in church.

In the Eastern church the cassock's equivalent is called a rhason.

CASTE, group of people having a specific social rank, defined generally by descent, marriage, commensality, and occupation.

Although the term *caste* is applied to hierarchically ranked groups in many different societies around the world, the caste system in its most developed form is found in India. The word (from the Portuguese *casta*, meaning "race" or "lineage") was first applied to Indian society by Portuguese travelers in the 16th century. A roughly analogous word used in many Indian languages is JĀTI ("birth group"). There are about 3,000 castes and more than 25,000 subcastes in India, some with several hundred members and others with millions.

In traditional Brahminical law books, and in much popular usage, Indian society is divided into four VARNAS (Sanskrit: "class," or "color"). At the top of the hierarchy are the BRAHMINS (priests and scholars), followed in rank order by the KSATRIYAS (warriors and rulers), the VAIŚYAS (merchants, traders, and farmers), and the ŚŪDRAS (artisans, laborers, servants, and slaves). The members of each class are considered to be ritually polluted to varying degrees as a result of defilements brought about by their birth, occupations, dietary habits, and customs. Those who have the most defiling jobs are typically ranked beneath the Śūdras and called "untouchables" (now also known as DALIT, Harijans ["Children of God," the name preferred by MAHATMA GANDHI], or as members of the Scheduled castes, because of the special status accorded them by census authorities in British India). India's Muslims, Sikhs, and Christians also observe caste distinctions in varying degrees, though they generally place less emphasis on food TABOOS and inherited rank than on endogamy.

It is important to emphasize that the *varnāśrama* DHARMA system—a vision of society in which an individual's place (or at least, an individual man's place) could be ascertained by cross referencing his *varna* with his stage of life (ashram)—has always functioned more as an ideal than as reality. *Jāti*s, which are true social groupings, do not always align easily with *varna*s, and their rankings vary radically from area to area. Rulers, not Brahmins, have very often been regarded as occupying the pinnacle position in Indian society, and even their specifically religious importance sometimes outranks that of Brahmins. In South India, additionally, landholding Śūdras hold high social rank. Scholars often emphasize the role played by the British census in institutionalizing the idea that the particular hierarchical *varna* conception found in *The Laws of Manu* corresponds to social reality.

In *Manu* and elsewhere, concepts of pollution and purification are based on the idea that each caste group can maintain its status by regulating its contact with lower-ranking caste groups and with objects thought to be inherently impure. In early Brahminical circles great emphasis was traditionally placed on bodily hygiene and dietary restrictions. The latter practice could contribute to a store of "austerities" (TAPAS) conducive to attaining the spiritual goal of MOKSA, or release from the cycle of transmigration. An added factor was the value of AHIMSĀ ("noninjury"), or refusal to kill for nonsacrificial purposes.

A person can be vulnerable to external pollution and internal pollution (as by ingesting impure food) and can also be polluted by coming into contact with people who, because of their own hygienic and dietary habits, are impure. Since members of a given caste customarily prepare and eat food with each other, a polluted individual can, by association, pollute others of his caste. In this social dimension, then, pollution is the degree to which a caste allows practices that a ritually and socially superior caste group does not permit its members. Each caste maintains its own standards, infractions of which are adjudicated and punished by the caste itself. While external pollution can be washed off with water, internal pollution requires another means of purification, normally imposed by tradition but, on occasion, by decision of the caste assembly (*sabhā*). Purification rites can include a fine or penalty paid by giving a feast for caste members or Brahmins. A common purification rite is the consumption of a cleansing agent whose constituents include cow's milk, butter, curds, dung, and urine.

Rigidities of caste have lessened in the 20th century, partly owing to Gandhi's influence and to the efforts of successive Indian governments to abolish caste rituals, remove legal restrictions from untouchables, and promote the welfare of the lower castes in general. Particularly since India gained independence in 1947, and especially in urban settings, there has been considerable social mobility among castes. This usually takes the form of a *jāti* trying to associate itself with a higher-ranked *varna* by adopting the customs, rituals, and attitudes found in the Brahminical SCRIPTURES, a process that has been called Sanskritization.

Urbanization and industrialization have also increased Indian social mobility and thereby modified the caste system. Modern transportation facilities, workplaces, and housing have brought Indians of all castes into close and unavoidable contact. As a result, prohibitions on many forms of personal contact between castes have been relaxed or abandoned entirely in urban areas, at least in public places. Declining specialization in traditional occupations has further eroded the caste system, particularly in the more industrialized areas, though new occupations sometimes tend to generate new caste rankings rather than dismantle caste altogether. In some instances "affirmative action" measures have also tended to perpetuate caste, though in new forms, as caste groups have joined to form bloc-voting pressure groups that compete in politics and vie for control of economic opportunities and social-welfare services. Particularly important are provisions regulating access to education and government jobs. Therefore, despite movements for reform, caste alliances still remain a powerful political and social force in India, and caste considerations remain strong in the countryside, where the majority of India's people live.

CATACOMB, *Latin* catacumba, *Italian* catacomba, subterranean cemetery composed of galleries or passages with side recesses for tombs. The term, of uncertain origin, seems to have been applied first to the subterranean cemetery under the BASILICA of San Sebastiano (on the Appian Way near Rome), which was reputed to have been the temporary resting place of the bodies of Saints PETER and PAUL in the last half of the 3rd century. The word came to refer to all the subterranean cemeteries around Rome. The early Christian catacombs of Rome are located in a rough circle about three miles from the center of the city. About 40 chambers are known, and most are found near the main roads leading into the city.

*Catacomb of Domitilla in Rome showing a passage with
side recesses for tombs*
Fototeca Unione, American Academy in Rome

In the early Christian communities of the Roman Empire, catacombs served many functions in addition to burial. Funeral feasts were celebrated in family vaults on the day of burial and on anniversaries. The EUCHARIST, which accompanied funerals in the early church, was celebrated there. In some catacombs, larger halls and connected suites of chapels were, in effect, shrines to saints and martyrs. A famous example is the Triclia in the catacomb of St. Sebastian, to which countless pilgrims came to partake of memorial meals (*refrigeria*) in honor of Saints Peter and Paul and to scratch prayers to them on the walls.

The catacombs also, because of their intricate layout and access by secret passages to sand quarries and open country, could be used as hiding places during times of persecution and civil commotion. There seems, however, to be no truth in the widespread belief that early Christians used the catacombs as secret meeting places for worship. By the 3rd century CE there were more than 50,000 Christians in Rome, and 50,000 persons could hardly go out to the catacombs in secret. Furthermore, worship of any kind would seem out of the question in the long, narrow corridors of the catacombs, and even the largest of the tomb chambers hardly holds 40 persons. Finally, Christians and pagans alike regarded death as unclean, so that, while memorial meals or masses for the dead might be celebrated there, regular public worship in such a place would be unlikely.

Catacombs were by no means a Christian or an exclusively Roman invention. The custom of burying the dead in underground rock chambers goes far back into antiquity. Catacombs are found all over the Mediterranean world.

CATECHISM, a manual of religious instruction usually arranged in the form of questions and answers used to instruct the young, to win converts, and to testify to the faith. The term catechism was evidently first used for written handbooks in the 16th century.

After the invention of printing and the REFORMATION, catechisms became much more important, both in PROTESTANTISM and ROMAN CATHOLICISM. These catechisms were influenced by the medieval catechism, which had concentrated upon the meaning of faith (the APOSTLES' CREED), hope (the LORD'S PRAYER), and charity (the TEN COMMANDMENTS). The later catechisms usually included discussions of these three subjects and added others.

Perhaps the most influential book produced by any Reformer was MARTIN LUTHER'S Small Catechism (1529), which added discussions of BAPTISM and the EUCHARIST to the usual three subjects. JOHN CALVIN published a catechism in 1542 intended for children. The HEIDELBERG CATECHISM (1563) of Caspar Olevianus and Zacharias Ursinus (revised by the SYNOD OF DORT in 1619) became the most widely used catechism in the Reformed churches. The standard PRESBYTERIAN catechisms have been the Westminster Larger and Shorter Catechisms, completed in 1647.

The Anglican catechism is included in THE BOOK OF COMMON PRAYER. The first part was probably prepared by Thomas Cranmer and Nicholas Ridley in 1549 and was modified several times before 1661. A second part, discussing the meaning of the two SACRAMENTS, was prepared in 1604 in response to a suggestion of the Puritan faction of the Hampton Court Conference.

The most famous Roman Catholic catechism was one by PETER CANISIUS, a JESUIT, first published in 1555, which went through 400 editions in 150 years. In more recent times, well-known Roman Catholic catechisms have included the Baltimore Catechism (1885) in the United States and *A Catechism of Christian Doctrine* ("Penny Catechism") in England (1898). In 1992 the Vatican issued a new universal *Catechism of the Catholic Church* that summarized the church's doctrinal positions and teachings since the SECOND VATICAN COUNCIL (1962–65).

In reaction to the work of the Jesuits and the REFORMED CHURCH among the Orthodox, PETER MOGILA composed *The Orthodox Confession of Faith* in the form of a catechism. It was approved at a provincial SYNOD in 1640 and standardized by the synod of Jerusalem in 1672. By order of the Russian tsar Peter I the Great, a smaller Orthodox catechism was prepared in 1723.

CATECHUMEN \,ka-tə-'kyü-mən, 'ka-tə-,\, a person who receives instruction in the Christian religion in order to be baptized. As the number of GENTILES in the early church increased, instruction in the Christian faith became more necessary, and by the 4th century, with the rise of HERESY, detailed doctrinal teaching was given. By this time the postponement of BAPTISM had become general, and, therefore, a large proportion of Christians belonged to the catechumenate. Catechumens were permitted to attend the first part of the liturgy ("Liturgy of the Catechumens") but were dismissed before the "Liturgy of the Faithful" (the liturgy of the EUCHARIST). As infant baptism became general, the catechumenate decreased. The baptismal rites now used are adaptations of rites intended for the reception of adult catechumens.

CATHARI \\'ka-thə-ˌrī, -ˌrē\\, *also spelled* Cathars \\'ka-ˌthärz\\ (from Greek: *katharos*, "pure"), heretical Christian sect that flourished in western Europe in the 12th and 13th centuries (*see also* ALBIGENSES). The Cathari professed a dualist doctrine that there are two principles, one good and the other evil, and that the material world is evil. Similar views were held in the Balkans and the Middle East by the PAULICIANS and the BOGOMILS.

Isolated groups of such believers appeared in western Germany, Flanders, and northern Italy in the first half of the 11th century, and their numbers grew rapidly in the mid-12th century. About this time the Bogomil church was reorganizing itself, and Bogomil missionaries, as well as Western dualists returning from the Second Crusade (1147–49), were at work in the West. From the 1140s the Cathari were an organized church with a hierarchy, a liturgy, and a system of doctrine. About 1149 the first bishop established himself in the north of France; a few years later he established colleagues at Albi and in Lombardy. The status of these bishops was confirmed and the prestige of the Cathar church enhanced by the visit of the Bogomil bishop Nicetas in 1167. In the following years more bishops were set up, until by the turn of the century there were 11 bishoprics in all, 1 in the north of France, 4 in the south, and 6 in Italy.

The groups emphasized different doctrines, but all agreed that matter was evil. Humans were aliens and sojourners in an evil world; their aim must be to free their spirit, which was in its nature good, and restore it to communion with God. There were strict rules for fasting, including the prohibition of meat. Sexual intercourse was forbidden; complete renunciation of the world was called for.

The extreme ASCETICISM made the Cathari a church of the elect, and yet in France and northern Italy it became a popular religion. This success was achieved by the division of the faithful into two bodies: the "perfect" and the "believers." The perfect were set apart from the mass of believers by a ceremony of initiation, the *consolamentum*. They devoted themselves to contemplation and were expected to maintain the highest moral standards. The believers were not expected to attain the standards of the perfect.

The Cathar doctrines of creation led them to rewrite the biblical story. They viewed much of the OLD TESTAMENT with reserve; some of them rejected it altogether. The orthodox doctrine of the INCARNATION was rejected. JESUS was merely an angel; his human sufferings and death were an illusion. They also severely criticized the worldliness and corruption of the ROMAN CATHOLIC church.

The Cathar doctrines struck at the roots of both orthodox CHRISTIANITY and the political institutions of Christendom, and the authorities of church and state united to attack them. POPE INNOCENT III (1198–1216) attempted to force Raymond VI, count of Toulouse, to join him in putting down the movement, but the papal legate was murdered in January 1208; the count was generally thought to have been an accessory to the crime. The Albigensian Crusade was proclaimed against the heretics, and an army led by a group of barons from northern France ravaged Toulouse and Provence and massacred the inhabitants, both Cathar and Catholic. A more orderly persecution of Cathars, later sanctioned by St. Louis IX, in alliance with the nascent INQUISITION, was more effective. In 1244 the great fortress of Montségur near the Pyrenees, a stronghold of the perfect, was captured and destroyed. Many of the French Cathari fled to Italy, where persecution was more intermittent. The hierarchy faded out in the 1270s; the movement lingered and finally disappeared early in the 15th.

CATHBAD \\'kȧ-fə, 'kȧth-vəth\\, *also spelled* Cathbhadh, in the Irish sagas, the great DRUID of Ulster and, in some legends, the father of King CONCHOBAR MAC NESSA (Conor).

Cathbad was able to divine the signs of the days, thus to determine auspicious or inauspicious activities for certain days. According to one tradition, the queen Nessa once consulted Cathbad, asking him what the day was auspicious for; Cathbad answered that it was auspicious for begetting a king upon a queen, and Conchobar was conceived in their subsequent union. When Conchobar reached manhood, none in Ulster was allowed to speak before he had spoken, but Conchobar never spoke before Cathbad had spoken—giving Cathbad precedence over the king. Cathbad acted as the king's advisor and is referred to as a teacher, supporting Julius Caesar's assertion that the Gallic Druids served as repositories of traditional knowledge.

CATHEDRAL, in Christian churches that have an episcopal form of church government, the church in which a residential BISHOP has his official seat or throne, the cathedra. Cathedral churches are of different degrees of dignity. There are cathedral churches of simple diocesan bishops, of ARCHBISHOPS or METROPOLITANS, of PRIMATES, PATRIARCHS, and, in ROMAN CATHOLICISM, of the POPE. A cathedral church is not necessarily large and magnificent, although most cathedrals have become so.

In the Roman Catholic church, CANON LAW makes no architectural conditions for a cathedral. The only canonical requirement is that a cathedral should be consecrated and adequately endowed. The pope has the right to designate a cathedral, although the choice of the bishop of the DIOCESE or his decision to build a cathedral is normally approved. The bishop must be present in his cathedral on certain holy days and normally must perform ORDINATIONS there.

In Eastern Orthodoxy, the cathedral is the main church in a city where the bishop resides and where he celebrates the liturgy on festival occasions. In Russia, where the dioceses have always been few and have covered a vast area, the main church in any large town became known as a cathedral (*sobor*), even though no bishop was in residence there. The principal church of a large monastery also assumed the same name.

CATHERINE OF SIENA, SAINT \\'ka-thə-rən . . . sē-'e-nə\\, *original name* Caterina Benincasa (b. March 25, 1347, Siena, Tuscany—d. April 29, 1380, Rome; canonized 1461; feast day April 29), patron saint of Italy who played a major role in returning the PAPACY from Avignon to Rome (1377). She was declared a doctor of the church in 1970.

Catherine became a tertiary (a member of a monastic third order who takes simple vows and may remain outside a CONVENT or monastery) of the DOMINICAN order (1363) in Siena. When Florence was placed under an interdict by Pope Gregory XI (1376), Catherine determined to take public action for peace within the church and Italy and to encourage a crusade against the Muslims. She went as an unofficial mediator to Avignon with her confessor and biographer Raymond of Capua. Her mission failed, and she was virtually ignored by the pope, but while at Avignon she promoted her plans for a crusade.

It became clear to her that the return of Pope Gregory XI to Rome—an idea that she did not initiate and had not strongly encouraged—was the only way to bring peace to Italy and thus facilitate a crusade. At her encouragement, Gregory moved the papacy to Rome in 1377 (where he died the next year). Catherine went to Rome in November of

St. Catherine of Siena; illustration from the Dialogo della divina provvidenza, *1504*
Culver Pictures

1378, probably at the invitation of Pope Urban VI (1378–1417), whom she helped in reorganizing the church. From Rome she sent out letters and exhortations to gain support for Urban in his struggles with the ANTIPOPE Clement VII.

Catherine's writings, all of which were dictated to her disciples, include about 380 letters, 26 prayers, and the four treatises of *Il libro della divina dottrina*, better known as the *Dialogo della divina provvidenza* (*c.* 1475). A complete edition of Catherine's works together with her biography by Raymond was published in Siena (1707–21).

CATHOLIC (from Greek: *katholikos*, "universal"), the characteristic that, according to ecclesiastical writers since the 2nd century, distinguished the Christian church at large from local communities or from heretical and schismatic sects. A notable exposition of the term as it had developed during the first three centuries of CHRISTIANITY was given by ST. CYRIL OF JERUSALEM in his *Catecheses* (348): the church is called catholic on the ground of its worldwide extension, its doctrinal completeness, its adaptation to the needs of men of every kind, and its moral and spiritual perfection. (*See* NICENE CREED.)

The theory that what has been universally taught or practiced is true was first fully developed by ST. AUGUSTINE in his controversy with the Donatists. It received classic expression in a paragraph by St. Vincent of Lérins in his *Commonitoria* (434), from which is derived the formula: "What all men have at all times and everywhere believed must be regarded as true."

Confusion in the use of the term has been inevitable, be-cause various groups that have been condemned by the Roman Catholic church as heretical or schismatic never retreated from their own claim to catholicity. Not only the Roman Catholic church but also the Eastern Orthodox, the Anglican, and a variety of national and other churches claim to be members of the holy catholic church, as do most major Protestant churches.

CECROPS \'sē-ˌkräps\, traditionally the first king of Attica in ancient Greece. He was said to have instituted the laws of marriage and property and a new form of worship. The introduction of bloodless sacrifice, the burial of the dead, and the invention of writing were also attributed to him. He acted as arbiter during the dispute between the deities ATHENA and POSEIDON for the possession of Attica. Cecrops was represented as human in the upper part of his body, while the lower part was shaped like a snake.

CELIBACY, abstention from sexual intercourse or from marriage, usually in association with the role of a religious official or devotee. The term is typically applied only to those for whom the unmarried state is the result of a sacred vow, act of renunciation, or religious conviction. Celibacy has existed in some form or another throughout the history of religions. Wherever celibacy has appeared, it has generally accompanied the view that the religious life is essentially different or even alienated from the normal structures of society and the normal drives of human nature.

Celibacy can be either permanent or temporary. Examples of permanent celibacy can be found in the lives of monks and nuns in CHRISTIANITY or in the rituals of HINDUISM performed by a SANNYASI (world renouncer). These rituals serve to separate the *sannyasi* from his life as a householder, underscoring the true significance of celibacy: it is a state in opposition to that which governs domestic life.

Celibacy in ancient civilizations.   In the great civilizations of antiquity celibacy emerged in various contexts. The requirement that the VESTAL VIRGINS of Rome remain celibate for at least the 30 years of their service indicates that celibacy had some place in a very ancient stratum of ROMAN RELIGION. Celibacy was especially characteristic of priest-devotees of the Great Mother cults. The well-organized PRIESTHOOD of the religion of ISIS, for example, represented sacerdotalism (that is, the belief that priests serve as essential mediators between humans and the divine); and sexual abstinence was an absolute requirement for those who celebrated her holy mysteries.

Similarly, Manichaeans, Gnostics, and Hermeticists typically had an inner circle requiring strict continence. Thus, many important religious movements in the classical world envisioned continence as an ideal and set the stage for Christian celibacy and MONASTICISM.

Celibacy in the religions of Asia.   In Hinduism, celibacy is not associated with the priesthood, which is hereditary. Prominent, however, among the religious personages of India are the *sadhus*, "holy men," who live a life free of possessions and family obligations. The *sadhus* have no institutions or organizations. Many *sadhus*, male and female, become celibates after marriage or widowhood; others early in life. The *sadhu* is one who has left the type of life ruled by the order of DHARMA (cosmic and societal law—*i.e.*, of CASTE, family, money, state, and all their responsibilities and privileges) in order to seek MOKṢA (final liberation).

Although celibacy is postulated for Buddhist clergy everywhere, there have been and are liberal exceptions, such as the married monks of pre-20th-century Ceylon (Sri Lanka) and those of some of the Japanese clergies. Since the vows of the Buddhist monk in principle are not permanent, the theoretical emphasis on celibacy has become academic in many parts of Asia, and, in fact, some VAJRAYĀNA schools have allowed sexual intercourse as an esoteric ritual that contributes to the attainment of release.

Chinese TAOISM has monastics and independent celibate adepts. SHINTŌ in Japan has no monks or celibate priesthood; instead, especially in premodern times, it has embraced shamaneses "married" to the shrine god and celibate priestesses in major shrines.

Celibacy in the major monotheisms. Permanent celibacy is of little significance in JUDAISM. There were, however, prescribed periods of sexual abstinence in connection with rituals and sacrifices and while engaging in HOLY WARS. It seems that in post-Old Testament times, some members of the ESSENE sect rejected marriage.

In ISLAM, too, celibacy does not play an important role. A basic social teaching in Islam is the encouragement of marriage, and the QUR'AN regards celibacy as something exceptional. However, many SUFIS preferred celibacy, and some even regarded women as an evil distraction from piety, although celibacy was exceptional even among members of these mystical orders.

Celibacy first appears in Christianity out of apocalyptic expectations (*see* MILLENNIALISM). It was believed among the original Christians that the present age was ending, that the KINGDOM OF GOD was at hand, and that in the new age there would be no marriage. The regional Council of Elvira in Spain (*c.* 306 CE) decreed that all priests and bishops, married or not, should abstain from sexual relations. The position of the Eastern churches was made clear by the decrees of the Quinisext Council in 692: bishops must be celibate, but ordained priests, deacons, and subdeacons could continue already established marriages.

In the 10th and 11th centuries, church lands became secularized, and many priests married or lived in concubinage. Not only the practice but also the principles of clerical celibacy were challenged. The first and second LATERAN COUNCILS (1123 and 1139) put an end to the legality of theoretically continent clerical marriages. They declared priestly orders an impediment to valid marriage and vice versa. This is still the official position within ROMAN CATHOLICISM, although exceptions have been made for some men who were married prior to their conversion to Roman Catholicism and then became Catholic priests. Although the SECOND VATICAN COUNCIL (1962–65) permitted a married diaconate, Pope Paul VI issued an ENCYCLICAL, *Sacerdotalis Caelibatus* (June 23, 1967), reaffirming the traditional law of celibacy for priests.

The churches of the REFORMATION (Lutheran, Anglican, Reformed, and others) do not require clerical celibacy. *See also* ASCETICISM; RITUAL; RITES OF PASSAGE.

CELTIC CHURCH, the early Christian church in the British Isles, founded in the 2nd or 3rd century. It contributed to the conversion of the Anglo-Saxons in the 7th century, but its organization gave way to that of Rome. It survived in Wales until the 11th century and in Scotland and Ireland until the 12th.

CELTIC RELIGION, religious beliefs and practices of the ancient Celts.

Because of their great reverence for the art of memory, the pre-Christian Celts themselves left no writings. Other than a few inscriptions, the principal sources of modern information about them are contemporary Greek and Latin writers, notably Poseidonius, Lucan, and Julius Caesar. Insight can also be gleaned from the sagas and myths, particularly of Ireland and Wales, that were recorded by native Christian monks centuries later.

Little is known about the religious beliefs of the Celts of Gaul. They believed in a life after death, for they buried food, weapons, and ornaments with the dead. The DRUIDS, the early Celtic PRIESTHOOD, taught the doctrine of transmigration of souls and discussed the nature and power of the gods. The Irish believed in an otherworld, imagined sometimes as underground and sometimes as islands in the sea. The otherworld was variously called "the Land of the Living," "Delightful Plain," and "Land of the Young" and was believed to be a country where there was no sickness, old age, or death, where happiness lasted forever, and where a hundred years were as one day. But this "delightful plain" was not accessible to all. Donn, god of the dead and ancestor of all the Irish, reigned over Tech Duinn, which was imagined as on or under Bull Island off the Beare Peninsula, and to him all men returned except the happy few.

According to Caesar, the god most honored by the Gauls was "Mercury," and this is confirmed by numerous images and inscriptions. His Celtic name is not explicitly stated, but it is implied in the place-name Lugudunon ("the fort or dwelling of the god Lugus") by which his numerous cult centers were known and from which the modern Lyon, Laon, and Loudun in France, Leiden in The Netherlands, and Legnica in Poland derive. The Irish and Welsh cognates of LUGUS are Lugh and LLEU, respectively, and the traditions concerning these figures mesh with those of the Gaulish god. Caesar's description of the latter as "the inventor of all the arts" might almost have been a paraphrase of Lugh's conventional epithet *samildánach* ("possessed of many talents"). Another important god is CERNUNNOS, the stag-horned, shamanistic Lord of the Animals. Stags play an integral part in the Celtic literature recorded in the early Christian period, apparently embodying the attributes of the SHAMAN. Many other animals, including the raven, the crane, and the bull are accorded divine significance.

Among the female deities, the goddess of mares, variously called EPONA (Gaul), MACHA (Ireland), and RHIANNON (Britain), is a very powerful force, as is the crow goddess Morrígan. These two figures seem to have ruled most closely the fortunes of king and tribe, the former personifying fertility, the latter, death and rebirth.

Goddesses frequently manifested themselves in triple aspects or in groups of three. Examples include the Gallic Matronae, or three mothers; the Irish BRIGITS, who rule over poetry, healing, and metalcraft; and the "great queen" Morrígan, whose three aspects represent death-prophecy, battle-panic, and death-in-battle. According to Lucan, the Gauls also had a triple god in whose honor they practiced HUMAN SACRIFICE. His aspects comprise thunder, war, and a mysterious bull, which may represent fertility.

Celtic worship centered upon the interplay of the "otherworld," or divine element, with the land and the waters. Wells, springs, rivers, and hills were believed to be inhabited by guardian spirits, usually female, and the names of these spirits live on in many place-names still. The land itself was regarded anthropomorphically as feminine. The ocean, which was ruled by the god Manannán, was also, particularly in British and Irish COSMOLOGY, a force of great magic and mystery.

Based on a fluid cosmology in which shape-shifting and magic bonds between humans and other creatures are com-

Graveyard in Al-Qayrawān, Tunisia
Georg Gerster—Photo Researchers

monplace, Celtic myths point to a strong belief in the transmigration of souls. Such artifacts as the Gundestrup Caldron (found in Denmark) and the so-called Paris relief depict scenes of shamanistic ritual, and much of Celtic poetry well into the Christian period reflects a preoccupation with transformations and animal consciousness.

Caesar stated that the Druids avoided manual labor and paid no taxes, so that many were attracted to join the order. They learned great numbers of verses by heart; some studied for as long as 20 years; they thought it wrong to commit their learning to writing but used the Greek alphabet for other purposes. Archaeological finds include post-holes from small, wooden buildings that contained sacred enclosures within. Remains of humans and animals (perhaps victims of sacrifice) also have been discovered in the Celtic areas—some in the vicinity of towns. These sacred buildings were destroyed during the Roman conquest, and Romano-Celtic temples took their place.

Irish cult life revolved around seasonal observances. One of the two major yearly festivals was SAMHAIN (on November 1), which marked the summer's end and served both as the New Year's festival and as the Feast of the Dead. The other was BELTANE, or Bel's Fire (May 1). Both festivals involved huge bonfires. Other, lesser feasts included those of IMBOLC (February 1), the beginning of the spring season sacred to the goddess Brigid, and LUGNASAD (August 1), the feast of the marriage of Lugus and the day of the harvest fair. CHRISTIANITY eventually absorbed and incorporated these great festivals.

CEMETERY, a place set apart for burial or entombment of the dead. Reflecting geography, religious beliefs, social attitudes, and aesthetic and sanitary considerations, cemeteries may be simple or elaborate. They may also be regarded as "holy fields" or prohibited areas. In countries such as Japan and Mexico cemeteries are festival places on certain occasions set aside to honor the dead. In other countries and among other religious groups, they are simple and stark and generally shunned.

In most cultures, providing a place for the dead was originally a family obligation because of the widespread belief that ties of KINSHIP last beyond death. Having a family mausoleum or graveyard is a custom that has endured in many parts of the world. Their locations have often been selected with great care: In China FENG-SHUI ("augury") experts picked sites calculated to provide "good wind and water"; Koreans hired geomancers to divine auspicious locations, out of the range of vision of "baleful spirits." Even when the tribe or the community took over the obligation, burial in the communal graveyard was a jealously guarded privilege. Strangers could dwell in towns and cities but could not be buried there. Special cemeteries for criminals, foreigners, and the poor were set up by many, including the ancient Jews and Romans. In Europe from the medieval period until well into the 19th century, convicted witches, murderers, and suicides were excluded from cemeteries.

Sanitary precautions have influenced the nature and location of cemeteries. Romans and Jews, for example, regarded cemeteries as hazardous or ritually unclean and established their graveyards outside the walls of Rome and Jerusalem. Christians, on the other hand, had no such concern, and, when they were allowed to practice their religion freely, they buried the dead in churches and churchyards.

By the middle of the 18th century the consequences of overcrowded churchyard burial and the lack of adequate space for further burial within city limits had become a matter of public apprehension. In the churchyards, coffins were placed tier above tier in the graves until they were within a few feet (or sometimes even a few inches) of the surface, and the level of the ground was often raised to that of the lower windows of the church. To make room for fresh interments, the sextons had recourse to the surreptitious removal of bones and partially decayed remains, and in some cases the contents of the graves were systematically transferred to pits adjacent to the site, the gravediggers appropriating the coffin plates, handles, and nails to be sold as waste metal. As a result of these practices, the neighborhoods of the churchyards were usually unhealthy and their sight intolerable.

From 1860 churchyard burials have gradually been discontinued in many countries. More common now are memorial parks where the graves may be marked with flat metal markers instead of the customary gravestones. In the United States there continue to be public cemeteries, cooperative cemeteries, church cemeteries, and large, mutually owned cemeteries. In addition to state, county, and municipal cemeteries, the federal government operates a complex of national cemeteries in the United States and abroad for military servicemen and members of their families. In the modern cemetery, lots are sold by the government, religious, commercial, or other organization that has charge. A fee is charged for perpetual care, and a charge is made for opening the grave and other duties performed by the sexton or superintendent. *See also* FUNERARY CUSTOMS.

CENOBITIC MONASTICISM \,se-nə-'bi-tik, ,sē-\, form of MONASTICISM based on "life in common" (Greek: *koinobion*), as distinct from eremetic (IDIORRHYTHMIC) monasticism, the solitary lifestyle of HERMITS. Cenobitic monasticism is characterized by strict discipline, regular worship, and manual work. The Egyptian saint PACHOMIUS was the author of the first cenobitic rule, which was later developed by ST. BASIL THE GREAT. Cenobitic monasticism was introduced in the West by ST. BENEDICT OF NURSIA and became the norm of the BENEDICTINE order. In the East its major centers were the monastery of Stoudios in Constantinople (now Istanbul in Turkey) and several communities on Mount Athos, in Greece.

CENOTE \si-'nō-tē\ (from Yucatec Maya: *ts'onot*), natural well or reservoir, common in the Yucatán Peninsula, associated with PILGRIMAGES and the cult of the rain gods, or CHACS. In ancient times, notably at Chichén Itzá, precious objects, such as jade, sacrificial knives, masks, plates made of gold and copper, and incense and also human beings, including children, were thrown into the cenotes as offerings. A survivor was believed to bring back a message from the gods about the year's crops.

CENTAUR, *Greek* kentauros, in Greek mythology, a race of creatures, part horse and part man, dwelling in the moun-

Centaur fighting a Lapith, detail of a metope of the Parthenon of Athens; in the British Museum
Hirmer Fotoarchiv, Munchen

tains of Thessaly and Arcadia. The centaurs were said to be the offspring of IXION, king of the Lapiths, and the goddess Nephele, whom he had raped under the impression that she was HERA. They were best known for their fight (centauromachy) with the Lapiths, which resulted from their attempt to carry off the bride of PIRITHOUS, son of Ixion. They lost the battle and were driven from Mount Pelion. In later Greek times they were often represented drawing the chariot of the wine god DIONYSUS or bound and ridden by EROS, the god of love, in allusion to their drunken and amorous habits. They were wild, lawless, and inhospitable beings, the antithesis of culture. By contrast the king of the centaurs, CHIRON, was notable for being civilized and gentle, and was named as the tutor of numerous heroes.

In early art they were portrayed as human beings in front, with the body and hindlegs of a horse attached to the back; later, they were men only as far as the waist. There were no female centaurs in classical mythology.

CENTRAL CONFERENCE OF AMERICAN RABBIS (CCAR), organization of North American Reform RABBIS, founded by Rabbi ISAAC MAYER WISE in 1889. The organization is one of the largest publishers of Jewish liturgical matter, publishing Reform prayerbooks, hymnals, and rabbinic manuals. CCAR also publishes a quarterly journal on JUDAISM. Its membership, which consists of more than 1,600 rabbis, is divided into 12 regions covering the United States and Canada, with two additional regions; one is composed of Israel, and the other encompasses all areas not in North America or Israel.

CEPHALUS \'se-fə-ləs\, legendary ancestor of an Attic family, traditionally a great hunter. He was beloved by the goddess Dawn (EOS, or Aurora). With his hound, Laelaps (Hurricane), he overcame the fox of Teumessus that had ravaged Boeotia. The most popular tale about Cephalus in later Greek and Roman literature concerned his wife, Procris.

Cephalus' devotion to hunting aroused in her suspicions that she had a rival, so she followed him. Emerging suddenly from a thicket, she was fatally struck by her husband, who mistook her for his prey. Later legends, made Cephalus the founder of the Ionian island community of Cephallenia and linked him with the ancestry of ODYSSEUS.

CERES \'sir-ēz, 'sē-rēz\, in ROMAN RELIGION, goddess of the growth of food plants, worshiped either alone or in association with the earth goddess TELLUS. At an early date her cult was overlaid by that of the Greek goddess DEMETER, who was also widely worshiped in Sicily. On the advice of the Sibylline Books, a cult of Ceres, Liber, and Libera was introduced into Rome (according to tradition, in 496 BCE) to check a famine. The temple, built on the Aventine Hill in 493 BCE, became a center of plebeian religious and political activities and also became known for the splendor of its works of art. Destroyed by fire in 31 BCE, it was restored by Augustus. The three chief festivals of Ceres' cult all followed Greek lines.

CERINTHUS \sə-'rin-thəs\ (fl. c. 100 CE), Christian heretic whose errors, according to the theologian Irenaeus, led the apostle John to write his NEW TESTAMENT Gospel.

Cerinthus was probably born a Jew in Egypt. He was a teacher and founded a short-lived sect of Jewish Christians with Gnostic tendencies. He apparently taught that the world was created by ANGELS, from one of whom the Jews received their imperfect Law. The only New Testament writing that he accepted was the Gospel of Matthew. Cerinthus taught that JESUS, the offspring of JOSEPH and MARY, received Christ at his BAPTISM as a divine power revealing the unknown Father. This Christ left Jesus before the Passion and the RESURRECTION. Cerinthus admitted CIRCUMCISION and the SABBATH and held a form of millenarianism (see MILLENNIALISM).

CERNUNNOS \ker-'nü-nōs\ (Celtic: "Horned One"), deity in CELTIC RELIGION who was presumably worshiped as the "Lord of Wild Things." Cernunnos may have had a variety of names in different parts of the Celtic world, but his attributes were generally consistent. He wore stag antlers and was sometimes accompanied by a stag and by a sacred ram-horned serpent that was also a deity in its own right. He wore and sometimes also held a torque, the sacred neck ornament of Celtic gods and heroes. The earliest known depiction of a possible Cernunnos-type is found at Val Camonica, in northern Italy, which was under Celtic occupation from about 400 BCE. He was also portrayed on the Gundestrup Caldron, a ritual vessel found at Gundestrup in Jutland, Denmark, dating to about the 1st century BCE.

Cernunnos was worshiped primarily in Britain, although there are also traces of his cult in Ireland. The Christian church seems to have used him as a symbol of the ANTI-CHRIST; such a horned god figured in Christian ICONOGRAPHY and medieval manuscripts.

CHAC \'chäk\, Mayan god of rain, especially important in the Yucatán region of Mexico where he was depicted in Classic times (from about 100–900 CE) with protruding fangs, large round eyes, and a proboscis-like nose.

Like other major Mayan gods, Chac also appeared as four gods, the Chacs. The four gods were associated with the cardinal directions and their colors: white, north; red, east; black, west; and yellow, south.

At Chichén Itzá, in post-Classic times (about 900–1519 CE), HUMAN SACRIFICE became associated with the rain god, and the priests who held the arms and legs of the sacrificial victims were called *chac*s.

CHAKRA \'chə-krə, 'chä-\, *also spelled* cakra, *Sanskrit* cakra \'chə-krə\ ("wheel"), psychic-energy centers of the body. In certain forms of HINDUISM and BUDDHISM (see VAJRAYĀNA), chakras are conceived of as focal points where psychic forces and bodily functions merge and interact with each other. Among the 88,000 chakras in the human body, 6 major ones located roughly along the spinal cord and another located just above the crown of the skull are of principal importance. Each of these 7 major chakras (in Buddhism, 4) is associated with a specific color, shape, sense organ, natural element, deity, and MANTRA. Along with the heart chakra, the most important chakras are often considered to be the *mūlādhāra*, located at the base of the spine, and the *sahasrāra*, at the top of the head. The *mūlādhāra* encircles a mysterious divine potency (KUNDALINĪ) that the individual attempts, by yogic techniques, to raise from chakra to chakra until it reaches the *sahasrāra* and self-illumination results.

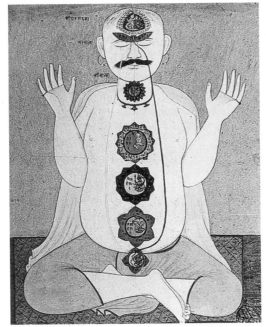
Hindu diagram of chakras
The Granger Collection

CHAKRAVARTIN \'chə-krə-'vär-tin\, *also spelled* Cakravartin, *Sanskrit* Cakravartin, the ancient Indian conception of the world ruler, derived from the Sanskrit *cakra*, "wheel," and *vartin*, "one who turns." Thus, a chakravartin may be understood as a ruler "whose movements are unobstructed."

Sources in BUDDHISM and JAINISM distinguish three types of secular chakravartin: *cakravāla cakravartin*, a king who rules over all four of the continents posited by ancient Indian cosmography; *dvīpa cakravartin*, a ruler who governs only one of those continents and is, therefore, less powerful than the first; and *pradeśa cakravartin*, a monarch who leads the people of only a part of a continent, the equivalent of a local king. Buddhist and Jain philosophers of this

193

period conflated the notion of the universal monarch with the idea of a king of righteousness and maintainer of moral law. The chakravartin was considered to be the secular counterpart of a Buddha.

CHALCEDON, COUNCIL OF \\'kal-si-,dän, kal-'sē-dən\\, the fourth ecumenical council of the Christian church, held in Chalcedon (modern Kadiköy, Turkey) in 451. It was attended by about 520 bishops or their representatives and was the largest and best-documented of the early councils. It approved the creed of Nicaea (325), the creed of Constantinople (381; subsequently known as the NICENE CREED), two letters of CYRIL OF ALEXANDRIA against NESTORIUS, which insisted on the unity of divine and human persons in Christ, and the *Tome* of POPE LEO I confirming two distinct natures in Christ and rejecting the MONOPHYSITE doctrine that Christ had only one nature.

Besides reinforcing canons of earlier church councils as well as declarations of some local SYNODS, the council issued disciplinary decrees affecting monks and clergy and declared Jerusalem and Constantinople patriarchates. The authority of the PATRIARCH of Constantinople—the "New Rome," where the emperor and the senate also resided—began with canon 28 of the Council of Chalcedon. Technically, the patriarch of Constantinople occupied the second rank—after the bishop of Rome—in a hierarchy of five major PRIMATES, which included also the patriarchs of Alexandria, Antioch, and Jerusalem.

CHALCHIUHTLICUE \\,chäl-chē-üt-'lē-kwā\\, *also spelled* Chalchihuitlicue (Nahuatl: "She Having a Skirt of Precious Green Stone"), *also called* Matlalcueye \\,mät-läl-'kwā-yā\\ ("She Having a Green Skirt"), Aztec goddess of rivers, lakes, streams, and other fresh waters. Wife (in some myths, sister) of the rain god TLALOC, in Aztec COSMOLOGY she ruled over the fourth of the previous suns; in her reign, corn was first used. Like other water deities, she was often associated with serpents.

CHALICE, cup used in the celebration of the Christian EUCHARIST. Both the statement of ST. PAUL about "the cup of blessing which we bless" (1 Corinthians 10:16) and the accounts in the first three Gospels indicate that special rites of consecration attended the use of the chalice from the beginning. It was not until the recognition of

Chalchiuhtlicue, carved stone, 4th–9th century CE
Giraudon—Art Resource

CHRISTIANITY by the Roman Empire in the 4th century that silver and gold became the usual materials for the chalice. In the Middle Ages the legend of the Holy Grail surrounded the origins of the eucharistic chalice with a magical aura.

CH'AN: *see* ZEN.

CHANG TAO-LING \\'jäŋ-'daü-'liŋ\\, *Pinyin* Zhang Daoling, *also called* Chang Ling (b. 34? CE, P'ei, Kiangsu, China—d. 156?, Hanchung), the founder and the first patriarch of the Taoist church in China.

Chang settled in the Szechwan area and there studied the TAO ("Way") sometime during the reign (125–144) of Emperor Shun-ti

"Chalice of Antioch," partially gilded silver, 4th–5th century CE
By courtesy of The Metropolitan Museum of Art, The Cloisters Collection, New York City

of the Eastern Han dynasty. Later he composed a Taoist work to propagate his cult, which attracted many followers among both the Chinese and the indigenous ethnic groups in Szechwan. Like other Taoists of his day Chang Ling promised physical immortality and longevity to his followers, but unlike the others, he emphasized the importance of religious organization. Thus he founded the first Taoist church, the T'IEN-SHIH TAO, or Way of the Celestial Masters, popularly known as the Way of the FIVE PECKS OF RICE because it required its members to contribute five pecks of rice a year, presumably for the upkeep of the organization.

Chang Ling's church was particularly attractive because of its emphasis on FAITH HEALING. Illness, it taught, was a result of sinful-mindedness, which could be most effectively cured by making confession to the minister in the church; purification of the soul formed the solid foundation of physical health.

Probably in imitation of the Han imperial throne, the patriarchate of the church was made hereditary. It passed from Chang Ling to his son Chang Heng and then to his distinguished grandson Chang Lu; they were collectively known as the Three Changs. Chang Lu succeeded even in establishing a Taoist theocratic state in Han-chung (modern Szechwan and part of Shensi) toward the end of the Han dynasty (c. 188–215). The basic text used for religious instruction in the Taoist church was the TAO-TE CHING of LAO-TZU; however, the famous Hsiang-erh commentary to Lao-tzu, traditionally attributed to Chang Ling, shows that this ancient philosophical treatise was interpreted to suit the religious needs of his church.

CHANG TSAI \\'jäŋ-'dzī\\, *Pinyin* Zhang Zai, *Wade-Giles romanization* Chang Heng-ch'ü \\-'həŋ-'chū̄\\ (b. 1020, Ch'ang-an, China—d. 1077, China), realist philosopher of the Sung dynasty, a leader in giving NEO-CONFUCIANISM a metaphysical foundation.

The son of a magistrate, Chang studied BUDDHISM and TAOISM but found his true inspiration in the Confucian

Classics. In his chief work, *Cheng-meng* ("Correct Discipline for Beginners"), he declared that the universe is a unity with myriad aspects, and all existence is an eternal integration and disintegration. *Ch'i* ("matter") is identified with ultimate reality. When *ch'i* is influenced by yang (male) elements, it floats and rises, dispersing its substance. When the yin (female) element is prevalent, *ch'i* sinks and falls, thus condensing and forming the concrete things of the world.

The one basic virtue is JEN ("humaneness"); in its various manifestations (*i.e.*, in various human relations) *jen* may become FILIAL PIETY toward parents or respect for an elder brother. Man was once *ch'i*, like all other aspects of the universe, and he has an original nature that is one with all the things of the world. His physical nature, however, derives from the physical form into which his *ch'i* has been dispersed. Moral self-cultivation consists in attempting to do one's duty as a member of society and as a member of the universe. One does not try to prolong or extend life. The superior person understands that "life entails no gain nor death any loss."

Chang influenced some of the most eminent later Neo-Confucian thinkers; the brothers Ch'eng Hao (1032–85) and Ch'eng I (1033–1107) were his pupils. His theory of mind was adopted by the great philosopher CHU HSI (1130–1200), and Wang Fu-chih (1619–92) developed Chang's philosophy into a system that has come to be recognized as one of the major achievements of Chinese thought.

CHANNING, WILLIAM ELLERY \'cha-niŋ\ (b. April 7, 1780, Newport, R.I.—d. Oct. 2, 1842, Bennington, Vt., U.S.), American author and moralist, Congregationalist and, later, Unitarian clergyman. Channing was a leading figure in the development of New England Transcendentalism and of organized attempts in the United States to eliminate slavery, drunkenness, poverty, and war.

Channing studied theology in Newport and at Harvard and soon became a successful preacher in various churches in the Boston area. From June 1, 1803, until his death he was minister of the Federal Street Church, Boston. Preferring to avoid abstruse points of doctrine, he preached morality, CHARITY, and Christian responsibilities. He became a popular speaker on ceremonial occasions and reached an even larger audience by writing for liberal Boston periodicals, one of which was *The Christian Disciple* (from 1824 called *The Christian Examiner*). In 1815 he was attacked by the orthodox Calvinist periodical *The Panoplist*, whose editor, Jedidiah Morse, denounced the Boston clergy as "Unitarian" rather than Christian. During the next five years Channing issued several defenses of his position, especially "Unitarian Christianity," a sermon delivered at an ORDINATION in Baltimore in 1819.

Reluctantly accepting the label of UNITARIANISM, he described his faith as "a rational and amiable system, against which no man's understanding, or conscience, or charity, or piety revolts." He did not wish to found a denomination, believing that a Unitarian orthodoxy would be just as oppressive as any other, but he formed (1820) a conference of liberal Congregational ministers, later (May 1825) reorganized as the American Unitarian Association.

Channing sympathized with several social and educational reform movements but did not believe that society could be improved by collective action. He denied that government—the only legitimate function of which was, in his view, maintaining public order—could advance the moral sensibility of the human race.

CHANUKAH: *see* HANUKKAH.

CHAOS, in early Greek COSMOLOGY, either the primeval EMPTINESS of the universe before things came into being or the abyss of Tartarus, the Underworld. Both concepts occur in the *Theogony* of Hesiod (*c.* 700 BCE). First there was Chaos in Hesiod's system, then GAEA and EROS. Chaos, however, did not generate Gaea; the offspring of Chaos were Erebus (Darkness) and NYX (Night).

In the later cosmologies Chaos generally designated the original state of things, however conceived. The modern meaning of the word is derived from Ovid, who saw Chaos as the original disordered and formless mass, from which the maker of the Cosmos produced the ordered universe. This concept of Chaos also was applied to the interpretation of the creation story in GENESIS 1 (to which it is not native) by the early CHURCH FATHERS.

CHAPLAIN, originally a priest or minister who had charge of a chapel, now a member of the clergy who is assigned to a special ministry. The title dates to the 8th century.

"Chaplain" owes its origin to the half-cape (Latin: *cappella*) of ST. MARTIN OF TOURS, which was the most renowned of the saints' relics owned by the Frankish kings of the Merovingian and Carolingian dynasties. The *cappella* gave its name to the royal oratory or chapel, as well as to the relics' custodians, the *cappellani*, or chaplains—royally appointed clerics who lived on the palace grounds and performed divine services for the court. In their duties the chaplains gradually became direct servants of the monarch and advisers in both ecclesiastical and secular matters.

The practice of kings appointing their own chaplains spread throughout western Christendom. Many of the royal chaplains were appointed to bishoprics and the highest offices in the church; and down to the present day the British monarchs have appointed their own royal chaplains.

In modern usage the term *chaplain* is not confined to any particular church or denomination. Clergy and ministers appointed to a variety of institutions and corporate bodies—such as cemeteries, prisons, hospitals, schools, colleges, universities, embassies, legations, and armed forces—usually are called chaplains.

Chaplains serve in the armed forces of most countries, generally as commissioned officers who are not required to bear arms. Protestant, Roman Catholic, and Jewish chaplains serve in the armed forces of the United States. A chaplain in the U.S. military must furnish or arrange for religious services and ministrations, advise on matters pertaining to religion and morality, administer religious education, and serve as counselor and friend to the personnel of the command, including those personnel who do not belong to his religious affiliation.

CHARISMA, attribute of awesome power and capacity ascribed by followers to the person and personality of extraordinarily magnetic leaders. Such leaders may be political and secular as well as religious. The term came into scholarly usage primarily through the works of the German sociologist MAX WEBER (1864–1920), especially his *Wirtschaft und Gesellschaft* (1921; *On Law in Economy and Society*), in which he postulated that charismatic authority was a form of authority distinct from those of tradition and law. Weber considered charisma to be essentially irrational.

CHARITY, in Christian thought, the highest form of love, signifying the reciprocal love between God and man that is made manifest in unselfish love of one's fellow men. ST. PAUL's classical description of charity is found in the NEW TESTAMENT (1 Corinthians 13). In Christian theology, charity (a translation of the Greek word *agapē*, also meaning "love") is most eloquently shown in the life, teachings, and death of JESUS CHRIST. ST. THOMAS AQUINAS identified charity as "the foundation or root" of the other Christian virtues.

Although the controversies of the REFORMATION dealt more with the definition of faith than with either hope or charity, the Reformers identified the uniqueness of God's *agapē* for man as unmerited love; therefore, they required that charity, as man's love for man, be based not upon the desirability of its object but upon the transformation of its subject through the power of divine *agapē*.

CHARON \'kar-ən, -,än\, in Greek mythology, the son of Erebus (Darkness) and NYX (Night), whose duty it was to ferry over the Rivers STYX and Acheron the souls of the deceased. In payment he received the coin that was placed in the mouth of the corpse at burial. In art Charon was represented as a grisly old man. In Etruscan he was known as Charun and appeared as a death DEMON, armed with a hammer. Eventually he came to be regarded as the image of death and of the world below. As such he survives in Charos the ANGEL of death in modern Greek folklore.

CHEMOSH \'kē-,mäsh\, ancient West Semitic deity, revered by the MOABITES as their supreme god. Little is known about Chemosh; although King SOLOMON of Israel built a SANCTUARY to him (1 Kings 11:7), the shrine was later abolished by King JOSIAH (2 Kings 23:13). The goddess ASTARTE was probably the cult partner of Chemosh. On the famous Moabite Stone, Chemosh received mention as the deity who brought victory over the Israelites to the Moabites.

CH'ENG-CHU SCHOOL \'chəŋ-'jü\, *Pinyin* Cheng-Zhu, *also called* Li-hsüeh \'lē-'shwe\ (Chinese: "School of Universal Principles"), *or* Tao-hsüeh \'daù-\ ("School of True Way"), Chinese school of NEO-CONFUCIAN philosophy in which cultivation of the self was integrated with social ethics and moral metaphysics; it derives its name from its leading philosophers, Ch'eng I and CHU HSI. Ch'eng I taught that the way to acquire knowledge of basic truths (LI) was to investigate those things in the world in which it is present; this investigation could take the form of induction, deduction, the study of history, or even political activities. Under the guidance of Chu Hsi, who maintained that moral cultivation entailed the rational investigation of all things in order fully to comprehend their essential principle (*li*), the school expanded to become the Rationalist school of Chinese philosophy, which dominated official circles until the Republican Revolution of 1911. Education, to the thinkers of this school, meant a self-cultivation of moral consciousness, the ultimate extent of which was the inner experience of feeling at one with universal principles. These men also made a commitment to reconstruct a moral society—to them the only conceivable foundation for good government. With missionary-like zeal, they engaged in propagation of this true way and formed moral-intellectual fellowships. The Ch'eng-Chu school was the primary opponent of the HSIN-HSÜEH (Lu-Wang) school, which encouraged a more introspective approach.

CH'ENG HAO AND CH'ENG I \'chəŋ-'haù . . . 'chəŋ-'ē\, Ch'eng I *also spelled* (Wade-Giles romanization) Ch'eng Yi, *Pinyin* Cheng Hao and Cheng Yi (respectively b. 1032 CE,

Honan, China—d. 1085, Honan; b. 1033, Honan—d. 1107, Honan), brothers who developed NEO-CONFUCIANISM into an organized school of philosophy. Ch'eng Hao influenced the idealist school of Neo-Confucianism, while Ch'eng I influenced the development of the rationalist school.

Ch'eng Hao was interested in both BUDDHISM and TAOISM as a young man. Later he studied CONFUCIANISM, passed his civil service examinations, and attained high office; but because he opposed the reforms of the innovator Wang An-shih (1021–86), he was dismissed from the government. He joined his brother in Honan, and a circle of disciples gathered around them.

After Ch'eng I passed his civil service examinations he served briefly as Imperial tutor (1069–70), but his stern conception of morality soon alienated those around him and he resigned. For most of his life he declined high office even as he criticized those in power. As a result, in 1097 his land was confiscated, his teachings barred, and he was banished to Fu-chou, in southwest China. Pardoned three years later, he was again censured in 1103. He was pardoned a second time in 1106, shortly before his death.

The two brothers built their philosophies primarily on the concept of LI—defined as the basic force, universal law, or truth underlying and governing all existence—an idea they brought to Neo-Confucianism from Buddhist and Taoist writings. While both agreed that exhaustive study of *li* is the best way to spiritual cultivation, Ch'eng Hao stressed calm introspection and taught that in his original state man was united with the universe, while Ch'eng I—whose philosophy was originally called Tao-hsüeh (School of True Way) but came to be called LI-HSÜEH (School of Universal Principle)—emphasized that the way to discover *li* is to investigate the myriad things of the universe in which *li* is present. Ch'eng I espoused many methods of investigation—induction, deduction, the study of history and other disciplines, and participation in human affairs.

Ch'eng Hao's stress on meditation influenced the later idealist school of Neo-Confucianism founded by LU HSIANG-SHAN (1139–93) and WANG YANG-MING (1472–1529). A decade after Ch'eng I's death CHU HSI (1130–1200) began to expand Ch'eng I's ideas into what came to be called the Ch'eng-Chu (after its two most important exponents) rationalist school of Chinese philosophy; it dominated official circles until the Republican Revolution of 1911.

CHENG-I TAO \'jəŋ-'ē-'daù\, *Pinyin* Zhengyidao (Chinese: "Way of Orthodox Unity"), Taoist sect, established during the end of the Sung Period (960–1279). During the centuries preceding the 1200s, the T'IEN-SHIH TAO (Way of the Celestial Masters), centered at Lung-hu Shan (Dragon-Tiger Mountain), had been eclipsed by the prestige of MAO SHAN. A revitalization occurred, however, when the 30th celestial master, Chang Chi-hsien, was four times summoned to court by the Sung emperor Hui-tsung, who hoped for support for his threatened reign. Chang Chi-hsien was credited with a renovation of the ancient sect, thereafter called Cheng-i tao, and with the introduction of the influential rites of the "five thunders" (*wu-lei*) into Taoist liturgy.

CHEN-JEN \'jən-'rən\, *Pinyin* zhenren (Chinese: "realized, perfected, or true man"), in TAOISM, a god or deified mortal; the term has been the official title of the head of the Cheng-i Taoist sect since the late 13th century.

The Taoist sage CHUANG-TZU used the term to refer to the Taoist ideal man who had achieved immortality and was immune to earthly desires and dangers.

CHEN TAO \\'jən-'daủ\\ (Chinese: "True Way"), one of the most recent and highly publicized of the new religions in Taiwan, founded by Chen Hong-min in Pei-pu, Hsin-chu county, Taiwan, in 1993.

Chen was a former professor of sociology at Chianan College of Pharmacology and Science when he received instruction from Chen Yu-hsia, a man he said was one of God's representatives on earth. With guidance from his mentor, Chen founded a religion that is an eclectic mixture of BUDDHISM, popular religion, CHRISTIANITY, and New Age Western cults with belief in extraterrestrial intervention in human affairs. Chen laid out a complex theology based on ideas of spiritual energy—a variation of Chinese *ch'i-kung* thought—modifying traditional Chinese popular ideas in accordance with his reading of Western physics and Asian and Western ideas of demonology. Preaching that much of the world is dominated by evil spirits, he integrated Christian millennialist and eschatological ideas into his theology, calling himself a prophet who was able to chart the course of the coming conflagration and the road to individual salvation. Pei-pu was the chosen place because, according to Chen, it was a place where spiritual energy created by God would flow from heaven to earth.

Chen developed his cult, published texts and works on his doctrine, and, according to some sources, convinced his followers to give him between $30,000 and $60,000 to gain passage aboard the spaceships—disguised as clouds—that would take them away after landing on earth in 1999. He also persuaded these followers to move to San Dimas, Calif., U.S., to await God's coming; they migrated in 1995. He then became convinced that Garland, Texas, would be the place where God would come, for to his ears "Garland" sounded like "Godland." He and his followers then moved to Texas in 1997.

Chen predicted that God would announce his plans and materialize on earth in human form, recognizable to Chen, on March 31, 1998. Before his incarnation—or, as Chen believed, simultaneous multi-incarnation—God would announce his formal SECOND COMING on channel 18 on television on March 25. When the day came and nothing happened, Chen revised his predictions. In the weeks that followed he relocated his cult, and many of the members returned to Taiwan or applied for legal immigrant status in the United States. *See also* NEW RELIGIOUS MOVEMENTS; MILLENNIALISM.

CHEN YESSU CHIAO-HUEI \\'jən-'ye-'sə-'chyaủ-'hwā\\ (Chinese: "True Jesus Church"), Chinese religious movement that evolved as a result of the Pentecostal charismatic revivals (1900–20) in the United States.

In 1917 a number of Christians from Shantung (Shandong) province in northeastern China listened to charismatic missionaries preaching, obtained materials, and then returned to Beijing where they began a church. The new church was built upon the teachings of the Pentecostal and Holiness churches in the United States but remained fiercely independent. This new church, the True Jesus Church, developed a theology that centered on the works of the HOLY SPIRIT as reflected in speaking in tongues, full immersion BAPTISM, and worship on the Hebrew SABBATH. The church also developed its own polity. The True Jesus Church expanded to the provinces along the China coast during the late 1910s and the 1920s and then took root in Taiwan in the late 1920s and the interior of the mainland in the late 1940s. After the Chinese Civil War (1945–49), the church was persecuted, and its community virtually disap-

peared from the mainland. However, Taiwan proved to be a safe haven, and the church developed there among Taiwanese and Hakka Chinese, among newly arrived immigrants from the Chinese mainland, and among the non-Chinese indigenous peoples of the island. It has become one of the largest independent churches operating on Taiwan and also has churches in the United States. In recent years the church's leaders have tried to renew their church in mainland China.

CHERUB, *plural* cherubim, in Jewish, Christian, and Islamic literature, a celestial winged being with human, animal, or birdlike characteristics who functions as a throne bearer of the deity. Derived from ancient Middle Eastern MYTHOLOGY and ICONOGRAPHY, these celestial beings serve important liturgical and intercessory functions in the hierarchy of ANGELS. The term most likely derives from the Akkadian *kāribu*, or *kūribu* (from the verb *karābu*, meaning "to pray," or "to bless").

Within JUDAISM, the OLD TESTAMENT descriptions of the cherubim emphasize their supernatural mobility and their cultic role as throne bearers of God, rather than any intercessory functions. In CHRISTIANITY the cherubim are ranked among the higher orders of angels and, as celestial attendants of God, continually praise him. Known as *karūbiyūn* in ISLAM, the cherubim continuously praise God by repeating the *tasbīḥ* ("Glory to Allāh") and dwell in peace in an area of the heavens that is inaccessible to attacks from IBLĪS, the devil.

CH'I \\'chē\\, *Pinyin* qi (Chinese: "breath," or "force"), in Chinese philosophy, the ethereal substance of which everything is composed. Early Taoist philosophers and alchemists regarded *ch'i* as a vital force associated with the breath and bodily fluids and developed techniques to alter and control the movement of *ch'i* within the body; their aim was to achieve physical longevity and spiritual power. Manipulation of *ch'i* is a central aspect of Chinese meditation, medicine, and MARTIAL ARTS.

Neo-Confucian philosophers of the Sung dynasty (960–1279 CE) regarded *ch'i* as emanating from the Great Ultimate (T'ai-chi) by way of LI, the prime ordering principle of the universe. This school, whose ideas predominate in traditional Chinese thought, held that *ch'i* was transformed through the yang (active) and yin (passive) modes into the Five Elements (*wu-hsing*; wood, metal, earth, water, and fire), which in turn formed the basic constituents of the physical universe. (*See also* YIN-YANG.)

CHICOMECOATL \\,chē-kō-mā-'kō-ä-təl\\ (Nahuatl: "Seven Snakes"), *also called* Xilonen ("[She] Went About/Lived [as an] Ear of Green Corn"), Aztec goddess of sustenance and corn, often the consort of the corn god, Centéotl, and one of the most ancient and important goddesses in the Valley of Mexico. Chicomecoatl is depicted with her body and face painted red, wearing a rectangular headdress or pleated fan of red paper, and often holding a double ear of corn in each hand.

CHIH-I \\'jə-'ē\\, *Pinyin* Zhiyi, *also called* Chih-k'ai \\-'kī\\ (b. 538, Hunan province, China—d. 597, Mount T'ien-t'ai, Chekiang province), Buddhist monk, founder of the eclectic T'ien-t'ai Buddhist sect, which was named for his monastery on Mount T'ien-t'ai in Chekiang, China. His name is frequently but erroneously given as Chih-k'ai.

Orphaned at 17, Chih-i turned to the monastic life. He

was a disciple of the great Buddhist master Hui-ssu from 560 to 567. Chih-i was intimately associated with the imperial government, first with the Ch'en dynasty in southern China and then with the Sui dynasty, which eventually reunified the country.

Confronted with the many varieties of Buddhist thought that existed in his time, Chih-i exhibited skill at compromise and classification. He regarded the various Buddhist doctrines as true and assumed they had all been present in the mind of Śākyamuni (the BUDDHA GOTAMA) from the time of his enlightenment. According to Chih-i, the Buddha unfolded his teachings in five periods, taking into account the capacity of his listeners: as they became more enlightened, they could absorb more profound doctrines. Chih-i believed the LOTUS SUTRA to be the Buddha's most advanced teaching, and Chih-i helped establish it as the most popular SCRIPTURE of east Asia.

He criticized both those who indulged in a purely intellectualized BUDDHISM and those who in reaction practiced a religion without a doctrinal base. His sect, which claimed more than 5,000,000 adherents in Japan in the late 20th century, was the leading sect in China in the 8th and 9th centuries.

CH'I-KUNG \\'chē-'gùŋ\\, *Pinyin* qigong ("ch'i work," or "working with the energy of ch'i"), loose set of physical and mystical techniques designed to reestablish bodily and spiritual health by regulating and manipulating the energy known as *ch'i*. These practices are related to ancient traditions often associated with TAOISM. It is, however, not exclusively Taoist and has similarities with traditional Chinese medicine, "inner alchemy," the martial arts, and T'ai-chi ch'uan. Having become wildly popular in post-Maoist China and other Chinese communities, it has taken on the characteristics of a revivalistic HEALING CULT promoted by various charismatic *ch'i-kung* masters.

CHILAM BALAM, BOOKS OF \\chē-'läm-bä-'läm\\, documents written in Yucatec MAYA with Spanish characters during the 17th and 18th centuries. A principal source of knowledge of ancient Mayan custom, the 12 surviving manuscripts contain myth, PROPHECY, medical lore, calendrical information, and historical chronicles. Those of Chumayel, Tizimín, and Maní (towns where they were written) are particularly important sources for scholars studying Mayan history. *Chilam Balam* means "spokesman of the jaguar."

CH'I-LIN \\'chē-'lin, -'lēn\\, *Pinyin* qilin, in Chinese mythology, a kind of unicorn whose rare appearance often coincides with the imminent birth or death of a sage or illustrious ruler. A *ch'i-lin* usually has a single horn on its forehead, a yellow belly, a multicolored back, the hooves of a horse, the body of a deer, and the tail of an ox. It is too gentle to tread upon or eat living vegetation.

The first *ch'i-lin* is said to have appeared in the garden of the legendary Huang-ti (Yellow Emperor) in 2697 BCE. Some three centuries later a pair of *ch'i-lin* were reported in the capital of Emperor YAO. Both events bore testimony to the benevolent nature of the rulers. A *ch'i-lin* was said to have appeared to the pregnant mother of CONFUCIUS, whereupon she coughed up an inscribed jade tablet that foretold the fu-

ture greatness of her son. Confucius' death was foreshadowed when a *ch'i-lin* was injured by a charioteer.

CHIMERA \\kī-'mir-ə, ki-\\, in Greek MYTHOLOGY, a fire-breathing female monster resembling a lion in the forepart, a goat in the middle, and a dragon behind. She devastated Caria and Lycia until she was slain by BELLEROPHON. In art the Chimera is usually represented as a lion with a goat's head in the middle of its back. The word is now used to denote a fantastic idea or figment of the imagination.

Chimera, interior of a black-figure cup, 7th century BCE
Deutsche Fotothek

CHINESE CLASSICS: *see* FIVE CLASSICS.

CHINESE RITES CONTRO-VERSY, a 17th–18th-century argument originating in China among ROMAN CATHOLIC missionaries about whether the ceremonies honoring CONFUCIUS and family ancestors were incompatible with Christian belief. The JESUITS believed that they probably were not and that they could be tolerated within certain limits; the DOMINICANS and FRANCISCANS took the opposite view and carried the issue to Rome. In 1645 the Congregation for the Propagation of the Faith, on the basis of a brief submitted by the Dominicans, condemned the rites. After considering the arguments of the Jesuits, however, the same congregation lifted the ban in 1656.

The continuing controversy was considered by eight popes and by the K'ang-hsi emperor. By the end of the 17th century, many Dominicans and Franciscans had come to share the Jesuits' opinion, but Rome disagreed. In a decree of 1704, reinforced by a bull in 1715, Clement XI banned the rites. Benedict XIV in 1742 reaffirmed the prohibition and forbade further debate. But a decree of Dec. 8, 1939, authorized Christians to take part in ceremonies honoring Confucius and to observe the ancestral rites. The SECOND VATICAN COUNCIL (1962–65) proclaimed the principle of admitting native ceremonies into the liturgy of the church whenever possible. *See also* MATTEO RICCI.

CHING-TSO \\'jiŋ-'dzwó\\, *Pinyin* jingzuo (Chinese: "quiet sitting"), meditation technique associated with NEO-CONFU-CIANISM. Influenced by both Taoist and Ch'an (ZEN) Buddhist forms of meditation, it involves sitting in a relaxed fashion with the intent of quieting the flow of discursive thought and the attainment of the original goodness of human nature (the condition of Confucian sagehood).

CHIRON \\'kī-,rän\\, in Greek mythology, leader of the CENTAURS, the son of the god CRONUS and Philyra, a nymph; his parentage set him apart from the other centaurs, who were sired by IXION. Chiron lived at the foot of Mount Pelion in Thessaly and was famous for his wisdom and knowledge of medicine. Many Greek heroes, including HERACLES, ACHILLES, JASON, and ASCLEPIUS, were instructed by him. Accidentally pierced by a poisoned arrow shot by Heracles, he suffered agony from the festering wound until he renounced his immortality in favor of PROMETHEUS and was placed among the stars as the constellation Sagittarius.

CHISHTĪYA \chish-'tē-ə\, Muslim SUFI order in India and Pakistan, named for Chisht, the village near Herat (in modern Afghanistan) in which the founder of the order, Abū Isḥāq of Syria, settled. The Chishtīya were brought to India by Khawāja Muʿīn al-Dīn Chishtī in the 12th century. Since the 16th century, Muʿīn al-Dīn's shrine in Ajmer, Rājasthān, has become the most frequented Muslim PILGRIMAGE site in the subcontinent; it also attracts Hindu devotees.

During the period of the Great SHAYKHS (c.1200–1356), a centralized network of Chishtīya monasteries (khanqahs) were established in the northern provinces of Rājputāna, the Punjab, and Uttar Pradesh. From the 14th century, these monasteries were provincial institutions where branches of the order took root, notably the Ṣābirīya branch in the 15th century at Rudawlī and the Niẓāmīya, revived in 18th century Delhi. Many of the teachers of the DEOBAND SCHOOL, founded in the 19th century, were Chishtīs.

Great emphasis was originally placed by the Chishtīya on the Sufi doctrine of the unity of being (waḥdat al-wujūd), oneness with God. Thus, material goods were rejected as distracting from the contemplation of God; no connection with the state was permitted; and pacifism was embraced. The recitation of the names of God, both aloud and silently (dhikr jahrī, dhikr khafī), formed the cornerstone of Chishtī practice. The order is still widely known for the performance of moving qawwālī songs at its assemblies. The order's prominence during the Mughal era (1520–1857) led it to permit ownership of property and other modifications of former practice.

CHʿIU CHʿU-CHI \'jyō-'jü-'jē\ (monastic name), Pinyin Qiu Chuji, original name Chʿang-chʿun \'chäŋ-'chŭn\, Pinyin Changchun (b. 1148, Chi-hsia, China—d. 1227, Beijing), Taoist monk and alchemist who journeyed from China to visit Genghis Khan, the famed Mongol conqueror, at his encampment north of the Hindu Kush mountains. The narrative of Chʿiu Chʿu-chi's expedition, The Travels of an Alchemist, written by his disciple-companion Li Chih-chʿang, vividly depicts the land and people between the Great Wall of China and Kābul (now in Afghanistan) and between the Yellow Sea and the Aral Sea.

Chʿiu Chʿu-chi was a member of a Taoist sect known for extreme ASCETICISM and for the doctrine of hsing-ming, which held that man's natural state had been lost but could be recovered through prescribed practices. In 1188 he was invited to give religious instruction to the Juchen dynasty emperor Shih Tsung, then reigning over northern China.

In 1215 the Mongols captured Beijing, and in 1219 Genghis Khan sent for Chʿiu Chʿu-chi. Having received an invitation from the Khan's brother, Temüge, who lived in northeastern Mongolia, he left Beijing, crossed the Gobi Desert, and visited Temüge's camp near Buir Nor. Chʿiu Chʿu-chi arrived in Samarkand, now in Uzbekistan, in midwinter (1221–22) and reached the Khan's Hindu Kush mountain camp in spring. He returned to Beijing in 1224.

CHʿOE SI-HYŎNG \'chœ-'sē-'hyəŋ\ (b. 1827, Korea—d. 1898, Seoul [now in South Korea]), second leader of the Korean apocalyptic antiforeign Tonghak (Chʿŏndogyo) religion, who helped organize the underground network that spread the sect after the 1864 execution of its founder, Chʿoe Che-u, for fomenting rebellion.

After Chʿoe Che-u's death, Chʿoe Si-hyŏng published in 1880 and 1881 the first two Tonghak SCRIPTURES, in which he expanded his predecessor's idea that all men are equal before heaven and must serve heaven, a principle onto which he grafted an ideal of public service. Meanwhile, he continued to preach the necessity of Korea's becoming as strong as the Western imperialist powers. In 1892 he mobilized his followers to stage a demonstration under the banner of "Expel the West, Expel the Japanese, and Inculcate Righteousness," and in 1894 he led the so-called Tonghak Revolt against the "corrupt government." The uprising was viciously suppressed, and in 1898 Chʿoe Si-hyŏng was finally arrested and executed, but not before Tonghak had spread throughout Korea.

CHOGYE-CHONG \'chō-'gye-'chŏn\, also known as Chogye, one of the largest Buddhist sects in Korea, founded by BOJO GUKSA (1158–1210). It was derived from Chʿan, the Chinese form of BUDDHISM, known as Sŏn in Korea and as ZEN in Japan. The Chogye-chong stressed the importance of studying the AVATAṂSAKA SŪTRA (Garland Sutra) and of meditation, with the goal of acquiring calmness of mind.

CHʿŎNDOGYO \'chən-'dō-'gyō\ (Korean: "Religion of the Heavenly Way"), Korean religion that combines elements of CONFUCIANISM, BUDDHISM, TAOISM, shamanism, and ROMAN CATHOLICISM. The movement was formerly called Tonghak ("Eastern Learning"). Converts to Chʿŏndogyo dedicate themselves to God by placing clean water on an altar in a ritual called chʿŏngsu. They are instructed to meditate on God, offer prayers (kido) upon leaving and entering their homes, dispel harmful thoughts, and worship God in church on Sundays.

The essence of Chʿŏndogyo is said to be contained in a formula (chumun) that is recited as the way to enlightenment: "May the creative power of the universe be within me in abundance. May heaven be with me and every creation will be done. Never forgetting this truth, everything will be known." The basic principle of Chʿŏndogyo is that "Man and God are one" (In-Nae-Chʿŏn); this oneness is realized by individuals through sincere faith in the unity of their own body and spirit and through faith in the universality of God.

Chʿŏndogyo was established by Chʿoe Che-u in 1860, after what he said was a direct inspiration from the Heavenly Emperor (Chʿŏnju). Chʿoe sought to effect change in the social order, a political course which resulted in his execution in 1864. Chʿoe Si-hyŏng, already prominent in the movement, took over the leadership but met a similar fate in 1898. The third leader, Son Pyŏng-hi, changed the name to Chʿŏndogyo in 1905. By the late 20th century there were some 3,000,000 adherents.

CHŎNG TO-JŎN \'chən-tō-'jən\ (d. 1398), Korean Neo-Confucian scholar who helped to overthrow the Koryŏ kingdom (918–1392 CE) and establish the Chosŏn kingdom (1392–1910 CE). He was of a nonaristocratic family and promoted Confucian learning and the rise of the bureaucratic class. With the fall of the Koryo patronage of BUDDHISM and the rise of the Chosŏn kingdom, he championed a sweeping reform of education and government along Neo-Confucian lines. Related to these reforms were his polemical writings against Buddhism, TAOISM, and other traditional shamanistic practices. Adhering to an exclusive Neo-Confucian political ideology and philosophical metaphysics, he condemned Buddhism and Taoism as being inherently antithetical to public-spirited service. Developments in later Buddhism and Taoism in Korea often represent an ameliorative response to these attacks.

CHOSEN PEOPLE: *see* ISRAEL.

CHOSEN WOMEN, *Quechua* Aclla Cuna, *or* Aklya Kona ("Virgins of the Sun"), in INCA religion, celibate women who lived in temples and prepared ritual food, maintained a sacred fire, and wove garments for the emperor and for ritual use. In the early 16th century the Virgins numbered several thousand and were governed by a high priestess, the Coya Pasca, a noblewoman believed to be the consort of the sun god. The Virgins were villagers selected for their beauty and talent at the age of 8 or 10 and shut up in the temples for six or seven years. Some became sacrificial victims, whereas others were made imperial concubines or the wives of nobles.

CHOU TUN-I \'zhō-'dùn-'ē\, *Pinyin* Zhou Dunyi, *also called* Chou Lien-Hsi \-'lyen-'shē\, *Pinyin* Zhou Lianxi (b. 1017, Ying-tao, Tao-chou, China—d. 1073, Nan-k'ang-ch'ing), Chinese philosopher considered the most important precursor of NEO-CONFUCIANISM.

Chou was born into a highly influential family and served in high governmental capacities throughout most of his life. He successively held the posts of magistrate, prefectural staff supervisor, professor of the directorate of education, and assistant prefect before resigning from office a year before his death.

In his reformulation of CONFUCIANISM, Chou drew from Taoist doctrines and elaborated on the I-CHING, or *Book of Changes*. His short treatise *T'ai-chi-t'u shuo* ("Explanation of the Diagram of the Great Ultimate") developed a metaphysics based on the idea that "the many are [ultimately] one, and the one is actually differentiated into the many." Chou combined Taoist schema of the universe with the *I-ching*'s concept of an evolutionary process of creation: originating from the Great Ultimate (which is simultaneously the Non-Ultimate) are yin (tranquillity) and yang (movement). The interactions of yin and yang then give rise to the Five Elements (fire, earth, water, metal, and wood), and the integration and union of all of the preceding entities give rise to the male and female elements, which in turn are the cause of the production and evolution of all things. When humans react to the external phenomena thus created, the distinction between GOOD AND EVIL emerges in their thought and conduct.

In a treatise entitled *T'ung-shu* ("Explanatory Text"), Chou's restatement and reinterpretation of Confucian doctrines laid the basis for the ethics of later Neo-Confucianism. The sage, or superior man, reacts to external phenomena according to the principles of propriety, humanity, righteousness, wisdom, faithfulness, and tranquillity. Chou viewed sincerity as the foundation of human moral nature, the source of one's ability to distinguish good from evil, and thus also of one's ability to perfect oneself.

Chou's work laid the foundation for the more systematic exposition of Neo-Confucianism provided by his later disciples, especially CHU HSI (1130–1200). Because of his efforts, the *I-ching* was revered as a Confucian classic by Chu and other Neo-Confucianists of the late Sung dynasty.

CHRIST, CHURCH OF, any of several conservative Protestant churches, found chiefly in the United States. Each church is known locally as a Church of Christ, and its members as Christians; and each church is autonomous in government, with elders, deacons, and a minister or ministers. There is no organization beyond the local church.

The early history of this group is identical with that of the DISCIPLES OF CHRIST. They developed from various religious movements in the United States in the early part of the 19th century, especially those led by Barton W. Stone and Thomas and ALEXANDER CAMPBELL. They pleaded for the BIBLE as the only standard of faith, without additional creeds, and for the unity of the people of God by the restoration of New Testament CHRISTIANITY. Refusing affiliation with any sect, they called themselves simply Christians.

Controversies developed among the Christians about the middle of the 19th century, principally over the scriptural authorization for organized MISSION societies and the use of instrumental music in worship. In 1906 in the federal census of religion there was added to the earlier listing of Disciples of Christ a new listing of Churches of Christ that enumerated those congregations opposing organized mission societies and instrumental music. The NEW TESTAMENT mentions neither, and, therefore, the Churches of Christ consider them to be unauthorized innovations.

After the division, the Churches of Christ continued to grow. Though the churches oppose organized mission societies, missionary work is supported by individual churches and is carried on in 100 foreign fields.

Sunday worship in the Churches of Christ consists of unaccompanied congregational singing, prayer, teaching, preaching, giving, and the Lord's Supper. Other worship and teaching services are held during the week.

CHRISTIAN CASTE, in India, the social stratification that persists among Christians, based upon CASTE membership at the time of an individual's own or of an ancestor's conversion. Indian Christian society is divided into groups geographically and according to denomination, but an additional factor is caste. Caste groups may worship and even dine together, but, as a rule, they do not intermarry.

The problem of reconciling change in religious belief with existing social tradition has dominated the history of CHRISTIANITY in India. The Syrian Christians along the Malabar coast trace their origin to the legendary visit of ST. THOMAS the Apostle, early in the 1st century CE. Many of his converts were of high birth, and after conversion they continued to be accorded a mid-rank status by the Hindu society that surrounded them.

With the arrival of Europeans from the 16th century onward, other groups of Christian converts emerged. Portuguese missionaries converted thousands of fisherfolk who then had little in common with the Syrian Christians. Roberto de Nobili (16th–17th century), a JESUIT of noble birth, took a different path by understanding his position to correspond to that of a BRAHMIN ascetic. Becoming expert in Sanskrit and Tamil, he hoped for India's large-scale conversion to Christianity by way of an appeal to its scholars. He sought to dissociate himself from the Portuguese missionaries who were converting the fisherfolk. These practices gave him acceptance among the Indian upper classes, but brought him into conflict with his own church.

In the 19th century, Protestant missionaries arrived in India in large numbers. They insisted on social reform along with religious conversion; the result was that most of their converts were from the lowest social classes.

Caste distinctions among contemporary Indian Christians are breaking down at about the same rate as those among Indians of other faiths. In some instances the old traditions persist, and there are ROMAN CATHOLIC churches where members of each caste sit together for worship.

CHRISTIAN FUNDAMENTALISM, conservative movement in American PROTESTANTISM arising out of the MILLENNIALISM of the 19th century and emphasizing as fundamental to CHRISTIANITY the literal interpretation and absolute inerrancy of the SCRIPTURES, the imminent and physical SECOND COMING of JESUS CHRIST, the VIRGIN BIRTH, the RESURRECTION, and the ATONEMENT.

The roots of fundamentalism lie in the American millenarian movement. In the 1830s and '40s there were numerous outbreaks of ADVENTIST excitement. They were eventually channeled into a movement largely through the Niagara Bible Conference. Initiated by James Inglis, a New York City BAPTIST minister, the conference continued under James H. Brookes (1830–97), a St. Louis, Mo., PRESBYTERIAN minister and editor of the influential millenarian periodical *The Truth*. The group held annual summer conferences until 1899.

By the end of the century the movement had emerged as an alternative to, and escape from, labor unrest, social discontent, the rising tide of ROMAN CATHOLIC immigration, and the challenges posed by the rise of liberal BIBLICAL CRITICISM. Growing numbers of Protestant clergy and laity turned to some form of millenarianism, and the evangelist Dwight L. Moody (1837–99) provided in his Northfield conferences an influential platform for millenarian expression.

The high point of millenarian influence upon the conservative tradition within evangelical Protestantism occurred when millenarians cooperated with other defenders of the inerrancy of the BIBLE, notably a group of conservative scholars from the Princeton Theological Seminary in New Jersey, in founding the American Bible League in 1902 and in writing a series of 12 pamphlets entitled *The Fundamentals*. The pamphlets, published between 1910 and 1915, attacked the current theories of biblical criticism and reasserted the authority of the Bible.

At the end of World War I, the millenarians held a number of conferences in New York City and Philadelphia that encouraged the formation of a larger and more comprehensive organization in 1919, the World's Christian Fundamentals Association. In spite of vigorous leadership, however, the association never prospered.

The liberal, or modernist, tendency that was their target had been of slight importance before the turn of the century. After that, however, the methods of "higher criticism" had begun to pervade the universities and the seminaries. By 1914, among the Episcopal, Methodist, Baptist, and Presbyterian denominations in the North, liberalism had gained many adherents. The battle to prevent the reception and spread of these new views had

Dwight L. Moody, detail from a drawing by Charles Stanley Reinhart; in Harper's Weekly, *March 1876*
By courtesy of the Library of Congress, Washington, D.C.

been lost. During the 1920s it only remained to be decided whether the liberals could be forced out of the denominations.

Not every Protestant denomination was affected by intellectual controversy during the 1920s. Serious controversy did erupt, however, among the northern Baptists and the Presbyterians in the northern states. Within the Presbyterian church, conservatives had, with the help of the millenarians, imposed a set of essential doctrines upon the denomination in 1910. To avoid a SCHISM within the Presbyterian church in the United States, a Commission of Fifteen was appointed to work out a compromise. Their report held that the Presbyterian denomination had traditionally tolerated a diversity of opinion and rejected the right of the General Assembly to determine which were the essential doctrines of the Christian faith. The report virtually destroyed the conservatives' position within Presbyterianism.

Displeasure with the teaching of evolution, as well as anxiety over the spread of biblical criticism, gained popular momentum in the 1920s, however. Fundamentalists, believing that the Bible could not be reconciled with the view of the origin of life put forward by Charles Darwin, opposed evolution; and antievolution crusaders lobbied for legislation to prevent the teaching of evolution in the public schools.

During the 1930s and '40s the institutional structure of modern fundamentalism developed. Some fundamentalist Presbyterians and Baptists broke away from their denominations to form new churches. Many fundamentalists joined a congregation of one of the smaller sects that had remained faithful to the creed of biblical literalism and premillennialism, such as the PLYMOUTH BRETHREN and the Evangelical Free Church, or one of the many independent Bible churches and tabernacles that arose during that period. Much of the structure of modern fundamentalism is provided by Bible institutes and Bible colleges. Many of these schools operate very much like denominational headquarters and provide a bond between otherwise isolated congregations.

The most significant influences upon the fundamentalist and evangelical churches in America since World War II have been the prosperity of the postwar decades, the religious revival of the 1950s, and the alleged threat of communist subversion. The issue of communism that preoccupied the American public during the 1950s closely resembled the traditional concerns of fundamentalism—namely, biblical criticism and evolution—which fundamentalists believed came from abroad, seemed to spread uncontrollably and subversively, and tended to undermine Christianity. The anticommunist activities of the mid-20th century virtually duplicated the history of the antievolution crusade of the 1920s.

In the late 20th century, while fundamentalist beliefs had not changed significantly since the Niagara Conference, the method of disseminating those beliefs had. Evangelists such as BILLY GRAHAM had paved the way for televangelists, and the fundamentalist movement became highly effective in using television broadcasting to reach its followers. The movement also had success creating political change desired by its members through such organizations as the Moral Majority, a fundamentalist citizens' organization under the leadership of Baptist minister Jerry Falwell. The "Christian right," as the movement was sometimes called, campaigned against legalized abortion, homosexual rights, and the women's Equal Rights Amendment, and for legalized school prayer.

CHRISTIANITY

Christianity is the religion that traces its origins to Jesus of Nazareth, whom it affirms to be the chosen one (Christ) of God. Christianity is the religion of one-third of the population of the earth.

Nearly 2,000,000,000 people are identified in some way or other with the Christian movement, with substantial populations on every continent. Despite its representation and support in many lands today, Christianity has been principally a Western phenomenon. Yet the influence of Christianity extends beyond the borders of traditional Christendom. It has affected other religions, as it has been affected by them, and its ethos continues to shape the characters of individuals and nations that no longer live by its creed.

HISTORY OF CHRISTIANITY

Christianity begins with JESUS CHRIST. The effects of his life, the response to his teachings, and the experience of his death and RESURRECTION were the beginnings of the Christian community. When PETER, Christ's APOSTLE, is represented in the NEW TESTAMENT as confessing that Jesus is "the Christ, the Son of the living God," he speaks for the Christianity of all ages. And it is in response to this CONFESSION that Jesus is described as announcing the foundation of the Christian church: "You are Peter, and on this rock I will build my church, and the powers of death shall not prevail against it."

The ministry of Jesus.   The Gospels represent Jesus as calling God "Father"; the God whom Jesus proclaimed and revealed was the forgiving Father in the PARABLE of the prodigal son (Luke 15:11 ff.), but he was also the wrathful king in the parable of the unmerciful servant (Matthew 17:23 ff.). Rather than mitigating the holiness of God and the severity of his judgment as described in the OLD TESTAMENT, Jesus made God's requirements even more stringent (Matthew 5–7). (That is, Jesus' message in this passage warns that the "outer" purity caused by following the laws of Leviticus is no longer sufficient for God—a purity of thought is also necessary for God.) Through Jesus' message God was conveying a threat, a demand, and a promise, all at once. Paradoxically, both the rigor and the tenderness of God received greater emphasis in his proclamation than they had before.

The Crucifixion, mosaic from the basilica of San Marco, Venice
Alinari—Art Resource

CONTENTS

This was partly due to the close connection in Jesus' message between the picture of God and the announcement of the KINGDOM OF GOD. "The kingdom of God is like . . ."—these words form the introduction to many of the parables in which Jesus described the kingly activity of God. By "kingdom" he seems to have meant not principally the realm of God but the reign of God: not a country or territory but a divine activity and a relation. (It is therefore foreign to Jesus' teaching when Christians speak of their "building the kingdom.") Clearly, Jesus directed his hearers to that which was to come when he spoke to them about the kingdom—they did not and could not take possession of the kingdom in their time. In this sense it is valid to describe Jesus' view of the kingdom as futuristic. But there are also statements in the Gospels, and not merely in the Fourth Gospel (John), that have no meaning unless this coming kingdom, while not yet fully arrived, was at least beginning. Jesus himself appears in the Gospels as the herald, but also as the sign and the bringer of the kingdom. Jesus brought the kingdom, and the kingdom was bringing Jesus: this is the only way to summarize the relation between Jesus' coming and the coming of the kingdom according to the Gospels. Therefore he could say to his enemies that the kingdom was "in the midst of you" (Luke 17:21; not "within you"); for he himself was the sign of the kingdom in their midst. God's reign was working in hidden ways, but one day soon it would come out of its hiding. Until then only some were privileged to know "the secrets of the kingdom of heaven" (Matthew 13:11). Hence it was with the announcement of the kingdom that Jesus began his public preaching (Mark 1:15).

Joined directly to this announcement of the kingdom in that earliest account of Jesus' preaching was the invitation to repent and to believe the Gospel. Repentance meant a change of mind, a break with the past and a new direction. The promises of the kingdom were not for those who boasted of their moral goodness before God but for those who were genuinely sorry for their SINS (Luke 18:9–14). Some of the strongest words in the Gospels are those in which Jesus denounced the pride of religious men in his time, with their claims upon God and the inner corruption of their hearts (Matthew 23:25–28). Because such claims and such corruption were not restricted to Jesus' contemporaries, these denunciations and this invitation to repentance and faith formed a continuing part of the Christian witness. One of the purposes of Jesus' stress upon the severity of God's demands was to bring about the kind of awareness out of which true repentance would issue. But the call to repentance was also an invitation to "believe the Gospel." The kingdom was a gift of God's good pleasure

(Luke 12:32), and the God who laid his demands upon humans was also the God whose purpose it was to forgive them their sins. Hence the only response proper to his invitation and his generosity was the response of faith, described by Jesus as resembling the trust of children (Mark 10:15).

The primary commandment was to believe in God and to love him. Next to this commandment, Jesus put the "second commandment" (Mark 12:31) of love toward one's neighbor. In enjoining such love, Jesus insisted that outward performance did not suffice. Not merely murder but even hatred was prohibited, and not merely adultery but even lust (Matthew 5:21–30). What was revolutionary about Jesus' ethic of the kingdom was this insistence upon purity of thought as well as action, coupled as it was with his primary emphasis upon the mercy and righteousness of God. Other issues do appear in the Gospels—*e.g.*, Jesus also spoke of marriage, of religious and cultic duties, of prayer and thanksgiving, of spiritual blindness and the illumination of God. But if there are any overarching themes to be found in Jesus' teachings, these themes center around God, the kingdom of God, and the call to repentance, and faith and love for one's neighbor.

The mission of Jesus. In the Gospels Jesus is described as having had the sense that God had called him for a special duty, but the descriptions of that sense of duty are not uniform. This has led New Testament scholars to concern themselves with the problem of development in the messianic consciousness of Jesus. Two questions are uppermost in that problem: Is the identification of Jesus as the MESSIAH in the Gospels principally a construction by the later church, read back into the career of Jesus? If not, when and under what circumstances did Jesus come to think of himself as the appointed Messiah? LUKE'S Gospel even makes this identification a part of its infancy narratives (Luke 2:26), while JOHN'S Gospel

credits it to ANDREW, the first of the disciples to be called (John 1:41). The title "Messiah" came from the Old Testament but had undergone further development in the period immediately preceding the time of Jesus, although it must be stated that the term was by no means as prominent among Jews as Christians often tend to suppose. Among many of the common people the title had come to represent their hope for deliverance—deliverance either from sin, or, at least, from the Romans. That hope for deliverance, coupled as it was with imaginative expectations of radical changes in the order of things, seems to have arisen with new fervor each time a new national or religious leader appeared, as happened, for example, when JOHN THE BAPTIST began his ministry (Luke 3:15); and with the coming of Jesus as a religious teacher and worker of mira-

The Resurrection of Lazarus, *one of the miracles performed by Christ (John 11:1–44), oil painting by Vincent van Gogh, 1890; in the Van Gogh Museum, Amsterdam*
The Granger Collection

cles, new speculation was raised as to whether he might not be the promised one (Matthew 16:14). The story of the entry into Jerusalem told by all four Gospels (see Matthew 21:1 ff.) and the account of the feeding of the five thousand in John's Gospel (John 6:14, 15) both disclose the character of the popular hope as Jesus stirred it up once more.

But Jesus not only stimulated this hope, he also reinterpreted it. In the expectations of ISRAEL there were many elements, two of which were the expectations of the Messiah, the Son of DAVID, who would restore the lost glory of his father's kingdom; and the idea, summarized most fully in Isaiah 53, that God's purposes for Israel could not achieve their fulfillment except through the suffering of God's servant. It is not altogether clear how closely or how often these two elements had ever been combined in previous versions of the messianic ideal, but the reactions of Jesus' contemporaries and disciples seem to suggest that the combination had rarely if ever been a part of Israel's hope. From the sources it is evident that such a combination eventually determined Jesus' own conception of his mission. Immediately after the great messianic disclosure at Caesarea Philippi (Matthew 16:16), Jesus goes into a discussion of the CRUCIFIXION (Matthew 16:21 ff.). The combination, significantly, comes out most clearly in one of the post-Resurrection scenes (Luke 24:26, 27), where the disciples learned to identify the Davidic king with the suffering servant. It may be the intent of the Gospels to say that fear of the political interpretation of the Messiah led Jesus to disclose his messianic mission to his disciples only gradually, until the course of the terminal events at Jerusalem should make any such political interpretation impossible. But some scholars have taken the Gospels to be saying that the full meaning of his messianic vocation only came upon Jesus over a period of time and that part of this meaning was his realization that the Messiah had to suffer and die. One problem with this notion of development is the difficulty encountered with any attempt to fix chronological sequence on the Gospels, and thus on the career and inner life of Jesus.

A special problem in the interpretation of Jesus' vocation is the so-called "messianic secret." Among the first to recognize Jesus as the Christ in the Gospels were the DEMONS (Luke 4:41), whom he then charges to keep silent. Mark attaches a passage in which Christ admonishes silence from his disciples at both Caesarea

Philippi (Mark 8:30) and the TRANSFIGURATION (Mark 9:9). In Matthew and even more in John, on the other hand, Jesus is quite overt about his declarations (John 4:25, 26). Which of these portrayals more accurately represents the usual attitude of Jesus toward the matter of his messianic character? Some critics maintain on the basis of this and other evidence that Jesus never thought of himself as the Messiah at all: He suppressed the messianic hopes of others as much as he could, but, as part of the process of glorification that took place in the memories of his followers after his death, the disciples ascribed to him messianic claims that he had never made for himself. The majority of interpreters, however, trace the identification of Messiah and suffering servant to Jesus himself, even though they differ widely on the extent to which that identification remained Jesus' private secret until near the end. At least in part, the answer to these and related questions will depend upon one's attitude not only toward the New Testament but toward Jesus himself. For those Christians whose view of Jesus is determined by the decisions on dogma made by the ancient church, the question should read: How did the limited human nature of Jesus Christ in the days of his sojourn on earth share in that full awareness of his mission from the Father that was a continual part of his unlimited divine nature? According to his divine nature, he was omniscient and always knew himself to be the Christ, whether or not this awareness was always complete in his human nature. Passages such as Mark 13:32—in which Christ claims that the hour of the passing away of heaven and earth are known by "no man, no, not the ANGELS which are in heaven, neither the Son, but the Father"—would then have to apply only to his human nature, not to the person of Christ as a whole.

As already mentioned, part of the messianic ideal that Jesus' contemporaries cherished was the expectation that a radical change was in the offing, to affect not only political and national destiny but the arrangement of the universe itself. Jewish apocalyptic literature gave vivid voice to this expectation in language that often finds echoes in the Gospels, and these expectations continue to be the subject of debate among students of the New Testament. Some scholars maintain that Jesus shared the apocalyptic beliefs of his time and that he confidently expected the end of the world to come in the near future. Accordingly, his death was the way he expected the coming of the end to be set in motion. Other scholars of the Gospels claim that the ESCHATOLOGY of Jesus, his view of the last things on earth, was a "realized eschatology." This means that the dramatic language of his apocalyptic utterances was intended to describe the "end" of human history—not the end understood as termination but the end understood as purpose, the appearance in human history of that which interprets, redeems, and judges it. In other words, Jesus was not talking about a finish so much as he was talking about a continuing feature of life seen under the judgment of God. A third way to interpret these utterances has been to say that in Jesus' own message both elements were present. Those in which "end" meant primarily "termination" found their way chiefly into the SYNOPTIC GOSPELS, while John's Gospel contains those that speak of the "end" as the continuing judgment of God. Again, a decision among these interpretations depends upon one's picture of Jesus. Traditional Christian doctrine, whether that of ROMAN CATHOLICISM, EASTERN ORTHODOXY, or PROTESTANTISM, forbids any interpretation that would either ascribe error to Christ's expectations or deny the ultimate termination of human history.

The title "Son of Man" was one of the symbols appearing in Jewish apocalyptic writings, and the Gospels frequently put it into the sayings of Jesus. Sometimes it merely takes the place of the personal pronoun "I," as is evident from a comparison of Matthew 16:13 with Luke 9:18 and from other sets of parallel passages. At other times it is merely equivalent to "man," which may indeed have been the original term in sayings like Mark 2:28. In some passages it may even refer, as it perhaps did in Psalms 8:4 (a passage applied in Hebrews 2:6–9 to the person of Jesus Christ), to man in his lowliness. But in some places it clearly carries the connotation it acquired in Jewish apocalyptic writings, possibly under the influence of Persian thought, of God's representative, anointed to bring in his kingdom. This connotation was most prominent in sayings like Matthew 24:27, 30, and it may be that Jesus used it deliberately to avoid the title "Messiah." "Son of Man" appears in the Gospels approximately 80 times, carrying one of several of these connotations. The fact that Jesus used the title in the third person certainly does not prove, as some have contended, that he did not regard himself as the Son of Man; this was merely general Semitic usage, prevalent in Arabic even today. The implications of terms like "kingdom," "Son of Man," and "end" are therefore more complex than has often been realized, combining meanings that later interpreters have falsely set in opposition to one another.

The influence of Jesus on the Gentiles. Concerning the attitude and relation of Jesus to non-Jews we know very little. His use of a SAMARITAN in the familiar parable of Luke 10:30–35 and the later reports of his other contacts with this hated semi-Jewish people suggest that he had made an impression upon the memory of his followers by his freedom from the sort of parochialism that had often marked his people. What he said about "the rulers of the GENTILES" (Matthew 20:25) indicates how geographically limited his career was. The people spoken of in John 12:20, were not "Greeks," but Hellenistic Jews or perhaps Jewish proselytes of Greek descent. In other contacts with non-Jews he is reported to have healed the daughter of the Syrophoenician woman (Mark 7:24 ff.) and the servant of the centurion (Matthew 8:11). It would seem that Jesus then had envisioned what the prophets had also predicted, that the kingdom of God would be universal, not restricted to the Jewish people; but apparently he saw that this would happen only after his death. In the closing scene of Matthew's Gospel (Matthew 28:19) as well as in the opening scene of the Acts (the ACTS OF THE APOSTLES 1:8), the risen Lord is portrayed as commanding that his followers bear witness to him throughout the Gentile world. But, despite these and other indications of Jesus' personal perspective, it was as an adherent of JUDAISM that he lived and among Jews that he was both accepted and rejected.

Opposition. The hostility to Jesus appears to have stemmed from diverse motives. He had repeatedly manifested an independence and "authority" in relation to the law of the Old Testament that was heretical to the religious leaders of his people. Some of them saw their position threatened by the support he had among the people. The vigorous denunciations he had directed against injustice and hypocrisy had undoubtedly earned him the hatred of others, while the cleansing of the temple (Matthew 21:12) was a dramatic indication to them of how far he was willing to go.

From a report preserved in John 11:47 ff., it appears that Jesus' miracles, his proclamation of the coming kingdom, and the attention he was receiving had become politically embarrassing to the Jewish leaders, who enjoyed considerable local autonomy under Roman rule and were fearful of losing it if there were an insurrection. It also seems plausible that the people turned against him because of his consistent refusal to lead such an insurrection. Jesus himself believed that the will of his Father for the kingdom could not come to pass except by his death, and he went up to Jerusalem to die in obedience to that will. Hence it is true that the cross was imposed upon him by his enemies, but it is also true that he voluntarily took upon himself the death of the cross (John 10:18).

Early Christianity. Jesus was a Jew, as were all the Apostles. Thus the earliest Christianity is in fact a movement within Judaism; the very acknowledgment of Jesus as "the Christ" means the confession that he is the fulfillment of the promises originally made to ABRAHAM, ISAAC, and JACOB. But the Christian gospel encountered opposition within Judaism, just as Jesus had, and soon it turned toward the Gentile world. Ideologically, this required Christian thought to shift from Judaism and to define the Gospel as both the correction and the fulfillment of Greek and Roman philosophy. This definition was the assignment of the Christian APOLOGISTS of the first three centuries. Politically, the Christian expansion into the Greco-Roman world and its rejection of such religious practices as the worship of Caesar brought upon the early Christians the suspicion of their fellow citizens and persecution by the Roman authorities. Despite this early hostility, Christian churches continued to arise in many portions of the Roman Empire, attracting Romans of every social class.

The inward growth of the Christian community matched this outward growth in numbers and prestige. Christians celebrated and shared the GRACE and power given in Christ by participating in the rites he had instituted, especially BAPTISM and the EUCHARIST. They recited the events of his life, exhorting, teaching, and urging one another to prepare for his coming again, which they apparently hoped to see very soon. In this hope they set themselves consciously apart from the way of life that characterized "the world" in its terminal stages.

From the very outset the Christian community was a community of structure. Its remembrance and celebration followed a pattern that was indeed fluid in some of its details but was nonetheless fixed in its basic outline. Similarly, the office of the Apostles, traced by the primitive church to the ordinance of the risen Christ himself, was the basis for the earliest structures of administrative and pastoral organization. Furthermore, the collections of the sayings and deeds of Jesus were combined with the writings of the Apostles to form a body of Christian sacred writings. From these primitive structures emerged the threefold system of apostolic authority in bishop, creed, and biblical canon, with which the early church met the challenge of preserving its continuity despite the death of the Apostles and the postponement of the Lord's return.

Even in these early centuries the Christian movement was plagued by faction and torn by strife. The New Testament itself bears marks of the strife provoked by early exponents of a Christian form of GNOSTICISM, who interpreted the Gospel to conform with their theories of sin and salvation. The flowering of Gnosticism within Christianity occurred during the 2nd century, when BASILIDES and VALENTINUS arose to claim that true apostolic Christianity had been transmitted secretly to them and their followers rather than to the church, with its bishops and SCRIPTURES. Though differing from these Gnostics in significant ways, MARCION OF

Jesus washing St. Peter's feet, detail from a medieval manuscript; in the Biblioteca Palatina, Parma, Italy
Erich Lessing—Art Resource

PONTUS also purported to be the restorer of apostolic, especially Pauline, doctrine and practice. And the doctrine of MONTANISM, which claimed that the church had forsaken the pristine holiness of the Apostles and had become too worldly, asserted that the promise of the "counselor" given in the last discourses of Jesus in St. John had been fulfilled in the life and teachings of the prophet MONTANUS.

Thus, the crystallization of bishop, creed, and canon as the triple norm of apostolic Christianity was accentuated, if not actually hastened, by the need for a definition of orthodoxy against these unorthodox movements and schisms. As it resisted both a syncretism that would have absorbed it into a universal world-religion and a particularism that would have restricted it to the select few, Christianity asserted that it was catholic, or universal, in its message and appeal. It was, of course, catholic in principle long before it became catholic in fact. The features that would characterize the Christianity of the first three centuries as "catholic"—the gospel of a Savior who had died for the entire world; a message communicated in the Koine, or common Greek, that had become the universal literary language of the empire; a polity that coordinated local responsibility with ecumenical concern, especially through the growing prestige of the bishop in the capital city of the Roman *oikoumene*; and a participation in the spirit of Greco-Roman classicism that nevertheless remained open to both the ancient oriental and the new Germanic cultures—all showed Christianity as being both possessed of an identity and able at the same time to encompass universality.

Little is recorded about the Christians of these centuries; both their number and their names remain largely unknown. Those whose names have become part of the historical record are the bishops, heretics, and saints—these categories are not mutually exclusive—who attracted more than the usual attention in their own time and thus became the spokesmen to later times for the silent in the land. Thus TERTULLIAN, who died about 220, has come to epitomize the church's radical rejection of the world and its culture, as CLEMENT OF ALEXANDRIA, who died in almost the same year, and ORIGEN, who died about 254, are the recurring symbols of the Christian conviction that Christ is "the desire of all nations" and the answer to the quest of the philosophers. In the thought of IRENAEUS (d. *c.* 200) the Christianity of the 2nd century produced a system that summarized many of its fundamental beliefs about the renewal and redemption accomplished in Christ. From the history of the use of these names it is clear how easily they can all become clichés, but behind the clichés is the struggle of Christianity during the first three centuries of its history to be faithful to the deposit of its faith and relevant to its world, and to be both at the same time.

The picture of Christ in the early church: the Apostles' Creed.   Even before the writings we know as the Gospels were written, Christians were reflecting upon the meaning of what Jesus had been and what he had said and done. To comprehend the faith of the early church regarding Christ, we must turn to the writings of the New Testament, where that faith found embodiment. It was also embodied in brief confessions or creeds, but these have not been preserved for us complete in their original form. What we have are fragments of those confessions

Apostolic voyages

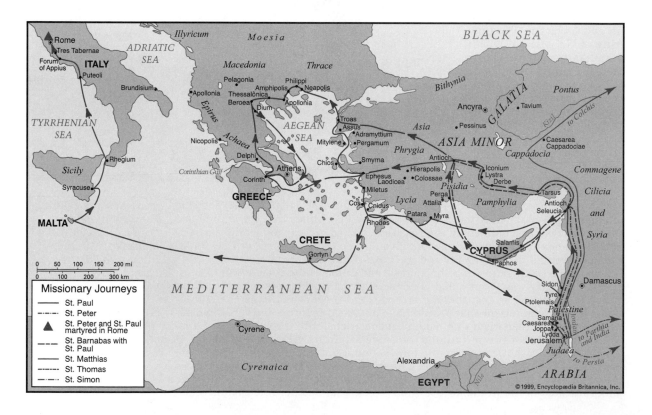

or creeds in various books of the New Testament, snatches from them in other early Christian documents, and later forms of them in Christian theology and liturgy. The so-called Apostles' Creed is one such later form. It did not achieve its present form until quite late; just how late is a matter of controversy. But in its earliest ancestry it is very early indeed, perhaps dating back to the 1st century. And its confession regarding Christ is probably the earliest core, around which later elaborations of it were composed. Allowing for such later elaborations, we may say that in the Apostles' Creed we have a convenient summary of what the early church believed about Christ amid all the variety of its expression and formulation. The creeds were a way for Christians to explain what they meant by their acts of worship. When they put "I believe" or "We believe" at the head of what they confessed about God and Christ, they meant that their declarations rested upon faith, not merely upon observation.

> ◆ **I believe in God, the Father Almighty,**
> **the Creator of heaven and earth,**
> **and in Jesus Christ, his only Son, our Lord:**
> **Who was conceived by the Holy Spirit,**
> **born of the Virgin Mary,**
> **suffered under Pontius Pilate, was crucified, died,**
> **and was buried.**
> **He descended into hell.**
> **The third day He arose again from the dead.**
> **He ascended into heaven and sits at the**
> **right hand of God the Father Almighty,**
> **Whence He will come to judge the living and**
> **the dead.**
> **I believe in the Holy Spirit,**
> **the holy catholic church,**
> **the communion of saints,**
> **the forgiveness of sins,**
> **the resurrection of the body,**
> **and the life everlasting.**
> **Amen.** ◆

Preexistence. The statement "I believe" also indicated that Christ was deserving of worship and faith and that he was therefore on a level with God. At an early date, possibly as early as the words of Paul in Philippians 2:6–11, Christian theology began to distinguish three stages in the career of Jesus Christ: his preexistence with the Father before all things; his INCARNATION and humiliation in "the days of His flesh" (Hebrews 5:7); and his glorification, beginning with the Resurrection and continuing forever.

Probably the most celebrated statement of the preexistence of Christ is the opening verses of the Gospel of St. John. Here Christ is identified as the incarnation of that Word (LOGOS) through which God made all things in the beginning, a Word existing in relation to God before the creation. The sources of this doctrine have been sought in Greek philosophy, both early and late, as well as in the Jewish thought of PHILO JUDAEUS and of the Palestinian RABBIS. Whatever its source, the doctrine of the Logos in John is distinctive by virtue of the fact that it identifies the Logos with a specific historical person. Other writings of the New Testament also illustrate the faith of the early Christians regarding the preexistence of Christ. The opening chapters of both Colossians and Hebrews speak of Christ as the preexistent one through whom all things were created, therefore as distinct from the created order of things in both time and preeminence; the preposition "before" in Colossians 1:17 apparently refers both to his temporal priority and to his superior dignity. Yet before any theological reflection about the nature of this preexistence had been able to find terms and concepts, the early Christians were worshiping Christ as divine. Philippians 2:6–11 may be a quotation from a HYMN used in such worship. Theological reflection told them that, if this worship was legitimate in a religion that continued to insist on MONOTHEISM, he must have existed with the Father "before all ages."

Jesus Christ. By the time the text of the creed was established, "Jesus Christ" was the usual designation for the Savior. Originally, of course, "Jesus" (the hellenized form of "Joshua") had been his given name, meaning "Yahweh saves" or "Yahweh will save" (Matthew 1:21), while "Christ" was the Greek translation of the title "Messiah." Some passages of the New Testament still used "Christ" as a title (*e.g.,* Luke 24:26; 2 John 7), but it is evident from Paul's usage that the title became simply a proper name very early. Most of the Gentiles took it to be a proper name, and it was as "Christians" that the early believers were labeled (Acts 11:26). In the most precise language, the term "Jesus" was reserved for the earthly career of the Lord, but it seems from liturgical sources such as Philippians 2:10 that it may actually have been endowed with greater solemnity than the name "Christ." Within a few years after the beginnings of the Christian movement, Jesus, Christ, Jesus Christ, and Christ Jesus could be used almost interchangeably, as the textual variants in the New Testament indicate. Only in modern times has it become customary to distinguish sharply among them for the sake of drawing a line (which often seems quite arbitrary) between the Jesus of history and the Christ of faith.

God's only Son. The declaration that Jesus Christ is the Son of God is one of the most universal in the New Testament, most of whose books refer to him that way. The Gospels do not quote him as using the title for himself in so many words, although sayings like Matthew 11:27 ("All things are delivered unto me of my Father: and no man knoweth the Son, but the Father . . .") come close to it. There are some instances—for example, the SERMON ON THE MOUNT (Matthew 5:9)—where the usage of the Gospels appears to echo the more general implications of divine sonship in the Old Testament as a prerogative of Israel or of the true believer. Usually, however, it is evident that the Evangelists, like Paul, meant some special honor by the name. The Evangelists associated the honor with the story of Jesus' baptism (Matthew 3:17) and Transfiguration (Matthew 17:5), Paul with the faith in the Resurrection (Romans 1:4). From this association some have argued that "Son of God" in the New Testament never referred to the preexistence of Christ. But it is clear in John and in Paul that this implication was not absent, even though it was not as prominent as it became soon thereafter.

The Nativity *by Piero della Francesca, wood panel, 1475; in the National Gallery, London*
The Granger Collection

What made the implication of preexistence more prominent in later Christian use of the term "Son of God" was the clarification of the doctrine of the TRINITY, where "Son" was the name for the eternal Second Person (Matthew 28:19). As the Gospels show, the application of the name "Son of God" to Jesus was offensive to the Jews, probably because it seemed to smack of Gentile POLYTHEISM. This also made it all too intelligible to polytheists, as early controversies indicate. Facing both the Jews and the Greeks, the apostolic church confessed that Jesus Christ was "God's only Son," antithetical to Jewish claims that the Eternal could have no sons and to Greek myths of divine procreation.

Our Lord. As passages like Romans 1:3 show, the phrase "Jesus Christ our Lord" was one of the ways the apostolic church expressed its understanding of what he had been and done. Luke even put the title into the mouth of the CHRISTMAS angel (Luke 2:11). From the way the name "Lord" (*Kyrios*) was employed during the 1st century it is possible to see several implications in the Christian use of it for Christ. The Christians meant that they did not accept the existence of a

Jesus carrying the cross, copper engraving by Martin Schongauer, 15th century
Foto Marburg—Art Resource

multitude of divine and lordly beings in the universe, but only one genuine *Kyrios* (1 Corinthians 8:5, 6). They meant that the Roman Caesar was not the lord of all, as he was styled by his worshipers, but that only Christ was Lord (Revelation 17:14). And they meant that YAHWEH, the COVENANT God of the Old Testament, whose name they pronounced as "Lord" (*Adonai*), had come in Jesus Christ to establish the new covenant ("For there is no difference between the Jew and the Greek: for the same Lord over all is rich unto all that call upon him. For whosoever shall call upon the name of the Lord shall be saved." Romans 10:12, 13). Like "Son of God," therefore, the name *Kyrios* was directed against both parts of the audience to which the primitive church addressed its proclamation. At times it stood particularly for the risen and glorified Christ, as in Acts 2:36; but in passages that echoed the Old Testament it was sometimes the preexistence that was being primarily emphasized (Matthew 22:44). Gradually "our Lord," like "Christ," became a common way of speaking about Jesus Christ (as it still is, especially among Roman Catholics), even when the speaker did not intend to stress his lordship over the world.

Incarnation and humiliation. *Conceived by the Holy Spirit, born of the Virgin Mary*—Earlier forms of the creed, reflected in the Niceno-Constantinopolitan Creed of 381, read: "Born of the Holy Spirit and of the Virgin Mary." The primary affirmation of this article is that the Son of God, the Word, had become human, or, as John's Gospel put it, "flesh" (John 1:14). Preexistence and incarnation presuppose each other in the Christian view of Jesus Christ. Hence the New Testament assumed Christ's preexistence when it talked about his becoming human; and, when it spoke of him as preexistent, it was ascribing this preexistence to Christ, about whom it was describing in the flesh. It may be that the reference in the creed to the Virgin Mary was intended to stress primarily her function as the guarantee of Christ's true humanity, as did the New Testament phrase "born of a woman" (Galatians 4:4), but the creed also intended to teach the supernatural origin of that humanity. Although it is true that neither Paul nor John makes reference to it, the teaching about the virginal conception of Jesus, apparently based upon Isaiah 7:14, was sufficiently widespread in the 1st century to warrant inclusion in both Matthew and Luke, as well as in creeds that date back to the 1st century. As it stands, the creedal statement is a paraphrase of Luke 1:35. In the New Testament the Holy Spirit was also involved in the baptism (Matthew 3:16) and the Resurrection (Romans 1:4) of Jesus.

Suffered under Pontius Pilate, was crucified, died, and was buried—To a reader of the Gospels, the most striking feature of the creed is probably its omission of that which occupied a major part of the Gospels, the story of Jesus' life and teachings. In this respect there is a direct parallel between the creed and the epistles of the New Testament, especially those of Paul. Judging by the amount of space they devoted to the Passion story, even the writers of the Gospels were apparently more interested in these few days of Jesus' life than they were in anything else he had said or done. The reason for this was the faith underlying both the New Testament and the creed, that the events of Jesus' Passion, death, and Resurrection were the events by which God had accomplished the salvation of human beings. The Gospels found their climax in those events, and the other material in turn led up to those events. The epistles applied those events to concrete situations in the early church. From the way Paul could speak of the cross (Philippians 2:6–11) and of "the night when he [Jesus] was betrayed" (1 Corinthians 11:23), it seems that before the Gospels came into existence the church commemorated the happenings associated with what came to be called HOLY WEEK. Some of the earliest Christian art was a portrayal of these happenings, as was the use of the sign of the cross to invoke divine blessing or to ward off evil—another indication of their importance in the cultic and devotional life of early Christianity. How did the cross effect our salvation? The answers of the New Testament and the early church to this question involved a variety of metaphors: Christ offered himself as a sacrifice to God; his life was a ransom for many; his death made us alive by trampling down the powers of death and hell; his suffering was an example to us when we must suffer; he was the Second Adam, creating a new humanity; his death shows us how much God loves us; and others. Every major ATONEMENT theory of Christian theological history discussed below was anticipated by one or another of these metaphors. The New Testament employed them all to symbolize something that could be described only symbolically, that "God was in Christ reconciling the world to himself, not counting their trespasses against them" (2 Corinthians 5:19).

He descended into hell—This phrase was probably the last to be added to the creed. Its principal source in the New Testament was the description in 1 Peter 3:18–20 of Christ's preaching to the spirits in prison. Originally the descent into hell may have been identified with the death of Christ, when he entered the abode of the dead. But in the time before it entered the creed, the descent was frequently taken to mean that Christ had gone to rescue the souls of the Old Testament faithful from the underworld, from what Western Catholic theology eventually called the *limbus patrum*. Among some of the CHURCH FATHERS the descent into hell had come to mean Christ's declaration of his triumph over the powers of hell. Despite its subsequent growth in importance, however, the doctrine of the descent into hell apparently did not form an integral part of the apostolic preaching about Christ in the way that the Crucifixion and the Resurrection did.

Glorification.   The third day he rose again from the dead—The writers of the New Testament nowhere made the Resurrection of Christ a matter for argument, but everywhere asserted it and assumed it. With it began that state in the history of Jesus Christ that was still continuing, his elevation to glory. They used it as a basis for three kinds of affirmations. The Resurrection of Christ was the way God bore witness to his Son, "designated Son of God in power according to the Spirit of holiness by his resurrection from the dead" (Romans 1, 4); this theme was prominent also in the book of Acts. The Resurrection was also the basis for the Christian hope of life after death (1 Thessalonians 4:14), and without it that hope was said to be baseless (1 Corinthians 15:12–20). The Resurrection of Christ was also the ground for admonitions to manifest a "newness of life" (Romans 6:4) and to "seek the things that are above" (Colossians 3:1). The writers of the New Testament themselves expressed no doubt that the Resurrection had really happened. But Paul's discussion in 1 Corinthians 15 and the response to his message in Athens as described in Acts 17:32 show that among those who heard the Christian message there was such doubt, as well as efforts to rationalize the Resurrection. The differences among the Gospels, and between the Gospels and Paul, suggest that from the outset a variety of traditions existed regarding the details of the Resurrection. But such differences only serve to emphasize how universal was the faith in the Resurrection amid this variety of traditions.

He ascended into heaven and sits at the right hand of God the Father Almighty—As indicated earlier, the narrative of the ASCENSION is peculiar to Luke and Acts, but other parts of the New Testament may refer to it. Ephesians 4:8–10 may be such a reference, but many interpreters hold that, for Paul, Resurrection was identical with Ascension. That, they maintain, is why Paul could speak of the appearance of the risen Christ to him in continuity with Christ's appearances to others (1 Corinthians 15:5–8) despite the fact that, in the chronology of the creed, the Ascension intervened between these appearances. Session at the right hand of the Father was apparently a Christian interpretation of Psalms 110:1. It implied the elevation—or, as the doctrine of preexistence became clearer, the restoration—of Christ to a position of honor with God. Taken together, the Ascension and the session were a way of speaking about the presence of Christ with the Father during the interim between the Resurrection and the Second Advent. From Ephesians 4:8–16, it is evident that this way of speaking was by no means inconsistent with another Christian tenet, the belief that Christ was still present in and with his church. It was, in fact, the only way to state that tenet in harmony with the doctrine of the Resurrection.

Whence He will come to judge the living and the dead—The creed concludes its Christological section with the doctrine of the Second Advent: the first Advent was a coming into the flesh, the Second Advent a coming in glory. Much controversy among modern scholars has been occasioned by the role of this doctrine in the early church. Those who maintain that Jesus erroneously expected the early end of the world have often interpreted Paul as the first of those who began the adjustment to a delay in the end, with John's Gospel as a more advanced stage of that adjustment. Those who hold that the imminence of the end was a continuing aspect of human history as Jesus saw it also maintain that this phrase of the creed was a statement of that imminence, without any timetable necessarily implied. From the New Testament it seems that both the hope of the SECOND COMING and a faith in the continuing presence of Christ belonged to the outlook of the apostolic church, and that seems to be what the creed meant. The phrase "the living and the dead" is a summary of passages like 1 Corinthians 15:51–52 and 1 Thessalonians 4:15–17.

In order to complete the confession of the creed regarding the glorification of Christ, the NICENE CREED added the phrase: "Of his kingdom there shall be no end." This was a declaration, apparently provoked by speculation on the basis of 1 Corinthians 15:28 that the end of history would mean the end of the rule of Christ, that Christ's return as judge would usher in the full exercise of his reign over the world. Such was the expectation of the apostolic church, based on what it knew and believed about Jesus Christ.

Established Christianity. In the first decades of the 4th century Christianity received a boon that shaped its history: toleration, recognition, and eventually establishment by the state. The emperor CONSTANTINE I the Great, for what appears to have been a mixture of personal and political motives, identified himself with the Christian movement. Except for a brief revival of traditional religions under Julian ("the Apostate"), who died in 363, Christianity, whether orthodox or heretical, was the religion of the Roman emperors thereafter, as it was of the Germanic tribes who eventually displaced and then "revived" the empire in the West. So it was that after Rome had fallen, Christianity preserved many of the values of Rome and thus provided later centuries with a link to classical culture.

Christian dogma, theology, and institutions: the ancient councils. The acceptance of Christianity by the Roman emperors helped to make possible the establishment of general councils as a means for adjudicating controversies in the areas of doctrine and discipline. The main lines of

Bronze paten (disk) combining the monogram of Christ (the Chi-Rho) with the Greek letters alpha and omega, which signify his divinity, Byzantine from the time of Constantine; at the Campo Santo Teutonico, Rome
Laurie Platt Winfrey, Inc.

orthodox Christian teaching about the person of Christ were set by the New Testament and the ancient creeds. But what was present there in a germinal form became a clear statement of Christian doctrine when it was formulated as dogma. In one way or another, the first six ecumenical councils were all concerned with the formulation of the dogma regarding the person of Christ—his relation to the Father, and the relation of the divine and the human in him. Such a formulation became necessary because teachings arose in the Christian community that seemed to threaten what the church believed and confessed about Christ. Both the dogma and the heretical teachings against which the dogma was directed are therefore part of the history of Jesus Christ.

Early heresies—From the outset Christianity has had to contend with those who offered unorthodox interpretations of the person and mission of Jesus. Both the New Testament and the early confessions of the church referred and replied to such interpretations. As the Christian movement gained adherents from the non-Jewish world, it had to explain Christ in the face of new challenges.

These unorthodoxies touched both the question of his humanity and the matter of his deity. A concern to safeguard the humanity of Jesus led some early Christians to teach that Jesus of Nazareth, an ordinary man, was adopted as the Son of God in the moment of his baptism or after his Resurrection; this movement was called ADOPTIONISM. Gnostics and others wanted to protect him against involvement in the world of matter, which they regarded as essentially evil, and therefore taught that he had only an apparent body, not a real one; they were called DOCETISTS. Most of the struggle over the person of Christ, however, dealt with the question of his relation to the Father. Some early views were so intent upon asserting Jesus' identity with the Father that the distinction of his separate personhood was lost and he became merely a manifestation of the one God. Because of this idea of Christ as a "mode" of divine self-manifestation, proponents of this view were dubbed "modalists"; from an early supporter of the view it was called "Sabellianism." Other interpretations of the person of Christ in relation to God went to the opposite extreme. They insisted so strenuously upon the distinctness of his person from that of the Father in order to safeguard the biblical insistence on monotheism that they subordinated him to the Father. Many early exponents of the doctrine of the Logos were also subordinationists, so that the Logos idea itself became suspect in some quarters. What was needed was a framework of concepts with which to articulate the doctrine of Christ's oneness with the Father and yet distinctness from the Father and thus to answer the question posed by the late 19th-century German theologian and historian of dogma Adolf von Harnack: "Is the Divinity which has appeared on earth and reunited men with God identical with that supreme Divinity which governs heaven and earth, or is it a DEMIGOD?"

The Council of Nicaea—That question forced itself upon the church through the teachings of ARIUS. He maintained that the Logos was the first of the creatures called into being by God as the agent or instrument through which he was to make all things. Christ was thus less than God, but more than man; he was divine, but he was not God. To meet the challenge of ARIANISM, which threatened to split the church, the newly converted emperor Constantine convoked in 325 the first ecumenical council of the Christian church at Nicaea. The private opinions of the attending bishops were anything but unanimous, but the opinion that carried the day was that espoused by the young presbyter ATHANASIUS, who later became bishop of Alexandria. The COUNCIL OF NICAEA determined that Christ was "begotten, not made," that he was therefore not creature but Creator. It also asserted that he was "of the same essence as the Father" (*homoousios to patri*). In this way the Council made clear its basic opposition to subordinationism, even though there could be, and were, quarrels about details. It was not equally clear how the position of Nicaea and of Athanasius differed from modalism. Athanasius asserted that it was not the Father nor the Holy Spirit but only the Son who became incarnate as Jesus Christ. But in order to assert this, he needed a more adequate terminology concerning the "persons" (to use later Latin terminology) in the Holy Trinity. So the settlement at Nicaea regarding the person of Christ made necessary a fuller clarification of the doctrine of the Trinity, and that clarification in turn made possible—and necessary—a fuller statement of the doctrine of the person of Christ.

The Council of Constantinople—Nicaea did not put an end to the controversies but only gave the parties a new rallying point. Doctrinal debate was complicated by the rivalry among bishops and theologians as well as by the intrusion of imperial politics that had begun at Nicaea. Out of the post-Nicene controversies came that fuller statement of the doctrine of the Trinity that was needed to protect the Nicene formula against the charge of failing to distinguish adequately between the Father and the Son. Ratified at the COUNCIL OF CONSTANTINOPLE in 381, that statement made official the terminology developed by the supporters of Nicene orthodoxy in the middle of the 4th century: one divine essence, three divine persons (*mia ousia, treis hypostaseis*). The three persons, Father, Son, and Holy Spirit, were distinct from one another but were equal in their eternity and power. Now it was possible to teach, as Nicaea had, that Christ was "of the same essence as the Father" without arousing the suspicion of modalism. Although this doctrine seemed to make problematical the unity of God, it did provide an answer to the first of the two issues confronted by the church in its doctrine of the person of Christ—the issue of Christ's relation to the Father. It now became necessary to clarify the second issue—the relation of the divine and the human within Christ.

The Councils of Ephesus and Chalcedon—By excluding several extreme positions from the circle of orthodoxy, the formulation of the doctrine of the Trinity in the 4th century determined the course of subsequent discussion about the person of Christ. It also provided the terminology for that discussion, since 5th-century theologians were able, within careful limits, to describe the relation between the divine and the human in Christ by analogy to the relation between the Father and the Son in the Trinity. The term that was found to express this relation in Christ was the term *physis*—meaning "nature." There were three divine persons in one divine essence and in one divine nature; such was the outcome of the controversies in the 4th century. But there were also two natures, one of them divine and the other human, in the one person Jesus Christ. Over the relation between these two natures the theologians of the 5th and 6th centuries carried on their controversies, on which the Second and Third Councils of Constantinople in 553 and in 680–81 pronounced in their decrees.

The abstract questions with which they sometimes dealt in those controversies, some of them almost unintelligible to a modern mind, must not be permitted to obscure the fact that a basic issue of the Christian faith was at stake: How can Jesus Christ be said to possess that identity with God that he must have to be our Savior, and yet be called our brother, as he truly must be to make his salvation available to us?

Alexandria and Antioch—During the half century after the Council of Constantinople several major points

Christ being tempted by the devil, Temptation of Christ, *engraving by Master LCZ (Lorenz Katzheimer),* c. *1492*

National Gallery of Art, Washington, D.C., Rosenwald Collection, B-11149

of emphasis developed in the doctrine of the person of Christ; characteristically, these are usually defined by the episcopal see that espoused them. There was a way of talking about Christ that was characteristic of the see at Alexandria. It stressed the divine character of all that Jesus Christ had been and done, but its enemies accused it of absorbing the humanity of Christ in his divinity. The mode of thought and language employed at Antioch, on the other hand, emphasized the true humanity of Christ; but its opponents maintained that in so doing it had split Christ into two persons, each of whom maintained his individual selfhood while they acted in concert with each other. Western theology was not as abstract as either of these alternatives. Its central emphasis was a practical concern for human salvation and for as harmonious a settlement of the conflict as was possible without sacrificing that concern.

Even more than had been the case in the 4th century, considerations of imperial politics were always involved in conciliar actions, together with the fear in countries like Egypt that Constantinople might come to dominate them. Thus a decision regarding the relation between the divine and the human in Christ could be simultaneously a decision regarding the political situation. Nevertheless, the settlements at which the councils of the 5th century arrived may be and are regarded as normative in the church long after their political setting has disappeared.

The conflict between Alexandria and Antioch came to a head when NESTORIUS, the PATRIARCH of Constantinople, taking exception to the use of the title "Mother of God" or, more literally, "God-Bearer" (THEOTOKOS) for the Virgin Mary, insisted that she was only "Christ-Bearer." In this insistence the Antiochian emphasis upon the distinction between the two natures in Christ made itself heard throughout the church. The Alexandrian theologians responded by charging that Nestorius was dividing the person of Christ, which they represented as so completely united that, in the famous phrase of Cyril, there was "one nature of the Logos which became incarnate." By this he meant that there was only one nature, the divine, before the Incarnation, but that after the Incarnation there were two natures indissolubly joined in one person; Christ's human nature had never had an independent existence. There were times when Cyril appeared to be saying that there was "one nature of the incarnate Logos" even after the Incarnation, but his most precise formulations avoided this language. The COUNCIL OF EPHESUS in 431 was one in a series of gatherings called to settle this conflict, some by one party and some by the other. It also made official and binding the designation of the Virgin Mary as "Theotokos."

The Council of Chalcedon—But the actual settlement was not accomplished until the calling of the COUNCIL OF CHALCEDON in 451. The basis of that settlement was the Western understanding of the two natures in Christ, as formulated in the *Tome* of POPE LEO I of Rome. Chalcedon declared: "We all unanimously teach . . . one and the same Son, our Lord Jesus Christ, perfect in deity and perfect in humanity . . . in two natures, without being mixed, transmuted, divided, or separated. The distinction between the natures is by no means done away with through the union, but rather the identity of each nature is preserved and concurs into one person and being." In this formula the valid emphases of both Alexandria and Antioch came to expression; both the unity of the person and the distinctness of the natures were affirmed. Therefore the decision of the Council of Chalcedon has been the basic statement of the doctrine of the person of Christ for most of the church ever since.

Emerging from this period, then, was an interpretation of the person of Christ that affirmed both his oneness with God and his oneness with humanity while still maintaining the oneness of his person. Interestingly, the liturgies of the church had maintained this interpretation at a time when the theologians of the church were still struggling for clarity, and the final solution was a scientifically precise restatement of what had been present germinally in the liturgical piety of the church. In the formula of Chalcedon that solution finally found the framework of concepts and of vocabulary that it needed to become intellectually consistent. In one sense, therefore, what Chalcedon formulated was what Christians had been believing from the beginning; in another sense it represented a development from the earlier stages of Christian thought.

Thus the classical Christian dogmas of the Trinity and the person of Christ emerged from the decisions of the councils in the 4th, 5th, and 6th centuries, dogmas that have been the criteria of Christian orthodoxy ever since. Christianity thus acquired an intellectual formulation that befitted its new status as the dominant religious force in the Mediterranean world. It acquired theological spokesmen also, whose speculations and systematizations, based upon Scripture and dogma, created the vocabulary and set the style for a Christian culture. Most prominent among these theologians in the West was AUGUSTINE of Hippo (354–430), whose *City of God* summarized the case for Christianity against competing faiths, and whose treatise *On the Trinity* combined fidelity to authority with philosophical reflection into a new synthesis. The Greek-speaking portions of the church were more richly endowed with theological leaders than was the Christian West. Athanasius defended the full deity of Christ against the Arians. BASIL, GREGORY OF NYSSA, and GREGORY OF NAZIANSUS, "the Cappadocian Fathers," refined and expanded the teachings of Athanasius into a more complete doctrine of the Trinity.

The Alexandrians and the Antiochians continued the controversies that had preceded Chalcedon, but they clashed as well now over how to interpret Chalcedon. The controversy over the MONOPHYSITES (those who believed Christ had one nature, which combined both the divine and human) and the Monothelites (those who accepted the orthodox position that Christ had two distinct natures but posited that he had only one will) was an effort to clarify the interpretation of Chalcedon, with the result that the extremes of the Alexandrian position were condemned just as the NESTORIAN extreme of the Antiochian had been.

The Church Fathers.   With Christianity's increased political recognition, MONASTICISM arose as a way to express the continuing separation of the church from the world. The figure of the hermit ANTHONY OF EGYPT, dramatically described in the biography of him by Athanasius, represented the Christianization of an ASCETICISM that had been at work in Egypt even before the coming of the gospel. A second stage in the development of monasticism was the rise of the communal or cenobitic form of the monastic life and the establishment of monasteries and CONVENTS, first in the Eastern section of the church through the work of PACHOMIUS and then much later (6th century) in the Western portion through the work of BENEDICT OF NURSIA. Instituted as a means of denying the world, monasticism became, through its role in the missionary enterprise and through its educational work, one of the principal means by which Christianity was able to spread. Another factor was the growth in the prestige and power of the bishop of Rome. Pope Leo I the Great (d. 461) made the primacy of the Roman bishop explicit both in theory and in practice and must be counted as one of the most important figures in the history of the centralization of authority in the church. The next such figure was GREGORY I the Great, pope from 590 to 604, whose work shaped the worship, the thought, and the structure of the church as well as its temporal wealth and power.

With the determination of the orthodox teaching of the church regarding the person of Christ, it still remained necessary to clarify the doctrine of the work of

Christ. While it had been principally in the East that the discussion of the former question was carried on, it was the Western church that provided the most detailed answers to the question: Granted that this is what Jesus Christ was, how are we to describe what it is that he did?

The most representative spokesman of the Western church on this question, as on most others, was Augustine. His deep understanding of the meaning of human sin was matched by his detailed attention to the meaning of divine grace. Central to that attention was his emphasis upon the humanity of Jesus Christ as assurance of human salvation, an emphasis to which he gave voice in a variety of ways. The humanity of Christ showed, for Augustine, how God elevated the humble; it was the link between human physical nature and the spiritual nature of God; it was the sacrifice that the human race offered to God; it was the foundation of a new humanity, re-created in Christ as the old humanity had been created in Adam—in these and other ways Augustine sought to describe the importance of the Incarnation for the redemption of humanity. By combining this stress upon the humanity of Christ as Savior with a doctrine of the Trinity that was orthodox but nevertheless highly creative and original, Augustine put his mark indelibly upon Western piety and theology.

The common theme in all these figures of speech concerning God and humanity was the desire to do two things simultaneously: to emphasize that the reunion was an act of God, and to safeguard the participation of humans in that act. Some theories current at the time were so "objective" in their emphasis upon the divine initiative that humans almost seemed to be pawns in the transaction between God in Christ and the Devil. Other theories so "subjectively" concentrated their attention upon human involvement and human response that the full scope of the redemption as a product of the divine initiative in grace could vanish from sight. It was to be in ANSELM OF CANTERBURY (d. 1109) that Western Christendom eventually found a theologian who could bring together elements from many theories into one doctrine of the atonement, summarized in his book, *Cur Deus homo?* (1099; "Why Did God Become Man?"). According to this doctrine, sin was a violation of the honor of God. God offered humans life if they rendered satisfaction for that violation; but the longer these humans lived, the worse their personal situation became. Only a life that was truly human and yet had infinite worth would have been enough to give such a satisfaction to the violated honor of God on behalf of the entire human race. Such a life was that of Jesus Christ, whom the mercy of God sent as a means of satisfying the justice of God. Because he was truly human, his life and death could be valid for humans; because he was true God, his life and death could be valid for *all* humans. By accepting the fruits of his life and death, humanity could receive the benefits of his satisfaction. With some minor alterations, Anselm's doctrine of atonement passed over into the theology of the Latin church, forming the basis of both Roman Catholic and orthodox Protestant ideas of the work of Christ. It owed its acceptance to many factors, not the least of them being the way it squared with the liturgy and art of the West. The crucifix has become the traditional symbol of Christ in the Western church, reinforcing and being reinforced by the satisfaction theory of the atonement.

Byzantine Christianity. Still a part of the universal church but increasingly isolated from the West by differences of language, culture, politics, and religion, Byzantine Christianity followed its own course in the shaping of the heritage of the early church. The Eastern churches never became as centralized in their polity as did the church in the West but developed the principle of the relative independence or "autocephaly" of each national church (*see* AUTOCEPHALOUS CHURCH). During the centuries when Western culture was striving to assimilate the German tribes, Constantinople, probably the most civilized city in Christendom, blended classical and Christian elements with a refinement that expressed itself in philosophy, the arts, statecraft, jurisprudence, and scholarship. A thinker such as Michael Psellus in the 11th century, who worked in several of these fields, epitomizes this synthesis. It was from Byzantine rather than from Roman missionaries that most of the Slavic tribes received Christianity; Byzantium was also the victim of Muslim aggressions throughout the period known in the West as the

Middle Ages. Following the pattern established by the emperors Constantine and Justinian, the relation between CHURCH AND STATE in the Byzantine empire was coordinated in such a way as to often subject the life and even the teaching of the church to the decisions of the temporal ruler—the phenomenon frequently, though oversimply, termed CAESAROPAPISM.

All these differences between the Eastern and the Western parts of the church, both the religious differences and those that were largely cultural or political, came together to cause the SCHISM between the two. It is not easy to date this schism, for the alienation between West and East erupted several times: in the 9th century through conflict over the MISSION to the Slavs; in the 11th century as a contest over rank and authority; in the 13th century with great vehemence in the Christian sack of Constantinople by the Fourth Crusade in 1204 and the establishment of the Latin patriarchate there; in the 15th century after the failure of the union of Florence and after the fall of Constantinople to the Turks. Whatever the date, the two divisions of the church have existed, both in spirit and in fact, for about half of Christian history, more than twice as long as PROTESTANTISM and ROMAN CATHOLICISM.

Papacy and empire. Conflict with the East was both a cause and an effect of the distinctive development of Western Christianity during the Middle Ages. If popes Leo I and Gregory I may be styled the architects of the medieval PAPACY, popes GREGORY VII (d. 1085) and INNOCENT III (d. 1216) should be called its master builders. Gregory VII reformed both the church and the papacy from within, establishing the canonical and moral authority of the papal office when it was threatened by corruption and attack; Innocent III made the papal claims to universality an ecclesiastical and political fact, exercising his authority at all levels of the life of the church in the 13th century. Significantly, both these popes were obliged to defend the papacy against the Holy Roman Empire and other temporal rulers. The battle between the church and the empire is a persistent theme in the history of medieval Christianity. Both the involvement of the church in feudalism and the participation of temporal rulers in the Crusades can be read as variations on this theme. Preoccupied as they often are with the history of the church as an institution and with the life and thought of the leaders of the church, the documentary sources of knowledge about medieval Christianity make it difficult for the historian to descry "the religion of the common man" during this period, but late 20th-century social history has made great progress in doing so. Both the "age of faith" depicted by neo-Gothic ROMANTICISM and the "dark ages" depicted by secularist and Protestant polemics are a gross oversimplification of history; only that historical judgment of medieval Christianity is valid that discerns how subtly faith and superstition can be blended in the piety and thought of medieval (and of modern) thinkers and of ordinary believers.

Medieval thought. No product of medieval Christianity has been more influential in the centuries since the Middle Ages than medieval thought, particularly the philosophy and theology of SCHOLASTICISM, whose outstanding exponent was THOMAS AQUINAS (d. 1274). The theology of scholasticism was an effort to harmonize the doctrinal traditions inherited from the Fathers of the early church and to relate these traditions to the intellectual achievements of classical antiquity. Because many of the early Fathers both in the East and in the West had developed their theologies under the influence of Platonic modes of thought, the reinterpretation of these theologies by scholasticism required that the doctrinal content of the tradition be disengaged from the metaphysical assumptions of Platonism. For this purpose the recovery of Aristotle—first through the influence of Aristotelian philosophers and theologians among the Muslims and eventually, with some help from Byzantium, through translation and study of the authentic texts of Aristotle himself—was providential to the scholastic theologians. Because it managed to

St. Francis and Episodes from His Life, *altarpiece panel by Bonaventura Berlinghieri, 1235; in the Church of San Francesco, Pescia, Italy*
Scala—Art Resource

combine a fidelity to Scripture and tradition with a positive, though critical, attitude toward the "natural" mind, scholasticism is a landmark both in the history of Christianity and in the history of Western culture. Very few theological systems have managed to play this dual role, which can be a symbol (depending upon one's own position) either of the Christianization of society and culture or of the betrayal of Christianity to the society and culture of the Middle Ages.

Scholastic theology, therefore, did not modify traditional ways of speaking about either the person or the work of Christ as sharply as it did, for example, some of the ways the Church Fathers had spoken about the presence of the body and blood of Christ in the Eucharist. The major contribution of the scholastic period (which dates from about the 6th century to the 17th century) to the Christian conception of Jesus Christ appears to lie in the way it managed to combine theological and mystical elements. Alongside the growth of Christological dogma and sometimes in apparent competition with it was the development of a view of Christ that emphasized personal union with him in addition to accurate concepts about him. Such a view of Christ appeared occasionally in the writings of Augustine, but it was in men like BERNARD OF CLAIRVAUX that it attained both its fullest expression and its most adequate harmonization with the dogmatic view. The relation between the divine and the human natures in Christ, as formulated in ancient dogma, provided the mystics, both men and women, with the ladder they needed to ascend through the man Jesus to the eternal Son of God, and through him to a mystical union with the Holy Trinity; this had been anticipated in the mystical theology of some of the Greek Fathers. At the same time the dogma saved MYSTICISM from the pantheistic excesses to which it might otherwise have gone; for the doctrine of the two natures meant that the humanity of the Lord was not an expendable element in Christian piety, mystical or not, but its indispensable presupposition and the continuing object of its adoration, in union with his deity. As a matter of fact, another contribution of the medieval development was the increased emphasis of ST. FRANCIS OF ASSISI (d. 1226) and his followers upon the human life of Jesus. These brotherhoods cultivated a more practical and ethical version of mystical devotion, to be distinguished from speculative and CONTEMPLATIVE mysticism. As expressed in the IMITATION OF CHRIST, a late medieval work that achieved wide circulation, their theme became the imitation of Christ in a life of humility and obedience. With it came a new appreciation of that true humanity of Christ which the dogma had indeed affirmed but which theologians had been perceived as being in danger of reducing to a mere dogmatic concept.

Adoration of the Lamb of God, surrounded by the Evangelists and 12 of the 24 elders, from a 10th-century Spanish commentary on the Apocalypse
The Pierpont Morgan Library—Art Resource

Reformation. It was the latter interpretation of scholasticism as a betrayal of Christianity that, in part, animated the Protestant REFORMATION. Protestantism differed from the various protest movements during the later Middle Ages by the thoroughness of its polemic against the ecclesiastical, theological, and sacramental developments of Western Catholicism. Initially the Protestant Reformers maintained the hope that they could accomplish the reformation of the doctrine and life of the church from within, but this proved impossible (again depending upon one's position) either because of the intransigency of the church or because of the extremism of the Protestant movements or because of the political and cultural situation—or for all of these reasons combined. The several parties of the Reformation may be conveniently classified according to the radicalism of their protest against medieval theology, piety, and polity. The Anglican Reformers (*see* ANGLICAN COMMUNION), as well as MARTIN LUTHER and his movement, were, in general, the most conservative in their treatment of the Roman Catholic tradition; JOHN CALVIN and his followers were less conservative; the ANABAPTISTS and other groups in the left wing of the Reformation were least conservative of all. Despite their deep differences, the various Reformation movements were almost all characterized by an emphasis upon the BIBLE, as distinguished from the church and its tradition, as the authority in religion; by an insistence upon the sovereignty of free grace in the forgiveness of sins; by a stress upon faith alone, without works, as the precondition of acceptance with God; and by the demand that the laity assume a more significant place in both the work and the worship of the church.

The attitude of most of the reformers toward the traditional conception of the person and work of Christ was conservative. Insisting for both religious and political reasons that they were orthodox, they altered very little in the Christological dogma. Luther and Calvin gave the dogma a new meaning when they related it to their doctrine of JUSTIFICATION by grace through faith. Because of his interpretation of sin as the captivity of the will, Luther also revived the patristic metaphor of the atonement as the victory of Christ; it is characteristic of him that he wrote hymns for both Christmas and Easter, but not for Lent. The new attention to the Bible that came with the Reformation created interest in the earthly life of Jesus, while the Reformation idea of "grace alone" and of the sovereignty of God even in his grace made the deity of Christ a matter of continuing importance.

In the ideas about the Lord's Supper set forth by HULDRYCH ZWINGLI, Luther thought he saw not only a weakening of the belief in the real presence but a threat to the orthodox doctrine of Christ, and he denounced those doctrines vehemently. As this controversy progressed, Luther interpreted the ancient dogma of the two natures to mean that the omnipresence of the divine nature was communicated to the human nature of Christ, and that therefore Christ as both God and man was present everywhere, and hence could be truly present in the bread and wine of the sacrament. Although he repudiated both Luther's and Zwingli's theories, Calvin was persuaded that the ancient Christological dogma was true to the biblical witness and he permitted no deviation from it. All this is evidence for the significance that "Jesus Christ, true God begotten of the Father from eternity, and also true man, born of the Virgin Mary," to use Luther's formula, had been retained in the faith and theology of all the reformers.

At one point the theology of the reformers did serve to bring together several facets of the biblical and the patristic descriptions of Jesus Christ. That was the doctrine of the threefold office of Christ, anticipated as early as the 4th century but systematized by Calvin and developed more fully in Protestant orthodoxy: Christ as prophet, priest, and king. Each of these symbolized the fulfillment of the Old Testament and represented one aspect of the church's continuing life. Christ as prophet fulfilled and elevated the prophetic tradition of the Old Testament, while continuing to fulfill his prophetic office in the ministry of the preaching of the Word. Christ as priest brought to an end the sacrificial system of the Old Testament by being both the priest and the victim, while he continued to function as intercessor with and for the church. Christ as king was the royal figure to whom the Old Testament had pointed, while exercising his rule among humans now through those whom he had appointed. In each of the three, Protestants differed from one another according to their theological, ethical, or liturgical positions. But the threefold office enabled Protestant theology to take into account the complexity of the biblical and patristic pictures of Christ as no oversimplified theory was able to do, and it is probably the chief contribution of the reformers to the theological formulation of the doctrine of the "office" or work of Christ.

The Reformation was originally launched as a movement within the established Christianity that had prevailed since Constantine. It envisaged neither schism within the church nor the dissolution of the Christian culture that had developed for more than a millennium. But by the time the Reformation was over, both the church and the culture had been radically transformed. In part this transformation was the consequence of the Reformation, in part it was the accompaniment of the Reformation. The voyages of discovery, the beginnings of a capitalistic economy, the rise of modern nationalism, the dawn of the scientific age, the culture of the Renaissance—all these factors, and others besides, helped to break up the "medieval synthesis." Among these factors, however, the Reformation was one of the most important, and certainly for the history of Christianity the most significant. For the consequences of the Reformation, not in intention but in fact, were a divided Christendom and a secularized West. Roman Catholicism, no less than Protestantism, has developed historically in the modern world as an effort to adapt historic forms to the implications of these consequences. Established Christianity, as it had been known in the West since the 4th century, ended after the Reformation, though not all at once.

Modern Christianity. Paradoxically, the end of "established Christianity" in the old sense resulted in the most rapid and most widespread expansion of Christianity and the Gospel in the history of the church. The Christianization of the Americas and the evangelization of Asia, Africa, and Australasia have given geographical substance to the Christian title "ecumenical." Growth in areas and in numbers, however, need not be equivalent to growth in influence. Despite its continuing strength throughout the modern period, Christianity has retreated on many fronts and has lost much of its prestige and authority.

During the formative period of modern Western history, roughly from the beginning of the 16th to the middle of the 18th century, Christianity participated in many of the movements of cultural and political expansion. The explorers of the New World were followed closely by missionaries—that is, when the two were not in fact identical. Protestant and Roman Catholic clergymen were prominent in politics, letters, and science. Although the RATIONALISM of the Enlightenment alienated many people from the Christian faith, especially among the intellectuals of the 17th and 18th centuries, those who were alienated often kept a loyalty to the figure of Jesus or to the teachings of the Bible even when they broke with traditional forms of Christian doctrine and life. Citing the theological conflicts of the Reformation and the political conflicts that followed upon these as evidence of the dangers of religious intolerance, representatives of the Enlightenment gradually introduced disestablishment, toleration, and religious liberty into most Western countries; in this movement they were joined by various Christian individuals and groups that advocated religious freedom not out of indifference to dogmatic truth but out of a concern for the free decision of personal faith.

The earliest criticism of orthodox dogma, however, had come in the age of the Reformation, not from the mainline reformers but from the left wing of the Reformation, from MICHAEL SERVETUS (1511?–53) and the Socinians. This criticism was directed against the presence of nonbiblical concepts and terms in the dogma, and it was intent upon safeguarding the true humanity of Jesus as a moral example. There were many inconsistencies in this criticism, such as the willingness of Servetus to call Jesus "Son of God" and the Socinian custom of addressing prayer and worship to him. But it illustrates the tendency, which became more evident in the Enlightenment, to use the Reformation protest against Catholicism as a basis for a protest against orthodox dogma as well. While that tendency did not

gain much support in the 16th century because of the orthodoxy of the reformers, later criticism of orthodox Christology was able to wield the "Protestant principle" against the dogma of the two natures, on the grounds that this was a consistent application of what the reformers had done. Among the ranks of the Protestant laity, the hymnody and the catechetical instruction of the Protestant churches assured continuing support for the orthodox dogma. Indeed, the doctrine of atonement by the vicarious satisfaction of Christ's death has seldom been expressed as amply within Roman Catholic theology and spirituality as it was in the hymns and CATECHISMS of both the Lutheran and the Reformed churches. During the period of PIETISM in the Protestant churches, this loyalty to orthodox teaching was combined with a growing emphasis upon the humanity of Jesus, also expressed in the hymnody of the time, and above all in the sacred music of Johann Sebastian Bach and George Frideric Handel.

When theologians began to criticize orthodox ideas of the person and work of Christ, therefore, they met with opposition from the common people. ALBERT SCHWEITZER dates the development of a critical attitude from the work of H.S. Reimarus (1694–1768), but Reimarus was representative of the way the Enlightenment treated the traditional view of Jesus. The books of the Bible were to be studied just as other books are, and the life of Jesus was to be drawn from them by critically sifting and weighing the evidence of the Gospels. The Enlightenment thus initiated the modern interest in the life of Jesus, with its detailed attention

Members of the congregation of the Jerusalem Church of Christ in Kawangware, a neighborhood of Nairobi, Kenya, at prayer
Press—Monkmeyer

to the problem of the relative credibility of the Gospel records. The leaders of Enlightenment thought did not make a sudden break with traditional ideas, but gave up belief in miracles, the VIRGIN BIRTH, the Resurrection, and the Second Advent only gradually. Their principal importance for the history of the doctrine of Christ consists in the fact that they made the historical study of the sources for the life of Jesus an indispensable element of any Christology.

The state of Christian faith and life within the churches during the 17th and 18th centuries both reflected and resisted the spirit of the time. Even though the Protestant Reformation had absorbed some of the reformatory energy within Roman Catholicism, the theology and morals of the church underwent serious revision in the Catholic COUNTER-REFORMATION. Fighting off the attempts by various countries, most notably perhaps in the Gallicanism of France, to establish national Roman Catholic churches, the papacy sought to learn from the history of the Reformation and to avoid the mistakes that had been made then. Protestantism, meanwhile, discovered that separation from Rome did not necessarily inoculate it against many of the trends it had denounced in Roman Catholicism. The confessional orthodoxy of the 17th century both in LUTHERANISM and in the Reformed churches displayed many features of medieval scholasticism, despite the attacks of the Reformers upon the latter.

Although the Enlightenment of the 18th century was the beginning of the break with orthodox teachings about Jesus Christ, it was only in the 19th century that this break attracted wide support among theologians and scholars in many parts of Christendom—even, for a while, among the Modernists of the Roman Catholic church. Two works of the 19th century were especially influential in their rejection of orthodox Christology. One was the *Life of Jesus* first published in 1835 by David Friedrich Strauss; the other, bearing the same title, was first published by Ernest Renan in 1863. Strauss's work paid more attention to the growth of Christian ideas—he called them "myths"—about Jesus as the basis for the picture we have in the Gospels, while Renan attempted to account for Jesus' career by a study of his inner psychological life in relation to his environment. Both works achieved wide circulation and were translated into other languages, including English. They took up the Enlightenment contention that the sources for the life of Jesus were to be studied as other sources are, and what they constructed on the basis of the sources was a type of biography in the modern sense of the word. In addition to Strauss and Renan, the 19th century saw the publication of a plethora of books about the life and teachings of Jesus. Each new hypothesis regarding the problem of the SYNOPTIC GOSPELS implied a reconstruction of the life and message of Jesus.

The fundamental assumption for most of this work on the life and teachings of Jesus was a distinction between the "Jesus

Celebration for the feast of St. John the Baptist in a church named for him in Texhuacán, Mex.
Miguel Sayago—Photo Researchers

of history" and the "Christ of faith." Another favorite way of putting the distinction was to speak of the religion of Jesus in antithesis to the religion about Jesus. This implied that Jesus was a man like other men but with a heightened awareness of the presence and power of God. Then the dogma of the church had mistaken this awareness for a metaphysical statement that Jesus was the Son of God, the Second Person of the Trinity, and had thus distorted the original simplicity of his message. Some critics went so far as to question the very historicity of Jesus, but even those who did not go that far questioned the historicity of some of the sayings and deeds attributed to Jesus in the Gospels—above all, the miracles and the declarations of identity with God.

In part this effort grew out of the general concern of 19th-century scholarship with the problem of the historicity of much of traditional history, but it also reflected the religious and ethical assumptions of the theologians. Many of them were influenced by the moral theories of Immanuel Kant in their estimate of what was permanent about the teachings of Jesus, and by the historical theories of George William Friedrich Hegel in the way they related the original message of Jesus to the Christian interpretations of that message by later generations of Christians. The ideas of evolution and of natural causality associated with the science of the 19th century also played a part through the naturalistic explanations of the biblical miracles. And the historians of dogma, climaxing in Adolf von Harnack (1851–1930), used their demonstration of the dependence of ancient Christology upon non-Christian sources for its concepts and terminology to reinforce their claim that Christianity had to get back from the Christ of dogma to the "essence of Christianity" in the teachings of Jesus about the fatherhood of God and the brotherhood of man.

During the political revolutions of the 18th, 19th, and 20th centuries, Roman Catholicism in France, EASTERN ORTHODOXY in Russia, and Protestantism in former European colonies in Africa were identified—by their enemies if not also by themselves—as part of the *ancien régime* and were nearly swept away with it. As the discoveries of science proceeded, they clashed with old and cherished notions about the universe and about humanity, many of which were passionately supported by various leaders of organized Christianity. The age of the revolutions—political, economic, technological, intellectual—was an age of crisis for Christianity. It was also an age of opportunity. The critical methods of modern scholarship, despite their frequent attacks upon traditional Christian ideas, helped to produce editions of the chief documents of the Christian faith, the Bible and the writings of the Fathers and Reformers, and to arouse an unprecedented interest in the history of the church. The 19th century has been called the great century in the history of Christian missions, both Roman Catholic and Protestant. By the very force of their attacks upon Christianity the critics of the church helped to arouse within the church new apologists for the faith, who creatively reinterpreted it in relation to contemporary philosophy and science.

At the beginning of the 20th century the most influential authorities on the New Testament were still engaged in the quest for the essence of Christianity and for the Jesus of history. But that quest led in the early decades of the 20th century to a revolutionary conclusion regarding the teachings of Jesus—namely, that he had expected the end of the age to come shortly after his death and that his teachings as laid down in the Gospels were an "interim ethic," intended for the messianic community in the brief span of time still remaining before the end. The effort to apply those teachings in modern life was criticized as a dangerous MODERNIZATION. This thesis of the "consistent eschatology" in Jesus' message was espoused by Johannes von Weiss (1863–1914) and gained wide circulation through the writings of Albert Schweitzer.

The years surrounding World War I also saw the development of a new theory regarding the composition of the Gospels. Because of its origin, this theory is usually called form criticism (German *Formgeschichte*). It stressed the forms of the Gospel narratives—parables, sayings, miracle stories, Passion accounts, etc.—as an indication of the ORAL TRADITION in the Christian community out of which the narratives came. While the attention of earlier scholars had been concentrated on the authenticity of Jesus' teachings as transmitted in the Gospels, this new theory was less confident of being able to separate the authentic from the later elements in the Gospel records, though various proponents of it did suggest criteria by which such a separation might be guided. The studies of form criticism made a life of Jesus in the old biographical sense impossible, just as consistent eschatology had declared impossible the codification of a universal ethic from the teachings of Jesus. Some adherents of form criticism espoused an extreme skepticism regarding any historical knowledge of Jesus' life at all, but the work of men like Martin Dibelius and even RUDOLF BULTMANN showed that such skepticism was not warranted by the conclusions of this study.

Influenced by these trends in New Testament study, Protestant theology by the middle of the 20th century was engaged in a reinterpretation of the Christology of the early church. Some Protestant churches continued to repeat the formulas of ancient dogma, but even there the critical study of the New Testament documents was beginning to call those formulas into question. The struggles of the evangelical churches in Germany under Adolf Hitler, which achieved forceful expression in the Barmen Declaration of 1934, caused some theologians to realize anew the power of the ancient dogma of the person of Christ to sustain faith, and some of them were inclined to treat the dogma with less severity. But even they acknowledged that the formulation of that dogma in static categories of person, essence, and nature was inadequate to the biblical emphasis upon actions and events rather than upon states of being. KARL BARTH for the Reformed tradition, Lionel Thornton for the Anglican tradition, and Karl Heim for the Lutheran tradition were instances of theologians trying to reinterpret classical Christology. While yielding nothing of their loyalty to the dogma of the church, Roman Catholic theologians like Karl Adam and KARL RAHNER were also endeavoring to state that dogma in a form that was meaningful to modernity. The doctrine of the work of Christ was receiving less attention than the doctrine of Christ's person. In much of Protestantism, the concentration of the 19th century upon the teachings of Jesus had made it difficult to speak of more than the prophetic office. The priestly office received least attention of all; and therefore, despite the support accorded to efforts like that of Gustaf Aulén to reinterpret the metaphor of the atonement as Christ's victory over his enemies, Protestant theology in the middle of the 20th century was still searching for a doctrine of the atonement to match its newly won insights into the doctrine of the person of Christ, especially its new emphases on his humanity and his personality.

From the history of Christianity both the critics and the adherents of the Christian movement can derive support for their ideas. To the critics of Christianity its history can prove that Christian faith was tied inseparably to worldviews that had been outmoded by modern discoveries and that therefore the churches were living fossils, doomed to become extinct as the full implications of science dawned upon an increasing number of believers. To the adherents of Christanity its history can prove the almost infinite adaptability of the Christian faith to a great diversity of societies, cultures, and philosophies, as well as its ability to convey the grace of God to people of every social station and cultural background. Yet Christianity is not simply an important element of the history of Western culture. It continues to claim the faith and obedience of hundreds of millions.

PRESENT STATE OF CHRISTENDOM

A map of the religions of the world at the end of the 20th century would reveal that Christianity was the most widely disseminated faith on earth. Virtually no nation has remained unaffected by Christian missions, although in many countries Christians are only a small fraction of the total population. Most of the countries of Asia and of Africa have Christian minorities, some of these, as in India, numbering many million. Yet such a map would continue to show the concentration of Christians in the domain of European or "Western" culture.

Roman Catholicism.   The Roman Catholics in the world outnumber all other Christians combined. They are organized in an intricate system that spans the life of the church from the local PARISH to the papacy. Under the central authority of the papacy, the church is divided into DIOCESES, whose bishops act in the name and by the authority of the pope but retain considerable administrative freedom within their individual jurisdictions. Similarly, the parish priest stands as the executor of papal and diocesan directives. Alongside the diocesan organization and interacting with it is a chain of orders, congregations, and societies; all of them are, of course, subject to the pope, but they are not as directly responsible to the bishop as are the local parishes. It would, however, be a mistake to interpret the polity of the Roman Catholic church in so purely an organizational manner as this. For Roman Catholic polity rests upon a belief in a mandate that is traced to the action of Jesus Christ himself, when he invested Peter, and through Peter his successors, with the power of the keys in the church. Christ is the invisible head of his church, and by his authority the pope is the visible head.

This interpretation of the origin and authority of the church determines both the attitude of Roman Catholicism to the rest of Christendom and its relation to the social order. Believing itself to be the true church of Jesus Christ on earth, it cannot deal with other Christian traditions as equals without betraying its own identity. This does not mean, however, that anyone outside the visible fellowship of the Roman Catholic church cannot be saved; nor does it preclude the presence of "vestiges of the church" in the other Christian bodies. During the 20th century, above all in the actions of the SECOND VATICAN COUNCIL (1962–65), the Roman Catholic church has increasingly concerned itself with its "separated brethren" both in Eastern Orthodoxy and in the several Protestant churches. Thus the ecumenical movement has evoked interest not only in the Protestant groups with which it began but Orthodoxy and Roman Catholicism as well. As the true church of Christ on earth, Roman Catholicism also believes itself responsible for the proclamation of the will of God as knowable by human reason to organized society and to the state. This role has often brought the church into conflict with the state throughout church history. Yet the political activities of individual churchmen, of whom Cardinal de Richelieu and Cardinal Mazarin are good illustrations, must not be confused with the fundamental obligation the church feels itself to have, believing itself to be the divinely ordained society to which is given responsibility for the moral law that is binding upon all; thus, the church feels itself to be responsible for giving this moral law to the nations and for working toward a social and political order in which both supernatural revelation and natural law can function.

Doctrine. The understanding that Roman Catholicism has of itself, its interpretation of the proper relation between the church and the state, and its attitude to other Christian traditions are all based upon Roman Catholic doctrine. In great measure this doctrine is identical with that confessed by orthodox Christians of every label, and consists of the Bible, the dogmatic heritage of the ancient church as laid down in the historic creeds and in the decrees of the ecumenical councils, and the theological work of the great doctors of the faith in East and West. If, therefore, the presentation of the other Christian traditions in this article compares them with Roman Catholicism, this comparison has a descriptive rather than a normative function; for to a considerable degree, Protestantism and Eastern Orthodoxy have defined themselves in relation to Roman Catholicism. In addition, as this article will attempt to show, most Christians past and present do have a shared body of beliefs about God, Christ, and the way of salvation.

Roman Catholic doctrine is more than this shared body of beliefs, as is that of each of the groups. Mention need only be made of the three distinctive doctrines that achieved definitive formulation during the 19th and 20th centuries: PAPAL INFALLIBILITY and the IMMACULATE CONCEPTION of and bodily ASSUMPTION of the Virgin Mary. On most other major issues of doctrine Roman Catholicism and Eastern Orthodoxy are largely in agreement, while Protestantism differs from both of them on several. For example, Roman Catholic theology treats the doctrine of the sacraments differently from the way Orthodox theology does; but in contrast to Protestantism, both Roman Catholic and Orthodox doctrine insist upon the centrality of the seven sacraments—baptism, confirmation, Eucharist, extreme unction, penance, matrimony, and holy orders—as channels of divine grace.

Liturgy. The Roman Catholic doctrine of the sacraments is a summary, in theological form, of that which is affirmed by Roman Catholic liturgy. The church is not merely an organization, nor is it a school of doctrine. It is the place where divine and human meet, as God approaches through grace and humans approach through worship. Hence the focus of Roman Catholic piety is the Eucharist, which is both a sacrament and a sacrifice. The obligations of church membership are also derived from the sacramental system, either as preparations for worthy participation in it or as expressions of the obedience sustained by it. Instruction in these obligations is the responsibility of Roman Catholic educational institutions, which, despite the low educational level of church members in many cultures, surpass any other system of schools in Christian history in both size and the excellence of their products. The missions of the church and its institutions of mercy, like the schools, are largely in the hands of religious orders.

Churches of Eastern Christendom. Roughly 214,000,000 Christians belong to the various Christian traditions of the East. Separated from the West, the Orthodox churches of the East have developed their own way for half of Christian history. Each national church is autonomous. The "ecumenical patriarch" of Constantinople is not the Eastern pope but merely the first in honor among equals in jurisdiction. Eastern Orthodoxy interprets the primacy of Peter, and therefore that of the pope, similarly as first among equals and thus denies the right of the pope to speak and act for the entire church by himself, without a church council and without his episcopal colleagues. Because of this polity, Eastern Orthodoxy has identified itself more intimately with national cultures and with national regimes than has Roman Catholicism. Therefore the history of church-state relations in the East has been very different from that in the West, because the church in the East has sometimes tended toward the extreme of becoming a mere instrument of national policy, while the church in the West has sometimes tended toward the opposite extreme of attempting to dominate the state.

During most of the 20th century, most Eastern Orthodox believers and churches lived under hostile regimes, in particular under Marxism-Leninism in the Soviet Union and the Balkans, and had to endure devastating persecution. The fall of those regimes in the final two decades of the 20th century, therefore, presented those churches with new opportunities, but also with new challenges.

The history of ecumenical relations between Eastern Orthodoxy and Protestantism during the 20th century was also different from the history of Protestant-Roman Catholic relations. The hope for an eventual healing of the East-West schism was symbolized by the fraternal meeting between Pope Paul VI of Rome and Patriarch Athenagoras I of Constantinople in Jerusalem in 1964, which resulted in the mutual withdrawal of the ancient EXCOMMUNICATIONS pronounced by each of these sees upon the other. Meanwhile, Orthodox churches were also making connections with the WORLD COUNCIL OF CHURCHES and the NATIONAL COUNCIL OF THE CHURCHES OF CHRIST IN THE U.S.A., and some Orthodox churches even established ties with the Anglican Communion and with the OLD CATHOLIC CHURCH.

Doctrinal authority for Eastern Orthodoxy resides in the Scriptures, the ancient creeds, the decrees of the first seven ecumenical councils, and the tradition of the church. The scope and content of this tradition are not specified; hence it is not always easy to discover just what the Eastern Orthodox churches teach on a particular doctrinal question. In addition to the two issues mentioned in the discussion of Roman Catholicism above, the chief dogmatic difference between Roman Catholic and Eastern Orthodox thought is on the Western doctrine of the procession of the Holy Spirit from the Father and Son, the so-called FILIOQUE, which the East rejects as an unwarranted addition to the Nicene Creed.

But "orthodoxy," in the Eastern use of the term, means primarily not a species of doctrine but a species of worship. The Feast of Orthodoxy on the first Sunday of Lent celebrates the end of the ICONOCLASTIC CONTROVERSY and the restoration to the churches of the ICONS, which are basic to Orthodox piety. In Orthodox churches (as well as in those Eastern churches that have reestablished communion with Rome), the most obvious points of divergence from normal Western practice are the right of the clergy to marry before ORDINATION, though bishops may not be married, and the administration to the laity of both species (bread and wine) in the Eucharist at the same time by the method of intinction (dipping bread in wine and offering this combined Eucharist to communicants).

Protestantism. Although there is a greater variety of thought and expression within both Roman Catholicism and Eastern Orthodoxy than outsiders usually recognize, both must appear monolithic when compared with Protestantism. Formulating a definition of Protestantism that would include all its varieties has long been the despair of Protestant historians and theologians, for there is greater diversity within Protestantism than there is between some forms of Protestantism and some non-Protestant Christianity. For example, an Anglican or a Lutheran high-churchman has more in common with an Orthodox theologian than he has with a BAPTIST theologian. Amid all this diversity, however, it is possible to define Protestantism formally as non-Roman Western Christianity and to divide most of Protestantism into four major confessions or confessional families—Lutheran, Anglican, Reformed, and Free Church.

Lutheranism. The largest of these non-Roman Catholic denominations in the West is the Lutheran church, whose worldwide membership totals approximately 76,000,000. The Lutheran churches in Germany, in the several Scandinavian countries, and in the Americas are distinct from one another in polity, but almost all of them are related through various national and international councils, of which the Lutheran World Federation is the most comprehensive. Doctrinally, Lutheranism sets forth its distinctive position in the BOOK OF CONCORD, especially in the AUGSBURG CONFESSION. A long tradition of theological scholarship has been responsible for the development of this position into many and varied doctrinal systems. Luther, as noted above, moved conservatively in his reformation of the Roman Catholic liturgy, and the Lutheran church, although it has altered many of his liturgical forms, has remained a liturgically traditional church. Most of the Lutheran churches of the world have participated in the ecumenical movement and are members of the World Council of Churches, but Lutheranism has not moved very often across its denominational boundaries to establish full communion with other bodies. That situation changed, however, with the Leuenberg Concord of 1973 in Europe and the establishment of full communion between the Evangelical Lutheran Church in America and three Reformed churches in 1997.

The prominence of Lutheran societies in the history of missions during the 18th and 19th centuries gave an international character to the Lutheran church; so did the development of strong Lutheran churches in North America, where the traditionally German and Scandinavian membership of the church was gradually replaced by a more cosmopolitan constituency.

Anglicanism. The ANGLICAN COMMUNION, with perhaps 64,000,000 members, is not only the ESTABLISHED CHURCH of England but the Christian denomination of many believers throughout the world. Like Lutheranism, Anglicanism has striven to retain whatever it could of the Catholic tradition of liturgy and piety, but after the middle of the 19th century the Catholic revival in Anglicanism went much further in the restoration of ancient liturgical usage as well as of the doctrinal tradition. Although the Catholic revival also served to rehabilitate the authority of tradition in Anglican theology generally, great variety continued to characterize the theologians of the Anglican Communion. Anglicanism is set off from most other non-Roman churches in the West by its retention of and its insistence upon the APOSTOLIC SUCCESSION of ordaining bishops. The Anglican claim to this apostolic succession, despite its repudiation by Pope Leo XIII in 1896, has largely determined the role of the Church of England in the discussions among the churches. Anglicanism has often taken the lead in inaugurating such discussions, but it has demanded the presence of the historic episcopate as a prerequisite to the establishment of full communion. During the 19th and 20th centuries many leaders of Anglican thought were engaged in finding new avenues of communication with industrial society and with modern intellectual thought. The strength of Anglicanism in the New World and in the younger churches of Asia and Africa has confronted this communion with the problem of deciding its relations to new forms of Christian life in these new cultures. As its centuries-old reliance upon the establishment in England has been compelled to retrench, Anglicanism has discovered new ways of exerting its influence and of expressing its message.

Presbyterian and Reformed churches. Protestant bodies that owe their origins to the reformatory work of John Calvin and his associates in various parts of Europe are often termed "Reformed," particularly in Germany, France, and Switzerland. In Britain and in the United States they have usually taken their name from their distinctive polity and have been called PRESBYTERIAN. They number about 40,000,000. They are distinguished from both Lutheranism and Anglicanism by the thoroughness of their separation from Roman Catholic patterns of liturgy, piety, and even doctrine. Reformed theology has tended to emphasize the sole authority of the Bible with more rigor than has characterized the practice of Anglican or Lutheran thought, and it has looked with deeper suspicion upon the symbolic and sacramental traditions of the Catholic centuries. Perhaps because of its stress upon biblical authority, Reformed Protestantism has sometimes tended to produce a separation of churches along the lines of divergent doctrine or polity, by contrast with the inclusive or latitudinarian churchmanship of the more traditionalistic Protestant communions. This understanding of the authority of the Bible has also led Reformed Protestantism to its characteristic interpretation of the relation between church and state, sometimes rather oversimply labeled theocratic, according to which those charged with the proclamation of the revealed will of God in the Scriptures (*i.e.*, the ministers) are to address this will also to civil magistrates. As the church is "reformed according to the word of God," so the lives of the individuals in the church are to conform to the word of God; hence the Reformed tradition has assigned great prominence to the cultivation of moral uprightness among its members. During the 20th century most of the Reformed churches of the world took an active part in the ecumenical movement.

Free churches. In the 19th century the term "free churches" was applied in Great Britain to those Protestant bodies that did not conform to the establishment, such as CONGREGATIONALISTS, METHODISTS, and Baptists (and Presbyterians in England); but since that time it has come into usage among the counterparts to these churches in the United States, where each of them has grown larger than its British parent body. As the Reformed denominations go beyond both Anglicanism and Lutheranism in their independence of Catholic traditions and usages, so the free churches have tended to reject some of the Catholic remnants also in classical Presbyterian worship and theology. Baptists and Congregationalists see the local congregation of gathered believers as the most nearly adequate visible representation of Christ's people on earth. The Baptists requirement of free personal decision as a prerequisite of membership in the congregation leads to the restriction of baptism to believers (*i.e,* those who have made and confessed such a decision of faith) and therefore to the repudiation of infant baptism; this in turn leads to the restriction of communion at the Eucharist to those who have been properly baptized. In Methodism the free church emphasis upon personal commitment leads to a deep concern for moral perfection in the individual and for moral purity in the community. The DISCIPLES OF CHRIST, a free church that originated in the United States, make the New Testament the sole authority of doctrine and practice in the church, requiring no creedal subscription at all; a distinctive feature of their worship is their weekly celebration of communion. Emphasizing as they do the need for the continuing reformation of the church, the free churches have provided leadership and support for the ecumenical movement. This cooperation, as well as the course of their own historical development from spontaneous movements to ecclesiastical institutions possessing many of the features that the founders of the free churches had originally found objectionable in the establishment, has made the question of their future role in Christendom a central concern of free churches on both sides of the Atlantic.

Other churches and movements.   In addition to these major divisions of Protestantism, there are other churches and movements not so readily classifiable; some of them are quite small, but others number millions of members. These churches and movements would include, for example, the SOCIETY OF FRIENDS, known both for their cultivation of the "inward light" and for their pacifism; the UNITARIAN and Universalist bodies, which do not consistently identify themselves as Christian; Pentecostal churches and churches of divine healing, which profess to return to primitive Christianity; and many independent churches and groups, most of them characterized by a free liturgy and a fundamentalist theology. Separately and together, these groups illustrate how persistent has been the tendency of Christianity since its beginnings to proliferate sects, heresies, and movements. They illustrate also how elusive is the precise demarcation of Christendom, even for those observers whose definition of normative Christianity is quite exact.

World distribution of Christianity

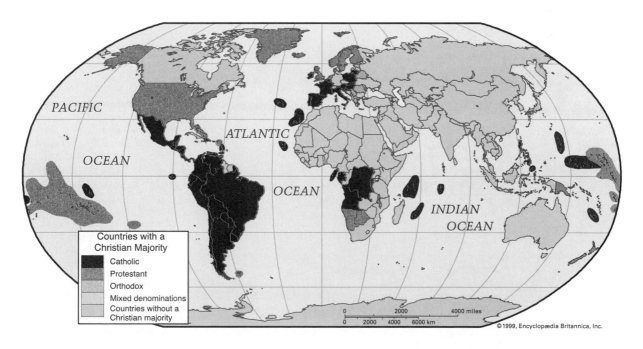

© 1999, Encyclopædia Britannica, Inc.

233

CHRISTIANITY, ART OF, art inspired by and often intended to offer instruction in the Christian faith. Because the history of Christian art is so extensive, tracing out its beginnings and influences to about the 6th century is all that is attempted in this article.

The earliest identifiably Christian art consists of a few 2nd-century wall and ceiling paintings in the Roman CATACOMBS (underground burial chambers), which continued to

A 3rd-century ceiling painting in the catacombs of SS. Peter and Marcellinus, Rome, shows the Good Shepherd in the center and panels illustrating the story of Jonah
Vincenzo Biolghini

be decorated in a sketchy style derived from Roman impressionism through the 4th century. They provide an important record of some aspects of the development of Christian subject matter. The earliest Christian ICONOGRAPHY tended to be symbolic. A simple rendering of a fish was sufficient to allude to JESUS CHRIST. Bread and wine invoked the EUCHARIST. During the 3rd and 4th centuries, in the catacomb paintings and in other manifestations, Christians began to adapt familiar pre-Christian prototypes to new meanings. The early figural representations of Christ, for instance, most often show him as the good shepherd by directly borrowing from a classical prototype. He was also sometimes depicted in the guise of familiar gods or heroes, such as APOLLO or ORPHEUS. Only later, when the religion itself had achieved some measure of earthly power, did he take on more exalted attributes. The earliest scenes from the life of Christ to be depicted were the miracles. The Passion, particularly the CRUCIFIXION itself, was generally avoided until the religion was well established.

The beginnings of Early Christian art date to the period when the religion was yet a modest and sometimes persecuted sect, and its flowering was possible only after 313, when the Christian emperor CONSTANTINE the Great decreed official toleration of CHRISTIANITY. Subsequent imperial sponsorship brought popularity, riches, and many converts from all classes of society. Suddenly the church needed to produce art and architecture on a more ambitious scale in order to accommodate and educate its new members and to reflect its new dignity and social importance.

Churches and shrines were soon being built throughout the empire, many sponsored by Constantine himself. These buildings were usually five-aisled BASILICAS, such as Old St. Peter's in Rome, or basilican-plan buildings centering upon a round or polygonal shrine, such as that in the Church of the Nativity in Bethlehem. Large-scale sculpture was not popular, but relief sculpture on sarcophagi and ivory carvings and book covers continued to be produced. The walls of the churches were decorated with paintings or mosaics to instruct the faithful. Painting also illustrated liturgical books and other manuscripts.

The art of this period had its roots in the classical Roman style, but it developed into a more abstract, simplified artistic expression. Its ideal was not physical beauty but spiritual feeling. The human figures thus became types rather than individuals and often had large, staring eyes, "the windows of the soul." Symbols were frequently used, and compositions were flat and hieratic, in order to concentrate on and clearly visualize the main idea. Although the art of the period intentionally departed from earlier NATURALISM, it sometimes has great power and immediacy.

CHRISTIANITY, ROOTS OF, the origins of the beliefs and practices of the Christian religion, which began in the Jewish community of Palestine. Though it attracted little attention among PAGANS and Jews at the beginning, CHRISTIANITY was by far the most important sectarian development of the Roman period. With the discovery of the DEAD SEA SCROLLS at QUMRĀN, the received view that Pharisaism was to be considered the mainstream of JUDAISM had to be revised sharply. In consequence, primitive Christianity, with its apocalyptic and eschatological interests, came to be viewed by many scholars no longer as a splinter group, peripheral to Jewish development, but, at least initially, as part of a broad range of attitudes within JUDAISM. JESUS himself, despite his criticisms of Pharisaic legalism, may now be classified as a PHARISEE with strong apocalyptic inclinations; he proclaimed that his intention was not to abrogate the TORAH, but to fulfill it. It is possible to envision a direct line of development from Jewish currents, both in Palestine and the Diaspora in the Hellenistic Age, to Christianity, particularly in the traditions of martyrdom, proselytism, MONASTICISM, MYSTICISM, liturgy, and such matters of religious philosophy as the doctrine of the LOGOS (Word) as an intermediary between God and the world and the synthesis of faith and reason. The SEPTUAGINT, in particular, played an important role: theoretically, in the transformation of Greek philosophy into the theology of the Church Fathers; and practically, in converting Jews and Jewish sympathizers to Christianity. The connection of nascent Christianity with the QUMRĀN groups may be seen in their DUALISM and apocalypticism; but there are differences, notably in the conception of the INCARNATION and in the relationship of the Son and the Father (*see also* ESSENE). Again, the Qumrān group constituted an esoteric and militant movement that enforced a community of goods and strict observance of the

TORAH, whereas Christianity was pacifist, was open to all, and represented a New COVENANT that looked away from Torah ritual and urged a voluntary community of possessions. In general, moreover, Christianity was more positively disposed toward Hellenism than was Pharisaism, particularly under the leadership of Paul, a thoroughly Hellenized Jew. (*See* PAUL THE APOSTLE, SAINT.)

When Paul proclaimed his ANTINOMIANISM (against Torah observance as a means of salvation) many Jewish followers of Jesus became Jewish Christians and continued to observe the Torah. Their two main groupings were the Ebionites—probably to be identified with those called minim, or "sectaries," in the Talmud—who accepted Jesus as the MESSIAH but denied his divinity, and the Nazarenes, who regarded Jesus as both messiah and God, but regarded the Torah as binding upon Jews alone. The percentage of Jews converted to any form of Christianity was extremely small, as can be seen from the frequent criticisms of Jews for their stubbornness by Christian writers.

There were four major turning points in the final break between Christianity and Judaism: (1) the flight of the Jewish Christians from Jerusalem to Pella across the Jordan in 70 CE and their refusal to continue the struggle against the Romans; (2) the institution by the patriarch GAMALIEL II of a prayer in the Eighteen BENEDICTIONS (*see* AMIDAH) against such heretics (*c.* 100 CE); and (3 and 4) the failure of the Christians to join the messianic leaders Lukuas-Andreas and BAR KOKHBA in the revolts against Trajan (115–117 CE) and Hadrian (132–135 CE), respectively.

CHRISTIAN SCIENCE, religious denomination founded in the United States in 1879 by MARY BAKER EDDY, author of the definitive statement of its teaching, *Science and Health with Key to the Scriptures.* About one-third of its nearly 3,000 congregations are located in 56 countries outside the United States, with membership concentrated in areas with strong Protestant traditions. It is widely known for its practice of spiritual healing.

Christian Science subscribes to the essential Christian belief in an omnipotent, purposeful God, accepts the revelatory authority (though not the verbal inerrancy) of the BIBLE, and holds the CRUCIFIXION and RESURRECTION of JESUS CHRIST to be the central event in history, indispensable to the redemption of mankind. It departs from traditional CHRISTIANITY in rejecting the deity (but not the divinity) of Jesus. His healing works, as well as his own victory over death and the grave, are regarded as demonstrating that all the ills and limitations of the mortal state can be overcome in proportion as one gains "the mind of Christ," *i.e.,* a rooted understanding of man's true spiritual status. This requires a penetration beyond material appearances to a spiritual order of being.

Once one accedes to the proposition that matter is created by God, Mrs. Eddy argued, one has made a fatal compromise with materialism, holding God responsible for all suffering in the universe (*see also* THEODICY). Christian redemption is therefore held to include regeneration from all phases of mortality, or "the flesh." Redemption from SIN is basic to this process, since sin in all its forms denies God's sovereignty by claiming that life, will, and mind evolve from brute matter rather than from Spirit. Mrs. Eddy saw the regenerative process as a long and demanding one, calling upon the Christian virtues of patience and humility, repentance and cross-bearing. The cure of disease through prayer is seen as a necessary element in a full redemption from the flesh.

Mary Baker Eddy
By courtesy of the Library of Congress, Washington, D.C.

A Christian Scientist is not compelled by the church to employ spiritual means for healing; it encourages members to obey public health laws, including quarantine regulations, report suspected contagious diseases, and follow immunization requirements where religious exemptions are not provided by law. They also generally employ the services of dentists and optometrists, and often those of physicians for such procedures as the setting of bones or the delivery of a child. Christian Scientists in need of nursing care can go to a Christian Science sanitorium or seek the services of a Christian Science nurse in the home. Those engaged in the full-time healing ministry are called Christian Science practitioners.

Systematic study and prayer are considered basic to the ongoing life of the denomination and the readiness of its members to meet the challenges of Christian healing. All Christian Science churches maintain Reading Rooms for this purpose. Central in this study is the "Bible lesson-sermon" composed of passages from the Bible and *Science and Health* on 26 rotating subjects. The lessons from these two books are studied daily and form the basis of the Sunday service, read by a first and second reader elected from the congregation. In this service there are no formally observed SACRAMENTS. Wednesday evening meetings include the sharing of healings and other experience by the congregation.

Christian Science has had significance out of proportion to its size. It is one of several lasting denominations indigenous to 19th-century America and reflects in its own way the emphasis of many American religious groups in the radical Reformed Protestant tradition on the revitalization of primitive Christianity. Yet Christian Science has aroused considerable controversy as well as misunderstanding by its view of creation as wholly spiritual, a view that breaks decisively with traditional Christian COSMOLOGY as well as with traditional scientific materialism.

In social terms, the Christian Science movement has increasingly been perceived as anticipating the development of feminism in the religious world. While not a feminist as such, Mrs. Eddy taught that the spiritual equality of men and women must have political and social effects. In the Christian Science movement as a whole, women have had significant roles as practitioners and church officers.

The church is widely known for *The Christian Science Monitor,* an international daily newspaper published in Boston, and for its international news broadcasts.

CHRISTIAN SOCIALISM, movement of the mid-19th century that attempted to apply the social principles of CHRISTIANITY to modern industrial life. The term was generally associated with the demands of Christian activists for a social program of political and economic action on behalf of all individuals, impoverished or wealthy, and the term was used in contradistinction to laissez-faire individualism. Later, Christian Socialism came to be applied in a general sense to any movement that attempted to combine the fundamental aims of socialism with the religious and ethical convictions of Christianity.

Early in the 19th century the French philosopher Henri de Saint-Simon expounded a "new Christianity" primarily concerned with the plight of the poor. Saint-Simonians believed that the keynote of social development would be a spirit of association, with religion as the dominating force, that would gradually supplant the prevailing spirit of egotism and antagonism in society.

The term Christian Socialism was first appropriated by a group of British men including FREDERICK DENISON MAURICE, novelist Charles Kingsley, and John Malcolm Ludlow, who founded a movement in England after the failure of the Chartist agitation of 1848. Ludlow enlisted other churchmen in an effort to promote the application of Christian principles in industrial organization. Stirred by the sufferings of the poor and by factory and workshop conditions, Ludlow's group vigorously criticized socially conservative Christianity and laissez-faire attitudes within the industrial sector. They joined forces with the cooperativist movement and financed several small cooperative societies. They also founded the Working Men's College in London. The movement as such dissolved in the late 1850s, however; numerous Christian Socialist organizations were formed in the 1880s and '90s in England.

In addition to the French Roman Catholic social movement long in existence, movements similar to Ludlow's took shape among French Protestants in the latter half of the 19th century. The Protestant Association for the Practical Study of Social Questions, founded in 1888, opposed bourgeois PROTESTANTISM while rejecting a strict, egalitarian socialism. In Germany the movement for Christian social action in the late 19th century became associated with violent anti-Semitic agitation, as in the case of Adolf Stoecker, a court preacher and a founder of the Christian Social Workers' Party. In the United States, Henry James, Sr., the father of novelist Henry James and philosopher William James, had argued the identity of the aims of socialism and Christianity as early as 1849. The Society of Christian Socialists was organized in 1889. The first years of the 20th century witnessed the rise of the SOCIAL GOSPEL movement, which was an outgrowth of Christian Socialism that stressed the social aspect of salvation.

CHRISTMAS (from Old English: *Cristes mæsse*, literally, "Christ's mass"), Christian festival celebrated on December 25, commemorating the birth of JESUS CHRIST. It is also a popular secular holiday.

According to a Roman almanac, Christmas was celebrated in Rome by 336 CE. In the eastern part of the Roman Empire, however, a festival on January 6 commemorated both the birth and the BAPTISM of Jesus, except in Jerusalem, where only the birth was celebrated. During the 4th century the celebration of Christ's birth on December 25 was gradually adopted by most Eastern churches. In the Armenian Church, a Christmas on December 25 was never accepted; Christ's birth is celebrated on January 6. After Christmas was established in the East, the baptism of Jesus was celebrated on EPIPHANY, January 6. In the West, however, Epiphany was the day on which the visit of the MAGI to the infant Jesus was celebrated.

The reason why Christmas came to be celebrated on December 25 remains uncertain, but most probably early Christians wished the date to coincide with the Roman festival marking the "birthday of the unconquered sun" (*natalis solis invicti*), the winter solstice, when the days again begin to lengthen. The traditional customs connected with Christmas have developed from several sources. In the Roman world the Saturnalia (December 17) was a time of merrymaking and exchange of gifts. December 25 was also regarded as the birth date of the Iranian god MITHRA. On the Roman New Year (January 1), houses were decorated with greenery and lights, and gifts were given to children and the poor. To these observances were added the German and Celtic Yule rites when the Teutonic tribes penetrated into Gaul, Britain, and central Europe. Food and good fellowship, the Yule log and Yule cakes, greenery and fir trees, and gifts and greetings all commemorated different aspects of this festive season. Fires and lights have always been associated with the winter festival, both pagan and Christian. Since the Middle Ages, evergreens have been associated with Christmas. Christmas is traditionally regarded as the festival of the family and of children, under the name of whose patron, SAINT NICHOLAS, or Santa Claus, presents are exchanged in many countries.

CHRISTOPHER, SAINT \\'kris-tə-fər\\ (fl. *c.* 3rd century; Western feast day July 25; Eastern feast day May 9), patron saint of travelers. Though one of the most popular saints, there is no certainty that he existed historically. Portrayed as a GIANT who helped travelers to cross rivers, he is the hero of many legends. In one legend a small child asked to be carried across the river, and in the middle of the river the child became so heavy that Christopher staggered under the burden, complained, and was told that he had borne upon his back the world and Him who created it. Hence, Christopher (Greek: "Christ-Bearer") is generally represented in art carrying the Christ child on his back. In 1969 his name was dropped from the calendar of the Roman Catholic church, and his feast day is no longer obligatory.

CHRYSOSTOM, SAINT JOHN \\'kri-sə-stəm, kri-'säs-təm\\ (b. *c.* 347 CE, Antioch, Syria—d. Sept. 14, 407, Comana, Helenopontus; Western feast day September 13; Eastern feast day November 13), early CHURCH FATHER, biblical interpreter, and archbishop of Constantinople; the zeal and clarity of his preaching earned him the Greek surname meaning "golden-mouthed."

John was brought up as a Christian and was intended for the law, but he also studied theology and gave up his profession to become a hermit-monk. His health gave way, and he returned to Antioch, becoming a priest there. For 12 years (from 386) he established himself as a great preacher. A sensational episode of this period was a riot in 387, when the citizens of Antioch treated the images of the emperors with disrespect and were threatened with reprisals; in a famous course of sermons, "On the Statues," Chrysostom brought his hearers to a frame of mind suitable both to the season, LENT, and to the danger of their situation.

In 398 Chrysostom was called to Constantinople to be its archbishop. He gained a large following among the people, but his castigation of the misuse of riches angered the wealthy and influential. He was concerned, above all, for the spiritual and temporal welfare of the needy and oppressed. He taught that personal property is not strictly private but a trust, and declaring that what was superfluous to one's reasonable needs ought to be given away.

An alliance against John was made by Eudoxia, the wife of the Eastern Roman emperor Arcadius, and the archbishop of the rival see of Alexandria, the powerful Theophilus. In 403 Theophilus convened a SYNOD that indicted John on a large number of charges, many of them purely frivolous or vexatious. Chrysostom refused to appear before the synod, whereupon it condemned him and professed to depose him from his see. Arcadius therefore banished Chrysostom to be kept in confinement at Cucusus in Armenia.

Chrysostom appealed his banishment to the bishop of Rome, Pope Innocent I; the latter, with the help of the Western emperor Honorius, attempted to intervene, but his efforts failed. In exile, however, John found it possible to keep up a lively correspondence and was still able to exert a measure of influence in his cause, and word came from Constantinople that he was to be removed to an even more remote place at the eastern end of the Black Sea. Chrysostom did not survive the journey. The official rehabilitation of John Chrysostom came in 438, when his relics were brought to Constantinople and were solemnly received by the then archbishop Proclus and the emperor Theodosius II, son of Arcadius and Eudoxia.

The most frequently used of the three eucharistic services in EASTERN ORTHODOXY is called the Liturgy of St. John Chrysostom, but the evidence upon which to base this theory of his having had anything to do with its composition is unconvincing.

CHTHONIC \ˈthä-nik\, of or relating to earth, particularly the Underworld. Chthonic figures in

Chuang-tzu, detail of an ink on silk
By courtesy of the National Palace Museum, Taiwan, Republic of China

Greek MYTHOLOGY included HADES and PERSEPHONE, the rulers of the Underworld, and the various heroes venerated after death; even ZEUS, the king of the sky, had earthly associations and was venerated as Zeus Chthonius. Oracles (prophecies) delivered through incubation (that is, whereby the inquirer slept in a holy precinct and received an answer in a dream) were believed to come from chthonian powers. In the symbolism and iconography of chthonic deities, snakes are often associated with such deities in world mythology; thus, divinities are often portrayed entwined with serpents.

CH'ÜAN-CHEN \ˈchwän-ˈjən\, *Pinyin* Quanzhen (Chinese: "Perfect Realization"), in TAOISM, sect founded in 1163 by WANG CHE. This sect came to the favorable attention of the Mongols, who had taken over in the North, and its second patriarch, Ch'iu Ch'ang-ch'un, was invited into Central Asia to preach to Genghis Khan. The sect enjoyed great popularity, and its establishment of celibate monks continued to be active into the 20th century, with the White

Cloud Monastery (Pai-yün kuan) at Beijing as headquarters.

CHUANG-TZU \ˈjwäŋ-ˈdzə̀\, *Pinyin* Zhuangzi, *personal name* (*Wade-Giles romanization*) Chou (b. *c.* 369 BCE—d. 286 BCE, the most significant of China's early interpreters of TAOISM, whose work (*Chuang-tzu*) is considered one of the definitive texts of Taoism and is thought to be more comprehensive than the TAO-TE CHING. Chuang-tzu's teachings also exerted a great influence on the development of Chinese BUDDHISM and had considerable effect on Chinese landscape painting and poetry.

Tradition says that Chuang-tzu was a native of the state of Meng; it is known that he was a minor official at Ch'i-yüan in his home state. He lived during the reign of Prince Wei of Ch'u and was therefore a contemporary of MENCIUS. According to Ssu-ma Ch'ien, Chuang-tzu's teachings were drawn primarily from the sayings of LAO-TZU, but his perspective was much broader. His literary and philosophical skills were used to refute the Confucianists and Mohists (followers of MO-TZU, who advocated universal love). In addition, he is reported to have written "The Old Fisherman," "Robber Chi," and "Opening Trunks," all attacks on CONFUCIANISM.

Chuang-tzu is best known through the book that bears his name, the *Chuang-tzu*, also known as *Nan-hua chen-ching* ("The Pure Classic of Nan-hua"). It is generally agreed that the first seven chapters, the "inner books," are, for the most part, genuine, whereas the "outer books" (chapters 8–22) and the miscellany (chapters 23–33) are largely spurious, even though it is possible that some passages may reflect Chuang-tzu's own hand.

The more vivid descriptions of his character come from the anecdotes in the later chapters of the book. He is portrayed as an unpredictable eccentric sage who seems careless about personal comforts or public esteem. The stories speak of his failure to mourn the death of his wife, or his refusal of an elaborate burial. Many of the stories of his eccentricities stem directly from his enlightened fatalism. Enlightenment for Chuang-tzu comes with the realization that everything in life is One, the TAO.

Chuang-tzu taught that what can be known or said of the Tao is not the Tao. It has no beginning or end, no limitations or demarcations. Life is subject to the eternal transformation of the Tao, in which there is no better or worse, no good or evil. Things should be allowed to follow their own course, and men should not value one situation over another. A truly virtuous man is free from the bondage of circumstance, personal attachments, tradition, and the need to reform his world. Accordingly, Chuang-tzu reputedly declined an offer to be prime minister of Ch'u because he did not want the entanglements of a court career.

The complete relativity of his perspective is forcefully expressed in one of the better-known passages of the *Chuang-tzu*:

> Once I, Chuang Chou, dreamed that I was a butterfly and was happy as a butterfly. I was conscious that I was quite pleased with myself, but I did not know that I was Chou. Suddenly I awoke, and there I was, visibly Chou. I do not know whether it was Chou dreaming that he was a butterfly or the butterfly dreaming that it was Chou. Between Chou and the butterfly there must be some distinction. This is called the transformation of things.

In the *Chuang-tzu*, the relativity of all experience is in constant tension with the unity of all things. When asked where the Tao was, Chuang-tzu replied that it was everywhere. When pushed to be more specific, he declared that it was in ants and, still lower, in weeds and potsherds; furthermore, it was also in excrement and urine. This forceful statement of the omnipresence of the Tao had its parallels in later Chinese Buddhism, in which a similar figure of speech was used to describe the ever-present Buddha.

CHUBB, THOMAS \\'chəb\\ (b. Sept. 29, 1679, East Harnham, Wiltshire, Eng.—d. Feb. 8, 1747, Salisbury, Wiltshire), self-taught English philosopher and proponent of DEISM.

The son of working-class parents, Chubb was apprenticed to a glovemaker and later worked for a tallow chandler. He read widely and began to write on RATIONALISM in the early 1700s; his first publication was an essay, "The Supremacy of the Father Asserted," written in 1715 in response to the Arian controversy. Chubb's other works, which include *Discourse Concerning Reason* (1731), *The True Gospel of Jesus Christ Vindicated* (1739), and *Discourse on Miracles* (1741), betray the deficiencies of his education, and he was often treated disparagingly by more erudite theologians. His tracts tended to limit the Christian religion to three fundamental tenets: belief in the divinely ordained moral law, belief in the need of sincere repentance for SIN, and belief in future rewards and punishments.

CHU HSI \\'jü-'shē\\, *Pinyin* Zhu Xi, *literary name* (hao) Yüan Hui \\'ywän-'hwā, 'ywen-\\, *or* Chung Hui \\'jùn-'hwā\\, *courtesy names* (tzu) Hui An, Ch'en Lang, Chi Yen, Hui Weng, Hsün Weng, *or* Yün Ku Lao-jen, *also called* Chu-tzu \\'jü-'dzə\\, *or* Chu-fu-tzu \\'jü-'fü-'dzə\\ (b. Oct. 18, 1130, Yu-hsi, Fukien province, China—d. April 23, 1200, China), Chinese philosopher whose synthesis of Neo-Confucian thought long dominated Chinese intellectual life.

Chu Hsi was the son of a local official. He was educated in the Confucian tradition by his father and passed the highest civil service examination at the young age of 18. Chu Hsi's first official position (1151–58) was as a registrar in T'ung-an, Fukien, where he reformed the management of taxation and police, improved the library and the standards of the local school, and drew up a code of proper formal conduct and ritual. Before proceeding to T'ung-an, Chu Hsi had studied in 1160 with Li T'ung, a thinker in the tradition of Sung CONFUCIANISM. Li had created a new metaphysical system to compete with Buddhist and Taoist phi-

losophy. Under his influence, Chu's allegiance turned definitely to Confucianism at this time.

After his assignment at T'ung-an ended, Chu Hsi did not accept another official appointment until 1179. He did, however, continue to express his political views in memorandums addressed to the emperor. In 1175 he held a famous philosophical debate with the philosopher LU HSIANG-SHAN (Lu Chiu-yüan) at which neither man was able to prevail. In contrast to Lu's insistence on the exclusive value of inwardness, Chu Hsi emphasized the value of inquiry and study, including book learning. In a number of works, including a compilation of the works of the Ch'eng brothers and studies of Chou-Tun-i (1017–73) and CHANG TSAI (1020–77), he expressed his esteem for these four philosophers, whose ideas he incorporated and synthesized into his own thought. In 1175 Chu Hsi and his friend Lü Tsu-ch'ien (1137–81) compiled passages from the works of the four to form their famous anthology, *Chin-ssu lu* (*Reflections on Things at Hand*). His enormously influential commentaries on the LUN-YÜ (*Analects*) of CONFUCIUS and on MENCIUS were both completed in 1177.

Chu Hsi also took a keen interest in history and directed a reworking and condensation of Ssu-ma Kuang's history, the *Tzu-chih t'ung-chien* ("Comprehensive Mirror for Aid in Government"), so that it would illustrate moral principles in government. The resulting work, known as the *T'ung-chien kang-mu* ("Outline and Digest of the General Mirror"), basically completed in 1172, served as the basis for the first comprehensive history of China published in Europe, J.-A.-M. Moyriac de Mailla's *Histoire générale de la Chine* (1777–85).

While serving as prefect (1179–81) in Nan-k'ang, Kiangsi, Chu Hsi rehabilitated the White Deer Grotto Academy, which had fallen to ruin. The prestige restored to it by Chu was to last through eight centuries.

In 1188 Chu Hsi wrote a major memorandum in which he restated his conviction that the emperor's character was the basis for the well-being of the realm. In 1189 he commenced an important commentary on TA-HSÜEH ("Great Learning"), a Confucian text on moral government, and he continued to work on *Ta hsüeh* for the rest of his life. Similarly, in 1189 he wrote a commentary on CHUNG-YUNG ("Doctrine of the Mean"). It was largely because of the influence of Chu Hsi that these two texts came to be accepted along with the *Analects* and *Mencius* as the FOUR BOOKS basic to the Confucian educational curriculum.

Near the end of his life, his enemies brought virulent accusations against him, and he was barred from political activity. Chu Hsi's reputation was rehabilitated soon after his death, however, and posthumous honors for him followed, culminating in the placement of his tablet in the Confucian Temple in 1241. In later centuries, rulers more authoritarian than those he had criticized made his system the sole orthodox creed, which it remained until the end of the 19th century.

Chu Hsi's philosophy emphasized logic, consistency, and the conscientious observance of classical authority, especially that of Confucius and his follower Mencius. Chu Hsi held that the universe has two aspects: the formless and the formed. The formless, or LI, is a principle or a network of principles that is supreme natural law and that determines the patterns of all created things. This law combines with the material force or energy called CH'I to produce matter, or things having form. In human beings the *li* (manifested as human nature) is essentially perfect, and defects—including vices—are introduced into the body and

SACRED PLACES

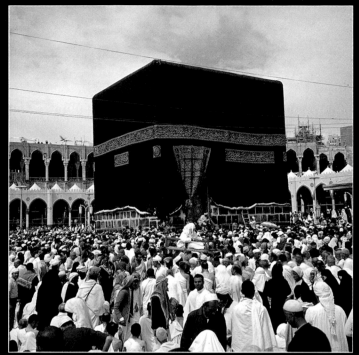

The Kaʻba in Mecca, Saudi Arabia, the holy city of Islam
Ruchan Arikan—Photo Researchers

The Yomei gate of the Shintō Tosho Shrine in Nikko, Japan
Scala—Art Resource

Buddhist shrine within the Shwe Dagon Pagoda, Yangôn (Rangoon), Myanmar
George Holton—Photo Researchers

(Left) Cathedral of St. Basil, Moscow; (opposite) Cao Dai Temple, Tay Ninh, Vietnam
(Left) K. Sholz—H. Armstrong Roberts, Inc.; (opposite) Photo Researchers

Legend

- Buddhism
- **Ch** Chinese religions[1]
- **C** Christianity, undifferentiated by branch[2]
- **E** Eastern Orthodox[3]
- **H** Hinduism
- **N** Independent churches of Eastern Christianity[4]
- **T** Indigenous (tribal) religions
- **I** Islam, predominantly Sunni
- Islam, predominantly Shi'ite
- **Ja** Japanese religions[1]
- **J** Judaism
- **K** Korean religions[1]
- Mormonism
- Sikhism
- **P** Protestantism
- **R** Roman Catholicism
- **X** Nonreligious
- No dominant religion
- Uninhabited

Footnotes:

[1] In certain eastern Asian areas, many of the people have plural religious affiliations. Chinese and Korean religions include Buddhism, Taoism, Confucianism, and folk cults. The Japanese religions include Shintō and Buddhism.

[2] Chiefly mingled Protestantism and Roman Catholicism, neither predominant.

[3] Including Greek and Russian Orthodox Christianity.

[4] Including Armenian, Coptic, Ethiopian, East and West Syrian.

RELIGIONS

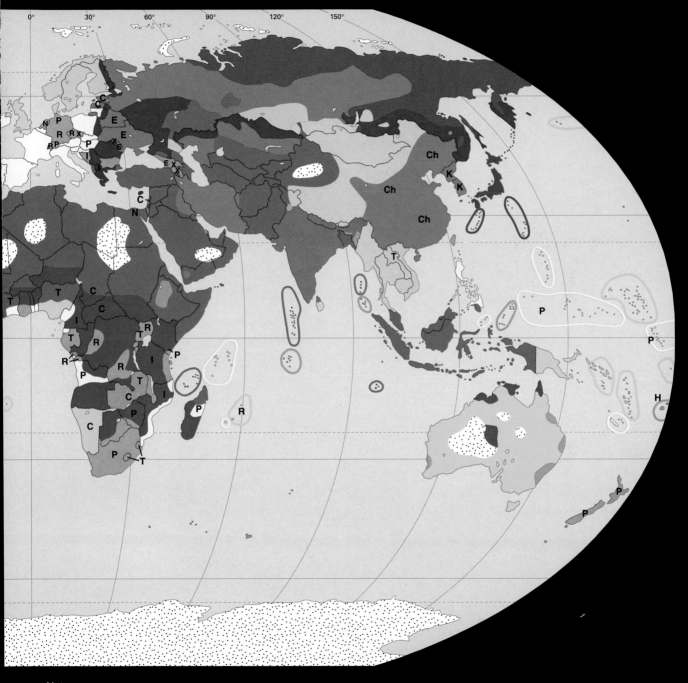

Note:
The majority of the inhabitants in each of the areas colored on the map share the religious tradition indicated. Letter symbols show religious traditions shared by at least 25 percent of the inhabitants within areas no smaller than 1,000 square miles. Therefore minority religions of city dwellers have generally not been represented.

The Sikh Golden Temple at Amritsar, Punjab, India
Photo Researchers

The Mīnākṣi-Sundareśvara Temple in Madurai, India
Photo Researchers

Dogon sacred cult site, Mali
Rene Gardi

Zoroastrian Temple of Fire, Naqsh-e Rostam, Iran
SEF—Art Resource

Rock-hewn tomb of Abba Salama (St. Frumentius), the first bishop of Ethiopia
Photo Researchers

Neolithic gallery grave, La Roche aux Fées, Essé, Ille-et-Vilaine, France

The Temple of Aphaea at Aegina, Greece
Paul Stepan—Vierow

Sainte-Chapelle, the royal chapel of Louis IX, Paris
A.F. Kersting

The Western Wall from the Second Temple, Jerusalem
A. Ramey—Woodfin Camp

mind through impurities of *ch'i*, or matter. Chu Hsi and his followers stressed the "investigation of things," by which they meant primarily the study of ethical conduct and of the revered FIVE CLASSICS. The study of ethical and metaphysical principles in turn constituted an ingredient both in building a personal faith and in advising emperors through whose self-cultivation order might be restored in the world.

CHU-HWEI HSUO, THE \'jü-'hwā-'shwȯ\, *also called* Tifang Huei \'dē-'fäṇ-'hwā\ (Chinese: "Local Church"), movement founded by Watchman Nee (1903–72) after study of the theology of the PLYMOUTH BRETHREN, an English independent church. Nee developed his own forms of church polity and his own theology, based on Brethren ideas, and the church gained followers on the Chinese mainland. After the revolution (1949) Nee and his church were persecuted harshly by the Chinese Communist Party. However, a lieutenant of Nee's, Witness Lee (1905–97), moved the church to Los Angeles, and other followers established themselves in Taiwan. In the years since 1949, the church has become a major independent Protestant entity in Taiwan and continues to have a strong base in the United States. It has also played a role in the redevelopment of independent forms of CHRISTIANITY in China.

CH'UN-CH'IU \'chùn-'chyō\, *Pinyin* Chunqiu (Chinese: "Spring and Autumn [Annals]"), the first Chinese chronological history, said to be the traditional history of Lu, as revised by CONFUCIUS. It is one of the FIVE CLASSICS (*Wu ching*) of CONFUCIANISM. The work is a complete month-by-month account of significant events that occurred during the reign of 12 rulers of Lu, Confucius' native state, beginning in 722 BCE and ending shortly before Confucius' death (479 BCE).

Among many who sought to discover profound meanings in the text was TUNG CHUNG-SHU (*c.* 179–*c.* 104 BCE), a great Han-dynasty Confucian, who claimed that the natural phenomena recorded in the book (*e.g.,* eclipse of the sun, shower of stars at night, drought) were intended as warnings to future leaders of what happens when rulers prove unworthy. Since Confucian scholars were the official interpreters of this and the other classics, the book was a means for imposing Confucian ideals on government.

The fame of *Ch'un-ch'iu* is mainly due to TSO-CHUAN, a commentary (*chuan*) by a scholar named Tso. Two other important commentaries on *Ch'un-ch'iu* are *Kung-yang chuan* and *Ku-liang chuan*. All three commentaries are listed among the alternative lists of the Nine, Twelve, and Thirteen Classics of Confucianism.

CHUNG-YUNG \'jùṇ-'yùṇ\, *Pinyin* Zhongyong, one of four ancient Confucian texts that, when published together in 1190 by CHU HSI, a great Neo-Confucian philosopher, became the famous *Ssu-shu* ("FOUR BOOKS"). *Chung-yung* was chosen by Chu Hsi for its metaphysical interest, which had already attracted the attention of BUDDHISTS and earlier NEO-CONFUCIANISTS. In his preface, Chu Hsi attributed authorship of the treatise (which was actually a chapter from LI-CHI, one of the FIVE CLASSICS of antiquity) to TZU SSU (K'ung Chi), a grandson of CONFUCIUS.

The two Chinese characters *Chung-yung* (often translated "doctrine of the mean") express a Confucian ideal that encompasses virtually every relationship and activity of a person's life: moderation, rectitude, objectivity, sincerity, honesty, truthfulness, propriety, equilibrium, and lack of prejudice. One must adhere unswervingly to the mean, or

center course, at all times. Such behavior conforms to the laws of nature, is the distinctive mark of the superior person, and is the essence of true orthodoxy.

CHÜN-TZU \'juen-'dzə̀\, *Pinyin* junzi (Chinese: "gentleman," literally "prince-son," or "noble son"), in the teachings of CONFUCIUS, the ideal of the high-minded man whose actions are guided by JEN (benevolence). The *chün-tzu* attains nobility by means of character rather than inheritance. Confucius envisaged a fellowship of noblemen as moral vanguards of society, whose mission was to redefine and revitalize those institutions, such as the family, that for centuries were believed to have maintained social solidarity and to have enabled people to live in harmony and prosperity.

CHURCH, in Christian doctrine, the Christian religious community as a whole, or a body or organization of Christian believers.

The Greek word *ekklesia*, which came to mean church, was originally applied in the classical period to an official assembly of citizens. In the SEPTUAGINT (Greek) translation of the OLD TESTAMENT (3rd–2nd century BCE), the term *ekklesia* is used for the general assembly of the Jewish people, especially when gathered for a religious purpose such as hearing the Law (*e.g.,* Deuteronomy 9:10, 18:16). In the NEW TESTAMENT it is used of the entire body of believing Christians throughout the world (*e.g.,* Matthew 16:18), of the believers in a particular area (*e.g.,* Acts 5:11), of the congregation meeting in a particular house—the "house-church" (*e.g.,* Romans 16:5), and also of the celestial "new Jerusalem" (*e.g.,* Revelation 21–22).

After the CRUCIFIXION of JESUS, his followers went forth to preach the Gospel and developed facilities for those who were converted. In time Christians established their own communities, modeled on the Jewish SYNAGOGUE. Gradually, the church worked out a governmental system based on the office of the bishop (episcopacy).

Various controversies threatened the unity of the church from its earliest history, but, except for small sects that did not ultimately survive, it maintained unity for several centuries. Since the SCHISM of the Eastern and Western churches in 1054 and the disruption of the Western church during the 16th-century Protestant REFORMATION, however, the church has been split into various bodies, most of which consider themselves either the one true church or at least a part of the true church.

A traditional means of discussing the nature of the church has been to consider the four marks, or characteristics, by which it is distinguished in the NICENE CREED: one, holy, catholic, and apostolic. The first, that of oneness or unity, appears to be contradicted by the divisions in the church. It has been held, however, that since BAPTISM is the rite of entry into the church, the church must consist of all baptized people, who form a single body irrespective of denomination. The holiness of the church derives from its creation by the HOLY SPIRIT. The term catholic originally meant the universal church as distinct from local congregations, but it came to imply the Church of Rome. Finally, apostolic implies that, in both its church and ministry, the church is historically continuous with the Apostles and thus with the earthly life of Jesus.

The fact that many Christians hold nominal beliefs and do not act like followers of Christ has been noted since the 4th century, when the church ceased to be persecuted. To account for this, ST. AUGUSTINE proposed that the real church is an invisible entity known only to God. MARTIN LUTHER used this theory to excuse the divisions of the church at the Reformation, holding that the true church has its members scattered among the various Christian bodies but that it is independent of any organization known upon earth. Many Christians, however, believing that Jesus intended to found one visible church here upon earth, have worked to restore the unity of the church in the ecumenical movement.

CHURCH AND STATE, concept that the religious and political powers in society are clearly distinct, though both claim the people's loyalty.

Early Christian theories. Before the advent of CHRISTIANITY, separate religious and political orders were not clearly defined in most civilizations. People worshiped the gods of the particular state in which they lived, religion in such cases being but a department of the state. In the case of the Jewish people, the revealed Law of the SCRIPTURE constituted the Law of ISRAEL. The Christian concept of the secular and the spiritual is founded on the words of Jesus: "Render unto Caesar the things that are Caesar's, and to God the things that are God's" (Mark 7:17). Two distinct, but not altogether separate, areas of human life and activity had to be distinguished; hence, a theory of two powers came to form the basis of Christian thought from earliest times.

In the early church the attitude of the Christian toward the political order was determined by the imminent expectation of the KINGDOM OF GOD; consequently, the importance of the existing political order was negligible. Orientation toward the coming Kingdom of God placed Christians in tension with the state, which occasionally made demands upon them that were in conflict with their faith. This contrast was developed most pointedly in the rejection of the Roman imperial cult and of certain state offices—above all,

Emperor Charlemagne, whose coronation in 800 by Pope Leo III led to a blurring of the division between church and state
By courtesy of Weidenfeld & Nicholson Ltd., photograph, Ann Munchow

that of judge—to which the power over life and death was professionally entrusted.

Despite the early Christian longing for the coming Kingdom, even the Christians of the early generations acknowledged the state as the bearer of order in the old AEON, which for the time being continued to exist. Two contrary views thus faced one another within the Christian communities. On the one hand, under the influence of Pauline missions, was the idea that the "ruling body"—*i.e.*, the existing political order of the Roman Empire—was "from God . . . for your good" (Romans 13:1–4) and that Christians should be "subject to the governing authorities." On the other hand was the apocalyptic identification of the imperial city of Rome with the great whore of Babylon (Revelation 17:3–7). The first attitude, formulated by PAUL, was decisive in the development of a Christian political consciousness. The second was noticeable especially in the subsequent history of radical Christianity and in radical Christian pacifism.

The Roman imperial period and following. The emperor CONSTANTINE I the Great (died 337 CE) granted himself, as "bishop of foreign affairs," certain rights to church leadership. These not only concerned the "outward" activity of the church but also encroached upon the inner life of the church—as in summoning and leading imperial councils to formulate fundamental Christian doctrine and to ratify their decisions.

It was EUSEBIUS OF CAESAREA (c. 260–c. 340), Constantine's court theologian, who formed the Orthodox understanding of the relationship of church and state. He saw the empire and the imperial church as sharing a close bond. In the center of the Christian empire stood the Christian emperor, who is God's representative on earth in whom God himself "lets shine forth the image of his absolute power." Through the possession of these characteristics the Christian emperor is the archetype not only of justice but also of the love of humankind (see CAESAROPAPISM).

Orthodox theologians have understood the coexistence of the Christian emperor and the head of the Christian church as *symphonia*, or "harmony." The church recognized the powers of the emperor as protector of the church and preserver of the unity of faith and limited its own authority to the purely spiritual domain of preserving the Orthodox truth and order in the church. The emperor, on the other hand, was subject to the spiritual leadership of the church as far as he was a son of the church.

By contrast, the historical development of the church in the Latin West, much influenced by ST. AUGUSTINE'S *De civitate Dei* (*The City of God*), produced a new entity, the Roman Church, the church of the bishop of Rome. The Roman Church's theocratic claim to dominion freely developed after the state and administrative organization of the Roman Empire in the West collapsed in the chaos following the fall of Rome in the 5th century CE. The Roman Church came to be viewed as the only guarantor of order, and the Roman popes used this power to develop an ecclesiastical state and to base this state upon a new theocratic ideology—the idea that the pope was the representative of JESUS CHRIST and the successor of ST. PETER.

It was in this context that the judicial pretense of the DONATION OF CONSTANTINE became possible. A fraudulent account of Constantine's conferring upon Pope Sylvester I (reigned 314–335) the primacy of the West, including the imperial symbols of rulership, the Donation attempted to retroactively reconstruct the history of the Roman PAPACY in order to explain and legitimate a number of important political developments and papal claims. These included the transfer of the capital of the Roman Empire to Byzantium in 330, the displacement of old Rome by the new Rome of the church, papal secular authority, and the papal right to create an emperor by crowning him.

The latter would be used to great effect when Pope Leo III crowned Charlemagne emperor of the Romans in 800. Charlemagne then claimed for himself the right to appoint the bishops of his empire, who were more and more involved in political affairs. These conflicting perspectives were the cause of interminable struggles between popes and rulers throughout the Middle Ages.

In the course of this development, the process of the feudalization of the church occurred. Ruling political leaders in this system occupied significant positions in the church; by virtue of patronage this development encompassed the whole imperial church. At the conclusion of this development, bishops in the Holy Roman Empire were simultaneously the reigning princes of their dioceses; they often were much more interested in the political tasks of their dominion than in the spiritual.

In the great church-renewal movement, which extended from the 10th century until the reign of Pope GREGORY VII in the late 11th century, the papal church rejected both the sacred position of the king and the temporal position of bishops, who were awarded their rights and privileges by the king. It proclaimed the freedom of the church from state authority, as well as its preeminence over worldly powers. This struggle, now remembered as the INVESTITURE CONTROVERSY, was fought out as a dramatic altercation between the papacy and the empire. The church was not able to gain a complete victory in terms of its claims to full authority over the worldly and the spiritual realms.

The Reformation and its consequences. With the weakening of the Holy Roman Empire, the European nation-states arose as opponents of the church. The 16th-century Reformation forced the church to focus on spiritual tasks and placed Reformation law and the legal powers of church leadership in the hands of the princes. Under King Henry VIII the English church broke away from papal supremacy, and in the German territories the reigning princes became, in effect, the legal guardians of the Protestant episcopate. Similar developments took place in the ROMAN CATHOLIC nation-states, such as Spain, Portugal, and France.

Various medieval sects (*e.g.*, CATHARI, WALDENSES, HUSSITES, and the Bohemian Brethren) had disseminated democratic ideas of the freedom and equality of Christians who held voluntary membership in a communion of saints. These ideas were reinforced during the Reformation by groups such as the HUTTERITES, MENNONITES, Schwenckfelders, and the followers of THOMAS MÜNTZER, who renounced aspects of the secular state such as military service and state offices and sought to found communist communities based on Christian ideals and radical pacifism. Many of their political ideas—at first bloodily suppressed by the Reformation and COUNTER-REFORMATION states and churches—were later prominent in the Dutch wars of independence (Eighty Years' War [1568–1648]) and in the English Revolution (the Revolution of 1688).

The Reformation's strivings toward a guarantee for the freedom of the church, the Enlightenment's ideas of natural law, and social revolutionary criticism against the wealthy ecclesiastical hierarchy came together in the separation of church and state proclaimed during the French Revolution in the latter part of the 18th century. This separation echoed developments that arose during and after the American Revolution from the struggle of the Puritans against the English Episcopal system and the English throne. The new Constitution of the United States sought to free the church of state supervision in order to allow it a maximum amount of freedom in the realization of its spiritual tasks.

CHURCH FATHER, any of the great bishops and other eminent Christian teachers of the early centuries whose writings remained as a court of appeal for their successors, especially in reference to controverted points of faith or practice.

CHURCH OF JESUS CHRIST OF LATTER-DAY SAINTS, largest denomination of the MORMON religion.

CH'U TZ'U \\'chü-'tsə\\, *Pinyin* Chuci (Chinese: "Words of the Ch'u"), compendium of ancient Chinese poetic songs from the southern state of Ch'u during the Chou dynasty. Collected in the 2nd century BCE by Wang I, many of the poems are attributed to the famous 4th-century state official and poet, Ch'u Yüan. Having shamanistic and political implications, these poems express the religious practices of the Ch'u people. Often associated with the development of TAOIST traditions that predate the Han Dynasty (which began about 200 BCE), some of the more renowned poems (the "Yuan-Yu," or "Far Off Journey," and the "Li-sao," or "On Encountering Sorrow") refer to the escape from human misery by means of an ecstatic celestial journey.

CILAPPATIKĀRAM \\'sē-lə-pə-tē-'kär-əm\\, *also spelled* Shilappadikaram, Tamil epic attributed to the Jain prince Iḷaṅkō Aṭikaḷ, in three books, set in the capitals of the three Tamil kingdoms: Pukār (the Cōḻa capital), Maturai (*i.e.*, MADURAI, the Pāṇṭiya [Pandya] capital), and Vañci (the Cēra capital). It dates to the age of the Pallavas (*c.* 300–500 CE).

The epic's hero is Kōvalaṉ, a young Pukār merchant. It narrates Kōvalaṉ's marriage to the virtuous Kaṇṇaki, his love for the courtesan Mātavi, and his consequent ruin and exile in Maturai—where he dies, unjustly executed for theft after trying to sell his wife's anklet to a wicked goldsmith who had stolen a similar anklet belonging to the queen. Kaṇṇaki comes running to the city and shows the king her other anklet, breaks it to prove it is not the queen's—Kaṇṇaki's contains rubies, and the queen's contains pearls—and thus proves Kōvalaṉ's innocence. Kaṇṇaki tears off one breast and throws it at the kingdom of Maturai, which goes up in flames. Such is the power of a faithful wife. The third book deals with the Cēra king's victorious expedition to the north to bring Himalayan stone for an image of Kaṇṇaki, now become a goddess of chastity (*paṭṭiṉi*).

The *Cilappatikāram* is a fine synthesis of mood poetry in the ancient Tamil *caṅkam* tradition and the rhetoric of Sanskrit poetry—even the epic's title is a blend of Tamil and Sanskrit. Included in the epic frame is an operatic blend of romantic lyric, the dialogues typical of the *caṅkam*-period text *Kalittokai* (containing poems of unrequited or mismatched love), choruses of folk songs, descriptions of cities and villages, technical accounts of dance and music, and strikingly dramatic scenes of love and tragic death. The *Cilappatikāram* is a detailed poetic witness to Tamil culture, its varied religions, its town plans and city types, the commingling of Greek, Arab, and Tamil peoples, and the arts of dance and music.

CIRCE \\'sər-sē\\, in Greek mythology, a sorceress, the daughter of HELIOS, the sun god, and of the ocean NYMPH Perse. She was able by means of drugs and incantations to change humans into wolves, lions, and swine. The Greek hero ODYSSEUS visited her island, Aeaea, with his companions, whom she changed into swine. But Odysseus, protected by an herb given him by HERMES, compelled her to restore them. He stayed with her for one year before resuming his journey. Greco-Roman tradition placed her island near Italy or located her on Mount Circeo.

CIRCUMCISION, the operation of cutting away all or part of the foreskin (prepuce) of the penis. The origin of the practice is unknown. The widespread ethnic distribution of circumcision as a ritual and the widely preferred use of a stone knife rather than a metal one suggest great antiquity. Wherever the operation is performed as a traditional rite, it is done either before or at puberty and sometimes, as among some Arab peoples, immediately before marriage.

Among the ancient Egyptians, boys were generally circumcised between the ages of 6 and 12 years. Among Ethiopians, Jews, and Muslims, the operation is performed shortly after birth (among Jews, on the eighth day after birth) or perhaps a few years after birth. Among most other peoples who practice it ritually the operation is performed at puberty. At any age the ritual operation is regarded as of the profoundest religious significance. For the Jews it represents the fulfillment of the COVENANT between God and ABRAHAM (GENESIS 17:10–14) that every male child shall be circumcised. That Christians were not obliged to be circumcised was first recorded biblically in Acts 15. The operation at puberty represents a beginning of the initiation into manhood and the leaving behind of childhood. For female circumcision *see* CLITORIDECTOMY.

CIST \'sist, 'kist\, *also called* stone chest, prehistoric European COFFIN containing a body or ashes, usually made of stone or a hollowed-out tree; also, a storage place for sacred objects. "Cist" has also been used to refer to the stone burial place itself, usually with several upright stone slabs supporting a flat roofing stone.

CISTERCIAN \sis-'tər-shən\, *byname* White Monk, *or* Bernardine \'bər-nər-din, -ˌdēn\, member of a ROMAN CATHOLIC monastic order that was founded in 1098 and named after the original establishment at Cîteaux (Latin: Cistercium), a locality in Burgundy. The order's founding fathers, led by St. Robert of Molesme, were a group of BENEDICTINE monks from the abbey of Molesme who were dissatisfied with the relaxed observance of their abbey and desired to live under the strictest interpretation of the Rule of ST. BENEDICT. The Cistercian regulations demanded severe asceticism and reintroduced

Egyptian circumcision, relief, tomb of Ankhmahor, Saqqārah, 6th dynasty (2345–2181 BCE)
Henri Stierlin—Ziolo

manual labor for monks, making it a principal feature of their life. Communities of nuns were added to the order about 1200.

Cistercian government was based on three features: (1) uniformity—all monasteries were to observe exactly the same rules and customs, (2) general chapter meeting—the ABBOTS of all houses were to meet in annual general chapter at Cîteaux, (3) visitation—each daughter house was to be visited yearly by the founding abbot. Each house preserved its internal autonomy, and each monk belonged for life to the house where he made his vows.

The Cistercians might have remained a relatively small family but for ST. BERNARD OF CLAIRVAUX, who joined Cîteaux as a novice in 1112 or 1113. In 1115 he was sent out as founding abbot of Clairvaux, and thenceforward the growth of the order was spectacular. At St. Bernard's death the total number of Cistercian abbeys was 338, of which 68 were direct foundations from Clairvaux.

With compact broad estates and with a large, disciplined, unpaid labor force, the Cistercians were able to develop all branches of farming. They played a large part in the economic progress of the 12th century and in the development of the techniques of farming and marketing. Be-

Cistercian abbot St. Bernard of Clairvaux, from a 15th-century altarpiece by the Florentine School
By courtesy of the Staatliche Museen zu Berlin

fore the close of the 12th century, however, many abbeys were breaking essential statutes by accumulating wealth. Discipline, too, was allowed to decline. The phenomenal expansion of the order made it impossible to maintain annual chapter and annual visitations of daughter houses. After the Protestant REFORMATION the Cistercian monks disappeared from northern Europe, and, where they survived, abbeys struggled for existence.

Nevertheless, reform movements took place in France during the 16th and 17th centuries. The most noteworthy reform is traced to Armand-Jean Le Bouthillier de Rancé, who became abbot of La Trappe in 1664. His reforms were so successful that strict monastic observance became popularly associated with the name TRAPPISTS. Before the modernizing reforms of the SECOND VATICAN COUNCIL (1962–65), the monks of the Order of the Reformed Cistercians of the Strict Observance (O.C.S.O.) slept, ate, and worked in common in perpetual silence. Since the 1960s, however, these practices have been modified.

Meanwhile, the original order, now known as the Cistercians of Common Observance (S.O.Cist.), after a more moderate reform begun in 1666, has continued.

CITPĀVAN \chit-'pä-vän\, *also called* Konkanasth, CASTE of BRAHMINS in Konkan (the area of Goa) and Maharashtra in western India. They rose to considerable eminence in Maharashtra as administrators during the rule of the peshwas of Pune (1713–1818), who belonged to that caste. The predominance among them of fair complexions and light-colored eyes has given rise to the speculation that they are descended from shipwrecked European sailors. While many Citpāvan Brahmins continue the administrative tradition, others are active in the professions and in scholarship.

CIVIL RELIGION, term coined by the American sociologist Robert Neelly Bellah to describe the shared symbolic heritage which binds a community together into a cohesive, moral unit. More widely, the term has come to refer to the symbolic and ritual structures which societies turn to when traditional religions retreat in the face of SECULARISM.

CIZIN \kē-'sēn\, *also spelled* Kisin (Yucatec Mayan: "One Who Farts"), Mayan (*see* PRE-COLUMBIAN MESO-AMERICAN RELIGIONS) god of earthquakes and death. He may have been one aspect of a malevolent Underworld deity who manifested himself under several names and guises (*e.g.*, Ah Puch, Xibalba, and Yum Cimil). In pre-Conquest manuscripts, Cizin is frequently depicted with the god of war in scenes of HUMAN SACRIFICE, while some codices show Cizin uprooting or destroying trees planted by CHAC, the rain god. Cizin is also often depicted in the codices as a dancing skeleton, holding a smoking cigarette. He is also known by his death collar, which partly consists of disembodied eyes dangling by their nerve cords. After the Spanish Conquest, Cizin became merged with the Christian devil, SATAN.

CLARE OF ASSISI, SAINT \'klar . . . ə-'si-sē, 'kler, -'sē-zē\, *also spelled* Clara \'klar-ə\, *Italian* Santa Chiara di Assisi (b. July 16, 1194, Assisi, duchy of Spoleto [Italy]—d. Aug. 11, 1253, Assisi; canonized 1255; feast day August 11), ABBESS and founder of the POOR CLARES (Clarissines).

Deeply influenced by ST. FRANCIS OF ASSISI, she refused to marry as her parents wished and fled (March 18, 1212) to the Porziuncola Chapel below Assisi, where Francis received her vows, thus marking the beginning of the Second Order of St. Francis. Many joined Clare, including her

mother and her sister St. Agnes. Soon the Poor Clares were housed in the church and convent of San Damiano, near Assisi, where Clare became abbess in 1216. Clare's great concern was to obtain a rule reflecting the spirit of Francis to replace the BENEDICTINE rule that Cardinal Ugolino (later Pope Gregory IX) had adapted for her order, which was eventually approved by Pope Innocent IV.

She was credited with many miracles in life and after death. Legends relate that she saved Assisi twice from invasion. In 1958 Pope PIUS XII declared her patron of television, alluding to an incident in her last illness when she miraculously heard and saw the Christmas midnight mass in the BASILICA of San Francesco on the far side of Assisi.

CLAROS \'klär-ˌós\, site of an oracular shrine of the Greek god APOLLO, near Colophon in Ionia, Asia Minor (now in Turkey). According to tradition, the shrine was founded by Manto, daughter of TIRESIAS. Prior to their utterances, the prophets drank from a pool within a cave. References to the Clarian ORACLE, which was especially celebrated during Roman times, have been found as far away as Britain.

CLEMENT, FIRST LETTER OF \'kle-mənt\, originally titled Letter to the Church of Corinth, a letter to the CHRISTIAN Church in Corinth from the church of Rome, traditionally ascribed to and almost certainly written by ST. CLEMENT I of Rome, *c.* 96 CE. It is extant in a 2nd-century Latin translation, which is possibly the oldest surviving Latin Christian work. Regarded as SCRIPTURE by many 3rd- and 4th-century Christians, it was transmitted in manuscripts with a sermon known as the *Second Letter of Clement*, written *c.* 125–140 by an unknown author.

The letter discusses the orders of the ministry, which it asserts were established by the APOSTLES at the will of God. The *First Letter* was an important influence on the development of the episcopal orders (BISHOPS, PRIESTS, deacons), and it has been used to support the doctrine of the APOSTOLIC SUCCESSION, according to which bishops represent a direct, unbroken line of succession from the Apostles.

CLEMENT I, SAINT, *byname* Clement of Rome, *Latin* Clemens Romanus (b. Rome?—d. end of 1st century CE, Rome; feast day November 23), first Apostolic Father, pope from 88 to 97, or from 92 to 101, supposed third successor of St. Peter.

According to TERTULLIAN, Clement was consecrated by PETER. Bishop ST. IRENAEUS of Lyon lists him as a contemporary of the APOSTLES and witness of their preaching. Bishop EUSEBIUS of CAESAREA dates his pontificate from 92 to 101. His martyrdom is legendary, and he has been hypothetically identified with the Clement mentioned in Philippians 4:3. His attribute is an anchor, to which he was tied and cast into the sea, according to spurious tales.

The authorship of the *Letter to the Church of Corinth* (1 Clement) has been traditionally ascribed to him. Still extant, it was written to settle a controversy among the Corinthians against their church leaders and reveals that Clement considered himself empowered to intervene (the first such action known by a bishop of Rome) in another community's affairs.

Clement is credited with transmitting to the church the *Ordinances of the Holy Apostles Through Clement* (APOSTOLIC CONSTITUTIONS), which, reputedly drafted by the Apostles, is the largest collection of early Christian ecclesiastical law; the constitutions are now believed, however, to have been written in Syria *c.* 380.

CLEMENT OF ALEXANDRIA, *Latin name* Titus Flavius Clemens (b. *c.* 150 CE, Athens—d. between 211 and 215; feast day December 4; Eastern feast day November 24), Christian APOLOGIST, missionary theologian to the Hellenistic world, and second known leader and teacher of the catechetical SCHOOL OF ALEXANDRIA.

Little is known of Clement's early life. As a student he traveled to Italy and in the eastern Mediterranean area. Converted to CHRISTIANITY by his last teacher, Pantaenus—reputedly a former Stoic philosopher and the first recorded president of the Christian catechetical school at Alexandria—Clement succeeded his mentor as head of the school about 180.

During the next two decades Clement was the intellectual leader of the Alexandrian Christian community: he wrote several ethical and theological works and biblical commentaries; he combatted GNOSTICISM; he engaged in polemics with Christians who were suspicious of an intellectualized Christianity; and he educated persons who later became theological and ecclesiastical leaders (*e.g.*, Alexander, bishop of Jerusalem).

According to Clement, philosophy was to the Greeks, as the Law of MOSES was to the Jews, a preparatory discipline leading to the truth, which was personified in the LOGOS. His goal was to make Christian beliefs intelligible to those trained within the context of the Greek *paideia* (educational curriculum) so that those who accepted the Christian faith might be able to witness effectively within Hellenistic culture. Clement's view, "One, therefore, is the way of truth, but into it, just as into an everlasting river, flow streams but from another place," prepared the way for the curriculum of the catechetical school under ORIGEN that became the basis of the medieval quadrivium and trivium (*i.e.*, the liberal arts).

Though much of Clement's attention was focused upon the reorientation of men's personal lives in accordance with the Christian gospel, his interest in the social witnessing of Christians also involved him in the political and economic forces that affected man's status and dignity. Clement alluded to the theory of the two cities, the city of heaven and the city of the earth. Like AUGUSTINE two centuries later in *The City of God*, Clement did not equate the city of heaven with the institutional church. According to Clement, the Christian was to live as a citizen of heaven and then, in an order of priorities, under the law as a citizen of the earth. If a conflict should arise between God and Caesar (*i.e.*, the state), the Christian was to appeal to the "higher law" of God. At one point Clement advocated the theory of the just cause for open rebellion against a government that enslaves people, as in the case of the Hebrews in Egypt. In this view he also anticipated Augustine's theory of the just war. He also struck at racism when it is considered a basis for slavery.

Because of the persecution of Christians in Alexandria under the Roman emperor Severus in 201–202, Clement was obliged to leave his position as head of the catechetical school and to seek sanctuary elsewhere. His position at the school was assumed by his young and gifted student Origen, who became one of the greatest theologians of the Christian church. Clement found safety with another of his former students, Alexander, bishop of Jerusalem.

The Greek church regarded Clement's views as too close to Origen's, some of which were considered heretical. In the Latin church he was regarded as a saint, and his feast day was celebrated on December 4 until 1586, when, because some of his views were questioned in regard to their orthodoxy, because of which Sixtus V deleted his name from the Roman martyrology.

CLEMENTIA \kle-'men-tē-ə\, in ROMAN RELIGION, personification of mercy and clemency. Her worship began with her deification as the celebrated virtue of Julius Caesar. The Senate in 44 BCE decreed a temple to Caesar and Clementia, in which the cult statue represented the two figures clasping hands. Tiberius was honored with an altar to his *clementia*, and the clemency of Caligula received yearly sacrifices. On coins the goddess was usually depicted standing, holding a patera (a dish used in sacrifices) and a scepter.

CLEOBIS AND BITON \'klē-ə-bis . . . 'bī-tən\, Biton *also spelled* Bito \'bī-tō\, in Greek myth, the sons of Cydippe, priestess of HERA, queen of the gods, at Argos, noted for their filial devotion and for their physical strength. During an Argive festival honoring Hera, Cydippe was called to the temple. When her oxen could not be found, the brothers took up the yoke of the wagon and conveyed her there themselves. Cydippe begged the goddess to grant them whatever was best for mortal men. They feasted and slept that night in the temple, but died in their sleep.

CLERGY, a body of ordained ministers in a CHRISTIAN church. In the ROMAN CATHOLIC church and in the churches of the ANGLICAN COMMUNION, the term includes the orders of bishop, priest, and deacon. Until 1972, in the Roman Catholic church, clergy also included several lower orders.

The Greek word *klēros* means literally "share" or "inheritance." Its use in patristic Greek to mean "church office" or "clergy" is sometimes traced to NEW TESTAMENT usages (such as in 1 Peter 5:3), in which *klēros* is thought to refer to the share or portion of the faithful assigned to each elder in a Christian community. Most Christian churches understand the clergy to be persons functioning within the PRIESTHOOD of all the people but ordained, or set aside, for particular service, especially in connection with eucharistic ministry.

A distinction between clergy and laity developed in the 2nd century, although the clerical ministry traces its beginnings to the commission of the Twelve Apostles and the Seventy for service. Over the centuries, the distinction between clergy and laity was emphasized by special privileges granted to the clergy. These privileges were later extended and codified by the Theodosian Code (438), but were eventually removed in most countries by legislation.

Within the Roman Catholic tradition, from the 4th century on, CELIBACY began to be enforced on priests. By the 12th century anyone taking vows as a deacon or priest also took a vow of celibacy. In the Eastern church, however, celibacy prevailed only for bishops. In the 20th century the permanent diaconate, open to married and single men, was once more restored within the Roman Catholic church.

Until the 20th century, in most Christian churches, the clergy was restricted to males. Gradually, however, many mainline Protestant churches began ordaining women.

CLIO \'klī-ō, 'klē-\, in Greek mythology, one of the nine MUSES, patron of history. Traditionally Clio reprimanded the goddess APHRODITE for her love for ADONIS. Aphrodite made her fall in love with Pierus, king of Macedonia. From that union was born HYACINTHUS, a young man of great beauty who was later killed by his lover, the god APOLLO. In art Clio was frequently represented with the heroic trumpet and the clepsydra (water clock).

CLITORIDECTOMY \ˌkli-tə-ri-ˈdek-tə-mē\, *also called* female circumcision, *or* excision, any of a range of ritual surgical procedures from a simple drawing of blood to infibulation (also called Pharoanic circumcision), which consists in removal of the clitoris, the labia minora, and the anterior two-thirds of the labia majora, the sides of which are joined leaving a small posterior opening.

The practice of female circumcision dates to ancient times and was traditionally performed to guard virginity and to reduce sexual desire. It is widely practiced in such places as New Guinea; Australia; the Malay Archipelago; Ethiopia, Egypt, and other parts of Africa; Brazil; Mexico; Peru; and by various Islamic peoples of the Middle East, Africa, western Asia, and India. Infibulation is common particularly in The Sudan, Somalia, and Nigeria. The operation is usually performed by a midwife. Especially with the more radical excision, consequences may include severe bleeding, tetanus and other infections, extreme pain, and death; urination and sexual intercourse may be painful. Where the practice of infibulation is common, women are reinfibulated after the birth of each child.

Groups in which clitoridectomy is practiced also usually practice male circumcision and view the ritual as a necessary ritual stage for passage into responsible adulthood.

COATLICUE \ˌkō-ät-ˈlē-kwä\ (Nahuatl: "Snake's Skirt," *i.e.,* "[She Who Has a] Skirt of Snakes"), Aztec earth goddess, symbol of the earth as creator and destroyer, mother of the gods and mortals. Her face consists of two fanged serpents; her skirt is of interwoven snakes (snakes symbolize fertility); her breasts are flabby (she nourished many); her necklace is of hands, hearts, and a skull; her hands and feet are claws (she feeds on corpses, as the earth consumes all that dies). Called also Teteoinnan ("Mother of the Gods") and Toci ("Our Grandmother"), she was one manifestation of the earth goddess. *See* PRE-COLUMBIAN MESO-AMERICAN RELIGIONS.

CODEPENDENT ORIGINATION: *see* PRATĪTYA-SAMUTPĀDA.

COFFIN, the receptacle in which a corpse is placed. The Greeks and Romans disposed of their dead both by burial

Coatlicue, stone sculpture
By courtesy of the Instituto Nacional de Antropologia e Historia, Mexico City

and by CREMATION. Greek coffins were urn-shaped, hexagonal, or triangular, with the body arranged in a sitting posture. The material used was generally burnt clay and in some cases had obviously been molded around the body and baked. In the Christian era stone coffins came into use. Romans who were rich enough had their coffins made of a limestone brought from Assus, in Asia Minor, which was commonly believed to "eat" the body (hence the term SARCOPHAGUS, or "flesh-eater"); rapid decomposition was thought to aid the passage of the soul to the afterlife.

The Egyptian coffins were the largest stone coffins known and were generally highly polished and covered with hieroglyphics that usually told a history of the deceased. MUMMY chests shaped to the form of the body were also used, being made of hardwood or painted papier-mâché; these also bore hieroglyphics.

Among the American Indians some tribes used roughhewn wooden coffins; others sometimes enclosed the corpse between the upper and lower shells of a turtle. In their tree and scaffold burial the Indians sometimes used wooden coffins or travois baskets or simply wrapped the body in blankets. Canoes, mounted on a scaffold near a river, were used as coffins by some tribes, while others placed the corpse in a canoe or wicker basket and floated it out into the stream or lake. The Aborigines of Australia generally used coffins of bark, but some tribes employed baskets of wickerwork.

COFFIN TEXTS, collection of ancient Egyptian funerary texts consisting of SPELLS or magic formulas painted on the burial COFFINS of the First Intermediate period (c. 2130–1939 BCE) and the Middle Kingdom (1938–c. 1600? BCE). The Coffin Texts, combined with the PYRAMID TEXTS from which they were derived, were the primary sources of the BOOK OF THE DEAD, which was in prominent use during the New Kingdom and Late period. These three collections represent the most extensive body of Egyptian religious literature available to modern scholars.

COHEN: *see* KOHEN.

COKHĀMELĀ \ˈchō-kä-ˈmä-lä\ (b. c. 1250–1300 CE, Mahārāshtra state, India—d. 1338, Mangalvedha, Mahārāshtra), poet-saint (*sant*) who is remembered as a composer of devotional songs (*abhang*) in Marathi to the Hindu deity Viṭṭhal. His songs are preserved through oral performance (KĪRTAN), old handwritten manuscripts, and modern printed collections. Cokhāmelā belonged to an UNTOUCHABLE caste (JĀTI), the MAHARS, and his own poetry, as well as the allusions and remembrances of others, highlights this important fact. HAGIOGRAPHY records that Cokhāmelā was miraculously born from a half-eaten mango that was given to Cokhāmelā's mother by Viṭṭhal disguised as a BRAHMIN. In another story the gods asked Cokhāmelā to purify heaven's nectar, which had been polluted by DEMONS. Only Cokhāmelā could purify the nectar because he had not been conceived by sexual intercourse; hence he received the name "Collection (*melā*) of Purity (*cokhā*)." Some songs attributed to Cokhāmelā, like the story about his name, lament his socially and religiously low status and challenge Hindu notions of purity and sacrality. In other songs he accepts the conditions of his "low" birth as justice for past sinful actions (KARMA). An understanding of VEDĀNTA pervades Cokhāmelā's compositions, a knowledge attributed to his relationship with his spiritual teacher and fellow Marāṭhī poet-saint NĀMDEV (1270?–1350? CE). Among Cokhāmelā's family members, his wife, son, sister, and brother-in-law are also remembered as poet-saints. Legend recalls that Cokhāmelā died when a wall he was building with other Mahārs collapsed on top of him. His family and friends asked Nāmdev how they might identify his bones from among those of the other workers. Nāmdev said, "You will know Cokhāmelā because you will hear Viṭṭhal's name vibrating in his bones."

COLETTE, SAINT \kȯ-'let\ (b. Jan. 13, 1381, Corbie, France—d. March 6, 1447, Ghent; canonized 1807; feast day March 6), ABBESS, reformer of the POOR CLARES and founder of the Colettine Poor Clares.

Colette entered the third order of St. Francis. Legend relates that in a vision, St. Francis directed her to restore the Poor Clares to the original severity of their rule. Despite initial opposition, her reform spread through Savoy, Burgundy, France, Flanders, and Spain, this was especially true after her death.

COLUMBUS PLATFORM, in REFORM JUDAISM, declaration issued by an important conference of American Reform rabbis in Columbus, Ohio (1937), supporting the use of traditional customs and ceremonies and the liturgical use of Hebrew. The platform also reemphasized the idea of Jewish peoplehood and represented a dramatic revision of Reform principles as stated in the PITTSBURGH PLATFORM of 1885.

COMANA \kə-'mä-nə\, modern Şahr, ancient city of Cappadocia in southern Turkey. Often called Chryse to distinguish it from Comana in Pontus, it was there that the cult of Ma-Enyo, a variant of the great west Asian MOTHER GODDESS, was celebrated with orgiastic rites. The service was carried on in an opulent temple by thousands of temple servants. The city, which was subordinate to the temple, was governed by the chief priest, usually a member of the reigning Cappadocian family, who ranked next to the king. Under the emperor Caracalla (reigned 211–217 CE), Comana became a Roman colony, and it continued to receive honors until the official recognition of Christianity.

COMMON LIFE, BRETHREN OF THE, religious community established in the late 14th century by Geert Groote at Deventer, in the Netherlands. Groote formed the brethren

from among his friends and disciples. After Groote's death, several followers became AUGUSTINIAN Canons and established the Congregation of Windesheim. These two communities became the principal exponents of DEVOTIO MODERNA, a school and trend of spirituality stressing meditation and the inner life and criticizing the highly speculative spirituality of the 13th and 14th centuries.

The brethren spread throughout the Netherlands, Germany, and Switzerland. They were self-supporting and lived a simple Christian life in common, with an absence of ritual. Among their chief aims were the education of a Christian elite and the promotion of the reading of devout literature. They produced finely written manuscripts and, later, printed books. They kept large schools in which the scholarship (but not the humanistic spirit) of the Italian Renaissance was found. Groote also founded the Sisters of the Common Life, devoted to education, the copying of books, and weaving.

The *devotio moderna* movement was seriously affected by the religious upheaval of the Protestant REFORMATION, and the brethren ceased to exist early in the 17th century.

COMMON PRAYER, THE BOOK OF, liturgical book used by churches of the ANGLICAN COMMUNION. First authorized for use in the Church of England in 1549, it was radically revised in 1552, with subsequent minor revisions in 1559, 1604, and 1662. The prayer book of 1662, with minor changes, has continued as the standard liturgy of most Anglican churches of the British Commonwealth. Outside the Commonwealth most churches of the Anglican Communion possess their own variants of the English prayer book.

The First Prayer Book of Edward VI was prepared primarily by Thomas Cranmer, who became archbishop of Canterbury in 1533. Intended as a compromise between old and new ideas, it aroused opposition from both conservatives and Reformers. The latter prevailed and in 1552 *The Second Prayer Book of Edward VI* was introduced. The revision changed the text and ceremonies in a Protestant direction. In 1553 the new Catholic queen, Mary, restored the old Latin liturgical books. After Elizabeth I became queen in 1558, the prayer book of 1552 was restored. It included a few small but significant changes, one which allowed for belief in the Real Presence of JESUS CHRIST in the EUCHARIST. The Puritans were dissatisfied and, on the accession of James I, their renewed demands for change resulted in some concessions in the prayer book of 1604.

The prayer book was proscripted under the Commonwealth and Protectorate. After the Restoration (1660) a revision of the prayer book was adopted (1662). After the Revolution of 1688, a revision of the prayer book was proposed in an attempt to reunite the Puritans with the ESTABLISHED CHURCH. That proposal failed, however, and further revisions were not attempted until the 20th century. Much controversy resulted from the revision of 1927–28; it was rejected by Parliament, which suspected "Romanizing" tendencies in changes proposed for the ministering of Holy Communion. The Church of England and most of those within the Anglican Communion did, however, develop a liturgy in contemporary language that was widely used; after much controversy it was fully adopted by the Church of England and the Protestant Episcopal Church in the United States at the end of the 1970s.

COMPANIONS OF THE PROPHET, Arabic Ṣaḥāba, or Aṣḥāb, in ISLAM, followers of MUHAMMAD who had personal contact with him; any Muslim who was alive in the

Concheros *dancer in San Miguel de Allende, Mex.*
Andrew Rakoczy—Monkmeyer

Prophet's lifetime and saw him may be reckoned among the Companions. The Companions, being eyewitnesses, are the most important sources of HADITH. The first four CALIPHS are the ṣaḥāba held in highest esteem among SUNNI Muslims; they are part of a group of 10 Companions to whom Muhammad promised paradise. The *muhājirūn* (those who followed the Prophet from MECCA to MEDINA), the ANṢĀR (the Medinese believers), and the *badrīyūn* (those who fought at the BATTLE OF BADR) are all considered Companions. (*See* HIJRA.) There are differing accounts of who belonged to the various groups.

SHĪʿITE Muslims disregard the ṣaḥāba, whom they consider responsible for the loss of the caliphate by the family of Muhammad's son-in-law ʿALĪ.

COMPARATIVE RELIGION, systematic study of the similarities and differences among religions. Comparative STUDY OF RELIGIONS was especially popular among Western scholars during the late 19th and early 20th centuries. In their search for similarities and differences, the standard measure, implicitly at least, was CHRISTIANITY, and the resulting comparisons were consequently biased toward theistic categories. Thus, the Hindu gods BRAHMĀ, VISHNU, and SHIVA were often compared to the TRINITY of Christianity, and the AVATARS of Vishnu were analyzed as similar to the INCARNATION of Christ. The rise of social evolution became a second major influence in comparative religion. Books characterizing religions as simple (primitive) or complex, nonrational or rational, cyclical or noncyclical, agricultural

or pastoral became very popular. The categories more often than not derived from an assumed progress of rationality, usually culminating in modern Western science and democracy. The development of typology and typological classifications provided a third method for comparing religion. Thus scholars often classed religions as solar, lunar, aquatic, cyclical, noncyclical, animist, natural, and revelatory. The ethnocentric bias of such analyses, together with the lack of theoretical agreement and the growth of specialization in the study of religion ultimately caused comparative religion to fall out of favor as a scholarly pursuit.

CONALL CERNACH \ˈkō-nəl-ˈkʸer-nək\, *also spelled* Conal, legendary warrior of Celtic myth who figures in the ULSTER CYCLE story *Bricriu's Feast* and many other stories. His name may be a cognate of CERNUNNOS, and he may be related to this Celtic god.

CONCHEROS \kȯn-ˈchā-rōs\, Mexican ritual dance that preserves many elements of PRE-COLUMBIAN MESO-AMERICAN religious ritual. It apparently originated in 1522, after the Spanish conquest of the Chichimec tribe, as a means of continuing ancient ritual. Dancers belong to an intertribal society organized as a military hierarchy; unlike most ritual dance societies, the *concheros* admits women. Members perform at seasonal festivals, notably at sites oriented north (Villa de Guadalupe), east (Amecameca), south (Chalma), and west (Los Remedios) of Mexico City, reflecting the ancient religious importance of the four cardinal directions. The dances are preceded by processions and invocations, and the paraphernalia include floral decorations, banners, and *concheros*, small lutes made from an armadillo shell.

CONCHOBAR MAC NESSA \ˈkä-nü-ər-mək-ˈne-sə, ˈkäŋ-kō-ər-\, *also known as* Conor \ˈkä-nər\, in ancient Irish Gaelic literature, the reputed king of the Ulaids of northeast Ireland from his seat at EMAIN MACHA about the beginning of the 1st century BCE. He figures prominently in the ULSTER CYCLE as the ideal Irish king.

In one story from the Ulster cycle (from *The Book of Leinster* [c. 1160]), Conor fell in love with the great beauty DEIRDRE. Deirdre, however, fell in love with Noíse, son of Uisnech. They eloped and fled to Scotland with Noíse's two brothers, where they lived idyllically until they were lured back to Ireland by the treachery of Conor. The sons of Uisnech were slain, causing revolt and bloodshed in Ulster. Deirdre took her own life by shattering her head against a rock to avoid falling into the hands of Conor.

CONCILIARISM \kən-ˈsi-lē-ə-ˌri-zəm\, in the ROMAN CATHOLIC church, a theory that a general council of the church has greater authority than the pope and may depose him. Conciliarism began with 12th- and 13th-century canonists attempting to set juridical limitations on the PAPACY.

The 15th century saw serious attempts to put the conciliar theories into practice. The COUNCIL OF CONSTANCE (1414–18) invoked the doctrine to depose three claimants to the papal throne; it then elected Pope Martin V, thereby effectively healing the Western (Great) SCHISM (1378–1417). Though this council is recognized by Rome as the 16th ecumenical council, neither was it convened by a legitimate pope nor was the decree *Sacrosancta* espousing conciliarism approved. The theory has continued to live, influencing doctrines that advocated restriction of papal power.

The FIRST VATICAN COUNCIL in 1870 explicitly condemned conciliarism. The SECOND VATICAN COUNCIL (1962–65) asserted that the pope as a member and the head of the college of bishops forms with it at all times an organic unity, especially when it is gathered in a general council.

CONCORD, BOOK OF, collected doctrinal standards of the Lutheran church, published in German (June 25, 1580) and in Latin (1584). Its publication climaxed 30 years of effort to heal the SCHISMS that had broken out in the Lutheran movement after MARTIN LUTHER'S death. After two political conferences (in 1558 and 1561) had failed to produce agreement, the Protestant princes of the Holy Roman Empire entrusted the project to several theologians, who produced the Formula of Concord, which was written primarily by Jakob Andreä and Martin Chemnitz and put in final form in 1577. The Book of Concord was subsequently compiled. It was not adopted in total by all Lutheran churches, but it has remained the standard of orthodox LUTHERANISM.

It consists of (1) a preface; (2) the three ecumenical creeds (APOSTOLIC, NICENE, and ATHANASIAN); (3) the Unaltered AUGSBURG CONFESSION (1530) and (4) its Apology (1531); (5) the SCHMALKALDIC ARTICLES (1536–37); (6) PHILIPP MELANCHTHON'S *Treatise on the Power and Primacy of the Pope* (1537); (7) Martin Luther's Small and Large CATECHISMS (1529); (8) the Formula of Concord (1577); and (9) the Catalogue of Testimonies (1580), an optional supplement of citations from the early CHURCH FATHERS.

CONCORDIA \kän-'kȯr-dē-ə\, in ROMAN RELIGION, goddess who was the personification of "concord," or "agreement," especially among members or classes of the Roman state. She had several temples at Rome, the oldest and most important one, dating from the middle of the 4th century BCE, located in the Forum. It was restored after the death of Gaius Gracchus and again by Augustus. Concordia often appeared on coins as a matron holding a CORNUCOPIA and either an olive branch or a patera (a dish used in sacrifices).

CONFESSING CHURCH, *German* Bekennende Kirche, movement within the German Protestant churches that developed during the 1930s from their resistance to Adolf Hitler's attempt to make the churches an instrument of National Socialist (Nazi) propaganda and politics.

Hitler's church party, the German Christians, gained control of the German Evangelical Church, a federation formed in 1933 of Lutheran, Reformed, and United territorial churches. Ludwig Müller, supported by the Nazis, was elected *Reichsbischof* ("imperial bishop"), upholding the Nazi doctrine of the racial superiority of so-called ARYANS.

In response, the Young Reforming Movement was formed within the churches under the leadership of Hanns Lilje, Martin Niemöller, and others. These founders believed that the doctrine of racial superiority ran counter to both Christian scriptures and the confessional writings of the REFORMATION. In November 1933 Niemöller founded the Pastors' Emergency League, which resisted the programs of the German Christians. The SYNOD OF BARMEN was held in May 1934, and its theological declaration transformed the defensive movement against Nazi control of the churches into an organized revival (*see* BARTH, KARL).

At the end of 1934, at the second synod of the Confessing Church at Dahlem, the church proclaimed its emergency law: the true church in Germany was that which accepted the Barmen Declaration, and, in any church in which the leadership was following the German Christian movement, ministers and parishes were to follow the orders of the Confessing Church. Thus, in practice, two Protestant churches developed in Germany, one under state control and the Confessing Church, which the state did not recognize. The Confessing Church, together with the churches of Bavaria, Württemberg, and Hanover (which had remained independent of Nazi rule), formed the provisional government of the German Evangelical Church.

In 1936 internal differences led the Lutheran territorial churches to form the Council of the Evangelical Lutheran Church in Germany, thus eroding the unity of the Confessing Church. The Reformed and United sections of the Confessing Church remained particularly active in protesting against the persecution of the Jews. Nazi pressure was gradually intensified, and increasingly the Confessing Church was forced underground. In 1937 Niemöller and other clergy were arrested. After the outbreak of World War II in 1939, the Confessing Church was seriously handicapped by the conscription of clergy and laity. Many founding members of the church were compelled to live abroad, and those who stayed in Germany faced imprisonment, and sometimes execution (*see* BONHOEFFER, DIETRICH). In 1948 the Confessing Church ceased to exist.

CONFESSION, in the Judeo-Christian tradition, the acknowledgment of sinfulness in public or private, regarded as necessary to obtain divine forgiveness.

The mission of the OLD TESTAMENT prophets was to awaken in the people a sense of sinfulness and an acknowledgment of their guilt, both personal and collective. Before the destruction of the TEMPLE OF JERUSALEM (70 CE), the sin offerings on the Day of Atonement (YOM KIPPUR) were prefaced by a collective expression of sinfulness (Leviticus 16:21), and, since the destruction of the Temple, the Day of Atone-

Penitent at confession with priest
Mimi Forsyth—Monkmeyer

ment has continued in JUDAISM as a day of prayer, fasting, and confession.

In the NEW TESTAMENT the public ministry of JESUS was prepared for by JOHN THE BAPTIST, whose BAPTISMS were accompanied by a public confession of sins. The practice of making a detailed confession to a BISHOP or PRIEST began fairly early in the church's history. In the 5th-century Roman church, the practice was to hear confessions at the beginning of LENT and to reconcile the penitents on Holy (MAUNDY) Thursday. Gradually the practice of reconciling, or absolving, sinners immediately after confession and before fulfillment of penance was introduced. By the end of the 11th century, only notorious sinners were reconciled on Holy Thursday. Often, those guilty of serious sins put off penance until death approached. To correct this abuse, the fourth LATERAN COUNCIL (1215) established the rule that every Christian should confess to a priest at least once a year.

The ROMAN CATHOLIC church teaches that penance is a SACRAMENT, instituted by Christ, in which a confession of all serious sins committed after baptism is necessary. The doctrine of the EASTERN ORTHODOX churches concerning confession agrees with that of the Roman Catholic church.

Most Protestants regard the general confession and ABSOLUTION of the communion service as sufficient preparation for the Lord's Supper. Among Lutherans, private confession and absolution survived the REFORMATION for a time but were eventually given up by most members. JOHN CALVIN also recognized the value of private confession and absolution for those troubled in conscience, but he denied that such confession was a sacrament or that it was necessary for the forgiveness of sins. In some Pentecostal and fundamentalist churches, confession of sins is an important part of the worship service. Most Protestants consider auricular or private confession to be unbiblical and consider confession viewed as a sacrament to be equally unbiblical. These Protestants stress that God alone can forgive sins.

CONFESSION OF FAITH, formal statement of doctrinal belief ordinarily intended for public avowal by an individual, a group, a congregation, a SYNOD, or a church; confessions are similar to creeds, although usually more extensive. They are especially associated with the churches of the Protestant REFORMATION.

The medieval Christian church did not attempt an official codification of its doctrine. The creeds inherited from antiquity (NICENE CREED) or formulated in the early Middle Ages (APOSTLES' CREED, ATHANASIAN CREED) were used in liturgical worship to confess the Christian faith. Certain doctrinal points were defined by councils as a result of doctrinal controversies. The heretical movements in the Middle Ages produced no comprehensive declarations of faith.

The Reformation in the 16th century led to the formulation of declarations which aimed at defining all the main points of the doctrinal system. Most of these documents were compiled with the purpose of expressing the church's doctrine; a few of them originally served other purposes (*e.g.*, Luther's CATECHISMS) but were soon given the rank of doctrinal standards. The first confessional documents of the Reformation were the drafts preceding the AUGSBURG CONFESSION of 1530. This example of the Lutherans was followed by other Reformation churches, and it was even followed by the COUNCIL OF TRENT (1545–63), whose decrees and canons, together with the *Professio fidei Tridentina* of 1564, were a codification of ROMAN CATHOLIC doctrine.

Other important Protestant confessions include the Formula of Concord (1577) and BOOK OF CONCORD (1580), the

Presbyterian WESTMINSTER CONFESSION (1648), and the Anglican THIRTY-NINE ARTICLES (1571).

CONFESSIONS, BOOK OF, compilation of creeds and CONFESSIONS OF FAITH that was prepared by a committee of the United PRESBYTERIAN Church in the U.S.A. and was adopted by that church in 1967. It includes the NICENE CREED, the APOSTLES' CREED, the Scots Confession (1560), the HEIDELBERG CATECHISM (1562), the Second Helvetic Confession (1566), the WESTMINSTER CONFESSION and the Westminster Shorter Catechism (1648), the Barmen Declaration (1934), and the new Confession of 1967.

The union that formed the United Presbyterian Church in the U.S.A. in 1958 had stipulated that the new church would draft "a brief contemporary statement of faith," that, it was assumed, would be a version of the Westminster Confession. The committee that began work on the project in 1959 soon found, however, that a simplified version of a 300-year-old confession would not suffice. The committee then secured permission to develop a Book of Confessions that would deal adequately with the problem of continuity and tradition.

The Confession of 1967 was designed explicitly to presuppose, continue, and supplement the historic creeds of the Book of Confessions without repeating their contents. The new creed was primarily concerned with the task of the church in the modern world. The Confession of 1967 also expresses clearly the church's conviction that critical study of the BIBLE is an aid to, rather than an attack upon, the use of the Bible in the church.

CONFIRMATION, in CHRISTIANITY, rite by which the relation between man and God established previously in BAPTISM is said to be confirmed (or strengthened and established in faith).

During the first several centuries of Christian history, when most of those who joined the church were adult converts from paganism, the baptism of these adults and the ceremony admitting them to the full rights of membership (equivalent to, but not yet called, confirmation) probably coincided. Early Christian theologians, therefore, closely connected the meaning and effects of confirmation with those of baptism. But as the baptism of infants rather than of adults became customary, a sharper distinction between baptism and confirmation became necessary.

The ROMAN CATHOLIC church views confirmation as a SACRAMENT instituted by JESUS CHRIST. It confers the gifts of the HOLY SPIRIT upon the recipient, who must be a baptized person at least seven years old. A BISHOP normally performs the rite, which includes the laying on of hands and anointing the forehead with chrism (consecrated oil).

In EASTERN ORTHODOXY, a child generally receives the three sacraments of baptism, confirmation (called chrismation), and the first communion all in the same service, administered by a PRIEST.

After the Protestant REFORMATION, the ANGLICAN COMMUNION and LUTHERANISM retained a form of confirmation. Lutheranism rejects the sacramental definition of confirmation and considers it a public profession of the faith into which the candidate was baptized as an infant. In both Anglicanism and Lutheranism, confirmation is usually preceded by instruction in the CATECHISM. Other Protestant bodies deny that confirmation is a sacrament, but they sometimes use the term confirmation for acceptance of baptized members into full membership of the church, including the right to receive Holy Communion.

CONFUCIANISM

Away of life propagated by CONFUCIUS in the 6th–5th century BCE and followed by the Chinese people for more than two millennia, Confucianism—a Western term that has no counterpart in Chinese—is a worldview, a social ethic, a political ideology, and a scholarly tradition. Although often grouped with the major HISTORICAL RELIGIONS, Confucianism differs from them by not being an organized religion. Nonetheless, it spread to other East Asian countries under the influence of Chinese literate culture and exerted a profound influence on spiritual and political life.

FORMATION OF THE CLASSICAL CONFUCIAN TRADITION

Confucius (551–479 BCE) lived in an era of political violence and social disintegration in China. As a master teacher concerned with modes of thought and action that could be potentially restorative of order and harmony, Confucius was said to have attracted 3,000 students, of whom 72 were close disciples. Believing in the perfectibility of all human beings, Confucius focused his teachings on his concept of JEN—variously translated as "love," "goodness," and "human-heartedness." In the most complete sense, *jen* signified supreme moral achievement and excellence in character in accord with LI (ritual norms) and the principles of *chung* (loyalty to one's true nature), *shu* (reciprocity), *yi* (righteousness), and HSIAO (filial piety). All of these principles make up the Confucian sense of TE or "virtue." The paradigmatic individual was the CHÜN-TZU (literally, "prince-son"), who in Confucius' view attained nobility by means of character rather than inheritance. Confucius found models of inspiration in legendary sage-kings who ruled by moral suasion rather than by might.

According to Han-fei-tzu (d. 233 BCE), shortly after Confucius' death his followers split into eight distinct schools, all claiming to be the legitimate heir to his legacy. Presumably each school was associated with or inspired by one or more of Confucius' disciples, which included Yen Yüan (or Yen Hui), TSENG-TZU, Tzu Kung, Tzu-hsia, and others. Yet the Confucians did not exert much influence in the 5th century BCE.

A century after Confucius' death, the Confucian attempt to moralize politics was not working; the disintegration of the Chou feudal ritual system and the rise

Vietnamese devotees at a Confucian shrine in Ho Chi Minh City light votive candles and incense

Van Bucher—Photo Researchers

of powerful hegemonic states reveal that wealth and power still spoke the loudest. The intellectual agenda was determined by the hermits (the early Taoists, *see* TAOISM), who left the world to create a sanctuary in nature in order to lead a contemplative life, and the realists (proto-Legalists), who played the dangerous game of assisting ambitious kings to gain wealth and power so that they could influence the political process. The Confucians refused to be identified with the interests of the ruling minority because their social consciousness impelled them to serve as the conscience of the people. Although they wanted to be actively involved in politics, they could not accept the status quo as the legitimate arena in which to exercise authority and power.

Mencius: The paradigmatic Confucian intellectual. MENCIUS is known as the self-styled transmitter of the Confucian Way. In his sophisticated argument against the physiocrats (who advocated the supremacy of agricultural labor), he employed the idea of the division of labor to defend those who labor with their minds, observing that service is as important as productivity. To him Confucians served the vital interests of the state as scholars, not by becoming bureaucratic functionaries but by assuming the responsibility of teaching the ruling minority humane government (*jen-cheng*) and the kingly way (*wang-tao*). In dealing with feudal lords, Mencius made it explicit that a true man cannot be corrupted by wealth, subdued by power, or affected by poverty.

Mencius' strategy for social reform was to change the language of profit, self-interest, wealth, and power by making it part of a moral discourse, with emphasis on rightness, public-spiritedness, welfare, and influence. Rather than arguing against profit, Mencius instructed the feudal lords to cultivate a common bond with their ministers, officers, clerks, and the seemingly undifferentiated masses. Only then, Mencius contended, would they be able to preserve their profit, self-interest, wealth, and power. He encouraged them to extend their benevolence and warned them that this was crucial for the protection of their families.

Mencius' appeal to the common bond among all people as a mechanism of government was predicated on his strong sense that the people are more important than the state and the state more important than the king and that the ruler who does not act in accordance with the kingly way is unfit to rule. Mencius insisted that an unfit ruler should be criticized, rehabilitated, or, as the last resort, deposed. Mencius' conception of politics was based upon his philosophical vision that human beings can perfect themselves through effort and that human nature is good. While he acknowledged the role of biological and environmental factors in shaping the human condition, he insisted that human beings become moral simply by willing to be so. Furthermore, Mencius asserted that if men fully realize the potential of their hearts, they will understand their nature; by understanding their nature, they will know Heaven.

Hsün-tzu: The transmitter of Confucian scholarship. If Mencius brought Confucian moral idealism to fruition, HSÜN-TZU (*c.* 300–*c.* 230 BCE) conscientiously transformed Confucianism into a realistic and systematic inquiry on the human condition, with special reference to ritual and authority. Hsün-tzu's penetrating insight into the shortcomings of virtually all the major currents of thought propounded by his fellow thinkers helped to establish the Confucian school as a forceful political and social movement.

Hsün-tzu underscored the centrality of self-cultivation. He defined the process of Confucian education as a ceaseless endeavor to accumulate knowledge, skills, insight, and wisdom. Because he saw human beings as prone to pursue the gratification of their passions, he firmly believed in the need for social constraints. Without constraints, social solidarity, the precondition for human well-being, would be undermined. The most serious flaw he saw in the Mencian commitment to the goodness of human nature was the practical consequence of neglecting the necessity of ritual and authority for the well-being of society.

Like Mencius, Hsün-tzu believed in the perfectibility of all human beings through self-cultivation, in humanity and rightness as cardinal virtues, in humane government as the kingly way, in social harmony, and in education. But his view of how these could actually be achieved was diametrically opposed to that of

Mencius. Hsün-tzu singled out human rationality as the basis for morality. Men become moral by voluntarily harnessing their desires and passions to act in accordance with society's norms. Although this is alien to human nature, it is perceived by the mind as necessary for both survival and well-being. A cultured person is by definition a fully socialized member of the human community, who has successfully sublimated his instinctual demands for the public good.

Hsün-tzu's insistence on objective standards of behavior may have ideologically contributed to the rise of authoritarianism, which resulted in the dictatorship of the Ch'in (221–206 BCE). Yet he was instrumental in the continuation of Confucianism as a scholarly enterprise, and he so significantly enriched the Confucian heritage that he was revered by the Confucians as the paradigmatic scholar for more than three centuries.

The Confucianization of politics. Confucianism before the emergence of TUNG CHUNG-SHU (c. 179–c. 104 BCE) was not particularly influential, but the gradual Confucianization of Han politics began soon after the founding of the dynasty. By the reign of Wu-ti (the Martial Emperor, 141–87 BCE), Confucianism was deeply entrenched in the central bureaucracy. It was manifest in such practices as the clear separation of the court and the government, often under the leadership of a scholarly prime minister, the process of recruiting officials through the dual mechanism of recommendation and selection, the family-centered social structure, the agriculture-based economy, and the educational network. Confucian ideas were also firmly established in the legal system as ritual became increasingly important in governing behavior, defining social relationships, and adjudicating civil disputes. Yet it was not until the prime minister Kung-sun Hung (d. 121 BCE) had persuaded Wu-ti to announce formally that the *ju* school alone would receive state sponsorship that Confucianism became an officially recognized Imperial ideology and state cult.

As a result Confucian Classics became the core curriculum for all levels of education. In 136 BCE Wu-ti set up at court five Erudites of the FIVE CLASSICS and in 124 BCE assigned 50 official students to study with them, creating a de facto Imperial university. By 50 BCE enrollment at the university had grown to 3,000, and by 1 CE those with a Confucian education staffed the bureaucracy. In the year 58 all government schools were required to make sacrifices to Confucius, and in 175 the court had the approved version of the Classics carved on large stone tablets.

The Five Classics. The compilation of the *Wu-ching* (The Five Classics) was a concrete manifestation of the coming of age of the Confucian tradition. Both pre-

Confucius receives a visitor during his travels
By courtesy of the Bibliotheque Nationale, Paris

Confucian texts, the SHU-CHING ("Classic of History") and the *Shih-ching* ("Classic of Poetry"), and contemporary Ch'in-Han material, such as certain portions of the LI-CHI ("Record of Rites"), were included.

The I-CHING ("Classic of Changes") combines divinatory art with numerological technique and ethical insight. According to the philosophy of change, the cosmos is a great transformation occasioned by the constant interaction of two complementary as well as conflicting vital energies, YIN AND YANG. The universe, which resulted from this great transformation, always exhibits both organismic unity and dynamism. The nobleman, inspired by the harmony and creativity of the universe, must emulate this pattern by aiming to realize the highest ideal of "unity of man and Heaven" through ceaseless self-exertion.

The *Shu-ching* presents kingship in terms of the ethical foundation for a humane government. The legendary Three Emperors (YAO, SHUN, and YÜ THE GREAT) all ruled by virtue. Their sagacity, filial piety, and dedication enabled them to create a political culture based on responsibility and trust. Their exemplary lives encouraged the people to enter into a covenant to achieve social harmony without punishment or coercion. Even in the Three Dynasties (Hsia, Shang, and Chou) moral authority, as expressed through ritual, was sufficient to maintain political order. The human continuum, from the undifferentiated masses to the enlightened, the nobility, and the sage-king, formed an organic unity as an integral part of the great cosmic transformation. For the Confucianist, politics means moral persuasion, and the purpose of the government is not only to provide food and maintain order but also to educate.

The *Shih-ching* underscores the Confucian valuation of common human feelings. The majority of its poetic verses give voice to emotions and sentiments of communities and persons from all levels of society expressed on a variety of occasions. The basic theme of this poetic world is mutual responsiveness.

The *Li-chi* shows society as a community of trust with emphasis on communication. Society organized by the four functional occupations—the scholar, farmer, artisan, and merchant—is, in the true sense of the word, a cooperation. As a contributing member of the cooperation each person is obligated to recognize the existence of others and to serve the public good. It is the king's duty to act kingly and the father's duty to act fatherly. If the king or father fails to behave properly, he cannot expect his minister or son to act in accordance with ritual.

The *Ch'un-ch'iu* ("Spring and Autumn Annals") emphasizes the significance of collective memory for communal self-identification. Historical consciousness is a defining characteristic of Confucian thought, which was in concert with the ancient Sinitic wisdom that reanimating the old is the best way to attain the new.

Tung Chung-shu: The Confucian visionary. Tung Chung-shu (c. 179–c. 104 BCE) was instrumental in developing an interpretation of Confucianism that came to be characteristic of the Han period. His work, *Ch'un-ch'iu fan-lu* ("Luxuriant Gems of the Spring and Autumn Annals"), is a metaphysical treatise in the spirit of the *I-ching*. Tung's elaborate worldview, which integrated Confucian ethics with naturalistic COSMOLOGY, developed out of his studies of the meaning of the five agents (metal, wood, water, fire, and earth), the correspondence of human beings and the numerical categories of heaven, and the sympathetic activation of things of the same kind, as well as his studies of cardinal Confucian values such as humanity, rightness, ritual, wisdom, and trustworthiness. His theory of mutual responsiveness between heaven and humanity provided the Confucian scholars with a higher law by which to judge the conduct of the ruler.

A reaction in favor of a more rational and moralistic approach to the Confucian Classics, known as the "Old Text" school, set in before the fall of the Hsi (Western) Han (25 CE). Yang Hsiung (c. 53 BCE–18 CE) in the *Fa-yen* ("Model Sayings"), a collection of moralistic aphorisms, and the *T'ai-hsüan ching* ("Classic of the Supremely Profound Principle"), a cosmological speculation, presented an alternative world view. This school, claiming its own recensions of authentic classical texts allegedly rediscovered during the Han period and written in an "old" script before the Ch'in unification, was widely accepted in the Eastern Han (25–220 CE).

As the study of the Classics became more refined and elaborate, Confucian scholasticism tended to become too professionalized to remain a vital intellectual force. Yet Confucian ethics exerted great influence on government, schools, and society at large. Toward the end of the Han period as many as 30,000 students attended the Imperial university, and a Confucian temple eventually stood in every one of China's 2,000 counties.

Confucian ethics in the Taoist and Buddhist context. Incompetent rulership, faction-ridden bureaucracy, a mismanaged tax structure, and domination by eunuchs toward the end of the Eastern Han period first prompted widespread protests by the Imperial university students. The court imprisoned and killed thousands of them and their official sympathizers in 169 CE, but the downward economic spiral made the life of the peasantry unbearable. The peasant rebellion, partly led by Confucian scholars, combined with open insurrections of the military, brought down the Han dynasty and thus put an end to the first Chinese empire. As the Imperial Han system disintegrated, barbarians invaded from the north. Northern China was controlled by rival groups, and a succession of states was established in the south. This period of disunity, from the early 3rd to the late 6th century, marked the decline of Confucianism, the emergence of an organized Taoist religion, and the spread of BUDDHISM.

Despite the prominence of Taoism and Buddhism among the cultural elite and the populace in general, Confucian ethics remained virtually inseparable from the moral fabric of Chinese society. Confucius continued to be universally honored as the paradigmatic sage. For example, the outstanding Taoist thinker Wang Pi (226–249) argued that Confucius, by not speculating on the nature of the Tao, had an experiential understanding of it superior to LAO-TZU'S. The Confucian Classics remained the foundation of all literate culture, and sophisticated commentaries were being produced throughout the age. The political forms of life also were distinctively Confucian, and in the south systematic attempts were made to strengthen family ties by establishing clan rules, genealogical trees, and ancestral rituals based on Confucian ethics.

The reunification of China by the Sui (581–618) and the restoration of lasting peace and prosperity by the T'ang (618–907) gave a powerful stimulus to the revival of Confucian learning. A definitive, official edition of the *Wu-ching* was published and Confucian rituals were implemented at all levels of governmental practice. An examination system was established based on literary competence; this made the mastery of the Confucian Classics a prerequisite for political success and was, therefore, perhaps the single most important institutional innovation in defining elite culture in Confucian terms.

The T'ang dynasty, nevertheless, was dominated by Buddhism and, to a lesser degree, by Taoism. One consequence in the development of Confucian thought was the rise of the metaphysically significant Confucian texts, notably CHUNG-YUNG ("Doctrine of the Mean") and *I-chuan* ("The Great Commentary of the Classic of Changes"), which appealed to some Buddhist and Taoist thinkers.

THE CONFUCIAN REVIVAL

The reemergence of Confucianism as the leading intellectual force involved both a creative response to the Buddhist and Taoist challenge and an imaginative reappropriation of classical Confucian insights.

The Sung masters. Under the Sung dynasty (960–1279), the decline of the aristocracy, the widespread availability of printed books, the democratization of education, and the full implementation of the examination system produced a new social class, the gentry, noted for its literary proficiency, social consciousness, and political participation. The outstanding members of this class, such as the classicists Hu Yüan (993–1059) and Sun Fu (992–1057), the reformers Fan Chung-yen (989–1052) and Wang An-shih (1021–86), the writer-officials Ou-yang Hsiu (1007–72) and Su Shih (pen name of Su Tung-p'o; 1036–1101), and the statesman-historian Ssu-ma Kuang (1019–86), contributed to the revival of Confucianism in education, politics, literature, and history.

The Confucian revival can be traced through a line of Neo-Confucian thinkers from CHOU TUN-I (1017–73) by way of SHAO YUNG (1011–77), CHANG TSAI (1020–77), the brothers CH'ENG HAO (1032–85) and CH'ENG I (1033–1107), and the great synthesizer CHU HSI (1130–1200). These men developed a comprehensive humanist vision in which cultivation of the self was integrated with social ethics and moral metaphysics. In the eyes of the Sung literati this new philosophy successfully applied the classical Confucian insights to the concerns of their own age.

Chou Tun-i articulated the relationship between the "great transformation" of the cosmos and the moral development of human beings. In his metaphysics, humanity, as the recipient of the highest excellence from heaven, is itself a center of cosmic creativity. He focused on the omnipresence of CH'I ("vital energy") and advocated the oneness of *li* ("principle") and the multiplicity of its manifestations, which is created as the principle expresses itself through the "vital energy."

Ch'eng Hao's definition of humanity as "forming one body with all things" was founded on his theme of mutuality between heaven and human beings, consanguinity between human beings, and harmony between humans and nature. To him the presence of T'ien-li ("Heavenly Principle") in all things as well as in human nature enables the human mind to purify itself in a spirit of reverence. Ch'eng I, following his brother's lead, formulated the famous dictum, "Self-cultivation requires reverence; the extension of knowledge consists in the investigation of things." By making special reference to KO-WU ("investigation of things"), he raised doubts about the appropriateness of focusing exclusively on the illumination of the mind in self-cultivation, as his brother seems to have done. The learning of the mind as advocated by Ch'eng Hao and the learning of the principle as advocated by Ch'eng I became two modes of thought in Sung Confucianism.

Chu Hsi, clearly following Ch'eng I's School of Principle, developed a pattern of interpreting and transmitting the Confucian Way that for centuries defined Confucianism in China, Korea, and Japan. Chu Hsi virtually reconstituted the Confucian tradition, giving it new structure, new texture, and new meaning. He was more than a synthesizer; through systematic interpretation he gave rise to a new Confucianism, known as NEO-CONFUCIANISM in the West but often referred to as LI-HSÜEH ("Learning of the Principle") in modern China.

The "Doctrine of the Mean" and the "Great Learning," two chapters in the *Li-chi*, had become independent treatises and, together with the *Analects* and *Mencius*, had been included in the core curriculum of Confucian education for centuries before Chu Hsi's birth. But by putting them into a particular sequence, the "Great Learning," the *Analects*, MENCIUS, and the "Doctrine of the Mean," synthesizing their commentaries, interpreting them as a coherent humanistic vision, and calling them the FOUR BOOKS, Chu Hsi fundamentally restructured the Confucian scriptural tradition. The Four Books, placed above the Five Classics, became the central texts for both primary education and civil service examinations in traditional China from the 14th century.

Chu Hsi defined the process of the investigation of things as a rigorous discipline of the mind to probe the principle in things. He recommended a twofold method of study: to cultivate a sense of reverence and to pursue knowledge. Reading, sitting quietly, ritual practice, physical exercise, calligraphy, arithmetic, and empirical observation all had a place in his pedagogical program. Under Chu Hsi's guidance, the White Deer Grotto in present Kiangsi province became the intellectual center of his age and provided a model for all schools in East Asia.

Confucian temple, Beijing, China
Rapho—Photo Researchers

LU HSIANG-SHAN (Lu Chiu-yüan, 1139–93) criticized Chu Hsi's theory of the investigation of things as fragmented and ineffective EMPIRICISM. Instead he advocated a return to Mencian moral idealism by insisting that establishing the "great body" (*i.e.*, Heaven-endowed nobility) is the primary precondition for self-realization. To him the learning of the mind as a quest for self-knowledge provided the basis upon which the investigation of things assumed its proper significance. Although Lu's challenge remained a minority position for some time, his learning of the mind later became a major intellectual force in Ming China (1368–1644) and Tokugawa Japan (1603–1867).

Confucian learning in the Chin, Yüan, and Ming dynasties. When the Mongols reunited China in 1279, the harsh treatment of scholars by the conquest Yüan dynasty (1206–1368) seriously damaged the well-being of the scholarly community, but outstanding Confucian thinkers emerged throughout the period. Hsü Heng (1209–81) was appointed by Kublai Khan as the president of the Imperial Academy, and he conscientiously introduced Chu Hsi's teaching to the Mongols and set the tone for the eventual success of the Confucianization of Yüan bureaucracy. In fact, it was the Yüan court that first officially adopted the Four Books as the basis of the civil service examination, a practice continued until 1905. Thanks to Hsü Heng, Chu Hsi's teaching prevailed in the Mongol period, but it was significantly simplified.

The hermit-scholar, Liu Yin (1249–93), on the other hand, allegedly refused Kublai Khan's summons in order to maintain the dignity of the Confucian Way. To him education was for self-realization. By taking seriously the idea of the investigation of things, Liu Yin put a great deal of emphasis on the learning of the mind. He applied philological methods to classical studies and advocated the importance of history. Liu Yin's contemporary Wu Cheng (1249–1333) further developed the learning of the mind. Wu assigned himself the task of harmonizing the difference between Chu Hsi and Lu Chiu-yüan. As a result, he reoriented Chu's balanced approach to morality and wisdom to accommodate Lu's existential concern for self-knowledge. This prepared the way for the revival of Lu's learning of the mind in the Ming dynasty (1368–1644).

WANG YANG-MING (1472–1529) was the most influential Confucian thinker after Chu Hsi. As a critique of excessive attention to philological details characteristic of Chu Hsi's followers, he allied himself with Lu Chiu-yüan's learning of the mind and advocated the precept of uniting thought and action. By focusing on the transformative power of the will, he inspired a generation of Confucian students to return to the moral idealism of Mencius.

Wang's primary concern was moral education, which he felt had to be grounded in the "original substance" of the mind. This he later identified as *liang-chih* ("good conscience"), by which he meant an innate knowledge or a primordial existential awareness that is possessed by every human being. Wang further suggested that good conscience as the Heavenly Principle is inherent in all beings from the highest spiritual forms to grass, wood, bricks, and stone. Because the universe consists of vital energy informed by good conscience, it is a dynamic process rather than a static structure. Human beings can learn to regard heaven and earth and the myriad things as one body by extending their good conscience to embrace an ever-expanding network of relationships.

Confucius, gouache on paper, c. 1770
The Granger Collection

Wang Yang-ming's dynamic idealism set the Confucian agenda for several generations in China. His followers, such as the communitarian Wang Chi (1498–1583), who devoted his long life to building a community of the like-minded, and the radical individualist Li Chih (1527–1602), who proposed to reduce all human relationships to friendship, broadened Confucianism to accommodate a variety of lifestyles.

The age of Confucianism: Yi-dynasty Korea, Tokugawa Japan, and Ch'ing China. Among all the dynasties, Chinese and foreign, the long-lived Yi in Korea (1392–1910) was undoubtedly the most thoroughly Confucianized. Since the 15th century, when the aristocracy (*yangban*) defined itself as the carrier of Confucian values, the penetration of court politics and elite culture by Confucianism had been unprecedented. Even today, as manifested in political behavior, legal practice, ancestral veneration, genealogy, village schools, and student activism, the vitality of the Confucian tradition is widely felt in South Korea.

Yi T'oegye (1501–70), the single most important Korean Confucian, helped shape the character of Yi Confucianism through his creative interpretation of Chu Hsi's teaching. Critically aware of the philosophical turn engineered by Wang Yang-ming, T'oegye transmitted the Chu Hsi legacy as a response to the advocates of the learning of the mind. As a result, he made Yi Confucianism at least as much a true heir to Sung learning as Ming Confucianism was.

Indeed, his *Discourse on the Ten Sagely Diagrams*, an aid for educating the king, offered a depiction of all the major concepts in Sung learning. His exchange of letters with Ki Taesung (1527–72) in the famous FOUR-SEVEN DEBATE, which discussed the relationship between Mencius' four basic human feelings—commiseration, shame, modesty, and right and wrong—and seven emotions, such as anger and joy, raised the level of Confucian dialogue.

In Japan, Chu Hsi's teaching, as interpreted by T'oegye, was introduced by YAMAZAKI ANSAI (1618–82). A distinctive feature of Yamazaki's thought was his recasting of native SHINTŌISM in Confucian terminology. The diversity and vitality of Japanese Confucianism was further evident in the appropriation of Wang Yangming's dynamic idealism by the samurai-scholars, notably KUMAZAWA BANZAN (1619–91). It is, however, in Ogyū Sorai's (1666–1728) determination to rediscover the original basis of Confucian teaching by returning to its pre-Confucian sources that a true exemplification of the independent-mindedness of Japanese Confucians is found. Although Tokugawa Japan was never as Confucianized as Yi Korea had been, virtually every educated person in Japanese society was exposed to the Four Books by the end of the 17th century.

The Confucianization of Chinese society reached its apex during the Ch'ing (1644–1911/12) when China was again ruled by a conquest (Manchu) dynasty. The Ch'ing emperors outshone their counterparts in the Ming in presenting themselves as exemplars of Confucian kingship. They transformed Confucian teaching into a political ideology, indeed a mechanism of control. Jealously guarding their Imperial prerogatives as the ultimate interpreters of Confucian truth, they undermined the freedom of scholars to transmit the Confucian Way.

MODERN TRANSFORMATION

The impact of Western culture has so fundamentally undermined the Confucian roots in East Asia that it has come to be widely debated whether or not Confucianism can remain a viable tradition in modern times. Beginning in the 19th century, Chinese intellectuals' faith in the ability of Confucian culture to withstand the impact of Western technology and political ideas became gradually eroded. The triumph of Marxism-Leninism as the official ideology of the People's Republic of China in 1949 relegated Confucian rhetoric to the background. The modern Chinese intelligentsia, however, maintained unacknowledged, sometimes unconscious, continuities with the Confucian tradition at every level of life—behavior, attitude, belief, and commitment. Indeed, Confucianism remains an integral part of the psycho-cultural construct of the contemporary Chinese intellectual as well as of the Chinese peasant. Meanwhile, rapid economic development in Asia has raised questions about how the typical East Asian institutions, still suffused with Confucian values—such as a paternalistic government, an educational system based on competitive examinations, an emphasis on loyalty and cooperation within the family, and local organizations informed by consensus—have adapted themselves to the imperatives of MODERNIZATION.

Some of the most creative and influential intellectuals in contemporary China have continued to think from Confucian roots. Although some of the most articulate intellectuals in the People's Republic of China criticize their Confucian heritage as the embodiment of authoritarianism, bureaucratism, nepotism, conservatism, and male chauvinism, others in China, Taiwan, Singapore, and North America have imaginatively established the relevance of Confucian humanism to China's modernization. The revival of Confucian studies in South Korea, Taiwan, Hong Kong, and Singapore has been under way for more than a generation, though Confucian scholarship in Japan remains unrivaled. Confucian thinkers in the West, inspired by religious pluralism and liberal democratic ideas, have begun to explore the possibility of a third epoch of Confucian humanism. They uphold that its modern transformation, as a creative response to the challenge of the West, is a continuation of its classical formulation and its medieval elaboration. Scholars in mainland China have also begun to explore the possibility of a fruitful interaction between Confucian humanism and democratic liberalism in a socialist context.

CONFUCIUS \kən-'fyü-shəs\, *Chinese* (Wade-Giles romanization) K'ung-fu-tzu \'kùŋ-'fü-'dzə̀\, *or* K'ung-tzu, *or* (Pinyin) Kongfuzi, *or* Kongzi, *original name* K'ung Ch'iu \'kùŋ-'chyü\, *literary name* Chung-ni \'jùŋ-'nē\ (b. 551 BCE, Ch'ü-fu, state of Lu [now in Shantung province, China]—d. 479, Lu], China's most famous teacher, philosopher, and political theorist, whose ideas have influenced the civilizations of all of eastern Asia. Confucius was not the founder of CON-FUCIANISM in the sense that the BUDDHA was the founder of BUDDHISM and JESUS CHRIST of CHRISTIANITY. Rather, Confucius considered himself a transmitter who consciously tried to reanimate the old in order to attain the new.

Confucius' ancestors were probably members of the aristocracy who had become poor commoners by the time of his birth. His father died when Confucius was only three years old. Instructed first by his mother, Confucius then distinguished himself as an indefatigable learner in his teens. He had served in minor government posts managing stables and keeping books for granaries before he married a woman of similar background when he was 19. It is not known who Confucius' teachers were, but he made a conscientious effort to find the right masters to teach him, among other things, ritual and music. His mastery of the six arts—ritual, music, archery, charioteering, calligraphy, and arithmetic—and his familiarity with the classical traditions enabled him to start a brilliant teaching career in his 30s.

Before Confucius, aristocratic families had hired tutors to educate their sons in specific arts, and government officials had instructed their subordinates in the necessary techniques; but he was the first person to devote his whole life to learning and teaching for the purpose of transforming and improving society. He believed that all human beings could benefit from self-cultivation. He inaugurated a humanities program for potential leaders, opened the doors of education to all, and defined learning not merely as the acquisition of knowledge but also as character building.

For Confucius, the primary function of education was to provide the proper way of training noblemen (CHÜN-TZU), a process that involved constant self-improvement and continuous social interaction. Although he emphatically noted that learning was "for the sake of the self" (the end of which was self-knowledge and self-realization), he found public service a natural consequence of true education. Confucius resisted the temptation to live apart from the human community, and opted to try to transform the world from within. For decades Confucius was actively involved in politics, putting his humanist ideas into practice through governmental channels.

Confucius and his followers considered themselves part of a scholarly tradition that had its origins two millennia previously, when the legendary YAO and SHUN created a civilized world through moral persuasion. Confucius' hero was Chou Kung, or the Duke of Chou (d. 1094 BCE), who was said to have helped consolidate and refine the "feudal" ritual system. This system was based on blood ties, marriage alliances, and old covenants, as well as on newly negotiated contracts, and was an elaborate system of mutual depen-

Confucius, Chinese paper album leaf, Sung dynasty
The Granger Collection

dence. The maintenance of interstate as well as domestic order was predicated on a shared political vision, namely, that authority lies in universal kingship, heavily invested with ethical and religious power by the mandate of heaven (*see* T'IEN-MING) and that social solidarity is achieved not by legal constraint but by ritual observance. Its implementation enabled the Chou dynasty to survive in relative peace and prosperity for more than five centuries. By Confucius' time, however, the system had been so undermined that political crises had precipitated a profound sense of moral decline.

Confucius' response was to address the issue of learning to be human. In so doing he attempted to redefine and revitalize the institutions that for centuries had been vital to political stability and social order: the family, the school, the local community, the state, and the kingdom. Not accepting the status quo, which held that wealth and power spoke the loudest, he felt that virtue (JEN, or Pinyin ren, "benevolence"), both as a personal quality and as a requirement for leadership, was essential for individual dignity, communal solidarity, and political order.

In his late 40s and early 50s, Confucius served first as a magistrate, then as an assistant minister of public works, and eventually as minister of justice in the state of Lu. It is likely that he accompanied King Lu as his chief minister on one of the diplomatic missions. Confucius' loyalty to the king, however, alienated him from the power holders of the time, the large Chi families, and his moral rectitude did not sit well with the king's inner circle. At 56, when he realized that his superiors were uninterested in his policies, Confucius left the country in an attempt to find another feudal state to which he could render his service. Despite his political frustration, he was accompanied by an expanding circle of students during this self-imposed exile of almost 12 years. His reputation as a man of vision and mission spread. At the age of 67 he returned home to teach, write, and edit classical works. According to the *Records of the Historian*, 72 of his students mastered the "six arts," and those who claimed to be his followers numbered 3,000. The earliest records of Confucius' life and thoughts are found in the text known as the *Lun-yü*, or *Analects*.

CONGREGATIONALISM, movement that arose among Protestant churches in England in the late 16th and early 17th centuries, emphasizing the right and duty of each congregation to make its own decisions about its affairs, independent of any higher human authority. Although this principle of church government is upheld by several modern denominations (*e.g.*, most BAPTISTS and the DISCIPLES OF CHRIST), the designation Congregationalist is usually reserved for those churches that hold the congregational polity to be their primary distinguishing characteristic.

Congregationalism developed as one wing of the broader movement known as PURITANISM. Congregationalists were concerned to put into practice the REFORMATION doctrine of the PRIESTHOOD of all believers. Congregationalists gained prestige when Oliver Cromwell aligned himself with this cause. Their political influence declined precipitously after

Cromwell's death in 1658. The Toleration Act of 1689 marked the beginning of a process that would finally grant full religious toleration to the Congregationalists along with all other religious dissenters.

In the Evangelical Revival (c. 1750–1815) Congregationalism gained a new vigor that was to increase throughout the 19th century. Congregationalists forged a strong tie with the Liberal Party. The Liberal victory of 1906 is generally seen as the peak of Congregational influence in English society and politics. Congregationalism also provided many prominent leaders for the ecumenical movement. In 1972 the majority of English Congregationalists and PRESBYTERIANS united to form the new United Reform Church.

Congregationalism achieved its greatest influence in the United States. It was transplanted to America in two forms very early in the colonial period. The "Pilgrims" of Plymouth Colony were separatistic Congregationalists; that is, they felt that realization of their ideal of church government required separation from the Church of England. The neighboring Puritans of Massachusetts Bay were nonseparatists, holding that the national church was capable of being reformed according to their ideal.

The adoption in 1662 of the Half-Way Covenant relaxing requirements for church membership was a response to declining church membership. The widespread revivalistic movement of the 1730s and 1740s, known as the GREAT AWAKENING, also helped replenish the membership rolls of New England's churches, but simultaneously it revealed a new division within American Congregationalism. The CALVINISM of the founding bodies was being replaced by an ARMINIAN theology that put greater emphasis on human efforts in attaining salvation. A general liberalizing of theological opinion continued in the Congregational Churches during the 19th century, with two results. First was the defection of many churches to UNITARIANISM. Second was Congregationalism's downplaying of the importance of conversion in Christian experience. The Kansas City Creed of 1913 is usually cited as the definitive statement of Congregationalism's break with its Calvinist past.

During the first half of the 19th century, the Congregationalists participated in a Plan of Union with the Presbyterians. The National Council of Congregational Churches, formed in 1871, was enlarged in 1931 through an affiliation with the smaller General Convention of the Christian Churches. In 1961 a further merger was effected with the Evangelical and Reformed Church to create the United Church of Christ. The Congregational tradition is now preserved in original name and form in only two or three small associations of churches.

As a rule, Congregationalists eschew binding creedal statements and view faith as a personal encounter with God. In worship the preached word is usually emphasized over the use of the SACRAMENTS. In common with most Protestant groups, Congregationalists accept only two sacraments, BAPTISM and the EUCHARIST. Communion is celebrated once or twice a month and is now usually open to "all believers." Baptism is not required for membership.

CONLAÍ \'kōn-ˌlī\, in Irish heroic tales, son of the most prominent hero of Ulster, CÚ CHULAINN, and of Aife (or Aoife), a warrior-queen of a magical land across the sea. Cú Chulainn overpowered Aife and asked her to bear him a son. He told her to send this son to him in Ulster with a ring as a token—the son was not to let himself be known and not to refuse combat to anyone. When Conlaí came as an unknown youth of seven in a bronze boat, the Ulster-

men tried to stop him and one by one were beaten. Even to Cú Chulainn, Conlaí refused to give his name. He won several fights against his father, who at last mortally wounded him. Only then did Conlaí reveal his identity.

CONSERVATIVE JUDAISM, a strand of JUDAISM that mediates between REFORM JUDAISM and ORTHODOX JUDAISM. Founded in 19th-century Germany as "Historical Judaism," or "the Historical School," the Conservative movement emphasizes the practice of the religious requirements of the TORAH (as does Orthodoxy), while fostering critical scholarship as well (as does Reform Judaism). The Historical School arose among German-Jewish theologians who advocated change but found Reform extreme. They parted company with Reform on some specific issues of practice and doctrine—observance of the dietary laws and belief in the coming of the MESSIAH, for example. But they also found Orthodoxy immobile.

The Historical School's emphasis on historical research in settling theological debates explains the name of the group. Arguing that its positions represented matters of historical fact rather than theological conviction, Conservative Judaism maintained that "positive historical scholarship" would prove capable of purifying and clarifying the faith, when joined to far stricter observance of the law than the Reformers required. Toward the end of the 19th century, in 1886, RABBIS of this same centrist persuasion organized the Jewish Theological Seminary of America, and from that rabbinical school the Conservative Movement developed. Conservative Judaism in America in the 20th century carried forward a centrist position and turned a viewpoint of intellectuals into a religious movement; indeed, by the middle of the 20th century it was the largest movement among American Judaisms.

Orthopraxy is used to refer to correct action and unfettered belief, as against Orthodoxy, right doctrine. In its strict observance to Torah, some would classify Conservative Judaism in America as an orthoprax Judaism defined through works, not doctrine.

CONSTANCE, COUNCIL OF \'kän-stəns\ (1414–18), 16th ecumenical council of the ROMAN CATHOLIC church. Following the election of two rival popes (Gregory XII in Rome and Benedict XIII in Avignon) in 1378 and the attempt at the Council of Pisa in 1409 to resolve the Western SCHISM by the election of a new pope, the church found itself with three popes. Under pressure from the Holy Roman emperor a council at Constance was convened principally to reunite Christendom but also to examine the teachings of JOHN WYCLIFFE and JAN HUS and to reform the church.

Political rivalries so divided the council delegates that a revolutionary system of voting was adopted, whereby each of the four power blocs (Italy, England, Germany, and France) was granted a single vote; later the CARDINALS were given a vote as a group, and still later Spain was empowered to vote. John XXIII (one of the three papal candidates) promised to resign if his rivals would do the same. Shortly after, he fled from Constance, hoping that this would deprive the council of its power and lead to its dissolution. The emperor insisted that the council continue, and it issued the decree *Sacrosancta*, affirming that a general council of the church is superior to the pope (see CONCILIARISM). John XXIII was then captured and deposed; Gregory XII agreed to abdicate provided he was permitted officially to convoke the council and so assert the legitimacy of his own line of popes, to which the council agreed; Benedict XIII was also deposed. In November 1417 the council elected Oddone Colonna, who became pope as Martin V, and the Great Schism was effectively healed. The authority of *Sacrosancta* has been a matter of dispute among scholars.

The council condemned 45 propositions of Wycliffe and 30 of Hus, who was declared an obstinate heretic and burned at the stake. Furthermore, the council adopted seven reform decrees. The Protestant REFORMATION has been attributed to the council's failure to effect stronger reforms.

CONSTANTINE I \'kän-stən-,tēn\, -,tīn\ *byname* Constantine the Great (b. Feb. 27, after CE 280?, Naissus, Moesia [now Niš, Yugos.—d. May 22, 337, Ancyrona, Bithynia [now Izmit, Tur.]), the first Roman emperor attested to have become a Christian.

Constantine's youth was spent at the imperial court of Diocletian. Constantine became emperor of the western portion of the empire in CE 312 after a series of civil wars and sole ruler of the entire Roman Empire in 324. Throughout his life Constantine ascribed his success to his conversion to CHRISTIANITY. He was personally committed to the religion by 313 when he issued the EDICT OF MILAN extending toleration to Christians. He addressed the COUNCIL OF NICAEA (325), which met to resolve a theological dispute. He rebuilt and enlarged Constantinople (formerly Byzantium), making it his permanent capital. His conversion influenced the relations of CHURCH AND STATE for centuries to come. Believing that he was God's chosen servant, he regarded himself as responsible to God for the good government of his church. Formerly a minority sect, Christianity became the official religion of the empire and was stimulated by the patronage of Constantine and his sons. Constantine is revered as a saint in EASTERN ORTHODOXY.

CONSTANTINE, DONATION OF, *Latin* Donatio Constantini, a document that discusses the supposed grant by the emperor Constantine the Great to Pope Sylvester I (314–335) and his successors of spiritual supremacy over the other great patriarchates and over all matters of faith and worship, as well as of temporal dominion over Rome and the entire Western Empire. It was claimed that the gift was motivated by Constantine's gratitude to Sylvester for miraculously healing his leprosy and converting him to CHRISTIANITY. Now universally admitted to be a forgery, it was regarded as genuine throughout the Middle Ages.

It was composed from various sources, especially the apocryphal *Vita S. Silvestri* ("Life of Saint Sylvester"). The earliest certain appeal to the document by a pope was made in 1054 by Leo IX in a letter to MICHAEL CERULARIUS, the PATRIARCH of Constantinople. From that time forward it was increasingly employed by popes and canonists in support of the papal claims. Although the validity of the document was sometimes questioned, its genuineness was first critically assailed during the Renaissance. In 1440 Lorenzo Valla proved that it was false and began a controversy that lasted until the end of the 18th century. Scholars now generally agree that the forgery was written between 750 and 800. Some believe that it was written in Rome, but others believe it was composed in the Frankish empire.

CONSTANTINOPLE, COUNCIL OF (381) \,kän-,stan-tə-'nō-pəl\, second ecumenical council of the Christian church, summoned by the emperor Theodosius I and meeting in Constantinople (Istanbul). Doctrinally, it promulgated what became known as the NICENE CREED; it also declared finally the Trinitarian doctrine of the equality of the HOLY SPIRIT with the Father and the Son. Among the council's canons was one giving the bishop of Constantinople precedence of honor over all other bishops except the bishop of Rome, "because Constantinople is the New Rome."

Though only eastern bishops had been summoned (about 150 in all), the Greeks claimed this council to be ecumenical. Pope Damasus I in Rome appears to have accepted the creed but not the canons, at least not that upon the precedence of Constantinople; Rome accepted the precedence of Constantinople, next to Rome, only during the life of the Latin Empire of Constantinople, created in the 13th century by the Fourth Crusade. In both East and West, nevertheless, the council came to be regarded as ecumenical.

CONSTANTINOPLE, COUNCIL OF (553), fifth ecumenical council of the Christian church, meeting under the presidency of Eutychius, PATRIARCH of Constantinople (Istanbul). The 14 ANATHEMAS issued by the council rejected NESTORIAN doctrine; the council also ratified an earlier condemnation of ORIGEN.

Pope Vigilius of Rome opposed the council and took SANCTUARY in a church from May to December, but he at last yielded and formally ratified the verdicts of the council on Feb. 23, 554. Even so, the Western church could not bring itself to accept the decrees of the council. In Africa, imperial troops were able to force acceptance. North Italian bishops refused their allegiance to the see of Rome and found support in France and Spain. The opposition hung on in northern Italy until the end of the 7th century.

CONSTANTINOPLE, COUNCIL OF (680), sixth ecumenical council of the Christian church, summoned by the emperor Constantine IV at Constantinople (Istanbul).

Some eastern Christians, forbidden to talk of the concept of one nature of Christ, thought to enforce the unity of the person of Christ by talking of one will (*thelema*) and one operation (*energeia*) from the two natures. Persons holding this view were called Monothelites. Sergius, PATRIARCH of Constantinople, and Honorius I, pope of Rome, appear to have embraced the Monothelite doctrine. The council of 680 condemned the Monothelites, among them Honorius, and asserted two wills and two operations.

CONSTANTINOPLE, COUNCIL OF (869–870), council of the Christian church, meeting in Constantinople (Istanbul). The Roman church eventually recognized it as the eighth ecumenical council, but the Eastern church for the most part denied its ecumenicity and continues to recognize only the first seven councils.

The council confirmed a Roman sentence of EXCOMMUNICATION against Photius, PATRIARCH of Constantinople, bringing to a head the so-called Photian SCHISM. (Photius was later reinstated in 879–880.) The council's canon (number 22) prohibiting lay interference in episcopal elections assumed great importance in the Western church's INVESTITURE CONTROVERSY in the 11th and early 12th centuries.

CONSUS \'kän-səs\, ancient Italian deity, cult partner of Ops. Some scholars have derived his name from the Latin verb *condere* ("to store away") on the presumption that he was a god of the granary or storage bin. He had a temple on the Aventine. In later times, Consus was only a secondary deity whose character was rather abstract. On his festival days, in August and December, horses and mules were crowned with garlands and given rest from work. In August the FLAMEN *Quirinalis* (priest of the god QUIRINUS) offered sacrifice, and the *pontifices* presided at horse and chariot races (in which mules took the place of horses).

CONTEMPLATIVE, religious movement that attempts to encourage—through prayer, meditation, and sometimes withdrawal from society—a mystical experience of god.

See also MONASTICISM; IDIORRYTHMIC MONASTICISM; CENOBITIC MONASTICISM.

CONVENT, residence of a religious order, particularly an order of NUNS. *See also* ABBEY.

COPTIC ORTHODOX CHURCH \'käp-tik\, *also called* Coptic Church, principal Christian church in Egypt. The people of Egypt before the Arab conquest in the 7th century identified themselves and their language in Greek as Aigyptios (Arabic *qibṭ*, Westernized as Copt); when Egyptian Muslims later ceased to call themselves Aigyptioi, the term became the distinctive name of the Christian minority. From the 5th century these Christians belonged to a MONOPHYSITE church, calling themselves simply the Egyptian Church. In the 19th and 20th centuries they began to call themselves Coptic Orthodox.

In the 4th and 5th centuries a theological conflict arose between the Copts and the Greek-speaking Romans, or Melchites ("Emperor's Men"), in Egypt over the COUNCIL OF CHALCEDON (451), which rejected Monophysite doctrine. After the Arab conquest, the Copts ceased speaking Greek, and the language barrier added to the controversy.

Apart from the Monophysite question, the Coptic and the EASTERN ORTHODOX churches agree in doctrinal matters. Arabic is now used in services for the lessons from the BIBLE and for many of the variable hymns; only certain short refrains are not in Arabic. The service books are written in Coptic (the Bohairic dialect of Alexandria), with the Arabic text in parallel columns.

The Coptic Orthodox Church developed a democratic system of government after the 1890s. The PATRIARCH and the 12 diocesan BISHOPS, with the assistance of community councils in which the laity is well represented, regulate the finances of the churches and schools and the administration of the rules relating to marriage, inheritance, and other matters of personal status. When the patriarch dies, an electoral college, predominantly of laymen, selects three monks at least 50 years of age as candidates, from whom the final choice is made by lot after prayer.

The patriarch of Alexandria resides in Cairo. The church has its own primary and secondary schools in many places in Egypt, as well as a strong Sunday-school program. There is an Institute of Coptic Studies in Cairo, a theological college connected with the institute, and a Coptic museum.

There is a Coptic Orthodox Church in Jerusalem, and there are a few other churches in the Holy Land, built in the 19th and 20th centuries, as well as a Coptic bishopric in Khartoum, Sudan. A large number of Coptic Orthodox churches exist in Australia and in the United States. The Ethiopian, Armenian, and Syrian Jacobite churches are in communion with the Coptic Orthodox Church.

CORDOVERO, MOSES BEN JACOB \,kȯr-dō-'ver-ō\ (b. 1522—d. 1570, Safed, Palestine [now Ẕefat, Israel]), Galilean RABBI who organized and codified the Zoharistic QABBALAH. He was the teacher of ISAAC LURIA.

Cordovero was a disciple of JOSEPH KARO. In *Pardes rimonim*, which he completed by the age of 27, and *Elimah rabati*, completed 10 years later, and in his extensive commentary on the SEFER HA-ZOHAR (the classic text of Jewish esoteric MYSTICISM), Cordovero attempted to summarize and synthesize Qabbalistic thought to that time and to put forth his own interpretive Qabbalistic system.

CORN MOTHER, *also called* Corn Maiden, mythological figure believed, among agricultural tribes in Meso-America and North America, to be responsible for the origin of maize.

The story of the Corn Mother is related in two main versions with many variations. In these versions she is either an old woman or a beautiful young woman who is able to feed her hungry tribe by producing corn in ways which, once discovered, are deemed disgusting. In the first version the Corn Mother is then accused of WITCHCRAFT. Before being killed by the tribe—by some accounts with her consent—she gives careful instructions about how to treat her corpse. Corn sprouts from the places over which her body was dragged or, by other accounts, from her corpse or burial site. In the second version, after her discovery she returns to her divine home, but her husband follows her, and she gives him seed corn and detailed instructions for its cultivation.

Similar stories of the immolation of a maternal figure or the insult to and flight of a beautiful maiden are told by the Indians in accounting for the origin of the buffalo, PEYOTE, certain medicinal herbs, and the SACRED PIPE.

Coptic papyrus of the Gospel According to John, 4th century
By courtesy of the British and Foreign Library Society, London

CORNUCOPIA \kȯr-nə-'kō-pē-ə, -nyə-\, *also called* horn of plenty, decorative motif, dating from ancient Greece, that symbolizes abundance. The motif originated as a curved goat's horn filled to overflowing with fruit and grain. It is emblematic of the horn possessed by Zeus's nurse, AMALTH-

AEA, a NYMPH, whose horn could be filled with whatever the owner wished.

CORONACH \'kȯr-ə-nək̲, 'kär-\, in Celtic tradition, choral lament or outcry for the dead; also, a funeral song sung or shrieked by Celtic women. Though observers have frequently reported hearing such songs in Ireland or in the Scottish Highlands, no such songs have been recorded.

CORPUS CHRISTI, FEAST OF \'kȯr-pəs-'kris-tē\, festival of the Western Christian church in honor of the Real Presence of the body (*corpus*) of JESUS CHRIST in the EUCHARIST. A movable feast, it is observed on the Thursday (or, in some countries, the Sunday) after Trinity Sunday. It originated in 1246 when Robert de Torote, bishop of Liège, ordered the festival celebrated in his DIOCESE. It did not spread until Jacques Pantaléon, formerly archdeacon of Liège, became pope as Urban IV; in 1264 he ordered the whole church to observe the feast. By the mid-14th century the festival was generally accepted, and in the 15th century it became, in effect, the principal feast of the church.

The PROCESSION became the feast's most prominent feature. Sovereigns and princes took part, as well as magistrates and members of guilds. In the 15th century the procession was customarily followed by the performance by guild members of miracle plays and mystery plays.

After the practice of adoring the Host was rejected in the REFORMATION, Protestant churches suppressed the festival.

CORYBANT \'kȯr-ə-ˌbant, 'kär-\, any of the wild, half-demonic beings who were mythical attendants of the ancient Oriental and Greco-Roman deity the GREAT MOTHER OF THE GODS. They were often identified or confused with the Cretan Curetes (attendants of the Greek god ZEUS) and were distinguished only by their Asiatic origin and by the more pronouncedly orgiastic nature of their rites. Accounts of the origin of the Corybantes vary, and their names and number differ from one authority to another. They apparently had a mystic cult, and a prominent feature of their ritual was a wild dance, which was claimed to have powers of healing mental disorder. It is possible that they originated as a mythical representation of the PRIESTHOOD.

COSMOGONY \käz-'mä-gə-nē\, type of myth that refers to the origin of the world. Cosmogony and CREATION MYTH are sometimes used as synonyms, though not all cosmogonies feature a creator.

Cosmogonic myths are concerned with origins in the sense of the foundation or validity of the world as it is. Creation stories in both nonliterate and literate cultures frequently speak of the act of creation as a fashioning of the earth out of raw material that was already present. A creation out of nothing occurs much less frequently.

Water has a special role in Asian and North American cosmogonies, where the creator (often an animal) is assisted by another figure, who dives for earth in the primordial ocean. The earth-diver helper sometimes develops into an opponent in other areas. This theme helps account for the fact that evil is constitutive of the cosmos without holding the creator responsible for it. Other widely diffused motifs are: the cosmogonic egg, found in the Pacific world, parts of Europe and southern Asia (*e.g.*, in HINDUISM); the world parents (usually in the image of sky and earth); and creation through sacrifice or through a primordial battle. Creation through the word of the creator also occurs outside the OLD TESTAMENT account (*e.g.*, in Polynesia).

The characteristics of a particular cosmogony often set the pattern for everything else in a tradition; other myths are often related to it or derived from it. Most cosmogonic accounts have certain formal features in common. They speak of irreconcilable opposites (*e.g.*, heaven and earth, darkness and light) and of events or things totally outside common perception and reason (*e.g.*, a "time" in which heaven and earth were not yet separated and darkness and light intermingled).

Human origins are usually linked immediately to the cosmogony. Humans, for instance, are placed on the earth by a god, or in some other way their origin is from heaven. Humans are sometimes said to have ascended from the depths of the earth (as with the Zuni, an American Indian people) or from a certain rock or tree of cultic significance. These images are often related to the idea of a realm of ancestors as the origin of newborn children. Humans are also said to be fashioned from the dust of the ground (as in GENESIS) or from a mixture of clay and blood (as in the Babylonian creation myth). In all cases humans have a particular place (because of their duties to the gods, their limitations, or even their gifts), though the harmony of humanity and other forms of nature is emphasized.

In most cosmogonic traditions the creation of humans is the final or culminating act. The condition of the cosmos prior to the arrival of humans is viewed as separate and distinct from the alterations that result from the beginning of the human cultural world. Creation is thus seen as a process of periods or stages, frequently in a three-stage model. The first stage consists of the world of gods or primordial beings; the second stage is the world of human ancestors; and the third stage is the human world. The three stages may be interrelated; for example, the gods may be the creators of humans or the ancestors of humans, or ancestors may undergo a transformation to become human.

Among innumerable tales of origin, one of the most common types is related to the origins of institutions. Certain initiation ceremonies or ritual acts are said to have originated in the beginning, in mythical times, this primeval moment of inception constituting their validity.

COSMOLOGY, type of myth or religious discourse dealing with the ordering of the world. As a cosmology does not necessarily deal with the origins of the world, it is distinct from COSMOGONY and CREATION MYTH. A cosmological myth typically tells of the origins of the culture that tells it and explains the basic ideological problems that concern it, such as the origin of death, the nature of society, and the relationship of men and women and of the living and the dead.

Geography and physical space typically enter into cosmological traditions, frequently by means of a symbolic identity between the divine world and the community's central temple or sacred site. Such an identity is witnessed in the sacred sites of the Algonquin, Sioux, and Blackfoot North American Indian tribes (*see* NATIVE AMERICAN RELIGIONS); the temple of BEL at Palmyra (in Syria); the KIVA of the Pueblo villages; the Buddhist STUPA; and Brahminic, Buddhist, and Mexican mountain temples. The cosmological scheme has been applied to Christian BASILICAS and churches—with square floor plans, overarching domes, and symbolic ornamentation—from as far back as the 6th and 7th centuries. The concept of a sacred space or area reserved for a particular deity or purpose is frequently encountered, as is the corollary theory that such designated areas could correspond to each other.

Cosmologies also frequently treat the structure of the universe and the shape of the earth. Micronesians generally believe in at least three vertically arranged levels of the universe: the earth proper, the underworld, and HEAVEN or the sky world. According to the Aztec cosmological ideas, the earth had the general shape of a great disk divided into four sections oriented to the four cardinal directions. To each of the four world directions were attached five of the 20 day-signs, a color, and certain gods. The fifth cardinal point, the center, was attributed to the fire god Huehuetéotl, because the hearth stood at the center of the house. This cosmic order is usually conceived as a divine order that is well intentioned toward humans and is working for their well-being as long as they are willing to insert themselves into this order, to follow it willingly, and not to upset it by perversion or rebellion.

COTYS \\'kō-tis\\, *also called* Cotytto \\kō-'ti-tō\\, Thracian goddess worshiped with orgiastic rites, especially at night. Her worship was apparently adopted publicly in Corinth (*c.* 425 BCE) and perhaps privately in Athens about the same time; it then included a baptismal ceremony. Later relief sculptures from Thrace showed her as a goddess of the hunt similar to ARTEMIS, but in literature she was instead compared with the Oriental-Greek-Roman Cybele (GREAT MOTHER OF THE GODS).

COUNTER-REFORMATION, *also called* Catholic Reformation, or Catholic Revival, in CHRISTIANITY, the ROMAN CATHOLIC efforts directed in the 16th and early 17th centuries both against the Protestant REFORMATION and toward internal renewal; the Counter-Reformation took place during roughly the same period as the Protestant Reformation, actually (according to some sources) beginning shortly before Martin Luther's NINETY-FIVE THESES (1517).

Early calls for reform grew out of criticism of the worldly attitudes and policies of the Renaissance popes and many of the clergy. New religious orders and other groups were founded to effect a religious renewal—*e.g.*, the Capuchins, the Ursulines, and especially the JESUITS. Later in the century, JOHN OF THE CROSS and TERESA OF ÁVILA promoted the reform of the CARMELITE order and influenced the development of the mystical tradition. FRANCIS DE SALES had a similar influence on the devotional life of the laity.

Saint John of the Cross, a leader of the Counter-Reformation, detail of an oil painting by Joaquin Canedo, 1795
By courtesy of the Museo Provincial, Valladolid, Spain; photograph, Mas, Barcelona

There was little significant papal reaction to the Protestants or to demands for reform from within the Roman Catholic church before mid-century. Pope Paul III (reigned 1534–49) is considered to be the first pope of the Counter-Reformation. It was he who in 1545 convened the COUNCIL OF TRENT, which met intermittently until 1563 and responded emphatically to the

issues at hand. Its doctrinal teaching was a reaction against the Lutheran emphasis on the role of faith and God's GRACE and against Protestant teaching on the number and nature of the SACRAMENTS. There was an attempt to regulate the training of candidates for the priesthood; measures were taken against luxurious living by the clergy and the appointment of relatives to church office.

The Roman INQUISITION, an agency established in 1542 to combat HERESY, was more successful in controlling doctrine and practice than similar bodies in those countries where Protestant princes had more power than the Roman Catholic church. Political and military involvement directed against Protestant growth is most clearly reflected in the policies of Emperor Charles V and in those of his son Philip II, who was associated with the Spanish Inquisition.

A major emphasis of the Counter-Reformation was an ongoing missionary endeavor in parts of the world that had been colonized by predominantly Roman Catholic countries. The work of such men as FRANCIS XAVIER and others in Asia and of missionaries in the New World produced millions of BAPTISMS, if not true conversions. There were also attempts to reconvert areas of the world that had once been Roman Catholic—*e.g.*, England and Sweden.

COVEN, group in which witches are said to gather. The coven traditionally is said to consist of 12 members and a devil as leader. The number is generally taken as a parody of Christ and his 12 disciples. An alternate theory, stressing a pre-Christian tradition of witches, explains 13 as the maximum number of dancers that can be accommodated in a nine-foot circle.

Each member of a coven is said to specialize in a particular branch of magic, such as bewitching agricultural produce, magical healing or infliction of disease, weather-magic, or love-magic. Many students of WITCHCRAFT, however, dismiss the theory of covens as unfounded and based on insufficient evidence. Nonetheless, contemporary witchcraft groups continue to use the term coven.

COVENANT, *Hebrew* berith \\bə-'rēt, 'brēt\\, in the OLD TESTAMENT, a term used variously to mean an agreement, alliance, compact, constitution, legal or diplomatic agreement, ordinance, pact, pledge, promise, testament, or treaty. A covenant may be either unilateral (with duties and obligations imposed upon only one party) or bilateral (with duties and obligations applied to both parties), and conditional (contingent upon one party performing certain actions) or unconditional. A bilateral covenant may be a "parity treaty," in which both parties are equal, or a "suzerainty treaty" (also called a "vassal treaty"), in which a dominant party offers or forces the treaty on a lesser party. The suzerainty treaty was typically the kind employed in the ancient Near East by great kings, who dictated terms and conditions to lesser kings and nations.

In the history of the Israelites, covenants are either struck or interdicted between an individual (who may be a king) and a nation (including ISRAEL), or between the Israelites and another nation (*e.g.*, Genesis 14:13; 21:22–32; Exodus 23:32; 34:12, 15; Deuteronomy 7:2, Joshua 9; Judges 2:2; 1 Samuel 11:1–2; 2 Samuel 3:12–13; 5:3; 1 Kings 5:12; 15:18–19, Jeremiah 34:8–18; Obadiah 7). A covenant may also be an agreement between individuals (*e.g.*, Genesis 31:44–54; 1 Samuel 18:3; 20:8; 23:18; 1 Kings 5:26; 20:34; Hosea 10:4), or it may refer to marriage or to a literal or figurative agreement between husband and wife (Malachi 2:14; Ezekiel 16:8; Proverbs 2:17).

The most theologically significant covenants in Hebrew SCRIPTURES are those in which YAHWEH (or ELOHIM)—who is mindful of his covenants with men (Genesis 9:15–17; Exodus 2:24; 6:4–5)—is an active party, or, sometimes, the only party. Covenant, in that instance, is his unilateral promise to an individual or nation; or it is a bilateral treaty or agreement he strikes with an individual or all Israel.

The most important unconditional unilateral covenants (understood as charters or promises) Yahweh grants are those with NOAH, ABRAHAM, ISAAC, JACOB, and DAVID. Yahweh tells Noah to build an ARK, with which he, his children, and pairs of other living creatures will be saved from destruction. Later, Yahweh promises Noah never again to destroy the earth by flood, and he sets his bow (the rainbow) in the sky as a reminder of this (Genesis 6:13–21; 7:1–5; 8:21–9:17). He promises Abraham that his descendants will be virtually innumerable and will inherit the Land of Israel, from the Wadi of Egypt to the Euphrates (Genesis 15:18–21; 22:15–18). He promises Jacob virtually innumerable progeny, that he and his progeny will be a blessing to all the other nations, and that he will return to the Land (Genesis 28:12–15, 32:11–12; 35:9–13; see also Genesis 46:3–4).

Yahweh also makes conditional covenants with Abraham and Isaac. Abraham, Ishmael, and Abraham's descendants through Isaac are to accept Yahweh as their God and to circumcise their sons; consequently, Abraham will inherit CANAAN and be the father of many nations (Genesis 17). Later, Yahweh promises Isaac that He will keep the covenant with Abraham if Isaac stays in the land of the Philistines (Genesis 26:3–5).

Yahweh gives an unconditional promise to David that his house, kingdom, and throne, through his son SOLOMON, are established forever, and Yahweh will not depart from them (e.g., 2 Samuel 7:11–16; 23:5; 1 Chronicles 17:12–14; 22:10; Psalms 89:3–4, 29–37; Jeremiah 33:17).

The most important bilateral covenant (as conditional suzerainty treaty or possibly loyalty OATH) in Hebrew scripture is the "great covenant" of SINAI/Horeb (Exodus 19:2–Numbers 10:11; Deuteronomy 4:10–20, 23–31, 44), which, in later traditions, is considered one mountain and one treaty (the covenant of Sinai). Yahweh offers the covenant to the Israelites, who agree to it. The Sinai Covenant is stated in Exodus 19–23 and ratified in Exodus 24 before the stipulation of its ordinances (Exodus 25:1–Num 10:11). It is reiterated by MOSES in Moab, where it is renewed (Deuteronomy 4: 23–24; 10:4;.28:1–29:29). After enjoining the people to observe Moses' law (i.e., the Sinai covenant [Joshua 23:6–8]) Joshua mediates an additional covenant at Shechem (Joshua 24: 1–28). The Sinai and Shechem covenants are determinative of and law for such subsequent religious traditions as Second Temple and RABBINIC JUDAISM.

COVENANT THEOLOGY, also called federal theology, type of Reformed (Calvinistic) theology emphasizing the biblical COVENANTS of works made by God with ADAM and the covenant of GRACE made between God and humanity through the grace of JESUS CHRIST. The covenants with ABRAHAM and MOSES were sometimes added. In Reformed theology, Christ was viewed as the second Adam, as he was described in the letters of the Apostle PAUL.

English Puritans of the 17th century incorporated the concept of the two covenants (law and grace) into what has been called a natural and a supernatural covenant. In the development of this theological movement, the 16th–17th-century English Puritan theologian William Ames's book *Medulla Theologiae* (*Marrow of Sacred Divinity*) influenced Reformed theology for nearly a century. The covenantal concept spread among Reformed groups in England,

Hindus honoring cows in the Gopāṣṭhamī Festival, Vrindaban, North India
John Stratton Hawley

Germany, Scotland, the Netherlands, and the New England colonies, where it was especially influential.

COW, SANCTITY OF THE, in HINDUISM, the belief that the cow is representative of divine and natural beneficence, and should therefore be protected and venerated.

The origin of the veneration of the cow can be traced to the early Vedic period. The Indo-European peoples who entered India in the 2nd millennium BCE were pastoralists; cattle had major economic significance that was reflected in VEDIC RELIGION. Though cattle were sacrificed and their flesh eaten in ancient India, the slaughter of milk-producing cows was increasingly prohibited, as in parts of the MAHĀBHĀRATA and MANU, and the milk-cow was already in the ṚG VEDA said to be "unslayable." The degree of veneration afforded the cow is indicated by the use in rites of healing, purification, and penance of the *pañcagavya*, the five products of the cow—milk, curd, butter, urine, and dung.

Subsequently, with the rise of the ideal of AHIMSĀ, being harmless to living creatures, the cow came to symbolize a life of nonviolent generosity. In addition, the cow was associated with motherhood and Mother Earth, owing to the fact that her products supplied nourishment. The cow was also early on identified with the BRAHMIN or priestly class, and killing the cow was sometimes equated (by Brahmins) with the heinous crime of killing a Brahmin. In the middle of the 1st millennium CE cow-killing was made a capital offense by the Gupta kings, and legislation against cow-killing persisted into the 20th century in many princely states where the monarch was Hindu.

Special associations align the cow with various deities, notably SHIVA (whose vehicle is a bull), INDRA (closely associated with Kāmadhenu, the wish-granting cow), KRISHNA (a cowherd in his youth), and goddesses in general (because of the maternal attributes of many of them).

Toward the end of the 19th century, especially in northern India, a Cow-Protection movement arose that strove to unify Hindus and distinguish them en bloc from Muslims by demanding that the government ban cow slaughter. This intertwining of political and religious purpose led periodically to anti-Muslim riots and eventually played a role in the partition of the Indian subcontinent in 1947.

CRANMER, THOMAS \'kran-mər\ (b. July 2, 1489, Aslacton, Nottinghamshire, Eng.—d. March 21, 1556, Oxford), the first Protestant archbishop of Canterbury (1533–56), adviser to the English kings Henry VIII and Edward VI. As archbishop, he put the English BIBLE in PARISH churches, drew up the BOOK OF COMMON PRAYER, and composed a litany that remains in use today. Denounced for promoting PROTESTANTISM by the CATHOLIC Mary I, he was convicted of HERESY and burned at the stake.

CREATIONISM, *also called* creation science, or scientific creationism, theory or doctrine that postulates that matter, the world, and the various forms of life, are the product of specific acts of creation by a transcendent, personal creator. Biblical creationism believes that the GENESIS story of God's six-day creation of all things is literally correct. Scientific creationists believe that a creator made all that exists, but they may not hold that the Genesis story is a literal history of that creation. Both types of creationists, however, believe that changes in organisms may involve changes within a species or downward changes (negative mutations), but they do not believe that any of these changes can lead to a species evolving into a higher or more complex species. Thus, the theory of human evolution from lower animals is disputed by all creationists.

Creationism grew after the publication in 1859 of Darwin's *Origin of Species*. Within two decades, most of the scientific community had accepted some form of organic evolution. Many religious leaders, however, feared that a less-than-literal reading of the biblical story of creation would result in a loss of faith; and well-known spokesmen for the cause—such as William Jennings Bryan—saw modern war and other purported signs of moral decay to be evidence of the damage brought about by the teaching of godless evolution. The issue was argued on a number of platforms, one of the most famous being the Scopes Trial (1925), in which a high-school teacher was convicted of unlawfully teaching the theory of evolution. In the United States, creationism faced a strong denial—in legal terms—in 1987, when the U.S. Supreme Court ruled that states may not require public schools to teach the creationist theory of human origin alongside evolution if such requirements are intended to promote RELIGIOUS BELIEF.

CREATION MYTH, *also called* COSMOGONY or cosmogonic myth, symbolic narrative of the beginning of the world as understood in a particular tradition and community. Creation myths are of central importance for the valuations of the world, for the orientation of humans in the universe, and for the basic patterns of life and culture. Certain rituals may have served as dramatizations of the creation myth, performed to underscore and highlight the effectiveness of the myth in ordering and safeguarding the culture and its way of life. In addition, a culture's modes of artistic expression—the gestures and dance of ritual and the imagery of the visual and verbal arts—find their models and meanings in the myths of creation.

Although creation myths are numerous, a few basic types may be distinguished. One of these, found in almost all parts of the world, is the belief in a supreme creator deity, usually characterized as omniscient and omnipotent, as having existed alone prior to the world's creation, and as having had a plan in creating the world. In many of these myths, the creator's plan is thwarted through some action of a creature. This rupture leads in some myths to the deity's departure from creation; in others it signifies the ambiguity of the world. In a contrasting cosmogonic view, the world emerges gradually through stages. In contrast to the supreme deity type, emergence myths emphasize the latent power in the earth and its components.

A third type of cosmogonic myth is that which sees the world as the offspring of primordial parents. The world-parents usually appear late in the narrative. The union of the parents is disrupted by the offspring. While reasons for this separation vary, it usually results in a cosmic order centered on the techniques and knowledge of human culture. Related to this type is one in which creation derives from a cosmic egg. This egg symbolizes unity and yet contains the

Creation of the sky, detail from the Creation Dome; Basilica of San Marco, Venice, Italy
Scala—Art Resource

possibilities of separation or creation. A fifth type of cosmogonic myth tells of an animal or devil who, at the bidding of the deity, dives into the primordial waters to secure a portion of earth on which life can survive.

CREED, an officially authorized, usually brief statement of the essential articles of faith of a religious community, often used liturgically in public worship or initiation rites. Creeds are similar to the so-called CONFESSIONS OF FAITH of some Protestant Christian churches, which are usually more extensive formulations.

Although RELIGIOUS BELIEFS frequently are not brought to the fully explicit level of creeds or confessions but are expressed in rituals and myths, liturgical formulas, sacred writings, codifications of law, or theological reflection, the cultural transmission of a religion frequently elicits the formation of formal creeds in an attempt to maintain the religion's identity amidst discontinuity and change. Only ZOROASTRIANISM, BUDDHISM, JUDAISM, CHRISTIANITY, ISLAM, and some modern movements of HINDUISM possess creeds in the full meaning of the word.

In most religions it is chiefly through liturgical expressions that religious faith is confessed and religious identity sustained. In the religions of the East, certain words and phrases function in part as creedal affirmations. LI (laws of appropriate behavior) and HSIAO (FILIAL PIETY) in CONFUCIANISM and TAO (the way) in TAOISM sum up important features of the religious tradition in which they are found. Also serving in some degree as a declaration of faith are the various MANTRAS of Hinduism, especially the Gāyatrī prayer from the ṚG VEDA that BRAHMIN youth learn as part of their initiation ceremony. In HĪNAYĀNA Buddhism a more properly creedal formulation is found in the early declaration of refuge in the BUDDHA, the doctrine, and the community.

Creedal statements are most numerous in the religions of the West. A central part of the life of every Muslim is profession of the SHAHĀDA, which confesses that only God is God and that MUHAMMAD is the prophet of God. In Judaism early creedal affirmations that were apparently confessed in a worship setting as part of an annual festival are preserved in Hebrew SCRIPTURE. In the medieval period efforts were made within Judaism to formulate creeds; of these, MAIMONIDES' creed, the THIRTEEN ARTICLES OF FAITH is the most significant, though it has never been officially recognized as normative. The confession of the oneness of God and of the RESURRECTION of the dead are the central declarations of Jewish belief, and these appear as parts of worship.

Christianity has given rise to numerous creeds. This is partly because the Christian church from the start possessed its distinctive gospel, or KERYGMA (proclamation), which was decidedly dogmatic in character. As early as the apostolic age this proclamation was beginning to crystallize in conventional acclamations (*e.g.*, "Jesus is Lord") and longer partly stereotyped summaries of belief. Creedal formulation in the West reached its summit with the APOSTLES' CREED, which is still used in baptismal ceremonies and public worship by most Protestants and Roman Catholics. Its present working probably goes back to the 8th century; however, it likely originated from earlier baptismal creeds, and in particular from the Old Roman Symbol, which in its essentials seems to go back to the 2nd century.

The NICENE CREED, designed as an authoritative norm of orthodox teaching, was formulated by the COUNCIL OF CONSTANTINOPLE in 381. This creed, also called the Niceno-Constantinopolitan Creed, is accepted in both the East and the West. Like the Apostles' Creed, the Nicene Creed was formulated in part to exclude heretical views, in particular the Arian HERESY that denied the equality of the Son with the Father. Thus, it affirmed that JESUS CHRIST is of one substance (HOMOOUSIAN) with the Father. Western churches also eventually adopted a FILIOQUE clause (never accepted in the East), which asserts that the Spirit proceeds from the Son as well as from the Father.

A third ecumenical creed in the West is the ATHANASIAN CREED, officially accepted by Roman Catholics, Anglicans, and Lutherans, although its use in liturgy has greatly declined in recent centuries. Strongly polemical in tone, it expounds on the nature of Christ and the TRINITY. It probably originated between 450 and 500 in southern France.

CREMATION, the practice of reducing a corpse to its essential elements by burning.

The practice of cremation on open fires was introduced to the Western world by the Greeks as early as 1000 BCE. They seem to have adopted cremation from some northern people as an imperative of war; corpses were incinerated on the battlefield, then the ashes were gathered up and sent to the homeland for ceremonial entombment. Cremation and inhumation subsequently alternated with one another as the preferred mode of burial in ancient Greece, perhaps in part due to the expense of the wood necessary for cremation in a time when local timber was scarce.

The Romans followed Greek and Trojan fashion in cremating their military heroes. In Virgil's epic poetry, the Romans covered the pyre with leaves and fronted it with cypresses; after it was set ablaze, troops shouting war cries circled it and cast trophies taken from their slain opponents into the fire. They poured the blood of animals on the flames, and, when the fires were quenched, washed the bones in wine and placed them in urns. Cremation became such a status symbol in Rome that constructing and renting space in columbariums (vaults or similar structures with niches in the walls to receive the ashes of the dead) became a profitable business. By about 100 CE, however, cremations in the Roman Empire were stopped, perhaps because of the spread of CHRISTIANITY. Although cremation was not explicitly prohibited among Christians, it was not encouraged because of the scarcity of wood, PAGAN associations attached to the practice, and concern that cremation might interfere with the promised RESURRECTION of the body and its reunion with the soul.

The ancient Scandinavians favored cremation, believing that it helped free the spirit from the flesh and also that it kept the dead from harming the living. Their practices paralleled the Greek and Roman epic cremations. After the Icelandic conversion to Christianity in 1000 CE, cremation was rare in western Europe until the 19th century, except in emergencies. During an outbreak of the Black Death in 1656, for example, the bodies of 60,000 victims were burned in Naples during a single week.

In HINDUISM in India, cremation is the preferred form of disposing of the dead. The placing of the body into fire is regarded as a kind of final sacrificial offering, and the burning of the body is often understood to begin the process of REINCARNATION: the soul is transported to the sky by the fire and smoke where it enters clouds, falls back to earth in the form of rain which in turn produces food and, in due course, is eaten and transformed into semen. The holy city of VARANASI (Benares) is especially known for its many cremation centers clustered along the banks of the sacred Gaṅgā (Ganges) River. In Tibet, cremation is usually reserved for the high lamas; in Laos it is for those who die

Cremation in Bali, Indonesia; bodies are hidden inside gilded papier-mâché cattle to confuse evil spirits
Ewing Krainin—Stockpile

"fortunately" (*i.e.*, of natural causes at the end of a peaceful and prosperous life).

Cremation in the modern manner is very different. Open fires are not used; instead, the body is placed in a chamber where intense heat transforms it in an hour or two to a few pounds of white, powdery ash that is disposed of in accordance with law and sentiment: scattered in a garden or some other preferred spot, placed in an urn and kept at home, or taken to a cemetery for burial in a small plot or placement in a columbarium.

Many Protestant churches have actively supported cremation; the Roman Catholic church has announced that it is not prohibited. Orthodox Jewish authorities, however, continue to declare it forbidden.

CRESCAS, ḤASDAI BEN ABRAHAM \'kres-käs\ (b. 1340, Barcelona?—d. 1410, Saragossa, Spain), Spanish philosopher, Talmudic scholar, and critic of the Aristotelian rationalist tradition in Jewish thought.

A merchant and Jewish communal leader in Barcelona (1367), Crescas became closely associated with the royal court of Aragon after the accession of John I (1387). Empowered to exercise over the Jewish community juridical and executive jurisdiction enumerated by Jewish law, he settled in Saragossa as the crown's chief RABBI.

Crescas' first known work is a chronicle of the massacres of JEWS (including his son) in Barcelona in 1391, written in the form of a letter to the Jewish community of Avignon (now in France). Motivated to reaffirm Jewish principles during severe persecution of the Jews in Spain, he wrote (1397–98) a treatise in "Refutation of the Principles of the Christians," a critique of 10 principles of CHRISTIANITY.

Crescas' closely reasoned critique of Aristotle and Jewish Aristotelian tradition, represented in particular by the 12th-century philosopher MAIMONIDES, is contained in his *Or Adonai* ("The Light of the Lord"), completed in 1410, in which he rejected traditional proofs for the existence of God, insisting that certainty in this matter rests only on the authority of the BIBLE in stating "Hear, O Israel: The Lord our God is one Lord" (Deuteronomy 6:4; *see* SHEMA).

CRIOBOLIUM \ˌkrī-ō-'bō-lē-əm\ (from Greek: *krios*, "ram" and *ballō*, "I throw, strike"), in the ancient religion of Asia Minor, the sacrifice of a ram and the bathing of a devotee in its blood, in the cult of the Phrygian deities ATTIS and Cybele, the GREAT MOTHER OF THE GODS. The ceremony may have been instituted on the analogy of the TAUROBOLIUM, or bull sacrifice, which it probably resembled. When it was performed in conjunction with the Taurobolium, the altar was usually inscribed to both the Great Mother and Attis, whereas the inscription was to the Mother alone when only the Taurobolium was performed.

CRONUS \'krō-nəs\, *also spelled* Cronos, *or* Kronos, in ancient GREEK RELIGION, male deity, probably not widely worshiped in historical times, but who was later identified with the Roman god SATURN. His functions were connected with agriculture; in Attica his festival celebrated the harvest. It influenced the Roman Saturnalia. In art he was depicted as an old man holding an implement, probably originally a sickle but interpreted as a *harpē*, or curved sword.

In Greek mythology Cronus was the son of OURANUS (Heaven) and GAEA (Earth) and the youngest of the 12 TITANS. On the advice of his mother he castrated his father with a *harpē*, thus separating heaven from earth. He now became the king of the Titans and took for his consort his sister RHEA; she bore by him HESTIA, DEMETER, HERA, HADES, and POSEIDON, all of whom he swallowed because his parents had warned that he would be overthrown by his own child. When ZEUS was born, however, Rhea hid him in Crete and tricked Cronus into swallowing a stone instead. Zeus grew up, forced Cronus to disgorge his brothers and sisters, waged war on Cronus, and was victorious. After his defeat, Cronus became, in different versions of his story, either a prisoner in Tartarus or king of the Golden Age.

CROSIER, *also spelled* crozier, *also called* pastoral staff, staff with a curved top that is a symbol of the Good Shepherd and is carried by BISHOPS of the ROMAN CATHOLIC, ANGLICAN, and some European LUTHERAN churches and by ABBOTS and abbesses as an insignia of their office. It is made of metal or carved wood and is often very ornate. It was first mentioned as a sign of a bishop's ruling power in 633 at the fourth Council of Toledo and was gradually adopted throughout Christendom. Originally a staff with a cross, sphere, or tau cross on top, it acquired its present form by the 13th century.

Bishops of the Eastern churches carry the *baktēria* (*dikanikion*), a pastoral staff with either a tau cross or two serpents facing each other on top.

CROSS, the principal symbol of CHRISTIANITY, recalling the CRUCIFIXION of JESUS CHRIST and the redeeming benefits of his Passion and death.

There are four basic types of iconographic representations of the cross: the *crux quadrata*, or Greek cross, with four equal arms; the *crux immissa*, or Latin cross, whose base stem is longer than the other three arms; the *crux commissa,* in the form of the Greek letter tau (τ), sometimes called St. Anthony's cross; and *crux decussata,* named from the Roman *decussis,* or symbol of the number 10, also known as St. Andrew's cross. The many variations and ornamentations of processional, altar, and heraldic crosses, of carved and painted crosses in churches, graveyards, and elsewhere, are developments of these four types.

Cross forms were used as symbols long before the Christian era. Two pre-Christian cross forms have had some Christian usage. The ancient Egyptian hieroglyphic symbol of life—the ANKH, a tau cross surmounted by a loop and known as *crux ansata*—was extensively used on Coptic Christian monuments. The SWASTIKA, called *crux gammata,* composed of four Greek uppercase gammas (Γ), is marked on early Christian tombs as a veiled symbol of the cross.

Before the time of the emperor CONSTANTINE in the 4th century, Christians were cautious about portraying the cross lest it expose them to ridicule or danger. After Constantine converted to Christianity, he abolished crucifixion as a death penalty and promoted, as symbols of the faith, both the cross and the chi-rho monogram of the name of Christ. The symbols became immensely popular in Christian art and funerary monuments from *c.* 350.

For several centuries after Constantine, Christian devotion to the cross centered on the victory of Christ over the powers of evil and death, and realistic portrayal of his suffering was avoided. The earliest crucifixes (crosses containing a representation of Christ) depict Christ alive, with eyes open and arms extended. By the 9th century, however, artists began to stress the realistic aspects of Christ's suffering and death. Subsequently, Western portrayals of the Crucifixion exhibited an increasing finesse in the suggestion of pain and agony. Romanesque crucifixes often show a royal crown upon Christ's head, but later Gothic types replaced it with a crown of thorns. In the 20th century a new emphasis emerged in ROMAN CATHOLICISM, in which Christ on the cross is crowned and vested as a king and priest, and the marks of his suffering are much less prominent.

After the 16th-century Protestant REFORMATION, the Lutherans generally retained the ornamental and ceremonial use of the cross. The Reformed churches, however, resisted such use of the cross until the 20th century, when ornamental crosses on church buildings and on communion tables began to appear. *See also* TRUE CROSS; CRUCIFIXION.

CROSS, STATIONS OF THE, *also called* Way of the Cross, a series of 14 pictures or carvings portraying events in the Passion of JESUS CHRIST, from his condemnation by PONTIUS PILATE to his entombment.

The series of stations is as follows: (1) Jesus is condemned to death, (2) he is made to bear his cross, (3) he falls the first time, (4) he meets his mother, (5) Simon of Cyrene is made to bear the cross, (6) Veronica wipes Jesus' face, (7) he falls the second time, (8) the women of Jerusalem weep over Jesus, (9) he falls the third time, (10) he is stripped of his garments, (11) he is nailed to the cross, (12) he dies on the cross, (13) he is taken down from the cross, (14) he is placed in the sepulchre. The images are usually mounted on the inside walls of a church or chapel but may also be erected in such places as cemeteries, corridors of hospitals, and religious houses and on mountainsides.

The devotional exercise of visiting and praying in front of each of the 14 stations and meditating on the Passion of Christ stems from the practice of early Christian pilgrims who visited the scenes of the events in Jerusalem and walked the traditional route from the supposed location of

Good Friday procession stopping at the third station of the Way of the Cross in Jerusalem
David Harris

Pilate's house to Calvary. The origin of the devotion in its present form is not clear. The number of stations originally observed in Jerusalem was considerably smaller than 14. The FRANCISCANS long popularized the devotional practice.

CRUCIFIXION, an important method of capital punishment, particularly among the Persians, Seleucids, Jews, Carthaginians, and Romans from about the 6th century BCE to the 4th century CE. CONSTANTINE the Great, the first Christian emperor, abolished it in the Roman Empire in 337 CE, out of veneration for JESUS CHRIST, who tradition relates was a victim of crucifixion.

There were various methods of performing the execution. Usually, the condemned man, after being whipped, or "scourged," dragged the crossbeam of his cross to the place of punishment, where the upright shaft was already fixed in the ground. He was then bound fast with outstretched arms to the crossbeam or nailed firmly to it through the wrists. The crossbeam was then raised against the upright shaft and made fast to it about 9 to 12 feet from the ground. Next, the feet were tightly bound or nailed to the upright shaft. A ledge inserted about halfway up the upright shaft gave some support to the body; evidence for a similar ledge for the feet is rare and late. Over the criminal's head was placed a notice stating his name and his crime. Death, by exhaustion or by heart failure, could be hastened by shattering the legs (*crurifragium*) with an iron club to bring on shock or asphyxiation. Crucifixion was most frequently used to punish political or religious agitators, pirates, slaves, or those who had no civil rights.

Crucifixion of Jesus. The account of Jesus Christ's Crucifixion in the Gospels begins with his scourging. The Roman soldiers then mocked him as the "King of the Jews" by clothing him in a purple robe and a crown of thorns and led him slowly to Mount Calvary, or GOLGOTHA. At the place of execution he was stripped and then nailed to the cross, at least nailed by his hands; and above him at the top of the cross was placed the condemnatory inscription stating his crime of professing to be King of the Jews. (The Gospels differ slightly in the wording but are in accordance that the inscription was in "Hebrew," or Aramaic, as well as Latin and Greek.) On the cross Jesus hung for three hours. The soldiers divided his garments and cast lots for his seamless robe; various onlookers taunted him. Crucified on either side of Jesus were two convicted thieves, whom the soldiers dispatched at eventide by breaking their legs. The soldiers found Jesus already dead; but, to be certain, one of them drove a spear into his side, from which poured blood and water. He was taken down before sunset (in deference to Jewish custom) and buried in a rock-hewn tomb.

Crucifixion in art. The representation of Christ on the cross has been an important subject of Western art since the early Middle Ages. Concerned primarily with symbolic affirmations of eternal life, and repelled by the ignominy of the punishment, the early Christians did not represent the Crucifixion realistically before the 5th century; instead, the event was symbolized first by a lamb and, after the official recognition of CHRISTIANITY by the Roman state in the early 4th century, by a jeweled cross. By the 6th century, however, representations of the Crucifixion became numerous as a result of current church efforts to combat a HERESY that Christ's nature was not dual—human and divine—but simply divine and therefore invulnerable. These early Crucifixions nevertheless showed Christ alive, with open eyes and no trace of suffering, victorious over death. In the 9th century, Byzantine art began to show a dead Christ, with closed eyes, reflecting current concern with the mystery of his death and the nature of the INCARNATION. This version was adopted in the West in the 13th century with an ever increasing emphasis on his suffering.

Parallel to this development in the representation of Christ himself was the growth of an increasingly complex ICONOGRAPHY involving other elements traditionally included in the scene. The Virgin MARY and St. JOHN THE APOSTLE are frequently the only other figures included in the composition. In various expanded versions of the theme, however, there are several other pairs of figures, both historical and symbolic, that traditionally appear to the right and left of the cross—*e.g.*, the two thieves, one repentant, who were crucified with Christ; and small personifications of the sun and moon, which were eclipsed at the Crucifixion.

With the growth of devotional art at the end of the Middle Ages, depictions of the Crucifixion often portrayed the scene with gruesome realism. Renaissance art restored a calm idealization to the scene, however, which was preserved, with a more overt expression of emotion, in the Baroque period. Like most of Christian religious art, the theme of the Crucifixion suffered a decline after the 17th century; some 20th-century artists, however, have created highly individual interpretations of the subject.

CÚ CHULAINN \kü-'k̬ə-lən\, *also called* Cuchulain, Cuchulinn, *or* Cuchullin, in ancient Irish Gaelic literature, the central character of the ULSTER (Ulaid) CYCLE. He was the greatest of the warriors of the Red Branch, *i.e.*, the warriors loyal to Conor (CONCHOBAR MAC NESSA), who was reputedly king of the Ulaid of northeast Ireland at about the beginning of the 1st century BCE. Cú Chulainn, born as Sétanta, the son of the god LUGUS (Lugh) of the Long Arm and Dechtire, the sister of Conchobar, was of great size and beauty and won distinction for his exploits while still a child. His prowess was increased by the gift of seven fingers on each hand, seven toes on each foot, and seven pupils in each eye. Favored by the gods and exempt from the curse of periodic feebleness laid upon the men of Ulster, he performed superhuman exploits and labors. In times of rage he could become monstrously deformed and uncontrollable. *The Cattle Raid of Cooley* (*Táin Bó Cuailnge*) records his single-handed defense of Ulster at the age of 17 against the forces of MEDB (Maeve), queen of Connaught. According to the best-known legends, he was tricked by his enemies into an unfair fight and slain at the age of 27.

CULT, collective veneration or worship. In the West, cults are usually thought of as groups that have deviated from normative religions. Thus, the term cult has, in recent times, often been identified with new religions which are viewed as foreign, peculiar, or dangerous.

CULTURE HEROES, mythological figures who secure for humanity the various attributes of culture (acting either with or against the gods). The culture hero is often an animal or trickster figure, and such traditions are found in etiologic stories about how humans first learned to hunt, discovered tobacco, and so on (*see* TRICKSTER TALE).

The most frequent motif is that of the animal who steals fire from the gods for the benefit of humans. Frequently, such traditions lie behind etiologies of specific animal or plant characteristics; *e.g.*, the bat is black and blind because it stole fire and was singed by the flames and blinded by the smoke. In other tales, the animals oppose the acquisition of culture by humans and must be overcome by a human culture hero. A closely related theme is the myth of a life-giving tree or other healing magical plant, growing in paradise or some other inaccessible place, to which the culture hero must travel in order to gain a boon for humanity. He is frequently assisted by or has to overcome supernatural animals. *See also* PROMETHEUS.

CUPID \'kyü-pid\, ancient Roman god of love in all its varieties, identified with the Greek god EROS and the equivalent of AMOR in Latin poetry. According to myth, Cupid was the son of MERCURY, the winged messenger of the gods, and VENUS, the goddess of love; he usually appeared as a winged infant carrying a bow and a quiver of arrows, whose wounds inspired love or passion in his every victim. He sometimes wore armor like that of MARS, the god of war, perhaps to suggest ironic parallels between warfare and romance or to symbolize the invincibility of love.

Cupid was generally viewed as beneficent, on account of the happiness he imparted to couples both mortal and immortal. At the worst he was considered mischievous in his matchmaking, this mischief often directed by his mother, Venus. In one tale, her machinations backfired when she used Cupid in revenge on the mortal PSYCHE, only to have Cupid fall in love and make Psyche his immortal wife.

CUPSTONE \ˈkəp-ˌstōn\, in prehistoric European religion, an altar stone, megalithic tomb, or isolated stone slab incised with small cuplike markings. They are found mainly in Scandinavia and northern and central Germany. Dating primarily to Neolithic times (from about 7000 BCE to approximately 2300 BCE), cupstones carved in the Early Paleolithic Period and at the beginning of historical times have also been found. Although most scholars consider the cupstones to be solar symbols, there is still disagreement on their origin and purpose.

CURIA, ROMAN \ˈkyu̇r-ē-ə, ˈku̇r-\, *Latin* Curia Romana, the group of Vatican bureaus that assist the pope in the exercise of his primatial jurisdiction over the ROMAN CATHOLIC church. The Curia was given its modern form by Pope Sixtus V late in the 16th century. Its work has tra-

Cupid; statue in the Museo Archeologico Nazionale, Naples
Alinari—Art Resource

ditionally been associated with the members of the Sacred College of CARDINALS, acting either as a body or individually as administrators in the various bureaus. A reorganization, ordered by Pope Pius X, was incorporated into the *Code of Canon Law* (promulgated 1917). Further steps toward reorganization were begun by Pope Paul VI in the 1960s.

Responsibility for the coordination of curial activities belongs to the cardinal who, as secretary of state, directs both the Secretariat of State (or Papal Secretariat) and the Council for the Public Affairs of the Church. The various sacred congregations of the Curia are concerned with administrative matters. The Sacred Congregation for the Doctrine of the Faith is responsible for safeguarding the doctrine on faith and morals. This congregation is primarily intended to promote theological orthodoxy and to protect the rights of those accused of failure in this regard.

Other sacred congregations are those for the Oriental Churches, Bishops (formerly the Sacred Congregation of the Consistorial), the SACRAMENTS and Divine Worship (formerly Congregation of Rites), the Causes of Saints (concerned with procedures for BEATIFICATION and CANONIZATION and with the preservation of relics, once a responsibility of the now defunct Congregation of Rites), the Clergy (formerly the Sacred Congregation of the Council), Religious and Secular Institutes, Catholic Education (formerly the Sacred Congregation of Seminaries and Universities), and the Propagation of the Faith (also known as the Congregation for the Evangelization of Peoples).

The judicial branch of the Curia consists of three tribunals: the Apostolic Signatura (the highest judicial body), the Sacred Roman Rota (for judging ecclesiastical cases appealed to the Vatican, especially those concerning the nullity of marriage), and the Sacred Apostolic Penitentiary (for matters of conscience).

In addition there are various offices and three secretariats for Promoting Christian Unity, for Non-Christians, and for Non-Believers. Several permanent commissions reflect papal concern for scholarly studies; they include the Pontifical Commission for Biblical Studies and the Pontifical Commission for the Revision of the Code of CANON LAW.

CYBELE: *see* GREAT MOTHER OF THE GODS.

CYCLOPS \ˈsī-ˌkläps\ (Greek: "Round-eyed"), in Greek legend, any of several one-eyed GIANTS to whom were ascribed a variety of histories and deeds. In Homer the Cyclopes were cannibals, living a rude pastoral life in a distant land (traditionally Sicily), and in the *Odyssey* ODYSSEUS escapes death by blinding the Cyclops POLYPHEMUS. In Hesiod the Cyclopes were three sons of OURANUS and GAEA—Arges, Brontes, and Steropes (Bright, Thunderer, Lightener)—who forged the thunderbolts of ZEUS. Later authors made them the workmen of HEPHAESTUS and said that APOLLO killed them for making the thunderbolt that slew ASCLEPIUS.

The walls of several ancient cities (*e.g.,* Tiryns) of Mycenaean architecture were sometimes said to have been built by Cyclopes. Hence in archaeology the term cyclopean is applied to walling of which the stones are not squared.

CYPRIAN, SAINT \ˈsi-prē-ən\, *Latin in full* Thascius Caecilius Cyprianus \ˌsi-prē-ˈā-nəs\ (b. *c.* 200 CE, Carthage—d. Sept. 14, 258, Carthage; Western and Eastern feast day September 16; Anglican feast day September 26), early Christian theologian and bishop of Carthage who led the Christians of North Africa during a period of persecution from Rome. He became the first bishop-martyr of Africa.

Cyprian was born of non-Christian parents and was converted to CHRISTIANITY about 246. Within two years he was elected BISHOP of Carthage and early in 250 was confronted by the Decian persecution. After he went into hiding, thousands of Christians apostatized (rejected their faith). When the persecution began to diminish, the confessors—*i.e.,* those who had stood firm for their faith—reconciled the lapsed on easy terms. Cyprian returned to Carthage and at a council of bishops in May 251 was able to regain his authority. The decision of the council was that, though no one should be totally excluded from penance, those who truly had sacrificed (the *sacrificati*) should be readmitted only on their deathbeds; others were to be readmitted after varying periods of penance.

Three important principles of church discipline were thus established. First, the right and power to remit DEADLY SINS, even that of APOSTASY, lay in the hands of the church; second, the final authority in disciplinary matters rested with the bishops in council; and, third, unworthy members among the laity must be accepted in the New Israel of Christianity just as in the Old Israel of JUDAISM.

By 252 Cyprian had defeated internal enemies who had set up a rival bishop in Carthage. In 251 Cyprian had supported Bishop Cornelius against his rival for the PAPACY, Novatian, and had written on his behalf the treatise *On the Unity of the Catholic Church*, which stressed the centrality of the see of Peter (Rome) as the source of the episcopacy. Cyprian, however, had implied no acceptance of Roman jurisdictional prerogatives. When in 254 two Spanish congregations appealed to him against a decision by Stephen to restore bishops who had lapsed during the persecution, he summoned a council to consider the case. The council decided that the congregations had not only a right but a duty to separate themselves from a cleric who had committed a deadly sin such as apostasy.

Within months there was an even more serious dispute with Rome. Supporters of the excommunicated Novatian had been asserting against Cyprian that no forgiveness for lapsed Christians was possible. With the recovery of Cyprian's prestige, however, their threat began to fade and many of those whom they had baptized desired admittance to the church. Thus Stephen confronted the problem of whether the Novatian BAPTISM had been valid and decided that all baptism in the name of the TRINITY was valid. Cyprian held three councils in 255 and 256. The last decided unanimously that there could be no baptism outside the church. Behind this clash over rites lay the more fundamental question concerning the nature of the church. Though Rome emphasized the church's universal and inevitably mixed character on earth, the North Africans stressed its integrity under all circumstances. Cyprian's theology was based on the central idea of the uniqueness of the church and of its unity—that unity being expressed through the consensus of bishops, all equally possessing the HOLY SPIRIT and sovereign in their own sees. The church consisted of the people united to their bishop, with no "bishop of bishops" in Rome to occupy a higher seat.

A complete breach between Rome and Carthage was averted by Stephen's death on Aug. 2, 257. Meanwhile, persecution had been renewed by Emperor Valerian (253–260). On Aug. 30, 257, Cyprian was summoned before the proconsul and assigned an enforced residence. The next year, he was brought back to Carthage and condemned to death.

CYRENE \sī-'rē-nē\, in Greek mythology, a NYMPH, daughter of Hypseus (king of the Lapiths) and Chlidanope (a NAIAD). One day Cyrene wrestled a lion that had attacked her father's flocks. APOLLO, who was watching, fell in love with her and carried her off from Mt. Pelion, in Thessaly, to Libya. There he founded the city of Cyrene and made her its queen. Cyrene was the mother by Apollo of ARISTAEUS and Idmon the seer and by ARES of Diomedes of Thrace.

CYRIL AND METHODIUS, SAINTS \'sir-əl...mə-'thō-dē-əs\ (respectively b. c. 827, Thessalonica, Macedonia—d. Feb. 14, 869, Rome; b. c. 825, Thessalonica—d. April 6, 884, Moravia; feast day for both, Western church February 14; Eastern church May 11), brothers who for christianizing the Danubian Slavs and for influencing the religious and cultural development of all Slavic peoples received the title

"the apostles of the Slavs." Both were outstanding scholars, theologians, and linguists. The Cyrillic alphabet, which was probably developed by their later followers, was named after Saint Cyril.

CYRIL OF ALEXANDRIA, SAINT \'sir-əl\ (b. c. 375—d. June 27, 444; Western feast day June 27; Eastern feast day June 9), Christian theologian and BISHOP active in the complex doctrinal struggles of the 5th century.

He succeeded his uncle Theophilus as bishop of the see of Alexandria in 412 and came in conflict with the civil administration over the zeal with which he championed orthodoxy. He closed the churches of the Novatians, a schismatic sect. He also was involved in the expulsion of Jews from Alexandria following their attacks upon Christians. Riots ensued, and Cyril, who if not directly responsible at least had done nothing to prevent them, was forced to acknowledge the authority of the civil government.

Cyril's conflict with NESTORIUS was doctrinal but also reflected the Egyptians' fear that Constantinople might come to dominate them. The religious argument involved the relation of the divine and human within JESUS CHRIST. Cyril emphasized the unity of the two in one Person, while Nestorius so emphasized their distinctness that he seemed to be splitting Christ into two Persons acting in concert. The conflict came to the fore over Cyril's insistence that the Virgin MARY be called THEOTOKOS (Greek: "God-bearer") to describe the union of the two natures in the INCARNATION. Nestorius refused to accept this, and their dispute was referred to a general council at Ephesus in 431.

Armed with a commission to represent Pope Celestine I as well as himself, Cyril convened the council and condemned Nestorius. He had not waited, however, for the arrival of certain bishops from the East, particularly from the see of Antioch. When they did reach EPHESUS, they reconvened the council and condemned Cyril. Papal recognition of Cyril's council was eventually obtained, however, and Nestorius was banished as a heretic. Even so, the dispute continued, and peace in the church was only restored in 433, when Cyril accepted a statement, representing a compromise with Antioch, that emphasized the distinctness of the two natures within the one Person of Christ.

CYRIL OF JERUSALEM, SAINT (b. c. 315, Jerusalem—d. 386?, Jerusalem; feast day March 18), BISHOP of Jerusalem and doctor of the church who fostered the development of the "holy city" as a PILGRIMAGE center for all Christendom.

A senior PRESBYTER when he succeeded Maximus as bishop (c. 350), Cyril was exiled about 357 and at two later times from his see by the ARIANS. Many years later at the COUNCIL OF CONSTANTINOPLE (381) there was evidence that he might have been suspected by the strictly orthodox for his associations with the HOMOOUSIANS (moderate Arians), who had reinstated him as bishop at the Council of Seleucia (359). He retained his bishopric during the reign of Emperor Julian the Apostate (361–363).

Cyril's primary surviving work is a collection of 23 catechetical lectures (*Catecheses*) delivered to candidates for BAPTISM. The first 18, based on the Jerusalem baptismal creed, were given during LENT, and the concluding 5 instructed the newly baptized during the week after EASTER. Cyril's Eucharistic theology is an advance on that of earlier writers: it interprets the Lord's presence in the terms later echoed in the dogma of TRANSUBSTANTIATION and describes the rite in pronounced sacrificial language. Cyril was declared a doctor of the church in 1883.

DĀDŪ \'dä-ˌdü\ (b. 1544, Ahmadabad, Gujarat, India—d. *c.* 1603, Naraina, India), Hindu/Muslim saint who inspired the formation of a sect called the Dādū Panth.

A cotton carder by profession, Dādū became a religious wanderer and preacher, settling for periods of time at Sembhar, Amber, and finally at Naraina, all within range of Jaipur and Ajmer (Rajasthan state). Dādū rejected the authority of the VEDAS (earliest Hindu SCRIPTURES), CASTE distinctions, and all divisive, external forms of worship. Instead he concentrated on *japa* (repetition of the name of God) and such themes as the soul as bride of God. His followers have insisted on vegetarianism and abstention from alcohol, and there is a strong ascetic component of the Dādū Panth. Dādū's poetic aphorisms and devotional HYMNS, the vehicle of his teachings, were collected in a 5,000-verse anthology, *Bāṇī* ("Utterances"). They also appear along with selections from the other poet-saints (*sants*) KABĪR, NĀMDEV, Ravidās, and Haridās in a somewhat fluid verse anthology called *Pañcvāṇī* ("five [groups of] utterances"), which constitutes scripture for the Dādū Panth.

DAEDALA \'de-də-lə, 'dē-\, ancient festival of the Greek goddess HERA. The Daedala was celebrated on Mount Cithaeron. In the festival, a wooden image dressed as a bride was carried in procession, then burnt with sacrificed animals and a wooden sacrificial altar. A myth existed that ZEUS had won back the estranged Hera by arousing her jealousy with such an image. The Daedala involved a new "marriage" of the pair following reconciliation.

DAEDALUS \'de-də-ləs, 'dē-\ (Greek: "skillfully made"), mythical Greek architect and sculptor who was said to have built, among other things, the Labyrinth for King MINOS of Crete. Daedalus fell out of favor with Minos and was imprisoned; he fashioned wings out of wax and feathers for himself and for his son ICARUS and escaped to Sicily. Icarus, however, flew too near the sun, and his wings melted; he fell into the sea and drowned. The island on which his body was washed ashore was later named Icaria.

The Greeks of the historic age attributed to Daedalus buildings and statues the origins of which were lost in the past. Later critics ascribed to him such innovations as representing humans in statues with their feet apart and their eyes open. A phase of early Greek art, Daedalic sculpture, is named for him.

DAGAN \'dä-ˌgän\, *also spelled* Dagon, West Semitic god of crop fertility, worshiped extensively throughout the ancient Middle East. *Dagan* was the Hebrew and Ugaritic common noun for "grain," and the god Dagan was the mythical inventor of the plow. His cult is attested as early as about 2500 BCE, and, according to texts found at Ras Shamra (ancient UGARIT), he was the father of the god BAAL. Dagan had an important temple at Ras Shamra, and in Palestine, where he was particularly known as a god of the

Philistines, he had several sanctuaries, including those at Beth-dagon in Asher (Joshua 19:27), Gaza (Judges 16:23), and Ashdod (1 Samuel 5:2–7). At Ras Shamra, he was apparently second in importance only to EL, the supreme god, although his functions as a god of vegetation seem to have been transferred to Baal by about 1500 BCE.

DAGDA \'däg-thə\, *also called* Eochaid Ollathair ("Eochaid All-Father"), *or* In Ruad Ro-fhessa ("The Red [or Mighty] One of Great Wisdom"), in Irish myth, one of the leaders of the god-race, the TUATHA DÉ DANANN ("People of the Goddess Danu"). His name was explained by medieval Irish commentators as equivalent to *dag-día*, literally "good god," alluding to the many powers credited to him rather than to his moral character. The Dagda had an enormous appetite for both food and sex, which points to some connection in cult with the maintenance of fertility. He also possessed a cauldron that was never empty and had a huge club that had the power both to kill men and to restore them to life. The Dagda mated with the sinister war goddess MORRÍGAN and with the river goddess BOANN (Boyne). He was the father of the triple goddess BRIGIT and of the god of youth and beauty, Oenghus (also known as Mac ind Óg and in Gaul as MAPONOS).

DAHRĪYA \däh-'rē-ə\, in ISLAM, the unbelievers who contend that the course of time (Arabic: *dahr*) is all that governs their existence. They were so called because of a reference to them in the QUR'AN, in which they are repudiated for saying, "There is no other than our present life; we die and we live and nothing but the course of time destroys us" (Qur'an 45:24).

The Dahrīya are portrayed in Islamic theological literature as naturalists and materialists who deny the existence of anything that cannot be perceived by the senses. In the 11th century AL-GHAZĀLĪ traced their origin to ancient Greek philosophy and distinguished them from the naturalists (*ṭabī'īyūn*) who speak of a creating deity while the Dahrīya recognize only natural laws. Others described them as believers in a supreme power but not in a soul or DEMONS and ANGELS.

In the popular imagination of devout Muslims, Dahrīya are opportunists who conduct their lives according to their selfish desires; in this devout view, the Dahrīya do not make a distinction between humans and inanimate objects and are devoid of compassion and human feelings.

DAIGAK GUKSA \'ta-ˌgäk-'kük-ˌsä\, *also spelled* Taegak Kuksa, *secular name* Ŭich'ŏn \'ə̇-ē-'chən\ (b. 1055, Korea—d. 1101, Korea), Korean Buddhist priest who founded the Ch'ŏnt'ae sect of BUDDHISM.

A son of the Koryŏ king Munjong, Ŭich'ŏn became a Buddhist monk at age 11. In 1084 he went to China to study and collect Buddhist literature. He returned to Korea with the doctrines of the Chinese T'IEN-T'AI (Korean Ch'ŏnt'ae) sect of Buddhism. Ŭich'ŏn became the chief propagator of the sect in Korea; this sect attempted, with considerable popular success, to reconcile the conflicting doctrines of the two chief Buddhist sects in Korea, the Kyo, or Textual, School and the ZEN School. The Ch'ŏnt'ae doctrines stimulated the reorganization of the Zen school into the CHOGYE school, and these three sects (Chogye, Textual, and Ch'ŏnt'ae) henceforth became the three main divisions of Buddhism in Korea.

In Korea Ŭich'ŏn also applied himself to collecting, cataloging, and publishing Buddhist writings. He published some 4,750 books of Buddhist SCRIPTURES, including the second publication of the TRIPIṬAKA (a complete collection of Buddhist scriptures) in Korea and an authoritative catalogue of Buddhist sectarian writings.

DAJJĀL, AL- \al-dȧj-'jal\ (Arabic: "The Deceiver"), in Islamic ESCHATOLOGY, the ANTICHRIST who will come forth before the end of time; after a reign of 40 days or 40 years, he will be destroyed by JESUS CHRIST or the MAHDI ("Divinely Guided One") or both, and the world will submit to God.

Daedalus and Icarus, antique bas-relief; in the Villa Albani, Rome
Alinari—Art Resource

Al-Dajjāl first appears in pseudoapocalyptic Christian literature and is reworked in HADITH ascribed to MUHAMMAD. There he is described as a plump, one-eyed man with a ruddy face and curling hair and the Arabic letters *k-f-r* ("unbelief") on his forehead. Al-Dajjāl will appear during a period of great tribulation; he will be followed by the Jews and will claim to be God in Jerusalem. He will work false miracles, and most people will be deceived. At this moment will occur the SECOND COMING of Christ.

Tradition expects al-Dajjāl to appear in the East, possibly Khorāsān. In the meantime, he is said to be somewhere in the East Indies, on an island from which the sounds of dancing and beautiful music emanate. An alternate version states that al-Dajjāl is bound to a rock on an island in the sea and is fed by DEMONS.

DAKHMA \'dȧk-mä\ (Avestan: "tower of silence"), PARSI funerary tower erected on a hill for the disposal of the dead according to the ZOROASTRIAN rite. Such towers are about 25 feet high, built of brick or stone, and contain gratings on which the corpses are exposed. After the bones have been picked clean by vultures, they fall into a pit below, thereby fulfilling the injunction that a corpse must not suffer contact with either fire or earth.

DALAI LAMA \'dä-lī-'lä-mə, 'dä-lā-\, head of the dominant DGE-LUGS-PA (Yellow Hat) order of TIBETAN BUDDHISTS and, un-

til 1959, both spiritual and temporal ruler of Tibet.

The first of the line was Dge-'dun-grub-pa (1391–1475), founder of Tashilhunpo monastery of central Tibet. In accordance with the belief in reincarnate LAMAS which began to develop in the 14th century, his successors were conceived as his rebirths and came to be regarded as physical manifestations of the AVALOKITEŚVARA, the BODHISATTVA of compassion.

The second head of the order, Dge-'dun-rgya-mtsho (1475–1542), became the head abbot of the 'Bras-spungs (Drepung) monastery on the outskirts of Lhasa, which thenceforward was the principal seat of the Dalai Lama. His successor, Bsod-nams-rgya-mtsho (1543–88), while on a visit to the Mongol chief Altan Khan, received from that ruler the honorific title *ta-le* (Anglicized as "dalai"), the Mongolian equivalent of the Tibetan *rgya-mtsho*, which means "ocean" and presumably suggests breadth and depth of wisdom. The title was subsequently applied posthumously to the abbot's two predecessors. The Tibetans themselves call the Dalai Lama Rgyal-ba Rin-po-che ("Great Precious Conqueror").

The fourth Dalai Lama, Yon-tan-rgya-mtsho (1589–1617), was a great-grandson of Altan Khan and the only non-Tibetan Dalai Lama. The next Dalai Lama, Ngag-dbang-rgya-mtsho (1617–82), is commonly called the Great Fifth. He established, with the military assistance of the Khoshut Mongols, the supremacy of the Dge-lugs-pa sect over rival orders for the temporal rule of Tibet. During his reign the majestic winter palace of the Dalai Lamas, the Potala, was built in Lhasa. The sixth Dalai Lama, Tshangs-dbyangs-rgya-mtsho (1683–1706) was deposed by the Mongols and died while being taken to China under military escort.

The seventh Dalai Lama, Bskal-bzang-rgya-mtsho (1708–57), experienced civil war and the establishment of Chinese Manchu suzerainty over Tibet; the eighth, 'Jam-dpal-rgya-mtsho (1758–1804), saw his country invaded by Gurkha troops from Nepal but defeated them with the aid of Chinese forces.

The next four Dalai Lamas all died young, and the country was ruled by regents. They were Lung-rtogs-rgya-mtsho (1806–15), Tshul-khrims-rgya-mtsho (1816–37), Mkhas-grub-rgya-mtsho (1838–56), and 'Phrin-las-rgya-mtsho (1856–75).

The 13th Dalai Lama, Thub-bstan-rgya-mtsho (1875–1933), ruled with great personal authority. The successful revolt within China against its ruling Manchu dynasty in 1912 gave the Tibetans the opportunity to dispel the dis-

The 14th Dalai Lama
Alison Wright—Photo Researchers

united Chinese troops, and the Dalai Lama reigned as head of a sovereign state.

The 14th in the line of Dalai Lamas, Bstan-'dzin-rgya-mtsho, was born in 1935 in Tsinghai province, China, of Tibetan parentage. He was enthroned in 1940 but fled to exile in India with a group of 100,000 followers in 1959, the year of the Tibetan people's unsuccessful revolt against communist Chinese forces that had occupied the country since 1950. The Dalai Lama set up a government-in-exile in Dharmsala, India, in the Himalayan Mountains. In 1989 he was awarded the Nobel Prize for Peace in recognition of his nonviolent campaign to end Chinese domination of Tibet. He wrote a number of books on Tibetan Buddhism and an autobiography entitled *Freedom in Exile.*

DALIT \'də-lit\ ("the Oppressed"), preferred term of self-identification for those at the bottom of the CASTE hierarchy in India, also known as "untouchables," "outcastes," or members of the scheduled castes. Because Dalit refers to all forms of social and economic oppression, its use can also be extended to other suppressed peoples of India: tribal groups, religious minorities, women, and the poor of all castes. Primarily, however, the term, was popularized in protest movements of the 1970s as a positive, assertive expression of pride in the UNTOUCHABLE heritage. It has largely replaced the name Harijan, or "Children of God," which was Mahatma GANDHI's suggested substitute for untouchables but has seemed patronizing to Dalits themselves.

DAMASCUS DOCUMENT \də-'mas-kəs\, *in full* The Document of the New Covenant in the Land of Damascus, *also called* Zadokite Fragments, one of the most important extant works of the ancient community of Jews at QUMRĀN in Palestine. The community fled to the Judaean desert wilderness around Qumrān during Antiochus IV Epiphanes' persecution of Palestinian Jews from 175 to 164/163 BCE. Though a precise date for the composition of the *Damascus Document* has not been determined, it must have been written before the great Jewish revolt of 66–70 CE, which forced the Qumrān community to disband.

Two medieval manuscripts dating from the 10th and 12th centuries were discovered in 1896–97 in the storeroom of the Ezra Synagogue in Cairo. They were published under the title *Fragments of a Zadokite Work* because members of the Qumrān community also called themselves Sons of Zadok (the Righteous One). The subsequent discovery of extensive Hebrew fragments from caves IV and VI at Qumrān confirmed that the document was one of the major doctrinal and administrative codes of the sect.

The *Damascus Document* consists of two major sections. The "exhortation" sets forth the sect's religious teaching, emphasizing fidelity to God's COVENANT with Israel and strict observance of the SABBATH and other holy days.

It also introduces the sect's enigmatic leader, the Teacher of Righteousness, whom scholars have not been able to identify. Opposed by the Wicked Priest (possibly either of two HIGH PRIESTS of the Hasmonean dynasty in Jerusalem: Jonathan, 152–143/142 BCE, or Alexander Jannaeus, 103–76 BCE), the Teacher of Righteousness was persecuted and exiled. The sect believed that a messianic age would commence 40 years after the death of the Teacher. The second section contains a list of statutes dealing with vows and ritual purity, guidelines for community assemblies, the selection of judges, and the duties of the Guardian, who controlled the admission and instruction of new members.

DAMU \'dä-ˌmü\, in MESOPOTAMIAN RELIGION, Sumerian deity, city god of Girsu on the Euphrates River near Ur in the southern orchards region. Damu, son of Enki (Akkadian: EA), was a vegetation god, especially of the vernal flowing of the sap of trees and plants. His name means "the child," and his cult—apparently celebrated primarily by women—centered on the lamentation and search for Damu, who had lain under the bark of his nurse, the cedar tree, and had disappeared. The search ended when he reappeared out of the river.

The cult of Damu influenced and later blended with the similar cult of DUMUZI the Shepherd, a Sumerian deity worshiped by the central grasslands people. A different deity called Damu was a goddess of healing and the daughter of Nininsina of Isin.

DAN \'dan\, one of the 12 tribes of Israel that in biblical times constituted the people of ISRAEL. The tribe was named after the first of two sons born to JACOB (also called Israel) and Bilhah, the maidservant of Jacob's second wife, Rachel (Genesis 30:5–6). Nine of the other 11 tribes were also named after sons of Jacob, while 2 bear the names of Jacob's grandsons, children of JOSEPH (Joshua 16:4).

After the death of MOSES, the Israelites were led into the promised land by JOSHUA, who divided the territory among the 12 tribes (Joshua 13–19). The portion assigned to the tribe of Dan was a region west of Jerusalem (Joshua 19:40–48). At least part of the tribe later moved to the extreme northeast and took the city of Laish, renaming it Dan (Genesis 14:14; Joshua 19:47; Judges 18). As the northernmost Israelite city, it became a point of reference in the familiar phrase "from Dan to Beersheba."

The great hero of the Danites was SAMSON, who warred against the Philistine invaders until his betrayal by DELILAH (Judges 13–16). Dan was one of the TEN LOST TRIBES OF ISRAEL, which disappeared from history after the Assyrian conquest of Israel in 721 BCE (2 Kings 17:5–6; 18:9–12).

DANA \'dä-nə\, in MAHĀYĀNA ("Greater Vehicle") BUDDHISM, one of the six virtues (PĀRAMITĀS), *dana* being the virtue of generosity (*dana-pāramitā*).

DANAË \'da-nə-ˌē\, in Greek legend, daughter of Acrisius, king of Argos. Her father, having been warned by an oracle that she would bear a son by whom he would be slain, confined Danaë in a brass tower. But ZEUS descended to her in a shower of gold, and she gave birth to PERSEUS, whereupon Acrisius placed her and her infant in a wooden box and threw them into the sea. They were finally driven ashore on the island of Seriphus, where they were picked up by a fisherman named Dictys. His brother Polydectes, who was king of the island, fell in love with Danaë and married her. According to another story, Perseus, on his return with the head of MEDUSA, finding his mother persecuted by Polydectes, turned him into stone and took Danaë back with him to Argos. Latin legend represented her as landing on the coast of Latium and marrying Pilumnus or Picumnus, from whom TURNUS, king of the Rutulians, was descended. Danaë formed the subject of tragedies by Aeschylus, Sophocles, Euripides, Livius Andronicus, and Naevius. She personifies the earth suffering from drought, on which the fertilizing rain descends from heaven.

DANAUS \'da-nā-əs\, in Greek mythology, son of Belus, king of Egypt, and twin brother of Aegyptus. Driven out of Egypt by his brother, he fled with his 50 daughters (the Danaïds) to Argos, where he became king. Soon thereafter the 50 sons of Aegyptus arrived in Argos, and Danaus was forced to consent to their marriage with his daughters. Danaus, however, commanded each daughter to slay her husband on the marriage night. They all obeyed except Hypermestra, who spared Lynceus. Being unable to find suitors for the other daughters, Danaus offered them in marriage to the youths of the district. (According to another story, Lynceus slew Danaus and his daughters and seized the throne of Argos.) In punishment for their crime the Danaïds were condemned to the endless task of filling with water a vessel that had no bottom.

DAN FODIO, USUMAN \dän-fō-'dē-ō\, *Usuman also spelled* Uthman, *or* Usman, *Arabic* ʿUthmān ibn Fūdī \ùth-'màn-,i-bən-fü-'dē\ (b. December 1754, Maratta, Gobir, Hausaland [now in Nigeria]—d. 1817, Sokoto, Fulani empire) Fulani mystic, philosopher, and revolutionary reformer who created a new Muslim state, the Fulani empire, in what is now northern Nigeria.

Usuman's father, Muhammad Fodiye, was a scholar from the Toronkawa clan, which had emigrated from Futa-Toro in Senegal about the 15th century. While still young, Usuman moved south with his family to Degel, where he studied the QURʾAN with his father. Subsequently he moved on to other scholar relatives, traveling from teacher to teacher and reading extensively in the Islamic sciences. One powerful intellectual and religious influence at this time was his teacher in the southern Saharan city of Agadez, Jibrīl ibn ʿUmar, a radical figure whom Usuman both respected and criticized and by whom he was admitted to the Qādirī and other SUFI orders.

About 1774–75 Usuman began his active life as a teacher, and for the next 12 years he combined study with peripatetic teaching and preaching in Kebbi and Gobir, followed by a further five years in Zamfara. During this latter period he visited Bawa, the SULTAN of Gobir, from whom he won important concessions for the local Muslim community (including his own freedom to propagate ISLAM); he also appears to have taught the future sultan Yunfa.

Throughout the 1780s and '90s Usuman's reputation increased, as did the size and importance of the community that looked to him for religious and political leadership. Particularly closely associated with him were his younger brother, Abdullahi, who was one of his first pupils, and his son, Muhammad Bello, both distinguished teachers and writers. Significant support appears to have come from the Hausa peasantry, whose economic and social grievances and experience of oppression under the existing dynasties stimulated millenarian hopes and led them to identify him with the MAHDĪ (the Muslim messianic deliverer). Although he rejected this identification, he did share and encourage their expectations.

During the 1790s a division developed between his substantial community and the Gobir ruling dynasty. About 1797–98 Sultan Nafata issued a proclamation forbidding any but the SHAYKH—as Usuman had come to be called—to preach, forbidding the conversion of sons from the religion of their fathers, and proscribing the use of turbans and veils. In 1802 Yunfa succeeded Nafata as sultan, but he did not improve the status of Usuman's community. In February 1804 the Shaykh carried out a HIJRA ("migration") to Gudu, 30 miles to the northwest, like the prophet Muhammad, whose biography he frequently noted as having close parallels with his own. There he was elected IMAM (leader), and the new caliphate was formally established.

During the next five years the Shaykh's primary interests were the conduct of the JIHAD ("holy war") and the organization of the caliphate. He did not himself take part in military expeditions, but he appointed commanders, encouraged the army, handled diplomatic questions, and wrote widely on problems relating to the jihad and its justification. On this his basic position was clear and rigorous: the sultan of Gobir had attacked the Muslims; therefore he was an unbeliever and as such must be fought; and anyone helping an unbeliever was also an unbeliever.

As regards the structure of the caliphate, the Shaykh attempted to establish an essentially simple, nonexploitative system. He limited the central bureaucracy to a loyal and honest vizier, judges, a chief of police, and a collector of taxes; and he left the local administration in the hands of governors (emirs) selected from the scholarly class for their learning, piety, integrity, and sense of justice.

By 1805–06 the Shaykh's caliphal authority was recognized by leaders of the Muslim communities in Katsina, Kano, Daura, and Zamfara. When Alkalawa, the Gobir capital, finally fell at the fourth assault in October 1808, the main military objectives of the jihad had been achieved.

Although the jihad had succeeded, Usuman believed the original objectives of the reforming movement had been largely forgotten. In 1809–10 Bello moved to Sokoto, making it his headquarters, and built a home for his father nearby at Sifawa, where he lived surrounded by 300 students. In 1812 the administration of the caliphate was reorganized, the Shaykh's two principal viziers, Abdullahi and Bello, taking responsibility for the western and eastern sectors, respectively. The Shaykh, though remaining formally CALIPH, returned to teaching and writing.

Usuman was the most important reforming leader of the western Sudan region in the early 19th century. His importance lies partly in the stimulus that he, as a *mujaddid,* or renewer of the faith, gave to Islam throughout the region and partly in his work as a teacher and intellectual. In the latter roles he was the focus of a network of students and the author of a large corpus of writings in Arabic and Fulani that covered most of the Islamic sciences and still enjoy wide circulation and influence. Lastly, Usuman's importance lies in his activities as founder of a *jamāʿa,* or Islamic community, the Sokoto caliphate, which brought the Hausa states and neighboring territories under a central administration for the first time in history.

DANU \'thȧ-,nü, 'dȧ-\, *also spelled* Dana \'thȧ-nə, 'dȧ-\, in CELTIC RELIGION the mother of the Gods. The Irish god-race was called the TUATHA DÉ DANANN or People of the Goddess Danu. Welsh texts also mention her as a mother of mythological figures. Danu is probably identical with Anu and should be seen in the context of several figures of Divine Mothers from the Celtic areas of the Continent.

DAPHNE \'daf-nē\, in Greek mythology, the personification of the laurel (Greek *daphnē*), whose leaves, formed into garlands, were particularly associated with APOLLO. Traditionally, the special position of the laurel was connected with Apollo's love for Daphne, the beautiful daughter of a river god (probably Ladon) who lived in either Thessaly, the Peloponnese, or Syria. She rejected every lover, including Apollo. When the god pursued her, she prayed to the Earth or to her father to rescue her, whereupon she was transformed into a laurel. Daphne was also loved by Leucippus, who was killed because of Apollo's jealousy.

DAPHNEPHORIA \ˌdaf-nē-'fōr-ē-ə\, in GREEK RELIGION, festival held every ninth year at Thebes in Boeotia in honor of APOLLO Ismenius (after the Theban river called Ismenus) or Apollo Chalazius (god of hail). It consisted of a procession in which the chief figure was a boy who was of good family and whose parents were still alive. In front of the boy walked one of his nearest relatives, carrying an olive branch hung with laurel (*daphnē*) flowers and bronze balls and twined round with ribbons. Then followed the *Daphnēphoros* ("Laurel Bearer"), *i.e.*, the young priest of Apollo Ismenius. The *Daphnēphoros* also dedicated a bronze tripod in the temple of Apollo. According to tradition, the festival originated because of a vision sent to the Theban general Polematas, in which the Thebans were promised victory in their war against the Aeolians and the Pelasgians if the Daphnephoria were instituted.

DAPHNIS \'daf-nis\, legendary hero of the shepherds of Sicily and the reputed inventor of bucolic poetry. According to tradition, Daphnis was the son of HERMES and a Sicilian NYMPH and was found by shepherds in a grove of laurels (Greek *daphnē*). He later won the affection of a nymph, but, upon his proving unfaithful to her, she blinded him. Daphnis tried to console himself by playing the flute and singing shepherds' songs, but he soon died or was taken up to heaven by Hermes. According to Theocritus (fl. 270 BCE), Daphnis offended EROS and APHRODITE and, in return, was smitten with unrequited love; he died, although Aphrodite, moved by compassion, attempted to save him.

DĀR AL-ISLAM \där-ȧl-is-'lam\, in Islamic political ideology, the region in which ISLAM has ascendance; traditionally it has been matched with the Dār al-Ḥarb (abode of war), the region into which Islam could and should expand. This mental division of the world into two regions persisted even after Muslim political expansion had ended. *See* JIHAD.

DARAZĪ, MUHAMMAD IBN ISMĀʿĪL AL- \ȧl-ˌdar-a-'zē\ (b. Bukhara, Turkistan [now in Uzbekistan]—d. 1019/20), propagandist for the Ismāʿīlī sect of ISLAM and the man for whom the DRUZE religion is named.

Al-Darazī was probably at least part-Turkish and is believed to have traveled from Bukhara to Egypt as an Ismāʿīlī preacher in 1017/18. He gained favor with the Fāṭimid caliph AL-ḤĀKIM and, together with ḤAMZA IBN ʿALĪ and others, created a theology that was based upon the caliph's divinity. According to al-Darazī, the divine spirit that had been invested in ADAM had been transmitted through successive IMAMS to al-Ḥākim. When al-Darazī publicly proclaimed the doctrine in the principal mosque of Cairo, rioting ensued that probably led to his death. The Druze religion was named for al-Darazī because his preaching gave him preeminence among the founders, even though Ḥamza had led in organizing the movement.

DARBĀR SĀHIB: *see* GOLDEN TEMPLE.

DARDANUS \'där-də-nəs\, in Greek legend, the son of ZEUS and the Pleiad Electra, mythical founder of Dardania on the Hellespont. He was the ancestor of the Dardanians of the Troad. According to tradition, having slain his brother Iasius, or Iasion, Dardanus fled from Arcadia across the sea to Samothrace. When that island was visited by a flood, he crossed over to the Troad, a region surrounding Troy in Asia Minor. Being hospitably received by Teucer (ruler of Phrygia), he married Teucer's daughter Bateia and became the founder of the royal house of Troy.

DARQĀWĀ \där-'kä-wə\, brotherhood of SUFIS (Muslim mystics) founded in Morocco at the end of the 18th century by Mawlāy al-ʿArbī al-Darqāwī (c. 1737–1823). The order is an offshoot of the Shadhīlī Sufis; its doctrine is orthodox,

Apollo and Daphne, *sculpture by Gian Lorenzo Bernini, 1622–24; in the Borghese Gallery, Rome*
Scala—Art Resource

emphasizing devotion to, contemplation of, and union with God, attainable by frequent solitary prayer or in communal sessions where phrase repetition, poetry, song, and dance induce a state of ECSTASY. Members of the Darqāwā generally refuse to participate in public life. The order is found in Morocco, Algeria, Egypt, Lebanon, and Sri Lanka.

DARŚAN \'dər-shən, 'där-\, *also spelled (Hindi)* darshan, *Sanskrit* darśana ("viewing"), in Hindu worship, the beholding of a deity (especially in image form), revered person, or sacred object. The experience is often conceived to be intrinsically reciprocal and results in a blessing of the human viewer. The RATHAYĀTRĀS (car festivals), in which images of gods are taken in PROCESSION through the streets, enable even those who in former days were not allowed to enter the temple to have *darśan* of the deity. *Darśan* is also imparted by GURUS to their followers, by rulers to their subjects, and by objects of veneration such as PILGRIMAGE shrines to their visitors.

In Indian philosophy the term designates a point of view, the distinctive way in which each philosophical system looks at things, including its particular exposition of sacred SCRIPTURES and authoritative knowledge and its understanding of what constitutes proof. The orthodox account is that there are six such *darśan*s: *śankhya* and YOGA; NYĀYA and VAIŚEṢIKA; and MĪMĀMSĀ and VEDĀNTA. Other *darśan*s are also considered important, especially those of BUDDHISM and JAINISM.

DASAM GRANTH \'də-səm-'grən-tə, -'grənt\ (shortened version of Dasven Pātśah kā Granth; Punjabi: "Book of the Tenth Emperor"—*i.e.*, the tenth GURŪ, Gobind Singh), SIKH scriptural text that contains devotional hymns, biographical compositions associated with the life of Gurū GOBIND SINGH, a collection of legendary narratives, and miscellaneous fables. These are written in Braj Bhāṣā, Persian, Hindi, and Punjabi. The orthodox Sikh view attributes the entire corpus to Gurū Gobind Singh, but many scholars argue that a large part of the *Dasam Granth* was produced not by the Gurū himself but by others associated with his court at Anandpur.

The earliest extant manuscript of the *Dasam Granth* is dated 1713, and minor textual variations are found in the early manuscripts. An attempt was made to standardize the text in the 1890s, resulting eventually in the current print edition, a two-volume work containing 1,428 pages. The text is held in high reverence by Sikhs, owing especially to its connection with the tenth Gurū, the second most important figure in the tradition after Gurū NANAK. With the exception of a small set of compositions that have made their way into Sikh liturgy, however, Sikhs generally know little about the remaining contents. The better-known compositions in the *Dasam Granth* include the *Jāp Sāhib*, a meditation on the nature of God using his different names, the *Akāl Ustat*, a hymn in praise of God, the *Chaupai*, a hymn of supplication, and the *Zafar Nāmā*, Gurū Gobind Singh's letter of defiance addressed to the Mughal emperor Aurangzeb (reigned 1658–1707).

DASSEHRA \də-'shā-rä, -'sā-\, *also spelled* Dussehra, *or* Daśarā, series of Hindu festivals, involving PROCESSIONS, feasts, and dramatic recreations, celebrated at the time of the annual DURGĀ-PŪJĀ ("Worship of the Goddess"), from the first to the tenth days of the period of the waxing moon in the month of Āśvina (September/October), just at the end of the rainy season. The holiday centers around two mythological events, both having to do with the struggle of GOOD AND EVIL.

The first nine days of Dassehra, a period of the festival also known as Navarātrī-pūjā ("Nine-nights Worship"), are connected to the defeat of the buffalo-demon, Mahiṣa, by the great warrior goddess DURGĀ. Images of the goddess, depicted with ten arms in the act of killing the buffalo-demon, are ritually constructed, adorned, worshiped, paraded about, and finally disposed of in a river or other body of water. The sacrificing of goats or buffalo sometimes also accompanies this part of the festival.

The tenth day of the festival celebrates the defeat of the RĀVAṆA (a DEMON) at the hands of the god RĀMA and his army of monkeys. Figures of the two antagonists are erected on bamboo sticks, and the image of the demon is filled with firecrackers. At nightfall, the demon is exploded; the forces of good, embodied in Rāma, once more prevail.

DAVID \'dā-vid\ (b. Bethlehem, Judah—d. *c.* 962 BCE, Jerusalem), second of the Israelite kings, reigning *c.* 1000 to *c.* 962 BCE, who established a united kingdom over all ISRAEL. In Jewish tradition he became the ideal king around whose figure and reign clustered messianic expectations of the people of Israel and the later NEW TESTAMENT writers. He was also held in high esteem in the Islamic tradition.

An aide at the court of SAUL, Israel's first king, David was forced by Saul's jealousy to flee into southern JUDAH and Philistia, on the coastal plain of Palestine. He became the leader of other outlaws and refugees (1 Samuel 22:2; 27:1–12) and eventually had himself "invited" to become the successor to Saul as king (2 Samuel 2:1–4a; 5:1–5). David proceeded to conquer Jerusalem, held by the Jebusites, which he made the capital of the new united kingdom (2 Samuel 5:6–10; 1 Chronicles 11:4–9). He defeated the Philistines and annexed the coastal region and later became the overlord of many small kingdoms bordering on Israel, including Edom, Moab, and Ammon. David's reign lasted for about 40 years (2 Samuel 5:4; 1 Chronicles 29:27).

David's great success as a warrior was marred by family dissensions and political revolts. His third son, ABSALOM, murdered the eldest son, Amnon, and launched a rebellion that sent his father fleeing across the Jordan (2 Samuel 13:1–17:29). Eventually, Absalom's forces were defeated and he was killed (2 Samuel 18:15). Later David put down another revolt, this time by Sheba, the son of Bichri, of the tribe of BENJAMIN.

David was Israel's first successful king and was the founder of an enduring dynasty. He sought to win power over all Israel by establishing the city of Jerusalem as the center both of Israel's political power and of its worship (2 Samuel 6–7; 1 Chronicles 13; 16–17). On the political level this effort was not enough, for the kingdom was divided after the death of SOLOMON (1 Kings 11:26ff.; 2 Chronicles 10ff.); but on the religious and cultic level it did eventually succeed. Israel's God was named YAHWEH. David made this name the supreme name for deity in Jerusalem (previously perhaps "Salem"), to indicate his conquest of the city (2 Samuel 7:18–29; 1 Chronicles 17:16–27). All former names and titles of deity became attributes or titles of Yahweh—for example, EL 'Elyon (God Most High). While the Israelite name for God displaced all others, the substance of the worship remained similar; Yahweh was enthroned on ZION, and his king sat at his right hand as his regent.

In Israel's religious tradition the royal line, or "house," of David became a primary symbol of the bond between God and the nation; the king was the mediator between the deity and his people. The English word MESSIAH is derived from *hameshiach* ("the anointed one"), the title of the kings of the line of David (2 Samuel 1:14,16; 2:4; 5:3; 1 Kings 1:39). Thus, in later times of disaster, Israel began to wait for a new mediator of the power of God who would redeem the people and its land. By designating JESUS CHRIST as the son of David, CHRISTIANITY dramatized its conviction that this hope had been fulfilled.

DAVID, STAR OF, *Hebrew* Magen David ("Shield of David"), Magen *also spelled* Mogen, Jewish symbol composed of two overlaid equilateral triangles that form a six-pointed star. It appears on SYNAGOGUES, Jewish tombstones, and the flag of the State of Israel. The symbol—which historically was not limited to use by Jews—originated in antiquity, when it served as a magical sign or as a decoration. In the Middle Ages the Star of David appeared with greater frequency among Jews but did not assume any special religious significance; it is found as well on some medieval cathedrals. The term *Magen David*, which in Jewish liturgy signifies God as the protector (shield) of David, gained currency among medieval Jewish mystics, who attached magical powers to King DAVID'S shield just as earlier (non-Jewish) magical traditions had referred to the five-pointed star as the "seal of SOLOMON." Qabbalists popularized the use of the symbol as a protection against evil spirits. The Jewish community of Prague was the first to use the Star of David as its official symbol, and from the 17th century on the six-pointed star became the official seal of many Jewish communities and a general sign of JUDAISM, though it has no biblical or Talmudic authority. The star was almost universally adopted by Jews in the 19th-century as an emblem of Judaism. The yellow badge that Jews were forced to wear in Nazi-occupied Europe invested the Star of David with a symbolism indicating martyrdom and heroism.

DAYANAND SARASVATI \də-'yä-nən-də-,sə-rəs-'və-tē\, *also spelled* Dayanand Saraswati, *or* Dayānanda Sarasvatī, *original name* Mūla Śaṅkara (b. 1824, Tankāra, Gujarat, India—d. Oct. 30, 1883, Ajmer, Rajasthan), Hindu ascetic and social reformer who was the founder (1875) of the ARYA SAMAJ, a Hindu reform movement advocating a return to the temporal and spiritual authority of the VEDAS.

Dayanand received the education appropriate for a young Brahmin. At the age of 14 he accompanied his father on an all-night vigil at a SHIVA temple. While his father and some others fell asleep, mice, attracted by the offerings placed before the image of the deity, ran over the image, polluting it. The experience set off a profound revulsion in the young boy against what he considered to be senseless idol worship. His religious doubts were further intensified five years later by the death of a beloved uncle. In a search for a way to overcome the limits of mortality, he was directed first toward YOGA. Faced with the prospect of a marriage being arranged for him, he left home and joined the Sarasvatī branch of the Daśanāmi order of ascetics.

For the next 15 years (1845–60) he traveled throughout India in search of religious truth and finally became a disciple of Swami Birajanand, of Mathura. In 1863 Dayanand (the name taken by him at the time of his initiation as an ascetic) began preaching his vision of reinstating the purified VEDIC RELIGION that he considered to have existed in pre-Buddhist India.

Dayanand first attracted wide public attention for his views when he engaged in a public debate with orthodox Hindu scholars in Banaras (VARANASI) presided over by the maharaja of Banaras, but he also became well known for his debates with Christian missionaries. The first meeting establishing the Arya Samaj (Society of ARYANS [Nobles]) was held in Bombay on April 10, 1875. In 1877, in Banaras, he published his best-known work *Satyārth Prakāś* ("The Light of Truth"). Dayanand's zeal to restore the purity of Vedic practice created a theoretical framework that allowed him to espouse many important social reforms in the name of tradition; for example, he opposed child marriage (SATĪ) and strictures on the remarriage of widows as un-Vedic. He opened Vedic study to members of all CASTES and to women as part of a broader educational program in which he founded many educational and charitable institutions. The Arya Samaj also contributed greatly to the reawakening of a spirit of Indian nationalism in pre-Independence days.

Dayanand died after vigorous public criticism of a princely ruler, under circumstances suggesting that he might have been poisoned by one of the maharaja's supporters.

DAZHBOG \'däzh-,bōg\, Russian pre-christian deity. Dazhbog is mentioned in the *Kiev Chronicle* (*Povest vremennykh let*), a 12th- to 13th-century account of events and life in the Kievan state. The chronicle enumerates seven Russian pre-Christian divinities: PERUN, Volos, Khors, Dazhbog, STRIBOG, Simargla, and Mokosh. A Russian glossary to the 6th-century Byzantine writer John Malalas' *Chronographia* mentions a SVAROG, apparently the son of Dazhbog. Of all these figures only two, Perun and Svarog, are at all likely to have been common to all the Slavs.

DEADLY SIN, *also called* cardinal sin, any of the most serious class of SINS, usually numbering seven, dating to the early history of Christian MONASTICISM. A sin was classified as deadly not merely because it was a serious offense morally but because "it gives rise to others, especially in the manner of a final cause" or motivation (from the *Summa Theologica* of St. Thomas Aquinas). The traditional catalog is: (1) vainglory, or pride; (2) covetousness; (3) lust; (4) envy; (5) gluttony, which usually included drunkenness; (6) anger; and (7) sloth. The deadly sins were a popular theme in the morality plays and art of the Middle Ages.

DEAD SEA SCROLLS, several caches of ancient, mostly Hebrew, manuscripts found between 1947 and 1956 on the northwestern shore of the Dead Sea. These writings come from various sites and date from between 3rd century BCE and 2nd century CE. The term usually refers more specifically to manuscripts deposited in 11 caves in the vicinity of the ruins of QUMRĀN, which most scholars think was the home of a community to which the scrolls belonged. The relevant period of occupation of this site runs from *c.* 100 BCE to *c.* 68 CE, and the scrolls themselves nearly all date from 3rd to 1st century BCE. The 15,000 fragments (most of them tiny) represent the remains of between 800 to 900 original manuscripts. They are conventionally labeled by cave number and the first letter (or letters) of the Hebrew title—*e.g.*, 1QM = Cave 1, Qumrān, Milhamah (the Hebrew for "war"); or 4QTest = Cave 4, Qumrān, Testimonia (*i.e.*, a collection of proof-texts). Each manuscript has also been given an individual number.

The community at Qumrān has been identified with many Jewish sects of the time. Most scholars believe the community to have been ESSENES; some, however, believe them to have been a branch of SADDUCEES, or perhaps ZEALOTS. The group is believed to have fled, or been driven, to the Judean wilderness as a result of a dispute with the

Two columns of the Rule of the Community, *from the Dead Sea Scrolls*
By courtesy of the Palestine Archaeological Museum

priestly leaders in Jerusalem over the sacred calendar and matters of legal interpretation. At Qumrān this group not only preserved their beliefs but developed a sectarian worldview that rejected the rest of the Jewish people, espoused a highly dualistic view of the world (*i.e.*, sharply divided between GOOD AND EVIL, light and darkness), and looked for an imminent divine judgment of the wicked. They also cultivated a communal life of extreme ritual purity, necessitated by their rejection of the Temple cult. The history of this community may be glimpsed, though darkly, through the Scrolls. Calling itself the "Union," it was apparently founded by a messianic figure called the "Teacher of Righteousness." It may have been a splinter group from a wider movement. It offers a fascinating example of a Jewish messianic movement and a parallel to the early Christians. Other parallels between the two groups, such as certain teachings and a belief that SCRIPTURE foretold the history of their own times, have sometimes been thought to indicate a direct connection but can as easily be explained by the Jewish background common to both.

The importance of these texts, it has become clear, is that they represent a collection taken from a wider spectrum of Jewish belief and practice. A quarter of the texts are biblical manuscripts—to which can be added copies of works such as the books of Enoch, Jubilees, and Tobit, previously known and not thought to be sectarian (though in many cases it is difficult to be certain whether a particular text is sectarian or not). Thus, the scrolls tell about more than merely the sect that possessed them. Indeed, it has been argued that the Qumrān scrolls actually represent the contents of libraries from Jerusalem, hurriedly hidden shortly before the Roman siege of the city during the war of 66–73 and reflecting quite diverse Jewish origins. This is not an improbable explanation for the concealment of the scrolls, since the evidence connecting scrolls and the site of Qumrān is largely circumstantial, but the diversity of these scrolls is not as wide as this account would suggest. Clearly many scrolls do originate from outside the sect, and this realization makes the importance of the Scrolls to ancient JU-

DAISM even greater than if they were entirely sectarian.

The greatest interest remains with the sectarian writings, which can be classified as follows: (1) rules, or manuals, like the *Rule of the Community,* describing the doctrine, constitution, and regulations of the Union; and the War Scroll, which tells how the "children of light" finally conquer the "children of darkness"; (2) interpretations of biblical texts, such as commentaries on Isaiah, Habakkuk, Nahum, or Psalms; or groupings of texts by topic, such as the Florilegium or the MELCHIZEDEK Fragments—all of these typically relating scriptural passages to the sect and its times; (3) liturgical texts, including the *Songs of the Sabbath Sacrifice,* which focus on the angelic worship in the heavenly Temple (anticipating later Jewish mystical traditions), and the *Thanksgiving Hymns,* which express a powerful sense of human depravity redeemed through divine grace; (4) collections of laws, frequently dealing with cultic purity, such as the Halakhic Letter, the DAMASCUS DOCUMENT, and the Temple Scroll; and (5) ethical tracts (*e.g.*, several wisdom works, and the *Song of the Sage*).

This unique collection of sectarian and non-sectarian writings is the most important archive for late Second-Temple Judaism known. This is because it reflects the beliefs and practices of Jewish groups during a highly volatile period of Judean history. By contrast, the NEW TESTAMENT literature was written by and for both diaspora Jews and non-Jews; and the rabbinic writings stem from a later period and quite different circumstances.

Above all else, the Scrolls show the remarkable flexibility and variety of Jewish thought and practice, destroying any notion of a basically uniform "Judaism" at this time. They show that the notion of cultic holiness and sacrifice could be contemplated without the Temple, that different liturgical calendars (implying different times for festivals and different priestly rotas at the Temple) existed at the same time; that the distinction between ISRAEL and the GENTILES could be displaced by a notion of two predestined groups of saved and damned individuals; that the worship of the celestial Temple could be witnessed and described (foreshadowing a tradition of Jewish MYSTICISM); and that good works could replace sacrifice, even before the destruction of the Temple. But they also show what may have been more widely shared features of Judaisms of the period: a belief in the imminent culmination of history, the advent of a messianic figure, and the absolute necessity of complete obedience to the Law of Moses (however interpreted).

DEATH AND THE AFTERLIFE, complex of beliefs concerning death and its aftermath within various religions. For a description of many rituals surrounding death and its aftermath, *see* FUNERARY CUSTOMS.

Concepts of life and death. Belief in an afterlife is an idea with an extremely long history; there are Paleolithic burials dating as early as 50,000 BCE, indicating that various ideas were held about death and the state of the dead. The provision of these graves with food, ornaments, and tools implies a general belief that the dead continued to exist with the same needs as in this life. The fact that in Paleolithic burials the skeleton has often been found lying on

Monument to the Dead, *sculpture by Bartholomé, 1895; in the Père-Lachaise Cemetery, Paris*
Giraudon—Art Resource

Human substance and nature. The conception of death in most religions is closely related to the particular view held about the constitution of human nature. Two major traditions have provided the basic assumptions of religious eschatologies and have often found expression in mortuary rituals and funerary practice. In the integralistic view of human nature, the individual person is a psychophysical organism of which both the material and the nonmaterial constituents are essential. In this view death is the fatal shattering of personal existence. Although some element of the living person survives this disintegration, it has not been regarded as conserving the essential self or personality.

The consequences of this view can be seen in the beliefs concerning an afterlife of many religions. The ancient Mesopotamians and Greeks thought that after death only a shadowy wraith descended to the realm of the dead, where it existed miserably in dust and darkness. Similarly, in ancient JUDAISM the existence of the dead in *sheol* (the UNDERWORLD) was merely the shadow or echo of living. For most of the biblical writers this existence was without experience, either of God or of anything else.

Such a conception of humanity, in turn, has meant that, where the possibility of an effective afterlife has been envisaged, the idea of a reconstitution or RESURRECTION of the body has also often been involved; for it has been deemed essential to restore the psychophysical complex of personality. In ancient Egypt, provision was made for the eventual reconstitution in an elaborate mortuary ritual which included the mummification of the corpse to preserve it from disintegration. The early Jewish notion of *sheol*, along with the belief in the possibility of occasional miraculous restorations of dead individuals to life, provided a foothold for the later development of belief in the resurrection of the dead body at some time in the future.

The alternative view of human nature may be termed dualistic. It conceives of the individual person as comprising an inner, nonmaterial self or soul and a physical body. In many religions that expound this view of human nature, the soul is regarded as being essentially immortal and existing before the body was formed. At death the soul leaves the body, and its subsequent fate is determined by the manner in which it has fulfilled what the particular religion concerned has prescribed for the achievement of salvation. For example, Jewish apocalyptic literature developed a sharper distinction between body and soul than is evident in the biblical materials, and the latter was conceived of as existing separately in a disembodied state after death. Although at this point the doctrine of the resurrection of the body was not put aside, the shades of *sheol* came to be thought of as souls, and real personal survival—with continuity between life on earth and in *sheol*—was posited.

In some religions the soul's incarnation in the body is interpreted as a penalty incurred for some SIN or error com-

its side in a crouched position has sometimes been interpreted as evidence of belief in rebirth, since the posture of the corpse imitates the position of the child in the womb. The data, however, are sparse and difficult to interpret.

That death was sometimes regarded as transforming those who experienced it into a state of being different from—and sometimes even hostile to—that of those living in this world is evident in later mortuary rites and customs. Indeed, the proper performance of funerary rites was deemed essential by many peoples to enable the dead to depart to the place and condition in which they properly belonged. Failure to expedite their departure could have dangerous consequences. Many ancient Mesopotamian divinatory texts reveal a belief that disease and other misfortunes could be caused by dead persons deprived of proper burial. The idea that the dead had to cross some barrier that divided the land of the living from that of the dead also occurs in many religions: The Greeks and Romans believed that the dead were ferried across a river, the Acheron or STYX, by a boatman called CHARON, for whose payment a coin was placed in the mouth of the deceased; in ZOROASTRIANISM the dead cross the Bridge of the Requiter (Činvato Paratu). Bridges also figure in Muslim and Scandinavian eschatologies (speculations concerning the end of the world and the afterlife)—the Ṣirāṭ bridge and the bridge over the Gjöll River (Gjallarbrú)—and Christian folklore included a Brig o' Dread, or Brig o' Death.

It is significant that in few religions has death been regarded as a natural event. Instead, it has generally been viewed as resulting from the attack of some supernatural power or god. In Etruscan sepulchral art a fearsome being called Charun strikes the deathblow, and medieval Christian art depicted the skeletal figure of Death with a dart. In many mythologies death is represented as resulting from some primordial mischance. According to Christian theology, death entered the world through the ORIGINAL SIN committed by ADAM AND EVE, the progenitors of humankind.

mitted in primordial times or during the course of a previous incarnation. This view was taught in such mystical cults and philosophies of the Greco-Roman world as Orphism (an ancient Greek religious movement), GNOSTICISM (a system of thought that viewed spirit as good and matter as evil), Hermeticism (a Hellenistic esoteric occult movement), and MANICHAEISM (a system of thought founded by MANI in ancient Iran). It finds its most notable modern expression in HINDUISM and, in a subtly qualified sense, in BUDDHISM. Within these systems the idea of rebirth or REINCARNATION has inspired a cyclical view of time and produced esoteric explanations of how the soul becomes reborn into a physical body, whether human or animal.

Geography of the afterlife. The practice of burial may originally have prompted the idea that the dead lived beneath the ground. The mortuary cults of many peoples indicate that the dead were imagined as actually residing in their tombs and able to receive the offerings of food and drink made to them; *e.g.,* some graves in ancient Crete and UGARIT (Ras Shamra) were equipped with pottery conduits from the surface for LIBATIONS. Often, however, the grave has been thought of as an entrance to a vast, subterranean abode of the dead. In some religions this underworld has been conceived as an immense pit or cavern, dark and grim (*e.g., sheol,* the Mesopotamian *kur-nu-gi-a* ["land of no return"], the Greek HADES, and the Scandinavian HEL). Sometimes it is ruled by an awful monarch, such as the Mesopotamian god NERGAL, the Greek god Hades, or the YAMA of Hinduism and Buddhism. According to the view of human nature and destiny held in a particular religion, this underworld may be a gloomy, joyless place where the shades of all the dead merely survive, or it may be a place of awful torments where the damned suffer for their misdeeds.

In those religions in which the underworld has been conceived as a place of postmortem retribution, the idea of a separate abode of the blessed dead generally became necessary. Such an abode has various locations. In most religions it is imagined as being in the sky or in a divine realm beyond the sky (*e.g.,* in CHRISTIANITY, Gnosticism, Hinduism, and Buddhism); sometimes it has been conceived as the "Isles of the Blessed" (*e.g.,* in later Greek and Celtic mythology) or as a beautiful garden or paradise such as the *al-firdaws* of ISLAM. Christian eschatology, which came to conceive of both an immediate judgment and a final judgment, developed the idea of a PURGATORY where the dead expiated their venial sins in readiness for the final judgment. The 10 hells of Chinese Buddhist eschatology may be considered as purgatories, for in them the dead expiated their sins before being incarnated once more in this world.

Those religions that have taught the possibility of a happy afterlife have also generally devised forms of postmortem testing of merit for eternal bliss. In ancient Egypt the judgment of the dead finds graphic expression in the vignettes that illustrate the BOOK OF THE DEAD. The heart of the deceased is represented as being weighed against the symbol of MA'AT (Truth) in the presence of OSIRIS, the god of the dead. A monster named Am-mut (Eater of the Dead) awaits an adverse verdict. The judgment of the dead in other religions (*e.g.,* Christianity, Islam, Zoroastrianism, Orphism) is basically a test of orthodoxy or ritual status, although moral qualities were included to varying degrees.

Means of approach to the underworld. The idea that the dead had to make a journey to the underworld, to which they belonged, finds expression in many religions. The oldest evidence occurs in the Egyptian PYRAMID TEXTS (*c.* 2375–*c.* 2200 BCE). The journey is conceived in various images. The dead pharaoh flies up to heaven to join the sun god RE in his solar boat on his unceasing voyage across the sky; or he joins the circumpolar stars, known as the "Imperishable Ones"; or he ascends a ladder to join the gods in heaven. Later Egyptian funerary texts depict the way to the next world as beset by awful perils: fearsome monsters, lakes of fire, gates that cannot be passed except by the use of magical formulas, and a sinister ferryman who must be thwarted. Ancient Mesopotamian literature records the visit of the goddess ISHTAR to the realm of the dead, the way to which was barred by gates. At each gate the goddess was deprived of some article of clothing, so that she was naked when she finally came before ERESHKIGAL, the queen of the underworld. The stripping-off of her clothing may have represented the decomposition of the corpse.

Such myths most likely reflect a feeling that the dead cease to belong to the world of the living; they have become uncanny and dangerous, and their departure to the world of the dead must be expedited. To assist these journeys, various aids have been provided. Thus, on some Egyptian COFFINS of the 11th dynasty a plan of the "Two Ways" to the underworld was painted, and from the New Kingdom period (*c.* 1567–1085 BCE) copies of the Book of the Dead, containing SPELLS for dealing with perils encountered en route, were placed in the tombs. Orphic communities in southern Italy and Crete provided their dead with instructions about the next world by inscribing them on gold laminae deposited in the graves. Advice about dying was given to medieval Christians in a book entitled *Ars moriendi* ("The Art of Dying") and to Tibetan Buddhists in the *Bardo Thödol* ("Book of the Dead"). Chinese Buddhists were informed in popular prints of what to expect as they passed after death through the 10 hells to their next incarnation. More practical equipment for the journey to the next world was provided for the Greek and Roman dead: In addition to the money to pay Charon for their passage across the Styx, they were also provided with honey cakes for Cerberus, the three-headed dog that guarded the entrance to Hades.

DEBORAH \'de-bə-rə, -brə \, prophet and heroine in the OLD TESTAMENT (Judges 4 and 5), who inspired the Israelites to a mighty victory over their Canaanite oppressors; the "Song of Deborah" (Judges 5), putatively composed by her, is perhaps the oldest section of the BIBLE and is of great importance for providing a contemporary glimpse of Israelite civilization in the 12th century BCE. According to rabbinic tradition, she was a keeper of TABERNACLE lamps.

The two narratives of her exploit, the prose account in Judges 4 and the martial poem comprising Judges 5, differ in important details. The most obvious discrepancy is in the identity of the chief foe of the Israelites. Judges 4 makes him Jabin, king of Hazor (present Tell el-Qedah, about 3 miles southwest of Ḥula Basin), though a prominent part is played by his commander in chief, Sisera of Harosheth-hagoiim (possibly Tell el-'Amr, approximately 12 miles northwest of Megiddo). In the poem Jabin does not appear, and Sisera is an independent king of CANAAN.

Assuming that the account preserved in Judges 5 is the older (probably written in 1125 BCE), the reader can reconstruct the actual history of the events. Israel holds the wilder parts of the country, the hills and the forests, but the Israelite settlements in the central range are cut off from those in the northern hills by a chain of Canaanite (or possibly Egyptian) fortresses down the Plain of Esdraelon (between Galilee and Samaria). At the instigation of Deborah, a charismatic counselor (or judge) and prophet, Barak gathers the tribes of EPHRAIM, BENJAMIN, Machir (MANASSEH), ZEBU-LUN, ISSACHAR, and his own tribe of NAPHTALI. ASHER, DAN, Gilead (GAD), and REUBEN remain aloof. JUDAH and SIMEON are not mentioned (attesting to the antiquity of the poem). The Israelite clans fall on the enemy at Taanach; a thunder-storm, in which Israel sees the coming of God from MOUNT SINAI, strikes terror into the Canaanites; their fabled 900 chariots of iron are useless on the sodden ground; and the Kishon River, swollen by torrential rains, sweeps away the fugitives. Sisera escapes on foot, pursued by Barak, taking refuge in the tent of Heber the KENITE (the Kenites, a no-madic tribe, were supposedly at peace with Canaan); he is offered protection by Heber's wife, Jael; as he drinks a bowl of milk, she pierces his head with a tent peg and kills him (thus fulfilling Deborah's prophecy—that "the Lord will sell Sisera into the hand of a woman").

DEE, JOHN \\'dē\\ (b. July 13, 1527, London, Eng.—d. December 1608, Mortlake, Surrey), English alchemist, astrolo-ger, and mathematician.

After lecturing and studying in Europe between 1547 and 1550, Dee returned to England in 1551 and was granted a pension by the government. Dee became astrologer to the queen, Mary Tudor, and shortly thereafter was imprisoned for being a magician but was released in 1555. Besides prac-ticing ASTROLOGY and horoscopy in the court of Elizabeth I, he also gave instruction and advice to pilots and navigators exploring the New World. He was asked to name a propi-tious day for Elizabeth's coronation, and he gave her les-sons in the mystical interpretation of his writings.

In 1570 the first English translation of Euclid's work ap-peared; although it is credited to Sir Henry Billingsley, who became sheriff and later lord mayor of London, Dee proba-bly wrote part or all of it. He certainly wrote the preface, which encouraged interest in the mathematical arts.

Dee later toured Poland and Bohemia (1583–89), giving exhibitions of magic at the courts of various princes. He be-came warden of Manchester College in 1595.

DEIRDRE \\'dir-drē, -drə; 'dar-drā\\, *Old Irish* Deirdriu, in early Irish literature, the gentle and fair heroine of *The Ex-ile of the Sons of Usliu* (*Longes Mac n-Uislenn*), the great love story of the ULSTER CYCLE. First composed in the 8th or 9th century, the story was revised and under the title *The Fate of the Sons of Uisnech* (*Oidheadh Chloinne Uis-neach*) was combined in the 15th century with *The Fate of the Children of Tuireann* (*Oidheadh Chloinne Tuireann*) and *The Fate of the Children of Lir* (*Oidheadh Chloinne Lir*) into *The Three Sorrows of Storytelling* (*Tri Truaighe Scéalaigheachta*). The older version, preserved in *The Book of Leinster* (*c.* 1160), is more starkly tragic, less polished, and less romantic than the later version. It describes a Dru-id's foretelling, at Deirdre's birth, that many men would die on her account. Raised in seclusion, she grew to be a wom-an of astonishing beauty. King CONCHOBAR MAC NESSA fell in love with her, but Deirdre fell in love with Noíse, son of Uisnech. They eloped and fled to Scotland, but Conchobar (untruly) promised them safety in Ireland, and so they re-turned. The sons of Uisnech were slain, causing revolt and bloodshed in Ulster. Deirdre took her own life rather than belong to Conchobar. (The later version omits the first half of the story and expands the tragic ending by making Deir-dre live for a year with Conchobar, never smiling, before killing herself.)

The story was immensely popular in Ireland and Scot-land and survived to the 20th century in Scottish Gaelic oral tradition; its influence continued into the 20th centu-ry, when the Anglo-Irish writers, notably William Butler Yeats and John Millington Synge, dramatized the theme.

DEISM \\'dē-,i-zəm, 'dā-\\, an unorthodox religious attitude that found expression especially among a group of English writers beginning with Edward Herbert in the first half of the 17th century and ending with Henry St. John, 1st Vis-count Bolingbroke, in the middle of the 18th century. In general, Deism refers to the acceptance of a certain body of religious knowledge that is inborn or that can be acquired by the use of reason, as opposed to knowledge acquired through revelation or the teaching of any church. The pro-ponents of NATURAL RELIGION were strongly influenced by faith in human reason, distrust of religious claims of reve-lation that lead to dogmatism and intolerance, and an im-age of God as the rational architect of an ordered world.

Renaissance humanism had rejected the orthodox Chris-tian emphasis upon the corruption of reason through SIN and had affirmed a general faith that reason could discern universal religious and moral truths apart from any super-natural revelation or specific church teachings. Similarly, Deists argued that within the world's religions and the var-ious Christian churches there was a common rational core of universally accepted religious and moral principles. The early Deists asserted that differences of ritual and dogma were insignificant and should be tolerated. By the turn of the 17th century, however, a number of Deists, notably John Toland, the Earl of Shaftesbury, Matthew Tindal, Tho-mas Woolston, and Anthony Collins, came to reject the li-turgical practices and institutional trappings of ROMAN CA-THOLICISM as analogous to ancient PAGAN superstition. In place of the noxious "enthusiasm" and strict individual pi-ety of the Protestant sects, they sought to promote the so-ber moral striving and tolerance of the religion of reason.

In place of the orthodox Judeo-Christian conception of God as involved actively in shaping and sustaining human history, the Deists argued that after God's initial work of creation, he withdrew into detached transcendence, leaving the world to operate according to rational natural rules. Borrowing upon the prestige of Isaac Newton's vision of the universe as a mechanism obeying stable rational laws, they propounded variations on the classic argument from design wherein the existence of a rational creator is inferred from the evidence of the ordering of the world.

By the end of the 18th century, in addition to becoming a dominant religious attitude among English, French, and German intellectuals, Deism had crossed the Atlantic to shape the religious views of upper-class Americans. The first three presidents of the United States all subscribed to Deist beliefs.

DELIA \\'dē-lē-ə\\, quadrennial festival of the Ionians, held on Delos (hence the name) in honor of the Greek god APOL-LO. The local title was Apollonia. It later declined along with the political importance of Ionia but was revived in 426 BCE by the Athenians as part of their imperial policy.

DELILAH \\də-'lī-lə\\, in the OLD TESTAMENT, a central figure in the story of SAMSON (Judges 16). She was a Philistine who, bribed to entrap Samson, coaxed him into revealing that the secret of his strength was his long hair, whereupon she betrayed him to his enemies.

DELPHI \\'del-,fī\\, seat of the most important ancient Greek temple and oracle of APOLLO. It lay in the territory of Phocis on the steep lower slope of Mount Parnassus, about six miles from the Gulf of Corinth. Delphi was considered in ancient GREEK RELIGION to be the center of the world. According to ancient myth, ZEUS released two eagles, one from the east, the other from the west, and caused them to fly toward the center. They met at Delphi, and the spot was marked by a stone in the temple; this stone was known as the omphalos (navel). According to legend, the oracle at Delphi originally belonged to GAEA, the Earth goddess, and was guarded by the serpent PYTHON; later, Apollo slew Python and founded his own oracle there.

Delphi has been continuously inhabited from late Mycenaean times (14th century BCE), but its history really begins in the 6th century BCE, when the Sacred War of about 590 BCE destroyed the nearby town of Crisa, which had been taxing pilgrims, and opened free access to Delphi. The Delphic oracle was consulted not only on private matters but also on affairs of state, and its utterances often swayed national policy. It was also consulted whenever a colony was to be sent out from Greece proper, and so its fame spread to the limits of the Greek-speaking world.

In Roman times Delphi was frequently pillaged; Nero is said to have removed 500 statues from the vicinity. With the spread of CHRISTIANITY, the old SANCTUARY of Delphi fell

Ruins of the temple of Apollo at Delphi
Gianni Tortoli—Photo Researchers

Delilah shears Samson's locks; French manuscript illumination, c. 1250
The Granger Collection

into decay. Julian the Apostate attempted to restore the temple in the mid-4th century CE, but with little success.

The temple sanctuary was a large, roughly rectangular area enclosed by a wall. A sacred way lined with monuments and treasuries wound up through the sanctuary to the temple of Apollo itself. The monuments along the way were offerings to Apollo erected by states or individuals in thanks for favors bestowed by the god. The existing temple, of which only the foundation and some steps and a few columns are preserved, was built in the 4th century BCE. The Delphic oracle was in a chamber at the rear of the temple. Two earlier temples of Apollo on the site are known from their actual remains. Of the first, dating from about 600 BCE, some archaic capitals and wall blocks are preserved. This temple was burned in 548 BCE. Of the second temple, built at the end of the 6th century BCE, many wall blocks and some pediment sculptures are extant.

DEMA DEITY \ˈdā-mə\, any of several mythical ancestral beings of the Marind-Anim of southern New Guinea, the center of a body of mythology in which the decisive act is the slaying of a *dema* (ancestral) deity by the ancestral tribe. This act brings about the transition from the ancestral world to the human one. In many ancient myths, the creation of humans and their particular attributes—sexuality, the cultivation of food, and death—is a decisive break with the previous mode of existence, which was characterized by asexual reproduction, the spontaneous production of food, and immortality.

The most widely quoted example of such myths is the Ceramese (from Ceram, Indonesia) myth of Hainuwele, quoted by the Danish anthropologist Adolf E. Jensen. In this myth, a *dema* man named Amenta found a coconut speared on a boar's tusk and in a dream was instructed to plant it. In six days a palm had sprung from the nut and flowered. Amenta cut his finger and dripped his blood on the blossom. Nine days later a girl grew asexually from the blossom, and in three more days she became sexually mature. Amenta named her Hainuwele, which means Coconut Branch. During a major religious festival Hainuwele stood in the midst of the dance grounds and excreted valuable objects. After nine days of this activity, the *dema* men dug a hole in the middle of the dance ground, threw Hainuwele in, and danced the ground firm on top of her. Amenta dug up her corpse, dismembered it, and planted the pieces. These pieces gave birth to plant species previously unknown, especially tubers, which have since been the Ceramese's chief food. Another *dema* goddess forced the *dema* men to go through a labyrinth. Some became ordinary mortals; others changed into animals and spirits.

This mythic complex is characteristic of the culture of many tuber cultivators. The motif of death and dismemberment appears to reflect the fact that a tuber must be cut up and the pieces buried in order to be propagated.

DEMETER \di-'mē-tər\, in GREEK RELIGION, daughter of the deities CRONUS and RHEA, sister and consort of ZEUS, and goddess of agriculture.

Demeter is rarely mentioned by Homer, nor is she included among the Olympian gods, but she is probably an ancient goddess. Her primary myth centered on the story of her daughter PERSEPHONE, who was abducted by HADES. Demeter went in search of Persephone and, during her journey, revealed her secret rites to the people of Eleusis, who had hospitably received her. Her distress at her daughter's disappearance was said to have diverted her attention from the harvest and caused a famine. In addition to Zeus, Demeter had a consort, IASION (a Cretan), to whom she bore Plutus (Wealth; *i.e.*, abundant produce of the soil).

Demeter appeared most commonly as a grain goddess. The influence of Demeter, however, was not limited to grain but extended to vegetation generally and to all the fruits of the earth, except the bean. In that wider sense Demeter was akin to GAEA (Earth), with whom she had several epithets in common, and was sometimes identified with the GREAT MOTHER OF THE GODS (Rhea, or Cybele).

Another important aspect of Demeter was that of a divinity of the Underworld; she was worshiped as such at Sparta, and especially at the festival of Chthonia at Hermione in Argolis, where a cow was sacrificed by four old women. The epithets Erinys ("Raging") and Melaina ("the Black One") as applied to Demeter were localized in Arcadia and stress the darker side of her character.

Demeter also appeared as a goddess of health, birth, and marriage. A certain number of political and ethnic titles were assigned to her, the most important being Amphiktyonis, as patron goddess of the Amphictyonic League, well known in connection with the temple at DELPHI.

Among the agrarian festivals held in honor of Demeter were the following: (1) Haloa, apparently derived from *halōs* ("threshing floor"), begun at Athens and finished at Eleusis, where there was a threshing floor of Triptolemus, her first priest and inventor of agriculture; it was held in the month Poseideon (December). (2) Chloia, the festival of the grain beginning to sprout, held at Eleusis in the early spring (Anthesterion) in honor of Demeter Chloë ("the

Demeter of Cnidus, sculpture from the mid-4th century BCE

Green"), the goddess of growing vegetation. This festival is to be distinguished from the later sacrifice of a ram to the same goddess on the sixth of the month Thargelion, probably intended as an act of propitiation. (3) Proerosia, at which prayers were offered for an abundant harvest, before the land was plowed for sowing. It was also called Proarktouria, an indication that it was held before the rising of Arcturus. The festival took place, probably sometime in September, at Eleusis. (4) Thalysia, a thanksgiving festival held in autumn after the harvest in the island of Cos. (5) The THESMOPHORIA, a women's festival meant to improve the fruitfulness of the seed grain. (6) The Skirophoria held in midsummer, a companion festival.

Her attributes were connected chiefly with her character as goddess of agriculture and vegetation—ears of grain, the mystic basket filled with flowers, grain, and fruit of all kinds. The pig was her favorite animal, and as a chthonian (underworld) deity she was accompanied by a snake. In Greek art Demeter resembled HERA, but she was more matronly and of milder expression; her form was broader and fuller. She was sometimes riding in a chariot drawn by horses or dragons, sometimes walking, or sometimes seated upon a throne, alone or with her daughter.

DEMIGOD (male), *female* demigoddess, mythological being with more power than a mortal but less than a god.

DEMIURGE \'de-mē-,ərj\, *plural* Demiourgoi, a subordinate god who fashions and arranges the physical world. Plato adapted the term, which in ancient Greece had originally been the ordinary word for "craftsman" or "artisan," and which in the 5th century BCE had come to designate certain magistrates or elected officials.

Plato used the term in the dialogue *Timaeus*, an exposition of COSMOLOGY in which the Demiurge is the agent who takes the preexisting materials of CHAOS, arranges them according to the models of eternal forms, and produces all the physical things of the world, including human bodies. The Demiurge is sometimes thought of as the Platonic personification of active reason. The term was later adopted by some of the GNOSTICS, who, in their dualistic worldview, saw the Demiurge as one of the forces of evil, who was responsible for the creation of the despised material world and was wholly alien to the supreme God of goodness.

DEMON, *also spelled* daemon, from the Greek *daimōn*, in religions worldwide, any of numerous beings, powers, or principles that mediate between gods and humans.

In ancient Greece a *daimōn* was a supernatural power, and the term was employed almost interchangeably by Homer with *theos*, for a god, though *theos* emphasized the personality of a particular god, whereas *daimōn* referred to a more general, indistinct divine force. Hence, the term was regularly applied to sudden or unexpected supernatural interventions not attributable to any particular deity. It became commonly the power determining a person's fate, and an individual could have a personal *daimōn*. As early as Hesiod, the dead of the Golden Age became *daimōn*s; and later philosophical speculation envisaged them as lower than the gods (possibly mortal) but as superior to humanity.

In ZOROASTRIANISM, a hierarchy of demons (daevas) is headed by Angra Mainyu (later called AHRIMAN), the Evil, or Destructive, Spirit. The demons are in constant battle with AHURA MAZDĀ (later called Ormazd), the Good Lord. The hierarchy of demons in JUDAISM, which is rooted in ancient Middle Eastern and Zoroastrian demonology after the postexilic period (after 538 BCE), is quite varied. In Judaism, evil beings—in Hebrew *shedim*, meaning "demons" and applied to foreign gods, or *se'irim*, meaning "hairy demons"—often were believed to inhabit desert wastes, ruins, and graves and to inflict humanity with various physical, psychological, and spiritual disorders. The prince of these demons was called by different names: SATAN (the Antagonist), Belial (the spirit of perversion, darkness, and destruction), Mastema (Enmity, or Opposition), and others. Though the OLD TESTAMENT refers to Satan as the prosecutor of God's celestial court (Zechariah 3; Job 1–2), a hierarchy of demons under Satan or other princes of evil was developed in intertestamental literature and later Judaism.

The hierarchy of demons in CHRISTIANITY is based on various sources: Jewish, Zoroastrian, gnostic, and the indigenous religions that succumbed to Christian missionizing. In the NEW TESTAMENT, Jesus speaks of BEELZEBUB as the chief of demons and equates him with Satan. In the European Middle Ages and the REFORMATION period, various hierarchies of demons were developed, such as that associated with the seven DEADLY SINS: LUCIFER (pride), Mammon (avarice), ASMODEUS (lechery), Satan (anger), Beelzebub (gluttony), Leviathan (envy), and Belphegor (sloth).

In ISLAM the hierarchy of demons is headed by IBLĪS (the devil), who also is called *Shayṭān* (Satan) or *'aduw Allāh* ("Enemy of God"). Based to a great extent on Jewish and Christian demonology, Iblīs became the leader of a host of JINN, spiritual beings that generally bode evil.

In HINDUISM, the ASURAS (the Zoroastrian *ahura*s) are the demons who oppose the DEVAS (the gods). Among the various classes of *asura*s are *nāga*s (serpent demons), Ahi (the demon of drought), and Kaṃsa (an archdemon). Demons that afflict humans include the *rākṣasa*s (grotesque beings

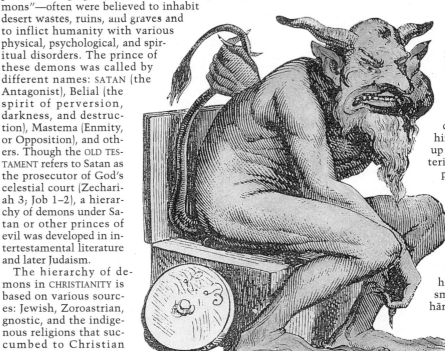

Belphegor, a biblical demon, French wood engraving, 19th century
The Granger Collection

who haunt cemeteries, impel the performance of foolish acts, and attack *sadhu*s (saintly men) and *piśaca*s (beings who haunt places where violent deaths have occurred).

Buddhists often view their demons as forces that inhibit the achievement of NIRVANA (bliss, or the extinction of desire); an important example is MĀRA, an arch tempter, who, with his daughters, Rati (Desire), Rāga (Pleasure), and Tanhā (Restlessness), attempted to dissuade Siddhārtha Gautama, the BUDDHA, from achieving his enlightenment. As MAHĀYĀNA (Greater Vehicle) Buddhism spread to Tibet, China, and Japan, many of the demons of the folk religions of these areas (*e.g.*, the Chinese *kuei-shen*; the Japanese *oni*) were incorporated into Buddhist beliefs.

DEMOPHON \'de-mə-ˌfän\, *also spelled* Demophoon, in Greek mythology, the son of Celeus, king of Eleusis. The goddess DEMETER, wandering in search of her daughter PERSEPHONE, became Demophon's nurse. She attempted to immortalize him by burning out his mortal parts but was surprised in the act by his mother, who thought that she was harming the boy. Incensed, Demeter quickly withdrew the child from the fire, thus leaving him susceptible to death; he grew up to be the first priest of her Mysteries. In another version the surprise resulted in Demophon's death in the flames.

DEOBAND SCHOOL \'dā-ə-ˌbənd\, *Urdu* Dār al-'Ulūm ("House of Learning"), the leading center of Islamic learning (MADRASA) in India. It was founded in 1867 by Muhammad 'Ābid Ḥusayn in the small town of Deoband in the Sahāranpur district of Uttar Pradesh. The theological position of Deoband is heavily influenced by the 18th-century Muslim reformer Shāh Walī Allāh and the early 19th-century Indian Wahhābīya. During the anti-British independence movement (1905–47), Deobandīs generally opposed partition of the country into Hindu and Muslim states. The school also inspired the Tablighī Jamā'at, a grassroots Muslim missionary movement of the 1920s.

The program of studies is highly traditional, stressing Ḥanafī jurisprudence (FIQH), Qur'ānic EXEGESIS (TAFSĪR), the study of traditions (HADITH), scholastic theology (KALĀM), and philosophy (*falsafa*). Modern disciplines are ignored, on the grounds that they are not relevant to a proper knowledge of ISLAM and can lead to sinful innovation (BID'A). Popular Muslim practices and beliefs are studied only in order to purify them of unorthodox accretions, but links with "sober" SUFI orders are maintained.

Deoband's enrollment of about 1,500 students represents all parts of the Muslim world. The *madrasa* boasts a library of 67,000 printed books and manuscripts in Arabic, Persian, and Urdu. A mosque, lecture halls, and student residences further serve the scholarly community. Its graduates have succeeded in establishing thousands of other Deobandī schools throughout the subcontinent.

DEREKH ERETZ \'der-e_k_-'er-ets\ (Hebrew: "correct conduct," or "way of the land"), *also spelled* Derekh Erez, in JUDAISM, decorum, dignified behavior, and gentlemanly conduct. Rabbinic scholars have applied the notion to all aspects of family life and marriage, to the qualities expected of a scholar, and to relationships between friends. *Derekh Eretz* applies also to one's manner of speaking, of eating, and of dressing and imposes on everyone the obligation of supporting himself so that others will not be unduly burdened. *Derekh Eretz* manifests itself in politeness toward others, whoever they be, and in genuine concern for their welfare. Two independent treatises on the subject are appended to the Babylonian Talmud (TALMUD BAVLI): *Derekh Eretz Rabba* ("the Great") and *Derekh Eretz Zuṭa'* ("the Minor").

DERVISH, *Arabic* darwīsh, any member of a Sufi fraternity, or *ṭariqa*. Within the Sufi fraternities, which were first organized in the 12th century, an established leadership and a prescribed discipline obliged the dervish postulant to serve his SHAYKH, or master, and to establish a rapport with him.

Dervishes
Culver Pictures

The postulant was also expected to learn the *silsila*, the spiritual line of descent of his fraternity.

The rituals of the Sufi brotherhoods stress the dervishes' attainment of hypnotic states and ecstatic trances through the DHIKR, the repeated recitation of a devotional formula in praise of God, and through such physical exertions as whirling and dancing. Dervishes can be either resident in community or lay members, both of these groups being generally drawn from the lower classes. In the Middle Ages, dervish communities played a vital role in religious, social, and political life in the central Islamic lands, but their monasteries now are often under government control, and their theological standing is discounted by orthodox theologians.

A wandering or MENDICANT dervish is called a FAKIR (Arabic: *faqīr*, "poor"). In mystical usage, the word refers to the human spiritual need for God, who alone is self-sufficient. Although of Muslim origin, the term has come to be applied in India to Hindus as well. Fakirs are generally regarded as holy men who are possessed of miraculous powers, such as the ability to walk on fire. While less influential in urban areas since the spread of education and technology, fakirs retain some hold over the people of the villages and the interior of India. Among Muslims the leading Sufi orders of fakirs are the CHISHTĪYA, QĀDIRĪYA, NAQSHBANDĪYA, and SUHRAWARDĪYA.

DEUCALION \dü-'kā-lē-,än, dyü-\, in Greek myth, the son of Prometheus, king of Phthia in Thessaly, and husband of Pyrrha; he was also the father of HELLEN, the mythical ancestor of the Greek race.

When ZEUS, the king of the gods, resolved to destroy all humanity by a flood, Deucalion constructed an ark in which, according to one version, he and his wife rode out the flood and landed on Mount Parnassus. Offering sacrifice and inquiring how to renew the human race, they were ordered to cast behind them the bones of their mother. The couple correctly interpreted this to mean they should throw behind them the stones of the hillside ("mother earth"), and did so. Those stones thrown by Deucalion became men, while those thrown by Pyrrha became women.

DEUS OTIOSUS \'dē-əs-,ō-shē-'ō-səs\ (Latin: "inactive god"), in the history of religions and philosophy, a HIGH GOD who has withdrawn from the immediate details of the governing of the world. The god has delegated all work on earth to ancestors or nature spirits, who act as mediators between the god and humans. This concept of god occurs widely in Africa, Melanesia, and South America.

In Western philosophy, the *deus otiosus* concept has been attributed to DEISM, a 17th–18th-century Western rationalistic religio-philosophical movement, in its view of a nonintervening creator of the universe. Although this stark interpretation was accepted by very few deists, many of their antagonists attempted to force them into the position of stating that after the original act of creation God virtually withdrew and refrained from interfering in the processes of nature and human affairs.

DEUTEROCANONICAL BOOKS \,dü-tə-rō-kə-'nä-ni-kəl, ,dyü-\, biblical literature accepted in the Roman Catholic and Eastern Orthodox canon but treated as APOCRYPHA by Jewish and Protestant canons; also, an authentic biblical work added to the canon later.

DEUTERONOMIC REFORM \,dü-tə-rə-'nä-mik, ,dyü-\, great religious reformation instituted in the reign of King JOSIAH of JUDAH (c. 640–609 BCE). It was so called because the book of the Law found in the TEMPLE OF JERUSALEM (c. 622 BCE), which was the basis of the reform, is considered by some scholars to be the same as the law code in the book of Deuteronomy (chapters 12–26). The reform consisted of removing PAGAN altars and idols from the Temple, destroying rural sanctuaries and fertility cults, and centralizing worship at the Temple of Jerusalem.

DEUTERONOMIST SOURCE \,dü-tə-'rä-nə-mist, ,dyü-\, *abbreviated* D, one of the hypothetical sources of a portion of the PENTATEUCH (the first five books of both the Jewish and the Christian BIBLES)—in particular, the source of the book of Deuteronomy, as well as JOSHUA, Judges, 1 and 2 Samuel, and 1 and 2 Kings. D uses a distinctive vocabulary and style of exhortation to call for Israel's conformity with the laws of Yahweh's COVENANT and to stress YAHWEH's election of ISRAEL as his special people.

In the name of MOSES, D states, "Here is God's law, which you will keep as your side of the contract that God made with you in bringing you out of Egypt and into the promised land." The book of Deuteronomy in its earliest phase came to light toward the end of the 7th century BCE, about 620, some 35 years prior to the destruction of the First TEMPLE OF JERUSALEM. At that time, Israel had spent more than a generation under Assyrian domination and was only just emerging from that cultural influence. The message of Deuteronomy and the books that flow from it, as stated by W. Lee Humphreys, is this: "Israel had prospered when it was loyal to the covenant and had suffered when it was disloyal. This pattern is revealed in the framework that was used to bind together the once separate stories about the federation's tribes and judges in the Book of Judges. . . . Loyalty to Yahweh and his stipulations brings life and security, gifts of the god who first called Israel into being from Egyptian slavery. Disloyalty will result only in death." *See also* ELOHIST SOURCE; YAHWIST SOURCE; PRIESTLY CODE.

DEVA \'dā-və, 'dē-\, *Iranian* daeva (Sanskrit: "divine"), in the VEDIC RELIGION of India, one of many divine powers, roughly divided on the basis of their identification with the forces of nature into sky, air, and earth divinities (*e.g.*, VARUṆA, INDRA, SOMA). In the monotheistic systems that emerged by the Late Vedic period, the *deva*s became subordinate to the one supreme being. During the Vedic period the gods were divided into two classes, the *deva*s and the ASURAS (in Avestan, *daeva*s and *ahura*s). In India the *deva*s came to be more powerful than the *asura*s, and the latter word eventually took on the meaning of DEMON. In Iran the reverse took place, and the *daeva*s were denounced as demons by ZOROASTER.

Buddhist COSMOLOGY posits the existence of three realms, in which the realm of the *devatā*s (gods and goddesses) is the highest of the six *gatis*, or destinies, of the lowest realm, the *kāmā-dhātu* ("realm of desire"). Within this destiny there are many heavens, each inhabited by many deities. Mythologically the most important are the Tuṣita Heaven where the future Buddha, MAITREYA, awaits the time for his coming to Earth; the Heaven of the Thirty-Three Gods, which is presided over by Inda (Sanskrit: INDRA; a deity sometimes called Sakka [Sanskrit: Śakra]); and the Heaven of the Four Guardian Kings, who are important protective deities in many Buddhist contexts.

DEVADĀSĪ \ˌdā-və-'dä-sē\ (Sanskrit: "female servant of a god"), group of women who dedicated themselves to the service of the patron god of the great temples in eastern and southern India.

This order or CASTE appears to date from the 9th and 10th centuries. The women attended the god—fanned the icon, honored it with lights, and sang and danced for the god's amusement—thus offering to the deity their auspicious presence. They played an important part in preserving elements of Hindu culture, for example, performing the great Sanskrit poem *Gītagovinda* for its hero KRISHNA in the temple dedicated to him in Puri. Devadāsīs' sons and daughters had equal rights of inheritance, an unusual practice among Hindu castes. Until the 20th century they were quite visible; about 1800 the main temple of Kanchipuram (Con-

jeeveram) had 100 Devadāsīs. As their occupation also involved temple prostitution, they came to be held in low social regard and have now largely disappeared.

DEVADATTA \ˌdā-və-'dət-tə\ (fl. 6th century BCE, India), Buddhist monk who sought to reform the SANGHA. Tradition relates that he was a cousin of the BUDDHA GOTAMA.

Devadatta is said to have joined the *sangha* in the 20th year of Gotama's ministry. Years later Devadatta proposed that the Buddha retire and hand over the leadership to him. This proposal was rejected, and Devadatta is said to have made three abortive attempts to bring about the death of the Buddha. The stories relate that Devadatta, sensing popular approval, proposed stricter ascetic rules for the *sangha* and when these were refused, he persuaded some 500 of the Buddha's followers to join in a secession. Nothing further is known about Devadatta's movement, but it may possibly be referred to under the name of the Gotamakas in the *Aṅguttara Nikāya* (a canonical text), for Devadatta's family name was Gotama.

DEVEQUT \ˌde-ve-'kùt\ (Hebrew: "attachment"), in Judaic QABBALAH texts, an adherence to or communion with God that stops short of mystical union. The notion of *devequt* apparently derived from the biblical reference to "loving the Lord your God, walking in all his ways, and holding fast to him" (Deuteronomy 11:22). As a fundamental concept of the Qabbalah, *devequt* was considered one of the three highest values and, for some, was equated with ECSTASY.

The Qabbalistic view of *devequt* as a privilege of the spiritual aristocracy was modified in HASIDISM, for, in its lower, or minor, stage, *devequt* found expression in the social sphere and was, in principle, open to every Hasid.

DEVĪ \'dā-vē\ (Sanskrit: "Goddess," "Lady," "Queen"), in HINDUISM, a general designation for "goddess," sometimes used as an honorific title for human women. The term has always been somewhat generic and is now often used in situations where it serves as a blanket designation for the local and often quite individual female divinities whose presences are felt in regions throughout India.

Historically, various goddesses are documented in the texts from the earliest layers of Hinduism. The VEDAS refer to goddesses who are associated with power, materiality, forces of nature, and speech, but not in a formulaic manner. Female energy in the forms of *prakṛti* ("matter"), *śakti* ("energy"), and MĀYĀ ("illusion") appear in later philosophical writings, but they are not thought of as being more than linguistically or abstractly feminine until the 5th and 6th centuries, when *purāṇic* texts such as the DEVĪ BHĀGAVATA PURĀṆA and the DEVĪ MĀHĀTMYA began to identify Devī, the Great Goddess, as the embodiment of matter, energy, and illusion. *See* ŚĀKTISM; DURGĀ; KĀLĪ.

DEVĪ BHĀGAVATA PURĀṆA \'dā-vē-'bä-gə-və-tə-pù-'rä-nə\, text of the devotional HINDUISM called ŚĀKTISM, in which the Great Goddess (Devī) is worshiped as primary. The *Devī Bhāgavata Purāṇa* is usually listed among the 18 "minor" or sectarian PURĀṆAS (encyclopedic compendiums whose topics range from COSMOGONY and COSMOLOGY to ritual instructions for worship of the gods). The date of its composition is unknown; scholars have dated it as early as the 6th century CE and as late as the 14th century. It was, in all probability, composed in Bengal, possibly over a period of time, by members of the local sect whose devotion centered on Devī.

The work is divided into 12 sections and 318 chapters. It opens (like other *Purāṇa*s) with an account of the creation of the universe—an act here attributed to Devī, who manifests herself in the form of three ŚAKTIS, or cosmic powers. The remainder of the text is largely given over to mythological accounts concerning various Hindu deities, usually featuring the Goddess (in one or another of her many manifestations), who is said to be the active force behind all the gods and the consort of the principal male divinities. The text also includes instructions for the worship of Devī and her sacred places and holy days, as well as various hymns and eulogies dedicated to her.

DEVĪ MĀHĀTMYA \'dā-vē-mə-'hät-myə\, Sanskrit text, written about the 5th or 6th century CE, that forms a portion of a larger work known as the *Mārkaṇḍeya-Purāṇa*. It is the first such text that revolves entirely around the figure of the Goddess (DEVĪ) as the primary deity.

While goddesses were worshiped in India before this period, the *Devī Māhātmya* is significant in that it is the earliest appearance in the high Sanskritic literary and religious tradition of a treatise in which the Goddess is elevated to a place of ultimate prominence. The work has been passed down as a self-contained text that is memorized and recited, word for word, as part of the religious practice of those Hindus who worship Devī as the highest divinity.

The *Devī Māhātmya* is also significant in that it regards various forms of the Goddess—ranging from the fearsome and dangerous KĀLĪ to the benign and gentle Śrī—as fundamentally unified. Chief among these forms is DURGĀ, a warrior figure whose salvific actions are recounted in this work. Durgā is depicted as aiding male deities, energizing them for the task of slaying the DEMONS. She is also active in her own right, most famously in her battle with the great buffalo-demon Mahiṣāsura. Durgā is described as having many arms, each of which wields a weapon, and riding a fierce lion. Although a conquering warrior, Durgā is also portrayed as beautiful and is sometimes referred to as "Mother," which displays the many-sided nature of this goddess.

DEVIL (from Greek: *diabolos*, "slanderer," or "accuser"), the spirit or power of evil. Though sometimes used for minor demonic spirits, the word devil generally refers to the prince of evil spirits and as such takes various forms in Western religions.

In the monotheistic Western religions, the devil is viewed as a fallen ANGEL who in pride has tried to usurp the position of the one and only God. In JUDAISM, and later CHRISTIANITY, the devil was known as SATAN. In the OLD TES-

Lucifer's Descent into Hell, *illumination from Queen Mary's Psalter*

TAMENT, Satan is viewed as the prosecutor of Yahweh's court, as in Job, chapters 1 and 2, but he is not regarded as an adversary of God. In postbiblical Judaism and in Christianity, however, Satan became known as the "prince of devils" and assumed various names: BEELZEBUB ("Lord of Flies") in Matthew 12:24–27, often cited as Beelzebul ("Lord of Dung"), and LUCIFER (the fallen angel of Light).

In Christian theology the devil's main task is to tempt humans to reject the way of life and redemption and to accept the way of death and destruction. The leader of the angels who have fallen from heaven because of pride, Satan has as his main adversary in legend and iconography the ARCHANGEL Michael, leader of God's heavenly hosts.

The theology of ISLAM is rich in references to IBLĪS, the personal name of the devil, who is also known as *ash-Shayṭān* ("The Demon") and *'aduw Allāh* ("Enemy of God"). Iblīs is an angel, a *jinn* (spiritual creature capable of good or evil), or an angel who was the leader of the *jinni*. In the QUR'AN, Iblīs first appears in the story of the creation of the world. He alone of the angels refuses God's order to bow before Adam, the first man. He is then cursed by God; his punishment is to come on the Day of Judgment, but until then he is empowered to tempt the unfaithful (but not true believers). Iblīs next appears as the tempter of ADAM AND EVE in the GARDEN OF EDEN. The questions of his SINS of pride and disobedience are especially important in the SUFI traditions, in which he is sometimes presented as a true monotheist who would bow only to God.

DEVIL'S ADVOCATE, *Latin* advocatus diaboli, in the ROMAN CATHOLIC church, the promoter of the faith who critically examines the life of and miracles attributed to an individual proposed for BEATIFICATION or CANONIZATION. Popular usage of the term "devil's advocate" derives from the fact that his presentation of facts includes everything unfavorable to the candidate. Sixtus V formally established the office in 1587.

DEVOTIO MODERNA, religious movement within ROMAN CATHOLICISM from the end of the 14th to the 16th century stressing meditation and the inner life, attaching little importance to ritual and external works. *Devotio moderna* (Latin: "modern devotion") originated in the Netherlands and spread south within Europe. Two communities—the BRETHREN OF THE COMMON LIFE and the AUGUSTINIAN Canons at Windesheim (near Zwolle, Holland)—became the principal exponents of *Devotio moderna*. The IMITATION OF CHRIST, traditionally attributed to THOMAS À KEMPIS, is a classic expression of the movement.

DGE-LUGS-PA \'gä-lük-bä\, *also spelled* Gelukpa (Tibetan: "Model of Virtue"), *also called* Yellow Hat Sect, since the

17th century the predominant BUDDHIST order in Tibet and the sect of the DALAI and PANCHEN LAMAS.

The Dge-lugs-pa sect was founded in the late 14th century by TSONG-KHA-PA, a member of the austere Bka'-gdams-pa school. Tsong-kha-pa's reforms included strict monastic discipline; CELIBACY and the prohibition of alcohol and meat; a higher standard of learning for monks; and the use of Tantric and magical rites in moderation. Three large monasteries were quickly established near Lhasa: at Dga'ldan (Ganden) in 1409, 'Bras-spungs (Drepung) in 1416, and Se-ra in 1419. The abbots of the 'Bras-spungs monastery first received the title Dalai Lama in 1578, and a period of struggle for the leadership of Tibet followed, principally with the Karma-pa sect. The Dge-lugs-pa eventually appealed for help to the Mongol chief Güüshi Khan, who secured their authority in Tibet. They continued to rule through their leader, the Dalai Lama, until the Chinese communists took over the country in 1950. During a popular revolt at Lhasa in 1959 the Dalai Lama escaped to India.

The name Yellow Hat refers to the distinctive yellow headdress adopted by the Dge-lugs-pa to distinguish themselves from the Karma-pa sect, whose monks wear red hats.

DHAMMAPADA \ˌdə-mə-'pä-də\ (Pāli: "Words of Doctrine," or "Way of Truth"), probably the best-known book in the Pāli Buddhist canon. It is an anthology of basic BUDDHIST teachings (primarily ethical teachings) in a simple aphoristic style. As the second text in the *Khuddaka Nikāya* of the SUTTA PIṬAKA, the *Dhammapada* appears in somewhat different versions in Prākrit, Sanskrit, and Chinese, and there are translations in other languages. More than half the verses are excerpted from other canonical texts and include many of the most famous Buddhist sayings; others come from the storehouse of pithy sayings drawn upon by much of Indian literature. The book is popular in Buddhist countries of both THERAVĀDA and MAHĀYĀNA traditions. In Sri Lanka it has been used for centuries as a manual for novices, and it is said that every monk can recite it from memory.

DHĀRAṆĪ \'där-ə-ˌnē\, in BUDDHISM and HINDUISM, a sacred verse of great efficacy, used by a common person as a verbal protective device or talisman and by a yogi (spiritual adept) as a support or instrument for concentration. The *dhāraṇī* is a short summary of the essential doctrine contained in a much longer sacred text and serves as an aid to its retention. Properly recited, the *dhāraṇī* conveys the same merit as reading the entire work. The meaning of a *dhāraṇī* is often very difficult to determine. A *dhāraṇī* may sound to the uninitiated like a string of meaningless words, but its accuracy is in fact carefully guarded when passed on from teacher to pupil. *Compare* MANTRA.

DHARMA \'dər-mə, 'där-\ (Sanskrit: "that which is established," thence "religion," "custom," "law," or "duty"), *Pāli* dhamma, key concept with multiple meanings in HINDUISM, BUDDHISM, and JAINISM.

In Hinduism dharma is the religious and moral law governing individual and group conduct and one of the four ends of life. One of its distinctive features is its contextual sensitivity. Although certain aspects of dharma are regarded as universal and perennial, others are to be followed according to one's class, status, and station in life. It constitutes the subject matter of the DHARMA SUTRAS, religious manuals that are the earliest source of Hindu law, and in the course of time was extended into lengthy compilations of law and custom, the DHARMA ŚĀSTRAS. The best-known *Dharma Śāstra* is the so-called *Laws of Manu*, which had become authoritative by the early centuries CE, but it remains a question whether it ever functioned in actual judicial practice until British authorities integrated certain aspects of it into colonial law.

In Buddhism, dharma is the universal truth common to all individuals at all times, as discovered and proclaimed by the BUDDHA GOTAMA. Dharma, the Buddha, and the SANGHA (the Buddhist monastic order) make up the TRIRATNA, or "three jewels," the primary sources of Buddhist doctrine and practice. In Buddhist metaphysics the term in the plural (dharmas) is used to describe the interrelated elements that make up the empirical world.

In Jain philosophy dharma, in addition to being commonly understood as moral virtue, also has the meaning—unique to Jainism—of an eternal "substance" (*dravya*), the supporting medium that allows beings to move.

DHARMAGUPTA \ˌdər-mə-'gȯp-tə, ˌdär-\, one of the so-called "18 schools" of Indian BUDDHISM. Named after the school's purported founder, the Dharmaguptakas (followers of Dharmagupta) were descendants of the Sthaviravāda lineage, which came into existence after the first major division of the Buddhist community. The Dharmaguptakas appear to have split away from the Mahīśāsaka school over a dispute concerning whether the BUDDHA GOTAMA should be considered a member of the monastic community or whether he stood outside of the community entirely. The Dharmaguptakas maintained that the Buddha was separate from the monastic community, and, as a result, gifts given to him alone would produce great merit. Similarly, the Dharmaguptakas also held that honoring Buddhist STUPAS, which often housed the corporeal remains of the Buddha or a fragment of a Buddhist text, produced much merit.

The Dharmaguptakas played a key role in the transmission of Buddhism through Central Asia, and there is evidence that the school was established in that region by the 3rd century CE. In addition, the Dharmaguptakas were important in the development of early Chinese Buddhism, and their *vinaya* (monastic rules) achieved a prominent place as the basis for MONASTICISM in many, if not all, centers of early Chinese Buddhism. Toward the middle of the 7th century the Chinese pilgrim HSÜAN-TSANG made his famous PILGRIMAGE to India in search of Buddhist SCRIPTURES. He wrote that the Dharmaguptaka *vinaya* was one of five *vinaya* still being studied among Buddhist practitioners he encountered, although the school's immediate followers were virtually nonexistent. As a result, by this time, the Dharmaguptakas had ceased to be an important Buddhist sect in India, surpassed by the growing number of SARVĀSTIVĀDIN, MAHĀSAṄGHIKA, and MAHĀYĀNA practitioners.

DHARMAKĪRTI \ˌdər-mə-'kir-tē, ˌdär-\ (fl. 7th century), Indian Buddhist philosopher and logician. He asserted that inference and direct perception are the only valid kinds of knowledge. According to him, the object of inference is the universal (*sāmānyalakṣaṇa*) and the object of perception—which may be perceived by the five senses, by the mind, by self-consciousness, or by the practice of YOGA—is the pure particular (*svalakṣaṇa*). Dharmakīrti claimed that every person is a transitory being and, in his turn, assumes the continuous existence of an individual.

DHARMA ŚĀSTRA \'dər-mə-'shäs-trə, 'där-\, *also spelled* Dharmaśastra, *or* Dharmashastra, *Sanskrit* Dharma-śāstra

("Teachings on Proper Conduct"), ancient Indian body of jurisprudence that survives in the family law of Hindus living in territories outside India (*e.g.*, Pakistan, Malaysia, East Africa) and has broader scope, subject to legislative modification, in India itself. *Dharma Śastra* is not primarily concerned with legal administration, though courts and their procedures are dealt with comprehensively, but with the right course of conduct in every dilemma. Some basic principles of Dharma Śastra are known to most Hindus brought up in a traditional environment. These include the principles that duties are more significant than rights, that women are under perpetual guardianship of their closest male relatives, and that the king (*i.e.*, the state) must protect the subjects from all harm, moral as well as material.

The *Dharma Śastra* literature, written in Sanskrit, exceeds 5,000 titles. It can be divided into three categories: (1) SŪTRAS (terse maxims); (2) SMṚTIS (shorter or longer treatises in stanzas); and (3) *nibandha*s (digests of *smṛti* verses from various quarters) and *vṛtti*s (commentaries upon individual continuous *smṛti*s). The *nibandha*s and *vṛtti*s are juridical works intended for legal advisers and exhibit much skill in harmonizing divergent *sūtra*s and *smṛti*s.

The techniques of the *Dharma Śastra* are mainly to state the ancient text, maxim, or stanza and to explain its meaning (where obscure), and to reconcile divergent traditions, if necessary by use of the traditional science of interpretation (MĪMĀṂSĀ). Where possible, *Dharma Śastra* permits custom to be enforced, if it can be ascertained and if its terms are not repugnant to the principles of life as understood by BRAHMINS (those of the priestly class). Brahmin ethics have given *Dharma Śastra* its color and provided a test under which many customs of the Hindu peoples could be administered by Hindu kings.

Dharma Śastra is equal in age to Jewish law, but its sources are more varied and less codified. It differs from Roman law in these respects but especially in its greater continuity and longevity. The British colonial administration in India affected the system of Hindu law by applying the traditional rules in a hard-and-fast way and by introducing the concept of precedent. Rapid social change, following foreign rule, required many adjustments to India's body of Hindu law. There was, for example, no provision in the *Dharma Śastra* for the development of judicial divorce or the allotting of equal shares to daughters along with sons in their fathers' estate at his death. Hence, first piecemeal and later comprehensive legislation, in 1955–56, altered the system of Indian law administered in the courts. Gradually, as judges lost familiarity with Sanskrit, the ancient texts began to be replaced with contemporary, cosmopolitan juridical and social concepts.

DHARMA SUTRA

DHARMA SUTRA \ˌdər-mə-'sü-trə, ˌdär-\, *Sanskrit* Dharma-sūtra ("text on dharma"), in HINDUISM, any of several manuals of human conduct that form the earliest body of religious law. They consist chiefly of strings (SŪTRA) of terse rules regarding human beings in their social, economic, and religious relations. Formulated in prose, they were intended to be committed to memory and expounded orally by teachers. Eventually these rules came to be interspersed with stanzaic verses in various meters, each generally giving the substance of the rule immediately preceding it. The verses themselves became increasingly popular and ultimately led to the appearance of works entirely in verse. These metrical versions of previously existing *Dharma Sutra*s came to be called DHARMA ŚASTRAS, though in modern times that term more commonly is used to denote the

whole body of customary rules and observances governing Hindu religious and social life.

DHARMA-ṬHĀKUR \'dər-mə-'tä-kûr, 'där-\, *also called* Dharma-Rāy, folk deity of eastern India of complex characteristics and obscure origins. Dharma-Ṭhākur is worshiped as the "high god" of a large number of villages of Raṛh, a region that comprises the greater part of modern West Bengal state. Dharma-Ṭhākur has no prescribed form; he is worshiped in the form of stones, as a wooden votive slab, or through a pair of wooden sandals. Among other attributes he is a fertility god and a healer of disease. Worship of him is correlated with SUN WORSHIP, and his annual worship, known as Dharma-pūjā, has been described as a kind of sympathetic magic to bring on the monsoon rains.

Scholars are not agreed on the origins of this worship. Some find in the deity and his worship a degenerate form of the Buddha and Buddhism; others trace the cult and deity to either pre-Aryan or tribal sources. Among the neighboring literate tribal peoples there are a number of cult practices and deities that share some of the characteristics of Dharma-Ṭhākur and his cult. The majesty and exploits of Dharma-Ṭhākur are presented in a major class of works in Bengali literature known as *Dharma-maṅgal*.

DHIKR \'thi-kər\, *also spelled* zikr \'zi-kər\ (Arabic: "remembrance," or "mention"), ritual prayer or litany practiced by Muslim mystics (SUFIS) to glorify God and achieve spiritual perfection. Based on the Qur'anic injunctions "Remind yourself [*udhkur*] of your Lord when you forget" (Qur'an 18:24) and "O you who believe! Remember [*udhkurū*] God often" (Qur'an 33:41), the *dhikr* is essentially a "remembering" of God by the frequent repetition of his names. Originally a simple recitation of the QUR'AN and various religious writings among ascetics and mystics, the *dhikr* gradually became a formula (*e.g.*, *lā ilāha illa 'llāh*, "there is no god but God"; *Allāhu akbar*, "God is greatest"; *al-ḥamdu lī'llāh*, "praise be to God"; *astaghfiru 'llāh*, "I ask God's forgiveness," *Allāh*; or simply *hū*, "He"), repeated aloud or softly, accompanied by prescribed posture and breathing. As the Sufi brotherhoods (ṬARĪQAS) were established, each adopted a particular *dhikr*, to be recited in solitude following each of the five obligatory daily prayers or as a community. The *ṭarīqa*s usually traced their litanies back to MUHAMMAD or one of his Companions through a chain of spiritual authorities. The *dhikr*, like *fikr* (meditation), is a method the Sufi may use to achieve oneness with God.

DHIMMA \'thi-mə\ (Arabic: "protection"), in ISLAM, protected status of non-Muslims within a Muslim state. Strictly speaking, such status is open only to the "People of the Book"—*i.e.*, Jews, Christians, and Zoroastrians. Dhimmis are not citizens, but they are guaranteed the right to life and property and are allowed to practice their religion, though a special tax is often levied and they may be subject to other legal restrictions. The institution has been the basis of official religious toleration within Islamic states.

ḌHOLĀ \dō-'lä\, *also called* Nal Purāṇa, oral epic that is sung in various Hindi dialects in honor of the goddess ŚAKTI and is performed in the western portion of Uttar Pradesh, as well as in parts of Rajasthan, Punjab, and Madhya Pradesh. Two major themes run through *Ḍholā*: the use of Śakta subjects (*see* ŚAKTISM) and the incorporation and validation of a much wider range of CASTE and gender images than is common in the dominant Sanskrit epics. Telling the story of Rājā Nal, his wives Motinī and Damayantī, and his son Ḍholā, the epic incorporates Śākta elements, for it is the goddess who responds to the devotion of the human actors and resolves the many problems encountered by its human heroes. Another Śākta element is the tantric magic of Nāth yogis that is used by the heroines as they work to resolve the conflicts created by their men. Caste and gender images reflect the multi-caste peasant farming communities where the epic is popular; Rājā Nal's friend and helper is a Gūjar (a herding caste), while as the epic unfolds, Rājā Nal is given or takes on various disguises, as a trader, an acrobat, an oil presser, a charioteer, a cripple, and a woman. These elements in the epic speak to its lower-caste singers (always male) and its rural audiences.

Ḍholā has recognizable narrative connections to the Nala-Damayantī story found in the MAHĀBHĀRATA as well as to the Rajasthani ballad known as Ḍholā-Mārū. Portions of the epic are found in chapbook literature, with some printed pieces dating to the late nineteenth century, but it is the oral performances, now also available on commercial tape cassettes, that are its primary form of transmission.

DHŪ AL-FAQĀR \ˌt͟hü-ál-fà-'kär\, in the mythology of ISLAM, the two-pointed magical sword that represents ʿALĪ, fourth CALIPH and son-in-law of MUHAMMAD. Originally owned by an unbeliever, al-ʿĀṣ ibn Munabbih, Dhū al-Faqār came into Muhammad's possession as booty from the BATTLE OF BADR (624). He in turn passed it on to ʿAlī, and the sword, said to have borne an inscription ending in the words *lā yuqtal Muslim bi-kāfir* ("no Muslim shall be slain for [the murder of] an unbeliever"), eventually rested with the ʿAbbāsid caliphs.

As ʿAlī's legendary status grew, the importance of his association with Dhū al-Faqār also increased. Particularly in legends surrounding the Battle of Ṣiffīn (657), Dhū al-Faqār, the two points of which were useful for blinding an enemy, is credited with enabling ʿAlī to decapitate or cut in half more than 500 men.

In Muslim countries, fine swords have traditionally been engraved with the phrase *lā sayfa illā Dhū al-Faqār* ("there is no sword but Dhū al-Faqār"), often with the addition *wa lā fatā illā ʿAlī* ("and there is no hero but ʿAlī").

DHYĀNADEV: *see* JÑĀNEŚVAR.

DHYĀNI-BUDDHA \'dyä-nē-ˌbùd-də, -ˌbü-də, -ˌbù-də\, in MAHĀYĀNA and VAJRAYĀNA (Tantric) BUDDHISM, any of a group of five "self-born" buddhas who have existed from the beginning of time, usually identified as VAIROCANA, AKṢOBHYA, Ratnasambhava, AMITĀBHA, and AMOGHASIDDHI.

The five are almost identically represented in art but are distinguished by characteristic colors, symbols, poses of hands, and the directions they face. Each of the five represents one of the five SKANDHAS, or mental and physical aggregates that make up the whole of cosmic as well as individual existence. Most of the other deities in the Buddhist pantheon are related to one of the five buddhas as members of his "family" and reflect his distinguishing characteristics, such as color, direction, and symbol. Each of the "self-born" buddhas is also said to have manifested himself as an earthly

buddha and as a BODHISATTVA. Each has his own consort, mount, sacred syllable, natural element, special sense organ and perception, and symbolic location in the human body.

In order to counter any tendency toward POLYTHEISM suggested by the fivefold scheme, some sects elevated one of the five, usually Vairocana, to the role of ĀDI-BUDDHA (first, or primal, Buddha). Sometimes a sixth deity is worshiped as the Ādi-Buddha. The Lamaist sects of Tibet identify the Ādi-Buddha as Vajradhara; some sects of Nepal give this role to Vajrasattva.

Dainichi Nyorai (Vairocana), wood sculpture by Unkei, 1175; in the Enjō-ji, Nara, Japan
Asuka-en

DIAMOND CUTTER SUTRA \'sü-trə\, *Sanskrit* Vajracchedikā-Sūtra, *Chinese* Chin-kang Ching, MAHĀYĀNA Buddhist text that is perhaps the best known of the 18 smaller "Wisdom" texts, which together with their commentaries are known as the PRAJÑĀPĀRAMITĀ. It takes the form of a dialogue between the BUDDHA GOTAMA as teacher and a disciple as questioner. The Chinese translation, *Chin-kang Ching* ("Diamond Sutra"), appeared about 400 CE.

The sutra expresses the *Prajñāpāramitā* emphasis upon the illusory nature of phenomena in these words: "Just as, in the vast ethereal sphere, stars and darkness, light and mirage, dew, foam, lightning, and clouds emerge, become visible, and vanish again, like the features of a dream—so everything endowed with an individual shape is to be regarded." As with most of the shorter (and later) *Prajñāpāramitā* texts, the ideas are not argued or explained but boldly stated, often in striking paradoxes. This, to some extent, is why the sutra is considered the Sanskrit work closest in spirit to the philosophy of ZEN.

Illustration and leaf from the Diamond Cutter Sutra

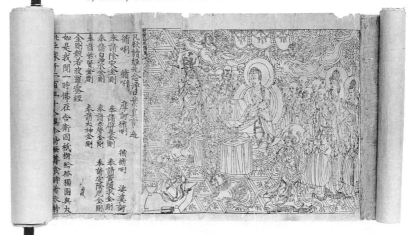

DIANA \dī-'a-nə\, in ROMAN RELIGION, goddess of wild animals and the hunt, virtually indistinguishable from the Greek goddess ARTEMIS. Her name is akin to the Latin words *dium* ("daylight sky") and *dius* ("lit by daylight"). She was also a goddess of domestic animals. As a fertility deity she was invoked by women to aid conception and delivery. There was probably no original connection between Diana and the moon, but she later absorbed Artemis' identification with both SELENE (Luna) and HECATE, a CHTHONIC (Underworld) deity; hence the characterization *triformis* sometimes used in Latin literature.

The most famous place of worship for the Italian goddess was the grove of Diana Nemorensis ("Diana of the Wood") on the shores of Lake Nemi at Aricia, near Rome. This was a shrine common to the cities of the Latin League. Associated with Diana at Aricia were EGERIA, the spirit of a nearby stream who shared with Diana the guardianship of childbirth, and the hero Virbius, who was said to have been the first priest of Diana's cult at Aricia.

At Rome the most important temple of Diana was on the Aventine. This temple housed the foundation charter of the Latin League and was said to date back to King Servius Tullius (6th century BCE). In her cult there Diana was also considered the protector of the lower classes, especially slaves; the Ides (13th) of August, her festival at Rome and Aricia, was a holiday for slaves. Another important center for the worship of Diana was at Ephesus, where the Temple of Artemis (or Diana) was one of the Seven Wonders of the World. In Roman art Diana usually appears as a huntress with bow and quiver, accompanied by a hound or deer.

Dido on her funeral pyre
Culver Pictures

DIAN CÉCHT \'dʸē-ən-'kʸākt\, one of the TUATHA DÉ DANANN, the gods of Celtic Ireland. He was the physician of the gods and father of Cian, who in turn was the father of the most important god, Lugh (*see* LUGUS). When NUADU, the king of the gods, had his hand cut off in the battle of MAG TUIRED, Dian Cécht fashioned him a silver hand that moved as well as a real hand. Dian Cécht's son Miach, however, was able to give Nuadu a functional human hand; Dian Cécht killed his son in a fit of jealousy.

Dian Cécht claimed to be able to restore any man who was mortally wounded. He did this by throwing the wounded into a well and pulling them out alive. This may refer to Celtic ritual involving ritual bathing or drowning.

DIASPORA, JEWISH \dī-'as-pə-rə, dē-\: *see* ISRAEL.

DIDACHĒ \'di-də-kē\ (Greek: "Teaching"), *also called* Teaching of the Twelve Apostles, the oldest surviving Christian church order, probably written in Egypt or Syria in the 2nd century. It presents a general program for instruction and initiation into the primitive church. Chapters 1–6 give ethical instruction concerning the two ways, of life and of death, and reflect an early Christian adaptation of a Jewish pattern of teaching in order to prepare CATECHUMENS (candidates for Christian BAPTISM). Chapters 7–15 discuss baptism, fasting, prayer, the EUCHARIST, how to receive and test traveling apostles and prophets, and the appointment of bishops and deacons. Chapter 16 considers the signs of the SECOND COMING of the Lord.

Some early Christian writers considered the *Didachē* to be canonical. It formed the basis of chapter 7 of the 4th-century APOSTOLIC CONSTITUTIONS, a collection of early Christian ecclesiastical law. It was known only through such references in early Christian works until a Greek manuscript of it, written in 1056, was discovered in Istanbul in 1873 by Philotheos Bryennios (1833–1914), an Eastern Church theologian and METROPOLITAN. From these discoveries, Bryennios published *The Teaching of the Twelve Apostles* (1883), with valuable notes of his own.

DIDO \'dī-dō\, *also called* Elissa \i-'li-sə\, in Greek legend, the reputed founder of Carthage, daughter of the Tyrian king Mutto (or Belus), and wife of Sychaeus (or Acerbas).

Her husband having been slain by her brother Pygmalion, Dido fled to the coast of Africa, where she purchased from a local chieftain, Iarbas, a piece of land on which she founded Carthage. The city soon prospered, and Iarbas sought Dido's hand in marriage. To escape from him, Dido constructed a funeral pyre, on which she stabbed herself before the people. Virgil, however, made Dido a contemporary of AENEAS, whose descendants founded Rome. Dido fell in love with Aeneas after his landing in Africa, and Virgil attributes her suicide to his abandonment of her at the command of JUPITER. Dido was identified with the Virgo Caelestis; *i.e.*, TANIT, the tutelary goddess of Carthage.

DIDYMA \'di-di-mə\, *also called* Didymi, or Branchidae, ancient SANCTUARY and seat of an oracle of APOLLO, located south of Miletus in modern Turkey. Before being plundered and burned by the Persians (*c.* 494 BCE), the sanctuary was in the charge of the Branchids, a priestly caste named after Branchus, a favorite youth of Apollo. After Alexander the Great conquered Miletus (334), the oracle was resanctified and the city administered the cult, annually electing a prophet. About 300 BCE the Milesians began to build a new temple, intended to be the largest in the Greek world. The annual festival held there, the Didymeia, became Panhellenic in the beginning of the 2nd century BCE.

DIEVS \\'dē-əfs\\ (Latvian), *also called* Debestēvs \\'de-bes-,tafs\\, *Lithuanian* Dievas \\'dʸē-'e-väs\\, *Old Prussian* Deivas, in BALTIC RELIGION, the sky god. Dievs and LAIMA, the goddess of human fate, determine human destiny and world order. Dievs is a wooer of SAULE, the sun. As pictured by the pre-Christian Balts, he is an Iron Age Baltic king who lives on a farmstead in the sky. Wearing a silver gown, pendants, and a sword, he occasionally rides down to earth, on horseback or in a chariot, to watch over farmers and their crops.

Dievs has two sons (Dieva dēli in Latvian; Dievo sūneliai in Lithuanian), who are known as the Heavenly Twins and the morning and evening stars. Like their Greek (DIOSCURI) and Vedic (Aśvins, or Nāsatyas) counterparts, Dieva dēli are skilled horsemen. They associate with Saules meita, the daughter of the sun, and when she is sinking into the sea with only her crown still visible, they come to her rescue.

In name, Dievs is cognate with the Vedic Dyaus-Pitṛ, the Latin Dies-piter (JUPITER), and the Greek ZEUS, denoting originally the bright daylight sky. The word *dievs* and its cognates were also used by the ancient Balts to denote god in general and in modern usage refer to the Christian God.

DIGAMBARA \\dē-'gəm-bə-rə\\ (Sanskrit: "Sky-clad"), in JAINISM, one of the two principal sects, whose ascetics, shunning all property, wear no clothes. The ascetics of the other sect, the ŚVETĀMBARA ("White-robed"), wear only simple white loincloths or robes.

The schism that gave rise to the two sects is traditionally said to have taken place following a migration of Jain monks southward from the Gaṅgā (Ganges) River or from Ujjain to Karnataka during a serious famine in the reign of Candragupta Maurya. Bhadrabāhu, the leader of the emigrants, insisted on the observance of nudity, thus following MAHĀVĪRA, the last of the Jain TĪRTHAṄKARAS (exemplars). Sthūlabhadra, the leader of the monks who remained behind in the north, allowed the wearing of white garments.

The philosophical doctrines of the two groups never significantly differed, and their members have continued to intermarry. Since the northern and southern branches lived at a distance from one another, however, variations in their ritual, mythology, and literature did arise. The most serious issue, the question of whether it was possible for a monk who owned property (*e.g.*, wore clothes) to achieve MOKṢA (spiritual release), led to the division into two sects in 80 CE (according to the Śvetāmbaras, 83 CE).

Other points of difference held by the Digambaras are (1) the belief that the perfect saint (*kevalin*) needs no food to stay alive, (2) the belief that Mahāvīra never married, (3) the view that no woman can reach *mokṣa* without being reborn as a man, and (4) the representation in their images of every Tīrthaṅkara as always naked, without ornaments, and with downcast eyes. Also, the Digambaras do not recognize the Śvetāmbara canon of religious texts but maintain that the early literature was gradually forgotten and lost completely by the 2nd century CE.

The Digambara influence on various political dynasties in southern India in roughly the 1st millennium CE was considerable, but it diminished in importance as devotional ŚAIVISM and VAIṢṆAVISM grew. The sect continues mainly in southern Maharashtra and Karnataka states.

DIGNĀGA \\dig-'nä-gə\\ (c. 480–540 CE), Buddhist logician and author of the *Pramāṇasamuccaya* ("Compendium of the Means of True Knowledge"), a work that laid the foundations of Buddhist logic. Dignāga gave a new definition of "perception": knowledge that is free from all conceptual constructions, including name and class concepts. In effect he regarded only pure sensation as perception. In his theory of inference he distinguished between inference for oneself and inference for the other and laid down three criteria of a valid middle term (*hetu*)—i.e., that it should "cover" the minor premise (*pakṣa*), be present in the similar instances (*sapakṣa*), and be absent in dissimilar instances (*vipakṣa*). In his *Hetucakra* ("The Wheel of 'Reason'"), Dignāga set up a matrix of nine types of middle terms, of which two yield valid conclusions, two contradictory, and the rest uncertain conclusions. Dignāga's tradition was further developed in the 7th century by DHARMAKĪRTI.

DĪKṢĀ \\'dēk-shä\\, rite of consecration that preceded the sacrifice in the VEDIC RELIGION of ancient India; in later and modern HINDUISM, the term denotes the initiation of a layman by his GURU (spiritual guide) into a religious sect.

In the SOMA sacrifices of the Vedic period, the lay sacrificer, after bathing, kept a daylong (in some cases up to a yearlong) silent vigil inside a special hut in front of a fire. He was dressed in garments of black antelope skin, which he also used to sit on, and at nightfall drank only cooked milk. The TAPAS (mystical heat that was a basis of all Indian ascetic practices) produced was considered to be a sign, and a means, of passing from the realm of the profane to that of the sacred. Like similar rites observed throughout the world, *dīkṣā* also carried with it the meaning of "rebirth," and the SCRIPTURES describing the ceremony made use of explicit symbolism, such as the "womb" of the hut.

At the end of the *soma* ritual, the sacrificer went through a reverse ceremony, the *avabhṛtha* ("concluding bath"), in which he again bathed, and his sacred garments, the ritual utensils, and the pressed shoots of the *soma* plant were all cast into the water.

In modern Hinduism, rites of consecration and initiation show many regional and sectarian variations. They are generally preceded by preparatory fasting, bathing, and dressing in new clothes and include in the act of initiation the placing of special marks on the body or forehead, taking on a new name, receiving from the preceptor a selected MANTRA (prayer formula), and worship.

DINAH \\'dī-nə\\, in the OLD TESTAMENT (Genesis 30:21; 34; 46:15), daughter of JACOB by Leah; Dinah was abducted and raped near the city of Shechem, by Shechem, son of Hamor the Hivite (the Hivites were a Canaanitish people). Because Shechem then wished to marry Dinah, Hamor suggested to Jacob that their two peoples initiate a policy of commercial and social intercourse. Dinah's brothers SIMEON and Levi pretended to agree to the marriage and the COVENANT if Shechem and all the other males of the city of Shechem were circumcised. After the operations, while the men were still weakened, Simeon and Levi attacked the city, killed all the males, and freed Dinah.

DĪN-I ILĀHĪ: *see* AKBAR.

DIOCESE \\'dī-ə-səs, -,sēs, -sēz\\, in some Christian churches, a territorial area administered by a BISHOP. The word originally referred to a governmental area in the Roman Empire, governed by an imperial VICAR. The original unit of ecclesiastical administration was the PARISH, which in the EASTERN ORTHODOX CHURCH still remains the designation of the area administered by the bishop, whereas the diocese is the larger area administered by the PATRIARCH. The use of these terms was fluid in the West until about the 13th century, from which time diocese meant the territory administered by a bishop. In the ROMAN CATHOLIC church only the pope can divide or merge dioceses or create new ones. All dioceses are divided into parishes, each with its own church; dioceses are also sometimes divided into rural deaneries, which contain several parishes.

DIOMEDES \,dī-ə-'mē-dēz\, in Greek legend, commander of 80 Argive ships and one of the most respected leaders in the Trojan War. His famous exploits include the wounding of APHRODITE, the slaughter of Rhesus and his Thracians, and seizure of the sacred image of the goddess ATHENA that protected Troy. After the war Diomedes returned home to find that his wife had been unfaithful (Aphrodite's punishment) and that his claim to the throne of Argos was disputed. He fled to Italy and founded Argyripa (later Arpi) in Apulia, eventually making peace with the Trojans. He was worshiped as a hero in Argos and Metapontum. According to Roman sources, his companions were turned into birds by Aphrodite, and, hostile to all but Greeks, they lived on the Isles of Diomedes off Apulia.

DIONE \dī-'ō-nē\, in Greek mythology, a consort and, in one remote region, cult partner of ZEUS, the king of the gods. Her name is the female form of Zeus. In the *Iliad* she is mentioned as the mother of the goddess APHRODITE by Zeus; in Hesiod's *Theogony*, however, she is simply identified as a daughter of OCEANUS. Other writers identified her as the mother of DIONYSUS.

DIONYSIUS THE AREOPAGITE \,dī-ə-'ni-shē-əs, -shəs; -'nī-sē-əs ... ,ar-ē-'ä-pə-,gīt\ (fl. 1st century CE), biblical figure, converted by St. PAUL THE APOSTLE at Athens (Acts 17:34), who acquired a notable posthumous reputation primarily through confusion with later Christians similarly named. In the 2nd century he was held to have been the first bishop of Athens.

About 500 CE, some writings were forged in his name: The so-called Pseudo-Dionysius, probably a Syrian monk, wrote a series of Greek treatises and letters for the purpose of uniting NEOPLATONIC philosophy with Christian theology and mystical experience. These writings established a Neoplatonic strain in medieval Christian doctrine and spirituality—especially in the Western Latin church—traces of which survive to the present time. Historical research has been unable to identify the author, who could have been one of several Christian writers familiar with the Neoplatonic system of the 5th-century Athenian Proclus.

The treatises "On the Divine Names," "On Mystical Theology,"

"On the Celestial Hierarchy," and "On the Ecclesiastical Hierarchy" comprise the bulk of the Dionysian corpus of writings, supplemented with 10 letters affecting a 1st-century primitive Christian atmosphere. Their doctrinal content forms a complete theology, covering the TRINITY and angelic world, the INCARNATION and redemption, and the last things (*see* ESCHATOLOGY), and provides a symbolic and mystical explanation of all that is. The system is essentially dialectical, or "crisis" (from the Greek word meaning "crossroads, decision"), theology—*i.e.*, the simultaneous affirmation and denial of paradox in any statement or concept relative to God. God's transcendence above all rational comprehension and categorical knowledge ultimately reduces any expression of the divinity to polar pairs of contraries: GRACE and judgment, freedom and necessity, being and nonbeing, time and eternity. The incarnation of the Word, or Son of God, in JESUS CHRIST, consequently, was the expression in the universe of the inexpressible, whereby the One enters into the world of multiplicity. Still, the human intellect can apply to God positive, analogous terms or names such as The Good, Unity, Trinity, Beauty, Love, Being, Life, Wisdom, or Intelligence, assuming that these are limited forms of communicating the incommunicable.

The "Divine Names" and "Mystical Theology" treat the nature and effects of CONTEMPLATIVE prayer—the disciplined abandonment of senses and intelligible forms to prepare for the immediate experience of "light from the divine darkness" and ecstatic union—in a manner and scope that make them indispensable to the history of Christian theology and piety. His treatises on the hierarchies, wherein he theorized that all that exists—the form of Christian society, the stages of prayer, and the angelic world—is structured as triads that are the images of the eternal Trinity, introduced a new meaning for the term hierarchy.

Dionysus, bas-relief sculpture; in the National Archaeological Museum, Naples
Alinari—Art Resource

DIONYSUS \,dī-ə-'nī-səs, -'nē-\, *also called* Bacchus \'ba-kəs, 'bä-\, *or (in Rome)* Liber, in GREEK RELIGION and in ROMAN RELIGION, a god of fruitfulness and vegetation, especially known as a god of wine and ecstatic dance. He was introduced to Greece from Thrace and Phrygia.

According to the most popular tradition, Dionysus was the son of ZEUS and SEMELE, a daughter of CADMUS (king of Thebes). HERA, the wife of Zeus, out of jealousy persuaded Semele to prove her lover's divinity by requesting him to appear in his real person. Zeus complied, but his power was too great for the mortal Semele, who was blasted with thunderbolts. Zeus, however, saved his son by sewing him up in his thigh, keeping him there until he reached maturity. Dionysus was then conveyed by the god HERMES to be brought up by bacchantes (Maenads, or Thyiads).

As Dionysus apparently represented the sap, juice, or lifeblood element in nature, lavish festal *or-*

gia (rites) called Dionysia (or BACCHANALIA) in his honor were widely instituted. According to tradition, Pentheus, king of Thebes, was torn to pieces by the bacchantes when he attempted to spy on their activities, while the Athenians were punished with impotence for dishonoring the god's cult. Forming *thyasi* (holy bands) and waving *thyrsoi* (fennel wands bound with vine leaves and tipped with ivy), the bacchantes danced by torchlight to the rhythm of the flute and the *tympanum*. While they were under the god's inspiration, they were believed to possess the ability to charm snakes and suckle animals, as well as preternatural strength that enabled them to tear living victims to pieces before indulging in a ritual feast (*omophagia*). The bacchantes hailed the god by his titles of Bromios (Thunderer), Taurokeros (Bull-Horned), or Tauroprosopos (Bull-Faced). The worship of Dionysus flourished in Asia Minor, particularly in Phrygia and Lydia, and his cult was closely associated with that of numerous Asiatic deities.

Although Dionysus was said to have descended to the UNDERWORLD to bring back his mother and was also associated with PERSEPHONE in southern Italy, any original connection between the god and the netherworld seems doubtful. He did, however, possess the gift of PROPHECY, and at DELPHI he was received by the PRIESTHOOD on almost equal terms with APOLLO. He had an oracle in Thrace and was later patron of a healing shrine at Amphicleia in Phocis.

The followers of Dionysus included spirits of fertility, such as the satyrs, and in his ritual the phallus was prominent. He often took on a animalistic shape and was associated with various animals. His personal attributes were an ivy wreath, the THYRSUS, and the kantharos, a large two-handled goblet. In early art he was represented as a bearded man, but later he was portrayed as youthful. Bacchic revels were a favorite subject with vase painters, though the private lodges of BACCHUS were rigorously suppressed throughout Italy by senatorial edict in 186 BCE.

DIOSCURI \,dī-ə-'skůr-ē, -'skyůr-; dī-'äs-kůr-ē, -kyůr-\ (from Greek: *Dioskouroi*, "Sons of Zeus"), *also called* Castor and Pollux, *or* Castor and Polydeuces, in Greek and Roman mythology, twin deities who aided shipwrecked sailors and received sacrifices for favorable winds. They were the children of LEDA and either ZEUS or Tyndareus, Leda's husband. According to some versions, Castor was the son of Tyndareus and thus a mortal, while Pollux was the son of Zeus.

The twins were renowned for their athletic ability. When Castor died, Pollux refused immortality in which his brother had no share. Zeus allowed them to remain together alternately in the heavens and the netherworld. Later he transformed them into the constellation Gemini.

The introduction of their cult at Rome goes back traditionally to 484 BCE. The building of their temple in the Forum followed a vow of Aulus Postumius at the battle of Lake Regillus, where, according to legend, the Dioscuri fought on the side of the Romans and carried the news of victory to Rome. In art the twins are represented as two youths, usually horsemen, holding spears and wearing helmets; their image appeared on early Roman coins.

DISCIPLES OF CHRIST, group of Protestant churches that originated in the religious revival movements of the American frontier in the early 19th century. The three major bodies are the Churches of Christ, the Christian Church (Disciples of Christ), and the Undenominational Fellowship of Christian Churches and Churches of Christ. Related churches exist outside the United States. All have attempt-

ed to restore what they believe to be the "ancient order" of the church and have repudiated "human creeds."

The Great Western Revival (1801) produced a variety of religious movements dedicated to overcoming the barriers of denominationalism through a return to primitive CHRISTIANITY. Two of these movements, located on the trans-Appalachian frontier and associated with the names of Thomas and ALEXANDER CAMPBELL and Barton W. Stone, merged in 1832 to become the Disciples of Christ. The new denomination grew rapidly with the frontier.

Despite the merger, the essential program of the Disciples—the unity of all Christians on the basis of NEW TESTAMENT faith and practice—failed to unite a divided PROTESTANTISM, and, in fact, proved to be divisive even within the movement. For the segment of Disciples that was to become the Churches of Christ, that platform meant that every aspect of faith, organization, and worship had to conform to New Testament prescription or precedent. Hence when societies for MISSIONS and for the publication of tracts appeared around 1849, and when churches began using reed organs during worship, charges of unscriptural innovation were raised. A division emerged during and after the American Civil War and was formally ratified by a request from the conservatives for a separate listing in the 1906 U.S. census (*see* CHRIST, CHURCH OF).

Following a very different path, the Christian Church (Disciples of Christ) gradually abandoned its primitivist platform and advocated instead a program of unity based on an already existing and generally recognized common faith in Christ. This branch of Disciples is the most widely known of the three. It participates in the National Council of Churches and the WORLD COUNCIL OF CHURCHES and generally supports the positions of these organizations. In 1985 the Disciples of Christ entered into an ecumenical partnership with the United Church of Christ.

While some congregations have experimented with liturgical forms, typical Christian Church worship still generally retains the basic elements of prayer, singing, preaching, and a weekly memorial observance of the Lord's Supper.

A number of congregations tracing their roots to the Disciples movement neither claim affiliation with the Christian Church (Disciples of Christ) denomination nor reject the use of musical instruments in worship. Most of these congregations continue to hold to a "Restoration" program. They began to separate from the Christian Church (Disciples of Christ) during and after World War I over such issues as ecumenical cooperation in missions, BIBLICAL CRITICISM, and the rising influence of liberal theology. As early as the 1920s alternative strategies for overseas missions were developed, Bible colleges were established to prepare a ministry true to the Restoration tradition, and in 1927 a separate annual gathering, the North American Christian Convention, was called. The division was formalized in the late 1960s when the Christian Church (Disciples of Christ) underwent restructuring, and many conservative congregations formally withdrew. As a group they continue to reject denominational status, retaining their group identity as a "movement" mainly through periodicals, annual conventions, and Bible colleges and seminaries.

The World Convention of Churches of Christ remains the only institutional manifestation of the common Disciples of Christ heritage. Organized in 1930, it meets every five years for worship and fellowship.

DIS PATER \'dis-'pā-tər\ (Latin: "Rich Father"), in ROMAN RELIGION, god of the infernal regions, the equivalent of the

Greek HADES, or PLUTO (Rich One). Also known to the Romans as Orcus, he was believed to be the brother of JUPITER. His wife, Proserpina (a Roman adaptation of the Greek PERSEPHONE), was identified with vegetation, being regarded as a goddess of death during her annual sojourn in the Underworld and of abundance during her term in the upper regions. Caesar claimed that the Celtic Gauls believed themselves to be descendants of Dis Pater.

DITCH, BATTLE OF THE, *Arabic* Al-Khandaq ("The Ditch"), early Muslim victory that ultimately forced the authorities at MECCA to recognize the political and religious strength of the Muslim community in MEDINA.

A Meccan army of 3,000 men had defeated the undisciplined Muslim forces at Uḥud, near Medina, in 625, wounding MUHAMMAD himself. In March 627, when they had persuaded a number of Bedouin tribes to join their cause, the Meccans brought a force of 10,000 men against Medina. Muhammad then resorted to tactics unfamiliar to the Arabs, who were accustomed to brief, isolated raids. Rather than sally out to meet the enemy in the usual way, he had a ditch dug around Medina (according to tradition he did so at the suggestion of a Persian convert, Salmān). The Meccan horsemen were disconcerted and soon bored, and the coalition of Bedouin tribes started breaking up. After an unsuccessful siege the Meccans dispersed. With the Muslim and Meccan forces now more evenly matched and the Meccans tiring of a war that was damaging their trade, Muhammad used his victory to negotiate greater concessions for the Muslims in a treaty at al-Ḥudaybiyya (628).

DĪVĀLĪ \di-'vä-lē, -'wä-\, *also spelled* Dīwālī, *or* Dīpāvali, one of the major religious festivals in HINDUISM, celebrated in India over a five-day period from the 13th day of the dark half of the lunar month Āśvina to the 2nd day of the light half of Kārttika. (The corresponding Gregorian dates usually fall in late October.) The name is derived from the Sanskrit term *dīpāvali*, or row of lights, for the lights that are lit on the new-moon night to bid the presence of LAKṢMĪ, the goddess of wealth. In Bengal, however, the goddess KĀLĪ is worshiped, and in northern India the festival also celebrates the return of RĀMA, SĪTĀ, Lakṣmaṇa, and HANUMĀN to the city of AYODHYA, where Rāma's rule of righteousness would commence.

During the festival, small earthenware lamps filled with oil are lighted and placed in rows along the parapets of temples and houses and set adrift on rivers and streams. The fourth day—the main Dīvālī festival day and the beginning of the lunar month of Kārttika—marks the beginning of the new year according to the Vikrama calendar. Merchants perform religious ceremonies and open new account books. It is generally a time for visiting, exchanging gifts, decorating houses, feasting, and wearing new clothes. Gambling is encouraged at this season, as a way of ensuring good luck for the coming year and in remembrance of Lord SHIVA and PĀRVATĪ's games of dice played on Mount Kailāsa, or similar contests between RĀDHĀ and KRISHNA. Ritually, in honor of Lakṣmī, the female partner always wins.

Dīvālī is also an important festival in JAINISM. For the Jain community, many of whose members belong to the merchant class, the day commemorates the passing into NIRVANA of MAHĀVĪRA, the most recent of the Jain TĪRTHAṄKARAS. The lighting of the lamps is explained as a material substitute for the light of holy knowledge that was extinguished with Māhavīra's passing. Since the 18th century Dīvālī has been celebrated in SIKHISM as the time GURŪ HARGOBIND returned to AMRITSAR from a supposed captivity in Gvalior—apparently an echo of Rāma's return to Ayodhya. Residents of Amritsar are said to have lit lamps throughout the city to celebrate the occasion.

DIVINATION, the practice of determining the hidden significance or cause of events by various natural, psychological, and other techniques. Found in all civilizations and in all areas, it is known in the Western world primarily in the form of ASTROLOGY.

Divinatory methods may be classified as inductive, interpretive, or intuitive. Inductive and interpretive divination are performed by inference from external facts. Manipulated accident is the essential dramatic element of interpretive divination. A diviner may randomly toss a bunch of selected objects on the ground and foretell the future by interpreting the final alignment of the objects where they fall. The casting of lots was common in classical antiquity and survives in the throwing of dice. The use of lots and number lore requires consultation of the I CHING in Chinese tradition.

In haruspication (the inspection of entrails), in scapulimancy (divination by the spealbone, or shoulder blade), and in divination by footprints in ashes, the diviner foretells the future by interpreting the visual appearance or condition of a particular object or objects. In the case of AUGURY and OMENS, the behavior and cries of birds, encounters with ominous animals, and so on are interpreted. Astrology, based upon observation of the heavenly bodies, is an inductive divining method of great antiquity. Other phenomena commonly subject to such interpretation include dreams, weather, and sequences of cards (*e.g.,* TAROT cards).

Intuitive divination depends for its results on sensory or motor automatisms or mental impressions. The prototype of the intuitive diviner is the SHAMAN who employs trance

Barotse basket diviner, who shakes various objects in a winnowing basket and interprets their final juxtaposition to determine the source and outcome of an illness
By courtesy of the Livingstone Museum, Republic of Zambia

states—either spontaneous, self-induced, or drug-induced—to achieve contact with superior forces and thereby gain insight into the future. Among sensory automatisms, crystal gazing is used to induce visions of future events. The OUIJA BOARD is a popular method of motor automatism.

DIVINE, FATHER, *also called* Major J. Devine, *byname of* George Baker (b. 1877?, Hutchinson's Island, near Savannah, Ga., U.S.—d. Sept. 10, 1965, Philadelphia, Pa.), American religious leader who in 1919 founded the PEACE MISSION movement.

Baker began preaching in Baltimore, Md., where he became known as "The Messenger" among his followers. After briefly returning to Georgia, he moved to New York City in 1915. He adopted the name Major J. Devine (later Divine) shortly thereafter and in 1919 established his first "heaven," or communal dwelling, in Sayville, Long Island, N.Y. His predominantly African-American following expanded rapidly in the 1930s and '40s, and more "heavens" were provided in other cities. Father Divine was regarded by his followers as God, and he did not permit them to smoke, drink liquor, or use cosmetics. The movement declined after his death.

DIVYĀVADĀNA \'di-,vyä-və-'dä-nə\ (Sanskrit: "Divine Avadāna"), important anthology of AVADĀNA (legendary material centering on the Buddha's explanations of events by a person's worthy deeds in a previous life) of the SARVĀSTIVĀDA ("Doctrine That All Is Real") school. The *Divyāvadāna* consists of 38 legends, including some about the great Buddhist emperor AŚOKA. In the Buddhist chronicles of Sri Lanka and the works of the northern Buddhist tradition—the *Divyāvadāna* and the *Aśokāvadāna*—he is extolled as a Buddhist emperor par excellence whose sole ambition was the expansion of BUDDHISM.

DOCETISM \dō-'sē-,ti-zəm, 'dō-sə-\ (from Greek *dokein*, "to seem"), in CHRISTIANITY, a HERESY and one of the earliest sectarian doctrines, affirming that Christ did not have a real or natural body during his life on earth but only an apparent or phantom one. Though its incipient forms are alluded to in the NEW TESTAMENT, such as in the Letters of John (*e.g.*, 1 John 4:1–3; 2 John 7), Docetism became more fully developed as an important doctrinal position of GNOSTICISM, developed from speculations about the imperfection or essential impurity of matter. More thoroughgoing Docetists asserted that Christ was born without any participation of matter and that all the acts and sufferings of his life, including the CRUCIFIXION, were mere appearances. They consequently denied Christ's RESURRECTION and ASCENSION into heaven. Milder Docetists attributed to Christ an ethereal and heavenly body but disagreed on the degree to which it shared the real actions and sufferings of Christ.

DODONA \dō-'dō-nə\, ancient SANCTUARY of the chief Greek god, ZEUS, in Epirus, Greece; the ceremonies held there had many remarkable and abnormal features. The earliest mention of it is in the *Iliad* (xvi, 234), where its priests are called the Selloi (or Helloi) and are described as "of unwashen feet, sleeping on the ground." Homer (*Odyssey*, xiv, 327) was the first to mention the oracle at Dodona. A tree (or trees) was reputed to give oracles, presumably through the rustling of its leaves and other sounds. Herodotus mentions priestesses, whom he describes as the givers of the oracles, doubtless under the god's inspiration. A further peculiarity of Dodona was the "bronze," a large gong set vibrating at every breeze by a scourge held in the hand of a figure standing over it; the persistent ringing passed into a Greek proverbial phrase—*Khalkos Dōdōnēs* ("Brass of Dodona")—for a continuous talker who has nothing to say.

DŌGEN \'dō-gen\, *also called* Jōyō Daishi \'jō-,yō-'dī-shē\, *or* Kigen Dōgen \kē-'gen-\ (b. Jan. 19, 1200, Kyōto, Japan—d. Sept. 22, 1253, Kyōto), Japanese Buddhist who introduced ZEN to Japan in the form of the SŌTŌ school.

Dōgen was ordained a monk at 13 and studied the holy SCRIPTURES of BUDDHISM on MOUNT HIEI, the center of Tendai (T'IEN-T'AI) Buddhism, without, however, fully satisfying his spiritual aspirations. Between 1223 and 1227 he studied meditation in China and gained enlightenment under the Zen master Ju-ching. Back in Japan again, he lived at various temples and worked for the spread of Zen practice. He spent his last years at Eihei Temple, which he founded. His first literary work, *Fukan zazen gi* (1227; "General Teachings for the Promotion of Zazen"), contains a brief introduction to the Zen practice. His chief work, *Shōbōgenzō* (1231–53; "Treasury of the True Dharma Eye"), containing 95 chapters and written over a period of more than 20 years, consists of his elaboration of Buddhist principles.

DOLMEN \'dōl-mən, 'dòl-, 'däl-\, prehistoric monument usually consisting of several stone slabs set edgewise to support a flat roofing stone. Designed as a burial chamber, the structure is typical of the Neolithic Period in Europe. Dolmens, although found in covered form as far east as Japan, are mainly confined to Europe, the British Isles, and northern Africa.

DOME OF THE ROCK, *Arabic* Qubbat al-ṣakhra, *also called* Mosque of Omar, shrine in Jerusalem that is the oldest extant Islamic monument. The rock over which the shrine was built is sacred to both Muslims and JEWS. In ISLAM, the Prophet MUHAMMAD is traditionally believed to have ascended into heaven from the site. In the tradition of JUDAISM, it is here that ABRAHAM, the progenitor and first PATRIARCH of the Hebrew people, is said to have prepared to sacrifice his son ISAAC. The Dome and the AL-AQSĀ MOSQUE are both located on the Temple Mount, which was previously the site of Solomon's Temple and its successors (see JERUSALEM, TEMPLE OF), an area known to Muslims as *al-ḥaram al-sharīf* (the Noble Sanctuary).

The Dome of the Rock was built between 685 and 691 CE by the CALIPH 'Abd al-Malik ibn Marwān as a MASHHAD, a shrine for pilgrims modeled after Christian *martyria*. It is rich with mosaic, faience, and marble, much of which was added several centuries after its completion. Basically octagonal, a wooden dome—approximately 60 feet in diameter and mounted on an elevated drum—rises above a circle of 16 piers and columns. Surrounding this circle is an octagonal arcade of 24 piers and columns. The outer walls repeat this octagon, each of the eight sides being approximately 60 feet wide and 36 feet high. Both the dome and the exterior walls contain many windows.

Its elaborate mosaics and Qur'anic inscriptions suggest that its original purpose was to openly declare Islamic doctrine about JESUS as a prophet, not the Son of God, and to display the Muslim triumph over the Byzantine and Persian empires. Christians and Muslims in the Middle Ages believed the Dome itself to be the Temple of SOLOMON (Templum Domini). The Knights TEMPLARS were quartered there in the Crusades, and Templar churches in Europe im-

Dome of the Rock in Jerusalem, built 685–691
D. Edwards—FPG

itated its plan. During the 20th century it became a symbolic focal point for the Palestinian nationalist cause against the Israeli government.

DOMINIC, SAINT \'dä-mə-ˌnik\ (b. *c.* 1170, Caleruega, Castile—d. Aug. 6, 1221, Bologna, Romagna; canonized July 3, 1234; feast day August 8), founder of the Order of Friars Preachers (O.P., also known as the DOMINICANS), a religious order of MENDICANT friars.

Domingo de Guzmán was born in Castile, possibly a year or two later than 1170, the traditional date. He studied at Palencia and then joined the canons regular (a religious community attached to the cathedral of a DIOCESE) of Osma about 1196. In 1203, Diego, bishop of Osma, took Dominic with him on a royal mission abroad.

This journey first made Dominic aware of the threat posed by the HERESY of the ALBIGENSES, or CATHARI, and their Manichaean teaching that two supreme beings rule spirit and matter respectively, so that whatever concerns the body—eating, drinking, procreation—is essentially evil, and the ideal is the renunciation of these things and even of life itself. Local feudal lords, especially the count of Toulouse, supported the Albigenses.

In 1206 the papal legates and preachers, depressed at their failure to convert the heretics back to orthodoxy, consulted the bishop and Dominic, who reasoned that the heretics would be regained only by an austerity equal to their own; preachers must tramp the roads barefoot and in poverty. This was the birth of Dominic's "evangelical preaching." A key part of his campaign was the establishment of a CONVENT of nuns at Prouille, formed in 1206 from a group of women converted from the heresy.

In 1208 the papal legate, Peter de Castelnau, was murdered by an emissary of the Count of Toulouse. A civil war ensued until 1213, when the Catholic party won. The Catholic party entered Toulouse, and Dominic and his friends were welcomed by the bishop, Foulques, and established as "diocesan preachers" in 1215.

From Foulques's charter in that year, Dominic's design for an order devoted to preaching developed rapidly. In 1215 he went to Rome with Foulques (bound for the Fourth LATERAN COUNCIL) to lay his plans before the pope, who, however, recommended adoption of the rule of one of the existing orders. (It was, perhaps, at this time that Dominic met FRANCIS OF ASSISI, and the friendship of the two saints is a strong tradition in both orders.) In the summer of 1216 Dominic was back at Toulouse conferring with his companions, now 16 in number. This meeting has been called the *capitulum fundationis* ("chapter, or meeting, of foundation"). The rule of St. Augustine was adopted, as well as a set of *consuetudines* ("customs") concerning the divine office, monastic life, and religious poverty; these are still the core of Dominican legislation. In July, INNOCENT III died, and his successor, Honorius III, granted Dominic formal sanction of his order.

In 1217 Dominic sent his men to Paris and to Spain, leaving two each at Toulouse and Prouille, while he and another went to Bologna and Rome. He placed his two principal houses near the universities of Paris and Bologna and decided that each of his houses should form a school of theology. This at once determined the role that the Dominicans would play in university studies.

At PENTECOST in 1220 the first general chapter of the order was held at Bologna, and a system of democratic representative government was devised. At the second general chapter, held on Pentecost in 1221, also at Bologna, the order was divided geographically into provinces.

Dominic was gifted in being able to conceive his ideal, to form his men to that ideal, and then to trust them completely. His leadership had great clarity of vision, firmness of command, and certainty of execution. Yet it was said that his gentleness was such that anyone who came to speak to him, even for reproof, went away happier.

DOMINICAN \də-'mi-ni-kən\, *byname* Black Friar, member of Order of Friars Preachers, one of the four great MENDICANT orders of the ROMAN CATHOLIC church, founded by St. Dominic in 1215. For a history of the order during Dominic's life, *see* DOMINIC, SAINT.

From the beginning the order has been a synthesis of the CONTEMPLATIVE life and the active ministry. The members live a community life, and a careful balance is maintained between democratically constituted chapters and strong but elected superiors. In contrast to the monastic orders that predated it, the Dominican order was not a collection of autonomous houses; it was an army of priests, organized in provinces under a master general. The individual belonged to the order, not to any one house, and could be sent anywhere at any time about its business; this innovation has served as a model for many subsequent bodies.

Within 40 years of the order's foundation, talented members were concentrated in the schools at Paris, Bologna, Cologne, and Oxford. Originally students of theology only, they were led by ALBERTUS MAGNUS and his pupil THOMAS AQUINAS to a study of the newly available works of Aristotle that had been transmitted to Europe by Muslim scholars, and to the integration of philosophy and theology. Meanwhile, the Dominicans pursued their vocation of preaching.

St. Dominic, detail of a 15th-century panel; in the National Archaeological Museum, Palermo, Italy
Anderson—Alinari from Art Resource

In southern France they spoke out against the ALBIGENSES and, in Spain and elsewhere, against the Moors and Jews. They evangelized in northern and eastern Europe, in the eastern Mediterranean, and in India. When the INQUISITION was established, Dominicans were entrusted with its execution. They were among the first and most energetic missionaries under the Spanish and Portuguese explorers and later under the French.

The Dominican order has continued its unswerving orthodoxy, based upon the teaching of Aquinas, and has steadfastly opposed novelty or accommodation in theology. The 19th and 20th centuries saw a tremendous development of congregations of Dominican sisters engaged in teaching, nursing, and charitable works.

DOMOVOY \də-mə-'voi\, in Slavic myth and folklore, a household spirit appearing under various names and having its origin in ANCESTOR WORSHIP. A *domovoy* dwells in any number of places in each home: near the oven, under the doorstep, in the hearth. He never goes out beyond the boundaries of the household.

The *domovoy* is the guardian of the family and its wealth, but he is partial to conscientious and hard-working people. Any displeasure the *domovoy* feels with the actions of its family is displayed in troubles with the farm animals or in strange knocks and grating noises in the house. These last, however, could just be the *domovoy* amusing himself. He can, in any case, be easily placated.

The *domovoy* sees to it that the various traditional proprieties are observed. He can foresee the future, and his groans and weeping or singing and jumping are interpreted as portents of evil or good. No household would consider moving to a new location without formally inviting the *domovoy* to join it. Similar to the *domovoy* are the *ovinnik*, which inhabits the drying-house, and the *gumenik*, which occupies the storehouse.

DÔN \'dōn\, the Welsh counterpart of the Irish goddess DANU, a Celtic mother-goddess. In the Irish tales Danu is the mother of the race of gods, while Dôn in the Welsh MABINOGION is mentioned as the mother of some of the more important characters and the sister of the magician-king MATH. Dôn's children included GWYDION, a master of magic, and Arianrhod. It was Arianrhod who was the mother of Lleu Llaw Gyffes (Lleu of the Dextrous Hand)—who is probably the Welsh form of the pan-Celtic deity LUGUS—and Dylan, who is presumably a god of the sea. Neither Gwydion nor Arianrhod seem to by very moral characters; for example, Arianrhod gives birth to Dylan and Lleu during a test of her virginity.

DONATISM \'dō-nə-,ti-zəm, 'dä-\, Christian movement in North Africa that broke with the Roman church in 312 over the election of Caecilian as bishop of Carthage. The name derived from their leader, Donatus (d. *c.* 355). The Donatists opposed state interference in church affairs, and, through the peasant warriors called Circumcellions, they had a program of social revolution combined with eschatological hopes. Martyrdom following a life of penance was the goal of the religiously minded Donatist. Despite almost continuous pressure from successive Roman, Vandal, and Byzantine rulers of North Africa, the Donatist church survived until the extinction of CHRISTIANITY in North Africa in the 7th century.

The ultimate causes of the SCHISM were both doctrinal and social. Throughout the 3rd century the African church had regarded itself as a body of the ELECT. A corollary of this view was the belief that the validity of sacerdotal acts depended on the presence of the HOLY SPIRIT in the minister and that a minister who was not in a state of GRACE could not administer a valid SACRAMENT.

In 311 Caecilian was elected bishop, but he was opposed by many because he allowed himself to be consecrated by a *traditor* bishop (one who had surrendered copies of SCRIPTURE to the authorities during Emperor Diocletian's persecution of Christians, beginning in 303). The PRIMATE of Numidia, Secundus of Tigisi, who had acquired in the previous 40 years the right of consecrating the bishop of Carthage, arrived in Carthage with 70 bishops and in solemn council declared Caecilian's election invalid.

The new emperor, CONSTANTINE the Great, ordered arbitration of the controversy. A commission of bishops under the bishop of Rome found Caecilian innocent of all charges on Oct. 2, 313. Donatus, who was the other candidate for bishop, appealed. Constantine summoned another council of bishops and again Caecilian was upheld and his position strengthened by a canon that ORDINATION was not invalid if it had been performed by a *traditor*. Despite further appeals by Donatus and his supporters, Constantine gave a final decision in favor of Caecilian in November 316.

The schism did not die out. In May 321 Constantine grudgingly granted toleration to the Donatists. The movement gained strength for several years, but in August 347 Emperor Constans I exiled Donatus and other leaders to Gaul, where Donatus died about 355.

When Julian the Apostate became emperor in 361, the exiled Donatists returned to Africa and were the majority Christian party for the next 30 years. Their opponents, however, now led by St. AUGUSTINE OF HIPPO, gained strength, and in 411 a council decided against the Donatists and for the Catholics. In 412 and 414 severe laws denied the Donatists civil and ecclesiastical rights; however, the Donatists expected hostility from the world and, thus, persecution did not obliterate the movement.

DÖNME \dœn-'me, *Angl* ˌdən-'mā\, *also spelled* Dönmeh (Turkish, literally, "convert"), sect of JUDAISM founded in Salonika (now Thessaloníki, Greece) in the late 17th century, after the conversion to ISLAM of SHABBETAI TZEVI, whom the sectarians believed to be the MESSIAH. The Dönme, who numbered about 15,000 in the late 20th century, are found primarily in Istanbul, Edirne, and İzmir, Turkey.

Shabbetai Tzevi had proclaimed himself the Messiah in 1648 and quickly gained financial support and a considerable following among Jews throughout the Holy Land, Europe, and North Africa. Early in 1666 he was arrested by Ottoman Turks and, faced with the choice of conversion or death, accepted Islam by the end of the year. The Dönme believed that the conversion of Shabbetai Tzevi was a step in the fulfillment of the messianic PROPHECY. They therefore also converted to Islam but secretly practiced various Judaic rites, preserved some knowledge of Hebrew, kept secret Hebrew names, forbade intermarriage with the Muslim population, and conducted their marriage and funeral rites in secret. Internally they split into a number of subsects, reflecting social distinctions and disputes over the successors to Shabbetai.

At the turn of the 20th century the Dönme, well represented in the professional classes, took an active part in the Young Turk movement and the revolution of 1908. After the Greco-Turkish War of 1921–22 the central Dönme community of Thessaloníki was moved to Istanbul, and a gradual process of assimilation set in. Contact with Jews was lost, and the Dönme themselves resisted Jewish attempts to return them to Judaism.

DORT, SYNOD OF \'dòrt\, assembly of the REFORMED CHURCH of the Netherlands that met at Dort (in full Dordrecht) from Nov. 13, 1618, to May 9, 1619. The SYNOD tried to settle disputes concerning ARMINIANISM. In 1610 the Dutch followers of JACOBUS ARMINIUS presented a Remonstrance in five articles that contained their theological views; thus, Dutch Arminians were also called REMONSTRANTS. They rejected the strict Calvinist doctrine of PREDESTINATION, the doctrine that God elects or chooses those who will be saved. Those who opposed the Remonstrants were the Gomarists, the followers of Franciscus Gomarus, a Dutch theologian who upheld a rigid CALVINISM.

The synod was attended by Gomarist Dutch delegates and also by delegates from Reformed churches in Germany, Switzerland, and England. The opening sessions dealt with a new Dutch translation of the BIBLE, a CATECHISM, and the censorship of books. The synod then called upon Remonstrants to express their beliefs, but they refused to accept the rules of the synod and eventually were expelled.

The synod then studied the theology of the Remonstrants and declared that it was contrary to SCRIPTURE. The canons of Dort were produced; they discussed the errors of

the Remonstrants that were rejected as well as the doctrines that were affirmed. The doctrines affirmed were that predestination is not conditional on belief; that Christ did not die for all; the total depravity of man; the irresistible GRACE of God; and the impossibility of falling from grace.

DOXOLOGY, an expression of praise to God. In Christian worship there are three common doxologies:

1. The greater doxology, or Gloria in Excelsis, is the Gloria of the ROMAN CATHOLIC and ANGLICAN masses, and in its hundreds of musical settings is usually sung in Latin. It is used in the Roman Catholic liturgy in a contemporary translation and, often in older translations, in many Anglican, Lutheran, and other Protestant worship services. The Latin text, from the *Roman Missal,* follows:

◆ *Gloria in excelsis Deo. Et in terra pax hominibus bonae voluntatis. Laudamus te. Benedicimus te. Adoramus te. Glorificamus te. Gratias agimus tibi propter magnam gloriam tuam. Domine Deus, Rex caelestis, Deus Pater Omnipotens. Domine Fili unigenite Jesu Christe. Domine Deus, Agnus Dei, Filius Patris. Qui tollis peccata mundi, miserere nobis. Qui tollis peccata mundi, suscipe deprecationem nostram. Qui sedes ad dexteram Patris, miserere nobis. Quoniam tu solus sanctus. Tu solus Dominus. Tu solus altissimus, Jesu Christe. Cum sancto Spiritu, in gloria Dei Patris.*
 Amen. ◆

The modern Roman Catholic English version reads:

◆ **Glory to God in the highest, and peace to his people on earth. Lord God, heavenly King, almighty God and Father, we worship you, we give you thanks, we praise you for your glory. Lord Jesus Christ, only Son of the Father, Lord God, Lamb of God you take away the sin of the world: have mercy on us; you are seated at the right hand of the Father: receive our prayer. For you alone are the Holy One, you alone are the Lord, you alone are the Most High, Jesus Christ, with the Holy Spirit in the glory of God the Father.**
 Amen. ◆

2. The lesser doxology, or Gloria Patri, is used in most Christian traditions at the close of the psalmody:

◆ **Glory be to the Father, and to the Son, and to the Holy Spirit, as it was in the beginning, is now, and ever shall be, world without end.**
 Amen. ◆

3. Metrical doxologies are usually variations upon the Gloria Patri. The most familiar in English is by the 17th-century Anglican bishop and hymn writer Thomas Ken:

◆ **Praise God, from whom all blessings flow;**
 Praise him, all creatures here below;
 Praise him above, ye heavenly host;
 Praise Father, Son, and Holy Ghost.
 Amen. ◆

Most Protestant churches use this form, often in conjunction with the presentation of TITHES and offerings.

DRAMA AND RELIGION, the presentation in theatrical form of religious concepts or the reenactment of events from the history or mythology of a religion. Most historians agree that drama emerged from religious ritual. At what precise point ritual became drama is uncertain, but formal drama is first known in the context of ancient Greek Dionysiac festivals. Certainly, religious festivals gave rise to dramatic expression by reenacting the passion and trials of the god or man-god on whom the religion centered. In Christian Europe, biblical plays became attached to particular festivities, notably the FEAST OF CORPUS CHRISTI. Similarly, the story of the assassination of the 7th-century Shi'ite hero AL-ḤUSAYN IBN 'ALĪ, grandson of the Prophet MUHAMMAD, was enacted at the Muslim festival of *ta'ziyah.* As in ancient Greece, these festivals extended over many days and involved the whole community.

With the disappearance of classical theater in the West, serious drama was reborn in the Middle Ages within the ROMAN CATHOLIC church. There, from early times, dramatic elements were introduced into certain offices, particularly at EASTER and CHRISTMAS. From this practice liturgical drama sprang. Performances took place inside churches, with the cast of clergy moving from place to place in the sanctuary. At first only Latin was used, though occasionally snatches of vernacular verse were included. Stories from the BIBLE and lives of the saints were dramatized; but as the scope of the dramas broadened, more plays were performed outside the church and used only the vernacular. Mystery plays, which enacted biblical episodes, and miracle plays, which offered a factual or fictitious depiction of a saint's life, developed from these roots.

In an example of a religious drama, a scene from a 1960 performance of the Passion play at Oberammergau in which Christ appears before Pilate and Herod
Bavaria-Verlag, Munich

The religious drama of ancient Greece, the temple drama of early India and Japan, the mystery cycles of medieval Europe, all have in common more than their religious content: when the theater is a place of worship, its drama goes to the roots of belief in a particular community. The dramatic experience becomes a natural extension of one's life both as an individual and as a social being.

DREAMING, THE, *also called* Dream-Time, *or* World Dawn, *Australian Aboriginal languages* Altjira, Altjiranga, Alcheringa, Wongar, *or* Djugurba, in the religion of Australian Aboriginal peoples, a mythological period of time that had a beginning but no foreseeable end, during which the natural environment was shaped and humanized by the actions of mythic beings. Many of these beings took the form of human beings or of animals; some changed their forms. They were credited with having taken long journeys and having established the local social order. Some were responsible for creating human life. In the Dreaming, humanity is regarded as part of nature, not fundamentally dissimilar to the mythic beings or to the animal species, all of which share a common life force.

Mythic beings of the Dreaming are eternal. Though in the myths some were killed or disappeared beyond the boundaries of the people who sang about them, and others metamorphosed into features such as rocky outcrops or waterholes or manifested as, or through, ritual objects, their essential quality remained undiminished. In Aboriginal belief, they are spiritually as much alive today as they ever were. The places where the mythic beings were believed to have performed some action or were turned into something else became sacred centers of ritual.

The expressions "Dreaming" or "Dream-Time" are approximate translations of *aljerreŋe,* a word in Aranda (an Aboriginal language spoken in the vicinity of Alice Springs in the Northern Territory), formed from *aljerre,* "dream," and *-ŋe,* "of, from."

DRESDEN CODEX \'drez-dən-'kō-,deks\: *see* MAYA CODICES.

DRUID, member of the learned class among the ancient Celts. They seem to have acted as priests, teachers, and judges. The earliest known records of the Druids come from the 3rd century BCE.

Julius Caesar is the chief source of information about the Druids, but he may have received some of his facts from the Stoic philosopher Poseidonius, whose account is often confirmed by early medieval Irish sagas. According to Caesar, there were two groups of men in Gaul that were held in honor, the Druids and the noblemen (*equites*). The Druids took charge of public and private sacrifices, and many young men went to them for instruction. They judged all public and private quarrels and decreed penalties. If anyone disobeyed their decree, he was barred from sacrifice, which was considered the gravest of punishments. One Druid was made the chief; upon his death, another was appointed. If several were equal in merit, the Druids voted, although they sometimes resorted to armed violence. Once a year they assembled at a sacred place in the territory of the Carnutes, which was believed to be the center of all Gaul.

Caesar also recorded that the Druids were exempt from warfare and paid no tribute. Attracted by those privileges, many joined the order voluntarily or were sent by their families. They studied ancient verse, natural philosophy, astronomy, and the lore of the gods, some spending as much as 20 years in training. The Druids' principal doctrine was that the soul was immortal and passed at death from one person into another.

The Druids were said to offer HUMAN SACRIFICES for those who were gravely sick or in danger of death in battle. Huge wickerwork images were filled with living men and then burned; although the Druids preferred to sacrifice criminals, they would choose other victims if necessary.

The Druids were suppressed in Gaul by the Romans under Tiberius (reigned 14–37 CE) and probably in Britain a little later. In Ireland they lost their priestly functions after the coming of CHRISTIANITY and survived as poets, historians, and judges (*filid, senchaidi,* and *brithemain*). Some scholars believe that the Hindu BRAHMIN in the East and the Celtic Druid in the West were lateral survivals of an ancient Indo-European PRIESTHOOD.

DRUZE \\'drüz\\, *also spelled* Druse, *Arabic* plural Durūz, *singular* Darazī, originating in ISLAM, a Middle Eastern religious sect characterized by an eclectic system of doctrines and by a cohesion and loyalty among its members that have enabled them to maintain through almost a thousand years of turbulent history their close-knit identity and distinctive faith. They numbered about one million in the late 20th century and lived mostly in Lebanon and Syria, with smaller communities in Israel and Jordan. They call themselves MUWAḤḤIDŪN ("unitarians").

The Druze permit no conversion, either away from or to their religion, and no intermarriage. Their religious system is kept secret not only from the outside world but in part even from their own number; only an elite of initiates, known as ʿUQQĀL ("knowers"), participate fully in the services and have access to the secret teachings of the *ḥikma,* the Druze religious doctrine. In times of persecution a Druze is allowed to deny his faith outwardly if his life is in danger. This concession, or TAQĪYA, is allowed according to *al-Taʿlīm* ("Instruction"), the anonymously written "catechism" of Druze faith.

It is not known to what extent this people was self-conscious and distinct before adopting their present religion. Druze religious beliefs developed out of Ismāʿīlī teachings. Various elements of JUDAISM, CHRISTIANITY, GNOSTICISM, NEOPLATONISM, and Iranian religion, however, are combined under a doctrine of strict MONOTHEISM. Propagation of the new religion began in Cairo in 1017 CE, led by Ḥamza ibn ʿAlī; it is from the name of Ḥamza's subordinate, Muhammad ad-Darazī, that the group derives its name. The eclectic belief system was organized into a doctrine of the soteriological divinity of AL-ḤĀKIM bi-Amr Allāh ("Ruler by the Command of Allāh"), the sixth CALIPH (996–1021) of the Fāṭimid dynasty of Egypt, whom they call al-Ḥākim bi-Amrih ("Ruler by His Own Command"). It is believed by the Druze that al-Ḥākim did not die but vanished and will one day return in triumph to inaugurate a golden age.

During the 20th century, the Druze have gained representation in the Lebanese parliament, allied themselves with the Baʿth party in Assad's Syria, and, unlike other Arabs, served voluntarily in the Israeli army. *See also* ISMĀʿĪLĪS.

DUALISM, in religion, belief in two supreme opposed powers or gods, or sets of divine or demonic beings, that control the world. Dualism is a phenomenon of major importance in the religions of the ancient world.

A certain kind of dualism is implied in many religions by the simple fact that the sacred is often considered to be radically different from and opposed to the profane. HINDUISM, for instance, posits an eternal dialectical tension between ultimate reality and the illusory world of phenomena. In Chinese TAOISM the entire inventory of opposing principles in the world is embraced in the dualistic doctrine of YIN-YANG.

In terms of MYTHOLOGY, most polytheistic religions recognize a class of supernatural beings (such as DEMONS, TITANS, or monsters) that are different from and antagonistic to the gods. Even within a single pantheon there may be noted a tension and a conflict between the celestial and the terrestrial or CHTHONIC gods (*e.g.,* the AESIR and the VANIR in Germanic mythology), or between constructive and destructive deities (*e.g.,* OSIRIS and SETH in EGYPTIAN RELIGION).

Another very characteristic type of religious dualism, exemplified in numerous cosmogonies worldwide, explains the introduction of evil into a previously perfect universe. In ancient Persia, ZOROASTER proclaimed an irreducible opposition between AHURA MAZDĀ, the Wise Lord (or Ormazd), and Angra Mainyu, the Evil Spirit (or AHRIMAN). According to Zoroaster, Ahriman freely chose to do evil, thus bringing misery, illness, and death into the world. Later Zoroastrianism presented Ormazd and Ahriman as two coeternal principles of good and evil—the Creator and the Destroyer. MANICHAEISM adopted this valuation and blended it with the movement's own myth of corrupted creation.

Under the influence of Iranian ESCHATOLOGY, some dualistic elements found their way into Jewish apocalyptic literature, but only in subordination to absolute MONOTHEISM. Although CHRISTIANITY accepts a radical difference between GOOD AND EVIL, it rejects a metaphysical dualism. The NEW TESTAMENT utilizes some old dualistic formulas, but in a different sense, denoting antithetical phases in the history of salvation.

DUBNOW, SIMON MARKOVICH \\'düb-,nȯf\\ (b. Sept. 10, 1860, Mstislavl, Russia [now in Belarus]—d. December 1941, Riga, Latvia, U.S.S.R.), Jewish historian who introduced a sociological emphasis into the study of Jewish history, particularly that of eastern Europe.

Early in his life, Dubnow ceased to practice Jewish rituals. He later came to believe that his vocation as a historian of JUDAISM was as true to the faith of his ancestors as were the Talmudic studies of his piously Orthodox grandfather. Largely a self-educated man who supported himself as a

Simon Dubnow, 1921
By courtesy of the YIVO Institute for Jewish Research, New York

teacher and writer, in 1882 he began his long association with the Russian-Jewish periodical *Voskhod* ("Rising"), to which he contributed many of his most famous scholarly and literary works. He left Russia in 1922 because of his hatred for Bolshevism and settled in Berlin. In 1933 he fled Germany because of the anti-Jewish policies of the Nazi government and sought refuge in Riga. He was killed during the deportation of most of Riga's Jewish population to extermination camps.

Dubnow was one of the first scholars to subject HASIDISM to systematic study; this work appeared in *Geschichte des Chassidismus* (1931; "History of Hasidism"). The mature fruit of Dubnow's historical studies is his monumental *Die Weltgeschichte des jüdischen Volkes*, 10 vol. (1925–30; "The World History of the Jewish People"; Eng. trans. *History of the Jews*), which is notable for its scholarship and cognizance of social and economic currents in Jewish history. According to Dubnow, the Jews not only are a religious community but also possess the distinctive characteristics of a cultural nationality and as such create their own forms of autonomous social and cultural life. As a cultural nationalist Dubnow rejected Jewish assimilation but at the same time believed that political ZIONISM was messianic and unrealistic.

DUKKHA \\'du̇k-kə\\ (Pāli), *Sanskrit* Duḥkha ("sorrow," "suffering," or "imperfection"), in Buddhist thought, the true nature of all existence. Suffering, its reality, cause, and means of suppression, formed the subject of the BUDDHA'S first sermon on the FOUR NOBLE TRUTHS. Recognition of the fact of suffering as one of three basic characteristics of existence—along with impermanence (ANICCA) and the absence of a self (*anattā*)—constitutes the "right knowledge" that is the first step on the EIGHTFOLD PATH that leads ultimately to enlightenment (NIRVANA). Three types of suffering are distinguished: they result, respectively, from torment, such as old age, sickness, and death; from the absence of pleasure; and from the necessity of giving up what one loves and has become attached to, because of the inescapable transitory quality of all phenomena.

DUMUZI-ABZU \\'du̇-mü-zē-'äb-ˌzü\\, in MESOPOTAMIAN RELIGION, Sumerian deity, city goddess of Kinirsha near Lagash in the southeastern marshland region. She represented the power of fertility and new life in the marshes. Dumuzi-Abzu corresponded to the Sumerian god Dumuzi of the central herding area, and thus around Eridu she was viewed as male and as son of Enki (Akkadian: EA, also called the Lord of Apsu).

DUMUZI-AMAUSHUMGALANA \\'du̇-mü-zē-ˌä-mä-'u̇-shu̇m-gä-'lä-nä\\, in MESOPOTAMIAN RELIGION, Sumerian deity especially popular in the southern orchard regions and later in the central grassland area. He was the young bridegroom of the goddess Inanna (Akkadian: ISHTAR), a fertility figure sometimes called the Lady of the Date Clusters. As such, he represented the power of growth and new life in the date palm. In Erech the marriage of Inanna, in her role as goddess of the storehouse, to Dumuzi-Amaushumgalana was essentially a harvest festival. Dumuzi-Amaushumgalana was essentially a form of Dumuzi, the Sumerian god of fertility and reproduction.

DUNS SCOTUS, JOHN \\'dənz-'skō-təs\\, *Latin given name* Joannes (b. *c.* 1266, Duns, Lothian, Scot.—d. Nov. 8, 1308, Cologne), influential FRANCISCAN realist philosopher and scholastic theologian.

Little is known of the life of Duns Scotus. Early 14th-century manuscripts offer little more than that John Duns was a Scot, from Duns, who belonged to the English province of FRIARS Minor (the order founded by FRANCIS OF ASSISI), that "he flourished at Cambridge, Oxford, and Paris and died in Cologne."

Jurisdictionally, the Scots belonged to the Franciscan province of England, whose principal house of studies was at the University of Oxford, and there Duns Scotus apparently spent 13 years (1288–1301) preparing for inception as master of theology. John Duns was ordained in 1291. From a date mentioned in the work's prologue, it is clear that in 1300 Duns Scotus was already at work on his monumental Oxford commentary on PETER LOMBARD'S *Sentences*, known as the *Ordinatio* or *Opus Oxoniense*. By June of 1301 he had completed all the requirements for the mastership in theology.

When the turn came for the English province to provide a candidate for the Franciscan chair of theology at the more prestigious University of Paris, Duns Scotus was appointed. One *reportatio* of his Paris lectures indicates that he began commenting on the *Sentences* there in the autumn of 1302 and continued to June 1303. Before the term ended, however, the university was affected by the feud between King Philip IV the Fair and Pope BONIFACE VIII. Scotus remained loyal to the pope and was exiled from France.

Where Duns Scotus spent the exile is unclear. He was back in Paris before the summer of 1304, for he was the bachelor respondent in the *disputatio in aula* (public disputation) when his predecessor, Giles of Ligny, was promoted to master. Duns Scotus was assigned as Giles' successor.

The period following Duns Scotus' inception as master in 1305 was one of great literary activity. Aided by associates and secretaries, he set to work to complete his *Ordinatio* and the less extensive but equally important *Quaestiones quodlibetales*—discussions of 21 questions organized under two main topics, God and creatures. Duns Scotus' renown depends principally on these two major works. The short but important *Tractatus de primo principio*, a compendium of what reason can prove about God, draws heavily upon the *Ordinatio*.

In 1307 Duns Scotus was appointed professor at Cologne. He may have been sent there for his own safety. Scotus pioneered the classical defense of the doctrine that MARY, the mother of JESUS, was conceived without ORIGINAL SIN (the IMMACULATE CONCEPTION); some felt, however, that this doctrine conflicted with the doctrine of Christ's universal redemption. Though his brilliant defense of the Immaculate Conception marked the turning point in the history of the doctrine, it was immediately challenged by secular and DOMINICAN colleagues. The secular master Jean de Pouilly, for example, declared the Scotist thesis not only improbable, but even heretical—this at a time when Philip IV the Fair had initiated HERESY trials against the wealthy Knights TEMPLARS. There seems to have been something hasty about Duns Scotus' departure for Cologne in any case. Duns Scotus lectured at Cologne until his death.

Duns Scotus left his *Ordinatio* and *Quodlibet* unfinished. Eager pupils completed the works, substituting materials from *reportationes examinatae* for the questions Duns Scotus left undictated. The critical Vatican edition begun in 1950 is aimed, among other things, at reconstructing the *Ordinatio* as Duns Scotus left it, with all his corrigenda, or corrections.

Despite their imperfect form, Duns Scotus' works were widely circulated. His claim that universal concepts are based on a "common nature" in individuals was one of the central issues in the 14th-century controversy between Realists and Nominalists concerning the question of whether general types are figments of the mind or are real. His strong defense of the PAPACY against the divine right of kings made him unpopular with the English Reformers of the 16th century for whom "dunce" (a Dunsman) became a word of obloquy, yet his theory of intuitive cognition suggested to JOHN CALVIN, the Genevan Reformer, how God may be "experienced."

DURAN, SIMEON BEN ZEMAH \dü-'rän\, *also called (by acronym)* Rashbaz \räsh-'bäth\ (b. 1361, Majorca, Balearic Islands [now part of Spain]—d. 1444, Algiers [Algeria]), first Spanish Jewish RABBI to be paid a regular salary by the community and author of an important commentary on *Avot* ("Fathers"), a popular ethical tractate in the TALMUD. Before the 14th century the rabbinical post had been almost invariably honorary; Duran set a precedent in accepting a salary. His commentary *Magen Avot* ("The Shield of the Fathers"), which influenced the great medieval Jewish

Durgā killing the demon Mahiṣāsura, watercolor; in the Victoria and Albert Museum, London
Art Resource

philosopher JOSEPH ALBO, is important for reducing the THIRTEEN ARTICLES OF FAITH of MOSES MAIMONIDES (1135–1204) to three essential dogmas: the existence of God, the divine origin of Jewish law, and the reality of divine reward and retribution.

DURGĀ \'dûr-gä\ (Sanskrit: "the Inaccessible"), in the mythology of HINDUISM, a principal form of the Goddess DEVĪ or ŚAKTI, and the wife of SHIVA. According to legend, Durgā was created for the slaying of the buffalo-demon Mahiṣāsura, by BRAHMĀ, VISHNU, Shiva, and the lesser gods who were otherwise powerless to overcome him. Embodying their collective energy (*śakti*), she is in one sense derivative from the male divinities and in another the true source of their inner power, and greater than any of them. Durgā was born fully grown and beautiful; nevertheless, she presents a fierce menacing form to her enemies. She is usually depicted riding a lion (sometimes shown as a tiger) and with 8 or 10 arms, each holding the special weapon of one or another of the gods, who gave them to her for her battle against the buffalo-demon. The DURGĀ-PŪJĀ, held annually in her honor, is one of the great festivals of northeastern India.

DURGĀ-PŪJĀ \'dûr-gä-'pü-jä\, in HINDUISM, one of the greatest festivals of northeastern India, held annually in September–October in honor of the goddess DURGĀ. Special images of the goddess are made that are worshiped for nine days, then immersed in water, all accomplished with large processions and much public and private festivity.

DURKHEIM, ÉMILE \dür-'kem, *Angl* 'dərk-,hīm\ (b. April 1858, Épinal, France—d. Nov. 15, 1917, Paris), French social scientist, widely regarded as the founder of the French school of sociology.

Durkheim was born into a Jewish family of very modest means. It was taken for granted that he would study to become a RABBI, like his father, but his outstanding success at school designated him as a candidate to the renowned École Normale Supérieure in Paris—the most prestigious teachers' college in France. Durkheim passed the stiff competitive examination for the École Normale in 1879. It is clear that his religious faith had vanished by then, though he had a strong bent toward moral reform. He looked to science and in particular to social science and profound educational reform as the means of avoiding the perils of social disconnectedness, or *anomie*, as he was to call this condition, in which norms for conduct were either absent, weak, or conflicting.

He passed the last competitive examination in 1882 and then accepted a series of provincial assignments as a teacher of philosophy at the state secondary schools of Sens, Saint-Quentin, and Troyes between 1882 and 1887. In 1887 he was appointed as lecturer at the University of Bordeaux, where he subsequently became professor and taught social philosophy until 1902.

In truth, Durkheim's vital interest did not lie in the study for its own sake of so-called primitive tribes, but rather in the light such a study might throw on the present. Much of what he thought and wrote stemmed from the events that he witnessed in his formative years. The latter half of the 19th century in France had seen the collapse of the Second Empire, the rise of the Paris Commune, the bloody repressions that followed the Commune's fall, and the later resurgence of nationalism and ANTI-SEMITISM. Durkheim was one of several young philosophers and scholars who became convinced that progress was not the necessary consequence of the development of science and technology. He perceived around him the prevalence of "anomie," a personal sense of rootlessness fostered by the absence of social norms. Material prosperity set free greed and passions that threatened the equilibrium of society. Durkheim's earlier works, including his doctoral thesis, *De la division du travail social* (1893; *The Division of Labor in Society*), and *Le Suicide* (1897; *Suicide*), articulated this view that ethical and social structures were being endangered by the advent of technology and mechanization.

The Dreyfus Affair—resulting from the false charge against a Jewish officer, Alfred Dreyfus, of spying for the Germans—erupted in the last years of the century, and the slurs aimed at Jews that accompanied it opened Durkheim's eyes to the latent hatred and passionate feuds hitherto half concealed under the varnish of civilization. He took an active part in the campaign to exonerate Dreyfus. He was not elected to the Institut de France, although his stature as a thinker suggests that he should have been named to that prestigious society. He was, however, appointed to the University of Paris in 1902 and made a full professor there in 1906.

More and more, the sociologist's thought became concerned with education and religion as the two most potent means of reforming humanity or of molding the new institutions required by the deep structural changes in society. He participated in numerous committees to prepare new curriculums and methods; worked to enliven the teaching of philosophy, which too long had dwelt on generalities; and attempted to teach teachers how to teach.

An important work of Durkheim's latter years dealt with the origin and nature of religion under the title of *Les Formes élémentaires de la vie religieuse* (1915; *The Elementary Forms of the Religious Life*). This text remains a classic in the study of religion; its thesis is that the object of religion is social life. It begins with a summary of theories and definitions of the ORIGIN OF RELIGION and ends with a brilliant reflection on the relation between SCIENCE AND RELIGION. Durkheim founded the SOCIOLOGY OF RELIGION, a discipline which taught that religion, including both belief and practice, was a representation in symbolic form of society. His DEFINITION OF RELIGION entailed both cognitive and moral elements and thus also established what is now known as the sociology of knowledge. Durkheim thought that the origin of religion could be found in the institution called "totemism." Although Lévi-Strauss has shown that this institution does not exist, Durkheim's book remains a monument in both sociology and the STUDY OF RELIGION.

The outbreak of World War I came as a cruel blow to Durkheim. His only son was killed in 1916, while fighting on the Balkan front. Durkheim died in November 1917.

Durkheim left behind him a brilliant school of researchers, including his nephew, MARCEL MAUSS. With Durkheim, sociology had become in France a seminal discipline that broadened and transformed the study of law, economics, linguistics, ethnology, art history, and history.

DVAITA \'dvī-tə\ (Sanskrit: "Dualism"), important school in the orthodox Hindu philosophical system of VEDĀNTA. Its founder was MADHVA, also called Ānandatīrtha (13th century). Already during his lifetime Madhva was regarded by his followers as an incarnation of the wind god Vāyu, who had been sent to earth by the lord VISHNU to save the good, after the powers of evil had sent the philosopher ŚAMKARA, an important proponent of the ADVAITA ("Nondualist") school.

In his expositions, Madhva maintains that Vishnu is the supreme God, thus identifying the BRAHMAN of the UPANISHADS with a personal God. There are in Madhva's system three eternal, ontological orders: that of God, that of soul, and that of inanimate nature. The existence of God is demonstrable by logic, though only SCRIPTURE teaches his nature. He is the epitome of all perfections and possesses a nonmaterial body, which consists of *saccidānanda* (being, spirit, and bliss). God is the efficient cause of the universe,

but Madhva denies that he is the material cause, for God cannot have created the world by splitting himself nor in any other way, since that contradicts the doctrine that God is unalterable; in addition, it is blasphemous to accept that a perfect God changes himself into an imperfect world.

Individual souls are countless in number and are of atomic proportions. They are a "portion" of God and exist completely by the grace of God and are totally subject to Him.

Ignorance, which for Madhva as for many other Indian philosophers means mistaken knowledge (*ajñāna*), can be removed or corrected by means of devotion (BHAKTI). Devotion can be attained in various ways: by solitary study of the scriptures, by performing one's duty without self-interest, or by practical acts of devotion. This devotion is accompanied by an intuitive insight into God's nature.

The present-day following of Dvaita has as its center a monastery at Udipi, in Karnataka state, which was founded by Madhva himself and has continued under an uninterrupted series of abbots.

DVIJA \'dvi-jä\ (Sanskrit: "twice-born"), in the Hindu social system, members of the three upper VARNAS, or social classes—the BRAHMINS (priests and teachers), KṢATRIYA (warriors), and VAISYA (merchants)—whose sacrament of initiation is regarded as a second or spiritual birth. The initiation ceremony (UPANAYANA) invests the male CASTE members with a sacred thread, a loop worn next to the skin over the left shoulder and across the right hip. The lowest Hindu *varṇa*, the SUDRA, and people whose status eludes the four-*varṇa* system altogether are regarded by it as theoretically ineligible to study or even to listen to the VEDAS. However, a vital tradition of protest against this and similar ideas has long existed in India. The position of women in the *dvija* system is anomalous. On the one hand, women are clearly marked by caste; on the other, high-caste women are not considered eligible for Vedic study according to traditional canons. Especially since the 19th century, increasing numbers of such women have challenged the traditional view, becoming students of Sanskrit and Vedic subjects, notably in India's public institutions of higher learning, chanting Vedic verses, and even offering their services as specialists in Brahminical rituals.

DYBBUK \'di-bək\, in Jewish FOLKLORE, a disembodied human spirit that, because of former SINS, wanders restlessly until it finds a haven in the body of a living person. Belief in such spirits was especially prevalent in 16th–17th-century eastern Europe. It was believed that only a miracle-working RABBI (BA'AL SHEM) could expel the harmful dybbuk through a religious rite of EXORCISM.

Isaac Luria (1534–72), laid the grounds for Jewish belief in a dybbuk with his doctrine of transmigration of souls (*gilgul*), which he saw as a means whereby souls could continue their task of self-perfection. His disciples went one step further with the notion of possession by a dybbuk.

DZIADY \'jä-də\, in SLAVIC RELIGION, all the dead ancestors of a family, the rites that are performed in their memory, and the day on which those rites are performed. *Dziady* take place three or four times a year; they are generally celebrated in the winter before the beginning of ADVENT and in the spring on the Sunday of Doubting THOMAS. A funeral feast (*pominki*) is prepared and attended by the family; the *dziady* themselves are addressed and invited to join their kinsmen. The *dziady*, however, are not considered family guardians and are never asked for favors or protection.

EA \'ā-ä\ (Akkadian), *Sumerian* Enki \'eŋ-
kē\, in MESOPOTAMIAN RELIGION, god of water
and a member of the triad of deities completed by ANU (Sumerian An) and BEL (ENLIL).
From a local deity worshiped in the city of
Eridu, Ea evolved into a major god, Lord of
Apsu, the fresh waters beneath the earth
(although Enki means literally "lord of the
earth"). In the Sumerian myth known as
"Enki and the World Order," Enki is said to
have fixed national boundaries and assigned
gods their roles. In another, Enki is the creator, having devised men as slaves to the
gods. In his original form, as Enki, he was
associated with semen and amniotic fluid,
and therefore with fertility. He was commonly represented as a half-goat, half-fish
creature, from which the modern astrological figure for Capricorn is derived.

Ea, the Akkadian counterpart of Enki,
was the god of ritual purification: ritual
cleansing waters were called "Ea's water."
Ea governed the arts of SORCERY and incanta-
tion. In some stories he was also the form-
giving god, and thus the patron of craftsmen
and artists; he was known as the bearer of
culture. As adviser to the king, Ea was a
wise god although not a forceful one. In
Akkadian myth, he appears frequently as a
clever mediator who could be devious and
cunning. He is also significant in Akkadian
mythology as the father of MARDUK, the national god of Babylonia.

EARTH MOTHER, in ancient and modern
nonliterate religions, the eternally fruitful
source of all things. The Earth Mother is
not necessarily a specific source of vitality
who must periodically undergo sexual intercourse, but is simply the mother; there is
nothing separate from her. All things come
from her, return to her, and are her.

The Earth Mother may transcend all
specificity and sexuality, manifesting herself in any form. In other mythological systems, however,
she may become the feminine earth, consort of the masculine sky; she is fertilized by the sky in the beginning and
brings forth terrestrial creation. In some agricultural traditions she is simply the earth and its fertility.

EASTER, *Latin and Greek* Pascha (from Hebrew: *Pesaḥ,*
"Passover"), principal festival of the Christian church year,
celebrating the RESURRECTION of JESUS CHRIST on the third day
after his CRUCIFIXION. The origins of Easter date to the beginnings of CHRISTIANITY, and it is probably the oldest Christian
observance after the SABBATH (originally observed on Saturday, later on Sunday); the Sabbath subsequently came to be
regarded as the weekly celebration of the Resurrection. According to the Anglo-Saxon historian BEDE, the name *Easter*
(Old English: *ēastre*) was taken from the name of a Germanic spring goddess Eostre, though evidence for such a deity is not otherwise known.

Date of Easter. Western Christians celebrate Easter on
the first Sunday after the full moon (the paschal moon) that
occurs upon or next after the vernal equinox (taken as
March 21). If the paschal moon, which is calculated from a

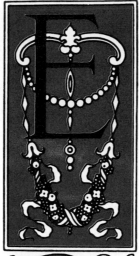

system of golden numbers and epacts and
does not necessarily coincide with the astronomical full moon, occurs on a Sunday,
Easter day is the succeeding Sunday. Easter,
therefore, can fall between March 22 and
April 25. This rule was fixed after much
controversy and uncertainty. In the EASTERN
ORTHODOX church, however, a slightly different calculation is followed, with the result that the Orthodox Easter, although
sometimes coinciding with that of the
West, can fall one, four, or five weeks later.

Religious observances. The festival of
Easter occurs on a particular Sunday, but its
importance is emphasized in the worship of
the church by the long preparation of LENT,
by HOLY WEEK, with its solemn services, and
by the following 50 days until PENTECOST
(Whitsunday). Easter is central to the whole
Christian year; not only does the entire ecclesiastical calendar of movable feasts depend upon its date but the whole liturgical
year of worship is arranged around it. In the
liturgical texts the emphasis is laid on its
being the Christian PASSOVER (the time of redemption).

By the time that the Christian liturgy had
begun to take shape (2nd century), the Sunday EUCHARIST was preceded by a vigil service of SCRIPTURE readings and psalms. In
this must be seen the origin of the Easter
Vigil service; from being a weekly observance the vigil has turned into an annual
one at Easter only. As it is now constituted
in the ROMAN CATHOLIC missal, this vigil
consists of the blessing of the new fire (a
practice introduced during the early Middle
Ages); the lighting of the paschal candle; a
service of lessons, called the prophecies; followed by the blessing of the font and BAP-
TISMS and then the MASS of Easter. A similar
form is used in some Lutheran and Anglican churches.

The connection of baptism with Easter is
of early date. During the church's first centuries the whole
of Lent was not only a time of penance but also the period
during which the CATECHUMENS were prepared for baptism,
which was given only once a year, at Easter. The catechumenate came to an end with the solemn baptisms of the
Easter vigil. This is the explanation of the present practice
of the long ceremony of blessing the font on Easter night
and of the great emphasis on baptism and its meaning and
the many allusions to it still present in the Easter services.

Among the Eastern Orthodox and Russian Orthodox
churches, perhaps even greater emphasis is laid on the central position of Easter. The vigil service is preceded by a
PROCESSION outside the church representing a fruitless
search for the body of Christ. Then comes the joyful announcement, "Christ is risen," followed by the Easter Eucharist. When the procession first leaves the church, there
are no lights anywhere, but on its return hundreds of candles and colored lamps are lighted to show the splendor of
Christ's Resurrection.

In PROTESTANTISM, Easter Sunday observances are the culminating point of a series of services held during Holy
Week, beginning with PALM SUNDAY. It is customary for the

Ea (seated) and attendant deities, Sumerian cylinder seal, c. 2300 BCE
By courtesy of the Pierpont Morgan Library, New York

Sacrament of Holy Communion to be administered during Holy Week, but the time of its observance varies. Many Protestant churches hold joint interdenominational GOOD FRIDAY services, prepared under the auspices of the local ministerial association. These services in many communities center on the traditional seven last "words" (or sayings) of Christ and are conducted from 12:00 noon to 3:00 PM with choirs and clergy of the participating denominations. This interdenominational pattern culminates in the Easter dawn service. The origin of the sunrise service is not known, but it would appear to be rooted in the Gospel narratives describing the Resurrection of Christ—*e.g.,* John 20, "Now on the first day of the week, Mary Magdalene came to the tomb early, while it was still dark."

Popular customs. Around the Christian observance of Easter as the climax of the liturgical drama of Holy Week and Good Friday, folk customs have collected, many of which have been handed down from the ancient symbolism of European and Middle Eastern pre-Christian spring festivals brought into relation with the resurrection theme. These customs have taken a variety of forms, in which, for example, eggs, formerly forbidden to be eaten during Lent, have been prominent as symbols of new life and resurrection. Thus, brightly colored or decorated eggs are hidden for children to find on Easter morning.

EASTERN ORTHODOXY, one of the major branches of CHRISTIANITY, characterized by its continuity with the apostolic church, its liturgy, and its territorial churches.

Eastern Orthodoxy is the large body of Christians who follow the faith and practices defined by the first seven ecumenical councils. The official designation of the church in Eastern Orthodox liturgical or canonical texts is "the Orthodox CATHOLIC Church." Because of the historical links of Eastern Orthodoxy with the Eastern Roman Empire and Byzantium (Constantinople), however, in English usage it is referred to as the "Eastern" or "Greek Orthodox"

church. These terms are sometimes misleading, especially when applied to Russian or Slavic churches and to the Orthodox communities in western Europe and America.

The SCHISM between the churches of the East and the West (1054) was the culmination of an estrangement that began in the first centuries of the Christian Era. At the time of the Schism of 1054, the membership of the Eastern Orthodox Church was spread throughout the Middle East, the Balkans, and Russia, with its center in Constantinople. The vicissitudes of history have greatly modified the internal structures of the Orthodox church, but, even today, the bulk of its members live in the same geographic areas. Missionary expansion toward Asia and emigration toward the West, however, have helped to maintain the importance of Orthodoxy worldwide.

The Orthodox church is a fellowship of "autocephalous" churches (governed by their own head bishops), with the Ecumenical PATRIARCH of Constantinople holding titular or honorary primacy. The number of AUTOCEPHALOUS CHURCHES has varied. Today there are many: the Church of Constantinople (Istanbul), the Church of Alexandria (Egypt), the Church of Antioch (with headquarters in Damascus, Syria), and the churches of Jerusalem, Russia, Ukraine, Georgia, Serbia, Romania, Bulgaria, Cyprus, Greece, Albania, Poland, the Czech Republic and Slovakia, and America. Several are de facto national churches, by far the largest being the Russian Church; however, it is not the criterion of nationality but rather the territorial principle that is the norm of organization in the Orthodox church.

All Orthodox credal formulas, liturgical texts, and doctrinal statements affirm the claim that the Orthodox church has preserved the original apostolic faith. The Orthodox church recognizes as ecumenical the seven councils of NICAEA (325), CONSTANTINOPLE (381), EPHESUS (431), CHALCEDON (451), CONSTANTINOPLE (553), CONSTANTINOPLE (680), and NICAEA (787) but considers that the decrees of several other later councils also reflect the same original faith (*e.g.,* the councils of Constantinople that endorsed the theology of ST. GREGORY PALAMAS in the 14th century). Finally, it recognizes itself as the bearer of an uninterrupted living tradition of true Christianity that is expressed in its worship, in the lives of the saints, and in the faith of the whole people of God. When expressing the beliefs of his church, the Orthodox theologian, rather than seeking literal conformity with any of these particular confessions, will rather look for consistency with SCRIPTURE and tradition, as it has been expressed in the ancient councils, the early Fathers, and the uninterrupted life of the liturgy.

The Greek Fathers of the church always implied that the phrase found in the biblical story of the creation of man Genesis 1:26), according to "the image and likeness of

God," meant that humans are not autonomous beings and that their ultimate nature is defined by relation to God, the human "prototype." Thus, the concept of SIN implies separation from God and the reduction of humans to a separate and autonomous existence, one deprived of both natural glory and freedom. In this perspective, "original sin" is understood not so much as a state of guilt inherited from Adam but as an unnatural condition of human life that ends in death. From this vicious circle of death and sin, humans are understood to be liberated by the death and RESURRECTION of JESUS CHRIST, which is actualized in BAPTISM and the sacramental life in the church. Hence the aim of the Christian is communion with God and deification. The church is regarded as a communion in which God and humans meet and a personal experience of divine life becomes possible.

The stress on Jesus Christ's identity with the preexistent Son of God, the LOGOS (Word) of the Gospel According to John, characterizes Orthodox Christology. Similarly, the liturgy consistently addresses the Virgin MARY as THEOTOKOS ("God-Bearer"); this term reflects the doctrine of Christ's unique divine Person, and Mary is thus venerated only because she is his mother "according to the flesh." The theopaschite formula ("God suffered in the flesh") became a standard of orthodoxy in the Eastern church, especially after the second Council of Constantinople (553). It implied that Christ's humanity was indeed real not only in itself but also for God, since it brought him to death on the cross, and that the salvation and redemption of humanity can be accomplished by God alone—hence the necessity for him to condescend to death, which held humanity captive.

Normally, the content of the Orthodox liturgy is directly accessible to the faithful through use of vernacular language in the liturgy, though liturgical conservatism leads to the preservation of antiquated languages. The liturgies of ST. JOHN CHRYSOSTOM and of ST. BASIL THE GREAT are most generally used in Orthodox worship. These liturgies differ only in the text of the eucharistic canon: their overall structures, established in the high Middle Ages, are identical. The church recognizes seven *mysteria*, or "SACRAMENTS": baptism, chrismation, communion, holy orders, penance, anointing of the sick (the "extreme unction" of the medieval West), and marriage. The underlying sacramental theology of the church is based on the notion that the ecclesiastical community is the unique mysterion, of which the various sacraments are the normal expressions.

EASTERN RITE CHURCH, *also called* Eastern Catholic church, any of a group of Eastern Christian churches that trace their origins to various ancient national or ethnic Christian bodies in the East but have established union or canonical communion with the Roman Apostolic See and, thus, with the ROMAN CATHOLIC church. In this union they accept the Roman Catholic faith, keep the seven SACRAMENTS, and recognize the POPE of Rome as supreme head of the church. The special status of the Catholic churches of the Eastern rite was guaranteed at the time of each rite's union with Rome and was approved again by the decree of the SECOND VATICAN COUNCIL (1962–65), in *De ecclesiis catholicis orientalibus*, promulgated on Nov. 21, 1964. In the late 20th century, the number of Eastern Catholics throughout the world numbered more than 12 million.

Despite the failure of the ecclesiastical authorities at the COUNCIL OF FERRARA-FLORENCE in 1439 to unite Christians of the East and West, the continued efforts of the proponents of Christian reunion, added to the missionary activities of

such monastic orders as the JESUITS, DOMINICANS, FRANCISCANS, and Capuchins, began to achieve some success. The Brest-Litovsk Union of 1596, under which all but two Ukrainian Orthodox bishops accepted the primacy of the pope, signaled the effective advent of Eastern rite churches.

Prior to this event, Eastern Catholics were few, limited to Italo-Albanians in southern Italy and Sicily, a large number of Maronites (Lebanese Christians of the Syro-Antiochene rite) who became associated with Rome in the 12th century, and some Armenians in the Syria-Lebanon region who also trace their relationship with Rome to the 12th century. A number of NESTORIANS were united with Rome in 1551, Ruthenians (an east-central European people) in 1595, Romanians of Transylvania in 1698, and Melchites (Syrian Christians of the BYZANTINE RITE) in 1724.

From the viewpoint of EASTERN ORTHODOXY, Eastern Catholics may be looked upon with suspicion, primarily because of the Latinizing influence found in their ranks. Hence the majority of Orthodox and Eastern independent churches characterize Eastern Catholics as "Uniate" churches. The expression Uniate is taken from Ukrainian *uniya*, a term coined by the opponents of the Brest-Litovsk Union. "Uniatism" implies hybridism, or the tendency for Latinization, and hence a betrayal of one's ancient and nationalistic tradition. Eastern rite churches prefer to be considered united churches rather than Uniate, with its negative implications.

Eastern Catholic rites permit a married clergy and the immediate admission of baptized infants to the sacraments of the EUCHARIST (the Lord's Supper) and CONFIRMATION.

The supreme head of the Eastern rite churches is the pope. The central organ of the Holy See is the Congregation for the Eastern Churches, the prefect of which is the pope, while a CARDINAL proprefect performs the ordinary functions of chairman. The Congregation is competent for the Eastern churches in all matters (except certain specified cases) and has exclusive jurisdiction in specified countries in eastern Europe and the Middle East. The individual Eastern Catholic churches are organized differently according to their historical and ethnic situation, the number of adherents, the degree of evolution, and so on.

Patriarchates comprise a certain number of DIOCESES of a single rite, under the jurisdiction of a PATRIARCH. The patriarchs, according to the Eastern CANON LAW, have special rights and privileges; in the general hierarchy they rank with the cardinals according to seniority (following the titular cardinal bishops of the suburban sees of Rome) and before all other bishops. In the late 20th century there were six Eastern Catholic patriarchates: one of Alexandria, for the Copts; three of Antioch, one each for the Syrians, Maronites, and Greek Melkites; one of Babylonia, for the Chaldeans; and one of Sis, or Cilicia, for the Armenians. The patriarchs of Babylonia and of Sis are called *katholikos*. Major archiepiscopates are those that govern a certain number of dioceses of their rite but whose territory has not yet been erected into a patriarchate. Metropolitanates govern ecclesiastical provinces independent of the patriarchates and major archiepiscopates and comprise a number of dioceses. One of them is the metropolis; and its archbishop, the METROPOLITAN, is the head of the whole metropolitanate. Eparchies correspond to the Latin dioceses. Although they are usually subject to one of the aforementioned higher organizations, a few are immediately subject to the Holy See or to a Latin metropolitan see.

The term "rite" in "Eastern Catholic rite" signifies not only liturgical ceremonies but the whole organization of particular churches. In the late 20th century, there were five distinct Eastern rite traditions—the Byzantine, the Alexandrian, the Antiochene, the Chaldean, and the Armenian—each (except the last) with two or more branches. The Byzantine rite affects the most persons and most territories worldwide. Its liturgy is based on the rite of St. James of Jerusalem and the churches of Antioch, as reformed by ST. BASIL and ST. JOHN CHRYSOSTOM. The liturgy is used by the majority of Eastern Catholics and by the Eastern Orthodox Church (which is not in union with Rome). The Coptic liturgy of the Alexandrian rite (known as the Liturgy of St. Mark) is derived from the Greek Liturgy of Alexandria, modified by several elements, including the Byzantine rite of St. Basil. The Antiochene rite can be traced to Book 8 of the APOSTOLIC CONSTITUTIONS and to the Liturgy of St. James of Jerusalem. The Chaldean rite, though derived from the Antiochene rite, is listed as a separate and distinct rite by the Sacred Congregation for the Eastern Churches. The ARMENIAN RITE, using the liturgical language of classical Armenian, is based on the Greek Liturgy of St. Basil, as modified by elements of the Antiochene rite.

ECCE HOMO

ECCE HOMO \'e-kē-'hō-mō, 'e-kā-, 'ek-sē-\ (Latin: "Behold the Man"), theme prevalent in western Christian art of the 15th to 17th century, so called after the words of PONTIUS PILATE to the Jews who demanded the CRUCIFIXION of JESUS (John 19:5). Paintings on this theme generally conform to one

Ecce Homo, *oil painting by Hiëronymus Bosch*
By courtesy of the Städelsches Kunstinstitut, Frankfurt am Main; photograph, Joachim Blauel, Munich

of two types: images of the head or half-figure of Jesus, or narrative depictions of the judgment hall scene. In either type, Christ is shown wearing a crown of thorns and purple robe placed on him by the Roman soldiers, and his face expresses compassion toward his accusers. In the narrative versions, two guards are often shown supporting the suffering figure while Pontius Pilate gestures toward Christ, illustrating his words.

ECHIDNA \i-'kid-nə\ (Greek: "Viper," "Snake"), in Greek mythology, a woman-serpent hybrid. Her parents were either the sea deities Phorcys and Ceto or Chrysaor, the son of MEDUSA, and Callirrhoë, the daughter of OCEANUS. Among Echidna's progeny by the 100-headed TYPHON were Ladon (the serpent who protected the Golden Apples of the HESPERIDES), the monster who protected the Golden Fleece, the HYDRA, the CHIMERA, and the hounds Orthus and Cerberus.

The SPHINX and the Nemean lion, both sired by Orthus, were also among her offspring.

ECHO, in Greek mythology, a mountain NYMPH, or oread. Ovid's *Metamorphoses* relates that Echo offended the goddess HERA by keeping her in conversation, thus preventing her from spying on one of Zeus's amours. To punish Echo, Hera deprived her of speech, except for the ability to repeat the last words of another. Echo's hopeless love for NARCISSUS, who fell in love with his own image, made her fade away until all that was left of her was her voice.

According to the Greek writer Longus, Echo rejected the advances of the god PAN; he thereupon drove the shepherds mad, and they tore her to pieces. GAEA buried her limbs but allowed her to retain the power of song.

ECK, JOHANN \'ek\, *original name* Johann Maier (b. Nov. 13, 1486, Egg, Swabia [Germany]—d. Feb. 10, 1543, Ingolstadt, Bavaria [Germany]), theologian who was MARTIN LUTHER'S principal ROMAN CATHOLIC opponent.

Early in his career Maier adopted the name of his home village, Egg (or Eck). He studied at the universities of Heidelberg, Tübingen, Cologne, and Freiburg im Breisgau. He was ordained to the PRIESTHOOD in 1508 and became a doctor of theology in 1510. In that year he became professor of theology at the University of Ingolstadt.

Eck was friendly with Luther until the appearance in 1517 of the latter's NINETY-FIVE THESES, which Eck assailed as heretical in a tract published in 1518. In the Leipzig disputation of 1519, Eck debated Luther on such topics as papal primacy and the infallibility of church councils. In 1520 Eck visited Rome, where he helped compose the papal bull *Exsurge Domine* (June 1520), in which Pope Leo X condemned 41 of Luther's theses and threatened EXCOMMUNICATION. Leo then commissioned Eck to publish and enforce the bull throughout Germany.

Eck went on to write extensively in defense of papal authority and traditional doctrine. Traveling throughout Europe, he organized Roman Catholic opposition to German PROTESTANTISM, and he drafted the Catholic refutation (1530) of the Lutheran creed contained in the AUGSBURG CONFESSION. Eck was a prolific writer in Latin, and his many works in that language are notable as learned defenses of the Roman Catholic faith. His treatise entitled *Enchiridion*

Against the Lutherans (1525) was a summary of contested Catholic beliefs, Protestant objections to them, and answers to these difficulties. The *Enchiridion* proved to be the most popular of Eck's works and went through 91 editions in various languages before 1600.

ECKHART, MEISTER \\'mīs-tər-'ek-ˌhärt\\, *English* Master Eckhart, *original name* Johannes Eckhart (b. *c.* 1260, Hochheim, Franconia [now in Germany]—d. 1327/28?, Avignon, France), DOMINICAN theologian and writer who was the greatest German speculative mystic.

Johannes Eckhart entered the Dominican Order when he was 15 and studied in Cologne, perhaps under the Scholastic philosopher ALBERTUS MAGNUS. The intellectual spirit there was influenced by the great Dominican theologian THOMAS AQUINAS, who had recently died. In his mid-30s, Eckhart was nominated VICAR (the main Dominican official) of Thuringia. Before and after this assignment he taught theology at Saint-Jacques's priory in Paris.

Eckhart wrote four works that are usually called "treatises." About the age of 40 he wrote the *Talks of Instruction*, on self-denial, the nobility of will and intellect, and obedience to God. The other works of this middle part of his life are the *Book of Divine Consolation*, dedicated to the Queen of Hungary, *The Nobleman*, and *On Detachment*.

In his mature teachings Eckhart described four stages of the union between the soul and God: dissimilarity, similarity, identity, and breakthrough. At first, God is all, the creature is nothing; at the ultimate stage, "the soul is above God." The driving power of this process is detachment.

1. Dissimilarity: "All creatures are pure nothingness. I do not say they are small or petty: they are pure nothingness." Whereas God inherently possesses being, creatures do not possess being but receive it derivatively.

2. Similarity: Man thus detached from the singular (individual things) discovers himself to be an image of God. Divine resemblance then emerges: the Son, image of the Father, engenders himself within the detached soul.

3. Identity: Eckhart's numerous statements on identity between God and the soul can be easily misunderstood. He never has substantial identity in mind, but God's operation and man's becoming are considered as one. God is no longer outside man, but he is perfectly interiorized.

4. Breakthrough: Identity with God is still not enough; to abandon all things without abandoning God is still not abandoning anything. Man must live "without why." He must seek nothing, not even God. For Eckhart, God exists as "God" only when the creature invokes him. Eckhart calls "Godhead" the origin of all things that is beyond God. "God and the Godhead are as distinct as heaven and earth." The soul is no longer the Son. The soul is now the Father: it engenders God as a divine person. "If I were not, God would not be God."

In his 60th year Eckhart was called to a professorship at Cologne. Heinrich von Virneburg—a FRANCISCAN, unfavorable to Dominicans, anyway—was the archbishop there, and it was before his court that the now immensely popular Meister Eckhart was first formally charged with HERESY. To a list of errors, he replied by publishing a Latin *Defense*. When ordered to justify a new series of propositions drawn from his writings, he declared: "I may err but I am not a heretic, for the first has to do with the mind and the second with the will!" The bull of Pope John XXII, dated March 27, 1329, condemns 28 propositions extracted from the two lists. Since it speaks of Meister Eckhart as already dead, it is inferred that Eckhart died some time before, perhaps in 1327 or 1328. It also says that Eckhart had retracted the errors as charged.

Although Eckhart's philosophy amalgamates Greek, Neoplatonic, Arabic, and Scholastic elements, it is unique. His doctrine, sometimes abstruse, always arises from one simple, personal mystical experience to which he gives a number of names. In the second half of the 20th century, there was great interest in Eckhart among some Marxist theorists and ZEN Buddhists.

ECSTASY (Greek: *ekstasis*, literally, "act of standing aside"), in MYSTICISM, the experience of an inner vision of God or of one's relation to or union with the divine. Various methods have been used to achieve ecstasy, which is a primary goal in most forms of religious mysticism. The most typical consists of four stages: (1) purgation (of bodily

The Ecstasy of St. Teresa, *marble and gilded bronze sculpture by Gian Lorenzo Bernini, 1645–52; in the Coronaro Chapel, Sta. Maria della Vittoria, Rome*
SCALA—Art Resource

desire); (2) purification (of the will); (3) illumination (of the mind); and (4) unification (of one's being or will with the divine). Other methods are: dancing (as used by the MAW-LAWĪYA, or whirling dervishes, a Muslim SUFI sect); the use of sedatives and stimulants (as utilized in some Hellenistic MYSTERY RELIGIONS); and the use of certain drugs, such as PEYOTE, mescaline, hashish, and LSD (in certain Islamic sects and modern experimental religious groups). Most mystics, both in the East and in the West, frown on the use of drugs.

In certain ancient Israelite prophetic groups, music was used to achieve the ecstatic state, in which the participants, in their accompanying dancing, were believed to have been seized by the hand of YAHWEH. The Pythia (priestess) of the Greek oracle at DELPHI often went into an ecstatic state during which she uttered sounds mystically revealed to her after drinking water from a certain spring. Her utterances were then interpreted by a priest to help answer the suppliant's question.

ECUMENISM \e-'kyü-mə-,ni-zəm, 'e-kyü-\, in CHRISTIANITY, the movement or tendency toward worldwide unity or cooperation. The term, of recent origin, emphasizes what is viewed as the universality of the Christian churches; it is derived from Greek *oikoumenē*, "the inhabited world"—in a NEW TESTAMENT context, as in Matthew 24:14, the site of God's reconciling mission to all people. The ecumenical movement seeks to recover the apostolic sense of the early church for unity in diversity, and it confronts the frustrations and difficulties of the modern pluralistic world.

The possibility of an ecumenical approach to Christianity increased in the 17th and 18th centuries, when English dissenting sects and Pietist groups on the Continent began to promote evangelistic, revivalistic, and missionary endeavor. This, along with the simultaneous effect of Enlightenment thought, broke down many of the traditional foundations that supported separate church structures. Additionally, the separation of CHURCH AND STATE in the United States signaled the need for civility and respect for religious rights in a land of many religions.

After the International Missionary Conference held at Edinburgh in 1910, Protestants began to use the term ecumenism to describe the gathering of missionary, evangelistic, service, and unitive forces. Roman Catholics used ecumenism to refer to the renewal of the whole life of the church, undertaken to make it more responsive to "separated churches" and to the needs of the world.

Early 20th-century ecumenism derived impetus from the convergence of three movements: international missionary conferences (PROTESTANT), beginning with the Edinburgh Conference and taking shape as an institution in the International Missionary Council (1921); the Faith and Order Conferences (on church doctrine and polity), commencing in the conference at Lausanne (1927); and the Life and Work Conferences (on social and practical problems), beginning with the Stockholm Conference (1925). The WORLD COUNCIL OF CHURCHES, a consultative and conciliar agent of ecumenism, working with national, denominational, regional, and confessional bodies, was inaugurated in Amsterdam in 1948. The International Missionary Council joined the World Council of Churches in 1961.

Protest movements against the developments that led to and continued in the World Council of Churches have produced an ecumenical convergence of their own. Most participants in this convergence prefer to be called "evangelical." In the United States the National Association of Evangelicals was formed in 1943, in large part to counter the Federal Council of Churches, which began in 1908 and reorganized as the National Council of Churches in 1950.

In 1961 POPE JOHN XXIII established the Secretariat for the Promotion of Christian Unity, and the Orthodox churches created the Pan-Orthodox Conference.

Roman Catholic ecumenism received definitions and momentum at the SECOND VATICAN COUNCIL (1962–64). The church gave the ecumenical movement new hope and language in the "Decree on Ecumenism" (1964), one of the classic ecumenical teaching documents. Another result of Vatican II was the establishment of a wide variety of international theological dialogues, commonly known as bilateral conversations. These include Roman Catholic bilaterals with Lutherans (1965), Orthodox (1967), Anglicans (1967), Methodists (1967), Reformed (1970), and the Disciples of Christ (1977). Topics identified for reconciling discussions include BAPTISM, the EUCHARIST, episcopacy and PAPACY, authority in the church, and mixed marriage.

Central to 20th-century ecumenism is the birth of united churches, which have reconciled formerly divided churches. The most heralded examples of this ecumenism are the United Church of Canada (1925), the Church of South India (1947), and the Church of North India (1970). Strategic union conversations were undertaken in the United States by the nine-church Consultation on Church Union (1960) and by such uniting churches as the United Church of Christ (1957), the Presbyterian Church, U.S.A. (1983), and the Evangelical Lutheran Church in America (1988).

EDDA \'e-də\, body of old Icelandic literature contained in two 13th-century books commonly distinguished as the *Prose*, or *Younger*, *Edda* and the *Poetic*, or *Elder*, *Edda*. It is the fullest and most detailed source for modern knowledge of Germanic mythology.

The *Prose Edda*. The *Prose Edda* was written by the Icelandic chieftain, poet, and historian Snorri Sturluson, probably in 1222–23. Being the only book actually called Edda, it is a textbook on poetics intended to instruct young poets in the difficult meters of the early Icelandic skalds (court poets) and to provide for a Christian age an understanding of the mythological subjects treated or alluded to in early poetry. It consists of a prologue and three parts. The section entitled *Gylfaginning* ("The Beguiling of Gylfi") describes the visit of Gylfi, a king of the Swedes, to ASGARD, the citadel of the gods. In answer to his questions, the gods tell Gylfi the Norse myths about the beginning of the world, the adventures of the gods, and the fate in store for all in the RAGNARÖK (Doom [or Twilight] of the Gods).

The *Poetic Edda*. The *Poetic Edda* is the name given to a later manuscript dating from the second half of the 13th century but containing older materials (hence its alternative title, the *Elder Edda*). It is a collection of anonymous mythological and heroic poems of unknown authorship, composed over a long period (800–1200 CE). They are usually dramatic dialogues in a terse, simple, archaic style that is in decided contrast to the artful poetry of the skalds. Many of the poems are quoted in the Prose Edda and must therefore be older.

The mythological cycle is introduced by *Vǫluspá* ("Sibyl's Prophecy"), which reviews the history of the gods, humans, and dwarfs, from the birth of the world to the death of the gods and the world's destruction.

It is followed by *Hávamál* ("Sayings of the High One"), a group of disconnected, fragmentary, didactic poems that sum up the wisdom of the divine wizard-king, ODIN. The latter part contains the myth of how Odin acquired the magical power of the runes (alphabetical characters) by hanging himself from a tree and suffering hunger and thirst for nine nights. The poem ends with a list of magic charms.

One of the finest poems is the humorous *Thrymskvida* ("Lay of Thrym"), in which the giant THRYM steals the hammer of THOR and demands the goddess FREYJA in marriage for its return. Thor himself journeys to Thrym, disguised as a bride—the "bride" proceeds to astonish the wedding party with her manners at the feast, where she consumes an ox, eight salmon, and three vessels of mead.

The second half of the *Poetic Edda* contains lays about the Germanic heroes. Except for the *Vǫlundarkvida* ("Lay of Völundr"; *i.e.*, Wayland the Smith) these are connected with the hero Sigurd (SIEGFRIED), recounting his youth, his marriage to Gudrun, his death, and the tragic fate of the Burgundians (Nibelungs). These lays are the oldest surviving poetic forms of the Germanic legend of deceit, slaughter, and revenge that forms the core of the great medieval German epic *Nibelungenlied*.

EDDY, MARY BAKER

EDDY, MARY BAKER \\'bā-kər-'e-dē\\ (b. July 16, 1821, Bow, near Concord, N.H., U.S.—d. Dec. 3, 1910, Chestnut Hill, Mass.), founder of CHRISTIAN SCIENCE.

A daughter of CONGREGATIONALISTS, Mary had limited formal education, but she began to write both prose and poetry at an early age. In 1843 she married George W. Glover, who died before the birth of their son, George. Because of her ill health, the boy was reared primarily by others and had little contact with his mother.

Suffering almost constantly from a spinal malady, she was preoccupied with questions of health. She experimented with homeopathy and in 1853 married Daniel Patterson, a dentist who shared this interest. Before their marriage ended in divorce in 1873, Mrs. Patterson sought out and was healed by Phineas P. Quimby of Portland, Maine, who performed remarkable cures without medication. She thought he had rediscovered the healing method of Jesus, and she lectured and wrote of it in regional periodicals. Despite subsequent official statements of her church denying any influence of Quimby, some scholars have considered him an important source of her views.

Soon after Quimby died her illness recurred, and in 1866 she suffered a severe fall but was healed after reading in the NEW TESTAMENT, which she marked as the point of her discovery of Christian Science. Separated from her husband, she spent several years in writing and evolving her system, teaching it to Hiram S. Crafts, Richard Kennedy, and others who subsequently became successful healers. In 1875 she published *Science and Health*, which was revised before her death as *Science and Health with Key to the Scriptures*. Regarded by her followers as divinely inspired, this work and the BIBLE formed the SCRIPTURE of the new faith. She soon held public meetings in Lynn, Roxbury, and Boston, Mass., and in 1877 married one of her followers, Asa G. Eddy (d. 1882).

Steps were taken to organize the First Church of Christ, Scientist, in Boston in 1879. In 1881 Mrs. Eddy founded the Massachusetts Metaphysical College, where she taught until it closed in 1889. Meetings in Boston moved in 1895 from rented halls to the newly dedicated Mother Church and then to its larger "extension" in 1906. Branch churches, following organizational directives issued by Mrs. Eddy and collected in the *Church Manual*, were started in other cities; their members often belonged also to the Mother Church in Boston.

A board of directors, set up by Mrs. Eddy, operated as the ruling authority according to the *Manual*, which is considered inspired and may not be amended. In 1883 she founded the monthly *Christian Science Journal*, in 1898 the weekly *Christian Science Sentinel*, and in 1908 *The Christian Science Monitor*, which has achieved a reputation as one of the leading daily newspapers in the United States. Among her major works are *Miscellaneous Writings* (1896), *Retrospection and Introspection* (1892), *Unity of Good* (1887), and *Rudimental Divine Science* (1908).

EDEN, GARDEN OF

EDEN, GARDEN OF, in JUDAISM and CHRISTIANITY, the biblical earthly paradise inhabited by the first created man and woman, ADAM AND EVE, prior to their expulsion for disobeying the commandments of God. The term *Eden* probably is derived from the Akkadian word *edinu*, borrowed from the Sumerian *eden*, meaning "plain." According to the Genesis story there were four rivers that flowed out of Eden to all areas of the world. Similar stories in Sumerian records indicate that an earthly paradise theme belonged to the MYTHOLOGY of the ancient Middle East.

In ISLAM a paradisal garden was the original home of Adam and his mate, but Eden (Arabic 'Adn) became the destination of the blessed after resurrection. The QUR'AN describes it as a place of multiple gardens and rivers where the righteous will be greeted by ANGELS, reunited with family members, dwell eternally in beautiful homes, and enjoy other luxurious heavenly rewards (see for example Qur'an 9:72, 13:23, and 35:33). Later Muslim scholars speculated that it was located in the highest ranks of the heavens.

EDWARDS, JONATHAN

EDWARDS, JONATHAN \\'ed-wərdz\\ (b. Oct. 5, 1703, East Windsor, Conn. [U.S.]—d. March 22, 1758, Princeton, N.J.), theologian, stimulator of the religious revival known as the "Great Awakening."

After a rigorous schooling at home, Edwards entered Yale College in New Haven, Conn., at the age of 13. He was graduated in 1720 but remained at New Haven for two years, studying divinity; he received the M.A. degree in 1723. In 1727 he became a pastor at his grandfather's church at Northampton, Mass.

Although he was the son of a minister, Edwards did not accept his theological inheritance passively. In his "Personal Narrative" he confesses that, from his childhood on, his mind "had been full of objections" against the doctrine of PREDESTINATION. Though he gradually worked through his intellectual objections, it was only with his conversion (early in 1721) that he came to a "new sense" of God's glory revealed in SCRIPTURE and in nature. This became the center of Edwards' piety: a direct, intuitive apprehension of God in all his glory, a sight and taste of Christ's majesty and beauty far beyond all "notional" understanding. What such a God does must be right; hence, Edwards' cosmic optimism. The acceptance and affirmation of God as he is and does and the love of God simply because he is God became central motifs in all of Edwards' preaching.

Upon his grandfather's death in 1729, Edwards became sole occupant of the Northampton pulpit, the most important in Massachusetts outside of Boston. In his first published sermon Edwards blamed New England's moral ills on its assumption of religious and moral self-sufficiency. Because God is the saints' whole good, faith, which abases man and exalts God, must be insisted on as the only means of salvation. The English colonists' enterprising spirit made them susceptible to a version of Arminianism; it minimized the disabling effects of ORIGINAL SIN, stressed FREE WILL, and tended to make morality the essence of religion.

Adam and Eve in the Garden of Eden, 15th-century book illustration in the Museo dell'Opera del Duomo, Florence, Italy
SCALA—Art Resource

per. The custom was that baptized but unconverted children of believers might have their own children baptized by "owning the COVENANT"; and, Northampton church followed the widespread practice of admitting to the EUCHARIST all who were thus "in the covenant," even if they knew themselves to be unconverted. Edwards gradually came to believe that the profession required for admission to full communion should be understood to imply genuine faith, not merely doctrinal knowledge and good moral behavior.

The public announcement of his position in 1749 precipitated a violent controversy that resulted in his dismissal. On July 1, 1750, Edwards preached his dignified and restrained "Farewell-Sermon." Though Edwards himself was defeated, his position finally triumphed and provided New England CONGREGATIONALISM with a doctrine of church membership more appropriate to its situation after disestablishment.

In 1751 Edwards became pastor of the frontier church at Stockbridge, Mass., and missionary to the Indians there. Hampered by language difficulties, illness, Indian wars, and conflicts with powerful personal enemies, he nevertheless discharged his pastoral duties and found time to write his famous work on the *Freedom of Will* (1754). By 1757 Edwards had finished his *Great Christian Doctrine of Original Sin Defended* (1758), which was mainly a reply to the English divine John Taylor of Norwich, whose works attacking CALVINISM had "made a mighty noise in America." In 1757 he accepted the presidency of the College of New Jersey (later Princeton University) and arrived there in January. He had hardly assumed his duties when he contracted smallpox and died.

Edwards' influence on the intellectual character of American PROTESTANTISM for a century after his death was very pronounced. In a general revolt against PURITANISM and Calvinism after the American Civil War (1861–65), Edwards' prestige declined. In the 1930s and after, he was rediscovered by theologians. Edwards' ability to combine religious intensity with intellectual rigor, the sweep of his theological vision, his emphasis on faith as an "existential" response to reality, and his insistence that love is the heart of religion are some of the reasons his life and writings are again being seriously studied.

Against these ideas Edwards also delivered a series of sermons on "Justification by Faith Alone" in November 1734. The result was a great revival in Northampton and along the Connecticut River valley in the winter and spring of 1734–35, during which period more than 300 of Edwards' people made professions of faith.

In 1740–42 came the GREAT AWAKENING throughout the colonies. George Whitefield, a highly successful evangelist in the English Methodist movement, and Gilbert Tennent, a PRESBYTERIAN minister from New Jersey, drew huge crowds; their "pathetical" (*i.e.,* emotional) sermons resulted in violent emotional response and mass conversions. The Awakening produced not only conversions and changed lives but also excesses, disorders, and ecclesiastical and civil disruptions. Though increasingly critical of attitudes and practices associated with the revival, Edwards maintained that it was a genuine work of God, which needed to be furthered and purified.

Meanwhile, Edwards' relations with his own congregation had become strained; one reason for it was his changed views on the requirements for admission to the Lord's Sup-

EGERIA \i-'jir-ē-ə, ē-\, in ROMAN RELIGION, a water spirit worshiped in connection with DIANA at Aricia and also with the Camenae in their grove outside the Porta Capena at Rome. Like Diana, she was a protectress of pregnant women and, like the Camenae, was considered to have prophetic powers. Traditionally she was the wife, or mistress, and adviser of the second king of Rome, Numa Pompilius, who established the grove at Rome and consorted with her there. Numa created Rome's religious institutions on her advice.

EGYPTIAN
RELIGION

The indigenous beliefs of ancient Egypt from predynastic times (4th millennium BCE) to the disappearance of the traditional culture in the first centuries CE constitute a display of remarkable continuity over so long a span of time.

KING, COSMOS, AND SOCIETY

The Egyptians conceived of the cosmos as including the gods and the present world—whose center was Egypt—and as being surrounded by the realm of disorder, from which order had arisen and to which it would finally revert. Disorder had to be kept at bay. The task of the king as the protagonist of human society was to retain the benevolence of the gods by maintaining order against disorder. This view of the cosmos formed a powerful political legitimation of the king and elite in their task of preserving order. The king was the center of human society, the recipient of god-given benefits including life itself, and the benevolent ruler of the world for humanity. He was ultimately responsible for the cults of the dead, for both his predecessors in office and the dead in general.

The king had a superhuman role, being a manifestation of a god or of various deities on earth. The king's principal original title, the HORUS name, proclaimed that he was an aspect of one of the chief gods, Horus, a sky god who was depicted as a falcon. Other identifications were added to this one, notably "Son of RE [the sun god]" and "Perfect God," both introduced during the 4th dynasty (c. 2575–2465 BCE), when the great PYRAMIDS were constructed. The epithet "Son of Re" placed the king in a close but dependent relation with the leading figure in the pantheon.

"Perfect God" (often rendered "Good God") indicated that the king had the status of a minor deity, for which he was "perfected" through accession to his office; it restricted the extent of his divinity and separated him from full deities. Some kings, notably Amenhotep III (reigned 1390–53 BCE), Ramses II (1279–13 BCE), and several of the Ptolemies (305–145 BCE), sought deification during their own lifetimes, while others, such as Amenemhet III (1818–c. 1770 BCE), became minor gods after their deaths. These very attempts at further deification show how restricted royal divinity actually was.

Adoration of the Rising Sun in the form of Re-Harakhty, c. 1150 BCE; in the British Museum, London

The Bridgeman Art Library International, Ltd.

The gods, the king, humanity, and the dead existed together in the cosmos, which Re the creator god had brought into being from the preexistent CHAOS. All living beings, except perhaps the creator, would die at the end of time. The sun god aged and needed to be rejuvenated and reborn daily. The ordered cosmos was surrounded by and shot through with disorder, which menaced most strongly at such times of transition as the passage from one year to the next or the death of a king. Thus, the king's role in maintaining order was cosmic and not merely social. His exaction of service from the people was necessary to the cosmos.

The concept of MA'AT ("order") was fundamental in Egyptian thought. The king's role was to set *ma'at* in place of *izfet* ("disorder"). *Ma'at* was crucial in human life and embraced notions of reciprocity, justice, truth, and moderation. *Ma'at* was personified as the creator's daughter, a goddess who received a cult of her own. The king's offering of *ma'at* to a deity encapsulated the relationship between humanity, the king, and the gods; as the representative of humanity, he returned to the gods the order that came from them and of which they were themselves part. *Ma'at* extended into the world of the dead. In the weighing of the heart after death, shown on papyri deposited in burials, the heart occupies one side of the scales and a representation of *ma'at* the other. The papyrus text asserts that the deceased behaved correctly on earth and did not overstep the boundaries of order, declaring that the person did not "know that which is not"—that is, things that were outside the created and ordered world.

GODS

Egyptian religion was polytheistic. The gods who inhabited the bounded and ultimately perishable cosmos varied in nature and capacity. The word *netjer* ("god") described a much wider range of beings than the deities of monotheistic religions, including what might be termed DEMONS. Gods were neither all-powerful nor all-knowing, but their power was immeasurably greater than that of human beings, and they had the ability to live almost indefinitely, to survive fatal wounds, to be in more than one place at once, and to affect people in visible and invisible ways.

Most gods were generally benevolent, but their favor could not be counted on, and they had to be propitiated and encouraged to inhabit their cult images so that they could receive the cult and further the reciprocity of divine and human. Some deities, notably such goddesses as NEITH, SEKHMET, and MUT, had strongly ambivalent characters. The god SETH embodied the disordered aspects of the ordered world, and in the 1st millennium BCE he came to be seen as an enemy who had to be eliminated (but would remain present).

The characters of the gods were not neatly defined. Most had a principal association, such as that of Re with the sun or that of the goddess HATHOR with women, but there was much overlap, especially among the leading deities. In general the more closely circumscribed a deity's character, the less powerful that deity was. All the main gods acquired the characteristics of creator gods. A single figure could have many names. Among those of the sun god the most important were KHEPRI (the morning form), ATUM (the old, evening form), and Re-Harakhty (the form of Re in association with Horus). There were three principal "social" categories of deity—gods, goddesses, and youthful deities, mostly male.

Deities had many manifestations, and most gods were associated with one or more species of animal. For gods the most important forms were the falcon and bull, whereas those for goddesses were the cow, cobra, vulture, and lioness. Rams were widespread, while some manifestations were as modest as the millipede of the god Sepa. Some gods were very strongly linked to particular animals, as SEBEK was with the crocodile and Khepri with the SCARAB beetle. THOTH had two animals, the ibis and the baboon. Some animal cults were only partly integrated with specific gods, notably the Ram of Mendes in the Delta and the APIS and MNEVIS bulls at Memphis and HELIOPOLIS, respectively. Changeable animal forms could express aspects of a deity's nature; some goddesses were lionesses in their fiercer aspect but were cats when mild.

These variable forms relate to aspects that were common to gods and people. The most significant of these were the KA, which was the vital essence of a person that survived the death of the body, the BA, which granted freedom of movement and the ability to take on different forms, principally in the next world, and the AKH, which was the transfigured spirit of a person in the next world.

Gods were also frequently represented as human, and many deities had only human form. Among these deities were very ancient figures such as the fertility god MIN and the creator and craftsman PTAH. The cosmic gods SHU, of the air and sky, and GEB, of the earth, had human form, as did OSIRIS, ISIS, and Nephthys, deities who provided a model of human society.

Gods having animal manifestations were shown with a human body and the head of their animal. The opposite convention, a human head and an animal body, was used for the king, who was shown as a SPHINX, which had a lion's body. Sphinxes could have a different type of head, notably that of a ram or falcon, associating the form with AMON and Re-Harakhty.

Demons were represented in more extravagant forms and combinations; these became common in the 1st millennium BCE. Among demons the most important figure was APOPIS, shown as a colossal snake, who was the enemy of the sun god in the god's daily cycle through the cosmos. Apopis existed outside the ordered realm; he had to be defeated daily, but, since he did not belong to the sphere of existence, he could not be destroyed.

Few myths have survived. The narratives that did survive include episodes of the rule of the sun god on earth, tales of the childhood of Horus in the delta marshes, and the Osiris myth and ones with similar themes but differently named protagonists. The rule of the sun god was followed by his withdrawal into the sky, motivated by his age and by the lack of tranquility in the world. One narrative recounts how Isis obtained a magical substance from Re's senile dribbling and fashioned from it a snake that bit him. To make her still the agony of the snakebite, he finally revealed to her the secret of his "true" name. A myth with varied realizations recounts how Re grew weary of humanity's recalcitrance and dispatched his daughter or "Eye" to destroy them. Later regretting his action, he arranged to have the bloodthirsty goddess tricked into drunkenness by spreading beer tinted the color of blood over the land.

CULTS

Most cults centered on the worship of an image of a deity, the daily tending of which was analogous to the pattern of human life. The shrine containing the im-

Anubis weighing the soul of the scribe Ani, in the Papyrus of Ani, from an Egyptian Book of the Dead, c. *1240 BCE* British Museum, London

age was opened at dawn, and then the deity was purified, greeted, praised, clothed, and fed. There were several further services, and the image was finally returned to its shrine for the night. This activity took place within the temple and was performed by a small group of priests. The daily cult was a state concern, conducted largely in isolation from the people.

The numerous festivals, however, allowed more direct interaction between people and the gods. The shrine and image of the deity were taken out from the SANCTUARY on a portable bark, carried among the people, and often brought to visit other temples. Questions were often asked of a deity, and responses might be given by a forward or backward movement of the bark carried on the priests' shoulders. Oracles, of which this was one form, were invoked by the king to obtain sanction for his plans, including military campaigns and important appointments. Although evidence is sparse, consultation with deities may have been part of religious interaction in all periods and for all levels of society. Festivals were also times of communal celebration and often of public reenactment of myths such as the death and vindication of Osiris at ABYDOS or the defeat of Seth by Horus at Idfū.

In the Late period (664–332 BCE) there was a vast expansion in animal cults. They involved a variety of practices centering on the mummification and burial of animals. The principal BULL CULTS focused on a single animal, which gave important oracles and was kept in a special shrine. The burial of an Apis bull was a major occasion involving vast expenditure. Some animals, such as the sacred ibis (connected with Thoth) were kept, and buried, in millions. The dedication of a burial seems to have counted as a pious act. The best-known area for these cults is the NECROPOLIS of northern Ṣaqqārah, which served the city of Memphis. Numerous species were buried there, and people visited the area to consult oracles, to spend the night in a temple area, and to receive a healing dream. A few people resided permanently in the animal necropolis in a state akin to monastic seclusion.

The main audience for the most important festivals of the principal gods of state held in capital cities may have been the ruling elite rather than the people as a whole. In the New Kingdom (c. 1539–c. 1075 BCE) these cities were remodeled as vast cosmic stages for the enactment of royal-divine relations and rituals. Despite the importance of temples and their architectural dominance, evidence does not point to mass participation in temple religion.

WORLD OF THE DEAD

The basic purpose of mortuary preparation was to ensure a safe and successful passage into the hereafter. Belief in an afterlife and a

Painted wooden stela of a musician playing the harp before Horus, c. 950–730 BCE; in the Louvre, Paris
Giraudon—Art Resource

passage to it is evident in predynastic burials, which are oriented to the west, the domain of the dead, and which include pottery grave goods as well as personal possessions of the deceased. The most striking development of later mortuary practice was mummification, which was an expression of the belief that the body must continue intact in order for the deceased to live in the next world (*see* MUMMY). Mummification evolved gradually from the Old Kingdom (*c.* 2575–*c.* 2130 BCE) until the early 1st millennium BCE, after which it declined. It was always too elaborate and costly to be available to the majority.

The next world was variously thought to be located in the area around the tomb (and consequently near the living); on the "perfect ways of the West," as it is expressed in Old Kingdom invocations; among the stars or in the celestial regions with the sun god; or in the underworld, the domain of Osiris. One prominent notion was of the "Elysian Fields," where the deceased could enjoy an ideal existence in a land of plenty. The journey to the next world was fraught with obstacles. It could be imagined as a passage by ferry past a succession of portals or through an "Island of Fire." The judgment after death was a subject often depicted from the New Kingdom onward. The related text, Chapter 125 of the BOOK OF THE DEAD, presented the dangers of the judgment, which assessed the deceased's conformity with *ma'at*. Those who failed the judgment would "die a second time" and would be cast outside the ordered cosmos. In the demotic story of Setna (3rd century BCE) this notion of moral retribution acquired overtones similar to those of the Christian judgment after death.

Because the recently deceased were believed to exert influence on the living, either for good or for bad, the offerings that were made to the dead were intended, among other purposes, to make them well disposed. People occasionally deposited with their offerings a letter telling the deceased of their problems and asking for assistance. This written communication with the dead was confined to the very few literate members of the population, but it was probably part of a more widespread oral practice. Some tombs of prominent people acquired minor cults, which may have originated in frequently successful outcomes to requests for assistance.

Offerings to the dead generally did not continue long after burial, and most tombs were robbed within a generation or so. Thus relations with dead kin probably focused on the recently deceased. Nonetheless, the dead were respected and feared more widely. The attitudes attested were almost uniformly negative. The dead were held accountable for much misfortune, both on a local, domestic level and in the broader context of the state. People were also concerned that, when they died, those in the next world would oppose their entry, because as newcomers they might oust the less-recently dead.

Sacred eye, faience fragment, 1st millennium BCE; National Maritime Museum, Haifa, Israel
Erich Lessing—Art Resource

EHUD \'ē-həd\, in the OLD TESTAMENT (Judges 3:12–4:1), son of Gera, the Benjaminite. Ehud was an Israelite hero who delivered his country from 18 years of oppression by the MOABITES. Ehud tricked Eglon, king of Moab, and killed him. He then led the tribe of EPHRAIM to seize the fords of the Jordan, where they killed about 10,000 Moabite soldiers. As a result, Israel enjoyed peace for about 80 years.

EID \'ēd\: *see* ʽID.

EIGHTFOLD PATH, fundamental Buddhist doctrine; *see* MĀRGA.

EILEITHYIA \ī-lī-'thī-ə\, Greek goddess of childbirth who hindered or facilitated the process according to her disposition. The earliest evidence for her cult is at Amnisus, in Crete, where excavations indicate that she was worshiped continuously from Neolithic to Roman times. In Homer she appears, sometimes in the plural, as a personification of birth pangs, and is described as the daughter of HERA, the consort of ZEUS. In later times Eileithyia tended to be identified with Hera or ARTEMIS, goddesses who were also associated with marriage and childbirth.

EISAI \'ā-'sī\ (b. 1141—d. 1215), Buddhist monk who contributed to the flowering of ZEN (Ch'an) BUDDHISM in Japan. Eisai, who founded the RINZAI school in 1191, was a Tendai monk who wished to restore pure Buddhism to Japan and with that aim visited China, first in 1168 and again in 1187. When he returned he taught a strict meditational system based on the use of the KOAN phrases. Unlike the Ch'an schools, Eisai also taught that Zen should defend the state and could observe ceremonial rules and offer prayers and incantations. These teachings influenced the warrior class and led to a Zen influence over the martial arts of archery and swordsmanship. Eisai founded Rinzai temples at Hakata in Krūshu (1191) and Kyōto (1215) and was appointed by the Shōgun Minamoto Yoriie as the head of the monastery of Kennin-ji in Kyōto in 1204. DŌGEN, the founder of the SŌTŌ Zen lineage, was one of his students.

EKNĀTH \'āk-,nāth, -,nät\, *also spelled* Ekanātha (b. 1544, Paithan, Mahārāshtra, India—d. 1599), Hindu poet-saint and mystic of the tradition of VAIṢṆAVISM. Eknāth is best known for his translations of various Sanskrit texts into Marathi (the local language of the Maharashtra region of central India), his authorship of others (*e.g.*, a *Rāmāyaṇa*) in that language, and his restored edition of the then-corrupted classic of Marathi literature, the *Jñāneśvarī* of JÑĀNEŚVAR. The object of his scholarship was to bring the means of salvation through devotion, or BHAKTI, within the reach and understanding of ordinary people, including outcastes and women.

Although himself a BRAHMIN, Eknāth came into conflict with some of the more orthodox Brahmins in his hometown of Paithan over the issue of CASTE. Eknāth insisted that there is no caste distinction in the eyes of God, and in his own life and writings he recognized no inherent difference between the Brahmin and the outcaste. His radical form of religious egalitarianism led him not only to argue that low-caste persons were eligible for God's grace but also to go so far as to claim in one of his compositions that "the dog and God are identical." Several temples dedicated to Eknāth exist to this day in Paithan—one at the site of his home and another near the place where he died in the Godāvari River.

EL \'el\ (Semitic: "God"), the chief deity of the West Semites. In the ancient texts from Ras Shamra (ancient UGARIT) in Syria, El (El the Bull) was described as the titular head of the pantheon, husband of ASHERAH, and father of all the other gods (except for BAAL). Although a venerable deity, he was not active in the myths, which primarily concerned his daughters and sons.

He was usually visually portrayed as an old man with a long beard and, often, two wings. Writers of the OLD TESTAMENT used the word El both as a general term for "deity" and as a synonym for YAHWEH.

ELEAZAR BEN JUDAH OF WORMS \,e-lē-'ā-zər-ben-'jü-də . . . 'wərmz, 'vȯrms\, *original name* Eleazar ben Judah ben Kalonymos, *also called* Eleazar Rokeaḥ (b. *c.* 1160, Mainz, Franconia [Germany]—d. 1238, Worms), Jewish RABBI, mystic, Talmudist, and codifier. Along with the SEFER ḤASIDIM (1538; "Book of the Pious"), of which he was a co-author, his voluminous works are the major extant documents of medieval German HASIDISM.

Eleazar was a member of the eminent Kalonymos family, which gave medieval Germany many of its spiritual leaders and mystics; another member of that family, the semi-legendary pietist JUDAH BEN SAMUEL, the Hasid of Regensburg, was his teacher and spiritual master. In 1196 two Christian crusaders broke into Eleazar's house and murdered his wife and two daughters, yet he continued to teach a doctrine of love of humanity. He became a rabbi at Worms in 1201 and in 1223 took part in a SYNOD at Mainz, which considered such questions as business relations with Christians and the inequitable exemptions of particularly favored Jews from the tax imposed by the government.

Eleazar was a man of great erudition who did not compartmentalize his knowledge of the QABBALAH and the TALMUD; rather, he tried to unify these opposing aspects of JUDAISM in his writings, often with strange results. His greatest work is his ethical code *Rokeaḥ* (1505; "Dealer in Spice"), for which he is sometimes known as Eleazar Rokeaḥ. The work is prefaced with a number of chapters dealing with the essential principles of Judaism, in which Eleazar attempts to explain mystical concepts, including the unity of God, in terms of HALAKHAH (Law). The work itself, which is not complete, contains some 497 sections addressed to every aspect of Jewish life, from SABBATH law, holiday rituals, and the marriage ceremony to penance for SINS, the latter a preoccupation of the German Hasidim.

Eleazar was an angelologist, not only in his mystic theories of theurgy (the art of persuading or compelling supernatural beings to one's bidding) but also in his writings on the *kavod* ("divine glory"). Eleazar believed that the *kavod*, a ruling ANGEL, was an emanation from God and the knowable aspect of him, while God himself was infinitely transcendent and unknowable. Eleazar also wrote TOSAFOT (commentaries) on a number of Talmudic tractates, as well as mystical commentaries on the five scrolls (Song of Solomon, Ruth, Lamentations, Ecclesiastes, and Esther) and on the PENTATEUCH.

ELECT, in CHRISTIANITY, those chosen for salvation by God; *see* PREDESTINATION.

ELECTRA \i-lek-trə\ (Greek: "Bright One"), in Greek myth, the daughter of AGAMEMNON and Clytemnestra who saved the life of her young brother ORESTES by sending him away when their father was murdered. When he later returned, she helped him to slay their mother and their mother's lover. Electra then married Orestes' friend Pylades. The plays of the same name written by Sophocles and Euripides and the *Choephoroi* by Aeschylus vary the theme in detail.

ELEUSINIA \\,el-yŭ-'si-nē-ə\\, ancient Greek festival in honor of the goddess DEMETER, unconnected with the ELEUSINIAN MYSTERIES despite the similarity of names. The Eleusinia, which included games and contests, was held every two years, probably in the month of Metageitnion (August–September). Every second festival had a particularly elaborate observance and was known as the Great Eleusinia. Its purpose was thanksgiving and sacrifice to Demeter for the gift of grain.

ELEUSINIAN MYSTERIES \\,el-yŭ-'si-nē-ən\\, most famous of the MYSTERY RELIGIONS of ancient Greece. According to the Homeric *Hymn to Demeter*, the goddess Demeter went in disguise to Eleusis in search of her daughter Kore (PERSEPHONE), who had been abducted by HADES. Befriended by the royal family of Eleusis, she agreed to rear the queen's son. She was, however, prevented by the queen's fear from making the boy eternally young. Thereupon she revealed her identity to the royal family and commanded that a temple be built for her into which she retired.

According to the *Hymn*, the Mysteries at Eleusis originated in the twofold story of Demeter's life—her separation from and reunion with her daughter and her failure to make the queen's son immortal. After Eleusis was incorporated, the city of Athens took responsibility for the festival, but the festival never lost its local associations.

The Mysteries began with the march of the *mystai* (initiates) in PROCESSION from Athens to Eleusis. The rites that they then performed in the Telesterion, or Hall of Initiation, were and remain a secret. Something was recited, something was revealed, and acts were performed, but there is no sure evidence of what the rites actually were, though some garbled information was given by later Christian writers. It is clear that neophytes were initiated in stages and that the annual process began with purification rites at what were called the Lesser Mysteries held at Agrai (Agrae) on the stream of Ilissos, outside of Athens, in the month of Anthesterion (February–March). The Greater Mysteries was celebrated annually in the month of Boedromion (September–October). It included a RITUAL BATH in the sea, three days of fasting, and completion of the still-myste-

Sculpture by Gian Lorenzo Bernini illustrating the base myth for the Eleusinian Mysteries, in which Persephone is abducted by Hades; sculpted in 1621–22, now in the Borghese Gallery, Rome
Anderson—Alinari from Art Resource

rious central rite. These acts completed the initiation, and the initiate was promised benefits in the afterlife.

ELIADE, MIRCEA \\,e-lē-'ä-də\\ (b. March 9, 1907, Bucharest, Rom.—d. April 22, 1986, Chicago, Ill., U.S.), historian of religions and man of letters, distinguished for his researches in the symbolic language used by various religious traditions and for his attempt to integrate their meaning into types of underlying primordial myths that provide the basis for mystical phenomena.

Eliade took an M.A. in philosophy from the University of Bucharest in 1928. He studied Sanskrit and Indian philosophy at the University of Calcutta (1928–31) and then lived for six months in the ASHRAM of Rishikesh in the HIMALAYAS. He earned his Ph.D. in 1933 with the dissertation *Yoga: Essai sur les origines de la mystique indienne* ("Yoga: Essay on the Origins of Indian Mysticism") and then taught the history of religions and Indian philosophy at Bucharest (1933–39). In 1945 he went to Paris as a visiting professor at the École des Hautes Études of the Sorbonne. In 1956 he joined the faculty of the University of Chicago. In 1961 he founded the journal *History of Religions*.

Eliade considered RELIGIOUS EXPERIENCE in traditional and contemporary societies as credible phenomena that he termed hierophanies (*i.e.*, manifestations of the sacred in the world). His "morphological analyses" traced the forms that these hierophanies have taken throughout the world and through time. Eliade's interpretation of traditional religious cultures and his analysis of the forms of mystical experience characterize his major works: *Traité d'histoire des religions* (1949; *Patterns of Comparative Religion*), *Le Mythe de l'éternel retour* (1949; *The Myth of the Eternal Return*), and *Le Chamanisme et les techniques archaïques de l'extase* (1951; *Shamanism: Archaic Techniques of Ecstasy*). He also expressed his views in works of fiction, notably the novels *Forêt interdite* (1955; *The Forbidden Forest*) and *The Old Man and the Bureaucrats* (1979). His works include two collections of essays, *The Quest: History and Meaning in Religion* (1969) and *Occultism, Witchcraft, and Cultural Fashion: Essays in Comparative Religion* (1976). He also wrote a three-volume work entitled *A History of Religious Ideas* (1978–85) and was editor in chief of the 16-volume *Encyclopedia of Religion* (1987).

Elijah's ascent into heaven, fresco, c. 1325; from the Kirkerup Church at Sealand, Denmark
The Granger Collection

ELIJAH \i-'lī-jə, ē-\, *also spelled* Elias, *or* Elia, *Hebrew* Eliyyahu (fl. 9th century BCE), Hebrew prophet who ranks with MOSES in saving the religion of YAHWEH from being corrupted by the nature worship of BAAL. Elijah's name means "Yahweh is my God" and is spelled Elias in some versions of the BIBLE. The story of his prophetic career in the northern kingdom of Israel during the reigns of Kings AHAB and Ahaziah is told in 1 Kings 17–19 and 2 Kings 1–2 in the OLD TESTAMENT. He is commemorated by Christians on July 20 and is recognized as a prophet by ISLAM.

The Israelite king Omri had allied himself with the Phoenician cities of the coast, and his son Ahab was married to JEZEBEL, daughter of Ethbaal, king of Tyre and Sidon. Jezebel propagated her native religion in a SANCTUARY built for Baal in the royal city of Samaria. This meant that the Israelites accepted Baal as well as Yahweh, putting Yahweh on a par with a nature-god celebrated often in an orgiastic cult.

Elijah was from Tishbe in Gilead. The narrative in 1 Kings relates how he suddenly appears during Ahab's reign to proclaim a drought in punishment of the cult of Baal. Later Elijah meets 450 prophets of Baal in a contest of strength on Mount Carmel to determine which deity is the true God of Israel. Sacrifices are placed on an altar to Baal and one to Yahweh. The PAGAN prophets' appeals to Baal to kindle the wood on his altar are unsuccessful, but Elijah's prayers to Yahweh are answered by a fire on his altar. This outcome is taken as decisive by the Israelites, who slay the priests and prophets of Baal under Elijah's direction. The drought thereupon ends with the falling of rain.

Elijah flees the wrath of Jezebel by undertaking a PILGRIMAGE to Mount Horeb (SINAI), where he is at first disheartened in his struggle and then miraculously renewed. In a further narrative, King Ahab has a man named Naboth condemned to death in order to gain possession of his vineyard. Elijah denounces Ahab for his crimes, asserting that all men are subject to the law of God and are therefore equals. Later Ahab's son, King Azariah, appeals to Baal to heal him of an illness, and Elijah once more upholds the exclusive rights of Yahweh by bringing down "fire from heaven." After bestowing his mantle on his successor, ELISHA, the prophet Elijah is taken up to heaven in a whirlwind.

Elijah's words proclaimed that there is no reality except the God of Israel, that there are no other beings entitled to the name of divinity. The acclamation of the people, "Yahweh, he is God," expresses a fully conscious MONOTHEISM, as it had never before perhaps been brought home to them. Elijah's deepest prophetic experience takes place on his pilgrimage to Horeb, where he learns that God is not in the storm, the earthquake, or the lightning. Nature, so far from being God's embodiment, is not even an adequate symbol. The transcendence of God receives here one of its earliest expressions. Elijah's story also expresses for the first time a thought that was to dominate Hebrew PROPHECY: salvation is bestowed only on those purified by God's judgment. The theme of the later prophets, that morality must be at the heart of ritual worship, is also taught by Elijah, who upholds the unity of law and religion.

ELIJAH BEN SOLOMON \i-'lī-jə-ben-'sä-lə-mən\, *in full* Elijah ben Solomon Zalman, *also called* by the acronym Ha-Gra \hä-'grä\ (b. April 23, 1720, Sielec, Lithuania, Russian Empire—d. Oct. 9, 1797, Vilna [now Vilnius, Lithuania]), the GAON ("excellency") of Vilna, and the outstanding authority in Jewish religious and cultural life in 18th-century Lithuania.

Born into a long line of scholars, Elijah traveled among the Jewish communities of Poland and Germany in 1740–45 and then settled in Vilna, which was the cultural center of eastern European Jewry. There he refused rabbinic office and lived as a recluse while devoting himself to study and prayer, but his reputation as a scholar had nonetheless spread throughout the Jewish world by the time he was 30. As a mark of nearly universal reverence, the title *gaon*, borne by the heads of the Babylonian academies and virtually extinct for many centuries, was bestowed upon him by the people.

Elijah's scholarship embraced mastery of every field of study in the Jewish literature. His vast knowledge of the TALMUD and MIDRASH and of biblical EXEGESIS, as well as of mystical literature and lore, was combined with a deep interest in philosophy, grammar, mathematics, astronomy, and folk medicine.

Elijah's most important contributions were his synoptic view of Jewish learning and his critical methods of study. In an age of narrow, puritanical piety, he broadened the con-

Elijah ben Solomon, engraving
Picture from the photographic archive of the Jewish Theological Seminary of America, New York, Frank J. Darmstaedter

ception of TORAH learning to include the natural sciences and asserted that a complete understanding of Jewish law and literature necessitated the study of mathematics, astronomy, geography, botany, and zoology. He encouraged translations of works on these subjects into Hebrew. Elijah also introduced the methods of textual criticism in the study of the BIBLE and the Talmud.

Elijah condemned HASIDISM as a superstitious and antischolarly movement and ordered the EXCOMMUNICATION of its adherents and the burning of their books. He became the leader of the Mitnaggedim (opponents of Hasidism) and was temporarily able to check the movement's spread in Lithuania. He was also mildly opposed to the HASKALAH, or Jewish Enlightenment. His writings, published posthumously, include commentaries and numerous annotations on the Bible, Talmud, Midrash, and other works.

ELIMELECH OF LIZHENSK \\,e-li-'me-le<u>k</u> . . . 'lē-zhensk\ (b. 1717—d. 1787, Lizhensk, Galicia [now in Poland]), Jewish teacher and author, one of the founders of HASIDISM in Galicia.

Elimelech was a disciple of Ṭov Baer, one of the early Hasidic leaders, and after Baer's death he settled in Lizhensk, which subsequently became an important Hasidic center. Elimelech emphasized the importance of the leader (ZADDIK, meaning "righteous one"), who, he believed, is mediator between God and the people and possesses authority

not only in the spiritual sphere but in all areas of life. Although the *zaddik* belongs to a higher world, he descends to the level of the community to redeem it, and his capacity to SIN is a necessary part of his mission of transforming evil into good. Elimelech's ideas are set forth in his treatise *No'am Elimelekh*, which was published after his death by his son Eleazar.

ELISHA \i-'lī-shə, ē-\, in the OLD TESTAMENT, Israelite prophet, the pupil of ELIJAH and also his successor (c. 851 BCE). He instigated and directed JEHU's revolt against the house of Omri, which was marked by a bloodbath at Jezreel in which King AHAB and his family were slaughtered.

The popular traditions about Elisha (2 Kings 2–13) sketch a charismatic, quasi-ecstatic figure, very similar to Elijah. Like his mentor, Elisha was a passionate exponent of the ancient religious and cultural traditions of ISRAEL, which both prophets felt to be threatened by the ruling dynasty of Omri, then in alliance with Phoenicia. As a prophet, Elisha was a political activist and revolutionary. He led a war that extinguished the house of Omri in Jerusalem as well as in Samaria (2 Kings 9–10).

In popular estimation Elisha always remains partly in the shadow of his master Elijah. The story of the beginning of his apprenticeship (1 Kings 19:19–21) and the account in which he becomes Elijah's heir and successor (2 Kings 2:8–18) both feature the prophetic "mantle," which carries connotations of power and authority. In the first, Elijah casts it upon his pupil; in the second, Elisha picks it up.

ELISHA BEN ABUYAH \i-'lī-shə-,ben-ä-'bü-yä\, *byname* Aḥer, early rabbinic authority, born prior to the destruction of the Second TEMPLE OF JERUSALEM (70 CE). While early in his career Elisha was an important and respected RABBI, he later was opposed as an apostate. He came to be so reviled that he generally is referred to simply as "the Other" (*Aḥrabbinicer*), a term used to designate a thing so repellent that even its name causes offense.

The paucity of early sources regarding Elisha and the extent to which all later sources presuppose his APOSTASY make it difficult to discern his true biography. The rabbinic literature paints a picture of a scholar with a broad education both in Jewish learning and Greek thought. He reportedly never ceased singing Greek songs and is said to have kept sectarian books hidden in his clothes, even while he was a rabbinic master.

Elisha's HERESY is said to have arisen from a mystical experience in which he, Ben Azzai, Ben Zoma, and AKIBA BEN JOSEPH entered paradise (Hagigah 14b [Talmud BAVLI]). The Bavli associates this experience with the emergence of what it sees as Elisha's heretical dualistic theology. The Talmud YERUSHALMI, by contrast, accuses Elisha of attempting to entice schoolchildren from the study of TORAH to more practical activities and, during the Hadrianic persecutions that followed the BAR KOKHBA revolt, of informing the Roman government against PHARISEES who continued to study and abide by Jewish law.

In his assigned role of the paradigmatic apostate, Elisha is charged with other heretical acts that define separation from the rabbinic community, such as riding through Jerusalem on a Day of ATONEMENT that coincided with the SABBATH and overstepping the Sabbath boundary. While the specifics of what Elisha actually did, or why, are lost, he is important in demonstrating how rabbinic culture viewed insider and outsider status and how it defined the character and results of apostasy.

ELLORA CAVES \e-'lōr-ə, -'lȯr-\, series of rock-cut temples of the Gupta
Period (c. 320–540 CE), near the village of Ellora, central Mahārāshtra
state, western India. The temples are
excavated out of rock cliffs and are of
Buddhist, Hindu, and Jain origins.
The most remarkable of the monuments is the Kailāsa Temple, 165 feet
long and 96 feet high, cut from a single outcropping of rock. It is extensively carved with sculptures of Hindu divinities and mythological
figures, many in erotic and volup-
tuous poses. The temple, dedicated
to the Hindu god SHIVA, was built in
the 8th century during the reign of
the Rāṣṭrakūṭas.

ELOHIM \,e-lō-'hēm, i-'lō-him\, *singular* Eloah (Hebrew: "God"), the God
of Israel in the OLD TESTAMENT.
Though Elohim is sometimes used
for other deities, such as the MOABITE
god CHEMOSH, the Sidonian goddess
ASTARTE, and also for other majestic
beings such as ANGELS, kings, judges

Carvings in a basalt cliff at the Ellora Caves, India
Kenneth Murray—Photo Researchers

(the Old Testament *shofeṭim*), and the MESSIAH, it is usually
employed in the Old Testament for the one and only God of
Israel, whose personal name was revealed to MOSES as
YHWH, or YAHWEH. When referring to Yahweh, *elohim* very
often is accompanied by the article *ha-*, to mean, in combination, "the God," and sometimes with a further identification *Elohim ḥayyim*, meaning "the living God."

Though plural in form, "Elohim" is commonly understood in the singular sense. The Israelites probably borrowed the Canaanite plural and made it singular in meaning in their cultic practices and theological reflections.

ELOHIST SOURCE \'e-lō-hist, i-'lō-\, *abbreviated* E, one
strand of four source texts that compose the PENTATEUCH
(the first five sections, or books, of both the Jewish and the
Christian BIBLES), identified for ELOHIM, the name for God
used therein. As an example, in the YAHWIST SOURCE (abbreviated J), along with YAHWEH as God's name, Moses' father-
in-law is called Reuel, the mountain is called Sinai, and the
people living in the region Palestine are referred to as
Canaanites. In a strand where God is called Elohim, Moses'
father-in-law is JETHRO, the mountain is Horeb, and the people living in the region Palestine are Amorites. Unlike J,
the Elohist source presents God as abstract and not directly
accessible. The Elohist prefers PROPHECY as the medium of
God's revelation, thus treating ABRAHAM as a prophet and
showing MOSES as the prophet who intercedes with God on
Israel's behalf.

E is generally thought to have been produced in the
northern kingdom of Israel in the 8th century BCE and later
to have been combined with J, yielding the source JE, identified where God is called "Yahweh Elohim"—*i.e.*, the Lord
God. *See also* DEUTERONOMIST SOURCE; PRIESTLY CODE.

ELYSIUM \i-'li-zhē-əm, -zē-\, *also called* Elysian Fields, *or*
Elysian Plain, in Greek mythology, originally the paradise
to which heroes on whom the gods conferred immortality
were sent. In Homer's writings the Elysian Plain was a land
of perfect happiness at the end of the earth, on the banks of

the Oceanus River. A similar description was given by Hesiod of the Isles of the Blessed. In the earlier authors, only
those specially favored by the gods entered Elysium and
were made immortal. Later Elysium became a place for the
blessed dead, and, from Pindar on (c. 500 BCE), entrance was
gained by a righteous life.

EMAIN MACHA \'e-vənʸ-'vȧ-ḵə\, the political center of the
northernmost of Ireland's provinces, Ulster, during mythical times. In the early Christian times (the 5th and 6th centuries) this region was known under the Old Irish name Ulaid (Latin: Ultonia; English: Ulster) centered on Emain
Macha near the modern-day town of Armagh. The place is
now called Navan Fort and is the site of a remarkable construction from the Iron Age, which probably had religious
significance.

Ulster is of special importance in the mythic history of
Ireland because its rulers and their champions played a
prominent role in the rich Irish sagas of the Middle Ages.
The semi-historical king CONCHOBAR (mac Nessa) reigned
from Emain Macha. He and his prodigious warriors of the
Red Branch, the most celebrated of whom was CÚ CHU-
LAINN, are the major figures of the ULSTER CYCLE. The best-
known and longest tale of this cycle is the *Táin Bó Cúailgne* (*The Cattle Raid of Cooley*), which recounts the invasion of Ulster by the other provinces, led by Queen MEDB of
Connaught (Connacht, the traditional western province;
literally, the "descendants of Conn") in pursuit of a won-
derful bull. Eventually the men of Connacht are repulsed
by the Ulstermen and their spectacular hero, Cú Chulainn.

The most successful Christian missionary in Ireland, the
5th-century Patrick, was predominantly based in Ulster
and was associated with its rulers. He established his ecclesiastical center near Emain Macha, at Armagh, which is
still the primatial see of both the Roman Catholic Church
in Ireland and of the Protestant Church of Ireland.

EMBALMING, the treatment of a dead body so as to steril-
ize it or to protect it from decay. For practical as well as

theological reasons a well-preserved body has long been a chief mortuary concern (*see* FUNERARY CUSTOMS). The application of spices and perfumed unguents to minimize putrefaction was so common a practice that the English word embalming had as its original meaning "to put on balm." Generally, however, the word is used to describe the introduction of agents into the body to ensure preservation.

The beginnings of the art and techniques of embalming are associated principally with ancient Egypt, where, as in parts of Asia and South America, a dry soil and climate encouraged its development. The early practice of wrapping the dead in cloth and burying them in charcoal and sand beyond the reach of the Nile waters preserved the corpses, which retained form and features for a long period.

Although it is held that embalming skill reached a peak during the New Kingdom period between 1738 and 1102 BCE, the most detailed description of methods used to prepare a MUMMY was given by the 5th-century-BCE Greek historian Herodotus. The most elaborate method, at first reserved for the royal dead, involved surgical procedures. The brain, intestines, and other vital organs were removed, washed in palm wine, and placed in vases, known as CANOPIC JARS, filled with herbs. The body cavities were filled with powder of myrrh and other aromatic resins and perfumes. The incisions were stitched, and the body was placed in nitre (potassium nitrate, or saltpetre) for 70 days, after which it was washed, wrapped in cotton bandages, dipped in a gummy substance, and finally coffined and entombed. In a less expensive procedure, oil of cedar was injected into the body, which was then placed in nitre for 70 days. When the body was removed, the oil was withdrawn along with fleshy parts of the body, so that only skin and bones remained. A third method, employed on the bodies of the poor, consisted of purging the intestines and covering the body with nitre for the prescribed period.

A number of other early peoples also practiced embalming of a sophisticated nature. Archaeologists have found evidence of a high degree of embalming skill in the burial chambers of the prehistoric Paraca Indians of Peru. The Guanches of the Canary Islands used methods much like those of the Egyptians, removing the viscera and filling the cavity with salt and vegetable powders. The Jívaro tribes of Ecuador and Peru took the additional precaution of ensuring the immortality of their chiefs by roasting their embalmed bodies over very low fires. In Tibet some bodies are still embalmed according to an ancient formula: the corpse is put in a large box and packed in salt for about three months, after which it is in a mummified condition.

Although there is evidence that some early Christians were embalmed, generally they rejected embalming as well as CREMATION, considering them PAGAN customs that mutilated the corpse. Such scruples were sometimes overcome by the desire to have an outstanding person linger on, a desire that was reinforced by the belief that the bodies of some of the devout were kept intact after death as a mark of divine favor. Consequently, some Christians were embalmed, a notable example being Charlemagne, whose embalmed and richly dressed corpse was placed in a sitting position in his tomb at Aachen after his death in 814.

EMDEN, JACOB ISRAEL \\'em-dən\\, *original name* Jacob ben Zebi, *also called* Yaabetz \\'yä-ˌbets\\ (b. June 4, 1697, Altona, Holstein [now in Germany]—d. April 19, 1776, Altona), RABBI and Talmudic scholar primarily known for his lengthy quarrel with Rabbi JONATHAN EYBESCHÜTZ, an antagonism that divided European Jewry.

Emden was thoroughly trained as a scholar of the TALMUD and also studied Latin and Dutch, though he believed that a Jew should pursue such secular subjects only during the twilight hours. Emden was a rabbi, serving four years in the city from which he took his name. After moving to Altona he established his own SYNAGOGUE and printing press and engaged in frequent disputes with members of the Jewish community. He attacked such people as the chief rabbi of the community, Ezekiel Katzenellenbogen, for his Talmudic decisions. When Katzenellenbogen died Jonathan Eybeschütz, a rabbi of great popularity and reputation in Europe, was chosen to take his place. Eybeschütz prescribed AMULETS to save women from death in childbirth, and one of the charms, with a prayer in cipher to SHABBETAI TZEVI, the most important of the Jewish false MESSIAHS, fell into Emden's hands. He publicly denounced the maker of the amulet (without specifying Eybeschütz) as a heretic deserving EXCOMMUNICATION, thereby initiating a long, often violent quarrel.

EMERALD BUDDHA, statue of the BUDDHA carved of green jasper and dating from around the 15th century.

The Emerald Buddha was originally at a temple in the town of Chiang Rai (now in Northern Thailand) until 1436, when it was removed to Chiang Mai. It was kept there until Setthathirat I, king of Chiang Mai and Laos, moved the statue to his capital, Vientiane (now in Laos), in 1560. There he built a majestic temple to house it. When King Rama I (reigned over Siam [now Thailand] 1782–1809) captured the town of Vientiane, he returned the Emerald Buddha to Thailand. Rama I established Bangkok as his capital, and in 1784 the image was placed there in the Temple of the Emerald Buddha.

The Emerald Buddha has seasonal costumes, which are changed ceremonially three times a year.

EMPIRICISM (from Greek *empeiria*, "experience"), in philosophy, an attitude expressed in a pair of doctrines: (1) that all concepts are derived from the experience to which they are applied; and (2) that all knowledge of matters of fact is based on, or derived from, experience. Accordingly, all claims to knowledge of the world can be justified only by experience.

Empiricism argues that knowledge derived from *a priori* reasoning (involving definitions or principles assumed) either does not exist or is confined to "analytical" truths, which have no content beyond the mere meanings of the words used to express them. Hence a metaphysics that seeks to combine the *a priori* validity of logic with a scientific content is impossible. Likewise there can be no "rational" method; the nature of the world cannot be discovered through pure reason or reflection.

The first Western empiricists were the ancient Greek Sophists, who concentrated their philosophical inquiries on such relatively concrete entities as human and society, rather than the speculative fields explored by their predecessors. Later ancient philosophers with empiricist tendencies were the Stoics and the Epicureans, although both were principally concerned with ethical questions. The majority of Christian philosophers in the Middle Ages were empiricists; for example, WILLIAM OF OCKHAM argued that all knowledge of the physical world is attained by sensory means.

The following ideas may be attributed to empiricist influence, although not all of them need be held by any particular empiricist thinker: (1) Experience is intelligible in isolation without reference to the nature of its object or to the circumstances of its subject. Hence an experience can be described without saying anything about the mind that has it, the thoughts that describe it, or the world that contains it. (2) The person who undergoes experience is in some sense the recipient of data that are imprinted upon his intelligence irrespective of his activity; the person brings nothing to experience, but gains everything from it. (3) All method is scientific method. To discover the nature of the world it is necessary to develop a method of experiment whereby all claims to knowledge are tested by experience, since nothing but experience can validate them. (4) REDUCTIONISM: All facts about the world are known by the experiences that confirm claims to knowledge as fact; hence no claims to knowledge of a transcendental world can have any foundation.

In the metaphysical sphere empiricism generates a characteristic view of causation. According to empiricist metaphysics the world consists of a set of contingently connected objects and situations, united by regularities rather than necessities, and unrelated to any transcendental cause or destiny. Science, according to this view, investigates connections, and its aim is to make predictions on the basis of observed regularities. Furthermore, judgments of value have no place in science, say the empiricists, as such judgments are subjective preferences of the investigator.

EMPTINESS, *also called* nothingness, *or* void, in MYSTICISM and religion, a state of "pure consciousness" in which the mind has been emptied of all particular objects and images; also, the undifferentiated reality (a world without distinctions and multiplicity) or quality of reality that the emptied mind reflects or manifests. The particular meanings of "emptiness" vary with the particular context and the religious or cultural tradition in which it is used. The concept, with a subjective or objective reference (sometimes the two are identified), has figured prominently in mystical thought in many historical periods and parts of the world. The emptying of the mind and the attainment of an undifferentiated unity is a theme that runs through mystical literature from the UPANISHADS (ancient Indian meditative treatises) to medieval and modern Western mystical works. The concepts of HSÜ in TAOISM, *sunyata* in MAHĀYĀNA BUDDHISM, and *En Sof* in Jewish mysticism are pertinent examples of "emptiness," or "holy nothing," doctrines. Buddhism, with its basic religious ultimate of NIRVANA, as well as its development of the *sunyata* doctrine, has probably articulated emptiness more fully than any other religious tradition; it has also affected some modern Western considerations of the concept. A good deal of 19th–20th century Western imaginative literature has been concerned with emptiness, as has a certain type of existentialist philosophy and some forms of the Death of God movement.

ENCYCLICAL, pastoral letter written by the POPE for the whole ROMAN CATHOLIC church on matters of doctrine, morals, or discipline. Although formal papal letters for the entire church were issued from the earliest days of the church, the first commonly called an encyclical was published by Benedict XIV in 1740. Encyclicals are normally addressed to the bishops of the church, but a few (notably *Pacem in terris* by John XXIII) have been addressed also to "all men of good will." The formal title of an encyclical consists of the first few words of the official text; the language is usually Latin, and the document is not considered to be infallible. *Compare* BULL.

ENDYMION \en-'di-mē-ən\, in Greek mythology, a beautiful youth who spent much of his life in perpetual sleep. Endymion's parentage varies among the different ancient references and stories, but several traditions say that he was originally the king of Elis. According to one tradition, ZEUS offered him anything that he might desire, and Endymion chose an everlasting sleep in which he might remain youthful forever. According to another version of the myth, Endymion's eternal sleep was a punishment inflicted by Zeus because he had fallen in love with Zeus's wife, HERA. In any case, Endymion was loved by SELENE, the goddess of the moon, who visited him every night while he lay asleep in a cave on Mount Latmus in Caria; she bore him 50 daughters. Another form of the myth represents Endymion as having been put to sleep by Selene herself so that she might enjoy his beauty undisturbed.

ENKIDU \'en-kē-ˌdü, 'eŋ-\, friend and companion of the Mesopotamian hero GILGAMESH. Their story is related in the *Epic of Gilgamesh,* which dates from the middle of the 2nd millennium BCE to the middle of the 1st millennium BCE. Enkidu was created as a wild man by the god ANU to act as a foil to Gilgamesh. After Gilgamesh defeats Enkidu, the two become friends (or sometimes Enkidu becomes the servant of Gilgamesh). Enkidu's death following the two heroes' de-

Endymion, in Greek myth, a youth of great beauty who sleeps eternally
Culver Pictures

feat of the Bull of Heaven motivated Gilgamesh's subsequent pursuit of immortality, the story of which forms the latter portions of the *Epic of Gilgamesh*.

ENLIL \'en-ˌlil\, Mesopotamian god of the atmosphere and a member of the triad of gods completed by ANU and EA. Enlil meant Lord Wind: both the hurricane and the gentle winds of spring were the breath issuing from his mouth or, later, his word or command. He was sometimes called Lord of the Air.

Although Anu held authority over the Sumerian pantheon, Enlil played a more important role: he embodied energy and force. Enlil was also the god of agriculture, who separated heaven and earth to make room for seeds to grow. He then invented the hoe and broke the hard crust of earth; men sprang forth from the hole. Another myth relates Enlil's rape of his consort Ninlil, a grain goddess, and his subsequent banishment to the underworld. This may reflect the agricultural cycle of fertilization, ripening, and winter inactivity. Enlil's cult center was Nippur. *See also* BEL.

ENNIN \'en-ˌnēn\, *original name* Mibu, *also called* Jikaku Daishi \ˌjē-'kä-kù-'dī-shē\ (b. 794, Tsuga District, Shimotsuke Province, Japan—d. Feb. 24, 864, Japan), Buddhist priest of the early Heian period, founder of the still-extant Sammon branch of the Tendai (T'IEN-T'AI) sect.

Ennin began his education at Dai-ji (*ji,* "temple"), entering the monastery of Enryaku-ji near Kyōto when he was 15. He became a disciple of the priest SAICHŌ, founder of the temple. Efforts were under way to harmonize BUDDHISM and SHINTŌ, and the emperor Nimmyō named Ennin to a large study mission to T'ang China, where Saichō's inspiration for Tendai had originated.

Ennin, returning home in 847, brought with him 559 volumes of Chinese Buddhist literature and many religious implements for Buddhist rituals. Ennin also brought back the method of musical notation for chants used in China, a system of curved and shaped lines and figures called neumes, whose use continues in Japan. Among his voluminous writings was a detailed journal of his Chinese travels.

It was also Ennin who introduced to Japanese Buddhism *nembutsu,* the practice of chanting the name of Amida (AMITĀBHA) Buddha, and this contributed to a new piety which developed in rural Japan. The Imperial Court recognized Ennin's contributions by naming him *daihosshi* ("great priest") in 848. Ennin's doctrines and teachings, stressing piety and the possibility of becoming a buddha in this life, influenced the course of Japanese Buddhism for centuries to come. The title *hōin daichi* (the highest priestly rank, in effect, "high priest of supreme wisdom") was posthumously conferred on him, and two years later he was given the honorific name Jikaku Daishi.

EOS \'ē-ˌäs\, in Greek mythology, the personification of the dawn. According to the poet Hesiod, she was the daughter of the TITAN Hyperion and the Titaness Theia and sister of HELIOS, the sun god, and SELENE, the moon goddess. By the Titan Astraeus she was the mother of the winds Zephyrus, Notus, and BOREAS, and of HESPERUS (the Evening Star) and the other stars; by TITHONUS of Assyria she was the mother of MEMNON, king of the Ethiopians. She bears in Homer's works the epithet Rosy-Fingered.

Eos was also represented as the lover of the hunter ORION and of the youthful hunter CEPHALUS, by whom she was the mother of PHAETHON. In works of art she is represented as a young woman, either walking fast with a youth in her arms

or rising from the sea in a chariot drawn by winged horses; sometimes, as the goddess who dispenses the dews of the morning, she has a pitcher in each hand.

EPHESUS, COUNCILS OF \'e-fə-səs\, three assemblies held in Asia Minor to resolve problems of the early Christian church.

In 190 Polycrates, bishop of Ephesus, convened a SYNOD to establish the 14th of Nisan (the date of the Jewish PASSOVER) as the official date of EASTER. Pope Victor I, preferring a Sunday as more convenient and desiring uniformity, repudiated the decision.

In 431 Pope Celestine I commissioned CYRIL OF ALEXANDRIA, to conduct proceedings against NESTORIUS. When the Eastern bishops (more sympathetic to Nestorius) arrived and learned that the council had been started without them, they set up a rival synod under John of Antioch and excommunicated Cyril. When Pope Celestine pronounced his EXCOMMUNICATION of Nestorius and ratified his deposition as bishop of Constantinople, the Emperor Theodosius II sided with Cyril. This council is known as the third ecumenical council of the church.

In 449 Emperor Theodosius II convened a council in Ephesus to uphold the MONOPHYSITE Eutyches in his battle against Flavian, patriarch of Constantinople, who championed the doctrine of two natures in Christ. Dioscorus (Cyril's successor at Alexandria) supported Eutyches and concurred in the anathematization of Flavian and other bishops over the protests of the papal legate. Dioscorus even attempted to excommunicate Pope Leo I, who referred to the gathering as the "Robber Synod."

EPHOD \'ē-ˌfäd, 'e-\, *also spelled* efod, part of the ceremonial dress of the HIGH PRIEST of ancient Israel described in the OLD TESTAMENT (Exodus 28:6–8; 39:2–5). It was worn outside the robe and probably kept in place by a girdle and by shoulder pieces, from which hung the breast piece (or pouch) containing the sacred lots, Urim and Thummim. Its association with the sacred lots indicates that the ephod was used for DIVINATION.

A similar vestment, made of linen, was worn by persons other than the high priest. Samuel wore the ephod when he served before the TABERNACLE at SHILOH (1 Samuel 2:18), as did David when he danced before the ARK at its entry into Jerusalem (2 Samuel 6:14).

EPHRAEM SYRUS, SAINT \'ē-frā-əm-'sī-rəs, -frē-\, *Syrian* Aphrem (b. *c.* 306, Nisibis, Mesopotamia—d. June 9, 373, Edessa, Osroëne; Western feast day June 9, Eastern feast day January 28), Christian theologian, poet, hymnist, and as doctrinal consultant to Eastern churchmen, the most authoritative representative of 4th-century Syriac CHRISTIANITY.

Deacon to Bishop James of Nisibis and tutor in theology, Ephraem went to teach at the academy in Edessa when his native town was ceded to the Persians in 363; his record of these events in verse, *Carmina Nisibena* ("Songs of Nisibis") constitutes a valuable historical source. Declining any higher office in the church (he escaped being consecrated bishop by feigning madness), he produced a wealth of theological literature. As a biblical exegete, Ephraem wrote commentaries on the OLD TESTAMENT books of GENESIS and EXODUS and annotated the important 2nd-century Syriac-Greek version of the NEW TESTAMENT, the *Diatessaron.* His favorite literary form was verse, in which he composed treatises, sermons, and HYMNS. Much of his hymnology was directed against the principal heresies of his day, particularly GNOSTICISM. Ephraem further emphasized devotion to the Virgin MARY, particularly her sinlessness and exemplary fidelity. Additional doctrinal themes integrated in his prose and poetry include the union of divinity and humanity in JESUS CHRIST; the essential function of the HOLY SPIRIT in prayer, especially in rendering Christ's actual Presence in the EUCHARIST; the RESURRECTION of all men, wherein he maintained the traditional Syriac belief that each individual would need to await the LAST JUDGMENT to gain heavenly beatitude. Ephraem's graphic description of heaven and hell contributed to the inspiration of Dante's *Divine Comedy*.

EPHRAIM \ 'ē-frē-əm \, one of the TWELVE TRIBES OF ISRAEL that in biblical times comprised the people of ISRAEL (Genesis 41:50–52; 48; Joshua 17:17; 18:5; Judges 1:23, 35). The tribe was named after one of the younger sons of JOSEPH, himself a son of JACOB.

After the death of MOSES, members of JOSHUA's tribe settled in the fertile, hilly region of central Palestine (Joshua 16:5–10). They gradually gained great power, for the Ephraimites acted as hosts to the tribal assemblies and had within their borders such religiously important centers as SHILOH and BETHEL (Judges 4:5; 7:24–25; 17:ff; 21:2; 1 Samuel 1:1–3).

In 930 BCE the tribe of Ephraim led the 10 northern tribes in a successful revolt against the south and established the Kingdom of Israel, with Jeroboam I, an Ephraimite, as king (1 Kings 11:26ff; 2 Chronicles 10). The seventh king of Israel, AHAB (reigned *c.* 874–*c.* 853 BCE), was also an Ephraimite (1 Kings 16:29). From about 745 BCE, the northern kingdom was often referred to as the Kingdom of Ephraim, a reflection of the tribe's importance (Isaiah 7:2–17; 11:13; Jeremiah 31:9, 18–20; Ezekiel 37:16–19). Assyrian conquerors overran the kingdom in 721 BCE, dispersing some of the inhabitants and gradually assimilating others, occurrences that account for the eventual disappearance of the tribe of Ephraim along with the nine other northern tribes (2 Kings 18:9–12). They have become known in legend as the TEN LOST TRIBES OF ISRAEL.

EPICLESIS \ e-pi-'klē-sis \ (Greek: "invocation"), in CHRISTIANITY, the portion of the prayer (anaphora) introducing the EUCHARIST that serves as a special invocation of the HOLY SPIRIT. In most Eastern Christian liturgies it follows the words of institution—the words used, according to the NEW TESTAMENT, by Jesus himself at the LAST SUPPER: "This is my body . . . this is my blood"—and has a clearly consecratory character. The epiclesis specifically asks that bread and wine be made the body and blood of Christ, and the actual change (Greek *metabolē*) is attributed to the Holy Spirit. It reflects the prevailing sacramental theology of the Eastern church, which interprets the effectiveness of the SACRAMENTS as an answer of God to the prayer of the church rather than as a result of the vicarious powers of a priest pronouncing the appropriate formula. The epiclesis also maintains the trinitarian character of the eucharistic prayer, which is addressed to the Father, commemorates the saving action of the Son, and invokes the power of the Spirit.

In the 14th century the epiclesis became an issue between Greeks and Latins because the Roman MASS did not invoke the Holy Spirit. Latin theology did not require the epiclesis since it was believed that the consecration of bread and wine and their TRANSUBSTANTIATION took place when the priest pronounced the words of institution.

The medieval Latin view was endorsed by the COUNCIL OF TRENT (1545–63), but the liturgical reforms adopted in ROMAN CATHOLICISM after the SECOND VATICAN COUNCIL (1962–65) have included the introduction of an epiclesis in the canon of the mass. This epiclesis, however, is placed before the words of institution so that the consecratory function of the latter can still be maintained.

EPICUREANISM \ ˌe-pi-kyu̇-'rē-ə-ˌni-zəm, ˌe-pi-'kyu̇r-ē- \, in a strict sense, the philosophy of the ancient Greek Epicurus (341–270 BCE); and in a broad sense, a system of ethics traceable to the principles of his philosophy. In physics, Epicureanism espouses atomism and a largely mechanical conception of causality, with the gods remaining extraneous; and, in ethics, the identification of good with pleasure and the absence of pain, utility and the limitation of desire, and a withdrawn and quiet life enriched by the company of friends.

Epicurus founded a school of philosophy in Athens. Because the society that he gathered round him included women as well as men, it frequently evoked public scandal and even persecution. Nonetheless, communities modeled on the original were founded throughout the Mediterranean world. The most significant revival of Epicureanism was the Christian interpretation developed by Pierre Gassendi in the 17th century.

The philosophic outlook of Epicurus was fundamentally ethical. For Epicurus the sole criterion of GOOD AND EVIL is sensation; so that "we declare pleasure to be the beginning and end of the blessed life." However, while every pleasure is in itself good, not all pleasures are to be chosen, since certain pleasures are produced by means which entail annoyances many times greater than the pleasures themselves. Thus pleasure as contemplated by Epicurus is not so much active enjoyment as the absence of pain.

According to Epicurus, the SOUL is a material body of fine parts and is distributed through the whole bodily structure. So long as it is protected by the body, it is capable of sensation and of communicating sensation to the body. When it leaves the body, it is dissipated into the primordial atoms of which it was compounded; the body, on the other hand, is no longer capable of sensation. Thus there can be no life to come, and death is not to be feared.

Epicurus holds that sensory perception is a purely material process. From the surface of all bodies there are continually being discharged images, hollow films of exceedingly fine texture, which in shape are exact replicas of the bodies. Sensation of such images is the sole source of knowledge, and all sensuous perceptions are true. Error can arise only when, beyond what is given in sensation, the mind forms an opinion that is afterward contradicted or unconfirmed. Epicurus does not deny the existence of the gods; rather he holds that "their existence is known to us by immediate apprehension." Fashioned of finer stuff than humankind, they dwell afar in the intermundial spaces, neither troubling human affairs nor troubled by them.

EPIMENIDES \ ˌe-pi-'me-nə-ˌdēz \ (fl. 6th century BCE?), Cretan seer, reputed author of religious and poetical writings. He conducted purificatory rites at Athens about 500 BCE according to Plato (about 600 according to Aristotle). All surviving fragments, including a line quoted by St. Paul (Titus 1:12), are attributable to other sources. Stories of his advanced age (157 or 299 years), his miraculous sleep of 57 years, and his wanderings outside the body have led some scholars to regard him as a legendary SHAMAN.

EPIPHANIUS OF SALAMIS, SAINT \,e-pə-'fā-nē-əs . . . 'sa-lə-məs\ (b. *c.* 315, Palestine—d. May 403, at sea; feast day May 12), bishop noted in the history of the early Christian church for his struggle against beliefs he considered heretical. His chief target was the teachings of ORIGEN, a major theologian in the Eastern church. The harsh attacks by Epiphanius, who considered Origen more a Greek philosopher than a Christian, did much to discredit Epiphanius' principles.

Epiphanius studied and practiced MONASTICISM in Egypt and then returned to his native Palestine, where he founded a monastery and became its superior. In 367 he was made bishop of Salamis (Constantia) in Cyprus. He spent the rest of his life in that post.

In 403 Epiphanius went to Constantinople (Istanbul) to campaign against the bishop there, ST. JOHN CHRYSOSTOM, who had been accused of sheltering four monks expelled from Alexandria for their Origenistic views. Becoming convinced of the falsity of this and related charges made by Bishop Theophilus of Alexandria (who wanted to depose John), Epiphanius set sail for Cyprus but died en route.

A zealous bishop and a revered ascetic, Epiphanius was lacking in moderation and judgment. These defects are reflected in his writings, of which the chief work is the *Panarion* (374–377). His works are valuable as a source for the history of theological ideas.

EPIPHANY (from Greek: *epiphaneia*, "manifestation"), festival celebrated on January 6; it is one of the three principal and oldest festival days of the Christian church (including EASTER and CHRISTMAS). In the Western church, it commemorates the first manifestation of JESUS CHRIST to the GENTILES, represented by the MAGI. In the Eastern church it commemorates the manifestation of his divinity, as it occurred at his BAPTISM in the Jordan River. In the West the evening preceding Epiphany is called Twelfth Night.

EPONA \'e-pō-nə\, the Gaulish version of a Celtic mare goddess who is also recognizable in the Welsh RHIANNON ("Great Queen") and the Irish MACHA.

In the Welsh and Irish stories, the goddess is strongly tied to the functions of kingship and fertility. Epona, whose name means "Divine Mare" or "Mare Goddess," was worshiped almost everywhere in the western part of the Roman Empire, her cult evidently being spread by the army, especially members of the cavalry.

ERASMUS, DESIDERIUS \i-'raz-məs\ (b. Oct. 27, 1469, Rotterdam, Holland [now in The Netherlands]—d. July 12, 1536, Basel, Switz.), European scholar who helped lay the groundwork for the historical-critical study of the past, especially in his studies of the Greek NEW TESTAMENT and the CHURCH FATHERS.

Erasmus was the illegitimate son of Roger Gerard, a priest. Erasmus entered the monastery of the AUGUSTINIAN canons regular at Steyn in 1485, where his monastic superiors discouraged his classical studies. Thus, after his ORDINATION to the PRIESTHOOD (April 1492), he was happy to escape the monastery by accepting a post as Latin secretary to the influential Henry of Bergen, bishop of Cambrai. The bishop was induced to send him to the University of Paris to study theology (1495). To support his classical studies, he began taking in pupils; from this period (1497–1500) date the earliest versions of those aids to elegant Latin—including the *Colloquia* and the *Adagia*—that before long would be in use in humanist schools throughout Europe.

In 1499 a pupil invited Erasmus to England. There he met Thomas More, who became a friend for life, and John Colet, the theologian and founder of St. Paul's School, London. Erasmus returned to the Continent with a Latin copy of St. Paul's Epistles and the conviction that "ancient theology" required mastery of Greek. By 1502 he had settled in Louvain (Brabant) and was reading ORIGEN and ST. PAUL in Greek. The fruit of his labors was *Enchiridion militis Christiani* (1503/04; *Handbook of a Christian Knight*). The *Enchiridion* was a manifesto of lay piety in its assertion that "monasticism is not piety."

Erasmus found an opportunity to travel to Italy as tutor to the sons of the future Henry VIII's physician. There he produced the monumental final version of *Adagia* and *De pueris instituendis* (published 1529), the clearest statement of Erasmus' enormous faith in the power of education.

The celebrated *Moriae encomium*, or *Praise of Folly*, written at Thomas More's house (1511), expresses a very different mood. For the first time the earnest scholar saw his own efforts along with everyone else's as bathed in a universal irony, in which foolish passion carried the day. In other works of about the same time Erasmus showed a new boldness in commenting on the ills of Christian society—popes who in their warlike ambition imitated Caesar rather than Christ; princes who hauled whole nations into war to avenge a personal slight; and preachers who looked to their own interests by pronouncing the princes' wars just. To remedy these evils Erasmus looked to education.

Erasmus, oil painting by Hans Holbein the Younger, 1523; in the Louvre, Paris
Giraudon—Art Resource

From about 1514 Erasmus' home base was Brabant. He joined the faculty of Louvain and was named honorary councillor to the 16-year-old archduke Charles, the future Charles V, for whom he wrote *Institutio principis Christiani* (1516; *The Education of a Christian Prince*) and *Querela pacis* (1517; *The Complaint of Peace*). It was at this time too that he completed his annotated Greek New Testament and began his *Paraphrases* of the books of the New Testament, each one dedicated to a monarch or a prince of the church.

From the very beginning of Martin Luther's challenge to papal authority, Erasmus' foes blamed him for inspiring Luther. In fact, Erasmus found much to admire in Luther's writings. When he quit Brabant for Basel (December 1521), he did so lest he be faced with a personal request from the emperor to write a book against Luther, which he could not have refused.

For Erasmus the root of the Protestant SCHISM was not theology but anticlericalism and lay resentment of the laws and "ceremonies" that the clergy made binding under pain of hell. As he wrote to Pope Adrian VI, whom he had known at Louvain, there was still hope of reconciliation, if the church would, for instance, grant the CHALICE to the laity and permit priests to marry.

When Adrian VI was succeeded by Clement VII, Erasmus could no longer avoid theological combat. *De libero arbitrio* (1524) defended the place of human free choice in the process of salvation and argued that the consensus of the church through the ages is authoritative in the interpretation of SCRIPTURE. In reply Luther wrote one of his most important theological works, *De servo arbitrio* (1525), to which Erasmus responded with a lengthy, two-part *Hyperaspistes* (1526–27).

In 1529, when Protestant Basel banned CATHOLIC worship altogether, Erasmus moved to the Catholic university town of Freiburg im Breisgau. He returned to Basel to see his manual on preaching (*Ecclesiastes*, 1535) through the press, and it was there he died.

ERATO \'er-ə-,tō\, in GREEK RELIGION, one of the nine MUSES, the patron of lyric and erotic poetry or hymns. She is often depicted playing a lyre.

ERECHTHEUM \,er-ek-'thē-əm\, Ionic temple of ATHENA, built during 421–407 BCE on the Acropolis at Athens, famous largely for its complexity and for the exquisite perfection of its details. The temple's Ionic capitals are the most

beautiful that Greece produced, and its distinctive porch, supported by caryatid figures, is unequaled.

The name, of popular origin, is derived from a shrine dedicated to the Greek hero Erichthonius. It is believed by some that the temple was erected in honor of the legendary

Erechtheum, on the Acropolis, Athens
Alison Frantz

king ERECHTHEUS. The temple contained a revered image of Athena Polias (Athena as goddess of the Acropolis), as well as altars to other gods and sacred objects. The architect was probably Mnesicles.

ERECHTHEUS \i-'rek-,thüs, -thē-əs\, legendary king and probably also a divinity of Athens. According to the *Iliad*, he was born from the corn land and raised by the goddess ATHENA, who established him in her temple at Athens. In later times only a great snake was thought to share the temple with Athena, and there is evidence that Erechtheus was or became a snake.

The earliest Athenian kings tended to have similar names suggesting a connection with the earth (*chthōn; e.g.*, Erichthonius, Erysichthon), to have been born of the earth and raised by Athena, and to have something serpentine about them. Snakes were often believed to embody earth or ancestor spirits, so that Athena's sharing her temple with Erechtheus, whom she herself nurtured, may have been the mythical way of expressing her guardianship of the ancient royal house of Athens and of the land itself and its fertility, with which the ancient understanding of kingship was intimately connected.

In his lost play *Erechtheus*, Euripides gave that king three daughters, one of whom was appropriately named Chthonia. At war with neighboring Eleusis and its ally King EUMOLPUS, Erechtheus learned from the god APOLLO that Athens would win if he sacrificed his daughter. He sacrificed Chthonia and Athens won but Erechtheus was destroyed by POSEIDON or by a thunderbolt from ZEUS.

ERESHKIGAL \ā-'resh-ˌkē-gəl\, in MESOPOTAMIAN RELIGION, goddess in the Sumero-Akkadian pantheon who was Lady of the Great Place (*i.e.*, the abode of the dead) and, in texts of the 3rd millennium BCE, wife of the god NINAZU (elsewhere accounted her son); in later texts she was the wife of NERGAL. Ereshkigal's sister was Inanna (Akkadian ISHTAR), and between the two there was great enmity. Ereshkigal reigned in her palace, on the watch for lawbreakers and on guard over the fount of life lest any of her subjects take of it and so escape her rule. Her offspring and servant was Namtar, the DEMON of Death. Her power extended to earth where, in magical ceremony, she liberated the sick possessed of evil spirits. Ereshkigal's cult extended to Asia Minor, Egypt, and southern Arabia. In Mesopotamia the chief temple known to be dedicated to her was at Cuthah.

ERIDU GENESIS \e-'rē-dü\, in the literature of MESOPOTAMIAN RELIGION, Sumerian epic primarily concerned with the creation of the world, the building of cities, and the flood. According to the epic, after the universe was created out of the primeval sea and the gods were given birth, the deities fashioned humans from clay to cultivate the ground, care for flocks, and perpetuate the worship of the gods.

Cities were soon built and kingship was instituted on Earth. Because of their noise-making, however, the gods determined to destroy mankind with a flood. Enki (Akkadian EA), who did not agree with the decree, revealed it to ZIUSUDRA (UTNAPISHTIM), a man well known for his humility and obedience. Ziusudra did as Enki commanded and built a huge boat, in which he successfully rode out the flood. Afterward, he prostrated himself before the gods An (ANU) and ENLIL (BEL), and, as a reward for living a godly life, was given immortality.

ERIGONE \i-'ri-gə-ˌnē\, in Greek mythology, daughter of Icarius, the hero of the Attic deme (township) of Icaria. Her father had been taught by the god DIONYSUS to make wine, and he gave some to several shepherds, who became intoxicated. Their companions, thinking they had been poisoned, killed Icarius and buried him under a tree. Erigone, guided by her dog Maera, found his grave and hanged herself on the tree. Dionysus sent a plague on the land, and all the maidens of Athens, in a fit of madness, hanged themselves. Icarius, Erigone, and Maera were set among the stars as Boötes (or Arcturus), Virgo, and Procyon, and to propitiate Icarius and Erigone, the festival called Aiora (the Swing) was instituted. During this festival various small images were swung from trees, and offerings of fruit were made. The story of Erigone may have been intended to explain the origin of this cult practice.

ERINYES \i-'ri-nē-ˌēz\, *singular* Erinys \i-'ri-nis, -'rī-\, *also called* Eumenides \yü-'me-ni-ˌdēz\ ("Kind Ones"), *or* Furies, in Greek mythology, goddesses of vengeance. They were probably personified curses but possibly were originally conceived of as ghosts of the murdered. A goddess Erinys appears in a Mycenaean text, but later sources referred to them in the plural. According to the Greek poet Hesiod they were the daughters of GAEA (Earth) and sprang from the blood of OURANUS; in the plays of Aeschylus they were the daughters of NYX (Night); in those of Sophocles they were the daughters of Erebos (Darkness) and of Gaea. Euripides was the first to speak of them as three in number. Later

writers named them Alecto ("Unceasing in Anger"), Tisiphone ("Avenger of Murder"), and Megaera ("Jealous"). They lived in the Underworld and ascended to earth to pursue the wicked. Because the Greeks feared to utter the dreaded name Erinyes, the goddesses were often addressed by the euphemistic names Eumenides or Semnai Theai ("Venerable Goddesses").

ERIS \'er-is, 'ir-\, in Greek mythology, the personification of strife, daughter of NYX, and sister and companion of ARES. Eris is best known for her part in starting the Trojan War. When she alone of the gods was not invited to the marriage of PELEUS and THETIS, she threw among the guests a golden apple inscribed "For the most beautiful." HERA, ATHENA, and APHRODITE each claimed it, and ZEUS assigned the decision to PARIS. Paris awarded the apple to Aphrodite, who then helped him win HELEN of Troy. In the war that resulted, Hera and Athena were implacable enemies of Troy.

EROS \'er-ˌäs, 'ir-\, in GREEK RELIGION, god of love. In the *Theogony* of Hesiod (fl. 700 BCE), Eros was a primeval god, son of CHAOS, the original primeval emptiness of the universe; but later tradition made him the son of APHRODITE by either ZEUS, ARES, or HERMES. Eros was god not simply of passion but also of fertility. His brother was Anteros, the god of mutual love, who was sometimes described as his opponent. The chief associates of Eros were Pothos and Himeros (Longing and Desire). In Alexandrian poetry he degenerated into a mischievous child. In archaic art he was represented as a beautiful winged youth but tended to be made younger and younger until, by the Hellenistic period, he was an infant. His chief cult center was at Thespiae in Boeotia, where the Erotidia were celebrated. He also shared a SANCTUARY with Aphrodite in the Acropolis at Athens.

ESAGILA \'ā-sä-'gē-lä\, most important temple complex in ancient Babylon, dedicated to the god MARDUK, the tutelary deity of that city. The temple area was located south of the huge ZIGGURAT called Etemenanki; it measured 660 feet on its longest side, and its three vast courtyards were surrounded by intricate chambers. The whole complex reflects centuries of building and rebuilding by the Babylonian kings, especially Nebuchadrezzar II (reigned 604–562 BCE). The tremendous wealth of Esagila was recorded by the Greek historian Herodotus, who is believed to have visited Babylon in the 5th century BCE. Babylon was excavated in 1899–1917 by German archaeologists; few objects of value, however, were found in Esagila, which had been thoroughly plundered in antiquity.

ESAU \'ē-ˌsȯ\, *also called* Edom \'ē-dəm\, in the OLD TESTAMENT, son of ISAAC and Rebekah, elder twin brother of JACOB, and in Hebrew tradition the ancestor of the Edomites.

At birth, Esau was red and hairy (Genesis 25:25), and he became a wandering hunter, while Jacob became a shepherd (Genesis 25:27). Although younger, Jacob dominated him by deception. At one time, when Esau was hungry, Jacob bought Esau's birthright (*i.e.*, the rights due him as the eldest son) for some soup (Genesis 25:29–34). When Isaac was dying, Jacob, with Rebekah's help, cheated Esau out of his father's blessing (Genesis 27:1–40). Esau would have killed Jacob, but Jacob fled (Genesis 27:41–45); when he returned 20 years later, Esau forgave him (Genesis 33:4).

The story was partly intended to explain why Israel (in the time of the United Monarchy) dominated the kingdom of Edom, although the latter was older.

ESCHATOLOGY \,es-kə-'tä-lə-jē\, the doctrine of last things, especially in JUDAISM, CHRISTIANITY, and ISLAM, concerning beliefs about the end of history, the resurrection of the dead, the LAST JUDGMENT, and related matters. Similar concepts are found in the religions of nonliterate peoples, ancient Mediterranean and Middle Eastern cultures, and Eastern civilizations.

By and large, eschatologies have appeared in two radically divergent forms, distinguished by their attitude toward time and history. In mythical eschatologies, so called after their characteristic representations of the eternal struggle between cosmos (order) and CHAOS (disorder), the meaning of history is found in a celebration of the eternity of the cosmos and the repeatability of the origin of the world. Historical eschatologies, on the other hand, are grounded not in a mythical primal happening but in datable events that are perceived as key experiences fundamental for the progress of history.

Historical eschatology is basic to the OLD TESTAMENT and thus enters into the structure of faith of those religions, primarily Judaism, Christianity, and Islam, that draw upon it. Old Testament eschatology consists in the conviction that the catastrophes that beset the people of Israel happened because of their disobedience to the laws and will of God. Subsequent conformity to the will of God would result in a return for the Jews to a final condition of righteousness and moral and material renewal, in which God's purpose would at last be fulfilled. Old Testament eschatology is closely bound to the concept of a redemptive history, in which the Jewish people are viewed as God's chosen instrument for the carrying out of his purpose and in which, upon the fulfillment of God's promises, the Jewish people would be the vehicle for both their own salvation and that of the world.

Christian eschatology is centered in the figure of JESUS CHRIST as the anticipation of the future KINGDOM OF GOD. Jesus is viewed as the MESSIAH of God, through whom and by whom the new age of God's redemption has been opened. The historical development of Christianity was marked by widely differing interpretations and degrees of acceptance of this original eschatology, however. Distinctions can be made between the hopes of messianism (directed toward a salvatory or vindicating figure to come), millenarianism (directed toward the prophesied 1,000-year Kingdom of Christ), and APOCALYPTICISM (directed toward the cataclysmic intervention of God in history). The eschatological views of Christianity also include a belief in the "restoration of all things," which some Christians, beginning with ORIGEN, have taken to include universal salvation.

ESSENE \i-'sēn, 'e-,sēn\, member of a religious sect or brotherhood that flourished in Palestine from about the 2nd century BCE to the end of the 1st century CE. Accounts given by the historians FLAVIUS JOSEPHUS, PHILO JUDAEUS, and Pliny the Elder sometimes differ in significant details, perhaps indicating a diversity that existed among the Essenes themselves.

The Essenes clustered in monastic communities that generally excluded women. Property was held in common, and all details of daily life were regulated by officials. The Essenes were never numerous; Pliny fixed their number at some 4,000 in his day. They meticulously observed the Law of MOSES, the SABBATH, and ritual purity (see TOHORAH). They also professed belief in immortality and divine punishment for SIN, but they denied the resurrection of the body. With few exceptions, they shunned Temple worship and lived ascetic lives of manual labor in seclusion. The sabbath was reserved for day-long prayer and meditation on the TORAH. OATHS were frowned upon, but once taken they could not be rescinded.

After a year's probation, proselytes received their Essenian emblems but could not participate in common meals for two more years. Those who qualified for membership were called upon to swear piety to God, justice toward men, hatred of falsehood, love of truth, and faithful observance of all other tenets of the Essene sect. Thereafter new converts were allowed to take their noon and evening meals in silence with the others.

Following the discovery of the DEAD SEA SCROLLS (late 1940s and 1950s) in the vicinity of Khirbet QUMRĀN, many scholars hold that the Qumrān community was Essenian.

ESTABLISHED CHURCH, church recognized by law as the official church of a state or nation and supported by civil authority. The church is not free to make changes in such things as doctrine, order, or worship without the consent of the state. In accepting such obligations, the church usually, though not always, receives financial support and other special privileges.

Among numerous examples of established churches or state religions are the following: the ANGLICAN church in England, LUTHERANISM in the Scandinavian countries, ROMAN CATHOLICISM in Italy and Spain, EASTERN ORTHODOXY in pre-Revolutionary Russia, JUDAISM in Israel, ISLAM in Saudi Arabia and Egypt, BUDDHISM in Thailand and Sikkim, and SHINTŌ in Japan before World War II. In pluralistic societies and under modern forms of government, religious establishment has tended to diminish in importance.

ESUS \'ē-səs\ (Celtic: "Lord," or "Master"), important Celtic deity, one of three mentioned by the Roman poet Lucan in the 1st century CE; the other two were TARANIS ("Thunderer") and TEUTATES ("God of the People"). Esus' victims, according to later commentators, were sacrificed by being ritually stabbed and hung from trees. A relief from the Cathedral of Notre-Dame in Paris portrays Esus as a bent woodman cutting a branch from a willow tree. This and a related relief from Trier, Germany, associate him with the sacred bull and with his accompanying three cranes or egrets.

ETANA EPIC \ā-'tä-nä\, ancient Mesopotamian tale concerned with the question of dynastic succession. In the beginning, according to the epic, there was no king on the earth; the gods thus set out to find one and apparently chose Etana, who proved to be an able ruler until he discovered that his wife, though pregnant, was unable to give birth, and thus he had no heir to the throne. The one known remedy was the birth plant, which Etana was required to bring down personally from heaven. Etana, therefore, prayed to the god SHAMASH, who heard his request and directed him to a mountain where a maimed eagle, languishing in a pit (into which it had been thrown as punishment for breaking a sacred pact), would help him obtain the special plant. Etana rescued the eagle, and as a reward it carried him high up into the sky.

The result of Etana's quest is uncertain because of the incomplete state of the texts. According to one fragment, Etana reached heaven and prostrated himself before the gods. There the text breaks off. According to another fragment, however, Etana either became dizzy or lost his nerve before reaching heaven and crashed to the ground. If Etana was successful, the myth may have been used to support early dynastic claims. Etana of the myth is probably the Etana who ruled Kish in southern Mesopotamia sometime in the first half of the 3rd millennium BCE.

ETHIOPIANISM \\,ē-thē-'ō-pē-ə-,ni-zəm\\, religious movement among sub-Saharan Africans that embodied the earliest stirrings toward religious and political autonomy in the modern colonial period. The movement was initiated in the 1880s when South African MISSION workers began forming independent all-African churches, such as the Tembu tribal church (1884) and the Church of Africa (1889). A former Wesleyan minister, Mangena Mokone, was the first to use the term when he founded the Ethiopian Church (1892). Among the main incentives for the movement were the frustrations experienced by Africans who were denied advancement in the hierarchy of mission churches, racial discontent, and the desire for a more African and relevant CHRISTIANITY and the restoration of tribal life.

The mystique of the term Ethiopianism derived from its occurrence in the BIBLE (where Ethiopia is also referred to as Kush, or Cush) and was enhanced when the ancient independent Christian kingdom of Ethiopia defeated the Italians at Adwa (Adowa) in 1896. The word therefore represented Africa's dignity and place in the divine dispensation and provided a charter for free African churches and nations of the future. Early Ethiopianism included tribalist, nationalist, and Pan-African dimensions, which were encouraged by association with independent American black churches and leaders with "back to Africa" ideas and an Ethiopianist ideology. This ideology was explicit in the thought of such pioneers of African cultural, religious, and political independence as E.W. Blyden and J.E. Casely-Hayford of Ghana.

Parallel developments occurred elsewhere and for similar reasons. In Nigeria the so-called African churches—the Native Baptist Church (1888), the formerly Anglican United Native African Church (1891) and its later divisions, and the United African Methodist Church (1917)—were important. Other Ethiopian-related movements included the Cameroun Native Baptist Church (1887); the Native Baptist Church (1898) in Ghana; in Rhodesia a branch (1906) of the African-American denomination, the AFRICAN METHODIST EPISCOPAL CHURCH, and Nemapare's African Methodist Church (1947); and in Kenya the Kenyan Church of Christ in Africa (1957), which was formerly Anglican.

Ethiopian movements played some part in the Zulu rebellion of 1906 and especially in the Nyasaland rising of 1915 led by John Chilembwe, founder of the independent Providence Industrial Mission. From about 1920, political activities were channeled into secular political parties and trade unions, and the use of the term Ethiopian then narrowed to one section of African independent religious movements. These Ethiopian-type churches originated by secession (and further sub-secessions) from a mission-connected church, which they resemble in beliefs, polity, and worship but from which they differ in certain cultural and ethnic practices. By the early 1970s the term Ethiopianism was not in popular use outside southern Africa.

ETHIOPIAN ORTHODOX CHURCH, *also called* Ethiopian church, independent Christian patriarchate in Ethiopia holding to MONOPHYSITE doctrine. The church recognizes the honorary primacy of the Coptic PATRIARCH of Alexandria. It is headquartered in Addis Ababa.

Ethiopia was Christianized in the 4th century CE by two brothers from Tyre—St. Frumentius, later consecrated the first Ethiopian bishop, and Aedesius. They won the confidence of King Ezana at Aksum (a powerful kingdom in northern Ethiopia) and were allowed to evangelize. Toward the end of the 5th century, nine monks from Syria, probably Monophysites, are said to have brought MONASTICISM to Ethiopia and encouraged the translation of the SCRIPTURES into the Ge'ez language. The Ethiopian church followed the Coptic church in continuing to adhere to the Monophysite doctrine after this doctrine had been condemned by the bishops of Rome and Constantinople.

In the 7th century the conquests of the Muslim Arabs cut off the Ethiopian church from contact with most of its Christian neighbors. The church absorbed various syncretic beliefs in the following centuries, but contact with the

Fourteenth-century church in Gorgora, Ethiopia
Alain Froissafdey—Atlas Photos

outside Christian world was maintained through the Ethiopian monastery in Jerusalem.

Beginning in the 12th century, the patriarch of Alexandria appointed the Ethiopian archbishop, known as the *abuna* (Arabic: "our father"), who was always an Egyptian Coptic monk; this created a rivalry with the native *itshage* (ABBOT general) of the strong Ethiopian monastic community. Attempts to shake Egyptian Coptic control were made from time to time, but not until 1950 was Basil, a native Ethiopian *abuna,* appointed, and in 1959 an autonomous Ethiopian patriarchate was established.

The Amhara and Tigray peoples of the northern and central highlands have historically been the principal adherents of the Ethiopian Orthodox church. Under the Amhara-dominated Ethiopian monarchy, the Ethiopian Orthodox church was declared to be the state church of the country, and it was a bulwark of the regime of Emperor Haile Selassie. Upon the abolition of the monarchy and the institution of socialism in the country beginning in 1975, the church was disestablished, its patriarch was removed, and the church was divested of its extensive landholdings. The church was placed on a footing of equality with ISLAM and other religions in the country, but it nevertheless remained Ethiopia's most influential religious body.

The clergy is composed of priests and deacons, who conduct the religious services, and *debtera,* who, though not ordained, perform the music and dance associated with church services and also function as astrologers, scribes, wizards, and fortune-tellers. Ethiopian Orthodox CHRISTIANITY blends Christian conceptions of God, saints, and ANGELS with non-Christian beliefs in benevolent and malevolent spirits. Considerable emphasis is placed on the OLD TESTAMENT. CIRCUMCISION is almost universally practiced; the Saturday SABBATH (in addition to Sunday) is observed by some devout believers; the ARK is an essential item in every church; and rigorous fasting is still practiced.

There are theological seminaries in Addis Ababa and Harer. Monasticism is widespread. Each community also has its own church school, which until 1900 was the sole source of education. The liturgy and scriptures are typically in Ge'ez, though both have been translated into Amharic, the principal modern language of Ethiopia. In the late 20th century the church had about 20,000,000 adherents in Ethiopia, with additional adherents spread through Eritrea, Jamaica, and Guyana.

ETRUSCAN RELIGION, beliefs and practices of the ancient people of Etruria, in Italy between the Tiber and Arno rivers west and south of the Apennines, whose urban civilization reached its height in the 6th century BCE. Many features of Etruscan culture were adopted by the Romans, their successors to power in the peninsula. Our knowledge and conjectures about Etruscan religion are chiefly dependent upon the later Roman commentaries.

Cosmology. The essential ingredient in Etruscan religion was a belief that human life was but one small meaningful element in a universe controlled by gods who manifested their nature and their will in every facet of the natural world, as well as in objects created by humans. Roman writers give evidence that the Etruscans regarded every bird and every berry as a potential source of knowledge of the gods and that they had developed an elaborate lore and attendant rituals for using this knowledge. Their myths explained the lore as having been communicated by the gods through a prophet, Tages, a miraculous child with the features of a wise old man, who sprang from a plowed

furrow in the fields of Tarquinii and sang out the elements of what the Romans called the *Disciplina Etrusca.*

The literary, epigraphic, and monumental sources provide a glimpse of a COSMOLOGY whose image of the sky with its subdivisions is reflected in consecrated areas on the earth and even in the viscera of animals. The concept of a sacred space or area reserved for a particular deity or purpose was fundamental, as was the corollary theory that such designated areas could correspond to each other. The celestial dome was divided into 16 compartments inhabited by the various divinities: major gods to the east, astral and terrestrial divine beings to the south, infernal and inauspicious beings to the west, and the most powerful and mysterious gods of destiny to the north. The deities manifested themselves by means of natural phenomena, principally by lightning and in the liver of animals (a bronze model of a sheep's liver found near Piacenza bears the incised names of divinities in its 16 outside divisions and in its internal divisions).

Divination. These conceptions are linked closely to the art of DIVINATION, for which the Etruscans were especially famous in the ancient world. Public and private actions of any importance were undertaken only after the gods had been interrogated; negative or threatening responses necessitated undertaking complex preventive or protective ceremonies. The most important form of divination was haruspicy, or hepatoscopy—the study of the details of the viscera, especially the livers, of sacrificial animals. Second in importance was the observation of lightning and of such other celestial phenomena as the flight of birds (also important in the religion of the Umbri and of the Romans). Finally, there was the interpretation of prodigies—extraordinary and marvelous events observed in the sky or on the earth. These practices, extensively adopted by the Romans, are explicitly attributed by the ancient authors to the religion of the Etruscans.

Gods and goddesses. The Etruscans recognized numerous deities (the Piacenza liver lists more than 40), and many are unknown today. Their nature was often vague, and references to them are fraught with ambiguity about number, attributes, and even gender. Some of the leading gods were equated with major deities of the Greeks and Romans, as may be seen especially from the labeled representations on Etruscan mirrors. Tin or TINIA was equivalent to ZEUS/JUPITER, Uni to HERA/JUNO, Sethlans to HEPHAESTUS/VULCAN, Turms to HERMES/MERCURY, Turan to APHRODITE/VENUS, and Menrva to ATHENA/MINERVA. But their characters and mythologies often differed sharply from those of their Greek counterparts. Menrva, for example, an immensely popular deity, was regarded as a sponsor of marriage and childbirth, in contrast to the virgin Athena. Many of the gods had healing powers, and many of them had the authority to hurl a thunderbolt. There were also deities of a fairly orthodox Greco-Roman character, such as Hercle (HERACLES) and Apulu (APOLLO), who were evidently introduced directly from Greece yet came to have their designated spaces and cults.

Temple architecture. Etruscan temples generally had a columniated, deep front porch and a cella that was flush with the podium on which it stood. The materials were frequently perishable (timber and mud brick, on a stone foundation) except for the abundant terra-cotta sculptures that adorned the roof. Especially well-preserved are the *acroteria,* or roof sculptures, from the Portonaccio temple at Veii (late 6th century BCE) representing Apulu and other mythological figures.

EUCHARIST, *also called* Holy Communion, or Lord's Supper, in CHRISTIANITY, a SACRAMENT commemorating the action of JESUS CHRIST at his LAST SUPPER with his disciples, when he gave them bread saying, "This is my body," and wine saying, "This is my blood." The story of the institution of the Eucharist by Jesus on the night before his CRUCIFIXION is reported in all of the SYNOPTIC GOSPELS.

The Eucharist has formed a central rite of Christian worship. However, although the Eucharist is intended as a symbol of the unity of the church and as a means of fostering that unity, it has been a source of disunity and contention as well. All Christians would agree that it is a memorial action in which the church recalls what Jesus Christ was, said, and did; they would also agree that participation in the Eucharist enhances and deepens the communion of believers not only with Christ but also with one another. The Eucharist is recognized by every Christian denomination as the central symbol of the death of Jesus Christ on the Cross. Most traditions teach that Jesus is present in the Eucharist in some special way, though they disagree about the mode, the locus, and the time of that presence.

According to the doctrine of ROMAN CATHOLICISM, the elements of bread and wine are "transubstantiated" into the body and blood of Christ; *i.e.*, their whole substance is converted into the whole substance of the body and blood, although the outward appearances of the elements, their "accidents," remain. Such practices as the adoration and reservation of the Host follow from this doctrine.

The eucharistic beliefs and practices of EASTERN ORTHODOXY differ principally in the area of piety and liturgy. The major difference is the use of leavened rather than of unleavened bread. While Roman Catholic theology maintains that the recitation of the words of institution constitutes the Eucharist as a sacrament, Eastern theology has taught that the invocation of the HOLY SPIRIT upon the elements (EPICLESIS) is part of the essential form of the Eucharist.

Among other Western Christians, those that adhere most closely to the traditions of Catholic eucharistic doctrine and practice are the Anglicans and the Lutherans. In the 16th century, LUTHERANISM unequivocally affirmed the Real Presence of the body and blood of Christ "in, with, and under" the bread and wine and emphasized that the reason for the Eucharist is the remission of SINS.

In Reformed Christianity, HULDRYCH ZWINGLI emphasized the memorial aspect of the Eucharist. JOHN CALVIN, however, taught a "real but spiritual presence" of the living Christ, but in the sacramental action rather than in the elements. In other traditions within PROTESTANTISM the sacraments have become "ordinances," not channels of GRACE but expressions of faith and obedience of the Christian community. Among BAPTISTS the practice of "close communion" has restricted the ordinance to those who are baptized properly, *i.e.*, as adults upon a profession of faith. The SOCIETY OF FRIENDS (Quakers) dropped the use of the Eucharist altogether in its reaction against formalism.

As a result of these variations in both doctrine and practice, the Eucharist has been a central issue in the discussions and deliberations of the ecumenical movement.

EUHEMERISM \yü-'hē-mə-,ri-zəm, -'he-\, approach to the STUDY OF RELIGION that seeks to establish a historical basis for mythical beings and events. Euhemerism is named for EUHEMERUS (fl. 300 BCE), a Greek mythographer who first established the tradition. Euhemerus is chiefly known by his *Sacred History*, a work in which he asserted that the Greek gods were originally heroes and conquerors who had earned a claim to veneration because of their benefactions to mankind.

This system spread widely. The early Christian CHURCH FATHERS adopted an attitude of modified Euhemerism, according to which classical mythology was to be explained in terms of mere men who had been raised to superhuman, demonic status because of their deeds. By this means Christians were able to incorporate myths from the culturally authoritative classical past into a Christian framework while defusing their religious significance—the gods became ordinary humans. The word euhemeristic is applied to such explanations of religion and mythology. There is some element of truth in this approach, for, among the Romans, the gradual deification of ancestors and emperors was a prominent feature of religious development. Thus, among some peoples, it is possible to trace family and tribal gods back to great chiefs and warriors. But it is not accepted by scholars as the sole explanation of the origin of gods.

EUHEMERUS \yü-'hē-mə-rəs, -'he-\, *also spelled* Euemeros, *or* Evemerus (fl. *c.* 300 BCE),

Celebrating the Eucharist, the priest consecrates the Host
Mimi Forsyth—Monkmeyer

Greek mythographer who established the tradition of seeking an actual historical basis for mythical beings and events. He lived at the court of Cassander, king of Macedonia, from about 301 to 297 BCE. He is chiefly known by his *Sacred History*, a philosophic romance based upon archaic inscriptions that he claimed to have found in his travels in various parts of Greece.

In this work he systematized for the first time an old Oriental (perhaps Phoenician) method of interpreting the popular myths; he asserted that the gods were originally heroes and conquerors who had earned a claim to the veneration of their subjects. This system spread widely, and the early Christians, especially, used it as a confirmation of their belief that ancient MYTHOLOGY was merely an aggregate of fables of human invention. The word euhemeristic is applied to such explanations of mythologies.

EUMOLPUS \yü-'mäl-pǝs\, mythical ancestor of the priestly clan of the Eumolpids at Eleusis in ancient Greece, the site of the ELEUSINIAN MYSTERIES. His name (meaning "good or strong singer"; *i.e.*, a priest who could chant his litanies clearly and well) was a personification of the clan's hereditary functions. His legend fluctuated so greatly that three identities for Eumolpus have been assumed:

1. Being a "sweet singer," he was connected with Thrace, the country of ORPHEUS. He was the son of the god POSEIDON and Chione ("Snow Girl"), daughter of the north wind, Boreas; after various adventures he became king in Thrace but was killed while helping the Eleusinians in their war against Erectheus of Athens.

2. As one of the originators of the Eleusinian Mysteries, he was an Eleusinian, a son of Gaia, father of Keryx, and the mythical ancestor of the Kerykes (Heralds).

3. Because Orpheus and his followers were closely connected with mysteries of all sorts, Eumolpus was believed to be the son, father, or pupil of Musaeus, a mythical singer closely allied with Orpheus.

EUROPA \yu̇-'rō-pǝ\, in Greek mythology, the daughter either of Phoenix or of Agenor, king of Phoenicia. The beauty of Europa inspired the love of ZEUS, who approached her in the form of a white bull and carried her away from Phoenicia to Crete. There she bore Zeus three sons: King MINOS of Crete, King Rhadamanthus of the Cyclades Islands and, according to some legends, Prince SARPEDON of Lycia. She later married the king of Crete, who adopted her sons, and she was worshiped under the name of Hellotis in Crete, where the festival Hellotia was held in her honor.

EURYDICE \yu̇-'ri-dǝ-sē\, in Greek mythology, the wife of ORPHEUS, whose unsuccessful attempt to retrieve her from HADES is the basis of one of the most popular Greek myths.

EUSEBIUS OF CAESAREA \yu̇-'sē-bē-ǝs\, *also called* Eusebius Pamphili (fl. 4th century, Caesarea Palestinae, Palestine), bishop, exegete, polemicist, and historian whose *Ecclesiastical History* is a landmark in Christian historiography.

Eusebius was baptized and ordained at Caesarea, where he was taught by the learned presbyter Pamphilus, from whom he derived the name "Eusebius Pamphili" (the son or servant of Pamphilus). Pamphilus was persecuted for his beliefs by the Romans and died in martyrdom in 310. Eusebius may himself have been imprisoned at Caesarea, and he was taunted many years later with having escaped by performing some act of submission.

Eusebius' fame rests on his *Ecclesiastical History*, which he probably began to write during the Roman persecutions and revised several times between 312 and 324. In this work Eusebius produced what may be called, at best, a fully documented history of the Christian church, and, at worst, collections of passages from his sources. In it he constantly quotes or paraphrases his sources, and he thus preserved portions of earlier works that are no longer extant. He enlarged his work in successive editions to cover events down to 324, the year before the COUNCIL OF NICAEA. Eusebius, however, was not a great historian. His treatment of HERESY, for example, is inadequate, and he knew next to nothing about the Western church.

Eusebius became bishop of Caesarea (in Palestine) about 313. About 318 the theological views of ARIUS became the subject of controversy. Expelled from Alexandria for heresy, Arius sought and found sympathy at Caesarea. Eusebius did not fully support either Arius or Alexander, bishop of Alexandria from 313 to 328, whose views appeared to tend toward Sabellianism (a heresy that taught that God was manifested in progressive modes as Father, Son, and HOLY SPIRIT). Eusebius wrote to Alexander, claiming that Arius had been misrepresented, and he also urged Arius to return to communion with his bishop. But events were moving fast, and at a strongly anti-Arian SYNOD at Antioch, Eusebius was provisionally excommunicated for Arian views. When the Council of Nicaea, called by the Roman emperor CONSTANTINE I, met later in the year, Eusebius was exonerated with the approval of the emperor.

Eusebius remained in the emperor's favor, and, after Constantine's death in 337, he wrote his *Life of Constantine*, a panegyric that possesses some historical value, chiefly be-

Europa being abducted by Zeus disguised as a bull, detail from an Attic krater (vessel used for mixing wine and water), 5th century BCE
By courtesy of the Museo Nazionale Tarquiniense, Tarquinia, Italy; photograph, Hirmer Fotoarchiv, Munchen

cause of its use of primary sources. Throughout his life Eusebius also wrote apologetic works, commentaries on the BIBLE, and works explaining the parallels and discrepancies in the Gospels.

EUTERPE \yü-'tər-pē\, in Greek mythology, one of the nine MUSES, patron of tragedy or flute playing. In some accounts she was the mother of Rhesus, the king of Thrace, whose father was sometimes identified as Strymon, the river god of Thrace.

EUTHYMIUS OF TŬRNOVO \yü-'thi-mē-əs . . . 'tər-nə-ˌvō\ (b. c. 1317—d. c. 1402), Orthodox PATRIARCH of Tŭrnovo (now Veliko Tŭrnovo), monastic scholar and linguist whose extensive literary activity spearheaded the late medieval renaissance in Bulgaria.

Bulgarian by birth, Euthymius joined the monastery of Kilifarevo, where he became the leading disciple of Theodosius, whom he succeeded as spokesman for HESYCHASM, the Byzantine movement of contemplative prayer. In 1375 he was elected patriarch of Tŭrnovo and PRIMATE of the Bulgarian ORTHODOX CHURCH, but he was forced into exile after the fall of Tŭrnovo to the Turks in 1393.

In order to promote orthodoxy, Euthymius began a reform of Church Slavic. The original, single Slavic tongue had splintered into distinct languages and dialects. Church Slavic, however, had by and large retained the grammatical and syntactical structure of the old 9th-century form and, by increasing divergence from the various Slavic idioms, in effect had become a dead language. The biblical and liturgical texts, moreover, had grown ambiguous through a series of coarse revisions and had occasioned the spread of heretical sects, principally the dualistic BOGOMILS, who held that the visible, material world was created by the devil.

Euthymius' reform followed his conviction that public morality and theological orthodoxy were essentially related to the accuracy and literary qualities of the sacred SCRIPTURES. Thus he revived an international Old Church Slavic with its Cyrillic written form but more intricately interwoven with the Greek rhetorical and emphatic style.

Applying his Hesychast background, Euthymius made this monastic culture the energy source of his theological and literary reform. Thus, the Bulgarian monastic centers of Paroria and Kilifarevo and the monk missioners, both native Slav and Greek refugee scholars, carried the Euthymian reform throughout eastern Europe.

EVAGRIUS PONTICUS \i-'va-grē-əs-'pän-ti-kəs\ (b. 346, Ibora, Pontus—d. 399, Cellia, Nitrian Desert, Egypt), Christian mystic and writer whose development of a theology of CONTEMPLATIVE prayer and ASCETICISM laid the groundwork for a tradition of spiritual life in both Eastern and Western churches.

Evagrius was a noted preacher and theological consultant in Constantinople (now Istanbul) when a personal spiritual crisis prompted him to become a monk. He soon withdrew into the Egyptian desert, where he spent the rest of his life evolving his mystical theology in theory and practice while he supported himself by copying manuscripts.

Historical research since 1920 has suggested that Evagrius produced the first major philosophical-theological exposition of monastic MYSTICISM by developing the Neoplatonic biblical theology of the 3rd-century Christian teacher ORIGEN. Evagrius' *Gnostic Centuries* emphasized that the essential function of spiritual beings is to experience union with God, the transcendent One, expressed as pure light.

Because of an original, alienating fault, man can find reconciliation only by an ascetical, self-mortifying process whereby the spirit regains its rule over matter. Only fragments remain of Evagrius' other written works.

His doctrine affected CHRISTIANITY in the Greek tradition through the 6th-century Neoplatonic philosopher–mystic PSEUDO-DIONYSIUS the Areopagite and the 7th-century mystical theologian Maximus the Confessor. In the Latin culture, he inspired the 5th-century writer John Cassian. Western Christianity, however, has long suspected Evagrius of HERESY. His teachings were denounced by the second general COUNCIL OF CONSTANTINOPLE in 553 as permeated with Origenist error. Nevertheless, he is considered the great doctor of mystical theology among the Syrians and other Eastern Christians, and his philosophy is sometimes seen as the Christian analogue of ZEN BUDDHISM.

EVANDER \ē-'van-dər\, in Roman legends, a migrant from Pallantium in Arcadia (central part of the Peloponnesus) who settled in Italy and founded a town named Pallantion, after his native place. The site of the town, at Rome, became known as the Palatine Hill, after his daughter Pallantia. Evander was the son of the goddess Carmentis (or Carmenta) and the god HERMES. Traditionally he instituted the LUPERCALIA and introduced some of the blessings of civilization, including writing.

EVANS-PRITCHARD, SIR EDWARD (EVAN) \'e-vənz-'pri-chərd\ (b. 1902, Crowborough, Sussex, Eng.—d. Sept. 11, 1973, Oxford, Oxfordshire), prominent English social anthropologist, especially known for his investigations of African cultures.

After studying modern history at the University of Oxford, Evans-Pritchard did postgraduate work in anthropology at the London School of Economics and Political Science. He then did fieldwork among the Azande and Nuer of southern Sudan. Two books about these peoples, *Witchcraft, Oracles, and Magic Among the Azande* (1937) and *The Nuer* (1940), made his reputation. In 1940 he and Meyer Fortes edited a volume of essays, *African Political Systems*, that revolutionized the study of "primitive" government. His *Theories of Primitive Religion* (1965) remains an authoritative and useful summary of the subject.

Under Evans-Pritchard's guidance, the Oxford school of social anthropology attracted students from many parts of the world, and he sponsored fieldwork in Africa and elsewhere as a member of the Colonial Social Science Research Council. He received numerous academic honors. He was a professor of social anthropology at Oxford and a fellow of All Souls College from 1946 to 1970, and he was subwarden from 1963 to 1965. He was knighted in 1971.

EVIL: *see* GOOD AND EVIL.

EVIL, PROBLEM OF, theological problem that arises for any philosophical or monotheistic religion that affirms the following three propositions: (1) God is omnipotent, (2) God is perfectly good, and (3) evil exists. If evil exists, it seems either that God wants to obliterate evil and is not able to—and thus his omnipotence is denied—or that God is able to obliterate evil but does not want to—and thus his goodness is denied.

The theological problem of evil can be solved logically by denying any one of these three propositions. William James attempted to solve the problem by regarding God as being perfectly good but having limited power. Some have defined the proposition of divine omnipotence to mean that God can do anything that is logically possible. The 17th-century German philosopher Gottfried Wilhelm Leibniz stated that, because God is limited to that which is logically possible, the existence of evil is necessary in this "best of all possible worlds." Orthodox CHRISTIANITY, however, has generally chosen to live with the tension involved in affirming all three propositions.

See THEODICY; MORALITY AND RELIGION.

EVIL EYE, glance believed to have the ability to cause injury or death to those on whom it falls; children and animals are thought to be particularly susceptible. Belief in the evil eye occurred in ancient Greece and Rome; is found in Jewish, Islamic, Buddhist, and Hindu traditions and in folk cultures and preliterate societies; and has persisted throughout the world into modern times.

The power of the evil eye is sometimes held to be involuntary. More frequently, however, malice toward and envy of prosperity and beauty are thought to be the cause. Thus, in medieval Europe—and sometimes still today—it was considered unlucky to be praised or to have one's possessions praised, so that some qualifying phrase such as "as God will" was commonly used.

Measures taken to ward off the evil eye may vary among cultures. Some authorities suggest that the purpose of ritual cross-dressing—a practice in the marriage ceremonies of parts of India—is to avert the evil eye. Asian children sometimes have their faces blackened, especially near the eyes, for protection. Among some Asian and African peoples the evil eye is particularly dreaded while eating and drinking, because the

Gregory VII lays a ban of excommunication on the clergy loyal to King Henry IV, drawing from the 12th-century chronicle of Otto von Freising; in the library of the University of Jena, Ger.
Leonard von Matt

soul is thought to be more vulnerable when the mouth is open; thus, the ingestion of substances is either a solitary activity or takes place only with the immediate family and behind locked doors. Other means of protection, common to many traditions, include the wearing of sacred texts, AMULETS, charms, and talismans (which may also be hung upon animals for their protection).

EXCOMMUNICATION, form of ecclesiastical censure by which a person is excluded from the communion of believers, the rites or SACRAMENTS of a church, and the rights of church membership, but not necessarily from membership in the church as such.

ROMAN CATHOLICISM distinguishes between two kinds of excommunication, that which renders a person *toleratus,* tolerated, and that which renders him *vitandus,* one who is to be avoided. The second and more severe form usually requires that the culprit be announced by name in public as

vitandus, in most cases by the Holy See itself; this is reserved for the gravest offenses. Both kinds of excommunication bar the excommunicated person from the sacraments of the church as well as from Christian burial. The actions that may incur excommunication from the Roman Catholic church include abortion, violation of the confidentiality of CONFESSION, profanation of the consecrated communion host, consecration of a bishop without Vatican approval, a physical attack on the pope, and HERESY and "abandoning the faith." If an excommunicated person confesses his SIN and undergoes penance for it, he is absolved; in some cases this ABSOLUTION may come from any priest, but in many others it is reserved to the bishop or even to the Holy See alone, save *in periculo mortis* ("in danger of death"). Excommunication should be distinguished from two related forms of censure, suspension and interdict. Suspension applies only to clergy and denies them some or all of their rights; interdict does not exclude a believer from the community of the faithful but forbids certain sacraments (such as baptism, marriage, or the anointing of the sick, depending on the type of interdict) and sacred offices, sometimes to an entire area.

Some churches do not use the term excommunication, preferring to speak of church discipline. Churches holding the Reformed order vest the authority for exercising discipline and, if need be, carrying out excommunication, in the session, which consists of the minister and the elders. LUTHERANISM has followed Martin Luther's CATECHISM in defining excommunication as the denial of the communion to public and obstinate sinners; the clergy and the congregation together have the right to exercise such discipline. Where a Congregational polity and the principle of "believers' baptism" are observed (*see* CONGREGATIONALISM), discipline is often very rigorous. In American denominations of the Free Church tradition, the term "churching" a sinner refers to excommunication.

EXEGESIS \ˌek-sə-ˈjē-sis, ˈek-sə-ˌjē-\ critical interpretation of a biblical text to discover its intended meaning. Various exegetical methods have been used in JUDAISM and CHRISTIANITY throughout their history, and doctrinal and polemical intentions have often influenced interpretive results; a given text may yield a number of very different interpretations according to the exegetical presuppositions and techniques applied to it. The study of these methodological principles themselves constitutes the field of HERMENEUTICS.

Interpretation of the BIBLE has always been considered a prerequisite for Jewish and Christian theological doctrine, since both faiths claim to be based upon the "sacred history" that makes up a major portion of the Bible. The other portions of the Bible—prophecy, poetry, proverbs, wisdom writings, epistles—are primarily reflections upon this sacred history and its meaning for the religious communities that grew out of that history. To that extent the nonhistorical writings of the Bible are themselves critical interpretations of the sacred history, and in large measure they form the basis for all other biblical exegesis.

The largest portion of the Bible is the Hebrew Bible, which is common to both Jews and Christians and is grounded in the history of the people of Israel. Christians add to this the NEW TESTAMENT (in contrast to the "Old Testament" of the Hebrew Bible), much of which is concerned with the interpretation of the Hebrew Bible in the light of the Christian community's experience of Jesus. Some Christians also include in their Bible the books of the APOCRYPHA that were excluded from the Hebrew Bible but that appeared in the SEPTUAGINT, sometimes considered to be of doctrinal value because the Septuagint was the "authorized version" of the early church.

Most forms of biblical exegesis employed in the modern era are applicable to many other bodies of literature. Textual criticism is concerned with establishing, as far as is possible, the original texts of the biblical books from the critical comparison of the various early materials available, including Hebrew manuscripts from the 9th century BCE onward and the Hebrew texts from the QUMRĀN community of the Dead Sea region, which date from the 3rd century BCE to the 2nd century CE. Other sources are the major translations of the Hebrew texts into Greek (the Septuagint), Syriac (the Peshitta), and Latin (the VULGATE). For the New Testament the textual materials are Greek manuscripts from the 2nd to the 15th century CE, ancient versions in Syriac, Coptic, Armenian, Georgian, Ethiopic, and other languages, and citations in the works of early Christian writers. These manuscripts are usually divided into various "families" of manuscripts that seem to lie within a single line of transmission.

Philological criticism is the study of the biblical languages in respect to grammar, vocabulary, and style, to ensure that they may be translated as faithfully as possible. Literary criticism classifies the various biblical texts according to their literary genre and attempts to use internal and external evidence to establish date, authorship, and intended audience. Tradition criticism attempts to analyze the various sources of the biblical materials in such a way as to discover the ORAL TRADITIONS that lie behind them and to trace their gradual development. Form criticism, a development of tradition criticism that in the 20th century became the dominant exegetical method, operates from the assumption that literary material, writ-

ten or oral, takes on certain forms according to the function the material serves within the community that preserves it. The content of a given narrative is an indication both of its form and of the narrative's use within the life of the community. Often a narrative will serve a variety of functions within various life settings over a period of time, and its proper analysis will reveal the development of the narrative into its final form.

Redaction criticism examines the way the various pieces of the tradition have been assembled into the final literary composition by an author or editor. The arrangement and modification of these pieces of tradition can reveal something of the author's intentions and the means by which he hoped to achieve them.

Historical criticism places the biblical documents within their historical context and examines them in the light of contemporary documents. In much the same way "history of religions" criticism compares the RELIGIOUS BELIEFS and practices expressed by the biblical texts to the trends discernible within world religion in general. The features of Israelite religion, for example, are often compared to those of other ancient Middle Eastern religions, while early Christianity may be compared to GNOSTICISM.

EXODUS \'ek-sə-dəs, 'eg-zə-\, second book of the PENTATEUCH, or Jewish BIBLE (the Christian OLD TESTAMENT). Exodus tells the story of how God liberated the children of Israel from slavery in Egypt through the prophet MOSES, his brother AARON, and his sister Miriam.

As recounted in the book of GENESIS, a famine had descended on the land of CANAAN, home of the Israelites, forcing them to seek refuge in Egypt. With the permission of the pharaoh, they settled in the land of Goshen, where they prospered and multiplied. After a lengthy period, however, a new pharaoh arose who was determined to enslave them.

Israelites crossing the Sea of Reeds in their Exodus from Egypt, illumination from a German Haggadah, 15th century
The Granger Collection

EXORCISM

Chapters 1:1–18:27 of Exodus tell the story of the liberation: 1:1–2:25 deal with the enslavement of the Israelites and the command of Pharaoh that all male infants born to the Hebrew women should be killed; 3:1–7:13 relate God's call to Moses to lead his people; 7:14–13:16, the plagues that persuaded the Egyptians to let the slaves leave and the PASSOVER rite celebrated on the eve of liberation; 13:17–15:21, the passage through the Sea of Reeds (traditionally mislocated as the Red Sea), which opened to allow the Israelites to pass and then closed over their Egyptian pursuers; 15:22–17:16, the way to Sinai; and 18:1–27, the organization of the people under Moses's administration.

Chapters 19:1–24:18 introduce the COVENANT between Israel and God reached at MOUNT SINAI: in 19:1–20:21 God appears and reveals the TEN COMMANDMENTS to Moses; 20:22–23:33 contain further rules and warnings; and 24:1–18 recount the Covenant ceremony. The last third of the book, chapters 25:1–40:38, describes in detail the TABERNACLE that the Israelites built for the worship of God in the wilderness, including its altars, basins, lamps, hangings, and priestly garments. Within this section of the book is the story (32:1–34:35) of the Israelites' betrayal of the Covenant and worship of the GOLDEN CALF and God's punishment and forgiveness on that occasion.

The book of Exodus accounts for the birth of Israel through the act of God, calling into being at Sinai a covenanted community formed out of a mixed multitude, guiding that people to the Promised Land to live under the laws of the Covenant and so form a kingdom of priests and a holy people. In Exodus God establishes his reliability as Israel's protector and savior, and he lays claim upon Israel's loyalty and obedience. In JUDAISM the Exodus is celebrated on the festival of Passover. The topic of the Exodus and God's intervention into history to form a holy community recurs through the liturgy and theology of Judaism and defines the principal motif throughout.

EXORCISM, ritual act addressed to evil spirits to force them to abandon an object, place, or person; technically, a ritual used in many traditions of CHRISTIANITY to expel DEMONS or spirits from persons who have come under their power.

In Christian tradition, Jesus expelled demons by a word and stated that this act was a sign of the coming of God's Kingdom. His followers, and others as well, drove out demons "in his name." In the first two centuries of the Christian era, the power of exorcism was considered a special gift that might be bestowed on anyone, lay or cleric. About 250 CE, however, there appeared a class of the lower clergy, called exorcists, who specialized in this function. About the same time, exorcism became one of the ceremonies preparatory to BAPTISM, and it has remained a part of the ROMAN CATHOLIC baptismal service.

In the THERAVĀDA Buddhist tradition, the Phi (Thailand) or NATS (Myanmar [Burma]) are expelled by specialists who are not monks.

EXTRINSICISM \ek-'strin-zə-ˌsi-zəm, -sə-\, in philosophy or theology, the tendency to place major emphasis on external matters rather than on allegedly more profound realities. In terms of morals and ethics, it tends to stress the external observance of laws and precepts, with lesser concern for the ultimate principles underlying moral conduct.

In Christian thought, this is illustrated by the tendency to define the church in terms of such exterior elements as its social structure and rituals rather than in terms of its spiritual elements.

EYBESCHÜTZ, JONATHAN \'ī-bə-ˌshœts\ (b. c. 1690, Kraków, Pol.—d. 1764, Altona, Holstein [now in Germany]), RABBI and religious scholar noted for his bitter quarrel

A saint, assisted by clerics, exorcising a demon from a possessed man, medieval woodcut
The Granger Collection

with Rabbi JACOB EMDEN, a dispute that split European Jewry and ended the effectiveness of rabbinic excommunication during Eybeschütz's time.

As a rabbi in a number of European towns, Eybeschütz became a celebrated master of the TALMUD, and he attracted a large, fiercely loyal corps of disciples. He was also learned in QABBALAH. When Eybeschütz accepted the pulpit in the triple community of Altona, Hamburg, and Wandsbek (then a domain of the Danish king), the women there hoped that his reputed mystic powers would save them from death in childbirth. He gave them AMULETS that were claimed to have contained, among other incantations, a prayer in cipher to SHABBETAI TZEVI (1626–76), the most famous of the false Jewish MESSIAHS, who had tried to abolish the Talmud. One of these amulets fell into the hands of

Rabbi Jacob Emden, a strict follower of the Talmud who publicly denounced the amulet's maker (without specifying Eybeschütz) as a heretic.

The Polish rabbinate sided with Eybeschütz and the German with Emden in a strident dispute that reflected a fundamental opposition between those who saw the pseudomessianic movement as a danger to JUDAISM and those who saw it as its fulfillment. Eybeschütz succeeded in maintaining his rabbinic post, if not in triumphing over Emden. The quarrel weakened rabbinic authority among the people, and repercussions were felt for a long time.

EZEKIEL \i-ˈzē-kē-əl\, *also spelled* Ezechiel, *Hebrew* Yeḥezqel (fl. early 6th century BCE), prophet-priest of ancient ISRAEL and the subject and partial author of an OLD TESTAMENT book that bears his name. Ezekiel's early oracles (from c. 592 BCE) in Jerusalem were pronouncements of violence and destruction; his later statements addressed the hopes of the Israelites exiled in Babylon. The faith of Ezekiel in the ultimate establishment of a new COVENANT between God and the people of Israel has had profound influence on the postexilic reconstruction and reorganization of JUDAISM.

Ezekiel's ministry was conducted in Jerusalem and Babylon in the first three decades of the 6th century BCE. These years saw the elimination of the state of JUDAH by the Babylonian empire under Nebuchadrezzar II (reigned 605–562 BCE). Jerusalem surrendered in 597 BCE. Israelite resistance was nevertheless renewed, and in 587–586 the city was destroyed after a lengthy siege. In both debacles and again in 582 large numbers of the surviving population were deported to Babylonia.

Before the first surrender of Jerusalem Ezekiel was a priest probably attached to the JERUSALEM TEMPLE staff. He was among those deported in 597 to Babylonia, where he was located at Tel-abib on the Kebar canal (near Nippur). Ezekiel's religious call came in July 592 when he had a vision of the "throne-chariot" of God. He subsequently prophesied until 585 and then was not heard of again until 572. His latest datable utterance can be dated about 570 BCE, 22 years after his first.

Ezekiel's earlier oracles to the Jews in Palestine were pronouncements of God's judgment on a sinful nation for its APOSTASY, declaring that Judah was guiltier than Israel had been and that Jerusalem would fall to Nebuchadrezzar and its inhabitants would be killed or exiled. According to Ezekiel, Judah trusted in foreign gods and foreign alliances, and Jerusalem was a city full of injustice.

After the fall of Jerusalem Ezekiel addressed himself more pointedly to the exiles and sought to direct their hopes for the restoration of their nation. Ezekiel prophesied that the exiles from both Judah and Israel would return to Palestine, leaving none in the Diaspora. In the imminent new age a new covenant would be made with the restored house of Israel, to whom God would give a new spirit and a new heart. The restoration would be an act of divine GRACE for the sake of God's name. Ezekiel's prophecies conclude with a vision of a restored Temple in Jerusalem. In contrast to those hoping for national restoration under a Davidic king, Ezekiel envisaged a theocratic community revolving around the Temple and its cult.

More than any of the classical biblical prophets Ezekiel was given to symbolic actions, strange visions, and even trances. He ate a scroll on which words of PROPHECY were written, in order to symbolize his appropriation of the message (3:1–3); he lay down for an extended time to symbolize

Israel's punishment (4:4ff); and he was apparently struck dumb on one occasion for an unspecified length of time (3:26). As other prophets had done before him, he saw the relationship of God to people as analogous to that of husband to unfaithful wife and therefore understood the collapse of the life of Judah as a judgment for essential infidelity. *See also* MERKABAH MYSTICISM AND HEKHALOT WRITING.

EZRA \ˈez-rə\, *Hebrew* ʿEzra (fl. 5th–4th century BCE, Babylon and Jerusalem), Jewish religious leader and reformer who returned from exile in Babylon to reconstitute the Jewish community on the basis of the TORAH. His work helped make JUDAISM a religion in which law was central, enabling the Jews to survive as a community when they were dispersed all over the world. Ezra has with some justice been called the father of Judaism; *i.e.*, the specific form the Jewish religion took after the BABYLONIAN EXILE.

Knowledge of Ezra is derived from the biblical books of Ezra and NEHEMIAH, supplemented by the Apocryphal book of 1 Esdras, which preserves the Greek text of Ezra and a part of Nehemiah. It is said that Ezra came to Jerusalem in the seventh year of King Artaxerxes (which Artaxerxes is not stated) of the Persian dynasty then ruling the area. Since he is introduced before Nehemiah, who was governor of the province of JUDAH from 445 to 433 BCE and again, after an interval, for a second term of unknown length, it is sometimes supposed that this was the seventh year of Artaxerxes I (458 BCE). Many scholars, however, now believe that the biblical account is not chronological and that Ezra arrived in the seventh year of Artaxerxes II (397 BCE), after Nehemiah had passed from the scene. Still others, holding that the two men were contemporaries, regard the seventh year as a scribal error and believe that perhaps Ezra arrived during Nehemiah's second term as governor.

When Ezra arrived in Judah, the Law was widely disregarded and public and private morality was at a low level. Moreover, intermarriage with foreigners posed the threat that the community would lose its identity. Ezra was a priest and "a scribe skilled in the law." He apparently had official status as a commissioner of the Persian government, and his title, "scribe of the law of the God of heaven," is best understood as "royal secretary for Jewish religious affairs," or the like. The Persians were tolerant of native cults but, in order to avert internal strife and to prevent religion from becoming a mask for rebellion, insisted that these be regulated under responsible authority. The delegated authority over the Jews of the satrapy (administrative area) "beyond the river," or west of the Euphrates River, was entrusted to Ezra; for a Jew to disobey the Law he brought was to disobey "the law of the king."

Ezra probably presented the Law to the people during the Feast of Tabernacles (SUKKOT) in the autumn, most likely in the year of his arrival. He also took action against mixed marriages and succeeded in persuading the people to divorce their foreign wives. His efforts reached their climax when the people engaged in solemn COVENANT before God to enter into no more mixed marriages, to refrain from work on the SABBATH, to levy on themselves an annual tax for the support of the Temple, regularly to present their TITHES and offerings, and otherwise to comply with the demands of the Law.

Nothing further is known of Ezra after his reforms. The 1st-century Hellenistic Jewish historian JOSEPHUS states that he died and was buried in Jerusalem. According to another tradition, he returned to Babylonia, where his supposed grave is a holy site.

FAFNIR \'fäf-nir, 'fäv-\, in Nordic mythology, name of the great dragon slain by Sigurd, the Norse version of the German hero SIEGFRIED. As told in the *Völsunga saga* ("Saga of the Volsungs"), Fafnir slew his father, Hreithmar, to obtain the vast amount of gold which Hreithmar had demanded of ODIN as a compensation for the loss of one of his sons. Odin gave the gold but put a curse on it. Full of greed, Fafnir changed into a dragon to guard his treasure and was later slain by the young hero Sigurd. Sigurd was spurred on by another brother of Fafnir, the blacksmith Regin. Once Sigurd, under the advice of Odin, had killed Fafnir, Regin asked him to cook the dragon's heart for him. Sigurd touched the heart as it was cooking to test if it was done and burned his thumb. He put his thumb into his mouth and was then able to understand the language of birds. (In this tale, knowledge is given to one who eats the heart of a dragon.) The birds told Sigurd that it was Regin's intention to kill him, so instead Sigurd killed Regin and left with Fafnir's treasure.

FA-HSIANG \'fä-'shyäŋ\, school of Chinese BUDDHISM derived from the Indian YOGĀCĀRA school.

FA-HSIEN \'fä-'shyen\, *Pinyin* Faxian, *original name* Sehi (fl. 399–414 CE), Chinese Buddhist monk whose PILGRIMAGE to India in 402 initiated Sino-Indian relations and whose writings give important information about the BUDDHISM of the period.

Sehi, who later adopted the name Fa-hsien ("Splendor of Religious Law"), was born at Shansi during the 4th century CE. Living at the time of the Eastern Chin dynasty, when Buddhism enjoyed an imperial favor seldom equaled in Chinese history, he was stirred by a profound faith to go to India, the fountainhead of Buddhism.

The historical importance of Fa-hsien is twofold. A famous record of his journeys—*Fo Kuo Chi* ("Record of Buddhist Kingdoms")—contains valuable information not found elsewhere concerning the history of Indian Buddhism during the early centuries CE. Because of his fairly detailed descriptions, it is possible to envision Buddhist India before it was overcome by the counter-reforms of HINDUISM and eclipsed by the Muslim invasion. He also strengthened Chinese Buddhism by helping provide a better knowledge of Buddhist sacred texts. After studying them for 10 years in India, he brought back to China a great number of copies of Buddhist texts and translated them from Sanskrit into Chinese. Among them, two of the most important were the *Mahāparinirvāṇa-sūtra*, a text glorifying the eternal, personal, and pure nature of NIRVANA—on which the Nirvana school in China then based its doctrines—and the rules of monastic discipline of the MAHĀSAṄGHIKA school.

In northwestern India, which he entered in 402, Fa-hsien visited the most important seats of Buddhist learning: Udyāna, Gandhāra, Peshāwar, and Taxila. Above all, however, he was attracted by eastern India, where the Buddha had

spent his life and had taught his doctrines. His pilgrimage was completed by visits to the most holy sites of the Buddha's life: Kapilavastu, where he was born; BODH GAYA, where he acquired the supreme enlightenment; Banares (VARANASI), where he preached his first sermon; and Kuśinagara, where he entered into *parinirvāṇa*. Everywhere Fa-hsien was amazed at the extraordinary flowering of the Buddhist faith.

Then he stayed a long time at Pāṭaliputra, conversing with Buddhist monks and studying Sanskrit texts with Buddhist scholars. When he had deepened his knowledge of Buddhism and was in possession of sacred texts that had not yet been translated into Chinese, he decided to go back to China. Fa-hsien took the sea route, first spending two years in Ceylon (now Sri Lanka), at that time one of the most flourishing centers of Buddhist studies.

FAITH, *Greek* pistis, *Latin* fides, a common synonym for religion. Faith is an inner attitude, conviction, or trust relating man to a supreme God or ultimate salvation. In religious traditions stressing divine GRACE, it is the certainty or attitude of love granted by God himself. In Christian theology, faith is the divinely inspired human response to God's relevation through JESUS CHRIST and, consequently, is of crucial significance. While in English usage, when one speaks of "the Christian faith" or "the Buddhist faith," the word is used as a synonym for religion, no definition actually allows for the identification of "faith" with "religion."

In biblical JUDAISM, "faith" is principally juridical; it is the faithfulness or truthfulness with which persons adhere to a treaty or promise and with which God and ISRAEL adhere to the COVENANT between them. In ISLAM and CHRISTIANITY, both rooted in this tradition, the notion of faith reflects that view. In Islam, faith (Arabic ĪMĀN) is what sets the believer apart from others; at the same time, it is ascertained that "None can have faith except by the will of Allāh" (Qur'an 10:100). In Christianity, ST. PAUL similarly asserts that faith is a gift of God (1 Corinthians 12:8–9), while the Letter to the Hebrews (11:1) defines faith (*pistis*) as "the assurance of things hoped for, the conviction of things not seen." Some scholars think that ZOROASTRIANISM, as well as Judaism, may have had some importance in the development of the notion of faith in Western religion; the prophet ZOROASTER (*c.* 628–*c.* 551 BCE) may have been the first founder of a religion to speak of a new, conscious religious choice on the part of humans for truth (*asha*).

The intellectual component of Christian faith is stressed by ST. THOMAS AQUINAS. A major issue of the PROTESTANT movement was the theological problem of JUSTIFICATION by faith alone. LUTHER stressed the element of trust, while CALVIN emphasized faith as a gift freely bestowed by God.

FAITH HEALING, recourse to divine power to cure mental or physical disabilities, either in conjunction with orthodox medical care or in place of it. Often an intermediary is involved, whose intercession may be all-important in effecting the desired cure. Sometimes the faith may reside in a particular place, which then becomes the focus of PILGRIMAGES for the sufferers.

In CHRISTIANITY, faith healing is exemplified especially in the miraculous cures wrought by JESUS (40 healings are attested) and by his APOSTLES. The early church later sanctioned faith healing through such practices as anointing and the IMPOSITION OF HANDS. Faith healing has also been associated with the intercessionary miracles of saints.

During the 19th and 20th centuries, faith healing has often motivated pilgrimages and healing services in many Christian denominations. The apparent healing gifts of individuals have also attracted wide attention: Leslie Weatherhead, Methodist pastor and theologian, and Harry Edwards, spiritualist, in England; Elsie Salmon, wife of a Methodist minister, in South Africa; Oral Roberts, a converted Methodist and mass-meeting evangelist, Agnes Sanford, wife of an Episcopal rector, and Edgar Cayce, a clairvoyant of Presbyterian background, in the United States. A different approach to the idea of divine healing is represented by the metaphysical healing movement in the United States called NEW THOUGHT. Phineas P. Quimby and MARY BAKER EDDY published numerous tracts exhorting their fol-

A faith healer ministers to a hopeful sufferer
Archive Photos

lowers to beliefs that stressed the immanence of God and a link between bodily ills and mistaken convictions. CHRISTIAN SCIENCE was unique in its view of sickness as a material state, subject to the transcendental power of the individual's spiritual being.

FAKHR AL-DĪN AL-RĀZĪ \ˈfä-ḵər-äd-ˈdēn-är-ˈrä-zē\, *in full* Abū ʿAbd Allāh Muhammad ibn ʿUmar ibn al-Ḥusayn Fakhr al-Dīn al-Rāzī (b. 1149, Rayy, Iran—d. 1209, near Herāt, Khwārezm), Muslim theologian and scholar, author of one of the most authoritative commentaries on the QURʾAN.

Al-Rāzī was the son of a preacher. After a broad education, in which he specialized in theology and philosophy, he traveled through present-day northwestern Iran and Turkmenistan and finally settled in Herāt (now in Afghanistan). Wherever he went, he debated with famous scholars and was patronized and consulted by local rulers. He wrote about 100 books and gained fame and wealth.

Al-Rāzī lived in an age of political and religious turmoil. The empire of the Baghdad CALIPHS was disintegrating; its numerous local rulers were virtually independent. Religious unity, too, had long since crumbled: in addition to the division of Islam into two major groups—the SUNNIS and the SHĪʿITES—countless small sects had developed, often with the support of local rulers, and SUFISM was gaining ground. Al-Rāzī attempted to reconcile a rationalistic theology and philosophy incorporating concepts taken from Aristotle and other Greek philosophers with the Qurʾan. This attempt inspired *al-Mabāḥith al-mashriqīya* ("Eastern Discourses"), a summation of his philosophical and theological positions, and several commentaries on IBN SĪNĀ (Avicenna), as well as his extremely wide-ranging commentary on the Qurʾan (*Mafātīḥ al-ghayb* or *Kitāb al-tafsīr al-kabīr*; "The Keys to the Unknown" or "The Great Commentary"), which ranks among the greatest works of its kind in Islam. Equally famous is his *Muḥaṣṣal afkār al-mutaqaddimīn wa-al-mutaʾakhkhirīn* ("Collection of the Opinions of Ancients and Moderns"), which was accepted from the first as a classic of KALĀM (Muslim theology). His other books, in addition to a general encyclopedia, dealt with subjects as varied as medicine, ASTROLOGY, geometry, physiognomy, mineralogy, and grammar.

Al-Rāzī was also a master of debate. His ability to refute arguments, together with his aggressiveness, self-confidence, irritability, and bad temper, made many enemies for him, and on occasion he could show extreme malice. He contrived to have his elder brother, who openly resented his success, imprisoned by the Khwārezm-Shāh (ruler of Turkistan); the brother died in prison. A famous preacher with whom he had quarreled was drowned by royal command. Some sources suggest further that al-Rāzī's death was not from natural causes but that he was poisoned by the Karrāmīya (a Muslim sect) in revenge for his attacks on them.

Al-Rāzī loved disputation so much that he went out of his way to present unorthodox and heretical religious views as fully and as favorably as possible, before refuting them. This habit gave his opponents grounds for accusing him of heresy. His thorough presentations of unorthodox views make his works a useful source of information about little-known Muslim sects.

FAKIR: *see* DERVISH.

FALASHA \fə-ˈlä-shə\, *also spelled* Felasha, Jewish Ethiopians. The Falasha call themselves House of Israel (Beta Israel) and claim descent from Menilek I, traditionally the son of the Queen of Sheba (Makeda) and King SOLOMON. Their ancestors, however, were probably local Agew peoples in Ethiopia who were converted by Jews living in southern Arabia. The Falasha remained faithful to JUDAISM after the conversion of the powerful Ethiopian kingdom of Aksum to CHRISTIANITY in the 4th century CE, and thereafter the Falasha were persecuted and forced to retreat to the area around Lake Tana, in northern Ethiopia. Despite Ethiopian Christian attempts to exterminate them in the 15th and 16th centuries, the Falasha partly retained their independence until the 17th century, when the emperor Susenyos crushed them and confiscated their lands. Their conditions improved in the late 19th and 20th centuries, at which time tens of thousands of Falasha lived in the region north of Lake Tana.

The Falasha have a BIBLE and a prayer book written in Ge'ez, the ancient Ethiopian language. They have no Talmudic laws, but they observe the SABBATH, practice CIRCUMCISION, have SYNAGOGUE services led by priests (*kohanim*) of the village, follow certain dietary laws of Judaism, observe many laws regarding ritual uncleanness, offer sacrifices on Nisan 14 in the Jewish religious year, and observe some of the major Jewish festivals.

From 1980 to 1992 some 45,000 Falasha fled drought- and war-stricken Ethiopia and emigrated to Israel. The number of Falasha remaining in Ethiopia was uncertain, possibly only a few thousand. The ongoing absorption of the Falasha community into Israeli society was a source of controversy and ethnic tension in subsequent years.

FALSE DECRETALS \di-'krē-təlz, 'de-krə-təlz\, a 9th-century collection of ecclesiastical legislation containing some forged documents. The principal aim of the forgers was to free the CHRISTIAN church from interference by the state.

A party had been formed in the Carolingian Empire to combat the subjection of the church to the state (*see* CHURCH AND STATE). Within this party was a group that became convinced that the use of legitimate means would never accomplish this purpose. They conceived that positive legislation of their demands could be projected into the past by attributing it to popes and kings long dead. Thus, they produced a number of falsifications of church law, of which the best known was the False Decretals.

The False Decretals—also called the Decretals of Pseudo-Isidore because their compilers passed as St. Isidore of Seville, a Spanish encyclopedist and historian—purports to be a collection of decrees of councils and decretals of popes (written replies on questions of ecclesiastical discipline) from the first seven centuries. The collection contains (1) the letters of the popes preceding the COUNCIL OF NICAEA (325) from Clement I to Miltiades, all of which are forgeries; (2) a collection of the decrees of councils, most of which are genuine, though the forged DONATION OF CONSTANTINE is included; (3) a large collection of letters of the popes from Sylvester I (died 335) to Gregory II (died 731), among which there are more than 40 falsifications.

As a collection, the False Decretals seems to have been used first at the Council of Soissons in 853. It was known at the end of the 9th century in Italy but had little influence there until the end of the 10th century. For the next few centuries, it was generally accepted by canonists, theologians, and councils as authentic. It was not until the 17th century that David Blondel, a Reformed theologian, clearly refuted its defenders. Since that time, research has concentrated on the origin, extent, and purpose of the falsification.

It is untrue to say that the False Decretals revolutionized CANON LAW, but the forgers did have a considerable influence. They seem to have helped to limit the power of archbishops, revive dormant privileges of the clergy, and revive the right of appeal of local bishops to the pope.

FAMA \'fä-mə, 'fä-\ (Latin), *Greek* Pheme, in Greco-Roman mythology, the personification of popular rumor. Pheme was more a poetic personification than a deified abstraction, although there was an altar in her honor at Athens. The Greek poet Hesiod portrayed her as an evildoer, easily stirred up but impossible to quell. The Athenian orator Aeschines distinguished Popular Rumor (Pheme) from Slander (Sykophantia) and Malice (Diabole). In Roman literature Fama was imaginatively conceived: Virgil described her (*Aeneid*, Book IV) as a swift, birdlike monster with as many eyes, lips, tongues, and ears as feathers, traveling on the ground but with her head in the clouds. According to Ovid in the *Metamorphoses*, she inhabited a reverberating mountaintop palace of brass.

FAMILIAR, in Western demonology, a small animal or imp kept as a witch's attendant, given to her by the devil or inherited from another witch. The familiar was a low-ranking DEMON that assumed an animal shape, such as that of a toad, a dog, an insect, or a black cat. Sometimes the familiar was described as an amalgam of several creatures.

The familiar was believed to subsist by sucking blood from a witch's fingers or from protuberances on her body such as moles or warts. During the European WITCHCRAFT trials of the 15th–17th century a suspected witch was searched for the "teats" by which she fed her familiar, and these, like the devil's brand marks, were considered sure signs of her guilt.

FAMILIST \'fa-mə-list\, member of Family of Love, religious sect of Dutch origin consisting of followers of Hendrik Niclaes, a 16th-century merchant. Niclaes' main activity was in Emden, East Friesland (1540–60). In his *Evangelium regni*, issued in English as *A Joyful Message of the Kingdom*, he invited all "lovers of truth" to join in a great fellowship of peace, giving up all contention over dogma and seeking to be incorporated into the body of Christ.

Niclaes gained many followers, among them the great publisher Christophe Plantin, who surreptitiously printed a number of Niclaes' works. Niclaes apparently made two visits to England, where his sect had the largest following. Elizabeth I issued a proclamation against the Family of Love in 1580, and James I believed it to have been the source of PURITANISM. The sect did not survive after the Restoration of the English monarchy in 1660, but according to GEORGE FOX some remaining Familists later became associated with the SOCIETY OF FRIENDS.

FAMILY OF LOVE, *formerly* Children of God, *or* Teens for Christ, religious group, generally considered to be part of the Jesus Movement, begun by David Berg, an itinerant preacher, in 1968. Originally called Teens for Christ, the group originated in California, U.S., and attracted alienated middle-class youth. Renamed Children of God by a journalist, the movement gained followers and spread to countries worldwide. Berg, who became known as Moses, withdrew from the day-to-day operations in the early 1970s but continued to communicate with members through "Mo letters," some of which were collected and published. In the early 1980s the group was renamed Family of Love.

Members of the group, which practices a form of charismatic CHRISTIANITY, generally live in communal colonies. Its ministry includes youth-oriented nightclubs, musical groups, street theatre, speaking in TONGUES (glossolalia), and aggressive proselytizing. Many of its practices, especially with regard to recruitment of new members, attracted criticism, including charges of brainwashing.

FANA \fə-'nä\, *Arabic* fanā' (literally, "passing away" or "cessation of existence"), in SUFISM, the complete denial of self and the realization of God that is one of the steps taken by the Muslim Sufi toward the achievement of union with God. Fana may be attained by constant meditation and by contemplation on the attributes of God, coupled with the denunciation of human attributes. When the Sufi succeeds in purifying himself entirely of the earthly world and loses himself in the love of God, it is said that he has "annihilated" his individual will and "passed away" from his own existence to live only in God and with God.

Many Sufis hold that fana alone is a negative state, for even though ridding oneself of earthly desires and recognizing and denouncing human imperfections are necessary for every pious individual, such virtues are insufficient for those who choose the path of Sufism. Through *fanā' 'an al-fanā'* ("passing away from passing away"), however, the Sufi succeeds in annihilating human attributes and loses all awareness of earthly existence; he then, through the GRACE of God, is revived, and the secrets of the divine attributes are revealed to him. Only after regaining full consciousness does he attain the more sublime state of *baqā'* (subsistence) and finally become ready for the direct vision of God.

FĀRĀBĪ, AL- \ȧl-fȧ-'rä-bē\, *in full* Muhammad ibn Muhammad ibn Ṭarkhān ibn Uzalagh al-Fārābī, *Latin name* Alpharabius \ˌal-fə-'rā-bē-əs\ *or* Avennasar \ˌa-və-'nä-sər\ (b. *c.* 878, Turkistan—d. *c.* 950, Damascus?), Muslim philosopher, one of the preeminent thinkers of medieval ISLAM. He was regarded in the Arab world as the greatest philosophical authority after Aristotle.

Al-Fārābī was of Turkic origin and is thought to have been brought to Baghdad as a child by his father, who was probably in the Turkish bodyguard of the CALIPH. Al-Fārābī was not a member of the court society, and he did not work in the administration of the central government. In 942 he took up residence at the court of the prince Sayf ad-Dawlah, where he remained, mostly in Ḥalab (modern Aleppo), until the time of his death.

Al-Fārābī's philosophical thinking was nourished in the heritage of the Arabic Aristotelian teachings of 10th-century Baghdad. He took the Greek heritage, as it had become known to the Arabs, and showed how it could be used to answer questions with which Muslims were struggling. To al-Fārābī, philosophy had come to an end in other parts of the world but had a chance for new life in Islam. Islam as a religion, however, was of itself not sufficient for the needs of a philosopher. He saw human reason as being superior to revelation. Religion provided truth in a sym-bolic form to nonphilosophers, who were not able to apprehend it in its more pure forms. Of the more than 100 works ascribed to him, the major part of al-Fārābī's writings were directed to the problem of the correct ordering of the state. Just as God rules the universe, so should the philosopher, as the most perfect kind of man, rule the state.

FARD, WALLACE D. \'färd\, *also called* Walli Farrad, Farrad Mohammed, F. Mohammed Ali, *or* Wallace Fard Muhammad (b. *c.* 1877, Mecca—d. 1934?), founder of the NATION OF ISLAM (sometimes called Black Muslim) movement in the United States.

Fard immigrated to the United States sometime before 1930. In that year, he established in Detroit the Temple of Islam as well as the University of Islam, which was the temple's school, and the Fruit of Islam, a corps of male guards. Fard preached that African-Americans must prepare for an inevitable race war and that Christianity was the religion of slaveowners. Accordingly, he gave his followers Arabic names to replace those that had originated in slavery. In 1934 he disappeared without a trace. Members of the movement believe Fard to be the incarnation of ALLĀH, and his birthday, February 26, is observed as Savior's Day.

FARRAKHAN, LOUIS \'fär-ə-ˌkän, 'far-ə-ˌkan\, *in full* Louis Abdul Farrakhan, *original name* Louis Eugene Walcott (b. May 11, 1933, Bronx, New York, N.Y., U.S.), African-American leader, from 1978, of the NATION OF ISLAM. A compelling orator whose rhetoric sometimes fell into overt racism and anti-Semitism, Farrakhan was effective in encouraging African-American self-reliance and unity.

Farrakhan grew up amid racial tensions in a Boston neighborhood. He attended Winston-Salem Teachers College for two years and afterward found work as a calypso guitarist-singer. In 1955 he converted from the Episcopal Church to the Nation of Islam, also called Black Muslims, the unorthodox form of Islam led by ELIJAH MUHAMMAD.

After assisting MALCOLM X at his mosque in Boston, he became minister there when Malcolm moved to New York

Louis Farrakhan addressing a crowd
UPI/Corbis—Bettmann

City. When Malcolm converted to SUNNI Islam, Farrakhan denounced and replaced him as minister of Mosque Number Seven in Harlem. Farrakhan later expressed regret at having contributed to the climate of antagonism toward Malcolm that preceded his assassination.

After Elijah Muhammad died in 1975, his son W. Deen Muhammad succeeded him as the principal IMAM, or leader, of the Nation of Islam and altered the organization's course by gradually integrating the estimated 50,000-member Nation into the orthodox Muslim community. In 1978, however, Farrakhan formed his own sect, which he again called the Nation of Islam and which continued or revived features of its predecessor. His followers often were recruited from the poor and alienated; they abstained from pork, intoxicants, and sexual promiscuity and wore distinctive, austere clothing. Farrakhan emphasized the importance of the family and the need for African-Americans to develop their own economic resources. He preached the inherent wickedness of whites, particularly Jews.

Though the separatism Farrakhan preached had encouraged nonparticipation in the political process, in 1983 he registered to vote and campaigned for the Reverend Jesse Jackson's candidacy for U.S. president. In later speeches he blamed the U.S. government for what he claimed was a conspiracy to destroy black people with AIDS and addictive drugs. Beginning in the late 1980s he cultivated a relationship with the Libyan dictator Muammar al-Qaddafi.

In 1995 Farrakhan was a prominent organizer of the "Million Man March" of African-American men in Washington, D.C. Several hundred thousand participants from throughout the United States affirmed their unity and pledged dedication to family values.

FASCHING \'fä-shiŋ\, ROMAN CATHOLIC Shrovetide CARNIVAL as celebrated in German-speaking countries. There are many regional differences in the name, duration, and activities of the carnival. It is known as Fasching in Bavaria and Austria, Fosnat in Franconia, Fasnet in Swabia, Fastnacht in Mainz and its environs, and Karneval in Cologne and the Rhineland. The beginning of the pre-Lenten season generally is considered to be EPIPHANY (January 6), but in Cologne, where the festivities are the most elaborate, the official beginning is marked on the 11th hour of the 11th day of the 11th month of the year. Merrymaking may get under way on the Thursday before LENT, but the truly rambunctious revelry associated with Fasching usually reaches its high point during the three days preceding ASH WEDNESDAY, culminating on Shrove Tuesday. The names of these final days also vary regionally.

Although the exact historical origins of Fasching are unclear, the observance of its rites is mentioned in Wolfram von Eschenbach's *Parzival* (early 13th century). It was a festival that originated in the cities—most notably Mainz and Speyer—and was already established in Cologne by 1234. Traditionally, it was not only a feast before Lent but also a time during which the rules and order of daily life were subverted. This gave rise to such customs as handing over the keys of the city to a council of fools or ceremoniously letting women rule. It also inspired noisy costumed parades and masked balls; satirical and often impertinent plays, speeches, and newspaper columns; and generally excessive behavior—all of which are still common elements of contemporary Fasching celebrations. After the REFORMATION, Protestant areas of Europe took exception to such Roman Catholic excesses, and carnival practices began to die out in those areas.

FASTING, abstinence from food or drink or both for ritualistic, mystical, ascetic, or other religious or ethical purposes. The abstention may be complete or partial, lengthy or of short duration. Fasting has been practiced by the founders and followers of many religions, by culturally designated individuals (*e.g.,* hunters or candidates for initiation rites), and by individuals or groups as an expression of protest against what they believe are violations of social, ethical, or political principles.

In the religions of ancient peoples and civilizations, fasting was a practice to prepare persons, especially priests and priestesses, to approach the deities. In the Hellenistic MYSTERY RELIGIONS (*e.g.,* the cult of ASCLEPIUS), the gods were thought to reveal their divine teachings in dreams and visions only after a fast that required the total dedication of the devotees. Among the pre-Columbian peoples of Peru, fasting often was one of the requirements for penance after an individual had confessed SINS before a priest. In many cultures the practice was considered a means to assuage an angered deity or to aid in resurrecting a deity who was believed to have died.

In various indigenous religions, fasting is practiced before and during a VISION QUEST (*e.g.,* among the North American Indian peoples of the Great Plains and the Pacific Northwest). Among the Evenk (Tungus) of Siberia, SHAMANS fast and train themselves to see visions and to control spirits. Priestly societies among the Pueblo Indians of the American Southwest fast during retreats before major ceremonies connected with seasonal changes. (*See* NATIVE AMERICAN RELIGIONS.)

Fasting for special purposes or before or during special sacred times is a characteristic of the major religions of the world. In JAINISM, fasting and meditation lead to trances that enable individuals to reach a transcendent state. Buddhist monks of the THERAVĀDA school fast on certain holy days (*uposatha*) of the month. In China prior to 1949, it was customary to observe a fixed period of fasting and abstinence before the sacrifice during the night of the winter solstice, a time when the heavenly Yang (positive energy) principle was believed to begin its new cycle. In India, Hindu sadhus (holy men) are admired for their frequent personal fasts for various reasons.

Among the major Western religions, only ZOROASTRIANISM prohibits fasting, because of its belief that such a form of ASCETICISM will not aid in strengthening the faithful in their struggle against evil. JUDAISM, CHRISTIANITY, and ISLAM emphasize fasting during certain periods. Judaism observes several annual fast days, primarily on days of penitence (such as YOM KIPPUR, the Day of Atonement) or mourning. Christianity, especially ROMAN CATHOLICISM and EASTERN ORTHODOXY, has observed a fast period during LENT, before EASTER, and during ADVENT, before CHRISTMAS. Among Roman Catholics the observance has been modified since the SECOND VATICAN COUNCIL (1962–65) to allow greater individual choice, with mandatory fasting only on ASH WEDNESDAY and GOOD FRIDAY during Lent. Protestant churches generally leave the decision to fast to individual church members. The month of RAMAḌĀN in Islam is a period of penitence and total fasting from dawn to dusk.

FATE, *Greek* Moira, *plural* Moirai, *Latin* Parca, *plural* Parcae, in Greek and Roman mythology, any of three goddesses who determined human destinies, and in particular the span of a person's life and his or her allotment of misery and suffering. Homer speaks of Fate (*moira*) in the singular as an impersonal power and sometimes makes its functions interchangeable with those of the Olympian gods. However, from the time of Hesiod (8th century BCE), the Fates were personified as three old women who spin the threads of human destiny. Their names were Clotho (Spinner), Lachesis (Allotter), and Atropos (Inflexible). Much later writers assigned the three different tasks: Clotho spun the "thread" of human fate, Lachesis dispensed it, and Atropos cut the thread (thus determining the moment of death). The Romans identified the Parcae, originally personifications of childbirth, with the three Greek Fates. The Roman goddesses were named Nona, Decuma, and Morta.

FĀTIḤA \\'fä-tē-ˌhä\\, *also called* fātiḥat al-kitāb (Arabic: "the opening of the book"), the "opening" or first chapter (SŪRA) of the QURʾAN. In contrast to the other *sūra*s, which are usually narratives or exhortations delivered by God, the seven verses of the *fātiḥa* form a short devotional prayer addressed to God and in oral recitation are ended with the word *amīn* ("amen"). Muslim tradition regards it as the essence of the Qurʾan. The *fātiḥa* has acquired broad ceremonial usage in ISLAM: it introduces each ritual bowing (*rakʿah*) in the five daily prayers (ṢALĀT), is recited at all Muslim sanctuaries, validates important resolutions, appears frequently on AMULETS, and is recited for the dead.

In North Africa, *fātiḥa* (or *fatḥa*) designates a prayer performed silently with arms outstretched, palms turned upward. The first *sūra* is not necessarily recited but was probably once part of the ceremony.

FĀṬIMA \\'fa-ti-mə\\, *also called* Al-Zahrāʾ (Arabic: "Shining One") (b. c. 605, Mecca, Arabia—d. 633, Medina), daughter of MUHAMMAD who in later centuries became the object of deep veneration by many Muslims, especially the SHIʿITES. Alone among Muhammad's sons and daughters, Fāṭima stood at the head of a genealogy that encompassed all of the Shiʿite IMAMS and that steadily enlarged through the generations.

To the Shiʿites she is particularly important as the wife of ʿAlī, whom they consider to be the legitimate heir of the authority of the prophet Muhammad and the first of their imams. The sons of Fāṭima and ʿAlī, ḤASAN and ḤUSAYN, are thus viewed by the Shiʿites as the rightful inheritors of the tradition of Muhammad. Thus, many traditions give her life more majesty that it had in reality. The ISMAʿĪLĪ Fāṭimid dynasty, which ruled North Africa, Egypt, and Syria between 909 and 1171, derived its name from hers.

Fāṭima accompanied Muhammad when he emigrated from Mecca to Medina in 622. Soon after her arrival in Medina she married ʿAlī, the son of one of the Prophet's uncles. Their first years were ones of material want. ʿAlī was often harsh with her, and Fāṭima brought her case before Muhammad himself; the Prophet took great satisfaction in being able to reconcile husband and wife. When in 632 Muhammad was facing his last illness, Fāṭima was there to nurse him. In general she avoided involvement in political affairs. Yet after Muhammad's death she had a sharp clash with Abū Bakr, who succeeded Muhammad as leader of the Islamic community, over property that she claimed Muhammad had left her. Abū Bakr refused to sanction her claim, and for six months she and ʿAlī refused to recognize his authority. It is not clear whether or not she had become reconciled to Abū Bakr by the time she died.

FAUNA \\'fȯ-nə\\, in ancient ROMAN RELIGION, a goddess of woodlands, fields, and flocks; she was the counterpart—variously the wife, sister, or daughter—of FAUNUS.

FAUNUS \\'fȯ-nəs\\, ancient Italian rural deity whose attributes in Roman times were identified with those of the Greek god PAN. Faunus was originally worshiped in the countryside as a bestower of fruitfulness on fields and flocks. He eventually became primarily a woodland deity, the sounds of the forest being regarded as his voice.

A grandson of SATURN, Faunus was typically represented as half man, half goat, a derivation from the Greek Satyr, in the company of similar creatures, known as Fauns. Like Pan, Faunus was associated with merriment, and his twice-yearly festivals were marked by revelry and abandon. At the LUPERCALIA, a festival held partly in his honor each February in Rome well into the Christian era, youths clothed as goats ran through the streets wielding strips of goatskin.

FAYḌ \\'fīḍ\\ (Arabic: "emanation"), in Islamic philosophy, the emanation of created things from God. The word is not used in the QURʾAN, which uses terms such as *khalq* ("creation") and *ibdāʿ* ("invention") in describing the process of creation. Early Muslim theologians dealt with this subject only in simple terms as stated in the Qurʾan, namely, that God had ordered the world to be, and it was. Later Muslim philosophers, such as AL-FĀRĀBĪ (10th century) and IBN SĪNA (11th century) under the influence of NEOPLATONISM conceived of creation as a gradual process. Generally, they proposed that the world came into being as the result of God's superabundance. The creation process takes a gradual course, which begins with the most perfect level and descends to the least perfect—the world of matter. The degree of perfection is measured by the distance from the first emanation, for which all creative things yearn. The soul, for example, is trapped in the body and will always long for its release from its bodily prison to join the world of spirit, which is closer to the first cause and therefore more perfect. God emanates not out of necessity but out of a free act of will. This process is spontaneous because it arises from God's natural goodness, and it is eternal because God is always superabundant.

AL-GHAZĀLĪ refuted the *fayḍ* theory on the grounds that it lowers God's role in the creation to mere natural causality. God, al-Ghazālī maintained, creates with absolute will and freedom, and theories of necessary overflowing and emanation lead logically to the denial of the absoluteness of the divine active will.

FEATHERED SERPENT, major deity of the ancient Meso-American pantheon. *See* QUETZALCÓATL; PRE-COLUMBIAN MESO-AMERICAN RELIGIONS.

FELICITAS \\fi-'li-sə-ˌtas\\, Roman goddess of good luck to whom a temple was first built in the mid-2nd century BCE. She became the special protector of successful commanders. Caesar planned to erect another temple to her, and it was built by the triumvir Marcus Aemilius Lepidus. The emperors made her prominent as symbolizing the blessings of the imperial regime.

FENG-HUANG \\'fəŋ-'hwäŋ\\, *Pinyin* fenghuang (Chinese: "phoenix"), in Chinese mythology, a creature whose rare appearance portends some great event or bears testimony to the greatness of a ruler. The *feng-huang* is also a popular symbol in Chinese alchemy and folk tradition. In systematized mythology, the *feng-huang* (phoenix) is the female counterpart of the male dragon. Tradition recounts an appearance of the *feng-huang* before the death of the legendary Yellow Emperor (HUANG-TI), who ruled China in the

27th century BCE. The bird has the breast of a goose, the hindquarters of a stag, the neck of a snake, the tail of a fish, the forehead of a fowl, the down of a duck, the marks of a dragon, the back of a tortoise, the face of a swallow, and the beak of a cock. It was reportedly about nine feet tall.

FENG-SHUI \'fəŋ-'shwā\, *Pinyin* fengshui ("wind-water"), traditional Chinese practice of geomancy, the arrangement of the human and social world in auspicious alignment with the forces of the cosmos (*i.e.*, the natural principles of CH'I, YIN-YANG, and *wu-hsiung*); it was developed during the Han dynasty (206 BCE–220 CE). The proper siting of graves, domestic buildings, and temples was a special concern in feng-shui, particularly the harmonious placement of such structures in relation to the twin powers of yin and yang, associated with bodies of water and mountains, respectively. Appropriate placement was done by feng-shui specialists, or diviners, who used a compasslike instrument to determine the precise cosmic forces affecting a site. Feng-shui was popular throughout all levels of Chinese society and continues to be used in both urban and rural communities in China and in the Chinese diaspora. It has gained a recent following in the United States, owing to the publication of a number of popular books on the subject.

FENRIR \'fen-rər\, *also called* Fenrisúlfr, monstrous wolf of Norse mythology. He was the son of the god LOKI and a giantess, Angerboda. Fearing Fenrir's strength and knowing that only evil could be expected of him, the gods bound him with a magical chain made of the sound of a cat's footsteps, the beard of a woman, the breath of fish, and other occult elements. When the chain was placed upon him, Fenrir bit off the hand of the god TYR. He was gagged with a sword and was destined to lie bound to a rock until the RAGNARÖK (Doomsday), when he will break his bonds and fall upon the gods. According to one version of the myth, Fenrir will devour the sun, and in the Ragnarök he will fight the chief god ODIN and swallow him. Odin's son Vidar will avenge his father, stabbing the wolf to the heart according to one account and tearing his jaws asunder in another. Fenrir figures prominently in Norwegian and Icelandic poetry of the 10th and 11th centuries, and the poets speak apprehensively of the day when he will break loose.

FER DÍAD \'far-ˌdē-əd\ (Old Irish: "Man of Smoke"), friend and foster brother of the legendary Irish warrior CÚ CHULAINN. He appears in the longest of the ULSTER CYCLE of hero tales, *The Cattle Raid at Cooley (Táin Bó Cuailnge)*, which deals with the conflict between Ulster and Connaught over possession of the famous brown bull of Cooley. Enlisted in the forces of Connaught, Fer Díad proceeds with the warrior-queen MEDB to seize the brown bull of Cooley from the Ulstermen; there he tragically engages in a three-day battle with Cú Chulainn and is defeated in the last moment.

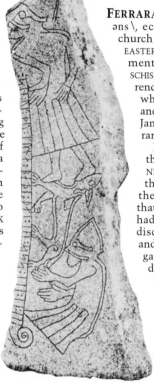

Fenrir attacking a warrior, possibly Odin, while another restrains him; engraved stone at Ledberg, Sweden
By courtesy of the Nordisk Presse Foto, Copenhagen

FERGUS \'fər-gəs\, mighty hero of Irish legend, and former king of Ulster. At the time of the battle between Connaught and Ulster in *The Cattle Raid at Cooley (Táin Bó Cuailnge)* MEDB (Maeve), while married to king Ailill, had an affair with Fergus, distinguished for his prodigious virility. In the tale Fergus, an exile from Ulster at the Connaught court, recalls for Medb and Ailill the heroic deeds of Cú Chulainn's youth.

FERIAE LATINAE \'fer-ē-ˌē-la-'tī-ˌnē\, in ROMAN RELIGION, the Festival of JUPITER Latiaris (Latialis), held in the spring each year on Mons Albanus (Monte Cavo), in the Alban Hills near Rome. Apparently antedating the foundation of Rome, it eventually was observed by all 47 members of the Latin League.

The ceremony was the initial responsibility of each newly chosen pair of Roman consuls, who offered milk as a LIBATION; the other cities sent cheese and sheep. A white heifer that had never been yoked was then sacrificed. Its flesh was consumed by the delegates of all the league communities on behalf of their constituents.

FERRARA-FLORENCE, COUNCIL OF \fə-'rär-ə-'flōr-əns\, ecumenical council of the ROMAN CATHOLIC church (1438–45) in which the Roman Catholic and EASTERN ORTHODOX churches tried to reach agreement on their doctrinal differences and end the SCHISM between them. The Council of Ferrara-Florence was a continuation of the Council of Basel, which Pope Eugenius IV transferred from Basel and which opened in Ferrara on Jan. 8, 1438. On Jan. 10, 1439, the council was moved from Ferrara to Florence when a plague hit Ferrara.

Discussions were held on PURGATORY and on the phrase FILIOQUE ("and from the Son") of the NICENE CREED, which sets forth the doctrine that the HOLY SPIRIT proceeds from both the Father and the Son. The Eastern Orthodox held that the Spirit proceeds from the Father only and had refused to accept the *Filioque*. After much discussion, they agreed to accept the *Filioque* and also the Roman Catholic statements on purgatory, the EUCHARIST, and papal primacy. The decree of union between the two groups (*Laetentur Caeli*) was signed on July 6, 1439. After their return to Constantinople, many of the Eastern Orthodox members repudiated the reunion.

Doctrinally, the council is of interest because of the exposition of the Catholic doctrines of purgatory and of the primacy and plenary powers of the pope set out in *Laetentur Caeli*.

FETIAL \'fē-shəl\, any of a body of 20 Roman priestly officials who were concerned with various aspects of international relations, such as treaties and declarations of war. Fetials were originally selected from the most noble families and served for life, but, like in all PRIESTHOODS, they could only submit advice, not make binding decisions.

According to the Roman historian Livy, after Rome had been injured by another state, four fetials were sent out to seek redress. One member, the *verbenarius*, carried herbs gathered from the Arx on the Capitoline Hill. Another member, called the *pater patratus*, served as the group's representative. Upon reaching the border of the offending state, the *pater patratus* first announced his mission and addressed a prayer to JUPITER in which he affirmed the justness of his errand. Crossing the border, he repeated the same form several times. If, after 30 days (some sources give 33), no satisfaction was given, the *pater patratus* harshly denounced the offending state and returned to Rome, where he reported to the Senate. If Rome decided to wage war, the *pater patratus* returned to the border, pronounced a declaration of war, and hurled across the boundary either a regular spear or a special stake sharpened and hardened in the fire. This ritual was supposed to keep Rome from waging an unjust or aggressive war. If, however, the hostile country was far away, the spear soon came to be cast upon a piece of land in front of the Temple of BELLONA in Rome; that land was treated as belonging to the enemy. Thus the ritual limitations were overcome, and the state entered into any wars that were seen to be to its advantage.

When treaties were concluded, the *verbenarius* and the *pater patratus* were sent to the other nation; after reading the treaty aloud, they pronounced a curse on Rome should that state be the first to break it. The ceremony was concluded by killing a pig with a flint implement. By the time of the late republic, the institution had faded out, although the emperor Augustus (63 BCE–14 CE) revived the group, ceremonially at least, and became a member himself in his effort to restore old Roman traditions.

FETISH, an object (such as a small carving of an animal) believed to have magical power to protect or aid its owner.

FEUERBACH, LUDWIG (ANDREAS) \'fȯi-ər-ˌbäk\ (b. July 28, 1804, Landshut, Bavaria [now in Germany]—d. Sept. 13, 1872, Rechenberg, Ger.), German philosopher and moralist remembered for his influence on Karl Marx and for his humanistic theology.

The fourth son of the eminent jurist Paul von Feuerbach, Ludwig abandoned theological studies to become a student of philosophy under G.W.F. Hegel for two years at Berlin. In 1828 he went to Erlangen to study natural science, and two years later his first book, *Gedanken über Tod und Unsterblichkeit* ("Thoughts on Death and Immortality"), was published anonymously. In this work Feuerbach attacked the concept of personal immortality and proposed a type of immortality by which human qualities are reabsorbed into nature. In his most important work, *Das Wesen des Christentums* (1841; *The Essence of Christianity*), Feuerbach posited the notion that man is to himself his own object of thought and that religion is nothing more than a consciousness of the infinite; thus God is merely the outward projection of man's inward nature. In the first part of his book, which strongly influenced Marx, Feuerbach analyzed the "true or anthropological essence of religion." He argued that the traditional aspects of God correspond to different needs in human nature. In the second section he contended that the view that God has an existence independent of human existence leads to a belief in REVELATION and SACRAMENTS, which are items of an undesirable religious materialism. Nonetheless, Feuerbach denied that he was an atheist.

Attacking religious orthodoxy during the politically turbulent years of 1848–49, Feuerbach was seen as a hero by many of the revolutionaries. His influence was greatest on such anti-Christian publicists as DAVID FRIEDRICH STRAUSS and Bruno Bauer. Some of Feuerbach's views were later endorsed by extremists in the struggle between CHURCH AND STATE in Germany and by those who, like Marx, led the revolt of labor against capitalism. Among his other works are *Theogonie* (1857) and *Gottheit, Freiheit, und Unsterblichkeit* (1866; "God, Freedom, and Immortality").

FIDEISM \'fē-ˌdā-ˌi-zəm\, a theological position extolling the primacy of faith by making it the ultimate criterion of truth and minimizing the power of reason to know religious truths. Strict fideists assign no place to reason in discovering or understanding fundamental tenets of religion. For them blind faith is supreme as the way to certitude and salvation. They defend such faith on various grounds—*e.g.*, mystical experience, revelation, subjective human need, and common sense. Some go so far as to assert that the true object of faith is the absurd, the nonrational, the impossible, or that which directly conflicts with reason. Such a position was approached in the philosophies of the 2nd-century North African theologian TERTULLIAN, the medieval English scholar WILLIAM OF OCKHAM, the 17th-century French philosopher Pierre Bayle, and more recently in the works of the 18th-century German philosopher Johann Georg Hamann and the 19th-century Danish philosopher SØREN KIERKEGAARD. This modern attitude is often motivated by our apparent inability to find rational solutions for the world's ills.

Moderate fideists generally assert that reason can or must play a role in the search for religious truths: some truths (*e.g.*, God's existence, moral principles) can be known by reason subsequently reinformed and clarified by faith. This position affirms that reason can, in some cases, partially comprehend religious truths after they have been revealed, or shows negatively that no contradiction is necessarily involved in them or that there is a rational basis for accepting truths of faith that the human mind cannot comprehend. Thus, the 17th-century French writer Blaise Pascal held that natural faculties are inadequate for religious certainty but suffice to justify religious faith in matters otherwise unknowable.

FIDES \'fī-dēz\, Roman goddess, the deification of good faith and honesty. Many of the oldest Roman deities were embodiments of high ideals (*e.g.*, HONOS, Libertas); it was the function of Fides to oversee the moral integrity of the Romans. Closely associated with JUPITER, Fides was honored with a temple built near his on the Capitoline Hill in 254 BCE. In symbolic recognition of the secret, inviolable trust between gods and mortals, attendants presented sacrificial offerings to her with covered hands.

In the later Roman period, she was called Fides Publica ("Public Faith") and was considered the guardian of treaties and other state documents, which were placed for safekeeping in her temple. There, too, the Senate often convened, signifying her importance to the state.

FILIAL PIETY, *Chinese* hsiao, *Pinyin* xiao, important concept in CONFUCIANISM, the virtue of devotion to one's parents, codified in the *Hsiao-ching* or *Classic of Filial Piety.* *See* HSIAO.

FILIOQUE \ˌfi-lē-'ō-kwā, ˌfī-, -kwē\ (Latin: "And from the Son"), clause affirming that the HOLY SPIRIT proceeds "from the Son" as well as from the Father. It was inserted into the NICENE CREED in Spain during the 6th century and gradually spread to all Western churches but was probably not used in Rome itself until 1014. The addition of the *Filioque* was one of the causes of the SCHISM between the Eastern and Latin churches that began in 1054. Eastern Christians continue to reject this addition, though now they do not generally regard it as heretical, especially if it is understood in the sense of "through the Son."

FINNEY, CHARLES GRANDISON \'fi-nē\ (b. Aug. 29, 1792, Warren, Conn., U.S.—d. Aug. 16, 1875, Oberlin, Ohio), American lawyer, president of Oberlin College, and a central figure in the wave of religious REVIVALISM of the early 19th century; he is sometimes called the first of the professional evangelists.

After teaching school briefly, Finney studied and then began practicing law. References in his studies to Mosaic institutions drew him to BIBLE study, and in 1821 he underwent a religious conversion. Finney dropped his law practice to become an evangelist and was licensed by the PRESBYTERIANS. Addressing congregations in the manner he had used earlier in pleading with juries, he fomented spirited revivals in the villages of upstate New York. His methods aroused criticism from theologians educated in the sterner traditions of eastern schools.

His revivals achieved spectacular success in large cities, and in 1832 he began an almost continuous revival in New York City as minister of the Second Free Presbyterian Church. His disaffection from Presbyterian theology and discipline, however, led his supporters to build for him the Broadway Tabernacle in 1834. The following year he became a professor of theology in a newly formed theological school in Oberlin, Ohio, dividing his time between that post and the Tabernacle. He left New York in 1837 to become minister of Oberlin's First Congregational Church, closely related to Oberlin College, where he was president from 1851 to 1866.

Finney, 1850
By courtesy of Oberlin College, Ohio

FINN MACCUMHAILL \'fin-mə-'kül\, *also spelled* Mac-Cool, in Irish Gaelic literature, a heroic character from tales and ballads known as the Fenian cycle, Fionn cycle, or Ossianic cycle. In these tales both Finn and his war band, the Fianna Éireann, figure prominently. An elite volunteer corps of warriors and huntsmen, skilled in poetry, the Fianna supposedly flourished under the reign of Cormac mac Airt in the 3rd century CE. The long-established Fenian lore attained greatest popularity about 1200, when the cycle's outstanding story, *The Colloquy of the Old Men* (*Acallam na Senórach*), was written down. The Fenian cycle remains a vital part of Irish FOLKLORE and contains many of the best-loved folk tales of the country.

An early tale, *The Boyish Exploits of Finn* (*Macgní-martha Finn*), tells how, after Cumhaill (Cool), chief of the Fianna, is killed, his posthumous son is reared secretly in a forest and earns the name Finn ("The Fair") by his exploits. He grows up to triumph over his father's slayer, Goll Mac-Morna, and to become head of the Fianna, which later includes his son Oisín (OSSIAN), the poet, his grandson Oscar, the handsome Diarmaid (Dermot), and his former clan enemy Goll MacMorna. The disintegration of the Fianna begins when Diarmaid elopes with Gráinne (Grace), a king's daughter whom Finn, as an old man, wishes to marry. Later, when Diarmaid is wounded, Finn lets him die for lack of water. The king and people finally turn against the overbearing Fianna, a conflict that culminates in the Battle of Gabhra, in which the Fianna is destroyed, Oscar is killed in battle, and Oisín survives but is lured away by a fairy princess to Tír na nÓg ("Land of Youths").

FINNO-UGRIC RELIGION \,fi-nō-'yü-grik, -'ü-grik\, pre-Christian RELIGIOUS BELIEFS and practices of the Finno-Ugric peoples, who inhabit regions of northern Scandinavia, Siberia, the Baltic area, and central Europe.

The geographic dispersion of the Finno-Ugric peoples is understood mainly through linguistic criteria, since historical and archaeological evidence is scanty. From their ancient home between the Ural Mountains and the Volga River they spread north about 5000–4000 BCE and south, east, and west perhaps a millennium later. Prominent among the many surviving groups are the Sami (Lapps) of the Arctic region, the Finns and the Estonians of the Baltic area, the Hungarians (or Magyars) of central Europe, and the Permic and Volga Finns of central and southern Russia.

Mythology. According to the most widespread Finno-Ugric account of the creation—the so-called earth-diver myth, found also in North America and Siberia—God commands a being (frequently the devil) to dive into the primeval sea and gather sand, from which God fashions the earth. A version of the myth of the creation of the world from an egg also is known in Estonia and Finland, where it is found in the KALEVALA.

Finno-Ugric descriptions of the cosmos entail a number of themes, the central components of which are the sky, the earth, and the Underworld: a stream or sea is said to encircle the round world; the canopy of the heavens pivots on the North Star; a world pole supports the sky; animals carry the earth; and an abyss in the sea swallows ships. The tradition of the god of the sky finds many expressions among the Finno-Ugric peoples, reflecting an ancient form altered by cultural contacts and environment. In the southeast, for example, Turkic influence is evident in the myths of a heavenly court, with servants acting as intermediaries between earthlings and the god of the sky. Also in the south, the sky god portrayed as "begetter" with the "earth mother" reflects an agricultural society, while in the Arctic the corresponding deities promote fishing, hunting, and herding. The HIGH GODS are typically distant and invisible, encountered in connection with specific rites.

Beliefs and practices. On a more intimate level, the patterns of daily life are closely tied to a system of GUARDIAN SPIRITS and spirits of the dead. The former are supranormal beings that appear in visions, auditory experiences, and other such occurrences, especially when a social norm involving a guardian-spirit sanction is broken. They are believed to "govern" and "own" a particular area, such as a cultural locality (*e.g.*, a household), a natural region (a forest or lake), or a natural element or phenomenon (fire or wind). In addition to propitiating these guardians of the world at large, each family privately venerates the spirits of its own ancestors, which are thought to protect family welfare. This cultic practice encompasses rites conducted at the moment of death, funeral preparations and committal of the body, celebrations in memory of an individual, annual collective memorials, offerings and prayers to the dead for subsistence, and occasional rites (*e.g.*, upon relocation or illness). In some groups, the memory of outstanding leaders and warriors is venerated in cultic fashion. The realm of the dead consists of the actual graveyard, envisioned as an underground village, and a distant land of the dead, far in the north, behind a burning stream.

Religious authorities included SHAMANS or seers, sacrificing priests, guardians of the SANCTUARY, professional weeping women, and the performers of wedding ceremonies. Cult centers ranged from the home sanctuary, perhaps a log structure, to a more communal fenced-off area in the forest, to sacrificial stones along the herding route. Mobile temples—images carried on special sleighs—were also used by the more mobile Finno-Ugric peoples.

FIQH \'fik\ (Arabic: "understanding"), Muslim jurisprudence, *i.e.*, the science of ascertaining the precise terms of the SHARĪʿA, or Islamic law. The collective sources of Muslim jurisprudence are known as USŪL AL-FIQH.

In classical Islamic theory, the four major sources from which law is derived are the QURʾAN, the SUNNA, IJMĀʿ (consensus of scholars), and QIYĀS (analogical deductions from these three). The *usūl*, systematized under AL-SHĀFIʿĪ (767–820), were the result of an Islamization of law that began about the 2nd century of the Muslim era (8th century CE).

Law existed apart from religion under the first four CALIPHS and the Umayyad dynasty and was generally administered through existing pre-Islamic institutions of Roman, Byzantine, Jewish, and Persian character. Pious Muslim scholars, who were later grouped into the legal schools of Iraq, Hejaz, and Syria, began to reinterpret the law in an Islamic light. Al-Shāfiʿī completed this Islamization process by establishing a norm for interpretation, the *usūl*, but the functions of the individual principles were fixed in legal theory by later scholars. During the 11th century *fiqh* became institutionalized in the curriculum of MADRASAS (Islamic colleges), and those specializing in jurisprudence were known as *fuqahāʾ* (plural of *faqīh*). The SUNNI and SHIʿITE branches of ISLAM each developed their own traditions of *fiqh*, and lively debates over points of law and their implementation in secular society are occurring at present. Since 1979 the Islamic Republic of Iran has recognized the Shiʿite *faqīh* constitutionally as the foremost religious and political authority in the country, a revolutionary doctrine developed by Ayatollah Khomeini in the 1960s and 1970s.

FIRE WALKING, religious ceremony practiced in many parts of the modern world, classical Greece, and ancient India and China. Fire walking most commonly is the practice of walking swiftly over a layer of embers spread thinly along the bottom of a shallow trench. Sometimes the devotees or priests or oracles have to walk through a blazing log fire. Instead of embers from a wood fire, there may be red-hot stones (Fiji and Mauritius), or embers may be poured over the devotee's head in a "fire bath," or the devotee may lash himself with a flaming torch.

Fire walking is said sometimes to ensure a good harvest, other times to purify the participants; a man accused of a crime or of falsehood may undergo the ordeal of fire to prove his innocence. Fire walkers believe that only those who lack faith will suffer from injuries. Devotees also undertake fire walking in fulfillment of vows.

Injuries from burns do occur, but they seem on the whole to be much less frequent than would be expected, especial-

ly as devotees do not apply any artificial preparation before the ordeal to protect their bodies.

FIRST-FRUITS CEREMONY, ceremony centered on the concept that the first fruits of a harvest belong to or are sanctified unto God (or gods).

Although the title signals that first-fruit offerings often are of agricultural produce, other types of offerings are also included under this heading. For instance, in the religions of some native northwest American tribes, there exists the belief that salmon were supernatural beings who voluntarily assumed piscine form to sacrifice themselves annually for the benefit of mankind. On being taken, the spirits of the fish returned to their home beneath the sea, where they were reincarnated if their bones were returned to the water. If offended, however, the salmon-beings would refuse to return to the river. Hence, there were numerous specific prohibitions on acts believed to offend them and observances designed to propitiate them.

The most characteristic motivation behind a first-fruits offering is the belief that, since all good things come from the divine, then a portion of those good things should be offered back to the divinity. Innumerable examples of such rites exist in the historical record. The ancient Greek THARGELIA festival, one of the primary rites dedicated to APOLLO at Athens, was a vegetation ritual named after the first bread baked from the newly harvested wheat. Similarly, in modern Sri Lanka at harvest time the Buddha is ceremonially offered a large bowl of milk and rice, while in SHINTŌ the first rice sheaves of the harvest are presented as offerings (*shinsen*) to the KAMI (god or sacred power) during agricultural and other festivals.

In JUDAISM, the first-fruits ceremony is known as SHAVUOT. The belief is that fruit trees live their own life and are to remain untrimmed for three years after they are planted. But even then their fruits cannot be enjoyed until God is given his share. Within classical Judaism, the idea of the first-fruits offering formed the center of sacrifice as a whole. The rationale for sacrifice is that everything belongs to God; the central point in the sacrifice was the sanctification of the offering, and the surrender of it to God. Its most immediate purpose was to serve as a form of taxation to the priests, since only they were considered holy enough to take possession of the offering following the rite. (*See also* PIDYON HA-BEN.)

The belief that all good things come from God, including the fertility of the fields, is widespread, and consequently first-fruit offerings are also a ubiquitous feature of the world's religions. Particularly if such offerings are taken as a characteristic form of sacrifice, the first-fruits ceremony may be seen as a category of fundamental importance to the study of religious ritual. (*See also* KWANZAA.)

FIVE CLASSICS, *Chinese* Wu-ching \'wü-'jiŋ\, *Pinyin* Wujing, five ancient Chinese books, all associated in some way with CONFUCIUS (551–479 BCE), that for 2,000 years have been invoked as authorities on Chinese society, law, government, education, literature, and religion. As such, their influence is without parallel in the long history of China. Chinese students, however, do not generally attempt the Five Classics without having first studied the shorter Confucian texts called *Ssu-shu* (Pinyin: Sishu; "FOUR BOOKS"). The Five Classics consist of the I-CHING ("Classic of Changes"), SHU-CHING ("Classic of History"), *Shih-ching* ("Classic of Poetry"), LI-CHI ("Collection of Rituals"), and CH'UN-CH'IU ("Spring and Autumn [Annals]").

In 136 BCE the Han ruler Wu-ti declared CONFUCIANISM to be the state ideology of China. Positions were thereupon established for the teaching of the Five Classics, and these continued to exist into the 20th century. In 124 BCE the Five Classics were accepted by the national university as its core curriculum. Proficiency in interpreting and expounding the texts became a requirement for all scholars in obtaining posts in the government bureaucracy.

FIVE PECKS OF RICE: *see* T'IEN-SHI TAO; TAOISM.

FIVE PILLARS OF ISLAM, *Arabic* Arkān al-Islam, the five duties incumbent on every Muslim according to the SHARĪʿA: SHAHĀDA, the Muslim profession of faith; ṢALĀT, or ritual prayer, performed in a prescribed manner five times each day; ZAKĀT, the alms tax levied to benefit the poor and the needy; ṢAWM, fasting during the month of Ramaḍān; and HAJJ, the major PILGRIMAGE TO MECCA. Though individually mentioned in the QURʾAN, the identification of five pillars (or foundations) actually occurs in the Hadith. According to one account, when MUHAMMAD was asked by JIBRĪL to define ISLAM, he answered by equating it with these five duties. Based on the SUNNA of the prophet, they were fully treated in FIQH manuals by the legal schools (*madhhabs*), which placed them in the category of worship (*ʿibādāt*).

Although SHIʿITE performance of these rituals does not differ greatly from that of the SUNNI, they do not always conceive of the rituals in the same way. Twelvers, for example, class *shahāda* under the theological category of *tawhīd* (doctrine relating to the "oneness" of God), not among *ʿibādāt*. Religious war (JIHAD), although not one of the Five Pillars of Islam, is seen as obligatory by Shiʿites, although these wars should only be defensive in nature until the Hidden IMAM returns. Other actions they consider "pillars" of worship are payment of the imam's tax (KHUMS), enjoining good actions, and prohibiting evil. All sects believe that by fulfilling their ritual obligations they will achieve rewards on earth and in the hereafter. *See also* ṬAHĀRA.

FLAGELLATION, the disciplinary or ritual practice of beating with whips. Ceremonial whippings or beatings are primarily concerned with rites of initiation, purification, and fertility, which often included other forms of physical suffering. Floggings and mutilations might or might not be self-inflicted. Beatings administered by masked impersonators of gods or ancestors are a feature of many North American Indian initiations. Ritual floggings were also known among the Spartans and in Rome.

In the early Christian church, flagellation apparently was used as punishment for disobedient clergy. From the 4th century, self-inflicted flagellation was practiced by both clergy and laity as a means of penance. In the early Middle Ages the laity became especially attracted by this devotional exercise. In the mid-13th century flagellant brotherhoods and PROCESSIONS composed of laymen and women, as well as clergy, began to be organized in Italy, and the practice spread into Germany and the Low Countries.

In the plague epidemic of the mid-14th century, flagellants sought to mitigate the divine judgment that was felt to be at hand. They formed groups and traveled about the country on foot. In two daily public ceremonies men whipped their backs and chests with leather thongs, while women chastised themselves in seclusion. In 1349 Pope Clement VI condemned flagellation, as did the COUNCIL OF CONSTANCE (1414–18). In Germany the flagellants became an organized sect and were a target of the INQUISITION. The

practice gradually subsided, but in the 16th century the JESUITS temporarily revived lay interest in self-inflicted flagellation, especially in the southern European countries.

Flagellation is also practiced by some SHIʿITE Muslims, who whip themselves on the holiday of ʿĀSHŪRĀʾ to commemorate the martyrdom of ḤUSAYN at the Battle of KARBALĀʾ (680 CE).

FLAMEN \ˈflā-mən\, *plural* flamines \ˈfla-mə-ˌnēz\, in ancient Rome, a priest devoted exclusively to the worship of one deity; the name perhaps meant originally "one who performs sacrifices," though the etymology of the word has been much disputed. Of the 15 *flamines*, the most important were Dialis, Martialis, and Quirinalis, who served JUPITER, MARS, and QUIRINUS, respectively. Chosen from the patrician class and supervised by the PONTIFEX *maximus*, or chief priest, the *flamines* had a distinctive dress, especially the *apex*, a conical cap. They offered daily sacrifices, and their lives were regulated by strict rules and prohibitions. The priests' wives, the *flaminicae*, served as their assistants and were also bound by ritual regulations. In imperial times, *flamines Divorum* ("priests of the Gods") were instituted for the worship of deified emperors both in Rome and in the empire's outlying provinces, where they often served as important representatives of the central government.

FLORA, in ROMAN RELIGION, the goddess of the flowering of plants. Titus Tatius (according to tradition, the Sabine king who ruled with Romulus) is said to have introduced her cult to Rome; her temple stood near the Circus Maximus. Her festival, called the Floralia, was instituted in 238 BCE. A representation of Flora's head, distinguished only by a floral crown, appeared on coins of the republic.

FOLKLORE, the sum total of traditionally derived and orally or imitatively transmitted literature, material culture, and custom of subcultures within predominantly literate and technologically advanced societies. In popular usage, the term folklore is sometimes restricted to the oral literature tradition.

Folklore studies began in the early 19th century. The first folklorists concentrated exclusively upon rural peasants, preferably uneducated, and a few other groups relatively untouched by modern ways (*e.g.*, Gypsies). Their aim was to trace preserved archaic customs and beliefs to their remote origins in order to trace the mental history of mankind. In Germany, Jacob Grimm used folklore to illuminate GERMANIC RELIGION of the Middle Ages. In Britain, Sir Edward Tylor, Andrew Lang, and others combined data from anthropology and folklore to "reconstruct" the beliefs and rituals of prehistoric man. The best-known work of this type is SIR JAMES FRAZER'S *The Golden Bough* (1890).

Large collections of material were amassed in the course of these efforts. Inspired by the Grimm Brothers, whose first collection of fairy tales appeared in 1812, scholars all over Europe began recording and publishing oral literature of many genres: fairy tales and other types of folktales, ballads and other songs, oral epics, folk plays, riddles, and proverbs. Similar work was undertaken for music, dance, and traditional arts and crafts; many archives and museums were founded. Often the underlying impulse was nationalistic; since the folklore of a group reinforced its sense of ethnic identity, it figured prominently in many struggles for political independence and national unity.

As the scholarship of folklore developed, an important advance was the classification of material for comparative

> Out set Riding Hood, so obliging and sweet,
> And she met a great Wolf in the wood,
> Who began most politely the maiden to greet,
> as tender a voice as he could.

> He asked to what house she was going, and why;
> Red Riding Hood answered him all:
> He said, "Give my love to your Gran; I will try
> "At my earliest leisure to call."

An illustration by Walter Crane of the folktale "Little Red Riding Hood"
Art Resource

analysis. Standards of identification were devised, notably for ballads (by F.J. Child) and for the plots and component motifs of folktales and myths (by Antti Aarne and Stith Thompson). Using these, Finnish scholars, led by Kaarle Krohn, developed the "historical-geographical" method of research, in which every known variant of a particular tale, ballad, riddle, or other item was classified as to place and date of collection in order to study distribution patterns and reconstruct "original" forms.

After World War II interest was no longer confined to rural communities, since it was recognized that cities too contained definable groups whose characteristic arts, customs, and values marked their identity; any group that expressed its inner cohesion by maintaining shared traditions qualified as a "folk," whether the linking factor be occupation, language, place of residence, age, religion, or ethnic origin. Emphasis also shifted from the past to the present, from the search for origins to the investigation of present meaning and function. In the view of "contextual" and "performance" analysis in the late 20th century, a particular story, song, drama, or custom is regarded as an event arising from the interaction between an individual and his or her social group, which fulfills some function and satisfies some need for both performer and audience.

FOMOIRE \ˈfō-vō-rʸə\, *also spelled* Fomhoire, in Irish myth, a race of demonic beings who posed a threat to the inhabitants of Ireland until they were defeated by the god-race, the TUATHA DÉ DANANN. The name Fomoire may mean "demons from below (the sea)," and their leader BALOR had one huge deadly eye. The most important of the gods, Lugh (*see* LUGUS), is the offspring of the marriage of a god, Cian, and the daughter of the monstrous Balor, and it is stated that originally the gods and the Fomoire were allies.

FOOLS, FEAST OF, popular festival during the Middle Ages, held on or about January 1, particularly in France, in which a mock bishop or pope was elected, ecclesiastical ritual was parodied, and low and high officials changed places. Such festivals were probably a Christian adaptation of the pre-Christian festivities of the Saturnalia (*see* SATURN). By the 13th century these feasts had become a burlesque of Christian morality and worship. In spite of repeated prohibitions and penalties imposed by the Council of Basel in 1431, the feasts did not die out until the 16th century.

FORMSTECHER, SOLOMON \ˈfȯrm-ˌste-kər\ (b. July 28, 1808, Offenbach, Hesse [Germany]—d. April 24, 1889, Offenbach), Jewish idealist philosopher who was RABBI at Offenbach from 1842. *Die Religion des Geistes* (1841; "The Religion of the Spirit") is a thorough systematization of JUDAISM. He argued there were only two basic religions: the religion of nature (paganism) and the religion of spirit (Judaism), the essence of which was ethical. Its ethics, adulterated by myth and art, were also disseminated by CHRISTIANITY and ISLAM but existed in purest form in Judaism.

FORTUNA \fȯr-ˈtü-nə, -ˈtyü-\, in ROMAN RELIGION, goddess of chance or lot who became identified with the Greek Tyche; the original Italian deity was probably regarded as the bearer of prosperity and increase. She was associated with the bounty of the soil and the fruitfulness of women. Frequently she was consulted in various ways regarding the future. Fortuna was worshiped extensively in Italy from the earliest times. At Praeneste her shrine was a well-known oracular seat, as was her shrine at Antium (*see* ORACLE). Fortuna is often represented bearing a CORNUCOPIA as the giver of abundance and a rudder as controller of destinies, or standing on a ball to indicate the uncertainty of fortune.

FOUR BOOKS, Chinese *Ssu-shu,* *Pinyin* Sishu, Confucian texts that were used as official subject matter for civil service examinations in China from 1313 to 1905. They serve to introduce students to Confucian literature. Students later turn to the more extensive *Wu-ching* (FIVE CLASSICS).

The publication of these four texts as a unit in 1190 with commentaries by CHU HSI, a great Neo-Confucian philosopher, helped to revitalize CONFUCIANISM in China. From 1415 onward knowledge of Chu's (and like-minded) commentaries was as indispensable to success in civil service examinations as knowledge of the texts themselves.

Even with its commentaries, the *Ssu-shu* is a modest volume, the four parts of which have no consistent order. The first, TA-HSÜEH, or Great Learning, is a short ethico-political treatise linking humane government with the personal integrity of rulers. The second, CHUNG-YUNG, or Doctrine of the Mean, is somewhat longer and more abstract than the other three books. It speaks of such things as the Way of Heaven, motion, spiritual beings, and religious sacrifices. For each of these two books (both direct excerpts from LI-CHI, one of the Five Classics), Chu Hsi wrote an individual preface. The third book, LUN-YÜ, or Analects, reputedly contains direct quotations from CONFUCIUS as recorded by his disciples, especially TSENG-TZU. It is considered the most reliable source of the Master's teachings. MENCIUS, the fourth and longest of the *Ssu-shu*, contains the teachings of Mencius, the most revered of all Confucian scholars.

FOUR NOBLE TRUTHS, *Pāli* Cattāri-Ariya-Saccāni, *Sanskrit* Catvāri-Ārya-Satyāni,

a brief formulation of Buddhist religious doctrine, expounded by BUDDHA GOTAMA in his first sermon at the deer park near Banares (VARANASI), India.

The four truths are (1) that existence is suffering (DUKKHA); (2) that this suffering has a cause (*samudaya*); (3) that it can be suppressed (*nirodha*); and (4) that there is a way (*magga*) to accomplish this, the noble EIGHTFOLD PATH. Though differently interpreted, these four truths are recognized by virtually all Buddhist schools.

FOUR-SEVEN DEBATE,

debate between the Korean Confucian Yi T'oegye (1501–70) and his disciple Ki Taesung (1527–72) via an exchange of letters. The debate concerned the relationship between MENCIUS' four basic human feelings (commiseration, shame, modesty, and right and wrong) and seven derived emotions (anger, joy, sorrow, pleasure, love, hatred, and desire) and raised the level of dialogue in CONFUCIANISM to a new height of intellectual and moral sophistication.

FOX, GEORGE \'fäks\ (b. July 1624, Drayton-in-the-Clay, Leicestershire, Eng.—d. Jan. 13, 1691, London),

English preacher and founder of the SOCIETY OF FRIENDS (or Quakers).

Fox was the son of a weaver in an English village. Probably apprenticed for a while to a cobbler, he may also have tended sheep, but there is little evidence of any adult business occupation or of much formal education. At the age of 18 he left home in search of religious counsel or experience and later reported in his *Journal* various personal RELIGIOUS EXPERIENCES or direct revelations, which he called "openings," that corrected, he believed, the traditional concepts of faith and practice in English religious life.

His religious background was apparently Puritan rather than strict Anglican, but he himself reacted even further than the Puritans from the formalism and traditionalism of the ESTABLISHED CHURCH. He placed the God-given inward light (inspiration) above creeds and SCRIPTURE and regarded personal experience as the true source of authority. His negative attitude to ecclesiastical customs was matched by a similar attitude toward some political and economic conventions (*e.g.*, OATHS, titles, and military service).

He began preaching to individuals or groups as he traveled on foot. In the northern counties of England, groups of Seekers (a 17th-century Puritan sect) welcomed him and his message. Local congregations were established, gathered both by Fox and by other itinerant preachers, who were called Publishers of Truth. Thus in the last years of the British Commonwealth (1649–60) the Society of Friends came into being (though it was called that only much later; its members were nicknamed Quakers).

Fox and his associates suffered public hostility and official constraint. Their contradiction of the ministers in the churches and their refusal to honor officials, to take oaths, or to pay TITHES caused Fox and his associates to be arrested and imprisoned with some frequency. Fox, in fact, suffered eight imprisonments between 1649 and 1673.

The restoration of the monarchy in 1660 led to special legislation against the Quakers and a widespread action against them. To meet this and other needs, George Fox encouraged local Quaker groups to organize into regular monthly and quarterly business meetings, which, with some central national meetings, became a permanent pattern of their church government. The continuing pressure was only intermittently eased until the Toleration Act of 1689, shortly before Fox's death, gave relief to the Quakers.

In 1669 Fox made a missionary visit to Ireland, and on his return he married one of his early converts, Margaret Fell. In the years 1671 to 1673 he traveled to the British colonies in the Caribbean and the North American mainland, strengthening and organizing the existing Quaker communities, especially in Maryland and Rhode Island. Shorter journeys in 1677 and 1684 took him to the Netherlands and a few other parts of northern Europe. About 1675 he dictated a running summary of his life that, with supplementary material, was posthumously edited and published as his *Journal*, the fullest account of the rise of Quakerism, as well as of Fox himself.

FRANCISCAN \fran-'sis-kən\,

member of a Christian religious order founded in the early 13th century by ST. FRANCIS OF ASSISI. The Franciscans actually consist of three orders. The First Order comprises priests and lay brothers who have sworn to lead a life of prayer, preaching, and penance. This First Order is divided into three independent branches: the Friars Minor (O.F.M.), the Friars Minor Conventual (O.F.M. Conv.), and the Friars Minor Capuchin (O.F.M. Cap.). The Second Order consists of cloistered nuns who belong to the Order of St. Clare (O.S.C.) and are known as POOR CLARES (P.C.). The Third Order consists of religious and laymen and laywomen who try to emulate Saint Francis' spirit in teaching, CHARITY, and social service. Strictly speaking, the latter order consists of the Third Order Secular, whose lay members live in the world without vows; and the Third Order Regular, whose members live in religious communities under vow. The Franciscans are the largest religious order in the ROMAN CATHOLIC church.

It was probably in 1207 that Francis felt the call to a life of preaching, penance, and total poverty. He was soon joined by his first followers, to whom he gave a short and simple rule of life. In 1209 he and 11 of his followers journeyed to Rome, where Francis received approval of his rule from POPE INNOCENT III. Under this rule, Franciscan friars could own no possessions of any kind, either individually or communally (*i.e.*, as the property of the order as a whole). The friars wandered and preached among the people, helping the poor and the sick. They supported themselves by working and by begging food, but they were forbidden to accept money either as payment for work or as alms. The impact of these street preachers and especially of their founder was immense, so that within 10 years they numbered 5,000. Affiliated with them were the Franciscan nuns, whose order was founded at Assisi in 1212 by St. Clare, who was under the guidance of St. Francis.

During the first years of the Franciscans, the example of Francis provided their real rule of life, but, as the order grew, it became clear that a revised rule was necessary. After preparing a rule in 1221 that was found too strict, Francis, with the help of several legal scholars, unwillingly composed the more restrained final rule in 1223. This rule was approved by Pope Honorius III.

Even before the death of Francis in 1226, conflicts had developed within the order over the observance of the vow of complete poverty. The rapid expansion of the order's membership had created a need for settled monastic houses, but it was impossible to justify these if Francis' rule of complete poverty was followed strictly. Three parties gradually appeared: the Zealots, who insisted on a literal observance of the primitive rule of poverty; the Laxists, who favored many mitigations; and the Moderates, or the Community, who wanted some form of communal possessions. Something of an equilibrium was reached while St. BONAVENTURE was minister general (1257–74). Sometimes called the second founder of the order, he provided a moderate interpretation of the rule. During this period the friars spread throughout Europe, while missionaries penetrated Syria and Africa. Simultaneously, the friars' houses in university towns such as Paris and Oxford were transformed into schools of theology that rapidly became among the most celebrated in Europe.

With the death of Bonaventure, the internal dissensions of the order flared up anew. The Zealots, who now became known as the Spirituals, demanded absolute poverty. Papal decisions favored the Community, or the Conventuals, and the Spirituals ceased to be a faction of importance in the order after 1325.

The latter part of the 14th century saw a great decline in the religious life of the friars. But throughout that century a series of reformers initiated groups of friars, known as Observants, living an austere life apart from the main body of Conventuals. Under the leadership of St. Bernardino of Siena and St. John of Capistrano, the Observants spread across Europe. Though several attempts were made to reconcile them with the Conventuals, the outcome was in fact a complete separation in 1517, when all the reform communities were united in one order with the name Friars Minor of the Observance, and this order was granted a completely independent and autonomous existence.

Death of St. Clare, founder of the Poor Clares order of Franciscan nuns, panel by the Master of Heiligenkreuz
Laurie Platt Winfrey

The union of the Observants was short-lived as several stricter groups arose. One of these reform groups, the Capuchins, founded in 1525, was separated as the third branch of the Franciscan Order in 1619. The other groups were finally reunited to the Observants by POPE LEO XIII in 1897, with new constitutions and the official title Order of Friars Minor. All three branches suffered in the French Revolution, but they revived during the 19th century.

St. Francis de Sales, detail from an oil painting by an unknown artist, 1618
BBC, Hulton Picture Library

FRANCIS DE SALES, SAINT \'fran-səs ... 'sālz, 'säl\, *French* Saint François de Sales (b. Aug. 21, 1567, Thorens-Glières, Savoy—d. Dec. 28, 1622, Lyon; canonized 1665; feast day January 24), ROMAN CATHOLIC bishop of Geneva who was active in the struggle against CALVINISM and cofounded the order of Visitation Nuns.

He was educated at the JESUIT college of Clermont in Paris (1580–88) and at Padua, Italy, where he received a doctorate in law (1591). After briefly practicing law he turned to religion and was ordained in 1593. Francis began intense missionary work in Chablais and rewon the bulk of the people of Chablais to Catholicism. He was consecrated bishop of Geneva on Dec. 8, 1602. In 1610, with St. Jane Frances de Chantal, he founded the Visitation of Holy Mary (the Visitation Nuns), which became principally a teaching order. He wrote the devotional classic *Introduction to a Devout Life* (3rd definitive edition, 1609), which emphasized that spiritual perfection is possible for people busy with the affairs of the world and not only for those who withdraw from society. Francis was the first to receive a solemn BEATIFICATION at St. Peter's, Rome (1661). In 1923 Pope Pius XI named him patron saint of writers.

FRANCIS OF ASSISI, SAINT \'fran-səs ... ə-'si-sē, ä-'sē-zē\, *Italian* San Francesco d'Assisi (b. 1181/82, Assisi, Duchy of Spoleto—d. Oct. 3, 1226, Assisi; canonized July 15, 1228; feast day October 4), founder of the FRANCISCAN orders of men and women and leader of the church reform movements of the early 13th century.

In his youth Francis learned Latin at the school near the church of San Giorgio. In 1202 he took part in a war between Assisi and Perugia, was held prisoner for almost a year, and on his release fell seriously ill. After his recovery, tradition states that he had a vision that bade him return to Assisi and await a call to a new kind of knighthood.

It is related that at the ruined chapel of San Damiano outside the gate of Assisi, he heard the crucifix above the altar command him: "Go, Francis, and repair my house which, as you see, is well-nigh in ruins." Taking this literally, he sold his horse and much of the cloth from his father's shop and tried to give the money to the priest at San Damiano. Angered, his father called him before the bishop. At this hearing Francis renounced material goods and family ties to embrace a life of poverty. He spent his time restoring the now-famous little chapel of St. Mary of the Angels (Santa Maria degli Angeli), the Porziuncola, near Assisi. There, on the feast of St. Matthias, Feb. 24, 1208, he heard the Gospel account of the mission of Christ to the Apostles: "Take no gold, nor silver, nor copper in your belts, no bag for your journey, nor two tunics, nor sandals, nor a staff; for the laborer deserves his food. And whatever town or village you enter, find out who is worthy in it, and stay with him until you depart" (Matthew 10:9–11).

Although he was a layman, Francis began to preach to the townspeople. Disciples were attracted to him, and he composed a simple rule of life for them. In 1209 they went to Rome and received the approval of POPE INNOCENT III for their rule of life. This event, which according to tradition occurred on April 16, marked the official founding of the Franciscan order. The early Franciscan rule of life, which has not survived, set as the aim of the new life, "To follow the teachings of our Lord JESUS CHRIST and to walk in his footsteps." This imitation of the life of Christ is the key to the character and spirit of St. Francis. To neglect it leaves an unbalanced portrait of the saint as a lover of nature, a social worker, an itinerant preacher, and a lover of poverty.

In 1212 Francis began a second order for women that became known as the POOR CLARES. For those who could not leave their families and homes he eventually (c. 1221) formed the Third Order of Brothers and Sisters of Penance, a lay fraternity that, without withdrawing from the world or taking religious vows, would carry out the principles of Franciscan life.

Probably in the late spring of 1212, Francis had set out for the Holy Land but was shipwrecked on the east coast of the Adriatic Sea and had to return. He went to Egypt, where the Crusaders were besieging Damietta, in 1219. News of disturbances among the friars in Italy forced Francis to return. There were now some 5,000 members of the men's order, yet it had little more than Francis' example and his brief rule of life to guide its increasing numbers. To handle the order's practical affairs, Francis appointed Peter Catanii as his vicar; after Peter's early death in 1221 he chose Elias of Cortona. Francis set about amplifying and revising the rule, which was approved by Honorius III in final form on Nov. 29, 1223. At this point Francis tended increasingly to withdraw from external affairs.

St. Francis of Assisi, detail of a fresco by Cimabue, late 13th century; in the lower church of San Francesco, Assisi, Italy
Alinari—Anderson from Art Resource

In the summer of 1224 Francis went to the mountain retreat of La Verna (Alvernia). There he prayed to know how best to please God; opening the Gospels for the answer, three times he came upon references to the Passion of Christ. Soon after, he is said to have had a vision of a SERAPH on a cross. Tradition is that the vision left not only a greater ardor of love in the inner man but marked him outwardly with the STIGMATA of Christ.

At his death Francis was buried temporarily in the church of San Giorgio, at Assisi. In 1230 his body was transferred to the lower church of the BASILICA in Assisi that was being erected in his memory by Elias.

FRANK, JACOB \'fraŋk\, *original name* Jacob Leibowicz (b. 1726, in Berezanka or Korolowka, Galicia, Pol. [now in Ukraine]—d. Dec. 10, 1791, Offenbach, Hessen [Germany]), Jewish false MESSIAH who claimed to be the reincarnation of SHABBETAI TZEVI (1626–76). The most notorious of the false messiahs, he was the founder of the antirabbinical Frankist, or Zoharist, sect.

An uneducated visionary, Frank appealed to many who awaited the resurrection of Shabbetai. About 1751 he proclaimed himself the messiah, and four years later, in Poland, he formed a sect that held that certain elect persons are exempt from the moral law. This sect abandoned JUDAISM for a "higher Torah" based on the SEFER HA-ZOHAR, the most important work in the QABBALAH. Hence its members also called themselves Zoharists. Their practices, including orgiastic rites, led the Jewish community to ban them as heretics in 1756. Protected by ROMAN CATHOLIC authorities, who saw in them a means of converting the Jews, the Frankists debated the rabbinate and claimed that the TALMUD should be discarded as blasphemous.

In the meantime, to preserve his following, Frank publicly committed his supporters to mass BAPTISM and was himself baptized in Warsaw, with Augustus III, king of Poland, acting as his godfather. The Frankists, however, continued their sectarian ways. As a result, the INQUISITION imprisoned Frank in the fortress of Częstochowa (1760). Freed by the conquering Russians in 1773, he eventually settled in Offenbach, dubbing himself baron. His followers supported him in a manner befitting nobility. Upon his death, he was succeeded by his daughter Eve, but the sect deteriorated rapidly, and descendants of those who were baptized merged with the Roman Catholic population.

FRANKEL, ZACHARIAS \'fräŋ-kəl\ (b. Sept. 30, 1801, Prague [now in Czech Republic]—d. Feb. 13, 1875, Breslau, Ger. [now Wrocław, Pol.]), RABBI and theologian, a founder of what became CONSERVATIVE JUDAISM.

After graduation from the University of Budapest in 1831, Frankel served as rabbi in several German communities, becoming chief rabbi of Dresden in 1836. During this period he developed a theology that he called positive-historical JUDAISM. It differed from Orthodoxy in its acceptance of scientific and historical research and in its willingness to make some liturgical changes. It differed from REFORM JUDAISM in that it sought to maintain traditional customs and adhere to the national aspects of Judaism.

In 1854 Frankel was chosen president of the newly organized Jewish theological seminary at Breslau. Through the faculty and students of Breslau seminary, Frankel's viewpoint became highly influential in central Europe. In the 20th century it took root in the United States, where, under the name of Conservative Judaism, it attained its greatest growth. Frankel's first major work, *Die Eidesleistung der Juden* (1840; "Oath-Taking by Jews"), attacked discrimination against Jews who testified in courts in Saxony. Frankel also published the classic *Vorstudien zur Septuaginta* (1841; "Preliminary Studies in the Septuagint"), in which he, the only major 19th-century Jewish scholar who wrote on the SEPTUAGINT, sought to show the necessary connection between Talmudic and Septuagintic EXEGESIS. Two works in Hebrew, *Darke ha-Mishnah* (1859; "Introduction to the Mishnah") and *Mebo ha-Yerushalmi* (1870; "Introduction to the Palestinian Talmud"; *see* YERUSHALMI), were major contributions to Jewish religious thought.

FRAVASHI \fra-va-'shē, frə-'vä-shē\, in ZOROASTRIANISM, the preexisting external higher soul or essence of a person (according to some sources, also of gods and ANGELS). Associated with AHURA MAZDĀ since the first creation, they participate in his nature. By free choice they descend into the world to suffer and combat the forces of evil, knowing their inevitable RESURRECTION at the final glory. Each person's *fravashi*, distinct from the incarnate soul, subtly guides toward the realization of that person's higher nature. The purified soul is united after death with its *fravashi*. Cosmically, the *fravashi*s are divided into three groups—the living, the dead, and the yet unborn. They are the force upon which Ahura Mazdā depends to maintain the cosmos against the DEMON host. Protecting the empyrean (sacred fire), they keep darkness imprisoned in the world.

In the PARSI festival Fravartigan, comprising the last 10 days of the year and culminating in its final night, each family honors the *fravashi*s of its dead with prayers, fire, and incense.

FRAZER, SIR JAMES GEORGE (b. Jan. 1, 1854, Glasgow, Scot.—d. May 7, 1941, Cambridge, Cambridgeshire, Eng.), British anthropologist, folklorist, and classical scholar, best remembered as the author of *The Golden Bough.*

Frazer entered Trinity College, Cambridge (1874), and became a fellow (1879). In 1907 he was appointed professor of social anthropology at Liverpool, but he returned to Cambridge soon after and remained there for the rest of his life.

His outstanding position among anthropologists was established by the publication in 1890 of *The Golden Bough: A Study in Comparative Religion* (enlarged to 12 vol., 1911–15; abridged edition in 1 vol., 1922; supplementary vol. *Aftermath*, 1936). The underlying theme of the work is Frazer's theory of a general development of modes of thought from the magical to the religious and, finally, to the scientific. Although the evolutionary sequence of magical, religious, and scientific thought is no longer accepted and Frazer's broad general psychological theory has proved unsatisfactory, his work enabled him to synthesize and compare a wider range of information about religious and magical practices than has been achieved subsequently by any other single anthropologist. His other works include *Totemism and Exogamy* (1910) and *Folk-Lore in the Old Testament* (1918).

FREEMASONRY \'frē-'mā-sən-rē, -,mā-\, teachings and practices of the secret fraternal order of Free and Accepted Masons, the largest worldwide secret society. Spread by the advance of the British Empire, FREEMASONRY remains most popular in Britain and in other countries originally within the empire.

Freemasonry evolved from the guilds of stonemasons and cathedral builders of the Middle Ages. With the decline of cathedral building, some lodges of operative (working) masons began to accept honorary members to bolster their declining membership. From a few of these lodges developed modern symbolic or speculative Freemasonry, which particularly in the 17th and 18th centuries, adopted the rites and trappings of ancient religious orders and of chivalric brotherhoods. In 1717 the first Grand Lodge, an association of lodges, was founded in England.

Freemasonry contains many of the elements of a religion; its teachings enjoin morality, CHARITY, and obedience to the law of the land. For admission the applicant is required to be an adult male believing in the existence of a Supreme Being and in the immortality of the soul. In practice, some lodges have been charged with prejudice against Jews, CATHOLICS, and nonwhites. Generally, Freemasonry in Latin countries has attracted freethinkers and anticlericals, whereas in the Anglo-Saxon countries, the membership is drawn largely from among white Protestants.

FREE WILL, the power or capacity within people to choose among alternatives or to act in certain situations independently of natural, social, or divine restraints. Free will is denied by those who espouse any of various forms of determinism. Arguments for free will are based on the subjective experience of freedom, on sentiments of guilt, on revealed religion, and on the universal supposition of responsibility for personal actions that underlies the concepts of law, reward, punishment, and incentive. In theology, the existence of free will must be reconciled with God's omniscience and goodness (in allowing humans to choose badly), and with divine GRACE, which is held to be necessary for any meritorious act.

FREUD, SIGMUND \'froid, *German* 'froͤt\ (b. May 6, 1856, Freiberg, Moravia, Austrian Empire [now Příbor, Czech Republic]—d. Sept. 23, 1939, London, Eng.), Austrian neurologist, founder of psychoanalysis.

Freud entered the University of Vienna in 1873 as a medical student and the General Hospital of Vienna in 1882. In 1885 he went to Paris to study with the neurologist Jean-Martin Charcot. Charcot's work with patients classified as hysterics introduced Freud to the possibility that mental disorders might be caused by purely psychological factors rather than by organic brain disease.

Upon his return to Vienna, Freud entered into a fruitful partnership with the physician Josef Breuer. They collaborated on *Studien über Hysterie* (1895; *Studies in Hysteria*), which contains a presentation of Freud's pioneering psychoanalytic method of free association. Via this method he developed theories concerning deeper layers of the mind, the unconscious. In 1899 he published *Die Traumdeutung* (*The Interpretation of Dreams*), in which he analyzed the highly complex symbolic processes underlying dream formation. Freud contended that dreams play a fundamental role in the psychic economy. The mind's energy—which Freud called libido and identified principally, but not exclusively, with the sexual drive—needed to be discharged to ensure pleasure and prevent pain and sought whatever outlet it might find. If denied the gratification provided by direct motor action, libidinal energy could seek its release through mental channels: that is, a wish can be satisfied by an imaginary wish fulfillment. All dreams, Freud claimed, are the disguised expression of wish fulfillments. Like neurotic symptoms, they are the effects of compromises in the psyche between desires and prohibitions in conflict with their realization.

In 1905 Freud's controversial study *Drei Abhandlungen zur Sexualtheorie* (*Three Essays on the Theory of Sexuality*) presented his discoveries concerning infantile sexuality and delineated the stages of psychosexual development, including the formation of the OEDIPUS complex, named for an element of the plot of Sophocles' *Oedipus Rex*. The universal applicability of the plot, Freud conjectured, lies in the desire of every male child to sleep with his mother and remove the obstacle to the realization of that wish, his father.

Freud also applied his psychoanalytic insights to mythological, anthropological, cultural, and religious phenomena. Among his most noted works in this vein are *Totem und Tabu* (1913; *Totem and Taboo*), *Das Unbehagen in der Kultur* (1930; *Civilization and Its Discontents*), and *Die Zu-kunft einer Illusion* (1927; *The Future of an Illusion*). In *Totem*, drawing on SIR JAMES FRAZER'S explorations of the Australian Aboriginals, he interpreted the mixture of fear and reverence for the totemic animal in terms of the child's attitude toward the parent of the same sex. The Aboriginals' insistence on exogamy was a complicated defense against the strong incestuous desires felt by the child for the parent of the opposite sex. Their religion was thus a phylogenetic anticipation of the ontogenetic Oedipal drama played out in modern man's psychic development. But whereas the latter was purely an intrapsychic phenomenon based on fantasies and fears, the former, Freud boldly suggested,

Freud, 1921

Mary Evans—Sigmund Freud Copyrights (courtesy of W.E. Freud)

was based on actual historical events. Freud speculated that the rebellion of sons against fathers for control of women had culminated in actual parricide. Ultimately producing remorse, this violent act led to ATONEMENT through incest taboos and the prohibitions against harming the father-substitute, the totemic object or animal. When the fraternal clan replaced the patriarchal horde, true society emerged. The totemic ancestor then could evolve into the more impersonal God of the great religions.

When Hitler invaded Austria in 1938, Freud was forced to flee to England. He died only a few weeks after World War II broke out, at a time when his worst fears about the irrationality lurking behind the facade of civilization were being realized. Freud's books were among the first to be burned, as the fruits of a "Jewish science," when the Nazis took over Germany.

FREY \frā\, *also spelled* Freyr (Old Norse: "Lord"), in GERMANIC RELIGION, one of the group of fertility deities called VANIR, who was brother and male counterpart of his sister FREYJA ("Lady") and son of the god Njörd. He was associated with peace and good crops. With his sister and father he was incorporated into the god-race called AESIR. The most famous story about him tells of his love and lust for the giantess GERD, who is wooed and won for him by his servant. He was worshiped most extensively in Sweden, where he was considered the progenitor of the royal line under the name Yngvi. His worship was believed to bring good weather and great wealth. Frey's sacred animal was the boar, and he rides one with golden bristles.

FREYJA \'frā-yə\ (Old Norse: "Lady"), in GERMANIC RELIGION, the most important goddess and one of the group of fertility deities called collectively VANIR. She was both sister and female counterpart of her brother FREY ("Lord"), and their father was the god of the wealth of the sea, Njörd. She was

called Sow and was connected with boars, as was her brother. She was also described as riding in a chariot drawn by cats. Her sexual promiscuity, natural in a fertility goddess, was alluded to often. It was told that half the slain belong to her and go to her dwelling, Folkvangr; the other half go to ODIN in VALHALLA. It is said that she taught a powerful magic, probably involving sexuality, to Odin and the AESIR. She wept tears of gold and owned a famous golden necklace (a sexual symbol) called Brísingamen, which was stolen by the trickster LOKI and recovered by HEIMDALL, the watchman of the gods.

Recently Freyja has been seen as the great goddess of the Scandinavian peoples rather than merely a fertility goddess.

FRIAR, one belonging to a ROMAN CATHOLIC religious order of MENDICANTS. The 10 mendicant orders are the DOMINICANS, FRANCISCANS, AUGUSTINIANS (Augustian HERMITS), CARMELITES, Trinitarians, Mercedarians, Servites, Minims, Hospitallers of St. John of God, and the Teutonic Order (the Austrian branch).

FRIENDS, SOCIETY OF, *byname* Quakers, Christian group that arose in mid-17th-century England, dedicated to living in accordance with the "Inward Light," or direct inward apprehension of God, without creeds, clergy, or other ecclesiastical forms.

There were meetings of the kind later associated with the Quakers before there was a group by that name. Small groups of Seekers gathered during the Puritan Revolution against Charles I to wait upon the Lord because they despaired of spiritual help from either the established Anglican Church or the existing Puritan bodies—Presbyterians, Congregationalists, and Baptists—through which most of them had already passed. To these Seekers came a band of preachers, mostly from the north of England, proclaiming the powers of direct contact with God. GEORGE FOX and James Nayler were perhaps the most eminent of these. Within a decade perhaps 20,000 to 60,000 had been converted from all social classes except the aristocracy and totally unskilled laborers.

The Puritan clergy were fierce in their opposition to the movement. The Restoration of Charles II in 1660 was only a change of persecutors for the Quakers. From the time of the Quaker Act of 1662 until the de facto toleration of James II in 1686, Friends were hounded by penal laws for not swearing OATHS, for not going to the services of the Church of England, for going to Quaker meetings, and for refusing to TITHE.

At the same time Quakers were converting and peopling America. In 1656 Quaker women preachers began work in Maryland and in the Massachusetts Bay Colony. The magistrates of Boston savagely persecuted the visitors and in 1659 and 1661 put four of them to death. Despite this, Quakerism took root in Massachusetts and flourished in

Rhode Island, where Friends for a long time were in the majority. The most famous Quaker colony was Pennsylvania, for which Charles II issued a charter to William Penn in 1681. Penn's "Holy Experiment" tested how far a state could be governed consistently with Friends' principles, especially pacifism and religious toleration.

The achievement of religious toleration in the 1690s coincided with a quietist phase in Quakerism that lasted until the 19th century. QUIETISM is endemic within Quakerism and emerges whenever trust in the Inward Light is stressed to the exclusion of everything else. The "public testimonies" of Friends from the very beginning included the plain speech and dress and refusal of tithes, oaths, and worldly courtesies. To these was added in a few years an explicit renunciation of participation in war; within the next century bankruptcy, marriage out of meeting, smuggling, and dealing in or owning slaves also became practices for which an unrepentant Friend would be disowned.

English Friends were active in the campaign to end the slave trade, and American Friends, urged on by John Woolman and others, emancipated their own slaves between 1758 and 1800. From the time of the American Revolution Quakers have been active in ministering to refugees and victims of famine—so much so that the entire Society of Friends is sometimes taken for a philanthropic organization. (This work was recognized in 1947 by the award of the Nobel Peace Prize to the AMERICAN FRIENDS SERVICE COMMITTEE and the (British) Friends Service Council.)

In the United States, as new yearly meetings were formed, ties with the London Yearly Meeting, the "mother" meeting, became weaker, and no American yearly meeting had a predominant position. The Philadelphia Yearly Meeting was sympathetic to evangelicalism; but many Friends, influenced by ELIAS HICKS (1748–1830), placed extreme emphasis on the Inward Light. The Hicksite separation spread to other yearly meetings that had to decide to which portion of the Philadelphia Yearly Meeting to write. A pastoral visit to the United States (1837–40) by the leading English evangelical Friend, Joseph John Gurney (one of the few systematic theologians ever produced in the Society of Friends), led to a further separation when the evangelical or "Gurneyite" New England Yearly Meeting disowned John Wilbur, an orthodox quietist Friend.

By 1900, Friends were divided into three groups. Yearly meetings of evangelical, or "orthodox," Friends were in fellowship with one another and with the London and Dublin yearly meetings. In the United States these Gurneyite meetings in 1902 formed the Five Years' Meeting (now the Friends United Meeting). The "conservative" American yearly meetings, in fellowship with one another, maintained traditional Quaker customs and mode of worship. The Hicksite yearly meetings, which formed the Friends General Conference in 1902, remained the most open to modern thought. During the century these divisions have been much softened.

Trust in the Inward Light is the distinctive theme of Quakerism. The Light is not to be confused with conscience or reason; it is rather that of God in everyone, which allows human beings an immediate sense of God's presence and will for them. It thus informs conscience and redirects reason. Meetings to worship God and await his word are essential to Quaker faith and practice, for it is in the pregnant silence of the meeting of true waiters and worshipers that the Spirit speaks. When someone has reached a new understanding that demands to be proclaimed, he or she speaks and thus ministers to the meeting, which weighs this "testimony" by its own experiences of God. Friends historically have rejected a formal or salaried clergy as a "hireling ministry."

But though Friends have no ORDINATION, they have always given a special place to Recorded Ministers (or Public Friends). Recorded Ministers are those whose testimony in local meetings has been officially recognized; they are free to "travel in the ministry" by visiting other meetings, should they be led to do so. Pastoral meetings maintain their Recorded Ministers, who also do much of the work of seeing to the relief of the poor, care of properties, and discipline of erring members.

FRIGG \'frig\, *also called* Friia \'frē-ə\, *or* Frea \'frā-ə\, in GERMANIC RELIGION, the wife of ODIN and mother of BALDER. She was a promoter of marriage and of fertility. In Icelandic stories, she tried to save her son's life but failed. Some myths depict her as the weeping and loving mother, while others stress her loose morals. Frigg was known also to other Germanic peoples, as Frija (in German) and Frea; her name survives in English in the word Friday.

FU HSI \'fü-'shē\, *Pinyin* Fu Xi, *formally (Wade-Giles romanization)* T'ai Hao \'tī-'haù\, *also called* Pao Hsi, *or* Mi Hsi, first of China's mythical emperors, said to have lived in the 29th century BCE. He was a divine being with a serpent's body, though in some representations he is a leaf-wreathed head growing out of a mountain or a man clothed with animal skins. A cultural hero, Fu Hsi is said to have discovered the trigrams used in DIVINATION and thus to have contributed to the development of writing. He domesticated animals, instituted marriage, offered the first open-air sacrifice to heaven, and taught his people to cook, to fish with nets, and to hunt with weapons made of iron. NÜ KUA, a frequent companion, was either his wife or sister.

Fu Hsi, painting on silk
By courtesy of the National Palace Museum, Taipei

FUJI, MOUNT \'fü-jē\, *Japanese* Fujisan \,fü-jē-'sän\, *also called* Fujiyama \,fü-jē-'yä-mä\, *or* Fuji no Yama \'fü-jē-,nō-'yä-mä\, highest mountain in Japan, rising to 12,388 feet near the Pacific coast in Yamanashi and Shizuoka *ken* (prefectures), central Honshu, about 60 miles west of Tokyo. It is a volcano that has been dormant since its last eruption in 1707 but is still generally classified as active by geologists. Mount Fuji, with its graceful conical form, has become famous throughout the world and is considered the sacred symbol of Japan.

Among the Japanese there is a sense of personal identification with the mountain.

Because it is considered a sacred mountain (one sect accords it virtually a soul), Mount Fuji is surrounded by temples and shrines; there are shrines even at the edge and the bottom of the crater. Climbing the mountain has long been a religious act, and tens of thousands of Japanese do so every year during the climbing season from July 1 to August 26. The ascent in early times was usually made in the white robes of a pilgrim, and until the Meiji Restoration women were not allowed to climb the mountain.

FULGENTIUS OF RUSPE, SAINT \fŭl-'jen-chē-əs, -chəs …'rəs-pē\ (b. *c.* 467, Telepte, North Africa—d. Jan. 1, 533, Ruspe; feast day January 1), African bishop of Ruspe and theological writer who defended orthodoxy in 6th-century Africa against ARIANISM.

Fulgentius became a monk, residing successively in Africa, Sicily, and Rome, then accepted the African bishopric of Ruspe on the Mediterranean coast (507). In 508 the Vandal king Thrasimund, a supporter of Arian beliefs, exiled 60 orthodox African bishops, who settled in Sardinia with Fulgentius as their leader and spokesman. Thrasimund recalled Fulgentius (515), but because of his orthodoxy, he was exiled again (517–523). Thrasimund's successor, Hilderich, allowed Fulgentius to return to Africa.

Eight of the numerous, essentially polemical writings (some speaking against SEMI-PELAGIANISM) ascribed to him elaborating orthodox views are known to be authentic.

FUNCTIONALISM, popular and widespread theory in the social sciences based on the premise that all aspects of society satisfy needs of various kinds for the long-term survival of the society. The theory is often used to explain why RELIGIOUS BELIEFS persist in a given society: religions persist because they fulfill certain indispensable needs (maintenance, integration, equilibrium) in a society or person. Thus, functionalism is often thought of as a causal explanation of religion.

Distinctions have been made within the theory between manifest functions, those consequences intended and recognized by participants in the system, and latent functions, which are neither intended nor recognized. Functionalism postulates that a social system has a functional unity in which all parts work together with some degree of internal consistency. It focuses on the conditions of stability, integration, and effectiveness of the system. Any process or set of conditions that does not contribute to the maintenance or development of the system is said to be dysfunctional. Some scholars have argued that there is a tautological nature to the premises of functionalism that precludes it from becoming an adequate theory.

FUNERARY CUSTOMS \'fyü-nə-,rer-ē\, ceremonial acts employed at the time of death and burial. Many of the beliefs and attitudes behind these practices are described in the article DEATH AND THE AFTERLIFE.

The disposal of the dead is almost always given special significance. As early as 50,000 BCE Paleolithic peoples, such as the Neanderthals and later groups, not only buried their dead but provided them with food, weapons, and other equipment, thereby implying a belief that the dead still needed such things in the grave. Funerary ritual provides the earliest evidence of religion in human history.

The process of dying and the moment of death have been regarded in many religions as occasions of the most serious crisis. The dying must be specially prepared for the experience. In China, for example, the head of a dying person was shaved, the body washed, and the nails pared. The person was placed in a sitting position to facilitate the exit of the soul. After the death relatives and friends called the soul to return, possibly to make certain that its departure from the body was definitive. In ROMAN CATHOLICISM the dying person makes a last CONFESSION to a priest, receives absolution, and is anointed with consecrated oil, which is known as "anointing of the sick" (formerly called extreme unction).

Preparation and disposal of the corpse. After death the corpse usually must be prepared for final disposal. Generally this preparation includes its washing and dressing in special garments and sometimes its public exposure. In some religions this preparation is accompanied by rites designed to protect the deceased from supernatural attack. Sometimes the purpose of the rites is to guard the living from the contagion of death or the malice of the dead, as it is often believed that the soul lingers about the body until the body is buried or completely decomposed.

The most elaborate known preparation of the dead took place in ancient Egypt. Because the Egyptians believed that the body was essential for a proper afterlife, a complex process of ritual embalmment was established. This process was intended not only to preserve the corpse from physical disintegration but also to reanimate it in the other world. One of the most significant of such rituals was the "opening of the mouth," in which a priest anointed the MUMMY, spoke incantations, and touched the mouth of the mummy with ritual objects, thereby restoring to the body its ability to see, breathe, and take nourishment.

The form of the disposal of the dead most generally used throughout the world has been burial in the ground. The mode of burial, however, has varied greatly. Sometimes the body is laid directly in the earth, with or without clothes and funerary equipment. It may be placed in either an extended or crouched position. Sometimes the corpse is oriented according to tradition, which may relate to the direction in which the land of the dead is thought to lie. The use of COFFINS dates from the early 3rd millennium BCE in Sumer and Egypt, and the use of a SARCOPHAGUS, elaborately carved with mythological scenes, became fashionable among the wealthier classes of Greco-Roman society.

In the ancient Near East the construction of stone tombs began in the 3rd millennium BCE and inaugurated a tradition of funerary architecture that produced such diverse monuments as the PYRAMIDS of Egypt, the Tāj Mahal, and the mausoleum of Lenin in Moscow. In Egypt the tomb was furnished to meet the needs of its inmate, sometimes to the extent that even toilet facilities were provided. Among many peoples the belief that some part of the deceased remains in the tomb even after the body decays has resulted in the tombs of certain holy persons being made into shrines, which thousands visit, hoping to find miracles of healing or to earn religious merit. Notable examples of such centers of PILGRIMAGE are the tombs of ST. PETER in Rome, MUHAMMAD in MEDINA, and, in ancient times, IMHOTEP at Ṣaqqārah, in Memphis, Egypt.

The funeral consists of conveying the deceased from home to the place of burial or CREMATION. This act of transportation has generally been made into a procession of mourners who lament the deceased, and it has often afforded an opportunity of advertising the person's wealth, status, or achievements. Many depictions of ancient Egyptian funerary processions graphically portray the basic pattern. The embalmed body of the deceased is borne on an ornate sledge, on which sit two mourning women. A priest precedes the bier, pouring LIBATIONS and burning incense. In the cortege are groups of mourning men and lamenting women, and servants carry the funerary furniture, which indicates the wealth of the dead person. In some Islamic countries friends carry the corpse on an open bier, generally followed by women relatives, lamenting with disheveled hair, and hired mourners. After a service in the mosque the body is interred with its right side toward MECCA.

In HINDUISM the funeral procession is made to the place of cremation and is preceded by a man carrying a firebrand kindled at the domestic hearth. A goat is sometimes sacrificed en route, and the mourners circumambulate the corpse, which is carried on a bier. Cremation is a ritual act, governed by careful prescriptions. The widow crouches by the pyre, on which in former times she might have died purposely (*see* SATĪ). After cremation the remains are gathered and often deposited in sacred rivers.

In JUDAISM the burial service is marked by simplicity, and the interment takes place as soon after death as possible. The body is prepared for the grave by the *ḥevra' qaddisha'* (the holy society) and is clad only in a simple shroud. Shrouds are normally of unadorned white linen, following the sumptuary ruling of the 1st-century-CE Rabbi GAMALIEL I (the Elder). To the shroud may be added the ṬALLIT used by the deceased, but with the fringes removed or cut, because the prescription governing their use applies only to the living. In Israel no coffin is used.

Postfunerary rites. Funerary rites do not usually terminate with the disposal of the corpse. Postfunerary ceremonies and customs generally have two not necessarily mutually exclusive motives: to mourn the dead and to purify the mourners. The mourning of the dead, especially by near relatives, has taken many forms. Wearing old or colorless dress, either black or white, shaving the hair or letting it grow long and unkempt, and abstaining from amusements have all been common practice.

In Judaism a mourning period of 30 days is observed, of which the first 7 (*shiv'a*) are the most rigorous. During the 11 months following a death the bereaved recite a synagogal DOXOLOGY (KADDISH) during the public service as an act of memorial. The doxology itself, entirely devoid of any mention of death, is a praise of God and a prayer for the establishment of the coming kingdom. It is also recited annually on the anniversary of the death (YAHRZEIT).

In some areas the belief that the spirit remains in this world until the corpse has completely decayed leads to extended periods of mourning, which may last for more than a year. In such cases a second burial rite often signals the end to this period: the remains of the deceased are exhumed from the tomb and deposited elsewhere, often in a community sepulchre. In rural Greece, where such rites are still practiced, it is believed that unusually slow decomposition indicates that the deceased is reluctant to leave this world; this is a dangerous state of affairs, and in such cases relatives may complete the process of decomposition themselves by scraping the remaining flesh from the bones.

A widespread custom is the funeral banquet, which may be held in the presence of the corpse before burial or in the tomb-chapel (in ancient Rome) or on the return of the mourners to the home of the deceased. Originally these meals might have grown out of sacrificial food offerings made to the deceased. In general the banquet celebrates life by bringing the survivors together for a common meal.

The purification of mourners is another powerful postfunerary concern. A corpse straddles the boundary between this world and the next, and as with most such liminal objects it is regarded as simultaneously powerful and polluting. All who come in contact with it therefore are in need of cleansing before they can rejoin normal society. Various forms of purification are prescribed, chiefly bathing and fumigation. PARSIS make a special point of cleansing the room in which the death occurred and all articles that had contact with the dead body (*see* ZOROASTRIANISM).

Commemorative rites. In Egypt MORTUARY TEMPLES or chapels were built, in which portrait images preserved the memory of the dead and offerings of food and drink were regularly made. In China an elaborate ancestor cult flourished. The ancestral shrine contained tablets, inscribed with the names of ancestors, which were revered and before which offerings were made. When the tablet of a newly deceased member was added to the collection, the oldest tablet was deposited in a chest containing still older ones. In India three generations of deceased ancestors are venerated at the monthly SRADDHA festival, at which mortuary offerings are made.

In early Christianity the bodies of martyrs were entombed in special chapels. The development of cults of martyrs and other saints in the medieval church centered on the veneration of their relics, which were often divided among several churches. The introduction of the doctrine of PURGATORY profoundly affected the postmortem care devoted to the ordinary dead. It was believed that the offering of the sacrifice of the MASS could alleviate the suffering of departed souls in purgatory. Consequently the celebration of masses for the dead proliferated, and wealthy Christians endowed monasteries or chantry chapels where masses were said regularly for the repose of their own souls or those of their relatives.

In many religions the dead are periodically commemorated. Buddhist China kept a Feast of Wandering Souls each year, designed to help unfortunate souls suffering in the next world. The Christian ALL SOULS' DAY, on November 2, which follows directly after ALL SAINTS' DAY, commemorates all the ordinary dead. Requiem masses are celebrated for their repose, and in many Catholic countries relatives visit the graves and place lighted candles on them.

Cult of the dead. Among many peoples it is customary to preserve the memory of the dead by placing images of them upon their graves or tombs. This sepulchral ICONOGRAPHY began in Egypt; the portrait statue of King Djoser (*c.* 2686–*c.* 2613 BCE), found in the worship chamber of the Step Pyramid, is the oldest known example. The images also provided a locus for the deceased's KA, the spiritual entity that was an essential element of the personality.

FURIES, the Roman goddesses of vengeance, identified with the Greek ERINYES.

FU-SHEN \'fü-'shən\, *Pinyin* Fushen, Chinese god of happiness, the deification of a 6th-century mandarin, Yang Ch'eng. The name also denotes the beneficent gods of Chinese myth.

Yang Ch'eng (or Yang Hsi-chi), who served the Liang Wu-ti emperor (reigned 502–549 CE) as a criminal judge in Hunan Province, was disturbed that the ruler was using dwarfs as servants and court entertainers. Yang admonished the emperor, pointing out that these unfortunate people were subjects, not slaves. The emperor thereupon called a halt to the practice. The grateful dwarfs set up images of their benefactor and offered sacrifice. The cult of Yang as god of happiness gradually spread throughout China.

GABAR \'ga-bər\, derogatory term used by Muslims in Iran to denote the country's small ZOROASTRIAN minority. The origin of the Persian word *gabar*, or *gabr*, is uncertain; perhaps most plausibly it has been conjectured to be a pre-Islamic borrowing of Arabic *kāfir* ("infidel"). The Zoroastrians who remained in Persia (modern Iran) after the Arab-Muslim conquest (7th century CE) purchased some toleration by paying the JIZYA ("poll tax"), which was abolished in 1882; but they were treated as an inferior race, had to wear distinctive garb, and were not allowed to ride horses or bear arms. Living for centuries in villages of central Iran, they have tended more recently to be concentrated in Kerman and Yazd, where Zoroastrians still maintain fire temples, and in Teheran. Long isolated, the Iranian Zoroastrians made contact with the PARSIS, the wealthy Zoroastrians of India, in the 15th century, and exchanged messages concerning religious lore. Since the 19th century the Parsis have taken a lively interest in improving the depressed condition of their Iranian coreligionists, remonstrating with the Iranian government over discrimination against Zoroastrians. Beginning with the reign of Reza Shah (1921–41), Iranian Zoroastrians enjoyed wider religious tolerance, but this was impeded by the Islamic revolution of 1978–79. They currently number a few thousand.

GABIJA \gä-bi-'yä\ (Lithuanian), *also called* Gabieta \gä-'bē-e-tä\, *Latvian* Uguns Māte \'ü-güns-'mä-te\, *Old Prussian* Panicke, in BALTIC RELIGION, the domestic hearth fire. In pre-Christian times a holy fire (*šventa ugnis*) was kept in tribal sanctuaries on high hills and riverbanks, where priests guarded it constantly, extinguishing and rekindling it once a year at the midsummer festival. Eventually this tradition was moved into the home as the *gabija*. Every evening the mistress of the house carefully tended the fire and prayed to it to ensure the family's good fortune. A new bride was given a fire from her mother's hearth in order that the *gabija* might provide an auspicious beginning for the new family.

GABRIEL \'gā-brē-əl\, *Hebrew* Gavri'el, *Arabic* Gibrā'īl, Jabra'il, *or* Jibril, in the BIBLE and the QUR'AN, one of the ARCHANGELS. Gabriel was the heavenly messenger sent to Daniel to explain the vision of the ram and the he-goat and to communicate the prediction of the Seventy Weeks. He also announced the birth of JOHN THE BAPTIST to ZECHARIAH and the birth of JESUS to MARY. It is because he stood in the divine presence that both Jewish and Christian writers generally speak of him as an archangel. Gabriel's feast is kept on September 29. His name and functions were taken over by ISLAM from Judaeo-Christian tradition. He is mentioned in the Qur'an only three times, but various epithets in that scripture are widely recognized as referring to him.

GAD \'gad\, one of the TWELVE TRIBES OF ISRAEL that in biblical times composed the people of ISRAEL. The tribe was

named after the elder of two sons born to JACOB and Zilpah, a maidservant of Jacob's first wife, LEAH (Genesis 30:10–11).

After entering the Promised Land, the tribe of Gad settled on land east of the Jordan River (Joshua 13:24–28), gained renown for its military spirit (1 Chronicles 12:8–15), and was one of the 10 northern tribes that formed a separate kingdom in 930 BCE with Jeroboam I as king (1 Kings 11:26ff). Following the Assyrian conquest of 721, the 10 tribes were partially dispersed and eventually assimilated by other peoples (2 Kings 17:5–6; 18:9–12). The tribe of Gad thus became one of the TEN LOST TRIBES OF ISRAEL.

GAEA \'jē-ə\, *also called* Ge \'jē\, Greek goddess of the earth. She was both mother and wife of OURANUS (Heaven), and it was the last child born of that union, CRONUS (a TITAN), who separated her from Ouranus (that is, separated Earth from Heaven). She was also mother of the other Titans, the Gigantes, the ERINYES, and the Cyclopes; hence literature and art sometimes made her the enemy of ZEUS, for the Titans and Gigantes threatened him. Gaea may have been originally a MOTHER GODDESS worshiped in Greece before the introduction of the cult of Zeus. Less widely worshiped in historic times, Gaea was described as the giver of dreams and the nourisher of plants and young children.

GAHANBAR \gä-ˌhän-'bär, gä-'hä-nä-'bär\, *also spelled* gahambar ("The Time of Storing [Merit]"), in ZOROASTRIANISM, any of six festivals, occurring at irregular intervals throughout the year, which celebrate the seasons as experienced in Iran. Globally, these are aligned with the six stages in the creation of the world: the heavens, water, the earth, the vegetable world, the animal world, and humanity. Each lasting five days, the Gahanbars are: Maidhyaōizaremaya (midspring), occurring 41 days after the New Year; 60 days later is Maidhyoishema (midsummer); 75 days later, Paitishhahya (harvest-time); 30 days later, Ayāthrima (possibly "Time of Prosperity"); 80 days later, Maidhyāirya (midwinter); and 75 days later, in the last five intercalary, or Gatha, days of the year, Hamaspathmaēdaya (vernal equinox).

PARSIS observe the Gahanbar festivals in two stages. Four liturgical rites are first celebrated: the Āfringān, being prayers of love or praise; the Bāj, prayers honoring YAZATAS (angels) or FRAVASHIS (guardian spirits); the Yasna, the central Zoroastrian rite, which includes the sacrifice of the sacred liquor, *haoma*; and the Pavi, prayers honoring God and his spirits, performed jointly by the priest and the faithful. A solemn feast then follows, in which the sacrificial offerings made in the preceding liturgies are consumed in ritual purity.

GALINTHIAS \gə-'lin-thē-əs\, in Greek mythology, a friend, or servant, of Alcmene, the mother (by ZEUS) of HERACLES. While Alcmene was in labor, Zeus's jealous wife, HERA, goddess of childbirth, was clasping her hands, thus by magic preventing delivery (by another variant, Hera sent EILEITHYIA to hold back the birth). To foil this, Galinthias rushed in to Hera and falsely announced that Alcmene had given birth to a son, so causing Hera to relax. Thus the charm was broken, and Alcmene gave birth to Heracles. As punishment, Hera transformed Galinthias into a weasel or (according to Ovid) a lizard. The goddess HECATE, however, took pity on her and took her as an attendant, and Heracles later made a SANCTUARY for her.

GALLERY GRAVE, long chamber grave, a variant of the collective tomb burials that spread into western Europe from the Aegean area during the final stage of the northern Stone Age (c. 2000 BCE). The tombs are often associated with divine ancestors and deities, who are depicted on the rock walls.

GALLI \\'ga-,lī\\, *singular* gallus \\'ga-ləs\\, priests, often temple attendants or wandering MENDICANTS, of the ancient Asiatic deity the GREAT MOTHER OF THE GODS, known as CYBELE or AGDISTIS in Greek and Latin literature. The *galli* were eunuchs attired in female garb, with long hair fragrant with ointment. Together with priestesses, they celebrated the Great Mother's rites with wild music and dancing until their frenzy culminated in self-scourging, self-laceration, or exhaustion. Self-emasculation by candidates for the PRIESTHOOD sometimes accompanied this delirium of worship.

The name *galli* may be Phrygian, from the two streams called Gallus, both tributaries of the Sangarius (now Sakarya) River, the waters of which were said to inspire religious frenzy. If the word is actually Phrygian, it may more plausibly descend from the Indo-European root of Greek *kolos*, "docked," and *kolobos*, "mutilated."

GAMALIEL I \\gə-'mä-lē-əl\\, *also called* Rabban Gamaliel \\rä-'bän\\ (*rabban*, "teacher") (fl. 1st century CE), important early rabbinic figure referred to in the Talmudic literature (*see* TALMUD) as Gamaliel ha-Zaqen ("the Elder"). He was the grandson of HILLEL and patriarch of the Jewish community of ISRAEL at the beginning of the 1st century CE. He was a teacher of Simeon of Mizpeh and other leading rabbis; Acts 22:3 states that the Apostle PAUL was his student. Regarding him, Mishnah Sotah 9:15 says: "When Rabban Gamaliel the Elder died, the glory of the TORAH came to an end, and cleanness and separateness perished."

GAMALIEL II, *also called* Gamaliel of Jabneh \\'jab-nə\\ (fl. 2nd century CE), important RABBI, a grandson of GAMALIEL I. It is to him that the name Gamaliel usually refers when it is used without further qualification. He succeeded JOHANAN BEN ZAKKAI as patriarch of the Jewish community of Israel about 80 CE. He was one of the greatest legal authorities of his generation and is frequently cited in the MISHNAH. Berakhot 27b–28a (Talmud BAVLI) reports that Gamaliel was involved in a disagreement regarding the JEWISH CALENDAR, a dispute that is said to have led to Gamaliel's temporary removal from the office of patriarch.

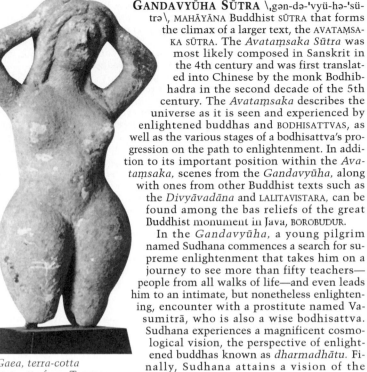

Gaea, terra-cotta statuette from Tanagra; in the Borély Museum, Marseille, France
Giraudon—Art Resource

GANDAVYŪHA SŪTRA \\,gən-də-'vyü-hə-'sü-trə\\, MAHĀYĀNA Buddhist SŪTRA that forms the climax of a larger text, the AVATAMSAKA SŪTRA. The *Avataṃsaka Sūtra* was most likely composed in Sanskrit in the 4th century and was first translated into Chinese by the monk Bodhibhadra in the second decade of the 5th century. The *Avataṃsaka* describes the universe as it is seen and experienced by enlightened buddhas and BODHISATTVAS, as well as the various stages of a bodhisattva's progression on the path to enlightenment. In addition to its important position within the *Avataṃsaka*, scenes from the *Gandavyūha*, along with ones from other Buddhist texts such as the *Divyāvadāna* and LALITAVISTARA, can be found among the bas reliefs of the great Buddhist monument in Java, BOROBUDUR.

In the *Gandavyūha*, a young pilgrim named Sudhana commences a search for supreme enlightenment that takes him on a journey to see more than fifty teachers—people from all walks of life—and even leads him to an intimate, but nonetheless enlightening, encounter with a prostitute named Vasumitrā, who is also a wise bodhisattva. Sudhana experiences a magnificent cosmological vision, the perspective of enlightened buddhas known as *dharmadhātu*. Finally, Sudhana attains a vision of the bodhisattva Samantabhadra and realizes that his own nature, and those of Samantabhadra, all buddhas, and all other existences in the cosmos are, in fact, one and infinitely interpenetrate one another.

GANDHI, MOHANDAS KARAMCHAND \\'gän-dē\\, *byname* Mahātmā ("Great-Souled") Gandhi \\mə-'hät-mə\\ (b. Oct. 2, 1869, Porbandar, India—d. Jan. 30, 1948, Delhi), leader of the Indian nationalist movement against British rule, considered to be the father of his country. He is internationally esteemed for his doctrine of nonviolent protest to achieve political and social progress.

Gandhi was reared by a deeply religious mother in a household that practiced VAIṢṆAVISM, and he developed a close, inspiring relationship with a Jain friend, Rajchandra Rajivbhai, whom he called Raychand. He hewed to his mother's vegetarianism when he began law studies in England in 1888. In quest of clerical work he went to South Africa (1893–1914) and was shocked at the racial discrimination there. He became an advocate for his fellow Indians in South Africa and undertook a series of challenges to the government that led to jail. He entered politics in India in 1919 to protest British sedition laws. He emerged as the head of the Indian National Congress and advocated a policy of noncooperation to achieve Indian independence under the general rubric of AHIMSĀ ("nonviolence"). In 1930 he led a march to the sea to protest the British-imposed tax on salt, and by the following spring the making of salt for personal use was permitted. Imprisoned throughout much of World War II, he negotiated with the British in August 1947 for an autonomous Indian state. In January 1948, however, he was assassinated by a right-wing Hindu fanatic.

The religious dimensions of Gandhi's life and thought are many. Gandhi's religious quest dated back to his childhood and the influence of his mother and of his homes at Porbandar and Rajkot, but it received a great impetus after his arrival in South Africa. His Quaker friends in Pretoria failed to convert him to Christianity, but they quickened his appetite for religious studies. He was fascinated by Tolstoy's writings on Christianity, read the QUR'AN in translation, and delved into Hindu scriptures and philosophy. The study of comparative religion, talks with scholars, and his own reading of theological works brought him to the conclusion that all religions were true and yet every one of them was imperfect because they were "interpreted with poor intellects, sometimes with poor hearts, and more often misinterpreted." Rajchandra, Gandhi's friend and spiritual mentor, convinced him of "the subtlety and profundity" of Hinduism, the religion of Gandhi's birth. And it was the BHAGAVAD GĪTĀ, which Gandhi had first read in London, that became his "spiritual dictionary" and exercised probably the greatest single influence on his life. Two Sanskrit words in the *Gītā* particularly fascinated him. One was *aparigraha* (nonpossession), which implied that man had to jettison the material goods that cramped the life of the spirit and to shake off the bonds of money and property. The other was *samabhava* (equability), which enjoined him to remain unruffled by pain or pleasure, victory or defeat, and to work without hope of success or fear of failure.

His personal devotions also tied him to the *Gītā* and RĀMĀYAṆA. The former presented an obvious challenge to his doctrine of *ahiṃsā* in KRISHNA's insistence that ARJUNA take up his weapon and fight. Gandhi solved this dilemma allegorically, by interpreting the intransigent yet intimately related enemy army of Arjuna's Kaurava kin as representing the "Satanic impulses" within each person. As he said, "Arjuna and others stand for the Godward impulses. The battlefield is our body." With such a credo he contextualized the struggle against the British Raj in cosmic terms, attempting to befriend the enemy and undermine him at the same time. This overarching strategy he called SATYĀGRAHA ("truth force," or "clinging to the truth"). His regard for truth as an ultimate principle was again a conviction he drew in part from his Hindu background, associating it especially with the phrase from the MAHĀBHĀRATA— *satyannāsti paro dharmaḥ* ("there is no religion [or duty] higher than

Mohandas K. Gandhi
Culver Pictures

truth"). Even Gandhi's devotion to Indian independence had religious overtones, for he understood "self-rule" (*svarāj*) not just politically but in connection with the sort of personal integrity that can only come with self-restraint and nonattachment, as taught in the *Gītā*.

GAṆEŚA \gə-'nā-shə\, *also spelled* Ganesha, *or* Ganesh, *also called* Gaṇapati, elephant-headed Hindu god, the son of SHIVA and PĀRVATĪ; also revered by Jains and important in the art, myth, and ritual of Buddhist Asia. Gaṇeśa, considered the remover of obstacles, is the first god invoked at the beginning of worship or of a new enterprise, and he is often positioned near thresholds and gateways. He is a patron of letters and learning, and he is the legendary scribe who wrote down the MAHĀBHĀRATA ("Great Epic of the Bhārata Dynasty") from Vyāsa's dictation. He is also called the chief of the *gaṇa*s (attendants of Shiva). Gaṇeśa is usually depicted colored red; he is pot-bellied, has one tusk broken, and has four arms that often hold a noose, a goad or axe, a pot of sweetmeats or jewels, and his broken tusk or a book. Thus, he displays a thoroughgoing mix of forbidding and welcoming traits, as is illustrated by the fact that he is sometimes thought of as creating obstacles and sometimes as removing them. Anomalously, he rides on a rat.

One account of his birth is that Pārvatī formed him from the rubbings of her body so that he might stand guard at the door while she bathed. When Shiva approached (unaware this was Pārvatī's son) he was enraged at being kept away from his wife and set his attendants against Gaṇeśa, whose head was cut off in the battle. To ease Pārvatī's grief, Shiva promised to cut off the head of the first creature that he came across and join it to the body. This was an elephant.

Although technically a subsidiary figure in the Hindu pantheon, Gaṇeśa's importance has advanced markedly during the 20th century. Gaṇeśa-caturthī, the festival celebrating his birth, falling on the fourth day (*caturthī*) of the lunar month Bhādrapada (August–September), was championed by the Indian independence leader Balgangadhar Tilak as a unifying public event. Gaṇeśa's largely nonsectarian identity has made him an appropriate focus for other recent expressions of Hindu life, especially in the Hindu diaspora.

GAṄGĀ RIVER \'gəŋ-gä\, *English* Ganges River \'gan-jēz\, great river of the plains of northern India, held sacred by people of the HINDU faith. In the myth told of the Gaṅgā, the river, personified as a goddess, originally flowed only in heaven (the Milky Way) until she was brought down by Bhagīratha to purify the ashes of his ancestors. She came down reluctantly, cascading first on the head of SHIVA, in order to break her fall, which would have otherwise shattered the Earth. Accordingly the Gaṅgā is recognized by many Hindus as one of Shiva's wives. Confluences are particularly holy, and the Gaṅgā's confluence with the JAMUNĀ (and mythical SARASVATĪ) at Allahabad (Hindi: Prayāg) is considered by many to be the most sacred spot in India. Every 12 years it becomes the focus of the KUMBH MELĀ, India's largest religious gathering.

In religious terms, the Gaṅgā river is regarded as the goddess Gaṅgā, a liquid, maternal form of ŚAKTI and one of the most benevolent divinities in the Hindu pantheon. Her mythology and geography tie her firmly to Shiva, both at her source and at Hardwar and VARANASI, but she is sometimes understood as a consort of VISHNU, a tie strengthened by her confluence with the Jamunā, sacred to KRISHNA. She is the archetype of sacred water. Her presence in water of any kind can be ritually invoked, and Gaṅgā water proper is highly prized in rites of healing and purification. It is sometimes claimed that a drop of Gaṅgā's water is sufficient to purify any sin. Because of her sacred embodiment of the cosmic water cycle, Hindus often desire to immerse the remains of the dead in the Gaṅgā.

GANIODA'YO \,gän-yō-'dī-yō\, *English* Handsome Lake (b. *c.* 1735, Ganawaugus, N.Y.—d. Aug. 10, 1815, Onondaga, N.Y., U.S.), Seneca Indian leader who developed a new religion for the Iroquois (*see* HANDSOME LAKE MOVEMENT). The cult was so successful that in the 20th century several thousand Indians still adhered to it.

Ganioda'yo became seriously ill in 1799 and, on his recovery, declared that he had been visited by three spirits who had revealed the will of the Great Spirit. From 1800, as an itinerant preacher of the religion that he called Gai'wiio ("Good Message"), he urged his people to refrain from adultery, drunkenness, laziness, and WITCHCRAFT. His combination of traditional beliefs and Christian ethics infused new energy into Iroquois culture at a period of crisis.

GANYMEDE \'ga-ni-,mēd\, *Greek* Ganymēdēs, in Greek mythology, the son of Tros (or LAOMEDON), king of Troy. Because of his unusual beauty, he was carried off either by the gods or by ZEUS, disguised as an eagle. According to a Cretan account, he was carried off by MINOS, to serve as the cupbearer for the gods. In compensation, Zeus gave Ganymede's father a stud of immortal horses (or a golden vine).

GAON \gä-'ōn\, *plural* geonim \ge-ō-'nēm\ (Hebrew: "majesty," or "excellence"), title accorded to the Jewish spiritual leaders and scholars who headed Talmudic academies that flourished from the 7th to the 13th century in Babylonia and Palestine. The chief concern of the *geonim* was to interpret and develop Talmudic Law and to safeguard Jewish legal traditions by adjudicating points of legal controversy. Their replies (RESPONSA) were quoted widely. The *geonim* continued a tradition of scholarship begun long before by the *soferim* (teachers and interpreters of biblical law) and kept alive in subsequent centuries by the *tannaim* (*see* TANNA) and *amoraim* (who, respectively, produced the MISHNAH and GEMARA; *see* AMORA).

A long-standing rivalry between the Babylonian and Palestinian *geonim* came to a head in the 10th century. SA'ADIA BEN JOSEPH, famous Babylonian *gaon* of the academy at Sura, bested his rival, Aaron ben Meir of Jerusalem, in a controversy involving calendar dates of Jewish festivals. Thereafter, the superiority of the Babylonian *geonim* was rarely

Garuḍa carrying Vishnu and Lakṣmī, South Indian bronze image, 18th century; in the Guimet Museum, Paris
Cliche Musees Nationaux, Paris

questioned. The prestige of the *geonim* gradually declined with the establishment of Talmudic academies elsewhere and the acceptance of local scholars as competent authorities on Jewish Law. After the gaonic period, the term *gaon* was used as a title of honor.

GARUḌA \'gə-rů-də\, in Hindu mythology, the bird and the *vāhana* (mount) of the god VISHNU. In the ṚG VEDA the sun is compared to a bird in its flight across the sky, and the association of the kitelike Garuḍa with Vishnu is taken by scholars as an indication of Vishnu's early origins as a sun deity. The mythological account of Garuḍa's birth identifies him as the younger brother of Aruṇa, the charioteer of the sun god, SŪRYA. Garuḍa's mother was held in slavery by a co-wife and her sons, who were NĀGAS, to which is attributed the lasting enmity between the eaglelike kite and the serpents. The *nāgas* agreed to release his mother if he could obtain for them a drink of the elixir of immortality, the *amṛta*. Garuḍa performed this feat and on his way back from the heavens met Vishnu and agreed to serve him as his vehicle and also as his emblem.

Garuḍa is described in one text as emerald in color, with a beak, roundish eyes, golden wings, and four arms and with breast, knees, and legs like those of the kite. He is also depicted anthropomorphically, with wings and hawklike features. Especially in South Indian temples to Vishnu, Garuḍa may often be seen resting atop a pillar that faces the sanctum.

Garuḍa traveled with the spread of HINDUISM to Nepal and to Southeast Asia, where he is frequently depicted on monuments. He is also associated with royalty in several Southeast Asian countries.

GAYŌMART \,ga-yō-'mart\, *Avestan* Gayō Maretan ("Mortal Life"), in later COSMOGONY of ZOROASTRIANISM, the first man and the progenitor of mankind. Gayōmart's spirit, with that of the primeval ox, lived for 3,000 years during the period in which creation was only spiritual. His mere existence immobilized AHRIMAN, the evil spirit who wanted to invade creation. Then AHURA MAZDĀ created Gayōmart incarnate—white and brilliant, shining like the sun—and put in him and the primeval ox, alone of all created things, a seed whose origin was in fire. Ahura Mazdā gave Gayōmart the boon of sleep for respite from the onslaught of Ahriman. But after 30 years of attacks, Ahriman destroyed Gayōmart. His body became the Earth's metals and minerals. Gold was his seed, and from it sprang the human race.

Geb falling away from intercourse with Nut, detail from the Papyrus of Tameniu

GEB \\'geb\\, *also called* Keb, in ancient EGYPTIAN RELIGION, the god of the earth, the physical support of the world. Geb and his sister, NUT, constituted the second generation in the Ennead (group of nine gods) of HELIOPOLIS. In Egyptian art Geb was often depicted lying by the feet of SHU, the air god, with Nut, the goddess of the sky, arched above them. Geb was usually portrayed as a man without any distinguishing characteristics, but at times he was represented with his head surmounted by a goose, the hieroglyph of his name. He was the third divine ruler among the gods; the pharaohs claimed to be descended from him, and therefore the royal throne was referred to as "the throne of Geb."

GEDALIAH, FAST OF \\gə-'däl-yə, ˌge-də-'lī-ə\\, a minor Jewish observance (on Tishri 3 [shortly after the fall equinox]; Zechariah 7:5; 8:19) that mournfully recalls the assassination of Gedaliah, Jewish governor of JUDAH and appointee of Nebuchadrezzar, the Babylonian king. Gedaliah, a supporter of JEREMIAH, was slain by Ishmael, a member of the former royal family of Judah. When the remaining Jews fled to Egypt, Jewish self-rule was thus effectively ended (2 Kings 25:22–26; Jeremiah 41:1ff.). Liturgically, the fast of Gedaliah follows the ritual of other fast days but adds certain penitential prayers. The festival is postponed one day if Tishri 3 falls on the SABBATH (Rosh Hashanah 18b).

GEFION \\'ge-vē-ˌȯn\\, *also spelled* Gefjun, in Nordic mythology, a minor goddess associated with unmarried women.

GEHENNA \\gi-'he-nə\\ (from Hebrew *Ge Hinnom,* "Valley of Hinnom"), *also called* Gehinnom \\gi-'hi-nəm\\, in Jewish and Christian ESCHATOLOGY, abode of the damned in the afterlife. Named in the NEW TESTAMENT in the word's Greek form (Geenna), Gehenna originally was a valley west and south of Jerusalem where children were burned as sacrifices to the AMMONITE god MOLOCH. This practice was carried out during the reigns of King SOLOMON in the 10th century BCE and King MANASSEH in the 7th century BCE and continued until the BABYLONIAN EXILE in the 6th century BCE. Gehenna later was made into a garbage center to discourage a reintroduction of such sacrifices.

The imagery of the burning of humans supplied the concept of "hellfire" to Jewish and Christian eschatology. Mentioned several times in the New Testament as a place in which fire will destroy the wicked, Gehenna also is noted in the TALMUD as a place of purification, after which one is released from further torture.

GEIGER, ABRAHAM \\'gī-gər\\ (b. May 24, 1810, Frankfurt am Main—d. Oct. 23, 1874, Berlin, Ger.), German-Jewish theologian, author, and the outstanding leader in the early development of REFORM JUDAISM.

In 1832 Geiger went to Wiesbaden as a RABBI and in 1835 helped to found the *Wissenschaftliche Zeitschrift für jüdische Theologie* ("Scientific Journal of Jewish Theology"), which he then edited. In 1838 he became a rabbi in Breslau (now Wrocław, Pol.). Remaining in Breslau until 1863, Geiger organized the Reform movement there and translated into German the works of JUDAH BEN SAMUEL HA-LEVI (1851), as well as writing his own magnum opus, *Urschrift und Übersetzungen der Bibel in ihrer Abhängigkeit von der innern Entwicklung des Judentums* (1857; "The Original Text and the Translations of the Bible: Their Dependence on the Inner Development of Judaism"). In this work, Geiger illustrated a basic idea of Reform Judaism: the Jewish religious consciousness grows and changes, and this development is reflected in succeeding editions and translations of the Bible.

GELUKPA: *see* DGE-LUGS-PA.

GEMARA \\gə-mä-'rä, gə-'mär-ə\\, rabbinic commentary on and interpretation of the MISHNAH.

GEMATRIA \\gə-'mä-trē-ə\\, the substitution of numbers for letters of the Hebrew alphabet, a favorite method of EXEGESIS used in QABBALAH to derive mystical insights into sacred writings or obtain new interpretations of the texts. GENESIS 28:12, for example, relates that in a dream JACOB saw a ladder (Hebrew *sullam*) stretching from earth to heaven. The numerical value of the word *sullam* in Hebrew is 130 (gematria assigns numeric equivalence only to consonants, and the word *sullam* has only three consonants in Hebrew, thus 60 + 30 + 40)—this is the same numerical value of Sinai (60 + 10 + 50 + 10)—so exegetes concluded that the Law revealed to MOSES on MOUNT SINAI is man's means of reaching heaven. Of the 22 letters in the Hebrew alphabet, the first 10 are given number values consecutively from 1 to 10, the next 8 from 20 to 90 in intervals of 10, while the final 4 letters equal 100, 200, 300, and 400, respectively. More complicated methods have also been used.

GEMILUT ḤESED \\gə-'mē-lùt-'ke-sed\\ (Hebrew: "bestowing kindness"), in JUDAISM, an attribute of God said to be imitated by those who in any of countless ways show personal kindness toward others. A Jew who does not manifest sensitive concern for others is considered no better than an atheist, regardless of his knowledge of the TORAH.

GENDER AND RELIGION, subject of critical importance to the modern STUDY OF RELIGION in that it concerns both biological sexuality and the stereotypes that form around cultural gender within a given religious and mythological system. Serious gender scholarship in the field of religion has tended to focus upon religious constructions of sexuality that transgress the polar circles of male and female, in order to investigate the possibilities of other sexualities (for instance, hermaphrodites) offered in various religions.

The so-called non-Western religions are not necessarily open to more liberal constructions of gender than are the great MONOTHEISMS (JUDAISM, CHRISTIANITY, and ISLAM); some of them are simply open to different constructions. Myths of androgyny—of creatures, human or divine, who are half female, half male—and of transsexuality—the transforming of a person of one biological sex into one of the other sex—sometimes support and sometimes deconstruct their own cultures' beliefs concerning gender. Myths of the origin of sexual differentiation generally affirm social boundaries; myths of transsexuality may subvert them, but do not always do so.

Gender is relatively easily sloughed off in some texts in which a male is entirely transformed into a female, with a female mentality and memory (aspects of cultural gender rather than sexuality); for instance, King Ila, the founder of the Hindu lunar dynasty, forgets everything about his male existence when he is magically transformed into a female who gives birth to the heir to the throne. Yet other texts seem to reflect a view of gender as astonishingly durable: the male merely assumes the outer form of the female, retaining his male essence, his male memory and mentality; thus the Hindu god VISHNU merely takes on the form of the enchantress Mohini to seduce the DEMONS and steal back the elixir of immortality. The sexual transformation of the body is distinct from the transformation of the mind, memory, and personality; even when physical sexuality changes, the gender of the mind may remain unchanged.

Some religions argue that gender is itself a lie, since it positions as natural and inevitable what is primarily cultural, learned, and transformable; but it is also true, since like any myth it is deeply embedded in our linguistic and narrative assumptions, and thus a powerfully compelling force that cannot be ignored.

GENESIS \'je-nə-sis\, *Hebrew* Bereshit ("In the Beginning"), the first book of the OLD TESTAMENT. Genesis narrates the primeval history of the world (chapters 1–11) and the patriarchal history of the Israelite people (chapters 12–50). The primeval history includes the stories of the creation, the GARDEN OF EDEN, CAIN and ABEL, NOAH and the Flood, and the TOWER OF BABEL. The patriarchal history begins with the divine promise to ABRAHAM that "I will make of you a great nation" (12:2) and tells the stories of Abraham (chapters 12–25) and his descendants: ISAAC and his twin sons JACOB and ESAU (chapters 26–36) and Jacob's family, principally JOSEPH (chapters 37–50), whose story tells how the Israelites came to be in Egypt. Their deliverance is narrated in the following book of EXODUS.

Genesis must thus be seen as a part of a larger unit of material traditionally understood to comprise the first five books of the BIBLE, called the TORAH, or Pentateuch. Scholars have identified three literary traditions in Genesis, as in Deuteronomy, usually identified as the YAHWIST, ELOHIST, and PRIESTLY strains. The Yahwist strain, so called because it used the name YAHWEH (JEHOVAH) for God, is a Judaean rendition of the sacred story, perhaps written as early as 950 BCE. The Elohist strain, which designates God as ELOHIM, is traceable to the northern kingdom of Israel and was written 900–700 BCE. The Priestly strain, so called because of its cultic interests and regulations for priests, is usually dated in the 5th century BCE and is regarded as the law upon which EZRA and NEHEMIAH based their reform. Because each of these strains preserves materials much older than the time of their incorporation into a written work, Genesis contains extremely old oral and written traditions.

GENESIS RABBAH \rä-'bä\, systematic EXEGESIS of the book of GENESIS produced by the Judaic sages about 450 CE, which sets forth a coherent and original account of that book. In Genesis Rabbah the entire narrative is formed so as to point toward the sacred history of ISRAEL, meaning the Jewish people—their slavery and redemption; their coming Temple in Jerusalem; and their exile and salvation at the end of time. The deeds of the founders supply signals for the children about what is to come. So the biographies of ABRAHAM, ISAAC, and JACOB also constitute a protracted account of Israel's later history.

GENIUS, *plural* genii, in classical ROMAN RELIGION, an attendant spirit of a person or place.

In its earliest meaning in private cult, the *genius* of the Roman housefather and the *iuno*, or *juno*, of the housemother were worshiped. In no early document is there mention of the *genius* or *iuno* of a dead person. The *genius* and *iuno* were probably the male and female forms of the family's, or clan's, power of continuing itself by reproduction, which were in the keeping of the heads of the family for the time being and passed at death to their successors.

Owing to the rise of individualism and also to the prevalence of Greek ideas concerning a guardian spirit, or *daimon*, the *genius* lost its original meaning and came to be a sort of personification of the individual's natural desires and appetites. The *genius* came to be thought of as a sort of guardian angel, a higher self; the poet Horace half-seriously said that only the *genius* knows what makes one person so different from another, adding that he is a god who is born and dies with each one of us. This individual *genius* was worshiped by each individual, especially on his birthday. A few inscriptions even mention the *genius* of a dead person, as Christian epitaphs sometimes speak of his angel.

To show reverence for the genius of another or to swear by it was a mark of deep respect; hence the *genius* of Augustus and of his successors formed objects of popular cult. Thus, to worship the *genius Augusti* avoided affronting the feeling against worshiping any living emperor, which remained fairly strong in Italy.

GENIZAH \gə-,nē-'zä, -'nē-zə\ (Hebrew: "hiding place"), in JUDAISM, a repository for timeworn sacred manuscripts and ritual objects, generally located in the attic or cellar of a SYNAGOGUE. In the Middle Ages most synagogues had a *genizah*, because ceremonial burial (often with the remains of a pious, scholarly Jew) was thought to be the only fitting manner of disposing of sacred documents.

In 1896 Solomon Schechter investigated a *genizah* in the old Ezra synagogue in Cairo. In time, some 90,000 manuscripts were uncovered there, a cache so priceless that biblical scholars subsequently referred to the site simply as "the *genizah.*" This vast collection of liturgical, legal, commercial, and literary documents revolutionized the study of the medieval history of Palestinian and Middle Eastern Judaism. The manuscripts from the Cairo *genizah* are now preserved in many of the great libraries of the world.

GENTILE, one who is not Jewish. *See* ISRAEL.

GEORGE, SAINT \'jòrj\ (fl. 3rd century CE; d. traditionally Lydda, Palestine [now Lod, Israel]; feast day April 23), early Christian martyr who during the Middle Ages became an ideal of martial valor and selflessness. He is the patron saint of England. The most famous legend told about him is the story of his rescuing a Libyan king's daughter from a dragon and then slaying the monster in return for a promise by the king's subjects to be baptized.

GERD \'gerd\, in Norse MYTHOLOGY, the daughter of the GIANT Gymir and the wife of FREY.

GERMANIC RELIGION

Beliefs and ritual practices of the Germanic-speaking peoples before their conversion to CHRISTIANITY are collectively termed Germanic religion. Germanic culture extended, at various times, from the Black Sea to Greenland, and Germanic religion played an important role in shaping European civilization.

THE BEGINNING OF THE WORLD

Two stories of the beginning of the world are told in the three poems of the Elder EDDA, which were synthesized by Icelandic poet Snorri Sturluson in his *Prose Edda*. Snorri added certain details that were probably taken from sources now lost. The first story relates that in the beginning there was nothing but the void, GINNUNGAGAP. ODIN and his two brothers Vili and Vé raised up the earth, presumably from the sea, and when the sun touched the rocks vegetation sprang up. The gods came upon two tree trunks, ASKR AND EMBLA, and they endowed them with breath, reason, hair, and fair countenance, thus creating the first human couple.

In the second story, a primal GIANT, YMIR (Aurgelmir), grew out of drops spurted from the rivers called Élivágar. The giant's two legs gave birth to a six-headed son, and under his arms grew a boy and a girl. A primeval cow Audhumla (Auðumla) was formed from drops of melting rime. Four rivers of milk flowed from her udders, on which the giant Ymir fed. She licked salty stones into the shape of a man; this was Buri (Búri), the grandfather of Odin and his brothers. These three slaughtered Ymir and formed the earth from his body: his bones became rocks, his skull the sky, his blood the sea, his hair the trees, and his brain the clouds.

A central point in the cosmos is the evergreen ash, YGGDRASILL, whose three roots stretch to the worlds of death, frost-giants, and men. When RAGNARÖK (the end of the world) approaches, the tree will shiver and, presumably, fall. Beneath the tree stands a well, the source of Odin's wisdom.

THE GODS

The gods can be divided roughly into two tribes, AESIR and VANIR. At one time there was war between them, but when neither side could score a decisive victory

Snorri Sturluson's Prose Edda, *14th-century Swedish manuscript*
Werner Forman—Art Resource

they made peace and exchanged hostages. In this way Njörd (Njörðr), his son FREY, and presumably his daughter, FREYJA, came to dwell among the Aesir in AS-GARD and to be accepted in their hierarchy.

Odin (Óðinn). Literary sources state that Odin was the foremost of the Aesir, but the limited occurrence of Odin's name in place-names seems to indicate that his worship was not widespread. Odin was essentially the sovereign god, whom the Germanic dynasties originally regarded as their divine founder. He was the god of inspired mental activity and poetic inspiration, and he was the one who brought the sacred mead of poetry to the world of the gods.

This beverage was first brewed from the blood of a wise god, KVASIR, who was murdered by dwarfs. It later came into the hands of a giant and was stolen by Odin, who flew from the giant's stronghold in the shape of an eagle, carrying the sacred mead in his crop to regurgitate it in the dwelling of the gods. Therefore, the early skalds designate poetry as "Kvasir's blood," or "Odin's theft."

Odin needs heroes in the otherworld to join him in the final battle against the forces of destruction at the time of Ragnarök. Therefore, fallen warriors on the battlefield are said to go to his castle VALHALLA, the "Hall of the Slain," where they live in bliss, training for the ultimate combat. He is a powerful magician, having hanged himself on the cosmic tree Yggdrasill for nine nights, pierced with a spear, to gain the mastery of the runes and the knowledge of magic SPELLS.

Odin was a shape-changer and was said to make spirit journeys to other worlds like a SHAMAN. As god of the dead he was accompanied by carrion beasts, two wolves and two ravens. These birds kept him informed of what happened in the world, adding to the knowledge he had acquired by relinquishing one eye in the well of Mímir under the tree Yggdrasill.

Thor (þórr). THOR was worshiped widely, especially toward the end of the pre-Christian period. He is essentially the champion of the gods, being constantly involved in struggles with the giants. Peasants worshiped Thor because he brought the rains that ensured good crops, and he seems to have been popular with warriors everywhere. He was well known as Thunor in the Saxon and Jutish areas in England; the Saxons on the mainland venerated him as Thunær.

On account of a shared association with thunder, the Germanic god *þunraz* (Thor) was equated with JUPITER by the Romans; hence, the name of the day, Thursday (German: *Donnerstag*), for *Jovis dies* (Italian: *giovedi*). Thor traveled in a chariot drawn by goats, and later evidence suggested that thunder was thought of as the sound of his chariot.

Balder (Baldr). BALDER, the god named in the west Norse sources as another son of Odin, was a favorite among the gods. Although nearly impervious to harm,

(Opposite page) One-eyed Odin astride his steed Sleipnir; (left) Thor, armed with his hammer, battles the World Serpent; illustrations from the Poetic Edda, 13th-century Icelandic manuscript
The Granger Collection

he was killed by the hand of the blind god Höd through a scheme of the trickster LOKI. In Danish sources, however, Balder and Höd were rivals for the hand of NANNA. After many adventures, Höd killed Balder with a sword. In order to secure vengeance, Odin raped a princess, Rinda (Rindr), who bore a son, Bous, who avenged Balder's death by killing Höd. Balder's name occurs rarely in place-names, and it does not appear that his worship was widespread.

Loki. Although he was counted among the Aesir, Loki's father was a giant (Fárbauti; "Dangerous Striker"). Loki seems to symbolize impulsive, but malicious, intelligence, and is a trickster figure who can change sex and shape at will. Thus, he can give birth as well as beget offspring. The eight-legged horse of Odin, SLEIPNIR, was born of Loki in the shape of a mare. He fought with HEIMDALL in the shape of a seal for the possession of Freya's precious Brísingamen necklace, and he sneaked into Freyja's residence in the form of a fly to steal the necklace for Odin. According to an early poem, Odin and Loki had mixed their blood as foster brothers.

Heimdall. The god Heimdall (Heimdal[l]r) is rather enigmatic. His antagonism with Loki, with whom he struggles for the possession of the Brísingamen necklace, results in their killing each other in the Ragnarök, according to Snorri. Heimdall is of mysterious origin: he is the son of nine mothers, said to be sisters, all of whom bear names of giantesses, though they are mostly identified with the storm waves. Heimdall lives in Himinbjörg ("Heavenly Fells"), at the edge of the world of the Aesir. He guards Bifrost, the rainbow bridge to Asgard, the home of the gods, against the giants. Another myth makes Heimdall the father of mankind. He consorted with three women, from whom descend the three classes of men—serf (thrall), freeman (karl), and nobleman (jarl).

Tyr. TYR (Týr, Tír) must have been a major god in early times. He is said to be a son of Odin, but, according to one early poem, he was the son of a giant. In Roman times, he was equated with MARS, and hence *dies Martis* (Mars' day; French: *mardi*) became Tuesday (Icelandic: *Týs dagr*). In the Ragnarök he will face the hellhound Garm (Garmr), and they will kill each other. Tyr's cult is remembered in place-names, particularly those of Denmark.

Frigg. FRIGG is the wife of Odin. In the southern Germanic sources she appears as Friia or Frea, the spouse of Wodan. Snorri depicted her as the weeping mother of Balder, but historian Saxo Grammaticus described her as unchaste and makes her misconduct responsible for the temporary banishment of Odin. In Snorri's "Ynglinga saga," Odin's brothers Vili and Vé share her during his absence in a polyandric relationship. She has been equated with VENUS, and her name survives in Friday (Old English: Frigedæg) from *dies Veneris*, Venus' day.

The Vanir. The Vanir represent a distinct group of gods associated with wealth, health, and fertility. The best-known Vanir—Njörd, Frey, and probably Freyja—came as hostages to the Aesir. In his *Germania*, Roman historian Tacitus described among this number a goddess, NERTHUS, who was worshiped on an island that was probably in the Baltic Sea. Whatever symbol represented her was kept hidden in a grove and taken around once a year in a covered chariot. During her pageant, there was rejoicing and peace, and all weapons were laid aside. Afterward, she was bathed in a lake and returned to her grove, but those who participated in her LUSTRATION were drowned in the lake as a sacrifice.

Njörd, the father of the god Frey and the goddess Freyja, was essentially a god of the sea. Before coming to the Aesir, he was supposed to have begotten his two children with his (unnamed) sister. Since such incestuous unions were not allowed among the Aesir, Njörd afterward married SKADI (Skaði), daughter of the giant Thjazi. Evidence from place-names shows that Njörd was worshiped widely in Sweden and Norway, and he was one of the gods whom Icelanders invoked when they swore their most sacred OATHS.

Tyr with the wolf Fenrir, 6th-century bronze plaque from Torslunds parish, Öland, Sweden; in the Statens Historiska Museet, Stockholm
Werner Forman—Art Resource

Frey. Frey ("Lord") was also called Yngvi or Yngvi-Freyr, and this name suggests that he was the eponymous father of the north Germans whom Tacitus calls Ingvæones (Ingævones). A comparatively late source tells how the idol of Frey was carried in a chariot to bring fertility to the crops in Sweden. In an early saga of Iceland, where crops were little cultivated, Frey still appears as the guardian of the sacred wheatfield. His name often is found as the first element of a place-name, especially in eastern Sweden; the second element often means "wheatfield," or "meadow." The center of his cult was UPPSALA, and he was once said to be king of the Swedes. He was said to be ancestor of the Ynglingar, the Swedish royal family.

Freyja. Frey's sister, Freyja, was the goddess of love, sexuality, wealth, and fertility. She practiced a disreputable kind of magic, called *seiðr*, which she taught Odin. She was known under various names, some obscure such as Mardöll, and others, such as Sýr ("Sow"), referring to her association with animals. Taking half of those who fall in battle, Freyja had some affinity with the deities of death.

This relation of fertility goddesses with the otherworld is already illustrated by the Germanic mother goddesses or matronae, whose cult was widespread along the lower Rhine in Roman imperial times. They are often represented with CHTHONIC (Underworld) symbols such as the dog, the snake, or baskets of fruit. The same applies to the goddess Nehalennia, worshiped near the mouth of the Scheldt River.

Guardian spirits. Medieval writers frequently allude to female guardian spirits called *dísir* and *fylgjur*. Sacrifice to the *dísir* was offered at the beginning of winter, involving a festive meal and apparently a private ceremony, suggesting that the *dísir* belonged to one house, one district, or one family. In an Eddic poem the *dísir* are described as "dead women," and they may have been dead female ancestors, assuring the prosperity of their descendants.

The elves (*álfar*) also stood in fairly close relationship to men. An Icelandic Christian poet of the 11th century described a sacrifice to the elves early in winter among the Swedes. The elves lived in mounds or rocks. An old saga tells how the blood of a bull was smeared on a mound inhabited by elves.

A good deal is told of land spirits (*landvoettir*). According to the pre-Christian law of Iceland, no one must approach the land in a ship bearing a dragonhead, lest he frighten the land spirits. An Icelandic poet, cursing the king and queen of Norway, enjoined the *landvoettir* to drive them from the land.

Dwarfs. Dwarfs (*dvergar*) were very wise and expert craftsmen who forged practically all of the treasures of the gods, in particular Thor's hammer. Snorri said that they originated as maggots in the flesh of the slaughtered giant Ymir. Four of them are supporting the sky, made of Ymir's skull. They may have been originally nature spirits or demonic beings, living in mountain caves, but they generally were friendly to man.

WORSHIP

Rites often were conducted in the open or in groves and forests. The HUMAN SACRIFICE to the tribal god of the Semnones, described by Tacitus, took place in a sacred grove; other examples of sacred groves include the one in which Nerthus usually resides. Tacitus does, however, mention temples in Germany, though they were probably few. Old English laws mention fenced places around a stone, tree, or other object of worship. In Scandinavia, sacrifice was brought to groves and waterfalls.

The word *hof*, commonly applied to temples in the literature of Iceland, seems to belong to the later rather than to the earlier period; one temple is described as having two compartments, one of which contained the images of the gods. Temples on the mainland of Scandinavia were probably built of wood, though the famous temple at Uppsala, Sweden, was said to have been covered in gold.

Sacrifice took different forms. A man might sacrifice an ox to a god or smear an elf mound with bull's blood. Roman authors mention the sacrifice of prisoners of war to the gods of victory. All kinds of cattle might be slaughtered, and blood might be sprinkled inside and outside dwellings; the meat was consumed and toasts were drunk to the gods. Every nine years a great festival was held at Uppsala, and sacrifice was conducted in a sacred grove that stood beside the temple. The victims, human and animal, were hung on trees. One of the trees in this grove was holier than all the others and beneath it lay a well into which a living man would be plunged.

ESCHATOLOGY AND DEATH CUSTOMS

No unified conception of the afterlife is known among the Germanic religions. Some may have believed that fallen warriors would go to Valhalla to live happily with Odin until the Ragnarök, but it is unlikely that this belief was widespread. Others seemed to believe that there was no afterlife. The presence of ships or boats in graves, and occasionally of chariots and horses, may suggest that the dead were thought to go on a journey to the otherworld. Some records imply that the dead needed company; a wife, mistress, or servant would be buried with them. Some stories suggest the existence of a belief in rebirth. On the whole, beliefs in afterlife seem rather gloomy: the dead pass, perhaps by slow stages, to a dark, misty world called NIFLHEIM (Niflheimr).

The final struggle. The end of the world is designated Ragnarök ("Fate of the Gods")—in German *Götterdammerung*, ("twilight of the gods"). Through their own efforts, and especially because of the strength of Thor, the gods have kept the DEMONS of destruction at bay. The wolf monster FENRIR and Loki have been chained, but they will break loose. Giants and other monsters will attack the world of gods and humans. Odin will fight the wolf and lose his life, to be avenged by his son Vidar (Víðarr), who will pierce the beast to the heart. According to another Eddic poem, the wolf will swallow Odin and, in revenge, his son will tear the jaws of the beast asunder. Thor will face the World Serpent, and they will kill each other. The sun will turn black, the stars vanish, and fire will play against the firmament. The earth will sink into the sea but will rise again, purified and renewed. Unsown fields will bear wheat. Balder and his innocent slayer, Höd, will return to inhabit the dwellings of gods. Worthy people will live forever in a shining hall thatched with gold.

GERSHOM BEN JUDAH \'ger-shəm-ben-'jü-də\ (b. *c.* 960, Metz, Lorraine [now in France]—d. 1028/40, Mainz, Franconia [Germany]), eminent rabbinical scholar who proposed a far-reaching series of legal enactments (*taqqanot*) that profoundly molded the social institutions of medieval European JUDAISM. He was called the light of the exile and also Rabbenu ("Our Teacher").

As head of the rabbinic academy at Mainz, he was a pioneer in bringing the learning of the Talmudic academies at Babylon and Palestine to western Europe. At synods of community leaders he proposed his *taqqanot*, which included the prohibition of polygamy (permitted by biblical and Talmudic law but already mostly unpracticed), and interdiction of the husband's right to divorce without the wife's consent.

He wrote many RESPONSA (authoritative answers to questions about Jewish law), worked on a critical text of the TALMUD and the Masora (6th–10th-century annotated texts) and transmitted to his students an extensive oral commentary on the Talmud. All subsequent rabbinic students in western Europe considered themselves, in the words of the renowned medieval French Jewish commentator RASHI (1040–1105), "students of his students."

GET \'get\, *also spelled* gett, *Hebrew* geṭ ("bill of divorce"), *plural* gittin \gē-'tēn, 'gi-tin\, Jewish document of divorce written in Aramaic according to a prescribed formula (day of the week, day of the month, and year reckoned from the creation of the world, city of husband's birth and its exact location, name of husband, city of husband's residence and its exact location, name of wife, city of wife's residence and its exact location, statement freeing wife to remarry whomsoever she chooses, signatures of two witnesses). Orthodox and Conservative Jews recognize it as the only valid instrument for severing a marriage bond. Rabbinic courts outside Israel require a civil divorce before a get is issued. Reform Jews disregard Talmudic divorce laws and hence require no get but simply accept the ruling of a civil divorce court as sufficient in itself.

A religious divorce becomes effective when the husband, having obtained a get from a rabbinic court, drops the document into the cupped hands of his willing wife in the presence of two witnesses and the three members of the court.

Though, strictly speaking, Jewish religious law permits a man to divorce his wife at any time for any reason, the rights of the women are protected by stipulations written into the marriage contract (*ketubbah*), and, since the 11th century, divorce has not been granted in the ASHKENAZI (German) rite without the wife's consent. In practice, therefore, the only basic requirement for divorce is the mutual consent of husband and wife.

Under certain special circumstances, such as APOSTASY, impotence, insanity, or refusal to cohabit, Jewish law entitles one party to compel the other to agree to a divorce.

GETHSEMANE \geth-'se-mə-nē\, garden across the Kidron Valley on the Mount of Olives (Hebrew *Har ha-Zetim*), a mile-long ridge paralleling the eastern part of Jerusalem, where JESUS is said to have prayed on the night of his arrest before his CRUCIFIXION. The name Gethsemane (Hebrew *gat shemanim*, "oil press") suggests that the garden was a grove of olive trees in which was located an oil press.

Though the exact location of Gethsemane cannot be determined with certainty, Armenian, Greek, Latin, and Russian churches have accepted an olive grove on the western slope of the Mount of Olives as the site. Another tradition locates Gethsemane at a place now called the Grotto of the Agony, near a bridge that crosses the valley. At another possible location, south of this site in a garden containing old olive trees, is a Latin church erected by FRANCISCAN monks on the ruins of a 4th-century church.

GHAYBA \'ḡī-bə\ (Arabic: "absence," or "concealment"), Islamic doctrine, especially among such SHIʿITE groups as the ITHNĀ ʿASHARĪYA, or "Twelvers." The term refers to the disappearance of the 12th and last IMAM (leader), MUHAMMAD AL-MAHDĪ AL-ḤUJJAH, in 878.

Ghayba is applied loosely to anyone whom God has withdrawn from the world and kept invisible to the eyes of ordinary men. The life of such a blessed person is thought to be miraculously prolonged by God through many generations. The Shiʿites maintain that their imams, even though invisible, still live and sometimes return to human society to maintain order and to guide their followers along the right path. The *ghayba* of the MAHDI ("divinely guided one") will end when the Mahdi finally appears in the last days of the world.

The Sufis understood *ghayba* to mean the absence in the heart of all thoughts except those of God. It is the *fanāʾ* ("passing away") of the carnal self, not a goal in itself but rather a stage that leads naturally to *ḥuḍūr* (presence) in God. (*See* SUFISM.)

GHAZĀLĪ, AL- \ˌäl-ḡä-'za-lē\, *also spelled* Al-Ghazzālī, *in full* Abū Ḥāmid Muhammad ibn Muhammad al-Ṭūsī al-Ghazālī (b. 1058, Ṭūs, Iran—d. Dec. 18, 1111, Ṭūs), Muslim theologian and mystic whose great work, *Iḥyāʾ ʿulūm al-dīn* ("The Revival of the Religious Sciences"), sought to reconcile the mysticism of SUFISM with the SUNNI tradition of Islamic learning.

Al-Ghazālī was educated in his native city, then in Jorjān, and finally at Nishapur, where his teacher was al-Juwaynī. After his teacher's death in 1085, al-Ghazālī was invited to go to the court of Niẓām al-Mulk, the powerful vizier of the Seljuq SULTANS, who in 1091 appointed him chief professor in the Niẓāmīyah college in Baghdad. While lecturing, al-Ghazālī was also mastering and criticizing the Neoplatonist philosophies of AL-FĀRĀBĪ and IBN SĪNĀ (Avicenna). He passed through a spiritual crisis, and in November 1095 he abandoned his career and left Baghdad on the pretext of going on PILGRIMAGE to MECCA. He disposed of his wealth and adopted the life of a poor Sufi, or mystic. After spending some time in Damascus and Jerusalem, with a visit to Mecca in November 1096, al-Ghazālī settled in Ṭūs, where Sufi disciples joined him in a virtually monastic communal life. In 1106 he was persuaded to return to teaching at the Niẓāmīyah college at Nishapur. A "renewer" of the life of ISLAM was expected at the beginning of each century, and his friends argued that he was the "renewer" for the century beginning in September 1106. He continued lecturing in Nishapur at least until 1110.

More than 400 works are ascribed to al-Ghazālī, but he probably did not write nearly so many. At least 50 genuine works are extant. Al-Ghazālī's greatest work is *Iḥyāʾ ʿulūm al-dīn*. In 40 "books" he explained the doctrines and practices of Islam and showed how these can be made the basis of a profound devotional life, leading to the higher stages of Sufism, or MYSTICISM. The relation of mystical experience to other forms of cognition is discussed in *The Niche for Lights*. Al-Ghazālī's abandonment of his career and adoption of a mystical, monastic life is defended in the autobiographical work *The Confessions of Al Ghazzali*.

His philosophical studies began with treatises on logic and culminated in the *Incoherence of the Philosophers*, in which he defended Islam against such philosophers as Ibn Sīnā who sought to demonstrate certain speculative views contrary to accepted Islamic teaching. In preparation for this major treatise, he published an objective account of *Maqāṣid al-falāsifah* ("The Aims of the Philosophers"; *i.e.*, their teachings). This book was influential in Europe and was one of the first to be translated from Arabic to Latin (12th century).

Most of his activity was in the field of jurisprudence and theology. Toward the end of his life he completed a work on general legal principles, *Al-Mustaṣfā* ("The Choice Part," or "Essentials"). His compendium of standard theological doctrine, *Al-Iqtiṣād fī al-i'tiqād* ("The Just Mean in Belief"), was probably written before he became a mystic, but there is nothing in the authentic writings to show that he rejected these doctrines, even though he came to hold that theology was inferior to mystical experience.

GHOST DANCE, either of two distinct religious movements that represented attempts of Native Americans (*see* NATIVE AMERICAN RELIGIONS) in the western United States to rehabilitate their traditional cultures. Both arose from Northern Paiute prophet-dreamers in western Nevada, who announced the imminent return of the dead (hence "ghost"), the ousting of the whites, and the restoration of Indian lands, food supplies, and way of life. These ends

---

Buckskin Ghost Dance dress with painted design of birds, turtle, and stars, Arapaho

Museum of the North American Indian, New York—The Bridgeman Art Library

would be hastened by the dances and songs revealed to the prophets in their visits to the spirit world and also by strict observance of a moral code that forbade war against Indians or whites. Many dancers fell into trances and received new songs from the dead they met in visions or were healed by Ghost Dance rituals.

The first Ghost Dance developed in 1869 around the trances of Wodziwob ("Gray Hair") and in 1871–73 spread to California and Oregon tribes; it soon died out or was transformed into other cults. The second derived from WOVOKA ("The Cutter"; *c.* 1856–1932), whose father, Tävibo ("White Man"), a Northern Paiute, had assisted Wodziwob. During a solar eclipse in January 1889, Wovoka had a vision of dying, speaking with God in heaven, and being commissioned to teach the new dance and to convey the millennial message that the dead would have a reunion with the living. Subsequently he displayed STIGMATA on hands and feet, which encouraged belief in him as a new MESSIAH, come to the Indians.

The Ghost Dance, a ritual round-dance conducted over four or five consecutive nights, spread to various tribes, including the Arapahoe, Caddo, Cheyenne, and Kiowa. It was also taken up by the Sioux, where its arrival coincided with the Sioux uprising of 1890 that culminated in their massacre by U.S. troops at Wounded Knee, S.D. The Ghost Dance was wrongly blamed for this uprising.

The second Ghost Dance continued in the 20th century in attenuated form among a few tribes. Both religious movements helped to reshape traditional shamanism (a belief system based on the healing and psychic transformation powers of the SHAMAN, or MEDICINE MAN).

GHOUL \'gül\, *Arabic* ghūl, in popular legend, demonic being believed to inhabit burial grounds and other deserted places. In ancient Arabic MYTHOLOGY, *ghūl*s belonged to a diabolic class of JINN (spirits) and were said to be the offspring of IBLĪS. They were capable of constantly changing form, but their presence was always recognizable by their unalterable sign: ass's hooves.

Considered female by the ancients, the *ghūl* was often confused with the *sila*, also female; the *sila*, however, was a witchlike species of jinn, immutable in shape. A *ghūl* stalked the desert, often in the guise of an attractive woman, trying to distract travelers, and, when successful, killed and ate them. The sole defense that one had against a *ghūl* was to strike it dead in one blow; a second blow would only bring it back to life again.

The *ghūl*, as a vivid figure in the Bedouin imagination, appeared in pre-Islamic Arabic poetry, notably that of Ta'abbata Sharran. In North Africa it was easily assimilated into an ancient Berber FOLKLORE already rich in DEMONS and fantastic creatures. Modern Arabs use *ghūl* to designate a human or demonic cannibal and frequently employ the word to frighten disobedient children.

Anglicized as "ghoul," the word entered English tradition and was further identified as a grave-robbing creature that feeds on dead bodies and on children. In the West ghouls are thought to assume disguises and to set fires at night to lure travelers away from the main roads.

GHULĀM AḤMAD, MĪRZĀ \'gü-lam-'aḵ-mad\ (b. *c.* 1839, Qādiān, India—d. May 26, 1908, India), Indian Muslim leader who founded an important Muslim sect known as the AḤMADĪYA.

The son of a prosperous family, Ghulām Aḥmad received an education in Persian and Arabic, after which he led a life of contemplation and religious study. He claimed to hear voices and declared in 1889 that he had had a revelation in which God had entitled him to receive *bayʿat* (an oath of allegiance). Soon he gathered a small group of devoted disciples. From this point on his influence and following steadily increased, as did opposition from the orthodox Muslim community.

Ghulām Aḥmad claimed not only that he was the Mahdi and a reappearance (*burūz*) of the Prophet MUHAMMAD but also that he was JESUS CHRIST and the Hindu god KRISHNA returned to earth. A number of his teachings were incorporated into the beliefs of the Aḥmadīya. While he made an attempt to copy the centralized missionary organizations and schools of the Christians, he had little interest in reconciling Christian and Muslim religious doctrine and evidently wanted only to be more effective in his struggle to supplant Western influences. After his death, his devotees formed a community of believers and elected a *khalīfa* (CALIPH) to lead them.

GHULĀT \'g̈ü-làt\ (Arabic, "extremists"), in ISLAM, a designation for sectarian groups holding beliefs not conforming to doctrines held by dominant SUNNI and SHIʿITE religious authorities. Their views are heterogeneous and include beliefs in God's human incarnation, ANTHROPOMORPHISM (*tashbīḥ*), the existence of prophets after MUHAMMAD, transmigration of souls (*tanāsukh*), and the disappearance (GHAYBA) and return (*rajʿa*) of messianic leaders.

The beginnings of the *ghulāt* are usually identified with ʿAbd Allāh ibn Sabā al-Ḥimyarī, a 7th-century convert from JUDAISM, who addressed ʿALĪ as God and maintained that ʿAlī never really died and would return from heaven to initiate a messianic age. Such beliefs appear to have developed in Iraq, where Jewish messianic movements were also proliferating, but were not considered "extreme" until several centuries later. Many *ghulāt* ideas came to be associated with ʿAlī (the fourth CALIPH) and other relatives of Muhammad, forming a doctrinal matrix for Shiʿite tenets. Thus, although Twelver (Imami) Shiʿite doctrine rejected anthropomorphism, divinization of the IMAMS, and transmigration, it embraced belief in the messianic 12th imam, the MAHDI, as an essential principle.

Some strands of SUFISM have been branded as "extreme," and in the late 20th century the term was also used pejoratively by proponents of the status quo to describe radical movements that were seeking to replace existing governments with new Islamic ones.

GIANT, huge mythical being, usually humanlike in form, often associated with barbarism and disorder. The term derives (through Latin) from the Giants (Gigantes) of Greek MYTHOLOGY, who were savage creatures often depicted with men's bodies terminating in serpentine legs. According to the Greek poet Hesiod, they were offspring of GAEA and OURANUS, born when Gaea (the Earth) absorbed the blood of Ouranus' severed genitals. The Gigantomachy was a desperate struggle between the Giants and the Olympians. The gods finally prevailed through the aid of HERACLES, and the Giants were slain. Many of them were believed to lie buried under mountains and to indicate their presence by volcanic fires and earthquakes. The Gigantomachy became a popular artistic theme, interpreted as a symbol of the triumph of Hellenism over barbarism, of good over evil.

Medieval European towns often had tutelary giants whose effigies were carried in PROCESSION. In London the giant figures of Gog and Magog are said to represent two Cor-

nish giants made captive by Brutus, the legendary founder of Britain. The 40-foot effigy of Druon Antigonus at Antwerp and the 22-foot figure of Gayant at Douai, France, preserve similar traditions.

In most European tales, giants appear as cruel and stupid, given to CANNIBALISM, and often one-eyed. Heroes who killed them often did so more by wit than by strength. Although kindly giants occur (*e.g.,* Rübezahl, who lived in the Bohemian forest), most were feared and hated; but marriages between their daughters and the hero were possible.

Hill figures, such as the giant of Cerne cut in the chalk near Cerne Abbas, Dorset, as well as megalithic monuments and long BARROWS, suggested giant builders of the past; and an ancient European tradition held that people had once been taller and stronger in a golden age.

GIDEON \'gi-dē-ən\, *also spelled* Gedeon, *also called* Jerubbaal \,jer-ə-'bāl, -'bäl, 'jer-ə-,\, *or* Jerobaal, a judge and hero-liberator of ISRAEL whose deeds are described in the Book of Judges. The author apparently juxtaposed two traditional accounts from his sources in order to emphasize Israel's MONOTHEISM and its duty to destroy IDOLATRY. Accordingly, in one account Gideon led his clansmen of the tribe of MANASSEH in slaying the MIDIANITES (Judges 6:11–7:25); but, influenced by the cult of his adversaries, he fashioned an idolatrous image from the spoils captured from the Midianites and induced Israel into immorality (Judges 8:24–28). In the parallel version he replaced the idol and altar of the local deity BAAL with the worship of YAHWEH, who consequently inspired Gideon and his clan to destroy the Midianites and their chiefs as a sign of Yahweh's supremacy over Baal (Judges 6:25–32). The story is also important for showing the development of a monarchy in Israel under Gideon's son Abimelech (Judges 9).

GIKATILLA, JOSEPH \,hē-kä-'tēl-yä\ (b. 1248, Medinaceli, Castile, Spain—d. *c.* 1305, Peñafiel), major Spanish Qabbalist whose writings influenced those of MOSES DE LEÓN, presumed author of the SEFER HA-ZOHAR ("Book of Splendor"), an important work of Jewish MYSTICISM. Gikatilla's early studies of philosophy and the TALMUD were a continuing influence on his attempt to reconcile philosophy with the QABBALAH.

Gikatilla was a pupil of Abraham Abulafia, a profound student of the Qabbalah. Under his influence, the 26-year-old Gikatilla wrote his seminal *Ginnat e'goz* ("Nut Orchard"), taking his title from the Song of Solomon 6:11. In Gikatilla's lexicon, the nut is an emblem of mysticism itself, while *Ginnat* employs the initial letters of three different names for methods of esoteric EXEGESIS. Gikatilla's book greatly influenced his contemporary and probable friend, Moses de León. Gikatilla was, in turn, influenced by the *Zohar,* as evidenced by his next major work, *Sha'are'ora* ("Gates of Light"), an account of Qabbalist symbolism.

GILGAMESH \'gil-gə-,mesh, gil-'gä-məsh\, the best known of all ancient heroes of MESOPOTAMIAN RELIGION.

The fullest extant text of the Gilgamesh epic is on 12 incomplete Akkadian-language tablets found at Nineveh in the library of the Assyrian king Ashurbanipal (reigned 668–627 BCE). The gaps that occur in the tablets have been partly filled by fragments found elsewhere. In addition, five short poems in Sumerian are known from tablets that were written during the first half of the 2nd millennium BCE; the poems have been entitled "Gilgamesh and Huwawa," "Gilgamesh and the Bull of Heaven," "Gilgamesh and Agga of

Kish," "Gilgamesh, Enkidu, and the Nether World," and "The Death of Gilgamesh."

The Gilgamesh of the poems and of the epic tablets was probably the Gilgamesh who ruled at Uruk in southern Mesopotamia sometime during the first half of the 3rd millennium BCE and who was thus a contemporary of Agga, ruler of Kish. Gilgamesh of Uruk was also mentioned in the Sumerian list of kings as reigning after the flood. There is, however, no historical evidence for the exploits narrated in poems and epic.

The Ninevite version of the epic begins with a prologue in praise of Gilgamesh, part divine and part human, the great builder and warrior, knower of all things on land and sea. In order to curb Gilgamesh's seemingly harsh rule, the god ANU caused the creation of ENKIDU, a wild man who at first lived among animals. Soon, however, Enkidu was initiated into the ways of city life and traveled to Uruk, where Gilgamesh awaited him. Tablet II describes a trial of strength between the two men in which Gilgamesh was the victor; thereafter, Enkidu was the friend and companion (in Sumerian texts, the servant) of Gilgamesh. In Tablets III–V the two men set out together against Huwawa (Humbaba), the divinely appointed guardian of a remote cedar forest, but the rest of the engagement is not recorded in the surviving fragments. In Tablet VI Gilgamesh, who had returned to Uruk, rejected the marriage proposal of ISHTAR, the goddess of love, and then,

Gilgamesh, ancient relief sculpture; in the Louvre, Paris
Alinari—Art Resource

with Enkidu's aid, killed the divine bull that she had sent to destroy him. Tablet VII begins with Enkidu's account of a dream in which the gods Anu, EA, and SHAMASH decided that he must die for slaying the bull. Enkidu then fell ill and dreamed of the "house of dust" that awaited him. Gilgamesh's lament for his friend and the state funeral of Enkidu are narrated in Tablet VIII. Afterward, Gilgamesh made a dangerous journey (Tablets IX and X) in search of UTNAPISHTIM, the survivor of the Babylonian flood, to learn from him how to escape death. He finally reached Utnapishtim, who told him the story of the flood and showed him where to find a plant that would renew youth (Tablet XI). But after Gilgamesh obtained the plant, it was seized by a serpent, and Gilgamesh unhappily returned to Uruk. An appendage to the epic, Tablet XII, relates the loss of objects called *pukku* and *mikku* (perhaps "drum" and "drumstick") given to Gilgamesh by Ishtar. The epic ends with the return of the spirit of Enkidu, who promised to recover the objects and then gave a grim report on the Underworld.

GINNUNGAGAP \'gin-ˌnüŋ-gä-ˌgäp, 'yin-\, in Norse and Germanic mythology, the void in which the world was created. The story is told, with much variation, in three poems of the *Elder* EDDA, and a synthesis of these is given by Snorri Sturluson in his *Prose Edda*.

GIRDLE TIE, *also called* Blood of Isis, in EGYPTIAN RELIGION, protective AMULET formed like a knot and made of gold, carnelian, or red glazed-ware. Most samples of the girdle tie have been found tied around the necks of mummies; the amulets were intended to protect the dead from all that was harmful in the afterlife.

GIRI \'gē-rē\ ("duty," "obligation"), traditional Japanese ideal of social obligation and reciprocity that still informs contemporary social life in Japan. A concept that developed in relation to feudal codes of behavior that defined the relationship between a lord and his subjects (especially the warrior class, or samurai), *giri* was a principle of loyalty and honor that demanded the repayment of social debts before any consideration was given to personal feelings, or *ninjō*. The plays of Chikamatsu Monzaemon (1653–1725) and the films of Ozu Yasujiro (1903–63) are especially illustrative of the moral tensions between *giri* and *ninjō*.

GITA PRESS \'gē-ˌtä\, HINDUISM's largest printer, publisher, and distributor of religious literature. Envisaged as the Hindu equivalent of a Christian Bible society, Gita Press was established on April 29, 1923, in the town of Gorakhpur by altruistic businessmen under the direction of Jayadayal Goyandka (1885–1965), who was joined several years later by Hanumanprasad Poddar (1892–1971). This nonprofit organization made nominally priced copies of Hindu sacred texts accessible on an unprecedented scale, with "neutral," simple-to-follow translations, abridgments, and commentaries written in the Hindi vernacular. The Gita Press's religious-text publication program has been the version of the Hindu canon most widely available in India during the past fifty years.

Distributed through Gita Press stores, mobile vans, and public outlets, the press's texts gained an established familiarity as sources of important textual material and as objects to be handled in prescribed, ritualistic ways. By the closing years of the 20th century, the press had published some 48 million copies of the RĀMCARITMĀNAS; 40 million copies of the BHAGAVAD GĪTĀ; 15 million copies of Hindu classics such as the PURĀṆAS and UPANISHADS; as well as a staggering 147 million scripture-based booklets, pamphlets, and tracts dealing with various topics relating to spiritual growth. These were written mostly by Poddar, Goyandka, and the present head trustee of the press, Swami Ramsukhdas (b. 1912).

The magazine *Kalyāṇ*, founded by Poddar in 1926, is perhaps one of Gita Press's best-known publications. The most widely read religious periodical ever published in India, *Kalyāṇ* currently has over 230,000 subscribers and an estimated pass-on rate of 10 times that figure. As such, the magazine remains at the forefront of populist efforts to proclaim

Hindu solidarity (*saṅgāṭhan*), pious self-identity, and "normative" cultural values.

GĪTAGOVINDA \\'gē-tə-gō-'vin-də\ (Sanskrit: literally, "Govinda of [*i.e.*, celebrated in] Song"), lyrical poem celebrating the romance of the divine cowherd KRISHNA and his beloved, RĀDHĀ. The poem was written in Sanskrit by JAYADEVA, who was attached to the Bengali court of King Lakṣmaṇa Sena (late 12th century). The name Govinda is a Middle Indo-Aryan descendant of Sanskrit *Gopendra* ("chief cowherd"), an epithet of Krishna.

The highly original form of the poem, which inspired many later imitations, intersperses the recitative stanzas with 24 songs, usually 8 stanzas in length. The religious drama of the worshiper's yearning for God is expressed through the idiom of Rādhā and Krishna's courtship and love. Central to the plot is the mutual longing of these two and the efforts of a go-between to reconcile the profligate Krishna with the sulking anger of his favorite lover, Rādhā. Ultimately this is achieved, and the poem concludes with a celebration of her "victory" over him. The *Gītagovinda* thus became a major document for religious communities whose piety focuses on Rādhā as much as on Krishna, such as the one established by CAITANYA, the 15th–16th-century Bengali saint.

The *Gītagovinda* is sung today at *bhajan* and KĪRTAN sessions (gatherings for devotion through song) throughout India. Until recently, it was also performed as temple dance, and its verses continue to inspire dances in various regional styles, especially BHĀRATA NĀṬYA and *Orissi*, wherever Indian culture flourishes. The *Gītagovinda* is one of the most frequently illustrated Indian texts.

GLAUCUS \\'glȯ-kəs\ (Greek: "Gleaming"), name of several figures in Greek mythology, the most important of whom were the following:

Glaucus, surnamed Pontius, was a sea divinity. Originally a fisherman and diver of Boeotia, he ate a magical herb and leaped into the sea and was changed into a god and endowed with the gift of PROPHECY. Another version made him spring into the sea for love of the sea god Melicertes, with whom he was often identified. In art he was depicted as a merman covered with shells and seaweed.

Glaucus of Potniae near Thebes was the son of SISYPHUS (king of Corinth) by his wife Merope and father of the hero BELLEROPHON. According to one legend, he fed his mares on human flesh and was torn to pieces by them.

Glaucus, the young son of the Cretan king MINOS and his wife Pasiphaë, fell into a jar of honey and was smothered. The seer Polyeidus discovered the child but on confessing his inability to restore him to life was shut up in a vault with the corpse. There he killed a serpent and, seeing it revived by a companion that laid a certain herb upon it, brought the dead Glaucus back to life with the same herb.

Glaucus, grandson of Bellerophon, was a Lycian prince who assisted PRIAM, king of Troy, in the Trojan War. When he found himself opposed in combat to his friend DIOMEDES, they ceased fighting and exchanged armor. Since the equipment of Glaucus was golden and that of Diomedes bronze, the expression "gold for bronze" (*Iliad*, vi, 236) came to be used proverbially for a bad exchange.

GNOSTICISM \\'näs-tə-ˌsi-zəm\, term based on the Greek word *gnosis* ("knowledge") and first coined in the 17th century by the Protestant Henry More. He understood Gnosticism to be false PROPHECY that seduces Christians to IDOLA-

Rādhā and Krishna in the garden, miniature in the Rajasthan style from a c. *1575 version of the* Gītagovinda
Scala—Art Resource

TRY, and he used the term to denigrate ROMAN CATHOLICISM by calling it "a spice of the old abhorred Gnosticism"—in short, he used the term as a generic term for ancient Christian HERESY. In the following centuries, church historians associated Gnosticism especially with the groups and teachings denounced by 2nd- and 3rd-century Christian heresy-fighters, notably IRENAEUS, CLEMENT OF ALEXANDRIA, TERTULLIAN, HIPPOLYTUS, EPIPHANIUS, and the Neoplatonist philosopher Plotinus. Reliance on these hostile reports led historians to describe Gnosticism as a radically dualistic, world-denying, and body-hating tradition that emphasized salvation through esoteric revelation and mystical spirituality. The term Gnosticism has also come to be used without much precision in psychology, literary studies, art, politics, and philosophy, to refer to any religion of salvation by mystical knowledge or any extreme form of DUALISM, especially anti-cosmic and ascetic forms of religious expression.

In the late 19th and 20th centuries, new acquaintance with Mandaeans and Manichaean texts, as well as discoveries of Coptic texts from Egypt, especially the Nag Hammadi codices, led to a reconsideration of Gnosticism. Rather than seeing it as a single tradition with one origin and line of development, the new evidence points toward enormous variety, leading to new groupings of texts and traditions, each with different intellectual and sociological histories.

Some of the Coptic texts represent lesser-known varieties of ancient CHRISTIANITY—for example, the *Gospel of Thomas* (a collection of the sayings of Jesus) or the *Gospel of Mary* (which portrays MARY MAGDALENE as a leading apostle). Both of these texts emphasize the importance of Jesus' teachings for salvation, not his death and RESURRECTION. Another category of texts belongs to groups with ties to the 2nd-century Christian teacher VALENTINUS, including a copy of his own writing *The Gospel of Truth*. Other texts are best considered as belonging to distinct religious traditions, especially Hermeticism, Mandaeism, and MANICHAEISM.

The materials with the best claim to the designation "Gnosticism" are the Sethian texts, first grouped together by Hans-Martin Schenke on the basis of intellectual and ritual similarities. Bentley Layton has strengthened the social-historical basis of this category by showing a connection between the Sethian texts and an ancient group known as the *gnostikoi* ("Gnostics").

Often characterized as "syncretistic," Sethian myth is a product of ancient urban pluralism. Sethian mythmakers shaped a distinctive view of the world out of the most prestigious religious and intellectual materials available to them. A good example is *The Apocryphon of John*, a grand narrative encompassing the nature of God and the divine world, the origins of the universe and humanity, the nature of evil, and salvation.

The Apocryphon of John envisions the transcendent God and the Divine Realm as an ideal of absolute goodness, truth, and stability. God is the divine source and ruler of everything above. Where Sethian myth departs radically from other ancient myth is in conceiving of a tragic rupture in the outpouring of divine being in creation. According to the story, the youngest of the heavenly beings, Sophia, decided to create alone without the knowledge or consent of the Spirit or her male partner. Sophia's child, the deficient product of her ignorance and passion, was ignorant, disobedient, and willfully arrogant. He created ARCHONS and ANGELS to serve him and falsely declared himself to be the only true God.

A dramatic retelling of the GENESIS creation story follows in which God appears as a wicked being who sought to dominate humanity unjustly by enslaving them to the passions and mortality of physical existence, withholding moral knowledge and eternal life. God was jealous of the humans because they were superior to him, created in the likeness of the true God above. Sophia had planted the divine spirit within them in order to save them from this unjust domination. Male and female saviors (including Christ) were sent from the world above to overcome the deception of the world rulers and instruct humanity in the knowledge of the true God and humanity's own divine nature. The saviors worked to protect people from the assaults of the wicked powers who rule the world. In the end, all humanity (except apostates) are destined for salvation. At death, they will leave the prison of the body and the world and return to the divine rule of the transcendent God, their true father.

According to this story, evil is primarily a matter of unjust rule, a rupture caused by disobedience to appropriate authority. The problem addressed by Sethian myth is a strongly perceived gap between the ideals of its age and the realities of lived experience. Sethian myth is the product not of rebellion but of a sense of betrayal. It shows a deep commitment to the values of its age, including an uncompromising belief in the goodness of God and a utopian desire for justice. But embedded in this message of hope for salvation is a sharp social criticism. For *The Apocryphon of John*, practices of spiritual development went hand-in-hand with condemnation of the injustices of the world.

The Sethians' biting criticism of the world order did not go unnoted. The myth's portrayal of the flawed nature of the world and its creator offended nearly everyone: Jewish RABBIS, Christian theologians, and Neoplatonic philosophers. In time, some Sethian thinkers (such as Marsanes and Allogenes) would soften their criticism and turn their focus more deeply upon the cultivation of inner spirituality and mystical knowledge. But the ire they aroused would leave them branded as the most exemplary form of heresy the Western world ever produced.

GOBIND SINGH \gō-'bin-də-'siŋ-gə, 'gō-,bind-'siŋ \, *original name* Gobind Rāi (b. 1666, Patna, Bihar, India—d. Oct. 7, 1708, Nānded, Maharashtra), 10th and last Sikh GURŪ (1675–1708), known for his creation of the KHĀLSĀ, a puri-

fied and reconstituted Sikh community, and for compiling the ĀDI GRANTH in its canonical form.

Gobind Singh was the son of Gurū TEGH BAHĀDUR and was born during one of his father's travels through India. He was brought to the Punjab in 1672 and given training in the martial arts. Gobind Singh had to deal with the tragedy of his father's execution in Delhi when he was nine years old, and as he entered adulthood he was at constant war with the surrounding chiefs in the Anandpur area. Under his leadership, however, the Sikh court at Anandpur flourished; at its height, 52 poets were in residence.

At the turn of the 18th century the Hindu chiefs opposing Gobind Singh sought the help of the Mughal authorities at nearby Sirhind, and in 1704 they forced the Sikhs out of Anandpur. In the melee that followed Gurū Gobind Singh's two elder sons died fighting, and his mother and two younger sons were captured. The sons were later executed by order of the governor of Sirhind, upon which his mother succumbed, in all likelihood from grief.

From his new base at Talwandi Sabo, now called Damdama, the Gurū wrote a defiant letter in verse, known as the *Zafarnāmā*, to Emperor Aurangzeb, accusing him of betraying proper ethical standards. The emperor invited the Gurū to meet him but died before the meeting could take place. In the battle of succession that ensued, Gurū Gobind Singh supported Prince Mauzam, and, after Mauzam became Emperor Bahādur Shah, Gobind Singh accompanied him on military campaigns to South India. The Gurū had hoped to have Bahādur Shah's permission to return to Anandpur, but, before that hope was realized, Gobind Singh became the target of an assassination attempt and died at the age of 42.

Through two monumental innovations, Gurū Gobind Singh had a profound impact on Sikh history. First, he established the Khālsā ("pure"), the egalitarian community that was to provide SIKHISM with its central political and religious definition and with the spirit necessary to pursue its military goals. Second, at the time of his death, he discontinued the office of the personal Gurū, decreeing that its authority should thereafer reside with the teachings of the *Ādi Granth*, now the *Srī Gurū Granth Sāhib*. Following his wishes, the community replaced the office of the Gurū with the twin principles of the Gurū Granth and the Gurū Panth ("the community as the Gurū"). The implications of this change were that the decisions (*gurmatā*) reached in a representative Sikh gathering (Sarbat Khālsā) meeting in the presence of the Gurū Granth have the sanction of the Gurū and are obligatory for the entire Sikh community.

GOD, common term for a male deity. *See also* DEUS OTIOSUS; GENDER AND RELIGION; MONOTHEISM; POLYTHEISM.

GODDESS, common term for a female deity. *See also* DEUS OTIOSUS; GENDER AND RELIGION; MONOTHEISM; POLYTHEISM.

GOD THE FATHER, superhuman, supernatural, intrinsically masculine being, embodying power and personality and presence. Most, though not all, religions invoke the existence and activity of a god or of gods, sometimes viewed as a person, sometimes as a power, but always as a purposive being and therefore animated by personality. This article describes the depictions and conceptions of God in the three major monotheist religions: JUDAISM, CHRISTIANITY, and ISLAM, for whom God is single and unique, merciful and just, and the image in which humans are created.

In the monotheist religions, God acts in the events ("history") of nations and persons. Ancient POLYTHEISMS generally identified the activities or embodiments of a god with the striking events in nature, and polytheistic gods were frequently consubstantial with nature. MONOTHEISMS, concomitantly, generally represent God as both above nature and as the creator of nature. The three major monotheisms further maintain that God makes himself known personally, not only as power, but with presence and personality, through self-revelation—through the TORAH revealed by God to MOSES at Sinai for Judaism, through JESUS CHRIST for Christianity, and through the revelation of the QUR'AN to the Prophet MUHAMMAD for Islam.

To the action and will of the powerful being are attributed the activities of nature and the fortunes of human beings. That is the point at which polytheism and monotheism have tended to part company. A religion of numerous gods may find many solutions to one problem, a religion of only one God presents one to many. The former attributes diverse activities to various gods, while the latter appeals to the will of one God to explain the meaning and purpose of all of life. That provokes a problem in the characterization of God on the part of monotheisms, as life can be unfair, rules may not be kept, and things happen at cross-purposes. To explain why, polytheisms adduce multiple causes of CHAOS, a god per anomaly. Diverse gods do various things, so it stands to reason that conflict results. Monotheism by nature explains many things in a single way. One God rules. Life is meant to be fair, and just rules are supposed to describe what is ordinary, all in the name of that one and only God.

So, in monotheism a simple logic governs, which limits ways of making sense of things. But that logic contains its own dialectic. If one true God has done everything, then, since he is God all-powerful and omniscient, all things are credited to, and blamed on, him. In that case he can be either good or bad, just or unjust—but not both. Monotheisms maintain that God is not only God but is also good (see also THEODICY; GOOD AND EVIL). The anomalies of the prosperity of the wicked and the suffering of the righteous then define the theological problematics of monotheisms but not of polytheisms. Christianity, Judaism, and Islam all concur that the conflict between God's will and the exercise of human FREE WILL forms the foundation for SIN and therefore also for suffering. The working system of the monotheisms finds its dynamic in the struggle between God's plan for creation—to create a perfect world of justice—and human will.

That dialectic embodies in a single paradigm the events contained in the sequences: rebellion, sin, punishment, repentance, and atonement; exile and return; or the disruption of world order and the restoration of world order. But at the end of time, all three religions agree, these anomalies will be resolved in a LAST JUDGMENT (see MILLENNIALISM) and in life eternal for those to whom God shows mercy.

GODI \'gō-dē\, *plural* godar \'gō-ˌdär\, pre-Christian priest in Scandinavia. At the time of Iceland's settlement, Norse people worshiped gods whom they called AESIR (Aesir, singular, Áss), and this religion has left behind an extensive mythology in Icelandic literature. It appears that this pre-Christian worship was organized around a distinct class of priest-chieftains, called *godar*, of whom there were about 40 in Iceland. In the absence of royal power in Iceland, the *godar* formed the ruling class in the country.

By the end of the settlement period, a general Icelandic assembly, called Althing, had been established and was held at midsummer on a site that came to be called Thingvellir. This assembly consisted of a law council (*lögrétta*), in which the *godar* made and amended the laws, and a system of courts of justice, in which householders, nominated by the *godar*, acted as judges. At the local level, three *godar* usually held a joint assembly in late spring, at which a local court operated, again with judges nominated by the *godar*.

By the end of the 10th century the Norwegians were forced by their king, Olaf I Tryggvason, to accept CHRISTIANITY. The king also sent missionaries to Iceland, who according to 12th-century sources were highly successful in converting the Icelanders. In 999 or 1000 the Althing made a peaceful decision that all Icelanders should become Christians. The *godar* retained their political role, however, and many of them probably built their own churches. Some were ordained, and as a group they seem to have closely controlled the organization of the new religion.

GODPARENT, *formally* sponsor (Latin: "person standing surety," or "one who guarantees another's good faith"), one who stands surety for another in the rite of Christian BAPTISM. In the modern baptism of an infant or child the godparent or godparents make profession of faith for the person being baptized (the godchild) and assume an obligation to serve as proxies for the parents if the parents either are unable or neglect to provide for the religious training of the child, in fulfillment of baptismal promises. In churches mandating a sponsor only one godparent is required; two (in most churches, of different sex) are permitted. Many Protestant denominations permit but do not require a child being baptized to have a sponsor.

The practice of sponsorship originated in the custom requiring that an adult convert who offered himself for the rite should be accompanied by a Christian known to the bishop—a Christian who could vouch for the applicant and undertake his supervision. The Greek word for the person undertaking this function was *anadochos*, to which the Latin *susceptor* is equivalent. The word sponsor in this ecclesiastical sense occurred for the first time in TERTULLIAN'S 2nd-century treatise *De Baptismo*. The anciently allowable practice of parents becoming sponsors for their own children was at last formally prohibited by the Council of Mainz (813 CE).

GOG AND MAGOG \'gäg . . . 'mā-ˌgäg\, in the BIBLE, hostile powers that are ruled by SATAN and will manifest themselves immediately before the end of the world (Revelation 20). Gog is joined by Magog in the biblical passage in REVELATION TO JOHN and in other Christian and Jewish apocalyptic literature, but elsewhere (Ezekiel 38; GENESIS 10:2) Magog is apparently the place of Gog's origin.

GOHEI \gō-'hā\, in SHINTŌ, paper or cloth offering made to a god, consisting of an upright stick to which is attached a strip of folded paper or cloth. The *gohei* also sometimes operates as a symbol of the KAMI (god, or sacred power) and indicates that the deity is present in the shrine.

GOIBNIU \'gȯvʸ-nʸü\ (Celtic: "Divine Smith"), *Welsh* Gofannon \gō-'vä-nōn\, ancient Celtic smith god. Goibniu figured in Irish tradition as one of a trio of divine craftsmen; the other two were Luchta the wright and Creidhne the metalworker. Goibniu was also the provider of the sacred otherworld feast, the Fled Goibnenn; he allegedly brewed the special ale thought to confer immortality on those who drank it. After the Christianization of Ireland he was metamorphosed into a legendary builder of churches as Gobbán Saer (Gobbán the Craftsman); as such he is still remembered in modern Celtic folk tradition. His Welsh equivalent, Gofannon, figured in the MABINOGION (a collection of medieval Welsh tales). It was believed that his help was vital in cleansing the plow at the end of the furrows.

GOLDEN CALF, idol worshiped by the Hebrews during the period of the EXODUS from Egypt in the 13th century BCE and during the age of Jeroboam I, king of Israel, in the 10th century BCE. Mentioned in Exodus 32 and 1 Kings 12 in the OLD

The Golden Temple of Amritsar
G. Reitz—De Wys Inc.

TESTAMENT, worship of the golden calf is seen as a supreme act of APOSTASY. The figure is probably a representation of the Egyptian bull god APIS in the earlier period and of the Canaanite god BAAL in the latter.

In Exodus 32 the Hebrews escaping Egypt asked AARON, the brother of MOSES, to fashion a golden calf during the long absence of Moses on Mt. Sinai. Upon returning from the mountain with the tablets of the Law, Moses had the idol melted down, pulverized, and mixed with water. The people were required to drink the mixture, an ordeal to separate the unfaithful (who later died in a plague) from the faithful (who lived). Defending the faith in the God revealed to Moses against the calf worshipers were the LEVITES, who became the priestly caste.

GOLDEN RULE, precept in the NEW TESTAMENT Gospel, Matthew (7:12): "So whatever you wish that men would do to you, do so to them . . . ." This rule of conduct is a summary of the Christian's duty to his neighbor and states a fundamental ethical principle. It recalls the command to "love the stranger (sojourner)," as found in Deuteronomy. It is not, however, peculiar to CHRISTIANITY. Its negative form is to be found in Tobit 4:15, in the writings of the two great Jewish scholars HILLEL (1st century BCE) and PHILO JUDAEUS (1st centuries BCE and CE), and in the *Analects* of CONFUCIUS (6th and 5th centuries BCE). It also appears in one form or another in the writings of Plato, Aristotle, Isocrates, and Seneca.

GOLDEN TEMPLE, *also called* Darbār Sāhib \dər-'bär-'sä-hib\ (Punjabi: "Honorable Court"), *also called* Harimandir \ˌhə-ri-'mən-dər\, *also spelled* Harmandir \ˌhər-'mən-dər\ (Punjabi: "Temple of God"), chief GURDWĀRĀ, or house of worship, of the Sikhs of India and their most important PILGRIMAGE site; it is located in the city of AMRITSAR, in Punjab state. The Golden Temple was founded by GURŪ RĀMDĀS (1574–81) and completed by his successor, Gurū ARJAN (1581–1606).

When Sikhs under the leadership of Gurū HARGOBIND (1606–44) decided to withdraw to the Shivalik hills, the control of the Golden Temple went into the hands of a rival group—the descendants of Prithī Chand (1558–1618), the elder brother of Gurū Arjan. In the late 1690s, however,

Gurū GOBIND SINGH was able to assert his authority over the Golden Temple. During the mid-18th century the temple served as the symbol of Sikh religio-political autonomy. The forces of Ahmad Shāh Abdālī, the Afghan invader, desecrated the complex in the 1760s, but the Sikhs rebuilt it. During the reign (1801–39) of Maharaja Ranjīt Singh the temple attained the features that have made it famous as a physical structure: its domes covered with gold-plated copper (hence, the "Golden Temple"), and its marble walls inlaid with precious stones.

The complex of buildings surrounding the Golden Temple includes the AKĀL TAKHAT, the Central Sikh Museum, the Sikh Reference Library, and the Teja Singh Samundari Hall, which houses the SHIROMAŅĪ GURDWĀRĀ PRABANDHAK COMMITTEE (although that body meets in the Akāl Takhat). In 1984, as a result of the Indian government's confrontation with Sikh separatists headquartered at Amritsar, government troops attacked the complex. The Golden Temple was damaged, and the Akāl Takhat and the Sikh Reference Library were completely destroyed. All have since been rebuilt.

GOLEM \'gō-ləm\, in Jewish FOLKLORE, image endowed with life. The term is used in the BIBLE (Psalms 139:16) and in Talmudic literature (SANHEDRIN 65b; GENESIS RABBAH 24:2) to refer to an embryonic or incomplete substance. In the Middle Ages many legends arose of wise men who could bring effigies to life by means of a charm or of a combination of letters forming a sacred word or one of the names of God. The letters, written on paper, were placed in the golem's mouth or affixed to its head. The letters' removal deanimated the golem. In early tales the golem

Golem (right) in the German horror film Der Golem *(1920)*
By courtesy of the Friedrich-Wilhelm Murnau-Stiftung; photograph, Museum of Modern Art Film Stills Archive, New York

was usually a perfect servant, his only fault being a too literal or mechanical fulfillment of his master's orders. In the 16th century the golem acquired the character of protector of the Jews in time of persecution but also had a frightening aspect. The most famous tale involves the golem created by the 16th-century rabbi Judah Löw ben Bezulel of Prague. When Bezulel's golem became uncontrollable and posed a threat to human lives it was destroyed, returning it to the dirt from which it was created. The legend was the basis for Gustav Meyrink's novel *Der Golem* (1915) and for a classic of German silent films (1920), which provided many details on the movement and behavior of man-made monsters that were later adopted in the popular American horror films on the Frankenstein theme. In recent years the golem folktale has inspired several books for children, including a Caldecott Medal-winning book, *Golem* (1996), by David Wisniewski.

GOLGOTHA \'göl-gə-thə, göl-'gä-thə\ (Aramaic: "Skull"), *also called* Calvary \'kal-və-rē\ (from Latin: *calva*, "bald head," or "skull"), skull-shaped hill in Jerusalem, the site of Jesus' CRUCIFIXION. It is referred to in all four Gospels. It lay outside the city walls of Jerusalem. Its exact location is uncertain, but most scholars prefer either the spot now covered by the Church of the HOLY SEPULCHRE or a hillock called Gordon's Calvary just north of the Damascus Gate.

GOLIATH \gə-'lī-əth\ (*c.* 11th century BCE), in the BIBLE (1 Samuel 17), the Philistine GIANT slain by DAVID. The Philistines had warred against SAUL, and Goliath came forth daily to challenge a warrior to single combat. Only David responded, and armed with a sling and pebbles he overcame Goliath. The Philistines, seeing their champion killed, lost heart and were easily put to flight. The giant's arms were placed in the SANCTUARY, and David took his sword with him in his flight from Saul (1 Samuel 21:1–9).

In another passage it is said that Goliath of Gath was slain by a certain Elhanan of Bethlehem in one of David's conflicts with the Philistines (2 Samuel 21:18–22).

GOOD AND EVIL, principles that are seen to stand in opposition, however they be defined. Good is sometimes taken to mean that which conforms to the moral order of the universe—that which leads to beauty, well-being, and happiness. Its converse, evil, is that which is morally reprehensible, wicked, or sinful and leads to pain and suffering in the world. Definitions of these words are typically circular, however, as contained within the definition is the very object of the definition. In the end, evil is frequently defined as being, or coming from, a self-existent principle antithetical to the principle of good.

Many religious systems have grappled with the problem of the existence of evil in a world thought to have been created by a God that is infinitely good (*see* THEODICY). In monotheistic religions evil does not originate within the divinity nor in general within a divine world as it does, for instance, in Gnosticism; it arises instead from the improper use of freedom by created beings. In monistic religions, which are based on the opposition between the One and the many, there is a notion of evil as being that which is caused by decay or fragmentation of the One.

GOOD FRIDAY, the Friday before EASTER, the day in HOLY WEEK on which the yearly commemoration of the CRUCIFIXION of JESUS CHRIST is observed. As early as the 2nd century, there are references to fasting and penance on this day by Christians, who, since the time of the early church, had observed every Friday as a fast day in commemoration of the Crucifixion.

In the Roman rite of the ROMAN CATHOLIC church, the liturgical service for Good Friday has been in approximately the same form for centuries. The liturgy, now celebrated after 3:00 PM, consists of three distinct parts: readings and prayers (including the Passion according to St. John), the veneration of the cross, and Holy Communion. Nonliturgical devotions such as the STATIONS OF THE CROSS and the Three Hours Service were introduced after the Protestant REFORMATION and are still observed in some places. The Three Hours Service consists of sermons, HYMNS, and prayers centered on Christ's "seven last words on the Cross." It takes place from 12 noon to 3:00 PM.

In the Eastern Orthodox churches, where Good Friday is known as Great Friday, the Matins service (usually celebrated on Thursday night) includes the reading of the Twelve Passion Gospel Readings taken from the various Passion accounts in the NEW TESTAMENT. No EUCHARIST service is celebrated. At Vespers there is a solemn reenactment of the burial procession of Christ, who is represented by the *epitaphion*, a piece of material bearing an image of the dead Savior.

In Lutheran and other Protestant churches various services are held, including the Three Hours Service and services with Holy Communion. In many areas concelebrated services take place among various denominations as an expression of Christian unity.

GORAKHNĀTH \'gör-ək-nät\, *also spelled* Gorakhnātha \'gör-ək-shə-'nä-tə\, *also called* Gorakṣanātha (fl. 11th century?, India), Hindu master yogi, commonly regarded as the founder of the Nāth or Kānphaṭa yogis, an order of ascetics that stresses the physical and spiritual disciplines of HAṬHA YOGA.

The details of his life are obscured by the numerous legends that have grown up around his supposedly miraculous powers. Apparently of a low-caste family, Gorakhnāth either was born in, or spent a good part of his lifetime in, the Punjab, traveling widely. He was said to have met with such other religious teachers as KABĪR and NĀNAK (though this is chronologically impossible) and to have popularized the practice of YOGA throughout India. Gorakhnāth is traditionally regarded as the disciple of MATSYENDRANĀTH, who is in turn understood by Nāth yogis as the first human GURU in their teaching succession. This connection is hagiographical shorthand (historically, Matsyendranāth probably preceded Gorakhnāth by at least three centuries), but it points to an important transition that Gorakhnāth instituted in tantric or SIDDHA practice, diverting its erotic, mystical heritage in the direction of austere Haṭha Yoga. Nonetheless, tantric worship (*see* TANTRIC HINDUISM) involving the use of sexual fluids is taught in several Sanskrit works attributed to Gorakhnāth, under the title *Gorakh Saṃhitā* ("Collections of Gorakh," 13th century?), alongside alchemy and Haṭha Yoga. Vernacular poetry attributed to Gorakhnāth, equally significant and anthologized under the title *Gorakh Bānī* ("Gorakh's Utterances"), emphasizes Haṭha Yoga.

GORDON, AARON DAVID \'gör-dən\, *Hebrew name* Aharon \ˌä-hä-'rōn\ (b. June 9/10, 1856, Troyanov, Ukraine—d. Feb. 22, 1922, Deganya, Palestine [now in Israel]), Zionist writer and philosopher who inculcated the idea of a return of Jews to Palestine as agriculturists.

After working as a minor official for the estate of Baron Horace Günzburg, a wealthy Russian Jew, Gordon, an ardent Zionist, emigrated to Palestine in 1904. He settled in the village of Petaḥ Tiqwa, refusing a job as librarian to work as a farm laborer in the belief that Jews could end the alienation caused by the Diaspora only if they returned to the Palestinian homeland and worked its soil. Gordon inspired other Jewish pioneers to establish Deganya (1909), Israel's first collective community, or kibbutz. At the end of World War I, Gordon went to Deganya, where his own example and ideals continued to influence the Jewish labor movement in Palestine. He became the ideologist of the ha-Po'el ha-Tza'ir ("The Younger Worker"), the first Palestinian Jewish Labor Party, which was later incorporated into the Mapai.

GORGON \ˈgȯr-gən\, monster figure in Greek mythology. Homer spoke of a single Gorgon—a monster of the Underworld. The later poet Hesiod increased the number of Gorgons to three—Stheno (the Mighty), Euryale (the Far Springer), and MEDUSA (the Queen)—and made them the daughters of the sea god Phorcys and of his sister-wife Ceto. Attic tradition regarded the Gorgon as a monster produced by GAEA, the Earth, to aid her sons against the gods.

Gorgon's head, carved marble mask, early 6th century BCE; in the Acropolis Museum, Athens
Alinari—Art Resource

In early classical art the Gorgons were portrayed as winged female creatures; their hair consisted of snakes, and they were round-faced and flat-nosed, with tongues lolling out and with large projecting teeth. Medusa was the only one who was mortal; hence, PERSEUS was able to kill her by cutting off her head. From the blood from her neck sprang Chrysaor and PEGASUS, her two offspring by POSEIDON. Medusa's severed head had the power of turning all who looked upon it to stone. Carved masks of the grotesque type of Gorgon's head were used as a protection against evil.

GORYŌ \gō-ˈryō\, in Japanese religion, vengeful spirits of the dead. In the Heian period (794–857 CE) goryō were spirits of nobility who had died as a result of political intrigue and who brought about natural disasters, diseases, and wars. The identities of the goryō were determined by DIVINATION or NECROMANCY. Many were appeased by being granted the status of gods (Japanese: goryō-shin, "goryō deities"). Later the belief arose that anyone could become a goryō by so willing at the moment of death or by meeting with accidental death under unusual circumstances. Various practices developed in the 9th–10th century to ward off the consequences of evil spirits, such as the Buddhist recitation of nembutsu (invoking the name of the Buddha Amida) to send angry spirits to Amida's paradise; the exorcising of spirits by SHUGEN-DŌ (mountain ascetic) rites; and the use of in-yo magic, derived from SHINTŌ and TAOISM. Belief in the power of goryō has survived, particularly among the rural population of Japan, and memorial services continue to be performed to appease victims of untimely death.

GOSPEL, any of four biblical narratives covering the life and death of JESUS CHRIST. Written, according to tradition, respectively by MATTHEW, MARK, LUKE, and JOHN (the four evangelists), they are placed at the beginning of the NEW TESTAMENT and make up about half the total text. The word gospel is descended from the Old English compound gōd-spel, meaning "good story," a rendering of the Latin evangelium and the Greek euangelion, meaning "good news" or "good telling." Since the late 18th century the first three have been called the SYNOPTIC GOSPELS, because the texts show a similar treatment of the life and death of Jesus Christ. In the writings of the apostle PAUL, which antedate all four written Gospels, the term gospel, sometimes in antithesis to law, refers to the entire Christian message.

GOSPEL MUSIC, American variation of HYMNS and hymn singing, originating in Protestant religious services. The melodies of gospel hymns, beginning in the 19th century, were similar to popular song melodies, with simple rhythms, harmonies, and major-key melodic lines.

Gospel's secondary development took place within urban settings during the post-Civil War Protestant revival movement. The services conducted by evangelist Dwight L. Moody, joined by singer-songwriter Ira D. Sankey, were important in spreading gospel music throughout the United States and Britain. The black gospel song reflected the collective improvisations of the African-American church congregation and the call-and-response rhetorical style of the gospel preacher. Congregational singing became a way of achieving climatic experiences of spiritual transcendence, often called spiritual possession, "shouting," or the "holy dance." Some white gospel groups tried to emulate the rhythmic energy of black gospel music, but country music performing techniques and barbershop quartet harmonies were more influential.

By the 1920s gospel had developed into a distinctive musical form that incorporated some secular elements and was considered by some observers to be the sacred counterpart to the blues. The early, pioneering gospel composers included the Reverend C.A. Tindley (1851–1933), followed by Lucie E. Campbell (1885–1963). Thomas A. Dorsey (1899–1993), often called the "Father of Gospel Music," wrote over one thousand songs. During the late 1920s Dorsey incorporated blues and jazz rhythms, coined the term gospel song, and by the mid-1940s had established the influential "Chicago school of gospel," in the city often regarded as the birthplace of the musical form.

In following years the Reverend William Herbert Brewster (1897–1987) attracted the attention of the top performers of gospel's classic era. Mahalia Jackson (1911–72), perhaps the greatest singer in gospel history, recorded Brewster's "Move On Up a Little Higher" in 1947, selling over one million copies. Others who traveled south to Brewster's church and home in Memphis, Tenn., included the Clara Ward (1924–73) Singers, Sam Cooke (1931–64) of the Soul Stirrers, and "Sister" Rosetta Tharpe (1915–73). Back in Chicago, pianist Roberta Martin (1907–69) developed the choral sound that defined the era, with her Roberta Martin Singers serving as a training ground for several legendary artists, including gospel singer James Cleveland (1931–91) and popular vocalist Dinah Washington (1924–63).

While gospel music remained veiled from mainstream popular culture for many years, today its profound influence and widespread popularity is undeniable. As one of the roots of American popular music, gospel's influence continues to expand around the world. In addition to the considerable success of several individual performers, gospel music "dynasties" such as the Winans and Hawkins families have guided the evolution of the music in recent years, drawing upon rhythm and blues, soul, jazz, and hiphop, while continuing the sacred traditions rooted in the music's origins.

GOTRA \'gō-trə\, lineage segment within an Indian CASTE that prohibits intermarriage by virtue of the members' descent from a common mythical ancestor, an important factor in determining possible Hindu marriage alliances. *Gotra* originally referred to the seven lineage segments of the BRAHMINS, who trace their derivation from seven ancient seers: Atri, Bharadvāja, Bhṛgu, Gotama, Kaśyapa, Vasiṣṭha, and Viśvāmitra. An eighth *gotra* was added early on, the Agastya, named after the seer intimately linked with the spread of Vedic HINDUISM in southern India. In later times the number of *gotra*s proliferated. KṢATRIYAS and VAIŚYAS also adopted the concept of *gotra* in a fashion, by assuming for their groups the *gotra* of their adjacent Brahmin *gotra*s or those of their GURUS, but this innovation was never very influential.

GRACE, *Greek* Charis, *plural* Charites, in GREEK RELIGION, one of a group of goddesses. The number of Graces varied in different legends, but usually there were three: Aglaia (Brightness), Euphrosyne (Joyfulness), and THALIA (Bloom). They are said to be daughters of ZEUS and HERA (or Eurynome, daughter of OCEANUS) or of HELIOS and Aegle, a daughter of Zeus. Frequently they were taken as goddesses of charm or beauty in general and hence were associated with APHRODITE, her attendant Peitho, and HERMES. In works of art they were represented in early times draped and later as nude female figures. Their chief cult centers were at Orchomenus in Boeotia, Athens, Sparta, and Paphos. The singular Gratia or Charis is sometimes used to denote the personification of Grace and Beauty.

GRACE, in Christian theology, the spontaneous, unmerited gift of the divine favor in the salvation of sinners, and the divine influence operating in man for his regeneration and sanctification. The English term is the usual translation for the Greek *charis*, which occurs in the NEW TESTAMENT about 150 times (two-thirds of these mentions are in writings attributed to PAUL).

The word *grace* is the central subject of three great theological controversies: (1) that of the nature of human depravity and regeneration, (2) that of the relation between grace and FREE WILL, and (3) that of the "means of grace" between ROMAN CATHOLICISM and PROTESTANTISM—*i.e.,* whether the granting of the divine grace is dependent on good works performed or dependent on the faith of the recipient.

Christian orthodoxy has taught that the initiative in the relationship of grace between God and man is always on the side of God. Once God has granted this "first grace," however, man does have a responsibility for the continuance of the relationship. Although the ideas of grace and of merit are mutually exclusive, neither AUGUSTINE nor the Protestant defenders of the principle of JUSTIFICATION by "grace alone" could totally avoid the question of reward or merit in the relationship of grace. In fact, some passages of the New Testament seem to use *charis* for "reward."

Catholics, EASTERN ORTHODOX, and some Protestants agree that grace is conferred through the SACRAMENTS, "the means of grace"; Reformed and Free Church Protestantism, how-

ever, have not bound grace as closely to the sacraments. BAPTISTS speak of ordinances rather than of sacraments and—as do evangelical Christians and those in the Reformed and Free Church traditions generally—insist that participation in grace occurs on the occasion of personal faith and not at all by sacramental observance.

GRAETZ, HEINRICH \'grets\ (b. Oct. 31, 1817, Xions, Prussia—d. Sept. 7, 1891, Munich, Ger.), author of the first standard history of the Jews.

Greatly influenced by his studies with the renowned scholar Rabbi SAMSON RAPHAEL HIRSCH, Graetz became a teacher at the Breslau (now Wrocław, Pol.) seminary in 1854. The seminary taught a CONSERVATIVE JUDAISM compatible with Graetz's belief that a Jewish theology should attempt to moderate between Orthodox literalism and Reform liberalism. He retained that post until the end of his life and also became an honorary professor at the University of Breslau in 1869.

Graetz's 11-volume *Geschichte der Juden von den ältesten Zeiten bis auf die Gegenwart* (1853–76; "History of the Jews from Oldest Times to the Present"; a condensed English version was published as *History of the Jews,* 6 vol., 1891–98) presents a picturesque and heroic account of the entire history of the Jewish people, emphasizing Jewish suffering and nationalistic aspirations. The work was widely translated and quickly became a standard work, greatly influencing future historians of JUDAISM.

GRAHAM, BILLY \'gram, 'grā-əm\, *byname of* William Franklin Graham, Jr. (b. Nov. 7, 1918, Charlotte, N.C., U.S.), American evangelist whose large-scale preaching tours, known as crusades, and friendship with numerous U.S. presidents brought him to international prominence.

The son of a prosperous dairy farmer, Graham attended rural public schools. He professed his "decision for Christ" at a revival meeting at the age of 16 and subsequently attended Bob Jones College (Cleveland, Tenn.) and Florida Bible Institute (near Tampa), both fundamentalist-Christian institutions. He began preaching in 1938 and was ordained as a Southern BAPTIST minister a year later. Following graduation from Florida Bible Institute in 1940, he took a B.A. in anthropology from Wheaton (Illinois) College.

Graham's reputation as an evangelist grew steadily during and immediately after World War II as a result of his radio broadcasts and tent revivals. By 1950 he was widely regarded as fundamentalism's chief spokesman. Through the Billy Graham Evangelistic Association he published his sermons and the magazine *Decision* (from 1960) and conducted the widely filmed and televised international revival crusades that became his hallmark.

First invited to the White House by Harry S. Truman in 1949, Graham later became a frequent guest of many succeeding presidents. He was awarded the U.S. Congressional Gold Medal in 1996.

GRĀMADEVATĀ \'grä-mə-'dā-və-ˌtä\ (Sanskrit: "village deity"), type of folk deity widely worshiped in rural India. The *grāmadevatā*s, often female figures, may have originated as agricultural deities; in South India and elsewhere they are propitiated with animal sacrifices to ward off and remove epidemics, crop failures, and other natural disasters.

The *grāmadevatā*s coexist side by side with the Brahminical gods of modern HINDUISM. Many *grāmadevatā*s are purely local deities. Spirits of the place (the crossroads, the boundary line), spirits of those who die a violent or untimely death, and tree and serpent spirits may also be treated as *grāmadevatā*s. They are worshiped in the form of earthenware ICONS or shapeless stones, established in simple shrines or on platforms set up under a village tree, and only occasionally in more imposing buildings.

An exceptional male village deity is Aiyaṇār, who in South India is the village watchman and whose shrine is always separate from those of the female goddesses. A similar male deity, known variously as Dharma-Ṭhakur, Dharma-Rāj, and Dharma-Rāy, is found in Bengali villages.

GREAT AWAKENING, religious revival in the British American colonies mainly between about 1720 and the 1740s. It was a part of the religious ferment that swept western Europe in the latter part of the 17th century and early 18th century, referred to as PIETISM and QUIETISM in continental Europe among Protestants and Roman Catholics and as Evangelicalism in England under the leadership of JOHN WESLEY (1703–91).

Conditions that prepared the way for the revival included an arid RATIONALISM in New England, formalism in liturgical practices, as among the Dutch Reformed in the Middle Colonies, and the neglect of pastoral supervision in the South. The revival took place primarily among the Dutch Reformed, CONGREGATIONALISTS, PRESBYTERIANS, BAPTISTS, and some members of the ANGLICAN COMMUNION, most of whom were Calvinists. The Great Awakening may be seen, therefore, as a development toward an evangelical CALVINISM.

Revival preachers emphasized the "terrors of the law" to sinners, the unmerited GRACE of God, and the "new birth" in JESUS CHRIST. One of the great figures of the movement was George Whitefield, an Anglican priest who was influenced by John Wesley but was himself a Calvinist. During 1739–40 he preached up and down the colonies to vast crowds. Although he gained many converts, he was attacked, as were other revival clergy, for stimulating emotional excesses and dangerous religious delusions.

JONATHAN EDWARDS was the great APOLOGIST of the Great Awakening. A Congregational pastor at Northampton, Mass., he preached JUSTIFICATION by faith alone with remarkable effectiveness. He also attempted to redefine the psychology of RELIGIOUS EXPERIENCE and to help those involved in the revival to discern what were true and false works of the Spirit of God.

The revival stimulated the growth of several educational institutions, including Princeton, Brown, and Rutgers universities and Dartmouth College. The increase of dissent from the established churches during this period led to a broader toleration.

A revival known as the Second Great Awakening began in New England in the 1790s. Generally less emotional than the first, the Second Awakening led to the founding of colleges and seminaries and to the organization of MISSION societies. Kentucky was also influenced by a revival during this period. The custom of camp-meeting revivals developed out of the Kentucky revival and was an influence on the American frontier during the 19th century.

GREAT MOTHER OF THE GODS, *also called* Cybele \'si-bə-lē, in Byron's work si-'bē-lē \, Cybebe \'si-bə-bē \, *or* Agdistis \ag-'dis-tis \, ancient Oriental and Greco-Roman deity, known by a variety of local names; the name Cybele or Cybebe predominates in Greek and Roman literature from about the 5th century BCE onward. Her full official Roman name was Mater Deum Magna Idaea ("Great Idaean Mother of the Gods").

Legends agree in locating the rise of the worship of the Great Mother in the area of Phrygia in Asia Minor (now in west-central Turkey), and in classical times her cult center was at Pessinus, on Mount Dindymus, or Agdistis. The Greeks saw in the Great Mother a resemblance to their goddess RHEA and finally identified the two completely.

During Hannibal's invasion of Italy in 204 BCE, the Romans followed a Sibylline PROPHECY that the enemy could be expelled and conquered if the "Idaean Mother" were brought to Rome, together with her sacred symbol, a small stone reputed to have fallen from the heavens. Her identification by the Romans with the goddesses Maia, Ops, Rhea, TELLUS, and CERES contributed to the establishment of her worship on a firm footing. By the end of the Roman Republic it had attained prominence, and under the empire it became one of the most important cults in the Roman world.

In all of her aspects—Roman, Greek, and Oriental—the Great Mother was characterized by essentially the same qualities, most importantly her universal motherhood. She was the great parent not only of gods but also of human beings and beasts. She was called the Mountain Mother, and special emphasis was placed on her maternity over wild nature. Her mythical attendants, the Corybantes, were wild, half-demonic beings. Her priests, the GALLI, castrated themselves on entering her service. The self-mutilation was justified by the myth that her lover ATTIS had emasculated himself under a pine tree, where he bled to death. At Cybele's festival (March 15–27), a pine tree was brought to her shrine, where it was honored as a god and adorned with violets considered to have sprung from the blood of Attis. On March 24, the "Day of

Cybele, terra-cotta statuette from Camirus, Rhodes, early 5th century BCE
By courtesy of the trustees of the British Museum

Blood," her chief priest, the *archigallus*, drew blood from his arms and offered it to her, while the lower clergy whirled madly and slashed themselves to bespatter the altar and the sacred pine with their blood. On March 27 the silver statue of the goddess was borne in PROCESSION and bathed in the Almo, a tributary of the Tiber River.

Roman citizens were at first forbidden to take part in the ceremonies—a ban that was not removed until the time of the empire. Though her cult sometimes existed by itself, in its fully developed state the worship of the Great Mother was accompanied by that of Attis. The Great Mother was especially prominent in the art of the empire. She usually appears with mural crown and veil, seated on a throne or in a chariot, and accompanied by two lions.

GREAT SANHEDRIN \san-'he-drən, sän-; san-'hē- \, supreme Jewish legislative and judicial court in Jerusalem under Roman rule.

GREEK RELIGION

The beliefs of the ancient Hellenes about the gods and their relationship with humanity were codified from the time of Homer (c. 8th century BCE) to the reign of the emperor Julian (4th century CE). During this period the influence of ancient Greek religion spread as far west as Spain, east to the Indus River, and throughout the Mediterranean world. Its effect was most marked on ROMAN RELIGION, which identified its deities with the Greek. Under CHRISTIANITY, Greek heroes and even deities survived as saints. The rediscovery of Greek literature during the Renaissance and, above all, the novel perfection of classical sculpture produced a revolution in taste that had far-reaching effects on Christian religious art. The most striking characteristic of Greek religion was the belief in a multiplicity of anthropomorphic deities, coupled with a minimum of dogmatism.

The Greeks had numerous beliefs about their gods, but the sole requirement was to believe that the gods existed and to perform ritual and sacrifice, through which the gods received their due. If a Greek went through the motions of piety, he risked little, since no attempt was made to enforce orthodoxy, a religious concept almost incomprehensible to the Greeks. The Greeks had no word for religion itself, the closest approximations being *eusebeia* ("piety") and *threskeia* ("cult"). The large corpus of myths concerned with gods, heroes, and rituals embodied the worldview of Greek religion and remains its legacy. Most Greeks "believed" in their gods in roughly the modern sense of the term, and they prayed in a time of crisis not merely to the "relevant" deity but to any deity on whose aid they had established a claim by sacrifice. To this end, each Greek polis (city-state) had a series of public festivals throughout the year that were intended to ensure the aid of all the gods who were thus honored. They reminded the gods of services rendered and asked for a quid pro quo. Particularly in times of crisis the Greeks, like the Romans, were often willing to add deities borrowed from other cultures.

HISTORY

Greek religion as it is currently understood probably resulted from the mingling of RELIGIOUS BELIEFS and practices between the incoming Greek-speaking peoples who arrived from the north during the 2nd millennium BCE and the indige-

The first meeting of Zeus and Hera, metope from a Greek temple at Selinus, Sicily, c. 470–460 BCE
The Granger Collection

nous inhabitants whom they called "Pelasgi." The incomers' pantheon was headed by the Indo-European sky god variously known as ZEUS (Greek), Dyaus (Indian), or JUPITER (Roman Dies-pater). Once in Greece, divinities from different pantheons came to be associated with one another; the Olympians were identified with local deities or assigned as consorts to the local god or goddess.

Sometime before the Homeric poems took their present form, the cult of the god DIONYSUS reached Greece, traditionally from Thrace and Phrygia. His devotees, known as *maenads* (literally "mad women"), armed with *thyrsoi* (wands tipped with a pine cone and wreathed with vine or ivy), were reputed to wander in *thiasoi* (revel bands) about mountain slopes, such as Cithaeron or Parnassus; the practice persisted into Roman imperial times. They were also supposed, in their ECSTASY, to practice *sparagmos*, the tearing of living victims to pieces and feasting on their raw flesh (*ōmophagia*).

Festivals were expressive of religion's social aspect and attracted large gatherings (*panēgyreis*). Mainly agrarian in origin, they were seasonal in character, held often at full moon and on the 7th of the month in the case of APOLLO, and always with a sacrifice in view. Some festivals of Athens were performed on behalf of the polis and all its members. Many of these seem to have been originally the cults of individual noble families who came together at the *synoikismos*, the creation of the polis of Athens from its small towns and villages. There were no "priests of the gods," or even priests of an individual god; one became a priest of one god at one temple. Except for these public festivals, anyone might perform a sacrifice at any time. The priest's role was to keep the temple clean; he was usually guaranteed some part of the animal sacrificed.

Popular religion flourished alongside the civic cults. Peasants worshiped the deities of the countryside, such as the Arcadian goat-god PAN, who prospered the flocks, and the NYMPHS (who, like EILEITHYIA, aided women in childbirth) inhabiting caves, springs (NAIADS), trees (Dryads and Hamadryads), and the sea (NEREIDS). They also believed in quasi-divinities such as Satyrs and the equine Sileni and CENTAURS. Among the more popular festivals were the rural Dionysia, which included a phallus pole; the ANTHESTERIA, when new wine was broached and offerings were made to the dead; the Thalysia, a harvest celebration; the THARGELIA, when a SCAPEGOAT (*pharmakos*) assumed the communal guilt; and the Pyanepsia, a bean feast in which boys collected offerings to hang on the *eiresiōne* ("wool pole"). Women celebrated the THESMOPHORIA in honor of DEMETER and commemorated the passing of ADONIS with laments and miniature gardens, while images were swung from trees at the Aiora to get rid of an ancient hanging curse.

BELIEFS, PRACTICES, AND INSTITUTIONS

The gods. The early Greeks personalized every aspect of their world, natural and cultural, and their experiences in it. The earth, the sea, the mountains, the rivers, custom-law (*themis*), and one's share in society and its goods were all seen in personal as well as naturalistic terms. In Hesiod, what could be distinguished as anthropomorphic deities and personalizations of natural or cultural phenomena both beget and are begotten by each other. HERA is of the first type—goddess of marriage but not identified with marriage. Earth is evidently of the second type, as are, in a somewhat different sense, EROS and APHRODITE (god and goddess of sexual desire) and ARES (god of war). These latter are personalized and anthropomorphized, but their worshipers may be "filled" with them. Some deities have epithets that express a particular aspect of their activities; for instance, Zeus is known as Zeus Xenios in his role as guarantor of guests.

In Homer the gods constitute essentially a super-aristocracy. The worshipers of these gods do not believe in reward or punishment after death; one's due must come in this life. Every success shows that the gods are well disposed, for the time being at least; every failure shows that some god is angry, usually as a result of a slight, intended or unintended, rather than from the just or unjust behavior of one mortal to another. The Greeks knew what angered their mortal aristocracy and extrapolated from there. Prayer and sacrifice, however abundant, could not guarantee that the gods would grant success. The gods might prefer peace on

Olympus to helping their worshipers—sacrifice, though necessary, was not sufficient.

In Homer, *hērōs* denotes the greatest of the living warriors. The cults of these mighty men developed later around their tombs. Heroes were worshiped as the most powerful of the dead, who were able, if they wished, to help the inhabitants of the polis in which their bones were buried. Thus, the Spartans brought back the bones of ORESTES from Tegea. Historical characters might be elevated to the status of heroes at their deaths. It is power, not righteousness, that distinguishes the hero. Since they are the mightiest of the dead, heroes receive offerings suitable for CHTHONIC (Underworld) deities.

Cosmogony. Of several competing cosmogonies in archaic Greece, Hesiod's *Theogony* is the only one that has survived in more than fragments. It records the generations of the gods from CHAOS through Zeus and his contemporaries to the gods who had two divine parents (*e.g.,* Apollo and ARTEMIS, born of Zeus and LETO) and the mortals who had one divine parent (*e.g.,* HERACLES, born of Zeus and Alcmene). Hesiod uses the relationships of the deities, by birth, marriage, or treaty, to explain why the world is as it is and why Zeus, the third supreme deity of the Greeks, has succeeded in maintaining his supremacy—thus far—where his predecessors failed. Essentially, Zeus is a better politician and has the balance of power, practical wisdom, and good counsel on his side.

The tholos (circular structure) built c. 390 BCE at Marmaria, the Sanctuary of Athena at Delphi, Greece
Noboru Komine—Photo Researchers

The divine world of the Greeks was bisected by a horizontal line. Above that line were the Olympians, gods of life, daylight, and the bright sky; below it were the chthonic gods of the Underworld and the dead and of the mysterious fertility of the earth. The Olympians kept aloof from the Underworld gods and from those who should be in their realm. Mortals could approach the Underworld figures through prayer or sacrifice, but they did so cautiously, as these were dangerous and frightening powers.

Eschatology. In Homer only the gods were by nature immortal, but ELYSIUM was reserved for their favored sons-in-law, whom they exempted from death. Heracles alone gained a place on Olympus by his own efforts. Ordinarily death was a hateful state, for the dead were regarded as strengthless doubles who had to be revived with drafts of blood, mead, wine, and water in order to enable them to speak. They were conducted, it was believed, to the realm of HADES by Hermes; but the way was barred, according to popular accounts, by the river STYX. Across this, CHARON ferried all who had received at least token burial, and coins were placed in the mouths of corpses to pay the fare. Originally only great wrongdoers like IXION, SISYPHUS, and Tityus, who had offended the gods personally, were punished in Tartarus.

Shrines and temples. In the earliest times deities were worshiped in natural spaces such as groves, caves, or mountain tops. Mycenaean deities shared the king's palace. Fundamental was the precinct (*temenos*) allotted to the deity, containing the altar, temple (if any), and other sacral or natural features, such as the sacred olive in the *temenos* of Pandrosos on the Athenian Acropolis. *Naoi* (temples—literally "dwellings"—that housed the god's image) were already known in Homeric times and were of wood and simple design. Limestone and marble replaced wood by the end of the 7th century BCE, when temples became larger and were constructed with rows of columns on all sides. The image, crude and wooden at first, was placed in the central chamber (*cella*), which was open at the eastern end. No ritual was associated with the image itself, though it was sometimes paraded. Hero shrines were far less elaborate and had pits for offerings. Miniature shrines also were known.

Most oracular shrines included a subterranean chamber, but no trace of such has been found at DELPHI, though the Pythia was always said to "descend." The temple of ASCLEPIUS, the god of healing, at Epidaurus was furnished with a hall where the sick were advised in dreams. DIVINATION was also widely practiced in Greece. Augurs interpreted the flight of birds, while dreams, and even sneezes, were regarded as ominous. Seers also divined from the shape of altar smoke and the conformation of victims' entrails.

Festivals and rites. The precise details of many festivals are obscure. Among the more elaborate was the PANATHENAEA, which was celebrated at high summer, and every fourth year (the Great Panathenaea) on a more splendid scale. Its purpose, besides offering sacrifice, was to provide the ancient wooden image of ATHENA, housed in the "Old Temple," with a new robe woven by the wives of Athenian citizens. The Great Panathenaea included a PROCESSION, a torch race, athletic contests, mock fights, and bardic recitations. The Great Dionysia was celebrated at Athens in spring. At the end of the ritual the god's image was escorted to the theater of Dionysus, where it presided over the dramatic contests. It, like its rural counterpart, included phallic features.

Sacrifice was offered to the Olympian deities at dawn at the altar in the *temenos*, which normally stood east of the temple. Representing as it did a gift to the gods, sacrifice constituted the principal proof of piety. The gods were content with the burnt portion of the offering, while the priests and worshipers shared the remainder of the meat. Different animals were sacred to different deities—*e.g.*, heifers to Athena, cows to Hera, pigs to Demeter, bulls to Zeus and Dionysus, dogs to HECATE, game and heifers to Artemis, horses to POSEIDON, and asses to Priapus—though the distinctions were not rigorously observed. Included in the Homeric cult were the practices of ritual washing before sacrifice, sprinkling barley grains, and making token offerings of hair. Victims were required to be free of blemish, or they were likely to offend the deity. Sacrifice also was made to chthonic powers in the evening. Black animals were offered, placed in pits, and the meat was entirely burned. Sacrifice preceded battles, the conclusion of treaties, or similar events. Bloodless sacrifices (*e.g.*, of agricultural goods) were made to some deities and heroes.

Prayers normally began with compliments to the deity, followed by discreet references to the petitioner's piety, and ended with his special plea. Processions formed part of most gatherings (*panēgyreis*) and festivals. The Panathenaic procession, for example, set out from the Pompeion (sacred storehouse) at dawn, headed by maiden basket-bearers (*kanēphoroi*), who carried the sacred panoply. Elders bore boughs (*thallophoroi*) while youths (*ephēboi*) conducted the victims for sacrifice, and cavalry brought up the rear. Athena's robe was spread on the mast of a wheeled ship.

MYTHOLOGY

Greek religious myths are concerned with gods or heroes in their more serious aspects or are connected with ritual. They include cosmogonical tales of the genesis of the gods and the world out of Chaos, the successions of divine rulers, and the internecine struggles that culminated in the supremacy of Zeus, the ruling god of Olympus. They also include the long tale of Zeus's amours with goddesses and mortal women, which usually resulted in the births of younger deities and heroes. The goddess Athena's unique status is implicit in the story of her motherless birth (she was born directly from Zeus); and the myths of Apollo explain that god's sacral associations, describe his remarkable victories over monsters and gi-

ants, and stress his jealousy and the dangers inherent in immortal alliances.

Some myths are closely associated with rituals, such as the account of the Curetes drowning out the infant Zeus's cries by clashing their weapons, or Hera's annual restoration of her virginity by bathing in the spring Canathus. Some myths about heroes and heroines also had a religious basis. Myths were viewed as embodying divine or timeless truths, whereas legends (or sagas) were quasi-historical. Hence, famous events in epics, such as the Trojan War, were generally regarded as having really happened, and heroes and heroines were believed to have actually lived. Earlier sagas, such as the voyage of the ARGONAUTS, were accepted in a similar fashion. Most Greek legends were embellished with folktales and fiction, but some certainly contain a historical substratum. Such are the tales of the various sacks of Troy, a fact supported by archaeological evidence, and the labors of Heracles, which may suggest Mycenaean feudalism. Again, the legend of the MINOTAUR (a being part human, part bull) could have arisen from exaggerated accounts of bull-leaping in ancient Crete.

In another class of legends, heinous offenses, such as attempting to make love to a goddess against her will, grossly deceiving the gods, or assuming their prerogatives, were punished by everlasting torture in the Underworld. The consequences of social crimes, such as murder or incest, were also described in legend (*e.g.,* the story of OEDIPUS, who killed his father and married his mother), and may have been intended to communicate and reinforce social values. Legends likewise could be employed to justify existing political systems or to bolster territorial claims.

Types of myths in Greek culture. *Myths of origin.* Myths of origin represent an attempt to render the universe comprehensible in human terms. Greek CREATION MYTHS (cosmogonies) and views of the universe (cosmologies) were more systematic and specific than those of other ancient peoples. Yet their very artistry serves as an impediment to interpretation, since the Greeks embellished the myths with folktale and fiction told for its own sake. Thus, though the aim of Hesiod's *Theogony* is to describe the ascendancy of Zeus (and, incidentally, the rise of the other gods), the inclusion of such familiar themes as the hostility between the generations, the enigma of woman (PANDORA), the exploits of the friendly trickster (PROMETHEUS), or struggles against powerful beings or monsters like the TITANS (and, in later tradition, the GIANTS) enhances the interest of an epic account.

According to Hesiod, four primary divine beings first came into existence: the Chaos, GAEA (Earth), Tartarus, and Eros (Sexual Attraction). The creative process began with the forcible separation of Gaea from her consort OURANUS (Heaven) in order to allow her progeny to be born: their son CRONUS cut off Ouranus' genitals with a weapon supplied him by his mother. Thereby Heaven was separated from Earth and life was free to develop between the two.

According to Greek cosmological concepts, the Earth was viewed as a flat disk afloat on the river of Ocean. The Sun (HELIOS) traversed the heavens like a charioteer and sailed around the Earth in a golden bowl at night. Natural fissures were popularly regarded as entrances to the subterranean house of Hades, home of the dead.

Myths of the ages of the world. From a very early period, Greek myths seem open to criticism and alteration on grounds of morality or of misrepresentation of known facts. In the *Works and Days*, Hesiod makes use of a scheme of Four Ages (or Races): Golden, Silver, Bronze, and Iron. These races or ages are separate creations of the gods, the Golden Age belonging to the reign of Cronus, the subsequent races the creation of Zeus. Those of the Golden Age never grew old, were free from toil, and passed their time in jollity and feasting. When they died, they became guardian spirits on Earth.

Why the Golden Age came to an end Hesiod failed to explain, but it was succeeded by the Silver Age. After an inordinately prolonged childhood, the men of the Silver Age began to act presumptuously and neglected the gods. Consequently, Zeus hid them in the Earth, where they became spirits among the dead.

Zeus next created the men of the Bronze Age, men of violence who perished by mutual destruction. At this point the poet intercalates the Age (or Race) of Heroes. Of these heroes the more favored (who were related to the gods) reverted to a kind of restored Golden Age existence under the rule of Cronus (forced into honorable exile by his son Zeus) in the Isles of the Blessed.

The final age, the antithesis of the Golden Age, was the Iron Age, during which the poet himself had the misfortune to live. But even that was not the worst, for he believed that a time would come when infants would be born old, and there would be no recourse left against the universal moral decline. The presence of evil was explained by Pandora's rash action in opening her fabled box, which in turn was occasioned by Prometheus' theft of fire.

Myths of the gods. Myths about the gods described their births, victories over monsters or rivals, love affairs, special powers, or connections with a cultic site or ritual. As these powers tended to be wide, the myths of many gods were correspondingly complex. Thus, the Homeric hymns to Demeter, a goddess of agriculture, and to the Delian and Pythian Apollo describe how these deities came to be associated with sites at Eleusis, Delos, and Delphi, respectively. Similarly, myths about Athena, the patroness of Athens, tend to em-

(Above) Athena with her attribute, the owl, Greek bronze statuette c. 460 BCE; (right) the birth of Athena from the forehead of Zeus, Greek black-figured vase, 6th century BCE; in the Louvre, Paris

The Granger Collection; Giraudon—Art Resource

phasize the goddess' love of war and her affection for heroes and the city of Athens; and those concerning HERMES (the messenger of the gods), Aphrodite (goddess of love), or Dionysus describe Hermes' proclivities as a god of thieves, Aphrodite's lovemaking, and Dionysus' association with wine, frenzy, miracles, and even ritual death. Poseidon (god of the sea) was unusually atavistic, in that his union with earth and his equine adventures appear to hark back to his pre-marine status as a horse or earthquake god. It is uncertain whether Homer knew of the judgment of PARIS; but he knew the far from trivial consequences for Troy of the favor of Aphrodite and the bitter enmity of Hera and Athena, which the judgment of Paris was composed to explain.

Of folk deities, the nymphs personified the life in water or trees and were said to punish unfaithful lovers. Water nymphs (Naiads) were reputed to drown those with whom they fell in love, such as Hylas, a companion of Heracles. Even the gentle MUSES (goddesses of the arts and sciences) blinded their human rivals, such as the bard THAMYRIS. Satyrs and Sileni (folk deities with bestial features) were the nymphs' male counterparts. Like sea deities, Sileni possessed secret knowledge that they would reveal only under duress. Charon, the grisly ferryman of the dead, was also a popular figure of folktale.

Antique relief sculpture, possibly a depiction of the Eleusinian Mysteries
Alinari—Art Resource

Myths of heroes. Hero myths included elements from tradition, folktale, and fiction. Episodes in the Trojan cycle, such as the departure of the Greek fleet from Aulis or THESEUS' Cretan expedition and death on Scyros, may belong to traditions dating from the Minoan-Mycenaean world. On the other hand, events described in the *Iliad* probably owe far more to Homer's creative ability than to genuine tradition. Even heroes like ACHILLES, HECTOR, or DIOMEDES are largely fictional, though doubtlessly based on legendary prototypes. The *Odyssey* is the prime example of the wholesale importation of folktales into epic. Certain heroes—Heracles, the DIOSCURI (the twins Castor and Pollux), Amphiaraus (one of the Argonauts), or HYACINTHUS (a youth loved by Apollo and accidentally killed)—may be regarded as partly legend and partly religious myth. Thus, whereas Heracles, a man of Tiryns, may originally have been a historical character, the myth of his demise on Oeta and subsequent elevation to full divinity is closely linked with a cult. In time, Heracles' popularity was responsible for connecting his story with the Argonauts, an earlier attack on Troy, and with Theban myth.

Myths of seasonal renewal. Certain myths, in which goddesses or heroes were temporarily incarcerated in the Underworld, were allegories of seasonal renewal. Perhaps the best-known myth of this type is the one telling how Hades, the god of the Underworld, carried PERSEPHONE off to be his wife, causing her mother Demeter, the goddess of grain, to allow the earth to grow barren out of grief. Because of her mother's grief, Zeus permitted Persephone to spend four months of the year in the house of Hades and eight in the light of day. In less benign climates, she was said to spend six months of the year in each. Rarely, however, was the seasonal interpretation the only meaning of the myth; the tradition surrounding Persephone, for instance, was also concerned with the rituals and experiences involved in a girl's marriage and arrival at adult womanhood.

See also MYSTERY RELIGIONS.

GREGORIAN CHANT, liturgical music of the ROMAN CATHOLIC church, sung in unison and used to accompany the text of the MASS and the canonical hours (also known as the divine office). Gregorian chant is named after ST. GREGORY I the Great, pope from 590 to 604. It was collected and codified during his reign.

The Ordinary of the mass includes those texts that remain the same for each mass. Those sung by the choir are, in the Latin mass, the Kyrie, Gloria, Credo, Sanctus (sometimes divided into Sanctus and Benedictus), and AGNUS DEI. The chant of the Kyrie ranges from neumatic (patterns of one to four notes per syllable) to melismatic (unlimited notes per syllable) styles. The Gloria appeared in the 7th century. The psalmodic recitation—*i.e.*, using psalm tones, simple formulas for the intoned reciting of psalms—of early Glorias attests to their ancient origin. Later Gloria chants are neumatic. The melodies of the Credo, accepted into the mass about the 11th century, resemble psalm tones. The Sanctus and Benedictus are probably from apostolic times. The usual Sanctus chants are neumatic. The Agnus Dei was brought from the Eastern church in the 7th century and is basically in neumatic style.

The Proper of the mass is composed of texts that vary for each mass in order to bring out the significance of each feast or season. The Introit is a processional chant that was originally a psalm with a refrain sung between verses. By the 9th century it had received its present form: refrain in a neumatic style—a psalm verse in psalm-tone style—refrain repeated. The Gradual, introduced in the 4th century, also developed from a refrain between psalm verses. Later it became: opening melody (chorus)—psalm verse or verses in an embellished psalmodic structure (soloist)—opening melody (chorus), repeated in whole or in part. The Alleluia is of 4th-century Eastern origin. Its structure is somewhat like that of the Gradual. The Tract replaces the Alleluia in penitential times; it is a descendant of SYNAGOGUE music.

The canonical hours, as observed by monastic communities, consist of eight prayer services: Matins, Lauds, Prime, Terce, Sext, None, Vespers, and Compline. Each includes antiphons or refrains, short texts that precede or follow each psalm and are set mostly in syllabic chant.

GREGORIAN REFORM, an attempt by POPE GREGORY VII (reigned 1073–85) to reform the medieval Western church, especially by prohibiting lay investiture. Gregory also brought about internal ecclesiastical reforms through innovations in CANON LAW.

GREGORY I, SAINT \'gre-gə-rē\, *byname* Gregory the Great (b. *c.* 540, Rome—d. March 12, 604, Rome; feast day March 12), architect of the medieval PAPACY (reigned 590–604), a notable theologian who was also an administrative, social, liturgical, and moral reformer.

Gregory's great-grandfather was Pope Felix III (reigned 483–492), and Pope Agapetus I (reigned 535–536) also may have been related to him. About 572 Gregory became *praefectus urbis* (urban prefect; *i.e.*, the administrative president of Rome), a position he relinquished only two years later. Having a great interest in MONASTICISM, Gregory converted the palace at Caelian Hill, which he had inherited, into St. Andrew's Monastery. He then utilized his large inheritance for the establishment of six additional monasteries on his other holdings in Sicily. Gregory served as papal nuncio to Constantinople from 579 until about 584.

After sincere efforts to evade election to the papacy, Gregory was elected to that position in 590. He immediately devoted himself to alleviating the misery of the populace and of the refugees fleeing the Lombard invasion of Italy. Gregory I had grain sent from Sicily and used the revenues from church property to aid those who were starving. His devotion to social concerns was succinctly stated in one of his letters (Epistle I:44): "We do not want the treasury of the church defiled by disreputable gain."

His efforts to reform and save the church in Italy, which was endangered spiritually as well as materially, began with the attempt to slowly catholicize the Arian Lombards. He protested against the oppressive fiscal policies of the Byzantine exchequer, which so harshly taxed the people that they sometimes had to sell their children or emigrate into areas controlled by the Lombards. The Lombards, in turn, so extorted the pope on their behalf that he called himself the "paymaster of the city." Not until 598 did this conflict even temporarily abate.

In 602 Phocas, a Thracian centurion in the imperial army, managed to get himself elected emperor. He had Emperor Maurice, Empress Constance, the couple's five sons—the oldest was the godson of the pope—and three daughters executed. Phocas gained the pope's approval of his Lombard policy and was thus able to act with increasing terror, for Gregory's blessing was tantamount to ABSOLUTION for all offenses. This action established a precedent that was followed by many popes. Phocas recognized the papal primacy of jurisdiction in the church and gave Gregory the impression of subordination. The Roman papacy valued such an attitude and in doing so overlooked other matters, including even the character of those with whom it came to terms.

A reign of anarchy under Phocas spelled the end of the late Roman era. Gregory clearly recognized the importance of the migrating peoples of the West, who were hardly or not at all Christianized, and that the future of the church of the West lay with them. He intensified his connections with Theodolinda, the Catholic Bavarian wife of the Lombard king Agilulf, whose son Adaloald became Catholic only in 615, and with Brunhild, the powerful Merovingian queen. In 596, under the protection of Brunhild, he initiated one of the greatest acts of his pontificate, the establishment of MISSIONS in England. He appointed AUGUSTINE (later first archbishop of Canterbury) and a band of 40 monks to begin the work in England. The later English missionary monks St. Willibrord (658–739) and ST. BONIFACE (*c.* 675–754) were able to conduct their missionary campaigns on the European continent because of the efforts of Gregory in regard to England. Gregory sometimes advocated a war of aggression against heathens in order to Christianize them. The earliest war benediction originated with Gregory; he has become, along with ST. AUGUSTINE (354–430), a precedent setter for the ecclesiastical war ideology of the Middle Ages.

With the consolidation of the patrimony of Peter (lands controlled by the papacy), Gregory, without realizing it himself, became the founder of the later Papal States and of the temporal papal authority. According to his view, the patrimony of Peter ought to be at the immediate disposal of the church and of the poor.

Because of his concern for people, he tried to make their faith more intelligible to themselves by popularizing miracles and the concept of PURGATORY and by encouraging a reform of the mass—from which came the GREGORIAN CHANT. For his theology, Gregory was deeply indebted to St. Augustine of Hippo. Estimations of his character have ranged from ecclesiastical adulation to sharp criticism.

Gregory's body lies buried in St. Peter's Basilica in Rome. He had forbidden veneration of his corpse under penalty of EXCOMMUNICATION.

GREGORY II CYPRIUS \'si-prē-əs\, *original name* George of Cyprus (b. 1241, Cyprus—d. 1290, Constantinople, Byzantine Empire [now Istanbul, Tur.]), Greek Orthodox PATRIARCH of Constantinople (1283–89) who strongly opposed reunion of the EASTERN ORTHODOX and ROMAN CATHOLIC churches.

In the beginning of his career as a cleric in the Byzantine imperial court, Gregory supported the policy of both his emperor, Michael VIII Palaeologus, and the patriarch of Constantinople, John XI Becchus, favoring a union between the two churches. With the accession in 1282 of the anti-unionist emperor Andronicus II Palaeologus, Gregory reversed his position and opposed Becchus. When mounting pressure on Becchus forced him to resign, Gregory was named to succeed him as Gregory II.

Gregory's stand against Becchus and against the theology of the Roman Catholic church led him to write *Tomos pisteos* ("Tome on Faith"), which refuted the Latin position that the HOLY SPIRIT proceeded from God the Son as well as God the Father. The text, however, was denounced as unorthodox by the patriarchs of Alexandria and Antioch. It and a subsequent work of APOLOGETICS (*Homologia*) antagonized both the enemies and supporters of reunion. Continued criticism from the exiled Becchus forced Gregory to resign as patriarch in 1289 and retire to a monastery, where he died.

GREGORY VII, SAINT, *original name* Hildebrand, *Italian* Ildebrando (b. c. 1020, near Soana, Papal States—d. May 25, 1085, Salerno, Principality of Salerno; canonized 1606; feast day May 25), one of the great reform popes of the Middle Ages (reigned 1073–85).

Hildebrand began his education at the Monastery of St. Mary in Rome, where his uncle was ABBOT. One of his teachers at the Schola Cantorum, Giovanni Graziano, later became Pope Gregory VI and took Hildebrand into his service. In 1046 Hildebrand accompanied his deposed patron into exile in Germany. He was called back to Rome by Pope Leo IX (reigned 1049–54) and there was one of the groups of reformers that Leo was assembling. Hildebrand became a CARDINAL and archdeacon of Rome.

Elected by acclamation (April 22, 1073) to succeed Alexander II, Gregory made reform and renewal of the church the goal of his reign. He began an attack on the chief problems of the church: SIMONY (selling or purchasing ecclesiastical offices) and nicolaitism (clerical marriage or concubinage). Because he found it difficult to work through the bishops, he tended to centralize authority. He used papal legates (representatives) freely and insisted on their precedence over local bishops.

Gregory is chiefly known for his contest with the German emperor Henry IV (1050–1106) over lay investiture (the right of lay rulers to grant ecclesiastical officials the symbols of their authority). The pope's Roman SYNOD of 1075 began the long conflict that was to go beyond his lifetime. At that synod Gregory excommunicated five of Henry's advisers. In late 1075 Henry gave support to the antireform party in Milan and placed a new bishop in the position of the legitimate bishop.

Although Gregory had written to Henry in December 1075, holding out the possibility of negotiations on the issue, Henry openly defied Gregory. Gregory excommunicated Henry and declared him deposed. The number of Henry's partisans dwindled, and in Germany plans were begun to elect another king. Henry was to leave the decision of his case to the pope, who was to come to a meeting of the magnates at Augsburg on Feb. 2, 1077. He was expected to repudiate his rebellion against the pope and to urge his advisers who had been excommunicated to seek ABSOLUTION.

Early in 1077 Gregory went north to cross the Alps and heard that Henry was hastening to Italy. Alarmed, the pope withdrew to the castle of Canossa, a stronghold of his supporter, Matilda, countess of Tuscany. Henry, however, was coming not as a foe but as a suppliant. For three cold January days he stood outside the castle pleading for absolution, while the nobles and bishops of Germany were awaiting the pope at Augsburg. The priest in Gregory prevailed over the politician, and he relented and absolved Henry from EXCOMMUNICATION.

Henry promptly regarded himself as legitimate king again, and Gregory had to write to the German magnates explaining his action. The Germans canceled the Augsburg meeting and called for another gathering. Gregory sent legates who pleaded with the assembled nobles and bishops not to proceed with an election until the pope could be present. The magnates went ahead, however, and elected Rudolf of Rheinfelden, thus precipitating a bloody civil war. Gregory tried to mediate between Henry and Rudolf, but by 1080 the pope was convinced that Henry was intransigent and once more excommunicated him and declared him deposed. This meant war. Henry had the support of his faction in Germany and that of the Lombard antireform party. Gregory sought the aid of the formidable Robert Guiscard, duke of Apulia and Calabria (c. 1015–85). Henry's German bishops met at Brixen (Italy) and declared Gregory deposed. To replace him they chose Guibert, archbishop of Ravenna, who took the name Clement III (1080, 1084–1100).

When Rudolf of Rheinfelden was killed at the Battle of the Elster (1080), Henry came over the Alps and besieged Rome. Gregory held a synod at the Lateran in November 1083 to attempt a settlement, but this failed, and on March 21, 1084, Henry's troops took the city. Gregory sought refuge in the Castel Sant'Angelo and suffered the chagrin of seeing Guibert of Ravenna crowned in St. Peter's. Guibert in turn crowned Henry emperor. Robert Guiscard, back from an unsuccessful attempt on the Byzantine Empire, marched on Rome and rescued Gregory, but in the fighting a large part of the city was burned down. Gregory, now unpopular with the embittered Romans, left with Guiscard.

GREGORY OF NAZIANZUS, SAINT \,na-zē-'an-zəs\ (b. c. 330, Arianzus, near Nazianzus, in Cappadocia, Asia Minor [now in Turkey]—d. c. 389, Arianzus; Eastern feast day January 25 and 30; Western feast day January 2), CHURCH FATHER whose defense of the doctrine of the TRINITY made him one of the greatest champions of orthodoxy against the heresy of ARIANISM.

Gregory's father, a convert to CHRISTIANITY, served as bishop of his native city, Nazianzus (the exact location of which is not known). Gregory thus grew up in a Christian and clerical family. Nevertheless, he received a classical as well as religious education. He was a close friend of BASIL, later bishop of Caesarea. Soon after returning to Cappadocia, Gregory joined the monastic community that Basil had founded in Pontus. The two friends collaborated in editing the *Philocalia*, an anthology of theological and devotional selections from the works of ORIGEN.

In 362 Gregory accepted ORDI-NATION to the PRIESTHOOD to as-sist his father, though he went to Annesi for further prepara-tion and remained there until the following EASTER. For the next 10 years he worked at Na-zianzus supporting Basil—who was first PRESBYTER and from 370 to 379 bishop of Caesarea—in his struggles with personal ri-vals, with Arians, and with the Arian emperor Valens. Basil was attempting to retain control of the church in at least part of the new province of Cappadocia Se-cunda, which had been created by Valens to diminish orthodox authority. Gregory, under pres-sure from Basil to assist him in this conflict, reluctantly accept-ed consecration (372) to the episcopate for the village of Sasima. He never took posses-sion of the bishopric, however. He briefly administered the church of Nazianzus again after his father's death in 374, but, when a successor was installed in that bishopric, Gregory re-tired to a monastery in Isauria, in south-central Anatolia.

After the death of Valens in 378 and that of Basil in 379, Gregory became the outstand-

St. Gregory of Nazianzus, detail of a mosaic in the Palatine Chapel, Palermo, Italy, 12th century
Anderson—Alinari from Art Resource

\'ni-sə\, *Latin* Gregorius Nysse-nus (b. *c.* 335, Caesarea, in Cap-padocia, Asia Minor [now Kay-seri, Tur.]—d. *c.* 394; feast day March 9), philosophical theolo-gian and mystic, leader of the orthodox party in the 4th-centu-ry Christian controversies over the doctrine of the TRINITY.

Gregory was more deeply in-fluenced by his philosophical training than by the other two Cappadocian Fathers of the Church, his brother BASIL OF CAE-SAREA and their friend GREGORY OF NAZIANZUS. He began his adult life as a teacher of rhetoric and is usually believed to have been married, although the strictures on marriage in his treatise *On Virginity* seem to imply the contrary. In the 360s he turned to religious studies and Christian devotion, per-haps even to the monastic life, under Basil's inspiration and guidance. As part of Basil's struggle with Bishop Anthimus of Tyana—whose city became the metropolis (civil and there-fore ecclesiastical capital) of western Cappadocia in 372— Gregory was consecrated as bishop of Nyssa, a small city in

ing spokesman of the Nicene party that accepted the de-crees of the COUNCIL OF NICAEA of 325. He was invited to take charge of the Nicene congregation at Constantinople, a city torn by sectarian strife. His Chapel of the Resurrec-tion (Greek: Anastasia) became the scene of the birth of Byzantine Orthodoxy—*i.e.*, the post-Nicene theology and practice of the majority of Eastern Christianity. A religious adventurer, Maximus the Cynic, however, was set up as a rival to Gregory by bishops from Egypt, who broke into the Anastasia at night for a clandestine consecration.

When the new emperor, Theodosius, came east in 380, the Arian bishop of Constantinople, Demophilus, was ex-pelled, and Gregory was able to take over the Great Church (probably the earlier BASILICA on the site of the present-day HAGIA SOPHIA). The council (later recognized as the second ecumenical council) that met at Constantinople in 381 was prepared to acknowledge Gregory as bishop of Constantino-ple; but, on the arrival of Bishop Timothy of Alexandria, his position was challenged on technical grounds. Weary of in-trigues, Gregory withdrew after an eloquent farewell dis-course. The council, however, supported his policies and endorsed the Trinitarian doctrine of three equal Persons (Father, Son, and HOLY SPIRIT) as taught by Gregory and ex-pressed in the "creed commonly called the Nicene."

For the rest of his life Gregory lived quietly on the family property at Arianzus near Nazianzus, except for a brief peri-od as administrator of the Church of Nazianzus during a vacancy. He continued his interest in church affairs through correspondence, including letters against the HERE-SY of Apollinaris, who denied the existence of a human soul in Christ.

the new province of Cappadocia Secunda, which Basil wished to retain in his ecclesiastical jurisdiction. In 375, however, Gregory was accused of maladministration by the provincial governor as part of the campaign of the Roman emperor Valens to promote ARIANISM. Gregory was deposed in 376 by a SYNOD of bishops and banished. But on Valens' death in 378 his congregation welcomed him back to Nyssa enthusiastically.

After his return to his DIOCESE he was active in the settle-ment of church affairs. In 379 he attended a council at An-tioch and was sent on a special MISSION to the churches of Arabia (*i.e.*, Transjordan); his visit to Jerusalem on this oc-casion left him with a dislike for the increasingly fashion-able PILGRIMAGES, an opinion he expressed vigorously in one of his letters. In 381 he took part in the General (second ec-umenical) Council at Constantinople and was recognized by the emperor Theodosius as one of the leaders of the or-thodox communion in Cappadocia. He had become the leading orthodox theologian in Asia Minor in the struggle against the Arians.

Gregory was primarily a scholar, whose chief contribu-tion lay in his writings. Besides controversial replies to her-etics, particularly the Arians—in which he formulated the doctrine of the Trinity (Father, Son, and HOLY SPIRIT) that emerged as a clear and cogent answer to Arian question-ing—he completed Basil's *Hexaëmeron* ("Six Days"), ser-mons on the days of the Creation, with *The Creation of Man*, and he produced a classic outline of orthodox theolo-gy in his *Great Catechesis*. His brief treatise *On Not Three Gods* relates the Cappadocian Fathers' theology of three Persons in the Godhead (*i.e.*, the Trinity) to Plato's teachings of the One and the Many. As a Christian Platonist, Gregory shared Origen's conviction that man's material nature is a result of the Fall of Man and also Origen's hope for ultimate universal salvation.

Platonic and Christian inspiration combine in Gregory's ascetic and mystical writings, which have been influential in the devotional traditions of the EASTERN ORTHODOX church and (indirectly) of the Western church. In his mystical *Life of Moses*—which treats the journey of the Hebrews from Egypt to MOUNT SINAI as a pattern of the progress of the soul through the temptations of the world to a vision of God—Gregory's teaching that the spiritual life is not one of static perfection but of constant progress may be seen.

GṚHYA SŪTRA \'gri-hyə-'sü-trə\, in HINDUISM, any of the religious manuals that detail the domestic (*gṛhya*) religious ceremonies that are to be performed by the householder over his own fire. They make up, together with the ŚRAUTA SŪTRAS (which deal with the grand Vedic sacrifices) and the DHARMA SUTRAS (which deal with rules of conduct), the KALPA SŪTRAS. The *Gṛhya Sūtra*s describe the ceremonies (SAMSKĀRAS) that mark each stage of a man's life, from the moment of his conception to his final death rites; the five daily sacrifices (*mahāyajña*); seasonal ceremonies; and those observed on special occasions, such as house building or cattle breeding.

GRIFFIN, *also spelled* griffon, *or* gryphon, composite mythological creature with a lion's body (winged or wingless) and a bird's head, usually that of an eagle. The griffin was a favorite decorative motif in the ancient Middle Eastern and

The griffin, French woodcut, 1533
The Granger Collection

Mediterranean lands. Probably originating in the Levant in the 2nd millennium BCE, the griffin had spread throughout western Asia and into Greece by the 14th century BCE. The griffin was shown either recumbent or seated on its haunches, often paired with the sphinx; its function may have been protective.

In the Iron Age the griffin was again prominent in both Asia and Greece. Apparently the griffin was in some sense sacred, appearing frequently in SANCTUARY and tomb furnishings. Its precise nature or its place in cult and legend remains unknown.

GROLIER CODEX \'grōl-yər-'kō-,deks\: *see* MAYA CODICES.

GUARDIAN SPIRIT, supernatural teacher, frequently depicted in animal form, who guides an individual through advice and songs; the belief in guardian spirits is widely diffused among the North American Indians.

In some traditions the guardian manifests itself in a dream or by other portents. In other traditions the individual sets out to discover his guardian by undertaking a VISION QUEST. Among the South American Indians, possession of a guardian spirit is limited to SHAMANS who have ingested hallucinogenic plants.

GUHYASAMĀJA TANTRA \'gù-hyə-sə-'mä-jə-'tən-trə\ (Sanskrit: "Treatise on the Sum Total of Mysteries"), *also called* Tathāgataguhyaka \tə-'tä-gə-tə-'gù-hyə-kə\ ("The Mystery of Tathāgatahood [Buddhahood]"), oldest and one of the most important of all Buddhist TANTRAS. These are the basic texts of the Tantric form of BUDDHISM.

The *Guhyasamāja Tantra* is ascribed by tradition to the sage ASAṄGA. Much of its symbolism, appearing at the beginning of the VAJRAYĀNA tradition (3rd–6th century CE), exercised a normative influence over that tradition's development. The first of 18 chapters presents the text's MANDALA, a visual image used in ritual and meditation and understood as the symbolic embodiment of a Tantric text. Other chapters present sexual and horrific symbolism, spiritual techniques, the nature of enlightened consciousness, and other central Tantric concerns.

GUṆASTHĀNA \'gù-nəs-'tä-nə\ (Sanskrit: "level of virtue"), in JAINISM, any of the 14 stages of spiritual development through which a soul passes on its way to MOKṢA (spiritual liberation from SAMSĀRA, or mundane existence coupled with endless transmigration).

The initial levels of development are: (1) *mithyā-dṛṣṭi*, "false views," in which the soul remains deluded; (2) *sāsvādana*, "mixed taste," a stage that is no longer than a single instant in duration through which the soul passes when it falls back to the state of *mithyā-dṛṣṭi*; (3) *samyak-mithyātva*, "truth and falsehood," a transitory state occurring during a rise to the fourth *guṇasthāna* or a regression to the first, during which both correct and incorrect views are manifest; (4) *samyak-dṛṣṭi*, "correct views," the state of possessing true vision and considered to be the first true level on the upward progression to *mokṣa*; (5) *deśa-virata*, "partial cessation," the level attained by taking the vows (*vratas*) prescribed for laity; (6) *sarva-virata*, "full cessation," the level attained by taking the vows of total restraint (the *mahāvratas* or "great vows") prescribed for mendicants; (7) *apramatta-virata*, "cessation without any relapses."

In the following seven stages, the aspirant enters the holy life. Stages 8, 9, and 10 (*apūrva-karaṇa, anivṛtti-karaṇa*, and *sūkṣma-sāmparāya;* respectively "the pursuit of that which has never before been experienced," "the pursuit of non-return [to *saṃsāra*], and "transition to the subtle state") comprise the levels at which the aspirant may either suppress or eliminate specific types of passions; (11) *upaśānta-moha,* "the quelling of delusion," a state of attainment at which specific passions are merely suppressed, causing an inevitable fall to the lower stages because an aspirant must eliminate passions, not merely quell them; (12) *kṣīṇa-moha,* "the destruction of delusion," the stage wherein passions are entirely eliminated, causing the soul to inevitably proceed to the higher stages of attainment; (13) *sayoga-kevalin,* "emancipation while still embodied," the stage of an ARHAT, *kevalin,* JINA, or TĪRTHAṄKARA. The 14th state, *ayoga-kevalin,* is the stage attained just prior to death, when all action (the ultimate cause of bondage to *saṃsāra*) comes to an end.

Symbolic meeting of the first Sikh Gurū, Nānak (d. 1539) with the 10th and last Gurū, Gobind Singh (d. 1708). Painting of the Guler school, c. 1820; in the collection of Mohan Singh, Punjab, India
By courtesy of the Victoria and Albert Museum, London

GURDĀS, BHĀĪ \gŭr-'däs\, *in full* Bhāī Gurdās Bhallā (b. *c.* 1550–d. 1637), most famous of all Sikh poets and theologians apart from the 10 GURŪS (the founders and early leaders of the Sikh community). *Bhāī* is an honorific title meaning "brother."

Bhāī Gurdās' fame rests on being the scribe of the *Kartārpur Pothī,* the manuscript of Sikh SCRIPTURE prepared during the time of Gurū ARJAN. Gurdās also composed original works of poetry that are highly regarded within SIKHISM. His compositions include 40 (some scholars say 39) *vār*s (ballads) in Punjabi and 556 *kabitt*s (short poems) in Braj Bhāṣā (a western dialect of Hindi). The *vār*s enjoy semicanonical status and are among the only compositions outside the sacred scriptures that Sikhs are allowed to recite and sing within the confines of the GURDWĀRĀS, or houses of worship. They also are a significant resource for understanding the early Sikh community.

GURDJIEFF, GEORGE IVANOVITCH \gər-'jē-əf, -'jēf, -'jef\, *original name* George S. Georgiades (b. 1872?, Alexandropol, Armenia, Russian Empire [now Kumayri, Armenia]—d. Oct. 29, 1949, Neuilly, near Paris, France), Greco-Armenian mystic and philosopher who founded an influential quasi-religious movement.

Gurdjieff is thought to have spent his early adult years traveling in northeast Africa, the Middle East, India, and especially Central Asia, learning about various spiritual traditions. He moved to Moscow about 1913 and began teaching there and in Petrograd (St. Petersburg), returning to the Caucasus at the outbreak of the Russian Revolution in 1917. Gurdjieff taught that human life as ordinarily lived is similar to sleep; an individual who managed to transcend the sleeping state could reach remarkable levels of vitality and awareness.

Joined by some followers, Gurdjieff established the Institute for the Harmonious Development of Man in 1919 at Tiflis (now Tbilisi), Georgia; it was reestablished at Fontainebleau, France, in 1922. Its members, many from prominent backgrounds, lived a monastic life, except for occasional banquets, at which Gurdjieff would engage in probing dialogue and at which his writings were read. Ritual exercises and dance were also part of the regimen, often accompanied by music composed by Gurdjieff and an associate. Performers from the institute appeared in Paris in 1923 and in four U.S. cities the following year and brought considerable attention to Gurdjieff's work. A disciple named P.D. Ouspensky introduced Gurdjieff's teachings to Western readers. The Fontainebleau center was closed in 1933, but Gurdjieff continued teaching in Paris until his death.

GURDWĀRĀ \gŭr-'dwä-rä\ (Punjabi: "doorway to the Gurū"), place of worship of the Sikhs.

The key area of a *gurdwārā* is a spacious room housing the *Srī Gurū Granth Sāhib* (also known as the ĀDI GRANTH), the Sikh scripture. The community gathers here to participate in devotional activity that typically includes recitation (*pāth*) of scripture, singing of scripture to musical accompaniment (*kīrtan*), and its exegesis (*kathā*). Toward the closing of the devotional session, a supplication (*ardās*) is made in which the Sikhs remember their history, seek divine blessings in dealing with their current problems, and reaffirm their vision of establishing a state in which Sikhs shall rule (Khālsā Rāj). The service ends with a hymn read from the *Srī Gurū Granth Sāhib,* which is interpreted to be the divine reply (*hukam*) to the congregation's supplication. The *gurdwārā* also has a community kitchen (*langar*) attached to it, in which meals are prepared and served to the congregation.

Sikhs call the *gurdwārā* gathering *diwān*, a Persian word meaning "court." Having paid respects to the *Srī Gurū Granth Sāhib* and participated in ritual glorification of God, they then discuss day-to-day problems facing the community. Activities at the *gurdwārā* thus become a fair indicator of concerns and tensions within the community at a particular time.

The *gurdwārā*s associated with the Sikh Gurūs' lives or their activities serve as centers for Sikh pilgrimage. The leading *gurdwārā*s among these are the Golden Temple in Amritsar; the five Takhats located in Amritsar, Anandpur, Damdamā, Patnā, and Nanded; and the birth place of Gurū Nānak at Nankānā, now in Pakistan.

GURU \'gür-ü\ (Sanskrit, from the adjective *guru*, meaning "heavy," "weighty," hence, "respected," "venerable"), in HINDUISM, a personal spiritual teacher or guide who has attained spiritual insight. From at least the time of the UPANISHADS, India has stressed the importance of the tutorial method in religious instruction. In the educational system of ancient India, knowledge of the VEDAS was personally transmitted through oral teachings from the guru to his pupil. During this period it was customary for male pupils to live at the home of their gurus and to serve them with obedience and devotion.

Later, with the rise of the BHAKTI movement, which stressed devotion to a personalized deity, the guru became an even more important figure. He could be venerated as the leader or founder of a sect and was also considered to be the living embodiment of the spiritual truth and, thus, identified with the deity. The tradition of willing service and obedience to the guru has continued to the present day. The guru prescribes spiritual disciplines and, at the time of initiation, instructs students in the use of the MANTRA to assist in meditation; often one's guru is treated with the same respect paid the deity during worship.

For centuries at least, women have been sought out as gurus by devotees of both sexes, but until recent times they have infrequently established lineages of their own, owing in part to the fact that patrilineal succession is the norm throughout almost all of India. Another important contemporary development is the transnational circulation of Hindu gurus, not only because they have become magnets for disciples not born Hindu (as with the Beatles and other celebrities and western devotees, starting in the late 1960s) but also because such a claim to international appeal has become one of the most important elements for increasing a guru's prestige in India itself.

GURŪ \'gür-ü\ (Punjabi: "Preceptor"), in SIKHISM, within the compositions of NĀNAK (1469–1539), the founder of that tradition, the word Gurū is used to designate God. In the later tradition, however, Nānak, as the bearer of God's revelation, is called the Gurū, and so are his nine successors. As a result, SIKHISM gives special meaning to the general sense of the word GURU in Indian languages: teacher. Sikh belief insists on the unity of Gurūship; the 10 Gurūs are thus seen as representing one light. In Nānak's compositions, God is presented as the Supreme Lord of the Universe. Extending this royal metaphor, the Gurū was seen as responsible for both the spiritual (*dīn*) and the temporal (*dunīyā*) concerns of the community. In 1708, GOBIND SINGH, the 10th Gurū, discontinued the office and vested its authority in

the ĀDI GRANTH, thus elevating the Sikh SCRIPTURE to the status of Sri Gurū Granth Sahib.

The 10 Sikh Gurūs and the dates of their reigns were:
1. Nānak (1469–1539).
2. AṄGAD (1539–52), a disciple of Nānak, traditionally given credit for developing Gurmukhi, the script used to write down the Sikh scriptures.
3. AMAR DĀS (1552–74), a disciple of Aṅgad.
4. RĀMDĀS (1574–81), the son-in-law of Amar Dās and the founder of the city of AMRITSAR.
5. ARJAN (1581–1606), the son of Rāmdās and the builder of the GOLDEN TEMPLE (Darbār Sāhib), the most famous place of PILGRIMAGE for the Sikhs.
6. HARGOBIND (1606–44), the son of Arjan.
7. HARI RĀI (1644–61), the grandson of Hargobind.
8. HARI KISHAN (1661–64), the son of Hari Rāi; he died of smallpox at the age of eight.
9. TEGH BAHĀDUR (1664–75), the son of Hargobind.
10. GOBIND SINGH (1675–1708), the son of Tegh Bahādur.

GUYON, JEANNE-MARIE BOUVIER DE LA MOTTE, MADAME DU CHESNOY \gwʸē-'yòⁿ . . . dǖ-shen-'wä\, *née* Bouvier de La Motte, *byname* Madame Guyon (b. April 13, 1648, Montargis, France—d. June 9, 1717, Blois), French mystic, a central figure in the theological debates of 17th-century France through her advocacy of QUIETISM.

At 16 she married Jacques Guyon, lord du Chesnoy, but, at the death of her husband in 1676, she turned toward mystical experiences. Led through a long cycle of personal religious developments by the Barnabite friar François Lacombe, she left her children and began travels with Lacombe to Geneva, Turin, and Grenoble (1681–86). The heterodox nature of her teachings—which tended to exclude the external world and the mechanisms of the church—aroused the suspicions of local bishops, and she was regularly forced to move on. During this period she published the most important of her many writings: the *Moyen court et très facile de faire oraison* (1685; "The Short and Very Easy Method of Prayer"). In 1687 Lacombe was put in prison, where he died, and Guyon was arrested in 1688 but was released after a few months at the intervention of the second wife of Louis XIV.

After her release, Guyon attracted her greatest disciple, the influential Abbé de Fénelon (1651–1715). By 1694 Fénelon's writings, colored by quietism, had generated a great alarm; and, in the midst of complicated political and religious maneuvers, a conference met at Issy (1695), at which Fénelon defended Guyon's teachings. Quietism, however, was officially condemned by the ROMAN CATHOLIC church, and Guyon was imprisoned. After her release from prison (1703), she lived and wrote quietly at Blois.

Her writings were published from 1712 to 1720 (45 vol., reprinted 1767–90).

GWYDION \'gwi-dē-ən\, in the Welsh MABINOGION, a son of the goddess DÔN, a master of magic and poetry and a somewhat dubious character. He assisted in raping a virgin servant girl of his uncle, King Math; for his punishment he was made to live as a stag, a sow, and a wolf with the rapist as his counterpart—the two producing children together. Later, however, he was the cunning protector of his sister Aranrhod's unwanted child Lleu Llaw Gyffes, probably the Welsh version of the pan-Celtic deity LUGUS. Aranrhod gave birth to Lleu during a test of her virginity and Gwydion had to trick her into giving him a name and weapons, apparently the duties of a mother.

ḤABAD \k̲ä-'bäd\, Jewish movement and its doctrine, an offshoot of the religious and social movement known as HASIDISM; its name derives from the initial letters of three Hebrew words: *ḥokhmah* ("wisdom"), *binah* ("intelligence"), and *da'at* ("knowledge"). Ḥabad follows the common Hasidic themes of DEVEQUT ("attachment"), *ḥitlahavut* ("enthusiasm"), and *kawwana* ("devotion"), but it elevates the importance of the intellect in spiritual endeavors. Adherence to divine commandments (TORAH) is encouraged, but excessive ASCETICISM is discouraged. The leaders (ZADDIKS, or *tzaddiqim*) of Ḥabad Hasidism tend to be teachers and spiritual guides rather than miracle workers. The strongest opposition to Ḥabad was based on the charge that it leaned toward PANTHEISM. (*See also* QABBALAH AND JEWISH MYSTICISM.)

The first leader of Ḥabad was Rabbi Shneur Zalman, a prolific writer of 18th-century Lyady, Russia, whose *Liqqute amarim* ("Collections of Sayings")—popularly known as *Tanya* ("There Is a Teaching") from its opening word—contains the theoretical doctrine of the movement and is an interpretation of Qabbalah. His five-volume version of Joseph Karo's legal code, SHULḤAN 'ARUKH, attracted numerous followers and several outstanding leaders.

Shneur's descendants became the spiritual leaders of the Lubavitcher Hasidim, who migrated from Lyubavichi in Russia and set up headquarters in New York City. The group is noted for its support of schools, orphanages, and study groups and for various other activities that foster Jewish religious life in all its manifestations.

ḤABDALAH \,häv-dä-'lä, häv-'dȯ-lə\ (Hebrew: "Separation" or "Distinction"), ceremony in Jewish homes and in SYNAGOGUES concluding the SABBATH and religious festivals. The main liturgical text for the ASHKENAZI version of the Habdalah is to be found in *Arba'ah Turim* (*The Tur*), Orah Hayyim 296:1. The ceremony consists of BENEDICTIONS that are recited over a cup of wine (and, on the night of the Sabbath, over spices and a braided candle) to praise God, who deigned to sanctify these days and thus "separate" them from routine weekdays. If a festival begins at the closing of the Sabbath, no spices are used, the candle lit for the festival replaces the Sabbath candle, and a special form of the Habdalah is combined with the special benediction (KIDDUSH) that ushers in the festival.

ḤACHIMAN \'hä-chē-,män\, one of the most popular SHINTŌ deities of Japan. He is the patron deity of the Minamoto clan and of warriors in general and is often referred to as the god of war. Hachiman is commonly regarded as the deification of Ōjin, the 15th emperor of Japan. Hachiman shrines are most frequently dedicated to three deities: Hachiman as Ōjin, his mother the empress Jingō, and the goddess Hime-gami.

The first shrine to Hachiman, the Usa Hachiman-gū in Ōita prefecture, was established in 725 CE. The deity is im-

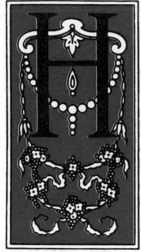

mensely popular throughout Japan, and half the registered Shintō shrines are dedicated to him. During the Nara period (710–784) Hachiman was accepted as a Buddhist divinity and came to be known as Hachiman Daibosatsu (Great Buddha-to-be). He was consulted as an oracle before the building of the colossal Buddha image at TŌDAI TEMPLE and, as guardian deity of the temple, has his own shrine within the temple compound.

ḤADAD \'hä-,däd, 'hä-,dad\, *also spelled* Had, Hadda, *or* Haddu, *in the Old Testament* Rimmon \'ri-mən\, West Semitic god of storms, thunder, and rain. His attributes were identical with those of ADAD of the Assyro-Babylonian pantheon. He was the chief BAAL ("lord") of the West Semites in north Syria, along the Phoenician coast, and along the Euphrates River. As Baal-Hadad he was represented as a bearded deity, often holding a club and thunderbolt and wearing a horned headdress. He was the consort of ATARGATIS in Syria and the bull was his symbolic animal.

ḤADES \'hā-dēz\, *Greek* Aïdes ("the Unseen"), *also called* Ploutos \'plü-təs, -,täs\, *or* Pluto \'plü-tō\, *or* Pluton \'plü-,tän\ ("the Rich" or "The Giver of Wealth"), in GREEK RELIGION, son of the TITANS CRONUS and RHEA, and brother of ZEUS and POSEIDON. After Cronus was killed, the kingdom of the Underworld fell by lot to Hades. There he ruled with his queen, PERSEPHONE, over the infernal powers and over the dead, in what was often called "the House of Hades," or simply Hades. Though he supervised the trial and punishment of the wicked after death, he was not normally one of the judges in the Underworld; nor did he personally torture the guilty, a task assigned to the Furies (ERINYES). Hades was stern and pitiless, unmoved by prayer or sacrifice.

He was usually worshiped under a euphemistic epithet such as Clymenus ("the Illustrious") or Eubuleus ("the Giver of Good Counsel"). His title PLUTO or Pluton may have originated through Hades' partial amalgamation with a god of the earth's fertility, or because he gathered all living things into his treasury at death.

The word Hades is used in the SEPTUAGINT to translate the Hebrew word *sheol*, denoting a dark region of the dead. Tartarus, originally an abyss far below Hades and the place of punishment in the lower world, later lost its distinctness and became almost a synonym for Hades.

ḤADITH \ha-'dēth\ (Arabic: "speech," "talk," "report," or "account"), the spoken traditions attributed to the Prophet MUHAMMAD, his family, and COMPANIONS OF THE PROPHET, which are revered in ISLAM as a major source of religious law and moral guidance. The development of Hadith was a vital element during the first three centuries of Islamic history.

Hadith embodies the SUNNA (right custom) of the community of Muslims. Every complete Hadith formulation consists of two parts, the text proper and the ISNĀD (chain of transmitters), which precedes it—*e.g.*, "It has been related to me by Yaḥyā on the authority of Mālik on the authority of Nāfiʿ on the authority of ʿAbd Allāh ibn ʿUmar that the Prophet said: 'If someone sells a palm tree which has been fertilized, its fruit belongs to the seller, unless the buyer stipulate it for himself.'"

This literary form came into being early in the 2nd century of the HIJRA (soon after 720 CE). The emergence of such traditions was mainly due to the activity of the so-called traditionists, who tried to base the Islamic way of life not on custom as it had developed in the centers of the Muslim world but on individual precedents going back to the Prophet. This led to a wholesale creation of traditions with ever more elaborate isnāds. As a result, most of the early opinions held on the religious law and dogma of Islam as well as on its early history (which provided legal and political precedents), not to mention prophecies expressing political and other expectations, were cast in the form of traditions, which often attempted to conceal their underlying tendencies. Once the Prophet's personal example became established as the universal Muslim norm (sunna), however, Muslim scholars attempted to determine forgeries or doubtful reports among the existing body of Hadiths. They were bound in principle to accept any textually reliable Hadith and had to restrict themselves principally to the scrutiny of isnāds.

All acceptable Hadiths therefore fall into three general categories: ṣaḥīḥ (sound), those with a reliable and uninterrupted chain of transmission and a matn (text) that does not contradict orthodox belief; ḥasan (good), those with an incomplete isnād or with transmitters of questionable authority; and daʿīf (weak), those whose matn or transmitters are subject to serious criticism.

Isnāds are further evaluated according to the completeness of their chains: they may be unbroken and reliable all the way back to Muhammad (musnad) yet very short (ʿālī), implying less likelihood of error; they may lack one authority in the chain of transmitters or may be missing two or more transmitters (muʿḍal) or may have an obscure authority, referred to simply as "a man" (mubham).

The transmitters themselves, once established in the historical record as reliable men or women, determine further categories; the same tradition may have been handed down concurrently through several different isnāds (mutawātir), indicating a long and sound history, or a Hadith may have been quoted by three different trustworthy authorities (mashhūr) or by only one (āḥād).

Many scholars produced collections of Hadith, the earliest compilation being the great Musnad of AḤMAD IBN ḤAN-BAL, arranged by isnād. Six large collections, known as al-kutub al-sitta ("the six books"), arranged by matn—those of AL-BUKHĀRĪ (d. 870), MUSLIM IBN AL-ḤAJJĀJ (d. 875), Abū Dāʾūd (d. 888), AL-TIRMIDHĪ (d. 892), Ibn Mājā (d. 886), and al-

Hachiman, woodblock print
By courtesy of the Museum für Volkerkunde, Vienna

Nasāʾī (d. 915)—came to be recognized as canonical in SUNNI Islam, though the books of al-Bukhārī and Muslim enjoy a prestige that virtually eclipses the other four. SHIʿITES make selective use of these books but esteem the collected sayings (akhbār) of the IMAMS most highly. Four of these collections are canonical: al-Kulaynī's (d. 940), Ibn Bāb-ūya's (d. 991), and two by al-Ṭūsī (d. 1068).

In critical scholarship, Hadith constitutes the main source for the study of doctrinal development during the first few centuries of Islam. It has been one of the core subjects studied in religious colleges (MADRA-SAS) since the Middle Ages, and it was an area of learning in which women scholars were active.

HAFṬARAH \ˌhäf-tä-ˈrä, häf-ˈtȯr-ə\, plural Haftarot \ˌhäf-tä-ˈrōt\, or Haftarahs (Hebrew: "Conclusion"), in JUDAISM, the passage from the Prophets that is read in the SYNA-GOGUE to complement the reading from the PENTATEUCH on the SABBATH and on festival and fast days. The practice of declaiming prophetic passages after Pentateuchal ones is well attested from ancient times. Although the Pentateuch is read from start to finish through the liturgical year, the prophetic readings consist of selected sections; only Obadiah, which accompanies Genesis 32:4–36:43, and the book of Jonah, read at the afternoon service on YOM KIPPUR, are declaimed start to finish.

Two criteria are used in choosing the prophetic complement to the Pentateuch. First, the prophetic passage may deal with the same theme as the Pentateuchal one. For instance, the "Song of Deborah," included in Judges 4:4–5:31, serves as the Hafṭarah for Exodus 13:17–17:16, involving the "Song of Moses." The Hafṭarah for Numbers 13:1–15:41, which deals with the 12 agents of Moses sent to spy out the land of Israel before the Israelite entry, is matched by Joshua 2:1–24, the account of Joshua's counterpart mission. Second, for about a third of the liturgical occasions, the Hafṭarah is chosen by the criterion of the special status of a given Sabbath within the year. For example, the advent of the NEW MOON requires a particular prophetic passage. Likewise, over a 10-week period in the summer, a time of mourning (commemorating events such as the destruction of the Temple on the ninth of Av [late July or early August]) and of preparation (for ROSH HASHANAH and Yom Kippur), the Hafṭarah comprises three readings that focus on prophets' warnings against Israelite SIN and seven selections that contain prophets' messages of consolation on the occasion of national mourning.

The reading of the prophetic portion follows that of the Pentateuchal one and forms a complementary part of the declamation of the TORAH, upon which synagogue worship on Sabbaths, festivals, and fast days is centered. While the Pentateuchal portion is read from a Torah scroll, which lacks vowels and indications of musical intonation, the

Traditional Seder accoutrements for Passover: matzah, Seder plate, wine cup, and Haggadah
Lambert—Archive Photos

Haftarah is read from an ordinary printed book and includes both. The Haftarah is given its own musical system, different from that of the Pentateuch. Any qualified Israelite may be called to recite the Haftarah. It is customary that when a child reaches puberty (age 12 for girls, 13 for boys), she or he is called to the Torah to take a place as a responsible member of the community of Israel and to recite the Haftarah of that occasion.

HAGAR \'hā-ˌgär, -gər\, *also spelled* Agar \'ā-ˌgär\, in the OLD TESTAMENT, Abraham's concubine and the mother of his son Ishmael. Purchased in Egypt, she served as a maid to Abraham's childless wife, SARAH, who gave her to ABRAHAM to conceive an heir (Genesis 16:1–4a). When Hagar became pregnant, she grew arrogant; with Abraham's permission, Sarah treated her so harshly that she fled into the wilderness (Genesis 16:4b–6). There, by a spring of water, she was found by an ANGEL, who told her to return home and promised her that she would have many descendants through a son, Ishmael; he would grow up to be a "wild ass of a man," in constant struggle with all other men. Hagar returned home to bear her child (Genesis 16:7–15).

About 14 years after the birth of Ishmael, ISAAC was born to Sarah (Genesis 21:1–4). One day Sarah saw Isaac and Ishmael playing together and, fearing that Ishmael would also become an heir, sent the son and mother into the desert (Genesis 21:9–14). There God sustained them and was with Ishmael until he grew up (Genesis 21:15–21). The Jews believed that Ishmael was the ancestor of a number of Be-

douin peoples dwelling in southern Palestine (Genesis 25:12–18). There are also legends stating that Ishmael was an ancestor of MUHAMMAD.

HAGGADAH \ˌhä-gä-'dä, hə-'gä-də\ (Hebrew: "Narrative"), in JUDAISM, the text that guides the performance of the ritual acts and prayers at the SEDER celebrating PASSOVER.

Celebrated on the 15th of the lunar month of Nisan, the first full moon after the vernal equinox, the Seder involves eating MATZAH (unleavened bread) and maror (bitter herbs), drinking four cups of wine, and reciting the story of the EXODUS. Songs are usually sung and psalms recited. The Haggadah's narrative explains the foods and practices of the rite. While its contents have evolved over the ages and continue to evolve today, with prayers and rites added in response to contemporary events, the HOLOCAUST and the advent of the State of Israel, for example, the Haggadah of Passover always involves certain fixed elements of the Seder rite.

HAGGADAH, *Aramaic* Aggadah: *see* HALAKHAH AND HAGGADAH.

HAGIA SOPHIA \'hä-gē-ə-sō-'fē-ə, 'ha-; 'hā-jē-ə-, *Modern Greek* 'ä-ɡē-ä-sō-'fē-ä\, *also called* Church of the Holy Wisdom, *Turkish* Ayasofya, cathedral, one of the world's great monuments, built at Constantinople (now Istanbul) under the direction of the Byzantine emperor JUSTINIAN I. The structure, a domed BASILICA, was built in the amazingly short time of about six years and was completed in 537 CE.

The original church is said to have been built by Constantine in 325 on the foundations of a PAGAN temple. The architects were Anthemius of Tralles and Isidore of Miletus. It was enlarged by the emperor Constans and rebuilt after the fire of 415 by Theodosius II. The church was burned again in the Nika Insurrection of 532 and reconstructed by Justinian. The structure now standing is essentially the 6th-century edifice, although an earthquake tumbled the dome in 559, after which it was rebuilt to a smaller scale and the whole church reinforced from the outside. It was restored again in the mid-14th century. In 1453 it became a mosque with MINARETS, and a great chandelier was added. In 1935 it was made into a museum. The walls are still hung with Muslim calligraphic disks. The beautiful mosaics of the church are considered to be the main source of knowledge about the state of mosaic in the time shortly after the end of the ICONOCLASTIC CONTROVERSY.

HAGIOGRAPHY \ˌha-gē-'ä-grə-fē, ˌhā-, -jē-\, the body of literature describing the lives and veneration of saints. The literature of hagiography in CHRISTIANITY embraces acts of the martyrs (*i.e.*, accounts of their trials and deaths); biographies of saintly monks, bishops, princes, or virgins; and accounts of miracles connected with saints' tombs, relics, ICONS, or statues.

Hagiographies have been written from the 2nd century CE to instruct and edify readers and glorify the saints. In the Middle Ages it was customary to read aloud biographies of the principal saints on their feast days. Other works of hagiography told the stories of a class of saints, such as EUSEBIUS OF CAESAREA's account of the martyrs of Palestine (4th century CE) and Pope GREGORY I the Great's *Dialogues*, a collection of stories about SAINT BENEDICT OF NURSIA and other 6th-century Latin monks. Perhaps the most important hagiographic collection is the *Legenda aurea* (*Golden Legend*) of JACOBUS DE VORAGINE in the 13th century. Modern critical hagiography began in 17th-century Flanders with the JESUIT ecclesiastic Jean Bolland and his successors, who became known as Bollandists—it is the Bollandists who are responsible for the great edition of the ACTA SANCTORUM.

The hagiographer has a threefold task: to collect all the material relevant to each particular saint, to edit the documents according to the best methods of textual criticism, and to interpret the evidence by using literary, historical, and any other pertinent criteria.

HAI BEN SHERIRA \'hī-ben-shā-'rir-ä\ (b. 939—d. March 23, 1038), last outstanding Babylonian GAON, or head, of a great Talmudic academy, remembered for the number, range, and profundity of the RESPONSA (authoritative answers to questions concerning interpretation of Jewish law) he wrote.

Hai, whose family traced its origin back to the Davidic dynasty, was fourth in a direct line to occupy the *gaon*ate of Pumbedita (Babylonia), situated in Baghdad from the late 9th century on. He assisted his father, Sherira ben Ḥanina, in teaching and later as chief of court of the academy. They were both imprisoned briefly (997) on false charges; when they were freed, Hai's father appointed him *gaon* (998).

Close to a thousand *responsa* written by Hai, equaling the number of extant *responsa* written by all other *geonim*, are extant. He couched them in the same languages (Hebrew, Aramaic, or Arabic) in which the questions were written. On occasion, when no Talmudic citation can be found, his answers employ non-Jewish authorities. Hai steered a middle course between rationalism and more esoteric doctrines, allowing the QABBALAH validity insofar as its components are Talmudic but castigating it when it proposes miracle-making formulas by using the names of God. He was eulogized by the Judeo-Spanish poets Solomon ibn Gabirol and SAMUEL HA-NAGID as one who left no children but countless disciples in all countries of the world.

HAIL MARY, *Latin* Ave Maria, *also called* Angelic Salutation, a principal prayer of the ROMAN CATHOLIC church, comprising three parts addressed to the Virgin MARY. The following are the Latin text and an English translation:

◆ Ave Maria, gratia plena;
Dominus tecum:
Benedicta tu in mulieribus et benedictus
fructus ventris tui [Jesus].
Sancta Maria, Mater Dei,
Ora pro nobis peccatoribus, nunc et in hora
mortis nostrae.
Amen.

Hail Mary, full of grace;
The Lord is with thee:
Blessed art thou among women and blessed is
the fruit of thy womb, Jesus.
Holy Mary, Mother of God,
Pray for us sinners, now and at the hour
of our death.
Amen. ◆

The first part, the words of the ARCHANGEL GABRIEL (Luke 1:28), appears in liturgies as early as the 6th century. The second part, the words of Elizabeth (Luke 1:42), was added to the first part by about 1000 CE. The closing petition came into general use during the 14th or 15th century and received its official formulation by Pope Pius V in 1568.

The prayer has been set to music many times, most notably by Franz Schubert and also by Charles Gounod (the latter's work is superimposed on Johann Sebastian Bach's *Prelude in C Major*).

HAJJ \'häj\, *also spelled* hadj, in ISLAM, the PILGRIMAGE to the holy city of MECCA in Saudi Arabia, which every adult Muslim of either gender must make at least once in his or her lifetime if able to do so. The hajj is the fifth of the required practices and institutions known as the FIVE PILLARS OF ISLAM. The pilgrimage rites begin on the 7th day of Dhū al-Ḥijja (the last month of the Islamic year) and end on the 12th day.

The hajj is incumbent on every Muslim who is physically and financially able to make the pilgrimage, but only if their absence will not place a hardship on the family. One may perform the hajj by proxy, appointing a relative or friend going on the pilgrimage to "stand in" for one.

The pattern of pilgrimage rites was established by the Prophet MUHAMMAD, but Islamic tradition traced their origins to ADAM, ABRAHAM, and his family (HAGAR and Ishmael). These sacred ancestors were reportedly instructed in the rites by the ANGELS. For Muhammad, the hajj was one of his last public acts of worship before his death in 632.

Pilgrims about 6 miles from Mecca enter the state of holiness and purity known as *iḥrām* and don the *iḥrām* garments, consisting for men of two white seamless sheets

Interior of the Hagia Sophia, reconstructed in 537, Istanbul, Turkey
Hirmer Fotoarchiv, Munich

that are wrapped around the body. The dress requirements for women are less stringent, though still within the bounds of modesty. Pilgrims cut neither their hair or nails until the pilgrimage rite is over. A pilgrim enters Mecca and walks seven times around the sacred shrine called the KAʿBA, in the Great Mosque, kisses or touches the Black Stone (al-ḥajar al-aswad) in the Kaʿba, prays twice in the direction of the Station of Abraham (MAQĀM Ibrāhīm) and the Kaʿba, and runs seven times between the minor prominences of Mount Ṣafā and Mount Marwa. On the 7th of Dhū al-Ḥijja the pilgrim is reminded of his or her duties. At the second stage of the ritual, which takes place between the 8th and the 12th days of the month, the pilgrim visits the holy places outside Mecca—Jabal ar-Raḥma, Muzdalifa, Minā—and sacrifices an animal in commemoration of Abraham's sacrifice. This sacrifice inaugurates the great Feast of Sacrifice (ʿĪd al-Aḍḥā), which is observed by Muslims everywhere. The male pilgrim's head is usually shaved then, and, after throwing seven stones at each of the three pillars at Minā on three successive days (the pillars exemplify various devils), the pilgrim returns to Mecca to perform the farewell ṭawāf, or circling, of the Kaʿba before leaving the city.

Only a small fraction of the world's Muslims have actually ever completed this ritual obligation. Since the 1980s, about 2,000,000 persons perform the hajj each year, and the modern government of Saudi Arabia has invested substantial resources in refurbishing the holy places and managing the swelling flow of pilgrims. Though Muslims have attributed a variety of meanings to the hajj through the centuries, many today see it as a unifying force in Islam that brings followers of diverse background together in religious celebration. Believers who have made the pilgrimage may add the title ḥājj or ḥājjī to their names.

ḤĀKIM, AL- \àl-ʿk̲ä-kim\, in full al-Ḥākim bi-Amr Allāh (Arabic: "Ruler by God's Command"), called by Druzes al-Ḥākim bi-Amrih ("Ruler by His Own Command") (b. 985—d. 1021?), sixth ruler of the Egyptian SHIʿITE Fāṭimid dynasty, noted for his eccentricities and cruelty, especially his persecutions of Christians and Jews. He is held by adherents of the DRUZE religion to be a divine incarnation.

Al-Ḥākim was named CALIPH in 996. His policies proved to be arbitrary and harsh. His religious persecutions affected SUNNI Muslims as well as Jews and Christians. At times, however, his administration was tolerant. During famines he distributed food and tried to stabilize prices. He also founded mosques and patronized scholars and poets. In 1017 he began to encourage the teachings of some Ismāʿīlī missionaries, who held that he was the incarnation of divinity. The Druze religion developed from these teachings. Al-Ḥākim mysteriously vanished while taking a walk in the hills outside Cairo on the night of Feb. 13, 1021.

HAKUIN \ʿhä-kù-ₑēŋ\, also called Hakuin Ekaku \-ʾe-kä-kù\, original name Iwajirō (b. Jan. 19, 1686, Hara, Suruga province, Japan—d. Jan. 18, 1769, Hara), priest, writer, and artist who helped revive the RINZAI sect of ZEN Buddhism in Japan.

Hakuin joined the Rinzai Zen sect about 1700. He subsequently became an itinerant monk, during which time he experienced what he considered to be enlightenment. BUDDHISM in Japan had been largely coopted by the Tokugawa shogunate, but while many priests sought personal advancement, Hakuin lived in great poverty among his peasant parishioners. He attracted a large following that became a new foundation for Rinzai Zen in Japan.

Hakuin taught that direct knowledge of the truth is available to all, even the lowliest, and that a moral life must accompany religious practice. He utilized KOANS to aid meditation and invented the well-known paradox of contemplating the sound of one hand clapping. His writings include Keisō dokozui ("Poisonous Stamens and Pistils of Thorns"), intended for advanced students of Zen; he also is known as an artist and calligrapher.

ḤĀL \ʿhal\ (Arabic: "condition"), plural aḥwāl, in SUFISM, a spiritual state of mind that comes to the Sufi from time to time during his journey toward God. The aḥwāl are graces of God that cannot be acquired or retained through an individual's own efforts. When the soul is purified of its attachments to the material world, it can only wait patiently for those gifts, which, when they come, fill the Sufi with the desire to continue his journey with new energy and higher expectations.

The aḥwāl are distinguished by most Sufis from the MAQĀMS (spiritual stages) in two main aspects. First, the aḥwāl are usually transitory; second, while aḥwāl denote a gratuitous favor of God, maqāms are granted solely on merit and efforts.

Though the Sufis spoke of hundreds of aḥwāl, the following are among those most often referred to: (1) The ḥāl of murāqaba ("watching") fills the Sufi with either fear or joy according to the aspect of God revealed to him. (2) The ḥāl of qurb ("nearness") is a state that enables the Sufi to become unconscious of his own acts and to see God's acts and bounties toward him. (3) The ḥāl of wajd ("ecstasy") is a state described by the Sufi as a sensation that encounters the heart and produces such varied effects as sorrow or joy, fear or love, contentment or restlessness. (4) In the ḥāl of sukr ("intoxication") the Sufi, while not totally unaware of the things that surround him, becomes half-dazed because his association with God dims his sight of other things. The overpowering sense of the beloved in this state destroys the mystic's ability to distinguish between physical pain and pleasure. Ṣaḥw ("sobriety") immediately follows sukr, but the memories of the previous experience remain vivid and become a source of immense spiritual joy. (5) The ḥāl of wudd ("intimacy") is characterized by "the removal of nervousness, together with the persistence of awe." The Sufi becomes calm, contented, and reassured, but the overwhelming sense of the divine presence fills his heart with the kind of awe that is free from fear.

The concept of aḥwāl is rooted historically in the pre-Islamic religions of the Near Eastern–Mediterranean region. By the 11th century it had become a standard subject of Sufi discourse.

HALAKHAH AND HAGGADAH \ₕhä-lä-ʿk̲ä, hä-ʾlä-k̲ə . . . ₕhä-gä-ʾdä, hə-ʾgä-də\, in RABBINIC JUDAISM, the systems of thought that have been organized into normative law and lore, respectively. The halakhah, a species of the generic "law" finds its counterpart and complement in the haggadah, "lore"—the two native categories joining to form the Oral TORAH. Norms of behavior defined in the halakhah differ from norms of belief found in the haggadah in the way they are set forth. The former are presented topically and analytically, the latter exegetically or propositionally. The halakhah uses small and particular rules in order to speak to the everyday concerns of ordinary Jews, while the haggadah speaks in general terms to the world at large. The halakhah addresses the internal state of Israel (the people; i.e., the Jews) in relationship with God, whereas the haggadah treats externalities. Categorically, the haggadah faces outward, correlating and showing the relationship of humanity in general and Israel in particular. The theological system of a just world order answerable to one God that animates the haggadah sets forth the parallel stories of humanity and Israel—each of these stories begins with Eden (which parallels the Land of Israel for the Jewish people), is marked by SIN and punishment (Adam's and Israel's respective acts of rebellion against God, the one through disobedience, the other through violating the Torah), and then features exile for the purpose of bringing about repentance and ATONEMENT (Adam from Eden, Israel from the land).

The classical statements of the halakhah occur in the MISHNAH, TOSEFTA, and two TALMUDS. Scriptural EXEGESIS and narratives are the principal media for thought about theological issues, and these occur in various compilations of the MIDRASH. However, both Talmuds contain ample components of haggadah, and some Midrashic compilations, particularly those devoted to EXODUS, Leviticus, Numbers, and Deuteronomy, attend to halakhic problems.

The halakhah identifies what is implicit in the facts set forth in SCRIPTURE, picking out the indicative traits that open the way to generalization and to identification of the principle embodied by the case. Then the halakhah of the Oral Torah regularizes, orders, systematizes, classifies, and, above all, places the discrete facts into an overall hierarchy, shaped into a single cogent structure. The halakhah shows how the structure sustains a working system. The haggadah, by contrast, focuses upon matters of RELIGIOUS BELIEF and experience, taking up large issues of life.

The haggadah works out the implications of the conviction that the one and only God who created heaven and Earth has established a world order of justice. It wants to know how to explain the way things are in contrast to how they are supposed to be. The halakhah asks how, in the construction of the godly community, justice shapes world order as the Torah requires. It spells out the norms for that holy community, which now and in the world to come, Israel is supposed to embody. Only together, each complementing the other, do the halakhah and the haggadah define JUDAISM.

HALDI \\'k̲al-dē\\, the national god of the ancient kingdom of Urartu, which ruled the plateau around Lake Van, now eastern Turkey, from about 900 to about 600 BCE. Haldi was represented as a man, with or without wings, standing on a lion; in the absence of religious texts his attributes are otherwise unknown. A Urartian temple at ancient Muṣaṣir dedicated to Haldi and to the goddess Bagbartu, or Bagmashtu, was captured and plundered by Sargon II of Assyria in 714 BCE; it is shown on a relief from his palace as a gabled building with a colonnade—one of the oldest known buildings to make use of that architectural form.

ḤALLĀJ, AL- \\,al-k̲a-'làj\\, *in full* Abū al-Mughīth al-Ḥusayn ibn Manṣūr al-Ḥallāj (b. c. 858, Ṭūr, Iran—d. March 26, 922, Baghdad), controversial Muslim writer and teacher of SUFISM.

According to tradition, al-Ḥallāj's grandfather was a ZOROASTRIAN and a descendant of Abū Ayyūb, a COMPANION OF THE PROPHET, Muhammad. At an early age al-Ḥallāj went to live in the city of Wāsiṭ, an important Iraqi center for trade and Arab culture. His father had become a Muslim and may have supported the family by carding wool.

Al-Ḥallāj was attracted to an ascetic way of life at an early age. Not satisfied with merely having learned the QUR'AN

by heart, he was motivated to understand its deeper and inner meanings. During his adolescence, at a time when Islamic MYSTICISM was in its formative period, he began to withdraw from the world and to seek the company of individuals who were able to instruct him in the Sufi way. His teachers were highly respected among the masters of Sufism. Studying first under Sahl at-Tustarī, who lived a solitary life in the city of Tustar in Khuzistan, al-Ḥallāj later became a disciple of 'Amr ibn 'Uthmān al-Makkī of Basra. During this period he married the daughter of the Sufi Abū Ya'qūb al-Aqṭa'. He concluded his instruction in the mystical way under Abū al-Qāsim al-Junayd of Baghdad.

During the next period of his life (c. 895–910), al-Ḥallāj traveled extensively and preached, taught, and wrote. He made a PILGRIMAGE to MECCA, where he followed a strict discipline for a year. In his journeys he attracted many disciples, some of whom accompanied him on a second pilgrimage to Mecca. Afterward, he returned to Baghdad and then set out for a mission to a territory hitherto not penetrated by Islam—India and Turkistan. Following a third pilgrimage to Mecca, he again returned to Baghdad (c. 908).

Al-Ḥallāj's propensity for travel and his willingness to share his mystical experiences with all who would listen were considered breaches of discipline by his Sufi masters. His travel for missionary purposes was suggestive of the subversive activity of the QARMAṬIANS (a SHI'ITE movement), whose acts of terrorism and whose missionaries were undermining the authority of the central government. Through his wife's family, he was suspected of having connections with the Zanj rebellion in southern Mesopotamia that was carried out by oppressed black slaves inspired and led by outside dissidents. The alleged involvement of al-Ḥallāj in an attempt at political and moral reform upon his return to Baghdad was an immediate factor in his arrest.

Al-Ḥallāj has been identified as an "intoxicated" Sufi—*i.e.*, those who, in the moment of ECSTASY, are so overcome by the presence of the divine that they lose awareness of personal identity and merge with ultimate reality. In that exalted state, such Sufis are given to using extravagant language. Not long before his arrest al-Ḥallāj is said to have uttered the statement "Anā al-ḥaqq" ("I am the Truth"—*i.e.*, God), which provided cause for the accusation that he had claimed to be divine. Such a statement was highly inappropriate in the view of most Muslims. There was no consensus about al-Ḥallāj, however. The long, drawn-out trial proceedings were marked by indecision. After a lengthy period of confinement (c. 911–922) in Baghdad, al-Ḥallāj was eventually crucified and tortured to death. A large crowd witnessed his execution. He is remembered to have endured gruesome torture calmly and courageously and to have uttered words of forgiveness for his accusers.

HALLEL \\hä-'lāl\\ (Hebrew: "Praise"), in JUDAISM, liturgical designation for Psalms 113–118 ("Egyptian Hallel") as read in SYNAGOGUES on festive occasions. In ancient times Jews recited these hymns on the three PILGRIM FESTIVALS, when they offered their sacrifices in the TEMPLE OF JERUSALEM.

A BENEDICTION usually precedes and follows recitation of the Psalms, but the preceding benediction is omitted on the eve of PASSOVER (Pesaḥ). The TALMUD stipulates that a reading from the Book of Esther should replace the Hallel on PURIM. In time the term Hallel came to mean the "Great Hallel," Psalm 136, which is used in the morning service on the SABBATH, festivals, and during the Passover SEDER. The "half-Hallel" (parts of Psalms 115 and 116 are omitted) is used on the last six days of Passover and on the NEW MOON.

HALLELUJAH \,ha-lə-'lü-yə\, *also spelled* alleluia \,a-lə-\, Hebrew liturgical expression meaning "praise ye Yah" ("praise the Lord"). It appears in the Hebrew BIBLE in several psalms, usually at the beginning or end of the psalm or in both places. In ancient JUDAISM the hallelujah was probably chanted as an antiphon by the LEVITE choir. In the NEW TESTAMENT it appears only in Revelation 19, where it occurs four times. It was translated in the SEPTUAGINT (Jewish Greek version of the Bible made in the pre-Christian period) and became "alleluia" in the VULGATE (4th-century Christian Latin version). The early Christians adopted the expression in their worship services, and it appeared often in EASTERN ORTHODOX, ROMAN CATHOLIC, and ANGLICAN and some other PROTESTANT liturgies and in HYMNS.

HALLOWEEN, *also called* All Hallows' Eve, holy or hallowed evening observed on October 31, the eve of All Saints' Day.

In ancient Britain and Ireland, the Celtic festival of SAMHAIN Eve was observed at the end of summer; later the date of observance was fixed upon October 31. This date was the eve of the Celtic new year. All fires were extinguished and a new ceremonial fire was kindled from which all hearth fires were relit. The date was connected with the return of herds from pasture, and laws and land tenures were renewed. The souls of the dead were supposed to revisit their homes on this day. In addition, Halloween was thought to be the most favorable time for DIVINATIONS concerning marriage, luck, health, and death.

The pre-Christian observances influenced the Christian festival of All Hallows' Eve, celebrated on the same date. Gradually, Halloween became a secular observance, and many customs and practices developed. In Scotland young people assembled for games to ascertain which of them would marry during the year and in what order the marriages would occur. Many Halloween customs have become games played by children.

Immigrants to the United States, particularly the Irish, introduced secular Halloween customs that became popular in the late 19th century, notably mischief-making by boys and young men. More recently, the occasion has come to be observed mainly by small children, who go from house to house, often in costume, demanding "Trick or treat" (the treat, usually candy, is generally given and the trick rarely played).

A common symbol of Halloween is the jack-o'-lantern (an expression that originally alluded to a lantern-carrying night watchman). It is a hollowed-out pumpkin with openings cut in it to suggest a face and with a lighted candle fixed inside. In Scotland a turnip was used, but the native pumpkin was substituted in the United States.

HALO, *also called* nimbus, in art, radiant circle or disk surrounding the head of a holy person, a representation of spiritual character. In Hellenistic and Roman art the sun god HELIOS and Roman emperors often appear with a crown of

The Angel with the Millstone *depicted with a halo, illumination from the Bamberg Apocalypse, c. 1007*
By courtesy of the Staatsbibliothek Bamberg, Germany

rays. Because of its pagan origin, the form was avoided in EARLY CHRISTIAN ART, but a simple circular nimbus was adopted by Christian emperors for their official portraits. From the middle of the 4th century, Christ was also shown with this imperial attribute, as was his symbol, the Lamb of God, from the end of the 4th century. In the 5th century it was sometimes given to ANGELS, but it was not until the 6th century that it became customary for the Virgin MARY and other SAINTS. For a time in the 5th century, living persons of eminence were depicted with a square nimbus.

The halo was used regularly in representations of Christ, the angels, and the saints throughout the Middle Ages. Often Christ's halo is quartered by the lines of a cross or inscribed with three bands, interpreted to signify his position in the TRINITY. From the 15th century, however, with the growth of naturalism in Renaissance art, the nimbus created problems in representation, and this led to its decline in Italian art in the 16th century and to its abandonment by Michelangelo and Titian. In Flemish painting of the 15th century, it began to be represented as rays of light, and this form was adopted by Italian artists of the late 16th century, notably Tintoretto, as a realistically rendered light emanating from the holy person's head. This interpretation was the standard one in the Baroque period and in most later religious works.

The halo is also found in Buddhist art of India, appearing from the late 3rd century CE. It is believed that the motif was brought to the East by Greek invaders.

HALTIA \'häl-tē-ä\, Balto-Finnic domestic spirit who oversees the household and protects it from harm.

In Finland the *haltia* was usually the spirit of the first person to lay claim to a site, by lighting a fire on it or by building a house on it or in some cases by being the first person to die there. The *haltia* was believed to resemble such a person in every way, including sex, age, dress, and mannerisms. The dominant idea was that a person, once laying claim to a piece of land, would always remain in charge of it. A *haltia* could even be brought to a new site from the previous one, either with the fire kept alive and transferred or by taking ashes from the old to the new site.

The *haltia* was the prime moral force of the household, who saw to it that norms were observed and expressed his displeasure at fighting, swearing, drinking, and other forms of socially disapproved conduct.

Other buildings on a farmstead also had their tutelary spirits. The barn spirit watched over the animals, the threshing-house spirit saw to it that the fire for drying grain was kept burning, and the mill spirit kept the miller awake to keep the mill running.

The Finnish *haltia* tradition has been influenced more recently by Swedish customs concerning the *tomte*, who appears in Finnish as *tonttu*. He is usually depicted as a bearded old man dressed in gray with a red stocking cap, with functions quite similar to those of the *haltia*. In some cases it is difficult to distinguish the household spirit from the *maahiset*, which is considered to be the aboriginal guardian of the land before human settlement.

HAMĀS \ha-'mas\, *acronym of* Ḥarakat-al-Muqāwama al-Islamiyya, *English* Islamic Resistance Movement, militant Palestinian Islamic movement in the West Bank and Gaza Strip, founded in 1987, that is dedicated to the destruction of Israel and the creation of an Islamic state in Palestine. Ḥamās has opposed peace accords between Israel and the Palestine Liberation Organization (PLO).

From the late 1970s Islamic activists connected with the pan-Arab MUSLIM BROTHERHOOD established a network of charities, clinics, and schools in Gaza and were active in many mosques; their activities in the West Bank generally were limited to the universities. The Muslim Brotherhood's activities in the West Bank and Gaza were usually nonviolent, but a number of small groups in the occupied territories began to call for JIHAD, or holy war, against Israel. In December 1987, at the beginning of the Palestinian *intifāḍa* (uprising) against Israeli occupation, Ḥamās was established by members of the Muslim Brotherhood and religious factions of the PLO, and the new organization quickly acquired a broad following. In its 1988 charter Ḥamās maintained that Palestine is an Islamic homeland that should never be surrendered to non-Muslims and that waging jihad to liberate Palestine is the duty of Palestinians. This position brought it into conflict with the PLO, which in 1988 recognized Israel's right to exist.

Ḥamās' armed wing, the 'Izz al-Dīn al-Qassām Forces, began a campaign of terrorism against Israel. Israel imprisoned the founder of Ḥamās, Sheikh Aḥmad Yāsīn, in 1991 and arrested hundreds of Ḥamās activists. Ḥamās denounced the 1993 peace agreement between Israel and the PLO and, along with the Islamic jihad group, subsequently intensified its terror campaign by the use of suicide bombers. The PLO and Israel responded with harsh security and punitive measures, although PLO chairman Yāsir 'Arafāt sought to include Ḥamās in the political process, appointing Ḥamās members to leadership positions in the Palestinian Authority.

ḤAMZA IBN 'ALĪ \'ham-zə-,i-bən-á-'lē\, *in full* Ḥamza ibn 'Alī ibn Aḥmad, *also called* az-Zūzanī (b. 985—d. after 1021), one of the founders of the DRUZE religion. After entering Egypt in 1017 he became a spokesman for the religious convictions of AL-ḤĀKIM, the Fāṭimid CALIPH, who was already accorded the position of IMAM, a divinely appointed and authoritative spokesman for ISLAM. Al-Ḥākim then claimed to be the embodiment of the Godhead—a state beyond name and beyond good and evil. Ḥamza in turn assumed the position of imam.

Considerable resistance to these doctrines appeared when they were first preached in 1017, and Ḥamza went into hiding until 1019, when al-Ḥākim was able to move vigorously to support the new religious movement. Near Cairo, Ḥamza began to build a strong missionary organization. Cosmic ranks were given to members of its hierarchy, and a class of missionaries was organized to spread the teachings. Ḥamza claimed to be representing an independent religion that superseded traditional Islam. Al-Ḥākim disappeared in mysterious circumstances in 1021, and, much persecuted, the Druze cult all but ceased to exist in Egypt. Ḥamza from hiding claimed that al-Ḥākim had only withdrawn to test the faith of his followers. Ḥamza's teach-

ings later provided the ideological foundation for many peasant revolts in Syria.

ḤANAFĪ LEGAL SCHOOL \'ha-nə-fē\, in ISLAM, one of the four SUNNI schools of religious law, incorporating the legal opinions of the ancient Iraqi schools of al-Kūfa and Basra. Ḥanafī legal thought (*madhhab*) developed from the teachings of the theologian IMAM ABŪ ḤANĪFA (c. 700–767) by such disciples as Abū Yūsuf (d. 798) and Muhammad al-Shaybānī (749/750–805) and became the official system of Islamic legal interpretation of the 'Abbāsids, Seljuqs, and Ottomans. Although the Ḥanafīs acknowledge the QUR'AN and HADITH as primary sources of law, they are noted for the acceptance of personal opinion (*ra'y*) in the absence of precedent. It is the most widespread Muslim legal school; and it currently predominates in Central Asia, India, Pakistan, Turkey, and the countries of the former Ottoman Empire. Even in Muslim countries with secular law codes, the Ḥanafī school prevails in personal status law (marriage, divorce, and inheritance).

ḤANBALĪ LEGAL SCHOOL \'han-bə-lē\, in ISLAM, the most scripturalist of the four SUNNI schools of religious law. Based on the teachings of AḤMAD IBN ḤANBAL (780–855), the Ḥanbalī legal school (*madhhab*) emphasized virtually complete dependence on the divine in the establishment of legal theory and rejected personal opinion (*ra'y*), analogy (QIYĀS), except in special cases, and the Hellenistic dogma of the MU'TAZILA school of theology, on the grounds that human speculation is likely to introduce sinful innovations (BID'A). The school thus relied mainly on a literal reading of the QUR'AN and HADITH in formulating legal decisions. Popular in Iraq and Syria until the 14th century, the traditionalist Ḥanbalī legal approach was revived in the 18th century through the teachings of Ibn Taymīyah (1263–1328) in the Wahhābīya movement of central Arabia. This *madhhab* has since become the official legal school of 20th-century Saudi Arabia.

HANDS, IMPOSITION OF, *also called* laying on of hands, ritual act in which a priest or other religious functionary places one or both hands palms down on the top of another person's head, usually while saying a prayer or blessing. The imposition of hands was first practiced in JUDAISM and was adopted by CHRISTIANITY. In the Hebrew BIBLE it is associated with three interrelated ideas: consecration (*i.e.*, setting apart for the service of God), transmission of a divine gift, and identification (the means whereby an offerer was linked with his sacrifice).

In the NEW TESTAMENT the same ideas are present; all of these ideas are connected with ORDINATION and BAPTISM, in both of which the imposition of hands is a standard part of the ritual. The New Testament further indicates that the imposition of hands conveyed a blessing and was a means of healing. The early Christian church added two more uses: the imposition of hands for the blessing of CATECHUMENS and for the reconciliation of penitents and heretics. The modern church has preserved its use in the rites of ordination and CONFIRMATION.

HANDSOME LAKE MOVEMENT, *also called* Longhouse Religion, or Gai'Wiio (Seneca: "Good Message"), longest-established prophet movement in North America. Its founder was Ganioda'yo, a Seneca chief whose name meant "Handsome Lake"; his trance revelations in 1799 transformed the demoralized Seneca. Their Christian beliefs included a personal creator-ruler, a devil, heaven, hell, and judgment; Jesus was identified with a local mythological figure. Seneca divinities were retained as ruling ANGELS, rituals were reduced to four transformed dance feasts, and the longhouse was modified into a "church." A puritan and modernizing ethic attacked alcohol and WITCHCRAFT, banned further land sales, encouraged the men to practice plow agriculture and animal husbandry, and stressed stability of the nuclear family.

Ganioda'yo's teaching spread among the Iroquois and later became embodied in the "Code of Handsome Lake," which is still recited once in two years by authorized "preachers" in some 10 longhouses providing for about 5,000 adherents on Iroquois reservations in the United States and Canada. The religion serves to maintain Indian identity and has shown some growth in the 20th century.

Lighting the Hanukkah candles
Janice Rubin—Black Star

ḤANĪF \ha-'nēf, hä-\, in the QUR'AN, an Arabic designation for true monotheists (especially ABRAHAM) who were not Jews, Christians, or worshipers of idols. The word appears to have been borrowed from a Syriac word meaning "heathen" and, by extension, designating a Hellenized person of culture. There is no evidence that an organized ḥanīf religion existed in pre-Islamic Arabia, but there were certain individuals who, having repudiated the old gods, prepared the way for ISLAM but embraced neither JUDAISM nor CHRISTIANITY. In this sense, some of Muhammad's relatives, contemporaries, and early supporters were called ḥanīfs—for example, Waraqa ibn Nawfal, a cousin of the Prophet's first wife, KHADĪJA, and Umayya ibn Abī al-Ṣalt, an early 7th-century Arab poet.

ḤANIWA \'hä-nē-ˌwä\ ("circle of clay"), unglazed terra-cotta cylinders and hollow sculptures that were arranged on and around the mounded tombs (*kofun*) of the Japanese elite in the Tumulus period (*c.* 250–552 CE). The first and most common *haniwa* were barrel-shaped cylinders used to mark the borders of a burial ground. Later, in the early 4th century, the cylinders were surmounted by sculptural forms such as figures of warriors, female attendants, dancers, birds, animals, boats, military equipment, and even houses. It is believed that the figures symbolized continued service to the deceased in the other world.

Haniwa were mass-produced during the 6th century, but thereafter the introduction of BUDDHISM and the practice of CREMATION caused a decline in the building of tumuli and, thus, in the production of *haniwa*.

ḤANNAH \'ha-nə\, *also spelled* Anna (11th century BCE), mother of Samuel, the Jewish judge. Childless in her marriage to Elkanah, Hannah prayed for a son, promising to dedicate him to God (1 Samuel 1:1–11). Her prayers were answered, and she brought the child Samuel to SHILOH for religious training (1 Samuel 1:12–28). In the TALMUD she is named as one of seven prophetesses (Megillah 14a), and her prayer is in the ROSH HASHANAH first-day service, exemplifying successful petitions to God.

HANUKKAH \'k̲ä-nə-kə, 'hä-; ˌk̲ä-nü-'kä\ (Hebrew: "Dedication"), *also called* Feast of Dedication, Feast of Lights, *or* Feast of the Maccabees, in JUDAISM, an observance commemorating the rededication (164 BCE) of the Second TEMPLE OF JERUSALEM after its desecration three years earlier by order of Antiochus IV Epiphanes (1 Maccabees 4:56–59; "Feast of the Dedication" in John 10:22). The distinctive rite of lighting the MENORAH also recalls the TALMUD story of how the small supply of nondesecrated oil—enough for one day—miraculously burned in the Temple for eight full days until new oil could be obtained (Shabbat 21b). Beginning on Kislev 25 (in December), Hanukkah is celebrated for eight days; during this time, the ceremonial candles are lit, gifts are exchanged, and children play games.

HANULLIM \'hän-'əl-'lēm\, *also called* Hanunim ("Sky Lord"), ancient Korean HIGH GOD or Sky Father who was held to be the progenitor of the Korean people. Drawing upon Chinese ideas of SHANG-TI ("Supreme Ruler") and T'IEN ("Heaven"), as well as on Confucian ideals of FILIAL PIETY, Hanullim was seen as a benevolent deity and divine ruler whose son, Tan-gun, gave rise to the human race and kingly order of society. Mythology associated Hanullim with the polestar, and he was traditionally worshiped as a tutelary mountain spirit. Hanullim has been syncretistically associated with the Abrahamic creator god by Christians and Muslims in modern Korea.

HANUMĀN \'hə-nü-ˌmän, ˌhə-nü-'män\, in the mythology of HINDUISM, the divine monkey chief, a central figure in the great Hindu epic the RĀMĀYAṆA ("The Acts of Rāma"). Hanumān is the child of a nymph by the wind god; accompanied by a host of monkeys, he aided RĀMA in recovering his wife, SĪTĀ, from the demon RĀVAṆA. His heroic exploits are many. He acted as Rāma's spy in the midst of the demon's kingdom; when he was discovered and his tail set on fire, he burnt down large parts of their city, Laṅkā. Hanumān flew to the HIMALAYAS and carried back the mountain of medicinal herbs to restore Rāma's grievously wounded brother Lakṣmaṇa.

A beneficent guardian, Hanumān is worshiped in the form of a monkey with a red face, who stands erect like a human and often displays an erect tail. Temples in his honor are numerous and ever increasing in influence, just as images of Hanumān have in recent years tended to become monumental in size. Hanumān's ability to change size at will and travel to distant realms aligns him with shamanic figures worldwide. His great physical strength makes him the patron saint of wrestlers and others, but it is the combination of this brute strength with an equally adamantine quality of faithfulness—both to Rāma and Sītā and to his own devotees—that has caused him to become one of Hinduism's most important deities in the course of the last millennium. In a heroically liminal style, then, he is both the recipient of intense BHAKTI and its exemplar.

HAN YÜ \ˈhän-ˈyüe\, *Pinyin* Han Yu, *also called* Han Wen-Kung \ˈhän-ˈwən-ˈgüŋ\ (b. 768, Teng-chou, Honan Province, China—d. 824, Ch'ang-an), T'ang period master of Chinese prose, outstanding poet, and the first proponent of what later came to be known as NEO-CONFU-CIANISM.

An orphan, Han initially failed his civil service exams because the examiners refused to accept his unconventional prose style, but he eventually entered the bureaucracy and served in several high government posts. At his death he was honored with the title of president of the ministry of rites and the epithet "Prince of Letters."

At a time when its popularity had greatly declined, Han began a defense of the Confucian doctrine. He attacked TAOISM and BUDDHISM, which were then at the height of their influence. He castigated the emperor for paying respect to the supposed finger bone of the Buddha, an act that almost cost Han Yü his life and because of which he was banished to South China for a year. In defending CONFUCIANISM, Han quoted extensively from the MEN-CIUS, the TA-HSÜEH ("Great Learning"), the *Chung-yung* ("Doctrine of the Mean"), and the I-CHING ("Classic of Changes"), works that hitherto had been somewhat neglected. In so doing, he laid the foundations for later Neo-Confucianists who took their basic ideas from these books.

Han advocated the adoption of the free, simple prose of the early philosophers, a style unlike the mannered and elaborate verselike regularity of the parallel prose that was

Hanumān carrying a mountain of healing herbs, detail of a Mughal painting, late 16th century
By courtesy of the Smithsonian Institution, Freer Gallery of Art, Washington, D.C.

Han Yü, portrait by an unknown artist
By courtesy of the Collection of the National Palace Museum, Taipei, Taiwan, Republic of China

prevalent in Han's time. His own essays (*e.g.*, "On the Way," "On Man," "On Spirits") became the most famous models of the prose style he espoused.

HAOMA \ˌhaú-ˈmä, ˈhaú-mə\, in ZOROASTRIANISM, sacred plant and the drink made from it. The preparation of the drink from the plant by pounding and the drinking of it are central features of Zoroastrian ritual. *Haoma* is also personified as a divinity. It bestows essential vital qualities—health, fertility, husbands for maidens, even immortality. The source of the earthly *haoma* plant is a shining white tree that grows on a paradisiacal mountain. Sprigs of this white *haoma* were brought to earth by divine birds.

Haoma is the Avestan cognate of the Sanskrit SOMA. The near identity of the two in ritual significance is considered by scholars to point to a salient feature of an Indo-Iranian religion antedating Zoroastrianism.

HAPI \ˈhä-pē\, in ancient EGYPTIAN RELIGION, personification of the annual inundation of the Nile River. Hapi was the most important among numerous personifications of aspects of natural fertility, and his dominance increased during Egyptian history. Hymns were composed in his honor, but he had no temples or formal cult, except at the narrows of Jabal al-Silsila in the south, where shrines were built and offerings were cast annually into the river's rising waters. Hapi was represented as a fat man with swelling, pendulous breasts, dressed in a belt suitable to a marsh dweller or servant. This form, which was originally common to many personifications, became identified increasingly closely with Hapi.

ḤAQĪQA \hä-ˈkē-kə\ (Arabic: "reality," "truth"), in the mystical terminology of ISLAM, the knowledge the Sufi acquires when the secrets of the divine essence are revealed to him at the end of his journey toward union with God (*see* SUFISM). The Sufi must first reach the state of *fanā'* ("passing away of the self"), in which he becomes free from attachment to the earthly world and loses himself entirely in God. After he is awakened from that state he attains the state of *baqā'* ("subsistence"), and *ḥaqīqa* is revealed to him.

The Sufis called themselves *ahl al-ḥaqīqa* ("the people of truth") to distinguish themselves from *ahl al-sharī'a* ("the people of religious law"). They used the label to defend themselves against accusations by scripturalist Muslims that Sufis deviated from Islamic laws and principles laid down in the QUR'AN and HADITH. Such accusations, the Sufis maintained, were made because the scripturalists relied too much on the external meaning of religious texts and did not seek the inner meaning of Islam.

HARAI \hä-'rī\, *also spelled* harae, barai, *or* barae (Japanese: "purification"), in Japanese religion, any of numerous SHINTŌ purification ceremonies. *Harai* rites, and similar *misogi* exercises using water, cleanse the individual so that he may approach a deity or sacred power (KAMI). Salt, water, and fire are the principal purificatory agents. Many of the rites are traditionally explained as the method used by Izanagi (the mythical creator of Japan) to rid himself of the polluting effect of seeing the decaying body of his wife and sister, Izanami, in the land of the dead.

The rites are observed before entering a temple, taking part in worship, beginning a festival, or taking out a religious procession. The simpler rites consist of washing the hands or rinsing the mouth or having the priest shake the *harai-gushi*, a wooden wand to which are attached folds of paper. Priests participating in public ceremonies are required to undergo much more extensive purification in which they must regulate the body (bathing, diet, abstention from stimulants), heart, environment, and soul. Great purification ceremonies called *ō-harai* are held twice a year, on June 30 and December 31, and at times of national disasters to purge the country from SINS and impurities.

ḤARAM \'här-əm\ (Arabic: "sacred place," or "sanctuary"), in ISLAM, a sacred place or territory. The principal *haram*s are in MECCA, MEDINA, Jerusalem, and, for SHI'ITES, KARBALĀ' (Iraq). At Mecca the *haram* encompasses the territory traversed by pilgrims engaged in the HAJJ (great PILGRIMAGE) and 'umra (lesser pilgrimage), including the KA'BA and Al-Ḥaram Mosque, Ṣafā and Marwā, Minā, and the plain of 'Arafāt. Medina's *haram* contains the Prophet's mosque-tomb. Jerusalem's "noble *haram*" (*al-haram al-sharīf*) consists of the area of the Temple Mount where the AL-AQṢĀ MOSQUE and the DOME OF THE ROCK stand. At Karbalā' the mosque-tomb of AL-ḤUSAYN IBN 'ALĪ (d. 680), the third IMAM, is the foremost *haram*. In general any mosque or shrine can be considered to possess a *haram*.

Such sacred places are regarded as focal points of divine blessing, usually mediated by a holy man or woman. According to the HADITH, Mecca's *haram* was consecrated when God created heaven and earth. MUHAMMAD was remembered to have declared that he had sacralized Medina just as ABRAHAM had once sacralized Mecca. *Ḥaram*s are "forbidden" areas set apart from the mundane human landscape by codes for ritualized behavior, which include bans on bloodshed, violence, uprooting trees, sexual activity, menstruating women, elimination of bodily wastes, offensive behavior, and, especially in Mecca and Medina, non-Muslims. Unlike in ancient Near Eastern temples and pre-Islamic Arabian sanctuaries, sacrifices are conducted in areas removed from the main centers of worship. In Mecca they are conducted near Minā, in a valley between the Al-Ḥaram Mosque and 'Arafāt. *Ḥaram* visitors are expected to observe rules of ritual purity, remove shoes, cross the threshold with the right foot first, and salute the shrine upon entrance. Hajj rites require the most complex procedures for attaining the holy state known as *iḥrām* before entering Mecca's precincts. Because of the holiness of such locations, God is believed to multiply rewards for virtuous acts in them just as he multiplies punishments for transgressions. Moreover, burial in or near a *haram* earns the deceased blessings in the afterlife.

Ḥaram territories are not necessarily enclosed by distinctive architecture. However, core *haram* sites and mosques are usually delimited by monumental features such as enclosure walls, arcades, ceremonial gateways, MINARETS, QIB-LA niches (*mihrāb*s), and domes. There may also be elaborate displays of Qur'anic calligraphy and geometric decorations in stone, stucco, brick, or adobe. In more mundane contexts *haram* has been used to denote the inviolability of a house, a man's wife, and even a secular university. *See also* SACRED SPACE.

HARE KRISHNA: *see* ISKCON.

HARGOBIND \ˌhər-'gō-bin-də, ˌhär-, -bind\ (b. 1595—d. 1644, Kīratpur, in the Himalayan foothills), in SIKHISM, sixth GURŪ (1606–44). Hargobind took over the leadership of the Sikh community in 1606 after the execution of his father, Gurū ARJAN, at Lahore, under the orders of the Mughal emperor Jahāngīr. At his succession ceremony Hargobind is believed to have defiantly borne two swords, symbolizing his twin authority as temporal (*mīri*) and spiritual (*pīri*) head of the community. A rapprochement was worked out with Jahāngīr whereby for a time Gurū Hargobind was left unperturbed in his regional sphere at AMRITSAR; during this period the Akāl Takhat and a fort (Mukhlispur, later called Lohgarh) were erected at Amritsar. But with the ascent of Shāh Jahān to the Mughal throne in 1628 problems began again, and continued skirmishes with Mughal troops led to the eventual departure of Gurū Hargobind from the Punjab plains to the Siwālik hills. There he established Kīratpur ("Town of Praise") in the Hindu principality of Hindūr, where he spent the remaining years of his life.

HARIBHADRA \ˌhə-rē-'bə-drə\, *also called* Haribhadra Sūri \sü-'rē\ (fl. 8th century), one of the noncanonical Jain authors, known for his works in Sanskrit and Prākrit on Jain doctrine and ethics, and for his commentaries (*see* JAINISM).

Haribhadra was born into the BRAHMIN CASTE in Cittaur, India, and received a thorough education in the Sanskrit classics. On adopting the Jain faith, he entered a ŚVETĀMBARA order of monks. Haribhadra is best known for his *Ṣaḍdarśanasamuccaya*, which deals with the six philosophical systems of India. He also wrote on logic and YOGA.

HARIHARA \'hə-rē-'hə-rə\, *also spelled* Hari-Hara, in HINDUISM, a syncretic deity combining the two major gods, VISHNU (Hari) and SHIVA (Hara). This dual form found special favor in Cambodia, where inscriptions and images of the 6th–7th century are known. In images of Harihara, the right half is depicted as Shiva and the left as Vishnu. The visage of the Shiva half is awesome, befitting his function as destroyer, and its hands hold the *triśūla* ("trident"); the Vishnu side is "pacific," appropriate to the preserver role of that deity. Half the headdress is shown with Shiva's matted locks and half as Vishnu's crown, and half of Shiva's third eye is visible. Many Hindus regard forms such as Harihara and ARDHANĀRĪŚVARA as aids in a process of spiritual growth whereby all representations of the divine are found to be partial and, if taken in isolation, misleading.

HARI KISHAN \'hə-rē-'ki-shən\, *also spelled* Har Krishan (b. 1656, Kīratpur—d. 1664, Delhi), in SIKHISM, eighth GURŪ (1661–64) who was installed at five years of age and reigned for only three years. Before his death from smallpox, he is said to have nominated his granduncle TEGH BAHĀDUR as his successor, a decision that had great significance in Sikh history because of Tegh Bahādur's effectiveness as Gurū.

HARI RĀĪ \'hə-rē-'rä-ē\ (b. 1630, Punjab, India—d. 1661, Punjab), in SIKHISM, seventh GURŪ (1644–61). Hari Rāī was nominated to be the Gurū by his grandfather Gurū HAR-GOBIND (Gurū from 1606 to 1644), and he provided leadership to the Sikh community during a difficult phase in its history. The Sikhs had been forced out of AMRITSAR, their center in the Punjab plains, in the early 1630s, and were still in the process of settling down in the Siwālik hills. There was also internal strife. Gurū Hari Rāi attempted to avoid confrontation with the Mughal authorities, but was dragged into it when he was accused of supporting Dārā Shikōh, the liberal Mughal prince, who lost the battle of sucession to his more orthodox brother, Aurangzeb. Gurū Hari Rāi's lasting achievement came in the form of his travels to the Malwa area, where he brought the local Brār tribes into the Sikh fold. They were the first Sikhs to establish their political supremacy in the middle decades of the 18th century.

HĀRITĪ \'hä-rē-ˌtē\, *Japanese* Kishi-Mojin \'kē-shē-'mȯ-jēn\, in BUDDHIST mythology, a child-devouring ogress who is said to have been converted from her cannibalistic habits by the BUDDHA GOTAMA to become a protectress of children and sometimes of women in childbirth as well. The Buddha hid the youngest of Hārītī's 500 children under his begging bowl, and thus made her realize the sorrow she was causing other parents. Hārītī is usually represented carrying a child, a pomegranate, or a CORNUCOPIA. Her cult traveled from India north into Central Asia, China, and Japan.

HARMONIA \här-'mō-nē-ə\, in Greek mythology, the daughter of ARES and APHRODITE, according to the Theban account; in Samothrace she was the daughter of ZEUS and the Pleiad Electra. She was carried off by CADMUS, and all the gods attended the wedding. Cadmus or one of the gods presented the bride with a robe and necklace, the work of HEPHAESTUS. This necklace brought misfortune to all who possessed it; it led to the death of the hero Amphiaraus, his wife Eriphyle, their son ALCMAEON, and Alcmaeon's father-in-law Phegeus and his sons. Both Harmonia and Cadmus were ultimately metamorphosed into snakes.

Harmonia is also the name given to the Greek personification of the order and symmetry of the universe.

HARPY \'här-pē\, in Greek mythology, a fabulous creature, probably a wind spirit. In Homer's *Odyssey* they were winds that carried people away. Elsewhere they were sometimes connected with the powers of the Underworld. Homer mentions one Harpy called Podarge (Swiftfoot). Hesiod mentions two, Aello and Okypete (Stormswift and Swiftwing).

Later, especially in the legend of JASON and the ARGONAUTS, they were represented as birds with the faces of women, horribly foul and loathsome. They were sent to punish the Thracian king Phineus for his ill-treatment of his children, but CALAIS AND ZETES, the sons of BOREAS, finally delivered him.

HARRIS MOVEMENT \'har-əs\, largest mass movement toward CHRISTIANITY in West Africa, named for the prophet William Wadé Harris (c. 1850–1929), a Grebo of Liberia and a teacher-catechist in the American Episcopal mission.

While in prison for a political offense in 1910, Harris was commissioned in a vision to become a preacher; he then traveled along the coast, reaching Ghana by 1914. The French colonial government of the Ivory Coast deported him to Liberia in 1915. An estimated 120,000 followers were baptized, adopted the SABBATH, built churches, and waited in anticipation for the white teachers who, as Harris promised, would come to teach them the BIBLE.

In western Ghana the Methodists and Roman Catholics each benefited by some 9,000 converts and CATECHUMENS in 1914–20, and a follower, John Swatson, pioneered Anglican work. British METHODISM sent missionaries to the Ivory Coast in 1924 and had gained 32,000 members by 1926. Other Harris converts developed a wide range of Harris independent churches, such as the Church of the Twelve Apostles in Ghana; the loosely grouped Églises Harristes, which, in the 20th century, had some 100,000 adherents in the Ivory Coast; and other, more syncretic, groups.

HARUSPICES \hə-'rəs-pə-ˌsēz\, ancient Etruscan diviners whose art consisted primarily in deducing the will of the gods from the appearance presented by the entrails of sacrificial animals. They also interpreted all portents or unusual phenomena of nature, especially thunder and lightning, and prescribed the expiatory ceremonies after such events.

Harpy from a tomb frieze from the acropolis of Xanthus, Asia Minor, c. 500 BCE; in the British Museum
Hirmer Fotoarchiv, Munchen

The art was practiced in Rome by Etruscans, but, although of great importance, especially under the early republic, it never became a part of the state religion. Under the empire there existed a collegium of 60 haruspices who were salaried expert advisers.

HĀRŪT AND MĀRŪT \ha-'rüt . . . ma-'rüt\, in the mythology of ISLAM, two ANGELS who unwittingly became masters of evil. A group of angels, observing the SINS being committed on earth, began to ridicule man's weakness. God declared that they would act no better and proposed that some angels be sent to earth to see how well they could resist IDOLATRY, murder, fornication, and wine. No sooner did Hārūt and Mārūt, the angels chosen, alight on earth than they were seduced by a beautiful woman. Then, discovering that there was a witness to their sin, they killed him.

The angels in heaven then admitted that God was right. Hārūt and Mārūt chose to be punished on earth rather than in hell and were condemned to hang by their feet in a well in Babylonia until the Day of Judgment.

Hārūt and Mārūt are first mentioned in the QUR'AN (2:102) as two angels purveying evil in Babylon, and the legend probably appeared to explain how they happened to be in that position. The story itself parallels a Jewish legend about the fallen angels Shemḥazaī, 'Uzza, and 'Aza'el. The names Hārūt and Mārūt appear to be related to those of Haruvatāt and Ameretāt, ZOROASTRIAN archangels.

ḤASAN \'hȧ-sȧn, ka-'san\, *in full* Ḥasan ibn 'Alī ibn Abī Ṭalib (b. 624, Arabia—d. 680, MEDINA), a grandson of the Prophet MUHAMMAD, the elder son of Muhammad's daughter FĀṬIMA. He belongs to the group of the five most holy persons of the SHI'ITES, those over whom Muhammad spread his cloak while calling them "The People of the House" (AHL AL-BAYT). After his father, 'ALĪ, he was considered by many of his contemporaries to be the rightful heir to Muhammad's position of leadership.

As a child Ḥasan lived with Muhammad for seven years, and after the latter's death in 632 he was politically inactive until the end of the reign of the caliph 'UTHMĀN IBN 'AF-FĀN. 'Uthmān was murdered in 656, and 'Alī became the next CALIPH. In the civil wars that soon broke out Ḥasan was sent to the Iraqi city of Kūfah to secure acceptance of 'Alī's rule and, if possible, obtain military aid. Later he fought in the Battle of Ṣiffīn, which, although not a defeat, did mark the beginning of a steady deterioration in 'Alī's position. After 'Alī was murdered in 661, never having chosen a successor, a large number of his followers pledged their loyalty to Ḥasan, and Ḥasan himself stressed his own close connections with the Prophet Muhammad.

When Mu'āwiya I, the governor of Syria and the man who had led the rebellion against 'Alī, refused to acknowledge Ḥasan as caliph and began to prepare for war, Ḥasan was able to offer considerable resistance. He dispatched a force to meet Mu'āwiya and then himself headed a larger force. With little money left, Ḥasan, not a warlike person, was plagued by defections from his army. Although some of his followers resented it fiercely, he opened peace negotiations and later in 661 abdicated the caliphate to Mu'āwiya. Ḥasan ibn 'Alī obtained a generous pension and was allowed to live quietly the rest of his life in Medina.

ḤASAN AL-BAṢRĪ, AL- \ȧl-'hȧ-sȧn-ȧl-bȧs-'rē\, *in full* Abū Sa'īd ibn Abī al-Ḥasan Yasār al-Baṣrī (b. 642, Medina, Arabia [now in Saudi Arabia]—d. 728, Basra, Iraq), deeply pious and ascetic Muslim who was one of the most important figures in early ISLAM.

One year after the Battle of Ṣiffīn (657) Ḥasan moved to Basra, a military camp town situated 50 miles northwest of the Persian Gulf. As a young man he participated in the expeditions that led to the conquest of eastern Iran. After his return to Basra, Ḥasan became a central figure in the religious, social, and political upheavals brought about by internal conflicts within the Muslim community. The years 684–704 marked the period of his great preaching activity. The few remaining fragments of his sermons, which are among the best examples of early Arabic prose, indicate that, for Ḥasan, the true Muslim must not only refrain from committing SIN but must live in a state of lasting anxiety, brought about by the certainty of death and the uncertainty of his destiny in the hereafter. The practice of religious self-examination (*muḥāsaba*), which led to avoiding

evil and doing good, coupled with a wariness of the world, marked Ḥasan's piety and influenced later ascetic and mystical attitudes in Islam.

The enemy of Islam, for Ḥasan, was not the infidel but the hypocrite (*munāfiq*) who took his religion lightly. In the debate between freedom and determinism, he took the position that humans are totally responsible for their actions, and he systematically argued this position in an important letter written to the Umayyad CALIPH 'Abd al-Malik. His letter, which is the earliest extant theological treatise in Islam, attacks the widely held view that God is the sole creator of man's actions. His political opinions, which were extensions of his religious views, often placed him in precarious situations. During the years 705–714 Ḥasan was forced into hiding for criticizing the policies of the powerful governor of Iraq, al-Ḥajjāj. It is said that when he died the people of Basra were so involved with the observance of his funeral that no afternoon prayer was said in the mosque because no one was there to pray.

Al-Ḥasan al-Baṣrī was known to his own generation as an eloquent preacher, a paragon of Muslim piety, and an outspoken critic of the political rulers of the Umayyad dynasty. Among later generations he has also been remembered for his religious ASCETICISM. Muslim mystics have counted him as one of their first and most notable spiritual masters. Both the MU'TAZILA (philosophical theologians) and the Ash'arīya (followers of the theologian AL-ASH'ARĪ), the two most important theological schools in early Sunni Islam, consider Ḥasan one of their founders.

ḤASAN-E ṢABBĀḤ \ha-'san-ā-sab-'bäh\ (d. 1124, Daylam, Iran), leader of an Islamic sect, the Nizārī ISMĀ'ĪLĪS, and commonly believed to be the founder of the order known as the Assassins.

Ḥasan studied theology in the Iranian city of Rayy and about the age of 17 adopted the Ismā'īlī faith, after which he rose in the Ismā'īlī organization. In 1076 he went to Egypt, probably for further religious training, remaining there for about three years. When he returned to Iran he traveled widely in an effort to further Ismā'īlī interests. He made a number of converts and in 1090, with the aid of converts made within its garrison, was able to seize the great fortress of Alamūt in Daylam, a Seljuq province on the southern shores of the Caspian Sea. After further turmoil, Ḥasan settled down to the leadership of a territorially scattered yet cohesive state. After the last major siege of Alamūt by the Sunni Seljuqs (1118), Ḥasan was able to live out his life in peace. Claiming to be the *Ḥujja* (proof), a living agent of the hidden IMAM, he led an ascetic existence and imposed a puritanical regime at Alamūt—when one of his sons was accused of murder and the other of drunkenness, he had them both executed. He wrote an autobiography and a number of theological treatises (none of which is extant in its original form), stressing the need for absolute authority in matters of religious faith, a doctrine widely accepted by contemporary Nizārīs.

HASIDEAN \‚hä-sə-'dē-ən, ‚ha-\, *Hebrew* Ḥasid \kä-'sēd; 'kä-sid, 'hä-\, *or* Chasid ("Pious One"), *plural* Hasidim \‚kä-sē-'dēm; kä-'sē-dəm, hä-\, *or* Chasidim, member of a Jewish sect of uncertain origin, noted for uncompromising observance of Judaic Law. The Hasideans joined the Maccabean revolt against the Hellenistic Seleucids (2nd century BCE) to fight for religious freedom and stem the tide of paganism (1 MACCABEES 2:42). They had no interest in politics as such, and, withdrawing from the Maccabean cause as soon as they had regained their religious freedom, they fell into disfavor with the Hasmonean rulers.

Tradition pictures them as so devoted to Judaic Law that martyrdom and torture were willingly preferred to the slightest violation of the SABBATH. No one can say for sure whether the Hasidim mentioned in the TALMUD were Hasideans or not. Historians tend to explain the disappearance of the Hasideans as a gradual merging with the PHARISEES. The Hasideans may also have had a doctrinal influence on the ESSENES. In later history two more groups would take the name "pious ones:" Jewish mystics in 12th-century Germany, called the "Hasidei Ashkenaz," and the modern Hasidic religious movement that began in 18th-century Poland.

HASIDISM \'hä-sə-,di-zəm, 'k̲ä-, 'ha-\, Jewish religious movement that originated in Eastern Europe in the mid-18th century and persists to this day in Europe, the United States, and Israel.

A form of JUDAISM in the mystical tradition of the QABBALAH, Hasidism took shape around the figures of holy men, or *ba'ale shem* ("masters of the name"), who were believed to possess a special bond with God and to exercise miraculous powers. The principal figure of Hasidism at the outset, Israel ben Eliezer, also called BA'AL SHEM ṬOV ("Master of the Good Name"), was one such charismatic leader. In the Hasidic tradition the master, or ZADDIK ("righteous man"), also called a Rebbe, was believed to enjoy a direct connection to God and attracted a circle of disciples, who were called Hasidim ("loyalists"). Each circle of Rebbe and Hasidim established its own traditions of intense prayer and ecstatic religious expression.

Ben Eliezer and his Hasidim, particularly Dov Baer of Mezhirech and JACOB JOSEPH OF POLONNOYE, attracted a considerable following. With ben Eliezer's death about 1760, the movement spread from Volhynia (northwestern Ukraine) southward further into Ukraine and Podolia, northward into Belorussia and Lithuania, westward into Galicia and central Poland, and elsewhere. Early in the movement, Hasidim also traveled to and settled in the Land of Israel, locating itself in Safed and Tiberias. Hasidism continued to spread in its third generation (1773–1815), and its decentralized leadership—combined with a great diversification of the modes of thought and way of life among the various and far-flung Hasidic communities—rendered the movement diverse.

By the 1830s Hasidism predominated among the Jews in Ukraine, Galicia, and Poland and was well represented in Belorussia-Lithuania and Hungary. Opposition to Hasidism in Lithuania was led by Elijah ben Solomon Zalman, GAON of Vilna, who criticized its ecstatic and miraculous emphases. The center of Hasidism remained in Eastern Europe until 1939; masses of Hasidim and most of the Rebbes perished in the HOLOCAUST, but some few escaped to the State of Israel or to the United States, thereby establishing the movement overseas. The single most influential contemporary Hasidic community is called Ḥabad (an acronym formed from the beginning letters of the Hebrew words *ḥokhmah, binah,* and *da'at*—meaning wisdom, understanding, and knowledge). Derived originally from Lubavich, Ḥabad now thrives in Brooklyn, N.Y., and throughout the world.

Traditionally, the Hasidim looked to the zaddik, who not only worked miracles but also served as moral instructor. He would expound his TORAH at his table, surrounded by his followers. The court of the Rebbe formed the center of a

Hasidic Jews—a father and a son—from Williamsburg, Brooklyn, New York City
Eugene Gordon—Photo Researchers

community, and the Hasidim would come to the court on the holy days.

While affirming the theological principles of RABBINIC JUDAISM, the Hasidic masters placed their own distinctive imprint upon them. They taught that it is a religious duty to rejoice and that depression and sorrow should be avoided; they laid heavy emphasis upon song and dance, optimism, joy, and enthusiasm, and they instilled their teachings through PARABLES. Religious duties, they taught, must be carried out in a spirit of love and fear of God; prayer without love and fear cannot reach God. The deed is valuable but requires a spirit of devotion. Prayer serves not to petition or supplicate God but as a ladder by means of which one ascends to a relationship of union with God. There are no barriers between God and man, all is created out of God's essence. Since not everyone can accomplish spiritual goals unaided, the special gifts of the zaddik come into play; he, in particular, realizes the highest goals of the holy way of life.

Hasidism produced about 3,000 works of literature, from the late 18th century, beginning with *Toledot Yaakov Yosef* (1780), by JACOB JOSEPH OF POLONNOYE, and the published teachings of Dov Baer of Mezhirech a year later; in the 19th century anthologies of Hasidic stories were produced and circulated widely. In the 20th century the philosopher MARTIN BUBER presented Hasidism as a religious movement affording direct encounter between man and God. The theology of Abraham J. Heschel also recapitulates Hasidic teachings within the framework of 20th century PHILOSOPHY OF RELIGION.

HASKALAH \,häs-kä-'lä\ (Hebrew: "Reason," or "Intellect"), *also called* Jewish Enlightenment, late 18th- and 19th-century intellectual movement among the Jews of central and eastern Europe that attempted to acquaint Jews with the European and Hebrew languages and with secular education and culture as supplements to traditional Talmudic studies. Though the Haskalah owed much of its inspiration and values to the European Enlightenment, its roots, character, and development were distinctly Jewish. When the movement began, Jews lived mostly in PALES of settlement and ghettos and followed a form of life that had evolved after centuries of segregation and discriminatory legislation. A move toward change was initiated by a relatively few "mobile Jews" (mainly merchants) and "court Jews" (agents of various rulers and princes).

The early proponents of Haskalah were convinced that Jews could be brought into the mainstream of European culture through a reform of traditional Jewish education and a breakdown of ghetto life. This meant adding secular subjects to the school curriculum, adopting the language of the larger society in place of Yiddish, abandoning traditional garb, reforming SYNAGOGUE services, and taking up new occupations.

Though basically rationalistic, Haskalah also exhibited such romantic tendencies as a desire to return to nature, a high regard for manual work, and an aspiration to revive a glorious and better past. Haskalah advocated the study of Jewish history and the ancient Hebrew language as a means of reviving a Jewish national consciousness; these values and attitudes later merged with those of the Jewish nationalist movement known as ZIONISM. More immediately, Haskalah's call to modernize the Jewish religion provided the impetus for the emergence of REFORM JUDAISM in Germany in the early 19th century.

ORTHODOX JUDAISM opposed the Haskalah movement from the start because of its repudiation of the traditional Jewish way of life, which threatened to destroy the tightly knit fabric of Judaism and to undermine religious observance. There was particular distrust of a rationalistic ideology that seemed to challenge rabbinic orthodoxy and the important role of Talmudic studies in Jewish education. Nonetheless, eventually Orthodoxy admitted a minimum of secular studies and the use of local vernaculars. But other fears were justified, for some aspects of the Haskalah did in fact lead to assimilation and a weakening of Jewish identity and historical consciousness.

In Germany Yiddish was rapidly abandoned and assimilation was widespread, but interest in Jewish history revived and gave birth to modern critical historico-philological Jewish studies. In the Austrian Empire a Hebrew Haskalah developed that promoted Jewish scholarship and literature. The adherents of Haskalah fought rabbinic orthodoxy and especially HASIDISM, the mystical and pietistic tendencies of which were attacked bitterly. In Russia some followers of Haskalah hoped to achieve "improvement of the Jews" by collaborating with the government plan for educational reform, but the increasingly reactionary and anti-Semitic policies of the tsarist regime drove some Jews to support the revolutionary movement, others to support nascent Zionism.

As the impossibility of establishing an integral, worldwide Hebrew culture became evident, a rising ANTI-SEMITISM made many of the movement's expectations appear unrealistic. By the end of the 19th century, some ideals of Haskalah had become permanent features of Jewish life,

Hathor flanked by the Hare Nome goddess and King Menkaure, 4th dynasty
By courtesy of the Museum of Fine Arts, Boston, the Harvard-Boston Expedition

while others were abandoned. Overall, Haskalah helped to create a middle class that was loyal to Jewish traditions and yet part of modern Western civilization.

HAṬHA YOGA \ˈhə-tə-ˈyō-gə, ˈhä-\ (Sanskrit: "Discipline of Force"), school of YOGA that stresses mastery of the body as a way of attaining a state of spiritual perfection in which the mind is withdrawn from external objects. Haṭha Yoga traces its origins especially to GORAKHNĀTH, the legendary 11th-century founder of the Nāth or Kānphaṭa Yogīs, but it grew out of yogic traditions dating back at least as far as PATAÑJALI (3rd century BCE?).

Haṭha Yoga places great importance on diet, purificatory processes, regulation of breathing (PRĀṆĀYĀMA), and the adoption of bodily postures called ĀSANAS, which structure a program of physical exertion. A common *āsana* is the *padmāsana* ("lotus posture"), in which the crossed feet rest on the opposite thighs. This is the position in which many Hindu and Buddhist gods are often depicted but it is only one of dozens described in Haṭha Yoga treatises. The "salute to the sun" is a well-known sequence of 12 *āsana*s performed in a fluid movement.

Haṭha Yoga has grown in popularity in the West as a form of exercise conducing to strength, flexibility, bodily relaxation, and mental concentration. Its true object, however, is to awaken the dormant energy (ŚAKTI) of SHIVA that animates the subtle body but is concealed behind the gross human frame. The subtle anatomy containing it is variously described, usually as a series of lotiform CHAKRAS ("wheels") rising from the anal/genital area to the top of the head. Through the forceful (*haṭha*) suppression of physical and mental activity, the female *śakti* is enabled to rise along the chakras and unite with the male Shiva in the uppermost chakra, a union indistinguishable from enlightenment and even immortality.

HATHOR \ˈhä-tȯr\, *also called* Athyr \ä-ˈthir\, in ancient EGYPTIAN RELIGION, goddess of the sky, of women, and of fertility and love. Hathor's worship originated in predynastic times (4th millennium BCE). The name Hathor means "estate of Horus" and may not be her original name. Her principal animal form was that of a cow, and she was strongly associated with motherhood. Hathor was closely connected with the sun god RE of HELIOPOLIS, whose "eye" or daughter she was said to be. In her cult center at Dandarah in Upper Egypt she was worshiped with HORUS.

There were cults of Hathor in many towns in Egypt and abroad, for she was the patroness of foreign parts and of minerals won from the desert. At Dayr al-Baḥrī, in the NECROPOLIS of Thebes, she became "Lady of the West." In the Late Period (1st millennium BCE) women aspired to be assimilated with Hathor in the next world, as men aspired to become OSIRIS. The Greeks identified Hathor with their APHRODITE.

HATTIAN RELIGIONS \\'ha-tē-ən\\: *see* ANATOLIA, RELIGIONS OF.

HAUHAU \\'haù-,haù\\, member of Pai Marire (Maori: "Good and Peaceful Religion"), a religio-military cult among the Maori of New Zealand that arose during the Maori Wars of the 1860s. The movement was founded in 1864 by Te Ua Haumene, who claimed to have been visited by the ANGEL GABRIEL (in 1862) and to have been moved by the experience to sacrifice his child in repentance for the straying of the Maori people.

Combining Jewish, Christian, and Maori religious tenets, the movement held that the Maori were a new chosen people. Their immediate task was to drive the Europeans from New Zealand and to recover their ancestral lands. The adherents of Pai Marire were assured by their leader that shouting the words "Pai Marire, hau, hau!" (or "hapa, hapa!") in battle would protect them from European bullets. In 1864–65, large-scale European confiscation of Maori land drove many Maori into the ranks of armed dissidents, and Hauhau became a common label for these people. Fighting continued until 1872. By then Pai Marire itself had dwindled, but similar patterns of RELIGIOUS BELIEF have continued among the Maori.

HAVDALA: *see* HABDALAH.

HAYASHI RAZAN \\hä-'yä-shē-rä-'zän\\, *original name* Hayashi Nobukatsu, *Buddhist name* Dōshun \\'dō-,shün\\ (b. August 1583, Kyōto, Japan—d. Feb. 4, 1657, Edo [now Tokyo]), Japanese scholar who established the NEO-CONFUCIANISM of CHU HSI as the official doctrine of the Tokugawa shogunate (ruled 1603–1867). Hayashi also reinterpreted SHINTŌ from the point of view of Chu Hsi's philosophy, laying the foundation for the Confucianized Shintō of later centuries.

Hayashi began as a student of BUDDHISM but became a devoted adherent of Neo-Confucianism. In 1604 he became a pupil of the Confucian scholar Fujiwara Seika and on his recommendation was employed by the shogunate, beginning in 1607. He served the first four Tokugawa shoguns, tutoring them in Neo-Confucianism and history. At the same time he was engaged in scholarly activities and in the drafting of diplomatic documents. Hayashi's philosophy, with its emphasis on loyalty, on a hierarchical social and political order, and on a static conservative point of view, proved to be a powerful support for the newly established government in its relations with the restless feudal lords. In 1630 the third shogun gave Hayashi an estate in the capital city of Edo, where he founded an academy.

Hayashi's third and fourth sons, also employed by the shogunate, collaborated with their father in compiling histories; after his death they assembled the *Hayashi Razan bunshū* ("Collected Works of Hayashi Razan") and the *Razan Sensei shishū* ("Master Razan's Poems"), republished in two volumes in 1918 and 1921. His grandson was given the title *daigaku-nokami* ("head of the state university"), which was then handed down to the subsequent heads of the Hayashi family until the late 19th century.

HEALING CULT, religious group or movement that places major, or even exclusive, emphasis on the treatment or prevention by nonmedical means of physical or spiritual ailments, which are often seen as manifestations of evil. Such cults are generally centered on certain shrines or holy places, certain organizations, or particular persons.

PILGRIMAGE to a sacred place and devotion before a sacred object is a major means of religious healing. From earliest times, healing and healing cults have been associated with springs and other sources of water. As in the spa therapy (bathing in mineral waters) of contemporary health resorts, so thermal and mineral springs were conceived to be curative in ancient times. There is evidence of Neolithic and Bronze Age devotion at the sites of a variety of such springs in western Europe (*e.g.*, Grisy and Saint-Sauveur in France; Forlì, Italy; Saint Moritz, Switz.). Every country in which they occur has healing traditions associated with such springs. In ancient Greece the most famous shrines were at Thermopylae and near Aedepses. In ancient Rome, the springs at Tibus and the hot sulfur wells of Aquae Abulae were well known. In the Middle East, Callirrhoe, where Herod attempted to find relief from his fatal illness, was perhaps the best known; in ancient Egypt many of the temples dedicated to the god ASCLEPIUS were near mineral springs.

Elaborate cultic practices surround those sources of water that have been the scenes of epiphanies or in which divinities are believed to dwell. The most famous Western example of this type of shrine is that at LOURDES in France, where the Virgin MARY is believed to have appeared to Marie-Bernarde Soubirous in a series of visions in 1858 and to have indicated a miraculously flowing stream that would heal the ill (*see* BERNADETTE OF LOURDES). A number of other European water shrines are associated with epiphanies of Mary (*e.g.*, the Shrine of the MADONNA of the Baths at Scafati, Italy). Many streams and wells are believed to have healing powers on the feast of the Conception of St. JOHN THE BAPTIST. More frequently, however, it is minor local water spirits (NYMPHS, water serpents, etc.) or wells and streams blessed by saints or other holy men to which devotion is made and from which healing is expected after immersion.

Certain great landmark rivers, the scene of both civic cults and private devotions, are believed to have general therapeutic and apotropaic powers. By immersion in the Euphrates (Iraq), the Pharpar (Damascus, Syria), the Jordan (Israel), the Tiber (Italy), the Nile (Egypt), or the GAṄGĀ, Jamunā, or Sarasvatī (all in India), one might be cured of disease, purified from transgression, or protected against future disorders.

Healing may be accomplished by those who derive powers from their office, such as priests and kings. More frequently, however, individuals are believed to cure by means of a special gift or sacred commission. This power may be revealed in a vision, it may be sought after, or it may be accidentally discovered that an individual possesses such abilities.

Almost every religious founder, saint, and prophet has been credited with the ability to heal—either as a demonstration of or as a consequence of his holiness. In every culture there are also specialists (*e.g.*, SHAMANS, medicine men, folk doctors) who have gone through extraordinary initiations that confer curative powers upon them. Some work within an established religious tradition but concentrate their energies primarily upon healing (*e.g.*, Christian faith healers of the 19th and 20th centuries, such as John of Kronstadt, Leslie Weatherhead, Edgar Cayce, and Oral Roberts). Others have founded their own religious communities that maintain a focus on healing (*e.g.*, Phineas P. Quimby and the NEW THOUGHT movement, MARY BAKER EDDY and CHRISTIAN SCIENCE, and the various independent churches of Africa).

HEART SUTRA \'sü-trə\, *Sanskrit* Prajñāpāramitāhṛdaya-sūtra \'prəg-ˌnyä-'pär-ə-mē-ˌtä-'hri-də-yə-\ ("*Sūtra* on the Heart of the *Prajñāpāramitā*"), extremely brief distillation of the teachings in the PRAJÑĀPĀRAMITĀ ("Perfection of Wisdom"). It has been much reproduced and recited throughout many parts of Asia. In the space of a single page (some versions adding an introductory and a concluding paragraph), in words placed in the mouth of the BODHISATTVA of compassion, AVALOKITEŚVARA, and in a series of terse paradoxes, the *sūtra* asserts the essentials of MAHĀYĀNA Buddhist doctrine from the point of view of the *Prajñāpāramitā* emphasis on "emptiness."

HEAVEN, the dwelling place of God, gods, or other superhuman beings and the abode or state of being of the saved, the ELECT, or the blessed in the afterlife or in the time after the LAST JUDGMENT. The term also designates the celestial sphere or spheres in contrast to the earth and to the Underworld. As celestial space, heaven also is the place of the sun, moon, planets, and stars, all of which give and symbolize light, a quality of the sacred and the good, as opposed to darkness, the quality of the Underworld and evil.

In the OLD TESTAMENT heaven is regarded as the abode of YAHWEH; because he also is heaven's creator, he transcends the celestial sphere. Until the 3rd–2nd century BCE, Israelites generally believed that all men (good and evil) slept in Sheol, the Underworld, which was a place of neither pain nor pleasure, punishment nor reward. In later JUDAISM, however, heaven came to be viewed as the postmortem destination of the righteous, who would be resurrected to live with God. Emerging from this matrix, CHRIS-

The Angel Shows John the Heavenly Jerusalem, *from the* Apocalypse of St. John, c. *1020*
By courtesy of the Staatsbibliothek Bamberg, Germany

TIANITY viewed heaven as the destination of the true believers and followers of Christ. Some of the more recent interpretations view heaven symbolically as a state of life with Christ, rather than as a place to which the elect or the saved go after death.

ISLAM, influenced by Judaism and Christianity, views heaven as a place of joy and bliss to which faithful Muslims go, according to the will of ALLĀH (God). In the QUR'AN, there are references to the belief that everyone must go through or pass by hell before reaching heaven.

In the Eastern religions, concepts of heaven vary considerably, some being similar to Western religious views and others being very dissimilar. The Chinese heaven (T'ien) is the guardian of both the moral laws of mankind and the physical laws of nature. T'ien also is synonymous with the divine will. In some MAHĀYĀNA Buddhist sects, such as the PURE LAND sect, heaven is a "Western Paradise" for those who have received the saving GRACE of the savior AMITĀBHA, a buddha who vowed to save all living creatures. In THERAVĀDA Buddhism, MAHĀMĀYĀ, the Buddha Gotama's mother, ascended into heaven immediately after his birth. In HINDUISM and BUDDHISM there are varied concepts of heaven.

HEBAT \'ke-ˌbät\, *also spelled* Hepa \'ke-ˌpä\, *or* Hepatu \ke-'pä-ˌtü\, in the religions of Asia Minor, a Hurrian goddess, the consort of the weather god TESHUB.

Hebat was called Queen of Heaven and was assimilated by the Hittites to their national goddess, the sun goddess of the city of Arinna. Teshub and Hebat had cult centers at Kummanni (classical COMANA Cappadociae) and at Aleppo (Ḥalab) and other cities in the region of the Taurus Mountains. Hebat is represented as a matronly figure standing on a lion or seated on a throne. She survived during Hellenistic times as Hipta, a goddess of Lydia and Caria. Her name has been compared to Hebrew Ḥawwa (Eve) and with the Greek HECATE. *See also* ANATOLIAN RELIGIONS.

HEBE \'hē-ˌbē\ (Greek: *hēbē*, "puberty," or "adolescence"), daughter of ZEUS and his wife HERA. In Homer she was a divine domestic, appearing most often as cupbearer to the gods. As the goddess of youth she was generally worshiped along with her mother, of whom she may have been regarded as an emanation or specialized form. She was also associated with HERACLES, whose bride she became when he was received into heaven. Her major centers of worship were Phlious and Sicyon, where she was called Ganymeda and Dia.

HEBRAIC LAW, body of ancient Hebrew law codes found in various places in the OLD TESTAMENT. These are similar to earlier law codes of ancient Middle Eastern monarchs, which typically claimed the authority of divine command. Two types of law are noted in the Hebrew codes: (1) casuistic, or case, law, which contains a conditional statement and a type of punishment to be meted out, and (2) apodictic law, which contains regulations in the form of divine commands (*e.g.*, the TEN COMMANDMENTS).

The Hebraic law codes incorporated in the Old Testament include (1) the Book of the COVENANT, or the Covenant Code, (2) the Deuteronomic Code, and (3) the PRIESTLY CODE. The Book of the Covenant is found in EXODUS 20:22–23:33. The Covenant Code is divided into (1) a prologue, (2) laws on the worship of YAHWEH, (3) laws dealing with persons, (4) property laws, (5) laws concerned with the continuance of the Covenant, and (6) an epilogue, with warnings and promises. The *lex talionis* (the law of retribution)—namely, the "eye for an eye, a tooth for a tooth" law—is found here, though the substitution of financial compensation or a fine for the literal punishment was allowed.

The Deuteronomic Code, found in Deuteronomy, chapters 12–26, is a reinterpretation or revision of Israelite law, based on historical conditions as interpreted by the 7th-century-BCE historians known as the Deuteronomists. Discovered in the Temple at Jerusalem in 621 BCE, the Deuteronomic Code attempted to purify the worship of Yahweh from Canaanite and other influences. The greatest SIN was considered to be APOSTASY, or the rejection of faith, the penalty for which was death. The Deuteronomic Code is divided into (1) statutes and ordinances, especially related to dealings with the Canaanites and worship in the Temple in Jerusalem alone, (2) laws (known as sabbatical laws) concerned with the year of release from obligations, especially financial, (3) regulations for leaders, (4) various civil, cultic, and ethical laws, and (5) an epilogue of blessings and curses.

The Priestly Code, containing a major section known as the Code of Holiness (in Leviticus, chapters 17–26), is found in various parts of Exodus, all of Leviticus, and most of Numbers. Emphasizing ceremonial, institutional, and ritualistic practices, the Priestly Code comes from the postexilic period (*i.e.*, after 538 BCE). Though most of the laws of the Code of Holiness probably come from the preexilic period, the laws reflect a reinterpretation encouraged by the exile experiences in Babylon. Purity of worship of Yahweh is emphasized.

HEB-SED FESTIVAL \'heb-,sed\, *also called* Sed festival, one of the oldest feasts of Egypt, celebrated by the king after 30 years of rule and repeated every three years thereafter. It is believed the ceremonies represented a ritual reenactment of the unification of Egypt accomplished by Menes. From numerous wall reliefs and paintings and from the Heb-Sed court in the Step PYRAMID complex of Djoser at Ṣaqqārah, much information has been gleaned about the festival. The king first presented offerings to a series of gods and then was crowned, first with the white crown of Upper Egypt and then with the red crown of Lower Egypt. Finally, dressed in a short kilt with an animal's tail in back, the king ran a ritual course four times and was then carried away in a great PROCESSION to visit the chapels of the gods HORUS and SETH.

HECATE \'he-kə-tē, *in the works of Shakespeare and Milton usually* 'he-kət\, goddess accepted at an early date into GREEK RELIGION but probably derived from the Carians in southwest Asia Minor. In Hesiod she is the daughter of the TITAN Perses and the NYMPH Asteria and has power over heaven, earth, and sea; hence, she bestows wealth and all the blessings of daily life.

Hecate was the chief goddess presiding over magic and SPELLS. She witnessed the abduction of Demeter's daughter PERSEPHONE to the Underworld and, torch in hand, assisted in the search for her. Thus, pillars called Hecataea stood at crossroads and doorways, perhaps to keep away evil spirits. Hecate was represented as single-formed, clad in a long robe, holding burning torches; in later representations she was triple-formed, with three bodies standing back to back, probably so that she could look in all directions at once from the crossroads.

HECTOR \'hek-tər\, in Greek legend, the eldest son of the Trojan king PRIAM and his queen HECUBA. He was the husband of ANDROMACHE and the chief warrior of the Trojan army. In Homer's *Iliad* he is represented as an ideal warrior, a good son, a loving husband and father, and a trusty friend. He is an especial favorite of APOLLO, and later poets even described him as son of that god. His chief exploits during the Trojan War were his defense of the wounded SARPEDON, his fight with Ajax, son of Telamon, and the storming of the Greek ramparts. Patroclus, the friend of ACHILLES who came to the help of the Greeks, was slain by Hector with the help of Apollo. Then Achilles, to revenge his friend's death, returned to the war, slew Hector and dragged his body behind his chariot to the camp and afterward round the tomb of

Patroclus. APHRODITE and Apollo preserved it from corruption and mutilation. Priam, guarded by HERMES, went to Achilles and prevailed on him to give back the body, which was buried with great honor. Hector was worshiped as a hero in the Troad (Greek Troias; "Land of Troy," the northwestern projection of Asia Minor into the Aegean Sea) and also at Tanagra, east of Thebes.

HECUBA \'he-kyə-bə\, *Greek* Hekabe, in Greek legend, the principal wife of the Trojan king PRIAM, mother of HECTOR, and daughter, according to some accounts, of the Phrygian king Dymas. When Troy was captured by the Greeks, Hecuba was taken prisoner. Her fate was told in various ways, most of which connected her with the promontory Cynossema (Dog's Monument) on the Hellespont. According to Euripides (in the *Hecuba*), her youngest son, Polydorus, had been placed under the care of Polymestor, king of Thrace. When the Greeks reached the Thracian Chersonese (ancient region comprising the modern Gallipoli Peninsula) on their way home, she discovered that her son had been murdered and in revenge put out the eyes of Polymestor and murdered his two sons. Later she was turned into a dog, and her grave became a mark for ships.

HEGIRA: *see* HIJRA.

HEIDELBERG CATECHISM \'hī-dəl-,bərg\, Reformed confession of faith; it was written in 1562 primarily by Caspar Olevianus, the superintendent of the Palatinate church, and Zacharias Ursinus, a professor of the theological faculty of the University of Heidelberg. It was accepted at the annual SYNOD of the Palatinate church in 1563.

The Heidelberg CATECHISM was prepared as part of a reform program of the Palatinate (now part of Germany). Although the elector of the Palatinate, Frederick III, preferred the Reformed faith, he hoped to conciliate the contending Protestant groups, which included the orthodox Lutheran party and the more moderate Lutheran followers of PHILIPP MELANCHTHON. The authors of the Catechism sought to bring their Reformed statements as near to the moderate Melanchthonian–Lutheran position as they could. The controversial doctrine of PREDESTINATION was very mildly stated. The strength and appeal of the catechism was the fact that it was a practical and devotional work, rather than an intellectual, dogmatic, or polemical one.

Although the Heidelberg Catechism failed to conciliate the Protestant groups in Germany, it was widely used. It has been translated into more than 25 languages.

HEIMDALL \'hām-,däl\, *Old Norse* Heimdallr \-,dä-lər\, in Norse mythology, the watchman of the gods. Called the shining god and whitest-skinned of the gods, Heimdall dwelt at the entry to ASGARD, where he guarded Bifrost, the rainbow bridge. He required less sleep than a bird, could see 100 leagues, and could hear grass growing in the meadows and wool growing on sheep. Heimdall kept the horn, Gjallarhorn, which could be heard throughout heaven, earth, and the lower world; it was believed that he would sound the horn to summon the gods when their enemies, the GIANTS, drew near at the RAGNARÖK, the end of the world of gods and humans. When that time came, Heimdall and his enemy LOKI would slay each other.

HEI TIKI \'hā-'tē-kē\, small neck pendant in the form of a human fetus, used by the Maori of New Zealand as a fertility symbol. Usually carved of green nephrite or a jadelike stone called *pounamu* that is found along the western coast of the South Island, *hei tiki*s normally are worn only by women. The object is believed to possess powers that increase as it is passed from generation to generation. According to one idea, the *hei tiki* protects its wearer against the vengeful spirits of stillborn infants, who have been deprived of the chance to live. Another theory holds that the figure represents the Polynesian god Tiki, the creator of life. To the Maori the greatest value of these pendants lies in their possession of magical powers and in the prestige acquired from previous owners.

HEKA \\'he-kä\\, *also spelled* Hike \\'hē-kā\\, in ancient EGYPTIAN RELIGION, the personification of one of the attributes of the sun god Re; the term is usually translated as "magic," or "magical power," though its exact meaning remains obscure. Heka was believed to accompany RE in his solar boat on its daily trip across the heavens; it could also be given to and used by humans. Consequently, the Egyptians believed that Heka could be used to procure the favor of the gods, to acquire what was ordinarily unobtainable, or to prevent the return of the dead to this world.

Hei tiki *from New Zealand*
By courtesy of the trustees of the British Museum

HEL \\'hel\\, in Norse mythology, originally the name of the world of the dead; it later came to mean the goddess of death. Hel was one of the children of the trickster god LOKI, and her kingdom was said to lie downward and northward. It was called NIFLHEIM, or the World of Darkness, and appears to have been divided into several sections, one of which was Náströnd, the shore of corpses. There stood a castle facing north; it was filled with the venom of serpents, in which murderers, adulterers, and perjurers suffered torment, while the dragon Nidhogg sucked the blood from their bodies. Mention is made in an early poem of the nine worlds of Niflheim. It was said that those who fell in battle did not go to Hel but to the god ODIN, in VALHALLA, the hall of the slain.

HELEN \\'he-lən\\, *Greek* Helene \\hə-'lēn, -'län\\, in Greek mythology, the most beautiful woman of Greece and the indirect cause of the Trojan War. She was daughter of ZEUS, either by LEDA or by NEMESIS, and sister of the DIOSCURI. She was also the sister of Clytemnestra, who married AGAMEMNON, and wife of MENELAUS, Agamemnon's younger brother. Helen eloped with PARIS, son of the Trojan king Priam; the couple fled to Troy. When Paris was slain, she married his brother Deïphobus, whom she betrayed to Menelaus when Troy was subsequently captured. She and Menelaus then returned to Sparta, where they lived until their deaths.

According to a variant of the story, Helen, in widowhood, was driven out by her stepsons and fled to Rhodes, whose queen, Polyxo, hanged her in revenge for the loss of her husband Tlepolemus in the Trojan War.

The poet Stesichorus, however, related in his second version of her story that she and Paris were driven ashore on the coast of Egypt and that Helen was detained there by King Proteus. The Helen carried on to Troy was thus a phantom, and the real one was recovered by her husband from Egypt after the war. This version of the story was used by Euripides in his play *Helen*.

Helen had a festival at Therapnae in Laconia; she also had a temple at Rhodes, where she was worshiped as Dendritis (the tree goddess). Like her brothers, the Dioscuri, she was a patron deity of sailors.

HELENA, SAINT \\'he-lə-nə\\, *also called* Helen (b. *c.* 248, Drepanon?, Bithynia, Asia Minor—d. *c.* 328, Nicomedia; Western feast day August 18; Eastern feast day [with CONSTANTINE] May 21), Roman empress who was the reputed discoverer of the TRUE CROSS upon which JESUS CHRIST was crucified.

Helena was married to the Roman emperor Constantius I Chlorus, who renounced her for political reasons. When her son Constantine I the Great became emperor, he made her empress dowager, and under his influence she later became a Christian. She was devoted to her eldest grandson, Crispus Caesar, whom Constantine made titular ruler of Gaul, but a mysterious embroilment in the imperial family culminated with the execution of Crispus and Fausta, Constantine's second wife and Crispus' stepmother. Immediately afterward Helena made a PILGRIMAGE to the Holy Land. She caused churches to be built on the reputed sites of the Nativity and of the ASCENSION.

Before 337 it was claimed in Jerusalem that the cross of Jesus Christ had been found during the building of Constantine's church on GOLGOTHA. Later in the century Helena was credited with the discovery. Many subsequent legends developed, and the story of the "invention," or the finding of the cross, enhanced by romances and confusions with other Helens, became a favorite throughout Christendom.

HELENUS \\'he-lə-nəs\\, in Greek mythology, son of King PRIAM of Troy and his wife HECUBA, brother of HECTOR and twin of the prophetess CASSANDRA. According to Homer he was a seer and warrior. After the death of PARIS in the Trojan War, Helenus paid suit to HELEN but was rejected and withdrew in indignation to Mt. Ida, where he was captured by the Greeks. Other accounts, however, relate that ODYSSEUS captured him, or he surrendered voluntarily in disgust at the treacherous murder of ACHILLES. He told the Greeks that in order to capture Troy they must do three things: gain possession of the Trojans' image of Pallas ATHENA (the PALLADIUM), obtain the bow of HERACLES, and have the bones of Achilles' son NEOPTOLEMUS. Helenus and ANDROMACHE, his brother Hector's widow, were later taken by Neoptolemus to Epirus. After Neoptolemus' death, Helenus married Andromache and became ruler of the country.

HELIOPOLIS \\,hē-lē-'ä-pə-lis\\ (Greek), *Egyptian* Iunu \\'yü-,nü\\, *or* Onu \\'ō-,nü\\ ("Pillar City"), *biblical* On \\'ōn, 'än\\, one of the most ancient Egyptian cities and the seat of worship of the sun god, RE. Its great TEMPLE of Re was second in size only to that of AMON at Thebes, and its PRIESTHOOD wielded great influence, particularly during the 5th dynasty, when the worship of Re became the state cult. In the New Kingdom the temple of Re-Horakhte became the repository of royal records.

HELIOS \\'hē-lē-əs, -,ōs\\, in GREEK RELIGION, the sun god. He drove a chariot daily across the sky and sailed around the northerly stream of Ocean each night in a huge cup. In classical Greece, Helios was especially worshiped in Rhodes, where from at least the early 5th century BCE he was regarded as the chief god, to whom the island belonged. His worship spread as he became increasingly identified with other deities, often under Eastern influence. From the 5th century BCE APOLLO was more and more interpreted as the sun god in Greece.

HELL, the abode or state of existence of beings that are damned to postmortem punishment. The word *hell*, like cognate words in other Germanic languages, is descended from a Common Germanic name for the abode of the dead that was transferred to Christian concepts of a place reserved for the souls of the damned.

The concept of a state of being or place that separates the good from the evil or the living from the dead is found in most religions of the world. The dwelling place of the dead as the destiny of the soul might be a gloomy subterranean realm or a distant island (*e.g.*, the Greek HADES); a deep abyss in the lower world in which the souls of persons are punished (*e.g.*, the Greek Tartarus); a dark region in the lower world in which both good and evil souls continue to exist as shades in constant thirst (*e.g.*, the ancient Israelite Sheol); an Underworld of cold and darkness (*e.g.*, the Norse NIFLHEIM, also called HEL); a celestial dwelling place in which the souls of the departed reside (as with the Pueblo Indians, who upon death become clouds); or a nebulous existence in which the soul might eventually fade into nonexistence (as with the Native American hunting tribes).

The view that hell is the final dwelling place of the damned after a LAST JUDGMENT is held by ZOROASTRIANISM, JUDAISM, CHRISTIANITY, and ISLAM. In Zoroastrianism, the soul at death waits three nights to be judged and on the fourth day goes to the Bridge of the Requiter, where its deeds in life are weighed. If the good outweighs the evil, the soul crosses the bridge, which becomes broad, and goes to heaven; if the evil deeds are greater, the bridge becomes too narrow to cross and the soul falls into a freezing and malodorous hell to suffer torment and chastisement until the RESURRECTION. For those whose good and evil deeds are equal is reserved *hamēstagān* ("the place of the mixed"), wherein such souls suffer from both heat and cold.

Judaism, as it developed from Hellenistic times, viewed hell in terms of GEHENNA, an infernal region of punishment for the wicked. The Christian view of hell, based on Jewish concepts, regarded hell as the fiery domain of the DEVIL and his evil angels, a place of eternal damnation for those who have lived a life of SIN and who thereby deny God. Some early Christian thinkers, such as ORIGEN of Alexandria and GREGORY OF NYSSA, questioned the eternity of hell and the literalistic view that hell was a place of a fiery afterlife. The majority of Christian thinkers, however, taught that hell is a state of punishment for those who die unrepentant of their sins. Some modern theologians have again questioned the literalistic view but still hold that hell is, at least, a state of separation of the wicked from the good.

Islam, basing its concepts of hell, *Jahannam*, on Zoroastrianism, Judaism, and Christianity, describes it as a huge crater of fire beneath a narrow bridge that all souls must pass over to go to paradise. The damned fall from the bridge and suffer torments, unless God wills otherwise.

In HINDUISM, hell is only one stage in a career of the soul. Because all actions have consequences and because of REINCARNATION, the time spent in one or more of the 21 hells beneath the netherworld is not eternal. Eventually, the soul

Helios in his chariot, relief sculpture from Troy
By courtesy of the Staatliche Museen zu Berlin

will return to the World (or Ultimate) Soul, even though it takes many life periods to do so. The JAINA hell (*bhumis*) is a place where DEMONS torture sinners until any evil accumulated during their lives has been exhausted. In BUDDHISM, multiple hells correspond to *karmavacara*, the cosmic realm in which the five senses may be experienced in a variety of bodies and perceptions.

HELLEN \'he-lən\, in Greek mythology, king of Phthia (at the northern end of the Gulf of Euboea) and grandson of the god Prometheus; he was the eponymous ancestor of all true Greeks (Hellenes). The Hellenes consisted of the Aeolians, Dorians, Ionians, and Achaeans, traditionally descended from and named for Hellen's sons, Aeolus and Dorus, and grandsons, Ion and Achaeus.

HELLENISTIC RELIGION, any of various systems of beliefs and practices of eastern Mediterranean peoples from the period of the Greco-Macedonian conqueror Alexander the Great (356–323 BCE) to the period of CONSTANTINE, the first Christian Roman emperor (d. 337 CE).

The empire that Alexander established constituted most of Europe, the Mediterranean, the Middle East, Africa, Persia, and the borderlands of India. The political and economic unification of such a vast territory opened the way for religious interchange between East and West. Almost every so-called Hellenistic religion occurred in both its homeland and in diasporic centers—the foreign cities in which its adherents lived in minority groups. For example, ISIS (Egypt), BAAL (Syria), the GREAT MOTHER (Phrygia), YAHWEH (Palestine), and MITHRA (Kurdistan) were worshiped in their native lands as well as in Rome and other centers.

In many cases the imposition of Greco-Roman political and cultural forms in disparate regions prompted a conscious revival of ancient religious practices, which became linked to nationalistic or messianic movements seeking to overthrow the foreign oppressors (*e.g.*, the Maccabean rebellion against Jewish hellenizing parties and the Syrian overlords in 167–165 BCE). Among the dispersed groups, however, ties to the homeland tended to weaken with successive generations, and religion shifted its focus from national prosperity to individual salvation. In terms of transmission, the diasporic groups may be seen as shifting from "birthright" to "convinced" religion (*i.e.*, from a religion into which one is born to a religion which one chooses to follow).

The archaic religions of the Mediterranean world had been primarily religions of etiquette, in which the interrelationships among people, between the people and the gods, between individuals and the state, and between the living and the dead were all seen to mirror the divine order of the cosmos, which in turn was discernible through ASTROLOGY, DIVINATION, oracles, and other occult practices. In the Hellenistic period such an emphasis on conformity no longer spoke to the needs of displaced and subjugated peoples. The formerly revered law and order of the cosmos came to be viewed as an evil, perverse, and confining structure from which the believer sought to be liberated. Most Hellenistic religions offered a highly dualistic COSMOLOGY in which the earthly realm in all its aspects—from despotic rulers to one's own body—constituted the imprisoning power of evil over the soul. Liberation was attainable through cultic activity, secret knowledge (*gnōsis*), and divine intervention (*see* GNOSTICISM).

The esotericism to which these changes led, emphasizing radical reinterpretation of the sacred texts and rigid codification of dogma, creeds, and means of admission, was met with deep suspicion by the Greco-Roman authorities. Attempts were made to expel foreigners or suppress foreign worship, and the emperor Augustus, among others, sought to revive traditional Roman religious practices. Externally, the heightened tension between Greco-Roman authority and the "new" Eastern religions expressed itself in wars, riots, and persecutions. The emergence of "emperor worship" with the deification of Augustus in 14 CE further escalated the animosity.

The dominant feature of the decline of Hellenistic influence was the rapid spread of CHRISTIANITY throughout the Roman Empire, culminating in the conversion of the emperor Constantine in 313. In this period the various Hellenistic cults were persecuted and eventually extinguished, although their influence continued even within Christianity. Hellenistic philosophy (Stoicism, Cynicism, Neo-Aristotelianism, Neo-Pythagoreanism, and Neoplatonism) provided key formulations for Jewish, Christian, and Muslim thought through the 18th century. Hellenistic magic, theurgy, astrology, and alchemy remained influential until modern times in both East and West. And many formal aspects of Hellenistic religion—from art and architecture to modes of worship to forms of literature—persist in the Jewish and Christian traditions today. (*See also* GREEK RELIGION.)

HELLER, YOM TOV LIPMANN BEN NATHAN HA-LEVI \'he-lər\ (b. 1579, Wallerstein, Bavaria [Germany]—d. Sept. 7, 1654, Kraków, Pol.), Bohemian Jewish RABBI and scholar who is best known for his commentary on the MISHNAH. He also had extensive knowledge of mathematics, the sciences, and other secular subjects.

Heller studied at the YESHIVA of Judah Loew ben Bezalel and was appointed a *dayan* (judge) in Prague at the age of 18. He served as a rabbi to communities in Moravia and Vienna, but he was recalled to Prague in 1627 to the office of the chief rabbinate. At this time, the Holy Roman emperor Ferdinand II had imposed heavy taxes on the Jews of Bohemia. The chief rabbi was responsible for overseeing the collection of the tax, a task that aroused bitter opposition within the Jewish community and made Heller the object of false accusations, for which he was heavily fined and briefly imprisoned; he was also forbidden to serve the rabbinate anywhere within the empire.

Later, while serving as a rabbi in Vladimir, Volhynia, Pol., Heller fought for the renewal of a decree preventing the purchase of rabbinical offices, SIMONY being a practice at that time. This aroused the anger of some of the wealthier Jews, who succeeded in obtaining a decree from the governor ordering Heller's expulsion. Although the decree was eventually rescinded, in 1643 Heller accepted an appointment to the chief rabbinate in Kraków, where he lived the remainder of his life.

Among Heller's many written works are an autobiography, *Megillat eyva* ("Scroll of Hate"; first published in 1818), which documented the various communities in which he had lived and included accounts of massacres of Jews in Prague (1618) and the Ukraine (1643). The most famous of his many religious works is his commentary on the Mishnah, *Tosafot Yom Ṭov* (1614–17, 2nd ed. 1643–44; "The Additions of Yom Ṭov"). In Heller's work on Obadiah of Bertinoro's commentary on the Mishnah, Heller explicated Bertinoro's sources, even as he criticized his conclusions regarding HALAKHAH.

HELWYS, THOMAS \'hel-wis\ (b. c. 1550—d. c. 1616), English Puritan leader, member of a Separatist group that emigrated to Amsterdam (1608), where he helped organize the first BAPTIST church.

Returning to England (1611/12) to witness to his belief in adult BAPTISM and greater individual moral responsibility (against extreme Calvinist PREDESTINATION), Helwys established the first General Baptist congregation in London. He was imprisoned for advocating universal religious tolerance and the independence of the church from state control.

HEMACANDRA \,hā-mə-'chən-drə\, *also called* Hemacandra Sūri \-'sü-rē\, *original name* Candradeva (b. 1088, Dhandhuka, Gujarāt, India—d. 1172, Gujarāt), Jain sage and Indian author who gained privileges for his religion from Siddharāja Jayasimha, one of the greatest kings of Gujarāt. With his eloquence and vast erudition, Hemacandra succeeded in converting the successor king Kumārapāla, thus firmly entrenching JAINISM in Gujarāt.

As with the birth accounts of many Indian pundits, Hemacandra's birth is said to have been attended by OMENS and supernatural occurrences—*e.g.*, when the child was taken to a Jain temple, the priest Devacandra noticed he had numerous auspicious signs on his person and convinced the parents to let him teach the boy.

Candradeva was ordained in 1110, changing his name to Somacandra. In 1125 he became an adviser to King Kumārapāla and wrote the *Arhannīti* ("Jain Politics"). A prodigious writer, he produced Sanskrit and Prākrit grammars, textbooks on practically every branch of Indian philosophy and science, and several poems, including the *Triṣaṣṭiśalākāpuruṣa-carita* ("Lives of the 63 Great Personages"), an epic in Sanskrit. His works became classics, setting new and higher standards for Sanskrit learning.

The thread of Jain doctrine weaves itself through all his writings. When he had at last attained the rank of *ācārya* (teacher), he changed his name to Hemacandra. At the end of his life, in accordance with Jain tradition, he fasted to death (a rite known as *sallekhanā*).

HEPHAESTUS \hi-'fes-təs\, *also spelled* Hephaistos, in GREEK RELIGION, the god of fire. Originally a deity of Asia Minor and the adjoining islands (in particular Lemnos), he had an important place of worship at the Lycian Olympus. Born lame or crippled at an early age, Hephaestus was cast from

heaven in disgust by his mother, HERA, and again by his father, ZEUS, after a family quarrel. His consort was APHRODITE or Charis, the personification of grace.

As god of fire, Hephaestus became the divine smith and patron of craftsmen; the natural volcanic or gaseous fires already connected with him were often considered to be his workshops. His cult reached Athens not later than about 600 BCE and arrived in Campania not long afterward. In art Hephaestus was generally represented as a middle-aged, bearded man.

HERA \'hir-ə, 'her-\, in GREEK RELIGION, a daughter of the TITANS CRONUS and RHEA, sister-wife of ZEUS, and queen of the Olympian gods. Hera was worshiped throughout the Greek world and played an important part in Greek literature, appearing most frequently as the jealous and rancorous wife of Zeus and pursuing with vindictive hatred the heroines who were beloved by him. From early times Hera was believed to be the sole lawful wife of Zeus; she superseded DIONE (a female form of the name Zeus), who shared with him his ancient oracle at DODONA in Epirus.

In general, Hera was worshiped in two main capacities: as consort of Zeus and queen of heaven and as goddess of marriage and of the life of women. The second sphere naturally made her the protectress of women in childbirth, and at Athens and Argos she bore the title of EILEITHYIA, normally the name of the goddess of birth. She was patron of the cities Argos and Samos, which gave her a position corresponding to that of ATHENA at Athens. Although her Argive ritual was markedly agricultural, she also had a celebration there called the Shield, and there was an armed PROCESSION in her honor at Samos. The animal sacred to Hera was the cow. Her sacred bird was first the cuckoo, later the peacock. She was represented as a majestic and severe, though youthful, matron.

HERACLEON \hə-'ra-klē-ən\ (fl. 2nd century CE), leader of an Italian gnostic school. Diverging from his contemporaries VALENTINUS and Ptolemaeus, Heracleon sought a conservative expression of GNOSTICISM divested of radical oriental theories; accordingly, in the first known exegetical commentary on the Gospel According to St. John, he expounded with allegorical emphasis his central doctrine of the three levels of being: JESUS CHRIST as the incarnate form of a fallen spirit or DEMIURGE representing the "psychic" level that is intermediate between the superior or "pneumatic" category (Greek: "spirit," comprising the "plenitude" of the Father) and the base level of the material world formed by the demigod of evil.

HERACLES \'her-ə-,klēz\, *Greek* Herakles, *Roman* Hercules \'hər-kyə-,lēz\, most famous Greco-Roman legendary hero.

Head of Hera from the votive group in the Heraeum at Olympia; in the Archaeological Museum, Olympia, Greece
Foto Marburg

Traditionally, Heracles was said to be the son of ZEUS and Alcmene, granddaughter of PERSEUS. Zeus swore that the next son born of the Perseid house should become ruler of Greece, but by a trick of Zeus's jealous wife, HERA, another child, the sickly Eurystheus, was born first and became king; when Heracles grew up, he had to serve him and also suffer the vengeful persecution of Hera. His first exploit was the strangling of two serpents that she had sent to kill him in his cradle.

Later, Heracles waged a victorious war against the kingdom of Orchomenus in Boeotia and married Megara, one of the royal princesses. But he killed her and their children in a fit of madness sent by Hera and, consequently, was obliged to become the servant of Eurystheus. It was Eurystheus who imposed upon Heracles the famous Labors, later arranged in a cycle of 12, usually as follows: (1) the slaying of the Nemean lion, whose skin he thereafter wore; (2) the slaying of the nine-headed HYDRA of Lerna; (3) the capture of the elusive hind (or stag) of Arcadia; (4) the capture of the wild boar of Mt. Erymanthus; (5) the cleansing, in a single day, of the cattle stables of King AUGEAS of Elis; (6) the shooting of the man-eating birds of the Stymphalian marshes; (7) the capture of the bull that terrorized the island of Crete; (8) the capture of the man-eating mares of King Diomedes of the Bistones; (9) the taking of the girdle of Hippolyte, queen of the AMAZONS; (10) the seizing of the cattle of the three-bodied GIANT Geryon, who ruled the island Erytheia in the far west; (11) the bringing back of the golden apples kept at the world's end by the Hesperides; and (12) the fetching up from the lower world of the triple-headed dog Cerberus, guardian of its gates.

Having completed the Labors, Heracles undertook further enterprises, including warlike campaigns. He also successfully fought the river god Achelous for the hand of Deianeira. As he was taking her home, the CENTAUR Nessus tried to abduct her, and Heracles shot him with one of his poisoned arrows. The Centaur, dying, told Deianeira to preserve the blood from his wound, for anyone wearing a garment rubbed with it would love her forever. Several years later Heracles fell in love with Iole, daughter of Eurytus, king of Oechalia. Deianeira, realizing that Iole was a dangerous rival, sent Heracles a garment smeared with the blood of Nessus. The blood proved to be a powerful poison instead, and Heracles in agony ascended a pyre on Mt. Oeta (modern Greek Oiti) and set it alight; his mortal part was consumed and his divine part ascended to heaven. There he was reconciled to Hera and married HEBE.

Heracles and his exploits have remained a popular subject to the present, even to their depiction in motion pictures and television series. Traditionally Heracles was represented as an enormously strong man, a huge eater and drinker, very amorous, and generally kindly but with occasional outbursts of brutal rage. His characteristic weapon

Heracles breaking the horns of the hind of Arcadia, flanked by Athena and Artemis, Greek vase painting, c. 540 BCE

was the bow but frequently also the club. In Italy he was worshiped as a god of merchants and traders, although others also prayed to him for his gifts of good luck or rescue from danger.

HERAEUM \hi-'rē-əm\, in ancient Greece, a TEMPLE or SANCTUARY dedicated to the goddess HERA. The most important of these was the Argive Heraeum, five miles northeast of Argos, where Hera's cult was established at an early date. A number of successive temples occupied that site, the last and best known of which was a limestone structure in the Doric order designed by the architect Eupolemos (423 BCE). It housed a famous gold and ivory statue of the goddess by Polyclitus the Elder. Other major *heraea* were at OLYMPIA and Samos in Greece, and at Lacinium, near Crotone, in southern Italy. Only ruins of any of these survive.

HERESY, doctrine or system rejected as false by religious authority. The term heresy is found frequently in the history of CHRISTIANITY. It also has been used among JEWS, although they have not been as intense as Christians in their punishment of heretics. The concept and combating of heresy is also important in ISLAM, BUDDHISM, and HINDUISM.

Heresy differs from schism in that the schismatic may be doctrinally orthodox but severs himself from the church. The Greek word *hairesis* (from which heresy is derived) was originally a neutral term that signified the holding of a particular set of philosophical opinions. Once appropriated by Christianity, however, the term heresy began to convey disapproval as the church regarded itself as the custodian of a divinely imparted revelation. Thus, any interpretation that differed from the official one was necessarily "heretical" in a pejorative sense.

This attitude of hostility to heresy is evident in the NEW TESTAMENT itself. Christian writers of the 2nd century appealed to the prophets and APOSTLES as sources of authoritative doctrine, and IRENAEUS and TERTULLIAN laid great stress on "the rule of faith," which was a loose summary of essential Christian beliefs handed down from apostolic times.

Later, the church council became the instrument for defining orthodoxy and condemning heresy. Eventually, in the Western church, the doctrinal decision of a council had to be ratified by the POPE to be accepted.

Historically, the major means that the church had of combating heretics was to excommunicate them. In the 12th and 13th centuries, however, the INQUISITION was established to combat heresy; heretics who refused to recant after being tried by the church were handed over to the civil authorities for punishment, usually execution.

A new situation came about in the 16th century with the REFORMATION and the consequent breakup of Western Christendom's doctrinal unity. The ROMAN CATHOLIC church, satisfied that it is the true church armed with an infallible authority, occasionally denounces doctrines or opinions that it considers heretical. With the gradual growth of toleration and the 20th-century ecumenical movement, most Protestant churches have drastically revised the notion of heresy; it is not now thought inconsistent for a person to maintain the doctrines of his or her own communion while not regarding as heretics those who hold different views. The Roman Catholic church, too, draws a distinction between those who willfully and persistently adhere to doctrinal error and those who embrace it through no fault of their own, *e.g.,* as a result of upbringing in another tradition.

HERM \'hərm\, *Greek* herma \'hər-mə\, in GREEK RELIGION, sacred object of stone connected with the cult of HERMES. According to some scholars, Hermes' name may be derived from the Greek word *herma* (used in Homer with the meaning "prop, support" [as for a ship drawn up onto the shore], though perhaps with the original sense "stone, rock"), but the cult of Hermes is considerably older than the earliest known references to herms. These objects came to be replaced either by statues or by pillars that were generally square and tapering toward the bottom so as to suggest the human figure. These were usually surmounted by the head of Hermes and had an erect phallus. They were used not only as cult objects but also for a variety of other purposes, for example, as milestones or boundary marks. They were regarded with respect, if not actually worshiped. In 415 BCE, shortly before an important military expedition to Sicily by the Athenians, most of the herms in Athens were emasculated during the night. The SACRILEGE was supposed by many to have been committed by the Athenian general Alcibiades. Alcibiades was sentenced to death in absentia, but fled to Sparta. The charge of corrupting the youth of Athens that was leveled against Alcibiades' teacher Socrates may have been based in part upon this incident.

Herms also occur in Roman sculpture and may have heads of the forest god SILVANUS or the chief god, JUPITER Terminus. In later times, all manner of fanciful herms were used as ornaments; both single and double herms existed, and the heads were not always those of gods.

HERMAPHRODITUS \hər-ˌma-frə-'dī-təs\, in Greek mythology, a being partly male, partly female. The idea of such a being originated in the East; in the Greek area it appeared in Cyprus, and, although it was a favorite subject in later Greek art, it was of no importance as a Greek cult. A legend of the Hellenistic period made Hermaphroditus a beautiful youth, the son of HERMES and APHRODITE. The NYMPH of the fountain of Salmacis in Caria became enamored of him and entreated the gods that she might be forever united with him. The result was the formation of a being half man, half woman.

HERMENEUTICS \,hər-mə-'nü-tiks, -'nyü-\, the study of the general principles of biblical interpretation. For both Jews and Christians throughout their histories the primary purpose of hermeneutics, and of the exegetical methods employed in interpretation, has been to discover the truths and values of the BIBLE.

The sacred status of the Bible in JUDAISM and CHRISTIANITY rests upon the conviction that it is a receptacle of divine revelation. This understanding of the Bible as the word of God, however, has not generated one uniform hermeneutical principle for its interpretation. Some persons have argued that the interpretation of the Bible must always be literal because the word of God is explicit and complete; others have insisted that the biblical words must always have a deeper "spiritual" meaning because God's message and truth are self-evidently profound. Still others have maintained that some parts of the Bible must be treated literally and some figuratively. In the history of biblical interpretation, four major types of hermeneutics have emerged: the literal, moral, allegorical, and anagogical.

Literal interpretation asserts that a biblical text is to be interpreted according to the "plain meaning" conveyed by its grammatical construction and historical context. The literal meaning is held to correspond to the intention of the authors. This type of hermeneutics is often, but not necessarily, associated with belief in the verbal inspiration of the Bible, according to which the individual words of the divine message were divinely chosen. Extreme forms of this view are criticized on the ground that they do not account adequately for the evident individuality of style and vocabulary found in the various biblical authors. JEROME, an influential 4th-century biblical scholar, championed the literal interpretation of the Bible in opposition to what he regarded as the excesses of allegorical interpretation. The primacy of the literal sense was later advocated by such diverse figures as THOMAS AQUINAS, Nicholas of Lyra, John Colet, MARTIN LUTHER, and JOHN CALVIN.

Moral interpretation seeks to establish exegetical principles by which ethical lessons may be drawn from the various parts of the Bible. Allegorization was often employed in this endeavor. The *Letter of Barnabas* (c. 100 CE), for example, interprets the dietary laws prescribed in the Book of Leviticus as forbidding not the flesh of certain animals but rather the vices imaginatively associated with those animals.

Allegorical interpretation interprets the biblical narratives as having a second level of reference beyond those persons, things, and events explicitly mentioned in the text. A particular form of allegorical interpretation is the typological, according to which the key figures, main events, and principal institutions of the OLD TESTAMENT are seen as "types" or foreshadowings of persons, events, and objects in the NEW TESTAMENT. In this theory, interpretations such as that of Noah's ARK as a "type" of the Christian church have been intended by God from the beginning.

Anagogical, or mystical, interpretation seeks to explain biblical events as they relate to or prefigure the life to come. Such an approach to the Bible is exemplified by the Jewish QABBALAH, which sought to disclose the mystical significance of the numerical values of Hebrew letters and words. A chief example of such mystical interpretation in Judaism is the medieval *Zohar*. In Christianity, many of the interpretations associated with MARIOLOGY fall into the anagogical category.

Shifts in hermeneutical emphases reflected broader academic and philosophical trends: historical-critical, existential, and structural interpretation have figured prominently during the 20th century. On the nonacademic level, the interpretation of prophetic and apocalyptic biblical material in terms of present-day events remains a vigorous pursuit in some circles. *See also* INTERPRETATION.

HERMES \'hər-,mēz\, Greek god, son of ZEUS and Maia; often identified with the Roman MERCURY. The earliest center of his cult was probably Arcadia, where Mount Cyllene was reputed to be his birthplace. There he was especially worshiped as the god of fertility, and his images were ithyphallic.

Both in literature and cult Hermes was constantly associated with the protection of cattle and sheep, and he was often closely connected with deities of vegetation, especially PAN and the NYMPHS. In the *Odyssey*, however, he appears mainly as the messenger of the gods and the conductor of the dead to HADES. Hermes was also a dream god, and the Greeks offered to him the last LIBATION before sleep. As a messenger he may also have become the god of roads and doorways, and he was the protector of travelers (and hence both merchants and thieves). Treasure casually found was his gift, and any stroke of good luck was attributed to him. In many respects he was APOLLO's counterpart; like him, Hermes was a patron of music and was credited with the invention of the kithara and sometimes of music itself. He was also god of eloquence and presided over some kinds of popular DIVINATION.

The sacred number of Hermes was four, and the fourth day of the month was his birthday. In archaic art he was portrayed as a full-grown and bearded man, clothed in a long tunic and often wearing a cap and winged boots. Sometimes he was represented in his pastoral character, bearing a sheep on his shoulders; at other times he appeared as the messenger of the gods with the *kērykeion*, or herald's staff, which was his most frequent attribute. From the latter part of the 5th century BCE he was portrayed as a nude and beardless youth, a young athlete.

HERMETIC WRITINGS \hər-'me-tik\, *also called* Hermetica, works of revelation on occult, theological, and philosophical subjects ascribed to the Egyptian god THOTH (Greek Hermes Trismegistos [Hermes the Thrice-Greatest]), who was believed to be the inventor of writing and the patron of all the arts dependent on writing. The collection, written in Greek and Latin, probably dates from the middle of the 1st to the end of the 3rd century CE. It was written in the form of dialogues and falls into two main classes: "popular" Hermetism, which deals with ASTROLOGY and the other occult sciences; and "learned" Hermetism, which is concerned with theology and philosophy.

From the Renaissance until the end of the 19th century, popular Hermetic literature received little scholarly attention. More recent study, however, has shown that its development preceded that of learned Hermetism and that it reflects ideas and beliefs that were widely held in the early Roman Empire and are therefore significant for the religious and intellectual history of the time.

In the Hellenistic age there was a growing distrust of traditional Greek RATIONALISM and a breaking down of the distinction between SCIENCE AND RELIGION. In this period the works ascribed to Hermes Trismegistos were primarily on astrology; to these were later added treatises on medicine, alchemy (*Tabula Smaragdina* ["Emerald Tablet"], a favorite source for medieval alchemists), and magic. The underlying concept of astrology—that the cosmos constituted a unity and that all parts of it were interdependent—was basic also to the other occult sciences. To make this principle effective in practice (and Hermetic "science" was intensely utilitarian), it was necessary to know the laws of sympathy and antipathy by which the parts of the universe were related. The aim of Hermetism was the deification or rebirth of man through the knowledge (*gnosis*) of the one transcendent God, the world, and men.

The theological writings are represented chiefly by the 17 treatises of the *Corpus Hermeticum*, by extensive fragments in the writings of Stobaeus, and by a Latin translation of the *Asclepius*, preserved among the works of Apuleius. Though the setting of these is Egyptian, the philosophy is Greek. The Hermetic writings, in fact, present a fusion of Eastern religious elements with Platonic, Stoic, and Neo-Pythagorean philosophies. It is unlikely, however, that there was any well-defined Hermetic community, or "church."

Hermetism was extensively cultivated by the Arabs, and through them it reached and influenced the West. There are frequent allusions to Hermes Trismegistos in late medieval and in Renaissance literature. The "closed" nature of some of the writings led to the word "hermetic" being used in Renaissance literature for something that is perfectly sealed, a meaning that is retained in modern science.

HERMIT, *also called* eremite \\'er-ə-ˌmīt\\ (from Greek: *erēmítēs*, "living in the desert"), one who retires from society, primarily for religious reasons, and lives in solitude. In CHRISTIANITY the word hermit is used interchangeably with anchorite, although the two were originally distinct: an anchorite selected a cell attached to a church or near a populous center, while a hermit retired to the wilderness.

The first Christian hermits appeared by the end of the 3rd century in Egypt in reaction to the persecution of Christians by the Roman emperor Decius, fleeing into the desert and leading a life of prayer and penance. Paul of Thebes, who fled to the desert about 250, has been considered the first hermit.

The austerities and other extremes of the early hermits' lives were tempered by the establishment of cenobite (common life) communities. The foundation was thus laid in the 4th century for the institution of MONASTICISM. The eremitic life eventually died out in Western Christianity, but it has continued in Eastern Christianity. *See also* IDIORRHYTHMIC MONASTICISM.

HERO AND LEANDER \\'hir-ō . . . lē-'an-dər, 'hē-rō\\, two lovers celebrated in Greek legend. Hero, virgin priestess of APHRODITE at Sestos, was seen at a festival by Leander of Abydos; they fell in love, and he swam the Hellespont at night to visit her, guided by a light from her tower. One stormy night the light was extinguished, and Leander was drowned; Hero, seeing his body, drowned herself.

HERZL, THEODOR (b. May 2, 1860, Budapest, Hungary, Austrian Empire [now in Hungary]—d. July 3, 1904, Edlach, Austria), founder of the political form of ZIONISM, a movement to establish a Jewish homeland.

Herzl received his license to practice law in 1884 but chose to devote himself to literature. For a number of years he was a journalist and playwright. A profound change began in Herzl's life when he was appointed Paris correspondent for the Viennese *Neue Freie Presse*. He arrived in Paris with his wife in the fall of 1891 and was shocked to find in the homeland of the French Revolution the same ANTI-SEMITISM with which he had become so familiar in Austria.

The Dreyfus affair in France crystallized Herzl's belief that assimilation was of no use for Jews. In the Dreyfus case, French military documents had been given to German agents, and a Jewish officer named Alfred Dreyfus had been falsely charged with the crime. The ensuing political controversy produced an outburst of anti-Semitism among the French public. Herzl said in later years that it was the Dreyfus affair that had made a Zionist out of him. So long as anti-Semitism existed, assimilation would be impossible, and the only solution for the majority of Jews would be organized emigration to a state of their own.

Herzl went to London in an effort to organize the Jews there in support of his program. Despite his personal magnetism, he found that his efforts to influence Jewish leaders in England were of little avail and therefore decided to organize a world congress of Zionists in the hope of winning support from the masses of Jews in all countries. The congress was held in Basel at the end of August 1897 and was attended by about 200 delegates, mostly from central and eastern Europe and Russia along with a few from western Europe and the United States.

The seven remaining years of his life were devoted to the furtherance of the Zionist cause. He established a Zionist newspaper, *Die Welt*, published as a German-language weekly in Vienna. He negotiated unsuccessfully with the Sultan of Turkey for the grant of a charter that would allow Jewish mass settlement in Palestine on an autonomous basis. He then turned to Great Britain, which seemed favorable to the establishment of a Jewish settlement in British territory in the Sinai Peninsula. When this project failed, the British proposed Uganda in East Africa. This offer, which he and some other Zionists were willing to accept, aroused violent opposition at the Zionist congress of 1903, particularly among the Russians. Herzl was unable to resolve the conflict. He died of a heart ailment at Edlach, near Vienna. He was buried in Vienna, but, in accordance with his wish, his remains were removed to Jerusalem in 1949 after the creation of the Jewish state and entombed on a hill west of the city now known as Mt. Herzl.

HESCHEL, ABRAHAM JOSHUA \\'he-shəl\\ (b. 1907, Warsaw, Pol., Russian Empire [now in Poland]—d. Dec. 23, 1972, New York, N.Y., U.S.), Jewish theologian and philosopher, noted for his presentation of the prophetic and mystical aspects of JUDAISM from which he attempted to construct a modern PHILOSOPHY OF RELIGION.

After a traditional Jewish education Heschel went on to higher studies at the University of Berlin and the Hochschule für die Wissenschaft des Judentums in Berlin. He taught at the latter school; at the Jüdisches Lehrhaus at Frankfurt am Main, Ger.; at the Institute of Jewish Studies in Warsaw (after being deported from Nazi Germany in 1938); at the Institute for Jewish Learning in London; at Hebrew Union College in Cincinnati, Ohio, U.S.; and at the Jewish Theological Seminary of America in New York City.

Heschel sought to evoke the inner depth of devotion and spontaneous response that he discerned in traditional Jewish piety. He also emphasized social action as an expression of pious ethical concerns and was at the forefront of protests and demonstrations in the 1960s and '70s intended to secure equal rights for African-Americans and to end the U.S. military intervention in Vietnam.

Among his works are *The Earth Is the Lord's* (1950); *Man Is Not Alone: A Philosophy of Religion* (1951); *The Sabbath: Its Meaning to Modern Man* (1951); *Man's Quest for*

God: Studies in Prayer and Symbolism (1954); *God in Search of Man: A Philosophy of Judaism* (1956); and *The Prophets* (1962; originally published in German in 1936).

HESPERIDES \he-'sper-ə-ˌdēz\, *singular* Hesperis \'hes-pə-ris\, in Greek mythology, maidens who guarded the tree bearing golden apples that GAEA gave to HERA at her marriage to ZEUS. Their name is a derivative of Greek *hesperos*, "evening, the evening star," or *hespera*, "evening, west." They were usually three in number, Aegle, Erytheia, and Hespere (or Hesperethusa), but by some accounts were as many as seven. They were said to live among the HYPERBOREANS. HERACLES later stole the apples or had Atlas get them for him. The golden apples that APHRODITE gave to Hippomenes before his race with ATALANTA were from the garden of the Hesperides.

HESPERUS \'hes-pə-rəs\, *Greek* Hesperos, *also called* Vesper \'ves-pər\, in Greco-Roman mythology, the evening star, son or brother of ATLAS. He was later identified with the morning star, Phosphorus (Latin: Lucifer), the bringer of light. Hesperus is variously described as the father of the HESPERIDES or of their mother, Hesperis.

HESTIA \'hes-tē-ə, -chə\, in GREEK RELIGION, goddess of the hearth, daughter of CRONUS and RHEA, and one of the 12 Olympian deities. When the gods APOLLO and POSEIDON became suitors for her hand she swore to remain a maiden forever, whereupon ZEUS, the king of the gods, bestowed upon her the honor of presiding over all sacrifices.

She was worshiped chiefly as goddess of the family hearth; but she had also, at least in some states, a public cult at the civic hearth in the *prytaneion*, or town hall. Hestia was closely connected with Zeus, god of the family in its external relation of hospitality and its internal unity. She was also associated with HERMES, the two representing domestic life on the one hand, and business and outdoor life on the other. In later philosophy Hestia became the hearth goddess of the universe.

HESYCHASM \'he-sē-ˌka-zəm\, in Eastern CHRISTIANITY, type of monastic life in which practitioners seek divine quietness (Greek: *hēsychia*) through the contemplation of God in uninterrupted prayer. Such prayer, involving the entire human being—soul, mind, and body—is often called "pure," or "intellectual," prayer or the Jesus prayer. In the late 13th century, St. Nicephorus the Hesychast produced a "method of prayer," advising novices to fix their eyes during prayer on the "middle of the body," in order to achieve a more total attention, and to "attach the prayer to their breathing." This practice was violently attacked in the first half of the 14th century by Barlaam the Calabrian, who called the Hesychasts *omphalopsychoi*, or people having their souls in their navels.

ST. GREGORY PALAMAS (1296–1359), a monk of Mt. Athos and later archbishop of Thessalonica, defended the Hesychast monks. In his view the human body, sanctified by the SACRAMENTS of the church, is able to participate in the prayer. The teachings of Palamas were confirmed by the Orthodox church in a series of councils held in Constantinople (1341, 1347, 1351). Hesychast spirituality is still practiced by Eastern Christians and once had wide popularity in Russia through the publication of a collection of Hesychast writings, known as the PHILOKALIA, in 1782.

HEVAJRA \hā-'vəj-rə\, *Tibetan* Kye-rdo-rje \'kʸā-dōr-jā\, *Mongolian* Kevajra, in northern BUDDHISM, a fierce protective deity, the *yab-yum* (in union with his female consort, Vajrayoginī) form of the fierce protective deity Heruka. Hevajra is a popular guardian deity in Tibet. His worship is the subject of the *Hevajra* TANTRA, a SCRIPTURE that helped bring about the conversion of the Mongol emperor Kublai Khan (1215–94).

Hevajra is represented in art as blue, with a headdress of skull crowns topped by a figure of the buddha AKṢOBHYA. He is characteristically shown with 8 heads, 4 legs, and 16 arms. The arms on the left hold skull cups containing various divinities, the ones on the right their steeds.

HEX SIGN, emblem painted on a barn, especially in the regions of southeastern Pennsylvania settled by German immigrants. Usually round, with colorful, simple floral and geometric motifs, they are said to protect farm animals from misfortunes resulting from witches' SPELLS and especially from the EVIL EYE.

HEZEKIAH \ˌhe-zə-'kī-ə\, *Hebrew* Ḥizqiyya \ḵēz-'kē-yä\, *Greek* Ezekias \ˌā-zā-'kē-äs\ (fl. late 8th and early 7th centuries BCE), son of AHAZ, and the 13th successor of DAVID as king of JUDAH at Jerusalem (2 Kings 18:1–2; 2 Chronicles 29:1). The dates of his reign are often given as about 715 to about 686 BCE, but inconsistencies in biblical and Assyrian cuneiform records have yielded a wide range of possible dates.

Hezekiah with a water clock, illustration from a French Bible, 13th century
The Granger Collection

Hezekiah reigned at a time when the Assyrian empire was consolidating its control of Palestine and Syria. His father had placed Judah under Assyrian suzerainty in 735 BCE (2 Kings 16:10ff.). Hezekiah may have taken part in a rebellion, which the Assyrians apparently crushed in the year 710. He may have been the leader of a further rebellion in Palestine, which gained the support of Egypt (2 Kings 18:8, 21). In preparing for the inevitable Assyrian campaign to retake Palestine, Hezekiah strengthened the defenses of his capital, Jerusalem (2 Chronicles 32:5), and dug out the famous Siloam tunnel (2 Kings 20:20, 2 Chronicles 32:30), bringing the water of the Gihon springs to a reservoir inside the city wall.

The rebellion was finally put down in 701 BCE, Judah was overrun, 46 of its walled cities fell, and much conquered Judaean territory was placed under the control of neighboring states (2 Kings 18:13). While the city of Lachish was under siege, Hezekiah sought to spare Jerusalem itself from capture by paying a heavy tribute of gold and silver to the

Assyrian king, who nevertheless demanded the city's unconditional surrender (2 Kings 18:19–35; 19:8–13; 2 Chronicles 32:9–19; Isaiah 36). At this point Jerusalem was unexpectedly spared, according to some traditions, by a plague that decimated the Assyrian army (according to the SCRIPTURE, an ANGEL saved Jerusalem; 2 Kings 19:35; 2 Chronicles 32:21). This event gave rise to the belief in Judah that Jerusalem was inviolable, a belief that lasted until the city fell to the Babylonians a century later.

HICKS, ELIAS \'hiks\ (b. March 19, 1748, Hempstead Township, Long Island, N.Y., U.S.—d. Feb. 27, 1830, Jericho, Long Island, N.Y.), early advocate of the abolition of slavery in the United States and a liberal QUAKER preacher whose followers were one of two factions created by the schism of 1827–28 in American Quakerism.

After assisting in ridding the SOCIETY OF FRIENDS (Quakers) of slavery, Hicks worked for general abolition. He urged a boycott of the products of slave labor, advocated establishment of an area in the Southwest as a home for freed slaves, and helped secure legislation that brought an end to slavery in New York state. In 1811 the first of several editions of his *Observations on the Slavery of the Africans and Their Descendants* was published.

One of the first to preach progressive revelation, which allowed for continuing revision and renewal of doctrinal beliefs, Hicks in 1817 successfully opposed the adoption of a set creed by the Society of Friends at the Baltimore Yearly Meeting. He was subsequently called a heretic for his opposition to Evangelicalism, which stressed established beliefs, and he was held responsible by some for the Quaker schism of 1827–28. After this separation Hicks's followers called themselves the Liberal branch of the Society of Friends, but orthodox Quakers labeled them Hicksites. The Hicksites became increasingly isolated from other Quakers until the 20th century, when mutual cooperation began to prevail.

HIEI, MOUNT \'hē-ā\, *Japanese* Hiei-zan \'hē-ā-ˌzän\, mountain (2,782 feet [845 meters] high) near Kyōto, the location of the Enryaku Temple, a Tendai Buddhist monastery complex built by the monk SAICHŌ (767–822). When Sannō (Japanese: "Mountain King"; the mountain's KAMI, or SHINTŌ deity) became identified with the Buddha Śākyamuni (Japanese: Shaka; the principal figure of Tendai BUDDHISM), the Sannō Shintō school emerged, based on the Tendai belief in Buddhist unity. Thus, Shaka was identical to Dainichi Nyorai (the Buddha VAIROCANA), and Sannō to AMATERASU (the Shintō sun goddess). Imperial patronage made the Hiei monastery one of the most powerful centers of Buddhist learning in Japan. HŌNEN and many other famous monks who later established their own schools came there for training.

HIEROPHANT \'hī-ə-rə-ˌfant, hī-'er-ə-fənt\, *Greek* hierophantēs ("displayer of holy things"), chief of the Eleusinian cult, the best known of the MYSTERY RELIGIONS of ancient Greece. His principal job was to display the sacred objects during the celebration of the mysteries and to explain their secret symbolic meaning to the initiates. At the opening of the ceremonies he proclaimed that all unclean persons must stay away, a rule that he had the right to enforce.

Usually an old, celibate man with a forceful voice, he was selected from the Eumolpids, one of the original clans of the ancient Greek city of Eleusis, to serve for life. Upon taking office he symbolically cast his former name into the sea and was thereafter called only *hierophantēs*. During the

ceremonies he wore a headband and a long, richly embroidered purple robe.

HIEROS GAMOS \'hē-ə-ˌrȯs-'gä-ˌmȯs\ (Greek: "sacred marriage"), sexual relations of fertility deities in myths and rituals, characteristic of societies based on cereal agriculture, especially in the Middle East. At least once a year humans representing the deities engaged in sexual intercourse, which guaranteed the fertility of the land, the prosperity of the community, and the continuation of the cosmos.

As ritually expressed, there were three main forms of the *hieros gamos:* between god and goddess (most usually symbolized by statues); between goddess and priest-king (who assumed the role of the god); and between god and priestess (who assumed the role of the goddess). In all three forms there was a relatively fixed form to the ritual: a PROCESSION that conveyed the divine actors to the marriage celebration; an exchange of gifts; a purification of the pair; a wedding feast; a preparation of the wedding chamber and bed; and the secret nocturnal act of intercourse. In some traditions this appears to have been an actual physical act between sacred functionaries who impersonated the deities; in other traditions it appears to have been a symbolic union. On the following day the marriage and its consequences for the community were celebrated.

Some scholars have applied the term *hieros gamos* to all myths of a divine pair (*e.g.*, heaven–earth) whose sexual intercourse is creative. The term, however, should probably be restricted only to those agricultural cultures that ritually reenact the marriage and that relate the marriage to agriculture, as in Mesopotamia, Phoenicia, CANAAN, Israel (the Song of SOLOMON has been suggested to be a hierogamitic text), Greece, and India.

HIGH GOD, *also called* Sky God, a type of supreme deity found among many indigenous peoples of North and South America, Africa, northern Asia, and Australia. A High God is conceived as being utterly transcendent, living in or identified with the sky and removed from the world that he created. Among North American Indians and central and southern Africans, thunder is thought to be his voice, and in Siberia the sun and moon are considered his eyes. He is connected with food and heaven among American Indians.

The High God sometimes is conceived as masculine or sexless, although in a number of traditions, especially in Meso-America, he is a balanced combination of male and female powers and identity. He is the sole creator of heaven and earth. Although he is omnipotent and omniscient, he is thought to have withdrawn from his creation and therefore to be inaccessible to prayer or sacrifice. If he is invoked, it is only in times of extreme distress, but there is no guarantee that he will hear or respond. His name often is revealed only to initiates, and to speak it aloud is thought to invite disaster or death; his most frequent title is Father. In some traditions he is a transcendent principle of divine order; in others he is senile or impotent and is replaced by a set of more active deities.

Some scholars consider the conception of the High God to be very old, preceding the creation of particular pantheons, while some see him as a recent development stimulated by monotheistic missionaries of CHRISTIANITY. In recent times the figure of the High God has been revived among some African messianic groups.

HIGH PLACE, *Hebrew* bamah, *or* bama \'bä-ˌmä, bä-'mä\, Israelite or Canaanite open-air shrine usually erected on an elevated site. Prior to the conquest of CANAAN (Palestine) by the Israelites in the 12th–11th century BCE, the high places served as shrines of Canaanite deities, the BAALS (Lords) and the Asherot (Semitic goddesses). In addition to an altar, *maṣṣebot* (stone pillars representing the presence of the divine, *see* MAṢṢEBA) and *asherim* (upright wooden poles symbolizing the female deities) often were erected on the high places, which sometimes were located under a tree or grove of trees. Other accoutrements sometimes associated with the *bamah* were *ḥammanim*, small incense altars. The high place at Megiddo in Israel is one of the oldest known high places, dating from about 2500 BCE.

Because the Israelites had associated the divine presence with elevated places (*e.g.*, MOUNT SINAI), they used Canaanite high places to worship YAHWEH. Canaanite agricultural fertility rites and practices were adopted by the previously nomadic Israelites, often in a syncretic fashion with Yahweh replacing Baal. A strong reaction to the adoption of such rites led to protests by Israelite judges and prophets from the 12th to the late 7th century BCE, when the DEUTERONOMIC REFORM of 621 led to the extirpation of the many local high places as sites of worship. The TEMPLE OF JERUSALEM on Mount ZION thus became the only legitimate high place in the Israelite religion, and the name *bamah* became a term of reproach and contempt.

HIGH PRIEST, *Hebrew* kohen gadol, in JUDAISM, the chief religious functionary in the TEMPLE OF JERUSALEM, whose unique privilege was to enter the HOLY OF HOLIES (inner sanctum) once a year on YOM KIPPUR in order to burn incense and sprinkle sacrificial animal blood, thereby expiating his own SINS and those of the people of Israel (Leviticus 16). The high priest had overall charge of Temple finances and administration, and in the early period of the Second Temple he collected taxes and maintained order as the recognized political head of the nation (*e.g.*, 1 Maccabees 10:20; 14:41; 16:23–24). The high priest could not mourn the dead, had to avoid defilement incurred by proximity to the dead, and could marry only a virgin (Leviticus 21:10–15). The office was normally hereditary and for life. In the 2nd century

BCE, however, bribery led to several reappointments, and the last of the high priests were appointed by government officials or chosen by lot. According to tradition, 18 high priests served in Solomon's Temple (*c.* 960–586 BCE) and 60 in the Second Temple (516 BCE–70 CE). Since that time, there has been no Jewish high priest, for national sacrifice was permanently interrupted with the destruction of the Second Temple.

ḤIJĀB \hi-'jab\ (Arabic: "cover," or "barrier"), in ISLAM a term that has three distinct meanings. The first meaning of *ḥijāb* refers to the garment worn by Muslim women in conformity to Islamic dress code. (*See* PURDAH.)

Another meaning of *ḥijāb* refers to an amulet designed to deter evil or enhance good fortune. Among Muslims it usually consists of a miniature Qur'an; selected Qur'anic verses; or the names of God, the Prophet Muhammad, angels, or other supernatural beings. Some consist of magic squares containing numerical formulas. Usually these *ḥijāb* are placed in a case and worn on the body or attached to some piece of property.

The meaning for *ḥijāb* within Sufi terminology refers to the veiling of the divine face. (*See* MUSHĀHADA.)

HIJIRI \hē-'jē-rē\ (Japanese: "sage"), in Japanese religions, a man of great personal magnetism and spiritual power. *Hijiri* has been used to refer to sages of various traditions: the SHAMAN, the SHINTŌ mountain ascetic, the Taoist magician, the Buddhist reciter, or, most characteristically, the wandering priest who operates outside the orthodox Buddhist tradition to meet the religious needs of the common people.

HIJRA \'hij-rə\, *English* Hegira \hi-'jī-rə, 'he-jə-rə\, *or* Hejira, (Arabic: "Emigration"), the Prophet Muhammad's migration (622 CE) from MECCA to MEDINA in order to escape persecution and establish an organized community under his leadership. The date represents the starting point of the Muslim era. MUHAMMAD himself dated his correspondence, treaties, and proclamations after other events of his life. It was 'Umar I, the second CALIPH, who in the year 639 CE (AH 17) introduced the Hijra era (now denoted by the initials AH, for Latin Anno Hegirae, "in the year of the Hijra"). 'Umar started the first year AH with the first day of the lunar month of Muḥarram, which corresponded to July 16, 622. In 1677–78 (AH 1088) the Ottoman government, still keeping the Hijra era, began to use the solar year of the Julian calendar, eventually creating two different Hijra era dates.

The term *hijra* has also been applied to the emigrations of the faithful to Ethiopia and of Muhammad's followers to Medina before the capture of Mecca. Muslims who later quitted lands under Christian rule were also called *muhā-jirūn* ("emigrants"). The most honored *muhājirūn*, considered among the COMPANIONS OF THE PROPHET, are those who emi-

Muslim women from Indonesia wearing the traditional head covering, or ḥijāb
Reuters—Enny Nuraheni—Archive Photos

grated with Muhammad to Medina. Muhammad praised them highly for having forsaken their native city to follow him and promised that God would favor them. They remained a separate and greatly esteemed group in the Muslim community, both in Mecca and in Medina, and assumed leadership of the Muslim state, through the caliphate, after Muhammad's death.

As a result of the Hijra, another distinct body of Muslims came into being, the *anṣār* ("helpers"); these were Medinese who aided Muhammad and the *muhājirūn*. The *anṣār* were members of the two major Medinese tribes, the feuding al-Khazraj and al-Aws, whom Muhammad had been asked to reconcile when he was still a rising figure in Mecca. They came to be his devoted supporters, constituting three-fourths of the Muslim army at the BATTLE OF BADR (624). When no one of their number was chosen to the caliphate to succeed Muhammad, they declined in influence.

Hijra subsequently received attention as a topic in Islamic jurisprudence (FIQH). The legal schools allowed that should Muslims find themselves ruled by non-Muslims they can, if able, combat them in jihad or emigrate to Muslim territory, the DĀR AL-ISLAM. Thus Muslims emigrated to North Africa from Spain during the Christian Reconquista, and from India to Pakistan after partition (1947). The modern state of Saudi Arabia grew out of fortress communities in central Arabia called *hijra*s from which Saudi-Wahhābī forces launched attacks against neighboring tribes and settlements. In SUFISM, however, *hijra* was used to describe the journey from the world of sensual distractions inward to the spiritual world of the heart.

HILARIA \hi-'lar-ē-ə, -'ler-\, in Roman and HELLENISTIC RELIGION, day of merriment and rejoicing in the Cybele-Attis cult and in the Isis-Osiris cult, March 25 and November 3, respectively. It was one of several days in the festival of CYBELE that honored ATTIS, her son and lover: March 15, his finding by Cybele among the reeds on the bank of the River Gallus; March 22, his self-mutilation; March 24, fasting and mourning at his death; and March 25, the Hilaria, rejoicing at his RESURRECTION. The Hilaria of the Isis-Osiris cult marked the resurrection of OSIRIS, husband of ISIS.

HILDEGARD, SAINT \'hil-də-ˌgärd\, *byname* Sibyl of the Rhine (b. 1098, Böckelheim, West Franconia—d. Sept. 17, 1179, Rupertsberg, near Bingen; traditional feast day September 17), German ABBESS and visionary mystic.

Hildegard was of noble birth and was educated at the BENEDICTINE cloister of Disibodenberg, where she became prioress in 1136. Having experienced visions since she was a child, at the age of 43 she consulted her confessor, who in turn reported the matter to the archbishop of Mainz. A committee of theologians subsequently confirmed the authenticity of Hildegard's visions, and a monk was appointed to help her record them in writing. The finished work, *Scivias* (1141–52), consisted of 26 visions, prophetic and apocalyptic in form, treating the church, the relationship between God and humankind, and redemption. About 1147 she left Disibodenberg with several of her nuns to found a new CONVENT at Rupertsberg, where she continued to issue prophecies and to record her visions in writing.

Her other writings include lives of saints, two treatises on medicine and natural history, and extensive correspondence, containing further prophecies and allegorical treatises. Though her earliest biographer proclaimed her a saint and miracles were reported during her life and at her tomb, she has not been formally canonized. She is, however, listed as a saint in the Roman Martyrology and is honored on her feast day in certain German DIOCESES.

HILLEL \'hi-ˌlel, -ˌläl, -ˌləl; hē-'lel\, *also known as* Hillel the Elder, legal scholar and founder of a school in Jerusalem during the time of Herod the Great (late 1st century BCE); he is recognized by later JUDAISM as one of the chief architects of RABBINIC JUDAISM. Born in Babylonia, Hillel is said to have gone to Israel to further his studies. In addition to his legal statements, he is credited with developing a system of biblical interpretation represented by seven fixed hermeneutical principles. The meaning of these principles, their actual association with Hillel, and their relationship to the 13 hermeneutical principles ascribed to the later authority ISHMAEL BEN ELISHA are all subjects of speculation.

While a large corpus of Talmudic material purports to depict Hillel's teaching and personality, a chronological survey of these sources suggests the extent to which they are the creations of a mature rabbinism interested in fleshing out the story of an early and important forebear. Thus, while the earliest rabbinic texts, the MISHNAH and TOSEFTA, report only a few legal statements in Hillel's name, later Talmudic sources provide numerous accounts depicting his life story and personality.

Four areas of Hillel's legal concern appear in the earliest layers of rabbinic law and so may be authentic to him. First, he argues that, once a woman finds that she is menstruating, she is to be deemed unclean retroactively, back to the last point at which she was known to be clean. Second, he disputes with Shammai the quantity of dough one may make without incurring liability to the separation of dough-offering. Third, in one of his best-known legal debates, Hillel argues that the PASCHAL LAMB may be sacrificed on the SABBATH (in Talmudic sources, Hillel's treatment of this issue is said to have led to his appointment as PATRIARCH). Fourth, ruling on economic matters, Hillel asserts that the buyer of a home within a walled city may not hide from the seller so as to avoid the right of repurchase mandated by Leviticus 25:29; he stands behind a method of circumventing Scripture's Sabbatical remission of debts; and he proscribes trading in futures, which he deems to involve earning forbidden interest.

Mishnah Abot 1:12 records one of Hillel's best-known statements, his enjoinder to all Jews to "Be disciples of AARON, loving peace and pursuing peace, loving people and drawing them near to the Torah."

Two contradictory stories survive to explain Hillel's move from Babylonia to Palestine. One holds that he went as a learned man in order to answer certain questions of law (Y. Pesahim 6:1). The other reports that he did not study at all until he arrived in the land of Israel at 40 years of age (GENESIS RABBAH 100:24). Subsequently, he studied for 40 years and served as patriarch for 40 years, like MOSES dying at the age of 120. Thus, the RABBIS see in Hillel the perfect paradigm of scholar and communal leader, a model for all future generations.

HILLEL BEN SAMUEL \ben-'sam-yu̇-wəl\, *also called* El-Al ben Shachar \el-'al-ben-'shä-ˌkär\ (b. *c.* 1220—d. *c.* 1295), physician, scholar of the TALMUD, and philosopher who defended the ideas of MAIMONIDES during the "years of controversy" (1289–90), when his work was attacked; Hillel ben Samuel denounced in turn the adherents of IBN RUSHD (Averroës), asserting that they precipitated the controversy through their denial of the immortality of the individual human soul.

Bāhubali is bathed with milk by Jains every 12 years, Sravana Belgola, Karnātaka, India

Russian Orthodox wedding, St. Petersburg, Russia
Sylvain Grandadam—Photo Researchers

Japanese bride is dressed for a Shintō wedding ceremony

Muslim ablutions before prayers, Dome of the Rock, Jerusalem

Sunday services at the Crystal Cathedral, Garden Grove, Calif.

Zapotec boy adds a candle to a shrine, Oaxaca, Mex.

Lighting the candles of the Hanukkah menorah

Ritual exorcism, Sri Lanka

Group baptism in the Pacific Ocean

Shintō priest blesses children at the Seven-Five-Three festival, Meiji Shrine, Tokyo
© Cameramann International, Ltd.

Hindu Chariot Festival of the Jagannāth temple, Puri, Orissa, India
© Dinodia—Dinodia Picture Agency

*(Above) Buddhist funeral
ceremony, South Korea*
Kim Newton—Woodfin Camp

*(Right) Funeral
procession with brass
band, New Orleans, La.*
Fred Maroon—Photo Researchers

*(Far right) Hindus bathe in
the sacred waters of the
Gaṅgā (Ganges) at
Varanasi, India*
Porterfield/Chickering—Photo
Researchers

Pope John Paul II baptizes an infant in the Sistine Chapel, Vatican City
Reuters—Plinio Lepri/Archive Photos

Reputed to have lived in Verona, Naples, and Capua, and later in Barcelona, Hillel ben Samuel wrote his major work, *Tagmule ha-nefesh* (1288–91; "The Rewards of the Soul"), to rebut Ibn Rushd's theory of the soul. In it, he holds that the soul is composed of "formal substance" that derives from the universal soul and that both are immortal.

ḤILLĪ, AL- \ȧl-ḵi-'lē\, *in full* Jamāl al-Dīn Ḥasan ibn Yūsuf ibn ʿAlī ibn Muṭahhar al-Ḥillī (b. Dec. 15, 1250, Ḥilla, Iraq—d. Dec. 18, 1325), Muslim theologian and expounder of SHIʿITE doctrines.

Al-Ḥillī studied law, theology, and the *uṣūl*, or principles of the faith, in the city of Ḥilla, an important center for Shiʿite learning in the SUNNI territory of the ʿAbbāsid caliphate (the second Arab dynasty). A scion of a family of Shiʿite theologians, he became known as the "wise man of Ḥilla." He also studied philosophy with Naṣīr al-Dīn al-Ṭūsī (d. 1274), a noted philosopher of his time.

Among al-Ḥillī's more than 500 scholarly works on the Islamic faith are the *Treatise on the Principles of Shiʿite Theology* (1928) and the *Sharḥ tajrīd al-iʿtiqād*. These are standard references on Twelver Shiʿite beliefs and are still used as textbooks in Iran.

Attracted by the religious freedom of the Mongol Il-Khanid dynasty (the descendants of Hülegü, who sacked Baghdad in 1258), al-Ḥillī emigrated to Iran in 1305. There he was responsible for converting Öljeytü, the eighth Il-Khanid of Iran, from Sunnism to Shiʿism. In 1305 Shiʿism was proclaimed the state religion of Iran. Al-Ḥillī was buried in MASHHAD (Meshed), Persia.

HIMALAYAS \ˌhi-mə-'lā-əz, hi-'mä-lə-yəz\, *Sanskrit* Himālaya, great mountain system of Asia forming a barrier between the Tibetan Plateau to the north and the alluvial plains of the Indian subcontinent to the south. Hindu mythology states that the Himalayas are the foothills of MOUNT MERU, the golden abode of the gods.

The Himalayan ranges contain 30 mountains rising to heights greater than 24,000 feet above sea level, including Mount Everest, the world's highest peak, which reaches an elevation of 29,028 feet. The mountains extend from Jammu and Kashmir eastward to Namcha Barwa peak in Tibet, near its southern border with India. Between these western and eastern extremities lie several Indian states and the Himalayan kingdoms of Nepal and Bhutan.

The Himalayas are the site of many of the most important shrines of HINDUISM and BUDDHISM. In Kashmir, SHIVA is worshiped in the Amarnāth cave in the form of a linga that is a stalagmite of ice. Thousands of pilgrims come yearly to this place, where the god is thought to have imparted the secret of immortality. Shiva and his divine consort are said to dwell on Mount Kailāsa. Other Himalayan holy sites include Badrīnāth, an uninhabited village and shrine situated along a headstream of the Gaṅgā (Ganges) River which is the site of a temple that contains a shrine of Badrīnāth, or VISHNU, that has been a well-known PILGRIMAGE center for

Peak in the Himalayas
Keith Gunnar—Photo Researchers

more than 2,000 years; Krimchi, a group of four Shiva temples situated six miles north of the town of Udhampur, itself the home of the important shrine of Vaiṣṇo Devī; and Gurkha, a town of central Nepal known for its shrine of GORAKHNĀTH, the patron saint of the region, as well as a temple to the Hindu goddess Bhavānī (DEVĪ).

HIMORAGI \hē-mȯ-'rä-gē\ ("offerings to the gods"), in Japanese Shintō tradition, sacred areas or ritual precincts marked off by rocks, tree branches, and hemp ropes. This kind of special cordoned-off natural space serves as a temporary SANCTUARY for KAMI spirits and is the predecessor for all forms of Shintō shrines.

HĪNAYĀNA \hē-nə-'yä-nə\ (Sanskrit: "Lesser Vehicle"), in BUDDHISM, more orthodox, conservative school; the name Hīnayāna is pejorative and was applied by the followers of the MAHĀYĀNA (meaning "Greater Vehicle") Buddhist tradition in ancient India. The name reflected the Mahāyānists' evaluation of their own tradition as a superior method, but the name was not accepted by the conservative schools as referring to a common tradition.

Most of the major Hīnayāna schools (traditionally 18 in number) predate the emergence of the Mahāyāna. After the rise of the Mahāyāna in about the 1st century CE, the Hīnayāna schools continued to prosper. However, the Theravādins are the only Hīnayāna-type school that maintained a strong position after the collapse of Indian Buddhism in the 13th century. *See* THERAVĀDA.

HINDU CALENDAR, dating system used in India from about 1000 BCE and still used to establish dates of the Hindu religious year. It is based on a year of 12 lunar months; *i.e.*, 12 full cycles of phases of the Moon. The discrepancy between this year of about 354 days and the solar year of about 365 days is partially resolved by intercalation of an extra month every 30 months.

HINDUISM

The beliefs and practices of Hindus are expressed in a series of characteristic doctrinal, ritual, social, narrative, and poetic forms.

INTRODUCTION

The term Hinduism.   The English term *Hinduism* was coined by British writers in the first decades of the 19th century and became familiar as a designator of religious ideas and practices distinctive to India with the publication of such books as Sir Monier-Williams' *Hinduism* (1877). Initially it was an outsiders' word, building on centuries-old usages of the word Hindu. Early travelers to the Indus Valley, beginning with the Greeks, spoke of its inhabitants as "Hindu" (Greek: *'indoi*), and in the 16th century residents of India themselves began very slowly to employ the term to distinguish themselves from the "Turks"—*i.e.*, descendants of people who came to India from Central Asia. Gradually the distinction became primarily religious, as opposed to ethnic, geographic, or cultural.

Since the late 19th century, Hindus have reacted to the term Hinduism in several ways. Some have rejected it in favor of indigenous formulations. Those preferring the terms VEDA or VEDIC RELIGION want to embrace an ancient textual core and the tradition of BRAHMIN learning that preserved and interpreted it. Those preferring the term SANATANA DHARMA ("eternal law," or as Philip Lutgendorf has playfully suggested "old-time religion") emphasize a more catholic tradition of belief and practice (such as worship through images, dietary codes, and the veneration of the cow) not necessarily mediated by Brahmins. Still others, perhaps the majority, have simply accepted the term Hinduism or its analogues in various Indic languages, especially *hindū dharma*.

From the early 20th century onward, textbooks on Hinduism were written by Hindus themselves, often under the rubric of *sanatana dharma*. These efforts at self-explanation were and are intended to set Hinduism parallel with other religious traditions and to teach it systematically to Hindu youths. They add a new layer to an elaborate tradition of ĀGAMAS and *śāstra*s expositing practice and doctrine that dates back well into the 1st millennium CE. The roots of this tradition can be traced back much farther—textually, to the schools of commentary and debate preserved in epic and Vedic writings dating to the 2nd millennium BCE; and visually, through YAKṢAS (luminous spirits associated with specific locales and

Ablutions and devotions performed by worshipers in the Gaṅgā River at Varanasi, India
Mimi Forsyth—Monkmeyer

CONTENTS

natural phenomena) and NĀGAS (snakelike divinities) worshiped about 400 BCE–400 CE to veneration of goddesses, as seems to be implied by the female terra-cotta figurines found ubiquitously in excavations of INDUS VALLEY CIVILIZATION (3rd–2nd millennia BCE) sites. In recognition of these ancient sources, present-day Hindus often assert that Hinduism is the world's oldest religion.

General nature of Hinduism. More strikingly than any other major religious community, Hindus accept and indeed celebrate the complex, organic, multi-leveled, and sometimes internally inconsistent nature of their tradition. This expansiveness is made possible by the widely shared Hindu view that truth or reality cannot be encapsulated in any creedal formulation. As many Hindus affirm through the prayer "May good thoughts come to us from all sides," truth is of such a nature that it must be multiply sought, not dogmatically claimed.

Anyone's view of the truth—even that of a GURU regarded as possessing superior authority—is fundamentally conditioned by the specifics of time, age, gender, state of consciousness, social and geographic location, and stage of attainment. These perspectives enhance a broad view of religious truth rather than diminish it; hence there is a strong tendency for contemporary Hindus to affirm that tolerance is the foremost religious virtue. On the other hand, even cosmopolitan Hindus living in a global environment recognize and prize the fact that their religion has developed in the specific geographic, social, historical, and ritual climates of the Indian subcontinent. Religious practices and ideological formulations that emphasize this fact—from benign PILGRIMAGES to the violent edge of Hindu nationalism—affirm a strong connection to the Hindu homeland. Such a tension between universalist and particularist impulses has long animated the Hindu tradition. When Hindus speak of their religious identity as *sanatana dharma*, a formulation made popular late in the 19th century, they emphasize its continuous, seemingly eternal (*sanatana*) existence and the fact that it describes a web of customs, obligations, traditions, and ideals (DHARMA) that far exceeds the recent Christian and Western secularist tendency to think of religion primarily as a system of beliefs. A common way in which English-speaking Hindus often distance themselves from that is to insist that Hinduism is not a religion but a way of life.

Five tensile strands. Across the sweep of Indian religious history over the past two millennia, at least five elements have given shape to the Hindu religious tradition: doctrine, practice, society, story, and devotion. None of these is univocal; no Hindu would claim that they correspond to the FIVE PILLARS OF ISLAM. Rather, to adopt a typical Hindu metaphor, they relate to one another as strands in an elaborate braid. Moreover, each strand develops out of a history of conversation, elaboration, and challenge. Hence, in looking for what makes the tradition cohere, it is sometimes better to locate major points of tension than to expect clear agreements on Hindu thought and practice.

Doctrine. The first of the five strands that weave together to make Hinduism is doctrine, as enunciated and debated in a vast textual tradition anchored to the Veda ("Knowledge"), the oldest core of Hindu religious utterance, and organized through the centuries primarily by members of the learned Brahmin CASTE. Here several characteristic tensions appear. One concerns the status of the One in relation to the Many—issues of POLYTHEISM, MONOTHEISM, and monism—or of supernal truth in relation to its embodied, phenomenal counterpart. Another tension concerns the disparity between the world-preserving ideal of dharma (proper behavior defined in relation to the gods and society) and that of MOKṢA (release from an inherently flawed world). A third tension exists between one's individual destiny, as shaped by KARMA (action in this and other lives), and any person's deep bond to family, society, and the divinities associated with them.

Practice. The second strand in the fabric of Hinduism is practice. Many Hindus, in fact, would place this first. Despite India's enormous diversity, a common grammar of ritual behavior connects various places, strata, and periods of Hindu life. While it is true that various elements of Vedic ritual survive in modern practice, especially in life-cycle rites (*see* SAṂSKĀRA), and serve a unifying function, much more influential commonalities appear in the ritual vocabulary of the worship of God in the form of an ICON, or image (PRATIMĀ, *mūrti*, etc.).

Broadly, this is called PŪJĀ ("praising [the deity]"). It echoes conventions of hospitality that might be performed for an honored guest, and the giving and sharing of food is central. Such food is called PRASĀDA (in Hindi, *prasād*: "grace"), reflecting the recognition that when human beings make offerings to deities, the initiative is not really theirs. They are actually responding to the generosity that bore them into a world fecund with life and auspicious possibility. The divine personality installed as a home or temple image receives *prasāda*, tasting it (Hindus differ as to whether this is a real or symbolic act, gross or subtle) and offering the remains to worshipers. Consuming these leftovers, worshipers accept their creaturely status as beings inferior to and dependent upon the divine. An element of tension arises because the logic of *pūjā* and *prasāda* would seem to accord all hu-

Vishnu on the serpent Śeṣa, c. 500 CE, Deogarh, Madhya Pradesh, India
Borromeo—Art Resource

mans an equally ancillary status with respect to God, yet exclusionary rules have often been sanctified rather than challenged by *prasāda*-based ritual. Specifically, lower-caste people and those perceived as outsiders or carriers of pollution have historically been forbidden to enter certain Hindu temples, a practice that continues in some instances even today.

Society. The third aspect that has served to organize Hindu life is society. Since the scholar al-Bīrūnī traveled to India in the early 11th century, visitors have been struck by an unusually well stratified (if locally variant) system of social relations that has come to be called familiarly the caste system. While it is true that there is a vast slippage between the ancient vision of society as divided into four ideal classifications (VARṆAS) and the thousands of endogamous birthgroups (JĀTIS, literally "births") that constitute Indian society in reality, few would dispute that Indian society is notably plural and hierarchical in its organization. This has to do with an understanding of truth or reality as being similarly plural and multilayered, whether one understands the direction of influence to proceed from social fact to religious doctrine or vice versa. Seeking its own answer to this conundrum, a well-known Vedic hymn (ṚG VEDA 10.90) describes how in the beginning of time a primordial person underwent a process of sacrifice that produced a four-part cosmos and its human counterpart, a four-part social order.

As in the realms of doctrine and religious practice, so also in this social domain there is a characteristic tension. Ideally, we have the humble, even-handed view that each person or group approaches truth in a way that is necessarily distinct, reflecting its own perspective. Only by allowing each to speak and act in such terms can a society constitute itself as a proper representation of truth or reality. Yet this pluriform, context-sensitive habit of thought can too easily be used to legitimate a social-system that enshrines privilege and prejudice. If it is believed that no standards apply universally, one group can too easily justify its dominance over another. Historically, therefore, certain Hindus have been able to espouse tolerance at the level of doctrine but practice intolerance in the social realm: caste discrimination. Responding to such oppression, especially when justified by allegedly Hindu norms, lower-caste groups have sometimes insisted, "We are not Hindus!" Yet their own communities may enact similar inequalities, and their religious practices and beliefs often continue to tie them to the greater Hindu fold.

Story. Another dimension drawing Hindus into a single community of discourse is narrative. For at least two millennia, people in almost all corners of India—and now well beyond—have responded to certain prominent stories of divine play and of interactions between gods and humans. These concern major figures in the Hindu pantheon: KRISHNA and his lover RĀDHĀ, RĀMA and his wife SĪTĀ and brother Lakṣmaṇa, SHIVA and his consort PĀRVATĪ (or, in a different birth, SATĪ), and the Great Goddess DURGĀ, or DEVĪ as a slayer of the buffalo demon Mahiṣāsura. Often such narratives illustrate the interpenetration of the divine and human spheres, with deities such as Krishna and Rāma entering entirely into the human drama. Many tales focus in different degrees on dharmic exemplariness, genealogies of human experience, forms of love, and the struggle between order and chaos or duty and play. In performing and listening to these stories, Hindus have often experienced themselves as members of a single imagined family.

Yet simultaneously these narratives serve as an arena for articulating tensions. Women performers sometimes tell the RĀMĀYAṆA as the story of Sītā's travails at the hands of Rāma rather than as a testament of Rāma's righteous victories. The virtues of Rāma's enemy RĀVAṆA, even supplanting those of Rāma himself, may be emphasized in South Indian performances. And lower-caste musicians of North India present epics such as ĀLHĀ or ḌHOLĀ, enacting their own experience of the world rather than playing out the upper-caste milieu of the MAHĀBHĀRATA, which these epics nonetheless echo. To the broadly known pan-Hindu, male-centered narrative traditions, these variants provide both resonance and challenge.

Devotion. Finally, there is a fifth strand that contributes to the complex unity of Hindu experience through time: BHAKTI ("sharing," or "devotion"), a broad tradition of loving God that is especially associated with the lives and words of vernacular poet-saints throughout India. Devotional poems attributed to these figures, who represent both sexes and all social classes, have elaborated a store of images to which access can be had in a score of languages. Individual poems are sometimes strikingly similar from one language or century to another, without there being any trace of mediation through the pan-Indian, distinctly upper-caste language Sanskrit. Often, individual motifs in the lives of *bhakti* poet-saints also bear strong family resemblances. Because *bhakti* verse first appeared in Tamil (*c.* 6th century), in South India, *bhakti* is sometimes attributed to a muse or goddess who spent her youth there, aging and revivifying as she moved northward into other regions with different languages. With its central affirmation that religious enthusiasm is more fundamental than rigidities of practice or doctrine, *bhakti* provides a common challenge to other aspects of Hindu life. At the same time, it contributes to a common Hindu heritage—in part, a common heritage of protest.

CENTRAL CONCEPTIONS

In the following sections, we will take up various aspects of this complex whole, proceeding in a fashion that allows us to develop a measure of historical perspective on the development of the Hindu tradition. This approach has its costs, for it may seem to give priority to aspects of the tradition that appear in its earliest extant texts. These owe their preservation primarily to the labors of up-

Śaivite sadhu
Earl Scott—Photo Researchers

per-caste men, especially Brahmins, and often tell us far too little about the perspectives of others. Particularly early on, readers must therefore read both with and against the grain, noting silences and imagining rebuttals to skewed visions of the experiences of women, regional communities, and people regarded by Brahmins as being of low status—all of whom nowadays call themselves Hindus or identify with groups that can sensibly be placed within the broad Hindu span.

Veda, Brahmins, and issues of religious authority.   For members of the upper castes, a principal characteristic of Hinduism has traditionally been a recognition of the Veda, the most ancient body of Indian religious literature, as an absolute authority revealing fundamental and unassailable truth. The Veda is also regarded as the basis of all the later śāstric texts used in Hindu doctrine and practice, including, for example, the medical corpus known as ĀYURVEDA. Parts of the Veda are quoted in essential Hindu rituals (*e.g.*, weddings), and it is the source of many enduring patterns of Hindu thought, yet its contents are practically unknown to most Hindus, and it is seldom drawn upon for literal information or advice. Still, it is venerated from a distance by most Hindus, and groups who reject its authority outright (as in BUDDHISM and JAINISM) are regarded by Hindus as unfaithful to their common tradition.

Another characteristic of much Hindu thought is its special regard for Brahmins as a priestly class possessing spiritual supremacy by birth. As special manifestations of religious power and as bearers and teachers of the Veda, Brahmins have often been considered to represent an ideal of ritual purity and social prestige. Yet this has also been challenged, either because of competing claims to religious authority—especially by kings and rulers—or because Brahminhood is regarded as a status attained by depth of learning, not birth. Evidence of both these challenges can be found in Vedic literature itself, especially the UPANISHADS, and *bhakti* literature is full of vignettes in which the small-mindedness of Brahmins inversely mirrors the true depth of RELIGIOUS EXPERIENCE.

Doctrine of ātman-Brahman.   Hindus believe in an uncreated, eternal, infinite, transcendent principle that, "comprising in itself being and non-being," is the sole reality, the ultimate cause and foundation, source, and goal of all existence. This ultimate reality may be called BRAHMAN. As the All, Brahman either causes the universe and all beings to emanate from itself, transforms itself into the universe, or assumes the appearance of the universe. Brahman is in all things and is the self (ĀTMAN) of all living beings. Brahman is the creator, preserver, or transformer and reabsorber of everything. Hindus differ, however, as to whether this ultimate reality is best conceived as lacking attributes and qualities—the impersonal Brahman—or as a personal God, especially VISHNU, Shiva, or the Goddess (these being the preferences of adherents called Vaiṣṇavas, Śaivas, and Śāktas, respectively). The conviction of the importance of a search for a One that is the All has been embedded in India's spiritual life for more than 3,000 years.

The pantheon.   Hindus typically focus their worship of the One on a favorite divinity (*iṣṭadevatā*); they do not, however, insist that there is anything exclusive in that choice. Although a range of deities may be so worshiped, many Hindus worship Vishnu and Shiva. Vishnu is often regarded as a special manifestation of the preservative aspect of Supreme Reality, while Shiva is regarded as the manifestation of the destructive aspect. Another deity, BRAHMĀ, whose name is a masculine inflection of the noun Brahman, is the creator and remains in the background as a DEMIURGE. These three great figures (Brahmā, Vishnu, and Shiva) constitute the so-called Hindu trinity (TRIMŪRTI). This conception was an early attempt to harmonize the conviction that the Supreme Power is singular with the plurality of gods addressed in daily worship. The *trimūrti* is still seen in Hindu theological writing, but it is virtually absent in practice, since Brahmā is rarely worshiped. Much closer to lived religion is another attempt to make sense of the pantheon, in which the Great Goddess (known variously as Devī, Durgā, or ŚAKTI) replaces Brahmā as the third element in a trinity (*see* DEVĪ MĀHĀTMYA; ŚĀKTISM).

Karma, saṃsāra, and mokṣa.   Hindus generally accept the doctrine of transmigration and rebirth and the complementary belief in karma ("action"), the idea that prior acts condition a being in subsequent forms of life. The whole process of rebirths is called SAMSĀRA, a cyclic process with no clear beginning or end that encompasses lives of perpetual, serial attachments. Actions (karma), if generated by desire and an appetite for results, propel the system forward and bind one's spirit (JĪVA) to an endless series of births and deaths unless a person is able to control the root cause of interested action, desire. Desire motivates any social interaction (particularly when involving sex or food), resulting in the mutual exchange of good and bad karma. In one prevalent view, the very meaning of salvation is one's final emancipation (mokṣa) from this morass, an escape from the impermanence that is an inescapable feature of mundane existence. In this view the only goal is the one permanent and eternal principle: the One, God, Brahman, which is totally opposite to phenomenal existence. People who have not fully realized that their being is identical with Brahman are thus seen as deluded. Fortunately, the very structure of human experience teaches the ultimate identity between Brahman and the kernel of human personality, the selfhood called ātman. One may learn this lesson by different means: by realizing one's essential sameness with all living beings, by responding in love to a personal expression of the divine, or by coming to appreciate that the competing attentions and moods of one's waking consciousness are grounded in a transcendental unity. We have a taste of this unity in our daily experience of deep, dreamless sleep.

Dharma and the three paths.   Hindus disagree about the best way (MĀRGA) to attain such release and concede that no "one size fits all." Three paths to salvation are presented in an extremely influential religious text, the BHAGAVAD GĪTĀ ("Song of God"; c. 100 CE). These three are (1) the karma-mārga ("path of duties"), the disinterested discharge of ritual and social obligations, (2) the jñāna-mārga ("path of knowledge"), the use of meditative concentration preceded by a long and systematic ethical and contemplative training (YOGA) to gain a supraintellectual insight into one's identity with Brahman, and (3) the bhakti-mārga ("path of devotion"), love for a personal God. These ways are regarded as suited to various types of people, but they are interactive and potentially available to all.

Although the pursuit of mokṣa is institutionalized in Hindu life through ascetic practice and the ideal of withdrawing from the world at the conclusion of one's life, such practices of withdrawal are explicitly denigrated in the Bhagavad Gītā itself. Because action is inescapable, these three disciplines are better thought of as simultaneously achieving the goals of world maintenance (dharma, doing one's duty) and world release (mokṣa). Through the suspension of desire and ambition and through a taste for the fruits (phala) of one's actions, one is enabled to float free of life while engaging it fully. This matches the goals of most Hindus, these being: to execute properly one's social and ritual duties; to support one's caste, family, and profession; and to do one's part to achieve a broader stability in the cosmos, nature, and society. The designation of Hinduism as sanatana dharma emphasizes this goal of maintaining personal and universal equilibrium, while at the same time calling attention to the role played by the performance of traditional (sanatana) religious practices in achieving that goal. Such tradition is understood to be inherently pluriform, since no one person can occupy all the social, occupational, and age-defined roles that are requisite to maintaining the health of the life-organism as a whole. Hence universal maxims (e.g., AHIMSĀ, the desire not to harm) are qualified by the more particular dharmas that are appropriate to each of the four major varṇas, or classes of society: Brahmins (priests), KṢATRIYAS (warriors and kings), VAIŚYAS (the common people), and ŚŪDRAS (servants). These four rather abstract categories are further superseded by the more practically applicable dharmas appropriate to each of the thousands of particular castes (jātis). And these, in turn, are cross-referenced to obligations appropriate to one's gender and stage of life (āśrama). In principle, then, Hindu ethics are exquisitely context-sensitive, and Hindus expect and celebrate a wide variety of individual behavior.

Āśramas: the four stages of life.   In the West, the so-called life-negating aspects of Hinduism—rigorous disciplines of Yoga, for example—have often been overemphasized. The polarity of ASCETICISM and sensuality, which assumes the form of a conflict between the aspiration for liberation and the heartfelt desire to have descendants and continue earthly life, manifests itself in Hindu social life as the tension between the different goals and stages of life. For many centuries, the relative value of an active life and the performance of meritorious works (*pravṛtti*) as opposed to the renunciation of all worldly interests and activity (*nivṛtti*) has been a debated issue. While philosophical works such as the Upanishads placed emphasis on renunciation, the dharma texts argued that the householder who maintains his sacred fire, begets children, and performs his ritual duties well also earns religious merit. Nearly 2,000 years ago these texts elaborated the social doctrine of the four *āśrama*s (*see* ASHRAM; stages of life). It held that a male member of the three higher classes should first become a chaste student (*brahmacārī*); then become a married householder (*gṛhastha*), discharging his debts to his ancestors by begetting sons and to the gods by sacrificing; then retire to the forest to devote himself to spiritual contemplation; and finally, but not mandatorily, become a homeless wandering ascetic (SANNYĀSĪ). The situation of the forest dweller was often omitted or rejected in practical life.

Although the status of a householder was often extolled and some authorities, regarding studentship a mere preparation for this next *āśrama*, went so far as to brand all other stages inferior, there were always people who became wandering ascetics immediately after studentship. Theorists were inclined to reconcile the divergent views and practices by allowing the ascetic way of life to those who are, owing to the effects of restrained conduct in former lives, entirely free from worldly desire, even if they had not gone through the prior stages.

Shrine to Vishnu in a Hindu temple in New York City
Katrina Thomas—Photo Researchers

The texts describing such life stages were written by men for men; they paid scant attention to paradigms for women. The MANU-SMṚTI (200 BCE–300 CE; "Laws of Manu"), for example, was content to regard marriage as the female equivalent to initiation in the life of a student, thereby effectively denying that the student stage in life is appropriate for girls. Furthermore, in the householder stage a woman's purpose was summarized as service to her husband. What we know of actual practice, however, challenges the idea that these patriarchal norms were ever perfectly enacted or that women entirely accepted them. While some women became ascetics (*sannyāsinī*s), many more focused their religious lives on realizing a state of blessedness (*kalyāṇa*) that is understood to be at once this-worldly and expressive of a larger, cosmic well-being. Women have often directed the cultivation of the auspicious (*śrī*) life-giving force (*śakti*) they possess to the benefit of their husbands and families, but as an ideal it has independent status.

SACRED TEXTS

Vedas. *Importance and components of the Veda.* The Veda ("Knowledge") is a collective term for the sacred SCRIPTURES of the Hindus. Since about the 5th century BCE, the Veda has been considered the creation of neither human nor god; rather, it is regarded as the eternal truth that was in ancient times directly revealed to or "heard" by gifted and inspired seers (*ṛṣis*) who uttered it in the most perfect human language, Sanskrit. Although most of the religion of the Vedic texts, which revolves around rituals of fire sacrifice, has been eclipsed by other aspects of Hindu doctrine and practice, parts of the Veda are still memorized and recited as a religious act of great merit.

The Veda is the product of early inhabitants of the Indian subcontinent who referred to themselves as ARYAN (*ārya*, "noble"). It represents the particular interests of the two classes of Aryan society—the priests (Brahmins) and the warrior-kings (Kṣatriyas)—who ruled over the far more numerous peasants (Vaiśyas). Because it is the literature of a ruling class, it probably does not represent all the myths and cults of the early Indo-Aryans, let alone those of non-Aryans.

Krishna, from Orissa, India, c. 1800; ivory with traces of polychrome
Archive Photos

Vedic literature ranges from the Ṛg Veda (composed *c.* 1200 BCE) to the Upanishads (composed *c.* 700 BCE–100 CE). The most important texts are the four collections (Saṃhitās) known as the Veda or Vedas (*i.e.*, "Book[s] of Knowledge"): the Ṛg Veda ("Wisdom of the Verses"), the YAJUR VEDA ("Wisdom of the Sacrificial Formulas"), the SĀMA VEDA ("Wisdom of the Chants"), and the ATHARVA VEDA ("Wisdom of the Atharvan Priests"). Of these, the Ṛg Veda is the oldest. In the Vedic texts that succeeded these earliest compilations, the BRĀHMAṆAS (discussions of Vedic ritual), *Āraṇyaka*s (books studied in the forest), and Upanishads (secret teachings concerning cosmic correlations), the interest in the early Ṛg Vedic gods wanes, and these gods become little more than accessories to Vedic ritual. Polytheism begins to be replaced by a sacrificial PANTHEISM of PRAJĀPATI ("Lord of Creatures"), who is the All. In the Upanishads Prajāpati merges with the concept of Brahman, the supreme reality and substance of the universe, replacing any specific personification, thus transforming the mythology into abstract philosophy.

Together, the components of each of the four Vedas—the Saṃhitās, *Brāhmaṇa*s, *Āraṇyaka*s, and Upanishads—constitute the revealed scripture of Hinduism, or ŚRUTI ("heard"). All other works—in which the actual doctrines and practices of Hindus are encoded—are recognized as having been composed by human authors and are thus classed as *smṛti* ("remembered"). The categorization of Veda, however, is capable of elasticity. First, *śruti* is not exactly closed; Upanishads, for example, have been composed until recent times. Second, the texts categorized as *smṛti* inevitably claim to be in accord with the authoritative *śruti* and, thus, worthy of the same respect and sacredness. In all this, the important thing to grasp is that the category of Veda functions as a symbol of authority and hallowed tradition.

The Ṛg Veda.   The religion reflected in the Ṛg Veda is a polytheism mainly concerned with the propitiation of divinities associated with the sky and the atmosphere. The old Indo-European sky father Dyaus was little regarded by the time the hymns of the Ṛg Veda were composed. More important were such gods as INDRA, VARUṆA (the guardian of the cosmic order), AGNI (the sacrificial fire), and SŪRYA (the sun).

The main ritual activity referred to in the Ṛg Veda is the SOMA sacrifice. Scholars disagree as to whether the *soma* beverage was a hallucinogen derived from the fly agaric mushroom native to mountain climates or (perhaps more likely) a stimulant squeezed from ephedra, a desert shrub. The Ṛg Veda contains a few clear references to animal sacrifice, which probably became more widespread later. There is doubt whether the priests formed a separate class at the beginning of the Ṛg Vedic period. If they did, the prevailing loose class boundaries made it possible for a man of nonpriestly parentage to become a priest. By the end of the period, however, they had become a separate class of specialists, the Brahmins (*brāhmaṇa*s), who claimed superiority over all the other social classes, including the Rājanyas (later Kṣatriyas), the warrior-kings.

The Upanishads.   The phase of Indian religious life roughly between 700 and 500 BCE was the period of the beginnings of philosophy and mysticism marked by the early Upanishads ("Connection," or "Correspondence"). With the Upanishads, the earlier emphasis on ritual was challenged by a new emphasis on knowledge alone—primarily, knowledge of the interconnectedness and ultimate identity of all phenomena, which merely appear to be separate. Historically, the most important of the Upanishads are the two oldest, the *Bṛhadāraṇyaka* ("Great Forest Text") and the *Chāndogya* (pertaining to the Chandogas, a class of priests who intone hymns at sacrifices), both of which are compilations that record the traditions of sages of the period, notably YĀJÑAVALKYA.

A primary motive of the Upanishads is a desire for mystical knowledge that would ensure freedom from *punarmṛtyu* ("re-death"). Throughout the later Vedic period, the idea that the world of heaven was not the end—and that even in heaven death was inevitable—had been growing. For Vedic thinkers, apprehension about the impermanence of religious merit and its loss in the hereafter, as well as the anticipation of the transience of any form of existence after death, culminating in the much-feared prospect of repeated death, assumed the character of an obsession. The *Brāhmaṇa*s laid out a largely ritual program for escaping and conquering death and achieving a full, integrated life. The *Bṛhadāraṇyaka*, however, placed more emphasis on the knowledge of the cosmic connection that formed the underpinnings of ritual. When the doctrine of the identity of *ātman* (the self) and Brahman was established in the Upanishads, the true knowledge of the self and the realization of this identity were (by those sages who were inclined to meditative thought) set above the ritual method.

In the following centuries the main theories connected with the divine essence underlying the world were harmonized and combined, and the tendency was to extol one god as the supreme Lord and Originator (ĪŚVARA), who is at the same time Puruṣa, Prajāpati, Brahman, and the inner self (*ātman*) of all beings. For those who worshiped him, he became the goal of identificatory meditation, which leads to complete cessation of phenomenal existence and becomes the refuge of those who seek eternal peace. The philosopher ŚAṂKARA (*c.* 800 CE) exercised enormous influence on subsequent Hindu thinking through his elegant synthesis of the nontheistic and theistic aspects of Upanishadic teaching. In his commentaries on several of the Upanishads, he distinguished between NIRGUṆA (without attributes) and SAGUṆA (with attributes) aspects of Brahman, that ultimate reality whose relation to the phenomenal world can best be described as nondual (ADVAITA). This "nonrelationship" states the world's deepest truth.

The origin and the development of the belief in the transmigration of souls are very obscure. A few passages suggest that this doctrine was known even in the days of the Ṛg Veda, but it was first clearly propounded in the *Bṛhadāraṇyaka*. There it is stated that normally the soul returns to earth and is reborn in human or animal form. This doctrine of *saṃsāra* (REINCARNATION) is attributed to the sage Uddālaka Āruṇi, who is said to have learned it from a Kṣatriya chief. In the same text, the doctrine of karma (actions), according to which the soul achieves a happy or unhappy rebirth according to its works in the previous life, also occurs for the first time, attributed to the teacher and sage Yājñavalkya. Both doctrines appear to have been new and strange ones, circulating among small groups of ascetics who were disinclined to make them public, but they must have spread rapidly, for in the later Upanishads and in the earliest Buddhist and Jain scriptures they are common knowledge.

Sūtras, śāstras, and smṛtis. Among the texts inspired by the Veda are the DHARMA SUTRAS, or manuals on dharma, which contain rules of conduct and rites as they were practiced in a number of branches of the Vedic schools. Their principal contents address duties at various stages of life, or *āśrama*s (studenthood, householdership, retirement, and asceticism); dietary regulations; offenses and expiations; and the rights and duties of kings. They also discuss purification rites, funerary ceremonies, forms of hospitality, and daily oblations. Finally, they mention juridical matters. The more important of these texts are the *sūtra*s of the BUDDHA GOTAMA, Baudhāyana, and Āpastamba. Although the relationship is not clear, the contents of these works were further elaborated in the more systematic DHARMA ŚĀSTRAS, which in turn became the basis of Hindu law.

Hanumān, chief among monkeys, goes to Laṅkā, episode in the Bhāgavata Purāṇa, *17th-century Indian miniature from Malwa*
Borromeo—Art Resource

First among them stands the *Dharma Śāstra* of Manu, also known as the MANU-SMṚTI ("Tradition [or Laws] of Manu"), with 2,694 stanzas divided into 12 chapters. It deals with various topics such as COSMOGONY, definition of dharma, the SACRAMENTS, initiation and Vedic study, the 8 forms of marriage, hospitality and funerary rites, dietary laws, pollution and purification, rules for women and wives, royal law, 18 categories of juridical matters, and religious matters, including donations, rites of reparation, the doctrine of karma, the soul, and punishment in hell. Law in the juridical sense is thus completely embedded in religious practice. The framework is provided by the model of the four-*varṇa* society. The influence of the *Dharma Śāstra* of Manu as a statement of ideal norms has been very great, but there is no evidence that it was ever employed as a working legal code in ancient India. Second only to Manu is the *Dharma Śāstra* of Yājñavalkya; its 1,013 stanzas are distributed under the three headings of good conduct, law, and expiation.

The *śāstra*s are a part of the SMṚTI ("remembered," or traditional) literature, which, like the *sūtra* literature that preceded it, stresses the religious merit of gifts to Brahmins. Because kings often transferred the revenues of villages or groups of villages to Brahmins, either singly or in corporate groups, the status and wealth of the priestly class rose steadily. In *agrahāra*s, as the settlements of Brahmins were called, Brahmins were encouraged to devote themselves to the study of the Vedas and to the subsidiary studies associated with them; but many Brahmins also developed the sciences of the period, such as mathematics, astronomy, and medicine, while others cultivated literature.

Epics and Purāṇas. During the centuries immediately preceding and following the beginning of the Christian Era, the recension of the two great Sanskrit epics, the *Mahābhārata* and the *Rāmāyaṇa*, took shape out of existing material, such as heroic epic stories, mythology, philosophy, and above all the discussion of the problem of dharma. Much of the material of which the epics were composed dates back into the Vedic period; the rest continued to be added until well after 1000 CE. The actual composition of the Sanskrit texts, however, dates to the period from 500 BCE to 400 CE for the *Mahābhārata* and to the period from 200 BCE to 200 CE for the *Rāmāyaṇa*.

The Mahābhārata. The *Mahābhārata* ("Great Epic of the Bhārata Dynasty"), a text of some 100,000 verses attributed to the sage Vyāsa, was preserved both orally and in manuscript form for centuries. The central plot concerns a great battle between the five sons of Pāṇḍu (called the PĀṆḌAVAS) and the sons of Pāṇḍu's brother Dhṛtarāṣṭra. Pāṇḍu had been placed under a curse: to have intercourse with any of his wives would cause his death. One wife, however, Kuntī, had a boon that permitted her to conceive through use of a MANTRA. Thus, Kuntī invoked the gods to allow her to conceive the Pāṇḍavas: the five brothers are ARJUNA, conceived of Indra; Yudhiṣṭhira, conceived of Dharma; Bhīma, conceived of Vāyu; and the twins, Nakula and Sahadeva, conceived of the Aśvins. The battle eventually leads to the destruction of the entire race, save one survivor who continues the dynasty. The epic is deeply infused with religious implications, and the battle itself is sometimes understood as a great sacrifice. There are, moreover, many passages in which dharma is systematically treated, so that Hindus regard the *Mahābhārata* as one of the *Dharma Śāstra*s. Religious practice takes the form of Vedic ritual (on official occasions), pilgrimage, and, to some extent, adoration of gods. Apart from the *Bhagavad Gītā* (part of book 6 of the *Mahābhārata*) much of the didactic material is found in the Book of the Forest (book 3), in which sages teach the exiled heroes, and in the Book of Peace (book 12), in which the wise Bhīṣma expounds on religious and moral matters.

In the *Mahābhārata* the Vedic gods have lessened in importance, surviving principally as figures of FOLKLORE. Prajāpati of the Upanishads is popularly personified as the god Brahmā, who creates all classes of beings and dispenses boons. Of far greater importance in the *Mahābhārata* is Krishna. In the epic he is primarily a hero, a leader of his people, and an active helper of his friends, yet at a grander, subtler level it is he who superintends the battle-sacrifice as a whole. Krishna's biography appears primarily elsewhere—in the *Harivaṃśa* (1st–3rd centuries CE?) and various PURĀṆAS—and there his divinity shows through more obviously than in the epic. Although he is occasionally identified with Vishnu in the *Mahābhārata*, he is mostly a chieftain, a counsellor, and an ally of the Pāṇḍavas, the heroes of the epic. He helps the Pāṇḍava brothers to settle in their kingdom and, when the kingdom is taken from them, to regain it. In the process he emerges as a great teacher who reveals the *Bhagavad Gītā*, arguably the most important religious text in Hinduism today. In the further development of Krishna worship, this dharmic aspect somewhat recedes, making way for the idyllic story of Krishna's boyhood, when he played with and loved young cowherd women (*gopī*s) in the village while hiding from an uncle who threatened to kill him. The influence of this theme on art has been profound. But even in the *Mahābhārata*, where it is often said that Krishna becomes incarnate in order to sustain dharma when it wanes and in order to combat *adharma* (forces contrary to dharma), he commits a number of deeds in direct violation of the warrior ethic and is indirectly responsible for the destruction of his entire family. This adharmic shadow is also cast in the Purāṇic idyll because the *gopī*s he woos are the wives of other men. In both cases, Krishna's actions illuminate levels of truth that go deeper than any conventional dharma—either a subtle dharma inscrutable to players immersed in the *Mahābhārata*'s epic battle or a quality of divine playfulness that characterizes the deepest rhythms of the cosmos itself.

Far remoter than Krishna in the *Mahābhārata* is Shiva, who also is hailed as the supreme god in several myths recounted of him, notably the Story of the Five Indras, Arjuna's battle with Shiva, and Shiva's destruction of the sacrifice of Dakṣa. The epic is rich in information about sacred places, and it is clear that making pilgrimages and bathing in sacred rivers constituted an important part of religious life. Occasionally these sacred places are associated with sanctuaries of gods. More frequent are accounts of mythical events concerning a particular place and enriching its sanctity. Numerous descriptions of pilgrimages (*tīrthayātrā*s) give the authors opportunities to detail local myths and legends. In addition to these, countless edifying stories shed light on the religious and moral concerns of the age. Almost divine are the towering ascetics capable of fantastic feats, whose benevolence is sought and whose curses are feared.

The Rāmāyaṇa.   The classical narrative of Rāma is recounted in the Sanskrit epic *Rāmāyaṇa*, whose authorship is attributed to the sage Vālmīki. Rāma is deprived of the kingdom to which he is heir and is exiled to the forest; his wife Sītā and his brother Lakṣmaṇa accompany him. While there, Sītā is abducted by Rāvaṇa, the demon king of Laṅkā. In their search for Sītā, the brothers ally themselves with Sugrīva, a monkey king whose chief, HANUMĀN (an important deity in modern Hinduism), finds Sītā in Laṅkā. In a cosmic battle, Rāvaṇa is defeated and Sītā rescued. When Rāma is restored to his kingdom, the populace casts doubt on Sītā's chastity during her captivity. Rāma banishes Sītā to a hermitage, where she bears him two sons and eventually dies by reentering the earth from which she had been born. Rāma's reign becomes the prototype of the harmonious and just kingdom to which all kings should aspire; Rāma and Sītā set the ideal of conjugal love; Rāma's relationship to his father is the ideal of filial love; and Rāma and Lakṣmaṇa represent perfect fraternal love. Everything in the myth is designed to show harmony, which after being disrupted is at last regained—or so, at least, Vālmīki would have it. This accords with the fact that in all but its oldest form (before *c.* 1st century CE), the *Rāmāyaṇa* identifies Rāma with Vishnu.

Yet there are deep fissures: Rāma's killing of Vālī in violation of all rules of combat and his banishment of the innocent Sītā are troublesome to subsequent tradition. The problems of the "subtlety" of dharma and the inevitability of its violation, central themes in both the *Rāmāyaṇa* and the *Mahābhārata*, have remained the locus of argument throughout Indian history, both at the level of abstract philosophy and in local performance traditions. In Kerala, for instance, men of the low-ranked artisan caste worship Vālī through rites of dance-possession that implicitly protest their ancestors' deaths as soldiers conscripted by high-caste leaders such as Rāma. And throughout India women performers have shifted the thrust of various episodes, emphasizing Sītā's story—her foundling infancy, her abduction by Rāvaṇa, her trial by fire, her childbirth in exile—thereby openly challenging Rāma. In the words of a Bengali women's song translated by Nabaneeta Dev Sen, "Five months pregnant, Sītā was in the royal palace, and a heartless Rāma sent her off to the forest!"

The *Mahābhārata* and the *Rāmāyaṇa* have also made an impact in Southeast Asia, where their stories have been continually retold in vernacular, oral, and visual versions. As for India, even today the epic stories and tales are part of the early education of almost all Hindus; a continuous reading of the *Rāmāyaṇa*—whether in Sanskrit or in a vernacular version such as that of TULSĪDĀS (16th century)—is an act of great merit, and the enacting of Tulsīdās' version of the *Rāmāyaṇa*, called the RĀMCARITMĀNAS, is an annual event across the northern part of the subcontinent. The *Rāmāyaṇa*'s influence is expressed in a dazzling variety of local and regional performance traditions—story, dance, drama, art—and extends to the spawning of explicit "counter epics," such as those published by the Tamil separatist E.V. Ramasami beginning in 1930.

The Bhagavad Gītā. The *Bhagavad Gītā* ("Song of God") is perhaps the most influential of any single Indian religious text, although it is not strictly classed as *śruti*, or revelation. It is a brief text, 700 verses divided into 18 chapters, in quasi-dialogue form. When the opposing parties in the *Mahābhārata* war stand ready to begin battle, Arjuna, the hero of the favored party, despairs at the thought of having to kill his kinsmen and lays down his arms. Krishna, his charioteer, friend, and adviser, thereupon argues against Arjuna's failure to do his duty as a noble. The argument soon becomes elevated into a general discourse on religious and philosophical matters, at the climax of which Krishna reveals his infinite, supernal form as Time itself. The text is typical of Hinduism in that it is able to reconcile different viewpoints, however incompatible they seem to be, and yet emerge with an undeniable character of its own. In its way, it does constitute ŚRUTI ("what is heard"), since Arjuna receives its teachings from the divine Krishna.

The Purāṇas. The Gupta Period (*c.* 320–540) saw the first of the series (traditionally 18) of often-voluminous texts that treat in encyclopedic manner the myths, legends, and genealogies of gods, heroes, and saints. Along with the epics, to which they are closely linked in origin, the *Purāṇas* became the scriptures of the common people; they were available to everybody, including women and members of the lowest order of society (Śūdras), and were not, like the Vedas, supposedly restricted to initiated men of the three higher orders. The origin of much of their contents may be non-Brahminical, but they were also accepted by Brahmins, who thus brought new elements into Vedic religion. For example, goddesses are rarely discussed in the Veda, yet they rose steadily in recognition in Purāṇic mythology. The *Devī Māhātmya* ("Glorification of the Goddess"), which belongs to the genre, dates to the 5th or 6th century CE, and the DEVĪ BHĀGAVATA PURĀṆA is sometimes regarded as being almost as old.

In other *Purāṇa*s Vishnu and Shiva establish their primacy. Both are known in the Vedas, though they play only minor roles: Vishnu is the god who, with his three strides, established the three worlds (heaven, atmosphere, and earth) and thus is present in all three orders; and Rudra-Shiva is a mysterious god who must be propitiated. Purāṇic literature reveals various stages in which these two gods progressively attract to themselves the identities of other popular gods and heroes: Vishnu assumes the powers of gods who protect the world and its order, Shiva the powers that are outside and beyond Vishnu's range. To these two is often added Brahmā; although still a cosmic figure, Brahmā appears in the *Purāṇa*s primarily to appease over-powerful sages and demons by granting them boons.

Myths of time and eternity. Purāṇic myths develop around the notion of YUGA (world age). The four *yuga*s, Kṛta, Tretā, Dvāpara, and Kali—they are named after the four throws, from best to worst, in a dice game—constitute a *mahāyuga* ("large *yuga*") and are periods of increasing deterioration. Time itself deteriorates, for the ages are successively shorter. Each *yuga* is preceded by an intermediate "dawn" and "dusk." The Kṛta *yuga* lasts 4,000 god-years, with a dawn and dusk of 400 god-years each, or a total of 4,800 god-years; Tretā a total of 3,600 god-years; Dvāpara 2,400 god-years; and Kali (the current *yuga*) 1,200 god-years. A *mahāyuga* thus lasts 12,000 god-years and observes the usual coefficient of 12, derived from the 12-month year, the unit of creation. Since each god-year lasts 360 human years, a *mahāyuga* is 4,320,000 years long in human time. Two thousand *mahāyuga*s form one *kalpa* (eon), which is itself but one day in the life of Brahmā, whose full life lasts 100 years; the present is the midpoint of his life. Each *kalpa* is followed by an equally long period of abeyance (*pralaya*), in which the universe is asleep. Seemingly the universe will come to an end at the end of Brahmā's life, but Brahmās too are innumerable, and a new universe is reborn with each new Brahmā.

MAJOR TRADITIONS OF AFFILIATION

Vaiṣṇavism. VAIṢṆAVISM is the worship of Vishnu and his various incarnations. During a long and complex development from Vedic times, there arose many Vaiṣṇava groups with differing beliefs and aims. Some of the major Vaiṣṇava groups include the Śrī Vaiṣṇavas and Dvaitins ("[Theological] Dualists") of South India, the followers of the teachings of the philosopher VALLABHA in western India, and several Vaiṣṇava groups in Bengal in eastern India, who follow teachings derived from those of the saint CAITANYA. The majority of Vaiṣṇava believers, however, take what they like from the various traditions and blend it with various local practices.

In the Veda, Vishnu is the god who penetrates and traverses the triple spaces of the universe to make their existence possible. All beings are said to dwell in his three strides or footsteps (*tri-vikrama*); his highest step, or abode, is beyond mortal ken in the realm of heaven. Vishnu is the god who serves as the pillar of the universe and is identified with sacrifice, which attempts by ritual means to open channels between the several levels of the universe. Vishnu imparts his all-pervading power to the sacrificer, who imitates his strides and so identifies himself with the god, thus conquering the universe and attaining "the goal, the safe foundation, the highest light" (*Śatapatha Brāhmaṇa*).

In the centuries preceding the beginning of the Common Era, Vishnu became the Īśvara (immanent deity) of his special worshipers, fusing with the Puruṣa-Prajāpati figure; with Nārāyaṇa, whose cult discloses a prominent influence of ascetics; with Krishna, who in the *Bhagavad Gītā* revealed a form of dharma-affirming devotional religion, in principle accessible to everyone; and with VĀSUDEVA, adored by a group known as the PĀÑCARĀTRAS.

The extensive mythology attached to Vishnu consists largely of his incarnations (AVATARS, literally "descents" into this world). Although the notion of incarnation is found elsewhere in Hinduism, it is basic to Vaiṣṇavism. The concept is particularly geared to the social role of Vishnu; whenever dharma is in danger, Vishnu departs from his heaven, Vaikuṇṭha, and incarnates himself in an earthly form to restore the proper order. Each incarnation has a particular mythology.

The classical number of these incarnations is 10, ascending from theriomorphic (animal form) to fully anthropomorphic manifestations. In their most familiar version, these are fish (Matsya), tortoise (Kūrma), boar (VARĀHA), man-lion (NARASIMHA), dwarf (VĀMANA), Rāma with the ax (PARAŚURĀMA), King Rāma, Krishna, the Buddha Gotama, and the future incarnation, KALKĪ.

A god thus active for the good of society and the individual inspires love. Vishnu has indeed been the object of devotional religion (*bhakti*) to a marked degree, but he is especially worshiped in his incarnations as Krishna and Rāma. The god rewards devotion with his grace, through which the votary may be lifted from transmigration to release or, more crucially, into Vishnu's intimate presence. Like most other gods, Vishnu has his especial entourage: his wife is LAKṢMĪ, or Śrī, the lotus goddess, granter of beauty, wealth, and good luck. She came forth from the primordial MILK-OCEAN when gods and demons churned it to recover from its depths the ambrosia or elixir of immortality, *amṛta.* At DĪVĀLĪ, or Dīpāvalī, the festival many Hindus regard as beginning the commercial year, special worship is paid to her for success in personal affairs. Vishnu's mount is the bird GARUDA, archenemy of snakes, and his emblems—which he carries in his four hands—are the lotus, club, discus (as a weapon), and conch shell.

Whatever justification the different Vaiṣṇava groups offer for their philosophical position, all Vaiṣṇavas believe in God as a person with distinctively high qualities and worship him through his manifestations and representations. Vaiṣṇava faith is essentially monotheistic, whether the object of adoration be Vishnu-Nārāyaṇa or one of his avatars, such as Rāma or Krishna. Preference for any one of these manifestations is largely a matter of tradition. Thus,

Umā-Maheśvara Mūrti—Shiva with Pārvatī, c. 10th–11th century, Rajasthan, India
Archive Photos

most South Indian Śrī Vaiṣṇavas prefer Vishnu or Śrī; North Indian groups tend to worship Krishna and his consort Rādhā or Rāma and his consort Sītā. While most Hindus would acknowledge the overarching avatar framework as a way of organizing the Vaiṣṇava side of the pantheon, more encompassing commitments to Rāma or Krishna are also possible, as in the *Bhāgavata Purāṇa*'s frequently quoted dictum "Krishna himself is God."

A pronounced feature of Vaiṣṇavism is the strong tendency to devotion (*bhakti*), a passionate love and adoration of God, a complete surrender. The widespread *bhakti* movement seems a natural corollary of the Vaiṣṇava ideal of a loving personal God and aversion to a conception of salvation that puts an end to all consciousness or individuality. The belief expressed in the *Bhagavad Gītā*—that those who seek refuge in God with all their being will, by his benevolence and grace (*prasāda*), win peace supreme, the eternal abode—was generally accepted: *bhakti* will result in divine intercession with regard to the consequences of one's deeds. A more radical position was embraced by certain followers of the 11th–12th-century theologian RĀMĀNUJA. They held that the efficaciousness of human action is limited to self-surrender (PRAPATTI); all the rest is Vishnu's grace. Equally radical—even paradoxical—forms of *bhakti* thrive in Śaiva and Śākta soil.

Śaivism.   The character and position of the Vedic god Rudra—called Shiva, "the Mild or Auspicious One," when the gentler side of his ambivalent nature is emphasized—remain clearly perceptible in some of the important features of the great god Shiva, who together with Vishnu and the Great Goddess (Devī, Durgā, or Śakti) came to dominate Hinduism. During a development from ancient, possibly pre-Vedic times, many different groups within ŚAIVISM arose. Major groups such as the Kashmir Śaivas and the Śaiva Siddhāntins and VĪRAŚAIVAS of southern India contributed the theological principles of Śaivism, and Śaiva worship became an amalgam of pan-Indian Śaiva philosophy and local forms of worship.

In the minds of ancient Indians, Shiva seems to have been especially associated with the uncultivated, dangerous, and much-to-be-feared aspects of nature. Shiva's character lent itself to being split into partial manifestations—each said to represent only one aspect of him—as well as to assimilating divine or demoniac powers of a similar nature from other deities. Already in the Ṛg Veda, appeals to him for help in case of disaster—of which he might be the originator—were combined with the confirmation of his great power. In the course of the Vedic period, Shiva—originally a ritual and conceptual outsider yet a mighty god whose benevolent aspects were emphasized—gradually gained access to the circle of respectable gods who preside over various spheres of human interest. Many characteristics of the Vedic Prajāpati (the creator), of Indra with his sexual potency, and of Agni (the great Vedic god of fire) have been integrated into the figure of Shiva.

In those circles that produced the Śvetāśvatara Upanishad (*c.* 200 BCE), Shiva rose to the highest rank. In its description of Shiva, he is the ultimate foundation of all existence and the source and ruler of all life, who, while emanating and withdrawing the universe, is the goal of that identificatory meditation that leads to a state of complete separation from phenomenal existence. While Vishnu came to be seen as an ally and advocate of humankind, Rudra-Shiva developed into an ambivalent and many-sided lord and master. As Paśupati ("Lord of Cattle"), he took over the fetters of the Vedic Varuṇa; as Aghora ("To Whom Nothing Is Horrible"), he showed the uncanny traits of his nature (evil, death, punishment) and also their opposites. Shiva might be the sole principle above change and variation, yet he did not sever his connections with innumerable local deities, some of them quite fearsome. Whereas Vishnu champions the cause of the gods, Shiva sometimes sides with the demons.

Shiva exemplifies the idea that the Highest Being encompasses semantically opposite though complementary aspects: the terrible and the mild, creation and reabsorption, eternal rest and ceaseless activity. These seeming contradictions make Shiva a paradoxical figure, transcending humanity and assuming a mysterious sublimity of his own. Although Brahmin philosophers like to emphasize his ascetic aspects and TANTRIC HINDUS his sexuality, the seemingly opposite strands of his nature are generally accepted as two sides of one character.

Shiva interrupts his austerity and asceticism (TAPAS), which is sometimes described as continuous, to marry Pārvatī—he is even said to perform ascetic acts in order to win her love—and he combines the roles of lover and ascetic to such a degree that his wife must be an ascetic (Yogi) when he devotes himself to austerities and a lustful mistress when he is in his erotic mode. Various Śaiva myths show that both chastity and the loss of chastity are necessary for fertility and the intermittent process of regeneration in nature, and ascetics who act erotically are a familiar feature of Hindu lore. By their very chastity, ascetics accumulate (sexual) power that can be discharged suddenly and completely so as to produce remarkable results, such as the fecundation of the soil. Krishna's irrepressible sexuality often has a certain idyllic cast, as represented through the metaphor of love beyond the bonds of marriage, whereas Shiva's complex sexuality plays itself out within the various facets of his marriage to Pārvatī. That marriage becomes a model of conjugal love, sanctifying the forces that carry on the human race.

Many of Shiva's poses express positive aspects of his nature: as a dancer, he is the originator of the eternal rhythm of the universe; he catches the waters of the heavenly GANGĀ (Ganges) River, which destroy all sin; and he wears in his headdress the crescent moon, which drips the nectar of everlasting life. Yet he is unpredictable. He is the hunter who slays and skins his prey and dances a wild dance while covered with the bloody hide. Far from society and the ordered world, he sits on the inaccessible Himalayan plateau of Mount Kailāsa, an austere ascetic averse to love who burns KĀMA, the god of love, to ashes with a glance from the third eye—the eye of insight beyond duality—in the middle of his forehead. Snakes seek his company and twine themselves around his body. He wears a necklace of skulls. He sits in meditation, with his hair braided like a hermit's, his body smeared white with ashes. These ashes recall the burning pyres on which the *sannyāsī*s (renouncers) take leave of the social order of the world and set out on a lonely course toward release, carrying with them a human skull. And, at the end of the eon, he will dance the universe to destruction. Nevertheless, he is invoked as Shiva, Śambhu, Śaṃkara ("the Auspicious One," or "the Peaceful One"), for the god that can strike down can also spare.

The form in which Shiva is most frequently worshiped is the among the sturdiest, plainest imaginable: an upright rounded post called a LIṄGA ("sign"), usually made of stone. Commentators often observe that its erect male sexuality is counterbalanced by the horizontal plane (YONI)—bespeaking female sexuality—in which it is often set. Yet the sexual dimension is not primary for most devotees, for whom the *liṅga*'s aniconic form simply marks Shiva's inscrutable stability.

Śāktism. The term ŚĀKTISM stands alongside Vaiṣṇavism or Śaivism as a way of designating a third aspect of Hindu religion that is indisputably ancient and influential: the worship of goddesses, especially when they are understood as expressions or aspects of a single Goddess (Devī) or Great Goddess (Mahādevī). This Goddess personifies a power, or energy (Śakti), present throughout the universe and challenges any notion of the feminine as passive or quiescent. She can be related to a widely dispersed tradition that associates forceful female deities, many inhabiting particular locales, with the offering of animal sacrifices. Such deities are summarized in the legendry of the *śākta pīṭhā*s ("seats of power") that are said to have been established when various parts of the dismembered goddess Satī, consort of Shiva, fell there. The texts often consider that there are 108 of these PĪṬHAS, extending throughout all of India and commemorated by a network of temples.

The power and variousness of the Great Goddess is expressed in her primary myth of origin, as recorded in the *Devī Māhātmya*. The text explains that the gods found themselves powerless in the face of opposing forces, especially a primordial buffalo demon (Mahiṣāsura), and pooled their angry energies to create a force capable of triumphing over such unruly, evil powers. The Great Goddess, summarizing and concentrating their various energies, emitted a menacing laugh, drank wine, refused the buffalo's overtures of marriage, and vanquished him utterly from atop her lion mount, piercing his chest with her trident and decapitating him with her discus. Devī's victory is memorialized in a series of sculptures that began to appear in the Gupta and Pallava periods (4th–8th centuries), contemporary with the *Devī Māhātmya*.

In a fashion loosely comparable to the process of gathering disparate divine energies that is so prominent in Devī's myth of origins, regional and local goddesses from all over South Asia have for centuries been found to exemplify the person and mythology of an overarching Goddess who offers maternal nurturance to the earth (one of her personas) and her devotees but is death to threatening outsiders. Yet these goddesses retain their local power as mothers guarding particular places and lineages. A key concept in enunciating the nature of this connection is *śakti*—power personified as female. *Śakti* may be associated with males, as in Devī's origination myth or in the depiction of goddesses as consorts, but in its essence it eludes the categories constructed by men. Thought to possess both natural and ritual force and to be embodied in human women, *śakti* as a description of divinity expresses (among other things) a recognition that women are far more powerful than their social position usually indicates. Hence texts such as the *Devī Bhāgavata Purāṇa* effectively feminize the older, all-male *trimūrti* by placing the Goddess, not Brahmā, alongside and indeed above Vishnu and Shiva.

Like any category that attempts to name broad traditions of belief and practice, Śāktism (like Vaiṣṇavism and Śaivism) is imprecise. With Śāktism, however, this is especially so, since the ancient āgamic traditions of ritual and theological practice solidified primarily around male deities— Vishnu and Shiva. Nonetheless, several motifs are particularly salient in contributing to a Śākta religious orientation. One is the close parallel between Purāṇic tales of the Great Goddess eagerly shedding and drinking blood and the ritual motif of blood sacrifice, an exchange of Śakti that has apparently been a singular feature of goddess worship throughout India from earliest times. Another is the enduring association between various forms of the Goddess and pots, especially those seen to be overflowing with vegetation, and the great tendency of widely disparate goddesses to express themselves by possessing their devotees. All of these display the organic energy of *śakti*. Yet the roles Śakti assumes as the enabling power of all beings remain various, and especially in early texts, are depicted as both horrific and benign.

The Great Goddess's role is different in the various systems. She may be seen as the central figure in a philosophically established doctrine, the dynamic aspect of Brahman, producing the universe through her MĀYĀ, or mysterious power of illusion; a capricious demoniac ruler of nature in its destructive aspects; a benign mother goddess; or the queen of a celestial court. There is a comprehensive Śāktism that identifies the goddess (usually Durgā) with Brahman and worships her as the ruler of the universe by virtue of whom even Shiva exists. As Mahāyoginī ("Great Mistress of Yoga"), she produces, maintains, and reabsorbs the world. In Bengal's devotion to the goddess KĀLĪ, she demands bloody sacrifices from her worshipers lest her creative potency fail her. Kālī worshipers believe that birth and death are inseparable, that joy and grief spring from the same source, and that the frightening manifestations of the divine should be faced calmly.

A yoga chart showing the kuṇḍalinī *serpent coiled asleep in the human body, Indian drawing,* c. *18th–19th century*
The Granger Collection

The Great Goddess also manifests herself as the divine consort. As ARDHANĀRĪŚ-VARA ("the Lord Who Is Half Female"), Shiva shares ultimate reality with her and presides over procreation. Accordingly, Śāktas—often closely associated with Śaivism—hold that creation is the result of the eternal lust of the divine couple. Thus a man who is blissfully embraced by a beloved woman who is Pārvatī's counterpart assumes Shiva's personality and, liberated, participates in the joy of Shiva's amorous sport. Similarly, in all his incarnations Vishnu is united with his consort, Lakṣmī. The sacred tales of his relations with her manifestations cause his worshipers to view human devotion as parallel to the divine love and hence as universal, eternal, and sanctified. In his supreme state, Vishnu and his *śakti* are indissolubly associated with one another, forming a dual divinity called Lakṣmī-Nārāyaṇa. Thus in art Lakṣmī often rests on Vishnu's bosom.

MODES OF RELIGIOUS PRACTICE

Tantrism. There is a close connection between Śākta persuasions and Tantrism, but they are not the same thing. Tantrism is the search for spiritual power and ultimate release by means of the repetition of sacred syllables and phrases (mantras), symbolic drawings (MANDALAS), and other secret rites elaborated in the texts known as TANTRAS ("looms"). Based especially on convictions about divine creative energy (*śakti*) as experienced in the body, Tantrism is a method of conquering transcendent powers and realizing oneness with the divine by yogic and ritual means. It appears in both Buddhism and Hinduism from the 5th century CE onward, coloring many religious trends and movements.

Tantrics take for granted that all factors in both the macrocosm and the microcosm are closely connected. The adept (*sādhaka*) is almost always understood as a man, who performs the relevant rites on his own body, transforming its normally chaotic state into a "cosmos." The macrocosm is conceived as a complex system of powers that by means of ritual-psychological techniques can be activated and organized within the individual body of the adept.

According to Tantrism, concentration is intended to evoke an internal image of the deity and to resuscitate the powers inherent in it so that the symbol changes into mental experience. This "symbolic ambiguity" is also much in evidence in the esoteric interpretation of ritual acts performed in connection with images, flowers, and other cult objects and is intended to bring about a transfiguration in the mind of the adept. Mantras (sacred utterances, such as *hūṃ*, *hrīṃ*, and *klaṃ*) are also an indispensable means of entering into contact with the power they bear and of transcending normal mundane existence. Most potent are the monosyllabic, fundamental, so-called *bīja* ("seed") mantras, which constitute the main element of longer formulas and embody the essence of divine power as the eternal, indestructible prototypes from which everything phenomenal derives its existence. The cosmos itself owes its very structure and harmony to them. Also important is the introduction of spiritual qualities or divine power into the body by placing a finger on the spot relevant to each (accompanied by a mantra).

Tantrics are often classified as being of two types: "right handed" or "left handed." The former confine to the sphere of metaphor and visualization what the latter enact literally. Tantrics who follow the right-hand path value Yoga and *bhakti* and aspire to union with the Supreme by emotional-dynamic means, their Yoga being a self-abnegation in order to reach a state of ecstatic bliss in which the passive soul is lifted up by divine grace. They also adopt a Tantric Mantra Yoga, as described above, and a HAṬHA YOGA ("Discipline of Force"). Haṭha Yoga incorporates normal yogic practices—abstinences, observances, bodily postures, breath control that requires intensive training, withdrawal of the mind from external objects, and concentration, contemplation, and identification that are technically helped by MUDRĀS (*i.e.*, ritual intertwining of fingers, or gestures expressing the metaphysical aspects of ceremonies or of the transformation effected by mantras). Haṭha Yoga goes on to involve vigorous muscular contractions, internal purifications (*e.g.*, washing out stomach and bowels), shaking the abdomen, and certain forms of strict self-discipline. The whole process is intended to control the "gross body" in order to free the "subtle body."

The left-hand Tantric practice (*vāmācāra*) consciously violates all the TABOOS of conventional Hinduism, both for the purpose of helping the adepts to understand their provisional nature and to work from the base of strength provided by the sensory capabilities inherent in bodily existence. For the traditional five elements (*tattva*s) of the Hindu cosmos, these Tantrics substitute the five "m"s: *māṃsa* (flesh, meat), *matsya* (fish), *madya* (fermented grapes, wine), *mudrā* (frumentum, cereal, parched grain, or gestures), and *maithuna* (fornication). This latter element is made particularly antinomian through the involvement of forbidden women, such as one's sister, mother, the wife of another man, or a low-caste woman, who is identified with the Goddess. Menstrual blood, strictly taboo in conventional Hinduism, is also used at times. Such rituals, which are described in Tantric texts and in tracts against Tantrics, have made *tantra* notorious among many Hindus. It is likely, however, that such rituals have never been regularly performed except by a relatively small group of highly trained adepts; the usual (right-handed) Tantric ceremony is purely symbolic and even more fastidious than the *pūjā*s in Hindu temples.

All forms of *tantra* seek to realize the unity of flesh and spirit, the interconnection of the human and the divine, and the experience of transcending time and space. The goal of surpassing the phenomenal duality of spirit and matter and recovering the primeval unity is often conceived as the realization of the identity of God and his Śakti—the core mystery of Śāktism. Ritual practice is varied. Extreme Śākta communities perform the secret nocturnal rites of the *śrīcakra* ("wheel of radiance"; described in the *Kulārṇava Tantra*), in which they avail themselves of the natural and esoteric symbolic properties of colors, sounds, and perfumes to intensify their sexual experiences. Or, in experiencing "the delectation of the deity," the male adept worships the mighty power of the Divine Mother by making a human woman the object of sexual worship, invoking the Goddess into her and cohabiting with her until his mind is free from impurity. The texts reiterate how dangerous these rites are for those who are not initiated, and most Śākta Tantrics probably do not exemplify this left-handed type.

As if to make this point clear, Tantric practice in general has sometimes been described as comprising not two contrasting types—left and right—but three. According to this taxonomy a Tantric may be either *paśu* (bestial), *vīra* (heroic), or *divya* (divine). Of these, only the *vīra* type is left-handed, consuming the five substances as literally enjoined in the texts. *Paśu*s, by contrast, use physical substitutes—*e.g.*, they imbibe coconut milk rather than wine and surrender to the feet of the Goddess (or another deity) rather than submitting to ritual intercourse. Sometimes they are classed in the right-handed group, but sometimes their *bhakti* approach is felt to exempt them from the left/right dichotomy altogether. Finally, there are the *divya* adepts, right-handed Tantrics who use not physical but mental substitutes. Instead of drinking wine, they taste the nectar that flows down from the body's uppermost "center," the *sahasrāra cakra*, when its snakelike physical energy (KUNDALINĪ) has risen from its anal base to its cranial apex, in the process being refined into a subtle, spiritual form. This then is interpreted as the true love-juice from the play of Shiva and Śakti in union, which *divya* adepts experience not through ritualized intercourse but through meditation.

As in most religious communities, such oscillations between visible expression and inner meaning form a major dimension of Hindu life. The Tantric tradition exploits this dynamic exquisitely, yet few would doubt that it is exceptional. Publicly enacted rituals such as temple ceremonies, processions, pilgrimage, and home worship—each, admittedly, with possibilities for interpretation that are all its own—form the backbone of Hindu practice. To these we now turn, beginning with a set of rituals that many Hindus regard as the most important of all.

Domestic rites. The fire rituals that served as the core of Vedic religion have long since been supplanted in most Hindu practice by image worship, whether in home or temple settings, and by various forms of devotionalism. Yet in the arena of domestic (*gṛhya*) ritual one can still see formulas and sequences that survive from the Vedic period. The domestic rituals include five obligatory daily offerings: (1) offerings to the gods (food taken from the meal), (2) a cursory offering (*bali*) made to "all beings," (3) a libation of water and sesame, offered to the spirits of the deceased, (4) hospitality, and (5) recitation of the Veda. Although some traditions prescribe a definite ritual in which these five "sacrifices" are performed, in most cases the five daily offerings are merely a way of speaking about one's religious obligations in general.

The morning and evening adorations (*sandhyā*), a very important duty of the traditional householder, are mainly Vedic in character, but they have, by the addition of Purāṇic and Tantric elements, become lengthy rituals. If not shortened, the morning ceremonies consist of self-purification, bathing, prayers, and recitation of mantras, especially the *gāyatrī mantra* (Ṛg Veda 3.62.10), a prayer for spiritual stimulation addressed to the sun. The accompanying ritual comprises (1) the application of marks (TILAKS) on the forehead, characterizing the adherents of a particular religious community, (2) the presentation of offerings (water and flowers) to the Sun, and (3) meditative concentration. There are Śaiva and Vaiṣṇava variants, and some elements are optional. The observance of the daily obligations, including the care of bodily purity and professional duties, leads to mundane reward and helps to preserve the state of sanctity required to enter into contact with the divine.

A second major aspect of domestic rites comprises life-cycle rituals. These sacraments (*saṃskāra*) of refinement and transition are intended to make a person fit for a certain purpose or for the next stage in life by removing taints (sins) or by generating fresh qualities. In antiquity there was a great divergence of opinion about the number of RITES OF PASSAGE, but in later times 16 came to be regarded as the most important. Many of the traditional *saṃskāra*s cluster in childhood, extending even before birth to conception itself. The impregnation rite, consecrating the supposed time of conception, consists of a ritual meal of pounded rice (mixed "with various other things according to whether the married man desires a fair, brown, or dark son; a learned son; or a learned daughter"), an offering of rice boiled in milk, the sprinkling of the woman, and intercourse; all acts are also accompanied by mantras. In the third month of pregnancy, the rite called *puṃsavana* (begetting of a son) follows. The birth is itself the subject of elaborate ceremonies, the main features of which are an oblation of *ghī* (clarified butter) cast into the fire; the introduction of a pellet of honey and *ghī* into the newborn child's mouth, which according to many authorities is an act intended to produce mental and bodily strength; the murmuring of mantras for the sake of a long life; and rites to counteract inauspicious influences. Opinions vary as to when the name-giving ceremony should take place; in addition to the personal name, there is often another one that should be kept secret for fear of sinister designs against the child. However that may be, the defining moment comes when the father utters the child's name into its ear.

A hallmark of these childhood *saṃskāra*s, as one can see, is a general male bias and the conscripting of natural processes into a person evoked by cultural means and defined primarily by male actors. In the birth ritual (*jātakarma*) the manuals direct the father to breathe upon his child's head, in a transparent ritual co-opting of the role that biology gives the mother. In practice, however, the mother may join in this breathing ritual, thereby complicating the simple nature-to-culture logic laid out in the texts.

Going still further against the patriarchal grain, there exists an array of life-cycle rites that focus specifically upon the lives of girls and women. In South India, for instance, one finds an initiation rite (*viḷakkiṭu kalyāṇam*) that corresponds roughly to the male initiation called *upanayana*, and that gives girls the authority to light oil lamps and thereby become full participants in proper domestic worship. There are also rites celebrating first MENSTRUATION and marking various moments surrounding childbirth. Typically women themselves act as officiants.

In modern times many of the textually mandated *saṃskāra*s (with the exceptions of impregnation, initiation, and marriage) have fallen into disuse or are performed in an abridged or simplified form without Vedic mantras or a priest. For example, the important *upanayana* initiation should by rights be held when an upper-caste boy is between the ages of 8 and 12, to mark his entry into the ritual community defined by access to Vedic learning. In this rite he becomes a "twice-born one," or DVIJA, and is invested with the sacred thread (*upavīta; see* UPANAYANA). Traditionally, this was the beginning of a long period of Vedic study and education in the house and under the guidance of a teacher (guru). In modern practice, however, the haircutting ceremony—formerly performed in a boy's third year—and the initiation are often performed on the same day, and the homecoming ceremony at the end of the period of Vedic study often becomes little more than a formality, if it is observed at all. More extreme still, the *upanayana* might also be ignored until it is inserted as a prelude to marriage.

Wedding ceremonies, the most important of all *saṃskāra*s, have not only remained elaborate (and often very expensive) but have also incorporated various elements—among others, propitiations and expiations—that are not indicated in the oldest sources. In ancient times there already existed great divergences in accordance with local customs or family or caste traditions. However, the following practices are usually considered essential. The date is fixed after careful astrological calculation; the bridegroom is conducted to the home of his future parents-in-law, who receive him as an honored guest; there are offerings of roasted grain into the fire; the bridegroom has to take hold of the bride's hand; he conducts her around the sacrificial fire; seven steps are taken by bride and bridegroom to solemnize the irrevocability of the unity; both are, in procession, conducted to their new home, which the bride enters without touching the threshold.

Of eight forms of marriage recognized by the ancient authorities, two have remained in vogue: the simple gift of a girl and the legalization of the alliance by means of a marriage gift paid to the bride's family. Yet it is noteworthy that the payment of a dowry—often very large—to the groom has become far more typical. In the Vedic period, girls do not seem to have married before they reached maturity, but that too changed over time. By the 19th century child marriage and customary upper-caste bars to the remarriage of widows (often a pressing issue if young girls were married to much older men) had become urgent social concerns in certain parts of India. These practices have abated since the mid-19th century, but laws against child marriage have been required, and they are sometimes flouted even today.

The traditional funeral method is CREMATION (which involves the active participation of members of the family of the deceased), but burial or immersion is more appropriate for those who have not been so tainted by life in this world that they require the purifying fire (*i.e.,* children) and those who no longer need the ritual fire to be conveyed to the hereafter, such as ascetics who have renounced all earthly concerns. An important and meritorious complement of the funeral offices is the *śrāddha* ceremony, in which food is offered to Brahmins for the benefit of the deceased. Many people are solicitous to perform this rite at least once a year even when they no longer engage in any of the five obligatory daily offerings.

Temple worship. Image worship takes place both in small household shrines and in the temple. Many Hindu authorities claim that regular temple worship to one of the deities of the devotional cults procures the same results for the worshiper as did the performance of

Hindu wedding ceremony in Suriname
Porterfield/Chickering—Photo Researchers

the great Vedic sacrifices, and one who provides the patronage for the construction of a temple is called a "sacrificer" (*yajamāna*). More to the point, once they have been enlivened by a mantric process of ritual inauguration, the images (*mūrti*) installed in temples, shrines, and homes are regarded as participating in the actual substance of the deities they represent. Some are even said to be self-manifest (*svayambhū*). Hence to encounter them with the proper sentiment (*bhāva*) is to make actual contact with the divine. This happens through paradigmatic acts such as *darśan*, the reciprocal act of both "seeing" and being seen by the deity; ĀRATĪ, the illumination of the image and the receiving of that light by worshipers; and *prasāda*, food offerings which, after being partially or symbolically consumed by the deity, return to the worshipers as blessings from the divine repast.

The erection of a temple is a meritorious deed recommended to anyone desirous of heavenly reward. The choice of a site, which should be serene and lovely, is determined by ASTROLOGY and DIVINATION as well as by its location with respect to human dwellings; for example, a SANCTUARY of a benevolent deity should face the village. Temples vary greatly in size and artistic value, ranging from small village shrines with simple statuettes to the great temple-cities of South India whose boundary walls, pierced by monumental gates (*gopura*), enclose various buildings, courtyards, pools for ceremonial bathing, and sometimes even schools, hospitals, and monasteries. From the point of view of construction, there is no striking difference between Śaiva and Vaiṣṇava sanctuaries, but they are easily distinguishable by their central objects of worship (*e.g., mūrti, liṅga*), the images on their walls, the symbol fixed on their finials (crowning ornaments), and the presence of Shiva's bull, NANDĪ, or Vishnu's bird, Garuḍa (the theriomorphic duplicate manifestations of each god's nature), in front of the entrance.

Worship in Hindu temples takes place on a spectrum that runs from ceremonies characterized by fully orchestrated congregational participation to rituals focused almost entirely on the priests who act as the deities' ritual servants to episodic acts of prayer and offering initiated by families or individual worshipers. Sometimes worshipers assemble to meditate, to take part in singing and chanting, or to listen to an exposition of doctrine. The *pūjā* (worship) performed in public "for the well-being of the world" is, though sometimes more elaborate, largely identical with that executed for personal interest. It consists essentially of an invocation, a reception, and the entertainment of God as a royal guest. Paradigmatically, it involves 16 "attendances" (*upacāra*s): an invocation by which the omnipresent God is invited to direct his/her attention to the particular worship; the offering of a seat, water (for washing the feet and hands and for rinsing the mouth), a bath, a garment, a sacred thread, perfumes, flowers, incense, a lamp, food, homage, and a circumambulation of the image and dismissal by the deity. *Darśan, āratī,* and *prasāda* emerge as significant features of these "attendances," whether experienced at specific times of day (such as the eight "watches" that are observed in many Krishna temples) or according to a freer, perhaps sparser schedule. In front of certain temples, ritual possession sometimes also occurs.

Sacred times and places. *Festivals.* Hindu festivals are combinations of religious ceremonies, semiritual spectacles, worship, prayer, lustrations, processions (to set something sacred in motion and to extend its power throughout a certain region), music, dances, eating, drinking, lovemaking, licentiousness, feeding the poor, and other activities of a religious or traditional character. The functions of these activities are clear from both literary sources and anthropological observation: they are intended to purify, avert malicious influences, renew society, bridge over critical moments, and stimulate, celebrate, and resuscitate the vital powers of nature (and hence the term *utsava,* which means both the generation of power and a festival).

Calendrical festivals refresh the mood of the participants, further the consciousness of the participants' power, help to compensate for any sensations of fear or inferiority in relation to the great forces of nature, and generally enable participants as individuals and communities to align their own hopes with the rhythms of the cosmos. Hindu festivals are anchored in a lunar calendar that is brought into conformity with the solar calendar every three years by the addition of an intercalary month, the anomalous status of which renders it a particular focus of ritual attention. There are also innumerable festivities in honor of specific gods, celebrated by individual temples, villages, and religious communities.

Hindu festival calendars are so varied from region to region that it is difficult to describe them briefly. Merely as example, we introduce two festivals that function roughly as New Year's rites throughout much of northern and central India. The first is HOLĪ, a saturnalia connected with the spring equinox and, in western India, with the wheat harvest. The mythical tradition of the festival describes how young Prahlāda, in spite of his demonic father's opposition, persisted in worshiping Vishnu and was carried into the fire by the female demon Holikā, who believed herself to be immune to the ravages of fire. Through Vishnu's intervention, however, Prahlāda emerged unharmed, while Holikā was burned to ashes. The bonfires are intended to commemorate this event or rather to reiterate the triumph of virtue and religion over evil and sacrilege. This explains why objects representing the sickness and impurities of the past year (many people calculate the new year as beginning immediately after Holī) are thrown into the bonfire, and it is considered inauspicious not to look at it. Moreover, people pay or forgive debts, and try to rid themselves of the evils, conflicts, and impurities that have accumu-

Temple dedicated to the sun god Sūrya, showing a wheel of his sky-chariot, c. 1238–58, Konārak, Orissa, India
George Holton—Photo Researchers

lated during the prior months, translating the conception of the festival into a justification for dealing anew with continuing situations in their lives. Various enactments of chaos (*e.g.*, the throwing of colored water), reversal (a ritualized battle in which women wield clubs and men defend themselves with shields), and extremity (FIRE WALKING through the Holī bonfire) constitute the "body" of Holī. These contrast vividly with the decorous reaffirmations of social relations that ensue when they are done: people bathe, don clean clothing, and visit family and gurus. There are local variants on Holī; for example, among the MARĀṬHĀS, heroes who died on the battlefield are "danced" by their descendants, sword in hand, until the descendants become possessed by the spirits of the heroes. In Bengal and Braj, swings are made for Krishna.

An even more widely celebrated New Year festival called DĪVĀLĪ, or Dīpāvali, occurs on the

Temple dedicated to Shiva and Pārvatī, c. 1200, Halebīd, Karnataka, India
Porterfield/Chickering—Photo Researchers

new moon of the month of Kārttika in mid-autumn. It involves ceremonial lights welcoming Lakṣmī, the goddess of wealth and good fortune; fireworks said to chase away the spirits of wandering ghosts; and gambling, an old ritual custom intended to secure luck for the coming year. Like Holī, it concludes with an affirmation of ritual, social, and calendrical order; special attention is given to honoring cattle and to celebrating and sampling the fall harvest.

Pilgrimages. Like processions, pilgrimages (*tīrthayātrā*) to holy rivers, mountains, forests, and cities were already known in Vedic and epic times and remain today one of the most remarkable aspects of Indian religious life. It is often said that pilgrimage is a layperson's renunciation (*sannyāsa*): it is physically difficult, it means leaving behind the array of duties and pleasures associated with home and family, and it has for centuries been a major aspect of the lives of many ascetics. Various sections of the *Purāṇa*s eulogize temples and the sacredness of places situated in beautiful scenery or wild solitude (especially the HIMALAYAS). The whole of India is considered holy ground that offers everyone the opportunity to attain religious fulfillment, but certain sites have for many centuries been regarded as possessing exceptional holiness. The Sanskrit *Purāṇa*s often mention Ayodhya, Mathura, Hardwar, VARANASI (Banaras), Kanchipuram, Ujjain, and Dvaraka, but at the same time strong regional traditions create very different lists. The reason for the sanctity of such places derives from their location on the bank of a holy river (especially the Gaṅgā), from their connection with figures of antiquity who are said to have lived there, or from the local legend of a manifestation of a god. Many places are sacred to a specific divinity; the district of Mathura, for example, encompasses many places of pilgrimage connected with Krishna, especially VRINDĀBAD (Vṛndāvana) and Mount Govardhan. Pilgrimages to Gaya, Hardwar, and Varanasi are often undertaken for the sake of the welfare of deceased ancestors. In most cases, however, devotees hope for increased well-being for themselves and their families in this life (often in response to the fulfillment of a vow), for deliverance from sin or pollution, or for emancipation from the world altogether (*mokṣa*). The last prospect is held out to those who, when death is near, travel to Varanasi to die near the Gaṅgā.

On special occasions, be they auspicious or, like a solar eclipse, inauspicious, the devout crowds increase enormously. The most impressive of these is the KUMBH MELA, the world's most massive religious gathering (10 million pilgrims at Hardwar in 1998). The Kumbh Mela is largest when held at the confluence of the Gaṅgā and JAMUNĀ rivers at Prayāg (Allahabad) every 12 years. These and other pilgrimages have contributed much to the spread of religious ideas and the cultural unification of India.

The geography of Hindu pilgrimage is in a process of constant evolution. The mountain deities Vaiṣṇo Devī (in the Himalayas) and Aiyappan (in the Nilgiri Hills) attracted vastly increased numbers of pilgrims toward the end of the 20th century, as did gurus such as SATHYA SAI BABA at his centers in Andhra state and near Bangalore. Yet traditional Vaiṣṇava shrines such as Puri and TIRUPATI and Śaiva sites such as Amarnāth have kept pace. Given their typically fluid sense of the boundaries between Hinduism and other faiths, Hindus also flock to Muslim, Jain, and Christian places of pilgrimage; sacred and secular tourism (to destinations such as the Taj Mahal) are often combined.

REGIONAL EXPRESSIONS OF HINDUISM

Many of the most important magnets for Hindu pilgrimage are regional in focus—*e.g.*, Śrīrangam for Tamil Nadu, PANDHARPUR for Maharashtra, or Gaṅgāsāgar for Bengal. Similarly, Hindu life is expressed in a variety of "mother tongue" languages that contrast vividly to pan-Indian Sanskrit. The localized sacred literatures are related in complex ways to Sanskrit texts and, crucially, each other.

Of the four primary Dravidian literatures—Tamil, Telugu, Kannada, and Malayalam—the oldest and best known is Tamil. The earliest preserved Tamil literature, the so-called *Caṅkam*, or *Saṅgam*, poetry anthologies, dates from the 1st century BCE. These poems are classified by theme into *akam* ("interior," primarily love poetry) and *puṟam* ("exterior," primarily about war, the poverty of poets, and the deaths of kings). The *bhakti* movement has been traced to Tamil poetry, beginning with the poems of the devotees of Shiva (Nāyaṉārs) and the devotees of Vishnu (Āḻvārs). The Nāyaṉārs, who date from about 500–750 CE, composed hymns addressed to the local manifestations of Shiva in which they "dance, weep, worship him, sing his feet." The most famous Nāyaṉār lyricists are Appar (whose words were just quoted, from Indira Peterson's translation), Campantar, and Cuntarar; their hymns are collected in the *Tevāram* (*c.* 11th century).

More or less contemporary were their Vaiṣṇava counterparts, the Āḻvārs, including the poetess ĀṆṬĀḶ, the untouchable-caste poet TIRUPPAN, and the farmer-caste Nammāḻvār, who is held to be the greatest. Whether Śaiva or Vaiṣṇava, their devotion exemplifies the *bhakti* movement, which values direct contact between human beings and God (especially as expressed in song), challenges rigidities of caste and ritual, and celebrates the experience of divine grace. These saints became the inspiration for major theological systems: the Śaivas for the Śaiva Siddhānta, the Vaiṣṇavas for VIŚIṢṬĀDVAITA. In Kannada the same movement was exemplified by poet-saints such as BASAVA and MAHĀDEVĪ, whose utterances achieved great popularity. Their religion, Vīraśaivism, was perhaps the most "protestant" version of *bhakti* religion.

New Dravidian genres continued to evolve into the 17th and 18th centuries, when the Tamil Cittars (from the Sanskrit SIDDHA, "perfected one"), who were eclectic mystics, composed poems noted for the power of their naturalistic diction. The Tamil sense and style of these poems belied the Sanskrit-derived title of their authors, a phenomenon that could stand as a symbol of the complex relationship between Dravidian and Sanskrit religious texts.

From middle India northward one encounters Indo-Aryan vernaculars related to Sanskrit, including Bengali, Hindi (the most important literary dialects of which are Brajbhāṣā and Avadhī and which bleeds into Urdu, with its increased Perso-Arabic content), Punjabi, Gujarati, Marathi, Oriya, Kashmiri, Sindhi, Assamese,

Nepali, Rajasthani, and Sinhalese. Most of these languages began to develop literary traditions around 1000 CE.

Marathi was the first to develop a substantial corpus of *bhakti* poetry and HAGIOGRAPHY, starting with the 13th–14th-century Vaiṣṇava saints JÑĀNEŚVAR and NĀMDEV, both of whom especially praised the deity Viṭṭhal (Viṭhobā) of Pandharpur, as did Jñāneśvar's sister Muktābāī and the untouchable saint COKHĀMELĀ (14th century). TUKĀRĀM (17th century), with his searchingly autobiographical poems, was to become the most famous of these Vārkarī (literally, "Pilgrim") poets.

Religious poetry of enduring significance in Hindi starts with a collection of antinomian, Haṭha Yoga *bānī* (utterances) attributed to GORAKHNĀTH in perhaps the 14th century and continues with the interior-oriented, iconoclastic poet-saint Kabīr (15th century). The earliest dated manuscripts for Hindi *bhakti* emerge toward the end of the 16th century, placing Kabīr alongside NĀNAK (the founder of SIKHISM) in one collection and alongside SŪRDĀS (16th-century Krishna lyricist) in another. The earliest hagiographies (*c.* 1600), written by Anantadās and Nābhādās, tend to firm up this distinction between *sant*s like Nānak or Kabīr and Vaiṣṇavas like Sūrdās or MĪRĀBĀĪ, though not absolutely. Sūrdās with his *Sūrsāgar* ("Sūr's Ocean") and Tulsīdās (16th–17th century) with his *Rāmcaritmānas* ("Sacred Lake of the Acts of Rāma") vie for the honor of being Hindi's greatest poets. Mīrābāī is equally well known, though the corpus of romantic Krishna poetry attributed to her is almost completely unattested before the 19th century and shows evidence of complex patterns of oral transmission in Gujarati, Rajasthani, and Brajbhāṣā. Hindi poets such as Sūrdās and the low-caste leatherworker Ravidās mention the Marathi poet Nāmdev, showing the importance of cross-regional affiliations, and Nāmdev has an independent corpus of poetry in Hindi and Punjabi.

Although the earliest Hindu text in Bengali is a mid-15th-century poem about Rādhā and Krishna, medieval texts in praise of gods and goddesses, known as MAṄGAL-KĀVYAS, must have existed in oral versions long before that. In later Bengal Vaiṣṇavism, the emphasis shifts from service and surrender to mutual attachment and attraction between God (*i.e.*, Krishna) and humankind: God is said to yearn for the worshiper's identification with himself, which is his gift to the wholly purified devotee. Thus, the highest fruition of *bhakti* is admission to the eternal sport of Krishna and his beloved Rādhā, which is sometimes glossed as the mutual love of God and the human soul. The best-known poets in this vein are the Bengali Caṇḍīdās (*c.* 1400) and the Maithili poet Vidyāpati (*c.* 1400). The greatest single influence was Caitanya, who in the 16th century renewed Krishnaism with his emphasis on community chanting and celebration (*saṃkīrtan*) and his dedication to what he saw as the renaissance of Vaiṣṇava culture in Braj, where Krishna is thought to have spent his youth. Caitanya left next to no writings of his own, but he inspired many hagiographies, among the more important of which is the *Caitanya Caritāmṛta* ("Nectar of Caitanya's Life") by Krishna Dās (born 1517). Almost equally influential, in a very different way, were the songs of RĀMPRASĀD SEN (1718–75), which honor Śakti as mother of the universe and are still in wide devotional use. The Śākta heritage was continued in the poetry of Kamalākānta Bhaṭṭācārya (*c.* 1769–1821) and eventually culminated in the ecstatic RAMAKRISHNA PARAMAHAMSA (1836–86), whose inspiration caused VIVEKANANDA to establish the Rāmakrishna Maṭh in India and the VEDĀNTA Society in the West.

Numerous important works of Hindu literature are omitted from this brief survey, not only in the five regional languages we have mentioned but even more so in Gujarati, Telugu, Maliyalam, and a host of others. We have focused primarily on *bhakti* lyrics, but these are complemented by a range of vernacular epics, such as the Tamil, Telugu, and Bengali *Rāmāyaṇa*s of Kampan, Buddharāja, and Kṛttibāsa (11th–14th centuries), respectively, and the highly individual *Mahābhārata* of the 16th-century Kannada poet Gadugu. The Tamils composed their own epics, notably Ilaṅkō Aṭikaḷ's CILAPPATIKĀRAM ("The Lay of the Anklet") and its sequel, *Maṇimekhalai* ("The Jeweled Girdle"). In Telugu there is the great Palnāḍu Epic; Rajasthani has an entire epic cycle about the hero Pabuji; and Hindi has its *Ālhā* and *Ḍholā*, the latter with a lower-caste base and focusing on the goddess Śakti.

This only begins to scratch the surface of a massive "literature" of oral performance that includes dance and theatre. Almost all of it is ritually circumscribed in some way, and some is actually performed in temple contexts, but that is not to underestimate the importance of a poem of Sūrdās or Kabīr that gets sung by a blind singer moving from car to car on a local train on the vast plains of North India. Nor is it meant to understate the influence of cassette recordings of devotional songs in a host of regional languages or the evident power of nationally televised Hindi versions of the *Mahābhārata, Rāmāyaṇa,* and *Bhāgavata Purāṇa.* Rāmānand Sāgar's *Rāmāyaṇa* (1987–88), which claimed a heritage including versions of the epic in a dozen languages but drew mainly from Tulsīdās' *Rāmcaritmānas,* was easily the most-watched program ever aired on Indian television. The vast majority of India's population is reported to have seen at least one weekly episode, and many people were loathe to miss a single one.

SOCIAL CORRELATES OF RELIGION

Caste. The origin of the so-called caste system is not known with certainty. Hindus attribute the proliferation of the castes (*jātis*) to the subdivision of the four classes, or *varṇas,* due to intermarriage (which is prohibited in Hindu works on dharma). Modern theorists, however, tend to assume that castes arose from differences in family ritual practices, racial distinctions, and occupational differentiation and specialization. Many modern scholars doubt whether the simple *varṇa* system was ever more than a theoretical socioreligious ideal and have emphasized that the highly complex division of Hindu society into nearly 3,000 castes and subcastes was probably in place even in ancient times.

In general, a caste is an endogamous hereditary group of families bearing a common name, often claiming a common descent, as a rule professing to follow the same hereditary calling, and maintaining the same customs. Moreover, tribes, guilds, or religious communities characterized by particular customs—for example, the Vīraśaivas—could easily be regarded as castes. The status of castes varies in different localities, and especially in urban settings social mobility is possible.

Traditional Hindus are inclined to emphasize that the ritual impurity and "untouchability" inherent in these groups does not essentially differ from that temporarily proper for mourners or menstruating women. This, and the fact that some exterior group or other might rise in estimation and become an interior one or that individual outcastes might be well-to-do, does not alter the fact that the spirit of exclusiveness was in the course of time carried to extremes. The lower, or scheduled, castes were subjected to various socioreligious disabilities before mitigating tendencies helped bring about reform. After India's independence, social discrimination was prohibited, the practice of untouchability was made a punishable offense, and various programs of social amelioration were instituted, including the reservation of a certain percentage of places in educational institutions and government jobs for lower-caste applicants. Before that time, however, scheduled castes were often openly barred from the use of temples and other religious institutions and from public schools, and these groups faced many oppressive restrictions in their relations with individuals of higher caste. Hindu texts such as the *Manu-smṛti* were seen to justify low social status, explaining it as the inevitable result of sins in a former life.

Social protest. For many centuries India has known religious communities dedicated in whole or in part to the elimination of caste discrimination. Many have been guided by *bhakti* sentiments, including the Vīraśaivas, Sikhs, Kabīr Panthīs, Satnāmīs, and Rāmnāmīs, all of whom bear

Sadā Shiva with Nandī and the flowing Gaṅgā, Bikaner school, mid-17th century; Guimet Museum, Paris
Giraudon—Art Resource

a complicated relation to the greater Hindu fold. A major theme in *bhakti* poetry throughout India has been the ridicule of caste and the etiquette of ritual purity that relates to it, although this element is stronger on the *nirguṇa* side of the *bhakti* spectrum than the *saguṇa*.

Other religions have provided members of low-ranked castes with a further hope for escaping social hierarchies associated with Hindu practice. Sikhism has already been mentioned. ISLAM played this role in Kerala from the 8th century onward and elsewhere in India since the 12th century, although certain convert groups have retained their original caste organization even after embracing Islam. CHRISTIANITY has exercised a similar force, serving for centuries as a magnet for disadvantaged Hindus. And in 1956 B.R. Ambedkar, the principal framer of the Indian constitution and a member of the scheduled MAHAR caste, abandoned Hinduism for Buddhism, eventually to be followed by millions of his lower-caste followers. Yet many Ambedkarite DALITS ("the Oppressed") continue to venerate saints such as Kabīr, Cokhāmelā, and Ravidās who figure in the general lore of Hindu *bhakti*. Other Dalits, especially members of the CAMĀR caste (traditionally leatherworkers), have gone further, identifying themselves explicitly as Ravidāsīs, creating a scripture that features his poetry, and building temples that house his image. Still other Dalit communities have claimed since the early 20th century that they represent India's original religion (*ādi dharma*), rejecting caste-coded Vedic beliefs and practices as perversions introduced by Aryan invaders in the 2nd millennium BCE.

Renunciants and the rejection of social order.   Another means of rejecting the social order that forms the background for significant portions of Hindu belief and practice is the institution of renunciation. The rituals of *sannyāsa*, which serve archetypally as gateway to a life of religious discipline, often mimic death rituals, signifying the renouncer's understanding that she or, more typically, he no longer occupies a place in family or society. Other rituals serve a complementary function, inducting the initiate into a new family—the alternative family provided by a celibate religious order, usually focused on a guru. In principle this family should not be structured along the lines of caste, and the initiate should pledge to renounce commensal dietary restrictions. In practice, however, some dietary restrictions remain in India's most influential renunciant communities (though not in all), and certain renunciant orders are closely paired with specific communities

World distribution of Hinduism

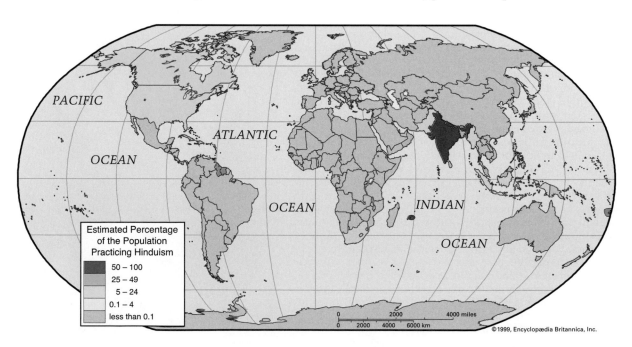

Estimated Percentage of the Population Practicing Hinduism

	50 – 100
	25 – 49
	5 – 24
	0.1 – 4
	less than 0.1

©1999, Encyclopædia Britannica, Inc.

of householders. This crystallizes a pattern that is loosely present everywhere. Householders and renouncers offer each other mutual benefits, with the former dispensing material substance to the theoretically propertyless renunciants while the latter dispense religious merit and spiritual guidance in return. Such an enactment of the values of dharma and *mokṣa* is symbiotic, to be sure, but that does not serve to domesticate renunciants entirely. Their existence questions the ultimacy of anything tied to caste, hierarchy, and bodily well-being.

HINDUISM AND THE WORLD BEYOND

Hinduism and religions of Indian origin.   Hinduism, Buddhism, and JAINISM originated out of the same milieu: the circles of world renouncers of the 6th century BCE. Although all share certain non-Vedic practices (such as renunciation itself and various yogic meditational techniques) and doctrines (such as the belief in rebirth and the goal of liberation from perpetual transmigration), Buddhists and Jains do not accept the authority of the Vedic tradition and therefore are regarded as less than orthodox by Hindus. Especially in the 6th–11th centuries there was strong and sometimes bloody competition for royal patronage among the three communities—with Brahmins representing Hindu values—as well as between Vaiṣṇavas and Śaivas. In general the Brahmin groups prevailed. In a typically absorptive gesture, Hindus in time recognized the Buddha as an incarnation of Vishnu—usually the ninth—but this was often qualified by the caveat that Vishnu assumed this form to mislead and destroy the enemies of the Veda. Hence, the Buddha avatar is rarely worshiped by Hindus, though often highly respected. At an institutional level, certain Buddhist shrines, such as the one marking the Buddha's Enlightenment at BODH GAYĀ, have remained partly under the supervision of Hindu ascetics and are visited by Hindu pilgrims.

After the rise of Buddhological studies in the West combined with the archaeological discoveries and restorations that began at the end of the 19th century, thus clarifying the ecumenical achievements of the Buddhist emperor AŚOKA, the Republic of India adopted the lion capital of the pillar found at Sarnath, which marked the place of the Buddha's first teaching, as its national emblem. Hinduism has so much in common with Jainism, which until recently remained an Indian religion, especially in social institutions and ritual life, that nowadays many Hindus tend to consider it a Hindu sect. The points of difference—*e.g.*, a stricter practice of *ahiṃsā* and the absence of sacrifices for the deceased in Jainism—do not give offense to orthodox Hindus. Moreover, many Jain laypeople worship images as Hindus do, though with a different rationale. There are even places outside India where Hindus and Jains have joined to build a single temple, sharing the worship space.

Hinduism and Islam.   Hindu relations with Islam and Christianity are in some ways quite different from the ties and tensions that bind together religions of Indian origin. Hindus live with a legacy of domination by Muslim and Christian rulers that stretches back many centuries—in North India, to the Delhi Sultanate established at the beginning of the 13th century. It is hardly the case that Muslim rule was generally loathsome to Hindus. Direct and indirect patronage from the Mughal emperors AKBAR (1542–1605) and Jahāngīr (1569–1627), whose chief generals were Hindu Rājpūts, laid the basis for the great burst of Krishnaite temple and institution building that transformed the Braj region beginning in the 16th century. Yet there were periods when the political ambitions of Islamic rulers took strength from iconoclastic aspects of Muslim teaching and led to the devastation of many major Hindu temple complexes, from Mathura and Varanasi in the north to Chidambaram and MADURAI in the far south; other temples were converted to mosques. Episodically, since the 14th century, this history has provided rhetorical fuel for Hindu warriors eager to assert themselves against Muslim rivals. The bloody partition of the South Asian subcontinent into India and Pakistan in 1947 added a new dimension. Mobilizing Hindu sensibilities about the sacredness of the land as a whole, extremists have sometimes depicted the creation of Pakistan as a rape of the body of India, in the process demonizing Muslims who remain within the political boundaries of India.

These strands converged at the end of the 20th century in a campaign to destroy the mosque built in 1528 by a lieutenant of the Mughal emperor Bābar in Ayodhya, a city that has since the 2nd century been identified with the place so named in the *Rāmāyaṇa*, where Rāma was born and ruled. In 1992 Hindu militants from all over India, who had been organized by the Vishwa Hindu Parishad (VHP: "World Hindu Council"), the Rashtriya Swayamsevak Sangh (RSS: "National Volunteer Alliance"), and the BHARATIYA JANATA PARTY (BJP: "Indian People's Party"), destroyed the mosque in an effort to "liberate" Rāma and establish a huge "Rāma's Birthplace Temple" on the spot. In the aftermath, several thousand people—mostly Muslims—were killed in riots that spread across North India.

The conflict in Ayodhya illustrated some of the complexities of Hindu-Hindu and Hindu-Muslim relations. The local police force, having been largely purged of its Muslim members shortly after partition and independence, was largely inactive. Certain leaders from Ayodhya's several communities of Hindu ascetics joined the militants, while others regarded the militants' actions as an outsiders' takeover that was injurious to their own standing and integrity. Local Muslims, who had for centuries lived at peace with Hindu neighbors, reflected bitterly on the fact that Hindu mobs also attacked an outlying shrine to a Muslim *pīr* (holy man) whose annual festival (*'urs*) typically attracted even more Hindu worshipers than Muslims. A Delhi-based artists' collective, echoing a lament that was voiced by millions of Hindus, mounted an exhibition called "We Are All Ayodhya," which documented the city's vividly multireligious history and traveled both in India and abroad.

Hinduism and Christianity.   Relations between Hinduism and Christianity have also been shaped by unequal balances of political power and cultural influence. Although communities of Christians have lived in South India since the middle of the 1st millennium, the great expansion of Indian Christianity followed the efforts of missionaries working under the protection of British colonial rule. Their denigration of selected features of Hindu practice—most notably, image worship, *satī*, and child marriage (the first two had also been criticized by Muslims)—was shared by certain Hindus. Beginning in the 19th century and continuing to the present, a movement that might be called neo-Vedānta has emphasized the monism of certain Upanishads, decried "popular" Hindu "degenerations" such as the worship of idols, acted as an agent of social reform, and championed dialogue between other religious communities.

Relations between Hindus and Christians are complicated. Many Hindus are ready to accept the ethical teachings of the Gospels, particularly the SERMON ON THE MOUNT (whose influence on GANDHI is well-known), but reject the theological superstructure. They are apt to regard Christian conceptions about love and its social consequences as a kind of *bhakti* and to venerate Jesus as a saint, yet many resent the organization and the exclusiveness of Islam and Christianity, considering these as obstacles to harmonious cooperation. They subscribe to Gandhi's opinion that missionaries should confine their activities to humanitarian service and look askance at conversion, finding also in Hinduism what might be attractive in Christianity. Such sentiments took an unusually extreme form at the end of the 20th century when Hindu activists attacked Dalit Christians and their churches in various parts of India, especially Orissa and Gujarat. A far more typical sentiment is expressed in the eagerness of Hindus of all social stations, especially the middle class, to send their children to high-quality (often English-language) schools established and maintained by Christian organizations.

Diasporic Hinduism.   Since the appearance of Swami Vivekananda at the World's Parliament of Religions in Chicago in 1893 and the subsequent establishment of the Vedānta Society in various American and British cities, Hinduism has had a growing missionary profile outside the Indian subcontinent. Conversion as understood by Christians or Muslims is usually not the aim. As seen in the Vedānta Society, Hindu perspectives are held to be sufficiently capacious that they do not require new adherents to abandon traditions of worship with which they are familiar, merely to see them as part of a greater whole. The Vedic formula "Truth is one, but scholars speak of it in many ways" (*ekam sat vipra bahudhā* *vadanti*) is much quoted. Many transnational Hindu communities, including Radhasoami, TRANSCENDENTAL MEDITATION, Siddha Yoga, the SELF-REALIZATION FEL-LOWSHIP, the Sathya Sai Baba Satsang, and the International Society for Krishna Consciousness (ISKCON, popularly called Hare Krishna), have tended to focus on specific gurus, particularly in their stages of most rapid growth. They frequently emphasize techniques of spiritual discipline more than doctrine. Of the groups just mentioned, only ISKCON has a deeply exclusivist cast—which makes it, in fact, generally more doctrinaire than the Gauḍīya Vaiṣṇava lineages out of which its founding guru, A.C. Bhaktivedanta, emerged.

At least as important as these guru-centered communities in the increasingly international texture of Hindu life are communities of Hindus who have emigrated from South Asia to other parts of the world. Their character differs markedly according to region, class, and the time at which emigration occurred. Tamils in Malaysia celebrate a festival to the god Murukan (Thaipusam) that accommodates body-piercing vows long outlawed in India itself. Formerly indentured laborers who settled in the Caribbean island Trinidad in the mid-19th century have tended to consolidate doctrine and practice from various locales in Gangetic India, with the result that Rāma and Sītā have a heightened profile. Many migrants from rural western India, especially Gujarat, became urbanized in East Africa in the late 19th century and have now resettled in Britain. Like those Gujaratis who came directly to the United States from India since the liberalization of U.S. immigration laws in 1965, once abroad they are more apt to embrace the reformist guru-centered SWĀMĪNĀRĀYAṆ faith than they would be in their native Gujarat, though this is by no means universal.

Professional-class emigrants from South India have spearheaded the construction of a series of impressive Śrī Vaiṣṇava-style temples throughout the United States, sometimes taking advantage of financial and technical assistance from the great Vaiṣṇava temple institutions at Tirupati. The siting of some of these temples, such as the Penn Hills temple near Pittsburgh, Pennsylvania, reveals an explicit desire to bring forth resonances of Tirupati's natural environment on American soil. Similarly, Telugu-speaking priests from the Tirupati region have been imported to serve at temples such as the historically important GAṆEŚA temple, constructed from a preexisting church in Queens, New York City, in 1975–77. Yet the population who worship at these temples tends to be far more mixed than one would find in India. This produces sectarian and regional eclecticism on the one hand—images and shrines that appeal to a wide variety of devotional tastes—and on the other hand a vigorous attempt to establish doctrinal common ground. As Vasudha Narayanan has observed, educational materials produced at such temples typically hold that Hinduism is not a religion but a way of life, that it insists in principle on religious tolerance, that its Godhead is functionally trinitarian (the male *trimūrti* of Brahmā, Vishnu, and Shiva is meant, although temple worship is often very active at goddesses' shrines), and that Hindu rituals have inner meanings consonant with scientific principles and conducive to good health.

Pacific and ecumenical as this sounds, members of such temples are also important contributors to the VHP, whose efforts since 1964 to find common ground among disparate Hindu groups have sometimes also contributed to displays of Hindu nationalism such as were seen at Ayodhya in 1992. As the 21st century opens, there is a vivid struggle between "left" and "right" within the Hindu fold, with diasporic groups playing a more important role than ever before. Because of their wealth and education, because globalizing processes lend them prestige and enable them to communicate constantly with Hindus living in South Asia, and because their experience as minorities tends to set them apart from their families in India itself, their contribution to the evolution of Hinduism is sure to be a very interesting one. As we have seen, "Hinduism" was originally an outsider's word, and it designates a multitude of realities defined by period, time, sect, class, and caste. Yet the veins and bones that hold this complex organism together are not just chimeras of external perception. Hindus themselves—particularly diasporic Hindus—affirm them, accelerating a process of self-definition that has been going on for millennia.

HINDU MAHĀSABHĀ

HINDU MAHĀSABHĀ \'hin-dü-mə-,hä-'sə-bə, -mə-'hä-sə-'bä\ (Hindi: "Great Assembly of Hindus"), organization founded in 1915 as a confederation of a number of previously existing groups that had arisen in Bengal and the Punjab to lobby for what they perceived as Hindu political interests.

Established in a period when Muslim nationalism had a considerable impact on South Asia (the All India Muslim League was founded in 1906), the Mahāsabhā envisioned an Indian nation responsive to the customs and ideals of its Hindu majority. Yet its leaders differed on how this could best be achieved. One early leader, Lajpat Rai, proposed a partition of the subcontinent between Hindus and Muslims, while another pillar, Madan Mohan Malaviya, the founder of Banaras Hindu University, continued active in the more inclusive and secular Congress Party led by Jawaharlal Nehru and MOHANDAS GANDHI.

In the 1930s and '40s the Mahāsabhā came under the influence of Vinayak Damodar Savarkar (1883–1966), one of the most important ideologues of Hindu religious nationalism. In addition to his stand on other political issues (the protection of cows, CASTE reforms, and the adoption of Hindi as the national language), Savarkar argued that from among all of India's diverse religious groups "only the Hindus are a nation because they are bound by a common culture, common language (Sanskrit) and common religion." He further claimed that India was a "Hindu holyland" and those who did not accept it as such should be considered mere "guests" in that nation upon independence.

In 1931 Savarkar merged the youth wing of his Mahāsabhā with the militant Hindu nationalist group,

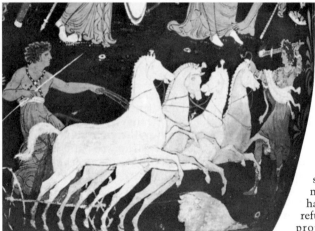

Hippolytus in his chariot, detail from a Greek vase
By courtesy of the trustees of the British Museum

the Rashtriya Swayamsevak Sangh, or RSS, a group to which the Mahāsabhā maintained close ties and one that survives to this day. When Gandhi was assassinated by a member of the Mahāsabhā in 1949, the group was banned and soon thereafter became for all intents and purposes defunct.

HINDUTVA \hin-'dùt-və\ (Sanskrit and Hindi: "Hinduness"), concept of Indian cultural, national, and religious identity first articulated in a book written by the Hindu nationalist leader Vinayak Damodar SAVARKAR while he was in prison for sedition in 1922. It has subsequently become the centerpiece of the Hindu nationalist movement in all its forms.

Savarkar defined a Hindu as "a person who regards the land of Bharat Varsha [India], from the Indus to the Seas, as his Father-Land as well as his Holy-Land," and *hindutva* embodied that identity. The term thus conflates a geographically based religious, cultural, and national identity: a true "Indian" is one who partakes of this "Hindu-ness."

Some Indians insist, however, that *hindutva* is primarily a cultural term to refer to the traditional and indigenous heritage of the Indian nation-state, and they compare the relationship between *hindutva* and India to that of ZIONISM and Israel. According to this view, even those who are not religiously Hindu but whose religions originated in India—Jains, Buddhists, Sikhs, and others—share in this historical, cultural, and national essence. Those whose religions were imported to India, meaning primarily the country's Muslim and Christian communities, may fall within the boundaries of *hindutva* only if they subsume themselves into the majority culture.

Hindutva has become the rallying cry of the Hindu nationalist movement, which achieved a large measure of political success in the 1980s and '90s. Its meaning and ramifications are controversial and disputed, especially by many Muslims living in India and by the advocates of an Indian nationalism based on secular principles.

HIPPOLYTUS \hi-'pä-lə-təs\, minor divinity in GREEK RELIGION. At Athens he was associated with APHRODITE, the goddess of love; at Troezen, girls dedicated a lock of their hair to him prior to marrying. To the Greeks his name suggested that he was destroyed by horses.

In Euripides' tragedy *Hippolytus* he was son of THESEUS, king of Athens, and the AMAZON Hippolyte. Theseus' queen, Phaedra, fell in love with Hippolytus. He reacted to her advances with such revulsion that she killed herself, leaving a note accusing Hippolytus of having attacked her. Theseus, refusing to believe Hippolytus' protestations of innocence, banished him and called down upon him one of the three curses the sea god POSEIDON had given to him. Poseidon sent a sea monster that frightened Hippolytus' horses until he could no longer control them. They smashed the chariot and dragged their master to death.

HIRATA ATSUTANE \hē-'rä-tä-,ä-tsû-'tä-nä\ (b. Sept. 25, 1776, Akita, Japan—d. Oct. 4, 1843, Akita), thinker and leader of the Japanese Restoration SHINTŌ (also known as Fukko Shintō) school. His thought, stressing the divine nature of the emperor, exerted a powerful influence on royalists who fought for the restoration of imperial rule during the second half of the 19th century.

At the age of 20, Hirata moved to Edo (modern Tokyo). He studied NEO-CONFUCIANISM but turned to Shintō, becoming a disciple of MOTOORI NORINAGA, one of the pioneers of the National Learning (KOKUGAKU) movement. Hirata attempted to develop a Shintō theological system that would provide normative principles for social and political action. In his later years he became increasingly critical of the Tokugawa shogunate's reduction of the emperor to a powerless symbol; as a result Hirata was confined to his birthplace for the rest of his life.

Hirata preached Japan's natural superiority as the land of the gods, who transmit the "True Way" to Japan through the imperial line. Despite his nationalism and xenophobia, he accepted certain features of Western science he learned through Chinese translations, even drawing on theology written by JESUIT missionaries in China.

HIRSCH, SAMSON RAPHAEL \'hirsh, 'hərsh\ (b. June 20, 1808, Hamburg [Ger.]—d. Dec. 31, 1888, Frankfurt am Main, Ger.), major Jewish religious thinker and founder of Trennungsorthodoxie (Separatist Orthodoxy), or Neo-Orthodoxy, a theological system that helped make ORTHODOX JUDAISM viable in Germany.

Hirsch was a RABBI successively in Oldenburg, Emden, Nikolsburg, and Frankfurt am Main. While still chief rabbi at Oldenburg, he published *Neunzehn Briefe über Judenthum* (1836; *Nineteen Letters of Ben Uziel*), in which he expounded Neo-Orthodoxy. This system required two chief courses of action: (1) an educational program that combined strict training in the TORAH with a modern secular education—so that Orthodoxy could withstand the challenge of REFORM JUDAISM; and (2) a separation of Orthodox congregations from the larger Jewish community when the latter deviated from a strict adherence to Jewish tradition. In 1876 Hirsch was a prime mover in getting the Prussian parliament to pass a law permitting Jews to secede from the state-recognized Jewish religious community (which Hirsch considered unfaithful to the Torah) and to establish separate congregations. Among his many works are *Horeb, Versuche über Jissroéls Pflichten in der Zerstreuung* (1837; "Essays on the Duties of the Jewish People in the Diaspora"), an Orthodox textbook on JUDAISM, and commentaries on the PENTATEUCH (1867–78). He founded (1855) and edited the monthly *Jeshurun* (the poetic name for Israel). Six volumes of his essays were published in 1902–12.

HIRSCH, SAMUEL \'hirsh, 'hərsh\ (b. June 8, 1815, Thalfang, near Trier, Prussia [now Germany]—d. May 14, 1889, Chicago, Ill., U.S.), religious philosopher, RABBI, and a leading advocate of radical REFORM JUDAISM. He was among the first to propose holding Jewish services on Sunday.

Educated at the universities of Bonn, Berlin, and Leipzig, Hirsch became rabbi at Dessau in 1838 but was forced to resign (1841) because of his views. From 1843 to 1866 he served as chief rabbi of the Grand Duchy of Luxembourg. Called to Philadelphia in 1866 to succeed David Einhorn as head of the Reform Congregation Keneseth Israel, he remained in that position for 22 years. He was elected president of the rabbinical conference held in Philadelphia in 1869 and in that capacity helped formulate the principles of Reform Judaism. The conference proclaimed that the dispersal of the Jews was part of a divine plan to lead all nations of the world to the true knowledge and worship of God. For Hirsch, Judaism was not law but doctrine, which was expressed in symbolic ceremonies that should change as needs require. His most ambitious work was *Religionsphilosophie der Juden*, 2 vol. (1842).

HISBA \'his-bə\, in the law and custom of ISLAM, the practice of overseeing public morality and, especially, fair trading in the marketplace. This custom became especially developed during the time of the 'Abbāsid dynasty when the responsibility for the practice of *hisba* was bestowed upon the *muhtasib*. The *muhtasib* was charged with regulating daily affairs and was the officer that the small craftsman or merchant turned to first. He was responsible for bringing wrongdoers to justice and for punishing drunkards and the unchaste with flogging. He also had the duty to amputate the hands of thieves caught in the act. *Hisba* is a practice thus designed to promote Islamic morals in the Muslim community.

HISTORICAL RELIGION, religion that entails history and linear time as an essential element in its concept of community, salvation, and truth. The 19th-century Pan-Babylonian school used the concept to draw a distinction between biblical and Hellenistic religious concepts of historical and cyclical time, and the distinction made by the school—"Jerusalem/Athens"—remains popular to this day. Historical religion is usually identified with JUDAISM and CHRISTIANITY in contrast to cyclical/mythical religions such as HINDUISM, BUDDHISM, and TAOISM. The concept was often used to draw a distinction between what was seen as the truth of historical religions as opposed to mythical religions of non-Western cultures. It is no longer in use in contemporary studies of religion.

HISTORICISM \hi-'stȯr-ə-,si-zəm, -'stär-\, view that the law of existence is change. Historicism emerged in the 19th century as an alternative to Enlightenment thinking concerning the universal nature of reason and morality in human existence. Historicism posited that as reason and morality were in themselves products of history, they too were subject to change. Historicism also opposed any transcendental norms or metaphysical principles. Values, religion, morality, and reason itself were subject to historical contexts and thus explained by contextual description. This objective and autonomous view of history gave rise to the establishment of history as an independent academic discipline separate from philosophy and theology. The rise of historiography had an important impact on the STUDY OF RELIGION as an academic inquiry. The historical-contextual method became the framework for biblical studies and what eventually became known as the history of religions, which attempted a value-free, or objective, approach to the study of religion.

The notion that all human events are historically constituted contained the seed of historical RELATIVISM and the inevitable conclusion that given the historicist law of change there could be no such thing as value-free historical analysis. To posit such a principle contradicted the law of existence as change. The late 20th-century emergence of a "new historicism," or "neo-historicism," emphasizes the radical notion that all knowledge is relative to the standpoint of the author. Thus, theory is introduced once again as crucial to the study of other social and cultural histories and the history of everyday life. *See also* INTERPRETATION.

HISTORY OF RELIGIONS: *see* RELIGIONSGESCHICHTLICHE SCHULE.

HITOGAMI \hē-,tō-'gä-mē\ (Japanese: "man-god"), category of Japanese RELIGIOUS BELIEF and practice that depends on the close relationship between a deity and his transmitter, such as a seer or a SHAMAN. As a religious system, *hitogami* is based on personal faith and contrasts with the UJIGAMI ("guardian deity") system, which is dependent on family or geographic origin. The *hitogami* type of belief is evident in the deification of heroes such as HACHIMAN and Tenjin, god of calligraphy; in the ecstatic singing and dancing of Japanese festival processions; and in the charismatic leadership of some of the new religions of Japan.

HITO-NO-MICHI \hē-'tō-ˌnō-'mē-chē\ (Japanese: "Way of Man"), Japanese religious sect founded by Miki Tokuharu (1871–1938); it was revived in a modified form after World War II as PL KYŌDAN (from the English words "perfect liberty" and a Japanese term for "religious body"). Hito-no-michi was a development of an earlier religious movement, Tokumitsu-kyō, named after its founder, Kanada Tokumitsu (1863–1919), who taught that the sufferings of his followers could be transferred to him by divine mediation and that he would vicariously endure their troubles.

Hito-no-michi was compelled by the government to affiliate itself with one of the SECT SHINTŌ denominations, Fusō-kyō; but its unorthodox teachings and growing strength (in 1934 it claimed a membership of 600,000) aroused the disfavor of the government. In 1937 the sect was ordered disbanded, and Miki Tokuharu and his son Miki Tokuchika were jailed. Tokuchika was released from prison in 1945 and shortly afterward established PL Kyōdan.

HITTITE RELIGIONS \'hi-ˌtīt\: *see* ANATOLIA, RELIGIONS OF.

HOLDHEIM, SAMUEL \'hȯlt-ˌhīm\ (b. 1806, Kempen, Prussia [now Kępno, Poland]—d. Aug. 22, 1860, Berlin), German RABBI, founder and leader of radical REFORM JUDAISM.

From 1836 to 1840 Holdheim officiated as a rabbi at Frankfurt an der Oder. In 1840 he went as *Landesrabbiner* (rabbi of a whole province) to Mecklenburg-Schwerin. Three years later he published *Ueber die Autonomie der Rabbinen* ("The Autonomy of the Rabbis"), in which he concluded that Jewish marriage and divorce laws were obsolete because they represented the national aspect of JUDAISM (no longer valid) as against its enduring religious aspect. Such laws, he held, should be superseded by the laws of the state, for Judaism is a religion only, whose essence is in biblical ethics and doctrine. During the rabbinical conferences of 1844–46, which elaborated the ideology of Reform Judaism, Holdheim played a dominant role.

In 1847 he became rabbi of the Jüdische Reformgenossenschaft ("Congregation of the Jewish Reform Alliance") in Berlin, where, for Reform Jews, he established Sunday as the day of worship and, except for Rosh Hashanah, abolished the keeping of the second day of holidays. Holdheim's writings form part of the classical literature of Reform Judaism.

ḤOL HA-MOʻED \'kȯl-ˌhä-mō-'äd\ (from Hebrew *ḥol,* "weekday," and *ha-moʻed,* "[of] the festival"), *also spelled* hol hamoed, *or* chol hamoed, in JUDAISM, the lesser festive days or semiholidays that occur between the initial and final days of the PASSOVER (Pesaḥ) and SUKKOT religious holidays. The number of *ḥol ha-moʻed* days is regulated by the locale. The principal ceremonies (such as the eating of MATZAHS) are observed during *ḥol ha-moʻed,* but not all work is forbidden. Marriages are postponed until after the festival, lest the one occasion interfere with the other.

HOLĪ \'hō-lē\, Hindu spring festival celebrated throughout North India on the full-moon day of Phālguna (February–March). The festival has many characteristics of a saturnalia, like CARNIVAL in certain Christian countries. Participants throw colored waters and powders on one another, and, on this one day only, license is given for the usual rankings of CASTE, gender, status, and age to be reversed. In the streets the celebrations are often marked by ribald language and behavior, but at its conclusion, when everyone bathes, dons clean white clothes, and visits friends, teach-

ers, and relatives, the ordered patterns of society are reasserted and renewed.

The festival is particularly enjoyed by worshipers of KRISHNA. Its general frivolity is considered to be in imitation of Krishna's play with the *gopīs* (wives and daughters of cowherds), and in Braj (also spelled Braja or Vraja), rituals of reversal culminate in a battle in which the women of RĀDHĀ's natal village pummel the men of Krishna's village with staves; the men defend themselves with shields. A major expression of Holī's mood of relaxation is the Ḍolay-ātrā ("swing festival"), in which images of the gods are placed on specially decorated platforms and are swung to the accompaniment of cycles of songs sung only in this spring season. But the most memorable rite in many locales is the kindling of an early-morning bonfire, which represents the burning of the demoness Holikā (or Holī), sister of Hiraṇyakaśipu, who had enlisted her in his attempt to kill his son Prahlāda. It was Prahlāda's unshakable devotion to VISHNU that had alienated him from his family. The burning of Holikā prompts worshipers to remember how Vishnu (in the form of a lion-man) attacked and killed Hiraṇyakaśipu, showing that faith prevails.

HOLIDAY (from "holy day"), originally, a day of dedication to religious observance; in modern times, a day of either religious or secular commemoration. Many holidays of the major WORLD RELIGIONS tend to occur at the approximate dates of more ancient festivals. In the case of CHRISTIANITY, this is sometimes owing to the policy of the early church of scheduling Christian observances at dates when they would eclipse pre-Christian ones—a practice that proved more efficacious than merely prohibiting the earlier celebrations. In other cases, the similarity of the date is due to the tendency to celebrate turning points of the seasons or to a combination of the two factors.

HOLINESS MOVEMENT, fundamentalist religious movement that arose in the 19th century among Protestant churches in the United States, characterized by a doctrine of sanctification centering on a postconversion experience. The numerous Holiness churches that arose during this period range from quasi-Methodist sects to groups that are similar to Pentecostal churches.

The movement traces back to JOHN WESLEY, the founder of METHODISM, who issued a call to Christian "perfection." Perfection was to be the goal of all who desired to be *altogether* Christian; it implied that the God who is good enough to forgive SIN (justify) is great enough to transform the sinner into a saint (sanctify), thus enabling him to be free from outward sin as well as from "evil thoughts and tempers," in short, to attain to a measure of holiness.

From the outset, the motto of colonial American Methodism was "to spread Christian holiness over these lands." But, in practice, the doctrines of holiness and perfectionism were largely ignored by American Methodists during the early decades of the 19th century. In 1843 about two dozen Holiness ministers withdrew from the Methodist Episcopal Church to found the Wesleyan Methodist Church of America, as sizable numbers of Protestants from the rural areas of the Midwest and South were joining the Holiness movement. These people had a penchant for Puritan-like codes of dress and behavior. Most of them had little sympathy for Christians preoccupied with wealth, social prestige, and religious formalism.

Between 1880 and World War I a number of new Holiness groups emerged. Some, such as the Church of God (Anderson, Ind.), were established to protest against bureaucratic denominationalism. Others, such as the Christian and Missionary Alliance and the CHURCH OF THE NAZARENE, were organized to serve the spiritual and social needs of the urban poor, who quite frequently were ignored by the middle-class congregations representing the mainstream of PROTESTANTISM. Almost all of these Holiness bodies arose in order to facilitate the proclamation of a second-blessing experience of sanctification with its concomitants—a life of separation and practical holiness.

Several of these Holiness groups demonstrated a capacity for sustained growth. Among these are the "older" denominations—the Wesleyan Methodist Church and the Free Methodist Church of North America (founded 1860)—as well as the newer ones: the Church of God (Anderson, Ind.), the Christian and Missionary Alliance, the SALVATION ARMY, and the Church of the Nazarene. The Church of the Nazarene, which claims nearly a third of the total membership of the Holiness movement, is generally recognized as being its most influential representative.

Contemporary Holiness churches tend to stand closer, doctrinally speaking, to fundamentalism than to their Methodist antecedents. Their tenets include such conservative evangelical beliefs as "plenary inspiration" (verbal inspiration of the whole BIBLE), "Christ's ATONEMENT for the entire human race," and "the personal SECOND COMING of Christ." Although the doctrinal statements of a few churches—Church of the Nazarene and Christian and Missionary Alliance—contain brief allusions to divine healing and Pentecostal experience, they should be distinguished from the Pentecostal movement.

HOLOCAUST \ˈhä-lə-ˌkȯst, ˈhō-\, *Hebrew* Sho'Ah, *or* Ḥurban, the 12 years (1933–45) of Nazi persecution of Jews and other minorities; it climaxed in the "final solution" (*die Endlösung*), the attempted extermination of European Jewry.

This near destruction of European Jewry during World War II has raised fundamental theological issues for the Jewish people and others. Not least, it has forced a reconsideration of the basic theological premises of JUDAISM. Given the Jewish belief that history and events can be seen as the revelation of God's plan, especially for the Jewish people, an event of such horror as the Holocaust has called into question other core beliefs, such as the belief in an omnipotent and loving God and the existence of a specific, caring relationship between God and Israel, usually expressed through the notion of COVENANT.

Owing to the complexity of the theological and metaphysical issues relating to the Holocaust, and the differing premises that individual thinkers and communities bring to these matters, it is not surprising that many different, often incompatible "answers" and "explanations" to the conundrum have been offered. So, for example, more radical scholars of theology such as Richard Rubinstein and Arthur A. Cohen and Irving Greenberg have argued that the Holocaust requires theological revisions within Judaism and changes in the HALAKHAH (Jewish law). An example of a proposed change to *halakhah* would be changing the criteria for who is or is not Jewish. By halakhic standards only one born to a Jewish mother is considered Jewish, but many individuals in Nazi Germany who were identified as Jews and killed had Jewish fathers and GENTILE mothers. Some scholars have proposed to change *halakhah* to define a Jew as someone with one Jewish parent, whether father or mother, allowing those who were murdered for Jewishness to be counted as Jewish.

Theological conservatives such as Eliezer Berkovits, Jacob Neusner, and the Lubavitcher Rebbe (that is, the Rabbi Menachem Mendel Schneerson; 1902–94), however, have argued that no such changes are necessary. Neusner, Schneerson, and Berkovits have all held that within Judaism there already exist paradigms that answer the problem (for instance, the story of Job may be seen as a way to understand the PROBLEM OF EVIL in instances where the innocent suffer).

Inmates of the Buchenwald concentration camp, near Weimar, Ger., 1945. During the Holocaust thousands of slave laborers died at Buchenwald from overwork, disease, and malnutrition.
Culver Pictures

The actual situation, however, if judged on the grounds of philosophical and theological arguments produced by both sides of the debate, is that neither has made a compelling case for its claims. Neither Rubinstein's endorsement of the "death of God," Cohen's call for a diminished idea of a God who cannot interfere in human affairs, Greenberg's declaration that "the covenant has been broken," Berkovit's recycling of the "Free-Will Defense," nor the Lubavitcher Rebbe's conservative qabbalistic pronouncements on the Holocaust as a *tikkun* (an act that creates the possibility of worldly and cosmic "repair") flow necessarily from the event itself. All of these and other denominational expositions are extrinsic to the reality of the death camps.

One issue in particular has become important to the theological conversation: the uniqueness of the Holocaust. Those who would make theologic and halakhic changes feel that because the Holocaust is a unique historical event the response to it must be novel and innovative as well. Alternatively, those who oppose change tend to view the Holocaust as just another case of anti-Semitism, if on a larger scale, or as another instance of the more general condition of "man's inhumanity to man." However, any theological position, given the present state of the theological dialogue, is compatible with the singularity of Sho'Ah. Religious conservatives who intuitively reject the uniqueness of the Holocaust on the usually implicit grounds that such an unequivocal conclusion would necessarily entail ominous alterations in the inherited halakhic tradition are simply mistaken. One can adopt without self-contradiction an unexceptional conservative theological posture while accepting the contention that the destruction of European Jewry was an event unparalleled in history. Conversely, the theological radicals who hold that the singularity of the Holocaust necessarily entails theologic transformations and Halakhic changes have not shown this to be the case. They have merely assumed it. It may be that one of these alternative positions is true, but so far neither side has made a convincing case.

In analyzing the concept of "uniqueness" one needs to specify more precise conditions of what this concept means, *i.e.*, to show that the Holocaust is unique in respect of conditions a, b, c, etc. In applying this approach many scholars argue that the Holocaust is unique by virtue of the fact that never before has a state set out, as a matter of not just intentional principle but of actualized policy, to annihilate every man, woman, and child identified as belonging to a specific people. It is this that defines the uniqueness of the Holocaust.

Given this definition of uniqueness two conclusions follow. First, historical study would confirm that the Holocaust is without real precedent. Second, crucially, the basis of this uniqueness—the Nazi's intention to murder every Jewish man, woman, and child without exception—does not necessarily require theological transformations within Judaism, because what makes the Holocaust distinctive does not carry any particular status within Judaism. To return to the example already given, the Third Reich, according to the Nuremberg Laws, defined a person as Jewish if he or she had one Jewish parent (and, unlike in Judaism, whether father or mother), and indeed relationships less close caused one to be considered Jewish by the Third Reich. But, this has no relevance to the internal Jewish discussion based on traditional Jewish principles and values of "who is a Jew." It may be that there are significant, even compelling grounds, for altering the classical definition of "who is a Jew" in our time, but one such ground, at least in

Jewish theology, cannot be Nazi racial theory and its various corollaries.

Finally, given the value system of Judaism, it must be recognized that, if the Holocaust is counted as negative theological evidence, then the creation of the state of Israel three years later should be counted as positive evidence. That is, the larger history of the Jewish people, of which the Holocaust is only a segment, must be appropriately accounted for as part of any broad theological judgment. How to do this is a complicated issue, for it is not a simple matter—it may even be impossible—to assign evidentiary value to specific historical events. This fact among others shows how very difficult it actually is to think through the theological implications of the Holocaust. *See also* JUDAISM: 20TH-CENTURY JUDAISMS BEYOND THE RABBINIC FRAMEWORK and JUDAISM: AMERICAN JUDAISM OF HOLOCAUST AND REDEMPTION.

HOLY, *also called* sacred, term often used to define the unique characteristics of religion as an experience or as a distinct phenomenon. It is frequently used in opposition to the profane. The classic theological treatise on the holy remains Rudolf Otto's *The Idea of the Holy* (1923). Otto thought of the holy in Kantian terms—that is, as a religious *a priori* (a self-evident truth). He described the history of religions as ideograms, or symbolic representations, of a numinous, transcendental reality called the holy in all of its mysterious, fascinating, awesome, and repellent aspects. MIRCEA ELIADE developed the concept of the holy as having a paradoxical ontological relation with the profane in *The Sacred and the Profane* (1959).

EMILE DURKHEIM'S *The Elementary Forms of the Religious Life* (1915) remains the classical theoretical statement of the opposition between the sacred and the profane as representations of social life. The sacred marks an absolute division from the profane that is both cognitive and moral in its representations of the social life. Many scholars have pointed out that the distinction between the sacred and the profane cannot be applied across all religions. Moreover, they have challenged the theoretical adequacy of the concepts as useful for the STUDY OF RELIGION.

HOLY LANCE, RELIC discovered in June 1098 during the First Crusade by Christian Crusaders at Antioch, in Syria. It was said to be the lance that pierced the side of JESUS CHRIST at the CRUCIFIXION. The recovery of the relic inspired the crusaders to take the offensive against the Muslims, routing them in battle and securing Christian possession of Antioch. Disputes about the authenticity of the lance, however, caused dissension among the Crusaders, and its discoverer, Peter Bartholomew, was eventually discredited.

HOLY OF HOLIES, *Hebrew* Qodesh ha-Qadashim, *also called* Devir, innermost and most sacred area of the ancient TEMPLE OF JERUSALEM, accessible only to the Israelite HIGH PRIEST. Once a year on YOM KIPPUR he was permitted to enter the square, windowless enclosure to burn incense and sprinkle sacrificial animal blood. By this act, the most solemn of the religious year, the high priest atoned for his own SINS and those of the PRIESTHOOD.

The Holy of Holies was located at the west end of the Temple, and in Solomon's Temple it enshrined the ARK OF THE COVENANT, a symbol of Israel's special relationship with God. At the entrance to the Holy of Holies stood a small cedar altar overlaid with gold. After his conquest of Jerusalem in 63 BCE Pompey desecrated the Temple by daring to enter the Holy of Holies.

The Holy Spirit, represented as a dove, descends on the disciples at Pentecost; woodcut by Albrecht Dürer, 1511
The Bridgeman Art Library—private collection

HOLY SEPULCHRE, tomb in which JESUS CHRIST was buried and name of the church built on the traditional site of his CRUCIFIXION and burial. According to the BIBLE, the tomb was close to the place of Crucifixion (John 19:41–42), and so the church was planned to enclose the site of both.

The Church of the Holy Sepulchre lies in the northwest quarter of the Old City of Jerusalem. CONSTANTINE the Great first built a church on the site. It was dedicated about 336 CE, burned by the Persians in 614, restored by Modestus (ABBOT of the monastery of Theodosius, 616–626), destroyed by the caliph al-Ḥākim bī-Amr Allāh (*see* HAKIM, AL-) about 1009, and restored by the Byzantine emperor Constantine Monomachus. In the 12th century the Crusaders carried out a general rebuilding of the church. Since that time, frequent repair, restoration, and remodeling have been necessary. The present church dates mainly from 1810. Various Christian groups, including the Greek, Roman, Armenian, and Coptic churches, control parts of the present church and conduct services regularly.

This site has been continuously recognized since the 4th century as the place where Jesus died, was buried, and rose from the dead. Whether it is the actual place, however, has been hotly debated. It cannot be determined that Christians during the first three centuries could or did preserve an authentic tradition as to where these events occurred. Another question involves the course of the second north wall of ancient Jerusalem. Some archaeological remains on the east and south sides of the Church of the Holy Sepulchre are widely interpreted to mark the course of the second wall. If so, the site of the church lay just outside the city wall in the time of Jesus, and this could be the actual place of his Crucifixion and burial. No rival site is supported by any real evidence.

HOLY SPIRIT, *also called* Paraclete, *or* Holy Ghost (from Old English: *gast*, "spirit"), in Christian belief, third Person of the TRINITY. The GOSPELS record a descent of the Holy Spirit on JESUS CHRIST at his BAPTISM, and numerous outpourings of the Spirit are mentioned in THE ACTS OF THE APOSTLES, in which healing, PROPHECY, the expelling of DEMONS (EXORCISM), and speaking in tongues (glossolalia) are particularly associated with the activity of the Spirit.

Christian writers have seen in various references to the Spirit of YAHWEH in the OLD TESTAMENT an anticipation of the doctrine of the Holy Spirit. The Hebrew word *ruaḥ* (usually translated "spirit") is often found in texts referring to the free and unhindered activity of God, either in creating or in revitalizing creation, especially in connection with the prophetic word or messianic expectation. There was, however, no explicit belief in a separate divine person in biblical Judaism; in fact, the NEW TESTAMENT itself is not entirely clear in this regard. One suggestion of such belief is the promise of another helper, or intercessor (paraclete), that is found in the Gospel According to John.

The definition that the Holy Spirit was a distinct divine Person equal in substance to the Father and the Son and not subordinate to them came at the COUNCIL OF CONSTANTINOPLE in 381 CE, following challenges to its divinity. The Western church has since viewed the Holy Spirit as the bond, the fellowship, or the mutual CHARITY between Father and Son; they are absolutely united in the Spirit. The relationship of the Holy Spirit to the other Persons of the Trinity has been described in the West as proceeding from both the Father and the Son, whereas in the East it has been held that the procession is from the Father through the Son.

From apostolic times, the formula for baptism has been Trinitarian. CONFIRMATION (in the Eastern ORTHODOX CHURCH, chrismation), although not accepted by most Protestants as a SACRAMENT, has been closely allied with the role of the Holy Spirit in the church. The Eastern Orthodox church has stressed the role of the descent of the Spirit upon the worshiping congregation and upon the eucharistic bread and wine in the prayer known as the EPICLESIS.

HOLY WAR, any war fought by divine command or for a religious purpose. The concept of holy war is found in the BIBLE (*e.g.,* the Book of Joshua) and has played a role in many religions. *See also* JIHAD.

HOLY WATER, in the Eastern Christian and ROMAN CATHOLIC churches, water that has been blessed and is used to convey a blessing to churches, homes, persons, and objects.

In the early Christian community the "living" water of rivers and streams was preferred for BAPTISM and apparently received no special blessing. By the time of the 4th century the still waters of the baptismal font or pool were exorcised and blessed with the sign of the cross. Other water was blessed for the use of the faithful as a means of warding off the unclean spirit and as a safeguard against sickness and disease. In the course of time this blessed, or holy, water was used as a reminder of baptism by the faithful on entering the church and by the celebrant in sprinkling the congregation before the Sunday MASS.

HOLY WEEK, in the Christian church, week between PALM SUNDAY and EASTER, a time of devotion to the passion of JESUS CHRIST. In the Greek and Roman liturgical books it is called the Great Week because great deeds were done by God during this week. The name Holy Week was used in the 4th century by ATHANASIUS, bishop of Alexandria, and Epiphanius, bishop of Constantia. Originally only Friday and Saturday were observed as holy days; later Wednesday was added as the day on which Judas plotted to betray Jesus, and by the beginning of the 3rd century the other days of the week had been added. The pre-Nicene church celebrated one great feast, the Christian PASSOVER, on the night between Saturday and Easter Sunday morning. By the later 4th century the various events were separated and commemorated on the days of the week on which they occurred: Judas' betrayal and the institution of the EUCHARIST on MAUNDY THURSDAY; the passion and death of Christ on GOOD FRIDAY; his burial on Saturday; and his RESURRECTION on Easter Sunday.

The Holy Week observances in the Roman missal were revised according to the decree *Maxima Redemptoris* (Nov. 16, 1955) to restore the services to the time of day corresponding to that of the events discussed in SCRIPTURE.

HOMOOUSIAN \ˌhō-mō-'ü-sē-ən, ˌhä-, -'ü-zē-\, in CHRISTIAN-ITY, adherent of the doctrine formulated at the COUNCIL OF NICAEA (325) that God the Son and God the Father are of the same substance. The council, presided over by the emperor CONSTANTINE, intended the condemnation of ARIANISM, which taught that Christ was more than human but not truly divine. The use of *homoousios* (Greek: "of the same substance," or "of one essence") in the Creed of Nicaea was meant to put an end to the controversy, but Arianism revived within the church, and it was not until 381 at the second ecumenical council (first COUNCIL OF CONSTANTI-NOPLE) that a creed (also containing the word *homoousios*, and eventually called the NICENE CREED) was accepted as a definitive statement of orthodox belief.

HŌNEN \'hō-nen\, *original name* Seishimaru, later Genkū, *also called* Hōnen Shōnin, Enkō Daishi, *or* Ganso (b. May 13, 1133, Inaoka, Mimasaka province [now Kume, Okayama prefecture], Japan—d. Feb. 29, 1212, Kyōto), Buddhist priest, founder of the PURE LAND (Jōdo) Buddhist sect of Japan. He was instrumental in establishing Pure Land pietism as one of the central forms of BUDDHISM in Japan.

At the age of 15 Hōnen was sent to MOUNT HIEI, the monastic center of the Tendai (Chinese: T'IEN-T'AI) sect of Buddhism. The center prospered externally in wealth and prestige but suffered internally from the power struggles of ambitious ABBOTS and the moral and spiritual corruption of the priests. Along with other serious-minded young priests, Hōnen came under the influence of the Pure Land doctrine, which taught salvation by the mercy of Amida (Sanskrit: AMITĀBHA) Buddha. Hōnen was greatly inspired by the *Ōjōyōshū* ("Essentials of Salvation"), written by a 10th–11th-century Japanese Buddhist, Genshin, and the *Kuan-ching-su* ("Commentary on the Meditation Sutra"), by a 7th-century Chinese Pure Land master, Shan-tao (Japanese: Zendō). In 1175 Hōnen proclaimed his message that the one and only thing needed for salvation is *nembutsu* (calling the name of Amida).

In Hōnen's main work, the *Senchaku hongan nembutsu-shū* ("Collection on the Choice of the *Nembutsu* of the Original Vow") written in 1198, he classified all the teachings of Buddhism under two headings: Shōdō ("Sacred Way") and Jōdo ("Pure Land"). According to Hōnen, Buddha, confident of man's inner character, had shown men the Sacred Way to Enlightenment, which enables them to be emancipated from this world of lust and delusion and to attain the other world of ultimate peace. Hōnen, convinced of his own "sinful and avaricious" nature, however, came to the conclusion that, although it was theoretically possible, it was practically impossible for him and others like him to follow the Sacred Way. Thus, Hōnen felt that the only alternative was to trust in the Original Vow (*hongan*) of Amida Buddha, the lord of the Sukhāvatī (Sanskrit: "Pure Land"), who is said to assure salvation to the believer who calls upon Amida's holy name.

Hōnen established his headquarters in the midst of the secular city of Kyōto, away from ecclesiastical establishments, and gathered together devoted disciples, including SHINRAN, who was to become the founder of the True Pure Land (Jōdo Shin) sect. Hōnen and his followers accepted the legendary periodization of Buddhist history, according to which the first 1,000 years following the demise of the Buddha is the period of the "perfect law" (*shōbō*), in which the true teaching prospers; the second 1,000 years is the period of the "copied law" (*zōbō*), in which piety continues but true teaching declines; and the last 1,000 years is the period of the "end of law" (MAPPŌ), in which Buddhism declines and the world is destined to be overwhelmed by vice and strife. It is to be noted that, according to the accepted calculation of Japanese Buddhists, the last period began in 1051 CE. As though to substantiate this view of history, Japanese society during the 12th century suffered from political instability and social disintegration that resulted in the establishment of feudal government under the leadership of the warrior class. Understandably, Hōnen's simple teaching found eager followers among the various levels of Japanese society of that time.

Although he insisted on faith in Amida and the recitation of the name as the best way to salvation, Hōnen, an intrepid but nonaggressive person, was markedly tolerant and nonpolemical, urging his followers to respect the other Buddhas and other Buddhist ways of faith and practice. (Hōnen was also especially careful to warn against the temptation of accompanying the *nembutsu* with an immoral life or of believing that its recitation removes the stain of violations of the Buddhist life-discipline or other immoral acts.) Still, the popularity of the faith in the Pure Land of Amida Buddha aroused jealousy from the established schools of Buddhism and led to Hōnen's banishment. With his immediate disciples, he was forced to leave the capital in 1207 (and some of his disciples were beheaded). Compelled to use a nonclerical name, he called himself Fujii Motohiko and proved to be an effective evangelist even during his exile to the island of SHIKOKU. He was permitted to leave Shikoku at the end of the year but not to return to Kyōto until 1211, when he received a warm popular welcome. He died in Kyōto the following year.

Hōnen combined the cultured heritage of the established Buddhism with the pioneering spirit of the new Buddhism of the 13th century. The movement he founded continues to be one of the most influential schools of Japanese Buddhism, and the far more numerous Jōdo Shin founded by his disciple Shinran adds still more to the Pure Land influence that he initiated.

HONJI-SUIJAKU \'hȯn-ˌjē-'sü-ē-ˌjä-kü\ (Japanese: "original substance, manifest traces"), Chinese Buddhist idea that was transmitted to Japan, greatly influencing the SHINTŌ understanding of deity, or KAMI. As developed in the medieval period, the theory reinterpreted Japanese *kami* as the "manifest traces" of the "original substance" of BUDDHAS or BODHISATTVAS. Ryōbu ("Dual Aspect") Shintō is particularly expressive of this principle, and the Yui-itsu school of Shintō chauvinistically reversed the formula to make Japanese *kami* the "original substance." This principle generally allowed for the pervasive blending of Shintō and Buddhist divinities and practices, a characteristic of Japanese religious life that continues in contemporary Japan.

HONOS \ˈhō-ˌnäs\, ancient Roman deified abstraction of honor, and particularly of honor perceived as military virtue. The earliest shrine of this deity in Rome was perhaps built not earlier than the 3rd century BCE and was located just outside the Colline Gate. A double TEMPLE of Honos and Virtus stood outside the Porta Capena, and another, built by Marius (d. 86 BCE), was probably located on the Capitoline Hill.

HOOKER, RICHARD \ˈhu̇-kər\ (b. March 1554?, Heavitree, Exeter, Devon, Eng.—d. Nov. 2, 1600, Bishopsbourne, near Canterbury, Kent), theologian who created a distinctive ANGLICAN theology. In 1568 he entered Corpus Christi College at Oxford, where he was trained in the traditions of Genevan PROTESTANTISM. Leading scholars at Oxford were, however, loyal to the Anglican *Book of Common Prayer* and used the vestments demanded by ecclesiastical law. Hooker looked beyond CALVINISM and read widely in scriptural interpretation, the early CHURCH FATHERS, and Renaissance THOMISM (the philosophical school influenced by the thought of ST. THOMAS AQUINAS).

Hooker became a scholar of Corpus Christi College in 1573 and took his M.A. in 1577. In the same year he became a fellow of his college. In 1585 he was elected master of the Temple. With the defeat of the Spanish Armada in 1588, the Church of England passed beyond the crisis of the threat of ROMAN CATHOLICISM. Now the threat was that of Calvinism, not only in doctrine but in ecclesiastical organization as well. The reformers' hold on general sympathy was so strong that even the bishops were lukewarm about suppressing them and allowed their growth to increase unchecked. In June 1572 radical religious reformers had issued *An Admonition to the Parliament,* which, though Queen Elizabeth I forbade its consideration by Parliament, became the platform of the PURITANS. The leading bishops were alarmed by the influence of the *Admonition,* and the Archbishop of Canterbury turned to John Whitgift, vice chancellor of the University of Cambridge, to reply to it. Whitgift was answered in turn by Thomas Cartwright, professor at Cambridge and the leading Puritan clergyman. The controversy was continued in a whole series of books. Hooker set himself the task of replying to the *Admonition.* After he ceased to be master of the Temple in 1591, he took up residence at his father-in-law's house and wrote his masterpiece, *Of the lawes of ecclesiasticall politie.* The *Politie* was to be a work of eight books, but the fifth book (1597) was the last one to appear in Hooker's lifetime.

In the *Politie,* Hooker defended the Elizabethan church against Roman Catholics and Puritans alike. He upheld the threefold authority of the Anglican tradition—BIBLE, church, and reason. Roman Catholics put Bible and tradition on a parity as the authorities for belief, while Puritans looked to SCRIPTURE as sole authority. Hooker avoided both extremes, allowing to Scripture absolute authority when it spoke plainly and unequivocally; where it was silent or am-

Richard Hooker; engraving by E. Finden after a print by W. Hollar

biguous, wisdom would consult the tradition of the church; but he insisted that a third element lay in human reason, which should be obeyed whenever both Scripture and tradition needed clarification or failed to cover some new circumstance. In his view, the Puritans adopted an impossible position; they claimed to be loyal to the Queen while repudiating the Queen's church.

According to tradition Hooker served the churches at Drayton Beauchamp and Boscombe following his term as master of the Temple, but more probably he received his salary as a VICAR but allowed a lesser clergyman to perform the duties that the PARISH required. In 1595 he accepted an appointment as vicar of Bishopsbourne, near Canterbury.

HORA \ˈhōr-ə, ˈhȯr-\, *plural* Horae \ˈhōr-ˌē, ˈhȯr-, -ˌī\, in Greek mythology, any of the personifications of the seasons and goddesses of natural order; in the *Iliad* they were the custodians of the gates of Olympus. According to Hesiod, the Horae were the children of ZEUS and THEMIS, and their names (Eunomia, Dike, Eirene—*i.e.,* Good Order, Justice, Peace) indicate the extension of their functions from nature to the events of human life. At Athens they were apparently two in number: Thallo and Carpo, the goddesses of the flowers of spring and of the fruits of summer. Their yearly festival was the Horaea. In later mythology the Horae became the four seasons, daughters of the sun god, HELIOS, and the moon goddess, SELENE, each represented with the conventional attributes. Subsequently, when the day was divided into 12 equal parts, each of them took the name Hora.

HOROSCOPE, in ASTROLOGY, chart of the heavens, showing the relative positions of the Sun, the Moon, the planets, and the ascendant and midheaven signs of the zodiac at a specific moment in time. A horoscope is used to provide information about the present and to predict events to come.

An individual's horoscope usually plots the positions at the moment of birth and is used by astrologers to analyze character, as well as—in conjunction with other astrological data—to predict the future. This is in accordance with the belief that each celestial body has its own mythological character, modified according to its geometric relationship with the other celestial bodies at a given moment. Everything in the universe being interrelated, these bodies exert an influence, particularly on the newborn. In casting a horoscope, the heavens are commonly represented by a circle divided into 12 sections, called houses. Each of these houses is assigned several aspects of human life, such as wealth or marriage. The planet that falls within a particular house is said to influence matters pertaining to that house.

HORUS \\'hōr-əs, 'hȯr-\\, *Egyptian* Hor \\'hōr, 'hȯr\\, *or* Har \\'här\\, in ancient EGYPTIAN RELIGION, god in the form of a falcon whose eyes were the sun and the moon. Falcon cults were widespread in Egypt. At Nekhen (Greek: Hierakonpolis), however, the conception arose that the reigning king was a manifestation of Horus and, after Egypt had been united by the kings from Nekhen, this conception became a generally accepted dogma. The first of the Egyptian king's five names was the Horus name—*i.e.*, the name that identified him with Horus.

From the 1st dynasty (*c.* 2525–2775 BCE), Horus and the god SETH were perpetual antagonists who were reconciled in the harmony of Upper and Lower Egypt. In the myth of OSIRIS, who became prominent about 2350 BCE, Horus was the son of Osiris. He was also the opponent of Seth, who murdered Osiris and contested Horus' heritage, the royal throne of Egypt. Horus finally defeated Seth, thus avenging his father and assuming the rule. In the fight his left eye (*i.e.,* the moon) was damaged and was healed by the god THOTH. The figure of the restored eye (the *wedjat* eye) became a powerful AMULET.

Horus appeared as a local god in many places and under different names and epithets: for instance, as Harmakhis (Har-em-akhet, "Horus in the Horizon"); Harpocrates (Har-pe-khrad, "Horus the Child"); Harsiesis (Har-si-Ese, "Horus, Son of Isis"); Harakhty ("Horus of the Horizon," closely associated with the sun god RE); and, at Kawm Umbū (Kom Ombo), as Haroeris (Harwer, "Horus the Elder"). Ho-

Horus offering a libation, bronze statue, 22nd dynasty (c. 800 BCE); in the Louvre, Paris
Giraudon—Art Resource

rus was later identified by the Greeks with APOLLO, and Edfu was called Apollinopolis ("Apollo's Town") in the Greco-Roman period.

In the Ptolemaic period the vanquishing of Seth became a symbol of Egypt triumphing over its occupiers. At Edfu, where rebellions frequently interrupted work on the temple, a ritual drama depicting Horus as pharaoh spearing Seth in the guise of a hippopotamus was enacted.

HOSEA \\hō-'zā-ə, -'zē-\\, *also spelled* Osee, *Assyrian* Ausi, in the OLD TESTAMENT (2 Kings 15:30; 17:1–6), son of Elah and last king of Israel (*c.* 732–724 BCE). He became king through a conspiracy in which his predecessor, Pekah, was killed. The Assyrian king Tiglath-pileser III claimed that he made Hosea king, and Hosea paid an annual tribute to him. After Tiglath-pileser died (727), Hosea revolted against the new Assyrian king, Shalmaneser, who then invaded Israel, took Hosea prisoner, and besieged Samaria. When the city fell three years later, many of Israel's citizens were deported to Assyria, and the Assyrians ruled in Israel.

HŌTOKU \\'hō-tȯ-kù\\ (Japanese: "requital of a kindness"), semireligious movement among Japanese peasants initiated in the 19th century by Ninomiya Sontoku (1787–1856). He combined a nonsectarian ethic of cooperation with practical economic measures such as crop rotation and famine relief. Hōtoku emphasized the debt owed to gods, nature, ancestors, emperor, and parents. This debt could be repaid only through frugality and conformity with the cosmic order, which was equated with moral sincerity. Ninomiya Sontoku's teachings were disseminated by his followers and played an important part in shaping 19th- and 20th-century Japanese popular morality.

HOU-CHI \\'hō-'jē\\, *Pinyin* Hou Ji, in Chinese mythology, Lord of Millet Grains, who was worshiped for the harvests that he provided. Conceived when his childless mother stepped on the toeprint of a god, he was reared in a forest by birds and animals and served as minister of agriculture in prehistoric times. Sacrifices in his honor were offered by rulers of the Hsia dynasty (22nd–18th/19th century BCE) and of the later Chou dynasty (600–255 BCE), which claimed him as their ancestor.

HRUNGNIR \\'hrüŋ-nir\\, in Norse mythology, GIANT who fought a single combat with THOR. Hrungnir was made of stone, and his weapons were a shield and a whetstone. Thor's helper Thjalfi tricked Hrungnir into lowering his shield by telling him that Thor would attack from underneath. Thus Hrungnir was standing on his shield and was unprotected when Thor threw his hammer. Hrungnir threw his whetstone, but Thor's hammer shattered the whetstone and killed the giant. The dead giant's leg pinned Thor to the ground, and a piece of whetstone was lodged in his head. Only Magni ("Strength"), a son of Thor, was able to move the leg of the giant off Thor. This duel, which is said to be the first fought between Thor and a giant, is seen as a mythic prototypical duel, which was an important institution in the Viking age.

HSIAO \\'shyaù\\, *Pinyin* xiao, *Japanese* kō \\'kō\\ (Chinese: "filial piety"), in CONFUCIANISM, the attitude of obedience, devotion, and care toward one's parents and elder family members that is the basis of individual moral conduct and social harmony. *Hsiao* consists in putting the needs of parents and family elders over self, spouse, and children, deferring to parents' judgment, and observing toward them the prescribed behavioral proprieties (LI).

Hsiao was originally rooted in the hierarchical ideology of Chinese feudalism, but CONFUCIUS raised it to a moral precept by citing it as the basis of JEN ("humanity"), the cultivated love of other people that was the Confucian moral ideal. He delineated the importance of *hsiao* for both family harmony and sociopolitical stability and facilitated its practice by reemphasizing the rites and behaviors associated with it.

The concept, rendered *kō*, was adopted in Japan during the 17th century, when Confucianism became the official doctrine of the Tokugawa shogunate.

HSIEN \'shyen\, *Pinyin* xian (Chinese: "immortal being"), in Chinese TAOISM, practitioner who has achieved immortality. Early Taoist sages referred to immortal beings with magical powers, perhaps allegorically; some followers interpreted these references literally and devoted themselves to discovering the "drug of immortality" and prolonging their lives through breath control, yogalike exercises, and abstention from grains. Adepts in these practices, though appearing to die, were believed to achieve physical immortality and admission to heavenly realms inaccessible to the spirits of mere mortals. The pursuit of this state fostered Taoist alchemical and other esoteric techniques and lore.

HSIN-HSÜEH \'shin-'shwe\, *Pinyin* Xinxue (Chinese: "Mind-Heart Teaching," or "School of Mind"), Chinese NEO-CONFUCIAN movement associated with LU HSIANG-SHAN (Lu Chiu-yüan; 1139–93) and WANG YANG-MING (1472–1529). In contrast with Chu Hsi's (1130–1200) School of Principle, this school taught that the awareness and activation of the ruling principle of life is attained by mental introspection and not through the examination of external reality. Wang Yang-ming's subjectivist development of the school especially reveals the influence of Buddhist ideals of meditative insight, the centrality of the moral ideal of "extending the good," and an emphasis on the basic unity of mind and body, thought and action.

HSI-WANG-MU \'shē-'wäŋ-'mü\, *Pinyin* Xiwangmu (Chinese: "Queen Mother of the West"), in the folk mythology of TAOISM in China, queen of the immortals in charge of female spirits who dwell in a fairyland called Hsi-hua ("West Flower"). The queen was a former mountain spirit transformed into a beautiful woman. Her garden was filled with rare flowers, extraordinary birds, and the flat peach (*p'an-t'ao*) of immortality. These stories were based on an earlier Han period mythology in which she was the goddess of the sacred mountain K'un-lun.

According to myth, Hsi-wang-mu's birthday is celebrated by the PA-HSIEN ("Eight Immortals") with a grand banquet during which Hsi-wang-mu serves special delicacies: bear paws, monkey lips, and dragon liver. *P'an-t'ao* are offered as the last course. A Taoist romance relates that during a visit to Wu-ti, emperor of the Han dynasty, Hsi-wang-mu gave him the famous peach of immortality. He was anxious to bury the stone, but she discouraged him, saying that Chinese soil was not suitable and, in any case, the tree bloomed only once in 3,000 years.

HSI-YU CHI \'shē-'yō-'jē\, *Pinyin* Xiyouji ("Record of a Journey to the West"), foremost Chinese comic novel, written by the long-anonymous Wu Ch'eng-en (1500–c. 1582).

Based on the actual 7th-century PILGRIMAGE of the Buddhist monk HSÜAN-TSANG (602–664) to India in search of sacred texts, the story was already a part of Chinese folk and literary tradition in the form of colloquial stories, a poetic novelette, and a six-part drama when Wu Ch'eng-en formed it into his novel. The novel is composed of 100 chapters. The first seven deal with the birth of a monkey from a stone egg and his acquisition of magic powers; five relate the story of Hsüan-tsang, known as Tripitaka, and the origin of his mission to the Western Paradise; while the bulk of the novel recounts the adventures that befall Tripitaka and his entourage of three animal spirits—the magically gifted Monkey, the slow-witted and clumsy Pigsy, and the fish spirit Sandy—on their journey to India, culminating in their attainment of the sacred scrolls. This novel has many levels of religious and philosophical interpretation from the perspectives of BUDDHISM, TAOISM, and NEO-CONFUCIANISM. Besides the overt Buddhist theme, the novel also displays Taoist and Neo-Confucian ideas of self-cultivation.

HSÜ \'shū\, *Pinyin* xu (Chinese: "emptiness"), in TAOISM, a state of being that is characterized by total tranquility and transcendence of self, through which individual consciousness becomes one with the Tao; the TAO can be understood only through individual experience of *hsü*.

CONTEMPLATIVE Taoists attain *hsü* by stilling their thought processes and emotions, which they regard as corruptions of the Tao. Many schools of Taoism have made use of breath-control techniques in order to quiet the mind; the more elaborate systems, requiring years of practice, were condemned by some as being contrary to the Tao, which is beyond human striving.

HSÜAN \'shwän\, *Pinyin* xuan (Chinese: "dark," or "mysterious"), common term in most forms of Chinese religion and philosophy that connotes a hidden or occult dimension to some aspect of experience or reality. First used metaphysically in the TAO-TE CHING, it is an idea that is given mystical significance in many aspects of later Taoist and Buddhist tradition. *See also* HSÜAN-HSÜEH.

HSÜAN-HSÜEH \'shwän-'shwe\, *Pinyin* Xuanxue ("Dark Learning"), intellectual movement among Chinese scholars that arose in the 3rd and 4th centuries CE during a period of widespread disenchantment with contemporary CONFUCIANISM. The movement found its scriptural support in drastically reinterpreted Confucian sources as well as in texts of TAOISM. Wang Pi (226–249 CE) is regarded as the school's founder.

The movement was grounded in the assumption that all temporally and spatially limited phenomena—anything "nameable"; all movement, change, and diversity; in short, all "being"—is produced from and sustained by one impersonal principle, which is unlimited, unnameable, unmoving, unchanging, and undiversified. Hsüan-hsüeh concentrated on the question of whether this ultimate reality was Being (YU) or Not-Being (WU) and whether the principle (LI) underlying a thing was universal or particular. The school came to reign supreme in cultural circles and represented the more abstract, unworldly, and idealistic tendency in early medieval Chinese thought.

The proponents of Hsüan-hsüeh regarded themselves as true Confucians and interpreted CONFUCIUS as an enlightened sage who had inwardly recognized the ultimate reality but had kept silent about it in his worldly teachings, knowing that these mysteries could not be expressed in words.

473

Hence, his doctrine was supposed to be a mere set of ad hoc rules intended to answer the practical needs of the times. This concept of "hidden saintliness" and the expedient character of the canonical teachings came to play a very important role in upper-class BUDDHISM. Under the influence of Hsüan-hsüeh, likewise, early Chinese Buddhist philosophers directed their attention chiefly to Being and Non-being. The question of universality and particularity, or of one and many, led to the development of truly Chinese Buddhist schools, whose concern was the relationship between principle, which combines all things as one, and facts, which differentiate things into the many.

HSÜAN-TSANG \'shwän-'dzäŋ\, *Pinyin* Xuanzang, *original name* Ch'en I, ho*norary epithet* San-tsang, *also called* Much'a T'i-p'o, *Sanskrit* Mokṣadeva (b. 602, Ch'en-lu, China—d. 664, China), Buddhist monk and Chinese pilgrim to India who founded the Wei-shih ("Ideation Only") school.

Born into a family of scholars, Hsüan-tsang received a classical Confucian education in his youth but became interested in the Buddhist SCRIPTURES and soon converted to BUDDHISM. He traveled to Ssu-ch'uan (modern Szechwan) and began studying Buddhist philosophy. He was soon troubled by numerous discrepancies and contradictions in the texts. Not finding any solution from his Chinese masters, he decided to go to India to study at the fountainhead of Buddhism. Being unable to obtain a travel permit, he left Ssu-ch'uan by stealth in 629. On his journey he traveled north, passing through such oasis centers as Tashkent and Samarkand, then beyond the Iron Gates into Bactria, across the Hindu Kush, and into Kashmir in northwest India. From there he sailed down the GAṄGĀ (Ganges) River to Mathura, then on to the holy land of Buddhism in the eastern reaches of the Gaṅgā, where he arrived in 633.

In India, Hsüan-tsang visited all the sacred sites connected with the life of the BUDDHA GOTAMA, and he journeyed along the coasts of the subcontinent. The major portion of his time, however, was spent at the Nālandā monastery, the great Buddhist center of learning, where he perfected his knowledge of Sanskrit, Buddhist philosophy, and Indian thought. Hsüan-tsang's reputation as a scholar was such that the king in northern India wanted to meet him. Owing to that king's patronage, Hsüan-tsang's return trip to China, begun in 643, was greatly facilitated.

Hsüan-tsang returned to Ch'ang-an, the T'ang capital, in 645, after an absence of 16 years. He was accorded a tumultuous welcome at the capital. Hsüan-tsang spent the remainder of his life translating the Buddhist scriptures, which numbered 657 items packed in 520 cases, that he had brought back from India. He was able to translate only a small portion of these, but his translations included some of the most important MAHĀYĀNA scriptures.

Hsüan-tsang's main interest was the philosophy of the YOGĀCĀRA (Vijñānavāda) school, and he and his disciple K'uei-chi (632–682) began the Wei-shih school in China. Its doctrine was set forth in Hsüan-tsang's *Ch'eng-wei-shih lun* ("Treatise on the Establishment of the Doctrine of Consciousness Only"), a translation of the essential Yogācāra writings, and in K'uei-chi's commentary. The main thesis of this school is that the whole world is but a representation of the mind. While Hsüan-tsang and K'uei-chi lived, the school achieved some degree of eminence, but with the passing of the two masters the school rapidly declined. A Japanese monk, Dōshō, arrived in China in 653 to study under Hsüan-tsang. He later introduced the doctrines of Wei-shih into Japan. During the 7th and 8th centuries, this school, called Hossō by the Japanese, became the most influential of all the Buddhist schools in Japan.

In addition to his translations, Hsüan-tsang composed the *Ta-T'ang Hsi-yü-chi* ("Records of the Western Regions of the Great T'ang Dynasty"), the great record of the various countries he passed through during his journey. Hsüan-tsang's travels were later dramatized in a folk tradition that culminated in the 16th century in Wu Ch'eng-en's great novel *The Journey to the West.*

HSÜN-TZU \'shün-'dzə\, *Pinyin* Xunzi, *original name* Hsün K'uang \-'kwäŋ\, *honorary name* Hsün Ch'ing \-'chiŋ\ (b. *c.* 300 BCE, Chao Kingdom, China—d. *c.* 230 BCE, Lanling, Ch'u Kingdom, China), philosopher who was one of the three great philosophers of the Classical period of CONFUCIANISM in China. He elaborated and systematized the work undertaken by CONFUCIUS and MENCIUS, and the strength he thereby gave to that philosophy has been largely responsible for its continuance as a living tradition for over 2,000 years. Little is known of his life save that he belonged for some years to the Chi-hsia academy of philosophers maintained in Ch'i by the ruler of that eastern state, and that, later, because of slander, he moved south to the state of Ch'u, where he became magistrate of a small district in 255 BCE and later died in retirement.

Hsün-tzu's major work, known today as the *Hsün-tzu*, is a milestone in the development of Chinese philosophy. In his book he introduced a rigorous writing style that emphasized topical development, sustained reasoning, detail, and clarity.

Hsün-tzu's most famous dictum is that "the nature of man is evil; his goodness is only acquired training." Human nature at birth, he maintained, consists of instinctual drives which, left to themselves, are selfish, anarchic, and antisocial. Society as a whole, however, exerts a civilizing influence upon the individual, gradually training and molding him until he becomes a disciplined and morally conscious human being. Of prime importance in this process are the LI (ceremonies and ritual practices, rules of social behavior, traditional mores) and music (which he regarded as having a profound moral significance).

Hsün-tzu's view of human nature was radically opposed to that of Mencius, who had optimistically proclaimed the innate goodness of man. Both thinkers agreed that all men are potentially capable of becoming sages, but for Hsün-tzu this meant that every man can learn from society how to overcome his initially antisocial impulses. Thus began what became one of the major controversies in Confucian thought, and in later centuries Mencius' growing prominence led to a neglect of Hsün-tzu's work.

During this time, a period of great change and instability, the historical *li* (ritual practices) were being abandoned by an increasingly agnostic intelligentsia. Hsün-tzu believed that these ritual practices were too important to be lost because they were a culturally binding force for a people whose existence depended on cooperative economic efforts. Further, those practices were important to the individual because they provided an aesthetic and spiritual dimension to one's life. By his insistence on the necessity of cultural continuity for both a person's physical and psychological well-being, Hsün-tzu provided an ethical and aesthetic philosophical basis for these ritual practices as their religious foundation was weakening.

The *li* are accordingly the basic stuff out of which he builds the ideal society as described in his book, and the scholar-officials who are to govern that society have as their primary function the preservation and transmission of these ritual practices. Like all early Confucians, Hsün-tzu was opposed to hereditary privilege, advocating literacy and moral worth as the determinants of leadership positions; and these determinants were to have as their foundation a demonstrated knowledge of the high cultural tradition—the *li*. The *li* were to be employed by scholars to ensure that everyone was in a place, and officials were to employ the *li* to ensure that there was a place for everyone.

Hsün-tzu engaged in polemic with rival schools, and he bitterly lamented the lack of a centralized political authority that could impose ideological unity from above. Indeed, he was an authoritarian who formed a logical link between Confucianism and the totalitarian Legalists; among his students were two of the most famous Legalists, the theoretician Han Fei-tzu (*c.* 280–233 BCE) and the statesman Li Ssu (*c.* 280–208 BCE). Both of these men earned the enmity of later Confucian historians, and their reputations have also negatively affected the evaluation of their teacher. For several centuries after Hsün-tzu's death, his influence remained greater than that of Mencius. Only with the rise of NEO-CONFUCIANISM in the 10th century CE did his influence begin to wane, and not until the 12th century was the triumph of Mencius formalized by the inclusion of the *Mencius* among the Confucian classics. Hsün-tzu was declared heterodox. Only recently have his works emerged from this period of neglect.

HU, SIA, AND HEH \ˈhü-ˈsē-ə…ˈheh\, Heh *also called* Neheh, in EGYPTIAN RELIGION, deified abstractions personifying, respectively, "creative command" (or "authoritative utterance"), "perception" (or "intelligence"), and "eternity." They were all essential forces in the creation and continuance of the cosmos. Hu and Sia served as crew members in the solar bark of the sun god RE. They were represented in an undistinctive form as bearded men and also served as bearers of the eye of the god HORUS. In the text known as the "Memphite Theology" they personified the tongue and the heart of the god PTAH. They were also regarded as two of the divine attributes of every king. Heh was the personification of infinite space and was portrayed as a squatting man with a sun disk on his head, bearing the symbols of many years of life and of happiness.

HUACA \ˈwä-kä\, *also spelled* wak'a (Quechua: "sacredness," or "holiness"), ancient INCA and modern Quechua and Aymara religious concept that refers to gods, sacred ritual, the state of being after death, or any sacred object. *Huaca* means "burial place," spirits that either inhabit or actually are physical phenomena such as waterfalls, mountains, or man-made shrines. These shrines, which are found throughout the Inca territory from Ecuador to Chile, range from stones piled in a field (*apachitas*) to stepped PYRAMIDS that were once topped with canopies and carved images.

Huang-ti, illustration from Li-tai ku-jen hsiang-tsan *(1498 edition)*
By courtesy of the University of Hong Kong

HUAI-NAN-TZU \ˈhwī-ˈnän-ˈdzə̀\, *Pinyin* Huainanzi (Chinese: "Master Huai-nan"), Chinese Taoist classic written *c.* 139 BCE under the patronage of the nobleman Huai-nan-tzu (Liu An). The writing is an important statement of the Han period (HUANG-LAO) TAOISM concerned with COSMOLOGY, astronomy, and statecraft. The *Huai-nan-tzu* states that the TAO originated from vacuity, and vacuity produced the universe, which in turn produced the material forces. The material forces combined to form yin and yang, which in turn give rise to the myriad things. In its broad outline, this COSMOGONY and cosmology have been retained as orthodox doctrine by Taoist philosophers and also by later Confucianists. The *Huai-nan-tzu* introduces such ideas as immortality on earth and the physical techniques, such as breathing, used to achieve it (*see* HSIEN).

HUANG-LAO \ˈhwäŋ-ˈlaù\, *Pinyin* Huanglao, political ideology drawing on the art of rulership attributed to the legendary Yellow Emperor (HUANG-TI) and the founder of TAOISM, LAO-TZU. This method of governance, which stressed the principles of reconciliation and noninterference, overtook Legalism as the dominant ideology of the imperial court in the early years of the Western Han (206 BCE–25 CE).

The Huang-Lao masters venerated Lao-tzu as a sage whose instructions, contained in his cryptic book TAO-TE CHING, describe the perfect art of government. Huang-ti was depicted as a ruler of the Golden Age who achieved his success because he applied his teachers' precepts to government. From the court of the king of Ch'i (in present-day Shantung province), where they were already expounding the *Tao-te ching* in the 3rd century BCE, the teachings of the Huang-Lao masters soon spread throughout learned and official circles in the capital. Many early Han statesmen became disciples and attempted to practice government by inaction (WU-WEI); among them were also scholars who cultivated esoteric arts. Although their doctrine lost its direct political relevance during the reign of the emperor Wu-ti (141/140–87/86 BCE), their teachings concerning both ideal government and practices for prolonging life continued to evoke considerable interest and constituted perhaps the earliest truly Taoist movement of which there is clear historical evidence.

HUANG-TI \ˈhwäŋ-ˈdē\, *Pinyin* Huangdi (Chinese: "Yellow Emperor"), third of ancient China's mythological emperors, culture hero and patron saint of TAOISM, associated with the HUANG-LAO Taoism of the Han period.

Huang-ti is reputed to have been born about 2704 BCE and to have begun his rule as emperor in 2697. Tradition states that his reign saw the introduction of wooden houses, carts, boats, the bow and arrow, and writing. Huang-ti himself defeated "barbarians" in a great battle somewhere in what is now Shansi—the victory winning him the leadership of tribes throughout the Huang Ho (Yellow River) plain. Some also credit him with the introduction of governmental institutions and the use of coined money. Huang-ti's wife was reputed to have taught women how to breed silkworms and weave fabrics of silk.

Huang-ti is held up in some ancient sources as a paragon of wisdom whose reign was a golden age. In accordance with a dream, he sought to institute an ideal kingdom whose tranquil inhabitants would live in harmonious accord with the natural law and possess virtues remarkably like those espoused by early Taoism. Upon his death he became an immortal.

HUA-YEN \'hwä-'yan\ (Chinese: "Flower Ornament"), *Japanese* Kegon, philosophical tradition of BUDDHISM. The school was founded in China in the late 6th–7th century by Fa-shun and further systematized in the 7th–8th century by Fa-tsang. It continued in China until the 10th century, after which it began to decline. The doctrine first reached Japan from China about 740, carried by two of Fa-tsang's pupils, Chen-hsiang (Japanese: Shinshō) and Tao-hsüan (Japanese: Dōsen), and by a southern Indian, Bodhisena.

The name Hua-yen is a translation of the Sanskrit *avataṃsaka* ("garland," or "wreath"), after the school's chief text, the *Avataṃsaka Sūtra*. This text, preserved in both Tibetan and Chinese versions, deals with the Buddha VAIROCANA. The school held that no element of the universe has a separate and independent existence apart from the whole but rather that each reflects all the others and that Vairocana is at the center of the universe.

The totalistic principle of the Kegon school caught the attention of the reigning Japanese emperor, Shōmu, who is credited with founding TŌDAI TEMPLE, which was the largest and most powerful monastery in Japan during the Nara period (710–784). In 752 Shōmu dedicated the Daibutsu, the colossal bronze image of Vairocana, the "Great Sun Buddha," at Tōdai Temple, and many of the ritual objects used in the consecration ceremony are preserved in the monastery treasury, the Shōsō-in.

HUBRIS \'hyü-bris\, *also spelled* hybris \'hī-bris\, in classical Greek ethical and religious thought, violent behavior suggesting impious disregard of the limits governing human action in an orderly universe. It is the SIN to which the great and gifted are most susceptible, and in Greek tragedy it is usually the hero's downfall.

ḤUDŪD \hü-'düd\ (Arabic: "the boundaries," or "prohibitions"), *singular* ḥadd \'hàd,\ in Islamic law, a class of penal laws set forth in the QUR'AN and the SUNNA, and elaborated by the Sunni and Shi'ite legal schools. It includes theft, adultery, defamation, highway robbery, consumption of alcohol, APOSTASY, and rebellion. Corporal punishment ranging from flogging (for more minor offenses) and amputation (for theft) to death (for adultery, apostasy, and rebellion) are imposed against those found legally guilty of these offenses. Imposition of these punishments must be by qualified legal authorities and are subject to strict rules of evidence.

The *ḥudūd* have not been consistently applied in Muslim societies, where customary laws often apply instead. In many modern Muslim nations such offenses are regulated by civil law adopted from the west. The *ḥudūd* punishments, however, have been applied unevenly during the 20th century by the governments of Saudi Arabia, Pakistan, Sudan and Iran. Islamists who call for the establishment of theocratic government usually include imposition of the *ḥudūd* as a primary objective. The *ḥudūd* are also at the center of human-rights debates in many Muslim countries.

In the DRUZE religion, *ḥudūd* represents the five cosmic principles that are emanations from God, the One. AL-ḤĀKIM, the 11th-century Fāṭimid CALIPH of Egypt, stands at the center of the universe as the embodiment of the One. ḤAMZA IBN 'ALĪ, a contemporary of al-Ḥākim, systematized the Druze religion and presented himself as the direct human link to the One; he then established a hierarchy of universal principles, or *al-ḥudūd*, that would span the distance between the One and the mass of Druze believers.

Each principle had a human counterpart from among al-Ḥākim's contemporaries. Ḥamza himself became the first principle, or *ḥadd*, Universal Intelligence (al-'Aql); al-'Aql generated the Universal Soul (al-Nafs), embodied in Ismā'īl ibn Muhammad al-Tamīmī. The Word (al-Kalima) emanates from al-Nafs and is manifest in the person of Muhammad ibn Wahb al-Qurashī. The fourth successive principle is the Preceder (al-Sābiq, or Right Wing [al-Janāḥ al-Ayman]), embodied in Salāma ibn 'Abd al-Wahhāb al-Sāmirrī; and the fifth is the Succeeder (al-Tālī, or Left Wing [al-Janāḥ al-Aysar]), personified by al-Muqtanā Bahā' al-Dīn. Each of these principles, the true *ḥudūd*, also had false counterparts, in turn embodied by various contemporaries of al-Ḥākim. The tension between the two sets of *ḥudūd* represented the conflict of GOOD AND EVIL in the world, to be resolved by al-Ḥākim's eventual support of the true *ḥudūd*.

HUI-NENG \'hwā-'nəng\, *Pinyin* Huineng (b. 638, southwest Kwangtung, China—d. 713, Kwangtung), sixth great patriarch of ZEN (Ch'an in Chinese) BUDDHISM and founder of the Southern school, which became the dominant school of Zen, both in China and in Japan.

As a young and illiterate peddler of firewood, Hui-neng heard the DIAMOND SUTRA and traveled 500 miles to North China where the fifth Ch'an patriarch, Hung-jen (601–674), was expounding this text. According to legend, in a dramatic poetry contest in 661 the senior monk, Shen-hsiu (605?–706), wrote, "The mind is the stand of a bright mirror. . . . / Do not allow it to become dusty," but Hui-neng wrote, "Buddha-nature is forever clear and pure, / Where is there any dust?" Thereupon the fifth patriarch transmitted the law to Hui-neng.

Hui-neng returned to South China and in 676 reached Canton, where he was ordained PRIEST. In a sermon that has been recorded as the *Liu-Tsu t'an-ch'ing* ("Platform Scripture of the Sixth Patriarch"), he declared that all people possess the buddha-nature and that one's nature is originally pure. Instead of reading scriptures, building temples, making offerings, reciting the name of the BUDDHA GOTAMA, and praying for rebirth in paradise, one should simply seek to discover one's own nature, in which all buddhas and Buddhist doctrines are immanent. The traditional method of sitting in meditation is useless for discovering this nature, for tranquillity is not motionlessness but is the state of having an unperturbed inner nature and an absence of erroneous thought. If one sees one's own nature, enlightenment will follow—suddenly, without external help.

In pronouncing this radical doctrine of sudden enlightenment, Hui-neng rejected traditional Buddhist concepts and created a wide schism between his Southern school and the Northern school led by Shen-hsiu, who advocated gradual enlightenment.

HUITZILOPOCHTLI \,wēt-sē-lō-'pōcht-lē\, *also spelled* Uitzilopochtli (from Nahuatl *huitzilin*, "hummingbird," and *opochtli*, "left side," or "left hand"), Aztec sun and war god. His other names included Xiuhpilli ("Turquoise

Prince") and Totec ("Our Lord"). His *nahual*, or animal disguise, was the eagle.

Traditionally, Huitzilopochtli was thought to have been born on the Coatepec, Serpent Mountain, near the city of Tula. His mother, COATLICUE, an earth goddess, conceived him after having kept in her bosom a ball of fine feathers (*i.e.*, the soul of a warrior) that fell from the sky. His brothers, the Centzon Huitznáua ("Four Hundred Southerners"), stars of the southern sky, and his sister Coyolxauhqui, a moon goddess, decided to kill Coatlicue. When the siblings attacked Serpent Mountain, she gave birth to the adult warrior Huitzilopochtli who exterminated them with his weapon, the *xiuhcóatl* ("turquoise snake").

Huitzilopochtli supporting the southern quarter of the heavens, illustration in the Codex Borgia, 14th–16th century
Biblioteca Apostolica Vaticana

priests also burned a huge bark-paper serpent symbolizing the god's primary weapon.

The Aztecs also believed that the sun god needed human blood and hearts as daily nourishment. Some sacrificial hearts were offered to the sun *quauhtlehuanitl* ("eagle who rises") and burned in the *quauhxicalli* ("the eagle's vase"). Warriors who died in battle or in sacrifice were believed to form part of the sun's retinue; then, after four years, they went to live forever in the bodies of hummingbirds.

Huitzilopochtli's high priest, the Quetzalcóatl Totec Tlamacazqui ("Feathered Serpent, Priest of Our Lord"), was, with the god TLALOC'S high priest, one of the two heads of the Aztec clergy.

HUMAN SACRIFICE, offering of the life of a human being to a deity. The occurrence of human sacrifice can usually be related to the recognition of blood as the sacred life-force in humans. Bloodless forms of killing, however, such as strangulation and drowning, have been used in some cultures. The killing of a human being, or the substitution of an animal for a person, has often been part of an attempt to effect communion with a god and thus to participate in his divine life. The offering of human life, as the most valuable material for sacrifice, has also occurred in attempts at expiation. There are two primary types of human sacrifice: the offering of a human being to a god, and the entombment or slaughter of servants or slaves intended to accompany the deceased into the afterlife.

The latter practice is the more common. In various places in Africa, where human sacrifice was connected with ANCESTOR WORSHIP, some of the slaves of the deceased were buried alive with him, or they were killed and laid beneath him in his grave. The Dahomey made especially elaborate sacrifices at the death of a king. Excavations in Egypt and elsewhere in the Middle East have revealed that numerous servants were at times interred with the rest of the funerary equipment of a member of the royal family in order to provide that person with a retinue in the next life. The Chinese practice of burying the emperor's retinue with him continued intermittently until the 17th century.

The sacrificial offering of human beings to a god has been well attested only in a few cultures. In what is now Mexico the belief that the sun needed human nourishment led to the sacrifice of thousands of victims annually in the Aztec and Nahua calendrical corn ritual. The INCAS confined such wholesale sacrifices to the accession of a ruler. The burning of children seems to have occurred in Assyrian and Canaanite religions and at various times among the Israelites. Among the African Ashanti, the victims sacrificed as first-fruit offerings during the Festival of New Yams were usually criminals, though slaves also were killed.

Other myths presented Huitzilopochtli as the divine leader of the tribe during the long migration that brought the Aztecs from Aztlan, their traditional home, to the Valley of Mexico. His image, in the form of a hummingbird, was carried upon the shoulders of the priests, and at night his voice was heard giving orders. The god's first shrine in the valley of Mexico was built on a spot where priests found an eagle poised upon a rock.

Representations of Huitzilopochtli usually showed him as a warrior with a headdress of parrot and quetzal feathers and a hummingbird device on his back. His legs, arms, and the lower part of his face were blue; the upper half of his face was black. He wore earplugs of cotinga feathers and brandished a round shield and a turquoise snake staff.

The fifteenth month of the ceremonial year, Panquetzaliztli ("Feast of the Raising of Banners"), was dedicated to Huitzilopochtli. During the month, warriors and maidens and pleasure girls danced by night on the plaza in front of the god's temple. War prisoners or slaves were bathed in a sacred spring at Huitzilopochco (modern Churubusco, in Mexico City) and were then sacrificed at a place called "the god's ball court" (Teotlachco) and at other locations. The

Accusations of human sacrifice in ancient and modern times have been far more widespread than the ritual practice ever was. The ancient Greeks told many myths that involved human sacrifice, which has led some researchers to posit that rites among the Greeks and Romans that involved the killing of animals may have originally involved human victims; to date, however, archaeological evidence does not support this claim. Some early Christians were falsely accused of CANNIBALISM, consuming sacrificial victims at nocturnal feasts, a misunderstanding probably due to the secrecy surrounding the Eucharistic rite and the use of the words "body" and "blood." From the Middle Ages until quite recently, Jews were often maliciously accused of having sacrificed Christian children at the PASSOVER, an accusation which has been termed the blood libel.

ḤUNAYN IBN ISḤĀQ \'k̲u-nīn-ˌi-bən-i-'shäk\, *Latin name* Johannitius \ˌyō-hə-'ni-shē-əs, -shəs\ (b. 808, al-Ḥīra, near Baghdad, Iraq—d. 873, Baghdad), Arab scholar whose translations of Plato, Aristotle, Galen, Hippocrates, and the Neoplatonists made accessible to Arab philosophers and scientists the most significant sources of Greek thought and culture.

Ḥunayn was a NESTORIAN Christian who studied medicine in Baghdad and became well versed in ancient Greek. He was appointed by CALIPH al-Mutawakkil to the post of chief physician to the court, a position that he held for the rest of his life. He traveled to Syria, Palestine, and Egypt to gather ancient Greek manuscripts, and, from his translators' school in Baghdad, he and his students transmitted Arabic and (more frequently) Syriac versions of the classical Greek texts throughout the Islamic world. Especially important are his translations of Galen, most of the original Greek manuscripts of which are lost.

HUNG HSIU-CH'ÜAN \'hu̇ŋ-'shyō-'chwän\, *Pinyin* Hong Xiuchuan (b. Jan. 1, 1814, Fu-yüan shui, Kwangtung, China—d. June 1, 1864, Nanking), Chinese religious prophet and leader of the TAIPING REBELLION (1850–64).

Though from an early age Hung showed signs of great intelligence, he failed the Confucian civil service examination several times. After failing for the third time, in 1837, he suffered an emotional collapse. During a delirium that lasted several days he imagined himself to be in the presence of a venerable old man with a golden beard. The old man complained that the world was overrun by evil DEMONS, and he gave Hung a sword and seal to use in eradicating the bad spirits. Hung also believed himself to have encountered a middle-aged man who aided and instructed him in the extermination of demons.

When Hung recovered he returned to his occupation as a village schoolteacher. In 1843 he took the examination for the fourth and last time and again failed. Shortly after this, Hung reexamined a work entitled *Ch'üan-shih liang-yen* ("Good Words for Exhorting the Age"), which had been given him on his visit to Canton in 1837. The work explained the basic elements of CHRISTIANITY, and in it Hung discovered the explanation for his visions. He realized that during his illness he had been transported to heaven. The old man he had spoken with was God, and the middle-aged man was JESUS CHRIST. Hung further understood that he was the second son of God, sent to save China. He baptized himself, prayed to God, and from then on considered himself a Christian.

Hung began to propagate the new doctrine among his friends and relatives. One of his most important converts was his schoolmate Feng Yün-shan. In 1844 Hung lost his job because he had destroyed the tablets to CONFUCIUS in the village school where he was teaching, and Feng accompanied him on a preaching trip to neighboring Kwangsi Province. Hung returned from Kwangsi after a few months, but Feng remained, establishing the Pai Shang-ti hui (God Worshipers' Society), devoted to Hung's new doctrines. From his narrow understanding of Christianity, Hung stressed a wrathful OLD TESTAMENT God, one who was to be worshiped and obeyed. He demanded the abolition of evil practices such as opium smoking, gambling, and prostitution and promised an ultimate reward to those who followed the teachings of the Lord.

Shortly thereafter Hung joined Feng and the God Worshipers and was immediately accepted as the new leader of the group. Conditions in the countryside were deplorable, and sentiment ran high against the foreign Manchu rulers of China. As a result, Hung and Feng began to plot the rebellion that finally began in July 1850. On Jan. 1, 1851, Hung's 37th birthday, he proclaimed his new dynasty, the T'ai-p'ing t'ien-kuo (Heavenly Kingdom of Great Peace) and assumed the title of T'ien-wang, or Heavenly King. As the Taipings pressed north through the Yangtze River Valley, they grew from a ragged band of a few thousand to a fanatical but highly disciplined army of more than a million, divided into separate divisions of men and women soldiers. Men and women were considered equal by the Taipings but were allowed no contact with one another—even married couples were forbidden sexual intercourse.

Hung's army captured Nanking on March 10, 1853, and he decided to make the city his permanent capital, renaming it T'ien-ching (Heavenly Capital). Meanwhile, Feng had died en route to Nanking, and Hung had placed much power in the hands of his minister of state, Yang Hsiu-ch'ing. Eventually Yang began to usurp Hung's prerogatives as supreme leader. To legitimize his authority, Yang occasionally lapsed into trances in which his voice supposedly became that of the Lord's. In one of his trances, Yang claimed that the Lord demanded Hung be whipped for kicking one of his concubines. On Sept. 2, 1856, Hung had Yang murdered by Wei Ch'ang-hui, another Taiping general, who in turn was killed at Hung's behest.

After this, Hung withdrew from all government matters and entrusted affairs of state to his incompetent elder brothers. By 1862, when Hung's generals were telling him that he ought to abandon Nanking, he refused, stating that he trusted in divine guidance. On June 1, 1864, Hung, despairing after a lingering illness, committed suicide. His young son succeeded him on the throne. The city finally fell on July 19, 1864, and government troops initiated a terrible slaughter in which more than 100,000 people were said to have been killed. Sporadic Taiping resistance continued in other parts of the country until 1866.

HUN-TUN \'hu̇n-'du̇n\, *Pinyin* hundun (Chinese: "chaos," or "primal lump"), ancient term that alludes to the spontaneous creation of the world from a primordial CHAOS, imagined sometimes as a kind of primal wonton, a lumpish sac of cosmic stuff, or a primal gourd. The theme was important in early Taoist texts like the TAO-TE CHING and the CHUANG-TZU and refers to the ideal of the sage who attempts through physiological and mental methods to reverse the process of creation and return to the original condition of chaotic wholeness—*hun-tun*, or *p'u*, the "uncarved block." In later sectarian TAOISM the theme of *hun-tun* had both positive and negative connotations and was incorporated

Jewish wedding with bride (left) and groom under a ḥuppah, detail from an illustrated German manuscript, c. 1272
The Granger Collection

into elaborate new mythologies (often influenced by BUDDHISM), liturgical practices of community renewal, and routines of introspective meditation by Taoist priests and alchemical adepts.

ḤUPPAH \kü-'pä, 'ku̇-pə\, *also spelled* chuppah, *plural* ḥuppot \kü-'pōt\, *or* ḥuppahs, in a Jewish wedding, the portable canopy beneath which the couple stands while the ceremony is performed. Depending on the local custom and the preference of the bride and groom, the *ḥuppah* may be a simple Jewish prayer shawl (TALLIT) suspended from four poles, a richly embroidered cloth of silk or velvet, or a flower-covered trellis. In ancient times *ḥuppah* signified the bridal chamber, but the canopy now symbolizes the home to be established by the newlyweds. In popular usage the term *ḥuppah* may also refer to the wedding ceremony itself.

HURRIAN RELIGIONS \'hu̇r-ē-ən\: *see* ANATOLIA, RELIGIONS OF.

HUS, JAN \'həs, 'hu̇s\, *also spelled* Huss (b. *c.* 1370, Husinec, Bohemia [now in Czech Republic]—d. July 6, 1415, Konstanz [Germany]), the most important 15th-century Czech religious Reformer, whose work anticipated the Lutheran REFORMATION by a full century.

About 1390 Hus enrolled in the University of Prague, and two years after his graduation in 1394 he received his master's degree and began teaching at the university. He became dean of the philosophical faculty there in 1401.

In that same year JOHN WYCLIFFE'S works and theological writings became available in Prague, and Hus was particularly impressed by Wycliffe's proposals for reform of the ROMAN CATHOLIC clergy. The clerical estate owned about one-half of all the land in Bohemia, and the wealth and simoniacal practices of the higher clergy aroused jealousy and resentment among the poor priests. The peasantry, too, represented the church as one of the heaviest land taxers. There was thus a basis of potential support for any movement to reform the church. Attempts at reform had been made by the Bohemian king Charles IV, and Wycliffe's works were the chosen weapon of the national reform movement founded by Jan Milíč of Kroměříž (d. 1374).

In 1391 Milíč's pupils founded the Bethlehem Chapel in Prague, where public sermons were preached in Czech (rather than in Latin) in the spirit of Milíč's teaching. From 1402 Hus was in charge of the chapel, which had become the center of the growing national reform movement. He became increasingly absorbed in public preaching and eventually emerged as the popular leader of the movement. Despite his extensive duties at the Bethlehem Chapel, Hus continued to teach in the university faculty of arts and became a candidate for the doctor's degree in theology.

In 1403 a German university master, Johann Hübner, drew up a list of 45 articles from Wycliffe and had them condemned as heretical; the articles were henceforth regarded as a test of orthodoxy. The principal charge against Wycliffe's teaching was his tenet of remanence—*i.e.*, that the bread and wine in the EUCHARIST retain their material substance. Wycliffe also declared the SCRIPTURES to be the sole source of Christian doctrine. Hus did not share all of Wycliffe's views, but several members of the reform party did, among them Hus's teacher, Stanislav of Znojmo, and his fellow student, Štěpán Páleč.

Since 1378 the Roman Catholic church had been split by the Great SCHISM, during which the papal jurisdiction was divided between two popes. The Council of Pisa (1409) was called to dethrone the rival popes and to reform the church. The archbishop of Prague, Zbyněk Zajíc, opposed the Council and in so doing had the support of the German masters of the University of Prague, while Hus and the Czech masters supported the Council. The German masters had a voting majority in university affairs until King Wenceslas in January 1409 gave a predominance of votes to the Czech masters, and the resulting exodus of Germans to several German universities left Hus as rector of the now Czech-dominated university.

The final break between Archbishop Zbyněk and Hus occurred when the Council of Pisa ineffectually deposed both Pope Gregory XII and the ANTIPOPE Benedict XIII and in their place elected Alexander V. The archbishop and the higher clergy in Bohemia remained faithful to Gregory, whereas Hus and the reform party acknowledged the new pope. The archbishop, through a large bribe, induced Alexander to prohibit preaching in private chapels. Hus refused to obey the pope's order, whereupon Zbyněk excommunicated him, though Hus continued to preach at the Bethlehem Chapel and to teach at the University of Prague.

479

Jan Hus at the stake in 1415, colored Bohemian woodcut, 1563
The Granger Collection

Karbalāʾ, Iraq), SHIʿITE Muslim hero and martyr, grandson of the Prophet MUHAMMAD and son of ʿALĪ (the fourth Islamic CALIPH) and FĀṬIMA, daughter of Muhammad. He is revered by Shiʿite Muslims as the third IMAM (after ʿAlī and Ḥusayn's older brother, ḤASAN).

After the assassination of their father, Ḥasan and Ḥusayn acquiesced to the rule of the first Umayyad caliph, Muʿāwiya, from whom they received pensions. Ḥusayn, however, refused to recognize the legitimacy of Muʿāwiya's son and successor, Yazīd (April 680). Ḥusayn was then invited by the townsmen of Kūfa, a city with a Shiʿite majority, to revolt against the Umayyads. Ḥusayn set out for Kūfa with a small band of relatives and followers. The governor of Iraq, on behalf of the caliph, sent 4,000 men to arrest Ḥusayn and his band. They trapped Ḥusayn near the banks of the Euphrates River (October 680) at KARBALĀʾ. When Ḥusayn refused to surrender, he and his escort were slain, and Ḥusayn's head was sent to Yazīd in Damascus.

In remembrance of the martyrdom of Ḥusayn, Shiʿite Muslims observe the 10th day of Muḥarram (the date of the battle according to the Islamic calendar) as the culmination of the 10-day observance of tazia (taʿziyah), which coincides with ʿĀSHŪRĀ. Revenge for Ḥusayn's death was turned into a rallying cry that helped undermine the Umayyad caliphate and gave impetus to the rise of a powerful Shiʿite movement.

The details of Ḥusayn's life are obscured by the legends that grew up surrounding his martyrdom, but his final acts appear to have been intended to found a regime that would reinstate a "true" Islamic polity as opposed to what he considered the unjust rule of the Umayyads. His shrine in Karbalāʾ became one of the leading Shiʿite PILGRIMAGE centers, aside from MECCA and MEDINA. Many SUNNIS venerate him at his shrine in Cairo. Devotees hold that Ḥusayn possesses extraordinary powers of intercession and healing. During the 20th century he was regarded by Sunnis and Shiʿites alike as a revolutionary hero.

In 1412 the case of Hus's HERESY was revived owing to a new dispute over the sale of INDULGENCES that had been issued by Alexander's successor, John XXIII, to finance his campaign against Gregory XII. Their sale in Bohemia had been approved by King Wenceslas, who shared in the proceeds. Hus publicly denounced these indulgences and by so doing lost the support of Wenceslas. Hus's enemies then renewed his trial at the Curia, where he was declared under major EXCOMMUNICATION for refusing to appear. Hus left Prague in October 1412 and found refuge mostly in southern Bohemia in the castles of his friends. His enemies wrote a large number of polemical treatises against him, which he answered in an equally vigorous manner. He also wrote a large number of treatises in Czech and a collection of sermons entitled *Postilla*.

Invited to the COUNCIL OF CONSTANCE to explain his views and promised safe-conduct, Hus was arrested shortly after his arrival there. He was tried before the Council of Constance as a Wycliffite heretic, and in three public hearings he was allowed to defend himself and succeeded in refuting some of the charges against him. The council urged Hus to recant in order to save his life, but when he refused he was sentenced and burned at the stake.

ḤUSAYN IBN ʿALĪ, AL- \kù-ʹsīn-ˌi-bən-ä-ʹlē\ (b. January 626, Medina, Arabia [now in Saudi Arabia]—d. Oct. 10, 680,

HUSSITE \ʹhə-ˌsīt, ʹhù-\, any of the followers of the Bohemian religious reformer JAN HUS, who was condemned by the COUNCIL OF CONSTANCE (1414–18) and burned at the stake. After his death in 1415 many Bohemian knights and nobles published a formal protest and offered protection to those who were persecuted for their faith. The movement's chief supporters were Jakoubek of Stříbro (died 1429), Hus's successor at the Bethlehem Chapel in Prague; Václav Koranda, leader of the Taborites (extreme Hussites named for the city of Tábor, their stronghold some 50 miles south of Prague); and Jan Želivský, who organized the extreme reform party in Prague.

The Hussites broke with Rome over two key issues: the use of a Czech liturgy and the administration of the EUCHARIST to the laity under the forms of both bread and wine.

(The doctrine supporting this was called Utraquism [from the Latin *utraque*, "each of two"] and the more moderate Hussites were called UTRAQUISTS.)

Under King Wenceslas (Václav) IV of Bohemia, the movement spread widely. In 1419, however, he died and was succeeded by his half brother Sigismund, king of the Romans and of Hungary. The Hussites would have acknowledged Sigismund had he accepted the Four Articles of Prague that Jakoubek had formulated: (1) freedom of preaching; (2) communion in both kinds; (3) poverty of the clergy and expropriation of church property; (4) punishment of notorious sinners. In 1420, however, Sigismund, who had failed to get possession of Prague, published a bull of Pope Martin V proclaiming a crusade against the Hussites. The Hussite union, which included the municipalities of Prague and other cities and the chief military power of Bohemia, deposed Sigismund and repelled two crusading attacks against Prague. Various crusades and battles against the Hussites failed for the next several years. In 1427 the Hussites, led by Prokop Holý, began a more revolutionary, rather than defensive, political program. Pope Martin V organized another crusade against them but did not live to see it decisively beaten by the Hussites in 1431.

Peace negotiations began in 1431, when the Council of Basel of the ROMAN CATHOLIC church agreed to negotiate with the Hussites on an equal basis, which Pope Martin V had refused to do. A Hussite delegation spent three months in Basel in 1433 discussing the Four Articles of Prague. The Council then sent a mission to Prague, which granted communion in both kinds to the Hussites. This grant split the Hussites, since the Utraquists were willing to make peace on these terms, but the more radical Taborites were not. Utraquists and Catholics then joined forces to defeat the Taborites in a battle at Lipany in 1434, which ended the Taborites' influence.

The Utraquist Hussites then resumed peace negotiations, and in July 1436 they obtained a peace treaty (the Compact of Iglau) that ensured all the principal gains of the war: communion in both kinds, the expropriation of church lands (which broke the economic power of the Roman Catholic church in Bohemia), and an independent Bohemian Catholic church under Jan Rokycana as its elected archbishop. Although association with the Roman Catholic church continued, the church of the Utraquist Hussites survived SCHISMS and periodic persecutions until *c.* 1620, when it was finally absorbed by the Roman Catholics.

In the mid-15th century the UNITAS FRATRUM (Unity of Brethren) movement began in Bohemia among some of the Hussites, and it established its own independent organization in 1467. During the REFORMATION, the Unitas Fratrum was in contact with Lutheran and Reformed Protestants. Eventually, however, Bohemian and Moravian PROTESTANT-ISM was suppressed, and the Roman Catholic COUNTER-REFORMATION was victorious after 1620, when the Protestant barons were defeated at the Battle of the White Mountain during the Thirty Years' War.

Remnants of the Unitas Fratrum remained, however, and in 1722 a group of them fled Moravia and settled on the estate of Count Nikolaus Ludwig von Zinzendorf in Saxony. A number of exiles from Moravia and Bohemia followed, and they formed the community of Herrnhut, where they were organized as the MORAVIAN CHURCH. There is also some continuity with 20th-century Czech Protestantism.

HUTTERITE \'hə-tə-ˌrīt, 'hü-\, member of the Hutterian Brethren, an ANABAPTIST sect that found refuge from perse-cution in Moravia and the Tirol; it stressed community of goods on the model of the primitive church in Jerusalem. The community, which acquired the name of its charismatic Austrian leader, Jakob Hutter (who was tortured and burned as a heretic in 1536), still survives, mostly in the western sections of the United States and Canada, with a population of about 20,000. In colonies of 60 to 150 persons, they operate collective farms (*Bruderhof*) and, not unlike the Old Order AMISH, remain aloof from outside society, taking no part in politics. Children are educated inside the colony until age 14 or until a minimum age decreed by state or province.

Persecutions drove the Hutterites to Hungary, the Ukraine, and in the 1870s to South Dakota; during World War I, when persecuted because of their pacifism, they migrated to Canada. After the war, many returned to the United States. Their high annual birth rate (45.9 per 1,000) has necessitated new colonies, sometimes to the displeasure of neighbors who distrust their communal life, object to their pacifism, and generally misunderstand their way of life. Some areas have passed legislation to hinder the growth of Hutterite colonies.

HUYNH PHU SO \'hü-yən-'pü-'sō\, Huynh *also spelled* Huyen, *also called* Dao Khung \'daù-'kủŋ\, *or* Phat Song \'pät-'sóŋ\ (b. 1919, Hoa Hao, Cochinchina [now in Vietnam]—d. 1947, Long Xuyen), Vietnamese philosopher, Buddhist reformer, and political activist, founder (1939) of the religion Phat Giao Hoa Hao, more simply known as Hoa Hao.

Sickly in his youth, Huynh Phu So was educated by a Buddhist monk and at the age of 20 was apparently miraculously cured. He then set about preaching the reform of BUDDHISM, advocating a return to THERAVĀDA Buddhism from the MAHĀYĀNA form prevalent in Vietnam, and stressing austerity, simple worship, and personal salvation. Hoa Hao is an amalgam of Buddhism, ANCESTOR WORSHIP, animistic rites, elements of CONFUCIANISM, and indigenous Vietnamese practices. Its adherents have their own flag and their own special holidays.

Huynh Phu So traveled throughout Vietnam practicing herbal healing and acupuncture, becoming known as Dao Khung ("Mad Monk"). He predicted with accuracy the fall of France in World War II, the Japanese invasion of Indochina, and the intervention of the United States at a later date. His success as a prophet led his followers to call him the Phat Song ("Living Buddha").

As his fame and his adherents increased, his inflammatory speeches brought him to the attention of the French colonial authorities. Exiled from one Vietnamese province after another, he continued to draw disciples. Finally he was committed to a mental institution, where he converted his doctor to his philosophy. The French tried to exile him to Laos, but he was kidnapped by Japanese agents in 1942 and held prisoner in Saigon (now Ho Chi Minh City).

After the war, disagreement, first with the French and then with the communist Viet Minh, made the Hoa Hao sect an aggressive religio-political-military cult. Huynh Phu So was abducted and executed after a trial in Long Xuyen. Many of the Hoa Hao faithful, refusing to believe that he died, predict his return in a time of crisis.

HVARENAH \'k̲vär-ə-näh\, *also spelled* khvarenah, in ZORO-ASTRIANISM, attribute of kingly glory. *Hvarenah* is thought of as a shining HALO that descends upon a leader and renders him sacred. The king thus proclaims himself divine and is authorized to rule with absolute power in the name of God. The *hvarenah* is the precursor of the nimbus of the Roman emperors and hence of the crown worn by European kings.

HWARANGDO \\'hwä-'räŋ-'dō\ (Korean: "Way of the Flower of Young Men"), unique military and philosophical code developed in the ancient Korean state of Silla around the 6th century CE. The Hwarangdo provided the basis for training of the elite society of youths known as the *hwarang*; this training placed almost equal emphasis on academic and martial skills.

The *hwarang* warriors played an instrumental role in Silla's conquest of the rest of the Korean peninsula and in the establishment of the Unified Silla dynasty (668–935). Each *hwarang* was composed of young Silla men of aristocratic birth, sometimes numbering in the thousands, who grouped themselves under a single leader. The *Hwarang*'s members prayed for the welfare of the state by visiting beautiful mountains and rivers and engaging in ritual songs and dances. They also chanted the *hyangga*, a special Silla poem that had a religious flavor. The *sesok o-kye* ("five commandments"), apparently derived from the teachings of CONFUCIANISM and BUDDHISM, taught the values of loyal service to the king, FILIAL PIETY, faithfulness to friends, courage in battle, and the evil of indiscriminate killing. The Hwarangdo began to decline with the disintegration of Silla rule, and the *hwarang* were officially disbanded during the Yi dynasty (1392–1910). Interest in the Hwarangdo was renewed in the second half of the 20th century with one style of modern Korean martial arts that is known as *hwarangdo*.

Hygieia, classical bas-relief
By courtesy of the trustees of the British Museum

HYACINTHUS \\hī-ə-'sin-thəs\, in Greek mythology, young man of Amyclae in Laconia. His great beauty attracted the love of APOLLO, who killed him accidentally while teaching him to throw the discus; in other versions of the myth Zephyrus (or BOREAS) out of jealousy deflected the discus so that it hit Hyacinthus on the head and killed him. Out of his blood there grew the flower called *hyacinthos* (not the modern hyacinth), the petals of which were marked with the mournful exclamation AI, AI ("Alas").

The death of Hyacinthus was celebrated at Amyclae by the second most important of Spartan festivals, the Hyacinthia, in the Spartan month Hyacinthius. It was probably an early summer festival; it lasted three days, and the tone of the rites gradually passed from mourning for Hyacinthus to rejoicing in the majesty of Apollo.

HYADES \\'hī-ə-,dēz\, in Greek mythology, five (or more) sisters of the PLEIADES who nursed the infant DIONYSUS and as a reward were made the five stars in the head of the constellation Taurus, the bull. According to another version, they so bitterly lamented the death of their brother Hyas that ZEUS, out of compassion, changed them into stars. Their name means the Rainers, since they rose in October and set in April and were thus prominent in the sky during the rainy season.

HYDRA \\'hī-drə\, in Greek mythology, offspring of TYPHON and ECHIDNA, a gigantic monster with nine heads (the number varies), the center one immortal. Its haunt was the marshes of Lerna near Argos. The destruction of Hydra was one of the 12 Labors of HERACLES, which he accomplished with the assistance of IOLAUS. As one head was cut off, two grew in its place; therefore, they finally burned out the roots with firebrands and at last severed the immortal head from the body. The arrows dipped by Heracles in the poisonous blood inflicted fatal wounds.

HYGIEIA \\hī-'jē-ə\, in GREEK RELIGION, goddess of health. The oldest traces of her cult are at Titane, west of Corinth, where she was worshiped together with ASCLEPIUS, the god of medicine. At first no special relationship existed between her and Asclepius, but gradually she came to be regarded as his daughter; later literature, however, makes her his wife. The cult of Hygieia spread concurrently with his and was introduced at Rome from Epidaurus in 293 BCE, when she was gradually identified with SALUS. In later times Hygieia and Asclepius became protecting deities. Hygieia's animal was a serpent, sometimes shown drinking from a saucer held in her hand.

HYMEN \'hī-mən\, *also called* Hymenaeus \ˌhī-mə-'nē-əs\, in GREEK RELIGION, the god of marriage, whose name derives from a word in the refrain of an ancient marriage song; some scholars believe it was originally the same word as *hymēn* ("hymenal membrane"), and formed part of a mock lament for the loss of the bride's vriginity. The god Hymen was usually held to be a son of APOLLO by a MUSE, perhaps Calliope; other accounts made him the son of DIONYSUS and APHRODITE. In Attic legend he was a beautiful youth who rescued a group of women, including the girl he loved, from a band of pirates. As a reward he obtained the girl in marriage, and their happy life caused him ever afterward to be invoked in marriage songs.

HYMIR \'hǖ-mir, 'hü-\, *also spelled* Hymer, in Norse mythology, GIANT who was the father of the god TYR. Hymir owned a large kettle and it was to get this that Tyr and THOR paid a visit to him. During that visit Thor went fishing with Hymir and caught the monstrous World Serpent. According to one version Thor killed the monster, but according to another Hymir cut his line just when the two mighty enemies were looking at each other. This scene is one of the most popular in Viking-age art and is often referred to in poetry.

HYMN (Greek: *hymnos,* "song of praise," in honor of gods, heroes, or famous men), strictly, a song used in Christian worship, usually sung by the congregation and characteristically having a metrical, strophic (stanzaic), non-biblical text. Similar songs, also generally termed hymns, exist in all civilizations.

Christian hymnody derives from the singing of psalms in the Hebrew Temple. The earliest fully preserved text (*c.* 200 CE or earlier) is the Greek "Phos hilarion" ("Go, Gladsome Light"). Hymnody flourished earliest in Syria, where the practice was possibly taken over from the singing by Gnostics and Manichaeans of hymns imitating the psalms. The Byzantine church adopted the practice; in its liturgy, hymns maintain a much more prominent place than in the Latin liturgy; and Byzantine hymnody developed complex types such as the *kanōn* and *kontakion.* Saint Ephraem—a 4th-century Mesopotamian deacon, poet, and hymnist— has been called the "father of Christian hymnody."

In the West, St. Hilary of Poitiers composed a book of hymn texts in about 360. Not much later ST. AMBROSE of Milan instituted the congregational singing of psalms and hymns, partly as a counter to the hymns of the Arians, who were in doctrinal conflict with orthodox CHRISTIANITY. In poetic form (iambic octosyllables in four-line stanzas), these early hymns—apparently sung to simple melodies— derive from Christian Latin poetry of the period. By the late Middle Ages trained choirs had supplanted the congregation in the singing of hymns. Although new, often more ornate melodies were composed and many earlier melodies were elaborated, one syllable of text per note was usual. Some polyphonic hymn settings were used, usually in alternation with plainchants, and were particularly important in organ music.

Congregational singing in the liturgy was reestablished only during the REFORMATION, by the Lutheran church in Germany. The early chorale, or German hymn melody, was unharmonized and sung unaccompanied, although harmonized versions, used by varying combinations of choir, or-

gan, and congregation, appeared later. Some were newly composed, but many drew upon plainsong, vernacular devotional song, and secular song. The pattern of secular lyrics also influenced the hymn texts of MARTIN LUTHER and his contemporaries. PIETISM brought a new lyrical and subjective note into German hymnody in the 17th and 18th centuries, among both Lutherans and other groups, such as the MORAVIAN CHURCH. Swiss, and later, French, English, and Scottish CALVINISM promoted the singing of metrical translations of the psalter, austerely set for unaccompanied unison singing.

European hymnody has been largely influenced by Lutheran models, although in Italy the Waldensian church cultivates congregational hymnody influenced by local folksong and operatic styles. The COUNTER-REFORMATION in the mid-16th century stimulated the composition of many fine ROMAN CATHOLIC hymns, and a renewal of interest in the late 19th century eventually led, in England, to the *Westminster Hymnal* (1940). The reintroduction of congregational singing during MASS in the late 1960s also proved a stimulus to the composition of new hymns and led to the adoption of many hymns from non-Catholic sources.

HYPERBOREAN \ˌhī-pər-'bōr-ē-ən, -'bȯr-, -bȯ-'rē-ən\, in GREEK RELIGION, one of a mythical people intimately connected with the worship of APOLLO at DELPHI and of ARTEMIS at Delos. The name *Hyperboreoi* was conventionally taken by the Greeks as alluding to BOREAS, the north wind, and their home was placed in a paradisal region beyond the north wind. They lived for 1,000 years; if any desired to shorten that period, he decked himself with garlands and threw himself from a rock into the sea. According to Herodotus, several Hyperborean maidens had been sent with offerings to Delos, but, the offerings having been delivered, the maidens died. Thereafter the Hyperboreans wrapped their offerings in wheat straw and requested their neighbors to hand them on, from nation to nation, until they finally reached Delos.

HYPNOS \'hip-nəs, -ˌnōs\, Greek god of sleep. Hypnos was the son of NYX (Night) and the brother of Thanatos (Death). He is variously described as living in the Underworld, in the land of the Cimmerians, or in a dark, misty cave on the island of Lemnos. The waters of LETHE, the river of forgetfulness and oblivion, flowed through this chamber. Hypnos lay on his soft couch, surrounded by his many sons, who were the bringers of dreams. Chief among them were MORPHEUS, who brought dreams of men; Icelus, who brought dreams of animals; and Phantasus, who brought dreams of inanimate things.

In Homer's *Iliad,* Hypnos is enlisted by HERA to lull ZEUS to sleep so that she can aid the Greeks in their war against Troy. As a reward for his services, Hypnos is given Pasithea, one of the GRACES, to wed.

HYSTASPES \hi-'stas-pēz\, *also called* Gushtasp, *or* Vishtāspa (fl. 7th and 6th centuries BCE), protector and follower of the Iranian prophet ZOROASTER. Son of Aurvataspa (Lohrasp) of the Naotara family, Hystaspes was a local ruler (*kavi*) in a country called in the AVESTA Aryana Vaejah, which may have been a Greater Chorasmian state abolished by the Achaemenid king Cyrus II the Great in the mid-6th century BCE. Hystaspes' son, known by his Greek name Darius, became king of the Persian Empire. There is some uncertainty as to whether this Hystaspes is the same as the Vishtāspa of the Zoroastrian texts.

483

IACCHUS \ī-'a-kəs\, *also spelled* Iakchos, minor deity associated with the ELEUSINIAN MYSTERIES, the best known of the ancient Greek MYSTERY RELIGIONS. On the day preceding the commencement of the mysteries, Iacchus' name was invoked with the names of the earth goddess DEMETER and her daughter Kore (PERSEPHONE) during the PROCESSION from Athens to Eleusis. Probably originally a personification of the ritual invocation (*Iakch' ō Iakche*), Iacchus was variously identified. According to some sources he was synonymous with Bacchus (DIONYSUS), whose name was similar to his. Iacchus was also regarded as the son of ZEUS and Demeter (or sometimes as her consort) and differentiated from the Theban Bacchus (Dionysus), who was the son of Zeus and SEMELE. Still other traditions identified Iacchus as the son of Kore or of Dionysus. In art Iacchus was portrayed holding a torch and leading the celebrants.

I AM MOVEMENT, religious movement in the United States that taught that the Mighty I Am is the source of power and of all necessary things. It was begun in the 1930s by Guy Ballard (1878–1939), a mining engineer, and his wife, Edna (1886–1971). The name of the movement came from the Bible verse (Exodus 3:14) in which God replies to MOSES, "I am who I am."

The Ballards taught that the power of the Mighty I Am was available to individuals through many Ascended Masters, the principal ones being JESUS and St. Germain. The Ascended Masters spoke through their special representatives on earth, the Accredited Messengers, who were Edna and Guy Ballard and their son, Donald.

Guy Ballard's professed first meeting with St. Germain, said to have taken place in 1930 at Mount Shasta in northern California, was recounted in his book, *Unveiled Mysteries* (1934). St. Germain was said to have lived on earth and been reincarnated several times as persons such as Samuel in the Old Testament and Francis Bacon of England. According to Ballard, St. Germain took him backward in time and revealed many of Ballard's previous lives (he had been George Washington). Ballard was introduced to many mysteries, and it was revealed to him how the Ascended Masters would work through the Accredited Messengers on earth.

In 1934 the Ballards began holding classes in Chicago and other cities in which messages were given through the Ballards from the Ascended Masters. In the early part of the movement the Ballards' religious presentations and lifestyle were quite simple, but as the movement gained followers and financial success, more elaborate meetings were developed. During the most successful period, in 1938, the movement was estimated to have from one to three million members. Local organizations were formed to carry on the movement, and a monthly periodical, *The Voice of the I Am*, was published.

The Ballards were increasingly criticized by the press and were accused of fraud. In 1939 Guy Ballard announced that

he had been instructed by St. Germain to suspend all public meetings. When Guy Ballard died on Dec. 29, 1939, Mrs. Ballard had his body cremated and on Jan. 1, 1940, announced that Ballard was now an Ascended Master. News of his death, however, led many followers to leave the movement, since the Ballards had taught that the ascension, the liberation forever from the physical body and from reincarnation, would come without the experience of physical death. Edna Ballard carried on as leader of the movement and often reported messages from her late husband.

In 1940 Edna, Donald, and other leaders in the movement were indicted for fraud. Edna and Donald were convicted on several counts, but the U.S. Supreme Court in 1946 set aside the indictment on a technicality. The movement initially declined, but, after some rebuilding, there are some 300 I Am centers worldwide.

IASION \ī-'ā-zē-ən\, *also called* Iasios \ī-'ā-zē-əs\, in Greek mythology, Cretan youth loved by DEMETER, who lay with him in a fallow field that had been thrice plowed. Their son was Plutus. According to another version, Iasion attempted to rape the goddess and was struck by lightning hurled by ZEUS.

IBLĪS \i-'blēs\, in ISLAM, the personal name of the devil, probably derived from the Greek *diabolos*. Iblīs is also referred to as *ʿadūw Allāh* (enemy of God), *ʿadūw* (enemy), or, when he is portrayed as a tempter, *al-Shayṭān* (DEMON).

At the creation of humans, God ordered all his ANGELS to bow down in obedience before Adam. Iblīs refused, claiming he was a nobler being since he was created of fire, while man came only of clay. For this exhibition of pride and disobedience, God threw Iblīs out of heaven. His punishment, however, was postponed until the Judgment Day, when he and his host will have to face the eternal fires of hell; until that time he is allowed to tempt all but true believers to evil. Iblīs entered the GARDEN OF EDEN and tempted Eve to eat of the tree of immortality, causing both ADAM AND EVE to forfeit paradise. Disguised as the *hātif*, the mysterious voice of Arab mythology, Iblīs tempted ABRAHAM when he was about to sacrifice his own son, and also tempted ʿALĪ, Muhammad's son-in-law, unsuccessfully trying to keep him from performing the ritual washing of the Prophet's dead body.

Iblīs has long been a figure of speculation among Muslim scholars, who have been trying to explain the ambiguous identification of Iblīs in the QURʾAN as either angel or *jinnī*, a contradiction in terms, as angels are created of light (*nūr*) and are incapable of SIN, while JINN are created of fire (*nār*) and can sin. Traditional explanations include the claim that Iblīs was simply a *jinnī* who inappropriately found himself among the angels in heaven, that he was an angel sent to earth to do battle with the rebellious *jinn* who inhabited the earth before man was created, and that he was himself one of the terrestrial *jinn* captured by the angels during their attack and brought to heaven.

Many Sufis (see SUFISM) regarded Iblīs as a figure of disobedience, but some saw him as a model for the perfect monotheist and lover of God because of his refusal to bow down to Adam and because of his separation from his beloved. Aḥmad AL-GHAZĀLĪ (d. 1126) reportedly said, "Who does not learn TAWḤĪD [proclaiming God's oneness] from SATAN is an infidel."

IBN ʿABBĀD \ˌi-bən-ab-ˈbäd\, in full Abū ʿabd Allāh Muhammad ibn Abī Isḥāq Ibrāhīmī al-Nafzī al-Ḥimyarī al-Rundī (b. 1333, Ronda, Spain—d. 1390, buried Bāb al-Futūḥ, Morocco), Islamic theologian who became the leading mystical thinker of North Africa in the 14th century.

Ibn ʿAbbād immigrated to Morocco at an early age to attend the famous MADRASAS (religious colleges), where he abandoned legal studies in a quest for mystical knowledge. In 1359 he settled in the town of Salé and became an adherent of the SHĀDHILĪYA order of mystics, which emphasized a personal commitment to SUFISM and institutionalized spiritual ASCETICISM. The order's spread and popularity in North Africa owed much to Ibn ʿAbbād's teachings and writings. Because the order and Ibn ʿAbbād represented moderate mystical tendencies, there was no conflict between them and the traditional SUNNI religious authorities of Morocco, and in 1375 he was appointed an IMAM (leader of public prayers) by the ruler of Morocco. As a scholar, Ibn ʿAbbād was especially noted for two collections of his correspondence, which contain spiritual directions and instructions to his followers.

IBN ʿABD AL-WAHHĀB, MUHAMMAD \ˌi-bən-ˌäb-dŭl-wa-ˈhäb\ (b. 1703, ʿUyaynah, Arabia [now in Saudi Arabia]—d. 1792, Al-Dirʿīya), theologian and founder of the Wahhābī movement, which attempted a return to the true principles of ISLAM.

Having completed his formal education in MEDINA, in Arabia, ʿAbd al-Wahhāb taught for four years in Basra, Iraq, and in Baghdad married an affluent woman whose property he inherited when she died. In 1736, in Iran, he began to teach against what he considered to be the extreme ideas of various exponents of the doctrines of SUFISM. On returning to his native city, he wrote the Kitāb al-tawḥīd ("Book of Unity"), the main text for Wahhābī doctrines. His followers call themselves MUWAḤḤIDŪN, or "Unitarians"; the term Wahhābī is generally used by non-Muslims and opponents.

ʿAbd al-Wahhāb's teachings have been characterized as puritanical and traditional, representing an attempt to reconstruct the early era of the Islamic religion. He made a clear stand against all innovations (BIDʿA) in Islamic faith because he believed them to be reprehensible, insisting that the original grandeur of Islam could be regained if the Islamic community would return to the principles enunciated by the Prophet MUHAMMAD. Wahhābī doctrines, therefore, do not allow for an intermediary between the faithful and Allāh and condemn any such practice as POLYTHEISM. The decoration of mosques, the popular cult of saints, SHIʿITE devotion to the IMAMS, and even the smoking of tobacco were condemned.

When the preaching of these doctrines led to controversy, ʿAbd al-Wahhāb was expelled from ʿUyayna in 1744. He then settled in Al-Dirʿīya, the provincial capital of Ibn Saʿūd, the ruler of the Najd region (now in Saudi Arabia). The spread of Wahhābīsm originated from the alliance between ʿAbd al-Wahhāb and Ibn Saʿūd, who, by initiating a campaign of conquest that was continued by his heirs, made Wahhābīsm the dominant force in Arabia from 1800.

IBN AL-ʿARABĪ \ˌib-nŭl-är-ä-ˈbē\, in full Muḥyi al-Dīn Abū ʿAbd Allāh Muḥammad ibn ʿAlī ibn Muhammad ibn al-ʿArabī al-Hātimī al-Ṭāī ibn al-ʿArabī, also called al-Shaykh al-Akbar \ˌäl-ˈshik̲-äl-ak-ˈbär\ (b. July 28, 1165, Murcia, Valencia—d. Nov. 16, 1240, Damascus), celebrated Muslim mystic-philosopher who gave the esoteric, mystical dimension of Islamic thought its first full-fledged philosophic expression.

Ibn al-ʿArabī was educated in Seville, then an outstanding center of Islamic culture and learning. He stayed there for 30 years, studying traditional Islamic sciences. During those years he traveled a great deal in Spain and North Africa in search of masters of the Sufi (mystical) Path (see SUFISM) who had achieved great spiritual progress. During one of these trips he had a dramatic encounter with the great Aristotelian philosopher IBN RUSHD (Averroës; 1126–98) in the city of Córdoba. After the early exchange of only a few words, it is said, the mystical depth of the boy so overwhelmed the old philosopher that he began trembling.

In 1198, while in Murcia, he had a vision in which he was ordered to leave Spain and set out for the East. The first notable place he visited on this journey was MECCA (1201), where he "received a divine commandment" to begin his major work al-Futūḥāt al-Makkīya ("The Meccan Revelations"), which was to be completed much later in Damascus. In 560 chapters, it is a personal encyclopedia extending over all the esoteric sciences in ISLAM as Ibn al-ʿArabī understood and had experienced them, together with valuable information about his own inner life.

It was also in Mecca that he became acquainted with a young girl of great beauty who, as a living embodiment of the eternal sophia (wisdom), was to play in his life a role much like that which Beatrice played for Dante. Her memory was eternalized by Ibn al-ʿArabī in a collection of love poems (Tarjumān al-ashwāq; "The Interpreter of Desires"), upon which he himself composed a mystical commentary. His pantheistic expressions drew down on him the wrath of Muslim authorities, some of whom prohibited the reading of his works at the same time that others were elevating him to the rank of the prophets and saints.

After Mecca, he visited Egypt (also in 1201) and then Anatolia, where, in Qunya, he met Ṣadr al-Dīn al-Qūnawī, who was to become his most important follower and successor in the East. From Qunya he went on to Baghdad and Aleppo. By the time his long PILGRIMAGE had come to an end at Damascus (1223), his fame had spread all over the Islamic world. Venerated as the greatest spiritual master, he spent the rest of his life in Damascus in contemplation, teaching, and writing. During his Damascus days he composed (1229) one of the most important works in mystical philosophy in Islam, Fuṣūṣ al-ḥikam ("The Bezels of Wisdom"). Its importance as an expression of his mystical thought in its most mature form cannot be overemphasized. Starting in the 14th century his ideas flourished among Sufis in India and later in Indonesia.

IBN AL-FĀRIḌ \ˌib-näl-ˈfär-id\, in full Sharaf al-Dīn Abū Ḥafṣ ʿUmar ibn al-Fāriḍ (b. March 22, 1181 or March 11, 1182, Cairo—d. Jan. 23, 1235, Cairo), Arab poet whose expression of Sufi MYSTICISM is regarded as the finest in the Arabic language.

Son of a Syrian-born inheritance-law functionary, Ibn al-Fāriḍ studied for a legal career but abandoned law for a solitary religious life in the Muqaṭṭam hills near Cairo. He spent some years in or near MECCA, where he met the renowned Sufi Abū Ḥafṣ ʿUmar AL-SUHRAWARDĪ of Baghdad (d.

1234). Venerated as a saint during his lifetime, Ibn al-Fāriḍ was buried in the Muqaṭṭam hills, where his tomb is still visited. In later times his verse became the subject of controversy. Some religious authorities accused him of favoring pantheistic ideas, similar to those of IBN AL-ʿARABĪ, which were held to undermine the SHARĪʿA and to be conducive to infidelity. In the end, his saintly status was redeemed with the assistance of the Mamlūk sultan Qāʾit Bāy (d. 1496).

Many of Ibn al-Fāriḍ's poems are *qaṣīda*s ("odes") on the lover's longing for reunion with his beloved. He expresses through this convention his yearning for a return to Mecca and, at a deeper level, a desire to be assimilated into the spirit of MUHAMMAD, first projection of the Godhead. He developed this theme at length in *Naẓm al-sulūk* (Eng. trans. by A.J. Arberry, *The Poem of the Way*, 1952). Almost equally famous is his "Khamrīya" ("Wine Ode"; Eng. trans., with other poems, in Reynold Alleyne Nicholson's *Studies in Islamic Mysticism* [1921] and in *The Mystical Poems of Ibn al-Fāriḍ*, translated by A.J. Arberry [1956]), which describes the effects of the wine of divine love. *See also* SUFISM.

IBN AL-JAWZĪ

IBN AL-JAWZĪ \,ib-nùl-jaù-'zē\, *in full* ʿAbd al-Raḥmān ibn ʿAlī ibn Muhammad Abū al-Farash ibn al-Jawzī (b. 1126, Baghdad—d. 1200, Baghdad), jurist, theologian, historian, preacher, and teacher who became an important figure in the Baghdad establishment and a leading spokesman of traditionalist Sunni ISLAM (*see* SUNNA).

Ibn al-Jawzī received a traditional religious education and chose a teaching career, becoming by 1161 the master of two religious colleges. A fervent adherent of Ḥanbalī doctrine (one of the four schools of Islamic law), he was a noted preacher whose sermons were conservative in viewpoint and supported the religious policies of the Baghdad ruling establishment. In return he was favored by the CALIPHS, and by 1178/79 he had become the master of five colleges and the leading Ḥanbalī spokesman of Baghdad.

In the decade 1170–80 he attained the height of his power. Becoming a semiofficial inquisitor, he constantly searched for doctrinal heresies. He was particularly critical of Sufis (Muslim mystics; *see* SUFISM) and of SHIʿITE scholars. His zeal antagonized many liberal religious scholars. The arrest in 1194 of Ibn Yūnus, his old friend and patron, marked the end of Ibn al-Jawzī's career and his close links with governmental circles. In that year he was arrested and exiled to the city of Wāsiṭ. He was partially rehabilitated on the eve of his death and allowed to return to Baghdad.

Ibn al-Jawzī's scholarly works reflected his adherence to Ḥanbalī doctrine. Much of his work was of a hagiographical and polemical nature. Of particular interest was his *Ṣifat al-Ṣafwah* ("Attributes of Mysticism"), an extensive history of MYSTICISM, which argued that the true mystics were those who modeled their lives on the COMPANIONS OF THE PROPHET. *See also* ḤANBALĪ LEGAL SCHOOL.

IBN ʿAQĪL

IBN ʿAQĪL \,i-bən-a-'kēl\, *in full* Abū al-Wafāʾ ʿAlī ibn ʿAqīl ibn Muhammad ibn ʿAqīl ibn Aḥmad al-Baghdādī az-Ẓafarī (b. 1040, Baghdad—d. 1119), Islamic theologian and scholar of the Ḥanbalī school, the most traditional of the schools of Islamic law. His thoughts and teachings represent an attempt to give a somewhat more liberal direction to Ḥanbalism.

In 1055–66 Ibn ʿAqīl received instruction in Islamic law according to the tenets of the Ḥanbalī school. During these years, however, he also became interested in liberal theological ideas that were regarded as reprehensible by his traditionalist Ḥanbalī teachers. These ideas represented two diverse trends within Islamic thought—that of the Muʿtazilites, those who sought to understand and interpret religious doctrine according to the canons of logical inquiry and reason, and that of the teachings of the mystic AL-ḤALLĀJ, especially his concept of unity of phenomena (*waḥdat al-shuhūd*), a doctrine that attempted to accommodate the idea of unity (TAWHĪD) of SUFISM and the scripturalist theologians' concern with the revealed law (*sharʿ*).

Ibn ʿAqīl's attraction to these ideas weakened his standing in the conservative Ḥanbalī community of Baghdad. He aroused further animosity when in 1066 he attained a professorship at the important mosque of al-Mansūr. The professional jealousy of those theologians who had been passed over, coupled with his espousal of innovative and controversial doctrines, led to Ibn ʿAqīl's persecution. After the death of his influential patron, Abū Manṣūr ibn Yūsuf, in 1067 or 1068, he was forced to retire from his teaching position. Until 1072 he lived in partial retirement under the protection of Abū Manṣūr's son-in-law, a wealthy Ḥanbalī merchant. The controversy over his ideas came to an end in September 1072, when he was forced to retract his beliefs publicly before a group of scripturalist theologians. This retraction may have been based on expediency and was in keeping with the recognized practice of TAQĪYA (precautionary dissimulation).

Ibn ʿAqīl spent the rest of his life in the pursuit of scholarship. His most famous work was the *Kitāb al-funūn* ("Book of Sciences"), an encyclopedia covering a large variety of subjects. This work was said to have included between 200 and 800 volumes, all but one of which have been lost. *See also* ḤANBALĪ LEGAL SCHOOL.

IBN BĀBAWAYH

IBN BĀBAWAYH \,i-bən-'bä-baù-,wī\, *also spelled* Ibn Babūyā, *in full* Abū Jaʿfar Muhammad ibn Abū al-Ḥasan ʿAlī ibn Ḥusayn ibn Mūsā al-Qummī, *also called* al-Ṣadūq \àl-sa-'dük\ (b. c. 923, Khorāsān province, Iran—d. 991, Rayy), Islamic religious scholar, author of one of the "Four Books" that are the basic authorities for the doctrine of Twelver Shiʿites (ITHNĀ ʿASHARĪYA).

According to legend Ibn Bābawayh was born as the result of special prayers to the MAHDI (the Shiʿite deliverer). In 966 he left Khorāsān for Baghdad, possibly attracted by the Shiʿite inclination of the Būyid dynasty that ruled there. Within a short time he was recognized as the spokesman and leading intellectual figure of Twelver Shiʿites.

More than 200 separate works have been attributed to Ibn Bābawayh, although only a few are now extant. His *Risālat al-iʿtiqādāt* (*Shiʿite Creed*, 1942) is important for the study of the doctrinal development of Shiʿism. His works are still widely used wherever Twelver Shiʿites are found.

IBN BĀJJA

IBN BĀJJA \,i-bən-'ba-jə\, *also called* Avempace \,ä-vəm-'pä-sä\, *in full* Abū Bakr Muhammad ibn Yahyā ibn al-Ṣāyigh al-Tujībī al-Andalusī al-Saraqustī (b. c. 1095, Zaragoza, Spain—d. 1138/39, Fès, Morocco), earliest known representative in Spain of the Arabic Aristotelian-Neoplatonic philosophical tradition and a forerunner of the scholar IBN ṬUFAYL and of the philosopher IBN RUSHD (Averroës).

Ibn Bājja's chief philosophical tenets seem to have included belief in the possibility that the human soul could become united with the Divine. This union was conceived as the final stage in an intellectual ascent beginning with the impressions of sense objects that consist of form and matter and rising through a hierarchy of spiritual forms (*i.e.*, forms containing less and less matter) to the Active Intellect, which is an emanation of the deity. Many Muslim biographers consider Ibn Bājja to have been an atheist.

Ibn Bājja's most important philosophical work is *Tadbīr al-mutawaḥḥid* ("The Regime of the Solitary"), incomplete at his death. He also wrote a number of songs and poems and a treatise on botany; he is known to have studied astronomy, medicine, and mathematics.

Unlike his predecessor AL-FĀRĀBĪ, Ibn Bājja is silent about the philosopher's duty to partake of the life of the city. He appears to argue that the aim of philosophy is attainable independently from the philosopher's concern with the best city and is to be achieved in solitude or, at most, in comradeship with philosophic souls. Unlike IBN SĪNĀ (Avicenna), who prepared the way for him by clearly distinguishing between theoretical and practical science, Ibn Bājja is concerned with practical science only insofar as it is relevant to the life of the philosopher. He is contemptuous of allegories and imaginative representations of philosophic knowledge and silent about theology, and he shows no concern with improving the multitude's opinions and way of life.

IBN DAUD, ABRAHAM BEN DAVID HALEVI \,i-bən-'da-ūd\, *also called* Rabad I \rä-'bäd, 'ra-bad\ (b. *c.* 1110, Toledo, Castile—d. *c.* 1180, Toledo), physician and historian who was the first Jewish philosopher to draw on Aristotle's writings in a systematic fashion.

Ibn Daud wrote his history *Sefer ha-kabbala* ("Book of Tradition") in answer to an attack on rabbinic authority by the Karaites, a Jewish sect that considered only SCRIPTURE as authoritative, not the Jewish oral law as embodied in the TALMUD. Thus, he attempted to demonstrate an unbroken chain of rabbinic tradition from MOSES, providing much valuable information about contemporary Spanish Jewry, their SYNAGOGUES, and their religious practices.

Deriving his Aristotelianism from the 11th-century physician and philosopher IBN SĪNĀ (Avicenna) and other Islamic writers, Ibn Daud intended his major philosophic work, *Sefer ha-emuna ha-rama* ("Book of Sublime Faith") as a solution to the problem of FREE WILL. Divided into three sections dealing with physics and metaphysics, religion, and ethics, the *Emuna ha-rama* was eclipsed by the more precise Aristotelian writings of the 12th-century rabbi MOSES MAIMONIDES.

IBN EZRA, ABRAHAM BEN MEIR \,i-bən-'ez-rə\ (b. 1092/93, Tudela, Emirate of Saragossa—d. 1167, Calahorra, Spain), poet, grammarian, traveler, Neoplatonic philosopher, and astronomer, best known as a biblical exegete whose commentaries contributed to the Golden Age of Spanish JUDAISM.

As a young man he lived in Muslim Spain. He was on friendly terms with the eminent poet and philosopher JUDAH HA-LEVI, and he traveled to North Africa and possibly to Egypt. Primarily known as a scholar and poet up to that point, about 1140 Ibn Ezra began a lifelong series of wanderings throughout Europe, in the course of which he produced distinguished works of biblical EXEGESIS and disseminated biblical lore.

His biblical commentaries include expositions of the BOOK OF JOB, the Book of Daniel, Psalms, and, most important, a work produced in his old age, a commentary on the PENTATEUCH. Although his exegeses are basically philological, he inserted enough philosophical remarks to reveal himself to be a Neoplatonic pantheist. At the same time,

he believed that God gave form to uncreated, eternal matter, a concept somewhat at odds with Neoplatonic doctrine. His commentary on the Pentateuch is sometimes ranked with the classic 11th-century commentaries by RASHI on the TALMUD.

Ibn Ezra translated the Hispano-Hebrew grammarians from Arabic and wrote grammatical treatises. He also had a good knowledge of astronomy and cast HOROSCOPES, and he believed in numerological MYSTICISM as well.

IBN FALAQUERA \'i-bən-,fä-lä-'kä-rä\, *in full* Shemtob ben Joseph ibn Falaquera, Falaquera *also spelled* Palquera \päl-'kä-rä\ (b. *c.* 1225—d. *c.* 1295), Spanish-born Jewish philosopher and translator who propagated a reconciliation between Jewish Orthodoxy and philosophy and defended MAIMONIDES against the attacks of traditionalists. His works include *Dialogue Between a Philosopher and a Man of Piety*; an ethical treatise known as *The Balm of Sorrow*; an introduction to the study of the sciences entitled *Reshit ḥokhma* ("The Beginning of Wisdom"); *Sefer ha-maʿalot* ("Book of Degrees"), which advocates the Neoplatonic ideal of the CONTEMPLATIVE life; a commentary on Maimonides' *Guide of the Perplexed* under the title *More ha-more* ("Guide of the Guide"); and an abstract of Ibn Gabirol's influential *Fons vitae* in Hebrew.

IBN ḤANBAL, AḤMAD \,i-bən-'ḵän-bəl\ (b. 780, Baghdad—d. 855, Baghdad), Muslim theologian, jurist, and martyr. He was the compiler of the traditions (HADITH) of the Prophet MUHAMMAD and formulator of the Ḥanbalī, the most strictly scripturalist of the four Sunni Islamic schools of law.

When Ibn Ḥanbal was 15 he began to study the Hadith of the Prophet Muhammad, supplementing his study with travels to the cities of Kufa and Basra in Iraq and MECCA, Hijaz, and MEDINA in Arabia. He also traveled to Yemen and Syria. He made five PILGRIMAGES to Mecca, three times on foot. Ibn Ḥanbal led a life of ASCETICISM and self-denial, winning many disciples. Two of his children were well known and closely associated with his intellectual work: Ṣāliḥ (d. 880) and ʿAbd Allāh (d. 903).

The inquisition, known as *al-miḥna*, was inaugurated in 833, when the CALIPH al-Maʾmūn made obligatory upon all Muslims the belief that the QURʾAN was created, a doctrine espoused by the Muʿtazilites (a rationalist school that argued that reason was equal to revelation as a means to religious truth).

Ibn Ḥanbal refused to subscribe to the Muʿtazilī doctrine and was imprisoned. In 833 Ibn Ḥanbal was tried before the caliph al-Muʿtaṣim for three days, and upon his continued refusal to recant he was flogged until fears of popular protest brought the torture to an end. After his release Ibn Ḥanbal did not resume his lectures until the inquisition was publicly proclaimed at an end.

The inquisition continued under the next caliph, al-Wāthiq, but Ibn Ḥanbal was no longer molested, in spite of attempts on the part of his opponents to persuade the caliph to persecute him. The new caliph, like his predecessor, was most likely influenced by the threat of a popular uprising should he lay hands on a man popularly held to be a saint. The momentum of the inquisition carried it two years into the reign of al-Mutawakkil, who finally put an end to it in 848.

The most important of Ibn Ḥanbal's works is his collection of the Hadith of the Prophet Muhammad and his Companions. This collection, the *Musnad*, was once believed to have been compiled by the author's son ('Abd Allāh), but there is now evidence that the work was compiled and arranged by Ibn Ḥanbal himself. These traditions were considered by Ibn Ḥanbal as a sound basis for argument in law and religion.

Historical scholarship regarding Ibn Ḥanbal and his school has suffered from a lack of sufficient documentation, among other things. Too much stress has been laid on the influence of the teachings of Shāfi'ī, the founder of the SHĀFI'Ī LEGAL SCHOOL, whom Ibn Ḥanbal apparently met only once. He had a high respect for Shāfi'ī but also for the other great jurists who belonged to other schools of law, without, for that matter, relinquishing his own independent opinions. He was against codification of the law, maintaining that canonists had to be free to derive the solutions for questions of law from scriptural sources, namely the Qu'ran and the SUNNA (the body of Islamic custom and practice based on Muhammad's words and deeds). It was to this end that he compiled his great *Musnad*, wherein he registered all the traditions considered in his day acceptable as bases for the solution of questions, along with the Qu'ran itself.

The fact that the Ḥanbalī school was organized at all was due to the impact of Ibn Ḥanbal on his time. The other Sunni schools were already prospering in Baghdad when the Ḥanbalī school sprang up in their midst, drawing its membership from theirs. The lateness of the hour accounts for the relatively small membership attained by the Ḥanbalī school compared with the older schools. Size notwithstanding, in the Middle Ages the school acted as a spearhead of traditionalist Sunnism in its struggle against RATIONALISM. One of Ibn Ḥanbal's greatest followers, IBN TAYMĪYA (1263–1328), was claimed by both the Wahhābīya, a reform movement founded in the Arabian peninsula during the 18th century, and the modern Salafīya movement, which arose in Egypt and advocated the continued supremacy of Islamic law but with fresh interpretations to meet the community's changing needs. Ibn Ḥanbal himself is among the fathers of ISLAM whose names have constantly been invoked against rationalist movements down through the ages. *See also* ḤANBALI LEGAL SCHOOL.

IBN ḤAZM \,i-bən-'ḳȧ-zəm\, *in full* Abū Muhammad 'Alī ibn Aḥmad ibn Sa'īd ibn Ḥazm (b. Nov. 7, 994, Córdoba, Caliphate of Córdoba—d. Aug. 15, 1064, Manta Līsham, near Seville), Muslim historian, jurist, and theologian of Islamic Spain, famed for his literary productivity, breadth of learning, and mastery of the Arabic language.

Ibn Ḥazm was born into a notable family that claimed descent from a Persian client of Yazīd, the brother of Mu'āwiya, the first of the Umayyad dynasty rulers in Syria; scholars, however, tend to favor evidence that he was of Iberian Christian background. Ḥazm, his great-grandfather, probably converted to ISLAM, and his grandfather Sa'īd moved to Córdoba, the capital of the caliphate. Aḥ-mad, his father, held a high position under al-Manṣūr and his successor, al-Muẓaffar, who ruled in the name of the CALIPH Hishām II.

Upon the death of al-Muẓaffar in 1008 CE a bloody civil war erupted and continued until 1031, when the caliphate was abolished and replaced by a large number of petty states. The family was uprooted, and Aḥmad died in 1012; Ibn Ḥazm continued to support Umayyad claimants to the office of caliph, for which he was frequently imprisoned.

By 1031 he began to express his convictions and activistic inclinations through literary activity, becoming a very

controversial figure. According to one of his sons, he produced some 80,000 pages of writing, making up about 400 works. Fewer than 40 of these works are still extant. The varied character of his literary activity covers an impressive range of jurisprudence, logic, history, ethics, COMPARATIVE RELIGION, and theology. Probably best known for his work in jurisprudence and theology, for which the basic qualification was a thorough knowledge of the QUR'AN and HADITH, he became one of the leading exponents of the Ẓāhirī (literalist) school of jurisprudence (*see* ẒĀHIRĪYA). Though his legal theories never won him many followers, he creatively extended the Ẓāhirī principle to the field of theology. He made a comparative study on the religious pluralism of his day, which is among the earliest of such studies and is highly regarded for its careful compilation of historical detail.

An activist by nature with a deep sense of the reality of God, Ibn Ḥazm lived very much in the political and intellectual world of his times; however, he was very much a nonconformist. He conversed and debated with the leading contemporaries of his area, to whom he exhibited a thirst for knowledge as well as uncompromising convictions. Most observant, careful in analysis, meticulous in detail, and devoted to the clarity of his positions, he demanded the same of others. In his writings he attacked deceit, distortion, and inconsistency; but at the same time Ibn Ḥazm exhibited a sensitive spirit and expressed profound insights about the dimensions of human relationships.

He was shunned and defamed for his political and theological views. When some of his writings were burned in public, he said that no such act could deprive him of their content. Although attacks against his thought continued after his death, various influential defenders appeared. He was frequently and effectively quoted, so much so that the phrase "Ibn Ḥazm said" became proverbial. *See also* FIQH; KALĀM.

IBN ISḤĀQ \,i-bən-ē-'shäk\, *in full* Muhammad ibn Isḥāq ibn Yasār ibn Khiyār (b. *c.* 704, MEDINA, Arabia—d. 767, Baghdad), Arab biographer of the Prophet MUHAMMAD whose book, in a recension by Ibn Hishām, is one of the most important sources on the Prophet's life.

Ibn Isḥāq was the grandson of an Arab prisoner captured by Muslim troops in Iraq and brought to Medina, where he was freed after accepting ISLAM. Ibn Isḥāq's father and two uncles collected and transmitted information about Muhammad in Medina, and Ibn Isḥāq soon became an authority on the Prophet's campaigns.

He studied in Alexandria and subsequently moved to Iraq, where he lived in the Jazīra and Ḥīra regions and finally in Baghdad. Informants met on these travels furnished him with much of the information for his *Sīra*, or life, of Muhammad (later revised by Ibn Hishām). This extensive biography covers Muhammad's genealogy and birth, the beginning of his mission and of the revelation of the QUR'AN, and his migration to Medina and campaigns of conquest, and it concludes with his death. Citations from the *Sīra* also appear in the works of Arabic historians such as AL-ṬABARĪ.

Ibn Isḥāq was criticized by some Muslim scholars, including the jurist MĀLIK IBN ANAS. AḤMAD IBN ḤANBAL, however, did accept Ibn Isḥāq as an authority for the campaigns. But, on the grounds that Ibn Isḥāq was not always exact enough in naming his authorities, Ibn Ḥanbal was not willing to accept the *Sīra* in regards to traditions about the Prophet having legal force.

IBN KATHĪR \‚i-bən-ka-'thir\, *in full* 'Imād al-Dīn Ismā'īl ibn 'Umar ibn Kathīr (b. *c.* 1300, Bursa, Byzantine Empire— d. February 1373, Damascus), Muslim theologian and historian who became one of the leading intellectual figures of 14th-century Syria.

Ibn Kathīr was educated in Damascus and obtained his first official appointment in 1341, when he joined an inquisitorial commission formed to determine certain questions of HERESY. Thereafter he received various semiofficial appointments, culminating in June/July 1366 with a professorial position at the Great Mosque of Damascus.

As a scholar, Ibn Kathīr is best remembered for his 14-volume history of ISLAM, *al-Bidāya wa'l-nihāya* ("The Beginning and the End"), a work that formed the basis of a number of writings by later historians. Ibn Kathīr was also a noted student of HADITH; his *Kitāb al-jāmi'* is an alphabetical listing of the COMPANIONS OF THE PROPHET and the sayings that each transmitted and is thus a reconstruction of the chain of authority for each Hadith.

IBN KHALDŪN \‚i-bən-ķal-'dün\, *in full* Walī al-Dīn 'Abd al-Raḥmān ibn Muhammad ibn Muhammad ibn Abī Bakr Muhammad ibn al-Ḥasan ibn Khaldūn (b. May 27, 1332, Tunis—d. March 17, 1406, Cairo), great Arab historian, who developed one of the earliest nonreligious philosophies of history, contained in his masterpiece, the *Muqaddima* ("Introduction to History").

After completing his formal education Ibn Khaldūn was, at the age of 20, given a post at the court of Tunis, followed three years later by a secretaryship to the SULTAN of Morocco. After two years of service, however, he was suspected of participation in a rebellion and was imprisoned. After his release he again fell into disfavor and decided to leave Morocco for Granada, whose prime minister, the brilliant writer Ibn al-Khatīb, was a friend. But, according to Ibn Khaldūn, "enemies and intriguers" turned Ibn al-Khatīb against him; it can be conjectured that the task of these enemies must have been greatly facilitated by the apparent jealousy between the two most brilliant Arab intellectuals of the age. Ibn Khaldūn found it necessary to leave, and he returned to Africa. (Later he would return to Granada to make an unsuccessful effort to save Ibn al-Khatīb from being killed by order of its ruler.)

The following 10 years saw him change employment frequently. During this period he served as prime minister and in other administrative capacities, led a punitive expedition, and spent some time "studying and teaching." This extreme mobility is partly explained by the instability of the times, as the Almohad Empire, which had embraced the whole of North Africa and Muslim Spain, had broken down in the middle of the 13th century. But in Ibn Khaldūn's case a certain restlessness and a capacity to make enemies might also be suspected.

In 1375 Ibn Khaldūn sought refuge with the tribe of Awlād 'Arīf, who lodged him and his family in the safety of a castle in Algeria. There he spent four years, writing his massive masterpiece, the *Muqaddima*. His original intention, which he subsequently achieved, was to write a universal history of the Arabs and Berbers, but before doing so he judged it necessary to discuss historical method, with the aim of providing the criteria necessary for distinguishing historical truth from error. This led him to formulate what the 20th-century English historian Arnold Toynbee has described as "a philosophy of history which is undoubtedly the greatest work of its kind that has ever yet been created by any mind in any time or place."

But Ibn Khaldūn went even further. His study of the nature of society and social change led him to evolve what he clearly saw was a new science, which he called *'ilm al-'umrān* ("the science of culture"). Many would claim that Book I of the *Muqaddima* sketches a general sociology; Books II and III a sociology of politics; Book IV, a sociology of urban life; Book V, a sociology of economics; and Book VI, a sociology of knowledge. The work is held together by the central concept of *'asabīya*, or "tribal cohesion." It is this form of social cohesion, which arises spontaneously in tribes and other small KINSHIP groups, but which can be intensified and enlarged by a religious ideology, that provides the motive force that carries ruling groups to power.

During his stay in Algeria, Ibn Khaldūn not only completed the first draft of the *Muqaddima* but also wrote part of his massive history, *Kitab al-'ibar*, the best single source on the history of Muslim North Africa. He then returned to Tunis. Once more he aroused both the jealousy of a prominent scholar and the suspicion of the ruler, and he left for Egypt, ostensibly for the purpose of performing the PILGRIMAGE to MECCA. A few days after his arrival in Cairo he started teaching at al-Azhar, the famous Islamic university. Shortly afterward, the new Mamlūk ruler of Egypt, Barqūq, with whom he was to remain on fairly good terms, appointed him to a professorship of jurisprudence, and later he made him a judge. Barqūq also successfully interceded with the ruler of Tunis to allow Ibn Khaldūn's family to rejoin him, but the ship carrying them foundered in the port of Alexandria, drowning all on board.

Ibn Khaldūn took his judicial duties quite seriously and attempted to reform the numerous abuses that had developed in the administration of justice. Once again, trouble ensued and he was dismissed. But he was given another professorship and spent his time teaching, writing, and revising his *Muqaddima*. He was also able to perform the pilgrimage to Mecca.

When the Tatars, led by Timur, invaded Syria in 1400, the new sultan of Egypt, Faraj, went out to meet them, taking Ibn Khaldūn and other notables with him. Shortly thereafter, the Mamlūk army returned to Egypt, leaving Ibn Khaldūn in besieged Damascus. The historian used all his accumulated worldly wisdom to secure from Timur a safe-conduct for the civilian employees left in Damascus and permission for himself to return to Egypt, where he remained until his death in 1406.

IBN RUSHD \‚i-bən-'rùsht\, *also called* Averroës, *medieval Latin* Averrhoës, *Arabic in full* Abū al-Walīd Muhammad ibn Aḥmad ibn Muhammad ibn Rushd (b. 1126, Córdoba— d. 1198, Marrakech, Almohad Empire), Islamic religious philosopher who integrated Islamic traditions and Greek thought in a series of summaries and commentaries on most of Aristotle's works (1162–95) and on Plato's *Republic*, which exerted considerable influence for centuries. He wrote the *Decisive Treatise on the Agreement Between Religious Law and Philosophy (Faṣl); Examination of the Methods of Proof Concerning the Doctrines of Religion (Manāhij);* and *The Incoherence of the Incoherence (Tahāfut al-tahāfut),* all in defense of the philosophical STUDY OF RELIGION (1179–80).

Ibn Rushd was born into a distinguished family of jurists. Thoroughly versed in the traditional Muslim sciences (especially EXEGESIS of the QUR'AN and HADITH, and FIQH, or Law), trained in medicine, and accomplished in philosophy, he rose to be chief *qāḍī* (judge) of Córdoba. After the death of the philosopher IBN ṬUFAYL, Ibn Rushd succeeded him as personal physician to the CA-LIPHS Abū Yaʿqūb Yūsuf in 1182 and his son Abū Yūsuf Yaʿqūb in 1184. In 1169 Ibn Ṭufayl had introduced Ibn Rushd to Abū Yaʿqūb, who requested that he provide a badly needed new interpretation of Aristotle's philosophy, a task to which he devoted many years of his life.

Between 1169 and 1195 Ibn Rushd wrote a series of commentaries on most of Aristotle's works (*e.g.*, the *Organon, De anima, Physica, Metaphysica, De partibus animalium, Parva naturalia, Meteorologica, Rhetorica, Poetica,* and the *Nicomachean Ethics*). Aristotle's *Politica* was inaccessible; therefore he wrote a commentary on Plato's *Republic.* Ibn Rushd's commentaries exerted considerable influence on Jews and Christians in the following centuries. He was able to present competently Aristotle's thought and to add considerably to its understanding. He ably and critically drew upon the ideas of the classical commentators Themistius and Alexander of Aphrodisias and the *falāsifa* (Muslim philosophers) AL-FĀRĀBĪ, IBN SĪNĀ (Avicenna), and his own countryman IBN BĀJJA (Avempace).

His own first work, *General Medicine* (*Kulliyāt,* Latin *Colliget*), was written between 1162 and 1169. Only a few of his legal writings and none of his theological writings are preserved. Undoubtedly his most important writings are three closely connected religious-philosophical polemical treatises, composed in the years 1179 and 1180: the *Faṣl;* its *Appendix: Manāhij;* and *Tahāfut al-tahāfut.* In the first two Ibn Rushd stakes a bold claim: Only the metaphysician employing certain proof (syllogism) is capable and competent (as well as obliged) to interpret the doctrines contained in the prophetically revealed law (Sharʿ or SHARĪʿA), and not the Muslim *mutakallimūn* (dialectic theologians), who rely on dialectical arguments. To establish the true, inner meaning of RELIGIOUS BELIEFS and convictions is the aim of philosophy in its quest for truth. This inner meaning must not be divulged to the masses, who must accept the plain, external meaning of SCRIPTURE contained in stories, similes, and metaphors. The third work is devoted to a defense of philosophy against his predecessor AL-GHAZĀLĪ's telling attack.

Ibn Rushd pursued his philosophical quest in the face of strong opposition from the *mutakallimūn,* who, together with the jurists, occupied a position of great influence. This may explain why Abū Yūsuf—on the occasion of a JIHAD against a coalition of Christians—dismissed him from high office and banished him to Lucena in 1195. But his disgrace

Ibn Rushd (Averroës), depicted on a Spanish postage stamp
Culver Pictures

was short-lived—though long enough to cause him acute suffering—since the caliph recalled him after his return to Marrakesh.

There is only one truth for Ibn Rushd, that of the religious law, which is the same truth that the metaphysician is seeking. Ibn Rushd stated explicitly and unequivocally that religion is for all three classes; that the contents of the Sharīʿa are the whole and only truth for all believers; and that religion's teachings about reward and punishment and the hereafter must be accepted in their plain meaning by the elite no less than by the masses. Accepting Aristotle's division of philosophy into theoretical (physics and metaphysics) and practical (ethics and politics), he finds that the Sharīʿa teaches both to perfection: abstract knowledge commanded as the perception of God, and practice—the ethical virtues the law enjoins (*Commentary on Plato's Republic*). As a Muslim, Ibn Rushd insists on the attainment of happiness in this and the next life by all believers. As a philosopher he distinguishes between degrees of happiness and assigns every believer the happiness that corresponds to his intellectual capacity. Everyone is entitled to his share of happiness. The Sharīʿa of ISLAM demands that the believer should know God. This knowledge is accessible to the naive believer in metaphors, the inner meaning of which is intelligible only to the metaphysician with the help of demonstration.

IBN SHEM TOV, JOSEPH BEN SHEM TOV \ˌi-bən-ˈshem-ˈtȯb̲, -ˈtȯv \ (b. *c.* 1400—d. *c.* 1480), Jewish philosopher and Castilian court physician who attempted to reconcile Aristotelian ethical philosophy with Jewish religious thought, best exemplified by his influential *Kevod Elohim* (written 1442; "The Glory of God"). Here he argued that answers sought through philosophical inquiry can be valuable in one's quest for religious knowledge and that even religious principles should be subjected to such inquiry. Although as a philosopher he advocated intellectual pursuits, Joseph maintained that the immortality of the soul was assured not by intellectual development but by conscientious religious observance. He also upheld the value of MYSTICISM and intuition in the understanding of religious precepts.

IBN SĪNĀ \ˌi-bən-ˈsē-nä \, *also called* Avicenna \ˌa-və-ˈse-nə \, *Arabic in full* Abū ʿAlī al-Ḥusayn ibn ʿAbd Allāh ibn Sīnā (b. 980, Bukhara, Iran—d. 1037, Hamadan), Iranian physician, the most famous and influential of the philosopher-scientists of ISLAM. He was particularly noted for his contributions in the fields of Aristotelian philosophy and medicine. He composed the *Kitāb al-shifāʾ* ("Book of Healing"), a vast philosophical and scientific encyclopedia, and the *Canon of Medicine,* which is among the most famous books in the history of medicine.

Ibn Sīnā received his earliest education in Bukhara under the direction of his father. Since his father's house was a meeting place for learned men, from his earliest childhood Ibn Sīnā was able to profit from the company of the outstanding masters of his day. By the age of 10 he had memorized the QURʾAN and much Arabic poetry. Thereafter, he studied logic and metaphysics. He read avidly and mastered Islamic law, then medicine, and finally metaphysics. Particularly helpful in his intellectual development was his access to the rich royal library of the Sāmānids—the first great native dynasty that arose in Iran after the Arab conquest—as the result of his successful cure of the Sāmānid prince, Nūḥ ibn Manṣūr. By the time he was 21 he was accomplished in all branches of formal learning and had already gained a reputation as an outstanding physician. His services were also sought as an administrator, and for a while he even entered government service as a clerk.

This was one of the tumultuous periods of Iranian history, when new Turkish elements were replacing Iranian domination in Central Asia, and local Iranian dynasties were trying to gain political independence from the ʿAb-

Ibn Sīnā (Avicenna), postage stamp from Qatar, 1971
The Granger Collection

bāsid caliphate in Baghdad (in modern Iraq). Fleeing political upheaval, Ibn Sīnā left for central Iran, then continued further to Hamadan in west-central Iran, where Shams al-Dawla was ruling. This journey marked the beginning of a new phase in Ibn Sīnā's life. He became court physician and enjoyed the favor of the ruler to the extent that twice he was appointed vizier. As was the order of the day, he also suffered political reactions and intrigues against him and was forced into hiding for some time; at one time he was even imprisoned.

This was the period when he began his two most famous works. *Kitāb al-shifāʾ* examines logic, the natural sciences, including psychology, the *quadrivium* (geometry, astronomy, arithmetic, and music), and metaphysics. His thought in this work owes a great deal to Greek influences, especially Aristotle, and to NEOPLATONISM. His system rests on the conception of God as the necessary existent: in God alone essence—what he is—and existence—that he is—coincide. There is a gradual multiplication of beings through a timeless emanation from God as a result of his self-knowledge. *The Canon of Medicine* (*Al-Qānūn fī al-ṭibb*) is a systematic encyclopedia based on the achievements of Greek physicians of the Roman imperial age and on other Arabic works and, to a lesser extent, on his own experience. Occupied during the day with his duties at court as both physician and administrator, Ibn Sīnā spent almost every night with his students composing these and other works and carrying out general philosophical and scientific discussions related to them. Even in hiding and in prison he continued to write.

In 1022 Shams al-Dawla died, and Ibn Sīnā, after a period of difficulty that included imprisonment, fled to Iṣfahān

(about 250 miles south of Tehran), where he spent the last 14 years of his life in relative peace. He was highly esteemed by ʿAlāʾ al-Dawla, the ruler, and by his court. Here he finished the two major works he began in Hamadan and wrote most of his nearly 200 treatises; he also composed the first work on Aristotelian philosophy in the Persian language and the masterly summary of his "Book of Healing" called *Kitāb al-najāt* ("Book of Salvation"). During this time he composed his last major philosophical opus and the most "personal" testament of his thought, *Kitāb al-ishārāt waʾl-tanbīhāt* ("Book of Directives and Remarks"). In this work he described the mystic's spiritual journey from the beginnings of faith to the final stage of direct and uninterrupted vision of God. When an authority on Arabic philology criticized him for his lack of mastery in the subject, he spent three years studying it and composed a vast work called *Lisān al-ʿarab* ("The Arabic Language"), which remained in rough draft until his death. Accompanying ʿAlāʾ al-Dawlah on a military campaign, Ibn Sīnā fell ill and, despite his attempts to treat himself, died from colic and exhaustion.

In the Western world, Ibn Sīnā's "Book of Healing" was translated partially into Latin in the 12th century, and the complete *Canon* appeared in the same century. His thought, blended with that of AUGUSTINE, was a basic component of the thought of many of the medieval SCHOLASTICS, especially in the FRANCISCAN schools. In medicine the *Canon* became the medical authority for several centuries, and Ibn Sīnā enjoyed an undisputed place of honor equaled only by the early Greek physicians Hippocrates and Galen. In the East his dominating influence in medicine, philosophy, and theology is still alive within the circles of Islamic thought.

IBN TAYMĪYA \ˌi-bən-tī-ˈmē-ä\, *in full* Taqī al-Dīn Abū al-ʿAbbās Aḥmad ibn ʿAbd as-Salām ibn ʿAbd Allāh ibn Muhammad ibn Taymīya (b. 1263, Harran, Mesopotamia—d. Sept. 26, 1328, Cairo), one of Islam's most forceful religious thinkers who, as a member of the Pietist school founded by IBN ḤANBAL, sought the return of ISLAM to its sources, the QURʾAN and the SUNNA. He is also the source of the Wahhābīya, a mid-18th-century traditionalist movement of Islam in Arabia.

Ibn Taymīya was born in Mesopotamia. Educated in Damascus, where he had been taken in 1268 as a refugee from the Mongol invasion, he later steeped himself in the teachings of the Pietist school. Though he remained faithful throughout his life to that school, he also acquired an extensive knowledge of contemporary Islamic sources and disciplines: the Qurʾan, the HADITH, jurisprudence (FIQH), dogmatic theology (KALĀM), philosophy, and Sufi theology. As early as 1293 Ibn Taymīya came into conflict with local authorities for protesting a sentence, pronounced under religious law, against a Christian accused of having insulted the Prophet. In 1298 he was accused of ANTHROPOMORPHISM and of criticizing the legitimacy of dogmatic theology.

During the great Mongol crisis of the years 1299 to 1303, and especially during the occupation of Damascus, he led the resistance party and denounced the suspect faith of the invaders and their accomplices. During the ensuing years Ibn Taymīya was engaged in intensive polemic activity: either against the Kasrawān SHĪʿITES in Lebanon; the Rifāʿīya, a Sufi (*see* SUFISM) religious brotherhood; or the *ittiḥādīya* school, which taught that the Creator and the created become one, a school that grew out of the teaching of IBN AL-ʿARABĪ (d. 1240).

In 1306 he was summoned to explain his beliefs to the governor's council, which, although it did not condemn him, sent him to Cairo; there he appeared before a new council on the charge of anthropomorphism and was imprisoned in the citadel for 18 months. Soon after gaining his freedom, he was confined again in 1308 for several months in the prison of the QĀḌĪS (Muslim judges who exercise both civil and religious functions) for having denounced the worship of saints as being against religious law (SHARĪʿA).

He was sent to Alexandria under house arrest in 1309, the day after the abdication of the SULTAN Muhammad ibn Qalāwūn and the advent of Baybars II al-Jāshnikīr, whom he regarded as a usurper and whose imminent end he predicted. Seven months later, on Ibn Qalāwūn's return, he was able to return to Cairo. But in 1313 he left Cairo once more with the sultan, on a campaign to recover Damascus, which was again being threatened by the Mongols.

Ibn Taymīya spent his last 15 years in Damascus. Promoted to the rank of schoolmaster, he gathered around him a circle of disciples from every social class, the most famous of whom was Ibn Qayyim al-Jawzīya (d. 1350). Accused of supporting a doctrine that would curtail the ease with which a Muslim could traditionally repudiate a wife, Ibn Taymīya was incarcerated on orders from Cairo in the citadel of Damascus from August 1320 to February 1321. In July 1326 Cairo again ordered him confined to the citadel for having continued his condemnation of saint worship, in spite of the prohibition forbidding him to do so. He died in prison and was buried in the Sufi cemetery amid a great public gathering. His tomb still exists and is widely venerated.

Ibn Taymīya left a considerable body of work—often republished in Syria, Egypt, Arabia, and India—that extended and justified his religious and political involvements and was characterized by its rich documentation, sober style, and brilliant polemic. In addition to innumerable *fatwās* (legal opinions based on religious law) and several professions of faith, two works particularly meriting attention are his *Al-Siyāsa al-sharʿīya* ("Treatise on Juridical Politics") and *Minhāj al-sunna* ("The Way of Tradition"), the richest work of comparative theology surviving from medieval Islam.

Ibn Taymīya desired a return to the sources of the Muslim religion, which he felt had been altered too often, to one extent or another, by the different religious sects or schools. The IJMĀʿ, or community consensus, had no value in itself, he insisted, unless it rested on the Qurʾan and the sunna. His traditionalism, however, did not prevent Ibn Taymīya from allowing analogical reasoning (QIYĀS) and the argument of utility (*maṣlaḥa*) a large place in his thought, on the condition that both rested on the objective givens of revelation and tradition. Only such a return to sources, he felt, would permit the divided and disunited Muslim community to regain its unity.

Concerning practices, Ibn Taymīya believed that one could only require, in worship, those practices inaugurated by God and his Prophet and that one could only forbid, in social relations, those things forbidden by the Qurʾan and the sunna. Thus, on the one hand, he favored a revision of the system of religious obligations and a brushing aside of condemnable innovations (*bidʿa*), and, on the other, he constructed an economic ethic that was more flexible on many points than that espoused by the contemporary schools.

Ibn Taymīya is the source of the Wahhābīya, a strictly traditionist movement founded by MUHAMMAD IBN ʿABD AL-

WAHHĀB (d. 1792). Ibn Taymīya also influenced various reform movements that have posed the problem of reformulating traditional ideologies by a return to sources. *See also* ḤANBALĪ LEGAL SCHOOL.

IBN TIBBON, JUDAH BEN SAUL \\,i-bən-'ti-bən\\ (b. 1120, Granada, Spain—d. *c.* 1190, Marseille, France), Jewish physician and translator of Jewish Arabic-language works into Hebrew. He was also the progenitor of several generations of important translators.

Persecution of the Jews forced Judah to flee Granada in 1150, and he settled in Lunel, in southern France, where he practiced medicine. In his Hebrew versions, which became standard, Judah made accessible various classic philosophical works by Arabic-speaking Jews who had utilized the concepts of both Muslim and Greek philosophers. Thus, Judah's translations served to disseminate Arabic and Greek culture in Europe. In addition he often coined Hebrew terms to accommodate the ideas of the authors he was translating.

Among his outstanding renditions from Arabic into Hebrew are *Amanat wa-i'tiqadat* of SA'ADIA BEN JOSEPH (882–942), a Jewish philosophical classic discussing the relationship between reason and divine revelation, translated as *Sefer ha-emunot we-ha-de'ot* (1186; *Beliefs and Opinions*, 1948); *Al-Hidayah ilā farā'id al-qulūb* by the rabbinic judge BAHYA BEN JOSEPH IBN PAKUDA, a widely read classic of Jewish devotional literature which examines the ethics of a man's acts and the intentions that give the acts meaning, translated as *Ḥovot ha-levavot* (*Duties of the Heart*, 1925–47); and *Sefer ha-Kuzari* ("Book of the Khazar") by the Spanish Hebrew poet JUDAH HA-LEVI (*c.* 1085–*c.* 1141), which recounts in dialogue form the arguments presented before the king of the Khazars by a rabbi, a Christian, a Muslim scholar, and an Aristotelian philosopher, with the subsequent conversion of the king to JUDAISM.

Judah ben Saul ibn Tibbon also translated the grammar of Abū al-Walīd Marwān ibn Janāḥ (*c.* 990–*c.* 1050), which became a basis for the work of future Hebrew grammarians. In addition, he wrote a well-known ethical will, *Musar Ab* (*c.* 1190; "A Father's Admonition"), to his son SAMUEL BEN JUDAH IBN TIBBON, who subsequently also became a noteworthy translator.

IBN TIBBON, MOSES BEN SAMUEL (b. Marseille, France, fl. 1240–83), Jewish physician, who like his father, SAMUEL BEN JUDAH IBN TIBBON, and his paternal grandfather, JUDAH BEN SAUL IBN TIBBON, was an important translator of works from the Arabic language into Hebrew. His translations helped to disseminate Greek and Arab culture throughout Europe. Besides his original works, which included commentaries with an allegorical bias on the PENTATEUCH, the Song of Songs, and Haggadic passages (those not dealing with Jewish law; *see* HALAKHAH AND HAGGADAH) in the TALMUD, he also translated Arabic-language works by Jews and Arabs dealing with philosophy, mathematics, astronomy, and medicine.

Following the family tradition, he translated from the Arabic a number of works by the medieval Jewish philosopher MOSES MAIMONIDES (1135–1204), notably portions of Maimonides' commentary on the MISHNAH and his *Sefer ha-mitzwot*, an analysis of the 613 commandments of the Pentateuch.

Among the Arabic writings, Moses translated the commentaries on Aristotle by IBN RUSHD (Averroës); a medical digest by the Persian philosopher and physician IBN SĪNĀ (Avicenna); and a philosophical work (known in English as the "Book of Principles") by the Muslim philosopher and Aristotelian disciple AL-FĀRĀBĪ (878–950). Moses also translated Euclid's *Elements*.

IBN TIBBON, SAMUEL BEN JUDAH (b. *c.* 1150, Lunel, France—d. *c.* 1230, Marseille), Jewish translator and physician whose most significant achievement was an accurate and faithful rendition from the Arabic into Hebrew of MAIMONIDES' classic *Dalālat al-ḥā'irīn* (Hebrew *More nevukhim*; English *The Guide of the Perplexed*).

From his father, JUDAH BEN SAUL IBN TIBBON, Samuel received a thorough grounding in medicine, Jewish law and lore, and Arabic. Like his father, Samuel earned his living as a physician; he also traveled extensively in France, Spain, and Egypt.

After corresponding with Maimonides to elucidate difficult passages in the *Guide*, in about 1190 Samuel published his translation. This work, which interprets SCRIPTURE and rabbinic theology in the light of Aristotelian philosophy, has had an influence on both Jewish and Christian theologians. In the translating process, Samuel enriched the Hebrew language through the borrowing of Arabic words and the adoption of the Arabic practice of forming verbs from substantives.

He also translated Maimonides' treatise on resurrection and his commentary on *Pirqe avot* ("Sayings of the Fathers"), which appears in the TALMUD; in addition, he translated the works of several Arabic commentators on the writings of Aristotle and Galen.

IBN ṬUFAYL \\,i-bən-tù-'fīl\\, *in full* Abū Bakr Muhammad ibn 'Abd Al-Malik ibn Muhammad ibn Muhammad ibn Ṭufayl al-Qaysī (b. 1109/10, Guádix, Spain—d. 1185/86, Marrakech, Morocco), Andalusian philosopher and physician who is known for his *Ḥayy ibn Yaqẓān* (*c.* 1175; "Living Son of the Wakeful One"), a romance in which he describes the self-education and gradual philosophical development of a man who passes the first 50 years of his life in complete isolation on an uninhabited island. Its moral was that a philosopher must educate himself in the ways of nonphilosophers and understand the incompatibility between philosophical life and the life of the multitude, which must be governed by religion and divine laws. Otherwise, his ignorance will lead him to actions dangerous to the well-being of both the community and philosophy. In addition to his works on philosophy Ibn Ṭufayl wrote a number of medical treatises in Arabic and he served as the court physician and general adviser to the ALMOHAD ruler Abū Ya'qūb Yūsuf from 1163 to 1184.

IBN TŪMART \\,i-bən-'tü-märt\\, *in full* Abū 'Abd Allāh Muhammad ibn Tūmart (b. *c.* 1080, Anti-Atlas Mountains, Morocco—d. August 1130), Berber religious reformer and military leader who founded the al-Muwaḥḥidūn confederation in North Africa (*see* ALMOHADS), which led to an Islamic empire that extended from North Africa into Spain and persisted until 1269. After visiting Córdoba (1106) Ibn Tūmart traveled eastward to MECCA and Baghdad, where he reportedly had an encounter with the famed scholar and mystic AL-GHAZĀLĪ. After returning to the Maghrib in 1120, he proclaimed himself to be the MAHDI and led a successful revolt against the Almoravid dynasty. The doctrine he taught combined a strict conception of the unity of God with a program of juridical and puritanical moral reform, based on a study of the QUR'AN and of tradition.

The Fall of Icarus, *engraving by Bernard Picart, 1731*
The Granger Collection

ICARUS \'i-kə-rəs\, in Greek mythology, son of the great inventor DAEDALUS. Daedalus fashioned wings for Icarus of feathers and wax so that he could fly, and he cautioned his son not to fly too close to the sun or to the ocean. Icarus disregarded his advice and perished when he soared too high and the heat of the sun melted the wax that held the wings together, plunging him into the ocean.

I-CHING \'ē-'jiŋ\, *Pinyin* Yijing, *also spelled* Yi Ching (Chinese: "Classic of Changes," or "Book of Changes"), ancient Chinese text, one of the FIVE CLASSICS (*Wu-ching*) of CONFUCIANISM. The main body of the work has traditionally been attributed to Wen-wang (fl. 12th century BCE), sage and father of the founder of the Chou dynasty, and contains a discussion of the divinatory system used by the Chou dynasty wizards. A supplementary section of "commentaries" is believed to be the work of authors of the Warring States period (475–221 BCE) and represents an attempt to explain the world and its ethical principles, applying a largely dialectic method. Han dynasty Confucianists (c. 2nd century BCE), influenced by the Taoist quest (*see* TAOISM) for immortality, justified their use of *I-ching* by attributing certain of its commentaries to CONFUCIUS, preparing the way for its inclusion among the Five Classics of antiquity.

Though the book was originally used for DIVINATION, its influence on Chinese thought and its universal popularity are due to a system of COSMOLOGY that involves humans and nature in a single system. The uniqueness of the *I-ching* consists in its presentation of 64 symbolic hexagrams that, properly understood and interpreted, are said to contain profound meanings applicable to daily life. The hexagrams are formed by joining in pairs, one above the other, eight basic trigrams (*pa-kua*). Each trigram has a name, a root meaning, and a symbolic meaning. The legendary emperor FU HSI (24th century BCE) is said to have discovered these trigrams on the back of a tortoise. Wen-wang is generally credited with having formed the hexagrams.

In practice, one creates a hexagram by casting lots in one of several ways. The hexagram is built up from the bottom, line by line, by successive lots. Solid lines have the number nine, broken lines have the number six. Solid lines represent yang (the male cosmic principle), while broken lines represent yin (the female cosmic principle). The *I-ching* text first explains each line separately, then gives an overall interpretation of the unit. The text is often expressed in cryptic, thought-provoking language, thus allowing the user great leeway in interpreting its significance.

ICON, in EASTERN ORTHODOX tradition, a representation of sacred personages or events in mural painting, mosaic, or wood. After the legitimizing of the use of icons at the COUNCIL OF NICAEA (787) following a lengthy struggle with the Iconoclasts, and a renewed ICONOCLASTIC CONTROVERSY in the 8th–9th century, which disputed the religious function and meaning of icons, the Eastern church formulated the doctrinal basis for their veneration: since God had assumed material form in the person of JESUS CHRIST, he also could be represented in pictures. Icons are considered an essential part of the church and are given special liturgical veneration. They also serve as mediums of instruction for the uneducated faithful through the ICONOSTASIS, a screen shielding the altar, covered with icons depicting scenes from the NEW TESTAMENT, church feasts, and popular saints. In the classical Byzantine and Orthodox tradition, iconography's function is to express symbolically in line and color the theological teaching of the church. Icon production was important in Constantinople, Mount Athos in Greece, in Crete, and in many areas of Russia, Ukraine, and the Balkans. Icons continue to form an important part of the artistic tradition of these areas. *See also* ART AND RELIGION.

ICONOCLASM \ī-'kä-nə-ˌkla-zəm\, destruction of religious images. Usually stemming from a monotheistic theological standpoint which rejects the validity of idols or other religious images, iconoclasm has played an important role in the history of CHRISTIANITY, particularly with regard to the relations between the Eastern and Western churches (*see* ICONOCLASTIC CONTROVERSY). In modern times, iconoclasm has played a role in the conflicts between Muslims and Hindus in India. *See also* ICON.

ICONOCLASTIC CONTROVERSY \ī-ˌkä-nə-'klas-tik\, a dispute over the use of religious images (ICONS) in the Byzantine Empire in the 8th and 9th centuries. The Iconoclasts (those who rejected images) objected to icon worship for several reasons, including the OLD TESTAMENT prohibition against images (EXODUS 20:4) and the possibility of IDOLATRY. The defenders of icon worship insisted on the symbolic nature of images and on the dignity of created matter.

In the early church, the making and veneration of portraits of Christ and the saints were opposed. The use of icons, nevertheless, steadily gained in popularity, especially in the eastern provinces of the Roman Empire. Toward the end of the 6th century and in the 7th, icons became the object of an officially encouraged cult. Opposition to such practices became particularly strong in Asia Minor. In 726 the Byzantine emperor Leo III took a public stand against icons; in 730 their use was prohibited. This opened a persecution of icon worshipers that was severe in the reign of Leo's successor, Constantine V (741–775).

In 787, however, the empress Irene convoked the seventh ecumenical council at Nicaea (*see* NICAEA, COUNCIL OF) at which ICONOCLASM was condemned and the use of images was reestablished. The Iconoclasts regained power in 814 after Leo V's accession, and the use of icons was again forbidden at a council (815). The second Iconoclast period ended with the death of the emperor Theophilus in 842. In 843 his widow, Theodora, finally restored icon veneration, an event still celebrated in the EASTERN ORTHODOX church as the Feast of Orthodoxy.

ICONOGRAPHY \ˌī-kə-ˈnä-grə-fē\, the science of identification, description, classification, and interpretation of symbols, themes, and subject matter in the visual arts. The term can also refer to the artist's use of this imagery in a particular work. The earliest iconographical studies, published in the 16th century, were catalogs of emblems and symbols collected from antique literature and translated into pictorial terms for the use of artists. The most famous of these works is Cesare Ripa's *Iconologia* (1593). Extensive iconographical study did not begin in Europe until the 18th century, however, when it consisted of the classification of subjects and motifs in ancient monuments.

In the 19th century, iconography became divorced from archaeology and was concerned primarily with the incidence and significance of religious symbolism in Christian art. In the 20th century, investigation of Christian iconography has continued, but the secular and classical iconography of European art has also been explored, as have the iconographic aspects of Eastern religious art.

ICONOSTASIS \ˌī-kə-ˈnä-stə-sis, ī-ˈkä-nə-ˌsta-sis\, in Eastern Christian churches of Byzantine tradition, a solid screen of stone, wood, or metal, usually separating the SANCTUARY from the nave. The iconostasis had originally been some sort of simple partition between the altar and the congregation; it then became a row of columns, and the spaces between them were eventually filled with ICONS. In later churches it extends the width of the sanctuary and is covered with panel icons. The iconostasis is pierced by a large, or royal, door and curtain in the center, in front of the altar, and two smaller doors on either side. It always includes the icon of the INCARNATION (MARY with JESUS CHRIST as a child) on the left side of the royal door and the SECOND COMING of Christ the Pantocrator (Christ in majesty) on the right. Icons of the four Evangelists (*see* MATTHEW; MARK; LUKE; JOHN), the ANNUNCIATION, and the LAST SUPPER cover the royal doors themselves. Representations of the ARCHANGELS GAB-

The eight kua, *trigrams from the* I-ching
The Granger Collection

RIEL and Michael, the Twelve Apostles, the feasts of the church, and the prophets of the OLD TESTAMENT are arranged on the iconostasis in complicated patterns, with all figures facing the royal doors.

In various parts of the modern Orthodox world, there is a tendency to restore the communal character of the EUCHARIST, which was partially broken by the development of the iconostasis, by either suppressing the iconostasis or giving it a lighter form.

'ĪD \ˈēd\ (Arabic), *Syriac* 'Ida ("Festival, Holiday"), *Turkish* Bayram, *also spelled* Eid, either of the two canonical festivals of ISLAM distinguished by the performance of communal prayer (SALĀT) at daybreak on the first day. The first of these celebrations, according to the calendar, is the 'Īd al-Fiṭr (al-'Īd al-Ṣaghīr; Küçük Bayram; "Festival of Breaking Fast," or "Minor Festival"), which immediately follows the fasting month of RAMAḌĀN and occupies the first three days of the 10th month, Shawwāl. It is a time of official receptions and private visits, when friends congratulate one another, and people exchange presents, wear new clothes, and visit the graves of relatives.

The second festival, the 'Īd al-Aḍḥā (al-'Īd al-Kabīr; Kur-

IDEOLOGY

ban Bayram; "Sacrificial Feast," or "Major Festival"), falls on the 10th and the following three days of the last month of the year, Dhū al-Ḥijja. Throughout the Muslim world, all who can afford it sacrifice at this time a legal animal (sheep, goat, camel, or cow) and then divide the flesh equally among themselves, the poor, and friends and neighbors. This commemorates the ransom with a ram of Ibrāhīm's (ABRAHAM'S) son Ismāʿīl (Ishmael)—rather than ISAAC, in Judeo-Christian tradition. It marks the culmination of the HAJJ rites.

IDEOLOGY, term with a variety of meanings, often identified with religion, RELIGIOUS LANGUAGE, values, beliefs, and ideas represented in the arts. Ideology is often viewed as the criterion for what is true and good in a society, the collective mentality of a society concerning its values and attitudes toward life, death, work, and happiness. This loose sense of ideology is often tightened to refer to the dominant intellectual set of ideas or conceptual forms of a culture or religion. Thus, ever since Karl Marx and Friedrich Engels, ideology marks the ideas belonging to the ruling elite: "The ideas of the ruling class are in every epoch the ruling ideas, *i.e.,* the class which is the ruling material force of society, is at the same time its ruling intellectual force." Ideology is, therefore, related to power in its various political and economical forms. Religion (culture) has its origins and its persistence in the elite of a society. Many scholars in the cultural sciences, however, have demonstrated that the notion of a dominant ideology is false. It is often the case that the ideology of a dominant class is not practiced by other classes in the same society. The term is also used in a broader sense, as elucidated by French sociologist ÉMILE DURKHEIM, signifying the conceptual representations of a social system. In either usage it is usually related to functionalist theories of culture that view ideology as functioning to maintain and provide coherence in the life of a society. Ideology is always a more encompassing term than religion since it usually includes such cultural phenomena as humanism, SECULARISM, Nazism, CIVIL RELIGION, and even Marxism as instances of ideological forms of social life.

IDIORRHYTHMIC MONASTICISM \ˌi-dē-ō-ˈrith-mik\, *also called* eremitic monasticism \ˌer-ə-ˈmi-tik\ (from Greek: *erēmitēs*, "living in the desert"), the original form of monastic life in CHRISTIANITY, as exemplified by ST. ANTHONY OF EGYPT (*c.* 250–355). It consisted of a total withdrawal from society, normally into the desert, and the constant practice of mental prayer. The CONTEMPLATIVE and mystical trend of eremitic MONASTICISM is also known as HESYCHASM. In the Christian East the "idiorrhythmic" system (from Greek: *idios,* "particular"; *rhythmos,* "manner") always coexisted with CENOBITIC MONASTICISM. It is still practiced on modern Mount Athos, Greece. *See also* HERMIT.

IDOL, image or statue of a deity fashioned to be an object of worship. Within some religions—most prominently ISLAM, JUDAISM, and CHRISTIANITY—the worship of idols is rejected, and hence the term is pejoratively applied to the cultic images of other religious traditions. Idols, however, are a widespread feature of the world's religions, past and present. The veneration of images has taken a wide variety of forms, from the treatment of the image as if it were the god himself (*i.e.,* ancient Mesopotamia and Greece) to the belief that the image is properly treated merely as an object of meditation and does not

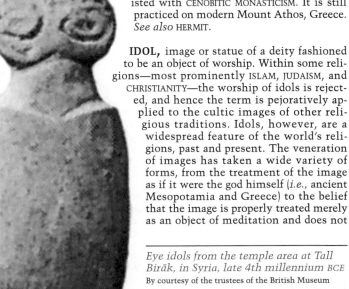

Eye idols from the temple area at Tall Birāk, in Syria, late 4th millennium BCE
By courtesy of the trustees of the British Museum

496

share in the substance of the deity itself (as in some sects within JAINISM).

Veneration of idols plays a central role in the religions of South Asia, including Jainism, BUDDHISM, and HINDUISM. Hinduism includes worship or service to an image or representation of the deity; known as PŪJĀ, the worship consists of a ritual in which the deity is invoked into an image that is established in either the home or temple, is honored, and is then dismissed out of the idol. The main purpose of the *pūjā* ritual is communion with the deity, which is meant to lead to a more permanent and closer relationship between the worshiper and God.

IDOLATRY, in JUDAISM, CHRISTIANITY, and ISLAM, the worship of someone or something other than God as though it were God. A reflection of the strength of the prohibition of this practice in monotheism is its listing as the first of the biblical TEN COMMANDMENTS: "You shall have no other gods before me."

Several forms of idolatry have been distinguished. Gross, or overt, idolatry consists of explicit acts of reverence addressed to a person or an object—the sun, the king, an animal, a statue. A person commits a more subtle idolatry, however, when, although overt acts of adoration are avoided, he or she attaches to a creature the confidence, loyalty, and devotion that properly belong only to the Creator.

In Judaism, the prophetic denunciation of idolatry as the "worship of sticks and stones," as Judaism characterized prayer to an object people have made with their own hands, obscured what is at stake in the graven image (the representation of divinity in concrete ways) but defined Judaism's dealings with the world. Judaism rejected all images and forms of god and defined all those outside the Jewish faith as idolators. In RABBINIC JUDAISM an extensive corpus of law regulated Israelite dealings with idolators on their festivals and forbade Israelites from deriving any benefit whatsoever from commerce with GENTILES on their festival days; the remainder of a bottle of wine opened and used for a LIBATION could not be consumed by Israelites; Gentiles, defined as idolators, could not touch wine intended for Israelite use, lest they make a libation of a few drops from it.

At the same time, certain schools of Christian thought have insisted upon the principle of mediation and have rejected the charge that attachment to a mediating agency is automatically idolatrous. Christians are not in agreement about the agents of mediation—*e.g.*, about the role of the Virgin MARY and of the other saints. But where such mediation is acknowledged to be present, it is also generally acknowledged that reverence shown toward it applies not to the agent himself but to the one for whom the agent stands. A special instance is the human nature of JESUS CHRIST (which is worthy of divine worship because of its inseparable union with the Second Person of the Holy TRINITY) and the consecrated Host in the EUCHARIST (which, by Roman CATHOLIC doctrine, may properly be adored because it has been changed into the very body of Christ).

In Islam, idolatry is generally conceived to be in contradiction to the command to worship only one god. As such, it is an expression of POLYTHEISM (SHIRK, literally, "attributing partners to God") and disbelief (KUFR, literally, "ingratitude"), in opposition to what Muslims construe to be true religion. The QUR'AN recognizes ABRAHAM as the ancestral opponent of idolatry, and it uses the term pejoratively in attacking the beliefs of Prophet MUHAMMAD's opponents. Indeed, one of Muhammad's first acts after winning control of Mecca in 630 CE was reported to have been the destruc-

tion of hundreds of idols housed in the KA'BA. Idol plundering and smashing thereafter became a recurrent theme in historical accounts of Islamic conquests.

As in Christianity, Muslim religious authorities employed the term to disparage the beliefs and practices of other Muslims. SUNNIS accused SHI'ITES of idolatry for their devotion to the IMAMS, and SUFISM came under suspicion because of the authority claimed by the SHAYKHS and the widespread veneration of Sufi holy men and women. Sufi writers, particularly in the Persian tradition, turned the tables on their accusers by using metaphors of idolatry favorably to express their absorption in God, for they saw in all created forms, including idols, signs of God's unity and love. Modern Islamic reform movements, however, draw upon the negative associations of the term to condemn materialism and any humanistic ideology that fails to recognize God's unity and sovereignty.

In the 18th and 19th centuries, the term "idolatry" was used in European scholarship to classify any non-Western, non-monotheistic religion. The term is no longer used this way in the humanities and social sciences.

IDOMENEUS \ī-'dä-mə-ˌnüs, ˌī-də-mə-'nē-əs\, in Greek legend, son of DEUCALION, grandson of MINOS and Pasiphaë, and king of Crete. He courted HELEN and took a distinguished part in the Trojan War. According to the *Odyssey*, he returned home safely, but a later tradition relates that he was overtaken by a violent storm and vowed to sacrifice to POSEIDON the first living thing that met him when he reached home. The first to greet him was his son, whom he thus slew; as a result, a plague developed, and Idomeneus was driven out. He fled to the district of Sallentum in Calabria and subsequently to Colophon in Asia Minor, where he settled near the Temple of the Clarian APOLLO.

IDRĪS \i-'drēs\, an immortal figure in Islamic legend, mentioned in the QUR'AN as a prophet. According to early Islamic stories, Idrīs appeared sometime between ADAM and NOAH and transmitted divine revelation through several books. He did not die but was taken bodily to paradise to spend eternity with God. Popular legend also credits him with the invention of writing and sewing and of several forms of DIVINATION. He is regarded as the patron saint of craftsmen and Muslim knights.

The name Idrīs has been variously identified by scholars as derived from the biblical EZRA, the Christian Apostle ANDREW, and Alexander the Great's cook Andreas. Later Muslim legend associated him with the biblical ELIJAH or Muslim AL-KHIḌR. Parallels have also been drawn between the biblical Enoch and Idrīs, on the basis of several striking similarities: both are pious men taken physically to paradise, and both live a reputed 365 years. Idrīs (and Enoch) has also been woven into the Islamic mythology surrounding the Greco-Egyptian god Hermes Trismegistos as the first incarnation of the tripartite Hermes.

IDUN \'ē-ˌthùn, *Angl* -ˌdün\, *also spelled* Idunn, *or* Iduna \'ē-ˌthü-nə, *Angl* 'ē-ˌdü-nə, i-'dü-\, in Norse mythology, the wife of Bragi, the god of poetry. She was the keeper of the magic apples of immortality, which the gods must eat to preserve their youth. When, through the cunning of LOKI, the trickster god, she and her apples were seized by the GIANT Thiassi and taken to the realm of the giants, the gods quickly began to grow old. They then forced Loki to rescue Idun, which he did by taking the form of a falcon, changing Idun into a nut, and flying off with her in his talons.

IFA \\'ē-fä\\, among the Yoruba of Africa, orally transmitted system of DIVINATION. In this system the Ifa priests throw beans onto a board. The beans fall in a series of complex patterns that the diviners key to folktales, whose contents are then applied to the particular situation at hand.

IFRIT \\'i-,frēt, ə-'frēt\\, *also spelled* afreet, afrit, afrite \\'a-,frēt, ə-'\\, *or* efreet \\'e-,frēt, ə-'\\, *Arabic* (male) 'ifrīt, *or* (female) 'ifrīta, in Islamic mythology, a class of infernal JINN (spirits below the level of ANGELS and devils) noted for their strength and cunning. An *ifrit* is an enormous winged creature of smoke, either male or female, who lives underground and frequents ruins. *Ifrits* live in a society structured along ancient Arab tribal lines, complete with kings, tribes, and clans. They generally marry one another, but they can also marry humans. While ordinary weapons and forces have no power over them, they are susceptible to magic, which humans can use to kill them or to capture and enslave them. As with the jinn, an *ifrit* may be either a believer or an unbeliever, good or evil, but he is most often depicted as a wicked and ruthless being.

The rare appearance of the term *ifrit* in the QUR'AN and in HADITH is always in the phrase "the *ifrit* of the jinn" and probably means "rebellious." The word subsequently came to refer to an entire class of formidable, rebellious beings, but, in the confused world of Underworld spirits, it was difficult to differentiate one from another. The *ifrit* thus became virtually indistinguishable from the *mārid*, also a type of wicked and rebellious DEMON.

IGLESIA NI KRISTO \\ē-'glä-syä-nē-'krēs-tō\\ (Tagalog: "Church of Christ"), Kristo *also spelled* Cristo, the largest entirely indigenous Christian church in the Philippines. Its members assert that the early Christian church was restored in God's chosen people, the Filipinos, when Felix Manalo launched this church in 1914. Rapid growth after 1945 produced some 600,000 members by the late 20th century and a wealthy centralized organization. Strong discipline from the leaders dictates a literal interpretation of the BIBLE and suggests individual contributions and the casting of votes, making the church a substantial political power. Unitarian in theology and Philippine in its languages, liturgy, and music, the church represents a popular Filipino nationalist movement for spiritual independence. (*See also* NEW RELIGIOUS MOVEMENTS.)

IGUVINE TABLES \\'i-gyə-,vīn, -vin\\, a set of seven inscribed bronze tables found in 1444 at Iguvium (modern Gubbio, Italy), an Umbrian town. The tables are written in the Umbrian language, four and part of a fifth using the Umbrian script, the rest Latin characters. The earliest appear to date from the 3rd or 2nd century BCE, the latest from the early part of the 1st century BCE. These tables give the liturgy of the Fratres Atiedii, a brotherhood of priests, and are of great value for the study of ancient Italic language and religion.

The first table contains regulations for the purification of the sacred mount or citadel of Iguvium and for the LUSTRATION (purification) of the people. Tables six and seven contain essentially the same material as the first, but in greatly

A wand used in the Ifa divination cult among the Yoruba of Nigeria. The wand is tapped against the Ifa board to summon the required orisha, *or deity*
Werner Forman Archive—Private Collection

expanded form and in somewhat later language. The second, third, and fourth tables describe several different sacrifices, many of the details of which are quite obscure. The fifth table deals with administrative details of the brotherhood and ends with a statement of mutual obligations between the Fratres Atiedii and 2 of the (originally) 10 divisions of the Iguvine people.

IJMĀ' \ij-'ma\ (Arabic: "agreeing upon," or "consensus"), the universal and infallible agreement of the Muslim community, especially of Muslim scholars, on any Islamic principle, at any time. The consensus—based on the HADITH that states, "My people will never agree in an error"—constitutes the third of the four sources of Islamic jurisprudence, the *uṣūl al-fiqh*, as first systematized by ABŪ 'ABD AL-LĀH AL-SHĀFI'Ī (d. 820). In effect, *ijmā'* has been the most important factor in defining the meaning of the other *uṣūl* and thus in formulating the doctrine and practice of the Muslim community. Twelver SHI'ITE jurisprudence, however, maintains that *ijmā* must admit the opinion of the hidden IMAM before having validity.

In Muslim history *ijmā'* has always had reference to consensuses reached in the past, near or remote, and never to contemporaneous agreement. It is thus a part of traditional authority and has from an early date represented the Muslim community's acknowledgment of the authority of the beliefs and practices of MUHAMMAD'S city of MEDINA.

Ijmā' also has come to operate as a principle of toleration of different traditions within ISLAM. It thus allows the four Sunni legal schools (*madhab*s) equal authority and has probably validated many non-Muslim practices taken into Islam by converts.

In modern Muslim usage, *ijmā'* has lost its association with traditional authority and appears as a democratic institution and an instrument of reform. *See also* IJTIHĀD; MUHAMMAD AL-MAHDI.

IJTIHĀD \,ij-tē-'had\ (Arabic: "effort," or "application, diligence"), in Islamic law, the independent or original interpretation of problems not precisely covered by the QUR'AN, HADITH, and IJMĀ' (scholarly consensus). In the early Muslim community every adequately qualified jurist had the right to exercise such original thinking, mainly *ra'y* (personal judgment) and QIYĀS (analogical reasoning), and those who did so were termed *mujtahid*s. But with the crystallization of legal schools (*madhab*s) and codification of law under the 'Abbāsids (reigned 750–1258), SUNNI authorities concurred at the beginning of the 10th century CE that the principal legal issues had been settled, though the "gates of *ijtihād*" were never actually closed as has been maintained by some Sunni Muslim and many Western scholars. The SHI'ITES attribute even greater significance to *ijtihād* and still recognize their leading jurists as *mujtahid*s. In Shi'ite Iran, the *mujtahid*s act as guardians of the official doctrine, and in committee they may veto any law that infringes on Islamic ordinances. Indeed, since the revolution of 1978–79 religious and political affairs in Iran have been governed largely by Shi'ite *mujtahid*s, the foremost having been Ayātollāh KHOMEINI, who inspired the overthrow of Mohammad Reza Shah Pahlavi.

Several prominent Sunni scholars, such as IBN TAYMĪYA (1263–1328) and Jalāl al-Dīn al-Suyūṭī (1445–1505), declared themselves *mujtahid*s. In the 19th and 20th centuries Sunni reformist movements clamored for the reinstatement of *ijtihād* as a means of freeing ISLAM from harmful innovations (BID'AS) accrued through the centuries and as a

tool capable of adapting Islam to the requirements of life in a modern world.

IKHTILĀF \,ik-tē-'laf\ (Arabic: "disagreement"), in ISLAM, differences of opinion on religious matters. Such diversity is permissible as long as the basic principles of Islam are not affected. *Ikhtilāf* is thus the opposite of IJMĀ' (consensus). *Ikhtilāf* permits a Muslim to choose the interpretation of religious teachings that best suits his own circumstances and causes the least harm. Two famous sayings from HADITH in favor of *ikhtilāf* were attributed to the Prophet MUHAMMAD: "Difference of opinion in the Muslim community is a sign of divine favor"; and "It is a mercy of God that the theologians differ in opinion."

Ikhtilāf thus allowed Islam to develop four equally orthodox legal schools: the MĀLIKĪ, the ḤANAFĪ, the SHĀFI'Ī, and the ḤANBALĪ, within each of which there have been diverse interpretations of the same religious texts. Among Twelver SHI'ITE jurists, diverse legal interpretations are also considered to be valid pending the return of the hidden IMAM, who alone has the authority to finally settle the question of conflicting opinions.

IKHWĀN \ik-'wän\ (Arabic: "Brethren"), in Arabia, members of a religious and military brotherhood that figured prominently in the unification of the Arabian Peninsula under Ibn Sa'ūd (1912–30); in modern Saudi Arabia they constitute the National Guard.

Ibn Sa'ūd began organizing the Ikhwān in 1912 with hopes of making them a reliable and stable source of an elite army corps. In order to break their traditional tribal allegiances and feuds, the Ikhwān were settled in colonies known as HIJRA. These settlements, established around desert oases, further forced the Bedouin to abandon their nomadic way of life. Their populations ranged from 10 to 10,000 and which offered tribesmen living quarters, mosques, schools, agricultural equipment and instruction, and arms and ammunition. Most important, religious teachers were brought in to instruct the Bedouin in the essential precepts of ISLAM as taught by the religious reformer IBN 'ABD AL-WAHHĀB in the 18th century. Consequently, the Ikhwān became arch-traditionalists.

Beginning in 1919, the Ikhwān were responsible for numerous military victories in Arabia and Iraq. In 1924, when SHARĪF Ḥusayn was proclaimed CALIPH in MECCA, the Ikhwān labeled the act heretical and accused Ḥusayn of obstructing their performance of the PILGRIMAGE to Mecca. They then moved against Transjordan, Iraq, and the Hijaz simultaneously, besieged al-Ṭā'if outside Mecca, and massacred several hundred of its inhabitants. Mecca fell to the Ikhwān, and, with the subsequent surrenders (1925) of Jidda and MEDINA, they won all of the Hijaz for Ibn Sa'ūd. The Ikhwān were also instrumental in securing the provinces of Asir, just south of the Hijaz on the coast (1920), and Ḥā'il, in the north of the peninsula, along the borders of Transjordan and Iraq (1921).

By 1926 the Ikhwān were becoming uncontrollable, attacking Ibn Sa'ūd for such technological innovations as telephones and automobiles. Rising in open rebellion, they were eventually forced to surrender in January 1930 and their leaders were imprisoned.

Not all of the Ikhwān revolted. Those who had remained loyal to Ibn Sa'ūd stayed on the *hijra*s, continuing to receive government support, and were still an influential religious force. They were eventually absorbed into the Saudi Arabian National Guard. *See also* MUSLIM BROTHERHOOD.

IKHWĀN AL-ṢAFĀʾ \ik-'wän-àl-sa-'fa\ (Arabic: "Brethren of Purity"), secret Arab confraternity, founded at Basra, Iraq, that produced a philosophical and religious encyclopedia, *Rasāʾil ikhwān al-ṣafāʾ wa-khillān al-wafāʾ* ("Epistles of the Brethren of Purity and Loyal Friends"), sometime in the second half of the 10th century CE.

Neither the identity nor the period of the Ikhwān al-Ṣafāʾ have been definitively established, but the various authors of the *Rasāʾil* do seem to reflect the doctrinal position of the ISMĀʿĪLĪS, a radical SHIʿITE Muslim sect influenced by MANICHAEISM and NEOPLATONISM, which preached an esoteric interpretation of the QURʾAN open only to initiates. The Ikhwān al-Ṣafāʾ, like all other Islamic philosophers, attempted to naturalize Greek philosophy by following a fairly orthodox Neoplatonic position and admitting Hermetic, Gnostic, astrological, and occult sciences on a large scale. They believed that their absorption of ancient wisdom enabled them to fathom the esoteric meaning of revelation.

According to the Ikhwān al-Ṣafāʾ, individual human souls emanate from the universal soul and rejoin it after death; the universal soul in its turn will be united with God on the day of the LAST JUDGMENT. The *Rasāʾil* are thus intended to purify the soul of misconceptions and lead it to a clear view of the essence of reality, which in turn will provide for happiness in the next life. To accomplish this enlightenment, the *Rasāʾil* are structured theoretically to lead the soul from concrete to abstract knowledge. There is also an important summary of the whole encyclopedia, *al-Risāla al-jāmiʿa*. *See also* GNOSTICISM; NEOPLATONISM.

IK OANKĀR \'ik-'ōŋ-kär\, *also spelled* Ek Omkār (Punjabi: "God is One"), expression or invocation that opens the ĀDI GRANTH, the primary SCRIPTURE of SIKHISM. The expression is a compound of the numeral 1 and the letter that represents the sound "o" in Gurmukhī, the writing system developed by the Sikhs for their sacred literature. Referring to the Sikh understanding of the absolute monotheistic unity of God, the expression is the central symbol of Sikhism.

Oankār corresponds to the Sanskrit term OM, which in the Hindu tradition is regarded as a sacred, mystical syllable that encapsulates all other MANTRAS, or sacred formulas, and represents the totality of the universe. GURŪ NĀNAK, the founder of the Sikh tradition, wrote a long composition entitled *Oankār*, in which he attributed the origin and sense of speech to the Divinity, who is thus the "*Om*-maker." Some Sikhs object to any suggestion that *Oankār* is the same as *Om* and rather view *Oankār* as pointing to the distinctively Sikh theological emphasis on the ineffable quality of God, who is described as "the Person beyond time," "the Eternal One," or "the One without form."

Recently, *Ik Oankār* has become an emblem of Sikh identity. Sikh men and women wear jewelry that features the *Ik Oankār* and have it inscribed on their cars or on the main entrance of their homes.

ILLUMINATO (Italian: "Enlightened"), *plural* Illuminati, *Spanish* Alumbrado, a follower of a mystical movement in Spain during the 16th and 17th centuries. Its adherents claimed that the human soul, having attained a certain degree of perfection, was permitted a vision of the divine and entered into direct communication with the Holy Spirit. From this state the soul could neither advance nor retrogress. Consequently, participation in the liturgy, good works, and observance of the exterior forms of religious life were unnecessary for those who had received the "light." The Illuminati came primarily from among the reformed FRANCISCANS and the JESUITS, but their doctrines seem to have had an influence on all classes of people. The extravagant claims made for their visions and revelations caused them to be relentlessly persecuted. The Inquisition issued edicts against them on three occasions (1568, 1574, and 1623).

ʿILM AL-ḤADĪTH \'ilm-àl-hà-'dēth\: *see* HADITH.

ILMARINEN \'ēl-mä-ˌrē-nen\, in Finnish mythology, creator-smith credited in the KALEVALA with forging the "lids of heaven" when the world was created and with fashioning the mythical SAMPO. Ilmarinen forged the *sampo* for Louhi, the goddess of the Underworld, but then stole it back; when Louhi pursued, the *sampo* was destroyed. In another source Ilmarinen is described as the god of wind and good weather.

ILOS \'ī-ləs\, in Greek mythology, the founder of Ilion (Troy). Ilos (or Zacynthus, a Cretan name) has been identified either as the brother of Erichthonius or as the son of Tros and grandson of Erichthonius. The King of Phrygia gave Ilos a spotted cow as a wrestling prize, with the advice that he should found a city wherever the cow first lay down. The animal chose the hill of ATE, where Ilos marked out the boundaries of Ilion. After praying for a sign from ZEUS, Ilos was sent the PALLADIUM, a statue of Pallas ATHENA, for which he built a temple. Ilos' son LAOMEDON succeeded him as ruler of the city, and his grandson PRIAM was the last king of Ilion.

ILUMQUH \i-'lùm-kü\ (Arabic: "God Is Power"), *also called* Wadd, ʿAmm, *and* Sin, Arabian god who was associated with the moon and was greater than the two other principal astral deities of South Arabia, the goddess Shams and the god ʿAthtar, who were associated with the sun and the planet VENUS, respectively. Ilumquh, protector of cities and the patron god of South Arabia's capital cities, was linked to various temples and was called father in reference to ʿAthtar Venus and to each of the peoples of South Arabia. Ilumquh had many names and epithets, sometimes more than one in a single district. He was, for example, called Wadd ("Love") in Maʿīn, ʿAmm ("Uncle") in Qatabān, and Sin (a name also used in Babylonia) in Ḥaḍramawt.

There were PILGRIMAGES to his temples where ABLUTIONS and offerings were made and certain rules of abstinence and purity were followed. Divine guidance from the three gods was sought and later acknowledged in writing, and undertakings were determined by the response of the oracles. Sometimes documents were deposited in the temples for safekeeping.

IMAM \i-'mäm\, *Arabic* imām ("leader," or "exemplar"), head of the Muslim community. The title is used in the QURʾAN several times to refer to leaders and to ABRAHAM. The origin and basis of the office of imam was conceived differently by various sections of the ISLAMIC community, this difference providing part of the political and religious basis for the split into SUNNI and SHIʿITE Islam. Among Sunnis, imam was synonymous with CALIPH (*khalīfa*), designating the successor of MUHAMMAD, who assumed his administrative and political, but not religious, functions. He was appointed by men and, although liable to error, was to be obeyed even though he personally sinned, provided he maintained the ordinances of Islam.

After the death (661) of ʿALĪ, the fourth caliph and Muhammad's son-in-law, political disagreement over succession to his office propelled the Shi'ite imam along a separate course of development, as partisans of 'Alī attempted to preserve leadership of the entire Muslim community among the descendants of 'Alī. In Shi'ite Islam, the imam became a figure of absolute spiritual authority and fundamental importance. 'Alī and the successive imams, who are believed by Shi'ism to be the sole possessors of secret insights into the QUR'AN given them by Muhammad, became viewed under Neoplatonic influences of the 9th–10th centuries CE as men illumined by the Primeval Light, God, and as divinely appointed and preserved from SIN. They alone, and not the general consensus of the community (IJMĀ') essential to Sunni Islam, determined matters of doctrinal importance and interpreted revelation. With the historical disappearance (GHAYBA) of the last imam there arose a belief in the hidden imam, who is identified with the MAHDI.

Imam has also been used as an honorary title, applied to such figures as the theologians ABŪ ḤANĪFA, AL-SHĀFI'Ī, MĀLIK IBN ANAS, AḤMAD IBN ḤANBAL, AL-GHAZĀLĪ, and MUHAMMAD 'ABDUH. The title also is given to Muslims who lead prayers in mosques.

IMAN \,ē-'man\ (Arabic: "belief" or "faith"), in ISLAM, the internal belief in God and his prophet, MUHAMMAD; this is expressed in the SHAHĀDA: "There is no god but God; Muhammad is the prophet of God." In addition to these tenets, *iman* comprises belief in God's ANGELS, in the QUR'AN as holy utterance, in the prophets, and in the doctrine that GOOD AND EVIL are predestined. *Iman* is held to come from God, as no man can have faith except by the will of Allāh. ABŪ ḤANĪFA, the great Muslim jurist and theologian, said of *iman*: it is "confessing with the tongue, believing with the mind, and knowing with the heart."

IMBOLC \'im-,bȯlg, -,bȯ-ləg\, *also called* Oimelc \'ȯ-,mʸelg, -,mʸe-ləg\ (Middle Irish, probably literally, "milking"), ancient Celtic religious festival, celebrated on February 1 to mark the beginning of spring. The festival apparently was a feast of purification for farmers and has been compared to the Roman LUSTRATIONS. Imbolc was associated with the goddess Brigid, and after the Christianization of Europe the day of the festival became the feast day of ST. BRIGIT.

IMHOTEP \im-'hō-,tep\, *Greek* Imouthes \i-'mü-,thēz\ (fl. 27th century BCE, Memphis, Egypt), vizier, sage, architect, astrologer, and chief minister to Djoser (reigned 2630–2611 BCE), the second king of Egypt's third dynasty, who was later worshiped as the god of medicine in Egypt and in Greece, where he was identified with the Greek god ASCLEPIUS. Considered the designer of the first temple of Edfu, on the upper Nile, he is credited with initiating the Old Kingdom (c. 2575–c. 2130 BCE) as the architect of the step PYRAMID built at the NECROPOLIS of Ṣaqqārah in the city of Memphis. The oldest extant monument of hewn stone known to the world, the pyramid consists of six steps and attains a height of 200 feet (61 m).

Although no contemporary account has been found that refers to Imhotep as a practicing physician, Imhotep's reputation as the reigning genius of the time, his position in the court, his training as a scribe, and his becoming known as a medical DEMIGOD only 100 years after his death are strong indications that he must have been a physician of considerable skill. Not until the Persian conquest of Egypt in 525 BCE was Imhotep elevated to the position of a full deity. He replaced Nefertum in the great triad of Memphis, which he shared with his mythological parent—his father, PTAH, the creator of the universe, and his mother, SEKHMET, the goddess of war and pestilence. Imhotep's cult reached its zenith during Greco-Roman times, when his temples in Memphis and on the island of Philae (Arabic: Jazirat Filah) in the Nile were often crowded with sufferers who prayed and slept there so that the god might reveal remedies to them in their dreams.

Imhotep reading a papyrus roll
By courtesy of the Staatliche Museen zu Berlin, Agyptisches Museum

IMITATION OF CHRIST, *Latin* Imitatio Christi, a Christian devotional book written between 1390 and 1440. Although its authorship is a matter of controversy, the book is linked to THOMAS À KEMPIS. Whatever the identity of the author, he was a representative of the DEVOTIO MODERNA and its two offshoots, the BRETHREN OF THE COMMON LIFE and the Congregation of Windsheim.

The *Imitation of Christ* in part I gives "exhortations useful for spiritual living," while part II admonishes the reader to be concerned with the spiritual side of life rather than with the materialistic, and part III affirms the comfort that results from being centered in Christ. Finally, it shows in part IV how an individual's faith has to be strengthened through the EUCHARIST, or Holy Communion. The simplicity of the book's language and the direct appeal to the religious sensitivity of the individual are perhaps the primary reasons why this book has been so deeply influential.

IMMACULATE CONCEPTION

IMMACULATE CONCEPTION, ROMAN CATHOLIC dogma asserting that MARY, the mother of JESUS CHRIST, was preserved free from the effects of the SIN of ADAM (usually referred to as "original sin") from the first instant of her conception. The doctrine seems to have arisen from a general acceptance in the early church of Mary's holiness. Especially after Mary had been solemnly declared to be the mother of God at the Council of Ephesus in 431, most theologians doubted that one who had been so close to God could have actually committed sinful acts.

The view that Mary had been spared also from the disposition to evil inherent in ORIGINAL SIN was not clearly articulated until the 12th century, when considerable debate was centered on an English celebration of Mary's conception. The discussion was clouded by medieval views of the biological aspects of conception and by a concern that the belief in the universal redemption effected by Jesus should not be threatened. The latter concern was countered not long after by the FRANCISCAN theologian JOHN DUNS SCOTUS, who argued that Christ's redemptive GRACE was applied to Mary to prevent sin from reaching her soul. Mary's privilege, thus, was the result of God's grace and not of any intrinsic merit on her part. It was not, however, until Dec. 8, 1854, that PIUS IX declared in the bull *Ineffabilis Deus* that the doctrine was revealed by God and hence was to be firmly believed as such by all Catholics. The feast of the Immaculate Conception is celebrated on December 8.

IMMORTALITY, the continuity of existence after the death of the body, or, the state of not being subject to death. *See* DEATH AND AFTERLIFE.

IMPRIMATUR \ˌim-prə-ˈmä-tür\ (Latin: "let it be printed"), in the ROMAN CATHOLIC church, a permission, required by contemporary CANON LAW and granted by a bishop, for the publication of any work on SCRIPTURE or, in general, any writing containing something of peculiar significance to religion, theology, or morality. Strictly speaking, the imprimatur is nothing more than the permission. But because its concession must be preceded by the favorable judgment of a censor (*nihil obstat*: "nothing hinders [it from being printed]"), the term has come to imply ecclesiastical approval of the publication itself. Nevertheless, the imprimatur is not an episcopal endorsement of the content, nor is it a guarantee of doctrinal integrity. It does, however, indicate that nothing offensive to faith or morals has been discovered in the work.

IMRAM \ˈēm-rəv\ (Old Irish Gaelic: "rowing about," or "voyaging"), *plural* imramha \-rə-və\, in early Irish literature, a story about an adventurous voyage. Stories of this type include

Inari, wood figurine, Tokugawa period (1603–1867)
By courtesy of the Guimet Museum, Paris

tales of Irish saints traveling to Iceland or Greenland, as well as fabulous tales of PAGAN heroes journeying to the otherworld (*echtrae*). An outstanding example of an *imram* is *Imram Brain*, or *The Voyage of Brân*, which describes a trip to the enchanted Land of Women. After what seems to be a year, BRÂN and his colleagues return home to discover that their voyage had lasted longer than any memories and was recorded only in ancient sources.

INANNA: *see* ISHTAR.

INARI \ē-ˈnä-rē\, in Japanese mythology, god who protects rice cultivation and furthers prosperity. The patron deity of swordsmiths, Inari is worshiped particularly by merchants and tradesmen and is also associated with brothels and with entertainers.

In SHINTŌ legends Inari is identified with Uka no Mitama no Kami ("August Spirit of Food"), son of the storm god, SU-SANOO, but in some Shintō shrines is associated with the goddess of food, UKEMOCHI NO KAMI. Inari's depictions vary from a bearded man riding a white fox to a woman with long hair, carrying sheaves of rice.

The fox is sometimes identified with the messenger of Inari, and statues of foxes are found in great numbers both inside and outside shrines dedicated to the rice god. Other characteristics of Inari shrines are their deep red buildings, long rows of votive TORII (gateways), and the *hōshu-no-tama* (a pear-shaped emblem surmounted by flamelike symbols).

INCA: *see* PRE-COLUMBIAN SOUTH AMERICAN RELIGIONS.

INCARNATION, central Christian doctrine that God assumed a human nature and became a man in the form of JESUS CHRIST, the Son of God and the second Person of the TRINITY. The doctrine maintains that the divine and human natures of Jesus do not exist beside one another in an unconnected way but rather are joined in a personal unity that has traditionally been referred to as the hypostatic union. The union of the two natures has not resulted in their diminution or mixture; rather, the identity of each is believed to have been fully preserved.

The word Incarnation (from the Latin *caro*, "flesh") may be most closely related to the claim in the prologue of the Gospel According to John that the Word became flesh, that is, assumed human nature. The essence of the doctrine of the Incarnation is that the preexistent Word has been embodied in the man Jesus of Nazareth, who is presented in John as being in close personal union with God, whose words Jesus is speaking when he preaches the gospel.

Belief in the preexistence of Christ is indicated in various letters of the NEW TESTAMENT but particularly in the Letter of Paul to the Philippians in which the Incarnation is presented as the emptying of Christ Jesus, who was by nature God and equal to God (*i.e.*, the Father) but who took on the nature of a slave and was later glorified by God.

The development of a more refined theology of the Incarnation resulted from the response of the early church to various divergent interpretations of the divinity of Jesus and the relationship of the divine and human natures of Jesus. The COUNCIL OF NICAEA (325 CE) pronounced that Christ was "begotten, not made" and that he was therefore not creature but Creator. The basis for this claim was the doctrine that he was "of the same substance as the Father." The doctrine was further defined by the COUNCIL OF CHALCEDON (451 CE), at which it was declared that Jesus was perfect in deity and in humanity and that the identity of each nature was preserved in the person of Jesus Christ.

Subsequent theology has worked out the implications of this definition, although there have been various tendencies emphasizing either the divinity or the humanity of Jesus. It has commonly been accepted that the union of the human nature of Christ with his divine nature had significant consequences for his human nature. The union of the two natures has been viewed by theologians as a gift for other humans, both in terms of its benefit for their redemption from SIN and in terms of the appreciation of the potential goodness inherent in human activity.

INCUBUS, DEMON in male form that seeks to have sexual intercourse with sleeping women. The corresponding spirit in female form is called a SUCCUBUS. The Latin nouns *incubus* and *incubo* ("demon" or "nightmare") are derivatives of the verb *incubare* ("to lie upon," "to weigh upon," "to keep a jealous watch over"), and usages of the words in classical and post-classical Latin played upon these various senses. The earliest explicit use of *incubus* to refer to a dream with sexual content is in the writing of ST. AUGUSTINE. Medieval writers narrowed the meaning of *incubus* to a demon seeking intercourse with sleeping women. Union with such a being was supposed by some to result in the birth of witches, demons, and deformed human offspring. Parallels exist in many cultures.

INDEX OF FORBIDDEN BOOKS (Latin: Index Librorum Prohibitorum), list of books once forbidden by ROMAN CATHOLIC church authority as dangerous to the faith or morals of Catholics. Its publication ceased in 1966.

Compiled by official censors, the *Index* attempted to prevent the contamination of the faith or the corruption of morals through the reading of theologically erroneous or immoral books. It was not, therefore, equivalent to the total legislation of the church regulating reading by Roman Catholics; nor was it ever a complete catalog of forbidden reading. Until 1966, CANON LAW prescribed two main forms of control over literature: the censorship of books by Roman Catholics in advance of publication, in regard to matters of faith and morals (a practice still followed); and the condemnation of published books judged to be harmful.

The origin of the church's legislation concerning the censorship of books is unclear. The decree of Pope Gelasius I about 496, which contained lists of recommended as well as banned books, has been described as the first Roman Index. The first catalog of forbidden books to include in its title the word index, however, was published in 1559 by the Sacred Congregation of the Roman INQUISITION. The list was suppressed in June 1966.

INDIAN SHAKER CHURCH, Christianized movement among Northwest American Indians; it is not connected with the SHAKER communities developed from the teachings of ANN LEE. In 1881 near Olympia, Wash., John Slocum, a Roman Catholic Squaxon logger, reported that he had visited heaven while in a coma and was commissioned to preach a new way of life. The following year his wife, Mary, experienced a shaking paroxysm that was interpreted as the Spirit of God curing John of a further illness. The Shaker Church they founded attempted to replace traditional Indian cures with spiritual healing through shaking and dancing rituals. *See* NATIVE AMERICAN RELIGIONS.

Christian elements of the Indian Shaker Church include belief in the TRINITY and Sunday worship in plain churches furnished with a prayer table, handbells, and many crosses. Direct revelations replace the BIBLE, but a secession group cooperating with white evangelicals accepts the Bible and the preaching of sermons. Earlier persecutions ceased after the church was incorporated in Oregon (1907), Washington (1910), and California (1932). A loose organization in the late 20th century united more than 20 congregations having some 2,000 adherents.

INDRA \\'in-drə\\, chief of the Vedic gods of India and patron of warriors.

Indra's weapons are lightning and the thunderbolt, and he is strengthened for his feats by drinks of the elixir SOMA, a major offering of Vedic sacrifice. Among his allies are the Maruts, sons of RUDRA, who ride the clouds and direct storms; the Aśvins, twin horsemen; and VISHNU, who later evolved into one of the principal gods of HINDUISM. In a struggle of cosmic proportions to which the VEDAS often refer, Indra wields his thunderbolt to defeat the demonic Vṛtra ("Obstacle"), releasing the waters and cattle it holds captive and thus establishing the conditions requisite for order and prosperity. In later Hinduism, Indra plays a much reduced role—as god of rain, regent of the heavens, guardian of the east and, perhaps most important, as a symbol of cosmologies and religious sensibilities now superseded. Indra also plays a subservient role in BUDDHISM and is defeated by KRISHNA in a battle at Mount Govardhana. In both cases, Indra's subordination signifies that propitiatory rites directed to deities conceived as external beings are passé. These are replaced by a redemptive order that focuses instead on the immediate realm of human experience. In the mythology of JAINISM, Indra assumes a similarly peripheral position, receiving into his hands the hair of the Jain prophet MAHĀVĪRA when he cut it off to signify his renunciation of the world.

Indra is father to ARJUNA, hero of the MAHĀBHĀRATA war. He is sometimes referred to as "the thousand-eyed," because of the thousand marks on his body resembling eyes (actually YONIS, or symbols of the female sexual organ), a result of a curse placed by a sage whose wife Indra seduced. In painting and sculpture he is often depicted riding on his white elephant Airāvata.

INDULGENCE, in ROMAN CATHOLICISM, a partial remission of temporal punishment due for a SIN after the sin has been forgiven through the SACRAMENT of penance. The theology of indulgences is based upon the concept that, even though the crime of sin and its eternal punishment are forgiven in the sacrament of penance, divine CHARITY and justice demand that the sinner pay for his crime either in this life or in PURGATORY.

The history of indulgences is intimately bound up with the penitential discipline of the early Christian church. The sacrament of penance (*see* CONFESSION) was frequently referred to as a second and more laborious BAPTISM in which the penitent endeavored to free themselves not only of the guilt of sin but of the temporal punishment as well. To this end fixed penances (canonical) were assigned to compensate the debt of punishment contracted by sin. Later, in the early Middle Ages, there developed procedures to commute the protracted canonical penance by substituting periods of fasting (usually of 40 days, a quarantine), special private prayers, almsgiving, and payments of money that was to be used for religious purposes. The first to grant a plenary, or absolute, indulgence was Pope Urban II on the occasion of the First Crusade (1095); the indulgence decree reads: "Whosoever out of pure devotion and not for the sake of gaining honor or money, shall go to Jerusalem to liberate the Church of God, may count that journey in lieu of all penance."

After the 12th century, references to indulgences became more frequent. Innocent II granted a 40-day indulgence for visiting and contributing to the adornment of the great church at Cluny (1132), and soon every church of any importance had its own indulgence to further the work of construction. The evident lack of proportion between the small sums of money contributed and the debt of punishment remitted posed a problem for the great speculative theologians of the age. Their solution was that money contributions and other pious works were not to be considered as substitutes for the canonical penance but rather as conditions for gaining the indulgence. The debt of punishment was paid from the church's treasury of merits.

The practice of demanding an offering as a necessary condition for certain indulgences inevitably prepared the way for serious abuses. Not a little of the money collected found its way into the pockets of greedy ecclesiastics and professional collectors (quaestores). And it is at least possible that preachers went beyond the limits of the doctrine, misleading the more credulous into believing that the indulgence was a substitute for true sorrow and confession. It would appear also that the frequently used expression ab omni culpa et poena—"from all guilt and punishment"—contributed to the misconception.

Martin Luther's NINETY-FIVE THESES (1517) were in part a protest against the wayward employment of indulgences and helped spark the Indulgence Controversy. Not until the COUNCIL OF TRENT (1562), however, was an end put to abuses connected with the practice of indulgences. The name and office of quaestor was abolished along with its privileges. Five years later, Pius V revoked all indulgences for which money payments or alms were prescribed and ordered the bishops to destroy all briefs in which such indulgences were granted. The Roman Catholic church nevertheless still held to its doctrine that the debt of punishment could be paid from the church's treasury of merits.

In current Roman Catholic doctrine and practice, in order to gain an indulgence the person must be in the state of GRACE (i.e., he must have no unabsolved mortal sin upon his conscience), he must have the intention of gaining the indulgence, and he must personally fulfill the prescribed good work. Indulgences may be applied to the souls of the dead. In such cases, however, the church cannot grant directly; indulgences can be offered for the dead only per modum suffragii (i.e., in supplication), not per modum absolutionis (i.e., as a grant).

INDUS VALLEY CIVILIZATION \'in-dəs\, *also called* Harappan civilization \hə-'ra-pən\, earliest known urban culture of the Indian subcontinent, first identified in 1921

at Harappā in the Punjab and then in 1922 at Mohenjo-daro, near the Indus River in the Sindh, now both in Pakistan. Subsequently, vestiges of the civilization were found as far apart as Sutkāgen Dor, near the shore of the Arabian Sea, 300 miles west of Karachi, and Rupar at the foot of the Shimla Hills, 1,000 miles to the northeast. Later exploration established its existence southward down the west coast as far as the Gulf of Cambay, 500 miles southeast of Karachi and as far east as the JAMUNĀ Basin, 30 miles north of Delhi.

The civilization is known to have comprised two large cities, Harappā and Mohenjo-daro, and over 100 towns and villages, often of relatively small size. The two cities were each over 3 miles in circuit, and their outstanding magnitude, coupled with a standard system of weights, as well as a common script over the entire culture, suggests to some scholars a single great empire or some form of centralized control. Other scholars see a system of independent city-states as a more likely form of polity in this period. Other comparably large cities have been found since the initial discovery of Harappā and Mohenjo-daro. The civilization was literate, and its script, with some 250 to 500 characters, has yet to be deciphered, despite a plethora of claims. Decipherment attempts have primarily focused on Dravidian and Indo-Aryan (and to a lesser extent Munda) languages from the subcontinent, as well as other languages outside South Asia such as Sumerian. No two decipherment attempts have been consistent, and we remain unsure of the linguistic affiliation of the Indus Valley inhabitants. The nuclear dates of the civilization appear to be about 2500–1700 BCE, though southern sites may have lasted later in the 2nd millennium BCE. The Indus Valley civilization maintained active trade contacts extending into Iran, Afghanistan, and the Gulf of Oman.

Perhaps the best-known artifacts of the Indus civilization are a number of small seals, generally made of steatite, which are distinctive in kind and unique in quality, depicting a wide variety of animals, both real—such as elephants, tigers, rhinoceroses, and antelopes—and fantastic, often composite, creatures. Sometimes human forms are included. A few small examples of Indus stone sculpture have been found, as well as large numbers of small terra-cotta figures of animals and humans. Among these, female figurines are particularly ubiquitous, causing some scholars to speculate that the worship of goddesses was a main feature of Indus religion.

Certain figures and scenes depicted on the Indus seals have led to speculation about many other connections to Hindu religion as it later developed. In one seal, for example, a figure emerging from a *pīpal* tree—sacred to Hindus—appears to be under worship. In another, a figure seated cross-legged seems to be venerated by two ancillary figures whose backs and heads are shielded by great snakes, after the manner of NĀGAS. In still another, a similarly seated figure rests hands on knees as if in the lotus position (*padmāsana*) familiar to yogic practice, and some observers have seen him to be an early version of SHIVA, the great ascetic who is exemplary in his ability both to store and restrain male erotic power.

The exact relation between Indus and Indo-Aryan religious cultures is still unsolved. The consensus among most Western and some Indian scholars, based primarily on philological and linguistic evidence, is that the ARYANS entered the subcontinent sometime after the decline of the Mature Harappan phase, or after 2000 BCE. A growing number of primarily South Asian archaeologists and scholars, however, consider that the Indus Valley may have been an Indo-Aryan civilization, or at least in co-existence with the Vedic culture. The issue is likely to remain contested until the Indus script is deciphered.

INNER LIGHT, *also called* Inward Light, the distinctive theme of the SOCIETY OF FRIENDS (Quakers), the direct awareness of God that allows a person to know God's will for him. It was expressed in the 17th century in the teachings of GEORGE FOX, founder of the Friends, who had failed to find spiritual truth in the English churches and who finally experienced a voice saying, "There is one, even Christ Jesus, that can speak to thy condition." A phrase used by Fox, "that of God in every man," is often used to describe the Inner Light. ROBERT BARCLAY, Scottish author of the influential systematic statement of the doctrines of the Friends, *An Apology for the True Christian Divinity* (1678), stated that "the Inner Light is never separated from God nor Christ; but wherever it is, God and Christ are as wrapped up therein." Most Friends believe that the Inner Light is not simply a mystical experience but should result in a person's working for the good of others.

INNOCENT III \\'i-nə-sənt\\, *original name* Lothair of Segni, *Italian* Lotario di Segni (b. 1160/61, Gavignano Castle, Campagna di Roma, Papal States—d. July 16, 1216, Perugia), pope from 1198 to 1216, under whom the medieval PAPACY reached the height of its prestige and power.

Lothair studied theology in Paris and CANON LAW in Bologna. In 1190 Pope Clement III (1187–91) raised him from subdeacon to CARDINAL deacon, but he played no prominent part in the government of the church during the pontificate of Celestine III (1191–98). On the day of Celestine's death, Jan. 8, 1198, Lothair was unanimously elected pope after only two ballots; he was ordained priest on February 21 and on the next day was consecrated as bishop of Rome.

At the time of his accession, Rome was practically independent of papal government, but Innocent soon succeeded in reasserting papal rights there. Within a few years he had pacified the rival aristocratic factions and won over most of the people. Moreover, he had been very successful in restoring papal government to the Papal States and had added to them the Duchy of Spoleto and the March of Ancona.

When the princes of the Holy Roman Empire split over the election of a new German king, one party electing the brother of the deceased emperor, Philip of Hohenstaufen, duke of Swabia, the other electing the duke of Brunswick, who was to be known as Otto IV, Innocent favored Otto because he distrusted the policies of Philip's family. Additionally, Innocent had no desire to see Frederick as emperor as that would reunite the empire with Sicily. Philip, however, was so successful against Otto that Innocent after a few years found it necessary to resume negotiations with him. But Philip was murdered in 1208, and Otto IV was then crowned emperor by Innocent III.

In a short time, Otto managed to alienate the Pope by his pursuit of plans and actions hostile to papal sovereignty in the Papal States and aiming at the reunion of the empire and Sicily. Innocent excommunicated him after he had embarked on the conquest of the Sicilian kingdom and turned to the young Frederick of Sicily. He gave his support to the German election of 1212, and in 1216 Frederick II, as king of Germany, promised to transfer full rule over Sicily to his infant son Henry.

Meanwhile, Frederick, with the help of King Philip II Augustus of France, had triumphed over Otto IV and over Ot-

to's uncle and ally, King John of England, at the Battle of Bouvines (1214). John had been excommunicated by Innocent for his refusal to recognize as archbishop of Canterbury Cardinal Stephen Langton, who had been elected by the monks of the cathedral in accordance with the Pope's wishes. In order to forestall French invasion of England, John declared England a fief of the Holy See (1213). When John was forced to sign Magna Carta and then complained to the Pope as to his feudal overlord, Innocent annulled the charter as having been extorted. Innocent considered Magna Carta an attempt at feudal insurrection against rightful royal authority.

Innocent presided over the Fourth Crusade of 1202–04, and when it was diverted to Constantinople, chiefly to suit Venetian interests and against the will of the Pope, he nevertheless accepted the fait accompli because he mistakenly believed that the establishment of the Latin Empire and patriarchate of Constantinople would bring about a lasting reunion between the Eastern and Western churches. The other crusade of his reign was launched, with his approval, against the ALBIGENSES, who denied the SACRAMENTS and the authority of the ecclesiastical hierarchy. The Pope's decision opened an unhappy chapter in the history of the church by placing under supreme ecclesiastical leadership the repression of HERESY by force. Although he never demanded the death sentence against heretics, he had little success in limiting the bloodshed and devastation.

Innocent encouraged the desire to live in apostolic poverty wherever he found it among the ROMAN CATHOLIC clergy and laity. In granting lay and clerical communities—such as the DOMINICANS and the first community of ST. FRANCIS OF ASSISI—permission to preach and teach, Innocent went far beyond what the popes of the 12th century had thought possible, inaugurating the MENDICANT orders.

He presided over the fourth LATERAN COUNCIL (1215), which promulgated the dogma of TRANSUBSTANTIATION, bound every Catholic to CONFESSION at least once a year and communion at EASTER time, and enacted important reforms of clergy and laity. A far-reaching centralization of church government is particularly reflected by Innocent's unlimited claim to fill all vacancies of ecclesiastical offices.

INOUE ENRYŌ \\ē-'nō-ü-e-'en-'ryō\\ (b. March 18, 1858, Echigo Province, Japan—d. June 6, 1919, Dairen, Manchuria), Japanese philosopher and educator who attempted to reinterpret Buddhist concepts so that they would be accessible to Western philosophers.

After attending the school for priests at the Higashihongan-ji, the main temple of the Jōdo-Shinshū (True PURE LAND sect) in Japan, Inoue enrolled in Tokyo Imperial University, where he graduated from the department of philosophy in 1885. Critical of what he considered the excessive Westernization of Japan, especially the conversion of many governmental leaders to CHRISTIANITY, he founded (1887) the Tetsugaku kan (Philosophical Institute) to promote the study of BUDDHISM. Inoue's belief that Buddhism epitomized Oriental philosophy gained many adherents, and with their aid he began to publish the highly nationalistic magazine *Nihonjin* ("The Japanese") and embarked on a series of lecture tours throughout Japan and Europe.

In his later life Inoue conducted an educational campaign to overcome superstitions inspired by folkloric interpretations of Japanese mythology. For this purpose he established the Ghost Lore Institute in Tokyo and gained the sobriquet "Doctor Obake," or "Doctor Ghost." He died while on a speaking tour in Manchuria.

The expulsion of the Jews from Spain during the Spanish Inquisition; Jews plead before Queen Isabella, while Torquemada (holding a cross) argues for expulsion; painting by Solomon A. Hart
Culver Pictures

INQUISITION, in ROMAN CATHOLICISM, a papal judicial institution that combated HERESY as well as alchemy, WITCHCRAFT, and SORCERY and wielded much power in medieval and early modern times. The name is derived from the Latin verb *inquiro* ("investigate, inquire into").

After the Roman church had consolidated its power in the early Middle Ages, heretics came to be looked upon as enemies of society. With the appearance of large-scale heresies in the 11th and 12th centuries—notably among the CATHARI and WALDENSES—Pope Gregory IX in 1231 instituted the papal Inquisition for the arrest and trial of heretics.

The inquisitorial procedure gave a person suspected of heresy time to confess and absolve himself; failing this, the accused was brought before the inquisitor and interrogated and tried, with the testimony of witnesses. The use of torture to obtain confessions and the names of other heretics was authorized in 1252 by Innocent IV. On admission or conviction of guilt, a person could be sentenced to any of a wide variety of penalties, ranging from simple prayer and fasting to confiscation of property and imprisonment, even for life. Condemned heretics who refused to recant, as well

as those who relapsed after condemnation and repentance, were turned over to the secular arm, which alone could impose the death penalty.

The medieval Inquisition functioned only in a limited way in northern Europe; it was most employed in northern Italy and southern France. During the Reconquista in Spain, the Catholic powers used it only occasionally; but, after the Muslims had been driven out, the Catholic monarchs of Aragon and Castile requested a special institution to combat apostate former Jews and Muslims as well as such heretics as the Alumbrados. Thus in 1478 Pope Sixtus IV authorized the Spanish Inquisition.

The first Spanish inquisitors, operating in Seville, proved so severe that Sixtus IV had to interfere. But the Spanish crown now had in its possession a powerful weapon, and the efforts of the Pope to limit the powers of the Inquisition were without avail. In 1483 he was induced to authorize the naming by the Spanish government of a grand inquisitor for Castile, and during the same year Aragon, Valencia, and Catalonia were placed under the power of the Inquisition. The first grand inquisitor was the DOMINICAN Tomás de Torquemada, who has become the symbol of the inquisitor who uses torture and confiscation to terrorize his victims. The number of burnings at the stake during his tenure has been exaggerated, but it was probably about 2,000.

The Spanish Inquisition was introduced into Sicily in 1517, but efforts to set it up in Naples and Milan failed. The emperor Charles V in 1522 introduced it into the

Netherlands, where its efforts to wipe out PROTESTANTISM were unsuccessful. The Inquisition in Spain was suppressed by Joseph Bonaparte in 1808, restored by Ferdinand VII in 1814, suppressed in 1820, restored in 1823, and finally suppressed in 1834.

A third variety of the Inquisition was the Roman Inquisition, established in 1542 by Pope Paul III to combat Protestantism in Italy. It was governed by a commission of six CARDINALS, the Congregation of the Inquisition, which was thoroughly independent and much freer from episcopal control than the medieval Inquisition had been. Under Paul III (1534–49) and Julius III (1550–55), the action of the Roman Inquisition was not rigorous, and the moderation of these popes was imitated by their successors with the exceptions of Paul IV (1555–59) and Pius V (1566–72). Under Paul IV the Inquisition alienated nearly all parties. Although Pius V (a Dominican and himself formerly grand inquisitor) avoided some of the worst excesses of Paul IV, he nevertheless declared that questions of faith took precedence over all other business and made it clear that his first care would be to see that heresy, false doctrine, and error were suppressed.

After Protestantism had been eliminated as a serious danger to Italian religious unity, the Roman Inquisition became more and more an ordinary organ of papal government concerned with maintaining good order as well as purity of faith among Catholics. In his reorganization of the ROMAN CURIA in 1908, PIUS X dropped the word Inquisition, and the congregation charged with maintaining purity of faith came to be known officially as the Holy Office. In 1965 Pope Paul VI reorganized the congregation along more democratic lines and renamed it the Congregation for the Doctrine of the Faith.

INSTITUTES OF THE CHRISTIAN RELIGION, *Latin* Christianae Religionis Institutio, *French* Institution de la Religion Chrétienne, John Calvin's masterpiece, a summary of biblical theology that became the normative statement of the Reformed faith. It was first published in 1536 and was revised and enlarged by Calvin in several editions before the definitive edition was published in 1559.

The first edition, written in Latin and published in Basel, where Calvin was in exile, included a dedication to the French king Francis I. Calvin intended his work to be a statement of French Protestant beliefs that would refute the king, who was persecuting French Protestants and incorrectly calling them ANABAPTISTS (radical Reformers who wished to separate the church from the state). It consisted of six chapters that discussed the TEN COMMANDMENTS, the APOSTLES' CREED, the LORD'S PRAYER, the SACRAMENTS of BAPTISM and the Lord's Supper (EUCHARIST), disputed sacraments, and Christian liberty. Most of the themes of Calvin's mature thought were in the first edition.

The first French edition, prepared by Calvin and published in Basel in 1541, was the first great work in argumentative French prose. The final edition, in Latin and published in Geneva in 1559, was more than four times longer than the first edition. It was organized into FOUR BOOKS concerning Creator, Redeemer, Spirit, and church. The dominating themes dealt with God's sovereignty, his GRACE, and his redemption of undeserving sinners. This edition was published in French (1560), in English (1561), and eventually in many other languages.

INTI \\'in-tē\\, *also called* Apu-Punchau, in Inca religion, the sun god, head of the state cult, and the ancestor of the In-

cas. He was usually represented in human form, his face a gold disk from which rays and flames extended. Inti's sister and consort was the moon, Mama-Kilya (or Mama-Quilla), portrayed as a silver disk with human features.

Inti-raymi, a festival in honor of Inti held in June (after the Spanish conquest, in May or June to coincide with the FEAST OF CORPUS CHRISTI), was celebrated with animal sacrifices and ritual dances. *See also* PRE-COLUMBIAN SOUTH AMERICAN RELIGIONS.

INVESTITURE CONTROVERSY \\in-'ves-tə-,chůr, -chər, -,tyůr\\, power struggle between the PAPACY and the Holy Roman Empire during the late 11th and early 12th centuries. It began with a dispute about the lay investiture of bishops and ABBOTS. Such PRELATES held land and often exercised secular as well as ecclesiastical functions; for this reason, lay overlords had an interest in their appointment and frequently invested (formally presented) them with the symbols of their various offices.

Because POPE GREGORY VII'S condemnation (1075) of lay investiture immediately preceded his dispute with the German king and Holy Roman emperor Henry IV (reigned 1056–1106), historians have given to the quarrel and its aftermath the name Investiture Controversy; but the real conflict between Henry IV and Gregory, the main disputants, involved the issue of whether the pope or the emperor should dominate the church. The political results of their struggle were far-reaching. In Germany the power of the aristocracy, at the expense of the monarchy, was permanently enhanced, while in northern Italy the rise of the Lombard communes with papal support weakened imperial authority there. Gradually, the extreme papalists widened their opposition to any lay control over the episcopate. In 1106 Henry I of England renounced the practice of investing prelates with the symbols of their office, and in return the church conceded that homage to the king should precede episcopal consecration. A similar compromise was effected by the CONCORDAT OF WORMS (1122) between the emperor Henry V and Pope Calixtus II; and in Germany (but not in Burgundy or Italy) the emperor also acquired the right to have elections conducted in his presence.

IO \\'ī-ō\\, in Greek mythology, daughter of Inachus, the river god of Argos. Under the name of Callithyia, Io was regarded as the first priestess of HERA, the wife of ZEUS. Zeus fell in love with her and, to protect her from the wrath of Hera, changed her into a white heifer. Hera persuaded Zeus to give her the heifer and set ARGUS PANOPTES ("the All-Seeing") to watch her. Zeus thereupon sent the god HERMES, who lulled Argus to sleep and killed him. Hera then sent a gadfly to bother Io, who therefore wandered all over the Earth, crossed the Ionian Sea, swam the strait that was thereafter known as the Bosporus (meaning Ox-Ford), and at last reached Egypt, where she was restored to her original form and became the mother of Epaphus.

Io was thus identified with the Egyptian goddess ISIS, and Epaphus with APIS, the sacred bull. Epaphus was said to have been carried off by order of Hera to Byblos in Syria, where he was found again by Io. This part of the legend connects Io with the Syrian goddess ASTARTE. Both the Egyptian and the Syrian parts reflect interchange with the East and the identification of foreign with Greek gods.

IOLAUS \\,ī-ə-'lā-əs\\, ancient Greek hero, the nephew, charioteer, and assistant of HERACLES. He was the son of Iphicles, himself half brother of Heracles by the same mother. Iolaus

The sacrifice of Iphigeneia, fresco from the House of the Tragic Poet, Pompeii, c. 30 CE; in the National Archaeological Museum, Naples, Italy
The Bridgeman Art Library International

aided Heracles in his second labor, the slaying of the HYDRA and its ally the crab. He also went with him to the west to capture the cattle of the GIANT Geryon. Hence he was associated with various places in Sicily and, later, in Sardinia. Iolaus had a hero cult at Thebes, but elsewhere he was worshiped only in conjunction with Heracles.

IPHIGENEIA \,i-fə-jə-'nī-ə\, in Greek mythology, eldest daughter of AGAMEMNON and his wife Clytemnestra. Her father had to sacrifice her to the goddess ARTEMIS in order that the Achaean fleet might be delivered from the calm (or contrary winds) by which Artemis was detaining it at Aulis and proceed on its way to the siege of Troy.

Iphigeneia served as a key figure in certain Greek tragedies: in the *Agamemnon* of Aeschylus, in the *Electra* of Sophocles, in Euripides' unfinished *Iphigeneia in Aulis*, and in his earlier play *Iphigeneia in Tauris*, in which she was saved by Artemis, who substituted a hind. Variants of her story are found in later authors. In some localities she was identified with Artemis, and some ancient writers claimed that Iphigeneia was originally the goddess HECATE.

IQBĀL, MUHAMMAD \'ik-,bäl\ (b. Nov. 9, 1877, Siālkot, Punjab, India [Pakistan]—d. April 21, 1938, Lahore, Punjab), Indian poet and philosopher, known for his influential efforts toward the establishment of a separate Muslim state.

Early life and career. Iqbāl was educated at Government College, Lahore. In Europe from 1905 to 1908 he earned his degree in philosophy from the University of Cambridge, qualified as a barrister in London, and received a doctorate from the University of Munich. His thesis, *The Development of Metaphysics in Persia*, revealed some aspects of Islamic MYSTICISM formerly unknown in Europe.

On his return from Europe, he gained his livelihood by the practice of law, but his fame came from his Persian- and Urdu-language poetry, which was written in the classical style for public recitation. Through poetic symposia and in a milieu in which memorizing verse was customary, his poetry became widely known, even among the illiterate. Almost all the cultured Indian and Pakistani Muslims of his and later generations have had the habit of quoting Iqbāl.

The recurrent themes of Iqbāl's poetry are a memory of the vanished glories of ISLAM, a complaint about its present decadence, and a call to unity and reform. Reform can be achieved by strengthening the individual through three successive stages: obedience to the law of Islam, self-control, and acceptance of the idea that everyone is potentially a vicegerent of God (*nā'ib*, or *mu'min*). Furthermore, the life of action is to be preferred to ascetic resignation.

Notoriety came in 1915 with the publication of his long Persian poem *The Secrets of the Self*. In this work he presents a strong condemnation of the self-negating QUIETISM (*i.e.*, the belief that perfection and spiritual peace are attained by passive absorption in contemplation of God and divine things) of classical Islamic mysticism; his criticism shocked many and excited controversy. Iqbāl and his admirers steadily maintained that creative self-affirmation is a fundamental Muslim virtue.

The dialectical quality of his thinking was expressed by the next long Persian poem, *The Mysteries of Selflessness* (1918). The Muslim community, as Iqbāl conceived it, ought to teach and encourage generous service to the ideals of brotherhood and justice. The mystery of selflessness was the hidden strength of Islam. Ultimately, the only satisfactory mode of active self-realization was the sacrifice of the self in the service of causes greater than the self. The paradigm was the life of the Prophet MUHAMMAD and the devoted service of the first believers. In 1922 he was knighted by the British Crown in recognition of his achievements.

Later, he published three more Persian volumes. *Payāme Mashriq* (1923; "Message of the East") affirmed the universal validity of Islam. In 1927 *Zabūr-e 'Ajam* ("Persian Psalms") appeared. *Jāvīd-nāmeh* (1932; "The Song of Eternity") is considered Iqbāl's masterpiece. Its theme is the ascent of the poet, guided by the great 13th-century Persian mystic Jalāl al-Dīn al-Rūmī, through all the realms of thought and experience to the final encounter.

Iqbāl's later publications in Urdu were *Bāl-e Jibrīl* (1935; "Gabriel's Wing"), *Zarb-e kalīm* (1937; "The Blow of Moses"), and the posthumous *Armaghān-e Hijāz* (1938; "Gift of the Hejaz"), which contained verses in both Urdu and Persian. He is considered the greatest poet in Urdu of the 20th century.

Philosophical position and influence. His philosophical position was articulated in *The Reconstruction of Religious Thought in Islam* (1934), a volume based on six lectures delivered at Madras, Hyderābād, and Alīgarh in 1928–29. He argued that a rightly focused man should unceasingly generate vitality through interaction with the purposes of the living God. The Muslim community ought, through the exercise of IJTIHĀD—the principle of legal advancement—to devise new social and political institutions. He also advocated a theory of IJMĀ'—consensus. Iqbāl tended to be progressive in adumbrating general principles of change but conservative in initiating actual change.

During the time that he was delivering these lectures, Iqbāl began working with the Muslim League. At the annual session of the league at Allahābād, in 1930, he gave the presidential address, in which he made a famous statement that the Muslims of northwestern India should demand status as a separate state.

After a long period of ill health, Iqbāl died in April 1938 and was buried in front of the great Bādshāhī Mosque in Lahore. Two years later, the Muslim League voted for the idea of Pakistan. He has been acclaimed as the father of that country, and every year Iqbāl Day is celebrated by Pakistanis.

IRANIAN RELIGIONS, ANCIENT, diverse beliefs and practices of a culturally and linguistically related group of peoples who inhabited the Iranian Plateau and its borderlands, as well as areas of Central Asia from the Black Sea to Khotan (modern Ho-t'ien, China). The northern Iranians (referred to generally as Scythians [Saka] in classical sources), who occupied the steppes, differed significantly from the southern Iranians. In religion and culture both the northern and southern Iranians had much in common with the ancient Indo-Aryans, although there was much borrowing from Mesopotamia as well, especially in western Iran.

One prominent feature of ancient Iranian religion was the notable influence of the MAGI, members of a priestly tribe originating in Media in northwestern Iran. The Magi's origin is unclear, but according to classical sources they presided at all religious ceremonies, where they chanted "theogonies," accounts of the origin and descent of the gods. They eventually became the official PRIESTHOOD of the Persian empire and were probably responsible for articulating a thoroughly dualist ideology and contributing to ZORO-ASTRIANISM its preoccupation with ritual purity.

Major deities. The early forms of the Iranian pantheon embraced two major groups of deities, the *daiva*s ("heavenly ones") and the *ahura*s. Among many Iranians and in Zoroastrianism the *daiva*s were regarded as DEMONS, but this belief was not pan-Iranian. The *ahura*s ("lords") were certain lofty sovereign deities, in contradistinction to the other deities called *bagha* ("the one who distributes") and YAZATA ("the one to be worshiped").

AHURA MAZDĀ ("Wise Lord") was probably the chief god of the pre-Zoroastrian pantheon. In both the religion of ZORO-ASTER and that of the Persian emperors Darius and Xerxes he is the creator of the universe and the one who establishes and maintains the cosmic and social order. As his name implies, he seems to have been sought by his worshipers for wisdom and insight, and may have been the object of a personal devotion that was lacking with other deities.

MITHRA is the next most important deity and may even have occupied a position of near equality with Ahura Mazdā. He was associated with the Sun, and in time the name Mithra became a common word for "Sun." Mithra functioned preeminently in the ethical sphere; he was the god of the covenant, who oversaw all solemn agreements that people made among themselves. As a sovereign deity, Mithra bore the epithet *varu-gavyūti* ("one who [presides over] wide pasture lands")—*i.e.*, one who keeps under his protection the territories of those who worship him and abide by their covenants. In later times Mithra gave his name to MITHRAISM, a MYSTERY RELIGION.

There was a powerful goddess whose full name was Ardvī Sūrā Anāhitā, literally "the damp, strong, untainted." She appears to have been a combination of two originally distinct divinities. First, Ardvī Sūrā is the Iranian name of a river goddess who flows from Mount Hukarya and brings fresh water to the earth. Second, ANĀHITI (probably "untaintedness, purity") was a goddess with martial traits, the patroness of Iranian heroes and legendary rulers, whose cult seems to have been popular originally in northeastern Iran. In addition, she was important for fertility.

The war deity Vrthraghna was equated in post-Achaemenian times with HERACLES and was a favorite deity of monarchs, some of whom took his name, which means "the smashing of resistance or obstruction"; he bore the epithet *bara-khvarnah*, "bearing the glory." Among all the deities, Vrthraghna preeminently possessed the power to undergo various transformations. 10 different forms have been recorded: the Wind (the god Vāyu), bull, stallion, rutting camel, wild boar, a 15-year-old man (15 was considered to be the ideal age), falcon, ram, goat, and hero.

RASHNU was an ethical deity, the divine judge who ultimately presided over legal disputes among men. He was invoked as the one who "best smite(s), who best destroy(s) the thief and the bandit at this trial." In particular, he appears to have been the god of OATHS and ordeals administered during trials.

Astral deities figured prominently in ancient Iranian religion, and the most important seem to have been TISHTRYA and Tīri. Tishtrya was identified with the star Sirius, and his principal myth involves a battle with a demonic star named APAUSHA ("Nonprosperity") over rainfall and water. In a combat that was reenacted in a yearly equestrian ritual, Tishtrya and Apausha, assuming the forms of a white stallion and a horse of horrible description, respectively, battle along the seashore. Initially Apausha is victorious, but after receiving worship Tishtrya conquers him and drives him away. Tishtrya then causes the cosmic sea to surge and boil, and a star, Satavaisa (Fomalhaut), rises with the mists that are blown by the wind in the form of "rain and clouds and hail to the dwelling and the settlements (and) to the seven continents." As one of the stars "who contains the seeds of waters" (*i.e.*, who causes rain), Tishtrya was also intimately connected with agriculture. He battled and defeated the shooting stars (identified as witches), especially one called "Bad Crop" (Duzhyāryā). In Zoroastrianism, Tishtrya was identified with the western Iranian astral deity, Tīri (Mercury in Sāsānian astronomy); a very important agricultural festival, the Tīragān, as well as the 4th month and the 13th day of the Zoroastrian calendar, bears his name.

Cultic practices, worship, and festivals. The Iranians did not make images of their deities, nor did they build temples to house them, preferring to worship in the open. Worship was performed primarily in the context of a central ritual called *yazna*, which is still performed by Zoroastrians. The *yazna* was a festive meal, the sacrificer being the host and the deity the guest. As such it followed the established rules of hospitality: the guest was sent an invitation; on his arrival he was greeted, shown to a seat, given meat and a drink, and entertained with song extolling his great deeds and virtues. Finally, the guest was expected to return the hospitality in the form of a gift. It is likely that from a very early period a priest, the *zautar* (Vedic *hotar*), was required to carry out the *yazna* properly.

In ancient Iran, fire was at once a highly sacred element and a manifestation of the deity. Since burned offerings were not made, the role of Ātar (Fire) was principally that of intermediary between heaven and earth (*compare* AGNI). Fire was always treated with utmost care as a sacred element. Whether in the household hearth or, at a later period, in fire temples, the sacred fire had to be maintained with proper fuel, kept free from polluting agents, and above all never permitted to go out or be extinguished.

More important than the meat offering of an animal victim was the preparation of the divine drink *hauma* (*compare* SOMA), which was regarded both as a sacred drink and as a powerful deity. Probably the greatest part of the *yazna* was devoted to the pressing of the *hauma*. The juice, described as yellow, was filtered and mixed with milk, and perhaps with water too, to cut the bitter taste. The resulting drink was a mind-altering drug believed to inspire the drinker with insight into truth. Also, *hauma*, invoked for victory, was taken as a stimulant by warriors going into battle, and various heroes of Iranian myth and legend are remembered as primary practitioners of its cult.

IRENAEUS, SAINT \ˌī-rə-ˈnē-əs, -ˈnā-\ (b. *c.* 120/140, Asia Minor—d. *c.* 200/203, probably Lyon; Western feast day June 28; Eastern feast day August 23), bishop of Lugdunum (Lyon) and leading Christian theologian of the 2nd century.

Irenaeus was born of Greek parents in Asia Minor. As a child he heard and saw Polycarp, the last known living connection with the APOSTLES. After persecutions in Gaul in 177 Irenaeus succeeded the martyred Pothinus as bishop of Lugdunum. According to EUSEBIUS OF CAESAREA, Irenaeus, prior to his becoming bishop, had served as a missionary to southern Gaul and as a peacemaker among the churches of Asia Minor that had been disturbed by HERESY.

The era in which Irenaeus lived was a time of expansion and inner tensions in the church. In many cases Irenaeus acted as mediator between factions. The churches of Asia Minor continued to celebrate EASTER on the Jewish PASSOVER, whereas the Roman church maintained that Easter should always be celebrated on a Sunday (the day of the RESURRECTION of Christ). Mediating between the parties, Irenaeus stated that differences in external factors, such as dates of festivals, need not destroy church unity.

In spite of these conciliatory policies, Irenaeus adopted a totally negative and unresponsive attitude toward Marcion (*see* MARCIONITE), a schismatic leader in Rome, and toward GNOSTICISM. Because Gnosticism was overcome through the efforts of the early CHURCH FATHERS, among them CLEMENT OF ALEXANDRIA and Irenaeus, Gnostic writings were largely obliterated. In reconstructing Gnostic doctrines, therefore, modern scholars have relied to a great extent on the writings of Irenaeus, who summarized the Gnostic views before attacking them. The discovery of the Gnostic library near Najʿ Ḥammādī (in Egypt) in the 1940s proved him to have been extremely precise and quite fair in his report of the doctrines he rejected.

All his known writings are devoted to the conflict with the Gnostics. His principal work consists of five books in a work entitled *Adversus haereses*. Originally written in Greek about 180, "Against Heresies" is now known in its entirety only in a Latin translation. A shorter work, *Demonstration of the Apostolic Preaching*, also written in Greek, is extant only in an Armenian translation.

Irenaeus asserted the validity of the Hebrew BIBLE (the OLD TESTAMENT), which the Gnostics denied, claiming that it upheld the laws of the Creator God of wrath. Though Irenaeus did not actually refer to two testaments, one old and one new, he prepared the way for this terminology. He asserted the validity of the two testaments at a time when concern for the unity and the difference between the two parts of the Bible was developing. Many works claiming scriptural authority, which included a large number by Gnostics, flourished in the 2nd century; by his attacks on the Gnostics, Irenaeus helped to establish a canon of SCRIPTURES.

The development of the APOSTLES' CREED and the office of bishop also can be traced to his conflicts with the Gnostics. Because the Gnostics denied that the God revealed in the NEW TESTAMENT was the Creator, the first article of the creed

was for polemical reasons directly connected with GENESIS ("In the beginning God created the heavens and the earth"). Irenaeus refers to the creed as a "Rule of Truth" used to combat heresy.

IRIS \ˈī-rəs\ (Greek: "Rainbow"), in Greek mythology, the personification of the rainbow and a messenger of the gods. According to the poet Hesiod, she was the daughter of Thaumas and the ocean NYMPH Electra, and had the duty of carrying water from the River STYX in a ewer whenever the gods had to take a solemn OATH. The water would render unconscious for one year any god or goddess who lied. In art, Iris was normally portrayed with wings, and her attributes were the herald's staff and a vase.

ISAAC \ˈī-zək\, *Hebrew* Yitzḥaq, *Arabic* Isḥāq, in the OLD TESTAMENT, second of the patriarchs of ISRAEL, the only son of ABRAHAM and SARAH, and father of ESAU and JACOB (GENESIS 21:1–28:9; 35:27–29). Although Sarah was past the age of childbearing, God promised Abraham and Sarah that they would have a son, and Isaac was born (Genesis 18:1–21; 21:1–7). Later, to test Abraham's obedience, God commanded Abraham to sacrifice the boy (Genesis 22:1–2). Abraham made all the preparations for the ritual sacrifice, but God spared Isaac at the last moment and substituted a ram in his place (Genesis 22:3–14). The story of Abraham's acqui-

The sacrifice of Isaac, from the Psalter of Ingeburg of Denmark, 1210; in the Condé Museum, Chantilly, France
Giraudon—Art Resource

escence to God's command to sacrifice Isaac was used in the early Christian church as an example of faith (Hebrews 11:17) and of obedience (James 2:21). In later Jewish tradition the sacrifice of Isaac was cited in appeals for the mercy of God.

In later Jewish tradition, Abraham asked God to recall his mercy at the binding of Isaac (or AKEDAH) when Isaac's descendants became inclined to transgressions and evil deeds (LEVITICUS RABBAH 29:9). One source says that Isaac was born on the PASSOVER, and through his birth many barren women became fertile (Rosh Hashanah 11a). According to another tradition, God commanded Abraham to sacrifice Isaac in response to Satan's accusation that Abraham made no sacrifice at Isaac's birth. In a similar version, it was Isaac who suggested his own sacrifice to counter Ishmael's boast that he was more virtuous because he had volunteered for CIRCUMCISION at age 13, when he could have resisted, whereas Isaac had been circumcised in infancy (Sanhedrin 89b; GENESIS RABBAH 55:4).

In the Christian NEW TESTAMENT, Paul uses Isaac to prefigure both JESUS CHRIST (Galatians 3:16) and his followers (Galatians 4:22–31), who are children of the "free woman" (Sarah, as opposed to the slave, HAGAR). The epistle to the Hebrews interprets the binding of Isaac as an example of Abraham's faith and as a prefigure to Christ's death and RESURRECTION (Hebrews 11:17–19).

In ISLAM, Ibrahim (Abraham), Ishāq (Isaac) and Ya'qūb (Jacob) are prophets and Godly men (QUR'AN, surah 29:27). The story of Ishāq's binding does not specifically mention his name (37:99–110), giving rise to a fierce controversy among later Islamic scholars at to whether is was Ismā'īl (Ishmael) or Ishāq who was offered. Many Muslims trace their ancestry to Ibrahim through Ismā'īl, but some (the Persians) through Ishāq.

ISAIAH \ī-'zā-ə, -'zī-\, *Hebrew* Yesha'yahu ("God Is Salvation") (fl. 8th century BCE, Jerusalem), prophet after whom the biblical Book of Isaiah is named (only some of the first 39 chapters are attributed to him), a significant contributor to both Jewish and Christian traditions.

Of Isaiah's origins it is known only that his father's name was Amoz. Whatever his family circumstances may have been, in his youth he came to know the face of poverty, the debauchery of the rich, and the other inequities and evils of human society. He was thoroughly schooled in the forms and language of prophetic speech and was particularly well acquainted with the prophetic tradition known to his slightly older contemporary, AMOS.

The earliest recorded event in his life is his call to PROPHECY as now found in the sixth chapter of the Book of Isaiah; this occurred about 742 BCE. The vision (probably in the JERUSALEM TEMPLE) that made him a prophet commissioned him to condemn his own people and watch the nation crumble and perish. As he tells it, he was only too aware that, coming with such a message, he would experience bitter opposition, willful disbelief, and ridicule—in order to withstand this he would have to be inwardly fortified.

Theologically, Isaiah leans heavily on Israelite tradition and shows his acquaintance with the thoughts of Amos. Isaiah also believed that a special bond united ISRAEL and its God. Since patriarchal times there had been a solemn COVENANT between them: Israel was to be God's people and he their God. Isaiah honored this ancient tradition; but, more significantly, he shared the conviction of Amos that this arrangement was contingent on the people's conduct. Misbehavior could cancel that Covenant, and had in fact done so.

As Isaiah knew him, Israel's God was more concerned about people than about proper ritual performance. Isaiah's theology included the sometimes comforting view that God shapes history, traditionally entering the human scene to rescue his people from national peril. But God could intervene quite as properly to chastise his own aberrant nation, and he could employ a human agent (*e.g.*, a conquering foe) to that end. Isaiah's call to prophecy roughly coincides with the beginning of the westward expansion of the Assyrian empire under the victorious generalship of Tiglath-pileser III (reigned 745–727 BCE). Isaiah could clearly see in Assyria the instrument of God's wrath.

If chapter 6 of the Book of Isaiah marks the beginning of his career as prophet, the judgment oracle about the conquest of Jerusalem in chapter 22 probably brings his grim story to a close. Quite unexpectedly the Assyrians have lifted the siege and departed, and the amazed defenders of Jerusalem, flushed and jubilant, give way to celebration; Isaiah cannot share the holiday spirit since for him there has been only a postponement. Nothing has changed, and in his "valley of vision" he sees the day of rout and confusion that God yet has in store for ZION.

The historical allusions in the scattered chapters of Isaiah's work agree with the title verse, according to which he was a contemporary of the Judaean kings UZZIAH, Jotham, AHAZ, and HEZEKIAH. At least a part of chapter 7 refers to the event of the year 734 when EPHRAIM and Syria jointly threatened King Ahaz of JUDAH. In 732 Tiglath-pileser conquered Damascus, and in 722 Samaria, the capital of Ephraim, fell to King Sargon of Assyria. By the end of the century (701) Sennacherib had laid siege to Jerusalem—and had subsequently withdrawn. Chapters 1:4–8; 10:27–34; 28:14–22; 30:1–7; and 31:1–4 point to those difficult days when Jerusalem was beleaguered and King Hezekiah feverishly sought help from Egypt. Isaiah, by contrast, looked neither to allies nor to armaments for security. If it is God who decides the destiny of nations, security is for God to grant and for men to deserve.

Although Isaiah was far from popular in his day, he does appear to have attracted some followers; these may have been the circle that kept alive the nucleus of what was to become, through a developing tradition, the biblical Book of Isaiah. The Greek translation of Isaiah by Jewish scholars (the SEPTUAGINT), accomplished before the Christian Era, reflects a developing tradition of interpretation; it renders the Hebrew *'alma* ("young woman") as *parthenos* ("virgin") in the verse (7:14) about Immanuel, thus drawing Isaiah further into the messianic ring. Now it is a virgin who "shall conceive and bear a son." The Christian Gospels lean more heavily on the Book of Isaiah than on any other prophetic text. Beyond any denominational differences is the utopian dream, the "swords-into-plowshares" passage in Isaiah 2.

ISE, GRAND SHRINE OF \'ē-se, *Angl* 'ē-sā\, *or* Ise-daijingū \-,dī-'jēŋ-gū\, *or* Ise-jingū, *or* Ise-no-Jingū, *or* Ise Shrine, most important SHINTŌ temple in Japan, located in Ise in southern Honshu. It is the main center of the worship of AMATERASU, the sun goddess and traditional progenitor of the Japanese imperial family. Traditionally it was founded in 4 BCE by Himiko, the first known ruler of Japan.

The Grand Shrine consists of an Inner and an Outer shrine, about 4 miles apart. The Sacred Mirror, one of the Three Sacred Treasures of Japan (Sanshu no Jingi), is preserved in the Inner shrine. The Outer Shrine (Gekū), founded in the late 5th century, is dedicated to Toyuke (Toyouke)

Ōkami, the god of food, clothing, and housing. The supreme priestess, *saishu* ("chief of the religious ceremonies") ranks above the supreme priest, the *dai-guji*; formerly this office was filled by an unmarried princess of the imperial family. At both shrines the main building is a thatched hut built with unpainted Japanese cypress (*hinoki*). From the 7th century to the early 17th century the buildings were reconstructed every 20 years; since then they have been rebuilt every 21 years. PILGRIMAGES to the shrines are popular.

ISE SHINTŌ \\'ē-se-'shēn-₁tō, *Angl* 'ē-sā-'shin-tō\\, *also called* Watarai Shintō \\,wä-tä-'rī-\\, school of SHINTŌ established by priests of the Watarai family who served at the Outer Shrine of the ISE SHRINE (Ise-jingū) associated with the imperial tradition. Ise Shintō establishes purity and honesty as the highest virtues, realizable through RELIGIOUS EXPERIENCE.

The school began in the Kamakura period (1192–1333) as an attempt to emancipate Shintō from the domination of Buddhist thought; it declared that the Buddhas and BODHISATTVAS were manifestations of Shintō KAMI. Later, Confucian elements were added. The theology of Ise Shintō was summarized in a five-volume apologia, the *Shintō gobusho*, which appeared in the 13th century.

ISHBOSHETH \\ish-'bō-shəth, -shət\\, *also spelled* Isboseth, *also called* Ishbaal \\ish-'bāl, -'bäl\\, *or* Eshbaal (fl. 11th century BCE), in the OLD TESTAMENT (2 Samuel 2:8–4:12), fourth son of King SAUL and the last representative of his family to be king over ISRAEL (the northern kingdom, as opposed to the southern kingdom of JUDAH). His name was originally Ishbaal (Eshbaal; 1 Chronicles 8:33; 9:39), meaning "man of BAAL." *Baal*, which could mean "master," was a title of dignity. Because the name came to be increasingly associated with Canaanite gods, Hebrew editors later substituted *bosheth*, meaning "shame," for *baal*.

Ishbosheth was proclaimed king of Israel by Abner, Saul's cousin and commander in chief, who then became the real power behind the throne. The House of Judah, however, followed DAVID, and war broke out between the two kingdoms. When Abner took Rizpah, one of Saul's concubines, Ishbosheth objected, because Abner's action was a symbolic usurpation of power. Abner then defected to David, leaving the northern tribes without effective leadership, and Ishbosheth was soon murdered by two of his captains.

Scholars believe that Ishbosheth was quite young when he became king and that his reign equaled that of David at Hebron, about seven and a half years.

ISHKUR \\'ish-₁kùr\\, in MESOPOTAMIAN RELIGION, Sumerian god of the rain and thunderstorms of spring. He was the city god of Bit Khakhuru (perhaps to be identified with modern al-Jidr) in the central grasslands region.

Ishkur closely resembled NINHAR (Ningubla) and was imagined in the form of a great bull and the son of NANNA (Akkadian Sin), the moon god. When he is portrayed in human shape, he often holds his symbol, the lightning fork. Ishkur's wife was the goddess Shala. In his role as god of rain and thunder, Ishkur corresponded to the other Sumerian deities ASALLUHE and NINURTA. He was identified by the Akkadians with their god of thunderstorms, ADAD.

ISHMAEL BEN ELISHA \\'ish-mā-əl-₁ben-i-'lī-shə, 'ish-mē-əl\\, one of the most important early rabbinic authorities, active at the beginning of the 2nd century CE. He is generally referred to simply as Ishmael, without the patronymic. In the MISHNAH, he often is portrayed in dispute with AKIBA BEN JOSEPH. Ishmael is known for 13 hermeneutical principles cited in his name, and his school is held to stand behind the midrashic compilations *Mekhilta de-Rabbi Ishmael* (on EXODUS), SIFRE TO NUMBERS, and part of SIFRE TO DEUTERONOMY. His actual association with these documents remains a matter of conjecture.

Ishmael is said to have been born to a wealthy priestly family and, as a youth, having been taken captive by the Romans, to have been ransomed by Joshua ben Hananiah, who recognized his scholarly potential and sent him back to Israel to study TORAH. Rabbinic texts depict him as exceedingly honest, charitable, and kindly. He reportedly said, "Be quick [in service] to a superior, kindly to the young, and receive everybody with joy" (Mishnah Abot 3:12). Later sources picture him in priestly service in the Second Temple, where he experienced the presence of God (Bavli Berakhot 7a):

> One time I went in to offer incense on the innermost altar, and I saw the Crown of the Lord, enthroned on the highest throne, and he said to me, "Ishmael, my son, bless me." I said to him, "May it be your will that your mercy overcome your anger and that your mercy prevail over your attributes, so that you treat your children in accord with the trait of mercy and in their regard go beyond the strict measure of the law." And he nodded his head to me. And from that story we learn that the blessing of a common person should not be negligible in your view.

Similarly, B. Berakhot 51a reports several folk traditions Ishmael is said to have been taught by the ANGEL Suriel, "the prince of the divine presence."

In biblical HERMENEUTICS, Ishmael is associated with the view that SCRIPTURE speaks in everyday language. He thus is said to have focused on the plain sense of the text, a position that stood in contrast to Akiba's interpretation of seemingly redundant words, of individual syllables of words, and even of single letters (B. Sanhedrin 51b).

ISHTAR \\'ish-₁tär\\ (Akkadian), *Sumerian* Inanna \\ē-'nän-₁nä\\, in MESOPOTAMIAN RELIGION, goddess of war and sexual love. Ishtar is the Akkadian counterpart of the West Semitic goddess ASTARTE. INANNA, an important goddess in the Sumerian pantheon, came to be identified with Ishtar, but it is uncertain whether Inanna is also of Semitic origin or whether, as is more likely, her similarity to Ishtar caused the two to be identified. In the figure of Inanna several traditions seem to have been combined: she is sometimes the daughter of the sky god An, sometimes his wife; in other myths she is the daughter of NANNA, god of the moon, or of the wind, ENLIL. In her earliest manifestations she was associated with the storehouse and thus personified as the goddess of dates, wool, meat, and grain; the storehouse gates were her emblem. She was also the goddess of rain and thunderstorms—leading to her association with An, the sky god—and was often pictured with the lion, whose roar resembled thunder. The power attributed to her in war may have arisen from her connection with storms. Inanna was also a fertility figure, and, as goddess of the storehouse and the bride of the god DUMUZI-AMAUSHUMGALANA, who represented the growth and fecundity of the date palm, she was characterized as young, beautiful, and impulsive—never as helpmate or mother.

From a fertility figure Ishtar evolved into a more complex character, a goddess of opposing forces: fire and fire-quenching, rejoicing and tears, fair play and enmity. The Akkadian Ishtar is also associated with the planet VENUS. In this manifestation her symbol is a star with 6, 8, or 16 rays within a circle. Delighting in bodily love, Ishtar was the protectress of prostitutes and the patroness of the alehouse. Part of her cult worship probably included temple prostitution, and her cult center, Erech, was a city filled with courtesans and prostitutes. Her popularity was universal in the ancient Middle East, and in many centers of worship she probably subsumed local goddesses. In later myth she was known as Queen of the Universe, taking on the powers of An, Enlil, and Enki.

ISIS \ˈī-səs\, *Egyptian* Aset \ˈä-set\, *or* Eset \ˈe-set\, one of the most important goddesses of ancient Egypt. Her name is the Greek form of an ancient Egyptian word that is perhaps associated with a word for "throne."

Little is known of Isis' early cult. In the PYRAMID TEXTS (*c.* 2350–*c.* 2100 BCE), she is the mourner for her murdered husband, the god OSIRIS. In her role as the wife of Osiris, she discovered and reunited the pieces of her dead husband's body, was the chief mourner at his funeral, and brought him back to life.

Isis hid her son, HORUS, from SETH, the murderer of Osiris, until Horus was fully grown and could avenge his father. She defended the child against many attacks from snakes and scorpions. But because Isis was also Seth's sister, she wavered during the eventual battle between Horus and Seth, and in one episode Isis pitied Seth and was beheaded by Horus during their struggle. The shelter she afforded her child gave her the character of a goddess of protection. But her chief aspect was that of a great magician, whose power transcended that of all other deities. Several narratives tell of her magical prowess, with which she could even outwit the creator god ATUM. She was invoked on behalf of the sick, and, with the goddesses Nephthys, NEITH, and SELKET, she protected the dead. She became associated with various other goddesses who had similar functions, and thus her nature became increasingly diverse. In particular, the goddess HATHOR and Isis became similar in many respects.

Isis was represented as a woman with the hieroglyphic sign of the throne on

Isis with Horus, bronze figurine of the Late Period; in the Egyptian Museum, Berlin
By courtesy of the Staatliche Museen Preussischer Kulturbesitz, Berlin

her head, either sitting on a throne, alone or holding the child Horus, or kneeling before a COFFIN. Occasionally she was shown with a cow's head. As mourner, she was a principal deity in all rites connected with the dead; as magician, she cured the sick and brought the dead to life; and, as mother, she was herself a life-giver.

The cult of Isis spread throughout Egypt. In Akhmīm she received special attention as the "mother" of the fertility god MIN. She had important temples throughout Egypt and Nubia. By Greco-Roman times she was dominant among Egyptian goddesses. Her cult reached much of the Roman world as a MYSTERY RELIGION. With Isis went Osiris and Horus the child, but Isis was the dominant figure. Many Egyptian monuments were imported to Rome to provide a setting for the principal Isis temple in the 1st century CE. The cult of Isis was probably influential on another level. The myth of Osiris shows some analogies with the Gospel story and, in the figure of Isis, with the role of the Virgin MARY. The ICONOGRAPHY of the Virgin and Child has evident affinities with that of Isis and the infant Horus. Thus, one aspect of Egyptian religion may have contributed to the background of early CHRISTIANITY.

ISKCON \ˈis-ˌkän\, *popularly called* Hare Krishna \ˈhär-ē-ˈkrish-nə, ˈhar-\, the International Society for KRISHNA Consciousness, a religious movement founded in the United States by A.C. BHAKTIVEDANTA Swami (Prabhupāda; 1896–1977) in 1966. The movement claims a lineage of spiritual masters dating to CAITANYA (1485–1533), whom it regards as an incarnation of the deity Krishna and his consort RĀDHĀ, and whose championing of religious enthusiasm it embraces. Its initial appeal was largely to "counterculture" Western youths, who could frequently be seen on city streets, their heads shaved and dressed in Hindu garments, chanting in the Caitanyite style and soliciting contributions from passersby. ISKCON adapts the Hindu ideology of CASTE by arguing (as certain ancient texts do) that the BRAHMIN status is determined by aptitude, rather than birth.

Humans are regarded as souls composed of Krishna's highest energy, with bodies of *māyā*, his lowest, material, and illusory energy. In order to achieve peace and happiness, believers are urged to return to their original relationship with Krishna (called Krishna Consciousness, after Caitanya's full name, Kṛṣṇa-Caitanya) through *bhakti-yoga.* This involves recognizing Krishna as the highest personality of godhead, whose servants perform his works with no thought of reward, and surrendering to Krishna and his representative, the spiritual master on earth. It also entails TABOOS against gambling, using intoxicants, eating meat, and engaging in illicit sex.

Hare Krishna temples are communes in which unmarried men and women live separately, with married couples having other quarters. Each temple has its own officers and supports itself by members' contributions, soliciting funds, and selling publications of the Bhaktivedanta Trust. Since the death of the founding GURU, temples obey an international governing commission. Of the governors, some are empowered as spiritual masters to initiate new members and oversee spiritual life in the temples.

In temple life Hare Krishna members assume Hindu customs and dress, but in the outer world they often pursue secular vocations. ISKCON has endured various schisms, notably its separation from the "City of God" founded as New Vṛndāvana in West Virginia. At the end of the 20th century its most active "mission fields" are the countries of the former Soviet Union, Africa, and India itself.

ISLAM

Major world religion that originated in the Middle East after JUDA- ISM and CHRISTIANITY; it was promulgated by the Prophet MU- HAMMAD in Arabia in the 7th century CE. The Arabic term *islām*, "surrender," illuminates the fundamental religious idea of Islam—that the believer (called a Muslim, from the active particle of *islām*) accepts "surrender to the will of ALLĀH." Allāh (Arabic: "God") is viewed as the sole God—the creator, sustainer, and restorer of the world. The will of Allāh, to which humankind must submit, is made known through the sacred SCRIPTURES, the QUR'AN (Koran), which Allāh revealed to his messenger, Muhammad. In Islam Muhammad is considered the last of a series of prophets (including ADAM, ABRA- HAM, MOSES, JESUS CHRIST, and others), and his message simultaneously consum- mates and abrogates the revelations attributed to earlier prophets.

Retaining its emphasis on an uncompromisng MONOTHEISM and a strict adher- ence to certain essential religious practices, the religion, which was first taught by Muhammad to a small group of followers, spread rapidly through the Middle East to Africa, Europe, the Indian subcontinent, the Malay Peninsula, and China. Although Islam encompasses many different ethnicities and many sectarian movements have arisen within it, all Muslims are ideally bound by a common faith and a sense of belonging to a single community.

THE LEGACY OF MUHAMMAD

From the very beginning of Islam, Muhammad inculcated a sense of communal identity and a bond of faith among his followers that was intensified by their ex- periences of persecution as a nascent community in Mecca. The conspicuous socioeconomic content of Islamic religious practices cemented this bond of faith. In 622 CE, when the Prophet migrated to MEDINA, his preaching was soon accepted, and the community-state of Islam emerged. During this early period, Islam ac- quired its characteristic ethos as a religion uniting in itself both the spiritual and temporal aspects of life and seeking to regulate not only an individual's relation- ship to God (through that individual's conscience) but human relationships in a social setting as well. Thus, there is not only an Islamic religious institution but also an Islamic law, state, and other institutions governing society. Not until the

The way of the pilgrims to the Ka'ba in Mecca, ceramic tiles from İznik, Turkey, Ottoman period; in the Louvre, Paris
Erich Lessing—Art Resource

515

ISLAM

20th century were the religious (private) and the secular (public) distinguished by some Muslim thinkers and separated formally, as in Turkey.

This dual religious and social character of Islam, expressing itself as a religious community commissioned by God to bring its own value system to the world through the JIHAD ("holy war" or "holy struggle"), explains much of the astonishing success of the early generations of Muslims. Within a century after the Prophet's death in 632 CE they had brought a large part of the globe—from Spain across Central Asia to India—under a new Arab Muslim empire.

The period of Islamic conquests and empire building marks the first phase of the expansion of Islam as a religion. Islam's essential egalitarianism within the community of the faithful and its official discrimination against the

followers of other religions won rapid converts. Jews and Christians were assigned a special status as communities possessing scriptures and called the "people of the Book" (AHL AL-KITĀB) and, therefore, were allowed religious autonomy. They were, however, required to pay a per capita tax called JIZYA. Members of other faiths were required either to accept Islam or to die. The same status of the people of the Book was later extended to Zoroastrians and Hindus, but many people of the Book eventually joined Islam in order to escape the disability of the *jizya*. A much more massive expansion of Islam after the 12th century was inaugurated by the Sufis (Muslim mystics), who contributed significantly to the spread of Islam in India, Central Asia, Turkey, and sub-Saharan Africa.

Besides the jihad and Sufi missionary activity another factor in the spread of Islam was the far-ranging influence of Muslim traders, who not only introduced Islam quite early to the Indian east coast and South India but who proved as well to be the main catalytic agents (besides the Sufis) in converting people to Islam in Indonesia, Malaya, and China. Islam was introduced to Indonesia in the 14th century, hardly having time to consolidate itself there politically before coming under Dutch colonial domination.

The vast variety of cultures embraced by Islam (estimated to total more than one billion persons worldwide) has produced important internal differences. All segments of Muslim society, however, are bound by a common faith and a sense of belonging to a single religious community. Despite the loss of political power during the period of Western colonialism in the 19th and 20th centuries, the concept of the Islamic community (*umma*) became stronger. Islam inspired various Muslim peoples in their struggles to gain political freedom in the mid-20th century, and the idealized unity of the community contributed to later attempts at political solidarity.

SOURCES OF ISLAMIC DOCTRINAL AND SOCIAL VIEWS

Islamic doctrine, law, and thinking in general are based on four sources, or fundamental principles (*uṣūl*): (1) the Qur'an, (2) the SUNNA (traditions), (3) IJMĀʿ (consensus), and (4) IJTIHĀD (individual thought).

The Qur'an ("Reading," or "Recitation") is regarded as the Word, or Speech, of God delivered to Muhammad by the angel GABRIEL. Divided into 114 SŪRAS (chapters) of unequal length, it is the fundamental source of Islamic teaching. The *sūras* revealed at Mecca during the earliest part of Muhammad's career are concerned with ethical and spiritual teachings and the Day of Judgment. The *sūras* revealed to the Prophet at Medina at a later period are concerned with social legislation, worship, and the politico-moral principles for constituting and ordering the community. The word sunna ("a well-trodden path") was used by pre-Islamic Arabs to denote their tribal or common law; in Islam it came to mean the example of the Prophet; *i.e.*, his words and deeds as recorded in compilations known as HADITH.

Hadith (a "Report," or collection, of sayings attributed to the Prophet and members of the early Muslim community) provides written documentation of the words and deeds of the Prophet and his followers. Six Hadith collections, compiled in the 9th century CE, or the 3rd century AH (*Anno Hegirae*, meaning "in the year of the HIJRA"; *see below* Sacred places and days: Holy days), came to be regarded as especially authoritative by the largest branch of Islam, the SUNNI. Another large branch, the SHIʿITE, has its own Hadith collections, in which, in addition to the Prophet, the IMAMS are of central importance.

The doctrine of *ijmāʿ*, or consensus, was introduced in the 2nd century AH (8th century CE) in order to standardize legal theory and practice and to overcome individual and regional differences of opinion. Though conceived as a "consensus of scholars," in actual practice *ijmāʿ* was a more fundamental operative factor. From the 3rd century AH points on which consensus was reached in practice were considered closed and further substantial questioning of them prohibited. Accepted interpretations of the Qur'an and of the actual content of the sunna (*i.e.*, Hadith and theology) all rest finally on the *ijmāʿ*.

Ijtihād, meaning "to endeavor," or "to exert effort," was required to find the legal or doctrinal solution to a new problem. In the early period of Islam, because *ijtihād* took the form of individual opinion (*ra'y*), there was an abundance of conflicting and chaotic opinions. In the 2nd century AH *ijtihād* was replaced by QIYĀS (reasoning by strict analogy), a formal procedure of deduction based on the texts of the Qur'an and the Hadith. The transformation of *ijmāʿ* into a conservative mechanism and the acceptance of a definitive body of Hadith virtually closed the "gate of *ijtihād*" in the Sunni tradition. Nevertheless, certain outstanding Sunni thinkers (*e.g.*, AL-GHAZĀLĪ, d. 1111 CE) and many Shi'ite jurists continued to claim the right of new *ijtihād* for themselves, and reformers of the 18th and 19th centuries, because of modern influences, have caused this principle once more to receive wider acceptance.

DOCTRINES OF THE QUR'AN

God. The doctrine concerning God within the Qur'an is rigorously monotheistic: God is one and unique; he has no partner and no equal. Muslims believe that there are no intermediaries between God and the creation that he brought into being by his sheer command: "Be." Although his presence is believed to be everywhere, he does not inhere in anything. He is the sole creator and the sole sustainer of the universe, wherein every creature bears witness to his unity and lordship. But he is also just and merciful: his justice ensures order in his creation, in which nothing is believed to be out of place, and his mercy is unbounded and encompasses everything. His creation and ordering of the universe is viewed as the act of prime mercy for which all things sing his glories. The God of the Qur'an, while described as majestic and sovereign, is also a personal God; whenever a person in need or distress calls to him, he responds. Above all, he is the God of guidance and shows everything, particularly human beings, the right way, "the straight path."

This picture of God—wherein the attributes of power, justice, and mercy interpenetrate—is related to Judaism and Christianity, whence it is derived with certain modifications, and also to the concepts of pre-Islamic Arabia, to which it provided an effective answer. One traditional Arabic RELIGIOUS BELIEF had been in a blind and inexorable fate over which man had no control. For this powerful but insensible fate the Qur'an substituted a provident and merciful God while rejecting IDOLATRY and all divinities that the Arabs worshiped in their sanctuaries (ḤARAMS), the most prominent of which was the KA'BA in Mecca itself.

The universe. In order to prove the unity of God, the Qur'an lays frequent stress on the design and order in the universe. There are no gaps or dislocations in nature. Order is explained by the fact that every created thing is endowed with a definite and defined nature whereby it falls into a pattern. This nature, though it allows every created thing to function as part of a whole, sets limits; and this idea of the limitedness of everything is one of the most fixed points in both the COSMOLOGY and theology of the Qur'an. The universe is viewed as autonomous, in the sense that everything has its own inherent laws of behavior, but not as autocratic, because the patterns of behavior have been endowed by God and are strictly limited. Thus, every creature is limited and "measured out" and hence depends on God, who alone reigns unchallenged in the heavens and the earth, is unlimited, independent, and self-sufficient.

The human condition. According to the Qur'an, God created two apparently parallel species of creatures, humans and JINN, the one from clay and the other from fire. About the *jinn*, however, the Qur'an says little, although it is implied that the *jinn* are endowed with reason and responsibility but are more prone to evil than humans. It is with the human being that the Qur'an, which describes itself as a guide for the human race, is centrally concerned (*e.g.*, Q 2:185). The Jewish and Christian story of the Fall of Adam (the first man) is accepted, but the Qur'an states that God forgave Adam his act of disobedience, which is not viewed in the Qur'an as ORIGINAL SIN (Q. 20:122–123).

A page from the Qur'an, on paper, Arabia, 16th century

The Pierpont Morgan Library—Art Resource

In the story of human creation, angels, who protested to God against such creation, lost in a competition of knowledge against Adam (Q 2:30–34). The Qur'an, therefore, declares humans to be the noblest creatures of all creation—those who bore the trust (of responsibility) that the rest of God's creation refused to accept. The Qur'an thus reiterates that all nature has been made subservient to humans: nothing in all creation has been made without a purpose, and people themselves have not been created "in sport," their purpose being service and obedience to God's will.

Despite this lofty station, however, human nature is frail and faltering. Whereas everything in the universe has a limited nature, and every creature recognizes its limitation and insufficiency, humans are viewed as rebellious and full of pride, arrogating to themselves the attributes of self-sufficiency. Pride is thus viewed as the cardinal sin of humankind, because by not recognizing in itself essential creaturely limitations humankind becomes guilty of ascribing to itself partnership with God (a form of SHIRK, or associating a creature with the Creator) and of violating the unity of God. True faith (*īmān*) thus consists in belief in the immaculate Divine Unity, and Islam in submission to the Divine Will.

Satan, sin, and repentance.   The being who became SATAN (Shayṭān, or IBLĪS) had previously occupied a high station but fell from divine grace by his act of disobedience in refusing to honor Adam when he, along with other angels, was ordered to do so; his act of disobedience is construed by the Qur'an as the sin of pride (Q 2:34). Since then, his work has been to beguile humans into error and sin. Satan's machinations will cease only on the Last Day.

The whole universe is replete with signs of God; the human soul itself is viewed as a witness to the unity and grace of God. The messengers and prophets of God have, throughout history, been calling humankind back to God. Yet very few have accepted the truth; most have rejected it and have become disbelievers (*kāfir*, plural *kuffār:* "ungrateful"—*i.e.*, to God), and when a person becomes so obdurate, his or her heart is sealed by God. Nevertheless, it is always possible for a sinner to repent (*tawba*) and to achieve redemption by a genuine conversion to the truth. Genuine repentance has the effect of removing all sins and restoring people to the state of sinlessness in which they started their lives.

Prophecy.   Prophets are specially elected by God to be his messengers. The Qur'an requires recognition of all prophets as such without discrimination, yet they are not all equal, some of them being particularly outstanding in qualities of steadfastness and patience under trial. Abraham, NOAH, Moses, and Jesus were such great prophets. As vindication of the truth of their mission, God often vested them with miracles: Abraham was saved from fire, Noah from the deluge, and Moses from the Pharaoh. Not only was Jesus born from the Virgin MARY but, in Islamic belief, God also saved him from CRUCIFIXION at the hands of the Jews.

All prophets are human and never part of divinity (except in Islamic THEOSOPHY and PANTHEISM); they are simply recipients of revelation from God. God never speaks directly to a human: he sends an angel messenger to him, makes him hear a voice, or inspires him. Muhammad is accepted as the last prophet in the series and its greatest member, for in him all the messages of earlier prophets were consummated. He had no miracles except the Qur'an, the like of which no human can produce. (Soon after the Prophet's death, however, a plethora of miracles was attributed to him by Muslims.) The angel Gabriel brought the Qur'an down to the Prophet's heart. Gabriel is represented by the Qur'an as a spirit, but the Prophet could sometimes see and hear him. According to early traditions, the Prophet's revelations occurred in a state of trance, when his normal consciousness was in abeyance. This phenomenon at the same time was accompanied by an unshakable conviction that the message was from God, and the Qur'an describes itself as the transcript of a heavenly "Mother Book" (Q 43:3–4) written on a "Preserved Tablet" (Q 85:21–22).

Eschatology.   Because not all requital is meted out in this life, a final judgment is necessary to bring it to completion. On the Last Day, when the world will come to an end, the dead will be resurrected, and a judgment will be pronounced on every person in accordance with his deeds. Although the Qur'an in the main speaks of a personal judgment, there are several verses that speak of the RESURRECTION of distinct communities that will be judged according to "their own book" (Q 45:27–29). The actual evaluation, however, will be for every individual, whatever the terms of reference of his performance. Those condemned will burn in hellfire, and those who are saved will enjoy the abiding pleasures of paradise. Besides suffering in physical fire, the damned will also experience fire "in their hearts"; similarly, the blessed, besides physical enjoyment, will experience the greatest happiness of divine pleasure.

Social service.   Because the purpose of human existence, as for every other creature, is submission to the divine will, God's role is that of the commander. Whereas the rest of nature obeys God automatically, humans alone possess the choice to obey or disobey. With the deep-seated belief in Satan's existence, the human's fundamental role becomes one of moral struggle, which constitutes the essence of human endeavor. Recognition of the unity of God does not simply rest in the intellect but also entails consequences in terms of the moral struggle, which consists primarily in freeing oneself of narrowness of mind and smallness of heart. One must go outside of oneself and expend one's best possessions for the sake of others.

The doctrine of social service, in terms of alleviating suffering and helping the needy, constitutes an integral part of the Islamic teaching. Praying to God and other religious acts are deemed to be a mere facade in the absence of active welfare service to the needy. It is Satan who whispers into people's ears that by spending for others they will become poor. God, on the contrary, promises prosperity in exchange for such expenditure, which constitutes a credit with God and grows much more than money that is invested in usury. Hoarding of wealth without recognizing the rights of the poor invites the most dire punishment in the hereafter and is declared to be one of the main causes of the decay of societies in this world. The practice of usury is forbidden.

With this socioeconomic doctrine cementing the bond of faith, the idea of a closely knit community of the faithful who are declared to be "brothers unto each other" emerges (Q 49:10). Muslims are described as "the middle community bearing witness on mankind" (Q 2:143), "the best community produced for mankind," whose function it is "to enjoin good and forbid evil" (Q 3:110). Cooperation and "good advice" within the community are emphasized, and opponents from within the community are to be fought and reduced with armed force if issues cannot be settled by persuasion and arbitration.

Because the mission of the community is to "enjoin good and forbid evil" so that "there is no mischief and corruption" on earth, the doctrine of jihad is the logical outcome. For the early community it was a basic religious concept. The object of jihad is not the forced conversion of individuals to Islam but rather the gaining of political control over the collective affairs of societies to run them in accordance with the principles of Islam. Individual conversions occur as a by-product of this process when the power structure passes into the hands of the Muslim community. In fact, according to strict Muslim doctrine, conversions "by force" are forbidden, and it is also strictly prohibited to wage wars for the sake of acquiring worldly glory, power, and rule. With the establishment of the Muslim empire, however, the doctrine of the jihad was modified by the leaders of the community. Their main concern became the consolidation of the empire and its administration, and thus they interpreted the teaching in a defensive rather than in an expansive sense. The KHĀRIJITES, who held that "decision belongs to God alone," insisted on continuous and relentless jihad, but they were virtually destroyed during internecine wars in the 8th century.

Distinction and privileges based on tribal rank or race were repudiated in the Qur'an and in the celebrated "Farewell Pilgrimage Address" of the Prophet shortly before his death. All men are therein declared to be "equal children of Adam," and the only distinction recognized in the sight of God is said to be based on piety and good acts. The age-old Arab institution of intertribal revenge (tha'r)—whereby it was not necessarily the killer who was executed but a person equal in rank to the slain person—was rejected. The pre-Islamic ethical ideal of manliness was modified and replaced by a more humane ideal of moral virtue and piety.

FUNDAMENTAL PRACTICES AND INSTITUTIONS OF ISLAM

The five pillars. During the earliest decades after the death of the Prophet, certain basic features of the religio-social organization of Islam were singled out to serve as anchoring points for the community's life. They were formulated as the "Pillars of Islam" (for a fuller exposition *see* ISLAM, PILLARS OF; SHAHĀDA; ṢALĀT; ZAKĀT; ṢAWM; ḤAJJ).

The shahāda, or profession of faith. The first pillar is the profession of faith: "There is no god but God; Muhammad is the prophet of God," upon which depends the membership in the community. The profession of faith must be recited at least once in one's lifetime, aloud, correctly, and purposively, with an understanding of its meaning and with an assent from the heart. From this fundamental belief are derived beliefs in (1) ANGELS (particularly Gabriel, the Angel of Revelation), (2) the revealed books (the Qur'an and the sacred books of Jewish and Christian revelation described in the Qur'an), (3) a series of prophets (among whom figures of the Jewish and Christian tradition are particularly eminent—although it is believed that God has sent messengers to every nation), and (4) the Last Day (Day of Judgment).

Prayer. The second pillar consists of five daily prayers, *ṣalāt*, performed facing toward the Kaʿba in Mecca. These prayers may be offered individually if one is unable to go to the mosque. The first prayer is performed before sunrise, the second just after noon, the third later in the afternoon, the fourth immediately after sunset, and the fifth before retiring to bed. Before a prayer, ABLUTIONS, including the washing of hands, face, and feet, are performed. The noon prayer on Fridays is the chief congregational prayer.

The zakāt. The third pillar is the obligatory tax called *zakāt* ("purification," indicating that such a payment makes the rest of one's wealth religiously and legally pure). This is the only permanent tax levied by the Qur'an and is payable annually on food grains, cattle, and cash after one year's possession. *Zakāt* is collectable by the state and is to be used primarily for the poor, but the Qur'an mentions other purposes: ransoming Muslim war captives, redeeming chronic debts, paying tax collectors' fees, jihad (and, by extension, education and health), and creating facilities for travelers.

Fasting. The obligation to fast (*ṣawm*) during the month of RAMAḌĀN, laid down in the Qur'an (2:183–185), is the fourth pillar of the faith. Fasting begins at daybreak and ends at sunset, and during the day eating, drinking, and smoking are forbidden. The elderly and the incurably sick are exempted through the daily feeding of one poor person.

The hajj. The fifth pillar is participation in the annual pilgrimage (hajj) to Mecca prescribed for every Muslim once in a lifetime—"provided one can afford it" and provided there are enough provisions for the family in the pilgrim's absence. A special service is held in the Sacred Mosque on the 7th of the month of Dhū al-Ḥijja (last in the Muslim year). Pilgrimage activities begin by the 8th and conclude on the 12th or 13th. The principal activities consist of walking seven times around the Kaʿba, a shrine within the mosque; kissing and touching the Black Stone (al-Ḥajar al-Aswad); and ascending and running between Mt. Ṣafā and Mt. Marwa (which are now, however, mere elevations) seven times. At the second stage of the ritual pilgrims proceed from Mecca to Minā, a few miles away; from there they go to ʿArafāt, where they must hear a sermon and spend one afternoon. The last rites consist of spending the night at Muzdalifa (between ʿArafāt and Minā) and offering sacrifice on the last day of *iḥrām*, which is the ʿĪD ("festival") of sacrifice.

By the early 1990s the number of visitors to Mecca on the occasion was estimated to be about 2,000,000, approximately half of them from non-Arab countries. All Muslim countries send official delegations, a fact that is being increasingly exploited for organizing religio-political congresses. At other times in the year it is considered meritorious to perform the lesser pilgrimage (ʿUMRA), which is not, however, a substitute for the hajj pilgrimage.

Sacred places and days. The most sacred place for Muslims is the Sacred Mosque at Mecca, which contains the Kaʿba, the object of the annual pilgrimage and the site toward which Muslims direct their daily prayers. It is much more than a mosque; it is believed to be "God's Sacred House," where heavenly bliss and power touch the earth directly. The Prophet's mosque in Medina, where Muhammad and the first CALIPHS are buried, is the next in sanctity. Jerusalem follows in third place as the first QIBLA (*i.e.*, direction in which the Muslims faced to offer prayers, before the *qibla* was changed to the Kaʿba) and as the place from where

A schematic view of Medina, second holiest city in Islam, ceramic tile from the Mamlūk period, 16th century; in the Museum of Islamic Arts, Cairo
Werner Forman Archive—Art Resource

Muhammad, according to tradition, made his ascent (MIʿRĀJ) to heaven. For the Shiʿites, KARBALĀʾ in Iraq (the place of martyrdom of ʿAlī's son, Ḥusayn) and MASH-HAD in Iran (where Imam ʿALĪ AL-RIḌĀ is buried) constitute places of special veneration where the Shiʿites make pilgrimages.

Shrines of Sufi saints. For Muslims in general, shrines of Sufi saints are particular objects of reverence and even veneration. In Baghdad the tomb of the most venerated Sufi saint, ʿABD AL-QĀDIR AL-JĪLĀNĪ, is visited every year by large numbers of pilgrims from all over the Muslim world. The shrine of Muʿīn al-Dīn Chisti in Ajmer (northern India) draws thousands of pilgrims annually, including Hindus and Christians as well as Muslims.

The mosque. General religious life is centered around the mosque, and in the days of the Prophet and early caliphs the mosque was the center of all community life. Small mosques are usually supervised by the imam (one who administers the prayer service) himself, although sometimes also a MUEZZIN (prayer-time announcer) is appointed. In larger mosques, where Friday prayers are offered, a *khaṭīb* (one who gives the *khuṭba*, or sermon) is appointed for Friday service. Many large mosques also function as religious schools and colleges.

Holy days. The Muslim calendar (based on the lunar year) dates from the emigration (hijra) of the Prophet from Mecca to Medina in 622 CE. Subsequent dates

Pilgrims surround the Ka'ba in the Great Mosque in Mecca
Mehmet Biber—Photo Researchers

are designated AH, *Anno Hegirae*. The two feast days in the year are the ʿīds, ʿĪd al-Fiṭr (the feast of breaking the fast), celebrating the end of the month of Ramaḍān, and ʿĪd al-Aḍḥā (the feast of sacrifice), marking the end of the pilgrimage. Other sacred times include the "night of determination" (Laylat al-Qadr, believed to be the night in which God makes decisions about the destiny of individuals and the world as a whole) and the night of the ascension of the Prophet to heaven (Laylat al-Isrāʾ waʾl-Miʿrāj). The Shiʿites observe the 10th of Muḥarram (the first month of the Muslim year) to mark the day of the martyrdom of Ḥusayn. Muslims also celebrate the birth/death anniversaries of various saints in a festival called *mūlid* ("birthday"), or *ʿurs* ("nuptial ceremony"). The saints are believed to reach the zenith of their spiritual life on this occasion.

ISLAMIC THOUGHT

Islamic theology (KALĀM) and philosophy (*falsafa*) are two traditions of learning developed by Muslim thinkers who were engaged, on the one hand, in the rational clarification and defense of the principles of the Islamic religion (*mutakallimūn*) and, on the other, in the pursuit of the ancient (Greco-Roman) sciences (*falāsifa*). These thinkers took a position that was intermediate between the traditionalists, who remained attached to the literal expressions of the primary

sources of Islamic doctrines (the Qurʾan and the Hadith) and who abhorred reasoning, and those whose reasoning led them to abandon the Islamic community altogether. The status of the believer in Islam remained in practice a juridical question, not a matter for theologians or philosophers to decide. Except in regard to the fundamental questions of the existence of God, Islamic revelation, and future reward and punishment, the juridical conditions for declaring someone an unbeliever or beyond the pale of Islam were so demanding as to make it almost impossible to make a valid declaration of this sort about a professing Muslim. In the course of Islamic history representatives of certain theological movements, who happened to be jurists and who succeeded in converting rulers to their cause, made those rulers declare in favor of their movements and even encouraged them to persecute their opponents. Thus there arose in some localities and periods a semblance of an official, or orthodox, doctrine.

Origins, nature, and significance of Islamic theology. The beginnings of theology in the Islamic tradition in the second half of the 7th century are not easily distinguishable from the beginnings of a number of other disciplines—Arabic philology, Qurʾanic interpretation, the collection of the sayings and deeds of the prophet Muhammad, jurisprudence, and historiography. During the first half of the 8th century a number of questions centering on God's unity, justice, and other attributes and relevant to man's freedom, actions, and fate in the hereafter formed the core of a more specialized discipline, which was called *kalām* ("speech"). The term *kalām* has come to include all matters directly or indirectly relevant to the establishment

The Mosque of Omar (Dome of the Rock) in Jerusalem, built in the 7th century on the site where the Prophet Muhammad is said to have ascended to heaven
Photo Researchers

and definition of religious beliefs. Despite various efforts by later thinkers to fuse the problems of *kalām* with those of philosophy (and MYSTICISM), theology preserved its relative independence from philosophy and other nonreligious sciences. It remained true to its original traditional and religious point of view, confined itself within the limits of the Islamic revelation, and assumed that these limits as it understood them were identical with the limits of truth.

The pre-Islamic and non-Islamic legacy with which early Islamic theology came into contact included almost all the religious thought that had survived and was being defended or disputed in Egypt, Syria, Iran, and India. It was transmitted by learned representatives of various Christian, Jewish, Manichaean, Zoroastrian, Indian (Hindu and Buddhist, primarily), and Ṣābian communities and by early converts to Islam conversant with the teachings, sacred writings, and doctrinal history of the religions of these areas.

By the 9th century Islamic theology had coined a vast number of technical terms, and theologians (*e.g.*, al-Jāḥiẓ, d. *c.* 868) had forged Arabic into a versatile language of science; Arabic philology had matured; and the religious sciences (jurisprudence, the study of the Qur'an, Hadith, criticism, and history) had developed complex techniques of textual study and interpretation. The 9th-century translators availed themselves of these advances to meet the needs of patrons. Apart from demands for medical and mathematical works, the translation of Greek learning was fostered by the early ʿAbbāsid caliphs (8th–9th century) and their viziers as additional weapons (the primary weapon was theology itself) against perceived threats from Manichaeanism and other ideas that went under the name *zandaqa* ("heresy" or "atheism").

Theology and dissent. Despite the notion of a unified and consolidated community, serious differences arose within the Muslim community immediately after the Prophet's death. According to the sunnis, or traditionalist faction—who today constitute the majority of Islam—the Prophet had designated no successor. Thus, the Muslims at Medina decided to elect their own chief. Because he would not have been accepted by the QURAYSH tribe of Mecca, the Prophet's own tribe, the *umma*, or Muslim community, would have disintegrated. Therefore, two of Muhammad's fathers-in-law, who were highly respected early converts as well as trusted lieutenants, prevailed upon the Medinans to join the rest of the Muslim community in electing a single leader, and the choice fell upon Abū Bakr, father of the Prophet's favored wife, 'Ā'isha. All of this occurred before the Prophet's burial (under the floor of 'Ā'isha's hut, alongside the courtyard of the mosque).

According to the Shi'ites, or "Partisans," of 'ALĪ, the Prophet had designated as his successor his cousin and son-in-law, 'Alī ibn Abī Ṭālib, husband of his daughter FĀṬIMA and father of his only surviving grandsons, ḤASAN and ḤUSAYN. His preference was general knowledge; yet, while 'Alī and the Prophet's closest kinsmen were preparing the body for burial, Abū Bakr, 'Umar, and Abū 'Ubayda from Muhammad's Companions in the Quraysh tribe met with the leaders of the Medinans and agreed to elect the aging Abū Bakr as the successor (khalīfa, hence "caliph") of the Prophet. 'Alī and his kinsmen were dismayed but agreed for the sake of unity and because 'Ali was still young to accept the fait accompli.

After the murder of 'Uthmān, the third caliph, 'Alī was invited by the Muslims at Medina to accept the caliphate. Thus 'Ali became the fourth caliph (reigned 656–661), but the disagreement over his right of succession brought about a major SCHISM in Islam, between the Shi'ites—those loyal to 'Alī—and the Sunnis, or traditionalists. Although their differences were in the first instance primarily political, arising out of the question of leadership, significant theological differences developed over time.

During the reign of the third caliph, 'Uthmān, certain rebellious groups had accused the caliph of nepotism and misrule, and the resulting discontent had led to his assassination. The rebels then recognized 'Alī as ruler, but they later deserted him and fought against him, accusing him of having committed a grave sin in submitting his claim to the caliphate to arbitration. The word khāraju, from which khārijī is derived, means "to withdraw"; thus the rebels, who believed in active secession from or dissent against a state of affairs they considered to be gravely impious, became known as the Khārijites.

The basic doctrine of the Khārijites was that a person or a group who committed a grave error or sin and did not sincerely repent ceased to be Muslim. Mere profession of the faith—"there is no god but God; Muhammad is the prophet of God"—did not make a person a Muslim unless this faith was accompanied by righteous deeds. In other words, good works were an integral part of faith and not extraneous to it. The second principle that flowed from their aggressive idealism was militancy, or jihad, which the Khārijites considered to be among the cardinal principles, or pillars, of Islam.

Because the Khārijites believed that the basis of rule was righteous character and piety alone, any Muslim, irrespective of race, color, or sex, could, in their view, become ruler—provided he or she satisfied the conditions of piety. This was in contrast to the claims of the Shi'ite sect (the party of 'Alī) that the ruler must belong to the family of the Prophet and follow the sunna (the Prophet's way) and that the head of state must belong to the Prophet's tribe, i.e., the Quraysh.

As a consequence of translations of Greek philosophical and scientific works into Arabic during the 8th and 9th centuries and the controversies of Muslims with thinkers from GNOSTICISM, MANICHAEINISM, BUDDHISM, and Christianity, a more powerful movement of rational theology emerged; its representatives are called the MU'TAZILA ("those who stand apart," a reference to the fact that they dissociated themselves from extreme views of faith and infidelity). On the question of the relationship of faith to works, the Mu'tazila—who called themselves "champions of God's unity and justice"—taught, like the Khārijites, that works were an essential part of faith but that a person guilty of a grave sin, unless he repented, was neither a Muslim nor yet a non-Muslim but occupied a "middle ground." They further defended the position, as a central part of their doctrine, that humans were free to choose and act and were, therefore, responsible for their actions. They claimed that human reason, independent of revelation, was capable of discovering what is good and what is evil, although revelation corroborated the findings of reason. Revelation had to be interpreted, therefore, in conformity with the dictates of rational ethics.

In the 10th century a reaction began against the Mu'tazila that culminated in the formulation and subsequent general acceptance of another set of theological propositions that became Sunni, or orthodox, theology. The concept of the community so vigorously pronounced by the earliest doctrine of the Qur'an gained both a new emphasis and a fresh context with the rise of Sunnism. An abundance of tradition (Hadith) came to be attributed to the Prophet to the effect that Muslims must follow the majority's way, that minority groups are all doomed to hell, and that God's protective hand is always on (the majority of) the community, which can never be in error. Under the impact of the new Hadith, the community, which had been charged by the Qur'an with a mission and commanded to accept a challenge, now became transformed into a privileged one that was endowed with infallibility. The dominant Sunni theological school, the Ash'arīya (named after ABŪ AL-ḤASAN AL-ASH'ARĪ, d. c. 935/936) displaced the Mu'tazila and successfully refuted key points of their theology. As a result Sunni theology became identified with the views that Muslim sinners remain Muslims, that GOOD AND EVIL alike are from God but that humans nevertheless acquire responsibility for their actions, that the Qur'an is the uncreated word of God, and that the qualities ascribed to God and the hereafter by the Qur'an are real—i.e., they cannot be reasoned away as the Mu'tazila argued.

At the same time, while condemning schisms and branding dissent as heretical, Sunnism also developed the opposite trend of accommodation, catholicity, and synthesis. A putative tradition of the Prophet that says "differences of opinion among my community are a blessing" was given wide currency. This principle of toleration ultimately made it possible for diverse sects and schools of thought—notwithstanding a wide range of differences in belief and practice—to recognize and coexist with each other.

Besides the Sunni, the Shi'ite sect is the only important surviving sect in Islam. As noted above, initially it was a movement of protest against Umayyad hegemony. Gradually, however, Shī'ism developed a theological content for its political stand. Probably under Gnostic (esoteric, dualistic, and speculative) and old Iranian (dualistic) influences, the figure of the political ruler, the imam (exemplary "leader"), was transformed into a metaphysical being, a manifestation of God and the primordial light that sustains the universe and bestows true knowledge on man. Through the imam alone the hidden and true meaning of the Qur'anic revelation could be known, because the imam alone was infallible. The Shi'ites thus developed a doctrine of esoteric knowledge that was adopted also, in a modified form, by the Sufis, or Islamic mystics (see SUFISM). The predominant Shi'ite com-

Worldwide distribution of Islam

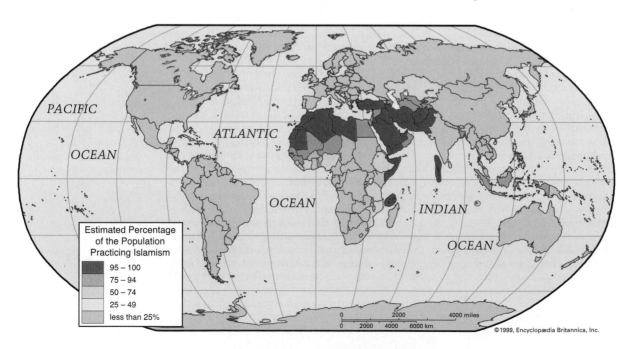

Estimated Percentage
of the Population
Practicing Islamism

95 – 100
75 – 94
50 – 74
25 – 49
less than 25%

©1999, Encyclopædia Britannica, Inc.

munity, the Ithna ʿAsharīya (Twelvers), recognizes 12 such imams, the last (Muhammad al-Mahdī al-Ḥujja) having disappeared in the 9th century. Since that time, the *mujtahid*s (*i.e.,* the Shiʿite jurists) have been able to interpret law and doctrine under the putative guidance of the imam, who will return near the end of time to fill the world with truth and justice.

On the basis of their doctrine of imamology, the Shiʿites emphasize their idealism and transcendentalism in conscious contrast with Sunni pragmatism. Thus, whereas the Sunnis believe in the *ijmāʿ* (consensus) of the community as the source of decision making and workable knowledge, the Shiʿites believe that knowledge derived from fallible sources is useless and that sure and true knowledge can come only through contact with the infallible imam.

Besides the main body of Twelver Shiʿites, Shiʿism has produced a variety of other sects, the most important of them being the ISMĀʿĪLĪS. Instead of recognizing Mūsā as the seventh imam, as did the main body of the Shiʿites, the Ismāʿīlīs upheld the claims of his elder brother Ismāʿīl. One group of Ismāʿīlīs, called Seveners (Sabʿīya), considered Ismāʿīl the seventh and last of the imams. The majority of Ismāʿīlis, however, believed that the imamate continued in the line of Ismāʿīl's descendants.

In Ismāʿīlīte theology, the universe is viewed as a cyclic process, and the unfolding of each cycle is marked by the advent of seven "speakers"—messengers of God with scriptures—each of whom is succeeded by seven "silents"—messengers without revealed scriptures; the last speaker (the Prophet Muhammad) is followed by seven imams who interpret the will of God to man and are, in a sense, higher than the Prophet because they draw their knowledge directly from God and not from the Angel of Revelation. During the 10th century certain Ismāʿīlī intellectuals formed a secret society called the Brethren of Purity, which issued a philosophical encyclopedia, *The Epistles of the Brethren of Purity,* aiming at the liquidation of the particular religions in favor of a universalist spirituality.

Islamic mysticism, or Sufism, emerged out of early ascetic reactions on the part of certain religiously sensitive personalities against the general worldliness that had overtaken the Muslim community and the purely "externalist" expressions of Islam in law and theology. These persons stressed the Muslim qualities of moral motivation, contrition against excessive worldliness, and "the state of the heart" as opposed to the legalist formulations of Islam. For a complete exposition of Sufi history, beliefs, and practices, *see also* SUFISM.

For religions based on Islam or Islamic in nature, *see* DRUZE; YAZĪDĪ; BĀBISM; BAHĀʾĪ FAITH; AḤMADĪYA; ISLAM, NATION OF; QARMATIANS.

Islamic philosophy. The origin and inspiration of philosophy in Islam are quite different from those of Islamic theology. Philosophy developed out of and around the nonreligious practical and theoretical sciences; it recognized no theoretical limits other than those of human reason itself; and it assumed that the truth found by unaided reason does not disagree with the truth of Islam when both are properly understood. Islamic philosophy was not a handmaid of theology. The two disciplines were related, because both followed the path of rational inquiry and distinguished themselves both from traditional religious disciplines and from mysticism, which sought knowledge through practical, spiritual purification.

The first Muslim philosopher, AL-KINDĪ, who flourished in the first half of the 9th century, was a diligent student of Greek and Hellenistic authors in philosophy, and his conscious, open, and unashamed acknowledgment of earlier contributions to scientific inquiry was foreign to the spirit, method, and purpose of the theologians of the time. Devoting most of his writings to questions of natural philosophy and mathematics, al-Kindī was particularly concerned with the relation between corporeal things—which are changeable, in constant flux, and as such unknowable—on the one hand and the permanent world of forms (spiritual or secondary substances)—which are not subject to flux yet to which man has no access except through things of the senses—on the other. He insisted that a purely human knowledge of all things is possible through the use of various scientific devices, the study of mathematics and logic, and the assimilation of the contribu-

Muslim men in the upper gallery of the main mosque in Delhi, India, at prayer for the holiday of 'Īd al-Fiṭr
Reuters—Corbis–Bettmann

tions of earlier thinkers. The existence of a supernatural way to this knowledge in which all these requirements can be dispensed with was acknowledged by al-Kindī: God may choose to impart it to his prophets by cleansing and illuminating their souls and by giving them his aid, right guidance, and inspiration; and they, in turn, communicate it to ordinary men in an admirably clear, concise, and comprehensible style. This is the prophets' "divine" knowledge, characterized by a special mode of access and style of exposition. In principle, however, this very same knowledge is accessible to man without divine aid, even though "human" knowledge may lack the completeness and consummate logic of the prophets' divine message.

Reflection on the two kinds of knowledge—the human knowledge bequeathed by the ancients and the revealed knowledge expressed in the Qur'an—led al-Kindī to pose a number of themes that became central in Islamic philosophy: the rational-metaphorical EXEGESIS of the Qur'an and the Hadith; the identification of God with the first being and the first cause; creation as the giving of being and as a kind of causation distinct from natural causation and Neoplatonic emanation; and the immortality of the individual soul.

The philosopher whose principal concerns, method, and opposition to authority were inspired by the extreme Mu'tazila was the physician Abū Bakr al-Rāzī (9th–10th century). He was intent on developing a rationally defensible theory of creation that would not require any change in God or attribute to him responsibility for the imperfection and evil prevalent in the created world. To this end, he expounded the view that there are five eternal principles—God; Soul; prime matter; infinite, or absolute, space; and unlimited, or absolute, time—and explained creation as the result of the unexpected and sudden turn of events (*falta*). *Falta* occurred when Soul, in her ignorance, desired matter and the good God eased her misery by allowing her to satisfy her desire and to experience the suffering of the material world, then giving her reason to make her realize her mistake and to deliver her from her union with matter, the cause of her suffering and of all evil.

AL-FĀRĀBĪ (9th–10th century) saw that theology and the juridical study of the law were derivative phenomena that function within a framework set by the prophet as lawgiver and founder of a human community. In this community, revelation defines the opinions the members of the community must hold and the actions they must perform if they are to attain the earthly happiness of this world and the supreme happiness of the other world. Philosophy could not understand this framework of religion as long as it concerned itself almost exclusively with its truth content and confined the study of practical science to individualistic ethics and personal salvation.

In contrast to al-Kindī and al-Rāzī, al-Fārābī recast philosophy in a new framework analogous to that of the Islamic religion. The sciences were organized within this philosophic framework so that logic, physics, mathematics, and metaphysics culminated in a political science whose subject matter was the investigation of happiness and how it could be realized in cities and nations. Philosophical cosmology, psychology, and politics were blended by al-Fārābī into a political theology whose aim was to clarify the foundations of the Islamic community and to defend its reform in a direction that would promote scientific inquiry and encourage philosophers to play an active role in practical affairs.

In al-Fārābī's lifetime the fate of the Islamic world was in the balance. The Sunni caliphate's power extended hardly beyond Baghdad, and it appeared quite likely that the various Shi'ite sects, especially the Ismā'īlīs, would finally overpower it and establish a new political order. Of all the movements in Islamic theology, Ismā'īlī theology was the one that was most clearly and extensively penetrated by philosophy. Yet its Neoplatonic cosmology, revolutionary background, ANTINOMI-ANISM (antilegalism), and general expectation that divine laws were about to become superfluous with the appearance of the qā'im (the imam of the "resurrection") all militated against the development of a coherent political theory to meet the practical demands of political life and present a viable alternative to the Sunni caliphate. Al-Fārābī's theologico-political writings helped point out this basic defect of Ismā'īlī theology. Under the Fāṭimids in Egypt (969–1171), Ismā'īlī theology modified its cosmology in the direction suggested by al-Fārābī, returned to the view that the community must continue to live under the divine law, and postponed the prospect of the abolition of divine laws and the appearance of the qā'im to an indefinite point in the future.

One indicator of al-Fārābī's success is the fact that his writings helped produce a philosopher of the stature of IBN SĪNĀ (also spelled Avicenna; d. 1037), whose versatility, imagination, inventiveness, and prudence shaped philosophy into a powerful force that gradually penetrated Islamic theology and mysticism and Persian poetry in eastern Islam. Following al-Fārābī's lead, Ibn Sīnā initiated a full-fledged inquiry into the question of being, in which he distinguished between essence and existence. He argued that the fact of existence cannot be inferred from or accounted for by the essence of existing things and that form and matter by themselves cannot interact and originate the movement of the universe or the progressive actualization of existing things. Existence must, therefore, be due to an agent-cause that necessitates, imparts, gives, or adds existence to essence. To do so, the cause must be an existing thing and must coexist with its effect. The universe consists of a chain of actual beings, each giving existence to the one below it and responsible for the existence of the rest of the chain below it. Because an actual infinite is deemed impossible by Ibn Sīnā, this chain as a whole must terminate in a being that is wholly simple and one, whose essence is its very existence, and who is therefore self-sufficient and not in need of something else to give it existence.

By the 12th century the writings of al-Fārābī, Ibn Sīnā, and al-Ghazālī, a Sufi theologian who offered a critical account of the theories of Ibn Sīnā and other Muslim philosophers, had found their way to the West. A philosophical tradition emerged, based primarily on the study of al-Fārābī. It was critical of Ibn Sīnā's philosophic innovations and not convinced that al-Ghazālī's critique of Ibn Sīnā touched philosophy as such, and it refused to acknowledge the position assigned by both to mysticism. The survival of Islamic philosophy in the West required extreme prudence, emphasis on its scientific character, abstention from meddling in political or religious matters, and abandonment of the hope of effecting extensive doctrinal or institutional reform.

IBN BĀJJA (Avempace; d. 1138/39) initiated this tradition with a radical interpretation of al-Fārābī's political philosophy that emphasized the virtues of the perfect but nonexistent city and the vices prevalent in all existing cities. He concluded that the philosopher must order his own life as a solitary individual, shun the company of nonphilosophers, reject their opinions and ways of life, and concentrate on reaching his own final goal by pursuing the theoretical sciences and achieving intuitive knowledge through contact with the Active Intelligence. The multitude lives in a dark cave and sees only dim shadows. The philosopher's duty is to seek the light of the sun (the intellect). To do so, he must leave the cave, see all colors as they truly are and see light itself, and finally become transformed into that light. Philosophy, he claimed, is the only way to the truly blessed state, which can be achieved only by going through theoretical science, even though it is higher than theoretical science.

To IBN RUSHD (Averroës; d. 1198) belongs the distinction of presenting a solution to the problem of the relation between philosophy and the Islamic community in the West. The intention of the divine law, he argued, is to assure the happiness of all members of the community. This requires everyone to profess belief in the basic principles of religion as enunciated in the Qur'an, the Hadith, and the *ijmā'* (consensus) of the learned and to perform all obligatory acts of worship. Beyond this, the only just requirement is to demand that each pursue knowledge as far as his natural capacity and makeup permit. The divine law directly authorizes philosophers to pursue its interpretation according to the best—*i.e.*, demonstrative or scientific—method, and theologians have no authority to interfere with the conduct of this activity or to judge its conclusions. Thus, theology must remain under the constant control of philosophy and the supervision of the divine law, so as not to drift into taking positions that cannot be demonstrated philosophically or that are contrary to the intention of the divine law.

See also IBN ṬUFAYL.

These philosophical developments were in time met with a resurgent traditionalism, which found effective defenders in men such as IBN TAYMĪYA (13th–14th century), who employed a massive battery of philosophic, theological, and legal arguments against every shade of innovation and called for a return to the beliefs and practices of the pious ancestors. These attacks, however, did not deal a decisive blow to philosophy as such. It rather drove philosophy underground for a period, only to re-emerge in a new garb. Contributing to this development was the renewed vitality and success of the program formulated by al-Ghazālī for the integration of theology, philosophy, and mysticism into a new kind of philosophy called wisdom (*ḥikma*). It consisted of a critical review of the philosophy of Ibn Sīnā, preserving its main external features (its logical, physical, and, in part, metaphysical structure, and its terminology) and introducing principles of explanation for the universe and its relation to God based on personal experience and direct vision.

The critique of Aristotle that had begun in Mu'tazilī circles and had found a prominent champion in Abū Bakr al-Rāzī was provided with a far more solid foundation in the 10th and 11th centuries by the Christian theologians and philosophers of Baghdad, who translated the writings of the Hellenistic critics of Aristotle (*e.g.*, John Philoponus) and made use of their arguments both in commenting on Aristotle and in independent theological and philosophic works. Their theologically based anti-Aristotelianism spread among Jewish and Muslim students of philosophy in the 12th century, such as Abū al-Barakāt al-Baghdādī (d. *c.* 1175) and Fakhr ad-Dīn al-Rāzī. These theologians continued and intensified al-Ghazālī's attacks on Ibn Sīnā and Aristotle. They suggested that a thorough examination of Aristotle had revealed to them, on philosophic grounds, that the fundamental disagreements between Aristotle and the theologies based on the revealed religions represented open options and that Aristotle's view of the universe was in need of explanatory principles that could be readily supplied by theology. This critique provided the framework for the integration of philosophy into theology from the 13th century onward.

Although it made use of such theological criticisms of philosophy, the new wisdom took the position that theology did not offer a positive substitute for and was incapable of solving the difficulties of Aristotelian philosophy. It did not question the need to have recourse to the Qur'an and the Hadith to find the right answers; it did, however, insist (on the authority of a long-standing mystical tradition) that theology concerns itself only with the external expressions of this divine source of knowledge. The inner core was reserved for the adepts of the mystic path, whose journey leads to the experience of the highest reality in dreams and visions. Only the mystical adepts are in possession of the one true wisdom, the ground of both the external expressions of the divine law and the phenomenal world of human experience and thought.

AL-SUHRAWARDĪ (12th century), the first master of the new wisdom, called it the "Wisdom of Illumination." He concentrated on the concepts of being and nonbeing, which he called light and darkness, and explained the gradation of beings as according to the strength, or perfection, of their light. This gradation forms a single continuum that culminates in pure light, self-luminosity, self-awareness, self-manifestation, or self-knowledge, which is God, the light of lights, the true One. The stability and eternity of this single continuum result from every higher light overpowering and subjugating the lower, and movement and change along the continuum result from each of the lower lights desiring and loving the higher.

Al-Suhrawardī's doctrine claims to be the inner truth behind the exoteric (external) teachings of both Islam and Zoroastrianism, as well as the wisdom of all ancient sages, especially Iranians and Greeks, and of the revealed religions as well. This neutral yet positive attitude toward the diversity of religions was to become one of the hallmarks of the new wisdom. Different religions were seen as different manifestations of the same truth, their essential agreement was emphasized, and various attempts were made to combine them into a single harmonious religion meant for all humankind.

The Scribe, *detail of a miniature in an Arabic manuscript, 13th century, Baghdad*
The Granger Collection

The account of the doctrines of IBN AL-'ARABĪ (12th–13th century) belongs properly to the history of Islamic mysticism. Yet al-'Arabī's impact on the subsequent development of the new wisdom was in many ways far greater than that of al-Suhrawardī. This is true especially of his central doctrine of the "unity of being" and his distinction between the absolute One, which is undefinable truth (*ḥaqq*), and his self-manifestation (*ẓuhūr*), or creation (*khalq*), which is ever new (*jadīd*) and in perpetual movement, a movement that unites the whole of creation in constant renewal. At the very core of this dynamic edifice stands nature, the "dark cloud" (*'amā'*) or "mist" (*bukhār*), as the ultimate principle of things and forms: intelligence, heavenly bodies, and elements and their mixtures that culminate in the perfect man. This primordial nature is the "breath" of the merciful God in his aspect as Lord. It flows throughout the universe and manifests truth in all its parts. It is the first mother through which truth manifests itself to itself and generates the universe. And it is the universal natural body that gives birth to the translucent bodies of the spheres, to the elements, and to their mixtures, all of which are related to that primary source as daughters to their mother.

After Ibn al-ʿArabī, the new wisdom developed rapidly in intellectual circles in eastern Islam. Commentators began the process of harmonizing and integrating the views of the masters. Great poets made them part of every educated man's literary culture. Mystical fraternities became the custodians of such works, spreading them into Central Asia and the Indian subcontinent and transmitting them from one generation to another. Following the Mongol khan Hülagü's entry into Baghdad (1258), the Twelver Shiʿites were encouraged by the Il Khanid Tatars and Naṣīr al-Dīn al-Ṭūsī (the philosopher and theologian who accompanied Hülagü as his vizier) to abandon their hostility to mysticism. Muʿtazilī doctrines were retained in their theology. Theology, however, was downgraded to "formal" learning that must be supplemented by higher things, the latter including philosophy and mysticism, both of earlier Shiʿite (including Ismāʿīlī) origin and of later Sunni provenance. Al-Ghazālī, al-Suhrawardī, Ibn al-ʿArabī, and Ibn Sīnā were then eagerly studied and (except for their doctrine of the imamate) embraced with little or no reservation. This movement in Shiʿite thought gathered momentum when the leaders of a mystical fraternity established themselves as the Ṣafavid dynasty (1501–1732) in Iran, where they championed Twelver Shiʿism as the official doctrine of the new monarchy. During the 17th century Iran experienced a cultural and scientific renaissance that included a revival of philosophic studies. There, Islamic philosophy found its last creative exponents. The new wisdom as expounded by the masters of the school of Eṣfahān (Iṣfahān) radiated throughout eastern Islam and continued as a vital tradition until modern times. *See also* MĪR DĀMĀD; MULLĀ ṢADRĀ.

The new wisdom lived on during the 18th and 19th centuries, conserving much of its vitality and strength but not cultivating new ground. It attracted able thinkers such as Shāh Walī Allāh of Delhi and Hādī Sabzevārī and became a regular part of the program of higher education in the cultural centers of the Ottoman Empire, Iran, and the Indian subcontinent, a status never achieved by the earlier tradition of Islamic philosophy. In collaboration with its close ally Persian mystical poetry, the new wisdom determined the intellectual outlook and spiritual mood of educated Muslims in the regions where Persian had become the dominant literary language.

The Sankore Mosque in Timbuktu, Mali, an important center for Islamic studies from the 14th century
Stephenie Hollyman—Photo Researchers

The wholesale rejection of the new wisdom in the name of simple, robust, and more practical piety (which had been initiated by Ibn Taymīya and which continued to find exponents among jurists) made little impression on its devotees. To be taken seriously, reform had to come from the devotees' own ranks and be espoused by such thinkers as the eminent theologian and mystic of Muslim India Aḥmad Sirhindī (16th–17th century)—a reformer who spoke their language and attacked Ibn al-ʿArabī's "unity of being" only to defend an older, presumably more orthodox form of mysticism. Despite some impact, however, attempts of this kind remained isolated and were either ignored or reintegrated into the mainstream until the coming of the modern reformers. The 19th- and 20th-century reformers JAMĀL AL-DĪN AL-AFGHĀNĪ, MUHAMMAD ʿABDUH, and MUHAMMAD IQBĀL were initially educated in this tradition, but they rebelled against it and advocated radical reforms.

The modernists attacked the new wisdom at its weakest points; that is, its social and political norms, its individualistic ethics, and its inability to speak intelligently about social, cultural, and political problems generated by a long period of intellectual isolation and further complicated by the domination of the European powers. Unlike the earlier tradition of Islamic philosophy from al-Fārābī to Ibn Rushd, which had consciously cultivated political science and investigated the political dimension of philosophy and religion and the relation between philosophy and the community at large, the new wisdom from its inception lacked genuine interest in these questions, had no appreciation for political philosophy, and had only a benign toleration for the affairs of the world.

None of the reformers was a great political philosopher. They were concerned with reviving their nations' latent energies, urging them to free themselves from foreign domination, and impressing on them the need to reform their social and educational institutions. They also saw that all this required a total reorientation, which could not take place so long as the new wisdom remained not only the highest aim of a few solitary individuals but also a social and popular ideal as well. Yet as late as 1917, Iqbāl found that "the present-day Muslim prefers to roam about aimlessly in the valley of Hellenic-Persian mysticism, which teaches us to shut our eyes to the hard reality around, and to fix our gaze on what is described as 'illumination.' " His reaction was harsh: "To me this self-mystification, this nihilism, *i.e.*, seeking reality where it does not exist, is a physiological symptom, giving me a clue to the decadence of the Muslim world."

To arrest this decadence and to infuse new vitality into a society in which they were convinced religion must remain the focal point the modern reformers advocated a return to the movements and masters of Islamic theology and philosophy antedating the new wisdom. They argued that these, rather than the "Persian incrustation of Islam," represented Islam's original and creative impulse. The modernists were attracted in particular to the views of the Muʿtazila: affirmation of God's unity and denial of all similarity between him and created things; reliance on human reason; emphasis on man's freedom; faith in man's ability to distinguish between good and bad; and insistence on man's responsibility to do good and fight against evil in private and public places. They were also impressed by the traditionalists' devotion to the original, uncomplicated forms of Islam and by their fighting spirit, as well as by the Ashʿarīs' view of faith as an affair of the heart and their spirited defense of the Muslim community from extreme expressions of RATIONALISM and sectarianism alike. In viewing the scientific and philosophic tradition of Eastern and Western Islam prior to the Tatar and Mongol invasions, they saw an irrefutable proof that true Islam stands for the liberation of man's spirit, promotes critical thought, and provides both the impetus to grapple with the temporal and the demonstration of how to set it in order. These ideas initiated what was to become a vast effort to recover, edit, and translate into the Muslim national languages works of earlier theologians and philosophers, which had been long neglected or known only indirectly through later accounts.

The modern reformers insisted, finally, that Muslims must be taught to understand the real meaning of what had happened in Europe, which in effect meant the understanding of modern science and philosophy, including modern social and political philosophies. Initially, this challenge became the task of the new universities in the Muslim world. In the latter part of the 20th century, however, the originally wide gap between the various programs of theological and philosophic studies in religious colleges and in modern universities narrowed considerably. *See* AL-AZHAR UNIVERSITY; ALĪGARH MUSLIM UNIVERSITY.

SOCIAL AND ETHICAL PRINCIPLES

Family life. A basic social teaching of Islam is the encouragement of marriage, and the Qur'an regards CELIBACY as something definitely exceptional, to be resorted to only under economic stringency. Thus, MONASTICISM as a way of life is severely criticized by the Qur'an. Many Sufis, on the other hand, prefer celibacy, and some even regard women as an evil distraction from piety, although marriage remains the normal practice also with Sufis.

Polygamy, which was practiced in pre-Islamic Arabia, is permitted by the Qur'an, which, however, limits the number of simultaneous wives to four, and this permission is made dependent on the condition that justice be done among co-wives (Q 4:3). Medieval law and society regarded this "justice" to be primarily a private matter between a husband and his wives, although the law did provide redress in cases of gross neglect of a wife. The right to divorce was also vested basically in the husband, who could unilaterally repudiate his wife, although the woman could also sue her husband for divorce before a court on certain grounds.

The virtue of chastity is regarded as of prime importance by Islam. The Qur'an advances its universal recommendation of marriage as a means to ensure a state of chastity (*iḥsān*), which is held to be induced by a single free wife. The Qur'an states that those guilty of adultery are to be severely punished with 100 lashes (Q 24:2). Tradition has intensified this injunction and has prescribed this punishment for unmarried persons, while married adulterers are to be stoned to death. A false accusation of adultery is punishable by 80 lashes.

The general ethic of the Qur'an considers the marital bond to rest on "mutual love and mercy," and the spouses are said to be "each other's garments" (Q 2:187). The detailed laws of inheritance prescribed by the Qur'an also tend to confirm the idea of a central family—husband, wife, and children, along with the husband's parents (Q 4:7–12). Easy access to polygamy (although the normal practice in Islamic society has always been that of monogamy) and easy divorce on the part of the husband led, however, to frequent abuses in the family. In recent times most Muslim countries have enacted legislation to tighten marital relationships.

The right of parents to good treatment is stressed in Islam, and the Qur'an extols FILIAL PIETY, particularly tenderness to the mother, as an important virtue (Q 46:15–17). One who murders his father is automatically disinherited. The tendency of the Islamic ethic to strengthen the immediate family on the one hand and the community on the other at the expense of the extended family or tribe has not prevailed, however. With urbanization, the nuclear family bond has become more prominent, but tribal indentities still prevail in the Arabian Peninsula and areas of Iraq, Syria, Jordan, and North Africa. So strong, indeed, has been the patriarchal family group ethos that in most Muslim societies daughters are not given the inheritance share prescribed by the sacred law in order to prevent disintegration of the joint family's patrimony.

The state. Because Islam draws no absolute distinction between the religious and the temporal spheres of life, the Muslim state is by definition religious. The main differences between the Sunni, Khārijite, and Shi'ite concepts of rulership have already been pointed out above. Although the office of the Sunni caliph is religious, he has no authority either to define dogma or to legislate. He is the chief executive of a religious community, and his primary function is to implement the sacred law and work in the general interests of the community. He himself is not above the law and if necessary can even be deposed, at least in theory.

Sunni political theory is essentially a product of circumstance—an after-the-fact rationalization of historical developments. Thus, while Shi'ite legitimism restricted rule to ʿAlī's family and Khārijite democratism allowed rulership to anyone, even to "an Ethiopian slave," Sunnism held the position that "rule belonged to the Quraysh" (the Prophet's tribe)—the condition that actually existed. Again between the extremes represented by the Khārijites, who demanded rebellion against what they considered to be unjust or impious rule, and the Shiʻites, who raised the imam to a metaphysical plane of infallibility, the Sunnis took the position that a ruler has to satisfy certain qualifications but that his rule cannot be upset by small issues. Indeed, in reaction to the civil wars started by the Khārijites, Sunnism drifted more and more toward conformism and actual toleration of injustice.

The first step taken in this direction by the Sunni was the enunciation that "one day of lawlessness is worse than 30 years of tyranny." This was followed by the principle that "Muslims must obey even a tyrannical ruler." Soon the SULTAN (ruler) was declared to be the "shadow of God on earth." No doubt the principle was also adopted—and insisted upon—that "there can be no obedience to the ruler in disobedience of God"; but there is no denying the fact that the Sunni doctrine came to be more and more heavily weighted on the side of political conformism. This change is also reflected in the principles of legitimacy. Whereas early Islam had confirmed the pre-Islamic democratic Arab principle of rule by consultation (SHŪRĀ) and some form of democratic election of the leader, that practice gave way to dynastic rule with the advent of the Umayyads. The *shūrā* was not developed into an institutionalized form but was, indeed, quickly discarded. Soon the principle of "might is right" came into being, and later theorists frankly acknowledged that actual possession of effective power is one method of the legitimization of power.

In spite of this development, the ruler could not become absolute, as a basic restraint was placed on him by the SHARĪʻA (the Islamic legal and moral code) under which he held his authority and which he was bound to execute and defend dutifully. When, in the latter half of the 16th century, the Mughal emperor AKBAR in India wanted to arrogate to himself the right of administrative-legal absolutism, the strong reaction of the religious conservatives thwarted his attempt. In general, the *ʻulamāʼ* (religious scholars and jurists) jealously upheld the sovereign position of the Sharīʻa against political authority.

The effective shift of power from the caliph to the sultan was, again, reflected in the redefinition of the functions of the caliph. It was conceded that, if the caliph administered through *wazīr*s (viziers or ministers) or subordinate rulers (*amīr*s), it was not necessary for him to embody all the physical, moral, and intellectual virtues theoretically insisted upon earlier. In practice, however, the caliph was no more than a titular head from the middle of the 10th century onward, when real power passed to self-made and adventurous *amīr*s and sultans, who used the caliph's name merely for legitimacy.

Education. Muslim educational activity began in the 8th century, primarily in order to disseminate the teaching of the Qurʼan and the sunna of the Prophet. The first task in this endeavor was to record ORAL TRADITIONS and collect written manuscripts. This information was systematically organized in the 8th–9th century CE, and by the 9th–early 10th century CE a sound corpus was agreed upon. This vast activity of "seeking knowledge" (*ṭalab al-ʻilm*) resulted in the creation of specifically Arab sciences of tradition, history, and literature.

When the introduction of the Greek sciences—philosophy, medicine, and mathematics—created a formidable body of lay knowledge, its reaction with the traditional religious base resulted in the rationalist theological movement of the Muʻtazila. Based on the Greek legacy, from the 9th to the 12th century CE a brilliant philosophical movement flowered and presented a challenge to the emerging Sunni consensus on the issues of the eternity of the world, the doctrine of revelation, and the status of the Sharīʻa.

Sunni scripturalists met the challenge positively by formulating a religious dogma. At the same time, however, for fear of HERESY, they began to draw a sharp distinction between religious and secular sciences. The custodians of the Sharīʻa developed an unsympathetic attitude toward the secular disciplines and excluded them from the curriculum of the MADRASA (college) system. This exclusion proved fatal, not only for those disciplines but, in the long run, for religious thought in general because of the lack of intellectual challenge and stimulation. A typical *madrasa* curriculum included logic, Arabic literature, law, Hadith, Qur'an commentary, and theology. Despite sporadic criticism from certain quarters, the *madrasa* system remained impervious to change.

One important feature of Muslim education was that primary education (which consisted of Qur'an reading, writing, and rudimentary arithmetic) did not feed candidates to institutions of higher education, and the two remained separate. In higher education, emphasis was on books rather than on subjects and on commentaries rather than on original works. This, coupled with the habit of learning by rote (which was developed from a tradition that encouraged learning more than thinking), impoverished intellectual creativity still further.

Despite these grave shortcomings, however, the *madrasa* produced one important advantage. Through the uniformity of its religio-legal content, it gave the *'ulamā'* the opportunity to effect that overall cohesiveness and unity of thought and purpose that, despite great variations in local Muslim cultures, has become a palpable feature of the world Muslim community. This uniformity has withstood even the tensions created against the seats of formal learning by Sufism through its distinctive disciplines and its own centers.

In contrast to the Sunnis, the Shi'ites continued seriously to cultivate philosophy, which developed a strong religious character. Indeed, philosophy has enjoyed an unbroken tradition in Persia down to the present and has produced some highly original thinkers. Both the Sunni and the Shi'ite medieval systems of learning, however, have come face to face with the greatest challenge of all—the impact of modern education and thought from the West.

The organization of education as an institution developed naturally in the course of time. Evidence exists of small schools already established in the first century of Islam that were devoted to reading, writing, and instruction in the Qur'an. These schools of "primary" education were called *kuttāb*s. The well-known governor of Iraq at the beginning of the 8th century, the ruthless al-Ḥajjāj, had been a schoolteacher in his early career. When higher learning in the form of tradition grew in the 8th and 9th centuries, it was centered around learned men to whom students traveled from far and near and from whom they obtained a certificate (*ijāza*) to teach what they had learned. Women were excluded from *madrasa*s, but in urban areas they had access to learning at mosques. Women in scholarly families sometimes became renowned teachers, especially of Hadith. Through the munificence of rulers, princes, and even wealthy female patrons, large private and public libraries were built, and schools and colleges arose. In the early 9th century a significant incentive to learning came from translations made of scientific and philosophical works from the Greek (and partly Sanskrit) at the famous *bayt al-ḥikmah* ("house of wisdom") at Baghdad, which was officially sponsored by the caliph al-Ma'mūn. The Fāṭimid caliph AL-ḤĀKIM set up a *dār al-ḥikmah* ("hall of wisdom") in Cairo in the 10th–11th century. With the advent of the Seljuq Turks, the famous vizier Niẓām al-Mulk created an important college at Baghdad, devoted to Sunni learning, in the latter half of the 11th century. One of the world's oldest surviving universities, al-Azhar at Cairo, was originally established by the Fāṭimids, but Saladin (Ṣalāḥ ad-Dīn al-Ayyūbī), after ousting the Fāṭimids, consecrated it to Sunni learning in the 12th century. Throughout subsequent centuries, colleges and quasi-universities arose throughout the Muslim world from Spain (whence Islamic philosophy and science were transmitted to the Latin West) across Central Asia to India.

In Turkey a new style of *madrasa* came into existence; it had four wings, for the teaching of the four schools of Sunni law. Professorial chairs were endowed in large colleges by princes and governments, and residential students were supported by college endowment funds. A myriad of smaller centers of learning were endowed by private donations.

Cultural diversity. Underneath unity of law and creed, the world of Islam harbours a tremendous diversity of cultures, particularly in the outlying regions. The expansion of Islam can be divided into two broad periods. In the first period of the Arab conquests the assimilative activity of the conquering religion was far-reaching. Although Persia resurrected its own language and a measure of its national culture after the first three centuries of Islam, its culture and language had come under heavy Arab influence. Only after Ṣafavid rule installed Shi'ism as a distinctive creed in the 16th century did Persia regain a kind of religious autonomy. The language of religion and thought, however, continued to be Arabic.

In the second period, the spread of Islam was not conducted by the state with 'ulamā' influence but was largely the work of Sufi missionaries. The Sufis, because of their latitudinarianism, compromised with local customs and beliefs and left a great deal of the pre-Islamic legacy in every region intact. Thus, among the Central Asian Turks, shamanistic practices were absorbed, while in Africa the holy man and his *barakah* (an influence supposedly causing material and spiritual well-being) survive. In India there are large areas geographically distant from the Muslim religio-political centre of power in which customs are still Hindu and even pre-Hindu and in which people worship a motley of saints and deities in common with the Hindus. The custom of SATĪ, under which a widow burned herself alive along with her dead husband, persisted in India even among some Muslims until late into the Mughal period. The 18th- and 19th-century reform movements strove to "purify" Islam of these accretions and superstitions.

Indonesia affords a striking example of this phenomenon. Because Islam arrived late and soon came under European colonialism, the Indonesian society has retained its pre-Islamic world view beneath an overlay of Islamic practices. It keeps its customary law (called *adat*) at the expense of the Sharī'a; many of its tribes are still matriarchal; and culturally the Hindu epics RĀMĀYAṆA and MAHĀBHĀRATA hold a high position in national life. Since the 19th century, however, orthodox Islam has gained steadily in strength because of fresh contacts with the Middle East.

Apart from regional diversity, the main internal division within Islamic society is between urban and village life. Islam originated in the two cities of Mecca and Medina, and as it expanded its peculiar ethos appears to have developed mainly in urban areas. Culturally, it came under a heavy Persian influence in Iraq, where the Arabs learned the ways and style of life of their conquered people. The custom of veiling women (the PURDAH, which originally arose as a sign of aristocracy but later served the purpose of segregating women from men), for example, was acquired in Iraq.

Another social trait derived from outside cultures was the disdain for agriculture and manual labor in general. Because the people of the town of Medina were mainly agriculturists, this disdain could not have been initially present. In general, Islam came to appropriate a strong feudal ethic from the peoples it conquered. Also, because the Muslims generally represented the administrative and military aristocracy and because the learned class (the 'ulamā') was an essential arm of the state, the higher culture of Islam became urban based.

This city orientation explains and also underlines the traditional cleavage between the orthodox Islam of the 'ulamā' and the folk Islam espoused by the Sufi orders of the countryside. In the modern period, the advent of education and rapid industrialization threatened to make this cleavage still wider. With the rise of a strong and widespread fundamentalist movement in the second half of the 20th century, this dichotomy has decreased.

Women in Jakarta, Indon., at prayer as a child looks on, at the end of the holy month of Ramaḍān
Reuters/Supri/Archive Photos

ISLAM, ART OF, artistic works created in the Islamic tradition. Although the Arabs had limited visual art, they did have a well-developed poetic art, which had been brought to full maturity and in which they took great pride. Some elements of Islamic art were borrowed from Persia and Byzantium. Whatever elements the Arabs borrowed they Islamized in a manner that fused them into a homogeneous spiritual-aesthetic complex. The most important principle governing art was ANICONISM; *i.e.*, the religious prohibition of figurization and representation of living creatures. Underlying this prohibition is the assumption that God is the sole author of life and that a person who produces a likeness of a living being seeks to rival God. Hence, in Islamic

Woman playing a lute, border decoration of a page of calligraphy, School of Herat, album 1262; in the Topkapi Palace Museum, Istanbul, Turkey
Scala—Art Resource

aniconism two considerations are fused together: rejection of such images that might become idols (these may be images of anything) and rejection of figures of living things.

This basic principle has, however, undergone modifications. First, pictures were tolerated if they were confined to private apartments and harems of palaces. This was the case with some members of the Umayyad and 'Abbāsid dynasties, Turks, and Persians—in particular with the SHI'ITES, who have produced an abundance of pictorial representations of the holy family and of MUHAMMAD himself. Second, in the field of pictorial representation, animal and human figures are combined with other ornamental designs such as geometrical patterns and arabesques—stressing their ornamental nature rather than representative function. Third, for the same reason, in sculptural art they appear in low relief. In other regions of the Muslim world—in North Africa, Egypt, and India (except for Mughal palaces)—representational art was strictly forbidden.

Much more important than sculptural art were paintings, particularly frescoes and later Persian and Perso-Indian miniatures. Frescoes are found in the Umayyad and 'Abbāsid palaces and in Spain, Iran, and the harem quarters of the Mughal palaces in India. Miniature paintings, introduced in Persia, assumed much greater importance later in Mughal India and Turkey. Miniature painting was closely

associated with the art of book illumination, and this technique of decorating the pages of the books was patronized by princes and other patrons from the upper classes.

ISLAM, NATION OF, *also called* American Muslim Mission, *or* World Community of al-Islam in the West, *or* Black Muslim movement, religious and cultural community that evolved in the 20th century in the United States out of various African nationalist organizations in America. Prominent among these precursor groups was the MOORISH SCIENCE TEMPLE OF AMERICA, founded in Newark, N.J., in 1913 by Prophet Drew Ali. The secular Universal Negro Improvement Association, founded in 1914 by Marcus Garvey, also espoused principles later adopted by the Black Muslims.

The movement proper was founded by WALLACE D. FARD, believed to have been an orthodox Muslim born in MECCA around 1877. He immigrated to the United States in 1930 and established a temple (or mosque) in Detroit a year later.

Most of Fard's initial followers were African-American migrants from the southern United States who had clustered together in the ghettos of the great northern industrial cities. They believed Fard to be an incarnation of ALLĀH who had come to liberate what he called the "Lost-Found Nation of ISLAM in the West." Fard promised that if they would heed his teachings and learn the truth about themselves, they would overcome their white "slave masters" and be restored to a position of dignity and primacy among the peoples of the world.

The chief developer of the movement was ELIJAH MUHAMMAD, who became leader of what had come to be called the Nation of Islam after Fard's mysterious disappearance in 1934. Shortly thereafter Muhammad founded the movement's second temple in Chicago. The movement spread slowly at first, but after World War II the Nation of Islam responded to the pent-up frustrations of African-Americans and offered those frustrations a militant, if avowedly nonviolent, expression. Soon there were mosques in all larger cities with sizable African-American populations.

Under Muhammad's leadership, the Nation of Islam professed the moral and cultural superiority of those of African descent, who were seen as destined by Allāh to assume cultural and political leadership of the earth. African-Americans were enjoined to give up CHRISTIANITY, which was regarded as the white man's chief stratagem for the enslavement of nonwhite people. The white race was presented as a race of devils whose time was coming to an end. African-Americans were urged to work together to reclaim their fallen (criminals, drug addicts), learn their true history, strive for economic independence, and prepare for the final struggle between GOOD AND EVIL.

During the 1960s the movement achieved national prominence through the personality of MALCOLM X, Elijah Muhammad's spokesman, whose forceful articulations of racial pride and Muslim principles made him a cultural hero, especially among African-American youth. Disagreements among the sect hierarchy eventually led to Malcolm's suspension and to the establishment of a rival group, the Muslim Mosque, Inc., under his leadership. Disputes between the two groups were a contributing factor to Malcolm's assassination in 1965.

A series of changes in the social, intellectual, and spiritual direction and development of the Nation of Islam was effected in the late 1970s under the leadership of Elijah Muhammad's successor, his son Warith Deen (or Wallace D.) Muhammad. During this period all precepts of color-consciousness, racism, and the deification of Fard were repudiated, and the organization was renamed the American Muslim Mission. In May 1985 W.D. Muhammad announced the dissolution of the Mission in order that its members might become a part of the worldwide orthodox Islamic community. The leadership and organization of the movement thus came to an end, although its network of mosques and their attendant religious, educational, and economic programs continued to function.

A splinter group based in New York City and under the leadership of LOUIS FARRAKHAN retained both the name and the founding principles of the Nation of Islam.

ISLAM, PILLARS OF: *see* FIVE PILLARS OF ISLAM.

ISLAMIC CASTE, any of the units of social stratification that developed among Muslims in India and Pakistan as a result of the proximity of Hindu culture. Most South Asian Muslims were recruited from the Hindu population; despite the egalitarianism of ISLAM, the converts persisted in their Hindu social habits. Hindus, in turn, accommodated the Muslim ruling class by giving it a status of its own.

In South Asian Muslim society a distinction is made between the *ashrāf* (Arabic, plural of *shārīf*, "nobleman"), who are supposedly descendants of Muslim Arab immigrants, and the non-*ashrāf*, who are Hindu converts. The *ashrāf* group is further divided into four subgroups: (1) SAYYIDS, originally, descendants of MUHAMMAD through his daughter FĀṬIMA and son-in-law 'ALĪ, (2) SHAYKHS (Arabic: "chiefs"), mainly descendants of Arab or Persian immigrants but including some converted Rājputs, (3) Pashtuns, members of Pashto-speaking tribes in Afghanistan and northwestern Pakistan, and (4) Mughals, persons of Turkish origin, who came into India with the Mughal armies.

The non-*ashrāf* Muslim CASTES are of three levels of status: at the top, converts from high Hindu castes, mainly Rājputs, insofar as they have not been absorbed into the shaykh castes; next, the artisan caste groups, such as the Julāhās, originally weavers; and lowest, the converted UNTOUCHABLES, who have continued their old occupations.

ISLAMISM \is-'lä-,mi-zəm, iz-, -'la-; 'iz-lə-, 'is-\, popular reformist movement throughout the Islamic world. Islamism has as its goal the reordering of government and society in accordance with the law of ISLAM. Islamist parties can be found in nations throughout the Muslim world including Algeria, Egypt, Pakistan, Afghanistan, and Turkey. Although there are regional differences among the various Islamist groups, there are a number of common traits, especially the belief that Islam is a comprehensive ideology that offers a blueprint for the social and political order.

Islamism is primarily an urban phenomenon and one brought on by the urbanization of the Muslim world. It is not, however, motivated by the discontent of the poor or of displaced peasants but rather is a movement of lower-middle- and middle-class professionals. Many Islamists are university graduates, some with degrees from Western institutions. Among the ranks of the Islamist parties are doctors, educators, engineers, lawyers, and scientists. There are also *'ulamā* (religious teachers) in the leadership, and all Islamists possess at least some knowledge of the holy texts.

Although not uniform throughout the Muslim world, Islamism is characterized by a number of shared values. The most important trait is a rejection of Western models of government and economics, both capitalism and communism. Islamists tend to believe that Muslim society has been corrupted by the SECULARISM, consumerism, and materialism of the West. As a consequence, Islamists generally advocate a new HIJRA (sacred emigration), a flight from the corrupting influence of an alien, Western culture.

Islamism is not a completely negative ideology, however, and the Hijra itself can be seen as a flight toward a better Muslim society. Islamists look back to the golden age of Islam, before the arrival of the Westerners, and hope to restore the traditional values and social relations that characterized that golden age. It is Islam itself that holds the key to societal reform because it is not just a collection of beliefs and rituals but an all-embracing ideology to guide public and private life. Islamists, therefore, look to the teachings of Islam and, especially, to Islamic law (SHARĪ'A) as the key to the creation of a better social order.

Among the economically and politically disaffected populations of the Islamic world a radical Islamism has emerged. Among the more well-known groups are Hamas in Palestine, Hezbollah in Lebanon, and the Taliban in Afghanistan. Although these groups have been accused of terrorist acts, Islamism itself is not intrinsically violent and can be a movement of peaceful social and political reform.

ISMĀ'ĪL I \,is-mä-'ēl\, *also spelled* Esmāʿīl I (b. July 17, 1487, Ardabīl?, Azerbaijan—d. May 23, 1524, Ardabīl, Safavid Iran), shah of Iran (1501–24) and religious leader who founded the Safavid dynasty and converted Iran from the SUNNI to the SHĪʿITE branch of ISLAM.

According to tradition, Ismāʿīl was descended from an IMAM. His father, leader of a Shiʿite group known as the Kizilbash (Red Heads), died in battle against the Sunnis when Ismāʿīl was only a year old. Fearful that the Sunnis, the majority sect, would wipe out the entire family, Shiʿite supporters kept family members hidden for a number of years.

Ismāʿīl emerged at the age of 14 to take his father's position as head of the Kizilbash. He quickly established a base of power in northwestern Iran, and in 1501 he took the city of Tabriz and proclaimed himself shah (Persian: "king") of Iran. In a succession of swift conquests he brought all of modern Iran and portions of present-day Iraq under his rule. In 1510, Ismāʿīl defeated the Sunni Uzbek tribes in what is now Uzbekistan. Muhammad Shaybānī, leader of the Uzbeks, was killed trying to escape, and Ismāʿīl had his skull made into a jeweled drinking goblet.

The Shiʿite branch of Islam was proclaimed by Ismāʿīl the established religion. The fact that much of the population considered him a Muslim saint as well as shah facilitated the process of conversion. Ismāʿīl's action provoked the Ottoman Turks. Religious friction grew after the Turkish ruler SULTAN Selīm I executed large numbers of his Shiʿite subjects as heretics and potential spies. In 1514 the Ottomans invaded northwest Iran and defeated Ismāʿīl's army. Ismāʿīl was wounded and nearly captured as he tried to rally troops. The warfare continued as a long series of border skirmishes, but Ismāʿīl remained strong enough to prevent further inroads by the Ottomans. In 1517 Ismāʿīl moved northwest, subduing the Sunni tribes in what is now Georgia. The basic conflict between the Shiʿite empire Ismāʿīl had founded and the Sunni Ottomans in the west and the Sunni Uzbek tribes in the east continued for more than a century. Ismāʿīl died at the age of 36, but the Safavid dynasty ruled Iran for two centuries, until 1722.

ISMĀ'ĪLĪS \,is-mä-'ē-lēz, ,iz-\, a sect of the SHĪʿITES that was most active as a religio-political movement in the 9th–13th centuries through its subsects, the Fāṭimids, the Qarāmiṭa (QARMATIANS), and the Assassins.

The Ismā'īlīs came into being after the death of JA'FAR IBN MUHAMMAD (765), the sixth IMAM, or spiritual successor to the Prophet, who was recognized by the Shi'ites. Ja'far's eldest son, ISMĀ'ĪL, was accepted as his successor only by a minority, who became known as the Ismā'īlīs. Those who accepted Ja'far's younger son, Mūsā al-Kāẓim, as the seventh imam and acknowledged his successors through the 12th imam became known as the ITHNĀ 'ASHARĪYA, or Twelvers, the largest of the Shi'ite sects. Certain of the Ismā'īlīs (known as Wāqifīya, or Stoppers) believed Ismā'īl to have been the seventh and last imam and were designated as SEVENERS (Sab'īya), while the majority of Ismā'īlīs believed the imamate continued in the line of the Fāṭimid CALIPHS. The Seveners later claimed that Ismā'īl's son Muhammad al-Tamm was expected to return at the end of the world as the MAHDI ("divinely guided one").

Ismā'īlī doctrine, formulated during the late 8th and early 9th centuries, stressed the dual nature of Qur'anic interpretation, exoteric and esoteric, and, like MANICHAEISM, made a corresponding distinction between the ordinary Muslim and the initiated Ismā'īlī. The secret wisdom of the Ismā'īlīs was accessible only through a hierarchical organization headed by the imam and was spread by dā'īs (missionaries), who introduced believers into the elite through graded levels. The *Rasā'il ikhwān al-ṣafā' wa khillān al-wafā'* ("Epistles of the Brethren of Purity and Loyal Friends"), a 10th-century philosophical and religious encyclopedia influenced by NEOPLATONISM, was said to have been composed by a secret society connected with the Ismā'īlīs.

The Ismā'īlīs became active in the second half of the 9th century in southern Iraq under the leadership of Ḥamdān Qarmaṭ. This branch of the sect, which came to be known as the Qarāmiṭa, established itself in Iraq, Yemen, and especially Bahrain, during the 9th–11th centuries. In Tunis, 'Ubayd Allāh established himself as the first Fāṭimid caliph in 909, claiming descent—through a line of "hidden imams"—from Muhammad, son of Ismā'īl, and through him from FĀṬIMA, daughter of the Prophet, whence the dynastic name. The Fāṭimids conquered Egypt in 969, founding Cairo as their capital; while they did not succeed in converting the bulk of their subjects during their rule of two centuries, they did create a widespread Ismā'īlī missionary network with followers all over the Islamic world.

A fatal schism split the movement over the succession to the Fāṭimid caliph al-Mustanṣir (d. 1094). The Egyptian Ismā'īlīs recognized his son al-Musta'lī, but the Ismā'īlīs of Iran and Syria upheld the claims of his older son, Nizār; hence, there are two branches of Fāṭimids, the Musta'līs and the Nizārīs.

When Ismā'īlīya came to an end in Egypt with the deposition of the last Fāṭimid caliph by Saladin in 1171, the Musta'lī Ismā'īlīs survived in Yemen. They had not recognized any Fāṭimid after al-Āmir, al-Musta'lī's son, and believed that al-Āmir's infant son al-Ṭayyib remained alive and that the line of the imams was hidden until a future time. In the interim they are governed by the chief dā'ī. In the 16th century the dā'ī of a major branch of the Musta'līs relocated in India. Today his successor resides in Surat, in Gujarāt district. His followers in India are usually known as Bohrās.

The Nizārīs, led by ḤASAN-E ṢABBĀḤ, gained control of a number of fortresses in Iran and Syria, the chief being Alamūt (1090). Known as Assassins, they remained in political power through the 13th century until displaced by the Mongols and the Mamlūks. The Nizārīs survived, though in two rival lines. The minor line died out by the 18th century, while the major line, led by an imam called

the Aga Khan, moved from Iran to India in 1840. The Aga Khan has a following, estimated in the millions, in India and Pakistan and in parts of Iran, Africa, and Syria.

The DRUZE, a hill people living in modern southern Lebanon, neighboring Syria, and Israel, separated from the main body of the Ismā'īlītes early in the 11th century. They then formed a special closed religion of their own, which acknowledged the imams as incarnations of the godhead.

ISMĀ'ĪL SHAHĪD, MUHAMMAD \,is-mȧ-'ēl-shȧ-'hēd\ (b. April 29, 1779, Phulat, India—d. May 6, 1831, Balakote), Indian Muslim reformer who attempted to purge IDOLATRY from Indian ISLAM and who preached holy war against the Sikhs and the British.

As a preacher in Delhi, Ismā'īl Shahīd attracted attention for his forceful preaching against such popular rituals as grave worship, the veneration of saints, and other practices regarded as heretical. Returning from a PILGRIMAGE to MECCA in 1823, he began to preach holy war (JIHAD) against the Sikhs who had been oppressing their Muslim subjects. In 1824–26 Ismā'īl accompanied a voluntary force of Muslim warriors led by Sayyid Ahmad to fight a holy war against the Sikhs in the Punjab. Ismā'īl assumed leadership of the *mujāhidīn* (holy warriors) in 1830, when they were driven out of their stronghold of Peshāwar. The Muslims were destroyed by a superior Sikh force at the battle of Balakote, on May 6, 1831, where Ismā'īl lost his life.

ISNĀD \is-'nad\ (Arabic, from the root s-n-d, "to support, base, base a tradition on"), in ISLAM, a list of authorities who have transmitted a report (HADITH) of a statement, action, or approbation of MUHAMMAD, one of his Companions (Ṣaḥāba), or of a later authority (*tābi'*); its reliability determines the validity of a Hadith. The *isnād* precedes the actual text (*matn*) and takes the form, "It has been related to me by A on the authority of B on the authority of C on the authority of D (usually a COMPANION OF THE PROPHET) that Muhammad said. . . ."

During and after Muhammad's lifetime, Hadiths were quoted by his Companions and contemporaries and were not prefaced by *isnād*s; only about 700 CE did the *isnād* appear to enhance the weight of its text. In the 2nd century AH (after 720 CE), when the example of the Prophet as embodied in Hadiths—rather than local custom as developed in Muslim communities—was established as the norm (SUNNA) for an Islamic way of life, a wholesale creation of Hadiths, all "substantiated" by elaborate *isnād*s, resulted. Since Hadiths were the basis of virtually all Islamic scholarship, especially Qur'anic EXEGESIS (TAFSĪR) and legal theory (FIQH), Muslim scholars had to determine which were authentic. They did so by scrutinizing the *isnād*s, rating each Hadith by the completeness of its chain of transmitters and the reliability and orthodoxy of its authorities.

Early compilations of the most reliable Hadiths (known as *musnad*s) were classified according to the Companion of Muhammad to whom they were attributed. Most notable of these was the *Musnad* of AḤMAD IBN ḤANBAL (d. 855), incorporating about 29,000 traditions. *Musnad*s proved difficult to use efficiently, however, and later compilations, known as *muṣannaf*, grouped Hadiths according to subject matter. Shi'ite Hadith, compiled later than the six canonical Sunni collections, often include the names of the IMAMS in the *isnād*, since these are believed to be the most reliable means of transmission.

ISRĀ' \is-'ra\: *see* MI'RĀJ.

ISRAEL, in JUDAISM, either of the kingdoms of the OLD TESTAMENT or the social group formed by the practitioners of that faith. The general usage refers to the modern state formed in 1948.

In the ancient historical sense, Israel means either of two political units in the Old Testament: the united kingdom of Israel under the kings SAUL, DAVID, and SOLOMON that lasted from about 1020 to 922 BCE; or the northern kingdom of Israel, including the territories of the 10 northern tribes (i.e., all except JUDAH and part of BENJAMIN), that was established in 922 BCE as the result of a revolt led by Jeroboam I. The southern kingdom, ruled by the Davidic dynasty, was thereafter referred to as Judah. The later kingdom's history was one of dynastic instability, with only two prolonged periods of stable government, under Omri (reigned 876–869 or c. 884–c. 872 BCE) and AHAB (c. 874–c. 853 BCE) and the JEHU dynasty (c. 842–746 BCE). In the 8th century BCE the northern kingdom was overrun by the Neo-Assyrian Empire, with Samaria, the capital, falling in 722/721.

The Israel social group refers to a people deemed to continue the genealogy and heritage of the Israel of whom the Hebrew SCRIPTURES speak—i.e., on one side, the descendants of ABRAHAM and SARAH, and, on the other side, those who continue the faith of that people who received the TORAH at MOUNT SINAI. In RABBINIC JUDAISM, Israel encompassed all those who knew and worshiped the one and only God, and "the Gentiles"—from the Latin word gens, meaning nation—were comprised entirely by idolators. In medieval times ISLAM and CHRISTIANITY were included among the monotheist religions as well, thus a Gentile may not necessarily be considered irreligious or idolatrous. To the concept of Israel as the continuing embodiment of the Scripture's narrative is added the idea that God has chosen Israel from among all the nations ("Gentiles"), has sanctified Israel, and has given Israel particular responsibilities and commandments that distinguish this people from the nations.

Israel in Judaism, therefore, refers to the holy people, whom God singled out for the redemption of mankind, variously represented in both the written Torah (PENTATEUCH) and the oral Torah (MISHNAH) as an extended, holy family, a people or nation chosen by God for sanctification and service, to be his community and venue on earth. One antonym for Israel is Gentile. Another is Adam. Israel is Adam's counterpoint, the other model for Man. Israel came into existence in the aftermath of the failure of Creation and the Fall of Man—in the restoration that followed the Flood, God called upon Abraham to found a supernatural social entity to realize his will in creating the world. Called, variously, a family, a community, a nation, and a people, above all, Israel forms God's resting place on earth. This definition of Israel cannot be confused with any secular meanings attributed to the same word, e.g., any nation or ethnic entity. The use of Israel to refer to "the state of Israel" has no basis in the theology of Judaism. In the liturgy of Judaism Israel means, and can only mean, "the holy people," wherever located, whatever their political condition.

At the most profound level, in Judaism Israel means those destined to rise from the dead and enjoy the world to come. And these are the ones who have no portion in the world to come: (1) He who says, the resurrection of the dead is a teaching which does not derive from the Torah, (2) and says the Torah does not come from heaven; and (3) is an Epicurean. Tosefta-tractate Sanhedrin 12:9 adds to this list the rejection of the yoke of the commandments, the denial of the COVENANT, and the perversion of the Torah by maintaining that God did not reveal it. The upshot is, to be Isra-

el is to rise from the dead to the world to come. Gentiles, by contrast, are not going to be resurrected when the dead are raised, but those among them who bear no guilt for their SINS also will not be judged for eternal damnation, so Yerushalmi-tractate Shebiit 4:10 IX: "Gentile children who did not act out of FREE WILL and Nebuchadnezzar's soldiers who had no choice but to follow the orders of the evil king will not live after the resurrection of the dead but will not be judged for their deeds."

The secular political sense of Israel and even "the Jews" occurs only very rarely in the oral Torah. In the oral Torah Israel bears three meanings: (1) family—a social entity different from the nations because it is formed by a common genealogy; (2) nation among nations; and (3) Israel as sui generis, different in its very category from all other nations.

Scripture told the story of Israel—a man, JACOB. His children therefore are the children of Jacob. That man's name was also Israel, and it followed his extended family would be the children of Israel. By extension upward, Israel formed the family of Abraham and Sarah, ISAAC and Rebecca, Jacob and LEAH and Rachel. Israel therefore invoked the metaphor of genealogy to explain the bonds that linked persons unseen into a single social entity; the shared traits were imputed, not empirical. That social metaphor of Israel—a simple one, really, and easily grasped—bore consequences in two ways. First, children in general are admonished to follow the good example of their parents. The deeds of the patriarchs and matriarchs therefore taught les-

On the festival of Simḥat Torah, the Scroll of the Law is shown to the congregation of a Tunisian synagogue
BBC Hulton Picture Library

sons on how the children were to act. Of greater interest in this context—Israel lived twice: once in the patriarchs and matriarchs, a second time in the life of the heirs as the descendants relived those earlier lives. The stories of the family were carefully reread to provide the meaning of the latter-day events of the descendants of that same family. Accordingly, the lives of the patriarchs signaled the history of Israel.

The theory of Israel as sui generis produced a political theory in which Israel's sole legitimate ruler is God, and whoever legitimately governs does so as God's surrogate. Here is a brief statement, framed out of the materials of LEVITICUS RABBAH, of the successor-documents' political theory and theological creed. The theory is as follows: God loves Israel, so gave them the Torah, which defines their life and governs their welfare. Israel is alone in its category (sui generis), proved by the fact that what is a virtue to Israel is a vice to the nation, life-giving to Israel, poison to the Gentiles. True, Israel sins, but God forgives that sin, having punished the nation on account of it. Such a process has yet to come to an end, but it will culminate in Israel's complete regeneration. Meanwhile, Israel's assurance of God's love lies in the many expressions of special concern, for even the humblest and most ordinary aspects of the national life: the food the nation eats, the sexual practices by which it procreates. These life-sustaining, life-transmitting activities draw God's special interest, as a mark of his general love for Israel. Israel then is supposed to achieve its life in conformity with the marks of God's love.

ISRAELI, ISAAC BEN SOLOMON \iz-'rā-lē\, *Arabic* Abū Ya-'qūb Isḥaq ibn Sulaymān al-Isrā'īlī, *also called* Isaac the Elder (b. 832/855, Egypt—d. 932/955, Al-Qayrawān, Tunisia), Jewish physician and philosopher, widely reputed in the Middle Ages for his scientific writings and regarded as the father of medieval Jewish NEOPLATONISM.

Israeli first gained note as an oculist, maintaining a practice near Cairo until about 904, when he became court physician in Al-Qayrawān to the last Aghlabid prince, Ziyādat Allāh. He also studied medicine under Isḥāq ibn 'Amrān al-Baghdādī, with whom he sometimes has been confused.

Some five years after his arrival, Israeli entered into the service of AL-MAHDĪ, the founder of the North African Fāṭimid dynasty (909–1171). At the request of the CALIPH, Israeli wrote eight medical works in Arabic, later translated into Latin. Israeli's scientific works include treatises on fevers, urine, pharmacology, ophthalmology, and ailments and treatments. He wrote also on logic and psychology, showing particular insight in the field of perception.

Of his philosophical writings, *Kitāb al-ḥudūd* (Hebrew: *Sefer ha-gevulim*, "The Book of Definitions") is best known. Beginning with a discussion of Aristotle's four types of inquiry, Israeli goes on to present 56 definitions, including wisdom, intellect, soul, nature, reason, love, locomotion, and time. Others of his philosophical works include *Sefer ha-ru'aḥ ve-ha-nefesh* ("Treatise on Spirit and Soul") and *Kitāb al-jawāhir* ("Book of Substances"). Israeli's interpretation of eschatological matters in the light of Neoplatonic MYSTICISM was to influence Solomon ibn Gabriol in the 10th century and later Jewish philosophers.

ISRĀFĪL \,is-rà-'fēl\: *see* ANGEL, ISLAM.

ISSACHAR \'i-sə-,kär\, one of the 12 tribes that in biblical times constituted the people of ISRAEL. The tribe was named after the fifth son born to JACOB and his first wife, LEAH (GEN-

ESIS 30:17–18). The tribe of Issachar occupied land lying west of the Jordan River and southeast of the southern tip of the Sea of Galilee (JOSHUA 19:17–23). After the death of King SOLOMON (922 BCE), Issachar was one of the 10 northern tribes that established the independent Kingdom of Israel (1 Kings 11:26ff; 2 Chronicles 10); dispersed to other regions after the Assyrian conquest of 721 BCE (2 Kings 17:5–6; 18:9–12), these tribes eventually became known as the TEN LOST TRIBES OF ISRAEL.

ISSERLES, MOSES BEN ISRAEL \ē-'ser-les\, *acronym* Rema (b. *c.* 1525, Kraków, Pol.—d. May 1, 1572, Kraków), Polish-Jewish RABBI and codifier who, by adding notes on customs of the ASHKENAZI to the great legal digest SHULḤAN 'ARUKH of codifier JOSEPH KARO, made it an authoritative guide for Orthodox Jews down to the present day.

Isserles became the head of the great YESHIVA (institution of Jewish learning) in Kraków while still a young man. Until his time, most great codifications of Jewish law had been written by Sephardim, *i.e.*, Jews of Spanish and Portuguese descent. Therefore many eastern European customs (*minhagim*) had been ignored, making the Sephardic codes increasingly unacceptable to the Ashkenazim, the Jews of German-Polish descent. When Joseph Karo published *Shulḥan 'arukh* (1565; "The Well-Laid Table"), its Sephardic bias provoked Isserles to write a commentary entitled *Mappa* ("The Tablecloth"), first published in Kraków in 1571 as notes to an edition of *Shulḥan 'arukh*. This commentary, which extensively utilized Ashkenazic customs, made the *Shulḥan 'arukh* acceptable all over the Jewish world.

ISTHMIAN GAMES \'is-mē-ən\, in ancient Greece, a festival of athletic and musical competition in honor of the sea god POSEIDON, held in the spring of the second and fourth years of each Olympiad at his SANCTUARY on the Isthmus of Corinth. Legend attributed the origin of the Games either to SISYPHUS, king of Corinth, or to THESEUS. Open to all Greeks, the Isthmian Games were especially popular with Athenians. The victors' prize, originally a crown of dry wild celery, was changed to a pine wreath in Roman times, the pine being sacred to Poseidon. The festival died out when CHRISTIANITY became dominant in the 4th century CE.

ISTIḤSĀN \,is-tih-'san\ (Arabic: "to approve," or "to sanction"), among Muslim jurists, the use of one's own judgment to determine the best solution to a religious problem that cannot be solved by citing sacred texts. Proponents of *istiḥsān* believe MUHAMMAD sanctioned this procedure when he said: "Whatever true Muslims prefer, is preferable in the eyes of God." Most religious authorities restrict the use of *istiḥsān* to cases that cannot be satisfactorily solved by applying such other well-established norms as analogy (QIYĀS) and consensus of opinion (IJMĀ'). Certain prominent jurists, however, among them AL-SHĀFI'Ī (d. 820), forbade the use of *istiḥsān* altogether, fearful that true knowledge and correct interpretation of religious obligations would suffer from arbitrary judgments infused with error. The followers of ABŪ ḤANĪFA (d. 767) held the modified view that *istiḥsān* is in fact a form of analogy because any judgment about what is best necessarily follows careful consideration of all alternative solutions. *See also* FIQH.

ĪSVARA \'ēsh-və-rə\ (Sanskrit: "Lord"), in HINDUISM, God understood as a person, contrasting with the impersonal transcendent BRAHMAN. The title is particularly favored by devotees of the god SHIVA; the comparable term *Bhagavān* (also meaning "Lord") is more commonly used by Vaiṣṇavas (followers of the god VISHNU). Particular communities within the Hindu fold differ in their understanding of the relation between Īśvara and Brahman. Theistic communities tend to argue that these two are one and the same, or even that the personal representation is superior; others, including some adherents of ADVAITA VEDĀNTA, argue that Īśvara is a limited and ultimately inadequate representation of Brahman.

ITHNĀ ʿASHARĪYA \ˌith-na-à-shà-ʾrē-ə\, *also called* Imāmīs, *English* Twelvers, the largest division of Shiʿism (*see* SHĪʿITE), believing in a succession of 12 IMAMS, leaders of the religion after the death of MUHAMMAD, beginning with ʿAlī ibn Abī Ṭālib, fourth CALIPH and the Prophet's son-in-law. Today they compose about 10 percent of the world Muslim population (close to 100 million).

Each imam—ʿAlī, his sons ḤASAN and ḤUSAYN, ʿAlī Zayn al-ʿĀbidīn, Muhammad al-Bāqir, Jaʿfar al-Ṣādiq, Mūsā al-Kāẓim, ʿAlī ar-Riḍā, Muhammad al-Jawād, ʿAlī al-Hādī, Ḥasan al-ʿAskarī, and MUHAMMAD AL-MAHDĪ AL-ḤUJJAH—was chosen from the family of his predecessor, not necessarily the eldest son but a descendant deemed spiritually pure. The last imam recognized by the Ithnā ʿAsharīya disappeared in 873 and is thought to be alive and in hiding, ready to return at the LAST JUDGMENT (*see* GHAYBA). As the 12 imams are seen as preservers of the religion and the only interpreters of the esoteric meanings of law and theology, a cult has grown around them, in which they are thought to influence the world's future. Indeed, Twelvers doctrine maintains that the world cannot exist without an imam. PILGRIMAGES to their tombs secure special rewards and are legitimate substitutes for pilgrimages to MECCA. In the time from the disappearance of the imam to the Mongol invasion (*c.* 1050), a body of literature known as HADITH (also called *akhbār*) was collected in support of Twelver beliefs. Like SUNNIS, Twelvers believe in God's absolute unity, the office of PROPHECY, and the Last Judgment. They also regard belief in God's justice and in the imams as essential.

Ithnā ʿAsharīya became the state religion of Iran under the Ṣafavīd dynasty (1501–1736), which claimed descent from the 7th imam and added the words "I testify that ʿAlī is the *walī* [friend] of God" to the Muslim profession of faith (SHAHĀDA). Besides Iran, Twelvers constitute majorities in Iraq and Bahrain. Sizeable communities also live in Lebanon, Kuwait, eastern Saudi Arabia, Afghanistan, and South Asia.

ITŌ JINSAI \ʾē-tō-ʾjēn-ˌsī\ (b. Aug. 30, 1627, Kyōto, Japan— d. April 4, 1705, Kyōto), sinologist, philosopher, and educator who helped found the KOGAKU ("Study of Antiquity"), which opposed the official NEO-CONFUCIANISM of Tokugawa Japan (*see* HAYASHI RAZAN). He advocated a return to classical Confucian teaching.

The son of a lumberman, Itō turned his hereditary business over to his younger brother in order to devote himself to teaching and scholarship. He and his son Itō Tōgai (1670–1736) founded the Kogi-dō ("School for Study of Ancient Meaning") in Kyōto. It was run by his descendants until 1904, when it was absorbed into the school system.

The outline of Itō's thought is in a work called *Gōmōjigi* (1683), a commentary on the analects of the Chinese philosophers CONFUCIUS and MENCIUS. Itō looked to what he saw as the underlying truths of Confucian thought for inspiration in developing a rational, as against an authoritarian, basis for human morality and the pursuit of happiness.

ITZAMNÁ \ˌēt-säm-ʾnä\ (Mayan: "Iguana House"), principal pre-Columbian Mayan deity. (*See* PRE-COLUMBIAN MESO-AMERICAN RELIGIONS.) He was ruler of the opposing forces of heaven, earth, day, and night, and a culture hero who gave humankind writing and the calendar and was patron deity of medicine. He frequently appeared as four gods called Itzamnás, who encased the world. The Itzamnás were associated with the points of the compass and their colors (east, red; north, white; west, black; and south, yellow). MAYA rulers held a two-headed ceremonial bar that represented Itzamná's cosmic powers as east-day-life and west-night-death. *See also* BACAB.

IXCHEL \ēsh-ʾchel\, *also spelled* Ix Chel, Mayan moon goddess. Ixchel was the patroness of womanly crafts but was often depicted as an evil old woman and had unfavorable aspects. She may have been a manifestation of the god ITZAMNÁ.

IXION \ik-ʾsī-ən, ʾik-sē-ən\, in Greek legend, son either of the god ARES or of Phlegyas, king of the Lapiths in Thessaly. He murdered his father-in-law and could find no one to purify him until ZEUS did so and admitted him as a guest to Olympus. Ixion then tried to seduce Zeus's wife HERA, but Zeus substituted for her a cloud (Nephele), by which Ixion became the father of the CENTAURS. Zeus, to punish him, bound him on a fiery wheel, which rolled unceasingly through the air or, according to another tradition, through the Underworld.

IZANAGI AND IZANAMI \ē-ʾzä-ˌnä-gē . . . ē-ʾzä-ˌnä-mē\ (Japanese: "He Who Invites" and "She Who Invites"), in the Japanese CREATION MYTH, the eighth pair of brother and sister gods to appear after heaven and earth separated out of CHAOS. By standing on the floating bridge of heaven and stirring the primeval ocean with a heavenly jeweled spear, they created the first land mass.

Their first attempt at sexual union resulted in a deformed child, Hiruko ("Leech Child," known in later SHINTŌ mythology as the god Ebisu), and they set him adrift in a boat. Attributing the mistake to a ritual error on the part of Izanami, they began again and produced numerous islands and deities. In the act of giving birth to the fire god, Kagutsuchi (or Homusubi), Izanami was fatally burned and went to Yomi, the land of darkness. Izanagi followed her there, but she had eaten the food of that place and could not leave. She became angry when he lit a fire and saw her rotting and covered with maggots, and the two were divorced.

As Izanagi bathed in the sea to purify himself from contact with the dead, the sun goddess AMATERASU was born from his left eye, the moon god Tsukiyomi was born from his right eye, and the storm god SUSANOO was born from his nose. Izanagi's bath is regarded as the founding of the purification practices of Shintō. *See* HARAI.

ʿIZRĀ'ĪL \ˌiz-rà-ʾēl\: *see* ANGEL, ISLAM.

IZUMO SHRINE \ʾē-zü-mȯ, *Angl* ē-ʾzü-mō\, *also called* the Grand Shrine of Izumo, *Japanese* Izumo-taisha \-ʾtī-shä\, Shintō shrine in Taisha. The oldest Shintō shrine in Japan, the Grand Shrine attracts pilgrims throughout the year. Its present buildings, constructed largely in the late 19th century, cover an area of 40 acres and are approached through an avenue of pines. The temple complex contains a valuable art collection and is enclosed by hills on three sides.

JACOB \'jā-kəb\, *Hebrew* Ya'aqov, *Arabic* Ya'qūb, *also called* Israel \'iz-rē-əl, -rā-\, *Hebrew* Yisra'el, *Arabic* Isrā'īl, Hebrew patriarch who was the grandson of ABRAHAM, the son of ISAAC and Rebekah, and the traditional ancestor of the people of Israel. Stories about Jacob in the BIBLE begin at GENESIS 25:19.

Jacob was the younger twin brother of ESAU, who was the ancestor of Edom and the Edomites (Genesis 25:30; 32:3; 36). The two are representatives of two different grades of social order, Jacob being a pastoralist and Esau a nomadic hunter (Genesis 25:27). During her pregnancy, Rebekah was told by God that she would give birth to twins; each of them would found a great nation, and Esau, the elder, would serve his younger brother (Genesis 25:23). As it turned out, Jacob managed to obtain both Esau's birthright and, by deception, Isaac's blessing (25:29–34; 27:1–40). Jacob then fled his brother's wrath and went to take refuge with the Aramaean tribe of his ancestors at Haran in Mesopotamia (27:43; 28:10). The stories about Jacob's birth and his acquisition of the birthright provide a thinly veiled apology for the relation between Edom (Esau) and Israel in Davidic times. Edom, the older nation, was made subject to Israel by David (2 Samuel 8:8ff.).

Arriving at his uncle Laban's home in Haran, Jacob fell in love with his own cousin, Rachel, but Laban tricked Jacob into first marrying Rachel's older sister, LEAH, and extracted from him 14 years of labor (Genesis 29–30). After Jacob amassed a large amount of property, he set out with his wives and children to return to CANAAN. On the way Jacob wrestled with a mysterious stranger, a divine being, who changed Jacob's name to Israel (Genesis 32:22–32). Jacob then met and was reconciled with Esau and settled in Canaan (Genesis 33).

Jacob had 13 children, 10 of whom were founders of tribes of Israel: REUBEN, SIMEON, Levi (*see* LEVITE), JUDAH, DAN, NAPHTALI, GAD, ASHER, ISSACHAR, ZEBULUN, DINAH, JOSEPH and BENJAMIN (Genesis 29:31–30:24; 35:16–18). Late in his life, a famine prompted Jacob and his sons to migrate to Egypt, where he was reunited with his son Joseph, who had disappeared some years before (Genesis 42:1–47:12). Jacob died in Egypt at the age of 147 and was buried in Canaan at Hebron (Genesis 49:29–50:14).

In JUDAISM, the RABBIS take great pains to reinterpret Jacob's deviousness positively and to further discredit Esau. Jacob becomes identified with all of later Israel and Esau (likewise Laban) with Rome (Genesis Rabbah 63:6–10; 70:19). According to the rabbis, Jacob did not "steal" the birthright, but took it from unworthy and unsuitable Esau in order to offer sacrifices himself (Genesis Rabbah 63:13; Numbers Rabbah 4:8). Jacob also stands in contrast to Abraham and Isaac who, although righteous themselves, both had sons who were dishonorable. Jacob is hence the greatest patriarch (Genesis Rabbah 76:1).

In ISLAM, in the QUR'AN, MUHAMMAD initially is not clear as to who is Ya'qūb's (Jacob's) father, Ishāq (Isaac) or Ibrahim

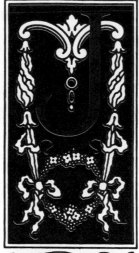

(Abraham; sūra 11:71). He later includes Ismaā'īl (Ishmael) as one of Jacob's fathers (along with Abraham and Isaac) and recognizes Jacob as the father of the Tribes (sūra 2:132–136). Jacob was a prophet (sūra 19:49) who cautioned his sons to remain faithful to the law of Abraham. Extra-Qur'anic sources say that he fought with his brother Esau in the womb but agreed to be born second in order to spare his mother.

JACOB BEN ASHER \'jä-kəb-ben-'a-shər\ (b. 1269?, Cologne? [Germany]—d. 1340?, Toledo, Castile [Spain]), Jewish scholar whose codification of Jewish law was considered standard until the publication in 1565 of the SHULḤAN 'ARUKH ("The Well-Laid Table") by JOSEPH KARO.

In 1303 Jacob immigrated to Spain with his brothers and father, the great codifier ASHER BEN JEHIEL, who became chief RABBI of Toledo. Jacob never became a rabbi and likely eked out an existence as a moneylender.

Jacob is best known for his code *Arba'a ṭurim* ("Four Rows"; first published in its entirety in 1475 and also known as *Ṭur*), which systematically divided all Jewish law into four "rows," or classes, a new arrangement that became classic. He is therefore called Ba'al ha-Ṭurim ("Master of the Rows"). His four divisions are: (1) *Oraḥ ḥayyim* ("Path of Life"), dealing with laws governing prayer and ritual; (2) *Yore de'a* ("Teacher of Knowledge"), setting forth the laws concerning things that are permitted or forbidden, such as dietary laws; (3) *Even ha-'ezer* ("Stone of Help"), containing the laws governing family relations, such as marriage and divorce; and (4) *Ḥoshen mishpaṭ* ("Breastplate of Judgment"), epitomizing civil and criminal law. Jacob eliminated all laws and customs that had been rendered obsolete by the destruction of the Second Temple (70 CE; *see* JERUSALEM, TEMPLE OF).

Jacob's digest became, after the BIBLE, the most popular work among 15th-century Jews and the usual basis for rabbinic decisions. It departed from earlier codes by basing the preponderance of its laws on decisions by post-Talmudic rabbinical authorities rather than on the TALMUD itself.

JACOB JOSEPH OF POLONNOYE \'jä-kəb-'jō-səf, -zəf ... pə-'lȯn-nə-yə\, *in full* Jacob Joseph Ben Tzevi Ha-Kohen Katz of Polonnoye (d. *c.* 1782), RABBI and preacher, the first theoretician and literary propagandist of Jewish HASIDISM.

Jacob Joseph was a rabbi in the large Jewish community at Shargorod, in Podolia (in modern Ukraine); after he came under the influence of the BA'AL SHEM ṬOV he was expelled (*c.* 1748). He was subsequently rabbi of Rashkov, Nemirov, and ultimately, of Polonnoye, where he remained until his death.

His first and main work was the controversial *Toldot Ya'aqov Yosef* (1780; "History of Jacob Joseph"), which related the teachings of the Ba'al Shem Ṭov and criticized traditional Jewish leadership and values. The work provoked anti-Hasidic sentiment and was burned by some opponents. Other works include homilies and commentary on books of the BIBLE, including *Ben Porat Yosef* (1781; "Joseph Is a Fruitful Vine") on Genesis; *Ẓefenat Pa'ne'aḥ* (1782) on Exodus; and *Ketonet Passim* ("Coat of Many Colors") on Leviticus and Numbers.

JACOBUS DE VORAGINE \jə-'kō-bəs-də-vō-'ra-ji-nē\, *also called* Jacob of Voragine (b. 1228/30, Varazze, near Genoa [Italy]—d. July 13/14, 1298, Genoa), archbishop of Genoa, chronicler, and author of the *Golden Legend*.

Jacobus became a DOMINICAN in 1244. After gaining a reputation as a preacher and theologian, he was provincial of Lombardy (1267–78 and 1281–86) and archbishop of the independent city of Genoa from 1292 until his death. He was beatified in 1816 for his work as a peacemaker between rival Italian political factions—the Guelphs (pro-papal party) and the Ghibellines (pro-imperial)—and his feast day in the Dominican order is July 13.

His works include sermons on Gospel readings, saints' days, and the Virgin MARY; a chronicle of Genoa; and the *Legenda aurea* (*Golden Legend*, also known as the *Lombardica historia*). This book is a collection of saints' lives (*see also* HAGIOGRAPHY), of accounts of events in the lives of JESUS CHRIST and of the Virgin Mary, and of information about holy days and seasons, the whole arranged as readings (Latin: *legenda*) for the church year. Immensely popular in the Middle Ages, it was translated into all western European languages and gradually much enlarged. William Caxton's translation was one of the first books printed in English (1483). Its miraculous stories and lack of historical perspective rendered the book unacceptable at the Reformation; after the rise of the new learning it was no longer consulted as a historical reference.

Jacob's Ladder, Jacob's dream of angels climbing to Heaven, Avignon school, 14th–15th century; in the Musée du Petit Palais, Avignon, France
Giraudon—Art Resource

JADE EMPEROR, *Wade-Giles* Yü-ti \'yē-'dē\, *Pinyin* Yudi, *also called* Yü-huang \'hwäŋ\ (Chinese: "Jade August One"), most revered and popular of Chinese deities in TAOISM and folk religion. In the Taoist pantheon, he is an impassive sage-deity, but he is popularly viewed as a celestial sovereign who guides human affairs and rules an enormous heavenly bureaucracy analogous to the Chinese Empire.

The worship of the Jade Emperor was officially sanctioned by the Taoist emperors of the Sung dynasty (960–1279 CE), who renamed him Yü-huang-shang-ti (Jade August Supreme Lord) and accorded him a status equivalent to that of the supreme power of Heaven. The Jade Emperor is usually depicted on a throne wearing the Imperial dragon-embroidered robes and beaded bonnet, holding a jade ceremonial tablet.

JA'FAR IBN MUHAMMAD \'jä-fär-ˌi-bən-mu̇-'hȧ-məd\, *also called* Ja'far al-Ṣādiq \ȧs-sȧ-'dēk\ (Arabic: "Ja'far the Trustworthy") (b. 699/700 or 702/703, Medina, Arabia [now in Saudi Arabia]—d. 765, Medina), sixth IMAM, or spiritual successor to the

Prophet MUHAMMAD, of the SHI'ITE branch of ISLAM and the last to be recognized as imam by all the Shi'ite sects.

Ja'far was the son of Muhammad al-Bāqir, the fifth imam, and great-grandson of the fourth CALIPH, 'ALĪ, who is considered to have been the first imam and founder of Shi'ism. On his mother's side, Ja'far was descended from the first caliph, Abū Bakr, whom Shi'ites usually consider a usurper.

The Shi'ites felt that the political leadership of Islam exercised by the caliph should belong to the direct descendants of 'Alī, and this political leadership was not clearly separated from religious leadership. To the end of the Umayyad regime, the caliphs sometimes preached in the mosque, using the sermon to reinforce their authority. Consequently, after his father's death, sometime between 731 and 743, Ja'far became a possible claimant to the caliphate and a potential danger to the Umayyads.

The Umayyad regime was already threatened by other hostile elements. The successful revolt of 749–750 that overthrew the Umayyads was under the leadership of the 'Abbāsid family, descended from one of the Prophet's uncles; and they, not the family of 'Alī, founded the new ruling dynasty. The new caliphs were, understandably, worried about Ja'far. Al-Manṣūr (reigned 754–775) wanted him in his new capital, Baghdad, where he could keep an eye on him, but Ja'far preferred to stay in MEDINA. After the defeat and death of the 'Alid rebel Muhammad ibn 'Abd Allāh in 762, however, Ja'far thought it prudent to obey the caliph's summons to Baghdad. After a short stay, he convinced al-Manṣūr that he was no threat and was allowed to return to Medina, where he died.

Ja'far was both politically astute and intellectually gifted. He gathered around him learned pupils including ABŪ ḤANĪFA and MĀLIK IBN ANAS (founders of two of the four recognized Islamic legal schools, the ḤANAFĪ and MĀLIKĪ) and WĀṢIL IBN 'ATA' (founder of the MU'TAZILA school of theology). Equally famous was Jābir ibn Hayyān, the alchemist known in Europe as Geber, who credited Ja'far with many of his scientific ideas. As to the manuscripts of half a dozen works bearing Ja'far's name, scholars generally regard them as spurious.

Various Muslim writers have ascribed three fundamental religious ideas to him. First, he adopted a middle road about the question of PREDESTINATION, asserting that God decreed some things absolutely but left others to human agency—a compromise that was widely adopted. Second, in the science of HADITH, he proclaimed that what was contrary to the QUR'AN should be rejected, whatever other evidence might support it. Third, he described Muhammad's prophetic mission as a ray of light, created before Adam and passed on from Muhammad to his descendants.

Shi'ite divisions date from Ja'far's death. His eldest son, Ismā'īl, predeceased him, but the "Seveners," represented today chiefly by the Ismā'īlites, argued that Ismā'īl merely disappeared and would reappear one day. Three other sons also claimed the imamate; of these, Mūsā al-Kāzim gained widest recognition. Shi'ite sects not recognizing Ismā'īl are mostly known as "Twelvers"; they trace the succession from Ja'far to the 12th imam, who disappeared and is expected to return at the LAST JUDGMENT.

JA'FARI LEGAL SCHOOL \jä-fà-'rē\, creation of the great Persian conqueror Nadir Shah (1688–1747), the Ja'fari Legal School was a proposed fifth *madhhab* (legal school) to be equal in status to the existing four orthodox, SUNNI legal schools (the ḤANAFĪ, ḤANBALĪ, MĀLIKĪ, and SHĀFI'Ī LEGAL SCHOOLS). After eliminating the last of the Ṣafavid puppet kings of Iran and successfully expanding the borders of Iran, Nadir focused on religious reform for his realm. The proposed reform would create a new legal school named after the widely respected sixth SHI'ITE imam, Ja'far al-Sadiq. Nadir hoped to integrate Shi'ite ISLAM with orthodox Sunni Islam and to see a fifth station established in Mecca for the celebration of the rites of the new school. To accomplish this reform, some of the fundamental Shi'ite teachings were to be abandoned. The new school would suspend belief in the divinity of the imams and would abandon the practice of the vilification of the first three CALIPHS and, instead, accept their legitimacy. Although Nadir's reforms received some support at a council he called and were accepted by Iraqi religious authorities under compulsion by Nadir, the teachings of the new school were clearly unacceptable to both Shi'ite and Sunni Muslims and the reform itself was a dismal failure.

JAGANNĀTH \'jə-gə-ˌnät\, *also spelled* Jagannātha (Sanskrit: "Lord of the World"), form under which the Hindu god KRISHNA is worshiped at Puri, Orissa, one of the most famous religious centers of India. The 12th-century temple of

The great temple of Jagannāth, Puri, Orissa, India
H. Miller—Shostal

Jagannāth in Puri, to many Hindus the eastern point on the sacred compass that is India, towers above the town. In its sanctuary, rough-hewn wooden images represent Jagannāth, his brother Balabhadra (BALARĀMA), and his sister Subhadrā. Modern representations made in Puri of the 10 AVATARS (incarnations) of VISHNU often show Jagannāth as one of the 10, in place of the more usually accepted Buddha.

Jagannāth's most important yearly festival is the Chariot Festival (RATHAYĀTRĀ), which takes place on the second day of the bright fortnight of Āṣāḍha (June–July). The image is placed in a wagon so heavy that the efforts of thousands of devotees are required to move it to the "country house" of the god, a temple outside the city, where the deities reside for a week. Balabhadra and Subhadrā travel in smaller carts. Reports of these processions in the past have been much exaggerated, although accidents are common and occasionally pilgrims attempt to throw themselves under the wagon in hopes of attaining instant salvation. The English word *juggernaut,* with its connotation of a force crushing whatever is in its path, is derived from this festival.

JAHANNAM \jä-'hä-näm\, in ISLAM, hell, described somewhat ambiguously in the QUR'AN and by MUHAMMAD. In one version, hell seems to be a fantastic monster that God can summon; in another description, it is a crater of concentric circles on the underside of the world that all souls must cross in order to enter paradise by way of a bridge, narrow as a razor's edge. Punishment in hell is graded and varied according to offenses, and sinners are released only when God wills.

Muslim theologians have attempted to clarify the problems inherent in the Qur'anic description of hell. IBN SĪNĀ (Avicenna), for example, speaks of hell as a state in which souls retain sensual lusts but suffer because they have no bodies with which to fulfill their desires.

JĀHILĪYA \ˌja-hi-'lē-ə\, in ISLAM, the period preceding the revelation of the QUR'AN to the Prophet MUHAMMAD. In Arabic the word means "ignorance" or "barbarism" and indicates a negative Muslim evaluation of pre-Islamic life and culture in Arabia as compared to the teachings and practices of Islam. The term has a positive connotation only in literature; pre-Islamic Arabic poetry is esteemed by Muslims for its precise and rich vocabulary, sophisticated metrical structures, and fully developed systems of rhyme and thematic sequence. In the writings of modern Islamists, such as ABŪ'L-AʿLĀ MAWDŪDĪ and Sayyid Quṭb, it is used to label societies that have fallen under the corrupting influences of Western SECULARISM. Muslims are called upon to resist this "new jāhilīya" and bring about instead a new moral order that submits to divine will.

JAINA \'jī-nə\, byname of the Federation of Jain Associations in North America, the umbrella organization for all the local congregations and centers of Jains living in the United States and Canada. The first local center for JAINISM in North America was established in New York City in 1966. JAINA was started in 1981 by the Jain Center of Southern California in conjunction with the centers in Cleveland, San Francisco, and Washington, D.C., and held its first national convention that year in Los Angeles. The aim of JAINA is to foster cooperation and unity among the various Jain national organizations and local centers in North America and to address issues of concern to the whole Jain community, especially as it interacts with the broader North American society. As of 1998 JAINA con-sisted of 54 member local centers (49 in the United States, 5 in Canada) and 10 affiliated national organizations, representing the majority of the estimated 40,000–60,000 Jains living in North America. Activities of JAINA include publishing a quarterly magazine, *Jain Digest;* organizing biennial conventions; supporting youth activities; organizing tours by Jain scholars and teachers from India; coordinating a matrimonial service for arranged marriages; publishing educational materials; publishing guidelines for Jain temples in North America; and establishing computer-based information networks.

JAINA VRATA \'jī-nə-'vrə-tə\ (Sanskrit: "vow"), in JAINISM, any of the vows that govern the activities of monks, nuns, and the lay community. The *mahāvrata*s, or five "Great Vows," are undertaken for life only by renouncers. They are (1) non-violence, (2) adhering to the truth, (3) not stealing, (4) sexual purity, and (5) renouncing possessions.

A lay member is not expected to be able to observe such vows strictly while living the life of a householder. If one has passed through the preliminary stages of spiritual discipline (the GUṆASTHĀNAS), one may promise to observe 12 vows for a stated period of time and may renew the pledge.

For a lay member, the first five vows are termed *anuvrata*s ("little vows") and are more moderate versions of the mendicant's *mahāvrata*s: abstaining from gross violence, falsehood, and stealing; sexual fidelity to one's own spouse; and ownership of as little as possible. The remaining vows are the three *guṇavrata*s (intended to help reinforce the *anuvrata*s; they include very specific restrictions on the locus of one's activities as well as acts that might potentially increase one's karmic store), and the four *śikṣāvrata*s, "vows of spiritual discipline," which govern four different types of ritual activity. These include (1) narrowing one's locus of activity as much as possible, (2) equanimity, (3) fasting, and (4) proper donation. There is also one final vow, termed *sallekhanāvrata,* to die in meditation during self-starvation when the observance of other vows is no longer physically possible due to old age, famine, personal calamity (such as capture), or to a terminal illness.

JAIN CANON, the sacred texts of JAINISM whose authenticity is disputed between sects. The SVETAMBARA canon consists principally of 45 works divided as follows: (1) 11 Aṅgas, the main texts—a 12th has been lost for at least 14 centuries; (2) 12 Upāṅgas, or subsidiary texts; (3) 10 Prakīrṇakas, or assorted texts; (4) 6 *Cheda Sūtras* on the rules of the ascetic life; (5) 2 *Cūlikā Sūtras* on cognition and epistemology; and (6) 4 *Mūla Sūtras* on miscellaneous topics. Svetambara, however, originally accepted a canon of 71 works derived from a 5th-century Council of Valabhī.

The Svetambara works cover a variety of topics, including a list of the TIRTHANKARAS, or Jinas (Jain saviors), their exploits and teachings, and doctrines. Some of the Aṅgas contain supposed dialogues between MĀHAVĪRA, the most recent Tirthankara, and his followers. Others are said to retain some of the earliest parts of the canon, which appears to have been preserved originally in oral form. The canon is written in the Prākrit dialect, though from the Gupta period (4th–6th century CE) Jain writers have used Sanskrit.

The DIGAMBARA sect disputes the authenticity of the entire Svetambara canon. The Digambara believe that the original is lost but that the substance of Jain doctrine has been preserved in a variety of religious and philosophic texts written by various leaders and scholars of the Jain community over the centuries.

JAINISM

A religion and philosophy of India, Jainism was founded in about the 6th century BCE by Vardhamāna. Known as MAHĀVĪRA ("Great Hero"), he is considered to be the 24th of the TĪRTHAṄKARAS ("Ford-makers"), or JINAS ("Conquerors"; whence the name Jainism), the great religious figures on whose example the religion is centered. Jainism was founded in protest against the orthodox Vedic (early Hindu) ritualistic cult of the period; its earliest proponents may have belonged to a sect that rebelled against the idea and practice of taking life prevalent in the Vedic animal sacrifice.

The name Jainism derives from the Sanskrit *ji*, "to conquer." It refers to the battle that Jain ascetics must fight against the passions and bodily senses in order to gain omniscience and the complete purity of soul that represents the highest religious goal in the Jain system. The ascetic who achieves this omniscience and purity is called a Jina (literally, "Conqueror" or "Victor"), and adherents to the tradition are called Jainas, or Jains.

HISTORICAL BACKGROUND

According to Jains their faith is eternal and has been revealed through the successive ages of the world by the Tīrthaṅkaras, each of whom attained perfection and absolute freedom, breaking free from the cycle of rebirths, and then preached Jainism to the world. The first Tīrthaṅkara, Ṛṣabha, is thus the traditional founder of Jainism, but though his name occurs in the VEDAS and the PURĀṆAS (Hindu sacred literature) very little else is known of him; nor is there historical evidence of the other Tīrthaṅkaras until Pārśva, the 23rd in the line, who is thought to have died in the late 8th century BCE.

Historians regard the actual founder of Jainism to be Mahāvīra, who was born *c.* 599 BCE near Patna in what is now Bihar state. His father was a ruling Kṣatriya, chief of the Nāta, or Jñātṛ, clan. Mahāvīra was an elder contemporary of Siddhārtha Gotama (the Buddha) and is referred to in writings of BUDDHISM as Nātaputra ("Son of the Nāta"). When he was about 28 years of age he took up the life of an ascetic. After years of hardship and meditation he attained enlightenment; thereafter he preached Jainism for about 30 years and died at Pāvāpurī (also in Bihar) in

Colossal statue of Bāhubali, the son of Ṛṣabha, the founder of Jainism, at Śravaṇa Beḷgoḷa, Karṇāṭaka, 10th century
Porterfield/Chickering—Photo Researchers

527 BCE. Pāvāpurī has been, since then, one of the chief places of Jain pilgrimage; Dīvālī, a major autumn festival for Hindus, is for Jains a day of great PILGRIMAGE for Mahāvīra.

Jainism has never been torn by philosophic dispute, but from the beginning it was subject to schismatic movements. In the 4th or 3rd century BCE the Jains began to split into two sects on points of rules and regulations for monks, a rift which was complete at least by the end of the 1st century CE. The DIGAMBARAS ("Sky-clad"; *i.e.*, naked) hold that an adherent should own nothing, not even clothes. They also believe that salvation is not possible for women. The ŚVETĀM-BARAS ("White-robed") differ from them on these points.

IMPORTANT FIGURES OF JAIN LEGEND

Sixty-three significant figures form the focus of Jain legend and story. The most important of these are the 24 Tīrthaṅkaras, perfected human beings who appear from time to time to preach and embody the Jain religious path; they represent the highest religious attainment for Jains. The Tīrthaṅkaras, along with 12 *cakra-vartin*s ("world conquerors"), nine VĀSUDEVAS (counterparts of Vāsudeva, the patronymic of KRISHNA), and nine *baladeva*s (counterparts of BALARĀMA, the elder half-brother of Krishna), constitute a list of 54 *mahāpuruṣa*s ("great souls"), to which were later added nine *prativāsudeva*s (enemies of the *vāsudeva*s). Other, more minor, figures include nine *nārada*s (counterparts of the deity Nārada, the messenger between gods and humans), 11 RUDRAS (counterparts of the Vedic god Rudra, from whom SHIVA is said to have evolved), and 24 *kāmadeva*s (gods of love), all of which show how Jain thinkers consciously shaped the faith to incorporate but supersede its precursor from HINDUISM.

Subordinated to these figures are the gods, who are classified into four groups: the *bhavanavāsī*s (gods of the house), the *vyantara*s (intermediaries), the *jyotiṣ-ka*s (luminaries), and the *vaimānika*s (astral gods). These, in turn, are divided into several subgroups. Other gods and goddesses include the 64 *dikkumārī*s (maidens of the directions), who act as nurses to a newborn Tīrthaṅkara.

DOCTRINES OF JAINISM

The Jain's religious goal is the complete perfection and purification of the soul. This can occur only when the soul is in a state of eternal liberation from and non-attachment to corporeal bodies. Liberation of the soul is impeded by the accumulation of karma, comprised of bits of material, generated by a person's actions, that bind themselves to the soul and consequently bind the soul to material bodies through many births; this has the effect of thwarting the full self-realization and freedom of the soul.

Time and the universe. Time, according to the Jains, is eternal and formless. It is conceived as a wheel with 12 spokes called *ārā*s ("ages"), six making an ascending arc and six a descending one. In the ascending arc (*utsarpiṇī*), humans progress in knowledge, age, stature, and happiness, while in the descending arc (*avasarpiṇī*) they deteriorate. The two cycles joined together make one rotation of the wheel of time, which is called a *kalpa*.

The world is eternal and uncreated. Its constituent elements are the six substances (*dravyas*), namely, soul, matter, time, space, the principles of motion, and the arrest of motion. These are eternal and indestructible, but their conditions change constantly.

Jains divide the inhabited universe into five parts. The lower world (*adholoka*) is subdivided into seven tiers, each one darker and more torturous than the one above it. The middle world (*madhyaloka*) consists of numberless concentric continents separated by seas, the center continent of which is called Jambudvīpa. Human beings occupy Jambudvīpa, the second continent, and half of the third. The locus of Jain activity, however, is Jambudvīpa, the only continent on which it is possible for the soul to achieve liberation. The celestial world (*ūrdhvaloka*) consists of two categories of heaven: one for the souls of those who may or may not have entered the Jain path and one for the souls of those who are far along on the path and are close to the time of their emancipation. At the apex of the occupied universe is the *siddha-śilā*, the crescent-shaped abode of liberated souls (SIDDHAS). Finally, there are some areas inhabited solely by *ekendriyas*, organisms that have only a single sense. Although *ekendriyas* permeate all parts of the occupied universe, there are places where they are the only living beings.

Jīva and ajīva. Jain reality is constituted by JĪVA (*i.e.*, "soul," or "living substance") and *ajīva* (*i.e.*, "non-soul," or "inanimate substance"). *Ajīva* is divided into two categories: (1) nonsentient and material and (2) nonsentient and nonmaterial. All but *jīva* are without life.

The essential characteristics of *jīva* are consciousness (*cetanā*), bliss (*sukha*), and energy (*vīrya*). In its pure state, *jīva* possesses these qualities in infinite measure. The souls, infinite in number, are divisible in their embodied state into two main classes, immobile and mobile, according to the number of sense organs possessed by the body they inhabit. The first group consists of souls inhabiting im-

Ṛṣabha with the other 23 Tīrthaṅkaras, cast bronze from Akota, Gujarāt, 9th century; in the Baroda Museum
Borromeo—Art Resource

measurably small particles of earth, water, fire, and air, plus the vegetable kingdom, which possess only the sense of touch. The second group comprises souls
that inhabit bodies that have between two and five sense organs. The Jains believe that the four elements (earth, water, fire, and air) also are animated by souls.
Moreover, the universe is full of an infinite number of minute beings, *nigoda*s,
which are slowly evolving.

A *jīva* is formless and genderless and cannot be perceived by the senses. A soul
is not all-pervasive but can, by contraction or expansion, occupy various amounts
of space. Like the light of a lamp in a small or a large room, it can fill both the
smaller and larger bodies it occupies. While the soul assumes the exact dimensions of the body it occupies, it is not identical with that body.

Matter (*pudgala*) has the characteristics of touch, taste, smell, and color. Its essential characteristic is lack of consciousness. The smallest unit of matter is the
atom (*paramāṇu*). Heat, light, and shade are forms of fine matter.

The nonsentient, nonmaterial substances are the principles of motion and its
arrest, space, and time. They are always pure and are not subject to defilement.
The principles of motion and its arrest permeate the universe; they do not exist
independently but, rather, form a necessary precondition for any object's movement or coming to rest. Space is infinite, all-pervasive, and formless and provides
accommodation for the entire universe. It is divided into occupied (*i.e.*, the universe) and unoccupied portions. Time is said to consist of innumerable eternal
and indivisible particles of "noncorporeal substance" that never mix with one another but that fill the entire universe. Thus, the nonsentient, nonmaterial substances form the context within which occurs the drama of a *jīva*'s struggle to extricate itself from involvement with matter.

Karma. The fundamental tenet of Jain doctrine is the belief that all phenomena are linked together in a universal chain of cause and effect. Every event has a
definite cause behind it. By nature each soul is pure, possessing infinite knowledge, bliss, and power; however, these faculties are restricted from beginningless
time by foreign matter coming in contact with the soul. Fine foreign matter producing the chain of cause and effect, of birth and death, is karma, conceived of as
a fine atomic substance and not a process as in Hinduism. To be free from the
shackles of karma, a person must stop the influx of new karma and eliminate
what has been acquired.

Karmic particles are acquired as the result of intentional action tinged with
passionate expression. Acquired karma can be annihilated through a process
called *nirjarā*, which consists of fasting, not eating certain kinds of food, control
over taste, resorting to lonely places, mortifications of the body, ATONEMENT and
expiation for SINS, modesty, service, study, meditation, and renunciation of the
ego. *Nirjarā* is, thus, the calculated cessation of passionate action.

A soul passes through various stages of spiritual development before becoming
free from all karmic bondages. These stages of development (GUṆASTHĀNAS) involve progressive manifestations of the innate faculties of knowledge and power
and are accompanied by decreasing sinfulness and increasing purity.

*Jīva*s become imprisoned in a succession of bodies owing to their connection
with karmic matter. These embodied souls bear different colors or tints (LEŚYĀ),
varying according to the merits or demerits of the particular being. This doctrine
of *leśyā*, peculiar to Jainism, seems to have been borrowed from the Ājīvika doctrine of six classes of bodies, expounded by Gośāla Maskarīputra. The six *leśyā*s
in Jainism are, in the ascending order of man's spiritual progress, black, blue, gray,
fiery red, lotus-pink (or yellow), and white.

Theories of knowledge as applied to liberation. In Jain thought, four stages of
perception—observation, will to recognize, determination, and impression—lead
to a subjective cognition (*matijñāna*), the first of five kinds of knowledge (*jñāna*).
The second kind of knowledge is *śrutajñāna*, derived from the SCRIPTURES and general information. Both of these are mediated cognition, based on external conditions perceived by the senses. There are three kinds of immediate knowledge—
avadhi (supersensory perception), *manaḥparyāya* (reading the thoughts of others), and *kevala*, which is the stage of omniscience. *Kevala* is necessarily accom-

panied by freedom from karmic obstruction and by direct experience of the soul's pure form unblemished by its attachment to matter. Omniscience is the foremost attribute of a liberated *jīva*, the emblem of its purity; thus, a liberated soul, such as a Tīrthaṅkara, is called a *kevalin* ("possessor of omniscience").

According to Jainism, YOGA, the ascetic physical and meditative discipline of the monk, is the means to the attainment of omniscience and thus to MOKṢA, or liberation. *Yoga* is the cultivation of true knowledge of reality, faith in the teachings of the Tīrthaṅkaras, and pure conduct; it is, thus, intimately connected to the three jewels (*ratnatraya*) of right knowledge, right belief, and right conduct (respectively, *samyagjñāna*, *samyagdarśaṇa*, and *samyakcāritra*).

Jain ethics. The *ratnatraya* constitute the basis of Jain ethics. Right knowledge, faith, and conduct must be cultivated together; none of them can be achieved in the absence of the others. Right faith leads to calmness or tranquillity, detachment, kindness, and the renunciation of pride of birth, beauty of form, wealth, scholarship, prowess, and fame. Right faith leads to perfection only when followed by right conduct. Yet, there can be no virtuous conduct without right knowledge, which consists of clear distinction between the self and the nonself. Knowledge of scriptures is distinguished from inner knowledge. Knowledge without faith and conduct is futile. Without purification of mind, all austerities are mere bodily torture. Right conduct is thus spontaneous, not a forced mechanical quality. Attainment of right conduct is a gradual process, and a householder can observe only partial self-control; when he becomes a monk, he is further able to observe more comprehensive rules of conduct.

Two separate courses of conduct are laid down for the ascetics and the laity. In both cases the code of morals is based on the doctrine of AHIMSĀ, or NONVIOLENCE. Since thought gives rise to action, violence in thought merely precedes violent

Chaumukha temple (1438) at Ranakpur, Rājasthān, a principal Jain pilgrimage site; the temple contains 1,444 intricately carved marble pillars
Porterfield/Chickering—Photo Researchers

behavior. Violence in thought, then, is the greater and subtler form of violence, because it arises from ideas of attachment and aversion, grounded in passionate states, which result from negligence or lack of care in behavior. Jainism enjoins avoidance of all forms of injury, whether committed by body, mind, or speech.

RITUAL PRACTICES AND RELIGIOUS AND SOCIAL INSTITUTIONS

The monks and their practices. The Śvetāmbara sect acknowledges two classes of monks: *jinakalpin*s, who wander naked and use the hollows of their palms as alms bowls; and *sthavirakalpin*s, who retain minimal possessions such as a robe, an alms bowl, a broom, and a *mukhavastrikā* (a piece of cloth held over the mouth to protect against the ingestion of small insects). An ascetic must obey the "great vows" (*mahāvrata*s) to avoid injuring any life-form, lying, stealing, having sexual intercourse, or accepting personal possessions. To help them live out their vows, ascetics' lives are carefully regulated in all details by specific ordinances and by the oversight of their superiors.

Among the Digambara sect, a full-fledged monk remains naked, though there are lower-grade monks who wear a loincloth and keep with them one piece of cloth not more than one and one-half yards long. Digambara monks use a peacock-feather duster and water gourd, live apart from human habitations, and beg and eat only once a day, using the palm of one hand as an alms bowl.

Eight essentials noted for the conduct of monks include the three *gupti*s (care in thought, speech, and action) and the five *samiti*s (kinds of vigilance over conduct). The six *āvaśyaka*s, or obligations, are equanimity; praise of the Tīrthaṅkaras (Jinas); obeisance to the Jinas, teachers, and scriptures; atonement; resolution to avoid sinful activities; and meditation.

The type of austerities in which a monk engages, the length of time he engages in them, and their severity are carefully regulated by his preceptor, who takes into account the monk's spiritual development, his capacity to withstand the austerities, and his ability to understand how they help further his spiritual progress at a given time. The culmination of a monk's ascetic rigors is the act of *sallekhanā*, in which he lies on one side on a bed of thorny grass and ceases to move or take food, ultimately starving to death. This act of ritual starvation is the ultimate act of nonattachment, in which the monk lets go of the body for the sake of his soul. The ascetic's preparatory rigors, which point to and culminate in this act, generally take 30 years or more to perform. Although it is a tenet of Jain doctrine that no one can achieve liberation in this corrupt time, it is thought that the act of *sallekhanā* nevertheless has value, because it can improve a soul's spiritual situation in the next birth.

Religious disciplines of the laity. The life of a lay votary is a preparatory stage to the rigors of ascetic life. The lay votary is enjoined to observe eight primary behavioral qualities (which usually include the avoidance of meat, wine, honey, fruits, roots, and night eating) and 12 vows. The *aṇuvrata*s ("little vows") are vows to abstain from gross violence, falsehood, and stealing; to be content with one's own wife; and to limit one's possessions. The other sets of vows are supplementary in nature, meant to strengthen and protect the *aṇuvrata*s. They involve avoidance of unnecessary travel, harmful activities, and the pursuit of pleasure; fasting and control of diet; offering of gifts and service to monks, the poor, and fellow believers; and voluntary death if the observance of vows proves impossible.

The *sāmāyika*, a lay meditative and renunciatory ritual of limited duration, aims at strengthening equanimity of mind and resolve to pursue the spiritual discipline of the Jain DHARMA (religious and moral law). This ritual brings the lay votary close to the demands required of an ascetic for a limited time. It may be performed in a person's own house, in a temple, in a fasting hall, or before a monk.

Eleven PRATIMAS, or stages of a householder's spiritual progress, are listed. Medieval writers conceived *pratima* (literally, "statue") as a regular series leading to higher stages of spiritual development. The last two stages lead logically to renunciation of the world and assumption of the ascetic life.

Sacred times and places. *Festivals and fairs.* The principal Jain festivals are connected with the five major events in the life of each Tīrthaṅkara. These mark the occasions of the Tīrthaṅkara's descent into his mother's womb, birth, renunciation, attainment of omniscience, and final emancipation.

The most popular Jain festival is PARYUṢAṆA, which occurs in the months of Śrāvaṇ and Bhādrapad (August–September). Paryuṣaṇa literally means staying at one place during the monsoon season, and is characterized by pacification by forgiving and service with wholehearted effort and devotion. On the last day of the festival, Jains distribute alms to the poor and take a Jina image in procession through the streets. Confession is performed during the festival to remove all ill feelings about conscious or unconscious misdeeds during the past year.

Twice a year, for nine days (March–April and September–October), a fasting ceremony known as *olī* is observed. These are also the eight-day festivals corresponding to the mythical celestial worship of images of the Jinas.

On the full-moon day of the month of Kārttika (October–November), Jains commemorate the Nirvāṇa of Mahāvīra by lighting lamps. Five days later is

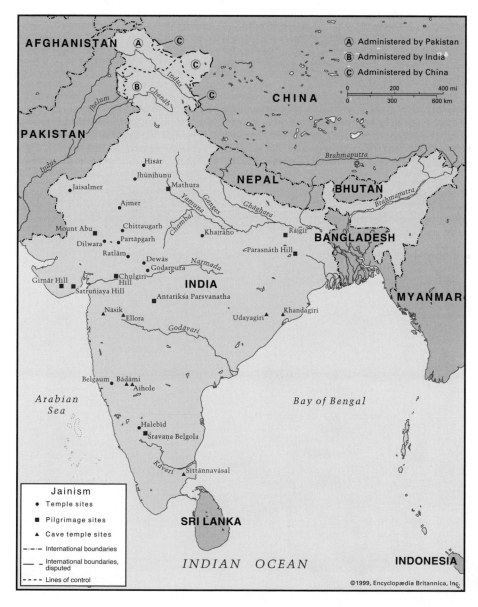

Principal Jain temples and pilgrimage sites

Jñānapañcamī (literally, "The Fifth Level of Knowledge," *i.e., kevala*), which the Jains celebrate with temple worship and with worship of the scriptures. Mahāvīra Jayanti, the birthday of Mahāvīra, is celebrated in early April or during the Paryuṣaṇa festival. The Jains also celebrate a number of festivals in common with Hindus, such as Holi (spring festival), Navaratra (nine nights festival), and PONGAL (a South Indian NEW YEAR FESTIVAL).

Pilgrimages and shrines. The erection of shrines and the donation of religious manuscripts are regarded as pious acts. Most villages or towns inhabited by Jains have at least one Jain shrine; some have become pilgrimage sites. Lists of these shrines have been composed, and the most noteworthy shrines are offered adoration in daily worship.

Places of pilgrimage were created at sites marking the principal events in the lives of Tīrthaṅkaras. Parasnāth Hill and Rājgīr in Bihār and Śatruñjaya and Girnār hills on the Kāthiāwār Peninsula are among such important ancient pilgrimage sites. Other shrines that have become pilgrimage destinations are Śravaṇa Beḷgoḷa in Karṇāṭaka, Mounts Ābu and Kesariajī in Rājasthān, and Antarikṣa PĀRŚVANĀTHA in Akola district, Mahārāshtra.

Several Jain cave temples, dating from as early as the 2nd century BCE, have been discovered and excavated. Cave temples are found at Udayagiri and Khandagiri, in Orissa; Rājgīr, in Bihār; Aihole, in Karṇāṭaka; Ellora, in Mahārāshtra; and Sittānnavāsal in Tamil Nādu.

Temple worship and observance. Temple worship is mentioned in early texts that describe gods worshiping Jina images and relics in heavenly eternal shrines. Worship, closely associated with the obligatory rites of the laity, is offered to all liberated souls, to monks, and to the scriptures. Though Tīrthaṅkaras remain unaffected by offerings and worship, such actions serve as a form of meditative discipline for the votary offering them. Daily worship includes recitation of the

Devotees worship at the Śravaṇa Beḷgoḷa shrine by washing the image and making offerings to it
Paul Stepan—Photo Researchers

names of the Jinas and idol worship by bathing the image and making offerings to it. Śvetāmbaras decorate images with clothing and ornaments. The worshiper also chants HYMNS of praise and prayers and mutters sacred formulas. A long-standing debate within both Jain communities over the centuries has concerned the relative value of external acts of worship and internalized acts of mental discipline and meditation.

Domestic rites and rites of passage. Early Jain literature is silent about domestic rites and RITES OF PASSAGE marking the main events in a person's life. These rituals are modeled mainly on the 16 Hindu SAṂSKĀRAS, which include conception, birth, naming, first meal, TONSURE, investiture with the sacred thread, beginning of study, marriage, and death. They are first discussed in Jinasena's 9th-century work, *Ādipurāṇa.*

CANONICAL AND COMMENTARIAL LITERATURE

The original, unadulterated teachings of the Jinas are said to be contained in 14 texts, called the *Pūrva*s ("Foundations"), which are now lost. Śvetāmbaras and Digambaras agree that a time will come when the teachings of the Jinas will be completely lost; Jainism will then disappear from the earth and reappear at an appropriate point in the next time cycle (*kalpa*). The two sects disagree, however, about the extent to which the corruption and loss of the Jinas' teachings has already occurred. Consequently, the texts for each sect differ.

The Śvetāmbaras follow an extensive canon (ĀGAMA) as the repository of their tradition, which they believe is based upon compilations of Mahāvīra's discourses by his disciples. This canon preserves the teachings of Mahāvīra in an imperfect way, as it is thought to be mixed with much that was not said by the Jina. Western scholars have fixed the number of texts in this canon at 45, divided into six groups: the 11 *Aṅga*s ("Parts"; originally there were 12, but one, the *Dṛṣṭivāda*, has been lost), 12 *Upāṅga*s (subsidiary texts), four *Mūla-sūtra*s (basic texts), six *Cheda-sūtra*s (concerned with discipline), two *Cūlikā-sūtra*s (appendix texts), and 10 *Prakīrṇaka*s (mixed, assorted texts). The *Aṅga*s contain several dialogues, mainly between Mahāvīra and his disciple Indrabhūti Gautama, presumably recorded by the disciple Sudharman, who transmitted these teachings to his own disciples.

Bhadrabāhu, whom tradition credits with being the last Jain sage to know the contents of the *Pūrva*s, is asserted to be the author of the *Niryukti*s, the earliest commentaries on the Jain canonical texts. These concise, metrical commentaries, written in Prākrit, gave rise to an expanded corpus comprising texts called *Bhāṣ-ya*s and *Cūrṇi*s. These were composed between the 4th and 7th centuries and contain many ancient Jain historical and legendary traditions, along with a large number of popular stories brought into the service of Jain doctrine. The *Bhāṣya*s and *Cūrṇi*s, in turn, gave rise in the medieval period to a large collection of Sanskrit commentaries. HARIBHADRA, Śīlāṅka, Abhayadeva, and Malayagiri are the best-known authors of such commentaries.

Digambaras give canonical status to two works in Prākrit: the *Karmaprābhṛta* ("Chapters on *Karma*") and the *Kaṣāyaprābhṛta* ("Chapters on the Passions"). The *Karmaprābhṛta,* based on the now-lost *Dṛṣṭivāda* text, deals with the doctrine of *karma* and was committed to writing by Puṣpadanta and Bhūtabalin in the mid-2nd century; the *Kaṣāyaprābhṛta,* compiled by Guṇadhara from the same source at about the same time, deals with the passions that defile and bind the soul. Later commentaries by Vīrasena (8th century) and his disciple JINASENA (9th century) on the *Kaṣāyaprābhṛta* are also highly respected by Digambaras.

MODERN DEVELOPMENTS

In modern times, Śvetāmbara Jainism has maintained a more effective organization and has a larger monastic community than its Digambara counterpart. Jains have traditionally been professional and mercantile people. These trades have made them adaptable to other environments and societies besides those of India. Many Jains have emigrated overseas, and this has had the result of increasing international awareness of Jainism.

JAJMĀNĪ SYSTEM

JAJMĀNĪ SYSTEM \jəj-'mä-nē, yəj-\ (Hindi, deriving from the Sanskrit *yajamāna*, "sacrificial patron who employs priests for a ritual"), reciprocal social and economic arrangements between families of different CASTES within a village community in India, by which one family exclusively performs certain services for the other, such as ministering to the ritual, barbering, or providing agricultural labor, and expects to receive pay, protection, and employment security in return. These relations are supposed to continue from one generation to another, and payment is normally made in the form of a fixed share in the harvest rather than in cash. The patron family itself can be the client of another whom it patronizes for certain services and by whom it is in turn patronized for other services. The hereditary character allows for certain forms of bond labor, since it is the family obligation to serve its hereditary patrons.

The extent to which this system has ever truly operated in the Indian countryside is a matter of considerable debate. The *jajmānī* ideal is suspect as the anthropological analog of the same theoretical system presented by texts that describe a unified, conflict-free, reciprocal, and hierarchically weighted system of interrelated *varṇas*. While aspects of *jajmānī* relationships have been clearly attested in both past and present, and the influence of the *jajmānī* ideal is something to be reckoned with, these are undeniably and increasingly accompanied by litigation, harassment, boycott, violence, political maneuvering, and a variety of monetized exchanges.

JALĀL AL-DĪN AL-RŪMĪ

\jə-'läl-ùd-'dēn-är-'rü-mē\, *also called* Mawlānā \'maù-ˌlä-ˌnä\ (b. *c*. Sept. 30, 1207, Balkh, Ghūrid empire [now in Afghanistan]—d. Dec. 17, 1273), the greatest Sufi mystic (*see* SUFISM) and poet in the Persian language, famous for his lyrics and for his didactic epic *Masnavī-ye Ma'navī* ("Spiritual Couplets").

Tomb of Jalāl al-Dīn al-Rūmī; Konya, Turkey
Fred J. Maroon—Photo Researchers

Jalāl al-Dīn's father, Bahā' al-Dīn Walad, was a noted mystical theologian, author, and teacher. Mainly because of the threat of the approaching Mongols, Bahā' al-Dīn and his family left their native town about 1218. After a PILGRIMAGE to MECCA and journeys through the Middle East, Bahā' al-Dīn and his family reached Anatolia (Rūm, hence the surname Rūmī), a region that enjoyed peace and prosperity under the rule of the Turkish Seljuq dynasty. After a short stay at Laranda (Karaman) they were called to the capital, Konya, in 1228. Here, Bahā' al-Dīn Walad taught at one of the numerous MADRASAS (religious schools); after his death in 1231 he was succeeded in this capacity by his son.

A year later, Burhān al-Dīn Muḥaqqiq, one of Bahā' al-Dīn's former disciples, arrived in Konya and acquainted Jalāl al-Dīn more deeply with some mystical theories that had developed in Iran. Burhān al-Dīn, who contributed considerably to Jalāl al-Dīn's spiritual formation, left Konya about 1240. Jalāl al-Dīn is said to have undertaken one or two journeys to Syria; there he may have met IBN AL-'ARABĪ, the leading Islamic theosophist whose interpreter and stepson, Ṣadr al-Dīn al-Qunawī, was Rūmī's colleague and friend in Konya.

The decisive moment in Rūmī's life occurred on Nov. 30, 1244, when in the streets of Konya he met the wandering DERVISH Shams al-Dīn ("Sun of Religion") of Tabrīz, whom he may have first encountered in Syria. Shams al-Dīn's overwhelming personality revealed to Jalāl al-Dīn the mysteries of divine majesty and beauty. For months the two mystics lived closely together, and Rūmī neglected his disciples and family until his entourage forced Shams to leave the town in February 1246. Jalāl al-Dīn was heartbroken; his eldest son, Sulṭān Walad, eventually brought Shams back from Syria. The family, however, could not tolerate the close relation of Jalāl al-Dīn with his beloved, and one night in 1247 Shams disappeared forever. It has been established that he was indeed murdered, not without the knowledge of Rūmī's sons, who hurriedly buried him close to a well that is still extant in Konya.

This experience turned Rūmī into a poet. His mystical poems—about 30,000 verses and a large number of *robā'īyāt* ("quatrains")—reflect the different stages of his love, until, as his son writes, "he found Shams in himself, radiant like the moon." The identification of lover and beloved is expressed by his inserting the name of Shams instead of his own pen name at the end of most of his lyrical poems.

A few years after Shams al-Dīn's death, Rūmī experienced a similar rapture in his acquaintance with an illiterate goldsmith, Ṣalāḥ al-Dīn Zarkūb. This love again inspired Jalāl al-Dīn to write poetry. After Ṣalāḥ al-Dīn's death, Ḥusām al-Dīn Chelebi became his spiritual love and deputy. Rūmī's main work, the *Masnavī-ye Ma'navī*, was composed under his influence. Ḥusām al-Dīn had asked him to follow the model of the poets 'Aṭṭār and Sanā'i, who had laid down mystical teachings in long poems, interspersed with anecdotes, fables, stories, proverbs, and allegories. Jalāl al-Dīn thus composed nearly 26,000 couplets of the *Masnavī* during the following years. The *Masnavī* reflects the experience of divine love; both Ṣalāḥ al-Dīn and Ḥusām al-Dīn were, for Rūmī, renewed manifestations of Shams al-Dīn, the all-embracing light. He called Ḥusām al-Dīn, therefore, Ḍiyā' al-Ḥaqq ("Light of the Truth").

Rūmī lived for a short while after completing the *Masnavī*. He always remained a respected member of Konya society, and his company was sought by the leading officials as well as by Christian monks. Ḥusām al-Dīn was his successor and was in turn succeeded by Sulṭān Walad, who organized the loose fraternity of Rūmī's disciples into MAW-LAWĪYA, known in the West as the Whirling Dervishes because of the mystical dance that constitutes their principal ritual. Sulṭān Walad's poetical accounts of his father's life are the most important source of knowledge of Rūmī's spiritual development.

In addition to his poetry, Rūmī left a small collection of letters and occasional talks as they were noted down by his friends; in the collection, known as *Fīhi mā fīhi* ("There is in it what is in it"), the main ideas of his poetry recur. Rūmī's influence on Turkish cultural life can scarcely be overstated; his mausoleum, the Green Dome, today a museum in Konya, is still a place of pilgrimage for thousands.

JAMAʿAT-I ISLAMI \\'jȧ-mȧ-ȧt-ē-is-'lȧ-mē\\ (Arabic: "Islamic Society"), religious party founded in British-controlled India (now Pakistan) in 1941 by Mawlana ABŪʾL-AʿLĀ MAWDŪDĪ (1903–79). The party was established to reform society in accordance with the faith and drew its inspiration from the model of the prophet MUHAMMAD's original Muslim community. It called for moral reform and political action but was not concerned with questions of nationalism or national boundaries because ISLAM is a universal religion. The Jamaʿat was to provide an alternative to the practices of the Sufi Brotherhoods and was designed to create an elite of educated and devout Muslim leaders that would direct the way toward the revival of Islam. (See SUFISM.)

Although a religious party, the Jamaʿat has not remained apart from political activity in Pakistan. Mawdūdī had opposed an independent Pakistan but, yielding to political reality, he focused his, and the party's, attention on Pakistan in 1947 until his retirement in 1972. In 1953, the Jamaʿat led a violent campaign against the Ahmadiyya sect that led to 2,000 deaths. For much of the next two decades, the party remained the voice of the ʿULAMĀʾ and was active in opposition politics although it did support the wars with India in 1965 and 1971. After the overthrow of Zulfiqar Ali Bhutto in 1977, the Jamaʿat supported General Zia ul-Haq's Islamization program but opposed his effort to ban student unions. More recently, members of the Jamaʿat supported Saddam Hussein during the Gulf War. They have been active in electoral politics and have sponsored legislation in the senate, both efforts having met with mixed success. The Jamaʿat remains active in its efforts to reform society according to Islamic law and took part in anti-government demonstrations before the fall of the Benazir Bhutto government in 1996.

JAMĀL AL-DĪN AL-AFGHĀNĪ \\jȧ-'mäl-ȯl-'dēn-ȯl-af-'gä-nē\\, *in full* Jamāl al-Dīn al-Afghānī al-Sayyid Muhammad ibn Ṣafdar al-Ḥusayn (b. 1838, Asadābād, Persia [now Iran]—d. March 9, 1897, Constantinople [now Istanbul, Turkey]), Muslim politician, political agitator, and journalist whose belief in the potency of a revived Islamic civilization in the face of European domination significantly influenced the development of Muslim thought in the 19th and early 20th centuries.

Some scholars believe that Afghānī was not an Afghan but a Persian SHIʿITE. An appreciable part of Afghānī's activities took place in areas where Sunnism was predominant, and it was probably to hide his Persian and Shiʿite origins, which would have aroused suspicion among SUNNIS, that he adopted the name Afghānī. As a young man he seems to have visited KARBALĀʾ and al-Najaf, the Shiʿite centers in southern Mesopotamia, as well as India and perhaps Istanbul. The intellectual currents with which he came in contact made him early into a religious skeptic.

From the death in 1863 of the famous Dōst Muhammad Khān, who had ruled for more than 20 years, Afghanistan had been the scene of civil wars occasioned by the quarrels of his sons over the succession. In 1866 one of these sons, Shīr ʿAlī Khān, was established in the capital, Kābul, but two of his brothers, Muhammad Afḍal Khān and Moḥammad Aʿẓam Khān, were threatening his tenure. In January 1867 Shīr ʿAlī was defeated and expelled from Kābul, where Afḍal and, upon his death shortly afterward, Aʿẓam reigned successively in 1867–68. At the end of 1866 Aʿẓam captured Qandahār, and Afghānī immediately became Aʿẓam's confidential counselor, following him to Kābul. He remained in this position until Aʿẓam was in turn deposed by Shīr ʿAlī in September 1868. Shīr ʿAlī expelled Afghānī from his territory two months later.

Afghānī next appeared in Istanbul in 1870, where he gave a lecture in which he likened the prophetic office to a human craft or skill. This view gave offense to the religious authorities, who denounced it as heretical. Afghānī had to leave Istanbul and in 1871 went to Cairo, where for the next few years he attracted a following of young writers and divines, among them MUHAMMAD ʿABDUH, who was to become the leader of the modernist movement in ISLAM, and Saʿd Pasha Zaghlūl, founder of the Egyptian nationalist party, the Wafd. Again, a reputation for HERESY and unbelief clung to Afghānī. The ruler of Egypt then was the Khedive Ismāʿīl, whose financial mismanagement led to pressure by his European creditors and great discontent among all his subjects by the mid-1870's. In response to French and British pressure, his suzerain, the Ottoman SULTAN, deposed him in June 1879. During this period Afghānī attempted to gain and manipulate power by organizing his followers in a Masonic lodge, of which he became the leader, and by delivering fiery speeches against Ismāʿīl, hoping to attract thereby the favor and confidence of Tawfīq, Ismāʿīl's son and successor; but the latter, reputedly fearing that Afghānī was propagating republicanism in Egypt, ordered his deportation in August 1879.

Afghānī then went to Hyderābād and later, via Calcutta, to Paris, where he arrived in January 1883. Together with his former student ʿAbduh, Afghānī published an anti-British newspaper, *al-ʿUrwa al-wuthqā* ("The Strongest Link"), which claimed (falsely) to be in touch with and have influence over the Sudanese Mahdi (*see* MAHDIST), a messianic bearer of justice and equality expected by some Muslims in the last days. He also engaged Ernest Renan, the French historian and philosopher, in a famous debate concerning the position of Islam regarding science. He tried unsuccessfully to persuade the British government to use him as intermediary in negotiation with the Ottoman sultan, Abdülhamid II, and then went to Russia, where his presence is recorded in 1887, 1888, and 1889 and where the authorities seem to have employed him in anti-British agitation directed to India. Afghānī next appeared in Iran, where he again attempted to play a political role as the shah's counselor and was yet again suspected of heresy. The shah, Nāṣir al-Dīn Shāh, became very suspicious of him, and Afghānī began a campaign of overt and violent opposition to the Iranian ruler. Again, in 1892, his fate was deportation. For this, Afghānī revenged himself by instigating the shah's murder in 1896. It was his only successful political act.

From Iran, Afghānī went to London, where he stayed briefly, editing a newspaper that attacked the shah. He then went to Istanbul, in response to an invitation made by an agent of the sultan. The sultan may have hoped to use him in pan-Islamic propaganda, but Afghānī soon aroused suspicion and was kept inactive, at arm's length and under observation. His burial place was kept secret, but in 1944 what was claimed to be his body, owing to the mistaken impression that he was an Afghan, was transferred to Kābul, where a mausoleum was erected for it.

JAMES, SAINT \'jāmz\, *also called* James, Son of Zebedee, *or* James the Great (b. Galilee, Palestine—d. *c.* 44 CE, Jerusalem; feast day July 25), one of the Twelve APOSTLES, JESUS' innermost circle, and the only apostle whose martyrdom is recorded in the NEW TESTAMENT (Acts 12:2).

James and his younger brother, the apostle JOHN, were, with PETER and ANDREW, the first four disciples whom Jesus called (Mark 1:16–19). His question "Tell us, when will this [the end of time] be, and what will be the sign when these things are all to be accomplished?" sparks Jesus' eschatological discourse in Mark 13. As a member of the inner circle, James is said to have witnessed the raising of Jairus' daughter (Mark 5:37, Luke 8:51), the TRANSFIGURATION (Mark 9:2), and Jesus' agony in the Garden of GETHSEMANE (Mark 14:33, Matthew 26:37). James was beheaded by order of King Herod Agrippa I of Judaea; Spanish tradition holds that he evangelized in Spain and that his body was taken to Santiago de Compostela, where his shrine attracts pilgrims from all over the world.

JĀMĪ \'jò-,mē\, *in full* Mawlanā Nūr al-Dīn 'Abd al-Raḥmān ibn Aḥmad (b. Nov. 7, 1414, district of Jam—d. Nov. 9, 1492, Herāt, Timurid Afghanistan), Persian scholar, mystic, and often regarded as the last great mystical poet of Iran.

Jāmī spent his life in Herāt except for two brief PILGRIMAGES to Mashad (Iran) and the Hijaz. During his lifetime his fame as a scholar resulted in numerous offers of patronage by many Islamic rulers. He declined most of these offers, preferring the simple life of a mystic and scholar to that of a court poet. His prose deals with a variety of subjects ranging from Qur'anic commentaries to treatises on SUFISM and music. Perhaps the most famous is his mystical treatise *Lava'iḥ* (*Flashes of Light*), a clear and precise exposition of the Sufi doctrines of *waḥdat al-wujūd* (the existential unity of Being), together with a commentary on the experiences of other famous mystics.

Jāmī's poetical works express his ethical and philosophical doctrines. His poetry is fresh and graceful and is not marred by unduly esoteric language. His most famous collection of poetry is a seven-part compendium entitled *Haft Awrang* ("The Seven Thrones," or "Ursa Major"), which includes *Salmān o-Absāl* and *Yūsof o-Zalīkhā.*

JAMUNĀ \'jə-mů-nə\, *also called* Jamnnā, Jumna, *or* Yamunā, river in Uttar Pradesh state, northern India, rising in the HIMALAYAS near Jamnotri. Near Allahabad (Prayāga), after a course of about 855 miles, the Jamunā joins the GAŃGĀ (Ganges) River; their confluence is a sacred place to Hindus and is thought to include a third river, now invisible, called the SARASVATĪ. The Jamunā is regarded as a goddess by Hindus, and in that role is often understood and pictured as the Gańgā's sister; both are liquid forms of the power (*śakti*) associated with goddesses in general. Since the Jamunā is the central artery of the Braj region, where KRISHNA is believed to have spent his youth, the river has a special association with him. Many of the most famous episodes in his childhood, such as his defeat of the black snake Kāliya or his

St. James, detail from a 12th-century mural; in the monastery of Eski Gümüs, Turkey
Sonia Halliday

bathing games with the milkmaid *gopī*s, took place on her banks or in her waters.

JANAM SĀKHĪ \'jə-nəm-'sä-kē\ (Punjabi: "life story"), hagiographic genre of Punjabi prose celebrating the life and works of GURŪ NĀNAK, the founder of the Sikh tradition (*see* SIKHISM). In all likelihood, *sākhī* traditions began to appear in oral form soon after the death of Nānak in the 16th century, if not before. The earliest extant written versions, however, can be traced back only to the mid-17th century. Nānak's poetic compositions often provide the themes of these stories. The biographer's effort is then to explain the narrative context that produced the Gurū's thought or utterance. Every effort is made to present Nānak as the greatest teacher and spiritual master of the age, but many observers have felt that the resulting stories do not always faithfully support Nānak's own positions on issues of belief and practice, as enunciated in his own compositions.

JANMĀṢṬAMĪ \,jən-'mäsh-tə-,mē\, Hindu festival celebrating the birth (*janma*) of the god KRISHNA (Kṛṣṇa) on the eighth (*aṣṭamī*) day of the dark fortnight of the month of Bhādrapada (August–September). The eighth also has significance in the Krishna legend, as he is usually regarded as the 8th of 10 AVATARS (incarnations) of Lord VISHNU and the eighth child of his mother, Devakī.

The occasion is observed with particular splendor in Mathura and VRINDĀBAD, the scenes of Krishna's childhood and early youth. The preceding day devotees keep a vigil and fast until midnight, the traditional hour of his birth. Then or on the following morning the image of Krishna is bathed in five sacred fluids, including water from the River Jamunā, and milk; dressed in especially regal clothes; and worshiped. Temples and household shrines are decorated with leaves and flowers; sweets are first offered to the god and then distributed as PRASĀDA (the god's favor) to all the members of the household. The devotees of Krishna commemorate the events of his birth in various ways, including the *rās līlā* plays in which episodes relating to his birth are reenacted. On the morning of the day following Krishna's midnight birth, some temples witness scenes of joyful abandon in which devotees take the role of cowherds congratulating Krishna's foster parents, Nanda and Yaśodā, on the birth of their baby boy and raining turmeric-dyed curd on one another. There are several regional variations on this theme. In many places pots of milk are hung from tall poles in the streets, and men form human pyramids to reach and break the pots—this in imitation of Krishna's childhood play with the cowherd boys, when they stole the curds hung out of reach by their mothers. The festival is generally a time for group singing and dancing and is calculated as the beginning of the liturgical year by members of the VALLABHA SAMPRADĀYA.

JANSEN, CORNELIUS OTTO \'yän-sən, *Angl* 'jan-sən\ (b. Oct. 28, 1585, Acquoi, near Leerdam, Holland—d. May 6, 1638, Ypres, Flanders, Spanish Netherlands [now in Belgium]), Flemish leader of the ROMAN CATHOLIC reform movement known as Jansenism.

Jansen entered the University of Louvain in 1602 to study theology. According to the custom adopted by the humanists of the Renaissance, Jansen Latinized his name to Cornelius Jansenius. He was deeply influenced by the thought of Michael Baius, who held that man is affected from his birth by the SIN of ADAM, that his instincts lead him necessarily to evil, and that he can be saved only by the GRACE of JESUS CHRIST, accorded to a small number of the ELECT who have been chosen in advance and destined to enter the kingdom of heaven. This doctrine, inspired by writings of ST. AUGUSTINE, also attracted another student, a Frenchman named Jean Duvergier de Hauranne. The two young men decided to revive theology, which they believed the theologians of the Sorbonne had reduced to subtle and vain discussions of SCHOLASTICISM.

In 1611 Jansen followed Duvergier to Bayonne, where he directed the episcopal college from 1612 to 1614. For three years afterward he dedicated himself to the study of the writings of the early CHURCH FATHERS. In 1617 Jansen returned to Louvain, where he directed the college of Sainte-Pulchérie, created for Dutch students. Jansen undertook a thorough study of the works of Augustine, and devoted himself most particularly to those texts drafted to combat the doctrine of PELAGIUS, who had held that, in spite of the fault committed by Adam, man continues to be entirely free to do good and to obtain salvation by means of his own merits. Jansen then began his great work, the *Augustinus*. For him, the divine grace that alone can save man is not due at all to his good actions but a gratuitous gift by means of which Christ leads the elect to eternal life; the multitude is doomed to damnation. He also wrote commentaries on the evangelists and on the Old Testament—notably on the PENTATEUCH—as well as a "Discourse on the Reformation of the Inner Man." He was likewise the author of pamphlets directed against the Protestants.

Having acquired the degree of doctor in theology at Louvain, Jansen became the rector of that university in 1635, and in 1636 he became bishop of Ypres. A short time later he died of the plague. In 1640 his friends published at Louvain the work he had dedicated to St. Augustine, under the title *Augustinus Cornelii Jansenii, Episcopi, seu Doctrina Sancti Augustini de Humanae Naturae, Sanitate, Aegritudine, Medicina adversus Pelagianos et Massilienses* ("The

Augustine of Cornelius Jansen, Bishop, or On the Doctrines of St. Augustine Concerning Human Nature, Health, Grief, and Cure Against the Pelagians and Massilians").

In a bull of 1642, Pope Urban VIII forbade the reading of the *Augustinus*, which had been published without the authorization of the Holy See. Five propositions in the *Augustinus* were condemned by Pope Innocent X in 1653, and by his successor, Alexander VII. The bishops of France were required to make all of the priests, monks, and nuns sign a formulary conforming to the pontifical decisions. But Duvergier de Hauranne, who had become the abbé of Saint-Cyran, had taught the doctrine of Jansen to the nuns of the abbey of Port-Royal. This CONVENT became a focus of resistance against the JESUITS, who, having obtained the pontifical decisions in their favor, intended to impose them.

Although Louis XIV was determined to eliminate the Jansenists as a threat to the unity of his kingdom, there was a temporary peace after Clement IX became pope in 1667, and the conflict ceased to be a major concern when the PAPACY and the French Roman Catholic church clashed on Gallicanism. But after that conflict was settled, Louis XIV obtained from Clement XI in 1705 a bull that renewed the earlier condemnations. In 1709 Louis XIV ordered the dispersal of the nuns of Port-Royal into diverse convents, and he had the abbey destroyed in 1710. He then obtained in 1713 the bull *Unigenitus Dei Filius*, which condemned 101 propositions of the exiled Jansenist theologian Pasquier Quesnel. The promulgation of *Unigenitus* as French law in 1730 began the decline of the Jansenist party.

In 1723 followers of Jansen's views established an autonomous Jansenist church at Utrecht, Holland, which still existed in the late 20th century. Jansenism also spread to Italy, where in 1786 the SYNOD of Pistoia, which was later condemned, propounded extreme Jansenist doctrines.

JANUS \'jā-nəs\, in ROMAN RELIGION, the spirit of doorways (*januae*) and archways (*jani*). The worship of Janus traditionally dated back to Romulus and a period even before the actual founding of the city of Rome. There were many *jani* (*i.e.*, ceremonial gateways) in Rome; these were usually freestanding structures that were used for symbolically auspicious entrances or exits. It was believed that there were lucky and unlucky ways for a departing Roman army to march through a *janus*. The most famous *janus* in Rome was the Janus Geminus, which was actually a shrine of Janus at the north side of the Forum. It was a simple rectangular bronze structure with double doors at each end. Traditionally, the doors of this shrine were left open in time of war and were kept closed when Rome was at peace. According to the Roman historian Livy, the gates were closed only twice in the long period between Numa Pompilius (7th century BCE) and Augustus (1st century BCE).

Some scholars regard Janus as the god of all beginnings and believe that his association with doorways is derivative. He was invoked as the first of any gods in regular liturgies. The beginning of the day, month, and year, both calendrical and agricultural, were sacred to him. The month of January is named for him, and his festival took place on January 9, the Agonium.

Janus was represented by a double-faced head, and he was represented in art either with or without a beard. Occasionally he was depicted as four-faced—as the spirit of the four-way arch.

JASON \'jā-sən\, in Greek mythology, leader of the ARGONAUTS and son of Aeson, king of Iolcos in Thessaly. His father's half-brother PELIAS seized Iolcos, and thus for safety Jason was sent away to CHIRON, a CENTAUR. Returning as a young man, Jason was promised his inheritance if he fetched the Golden Fleece for Pelias. Jason gathered the Argonauts and, after many adventures, obtained the fleece with the help of the sorceress MEDEA, whom he married. On their return Medea murdered Pelias, but she and Jason were driven out by Pelias' son and had to take refuge with King Creon of Corinth. Later Jason deserted Medea for Creon's daughter; this desertion and its consequences formed the subject of Euripides' *Medea*.

JĀṬ \'jät\, *also spelled (Punjabi)* Jaṭ, major group of farmers in northern India and Pakistan. Their sense of group solidarity, pride, and self-sufficiency have been historically significant in many ways, as, for instance, during the rule of the Mughal emperor Aurangzeb (late 17th century), when Jāṭ leaders captained uprisings in the region of Mathura. A Jāṭ kingdom established at nearby Bharatpur in the 18th century became a principal rival for declining Mughal power, its rulers apparently seeing themselves as defenders of Hindu ways against the Muslim Mughals. Jāṭs living toward the western side of the Jāṭ region tend to be Muslim, and those inhabiting eastern Punjab are primarily Sikh. Numerically, Jāṭs form the largest percentage of the Sikh community and therefore vie for leadership of the faith with urban Khatrīs, the group to which all 10 GURŪS belonged. Some scholars attribute Sikh military tradition largely to its Jāṭ heritage.

JĀTAKA \'jä-tə-kə\ (Pāli and Sanskrit: "Story of a Birth," akin to Sanskrit *jāta*, "born," *jāti*, "birth"), any of the extremely popular stories of former lives of the BUDDHA GOTAMA that are preserved in all branches of BUDDHISM. Some *Jātaka* tales are scattered in various sections of the Pāli canon, including a group of 35 that constitute the last book, the *Cariyā Piṭaka* ("Basket of Conduct"), of the *Khuddaka Nikāya*. Beyond this, a Sinhalese commentary of the 5th century that is questionably attributed to Buddhagosa and called the *Jātakaṭṭhavaṇṇanā* gathers together 547 *Jātaka* stories.

Each tale begins by noting the occasion that prompted its telling and ends with the Buddha disclosing his identity. In whatever form the Buddha appears, he exhibits some virtue that the tale thereby inculcates. Many *Jātaka*s have parallels in the MAHĀBHĀRATA ("Great Epic of the Bhārata Dynasty"), the *Pañca Tantra* (animal fables), and the PURĀṆAS. Some turn up again in such places as Aesop's fables. The *Jātaka* stories have also been illustrated frequently in sculpture and painting throughout the Buddhist world. *See also* VESSANTARA JĀTAKA.

JĀTI \'jä-tē\, *also spelled* jāt, CASTE, in Hindu society. The Sanskrit word *jāti* means literally "birth," and by extension "the position in the community assigned to one by virtue of one's birth." Sociologically, *jāti* has come to be used universally to indicate a caste group among Hindus.

A sharp distinction should be made between *jāti*, as a limited endogamous group of families, often regionally defined and embracing only a certain set of characteristic occupations, and VARṆA, the "classical" four-part model of social organization articulated in various Vedic and post-Vedic texts. The relation between these two has never been simple, and the ranking of *jāti*s in relation to one another often diverges markedly from one area of India to another. Since the 19th century, Hindu social reformers, such as

GANDHI, have been eager to challenge the notion that birth should be the key determinant of a society that functions through a natural complementing of its constituent functions. Thinking such an idealist approach unrealistic and doomed to failure, other reformers, such as B.R. AMBEDKAR, have insisted that birth groups—since they exist—be granted separate, differential rights and privileges as a strategy for remedying social injustice.

JAYADEVA \ˌjä-yə-'dā-və\: *see* GĪTAGOVINDA.

JEHOIACHIN \ji-'hȯi-ə-ˌkin\, *also spelled* Joachin, *Hebrew* Joiachin, in the OLD TESTAMENT (2 Kings 24), son of King JEHOIAKIM and king of JUDAH. He came to the throne at the age of 18 and reigned three months. He was forced to surrender to Nebuchadrezzar II and was taken to Babylon (597 BCE), along with 10,000 of his subjects. He was released nearly 40 years later.

JEHOIAKIM \ji-'hȯi-ə-ˌkim\, *also spelled* Joakim, in the OLD TESTAMENT (2 Kings 23:34–24:17; Jeremiah 22:13–19; 2 Chronicles 36:4–8), son of King JOSIAH and king of JUDAH (*c.* 609–598 BCE). Enthroned after his younger brother Jehoahaz (or Shallum) was taken to Egypt by the Egyptian conqueror Necho, Jehoiakim reigned under Egyptian protection for some time and paid heavy tribute. When the new Chaldean Empire under Nebuchadrezzar II defeated Egypt at the Battle of Carchemish (605), however, Jehoiakim changed his allegiance to Nebuchadrezzar. He remained loyal for three years but then revolted; after several battles and invasions, Nebuchadrezzar succeeded in besieging Jerusalem (598). Jehoiakim died at this time, but the circumstances of his death remain uncertain.

JEHORAM \jə-'hō-rəm\, *also called* Joram \'jō-rəm\, *Hebrew* Yehoram, *or* Yoram, one of two contemporary OLD TESTAMENT kings.

Jehoram, the son of AHAB and JEZEBEL and king (*c.* 850–*c.* 842 BCE) of ISRAEL (2 Kings 1:17; 3:1–2), maintained close relations with JUDAH. Together with JEHOSHAPHAT, king of Judah, Jehoram unsuccessfully attempted to subdue a revolt of Moab against Israel (2 Kings 3:1–27). As had his father, Jehoram later endeavored to recover Ramoth-gilead from Hazael, king of Damascus. In this matter he was aided by his nephew Ahaziah, then king of Judah. Wounded during the fighting at Ramoth-gilead, Jehoram retired to Jezreel in Judah (2 Kings 8:28–29; 2 Chronicles 22:5–6). During his convalescence a revolution took place and JEHU was anointed king at Ramoth-gilead. Jehu then put to death all the members of Ahab's family including Jehoram, Jezebel, and Ahaziah (2 Kings 9:1–37; 2 Chronicles 22:7–9).

Jehoram, son of Jehoshaphat and king (*c.* 851–*c.* 842 BCE) of Judah, married ATHALIAH, daughter of Ahab, and was thus brother-in-law of the Jehoram of Israel.

JEHOSHAPHAT \ji-'hä-sə-ˌfat, -shə-\, *also called* Josaphat \'jä-sə-ˌfat\, *Hebrew* Yehoshaphat, king (*c.* 873–*c.* 849 BCE) of JUDAH during the reigns in ISRAEL of AHAB, Ahaziah, and JEHORAM, with whom he maintained close political and economic alliances (1 Kings 22:1ff.; 22:41–50). In Judah he reorganized the army and attempted to centralize political power through a series of religious and legal reforms (2 Chronicles 17:1–21:1).

JEHOVAH \ji-'hō-və\, Judeo-Christian name for God, derived from YHWH. The Masoretes, who from about the 6th to the 10th century worked to reproduce the original text of the Hebrew BIBLE, replaced the vowels of the Hebraic name YHWH with the vowel signs of the Hebrew words Adonai or ELOHIM. Thus, the artificial name Jehovah (YeHoWaH) came into being. *See* YAHWEH.

JEHOVAH'S WITNESS, an adherent of a millennialist sect (*see* MILLENNIALISM) that began in the United States in the 19th century and has since spread over much of the world; the group is an outgrowth of the International Bible Students Association founded in Pittsburgh, Pa., in 1872 by CHARLES TAZE RUSSELL.

The name Jehovah's Witnesses was adopted in 1931 by Russell's successor, Joseph Franklin Rutherford (Judge Rutherford; 1869–1942), who sought to reaffirm JEHOVAH as the true God and to identify those who witness in this name as God's specially accredited followers. Under his leadership, the democratic polity devised by Russell was replaced by a theocratic system directed from the society's headquarters in Brooklyn, N.Y.

Rutherford's policies were continued under his successor, Nathan Homer Knorr (1905–77). Knorr established the Watch Tower Bible School of Gilead (South Lansing, N.Y.) to train missionaries and leaders, decreed that all the society's books and articles be published anonymously, and set up adult education programs to train Witnesses to deliver their own apologetical talks. Under Knorr's direction a group of Witnesses produced a new translation of the Bible.

The Witnesses have little or no association with other denominations and maintain a complete separation from all secular governments. They regard world powers and political parties as the unwitting allies of SATAN. For this reason they refuse to salute the flag of any nation or to perform military services and almost never vote in public elections. Their beliefs also extend to religious denominations, and for many years they disavowed the use of such terms as minister, church, or congregation in their organizational structure. This attitude has changed, but they are still exclusive and insulated from the ecumenical movement of the 20th century. Their avowed goal is the establishment of God's Kingdom, the Theocracy, which they believe will emerge following ARMAGEDDON, their basis for this assumption being the apocalyptic books of the Bible, especially Daniel and the Book of Revelation. Theologically they hold that JESUS CHRIST is God's agent in establishing the Theocracy. The concept of a literal hell is rejected, as is the inevitability of eternal life. Death in certain instances can mean total extinction. Pastor Russell established 1874 as the year of Christ's "invisible return" and designated 1914 as the year of Christ's SECOND COMING and the end of the "times of the GENTILES." Date setting and PROPHECY among the Witnesses have given way, however, to a more contemporary analysis of modern life based on world events and what they regard as signs of the times.

Witnesses faced active persecution in Germany and other Axis countries during World War II as well as in several Allied countries where their work was banned. In the postcolonial era, they encountered hostility in a number of new African nations whose nationalism conflicted with the Watch Tower idea of theocracy.

The Witnesses meet in churches called Kingdom Halls, baptize by immersion, insist upon a high moral code in personal conduct, disapprove of divorce except on grounds of adultery, oppose blood transfusions on a scriptural basis, and have won many cases in the U.S. courts establishing their right to speak in accordance with their belief.

Most members of a local congregation, or "company," are kingdom publishers, who are expected to spend five hours a week at meetings in Kingdom Hall and spend as much time as circumstances permit in doorstep preaching. Pioneer publishers hold part-time secular jobs and try to devote 100 hours a month to religious service. Special pioneers are full-time, salaried employees of the society who should spend at least 150 hours a month in this work. Each Kingdom Hall has an assigned territory and each Witness a particular neighborhood to canvass. The sect takes great pains to keep records of the number of visits, back calls, Bible classes, and books and magazines distributed. Publishing activities include books, tracts, recordings, and periodicals, chief among which are a semimonthly magazine, the *Watchtower*, and its companion publication, *Awake!*, which during the early 1980s reached a circulation of more than 10,000,000 in some 80 languages.

JEHU \'jē-,hyü, 'jā-, -,hü\, *Hebrew* Yehu, king (*c.* 842–815 BCE) of Israel. He was a commander of chariots for the king of ISRAEL, AHAB, and his son JEHORAM, on Israel's fron-

Baptism by immersion of Jehovah's Witnesses
Archive Photos

Jehu prostrating himself before King Shalmeneser III of Assyria, Assyrian bas-relief sculpture known as the Black Obelisk; in the British Museum, London
Erich Lessing—Art Resource

tier facing Damascus and Assyria. During Jehoram's rule, Jehu accepted the invitation of the prophet ELISHA to overthrow the dynasty of Omri (started by Ahab's father).

Jehu's revolt, which extinguished the dynasty of Omri, took place at a time when the dynasty was already in decline. The narrator in 2 Kings is clearly in favor of Jehu, but within a century the prophet HOSEA would cite the bloodbath in Jezreel, capital of the northern kingdom of Israel, as reason for the imminent end of the kingdom (1:4–5). Jehu's success ended the standing Phoenician alliance, and Israel alone was no match for the incursions of Shalmeneser III of Assyria, who moved westward in 841 BCE. The second scene in the famous Black Obelisk in the British Museum shows Jehu making his obeisance before the great king.

JELLINEK, ADOLF \'ye-li-,nek\ (b. June 26, 1821, Drslavice, Moravia, Austrian Empire [now in Czech Republic]—d. Dec. 29, 1893, Vienna), RABBI and scholar who was the most forceful Jewish preacher of his time in central Europe.

From 1845 to 1856 Jellinek preached in Leipzig and from 1856 to 1893 in Vienna. More than 200 of his sermons were published (three volumes, 1862–66, and nine smaller collections, 1847–82), and these works measurably affected the development of the art of Jewish preaching.

Jellinek's scholarly activities chiefly comprised studies of the Qabbalah and Midrashic literature (*see* QABBALAH AND JEWISH MYSTICISM; MIDRASH). He was an exponent of *Wissenschaft des Judentums* ("science of Judaism"), the analysis of Jewish literature and culture with the tools of modern scholarly research. He was the first to compare the SEFER HA-ZOHAR, the fundamental text of the Qabbalists, with the Hebrew texts of MOSES DE LEÓN. Deducing that Moses de León was the principal author of the *Zohar*, Jellinek also postulated that the *Zohar* was an attempt to counteract the rationalist trend among his educated contemporaries. In the Midrashic field, he edited treatises on ancient and medieval homilies and documents of messianic thinking, such as *Bet ha-Midrash* (1853–77; "The House of Study").

JEN \'rən\, *Pinyin* ren, in Confucian philosophy, fundamental virtue variously translated as humaneness, warmheartedness, or benevolence. Before Confucius' time *jen* was understood as the kindness of rulers to their subjects. It was gradually broadened to mean benevolence in general, and CONFUCIUS further changed it to connote perfect virtue, which includes all particular virtues and applies to all people. MENCIUS went on to say that *jen* is the distinguishing characteristic of man. During the Han period it was generally interpreted as love, and HAN YÜ in the T'ang period stressed it as love for all humanity.

Under the influence of BUDDHISM, the followers of NEO-CONFUCIANISM in the Sung and Ming dynasties extended *jen* to mean "forming one body with Heaven, Earth, and all things." Some Sung Neo-Confucianists took *jen* to be a state of consciousness. CHU HSI called it "the character of the mind and the principle of love," and WANG YANG-MING equated it with the "clear character" of innate knowledge. Seventeenth- and 18th-century Neo-Confucianists returned to an emphasis on its social and active aspects, but all Neo-Confucianists agreed that *jen*, or humanity, is a moral quality imparted by heaven, characterized by production and reproduction, and being both life-affirming and life-giving. Under the influence of Western science in the late 19th and early 20th centuries, modern Confucianists likened *jen* to electricity and ether, a dynamic force and an all-pervasive substance.

JEPHTHAH \'jef-thə\, a judge or regent (often a hero figure) of ISRAEL who dominates a narrative in the Book of Judges, where he is presented as an exemplar of faith for Israel in its monotheistic commitment to YAHWEH. Of the Israelite tribe in Gilead (present northwest Jordan), he was banished from his home and became the head of a powerful band of brigands (Judges 11:1–3). He successfully defeated the non-Israelite peoples of Hauran and Ammon but at the cost, according to the story, of having to sacrifice his daughter to Yahweh in fulfillment of a vow setting the price of victory (Judges 11:12–40), a possible mythological basis for dedicating certain Israelite women to virginity. Scholars interpret the story of Jephthah as an expression of the Book of Judges' theological significance; namely, that Israel's fortunes fluctuated depending on the degree of their fidelity to Yahweh.

JEREMIAH \,jer-ə-'mī-ə\, *Hebrew* Yirmeyahu, *Latin* Vulgate Jeremias \-'mī-əs\ (b. probably after 650 BCE, Anathoth, Judah—d. *c.* 570 BCE, Egypt), Hebrew prophet, reformer, and author of an OLD TESTAMENT book that bears his name.

Life and times. Jeremiah was born and grew up in the village of Anathoth, a few miles northeast of Jerusalem, in a priestly family (Jeremiah 1:1; *cf.* Joshua 21:18). In his childhood he must have learned the prophecies of HOSEA, whose influence can be seen in his early messages. The era in which he lived was one of transition for the ancient Near East. During Jeremiah's lifetime the foremost power was the Neo-Babylonian Empire, ruled by a Chaldean dynasty whose best known king was Nebuchadrezzar (Jeremiah 21:2). The small and comparatively insignificant state of JUDAH had been a vassal of Assyria and, when Assyria declined after two centuries of dominance, Judah asserted its independence for a short time (2 Kings 24:1; 2 Chronicles 36:13). Subsequently, Judah vacillated in its allegiance between Babylonia and Egypt and ultimately became a province of the Neo-Babylonian Empire (Jeremiah 37–39; 2 Kings 25; 2 Chronicles 36:1–21).

According to the biblical Book of Jeremiah, he began his prophetic career in 627/626—the 13th year of King JOSIAH'S reign (Jeremiah 1:2). Jeremiah's early messages to the people were condemnations of them for their false worship and social injustice, with summons to repentance. He proclaimed the coming of a foe from the north, symbolized by a boiling pot facing from the north in one of his visions, that would cause great destruction (Jeremiah 1:13ff.), though scholars have differed in their identification of the northern foe to which he was referring.

Jeremiah commended King Josiah for doing justice and righteousness, but denounced his son JEHOIAKIM harshly for his selfishness, materialism, and practice of social injustice. Early in the reign of Jehoiakim, Jeremiah delivered his famous "Temple sermon," of which there are two versions, one in Jeremiah, chapter 7, verses 1 to 15, the other in chapter 26, verses 1 to 24. He denounced the people for their dependence on the Temple for security and called on them to effect genuine ethical reform. He predicted that God would destroy the TEMPLE OF JERUSALEM, as he had earlier destroyed that of SHILOH, if they continued in their present path. Jeremiah was immediately arrested and tried on a capital charge, but was later acquitted.

Near the time of the Battle of Carchemish, in 605, when the Babylonians decisively defeated the Egyptians and the remnant of the Assyrians, Jeremiah delivered an oracle against Egypt. When Jehoiakim withheld tribute from the Babylonians (about 601), Jeremiah began to warn the Judaeans that they would be destroyed at the hands of those who had previously been their friends. When the King persisted in resisting Babylonia, Nebuchadrezzar sent an army to besiege Jerusalem. King Jehoiakim died before the siege began and was succeeded by his son, JEHOIACHIN, who surrendered the capital to the Babylonians on March 16, 597, and was taken to Babylonia with many of his subjects. The Babylonians placed on the throne of Judah a king favorable to them, Zedekiah (597–586 BCE), who was more inclined to follow Jeremiah's counsel than Jehoiakim had been but was weak and vacillating. After paying Babylonia tribute for nearly 10 years, however, the King made an alliance with Egypt. A second time Nebuchadrezzar sent an army to Jerusalem, which he captured in August 586.

Early in Zedekiah's reign, Jeremiah wrote a letter to the exiles in Babylonia, advising them not to expect to return immediately to their homeland, as false prophets were encouraging them to believe, but to settle peaceably in their place of exile and seek the welfare of their captors. When emissaries from surrounding states came to Judah in 594 to enlist Judah's support in rebellion against Babylonia, Jeremiah put a yoke upon his neck and went around proclaiming that Judah and the surrounding states should submit to the yoke of Babylonia, for it was YAHWEH who had given them into the hand of the King of Babylonia (Jeremiah 27).

Even to the time of the fall of Jerusalem, Jeremiah's message remained the same: submit to the yoke of Babylonia.

When Jerusalem finally fell, Jeremiah was entrusted to Gedaliah, a Judaean from a prominent family whom the Babylonians appointed as governor of the province of Judah. After Gedaliah was assassinated, Jeremiah was taken against his will to Egypt by some of the Jews who feared reprisal from the Babylonians. Even in Egypt he continued to rebuke his fellow exiles. Jeremiah probably died in about 570 BCE. According to a tradition that is preserved in extrabiblical sources, he was stoned to death by his exasperated fellow countrymen in Egypt.

Main teachings and prophecy. Jeremiah is noteworthy for his rich use of literary tools, especially of metaphor, simile, symbolic action, and drama to convey his message which is both of judgment (before the destruction of Jerusalem) and of comfort (to the exiles in Babylonia). The prophet is concerned with the immensity of evil in the nation and the just punishment that will surely follow. Hence, Jeremiah preaches inescapable divine justice: reward and punishment, repayment of GOOD AND EVIL, and the inevitable results of faithfulness and disobedience. These themes find expression in his metaphors (borrowed from Hosea) of the marriage and parental relationships, in which the wife is to submit to the husband and the children to the father (Jeremiah 2:2b–3; 19–25; 31:32). Likewise, Israel is to submit fully to God's covenantal law, responding to his love and free GRACE. Jeremiah freely denounces the foreign rulers and powers that threaten Israel or to whom Israel turns for aid (Jeremiah 4:7; 5:6; 8:17; 25:32), but he reserves his harshest judgment for Israel itself, whose rejection of God and worship of BAALS he likens to a prostitute cavorting with many lovers (Jeremiah 2:20; 3:1–3), a faithless wife (Jeremiah 3:20), wayward children (Jeremiah 3:21–22), and animals in heat (Jeremiah 2:23–24; 5:8).

In CHRISTIANITY, Jeremiah's most important prophecy concerning the future is that of the new COVENANT (Jeremiah 31:31–34; 32:38–40; cf. EZEKIEL 11:19). He prophesied of a time when Yahweh would make a covenant with Israel; Yahweh would write his law upon the hearts of men (rather than on tables of stone, as with the old Mosaic covenant), and all would know God directly and receive his forgiveness. This prophecy was very influential in some NEW TESTAMENT writings (Hebrews 8:8–13; 10:16–17) and lies behind the words attributed to Jesus at the LAST SUPPER: "This cup...is the new covenant in my blood" (Luke 22:20; cf. Matthew 26:28; Mark 14:24; John 13:34).

JERICHO \'jer-i-ˌkō\, *Arabic* Arīḥā \ä-'rē-hä\, town in the West Bank area occupied by Israel since 1967, on the west side of the Jordan River valley. It is one of the earliest continuous settlements in the world, dating perhaps from about 9000 BCE.

Jericho is famous in biblical history as the first town attacked by the Israelites under JOSHUA after they crossed the Jordan River (Joshua 6). OLD TESTAMENT Jericho has been identified in the mound known as Tall as-Sulṭān (at the source of the copious spring 'As-Sulṭān), which rises 70 feet above the surrounding plain. After the town's destruction by the Israelites the site was abandoned until the Iron Age, when (according to the biblical account) Hiel the Bethelite established himself there in the 9th century BCE (1 Kings 16:34). There was a sizable settlement in the 7th century BCE, ending perhaps at the time of the second BABYLONIAN EXILE in 586 BCE. The site was then finally abandoned, and later Jerichos grew up elsewhere; the site of the Roman and

Excavation of the Tall as-Sulṭān, ancient site of Jericho
By courtesy of the Jericho Excavation Fund

NEW TESTAMENT Jericho is approximately one mile south of that of the Old Testament town.

JEROME, SAINT, *Latin in full* Eusebius Hieronymus, *pseudonym* Sophronius

(b. *c.* 347, Stridon, Dalmatia—d. 419/420, Bethlehem, Palestine; feast day September 30), biblical translator and monastic leader, traditionally regarded as the most learned of the Latin Fathers.

Jerome was born of well-to-do Christian parents. His education, begun at home, was continued in Rome when he was about 12. There he studied grammar, rhetoric, and philosophy. He frequented the CATACOMBS and was baptized (*c.* 366), probably by Pope Liberius.

He spent the next 20 years in travel. At Treveris (now Trier), he was profoundly attracted to MONASTICISM. In Aquileia (Italy) he was linked with an ascetic elite grouped around Bishop Valerianus. When the group disbanded (*c.* 373), Jerome decided to go on a trip through the East. On reaching Antioch in 374, he composed his earliest known work, *De septies percussa* ("Concerning Seven Beatings"). There also, in mid-Lent 375, during a near-fatal illness, he had a celebrated dream, in which he was dragged before a tribunal of the Lord, accused of being a Ciceronian—a follower of the 1st-century-BCE Roman philosopher—rather than a Christian, and was severely lashed; he vowed never again to read or possess pagan literature.

In 375 Jerome began a two-year search for inner peace as a HERMIT in the desert of Chalcis. His response to temptation was incessant prayer and fasting; he learned Hebrew from a Jewish convert, studied Greek, had manuscripts copied for his library and his friends, and carried on a brisk correspondence. The crisis arrived when Chalcis became involved with ecclesiastical and theological controversies. Suspected of harboring heretical views (*i.e.*, Sabellianism, which emphasized God's unity at the expense of the distinct persons), Jerome insisted that the answer to ecclesiastical and theological problems resided in oneness with the Roman bishop. Pope Damasus did not respond, and Jerome quit the desert for Antioch.

In Antioch his host, EVAGRIUS, won Jerome over to the party of Bishop Paulinus, who was opposed by BASIL, the great orthodox bishop of Caesarea. Recognizing his importance—since Jerome was by now known as a scholar and a monastic figure of significance—Paulinus decided to ordain him. Jerome accepted (378) on two conditions: his monastic aspirations would not be prejudiced, and priestly functions would not be forced on him. He attended the exegetical lectures of Apollinaris of Laodicea and visited the Nazarenes (Jewish Christians) of Beroea to examine their copy of a Hebrew gospel purporting to be the original Gospel of Matthew.

Jerome spent almost three years (379–382) continuing his pursuit of scriptural studies. An enthusiastic disciple of GREGORY OF NAZIANZUS, Jerome also came to know GREGORY OF NYSSA and the theologian Amphilochius of Iconium at the COUNCIL OF CONSTANTINOPLE (381). Under such influences he improved his knowledge of Greek and developed an admiration for the EXEGESIS of ORIGEN. He translated 14 of Origen's homilies (sermons) on OLD TESTAMENT books into Latin. He also translated the church historian Eusebius' *Chronicon* (*Chronicles*) and continued it to the year 378.

But the most decisive influence on Jerome's later life was his return to Rome (382–385) as secretary to Pope Damasus. There he pursued his scholarly work on the BIBLE, revised the Old Latin version of the Gospels on the basis of the best Greek manuscripts at his command, and made his first revision of the Old Latin Psalter based on a few SEPTUAGINT manuscripts. But his preaching in support of the monastic life and his relationship with the ascetic coterie, his castigation of Roman clergy, lax monks, and hypocritical virgins, and his correction of the gospel text provoked a storm of criticism and calumny, and in August 385 he left Rome in bitter indignation and made his way to the Holy Land. He settled in Bethlehem, where by 389 a wealthy Roman patroness built a monastery for men under Jerome's direction, three cloisters for women under her own supervision, and a hostel for pilgrims. Here Jerome lived, except for brief journeys, until his death.

The literary legacy of Jerome's last 34 years is the outgrowth of contemporary controversies, Jerome's passion for SCRIPTURE, and his involvement in monastic life. An anti-Origen movement in the east, fanned by the bishop EPIPHANIUS, turned Jerome not only against the views of Origen—whose 39 sermons on LUKE he had translated *c.* 389–392—but against his friends Bishop John of Jerusalem and Rufinus. His petulance in correspondence with ST. AUGUSTINE, stemming from the African's strictures on Jerome's biblical efforts, imperiled their mutual respect, as well.

Jerome's biblical production in Bethlehem includes two works helpful to biblical scholars: *Liber locorum* ("Book of Places"); and *Liber interpretationis Hebraicorum nominum* ("Book of Interpretation of Hebrew Names"). Continuing his revision of the Old Latin version of the Septuagint based on Origen's *Hexapla* (an edition with the Hebrew text in Hebrew and Greek characters, and four different Greek versions arranged in six parallel columns), Jerome revised Ecclesiastes, Proverbs, the Song of Solomon, Chronicles, and Job, and to his Roman revision of the Psalms added Origen's diacritical notes. Between 391 and 406 he produced his Latin translation of the Old Testament, as well. This completed his contribution to the version of the Bible known as the VULGATE. His commentary on Ecclesiastes (c. 387) is a milestone in exegesis, because it is the first original Latin commentary that takes advantage of the Hebrew text. Perhaps Jerome's best commentaries are on the prophets of the Old Testament.

JERUSALEM, COUNCIL OF \jə-'rü-sə-ləm, -'rü-zə-\, conference of the Christian Apostles in Jerusalem about 50 CE which decreed that GENTILE Christians did not have to observe the Mosaic Law of the Jews. It was occasioned by the insistence of certain Judaic Christians from Jerusalem that Gentile Christians from Antioch in Syria obey the Mosaic custom of CIRCUMCISION. A delegation, led by the apostle PAUL and his companion Barnabas, was appointed to confer with the elders of the church in Jerusalem.

The ensuing apostolic conference (noted in Acts 15:2–35), led by the apostles PETER and JAMES, decided the issue in favor of Paul and the Gentile Christians. From this time onward Gentile Christians were not bound by the Levitical ceremonial regulations, except for the provisions of the so-called apostolic decree: abstention "from what has been sacrificed to idols and from blood and from what is strangled and from unchastity" (Acts 15:29).

JERUSALEM, TEMPLE OF, either of two temples at the center of worship and national identity in ancient Israel.

In the early years of the Israelite kingdom, the ARK OF THE COVENANT was periodically moved about among several sanctuaries, but after King DAVID'S capture of Jerusalem, the Ark was moved to that city. This action joined Israel's major religious object with the monarchy and the city itself into a central symbol of union of the Israelite tribes. As the site for a future temple, David chose Mount Moriah, or the Temple Mount, where it was believed ABRAHAM had built the altar on which to sacrifice his son ISAAC.

The First Temple was constructed during the reign of David's son, SOLOMON, and completed in 957 BCE. Other sanctuaries retained their religious functions, however, until JOSIAH (reigned c. 640–609 BCE) abolished them and established the Temple of Jerusalem as the only place of sacrifice in the Kingdom of JUDAH. The First Temple was built as an abode for the Ark and as a place of assembly. The Temple building faced eastward. It was oblong and consisted of three rooms: the porch, or vestibule (*'ulam*);

the main room of religious service, or Holy Place (*hekhal*); and the HOLY OF HOLIES (*devir*), the sacred room in which the Ark rested. A storehouse (*yaẓi'a*) surrounded the Temple except on its front (east) side.

The First Temple contained five altars: one at the entrance of the Holy of Holies, two others within the building, a large bronze one before the porch, and a large tiered altar in the courtyard. A huge bronze bowl, or "sea," in the courtyard was used for the priests' ABLUTIONS. Within the Holy of Holies, two cherubim of olive wood stood with the Ark; this innermost SANCTUARY was considered the dwelling place of the Divine Presence (Shekhina) and could be entered only by the HIGH PRIEST and only on YOM KIPPUR. Nebuchadrezzar II of Babylonia removed the Temple treasures in 604 BCE and 597 BCE and totally destroyed the building in 587/586. This destruction and the deportations of Jews to Babylonia in 586 and 582, which came to be seen as fulfillments of PROPHECY, established JUDAISM as an international religion whose adherents, nonetheless, continued to hope for the reestablishment of the independent Jewish state.

Cyrus II, founder of the Achaemenian dynasty of Persia and conqueror of Babylonia, in 538 BCE issued an order allowing exiled Jews to return to Jerusalem and rebuild the Temple. Work was completed in 515 BCE. The Second Temple, which was constructed as a modest version of the original building, was surrounded by two courtyards with chambers, gates, and a public square. It did not include the ritual objects of the First Temple. Ritual, however, was elaborate and was conducted by well-organized families of priests and LEVITES.

Orthodox Jews praying at the Western Wall, the last remnant of the Second Temple of Jerusalem
Jan Lukas—Photo Researchers

During the Persian and Hellenistic (4th–3rd century BCE) periods, the Temple generally was respected, and in part subsidized, by Judaea's foreign rulers. Antiochus IV Epiphanes, however, plundered it in 169 BCE and desecrated it in 167 BCE by commanding that sacrifices be made to ZEUS on an altar built for him. This final act touched off the Hasmonean revolt, during which Judas Maccabeus (*see* MACCABEES) cleansed and rededicated the Temple (the event celebrated in the annual festival of HANUKKAH). During the Roman conquest, Pompey entered (63 BCE) the Holy of Holies but left the Temple intact. In 54 BCE, however, Crassus plundered the Temple treasury. Of major importance was the rebuilding of the Second Temple begun by Herod the Great, king (37 BCE–4 CE) of Judaea. Construction began in 20 BCE and lasted for 46 years. The area of the Temple Mount was doubled and surrounded by a wall with gates. The Temple was raised, enlarged, and faced with white stone.

The rebellion against Rome that began in 66 CE soon focused on the Temple and effectively ended with the Temple's destruction on the 9th/10th of Av, 70 CE. All that remained of the Temple was a portion of the Western Wall (also called the Wailing Wall), which continues to be the focus of Jewish aspirations and PILGRIMAGE. Made part of the wall surrounding the Muslim DOME OF THE ROCK and AL-AQSA MOSQUE in 691 CE, it returned to Jewish control in 1967.

JESSE \\'je-sē\\, *also spelled* Isai \\'ī-ˌzī\\, in the OLD TESTAMENT, the father of King DAVID. Jesse was the son of Ohed, and the grandson of Boaz and Ruth (Ruth 4:22). He was a farmer and sheep breeder in Bethlehem (1 Samuel 17:15–18). David was the youngest of Jesse's eight sons (1 Samuel 16:11; 17:14). The appellation "son of Jesse" became a standard poetic metaphor in the BIBLE, expanded by phrases such as "root of Jesse" and "stump of Jesse" (Isaiah 11:1,10) expand the metaphor. All evoke the figure of David.

Because Jesus belonged to one of the family branches descended from King David (Matthew 1:6; Luke 3:31), it became customary for medieval artists to visually depict Jesus' genealogy as beginning with Jesse in such works as the stained-glass windows known as Jesse windows.

JESUIT \\'je-zù-it, -zhù-, -zyù-\\, member of the Society of Jesus (S.J.), a ROMAN CATHOLIC order of religious men, founded by ST. IGNATIUS OF LOYOLA, noted for its educational, missionary, and charitable works. The order was once regarded by many as the principal agent of the COUNTER-REFORMATION and later a leading force in modernizing the church.

The order grew out of the activity of Ignatius, a Spanish soldier who in 1539 drafted the first outline of the order's organization, which Pope Paul III approved on Sept. 27, 1540. The society introduced several innovations in the form of the religious life. Among these were the discontinuance of many medieval practices—such as regular penances or fasts obligatory on all, a common uniform, and the choral recitation of the liturgical office—in the interest of greater mobility and adaptability. Other innovations included a highly centralized form of authority with life tenure for the head of the order; probation lasting many years before final vows; gradation of members; and lack of a female branch. Particular emphasis was laid upon the virtue of obedience, including special obedience to the POPE. Emphasis was also placed upon flexibility, a condition that allowed Jesuits to become involved in a great variety of ministries in all parts of the world.

The society grew rapidly, and it quickly assumed a prominent role in the Counter-Reformation defense and revival of Catholicism. Almost from the beginning, education and scholarship became the principal work. The early Jesuits, however, also produced preachers and catechists who devoted themselves to the care of the young, the sick, prisoners, prostitutes, and soldiers; and they were often called upon to undertake the controversial task of confessor to many of the royal and ruling families of Europe. The society entered the foreign MISSION field within months of its founding. More Jesuits were to be involved in missionary work than in any other activity, save education. By the time of Ignatius' death in 1556, about 1,000 Jesuits were already working throughout Europe and in Asia, Africa, and the New World. By 1626 the number of Jesuits was 15,544; and in 1749 the total was 22,589.

The preeminent position of the Jesuits among the religious orders and their championship of the pope exposed them to hostility. In 1773 Pope Clement XIV, under pressure especially from the governments of France, Spain, and Portugal, issued a decree abolishing the order. The society's corporate existence was maintained in Russia, where political circumstances—notably the opposition of Catherine II the Great—prevented the canonical execution of the suppression. The demand that the Jesuits take up their former work, especially in the field of education and in the missions, became so insistent that in 1814 Pope Pius VII reestablished the society.

After the restoration, the order grew to be the largest order of male religious. Work in education on all levels continued to involve more Jesuits than any other activity; but the number of Jesuits working in the mission fields, especially in Asia and Africa, exceeded that of any other religious order. They were also involved in the field of communications, in social work, in ecumenical groups, and even in politics.

JESUS CHRIST \\'jē-zəs-'krīst, -zəz-\\, *also called* Jesus of Nazareth (b. *c.* 6 BCE, Judaea—d. *c.* 30 CE, Jerusalem), founder of the Christian faith and arguably the most important figure in the history of western civilization. To the faithful Christian, Jesus is the son of God and God incarnate whose sacrifice on the cross offers the promise of salvation and whose life and passion are the fulfillment of the Jewish Scriptures.

Although the earliest accounts of Jesus' life—the Synoptic Gospels of Matthew, Mark, and Luke and the more philosophical Gospel of John—are marked by inconsistencies and differing agendas and no independent account by contemporary authors exists, a picture of his life can be discerned from Scripture. According to Matthew, Jesus was born to the house of DAVID, as foretold in Jewish scripture and messianic traditions. He was born of Mary, the wife of the carpenter Joseph. According to Luke the birth occurred during the time of a census held by Augustus and according to Matthew during the reign of Herod the Great. Although the chronology of the Gospels is inconsistent, they do agree that Jesus was born in the town of Bethlehem, in support of Jewish messianic teachings, and raised in the Galilean town of Nazareth. Little is told of Jesus' early life except for the stories found in Luke concerning the presentation of Jesus at the Temple and the encounter of Jesus with the teachers in the Temple.

While his birth and youth, according to the evangelists, fulfilled scriptural prophecy, it was the adult ministry of Jesus that established the foundation of the faith. Once again the Gospels are not wholly consistent—differences in the length of the ministry and the number of visits to Jerus-

Jesus Christ as Ruler, with the Apostles and Evangelists (represented by the beasts), mosaic in the apse of Santa Pudenziana, Rome, 401–417 CE
De Antonis

alem exist—but a coherent picture of the ministry does emerge. It begins with the baptism of Jesus by JOHN THE BAPTIST. Indeed, Jesus recognized the importance of John's teachings and sought baptism from John. This episode has led to the suggestion that Jesus was a follower of John, and the affinities they had with the teachings of the ESSENES and related Judaic teachings lends some credence to this possibility. But, as John acknowledged, Jesus was the greater of the two and would go beyond John's own ministry. Jesus began to preach and recruited a number of disciples, including the twelve APOSTLES. Jesus' ministry was characterized by charismatic preaching exercised with great moral authority that in some ways challenged existing law but also, as Jesus says, fulfilled the law. His preaching, which was often in the form of parables, spoke of the coming of the kingdom of God and demanded repentance of the people in preparation for the coming of the kingdom. Jesus was also a healer—curing a woman of an effusion of blood, healing the sick, and raising Lazarus from the dead—often in apparent violation of Sabbath prohibitions and Jewish laws of purity (*see* TOHORAH). The Gospels also record that Jesus was a miracle worker and that he calmed the seas, changed water into wine, and fed a great multitude with a few loaves and fishes.

The final chapter of Jesus' life involved his visit to Jerusalem. His entry at PASSOVER, riding a donkey, was heavily symbolic and evoked the messianic traditions of Judaism. It was in this final, although possibly not first, visit to Jerusalem that Jesus probably came to the attention of the authorities as a result of the incident at the TEMPLE OF JERUSALEM, in which he cast out the various merchants, declaring the Temple a house of prayer and not a den of thieves. He was questioned by Jewish leaders who, according to the Gospels, sought to put him in the wrong over such issues as the proper attitude toward the secular authority and over

matters concerning resurrection. While in Jerusalem Jesus responded to the questions of the Scribes saying that the highest commandment is to love God. He also prophesied the impending destruction of Jerusalem and the world.

The most important events of his time in Jerusalem involved his LAST SUPPER and Passion, the events surrounding his trial and death. He established the new COVENANT by instituting the Eucharist and sharing the bread and wine—his body and blood—with the disciples, who were told to do this in his memory. He was betrayed by one of these disciples, JUDAS ISCARIOT, and condemned to death. For the Jewish authorities he was guilty of violating the law of Moses and blasphemy and for the Romans he was guilty of inciting the overthrow of Roman authority. Indeed, the Romans reserved the horrible punishment of CRUCIFIXION for their most dangerous political criminals. Recognizing himself as the suffering servant, Jesus quietly accepted his fate, forbidding his followers to defend him in the garden of GETHSEMANE when he was arrested and enduring his punishment. Suffering on the CROSS, he sought forgiveness for those around him and commended his soul to God. The sacrifice on the cross was followed by the burial and by the resurrection of Jesus three days later. Having risen, he met Mary Magdalene and other women before revealing himself to his disciples and commanding them to make disciples of all nations, baptizing them in the name of the Father, and of the Son, and of the Holy Spirit (Matthew 28:20).

To understand the teachings of Jesus fully, it is necessary to place him in the context of the JUDAISM of his time. Jesus was in many ways an observant Jew—honoring the Passover, attending the Temple, and adhering to biblical teaching. Furthermore, the apocalyptic fervor of the period, the beliefs of the QUMRĀN sect, and the teachings of the PHARISEES shed considerable light on the message of Jesus. During his lifetime there was a wide range of messianic teachings, from the violence of the ZEALOTS to the otherworldly teachings of the Essenes, which foresaw the coming of a savior from the house of David. Notions of the "son of man" as an eschatological figure were current in Jewish circles as well. The Pharisees, moreover, taught a doctrine that included bodily resurrection, ANGELS, and SATAN, and they held an eschatological outlook (see ESCHATOLOGY).

Although Jesus was a part of contemporary Judaism, he made these traditions uniquely his own. Reluctant to identify himself as the MESSIAH, he called himself the son of man and placed himself in the contemporary messianic context. His passion can best be understood in light of the suffering servant as prophesied in Isaiah, whose sacrifice atones for the sins of others. His calls to personal moral reform and repentance, too, must be seen in the context of the imminent coming of the kingdom of God that he preached. His moral reform is outlined in the "SERMON ON THE MOUNT," in which he taught that the kingdom of God awaits the peacemakers, the poor in spirit, and those who have suffered in Jesus' name. The kingdom is not for the hypocrites nor the weak in spirit nor is for those who worship idols or material possessions. Indeed, he asserts that one "cannot serve God and Mammon." (Matthew 6:24) and that one must love God. Drawn from Jewish tradition but made his own, the doctrine Jesus taught was one of repentance and moral reform, the love of God and service to his will—service that Jesus undertook with his passion on the cross. The passion, Christians believe, was rewarded with resurrection and thus offers the hope of salvation to all.

JETHRO \\'jeth-ˌrō\\, *also called* Reuel, *or* Hobab, in the OLD TESTAMENT, priest of Midian of the KENITE clan, with whom MOSES took refuge after he killed an Egyptian and whose daughter Moses married (EXODUS 3:1).

After the Exodus, Jethro visited the Hebrews and brought with him Moses' wife and sons. There he officiated at a sacrifice and suggested that Moses appoint able men to assist him in judging his people, thus founding the Hebrew judiciary (Exodus 18). Jethro's Kenite descendants settled in Judaean territory in the Negev.

JEWISH CALENDAR, religious and civil dating system of both ancient and modern JUDAISM, which is based upon both lunar and solar cycles.

In the Jewish calendar in use today, a day is counted from sunset to sunset, a week comprises seven days, a month contains 29 or 30 days, and a year has 12 lunar months and approximately 11 days (or 353, 354, or 355 days). In order to bring the calendar in line with the annual solar cycle, a 13th month of 30 days is intercalated in the 3rd, 6th, 8th, 11th, 14th, 17th, and 19th years of a 19-year cycle. Therefore, a leap year may total from 383 to 385 days. The Jewish Era in use today was popularly accepted about the 9th century CE and is based on biblical calculations placing the creation in 3761 BCE.

The names of the months of the year are derived from Babylonian terms. (Before the Exile, the names were in Hebrew. Only four of these Hebrew names are known today; those being Ethanim, Bul, Abib, and Ziv.) The months are ordered according to religious usage and are:

Nisan (Abib): March–April of the Western Gregorian calendar
Iyyar (Ziv): April–May
Sivan: May–June
Tammuz: June–July
Av: July–August
Elul: August–September
Tishri (Ethanim): September–October
Ḥeshvan, or Marḥeshvan (Bul): October–November
Kislev: November–December
Ṭevet: December–January
Shevaṭ: January–February
Adar: February–March

The 13th month of the leap year, Adar Sheni (or ve-Adar), is intercalated before Adar and so contains the religious observances normally occurring in Adar.

The civil calendar begins with the month of Tishri, the first day of which is the holiday of ROSH HASHANAH. The SABBATH is observed on the seventh day of the week (Saturday). The annual cycle of the religious calendar begins with the celebration of PASSOVER (Pesaḥ) on Nisan 15–22. The next major holiday of the year is that of SHAVUOT, celebrated on Sivan 6–7, the second of the PILGRIM FESTIVALS. The TEN DAYS OF PENITENCE begin with Rosh Hashanah on Tishri 1–2 and end with YOM KIPPUR on Tishri 10. The last of the major holidays, and the third of the Pilgrim Festivals is SUKKOT which is celebrated on Tishri 15–21.

The Jewish religious calendar also includes a series of minor holidays—so called because they are not accompanied by the proscription of work—and fasts. HANUKKAH is celebrated for eight days, beginning on Kislev 25, and is marked by the lighting of candles, feasting, songs, and the giving of gifts to children. The five fast days commemorate tragic events in Jewish history. They are Shiva' 'Asar be-Tammuz (FAST OF TAMMUZ 17); TISHA BE-AV (Fast of Av 9), which commemorates the destruction of the First and Second Temples in 586 BCE and 70 CE, respectively; Tzom Gedaliahu (Tishri 3); 'Asara be-Ṭevet (Fast of Ṭevet 10); and Ta'anit Esther (Fast of Esther; Adar 13). Also celebrated are LAG BA-OMER (Iyyar 18), usually observed as a school holiday, and ṬU BI-SHEVAṬ (Shevaṭ 15), in modern times associated with the planting of trees in Israel.

Since the establishment of the modern state of Israel in 1948, three other holidays have been added to the Jewish calendar. They are HOLOCAUST Day (Nisan 27), Remembrance Day (Iyyar 4), and Independence Day (Iyyar 5).

JEZEBEL \\'je-zə-ˌbel\\, *also spelled* Jezabel (d. c. 843 BCE), in the OLD TESTAMENT (1 and 2 Kings), the wife of AHAB, King of Israel; by interfering with the exclusive worship of the Hebrew god YAHWEH, disregarding the rights of the common people, and defying the great prophets ELIJAH and ELISHA, she provoked the internecine strife that enfeebled Israel for decades. She has come to be known as an archetype of the wicked woman.

Jezebel was the daughter of the priest-king Ethbaal, ruler of the coastal Phoenician cities of Tyre and Sidon (modern Ṣaydā, Lebanon). When she married Ahab (ruled c. 874–c. 853), she persuaded him to introduce the worship of the Tyrian god Baal-Melkart. She tried to destroy those who opposed her; most of the prophets of Yahweh were killed at her command. These actions provoked the wrath of Elijah; according to 1 Kings 17, he prophesied the onset of a severe drought as divine retribution. Some time later, Elijah had the BAAL priests slain after they had lost a contest with him;

when Jezebel heard of the slaughter, she angrily swore to have Elijah killed, forcing him to flee (1 Kings 18:19–19:3).

A few years later, Ahab perished in battle with the Syrians. Jezebel lived on for approximately another 10 years. Elijah's successor, Elisha, provoked civil war by causing a military commander named JEHU to be made king of Israel, though Jezebel's son JEHORAM then ruled. Jehu killed Jehoram and then went to Jezebel's palace. Expecting him, she adorned herself and, looking down from her window, taunted him. Jehu ordered her eunuchs to throw her out the window. Later, when he commanded that she be properly buried as a king's daughter, it was discovered that dogs had eaten most of her body.

JIBRĪL \ji-'brēl\, *also spelled* Jabrā'īl, in ISLAM, the ARCHANGEL who acts as intermediary between God and man and as bearer of revelation to the prophets, most notably to MUHAMMAD.

Muhammad himself could not at first identify the spirit that possessed him, and the QUR'AN mentions him by name only three times. Jibrīl, however, became Muhammad's constant helper, according to the HADITH and Ibn Isḥāq's *Sīra*. He and the archangel MĪKĀL purified Muhammad's heart in preparation for the Prophet's ascension to heaven (*mi'rāj*), and then Jibrīl guided him through the various levels until they reached the throne of God. When Muhammad recited a supposed revelation acknowledging the PAGAN goddesses AL-LĀT, al-'Uzzā, and Manāt, Jibrīl chastised him for presenting as divine a message inspired by the devil. Jibrīl also helped Muhammad in times of political crisis, coming to his aid at the BATTLE OF BADR (624) with thousands of ANGELS, then telling him to attack the Jewish tribes of Banū Qaynuqā' and Banū Qurayẓa.

Muhammad generally only heard the voice of his inspiration, but, according to 'Ā'ISHA, his wife, he saw Jibrīl twice "in the shape that he was created" and on other occasions as a man resembling Diḥya ibn Khalīfa al-Kalbī, a disciple of Muhammad. Others have described the archangel as having 600 wings, each pair so enormous that they crowd the space between East and West. Jibrīl has also been depicted as sitting on a chair suspended between heaven and earth. The popular image of Jibrīl is of an ordinary, turbaned man, dressed in two green garments, astride a horse or a mule.

Muslim traditions concerning Jibrīl largely concur with biblical accounts of the angel GABRIEL, but his special relationship with Muhammad inspired a large body of mythical detail. Jibrīl is said to have appeared at ADAM'S side after his expulsion from paradise and shown him how to write and work iron and raise wheat. Jibrīl later appeared in Egypt to help MOSES and to deceive the Egyptians into entering the Red Sea in pursuit of the Jews. His name figures in the preparation of charms and appears with those of the other archangels on the sides of magic squares.

JIGOKU \'jē-gò-kù\, in Japanese BUDDHISM, hell, a region popularly believed to consist of a number of hot and cold regions under the earth. Jigoku is ruled over by Emma-ō, the Japanese lord of death, who judges the dead. He is assisted in examining the dead by two disembodied heads on pillars at either side of him. The female head, Miru-me, can perceive the sinner's faults, while the male head, Kagu-hana, can detect any misdeed. Damnation is not eternal; the dead are sentenced to fixed periods of time, which can be shortened by the intervention of BODHISATTVAS.

The *Jigoku-zōshi*, a late 12th-century scroll, depicts the 8 great and the 16 lesser hells in both text and paintings.

JIHAD \ji-'häd\, *also spelled* jehad (Arabic: "fighting," or "striving"), in ISLAM, a key doctrine which calls upon believers to devote themselves to combating the enemies of their religion, both human and psychological, even if it means sacrificing their own material comforts and lives. As a doctrine of warfare, Islamic legal schools have offered various interpretations of when, how, and by whom it should be conducted. Generally, it may be offensive or defensive in nature, is subject to ethical injunctions upon combatants, and requires collective assent before it can be initiated. Alternately, Sufis (*see* SUFISM) have conceived of the "greater jihad" as combat against inner impulses and evil desires that prevent seekers from attaining spiritual renewal and a more intimate experience of God (*see* MUJĀHADA).

The classical juristic formulations of jihad, based on the QUR'AN and HADITH, were shaped by the experience of building both a community and an empire in a world of warring tribes and states. It was considered to be a duty that could be fulfilled in four ways: by the heart, the tongue, the hand, and the sword. The first is the "greater jihad" of the Sufis. The propagation of Islam through the tongue and hand is accomplished in large measure by supporting what is right and correcting what is wrong. The jihad of the sword, sometimes called the "lesser jihad," is to physically combat unbelievers and enemies of Islam. Believers who died in combat became martyrs and were guaranteed an esteemed place in paradise among the blessed. People of the Book (AHL AL-KITĀB)—Christians and Jews in particular—were shown special consideration in the jihad code. They could embrace Islam, or if they agreed to submit to Islamic rulers by paying poll and land taxes, they could assume the status of a "protected" (*dhimmi*) community within the House of Islam (DĀR AL-ISLAM).

Through much of Islamic history, wars against other Muslim states as well as non-Muslim ones, even those with significant political overtones, were labeled jihads to rally support and delegitimate opponents. In the 18th and 19th centuries it was invoked by Islamic movements in many regions, including the WAHHĀBĪS in the Arabian Peninsula, the Algerians in northern Africa, USMAN DAN FODIO (d. 1817) in western Africa, the MAHDISTS of the Sudan, the followers of Ahmad Barelewi (d. 1831) in the Northwest Frontier Province (now Pakistan), and the NAQSHBANDĪYA Sufis in the Caucasus and China. During the 20th century jihad was transformed into an ideological weapon to combat western influences and secular national governments and to establish an ideal Islamic society. It inspired the radical Islamist organizations opposed to the Egyptian government and Israeli occupation of the West Bank and southern Lebanon. Even Iraq, with an avowed secular regime, used jihad in its propaganda campaign against coalition forces involved in the 1990–91 Persian Gulf war.

JĪLĪ, AL- \àl-jē-'lē\, *in full* 'Abd al-Karīm Quṭb al-Dīn ibn Ibrāhīm al-Jīlī (b. 1365—d. c. 1424), mystic whose doctrines of the "perfect man" became popular throughout the Islamic world.

Little is known about al-Jīlī's personal life. Possibly after a visit to India in 1387, he studied in Yemen during 1393–1403. Of his more than 30 works the most famous is *Al-insān al-kāmil fi ma'rifat al-awākhir wa'l-awā 'il* (partial Eng. trans., R.A. Nicholson, *Studies in Islamic Mysticism*), which contains his complex doctrine of the perfect man. The work shows clearly the influence of the pantheistic Spanish mystic IBN AL-'ARABĪ (d. 1240).

Al-Jīlī maintained that the perfect man can achieve unity

with the Divine Being. This unity is experienced not only by the prophets, from ADAM to MUHAMMAD, but also by others who reach the highest level of being (wujūd) and become, as it were, the most select of the select. At this level all contradictions, such as being with non-being and vengeance with mercy, are resolved. In every age the perfect man manifests the outward appearance and inner essences of the Prophet Muhammad. The perfect man is thereby a channel through which the community can enjoy contact with the Divine Being. Al-Jīlī claimed that, in the town of Zabīd in Yemen in 1393, he had met the Prophet Muhammad, who then manifested himself through al-Jīlī as SHAYKH, or spiritual leader. Al-Jīlī's doctrine of the perfect man later developed into a belief that all holy men and mystics were able to achieve contact and unity with God.

JIMMU \ˈjēm-ˌmü\, *in full* Jimmu Tennō \-ˈten-ˌnō\, *original name* Kow-Yamato-Iware-Hiko no Mikoto, legendary first emperor of Japan and founder of the imperial dynasty. Japanese chronicles record that Jimmu, a descendant of the sun goddess AMATERASU and husband of a descendant of the storm god SUSANOO, moved eastward from Hyuga in 607 BCE along Japan's Inland Sea, subduing tribes as he went. Arriving in YAMATO, he established his center of power there. Modern historians agree that there was an aggressive movement of peoples from the west, but date it to the early Common Era.

Jimmu Tennō (the posthumous reign name by which he is generally known) is said to be buried in Unebi. A SHINTŌ shrine was erected there by the Japanese government in 1890, but he has never had much of a cult following, despite his importance as a link between the ruling family of Japan and the divine ancestors.

JINA: *see* TĪRTHAṄKARA.

JINASENA \ˌji-nə-ˈsā-nə\, in JAINISM, 9th-century DIGAMBARA monk, philosopher, and poet whose royal patron, Amoghavarṣa I, renounced his throne to become Jinasena's disciple late in life. Jinasena was a disciple of Vīrasena. His commentary on the *Kaṣāyaprābhṛta* (a canonical Jain work) is highly respected by Digambaras. His *Ādipurāṇa*, a HAGIOGRAPHY of Ṛṣabha and his two sons Bāhubali and Bharata, provides the first discussion of Jain domestic rites, as well as depicting and lending authority to the CASTE system existent among the Jain laity of his day.

JINJA \ˈjēn-jä, *Angl* ˈjin-jə\, in SHINTŌ, the place where the spirit of a deity is enshrined or to which it is summoned. Historically, *jinja* were located in places of natural beauty; in modern times, however, urban shrines have become common. Though they may vary from large complexes of buildings to small roadside places of prayer, they generally consist of three units: (1) the *honden* (also called *shinden*), the main sanctuary, where the spirit of the deity is enshrined, normally approached only by the priests; here are offered the prayers which "call down" the KAMI and subsequently send it away; (2) the *heiden* (hall of offerings), or *norito-den* (hall for reciting prayers), where religious rites are performed by the priests; and (3) the *haiden* (hall of worship), where the devotees worship and offer prayers. Large shrines may have additional structures, such as the *kagura-den* (stage for ceremonial dance), *shamusho* (shrine office), *temizu-ya* (ABLUTION basin for washing hands and mouth before worshiping), and also *komainu* (statues of guardian animals) and *tōrō* (stone or bronze lanterns given as offerings). The sacred compound is demarcated by an entrance gateway, or TORII.

From the Meiji Restoration in 1868 to the end of World War II, Shintō shrines were governed by the home ministry and subsidized by government funds. Following the disestablishment of STATE SHINTŌ, and the constitutional prohibition of subsidies, the shrines have depended for support on the offerings of their parishioners and other worshipers and on revenue from tourism and local services such as kindergartens. Many priests work at second jobs to maintain themselves and their families.

JINN \ˈjin\, *singular* jinni, *also called* genie, *Arabic* jinnī, in Arabic mythology, supernatural spirits below the level of ANGELS and devils. *Ghūl* (treacherous spirits of changing shape), ʿIFRĪT (evil spirits), and *siʿlā* (treacherous spirits of invariable form) constitute classes of jinn. Jinn are beings of flame or air who are capable of assuming human or animal form and are said to dwell in inanimate objects, underneath the earth, in the air, and in fire. They possess the bodily needs of human beings and can be killed, but they are free from all physical restraints. Jinn delight in punishing humans for any harm done them, intentionally or not, and are said to be responsible for many diseases and all kinds of accidents; however, those knowing the proper magical procedure can exploit the jinn to their advantage.

Belief in jinn was common in early Arabia, where they were thought to inspire poets and soothsayers. MUHAMMAD originally feared that his revelations might be the work of jinn, and official ISLAM held that they, like human beings, would have to face eventual salvation or damnation. Jinn, especially through their association with magic, have always been favorite figures in North African, Egyptian, Syrian, Persian, and Turkish FOLKLORE and are the center of an immense popular literature. In India and Indonesia they have entered local Muslim imaginations by way of the Qurʾanic descriptions and Arabic literature.

An example of a Shintō jinja, *the main building of the Inner Shrine at Ise*
By courtesy of the Kokusai Bunka Shinkokai, Tokyo

JINNAH, MUHAMMAD 'ALI \\'ji-ˌnä, 'ji-nə\\, *also called* Qā'id-e A'ẓam (Perso-Arabic: "Great Leader") (b. Dec. 25, 1876, Karāchi, India [Pakistan]—d. Sept. 11, 1948, Karāchi), Indian Muslim politician, founder and first governor-general (1947–48) of Pakistan.

Jinnah was the child of a prosperous merchant who sent him to England to acquire business experience. Jinnah, however, had made up his mind to become a barrister. He completed his formal studies in London and also made a study of the British political system, frequently visiting the House of Commons, being especially influenced by the liberalism of William E. Gladstone. Jinnah also took a keen interest in the affairs of India and in Indian students and worked in the campaign of the PARSI leader Dadabhai Naoroji, a leading Indian nationalist who was the first Indian to sit in the British House of Commons.

Jinnah returned to India in 1896 and started his legal practice in Bombay. He first entered politics by participating in the 1906 Calcutta session of the Indian National Congress. Four years later he was elected to the Imperial Legislative Council. Admiration for British political institutions and an eagerness to raise the status of India in the international community and to develop a sense of Indian nationhood among the peoples of India were the chief elements of his politics. At that time, he still looked upon Muslim interests in the context of Indian nationalism.

But, by the beginning of the 20th century, the conviction had been growing among the Muslims that their interests demanded the preservation of their separate identity rather than amalgamation in the Indian nation that would for all practical purposes be Hindu. Largely to safeguard Muslim interests, the All-India Muslim League was founded in 1906, and Jinnah joined it in 1913. When the Indian Home Rule League was formed, he became its chief organizer in Bombay and was elected president of the Bombay branch.

Jinnah consistently worked to bring about the political union of Hindus and Muslims. It was largely through his efforts that the Congress and the Muslim League began to hold their annual sessions jointly, to facilitate mutual consultation and participation. In 1916 the two organizations held their meetings in Lucknow, where the Lucknow Pact was concluded. Under the terms of the pact, the two organizations put their seal to a scheme of constitutional reform that became their joint demand vis-à-vis the British government.

Meanwhile, a new force in Indian politics had appeared in the person of MOHANDAS K. GANDHI. Opposed to Gandhi's Non-cooperation Movement and his essentially Hindu approach to politics, Jinnah left both the League and the Congress in 1920. After his withdrawal from the Congress, he used the Muslim League platform for the propagation of his views. When the failure of the Non-cooperation Movement and the emergence of Hindu revivalist movements led to antagonism and riots between the Hindus and Muslims, the league gradually began to come into its own. Among Jinnah's problems during the following years was to convince the Congress, as a prerequisite for political progress, of the necessity of settling the Hindu-Muslim conflict.

To bring about such a rapprochement was Jinnah's chief purpose during the late 1920s and early 1930s. He called for a federal form of government, greater rights for minorities, one-third representation for Muslims in the central legislature, separation of the predominantly Muslim Sind region from the rest of the Bombay province, and the introduction of reforms in the North-West Frontier Province. Many Muslims, however, thought that he was too nationalistic in his policy and that Muslim interests were not safe in his hands, while the Indian National Congress would not even meet the moderate Muslim demands halfway. The Punjab Muslim League repudiated his leadership and organized itself separately. In disgust, Jinnah decided to settle in England. From 1930 to 1935 he was in London, devoting himself to practice before the Privy Council. But when constitutional changes were in the offing, he was persuaded to return home to head a reconstituted Muslim League.

Soon preparations started for the elections under the Government of India Act of 1935. In the elections of 1937 the Congress obtained an absolute majority in six provinces, and the league did not do particularly well. The Congress decided not to include the league in the formation of provincial governments, and exclusive all-Congress governments were the result. Relations between Hindus and Muslims started to deteriorate.

Jinnah had originally been dubious about the practicability of Pakistan, an idea that Sir MUHAMMAD IQBĀL had propounded to the Muslim League conference of 1930; but before long he became convinced that a Muslim homeland on the Indian subcontinent was the only way of safeguarding Muslim interests. Accordingly he converted the Muslim League into a powerful instrument for unifying the Muslims into a nation. On March 22–23, 1940, in Lahore, the league adopted a resolution to form a separate Muslim state, Pakistan. Pitted against Jinnah were men of the stature of Gandhi and Jawaharlal Nehru, but ultimately both the Congress and the British government had no option but to agree to the partitioning of India. Pakistan thus emerged as an independent state in 1947. Jinnah became the first head of the new state.

JĪVA \\'jē-və\\ (Sanskrit: "life essence"), according to the philosophy of JAINISM, "living sentient substance," or "SOUL," as opposed to *ajīva*, or "nonliving substance."

Souls are eternal and infinite in number and are not the same as the bodies that they inhabit. In a pure state (*mukta-jīva*), souls rise to the top of the universe, where they reside with other perfected beings and are never again reborn. Most souls are, however, bound to SAMSĀRA (mundane earthly existence) because they are covered with a thin veil of good or bad KARMA, which is conceived as a kind of matter, accumulated by the emotions in the same way that oil accumulates dust particles.

*Jīva*s are categorized according to the number of sense organs that they possess. Humans, gods, and DEMONS possess the five sense organs plus intellect. Minute clusters of invisible souls, called *nigoda*s, belong to the lowest class of *jīva* and possess only the sense of touch, share common functions such as respiration and nutrition, and experience intense pain. The whole space of the world is packed with *nigoda*s. They are the source of souls to take the place of the infinitesimally small number that have been able to attain MOKṢA.

Hindu thinkers also employ the term *jīva*, using it to designate the soul or self that is subject to embodiment. Since many Hindu schools of thought do not regard selfhood as intrinsically plural, however, they typically understand these individual *jīva*s as parts, aspects, or derivatives of the unifying ontological principle ĀTMAN, which is in turn identified with BRAHMAN. In this usage, *jīva* is short for *jīva-ātman*, an individual living being. Schools differ as to whether the relation between *jīva*s and *ātman*/Brahman should be understood as nondual (ADVAITA), nondual in a qualified way (VIŚIṢṬĀDVAITA), or simply dual (DVAITA).

JIZŌ \jē-'zō\: *see* KṢITIGARBHA.

JIZYA \'jiz-yə\, *also spelled* jizyah, head or poll tax that early Islamic rulers demanded from their non-Muslim subjects.

Islamic law made a distinction between two categories of non-Muslim subjects—pagans and *dhimmis* ("protected peoples," or "peoples of the book" [AHL AL-KITAB]; *i.e.,* those peoples who based their RELIGIOUS BELIEFS on sacred texts, such as Christians, Jews, and Zoroastrians). The Muslim rulers tolerated the *dhimmis* and allowed them to practice their religion. In return for protection and as a mark of their submission, the *dhimmis* were required to pay a special poll tax known as the *jizya*. The rate of taxation and methods of collection varied greatly from province to province and were greatly influenced by local pre-Islamic customs. In theory the tax money was to be used for charitable purposes and the payment of salaries and pensions. In practice, however, the revenues derived from the *jizya* were deposited in the private treasuries of the rulers. The Ottomans usually used the proceeds of the *jizya* to pay their military expenses.

A convert to ISLAM, in theory, was no longer required to pay the *jizya*. The Umayyad CALIPHS (661–750), however, faced with increasing financial difficulties, demanded the *jizya* from recent converts to Islam as well as from the *dhimmis*. This discrimination against converts was a cause of the Abū Muslim rebellion (747) in Khorāsān and helped to precipitate the downfall of the Umayyads.

JÑĀNA \'gnä-nə, 'gnyä-\ ("knowledge"), in Hindu philosophy, a word with a range of meanings focusing on a cognitive event that proves not to be mistaken. In the religious realm it especially designates the sort of knowledge that is a total experience of its object, particularly the supreme being or reality, as contrasted with *vijñāna*, "knowing one thing from another," or "practical knowledge." The total cognitive experience of the supreme object sets the soul free from the transmigratory life and the polarities this imposes upon thought. Its opposite, *ajñāna* (also called *avidyā*), is the false apprehension of reality that keeps the soul from attaining release; it is a form of mistaken knowledge, which has a large measure of validity as far as the realities of the present world are concerned but conceals the truth of a reality outside it.

In the BHAGAVAD GĪTĀ, *jñāna yoga* ("the discipline of knowledge") is recognized as one of three complementary paths to religious fulfillment. It centers on the recognition of the distinction between the perduring self and its transitory embodiments, a recognition fundamentally facilitated by the presence of the divine KRISHNA, who reorients the knowledge of his doubting interlocutor and ultimate devotee, ARJUNA.

JÑĀNEŚVAR \dnyä-'nāsh-wər, gnyä-\, *also called* Jñānadeva, *or* Dhyānadev (b. *c.* 1271–75, India—d. 1296, Alandi, India), foremost among the mystical poets of Maharashtra, and composer of the *Bhāvārthadīpikā* (popularly known as the *Jñāneśvarī*), a translation and commentary in Marathi oral verse on the Sanskrit classic BHAGAVAD GĪTĀ. Jñāneśvar was both a Vārkarī, a devotee of the Vaiṣṇava (*see* VAIṢṆAVISM) deity Viṭṭhal (Viṭhobā), and a practitioner of the Śaiva (*see* ŚAIVISM) YOGA of the Nāths. Born into a family that had renounced society (SANNYĀSĪ), Jñāneśvar was considered an outcaste when his family returned to Alandi after years of living in seclusion. To reinstate their socio-religious status, the family obtained a certificate of purity from a Brahmin council in the village of Paithan. Poems attributed to another Marathi poet, NĀMDEV, provide the oldest description of Jñāneśvar's life. Three collections of Nāmdev's songs describe Jñāneśvar's birth and meeting with Nāmdev, their travels together through northern India to holy sites, and his entrance into what his followers believe to be a deathless state of meditation (SAMĀDHI) at Alandi. There is a small temple at Alandi where the saint is entombed.

Jñāneśvar, along with Nāmdev, is placed historically at the emergence of the Vārkarī ("Pilgrim") devotional school, a 700-year-old sect particular to Maharashtra that conducts annual circumambulatory PILGRIMAGES throughout Maharashtra, culminating at the Viṭṭhal temple in PANDHARPUR in early July. Jñāneśvar composed the *Amṛtānubhāva*, a work on Upanishadic philosophy, and the *Haripāṭha*, a song praising the name of Hari (VISHNU). His siblings, two brothers, Nivṛttināth and Sopānadev, and particularly his sister Muktābāī, are themselves highly respected saints of the Vārkarī tradition.

JOAB \'jō-,ab\ (fl. 1000 BCE), in the OLD TESTAMENT, a military commander under King DAVID, who was David's maternal uncle (2 Samuel 2:13). Joab led the party that captured Jerusalem and as a reward was appointed commander in chief of the army (1 Chronicles 11:6). He played a leading part in many of David's victories (2 Samuel 10:7; 12:26) and led the force that crushed the rebellion of David's son ABSALOM; subsequently he killed Absalom, although David had commanded that his life be saved (2 Samuel 18:5, 14). Joab showed his characteristic ruthlessness in the murder of two of his potential rivals, Abner and Amasa (2 Samuel 3:26–30; 20:9–10; 1 Kings 2:5). During David's last days, Joab supported the abortive bid for the throne by David's son Adonijah (1 Kings 1:5–8) and was executed by the successful SOLOMON (1 Kings 2:28–35).

JOACHIM OF FIORE \yō-'ä-kēm . . . 'fyō-rā\, Fiore *also spelled* Floris, *Italian* Gioacchino da Fiore (b. *c.* 1130/35, Celico, Kingdom of Naples [Italy]—d. 1201/02, Fiore), Italian mystic, theologian, biblical commentator, philosopher of history, and founder of the monastic order of San Giovanni in Fiore.

Joachim, after a PILGRIMAGE to the Holy Land, became a CISTERCIAN monk at Sambucina and in 1177 ABBOT of Corazzo (Sicily). About 1191 he retired into the mountains to follow the CONTEMPLATIVE life. Although claimed as a fugitive by the Cistercians, Joachim was allowed by Pope Celestine III to form the disciples who gathered around him into the Order of San Giovanni in Fiore in 1196.

He was summoned by Pope Lucius III in 1184 and urged to press on with the biblical EXEGESIS he had begun. This probably refers to the *Liber concordie Novi ac Veteris Testamenti* ("Book of Harmony of the New and Old Testaments"), in which Joachim worked out his philosophy of history, primarily in a pattern of "twos"—the concords between the two great dispensations (or Testaments) of history, the Old and the New. But already Joachim's spiritual experience was creating in his mind his "pattern of threes." If the *spiritualis intellectus* springs from the letter of the OLD TESTAMENT and NEW TESTAMENT, then history itself must culminate in a final age of the spirit that proceeds from both the previous ages. Thus was born his trinitarian philosophy of history in which the three Persons are, as it were, built into the time structure in the three ages or *status* of the Father, Son, and HOLY SPIRIT.

In the *Expositio in Apocalypsim* ("Exposition of the Apocalypse"), Joachim seeks to probe the imminent crisis of evil, as pictured in the apocalyptic symbols of ANTICHRIST, and the life of the spirit to follow. His third main work, the *Psalterium decem chordarum* ("Psaltery of Ten Strings"), expounds his doctrine of the TRINITY through the symbol of a 10-stringed psaltery. Here and in a lost tract he attacked the doctrine of "quaternity" (an overemphasis on the "one essence" of the Godhead that seems to separate it from the three Persons of the Trinity and so create a fourth), which he attributed to PETER LOMBARD.

Joachim's visual imagination is expressed in the unique *Liber figurarum* ("Book of Figures"; discovered in 1937), a book of drawings and figures thought to be a genuine work by most Joachim scholars today. Here his vision of the culminating age of history is embodied in trees that flower and bear fruit luxuriantly at the top; his doctrine of the Trinity is expressed in remarkable geometric figures.

In his lifetime Joachim was acclaimed as a prophet, gifted with divine illumination, and this is how he was seen by the first chroniclers after his death, though the condemnation of his tract against Peter Lombard by the fourth LATERAN COUNCIL in 1215 dimmed his reputation for a time. The Spiritual FRANCISCANS at mid-13th century and various other FRIARS, monks, and sects down to the 16th century appropriated his PROPHECY of a third age, but the debate as to whether he was orthodox or heretic continues today.

JOAN, POPE \'jōn\, legendary female pontiff who supposedly reigned, as John VIII, for slightly more than 25 months, from 855 to 858, between the pontificates of Leo IV (847–855) and Benedict III (855–858). It has subsequently been proved that a gap of only a few weeks fell between Leo and Benedict and that the story is entirely apocryphal.

One of the earliest extant sources for the Joan legend is the *De septem donis Spiritu Sancti* ("The Seven Gifts of the Holy Spirit"), written by the 13th-century French DOMINICAN Stephen of Bourbon, who dated Joan's election to approximately 1100. In this account the nameless pontiff was a clever scribe who became a papal notary and later was elected pope; pregnant at the time of her election, she gave birth during the PROCESSION to the Lateran, whereupon she was dragged out of Rome and stoned to death.

The story was widely spread during the later 13th century, mostly by FRIARS. Support for the version that she died in childbirth and was buried on the spot was derived from the fact that in later years papal processions used to avoid a particular street, allegedly where the event had occurred.

The name Joan was not finally adopted until the 14th century; other names commonly given were Agnes or Gilberta.

According to later legend Joan was an Englishwoman, but her birthplace was given as the German city of Mainz—an apparent inconsistency that some writers reconciled by explaining that her parents migrated to that city. She supposedly fell in love with an English Benedictine monk and, dressing as a man, accompanied him to Athens. Having acquired great learning, she moved to Rome, where she became CARDINAL and pope. From the 13th century the story appears in literature, including the works of the Benedictine chronicler Ranulf Higden and the Italian humanists Giovanni Boccaccio and Petrarch.

In the 15th century, Joan's existence was regarded as fact, even by the COUNCIL OF CONSTANCE in 1415. During the 16th and 17th centuries the story was used for Protestant polemics. It was the Calvinist David Blondel who made the first determined attempt to destroy the fable in his *Éclaircissement familier de la question: Si une femme a été assise au siège papal de Rome* (1647; "Familiar Enlightenment of the Question: Whether a Woman Had Been Seated on the Papal Throne in Rome").

JOAN OF ARC, SAINT \'jōn ... 'ärk\, *French* Jeanne d'Arc \zhän-'dȧrk\, *byname* The Maid of Orléans (b. *c.* 1412, Domrémy, Bar, France—d. May 30, 1431, Rouen; canonized May 16, 1920; feast day May 30; French national holiday, second Sunday in May), national heroine of France, a peasant girl who, believing that she was acting under divine guidance, led the French army in a momentous victory at Orléans that repulsed an English attempt to conquer France during the Hundred Years' War. Captured a year afterward, Joan was burned by the English and their French collaborators as a heretic. She became the greatest national heroine of France; her achievement was a decisive factor in the awakening of French national consciousness.

Satan leaves the presence of God to test Job, engraving by William Blake, 1825, for an illustrated edition of the Book of Job

By courtesy of the trustees of the British Museum—photograph, J.R. Freeman & Co., Ltd.

JOB, THE BOOK OF \'jōb\, OLD TESTAMENT book that is often counted among the masterpieces of world literature. It is found in the third section of the biblical canon known as the KETUBIM, or Writings. The book's theme is the eternal problem of unmerited suffering, and it is named after its central character, Job, who attempts to understand the sufferings that engulf him.

The Book of Job may be divided into two sections of prose narrative, consisting of a prologue (Chapters 1–2) and epilogue (Chapter 42:7–17); and intervening poetic disputation (Chapters 3–42:6). The prose narratives date to before the 6th century BCE, and the poetry has been dated between the 4th and the 6th century BCE. Chapters 28 and 32–37 were probably later additions.

The poetic disputations are set within the prose framework of an ancient legend that originated outside ISRAEL. This legend concerns Job, a prosperous man of outstanding piety. SATAN tests whether or not Job's piety is rooted merely in his prosperity. But faced with the appalling loss of his possessions, his children, and finally his own health, Job still refuses to curse God. Three of his friends then arrive to comfort him, and at this point the poetic dialogue begins, which probes the meaning of Job's sufferings. Job proclaims his innocence and the injustice of his suffering, while his friends argue that Job is so afflicted because of personal SIN. A final conversation between Job and God resolves the dramatic tension without, however, solving the problem of undeserved suffering. The speeches evoke Job's trust in the purposeful activity of God in the world, even though God's ways remain mysterious and inscrutable.

JOHANAN BEN ZAKKAI \jō-'ha-nən-ben-'za-kā-ˌī, -zä-'kī\, one of the most important early rabbinic authorities, who was active during the last years of the Second TEMPLE OF JERUSALEM and, after its destruction (70 CE), was founder and head of the rabbinic academy at Jamnia (now Yibna). He is named as the final link in the chain of authorities in Mishnah Abot that begins with MOSES and concludes with the early rabbinic movement. He is said to have received the traditions of the oral TORAH from Shammai and HILLEL, the latter of whom called him "father of wisdom" and "father of the coming generations" (Y. Nedarim 39b).

Later sources speak of Johanan's importance as a teacher of the leading 2nd-century sages and as a principal authority in establishing the foundations of the MISHNAH. But the Mishnah itself quotes in his name only a few matters of law concerning cultic cleanness and, in several cases, related to the impact of the destruction of the Temple on liturgical practices. Later Talmudic sources add a large number of stories about his life and work, commenting frequently on his piety. Among these materials, perhaps most famous is the depiction of his actions during the war with Rome in 70 CE. Unable to convince the Jews of Jerusalem to give up their fight for freedom from Roman dominion, Johanan reportedly escaped the besieged city in a coffin and went to the Roman camp. There he met with Vespasian, whom he announced would be made emperor of Rome, a prediction that almost immediately was fulfilled. In recognition of his wisdom, Vespasian is said to have granted Johanan the right to establish at Jamnia a center for study and religious observance (B. Gittin 56a–b).

Johanan is noted for his teaching (M. Abot 2:8), "If you have learned much Torah, do not puff yourself up on that account, for it was for that purpose that you were created." His devotion to study and piety is depicted at B. Sukkah 28a:

> They said about Rabban Yohanan ben Zakkai: He never engaged in idle chatter, he never went four cubits without words of Torah and without wearing his phylacteries, no one ever got to the study house before him, he never slept in the study house, neither a real nap nor a snooze, he never reflected upon holy matters while in filthy alleys, he never left anyone behind him in the study house when he went out, no one ever found him sitting and dreaming, but only sitting and repeating traditions, only he himself opened the door of his

house for his disciples, he never said anything that he had not heard from his master, and he never said, "Time has come to arise from studying in the study house," except for doing so on the eve of Passover and on the eve of the Day of Atonement [when liturgical obligations required this]. And that is how R. Eliezer, his disciple, conducted himself after him.

JOHN OF DAMASCUS, SAINT, *also called* Saint John Damascene, *Latin* Johannes Damascenus (b. *c.* 675, Damascus—d. Dec. 4, 749, near Jerusalem; Western feast day December 4), Eastern Christian monk and doctor of the Greek and Latin churches who stood in the forefront of the ICONOCLASTIC CONTROVERSY and was also a preeminent intermediary between Greek and medieval Latin cultures.

John of Damascus succeeded his father as one of the Muslim caliph's tax officials, and while still a government minister he wrote three *Discourses on Sacred Images, c.* 730, defending their veneration against the Byzantine emperor Leo III and the Iconoclasts. The Iconoclasts obtained a condemnation of John at the Council of Hieria in 754 that was reversed at the second COUNCIL OF NICAEA in 787.

Soon after 730, John became a monk at Mar Saba, near Jerusalem, and there passed the rest of his life studying, writing, and preaching, acquiring the name "the Golden Orator" (Greek: Chrysorrhoas, literally "the Golden Stream"). Among his approximately 150 written works the most significant is *Pēgē gnōseōs* ("The Source of Knowledge"), a synthesis of Christian philosophy and doctrine that was influential in directing the course of medieval Latin thought and that became the principal textbook of Greek Orthodox theology. Its "Exposition [*Ekthesis*] of the Orthodox Faith," through its translation into oriental languages and Latin, served both Eastern and Western thinkers not only as a source of logical and theological concepts but also, by its systematic style, as a model for subsequent theological syntheses by medieval Scholastics in the West.

A counterpart to *The Source of Knowledge* is John's anthology of moral exhortations, the *Sacred Parallels*, culled from biblical texts and from writings of the CHURCH FATHERS. Among his literary works are several intricately structured HYMNS for the Greek liturgy, although his reputation in liturgical poetry rests largely on his revision of the Eastern Church's hymnal, the *Octoēchos*.

JOHN OF THE CROSS, SAINT, *original name* Juan de Yepes y Álvarez (b. June 24, 1542, Fontiveros, Spain—d. Dec. 14, 1591, Ubeda; canonized 1726; feast day December 14), one of the greatest Christian mystics and Spanish poets, doctor of the church, reformer of Spanish MONASTICISM, and cofounder of the order of Discalced CARMELITES.

John became a Carmelite monk at Medina del Campo, Spain, in 1563 and was ordained a priest in 1567. ST. TERESA OF ÁVILA enlisted his help (1568) in her restoration of Carmelite life to its original observance of austerity. A year later, at Duruelo, he opened the first Discalced Carmelite monastery. Reform, however, caused friction within the order and led to his imprisonment in 1576 and again in 1577 at Toledo, where he wrote some of his finest poetry. Escaping in 1578, he later won high office in the order, becoming vicar provincial of Andalusia from 1585 to 1587. Late in his life the Discalced Carmelites were again troubled by dissension, and he withdrew to absolute solitude.

John schematized the steps of mystical ascent—a self-communion that in quietude leads the individual from the distractions of the world to the sublime peace of reunion between the soul and God. John's schematization combines a poetic sensitivity for the nuances of mystical experience with a theological and philosophical precision guided by his study of ST. THOMAS AQUINAS. By virtue of his intense poems such as "Cántico espiritual" ("The Spiritual Canticle") and "Noche obscura del alma" ("The Dark Night of the Soul"), he achieves preeminence in Spanish mystical literature, expressing the experience of the mystical union between the soul and Christ.

JOHN PAUL II, POPE,

Latin Johannes Paulus, *original name* Karol Wojtyła (b. May 18, 1920, Wadowice, Pol.), pope from 1978, the first Polish pope in the ROMAN CATHOLIC church's history and the first non-Italian pope in 456 years. From the beginning of his reign he was an active pontiff, undertaking extensive travels to Latin America and the Caribbean, the United States and Canada, Africa, various European countries, India, the Far East, and Australia. On social questions, John Paul II was a conservative pope who firmly endorsed traditional Catholic views, such as prohibitions against abortion, use of contraceptives, divorce, political officeholding by nuns and priests, and ORDINATION of women to the PRIESTHOOD. His strongly centralized leadership and conservative teachings on doctrine aroused some dissent among more liberal Roman Catholic clergymen in western Europe and the Western Hemisphere. However, John Paul also championed democracy and economic justice for the developing nations of the world.

JOHN THE APOSTLE, SAINT,

also called Saint John the Evangelist, *or* Saint John the Divine (fl. 1st century CE), in Christian tradition, the author of three letters, the Fourth Gospel, and the REVELATION TO JOHN in the NEW TESTAMENT (although this last work now appears in fact to have been a collection of separate units that were composed by unknown authors who lived during the last quarter of the 1st century). He played a leading role in the early church at Jerusalem.

The son of Zebedee, a Galilean fisherman, and Salome, John and his brother JAMES were among the first disciples called by Jesus. In the Gospel According to Mark, John is always mentioned after James and was no doubt the younger brother. His mother was among those women who ministered to the circle of disciples. John and his brother, together with Simon Peter, formed an inner nucleus of intimate disciples. In the Fourth Gospel the sons of Zebedee are mentioned only once, as being at the shores of the lake of Tiberias when the risen Lord appeared; whether the "disciple whom Jesus loved" (who is

St. John the Baptist, fresco by Pinturicchio, 1504–05; in the chapel of St. John the Baptist, the cathedral of Siena, Italy
Alinari—Art Resource

never named) mentioned in this Gospel is to be identified with John (also not named) is not clear from the text.

John's authoritative position in the church after the RESURRECTION is shown by his visit with PETER to Samaria to lay hands on the new converts there. It is to Peter, James (not the brother of John but "the brother of Jesus"), and John that PAUL submitted his Gospel for recognition.

John's subsequent history is obscure and passes into legend. At the end of the 2nd century, Polycrates, bishop of Ephesus, claims that John's tomb is at Ephesus, identifies him with the beloved disciple, and adds that he "was a priest, wearing the sacerdotal plate, both martyr and teacher." That John died in Ephesus is also stated by IRENAEUS, bishop of Lyon *c.* 180 CE, who says John wrote his Gospel and letters at Ephesus and Revelation at Patmos. During the 3rd century, two rival sites at Ephesus claimed the Apostle's grave. One eventually achieved official recognition, becoming a shrine in the 4th century.

Legend was also active in the West, being especially stimulated by the passage in Mark 10:39, with its hints of John's martyrdom. TERTULLIAN reports that John was plunged into boiling oil from which he miraculously escaped unscathed. During the 7th century, this scene was portrayed in the Lateran BASILICA and located in Rome by the Latin Gate; it is still annually commemorated on May 6. John's feast day otherwise is December 27. This belief that John did not die is based on an early tradition. In the original form of the apocryphal Acts of John (second half of the 2nd century) the Apostle dies; but in later traditions he is assumed to have ascended to heaven like ELIJAH.

The legends that contributed most to medieval ICONOGRAPHY are mainly derived from the Acts of John, also the source of the notion that John became a disciple as a very young man. Iconographically, the young, beardless type is early and came to be preferred in the medieval West. In the Byzantine world the evangelist is portrayed as old, with long, white beard and hair, usually carrying his Gospel. His symbol as an evangelist is an eagle. Because of the inspired visions of the book of Revelation the Byzantine churches entitled him "the Divine," a title which appears in Byzantine manuscripts of Revelation but not the Gospel. John is also (along with GREGORY OF NAZIANZUS) titled "the Theologian," as expositor of the doctrine of the TRINITY.

JOHN THE BAPTIST, SAINT (b.

Judaea—fl. early 1st century CE), Jewish prophet of priestly origin who preached the imminence of God's Final Judgment and baptized those who repented in self-preparation for it; he is revered in the Christian church as the forerunner of JESUS CHRIST.

The primary sources for information about John are the four GOSPELS (Matthew, Mark, Luke, and John), THE ACTS OF THE APOSTLES, and JOSEPHUS' *Antiquities of the Jews.* All four Gospels recognize in John the forerunner of Jesus and the herald of of the imminent KINGDOM OF GOD. Each tries to reconcile John's precedence in time and Jesus' acceptance of his message and of a BAPTISM of repentance from his hands (elements suggesting subordination to John) with the author's belief in Jesus as MESSIAH and Son of God. In the Gospels of Matthew and Mark, John is the prophet ELIJAH returned; in Luke's Gospel and his Acts of the Apostles, John is inaugurator of the time of fulfillment of PROPHECY. John, however, reduces the Baptist to a model Christian preacher and omits any description of Jesus' baptism.

John was born somewhere in Judaea (localized at 'En Kerem from at least 530 CE) to Zechariah, a priest of the order of Abijah, and his wife, Elizabeth, perhaps a relative of MARY, the mother of Jesus. His formative years were spent in the Judaean desert, where monastic communities, such as the ESSENES, and individual HERMITS often educated the young in their own ideals. In 27/28 or 28/29 John attained public notice as a prophet. His austere camel-hair garment was the traditional garb of the prophets, and his diet of locusts and wild honey represented either strict adherence to Jewish purity laws or the ascetic conduct of a NAZIRITE. His message was that God's wrathful judgment on the world was imminent and that the people should repent their SINS, be baptized, and produce appropriate fruits of repentance.

Although John had an inner circle of disciples, baptism was not an admission rite into this group. It was a rite that symbolized repentance in preparation for the coming world judgment and was to be accompanied, before and afterward, by a righteous life. It was hardly conceived as a SACRAMENT, in the Christian sense, conveying forgiveness, or as superseding JUDAISM and marking off a new people prepared for God's final Kingdom. The Jewish rite of baptism of converts differs fundamentally and is not its source. John's baptism probably symbolized not so much anticipated entrance into the Kingdom of God as submission to the coming world judgment, which was represented as a coming second "baptism" by the HOLY SPIRIT in a river of fire.

The discovery of the DEAD SEA SCROLLS has drawn attention to the numerous parallels between John's mission and that of the Essenes, with whom John may have received some of his religious training. Both were priestly in origin, ascetic, and with intense and, in many respects, similar expectations about the end of the world. But John neither belonged to nor intended to found any organized community; he did not stress study of the Mosaic Law; and his message was more widely directed than was that of the Essenes.

Jesus, who was baptized by John, saw in John the last and greatest of the prophets, the one who prepared for the coming of God's Kingdom (Mark 9, Matthew 11, Luke 7), and in many ways his ministry continued and developed John's. Whether John, who probably expected a divine Son of Man, recognized him in Jesus is not clear, but many of his disciples later followed Jesus.

Some time after baptizing Jesus, John was imprisoned and executed by Herod Antipas, ruler of Galilee and central Transjordan. Herod had married (illegally, by Jewish law) Herodias, the divorced wife of his half brother, after divorcing his first wife, the daughter of King Aretas IV of the Nabataeans. John's denunciation of this marriage doubtless convinced Herod of the danger that his Jewish subjects would combine with his semi-Arab subjects in opposition to him. According to the Gospel (Matthew 14:1–12; Mark 6:14–29), Herod's stepdaughter, Salome, prompted by her mother Herodias, demanded John's head as a reward for dancing for Herod and his guests. It is probable that John's followers recovered and buried his body and revered his tomb. The traditional burial site, at Sebaste (originally Samaria), near "Aenon by Salim," is attested from 360 onward. In 35–36, Herod was defeated by Aretas, an event popularly considered to have been divine vengeance on Herod for killing John.

JOHN XXIII, POPE, *original name* Angelo Giuseppe Roncalli (b. Nov. 25, 1881, Sotto il Monte, Italy—d. June 3, 1963, Rome), one of the most popular popes of all times (reigned 1958–63), who inaugurated a new era of the ROMAN CATHOLIC church by his openness to change, shown especially in his convoking of the SECOND VATICAN COUNCIL.

Roncalli was sent to prepare for the PRIESTHOOD at 11 and was sent to Rome for theological studies in 1900. Although his studies were interrupted by military duty, he was ordained in Rome on Aug. 10, 1904. He returned to the Seminario Romano for further study and eventually received a doctorate in CANON LAW.

For most of his life Roncalli toiled in relative obscurity, first as director of the Italian organization for the support of foreign MISSIONS, then as apostolic visitor to Bulgaria (1925–1935), and finally as apostolic delegate to Greece. Roncalli, by now an archbishop, was in 1944 named papal nuncio to Charles de Gaulle's newly liberated France. The post was particularly delicate at the time, as Roncalli's predecessor had cooperated with the hated Vichy government and there was a growing trend of radicalism among the younger French clergy. His success in carrying out the assignment was acknowledged by the PAPACY when he was named a CARDINAL by PIUS XII. Appointed Patriarch of Venice at the age of 71, after the death of Pius XII on Oct. 9, 1958, he was elected pope on the 12th ballot—clearly a compromise candidate acceptable because of his advanced years.

Soon after his coronation, John XXIII announced that he was summoning an ecumenical council, the first in almost a century. He was the first pope since the REFORMATION to acknowledge that Catholicism stood in need of reinvigoration and reform. Some of the Vatican cardinals sought to delay the council until it could be quietly dropped. But the Pope pushed on with his plan and lived long enough to preside over the first session of the second Vatican Council in the fall of 1962.

The council was convened as a pastoral council. No new dogmas were to be pronounced, though old doctrines and disciplines were to be reexamined. The council was to make a new start toward achieving Christian unity by putting aside the hostilities of the past and acknowledging a share of responsibility for the scandal of a divided CHRISTIANITY. John received EASTERN ORTHODOX, Anglican (*see* ANGLICAN COMMUNION), and PROTESTANT religious leaders with cordiality and made sure they were invited to send observers to the Vatican Council. He removed certain words offensive to Jews from the official liturgy of the church. He played down his own position as ruler of the Vatican and emphasized his role as "servant of the servants of God."

During the Cuban missile crisis of 1962, the Pope publicly urged both the United States and the Soviet Union to exercise caution and restraint and won the appreciation of both Pres. John F. Kennedy and Premier Nikita Khrushchev. His major ENCYCLICAL, *Pacem in Terris* ("Peace on Earth"), avoided the language of diplomacy and set forth the requirements for world peace in profoundly human terms. John suggested that peaceful coexistence between the West and the Communist East was not only desirable but was actually necessary if mankind was to survive. After his death in 1963 John's successor, Paul VI, instituted formal proceedings that could lead to his CANONIZATION.

JONATHAN \\'jä-nə-thən\\, in the OLD TESTAMENT (1 and 2 Samuel), eldest son of King Saul; his intrepidity and fidelity to his friend, the future king DAVID, make him one of the most admired figures in the BIBLE.

Jonathan is first mentioned in 1 Samuel 13:2, when he defeated a garrison of Philistines at Geba. Later he and his armor bearer captured the outpost at Michmash. The Israelites then attacked and defeated the Philistines. SAUL ordered a fast for one day, but the absent Jonathan was unaware of the order and ate wild honey. When Saul requested information about the war from God and there was no answer, Saul blamed the silence on Jonathan's breaking of the fast and would have killed him had not his own soldiers ransomed Jonathan.

When David became a member of Saul's household, he and Jonathan became friends. After Saul jealously turned against David, Jonathan attempted to reconcile them. Saul tried to enlist Jonathan's aid to kill David, but Jonathan remained David's friend and warned him. When the two met for the last time, they planned that David would be the next king of Israel and Jonathan his minister.

Saul, Jonathan, and Jonathan's brothers were killed in a battle against the Philistines at Mt. Gilboa. Despoiled and exposed by the Philistines, the bodies were buried in Jabesh. Years later, David reinterred the remains in the tomb of Kish in the land of BENJAMIN.

JONES, JIM \\'jōnz\\, *byname of* James Warren Jones (b. May 13, 1931, near Lynn, Ind., U.S.—d. Nov. 18, 1978, Jonestown, Guyana), American cult leader who promised his followers a utopia in South America after proclaiming himself MESSIAH of the People's Temple, a San Francisco-based evangelist group. He ultimately led his followers into a mass suicide, which came to be known as the Jonestown Massacre (Nov. 18, 1978). *See also* NEW RELIGIOUS MOVEMENTS.

In the 1950s and '60s in Indianapolis, Ind., Jones gained a reputation as a charismatic churchman, and, after moving his headquarters to northern California in 1965, he apparently became obsessed with power. In the face of mounting accusations by journalists and defectors from the cult that he was defrauding church members, Jones and hundreds of his followers emigrated to Guyana and set up an agricultural commune called Jonestown (1977). Jones is said to have confiscated passports and millions of dollars and manipulated his followers with physical and psychological threats.

On Nov. 14, 1978, U.S. Rep. Leo Ryan of California arrived in Guyana with a group of newsmen and relatives of cult members to conduct an unofficial investigation of alleged abuses. Four days later, as Ryan's party and 14 defectors from the cult prepared to leave from an airstrip near Jonestown, Ryan and 4 others were killed by Jones' followers. The same day, Jones commanded his followers to drink a fruit punch that had been laced with cyanide, and the vast majority of them obeyed. Jones died of a gunshot wound to the head, possibly self-inflicted. Guyanese troops reached Jonestown the next day, and the death toll of Jones' followers was eventually placed at 913 (including 276 children).

JÖRD \\'yœrth\\ (Old Norse: "Earth"), *also called* Fjörgyn \\'fyœr-gin\\, *or* Hlódyn \\'hlō-thin\\, in GERMANIC RELIGION, a giantess, mother of THOR and mistress of ODIN. In the late pre-Christian era she was believed to have had a husband of the same name, perhaps indicating her transformation into a masculine personality.

JÖRMUNGAND \\'yœr-mùn-ˌgänd\\, in GERMANIC RELIGION, the evil serpent that encircles the world and that is the chief enemy of THOR. Jörmungand is also called the world-serpent, Midgardsorm. Viking art frequently depicts Thor trying to haul Jörmungand into a boat. Legends relate that the serpent will be the cause of Thor's death at RAGNARÖK, the doom of the gods.

JOSEL OF ROSHEIM \\'yō-zəl, -səl . . . 'rōs-ˌhīm\\, *also called* Joselmann, *or* Joselin, of Rosheim, *or* Joseph Ben Gershon Loans (b. *c.* 1478, Alsace?—d. March 1554, Rosheim, Alsace [now in France]), famous *shtadlan* (advocate who protected the interests and pled the cause of the Jewish people). He prevented many acts of persecution.

Josel realized keenly the precarious status of German Jewry, which was caught between rival imperial, municipal, and Christian religious sovereignties. By his diplomatic skills, he found listeners at the imperial court, which, through him, sought to strengthen its own hold over the Jewish communities. Thus, when Rosheim's Jewish community was threatened in 1525 by marauding peasants, Jo-

Jim Jones
UPI—Corbis–Bettmann

sel, by a combination of bribery and persuasion, managed to save his city. Soon after the coronation in 1520 of the Holy Roman emperor Charles V, Josel presented him with a memorandum that convincingly refuted the popular accusation that the Jews were allies of the expanding Ottoman Empire; this document averted proposed anti-Semitic measures. In the same year, Josel persuaded the government that the Jews desired better relations with it and convoked an assembly of representatives of all German Jewish communities.

JOSEPH \'jō-səf, -zəf\, in the OLD TESTAMENT, son of the patriarch JACOB and his wife Rachel. According to tradition, his bones were buried at Shechem, oldest of the northern shrines. His story is told in GENESIS (37–50).

Joseph, most beloved of Jacob's sons, is hated by his envious brothers. Angry and jealous of Jacob's gift to Joseph, a resplendent "coat of many colors," the brothers sell him to a party of Ishmaelites, or MIDIANITES, who carry him to Egypt. There Joseph gains the favor of the pharaoh of Egypt by his interpretation of a dream and obtains a high place in the kingdom. His acquisition of grain supplies enables Egypt to withstand a famine. Driven by the same famine, his brothers journey from CANAAN to Egypt, where they prostrate themselves before Joseph but do not recognize him. After Joseph reconciles with his brothers, he invites Jacob's household to come to Goshen in Egypt, where a settlement is provided for the family and their flocks. His brothers' sale of Joseph into slavery thus proves providential, since it protected the family from famine. The family's descendants grew and multiplied into the Hebrews, who would eventually depart from Egypt for Israel.

The purpose of the story is to relate the preservation of Israel. Its people survive despite their foolishness and wickedness, indeed, ironically, in part because of these. The story is a testimony to the operation of divine providence: "you meant evil against me; but God meant it for good" (Genesis 50:20) sums up its moral. Even so, God had realized his end through the faithfulness of Joseph, true to Israel's ideals under all circumstances and ever mindful of his obligations to his people.

JOSEPH, SAINT (fl. 1st century CE, Nazareth, Galilee, region of Palestine; principal feast day March 19, Feast of St. Joseph the Worker May 1), in the NEW TESTAMENT, Jesus' earthly father, the Virgin MARY's husband, and in ROMAN CATHOLICISM patron of the universal church. His life is recorded in the Gospels, particularly Matthew and Luke.

Joseph was descended of King David. After marrying Mary, he found her already pregnant and, being "a just man and unwilling to put her to shame" (Matthew 1:19), decided to divorce her quietly; but an ANGEL told him that the child was the son of God and was conceived by the Holy Ghost. Obeying the angel, Joseph took Mary as his wife. After Jesus' birth at Bethlehem in Judaea, the holy family eventually settled in Nazareth (Matthew 2:22–23) in Galilee, where Joseph taught his craft of carpentry to Jesus. Joseph is last mentioned in the Gospels when he and Mary frantically searched for the lost Jesus in Jerusalem, where they found him in the Temple (Luke 2:41–48). The circumstances of Joseph's death are unknown, except that he probably died before Jesus' public ministry began and was dead before the CRUCIFIXION (John 19:26–27).

The 2nd-century *Protevangelium of James* and the 4th-century *History of Joseph the Carpenter* present him as a widower with children at the time of his betrothal to Mary,

contributing to the confusion over the question of Jesus' brothers and sisters. Although the veneration of Joseph seems to have begun in Egypt, the earliest Western devotion to him dates from the early 14th century, when the Servites, an order of MENDICANT FRIARS, observed his feast on March 19, the traditional day of his death. Among the subsequent promoters of the devotion was Pope Sixtus IV, who introduced it at Rome *c.* 1479, and the celebrated 16th-century mystic ST. TERESA OF ÁVILA. Joseph was declared patron of the universal church by POPE PIUS IX in 1870. In 1955 POPE PIUS XII established the Feast of St. Joseph the Worker as May 1 as a Christian countercelebration to the Communists' May Day.

JOSEPH OF ARIMATHEA, SAINT \ˌar-i-mə-'thē-ə\ (b. Arimathea, Samaria; fl. *c.* 30 CE; Western feast day March 17, Eastern feast day July 31), according to all four Gospels, secret disciple of JESUS, whose body he buried in his own tomb. In designating him a "member of the council," Mark 15:43 and Luke 23:50 suggest membership of the town council in Jerusalem. He held a high office and was the one to gain Pontius Pilate's permission to obtain Jesus' body for burial.

Joseph is accorded a long history in later literature. In the apocryphal *Gospel of Peter* (2nd century), he is a friend of Jesus and of Pilate. In the apocryphal *Gospel of Nicodemus* (or *Acts of Pilate*; 4th/5th century), Jews imprison Joseph after Jesus' burial, but he is released by the risen Christ, thus becoming the first witness of the RESURRECTION. In Robert de Boron's verse romance *Joseph d'Arimathie* (*c.* 1200), he is entrusted with the Holy Grail (cup) of the LAST SUPPER. A mid-13th-century interpolation relates that Joseph went to Glastonbury (in Somerset, Eng.), of which he is patron saint, as head of 12 missionaries dispatched there by the Apostle St. Philip.

JOSEPHUS, FLAVIUS \jō-'sē-fəs\ (b. 37/38 CE, Jerusalem—d. *c.* 100 CE, Rome), historian whose works provide an invaluable record of Roman-era Judaism. Born Joseph, the son of Matthias, into a priestly family in Jerusalem, Josephus fought against the Romans in the great war (66–73/74 CE), was captured by them, then spent the last three decades of his life as a free man in Rome. While in Rome he wrote three works in Greek that have survived: *Bellum Judaicum* ("Judean War" [75–79]); *Antiquitates Judaicae* ("Judean Antiquities" [93]), and *Contra Apionem* ("Against Apion"). These works provide by far the most important chronological and geographical guides for the study of JUDAISM in the Greco-Roman world, especially for the period 200 BCE to 75 CE. A contemporary of the Gospel writers, Josephus incidentally provides critical background for the student of Christian origins.

Josephus composed his copious historical material in the service of statements about Judaism. His expression of Judaism gives us unique insight into the views of one aristocrat, though we may safely assume that at least some of his class held similar views. The genius of this outlook is its fusion of biblical themes with core values of the Greco-Roman world. Josephus' fundamental position was that God controlled all human affairs, causing various world powers to rise and fall in succession. Evincing a special debt to the biblical books of Jeremiah and Daniel, he structured both the *War* and the *Antiquities* around this central theme: that several nations had risen and fallen in the past, and now God was with the Romans. In the future, the Jewish nation would itself achieve greatness, and signs of this

Josephus before Vespasian, detail of a manuscript miniature, 14th century
By courtesy of the Hessische Landesbibliothek, Fulda, Ger.

astronomy to the Egyptians. Josephus believed that Pythagoras, Plato, and other Greeks had borrowed from the philosopher Moses. In his own day, Josephus described the main Jewish groups—the Essenes, whom he most admired, along with the PHARISEES and Sadducees—as philosophical schools within the national philosophy. Repeatedly throughout his writings, he tackled such philosophical questions as the soul, afterlife, and the roles of fate and free will; he explicitly repudiated EPICUREANISM.

Josephus claimed that he wrote the seven-volume *Judean War* to combat the numerous anti-Jewish accounts that had appeared after the Jewish-Roman conflict of 66–73/74 CE. Those accounts had apparently presented the Roman victory as a triumph of the Roman gods over the Jewish God, and the revolt itself as an expression of the allegedly rebellious, antisocial character of the Jewish nation. Josephus directly challenged both propositions. He claimed that, although the Jews had been sorely pressed by incompetent governors, the people and their legitimate leaders were committed to peaceful existence in a Roman world under divine control. It was only a handful of demagogues among them who had engineered the fateful conflict, and these had now been punished. The Roman victory, further, was orchestrated by the God of the Jews, who used the Romans as he used all others, to achieve his ends. The Romans who formed Josephus' most immediate audience for the *War* must have been somewhat sympathetic in advance to bother with this book.

Josephus composed his major work, the 20-volume *Judean Antiquities*, for the same sort of friendly audience, now associated with one Epaphroditus, a Gentile named in the *Antiquities* as patron. Claiming that he had been pursued by Gentiles who were keenly interested in the history and political constitution of the Jews, Josephus finally acceded to their demanding request: he offered 10 volumes on the period from creation to the destruction of the First Temple (to the 6th century BCE) and another 10 on the period of the Second Temple (to 66 CE). This work spells out in detail the foundations and terms of the Jewish constitution, and then gives numerous examples, from Judea and abroad (even from Rome), of its universal effectiveness. The appendix known as the Life is a highly rhetorical depiction of Josephus' character, based on his ancestry and career as Galilean commander in the war.

In Josephus' final work, commonly known as *Against Apion* after the essay of that name contained within this work—Josephus further elaborated the age and nobility of the Jewish constitution, but in a systematic rather than chronological way, and in direct debate with the Jews' main literary opponents, most of whom came from Alexandria.

development were already to be seen in the adoption of Jewish ways by others. The proper human response to this state of affairs, exemplified most brilliantly in Josephus' commentary on the ESSENES, was to be scrupulously faithful to Jewish law and customs, while at the same time cooperating with the provisional powers then ruling. Josephus' view of history thus supported the aristocrats' comfortable world; in laying responsibility for the choosing of political leadership with God, this view enshrined the status quo and precluded the popular revolutionary sentiments that threatened ancient aristocracies.

Josephus also believed the Jews to possess the finest "constitution" in existence, one that epitomized the highest aspirations of the entire world. Discussion of optimal constitutions was widespread in Josephus' day, and had been since Plato and Aristotle. Josephus argued in his work that MOSES had crafted the Jewish constitution—that is, effectively, the TORAH—in harmony with the very principles of the universe. This remarkable constitution, which inexorably punished criminals and rewarded the virtuous, was known intimately by all Jews, even women and children. It perfectly balanced clemency and humaneness, even toward animals, with speedy and incorruptible justice.

Josephus also emphasized the philosophical character of the Judean constitution. Philosophy, at least as a generic pursuit, had a respected place in Josephus' world. He portrayed ABRAHAM as the first serious philosopher, who had discovered MONOTHEISM and also taught mathematics and

JOSHUA \ˈjä-shə-wə\, *also spelled* Josue \ˈjä-shü-ē\, *Hebrew* Yehoshua' ("Yahweh is Deliverance"), leader of the Israelite tribes after the death of MOSES. His story is told in the OLD TESTAMENT Book of Joshua.

Joshua was the personally appointed successor to Moses (Deuteronomy 31:1–8; 34:9) who led ISRAEL in the conquest of CANAAN after the EXODUS from Egypt. Leading the Israelites in an invasion across the Jordan River, he took the important city of JERICHO (Joshua 3–6) and then captured other towns in the north and south (Joshua 10:28–11:15) until most of Palestine was brought under Israelite control (Joshua 13:13; 15:63; 17:12–13). He divided the conquered lands among the TWELVE TRIBES OF ISRAEL and then bade farewell to his people, admonishing them to be loyal to the God of the COVENANT.

Scholars agree that Israel did not take Canaan by means of a single plan of conquest. It happened more gradually, through progressive infiltration and acculturation. This development went on for a couple of centuries, during which walled cities generally remained in Canaanite hands. Even if these cities were razed, Israel does not seem to have made military use of them; DAVID's occupation of Jerusalem was a first in this respect. The accounts of Joshua's campaigns tell of forays by a mobile community that increasingly constituted a force to be reckoned with in the open spaces between the walled cities.

The story of the book of Joshua conveys three complementary theological points: (1) Israel is YAHWEH's chosen people and he is their only sovereign, as demonstrated by Yahweh's liberation of Israel from slavery, re-forming them into his special and chosen people in the wilderness, and granting them the gift of the promised land of Canaan; (2) Yahweh, the God of Israel, is Lord of all that is (Joshua 2:11), as demonstrated by his taking the land from the Canaanites and giving it to the Israelites; (3) Yahweh is a God of grace, for the "conquest" is his supreme gift of protection and freedom.

JOSIAH \jō-'sī-ə\, *also spelled* Josias, king of JUDAH (*c.* 640–609 BCE), who set in motion a reformation that left an indelible mark on Israel's traditions (2 Kings 22–23:30).

Josiah ascended the throne at the age of eight after the assassination of his father, AMON, in 641. For a century, Judah had been a vassal of the Assyrian empire. Imperial policy imposed alien cults on Judah that suppressed or obscured the Israelite religious identity. After the death of King Nabopolassar, the Assyrian empire fell into chaos. Egypt also was weak, and Judah thus obtained an unusual degree of independence. About 621 Josiah launched a program of national renewal, centered on the TEMPLE OF JERUSALEM and inspired in large part by a book containing provisions relating to religious traditions of premonarchic times. The Temple was purged of all foreign cults and dedicated wholly to the worship of YAHWEH, and all local sanctuaries were abolished, sacrifice being concentrated at Jerusalem.

In Assyria, Babylonia led a coalition that sacked Nineveh. Intending to keep Mesopotamia divided, Necho, the Egyptian pharaoh, set out to aid the Assyrians. He landed a force on the territory of ISRAEL. King Josiah, in an attempt to reunify Judah and Israel under the aegis of Babylonia, challenged the pharaoh to battle; but "Necho slew him at Megiddo, when he saw him." Soon thereafter Assyria was completely eliminated, the Egyptians retreated, and Josiah's son, JEHOIAKIM, whom Necho had placed on the throne of Judah as a vassal, had to submit to Babylonia.

JÖTUN \'yœ-,tùn, 'yȯ-\, *also spelled* Jöten \-tən\, in GERMANIC RELIGION, race of GIANTS that lived in JÖTUNHEIM under one of the roots of YGGDRASILL. They were older than and ruled before the gods (AESIR), to whom they remained hostile. It was believed that RAGNARÖK, the destruction of this world and the beginning of a new one, would be brought about by a final battle between gods and giants.

JÖTUNHEIM \'yœ-,tùn, 'yȯ-\, *also known as* Utgard \'üt-,gärd\, in GERMANIC RELIGION, home of the gods and one of the three realms (with NIFLHEIM and ASGARD) into which a root of the world-tree YGGDRASILL extended.

JUBILEE, YEAR OF, *also called* Holy Year, in the ROMAN CATHOLIC church, celebration that is observed on certain special occasions and for one year every 25 years, under certain conditions, when a special INDULGENCE is granted to members of the faith by the pope and confessors are given special faculties, including the lifting of censures. It resembles the OLD TESTAMENT Jubilee—in which, every 50 years, the Hebrews celebrated a year of perfect rest, emancipated slaves, and restored hereditary property—but does not seem to be based on it.

POPE BONIFACE VIII established the Holy Year in 1300 as a centenary observance. In 1342 Clement VI reduced the interval to 50 years, and in 1470 Paul II further reduced it to 25 years. The year begins on CHRISTMAS Eve, with the opening of the Holy Doors at the Roman BASILICAS of St. Peter, St. John Lateran, St. Paul Outside-the-Walls, and St. Mary Major, and ends with their closing on the following Christmas Eve. Since 1500 the Jubilee has been extended to the whole world in the year following a Holy Year.

Since at least 1560, special jubilees have been declared. Special jubilees have been declared for a pope's 50th anniversary in the PRIESTHOOD (Pope Pius XI, 1929), at the close of the SECOND VATICAN COUNCIL (1965) to promote the knowledge and application of the council's achievements. Pope John Paul II designated the year 2000 as a Jubilee to commemorate two millennia of CHRISTIANITY and to explore the church's mission in the 3rd millennium.

JUDAH \'jü-də\, one of the TWELVE TRIBES OF ISRAEL, descended from Judah, the fourth son of JACOB and his first wife, LEAH (GENESIS 29:35). It is disputed whether the name Judah was originally that of the tribe or the territory it occupied.

After the Israelites took possession of the Promised Land, the tribe of Judah settled in the region south of Jerusalem (Joshua 15) and in time became the most powerful and most important tribe. It produced the kings DAVID and SOLOMON (1 Samuel 16:1; 16:12), and it was prophesied that the MESSIAH would come from among its members (Micah 5:2). Modern Jews trace their lineage to the tribes of Judah and BENJAMIN (absorbed by Judah) or to the tribe, or group, of clans of religious functionaries known as LEVITES, since the Assyrian conquest of the Kingdom of Israel in 721 BCE led to the dispersion of the 10 northern tribes (2 Kings 17:5–6; 18:9–12) and their assimilation by other peoples (*see* TEN LOST TRIBES OF ISRAEL).

The southern Kingdom of Judah thrived until 587/586 BCE, when the Babylonians carried off many of its inhabitants into exile (2 Kings 24–25). When the Persians conquered Babylonia in 538 BCE, Cyrus the Great allowed the Jews to return to their homeland (2 Chronicles 36:22–23; EZRA 1, 2), where they replaced the TEMPLE OF JERUSALEM that the Babylonians had destroyed (Ezra 3:1–13; 4:24–6:22). The history of the Jews from that time forward is predominantly the history of the tribe of Judah.

JUDAH BEN SAMUEL \'jü-də-ben-'sam-yù-wəl\, *also called* Judah the Hasid of Regensburg, *or* Yehuda the Hasid (d. 1217), semilegendary Jewish mystic and pietist, founder of the fervent, ultrapious movement of German HASIDISM and principal author of the ethical treatise SEFER HASIDIM (1538; "Book of the Pious"), possibly the most important extant document of medieval JUDAISM and a major work of Jewish literature. The Hasidic movement of Judah's time is not directly related to the 18th-century Hasidic movement founded by the BA'AL SHEM ṬOV.

Judah was the son of Samuel the Hasid, also a mystic, and belonged to the eminent Kalonymos family, which provided medieval Germany with many mystics and spiritual leaders. About 1195 he left Speyer for Regensburg, where he founded a YESHIVA (academy) and gathered such disciples as the mystic Eleazar of Worms (also a member of the Kalonymos family) and the codifiers Isaac ben Moses of Vienna and Baruch ben Samuel of Mainz.

The *Sefer Hasidim* is a compilation of the writings of Judah, his father Samuel, and Eleazar of Worms. Dealing with man's relations with God and his fellowman, his business practices, the SABBATH, social intercourse with GENTILES, penitence, and a host of other subjects, the book is a detailed manual of conduct. Judah also wrote a mystic work surviving only in citations dealing with the *kavod* ("divine glory"), the aspect of God that man can experience, as distinguished from the ultimate reality of God, which is beyond man's experience or comprehension. Judah was also the author of liturgies and RESPONSA.

JUDAH HA-LEVI \,hä-'lē-,vī, -'le-vē\, *in full* Yehuda ben Shemuel ha-Levi (b. *c.* 1075, Tudela, Kingdom of Pamplona [Navarre]—d. July 1141, Egypt), Jewish poet and religious philosopher. His works were the culmination of the development of Hebrew poetry within the Arabic cultural sphere. Among his major works are the poems collected in *Diwan*, the "Zionide" poems celebrating ZION, and the *Sefer ha-Kuzari* ("Book of the Khazar"), presenting his philosophy of JUDAISM in dialogue form.

At the time of Judah ha-Levi's birth, most of Spain, including his native town, was still under Muslim rule, but the Reconquista, the Christian sovereigns' struggle to regain their lost territories, was already under way. Judah ha-Levi, whose poetic gifts manifested themselves unusually early, spent his childhood in the Christian part of the country, but he felt himself drawn to Muslim Spain, then one of the principal cultural centers of Europe. He went to Andalusia in southern Spain some time before 1090, where he established contact with local Hebrew poets and intellectuals and attracted considerable attention. This period ended in 1090 when Granada was stormed by the ALMORAVIDS, North African Berber disciples of a zealous Muslim movement, who now established an orthodox and intolerant regime in Andalusia. It is not known with any certainty whether Judah ha-Levi witnessed the Almoravid invasion in Granada or elsewhere, but the event greatly influenced the remainder of his life and his worldview.

In the last years of his life he lived in Córdoba, which remained an important center of Jewish culture even in the period of decline. As old age approached, however, Judah ha-Levi felt an increasing need to travel to Jerusalem, writing about it at length in verse and prose. The epilogue of the Kuzari explains his attachment to Zion and sounds like a farewell to Spain. Among his many poems celebrating the Holy Land is "Zionide" ("Ode to Zion"), his most famous work and the most widely translated Hebrew poem of the Middle Ages. He also carried on a heated controversy in verse with the opponents of his Zionist ideas.

Judah ha-Levi left Spain in 1140. He planned first to embark for Egypt and then to proceed via the land route to Palestine. Aboard ship he composed a whole series of sea songs, which in both theme and mood represented a con-

siderable innovation in Hebrew literature. His ship entered Alexandria harbor on May 3, 1140, where he, along with a large Jewish party, was splendidly received. From Alexandria he went to Cairo, or Fustat, the city where lived Samuel ben Hananiah, the Nagid, or head, of all Egyptian Jews, and there he was further acclaimed. Judah ha-Levi felt deep awe and humility in the land in which some of the biblical miracles had occurred and at the same time a kind of delight in all the beauties that revealed themselves to him; he wrote prolifically and easily. But he certainly always bore in mind his sacred destination and was often disturbed by the thought that death might yet intervene.

He did not in fact go beyond Egypt, although it is not known what detained him there. He died in 1141 and was deeply mourned in Egypt.

Judah ha-Levi was strongly influenced by Arabian literature, elements of which he ingeniously assimilated. His great collection of poems entitled *Diwan* includes secular and religious poetry, both of which express passionate attachment to Zion (the Land of Israel). For the poet, the Holy Land was not only a site where the Jewish people would one day gather after their deliverance from exile; immigration and settlement in Palestine would also hasten the coming of the MESSIAH. He celebrated Jerusalem in song as had none of his medieval predecessors. He also expounded his views on the nature of Judaism in an Arabic prose work consisting of dialogues between a learned Jew and the Khazar king who was converted to Judaism in the 8th century. It was widely circulated in Hebrew translation under the title *Sefer ha-Kuzari*.

JUDAH HA-NASI \,hä-nä-'sē\, important figure in early RABBINIC JUDAISM, active at the end of the 2nd and beginning of the 3rd centuries CE. Tradition considered him to have been the redactor of the MISHNAH. Judah was the first of HILLEL's successors to carry the designation *ha-Nasi,* that is, "the patriarch," indicating his position as head of the Jewish community in the land of Israel. In the Mishnah, he generally is referred to simply as "Rabbi," that is, the rabbinic master par excellence.

While the TALMUDS declare that Judah prepared the Mishnah, the reality is more complex, and Judah's actual role is not known. The Mishnah itself contains no definitive statements about its own redaction, and Judah is cited there exactly as any other RABBI. Traditional scholarship has generally held that Judah did the final editing of a compilation prepared by MEÏR, who had continued the work of his teacher AKIBA BEN JOSEPH. None of this, however, can be verified on the actual evidence of the Mishnaic text.

Later sources frequently discuss Judah's life and pietistic teachings. He defined piety as follows (M. Abot 2:1):

> What is the straight path a person should choose
> for himself? Whatever is an ornament to the one
> who follows it and an ornament in the view of
> others. Be meticulous in a small religious duty as
> in a large one, for you do not know what sort of
> reward is coming for any of the various religious
> duties. And reckon the cost of carrying out a
> religious duty against the reward for doing it, and
> the reward for committing a transgression against
> the cost for doing it. And keep your eye on three
> things, so you will not come into the clutches of
> transgression: Know what is above you: an eye that
> sees, and an ear that hears, and all your actions are
> written down in a book.

JUDAISM

Areligion of ethical MONOTHEISM in the class of CHRISTIANITY and ISLAM—Judaism encompasses all the related religious systems that exhibit these common traits: (1) they maintain that God is unique and made manifest in his revelation of himself to MOSES in the TORAH at Mount Sinai; (2) they privilege the PENTATEUCH (the Five Books of Moses, also called the Torah) among the Israelite Scriptures; and (3) they regard the Jews, or at least some of the Jews who lived in later times and in other places, as the continuation of Scripture's "ISRAEL" in the Land of Israel.

THE TORAH

The Pentateuchal framework. The Pentateuch—consisting of the books of GENESIS, EXODUS, Leviticus, Numbers, and Deuteronomy—is written from the perspective of the loss and recovery of the Land of Israel between 586 and 450 BCE. These events of a long-ago past begin with the creation of the world, the making of man and woman, the fall of humanity through disobedience, and the flood that wiped out nearly all of humanity except for NOAH and his kin (making Noah the progenitor of all humanity). There then follows the decline of humanity from Noah to Abraham; the rise of humanity through ABRAHAM, ISAAC, JACOB (who is also called Israel), and the 12 sons of Jacob; the exile in Egypt; and the deliverance to Sinai. There, the scriptural narrative continues, God revealed the Torah to Moses, and that revelation contained the terms of the COVENANT, or contract, that God then made with Israel—*i.e.*, the family of Abraham, Isaac, and Jacob. The book of Genesis therefore narrates the story of creation and then of the beginnings of the family that would always constitute Israel: the children of Abraham, Isaac, and Jacob. The book of Exodus presents the story of the children of Israel's slavery in Egypt and how God redeemed them from Egyptian bondage and brought them to Sinai, there to make a covenant with them by which they would accept the Torah and carry out its rules. The book of Leviticus portrays the founding of the priests' service to God: that service being through the sacrifice of the produce of the Holy Land to which God had brought Israel. The book of Numbers provides an account of the wandering in the wilderness. The book of Deuteronomy then presents a reprise of the story, a long sermon by Moses looking back on

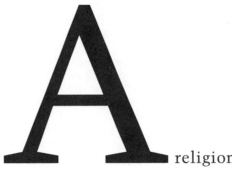

A boy carries the Torah scrolls enclosed in their embroidered case; the silver yad, or pointer, assists the reader in keeping his place in the text
Pinney—Monkmeyer

JUDAISM

CONTENTS

the history of Israel from the beginning of the wandering through the point of entry into the Promised Land, followed by a restatement of the rules of the covenant between Israel and God.

Thus, it follows that every Judaism, wherever and whenever created, believes that through the Scriptures of ancient Israel it can trace its beginnings to the creation of the world. Following the biblical record, each system maintains that God created the world and for ten dismal and declining generations, from Adam to Noah, despaired of creation. For ten generations, from Noah to Abraham, God waited for humanity to acknowledge the sovereignty of the one God, creator of heaven and earth. Finally came Abraham and SARAH; Abraham obeyed God's commandment to leave his home in the city of Ur in Chaldea (an area that would become known as Babylonia) and journey to the Promised Land. Thus, Israel begins with the experience of alienation: "Go from your country and your kindred and your father's house to the land that I will show you" (Genesis 12:1). Through their descendants Sarah and Abraham founded Israel, the people of the Lord, to whom, later at Sinai, God revealed the Torah, the complete record of God's will— initially for Israel (the Jewish people), but eventually for all humanity. The biblical record goes on to speak of DAVID, the king of Israel and founder of the ruling household, from which, at the end of time, the MESSIAH is destined to come forth. So Judaism tells the story of the world from the creation of ADAM AND EVE, through the revelation of the Torah at MOUNT SINAI, to the redemption of humanity through the Messiah at the end of time—a picture of the world, beginning, middle, and end. This account of the history of humanity and all creation derives from a people that traces its origins to the beginnings of history and yet thrives in the world today.

The Pentateuch includes a composite of materials by different authors, each of whom had his own viewpoint and intellectual traits. It must be remembered that it was only after the destruction of the First TEMPLE OF JERUSALEM in 586 BCE that the Torah—in this context, the Five Books of Moses—came into being, coming together as a pastiche of received stories, some old, some new, all revised to fulfill the purposes of the final authors and to explain the origins of Israel, the Jewish people. In light of Israel's ultimate destiny, which the authors took to be the loss and restoration of the Holy Land, the origins of the people in its land became meaningful. Israel began with its acquisition of the land, through Abraham; attained its identity as a people through the promise of the land, in the covenant of Sinai; and entered the land under JOSHUA. Israel's history then formed the story of how, because of its conduct on the land, Israel, in spite of the prophets' persistent warnings, lost its land, first in the north (Israel), then in the south (Judaea). Exiled in Babylonia, the authors of the Torah recast Israel's history into the story of the existence of the people, a conditional existence dependent on their carrying out a contract: do this, get that; do not do this, do not get that.

The Pentateuch as fully formulated comes from the small number of Israelite families who remembered the exile, survived in Babylonia, and then, toward the end of the 6th century BCE, began the return to ZION. To the priests who rebuilt the Temple and gave the Pentateuch its final form what mattered historically was the destruction of the First Temple (586 BCE), and, some three generations later, the restoration of Zion and the rebuilding of the Temple. To them the cult was the key, the Temple the nexus between heaven and earth. The Pentateuch set forth the priest's conception of a shared consciousness, a collective myth of a people subject to condition and stipulation, forever threatened with desolation, always requiring renewal—nothing was a given. Beginning at this time the Pentateuch, declaimed in the SYNAGOGUE from week to week, taught this one lesson of the human condition of Israel. The priests' Torah, the Pentateuch in its final statement, constituted the first and enduring Judaic paradigm, to which all Judaisms to come would either conform or object.

The Pentateuchal paradigm of all Judaisms.   A Judaic religion confronts an urgent question and supplies an answer that is self-evidently valid within the paradigm of Israel's exile and return as interpreted in the Pentateuch. Responding to the agenda framed by Scripture in the original encounter—death and resurrection, as interpreted in the destruction of the Temple and the later return to Zion—the question addressed by Judaic systems from the Pentateuch onward was, and would remain, "Who is Israel? And what rules define Israel as a social, and therefore political, entity?" In one way or another, Israel, the Jewish people wherever they lived, sought means of declaring itself distinct from its neighbors. However, this persistent stress on differentiation—the exclusion of the neighbors from the group, and vice versa—yields a preoccupation with self-definition that runs contrary to the situation of ancient Israel, with the unmarked cultural frontiers and constant trade among diverse groups that was characteristic of ancient times. At the formation of the Pentateuch, Israel was deeply affected by the shifts and changes in social, cultural, and political life. The problem of self-definition came to renewed expression when, more than a century after the formation of the Pentateuch under EZRA and NEHEMIAH, the Greeks under Alexander the Great conquered the entire Middle East (c. 330 BCE) and incorporated the Land of Israel into the international Hellenistic culture. And, when the war of independence fought by the Jews under the leadership of the MACCABEES (c. 160 BCE) produced an independent state for a brief period, that state found itself under the government of a Jewish court that accommodated itself to the international style of politics and culture.

So what made Israel separate in any sense from its neighbors? In fact, the principal propositions of the Pentateuchal Torah and the historical and prophetic writings of the century beyond 586 BCE—namely, Israel's heightened sense of its own social reality and its status as an elected people standing in a contractual or covenantal relationship with God—reveal the inner structure of the system. They express the paradigm's logic—which is not dictated by events, even in events selected and reworked—and apply its theological premises, not the hard data of Israel's common life in either Babylonia or the Land of Israel. The Pentateuchal system not only selected the events it would deem consequential, it dictated to whose experience those events would bear consequence. For from

(Opposite page) Frontispiece to Leviticus, 14th-century German Torah; (below) the rock-cut tombs of the Maccabees, Modi'im, Israel

(Opposite) The Granger Collection; (below) Erich Lessing—Art Resource

the perspective of a vast population of Israel—Jews who remained in the Land of Israel after 586, or in Babylonia after Cyrus' decree in 538 permitted return to Zion—the system spoke of events that simply never happened. For both groups, for different reasons, there was no alienation and consequently, no reconciliation—for these groups what was normative corresponded to the merely normal, they lived life like any other nation, wherever it happened to locate itself. As an example of a religious system creating a society, we can find few better instances than the power of the conception of Israel as expressed by the Pentateuch and associated writings after 586 BCE. It served to show people not only the meaning of what had happened but to also tell them what had happened: to create for Israelite society a picture of what it must be and therefore what it had been. That sense of heightened reality and intense focus on the identification of the nation as extraordinary represented only one possible meaning of events. However, we do not have access to any interpretation other than the system of the Torah and the prophetic and historical writings framed by the priests and given definitive statement under the auspices of Persia's Jewish viceroy in Jerusalem, Nehemiah, and his counsellor Ezra.

Since the Pentateuchal face of Judaism began as a paradigm, not as a set of actual events, the conclusions generated by the paradigm, derived not from reflection on things that happened but from the logic of the paradigm. Additionally, that same paradigm created expectations that could not be met, thereby renewing the resentment presented in the myth of exile within people who had never experienced the phenomena. At the same time the paradigm set the conditions for remission of resentment, and so resolving the crisis of exile with the promise of return. This self-generating, self-renewing paradigm formed the self-fulfilling prophecy that all Judaisms have offered as the generative tension and critical symbolic structure of their systems.

The Judaic system devised in the Pentateuch's basic structure by the priests not only addressed, but also created, a continuing, chronic social fact of Israel's life. So long as the people perceived the world in such a way as to make urgent the question that Scripture framed and answered, Scripture enjoyed a power of persuasion beyond all need for argument, imparting to it the self-evident status of God's revealed will to Israel. And that power lasted for a very long time. Scripture gained its own authority, however, independent of the circumstance of society, and the priests' paradigm of exile and return imposed itself even in situations where its fundamental premises hardly pertained. Accordingly, when the world imposed different questions upon them, Jews went in search of not only more answers—an additional Torah (hence the formation of the Judaism of the dual Torah)—but different answers (hence the formation, in modern times, of Judaic systems of a different character altogether). But even then, a great many Jews continued to envision the world through the original perspective of exile and return created in the aftermath of destruction and restoration—to see the world as a gift instead of a given, and themselves as chosen for a life of special suffering but also special reward.

The generative tension—precipitated by the interpretation of the Jews' life as exile and return—that had formed the critical center of the Torah of Moses remained. Therefore the urgent question "Who is Israel?" answered by the Torah retained its original character and definition, and the self-evidently valid answer—as read in the synagogue—retained its relevance. With the renewal, generation after generation, of that same resentment—the product of a memory of loss and restoration joined to the danger of a further loss in the here and now—the priests' authoritative answer did not lose its power to persist and to persuade. Scripture kept reminding people to ask the question, to see the world as described, in Scripture's mythic terms, through the experience of exile and return. To those troubled by the question of exile and return—that is, the chronic allegation that Israel's group-life did not constitute a given but formed a gift accorded on conditions and stipulations—the answer enjoyed the status of (mere) fact. For a small, uncertain people, who were captivated by a vision of distant horizons, behind and before such a powerful and immediate message was a map of meaning.

SECOND TEMPLE JUDAISMS, 450 BCE TO 70 CE

Ancient Israel's Scriptures yielded not only the priestly model but, in fact, three quite distinct points of emphasis; definitions of what, in the life of community, nation, and individual, mattered. The Judaisms that emerged from Scripture centered upon three types or points of emphasis: (1) the one that emerged from the priestly viewpoint, with its interest in sanctification, and so stressed doctrine, law, and a way of life; (2) the one that took a special interest in the wise conduct of everyday affairs, yielded by the wisdom-writings, with a stress on the here and now of ordinary life; and (3) the one that emphasized the meaning and end of history, produced by the prophetic angle of vision, with a focus on salvation. To describe the three basic sorts of Second Temple Judaisms, we turn first to the idealized type as it will have reached expression in generative symbol: (1) an altar for an offering, (2) a Torah-scroll, (3) a coin. The altar for the priestly ideal, the scroll of Scripture for the ideal of wisdom, and the coin marked "Israel's freedom: year one," for the messianic modality (drawing on a later messianic movement, the one led in 132–135 CE by BAR KOKHBA). The principal strands of ancient Israelite life come to realization in the distinct types of holy men we identify as priests, scribes, and messiahs, with their definitive activities in cult, school and government offices, and (ordinarily) the battlefield.

The priest described society as organized through lines of structure emanating from the Temple. His caste stood at the top of a social scale in which all things were properly organized, each with its correct name and proper place. The inherent sanctity of Israel, the people, came through genealogy to its richest embodiment in him, the priest. Food set aside for his rations at God's command possessed that same sanctity, as did the table at which he ate. To the priest the history produced by the sacred society of Israel was an account of what happened in, and (alas) on occasion to, the Temple.

To the sage, the life of society demanded wise regulation. Human relationships required guidance by the laws embodied in the Torah and best interpreted by the sage. Accordingly, the task of Israel was to construct a way of life in accordance with the revealed rules of the Torah, and so the sage, master of the rules, stood at the head of society. As for prophecy's insistence that the fate of the nation depended upon the faith and moral condition of society, history testified to the external context and inner condition of Israel, viewed as a whole. Both sage and

World distribution of Judaism

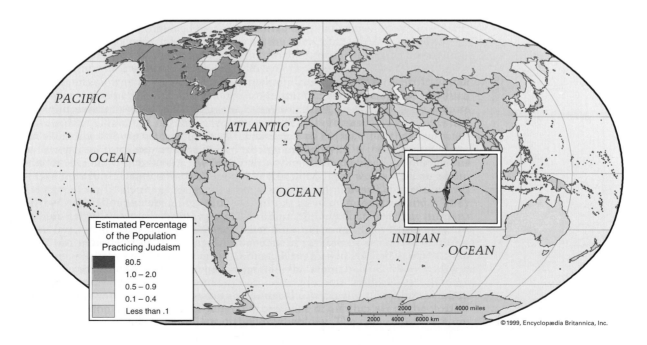

Estimated Percentage of the Population Practicing Judaism
- 80.5
- 1.0 – 2.0
- 0.5 – 0.9
- 0.1 – 0.4
- Less than .1

© 1999, Encyclopædia Britannica, Inc.

priest saw Israel from the aspect of eternity. But the nation lived out its life in the history of this world, among other peoples who coveted the very same land, within the politics of empires. It was the messiah's kingship that would resolve the issues of Israel's subordinated relationship to other nations and empires, establishing once for all time the correct context for priest and sage alike.

The social world of Second Temple Judaisms. Among a number of Judaic groups that distinguished themselves between 450 BCE and 70 CE, we have sufficient evidence to describe two sects in their broader social context, and not merely their statements of belief: first, the Judaic system, identified by some with the ESSENES, and put forth by the writings found at QUMRĀN; and second, the PHARISEES. Each in its way realized in sharp and extreme form the ideals of the normative system of the priests' Torah of Moses. The community-writings (assigned by some to the Essenes) of Qumrān and the writings of the Pharisees turned back to the PRIESTLY CODE and its generative symbols and myths. One encompassing example of that fact is the stress among both groups upon cultic cleanness and uncleanness. Each of these social groups defined itself around the eating of cultic meals in the state of cleanness prescribed in Leviticus for the Temple priest in the eating of his share of the Temple sacrifices.

Qumrān's Judaic system. The Judaism portrayed by the library discovered at Qumrān (*see* DEAD SEA SCROLLS) flourished in the last two centuries BCE to 68 CE. The main element of the library's worldview of Judaism was the conviction that the community formed the final remnant of Israel, and that God would shortly annihilate the wicked. These "converts" to the true faith would be saved and this "Israel" at Qumrān would endure because their founder, the Teacher of Righteousness, established a new contract or covenant between the community and God. The task of the community was to remain faithful to the covenant, endure the exile in the wilderness, and prepare for the restoration of the Temple in its correct form. So it recapitulated the history of Israel, seeing itself as the surviving remnant of some disaster that had destroyed the faith, and preparing for the restoration they anticipated would soon come—just as it had before. Therefore, we find in the Qumrān system a replication of the Judaic system of the PRIESTHOOD, with one important qualification. While the Judaic system represented by the Pentateuch laid great stress on the holy way of life, the Qumrān system added a powerful element of eschatological expectation and so combined the holy way of life with a doctrine of salvation at the end of time. The principal components of the scriptural composite—Torah-laws, prophetic historical interpretation, and sagacious rules on the conduct of everyday life—found counterparts in the library of the community as the Qumrān Judaism reworked the several strands into a distinctive and characteristic statement of its own.

The Qumrān library sets forth the Judaic system of a holy community in the here and now, awaiting an eschatological climax. The elements of the original paradigm are three: first, the notion of a saving remnant, a chosen few, which surely originated in the pattern of Israel that endured beyond 586 BCE; second, the conception of a community with a beginning, middle, and end, rather than a community that exists more or less permanently; third, the notion that the Israel at hand replicates the sanctification of the temple in its very being. These are large and encompassing principles, and within them we can make provision for the indicative traits of the Qumrān system. All commentators on the library of Qumrān have found the community's sense of itself striking: a people different, separate from the rest of Israel, the clean, saved few among the unclean many, the children of light. The fundamental notion that this small group constituted in microcosm the Israel that mattered rested on the premise that the "Israel" out there, the nation as a whole, live on condition and respond to stipulation. That "Israel" had failed; its people had become (in the mind of the followers at Qumrān) the children of darkness. Making such distinctions within the old Israel in favor of the new requires the conviction that the life of Israel is not a given, a fact of ordinary reality, but a status to be attained through appropriate regeneration, in context, sanctification. And that basic notion expresses the general pattern of the Pentateuchal structure: Israel is called and, out of nothing, in formed a very particular entity, subject to very special conditions: the children of light, as against the rest, the children of darkness. The prerequisite for such an acutely self-conscious understanding of one's people is the original and paradigmatic experience of national death and resurrection.

Pharisaic Judaism before 70 CE.   The Pharisees, who also stressed the observance of cultic rules of sanctification, were especially diligent in keeping the laws concerning the correct preparation of food, including the proper separation of a portion of the crops for the support of the priesthood and other scheduled castes (tithing). Scripture had specified a variety of rules on tithing and other agricultural offerings, in general holding that God owned a share of the crops, and God's share was to go to the holy castes (priests, LEVITES, as well as to the poor). In addition to making sure everything that was supposed to yield its portion to the castes did, the Pharisees obeyed those rules concerning the preparation of food that linked meals to the altar and its service. Scripture—the book of Leviticus—had furthermore laid down rules governing the sources and affects of uncleanness (*see also* TOHORAH). Such sources of uncleanness, specified in Leviticus 11–15, derive from the bodily flux of human beings, including excretions from sexual organs, and contact with certain deceased creatures, for example. The primary re-

Caves at Qumrān in which the Dead Sea Scrolls were discovered in 1947
Joel Fishman—Photo Researchers

sult of contact with such sources of uncleanness was not hygienic but, mainly, cultic: one affected by uncleanness could not enter the Temple. Therefore, for the authors of the Priestly Code, the concern for the cleanness or uncleanness of utensils and persons was rooted in the desire to protect the cult and the Temple against the dangers lurking in the sources of uncleanness. But the rules laid out in the MISHNAH that affect uncleanness—many of them going back to the earliest stratum of the Mishnaic system, before 70 CE, and, hence, many assume, to Pharisaic origins—deal primarily with domestic matters. The Pharisees maintained that Israel was meant to observe ritual purity in the home as well as the Temple, and recent archaeological findings show that many Pharisees did. (These findings include immersion pools [*miqvaot*] in homes.) The fundamental assumption was that one should eat not only food deriving from the altar, but meals eaten at home in a state of cultic cleanness. The further and more important assumption was that ordinary people, and not only priests, keep those rules. Put together, the two premises describe a group of lay people emulating priests, much on the order of the Qumrān Judaism, and treating their homes as temples, their tables as altars.

The Pharisaic stress on the sanctification of the home and the paradigmatic power of the Temple for the home suggests the Pharisees had a more extreme position on the priestly paradigm of the Pentateuch than the priests themselves. What the priests wanted for the Temple, the Pharisees wanted for the community at large, and so carried to a still more radical extreme the fundamental systemic position of the priests' Torah of Moses. Admittedly, we have little access to positions taken in the 1st century by the Pharisaic system on other matters, besides those represented in the GOSPELS and by the later RABBIS of the Mishnah. Still, one cannot imagine that the group took these positions only on the questions concerning cultic sanctification, as that was only a partial aspect of the complete system. The Qumrān Judaism presented a substantial account of the meaning and end of history; its doctrine of salvation spelled out in so many words the community's idea of Israel—or, rather of itself as the final remnant of Israel. What we know of the Pharisaic system allows us to characterize it also as a Judaism of sanctification—at least that—and permits us to identify that generative Pentateuchal paradigm of the 6th and early 5th centuries BCE. No wonder the Pharisees affirmed the eternity of the soul (as JOSEPHUS says) or the resurrection of the dead (as PAUL, himself a Pharisee before conversion to Christianity, is presented in Luke's ACTS). For the way of sanctification led past the uncleanness of the grave to the renewed purity of the living person, bringing purification out of the most unclean of all sources of uncleanness, the realm of death itself. Thus the pattern of everyday sanctification brought immediacy to the cosmic pattern of death and resurrection.

RABBINIC JUDAISM

Taking shape after 70 CE out of the union of the traditions of Pharisaism and of pre-70 scribes, RABBINIC JUDAISM—in the Mishnah, the Talmuds BAVLI and YERUSHALMI, and the MIDRASH—culminated in the doctrine of the dual Torah. That is, the Torah both oral and written, that God revealed to Moses at Mount Sinai. The Pharisees' belief system incorporated "Traditions of the Fathers," and to these later Rabbinic Judaism would assign the ORAL TRADITION from Sinai. This oral tradition, the doctrine held, was handed on from master to disciple in a chain extending from Moses down to the rabbis themselves. It was then preserved in the writing of the Mishnah, a philosophical law code; the Talmuds, which comment on the code; and the midrashic compilations, which interpret Scripture in accord with the rabbis' doctrines.

Rabbinic Judaism took shape in two stages: firstly, from 70 to the 4th century CE, as represented by the Mishnah (dating to *c.* 200 CE), commentaries on the Mishnah (which date from 200 to around 300 CE), and commentaries on the Scripture produced during that same period; and, secondly, by the two Talmuds—the Yerushalmi (dating to *c.* 400 CE) and the Bavli (dating to *c.* 600 CE), and the later midrashic compilations. The first stage set forth a Judaic religious system without reference to the challenge of Christianity; the second was a revision of the initial system, now responding to the challenge of Christianity's use of the canon and Scriptures of Judaism to prove and validate Christian beliefs. That second, fully articulated system of Judaism would then form the framework for all Judaisms until the 20th century (*see below:* Twentieth-century Judaisms beyond the Rabbinic framework). Some Judaisms took shape in response to the Rabbinic system and amplified it or added to its resources; others took shape as heresies defined by rejection of principal parts of that same system. But so long as Christianity, and later, Islam, set the critical issue confronting Israel, the holy people, Rabbinic Judaism defined the paramount, norm-setting Judaism.

The first phase of Rabbinic Judaism. As portrayed in the Mishnah, the first phase of Rabbinic Judaism—which was continuous with pre-70 Pharisaism—responded to the destruction of the Temple by maintaining that although the holiness of Israel, the people, had formerly centered on the Temple, it had endured and transcended the physical destruction of the building and the cessation of sacrifices. Thus, Israel the people was holy. The system created by Rabbinic Judaism instructed Israel to act as if there was a new Temple formed of Israel, with the Jewish people becoming the medium and instrument of God's sanctification. Joined with this new Pharisaic view of life was the substance of the scribal ideal, which stressed learning the Torah and carrying out its teachings. Like the scribes of old, the emerging system claimed it was possible to serve God not only through sacrifice but also through study of the Torah.

The way of life of Rabbinic Judaism, in its final definition, was the Pharisaic method, with its stress on the everyday sanctification of all Israel. The worldview and substance of that Judaism was the scribal message, with its stress on the Torah. Pharisaism stressed the universal keeping of the law, obligating every Jew to do what only the elite—the priests—were normally expected to accomplish. But, it was this doctrine of who actually constituted Israel that would at first glance seem fresh and unpredictable. The people who constituted Israel was surviving Israel: after the rupture marked by the destruction of the Temple the crisis centered attention on what had endured, persisting beyond the end: the people itself. In the life of a nation that had ceased to be a nation on its own land and then once more had regained that land, the calamity of the Temple's destruction represented once more the paradigm of the death and resurrection. Consequently after 70 CE the truly fresh and definitive component of the new system actually restated in contemporary terms the fixed and established doctrine with which the first Judaism, the Judaism of the Torah of Moses after 450 BCE, had commenced.

The initial statement of Rabbinic Judaism—the Mishnah—stresses sanctification, which is understood as the correct arrangement of all things, each in its proper category, and each called by its rightful name, just as at the creation. Everything (except the beasts that would be named by Adam) had been given its proper name—or, in the language of Scripture, been classified in its correct category. God then called the natural world very good and God sanctified it. The system of philosophy expressed through concrete and detailed Mishnaic law is a worldview that speaks of transcendent things, presenting a way of life in response to the supernatural meaning of what is done, and thus, a heightened and deepened perception of the sanctification of Israel in deed and in deliberation. Therefore sanctification means two things: first, the distinguishing of Israel in all its dimensions from the rest of the world and its ways; and second, the establishment of the stability of Israel in the world of nature and supernature, particularly when threatened by instability or disorder. Each principal topic of the Mishnah takes up a critical and indispensable moment or context of social being and fully expresses what the halakhic system (see HALAKHAH AND HAGGADAH) as a whole wishes to declare on that subject.

The world that the Mishnah addressed was hardly congruent to the worldview presented within the Mishnah. In the aftermath of Bar Kokhba's war against Rome in 132–135 CE, Jews were barred from Jerusalem and the Temple. Thus, at this time, there was no cult, no Temple, no holy city to which the Mishnaic laws applied. The laws of the Mishnah were formulated before the loss of the Temple, but the codification of the laws began after the Temple was gone. Therefore, at the very outset, a sizable proportion of the Mishnah dealt with matters to which the sages had no material access or practical knowledge of at the time of their work. We have seen that the Mishnah contains a division on the conduct of the cult (the fifth division), as well as one on the preservation of the cultic purity of the sacrificial system along the lines laid out in the book of Leviticus (the sixth division). In fact, a fair part of the second division takes up the conduct of the cult on special days—e.g., the sacrifices offered on the Day of Atonement (YOM KIPPUR), PASSOVER, and the like. Indeed, what the Mishnah wants to know about appointed seasons concerns the cult far more than it does the synagogue. The fourth division, on civil law, presents an elaborate account of a political structure and system of Israelite self-government that speaks of king, priest, Temple, and court. But in the time in which the 2nd-century authorities did their work it was not Jewish kings, priests, and judges who conducted the government of Israel in the Land of Israel but the Romans. So it would appear that well over half of the document speaks of the lost cult, Temple, government, and priesthood. Moreover, as we shall see, the Mishnah takes up a profoundly priestly and Levitical conception of sanctification. When we consider that the Temple lay in ruins, the city of Jerusalem was prohibited to all Israelites, and the Jewish government and administration that had been centered on the Temple and based its authority on the holy life there were dismantled, the fantastic character of the Mishnah's address to its own catastrophic day becomes clear. Much of the Mishnah speaks of matters not in being at the time of its creation, because the Mishnah wishes to make its statement on what really matters.

The Mishnah tells us something about how things were, but it tells us everything about how a small group of rabbinic sages wanted things to be. The document is orderly, repetitious, and careful in both language and message. It is small-minded, picayune, obvious, dull, and routine—everything its age was not. Standing in contrast with the world to which it speaks, the Mishnah's message is one of small achievements and modest hope intended to defy a world of large disorders and immodest demands. It offers this message to an Israelite world that could not shape affairs in any important ways and speaks to people who by no means willed the way things were. The Mishnah lays down a practical judgment on and in favor of a people who must go forth with the imagination and will to reshape their reality, regain a system, and reestablish an order upon which trustworthy existence is to be built.

The Mishnah's principal message is that humanity is at the center of creation, and as the head of all creatures upon earth, corresponds to God in heaven, in whose image humanity is made. The Mishnah makes this simple and fundamental statement by imputing the power to man to inaugurate and initiate those corresponding processes, sanctification and uncleanness, which play such a critical role in the Mishnah's account of reality. Human will, expressed through human deed, is the active power in the world. Will and deed constitute those actors of creation that work upon those neutral realms that are subject to either sanctification or uncleanness: the Temple and table, the field and family, the altar and hearth, as well as woman, time, space, and transactions in the material world and in the world above as well. An object, a substance, a transaction, even a phrase or a sentence is inert but may be made holy when its potential to be sanctified is aroused or generated by the interplay of man's will and deed. Each thing may either be treated as ordinary or (where relevant) made unclean by the neglect of the will and the inattentive acts of humankind. The entire system of uncleanness and holiness awaits the intervention of humanity, which imparts the capacity to become unclean upon what was formerly inert, or which removes the capacity to impart cleanness from what was formerly in its natural and powerful condition. Likewise, in the other ranges of reality humanity is at the center on earth, just as is God in heaven. People are God's counterpart and partner in creation, and, like God, they have power over the status and condition of creation, putting everything in its proper place, and calling everything by its rightful name.

Whereas the urgent question had previously been "Who is Israel?," when the answer was found by Judaism in the first Rabbinic

Roman soldiers carrying the menorah taken from the Temple of Jerusalem as war booty, 70 CE; detail of a relief on the Arch of Titus, Rome, 81 CE
Alinari—Art Resource

phase—that Israel is the surviving people faithful to the Covenant—the question then became "What can a man do?" Addressing itself to holy Israel, the Mishnah proceeded to answer that man, through will and deed, is master of this world, the measure of all things. When the Mishnah thinks of man it means Israel, the subject and actor of its system, and so the statement is clear: this man is Israel, who can do what he wills. In the aftermath of the two Roman wars (66–73 and 132–135 CE), the message of the Mishnah cannot have proved more pertinent—or poignant and tragic. The first stage of Rabbinic Judaism's formation therefore answered a single encompassing question: in the aftermath of the destruction of the holy place and holy cult, what remained of the sanctity of the priestly caste, the holy land, and, above all, Israel and its holy way of life? The answer was that sanctity persists, indelibly, in Israel, the people—in its way of life, in its land, in its priesthood, in its food, in its mode of sustaining life, in its manner of procreating and so sustaining the nation—and that sanctity would endure. But in time to come that answer found itself absorbed within a successor-system, one with its own points of stress and emphasis.

The second phase of Rabbinic Judaism. Rabbinic Judaism, which emerged about 70 CE and reached its final statement in the Talmud Bavli, took shape in response to both internal and external stimuli. Its internal set of questions derived from the character of the Mishnah itself, while its external questions came from the catastrophic political change the Jews underwent following the conversion of the Roman emperor CONSTANTINE I to Christianity in 312 and the subsequent establishment of the Christian religion as the religion of the state.

As soon as the Mishnah made its appearance in about 200 CE the vast labor of explaining its meaning and justifying its authority got under way. The Mishnah presented one striking problem in particular: it rarely cited scriptural authority for its rules. By omitting scriptural proof-texts, the Mishnah bore the implicit claim to an authority independent of Scripture, and in that striking fact the Mishnah set a new course for itself, raising problems for those who would apply its laws. From the time of the formation of ancient Israelite Scripture into a holy book, the Torah—after the return to Zion in Ezra's time (c. 450 BCE)—the established canon of revelation (whatever its contents) was with Scripture, in that proof-texts were cited alongside their own rules. Otherwise the new writings could find no ready hearing in Israelite culture.

Over the next 650 years after the formation of the Torah, four conventional ways to accommodate new writings, or new "tradition," to the established canon of received Scripture had come to the fore. First and simplest, a writer would sign a famous name to his book, attributing his ideas to Adam, Enoch, Jacob's sons, JEREMIAH, Baruch, or any number of others, down to Ezra. But the Mishnah bore no such attribution. Implicitly the Mishnah carried the further notion that sayings of people on the list of authorities from Moses to nearly their own day derived from God's revelation at Sinai. But no one made that premise explicit before the time of the Talmud Yerushalmi. Second, an author might also imitate the style of biblical Hebrew and so try to creep into the canon under the cloak of Scripture. But the Mishnah's authors ignore biblical syntax and style. Third, an author would surely claim his work was inspired by God, a new revelation for an open canon. The Mishnah, however, contains no claim that it forms part of the Torah of Sinai; that claim would be added only in the mid-3rd century by the compilers of the Pirke Abot ("The Sayings of Our Fathers"), which linked authorities of the Mishnah to Moses on Sinai. Fourth, at the very least, an author would link his opinions to biblical verses by including an EXEGESIS of the latter in line with the former so that Scripture would validate his views. The authorship of the Mishnah did so occasionally, but far more commonly stated on its own authority whatever rules it proposed to lay down.

The solution to the problem of the Mishnah's authority—that is, its relationship to Scripture—was worked out after its compilation and set forth in the subsequent writings of the rabbis, particularly in the Talmuds, the commentaries to the Mishnah. There were several ways in which the work of legitimization went forward, as represented by diverse documents that succeeded and dealt with the

A page of the tractate Makkot *of the fourth order,* Neziqin, *from the Vilna edition of the Bavli, or Babylonian Talmud, first printed 1880–86. It concerns the fate of a man who was convicted and escaped and how he is to be judged. The box surrounding the Mishnah and code numbers have been superimposed on the page. They indicate a variety of notes, commentaries, and references to Scripture and other Talmudic and Rabbinic sources that span hundreds of years of scholarship*
By courtesy of the Library of the Jewish Theological Seminary of America, New York; Frank J. Darmstaedter

Mishnah. The three principal forms of legitimization were: (1) The tractate Abot (*c.* 250 CE), which represents the authority of the sages cited in Abot as autonomous of Scripture. Abot claims the Mishnah requires no systematic support through exegesis of Scripture in light of Mishnaic laws. The authorities in Abot do not cite verses of Scripture, but what they say does constitute a statement of the Torah. (2) The book TOSEFTA (*c.* 400 CE), whose authors took the middle position that the Mishnah by itself provided no reliable information and all its propositions demanded linkage to Scripture, to which the Mishnah must be subordinate and secondary. Tosefta very commonly cites a passage of the Mishnah and then adds an appropriate proof text. (3) The far extreme, which states that everything in the Mishnah makes sense only as a (re)statement of Scripture or upon Scripture's authority. This stance was taken by the SIFRA, a post-Mishnaic compilation of exegeses on Leviticus, redacted at an indeterminate point, perhaps about 300 CE. The Sifra systematically demolishes the logic that sustains an autonomous Mishnah, for the Mishnah appeals to the intrinsic traits of things, and those traits allow for classification and hierarchization; it in no way depends on classification from external sources (not even Scripture). Sifra, however, demonstrates that the identification of the correct classification of things depends not upon the traits of things viewed in the abstract but upon the classification of things by Scripture. The framers of the Sifra thus recast the two parts of the Torah into a single coherent statement through unitary and cogent discourse. So the authorship of Sifra made its entire statement by choosing, for structure, a book of the Pentateuch—Leviticus—and, for form, an exegesis of a base-text of Scripture.

THE CHALLENGE OF CHRISTIANITY

Five fundamentally important events in the history of Judaism took place in the 4th and 5th centuries CE. All of them except for the last were well known in their day. These events were as follows: (1) the Christian conversion of the Roman emperor Constantine in 312; (2) the failure of the emperor Julian's (reigned 361–363) plan to rebuild the Temple of Jerusalem, seen by Israel as a sign of its reconciliation with God; (3) the beginning of the depaganization of the Roman Empire, including a program of attacks on PAGAN temples and, along the way, synagogues; (4) the Christianization of the majority of the population of Palestine (the land Jews believed God had set apart for the people of Israel); and (5) the creation of the Talmud Yerushalmi and of the compositions of Scriptural exegeses, in particular GENESIS RABBAH and LEVITICUS RABBAH (both part of midrash Rabbah). This world-historical change could not be absorbed into Israel's system of theories on the outsiders (GENTILES), in general, and the meaning of the history of the great empires, in particular. (That theory—coming from, among other places, the books of the prophets—contained the belief the God of Israel is revealed in the events of nations and the history of the world, and not only through the rhythms of nature. For example, when God was pleased with Israel, Israel was given self-rule. But the Pentateuch at Leviticus 26 and Deuteronomy 32–34 stated explicitly that Israel's rule by pagans was God's punishment of Israel's disobedient intransigence toward his covenant.)

Additionally, the Roman Empire under Christianity was fundamentally different in two ways from the Empire under pagan rulers. First, it shared Israel's reverence for exactly the same Holy Scriptures on which Jewry based its existence. So it was no longer a wholly other, entirely alien empire that ruled over the horizon. It was now a monotheist biblical empire, formerly persecuted and not so different from Israel in its basic convictions about the all important matters of time and eternity. The Christian emperors read the same Scriptures as the rabbis, so the challenge to Judaism was acute in a way that the pagan challenge had never been. Second, established policies of more than a half a millennium—from the time of the Maccabees' alliance with Rome to the start of the 4th century—now gave way. Pagan tolerance of Judaism and an accommodation with the Jews in their Holy Land (disrupted only by the Jews' own violation of the terms of the agreement in 66–73 and 132–135) was no longer a governing principle. Instead, there was intolerance of Judaism and persecution of Jews through attacks on their persons and property.

Given the political changes of the age, with their implications for the meaning and end of history as Israel would experience it, the fresh emphasis on salvation, the introduction of the figure of the Messiah as a principal teleological force, the statement of an eschatological teleology for the system as a whole—these constitute answers to questions that were raised by Christian theologians. These theologians held that the Christian triumph confirmed the Godhood of Jesus and thus the rejection of Israel and the end of Israel's hope for salvation at the end of time. The answer offered by Judaic sages was the Torah in its dual media, the affirmation of Israel as children of Abraham, Isaac, and Jacob, and the coming of the Messiah at the end of time. The questions and answers fit the challenge of the age.

Canon. The text-based answer to Christianity's ascent was revealed in the unfolding of the sages' canon as it pertained to the use of Scripture. The Mishnah and the exegetical literature that served it (*e.g.*, the Tosefta and the Talmuds) had followed a topical organizational pattern that arranged ideas by subject matter. However, in the 3rd and, especially, the later 4th centuries, writings entering the sages' canon took shape around the explanation of verses of Scripture, instead of around a set of topics.

From the 4th century the rabbis produced compositions of biblical exegeses that were collected into holy books. The making of such collections facilitated the next natural step in the process as precipitated by the appearance of the Mishnah. Christianity addressed the world (including the Jews) with a systematic exegetical apologetic—Matthew's and the other Gospels demonstrated a living exegesis showing how events in the life of Jesus fulfilled the prophecies of the shared Scripture (the OLD TESTAMENT). The Judaic task of creating a counterpart exegesis of the Mishnah was a pressing issue in the confrontation with Christianity; it became necessary to show in a systematic and orderly way how Scripture was to be read by Israel. In the Mishnah the sages had found a systematic exegesis of Scripture unnecessary since there was no contrary reading to theirs to present a challenge. But confronting the powerful Christian challenge made further indifference impolitic and impossible, and sages replied with their compositions of the Talmud and the midrashic compilations, restating their reading of Scripture in the face of the Christians' interpretation of God's message.

By the 4th century the Christian church had reached a consensus on the bulk of the NEW TESTAMENT canon, having earlier accepted the Old Testament. Accordingly, the issue of what constituted Scripture had come to the fore for Judaism, as Christianity focused the sages' attention on that larger matter of systematic exegesis. This issue was raised, for example, when the Christian scholar JEROME (d. 419/420) referred to the Jews' having a "second" Torah (meaning the oral Torah) that was not authoritative, and when a series of important fathers of the Christian church produced profoundly Christological exegeses of Scripture. It would be heightened when the sages, speaking on their own and to their chosen audience, went through pretty much the same processes. They explained the standing of that "second Torah" and produced not merely counterpart exegeses to those of the Christians but counterpart compilations of such exegeses as well.

Symbol.   As the generative symbol of the literary culture of the sages, the Torah stands for the system of Rabbinic Judaisms as a whole. The Torah was symbolic of the doctrine that Moses received the Torah at Mount Sinai in two media, written and oral. The written Torah was transmitted and is now contained in the Pentateuch. The oral Torah was formulated for ease in memorization and then transmitted through sages and their disciples, from Moses and Joshua to the most current generation of rabbis today.

That doctrine of the dual Torah, that is, of the Torah in two media, came about in response to the problem of explaining the standing and authority of the Mishnah. But broadening the symbol of the Torah was actually accomplished around the figure of the sage. The symbol of the Torah accounted for the sages' authority—the sage being the one in possession of God's oral law. Only later on in the pages of the Talmud Yerushalmi did the doctrine of the dual Torah reach expression. So in the evolution of the documents of the canon of Judaism, the generative symbol of Torah reveals a striking change. Beginning as a rather generalized account of how sages' teachings relate to God's will, the symbol of Torah gained concrete form in its application to the dual Torah, written and oral, Pentateuch and Mishnah. What once stood for a few specific books came to stand for all the teachings and laws of Israel, as well as the system that taught and promulgated those laws.

Torah thus took on a multiplicity of meaning: standing for a kind of human being, connoting a social status and group, and referring to a type of social relationship. It further came to denote a legal status, differentiating things and persons, actions and status, as well as "revealed truth." In all, the main points of insistence of the whole of Israel's life and history come to full symbolic expression in that single word. If people wanted to explain how they would be saved, they would use the word Torah. Torah stood for salvation and accounted for Israel's this-worldly condition and the hope, for both individual and nation alike, of life in the world to come. For the kind of Judaism under discussion, therefore, the word Torah stood for everything, symbolizing at once the whole.

After the appearance of the Mishnah, the Torah moved, in two significant stages, from standing for a concrete, material object, a scroll, to symbolizing a broad range of relationships. The first stage is marked off by tractate Abot, the second by the Talmud Yerushalmi. As to the former, Abot regards the study of Torah as what a sage does, while the substance of Torah is what a sage says, and likewise what a sage says falls into the classification of Torah. At issue in Abot is not Torah but the authority of the sage. It is the sage's standing that transforms a saying into a Torah-saying, placing it into the classification of Torah. Abot then stands as the first document of incipient Rabbinic Judaism—the doctrine wherein the sage embodies the Torah and is a holy man in the likeness and image of God, like Moses "our rabbi." So the claim that a saying falls into the category of Torah if a sage says it as Torah leads to the view that the sage himself is Torah incarnate.

To the rabbis the principal salvific deed was to "study Torah;" memorizing Torah-sayings by constant repetition, and, as the Yerushalmi itself amply testifies, for some sages this included profound analytic inquiry into the meanings of those sayings. The innovation alters the symbol such that the "study of Torah" is imparted with a material supernatural power. For example, by repeating words of Torah as incantations, the sage could ward off the angel of death, as well as accomplish other kinds of miracles. Mastery of Torah transformed the man engaged in Torah-learning into a supernatural figure, able to do things ordinary folk could not. The vast expansion of the category of "Torah" meant that through the transformation of the Torah from a concrete thing to a symbol, a Torah-scroll could be compared to a man of Torah, namely, a rabbi. It had been established that salvation would come from keeping God's will in general, as Israelite holy men had insisted for so many centuries. So it was a small step for rabbis to identify their particular corpus of learning, namely, the Mishnah and associated sayings, with God's will as expressed in Scripture, which was the universally acknowledged medium of revelation.

The symbolization of the Torah proceeded from its removal from the framework of material objects, or of its own contents, to its transformation into something quite different and abstract, distinct from the document and its teachings. Specifically, the Torah stands for something more when it comes to be identified with a living person, the sage, and endowed with those particular traits that the sage claimed for himself.

Teleology. The teleology of a system answers the question of a system's purpose and goal, presupposing that a system has a purpose or goal. Teleology explains why someone should do what the system requires, and what will happen if they do not. The Mishnah and its closely related successor documents, Abot and the Tosefta in particular, present a teleology without eschatological focus (that is, a teleology in which the messianic theme plays no considerable role). These books speak more commonly about preparing in this world for life in the world to come, and focus on the individual and his or her personal salvation, rather than the nation and its destiny at the end of time. By contrast, the Talmuds provide an eschatological and therefore messiah-centered teleology. Theirs is the more familiar teleology of Judaism, which, from the Talmud Yerushalmi onward, commonly explains the meaning of the Rabbinic system of Judaism by referring to the end of time and the coming of the Messiah.

Torah scroll
The Jewish Museum

The Mishnah's authors constructed a system of Judaism in which the entire teleological dimension reached full exposure while hardly invoking the person or functions of a messianic figure of any kind. The Mishnah's framers presented no elaborate theory of events, a fact fully consonant with their systematic points of insistence and encompassing concern: one by one, events do not matter. The philosopher-lawyers also exhibited no theory of history. Their conception of Israel's destiny was not historical but existential. They did not retell stories, or teach lessons called for by events. They taught that the future would be shaped by the character of Israel in the here and now; its loyalty to the Torah that marked its convenant with God in no way called upon historical categories of either narrative or didactic explanation to describe and account for the future. Therefore, the small importance attributed to the figure of the Messiah as a historical-eschatological figure is in full accord with the larger traits of the system as a whole. If, as in the Mishnah, what is important in Israel's existence was the ongoing process of sanctification and not a salvation understood as a one-time event at the end of time, then there was no reason to narrate history. Thus few formed the obsession about the Messiah so characteristic of Judaism in its later, Rabbinic mode, when a messianic focus formed, in large part, in response to the sudden ascent of Christianity.

The Talmudic reply to political events. With its political triumph, Christianity's explicit claims, now validated in the world-shaking events of the age, demanded a reply. The sages of the Talmud Yerushalmi provided it. Responding to the very specific points where the Christian challenge met old Israel's worldview head-on, the sages' doctrines reemphasized the biblical message that history teaches lessons. They restated the Pentateuchal-prophetic teaching that said Israel's covenant with God accounts for Israel's fate and they stressed the Pentateuchal theme that Israel was to make itself holy because the Lord God is holy and Israel was to be like God. The sages also taught that when Israel had made itself holy ("sanctified") God would respond by saving Israel from its lamentable situation among the nations and bring it back to the Land for judgment and entry into the world to come.

What did Israel's sages have to present as the Torah's answer to the cross, with its doctrine of the triumphant Christ, Messiah and king, ruler now of earth as of heaven? It was the Torah in three forms. The Torah was defined in the doctrine, first, as the status, as oral and memorized revelation, of the Mishnah, and, by implication, of other rabbinical writings. The Torah, moreover, was presented as the encompassing symbol of Israel's salvation. The Torah, finally, was embodied in the person of the Messiah who, of course, would be a rabbi. The outcome was a stunning success for that society for which the sages, and, in the sages' view, God, cared so deeply: eternal Israel "after the flesh" (*i.e.*, those who are Jewish by birth). In the rabbis' statement Judaism did endure in the Christian West, as the sages gave Israel a secure conviction of an Israel after the flesh, to which the Torah continued to speak. We know the sages' Judaism won because when, in turn, Islam gained its victory, Christianity throughout the Middle East and North Africa gave way, leaving only pockets of the faithful. But the sages' Judaism in those same vast territories retained the loyalty and conviction of the people of the Torah. The cross would rule only where the crescent did not, but the Torah of Sinai, sanctified Israel in time everywhere and always, and promised secure salvation for eternity.

RABBINIC JUDAISM'S SUCCESS IN WESTERN CIVILIZATION

The eventual success of Rabbinic Judaism in overcoming Christianity's challenge and holding the faith of its people cannot be attributed only to its power to recapitulate and systematize Scripture's system. Whatever the power of a well-crafted and cogent theology, in the end the political and social world also decided the fate of Rabbinic Judaism. Judaism endured in the Christian West, as well as in the Muslim East, for two reasons. First, Christianity and Islam permitted it, and second, Israel, the Jewish people, wanted it to endure.

The importance of the first of the two factors can be seen in the fate of paganism in the 4th century (and the fate in the 7th and 8th centuries under Islam of ZOROASTRIANISM and Sabianism, a religion that worshiped a moon deity at Harran in Assyria). It was not the intellectual power of sages alone that secured the long-term triumph of Judaism. It also was the Christian emperors' policy toward Judaism that afforded to Jews and their religion such toleration as they would enjoy then and thereafter. There may have been some incidents of ANTI-SEMITISM against Jews or their synagogues, but the religious worship of Judaism was never actually prohibited. Pagan sacrifice, by contrast, came under interdict in 341, and, while pagan festivals went on into the 5th century, the die had been cast.

But the Jews also remained faithful to Rabbinic Judaism because it contained the answers that allowed them to make sense of their world. The Judaism of the dual Torah constructed for Israel a world in which the loss of political sovereignty and the persistence of tolerated subordination within Islamic and Christian nations actually attested to Israel's importance and centrality in the human situation. So the long-term condition of the conquered people found more than mere explanation in that pattern which had defined God's will in the Torah for Israel beyond the first catastrophe and restoration. That generative experience of loss and restoration, death and resurrection, set forth by the first Scripture allowed Israel to maintain a renewed sense of its own distinctive standing among the nations of the world.

But while Judaism taught the Jews that Israel's subordinated position gave probative evidence of its true standing, Judaism also promised an eventual ascendancy: the low would be raised up, the humble placed into authority, the proud reduced, the world made right. So the Judaism of the dual Torah did more than react: it reassured and encouraged. For a long time that Judaism defined the politics and policy of the community. It instructed Israel, the Jewish people, on the rules for the formation of the appropriate world and it designed those attitudes and actions that would yield an Israel on one side subordinate and tolerated, but on the other proud and hopeful. The Judaism of the dual Torah began with the encounter of a successful Christianity and persisted in the face of a still more successful Islam. But for Israel, the Jewish people, that Judaism persevered long after the conditions that originally precipitated the positions and policies deemed normative, because that same Judaism not only reacted to, but also shaped Israel's condition in the world. In making a virtue of a policy of subordination that was not always necessary or even wise, the Judaism of the dual Torah defined the Jews' condition and set the limits to its circumstance.

The theology of Rabbinic Judaism. The theological beliefs of Rabbinic Judaism—the Judaism that had become the normative system—are as follows: God is one and unique, loving and just. Monotheism by nature explains many things in a single way. One God rules. Life is meant to be fair, and just rules should describe what is ordinary, all in the name of that one and only God. Thus, in monotheism a simple logic governs, limiting the ways of making sense of things. But that logic contains its own dialectics. If one true all-powerful and omniscient God has done everything, then all things are credited to, and blamed on, him. In that case he can be either good or bad, just or unjust—but not both. Responding to the generative dialectics of monotheism, the sages' dual Torah systematically reveals the justice of the one and only God of all creation. God is not only God but he is also good. Appealing to the facts of Scripture—the written part of the Torah—the sages constructed in the documents of the Oral part of the Torah a coherent theology, creating a cogent structure and logical system to expose the justice of God. The theology of the dual Torah presents a world order based on God's justice and equity. The categorical structure of the dual Torah encompasses God and humans, the Torah, and Israel and the nations. The working system of the dual Torah finds its dynamic in the struggle between God's plan for creation—to create a perfect world of justice—and man's will. That dialectic took the events contained in the sequences of rebellion, sin, punishment, repentance, and atonement; exile and return; and embodied them in a single paradigm: the disruption of world order and its subsequent restoration.

The four principles of the dual Torah's theology are as follows:

1. God formed creation according to a plan, which the Torah reveals. The facts

Illuminated page of the Mishne Torah, written by Moses Maimonides, c. *1351*
Giraudon—Art Resource

of nature and society set forth in that plan conform to a pattern of reason based upon justice, showing the world order. Those who possess the Torah (Israel) know God and those who do not (the Gentiles) reject him in favor of idols. What happens to each of these two sectors of humanity depends on their respective relationship with God. Israel in the present age is subordinate to the nations, because God has designated the Gentiles as the medium for penalizing Israel's rebellion, provoking Israel to repent through its subordination and exile. Private life and the public order conform to the principle that God rules justly in a perfected and static creation.

2. The perfection of creation, as realized in the rule of exact justice, is signified by the timelessness of the world of human affairs—this world conforms to a few enduring paradigms that transcend change (a theory known as the theology of history). Time is marked not by present, past, or future but only by the recapitulation of those patterns. Perfection is further embodied in the unchanging relationships of the social commonwealth (an idea known as the theology of political economy), assuring that scarce resources, once allocated, remain in stasis. A further indication of perfection lies on one side in how the components of creation complement one another, and on the other, the correspondence between God and man, who was made in God's image (known as theological anthropology).

3. Israel's public and personal condition marks flaws in creation. Perfection is disrupted by the sole power capable of standing on its own against God's power: man's FREE WILL. What man controls and God cannot coerce is man's capacity to form intention and therefore choose to either arrogantly defy God or humbly love God. Because man defies God, the sin that results from man's rebellion flaws creation and disrupts world order (a view known as theodicy, which defends the goodness of God despite evil in the world). The paradigm of Adam's rebellion in Eden governs; thus the act of arrogance leading to exile from Eden accounts for the condition of humanity. But, as in the original transaction of alienation and consequent exile, God retains the power to encourage repentance through the punishment of man's arrogance. In mercy, moreover, God exercises the power to respond to repentance with forgiveness; a change of attitude can evoke a counterpart change. Since he commands his own will, man also has the power to initiate the process of reconciliation with God, through an act of humility and repentance, man may restore the perfection of that order that his arrogance has marred.

4. God ultimately will restore the perfection that embodied his plan for creation. In this restoration death by reason of sin will die, the dead will be raised and judged for their deeds, and most of them, having been justified, will go on to eternal life in the world to come. The paradigm of man's restoration to Eden is realized in Israel's, the people's, return to the Land of Israel at the resurrection of the dead and the LAST JUDGMENT. In the language of the Mishnah tractate Sanhedrin, "All Israel has a portion in the world to come," meaning that Israel, the people, will be brought back to the land, judged, and (in most cases) granted eternal life in Eden. (This eschatological theology should not be confused with contemporary political and secular events.) In that world or age to come the sector of hu-

manity that knows God through the Torah will encompass all of humanity. Idolators will perish, and the humanity that comprises Israel at the end will know the one, true God and spend eternity in his light.

Here we have nothing other than the Pentateuch's paradigm of exile and return, beginning with the fall of Adam and the loss of Eden, and paralleled in the fall of Israel and the loss of the Land of Israel, Jerusalem, and the Temple. But the sages underscored that, as prophecy insisted, through return to God, Israel would recover and keep its Eden. And, they added, even now on certain occasions and through certain rites and practices on the Sabbath Israel could regain Eden for a moment. In the dual Torah the rabbis reworked Scripture's story, trying to translate its lessons into the organizational norms of the community of Israel. The law represented the conclusions drawn by sages from Scripture's story about humanity from Genesis through Israel in 586. Furthermore, the liturgy of synagogue and home recapitulates the characteristic modes of thought of the dual Torah and reworks its distinctive constructions of exemplary figures, events, and conceptions. In defining the religion the world calls "Judaism" and that calls itself "the Torah," sages have always maintained that they possessed the Torah revealed by God to Moses at Mount Sinai ("Moses received Torah at Sinai and handed it on to Joshua, Joshua to elders, and elders to prophets, and prophets handed it on to the men of the great assembly" [Mishnah Abot 1:1]). As a matter of fact, by making the theology of the dual Torah the pivot between the written Torah and the liturgy and piety of the faith, the sages were right in registering that claim.

Set forth baldly, Rabbinic Judaism takes up the critical theological heritage of the Hebrew Scriptures and hands it on to the age to come as an ordered, coherent, integrated system. Sages take as their task the recapitulation of the structure and system that they identify with the written Torah and encompass within that theology their own, as we see, very limited amplifications. For sages implicitly insist that those very ideas—that logic, this story of theirs—do recapitulate the ones set forth by the written Torah. Their heirs, in early medieval times, saw in the dual Torah, written and oral, a single coherent revelation: "the one whole Torah given by God to Moses, our rabbi, at Sinai." That apologetics, integral to the theology of the oral Torah, takes a critical position in nearly every line of every document. It defines the form of many documents and the generative energy of them all.

The hegemony of Rabbinic Judaism. In the history of Judaism from the 7th to the 20th centuries two facts attested to the power of Rabbinic Judaism. First, the Judaic system was able to absorb massive innovations in modes of thought and media of piety. Second, the same system defined issues so that heresies took shape in explicit response to its doctrines, showing that the system predominated to the extent that it dictated the character of its critics and enemies.

The power of the Judaism of the dual Torah and the cogency of the system is attested to by its capacity to both precipitate and also accommodate diverse Judaisms. Over the centuries, from the 4th to the present time, derivative systems took shape, restating in distinctive ways the fundamental convictions of the Judaism of the dual Torah, or adding their particular perspective or doctrine to that system.

Others attained heretical status specifically by rejecting important components of the received system—e.g., its doctrine of the dual Torah or of the Messiah as a sage and model of the Torah fully observed. So long as the self-evident truth of the established Judaism persisted for believers, each of these derivative systems—orthodox or heretical—had a relationship with that fundamentally paramount statement of matters. It was only when this received Judaism no longer enjoyed a virtually unique standing as the valid answer to urgent questions that Judaic systems took shape that were utterly out of phase with that system that had reached its initial version in the 4th century and its final one in the Talmud Bavli.

Within Rabbinic Judaism, however, most of the diverse systems found ample space for their beliefs without resorting to HERESY. Some of these systems concerned new doctrines which had to be brought into accord with the received ones. Among them, for example, was a massive rethinking of the very modes of thought of Judaism, which took shape over a long period of time, moving from mythic to philosophical thinking. The philosophical movement presents striking testimony to the power of the received system, for it set out to validate and vindicate the faith of that system, inclusive of the law and doctrine of the oral Torah. Each continuator-Judaism laid its stress on a received component of the original system or explicitly reaffirmed the whole of that system, while adding to it in interesting ways. All of the continuator-Judaisms claimed to stand in a linear and incremental relationship to the original. For example, they made constant reference to the established and authoritative canon or affirmed the importance of meticulous obedience to the law. Each one in its own way proposed to strengthen, purify or otherwise confirm the dual Torah of Sinai.

SUBSETS OF RABBINIC JUDAISM

New modes of thought and the advent of philosophical thinking.   Because of the character of Islamic culture, the rise of Islam brought important intellectual changes to Judaism. The system set forth by Rabbinic Judaism accommodated this new mode of thought. Specifically, Muslim theologians—who could read Greek (or who read Greek philosophy translated into Arabic)—developed a rigorous, abstract, and scientific mode of thought along philosophical lines, with special interest in a close reading of Aristotle, one of the founders of the philosophical tradition. Rabbinic Judaism, embodied in the great authorities of the Torah, naturalized philosophy within the framework of the dual Torah. While in ancient times a school of Judaic philosophy in the Greek-speaking Jewish world—represented by Philo of Alexandria (d. 45–50 CE)—read Scripture in a philosophical light, the sages of the Talmud did not follow that generalizing and speculative mode of thought. But as the Judaic intellectuals under Muslim rule faced the challenge of Muslim RATIONALISM and philosophical rigor, they read Scripture as well as the oral Torah in a new way, attempting to reconcile and accommodate

Hasidic Jews,
New York City
Photo Researchers

the one with the other. In medieval Islamdom and Christendom, no Judaic intellectuals could rest easy in an admission of conflict between Scripture and science in its philosophical form.

Thus, alongside study of Torah—the spending of one's life in learning the Talmud Bavli and later codes, commentaries, and rabbinical court decisions—a different sort of intellectual-religious life flourished in classical Judaism. It was the study of the tradition through the instruments of reason and the discipline of philosophy. The philosophical enterprise attracted small numbers of elitists and mainly served their specialized spiritual and intellectual needs. But they set the standard, and those who followed it included the thoughtful and the perplexed—those who took the statements of the tradition most seriously and intended through questioning and reflection, to examine and then effect them. The philosophers, moreover, did not limit their activities to study and teaching; they frequently occupied high posts within the Jewish community and served in the high society of politics, culture, and science outside the community as well. Though not numerous, the philosophers exercised considerable influence.

Philosophy flourished in a world of deep religious conviction—a conviction common to the several disparate religious communities. The issues of philosophy were set not by lack of belief but by deep faith; few, if any, denied the ideas of providence, a personal God, and a holy book revealed by God through his chosen messenger. Nearly everyone believed in reward and punishment, in a last judgment, and in a settling of accounts. The Jewish philosopher had to cope with problems imposed not only by the classical faith but also by the anomalous situation of the Jews themselves. How was philosophy to account reasonably for the homelessness of God's people, who were well aware that they lived as a minority among powerful, prosperous majorities of Christians or Muslims? If Torah were true, why did different revelations claiming to be based upon it—but to complete it—flourish while the people of the Torah suffered? Why, indeed, ought one remain a Jew when every day one was confronted by the success of the daughter religions? For a member of a despised minority conversion was always an inviting possibility, even under the best of circumstances. The search was complicated by the formidable appeal of Greek philosophy to medieval Christian and Islamic civilization. Philosophy's rationalism, openness, and search for pure knowledge challenged all revelations, and called into question all assertions of truth that were verifiable not through reason but only through appeals to a source of truth not universally recognized. Thus it seemed reason stood against revelation. Mysterious divine plans came into conflict with allegations of the limitless capacity of human reason: free inquiry might lead anywhere, and not necessarily to the synagogue, church, or mosque. And not just traditional knowledge, but the specific propositions of faith and the assertions of a holy book had to be measured against the results of reason. Faith or reason—this seemed to be the choice.

For the Jews, moreover, a formidable obstacle was posed by the very substance of their faith in a personal, highly anthropomorphic God who exhibited character traits not always in conformity with humanity's highest ideals and who in rabbinic hands looked much like the rabbi himself. Classical philosophical conundrums were further enriched by the obvious contradictions between belief in free will and belief in divine providence. Is God all-knowing? Then how can people be held responsible for what they do? Is God perfect? Then how can he change his mind or set aside his laws to forgive people? No theologian in such a cosmopolitan, rational age could permit the assertion of a double truth or a private, relative truth. There was little appeal in the notion that something could be true for one party and not for another, or that faith and reason were equally valid and yet contradictory. The holy book had to retain the upper hand. Two philosophers represent the best efforts of medieval Judaic civilization to confront these perplexities.

Maimonides (1135–1204). First is MOSES MAIMONIDES, who was a distinguished student of the Talmud and of Jewish law in the classical mode, a community authority, a great physician, and a leading thinker of his day. His achievement was to synthesize a Neoplatonic Aristotelianism with biblical revelation. His *The Guide of the Perplexed* (original Arabic title, *Dalālat al-ḥāʾirīn*, later known under its Hebrew title as the *More nevukhim*), compiled in 1190, was intended to reconcile the believer to the philosopher and the philosopher to faith. For him philosophy was not alien to religion but identical with it, for in the end truth was the sole issue. Faith is a form of knowledge; philosophy is the road to faith. His proof for the existence of God was Aristotelian. He argued from creation to Creator but accepted the eternity of the world. God becomes, therefore an "absolutely simple essence from which all positive definition is excluded" (Julius Guttmann, *Philosophies of Judaism: The History of Jewish Philosophy from Biblical Times to Franz Rosenzweig,* trans. by David Silverman [1964], p. 158). One can say nothing about the attributes of God. He is purged of all sensuous elements. One can say only that God is God, and nothing more, for God can only be known as the highest cause of being.

What then of revelation? Did God not say anything about himself? And if he did, what need is there for reasonings such as these? For Maimonides, prophecy, like philosophy, depends upon the active intellect (human intellectual and imaginative capabilities). Prophecy is a gift bestowed by God upon man. The Torah and commandments are clearly important, but ultimately are not beyond question or reasonable inquiry. They, however, survive the inquiry unimpaired. The Torah fosters a sound mind and body. The greatest good, however, is not to study Torah in the sense described earlier, but rather to know God—that is, to worship and love him. Piety and knowledge of Torah serve merely to prepare people for this highest achievement. The study of Torah loses its character as an end in itself and becomes a means to a philosophical goal. This constituted the most striking transformation of the old values.

Maimonides provided a philosophical definition of Judaism—a list of articles of faith he thought obligatory for every faithful Jew. These required beliefs are as follows: (1) that God exists, (2) he has absolute unity, (3) he is incorporeal, (4) he is eternal, (5) he must be worshiped exclusively, (6) he speaks through prophecy, (7) that Moses was the greatest of the prophets, (8) that the Torah is divine in origin, (9) that the Torah is eternally valid, (10) that God has knowledge of man's deeds, (11) that God will reward and punish mankind, (12) that God has promised to send a messiah, and (13) that God has promised to resurrect the dead. The esoteric words of the philosopher were thus transformed into a message of faith complex enough to sustain critical inquiry according to the canons of the day and simple enough to bear the weight of the faith of ordinary folk and to be sung in the synagogue, as the hymn entitled "Yigdal." The "God without attributes" remains guide, refuge, and stronghold.

Judah ha-Levi (1080–1141). JUDAH HA-LEVI was a poet and mystic who represented those Jews who did not concur with Maimonides' position; who found the philosophers presumptuous, inadequate, and incapable of investigating the truths of faith. But the critics of "philosophy" were themselves philosophers. Judah ha-Levi produced *Sefer ha-Kuzari* ("Book of the Khazar"), a work that comprised a set of dialogues between a king in search of true religion and advocates of the religious and philosophical positions of the day, including Judaism. (The monarch was the king of the Khazar [now southeastern Russia], a kingdom which did, in fact, adopt Judaism about the 8th century.) Judah ha-Levi objected to philosophy's indifference to the comparative merits of the competing traditions, since in philosophy's approach, religion is recommended, but which religion does not matter much. Such an indifference may have been tolerable for the majority religions in the West—Islam and Christianity—but not for a minority destined any day to have to die for their faith.

Judah ha-Levi argues that martyrdom such as Jews faced will not be evoked by the unmoved mover, the God anyone may reach through either revelation or reason. Only for the God of Israel will a Jew give up his or her life. By its nature, philosophy is insufficient for the religious quest. It can hardly compete with—let alone challenge—the history of the Jewish people, which records extraordinary events centering on God's revelation. What does philosophy have to do with Sinai, the land, or prophecy? On the contrary, in expounding religion to the king of the Khazars, the Jew begins not like the philosopher with a disquisition on divine attributes, nor like the Christian who starts with the works of creation and expounds the TRINITY, nor like the Muslim who acknowledges the unity and eternity of God. The Jew states: "I believe in the God of Abraham, Isaac, and Israel, who led the Israelites out of Egypt with signs and miracles; who fed them in the desert and gave them the Land, after having made traverse the sea and the Jordan in a miraculous way; who sent Moses with his Torah and subsequently thousands of prophets, who confirmed his law by promises to those who observed and threats to the disobedient. We believe in what is contained in the Torah—a very large domain" (Isaak Heinemann, "Judah Halevi, Kuzari," in *Three Jewish Philosophers,* ed. by Isaak Heinemann, Alexander Altmann, and Hans Lewy [1960], p. 33).

In *Sefer ha-Kuzari* the king then asks: Why did the Jew not say he believes in the creator of the world and in similar attributes common to all creeds? The Jew responds that the evidence for Israel's faith is Israel, the people, and its history and endurance, and not the kinds of reasonable truths offered by other traditions. The proof of revelation is the testimony of those who were there and wrote down what they heard, saw, and did. If so, the king wonders, what accounts for the despised condition of Israel today? The Jew compares Israel to the dry bones of EZE-KIEL: "These bones, which have retained a trace of vital power and have once been the seat of a heart, head, spirit, soul, and intellect, are better than bones formed of marble and plaster, endowed with heads, eyes, ears, and all limbs, in which there never dwelt the spirit of life" (ibid., p. 72). God's people is Israel; he rules them and keeps them in their present status: "Israel amid the nations is like the heart amid the organs: it is the most sick and the most healthy of them all . . . The relationship of the Divine power to us is the same as that of the soul to the heart. For this reason it is said, 'You only have I known among all the families of the earth, therefore I will punish you for all your iniquities' (AMOS 3:2) . . . Now we are oppressed, while the whole world enjoys rest and prosperity. But the trials which meet us serve to purify our piety, cleanse us, and to remove all taint from us" (ibid., p. 75).

The pitiful condition of Israel is, therefore, turned into the primary testimony and vindication of Israel's faith. That Israel suffers is the best assurance of divine concern since the suffering constitutes the certainty of coming redemption. In the end, the Jew parts from the king in order to undertake a journey to the Land of Israel, where he will seek perfection with God. The king objects to this. He thought that the Jew loved freedom, but will find himself in bondage by imposing upon himself those duties obligatory for a Jew residing in the Land of Israel. The Jew replies that the freedom he seeks is from the service of men and the courting of their favor. He seeks the service of one whose favor is obtained with the smallest effort: "His service is freedom, and humility before him is true honor." He therefore turns to Jerusalem to seek the holy life. There is no effort to identify Judaism with rational truth, but rather there is the claim that the life of the pious Jew stands above truth—indeed constituting the best testimony to it.

Judah ha-Levi proposes that the source of truth is biblical revelation and that this revelation was public, complete, and fully in the light of history. History, not philosophy, testifies to the truth and in the end constitutes its sole criterion. Philosophy claims that reason can find the way to God. Judah ha-Levi says that only God can show the way to God, and he does so through revelation, and therefore through history. For the philosopher, God is the object of knowledge. For Judah ha-Levi, God is the subject of knowledge. And Israel has a specifically religious faculty that mediates the relationship to God; in references the role of Israel among the nations is similar to the role of the heart among the organs. Judah ha-Levi seeks to explain the supernatural status of Israel. The religious faculty is Israel's peculiar inheritance and makes it the core of humanity. But while the rest of humanity is subject to the laws of nature, Israel is subject to supernatural, divine providence, manifested in reward and punishment. The very condition of the Jews, in that God punishes them, verifies the particular place of Israel in the divine plan. The teaching of prophecy returns in Judah ha-Levi's philosophy.

Judah ha-Levi and Maimonides were part of a number of important thinkers who attempted to meet the challenge of philosophy and of reason by constructing a comprehensive theological system. While they were much like the Muslim and Christian intellectuals in mentality, the Jewish philosophers had more in common with the Talmudic rabbis than with Gentile philosophers. The rabbis accepted the Bible and the Talmud and Mishnah as "the whole Torah," and so did the Jewish philosophers. Both groups devoted themselves to the articulation of the role of Torah in the life of Israel, to the meaning of the fate of Israel, and to the effort to form piety and shape faith. And for both reason was the means of reaching into Torah—of recovering and achieving truth. Both agreed that words could contain and convey the sacred, and, therefore, reason was, through the examination of the meaning and referents of words, the golden measure. They differed only in the object of reason; one studied law, the other, philosophy. Yet Maimonides, the complete and whole Jew, studied both and made a lasting impact upon the formation of not only both sorts of Judaic tradition but also of the pious imagination of the ordinary Jew. This is because he translated his philosophical and theological principles and convictions into his presentation of the concrete, practical law.

Media of piety—mysticism and Hasidism.   Not only did Rabbinic Judaism draw strength from new modes of thought, it also accommodated emphases in piety that placed a higher value on direct encounter with God and on spiritual gifts, even more than upon knowledge of the Torah. In mid-18th century Poland and Lithuania, HASIDISM, a mystical movement drawing upon the resources of the QAB-BALAH, began with emphases quite at variance with those of Rabbinic Judaism. Though Hasidism favors the holy man's direct encounter with God over the sages' meeting God in the Torah, it ultimately found a central place in its piety for Torah-study. Hasidism developed in mystic circles in Lithuania and Poland which carried on practices that marked them as different from other Jews—for example, special prayers, distinctive ways of observing certain religious duties, and the like. The first among the leaders of the movement of ecstatics and anti-ascetics, Israel ben Eliezer BA'AL SHEM ṬOV, "the Besht," worked as a popular healer. From the 1730s onward he traveled and attracted circles of followers in Podolia (a region in present-day western Ukraine), Poland, Lithuania, and elsewhere. When he

The Exodus, *carrying Holocaust refugees from Europe, lands at Haifa, Palestine, on July 18, 1947*
Archive France/Tallandier—
Archive Photos

died in 1760 he left behind a broad variety of disciples, followers, and admirers in southeastern Poland and Ukraine. Leadership of the movement passed to a succession of holy men, about whom stories were told and preserved. In the third generation, from the third quarter of the 18th century into the first of the 19th, the movement spread and took hold. Diverse leaders, holy men and charismatic figures called zaddikim, developed their own standing and doctrine.

Given the controversies that swirled about the movement, we would expect many of its basic ideas to have been new. But that was hardly the case. The movement drew heavily on available mystical books and doctrines, which from medieval times onward had won a place within the faith as part of the Torah. The Hasidic thinkers' emphasis on a given doctrine should not obscure the profound continuities between the modern movement and its medieval sources. To take one example of how the movement imparted its own imprint on an available idea, Menaḥem Mendel Schneerson of Lubavich notes that God's oneness—surely a given in all Judaisms—means more than that God is unique. It means that God is all that is: "There is no reality in created things. This is to say that in truth all creatures are not in the category of something or a thing as we see them with our eyes. For this is only from our point of view, since we cannot perceive the divine vitality. But from the point of view of the divine vitality which sustains us, we have no existence and we are in the category of complete nothingness like the rays of the sun in the sun itself. . . . From which it follows that there is no other existence whatsoever apart from his existence, blessed be he. This is true unification." (cited by Louis Jacobs, "Basic Ideas of Hasidism," *Encyclopaedia Judaica* [1972], vol. 7, col. 1404). Since all things are in God, the suffering and sorrow of the world cannot be said to exist. So to despair is to sin.

Hasidism laid great stress on joy and avoiding melancholy. It also maintained that religious deeds must be carried out in a spirit of devotion. The doctrine of Hasidism moreover held that, "In all things there are 'holy sparks' (*niẓoẓot*) waiting to be redeemed and rescued for sanctity through man using his appetites to serve God. The very taste of food is a pale reflection of the spiritual force which brings the food into being" (ibid., col. 1405). Before carrying out a religious deed, the Hasid would recite the formula, "For the sake of the unification of the Holy One, blessed be he, and his SHEKHINAH [presence in the world]." On that account they were criticized. But Hasidism was defined by the fundamental pattern of life and received worldview contained in the holy canon of Judaism. Hasidism therefore constituted a Judaism within Judaism—distinctive, yet related closely enough in its major traits to the Judaism of the dual Torah as to be indistinguishable except in trivial details. But one of these details mattered a great deal, and that is the doctrine of zaddikism: the ZADDIK, or holy man, had the power to raise the prayers of the followers and to work miracles. The zaddik was the means through which GRACE reached the world, as he was the one who controlled the universe through his prayers. The zaddik would bring humanity nearer to God and God closer to humanity. The Hasidim were well aware that this doctrine of the zaddik—the pure and elevated soul that could reach to that realm of heaven in which only mercy reigns—represented an innovation. As did the massive opposition to Hasidism organized by the great sages of the Torah of that time.

By the end of the 18th century this powerful opposition, led by the most influential figures of Eastern European Judaism, characterized Hasidism as heretical. Hasidism's stress on ECSTASY, visions, miracles of the leaders, and its enthusiastic way of life were seen as delusions, and the veneration of the zaddik was interpreted as worship of a human being. The stress on prayer to the denigration of study of the Torah likewise called into question the legitimacy of the movement. In this war Hasidism found itself anathematized, its books burned, and its leaders vilified: "They must leave our communities with their wives and children . . . and they should not be given a night's lodging; . . . it is forbidden to do business with them and to intermarry with them or to assist at their burial." Under these circumstances, no one could have anticipated Hasidism finding a place for itself in what would at some point be deemed Orthodoxy. But it did. By the 1830s Hasidism, which began as a persecuted sect, now defined the way of life of the Jews in

Theodor Herzl, the founder of Zionism
Archive Photos

A Jewish family from Yemen celebrates Passover
Popperfoto

the Ukraine, Galicia (now in modern day Poland and Ukraine), and central Poland, with offshoots in White Russia (present-day Belarus) and Lithuania on one side and Hungary on the other. Waves of emigration from the 1880s onward carried the movement to Western Europe, and, in the aftermath of World War II, to the United States as well as the state of Israel. Today the movement forms a powerful component of Orthodox Judaism, demonstrating Rabbinic Judaism's capacity to find strength by naturalizing once-alien modes of thought and media of piety.

HERETICAL SYSTEMS

Karaism and Shabbetaianism.

Whereas some religions—Roman Catholicism, for example—have central authorities that define what is orthodox belief, no such authority existed for the Judaism of the dual Torah. Yet still, as we shall see, the dual Torah did come to define what was orthodox for Judaism—as judged by the fact that nearly all movements considered heretical by Jews were formed in direct opposition to the system of the dual Torah, which, in its ascendancy, defined the limits of heresy, imposing its values and stresses upon the contrary-minded statements of the age.

In the age of the dual Torah's dominance of Judaism it is difficult to find evidence that the dual Torah faced heresies essentially alien to its structure and system. From the 4th to the 19th century in Christendom, and to the mid-20th century in the Muslim world, Judaic heresies commonly took a position on exactly the program and agenda of the Judaism of the dual Torah. What characterized a heresy then was the rejection of one or another of the definitive doctrines of the norm. Two systemic heresies addressed a fundamental plank in the platform of the Judaism of the dual Torah. KARAISM denied the myth of the dual Torah, and Shabbetaianism rejected the doctrine of the messiah as defined in the classical system and created a new doctrine within the received structure and system: a messiah outside of the law.

The indicative trait of the Judaism of the dual Torah was the doctrine that at Sinai God revealed the Torah to be transmitted thorough two media, written (the Pentateuch) and oral (which would eventually be written down in such canonical works as the Mishnah and Talmuds). Focusing upon that central belief, Karaism denied that God revealed to Moses at Sinai more than the written Torah, and explicitly condemned belief in an oral one. Karaism advocated the return to Scripture as against tradition, inclusive of rabbinic tradition. Although Karaism claimed to originate in biblical times and to derive its doctrine from the true priest, Zadok, the sect took shape in the 8th century in Babylonia in the period following the formation of the Talmud of Babylonia, on the one side, and the rise of Islam, on the other. The founder of the movement, ANAN BEN DAVID, claimed then to have recovered the original Torah of Moses. Ben David imposed rules concerning food that were stricter than the rabbis', and in other ways he legislated a version of the law of a more strict character than the Talmudic authorities admitted. The basic principle of Karaism was that Scriptures were to be studied freely, independently, and individually so that no uniformity of view could emerge. Given the stress placed by the Judaism of the dual Torah on the authority of the Talmud and related canonical documents, we could not find a more precise statement of the opposite view.

The Shabbetaian movement was a 17th-century messianic movement organized around the figure of SHABBETAI TZEVI (1626–76) and is important in that it defined the messiah not as a sage who kept and embodied the law as did the Judaism of the dual Torah, but as the very opposite. Shabbetaianism posited the messiah as a holy man who violated the law in letter and in spirit, but by doing so in a complete reversal of the sage-messiah of the Judaism of the dual Torah, the Shabbetaian movement, like Karaism, also paid its respects to the received system.

RABBINIC JUDAISM MEETS COMPETITION

Between the 4th and the 19th centuries, Rabbinic Judaism in its classical paradigm found the strength to absorb innovation in intellectual life and in piety and even to define the character of heresies. When politics revised the urgent question facing Israel, Rabbinic Judaism began to face competition from other Judaisms, including both those that continued its system and those that rejected it altogether. Specifically, in modern times in the West (though not in Muslim countries) the long-established system of Judaism formed in ancient days—the worldview and way of life, that was addressed to a distinctive Israel and was framed in response to urgent and perennial questions—lost its near-monopoly among Judaisms. That received Judaic system—built on the experience of exile and return and modified in the oral Torah to encompass the sanctification of the life of the people as the condition of the salvation of the nation at the end of time—competed with, and even gave way to, a number of systems. Some Judaisms, such as Reform and Orthodoxy, stood in direct continuation with the received system, revering its canon and repeating its main points. Others utterly rejected the mythic structure and system of the Judaism of the dual Torah. These are represented by Zionism—originally a political, and not a religious, system—and the American Judaism of HOLOCAUST and Redemption, a system that completely ignores the Torah as generative symbol. But, as we shall see, these two systems also recapitulate the original system's pattern of exile and return, one of them explicitly, the other structurally.

A political change in the circumstance of the Jews in central and western Europe as well as in the United States demanded a rethinking of "Who is Israel?" and what it meant to be Israel, because Christianity could no longer be used to define the terms of debate. The original paradigm—that of exile and return—had emerged out of an essentially political problem confronting the authors of the Torah, namely, defining Israel within the political hegemony of Christianity. In subsequent settings the Rabbinic paradigm served to create a powerful and definitive myth of "Who is Israel?" The thought of Jews about perennial questions was affected by a stunning shift in the political circumstance of Judaism in the West brought about by the American Constitution of 1787 and the French Revolution of 1789. What happened from the end of the 18th century was the secularization of political life and institutions. Earlier modes of organization had recognized differing groups, guilds, and classes as political entities, and the Jews had found a place among them. In the hierarchical scheme, with church, monarchy, and aristocracy in their "proper" alignment, other political entities could likewise find their location. With church disestablished, monarchy rejected, and aristocracy no longer dominant in politics, the political unit became (theoretically at least) the undifferentiated individual making up the nation-state. That theory left no room for a collective such as Israel, the Jewish people, when viewed as a political unit, though (again, in theory) there might be room for the Jewish individual alongside other undifferentiated individuals. This produced a considerable crisis for the Judaism of the dual Torah.

In the aftermath of the changes in Western politics in the 19th century, Jews indeed asked themselves whether and how they could be something in addition to Jewish, and initially that something invariably found expression in the name of the locale in which they lived, whether it be France, Germany, Britain, or the United States. Could one be both Jewish and, for instance, German? That ques-

The blessing of the Sabbath candles, a weekly ritual performed by women that marks the beginning and end of the Sabbath

Hershkowitz—Monkmeyer

tion found its answer in two givens: the datum of the received Judaism of the dual Torah and the datum that being German or French imposed certain clearly defined responsibilities as well.

The Jews had formerly constituted a distinct group and in Eastern Europe and the Muslim countries they continued to. Now in the West, however, they, in theory, formed part of an undifferentiated mass of citizens, all of them equal before and subject to the same law. The Judaism of the dual Torah rested on the political premise that the Jews were governed by God's law and formed God's people. The two political premises of the nation-state and of the Torah scarcely permitted reconciliation. The consequent Judaic systems in the 19th century, REFORM JUDAISM and ORTHODOX JUDAISM, each addressed issues regarded as acute and not merely chronic and alleged that they formed the natural next step in the unfolding of "the tradition," meaning the Judaic system of the dual Torah. The Judaic systems born in the 20th century did not make that claim, but they recapitulated that pattern, familiar from the very beginning of the Torah, that taught them what to expect and how to explain what happened.

The further political shift in the 20th century confronted Jews with a different and still more acute question: whether and how they could be human beings, if they were, or had been, Jewish. The 20th-century innovation of totalitarianism, whether Soviet-Communist or German-Nazi, made its imprint in full force upon the Judaic agenda. The question that then predominated became: where and how could the Jew endure? Its self-evident answer was: not among Gentiles, but only in the Jewish state, and this response produced one Judaism for the Jews of the state of Israel, and another, quite different one for the Jews of the Western democracies. Yet, at the threshold of the 21st century, it was only in those two environments that Jews found themselves free enough to ask such questions and receive such answers at all.

CONTINUATOR-JUDAISMS OF THE 19TH CENTURY

Reform Judaism. From the perspective of the political changes taking place following the American and French revolutions, the received system of the Judaism of the dual Torah answered only irrelevant questions and did not respond to acute ones. Secular nationalism conceived of society not as the expression of God's will for the social order under the rule of Christ and his Church or his anointed king (or emperor or tsar), but as the expression of popular will for the social order under the government of the people and their elected representatives—a considerable shift. When society does not form the aggregate of distinct groups—each with its place and definition, language and religion, but rather undifferentiated citizens (though male, white, and wealthy, to be sure)—then the Jews in such a society will have to work out a different order of Judaism altogether. That Judaism will have to frame a theory of "who is Israel?" that is consonant with the social situation of Jews who are willing to be different, but not so different that they cannot also be citizens. Both Reform and Orthodoxy responded to this concern. Each rightly claimed to continue the received "tradition," that is, the Judaism of the dual Torah.

The world at large no longer verified, as had the world of Christendom and Islamdom, the generative social category of Israel's life that saw Israel as supernatural entity. This raised the problem of defining what sort of entity Israel did constitute, what sort of way of life should characterize it, and what sort of worldview should explain it. This produced a new set of questions, and, in the nature of things, also self-evidently true answers. The American Reform rabbis, meeting in Pittsburgh in 1885 (*see also* PITTSBURGH PLATFORM), issued a clear and accessible statement of their Judaism:

> We recognize in the Mosaic legislation a system of training the Jewish people for its mission during its national life in Palestine, and today we accept as binding only its moral laws, and maintain only such ceremonies as elevate and sanctify our lives, but reject all such as are not adapted to the views and habits of modern civilization. . . . We hold that all such Mosaic and rabbinical laws as regular diet, priestly purity, and dress originated in ages and under the influence of ideas entirely foreign to our present mental and spiritual state. . . . Their observance in our days is apt rather to obstruct than to further modern spiritual elevation. . . . We recognize, in the modern era of universal culture of heart and intellect, the approaching of the realization of Israel's great messianic hope for the establishment of the kingdom of truth, justice, and peace among all men. We consider ourselves no longer a nation, but a religious community and therefore expect neither a return to Palestine, nor a sacrificial worship under the sons of Aaron, nor the restoration of any of the laws concerning the Jewish state.

Here we find a Judaism in theoretical formulation, answering the key questions, "Who is Israel? What is its way of life? How does it account for its existence as a distinct, and distinctive, group?" Israel once was a nation ("during its national life") but today is not. It once had a set of laws that regulated diet, clothing, and the like, which no longer apply, because Israel is not now what it was then. However, Israel forms an integral part of Western civilization. The reason to persist as a distinctive group was that the group has its work to do—namely, to realize the "messianic hope for the establishment of a kingdom of truth, justice, and peace." For that purpose Israel no longer constituted a nation. It formed a religious community.

Orthodox Judaism. The term Orthodoxy in connection with Judaism first surfaced in 1795, and covers all Jews who believe that God revealed the dual Torah at Sinai and that Jews must carry out the requirements of Jewish law contained in the Torah as interpreted by the sages through time. Obviously, so long as that position was believed and practiced by the generality of Jewry, Orthodoxy as a distinct and organized Judaism did not have to exist. The point at which two events took place is interesting: first, the recognition of the received system, "the tradition," as Orthodoxy, and second, the specifying of the received system as religion. The two of course go together. So long as the Judaism of the dual Torah enjoyed recognition as a set of self-evident truths, those truths did not add to something so distinct as "religion," but rather were a general statement of how things are: all of life explained and harmonized in one whole account.

Orthodox Judaism, founded in Germany in the mid-19th century in response to the success of Reform, mediates between the received Judaism of the dual Torah and the requirements of a life integrated in modern circumstances. Orthodoxy maintains the worldview of the received dual Torah, constantly citing its sayings and adhering, with only trivial variations, to the bulk of its norms for the everyday life. At the same time Orthodoxy holds that Jews adhering to the dual Torah may wear the same clothing as non-Jews wear instead of distinctively Jewish (even Judaic) clothing; they may live within a common economy and not practice distinctively Jewish professions (however these professions may be defined in a given setting); and they may, in diverse ways, take up a life not readily distinguished in important characteristics from that lived by people in general. So for Orthodoxy, a portion of Israel's life may prove secular, in that the Torah does not dictate and so sanctify all details under all circumstances. The Judaism of the dual Torah presupposed not only the supernatural entity Israel, but also a way of life that distinguished, in important ways, that entity from the social world at large. Orthodoxy accommodated Jews who valued the received way of life and worldview but who also planned to live in an essentially integrated social world. Therefore the difference between Orthodoxy and the system of the dual Torah comes to expression in social policy: integration, however circumscribed, versus the total separation of the holy people.

Orthodoxy addressed the same questions as Reform but gave different answers. Reform maintained that the distinctive way of life had to go, since the Jews no longer constituted the holy people living a distinct existence but instead formed a religious group as part of a larger nation-state. Orthodoxy held that the Torah made provision for areas of life in which a Jew could be something other than a Jew. For example on the important point of education, the institutions of the Judaism of the dual Torah commonly held that one should study only Torah. Orthodoxy in the West included study of the secular sciences in its curriculum as well. The Judaism of the dual Torah ordinarily identified particular forms of dress as

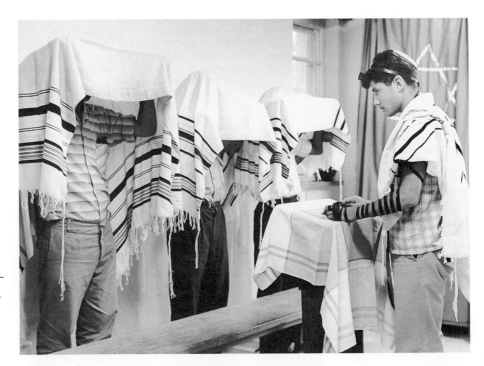

Israeli men cover their heads with the ṭallit, or prayer shawl, as a sign of respect during morning prayers
Roy Pinney—Monkmeyer

being Judaic. Orthodoxy required only the wearing of fringes (which could be concealed inside of a man's clothing) and a covering for the head. In these and in other ways Orthodoxy formed a fresh statement of the Judaism of the dual Torah, distinctive in its provision, for the Jew, of a life lived legitimately outside—though never in violation—of the Judaic norms. The distinction between adhering to the received system of the dual Torah and identifying with the mid-19th-century German Orthodox Judaism rested on such indicators as clothing, language, and above all, education.

Jews who kept the law of the Torah—for example, its strictures on food choices and the use of leisure time (to speak of the Sabbath and festivals in modern, secular terms)—crossed the boundary between the received Judaism and the new (if also traditional and received) Judaism of Orthodoxy when they sent their children to secular schools, in addition to or instead of solely Jewish ones, or when they included subjects outside of the sciences of the Torah in Jewish schools' curriculum. The notion that science, German, Latin, or philosophy deserved serious study was not alien to important exemplars of the received system of the dual Torah, but in the 19th century it felt wrong to those for whom the received system remained self-evidently right. Those Jews (including, as a rule such Jews as the Hasidim) did not send their children to Gentile schools, or include anything other than Torah-study in the curriculum of the Jewish schools. The Reformers held that Judaism could change, and that Judaism was a product of history. The Orthodox opponents denied that Judaism could change and insisted that Judaism derived from God's will at Mount Sinai and was eternal and supernatural, not historical and man-made. In these two convictions, of course, the Orthodox recapitulated the convictions of the received system. But in their appeal to the given traditional thought, they found some components of that system more persuasive than others, and in this picking and choosing, and the articulation of Judaism as a distinct religion autonomous of politics, society, and "the rest of life," the Orthodox entered the same world of self-conscious believing that the Reformers also explored.

TWENTIETH-CENTURY JUDAISMS BEYOND THE RABBINIC FRAMEWORK

Zionism. In the 20th century two Judaic systems dropped the theme of Torah altogether, while reworking the paradigm of exile and return that the Pentateuch set forth. Though neither of them are religious in any conventional sense, both have powerful influences among Jews who practice a Judaic religious system. The American Judaism of Holocaust and Redemption and ZIONISM both responded to political crises: one to the advent of anti-Semitism that denied Jews the right to live in Europe at all, the other to the reconstruction and re-ethnicization of the American cultural order in the late 1960s. Both of these Jewish systems—they cannot strictly speaking be called Judaic, that is, religious—continue the generative paradigm of exile and return.

Zionism was the Jews' self-emancipation, in response to the nations' (Gentiles') failed promises of Jewish emancipation. It framed its worldview and way of life for its definition of Israel in response to the lack, by the end of the 19th century, of political improvement in the Jews' status and condition. Zionism called for Jews to face the fact that, in the main, Gentiles hated Jews and so they must emancipate themselves. Founding a Jewish state where Jews could build their own destiny free of anti-Semitism, the Zionist worldview declared the simple proposition that the Jews form a people, one people, and should transform themselves into a political entity and build a Jewish state. Zionism came into existence with the founding of the Zionist Organization at the First Zionist Congress in Basel (August 29–31, 1897) and reached its fulfillment, and dissolution in its original form, with the founding of the state of Israel in May 1948. Zionism began with its definition of Israel: a people, one people, in a secular sense. Then came a worldview combining the diverse histories of Jews into a singular history of the Jewish people (nation), leading from the Land of Israel, through exile, back to the Land of Israel. This component of Zionism constituted an exact recapitulation of the biblical narrative, though it derived from a nationalist, not a religious, perspective. The way of life of the Zionist required participating in meetings, organizing within the local community, and attending national and international conferences in a focus of life's energy on the movement. After settlement in the Land itself became possible in 1903, Zionism defined the most noble way of living life as migration to the Land, and, for the socialist wing of Zionism, building a collective community (kibbutz). So, Zionism presented a complete and fully articulated Judaism, which was prior to the creation of the state of Israel in 1948, one of the most powerful and effective of them all.

Three main streams of theory flowed together in the formative decades. Aḥad Ha'am (1856–1927) laid stress on Zion as a spiritual center, uniting all of the Jewish people wherever they lived, and emphasizing spiritual preparation, ideological and cultural activities, and the long-term intellectual persuasion of the Jews to Zionist premises. A political stream began in 1897 and maintained that the Jews should provide for the emigration of their nation's masses from Eastern Europe to the land of Israel, or anywhere, as Europe was entering a protracted state of political disintegration and already long suffering from economic dislocation. The founder of Zionism, THEODOR HERZL (1860–1904) placed more importance on the requirement for legal recognition of a Jewish state than upon the location of the state, and, in doing so, he defined

Israeli soldiers in the Old City of Jerusalem during the 1967 Six-Day War
Archive Photos

Zionism as the practical salvation of the Jews through political means. Herzl stressed that the Jewish state would come into existence in the forum of international politics. The instruments of state—a political forum, a bank, a mode of national allegiance, a press, and a central body and leader—came into being in the aftermath of the First Zionist Congress. Herzl spent the rest of his life—less than a decade—seeking an international charter and recognition of the Jews' state. A third stream expressed a Zionist vision of socialism (or a socialist vision of Zionism): the Jewish state was to be socialist, and for its first three decades it was. The early theoretical formulation of socialist Zionism (before its near-total bureaucratization) emphasized that a proletarian Zionism would define the arena for the class struggle to be realized within the Jewish people. The socialist Zionists dominated the settlement of the Land of Israel and controlled its political institutions for three quarters of a century. They founded the labor unions, the large scale industries, the health institutions and organizations, the press, and the nascent army. They created the nation.

A Judaism entirely out of phase with the received system of the dual Torah, Zionism enunciated a powerful doctrine of Israel: The Jews form "a people, one people." Given the Jews' diversity, it was easier for people to concede the supernatural reading of Judaic existence than the national construction given to it. Scattered across the European countries and the Muslim world, Jews did not speak a single language, follow a single way of life, or adhere in common to a single code of belief and behavior. The Zionist worldview's central theme was the question of what made them a people, one people, and further validated their claim and right to a nation-state of their own. No facts of perceived society validated that view, since, except for a common fate, the Jews did not form a people, one people. True, in the Judaic system of the dual Torah and its continuators they commonly did. But these systems imputed to Israel, the Jewish people, a supernatural status, mission, and purpose, which Zionism did not. Zionist theory had the task of explaining how the Jews forming a unified people lead to the invention of "Jewish history," in which the past is read in a secular framework as a single and unitary story. Zionist theory showed how all the Jews came from one place, traveled together, and would return to that same place, and thus constituted one people as a matter of secular fact. Like Reform Judaism, Zionist theory derived strength from the study of history, and in time generated a great renaissance of Judaic studies, as the scholarly community of the nascent Jewish state took up the task at hand. The sort of history that emerged took the form of factual and descriptive narrative, but its selection of facts, its recognition of problems requiring explanation, and its choice of what did and did not matter all sprang from the larger program of nationalist ideology. So although the form was secular and descriptive, the substance was ideological in the extreme.

At the same time, Zionist theory explicitly rejected the precedent formed by that Torah, selecting not the history of the faith but the history of the nation, with Israel construed as a secular entity. Zionism defined episodes as linear Jewish history and appealed to those strung-together events, all of a given classification to be sure, as vindication for actions. This distinctive worldview explains a very particular way of life and defines for itself that Israel to which it wishes to speak. Like Reform Judaism, Zionism found the written component of the Torah more interesting than the oral. And in its search for a usable past, it turned to documents formerly neglected or treated as not authoritative—for instance, the books of Maccabees. Zionism went in search of heroes unlike those of the present—it sought warriors, political figures, and others who might provide a model for the movement's future, and for the projected state beyond. So instead of rabbis or sages, Zionism chose figures such as DAVID the warrior king, Judah Maccabee, who had led the revolt against the Syrian Hellenists, and SAMSON the powerful fighter—these provided the appropriate heroes for a Zionism that proposed to redefine Jewish consciousness and turn storekeepers into soldiers, lawyers into farmers, corner grocers into the builders and administrators of great institutions of state and government. The Judaism of the dual Torah treated David as a rabbi, but the Zionist system of Judaism saw him as a more worldly hero: a courageous nation-builder.

Yet the principal components of Zionism's worldview fit comfortably within the paradigm of the Torah, which stated, based on its own genealogical reasons, that the Jews form a people, one people, and should (when worthy) have the land back and build a state on it. It is not surprising that Zionism found ample precedent for its program in writings about the return to Zion as it linked today's politics to something very like God's will for Israel, the Jewish people, in ancient times. Thus, calling the newly formed Jewish city "Tel Aviv" invoked the memory of Ezekiel's reference to a Tel Aviv. Zionism would reconstitute the age of the return to Zion of Ezra and Nehemiah's era, and so carry out the prophetic promises. Again the mode of thought is entirely reminiscent of Reform Judaism's, which, to be sure, selected a different, mythic perfect world; a golden age other than the one that glistened so brightly to Zionism. Yet the points of continuity should not be overstated. Alongside the search of Scripture, Zionism articulated very clearly what it wished to find there. And what Zionism did not find, it deposited on its own, its own systemic design marking it as heresy: the celebration of the nation as a secular, not supernatural, category, and the imposition of the nation and its heroism in place of the heroic works of the supernatural God. This classic shift can be seen in the recasting of the verse of Psalms, which originally read "Who will retell the great deeds of God" and ended up reading "Who will retell the great deeds of Israel"—and that only typifies Zionism's profound revisioning of Israel's history. For Israel in its dual Torah (though not only in that Judaism) formed a supernatural entity; a social unit unlike any other on the face of the earth and all humanity divided into two parts: Israel and the (undifferentiated) nations. Moreover, the Judaism given literary expression in Constantine's day maintained that the one thing Israel should not do is arrogant deeds. That meant Israel waited with patience, loyalty, humility, and obedience for God to save it. The earliest pronouncements of a Zionist movement were received in the Jewish heartland of Eastern Europe like the tocsin of the coming messiah, but for that same reason they seemed as BLASPHEMY to the sages of the dual Torah. God will do it—or it will not be done. Considerable time would elapse before most of the avatars of the dual Torah could make their peace with Zionism, and some never did.

American Judaism of Holocaust and Redemption.   In the context of this article "the Holocaust" refers to the Nazi's murder of nearly six million Jewish children, women, and men in Europe in 1933 through 1945. The "Redemption" is the creation of the state of Israel. This Judaic system—an ethnic ideology, not a religious formulation built out of the Torah—flourishes in the United States and, from 1967, has been the principal force in the public life of American Jews. This Judaism stresses the unique complementary experiences of mid-20th century Jewry: the mass murder of six million European Jews in death factories, and the providential and redemptive meaning of the creation of the state of Israel three years after the massacre's end. The way of life of Holocaust and Redemptive Judaism requires actively raising money and political support for the state of Israel. Whereas Zionism held that Jews should live in a Jewish state, this system gives Jews living in the United States a reason and explanation for being Jewish. As a whole it presents an encompassing myth, linking the Holocaust to the state of Israel as an instructive pattern, and it moves Jews to follow a particular set of actions. Diverse Judaic systems flourish in the United States: Reform, Orthodoxy, Conservatism, RECONSTRUCTIONISM, as well as others less choate. But the American Judaism of Holocaust and Redemption exercises enormous power over the mind and imagination of Jewish Americans. It answers two separate and distinct urgent questions, the first addressed to the particular world of the Jews, the second to the world at large. The first question is, "Why should I be different, why should I be Jewish?" The second is, "How should I relate to the world at large?"

The Judaism of Holocaust and Redemption gives a powerful and critical answer to the question of why be Jewish: because you have no choice. It also explains that "Israel" should relate to the world at large through its own nation-state overseas, and in its distinctive and distinct communities at home. So American Judaism addresses the inner world as well as policy toward the outer world.

The two questions are connected—both emerge from the special circumstances of the Jewish American whose grandparents or great-grandparents immigrated to the United States or Canada. For that sort of American Jew, there is no common acknowledged core of RELIGIOUS EXPERIENCE by which "being Jewish" may be explained and interpreted. Also, because anti-Semitism has become less common than it was from the 1920s through the early 1950s, there is no common core of social alienation to account for the distinctive character of the group and explain why it must continue to endure. Indeed, many American Jews, though they continue to affirm their Jewishness, have no clear notion of how they are Jewish, or what their Jewish heritage demands of them. Judaism is, for this critical part of the American Jewish population, merely one reference point among many. For ideologists of the Jewish community, the most certain answer to the question "Why am I Jewish?," posed by the third generation, must be, "There is no real choice" since the Holocaust provides the answer: "Hitler considered you Jewish." The formative experiences of the Holocaust are now immediately accessible through emotions unmediated by sentiment or sensibility. These "Judaizing experiences" take the place of the Torah in nurturing an inner and distinctive consciousness of "being Jewish." So the Holocaust is made to answer the inner question of "Who are we, and why are we what we are and not something else?"

By the late 1960s third-generation American Jews—the grandchildren of the immigrants who were born between 1920 and 1940—had found the continuator-Judaisms of the synagogue conventional and irrelevant. These Judaisms did not address their questions and provide self-evidently valid answers. And how could those Judaisms serve, when they invoked experiences of learning and sensibility unavailable to American Jews beyond the immigrant generation and their children? Jews found that to make a model for viable life—an explanation of the world, and an account of how to live—out of those Judaisms, they had to give what they did not have. What was required was either memories few possessed or locating a road back to find memories, and very few found the will for this. The world of the everyday did not provide access to a worldview as subtle and alien as that of the Judaism of the dual Torah with its conception of humanity and Israel, let alone to the way of life formed within that worldview. How then to engage the emotions without the mediation of learning in the Torah that few possessed or wished to attain? And how to define a way of life that imparted distinction without great material difference? To put it bluntly, what distinctively Judaic way of life would allow devotees to eat whatever they wanted? The answer to the question of how to gain access to the life of feeling and experience that made one distinctive without leaving the person terribly different from everybody else emerged in the Judaic system of Holocaust and Redemption. This system presented an immediately accessible message that was cast in extreme emotions of terror and triumph, and its round of endless activity demanded only spare time. In all, the system of American Judaism realized in a poignant way the conflicting demands of Jewish Americans to be intensely Jewish (but only once in a while) but to not be too meaningfully different from others.

Three factors reinforced one another in turning the Judaism of Holocaust and Redemption into a set of self-evident and descriptive facts, truths beyond all argument and gave it a position of paramount importance among the bulk of the organized American Jewish community: the Six-Day War of 1967, the re-ethnicization of American life, and the transformation of the mass murder of European Jews into an event of mythic and world-destroying proportions. Why date the birth of the Judaism of Holocaust and Redemption so precisely as the 1967 war? People take the importance of the state of Israel in American Jewish consciousness as routine. But in the 1940s and '50s, American Jewry had yet to translate its deep sympathy for the Jewish state into political activity, or the shaping element for local cultural activity and sentiment. Likewise, the destruction of European Jewry did not right away become "the Holocaust," in contemporary Jewish consciousness. (The term "holocaust"—which originally meant a sacrifice wholly consumed by fire, or a burnt offering—was not actually used to refer to the Nazi death camps until the 1950s. The term became more common through its use by such writers as Elie Wiesel [b. 1928] in his 1958 work *Night*.) Additionally, the re-ethnicization of the Jews could not have taken the form that it did—a powerful identification with the state of Israel as the answer to the question of the Holocaust—without a single, catalytic event.

That event was the 1967 war between the state of Israel and its Arab neighbors. On June 5, after a long period of threat, the dreaded war of "all against one" began, and American Jews feared the worst. Six days later they faced an unimagined outcome, with the state of Israel holding territory on the Jordan River, the Nile, and the outskirts of Damascus. The trauma of the weeks preceding the war, when the Arabs promised to drive the Jews into the sea and no other power intervened or promised help, renewed for the third generation the nightmare of the second. Once more the streets and newspapers became the school for being Jewish. On that account the Judaism in formation took up a program of urgent questions—and answered them. In the 1930s and '40s, the age of Hitler's Germany and the murder of the European Jews in death factories, every day's newspaper brought lessons of Jewish history. Everybody knew that if he or she were in Europe, death would be the sentence for the "crime" of Jewish birth. And the world was indifferent. No avenues of escape were opened to the Jews who wanted to flee, and many roads to survival were deliberately blocked by anti-Semitic foreign service officials. Likewise, in 1967 the Arab states threatened to destroy the state of Israel and murder its citizens. The Israelis turned to the world, the world again ignored Jewish suffering, and a new Holocaust loomed. But this time the outcome was quite different. The entire history of the century at hand came under a new light as this moment of powerful and salvific weight placed everything that had happened from the beginning to the present into a fresh perspective.

The third generation now had found its memory and its hope, much as Zionism had invented a usable past. Its members could now confront the murder of the Jews of Europe, along with the exclusion and bigotry experienced by their parents and themselves. It was no longer necessary to avoid painful, intolerable memories. Now what had happened had to be remembered, because it bore within itself the entire message of the new day in Judaism. The binding of the murder of nearly six million Jews of Europe to the creation of the state of Israel transformed both events. One became "the Holocaust," the purest statement of evil in all of human history. The other became salvation in the form of "the first appearance of our redemption" (as the language of the Jewish prayer for the state of Israel has it). Accordingly, a moment of stark epiphany had captured the entire experience of the age and imparted to it that meaning and order that a religious system has the power to express as self-evident. For the third generation the self-evident system of American Judaism encompassed a salvific myth deeply and personally relevant to the devotees. At a single instant that myth made equal sense of both the world and the self, of what the newspapers had to say, and what the individual understood in personal life.

The distinctively American form of Judaism clearly connects to the Judaism of the dual Torah with its exact recapitulation of the pattern of the original Torah. The exile has its counterpart in the Holocaust, and the return to Zion is, in the Redemption, represented by the state of Israel. But American Judaism is not completely continuous; in fact it forms a heresy structurally out of phase with the Judaism of the dual Torah. In its stress upon the realization, in the here and now, of ultimate evil and salvation and in its mythicization of contemporary history, American Judaism offers a distinctively American, therefore a new and unprecedented, reading of the received tradition. This is by definition; when Jews have come to speak of fully realized salvation and an end of history, the result has commonly proved to be a new religion, connected to, but not continuous with, the received religion of Judaism.

RABBINIC AND OTHER JUDAISMS IN MODERN TIMES: CONTINUITY AND DISCONTINUITY

The 19th-century Judaisms, represented by Reform and Orthodoxy, made constant reference to the received system of the dual Torah; its writings, its values, its requirements, its viewpoints, and its way of life. The 20th-century Judaisms, Zionism and the American Judaism of Holocaust and Redemption, did not pretend to negotiate with Rabbinic Judaism or draw on its holy books. But there is a clear connection of all four Judaisms to the generative paradigm of the Torah—that experience of exile and return as announced in the time of Ezra. There are, of course, important differences between the continuator-Judaisms of the 19th century and the Judaic innovations of the 20th. Each Judaism born in the 19th century faced the task of validating the change affirmed by all of the borning Judaisms in one way or another. But all of those new Judaisms articulated a principle in which change guided relationships with the received system. And all the Judaisms recognized themselves as answerable, in diverse ways to be sure, to the received system, which continued to define the agenda of law and theology alike. We cannot point to a similar relationship between the new Judaisms of the 20th century and the received Judaism of the dual Torah. For none of them made much use of the intellectual resources of that system, found urgent, important issues within that system, or even regarded themselves as answerable to the Judaism of the dual Torah.

The 20th-century systems came to expression within the larger world—that of the nationalism of the smaller peoples of Europe and Zionism's rejection of the government of the international empires of Central and Eastern Europe—and, for American Judaism, the reframing, in American culture, of the policy governing social and ethnic difference. While these Judaic systems of believing and behaving did not draw extensively on the received Judaic system of the dual Torah, they did vastly overshadow in acceptance the Judaisms that did. From the 18th to the 20th century there was a radical attenuation of the bonds that joined the Jews to the Judaism of the dual Torah. The difference between the 20th-century Judaisms and the 19th-century ones was in the character of the ages in which they took shape. The Judaisms of the 19th century retained close and nurturing ties to the Judaism of the dual Torah, confronted its issues, drew heavily on its symbolic system, cited its texts as proof-texts, and eagerly referred to its sources in justification for the new formations. They looked backward and assumed responsibility toward that long past of the Judaism of the dual Torah, acknowledging its authority, accepting its program of thought, and acceding to its way of life—if only by way of explicit rejection. The Judaisms of the 20th century in common treated with entire disinterest the same received Judaism of the dual Torah. They looked forward and drew heavily upon contemporary systems of belief and behavior. But they turned to the received system of the dual Torah only adventitiously.

The difference between the 20th-century Judaisms and the 19th-century ones was much more than a century. It was the difference between the civilization of the West in its Christian form and that same civilization as it took new, secular forms altogether. With its interest in Scripture, messiah, and the long trends of history worked out in sanctification now for salvation at the end of days, what pertinence had the Judaism that was formed in response to Christianity? The new world imposed its own categories, including such organizing constructions as class struggle, the ideology of a homogeneously cultural and ethnic nation-state, and, in the United States and Canada, diverse and rootless people's search for ethnic identity. These issues characterized a world that had cast loose the moorings that had long held things firm and whole. What was left in the 20th century, for people with no relationship with the Judaism of the dual Torah, was a Judaic experience composed of politics on one side and raw emotions on the other. The ideologies of the 20th-century Judaisms came after the fact of experience and emotion. They explained the fact; they did not, as religions had done, transform feeling into sensibility and sentiment into an intellectual explanation of the world. The 20th-century systems represented by Zionism and the American Judaism of Holocaust and Redemption in common appeal to a self-evidence deriving from a visceral response to intolerable experience. Zionism formed into a single whole the experiences of remarkably diverse people living in widely separated places, showing that all those experiences formed a single fact—exclusion, victimization, and anti-Semitism—which Zionism could confront. American Judaism linked to an inchoate past the aspirations of a third and fourth generation of Jewish Americans who wanted desperately to be Jewish but in its own experience and intellectual resources could find slight access to something "Jewish." Emotion—of resentment in particular—formed the road within: for American Judaism, strong feelings about suffering and redemption; for Zionism, a powerful appeal to concrete deeds in the here and now by people who thought themselves helpless. Yet these Judaisms, so remote from the circumstance and substance of the generative system of the Torah, do not stand far from the starting point; for the contemporary Judaisms invoke exile and homecoming as the norm, just as stated in the Pentateuch: All have Eden in mind and eternal life in the mind's eye.

JUDAISM, ART OF, artistic works created in a Judaic context or intended to facilitate or accompany Jewish worship. Although the Second Commandment (Exodus 20:4; Deuteronomy 5:8), "You shall not make yourself a graven image, or any likeness of anything that is in heaven above, or that is in the earth beneath, or that is in the water under the earth," has been understood by some Jewish scholars as absolutely prohibiting any and all artistic representation, it can also be interpreted as a prohibition against the construction of such likenesses as were the object of worship in the cultural area in which the Israelites dwelt. Even in the BIBLE there are reports of artistic productivity in the construction of the tent SANCTUARY and its ritual vessels (Exodus 25–31) and of the TEMPLE OF JERUSALEM (I Kings 6–7).

Cecil Roth, the great art historian of JUDAISM, writes, "At every stage of their history the Jews . . . expressed themselves in various art forms which inevitably reflect contemporary styles and fashions. For purposes of cult and of religious observance . . . Jews have constantly produced . . . objects which appealed in some fashion to their aesthetic sense" (*Encyclopaedia Judaica* 3:499). The Talmudic sages, in BAVLI Shabbat 133b, recommended the use of lovely ornaments for religious observance. The biblical prohibitions against representing God in graven images tended to discourage the representation of the human form, especially in plastic arts. But in painting, drawing, and mosaics SYNAGOGUES of antiquity were elaborately decorated with all manner of images, including human. In ancient times the prohibition of graven images pertained principally to images meant to be worshiped; human and animal forms were otherwise accepted. Interestingly, the zodiac motif occurs in a number of synagogues, as do representations of the seasons. By medieval times, representational art was avoided, and nonrepresentational art became preferred.

Illuminated manuscripts from the medieval period in Europe were frequently decorated with biblical figures, some quite clearly copied from Christian prototypes. The Renaissance period saw the appearance of beautifully decorated Scrolls of Esther and *ketubbot* (KETUBAH, or marriage contracts). A fascinating mediating position in representational art is to be seen in a HAGGADAH in which the human figures have bird heads.

Given the general anti-iconic attitude, however, much of Jewish artistic endeavor has been directed toward the creation of ceremonial objects: KIDDUSH goblets, candelabra, spice boxes for the HABDALAH ceremony at the end of the SABBATH, ornamented containers for the mezuza, the silver crowns placed on the TORAH scrolls, and many other objects designed to embellish the performance of ritual acts.

JUDAS ISCARIOT \'jü-dəs-i-'skar-ē-ət\ (d. *c.* 30 CE), in CHRISTIANITY, one of the Twelve APOSTLES, notorious for betraying JESUS CHRIST. Judas' surname may have been an alteration of Latin *sicarius* ("murderer" or "assassin"), suggesting that he belonged to the Sicarii, the most radical Jewish group. Other than his apostleship, his betrayal, and his death, little is revealed about Judas in the Gospels. Always the last on the list of the Apostles, he was their treasurer.

There are variant traditions about Judas' death. According to Matthew 27:3–10, he repented after seeing Jesus condemned to death, then returned the silver and hanged himself (traditionally from the Judas tree). In Acts 1:18, he "bought a field with the reward of his wickedness; and falling headlong he burst open in the middle and all his bowels gushed out," implying that he threw himself down, rather than that he died accidentally. Apocryphal gospels developed the point in Acts that calls the spot of his death the place (field) of blood. The 1st–2nd-century Apostolic Father Papias is quoted to have given macabre details about Judas' death, presumably to show that Gospel prophecies were literally fulfilled. His account appears in numerous legends, particularly in Coptic works, and in medieval literature.

In Muslim polemic literature, however, Judas ceases to be a traitor; instead, he supposedly lied to the Jews in order to defend Jesus (who was not crucified). The 14th-century cosmographer Ibn Abī ʿAṣrūn maintains that Judas assumed Jesus' likeness and was crucified in his place. The 2nd-century apocryphal *Gospel of Judas* favorably evaluates him. His name has subsequently become associated with traitor (a Judas) and treacherous kiss (a Judas kiss).

JULIAN OF NORWICH \'jü-lē-ən . . . 'när-ij, -ich; 'nȯr-wich\, *also called* Juliana (b. 1342, probably Norwich, Norfolk, Eng.—d. after 1416), celebrated mystic whose *Revelations of Divine Love* is generally considered one of the most remarkable documents of medieval RELIGIOUS EXPERIENCE. She spent the latter part of her life as a recluse at St. Julian's Church, Norwich.

On May 13, 1373, Julian was healed of a serious illness after experiencing a series of visions of Christ's suffering and of the Blessed Virgin, about which she wrote two accounts; the second, longer version was composed 20 or 30 years after the first. Unparalleled in English religious literature, *Revelations* spans the most profound mysteries of the Christian faith—such as the problems of PREDESTINATION, the foreknowledge of God, and the existence of evil. The clarity and depth of her perception, the precision and accuracy of her theological presentation, and the sincerity and beauty of her expression reveal a mind and personality of exceptional strength and charm. Never beatified, Julian is honored on the unofficial feast day of May 13. A modern chapel in the Church of St. Julian is dedicated to her.

JUNAYD, SHAYKH \jù-'nīd\ (b. *c.* 1430, Iranian Azerbaijan?—d. March 4, 1460, near the Kura River), fourth head of the Ṣafavid order of Sufi mystics, who sought to transform the spiritual strength of the order into political power.

When Junayd's father died in 1447 he became the head of the Ṣafavid order, which had its capital at Ardabīl, Iran. Because he was a minor, he was placed under the guardianship of his paternal uncle, Shaykh Jaʿfar. Departing from previous custom, Junayd attempted to convert spiritual respect into temporal power, a policy that led to a split in the order. The moderate majority remained with Shaykh Jaʿfar, and the rest followed Junayd. Junayd was the first Ṣafavid leader to whom the term SULTAN, indicative of temporal rule, was applied. The arming of his *murīd*s (spiritual followers), who regarded him as an emanation of divinity, brought him into conflict with Jahān Shāh (d. 1467), the ruler of Azerbaijan, and resulted in the expulsion of Junayd and his followers from Ardabīl, the traditional center of the Ṣafavid order, in 1448.

Junayd then attempted to seek a new power base for his wing of the order. When Sultan Murad II, the Ottoman ruler, refused him sanctuary in his domains, Junayd led his followers to Aleppo (now in Syria) but was expelled by the authorities. He next attempted to settle along the southern shores of the Black Sea. In 1456 he led an unsuccessful campaign against the Christian Greek principality of Trabzon (now in Turkey). The attack was motivated by the desire for booty and to attract new recruits to his banner. After the failure of this expedition he sought refuge with the Turkish ruler Uzun Ḥasan, who received him and allowed him to remain in the city of Amid.

Junayd married Uzun Ḥasan's sister, Khadījah Begūm. This alliance revived the fortunes of the extremist wing of the Ṣafavid order and was in line with Uzun Ḥasan's policy of supporting Sufi orders (see SUFISM) to add legitimacy to his rule. Junayd sought an alliance with Uzun Ḥasan's SUNNI Turks, who were enemies of the SHI'ITE Jahān Shāh. On leaving Amid in 1459 to retake Ardabīl, Junayd was blocked by the superior forces of Jahān Shāh. Junayd and his 10,000 troops turned north to attack the Christian Circassians in Tabarsaran (in the Caucasus region), where he was killed in an ambush. His policies of military adventurism combined with Shi'ite and Sufi piety were continued by his son, Ḥaydar, and culminated eventually in the establishment of the Ṣafavid dynasty and of Twelver Shi'ite ISLAM in Iran under his grandson, ISMĀ'ĪL I.

JUNO \'jü-nō\, in ROMAN RELIGION, chief goddess and female counterpart of JUPITER, closely resembling the Greek HERA, with whom she was identified. With Jupiter and MINERVA, she was a member of the Capitoline triad of deities traditionally introduced by the Etruscan kings. Juno was connected with all aspects of the life of women, most particularly married life. As Juno Lucina, goddess of childbirth, she had a temple on the Esquiline from the 4th century BCE. In her role as female comforter she assumed various descriptive names. Individualized, she became a female guardian angel; as every man had his GENIUS, so every woman had her *juno*. Thus, she represented, in a sense, the female principle of life.

As her cult expanded she assumed wider functions and became the principal female divinity of the state. As Sospita, portrayed as an armed deity, she was invoked all over Latium, originally as a savior of women but eventually as savior of the state. As Juno Moneta (perhaps literally "the Warner"), she had a temple on the Arx (the northern summit of the Capitoline Hill) from 344 BCE; it later housed the Roman mint, and the words "mint" and "money" derive from the name. Her significant festivals were the MATRONALIA on March 1 and the Nonae Caprotinae, which was celebrated under a wild fig tree in the Campus Martius on July 7. Frequently she is portrayed as a standing matron of statuesque proportions and severe beauty, occasionally exhibiting military characteristics.

Juno, classical sculpture; in the Museo Archeologico Nazionale, Naples
Alinari—Art Resource

JUPITER \'jü-pə-tər\, *also called* Jove \'jōv\, *Latin* Iuppiter, Iovis, *or* Diespiter, chief ancient Roman and Italian god. Like ZEUS, the Greek god to whom he is etymologically related, Jupiter was a sky god. One of his most ancient epithets is Lucetius (from Latin *luc-*, "light"); and later literature has preserved the same idea in such phrases as *sub Iove*, "under the open sky." As Jupiter Elicius he was propitiated with a peculiar ritual to send rain in time of drought; as Jupiter Fulgur he had an altar in the Campus Martius, and all places struck by lightning were made his property and were guarded from the profane by a circular wall.

Throughout Italy he was worshiped on the summits of hills; thus, on the Alban Hill south of Rome was an ancient seat of his worship as Jupiter Latiaris, which was the center of the league of 30 Latin cities of which Rome was originally an ordinary member. At Rome itself on the Capitoline Hill was his oldest temple; here there was a tradition of his sacred tree, the oak, and here, too, were kept the *lapides silices*, pebbles or flint stones, which were used in symbolic ceremonies by the *fetiales*, the Roman priests who officially declared war or made treaties on behalf of the Roman state.

Jupiter was especially concerned with OATHS, treaties, and leagues, and in the presence of his priest the most ancient and sacred form of marriage (*confarreatio*) took place. The lesser deities Dius Fidius and FIDES were, perhaps, originally identical and certainly were connected with him. In Virgil's *Aeneid*, though Jupiter is in many ways as much Greek as Roman, he is still the great protecting deity who keeps the hero on the path of duty (PIETAS) toward gods, state, and family.

But this aspect of Jupiter gained a new force and meaning at the close of the early Roman monarchy with the building of the famous temple on the Capitol, of which the foundations are still to be seen. It was dedicated to Iuppiter Optimus Maximus (*i.e.*, Jupiter, the Best and Greatest), and with him were associated JUNO and MINERVA, in a fashion that clearly indicates a Greco-Etruscan origin, since the combination of three deities in one temple was foreign to the ancient ROMAN RELIGION, while it is found in both Greece and Etruria. The temple's dedication festival fell on September 13, on which day the consuls originally succeeded to office, accompanied by the Senate and other magistrates and priests. In fulfillment of a vow made by their predecessors, the consuls offered to Jupiter a white ox, his favorite sacrifice, and, after rendering thanks for the preservation of the state during the past year, they made the same vow as that by which their predecessors had been bound. Then followed the feast of Jupiter. In later times this day became the central point of the great Roman games. When a victorious army returned home the triumphal procession passed to this temple.

Throughout the Roman Republic this remained the central Roman cult; and in imperial times he became the protecting deity of the reigning emperor as representing the state, as he had been the protecting deity of the free republic. His worship spread over the whole empire.

JUPITER DOLICHENUS \\'jü-pi-tər-ˌdō-li-'kā-nəs\\, god of a Roman mystery cult, originally a local Hittite-Hurrian god of fertility and thunder worshiped at Doliche (modern Dülük), in southeastern Turkey. Later the deity was given a Semitic character, but, under Achaemenidian rule (6th–4th century BCE), he was identified with the Persian god AHURA MAZDĀ, thus becoming a god of the universe. Through Greek influence he was renamed ZEUS Oromasdes; and under that title he was closely associated with the cult of MITHRA, another Persian deity. The worship of Jupiter Dolichenus and of his consort was gradually carried west-

Jupiter, classical sculpture; in the Vatican Museum
Alinari—Art Resource

ward to Rome and other military centers, where it became extremely popular during the 2nd and 3rd centuries CE. In the Roman mystery religion he was believed to control military success and safety. In art Jupiter Dolichenus was usually represented standing on a bull and carrying the double ax and the thunderbolt.

JUSTIFICATION, in Christian theology, either (1) the act by which God moves a person from the state of SIN to the state of GRACE; (2) the change in a person's condition as he moves from a state of sin to a state of righteousness; or (3) especially in PROTESTANTISM, the act of acquittal whereby God gives contrite sinners the status of the righteous.

The term is a translation of the Greek *dikaiōsis* (Latin *justificatio*). Justification has had importance in the history of the church and of theology since the time of the Apostle Paul, who asserted that one becomes just before God not by works, nor even by obeying the commandments (the law of God, which in itself is good). A person stands before God as a sinner, entirely dependent on God's grace. It is God who calls the sinner righteous. This is no arbitrary pronouncement but is made with reference to JESUS CHRIST, "who was put to death for our trespasses and raised for our justification" (Romans 4:25). In this way, the sinner is acquitted from law, sin, and death; is reconciled with God; and is not merely declared but is truly made just.

In response, one should accept God's merciful judgment in Christ and place complete trust in the Lord; in short, have faith. The person who has been justified is tempted as before and therefore remains dependent on the grace of God. Faith must not be inactive, but a "faith working

through love" (Galatians 5:6); *i.e.*, one must authenticate religious faith by deeds of love.

The Greek Fathers of the church did not emphasize the doctrine of justification, but it became an important theological concept in the thought of AUGUSTINE during his controversy with the Pelagians, a group who were teaching an ethical self-sanctification by works. The doctrine received great stress in MARTIN LUTHER'S struggle against the concept of justification by works current in the late Middle Ages, a struggle that led to a reappraisal of Paul's doctrine of justification. It became a capital doctrine for the Reformers. The COUNCIL OF TRENT (1545–63) defined the ROMAN CATHOLIC position in terms that for the next several centuries drew the lines for opposition between Roman Catholics and Protestants in their understanding of the doctrine.

JUSTINIAN I \\jə-'sti-nē-ən\\, *Latin in full* Flavius Justinianus, *original name* Petrus Sabbatius (b. 483, Tauresium, Dardania [modern Serbia, Yugos.]—d. Nov. 14, 565, Constantinople [now Istanbul, Turkey]), Byzantine emperor (527–565), noted for his reorganization of the imperial government and his sponsorship of a codification of laws known as the *Codex Justinianus* (534).

A Latin-speaking Illyrian of peasant stock, Justinian took the name from his uncle, the emperor Justin I, to whom he owed his advancement. While still a young man, he went to Constantinople to be educated. When Justin became emperor in 518, Justinian was a powerful influence in guiding the policy of his elderly and childless uncle. He was legally adopted by Justin and held important offices. In 525 he received the title of caesar and, on April 4, 527, was made co-emperor with the rank of augustus. At the same time, his wife, the former actress Theodora, who exercised considerable influence over him, was crowned augusta. On Justin I's death Justinian succeeded him as sole emperor.

Justinian considered it his duty to regain provinces lost to the empire "through indolence," and he could not ignore the trials of ROMAN CATHOLICS living under Arian rule in Italy and in the Vandal kingdom of North Africa. He attacked North Africa in June 533. By the following March (534) his general Belisarius had mastered the kingdom and received the submission of the Vandal ruler Gelimer. Northern Africa was reorganized as part of the empire.

In Italy, Justinian found a situation particularly favorable to his ambitions. The Ostrogoth Theodoric, who toward the end of his reign had begun to persecute Catholics, had died. Furthermore, not only was there antagonism between Arian Goths and Catholic Italians, but there was a rift within the ranks of the Ostrogoths as well. Thinking that this was now his opportunity to support his fellow Catholics and to reassert direct control over the province, Justinian dispatched an army and sent Belisarius with a fleet to attack Sicily. After the defeat of the Ostrogothic king Witigis and the capture of Ravenna in 540, imperial rule was reestablished in Italy. Justinian hoped to restore the well-being of Italy by a series of measures, the Pragmatic Sanction of 554, but the country was so ravaged by war that a return to normal life proved impossible, and after his death part of the country was lost to the Lombard invaders.

In the Byzantine Empire, CHURCH AND STATE were indissolubly linked as essential aspects of a single Christian empire that was thought of as the terrestrial counterpart of the heavenly polity. It was therefore the duty of Justinian to promote the good government of the church and to uphold orthodox teaching. He forbade PAGANS, heretics, and SAMARITANS to teach any subject whatsoever, and he expelled pagan teachers from the once-famous Academy at Athens.

Justinian's main doctrinal problem was the conflict between the orthodox view accepted at the COUNCIL OF CHALCEDON (451), that the divine and human natures coexist in Christ, and the MONOPHYSITE teaching that spoke of "one nature of the incarnate LOGOS." Monophysitism was strongly held in Syria and Egypt and was closely allied to growing national feelings and resentment of Byzantine rule. Justinian, whose wife, Theodora, was a strong champion of the Monophysites, knew that any concessions to the eastern provinces would almost certainly alienate Rome and the West. Justinian tried to compel the orthodox Western bishops to arrive at a compromise with the Monophysites—even going so far as to hold Pope Vigilius against his will in Constantinople, forcing Vigilius to condemn some writings by such anti-Monophysite figures from Antioch as THEODORE OF MOPSUESTIA, Theodoret, and Ibas. (This event came to be known as the "Three Chapters Controversy.") The second COUNCIL OF CONSTANTINOPLE (553) also condemned the suspect writings. Justinian achieved noth-

Justinian I, detail of a 6th-century mosaic; in the Basilica of San Vitale, Ravenna
Alinari—Giraudon from Art Resource

ing, however; he did not conciliate the Monophysites, he enraged Antioch, and he aroused Rome particularly by his handling of Pope Vigilius and his attempt to determine doctrinal matters. The decrees of the council were not accepted by Vigilius' successors, and a SCHISM thus occurred between Rome and Constantinople that lasted until 610.

JUSTIN MARTYR, SAINT \'jəs-tin\ (b. *c.* 100, Flavia Neapolis, Palestine [now Nābulus]—d. *c.* 165, Rome [Italy]; feast day June 1), one of the most important of the Greek philosopher-Apologists in the early Christian church. His writings represent the first positive encounter of Christian revelation with Greek philosophy and laid the basis for a theology of history.

A pagan reared in a Jewish environment, Justin studied Stoic, Platonic, and other philosophies and then became a Christian in 132, possibly at Ephesus, near modern Selçuk, Turkey. Soon after 135 he began wandering from place to place proclaiming his newfound Christian philosophy. He spent a considerable time in Rome. Some years later, after debating with the cynic Crescens, Justin was denounced to the Roman prefect as subversive and condemned to death. Authentic records of his martyrdom survive.

Of the works bearing Justin's authorship and still deemed genuine are two *Apologies* and the *Dialogue with Trypho.* The first, or "Major Apology," was addressed about 150 to the Roman emperors Antoninus Pius and Marcus Aurelius. In the *First Apology,* Justin expresses the core of his Christian philosophy: the highest aspiration of both CHRISTIANITY and Platonic philosophy is a transcendent and unchangeable God; consequently, an intellectual articulation of the Christian faith would demonstrate its harmony with reason. Such a convergence is rooted in the relationship between human reason and the divine mind, both identified by the same term, LOGOS (Greek: "intellect," "word"), which enables man to understand basic truths regarding the world, time, creation, freedom, the human soul's affinity with the divine spirit, and the recognition of GOOD AND EVIL. Justin asserts that JESUS CHRIST is the INCARNATION of the entire divine *logos* and thus of these basic truths, whereas only traces of truth were found in the great works of the pagan philosophers. The purpose of Christ's coming into the world was to teach men the truth and save them from the power of DEMONS.

In the *Dialogue with Trypho,* Justin tries to prove the truth of Christianity to a learned Jew named Trypho. Justin attempts to demonstrate that a new COVENANT has superseded the old covenant of God with the Jewish people; that Jesus is both the MESSIAH announced by the OLD TESTAMENT prophets and the preexisting *logos* through whom God revealed himself in the Scriptures; and that the GENTILES have been chosen to replace Israel as God's CHOSEN PEOPLE.

Justin's distinctive contribution to Christian theology is his conception of a divine plan in history, a process of salvation structured by God, wherein the various historical epochs have been integrated into an organic unity directed toward a supernatural end; the Old Testament and Greek philosophy met to form the single stream of Christianity.

Justin's concrete description of the sacramental celebrations of BAPTISM and the EUCHARIST remain a principal source for the history of the primitive church. Justin serves, moreover, as a crucial witness to the status of the 2nd-century NEW TESTAMENT corpus, mentioning the first three Gospels and quoting and paraphrasing the letters of Paul and 1 Peter; he was the first known writer to quote from THE ACTS OF THE APOSTLES.

KA \\'kä\\, in ancient EGYPTIAN RELIGION, with BA and AKH, a principal aspect of the soul of a human being or of a god. The exact significance of *ka* remains a matter of controversy, chiefly for lack of an Egyptian definition. Written by a hieroglyph of uplifted arms, it seems originally to have designated the protecting divine spirit of a person, and later the personified sum of physical and intellectual qualities constituting an "individuality." The *ka* survived the death of the body and could reside in a picture or statue of a person.

KAʿBA \\'kà-bə\\, *also spelled* Kaaba, small shrine located near the center of the Great Mosque in MECCA and considered by Muslims everywhere to be the most sacred spot on earth. Muslims orient themselves toward this shrine during the five daily prayers, bury their dead facing its meridian, and cherish the ambition of visiting it on HAJJ, or pilgrimage, in accord with the command of God in the QURʾAN.

The cube-shaped structure, constructed of gray stone and marble, is oriented so that its corners roughly correspond to the points of the compass. The interior contains nothing but the three pillars supporting the roof and a number of suspended silver and gold lamps. During most of the year the Kaʿba is covered with an enormous cloth of black brocade, the *kiswa*.

Built into the eastern wall of the Kaʿba is the Black Stone of Mecca (Arabic: al-Ḥajar al-Aswad), an object of veneration that probably dates from the pre-Islamic religion of the Arabs. It now consists of three large pieces and some fragments, surrounded by a stone ring and held together with a silver band. According to popular Islamic legend, the stone was given to ADAM on his fall from paradise and was originally white but has become black by absorbing the SINS of the thousands of pilgrims who have kissed and touched it. In 930 it was carried away by adherents of the QARMATIAN sect and held for ransom for about 20 years.

Every Muslim who makes the pilgrimage is required to walk around the Kaʿba seven times, kissing and touching the Black Stone, or saluting it as they pass by. When the month of pilgrimages (Dhū al-Ḥijjah) is over, a ceremonial washing of the Kaʿba takes place; religious officials as well as pilgrims take part.

The early history of the Kaʿba is not well known, but it is certain that in the period before the rise of ISLAM it was revered as a sacred SANCTUARY and was a site of pilgrimage. The Qurʾan says of ABRAHAM and Ishmael that they "raised the foundations" of the Kaʿba. The exact sense is ambiguous, but Muslim legend has interpreted the phrase to mean that they rebuilt a shrine first erected by Adam of which only the foundations still existed. The Kaʿba has been destroyed, damaged, and subsequently rebuilt several times. Early in his prophetic ministry MUHAMMAD seems to have disregarded the Kaʿba, but, after his immigration to MEDINA and his difficulties there with the Jews, he changed the direction toward which the prayer is recited from Jerusalem

to the Kaʿba. When he took Mecca (630), he caused the idols within and surrounding the sanctuary to be destroyed and had the building cleansed of the pictures covering its interior. The Kaʿba has been the focal point of Muslim piety ever since.

In Sufi (*see* SUFISM) literature the true Kaʿba is identified with the heart of the seeker.

KABBALAH: *see* QABBALAH.

KABĪR \\kə-'bir\\ (fl. late 15th century, Varanasi, India—d. near Magahar?), iconoclastic Indian poet-saint revered alike by Hindus, Muslims, and Sikhs. Though Kabīr is often depicted in modern times as a harmonizer of Hindu and Muslim belief and practice, it would be more accurate to say that he was equally critical of both, often conceiving them as parallel to one another in their misguided ways. In his view, the mindless, repetitious, prideful habit of declaiming SCRIPTURE could be visited alike on VEDA or QURʾAN; the religious authorities doing so could be Brahmins or Qāzīs; meaningless rites of initiation could focus either on the sacred thread (*see* UPANAYANA) or on CIRCUMCISION. What really counted for Kabir was utter fidelity to the one deathless truth of life, which he associated equally with the designations Allah and Rām—the latter understood as a general Hindu name for the divine, not the hero of the RĀMĀYAṆA. Kabīr experienced this ineffable reality as simple or spontaneous (*sahaj*), and the sometimes openly paradoxical language he used to describe it suggests the formative influence of Nāth Yogī practices (*see* HAṬHA YOGA; GORAKHNĀTH). Kabīr's principal media of communication were songs called *pada*s and rhymed couplets (*dohā*s) sometimes called "words" (ŚABDAS) or "witnesses" (*sākhī*s). A number of these memorable couplets have become common coin among speakers of north Indian languages, amplified by others attributed to Kabīr since his death.

Kabīr's poetic personality differs somewhat according to the emphases of the religious traditions that revere him, and the same can be said for his HAGIOGRAPHY. For Sikhs he is a precursor and interlocutor of NĀNAK, the founding Sikh GURŪ; for Muslims he takes his place in Sufi lineages; for Hindus, he becomes a Vaiṣṇava with universalist leanings. But when one goes back to the poetry that can most reliably be attributed to Kabīr, only two aspects of his life emerge as truly certain: he lived most of his life in Banaras (now VARANASI), and he was a weaver (*julāhā*), a low-ranked CASTE that had become largely Muslim in Kabīr's time. His humble social station and his own combative reaction to any who would regard it as such have contributed to his celebrity among Dādū Pathīs, Ravidāsīs (*see* RAVIDĀS), and Radhasoamis (*see* RADHASOAMI SATSUNG) and helped shape the Kabīr Panth, a sect found across north and central India that draws its members especially but not exclusively from Scheduled Caste (working classes) people. The Kabīr Panth regards Kabīr as its principal GURU or even as a divinity—

Ka'ba, shrine in the Great Mosque at Mecca
Mehmet Biber—Rapho/Photo Researchers

truth incarnate. The broad range of traditions on which Kabīr has had an impact is testimony to his massive authority, even for those whose beliefs and practices he criticized so unsparingly. From early on, his presence in anthologies of north Indian BHAKTI poetry is remarkable.

KACHINA \kə-'chē-nə\, *Hopi* qacína, in Pueblo Indian religious practice, any of more than 500 ancestral spirits often associated with fertility who act as intermediaries between the human and divine. Kachinas reside with the tribe for half of each year and allow themselves to be seen by the community if the men perform a traditional ritual while wearing kachina masks. The being depicted on the mask is thought to be present with the performer, temporarily transforming him. Kachinas are also depicted in small, carved-wood dolls, which are presented to children both as playthings and as devices to teach the identities of the kachinas and the symbolism of their costumes. The identity of the spirit is depicted primarily by the applied color and elaborate feather, leather, and, occasionally, fabric ornamentation of its mask.

Hopi kachina doll, c. 1950
By courtesy of the Museum of the American Indian, Heye Foundation, New York City

KADDISH \'kä-dish\, *also spelled* Qaddish, in JUDAISM, a hymn of praise usually recited in Aramaic at the end of principal sections of SYNAGOGUE services. The nucleus of the prayer is the phrase "Glorified and sanctified be God's great name throughout the world which He has created according to His will. May He establish His kingdom in your lifetime and during your days." The congregation responds: "May His great name be blessed forever to all eternity."

Originally the Kaddish was recited in the rabbinical academies at the conclusion of public study or after the sermon of the preacher. In time it became a regular feature of the synagogue service. The prayer pleads for the realization of the messianic age; and, because the resurrection of the dead is associated with the coming of the MESSIAH, the Kaddish eventually became the prayer of mourners who recite it for 11 months and one day after the death of a parent or close relative.

KAGURA \'kä-gü-ˌrä\, in SHINTŌ, traditional style of music and dancing used in religious ceremonies. Tradition states that *kagura* originated in the performances of Amenouzume, the patron goddess of dancers. *Kagura* dances dedicated to native deities and performed at the imperial court or in villages before local Shintō shrines are in essence a symbolic reenactment of the propitiatory dance that lured the sun goddess AMATERASU from the cave in ancient myth. Although *kagura* dance has been influenced by later, more sophisticated dance forms, it is still performed much as it was 1,500 years ago, to religious chants accompanied by drums, brass gongs, and flutes.

The kind of music and ritual used exclusively in the imperial palace grounds is called *mi-kagura*, that in large Shintō shrines, *o-kagura*, and Shintō music for local shrines, *sato-kagura*. The music for *mi-kagura* ceremonies is divided into two types: one to praise the spirits or seek their aid (*torimono*), the other to entertain the gods (*saibari*). *Mi-kagura* is exclusively a male event, but Shintō female dancers (*miko*) are found in other shrines.

KAIBARA EKIKEN \'kī-bä-rä-e-'kē-ˌken\, Ekiken *also spelled* Ekken \'ek-ˌken\, *original name* Atsunobu (b. Dec. 17, 1630, Fukuoka, Japan—d. Oct. 5, 1714, Japan), philosopher, travel writer, and pioneer botanist of the early Tokugawa period (1603–1867) who popularized Confucian doctrines. He was the first to apply Confucian ethics to women and children and the Japanese lower classes.

Originally trained as a physician, he left the medical profession in 1657 to study the thought of the Neo-Confucian philosopher CHU HSI. Kaibara wrote about 100 philosophical works in which he stressed Chu Hsi's conception of the hierarchical structure of society. In his *Taigi roku* ("Grave Doubts"), however, he took issue with Chu Hsi's DUALISM in favor of a single creative force. In his *Dōji kun* ("Instructions for Children"), Kaibara tells parents to discipline their children severely, so that they might accept all that parents tell them, whether it is right or wrong. To Kaibara is usually attributed *Onna daigaku* ("The Great Learning for Women"), long considered the most important ethical text for women in Japan, which advocates women's obedience to their parents, parents-in-law, husband, and, if widowed, their eldest son. Kaibara's own wife, Tōken, was also a scholar, calligrapher, and poet, and it has been suggested that she was the real author of his books.

K'AI-FENG JEW \'kī-'fəŋ\, member of a former religious community in Honan province, China. It is likely that Jews entered K'ai-feng about 1127 from India or Persia, and the oldest known SYNAGOGUE in K'ai-feng was built in 1163. There is evidence that other Jewish communities existed in China for much more than 1,000 years, but only the history of the K'ai-feng Jews has been well documented.

In the early 17th century Chinese JESUITS learned of the existence of a community of monotheists living in the city of K'ai-feng. There was a large synagogue (with a HOLY OF HOLIES accessible only to the chief RABBI), and the community observed the SABBATH and major religious festivals, practiced CIRCUMCISION, read the TORAH, had Hebrew manuscripts, used name tablets rather than pictures in their synagogue, and abstained from eating pork. Their Chinese name, T'iao-chin chiao ("pick out the tendons"), refers to practices prescribed by Jewish dietary laws.

The religious life of the Jewish community in K'ai-feng was permanently disrupted by the protracted period of war and social upheaval that accompanied the establishment of the Ch'ing (Manchu) dynasty in 1644, which saw the destruction of the synagogue as well as Jewish records, books, and burial grounds. Though the synagogue was rebuilt in 1653, few members of the community were left who could read Hebrew by 1700. The last Chinese rabbi died in 1800. The community is presumed to have died out in the early 1900s.

KĀLACAKRA TANTRA \'kä-lə-'chə-krə-'tən-trə\ (Sanskrit: "Wheel of Time Tantra"), chief text of a distinctive school of Tantric BUDDHISM that arose in northwestern India in the 10th century. The work represents the final phase of Tantric Buddhism in India, just prior to the Muslim invasion, but it has retained its prominence in Tibet.

At the center of the text's MANDALA (ritual drawing) is an image of the deity Kālacakra, another manifestation of the Buddha AKṢOBHYA, either alone or embracing his consort Viśvamātṛ (Mother of the Universe). Surrounding them are more than 250 divine figures. The most notable innovation in this TANTRA is its astrological frame of reference. The figures constituting the mandala are identified with planets and stars, and the structure of the mandala is correlated with the temporal rhythms of the heavens.

KALĀM \kə-'läm\, in ISLAM, speculative theology. Kalām is short for 'ilm al-kalām, in Arabic, "knowledge of debate" or "science of discourse" on God. Those who practice kalām are known as mutakallimūn.

In its early stage, kalām was merely a defense of Islam against Christians, Manichaeans, and believers in other religions. As interest in philosophy grew among Muslim

Kālī, relief from Bherāghāṭ, near Jabalpur, Madhya Pradesh state, India, 10th century CE
Pramod Chandra

thinkers, kalām adopted the methodology of the Greek skeptics and the stoics and directed these against the Islamic philosophers who attempted to fit Aristotle and Plato into a Muslim context.

Several schools of kalām developed. The most significant was the MU'TAZILA, often described as the rationalists of Islam, who appeared in the 8th century. They believed in the autonomy of reason with regard to revelation and in the supremacy of reasoned ('aqlī) faith against traditional (naqlī) faith. The Mu'tazila championed the freedom of the human will, holding that it was against divine justice to either punish a good man or pardon an unrighteous one. The Ash'arīya, a school of kalām originating in the 10th century, was a mediation between the rationalization of the Mu'tazila and the ANTHROPOMORPHISM of the traditionalists and represented the successful adaptation of Hellenistic philosophical reasoning to Muslim orthodox theology. They too affirmed the freedom of the human will but denied its efficacy. Closely resembling but more liberal than the Ash'arīya was the al-Māturīdīya school, which also originated in the 10th century. See also ASH'ARĪ, ABŪ AL-ḤASAN AL-; KASB; MĀTURĪDĪYA.

KALEVALA \'kä-lä-,vä-lä\, Finnish national epic compiled from old Finnish ballads, lyrical songs, and incantations that were a part of Finnish ORAL TRADITION.

The Kalevala was compiled by Elias Lönnrot, who published the folk material in two editions (32 cantos, 1835; enlarged into 50 cantos, 1849). Kalevala, the dwelling place of the poem's chief characters, is a poetic name for Finland, meaning "land of heroes." The leader of the "sons of Kaleva" is VÄINÄMÖINEN, a powerful seer with supernatural origins, who is a master of the kantele, a harplike stringed instrument. Other characters include the smith ILMARINEN, one of those who forged the "lids of heaven" when the world was created; LEMMINKÄINEN, an adventurer-warrior and charmer of women; Louhi, the female ruler of POHJOLA, a powerful land in the north; and Kullervo, who is forced by fate to be a slave from childhood.

Among the main dramas of the poem are the creation of the world and the adventurous journeys of Väinämöinen, Ilmarinen, and Lemminkäinen to Pohjola to woo the beautiful daughter of Louhi, during which the miraculous SAMPO is forged and recovered for the people of Kalevala. Although the Kalevala depicts the conditions and ideas of the pre-Christian period, the last canto seems to predict the decline of traditional religions: the maid Marjatta gives birth to a son who is baptized king of Karelia, and Väinämöinen makes way for him, departing from Finland without his kantele and songs.

KĀLĪ \'kä-lē\ (Sanskrit, literally: "She Who Is Black"), major Hindu goddess whose ICONOGRAPHY, cult, and mythology commonly associate her with death, sexuality, violence, and, paradoxically in some of her later historical appearances, motherly love. Although depicted in many forms throughout South Asia (and now much of the world), Kālī is most often characterized as a black or blue goddess, partially or completely naked, with a long lolling tongue, a skirt or girdle of human arms, a necklace of decapitated heads, and multiple arms. She is often depicted standing or dancing on her husband, the god Shiva, who lies prostrate beneath her.

Kālī was originally most likely a deity of the tribal and mountain cultures of South Asia who was gradually appropriated and transformed, if never quite tamed, by the more traditional and public pan-Indian Sanskritic traditions. She makes her first major appearance in Sanskrit culture in the *Devī-Māhātmya* ("The Greatness of the Goddess," *c.* 6th century CE), where she springs from the angry brow of the goddess DURGĀ to slay the DEMON Raktabīja. Her paradoxical nature, deeds of violence and grace, and ecstatic secrets have since then been displayed, encoded, and meditated on in a wide range of Sanskrit, vernacular, and artistic media (PURĀNAS, TANTRAS, philosophical treatises, meditation manuals, sculpture, ritual theatre, vernacular songs) up until the present.

Kālī's cult has been particularly popular at different points of Indian history in Kashmir, Kerala, South India, Bengal, and Assam. She has thus inhabited a space "on the edges" of the subcontinent and culture in both a geographic and a doctrinal sense. The last three decades of the 20th century have seen a growing interest in Kālī's mythology and ritual in the West, particularly in the United States among feminist-oriented scholars and writers, who see Kālī as a symbol of feminine empowerment and radical embodiment, and "New Age" believers, who are often attracted to the positive and liberating roles that sexuality and theological paradox play in her more Tantric manifestations.

KALKĪ \ˈkəl-kē\, *also called* Kalkin \ˈkəl-kin\, tenth and final AVATAR (incarnation) of the Hindu god VISHNU, who is yet to appear. At the end of the present Kali age, when virtue and religion have disappeared into CHAOS and the world is ruled by unjust men, Kalkī will appear to destroy the wicked and usher in a new age. Often he is pictured as being seated on a white horse, with a naked sword in his hand, blazing like a comet. According to some myths, Kalkī's horse will stamp the earth with its right foot, causing the tortoise that supports the world to drop into the deep. Then Kalkī will restore the earth to its initial purity.

Certain aspects of the mythology of Kalkī contain motifs shared with millennial aspects of other religious traditions, especially the horsemen of the APOCALYPSE in CHRISTIANITY and the utopian locale Shambhālā in BUDDHISM. This place, described in Hindu accounts as

Kalkī, 17th-century Nepalese miniature; in a private collection
Pramod Chandra

the village in which Kalkī will be born and to which he will repeatedly return, is in TIBETAN BUDDHISM a secret mountain kingdom whose future ruler will inaugurate a worldwide golden age.

KALPA SŪTRA \ˈkəl-pə-ˈsü-trə\, any of several manuals of Hindu religious practice, a number of which emerged within the different schools of the VEDA. Each manual explains the procedures (*kalpa*) of its school as it applies to the sacrificial ritual (the *Śrauta Sūtra*s), the domestic ritual (the *Grhya Sūtra*s), and the conduct of life (the *Dharma Sutra*s). They are written in the short aphoristic style of the *sūtra* (literally "thread") so that they can be committed easily to memory. *Kalpa* is one of six fields of scholarly discipline known as Vedāngas ("accessories to the Vedas"). Regarded to be of human origin, they are considered *Smṛti* ("Tradition") as distinct from the Veda itself, which is *Śruti* ("Revelation").

KALVIS \ˈkäl-vis\, *also called* Kalvaitis, or Kalvelis (Lithuanian), *Latvian* Kalējs \ˈkä-lās\, in BALTIC RELIGION, the heavenly smith, usually associated with a huge iron hammer. Kalvis also seems to have been a dragon killer, a function in which he was superseded by the Christian St. George. Every morning Kalvis hammers a new sun for Aušrinė (Latvian: AUSEKLIS), the dawn, and a silver belt and golden stirrups for Dievo sūneliai (Latvian: Dieva dēli), the morning and evening stars.

Kalvis' extraordinarily large iron hammer, by whose aid the sun was said to have been freed from imprisonment, was honored by the Lithuanians as late as the turn of the 15th century.

KĀMA \ˈkä-mə\, in the mythology of India, the god of love. During the Vedic age, he personified cosmic desire, or the creative impulse, and is called the first-born of the primeval CHAOS that makes all later creation possible. In later periods he is depicted as a handsome youth, attended by heavenly nymphs, who shoots love-producing flower-arrows. His bow is of sugarcane, his bowstring a row of bees. Once directed by the other gods to arouse SHIVA's passion for PĀRVATĪ, he disturbed the great god's meditation on a mountaintop. Enraged, Shiva burned him to ashes with the fire of his third eye. Thus he became Ananga (Sanskrit: "the Bodiless"). Some accounts say Shiva soon relented and restored him to life after the entreaties of Kāma's wife, Rati. Others hold that Kāma's subtle, bodiless form renders him even more deftly omnipresent than he would be if constrained by bodily limitation.

The Sanskrit term *kāma* also refers to one of the four proper aims of human life—pleasure and love. A classic textbook on erotics and other forms of human pleasure, the *Kāma Sūtra*, is attributed to the sage Vātsyāyana.

KAMI \\'kä-'mē, *Angl* 'kä-mē\\, *plural* kami, object of worship in SHINTŌ and other indigenous religions of Japan, often translated as "god," "lord," or "deity" but also including other forces of nature which become objects of reverence and respect. The sun goddess AMATERASU Ōmikami, illustrious ancestors, and animate or inanimate things, such as plants, rocks, birds, beasts, and fish, may all be treated as *kami*. In early Shintō, the heavenly *kami* (*amatsukami*) were considered more noble than the earthly *kami* (*kunitsukami*), but in modern Shintō this distinction is no longer made. *Kami* are usually worshiped in their manifestations, or residences, in a symbolic object such as a mirror (*see* SHINTAI). Shintō myths speak of the "800 myriads of *kami*" to express the infinite number of potential *kami*, and new ones continue to be recognized.

KAMIDANA \\'kä-mē-,dä-nä\\ (Japanese: "god-shelf"), in SHINTŌ, a miniature shrine, the center of daily worship in a household or a shop. The *kamidana* usually consists of a small cupboard or shelf on which are displayed articles of veneration and daily offerings. At the center of the shrine stands the *taima*, an inscribed board from the main Shintō shrine, the GRAND SHRINE OF ISE, which represents a universal KAMI. On either side are various paper AMULETS (*o-fuda*) associated with local tutelary gods (*uji-gami*) and ancestral spirits. The *kamidana* may also include a *shimenawa*, a sacred rope of twisted rice straw traditionally used to demarcate a sacred area. Offerings of water, sake, food, and green twigs are placed daily at the front of the shrine, and prayers are offered for blessings on the household.

KAMMAṬṬHĀNA \\,kə-mə-'tä-nə\\ (Pāli: "basis of meditation"), *Sanskrit* karmasthāna, in THERAVĀDA Buddhist tradition, one of the objects of mental concentration or a stage of meditation employing it. According to *Visuddhi-magga* (a 5th-century-CE Pāli text by BUDDHAGHOSA), there are 40 *kammaṭṭhānas*; an individual should choose the object of mental concentration that is in accordance with his own character or inclination. Theravāda BUDDHISM classifies human dispositions into six: covetousness, anger, stupidity, trustfulness, wisdom, and reason. Each type of disposition has its appropriate objects for mental concentration among the *kammaṭṭhānas*. The meditation of *kammaṭṭhāna* is highly valued among Buddhist monks and is still practiced in Myanmar (Burma), Thailand, and other Southeast Asian countries.

KANIṢKA \\kə-'nish-kə\\, *also spelled* Kanishka, *Chinese* Chia-ni-se-chia, greatest king of the Kushān dynasty and patron of BUDDHISM.

Most of what is known about Kaniṣka derives from Chinese sources, particularly Buddhist writings. When Kaniṣka came to the throne is uncertain. His accession has been estimated as occurring between 78 and 144 CE; his reign is believed to have lasted 23 years. The year 78 marks the beginning of the Śaka era, a system of dating that Kaniṣka might have initiated.

Through inheritance and conquest, Kaniṣka's kingdom came to cover areas in modern-day Uzbekistan, the GAṄGĀ (Ganges) Valley, Tajikistan, central India, Pakistan, and possibly Chinese Turkistan. Contact between Kaniṣka and the Chinese in Central Asia may have inspired the transmission of Indian ideas, particularly Buddhism, to China; it is

known that Buddhism first appeared in China in the 2nd century CE.

As a patron of Buddhism Kaniṣka is chiefly noted for having convened the fourth great Buddhist council in Kashmir that marked the beginnings of MAHĀYĀNA Buddhism. At the council, according to Chinese sources, authorized commentaries on the Buddhist canon were prepared and engraved on copper plates. These texts have survived only in Chinese translations and adaptations. Kaniṣka was a tolerant king, and his coins show that he honored the Zoroastrian, Greek, and Brahmanic deities as well as the Buddha.

KANNON \\'kän-'nȯn\\, in Japanese BUDDHISM, the BODHISATTVA of infinite compassion and mercy. *See* AVALOKITEŚVARA.

KĀPĀLIKA AND KĀLĀMUKHA \\kä-'pä-li-kə . . . 'kä-lä-,mù-kə\\, members of either of two groups of Śaivite (*see* ŚAIVISM) ascetics most prominent in India from the 8th through 13th century, notorious for their practices of worship, which included the five tantric rites and animal and HUMAN SACRIFICE. They were successors of the PĀŚUPATAS, an early sect that worshiped SHIVA according to "animal" (*paśu*)— that is, antisocial—vows.

The Kāpālikas (worshipers of Kāpālin, the skull bearer, a name of Shiva) and the Kālāmukhas (black-faced, so called because of the black mark, or *tilaka*, customarily worn on their foreheads) were often confused. They were both designated as *mahāvratins* ("observers of the great vows"), referring to a 12-year vow of rigorous self-abnegation that was said to follow the sacrifice of a BRAHMIN or other high-ranking person, in imitation of Shiva's act of severing one of Brahmā's five heads. During this time ascetics ate and drank from the skull of the person so sacrificed and followed such extreme tantric practices as going naked, eating the flesh of the dead, smearing themselves with the ashes of corpses, and frequenting lonely CREMATION grounds where they meditated on the YONI, the symbol of the female sexual organ. Other Śaivites, in particular, were enraged by such practices.

Some otherwise puzzling sculptures on medieval Indian temples are sometimes explained as depicting Kāpālika ascetics. An inscription at Igatpuri in Nasik district (Maharashtra state) confirms that the Kāpālika were well established in that region in the 7th century; another important center was probably Śrīparvata (modern Nāgārjunīkoṇḍā), in Andhra Pradesh, and they apparently spread throughout India. In an 8th-century Sanskrit drama, *Mālatīmādhava*, the heroine narrowly escapes being sacrificed to the goddess Cāmuṇḍā by a pair of Kāpālika ascetics. Successors to the Kāpālikas in modern times are the Aghorīs, or Aghorapanthīs.

KAPILA \\'kə-pē-lə\\ (fl. 550 BCE?), Vedic sage who is often claimed, with others (especially Āsuri), as the founder of the system of Sāṃkhya, one of six schools of Vedic philosophy. He is not, however, the author of the text primarily responsible for giving the school its philosophical definition: Īśvarakṛṣṇa's *Sāṃkhya-kārikā* (*c*. 4th century CE).

According to Hindu sources, Kapila was a descendant of MANU, the primal human being, and a grandson of the creator-god BRAHMĀ or, alternatively, an AVATAR of VISHNU. The BHAGAVAD GĪTĀ pictures him as a recluse associated with yogic adepts (SIDDHAS). The Sāṃkhya system attributed to Kapila has had a considerable impact on the Hindu tradition as a whole, especially through its close association with YOGA, as symbolized in Kapila's own renunciant persona. For example, Sāṁkhya forms a notable part of the philosophical background of the *Bhagavad Gītā*. In mythology, Kapila is portrayed as an exemplar of yogic stringency. His HERMIT regimen is said to have produced in him an inner store of such intense heat that he was capable of reducing to ash the 60,000 sons of Sagara.

KAPLAN, MORDECAI MENAHEM \\'ka-plən\\ (b. June 11, 1881, Švenčionys, Lithuania—d. Nov. 8, 1983, New York, N.Y., U.S.), American RABBI, educator, theologian, and religious leader who founded the influential Reconstructionist movement in JUDAISM.

Kaplan was a visionary who thought it urgent that Judaism adapt to the crisis of modernity. Utilizing the disciplines of history and sociology, he defined Judaism as the evolving religious civilization of the Jewish people. With this definition, he resisted defining Judaism as solely a religion, whose beliefs and practices are timeless and unchanging. Rather, he understood Judaism as the civilization—the culture, languages, values, literature, and FOLKLORE, in addition to RELIGIOUS BELIEFS and ritual practices—of communities of Jewish people through the ages. He showed how all aspects of that civilization had evolved in response to the ever changing historical circumstances.

Based on that analysis, Kaplan argued that it is the responsibility of each generation of Jews to continue the ongoing evolution, reconstructing Judaism to meet contemporary challenges. Specifically, Kaplan sought to address the crisis in Jewish life caused by the political emancipation of the American Jews, who, for the most part, are primarily integrated within American culture. He advocated the formation of voluntary intensive communities in which Judaism could continue to flourish. Embracing the democratic values of the United States, he sought to reformulate Jewish beliefs and practices in ways that Jews would find compelling. He described God in naturalistic terms, eschewing supernatural miracles, as the Power that makes for salvation. He understood TORAH not as a one-time revelation at Sinai, but rather as the ongoing product of successive generations: quests for ultimate value and meaning. He advocated intensive ritual observance and prayer, because a civilization is transmitted through the values embedded in cultural forms, but he also urged that prayer and ritual be reinterpreted when they express values that are now repugnant. In this regard, he eliminated all chauvinistic references to the chosen status of the Jewish people. He also initiated gender equity in ritual practice, most dramatically by the introduction in 1922 of the bat mitzvah ceremony for girls.

KARAISM \\'kar-ə-ˌi-zəm\\, *also spelled* Karaitism, *or* Qaraism (from Hebrew: *qara*, "to read"), a Jewish religious movement that repudiated ORAL TRADITION as a source of divine law and defended the Hebrew BIBLE as the sole authentic font of religious doctrine and practice. Initially, supporters of the movement were called Ananites, after ANAN BEN DAVID, the first literary figure of the group, who worked out a code of life independent of the TALMUD. During the 9th or 10th century, the name Karaites was adopted to underscore the group's emphasis on a personal reading of the Bible.

The movement began in 8th-century Persia. Though its members were never numerous, it spread to Egypt and Syria and later into Europe by way of Spain and Constantinople. Karaism proclaimed the Bible to be self-explanatory and sanctioned personal interpretations of the SCRIPTURES. The movement, however, soon found it necessary to devel-op an oral tradition of its own in applying scriptural principles to daily life. Extreme ASCETICISM was practiced, the festival of HANUKKAH was suppressed, and great rigor was applied to dietary laws, ritual purity, fasting, clothing, and marriage (adherents were forbidden to marry outside the sect). An uncompromising MONOTHEISM led to the exclusion of traditional Jewish ritual objects such as phylacteries and mezuzahs.

The movement suffered from numerous SCHISMS and from a lack of competent scholars to defend its position on the Bible. SAʿADIA BEN JOSEPH (10th century) was an outspoken and effective opponent of Karaism and tried to exclude Karaites from Jewish communities. He and others, however, were forced by Karaism to develop Jewish philosophy and sharpen their EXEGESIS to defend rabbinic Judaism's use of oral tradition (and the Talmud in particular). These controversies produced a great mass of polemical literature in Hebrew and Aramaic, the largest collection of which is now in the St. Petersburg Public Library.

Karaites still exist today, about 10,000 of them living in or near Ramla, outside Tel Aviv–Yafo, and probably small enclaves survive in Poland and Russia. Their liturgy has little poetry but many readings of scriptural texts.

KARBALĀʾ \\'kär-bä-lä\\, *also spelled* Kerbela \\'kər-bə-lə\\, city, central Iraq. The city is Iraq's foremost holy city and lies 55 miles southwest of Baghdad.

The city's religious importance derives from the Battle of Karbalāʾ (680 CE) between SUNNI and SHIʿITE forces. Ḥusayn ibn ʿAlī, the Shiʿite leader and grandson of MUHAMMAD, was killed, and his tomb remains one of the greatest Shiʿite shrines and PILGRIMAGE centers. It was destroyed in 1801 but was soon rebuilt. Shiʿite Muslims consider burial in Karbalāʾ a sure means of reaching paradise; the city therefore has extensive cemeteries. The city is also a departure point for pilgrimages to MECCA. In the aftermath of the 1991 Persian Gulf War both the city and the shrine were devastated when Saddam Hussein's Republican Guard moved in to eradicate a widespread Shiʿite uprising in the region.

KARMA \\'kər-mə, 'kär-\\ ("act," "deed," or "task"), *Sanskrit* karman, *Pāli* kamma, in Indian philosophy, the impact of an individual's past actions on future lives, or REINCARNATIONS. The doctrine of karma reflects the conviction that this life is but one in a chain of lives (SAMSĀRA) and that it is significantly influenced by actions in a previous life. Such a system, in which actions in the present produce future reactions in kind, but sometimes with lapses in time or changes of medium, is offered as a simple description of moral reality; as a justification for the evident disparities in status that exist between beings, both human and otherwise; and as an impetus for virtuous behavior. But it is rarely well understood in the West that this "law of karma" has often been disputed in India, not only by those whose station in life is low, as might be expected, but by others as well.

Buddhists and Jains join Hindus in incorporating doctrines of karma as part of their common Indian legacy. Buddhists tend to interpret it strictly in terms of ethical cause and effect with a range of views about the mechanics of rebirth that contrast somewhat with those held by Hindus, since issues of enduring personhood pose different philosophical problems for Buddhists than they do for Hindus. For Jains, karma is not viewed as a process but as a fine particulate substance that produces the universal chain of cause and effect and of birth and death.

KARO, JOSEPH BEN EPHRAIM \\'kär-ō\\, Karo *also spelled* Caro, *or* Qaro, *also called* Maran \\'mär-än\\ (Aramaic: "Our Master") (b. 1488, Spain—d. March 24, 1575, Safed, Palestine [now Ẕefat, Israel]), Spanish-born Jewish author of the last great codification of Jewish law, the *Bet Yosef* ("House of Joseph"). Its condensation, the SHULḤAN ʿARUKH ("The Prepared Table," or "The Well-Laid Table"), is still authoritative for Orthodox Jewry.

When the Jews were expelled from Spain in 1492, Karo and his parents settled in Turkey. About 1536 he immigrated to Safed in Palestine, then the center for students of the TALMUD and the QABBALAH. Because of the partial disintegration in Jewish life after the Spanish expulsion, and the diversity of Talmudic authorities in different countries, Karo undertook two major works to standardize Judaism's customs and laws. The first and greater of his works was the commentary *Bet Yosef* on the codification *Arbaʿa ṭurim* (1475; "Four Rows") of JACOB BEN ASHER. Karo brought together the legal decisions of three leading representative Talmudists: MOSES MAIMONIDES, ISAAC BEN JACOB ALFASI, and Asher ben Jehiel. When he found disagreement among the three, Karo took the majority opinion as final. That procedure, however, gave a Sephardic bias to the work, because both Maimonides and Alfasi were Sephardic—*i.e.*, Jews of Spanish and Portuguese descent. In addition, Karo often decided difficult points of law on his own authority. Because of the complexity and erudition of the *Bet Yosef*, Karo produced a popular condensation, *Shulḥan ʿarukh* (1564–65). A corrective commentary by Moses Isserles entitled *Mappa* (1571; "The Tablecloth"), made Karo's code acceptable to Sephardic and Ashkenazic Jews alike.

Karo was also the author of a mystical diary, entitled *Maggid mesharim* (1646; "Preacher of Righteousness"), in which he recorded the nocturnal visits of an angelic being, the personification of the MISHNAH. His visitor spurred him to acts of righteousness and ASCETICISM, exhorted him to study the Qabbalah, and reproved him for moral laxities.

KARTĒR \\kär-'tēr\\, *also spelled* Kartir, *or* Karder (fl. 3rd century CE, Persia [now Iran]), influential HIGH PRIEST of ZOROASTRIANISM, whose aim was to purge Persia of all other religions, especially MANICHAEISM. What little is known of Kartēr comes from inscriptions on cliff faces, mostly dating from the reign of Shāpūr I (241–272). On more than 700 cliffs he proclaimed the fundamental doctrines of the religion of ZOROASTER.

Beginning his career under King Ardashīr I (ruled 224–241), Kartēr sought to restore the Mazdean religion (Zoroastrianism) into what he believed was its pure form. Under Shāpūr I, he held the title of *ehrpat* ("master of learning"). Later, under another king, Hormizd, he was elevated to the rank of *magaput*, or chief, of the MAGI of Hormizd, a title previously unknown to the Magi, the priestly caste of ancient Persia.

When Bahrām I (ruled 273–276) assumed the throne, Kartēr was at last afforded an opportunity to get rid of his archrival MANI, who had been protected by Shāpūr. Bahrām put Mani in prison, where he finally died. Kartēr managed to establish his version of orthodox Zoroastrianism and proceeded to persecute all other religions, especially the Zandīks (Zoroastrian heretics, perhaps Zurvanites), who insisted on interpreting the AVESTA in the light of their own thinking. After the death of Kartēr, a degree of religious tolerance gradually reasserted itself, and the many titles created for Kartēr or taken by him were recovered by other priests.

KASB \\'kä-səb\\ (Arabic: "acquisition"), a doctrine in ISLAM adopted by the theologian AL-ASHʿARĪ (d. 935) as a mean between PREDESTINATION and FREE WILL. According to al-Ashʿarī, all actions, good and evil, are originated by God, but they are "acquired" (*maksūb*, whence *kasb*) by men. As for the criticism that his *kasb* theory attributes evil to God, al-Ashʿarī explained that, by creating evil, God is not an evildoer.

Al-Ashʿarī chose the term *kasb* to avoid attributing *khalq* (creation) to anyone but God. His main concern was to maintain God's total omnipotence and at the same time allow humans a degree of responsibility for their actions. Al-Ashʿarī rejected the assertion of the MUʿTAZILA theological school, of which he had been a member, that humans have the power to will an act or its opposite. He maintained rather that humans have the power to will only the act, not the opposite: they do not initiate anything, but merely acquire what God has created. Thus human responsibility comes from the decision as to which actions one should acquire.

The *kasb* doctrine was regarded by many Muslim theologians as being indistinguishable from pure predetermination. Despite the efforts of al-Ashʿarī and his followers (the Ashʿarīya) to clarify *kasb*, it remained one of the most vague theories in Islamic theology, as the proverb *aḍaqq min kasb al-Ashʿarī* ("more subtle than the *kasb* of al-Ashʿarī") indicates.

KASHF \\'kä-shəf\\ (Arabic: "uncovering," "revelation"), in SUFISM, the privileged inner knowledge that mystics acquire through personal experience and direct vision of God. The truths revealed through *kashf* cannot be transmitted to those who have not shared with them the same experience. The Sufis regard *kashf* as the alternative to ʿILM ("knowledge"), which applies systematic theology, logic, and speculative philosophy to the study of the nature of God. Its place in Sufi discourse was secure by the time of al-Hujwiri (d. *c.* 1072), who wrote a treatise on Sufism called *Kashf al-mahjub* ("Revelation of Veiled Reality"). When the Muslim jurist and theologian AL-GHAZĀLĪ (d. 1111) felt that philosophy and speculative theology had failed him, he turned wholeheartedly to Sufism. After a period of mystical contemplation, he became certain that pure philosophical systems are contradictory and illusory and that the intellect should be used only to destroy trust in human logic. He concluded that *kashf* is the only means through which true and trustworthy knowledge can be attained and described it as "a light with which God floods the heart of the believer." *See also* GNOSTICISM; MYSTICISM.

KASHMIR ŚAIVISM \\'kash-ˌmir-'shī-ˌvi-zəm, 'kazh-\\, *also called* Pratyabhijñā (Sanskrit: "Recognition"), an important religio-philosophical system of India whose followers worship Lord SHIVA as the supreme reality. The school is idealistic and monistic, as contrasted with the realistic and dualistic school of ŚAIVA-SIDDHĀNTA.

The principal texts of the school are the *Śiva Sūtra*, which is said to have been revealed to Vasugupta; Vasugupta's *Spanda-kārikā* ("Verses on Activity"; 8th–9th century); Utpala's *Pratyabhijñā Śāstra* (*c.* 900; "Manual on Recognition"); Abhinavagupta's *Paramārthasāra* ("The Essence of the Highest Truth"), *Pratyabhijñāvimarśini* ("Reflections on Recognition"), and *Tantrāloka* ("Lights on the Doctrine"; 11th–12th century); and Kṣemarāja's *Śiva Sūtra Vimarśini* ("Reflections on the Aphorisms on Shiva"; 12th century).

Shiva is seen as the sole reality and both the material and efficient cause of the universe. His power is known in five aspects: *cit* ("consciousness"), ĀNANDA ("bliss"), *ichā* ("will"), *jñāna* ("knowledge"), and *kriyā* ("action"). For the adherents of Kashmir Śaivism, liberation comes about through intense meditation on the Lord and recognition of the identical nature of the individual soul and the Lord. (*Compare* ŚAIVISM.)

KASHRUTH \kä-'shrüt, 'kä-shrüth\, *also spelled* kashrut, *or* kashrus \'kä-shrùs\, *Hebrew* kashrūt ("fitness"), in JUDAISM, regulations that prohibit the eating of certain foods and require that other foods be prepared in a specified manner. The term also denotes the state of being KOSHER according to Jewish law. Most prescriptions regarding kashruth are found in the biblical Leviticus, Deuteronomy, GENESIS, and EXODUS.

In general, Jews observing kashruth may eat only those fish that have both fins and scales (*i.e.*, not shellfish), certain birds, and mammals that chew the cud and have cloven feet. These mammals and birds must be slaughtered according to a ritual (*shehitah*) that, if violated, makes the meat unfit for use. The slaughterer (*shohet*) recites a prayer and then makes an incision across the neck of the animal or fowl with a special knife that is razor-sharp and has a smooth edge with absolutely no nicks. The cutting must be made by moving the knife in a single swift and uninterrupted sweep and not by pressure or by stabbing. The cut severs the main arteries, rendering the animal unconscious and permitting the blood to drain from the body. Because animal blood may not be eaten, meat must undergo a ritual process of presoaking and "salting" (*meliḥa*) to draw off any blood that may remain within the meat after death. Objections have sometimes been raised to this method of slaughter on the grounds of cruelty, and in some European countries this resulted in legislation forbidding *shehitah*.

Strict separation of meat and dairy products is enjoined, both in eating and in preparation; these two types of food may not be eaten at the same meal and distinct sets of dishes, cutlery, utensils, and table linens must be used for meat and dairy products during the time of preparation. Some foods are "neutral" (PAREVE) and may be eaten freely with meat or milk. No restrictions apply to the use of vegetables and fruit. Ultra-Orthodox Judaism requires that non-Jews be excluded from the preparation of kosher wine. During the festival of PASSOVER (Pesaḥ), special laws exclude the use of leaven in bread and other baked goods. (*See also* TOHORAH.)

KAVA \'kä-və\, *also spelled* cava, *or* ava, euphoria-producing beverage that is made from the root of the pepper plant, principally *Piper methysticum* and is used in most of the South Pacific islands. It is yellow-green in color and somewhat bitter in taste, and the active ingredient is apparently alkaloidal in nature.

Consumption of the beverage takes place in the kava ceremony, which includes the ritual making and drinking of kava and a ceremonial feast. Occasions for the kava ceremony can be social, such as a gathering of chiefs, a visit of a chief from a neighboring island, or a gathering before battle, or it can be ceremonial, such as the conclusion of a public assembly presided over by a chief or king, the inauguration of a new chief, or a meeting with a god or gods for DIVINATION.

KĀVERĪ RIVER \'kä-və-rē\, *also spelled* Cauvery \'kô-və-rē\, sacred river of southern India, rising on Brahmagiri Hill in the Western Ghāts in Coorg district of Karnataka state, flowing in a southeasterly direction for 475 miles through Karnataka and Tamil Nadu states, and descending the Eastern Ghāts in a series of great falls. Before emptying into the Bay of Bengal south of Cuddalore, Tamil Nadu, it breaks into a large number of distributaries describing a wide delta called the "garden of southern India." Known to devout Hindus as Dakṣina Gaṅgā (Ganges of the South), it is celebrated for its scenery and sanctity in Tamil literature, and its entire course is considered holy ground.

In Karnataka, the river bifurcates twice, forming the sacred islands of Śrīraṅgapatnam and Śivasamudram, 50 miles apart. After sweeping past the historic rock of Tiruchchirappalli (Trichinopoly), the Kāverī breaks at Śrīraṅgam Island, a main PILGRIMAGE center. The only navigation on any part of the Kāverī course is in basketwork boats. Its main tributaries are the Kabbani, AMARĀVATI, Noyil, and Bhavāni rivers.

KEDESHA \'ke-de-shä\, *also spelled* kedeshah, *Akkadian* qadishtu, *Hebrew* qedesha, one of a class of sacred prostitutes found throughout the ancient Middle East, especially in the worship of the fertility goddess ASTARTE. These prostitutes, who often played an important part in official temple worship, could be either male or female. In Egypt, a god-

A kava ceremony being performed in Fiji
Jack Fields—Photo Researchers

dess named Qedeshu, Lady of Kadesh (Syria), was worshiped in the 19th and 20th dynasties (1292–c. 1075 BCE). On stelae she is shown nude, posed frontally on a lioness (or a leopard), holding arrows in her hands. Although Israelite prophets and reformers repeatedly denounced sacred prostitution, the early Israelites seem to have adopted the local Canaanite rites, which they apparently practiced publicly until the reform of King JOSIAH about 622 BCE.

KEGON: *see* HUA-YEN.

KEIZAN JŌKIN \ˈkā-zän-ˈjō-kēn\, *posthumous name* Jōsai Daishi (b. Nov. 13, 1268, Echizen province [now in Fukui prefecture], Japan—d. Sept. 22, 1325, Noto province [now in Ishikawa prefecture]), priest of the SŌTŌ sect of ZEN BUDDHISM, who founded the Sōji Temple (now rebuilt in Yokohama), one of the two head temples of the sect.

At the age of 12 Keizan entered the PRIESTHOOD at the Eihei Temple, the headquarters of the sect. After studying at the Daijō Temple, he became a teacher there, where he propagated the teachings of the Sōtō sect for 10 years. He then became the head priest of the Shogaku Temple.

Keizan gave the temple a new name, Shogaku-zan Sōji Temple, and affiliated it with the Sōtō sect in 1321. Later, when he preached to the emperor Go-Daigo on the Ten Questions on Buddhism, Sōji Temple became an imperial temple. Keizan devoted himself to establishing many temples, renewing the religious traditions of his sect, and popularizing the teachings of its founder, DŌGEN. Under him the Sōtō sect developed rapidly. Now called Taiso ("Great Master"), he is worshiped as the restorer of the sect.

KEKRI \ˈke-krē\, *also spelled* Keyri, *or* Käyri, in ancient Finnish religion, a feast day marking the end of the agricultural season that also coincided with the time when the cattle were taken in from pasture for the winter. Kekri originally fell on Michaelmas, September 29, but was later shifted to November 1, ALL SAINTS' DAY. In the old system of reckoning time, Kekri was a critical period between the old and new years when the ancestor spirits came to visit their former homes and the living held feasts honoring the dead. Food and drink were left for the spirits, the sauna was heated, and the dead were referred to as "holy men." The feast was generally restricted to the members of the family, but in some areas the occasion was also marked by the sacrifice of a sheep by the men of the entire village.

KENITE \ˈkē-ˌnīt\, member of a tribe of itinerant metalsmiths, mentioned several times in the OLD TESTAMENT, who were related to the MIDIANITES and the Israelites. The Kenites' name was derived from CAIN, whose descendants they were believed to be.

The father-in-law of MOSES, JETHRO, was a Kenite and was priest-leader of the tribe he led in the worship of YAHWEH, whom Moses later revealed to the Hebrews as their own God whom they had forgotten. Settling among the Israelites, AMALEKITES, and Canaanites, the Kenites apparently became absorbed into the tribe of JUDAH. Conservative groups of Kenites retained their nomadic way of life and beliefs and practices, however, and one such group, the RECHABITES (2 Kings), fought alongside the rebel and future king of Israel, JEHU, against the Omri dynasty.

KER \ˈkir\, *also spelled* Cer \ˈsir\, in ancient GREEK RELIGION, a destructive spirit. Popular belief attributed death and illness to the action of impersonal powers, often spoken of in the plural (Keres). *Ker* was also used as a word signifying an individual's doom. In the Attic festival of the ANTHESTERIA, the "Keres" (presumably spirits of the dead) were expelled at the end of the ceremony; thus some scholars have conjectured that this was the original meaning of the word.

KERYGMA AND CATECHESIS \kə-ˈrig-mə, ˈkir-ig-mə . . . ˌka-tə-ˈkē-sis\, in the theology of CHRISTIANITY, respectively, the initial proclamation of the gospel message and the oral instruction given before BAPTISM to those who have accepted the message. Kerygma refers primarily to the preaching of the Apostles, as recorded in the NEW TESTAMENT, that JESUS CHRIST, in fulfillment of the prophecies of the OLD TESTAMENT, was sent by God, preached the coming of the KINGDOM OF GOD, died, was buried, rose from the dead, and was raised to the right hand of God in heaven. To those who accepted this proclamation, the reward was salvation, or deliverance from SIN. Acceptance into the church required a turning away from a life of sin. Early Christian catechesis was concerned primarily with exhorting those preparing for baptism to follow the way of "life" as opposed to that of "death"; it was distinguished from the more doctrinal instruction that followed one's baptism. Catechesis was usually accompanied by self-denial and EXORCISM (an attempt to expel the devil from the potential convert).

The mode of teaching, geared to the general absence of literacy, was characterized by the use of formalized expressions (some of which are preserved in the New Testament). The emphasis given to the use of the APOSTLES' CREED (including its antecedents) and the LORD'S PRAYER as mnemonic devices, as well as the frequent use of numbered lists, is indicative of the rote nature of the instruction during the early medieval period. In the East, the connection between the liturgy and practical instruction had never been lost; this was not the case in the West, where only a minority understood Latin, the language of liturgy and theology.

In the 16th century, both PROTESTANTS and ROMAN CATHOLICS began to make extensive use of written manuals called CATECHISMS. By the 19th century the term catechetics referred to all religious education outside of that found in the liturgy and preaching. In reaction to the abstract catechesis of recent centuries, some in the 20th century have called for a "kerygmatic theology" that would be concerned more with the saving work of Jesus Christ than with speculative theology and would treat the Christian message as an event to be experienced rather than ideas to be studied.

KETUBAH \kə-tü-ˈbä, kə-ˈtü-bə\, *also spelled* ketubba, in JUDAISM, a formal Jewish marriage contract written in Aramaic and guaranteeing a bride certain future rights before her marriage. Since Jewish religious law permits a man to divorce his wife at any time for any reason, the ketubah was introduced in ancient times to protect a woman's rights and to make divorce a costly matter for the husband. The conditions stipulated in the document also guarantee the woman's right to property when her husband dies.

In Orthodox and Conservative congregations, the ketubah is a prerequisite for marriage. It must be signed by two witnesses not related to the couple or to each other and, in some congregations, by the bridegroom also. A summary of the conditions is often added in the vernacular, and this is usually read together with the formal document just before or during the marriage ceremony. The formula used by Conservative Jews obliges the couple to appear before a rabbinic court to settle marital disputes, precluding the possibility of immediate divorce in a state of high emotion.

Ketubah, Jewish marriage contract, from Utica, N.Y., 1864; in the Library of the Jewish Theological Seminary, New York City
Erich Lessing—Art Resource

KETUBIM \kə-tü-'vēm\ (Hebrew), *English* Writings, *Greek* Hagiographa \,ha-gē-'ä-grə-fə, ,hā-, -jē-\, the third division of the Hebrew BIBLE, or OLD TESTAMENT. The writings of the Ketubim are notoriously difficult to date. Divided into four sections, they include (1) the *poetical books* of the Psalms (compiled in the early Second Temple period), Proverbs (also compiled after the BABYLONIAN EXILE), and Job (composed *c.* 6th century BCE); (2) the *Megillot*, or *Scrolls*, comprising the Song of Solomon (perhaps postexilic), Ruth (exilic or postexilic), Lamentations of Jeremiah (perhaps soon after 587 BCE), Ecclesiastes (*c.* 3rd century BCE), and Esther (*c.* early 2nd century BCE); (3) *prophecy*, comprising the book of Daniel (*c.* early 2nd century BCE); and (4) *history*, including Ezra, Nehemiah, and 1 and 2 Chronicles (all *c.* 5th or 4th century BCE, perhaps composed as a unit).

The Ketubim were composed over a period stretching from before the Babylonian Exile in the early 6th century BCE to the middle of the 2nd century BCE. Unlike the TORAH and the NEBI'IM (Prophets), which were canonized as groups, each book of the Ketubim was canonized separately, often on the basis of its popularity.

KHADĪJA \ka-'dē-jä\ (d. 619, Mecca, Arabia [now Saudi Arabia]), the first wife of the Prophet MUHAMMAD, whom she met when she was the widow of a wealthy merchant and had become prosperous in the management of her own commercial dealings.

Having hired Muhammad as a business agent, Khadīja soon came to see him as a suitable husband. She had been married twice before and had children from each marriage. According to most sources she was about 40 and Muhammad about 25 when they married. That she bore him at least six children (including FĀTIMA, the wife of 'ALĪ), however, may suggest that she was younger. She gave Muhammad support and encouragement when he received his first revelations, after which she became the first convert to ISLAM according to some accounts. She remained loyal to him when many prominent Meccans began to oppose him. While she lived, Muhammad took no other wives.

KHAJRĀHO \kûj-'rä-hō\, *ancient name* Kharjuravāhaka, historical town, northern Madhya Pradesh state, central India. It is a famous tourist and archaeological site known for its sculptured temples dedicated to SHIVA, VISHNU, and Jain patriarchs.

Khajrāho was one of the capitals of the kings of the Chandela, who from the 9th to the 11th century CE developed a large realm, Jejākabhukti (Jijhoti), which at its height included almost all of what is now Madhya Pradesh state. The original capital extended over 8 square miles and contained about 85 temples, built by successive rulers from about 950 to 1050. In the late 11th century the Chandela, in a period of chaos and decline, moved to hill forts elsewhere. Kahjrāho continued its religious importance until the 14th century but was afterward largely forgotten; its remoteness probably saved it from the desecration that the Mughal conquerors generally inflicted on Hindu monuments. In 1838 a British army captain, T.S. Burt, employed by the Asiatic Society in Calcutta, came upon information that led him to the rediscovery of the complex of temples in the jungle in Khajrāho.

Of the area's original temples, about 20 are still reasonably well preserved. With a few exceptions, they are constructed of hard river sandstone. Both internally and externally the temples are richly carved with excellent sculptures that are frequently sensual and, in a few instances, sexually explicit. The temples are divided into three complexes, of which the western is the largest and best known, containing the magnificent Śaivite temple Kaṇḍārya Mahādeva (*c.* 1000), a 102-foot-high agglomeration of porches and turrets culminating in a spire.

KHALISTAN \'kä-li-,stän, ,kä-li-'stän\ (Punjabi: Khālistān, "Land of the Khālsā," meaning "pure"), in Sikh political ideology, autonomous Sikh homeland.

The declaration of the KHĀLSĀ by Gurū GOBIND SINGH in 1699 and the religio-political vision that came with it fired the Sikh imagination with the belief that it was their God-given right to rule the Punjab. In 1710, under the leadership of BANDĀ SINGH BAHĀDUR (d. 1716), Sikh forces captured Sirhind, the most powerful Mughal administrative center between Delhi and Lahore, and established a capital in nearby Mukhlispur ("City of the Purified"). They struck coins, designed an official seal, and issued letters of command invoking the authority of God and of the Gurūs. The belief that "the Khālsā shall rule" (*rāj karegā Khālsā*) was formally added to Sikh liturgical prayer at the time, and it remains an indivisible part of it. Although the Khālsā Rāj under Bandā Singh was short-lived, the idea found its realization in the early 19th century in the form of the kingdom of Maharaja Ranjīt Singh (1780–1839). Though the subsequent rapid decline of the Khālsā Rāj and its final loss to the British (1849) was a painful experience, it failed to extinguish many Sikhs' hope that the Khālsā Raj would yet return in some form.

In the protracted negotiations that preceded the partition of the Punjab in 1947 the idea of an independent Sikh state figured prominently. The Sikh population's lack of numerical strength in relation to other residents of the Punjab made this an unviable proposition, but it has resurfaced in various forms since. In the 1970s and '80s a violent secessionist movement to create Khalistan paralyzed the Punjab for a decade. It received support from the All India Sikh Students' Federation and was led most effectively by SANT JARNAIL SINGH BHINDRANWALE. The movement failed for a complex set of reasons, but the idea of a state of the Khālsā continues to be invoked twice a day in GURDWĀRĀS (temples), as Sikhs mention in prayer their responsibility to rule.

KHĀLSĀ \'käl-sä, 'ka̱l-\, term chosen by Gurū GOBIND SINGH in 1699 to designate the Sikh community. His declaration had three dimensions: it redefined the concept of authority within the Sikh community; it introduced a new initiation ceremony and code of conduct; and it provided the community with a new religio-political vision.

The early Sikh community had been shaped by three levels of authority: the *masand*s ("Gurū's deputies") were responsible for local congregations, the GURŪ was the active central authority, and the revealed word as recorded in Sikh scriptural text served as the symbolic base. With the establishment of the Khālsā, the authority of the *masand*s was eliminated. They were expected either to become members of the community on a par with all others or to leave the fold.

The initiation ceremony that Gurū Gobind Singh introduced, called *khande kī pāhul* (literally, "ceremony of the double-edged sword"—more commonly called *amrit pahul*, "the nectar ceremony"), was centered on a belief in the transformative power of the revealed word. It was recited while water for initiation was stirred with a double-edged sword. Every Sikh who had undergone the ceremony became a member of the Khālsā and was assigned the name Singh ("Lion") and was expected to observe a rigorous code of conduct (*rahit*) symbolized by the wearing of five items: *kes* (long hair), *kaṅghā* (a comb), *kachha* (a pair of shorts), *karhā* (a steel bracelet), and *kirpān* (a sword). The names of all these items begin with the Punjabi letter k and thus came to be known as the five Ks. The Singhs were also expected to foreswear tobacco, alcohol, and certain types of meat. Ideally, all Khālsā Sikhs were expected to undergo this ceremony.

In its third aspect the Khālsā embodied a concrete political agenda: the pledge to realize the rule of the Sikh community (Khālsā Rāj) in the Punjab. These three interlocking dimensions have made the institution of the Khālsā perhaps the most powerful force in shaping Sikh identity during the past three centuries. Initially a male institution, it is now open to women as well, although Khālsā authority remains firmly in male hands.

KHARĀJ \ka̱-'rȧj\, a special Islamic fiscal imposition that was demanded from recent converts to ISLAM in the 7th and 8th centuries.

The origin of the concept of the *kharāj* is closely linked to changes in the status of non-Muslims and of recent converts to Islam in newly conquered Islamic territories. The indigenous Jewish, Christian, or Zoroastrian populations were permitted to convert to Islam, while those who pre-

ferred not to convert were required to pay a special tribute, usually in the form of a poll tax or head tax known as the JIZYA. Those who did choose to convert would, in theory, be placed on an equal fiscal footing with other Muslims.

Under Islamic law, only original Muslims or converts to Islam could own land. Thus, there was incentive for non-Muslim cultivators to convert to Islam so that they could maintain their agricultural holdings. Upon conversion, the cultivators were required to pay the *'ushr* (or TITHE), a tax equivalent to one-tenth of their produce. But the Umayyad CALIPHS (reigned 661–750), faced with increasing financial problems, imposed a kind of *kharāj* on the land of recent converts in addition to their payment of *'ushr*. This extra imposition of the *kharāj* was unpopular, and many converts felt that it violated the egalitarian principles of Islam.

In Khorāsān, the northeastern province of Iran, the collection of the *kharāj* was one of the grievances that led to Abū Muslim's revolt in 747, which precipitated the downfall of the Umayyad caliphate. During the early years of the succeeding 'Abbāsid caliphate, the collection of the *kharāj* fell into disuse.

KHĀRIJITES \'ka̱r-i-ˌjīts, 'kär-\, *Arabic* Khawārij ("Separatists"), the earliest Islamic sect, which traces its beginning to a religio-political controversy over the caliphate.

After the murder of the third CALIPH, 'UTHMĀN, and the succession of 'ALĪ (Muhammad's son-in-law) as the fourth caliph, Mu'āwiya, the governor of Syria, sought to avenge the murder of 'Uthmān. After fighting the indecisive Battle of Ṣiffīn (July 657) against Mu'āwiya's forces, 'Alī was forced to agree to arbitration. This concession aroused the anger of a large group of 'Alī's followers, who believed that arbitration would be a repudiation of the Qur'anic dictum "If one party rebels against the other, fight against that which rebels" (49:9). A small number of these pietists withdrew (*kharajū*) to the village of Ḥarūrā' under the leadership of Ibn Wahb and, when arbitration proved disastrous to 'Alī, were joined near Nahrawān by a larger group.

These Khārijites, as they came to be known, were opposed equally to 'Alī's claims and to those of Mu'āwiya. Repudiating not only the existing caliphal candidates but all Muslims who did not accept their views, the Khārijites engaged in campaigns of harassment and terror. In the Battle of Nahrawān (July 658) Ibn Wahb and most of his followers were killed by 'Alī, but the Khārijite movement persisted in a series of uprisings that plagued both 'Alī (whom they assassinated) and Mu'āwiya (who succeeded 'Alī as caliph). In the period of civil war (*fitna*) following the death of the caliph Yazīd I (683), the Khārijites were the source of serious disruptions within the Umayyad domain and in Arabia. Subdued through the intensive campaigning of al-Ḥajjāj, the Khārijites did not stir again until the collapse of the Umayyads, and then their two major rebellions, in Iraq and Arabia, ended in defeat.

The Khārijites held that the judgment of God could be expressed only through the free choice of the entire Muslim community. They insisted that anyone, even a slave, could be elected caliph if he possessed the necessary qualifications, chiefly religious piety and moral purity. A caliph might be deposed upon the commission of any major SIN. The Khārijites thus set themselves against the legitimist claims to the caliphate of the tribe of QURAYSH (among the SUNNIS) and of 'Alī's descendants (among the SHI'ITES). As proponents of the democratic principle, the Khārijites drew to themselves many who were dissatisfied with the existing political and religious authorities.

The Khārijites were also known for their puritanism and fanaticism. Any Muslim who committed a major sin was considered an apostate. Luxury, music, games, and concubinage without the consent of wives were forbidden. Intermarriage and relations with other Muslims were strongly discouraged. The doctrine of justification by faith without works was rejected, and literal interpretation of the QUR'AN was insisted upon.

Within the Khārijite movement the Azāriqa of Basra were the most extreme subsect, separating themselves from the Muslim community and declaring death to all sinners and their families. The more moderate subsect of the Ibāḍīya, however, survived into the 20th century in Oman, Zanzibar, and scattered communities in North Africa, with about 500,000 members.

KHEPRI \'ke-prē\, morning form of the Egyptian sun god. *See* ATUM.

KHIDR, AL- \ȧl-'ki-dǝr\ (Arabic, literally, "the Green," derived from the earlier epithet *al-Khaḍir*, "the Green One"), a mythical Islamic figure endowed with immortality who became a popular saint, especially among sailors and Sufis.

The cycle of myths and stories surrounding al-Khiḍr originated in a narrative in the QUR'AN (18:60–82) that describes the long and arduous journey of Mūsā (MOSES) and his servant to the "meeting of the two seas." In the course of their travels, they lose a fish they had taken with them; a man of God appears, offering to help them in their search for the fish but performs seemingly senseless deeds along the way—he sinks a boat, kills a young man, then restores a wall in a city hostile to them. Mūsā questions what the man has done and receives a satisfactory explanation for everything; but by questioning, Mūsā forfeits the man's patronage. Arab commentators elaborated and embellished the Qur'anic story and named the "man of God" Khiḍr, claiming that he turned green as he dived into the spring of life, though variant interpretations identify Khiḍr with the vegetable world.

On a popular level, Khiḍr has been given a name (most frequently Balyā ibn Malkān), many different genealogies, and dates that have made him a contemporary of ABRAHAM or Alexander. Khiḍr's immortality and ability to assume a variety of local characteristics probably account for his popularity among Arabs, Turks, Iranians, and other Muslims, despite orthodox Islamic opposition. In Syria, Khiḍr became partially identified with St. George, who, according to a local tradition, is of Syrian birth; in India and Pakistan, Khiḍr is identified with a water deity (Khwādja Khiḍr) who protects mariners and river travelers; and, among the Sufis (*see* SUFISM), he is associated with their founders, who were often endowed with holiness and sainthood.

KHIRQA \'kir-kǝ\ (Arabic: "rag"), woolen robe traditionally bestowed by Sufi masters (*see* SUFISM) on those who had newly joined the Sufi path, in recognition of their sincerity and devotion. While most sources agree that the *khirqa* was a patched piece of cloth, there is no uniform description of the color or shape. Some described it as a blue woolen robe, and, since blue is the color of mourning, it signified the rejection of worldly pleasure. Others described it as white indicating purity.

The *khirqa* was a sign of *faqr* (poverty) and symbolized the devotee's vow to abandon the earthly world and to devote himself entirely to the love of God. It took a period of good work under the supervision of the SHAYKH (Sufi mas-

ter) for a novice to obtain the *khirqa*, which was then bestowed upon him in a special ceremony to mark his "entering upon the way of Truth."

There were different types of *khirqa*. The *khirqat al-irāda* ("robe of will") was given to those who entered the Sufi path fully aware of the difficult duties that they must undertake and prepared to accept and obey without question the shaykh's orders. The inferior *khirqat at-tabarruk* ("robe of benediction") was given to those whom the shaykh felt had the potential of surviving the tests that eventually would lead to their acceptance in the Sufi brotherhood, even if they did not yet know the full meaning of wearing the *khirqa*.

Investiture of a cloak recalls stories of the mantle worn by MUHAMMAD during his ascent (MI'RĀJ) and preserves the memory of the derivation of the term Sufi from woolen garments (*sūf*) worn by early ascetics. The ceremony was especially elaborate in eastern Islamic lands, but many Sufis rejected the idea of a universal attire as unnecessary. All Sufis agree that a real seeker of truth is known by his *ḥarqa* (inner flame), and that the *khirqa* is merely a symbol that should not be overvalued.

KHNUM \'knüm\, *also spelled* Khnemu \'kne-mü\, ancient Egyptian god of fertility, associated with water and with procreation. Khnum was worshiped from the 1st dynasty (c. 2925–2775 BCE) into the early centuries CE. He was represented as a ram with horizontal, twisting horns or as a man with a ram's head. Khnum was believed to have created humankind from clay like a potter; this scene was de-

Khnum (left) with Sekhmet and a human, from the Tomb of Nefertari, Luxor, Thebes, Egypt
Borromeo—Art Resource

picted in later times. The god's first main cult center was Herwer, near Al-Ashmūnayn in Middle Egypt. From the New Kingdom (1539–1075 BCE) on, however, he became the god of the island of Elephantine, near present-day Aswān, and was known as the lord of the surrounding First Cataract of the Nile River. At Elephantine he formed a triad of deities with the goddesses Satis and Anukis. Khnum also had an important cult at Esna, south of Thebes.

KHOMEINI, RUHOLLAH MUSAVI \ˌkō-mä-'nē\, Khomeini *also spelled* Khumayni *or* Khomeyni, Ruhollah *also spelled* Ruhallah, Musavi *also spelled* Musawi (b. Sept. 24, 1902, Khumayn, Iran—d. June 3, 1989, Tehrān), Iranian SHIʿITE cleric who led the revolution that overthrew Mohammad Reza Shah Pahlavi in 1979 and became Iran's ultimate political and religious authority for the next 10 years.

Khomeini was the grandson and son of mullahs, or Shiʿite religious leaders. When he was five months old, his father was killed on the orders of a local landlord. The young Khomeini was raised by his mother and aunt and then by his older brother. He was educated in various Islamic schools, and he settled in the city of QOM about 1922. About 1930 he adopted the name of his hometown, Khomeyn (also spelled Khumayn), as his surname. As a Shiʿite scholar and teacher, Khomeini produced numerous writings on Islamic philosophy, law, and ethics, but it was his outspoken opposition to Iran's ruler, Mohammad Reza Shah Pahlavi, his denunciations of Western influences, and his uncompromising advocacy of Islamic purity that won him his initial following in Iran. In the 1950s he was acclaimed as an ayatollah, or major religious leader, and by the early 1960s he had received the title of grand ayatollah, thereby making him one of the supreme religious leaders of the Shiʿite community in Iran.

In 1962–63 Khomeini spoke out against the shah's reduction of religious estates in a land-reform program and against the emancipation of women. His ensuing arrest sparked antigovernment riots, and, after a year's imprisonment, he was forcibly exiled from Iran on Nov. 4, 1964. He eventually settled in the Shiʿite holy city of Al-Najaf, Iraq, where he taught and continued to call for the shah's overthrow and the establishment of an Islamic republic in Iran.

From the mid-1970s Khomeini's influence inside Iran grew dramatically owing to mounting public dissatisfaction with the shah's regime. Iraq's ruler, Saddam Hussein, forced Khomeini to leave Iraq on Oct. 6, 1978. Khomeini then settled in Neauphle-le-Château, a suburb of Paris. When massive demonstrations, strikes, and civil unrest in late 1978 forced the departure of the shah from the country on Jan. 16, 1979, Khomeini arrived in Tehrān in triumph on Feb. 1, 1979, and was acclaimed as the religious leader of Iran's revolution. He appointed a government four days later and on March 1 again took up residence in Qom. In December a referendum on a new constitution created an Islamic republic in Iran, with Khomeini named Iran's political and religious leader for life.

Khomeini proved unwavering in his determination to transform Iran into a theocratically ruled Islamic state. Iran's Shiʿite clerics largely took over the formulation of governmental policy, while Khomeini arbitrated between the various revolutionary factions and made final decisions on important matters requiring his personal authority. First his regime took political vengeance, with hundreds of people who had worked for the shah's regime reportedly executed. The remaining domestic opposition was then suppressed. Iranian women were required to wear the veil, Western music and alcohol were banned, and the punishments prescribed by Islamic law were reinstated.

The main thrust of Khomeini's foreign policy was the adoption of an attitude of unrelenting hostility toward both superpowers, while in the meantime Iran tried to export its brand of Islamic fundamentalism to neighboring Muslim countries. Khomeini sanctioned Iranian militants' seizure of the U.S. embassy in Tehrān (Nov. 4, 1979) and their holding of American diplomatic personnel as hostages for more than a year. He also refused to countenance a peaceful solution to the Iran-Iraq war, which had begun in 1980 and which he prolonged in the hope of overthrowing Iraq's ruler, Saddam Hussein. Khomeini finally approved a cease-fire in 1988 that effectively ended the war.

Iran's course of economic development foundered under Khomeini's rule, and his pursuit of victory in the Iran-Iraq War ultimately proved futile. But Khomeini was able to retain his charismatic hold over Iran's Shiʿite masses, and he remained the supreme political and religious arbiter in the country until his death. His gold-domed tomb in Tehrān's Behesht-i Zahrāʾ cemetery has since become a shrine for his supporters. Ideologically, he is best remembered for having developed the concept of *vilāyat-i faqīh* ("guardianship of the jurist") in a series of lectures and tracts first promulgated during exile in Iraq in the late 1960s and '70s. He argued therein for the establishment of a theocratic government administered by Islamic jurists in place of corrupt secular regimes. The Iranian Constitution of 1979 embodies articles upholding this concept of juristic authority.

KHORRAM-DĪNĀN \ḵȯr-ˌram-dē-'nän\ (Persian: "Glad Religionists"), *also called* Khorramīyeh \ḵȯr-ˌra-mē-'yeh\, esoteric Islamic sect whose leader Bābak led a rebellion in Azerbaijan that lasted from 816 until 837.

The doctrinal beliefs of the Khorram-dīnān are not altogether clear. Although the sect accepted the general principles of ISLAM, its members also believed in transmigration of the soul and placed special emphasis on the Zoroastrian DUALISM of light and darkness (*see* ZOROASTRIANISM). They differed from SUNNI Muslims in that they believed in the SHIʿITE doctrine of the imamate (the belief that the religious community should be led by the descendants of the union of FĀṬIMA, the daughter of the Prophet MUHAMMAD, and ʿALĪ, the Prophet's nephew).

The Khorram-dīnān differed from most Shiʿites, however, in believing that the imamate should be hereditary in the person of Abū Muslim (d. 755), who had led a revolutionary movement in Khorāsān. According to some sources, Bābak, spiritual leader of the Khorram-dīnān, claimed, in the early 9th century, to be a descendant of Abū Muslim. Other sources, emphasizing the belief in transmigration of souls current among the Khorram-dīnān, maintain that Bābak claimed to possess the soul of Jawizān ibn Sahl, a former leader of the Khorram-dīnān. In 816 Bābak, believing that he had a divinely inspired mission to right the wrongs of the temporal world, led the Khorram-dīnān in open rebellion against the ʿAbbāsid CALIPHS that ruled from Baghdad. The rebellion lasted 20 years and was suppressed only in 837, when Bābak was captured. Although the rebellion died out with Bābak's execution in 838, the Khorram-dīnān survived as a sect until the 11th century.

KHUMS \'ḵùms\, in ISLAM, tax paid to an IMAM; *see also* FIVE PILLARS OF ISLAM.

KHUTBA \'ḵùt-bə\, in ISLAM, the sermon, delivered especially at a Friday service, at the two major Islamic festivals (ʿĪDS), at celebrations of saintly birthdays (MAWLIDS), and on extraordinary occasions. It is customarily delivered from a podium (*minbar*) situated by the QIBLA wall of the mosque in imitation of MUHAMMAD.

The *khutba* probably derived, though without a religious context, from the pronouncements of the *khaṭīb*, a prominent tribal spokesman of pre-Islamic Arabia. The *khaṭīb* expressed himself in prose extolling the nobility and achievements of his tribesmen and denigrating the weakness of the tribe's enemies. Even Muhammad presented himself as a *khaṭīb* after taking MECCA in 630. The first four CALIPHS, the Umayyad caliphs, and the Umayyad provincial governors all delivered *khutba*s in their respective areas, though the content of the speeches was no longer strictly exhortatory but dealt with practical questions of government and on political problems. Under the 'Abbāsids, the caliphs themselves no longer preached but assigned the function of *khaṭīb* to the religious judges (*qadis*). The pointed insistence of the 'Abbāsids on clearing Islam of the SECULARISM of the Umayyads probably helped strengthen the religious aspect of the *khutba*. *Khutba*s never completely lost their political aspects, however. In the 19th and 20th centuries they were used to legitimate the policies of national governments in Muslim countries and to criticize or condemn those governments, as well.

KIDDUSH \'ki-dəsh, -,dush, ki-'düsh\, *also spelled* Qiddush (Hebrew: "sanctification"), in JUDAISM, BENEDICTION and prayer recited over a cup of wine immediately before the meal on the eve of the SABBATH or of a festival; the ceremony acknowledges the sanctity of the day that has just begun. Chanting, or recitation, usually performed by the head of the household, may involve several or all members of the family, depending on the custom; each then sips wine from the cup, which was held in the right hand during the benediction. In the ASHKENAZI (German) tradition, two covered loaves of bread (*halloth*) on the table symbolize the double portion of MANNA gathered before the Sabbath by Israelites during their years of wandering in the wilderness. If no wine is available, bread may also be used as a substitute.

KIERKEGAARD, SØREN AABYE \'kir-kə-,gärd, -,gòr\ (b. May 5, 1813, Copenhagen, Den.—d. Nov. 11, 1855, Copenhagen), Danish religious philosopher and critic of RATIONALISM, regarded as the founder of existentialist philosophy.

Kierkegaard's father was a wealthy man who, during a period of grinding poverty in his youth, had solemnly cursed God for his indif-

Kiddush cup, engraved silver by Johann Georg Stenglin or Johann Gottfried Schleissner, 1749–51; in the Jewish Museum, New York, gift of Dr. Harry G. Friedman
Art Resource

Kierkegaard, drawing by Christian Kierkegaard, c. 1840; in a private collection
By courtesy of the Royal Danish Ministry of Foreign Affairs

ference to human suffering. Kierkegaard came to know of his father's sin and remained haunted by the elder Kierkegaard's conviction that God's curse lay on the family, a conviction that the deaths of Kierkegaard's mother and five of his six brothers and sisters seemed to confirm.

He went to the University of Copenhagen to study theology but neglected this in favor of philosophy. After the death of his father in 1838, he resumed his theological studies and two years later took his master's degree. At the same time he had become engaged to Regine Olsen but ultimately broke off the relationship and fled to Berlin, where he lived for half a year. This romance had a profound effect on Kierkegaard and furnished him with material for reflection in several of his books.

He returned from Berlin with the manuscript for *Enten-Eller: et-livs fragment* (1843; *Either/Or: A Fragment of Life*). *Either/Or* offers the alternatives of an aesthetic or an ethical view of life. Kierkegaard's belief in the necessity of making a fully conscious, responsible choice among the alternatives that life offers has become fundamental in all existential writing and thought. The book can be seen as a communication to Olsen, intended to explain and justify his attitude to her.

Frygt og baeven (1843; *Fear and Trembling*) deals with faith and with the idea of sacrifice. The starting point of *Fear and Trembling* is the story of ABRAHAM and ISAAC. Once more Kierkegaard examines the implications of his break with Olsen, a sacrifice, like that of Abraham, performed in obedience to what he saw as a higher duty, and, like Abraham's readiness to slay his son, an act that contravenes the laws of ethics. The problem is whether situations can be imagined in which ethics can be suspended by a higher authority—*i.e.*, by God, when God himself must be considered the essence of everything ethical. This problem—which Kierkegaard calls "the teleological suspension of the ethical"—led him to the conclusion that faith is essentially paradoxical.

In 1844 *Philosophiske smuler* (*Philosophical Fragments*) and *Begrebet angest* (*The Concept of Dread*) appeared. The former presents CHRISTIANITY as a form of existence that presupposes FREE WILL, without which everything becomes meaningless. With *The Concept of Dread*, Kierkegaard perceived that the discussion of freedom does not belong to the sphere of logic but to that of psychology, which cannot discuss freedom itself but can describe the state of mind that makes freedom possible. This state of mind is dread. Through experiencing dread, one leaps from innocence to sin, and, if the challenge of Christianity is accepted, from guilt to faith. Dread is thus sin's prelude, not its sequel.

In 1845 Kierkegaard brought out *Stadier paa livets vei* (*Stages on Life's Way*), which distinguishes the religious stage, or sphere, not merely from the aesthetic but also from the ethical. His next book, *Concluding Unscientific Postscript to the Philosophical Fragments. A Mimic-Pathetic-Dialectic Composition, an Existential Contribution* (1846) attacked Hegel's attempt to systematize the whole of existence, declaring that a system of existence cannot be constructed, since existence is incomplete and constantly developing.

Meanwhile, Kierkegaard had come to believe that God had appointed him to reveal the true nature of Christianity and to expose the ESTABLISHED CHURCH of Denmark, the clergy of which, in Kierkegaard's opinion, had become too comfortable in secular society. In the works that he now produced, particularly *Kjerlighedens gjerninger* (1847; *Works of Love*), *Christelige taler* (1848; *Christian Discourses*), *Sygdommen til døden* (1849; *The Sickness unto Death*), and *Indøvelse i Christendom* (1850; *Training in Christianity*), he depicted a Christianity sterner and more uncompromising than in any of his other writings.

It was not until several decades after Kierkegaard's death that the philosophical and artistic value of his work began to be fully appreciated, and it was not until the years between the two world wars that knowledge of Kierkegaard's work became widespread. The theology of the Swiss Protestant theologian KARL BARTH helped to escalate existentialist thinking, as did the philosophical thought of Karl Jaspers and Martin Heidegger and the Jewish religious thinker MARTIN BUBER. The crucial understanding of Kierkegaard's writing came in the post-World War II years, which seem to have created a more penetrating realization of such states as angst and suffering.

KIJA \\'kē-ˌjä\\, legendary Korean king of Chinese origin whose arrival in Korea with 5,000 rice- and barley-bearing refugees reputedly introduced Chinese civilization (and these new grains) to the Korean people. The band allegedly had fled China in 1111 BCE, refusing to serve the new Chou-dynasty ruler who had overthrown Kija's Shang-dynasty relatives. Many traditions credit Kija with certain cultural innovations, such as introducing the art of writing and instituting a code of law that punished murderers with a death like that which they inflicted on their victims. Other legends associate Kija's name with SORCERY and the fashioning of Korea's flat-topped, wide-brimmed national hat (*kat*).

KILESA \\ki-'lä-sə\\ (Pali), *Sanskrit* kleśa \\'klā-shə\\ ("affliction"), *also called* āsava \\'ä-sə-və\\ (Pāli), *Sanskrit* āsrava \\'äs-rə-və, 'äsh-\\ ("what flows out"), in the teaching of BUDDHISM, moral defilements that find individuals within the unsatisfying realm of continuing birth, death, and rebirth. In one formulation the eradication of *kilesa*, which are understood as the source of evil, is one of the four activities that are deemed essential to the attainment of release.

KIMBANGUIST CHURCH \\kim-'bäŋ-gü-ist\\, *French in full* Église de Jésus-Christ sur la terre par le prophète Simon Kimbangu ("Church of Jesus Christ on Earth Through the Prophet Simon Kimbangu"), largest independent African church and the first to be admitted (in 1969) to the WORLD COUNCIL OF CHURCHES. It takes its name from its founder, Simon Kimbangu (1889?–1951), a BAPTIST mission catechist of the Lower Congo region, who in April 1921 inaugurated a mass movement by miraculous healings and biblical teaching. In October 1921 he was charged with insurrection by Belgian colonial authorities and imprisoned for life.

The movement continued clandestinely as Ngunzism (Prophetism), and mass deportations during government persecutions only helped to spread it. Toleration was granted in 1957, and the church was formally established and legally recognized in 1959. This church spread widely in

Central Africa and developed a hierarchical organization under Kimbangu's three sons, with Nkamba, the prophet's birth and final burial place, called the New Jerusalem.

The church eschews politics and embraces a puritan ethic, rejecting violence, polygamy, magic and WITCHCRAFT, alcohol, tobacco, and dancing. Its worship is Baptist in form, though the institution of communion was not introduced until 1971. Extensive social services in agriculture, healing, education, youth work, and cooperatives make it a modernizing agency for a membership variously estimated at from 1,000,000 to 3,000,000. Many other smaller, more loosely organized groups in Central Africa also regard Kimbangu as God's special prophet.

KIM SISŬP \\'kēm-'shē-'sǝp\\, Korean author during the early Choson period (1392–1598). His five stories contained in the *Kŭmo sinwha* ("New Stories from Golden Turtle Mountain") are written in Chinese in the tradition of the *ch'uan-ch'i*. The subject material of these stories include love affairs between mortals and ghosts and dream journeys to the Underworld or to the Dragon Palace. He promoted the unity of CONFUCIANISM, TAOISM, and BUDDHISM but is especially remembered for his NEO-CONFUCIAN views.

KINDĪ, YA'QŪB IBN ISḤĀQ AL-ṢABĀḤ, AL- \\ˌàl-'kin-dē\\ (d. *c*. 870), the first outstanding Islamic philosopher, known as "the philosopher of the Arabs."

Al-Kindī was born of noble Arabic descent and flourished in Iraq under the CALIPHS al-Ma'mūn (813–833) and al-Mu'taṣim (833–842). He concerned himself not only with those philosophical questions that had been treated by the Aristotelian Neoplatonists of Alexandria but also with such subjects as ASTROLOGY, medicine, Indian arithmetic, logographs (word puzzles), the manufacture of swords, and cooking. He is known to have written more than 270 works (mostly short treatises), a considerable number of which are extant, some in Latin translations.

KINGDOM OF GOD, *also called* Kingdom of Heaven, in CHRISTIANITY, the spiritual realm over which God reigns as king, or the fulfillment on earth of God's will. The phrase occurs frequently in the NEW TESTAMENT, primarily used by JESUS CHRIST in the first three GOSPELS, and is referenced in the Lord's Prayer in the phrase, "Thy Kingdom come."

Though the phrase itself rarely occurs in pre-Christian Jewish literature, the idea of God as king was fundamental to JUDAISM, and Jewish ideas on the subject undoubtedly underlie, and to some extent determine, the New Testament usage. Behind the Greek word for kingdom (*basileia*) lies the Aramaic term *malkut*, which Jesus may have used. *Malkut* refers primarily not to a geographical area or realm nor to the people inhabiting the realm but, rather, to the activity of the king himself, his exercise of sovereign power. The idea might better be conveyed in English by an expression such as kingship, rule, reign, or sovereignty.

To most Jews of Jesus' time the world seemed so completely alienated from God that nothing would deal with the situation short of direct divine intervention on a cosmic scale. The details were variously conceived, but it was widely expected that God would send a supernatural, or supernaturally endowed, intermediary (the MESSIAH or Son of Man), whose functions would include a judgment to decide who was worthy to "inherit the Kingdom," an expression which emphasizes that the Kingdom was thought of as a divine gift, not a human achievement.

According to the first three Gospels, most of Jesus' miraculous actions are to be understood as prophetic symbols of the coming of the Kingdom, and his teaching was concerned with the right response to the crisis of its coming. The nationalistic tone of much of the Jewish expectation is absent from his teaching.

Scholarly opinion is divided on the question as to whether Jesus taught that the Kingdom had actually arrived during his lifetime. Possibly, he recognized in his ministry the signs of its imminence, but he nevertheless looked to the future for its arrival "with power." He may well have regarded his own death as the providential condition of its full establishment. Nevertheless, he seems to have expected the final consummation in a relatively short time (Mark 9:1). Thus, Christians were perplexed when the end of the world did not occur within a generation, as Paul, for example, expected. Christian experience soon suggested, however, that, as the result of Christ's RESURRECTION, many of the blessings traditionally reserved until the life of the age to come were already accessible to the believer in this age. Thus, though the phrase Kingdom of God was used with decreasing frequency, that for which it stood was thought of as partly realized here and now in the life of the church, which at various periods has been virtually identified with the Kingdom; the Kingdom of God, however, would be fully realized only after the end of the world and the accompanying LAST JUDGMENT.

The first king of Rome, Romulus, with his twin Remus and their wolf foster-mother, bronze sculpture; in the Museo Nuovo in the Palazzo dei Conservatori, Rome
Alinari—Art Resource

KING JAMES VERSION, *also called* Authorized Version, English translation of the BIBLE published in 1611 under the auspices of James I of England. Forty-seven scholars labored in six groups at three locations for seven years, utilizing previous English translations and texts in the original languages. The resulting translation had a marked influence on English style and was generally accepted as the standard English Bible for more than three centuries.

KINGS OF ROME, in ancient Roman tradition, series of kings who preceded the Republic. While some of these figures were historical, others are to be identified as characters within ancient Roman mythology.

Romulus, Rome's first king according to tradition, was the invention of later ancient historians. His name, which is not even proper Latin, was designed to explain the origin of Rome's name. His fictitious reign was filled with the sort of deeds expected of an ancient city founder and the son of a war god: He established Rome's early political, military, and social institutions and waged war against neighboring states. Romulus was also thought to have shared his royal power for a time with a Sabine named Titus Tatius. The name may be that of an authentic ruler of early Rome, perhaps Rome's first real king; nothing, however, was known about him in later centuries, and his reign was therefore lumped together with that of Romulus.

The names of the other six kings are authentic, but few reliable details are known about their reigns. However, since the later Romans wished to have explanations for their early customs and institutions, historians ascribed various innovations to these kings, often in stereotypical and erroneous ways. The three kings after Romulus are still hardly more than names, but the deeds that were ascribed to the last three kings can, to some extent, be checked by evidence from archaeology. Romulus was succeeded by the Sabine Numa Pompilius, whose reign was characterized by complete tranquility and peace. Numa was supposed to have created virtually all of Rome's religious institutions and practices. The tradition of his religiosity probably derives from the erroneous connection by the ancients of his name with the Latin word *numen,* meaning "divine power." Numa was succeeded by Tullus Hostilius, whose reign was filled with warlike exploits, probably because the name Hostilius was later interpreted to suggest hostility and belligerence. Tullus was followed by Ancus Marcius, who was believed to have been the grandson of Numa. His reign combined the characteristics of those of his two predecessors—religious innovations as well as warfare.

The last three kings were Lucius Tarquinius Priscus (Tarquin the Elder), Servius Tullius, and Lucius Tarquinius Superbus (Tarquin the Proud). According to tradition, the two Tarquins were father and son and came from Etruria. One tradition made Servius Tullius a Latin; another described him as an Etruscan named Mastarna. All three were supposed to have been great city planners and organizers (and this is a tradition that in fact has been confirmed by archaeology). Their Etruscan origin is rendered plausible by Rome's proximity to Etruria, by Rome's growing geographic significance, and by the public works that were carried out by the kings themselves and that were characteristic of contemporary Etruscan cities. It would thus appear that during the 6th century BCE some Etruscan adventurers took over the site of Rome and transformed it into a city along Etruscan lines.

KINGU \'kiŋ-ˌgü\, in Babylonian mythology, the consort of TIAMAT. The creation epic *Enuma elish* tells how Tiamat, determined to destroy the other gods, created a mighty army and set Kingu at its head. When Kingu saw MARDUK coming against him, however, he fled. After Tiamat's defeat, Kingu was taken captive and executed; the god Enki (EA) created humans from his blood.

KINSHIP, socially recognized relationship between people in a culture who are given the status of relatives by marriage, adoption, or other ritual.

Kinship is the broad-ranging term for all the relationships that people are born into or create later in life and that are considered binding in the eyes of their society. Although customs vary as to which bonds are accorded greater weight, their very acknowledgment defines individuals and the roles that society expects them to play.

All cultures recognize the structure of the nuclear family unit as a set of relations: brother/sister, husband/wife, father/son, maternal uncle/nephew, and so on. New families are formed or established families are augmented depending upon whether the newly married couple sets up a new household or remains with close kin of the bride or groom. Different arrangements along these lines form different kinds of families. A "stem" family is one in which only one child stays at home after marriage to care for the elderly parents and to work the land. This type was especially common in Japan, where farms were too small to be divided among numerous offspring. An extended family is formed when married sons and daughters remain at home or when others are brought into the family unit and made kin through adoption. A married couple may also adopt children, who then assume the societal position of their adoptive parents. Although the nuclear family unit is no doubt the oldest form of societal organization, a domestic family can be any group of kinsmen and spouses who share food and usually a common roof.

Patrifiliation identifies an individual with the father's side of the family, and matrifiliation is identification with one's mother. The terms connoting descent—patrilineal and matrilineal—derive from the same concept, with either the father or the mother acting as the primary ancestor. In a cognatic society, people acknowledge an equal responsibility to both sides of the family. All the persons connected to an individual through parent–child progressions are considered lineal ancestors (*e.g.*, grandparents and great-grandparents). Those linked less directly (*e.g.*, a parent's sibling or a sibling's child) are consanguineal kin. Cousins, aunts, uncles, nieces, and nephews fall into this category.

The nature of kinship is not limited to blood ties; some notable omissions are fictive, or ritual, kin relationships, which include ritual coparenthood (the Christian tradition of GODPARENTS); blood brotherhood, which is a forged bond of mutual trust and cooperation; and a Japanese custom known as *oyako-kankei*, or *oyabun-kobun*, which sets up an interdependency between those in need of economic aid and wealthy patrons. While motherhood can never be disputed, certain societies recognize three kinds of fatherhood: the genetic father; the "pater" (usually the mother's husband who may also be the genetic father) who gives the child its position in society; and the "genitor," who is a person believed to have contributed to the growth of the fetus in the womb.

The common thread that links all these relationships together under the umbrella term of "kinship" is societal recognition, so they are all subject in some degree to societal scrutiny, expectations, and control—particularly in sexual relationships.

Marriage creates many kinship bonds. Some marriages are arranged, others are entered into after a culturally shaped courtship. Monogamy, an exclusive sexual relationship between a man and a woman, is practiced in most areas. Polygyny, in which one man is married to several women at once, is practiced in some areas. Polyandry, seldom practiced, is the marriage of one woman and several men. The nearest approach to a universal rule found in all cultures is the incest prohibition, which forbids sexual intercourse between a parent and child, between siblings, or between other specified kin. So, although most cultures require that immediate kin approve a proposed marriage, men and women must look outside the immediate family for a spouse.

KĪRTAN \\'kir-tən\\, *also spelled* kīrtana \\'kir-tə-nə\\, form of musical worship or group devotion practiced by the sects of VAIṢṆAVISM (devotion to the god VISHNU) of Bengal. *Kīrtan* usually consists of a verse sung by a soloist and then repeated by a chorus, to the accompaniment of percussion instruments. Sometimes the singing gives way to the recitation of a religious poem, the repetition of God's name (*nām-kīrtan*), or dancing. Frequently *kīrtan* songs describe the love of the divine cowherder KRISHNA and his favorite, RĀDHĀ. An evening of *kīrtan* may last for several hours, often bringing about in the participants a state of religious exaltation. *Kīrtan* as a form of worship was popularized by the 15th–16th-century Bengal mystic CAITANYA, who continually strove for more direct emotional experience of God. More generally, the word *kīrtan* may also designate devotional singing and chanting across North India.

KITTEL \\'ki-təl\\, *plural* kittel, in JUDAISM, a burial shroud; also, a white robe worn in the SYNAGOGUE on such major festivals as ROSH HASHANAH and YOM KIPPUR. The RABBI wears it, as does the CANTOR, the blower of the SHOFAR, and male members of ASHKENAZI congregations. Before a SEDER dinner, the leader of the PASSOVER (Pesaḥ) service dons a kittel, and in Orthodox communities the bridegroom wears it at his wedding.

KIVA \\'kē-və\\ (Hopi *kíva*), semisubterranean ceremonial and social chamber found in the Pueblo American Indian villages of the southwestern United States, often containing colorful mural paintings decorating the walls.

A small hole in the floor of the kiva (sometimes carved through a plank of wood), called the *sípapu*, served as the symbolic place of origin of the tribe. Although its most important purpose is for ritual ceremonies, for which altars are erected, the kiva is also used for political meetings or casual gatherings. Women are almost always excluded.

The traditional round slope of the earliest kiva recalls the circular pit houses of the prehistoric basket-weaving culture from which these tribes, primarily Hopi and Zuni, are descended.

The kiva murals depict sacred figures or scenes from daily life. The style of these paintings tends to be geometric, with an emphasis on straight rather than curved lines and with the entire mural laid out in a linear pattern around the walls. The murals are painted on adobe plaster with warm, colorful pigments made from the rich mineral deposits of the area. Frequently the Indians plastered over an old mural to paint a new one on top; in recent years the several layers of a number of kiva murals have been unpeeled and restored. (See NATIVE AMERICAN RELIGIONS.)

KNOX, JOHN \\'näks\\ (b. *c.* 1514, near Haddington, Lothian, Scot.—d. Nov. 24, 1572, Edinburgh), foremost leader of the Scottish REFORMATION, who set the austere moral tone of the Church of Scotland and shaped the democratic form of government it adopted.

Almost nothing is known of Knox's life before 1540. It is

supposed that he trained for the PRIESTHOOD at the University of St. Andrews. He was in priest's orders by 1540 and was in 1543 known to be also practicing as an apostolic notary. Two years later Knox came into association with George Wishart, a Scottish Reformation leader, who converted him to the Reformed faith. Wishart was burned for HERESY in March 1546 by Cardinal David Beaton, archbishop of St. Andrews. Three months later, Beaton was murdered by Protestant conspirators who fortified themselves in St. Andrews castle. In April 1547, Knox went to St. Andrews, where he took up preaching for the first time. At the end of June 1547, the garrison of St. Andrews castle capitulated, and Knox and others were carried off to slavery. English intervention secured his release 19 months later, though with permanently broken health.

In England the Protestant government of Edward VI made Knox a licensed preacher and sent him north to propagate the Reformation in the turbulent garrison town of Berwick-upon-Tweed. He established a congregation there on Puritan lines. Early in 1551 he was given a new assignment in Newcastle and a little later was appointed to be one of the six royal CHAPLAINS whose duties included periodic residence at, and preaching before, the court.

In three respects Knox left his mark on the Church of England: he took part in the shaping of its articles; he secured the insertion into THE BOOK OF COMMON PRAYER of the so-called black rubric, which denies the corporal presence of

On the accession of Mary Tudor, a Roman Catholic, to the throne in 1553, Knox was one of the last of the Protestant leaders to flee the country. That the personal whim of a sovereign was permitted to settle the religion of a nation drove him to the conclusion that God-fearing magistrates and nobility have both the right and the duty to resist, if necessary by force, a ruler who threatens the safety of true religion. In 1554 Knox became minister of a congregation of English refugees, mainly Puritan, in Frankfurt am Main; but he remained there for only a few months. He then became minister of the growing congregation of English exiles in Geneva.

In Scotland matters reached a crisis in the spring of 1559 when the Queen Regent, the French-born Mary of Guise, summoned the Protestant preachers to appear before her. The Protestants replied by recalling Knox from Geneva and taking a defiant stance. By the end of June, Edinburgh was temporarily in Protestant hands, but the triumph was illusory and Knox knew it. At this juncture Henry II of France died and power fell into the hands of the Guises, the brothers of the Queen Regent. A French victory in Scotland would place Elizabeth and England in peril. It therefore behooved England to make common cause with the Scottish Protestants. In April of 1560, 10,000 English troops joined the Scottish Protestants, the Queen Regent died in Edinburgh castle, and the disheartened French gave up. By treaty, French and English troops were then withdrawn, leaving the victorious Scottish Protestants to set their own house in order. The Scots confession (prepared by Knox and three others) was adopted by the Scottish Parliament and papal jurisdiction was abolished.

Knox, aided by a committee of distinguished churchmen, composed the *First Book of Discipline* containing proposals for the constitution and finance of the REFORMED CHURCH. Worship was to be regulated by the *Book of Common Order* (also called Knox's Liturgy), according to which congregations were to be governed by elders elected annually by the people and the elders were to aid the minister to maintain firm moral discipline among the people. Ministers were to be elected by the people but to be ap-

Ruins of a Pueblo kiva, at Aztec Ruins National Monument, New Mexico
Bob Harper

Christ in the consecrated bread and wine used in Holy Communion and explains that kneeling at communion implies no adoration of the elements; and he was one of the chief foster fathers of English PURITANISM.

pointed only after rigorous examination of life and doctrine by their ministerial brethren. In the high place given to the laity, Knox's system contains the most essential element of later Presbyterianism.

Mary, Queen of Scots arrived in Scotland in 1561 and soon joined battle with Knox, who opposed her proposed marriage with Don Carlos of Spain. Mary, enraged at this intervention in affairs of state, charged Knox with treason, but the Privy Council refused to convict him. Knox further angered Mary in 1564 by marrying, without the royal assent, a distant relative of the Queen. In 1567 came Mary's ruin and abdication, and the country was plunged into a struggle between the supporters of the Queen and those of the regency. Knox was involved in the turmoil, but he suffered a paralytic stroke. When Edinburgh became a battleground between the factions in 1571, the leaders on both sides insisted on his removal to safety in St. Andrews, from where he returned in 1572 to die.

KOAN \\'kō-ˌän\\, *Japanese* kōan, in the ZEN (Chinese: Ch'an) BUDDHISM of East Asia, a succinct paradoxical statement or question used as a meditation discipline, particularly in the Japanese RINZAI sect. The effort to "solve" a koan is intended to exhaust the analytic intellect and the egoistic will, readying the mind to entertain an appropriate response on the intuitive level.

A characteristic example of the style is the well-known koan "When both hands are clapped a sound is produced; listen to the sound of one hand clapping." Sometimes the koan is set in question and answer form, as in the question "What is Buddha?" and its answer, "Three pounds of flax."

Koans—the word itself is borrowed from the Middle Chinese words ancestral to Modern Standard Chinese *kung-an*, "public notice," or "public announcement"—are based on anecdotes of Zen masters. There are said to be 1,700 koans in all. The two major collections are the *Pi-yen lu* (Chinese: "Blue Cliff Records"; Japanese: *Hekigan-roku*) and the *Wu-men kuan* (Japanese: *Mumon-kan*). *Compare* ZAZEN.

KOBDAS \\'gō-aù-ˌdēs\\, *also spelled* goavddis, in FINNO-UGRIC RELIGION, drum used for trance induction and DIVINATION by the Sami SHAMAN, or NOAIDE. The drum consisted of a wooden frame, ring, or bowl over which a membrane of reindeer hide was stretched. The hide was usually covered with figures of deities, tutelary spirits of the *noaide*, and otherworld localities, painted with the juice of alder bark. Metal trinkets, pieces of bone, teeth, or claws might be strung on the underside of the drum or around its outer edges. When used for divination, the *kobdas* was beaten with a hammer made of reindeer antler, which caused a triangular piece of bone or metal called an *arpa* to move along the surface of the drum. The *arpa* might be in the shape of a brass ring or even a frog, which represented the tutelary spirit of the *noaide* that went out to discover the things he wanted to know. From the movements of the *arpa*, the *noaide* divined the nature of illness and the location of lost or stolen objects. The use of the drum was limited to the Samis, Mansi (Voguls), and Khanty (Ostyaks) among the Finno-Ugric peoples, but similar divinatory practices with the aid of a sieve were known among the Finns and other Balto-Finnic groups.

KOGAKU \\'kò-gä-kù\\ (Japanese: "Study of Ancient Things"), one of three schools of NEO-CONFUCIAN studies that began in Japan in the Tokugawa period (1603–1867).

KOHEN \\kō-'hān, -'hen\\, *also spelled* cohen \\'kō-ən\\ (Hebrew: "priest"), *plural* kohanim \\ˌkō-hä-'nēm\\, in JUDAISM, a priest, one who is a descendant of Zadok, founder of the PRIESTHOOD when the First TEMPLE OF JERUSALEM was built by

SOLOMON (10th century BCE) and through Zadok related to AARON, the first Jewish priest, who was appointed to that office by his younger brother, MOSES. Though laymen such as GIDEON, DAVID, and Solomon offered sacrifice as God commanded, the Hebrew priesthood was hereditary in biblical times and was transmitted exclusively to male descendants of Aaron of the tribe of Levi.

In biblical times the Hebrew HIGH PRIEST (*kohen gadol*) headed a priestly hierarchy in Jerusalem. He had many privileges but was also bound by numerous restrictions. Until the time of King JOSIAH (7th century BCE), the high priest was anointed with oil before assuming office, and he alone could enter the HOLY OF HOLIES once a year to offer sacrifice on YOM KIPPUR.

Of lesser rank were his deputy and the military chaplain, who accompanied troops into battle. Other priests had charge of Temple finances or assumed administrative functions connected with the Temple, such as assigning duties to the lowest rank of priests (the kohanim), who, divided into 24 groups, took turns serving in the Temple. The Jewish priesthood reached its apogee during the period of the Second Temple.

During the post-Temple era, all priestly functions were necessarily curtailed, and priests lost most of their prerogatives. In the Diaspora, RABBIS replaced the kohanim as teachers and authorities on the Law, but the priesthood still belonged by right of blood to kohanim, who trace their lineage back to Aaron. Kohanim are granted first preference in the SYNAGOGUE in the reading of the TORAH and pronounce the priestly blessing over the congregation on festivals. They also officiate at the ritual whereby a father (only a father who is not a kohen, however) "redeems" his firstborn son from service to the Temple with an offering of five silver coins (usually returned as a gift to the child). A kohen must also preserve his ritual purity by avoiding contact with the dead and hence may not attend funerals, except those of close relatives. There are also certain restrictions regarding marriage. Rules and privileges pertaining to kohanim are disregarded by REFORM JUDAISM.

KOHLER, KAUFMANN \\'kō-lər\\ (b. May 10, 1843, Fürth, Bavaria [Germany]—d. Jan. 28, 1926, New York, N.Y., U.S.), German-American RABBI, one of the most influential theologians of REFORM JUDAISM in the United States.

Although his upbringing and early schooling were Orthodox, Kohler was strongly affected by the teachings of ABRAHAM GEIGER, one of the most prominent German leaders of Reform. Kohler's quest for the reconciliation of traditional faith with modern knowledge excluded him from the Jewish pulpit in Germany. He immigrated to the United States and was welcomed by the eminent Reform rabbi David Einhorn, whose daughter he married. He then became rabbi of Reform congregations in Detroit (1869–71), Chicago (1871–79), and, finally, New York City (1879–1903).

In 1885 Kohler convened the Pittsburgh rabbinical conference, which adopted a platform drafted by him that remains the classic expression of Reform principles and is a landmark in the history of American Judaism (*see* PITTSBURGH PLATFORM). From 1901 to 1906 Kohler served as an editor of the *Jewish Encyclopedia*, to which he contributed some 300 articles. In 1903 he became president of the Hebrew Union College (now Hebrew Union College–Jewish Institute of Religion) in Cincinnati, Ohio, a position he retained until 1921.

Kohler's primary work is *Jewish Theology Systematically and Historically Considered* (1918), which succinctly sets forth the teachings of Jewish theology; although Reform principles are promulgated, Orthodox and Conservative concepts are also sympathetically treated. The posthumous *Origins of the Synagogue and the Church* (1929) concerns the relationship of the Jews and early Christians and speculates that JESUS and JOHN THE BAPTIST were ESSENES.

KO HUNG \'gə-'hùŋ, 'gō-\, Pinyin Ge Hong, *also called* (Wade-Giles romanization) Pao-p'u-tzu \'baù-'pü-'dzə̀\ (b. 283? CE, Tan-yang, China—d. 343 CE, Tan-yang), prominent Taoist alchemist of China, who tried to combine the ethics of CONFUCIANISM with the occult doctrines of TAOISM.

He received a Confucian education but later grew interested in the Taoist cult of physical immortality (HSIEN). His monumental work, *Pao-p'u-tzu* ("He Who Holds to Simplicity"), is divided into two parts. The first part, "The 20 Inner Chapters," discusses alchemy and recommends sexual hygiene, special diets, and breathing and meditation exercises. The second part of the book, "The 50 Outer Chapters," shows Ko as a Confucianist who stresses the importance of ethical principles for the regulation of proper human relations and who severely criticizes the hedonism that characterized the Taoist individualists of his day.

KOJIKI \kò-'jē-kē\ (Japanese: "Records of Ancient Matters"), together with the NIHON SHOKI, the first written record in Japan, part of which is considered a sacred text of SHINTŌ. The *Kojiki* text was compiled from ORAL TRADITION in 712, and for lack of a native Japanese alphabet was written using Chinese characters to represent Japanese sounds.

The *Kojiki* includes myths, legends, and historical accounts of the imperial court from the earliest days of its creation up to the reign of Empress Suiko (628). Much of Shintō thought is based on interpretations of its mythology accounts. The religious and ethical values of the *Kojiki* were rediscovered and reevaluated by Moto-ori Norinaga (1730–1801), who wrote the complete "Annotation of the *Kojiki*" in 49 volumes.

KOKUGAKU \'kò-kù-,gä-kù\ (Japanese: "Study of National [*i.e.*, Japanese] Things"), a movement in late 17th- and 18th-century Japan that emphasized Japanese classical studies. The movement initially received impetus from the NEO-CONFUCIANISTS, but soon attempted a purge of all foreign influences, including BUDDHISM and CONFUCIANISM. The Kokugaku movement culminated in the Fukko (Restoration) school of SHINTŌ under the leadership of such men as Kamo Mabuchi, MOTOORI NORINAGA, and HIRATA ATSUTANE. The Shintō revival, Kokugaku movement, and royalist sentiments all combined in the Meiji period (1868–1912) in the restoration of imperial rule and the establishment of Shintō as a state cult.

KOKUTAI \,kòk-'tī, *Angl* 'kō-kü-,tī\ (Japanese: "national essence"), expression first used in the 18th century by MOTOORI NORINAGA to refer to the social and cultural values embodied in the SHINTŌ mythology of the KOJIKI. This ideal was appropriated in the first part of the 20th century to emphasize the religious and political unity of Japan as linked with STATE SHINTŌ and the imperial cult.

KOL NIDRE \'kòl-'ni-,drā, 'kōl-, -ni-'drā, -'ni-drə\ (Aramaic: "All Vows"), a prayer sung in Jewish SYNAGOGUES at the beginning of the service on the eve of YOM KIPPUR. The name, derived from the opening words, also designates the melody to which the prayer is traditionally chanted. Though equally ancient versions exist in Hebrew and Aramaic, the Aramaic is generally used in the predominant ASHKENAZIC and SEPHARDIC rites. The prayer begins with an expression of repentance for all unfulfilled vows, OATHS, and promises made to God during the year. Some Jewish authorities contend that even fulfilled vows are included since the act of vowing itself is considered sinful. The prayer was used as early as the 8th century.

The melody to which the Kol Nidre is sung in the Ashkenazic (German) rite became famous when the Protestant composer Max Bruch used it (1880) as the basis for variations for cello. The melody's origin is unknown; the earliest known mention of a specific—rather than an improvised—melody dates from the 16th century. The Sephardic (Spanish), Italian, and Oriental Jewish traditions use their own distinct melodies unrelated to the Ashkenazic melody.

KONJAKU MONOGATARI \'kòn-jä-kù-,mò-nò-'gä-tä-rē\ (Japanese: "Tales of Now and Then"), massive 12th-century collection of religious stories and folktales drawn from the Japanese countryside and from Indian and Chinese sources. These stories provide glimpses of how the common people spoke and behaved in an age marked by warfare and new religious movements.

KONKŌ-KYŌ \kòn-'kō-,kyō\, Japanese religious movement founded in the 19th century, a prototype of the new religious movements that proliferated in post-World War II Japan. The movement was founded in 1859 by Kawate Bunjirō, a farmer who lived in present-day Okayama Prefecture. He believed that he was appointed by the deity Konkō ("Bright Metal"; new name for the formerly malevolent deity Konjin) to act as a mediator (*toritsugi*) between god and mankind. The mediator takes on the pain and sufferings of his followers and transmits them to god. Succession to the mediatorship is reserved for male descendants of the founder. Konkō-kyō emphasizes the interdependence of god and man, which is likened to the relationship of parent and son. The group continues to be recognized as a denomination of SECT SHINTŌ and in 1978 claimed about 480,000 followers.

KOOK, ABRAHAM ISAAC \'kük\ (b. 1865, Greiva, Courland, Latvia—d. Sept. 1, 1935, Jerusalem), Jewish mystic, fervent Zionist, and first chief RABBI of Palestine under a British administration.

After serving as rabbi in a number of small towns in eastern Europe, in 1904 Kook became rabbi of the seaport city of Jaffa in Palestine, and he established a YESHIVA there. During World War I, Kook, who had left Palestine for a visit to Germany, was interned as an alien, but he escaped to England via Switzerland. He became rabbi of the congregation Machzike Hadath in London and in 1919 was appointed rabbi of the Ashkenazic communities in Jerusalem. In 1921 he was elected chief rabbi of Palestine, a post he held for the rest of his life.

A mystic by nature, Kook viewed Jewish national revival as part of the divine plan for strengthening faith against the rising tide of HERESY. He expounded this philosophy in several essays, many of which were published posthumously under the title *Orot ha-qodesh*, 3 vol. (1963–64; "Lights of Holiness").

Other important works are *Iggerot ha Re'ayah* (1962–65; "Letters"); *Orot* (1961; "Lights"); *Orot ha-Teshuvah* (1955; *Rabbi Kook's Philosophy of Repentance*, 1968); *Eretz Hefetz* (1930; "Precious Land"); *Eder ha-Yekar ve-Ikvei ha-*

ton (1967; "The Precious Mantle and Footsteps of the Flock"); *Shabbat ha-Areẓ* (1937); and *Mishpat Kohen* (1966).

KOREAN RELIGIONS, RELIGIOUS BELIEFS that include aspects of ancient indigenous agricultural and shamanistic traditions, TAOISM, BUDDHISM, and CONFUCIANISM imported from China, aspects of Chinese Buddhism (especially Ch'an [ZEN] tradition), ISLAM, CHRISTIANITY, and various eclectic new religious movements. But while Korea is a part of the East Asian cultural contingent heavily influenced by Chinese civilization, it has its own unique characteristics associated with eastern Siberian and central Asiatic shamanistic traditions that draw on cosmological symbolism associated with animals and the sun. Some of these distinctive characteristics are seen in the ancient myths associated with the establishment of the Korean peninsula and the creation of the Korean people, the most famous tales being those of Tan'gun, a semidivine man-animal descended from heaven, who became the patron god of the sacred Mt. Paegak and the Korean state.

Very early in Korean tradition there was an active interaction with the relatively more advanced Chinese civilization, a cultural differential that led to the adoption of a system of social values and a political order consciously modeled on Confucian thought and practice as developed by the Han dynasty. During the foundational Koguryo period (37 BCE–668 CE), the indigenous clan traditions developed elaborate rituals associated with the agricultural cycle of life—indeed, the harvest rite of the 10th month was associated not only with human and vegetal fertility but also with the maintenance of a unified political order. Other rites and magical practices, such as healing and exorcistic rituals, were performed at significant transitional moments in the celestial and seasonal round, and many were conducted by SHAMANS and shamanic political leaders or kings. Taoist magic and other talismanic and geomantic operations were often associated with these indigenous practices. These agricultural, shamanistic, and magical practices continue down to the present day in relation to rural traditions and popular urban rituals. After the 10th and 11th centuries, Chinese NEO-CONFUCIANISM and Ch'an Buddhism were especially influential at the elite levels of society, a situation that persisted until the 19th century and the impact of Western traditions.

During the last century one of the most active manifestations of Korean religious life was the efflorescence of voluntary "new religions" associated with the revelations and leadership of some powerful charismatic figure. The teachings of these new religions are often syncretistic and blend features of traditional Buddhism, Taoism, and Confucianism with an evangelical style of Christianity. One of the first and most influential of these new religions was the late 19th century CH'ŎNDOGYO ("Religion of the Heavenly Way"). Very active recently have been the Chondogwon or Evangelical Church, founded by Pak Tae-son in the 1950s, and the UNIFICATION CHURCH (known somewhat pejoratively in the West as the "Moonies" in reference to the founder SUN MYUNG MOON [b. 1920]).

KOSHER \'kō-shər\, *Hebrew* kāshēr \kä-'sher\ ("fit," or "proper"), in JUDAISM, the fitness of an object for ritual purposes. *See* KASHRUT.

KOTHAR \'kō-ˌthär\, *also called* Khasis \'k̠ä-sēs\, *or* Khayin \'k̠ä-yin\, ancient West Semitic god of crafts. Kothar was responsible for supplying the gods with weapons and for building and furnishing their palaces. During the earlier part of the 2nd millennium BCE, Kothar's forge was believed to be on the biblical Caphtor (possibly Crete), though later, during the period of Egyptian domination of Syria and Palestine, he was identified with the Egyptian god PTAH, patron of craftsmen, and his forge was thus located at Memphis in Egypt. According to Phoenician tradition, Kothar was also the patron of magic and inventor of magical incantations; in addition, he was believed to have been the first poet.

K'OU CH'IEN-CHIH \'kō-'chyen-'jə̇, -'jər\, *Pinyin* Kou Qianzhi (d. 448 CE, Northern Wei Empire, China), Taoist who organized many of the ceremonies and rites of TAOISM, reformulated its theology, and managed to establish it as the official state religion of the Northern Wei dynasty (386–534/535).

K'ou apparently began his career as a Taoist physician and hygienist. But in 415 he had a vision in which a spirit awarded him with the title of *t'ien-shih* ("celestial master") and charged him with eliminating excesses in Taoist rituals. Accordingly, K'ou began to attempt to curb the orgiastic practices and mercenary spirit that had become associated with Taoist rites and to place greater emphasis on hygienic ritual and good works. He gained many adherents and attracted the attention of Emperor T'ai-wu ti (reigned 423–452), who in 423 officially conferred the title of *t'ien-shih* on him. Subsequently the title was passed to the church's leader in an unbroken generational line. By conspiring with certain court officials, K'ou was able to have BUDDHISM, Taoism's chief competitor, proscribed and all its practitioners subjected to a bloody persecution. Taoism then became the official religion of the empire.

K'ou's efforts were only temporarily effective: Buddhism soon returned to China, stronger than ever. Moreover, because orgiastic Taoist rites were still noted as late as the T'ang dynasty (618–907), many observers view his reforms as transitory.

KO-WU \'gə-'wü\, *Pinyin* gewu (Chinese: "investigation of things"), Neo-Confucian practice associated with Chu Hsi's Li-hsüeh ("School of Principle"), which stressed the close examination and study of things, persons, and events in the world in order to arrive at an understanding of the inner "principle" (LI) of reality. Connected with the gradual awareness of *li* is the Neo-Confucian emphasis on moral commitment to social harmony and the material betterment of the real world.

KŌYA, MOUNT \'kȯi-ä\, sacred Japanese mountain, most notable for its association with KŪKAI (774–835), the founder of the SHINGON sect of Japanese BUDDHISM. Located in the present Wakayama Prefecture, it was traditionally said to be several days' journey on foot from Kyōto. After studying Tantric Buddhism in China for two years (804–806), Kūkai returned to his native Japan intent upon establishing an appropriate monastic center for engaging in meditation. According to one legend, Kūkai had vowed to build a monastic center for Shingon Buddhism in Japan, and he chose its location by hurling a three-pronged VAJRA (a kind of mythological weapon) into the air, while returning by sea from China. The *vajra*, according to legend, was discovered to have landed on Mount Kōya.

Mount Kōya was given to Kūkai in the year 816 by Emperor Saga after Kūkai had petitioned him for permission to build his monastery there. According to Kūkai, such a retreat needed to be set on a high mountaintop, far away from village temples or monasteries, so that meditation could be pursued properly. Kūkai proposed that his monastery be built in harmony with the natural surroundings unique to Mount Kōya. He viewed its eight peaks surrounding the central plateau as the eight petals of a lotus, and he imagined that both the outer mountain peaks and the inner buildings and chambers of his monastic center would form complementary, auspicious circles, highly symbolic in Shingon Buddhism. The monastic center was constructed over the course of many years and was not completed until after Kūkai's death. However, many believers hold that Kūkai remains alive deep inside the peaks of Mount Kōya in a meditative trance, awaiting the coming of the future Buddha, MAITREYA.

KRISHNA \'krish-nə\, *Sanskrit* Kṛṣṇa, one of the most popular of all Hindu divinities, widely worshiped as the eighth incarnation (AVATAR, or *avatāra*) of the Hindu god VISHNU and also as the supreme deity. Krishna is the focus of numerous BHAKTI (devotional) cults, which over the centuries have produced a wealth of religious poetry, music, and painting. The basic Sanskrit sources for the story of Krishna are the epic MAHĀBHĀRATA, the *Harivaṃśa* (1st–3rd centuries CE?, traditionally regarded as an appendix to the epic), and the PURĀṆAS, particularly the *Viṣṇu Purāṇa* and Books 10 and 11 of the BHĀGAVATA-PURĀṆA. They relate how Krishna (literally "black") was born into the Yādava clan, the son of Vasudeva and Devakī,

Krishna playing the flute; in the Victoria and Albert Museum, London
Art Resource

na is a particular focus of the extensive literature of love concerning Krishna and the *gopīs*. At length Krishna and his brother BALARĀMA returned to Mathura to slay the wicked Kaṃsa. Afterward, finding the kingdom unsafe, he led the Yādavas to the western coast of Kathiawar and established his court at Dvaraka. He married the princess Rukminī and took other wives as well.

Krishna refused to bear arms in the great war between the Kauravas and the PĀṆḌAVAS but offered a choice of his personal attendance to one side and the loan of his army to the other. The Pāṇḍavas chose the former, and Krishna thus served as charioteer for ARJUNA. After he had returned to Dvaraka, a brawl broke out one day among the Yādava chiefs, and Krishna's brother and son were slain in the course of the fray. As the god sat in the forest lamenting his loss, a huntsman, mistaking him for a deer, shot him and struck him in his one vulnerable spot, the heel, killing him.

Krishna's personality has distinguishable facets: Vāsudeva-Kṛṣṇa, the heroic Vṛṣṇi prince; Krishna Gopāla, the cowherd youth closely associated with the Braj (Vraja) region; and the epic figure who subtly superintends the vast ritual of battle described in the *Mahābhārata*. Historically, one sees a shift from a heroic and epic focus to a more amorous one, with increasing attention also paid to the intimate wonders of the divine child. At several levels, the loves surrounding Krishna become theaters for exploring the elaborate interplay between God and the human soul—sometimes literally, as in the *rās līlā* dramas that have for centuries depicted Krishna's "play" (LĪLĀ) in Braj.

sister of Kaṃsa, the wicked king of Mathura (in modern Uttar Pradesh). Kaṃsa, hearing a PROPHECY that he should be destroyed by Devakī's eighth child, tried to slay her children; but Krishna was smuggled across the Jamunā River to Gokula (or Vraja), where he was raised by the leader of the cowherds, Nanda, and his wife Yaśodā.

The child Krishna was adored for his mischievous pranks; he also performed many miracles and slew DEMONS. As a youth, the cowherd Krishna became renowned as a lover, the sound of his flute prompting the *gopīs* (wives and daughters of the cowherds) to leave their homes to dance ecstatically with him in the forests. His favorite among them was the beautiful RĀDHĀ, whose romance with Krish-

The rich variety of legends associated with Krishna's life has led to an abundance of representation in painting and sculpture. The child Krishna (Bālakṛṣṇa) is often depicted crawling on his hands and knees or dancing with joy, a ball of butter held in his hand. The divine lover (today the most common representation) is apt to be shown playing the flute, surrounded by adoring *gopīs*. In painting, Krishna is characteristically depicted with blue-black skin, wearing a yellow dhoti (loincloth) and a crown of peacock feathers. In the period from about 500 to 1500 CE, sculptors appear to have preferred above all the vision of Krishna as cosmic victor, taming the sky god INDRA at Mount Govardhana or the great snake (NĀGA) Kāliya at the Jamuna.

KROCHMAL, NACHMAN \'kròk̲-mȧl\, *also called (by acronym)* Ranak \rä-'näk\ (b. Feb. 17, 1785, Brody, Austrian Poland [now in Ukraine]—d. July 31, 1840, Tarnopol, Galicia, Austrian Empire [now Ternopil, Ukraine]), Jewish scholar and philosopher.

During his lifetime Krochmal published only a few essays; his unfinished *Moreh nevukhe ha-zeman* (1851; "Guide for the Perplexed of Our Time"), was edited and published posthumously by the eminent Jewish scholar Leopold Zunz (1794–1886). Krochmal's aim—like that of MOSES MAIMONIDES, whose work was quite influential for him—was to reconcile the traditions of JUDAISM with modern secular knowledge, which he sought to accomplish by tracing the Jewish spirit through its manifestations in history, literature, and religious philosophy. A major achievement of Krochmal's book is that it shifted attention from Judaism as an abstract religion to Judaism as a process expressed through the activities of a people.

KṢATRIYA \'kshȧ-trē-ȧ\, *also spelled* Kshattriya, Ksatriya, *or* Kshatriya, second highest in ritual status of the four VARNAS, or social classes, of Hindu India, traditionally the military or ruling class.

The earliest Vedic literature listed the Kṣatriya (holders of *kṣatra*, or authority) as first in rank, then the BRAHMINS (priests and teachers of law), next the VAIŚYA (merchant-traders), and finally the ŚŪDRA (artisans and laborers). Movements of individuals and groups from one class to another, both upward and downward, were not uncommon; a rise in status even to the rank of Kṣatriya was a recognized reward for outstanding service to the rulers of the day. The legend that the Kṣatriya were destroyed by PARAŚURĀMA, the sixth REINCARNATION of VISHNU, as a punishment for their tyranny is thought by some scholars to reflect a long struggle for supremacy between priests and rulers. Brahminic texts such as *The Laws of Manu* and most other DHARMA ŚĀSTRAS tend to report a Brahmin victory, but epic texts often read rather differently, and a good argument can be made that in social reality rulers have usually ranked first. The persistent representation of deities (especially Vishnu, KRISHNA, and RĀMA) as rulers underscores the point, as does the elaborate series of ritual roles and privileges pertaining to kings through most of Hindu history. These

Kuan-ti with his son Kuan-p'ing (left) and his squire Ch'ou-ts'ang; in the Religionskundliche Sammlung der Philipps-Universität, Marburg, Ger.
Foto Marburg—Art Resource

largely buttress the image of a ruler as preserver of DHARMA and auspicious wealth. In modern times, the Kṣatriya *varṇa* is held to include a broad class of CASTE groups, differing considerably in status and function, but united by their claims to rulership, the pursuit of war, or the possession of land. *See also* JĀTI.

KṢITIGARBHA \'kshi-ti-'gȧr-bȧ, -'gär-\ (Sanskrit: "Womb of the Earth"), BODHISATTVA who, though known in India as early as the 4th century CE, became immensely popular in China as Ti-ts'ang and in Japan as Jizō. He is the savior of the oppressed, the dying, and the dreamer of evil dreams, for he has vowed not to stop his labors until he has saved the souls of all the dead condemned to hell. In China, where he is considered the overlord of hell, stories about him are recounted in the SCRIPTURE *on Ti-ts'ang's Vows*, and he is especially associated with Chiu-hua Mountain, which is a favorite place of PILGRIMAGE. In Japan he does not reign over hell (the job of Emma-ō) but is venerated for the mercy he shows the departed and in particular for his kindness to dead children. His widespread worship in Central Asia is attested to by his frequent appearances on temple banners from the Uighur Autonomous Region of Sinkiang, China (Chinese Turkistan).

Kṣitigarbha is most commonly represented as a monk with a nimbus about his shaved head and with the *ūrṇā* (tuft of hair) between his eyebrows. He is depicted carrying the clerical staff (*khakkara*) with which he forces open the gates of hell, together with the flaming pearl (*cintāmaṇi*) with which he lights up the darkness.

KUAN-TI \'gwän-'dē\, *Pinyin* Guandi, *historical name* (Wade-Giles romanization) Kuan Yü, *also called* Kuan Kung \-'gùŋ\, *or* Wu-ti \'wü-'dē\, Chinese god of war and patron of numerous trades and professions. His control over evil spirits is so great that even actors who play his part in dramas share his power over DEMONS. Traditions that he had memorized a Confucian classic, the TSO-CHUAN, led the literati to adopt him as the god of literature, a post he now shares with another deity, WEN-TI.

Kuan Yü lived during the chivalrous era of the Three Kingdoms (3rd century CE) and has been romanticized in popular lore, in drama, and especially in the Ming dynasty novel *San-kuo yen-i*, in which he plays a role similar to that of Robin Hood. Kuan Yü was captured and executed in

219 CE, but his fame continued to grow as rulers conferred successively greater titles upon him. Finally, in 1594, a Ming dynasty emperor canonized him as god of war—protector of China and of all its citizens. Thousands of temples were constructed, each bearing the title Wu-miao (Warrior Temple) or Wu-sheng Miao (Sacred Warrior Temple). Sacrifices were offered on the 15th day of the second moon and on the 13th day of the fifth moon.

For a time the public executioner's sword was housed in Kuan-ti's temple. After a criminal was put to death, the magistrate in charge of executions worshiped in the temple, certain that the spirit of the dead man would not dare to enter the temple or even follow the magistrate home.

In the 17th century Kuan-ti's cult spread to Korea, where it was popularly believed that he saved the country from invasion by the Japanese.

KUAN-YIN \\'gwän-'yin, 'kwän-\\, in Chinese BUDDHISM, the BODHISATTVA of infinite compassion and mercy. *See* AVALOKITEŚVARA.

KUBABA \\kü-'bä-bä\\, goddess of the ancient Syrian city of Carchemish. In religious texts of the Hittite empire (*c.* 1400–*c.* 1190 BCE), she played a minor part. After the downfall of the empire her cult spread westward and northward, and she became the chief goddess of the neo-Hittite successor kingdoms from Cilicia to the Halys River.

Kubaba was represented as a dignified figure draped in a long robe, either standing or seated, and holding a mirror. Although her name was adopted by the Phrygians for their great MOTHER GODDESS in the form of Cybebe (CYBELE), the Phrygian goddess bore little resemblance to Kubaba in other respects.

KUBERA \\'kü-bā-rə\\, in Hindu mythology, the king of the YAKṢAS (nature spirits) and the god of wealth. He is associated with the earth, mountains, all treasures such as minerals and jewels that lie underground, and riches in general. According to most accounts he first lived in Laṅkā (Sri Lanka), but his palace was taken away from him by his half brother, RĀVAṆA, and he now resides in a beautiful mountain residence near SHIVA's home on Mount Kailāsa, where he is attended by all manner of genies.

Kubera is the guardian of the north and is usually depicted as a dwarfish figure with a large paunch, holding a money bag or a pomegranate, sometimes riding on a man. Also known as Vaiśrāvaṇa and Jambhala, he is a popular figure in Buddhist and Jain mythology as well. In Buddhist sculptures he is often shown accompanied by a mongoose.

KUEI \\'gwā\\, *Pinyin* gui (Chinese: "ghost," or "spirit"), in popular Chinese religion, a troublesome spirit that roams the world causing misfortune, illness, and death.

Kuei are malevolent spirits of individuals who were not properly buried or were denied the proper memorial offerings and hence cannot ascend to the spirit world. Protective rituals and talismans ward *kuei* away from the home, and the main entrance is usually screened by a protective "shadow wall."

KUFR \\'kü-fər\\, in ISLAM, unbelief, that is, lack of faith in God. *See also* BIDʿA; IMAN.

KUGA SORTA \\kü-'gä-sȯr-'tä\\ (Mari: "Big Candle"), pacifist and theocratic movement among the Mari (or Cheremis), a FINNO-UGRIC tribal people living chiefly in Mari El re-

public, Russia. The emergence of the movement around 1870 was an attempt by the Mari—who were nominally Christianized during the 16th–19th centuries—to resist Russian acculturation by a synthesis of their own religion with Christianity.

The movement takes its name from the large candle central to its worship. The ritual is conducted in houses or forest groves, without priests or images. An ascetic ethic includes TABOOS on certain foods and stimulants and enjoins love, tolerance, respect for nature, and rejection of modern goods and medicine. Adherents believe that Christ was the greatest of prophets. The Mari element contributes ancient marriage ceremonies, the cult of the dead, and a mythology of the spirit world.

KŪKAI \\'kü-ˌkī\\, *original name* Saeki Mao, *posthumous name* Kōbō Daishi (b. July 27, 774, Byōbugaura [modern Zen-tsūji], Japan—d. April 22, 835, Mount Kōya, near modern Wakayama), one of the best known and most beloved Buddhist saints in Japan, founder of the SHINGON school of BUDDHISM that emphasizes SPELLS, magic formulas, ceremonials, and masses for the dead.

As a youth Kūkai was trained in the Confucian FIVE CLASSICS. In 791, at the age of 17, he is said to have completed his first major work, the *Sangō shiiki* ("Essentials of the Three Teachings"), in which he proclaimed that Buddhism contained everything that was worthwhile in CONFUCIANISM and TAOISM, while it also showed more concern than either for man's existence after death. Kūkai went to China in 804 and met the great master of esoteric Buddhism, Hui-kuo (746–805; Japanese: Keika), and became the master's favorite disciple, receiving his secret teachings when he lay dying. Returning to Japan in 806, Kūkai was given imperial sanction to promulgate his new doctrines. In 816 he began building a monastery on MOUNT KŌYA. This grew into one of the largest and most vigorous monastic complexes in the country, and the Shingon sect became one of the most popular forms of Japanese Buddhism.

Kūkai was also a poet, an artist, and a calligrapher and, thus, had a profound influence on the development of Japanese religious art over the next two centuries. His major work, the *Jūjū shinron*, written in Chinese in a poetic style, classified Confucianism, Taoism, and all the existing Buddhist literature into 10 stages, the last and highest stage being that of Shingon philosophy. This work assured Kūkai a leading rank among the intellectual figures of Japanese Buddhism.

KUMĀRAJĪVA \\kù-'mär-ə-'jē-və\\ (b. 343/344 CE—d. 413), Buddhist scholar and seer, famed for his encyclopedic knowledge of Indian and Vedantic learning. He was one of the greatest translators of the SCRIPTURES of BUDDHISM from Sanskrit into Chinese and as a result was a major contributor to the dissemination of Buddhist ideas in China.

Before his ordination Kumārajīva studied HĪNAYĀNA Buddhism at Kashgar, in an area of central Asia that is now part of China. He was converted to the MĀDHYAMIKA school of Buddhism. Captured by Chinese raiders, he was taken prisoner and brought to the Chinese capital of Ch'ang-an in 401. There he gained the approval of the imperial family and headed a famous school of translators.

KUMAZAWA BANZAN \\'kü-mä-ˌzä-wä-'bän-ˌzän\\ (b. 1619, Kyōto, Japan—d. Sept. 9, 1691, Shimofusa), political philosopher and Japanese disciple of the Chinese NEO-CONFUCIAN philosopher WANG YANG-MING (d. 1529).

Born a *rōnin* ("masterless samurai"), Kumazawa showed such great promise that he was taken into the service of the great feudal lord of Okayama, Ikeda Mitsumasa, at the age of 15. Largely self-taught, Kumazawa was attracted to the ideas of Wang because of their anti-scholastic bent and emphasis on direct action. His common-sensical solutions to problems were held in great esteem, and in 1647 he was appointed chief minister of Okayama. His attempts to return to the barter economy of Japan's simpler past provoked opposition, and in 1656 Kumazawa was forced to resign; he spent the rest of his years in study and writing.

Devotees offering prayers in the river Gaṅgā during the Kumbh Mela festival
Reuters—Corbis-Bettmann

Writing in colloquial Japanese rather than the classical Chinese usually used for philosophical works, Kumazawa advocated advancement based on individual merit rather than on hereditary status, an increased government responsibility for economic life, and a relaxation of central control over the great feudal lords. His ideas caused such a fury in the government that Kumazawa was kept in custody or under surveillance for the rest of his life.

KUMBH MELA \'kům-bə-'mä-lä\, *also called* Kumbha Mela, *Hindi* Kumbh Melā, in HINDUISM, religious festival that is celebrated four times every 12 years, the site of the observance rotating between four PILGRIMAGE places on four sacred rivers: at Hardwar on the GAṄGĀ (Ganges) River, at Ujjain on the Śiprā, at Nāsik on the Godāvarī, and at Prayāg (Allahabad) at the confluence of the Gaṅgā, JAMUNA, and the mythical SARASVATĪ. Each site's celebration is based on particular zodiacal positions of the sun, moon, and Jupiter, the holiest time occurring at the exact moment these zodiacal conditions are fulfilled. Bathing at this moment is believed to generate the greatest religious merit, but the Kumbh time is regarded as being so holy that other bathing days are designated weeks or even months before and after this climactic time.

Tradition ascribes the Kumbh Mela's origin to the 8th-century philosopher ŚAMKARA, who sought to strengthen Hindu religion by instituting regular gatherings of learned ascetics for discussion and debate. Yet the Kumbh Mela's most important historical figures have been the *nāga akhāḍā*s, militant ascetic orders whose members formerly made their living as mercenary soldiers and traders. These *akhāḍā*s still monopolize the holiest spots at each Kumbh's most propitious moment, and although the government now enforces an established bathing order, history records bloody disputes between groups vying for precedence.

Aside from the *akhāḍā*s, attendees at the Kumbh Mela display the full spectrum of Hindu religious life, ranging from SADHUS (holy men) who remain naked the year round or practice the most severe physical disciplines to HERMITS who leave their isolation only for these pilgrimages and even to silk-clad teachers who spread their teachings using the latest technology. The religious organizations represented range from social welfare societies to political lobbyists. Vast crowds of disciples, friends, and spectators join the individual ascetics and organizations, making the Kumbh Mela the world's largest religious gathering—an estimated 10 million were drawn to Hardwar in April 1998.

The charter myth of the Kumbh Mela—attributed to the PURĀNAS but actually found in none of them—recounts how the gods and DEMONS fought over the pot (*kumbha*) of *amrta*, the elixir of immortality produced by their joint CHURNING OF THE MILK-OCEAN. During the struggle, drops of the elixir fell on the Mela's four earthly sites. At each Mela's climactic moment, the rivers are believed to turn back into that primordial nectar, giving pilgrims the chance to bathe in the essence of purity, auspiciousness, and immortality. The name *Kumbh* comes from this mythic pot of elixir but is also the name for Aquarius, the sign of the ZODIAC in which Jupiter resides during the Hardwar Mela.

KUNDAKUNDA \'kůn-də-'kůn-də\, 2nd-century Jain philosopher, the first to develop Jain logic (*see* JAINISM). His influential Prakrit works include the *Pravacanasāra* (on ethics), the *Samayasāra* (on fine entities), the *Niyamasāra* (on Jain monastic discipline), and six *Prabhṛta*s ("Chapters") on various religious topics.

KUṆḌALINĪ \ˌkún-də-'lē-nē\, *Sanskrit* kuṇḍala ("coil"), in some Tantric forms of YOGA, the cosmic energy that lies within everyone, pictured as a coiled serpent lying at the base of the spine. In the practice of Laya Yoga ("Discipline of Dissolution"), the adept is instructed to awaken the *kuṇḍalinī,* also identified with the deity ŚAKTI, through a series of techniques that combine prescribed postures, gestures, and breathing exercises. In the process the *kuṇḍalinī* passes upward through six centers, or CHAKRAS (Sanskrit: *çakras*). When the *kuṇḍalinī* arrives at the seventh chakra, at the top of the head, the practitioner experiences a feeling of bliss that registers the dissolution (*laya*) of the ordinary self into its eternal essence, ĀTMAN. This experience is also understood as the primordial union of the male and female cosmic principles, the former being represented by the *liṅga* of SHIVA and the latter by the *kuṇḍalinī* of his consort ŚAKTI. It is thus simultaneously a microcosmic, bodily occurrence and a universal one. (*See* HAṬHA YOGA.)

KÜNG, HANS \'kɐŋ, 'kúŋ\ (b. March 19, 1928, Sursee, Switz.), Swiss ROMAN CATHOLIC theologian whose controversial views led to his censorship by the Vatican.

Küng studied at Gregorian University in Rome and obtained a doctorate in theology from the Catholic Institute at the Sorbonne in 1957. He was ordained a priest in 1954, and he taught at the University of Münster (1959–60) and at the University of Tübingen (1960–96), where he also directed the Institute for Ecumenical Research from 1963. In 1962 he was named by POPE JOHN XXIII a *peritus* (theological consultant) for the SECOND VATICAN COUNCIL.

Küng's prolific writings questioned such traditional church doctrine as PAPAL INFALLIBILITY, the divinity of JESUS CHRIST, and the dogma of the Virgin MARY. In 1979 a Vatican censure that banned his teaching as a Catholic theologian provoked international controversy, and in 1980 a settlement was reached at Tübingen that allowed him to teach under secular rather than Catholic auspices.

KUO HSIANG \'gwȯ-'shyän\, *Pinyin* Guo Xiang (d. 312 CE, China), Chinese Neo-Taoist philosopher to whom is attributed a celebrated commentary on the CHUANG-TZU, one of the basic writings of TAOISM.

Kuo was a high government official. His *Chuang-tzu chu* ("Chuang-tzu Commentary") is thought to have been begun by another Neo-Taoist philosopher, Hsiang Hsiu. When Hsiang died, Kuo is said to have incorporated Hsiang's commentary into his own. For this reason the work is sometimes called the Kuo–Hsiang commentary.

Kuo deviated from LAO-TZU in interpreting TAO ("the Way") as nothingness. As nonbeing, Tao does not produce being—that is, it cannot be regarded as a first cause. Investigation of the cause of a thing ultimately arrives at something which has no cause, which is self-produced; ultimately, he therefore argued, everything produces itself spontaneously. The "self-transformation" of a thing as well as its existence is conditioned by other things and in its turn conditions them. Applying this general principle to human affairs, Kuo argued that social institutions and moral ideas must be changed when situations change. Kuo also interpreted the Taoist term "nonaction" (WU-WEI) to mean spontaneous action, not sitting still. Everything has a definite nature; if it follows its own way, it finds satisfaction and enjoyment; if it is not content with what is, and craves to be what it is not, then there is dissatisfaction and regret. The Perfect Man ignores all such distinctions as right and wrong, life and death; his happiness is unlimited.

KUROZUMI-KYŌ \ˌkú-rō-'zü-mē-ˌkyō\, "new religion" of Japan, named for its founder, Kurozumi Munetada (1780–1850), a SHINTŌ priest of the area that is now Okayama prefecture. The believers venerate the sun goddess AMATERASU as the supreme god and creator of the universe and consider the other traditional 8,000,000 Shintō KAMI to be her manifestations. Devotional activities include morning worship of the sun, with breathing exercises, described as "swallowing the sun," intended to bring about spiritual union with the sun and physical well-being. The movement was officially recognized as a Shintō sect in 1846 and reorganized under its present name in 1876. It is still recognized as a denomination of SECT SHINTŌ and in the late 20th century claimed over 200,000 followers.

KUSHUKH \'kú-ˌshúk̲\, *also spelled* Kushuh, the Hurrian moon god. Kushukh was regularly placed above the sun god, Shimegi; his consort was Niggal (the Sumero-Akkadian Ningal). His home was said to be the city of Kuzina (location unknown), and his cult was later adopted by the Hittites. As Lord of the OATH he had as his special function the punishment of perjury. He was represented as a winged man with a crescent on his helmet and sometimes standing on a lion; in this form he appears among the images of Hittite gods at the rock SANCTUARY of Yazılıkaya (near modern Boğazköy in Turkey). *See* ANATOLIAN RELIGIONS.

KUT \'küt\, trance ritual in Korean folk shamanism, directed to the repulsion of spirits who might cause harm. The ceremony attempts to bring good fortune and is sometimes used for healing purposes or to promote the welfare of an individual or a village. *See* SHAMAN; MUDANG.

KVASIR \'kvä-sir\, in Norse mythology, a poet and the wisest of all beings. Kvasir was born of the saliva of two rival groups of gods, the AESIR and the VANIR, when they performed the ancient peace ritual of spitting into a common vessel. He wandered around teaching and instructing, never failing to give the right answer to a question. Two dwarfs, Fjalar and Galar, who were weary of learning, killed Kvasir and distilled his blood in Odrerir, the magic caldron (whose name means "stirring up ecstasy"). When mixed with honey by the GIANT Suttung, his blood formed mead that gave wisdom and poetic inspiration to those who drank it. The story of Kvasir's murder is told by Snorri Sturluson in his EDDA.

KWANZAA \'kwän-zə\, *also spelled* Kwanza, African-American holiday, celebrated each year from December 26 to January 1; it is patterned after various African harvest festivals. The name was taken from the Swahili phrase *matunda ya kwanza* ("first fruits"). Kwanzaa was created in 1966 by Maulana Karenga, a black-studies professor at California State University at Long Beach, as a nonreligious celebration of family and social values. Each day of Kwanzaa is dedicated to one of seven principles: unity (*umoja*), self-determination (*kujichagulia*), collective responsibility (*ujima*), cooperative economics (*ujamaa*), purpose (*nia*), creativity (*kuumba*), and faith (*imani*). Each evening family members gather to light one of the candles in the *kinara*, a seven-branched candelabra, and discuss the principle for that day; often gifts are exchanged. On December 31 the family joins other members of the community for a feast, called the *karamu.*

KYŌHA SHINTŌ: *see* SECT SHINTŌ.

LAG BA-'OMER \'läg-bə-'ō-mər, -'bō-mər\, *also spelled* Lag B'Omer, *or* Lag be-Omer, in JUDAISM, minor observance falling on the 33rd day in the period of the counting of the *'omer* ("barley sheaves"); on this day semi-mourning ceases and weddings are allowed. One tradition has it that MANNA first fell from heaven on this day, another that a plague that raged among the followers of RABBI AKIBA BEN JOSEPH during *'omer* ceased on this day. In Meron in Upper Galilee, Israel, Orthodox Jews make a PILGRIMAGE to the burial site of the rabbi SIMEON BEN YOḤAI, and young children receive their first haircuts as part of a celebration that includes playing with bows and arrows (symbols of the rainbow) and dancing around a bonfire.

LAHMU AND LAHAMU \'läk̲-,mü . . . lä-'k̲ä-,mü\, in Mesopotamian mythology, twin deities, the first gods to be born from the CHAOS that was created by the merging of Apsu (the watery deep beneath the earth) and TIAMAT (the personification of the salt waters); this is described in the Babylonian mythological text *Enuma elish* (c. 12th century BCE).

Usually, Lahmu and Lahamu represent silt, but in some texts they seem to take the form of serpents, and some scholars believe that Lahmu and Lahamu may have been only synonyms of Tiamat. Lahmu and Lahamu do not seem to have played any significant part in subsequent myths, although they are considered the progenitors of ANSHAR AND KISHAR, who in turn give birth to more active gods.

LAIMA \'lī-mä\, *also called* Laima-Dalia \-dä-'lʸä\, in BALTIC RELIGION, goddess of fate, associated with the linden tree. Her name is a variant of a generic noun in Baltic languages (Lithuanian *laimė,* Latvian *laime*) meaning "luck," "fortune," or "happiness." Together with DIEVS, the sky, and SAULE, the sun, Laima determines the length and fortune of human life. In the course of each life she helps arrange marriages, oversees weddings, protects pregnant women, and appears at childbirth to pronounce each infant's destiny.

Revered as patroness of cows and horses, Laima decides the life span of plants and animals and determines the length of the day.

LAKṢMĪ \'lək-shmē\, *also spelled* Lakshmi, *also called* Śrī \'shrē\, HINDU and JAIN goddess of wealth and good fortune. The wife of VISHNU, she is said to have taken different forms in order to be with him in each of his INCARNATIONS. In the most widely received account of Lakṣmī's birth, she rose from the churning of the primal MILK-OCEAN, seated on a lotus blossom and holding another in her hand. Controversy arose between the gods and DEMONS over possession of her.

Lakṣmī is often represented in sculpture seated or standing on a lotus, full-breasted, broad-hipped, beneficently smiling, and sometimes being anointed or consecrated by a pair of elephants, a scene suggesting her royal authority and her association with fertilizing rains. In the Śrī Vaiṣṇava

sampradāya, she is also shown as a jewel upon the breast of her consort Vishnu. This recognizes her constant, heartlike presence with her mate and suggests the tender, mediating role she plays between the more austere Vishnu and his human devotees. Yet on the whole, Lakṣmī is worshiped independently. She is a major presence in poster art; in home and temple worship, especially on Fridays when she is honored along with other goddesses; and in various festivals. She is a principal object of worship during DĪVĀLĪ, when her presence is sought in homes, temples, and businesses for the whole of the year to come.

LALLĀ DED \'lä-lə-'dād\, *also known as* Lal Ded, *or* Lalles hvari, 14th-century Hindu poet-saint from Kashmir, who defied social convention in her search for God.

Legend tells of the harsh treatment LALLĀ DED received from her husband and mother-in-law and extols her patience and forbearance. Twelve years after being wed, she left her home in order to dedicate herself to SHIVA and became a wandering religious singer. Her poems and songs concern the longing for God and the joy she finds in the deity who lives within, as well as her disregard for conventional forms of worship such as image worship: "Temple and image, the two that you have fashioned, are no better than stone." Her highly emotional lyrics have become famous among the devotees of Shiva and are revered as being among the finest products of the poet-saints of the Hindu BHAKTI tradition.

LALITAVISTARA \'lə-li-tə-'vis-tə-rə\ (Sanskrit: "Detailed Narration of the Sport [of the Buddha]"), legendary life of the BUDDHA GOTAMA, written in a combination of Sanskrit and a vernacular language. Like the MAHĀVASTU, the subject matter of which has a number of similarities, the *Lalitavistara* contains late material but also preserves some very ancient passages. It shares with the Hindu PURĀṆAS similarities of style as well as the concept of a divine being's earthly activities as "sport," or "play." In this narrative it is especially with regard to the Buddha's conception and birth that this work adds to the miraculous and mythological elements of earlier accounts. The *Lalitavistara* is regarded as especially sacred in MAHĀYĀNA circles, and it has inspired a considerable amount of Buddhist art.

LAMA \'lä-mə\, *Tibetan* bla-ma ("superior one"), in TIBETAN BUDDHISM, a spiritual leader. Originally used to translate "GURU" (Sanskrit: "venerable one") and thus applicable only to heads of monasteries or great teachers, the term is now extended out of courtesy to any respected monk or priest.

Some lamas are considered REINCARNATIONS of their predecessors. These are termed *sprul-sku* lamas, as distinguished from "developed" lamas, who have won respect because of the high level of spiritual development they have achieved. The highest lineage of reincarnate lamas is that of the DALAI LAMA, who was, until his exile in 1959, the temporal ruler of Tibet. The title is given to the head of the DGE-LUGS-PA (Yellow Hat sect). He is considered the physical manifestation of the BODHISATTVA of compassion AVALOKITEŚ-VARA. The second highest line of succession is that of the Panchen Lama, head ABBOT of the Tashilhunpo monastery, believed to be the manifestation of the self-born Buddha AMITĀBHA. Other, lesser *sprul-sku* lamas are revered as reincarnations of great saints or teachers. The idea probably originated from the tradition of the 84 MAHĀSIDDHAS, or master yogins, many of whom were identified as manifestations of earlier sages, coupled with the accepted Buddhist belief in rebirth.

The process of discovering the rebirth of a reincarnated lama can be elaborate and exacting, particularly in the selection of a Dalai Lama. The rebirth may take place at any time, from days to years, following the death of the previous lama. Remarks made by the Dalai Lama before his death are frequently accepted as indications of a favored place for rebirth, as are any unusual signs that are observed during his death or during a birth thereafter. The state oracle at Nechung has also been consulted for the whereabouts of the newly born Dalai Lama. Often two or more candidates are subjected to a critical physical and mental examination, which includes recognition of personal belongings handled by the previous lama. In case of doubt, lots may be drawn. After selection, the young child is given extensive monastic training from an early age. During the years of search for and education of a newly incarnated lama, a regent is appointed to rule in his stead.

LAMASHTU \lä-'mäsh-ˌtü\ (Akkadian), *Sumerian* Dimme, in MESOPOTAMIAN RELIGION, most terrible of all female DEMONS, daughter of the sky god ANU (Sumerian: An), who slew children, drank the blood of men, and ate their flesh. She had seven names and was often described in incantations as the "seven witches." Lamashtu disturbed sleep and brought nightmares; she killed foliage and infested rivers

---

Relief of the Buddha as Siddhārtha competing at archery, inspired by the Lalitavistara; *from the temple complex of Borobuḍur, Indon., 750–850* CE

J. Powell, Rome

and streams; she bound the muscles of men, caused pregnant women to miscarry, and brought disease and sickness. Lamashtu was often portrayed on AMULETS as a lion- or bird-headed female figure kneeling on an ass; she held a double-headed serpent in each hand and suckled a dog at her right breast and a pig or another dog at her left breast.

LAMENT FOR THE DESTRUCTION OF UR \'ər, 'ür\, ancient Sumerian composition bewailing the collapse of the 3rd Dynasty of Ur (*c.* 2112–*c.* 2004 BCE) in southern Mesopotamia. The lament, primarily composed of 11 "songs" or stanzas of unequal length, begins by enumerating some of the prominent cities and temples of Sumer and the deities who had deserted them. In the second "song," the people of Ur and of other cities of Sumer are urged to set up a bitter lament. The third "song" relates that the goddess Ningal hears the pleas of the people of Ur, but she is not able to dissuade the gods ANU and ENLIL from their decision to destroy the city, and the remaining "songs" relate the devastating results of Ur's defeat in battle. The last stanza ends with a plea to NANNA, the husband of Ningal, that the city may once more rise up and that the people of Ur may again present their offerings to him.

LAMIA \'lā-mē-ə\, in Greek mythology, female DEMON who devoured children. According to late myths she was a queen of Libya who was beloved by ZEUS. When HERA robbed her of her children from this union, Lamia killed every child she could get into her power. She was also known as a fiend who, in the form of a beautiful woman, seduced young men in order to devour them.

LANDAU, EZEKIEL \'län-ˌdaů\ (b. Oct. 8, 1713, Opatów, Pol.—d. April 29, 1793, Prague), Polish RABBI and author of a much-reprinted book on Jewish law (HALAKHAH).

In 1734 Landau was appointed head of the rabbinical court at Brody, and in 1745 he became rabbi of Jampol, Podolia (then part of Poland). There he gained fame by his diplomacy in arbitrating the controversy between Rabbi JACOB EMDEN and Rabbi JONATHAN EYBESCHÜTZ. In 1755 he went to Prague as rabbi and remained there until his death. His Halakhic decisions (RESPONSA) were collected under the title *Noda' be-Yehuda* ("Known in Judah").

He was an implacable opponent of the two major currents of JUDAISM that arose in his generation: HASIDISM, which he opposed as sinfully ignorant, and HASKALAH, which he attacked as a threat to Jewish identity. Landau even went so far as to order the public burning of a famous Hasidic polemic, the *Toledot Ya'aqov Yosef* ("History of Jacob Joseph") of JACOB JOSEPH OF POLONNOYE (d. *c.* 1782).

LANGUAGE, RELIGIOUS, language that is usually understood as symbolic in nature, its hidden meanings needing to be decoded or translated. An explanation of religious language, however, really depends upon how we define religion and language. In general there are three basic approaches to the study of religious language. The first assumes that religion refers to some transcendent reality, usually called the sacred, or to all-encompassing questions in life, such as the meaning of life and death, good and evil, and suffering. The second approach views religion as basically expressive of emotions. With both of these approaches, religious language is not to be taken literally but is to be seen as symbols that stand for emotions that are noncognitive. The third approach denies that there is anything special about religious language. This theory, known as semantic theory, draws on LOGICAL POSITIVISM and claims that the meaning of religious language should be explained as part of ordinary language, in which meaning is determined by the truth conditions entailed by all languages.

Throughout most of the 20 century the truth conditions of language of the Logical Positivists were based on empirical verification. Semantic theory accordingly takes religious language literally, since the notion of "hidden meaning" does not make semantic sense. This, however, led to the conclusion that religious language can be neither true nor false, since many statements—*i.e.*, about the nature of God, on miracles, etc.—cannot be empirically verified. This in turn led to the search for hidden meanings on the part of other scholars of religious language. Thus, while the development of many theories of symbolic meaning can be traced back to the power of Logical Positivism in the domain of semantic theory, many contemporary theories of semantic-truth conditions no longer entail the empirical correspondence theory of truth as the basic principle of meaning. While most studies of religious language assume some notion of symbolic, and thus hidden, meaning, no agreement has been reached concerning what the hidden meaning of religious language refers to.

LAṄKĀVATĀRA SŪTRA \ləṇ-ˌkä-və-ˈtär-ə-ˈsü-trə\, *in full* Saddharma Laṅkāvatāra Sūtra (Sanskrit: "Sutra of the Appearance of the Good Doctrine in Laṅkā"), distinctive and influential philosophical discourse in the MAHĀYĀNA Buddhist tradition that is said to have been preached by the Buddha in the mythical city Laṅkā; it was first translated into Chinese in the 5th century. It teaches the doctrine of the YOGĀCĀRA (Vijñānavāda) school—that the world is an illusory reflection of an ultimate, undifferentiated mind and that this truth becomes an inner realization upon concentrated meditation. The thought of the *Laṅkāvatāra* provides some of the philosophical background of the ZEN (Ch'an) schools as well.

LAOCOÖN \lā-ˈä-kō-ˌän\, in Greek legend, seer and priest of the god Apollo; he was the son of Agenor of Troy or the brother of ANCHISES (the father of AENEAS). Laocoön offended APOLLO by breaking his OATH of CELIBACY and begetting children. Thus, while preparing to sacrifice a bull on the altar of the god POSEIDON (a task that had fallen to him by lot), Laocoön and his twin sons, Antiphas and Thymbraeus (also called Melanthus), were crushed to death by two great sea serpents, Porces and Chariboea (or Curissia or Periboea), sent by Apollo. An additional reason for his punishment was that he had warned the Trojans against accepting the wooden horse left by the Greeks. The legend found its most

Lao-tzu riding to the west on a water buffalo
Bildarchiv Foto Marburg der Philipps-Universitat—Art Resource

famous expressions in Virgil's *Aeneid* (ii, 109 *et seq.*) and in the Laocoön statue (now in the Vatican Museum) by three Rhodian sculptors, Agesander, Polydorus, and Athenodorus, dating probably from the 2nd century BCE.

LAOMEDON \lā-ˈä-mə-ˌdän\, legendary king of Troy and father of Podarces (later famous as King PRIAM of Troy). Laomedon refused to give APOLLO and POSEIDON their wages after they had built the walls of Troy for him. The gods therefore sent a pestilence and a sea monster to ravage the land, which could be delivered only by the sacrifice of the king's daughter Hesione. But HERACLES killed the monster and rescued the maiden on the understanding that Laomedon should give him his divine horses. When Laomedon later refused, Heracles returned with a band of warriors, captured Troy, and slew Laomedon and all his sons except Priam. Laomedon was buried near the Scaean Gate, and, according to legend, as long as his grave remained undisturbed the walls of Troy would remain impregnable.

LAO-TZU \ˈlaů-ˈdzə̇\, *Pinyin* Laozi (Chinese: "Master Lao," or "Old Master"), *also called* Li Erh \ˈlē-ˈər\, Lao Tun \-ˈdůn\, *or* Lao Tan \-ˈdän\, *deified as* Lao-chün, T'ai-shang Lao-chün, *or* T'ai-shang hsüan-yüan huang-ti (fl. *c.* 6th century BCE?, China), legendary first philosopher of Chinese TAOISM and alleged author of the TAO-TE CHING (*Lao-tzu*), a primary Taoist writing, though many modern scholars discount the possibility that the *Tao-te ching* was written by only one person. Lao-tzu is venerated as a philosopher by Confucianists and as a saint or god by later religious Taoists and was worshiped as an imperial ancestor during the T'ang dynasty (618–907).

The life of Lao-tzu. The principal source of information about Lao-tzu's life is a biography in the *Shih-chi* ("Historical Records") by Ssu-ma Ch'ien. This historian, who wrote about 100 BCE, says that Lao-tzu was a native of Ch'ü-jen, a village in the district of Hu in the state of Ch'u, which corresponds to the modern Lu-i in the eastern part of Honan province. His family name was Li, his proper name Erh, his appellation Tan. He was appointed to the office of *shih* at the royal court of the Chou dynasty (*c.* 1111–255 BCE). In ancient China the *shih* were scholars specializing in matters such as ASTROLOGY and DIVINATION and were in charge of sacred books.

Interspersed among these few historical details are legendary tales, including an account of Lao-tzu's voyage to the west. Realizing that the Chou dynasty was on the decline, the philosopher departed and came to the Hsien-ku pass, which was the entrance to the state of Ch'in. Yin Hsi, the legendary guardian of the pass (*kuan-ling*), begged him to write a book for him. Thereupon, Lao-tzu wrote a book in two sections of 5,000 characters, in which he set down his ideas about the TAO (literally "Way," the Supreme Principle) and the TE (its "virtue" or "power"): the *Tao-te ching.* Then he left, and "nobody knows what has become of him," says Ssu-ma Ch'ien. The *Tao-te ching,* however, cannot be the work of a single man; some of its sayings may date from the time of Confucius; others are certainly later; and the book as a whole dates from about 300 BCE. The name Lao-tzu seems originally to have designated a type of sage rather than an individual.

Hagiographical legends. Several hagiographies were written from the 2nd century CE onward that relate the history of the formation of religious Taoism (Tao-chiao). During the Eastern, or Later, Han dynasty (25–220 CE), Lao-tzu had already become a mythical figure who was worshiped by the people and occasionally by an emperor. Later, in religious circles, he became the Lord Lao (Lao-chün), revealer of sacred texts and savior of mankind. There were several stories about his birth, one of which was influenced by the legend of the miraculous birth of the BUDDHA GOTAMA. Lao-tzu's mother is said to have borne him 72 years in her womb and he is said to have entered the world through her left flank.

Two legends were particularly important in the creed of the Taoists. According to the first, the Lao-chün was believed to have adopted different personalities throughout history and to have come down to the earth several times to instruct the rulers in the Taoist doctrine. The second legend developed from the story of Lao-tzu's voyage to the west. In this account the Buddha was thought to be none other than Lao-tzu himself. During the 3rd century CE an apocryphal book was fabricated on this theme with a view to combating Buddhist propaganda. This book, the *Lao-tzu hua-hu ching* ("Lao-tzu's Conversion of the Barbarians"), in which BUDDHISM was presented as an inferior kind of Taoism, was condemned by the Chinese imperial authorities.

Lao-tzu has never ceased to be generally respected in all circles in China. To the Confucianists he was a venerated philosopher; to the people he was a saint or a god; and to the Taoists he was an emanation of the Tao and one of their greatest divinities.

LAR \\'lär\\, *plural* Lares, in ROMAN RELIGION, any of numerous tutelary deities. They were originally gods of the cultivated fields, worshiped by each household at a crossroads. Later the Lares were worshiped in the houses in association with the PENATES, the gods of the storeroom (*penus*); the household Lar (Familiaris) was conceived as the center of the family and of the family cult.

Originally each household had only one Lar. It was usually represented as a youthful figure, dressed in a short tunic, holding in one hand a drinking horn, in the other a cup. Under the empire, two of these images were commonly to be found, one on each side of the central figure of the GENIUS, of VESTA, or of some other deity. The whole group came to be called indifferently Lares or Penates. A prayer was said to the Lar every morning, and special offerings were made at family festivals.

The public Lares belonged to the state religion. Among these were included the *Lares compitales*, who presided over the crossroads (*compita*) and the whole neighboring district. They had an annual festival called the Compitalia.

The state had its own Lares, called *praestites*, the protecting patrons and guardians of the city. They had a temple and altar on the Via Sacra and were represented as men wearing a military cloak, carrying lances, seated, with a dog (the emblem of watchfulness) at their feet.

LAST JUDGMENT, general, or sometimes individual, judging of the thoughts, words, and deeds of persons by God, the gods, or by the laws of cause and effect.

In ancient EGYPTIAN RELIGION, a dead person's heart was judged by being placed on a balance held by ANUBIS. If the heart was light, thus indicating a person's comparative goodness, the soul was allowed to go to the blessed region ruled by OSIRIS, god of the dead. If the heart was heavy, the soul might be destroyed by a creature called the Devouress.

ZOROASTRIANISM, similarly, teaches that after death the soul waits for three nights by the grave and on the fourth day goes to the Bridge of the Requiter, where his deeds are weighed. If the good deeds outweigh the bad, the soul is able to cross the bridge to heaven; if the bad deeds outweigh the good, the bridge becomes too narrow for the soul to cross, and it plunges into the cold, dark abyss of hell. This is not the end, however, for there will be a final overthrow of AHRIMAN, the prince of DEMONS, by AHURA MAZDĀ, the Wise Lord, who will resurrect all men, preside over a Last Judgment, and restore the world to goodness.

Early Judaic writers emphasized a day of YAHWEH, the God of Israel, which is also called the day of the Lord. This day, which will be a day of judgment of Israel and all nations, will inaugurate the KINGDOM OF GOD. CHRISTIANITY, further developing the concept of the Last Judgment, teaches that it will occur at the Parousia (the SECOND COMING, or Second Advent, of Christ in glory), when all men will stand before a judging God.

In ISLAM the Day of Judgment is one of the five cardinal beliefs. After death, persons are questioned about their faith by two ANGELS: Munkar and Nakīr. If a person has been a martyr, his soul immediately goes to paradise; others go through a type of PURGATORY. At doomsday all persons will die and then be resurrected to be judged according to the records kept in two books, one containing a person's good deeds, and the other his evil deeds. According to the weight of the book that is tied around a person's neck, he will be consigned to paradise or hell.

LAST SUPPER, *also called* Lord's Supper, in the NEW TESTAMENT (Matthew 26:17–29; Mark 14:12–25; Luke 22:7–38; 1 Corinthians 11:23–25), final meal shared by Jesus and his disciples in an upper room in Jerusalem, the occasion of the institution of the EUCHARIST. In the biblical account, Jesus sent two of his disciples to prepare for the meal and met with all of them in the room. He told them that one of them would betray him. After blessing bread and wine and giving it to them to eat and drink, Jesus told them that it was his body and his blood.

The SYNOPTIC GOSPELS and the traditions of the church affirm that the Last Supper occurred on the PASSOVER, though the account of the CRUCIFIXION in the Gospel According to John indicates that the Last Supper could not have been a Passover meal. Two aspects of the Last Supper have been traditionally depicted in Christian art: Christ's revelation to his Apostles that one of them will betray him and their reaction to this announcement, and the institution of the SACRAMENT of the Eucharist with the communion of the Apostles. In early Christian art the presence of a fish on the table symbolizes the institution of the Eucharist. This symbol appeared in Western depictions of the communion of the Apostles until the 15th century, when a CHALICE and wafer were substituted for it.

LĀT, AL- \ˌäl-ˈlat\, North Arabian goddess to whom a stone cube at aṭ-Ṭāʾif (near MECCA) was held sacred as part of her cult. Two other North Arabian goddesses, Manāt (Fate) and al-ʿUzzā (Strong), were associated with al-Lāt in the QURʾAN. According to some traditions MUHAMMAD once recognized these three as goddesses, but a new revelation led him to abrogate the approving verses he had earlier recited and to abandon his attempt to placate Meccan PAGANS. Members of the tribe of QURAYSH circumambulated the KAʿBA in Mecca (now a central shrine of ISLAM in the Great Mosque in Mecca) chanting the praises of al-Lāt, al-ʿUzzā, and Manāt. Each of the three had main sanctuaries near Mecca that were sites of pious visits and offerings until Muhammad ordered them destroyed. The goddesses were also worshiped by various Arab tribes located as far away as Palmyra, Syria.

LATERAN COUNCIL \ˈla-tə-rən\, any of the five ecumenical councils of the ROMAN CATHOLIC church held in the Lateran Palace in Rome.

The first Lateran Council, the ninth ecumenical council (1123), was held during the reign of Pope Calixtus II. The council promulgated a number of canons (probably 22), many of which merely reiterated decrees of earlier councils. Much of the discussion was occupied with disciplinary or political decisions relating to the INVESTITURE CONTROVERSY settled the previous year by the Concordat of Worms; SIMONY was condemned, laymen were prohibited from disposing of church property, clerics in major orders were forbidden to marry, and uncanonical consecration of bishops was forbidden. There were no specific dogmatic decrees.

The second Lateran Council, the 10th ecumenical council (1139), was convoked by Pope Innocent II to condemn as schismatics the followers of Arnold of Brescia, a reformer and opponent of the temporal power of the pope, and to end the SCHISM created by the election of Anacletus II, a rival pope. Supported by ST. BERNARD DE CLAIRVAUX and later by Emperor Lothair II, Innocent was eventually acknowledged as the legitimate pope. The second Lateran Council declared invalid all marriages of those in major orders and of professed monks, canons, lay brothers, and nuns, and repudiated the heresies of the 12th century concerning holy orders, matrimony, infant BAPTISM, and the EUCHARIST.

The third Lateran Council, the 11th ecumenical council, was convoked in 1179 by Pope Alexander III and attended by 291 bishops who studied the Peace of Venice (1177), by which the Holy Roman emperor, Frederick I Barbarossa, agreed to withdraw support from his ANTIPOPE and to restore the church property he had seized. This council also established a two-thirds majority of the College of CARDINALS as a requirement for papal election and stipulated that candidates for bishop must be 30 years old and of legitimate birth. The CATHARI (or ALBIGENSES) were condemned as heretical, and Christians were authorized to take up arms against vagabond robbers.

The fourth Lateran Council, the 12th ecumenical council (1215), was convoked by Pope INNOCENT III and is generally considered the greatest council before Trent, involving more than 400 bishops, 800 abbots and priors, envoys of many European kings, and personal representatives of Frederick II (confirmed by the council as emperor of the West). The purpose of the council was twofold: reform of the church and the recovery of the Holy Land. The council ruled on such vexing problems as the use of church property, TITHES, judicial procedures, and patriarchal precedence.

It ordered Jews and Saracens to wear distinctive dress and obliged Catholics to make a yearly CONFESSION and to receive communion during the EASTER season. The council sanctioned the word TRANSUBSTANTIATION as a correct expression of eucharistic doctrine. The teachings of the Cathari and WALDENSES were condemned. Innocent also ordered a four-year truce among Christian rulers so that a new crusade could be launched.

The fifth Lateran Council, the 18th ecumenical council (1512–17), was convoked by Pope Julius II in response to a council summoned at Pisa by a group of cardinals who were hostile to the Pope. It restored peace among warring Christian rulers. The council affirmed the immortality of the soul and repudiated declarations of the councils of Constance and Basel that made church councils superior to the pope.

LATINUS \lə-ˈtī-nəs\, in Roman mythology, king of the aborigines in Latium and eponymous hero of the Latin race. He was believed to be either the son of the Greek hero ODYSSEUS and the enchantress CIRCE or the son of the Roman god FAUNUS and the NYMPH Marica. According to the *Aeneid*, the hero AENEAS landed at the mouth of the Tiber River and was welcomed by Latinus, the peaceful ruler whose daughter Lavinia he ultimately married.

LAUMA \ˈlaù-mä\ (Latvian), Lithuanian Laumė \ˈlaù-mä\, or Deivė \ˈdʸä-vä\, in Baltic FOLKLORE, fairy who appears as a beautiful naked maiden with long fair hair. *Lauma*s dwell in the forest near water or stones. Being unable to give birth, they often kidnap babies to raise as their own. Sometimes they marry young men and become excellent wives, perfectly skilled in all domestic work. They are noted as swift spinners and weavers, and, when they spin on Thursday evenings and launder after sunset on the other days, no mortal woman is allowed to do the same.

*Lauma*s are benevolent, motherly beings, helpful to orphans and poor girls, but they are extremely vindictive when angered, particularly by disrespectful men.

Among the Lithuanians, a *laumė* was sometimes called *laumė-ragana*, indicating that she may have been a prophetess (*ragana*) at one time. By the 18th century *laumė* was totally confused with *ragana* and came to denote a witch or hag capable of changing into a snake or toad. Not only could a *laumė* fly, she could also transform people into birds, dogs, and horses and dry up a cow's milk. Similarly, in modern Latvian *lauma* is a hag and *lauminet* means "to practice WITCHCRAFT."

LAZARUS, MORITZ \ˈlät-sä-rùs\ (b. Sept. 15, 1824, Filehne, Prussia [now Wieleń, Pol.]—d. April 13, 1903, Meran, Austria [now Merano, Italy]), Jewish philosopher and psychologist, a leading opponent of ANTI-SEMITISM and a founder of comparative psychology.

The son of a rabbinical scholar, Lazarus studied Hebrew literature and history, law, and philosophy at Berlin. He served as professor at Bern (1860–66), at the Kriegs Akademie in Berlin (1867–73), and at the Friedrich Wilhelm University (now Humboldt University of Berlin; 1873).

Lazarus' philosophy stated that truth must be sought in psychological investigation and the psychologist must study humanity from the historical or comparative standpoint, analyzing the elements that constitute the fabric of society. To further this *Völkerpsychologie*, he founded, with the philologist H. Steinthal, the journal *Zeitschrift für Völkerpsychologie und Sprachwissenschaft* (1859). His chief philosophical work is *Das Leben der Seele*, 3 vol. (1855–57; "The Life of the Soul").

In both 1869 and 1871 Lazarus was president of the Liberal Jewish synods at Leipzig and Augsburg. His works on Jewish subjects include *Treu und frei: Reden und Vorträge über Juden und Judenthum* (1887; "Faithful and Free: Speeches and Lectures About Jews and Judaism"); a monograph on the prophet JEREMIAH (1894); and *Die Ethik des Judentums*, 2 vol. (vol. 1, 1898; vol. 2, 1911; *The Ethics of Judaism*), which soon achieved the rank of a standard work.

Moritz Lazarus, 1892
By courtesy of the Staatsbibliothek Preussischer Kulturbesitz, Berlin

LEAH \'lē-ə, 'lā-ə\, *also spelled* Lia \'lī-ə\, in the OLD TESTAMENT, first wife of JACOB and the traditional ancestor of five of the TWELVE TRIBES OF ISRAEL. Leah was the mother of six of Jacob's sons: REUBEN, SIMEON, Levi (*see* LEVITE), ISSACHAR, ZEBULUN, and JUDAH (GENESIS 29:31–35; 30:17–20).

After Jacob had deprived his brother ESAU of his birthright and blessing (Genesis 25:29–34; 27:1–40), he took refuge in the household of his uncle Laban (Genesis 27:43; 28:1–5). There he fell in love with Laban's younger daughter, Rachel, working for Laban seven years to win her hand. On the night of the nuptial feast, however, Laban deceived him by sending in Leah; thus, Jacob was compelled to work another seven years for Rachel (Genesis 29:1-30). Jacob did not love Leah, but God consoled her with children before allowing Rachel to become pregnant. According to some traditions, she was buried in Hebron on the west bank of the Jordan River (Genesis 49:31).

LECTIONARY \'lek-shə-,ner-ē\, in CHRISTIANITY, a book containing portions of the BIBLE appointed to be read on particular days of the year. The word is also used for the list of such SCRIPTURE lessons. The early Christians adopted the Jewish custom of reading extracts from the OLD TESTAMENT on the SABBATH. They soon added extracts from the writings of the Apostles and Evangelists. During the 3rd and 4th centuries, several systems of lessons were devised for churches of various localities.

At first, the lessons were marked off in the margins of manuscripts of the Scriptures. Later, special lectionary manuscripts were prepared, containing in sequence the appointed passages. The Greek church developed two forms of lectionaries, one (*Synaxarion*) arranged in accord with the ecclesiastical year and beginning with EASTER, the other (*Mēnologion*) arranged according to the civil year (beginning September 1) and commemorating the festivals of various saints and churches. Other national churches produced similar volumes. Among the Western churches during the medieval period the ancient usage at Rome prevailed, with its emphasis on ADVENT.

During the 16th-century REFORMATION the LUTHERANS and Anglicans (*see* ANGLICAN COMMUNION) made changes in the

ROMAN CATHOLIC lectionaries, Luther including a greater proportion of doctrinal passages. In the Anglican church, the first edition of THE BOOK OF COMMON PRAYER assigned for each day a passage of the Old Testament and the NEW TESTAMENT to be read at both the morning and evening services. Nearly all the saints' days were dropped, and the new system assigned chapters of the Bible to be read consecutively.

LECTISTERNIUM \,lek-tə-'stər-nē-əm\ (Latin, from *lectum sternere*, "to spread a couch [with blankets or cushions]"), ancient Greek and Roman rite in which a meal was offered to gods and goddesses whose representations were laid upon a couch positioned in the open street. On the first occasion of the rite (399 BCE), which originated in Greece, couches were prepared for three pairs of gods: APOLLO and Latona, Hercules (*see* HERACLES) and DIANA, MERCURY and NEPTUNE. The feast, lasting for seven or eight days, was also celebrated by private individuals; the citizens kept open house, debtors and prisoners were released, and everything was done to banish sorrow. In later times, similar honors were paid to other divinities. The rite largely replaced the old Roman *epulum* and *daps*, in which the god was not visibly represented. In Christian times, the word was used for a feast in memory of the dead.

LEDA \'lē-də\, in Greek mythology, daughter of Thestius, king of Aetolia, and wife of Tyndareus, king of Lacedaemon; alternatively, mother by Tyndareus of Clytemnestra and Castor, one of the DIOSCURI. She was also believed to have been the mother (by ZEUS, who had approached her in the form of a swan) of the other twin, Polydeuces, and of HELEN of Troy, both of whom hatched from eggs. Variant tales gave divine parentage to both the twins and possibly also to Clytemnestra, with all three of them having hatched from the eggs of Leda, while others say that Leda bore the twins to her mortal husband, Tyndareus. Still other variants say that Leda may have hatched Helen from an egg laid by the goddess NEMESIS, who was similarly approached by Zeus in the form of a swan.

LEE, ANN \'lē\, *byname* Mother Ann (b. Feb. 29, 1736, Manchester, Eng.—d. Sept. 8, 1784, Watervliet, N.Y., U.S.), religious leader who brought the SHAKER sect from England to the American colonies.

The daughter of a blacksmith, she was a factory worker who in 1758 joined the Shaking Quakers, an offshoot of the Quakers. She married in 1762, an unhappy union that probably influenced her later doctrinal insistence on CELIBACY.

In 1770, during a period of religious persecution by the English authorities, she was imprisoned and while in jail became convinced of the truth of certain religious ideas perceived in a vision. She came to believe that sexual lust impeded Christ's work and that only through celibacy could men and women further his kingdom on earth. Four years later, commanded in another vision, Lee persuaded her husband, brother, and six other followers to emigrate to America. There, her followers founded a settlement in the woods of Niskeyuna (now Watervliet), near Albany (in present-day New York state). Beginning with converts from nearby settlements, the Shaker movement grew and began to spread throughout New England to embrace thousands. Mother Ann, as she came to be known, was believed to have ushered in the MILLENNIUM, for the Shakers asserted that, as Christ had embodied the masculine half of God's dual nature, so she embodied the female half.

In 1780 Mother Ann was imprisoned for treason because

of her pacifist doctrines and her refusal to sign an OATH of allegiance. She was soon released and in 1781–83 toured New England. According to witnesses, she performed a number of miracles, including healing the sick by touch.

LEI-KUNG \ˈlā-ˈgu̇ŋ\, *Pinyin* Leigong, *also called* Lei-shen \-ˈshən\ (Chinese: "Lord of Thunder"), Chinese Taoist and folk deity who, when so ordered by heaven, punishes earthly mortals guilty of secret crimes and evil spirits who have used their knowledge of TAOISM to harm human beings.

Lei-kung is depicted as a fearsome creature with claws, bat wings, and a blue body and wears only a loincloth. Lei-kung's assistants are those capable of producing other heavenly phenomena: lightning (Tien-mu), clouds (Yün-t'ung), rain (Yü-tzu), and winds (Feng-po, later transformed into the goddess Feng p'o-p'o).

LEMMINKÄINEN \ˈlem-mēn-ˌka-ē-nen\, hero of Finnish traditional songs. In these songs Lemminkäinen travels to an otherworldly place where he overcomes many obstacles such as a ditch full of burning rocks and a fence made of snakes. When he reaches his goal he must also succeed at a series of tests and best his host in a wizard's contest. The narrative up until this point is reminiscent of shamanistic tales of travels to the otherworld, but it takes a different turn when Lemminkäinen is killed. In some versions it is done with a hollow reed, in others with a snake, but in all tales he is killed with the only weapon against which he is defenseless. After Lemminkäinen's death, his mother goes to great lengths to retreive his body and she finally succeeds, but her attempts to revive it are successful in only a few versions of the story. This last part may show some Christian influence and also influence from the Nordic story of the death of BALDER.

LEMURES \ˈle-mə-ˌrās, ˈlem-yə-ˌrēz\, *also called* Larvae, in ROMAN RELIGION, wicked and fearsome specters of the dead. Appearing in grotesque and terrifying forms, they were said to haunt their living relatives and cause them injury. To propitiate these ghosts and keep them from the household, ritual observances called Lemuria were held yearly on May 9, 11, and 13. These Lemuria, reputedly instituted by Romulus in expiation of his brother's murder, required the father of every family to rise at midnight, purify his hands, toss black beans for the spirits to gather, and recite entreaties for the spirits' departure.

LENT, in the Christian church, period of penitential preparation for EASTER. In Western churches it begins on ASH WEDNESDAY, 6 weeks before Easter, and provides for a 40-day fast (Sundays are excluded), in imitation of Jesus Christ's fasting in the wilderness. In Eastern churches it begins eight weeks before Easter (both Saturdays and Sundays are excluded as fast days).

Since apostolic times a period of preparation and fasting has been observed before the Easter festival. It was a time of preparation of candidates for BAPTISM and a time of penance for sinners. In the early centuries fasting rules were strict, as they still are in Eastern churches. One meal a day was allowed in the evening, and meat, fish, eggs, and butter were forbidden. In the West these fasting rules have gradually been relaxed. The strict law of fasting among ROMAN CATHOLICS was dispensed with during World War II, and only Ash Wednesday and GOOD FRIDAY are now kept as Lenten fast days, though the emphasis on penitential practice remains.

LEO I, SAINT \ˈlē-ō\, *byname* Leo the Great (b. late 4th century, Tuscany?—d. Nov. 10, 461, Rome; Western feast day November 10, Eastern feast day February 18), pope from 440 to 461, master exponent of papal supremacy. His pontificate—which saw the disintegration of the Roman Empire in the West and the formation in the East of theological differences that were to split Christendom—was devoted to safeguarding orthodoxy and securing the unity of the Western church.

Consecrated on Sept. 29, 440, as successor to St. Sixtus III, Leo worked to suppress HERESY, which he regarded as the cause of corruption and disunity. The monk Eutyches of Constantinople had founded Eutychianism, a form of MONOPHYSITISM holding that Christ had only one nature, his human nature being absorbed in his divine nature. PATRIARCH Flavian of Constantinople excommunicated Eutyches, who then appealed to Leo. Leo sent Flavian (449) his celebrated *Tome*, which rejected Eutyches' teaching and argued that Christ's natures coexist and his INCARNATION reveals how human nature is restored to perfect unity with divine being. The Council (451) of Chalcedon (modern Kadıköy, Turkey), summoned to condemn Eutychianism, declared that Leo's *Tome* was the ultimate truth.

Leo held that papal power was granted by Christ to St. Peter alone and that that power was passed on by Peter to his successors. He cautioned the bishop of Thessalonica that, although he had been entrusted with office and shared Leo's solicitude, he was "not to possess the plenitude of power." Leo further enhanced the prestige of the PAPACY and helped to place Western leadership in its hands by dealing with invading barbarian tribes. He persuaded the Huns not to attack Rome in 452 and the Vandals not to sack Rome when they occupied it in 455. Leo was declared a doctor of the church by Pope Benedict XIV in 1754.

Leo I, detail of a miniature from an ecclesiastical calendar, 10th century
Biblioteca Apostolica Vaticana

LEO X, POPE, *original name* Giovanni de' Medici (b. Dec. 11, 1475, Florence—d. Dec. 1, 1521, Rome), one of the most extravagant of the Renaissance popes (reigned 1513–21), who made Rome a center of European culture and raised the PAPACY to significant political power in Europe. However, he depleted the papal treasury, and, by his response to the developing REFORMATION, he contributed to the dissolution of the unified Western church. Leo excommunicated MARTIN LUTHER in 1521.

LEO XIII, POPE, *original name* Vincenzo Gioacchino Pecci (b. March 2, 1810, Carpineto Romano, Papal States—d. July 20, 1903, Rome), head of the ROMAN CATHOLIC church (1878–1903) who brought a new spirit to the PAPACY, manifested in a more conciliatory position toward civil government, through care that the church not be opposed to scientific progress, and through an awareness of the pastoral and social needs of the times.

Pecci's family was of the lower nobility. After his early education in Viterbo and Rome he completed his studies at the Accademia dei Nobili Ecclesiastici (Academy of Noble Ecclesiastics) in Rome. In 1837 he was ordained a priest and entered the diplomatic service of the Papal States. He was made delegate (the equivalent of provincial governor) of Benevento in 1838 and was transferred in 1841 to the more important delegation of Perugia. In January 1843 he was appointed nuncio to Brussels and shortly after was consecrated an archbishop. But King Leopold I, considering him less docile than his predecessor, soon demanded his recall. He was then named, early in 1846, bishop of Perugia, a small DIOCESE to which he was confined for 32 years, despite his having been made a CARDINAL in 1853; his harsh judgment of the opposition in the Papal States to the Roman Revolution of 1848 and his concern to avoid useless conflicts with the Italian authorities after the annexation of Umbria in 1860 made Rome wrongly suspect him of liberal sympathies.

During this period of exile Pecci occupied himself with the renewal of Christian philosophy and studied particularly the writings of ST. THOMAS AQUINAS. He was also led to reconsider the problem of the relations between the church and modern society and became increasingly convinced of the mistake committed by ecclesiastical authorities in taking a fearful, negative attitude toward the aspirations of the times. In 1877 he was named camerlengo, the office of chief administrator of the church in the event that the pope dies.

At the death of PIUS IX in February 1878 Cardinal Pecci was elected on the third ballot. The age of the new pope and his delicate health caused speculation that his pontificate would be brief. But, in fact, he directed the church for a quarter of a century.

Pius IX had been a strong, conservative authoritarian, both in his governing of the church and in his opposition to the new Italian government that annexed the Papal States. Although the pontificate of Leo XIII had a new spirit, the new pope was as intractable as his predecessor on the principle of the temporal sovereignty of the pope and continued to consider the traditional doctrine of the Christian state as an ideal. He reacted strongly against secular liberalism. In church administration he continued to accentuate the centralization of authority in the papacy rather than in the national churches and reinforced the power of the nuncios (papal legates accredited as ambassadors to civil governments). He renewed the condemnations of rationalism—the theory that reason is the primary source of knowledge and of spiritual truth—and pursued with fresh vigor the reestablishment of the philosophy of St. Thomas Aquinas.

In other respects, however, Leo XIII's pontificate was characterized by change. In his relations with civil governments, Leo XIII showed his preference for diplomacy. He was also an intellectual sympathetic to scientific progress and to the need for the church to demonstrate itself open to such progress. In several instructions he recommended that CHURCH AND STATE live together in peace within the framework of modern society. The ENCYCLICAL *Rerum Novarum* ("Of New Things") in 1891 showed that the papacy had cautiously taken cognizance of the problems of the working class. He supported the organization of the Catholic laity and the attempt to create a link between the Anglican church and Rome (despite his rejection of the validity of Anglican ORDINATION). During the last years of his pontificate there was a hardening of church policy and a more reserved attitude toward Christian democracy.

LESHY \'lʸe-shə̇y\, in Slavic mythology, forest spirit. The *leshy* is a sportive spirit who enjoys playing tricks on people, though when angered he can be treacherous. He is seldom seen, but his voice can be heard in the forest laughing, whistling, or singing. When the *leshy* is spotted, he can be easily recognized; for, though he often has the appearance of a man, his eyebrows, eyelashes, and right ear are missing and his head is somewhat pointed. In his native forest the *leshy* is as tall as the trees, but, the moment he steps beyond, he shrinks to the size of grass.

The Ukrainians living in steppe country lack a fully articulated *leshy* and know about him from hearsay. Similar to the *leshy* are the field spirit (*polevoy*) and, perhaps, the water spirit (VODYANOY).

LEŚYĀ \'lāsh-yä\ (Sanskrit: "light," "tint"), according to JAINISM, the special aura of the soul that can be described in terms of color, scent, touch, and taste and that indicates the stage of spiritual progress reached by the creature, whether human, animal, demon, or divine. The *leśyā* is determined by the adherence of karmic matter to the soul, resulting from both good and bad actions. This adherence is compared to the way in which particles of dust adhere to a body smeared with oil.

The JĪVA, or soul, is classified according to the good or bad emotions that hold sway. Thus the *saleśī* ("having *leśyā*") are all those who are swayed by any of the emotions, and the *aleśī* are those liberated beings (SIDDHAS) who no longer experience any feelings—neither pain nor pleasure, nor even humor. The three bad emotions (ill will, envy, and untruthfulness) give the *leśyā* a bitter taste, a harsh or dull color, a smell that can be likened to the odor of a dead cow, and a texture rougher than the blade of a saw. The three good emotions (good will, union with goodness, and nondistinction) lend the aura the fragrance of sweet flowers, the softness of butter, a taste sweeter than fruit or honey, and a pleasing hue ranging from bright red to pure white.

LETHE \'lē-thē\ (Greek *lēthē*, literally, "act of forgetting," "forgetfulness," or "oblivion"), in Greek mythology, daughter of ERIS (Strife). Lethe is also the name of a river or plain in the Underworld.

In Orphism, it was believed that the newly dead who drank from the River Lethe would lose all memory of their past existence. The initiated were taught to seek instead the river of memory, MNEMOSYNE, thus securing the end of the transmigration of the soul. At the oracle of Trophonius near Lebadeia (modern Levadhia, Greece), which was thought to be an entrance to the Underworld, there were two springs called Lethe and Mnemosyne.

Aristophanes' *The Frogs* mentions a plain of Lethe. In Book X of Plato's *The Republic* the souls of the dead must drink from the "river of Forgetfulness" before rebirth. In the works of the Latin poets Lethe is one of the five rivers of the Underworld.

LETO \'lē-tō\, *Latin* Latona \lə-'tō-nə\, in classical mythology, TITAN daughter of Coeus and PHOEBE and mother of APOL-

LO and ARTEMIS. Leto, pregnant by ZEUS, sought a place of refuge to be delivered. She finally reached the isle of Delos, which, according to some, was a wandering rock borne about by the waves until it was fixed to the bottom of the sea for the birth of Apollo and Artemis. In later versions the wanderings of Leto were ascribed to the jealousy of Zeus's wife, HERA, who was enraged at Leto's bearing Zeus's children. The foundation of DELPHI followed immediately upon the birth of Apollo. Leto has been identified with the Lycian goddess Lada. She was also known as Kourotrophos (Rearer of Youths).

LEUCOTHEA \lü-'kä-thē-ə\ (Greek: "White Goddess [of the Foam]"), in Greek mythology, a sea goddess first mentioned in Homer's *Odyssey*, in which she rescues ODYSSEUS from drowning. She was identified with Ino, daughter of the Phoenician Cadmus; because she cared for the infant god DIONYSUS, the goddess HERA drove Ino (or her husband, ATHAMAS) mad so that she and her son, Melicertes, leaped into the sea. Both were changed into marine deities—Ino as Leucothea, Melicertes as Palaemon. The body of Melicertes was carried by a dolphin to the Isthmus of Corinth and deposited under a pine tree. There Melicertes' body was found by his uncle SISYPHUS, who removed it to Corinth and instituted the ISTHMIAN GAMES and sacrifices in his honor.

LEVI BEN GERSHOM \'lē-vī-ben-'gər-shəm, -səm\, *also called* Gersonides \gər-'sä-nə-ˌdēz\, Leo de Bagnols, Leo Hebraeus, *or* (*by acronym*) Ralbag \'räl-ˌbäg\ (b. 1288, Bagnols-sur-Cèze, France—d. 1344), French Jewish mathematician, philosopher, astronomer, and Talmudic scholar.

Levi's mathematical works, written between 1321 and 1343, dealt with such topics as arithmetical operations (*Sefer ha-mispar* ["Book of the Number"]), sine theorems for plane triangles and tables of sines (*De sinibus, chordis et arcubus* ["On Sines, Chords, and Arcs"]), and Euclidean geometry (*De numeris harmonicis* ["The Harmony of Numbers"]). Influenced by the works of Aristotle and IBN RUSHD (Averroës), Levi wrote *Sefer ha-hekkesh ha-yashar* (1319; Latin *Liber syllogismi recti;* "Book of Proper Analogy"), criticizing several arguments of Aristotle; he also wrote commentaries on the works of both philosophers.

Levi presupposed an audience familiar with these commentaries, medieval astronomical literature, and the works of Ibn Rushd when he wrote (1317–29) his major work, *Sefer milḥamot Adonai* ("The Book of the Wars of the Lord"; partial trans. *Die Kämpfe Gottes*, 2 vol.). The work treats the immortality of the soul; dreams, DIVINATION, and PROPHECY; divine knowledge; providence; celestial spheres and separate intellects and their relationship with God; and the creation of the world, miracles, and the criteria by which one recognizes the true prophet.

Leucothea giving Dionysus a drink from the horn of plenty, antique bas-relief; in the Lateran Museum, Rome
Alinari—Art Resource

Levi's work has been criticized because of his bold expression and the unconventionality of his thought, but he continued to exercise wide influence into the 19th century.

LEVITE \'lē-ˌvīt\, member of a group of clans of religious functionaries in ancient Israel who apparently were given a special religious status, conjecturally for slaughtering idolaters of the GOLDEN CALF during the time of MOSES (EXODUS 32:25–29).

There is no clear evidence that the Levites originally constituted a secular tribe that was named after Levi, the third son born to JACOB and his first wife, LEAH. Unlike the TWELVE TRIBES OF ISRAEL, the Levites were not assigned a specific territory of their own when the Israelites took possession of the Promised Land but rather 48 cities scattered throughout the entire country (Numbers 35:1–8). Moreover, their ranks may have included representatives of all the tribes. It is equally unclear what relationship existed between the Levites and the members of the PRIESTHOOD, who were descendants of AARON, himself a descendant of Levi. The priests of Aaron (*see* AARONIC PRIESTHOOD) clearly acquired sole right to the Jewish priesthood. Those who performed subordinate services associated with public worship were known as Levites. In this capacity, the Levites were musicians, gatekeepers, guardians, Temple officials, judges, and craftsmen.

LEVITICUS RABBAH \li-'vi-ti-kəs-rä-'bä\, compilation of 37 propositional compositions on topics suggested by the book of Leviticus, *c.* 450 CE, which argues that the rules of sanctification for the PRIESTHOOD deliver a message of the salvation of all Israel (*i.e.,* the Jewish people). The compilation makes no pretense at a systematic EXEGESIS of sequences of verses of SCRIPTURE, abandoning the verse-by-verse mode of organizing discourse; each of the 37 chapters is cogent in its own terms. The message of Leviticus Rabbah is that the laws of history may be known and that these laws focus upon the holy life of the community. If Israel obeys the laws of society aimed at Israel's sanctification, then the foreordained history, resting on the merit of the ancestors, will unfold as Israel hopes. Israel, for its part, can affect its destiny and effect salvation. The authorship of Leviticus Rabbah has thus joined the two great motifs, sanctification and salvation, by reading a biblical book, Leviticus, that is devoted to the former in the light of the requirements of the latter. In this way the authors made their fundamental point, that salvation at the end of history depends on sanctification in the here and now.

LI \'lē\, *Pinyin* li, CONFUCIAN concept often rendered as "ritual," "proper conduct," "ceremony," or "propriety." Originally, *li* denoted rites performed to sustain social and cosmic order. Confucians, however, reinterpreted it to mean formal social patterns that, in their view, the ancients had abstracted from cosmic models to order communal life. From customary patterns, *li* came to mean conventional norms, yielding a new concept of an internalized code of civility that defined proper human conduct. It is this concept that is detailed in the Confucian Classic called the LI-CHI ("Record of Rites"). Yet, even in this context, *li* transcends mere politeness or convention, for, as a derivative of natural order, it retains a cosmic role, harmonizing humans with nature.

LI \\'lē\\, *Pinyin* li, in Chinese NEO-CONFUCIAN thought, cosmological, metaphysical, and moral principle meaning "reason." It refers to the inner order of the physical universe and moral tradition. CHU HSI is the most famous philosopher to advance this concept.

LI AO \\'lē-'aù\\, *Pinyin* Li Ao (d. *c.* 844, China), Chinese scholar who helped reestablish CONFUCIANISM at a time when it was severely challenged by BUDDHISM and TAOISM, laying the groundwork for the Neo-Confucianists of the Sung dynasty (960–1279).

Li was a high official of the T'ang dynasty (618–907) who was apparently friends with or a disciple of the great Confucian stylist and thinker HAN YÜ. Unlike Han Yü, Li was much influenced by Buddhism, helping to integrate many Buddhist ideas into Confucianism and beginning the development of a metaphysical framework to justify Confucian ethical thinking; he insisted that questions of human nature and human destiny were central to Confucianism, ideas that became the core of later NEO-CONFUCIANISM. His quotations from the TA-HSÜEH ("Great Learning"), the CHUNG-YUNG ("Doctrine of the Mean"), and the I-CHING ("Classic of Changes") helped bring recognition to these previously obscure works. Finally, Li helped establish the importance of MENCIUS for later Neo-Confucians as almost the equal to that of CONFUCIUS.

LIBATION, act of pouring a liquid (frequently wine, but sometimes milk or other fluids) as a sacrifice to a deity.

LIBERALISM, THEOLOGICAL, form of religious thought that establishes religious inquiry on the basis of a norm other than the authority of tradition. It was an important influence in PROTESTANTISM from the mid-17th century through the 1920s.

The defining trait of this liberalism is a will to be liberated from the coercion of external controls and a consequent concern with inner motivation. The first overt evidence of this temper of mind came during the Renaissance, when curiosity about natural man and appreciation for the human spirit developed. The modern period of theological liberalism began, however, in the 17th century with René Descartes, who designated the thinking self as the primary substance from which the existence of other realities was to be deduced (except that of God), and thereby initiated a mode of thinking that remained in force through the 19th century and laid the ground for the presuppositions of this modern consciousness: (1) confidence in human reason, (2) primacy of the person, (3) immanence of God, and (4) meliorism (the belief that human nature is improvable and is improving). The many persons influencing religious thought in this period included the philosophers Benedict de Spinoza, Gottfried Wilhelm Leibniz, Gotthold Ephraim Lessing, John Locke, and Samuel Clarke.

The second stage of theological liberalism, ROMANTICISM, lasted from the late 18th century to the end of the 19th and was marked by the significance it placed on individual experience as a distinctive source of meaning. The American and French revolutions provided the symbol of this spirit of independence and dramatically exemplified it in political action. Jean-Jacques Rousseau and Immanuel Kant were the architects of Romantic liberalism. In theology, FRIEDRICH SCHLEIERMACHER, called the father of modern Protestant theology, was outstanding. Unlike Kant, who saw in moral will the clue to man's higher nature, Schleiermacher identified the feeling of absolute dependence as simultaneously that which "signifies God for us" and that which is distinctive in the religious response. Thus, self-consciousness becomes God-consciousness; the Christian is brought to this deeper vein of self-consciousness through the man Jesus, in whom the God-consciousness had been perfected.

ALBRECHT RITSCHL dominated liberal Protestant theology after Schleiermacher, and Wilhelm Herrmann and Adolf von Harnack were Ritschl's most prominent followers. In the United States, HORACE BUSHNELL was the most significant liberal theologian, along with WALTER RAUSCHENBUSCH, leader of the SOCIAL GOSPEL movement.

The third period of theological liberalism, MODERNISM, from the mid-19th century through the 1920s, was marked by the significance it placed on the notion of progress. The decisive events stimulating these interests were the Industrial Revolution and the publication of Charles Darwin's *Origin of Species* (1859). Modernists sought to bring religious thought into accord with modern knowledge and to solve issues raised by modern culture, and they transformed the study of Christian doctrine into the psychological, sociological, and philosophical study of RELIGIOUS EXPERIENCE, institutions, customs, knowledge, and values. Important figures during this period included Thomas Huxley, Herbert Spencer, William James, John Dewey, Shailer Mathews, Harry Emerson Fosdick, and ERNST TROELTSCH.

After the 1920s many theologically liberal ideas were challenged by neoorthodoxy, a theological movement in Europe and the United States that returned to the traditional language of Protestant orthodoxy and biblical faith centered in Christ, although it accepted modern critical methods of biblical interpretation.

LIBER AND LIBERA \\'lē-bər . . . 'lē-bə-rə\\, in ROMAN RELIGION, pair of cultivation deities of uncertain origin. Liber, though an old and native Italian deity, came to be identified with DIONYSUS. The triad CERES, Liber, and Libera (his female counterpart) represented in Rome, from early times and always under Greek influence, the Eleusinian DEMETER, Iacchus-Dionysus, and Kore (PERSEPHONE). At the festival of the Liberalia, held at Rome on March 17, the *toga virilis* was commonly assumed for the first time by boys who were of age. At the town of Lavinium, a month was consecrated to Liber, and the festival activities there were believed to make the seeds grow.

LIBERATION THEOLOGY, in late 20th-century ROMAN CATHOLICISM, movement centered in Latin America that sought to apply religious faith to the circumstances of the poor and the politically oppressed. It stressed both heightened awareness of the socioeconomic structures that caused social inequities and active participation in changing those structures.

Liberation theologians believed that God speaks particularly through the poor and that the BIBLE can be understood only when seen from the perspective of the poor. They perceived that the Roman Catholic church in Latin America was a church for and of the poor, a state fundamentally different from that of the church in Europe. In order to build this church, they established base communities, local Christian groups composed of 10 to 30 members each, that both studied the Bible and attempted to meet their parishioners' immediate needs for food, water, sewage disposal, and electricity. Many such base communities, led mostly by laypersons, sprang up throughout Latin America.

The birth of the movement is usually dated to the second Latin American Bishops' Conference, which was held in Medellín, Colombia, in 1968. The attending bishops issued a document affirming the rights of the poor and asserting that industrialized nations enriched themselves at the expense of Third World countries. The movement's seminal text, *Teología de la liberación* (1971; *A Theology of Liberation*), was written by Gustavo Gutiérrez, a Peruvian priest and theologian. Other leaders of the movement included Archbishop Oscar Arnulfo Romero of El Salvador (killed in 1980), Brazilian theologian Leonardo Boff, JESUIT scholar Jon Sobrino, and Archbishop Helder Câmara of Brazil.

The liberation theology movement gained strength in Latin America during the 1970s. Because of their insistence that ministry includes involvement in the political struggle of the poor against wealthy elites, liberation theologians were often criticized by those within the Roman Catholic church and others as naive advocates of Marxism and left-wing social activism. By the 1990s the Vatican, under Pope John Paul II, had begun trying to curb the movement's influence through the appointment of more conservative PRELATES in Brazil and elsewhere in Latin America.

LIBITINA \,li-bə-'tī-nə, -'tē-nə\, in ROMAN RELIGION, goddess of funerals. At her SANCTUARY in a sacred grove (perhaps on the Esquiline Hill), a piece of money was deposited whenever a death occurred. There the undertakers (*libitinarii*) had their offices, and there all deaths were registered for statistical purposes. The word Libitina thus came to be used for the business of an undertaker, funeral requisites, and, by poets, for death itself. Libitina was often mistakenly identified with VENUS Lubentia (Lubentina), an Italian goddess of gardens.

LI-CHI \'lē-'jē\, *Pinyin* Liji (Chinese: "Record of Rites"), one of the FIVE CLASSICS (WU-CHING) of Chinese Confucian literature, the original text of which is said to have been compiled by CONFUCIUS (551–479 BCE). The text was extensively reworked during the 1st century BCE by Elder Tai and his cousin Younger Tai.

Li-chi underscores moral principles and treats such subjects as royal regulations, ritual objects and sacrifices, education, music, and the doctrine of the mean (CHUNG-YUNG).

In 1190 CHU HSI, a NEO-CONFUCIAN philosopher, gave two chapters of *Li-chi* separate titles (*i.e.*, "Ta-hsüeh" and "Chung-yung") and published them together with two other CONFUCIAN texts under the name *Ssu-shu* ("FOUR BOOKS"). This collection is generally used to introduce Chinese students to Confucian literature.

LIEH-TZU \'lye-'dzə\, *Pinyin* Liezi (fl. 4th century BCE, China), legendary TAOIST master and presumed author of the Taoist work *Lieh-tzu*. Many of the writings attributed to Lieh-tzu have been identified as later forgeries.

Little is known of Lieh-tzu's life save that, like his contemporaries, he had a large number of disciples and roamed

through the different warring states into which China was then divided, advising kings and rulers. His work is distinguished stylistically by its wittiness and philosophically by its emphasis on determinism.

LIEH-TZU \'lye-'dzə\, *Pinyin* Liezi, Chinese Taoist classic bearing the name of Lieh-tzu, a legendary Taoist master. In its present form, the *Lieh-tzu* possibly dates from the 3rd or 4th century CE. The text echoes themes seen in the *Chuang-tzu*.

The *Lieh-tzu*'s "Yang Chu" chapter—named after a legendary figure of the 5th–4th century BCE, incorrectly identified as its author—acknowledges the futility of challenging the immutable and irresistible TAO (Way); it concludes that humans can look forward in this life only to sex, music, physical beauty, and material abundance, and even these goals are not always satisfied. Such fatalism implies a life of radical self-interest (a new development in TAOISM), according to which a person should make no sacrifice for the benefit of others.

LĪGO FEAST \'lē-gwȯ\, in BALTIC RELIGION, major celebration honoring the sun goddess, SAULE. It took place on St. John's Eve (June 23, Midsummer Eve). Bonfires were lighted and the young people leaped over them.

LIGUORI, SAINT ALFONSO MARIA DE' \äl-'fȯn-sō...lē-'gwȯ-rē\, Alfonso *also spelled* Alphonsus (b. Sept. 27, 1696, Marianella, Kingdom of Naples—d. Aug. 1, 1787, Pagani; canonized 1839; feast day August 1), Italian doctor of the church, one of the chief 18th-century moral theologians, and founder of the Redemptorists, a congregation dedicated primarily to PARISH and foreign MISSIONS.

After practicing law for eight years, he was ordained a priest in 1726. In 1732 he founded the Congregation of the Most Holy Redeemer, or the Redemptorists, at Scala. Dissension within the congregation culminated in 1777 when he was tricked into signing what he thought was a royal sanction for his rule but was actually a new rule devised by one of his enemies, thus causing the followers of the old rule to break away. In 1762 Pope Clement XIII made Alfonso bishop of Sant' Agata del Goti near Naples; he was obliged to resign the appointment in 1775 because of ill health. He was declared a doctor of the church by Pope PIUS IX in 1871, and in 1950 he was named patron of moralists and confessors by Pope PIUS XII.

Liguori's works include moral theology, best represented by his *Theologia moralis* (1748); ascetical and devotional writings, including *Visits to the Blessed Sacrament*, *The True Spouse of Jesus Christ* (for nuns), *Selva* (for priests), and *The Glories of Mary*—one of the most widely used manuals of devotion to the Virgin Mary; and dogmatic writings on such subjects as PAPAL INFALLIBILITY and the power of prayer. By the middle of the 20th century, his works had been translated into 60 languages. In theology Liguori is known as the principal exponent of equiprobabilism, a system of principles designed to guide those in doubt, whether they be free from or bound by a given civil or religious law.

LI-HSÜEH \'lē-'shwe\, *Pinyin* Lixue (Chinese: "School of Universal Principles"), school of NEO-CONFUCIAN philosophy, often called the Ch'eng-Chu after its leading philosophers, Ch'eng I and CHU HSI. The Li-hsüeh school stressed that the way to discover LI (conventional norms grounded in universal principles) is to investigate—by means of induction, deduction, the study of history, and participation in human affairs—the myriad things of the universe in which *li* is present.

LĪLĀ \'lē-lä\ (Sanskrit: "play," "sport," "spontaneity," or "drama"), in HINDUISM, a term that has several different meanings, most focusing in one way or another on the effortless or playful relation between the Supreme Reality and the contingent world. For the monistic philosophical tradition of VEDĀNTA, *līlā* refers to the manifestation of the Cosmic One, or BRAHMAN, expressed in every aspect of the empirical world. Some philosophers argue that *līlā* springs from the abundance of the Supreme Being's bliss, which provides a motive for creation.

In the devotional sects, *līlā* has other and more particular meanings. In the Śākta traditions, *līlā* is generally understood as a certain sweet and playful goodness that characterizes a universe whose essential nature is Śakti (the powerful, energetic principle) becoming Śakti. It is therefore associated with the goddesses LAKṢMĪ and Lalitā; one of the latter's names is Līlāvinodinī. The concept takes on other shadings and plays a central role in the thinking and practice of the Vaiṣṇava (*see* VAIṢṆAVISM) sects. In North India, the adventures of the god RĀMA, depicted in the epic RĀMĀYANA, are regarded as his "play," implying he entered the action as an actor might engage a drama—deeply involved, but with an element of freedom that prevents his being constrained by the "play" of life as lesser beings must be.

Among the worshipers of the god KRISHNA, *līlā* refers to the playful and erotic activities in which he sports with the young women of Braj (*gopīs*) and especially his favorite, RĀDHĀ, as they explore their mutual devotion. His interactions with others who surround him in this pastoral setting—whether heroic, playful, or deeply sad—also qualify as *līlā*. One of the most powerful images associated with this tradition is that of the circle (*rās*) dance, in which Krishna multiplies his form so that each *gopī* thinks it is she who is his partner. It provides the touchstone for a series of staged dramas called *rās līlā*s that replicate Krishna's paradigmatic "sports" so as to draw the devotees into an appropriate "mood" or emotion of love and *līlā* so that they experience the world itself in its true form as divine play. Similarly, the dramatic reenactment of the events of the *Rāmāyana* are known as Rām Līlā, celebrating his deeds in such a way as to draw devotees of this god into his cosmic play.

LILITH \'li-lith\, in Jewish FOLKLORE, female DEMON derived from the class of Mesopotamian demons called *lilû* (feminine: *lilītu*). In rabbinic literature Lilith is variously depicted as the mother of Adam's demonic offspring or as his first wife. The evil she threatened, especially against children, was counteracted by the wearing of an AMULET bearing

Lilith tempting Eve with an apple in the Garden of Eden, German woodcut, 1470
The Granger Collection

the names of the ANGELS. A cult of Lilith survived among some Jews as late as the 7th century CE.

LIMBO, in ROMAN CATHOLIC theology, border place between heaven and hell where dwell those souls who, though not condemned to punishment, are deprived of the joy of eternal existence with God in heaven. The concept of limbo probably developed in the Middle Ages. Two distinct kinds of limbo have been supposed to exist: (1) the *limbus patrum* ("fathers' limbo"), which is the place where the OLD TESTAMENT saints were thought to be confined until they were liberated by Christ in his "descent into hell"; and (2) the *limbus infantum*, or *puerorum* ("children's limbo"), which is the abode of those who have died without actual SIN but whose ORIGINAL SIN has not been washed away by BAPTISM. This "children's limbo" included not only unbaptized infants but also the mentally defective.

The question of the destiny of infants dying unbaptized presented itself to Christian theologians at a relatively early period. Generally speaking, the Greek Fathers of the Church inclined to optimism and the Latin Fathers to pessimism. Indeed, some of the Greek Fathers expressed opinions that are almost indistinguishable from the Pelagian view that children dying unbaptized might be admitted to eternal life, though not to the KINGDOM OF GOD. By contrast, ST. AUGUSTINE drew a sharp antithesis between the state of the saved and that of the damned. Later theologians followed Augustine in rejecting the notion of any final place intermediate between heaven and hell, but they otherwise were inclined to take the mildest possible view of the destiny of the irresponsible and unbaptized.

The Roman Catholic church in the 13th and 15th centuries made several authoritative declarations on the subject of limbo, stating that the souls of those who die in original sin only (*i.e.*, unbaptized infants) descend into hell but are given lighter punishments than those souls guilty of actual sin. The damnation of infants and also the comparative lightness of their punishment thus became articles of faith, but the details of the place such souls occupied in hell or the nature of their actual punishment remained undetermined. From the COUNCIL OF TRENT (1545–63) onward, there were considerable differences of opinion as to the extent of the infant souls' deprivation, with some theologians maintaining that the infants in limbo are affected with sadness because of a felt privation, and other theologians holding that the infants enjoy every kind of natural felicity, as regards their souls now and their bodies after the RESURRECTION. The concept of limbo has remained undefined and problematic and in the 20th century has increasingly been relegated to a marginal position in Roman Catholic theology.

LING \\'liŋ\\, *Pinyin* ling (Chinese: "numinous energy," or "magic power"), in Chinese popular religion, term used to refer to the effects achieved by supra-human agents such as gods, ancestors, and DEMONS. It is a particularly potent form of CH'I (matter-energy). The manifestation of *ling* is evidence of the active presence and efficacy of the divine realm. When associated with human beings, it can lead to their deification and to the emergence of devotional cults.

LIṄGA \\'liŋ-gə\\, *also spelled* liṅgam \\-gəm\\ (Sanskrit: "sign," "distinguishing symbol"), in HINDUISM, symbol of the god SHIVA, worshiped as an emblem of generative power.

The *liṅga* is the main object of worship in Śaivite temples (*see* ŚAIVISM) and the private shrines of Śaiva families throughout India. Historically, the *liṅga* was a representation of the phallus, as sculptures from the early centuries CE make clear, but many—probably most—modern Hindus do not think of the *liṅga* in these terms. In fact, the general stylization of the *liṅga* into a smooth cylindrical mass asserts a distinctively aniconic meaning, quite by contrast to the *mūrti*s (deities in image form) that serve otherwise as the most important foci of Hindu worship. This interplay is found in Śaivite temples themselves, where the *liṅga* is apt to be at the center, surrounded by a panoply of *mūrti*s. A sexual dimension remains in the most common form in which the *liṅga* appears today, where the lingam is placed in the center of a disc-shaped object called the YONI, a symbol of the female sexual organ, often associated with the goddess (ŚAKTI). The two together are a reminder that the male and female principles are forever inseparable and that together they represent the totality of all existence.

Liṅga, of a type known as a liṅgōdbhavamūrti, c. 900

Worship of the *liṅga* is performed with offerings of milk, water, fresh flowers, young sprouts of grass, fruit, leaves, and sun-dried rice. Among the most important of all *liṅga*s are the *svāyambhuva* ("self-originated") *liṅga*s, which are believed to have come into existence by themselves at the beginning of time; nearly 70 are worshiped in various parts of India. Another common icon in South India is the *liṅgōdbhavamūrti*, which shows Shiva emerging out of a fiery *liṅga*. This is a representation of the sectarian myth that the gods VISHNU and BRAHMA were once arguing about their respective importance when Shiva appeared in the form of a blazing pillar to quell their pride. Brahma took the form of a swan and flew upward to see if he could find the top of the pillar, and Vishnu took the form of a boar and dived below to find its source, but neither was successful, and both were compelled to recognize Shiva's superiority.

LING-PAO \\'liŋ-'baù\\, *Pinyin* Lingbao, form of TAOISM based upon one of the great Taoist scriptural traditions.

Ko Ch'ao-fu began composing the *Ling-pao ching* ("Classic of the Sacred Jewel") about 397 CE. He claimed that they had been first revealed to his own ancestor, the famous Ko Hsüan, early in the 3rd century. In these works the TAO is personified in a series of "celestial worthies" (*t'ien-tsun*), its primordial and uncreated manifestations. These in turn were worshiped by means of a group of liturgies, which, during the 5th century, became supreme in Taoist practice, completely absorbing the older, simpler rites of the T'IEN-SHI TAO ("Way of the Celestial Masters"). As each celestial worthy represented a different aspect of the Tao, so each ceremony of worship had a particular purpose, which it attempted to realize by distinct means. The rites as a whole were called *chai* ("retreat"), from the preliminary abstinence obligatory on all participants. They lasted a day and a night or for a fixed period of three, five, or seven days; the number of persons taking part was also specified, centering on a sacerdotal unit of six officiants. One's own salvation was inseparable from that of his ancestors; the Huang-lu chai (Retreat of the Yellow Register) was directed toward the salvation of the dead. Chin-lu chai (Retreat of the Golden Register), on the other hand, was intended to promote auspicious influences on the living. The T'u-t'an chai (Mud and Soot Retreat, or Retreat of Misery) was a ceremony of collective contrition; in Chinese civil law, confession resulted in an automatic reduction or suspension of sentence. These and other rituals were accomplished for the most part in the open, within a specially delimited sacred area, or altar (*t'an*), the outdoor complement of the oratory. The chanted liturgy, innumerable lamps, and clouds of billowing incense combined to produce in the participants a cathartic experience that assured these ceremonies a central place in subsequent Taoist practices.

LINUS \\'lī-nəs\\, *also spelled* Linos, in Greek mythology, the personification of lamentation. The name derives from the ritual cry *ailinos*, the refrain of a dirge.

According to an Argive story, Linus, child of APOLLO and Psamathe (daughter of Crotopus, king of Argos), was exposed at birth and was torn to pieces by dogs. In revenge, Apollo sent a Poine, or avenging spirit, which destroyed the Argive children. The hero Coroebus killed the Poine, and a festival, Arnis, otherwise called dog-killing day (*kunophontis*), was instituted, in which stray dogs were killed, sacrifice offered, and mourning made for Linus and Psamathe.

In a Theban variant, Linus was the son of OURANIA, muse of astronomy, and the musician Amphimarus, and he was himself a great musician. He invented the Linus song but was put to death by Apollo for presuming to be his rival.

A later, half-burlesque story related that Linus was the Greek hero HERACLES' music master and was killed by his pupil, whom he tried to correct.

LI SHAO-CHÜN \\'lē-'shaù-'jūen\\, *Pinyin* Li Shaojun (fl. 2nd century BCE, China), noted Chinese Taoist and occult practitioner (*fang-shih*) of the Han period. Li was the first known Taoist alchemist, the first to make the practice of certain hygienic exercises a part of Taoist rites, and the first to claim that a Taoist's ultimate goal was to achieve the status of HSIEN, or immortal sage.

In 133 BCE, Li persuaded the emperor Wu-ti that immortality could be achieved by eating from a cinnabar vessel that had been transmuted into gold. When that occurred, one would see the famous sages on P'eng-lai, the legendary isles of immortality. If one performed the proper rituals while gazing on these *hsien*, one would never die. The first step in the transmutation of cinnabar involved prayers to TSAO-CHÜN, the Furnace Prince. These prayers became an established part of some forms of later Taoist ritual, and shortly after Li's death, Tsao-chün came to be considered the first of the great Taoist divinities.

LITURGICAL MOVEMENT, 19th- and 20th-century effort in Christian churches to restore the active and intelligent participation of the people in the liturgy, or official rites, of CHRISTIANITY. The movement sought to make the liturgy both more attuned to early Christian traditions and more relevant to modern Christian life by simplifying rites, developing new texts (in the case of ROMAN CATHOLICISM, translating the Latin texts into the vernacular of individual countries), and reeducating both laity and clergy on their role in liturgical celebrations.

In the Roman Catholic church, the movement can be traced back to the mid-19th century, when it was initially connected with monastic worship, especially in the BENE-DICTINE communities in France, Belgium, and Germany. After about 1910, it spread to Holland, Italy, and England and subsequently to the United States. Changes introduced by POPE PIUS X that mark the beginning of the Liturgical Movement include his eucharistic decrees, which eased the regulations governing daily communion, his revival of the Gregorian plainsong, and his recasting of the breviary and of the missal.

POPE PIUS XII issued in 1947 the ENCYCLICAL *Mediator Dei*, in which he stressed the importance of liturgy and the need for people to participate. The reform of rites began with HOLY WEEK revisions in 1951 and 1955. The SECOND VATICAN COUNCIL (1962–65) recommended that Roman Catholics should actively take part in the liturgy; legislated the use of the vernacular for liturgies, overturning the traditional use of Latin as the sole liturgical language; and ordered the reform of all sacramental rites. A new LECTIONARY and calendar (the *Ordo Missae*) appeared in 1969, and a definitive Roman Missal was published in 1970.

Protestant churches have also revised texts and updated archaic expressions in their liturgical rites. The United Presbyterian Church published a liturgy for congregational use, the *Worshipbook*, in 1970. In 1978 the Lutheran Church in the United States published its revised *Lutheran Book of Worship*, offering more individual choices in liturgy and also an expanded variety of musical styles. In 1979 the Episcopal Church adopted a revised *Book of Common Prayer*, which offered a choice of texts, one preserving the traditional language.

LLEU \'hləi\, or Lleu Llaw Gyffes \-'hlaù-'gə-fes\: *see* LUGUS.

LLYR \'hlir\, in Celtic mythology, leader of one of two warring families of gods. In Welsh tradition, Llyr and his son Manawydan, like the Irish gods Lir and Manannán, were associated with the sea. Llyr's other children included BRÂN (Bendigeidfran), a god of bards and poetry; Branwen, wife of the sun god Matholwch, king of Ireland; and Creidylad (in earlier myths, a daughter of Lludd).

Hearing of Matholwch's maltreatment of Branwen, Brân and Manawydan led an expedition to avenge her. Brân was killed in the war, which left only seven survivors, among them Manawydan and Pryderi, son of PWYLL. Manawydan married Pryderi's mother, RHIANNON, and was thereafter closely associated with them.

LOGIA \'lō-gē-ə, -,ä\, hypothetical collection, either written or oral, of the sayings of JESUS, which might have been in circulation around the time of the composition of the SYNOPTIC GOSPELS. (The Greek word *logion*, which meant "oracular utterance" in Ancient Greek, was used in the plural form *logia* in the Greek of the SEPTUAGINT and NEW TESTAMENT to refer to bodies of sayings of sacred significance.) Most biblical scholars agree that MATTHEW and LUKE based their written accounts largely on The Gospel According to Mark, but both share a good deal of material that is absent from Mark. This shared material is largely made up of sayings attributed to Jesus, and this has led biblical scholars to hypothesize the existence of a source, perhaps the logia, from which the shared material is drawn.

The first references to the logia were made by Papias, a 2nd-century bishop of Hierapolis in Asia Minor, in his work *Logiōn kyriakōn exēgēseis* ("Interpretation of the Logia of the Lord"), and by other early Christian writers, such as Polycarp, a 2nd-century bishop of Smyrna in Asia Minor. According to EUSEBIUS, a 4th-century church historian, Papias wrote that the apostle Matthew arranged the logia of Jesus in an orderly form in Hebrew.

Some scholars contend that the logia was a collection of OLD TESTAMENT oracles predicting the coming of the MESSIAH, but this view has been challenged. In addition to the sayings of Jesus, Matthew and Luke share narrative material. Scholars have therefore hypothesized the existence of a kind of proto-gospel that incorporates the logia. Experts have called this hypothetical source Q (from German *Quelle*, "source"). The existence of the source Q is theoretical. Though the logia may not have been part of either Q or of the Old Testament messianic oracles, it is generally assumed that early Christians either wrote down or transmitted orally the sayings of Jesus, much as Jews of the period collected the sayings of respected RABBIS, and that this material was used by both Matthew and Luke.

LOGICAL POSITIVISM, *also called* Logical Empiricism, philosophical doctrine formulated in Vienna in the 1920s, according to which scientific knowledge is the only kind of factual knowledge and all traditional metaphysical doctrines are to be rejected as meaningless—that the "great unanswerable questions" about substance, causality, freedom, and God are unanswerable just because they are not genuine questions at all.

One fundamental element of Logical Positivism is the verification principle, which holds that a statement is meaningful only if it is either empirically verifiable or else tautological (*i.e.*, such that its truth arises entirely from the meanings of its terms). According to this principle, which gave what the positivists considered to be the touchstone of meaning, an assertion has meaning if and only if it is verifiable at least in principle by sense experience. Thus, religious and moral statements would be without literal significance, because there is no way in which they can be either justified or falsified (refuted). Such statements may influence feelings, beliefs, or conduct but not in the sense of being true or false and hence of imparting knowledge. A non-tautological statement has meaning only if some set of observable conditions is relevant to determining its truth or falsity; thus the meaning of a statement is the set of conditions under which it would be true.

In the years immediately after World War II this account of factual meaning was applied to theological statements, raising such questions as: What observable difference does it make whether it is true or false that "God loves us"?

Whatever tragedies occur, do not the faithful still maintain their belief? But if it is not possible to conceive of circumstances in which "God loves us" would have to be judged false, is not the statement factually empty or meaningless? This challenge evoked three kinds of response. Some Christian philosophers have declared it to be a non-challenge, on the ground that the positivists never succeeded in finding a precise formulation of the verification criterion that was fully satisfactory even to themselves. Among those who thought it necessary to face this challenge, one group granted that theological statements lack factual meaning and suggested that their proper use lies elsewhere, as expressing a way of looking at the world or a moral point of view and commitment. The other group claimed that THEISM is ultimately open to experiential confirmation. The theory of eschatological verification (developed by John Hick) holds that the belief in future postmortem experiences will be verified if true (though not falsified if false), and that in a divinely governed universe such experiences will take forms confirming theistic faith. Thus although the believer and the disbeliever do not have different expectations about the course of earthly history, they do expect the total course of the universe to be radically different. In the late 20th century attention has been directed to the multiple legitimate uses of language in the various language games developed within different human activities and forms of life; and it has been urged that RELIGIOUS BELIEF has its own autonomous validity, not subject to verificationist criteria. Statements about God and eternal life do not make true-or-false factual claims but express, in RELIGIOUS LANGUAGE, a distinctive attitude to life and way of engaging in it.

The basic problem that was never resolved concerning logical positivism is this: Is the verification principle itself meaningful? That is to say, is the principle itself verifiable?

LOGOS \'lō-gōs, 'lò-ˌgòs\ (Greek: "word," "reason," or "plan"), *plural* logoi, in Greek philosophy and theology, the divine reason implicit in the cosmos, ordering it and giving it form and meaning. Though the concept defined by the term logos is found in Greek, Indian, Egyptian, and Persian philosophical and theological systems, it became particularly significant in Christian writings and doctrines to describe or define the role of JESUS CHRIST as the principle of God active in the creation and the continuous structuring of the cosmos and in revealing the divine plan of salvation to man. It thus underlies the basic Christian doctrine of the preexistence of Jesus.

The idea of the logos in Greek thought harks back at least to the 6th-century-BCE philosopher Heracleitus, who discerned in the cosmic process a logos analogous to the reasoning power in man. Later, the Stoics, philosophers who followed the teachings of the thinker Zeno of Citium (4th–3rd century BCE), defined the logos as an active rational and spiritual principle that permeated all reality. They called the logos providence, na-

Forge stone incised with the face of Loki, his lips sewn, Horsens Fjord, Denmark; in the Werner Forman Archive, Arhus Kunstmuseum, Denmark
Art Resource

ture, god, and the soul of the universe, which is composed of many seminal logoi that are contained in the universal logos. PHILO JUDAEUS, a 1st-century-CE Jewish philosopher, taught that the logos was the intermediary between God and the cosmos, being both the agent of creation and the agent through which the human mind can apprehend and comprehend God. According to Philo and the Middle Platonists, the logos was both immanent in the world and at the same time the transcendent divine mind.

In the first chapter of The Gospel According to John, Jesus Christ is identified as "the Word" (Greek *logos*) incarnated, or made flesh. This identification of Jesus with the logos is based partly on the Jewish view that Wisdom is the divine agent that draws man to God and is identified with the word of God. The author of The Gospel According to John used this philosophical expression, which easily would be recognizable to readers in the Hellenistic world, to emphasize the redemptive character of the person of Christ. Just as the Jews had viewed the TORAH (the Law) as preexistent with God, so also the author of John viewed Jesus, but interprets the logos as inseparable from the person of Jesus and does not simply imply that the logos is the revelation that Jesus proclaims.

The identification of Jesus with the logos was further developed in the early church on the basis of Greek philosophical ideas. This development was dictated by the need to express the Christian faith in terms that would be intelligible to the Hellenistic world and to convey the view that CHRISTIANITY was superior to, or heir to, all that was best in pre-Christian philosophy. Thus, in their apologies and polemical works, the early Christian Fathers stated that Christ as the preexistent logos (1) reveals the Father to humankind and is the subject of the OLD TESTAMENT manifestations of God; (2) is the divine reason in which the whole human race shares, so that the 6th-century-BCE philosopher and others who lived with reason were Christians before Christ; and (3) is the divine will and word by which the worlds were framed.

LOKA \'lō-kə\ (Sanskrit: "world," "open space," "universe"), in the cosmography of HINDUISM, the universe or any particular division of it. The most common division of the universe is the *triloka*, or three worlds (heaven, earth, atmosphere; later, heaven, world, netherworld), each of which is divided into seven regions. Sometimes 14 worlds are enumerated: 7 above Earth and 7 below. The various divisions illustrate the Hindu concept of innumerable hierarchically ordered worlds. *Loka*s are often associated with particular divinities, a linkage that is carried over into BUDDHISM, with the deities replaced by Buddhas or BODHISATTVAS.

LOKI \'lō-kē\, in Norse mythology, cunning trickster who had the ability to change his shape and sex. Although his father was the GIANT Fárbauti, he was included among the AESIR (a tribe of gods). Loki was represented as the companion of the great gods ODIN and THOR, helping them with his clever plans but sometimes causing embarrassment and difficulty for them and himself. He also appeared as the enemy of the gods; he was the principal cause of the death of the god BALDER. Loki was punished by being bound to a rock. With the giantess Angerboda (Angrboda: "Distress Bringer"), Loki produced three evil progeny: HEL, the goddess of death; JÖRMUNGAND, the serpent surrounding the world; and FENRIR (Fenrisúlfr), the giant wolf that will swallow Odin at the end of the world. *See also* GERMANIC RELIGION.

The figure of Loki remains obscure; there is no trace of a cult, and the name does not appear in place-names.

LORD'S PRAYER, *Latin* Oratio Dominica, *also called* Pater Noster (Latin: "Our Father"), prayer taught by JESUS to his disciples and principal prayer used by all Christians in common worship. It appears in two forms in the NEW TESTAMENT, the shorter version in Luke 11:2–4 and the longer version in Matthew 6:9–13. In both contexts it is offered as a model of how to pray. Many scholars believe the version in Luke to be closer to the original, the extra phrases in Matthew's version having been added in liturgical use.

The Lord's Prayer resembles other prayers that came out of Jesus' time and contains three common Jewish elements: praise, petition, and a yearning for the coming KINGDOM OF GOD. It consists of an introductory address and seven petitions. The Matthean version used by the ROMAN CATHOLIC church is as follows:

◆ Our Father who art in Heaven,
 Hallowed be thy name;
 Thy Kingdom come;
 Thy will be done
 On earth as it is in heaven.
 Give us this day our daily bread;
 And forgive us our trespasses
 As we forgive those who trespass against us;
 And lead us not into temptation,
 But deliver us from evil. ◆

The English version of the Lord's Prayer used in many Protestant churches departs from the Roman Catholic version by use of "debts" and "debtors" rather than "trespasses" and "those who trespass against us," and adding the concluding DOXOLOGY (short formula of praise):

◆ For thine is the Kingdom
 And the power
 And the glory,
 Forever. ◆

This conclusion was probably added early in the Christian era, since it occurs in some early manuscripts of the Gospels and is used in both Roman Catholic and EASTERN ORTHODOX liturgies as an elaboration of the Lord's Prayer.

Biblical scholars disagree about Jesus' meaning in the Lord's Prayer. Some view it as "existential," referring to present human experience on earth, while others interpret it as eschatological, referring to the coming Kingdom of God. The prayer lends itself to both interpretations, and further questions are posed by the existence of different translations and the problems inherent in the process of translation. In the case of the term "daily bread," for example, the Greek word *epiousion*, which modifies "bread," has no known parallels in Greek writing and may have

meant "for tomorrow." The petition "Give us this day our daily bread" may thus be given the eschatological interpretation "Give us today a foretaste of the heavenly banquet to come." This interpretation is supported by Ethiopic versions and by ST. JEROME'S reference to the reading "bread of the future" in the lost Gospel According to the Hebrews.

LOTUS-EATER, *Greek plural* Lotophagoi, in Greek mythology, one of a tribe encountered by ODYSSEUS on his way back to Ithaca after the Trojan War. The local inhabitants invited Odysseus' scouts to eat of the mysterious plant. Those who did so were overcome by a blissful forgetfulness; they had to be dragged back to the ship and chained to the rowing-benches, or they would never have returned to their duties.

The Greeks called several non-narcotic plants *lōtos,* but the name may have been used in this case for the opium poppy, the ripe seedpod of which resembles the pod of the true lotus. The phrase "to eat lotus" is used metaphorically by numerous ancient writers to mean "to forget," or "to be unmindful."

LOTUS SUTRA \'sü-trə\, *Sanskrit* Saddharmapuṇḍarīka-sūtra \səd-'dər-mə-,pùn-də-'rē-kə-'sü-trə, -'där-\ ("Lotus of the Good Law [or True Doctrine] Sutra"), one of the earlier MAHĀYĀNA Buddhist texts venerated as the quintessence of truth by the East Asian T'IEN-T'AI (Japanese: Tendai) school and the Japanese NICHIREN sect.

In the *Lotus Sutra* the buddha spoken of has become the divine eternal buddha, who attained perfect enlightenment endless aeons ago. In keeping with this Buddhology, the goals of emancipation and sainthood are thought to be inferior expedients: here all beings are invited to become no less than fully enlightened buddhas through the grace of innumerable BODHISATTVAS.

Composed largely in verse, the *Lotus Sutra* has a total of 28 chapters and contains many charms and MANTRAS. It was first translated into Chinese *(Miao-fa lien-hua ching)* in the 3rd century CE and became extremely popular in China and Japan, where common belief held that the simple act of chanting it would bring salvation.

LOURDES \'lürd, 'lùrd\, PILGRIMAGE town, southwestern France, Hautes-Pyrénées *département,* Provence-Alpes-Côte-d'Azur region, southwest of Toulouse.

Situated at the foot of the Pyrenees and now on both banks of a torrent, the Gave de Pau, the town and its fortress formed a strategic stronghold in medieval times. The contemporary importance of Lourdes, however, dates from 1858 when, from February 11 to July 16, Marie-Bernarde Soubirous (*see* BERNADETTE OF LOURDES, SAINT), a 14-year-old girl, had numerous visions of the Virgin MARY in the nearby Massabielle grotto, on the left bank of the stream. The visions were declared authentic by the pope in 1862, and the veneration of Our Lady of Lourdes was authorized. The underground spring in the grotto, revealed to Bernadette, was declared to have miraculous qualities; and since then Lourdes has become a major pilgrimage center. Almost 3,000,000 pilgrims, about 50,000 of them sick or disabled, go there annually. The BASILICA, built above the grotto in 1876, eventually became overcrowded by the increasing number of pilgrims, and in 1958 an immense concrete underground church, seating 20,000, was inaugurated.

LOYOLA, SAINT IGNATIUS OF \ig-'nā-shē-əs, -shəs… lòi-'ō-lə\, *Spanish* San Ignacio de Loyola, *baptized* Iñigo (b.

1491, Loyola, Castile—d. July 31, 1556, Rome; canonized March 12, 1622; feast day July 31), Spanish theologian and one of the most influential figures in the Catholic COUNTER-REFORMATION of the 16th century, founder of the Society of Jesus (JESUITS) in Paris in 1534.

Born in the Basque province of Guipúzcoa the youngest son of a noble and wealthy family, in 1517 Ignatius became a knight in the service of a relative, Antonio Manrique de Lara, duke of Nájera and viceroy of Navarre. While defending the citadel of Pamplona against the French in 1521, Ignatius sustained a bad fracture of his right leg and damage to his left.

After treatment at Pamplona, he was transported tò Loyola, where he chose to undergo painful surgery to correct blunders made when the bone was first set. The result was a convalescence of many weeks, during which he read a life of Christ and a book on the lives of the saints. The version of the lives of the saints he was reading contained prologues to the various lives by a CISTERCIAN monk who conceived the service of God as a holy chivalry. After much reflection, he resolved to imitate the holy austerities of the saints in order to do penance for his sins.

In 1522 Ignatius went to Manresa, where he lived as a beggar, ate and drank sparingly, scourged himself, and for a time neither combed nor trimmed his hair and did not cut his nails. Daily he attended MASS and spent seven hours in prayer, often in a cave outside Manresa. While sitting by a river, he experienced what he described as a profound understanding. On this basis he sketched the fundamentals of *The Spiritual Exercises*, which he continued to revise until Pope Paul III approved it in 1548. *The Spiritual Exercises* is a manual of spiritual arms containing a vital and dynamic system of spirituality.

Ignatius left Barcelona on PILGRIMAGE in March 1523 and reached Jerusalem in September. He would have liked to settle there permanently, but the FRANCISCAN custodians of the shrines of the Latin church would not listen to this plan. After visiting Bethany, the Mount of Olives, Bethlehem, the Jordan, and Mount of Temptation, Ignatius left Palestine and reached Barcelona in March 1524.

Ignatius then decided to acquire a good education, convinced that a well-trained man would accomplish in a short time what one without training would never accomplish. He studied at Barcelona for nearly two years. In 1526 he transferred to Alcalá, and then Salamanca, each time acquiring disciples but meeting with charges of heresy; ultimately he was forbidden to teach until he had finished his studies. This prohibition induced Ignatius to leave his disciples and Spain.

From 1528 to 1535 he studied in Paris while living on alms. Eventually Ignatius won the M.A. of the university. He also gathered the companions who were to be cofounders with him of the Society of Jesus, among them FRANCIS XAVIER. On Aug. 15, 1534, they bound themselves by vows of poverty, chastity, and obedience, though as yet without the express purpose of founding a religious order.

Ignatius and most of his companions were ordained on June 24, 1537. Later, while in prayer, Ignatius seemed to see Christ with the cross on his shoulder and beside him God, who said, "I wish you to take this man for your servant," and Jesus took him and said, "My will is that you should serve us." On Christmas Day 1538 Ignatius said his first mass at the Church of St. Mary Major in Rome.

In 1539 the companions decided to form a permanent union, and in 1540 Pope Paul III approved the plan of the new order. Loyola was the choice of his companions for the

office of general of the order. The Society of Jesus developed rapidly under his hand. When he died there were about 1,000 Jesuits divided into 12 administrative units, called provinces. Loyola dispatched missionaries to Germany, India, the Congo, and Ethiopia. He founded the Roman College, embryo of the Gregorian University, and a German seminary. He also established a home for fallen women and one for converted Jews. In 1546 Loyola secret-

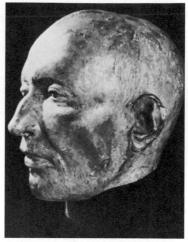

St. Ignatius of Loyola, death mask
By courtesy of the Archivum Romanum Societatis Iesu

ly received into the society Francis Borgia, duke of Gandía and viceroy of Catalonia. When word of this became public four years later it created a sensation. Borgia organized the Spanish provinces of the order and became the order's third general.

In the *Constitutions* of the Society of Jesus he decreed that his followers were to abandon some of the traditional forms of the religious life in favor of greater adaptability and mobility; they also renounced chapter government by the members in favor of a more authoritative regime. Loyola insisted on long and thorough training of his followers. Convinced that women are better ruled by women than by men, he excluded a female branch of the order.

Though frequently sick, he continued to direct the order until his death. He was beatified by Pope Paul V in 1609 and canonized by Pope Gregory XV in 1622. In 1922 he was declared patron of all spiritual retreats by Pope Pius XI.

LUCIFER \'lü-sə-fər\ (Latin: "Light Bearer"), *Greek* Phosphorus, *or* Eosphorus, in classical mythology, morning star (*i.e.*, the planet VENUS at dawn); personified as a male figure bearing a torch, Lucifer had almost no legend, but in poetry he was often herald of the dawn. In Christian times Lucifer came to be regarded as the name of SATAN before his fall. It was thus used by John Milton (1608–74) in *Paradise Lost*.

LUD \'lüd\, among the Votyaks and Zyryans, sacred grove where sacrifices were performed. The sacrificial ceremonies performed annually in the groves were usually centered on some ancient tree dedicated to a deity. The *lud*, surrounded by a high board or log fence, generally consisted of a grove of fir trees, a place for a fire, and tables for the sacrificial meal. The grove was so sacred that no unseemly behavior was allowed in its vicinity, and those with legitimate business at the enclosure had to bathe before entering it. People were forbidden to break even a branch from its trees, which was watched over by a special guardian whose position was hereditary. In some areas women and children were banned from the grove altogether. Each family had its own *lud*, and, in addition, there were great *lud*s at which the entire clan met for sacrificial feasts. All food had to be consumed on the premises, and the hides of the sacrificed animals were hung on the trees.

Similar sacrificial groves existed among most of the Finno-Ugrian peoples (*see* FINNO-UGRIC RELIGIONS). In the *keremet* of the Mordvins, sacrifices were made both upward to the sun or downward to the night. In groves of deciduous trees the HIGH GODS were worshiped, whereas the lower spirits lived in the fir groves. In the Cheremis *keremet* only the native language could be spoken because the deities would have been offended by foreign speech. Some of the groves were specifically dedicated to heroic ancestors, and carved images were reported present in the groves by the earliest travelers to the area.

The Finnish *hiisi* and Estonian *hiis* were apparently comparable groves. In Ingria sacred groves were still in use during the latter part of the 19th century, where prayers and offerings were directed to UKKO, a thunder god, and Sämpsä, a god of vegetation.

LUDI PUBLICI \\'lü-dē-'pü-blē-kē\\ (Latin: "public games"), ancient Roman spectacles, primarily consisting of chariot races and various kinds of theatrical performances, usually held at regular intervals in honor of some god; they are distinct from the gladiatorial contests (originally associated with funeral rites). A special magistrate presided over them. Oldest and most famous were the Ludi Romani, or Magni, dedicated to JUPITER and celebrated each year in September. Like the Ludi Apollinares (for APOLLO) and the Ludi Cereales (for CERES), they centered on the chariot races of the Circus Maximus. A special feature of the Megalensia, or Megalesia, held in April and dedicated to Cybele, the GREAT MOTHER OF THE GODS, were the *ludi scaenici*, consisting of plays and farces.

LUDLUL BEL NEMEQI \\'lùd-,lùl-'bāl-ne-'me-kē\\ (Akkadian: "Let Me Praise the Expert"), in the literature of ancient MESOPOTAMIAN RELIGION, philosophical composition concerned with a man who, seemingly forsaken by the gods, speculates on the changeability of men and fate. The composition, also called the "Poem of the Righteous Sufferer" or the "Babylonian JOB," has been compared to the biblical Book of Job.

LUGNASAD \\'lü-nə-sə, 'lùg̣-nə-səth\\, *also spelled* Lughnasadh, Celtic religious festival celebrated August 1 as the feast of the marriage of the god LUGUS; this was also the day of the harvest fair.

LUGUS \\'lü-gəs\\, *also called* Lug, or Lugh \\'lùg̣\\, in ancient CELTIC RELIGION, one of the major gods. He is probably the deity whom Julius Caesar identified with the Roman god MERCURY. His cult was widespread throughout the early Celtic world, and his name occurs as an element in many continental European and British place-names, such as Lyon, Laon, Leiden, and Carlisle (formerly Luguvallium, "Strong in the God Lugus").

According to Irish tradition, Lug Lámfota ("Lug of the Long Arm") was the sole survivor of triplet brothers all having the same name. At least three dedications to Lugus in plural form, Lugoues, are known from the European continent, and the Celtic affinity for trinitarian forms would suggest that three gods were likewise envisaged in these dedications. Lug's son, or rebirth, according to Irish belief, was the great Ulster hero, CÚ CHULAINN.

In Wales, as Lleu Llaw Gyffes ("Lleu of the Dexterous Hand"), he was also believed to have had a strange birth.

His mother was the virgin goddess Aranrhod ("Silver Wheel"). When her uncle, the great magician MATH, tested her virginity by means of a wand of chastity, she at once gave birth to a boy child, who was instantly carried off by his uncle GWYDION and reared by him. Aranrhod then sought repeatedly to destroy her son, but she was always prevented by Gwydion's powerful magic; she was forced to give her son a name and provide him with arms; finally, as his mother had denied him a wife, Gwydion created a woman for him from flowers.

Lug was also known in Irish tradition as Samildánach ("Skilled in All the Arts"). The variety of his attributes and the extent to which his calendar festival LUGNASAD on August 1 was celebrated in Celtic lands indicate that he was one of the most important of all the ancient Celtic deities.

LU HSIANG-SHAN \\'lü-'shyän-'shän\\, *Pinyin* Lu Xiang-shan, *also called* Lu Chiu-yüan \\-'jyō-'ywän, -'ywen\\, *courtesy name* (*tzu*) Tzu-ching, *literary name* (*hao*) Ts'ún-chai (b. 1139, Kiangsi, China—d. Jan. 10, 1193, China), idealist NEO-CONFUCIAN philosopher of the Southern Sung and rival of the rationalist CHU HSI. Lu's thought was revised and refined three centuries later by Wang Yang-ming. The name of their school is HSIN-HSÜEH, often called the Lu-Wang school, after its two great proponents. It was opposed to the other great school (and the one that was dominant), the LI-HSÜEH.

Lu held a number of government posts, but he devoted most of his life to teaching and lecturing. He taught that the highest knowledge of the TAO comes from the constant practice of inner reflection and self-education. In this process, man develops his original goodness, for human nature is basically good, or regains his goodness if it has been corrupted and lost through material desires (*wu yü*).

After his death, Lu's works were collected and published under the title of *Hsiang-shan hsien-sheng ch'üan-chi* ("Complete Works of Master Hsiang-shan"). In 1217 he was canonized as Wen-an, and in 1530 a tablet in his honor was placed in the Confucian temple of the Ming dynasty.

LU HSIU-CHING \\'lü-'shyō-'jiŋ\\, *Pinyin* Lu Xiujing (b. 406—d. 477 CE), scholar of TAOISM in South China who edited the revealed LING-PAO scriptures that became the basis for the most important ritualistic, or liturgical, traditions in religious TAOISM. His efforts to assemble Taoist texts and to unify Taoist rituals show the influence of BUDDHISM during the 5th century and led eventually to the creation of a coherent sectarian tradition and scriptural canon.

LUKE, SAINT \\'lük\\ (fl. 1st century CE), in Christian tradition, the author of both the third Gospel and THE ACTS OF THE APOSTLES, and a close companion of the Apostle PAUL. Luke may have accompanied Paul on several missionary journeys. His writing style indicates a cultivated literary background.

Information about his life is scanty. Luke is first mentioned in the letters of the Apostle Paul as the latter's "coworker" and as the "beloved physician." The former designation is the more significant one, for it identifies him as one of a professional cadre of itinerant Christian "workers," many of whom were teachers and preachers. His medical skills, like Paul's tentmaking, may have contributed to his livelihood. If Luke was the author of the third Gospel and the Acts of the Apostles, as is very probable, the course and nature of his ministry may be sketched in more detail. He excludes himself from those who were eyewitnesses of Christ's ministry. His participation in the Pauline mission, however, is indicated by the use of the first person in the "we" sections of Acts.

The "we" sections place the author with Paul during his initial mission into Greece (c. 51 CE). It is there that Luke later rejoins Paul and accompanies him on his final journey to Jerusalem (c. 58 CE). He appears with Paul on his prison voyage from Caesarea to Rome and again, according to 2 Timothy 4:11, at the time of the APOSTLE'S martyrdom in the imperial city (c. 66 CE).

The literary style of his writings and the range of his vocabulary mark him as an educated man. His intimate knowledge of the OLD TESTAMENT and the focus of interest in his writings favor, on balance, the view that he was a Jewish Christian who followed a Greek lifestyle and was comparatively lax in ritual observances. Writings from the latter half of the 2nd century provide further information. A number of them—ST. IRENAEUS' *Against Heresies*, the Anti-Marcionite Prologue to the Gospel, and the *Muratorian Canon* listing the books received as sacred by the Christians—identify Luke as the author of the third Gospel and Acts, identifying him as a man from Antioch, Syria, who wrote "moved by the Holy Spirit"—that is, as a prophet. Whether Luke is to be identified with the prophet Lucius mentioned in Acts 13:1 and with St. Paul's "fellow worker" (and kinsman) in Romans 16:21 is more questionable, although not impossible. Less than certain also is the comment of the prologue placing the writing of the Gospel and Luke's death in Greece; but, on the whole, it is more probable than the later traditions locating his literary work in Alexandria (or Rome) and his death in Bithynia. The identification of St. Luke as "a disciple of the Apostles" probably reflects the concern of the 2nd-century church to place all canonical Christian writings under an apostolic umbrella. Later notions that Luke was one of the 70 disciples appointed by the Lord, that he was the companion of Cleopas, and that he was an artist appear to be legendary. In liturgical tradition Luke's feast day is October 18.

Luke had a literary background and wrote in good idiomatic Greek. The Gospel bearing his name and the Acts of the Apostles were probably written during or shortly after the Jewish revolt (66–73 CE), although a somewhat later date is not inconceivable. Some scholars have also associated Luke with the Pastoral Letters and the Letter to the Hebrews, either as author or as amanuensis, because of linguistic and other similarities with the Gospel and the Acts. The Gospel and Acts were, in all likelihood, tagged with the name Luke when they were deposited in the library of the author's patron, Theophilus (Luke 1:3). Within a century there was a widespread tradition identifying that Luke with an otherwise insignificant physician and colleague of Paul. The tradition is on the whole consistent with the literary and historical character of the documents, and one may be reasonably certain that it is correct.

LUMBINĪ \lùm-'bē-nē\, grove near the southern border of modern-day Nepal where, according to Buddhist legend, Queen MAHĀMĀYĀ stood and gave birth to the future BUDDHA GOTAMA while holding onto a branch of a sal tree. The site is a popular destination of Buddhist PILGRIMAGE. There are two references to Lumbinī as the birthplace of the Buddha in Pāli SCRIPTURE, but the earliest canonical accounts of the birth are in Sanskrit scripture, the MAHĀVASTU (ii. 18) and the LALITAVISTARA (ch. 7), neither of which can be dated earlier than the 3rd or the 4th century CE. The discovery of an inscription recording the visit of AŚOKA, Maurya emperor of India from about 265 to 238 BCE, to the spot he considered the birthplace makes it probable that the legend was established at least as early as the 3rd century BCE.

LUNAR DEITY, any god or goddess related to or associated with the moon and its cycles.

LUNG-MEN CAVES \'lùŋ-'mən\, *Pinyin* Longmen, series of Chinese cave temples carved into the rock of a high river bank south of the city of Lo-yang, in Honan province. The temples were begun late in the Northern Wei dynasty (386–535) and construction continued sporadically through the 6th century and the T'ang dynasty (618–907).

The Northern Wei caves at Lung-men (including the often-cited Ku-yang cave and the Pin-yang cave) are intimate in scale, contain complex ICONOGRAPHY, and were elegantly crafted to create ethereal effects in the hard stone.

Stone sculptures in the Pin-yang cave, Lung-men, Northern Wei dynasty (386–535 CE)
Jimbunkagaku Kenkyusho, Kyoto

The BUDDHA images—clothed in the costume of the Chinese scholar, with a sinuous cascade of drapery falling over an increasingly flattened figure—provide the type form for what is known as the Lung-men style. Work at the site, which continued in a minor and sporadic way through later times, culminated in the T'ang dynasty with the construction of a cave shrine, known as Feng-hsien Ssu, of truly monumental proportions, carved out over the three-year period 672–675. The square plan measures about 100 feet on each side, and a colossal seated Buddha figure upon the back wall, flanked by attendant figures, is more than 35 feet high. (*See also* YÜN-KANG CAVES.)

LUNG-MEN TAOISM \\'lùŋ-'mən-'daù-,i-zəm\\, *Pinyin* Longmen (Chinese: "Dragon Gate"), offshoot of the Ch'üanchen, or Perfect Realization, school of TAOISM founded by WANG CHE. The Lung-men, or Northern, school resulted from the efforts of Wang Che's disciple, CHIU CHU-CHI (b. 1148—d. 1227), who was patronized by the Yüan emperor Tai-tzu (Genghis Khan). This sect, like Ch'üan-chen in general, promotes the spiritual cultivation of inner alchemy and was heavily influenced by Ch'an (ZEN) Buddhist practices. It continues today in Beijing at the PAI-YÜN KUAN, or Temple of the White Cloud; in Hong Kong; and in other Chinese communities of the diaspora.

LUN-YÜ \\'lùn-'ȳe\\, *Pinyin* Lunyu, *English* Analects \\'a-nə-,lekts\\ (Chinese: "Conversations"), one of four Confucian texts that, when published together in 1190 by the Neo-Confucian philosopher CHU HSI, became the great Chinese classic known as *Ssu-shu* ("FOUR BOOKS").

Lun-yü is considered by scholars to be the most reliable source of the doctrine of CONFUCIUS (551–479 BCE). It covers the basic ethical concepts of Confucius—*e.g.*, JEN ("benevolence"), CHÜN-TZU ("the superior man"), T'IEN ("Heaven"), CHUNG-YUNG (doctrine of "the mean"), LI ("proper conduct"), and *cheng-ming* ("adjustment to names"). The last argues that all phases of a person's conduct should correspond to the true significance of "names"; *e.g.*, marriage should be true marriage, not concubinage. In addition to many direct quotations attributed to Confucius, *Lun-yü* also contains homely glimpses of Confucius as recorded by his disciples.

LUPERCALIA \\,lü-pər-'kā-lē-ə, -'kāl-yə\\, ancient Roman festival that was conducted annually on February 15 under the superintendence of a corporation of priests called Luperci. The origins of the festival are obscure, although the likely derivation of its name from *lupus* (Latin: "wolf") has variously suggested connection with a primitive deity who protected herds from wolves and with the legendary she-wolf who nursed ROMULUS AND REMUS. As a fertility rite, the festival is also associated with the god FAUNUS.

Each Lupercalia began with the sacrifice by the Luperci of goats and a dog, after which two of the Luperci were led to the altar, their foreheads were touched with a bloody knife, and the blood wiped off with wool dipped in milk; then the ritual required that the two young men laugh. The sacrificial feast followed, after which the Luperci cut thongs from the skins of the victims and ran in two bands around the Palatine hill, striking with the thongs at any woman who came near them. A blow from the thong was supposed to render a woman fertile. In 494 CE the Christian church under Pope Gelasius I appropriated the day of this rite as the Feast of the Purification of the Blessed Virgin MARY. (That feast was later moved to February 2.) *See* CANDLEMAS.

LURIA, ISAAC BEN SOLOMON \\'lür-yä\\, *byname* Ha-Ari (Hebrew: "The Lion") (b. 1534, Jerusalem, Palestine, Ottoman Empire—d. Aug. 5, 1572, Safed, Syria [now Ẓefat, Israel]), founder of the Lurianic school of QABBALAH.

The main source for Luria's life story is an anonymous biography, *Toledot ha-Ari* ("Life of the Ari"), written or perhaps edited some 20 years after his death, in which factual and legendary elements are indiscriminately mingled. Legend has it that the prophet ELIJAH appeared to Luria's father and foretold the birth of the son, whose name was to be Isaac. According to the *Toledot*, Luria's father died while

Isaac was a child, and his mother then took him to Egypt to live with her well-to-do family. It was while in Egypt that he became versed in rabbinic studies, including HALAKHAH (Jewish law), and even wrote glosses on the *Sefer ha-Halakhot* of ISAAC BEN JACOB ALFASI.

While still a youth, Luria began the study of JEWISH MYSTICISM and lived for nearly seven years in seclusion at his uncle's home on an island in the Nile River. His studies concentrated on the SEFER HA-ZOHAR (late 13th–early 14th century), the central and revered work of the Qabbalah, but he also studied the early Qabbalists (12th–13th century). The greatest Qabbalist of Luria's time was MOSES BEN JACOB CORDOVERO of Safed (modern Ẓefat), in Palestine, whose work Luria studied while still in Egypt. During this period he wrote a commentary on the *Sifra di-tzeniʿuta* ("Book of Concealment"), a section of the *Zohar.*

Early in 1570 Luria journeyed to Safed, and he studied there with Cordovero. At the time of Luria's arrival, the group of Qabbalists gathered around Cordovero had already developed a unique style of living and observed special rituals, going out, for instance, into the fields to welcome the SABBATH, personified as the Sabbath Queen. With Luria's arrival, new elements were added to these excursions, such as communion with the souls of the zaddikim (men of outstanding piety; *see* ZADDIK) by means of special *kawwanot* ("ritual meditations") and *yihudim* ("unifications") that were in essence a kind of lesser redemption whereby the souls were lifted up from the *kelipot* ("shells"; *i.e.*, the impure, evil forms) into which they were banned until the coming of the MESSIAH.

Luria began to teach Qabbalah according to a new system and attracted many pupils. The greatest of these was Ḥayyim Vital, who later set Luria's teachings down in writing. Luria apparently looked upon himself as the Messiah ben Joseph, the first of the two messiahs in Jewish tradition, who is fated to be killed in the wars (of GOG AND MAGOG) that will precede the final redemption. In Safed there was an expectation (based on the *Zohar*) that the Messiah would appear in Galilee in the year 1575. He apparently expounded his teachings only in esoteric circles; not everyone was allowed to take part in these studies. While he devoted most of his time to the instruction of his pupils, he probably made his living in trade.

Luria composed three hymns for the Sabbath meals that became part of the Sephardic Sabbath ritual and were printed in many prayer books. The hymns are known as "Azamer be-she-vahim" ("I Will Sing on the Praises"), "Asader seʿudata" ("I Will Order the Festive Meal"), and "Bene hekh-ala de-khesifin" ("Sons of the Temple of Silver"). They are mystical, erotic songs about "the adornment (or fitting) of the bride"—*i.e.*, the sabbath, who was identified with the community of Israel—and on the other *partzufim: arikh anpin* (the long-suffering: the countenance of grace) and *zeʿir anpin* (the impatient: the countenance of judgment).

During his time in Safed Luria managed to construct a many-faceted and fertile Qabbalistic system from which many new elements in Jewish mysticism drew their nourishment. He set down almost none of his doctrine in writing, with the exception of a short text that seems to be only a fragment: his commentary on the first chapter of the *Zohar*—"Be-resh hormanuta de-malka"—as well as commentaries on isolated passages of the *Zohar* that were collected by Ḥayyim Vital, who attests to their being in his teacher's own hand. Luria died in an epidemic that struck Safed in August 1572.

Lurianic Qabbalah became the new thought that influenced all Jewish mysticism after Luria, competing with the Qabbalah of Cordovero. It played an important role in the movement of the false messiah SHABBETAI TZEVI in the 17th century and in the popular Hasidic movement a century later. It propounds a theory of the creation and subsequent degeneration of the world based on three concepts: *tzimtzum* ("contraction," or "withdrawal"), *shevirat ha-kelim* ("breaking of the vessels"), and *tiqqun* ("restoration"). God as the Infinite (En Sof) withdraws into himself in order to make room for the creation, which occurs by a beam of light from the Infinite into the newly provided space. Later the divine light is enclosed in finite "vessels," most of which break under the strain, a catastrophe whereby disharmony and evil enter the world. Hence comes the struggle to rid the world of evil and accomplish the redemption of both the cosmos and history. This event occurs in the stage of *tiqqun,* in which the divine realm itself is reconstructed, the divine sparks returned to their source, and Adam Qadmon, the symbolic "primordial man," who is the highest configuration of the divine light, is rebuilt. Man plays an important role in this process through various *kawwanot* used during prayer and through mystical intentions involving secret combinations of words, all of which is directed toward the restoration of the primordial harmony and the reunification of the divine name.

LUSTRATION \ˌləs-ˈtrā-shən\ (from Latin *lustratio*, "ritual cleansing"), any of various processes in ancient Greece and Rome whereby individuals or communities rid themselves of ceremonial impurity (*e.g.*, bloodguilt, pollution incurred by contact with childbirth or with a corpse) or simply

Martin Luther, oil painting by Lucas Cranach, 1526
By courtesy of the Nationalmuseum, Stockholm

of the profane or ordinary state, which made it dangerous to come into contact with sacred rites or objects. The methods varied from sprinkling with or washing in water, through rubbing with various substances, such as blood or clay, to complicated ceremonies, some of which involved confession of misdeeds. Fumigation was also used.

When a community was to be purified, different processes were used from culture to culture. The usual Greek method seems to have been to lead through the village certain persons or animals capable of absorbing the pollution and then to lead them out of the city. In Rome, purifying materials were led or carried around the person or community in question. Many noteworthy public rites were of this kind, such as the LUPERCALIA (around the Palatine hill) and the *amburbium* ("around the city").

LUTHER, MARTIN \lü-thər, *German* ˈlὑ-tər\ (b. Nov. 10, 1483, Eisleben, Saxony [Germany]—d. Feb. 18, 1546, Eisleben), preacher, biblical scholar, and linguist whose NINETY-FIVE THESES, an attack on various ROMAN CATHOLIC ecclesiastical abuses, precipitated the Protestant REFORMATION.

Luther was the son of a prosperous copper miner. In 1502 he graduated from the University of Erfurt, and he took his M.A. in 1505, after which he entered the monastery of the eremitical order of St. Augustine. He was ordained priest in

April 1507, and in 1508 he went to the University of Wittenberg, where he took his Doctorate of Theology in 1512 and received the chair of biblical theology.

After a long period of religious doubts and guilt at what he saw as his failure to obey God's Law, Luther found relief around 1518 through a sudden conviction that JUSTIFICATION came through FAITH; that salvation is a divine gift of grace; that Christ represents God's forgiving mercy; and that the soul, free from the burden of guilt, may serve God with a joyful obedience.

Luther was moved to public protest by a jubilee INDULGENCE, the ostensible purpose of which was the rebuilding of St. Peter's BASILICA in Rome. (Indulgences were the commutation for money of part of the penalty for SIN, as part of the penance which also required contrition and priestly ABSOLUTION. At no time did they imply that divine forgiveness could be bought or sold.) For Luther the provocation lay in extravagant claims made by a DOMINICAN indulgence salesman.

Luther drew up the Ninety-five Theses, and according to tradition (probably untrue), fastened them on the door of the Castle Church in Wittenberg, on Oct. 31, 1517. These were tentative opinions, to some of which Luther himself was not committed. The first thesis claimed that repentance involved the whole life of the Christian man, and the 62nd that the true treasure of the church was the most holy gospel of the glory and the GRACE of God. The closing section attacked those who refused to recognize that to be a Christian involved embracing the cross and entering heaven through tribulation. Luther sent copies of the theses to the archbishop of Mainz and to his bishop, but further copies were circulated. The archbishop forwarded the documents to Rome in December 1517, with the request that Luther be inhibited. The pope merely instructed the VICAR general of the AUGUSTINIANS to deal with Luther through the usual channels, and in October the CARDINAL Cajetan at Augsburg ordered him to recant.

In June 1520 there appeared the papal bull *Exsurge Domine* ("Lord, Cast Out") against 41 articles of Luther's teaching, followed by the burning of Luther's writings in Rome. Luther replied in a series of treatises issued in 1520, the second of which, *De captivitate Babylonica ecclesiae praeludium* ("A Prelude Concerning the Babylonian Captivity of the Church"), reduced to three (BAPTISM, the Lord's Supper [EUCHARIST], and penance) the seven SACRAMENTS of the church, denied MASS and attacked TRANSUBSTANTIATION, made vehement charges against papal authority, and asserted the supremacy of Holy SCRIPTURE and the rights of individual conscience. In January 1521 the pope issued the bull of formal EXCOMMUNICATION (*Decet Romanum Pontificem*), though it was some months before the condemnation was received throughout Germany.

On April 17, 1521, Luther appeared before civic and religious authorities at the DIET OF WORMS. When required to recant his assertions, he stated that he would not go against his conscience unless convinced of his error either by Scripture or by evident reason. The emperor cut short the proceedings and Luther was allowed to depart. Luther's enemies, nonetheless, salvaged something when a rump Diet passed the Edict of Worms. It declared Luther to be an outlaw whose writings were proscribed. The edict fettered his movements for the rest of his days. Luther departed to Wartburg, where he remained until March 1522. There he translated the NEW TESTAMENT into German (published in September 1522) which, like his later translation of the OLD TESTAMENT (1534), had deep and lasting influence on the language, life, and religion of the German people.

Luther deplored the use of violence, and he was dismayed by the evident social and political unrest in Germany. In 1523 he issued a treatise *Von weltlicher Obrigkeit* ("Of Earthly Government"), in which he distinguished between the two realms of spiritual and of temporal government, and stressed the sinfulness of rebellion against lawful authority. In May 1525, after the Peasants' War had broken out, he published the *Ermahnung zum Frieden* ("Exhortation for Freedom"), sympathizing with just grievances, but repudiating the notion of a so-called Christian rebellion and claiming that the worldly kingdom cannot exist without inequality of persons.

In June 1525 Luther married Katherina von Bora, a former nun. His home meant a great deal to him and was an emblem for him of Christian vocation, so that he included domestic life among the three hierarchies (or "orders of creation") of Christian existence in this world, the other two being political and church life. Later in 1525, faced with imminent political chaos, he wrote the brutal *Wider die räuberischen und mörderischen Rotten der andern Bauern* ("Against the Murdering and Thieving Hordes of Peasants"), which only served to confirm many peasants in their preference for radical ideology. Luther henceforth was occupied with divisions within the Reformation camp, particularly with regard to the Eucharist.

LUTHERANISM \ˈlü-thə-rə-ˌni-zəm\, branch of the Western Christian church that adopted the religious principles of MARTIN LUTHER. Lutheran churches often term themselves Evangelical as distinct from Reformed (Calvinist), but these uses are not always strictly applied.

Lutheranism cannot be defined or understood without some reference to the personal experience and the biblical studies of Luther, which came to voice in 1517 in his famous NINETY-FIVE THESES for debate over INDULGENCES and in his attack on the theology and sacramental practice of the late medieval church of the West. In 1521 Luther was excommunicated; his followers accepted the designation "Lutheran" in part against his will and in spite of the fact that it was filled, in many instances, with implications of derision and sectarianism. The Lutheran movement, a central element of the Protestant REFORMATION, spread through much of Germany and into Scandinavia, where it was established by law.

The theological vigor of Luther's generation gave way to an increasingly rigid orthodoxy in the late 16th and 17th centuries. This in turn precipitated a pietist reaction that asserted the need for living faith in addition to right doctrine. The Pietists encouraged missionary and charitable work in addition to devotional practice. Eighteenth-century Lutheranism was marked by rationalist influences. Orthodoxy was reasserted during the next century, notably by the Danish bishop and poet N.F.S. Grundtvig.

In America, Lutherans were among the earliest colonists to settle on the Delaware River, and they were followed by German colonists who settled especially in the present

Middle Atlantic states, the Shenandoah Valley, Georgia, and Nova Scotia, Canada. The spread of Lutheranism in the United States was extended by migrations to the western frontier and by the large immigrations during the 19th and early 20th centuries of Germans, Norwegians, Swedes, Danes, and Finns. Many of these immigrants settled in the Midwest, and from there later pushed on to the far West. These immigrants organized in congregations and later SYNODS according to their national origins. It was largely the prolongation of linguistic and ethnic barriers that prevented Lutheran union until well into the 20th century, when the advance into intra-Lutheran ecumenical relations became rapid.

Lutheran doctrinal statements are usually said to include nine separate formulations that together form the BOOK OF CONCORD. Three belong to the early Christian church—the APOSTLES' CREED, the NICENE CREED in its Western form, and the so-called ATHANASIAN CREED. Six derive from the 16th-century Reformation—the AUGSBURG CONFESSION, the Apology for the Augsburg Confession, the SCHMALKALDIC ARTICLES, Luther's two CATECHISMS, and the Formula of Concord. Only the three early creeds and the Augsburg Confession are recognized by all Lutherans. Luther's Catechisms have met almost universal acceptance, but many Lutheran churches rejected the Formula of Concord because of its strict and detailed doctrinal statements. The Augsburg Confession and Luther's Small Catechism may properly be said to define Lutheranism inclusively in its doctrinal aspect, though Lutherans may be divided on many issues raised since the Augsburg Confession of 1530.

The largest and one of the oldest of non-Roman Catholic, non-Orthodox families of Christians, Lutheranism is represented in most areas of the world, but its particular geographic orientation has been in northern and western Europe and in younger countries settled by Germans and Scandinavians. It has been represented with less strength in Switzerland, the Low Countries, and Scotland, where Reformed confessions predominated, and it has been a secondary influence in the former British empire and Commonwealth, where the ANGLICAN COMMUNION has prevailed.

Lutheranism acknowledges no world headquarters, but the vast majority of the world's Lutherans cooperate in the Lutheran World Federation, which has offices in Geneva.

LUWIAN RELIGIONS \ˈlü-ē-ən\: *see* ANATOLIAN RELIGIONS.

LUZZATTO, MOSHE ḤAYYIM \lüt-ˈtsät-tō\ (b. 1707, Padua, Venetian republic [Italy]—d. May 6, 1747, Acre, Palestine [now ʿAkko, Israel]), Jewish Qabbalist and writer, one of the founders of modern Hebrew poetry.

About 1727 Luzzatto wrote the drama *Migdal ʿoz* ("Tower of Victory"), but he early turned to Qabbalist studies—eventually becoming convinced that he was receiving divine revelation and, finally, that he was the MESSIAH. After being expelled by the Italian RABBIS, he moved to Amsterdam (1736), where he wrote his morality play *La-yesharim tehilah* (*Praise for Uprightness*) and an ethical work, *Mesilat yesharim* (1740; *The Path of the Upright*).

LYCAON \lī-ˈkā-ˌän\, in Greek mythology, legendary king of Arcadia. Traditionally, he was an impious and cruel king who tried to trick ZEUS into eating human flesh. The god was not deceived and in wrath caused a deluge to devastate the earth. The story of Lycaon was apparently told in order to explain an extraordinary ceremony, the Lycaea, held in honour of Zeus Lycaeus at Mount Lycaeus.

MAA-ALUSED \'mä-'ä-lü-ˌsed\, in Estonian folk religion, mysterious small folk living under the earth. Corresponding to these are the Finnish *maahiset* and Karelian *muahiset,* which refer both to the spirits and to an illness caused by them respectively.

These beings lead an existence quite parallel to that of people living on earth, except that up becomes down and right becomes left. In Finland the subterranean abode of the *maahiset* was believed to be a source of many kinds of skin disease, which were called by the same term. People came in contact with the *maa-alused* or *maahiset* either by chance or at the wish of these elf-like creatures themselves. Legends tell of distraught elves seeking help from humans in difficult cases of childbirth or illness. A human could marry an elf, but such a marriage eventually dissolved as the spouse returned to his or her former home.

The elf tradition is by no means homogeneous, carrying with it many often distinct concepts. Some scholars have considered the *maa-alused* to be spirits of the dead. Others place them in the realm of nature spirits. The elves are also thought of as overseers of certain localities, and in this sense they blend with the HALTIA, the household spirit, and function as supernatural guardians of moral order among the humans dwelling on their territory.

MAʿAMADOT \ˌmä-ä-mä-'dōt\ (Hebrew: "stands," or "posts"), 24 groups of laymen that witnessed the daily sacrifice in the Second TEMPLE OF JERUSALEM as representatives of the people. Gradually *maʿamadot* were organized in areas outside Jerusalem; some scholars view these village *maʿamadot* as representing the first step toward regular SYNAGOGUE worship.

Though public sacrifices were terminated when Jerusalem was destroyed in 70 CE, daily prayers called *maʿamadot* are still recited privately by many pious Jews.

MAʿAT \'mä-ˌät\, *also spelled* Mayet \'mä-ˌyet\, in ancient EGYPTIAN RELIGION, the personification of truth, justice, and the cosmic order. The daughter of the sun god RE, she was associated with THOTH, god of wisdom.

The ceremony of judgment of the dead (called the "Judgment of OSIRIS," named for Osiris, the god of the dead) was believed to focus upon the weighing of the heart of the deceased in a scale balanced by Maʿat (or her hieroglyph, the ostrich feather), as a test of conformity to proper values. The Hall of Double Justice where this occurred was so called from Maʿat's frequent appearances there as two identical goddesses.

In its abstract sense, *maʿat* was the divine order established at creation and reaffirmed at the accession of each new king of Egypt. In setting *maʿat,* "order," in place of *izfet,* "disorder," the king played the role of the sun god, the god with the closest links to Maʿat. Maʿat stood at the head of the sun god's bark as it traveled through the sky and the Underworld. Although aspects of kingship and of *maʿat*

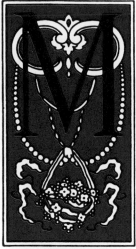

were at at various times subjected to both criticism and reformulation, the principles underlying these two institutions were fundamental to ancient Egyptian life and thought and endured to the end of ancient Egyptian history.

MABINOGION \mȧ-bē-'nȯg-yən, *Angl* ˌma-bə-'nō-gē-ən\, collection of 11 medieval Welsh tales based on MYTHOLOGY, FOLKLORE, and heroic legends. The name Mabinogion derives from a scribal error and is an unjustified but convenient term for these anonymous tales.

The finest of the tales are the four related stories known as "The Four Branches of the *Mabinogi,*" or "The Four Branches" (dating, in their present form, from the late 11th century), the only tales in which the word Mabinogi (meaning "Matters Concerning [the Family of?] Maponos") appears. Of great interest to Welsh studies are "The Four Independent Native Tales," which show minimal continental influence and include "Kulhwch and Olwen," "Lludd and Llefelys," "The Dream of Macsen," and "The Dream of Rhonabwy." The tales "Owein and Luned" (or "The Lady of the Fountain"), "Geraint and Enid," and "Peredur Son of Efrawg" parallel the French romances *Yvain, Erec,* and *Perceval* of Chrétien de Troyes.

MACCABEES \'ma-kə-ˌbēz\ (fl. 2nd century BCE, Palestine), in Jewish history, priestly family who organized a successful rebellion against the Seleucid ruler Antiochus IV Epiphanes and reconsecrated the TEMPLE OF JERUSALEM. The name Maccabee was a title of honor given to Judas, a son of Mattathias and the hero of the Jewish wars of independence, 168–164 BCE. Later, the name was extended to include the rest of his family.

There is no unanimity about the meaning of the title Maccabee. The Hebrew may be read as "Hammer," "Hammerer," or "Extinguisher."

Antiochus IV, who ruled Syria from 175 to 164/163 BCE, seized Judaea (or JUDAH) and sought to unify it with his other conquests by imposing a universal religion on the Hebrews. He forbade the observance of the SABBATH, the performance of sacrifice, the reading of the Law of MOSES, or the practice of CIRCUMCISION. In place of these practices Antiochus encouraged the development of cultural clubs called gymnasia, in which people gathered to study, to learn, and to enjoy each other's company. In 168 BCE, Antiochus invaded Jerusalem and desacralized the HOLY OF HOLIES in the Temple. A number of Jews, including Jason the HIGH PRIEST, chose to conform with the new trends, but when, on Dec. 25, 167 BCE, Antiochus rededicated the Temple in Jerusalem to the Greek god ZEUS, he touched off a rebellion.

The resistance was sparked when Mattathias, a priest in the village of Modiʿim, 17 miles northwest of Jerusalem, struck a Jew who was preparing to offer sacrifice to the new gods and killed the king's officer who was standing by. Mattathias then fled with his family to the hills. Many joined them there, and Mattathias was the first leader of the rebellion. Josephus gives Mattathias' great-grandfather the surname Asamonaios. From this title comes the name Hasmonean that was applied to the dynasty that descended from the Maccabees in the following century.

After the death of Mattathias (*c.* 166 BCE), his son Judas Maccabeus became the leader of the resistance movement. In December 164 BCE he recaptured Jerusalem. He then had priests cleanse the Holy Place and erect a new altar of unhewn stones. They then reconsecrated the SANCTUARY. The Hebrew word for this act, HANUKKAH ("Dedication"), is the name of the festival that commemorates the event. Judas next continued the war in Galilee and even Transjordan.

The war continued, however, and when Judas was killed in battle after more than five years of leadership, his brother Jonathan succeeded him as general. King Alexander Balas (also known as Alexander Epiphanes) made peace with Jonathan, and in 153 or 152 BCE he elected Jonathan as high priest in Jerusalem, but still the war continued. Jonathan died by treachery and was succeeded by his brother Simon. On his own initiative Simon brought peace and security to Jerusalem. He was the second Hasmonean high priest. In 135/134 BCE he was assassinated.

Simon's son John, known later as Hyrcanus I, remained as high priest in Jerusalem until his death in 104 BCE. He was able to consolidate and extend Jewish control, bringing Samaria into subjection and forcing the Idumaeans to accept JUDAISM.

MACEDONIANISM \,ma-sə-'dō-nē-ə-,ni,zəm\, *also called* Pneumatomachian heresy \,nü-mə-tə-'mä-kē-ən\, 4th-century Christian HERESY that denied the full personality and deity of the HOLY SPIRIT, arguing that the Holy Spirit was created by the Son and was thus subordinate to the Father and the Son. (In Orthodox Christian theology, God is one in essence but three in Person—Father, Son, and Holy Spirit, who are distinct and equal.) Those who accepted the heresy were called Macedonians but were also and more descriptively known as pneumatomachians, the "spirit fighters."

Some sources attribute leadership of the group to Macedonius, a semi-Arian who was twice bishop of Constantinople, but the writings of the Macedonians have all been lost, and their doctrine is known mainly from polemical refutations by Orthodox writers, particularly ST. ATHANASIUS of Alexandria (*Letters to Serapion*) and ST. BASIL of Caesarea (*On the Holy Spirit*). The second ecumenical COUNCIL OF CONSTANTINOPLE (381 CE) formally condemned the Macedonians and expanded the Creed of Nicaea to affirm the Orthodox belief in the Holy Spirit, "who with the Father and the Son together is worshiped and glori-

Ma'at, bronze figure dating to the 26th dynasty (664–525 BCE)

fied." The Macedonian heresy was suppressed by the emperor Theodosius I.

MACHA \'mä-ḵə\, in CELTIC RELIGION, one of three war goddesses. It is also a collective name for the three, who were also referred to as the three Morrígan. As an individual, Macha was known by a great variety of names, including Dana and Badb ("Crow," or "Raven"). She was the great EARTH MOTHER and a slaughterer of men, as was another of the trinity, Morrígan, or Black Annis, who survives in Arthurian legend as Morgan le Fay. The third goddess was Nemain.

MACUMBA \mə-'küm-bə\, Afro-Brazilian religion that is characterized by a marked syncretism of traditional African religions, European culture, Brazilian SPIRITUALISM, and ROMAN CATHOLICISM. Of the several Macumba sects, the most important are CANDOMBLÉ and Umbanda.

African elements in Macumba rituals include an outdoor ceremonial site, the sacrifice of animals (such as cocks), spirit offerings (such as candles, cigars, and flowers), and ritual dances. Macumba rites are led by mediums, who communicate in trance with holy spirits. Roman Catholic elements include use of the cross and the worship of saints, who are given African names such as Ogum (ST. GEORGE), Xangô (ST. JEROME), and Iemanjá (the Blessed Virgin MARY).

Candomblé, practiced in Bahia state, is considered to be the most African of the Macumba sects. Umbanda, practiced in urban areas such as Rio de Janeiro and São Paulo, also reflects Hindu and Buddhist influence; its appeal has spread to the white middle class. Macumba sects continue to flourish throughout Brazil.

MADDERAKKA \'mäd-dä-,räh-kä\, Sami goddess of childbirth. She is assisted by three of her daughters—Sarakka, the cleaving woman, Uksakka, the door woman, and Juksakka, the bow woman—who watch over the development of the child from conception through early childhood. Madderakka was believed to receive the soul of a child from VERALDEN-RADIEN, the world ruler deity, and to give it a body, which Sarakka would then place in the mother's womb. Uksakka was believed to aid in the actual childbirth; Juksakka would then take care of the child after birth. Sarakka was also thought of as the separating woman who made childbirth easier and was considered to be a deity of women in a more general sense, aiding them in concerns such as MENSTRUATION. (*See also* FINNO-UGRIC RELIGION.)

MĀDHAVA \'mä-də-və\, *also called* Mādhavācārya, *or* Vidyāraṇya (b. 1296?–d. 1386?, Sringeri, Karnataka, India), Hindu statesman and philosopher. He lived at the court of Vijayanagar, a southern Indian kingdom.

Mādhava became an ascetic in 1377 and was thereafter known as Vidyāraṇya. He was part author of *Jīvan-muktiviveka* and *Pañcadaśī*, works of VEDĀNTA philosophy; *Nyāya-mālāvistara*, a work on the Mīmāṃsā system, one of the earliest orthodox systems of Vedic philosophy; and *Parāśarasmṛtivyākhyā*, an elaborate comment on the *Parāśarasmṛti*. The influential *Sarvadarśanasaṃgraha* ("Compendium of All Philosophical Positions") is signed by Mādhava, but scholars differ as to whether its author is the same as the Mādhava described here. *See also* VEDIC RELIGION.

MADHVA \'mäd-və\, *also called* Ānandatīrtha \'ä-nən-də-'tir-tə\, *or* Pūrṇaprajña \'pür-nə-'prəg-nyə\ (b. *c.* 1199, Kalyānpur, near Udipi, Karnataka, India—d. *c.* 1278, Udipi), Hindu philosopher, exponent of DVAITA (DUALISM). His followers are called Mādhvas.

Born into a Brahmin family, as a youth he disappeared for a short time, according to tradition. After a four-day search his parents found him engaged in discourse with the learned priests of VISHNU; later, on a PILGRIMAGE to the sacred city of VARANASI (Benares), he walked on water, calmed rough sea, and became a "fisher of men." Similarities between his life story and narratives found in the Christian Gospels suggest that he may have been influenced during his youth by a group of NESTORIAN Christians who were residing at Kalyānpur.

Madhva set out to refute the nondualistic ADVAITA philosophy of ŚAMKARA (d. *c.* 750 CE), who believed the individual self to be a phenomenon and the absolute spirit (BRAHMAN) the only reality. Thus, Madhva rejected the venerable Hindu theory of MĀYĀ ("illusion"), which taught that only spirituality is eternal and the material world is illusory and deceptive. Madhva maintained that the simple fact that things are transient and ever-changing does not mean they are not real.

Departing from orthodox Hinduism, he believed in eternal damnation, offering a concept of heaven and hell, plus a Hindu PURGATORY of endless transmigration of souls. Madhva's cult outlawed temple prostitutes and offered figures made of dough as a substitute for blood sacrifices, and its adherents customarily branded themselves on the shoulder with a multiarmed figure of Vishnu.

During his lifetime, Madhva wrote 37 works in Sanskrit, mostly commentaries on Hindu sacred writings and treatises on his own theological system and philosophy.

The Grand-Duke's Madonna, *oil painting by Raphael, 1505; in the Pitti Palace, Florence*
SCALA—Art Resource

MĀDHYAMIKA \mäd-'yə-mi-kə\ (Sanskrit: "Intermediate," or "Middle Way"), important school in the MAHĀYĀNA Buddhist philosophy. Its name derives from its having sought a middle position between the realism of the SARVĀSTIVĀDA school and the idealism of the YOGĀCĀRA school. The most renowned Mādhyamika thinker was NĀGĀRJUNA (d. *c.* 250 CE), who developed *śūnyavāda*, the doctrine that all is void. Three of the most authoritative texts for the school are the *Mādhyamika Śāstra* (Sanskrit: "Treatise of the Middle Way") and the *Dvādaśa-dvāra Śāstra* ("Twelve Gates Treatise") by Nāgārjuna and the *Śataka Śāstra* ("One Hundred Verses Treatise"), which has been attributed to his pupil Āryadeva.

BUDDHISM in general assumed that the world is a cosmic flux of momentary interconnected events (DHARMAS), however the reality of these events might be viewed. Nāgārjuna sought to demonstrate that the flux itself could not be held to be real, nor could the consciousness perceiving it, as it itself is part of this flux. If this world of constant change is not real, neither can the cycle of death and rebirth be real, nor its opposite, NIRVANA. In the final analysis, reality can only be attributed to something entirely different from all that is known, which must therefore have no identifiable predicates and can only be styled the void (*śūnyatā*).

The basic Mādhyamika texts were translated into Chinese by KUMĀRAJĪVA in the 5th century, and the teachings were further systematized (as the SAN-LUN, or "Three Treatises," school) in the 6th–7th centuries by Chi-tsang. The school spread to Korea and was subsequently transmitted to Japan, as Sanron, in 625 by the Korean monk Ekwan.

MADONNA \mə-'dä-nə\ (Old Italian: "My Lady"), in Christian art, depiction of the Virgin Mary; the term is usually restricted to those representations that are devotional rather than narrative and that show her in a nonhistorical context and emphasize later doctrinal or sentimental significance. The Madonna is accompanied most often by the infant JESUS CHRIST, but there are several important types that show her alone.

Byzantine art developed a great number of Madonna types. All are illustrated on ICONS, and one or another type was usually pictured prominently on the eastern wall of Byzantine churches below the image of Christ; the location dramatized her role as mediator between Christ and the congregation. The major types of the Madonna in Byzantine art are the *nikopoia* ("bringer of victory"), a regal image of the Madonna and Child enthroned; the *hodēgētria* ("she who points the way"), showing a standing Virgin holding the Child on her left arm; and the *blacherniotissa* (from the Church of the Blachernes, which contains the icon that is its prototype), which emphasizes her role as intercessor, showing her alone in an orant, or prayer posture, with the Child pictured in a medallion on her breast. The Virgin also figured prominently as an intercessor in the group of the Deēsis, where she and ST. JOHN THE BAPTIST appear as intercessors on either side of Christ. The Virgin also appears in the more intimate types of the *galaktotrophousa*, in which she nurses the Child, and the *glykophilousa*, in which the Child caresses her cheek while she seems sadly to contemplate his coming Passion.

In the West, particularly with the spread of devotional images at the end of the Middle Ages, the theme of the Madonna was developed into a number of additional types, in general less rigidly defined than those of the East but often modeled on Byzantine types. As a rule, Western types of the Madonna sought to inspire piety through the beauty and tenderness rather than the theological significance of the subject. By far the most popular type in the West throughout the Renaissance and into the Baroque period was that derived from the *glykophilousa*. Though this type has many variants, it usually depicts a Virgin of grave expression, turning her gaze away from the playful Child.

Three major Madonna types showing the Virgin alone have theological significance. As the Madonna of mercy, a type that flourished in the 15th century, the Virgin spreads her mantle protectively over a group of the faithful. The *immacolata*, which in the 17th century emphasized her IMMACULATE CONCEPTION, shows her as a young girl descending from the heavens, supported by a crescent moon and crowned by stars. The Madonna of the ROSARY, shows the Virgin giving the rosary to ST. DOMINIC, founder of the order that spread its use.

The theme of the Madonna appeared less frequently in the major arts after the 17th century. Representations of the Madonna and Child, however, continued to be important in popular art into the 20th century, most following 16th- and 17th-century models.

MADRASA \\'mȧ-drə-sə\\ (Arabic: "school"), *Turkish* medrese, in Muslim countries, institution of higher education. Originating in the 10th century, the *madrasa* functioned until the 20th century as a theological seminary and law school, with a curriculum centered on the QUR'AN. It served to promote scripturalist Islamic learning in opposition to speculative or heretical movements. In addition to Islamic theology and law, Arabic grammar and literature, mathematics, logic, and, in some cases, natural science were studied in *madrasa*s. Limited exclusively to males, the schools offered free tuition, and food, lodging, and medical care were provided as well. Instruction usually took place in a courtyard and consisted primarily of memorizing textbooks and the instructor's lectures. The lecturer issued certificates to his students that constituted permission to repeat his words. Financed by donations from wealthy and powerful patrons, SUNNI *madrasa*s flourished in Damascus, Baghdad, Mosul, Cairo, and most other Muslim cities by the end of the 12th century. Leading SHI'ITE *madrasa*s are located in NAJAF, MASHHAD, and QOM. In the mid-20th century these *madrasa*s provided focal points for Iranian political activism; the religious leaders who established the Islamic Republic of Iran in 1979 studied and taught there.

MADRID CODEX \\mə-'drid-'kō-ˌdeks\\: *see* MAYA CODICES.

MADURAI \\ˌmä-dù-'rī\\, *formerly* Madura, city, south-central Tamil Nadu state, southeastern India. Situated on the Vaigai River, Madurai dates to the early centuries CE, if not before, and was the site of the Pāṇṭya (4th–11th century CE) capital, which centered on the great temple of Mīnākṣī (the "fish-eyed" goddess) and her consort Sundareśvara ("the beautiful lord"), who are ŚAKTI and SHIVA. Fourteenth-century Muslim invaders destroyed the temple complex except for its central shrines, but in the following century the Hindu rulers of Vijayanagara mounted a decades-long campaign of rebuilding. Major British construction projects obscured the city's original plan, a sacred diagram (YANTRA) emanating axially from the dwelling place of Mīnākṣī and Sundareśvara and incorporating the palace of the Pāṇṭya ruler. Within that space the amalgam of divine and human realms was represented as being possible, owing first to the self-manifestation of the deities as images and second to the dharmic guidance of their servant, the king. Often the city's design was described as a lotus, with its thoroughfares as petals and the Śakti-Shiva temple at the center.

MAELDÚIN \\'mīl-'dün^y\\, *also spelled* Mael Dúin, *or* Maeldun, hero of the longest of the Irish *immram* ("travel-tale"), known as *Immram Curaig Mael Dúin*. Maeldúin originally sets out on a journey when a DRUID advises him that he must find his father's killer. Maeldúin sees the man who killed his father at the first island he and his companions approach, but they are driven out to sea by a storm. They go on to encounter many wonders—during his journey Maeldúin visits no fewer than 31 islands.

Some of the islands contain strange beings—on one island the ants are as large as foals. Some islands are very structured; one is split in a black and a white half, where everything white becomes black on the other side and vice-versa. Another is divided by fences that correspond to the aristocratic hierarchy. On one island is a mill where half the corn of Ireland is ground, namely, all that which men begrudge one another. The island of women is difficult for the voyagers to leave. The queen throws a ball of yarn out to the boat each time they try to leave and every time they catch the ball they are obliged to stay another three months. At last they cut off the hand of the man who catches the ball and are saved.

On the penultimate island they meet a monk who stole treasures from his church and was guided to the rocky island and miraculously fed. He advises Maeldúin to reconcile himself with his father's killer. The next island is the same as the first they saw, and here the reconciliation takes place. Stories of travels at sea are part of the Irish literature and not all are as obviously Christian as this one. In the tale of St. Brendan (*Navigatio Brendani*) the theme has become completely Christian, and some of the wonders encountered by Brendan are also found in the earlier story of Maeldúin.

MAGGID \\mä-'gēd, 'mä-gid\\ (Hebrew: "preacher"), *plural* maggidim, any of the many itinerant Jewish preachers who flourished especially in Poland and Russia during the 17th and 18th centuries. Because RABBIS at that time preached only on the SABBATHS preceding PASSOVER and YOM KIPPUR, *maggidim* were in great demand throughout the year. Through their preaching, the *maggidim* were instrumental in spreading 18th-century HASIDISM. Rabbi Dov Baer of Mezhirich, who succeeded Ba'al Shem Ṭov as leader of the Hasidic movement, is known as the Great Maggid.

Closely associated with the *maggidim* were the *mokhiḥim* ("reprovers," or "rebukers"), who warned their listeners of severe punishments if they failed to observe the commandments. A heavenly being (or voice) that revealed secrets to a Jewish mystic was also called a *maggid*.

MAGI \\'mā-ˌjī, 'ma-\\, *singular* magus \\-gəs\\, originally, member of an ancient Median PRIESTHOOD specializing in cultic activities. The name is the Latinized form of *magoi*, the Greek transliteration of the Iranian original. From it the word magic is derived.

It is disputed whether the magi were from the beginning followers of ZOROASTER. They do not appear as such in the inscription of Bīsitūn, in which Darius the Great describes his speedy and final triumph over the magi who had revolted against his rule (522 BCE). Rather it appears that they constituted a priesthood serving several religions. The magi were a priestly CASTE during the Seleucid, Parthian, and Sāsānian periods; later parts of the AVESTA, such as the ritualistic sections of the *Vidēvdāt* (*Vendidad*), probably derive from them. From the 1st century CE the word in its Syriac form (*magusai*) was applied to magicians and soothsayers, chiefly from Babylonia, with a reputation for the most varied forms of wisdom. As long as the Persian empire lasted there was always a distinction between the Persian magi, who were credited with profound and extraordinary religious knowledge, and the Babylonian magi, who were often considered to be outright imposters. The word is thus used as a derogatory term for a traveling soothsayer in addition to its use as a title of respect.

MAGI, *singular* Magus, *also called* Wise Men, in Christian tradition, the noble pilgrims "from the East" who followed a miraculous guiding star to Bethlehem, where they paid homage to the infant JESUS as king of the Jews (Matthew 2:1–12). Eastern tradition sets the number of Magi at 12, but Western tradition sets their number at 3, probably based on the three gifts of "gold and frankincense and myrrh" presented to the infant.

The Gospel of Matthew relates how at Jerusalem the Magi attracted the interest of King Herod I of Judaea by announcing Jesus' birth. Herod extracted from them the place of Jesus' birth, requesting that they disclose the exact spot upon their return. An ANGEL in a dream, however, warned the Wise Men of Herod's intentions, and, after adoring the Christ Child, they returned to their own country.

Subsequent traditions embellished the narrative. As early as the 3rd century, they were considered to be kings, probably interpreted as the fulfillment of the PROPHECY in ISAIAH 60:3 ("And the GENTILES shall come to thy light, and

kings to the brightness of thy rising"). About the 8th century the names of three Magi—Bithisarea, Melichior, and Gathaspa—appear in a chronicle known as the *Excerpta latina barbari.* They have become known most commonly as Balthasar, Melchior, and Gaspar (or Casper). According to Western church tradition, Balthasar is often represented as a king of Arabia, Melchior as a king of Persia, and Gaspar as a king of India. Their supposed relics were transferred from Constantinople, possibly in the late 5th century, to Milan and thence to Cologne Cathedral in the 12th century. Devotion to the Magi was especially fervent in the Middle Ages. The Magi are venerated as patrons of travelers; their feast day is July 23.

The Adoration of the Magi—*i.e.*, their homage to the infant Jesus—early became one of the most popular themes in Christian art, the first extant painting on the subject being the fresco in the Priscilla CATACOMB of Rome dating from the 2nd century.

MAGIC, SCIENCE, AND RELIGION, categories used to depict different types of worldviews or developmental stages in the history of culture. Broadly speaking, the debate over the use of these categories comes down to the extent to which the terms should properly be distinguished from one another, and the basis for making such distinctions.

In the history of anthropology and COMPARATIVE RELIGION, three different understandings of these terms have emerged. The first views magic, religion, and science as different evolutionary stages in a single developmental progression. Within this approach, each term refers to a stage of cultural development. Magic, under this view, describes the worldview of so-called primitive or technologically underdeveloped societies. Among such peoples, magic is employed as a technique to explain and control the world in the absence of better methods for doing so. This stage gives way to a more sophisticated worldview, that of religion, wherein human beings have a more realistic view of their abilities to control the natural world, and the automatic workings of magic SPELLS give way to the worship of and dependence upon powerful superhuman entities (gods and goddesses). Finally, the third and most highly evolved stage, according to this view, is modern science, demonstrably more successful than magic or religion as an explanatory mechanism and means of controlling nature that then supersedes the magical and religious worldviews.

This evolutionary theory of human culture enjoyed wide currency in the 19th and early 20th centuries, particularly within the ethnographies of SIR EDWARD BURNETT TYLOR and SIR JAMES FRAZER and the social psychology of Sigmund Freud. It has since fallen into general disuse, however, in the face of criticism that it is prejudicial and teleological, fails to account for the complexity and diversity of culture, and drastically simplifies the variety of processes that make up historical development.

The second approach takes magic and science together and separates religion out as something intrinsically different. This approach begins from the premise that a kind of science is to be found in all cultures, though sometimes in a quite rudimentary form. Both magic and science share the assumption of "laws of nature"

An angel warns the Magi not to return to King Herod, 12th-century relief by Gislebertus in the cathedral of Saint-Lazare, Autun, France
Giraudon—Art Resource

and of causality; both attempt to operate on the world through the exploitation and manipulation of these laws. Therefore, magic is regarded as fundamentally similar to modern science, though it is based on a different belief system, identifies different laws of nature, and understands causality differently. Religion is, by contrast, relatively unconcerned with natural laws of cause and effect; rather, it is characterized by its moral and social concerns or is focused on ultimate meaning and therefore seeks to answer questions that science does not attempt to ask.

The third approach, finally, asserts that there is no necessary or real difference between the terms magic and religion, and often the proponents of this approach use the term magico-religious to signal this fundamental unity. This approach frequently asserts that the distinctions between magic and religion are often imposed by the outside observer: those operations which he feels to be truly religious are identified as such, but those things which seem fundamentally alien to his own value system are labeled as magical. Science, on the other hand, can be regarded as an empirically based technique; its findings are accepted as truth only when they can be replicated by others. Still, within science, the way in which findings are interpreted can change dramatically, that is, shifts in the paradigm, to use the language of philosophy of science scholar Thomas Kuhn, do occur. Also, for most nonscientists living in scientifically oriented cultures, science functions much like religion and magic does in other cultures—as a belief system or worldview whose claims are taken more or less on faith. Thus, within this approach, magic, science, and religion are all somewhat imprecise terms that refer to more or less different ways of viewing the world and operating in accordance with the rules which are believed to govern it. *See also* RELIGION, DEFINITION OF.

MAGNES, JUDAH LEON \\'mag-nəs\\ (b. July 5, 1877, San Francisco, Calif., U.S.—d. Oct. 27, 1948, New York, N.Y.), RABBI, religious leader, Zionist, and prime founder and first president of the Hebrew University of Jerusalem.

Magnes attended Hebrew Union College and was ordained a rabbi in 1900. After receiving a Ph.D. from the University of Heidelberg in 1902, Magnes returned to the United States and in 1904 became rabbi of a Reform SYNAGOGUE, Temple Israel of Brooklyn. From 1905 to 1908 he was secretary of the Federation of American Zionists. In 1906 he assumed the pulpit of the Reform temple Emanu-El in New York City. He founded Qehilla (Community) to unite the disparate elements of New York Jewry; its Bureau of Jewish Education (1910–41) had a profound effect for decades. A growing dissatisfaction with REFORM JUDAISM caused Magnes to resign from Emanu-El in 1910 and accept the pulpit of Temple B'nai Jeshurun, an Orthodox congregation. (*See* ORTHODOX JUDAISM.)

During World War I Magnes was a pacifist and drifted away from ZIONISM, whose leaders supported the Allied war effort. He joined the Joint Distribution Committee, which emphasized relief to Jews in Palestine rather than political activism there. At the war's end he went to Palestine and subsequently became the guiding spirit of the effort to establish the Hebrew University of Jerusalem. He devised the university's academic program and, when the institution was completed at Mt. Scopus in 1925, became chancellor. In 1935 he became the university's first president, a post he retained until his death.

Magnes also founded Iḥud (Unity), an association dedicated to the advancement of Arab-Jewish reconciliation,

and advocated an Arab-Jewish state that would be part of an Arab Federation.

MAGNIFICAT \\mag-'ni-fi-ˌkat, -ˌkät; män-'yi-fi-ˌkät\\, in CHRISTIANITY, the HYMN of praise by MARY, the mother of JESUS, found in Luke 1:46–55 and incorporated into the liturgical services of the Western churches (at Vespers) and of the Eastern Orthodox churches (at the morning services). Though some scholars have contended that this canticle was a song of Elizabeth (the wife of Zechariah and the mother of JOHN THE BAPTIST), most early Greek and Latin manuscripts regard it as the "Song of Mary."

It is named after the first word of its first line in Latin ("Magnificat anima mea Dominum," or "My soul magnifies the Lord"). Elaborate musical settings have been created for the Magnificat. It has been chanted in all eight modes of the plainsong and has been the subject of numerous other settings.

The following is the text of the Magnificat in the English Revised Standard Version:

◆ My soul magnifies the Lord,
   and my spirit rejoices in God my Savior,
   for he has regarded the low estate
     of his handmaiden.
For behold, henceforth all generations
   will call me blessed;
for he who is mighty has done great
   things for me,
and holy is his name.
And his mercy is on those who fear him
   from generation to generation.
He has shown strength with his arm,
he has scattered the proud in the
   imagination of their hearts,
he has put down the mighty from
   their thrones,
and exalted those of low degree;
he has filled the hungry with good things,
and the rich he has sent empty away.
He has helped his servant Israel,
in remembrance of his mercy,
as he spoke to our fathers,
to Abraham and to his posterity for ever. ◆

MAGOG \\'mā-ˌgäg\\, in biblical and apocalyptic literature, a hostile power associated with GOG.

MAG TUIRED \\'måg-'tù-rʸəth\\, *also spelled* Moytura, mythical plain in Ireland, which was the scene of two important battles. The first battle was between the Fir Bolg and the TUATHA DÉ DANANN, or race of gods. In this battle the Dé Danann overcame the Fir Bolg and won Ireland for themselves, but NUADU, the king of the gods, lost his hand in the battle. Because of this flaw, he was no longer permitted to be king. Bres, the beautiful son of a goddess and a FOMOIRE king, was chosen to rule in Nuadu's stead. Bres's reign was not successful because of his lack of generosity and kingly qualities. Nuadu was given a functional human hand by Mirach (*see* DIAN CÉCHT), and Bres was overthrown. Bres went to his father's family for aid and led a great army against the gods in the second battle of Mag Tuired. The gods had for a leader Lugh (*see* LUGUS), one of the most important Celtic gods, who won the battle and killed BALOR, the king of the Fomoire. The battle marks an end to the threat of the Fomoire in Irish myths and sagas.

MAHĀBHĀRATA

MAHĀBHĀRATA \mə-ˌhä-'bär-ə-tə\ (Sanskrit: "Great [Tale of the] Bhāratas"), one of the two major Sanskrit epics of India, valued for its high literary merit and its religious inspiration. The *Mahābhārata* consists of a mass of legendary and didactic material surrounding a central heroic narrative that tells of the struggle for supremacy between two groups of cousins—the Kauravas and the PĀṆḌAVAS. Together with the second major epic, the RĀMĀYAṆA, it is an important source of information about the evolution of HINDU-ISM during the period from about 400 BCE to 200 CE. Contained within the *Mahābhārata* is the BHAGAVAD GĪTĀ, which is the single most important religious text of Hinduism.

The poem is made up of almost 100,000 couplets—its length thus being about seven times that of the *Iliad* and the *Odyssey* combined—divided into 18 *parvan*s, or sections, to which has been added a supplement entitled *Harivaṃśa* ("Genealogy of the God Hari"—*i.e.*, Krishna-Vishnu). Authorship of the poem is traditionally ascribed to the sage Vyāsa, although it is more likely that he compiled existing material. The traditional date for the war that is the central event of the *Mahābhārata* is 3102 BCE, but most historians prefer a later date. The poem reached its present form about 400 CE.

The epic narrates a power struggle between the five Pāṇḍava brothers (Yudhiṣṭhira, Bhīma, ARJUNA, Nakula, and Sahadeva) and their cousins, the Kauravas. Forced into exile, the Pāṇḍavas jointly marry Draupadī and meet their cousin KRISHNA, who remains their friend and companion thereafter. The feud culminates in a great series of battles on the field of Kurukṣetra (north of modern Delhi, in Haryana state). All the Kauravas are annihilated, and, on the victorious side, only the five Pāṇḍava brothers and Krishna survive. Krishna dies at the hands of a hunter who mistakes him for a deer. The five brothers, along with Draupadī and a dog who joins them (Dharma, the god of justice, in disguise), set out for INDRA's heaven, yet only Yudhiṣṭhira, the son of Dharma, reaches its gate. After further tests of his faithfulness and constancy, Yudhiṣṭhira is finally reunited with his brothers and Draupadī to enjoy perpetual bliss.

The feud constitutes little more than a fifth of the total work and may once have formed a separate poem, the *Bhārata*. Interwoven with its episodes are the romance of Nala and Damayantī; the legend of SĀVITRĪ, whose devotion to her dead husband persuades YAMA, the god of death, to restore him to life; descriptions of places of pilgrimages; and many other myths and legends.

Above all, the *Mahābhārata* is an exposition on DHARMA (codes of conduct), including the proper conduct of a king, of a warrior, of a man living in times of calamity, and of a person seeking to attain emanci-pation from rebirth. The several centuries during which the epic took shape were a period of transition from the religion of Vedic sacrifice to the sectarian, internalized worship of later Hinduism, and different sections of the poem express varying and sometimes contradictory beliefs. Some sections, such as the *Nārāyaṇīya* (a part of Book XIII), the *Bhagavad Gītā* (Book VI), the *Anugītā* (Book XIV), and the later supplement, the *Harivaṃśa*, are important sources of early Vaiṣṇavite thought. There Krishna is identified with Lord VISHNU, and other AVATARS (incarnations) are also described.

MAHABODHI SOCIETY \mə-ˌhä-'bō-dē\, organization that was established to encourage BUDDHISM and Buddhist studies in India and abroad. The society was founded in Ceylon (now Sri Lanka) in 1891 by Anagarika Dharmapala; one of its original goals was the restoration of the Mahābodhi temple at BODH GAYĀ, Bihār state, India, the site of the BUDDHA GOTAMA's enlightenment.

The society has its headquarters in Calcutta and operates centers in several other cities in India and at Anuradhapura, Sri Lanka. An English-language journal, *The Maha Bodhi,* is published by the society.

MAHĀDEVĪ \mə-ˌhä-'dā-vē\, *also known as* Mahādevīyak-ka, 12th-century-CE Hindu poet-saint of the Karnataka region of India.

Married to a local king against her will, Mahādevī subsequently left her husband and renounced the world. Legend has it that she wandered naked, singing songs of passionate love for her "true husband," the god SHIVA. Some of her poems concern the irreconcilable conflict between secular and religious love and devotion: "Take these husbands who die, decay, and feed them to your kitchen fires!" Her devotional songs revolve around a theme typical of the Indian devotional tradition—the interplay between, on the one hand, love in separation and the longing for the divine lover, and on the other hand, love in union and the inexpressible bliss it brings: "When he's away I cannot wait to get a glimpse of him. Friend, when will I have it both ways, be with Him yet not with Him."

MAHĀMĀYĀ \mə-ˌhä-'mä-yä\, *also called* Māyā, mother of the BUDDHA GOTAMA; she was the wife of Rāja Śuddhodana.

In Buddhist legend, Mahāmāyā dreamt that a white elephant with six tusks entered her right side, which was interpreted to mean that she had conceived a child who would become either a world ruler or a buddha. After 10 lunar months she went to the Lumbinī grove outside the city of Kapilavastu. While she stood upright and held onto the branch of a sal tree (in the posture adopted by mothers of all buddhas), the child came

Mahāmāyā dreaming of the white elephant, Gandhāra relief, 2nd century CE
By courtesy of the trustees of the British Museum

forth from her right hip. Seven days after his birth (again, in accordance with the destiny of the mothers of all buddhas) she died and was reborn again in the Heaven of the Thirty-three Gods.

MAHAMUNI \mə-ˈhä-mü-nē\, brass Buddha statue (12 feet high), one of the most sacred images in Myanmar (Burma) and believed to be of great antiquity. Located in the Maha-muni, or Arakan, PAGODA south of the city of Mandalay, the statue was among the spoils of war brought from the Ara-kan Coast in 1784 by King Bodawpaya.

MAHAR \mə-ˈhär\, caste-cluster, or group of many endoga-mous CASTES, living chiefly in Mahārāshtra state, India, and in adjoining states. In the early 1980s the Mahar communi-ty was believed to constitute about 9 percent of the total population of Mahārāshtra—by far the largest, most wide-spread, and most important of all the officially designated Scheduled castes (formerly UNTOUCHABLES or Harijans) in the region.

Traditionally, Mahars lived on the outskirts of villages and served as village watchmen, messengers, street sweep-ers, removers of carcasses, and agricultural laborers. In the mid-20th century, Mahars began to migrate in large num-bers to urban centers (Bombay, Nāgpur, Pune [Poona], and Sholāpur), where they were employed as industrial labor-ers, mechanics, and bus and truck drivers. Mahars were unified by the eminent 20th-century leader BHIMRAO RAMJI AMBEDKAR, who urged them to militant political conscious-ness and to great educational improvement. Before his death in 1956, Ambedkar and hundreds of thousands of his Mahar followers converted to BUDDHISM in protest against their Hindu caste status.

MAHĀSANGHIKA \mə-ˌhä-ˈsəŋ-gi-kə\ (Sanskrit, from mahā-, "great" + sangha, "community, brotherhood [of monks]"), early Buddhist school in India that was a precur-sor of the MAHĀYĀNA tradition. The school's emergence about a century after the death of the BUDDHA GOTAMA (483 BCE) represented the first major schism in the Buddhist community. Traditional accounts of the second Buddhist council at Vaiśālī attribute the split to a dispute over mo-nastic rules between the Mahāsanghikas and the more con-servative Sthaviravādins. Later texts stress the Mahāsan-ghika beliefs regarding the nature of the Buddha—that there are a plurality of buddhas who are supramundane (lokottara) and that what passed for the Buddha Gotama in his earthly existence was only an apparition.

The school's influence spread from Vaiśālī to southern India, where it further divided into several subsects, of which the best known was the Lokottaravāda.

MAHĀSIDDHA \mə-ˌhä-ˈsid-də\ (Sanskrit: "great perfect one"), Tibetan grub-thob chen \ˈdùp-tōp-ˈchen\, in the Tantric, or esoteric, traditions of India and Tibet, a person who, by the practice of meditative disciplines, has attained SIDDHA (miraculous powers). See TANTRIC HINDUISM; TANTRIC BUDDHISM.

Both the Śaivites (followers of SHIVA) of Hindu India and the Tantric Buddhists of Tibet preserve legends of 84 ma-hāsiddhas who flourished up to the 11th century. (The number 84 is a conventional, mystical number represent-ing totality.) The lists of names vary considerably. All class-es of society and both sexes are represented, and many non-Indian names appear. The prominence of the 84 mahāsid-dhas reflects a synthesis during that period of the two reli-

gious traditions, combined with elements of HATHA YOGA, magic, and alchemy.

The 84 mahāsiddhas continue to be revered in Tibet. They are the authors of most of the Tantric works on magic and are the originators of spiritual lines of descent—from master to disciple—still honored. The most famous of the Tibetan mahāsiddhas is the great 8th-century Tantric mas-ter PADMASAMBHAVA.

MAHĀ-ŚIVARĀTRĪ \mə-ˈhä-ˌshi-və-ˈrä-trē\ (Sanskrit: "Great Night of Shiva"), in HINDUISM, the most important sectarian festival of the year for devotees of SHIVA. The 14th day of the dark half of each lunar month is specially sacred to Shiva, but when it occurs in the month of Māgha (Janu-ary–February) and, to a lesser extent, in the month of Phāl-guna (February–March), it is a day of particular rejoicing. The preceding day the participant observes a fast and at night a vigil during which a special worship of the LINGA is performed. The following day is celebrated with feasting and, among the members of the South Indian VĪRAŚAIVA sect, with the giving of gifts to the GURU.

MAHĀVAIROCANA SUTRA \mə-ˈhä-vī-ˈrō-chə-nə-ˈsü-trə\ (Sanskrit: "Great Illuminator Sutra"), Japanese Dainichi-kyō \dī-ˈnē-chē-ˌkyō\, text of Indian TANTRIC BUDDHISM that became a principal SCRIPTURE of the SHINGON sect. The text received a Chinese translation, under the title Ta-jih Ching, about CE 725, and its teachings were propagated a century later in Japan by KŪKAI. These teachings center upon Mahāvairocana (Japanese: Dainichi Nyorai), the su-preme cosmic buddha, whose body forms the universe. Through mystic rituals with an Indian flavor (even involv-ing Hindu deities), one is led to realize that all one's thoughts, words, and actions are in reality expressions of Mahāvairocana.

MAHĀVASTU \mə-ˌhä-ˈvəs-tü\ (Sanskrit: "Great Story"), legendary life of the BUDDHA GOTAMA, a late canonical work of the MAHĀSANGHIKA school. Its three sections treat the Buddha's former lives, the events from his entering the womb of MAHĀMĀYĀ to his enlightenment, and his first con-versions and the rise of the monastic community.

The central narrative of the text is frequently interrupted by JĀTAKAS, AVADĀNAS, and doctrinal discourses. The life of the Buddha itself is presented as a profusion of wondrous events. The Mahāvastu reflects a growth of ideas about BO-DHISATTVAS that was to continue in MAHĀYĀNA circles, but at the same time, like the LALITAVISTARA, it preserves many an-cient stories, traditions, and textual passages. The core of the work may go back to the 2nd century BCE, but much material was added in the centuries that followed.

MAHĀVIHĀRA \mə-ˈhä-vi-ˈhär-ə\, Buddhist monastery founded in the late 3rd century BCE in Anurādhapura, the ancient capital of Sri Lanka. The monastery was built by the Sinhalese king Devānampiya Tissa not long after his conversion to BUDDHISM. Though during the 12 ensuing cen-turies the other monasteries in Sri Lanka came to rival the Mahāvihāra in terms of size and influence, the Mahāvihāra monks played a central role through their preservation and development of the THERAVĀDA school of Buddhism and its Pāli textual tradition. Through a series of reforms spon-sored by Sinhalese kings during the 12th and 13th centu-ries, the Mahāvihāra community and the reformed version of the Theravāda/Pāli tradition with which it was associat-ed became the dominant religious force in Sri Lanka. The reformed Theravāda tradition continued to have its center at the Mahāvihāra as it spread from Sri Lanka and became an important force in Southeast Asian Buddhism.

MAHĀVĪRA \mə-ˌhä-'vē-rə\ (Sanskrit: "Great Hero"), *epithet* of Vardhamāna \ˌvər-də-'mä-nə, ˌvär-\ (b. *c.* 599 BCE, Kuṇḍagrāma, India—d. 527, Pāvāpurī), last of the 24 TĪRTHAṄKARAS (Jain saints), and the reformer of the Jain monastic community (*see* JAINISM). The traditions of the two main Jain sects record that Mahāvīra became a monk and followed an extremely ascetic life, attaining *kevala-jñāna*, the stage of omniscience or highest perception. Teaching a doctrine of austerity, Mahāvīra advocated NONVIOLENCE, vegetarianism, and the acceptance of the *mahāvrata*s, the five "great vows" of renunciation.

Mahāvīra appears to have been a younger contemporary of the BUDDHA GOTAMA. The son of a KṢATRIYA family, he grew up in Kuṇḍagrāma, a large city in the kingdom of Vaiśālī (modern Basarh, Bihār state), the area of origin of both JAINISM and BUDDHISM. His father was Siddhārtha, a ruler of the Nāta, or Jñātṛ, clan. According to one Jain tradition his mother was named Devānandā and was a member of the Brahmin class; other traditions name her Triśalā, Videhadinnā, or Priyakāriṇī, and place her in the Kṣatriya class.

The 6th century BCE was a period in which certain members of the Kṣatriya class opposed the cultural domination of the Brahmins, who used their positions as members of the highest class to make demands upon the lower CASTES. In particular, there was growing opposition to the large-scale Vedic sacrifices (YAJÑA), which involved the killing of many animals. Unnecessary killing had become objectionable to many thoughtful people of the time as a result of the spread of the doctrine of REINCARNATION, which linked animals and human beings in the same cycle of rebirth. Economic factors may also have encouraged the growth of the doctrine of nonviolence. Mahāvīra and his contemporary Siddhārtha Gotama, the Buddha, were two of the greatest leaders in the anti-Brahmin movement.

Mahāvīra apparently was reared in luxury, though as a younger son he could not inherit the leadership of the clan. At the age of 30, after he had married and had a daughter, he renounced the world and became a monk. According to legend, his parents had died by practicing the rite of *sallekhanā*—*i.e.*, voluntary self-starvation.

It is related that Mahāvīra used one garment for more than a year, but subsequently went about naked and kept

Mahāvīra enthroned, miniature from the Kalpa Sūtra, *15th century*
By courtesy of the Smithsonian Institution, Freer Gallery of Art, Washington, D.C.

no possessions—not even a bowl for obtaining alms or drinking water. He meditated day and night and lived in various places—workshops, cremation and burial grounds, and at the feet of trees. Trying to avoid all sinful activity, he especially avoided harming any kind of life, thus developing the doctrine of AHIṂSĀ, or noninjury. He kept numerous fast periods and never ate anything that was expressly prepared for him.

After 12 years of practicing such austerities, he attained *kevala-jñāna*, the highest stage of perception. The school of PĀRŚVANĀTHA, the 23rd Tīrthaṅkara, apparently had been waning in appeal; Mahāvīra revived and reorganized Jain doctrine and its monastic order, thus being credited as the founder of Jainism. Basing his doctrines, according to tradition, on the teachings of Pārśvanātha, a 9th-century-BCE teacher from Vārānāsī, Mahāvīra systematized earlier Jain doctrines—along with metaphysical, mythological, and cosmological beliefs—and also established the rules and guidelines for the monks, nuns, and laity of Jain religious life.

Mahāvīra's advocacy of nonviolence encouraged his followers to become strong advocates of vegetarianism, which in the course of time helped to bring about a virtual end to sacrificial killing in Indian rituals. His followers accept his five *mahāvrata*s: renunciation of killing, of speaking untruths, of greed, of sexual pleasure, and of all attachments to living beings and nonliving things.

Mahāvīra was given the title *jina*, or "conqueror" (*i.e.*, conqueror of enemies such as attachment and greed), which subsequently became a synonym for Tīrthaṅkara. He died, according to tradition, in 527 BCE at Pāvāpurī in Bihār state, leaving a group of followers who established Jainism, which, with its practice of nonviolence, has profoundly influenced Indian culture.

MAHĀYĀNA \mə-ˌhä-'yä-nə, ˌmä-hə-\ (Sanskrit: "Greater Vehicle"), one of the three major Buddhist traditions and the form most widely adhered to in China, Korea, Vietnam, and Japan. Mahāyāna BUDDHISM emerged about the 1st century CE from the ancient Buddhist schools as a more liberal and innovative interpretation of the Buddha's teachings. Mahāyānists differ from the conservatives (represented in the modern world by the Theravādins) in their views of Buddhas and related figures and in the goal that they set forth for Buddhist practitioners. Whereas THERAVĀDA Buddhists revere the BUDDHA GOTAMA as a real, historically situated being and focus their attention on him, Mahāyānists see Gotama as an earthly manifestation of a transcendent celestial buddha and affirm the accessibility and immediate religious importance of many different buddhas and celestial BODHISATTVAS. In addition, Mahāyānists do not believe that the ideal goal for a Buddhist practitioner is to become an ARHAT, or perfected saint; this they consider to be a limited, selfish goal. Rather, the goal is to attain the condition of a bodhisattva, or person who has approached the achievement of buddhahood but has postponed entrance into NIRVANA in order to work toward the salvation of all sentient beings. Thus, compassion, the chief virtue associated with the bodhisattva, is accorded an equal place with wisdom or insight, the virtue emphasized by the ancient schools. The merit accrued by buddhas and bodhisattvas is considered transferable to others, a concept that led to the development of devotional traditions, in which the faith of the practitioner plays a crucial role.

The Mahāyāna tradition encompasses a wide variety of schools and sects, including the MĀDHYAMIKA and YOGĀCĀRA philosophical schools of India, the great East Asian scholastic schools such as T'ien-t'ai (Tendai) and HUA-YEN (Kegon), the Ch'an (ZEN) schools of East Asia, the PURE LAND school of East Asia, and the NICHIREN sect in Japan.

The third major branch of Buddhism is the Esoteric branch, which includes the VAJRAYĀNA school, predominant in TIBETAN BUDDHISM, and the East Asian tradition represented by the SHINGON school, which persists in Japan. This branch accepts most aspects of Mahāyāna Buddhology and the basic principles of Mahāyāna doctrine, but these very distinctive schools and sects supplement the Mahāyāna orientation with important components of Esoteric teaching and ritual practice.

MAHDĪ, AL- \ál-'mä-dē, -'mä-hə-dē\ (Arabic: "Divinely Guided One"), in Islamic ESCHATOLOGY, a messianic deliverer who will fill the earth with justice and equity, restore true religion, and usher in a golden age lasting seven, eight, or nine years before the end of the world. The QUR'AN does not mention him, and almost no reliable HADITHS concerning the Mahdī can be adduced. Many SUNNI theologians accordingly question Mahdist beliefs, but such beliefs rise among the populace in times of crisis, and they form a necessary part of SHI'ITE doctrine.

The doctrine of the Mahdī seems to have gained currency during the religious and political upheavals of early ISLAM (7th and 8th centuries). In 686 AL-MUKHTĀR IBN ABŪ 'UBAYD AL-THAQAFĪ, leader of a revolt of non-Arab Muslims in Iraq, seems to have first used the doctrine by maintaining his allegiance to a son of 'ALĪ (Muhammad's cousin, son-in-law, and fourth CALIPH), Muhammad ibn al-Ḥanafīya, even after Ibn al-Ḥanafīya's death. Abū 'Ubayd taught that, as Mahdī, Ibn al-Ḥanafīya remained alive in his tomb in a state of occultation (GHAYBA) and would reappear to vanquish his enemies. In 750 the 'Abbāsid revolution made use of eschatological prophecies current at the time that the Mahdī would rise in Khorāsān in the east, carrying a black banner.

Belief in the Mahdī has tended to receive new emphasis in every time of crisis. Thus, after the battle of Las Navas de Tolosa (1212), when most of Spain was lost for Islam, Spanish Muslims circulated traditions ascribed to the Prophet foretelling a reconquest of Spain by the Mahdī. During the Napoleonic invasion of Egypt, a person claiming to be the Mahdī appeared briefly in Lower Egypt.

Because the Mahdī is seen as a restorer of the political power and religious purity of Islam, the title has tended to be claimed by social revolutionaries in Islamic society. North Africa in particular has seen a number of self-styled

Mahdīs, the most important of these being 'Ubayd Allāh, founder of the Fāṭimid dynasty (909); MUHAMMAD IBN TŪMART, founder of the Almohad movement in Morocco in the 12th century; and Muhammad Ahmad, the Mahdī of the Sudan who, in 1881, revolted against the Egyptian administration.

MAHDĪ, AL- \ùl-maḵ-'dē, -'mä-dē\ (Sudanese), *original name* Muhammad Ahmad ibn al-Sayyid 'Abd Allāh (b. Aug. 12, 1844—d. June 22, 1885, Omdurman, Sudan), creator of a vast Islamic state extending from the Red Sea to central Africa and founder of a movement that remained influential in The Sudan a century later. As a youth he moved from traditional SUNNI religious study to a mystical interpretation of ISLAM. In 1881 he proclaimed his divine mission to purify Islam and the governments that defiled it. His extensive campaign culminated in the capture of Khartoum (Jan. 26, 1885). He then established a theocratic state in The Sudan, with its capital at Omdurman.

Muhammad Ahmad was the son of a shipbuilder from the Dongola district of Nubia. Shortly after his birth, the family moved south to Karari, a river village near Khartoum. As a boy, Muhammad developed a love of religious study. Increasingly, he tended to a more mystic interpretation of Islam, in the Sufi tradition, through study of the QUR'AN and the practice of self-denial under the discipline of a religious brotherhood.

He joined the Sammānīya order and grew to manhood in a wholly Sudanese religious setting, purposely separating himself from the official ruling class. By now he had begun to attract his own disciples and, in 1870, moved with them to a hermitage on Abā Island in the White Nile, 175 miles south of Khartoum. His highly emotional and intransigent religious observance brought him into conflict with his SHAYKH (teacher), whom he reproved for worldliness. The exasperated *shaykh* expelled him from the circle of his disciples, whereupon Muhammad Ahmad, having vainly asked his teacher's pardon, joined the brotherhood of a rival *shaykh* within the same order.

The Sudan at this time was a dependency of Egypt, itself a province of the Ottoman Empire and governed by a multiracial, Turkish-speaking ruling class. In appearance, education, and way of life, the rulers contrasted starkly with their Sudanese subjects, and the situation was politically dangerous. Gradually, during 1880 and the first weeks of 1881, Muhammad Ahmad became convinced that the ruling class had deserted Islam and that the viceroy of Egypt was a puppet in the hands of unbelievers and thus unfit to rule over Muslims. In March 1881 he revealed to his closest followers that God had appointed him to purify Islam and to destroy all governments that defiled it. On June 29 he publicly assumed the title of the "Anticipated Mahdī" (al-Mahdī al-Muntazar), a figure who, according to tradition, would appear to restore Islam.

In less than four years al-Mahdī, who set out from Abā Island with a few followers (*see* ANSAR) armed with sticks and spears, was master of almost all the territory formerly occupied by the Egyptian government. By the end of 1883, his forces had annihilated three Egyptian armies sent against them. His fame reached responsive ears in Arabia to the north and as far west as Bornu (Nigeria). Al-Mahdī's crowning victory was the capture of Khartoum in 1885. After many of the citizens of Khartoum had been massacred, al-Mahdī made a triumphal entry into the city and led the prayers in the principal mosque.

The withdrawal of the British expedition, which had

failed to relieve Khartoum, left al-Mahdī free to consolidate his religious empire. He abandoned Khartoum and set up his administrative center at Omdurman, an expanded village of mud houses and grass-roofed huts on the left bank of the Nile, opposite Khartoum. He directed every aspect of community and personal life by proclamations, sermons, warnings, and letters. The political institutions, as well as the nomenclature of his government, were based insofar as practicable on those of early Islam. In the manner of the Prophet MUHAMMAD, he appointed four CALIPHS to be the living successors of the four earliest caliphs in Islamic history. Al-Mahdī referred to himself as "the successor to the apostle of God"—that is, successor to the Prophet Muhammad, but only in the sense of continuing his work. Al-Mahdī's rule was brief. He took ill, possibly of typhus, and died in June 1885, only 41 years old.

MAHDIST \'mä-dist\: *see* ANSAR.

MAHESH YOGI, MAHARISHI \mə-,hä-'rē-shē-'mä-hesh-'yō-gē, ,mä-hə-\ (b. 1911?, India), Hindu religious leader who introduced the practice of TRANSCENDENTAL MEDITATION (TM) to the West.

Little is known of the Maharishi's early life. He studied physics at the University of Allahābād and worked for a time in factories. He later left for the HIMALAYAS, where for 13 years he studied under GURU DEV, the founder of TM. When Guru Dev died in 1952, the Maharishi organized a movement to spread his teachings throughout the world; his first world tour took place in 1959 and brought him to the United States.

TM is a type of meditation, practiced twice a day, in which the subject mentally recites a special MANTRA (sacred sound or phrase). Concentration on the repeated utterances decreases mental activity, and as a result the subject is expected to reach a higher state of consciousness. The movement grew slowly until the late 1960s, when it was adopted by many of the spiritual seekers of that era.

MAHZOR \mäk̲-'zòr, 'mäk̲-zər\, *also spelled* machzor, *plural* mahzorim \,mäk̲-zò-'rēm\, *or* mahzors (Hebrew: "cycle"), originally a Jewish prayer book arranged according to liturgical chronology and used throughout the entire year. *Mahzor* has come to mean the festival prayer book, as distinguished from the SIDDUR, the prayer book used on the ordinary SABBATH and on weekdays.

Though the basic structure and prayers of the rites of the ASHKENAZI and SEPHARDI are essentially the same, religious hymns (*piyyutim*) composed by such celebrated medieval poets as Eleazar Kalir abound in the Ashkenazic *mahzor* but do not appear in Sephardic festive liturgies, which draw on the compositions of the great Spanish poets. Local ritual differences have given rise to somewhat different *mahzorim* within both the Ashkenazic and the Sephardic rites.

MAIMON, SALOMON \'mī-mòn\, *original name* Salomon ben Joshua (b. *c.* 1754, Nieśwież, Grand Duchy of Lithuania [now Nesvizh, Belarus]—d. Nov. 22, 1800, Nieder-Siegersdorf, Silesia), Jewish philosopher who combined an early and extensive familiarity of rabbinic learning with a proficiency in Hebrew. After acquiring a special reverence for MOSES MAIMONIDES, he took the philosopher's surname.

In 1770, before he was 20, Maimon wrote an unorthodox commentary on Maimonides' *More nevukhim* (*Guide of the Perplexed*) that earned him the hostility of fellow Jews. At 25 he wandered over Europe until he settled in Posen, Pol., as a tutor. In 1790 he was given residence on the estate of Count Friedrich Adolf, Graf von Kalckreuth, at Nieder-Siegersdorf. During the next decade he wrote his major philosophical works, including the autobiography edited for him by K.P. Moritz as *Salomon Maimons Lebensgeschichte* (1792; *Solomon Maimon: An Autobiography*) and his major critique of Kantian philosophy, *Versuch über die Transcendentalphilosophie* (1790; "Search for the Transcendental Philosophy").

By emphasizing the limits of pure thought, Maimon helped to advance philosophical discussion of the connection between thought and experience and between knowledge and faith. In his view there was religious and ethical value in the pursuit of truth, even though the goal itself was not completely attainable. His other major writings are *Philosophisches Wörterbuch* (1791; "Philosophical Dictionary"), *Über die Progressen der Philosophie* (1792; "On the Progresses of

Maharishi Mahesh Yogi (center) with George Harrison and John Lennon of the Beatles
Archive Photos—Popperfoto

Philosophy"), and *Kritische Untersuchungen über den menschlichen Geist* (1797; "Critical Investigations of the Human Spirit").

MAIMONIDES, MOSES \mī-ˈmä-nə-ˌdēz\, *original name* Moses ben Maimon \ben-mī-ˈmȯn\, *also called* Rambam \räm-ˈbäm\, *Arabic* Abū ʿImran Mūsā ibn Maymūn ibn ʿUbayd Allāh (b. March 30, 1135, Córdoba [Spain]—d. Dec. 13, 1204, Egypt), Jewish philosopher, jurist, and physician, the foremost intellectual figure of medieval JUDAISM. His monumental contributions in religion, philosophy, and medicine influenced Jewish and non-Jewish scholars alike.

Maimonides was born into a distinguished family of Córdoba, where citizens were accorded full religious freedom. But before Moses' 13th birthday the Islamic Mediterranean world was shaken by a revolutionary Islamic sect, the AL-MOHADS, who captured Córdoba in 1148, leaving the Jewish community faced with the alternative of submitting to IS-LAM or leaving the city. The Maimons remained in Córdoba for some 11 years, practicing their Judaism in private while disguising their ways in public.

When the double life proved too irksome, the family left the city about 1159 to settle in Fez, Morocco, where Moses continued his studies in rabbinics, Greek philosophy, and medicine. In 1165, however, RABBI Judah ibn Shoshan, with whom Moses had studied, was executed for practicing Judaism. The Maimon family moved again, this time to Palestine, then on to Egypt, settling in Fostat, near Cairo. There Jews were free to practice their faith openly.

Moses was soon left as the sole support of his family. He became a practicing physician. His fame as a physician spread rapidly, and he soon became the court physician to the SULTAN Saladin and his son al-Afḍal. He also continued a private practice and lectured before his fellow physicians at the state hospital. At the same time he became the leading member of the Jewish community, teaching in public and helping his people with various personal and communal problems.

Maimonides' earliest written work was the *Millot ha-Higgayon* ("Treatise on Logical Terminology"), a study of various technical terms employed in logic and metaphysics. Another of his early works was the "Essay on the Calendar" (Hebrew title: *Maʾamar haʿibur*). The first of his major works, begun at the age of 23, was his commentary on the MISHNAH, *Kitāb al-Sirāj*, written in Arabic. Maimonides' commentary clarified individual words and phrases, frequently citing relevant information in the fields of archaeology, theology, or science, and featured a series of introductory essays dealing with general philosophic issues touched on in the Mishnah. One of these essays summarizes the teachings of Judaism in a creed of THIRTEEN ARTICLES OF FAITH.

He completed the commentary on the Mishnah at the age of 33, after which he began his magnum opus, the code of Jewish law, on which he also labored for 10 years. Bearing the name of MISHNE TORAH ("The Torah Reviewed") and written in a lucid Hebrew style, the code offers a brilliant systematization of all Jewish law and doctrine. Maimonides wrote two other works in Jewish law of lesser scope: the *Sefer ha-mitzwot* ("Book of Precepts"), a digest of law for the less sophisticated reader, written in Arabic; and the *Hilkhot ha-Yerushalmi* ("Laws of Jerusalem"), a digest of the laws in the PALESTINIAN TALMUD that was written in Hebrew.

His next major work, on which he labored for 15 years, was his classic in religious philosophy, the *Dalālat al-ḥāʾir-*

īn (*The Guide of the Perplexed*), later known under its Hebrew title as the *More nevukhim*. A plea for what he called a more rational philosophy of Judaism, it was written in Arabic and sent as a private communication to his favorite disciple, Joseph ibn Aknin. The work was translated into Hebrew in Maimonides' lifetime and later into Latin and most European languages.

Maimonides also wrote occasional essays dealing with current problems that faced the Jewish community, and he maintained an extensive correspondence with scholars, students, and community leaders. Among his minor works are *Iggert Teman* ("Epistle to Yemen"), *Iggeret ha-shemad* or *Maʾamar Qiddush ha-Shem* ("Letter on Apostasy"), *Iggeret le-qahal Marsilia* ("Letter on Astrology," or, literally, "Letter to the Community of Marseille"), and works dealing with medicine, including a popular miscellany of health rules, dedicated to the sultan, al-Afḍal.

MAISON-CARRÉE \mä-ˌzȯⁿ-kä-ˈrā\, Roman TEMPLE at Nîmes, France. According to an inscription, it was dedicated to Gaius and Lucius Caesar, adopted sons of Augustus, and dates from the beginning of the Christian era.

The temple, 82 feet long by 40 feet wide, is one of the most beautiful monuments built in Gaul by the Romans. It houses a collection of Roman sculpture and classical fragments.

MAITREYA \mī-ˈtrā-yə\, in BUD-DHISM, a future buddha, presently a BODHISATTVA residing in the Tuṣi-ta heaven, who will descend to earth in order to renew preaching of the DHARMA when the teachings of the BUDDHA GOTA-MA have completely decayed. Maitreya is the earliest bodhisattva around whom a cult developed and is mentioned in SCRIPTURES from as early as the 3rd century CE.

The name Maitreya is derived from the Sanskrit *maitrī* ("friendliness"). In Pāli the name becomes Metteyya, in Chinese Mi-lo-fo, in Japanese Miroku, and in Mongolian Maidari; in Tibetan the bodhisattva is known as Byams-pa ("kind," or "loving"). His worship was especially popular during the 4th to 7th century, and his images are found throughout the Buddhist world. He is represented in painting and sculpture both as a bodhisattva and as a buddha, and he is frequently depicted seated in European fashion or with his ankles

Miroku (Maitreya) in meditation, Japanese gilt bronze figure, 7th century
The Cleveland Museum of Art, John L. Severance Fund, 50.86

loosely crossed. In some contexts, particularly, though not exclusively, in medieval China, the expectation of the coming of Maitreya came to be associated with peasant rebellions and the hope for the establishment of a new religion and social order.

MAKTAB \'mȧk-tȧb\, *also called* kuttāb (Arabic: "school"), Muslim elementary school. Until the 20th century boys were instructed in QUR'AN recitation, reading, writing, and grammar in *maktab*s, which were the only means of mass education. Girls had limited access to this level of learning, but it was not until the 19th century that their access to the *maktab* became usual. During the 20th century government-supported primary schools have tended to supplant the *maktab* in Muslim countries, providing education for both girls and boys. Some religious education is incorporated in the curriculum of government schools in most Muslim countries.

MALAKBEL \,mä-läk-'bäl\ (Hebrew: "Angel of Baal"), West Semitic sun god and messenger god, worshiped primarily in the ancient Syrian city of Palmyra; he was variously identified by the Greeks with ZEUS and HERMES and by the Romans with SOL. His name may have been of Babylonian origin, and he was considered the equivalent of the Babylonian sun god SHAMASH. Engravings on a marble altar from Palmyra depict the four annual stages in the life of Malakbel, symbolizing the yearly sequence of the sun. Most other representations portray Malakbel with Aglibol, the moon god.

MALĀMATĪYA \,mȧ-lȧ-mȧ-'tē-ə\, Sufi group that appeared in Sāmānid Iran during the 9th century (*see* SUFISM). The name *Malāmatīya* was derived from the Arabic verb *lāma* ("blame"). Malāmatī doctrines were based on the reproach of the carnal self and a careful watch over its inclinations to surrender to the temptations of the world. They often claimed as the basis of their philosophy the Qur'anic verse "I [God] swear by the reproachful soul," which, they said, clearly praised a self that constantly reproached its owner for the slightest deviation from the world of God. The reproachful self in Malāmatī terminology was the perfect self.

The Malāmatīya found value in self-blame, believing that it would be conducive to a true detachment from worldly things and to disinterested service of God. They feared the praise and respect of other persons. Piety, the Malāmatī believer said, is a private affair between a person and God. A Malāmatī believer further concealed his knowledge as a precaution against acquiring fame and strove to make his faults known, so that he would always be reminded of his imperfection. Toward others they were as tolerant and forgiving as they were strict and harsh on themselves.

While other Sufis revealed their *aḥwāl* (states of ECSTASY) and their joy over progressing from one MAQĀM (spiritual stage) to the next, the Malāmatīya kept their achievements and their feelings concealed. Sufis wore particular clothes, organized various orders, and assumed many titles; the Malāmatīya concealed their identities and belittled their achievements. In fact, Malāmatī doctrines were so different from those of most Sufi groups that a few Muslim scholars did not consider the Malāmatīya to be Sufis.

MALCOLM X \'mal-kəm-'eks\, *original name* Malcolm Little, *Muslim name* el-Hajj Malik el-Shabazz \el-'haj-mə-'lēk-el-shə-'baz\ (b. May 19, 1925, Omaha, Neb., U.S.—d. Feb. 21, 1965, New York, N.Y.), African-American militant leader who articulated concepts of racial pride and nationalism in the early 1960s. After his assassination, the widespread distribution of his life story—Alex Haley's *The Autobiography of Malcolm X* (1965) and the 1992 film *Malcolm X*, directed by Spike Lee—made him an ideological hero, especially among black youth.

Drawn to the doctrines of ELIJAH MUHAMMAD while serving a prison term, Malcolm X converted to the NATION OF ISLAM in 1946. After his release in 1952 he soon became the most effective speaker and organizer for the Nation of Islam. He was assigned to be minister of the important Mosque Number Seven in New York City's Harlem in 1954. He founded many new mosques and greatly increased the movement's membership. In 1961 he launched *Muhammad Speaks,* the official publication of the movement.

Malcolm X
AP—Wide World Photos

Speaking with bitter eloquence against the white exploitation of African-American people, Malcolm developed a brilliant platform style, which soon won him a large and dedicated following. He derided the civil-rights movement and rejected both integration and racial equality, calling instead for racial pride and self-reliance within a separatist African-American community. Because he advocated the use of violence for self-protection, his leadership was rejected by most civil-rights leaders, who emphasized nonviolent resistance to racial injustice.

Malcolm X described the assassination of President John F. Kennedy as a "case of chickens coming home to roost"—*i.e.,* an instance of the kind of violence that whites had long used against African-Americans. Malcolm's success had by this time aroused jealousy within the Black Muslim hierarchy, and, in response to his comments on the Kennedy assassination, Elijah Muhammad suspended Malcolm from the movement. In March 1964 Malcolm X left the Nation of Islam and announced the formation of his own religious organization. As a result of a PILGRIMAGE he took to MECCA in April 1964, he modified his views of separatism, declaring that he no longer believed whites to be innately evil and acknowledging his vision of the possibility of world brotherhood. In October 1964 he reaffirmed his conversion to Sunni Islam. Growing hostility between Malcolm's followers and the rival Black Muslims manifested itself in violence and threats against his life. He was shot to death at a rally of his followers at a Harlem ballroom. Three Black Muslims were convicted of the murder.

MĀLIK IBN ANAS \'mä-lik-,i-bən-a-'nas\, *in full* Abū 'Abd Allāh Mālik ibn Anas ibn al-Ḥārith al-Aṣbaḥī (b. *c.* 715, Medina, Arabia [now in Saudi Arabia]—d. 796, Medina), Muslim legist who played an important role in formulating early legal doctrines of ISLAM.

Few details are known about Mālik ibn Anas' life, most of which was spent in the city of MEDINA. He became learned in Islamic law and attracted a considerable number of students, his followers coming to be known as the Mālikī school of law. His prestige involved him in politics, and

The hand of God forestalls the sacrifice of Isaac by Abraham, Spanish Haggadah, c. 1300

Trickster Loki (center) causes the killing of the Norse god Balder by the blind god Höd
The Granger Collection

The god Tezcatlipoca, whose foot has been bitten off by the Earth Monster; Aztec Codex
Werner Forman Archive—Art Resource

Confucius
The Granger Collection

The Egyptian gods Horus (falcon-headed) and Mut
SEF—Art Resource

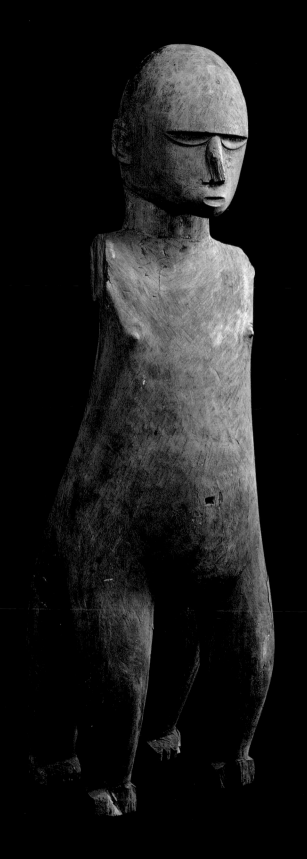

(Left) The god Tu, from the Gambier Islands, Polynesia; (above) Japanese depiction of a Buddhist arahant
(Left) Scala—Art Resource; (above) Art Resource

The Prophet Muhammad (his face undepicted out of respect) ascends into heaven
Art Resource

A page from Johannes Gutenberg's 42-line Latin Bible, c. 1455
The Granger Collection

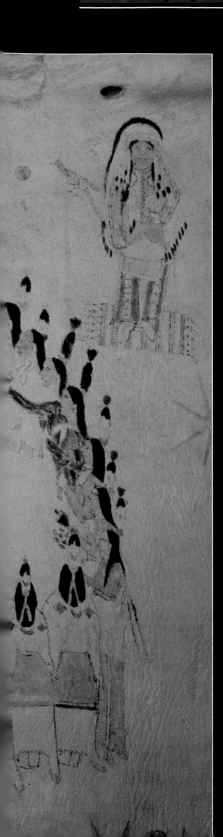

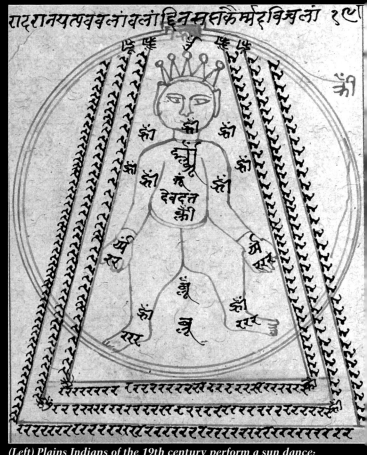

राद्रानयत्वबब्लांबलांहिनमसतकिमेंरविशलां १९

*(Left) Plains Indians of the 19th century perform a sun dance;
(above) Jain Tantric diagram*

(Left) Werner Forman Archive—Art Resource; (above) Image Select—Art Resource

Krishna beheads the demon Nikumbha

he declared during a rebellion that loyalty to the CALIPH was not a religious necessity since homage to him had been given under compulsion. However, Abbusid al-Mansūr (reigned 754–775), the caliph, was victorious, and Mālik received a flogging for his complicity. This only increased his prestige, and during later years he regained favor with the central government.

Mālik ibn Anas produced one major book—the *Muwaṭṭa'* ("The Leveled Path"). This is the oldest surviving compendium of Islamic law based on HADITHS from MUHAMMAD, his COMPANIONS, and their followers.

MĀLIKĪ LEGAL SCHOOL \'mä-li-kē\, *also called* Madhhab Mālik, *English* Malikites \'ma-lə-ˌkīts\, in ISLAM, one of the four Sunni schools of law, formerly the ancient school of MEDINA. Founded in the 8th century and based on the teachings of the imam MĀLIK IBN ANAS, the Mālikī legal school stressed local Medinese community practice (SUNNA), preferring traditional opinions (*ra'y*) and analogical reasoning (QIYĀS) to a strict reliance on HADITH as a basis for legal judgment. Hadith, however, was always applied, though arbitrarily. The Mālikī school, which once was predominant in Andalusia in Spain, currently prevails throughout northern and western Africa, in The Sudan, and in some of the Persian Gulf states.

MALINOWSKI, BRONISŁAW \ˌma-lə-'nȯf-skē, ˌmä-\ (b. April 7, 1884, Kraków, Poland, Austria-Hungary—d. May 16, 1942, New Haven, Conn., U.S.), one of the most important anthropologists of the 20th century. He is widely recognized as the founder of social anthropology and the development of FUNCTIONALISM.

Malinowski was the son of Lucjan Malinowski, a professor of Slavic philology at the Jagiellonian University in Kraków and a linguist of some reputation. Bronisław Malinowski's mother, Józefa, *née* Łącka, of a moderately wealthy land-owning family, was highly cultured and a good linguist. Although his early education was conducted largely at home, he subsequently attended the Jagiellonian University, completing his doctorate in philosophy in 1908, with physics and mathematics as subsidiaries. Happening upon SIR JAMES FRAZER's *Golden Bough* changed his course; in 1910 he entered the London School of Economics and Political Science where anthropology had been recently established as a discipline.

In 1914 he went to New Guinea. His six months' work among the Mailu on the south coast produced a monograph that was sufficient to earn him a doctor of science (D.Sc.) degree from the University of London in 1916. He moved to the nearby Trobriand Islands, where he worked for two years in 1915–16 and 1917–18, it was there that he discovered the now famous *kula* ritual that ranged between islands in the Pacific. The published works on agricultural economics; on sex, marriage, and family life; on primitive law and custom; and on magic and myth, drew heavily on his Trobriand data in putting forward theoretical propositions of basic significance and stimulus in the development of social anthropology. Writing in Polish for his own private record, Malinowski kept field diaries in which he exposed very frankly his problems of isolation and of his relations with New Guinea people.

After living in the Canary Islands and southern France, Malinowski returned in 1924 to the University of London as reader in anthropology; he became professor in 1927. In 1938 Malinowski went on sabbatical leave to the United States. When World War II was declared, he became Bishop Museum Visiting Professor of Anthropology at Yale University and then accepted a tenured appointment there. He was able to study peasant markets in Mexico in 1940 and 1941 and had plans for a study of social change in Mexican-Indian communities when he died in 1942. *Argonauts of the Western Pacific* (1922) and *Magic, Science and Religion* (1948) remain two of his most popular works.

MALLEUS MALEFICARUM \'ma-lē-əs-ma-lə-fi-'kā-rəm, 'mä-lē-ùs-,mä-lā-fē-'kä-rùm\ (Latin: "Hammer of Witches"), detailed legal and theological document (*c.* 1486) regarded as the standard handbook on WITCHCRAFT, including its detection and its extirpation, until well into the 18th century. Its appearance did much to spur on some two centuries of witch-hunting hysteria in Europe. The *Malleus* was the work of two DOMINICANS: Johann Sprenger, dean of the University of Cologne in Germany, and Heinrich Kraemer, professor of theology at the University of Salzburg, Austria, and inquisitor in the Tirol region of Austria.

In 1484 Pope Innocent VIII issued the bull *Summis Desiderantes*, in which he authorized Sprenger and Kraemer to extirpate witchcraft in Germany. The *Malleus* codified the FOLKLORE and beliefs of the Alpine peasants and was divided into three parts. In Part I the reality and the depravity of witches is emphasized, and any disbelief in demonology is condemned as HERESY. Because of the nature of the enemy, any witness, no matter what his credentials, may testify against an accused. Part II is a compendium of fabulous stories about the activities of witches—*e.g.*, diabolic compacts, sexual relations with devils (incubi and succubi), transvection (night-riding), and metamorphosis. Part III is a discussion of the legal procedures to be followed in witch trials. Torture is sanctioned as a means of securing confessions. Lay and secular authorities are called upon to assist the inquisitors in the task of exterminating those whom SATAN has enlisted in his cause.

The *Malleus* went through 28 editions between 1486 and 1600 and was widely accepted as authoritative on SATANISM and as a guide to Christian defense.

MANA \'mä-nə\ (Maori *mana*, or a cognate word in other Austronesian languages), among Melanesian and Polynesian peoples, supernatural force or power that may be ascribed to persons, spirits, or inanimate objects. Mana may be either good or evil, beneficial or dangerous. The term was first used in 19th-century scholarship during debates concerning the ORIGIN OF RELIGION. It was interpreted to be an impersonal, amoral, supernatural power that manifested itself in extraordinary phenomena and abilities. Anything distinguished from the ordinary (*e.g.*, an uncommonly shaped stone) could be possessed by mana.

Subsequent scholarship has challenged both the original description of mana and the conclusions drawn from it. Mana is by no means universal; it is not even common to all of Melanesia; many of the parallels that have been adduced have been found to be specious. Mana is not impersonal. It is never spoken of by itself but always in connection with powerful beings or things. Thus, mana would seem to be descriptive of the possession of power and not itself the source of power. Rather than being an impersonal power, mana is inextricably related to belief in spirits.

Among contemporary scholars a functionalist and political interpretation has been offered. Mana seems to be a symbolic way of expressing the special qualities attributed to persons of status and authority in a society, of providing sanction for their actions, and of explaining their failures.

MANALA \'mä-nä-ˌlä\, in Finnish mythology, the realm of the dead. The word is possibly derived from the compound *maan-ala*, "the space (or area) under the earth." It is also called TUONELA, the realm of Tuoni, and POHJOLA, derived from the word *pohja*, meaning "bottom" and also "north."

The Finnish Underworld and related concepts among other Finno-Ugric peoples, such as the *yabme-aimo* of the Sami, do not provide a consistent COSMOLOGY. Manala is often reached by crossing a fiery stream, the river of death, either over a narrow bridge or by a boat brought by a denizen of the otherworld. Manala is a dark, gloomy place ruled by the goddess Louhi, a fierce haglike creature with several vaguely defined sons, daughters, and servants in her retinue. Pohjola is similarly found in various forms in the underworld, but it is to the north and at the outer edges of the universe, outside the known world. In a more concrete sense the realm of the dead was where the dead were buried, and many of the descriptions of the Underworld depict the COFFINS and funerary shelters erected at the burial sites.

MANANNÁN MAC LIR \'má-nȧ-nän-ˌmák-'lʸirʸ\ (Middle Irish: "Manannán, Son of [the] Sea"), Irish sea god from whom the name of the Isle of Man allegedly derived. Manannán traditionally ruled an island paradise, protected sailors, and provided abundant crops. He gave immortality to the gods through his swine, which returned to life when killed; those who ate of the swine never died. He wore impenetrable armor and, carrying an invincible sword, rode over the waves in a splendid chariot. He and his Welsh equivalent, Manawydan, brother of the god BRÂN, apparently derived from an early Celtic deity.

MANASĀ \'mə-nə-ˌsä\, goddess of snakes, worshiped mainly in northeastern India, chiefly for the prevention and cure of snakebite and also for general prosperity. As the protector of children, she is often identified with the goddess Ṣaṣṭhī ("the Sixth," worshiped on the sixth day after birth). The written texts that contain her myth, the *Manasā-maṅgal*s, date from the 16th to 17th century but are probably based on an earlier ORAL TRADITION. Manasā is a goddess local primarily to Bengal who was later incorporated into the classical Hindu pantheon. She is probably related to the NĀGAS, a legendary half-human, half-serpent race in India.

MANASSEH \mə-'na-sə\, one of the 12 biblical tribes of Israel, named after a younger son of JOSEPH, son of JACOB.

After the exodus from Egypt, the tribe of Manasseh settled in central Palestine. When Israel was conquered by the Assyrians in the late 8th century BCE, many Israelites were carried off into slavery (2 Kings 18:9–12). In time the tribe of Manasseh was assimilated by other peoples and thus became one of the TEN LOST TRIBES OF ISRAEL.

MANASSEH BEN ISRAEL \mə-'na-sə-ben-'iz-rē-əl, -rā-əl\, Manasseh *also spelled* Menasseh, *original name* Manoel Dias Soeiro (b. 1604, Lisbon? [Portugal]—d. Nov. 20, 1657, Middelburg, Netherlands), major Hebraic scholar and the founder of the modern Jewish community in England.

Manasseh was born into a family of Marranos (Jews of Spain and Portugal who publicly accepted CHRISTIANITY but privately practiced JUDAISM). Ultimately the family emigrated to Amsterdam, where Manasseh became the RABBI of a Portuguese Jewish congregation in 1622.

Manasseh believed that the MESSIAH would return to lead the Jews to the Holy Land only after their dispersal throughout the world was achieved. He considered immigrating to Brazil in 1640 and reported the alleged discovery in South America of the TEN LOST TRIBES OF ISRAEL in *Esperança de Israel* ("Hope of Israel"). To support the settlement of Jews in Protestant England, where their presence had been officially banned since 1290, he dedicated the Latin edition of this work (1650) to the English Parliament. Manasseh's plea before Oliver Cromwell in 1655 for the formal recognition of Jewish settlement in England ultimately led to the granting of an official charter of protection to the Jews of England in 1664.

MANDAEANISM \man-'dē-ə-ˌni-zəm\ (from Mandaean: *mandayya*, "having knowledge"), ancient Middle Eastern religion still surviving in Iraq and Khuzistan (southwest Iran). The religion is usually treated as an instance of GNOSTICISM; it resembles MANICHAEISM in some respects. Most scholars date the beginnings of Mandaeanism to sometime during the first three centuries CE. Some, emphasizing the Babylonian elements in Mandaean magical texts, use of the Iranian calendar, and Iranian words in the Mandaic language, argue that Mandaeanism originated in southwestern Mesopotamia in early Christian or even pre-Christian times. Others argue for a Syro-Palestinian origin, based on the quasi-historical Mandaean document, the *Haran Gawaita*, which narrates the exodus from Palestine to Mesopotamia in the 1st century CE of a group called Nasoreans (the Mandaean priestly CASTE as opposed to Mandaiia, the laity). They also call attention to certain Mandaean affinities to JUDAISM: familiarity with OLD TESTAMENT writings; parallels to Jewish ethics, particularly the high value placed on marriage and procreation; and concern for cultic purity.

Mandaeanism stresses salvation of the soul through esoteric knowledge (gnosis) of its divine origin. In its cosmological superstructure, evil ARCHONS (rulers) obstruct the ascent of the soul through the heavenly spheres to reunion with the supreme deity. Unlike many Gnostic systems, however, Mandaeanism strongly supports marriage and forbids sexual license. The Mandaeans also developed an elaborate cultic ritual, particularly for BAPTISM. The Mandaeans viewed Jesus as a false MESSIAH but revered JOHN THE BAPTIST, who performed miracles of healing through baptism, which the Mandaeans viewed as a powerful process giving immortality and purification.

Among the more important extant Mandaean writings are: the *Ginza* ("Treasure," also known as the *Book of Adam*), a cosmological treatise; the *Book of John*, describing the activities of John the Baptist; the *Book of the Zodiac*, a collection of magical and astrological texts; and the *Baptism of Hibil Ziwa*, describing the purification of the heavenly savior of the Mandaeans.

MANDALA \'mən-də-lə\, *Sanskrit* maṇḍala ("circle," or "plan of the cosmos"), in TANTRIC HINDUISM and BUDDHISM, a symbolic diagram used in the performance of sacred rites and as an instrument of meditation. The mandala is a representation of the universe, a consecrated area that serves as a receptacle for the gods and as a collection point of universal forces. By mentally "entering" the mandala and "proceeding" toward its center, practitioners are by analogy guided through the cosmic processes of disintegration and reintegration.

In China, Japan, and Tibet mandalas are of two primary types, representing different aspects of the universe: the *garbha-dhātu* (Sanskrit: "womb world"; Japanese: *taizō-kai*), where movement is from the one to the many; and the *vajra-dhātu* (Sanskrit: "diamond [or thunderbolt] world";

Japanese *kongō-kai*), from the many into one. Mandalas may be painted on paper or cloth, drawn on prepared ground with white and colored threads or with rice powders, fashioned in bronze, or built in stone.

The mandala of a Tibetan *tanka* (cloth scroll painting) characteristically consists of an outer enclosure around one or more concentric circles, which in turn surround a square transversed by lines from the center to the four corners. In the center and the middle of each triangle are five circles containing symbols or images of divinities, most commonly the five "self-born" buddhas. Of the borders surrounding the mandala, the first is a ring of fire, which both bars entry to the uninitiated and symbolizes the burning of ignorance; next comes a girdle of diamonds, which stands for illumination; then a circle of eight graveyards, symbolizing the eight aspects of individuating cognition; next a girdle of lotus leaves, signifying spiritual rebirth; and, finally, at the center, the mandala itself, where the images are set.

Mandala of the Vairocana Buddha, Tibetan tanka *painting, 17th century*
By courtesy of the Newark Museum, New Jersey

MANDATE OF HEAVEN: *see* T'IEN MING.

MAṄGAL-KĀVYA \'məŋ-gəl-'kä-vyə\ (Bengali: "auspicious poem"), type of eulogistic verse in honor of a god or goddess in Bengal (India) and most often associated with a local Bengali deity—*e.g.,* MANASĀ, the goddess of snakes; Śītalā, the goddess of smallpox; or the folk god Dhama-Ṭhākur.

*Maṅgal-kāvya*s are most often heard at the festivals of the deities they celebrate. They tell the story of how a particular god or goddess succeeded in establishing his or her worship on earth. They are similar in form, written for the most part in the simple *payār* meter, a couplet form with rhyme scheme "aa bb," etc. Typical of *maṅgal*s is their earthy imagery, drawn from village, field, and river.

MANI \må-'nē\, *also called* Manes \må-'nē, 'mā-nēz\, *or* Manichaeus \ˌma-nə-'kē-əs\ (b. April 14, 216, southern Babylonia—d. 274?, Gundeshapur), Iranian founder of MANICHAEISM, which advocates a dualistic doctrine that viewed the world as a fusion of spirit and matter, the original contrary principles of GOOD AND EVIL, respectively.

Before Mani's birth, his father, Patek, a native of Hamadan, had joined a religious community practicing BAPTISM and abstinence. Information about his life appears to derive from his own writings and the traditions of his church. He grew up at his birthplace, speaking a form of eastern Aramaic. Twice, as a boy and young man, he saw in visions an ANGEL, the "Twin," who, the second time, called him to preach a new religion.

He traveled to India (probably Sind and Turan) and made converts. Favorably received on his return by the newly

crowned Persian king, Shāpūr I, he was permitted to preach his religion in the Persian empire. Under the reign of the Persian king Bahrām I, however, he was attacked by Zoroastrian priests and was imprisoned by the king at Gundeshapur (Belapet), where he died after undergoing a trial that lasted 26 days.

MANICHAEISM \'ma-nə-ˌkē-ˌi-zəm, ˌma-nə-'kē-\, dualistic religious movement founded in Persia in the 3rd century CE by MANI, who was known as the "Apostle of Light" and supreme "Illuminator." Manichaeism was long considered a Christian HERESY, but it was a religion in its own right that, because of the coherence of its doctrines and the rigidness of its structure and institutions, preserved throughout its history a unity and unique character.

With Mani's "annunciation" at the age of 24 he obeyed a heavenly order to manifest himself publicly and to proclaim his doctrines; thus began the new religion. From that point on, Mani preached throughout the Persian Empire. At first unhindered, he later was opposed by the king, condemned, and imprisoned. After 26 days of trials, which his followers called the "Passion of the Illuminator" or Mani's "crucifixion," Mani delivered a final message to his disciples and died (sometime between 274 and 277).

Mani viewed himself as the final successor in a long line of prophets, beginning with ADAM and including BUDDHA, ZOROASTER, and JESUS. He viewed earlier revelations as being limited because they were local and taught in one language to one people. Mani regarded himself as the carrier of a universal message destined to replace all other religions. Hoping to avoid corruption and to ensure doctrinal unity, he recorded his teachings in writing and gave those writings canonical status during his lifetime.

Mani encouraged the translation of his writings into other languages and organized an extensive mission program, so that Manichaeism rapidly spread from Egypt across northern Africa (where the young AUGUSTINE temporarily became a convert), reaching Rome in the early 4th century. The 4th century marked the height of Manichaean expansion in the West, with churches in southern Gaul and Spain. Vigorously attacked by both the Christian church and the Roman state, it almost disappeared from western Europe by the end of the 5th century, and, during the 6th century, from the eastern portion of the Empire. Within Persia the Manichaean community maintained itself in spite of severe persecutions, until Muslim 'Abbāsid persecution in the 10th century forced the transfer of the seat of the Manichaean leader to Samarkand (now in Uzbekistan).

A Manichaean missionary reached the Chinese court in 694, and in 732 an edict gave the religion freedom of worship in China. When East Turkistan was conquered in the

8th century by the Uighur Turks, one of their leaders adopted Manichaeism and it remained the state religion of the Uighur kingdom until its overthrow in 840. Manichaeism itself probably survived in East Turkistan until the Mongol invasion in the 13th century. In China it was forbidden in 843, but, although its followers were persecuted, it continued there at least until the 14th century.

Teachings similar to Manichaeism resurfaced during the Middle Ages in Europe in the so-called neo-Manichaean sects. Beliefs of the PAULICIANS (Armenia, 7th century), the BOGOMILS (Bulgaria, 10th century), and the CATHARI or Albigensians (France, 12th century) strongly resembled Manichaeism, though direct historical links to the religion of Mani are difficult to establish.

Mani sought to found a truly ecumenical and universal religion that would integrate into itself all the partial truths of previous revelations. However, beyond mere syncretism, it sought the proclamation of a truth that could be translated into diverse forms in accordance with the different cultures into which it spread. Thus, Manichaeism, depending on the context, resembles Iranian and Indian religions, CHRISTIANITY, BUDDHISM, and TAOISM.

Fragment of a wall painting presumably depicting (left) Mani, followed by members of the elect, from K'o-cha, China, 8th–9th century; in the Museum für Indische Kunst, Berlin
By courtesy of the Staatliche Museen Preussischer Kulturbesitz, Berlin

At its core, Manichaeism was a type of GNOSTICISM, teaching that life in this world is unbearably painful and radically evil. Inner illumination reveals that the soul which shares in the nature of God has fallen into the evil world of matter and must be saved by means of the spirit or intelligence (*nous*). To know one's self is to recover one's true self from ignorance because of its mingling with the body and with matter. In Manichaeism, to know one's self is to see one's soul as sharing in the nature of God and as coming from a transcendent world. Knowledge enables a person to realize that, despite his abject present condition in the material world, he does not cease to remain united to the transcendent world by eternal and immanent bonds with it. Thus knowledge is the only way to salvation.

The saving knowledge of the true nature and destiny of humanity, God, and the universe is expressed in Manichaeism in a complex mythology which stressed that the soul is fallen, entangled with evil matter, and then liberated by the spirit or *nous*. The myth unfolds in three stages: a past period in which there was a separation of the two radically opposed substances—Spirit and Matter, GOOD AND EVIL, Light and Darkness; a middle period (corresponding to the present) during which the two substances are mixed; and a future period in which the original duality will be re-established. At death the soul of the righteous person returns to paradise. The soul of the person who persisted in things of the flesh—fornication, procreation, possessions, cultivation, harvesting, eating of meat, drinking of wine—is condemned to rebirth in a succession of bodies.

Only a portion of the faithful followed the strict ascetic life advocated in Manichaeism. The community was divided into the ELECT, who felt able to embrace a rigorous rule, and the hearers who supported the elect with works and alms. The essentials of the Manichaean sacramental rites were prayers, almsgiving, and fasting. CONFESSION and the singing of hymns were also important in their communal life. The Manichaean scriptural canon includes seven works attributed to Mani. Portions of the Manichaean SCRIPTURES were rediscovered in the 20th century, mainly in Chinese Turkistan and Egypt.

MANIKKAVACAKAR \'mə-nē-kə-'və-sə-gər\, *also spelled* Manikkavasagar, 9th-century Hindu mystic and poet-saint of the Śaiva tradition (*see* ŚAIVISM).

Manikkavacakar was born of Brahmin parents in South India and became the chief minister to the king of Madura. Legend has it that, while on an errand for the king, Manikkavacakar had a vision of the god SHIVA and from that time on dedicated his life to the religious piety and devotional poetry, written in Tamil, that made him famous. His best-known work is the *Tiruvacakam*, or "Blessed Utterance," which became the inspiration for later devotional poetry in Tamil. The text, apparently influenced by the BHAGAVAD GĪTĀ, is a collection of poems and songs dedicated to Shiva, who is said to take on human form and teach the means to salvation to people of all classes. The work is revered by Tamil Śaivites, who commit its psalms to memory and daily sing its verses in temples and homes.

MAÑJUŚRĪ \,mən-'jü-shrē\, in MAHĀYĀNA BUDDHISM, the BODHISATTVA personifying supreme wisdom. His name in Sanskrit means "gentle, or sweet, glory"; he is also known as Mānjughoṣa ("Sweet Voice") and Vāgīśvara ("Lord of Speech"). In China he is called Wen-shu Shih-li, in Japan Monju, and in Tibet 'Jam-dpal.

Although SŪTRAS were composed in his honor by at least 250 CE, he does not seem to have been represented in Buddhist art before 400 CE. He is commonly shown wearing princely ornaments, his right hand holding aloft the sword of wisdom to cleave the clouds of ignorance and his left holding a palm-leaf manuscript of the PRAJÑĀPĀRAMITĀ.

His devotional cult spread widely in China in the 8th century, and Mount Wu-t'ai in Shansi province, which is dedicated to him, is covered with his temples. Though he is usually considered a celestial bodhisattva, some traditions endow him with a human history. He is said to manifest himself in many ways—in dreams; as a pilgrim on his sacred mountain; as an incarnation of the monk Vairocana, who introduced Buddhism into Khotan; as the Tibetan reformer Atīśa; and as the emperor of China.

MANNA \'ma-nə\, in biblical literature, one or more of the foods that sustained the Hebrews during the 40 years that intervened between their exodus from Egypt and their arrival in the Promised Land (Exodus 16). The word is perhaps derived from the question *man hu!* ("What is it?"; Exodus 16:15, 31). The manna was gathered and was used in part to prepare bread, and it was therefore referred to as "bread from heaven" (Exodus 16:4).

In the NEW TESTAMENT, Jesus spoke of himself as the "true bread from heaven" (John 6:32), and manna consequently is a Christian symbol for the EUCHARIST.

MANTRA \\'mən-trə, 'män-, 'man-\\, in HINDUISM and BUDDHISM, sacred utterance (syllable, word, or verse) that is considered to possess mystical or spiritual efficacy. Various mantras are either spoken aloud or merely sounded in one's thoughts, and they are either repeated continuously for some time or just sounded once. Some have no apparent verbal meaning, but they are thought to have a profound significance and are in effect distillations of spiritual wisdom. Thus, repetition of or meditation on a particular mantra can induce a trancelike state in the participant and can lead him to a higher level of spiritual awareness.

One of the most powerful and widely used mantras in Hinduism is the sacred syllable OM. The principal mantra in Buddhism is *om maṇi padme hūṃ* ("om, the jewel in the lotus, hūṃ"). Initiation into many Hindu sects involves the whispering of a secret mantra into the ear of the initiate by the GURU. Indeed, mantras are thought to be truly efficacious only when they are received verbally from one's guru or other spiritual preceptor.

MANTRAYĀNA \\,mən-trə-'yä-nə\\, important Indo-Tibetan movement within Buddhism; *see* VAJRAYĀNA.

MANU \\'mə-nü\\, in the mythology of India, first man and legendary author of an important Sanskrit code of law, the *Manu-smṛti*. In the VEDAS, Manu performs the first sacrifice. He is the first king, and most rulers of medieval India traced their genealogy to him, through either his son (the solar line) or his daughter (the lunar line).

The *Śatapatha Brāhmaṇa* recounts how Manu was warned by a fish, to whom he had done a kindness, that a flood would destroy the whole of humanity. He therefore built a boat, and when the flood came, he tied this boat to the fish's horn and was safely steered to a resting place on a mountaintop. When the flood receded, Manu performed a sacrifice, pouring oblations of butter and sour milk into the waters. After a year there was born from the waters a woman who announced herself as "the daughter of Manu." These two then became the ancestors of a new human race to replenish the earth. In the MAHĀBHĀRATA the fish is identified with the god BRAHMĀ, while in the *Purāṇa*s it is Matsya, the fish INCARNATION of the lord VISHNU.

In the cosmological speculations of later HINDUISM, a day in the life of Brahmā is divided into 14 periods called *manvantara*s ("Manu intervals"), each of which lasts for 306,720,000 years. In every secondary cycle the world is recreated, and a new Manu appears to become the father of the next human race. The present age is considered to be the seventh Manu cycle.

MANU-SMṚTI \\'mə-nü-'smri-tē\\ (Sanskrit: "Precepts of Manu"), traditionally, the most authoritative of the books of the Hindu code (DHARMA ŚĀSTRA) in India; its official title is *Mānava-dharma-śāstra*. It is attributed to the first man and lawgiver, MANU, and dates from the 1st century BCE.

The *Manu-smṛti* prescribes Hindu dharma—*i.e.*, that set of obligations incumbent on each individual as a member of one of the four social classes (VARṆAS) and engaged in one of the four stages of life (ASHRAMS). Its vast range of topics includes COSMOGONY, the sacraments (SAṂSKĀRAS), initiation (UPANAYANA) and study of the VEDA, social rites and obligations, dietary restrictions, pollution and means of purification, the conduct of women and wives, the law of kings, the doctrine of KARMA, the soul, and hell.

MAO SHAN \\'maủ-'shän\\, *Pinyin* Maoshan, in TAOISM, sacred mountain in Kiangsu province, associated with a 4th-century-CE apocalyptic visionary, Yang Hsi. Mao Shan is the traditional center of Shang-ch'ing Taoism.

Yang Hsi was visited by a group of perfected immortals (CHEN-JEN) from the heaven of Shang-ch'ing (Supreme Purity) between the years of 364 and 370, during which he received a new scriptural and hagiographic literature. The perfected announced that the prevailing social order was soon to end and that the rule of men on earth was to be replaced by a universal Taoist imperium. The 4th century was seen as a time of trials, given over to the reign of the demonic Six Heavens, at the end of which the earth was to be cleansed of evildoers by a cataclysm of fire and flood. At that time the Good would take refuge deep in the earth, in the luminous caverns of the perfected beneath such sacred mountains as Mao Shan. There they would complete the study of immortality already begun in their lifetimes, so as to be ready for the descent from heaven of the new universal ruler, Lord Li Hung, the "sage who is to come" (*housheng*). This was prophesied for the year 392.

Yang Hsi gave great consistency and consummate literary form to his comprehensive synthesis of many spiritual traditions, which has become known as the Mao Shan literature. Popular messianism was adapted to provide an encompassing framework and temporal cogency, and Buddhist concepts were merged into Yang's Taoist system. The perfected also dictated a "Taoicized" version of large portions of an early Buddhist compilation, the *Sutra in Forty-two Sections* (*Ssu-shih-erh chang ching*). Buddhist notions of PREDESTINATION and REINCARNATION were subtly blended with native Chinese beliefs in hereditary character traits and the clan as a single unit involving mutual responsibility on the part of all its members, living and dead. Furthermore, the Mao Shan revelations envisaged some reform of the practices of Taoism.

MAPONOS \\mä-'pō-nōs\\ ("Divine Son," or "Divine Youth"), *also called* Mabon \\'mä-bōn\\, *or* Mac ind Óg \\'mȧ-kən-'dōg\\, *or* Oenghus \\'ē-nəs, 'ȯin-g̅əs\\, Celtic deity, attested in Gaul but occurring mainly in northern Britain. He appears in medieval Welsh literature as Mabon, son of Modron, and he evidently figured in a myth of the infant god carried off from his mother when three nights old. His name survives in Arthurian romance under the forms Mabon, Mabuz, and Mabonagrain. His Irish equivalent was Mac ind Óg ("Young Son," or "Young Lad"), known also as Oenghus, who dwelt in Bruigh na Bóinne, the great Neolithic, and therefore pre-Celtic, passage grave of Newgrange (or Newgrange House). He was the son of DAGDA (or Daghda), chief god of the Irish, and of BOANN, the personified sacred river of Irish tradition.

MAPPŌ \\'mäp-ˌpō\\, in Japanese BUDDHISM, a version of the widespread notion of an age of degeneration that culminates a process of decline following the death of the BUDDHA GOTAMA. In different Buddhist contexts this process of decline was associated with different chronologies. According to one view that became very prominent in medieval Japan, the period following the death of the Buddha is divisible into three ages: the age of the "true law," the age of the "counterfeit law," and the age of the "degeneration of the law," or *mappō*. The first two periods were often thought to last 1,000 years each. Assuming the date of the Buddha Gotama's death to be 949 BCE, many Japanese Buddhists calculated that the age of *mappō*—which would last another 10,000 years—began about 1052 CE.

In the 12th and 13th centuries the Japanese experienced a number of crises that seemed to confirm that *mappō* had, in fact, begun. In this situation there arose Buddhist leaders who came to see *mappō* as a time in which the decline of the traditionally aristocratic religious and social order mandated new, less demanding forms of Buddhist practice that could make Buddhist goals accessible to all. The result was the formation, and great success, of new, distinctively Japanese PURE LAND sects that offered means of salvation (such as faith in the Buddha Amida [AMITĀBHA]) that were accessible to all who were open to receive them.

MAQĀM \mȧ-'käm\ (Arabic: "station," or "place of residence"), *plural* maqāmāt, in SUFISM, a spiritual stage that periodically marks the long path followed by Sufi mystics leading to the vision of and union with God. The Sufi progresses by means of his own MUJĀHADA (work, or self-mortification) and through the help and guidance of the masters (SHAYKHS). In each *maqām* the Sufi strives to purify himself from all worldly inclination and to prepare himself to attain an ever-higher spiritual level.

The order and number of the *māqams* are not uniform among all Sufis. The majority, however, agree on seven major *maqāms*: (1) the *maqām* of *tawba* (repentance); (2) the *maqām* of *wara'* (fear of the Lord), which is the dread of being veiled eternally from God; (3) the *maqām* of ZUHD (renunciation, or detachment); (4) the *maqām* of *faqr* (poverty); (5) the *maqām* of *ṣabr* (patience); (6) the *maqām* of *tawakkul* (trust, or surrender); (7) the *maqām* of *riḍā* (satisfaction), a state of quiet contentment and joy that comes from the anticipation of the long-sought union with God.

In other contexts, *maqām* is used to designate a shrine dedicated to a holy man or woman which devotees visit to obtain a cure or divine blessing (*boraka*). It also designates a stone near the KA'BA where, according to tradition, Ibrāhīm (ABRAHAM) stood to build that shrine.

MĀRA \'mär-ə\, in BUDDHISM, lord of the realm of desire who was, in traditional accounts, the Buddha's tempter. When the BODHISATTVA Gotama seated himself under the BODHI TREE to seek Enlightenment, Māra appeared first in the guise of a messenger stating that a rival, DEVADATTA, had usurped the throne from Gotama's family. Next Māra sent a great storm of ashes and darkness, frightening away the gods who had gathered to honor the future Buddha. He challenged Gotama's right to sit beneath the tree, provoking the future Buddha to call upon the earth to give witness to his previous charities. Māra sent his three daughters, Tṛṣṇā, Rati, and Rāga (Thirst, Desire, and Delight), to seduce Gotama, but to no avail. After the Buddha had achieved supreme Enlightenment, he experienced doubt that others could understand the truth, and Māra pressed him not to preach. But when the gods implored him to preach the law (DHARMA), the Buddha agreed.

In Buddhist lore Māra continued to tempt and challenge the Buddha and his followers. On the one hand, Māra, his daughters, and his other associates are often treated as beings who act externally. At the same time, they are often identified with the psychic impurities, defilements, and

The Buddha assaulted by Māra and his demon horde, relief sculpture from Gandhara, Pakistan
By courtesy of the Rijksmuseum voor Volkenkunde, Leiden, The Netherlands

vices that, according to Buddhist teaching, cause suffering and prevent release from the continuing process of birth, death, and rebirth.

MARABOUT \'mar-ə-,bü\, *Arabic* Murābiṭ, originally, in North Africa, member of a Muslim religious community living in a *ribāṭ*, a fortified monastery, serving both religious and military functions. Men who possessed certain religious qualifications, such as the reciters of the QUR'AN (QURRĀ'), transmitters of HADITH (*muḥaddithūn*), jurists of Islamic law (*fuqahā'*), and ascetics, lived in the *ribāṭ* and were held in honor by the people. When ISLAM spread to western Africa in the 12th century, its propagators became known as al-Murābiṭūn (ALMORAVIDS), and every missionary who organized a group of disciples became known as a *murābiṭ*. In the 14th century, when SUFISM pervaded Muslim religious life, the *murābiṭ*, in the Maghrib, came to designate any preacher calling for the formation of Sufi fraternities according to the "order" (ṬARĪQA) of Abū Madyan. Thus, the word lost all trace of its original meaning of military defense, and in Algeria *murābiṭ* came to be used for the tomb, usually domed, in which a pious man is buried.

MARCIONITE \'mär-shə-,nīt\, any member of a gnostic sect that flourished in the 2nd century CE. The name derives from MARCION OF PONTUS who, sometime after his arrival in Rome, fell under the influence of Cerdo, a gnostic Christian, whose stormy relations with the Church of Rome were the consequence of his belief that the God of the OLD TESTAMENT could be distinguished from the God of the NEW TESTAMENT—the one embodying justice, the other goodness. For accepting and propagating such ideas, Marcion was expelled from the church in 144 as a heretic, but the movement he headed became both widespread and powerful.

The basis of Marcionite theology was that there were two cosmic gods. A vain and angry creator god who demanded and ruthlessly exacted justice had created the material world of which humans, body and soul, were a part—a striking departure from the usual gnostic thesis that only the human body is part of creation, that the soul is a spark from the true but unknown superior God, and that the world creator is a demonic power. The other god, according to Marcion, was completely ineffable and bore no intrinsic relation to the created universe at all. Out of sheer goodness, he had sent his son JESUS CHRIST to save humans from the material world and bring them to a new home. Christ's sacrifice was a legalistic act that cancelled the claim of the creator God upon men. Marcion and his followers emphasized faith in the effect of Christ's act and practiced stern ASCETICISM to restrict contact with the creator's world while looking forward to eventual salvation in the realm of the extra-worldly God. They admitted women to the PRIEST-HOOD and bishopric. The Marcionites were considered the most dangerous of the gnostics by the established church. When Polycarp met Marcion at Rome he is said to have identified Marcion as "the firstborn of SATAN."

MARCION OF PONTUS \'mär-shē-ən, -shən\ (fl. 2nd century CE), Christian heretic. Although Marcion is known only through reports and quotations from his orthodox opponents, especially Tertullian's *Adversus Marcionem* ("Against Marcion"), the principal outlines of his teaching seem clear. His teaching made a radical distinction between the God of the OLD TESTAMENT (the Creator) and the Father of JESUS CHRIST (the God of Love).

According to Marcion, that distinction had been obscured at the very earliest stages of the Christian movement, and, among the Apostles, only Paul had understood it. Because the corruptions that had consequently been introduced into the life and message of the church and into the very text of the NEW TESTAMENT had to be expunged, Marcion edited his own versions of the biblical books. His collection of those books that he regarded as authoritative seems to have had some influence on the formation of the church's canon of the New Testament, and various elements of early Christian creeds, such as the widespread equation of Father with Creator, may have been formulated partly in response to his teachings.

MARDI GRAS \'mär-dē-ˌgrä, -ˌgrȯ\ (French: "Fat Tuesday"), festive day celebrated in France on the Tuesday (Shrove Tuesday) before ASH WEDNESDAY, which marks the close of the pre-Lenten season. In the United States the festival is most elaborately celebrated in New Orleans, La.

MARDUK \'mär-ˌdük\, in Mesopotamian religion, the chief god of the city of Babylon and the national god of Babylonia; as such he was eventually called simply BEL, or Lord. Originally he seems to have been a god of thunderstorms. The poem *Enuma elish*, dating from the reign of Nebuchadrezzar I (1124–03 BCE), refers to Marduk as the god of 50 names, each one that of a deity or of a divine attribute. After conquering the monster of primeval chaos, TIAMAT, he became "lord of the gods of heaven and earth." All nature, including humans, owed its existence to him; the destiny of kingdoms and subjects was in his hands.

Marduk's chief temples at Babylon were the ESAGILA and the Etemenanki, a ZIGGURAT with a shrine of Marduk on the top. In Esagila the *Enuma elish* was recited every year at the NEW YEAR FESTIVAL. The goddess named most often as the consort of Marduk was Zarpanit, or Zarbanit (She of the City Zarpan).

Marduk's star was JUPITER, and his sacred animals were horses, dogs, and especially a dragon with forked tongue, representations of which adorn his city's walls. On the oldest monuments Marduk is represented holding a spade or hoe. He is also pictured walking, or in his war chariot.

MĀRGA \'mär-gə\ (Sanskrit: "path"), in Indian religions, path, or way, of reaching salvation. HINDUISM articulates the following meanings: *jñāna-mārga*, the way of knowledge (study of philosophic texts and contemplation); *karma-mārga*, the way of action (proper performance of one's religious and ethical duties); and *bhakti-mārga*, the way of devotion and self-surrender to God. In the BHAGAVAD GĪTĀ the god KRISHNA praises all three means but favors *bhakti-mārga*, which was accessible to members of any class or CASTE.

In BUDDHISM the Eightfold Path (Sanskrit *Aṣṭāṅgika-marga*, Pāli *Aṭṭhaṅgika-magga*), a doctrine taught by the BUDDHA GOTAMA in his first sermon, is a fundamental element of Buddhist teaching. It is also called the Middle Path, as it steers a course between the sensual pleasures of the materialists and the self-mortification of the ascetics. Those who follow the Eightfold Path are said to be freed from the suffering that is an essential part of human existence and are led ultimately to NIRVANA, or Enlightenment.

The Eightfold Path consists of (1) right understanding—faith in the Buddhist view of the nature of existence in terms of the Four Noble Truths; (2) right thought—the resolve to practice the faith; (3) right speech—avoidance of falsehoods, slander, or abusive speech; (4) right action—abstention from taking life, stealing, and improper sexual behavior; (5) right livelihood—rejection of occupations not in keeping with Buddhist principles; (6) right effort—avoidance of bad and development of good mental states; (7) right mindfulness—awareness of the body, feelings, and thought; and (8) right concentration—meditation.

MARIA LEGIO \mə-'rē-ə-'lä-gē-ˌō\, *also called* Legio Maria, or Legion of Mary Church, largest African independent church with a ROMAN CATHOLIC background. It should not be confused with a less successful predecessor in Kenya, the Dini ya Mariam (Religion of MARY) of the 1950s.

Maria Legio originated with two Catholics of the Luo group, Simeon Ondeto and Gaundencia Aoko, who claimed to have received prophetic inspiration that directed them to reject traditional magic and divine healers and to form an all-African church to be named Maria Legio (after the Catholic Legion of Mary), which offered free healing by prayer and EXORCISM of evil spirits. The first year (1963) an estimated 90,000 Catholics and non-Christians, mostly Luo, joined the church; by 1970 membership had dropped to about 50,000.

Catholic worship, symbols, and hierarchy have been added to pentecostal features. The sect rejects Western and traditional medicines, alcohol, tobacco, and dancing but accepts polygamy and is strongly nationalistic. Internal tensions and difficulties with the Kenyan government have rendered the future of the church uncertain.

MAʿRIFA \'mä-ri-fə\ (Arabic: "interior knowledge"), in ISLAM, the mystical knowledge of God or the "higher realities" that is the ultimate goal of followers of SUFISM. Sufi mystics came to *maʿrifa* by following a spiritual path that later Sufi thinkers categorized into a series of "stations" that were followed by another series of steps, the "states," through which the Sufi would come to union with God. The acquisition of *maʿrifa* was not the result of learnedness but was a type of gnosis in which the mystic received illumination through the GRACE of God. The finest expressions of *maʿrifa* can be found in the poetry of the Sufis JALĀL AL-DĪN AL-RŪMĪ (1207–73) and IBN AL-ʿARABĪ (1165–1240). Although the pursuit of *maʿrifa* is most commonly associated with the Sufis, the search for *maʿrifa*—known also by the term *hikma*—became part of SHIʿITE ideology.

MARIOLOGY \ˌmar-ē-'ä-lə-jē\, in Christian, especially ROMAN CATHOLIC, theology, the study of doctrines concerning MARY, the mother of Jesus; the term also refers to the content of these doctrines.

MARK (THE EVANGELIST), SAINT \'märk\ (fl. 1st century CE; b. Jerusalem?—d. traditionally Alexandria, Egypt; Western feast day April 25, Eastern feast day September 23), traditional author of the second Synoptic Gospel. Data on his life found in the NEW TESTAMENT is fragmentary, and its historicity has been questioned. The only unquestionably reliable information is in Philemon 24, where a certain Mark is mentioned as one of ST. PAUL's fellow workers who sends greetings from Rome to the Christians of Colossae (near modern Denizli, Turkey), but the identity of this person is not indicated. That Mark was St. Barnabas' cousin in Colossians 4:10 may also be authentic.

Except for being referred to as John in Acts (12:25; 13:5, 13; and 15:37), elsewhere in the New Testament he is consistently called by his Latin surname Mark. According to Acts, his mother's house in Jerusalem was a center of Christian life (12:12), and he accompanied Barnabas and Paul to Antioch (12:25) (now Antakya, Turkey), where he became their assistant on a MISSION journey (13:5). When they arrived at Perga (near modern İhsaniye, Turkey), Mark left them and returned to Jerusalem (13:13). Subsequently, he sailed to Cyprus with Barnabas, never to be mentioned again in Acts. The dependability of the Acts account is questionable, for its author is particularly interested in explaining the breach between Paul and Barnabas, probably introducing Mark for this reason. In this, he contradicts Paul's account of their breach in Galatians 2:11–14.

Later tradition assumes that Mark was one of the 72 disciples appointed by JESUS (Luke 10:1) and identifies him with the young man fleeing naked at Jesus' arrest (Mark 14:51–52). The Egyptian church claims Mark as its founder, and, from the 4th century CE, the see of Alexandria has been called *cathedra Marci* ("the chair of Mark"). Mark is also claimed by the Italian cities of Aquileia and Venice, of which he is the patron saint. His symbol is the lion.

MARONITE CHURCH \'mar-ə-ˌnīt\, one of the largest Eastern-rite communities of the ROMAN CATHOLIC church, prominent especially in modern Lebanon; it is the only Eastern-rite church that has no non-Catholic or Orthodox counterpart. The Maronites trace their origins to St. Maron, or Maro (Arabic Mārūn), a Syrian HERMIT of the late 4th and early 5th centuries, and St. John Maron, or Joannes Maro (Arabic, Yūḥanna Mārūn), PATRIARCH of Antioch in 685–707, under whose leadership the invading Byzantine armies of Justinian II were routed in 684, making the Maronites a fully independent people.

There is evidence that for centuries the Maronites were Monothelites (those who maintained a HERESY that Christ had only one will). According to the medieval bishop William of Tyre, the Maronite patriarch sought union with the Latin patriarch of Antioch in 1182. A definitive consolidation of the union, however, did not come until the 16th century, brought about largely through the work of the JESUIT John Eliano. In 1584 Pope Gregory XIII founded the Maronite College in Rome, which flourished under Jesuit administration into the 20th century.

Hardy, martial mountaineers, the Maronites preserved their liberty and folkways. The Muslim caliphate (632–1258) could not absorb them, and two CALIPHS of the Umayyad dynasty (661–750) paid them tribute. Under the rule of the Ottoman Turks, the Maronites maintained their religion and customs under the protection of France, largely because of their geographic isolation. In the 19th century the Maronites achieved formal autonomy within the Ottoman Empire. Since the establishment of a fully independent Lebanon in 1943, they have constituted one of the two major religious groups in the country.

The immediate spiritual head of the Maronite church after the POPE is the "patriarch of Antioch and all the East," residing in Bkirkī, near Beirut. The church retains the ancient West Syrian liturgy, even though the vernacular tongue of the Maronites is Arabic. Contact with Rome has been close and cordial, but it was not until after the SECOND VATICAN COUNCIL that papal efforts to Latinize their rite ceased. Maronites are also found in southern Europe and North and South America, having emigrated in the 19th century under the pressure of persecutions.

MARPA \'mär-pä\, *also called* Mar-Pa of Lhobrag, *or* Dvags-Po Lha-Rje \'däk-bō-'hlä-jā, 'täk-\ ("Physician of Dvags-po") (b. 1012, Lhobrag, Tibet—d. 1096, Tibet), one of the foremost Tibetan translators of Indian VAJRAYĀNA (or Tantric) Buddhist texts, a significant figure in the revival of BUDDHISM in Tibet.

The chief source of information on the life of Marpa is a 14th-century biography written by the "Mad Yogin of Tsang." According to it, Marpa was born of wealthy parents. He had a violent nature and was sent to a Tibetan monastery to study Buddhism. Eventually he went to India, where he studied for 10 years under the Indian yogi Nāropa. Returning to Tibet, he married, began to teach, and assumed the life of a wealthy farmer. He undertook another period of study with Nāropa, this time for six years. When he returned to Tibet, he gathered disciples, among them Milarepa, who later played a critical role along with Marpa in founding the Bka'-brgyud-pa sect. After a third stay in India, Marpa spent the remainder of his life in Tibet.

Among Marpa's notable translations are several works included in the *Bka'-'gyur* and the *Bstan-'gyur*. He also introduced to Tibet the mystical songs (*dohā*s) of the Indian Tantric tradition (*see* TANTRIC HINDUISM), later used with great skill by Mi-la ras-pa and his followers.

MARS \'märz\, ancient Roman deity, in importance second only to JUPITER. Little is known of his original character, but by historical times he had developed into a god of war, and in Roman literature he was protector of Rome.

Mars's festivals at Rome occurred in the spring and the fall—the beginning and the end of both the agricultural and the military seasons. The month of March was especially filled with festivals wholly or partially in his honor; the members of the PRIESTHOOD of the SALII, who were particularly associated with Jupiter, Mars, and QUIRINUS, came out several times during the month to dance their ceremonial war dance in old-fashioned armor and chant a hymn to the gods. At the festival of the October Horse on October 15, a two-horse chariot race was held in the Campus Martius, and on October 19 the Armilustrium marked the purification of the arms of war and their storage for the winter. The god was invoked in the ancient hymn of the ARVAL BROTHERS, whose religious duties had as their object to keep off enemies of all kinds from crops and herds.

Until the time of Augustus, Mars had only two TEMPLES at Rome, one in the Campus Martius, the exercise ground of the army, the other outside the Porta Capena. Within the city he had a *sacrarium* ("shrine," or "sanctuary") in the *regia*, originally the king's house, in which his sacred spears were kept; upon the outbreak of war the consul had to shake the spears saying, *"Mars vigila"* ("Mars, wake up!").

Under Augustus, as Mars Ultor ("Mars the Avenger"), he became the personal guardian of the emperor in his role as avenger of Caesar. About 250 CE Mars became the most prominent of the *di militares* ("military gods") worshiped by the legions. In literature and art he is hardly distinguished from the Greek ARES.

MARSYAS \\'mär-sē-əs\\, mythological Greek figure of Anatolian origin. Marsyas found the oboe that the goddess ATHENA had invented and, after becoming skilled in playing it, challenged APOLLO to a contest with his lyre. When King MIDAS of Phrygia, who had been appointed judge, declared in favor of Marsyas, Apollo punished Midas by changing his ears into ass's ears. In another version the MUSES were the judges, and they awarded the victory to Apollo, who tied Marsyas to a tree and flayed him. In Rome a statue of Marsyas stood in the Forum; this was imitated by Roman colonies and came to be considered a symbol of autonomy.

MARTIN OF TOURS, SAINT \\'mär-tən, mär-'taⁿ . . . 'tu̇r\\ (b. 316 CE, Sabaria, Pannonia [now Szombathely, Hung.]—d. Nov. 8, 397, Candes, Gaul [France]; Western feast day November 11; Eastern feast day November 12), patron saint of France, father of MONASTICISM in Gaul, and the first great leader of Western monasticism. After 360 he founded a community of HERMITS at Ligugé, the first monastery in Gaul. In 371 he was made bishop of Tours, and outside that city he founded another monastery, Marmoutier, which he made into a great monastic complex to which European ascetics were attracted and from which apostles spread CHRISTIANITY throughout Gaul. During his lifetime, Martin acquired a reputation as a miracle worker, and he was one of the first nonmartyrs to be publicly venerated as a saint.

Mars, Etruscan statuette; in the Museo Archeologico, Florence

Alinari—Art Resource

MARTYR, in the strictest sense, one who voluntarily suffers death rather than deny his or her religion by words or deeds; such action is afforded special, institutionalized recognition in most major religions of the world. Contemporary usage of the term has come to include one who has died for his or her RELIGIOUS BELIEFS.

Judaism. The ideal of martyrdom in Judaism begins with ABRAHAM, who according to legend was cast into a lime kiln and saved from the fire by divine GRACE. The tradition was continued by ISAAC, who consented to be sacrificed by his father, and by Daniel, whose example—*i.e.*, of being thrown into a den of lions for refusing to obey an edict which forbade prayer— compelled the popular imagination. Readiness for martyrdom became a collective Jewish ideal during the Antiochene persecution and the MACCABEE's rebellion of the 2nd century BCE; the best-known episode was that of the mother and her seven sons (2 Maccabees 7). In Hadrian's time, pious Jews risked death to circumcise their sons, and RABBI AKIBA BEN JOSEPH embraced martyrdom to assert the right to teach the Law publicly. The TALMUD cites the majority opinion that one should pre-

fer martyrdom to three transgressions—idolatry, sexual immorality, and murder.

The MIDRASH on Lamentations 2:2 contains what is probably the oldest Jewish martyrology, the list of the Ten Martyrs. It was repeated in later *midrashim* and formed the theme of several liturgical elegies, including the *Eleh Ezkerah*, found in the YOM KIPPUR service. During the European persecutions of the later Middle Ages, chronological registers of martyrs were drawn up for use in SYNAGOGUE commemorative services. In 1296 Isaac ben Samuel of Meiningen began to collect these in the *Memorbuch* (published in 1898), covering the years 1096–1349. Martyrs are honored as *kedoshim* ("the holy ones"). Rabbi Shneur Zalman of Lyady, founder of ḤABAD Hasidism, considered the spirit of martyrdom (*mesirut nefesh*) to be the distinguishing quality of the Jewish people.

Christianity. The original meaning of the Greek word *martys* was "witness"; in this sense it is often used in the NEW TESTAMENT. Since the most striking witness that Christians could bear to their faith was to die rather than deny it, the word soon began to be used in reference to one who was not only a witness but specifically a witness unto death. This usage is present, at least implicitly, in Acts 22:20 and Revelation 2:13.

The first Christian martyrs were St. Stephen and ST. JAMES. Of the apostles the most important martyrs were PETER and PAUL, both put to death at Rome. Early in the 2nd century, Ignatius of Antioch described his own prospective martyrdom as a way of "attaining to God" and urged the Roman Christians not to make any effort to have him spared. In the sporadic persecutions of the first two centuries, martyrdoms were not especially frequent, but the martyrs were highly regarded by Christians. With the passage of time and with a fresh emphasis on martyrdom (often regarded as a substitute for BAPTISM) in the persecutions under Decius (250 CE) and Diocletian (303–311 CE), the authentic acts of the early martyrs were often replaced by legendary accounts (for instance, none of the versions of the death of Ignatius is genuine). The earliest surviving Christian martyrologies are the Syrian *Breviarium Syriacum* (411 CE) and the Hieronymian (mid-5th century), which purports to be by St. Jerome.

Islam. The Islamic designation *shahīd* (Arabic: "witness") is equivalent to and in a sense derivative of the Judeo-Christian concept of martyr. The full sense of "witness unto death" does not appear in the QUR'AN but receives explicit treatment in the subsequent HADITH literature, in which it is stated that martyrs, among the host of heaven, stand nearest the throne of God.

While details of the status accorded by martyrdom (*e.g.*, whether or not a martyr is exempt from certain rituals of burial) have been debated, it is generally agreed that the rank of *shahīd* comprises two groups of the faithful: those killed in JIHAD, or HOLY WAR, and those killed unjustly. The term is used informally to venerate anyone who dies in a pitiable manner (*e.g.*, in childbirth; in a strange land). Among the Shī'ite branch, the martyr most revered is ḤUSAYN IBN 'ALĪ (*c.* 629–680), whose death at the hands of the rival SUNNI faction under Yazīd is commemorated every year during the first 10 days of the month of Muḥarram.

Buddhism. While distinctly lacking a history of violent conflict with other faiths, BUDDHISM does recognize among its adherents a venerable class of martyrs. The JĀTAKA commentary on the former lives of the BUDDHA GOTAMA is in a sense a martyrology of the BODHISATTVA ("buddha-to-be") and his disciples, recounting their continual self-sacrifice and repeated deaths. In MAHĀYĀNA Buddhism, the decision by one destined to become a buddha in this or another life to postpone his own enlightenment to alleviate the suffering of others is regarded as martyrdom.

MARY \\'mer-ē, 'mar-ē, 'mā-rē\, *also called* Saint Mary, *or* Virgin Mary (fl. beginning of the Christian Era), the mother of JESUS, venerated in the Christian church since the apostolic age, and a favorite subject in art, music, and literature.

The first mention of Mary is the story of the ANNUNCIATION, which reports that she was living in Nazareth and was betrothed to JOSEPH (Luke 1:26 ff.); the last mention of her (Acts 1:14) includes her in the company of those who devoted themselves to prayer after the ASCENSION of Jesus into heaven. She appears in the following incidents in the Gospels: the Annunciation; the visit with Elizabeth, her kinswoman and the mother of John the BAPTIST (Luke 1:39 ff.); the birth of Jesus and his presentation in the Temple (Luke 2:1 ff.); the coming of the MAGI and the flight to Egypt (Matthew 2:1 ff.); the PASSOVER visit to Jerusalem (Luke 2:41 ff.); the marriage at Cana in Galilee (John 2:1 ff.); the attempt to see Jesus while he was teaching (Mark 3:31 ff.); and at the cross (John 19:26 ff.).

Probably the earliest allusion to Mary in Christian literature is the phrase "born of woman" in Galatians 4:4, which was written before any of the Gospels. The phrase is a Hebraic way of speaking about the essential humanity of a person. When applied to Jesus, therefore, "born of woman" asserted that he was a real man, in opposition to the attempt to deny that he had had a completely human life. Her role as mother takes precedence over any of the other roles assigned to her in devotion and in dogma. Those who defend the doctrine of the VIRGIN BIRTH usually maintain that Jesus' true humanity was made possible when Mary accepted her commission as the guarantee of the INCARNATION (Luke 1:38). This is the original source of the title Co-Redemptrix—indicating some participation with Christ in the re-

Mary as the Mother of Mercy, panel by Lippo Memmi (c. 1285–1361); in the dome of the Orvieto Cathedral, Italy
Anderson—Alinari from Art Resource

demption of mankind—assigned to Mary in ROMAN CATHOLIC theology, though the term has come to connote a more active role whose precise nature is still debated.

By far the most voluminous narratives about Mary in the NEW TESTAMENT are the infancy stories in the Gospels of Matthew and Luke. In their present form, both accounts make a point of asserting that Jesus was conceived in the womb of Mary without any human agency (Matthew 1:18 ff.; Luke 1:34 ff.); yet the many textual variants in Matthew 1:16, some of them with the words "Joseph begat Jesus," raises the question of whether such an assertion was part of Matthew's original account. The passages in Matthew and in Luke seem to be the only references to the matter in the New Testament. The apostle Paul nowhere mentions it; the Gospel According to Mark begins with Jesus as an adult; and the Gospel According to John does not allude to the virgin birth. It was the teaching of all the orthodox Fathers of the Church that Mary conceived Jesus with her virginity intact, a teaching enshrined in the early Christian creeds and concurred in by most Protestant churches and believers since the REFORMATION.

Various corollaries could be deduced from the assertion of Mary's virginity in the conception of Jesus, including the doctrine that she had remained a virgin in the course of his birth (the *virginitas in partu*) and the doctrine that she had remained a virgin until the end of her life (the *virginitas post partum*). The APOSTLES' CREED appears to teach at least the *virginitas in partu* when it says "born of the Virgin Mary." On a similar level, most theologians came to accept the view that Mary never did anything sinful. THOMAS AQUINAS taught that God suppressed and ultimately extinguished ORIGINAL SIN in her, apparently before she was born. This position, however, was opposed by the doctrine of the IMMACULATE CONCEPTION, systematized by DUNS SCOTUS and finally defined as Roman Catholic dogma by Pope PIUS IX in 1854. According to this dogma, Mary was not only pure in her life and in her birth, but "at the first instant of her conception was preserved immaculate from all stain of original sin" through the GRACE of God.

No account of the place and circumstances of Mary's death was universally accepted in the church, no burial place was acknowledged, and no miracles were credited to relics of her body. In 1950 Pope PIUS XII declared that "the Immaculate Mother of God, the ever Virgin Mary, when the course of her earthly life was run, was assumed in body and soul to heavenly glory."

MARY MAGDALENE, SAINT \\'mag-də-ˌlēn, -lin; ˌmag-də-'lē-nē\, *also called* Mary of Magdala (fl. 1st century CE, Palestine; feast day July 22), one of JESUS' most celebrated disciples, according to Mark 16:9–10 and John 20:14–17, the first person to see the resurrected Christ.

She is first mentioned when Jesus cleanses her of seven DEMONS (Luke 8:2 and Mark 16:9), probably implying that he cured her of a physical disorder. She was one of the women who accompanied and aided Jesus in Galilee (Luke 8:1–2), and all four canonical GOSPELS attest that she witnessed Jesus' CRUCIFIXION and burial; John 19:25–26 further notes that she stood by the cross. Having seen where Jesus was buried (Mark 15:47), she went with two other women on EASTER morning to the tomb to anoint the corpse. Finding the tomb empty, Mary ran to the disciples. She returned with ST. PETER, who, astonished, left her. Christ then appeared to Mary and, according to John 20:17, instructed her to tell the APOSTLES that he was ascending to God.

ORIGEN and other early interpreters usually viewed her as distinct from the Mary of Bethany, who anointed Jesus' feet and wiped them with her hair (John 12:3–7), and from the penitent woman whose SINS Jesus pardoned for anointing him in a like fashion (Luke 7:37–48). The Eastern church also distinguishes between the three, but after they were identified as one and the same by Pope Gregory I, Mary Magdalene's cult flourished in the West. Modern scholars feel that the three women are distinct.

Gnostics regarded her as a medium of secret revelation, so described in their *Gospel of Mary, Gospel of Philip,* and *Pistis Sophia.* According to Eastern tradition, she accompanied ST. JOHN THE EVANGELIST to Ephesus (near modern Selçuk, Turkey), where she died and was buried. French tradition claims that she evangelized Provence (now southeastern France) and spent her last 30 years in an Alpine cavern. Medieval legend relates that she was John's wife.

MASHHAD \\'mȧsh-hȧd, mə-'shad\\, *also spelled* Meshed \\mə-'shed\\, *or* Mashad (Arabic: "Martyr's Place"), city, northeastern Iran, lying 3,231 feet up in the valley of the Kashaf River. It is an important political and religious center, visited annually by more than 100,000 pilgrims.

The city is an offshoot of the ancient city of Tūs and owes its historical importance to the burial place and shrine of the CALIPH Hārūn al-Rashīd (d. 809 CE) and that of ʿALĪ AL-RIḌĀ (d. 818), the eighth IMAM of the Twelver SHIʿITE sect of ISLAM. Although Mashhad was severely damaged in a Mongol attack in 1220, the sacred buildings were partially spared, and traces of the earlier structures remain. Shah Rokh, the son of the conqueror Tīmūr (Tamerlane), did much to beautify Mashhad, and his wife erected a mosque that is one of the finest architectural achievements of Iran. In the 16th and 17th centuries, Mashhad was sacked by Turkmen and Uzbeks. It was restored by ʿAbbās I (reigned 1588–1629), who encouraged the PILGRIMAGE and beautified the city. Nādir Shah (reigned 1736–47) made it his capital and made several additions to its buildings. After Nādir's death, Mashhad became the capital of a small state controlled by his grandson. In 1975 Muhammad Reẓā Shah demolished many of the city's religious colleges (MADRASAS) as part of an urban development plan. This contributed to the unrest that brought about the downfall of his government in 1979.

MASHRIQ AL-ADHKĀR \\'mȧsh-rik-ȧl-ȧt̲h̲-'kȧr\\ (Arabic: "place where the uttering of the names of God arises at dawn"), temple or house of worship in the BAHĀʾĪ FAITH. The *mashriq* is characterized by a nine-sided construction, in keeping with the Bahāʾī belief in the mystical properties of the number nine. Free of ritual and clergy, the *mashriq* is open to adherents of all religions and offers a simple service of readings from the sacred Bahāʾī writings and the holy books of other faiths. The Bahāʾī faithful envision a *mashriq* in every sizeable community, serving as the focal point of a social center that would include a hospital, orphanage, dispensary, and school. The first *mashriq* was completed in 1907 in ʿIshqābād, modern Turkmenistan.

MASK, type of disguise, commonly an object worn over or in front of the face to hide the identity of the wearer. The features of the mask not only conceal those of the wearer but also project the image of another personality or being. This dual function is a basic characteristic of masks.

Cultures have made and used masks imbued with symbolism and ascribed spiritual power since the Stone Age. The greatest range of mask forms and functions occurs in Africa and in Oceania. Since the end of the 19th century masks have been exhibited and collected as art objects in their own right and as cultural artifacts.

In indigenous societies, masks are frequently associated with the ritual of SECRET SOCIETIES or with the high priest or MEDICINE MAN. Totemic practices, whereby a natural object such as an animal or bird is adopted as the emblem of a family line, has led to the evolution of totem masks such as those of the Native Americans of the northwestern coast of the United States and also of some African cultures.

Funerary masks and death masks in ancient Egypt were associated with the return of the spirit to the body. Such masks were generalized portraits and, in the case of nobility, were made of precious metals. Gold death masks also occur in Asia and in the INCA civilization. From Roman times onward, death masks were sometimes kept as portraits of the dead person. Masks as theatrical devices, to represent characters, evolved from religious traditions of ancient Greek civilization.

The deity Karura, bugaku mask, lacquer and painted wood, 14th century; in the Tō Temple, Kyōto, Japan
Tō-ji, Kyōto, Japan

MASORETIC TEXT \\,ma-sə-'re-tik\\ (from Hebrew: *māsōreth,* "tradition"), traditional text of the Hebrew BIBLE, meticulously assembled and supplied with diacritical marks to enable correct pronunciation. This monumental work was begun around the 6th century CE and completed in the 10th by scholars at Talmudic academies in Babylonia and Palestine, in an effort to reproduce, as far as possible, the original text of the Hebrew OLD TESTAMENT.

In Hebrew or Aramaic, they called attention to strange spellings and unusual grammar and noted discrepancies in various texts. Since texts traditionally omitted vowels in writing, the Masoretes introduced vowel signs to guarantee correct pronunciation. Among the various systems of vocalization that were invented, the one fashioned in the city of Tiberias, Galilee, eventually gained ascendancy. In addition, signs for stress and pause were added to the text to facilitate public reading of the SCRIPTURES in the SYNAGOGUE.

When the final codification of each section was complete, the Masoretes counted and noted down the total number of verses, words, and letters in the text and further indicated which verse, which word, and which letter marked the text's center, so that any future emendation could be detected. The rigorous care given the Masoretic text in its preparation is credited for the remarkable consistency found in Old Testament Hebrew texts since that

697

time. The Masoretic text is universally accepted as the authentic Hebrew Bible.

MASS, the celebration of the EUCHARIST in the ROMAN CATHOLIC church. The term mass is derived from the rite's Latin formula of dismissal, *Ite, missa est* ("Go, it is ended"). According to Roman Catholic teaching, the mass is a memorial in which the death and RESURRECTION of JESUS CHRIST are sacramentally reenacted; it is a sacrifice in which the body and blood of Jesus, under the appearances of bread and wine, are offered to God; and it is a sacred meal in which the community symbolically expresses its unity and its dependence upon God. The mass consists of two parts: the liturgy of the Word, which includes readings from SCRIPTURE and the homily (sermon), and the liturgy of the EUCHARIST, which includes the offertory, the eucharistic prayer (canon), and the communion. The rite was changed greatly after the SECOND VATICAN COUNCIL (1962–65), most conspicuously in the use of vernacular languages in place of Latin.

MAṢṢEBA \ˌmät-sā-ˈvä\, *also spelled* maẓẓevah, *or* matzeva (Hebrew: "tombstone," "monument"), *plural* maṣṣebot, maẓẓevoth, *or* matzevot, stone pillar erected on elevated ground beside a sacrificial altar. It was considered sacred to the god it symbolized and had a wooden pole (*ashera*) nearby to signify a goddess. After conquering the Canaanites, early Israelites appropriated these symbols until their use was outlawed as idolatrous (*e.g.,* Deuteronomy 16:21).

In the OLD TESTAMENT (Genesis 28:18–22; 2 Samuel 18:18; Joshua 4:20–23) *maṣṣeba* is used to designate a stone memorial, or monument, or, more specifically, a tombstone resting upright on a grave (Genesis 35:20). This latter meaning is retained in modern Hebrew.

MATH \ˈmäth\, in the Welsh collection of stories known as the MABINOGION, king of Gwynedd in the North. He is also the brother of DÔN, who is probably the Welsh counterpart of the Irish goddess DANU. Whenever at peace, it was necessary for Math to have his feet upon a virgin's lap. The virgin who held Math's feet was raped by one of his nephews, Gilfaethwy, and both he and his brother GWYDION were punished for the act by Math. Later, Math's niece Arianrhod (sister of Gilfaethwy and Gwydion) tried for the position of footholder, but during the test of her virginity she gave birth to two children, one of whom was LLEU.

Together with Gwydion, Math helped Lleu in many ways, creating an artificial wife, BLODEUEDD, for him and helping him to avenge her eventual unfaithfulness. Together with Gwydion, Math was responsible for the introduction of pigs—supposedly from the otherworld into North Wales—an aspect which points to a role as a fertility figure.

MATHA \ˈmə-tə\, any Hindu monastic establishment of world renouncers or *sannyasin*s. The first *matha*s were founded by the great teacher of ADVAITA Vedanta, ŚAMKARA, in the 8th century CE. Śaṃkara was said to have established four such *matha*s at the

strategic corners of India as bulwarks for Hindu missionary activity and as centers for the 10 religious orders of his group: the Govardhana Matha in Puri on the east coast for the Aranya and Vana orders; the Jyotih Matha, near Badrinath in the HIMALAYAS, for the GIRI, Parvata, and Sagara orders; the Sarada Matha in Dvaraka on the west coast of India for the Tirtha and Asrama orders; and the Srngeri Matha in South India for the Bharati, Puri, and Sarasvati orders. A fifth *matha*, the Saradapitha in Kancipuram near Madras, arose somewhat later.

Each of these *matha*s is ruled by a spiritual leader, or teacher, called a Śaṃkaracarya. The head of the Srngeri Matha is regarded by this sect as the *jagadguru* or spiritual master of the whole world. The Śaṃkaracaryas, who trace their spiritual lineage back to the great Śaṃkara, are almost universally respected in HINDUISM for their heritage, for their tradition of Sanskrit learning, and for their role as defenders of and spokesmen for the faith.

Other Hindu sects have also formed *matha*s. The Vaiṣṇava group called the ŚRĪ VAIṢṆAVAS established their own monastic centers in Srirangam, Melkote, and elsewhere from the time of the founder of their sect, Ramanuja. DVAITA, another Vaiṣṇava order with *matha*s throughout South India, traces its lineage back to the teacher MADHVA, an opponent of monistic Vedanta. In the 20th century the Ramakrishna Mission Society, a religiously inclusivistic reform group originally organized under the leadership of its founder Ramakrishna and his disciple VIVEKANANDA, also established *matha*s to house its monks and to act as centers for learning and the propagation of its teachings.

MATHER, COTTON \ˈma-thər, -thər\ (b. Feb. 12, 1663, Boston, Massachusetts Bay Colony [U.S.]—d. Feb. 13, 1728, Boston), American Congregational minister and author, supporter of the old order of the ruling clergy, who became the most celebrated of all New England Puritans.

The son of INCREASE MATHER and the grandson of John Cotton and Richard Mather, Cotton lived all his life in Boston. He entered Harvard at the age of 12. At 18 he received his M.A. degree from the hands of his father, who was president of the college.

Cotton Mather, portrait by Peter Pelham
By courtesy of the American Antiquarian Society, Worcester, Mass.

Mather once noted that his life was "a continual conversation with heaven," but he spent agonizing hours convinced that he was damned and equal time in ecstasies that he was not. For a while, he feared he could not enter the ministry because of a speech impediment. Returning to religious studies, he preached his first sermon in his father's church in August 1680 and in October another from his grandfather John Cotton's pulpit. He was formally ordained in 1685 and became his father's colleague.

He joined his father in cautioning judges against the use of "specter evidence" (testimony of a victim of WITCHCRAFT that he had been attacked by a specter bearing the appearance of someone he knew) in the witchcraft trials and in working for the ouster of Sir Edmund Andros as governor of Massachusetts. He was also a leader in the fight for inoculation against smallpox, incurring popular disapproval.

When Cotton inoculated his own son, who almost died from it, the whole community was wrathful, and a bomb was thrown through his chamber window. Various members of his family became ill, and some died.

Mather's interest in science and particularly in various American phenomena—published in his *Curiosa Americana* (1712–24)—won him membership in the Royal Society of London. His *Christian Philosopher* (1721) recognizes God in the wonders of the earth and the universe beyond; it is both philosophical and scientific and, ironically, anticipates 18th-century DEISM, despite his conservatism.

Cotton Mather wrote and published more than 400 works. His magnum opus was *Magnalia Christi Americana* (1702), an ecclesiastical history of America from the founding of New England to his own time. His *Manuductio ad Ministerium* (1726) was a handbook of advice for young graduates to the ministry: on doing good, on college love affairs, on poetry and music, and on style. His ambitious 20-year work on biblical learning was interrupted by his death.

MATHER, INCREASE (b. June 21, 1639, Dorchester, Massachusetts Bay Colony [U.S.]—d. Aug. 23, 1723, Boston), prominent Boston Congregational minister, author, and educator (*see* CONGREGATIONALISM).

Mather entered Harvard at the age of 12 and received his bachelor's degree at 17. At graduation, his attack on Aristotelian logic, basic to the Harvard curriculum, shocked the faculty and nearly resulted in his dismissal. On his 18th birthday he preached his first sermon in a village near his home and his second in his father's church in Dorchester. Soon he left for Dublin, where he entered Trinity College and received a master's degree the following June. Chosen a fellow at Trinity, he refused the post. He preached at various posts in England and was at Guernsey when the Puritan Commonwealth ended and Charles II was proclaimed king. On the appointment of a new governor for Guernsey, unsympathetic to NONCONFORMISTS, Increase left a comfortable living and soon sailed for Boston, where he became minister of North Church in 1661.

In 1683 Charles delivered an ultimatum to the Massachusetts colonists: to retain their charter with absolute obedience to the king or to have it revoked. Before an assembly of freemen, Mather proclaimed that an affirmative vote would be a SIN against God, for only to him should one give absolute obedience. The colonists refused submission, and the charter was subsequently revoked in 1686.

While James II was king, in 1688, Mather was sent as the representative of the colonists to thank him for his declaration of liberty to all faiths. He remained in England for several years, and, on the accession of William and Mary in 1689, he obtained from them the removal of the hated governor of Massachusetts, Sir Edmund Andros, and his replacement by Sir William Phipps. Increase's petition for the restoration of the old charter proved unsuccessful, but he was able to get a new charter in 1691. Both the new governor and the new charter, however, turned out to be unpopular. In 1685 Increase had been made president of Harvard, but he resigned in 1701, in part because of opposition to the new colonial charter.

Among his books is *An Essay for the Recording of Illustrious Providences* (1684), a compilation of stories showing the hand of divine providence in rescuing people from natural and supernatural disasters. Some historians suggest that this book conditioned the minds of the populace for the WITCHCRAFT hysteria of Salem in 1692. Despite the fact that Increase and his son COTTON MATHER believed in witches—

as did most of the world at the time—they suspected that evidence could be faulty and justice might miscarry. The case against a suspected witch rested on testimony that the victim had been attacked by a specter bearing the appearance of someone he knew, which the Mathers distrusted because a witch could assume the form of an innocent person. When this type of evidence was finally thrown out of court at the insistence of the Mathers and other ministers, the whole affair came to an end.

MATRONALIA \,ma-trə-'nā-lē-ə\, *also called* Matronales Feriae, in ROMAN RELIGION, ancient festival of JUNO, the birth goddess, celebrated annually by Roman matrons on March 1, the day on which a temple was dedicated to Juno. According to tradition, the cult was established by Titus Tatius, king of the Sabines. The Matronalia symbolized the sacredness of marriage and was mythically tied to the peace that followed the first marriages between Romans and Sabine women. The festival consisted of a procession of married women to the temple, where they made offerings to Juno. At home, offerings were supplemented by prayers for marital felicity. Wives received gifts from their husbands and gave a feast for their female slaves.

MATSURI \'mät-sü-‚rē\ (Japanese: "festival"), in general, any of a wide variety of civil and religious ceremonies in Japan; more particularly, the shrine festivals of SHINTŌ. *Matsuri* vary according to the shrine, the deity or sacred power (KAMI) worshiped, and the purpose and occasion of the ceremony. A *matsuri* generally falls into two parts: the solemn ritual of worship, followed by a joyous celebration.

The participants first purify themselves (*see* HARAI) by periods of abstinence, which may vary from hours to days, and by bathing (*misogi*), preferably in salt water. The *kami* is then requested to descend into its symbol or object of residence (SHINTAI) in a rite that consists of opening the inner doors of the shrine, beating a drum or ringing bells, and calling the *kami* to descend. Next the food offerings (*shinsen*) are presented and on occasion other offerings, *heihaku* (literally, "cloth," but including also paper, jewels, weapons, money, and utensils). Prayers (NORITO) are recited

Matsuri procession at the Shintō shrine Heian Jingu, Kyōto, Japan
Photo Researchers

by the priests. Individual worshipers offer branches of a sacred tree (*tamagushi*), and ceremonial music and dancing (*gagaku* and *bugaku*) are performed. The offerings are then withdrawn and the *kami* requested to retire.

The celebrations usually include a feast (*naorai*), in which the consecrated offerings of food and drink are consumed by priests and laymen, dancing, theatrical performances, DIVINATION, and athletic contests. The *kami* is frequently taken out in a procession in a portable shrine (*mikoshi*); thus, its presence blesses the locations along its route. Accompanying it in the procession are priests of the temple in full ceremonial dress; delegations of parishioners, musicians, and dancers dressed in ancient costumes; and floats (*dashi*). The floats are decorated cars shaped like mountains, shrines, or perhaps boats, either drawn by men or oxen or carried on men's shoulders.

MATSYENDRANĀTH \‚məts-yen-drə-'nä-tə\, *also called* Mīnanātha (fl. 10th century?, India), first human GURU of the NĀTHA cult.

Matsyendranāth's name appears on both the lists of the 9 *nātha*s ("masters") and the 84 *mahāsiddha*s ("great accomplished ones") common to HINDUISM and BUDDHISM. He was given semidivine status by his followers and identified with Avalokiteśvara-Padmapāni (a BODHISATTVA) by his Buddhist followers in Nepal and with the god SHIVA by his Hindu devotees. In Tibet he was known as Lui-pa. The name Mīna-nātha ("Fish-Lord") refers either to his receipt of spiritual instruction from Shiva while in the form of a fish or to his rescue of a sacred text from the belly of a fish.

Though an ascetic he succumbed, according to tradition, to the charms of two queens of Ceylon and had two sons, Pārosenāth and Nīmnāth, who were leaders of JAINISM. His leading disciple, GORAKHNĀTH, is commonly regarded as the founder of the Kānphaṭa Yogis, an order of religious ascetics who stress the practice of HAṬHA YOGA.

MATTHEW (THE EVANGELIST), SAINT \'math-yü\, *also called* Levi \'lē-‚vī\ (fl. 1st century CE, Palestine; Western feast day September 21, Eastern feast day November 16), one of the Twelve Apostles, traditional author of the first Synoptic Gospel. The Gospel According to Matthew was certainly written for a Jewish-Christian church in a strongly Jewish environment, but that this Matthew is definitely the synoptic author is seriously doubted. Tradition notes his ministry in Judaea, after which he supposedly missioned to the East, suggesting Ethiopia and Persia. Legend differs as to the scene of his MISSIONS and as to whether he died a martyr's death. Matthew's relics were reputedly discovered in Salerno (Italy) in 1080. His symbol is an ANGEL.

MĀTURĪDĪYA \mà-‚tür-ē-'dē-ə\, Muslim orthodox school of theology named after its founder, Abū Manṣūr Muhammad al-Māturīdī (d. 944). The Māturīdīya is similar in outlook to the school of AL-ASH'ARĪ (d. 935), the Ash'arīya, that has received more attention and praise as the champion of the true faith. The Māturīdīya is more popular in its home region, known historically as Transoxania (Central Asia).

The Māturīdī school is characterized by its reliance on the QUR'AN without reasoning or free interpretation. Its members argued that since MUHAMMAD himself had not used reason in this respect, it is an innovation (BID'A) to do so, and every innovation is a HERESY according to a well-known prophetic saying. The later Māturīdīya, however, acknowledged the possibility of problems for which there is no precedent in either the Qur'an or HADITH, and modified this rule, allowing for rational inferences when necessary.

The Māturīdīya entered the discussion of "compulsion" and "free will," which was at its peak in theological circles at the time of its founding. They followed a doctrine similar to that of the Ash'arīya, emphasizing the absolute omnipotence of God and at the same time allowing humans a minimum of freedom to act so that they may be justly punished or rewarded. In the later stages of its development, however, the Māturīdīya took an independent course and stated unequivocally that humans have the utmost freedom to act, a point of view derived directly from many verses in the Qur'an and the Hadith.

The Māturīdīya differed also from the Ash'arīya on the question of the "assurance of salvation." They held that a Muslim who sincerely performed his religious duties as prescribed by God in the Qur'an, and as explained and taught by his Prophet, is assured of a place in heaven. The Ash'arīya maintained that one is not saved unless God wills him to be saved, and that no one knows whether he is a believer or not, for only God can make such a decision.

MATZAH \'mät-sə\, unleavened bread eaten by Jews during the holiday of PASSOVER (Pesaḥ) in commemoration of their exodus from Egypt, when the rapid departure did not allow for the fermentation of dough. The Passover ritual requires that Jews eat matzahs at least on the first night of the celebration and that they eat no leavened bread throughout the entire holiday of Passover.

MAUNDY THURSDAY, *also called* Holy Thursday, the Thursday before EASTER, observed in commemoration of JESUS CHRIST's institution of the EUCHARIST. The English name is taken (via medieval French) from an anthem sung in ROMAN CATHOLIC churches on that day: "Mandatum novum do vobis" ("A new commandment I give to you"; John 13:34). In the early Christian church the day was celebrated with a general communion of clergy and people. At a special MASS the bishop consecrated the holy oils in preparation for the anointing of the neophytes at the BAPTISM on Easter night. Since 1956 Maundy Thursday has been celebrated in Roman Catholic churches with a morning liturgy for the consecration of the holy oils for the coming year and an evening liturgy in commemoration of the institution of the Eucharist, with a general communion. During the evening liturgy the hosts are consecrated for the communion on GOOD FRIDAY, and the celebrant ceremonially washes the feet of 12 men in memory of Christ's washing the feet of his disciples. Eastern Orthodox churches also have a ceremony of foot washing and blessing of oil on this day.

MAURICE, (JOHN) FREDERICK DENISON \'mȯr-is, mȯ-'rēs\ (b. Aug. 29, 1805, Normanston, Suffolk, Eng.—d. April 1, 1872, London), major English theologian of 19th-century Anglicanism and prolific author, remembered chiefly as a founder of CHRISTIAN SOCIALISM.

Prevented from graduation in law at Cambridge by his refusal to subscribe to the THIRTY-NINE ARTICLES, the Anglican CONFESSION OF FAITH, Maurice reversed his position by 1830 and attended Oxford. In the interim he had worked in London as a writer and an editor for literary journals and in 1834 published his only novel, *Eustace Conway*. That same year he was ordained and soon afterward became CHAPLAIN at Guy's Hospital in London. Elected professor of English literature and modern history at King's College, Cambridge, in 1840, he became professor of divinity and accepted the chaplaincy at Lincoln's Inn, a London academy of law, six years later. His reputation as a theologian was enhanced with the publication of his book *The Kingdom of Christ* (1838), in which he held the church to be a united body that transcended the diversity and partiality of individual men, factions, and sects. That view—subsequently regarded as presaging the 20th-century ecumenical movement—aroused the suspicions of orthodox Anglicans. Their misgivings were intensified in 1848, when he joined the moderate Anglicans Charles Kingsley, John Malcolm Ludlow, and others to found the Christian Socialist movement.

Opposition to Maurice grew after his *Theological Essays* of 1853 revealed his disbelief in the eternity of hell, and that year he was dismissed from his King's College post. Maurice planned and became the first principal of the Working Men's College (1854). In 1860 Maurice left the chaplaincy at Lincoln's Inn for St. Peter's Church. Elected to the Knightsbridge professorship of moral philosophy at Cambridge in 1866, he lectured on ethical subjects and wrote his celebrated *Social Morality* (1869). To this position, which he held until his death, he added the chaplaincy of St. Edward's Church at Cambridge in 1870.

MAUSS, MARCEL \'mōs\ (b. May 10, 1872, Épinal, France—d. Feb. 10, 1950, Paris), French sociologist and anthropologist whose contributions include a highly original comparative study of the relation between forms of exchange and social structure. His views on the theory and method of ethnology are thought to have influenced Claude Lévi-Strauss, A.R. RADCLIFFE-BROWN, E.E. EVANS-PRITCHARD, and Melville J. Herskovits, among others.

Mauss was the nephew of sociologist ÉMILE DURKHEIM, who contributed much to his intellectual formation. Mauss succeeded Durkheim as editor of the journal *L'Année Sociologique* ("The Sociological Year"). In 1902 he began his career as professor of primitive religion at the École Pratique des Hautes Études ("Practical School of Higher Studies"), Paris. He was a founder of the Ethnology Institute of the University of Paris (1925) and also taught at the Collège de France (1931–39). A political activist for many years, he supported Alfred Dreyfus in his famed court battle, aligned himself with the socialist leader Jean Jaurès, and assisted in founding the socialist daily *L'Humanité* (1904).

Among his earliest works was "Essai sur la nature et la fonction du sacrifice" (written with Henri Hubert, 1899; *Sacrifice: Its Nature and Function*). His most influential work is thought to be "Essai sur le don" (1925; *The Gift*). Concentrating on the forms of exchange and contract in Melanesia, Polynesia, and northwestern North America, the work explores the religious, legal, economic, mythological, and other aspects of giving, receiving, and repaying; it displays Mauss' concern with studying a limited segment of social phenomena viewed in its systematic entirety. Mauss also wrote on magic, the concept of self, mourning rites, and other topics. *Sociologie et anthropologie* (1950) is a collection of essays he published between 1904 and 1938.

MAWDŪDĪ, ABŪ'L-AʿLĀ \maù-'dü-dē\ (b. Sept. 25, 1903, Aurangābād, Hyderābād state [India]—d. Sept. 22, 1979, Buffalo, N.Y., U.S.), journalist and fundamentalist Muslim theologian who played a major role in Pakistani politics.

The son of a lawyer, Mawdūdī was given a traditional Islamic education at home in order to shield him from Western influences. In his adult years he became convinced that Muslim thinkers must be freed from the hold that Western civilization had over them, in favor of a code of life, culture, and political and economic system unique to ISLAM.

When Pakistan split off from India in 1947, his efforts were instrumental in guiding the new nation away from the SECULARISM of Western governments, and toward the formation of an Islamic state. Persistently Mawdūdī found himself in opposition to the Pakistani government. He was imprisoned from 1948 to 1950 and again from 1953 to 1955 and was under a sentence of death for a period in 1953.

Mawdūdī wrote on a very broad range of topics, including philosophy, Muslim jurisprudence, history, economics, sociology, and theology. He is best known for the thesis that God alone is sovereign, not human rulers, nations, or customs. Political power in this world exists in order to put the divinely ordained principles of the SHARĪʿA (the Islamic legal and moral code) into effect. Since Islam is a universal code for human life, moreover, the state must be all-embracing and must be left in the hands of Muslims, though non-believers should be allowed to live within the state as non-Muslim citizens (*see* DHIMMA). Since all Muslims share the same relationship to God, this state must be what Mawdūdī called a "theo-democracy," in which the whole community is called upon to interpret the divine law.

MAWLĀ: *see* MULLĀ.

MAWLAWĪYA \ˌmaù-lə-'wē-ə\, *Turkish* Mevleviya, fraternity of Sufi mystics founded in Konya (Qonya), Anatolia, by the Persian Sufi poet JALĀL AL-DĪN AL-RŪMĪ (d. 1273), whose popular title *mawlānā* (Arabic: "our master") gave the order its name (*see* SUFISM). The order, propagated throughout Anatolia, controlled Konya and environs by the 15th century and in the 17th century appeared in Constantinople (Istanbul). European travelers identified the Mawlawīya as dancing (or whirling) DERVISHES, based on their observations of the order's ritual prayer (DHIKR), performed spinning on the right foot to musical accompaniment.

After the dissolution of all Sufi brotherhoods in Turkey in 1925, the Mawlawīya survived in a few monasteries in Aleppo, Syria, and small towns in the Middle East. Special permission granted by the Turkish government in 1954 allowed the Mawlawī dervishes of Konya to perform their ritual dances for tourists during two weeks of every year. Despite opposition from the Turkish government, the order continued to exist as a religious body into the late 20th century. The tomb of al-Rūmī at Konya, although officially a museum, attracted a steady stream of devotees. In recent years branches of this order have been established in Europe and the Americas, and in 1996 an international Mevlevi foundation was inaugurated at the request of the order's leader, Celâlettin Celebi (d. 1996), to organize international meetings and publishing activities.

MAWLID \'maù-lid\, *also spelled* mawlūd, *or* mīlād, in ISLAM, the birthday of a holy figure, especially the birthday of the Prophet MUHAMMAD (Mawlid al-Nabī).

Muhammad's birthday, fixed by tradition as the 12th day of the month of Rabīʿ I, *i.e.*, the day of Muhammad's death, was not widely celebrated until about the 13th century. At the end of the 11th century in Egypt, the ruling Shiʿite Fāṭimids (descendants of ʿALĪ, the fourth CALIPH, through his wife FĀṬIMA, Muhammad's daughter) observed four *mawlids*, those of Muhammad, ʿAlī, Fāṭimah, and the ruling caliph. The festivals were simple PROCESSIONS of court officials, held in daylight, that culminated in the recitation of three sermons (KHUTBAS) in the presence of the caliph.

SUNNIS regard a *mawlid* celebration held in 1207 as the first *mawlid* festival. That occasion was organized by Muẓaffar al-Dīn Gökburī, brother-in-law of the Egyptian SULTAN Saladin, at Irbīl, near Mosul (Iraq). It closely parallels the modern *mawlid* in form. The day of Muhammad's birth was preceded by a month of merrymaking. Musicians, jugglers, and assorted entertainers attracted people from as far away as Baghdad and Niṣībīn (modern Nusaybin, Turkey); and Muslim scholars, jurists, mystics, and poets began arriving as much as two months in advance. Two days before the formal *mawlid* a large number of camels, sheep, and oxen were sacrificed, and on the eve of *mawlid* a torchlight procession passed through the town. On the morning of the *mawlid*, the faithful and the soldiery assembled to hear the sermon. The religious dignitaries were then honored with special robes, and all feasted at the prince's expense.

The *mawlid* festival quickly spread throughout the Muslim world, partly because of a contemporary corresponding enthusiasm for SUFISM, by which Islam became a personal experience. Many Muslim theologians could not accept the new festivities, branding them BID'AS, innovations possibly leading to SIN. The *mawlid*, indeed, betrayed a Christian influence; Christians in Muslim lands observed CHRISTMAS in similar ways, and Muslims often participated in the celebration. Modern revivalist Muslims such as the Wahhābīya still view the *mawlid* festivities as idolatrous.

*Mawlid*s, however, continue to be celebrated and have been extended to popular saints and the founders of Sufi brotherhoods. The *mawlid* poems, which relate Muhammad's life and virtues, are also widely popular outside the times of regular feasts. *Mawlid*s are also recited in commemoration of deceased relatives.

MAXIMUS THE CONFESSOR, SAINT \'mak-si-məs\ (b. *c.* 580, Constantinople—d. Aug. 13, 662, Lazica), the most important Byzantine theologian of the 7th century, whose commentaries on Pseudo-DIONYSIUS THE AREOPAGITE and on the Greek church fathers considerably influenced the theology and MYSTICISM of the Middle Ages.

A court secretary of the Eastern Roman emperor Heraclius I, Maximus became a monk *c.* 613 at a monastery near Chrysopolis in Bithynia. Fleeing to North Africa because of the Persian invasion of 626, he took part at Carthage (near modern Tunis) in the Monothelite controversy. Arguing that JESUS CHRIST had two wills as he had two natures, the divine and the human, Maximus was called to Rome, where he supported the condemnation of Monothelitism by a regional church council under Pope Martin I in 649. Maximus and Martin were arrested by the emperor Constans II in an intricate theological-political tactic, and, after imprisonment from 653 to 655, Maximus was tortured and exiled; he died in the wilderness near the Black Sea.

Throughout his approximately 90 major works Maximus developed a Christocentric theology and mysticism. His *Opuscula theologica et polemica* ("Short Theological and Polemical Treatises"), *Ambigua* ("Ambiguities" in the works of GREGORY OF NAZIANZUS), and *Scholia* (on Pseudo-Dionysius the Areopagite), mostly authentic, express Maximus' teaching on the transcendental, nonpredicable nature of the divinity, his intrinsic Trinitarian existence, and his definitive communication in Christ. In his *400 Capita de caritate* ("Four Hundred Chapters on Charity"), Maximus counseled a Christian humanism, integrating ASCETICISM with ordinary life and active CHARITY.

MAXIMUS THE GREEK, *also called* Maximus the Hagiorite (b. 1480, Árta, Greece—d. 1556, near Moscow), Greek Orthodox monk, humanist scholar, and linguist, whose

principal role in the translation of the SCRIPTURES and philosophical–theological literature into the Russian Church Slavic made possible the dissemination of Byzantine culture throughout Russia.

Maximus was educated in Paris, Venice, and Florence. When the Russian church requested from the patriarchate of Constantinople an expert to correct church texts that were used in Russia, Maximus was chosen for the mission. In Moscow, with the assistance of Russian secretaries, he translated original Greek canonical, liturgical, and theological texts into Church Slavic. The great literary output inspired a Slavic cultural movement and laid the groundwork for later Russian theology.

While in Moscow Maximus became involved in the factional controversy between the Nonpossessors (or Transvolgans), who believed that monasteries should not own property and who had liberal political views, and the Possessors (or Josephites), who held opposite opinions. The Nonpossessors came to be led by Maximus and Nil Sorsky, the Possessors by Joseph of Volokolamsk. Maximus took part in the preparation of a corrected and critical edition of the *Kormchaya kniga*, a Slavic version of the Byzantine ecclesiastical laws collected as the *Nomocanon*. In this work, he supported the ideas of the Nonpossessors, holding that the Church should practice poverty and desist from feudal exploitation of the peasantry. In 1525 Maximus was arrested on the charge of HERESY by Daniel, METROPOLITAN of Moscow and a Possessor. After a series of trials, he was condemned in 1531 and imprisoned for 20 years in the monastery of Volokolamsk, near Moscow, of which Joseph was ABBOT. While in detention, Maximus continued to produce theological works. When he emerged in 1551, his personal prestige was immense, but his political views were suppressed. During the last five years of his life, he retired to the Troitse-Sergiyeva Monastery, where he was buried and was subsequently venerated as a saint.

Among the works credited to him are commentaries on the Psalms and on THE ACTS OF THE APOSTLES and an anti-Latin church treatise entitled *Eulogy for the Holy Apostles Peter and Paul*. The *Eulogy* includes a criticism of Western CHRISTIANITY for fostering the doctrine of PURGATORY.

MĀYĀ \'mä-yä\ (Sanskrit: "illusion"), fundamental concept in HINDUISM, notably in the ADVAITA (Nondualist) school of the orthodox system of VEDĀNTA. *Māyā* originally denoted the power with which a god can make humans believe in an illusion; by extension it later came to mean the force that creates the cosmic illusion that the phenomenal world is real. For the Nondualists, *māyā* is the cosmic force that manifests the infinite BRAHMAN (the supreme being) as the finite phenomenal world. *Māyā* is reflected on the individual level by human ignorance (*ajñāna*) of the real nature of the self, which is mistaken for the empirical ego but which is in reality identical with Brahman.

MAYA \'mī-ə\: *see* PRE-COLUMBIAN MESO-AMERICAN RELIGIONS.

MAYA CODICES \'mī-ə-'kō-də-ˌsēz, -'kä-\, richly illustrated pre-Columbian Mayan hieroglyphic writings, only a few of which survived burning by the Spanish clergy during the 16th century. The texts are known today as the Madrid, Paris, Dresden, and Grolier codices.

The Madrid Codex (Latin Codex Tro-Cortesianus) is believed to be a product of the late Mayan period (*c.* 1400 CE), possibly a post-Classic copy of Classic Mayan scholarship. The Madrid Codex consists of 56 pages, inscribed on both sides, formed by folding and doubling a sheet made from the bark of a fig tree. Containing a wealth of information on ASTROLOGY and on DIVINATION, this codex has been of particular value in identifying the various Mayan gods and reconstructing the rites that ushered in new years. Also illustrated are Mayan crafts such as pottery and weaving and activities such as hunting. Found in two unequal sections (called the *Troano* and the *Cortesianus*) in two locations in Spain in the 1860s, the Codex is now housed in the Museum of America in Madrid.

The Paris Codex's Latin name, Codex Peresianus, comes from the name Perez, which was written on the torn wrappings of the manuscript when it was discovered in 1859 in the Bibliothèque Nationale in Paris. It is devoted almost entirely to Mayan ritual and ceremony. It is fragmentary and is composed of paper made from tree bark, fashioned in a long strip and folded like a screen. The 11 leaves provide 22 pages of columns of glyphs and pictures of the gods. It has been dated to between the Classic and Conquest periods of Mayan history.

The Dresden Codex (Latin Codex Dresdensis) contains astronomical calculations—eclipse-prediction tables, the synodical period of Venus—of exceptional accuracy. The Maya's reputation as astronomers is based largely on these figures. The codex was acquired by the Saxon State Library, Dresden, Saxony, and was published by Edward King, Viscount Kingsborough, in *Antiquities of Mexico* (1830–48). King erroneously attributed the codex to the Aztecs.

The Grolier Codex, possibly the oldest of the codices (it has been dated to the 13th century BCE), gets its name from the Grolier Club in New York, where it was first exhibited after its discovery in 1971. It contains portions of a table charting the movements of Venus. Initially treated with some skepticism, most authorities today accept its authenticity. Its current whereabouts are unknown.

MAZDAKISM \\'maz-də-ˌki-zəm\\, dualistic religion that rose to prominence in the late 5th century in Iran from obscure origins. According to some scholars, Mazdakism was a reform movement seeking an optimistic interpretation of the Manichaean DUALISM. Its founder appears to have been one Zaradust-e Khuragan; a connection has been sought between him and a Persian, Bundos, who preached a divergent MANICHAEISM in Rome under Diocletian at the end of the 3rd century. Other scholars see it as an internal development within Iranian religion. After the 5th century the religion came generally to be called after Mazdak (fl. late 5th century CE, Persia), its major Persian proponent. No Mazdakite books survive. Knowledge of the movement comes from brief mentions in Syrian, Persian, Arabic, and Greek sources.

According to Mazdakism, there exist two original principles, Good (or Light) and Evil (or Darkness). Light acts by

Drawing from the Madrid Codex showing the corn god (left) and the rain god, Chac
By courtesy of the Museo de America, Madrid

FREE WILL and design; Darkness, blindly and by chance. By accident the two became mixed, producing the world. There are three Light elements: water, fire, and earth. By their actions humans should seek to release the Light in the world; this is accomplished through moral conduct and ascetic life. They may not kill or eat flesh. They are to be gentle, kind, hospitable, and clement to foes. To encourage brotherly helpfulness and reduce causes of greed and strife, Mazdak sought to make property and women common. He converted to his faith the Sāsānid king Kavadh I (488–496 and 499–531), who introduced social reforms inspired by its tenets. These appear to have involved some liberalizing of marriage laws and of measures concerning property. These actions aroused the hostility of the nobles and the Zoroastrian clergy and led to the eventual suppression of Mazdakism. Nevertheless, the religion survived in secret into Islamic times (the 8th century).

McPHERSON, AIMEE SEMPLE \\mək-'fər-sən\\ (b. Oct. 9, 1890, near Ingersoll, Ont., Can.—d. Sept. 27, 1944, Oakland, Calif., U.S.), controversial U.S. Pentecostal evangelist and early radio preacher whose International Church of the Foursquare Gospel brought her wealth, notoriety, and a following numbering in the tens of thousands. Known as "Sister Aimee," she was a dynamic and attractive woman and retained the loyalty of her followers despite a third marriage that ended in divorce, a sensational five-week disappearance in 1926, and various grave but unproved charges against her. Her career reached its height in the late 1930s. She died from an overdose of barbiturates.

MECCA \\'me-kə\\, *Arabic* Makka, *formally* Makka al-Mukarrama ("Ennobled Mecca"), *ancient* Bakka, *or* Macoraba, city, western Saudi Arabia. Mecca is the most holy city of ISLAM; it was the birthplace of MUHAMMAD and is a religious center to which Muslims attempt a pilgrimage, or HAJJ, during their lifetime.

Mecca is located in the Ṣirāt Mountains, 45 miles inland from the Red Sea port of Jidda. The city centers upon the Al-Ḥaram Mosque and the sacred well of Zamzam, located inside. In the mosque's central courtyard is the KAʿBA, the holiest shrine of Islam, which has been destroyed and rebuilt several times. Other holy sites in and near Mecca include the hills of Safa and Marwa next to the Al-Ḥaram Mosque, where pilgrims reenact Hajar's (Hagar's) search for water for her son Ismaʾīl (Ishmael); the town of Mina, where pilgrims stone three pillars during the hajj rites; the plain of ʿArafat, where they assemble for midday prayers; and Mt. Hira, where Muhammad received his first revelations. During the month of pilgrimage (the Islamic month of Dhū al-Ḥijja), Mecca's population swells with the addition of about two million pilgrims. Only Muslims are permitted to reside in the city.

MEDB \'māv, 'm^{y}ethv\, *also spelled* Medhbh, legendary queen of Connaught (Connacht) in Ireland. In the Irish epic tale *Táin Bó Cúailnge* ("The Cattle Raid at Cooley") she led her forces against those of Ulster and fought in the battle herself. Originally Medb appears not to have been a historical queen but a fierce goddess with an insatiable sexual appetite. The list of her mates is impressive; at the time of the battle against Ulster, the king Ailill was her mate, but she also had an affair with the mighty hero FERGUS, distinguished for his prodigious virility. The name *Medb,* which is variously interpreted as: "the drunken one" or "she who intoxicates," is most likely a derivative of a Celtic adjective meaning "strong, intoxicating" (Middle Irish *medb*) or "drunken" (Welsh *meddw*).

MEDEA \mə-'dē-ə\, in Greek mythology, enchantress who helped JASON, leader of the ARGONAUTS, to obtain the Golden Fleece from her father, King Aeetes of Colchis. She had the gift of PROPHECY, and the character was perhaps the remnant of an early goddess. Her aid was invaluable to Jason in his quest, and she later married him.

The *Medea* of Euripides takes up the story at a later stage, after Jason and Medea had fled Colchis with the fleece and had been driven out of Iolcos because of the vengeance taken by Medea on King PELIAS of Iolcos (who had sent Jason to fetch the fleece). The play is set during the time that the pair lived in Corinth, when Jason deserted Medea for the daughter of King Creon of Corinth; in revenge, Medea murdered Creon, his daughter, and her own two sons by Jason and took refuge with King Aegeus of Athens. The Greek historian Herodotus related that from Athens Medea went to the region of Asia subsequently called Media, whose inhabitants thereupon changed their name to Medes.

MEDICINE MAN, member of a nonliterate society who is knowledgeable about the magic potencies of various substances (medicines) and skilled in the rituals in which they are administered, particularly for healing. The term has been used most widely in the context of indigenous American cultures.

Some medicine men (or women in some societies) undergo rigorous initiation to gain supernormal powers, while others are essentially learned experts. The medicine man commonly carries a kit of objects—such as feathers of valued birds, bones, suggestively shaped or marked stones, or hallucinogenic plants—that have magical associations; in some cases, the stones are considered to have been embedded in the body of the medicine man at his initiation.

MEDINA \mə-'dē-nə\, *Arabic* Al-Madīna, *formally* Al-Madīna Al-Munawwara ("The Luminous City"), *or* Madīnat Rasūl Allāh ("City of the Messenger of God [*i.e.,* Muhammad]"), *ancient* Yathrib, one of two most sacred cities of ISLAM, in Saudi Arabia some 278 miles from MECCA.

In 622 MUHAMMAD arrived at Medina from Mecca. This flight, known as the HIJRA, marks the beginning of the Muslim calendar. Soon afterward Muhammad drove out the Jews who had controlled the oasis. Thereafter known as Medina, the city prospered as the administrative capital of the steadily expanding Islamic state, a position it maintained until 661, when it was superseded in that role by Damascus. The city was sacked in 683 by the CALIPHS for its fractiousness.

The Ottomans, following their conquest of Egypt, held Medina from 1517 until the WAHHĀBĪS, a militant Islamic re-vivalist group, took the city in 1804. An Ottoman-Egyptian force retook it in 1812, and the Ottomans remained in effective control until 1912 with the resurgence of the Wahhābī movement under Ibn Saʿūd. Ottoman rule ceased during World War I, when the sharif Ḥusayn ibn ʿAlī, ruler of Mecca, revolted. Ḥusayn later came into conflict with Ibn Saʿūd, and in 1925 Medina fell to the Saʿūdī dynasty.

Medina is second only to Mecca as the holiest place of Muslim pilgrimage; the tomb of Muhammad in the Prophet's Mosque is among the most sacred shrines in the Islamic world. The first two SUNNI caliphs, Abū Bakr and ʿUmār, are also believed to be buried there, as are FĀṬIMA and several of the Shiʿite IMAMS. Other religious features of the oasis include the mosque of Qubāʾ, the first in Islamic history, from which the Prophet was vouchsafed a view of Mecca; the Mosque of the Two Qiblahs at al-Rimāḥ, commemorating the change of the prayer direction from Jerusalem to Mecca; the tomb of Ḥamza, uncle of the Prophet, and of his companions who fell in the Battle of Uḥud (625), in which the Prophet was wounded; and the cave in the flank of Uḥud, in which the Prophet took refuge on that occasion. Other mosques commemorate where he donned his armor for that battle; where he rested on the way there; where he unfurled his standard for the Battle of the Ditch; and the ditch itself, dug around Medina by Muhammad. All these spots are the object of pious visitation by all Muslims visiting Medina; they are forbidden to non-Muslims. In addition the city is also the site of the Islamic University, established in 1961.

MEDINA, CONSTITUTION OF, document based upon two agreements concluded between the clans of MEDINA and the Prophet MUHAMMAD soon after the HIJRA, or emigration to Medina in 622 CE. The agreements established the *muhājirūn, i.e.,* the early Muslims from MECCA who followed Muhammad, on a par with the eight clans of Medina (called the ANSAR, or "helpers"); collectively, the nine tribes formed the first Muslim community. The agreements also regulated the relations of the Muslims with the Jews who at that time inhabited Medina.

MEDITATION, mental exercise consisting in techniques of concentration, contemplation, and abstraction, regarded as conducive to heightened awareness or somatic calm.

Meditation in some form has been systematized in most great religions of the world. The Hindu philosophical school of YOGA prescribes an elaborate process for the purification of body, mind, and soul. In numerous religions, spiritual purification may be sought through the verbal or mental repetition of a prescribed efficacious syllable, word, or text (*e.g.,* the Hindu and Buddhist mantra; Islamic DHIKR; Christian Jesus prayer). The focusing of attention upon a visual image is a common technique; Tantric Buddhists of Tibet, for example, regard the MANDALA (Sanskrit: "circle") diagram as a collection point of universal forces, accessible to humans by meditation. Tactile and mechanical devices, such as the ROSARY and the PRAYER WHEEL, play a highly ritualized role in many contemplative traditions.

BUDDHISM places perhaps the greatest focus on meditation of any major religion. In that tradition, the practice of meditation—that is, mental concentration leading through a succession of stages—can lead to the final goal of spiritual freedom, NIRVANA. Meditation occupies a central place in Buddhism and combines, in its highest stages, the discipline of increased introversion with the insight brought about by wisdom, or *prajñā.*

Monks performing zazen, *a type of meditation in Zen Buddhism*
Paolo Koch—Photo Researchers

The object of concentration (the *kammaṭṭhāna*) may vary according to individual and situation. One Pāli text lists 40 *kammaṭṭhāna*s, including devices (such as a color or a light), repulsive things (such as a corpse), and recollections (as of the Buddha).

Four stages of concentration (called in Sanskrit *dhyāna*s) are distinguished: (1) detachment from the external world and a consciousness of joy and ease; (2) concentration, with suppression of reasoning and investigation; (3) the passing away of joy, with the sense of ease remaining; and (4) the passing away of ease also, bringing about a state of pure self-possession and equanimity. The *dhyāna*s are followed by four further exercises, the *samāpatti*s ("attainments"). They are described as (1) consciousness of infinity of space; (2) consciousness of the infinity of cognition; (3) concern with the unreality of things; and (4) consciousness of unreality as the object of thought.

The stages of Buddhist meditation show many similarities with Hindu Yoga, reflecting a common tradition in ancient India. The Buddhists, however, describe the culminating trancelike state as transient; final Nirvana requires the insight of wisdom. The various exercises and visualizations that are meant to develop wisdom focus on penetrating through to the true nature of reality, or to the discernment of the conditioned and unconditioned dharmas (elements) that make up all phenomena. Although meditation is important in all schools of Buddhism, it has developed characteristic variations within different traditions, and some schools, such as Zen, place more emphasis upon meditation. *See also* TRANSCENDENTAL MEDITATION.

MEDIUM, in OCCULTISM, person reputedly able to make contact with the world of spirits, especially while in a state of trance. A medium is the central figure during a SÉANCE and sometimes requires the assistance of an invisible go-between, or control. During a séance, disembodied voices are said to speak, either directly or through the medium.

MEDUSA \mə-'dü-sə, -'dyü-, -zə\, in Greek mythology, the most famous of the GORGONS. She was usually represented as a winged female creature whose hair consisted of snakes. Medusa was the only Gorgon who was mortal; hence PERSEUS was able to kill her by cutting off her head. From her

neck sprang Chrysaor and PEGASUS, her two sons by POSEIDON. The severed head, which had the power of turning into stone all who looked upon it, was given to ATHENA, who placed it in her shield; according to another account, Perseus buried it in the marketplace of Argos.

HERACLES is said to have obtained a lock of Medusa's hair (which possessed the same powers as the head) from Athena and to have given it to Sterope, the daughter of Cepheus, as a protection for the town of Tegea against attack; when exposed to view, the lock was supposed to bring on a storm, causing the enemy to flee.

MEGALITH \'me-gə-ˌlith\, huge, often undressed stone used in various types of Neolithic and Early Bronze Age monuments.

In Spain, Portugal, and the Mediterranean coast the most ancient of the cyclopean stone tombs was probably the DOLMEN, which consisted of several upright supports and a flat roofing slab, all covered by a protective mound of earth. In northern and western Europe, two principal plans developed from the dolmen: one, the passage grave, was formed by the addition of a long stone-roofed entrance passage to the dolmen itself; and the other, the long, coffinlike CIST or covered GALLERY GRAVE, consisted of a long, rectangular burial chamber with no distinct passageway. Many round and long barrows also were found to contain megalithic burial chambers.

Another form of megalithic monument was the menhir (from Breton *men*, "stone," and *hir*, "long"). Menhirs were simple upright stones, sometimes of great size, and were erected most frequently in western Europe, especially Brittany. Often they were placed together, forming circles, semicircles, or vast ellipses. Many were built in England, the best-known sites being STONEHENGE and Avebury in Wiltshire. Megalithic menhirs were also placed in parallel rows, called alignments. The most famous are the alignments at Carnnac, France, which include 2,935 menhirs. The alignments were probably used for ritual PROCESSIONS, and often a circle or semicircle of megaliths stood at one end.

Megalith at Avebury stone circle, Wiltshire, Eng.
J. Allan Cash

MEGILLAH \mə-'gi-lə\ (Hebrew: "Scroll"), any of five sacred books of the KETUBIM, in scroll form, that are read in the SYNAGOGUE in the course of certain festivals. The Song of Solomon (Song of Songs) is read on the SABBATH of PASSOVER week, the Book of Ruth on SHAVUOT, Lamentations of Jeremiah on TISHA BE-AV, Ecclesiastes on the Sabbath of the week of SUKKOT, and the Book of Esther on PURIM. (It must be noted that the phrase "the Megillah" refers to the scroll of Esther.) The reading of Esther on Purim is prescribed in the MISHNAH; other readings were introduced in post-Talmudic days.

Megillah (scroll of Esther) in a silver case, German, 17th century
By courtesy of the Jewish Museum, London; photograph, A.C. Cooper

MEHER BABA \'mā-hər-'bä-bä\, *also called* The Awakener, *original name* Merwan Sheriar Irani (b. Feb. 25, 1894, Poona, India—d. Jan. 31, 1969, Ahmednagar), spiritual master in western India with a sizable following both in that country and abroad. Beginning on July 10, 1925, he observed silence for the last 44 years of his life, communicating with his disciples at first through an alphabet board but increasingly with gestures.

He was born into a ZOROASTRIAN family of Persian descent. At age 19 he met an aged Muslim woman, Hazrat Babajan, the first of five "perfect masters" (spiritually enlightened, or "God-realized," persons) who over the next seven years helped him find his own spiritual identity. That identity was as the AVATAR of this age, by which he meant the periodic incarnation of God in human form. He placed himself among such universal religious figures as ZOROASTER, RĀMA, KRISHNA, BUDDHA GOTAMA, JESUS, and MUHAMMAD, declaring that all major religions are revelations of "the One Reality which is God."

In Meher Baba's COSMOLOGY the goal of all life is to realize the absolute oneness of God, from whom the universe emanated as a result of the whim of unconscious divinity to know itself as conscious divinity. In pursuit of consciousness, evolution of forms occurs in seven stages: stone or metal, vegetable, worm, fish, bird, animal, and human. Every individualized soul must experience all of these forms in order to gain full consciousness. Once consciousness is attained, the burden of impressions accumulated in these

forms prevents the soul from realizing its identity with God. To gain this realization the individual must traverse an inward spiritual path, eliminating all false impressions of individuality and eventuating in the knowledge of the "real self" as God.

Meher Baba saw his work as awakening the world through love to a new consciousness of the oneness of all life. To that end he lived a life of service that included extensive work with the poor, the physically and mentally ill, and many others.

Between 1931 and 1958 he made many visits to the United States and Europe. On one trip to the United States, in 1952, he established the Meher Spiritual Center in Myrtle Beach, S.C. A similar center, Avatar's Abode, was created at Woomby, Queensland, Australia, in 1958.

Meher Baba never sought to form a sect or proclaim a dogma; he attracted and welcomed followers of many faiths and every social class with a message emphasizing love and compassion, the elimination of the selfish ego, and the potential of realizing God within themselves. After his death his followers heeded his wish that they not form an organization, but continued to gather informally. His tomb at Meherabad, near Ahmednagar, has become a place of PILGRIMAGE for his followers throughout the world. His books include *Discourses* (5 vol., 1938–43; the earliest dictated on an alphabet board, the others by gesture), *God Speaks: The Theme of Creation and Its Purposes* (1955), and *The Everything and the Nothing* (1963).

MEÏR \mā-'ir\ (Hebrew: "the Enlightener"), important rabbinic authority of the second century CE and a leader in the period following the BAR KOKHBA revolt. He was a student of ISHMAEL BEN ELISHA and, later, AKIBA BEN JOSEPH. Meïr resided primarily in Tiberias but died in Asia. He is one of the most frequently cited RABBIS in the MISHNAH.

Later sources hold that Meïr was descended from proselytes and that his given name was Nehorai (Talmud Bavli Eruvin 13b). He reportedly was one of the five scholars ordained by Judah ben Bava during the persecutions following the Bar Kokhba revolt, though discussions of his ORDINATION by Akiba also are extant. After the persecution, he was a major figure in the newly convened academy at Usha, where he held a position of leadership over the SANHEDRIN.

Meïr's centrality in the formulation of the Mishnah is indicated by the Talmudic statement that anonymous Mishnaic rules represent Meïr's views based upon Akiba's teaching. While this statement is not literally true (the Mishnah reports numerous anonymous rules that disagree with statements of Meïr), it indicates Meïr's importance and the respect in which later authorities held him.

Talmudic stories report a number of tragedies in Meïr's life. His wife Beruryah was the daughter of the martyr Hananiah ben Teradyon. After the Bar Kokhba revolt, her sister was enslaved in a brothel, from which Meïr rescued her. Beruryah was known for her erudition and intelligence but reportedly was seduced by one of Meïr's students.

MEÏR OF ROTHENBURG \mā-'ir . . . 'rō-tən-,bůrk\, *original name* Meir Ben Baruch (b. *c.* 1215, Worms, Franconia [Germany]—d. May 2, 1293, Ensisheim Fortress, Alsace), great rabbinical authority of 13th-century German JUDAISM and one of the last great *tosaphists* (writers of notes and commentary; *see* TOSEFTA) of Rashi's authoritative commentary on the TALMUD.

Meir studied in Germany and later in France, where he witnessed, in 1242 or 1244, the public burning of 24 cartloads of Talmudic manuscripts, a disaster that inspired him to write a moving poem. On returning to Germany, he was RABBI in many communities but probably spent the longest time in Rothenburg, where he opened a Talmudic school. He became famous as an authority on rabbinic law and for nearly half a century acted as the supreme court of appeals for Jews of Germany and surrounding countries. In practice he was a strict Talmudist.

In 1286 Emperor Rudolph I attempted to abrogate Jews' political freedom by making them *servi camerae* ("serfs of the treasury"). While attempting to escape with his family and a group of followers, Rabbi Meir was apprehended and imprisoned for the rest of his life in an Alsatian fortress. Although the Jews raised a large ransom, it is generally believed that Meir refused it for fear of encouraging the government to imprison more rabbis for ransom. Fourteen years after his death, upon payment of a large ransom, his body was finally delivered for burial.

Although Meir wrote no single major work, his 1,500 or so extant RESPONSA (authoritative answers to questions regarding Jewish law and ritual) are rich with information about the community organization and social customs of medieval German Judaism. He also wrote many erudite Talmudic *tosaphoth* (notes). His main teachings, however, were included in numerous literary compositions by his disciples, such as the famous codifier ASHER BEN JEHIEL. These compositions became classical textbooks of law and ritual for ASHKENAZIC Jews of all subsequent generations.

MEKHILTA ATTRIBUTED TO RABBI ISHMAEL \mə-ˈkil-tə…ˈish-mä-əl, -mē-əl\, TANNA commentary on the book of EXODUS, usually dated to *c.* 300 CE. (Some scholars believe the text dates only as long ago as medieval times, which, if true, would take it well out of the era of the *tannaim.*) *Mekhilta* presents a composite of three kinds of materials concerning the book of Exodus. The first material is composed of ad hoc and episodic exegeses of some passages of SCRIPTURE. The second material is a group of propositional and argumentative essays in exegetical form, in which theological principles are set forth and demonstrated. The third material consists of topical articles, some of them sustained and many of them well crafted, about important subjects of the JUDAISM of the dual TORAH. (Within Jewish tradition, God revealed the Torah to MOSES in two media, writing and memory. The former is recorded in the PENTATEUCH. The latter is subsequently set down in documents from the MISHNAH through the TALMUD of Babylonia—thus, dual Torah.) The document forms a sustained address to the book of Exodus.

MELAMPUS \mə-ˈlam-pəs\, in Greek mythology, seer who as a child received the understanding of the language of birds after two young snakes, whose lives he had saved, licked his ears when he was asleep. He later helped his brother Bias to marry Pero, daughter of King Neleus of Pylos. According to another tradition, Melampus cured the insanity of the daughters of PROETUS, prince of Tiryns; he and Bias then married two of the daughters. According to Pausanias (2nd century CE), there was a shrine to Melampus at Aegosthena (Megarid) and an annual festival.

MELANCHTHON, PHILIPP \mə-ˈlaŋk-thən, *German* mä-ˈlänk-tòn\, *original name* Philipp Schwartzerd (b. Feb. 15, 1497, Bretten, Palatinate [Germany]—d. April 19, 1560, probably Wittenberg, Saxony [Germany]), author of the AUGSBURG CONFESSION of LUTHERANISM (1530), humanist, Reformer, theologian, and educator.

Melanchthon inherited from his parents a deep sense of piety, though he was also a firm believer in ASTROLOGY and demonology. Philipp's first tutor instilled in him a lifelong love of Latin and classical literature, and, at the Pforzheim Latin school, he had his name changed from Schwartzerd to its Greek equivalent, Melanchthon.

While at the universities of Heidelberg and Tübingen, Melanchthon explored scholastic thought, the rhetoric of the Dutch humanist Rudolf Agricola, and the nominalism of the English philosopher WILLIAM OF OCKHAM, in addition to SCRIPTURE and classical works. He then lectured on the classics and soon had six books to his credit, including "Rudiments of the Greek Language" (1518), a grammar that was to go through many editions. In 1518 he accepted an invitation to become the University of Wittenberg's first professor of Greek. Only four days after his arrival, he addressed the university on "The Improvement of Studies," boldly setting forth a humanistic program and calling for a return to classical and Christian sources in order to rejuvenate both theology and society.

Luther and Melanchthon responded to each other enthusiastically, and a deep friendship developed. Melanchthon committed himself wholeheartedly to the new evangelical cause, initiated when Luther circulated his NINETY-FIVE THESES. By the end of 1519 he had already defended scriptural authority against Luther's opponent JOHANN ECK, rejected (before Luther did) TRANSUBSTANTIATION, and made JUSTIFICATION by faith the keystone of his theology. He had also published seven more small books and had earned a theology degree at Wittenberg.

Philipp Melanchthon, engraving by Albrecht Dürer, 1526
By courtesy of the Staatliche Museen Kuperstichkabinett, Berlin

In spite of the fact that an imperial decree of death to those who supported Luther had been issued, in 1521 Melanchthon made sharp reply to the Sorbonne's condemnation of 104 of Luther's statements with "Against the Furious Decree of the Parisian Theologasters." His "Passion of Christ and Antichrist," in the same year, utilized woodcuts by Lucas Cranach (1472–1553) in a scathing criticism of the lifestyle of the pope. When Melanchthon hesitated to publish his lectures on Corinthians, Luther stole a copy and published them in 1521; in 1523 he did the same with Melanchthon's notes on John.

At the Diet of Augsburg (1530) Melanchthon was the leading representative of the REFORMATION, because Luther was in exile at Coburg Castle, and it was he who prepared the Augsburg Confession, which influenced every subsequent major credal statement in PROTESTANTISM. In the Confession he sought to be as inoffensive to ROMAN CATHOLICS as possible but forcefully stated the evangelical stance. In the ensuing negotiations over adoption of the confessional statement, he seemed to compromise, but the vigor of his Apology of the Confession of Augsburg (1531) belied any change. The Apology and Confession quickly became authoritative Lutheran statements of faith, as did his "Appendix on the Papacy," which was an addition to the Schmalkald Articles of 1536–37. In the "Appendix," Melanchthon refuted historically and theologically any papal primacy by divine right but accepted papal jurisdiction as a human right for the sake of peace, if the Gospel were permitted.

The year after Luther's death an attempt was made to unite the evangelicals and Roman Catholics in the provisional agreements of the Augsburg Interim. Melanchthon refused to accept the Interim until justification by faith was ensured as a fundamental doctrine. Then, for the sake of order and peace, he declared that those principles which did not violate justification by faith might be observed as adiaphora, or nonessentials. He allowed the necessity of good works to salvation, but not in the old sense of meriting righteousness; and he accepted the seven SACRAMENTS, but only as rites that had no inherent efficacy to salvation. His later years were occupied with controversies within the evangelical church and fruitless conferences with his Roman Catholic adversaries.

MELCHIZEDEK \mel-'ki-zə-,dek\, *also spelled* Melchisedech, in the OLD TESTAMENT, figure of importance in biblical tradition because he was both king and priest, was connected with Jerusalem, and was revered by ABRAHAM. He appears as a person only in an interpolated vignette (GENESIS 14:18–20) of the story of Abraham rescuing his kidnapped nephew, Lot, by defeating a coalition of Mesopotamian kings under Chedorlaomer.

In the episode, Melchizedek meets Abraham on his return from battle, gives him bread and wine (which has been interpreted by some Christian scholars as a precursor of the EUCHARIST, so that Melchizedek's name entered the canon of the Roman MASS) and blesses Abraham in the name of "God Most High" (in Hebrew El 'Elyon). In return, Abraham gives him a tithe of the booty.

Melchizedek is an old Canaanite name meaning "My King is [the god] Sedek" or "My King is Righteousness" (the meaning of the similar Hebrew cognate). Salem, of which he is said to be king, is very probably Jerusalem. Psalm 76:2 refers to Salem in a way that implies that it is synonymous with Jerusalem, and the reference in Genesis 14:17 to "the King's Valley" further confirms this identification. The god whom Melchizedek serves as priest is El 'Elyon, again a name of Canaanite origin, probably designating the high god of their pantheon.

For Abraham to recognize the authority and authenticity of a Canaanite priest-king is startling and has no parallel in biblical literature. This story may have reached its final formulation in the days of King David, serving as an apologia for David's making Jerusalem his headquarters and setting up the PRIESTHOOD there. Abraham's paying tribute to a Jerusalem priest-king then would anticipate the time when Abraham's descendants would bring tithes to the priests of Jerusalem ministering in the SANCTUARY at the Davidic capital. The story may also relate to the conflict between the LEVITE priests descended from Abraham and the Zadokite priests of Jerusalem, who later changed their allegiance to YAHWEH, the Hebrew god. The Zadokites monopolized the Jerusalem priesthood until forcibly taken away to Babylon, at which time Levite priests asserted their own hegemony;

the Melchizedek episode could reveal the reascendancy of Zadokite power.

The biblical account also poses textual problems. Abraham paying a tithe to Melchizedek is an interpretation, though a likely one, of the original biblical text, in which the matter is ambiguous; it seems incongruous that Abraham gives a tenth of the booty to Melchizedek and then refuses to take any of it for himself (Genesis 14:20–23). Again, some scholars have asserted that it would be unusual for an author of Davidic times to construct a narrative with a Canaanite protagonist.

Psalm 110, in referring to a future MESSIAH of the Davidic line, alludes to the priest-king Melchizedek as a prototype of this messiah. This allusion led the author of the Letter to the Hebrews in the NEW TESTAMENT to translate the name Melchizedek as "king of righteousness" and Salem as "peace," so that Melchizedek is made to foreshadow Christ, stated to be the true king of righteousness and peace. According to the analogy, just as Abraham, the ancestor of the Levites, paid tithes to Melchizedek and was therefore his inferior, so the Melchizedek-like priesthood of Christ is superior to that of the Levites. Furthermore, just as the Old Testament assigns no birth or death date to Melchizedek, so is the priesthood of Christ eternal.

MELCHIZEDEK PRIESTHOOD, in the Mormon church (CHURCH OF JESUS CHRIST OF LATTER-DAY SAINTS), higher of two PRIESTHOODS, concerned with spiritual rather than secular matters. *See also* MELCHIZEDEK.

MELEAGER \,me-lē-'ā-jər\, in Greek mythology, leader of the Calydonian boar hunt. The *Iliad* relates how Meleager's father, King OENEUS of Calydon, had omitted to sacrifice to ARTEMIS, who sent a wild boar to ravage the country. Meleager collected a band of heroes to drive it away and eventually killed it himself. The Calydonians and the Curetes (neighboring warriors who aided in the hunt) then quarreled over the spoils, and war broke out between them. At one point the Curetes besieged Calydon and were ready to take it when Meleager repulsed them. One tradition relates that Meleager's mother, Althea, had a vision that foretold that Meleager would live as long as a log that was on the fire; she snatched the log from the fire but later caused his death by burning it.

MELPOMENE \mel-'pä-mə-,nē\, in GREEK RELIGION, one of nine MUSES, patron of tragedy and lyre playing. In Greek art her attributes were the tragic mask and the club of HERACLES. According to some traditions, the SIRENS were born from the union of Melpomene with the river god Achelous.

MELQART \'mel-,kärt\, *also spelled* Melkart, or Melkarth, Phoenician god, chief deity of Tyre and of two of its colonies, Carthage and Gadir (Cádiz, Spain). He was also called the Tyrian BAAL (Lord). Under the name Malku he was equated with the Babylonian NERGAL, god of the Underworld and death. Melqart was usually depicted as a bearded figure, wearing a kilt and holding an Egyptian ANKH, symbol of life, and, as a symbol of death, a fenestrated ax. His SANCTUARY in Tyre, described by Herodotus (who called the temple that of HERACLES), was the scene of annual winter and spring festivals and is believed to have been the model for Solomon's temple in Jerusalem.

Melqart was probably equated with the sun, and Baal Hammon (Baal Amon), "Lord of the Incense Altar," was perhaps his title in that capacity. Baal Hammon was also the name of the chief god of Carthage, consort of the goddess TANIT.

MEMNON \'mem-ˌnän\, in Greek mythology, son of TITHONUS (son of LAOMEDON, king of Troy) and EOS and king of the Ethiopians. He was a hero, who, after the death of the Trojan warrior HECTOR, went to assist his uncle PRIAM, the last king of Troy, against the Greeks. He performed prodigies of valor but was slain by the Greek hero ACHILLES. According to tradition, ZEUS was moved by the tears of Eos and bestowed immortality upon Memnon. His companions were changed into birds, called Memnonides, that came every year to fight and lament over his grave. The combat between Achilles and Memnon was often represented by Greek artists, and the story of Memnon was the subject of the lost *Aethiopis* of Arctinus of Miletus (fl. *c.* 650 BCE).

In Egypt the name of Memnon was connected with the colossal (70-foot) stone statues of Amenhotep III near Thebes, two of which still remain. The more northerly of these was partly destroyed by an earthquake in 27 BCE, resulting in a curious phenomenon. Every morning, when the rays of the rising sun touched the statue, it gave forth musical sounds like the twang of a harp string. This was supposed to be the voice of Memnon responding to the greeting of his mother, Eos (goddess of dawn). After the restoration of the statue by the Roman emperor Septimius Severus (170 CE) the sounds ceased; they were attributed to the passage of air through the pores of the stone, caused chiefly by the change of temperature at sunrise.

MENAHEM \'me-nə-ˌhem, me-'nä-ḵem\, *also spelled* Manahem (fl. mid-8th century BCE), king of Israel whose 10-year reign was distinguished for its cruelty. Events of his rule are related in 2 Kings 15:14–22. About 746 BCE, Shallum ben Jabesh assassinated Zechariah, king of Israel, and established his throne in the region of Samaria. One month later Menahem advanced from Tirzah, the old royal city, against Shallum and killed him. Menahem assumed power but was not accepted by the district around the city of Tappuah; in revenge he slaughtered the city's inhabitants.

Toward the end of Menahem's reign, the Assyrian king Tiglath-pileser III (identified in the BIBLE as King Pul) advanced against Israel; he was deterred only by a large bribe, which Menahem extorted from his wealthy subjects. Israel remained subjugated to Assyria under Menahem's son and successor, Pekahiah, who was forced to continue tribute.

MENAT \'me-ˌnät\, in EGYPTIAN RELIGION, protective AMULET, usually hung at the back of the neck as a counterpoise to the necklace worn in the front. Frequently made of glazed ware and often found buried with the dead, it was a symbol of divine protection. Among women it fostered fruitfulness and health, while for men it signified virility.

MENCIUS \'men-chē-əs, -chəs\ (Latin), *Chinese* (Wade-Giles) Meng-tzu \'məŋ-dzə\, *or* (Pinyin) Mengzi, *original name* (Wade-Giles) Meng K'o \-'kə\, *posthumous name* Tsou-kung \'dzō-'gùŋ\, *or* Duke of Tsou (b. *c.* 372 BCE, ancient state of Tsou, China—d. *c.* 289, China), early Chinese philosopher whose development of orthodox CONFUCIANISM earned him the title "second sage."

Of noble origin, the Meng family settled in the state of Tsou, a minor state in the present province of Shantung. Tsou and Lu (the state of Confucius' origin) were adjacent states. Like CONFUCIUS, Mencius was only three when he lost his father. Mencius' mother paid special attention to the upbringing of her young son. A traditional story tells of her moving their home near a school, so that the boy should have the right kind of environmental influence, and of her encouraging her son to persevere in his studies. In China she has been for ages upheld as the model mother.

Mencius had for his mentor a pupil of TZU-SSU, who was himself the grandson of Confucius. In due time Mencius became a teacher himself and for a brief period served as an official in the state of Ch'i. He spent much time traveling, offering his advice and counsel to the various princes on government by JEN ("humaneness").

The Chou dynasty (*c.* 1111–256/255 BCE) was founded on the feudalistic principle of a sociopolitical hierarchy, with clearly defined prerogatives and obligations between those of high and low status. As time went on, however, ambition and intrigue resulted in usurpations and impositions, bringing on a condition of political and moral disorder. The age in which Mencius lived is known in Chinese history as the period of Warring States (475–221 BCE). Under such conditions, Mencius' lectures to the princes on virtuous personal conduct and humane government fell on deaf ears; yet he continued to speak his mind.

According to Mencius, the ruler was to provide for the welfare of the people in two respects: material conditions for their livelihood and moral and educational guidance for their edification. Mencius had worked out a definite program, recorded in the book of *Mencius*, to attain economic sufficiency for the common people. He also advocated light taxes, free trade, conservation of natural resources, welfare measures for the old and disadvantaged, and more nearly equal sharing of wealth. It was his fundamental belief that "only when the people had a steady livelihood would they have a steady heart."

Mencius
By courtesy of the National Palace Museum, Taipei, Taiwan, Republic of China

Mencius also emphatically reminded the princes of the responsibility that came to them with T'IEN MING (the mandate of heaven) to govern for the good of the people: "The people are the most important element in a nation; the spirits of the land and grain come next; the sovereign counts for the least." He also quoted from the SHU-CHING ("Classic of History"), one of the FIVE CLASSICS of Confucianism, the saying "Heaven sees as the people see; Heaven hears as the people hear." The outspoken sympathies of Mencius made him a champion of the common people and an advocate of democratic principles in government.

Mencius' sojourn covered several states, but nowhere did he find a prince willing to put his lofty principles of government into practice. His sense of disappointment grew with the years and finally brought him back to his native state of Tsou, where he devoted the remaining years of his life to the instruction of his pupils. The work *Mencius* is a collection of the records of the doings and sayings of the master by his disciples.

Confucius taught the concept of *jen* as the basic virtue of humanity. Mencius made the original goodness of human nature the keynote to his system. That the four beginnings, or "four principles" (*ssu-tuan*)—the feeling of commiseration, the feeling of shame, the feeling of courtesy, and the feeling of right and wrong—are all inborn in humans was a self-evident truth to Mencius; and the "four beginnings," when properly cultivated, will develop into the four cardinal virtues of *jen*, righteousness, decorum, and wisdom. This doctrine of the goodness of human nature on the part of Mencius has become an enduring topic for debate among the Chinese thinkers throughout the ages.

Mencius went further and taught that humans possess intuitive knowledge and intuitive ability and that personal cultivation consisted in developing one's mind. Mencius said: "He who has developed his mind to the utmost, knows his nature. Knowing his nature, he knows Heaven." Hence, all people could become like the great sage-kings YAO and SHUN, the legendary heroes of the archaic past.

While Mencius has always been regarded as a major philosopher, special importance was attributed to him and his work by the Neo-Confucianists of the Sung dynasty (960–1279 CE). For the last 1,000 years, Mencius has been revered among the Chinese people as the cofounder of Confucianism, second only to Confucius himself.

MENCIUS \\'men-chē-əs, -chəs\\ (Latin), *Chinese* (Wade-Giles) Meng-tzu \\'məŋ-dzə\\ (Pinyin) Mengzi, Chinese Confucian text, named for its author, that earned for the 4th-century-BCE philosopher Mencius the title *ya-sheng* ("second sage"). When CHU HSI published the *Mencius* together with three other Confucian texts (1190), he created the classic known as *Ssu-shu* ("FOUR BOOKS").

The book concerns government and maintains that the welfare of the common people comes before every other consideration. When a ruler no longer practices benevolence (JEN) and righteousness (*i*), the mandate of heaven (T'IEN MING) has been withdrawn, and he should be removed. Mencius also declared filial piety (HSIAO) to be the foundation stone of Chinese society. For him, the greatest act of *hsiao* was to honor parents; the greatest lack of *hsiao* was to have no offspring (so that ancestral rites are not perpetuated).

Mencius advances the doctrine that because humans are endowed by heaven, their nature tends toward good as naturally as water flows downhill. As proof, Mencius cited the natural love of children for their parents, the universal sense of right and wrong, and the spontaneous alarm one experiences when one sees a small child in danger. This doctrine of natural human goodness was attacked in the 3rd century BCE by HSÜN-TZU. Mencius's position, however, has long been accepted as an orthodox interpretation of CONFUCIANISM.

MENDELSSOHN, MOSES \\'men-dəl-sən, *German* -ˌzōn\\ (b. Sept. 26, 1729, Dessau, Anhalt [Germany]—d. Jan. 4, 1786, Berlin, Prussia), German-Jewish philosopher, critic of German literature, and BIBLE translator and commentator who greatly contributed to the efforts of Jews to assimilate to the German bourgeoisie. He was the grandfather of the composer Felix Mendelssohn.

Mendelssohn endeavored to combine JUDAISM with the RATIONALISM of the Enlightenment. He was one of the initiators of the HASKALAH or "Jewish Enlightenment." Through his advocacy of religious toleration and through the prestige of his own intellectual accomplishments, Men-

delssohn worked to emancipate German Jews from prevailing social, cultural, political, and economic restrictions.

Born Moses ben Menachem to an impoverished TORAH scribe, Menachem Mendel Dessau, he took the name Mendelssohn from the Hebrew *ben Mendel* ("the son of Mendel"). He studied the thought of John Locke, Gottfried von Leibniz, and Christian von Wolff in Berlin, and was versed in Hebrew, Latin, Greek, English, French, and Italian. His own works on aesthetics influenced the thought of Schiller, Goethe, Kant, and the playwight Lessing.

Mendelssohn published his first two books in 1755: *Philosophische Gesprache* ("Philosophical Speeches") and *Briefe über die Empfindungen* ("Letters on the Emotions"). In *Briefe* and in his later *Philosophische Schriften* (1761; "Philosophical Writings") he began his formulation of a new psychological theory that stressed the autonomy of aesthetics, logic, and ethics relative to each other. Mendelssohn's PHILOSOPHY OF RELIGION continued the classical rationalist tradition of the Enlightenment, emphasizing reason as the medium through which knowledge is fulfilled, and stressing that humanity is endowed with certain innate knowledge: its own goodness, the immortality of the soul, and the existence of God. He held that eternal truths are differentiated from historical or temporal truths: the former are self-evident, the latter require the verification of sense-perception. Mendelssohn's main philosophical work, *Phädon, oder über die Unsterblichkeit der Seele* (1767; "Phaedo, or on the Immortality of the Soul"), carries forth his argument for the immortality of the soul. Following Leibniz, Mendelssohn says that the soul by nature is imperishable, though its continued consciousness is not innate but granted by the goodness and justice of God. God's existence, Mendelssohn believed, was proven by a modified version of the ontological argument: humans are born knowing that God exists, knowledge that cannot come through sense perception or experience. Also, the concept of perfection necessitates existence, since a thing that does not exist is by definition incomplete and imperfect.

In 1770 Mendelssohn reluctantly engaged in a public dispute with the Swiss theologian J.C. Lavater over the right of Judaism to exist independently as a religion alongside CHRISTIANITY. Mendelssohn was tolerant of Christianity and appreciated its moral value, though he believed that it was based on irrational precepts contrary to natural law, which Judaism was not. Later, after working on a translation of the Psalms in 1774 and a German version of the PENTATEUCH written in Hebrew characters (1780–83), he embarked on a controversy regarding the separation of CHURCH AND STATE. In his *Jerusalem, oder über religiöse Macht und Jedentum* (1783; "Jerusalem, or on Religious Power and Judaism"), he argued that both church and state seek the same end, a good and just society. Only the state, however, must retain the powers of force in order to control people's actions; the church must care for people's souls by attending to their relationship with God.

MENDICANT, member of any of several ROMAN CATHOLIC religious orders who assumes a vow of poverty and supports himself or herself by work and charitable contributions. The mendicant orders surviving today are the DOMINICANS, FRANCISCANS, AUGUSTINIANS (Augustinian hermits), CARMELITES, Trinitarians, Mercedarians, Servites, Hospitallers of St. John of God, and the Teutonic Order.

ST. DOMINIC founded the Dominican order in 1216, and ST. FRANCIS OF ASSISI founded the Franciscan order in 1210. Within a generation of their deaths, their institutes had spread throughout Europe and into Asia. In the great cities of western Europe friaries were established, and in the universities theological chairs were held by Dominicans and Franciscans. Later in the 13th century they were joined by the Carmelites, Augustinian Hermits, and Servites.

Poverty was St. Francis' root idea, and there is little doubt that it was borrowed from him by St. Dominic and the other mendicant founders. St. Francis intended his FRIARS to live by the work of their hands and to have recourse to alms only when they could not earn their livelihood. But, as the friars soon came to be devoted to spiritual ministrations and as the communities grew larger, it became increasingly difficult for them to support themselves by personal work; and so begging came to play a greater role.

Francis' idea was that his friars should have no lands, no funded property, and no fixed sources of income. This ideal proved unworkable in practice. In the Dominican order and the others that started as mendicant it has been mitigated or even abrogated. Among the Franciscans it was the occasion of endless strife and was kept alive only by dint of successive reforms and fresh starts, each successful for a time but ultimately doomed. The Capuchins, a Franciscan offshoot, made the most permanently successful effort to maintain St. Francis' ideal; but even among them mitigations have had to be admitted.

MENELAUS \,me-nə-'lā-əs\, in Greek mythology, king of Sparta and younger son of ATREUS, king of Mycenae; the abduction of his wife, HELEN, led to the Trojan War. During the war Menelaus served under his elder brother AGAMEMNON. After the fall of Troy, Menelaus recovered Helen and brought her home. Menelaus was a prominent figure in the *Iliad* and the *Odyssey*; in the latter text he was promised a place in ELYSIUM after his death because he was married to a daughter of ZEUS.

MĖNESS \'me-nes\ (Latvian), Lithuanian Mėnuo \'mʸān-wȯ\, in BALTIC RELIGION, the moon, whose monthly renewal of strength is imparted to all growing things. The "young," or "new," moon, sometimes called Dievaitis (Lithuanian: "Little God," or "Prince"), is especially receptive to human prayers and is honored by farmers.

MENNONITE, member of a Protestant church rising out of the ANABAPTISTS and named for MENNO SIMONSZ., a Dutch priest.

Among the various Anabaptist groups, the Mennonites trace their origin particularly to the so-called Swiss Brethren, who formed their first congregation on Jan. 21, 1525. Persecution by the state church soon scattered the Swiss Brethren across Europe; their doctrinal views found quick response among many people. Menno Simonsz., a Dutch priest who joined the Anabaptist movement in 1536, gathered the scattered Anabaptists of northern Europe into congregations that were soon called by his name.

Mennonites found political freedom first in the Netherlands and northern Poland. By 1700 there were 160,000 baptized members in the Mennonite churches of the Netherlands, but membership declined to about 15,300 in 1837. Persecutions that continued in Switzerland into the 18th century drove many Mennonites to southern Germany, Alsace, the Netherlands, and the United States. A major SCHISM occurred (1693–97) when the Swiss Mennonite bishop left the Mennonites to form the AMISH Church in an attempt to preserve biblical discipline among the members. From the 17th to the 20th centuries, most Mennonites in Switzerland, southern Germany, and Alsace lived in semi-closed rural communities with a simple agrarian economy. Religiously, they were influenced by PIETISM. Starting in 1663, Mennonites immigrated to North America.

In 1788 the first of a long stream of Mennonites left northern Poland to settle in the Ukraine, where they acquired land and escaped military conscription. By 1835 about 1,600 families had settled in 72 villages. In 1860 a small group within the Mennonite community in Russia underwent a religious awakening and demanded stricter discipline for church members. They founded the Mennonite Brethren Church, some of whose members joined an exodus of Mennonites from Russia in the 1870s that was provoked by the loss of their exemption from military service. Many of these immigrants settled in the Middle West of the United States and in Manitoba, Can. By World War I the Mennonite settlements in Russia included more than 120,000 members. All Mennonite communities in Russia were either destroyed during World War II or dissolved by the Soviets soon after 1945. Mennonites today live scattered among the Russian population.

Until the late 19th century, most Mennonites in North America lived in rural communities and engaged in farming. They retained their German language, partly as a religious symbol and partly as insulation against their environment. In 1783 Mennonites in Lancaster county, Pa., were accused of treason for feeding destitute British soldiers. During the American Civil War, rather than fight, some hired substitutes or paid an exemption fee of $300 in the North and $500 in the South. Those who fought in the armed forces were usually excommunicated for doing so.

After 1850 the transition from the German language to English and the adoption of such institutions and practices as Sunday schools and evangelistic services led to a number of divisions among the Mennonites; some branches were also imported from Europe. The largest single body is the (Old) Mennonite Church; following are the General Conference Mennonite Church, the Mennonite Brethren, and the Old Order Amish. Most extreme are the Hutterian Brethren, who still live communally and practice community of goods; this relatively small group is concentrated in the upper Great Plains region of North America.

Mennonites believe in the doctrine of the TRINITY, affirm the SCRIPTURES (especially the NEW TESTAMENT) as their final authority for faith and life, and appeal to the pattern of the early church as their congregational model. They stress BAPTISM on CONFESSION OF FAITH and a symbolic understanding of the Lord's Supper. Some practice foot washing, a practice based on an act of Jesus with his disciples. The doctrines of nonconformity to the world, nonswearing of OATHS, nonresistance in lieu of military service, and church discipline are generally affirmed but not practiced universally. Mennonite worship services are sermon-centered. A simple liturgy surrounds the Gospel proclamation. In the late 20th century, however, there were many signs of experiment in worship similar to those found in other denominations.

Most Mennonite congregations are joined together into numerous conferences, seven of which are in North America, though some conservative Mennonites do not form conferences. Since 1925 there has been a Mennonite World Conference that meets every five years for fellowship, study, and inspiration but does not make decisions binding on its member bodies.

MENNO SIMONSZ. \'me-nō-'sī-mənz, -'sē-mȯns\, *in full* Menno Simonszoon, Simonsz. *also spelled* Simons (b.

1496, Witmarsum, Friesland—d. Jan. 31, 1561, near Lübeck, Holstein), Dutch priest, an early leader of the peaceful wing of Dutch Anabaptism, whose followers formed the MENNONITE church.

Menno was born into a Dutch peasant family. At an early age he was enrolled in a monastic school, possibly at the FRANCISCAN monastery in Bolsward, to prepare for the PRIESTHOOD. In March 1524 he was ordained at Utrecht and assigned to the PARISH at Pingjum near the place of his birth. In 1531 he became the village priest in his home parish at Witmarsum.

During his first year as priest Menno began to question the real presence of Christ in the bread and wine of the EUCHARIST. Antisacramental tendencies were prevalent in the Netherlands at that time, developed from the humanism of ERASMUS and the ethical concerns of the BRETHREN OF THE COMMON LIFE. These doubts led Menno to read both the BIBLE and the writings of MARTIN LUTHER for the first time. He soon agreed with Luther and the Swiss reformer HULDRYCH ZWINGLI that biblical authority ought to be primary in the life of the believer and in the church.

Menno's readings of the NEW TESTAMENT led him to the firm conviction that only persons of mature faith, who had acknowledged JESUS as lord and had counted the cost of following him, could be eligible for membership in the church and could be baptized. The GRACE of Christ was sufficient for children until they reached the age of accountability and made a conscious choice. The experience of conversion came to be central to all of Menno's life and theology.

On April 7, 1535, the Olde Klooster near Bolsward, which had been occupied by revolutionary ANABAPTISTS, fell to the state militia. Among those killed were members of Menno's congregation and Peter Simons, who may have been his brother. This prompted him to preach openly against the errors of the revolutionaries. In doing so he articulated with increasing clarity what he believed to be the true nature of a believers' church: pure doctrine, scriptural use of SACRAMENTS, ethical obedience, love of neighbor, a clear and open witness to the faith, and a willingness to suffer. This bold and outspoken ministry soon jeopardized his safety, and in January 1536 he went into hiding.

During a year in hiding he wrote "The Spiritual Resurrection," "The New Birth," and "Meditation on the Twenty-third Psalm." Late in 1536 or early 1537 he received believer's BAPTISM, was called to leadership by the peaceful Anabaptist group founded in 1534 by Obbe Philips, and was or-

Menno Simonsz., engraving by Christopher van Sichem, 1605–08
By courtesy of the Mennonite Library and Archives, North Newton, Kansas

dained by Obbe. From this time on he was in constant danger. In 1542 the Holy Roman emperor Charles V (1500–58) issued an edict against him, promising 100 guilders reward for his arrest.

From 1543 to 1544 Menno worked in East Friesland. The next two years, 1544–46, were spent in the Rhineland, after which he traveled from his new home base in Holstein until his death in 1561. At Holstein he wrote extensively and established a printing press to circulate Anabaptist writings. Although he was not the founder of the Mennonite Church nor the most articulate spokesman of early Anabaptist theology. His greatness lay rather in the leadership he gave to northern Anabaptism during its formative first generation.

MENORAH \mə-'nōr-ə\, in JUDAISM, multibranched candelabrum used in rites during the festival of HANUKKAH. Its essential feature has always been eight receptacles for oil or candles (one lit the first day, two the second, etc.) and a further receptacle for the *shammash* ("servant") light, which is set apart and used for kindling the other lights.

This menorah is an imitation of the seven-branched golden candelabrum of the TABERNACLE, which signified, among other things, the seven days of creation. The cup atop the central shaft, which is somewhat elevated to signify the SABBATH, was flanked by three lights on each side. The seven-branched menorah is mentioned in the TALMUD, and it has for centuries been used in art as an iconographic symbol signifying Judaism.

MEN-SHEN \'mən-'shən\, *Pinyin* Menshen, in Chinese mythology, two door gods whose images are posted on the two halves of the double front door of private homes to guarantee protection from evil spirits. Tradition reports that two T'ang dynasty generals stood guard against evil spirits during a serious illness of T'ai-tsung (reigned 626–649 CE). Their presence was so effective that the emperor ordered their pictures to be posted permanently on the imperial gates. At a later date another Men-shen was added and given custody of the rear door. During the New Year celebration, the images are traditionally refurbished in brilliant colors.

MENSTRUATION, periodic discharge from the vagina of blood, secretions, and disintegrating tissue that had lined the uterus. Menstruation takes place if the ovum (egg) released by the ovary has not been fertilized. Throughout the history of religions menstruation has frequently been the

Men-shen, Chinese painting on paper; in the Musée Guimet, Paris
Giraudon—Art Resource

focus of ritual prohibitions and mythic systems that focus on distinctions between the genders.

In many parts of New Guinea and island Melanesia male-female relationships were traditionally polarized. In New Guinea, men's cult secrecy, ritualized male homosexuality, elaborate men's initiation rituals, and the celebration of warfare were accompanied by belief in dangers emanating from women's bodies and by separation of the sexes. These peoples were preoccupied with growth and with the physical fluids and substances (e.g., menstrual blood, semen, vaginal fluids) that are agents of reproduction and growth, all being regarded as sources of power and danger. In the eastern Highlands this belief system was associated with ritualized nose- or penis-bleeding, ostensibly in imitation of menstruation, and there were accompanying myths of an ancient female power that fell into the hands of men.

Among certain Native American cultures, a girl who had her first menstruation was secluded in a menstrual lodge some distance from the village. Her hair was bound up in rolls, and she was only allowed to touch it with a small comb. Her face was painted red or yellow, and she wore undecorated clothing. She was not allowed to drink directly from a well but had to use a drinking tube, and she cleansed herself after the flow in a sweathouse. After a time—one or several months—she finished her seclusion with prayers in the evening on a hill. Then she returned to the village a full-grown woman.

MER \'mer\, among the Cheremis and Udmurts (also called Votyaks), district where people would gather periodically to hold religious festivals and perform sacrifices.

MERCURY \'mər-kyə-rē\, *Latin* Mercurius \mər-'kyùr-ē-əs\, in ROMAN RELIGION, god of merchandise and merchants, commonly identified with the Greek HERMES. His worship was introduced early, and his temple on the Aventine Hill in Rome was dedicated in 495 BCE. There he was associated with the goddess Maia, who became identified as his mother through her association with the Greek Maia, mother of Hermes. Both Mercury and Maia were honored in a festival on May 15, the dedication day of Mercury's temple on the Aventine (built about 500 BCE).

Mercury is sometimes represented as holding a purse, symbolic of his business functions. Usually, however, artists borrow the attributes of Hermes irrespective of their appropriateness and portray him wearing winged sandals or a winged cap and carrying a CADUCEUS (staff).

MERKABAH MYSTICISM AND HEKHALOT WRITINGS \,mer-kä-'vä . . . ,he-ḵä-'lōt\, Jewish mystic tradition of the early centuries CE that claims to afford knowledge of the hidden world of heaven, the GARDEN OF EDEN, GEHENNA, ANGELS and spirits, and the fate of the souls in the hidden

Mercury, classical statue; in the Uffizi, Florence, Italy
Alinari—Art Resource

world. Merkabah also provides revelations of the Throne (*Merkabah*) of God's Glory.

Focused on Ezekiel 1, with its vision of God on the throne of his chariot, Merkabah mysticism was kept secret from ordinary believers and was taught only to sages. Hekhalot literature carries forward the Merkabah tradition. Its principal texts are *Kehkahlot Rabbati*, attributed to Rabbi Ishmael, *Heikahlot Zutrati*, attributed to Rabbi Akiba, and *Sefer Keihkalot*, published as *Third Book of Enoch* or the *Hebrew Enoch*. These documents provide detailed descriptions of the world of the Chariot, the ecstatic ascent to that world, and the techniques used by practitioners of this form of mysticism to make the ascent. Magical techniques are involved. One who wishes to ascend must first adopt an ascetic character. Then, to achieve the mystic state, an individual self-induces a hyponotic state and recites ecstatic hymns, the texts of which are found in *Kehkahlot Rabbati*. Among them are songs concerning the holy creatures who bear the throne of God; the songs conclude with the sanctification language of Isaiah 6:3 as a fixed refrain. In this mystical doctrine, God is holy king, residing within walls of majesty, fear, and awe in palaces of silence; his traits are sovereignty, majesty, and holiness—a God who is far off and removed from human comprehension.

MERTON, THOMAS \'mərt-ən\, *original name of* Father M. Louis (b. Jan. 31, 1915, Prades, France—d. Dec. 10, 1968, Bangkok, Thailand), important 20th-century American ROMAN CATHOLIC monk, poet, and writer on spiritual and social themes.

Merton's early education was in England and France; after a year at the University of Cambridge, he entered Columbia University in New York City, where he earned degrees in 1938 and 1939. After teaching English at Columbia (1938–39) and at St. Bonaventure University (1939–41) near Olean, N.Y., he entered the Trappist Abbey of Gethsemani near Louisville, Ky. He was ordained in 1949. Merton's first published works were collections of poems, but international fame occurred after the publication of the autobiographical *Seven Storey Mountain* (1948). His early works were strictly spiritual, but in the early 1960s his writings moved more in the direction of social criticism, while many of his later works reveal an unusually deep insight into Oriental philosophy and MYSTICISM.

MERU, MOUNT \'mā-rü\, in Hindu mythology, golden mountain that stands in the center of the universe and is the axis of the world and the abode of the gods. Its foothills are the Himalayas. Mount Meru reaches down below the ground as far as it extends into the heavens. All of the principal deities have their own celestial kingdoms on or near it, where their devotees reside with them after death while awaiting their next REINCARNATION.

MESOPOTAMIAN RELIGIONS

RELIGIOUS BELIEFS and practices included in the category Mesopotamian are those of the Sumerians and Akkadians, who inhabited ancient Mesopotamia (modern Iraq) in the millennia before the Christian era. Their beliefs and practices form a single stream of tradition. Sumerian in origin, the tradition was added to and subtly modified by the Akkadians (Semites who emigrated into Mesopotamia from the west at the end of the 4th millennium BCE), whose own beliefs were in large measure assimilated to and integrated with those of their new environment.

BACKGROUND

Human occupation of Mesopotamia—"the land between the rivers" (*i.e.*, the Tigris and the Euphrates)—seems to reach back farthest in time in the north (Assyria), where the earliest settlers built their small villages some time about 6000 BCE. In the south (the area that was later called Sumer) the earliest settlements appear to have been founded about 5000 BCE. An early division of the country into small, independent city-states that formed a loosely organized league was followed by a unification by force under King Lugalzagesi (*c.* 2375–2350 BCE) of Uruk just before the Akkadian period. The unification was maintained by Lugalzagesi's successors, the kings of Akkad, who built it into an empire, and—after a brief interruption by Gutian invaders—by Utuhegal (*c.* 2116–*c.* 2110) of Uruk and the rulers of the 3rd dynasty of Ur (*c.* 2112–*c.* 2004 BCE). When Ur fell, about 2000 BCE, the country again divided into smaller units, with the cities Isin and Larsa vying for hegemony. Eventually Babylon established a lasting national state in the south, while ASHUR dominated a similar rival state, Assyria, in the north. From the middle of the 1st millennium onward, Assyria built an empire comprising, for a short time, all of the ancient Middle East. This political and administrative achievement remained essentially intact under the subsequent Neo-Babylonian and Persian kings down to Alexander the Great's conquest of the region (331 BCE).

MYTHS

The genre of myths in ancient Mesopotamian literature centers on praise that recounts and celebrates great deeds. The doers of the deeds (creative or otherwise

The demon Huwawa (Humbaba): the Gilgamesh epic relates how Gilgamesh and Enkidu cut off Huwawa's head; terracotta, 20th–16th century BCE, in the Louvre, Paris

Erich Lessing—Art Resource

decisive acts), and thus the subjects of the praise, are the gods. An example of such myths is "Dumuzi's Death," which relates how Dumuzi (the Akkadian TAM-MUZ, "Producer of Sound Offspring"), the power in the fertility of spring, dreamed of his own death at the hands of a group of deputies from the netherworld and how he tried to hide himself but was betrayed by his friend after his sister had resisted all attempts to make her reveal where he was.

A similar myth, "Inanna's Descent," relates how the goddess INANNA ("Lady of the Date Clusters") set her heart on ruling the netherworld and tried to depose her older sister, the queen of the netherworld, ERESHKIGAL ("Lady of the Greater Earth"). Her attempt failed, and she was killed and changed into a piece of rotting meat in the netherworld. Enki (the Akkadian, EA, "Lord of Sweet Waters in the Earth") brought Inanna back to life, but she was released only on condition that she furnish a substitute to take her place. On her return, finding her young husband Dumuzi feasting instead of mourning for her, Inanna was seized with jealousy and designated him as that substitute. Dumuzi tried to flee the posse of deputies who had accompanied Inanna, and with the help of the sun god Utu, who changed Dumuzi's shape, he managed to escape, was recaptured, escaped again, and so on, until he was finally taken to the netherworld. His sister Geshtinanna then went in search of him. The myth ends with Inanna decreeing that Dumuzi and his sister could alternate as her substitute, each of them spending half a year in the netherworld, the other half above with the living.

A third myth built over the motif of journeying to the netherworld is "The Engendering of the Moongod and his Brothers," which tells how ENLIL ("Lord Wind"), came upon Ninlil (the goddess of grain) as she was bathing in a canal. He lay with her and thus engendered the moon god Suen. For this offense Enlil was banished from Nippur and took the road to the netherworld. Ninlil, carrying his child, followed him. On the way Enlil took the shape first of the Nippur gatekeeper, then of the man of the river of the netherworld, and lastly of the ferryman of the river of the netherworld. In each such disguise Enlil persuaded Ninlil to let him lie with her to engender a son who might take Suen's place in the netherworld and leave him free for the world above. Thus, three further deities, all Underworld figures, were engendered: Meslamtaea ("He Who Comes Out of the Meslam Temple"), NINAZU ("Water Sprinkler" [?]), and Ennugi ("The God Who Returns Not").

In the myth "Enki and Ninhursag," Enki lay with NINHURSAG ("Lady of the Stony Ground") on the island of Dilmun (modern Bahrain), the territory which had been allotted to them. There Enki provided water for the future city of Dilmun, lay with Ninhursag, and left her. She gave birth to a daughter, Ninshar ("Lady Herb"), on whom Enki in turn engendered the spider Uttu, goddess of spinning and weaving. Ninhursag warned Uttu against Enki, but he, proffering marriage gifts, persuaded her to open the door to him. After Enki had abandoned Uttu, Ninhursag found her and removed Enki's semen from her body. From the semen seven plants sprouted forth. These plants Enki later saw and ate and thereby became pregnant from his own semen. Unable as a male to give birth, he fell fatally ill, until Ninhursag relented and—in her role as as birth goddess—placed him in her vulva and helped him to give birth to seven daughters, whom Enki then married off to various gods.

The creation of humans is also treated in the myths. The myth "Enki and Ninmah" relates how the gods originally had to toil for their food, dig irrigation canals, and perform other menial tasks until, in their distress, they complained to Enki's mother, Nammu, who took the complaints to Enki. Enki took the engendering clay of the Apsu, and, with the help of the womb goddesses and eight midwife goddesses led by Ninmah (another name for Ninhursag), he had his mother become pregnant with and give birth to humans so that they could relieve the gods of their toil. At the celebration of the birth, however, Enki and Ninmah both drank too much beer and began to quarrel. Ninmah boasted that she could impair human shape at will, and Enki countered that he could temper even the worst that she might do. So she made seven freaks, for each of which Enki found a place in society and a living. He then challenged her to alleviate the mischief he could do, but the creature he fashioned—a prematurely aborted fetus—was beyond help. The moral drawn by Enki was that both male and female contribute to the birth of a happy child. The aborted fetus lacked the contribution of the birth goddess in the womb.

Another myth, called from its opening word Lugal-e ("O King"), concerns Enlil's son, the rain god NINURTA. This myth begins with a description of the young king, Ninurta, sitting at home in Nippur when, through his general, reports reach him of a new power that has arisen in the mountains to challenge him—*i.e.*, Azag, son of ANU ("Sky") and Ki ("Earth"), who has been chosen king by the plants and is raiding the cities with his warriors, the stones. Ninurta sets out in his boat to give battle, and a fierce engagement ensues, in which Azag is killed. Afterward Ninurta reorganizes his newly won territory, builds a stone barrier—the near mountain ranges or foothills (the *hursag*)—and gathers the waters that used to go up into the mountains and directs them into the Tigris to flood it and provide plentiful irrigation water. The *hursag* he presents as a gift to his mother, who has come to visit him, naming her Ninhursag ("Lady of the *hursag*"). Lastly he sits in judgment on the stones who had formed the Azag's army. Some of them, who had shown special ill will toward him, he curses, and others he trusts and gives high office in his administration. These judgments give the stones their present characteristics so that, for example, the flint is condemned to break before the much softer horn, as it indeed does when the horn is pressed against it to flake it. Noteworthy also is the way in which order in the universe (*i.e.*, the yearly flood and other seasonal events) is seen—consonantly with Ninurta's role as "king" and leader in war—as relating to a reorganization of conquered territories.

AKKADIAN LITERATURE

The first centuries of the 2nd millennium BCE witnessed the demise of Sumerian as a spoken language and its replacement by Akkadian, which was not without its own literary tradition. Writing, to judge from Akkadian orthographic peculiarities, was very early borrowed from the Sumerians. By Old Babylonian times (*c.* 19th century BCE), the literature in Akkadian, partly under the influence of Sumerian models and Sumerian literary themes, had developed myths and epics of its own, among them the superb Old Babylonian GILGAMESH epic (dealing with the problem of death) as well as hymns, disputation texts (evaluations of elements of the cosmos and society), penitential psalms, and other genres. The quick rise of Sargon, the founder of the dynasty of Akkad (*c.* 2334–*c.* 2154 BCE), from obscurity to fame and his victory over Lugalzagesi of Uruk form the theme of several epic tales. The sudden eclipse of the Akkadian empire long after Naram-Sin, which was attributed to that ruler's pride and the gods' retaliation, is the theme of "The Fall of Akkad."

Other Akkadian epics include the ETANA EPIC, which tells how Etana, the first king, was carried up to heaven on the back of an eagle to obtain the plant of birth so that his son could be born. Also important are the epic tales about Sargon of Akkad, one of which, the birth legend, tells of his abandonment in a casket on the river by his mother (*compare* MOSES) and his discovery by an orchardman, who raised him as his son. Naram-Sin is the central figure in another tale dealing with that king's pride and also relating the destructive invasions by barbarous foes.

COSMOGONY AND COSMOLOGY

The Sumerian myths have relatively little to say about creation. A story about Gilgamesh refers in its introductory lines to the times "after heaven had been moved away from earth, after earth had been separated from heaven." The same notion that heaven and earth were once close together occurs also in a bilingual Sumero-Akkadian text from Ashur about the creation of humans. The actual act of separating them is credited to the storm

Pendant with archaic signs and the emblem of the goddess Inanna; in the Louvre, Paris
Erich Lessing—Art Resource

*Marduk, the chief god
of Babylon,* c. *1500* BCE
Corbis—Bettmann

god Enlil of Nippur in the introduction to a third tale that deals with the creation of the first hoe.

A fully elaborated cosmogonic and cosmological myth does not actually appear until Old Babylonian times. The *Enuma elish* tells of a beginning when all was a watery CHAOS and there was nothing but the sea, TIAMAT, and the sweet waters under ground, Apsu, who mingled their waters together. In their midst the gods were born. The first pair, LAHMU AND LAHAMU, represented the powers in silt; the next, ANSHAR AND KISHAR, those in the horizon. Anshar and Kishar engendered the god of heaven, Anu, and he in turn the god of the flowing sweet waters, Ea.

This tradition is known in a more complete form from an ancient list of gods called *An: Anum.* There, after a different beginning, Lahmu and Lahamu give rise to Duri and Dari, "the time-cycle"; and these in turn give rise to Enshar and Ninshar, "Lord and Lady Circle." Enshar and Ninshar engender the concrete circle of the horizon, Anshar and Kishar, probably conceived as silt deposited along the edge of the universe. Next was the horizon of the greater heaven and earth, and then—omitting an intrusive line—heaven and earth, probably conceived as two juxtaposed flat disks formed from silt deposited inward from the horizons.

The later generations of gods were dynamic creatures who contrast strikingly with the more sedate older generation. This contrast leads to a series of conflicts in which first Apsu is killed by Ea; then Tiamat, who was roused later to attack the gods, is killed by Ea's son MARDUK. It is Marduk, the hero of the story, who creates the extant universe out of the body of Tiamat. He cuts her in two, making half of her into heaven—to which she appoints sun, moon, and stars to execute their prescribed motions—and half into the earth. He pierces her eyes to let the Tigris and Euphrates flow forth, and then, heaping mountains on her body in the east, he makes the various tributaries of the Tigris flow out from her breasts. The remainder of the story deals with Marduk's organization of the cosmos, his creation of humans, and his assigning to the gods their various cosmic offices and tasks. The cosmos is seen to be structured and to function as a benevolent absolute monarchy.

GODS AND DEMONS

The gods were, as mentioned previously, organized in a polity of a primitive democratic cast. They constituted, as it were, a landed nobility, each god owning and working an estate—his temple and its lands—and controlling the city in which it was located. They also attended the general assembly of the gods, which was the highest authority in the cosmos, to vote on matters of collective import. The major gods also served as officers having charge of cosmic offices. Thus, for example, Utu, the sun god, was the judge of the gods, in charge of justice and righteousness generally.

Highest in the pantheon—and presiding in the divine assembly—ranked An (Akkadian: Anu), god of heaven, who was responsible for the calendar and the seasons as they were indicated by their appropriate stars. Next came Enlil of Nippur, god of winds and of agriculture and creator of the hoe. Enlil executed the verdicts of the divine assembly. Equal in rank to An and Enlil was the goddess Ninhursag (also known as Nintur and Ninmah), the goddess of stony ground; *i.e.,* the near mountain ranges in the east and the stony desert with its wildlife—wild asses, gazelles, and wild goats—in the west. She was also the goddess of birth. With these gods was joined—seemingly secondarily—Enki, god of the sweet waters of rivers and marshes; he was the cleverest of the gods, often appealed to by both gods and humans. Enlil's sons were the moon god, NANNA, or Sin; the god of thunderstorms, floods, and the plough, Ninurta; and the underworld figures Meslamtaea, Ninazu, and Ennugi. Sin's progeny were the sun god and judge of the gods, Utu (the Akkadian SHAMASH); the rain god ISHKUR (the Akkadian ADAD); and his daughter, the goddess of war, love, and the morning and evening star, Inanna (the Akkadian ISHTAR). Inanna's husband was the herder god Dumuzi. The netherworld was ruled by the goddess Ereshkigal and her husband NERGAL, a figure closely related to Meslamtaea and Ninurta. Earlier tradition mentions Ninazu as her husband.

DEMONS played little or no role in the myths or lists of the Mesopotamian pantheon. Their domain was that of incantations. Mostly, they were depicted as outlaws; the demoness LAMASHTU, for instance, was hurled from heaven by her father An because of her wickedness. The demons attacked humans by causing all kinds of diseases and were, as a rule, viewed as wind and storm beings. It was possible for a person to go to the law courts against the demons—*i.e.*, to seek recourse before Utu and obtain judgments against them. Various rituals for such procedures are known.

HUMAN ORIGIN, NATURE, AND DESTINY

Two different notions about human origin seem to have been current in ancient Mesopotamian religions. In the Sumerian "Myth of the Creation of the Hoe," Enlil removed heaven from earth in order to make room for seeds to come up. After he had created the hoe he used it to break the hard crust of earth in Uzumua ("the flesh-grower"), a place in the Temple of Inanna in Nippur. Here, out of the hole made by Enlil's hoe, humans grew forth. The other notion presented the view that humans were created from select "ingredients" by Enki, or by Enki and his mother Nammu, or by Enki and the birth goddess called, variously, Ninhursag, Nintur, and Ninmah. One Akkadian tradition, as represented by the "Myth of Atrahasis," had Enki advise that a god—presumably a rebel—be killed and that the birth goddess Nintur mix his flesh and blood with clay. This was done, after which 14 womb goddesses gestated the mixture and gave birth to 7 human pairs. The *etemmu* (ghost) of the slain god was left in human flesh. It is this originally divine part of humanity, the *etemmu*, that was believed to survive after death and pass into a shadowy afterlife in the netherworld.

CULTIC PRACTICES

In the cultic practices, humans fulfilled their destiny: to take care of the gods' material needs. They therefore provided the gods with houses (the temples) that were richly supplied with lands, which people cultivated for them. In the temple the god was present in—but not bounded by—a statue made of precious wood overlaid with gold. For this statue the temple kitchen staff prepared daily meals from victuals grown or raised on the temple's fields, in its orchards, in its sheepfolds, cattle pens, and game preserves, brought in by its fishermen, or delivered by farmers owing it as a temple tax. The statue was also clad in costly raiment, bathed, and escorted to bed in the bedchamber of the god, often on top of the temple tower, or ZIGGURAT.

At irregular intervals there were occasions for audiences with the god in which the king or other worshipers presented their petitions and prayers accompanied by appropriate offerings. These were mostly edibles, but they were often offered in costly containers. Appropriate gifts other than edibles were also acceptable—among them were cylinder seals for the god's use, superhuman in size, and equally outsized weapons.

Little is known concerning burial ritual. In late Early Dynastic times in Girsu two modes of burial were current. One was ordinary burial in a cemetery; the other, called laying the body "in the reeds of Enki," is not understood. It may have denoted the floating of the body down the river into the canebrakes. Elegists and other funerary personnel were in attendance and conducted laments seeking to give full expression to the grief of the bereaved and to propitiate the spirit of the dead. Later burial in a family vault under the dwelling house was common.

SACRED TIMES

During most of the 2nd millennium each major city had its own calendar. The months were named from local religious festivals celebrated in the month in question. Only by the 2nd millennium did the Nippur calendar attain general acceptance throughout the region. The nature of the festivals in these various sacred calendars sometimes reflected the cycle of agricultural activities, such as celebrating the ritual hitching up of the plows and, later in the year, their unhitching, or rites of sowing, harvesting, and other activities. During some of these festival periods the queen presented funerary offerings of barley, malt, and other agricultural products to the gods and to the spirits of deceased human administrators.

The cycles of festivals celebrating the marriage and early death of Dumuzi and similar figures in the spring were structured according to the backgrounds of the various communities of farmers, herders, or date growers. The sacred marriage (HIEROS GAMOS)—sometimes a fertility rite, sometimes a harvest festival with overtones of thanksgiving—was performed as a drama: the ruler and a high priestess took on the identity of the two deities and so ensured that their highly desirable union actually took place. In many communities the lament for the dead god took the form of a procession out into the desert to find the slain god, a PILGRIMAGE to the accompaniment of harps and heart-rending laments for the god.

Of major importance in later times was the NEW YEAR FESTIVAL, or Akitu, celebrated in a special temple out in the fields. Originally an agricultural festival con-

Major archaeological sites of Mesopotamia

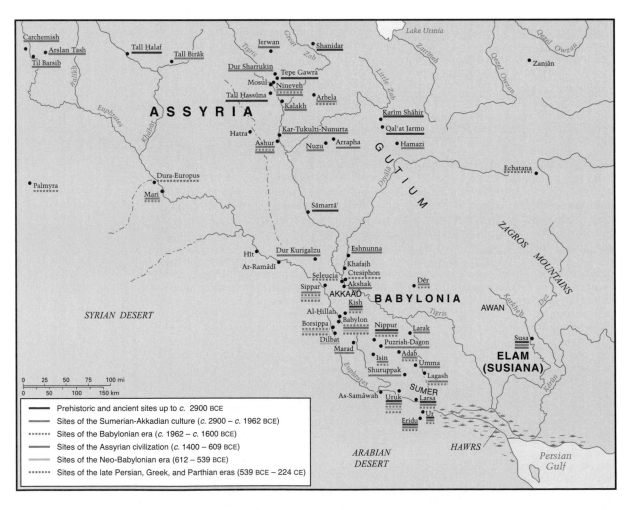

720

nected with sowing and harvest, it became the proper occasion for the crowning and investiture of a new king. In Babylon it came to celebrate Marduk's victory over Tiamat (*see above*, Cosmogony and Cosmology). Besides the yearly festivals there were also monthly festivals at new moon, the 7th, the 15th, and the 28th of the month. The last—when the moon was invisible and thought to be dead—had a distinctly funereal character.

Supreme responsibility for carrying out the cults was entrusted to the rulers. In certain periods the king was deified. All the rulers of the 3rd dynasty of Ur (*c.* 2112–*c.* 2004 BCE) and most of the rulers of the dynasty of Isin (*c.* 2020–*c.* 1800 BCE) were treated as embodiments of the dying god DAMU and invoked in the ritual laments for him. As a vessel of sacred power the king was surrounded by strict ritual to protect that power, and he was required to undergo elaborate rituals of purification if the power became threatened.

The individual temples were usually administered by officials called *sanga*s, who headed staffs of accountants, overseers of agricultural and industrial works on the temple estate, and priests (*gudu*s), who looked after the god as house servants. Among the priestesses the highest-ranking was termed *en* (Akkadian: *entu*). They were usually princesses of royal blood and were considered the human spouses of the gods they served, participating as brides in the rites of the sacred marriage. Other ranks of priestesses are known, most of which are considered orders of nuns. The best known are the votaries of the sun god, who lived in a cloister (*gagûm*) in Sippar.

SACRED PLACES

Mesopotamians worshiped in open-air sanctuaries, in chapels in private houses, or in small separate chapels located in the residential quarters of town, but the primary sacred place was the temple. Archaeology has traced the temple back to the earliest periods of settlement, and it is clear that from the Early Dynastic period onward the temple was considered the god's house or dwelling. In its more elaborate form such a temple would be built on a series of irregular artificial platforms, one on top of the other; by the 3rd dynasty of Ur, near the end of the 3rd millennium, these became squared off to form ziggurats. On the lowest of these platforms a heavy wall enclosed storerooms, the temple kitchen, workshops, and other such rooms. On the highest level, approached by a stairway, were the god's living quarters, centered in the cella, a rectangular room with an entrance door in the long wall near one corner. The god's place was on a podium in a niche at the short wall farthest from the entrance; benches with statues of worshipers ran along both long walls, and a hearth in the middle of the floor served for heating. Low pillars in front of the god's seat seem to have served as stoppers for a hanging that shielded him from profane eyes. Here, or in a connecting room, were the god's table, bed, and bathtub.

DIVINATION AND ASTROLOGY

There were many forms of DIVINATION in Mesopotamia. The forms most frequently used seem to have been incubation—sleeping in the temple in the hope that the god would send an enlightening dream—and hepatoscopy—examining the entrails, particularly the liver, of a lamb or kid sacrificed for a divinatory purpose, to read what the god had "written" there by interpreting variations in form and shape. In the 2nd and 1st millennia large and detailed handbooks in hepatoscopy were composed for consultation by the diviners. Apparently divination was an attempt to read the future from "symptoms" in the present, much as a physician recognizes the onset of a disease.

Related to the observation of unusual happenings in society or nature, but far more systematized, was ASTROLOGY. The movements and appearance of the sun, the moon, and the planets were believed to yield information about future events affecting the nation or, in some cases, the fate of individuals. HOROSCOPES, predicting the character and fate of a person on the basis of the constellation of the stars at his birth, are known to have been constructed in the late 1st millennium, but the art may conceivably be older.

MESSIAH \mə-'sī-ə\ (from Hebrew *mashiaḥ*, "anointed"), in JUDAISM, the eschatological redeemer of ISRAEL. It is widely supposed that Judaism is a messianic religion and that hope for the Messiah's appearance is the major focus of, and driving force behind, Jewish RELIGIOUS BELIEF and behavior. Indeed, two commonplace beliefs of western history are that, in 1st-century Palestine, enhanced Jewish anticipation of the Messiah's arrival was the backdrop for the emergence of CHRISTIANITY, and that it was the conflicting opinions about the Messiah's appearance, identity, activity, and implications that caused the division between Judaism and Christianity.

These assumptions, however, need qualification. Judaism's SCRIPTURE, the Hebrew BIBLE, contains no doctrine of an eschatological redeemer and does not use the term *messiah* to refer to one. Postbiblical Jewish texts—including the APOCRYPHA, PSEUDEPIGRAPHA, DEAD SEA SCROLLS, and the writings of PHILO and JOSEPHUS—use the term *messiah* infrequently and inconsistently. Based upon these texts there is no reason to think that the Jews of 1st-century Palestine were anticipating a messiah. Additionally, the idea of the Messiah is barely present in the MISHNAH, the foundation document of RABBINIC JUDAISM. A key reason for the unclarity about the Messiah in these texts is that the temple-centered religion practiced in Jerusalem and described in scripture, which dominated ancient Judaism and is the basis of all other forms of Judaism, provides no religious role for a savior. God alone is Israel's—and therefore humanity's—redeemer. In this religion, living according to God's design both ethically and ritually maintains Israel's relationship with God, which includes the forgiveness of SIN. "Levitical religion," as we might call it, offers no religious function for a messiah that is not already covered in some other way.

Of all the Jewish writings of the Second Temple period and the period immediately following the destruction of that temple, only the NEW TESTAMENT—which became Christianity's scripture—offers the rudiments of a coherent doctrine of the Messiah. Early Christian teaching about Jesus (though perhaps not Jesus' own teaching about himself) ultimately shifted the focus of redemption from God to the Messiah. Making the Messiah the medium of humanity's salvation altered the nascent religion's Judaic structure and produced a new religion.

Ancient and medieval rabbinic writings—as well as the SYNAGOGUE liturgy—contain the category of "messiah," but, as in earlier writings, the pictures in these varied literatures are not consistent. In the TALMUDS "the Messiah" is not an autonomous conception. Rather, it is a secondary category, subordinate to the generative and more central components of the rabbinic religious system. In this sense, for most forms of Judaism, the Messiah is present in, but not essential to, the workings of the Jewish religion. (An exception must be made for certain heretical Judaisms such as Shabbetaianism. *See* SHABBETAI, TZEVI).

Jewish religion is grounded in the experience of exile. For most of its history, Judaism has existed without a native center. Its scripture, theology, liturgy, practices, and most of its writings assume that Judaism's adherents are living as aliens, away from their native territory. Ancient Jews—certain that they were God's people always—drew creatively on their Israelite culture and heritage to develop two major responses to the twin challenges of national dislocation and chronic political oppression, particularly the loss of the Davidic dynasty and of Israel's political autonomy. The first was the hope for an ideal national leader—often, but not always, from the royal Davidic dynasty—whose work could range from leading the people home to an ideal kingdom to the establishment of a new cosmic order. The idea of "the Messiah," an individual savior or redeemer of Israel, derives from this conception. The messiah theme, therefore, is inextricably bound up with the notion of exile and the Jews' recovery of the land they regard as theirs inevitably has messianic overtones. By realizing the ancient promise of restoration, the establishment of a Jewish polity in the Land of Israel raises unprecedented questions about the religious meaning of return from exile in terms of classic Jewish ideas of the Messiah. *See* ZIONISM.

The second response was the establishment of "Levitical religion," a system of ethics and piety that both maintained and manifested the distinctive relationship between Israel and God. Although initially centered around the Temple and its cult, Levitical religion—particularly as adapted by rabbinic Judaism—could be performed anywhere.

These two responses are not mutually exclusive, but they are systemically independent of one another. Judaism is an extension of Levitical religion. The idea of an individual messiah existed alongside, but was never fully integrated into, the Levitical system of ethics and piety that constituted the core of rabbinic Judaism. Structurally, Judaism does not require a messiah to justify fulfilling the commandments. Indeed, a persistent strain of rabbinic teaching holds that the commandments will apply after the Messiah appears. Despite references to a restored Jerusalem and future heir of David, the synagogue liturgy celebrates God, not the Messiah, as Israel's redeemer and looks forward to the restoration of the Temple cult.

Because the category of the Messiah is extrinsic to the system of Jewish religious practice, it is subject to speculation. In the varied forms Judaism has taken over time, there was and remains a wide range of opinions about what the Messiah will be and do. These opinions in themselves do not constitute grounds for separation from Judaism. The figure of the Messiah surely is present in Jewish religious imagination, but hope for the Messiah's arrival is not the driving force of Jewish religious life.

For messianic figures in non-Judaic religions, *see* JESUS CHRIST; THE MAHDI; and MAITREYA BUDDHA.

METHODISM, movement founded by JOHN WESLEY in the 18th century, which survives in the form of the modern Methodist churches worldwide.

In 1738 Wesley, an Anglican clergyman, attended a religious meeting where he experienced an inward assurance of personal salvation he had not known before. Soon he was preaching among those who felt themselves neglected by the Church of England.

The Methodists formed a "society" within the Church of England. Wesley never wished them to leave the Anglican church, but after years of strained relations, the formal break came in 1795, four years after Wesley's death. In America the Methodist Episcopal Church was constituted as an autonomous body in 1784 under the guidance of Francis Asbury and Thomas Coke. Although the first Methodist itinerants did not arrive in America until shortly before the Revolution, by the middle of the 19th century the Methodists had more members than any other American denomination. This growth occurred especially on the frontier.

Methodists were organized locally into "classes" that enforced discipline, while a hierarchical structure with a strong central authority efficiently organized and supervised the itinerant preachers. The Methodist advance was temporarily halted in 1844 by the church's division into

Northern and Southern branches over the issue of slavery. After the Civil War both branches continued their rapid increase in numbers and in material resources. As Methodism gradually became assimilated to the general pattern of middle-class American PROTESTANTISM, a "holiness" movement emerged out of Methodism and then separated from it in the late 19th century. The Northern and Southern branches reunited in 1939, and further mergers took place later in the 20th century, but the independent holiness and pentecostal denominations that grew out of the HOLINESS MOVEMENT still exist. The African-American Methodist churches, which had been merged into a new central jurisdiction in 1939 (forming a separate but equal jurisdiction within the United Methodist Church), gradually became integrated after 1968. By 1974 all districts based on race had been abolished.

John Wesley, detail of an oil painting by Nathaniel Hone, 1766
National Portrait Gallery, London

Despite wide variations in belief, practice, and status, all Methodists accept the doctrines of historic CHRISTIANITY, without insistence on doctrinal conformity. They share an emphasis on those doctrines that indicate the power of the HOLY SPIRIT to confirm the faith of the believer and to transform one's personal life (especially the teaching about assurance and Christian perfection that is associated with John Wesley); a system of government by which all ministers are "in connection" with the central authority of the church; and an allegiance to John Wesley.

METHUSELAH \mə-ˈthü-zə-lə\, *also spelled* Methushael, OLD TESTAMENT PATRIARCH whose life span as recorded in GENESIS (5:27) was 969 years; he has survived in legend and tradition as the longest-lived human. Genesis tells nothing about Methuselah beyond sparse genealogical details: he was the great-great-great-great-grandson of SETH, the child of ADAM AND EVE (Genesis 5:6–21). He was the father of Lamech and the grandfather of NOAH (Genesis 5:25–32). All his forebears lived for between 895 and 962 years except for his father, Enoch, who lived to be 365. In 1 Chronicles 1:3 he is cited in the lineage of SAUL. In the Gospel of LUKE (3:23–38) the lineage of JOSEPH, the husband of MARY, is traced back 75 generations, through DAVID, Saul, ABRAHAM, ISAAC, and JACOB, to Methuselah, thence to Seth and Adam.

METROPOLITAN, in the ROMAN CATHOLIC, EASTERN ORTHODOX, and churches of the ANGLICAN COMMUNION, the head of an ecclesiastical province. Originally, a metropolitan was a bishop who resided in the chief city, or metropolis, of a civil province of the Roman Empire and administered a territorial area coextensive with a civil province. The first known use of the title in church conciliar documents was at the COUNCIL OF NICAEA in 325.

Following the pattern of civil government, the expanding church created ecclesiastical provinces, each headed by a metropolitan, who was assisted by his suffragan bishops, each of whom headed a DIOCESE within the province. This system has continued substantially unchanged. The metropolitan convokes and presides at provincial SYNODS, and he takes the chief part in the consecration of bishops. In Western medieval Roman Catholicism, especially since the 9th century, the rights of the metropolitans gradually disappeared in the framework of papal centralization.

In Slavic-speaking Orthodox churches the title metropolitan is used to designate those heads of autocephalous churches who do not carry the title "patriarch" and of a few important episcopal sees; in Greek-speaking Orthodox churches it may be given to all diocesan bishops, as distinct from their auxiliaries.

MICHAEL CERULARIUS \ˈmī-kəl-ˌser-yə-ˈlar-ē-əs\ (b. *c.* 1000, Constantinople [now Istanbul, Turkey]—d. Jan. 21, 1059, Madytus, near Constantinople), Greek Orthodox PATRIARCH of Constantinople who figured prominently in the events leading to the SCHISM of 1054.

Although Cerularius was educated for the civil service rather than for an ecclesiastical career, he was named patriarch in 1043 by the Byzantine emperor Constantine IX Monomachus. Cerularius' political ambition, coupled with his inflexible belief in the autonomy of the Eastern church, led him to thwart Constantine's attempts to ally the Byzantine and Roman empires in defense against the Normans. In 1052, partly in response to concessions that Constantine made to Pope Leo IX, Cerularius required the Latin churches in his DIOCESE to use the Greek language and liturgical practices; when they refused, he ordered them closed.

In 1054, when Pope Leo sent three legates to Constantinople to negotiate an alliance with the Byzantine Empire, Cerularius again obstructed Constantine's and Leo's efforts by refusing to meet with the legates. In the midst of these negotiations, however, Pope Leo died, and one of his legates, the French CARDINAL Humbert of Silva Candida, took advantage of the papal vacancy to retaliate against Cerularius. On July 16, 1054, Humbert entered Constantinople's cathedral, HAGIA SOPHIA, and excommunicated Cerularius and his clergy. In response, Cerularius convened a Holy SYNOD and excommunicated all the legates. Constantine's efforts to effect a reconciliation failed, and the schism between Rome and Constantinople was final.

Cerularius ultimately constrained Constantine to support the schism. He had less control, however, over Constantine's successor, Emperor Isaac I Comnenus, who dethroned Cerularius in 1058 and drove him into exile.

MICTLANTECUHTLI \ˌmēk-tlän-ˈtä-kùt-lē\, Aztec god of the dead, usually portrayed with a skull face. With his wife, Mictecacihuatl, he ruled Mictlan, the UNDERWORLD. The souls of those whose manner of death failed to call them to various paradises made a four-year journey, fraught with trials, through the nine hells of Mictlan. In the last, where Mictlantecuhtli dwelt, they suffered the horrors of the Underworld.

MIDAS \ˈmī-dəs\, in Greek and Roman myth, king known for his foolishness and greed. The stories of Midas were first elaborated in the Athenian satyr plays. The tales are familiar to modern readers through the late classical versions, such as those in Ovid's *Metamorphoses*.

According to the myth, Midas captured Silenus, the satyr and companion of the god DIONYSUS. For his kind treatment of Silenus, Midas was rewarded by Dionysus with a wish.

The king wished that all he touched might turn to gold, but when his food became gold and he nearly starved to death as a result, he realized his error. Dionysus then granted him release by having him bathe in the Pactolus River (near Sardis in modern Turkey), an action to which the presence of alluvial gold in that stream is attributed.

In another story the king was asked to judge a musical contest between APOLLO and the satyr MARSYAS. When Midas decided against Apollo, the god changed his ears into those of an ass. Midas concealed them under a turban and made his barber swear to tell no living soul. The barber, bursting with his secret, whispered it into a hole in the ground. He filled in the hole, but reeds grew from the spot and broadcast the secret—"Midas has ass's ears"—when the wind blew through them.

MIDDLE WAY, *Sanskrit* Madhyama-Pratipadā, *Pāli* Majjhima-Patipadā, in BUDDHISM, practices that are said to facilitate Enlightenment by avoiding the extremes of self-gratification and self-mortification. The term also refers to philosophical views that avoid the extremes of nihilism and eternalism. *See* MĀDHYAMIKA; EIGHTFOLD PATH.

MIDDOT \mē-'dōt\ (Hebrew: "measure," or "norms"), in Jewish HERMENEUTICS or biblical interpretation, methods or principles used to explicate the meaning of biblical words or passages to meet the exigencies of new situations. Though the rules, or norms, were probably developing in early Hellenistic JUDAISM, the first known *middot* were compiled by RABBI HILLEL in the 1st century BCE. Following the 7 norms compiled by Hillel were the 13 rules of Rabbi ISHMAEL BEN ELISHA (*c.* 100 CE) and the 32 rules of Rabbi Eliezer ben Yose the Galilaean (*c.* 150 CE). These *middot* remained normative in Judaism for more than 1,000 years.

MIDGARD \'mid-ˌgärd\, *Old Norse* Midgardr \'mēth-ˌgärthər\ ("Middle Abode"), *also called* Manna-Heim \'män-näˌhäm\ ("Home of Man"), in Norse mythology, the Middle Earth, the abode of mankind, made from the body of the first created being, the GIANT YMIR (Aurgelmir). According to legend, the gods killed Ymir, rolled his body into the central void of the universe, and began fashioning the Midgard. Ymir's flesh became the land, his blood the oceans, his bones the mountains, his teeth the cliffs, his hair the trees, and his brains became the clouds. Ymir's skull was held up by four dwarfs, Nordri, Sudri, Austri, and Vestri (the four points of the compass), and became the dome of the heavens. The sun, moon, and stars were made of scattered sparks that were caught in the skull.

MIDIANITE \'mi-dē-ə-ˌnīt\, *also called* Ishmaelite \'ish-mā-ə-ˌlīt, -mē-\, in the OLD TESTAMENT, member of a group of nomadic tribes related to the Israelites and most likely living in the northwestern regions of the Arabian Desert. According to the Book of Judges, the Israelite chieftain GIDEON drove the Midianites into western Palestine, after which they largely disappear from the biblical narrative.

According to the Book of GENESIS, the Midianites were descended from Midian, who was the son of ABRAHAM by his second wife, Keturah (Genesis 25:1–4). JETHRO, priest-leader of the Midianite subtribe known as the KENITES (Judges 1:16), and his daughter Zipporah (a wife of MOSES, Exodus 2:21), influenced early Hebrew thought: it was YAHWEH, the lord of the Midianites, who was revealed to Moses as the God of the Hebrews (Exodus 3:14). CIRCUMCISION was practiced by the Midianites before the Israelites (Exodus 4:25).

MIDRASH \mē-'dräsh, 'mi-ˌdräsh\ (Hebrew: "exposition," or "investigation"), in JUDAISM, an inquiry into the meaning of SCRIPTURE. The word has three related uses, referring (1) to the process of biblical interpretation and to the particular hermeneutical methods being applied ("doing midrash"), (2) to an interpretation of a specific passage of Scripture ("a midrash on GENESIS 1:1 suggests that God created many worlds prior to this one"), or (3) to a literary compendium of such interpretations presented in the form of a book (*e.g.,* SIFRA to Leviticus). The unique significance of midrashic interpretation emerges from the way in which it mediates scriptural teachings to Jews of successive generations, showing how Scripture speaks to the particular circumstance and needs of Jews in each age. By assuring the continued relevance of Scripture, midrash allows the inherited values of Judaism, revised according to the needs of each age, to continue to have importance and meaning.

Midrashic texts traditionally are classified as either Halakhic, concerning the legal sections of Scripture, or Haggadic, on the nonlegal portions. *See* HALAKHAH AND HAGGADAH. A better division is attentive to the particular interpretative method at play in each midrash compilation. The major compilations of the Talmudic period reveal three distinct approaches: verse-by-verse analyses, discursive treatment of specific biblical laws or stories, and elaborate theological essays based upon the exegetical reading of biblical texts. The first type, focused on the legal sections of the PENTATEUCH, was produced between *c.* 200 and 400 CE. It includes Sifra to Leviticus, Sifre to Numbers, Sifre to Deuteronomy, and MEKHILTA ATTRIBUTED TO RABBI ISHMAEL on EXODUS. The second type, of the late 4th and 5th centuries, includes GENESIS RABBAH, LEVITICUS RABBAH, and Pesiqta (Peskita) deRab Kahana on the LECTIONARY calendar of SYNAGOGUE TORAH readings. The third type is the product of the 6th and 7th centuries and includes Lamentations Rabbah, Song of Songs Rabbah, Esther Rabbah, and Ruth Rabbah.

MIḤNA \'mih-nə\, any of the Islamic courts of inquiry established about 833 CE by the 'Abbāsid CALIPH al-Ma'mūn (reigned 813–833) to impose the Mu'tazilite doctrine of a created QUR'AN on his subjects.

The Mu'tazilites, a Muslim theological school influenced by the rationalist methods of Hellenistic philosophy, taught that God was an absolute unity admitting of no parts. Consequently, because the Word is God and not a part of him, the Qur'an, as a verbal expression and thus a material thing removed from God, had to be created by God in order to be accessible to humans. In contrast, the traditionalist view held that the Qur'an was uncreated and external, essentially, that it had existed along with God since the beginning of time.

Al-Ma'mūn adopted the Mu'tazilite view and demanded that all judges and legal scholars in the empire submit to questioning to determine the soundness of their positions. Most acquiesced, utilizing the principle of *taqiya* (concealment of one's beliefs under duress) to avoid imprisonment. When al-Ma'mūn died, the two succeeding caliphs continued his policies, until about 848, when al-Mutawakkil (reigned 847–861) made the profession of the Mu'tazilite view of a created Qur'an punishable by death.

MIKVEH \mēk-'vä\, *also spelled* mikvah, *or* miqwe \'mikvə\ ("collection [of water]"), in JUDAISM, pool of natural water in which one bathes for the restoration of ritual purity. The Mishnah describes the requirements for ritually proper water and the quantity of water required for ritual cleansing before entering the temple. Converts are required by Halakhah (legal tradition) to undergo a RITUAL BATH. Males bathe each Friday and before major festivals, while women use the *mikveh* before their weddings, after childbirth, and following MENSTRUATION.

MILAN, EDICT OF \mi-'lan, mē-'län\, proclamation that established religious toleration for CHRISTIANITY within the Roman Empire. It was the outcome of a political agreement concluded in Milan between the Roman emperors CONSTANTINE I and Licinius in February 313. The proclamation, made for the East by Licinius in June 313, granted all persons freedom to worship whatever deity they pleased, and assured Christians of legal rights.

MILAREPA \'mē-lä-'rä-bä\ (b. 1040—d. 1123), one of the most famous and beloved of Tibetan Buddhist masters (SIDDHA). His life and accomplishments are commemorated in two main literary works.

The first is a biography by the "Mad Yogin of Tsang" that chronicles the major events in his life from birth, to Enlightenment, to death. According to this work, Milarepa studied black magic in his younger years in an attempt to gain revenge on a wicked uncle who had stripped his mother and sister of all their property, after having previously promised to look after them when Milarepa's father died. After a series of successful acts of destruction and revenge against his uncle and other family members, Milarepa is said to have undergone a crisis of conscience. Soon afterward, he sought out various Tibetan Buddhist masters, finally gaining acceptance as a full-fledged disciple under the guidance of the Tibetan master MARPA, founder of the Bka'-brgyud-pa sect. The lengthy relationship between Marpa and Milarepa is a significant element in the biography, since it emphasizes the necessity of, and intimate trust that develops in the student-disciple relationship in VAJRAYĀNA BUDDHISM. After his years of study with Marpa were completed, Milarepa sought out remote, isolated mountain retreats in which he practiced rigorous meditation, only occasionally would he visit Marpa. Milarepa continued the Bka'-brgyud-pa line, converting and teaching many disciples.

The second work of commemoration is a collection of Tantric songs entitled *The Hundred Thousand Songs of Milarepa*, which express the nature of Buddhist teaching. They also expand upon the climate and conditions of Milarepa's mountain ascetic retreats as well as the intense labors and ultimate joys of the ascetic life.

MILESIANS \mī-'lē-zhənz, -shənz\, in Irish mythical history, name for the people who drove the race of gods, the TUATHA DÉ DANANN, below ground. The Milesians are thus the ancestors of the Celtic population of Ireland and it is stressed that they had an ancient right to the island when they came. According to the Medieval Irish historians the gods were driven from the surface and into the old BURIAL MOUNDS, where they were supposed to live on. The word for burial mound is "side," pronounced "shee," and this word is used for the otherworld in Irish tales up to the present. Thus, a banshee means a "woman from the burial mound."

MILINDA-PAÑHA: *see* QUESTIONS OF MILINDA.

MILK-OCEAN, CHURNING OF THE, one of the central events in the ever-continuing struggle between the DEVAS (gods) and the ASURAS (demons, or titans), and a major aspect of Hindu COSMOGONY.

The gods, who had become weakened as a result of a curse by the irascible sage, Durvāsas, invited the *asuras* to help them recover the elixir of immortality, the *amṛta*, from the depths of the cosmic ocean. Mt. Mandara, a spur of the world axis, Mt. Meru, was torn out to use as a churning stick and was steadied at the bottom of the ocean by VISHNU in his aspect as the tortoise Kūrma. The *asuras* held the head of the NĀGA (serpent) Vāsuki, who was procured for a churning rope, and the gods held his tail. When Vāsuki's head hit the rocks and he vomited forth poison that threatened to fall into the ocean and contaminate the *amṛta*, the god Śiva took it and held it in his throat, a feat that turned his throat blue.

When the *amṛta* appeared, the gods and the *asuras* fought over its possession. After many adventures, it was finally consumed by the gods, who were thus restored in strength.

The Hindu myth of the churning of the milk-ocean
Victoria and Albert Museum, London—Art Resource

MILLENNIALISM

Literally, millennialism is the belief, expressed in the biblical Book of REVELATION TO JOHN, that Christ will establish a one-thousand year reign of the saints on earth before the LAST JUDGMENT (*compare* MILLENNIUM). More broadly defined, millennialists expect a time of supernatural peace and abundance here on earth. Millennialism offers a concrete vision of the fundamental eschatological belief that at the "end of time" God will judge the living and the (resurrected) dead. This belief in an ultimate divine justice has provided a solution to the problem of THEODICY in the face of suffering and oppression for countless generations of believers—Jews, Christians, Muslims, and Buddhists. It has, therefore, had immense appeal in every age. Whereas the name comes from the 1,000-year period, the key factor concerns not time but rather the earthly nature of the coming "new world": whether it is of a duration of 40 years or of 4,000, the transformation necessarily means an end to the current institutions of power and, therefore, gives all millennial beliefs a revolutionary quality that has made them unwelcome to those in positions of authority.

MILLENNIALISM AND SOCIETY

The key issue regarding millennialism's impact on society, however, is the matter of timing. As long as the day of redemption is not yet come, millennial hopes console the suffering and inspire patience (Revelation 13:10) and political quiescence; thus, they have a profoundly conservative influence. But driven by a sense of imminence (*see* apocalypticism), believers can become disruptive, even engaging in revolutionary efforts to overthrow an unjust sociopolitical order in an attempt to bring about the kingdom of "peace" for the meek and the defenseless. Thus, apocalyptic millennialism constitutes a powerful and volatile mixture, fascinating the hearts and minds of people throughout the ages. No matter how often the apocalyptic beliefs have been proven wrong (as has always been the case through the present), no matter how often the millennial efforts to establish God's kingdom on earth have led to disastrous results, apocalyptic expectations repeatedly revive. From the Jewish revolts against Rome that led to hundreds of thousands of deaths (in 3 and 66–73 or 74 CE and again in 132–135 CE) to the TAI-

The Sixth Trumpet: Army of Horsemen, illustrating a passage in Revelation to John 9:13–21; from a Spanish illuminated manuscript, 1220
The Granger Collection

PING REBELLION that led to the death of some 20–35 million people, such movements have a tendency to self-destruct in a most spectacular fashion. And yet, for all the costly failures, the appeal remains, and generation after generation finds devotees in search of the chimerical kingdom.

Apocalyptic millennialism, for all its dangers, offers immense rewards: believers find themselves at the center of the ultimate universal drama, where their every act has cosmic significance. Apocalyptic believers become semiotically aroused, finding cosmic messages in the smallest incident, in every coincidence. They can almost taste the fulfillment of their burning desire to see justice done—the good lavishly rewarded, the evil savagely punished. Finally, the approach of the end of time and the promise of the new world liberates believers from all earthly inhibitions: the fear of future punishment by those who now hold power vanishes, and a wide range of repressed feelings—sexual, emotional, psychological—bursts forth. Such a combination proves irresistible to many.

From their earliest manifestations, millennial beliefs bifurcated into imperial, hierarchical visions of the world to come—a kingdom ruled over by a just, if authoritarian, imperial figure who would conquer the forces of chaos and establish the true order of society—and a demotic vision of a world of holy anarchy, where there would be an end to dominion over man. Many world conquerors used millennial "savior" imagery to bolster their rule (notably, but by no means limited to, Cyrus the Great, Alexander the Great, Caesar Augustus, and Constantine the Great), and especially in the Muslim and Christian Middle Ages these imperial uses of millennial imagery proliferated. The demotic millennial vision, however, was marked by a profoundly anti-imperial, even anti-authoritarian, thrust. Indeed, one of the major strains of Hebrew messianic imagery foresaw a time when men shall beat the instruments of war and domination into instruments of peace and prosperity, each sitting under his own tree, enjoying the fruits of honest labor undisturbed (Isaiah 2:1–3, Micah 4:1–4). This millennialism foresaw the end of the rapacious aristocracy (the lion will lie down with the lamb) and the peace of the commoner and the manual laborer. Perhaps no idea in the ancient world, where aristocratic empires ruled over almost every area of cultivated land, held more subversive connotations.

Apostolic CHRISTIANITY demonstrates many of the key traits of apocalyptic millenarian groups of this second, demotic type: the rhetoric of the meek overcoming the powerful and arrogant to inherit the earth; the imminence of the Lord's Day of wrath and the coming Kingdom of Heaven; a leader and a following among common, working people; rituals of initiation into a group preparing for and awaiting the End; fervent spirituality and radical restructuring of community bonds; enthusiastic crowds; the prominence of women visionaries; and the shift from a disappointed messianic hope (CRUCIFIXION) to a revised expectation (SECOND COMING, or Parousia).

The only missing element, at that time prominent in several strains of Jewish millennialism (*e.g.*, the ZEALOTS), is violence; apparently this was subsumed (or sublimated) in the passion for martyrdom. Not for centuries would violence became a notable part of Christian millennialism (*e.g.*, the Circumcelliones of 4th-century North Africa).

The fundamental problem for early Christianity, as for all apocalyptic movements, was the passage of time which brought with it growing and eventually profound disappointment and humiliation. Those who did not abandon the movement (*e.g.*, by returning to observant JUDAISM) handled the delay of the Parousia by organizing communities and rituals that brought, proleptically, a foretaste of the coming world—for example, the EUCHARIST or the reading of Revelation. But above all, the passing of time called for a new temporal horizon. The End would come, but not now, not even soon, rather in the fullness of time, once the tasks assigned to the initiate by God—especially the spreading of the Gospels to the four corners of the world—were completed.

As Christianity evolved from a charismatic cult on the fringes of society into a self-perpetuating institution eager to live in harmony with Rome, the hopes of apocalyptic millenarianism embarrassed church leaders, who emphasized to Roman authorities that Jesus' kingdom was "not of this world." Whereas almost every prominent Christian writer from the movement's 1st century assumed a literal millennialism, by the late 2nd century ecclesiastical writers, striving to eliminate subversive millennialism from church doctrine, began an assault on millenarian texts (especially Revelation, the only text in the NEW TESTAMENT to speak explicitly of an earthly kingdom). ORIGEN, an early 3rd-century theologian, argued that the millennium was to be interpreted allegorically, not carnally; others attempted (successfully in the Eastern church) to eliminate Revelation from the canon altogether. With the advent of imperial Christianity, millenarianism was pushed to the very margins of acceptable Christian thought.

CALCULATING THE MILLENNIUM

Despite these efforts by the church hierarchy to remove millennialism from formal theology, apocalyptic fears and millennial hopes remained powerful among Christians high and low. Indeed, the very texts that anti-millenarian writers like JEROME wrote served as the basis for new forms of millennialism, such as the "Refreshment of Saints." (The Refreshment of Saints was seen as a brief period of respite [45 days] during which the saints who had survived the tribulations of the endtime would enjoy peace on this earth. Initially an exegetical problem [a "loose" 45 days unaccounted for], this concept became the basis of a whole range of millennial speculation about a period of earthly perfection.) Above all, charismatic prophets using apocalyptic calculations drawn from Daniel and Revelation continued to excite the faithful. Perhaps in recognition of this perennial appeal, church leaders compromised when dealing with those who remained deeply attached to hopes for a real millennium. As a result, as early as the 2nd century, two of the principal themes of medieval millennialism had already emerged: (1) the use of an anti-apocalyptic chronology to postpone the date of the End, thus encouraging patience; and (2) the transformation of the Roman Empire into a positive eschatological force.

To delay the end and reap the calming benefits of non-apocalyptic millennialism, theologians placed great weight on the idea of a "sabbatical millennium." This idea, by combining GENESIS 2:2–3 (six days of travail, SABBATH rest), with Psalm 90 (1,000 years is a day in the sight of the Lord), promised the thousand-year kingdom after 6,000 years. About 200 CE the first Christian chronology placed the INCARNATION of Christ in 5500 *Annus Mundi* (*Annus Mundi*, or AM, meaning the "the year of the world"; thus Christ was said to have been born 5,500 years after the creation of the earth). This marked the year 500 CE as the year 6000 and provided a buffer of some 300 years. As a result, when apocalyptic prophets announced the imminent End, conservative clerics could counter with the argument that centuries yet remained until the millennium. Documentary evidence for this chronological argument provides an indicator of the presence of popular apocalyptic rumors, which were countered by theologians trying to calm the panics such rumors incited. From our modern perspective, of course, such chronological temporizing merely postponed, indeed aggravated, apocalyptic millennialism. In the early 3rd century, another 300 years probably seemed like an immensely long time, but eventually the 6,000 years would be fulfilled.

At the same time as theologians tried to postpone millennial hopes, they also tried to remove Christian millennial hostility to the Roman empire. Thus, theologians took Paul's discussion of the timing of the End (2 Thessalonians 2:3) and interpreted his reference to an "obstacle" to the advent of the "man of iniquity" as meaning that as long as the Roman empire endured, the ANTICHRIST could not come. This pro-Roman ESCHATOLOGY would, after Christianity became imperial, produce the myth of the Last Emperor, a superhuman figure who would unite all of Christendom and rule in peace and justice for 120 years before abdicating his throne, thus removing the "obstacle" and bringing on the brief rule of the Antichrist (this myth is found in both the Tiburtine Sybil and Pseudo-Methodius). This imperial millennialism, which probably already influenced Constantine— the first "Last Emperor"—offered a powerful antidote to the subversive elements of popular millennialism. Its cosmic struggle was not the demotic holy anarchy opposing the evil empire of early Christianity but the authoritarian holy empire fighting anarchic chaos; instead of the aniconic monotheistic political ideal of "no king but God," it offered the iconic one of "one God, one king." Not surprisingly, this form of "top-down" millennialism found much favor among subsequent Christian theologians.

But both these approaches, however creative and successful among theologians, merely delayed the problem. Despite pre-Christian and Christian belief in *Roma eterna*, the empire (especially in the West) was vulnerable; and no matter how far away 6000 AM (500 CE) seemed from 5700 (200), it did not seem so far away in the 5900s (400s). Indeed, the western Roman empire faltered just as the year 6000 approached, turning both these anti-apocalyptic exegeses—the sabbatical chronology and the imperial "obstacle" to the Antichrist—into profoundly apocalyptic ones. At the beginning of the 5th century Jerome and AUGUSTINE, perceiving the danger posed by two such unstable eschatological "teachings," developed more stringent forms of opposition to millennialism. They reoriented Latin thought in two ways. Jerome, translating the work of the great imperialist, anti-millenarian theologian and chronographer, EUSEBIUS OF CAESAREA, introduced a new set of calculations that placed the Incarnation in 5199 AM (II), thus delaying the year 6000 AM another three centuries. He thereby made it possible for Latin chronographers to ignore the year 6000 AM I, since by his calculations it was really only 5701 AM II. At the same time he heaped ridicule and contempt on millennialists, believers in foolish tales of earthly delights, gluttony, and sexual promiscuity.

Augustine went still further, arguing that no historical event or chronology can be interpreted apocalyptically and that the millennium was not a future event but already in progress, already set in motion by Christ. To explain why the evils of war, hatred, injustice and poverty continued unabated, Augustine used the notion of the two cities. There was a "heavenly city," the celestial Jerusalem, where the millennium was already manifest, and a terrestrial Babylon, the time-bound city of violence and oppression in which the millennium was not visible. These two cities would coexist as a *corpus permixtum* (a mixed body) in every man (even saints) and in every society (even the church) until the eschaton (the consummation of history). Thus, Christian Rome and even the earthly church could not represent the perfection of eschatological fulfillment, and their historical fate had nothing to do with God's plans for human salvation. This teaching radically reoriented Christian eschatology: rather than await the coming kingdom on earth, one should await it at the very end of time. Augustine basically banned millennialism, or the belief in a coming KINGDOM OF GOD on earth, from Christian theology.

POPULAR AND UNDERGROUND MILLENNIALISM

This ban on millennial thought so dominated the official theological writings of the early Middle Ages that most modern historians think it disappeared entirely from Latin Christendom. Indeed, standard treatments of millennialism, unaware of the idea of the sabbatical millennium and the popular millennial discourse it opposed, tend to skip from Augustine (5th century) to JOACHIM OF FIORE (12th century), when the first formal theology that looked forward to the millennium reemerged. There are signs of millennialism, however, both in the activity of anti-ecclesiastical prophets like the "false" Christ of Bourges described in the 6th century by Gregory of Tours in his *History of the Franks* and in the anti-apocalyptic uses of chronology to oppose them. Gregory, for example, published his chronology for "those who despair at the coming end of the world." The implicit message was clear: Gregory wrote in the late 5700s, and, when arguing with the "saints" who emerged after the assassination of the false Christ and "gained quite an influence over the common people," Gregory and his colleagues could argue that there were more than two centuries to wait. But, of course, even this more remote date eventually drew near, and in the 8th century—the 5900s—the Anglo-Saxon monk BEDE THE VENERABLE and his Carolingian followers did for AM II what Jerome had done for AM I: they shifted the dating system again, this time to AD (*anno Domini*). Hence the year 6000 AM II, like the year 6000 AM I, passed unnoted by sources that spoke instead of AD 801.

And yet the relative silence in our documentation does not mean that there was no further discussion of the approaching 6000 AM II. Indeed, as in 6000 AM I (500 AD), the approach of 6000 brought an acute political crisis, with the occupation of the Byzantine throne by a woman (Irene). The "obstacle" of 2 Thessalonians had been removed. Charlemagne's response, to hold his imperial coronation on the first day of the year 6000 AM II (AD 801), unquestionably held millennial significance, despite the reluctance of the written sources to elaborate. The coronation was, in this sense, like the "Emperor's New Clothes": everyone in the court knew of the date AM, but no chronicler mentioned it. Ignorant of this tension, modern historians have analyzed this pivotal moment in Western history without any awareness of its millennial background, speaking only of the coronation of the year 800. (For the Carolingians, the new year began on Christmas Day, not on January 1, thus historians now give the year of Charlemagne's coronation as 800, whereas, at that time, it was considered the first day of 801.)

Charlemagne's coronation contributed two essential elements to subsequent European millennialism. First, it meant the "transfer" of the empire, with all its apocalyptic and millennial freight, including the notion of the last emperor, to the West. Numerous European kings claimed this messianic status, but the German emperors above all proved fascinated by the idea (*e.g.*, Otto III, Frederick I, and Frederick II). Second, the Carolingians shifted chronological hopes for the APOCALYPSE from 6000 AM to the year AD 1000, a date at once millennial (the end of the sixth age, dawn of the sabbatical era) and Augustinian (the end of the millennium since Christ). And, unlike the previous cases of a millennial date's advent, chronographers this time were unable to shift the chronology and avoid mentioning the apocalyptic date.

Germany and France of 1000 illustrate the two dynamics of millennial symbolism: Germany incarnates the "top-down" imperial version, while France displays a remarkable array of "bottom-up" populist expressions. Emperor Otto III manipulated every aspect of the imperial variety: he insisted on the *renovatio imperii Romani* (renewal of the empire of Rome, the "obstacle" to Antichrist); on PENTECOST of 1000 he opened Charlemagne's tomb (emperor of 6000); and he urged rulers throughout the Eastern regions (Poland, Hungary, and Scandinavia) to convert to Christianity. In contrast, King Robert II of France, the second ruler of a new and still uncertain dynasty and under ANATHEMA in 1000, presided over a kingdom marked by the social turmoil of a castellan revolution that neither the king nor most of the high aristocracy were capable of controlling. Here apocalyptic and millennial symbols were generated from below, especially in the earliest popular religious movement of the Middle Ages: the Peace of God. This conciliar movement, which mobilized huge crowds at open-air revivalist gatherings in the collective pursuit of God's peace on earth, may have been the earliest sustained millenarian movement that joined all levels of society together. It thus displays two key and consequential aspects of subsequent millennialism in the West: the vast revivalist gatherings and the sense of a social covenant. It appeared in two waves, in the decades before the millennia of the Incarnation (1000) and of the Passion (1033), respectively, first south of the Loire, then throughout France.

Of course, the two waves passed and, despite vast social covenants followed by years of jubilee-like abundance and peace, there was still no Parousia, still no millennium. A failure as a messianic voluntary movement, the Peace of God became the enforced "King's Peace," as the social covenant that had been based on an oral commitment and trust became a contract, a legal commitment enforced by written law. Yet apocalyptic expectations did not disappear in Western Europe; on the contrary, there was a sea change in millennial hopes. Instead of the pre-

Bede the Venerable
Art Resource

BEDE LEVENERABLE

Coronation of Charlemagne by Pope Leo III, from the 14th-century Grandes Chroniques de France
Art Resource

dominantly passive expectation of the earlier period, the passing of 1000 seems to have introduced, via the peace movement, a new and more aggressive form which sought to prepare the world for the End. Here we see the earliest forms of what Christian theologians today call "postmillennialism," or the notion that Christ will come after a millennial kingdom wrought and presided over by the saints, a kingdom toward which believers can and should work. While popular "messiahs" continued to appear (*e.g.,* Eon de l'Etoile and Tanchelm), the period after the year 1000 saw much vaster movements, often approved (at least initially) by ecclesiastical authorities—the popular crusades, the Capuchins, the FRANCISCANS, the flagellants. Some of these movements were popularly based, militant, and extremely hostile to ecclesiastical authority, the wealthy, Jews, intellectuals, etc., displaying the anger, paranoia, and violence that would dominate an entire strain of anti-modern Christian millennialism from the crusading pogroms to the Nazis.

But the more documentable, and in some ways more surprising, aspect of medieval millennialism was its use by lay and ecclesiastical elites to buttress their own authority. Starting with the GREGORIAN REFORM, papal reformers used apocalyptic imagery both to attack their enemies as the Antichrist and to wrap their own efforts in messianic promises. Similarly, royal and even comitial courts used eschatological prophecy as propaganda. Dynastic publicists often painted their patrons in the imagery of the Last Emperor; William I of Normandy consciously used themes from Revelation—his crown, his Domesday Book—to buttress his conquest of England. Supporters of Thierry of Alsace, count of Flanders, responded to the seemingly apocalyptic civil war of 1127–28 by disseminating prophecies claiming that his dynasty was the last barrier to the Antichrist. At the time of the Second Crusade a French prophet evoked the Tiburtine SIBYL to predict that Louis VII was to conquer the Orient in the fashion of Cyrus the Great of Persia. Similarly, Richard I of England and the German king Frederick I embarked on the Third Crusade inspired by apocalyptic prophecies.

MILLENNIALISM REVIVED

Millennial hopes and ambitions reached new levels as a result of the work of Joachim of Fiore (late 12th century). Joachim postulated that, by analogy with the TRINITY, there were to be three great states (*status*) of history: (1) that of the Father, which had been characterized by the vesting of righteousness in married persons; (2) that of the Son, during which an order of unmarried clerics served as the guardians of righteousness; and (3) that of the HOLY SPIRIT, the period of the "Refreshment of the Saints" after the Antichrist, in which the order of monks would bring an era of earthly peace and spiritual contemplation. Joachim was the first theologian to reject Augustine and return to the notion of a millennium to come, and his influence on subsequent millennial thought was immense.

The earliest historians of millennialism thought of Joachim as the first millennial thinker since the days when Augustine banned such ideas. He now appears to be the first formal thinker to articulate his millennialism in a way that could survive legitimately in writing. Had Augustine been present when the papal council declared Joachim's works acceptable, he would have denounced the decision loudly. Instead of a lone millenarian presence, then, Joachim's work is the literate articulation of a widespread oral discussion of millennialism at the turn of 1200, an oral discourse that had never ceased, despite its sudden ups and long downs, since well before Augustine. The spectacular success of the movements that could fuel themselves with Joachimite "age of the spirit" rhetoric illustrates the broad social stratum and the liveliness of the millennial religiosity.

Joachim revitalized every aspect of medieval millennialism: within decades of his death in 1202 prophecies attributed to him began to circulate that people identified (in profoundly un-Augustinian fashion) with current events. Franciscans and DOMINICANS, Holy Roman emperors and popes all became figures in vast and ever-shifting predictions of imminent apocalypse. Chronological calculations fixed on 1250, then on 1260, as the beginning of the new Age, producing new and fearsome forms of spirituality, like FLAGELLATION. The Franciscan order split over interpretations of Joachimite prophecy, one branch (the Community) becoming inquisitors, the other (the Spirituals), revolutionary millenarians. Angelic popes and messianic emperors vied among lay and clerical constituencies for a following. By the end of the 13th century millennialism had reached a fevered pitch, especially among Spiritual Franciscans and their lay spin-offs, the Apostolic Brethren, as well as among the more mystical elements of the BEGUINES (for example, Marguerite Porete) and the Beghards. The execution, in 1300, of some of the Apostolic Brethren, including their founder Gerard Segarelli, by Pope BONIFACE VIII set the stage for a particularly violent round of paranoid millennialism under the leadership of Fra Dolcino in the early 14th century.

In France the imagery of millennialism continued to influence political discourse throughout the remainder of the Middle Ages. The terrible catastrophes of the 14th century—the Hundred Years' War and the Black Death—renewed fervor for the final, divine intervention, including new and radical forms of flagellants. Writing immediately after the humiliating rout of the French knighthood and capture of the French king at Poitiers in 1356, the Franciscan John of Rupescissa prophesied that plagues would cut down the populace like the harvest in the fields, the poor would rise up against tyrants and the rich, the church would be stripped of its wealth, and Antichrists would arise in Rome and Jerusalem. At least one contemporary, the court historian Jean Froissart (d. 1400/01), seemed to think that Roquetaillade's prophecies inspired the Jacquerie (the insurrection of peasants against the nobility in northeastern France in 1358—so named from the nobles' habit of referring contemptuously to any peasant as Jacques, or Jacques Bonhomme). However, Rupescissa prophesied, the agony of the world would end by 1367, for a great reforming pope would come to power, and the king of France would again be elected Holy Roman emperor. Fulfilling his glorious role as a second Charlemagne, this worthy king would conquer the entire world and establish a millennial reign of peace and prosperity. Indeed, French kings bearing the name Charles were the subjects of particularly intense millennial prophecies throughout the late Middle Ages. A prophecy of 1380 pertaining to Charles VI was subsequently applied to Charles VII and Charles VIII and even (much later) to England's Charles II while he was in exile in France.

Despite such fundamentally conservative applications of millennial prophecies, the hopes and expectations aroused by the prospect of the Christian Apocalypse still offered the outlines of a powerful, if fundamentally impractical and hence ultimately suicidal, ideology of social revolution to the peasants and the urban poor of the late Middle Ages. The thousands of shepherds, or Pastoureaux, who swept through the French countryside in 1251 and again in 1320 were convinced that they were God's chosen instrument to free the Holy Land and thereby bring about the Parousia. While none of them ever reached the Holy Land, they traveled in bands about the kingdom, amazing some with their piety, but all the while slaughtering clerics, Jews, and university intellectuals. Similar apocalyptic ideas regarding the election of the poor to usher in God's kingdom, either by participating in a crusade of the poor or by rescuing the king in his hour of need, motivated other popular insurrections.

Modern historians, limited by the nature of the documentation, tend to emphasize in their analyses the kinds of "political," or imperial, millennialism that find expression in the sources. Popular and revolutionary millennialism, rarely reported except by hostile clerical sources or by later spokesmen eager to downplay millenarian origins, are more difficult to assess. If one limits oneself to only explicitly millenarian groups, the numbers are few until the period of the printing press; if one identifies such groups by their patterns, rather than by their own or others' claims about them, they are far more numerous than documentation indicates.

The Taborites were perhaps the most important millennial movement of the late Middle Ages and represent a transition to the new age of millennial movements in the Renaissance and the REFORMATION. Taking themes from the English reformer JOHN WYCLIFFE, Czech preachers began to rally the faithful to a program of radical, antipapal reform. JAN HUS, the most prominent of these men, was burned at the stake at the COUNCIL OF CONSTANCE (1415), strengthening the hand of the most radical, indeed millennial, of the Taborites, who targeted 1420 as the date of the End. For the next two decades the region was plagued with millennial wars that brought out the social and revolutionary elements of millennialism and ended in a national church, the HUSSITE Church, centered in Prague.

The approach of the year 7000 AM I (AD 1492/1500) brought with it a number of millennial currents. The fall of Constantinople in 1453 not only put an end to the last remnant of the Roman Empire from antiquity; it also provoked the appearance of a large number of books like the *Corpus Hermeticum*, purporting to convey "secret knowledge," to the West, thus reinvigorating the Joachimite tradition with Gnostic elements of an apolitical elitism that sought, through esoteric knowledge, to transform the world. One enthusiast of the proliferation of prophecy and knowledge was the explorer Christopher Columbus. At this point, especially with the assistance of the printing press, various strains of millennial prophecy proliferated throughout Europe. These new strains, linked to the Gnostic search for knowledge that could transform nature, had important implications for the emergence of modern science. In a sense, the Renaissance, with its belief in a new world in the making and its eagerness to embrace any new form of thinking, Christian or otherwise, may represent the first "New Age" movement, the first secular millennial movement on record.

From the Renaissance onward, European culture developed an ever-more-secular strain of millennialism. The longer God tarried, the more humans took over his job of bringing about the perfect kingdom. Here we find the utopian and scientific traditions and the radical democratic movements that gave us the French Revolution, radical socialism, and Marxist communism, as well as Nazism and, in a modified form, ZIONISM. Totalitarianism may be seen as the result of millennial movements that seize power and, in the failure of their millennial hopes, find themselves "forcing" the perfection of man.

PROTESTANT MILLENNIALISM

Popular millennial movements, however, returned in strength with the Protestant Reformation. Luther himself was not a millennial thinker (he was, after all, trained as an AUGUSTINIAN hermit), but he used powerful apocalyptic rhetoric, making the pope as Antichrist a staple of Protestant discourse. In so doing, he unleashed a wave of millennialism that covered the gamut from THOMAS MÜNTZER'S revolutionary Peasants' Revolt in Thuringia (1524–25), to the ANABAPTISTS who gathered in Münster in 1534 to see the heavenly Jerusalem descend to earth, to the HUTTERITES and MENNONITES. But the most powerful form of millennialism to emerge came from the British Isles after Henry VIII introduced PROTESTANTISM as the official religion in 1534. PURITANISM in both England and Scotland had strong millennial elements that eventually burst forth during the English Civil Wars (1642–51), unleashing a whole panoply of new millennial movements— Levelers, Diggers, Ranters, QUAKERS, and Muggletonians. Nor was the 17th century limited to Christian millennialism: 1666 saw the climax of the most widespread millennial movement in the history of Judaism, with the career of SHAB-

St. John's visions of the sixth angel (top) and seventh angel (bottom), from an English manuscript illumination of Revelation to John, c. 1250
The Granger Collection

BETAI TZEVI, whose messianic message ignited Jewish communities in both Muslim and Christian lands. Although RABBINIC JUDAISM has, like Catholicism, strong barriers against apocalyptic outbreaks, evidence of messianic activity can be found in almost every generation, and today, especially among religious Zionists, there are strong millennial currents.

The Puritan millennial strain came to America with the pilgrims and has, essentially, marked American religiosity ever since. The GREAT AWAKENING (1720–40s) and the Second Great Awakening (1795–1835) were both inspired by a form of millennial fervor derived from the teachings of Congregational pastor JONATHAN EDWARDS. Both the theological underpinnings and the emphasis on collective penitence, public weeping, and large crowds singing HYMNS reflect the characteristics of millennial moments from the times of the peace assemblies in Europe. According to some historians, the enthusiasm of the Great Awakening was redirected into the militant patriotism of the American Revolution, whose religious rhetoric was steeped in millennial themes. In addition to the more mainstream millennialism of the Great Awakenings, American millennialism gave birth to a wide range of new religious movements like the MORMONS, the SEVENTH-DAY ADVENTISTS, and the JEHOVAH'S WITNESSES. At the present time, these represent some of the most active religions in the world.

American Protestant millennialism split into two streams: the premillennialists (who believe that Jesus will come before the millennium and inaugurate it), and the postmillennialists (who believe that Jesus will come after the millennium inaugurated by an inspired mankind). The former tends to be catastrophic (the seven years before the advent of Jesus, known as the Tribulation, preceded by the Rapture of the saints, are marked by terrible catastrophes and by the coming of the Antichrist); whereas the latter tends to be progressive and gradualist. The former tends to be apolitical (only personal repentance and purification can prepare); the latter, politically active (through reform we can bring about the kingdom). In the late 19th century premillennialism gained the upper hand in much American millennial thinking, only to cede to postmillennialism reformism in the early decades of the 20th. The evangelical and fundamentalist reaction that developed in the 1910s and '20s was premillennial dispensationalist in nature; it was inspired by the work of John Nelson Darby (1800–82) and the Scofield Bible (1909), and it was committed to reversing the secularizing tendencies of reformist postmillennialism.

Premillennial Dispensationalism became extremely popular in Protestant circles in America, starting in the 1970s with the publication of Hal Lindsey's *The Late Great Planet Earth* (1972) and the "Rapture" film *A Thief in the Night* (1972). In the 1980s Edgar C. Whisenant published the pamphlet *88 Reasons Why the Rapture Will Happen in 1988*, starting off a range of Rapture predictions that have dotted the 1990s. The Y2K computer bug, set to go off on Jan. 1, 2000, triggered a whole new wave of apocalyptic thinking among premillennial preachers like Chuck Missler, Jack Van Impe, and Jerry Falwell and had the potential to be the great ecumenical apocalyptic prophecy of the age.

MILLENNIALISM OUTSIDE CHRISTIANITY

Finally, millennialism has an important non-Western component. ISLAM, as a religion of revelation, began as an apocalyptic movement anticipating a Day of Judgment, and it retains apocalyptic and millennial elements to this day, especially in SHIʿITE theology but also in many of the forms of popular religiosity that have emerged within it. In particular the Mujaddid tradition, which foresees a "renewer" at every century turn of the Muslim calendar (AH), appears to constitute—before the century has turned—a form of apocalyptic messianic expectation in the coming of the hidden MAHDI. Many indigenous movements, often anti-imperialist in nature, take on the full range of characteristics of millennialism. In the Western hemisphere, for example, native populations produced a wide range of millennial movements, from the HANDSOME LAKE MOVEMENT (c. 1800) to the GHOST DANCE cult of the prophet WOVOKA in the 1890s. Among some Pacific islanders the arrival of cargo-laden airplanes during World War II led to the emergence of CARGO CULTS and the belief that the proper rituals would bring precious "cargo" from the great bird in the sky. Modern UFO cults, many of which have strong millennial elements, represent a kind of postmodern cargo cult.

By far the most powerful non-Western millennial tradition is found in BUDDHISM, with the PURE LAND traditions and the expectation of MAITREYA, a kind of messianic final incarnation of the Buddha. Especially strong in China, but evident as well in Korea, Japan, Vietnam, and Myanmar (Burma), millennial strains of Buddhism have given birth to secret societies (*i.e.*, WHITE LOTUS) and some powerful popular movements, one of which toppled the Yüan dynasty in China in the 14th century, and another of which, the TAIPING REBELLION, almost toppled the Qing (Ch'ing) dynasty in the mid-19th century. By the time this last movement, itself a mixture of native Buddhist and imported Christian millennialism, was finally suppressed in 1864, some 20 million people were dead. The Boxer Rebellion of 1900 again demonstrated the power of millennial beliefs, especially the characteristic belief, shared by members of the Ghost Dance cult of North America and the Kartelite Cults of Africa, that certain incantations could render the believer invulnerable to bullets.

Millennial studies is still a young field. First launched by anthropologists who studied cargo cults after World War II, developed by medievalists like Norman Cohn and Marjorie Reeves, and refined theoretically by sociologists like Leon Festinger, it has become an international field of research. Because of the dynamics

Marshall Applewhite, the leader of the apocalyptic movement Heaven's Gate. Applewhite was among the 39 members of the cult who committed suicide at a house in Rancho Santa Fe, Calif., U.S., in 1997. The mass suicide was linked to the arrival of the Hale-Bopp comet in that year
Reuters—NBC Reuters TV—Archive Photos

of millennial manifestations—their brief intensity, their seemingly irrational passions, their range of responses to apocalyptic disappointment—they often demand counterintuitive thinking and call for a multidisciplinary approach that engages a wide range of fields and specialties. At the approach of the 3rd millennium the field proliferated not only among scholars but also among policy makers.

We are, however, not yet in a position to judge just how significant millennialism is as a historical factor. It unquestionably plays an important role in various forms of antimodern and anti-Western protests, but it also has played a key role in generating modernity. With its images of a perfected mankind, its emphasis on social egalitarianism and the dignity of manual labor, its undermining of monarchical authority, its spread of a sense of popular empowerment, millennialism has, even in failure, left a legacy of social transformation. Indeed, millennial movements may play an important role in the diffusion of new technology: in their initial stages they make widespread and innovative use of communications technology, as early Protestants made use of print and new religious movements take advantage of the World Wide Web. In later stages they often integrate new technology into the lifestyle of a community as it adjusts to the return of "normal time" and finds more durable, more economically viable, forms. Ironically, some of the most antimodern groups can, by the end of their apocalyptic journey, end up at the cutting edge of modernity.

For all its socially creative force, however, millennialism also has powerfully destructive tendencies. In some primarily antimodern forms, millennial movements can become highly authoritarian, suffused with conspiracist thinking, implacably opposed to imagined enemies (Jews, independent women, denominational opponents), and capable of staggering acts of violence and self-destruction. The Nazis, with their racist *tausendjähriges Reich,* represent the ultimate expression of this tendency. It is one of the main tasks of millennial studies to understand which factors indicate whether, in the period of disappointment, a group will turn peaceful or violent. In the meantime millennialism, with its power to fire the imagination and elicit passions, to move great numbers to extraordinary self-sacrifice, social creativity, and destructiveness, may be one of the most protean social and religious forces in the history of civilization.

MILLENNIUM, in Christian theology, the 1,000-year period when JESUS CHRIST will return and establish his kingdom on earth. Among early Christians the idea of MILLENNIALISM, or millenarianism, derived chiefly from Jewish eschatological expectations and usually implied the nearness of the triumph of Christians over the world.

The doctrine of the millennium is clearly present in the NEW TESTAMENT only in Revelation 20. According to the account of the vision there, SATAN was bound and thrown into a pit for 1,000 years. Martyrs were resurrected and reigned with Christ for the millennium. At the end of the period, Satan was loosed for a time to deceive the nations, but he was subsequently defeated. All the dead were then gathered for the final judgment.

Many different interpretations of the millennium have been given. Those Christians who believe that the SECOND COMING of Christ will begin the 1,000-year period of righteousness in the world have been called premillennialists. Others, known as postmillennialists, believe that eventually CHRISTIANITY will be accepted throughout the world, and a 1,000-year period of Christian righteousness will be climaxed by the return of Christ, the RESURRECTION of the dead, and the final judgment.

The more general use of the term to include expectations of material benefits to be enjoyed on earth in the near future means that a number of early Christian writers, especially those close to Jewish Christianity, can be called millenarians. Among such writers are the author of the Epistle of Barnabas, Papias, Justin, IRENAEUS, and the Jewish-Christian Gnostic CERINTHUS. The Montanists believed that the heavenly Jerusalem would soon be manifested in Phrygia and that their leader was the Paraclete promised in the Gospel of John. At the same time, more orthodox teachers continued to share a similar hope; Hippolytus tells of bishops in Syria and Pontus who led their flocks out into the desert to await Christ's coming.

By the time of the triumph of the church in the reign of CONSTANTINE such hopes were on the wane. The great Western theologian AUGUSTINE was a millenarian early in his career, but he later changed his views. At the Council of Ephesus (431) millenarian views were not condemned, but they were mentioned only to be ignored. In later times they arose sporadically when they could be used against the authority of the church; thus they flourished among spiritual enthusiasts during the Middle Ages and particularly at the time of the REFORMATION, when social and religious ferment worked together, especially among the various groups loosely denominated ANABAPTIST. The more conservative Reformers shared the Catholic view of the coming of Christ as primarily past rather than future, thus identifying the KINGDOM OF GOD on earth with the church, even though such an identification was hardly ever regarded as complete.

Throughout later Western history, the appeal of millennialism has tended to resurge in times of great social change or crisis. Sects arising out of the industrialization of the West include the SEVENTH-DAY ADVENTISTS, JEHOVAH'S WITNESSES, and the Latter-day Saints (MORMONS).

MILLER, WILLIAM \'mi-lər\ (b. Feb. 15, 1782, Pittsfield, Mass., U.S.—d. Dec. 20, 1849, Low Hampton, N.Y.), American religious enthusiast, leader of a movement called Millerism that sought to revive belief that the bodily arrival ("advent") of Christ was imminent.

Miller was a farmer, but he also held such offices as deputy sheriff and justice of the peace, and served as captain in the War of 1812. After years of BIBLE study he began to preach in 1831 that the present world would end "about the year 1843," his belief based primarily on a passage in the Book of Daniel (8:13–14). Miller estimated that between 50,000 and 100,000 believed in his views. When 1843 passed, some of his associates set Oct. 22, 1844, as the date of the SECOND COMING. This date brought the movement to a sharp climax. The last general conference met at Albany, N.Y., April 1845. Belief in the imminence of the Advent was restated, but no date was set and no church organization created.

There are two principal ADVENTIST bodies today—the Advent Christian Church, organized in 1861, and the much larger body of SEVENTH-DAY ADVENTISTS, organized in 1863—and several small Adventist bodies.

MILLET \'mi-let, -lət\ (Turkish: "religious community," "people," "nation," from Arabic: *milla*, "religion," "religious community"), according to the QUR'AN, the religion professed by ABRAHAM and other ancient prophets. In medieval Islamic states, the word was applied to certain non-Muslim minorities, mainly Christians and Jews. In the heterogeneous Ottoman Empire (c. 1300–1923), a *millet* was an autonomous self-governing religious community, organized under its own laws and headed by a religious leader. Each *millet* assumed responsibility for social and administrative functions not provided by the state, conducting affairs through a communal council (*meclisimilli*). From 1856 on, a series of imperial reform edicts introduced secular law codes for all citizens, and much of the *millet*s' administrative autonomy was lost. Subsequently, *millet*s were infused with European ideas of nationalism; thus, the word means "nation" in modern Turkish.

MĪMĀṂSĀ \mē-'mäm-sä, -'mäⁿ-sä\ (Sanskrit: "Reflection," or "Critical Investigation"), probably the earliest of the six orthodox systems (*darśaṇas*) of Indian philosophy.

The aim of Mīmāṃsā is to give rules for the interpretation of the VEDAS and to provide a philosophical justification for the observance of Vedic ritual. Because Mīmāṃsā is concerned with the earlier parts of the Vedas (called the Karmakāṇḍa), it is also referred to as Pūrva-Mīmāṃsā ("Prior Study"), or Karma-Mīmāṃsā ("Study of the Acts").

The earliest work of the system is the *Mīmāṃsā Sūtra* of Jaimini (c. 4th century BCE). A major commentary was written by Śabarasvāmī (1st century BCE?), whose most notable successors were Kumārila Bhaṭṭa and Prabhākara (7th/8th century CE). The goal of Mīmāṃsā is to provide enlightenment on DHARMA, which in this school is understood as the set of ritual obligations and prerogatives that, if properly performed, maintains the harmony of the world and furthers the personal goals of the performer. One must depend on revelation in the Veda, which is considered eternal, authorless, and absolutely infallible. If the Vedic command is implicit, one must judge from parallels; if a text fails to detail how a priest proceeds with an action, this detail must be provided from other texts. This concern with precise statement necessitates meticulous examination of the structure of a sentence conveying a command.

Although it was purely practical in origin, Mīmāṃsā became a powerful intellectual force. It has contributed to the direction, method, and content of Hindu erudition, and is traditionally credited with the defeat of BUDDHISM in India.

MIMIR \'mē-mir\, *Old Norse* Mímir, in GERMANIC RELIGION, the wisest of the gods of the tribe AESIR. Mimir was sent by the Aesir as a hostage to the rival gods (the VANIR), but he was decapitated and his head was returned to the Aesir. The god ODIN preserved the head in herbs, made it speak, and gained knowledge from it. According to another story, Mimir resided by a well that stood beneath one of the roots of YGGDRASILL, the WORLD TREE. That well, sometimes called Mímisbrunnr, contained one of Odin's eyes, which Odin had pledged in order to drink from the waters and receive wisdom. Another myth features a different Mimir, a smith who taught the hero SIEGFRIED his craft.

MIN \\'min\\, in ancient EGYPTIAN RELIGION, god of fertility and harvest, embodiment of the masculine principle; he was also worshiped as the Lord of the Eastern Desert. His cult originated in predynastic times (4th millennium BCE). Min was represented with phallus erect and a flail in his raised right hand. His cult was strongest in Coptos and Akhmīm (Panopolis), where great festivals were held celebrating his "coming forth" with a public procession and presentation of offerings. The lettuce was his sacred plant.

MINARET \\,mi-nə-'ret, 'mi-nə-,\\ (Arabic: "beacon"), tower from which the Muslim faithful are called to prayer five times each day by a MUEZZIN, or crier. With some notable exceptions in medieval Central Asia, Iran, and Iraq, such a tower is always connected with a mosque and has one or more balconies or open galleries. At the time of MUHAMMAD, the call to prayer was made from the highest roof in the vicinity of the mosque. The earliest minarets were former Greek watchtowers and the towers of Christian churches. The oldest minaret in North Africa is at al-Qayrawān, Tunisia. It was built between 724 and 727.

The upper parts of the minaret are usually richly decorated with carving. The number of minarets per mosque varies from one to as many as six. These towers were built to be visible from afar and to stamp a site with Islamic character.

MINERVA \\mi-'nər-və\\, in ROMAN RELIGION, goddess of handicrafts, the professions, the arts, and, later, war; she was identified with the Greek ATHENA. She was one of the Capitoline triad, in association with JUPITER and JUNO. Her shrine on the Aventine in Rome was a meeting place for guilds of craftsmen, including at one time dramatic poets and actors.

Her worship as a goddess of war encroached upon that of MARS. Pompey erected a temple to her out of the spoils of his Eastern conquests in recognition of her identificaton with the Greek Athena NIKE, bestower of victory. Under the emperor Domitian, who claimed her special protection, the worship of Minerva attained its greatest vogue in Rome.

MINISTRY, in CHRISTIANITY, office held by persons who are set apart by ecclesiastical authority to be ministers in the church or whose call to special vocational service in a church is afforded some measure of general recognition. The type of ministry varies in the different churches. That which developed in the early church and is retained by the ROMAN CATHOLIC, EASTERN OR-THODOX, OLD CATHOLIC, ANGLICAN, and some other churches is episcopal and is based on the three orders, or offices, of bishop, priest, and deacon.

Throughout much of the history of the church, the episcopal ministry was taken for granted, but the Protestant REFORMATION challenged the authority of the PAPACY and with it the authority of the episcopal ministry. MARTIN LUTHER introduced the concept of the PRIESTHOOD of all believers, which denied any special authority to the offices of the episcopacy, but he also retained the ordained ministry. Ministers were encouraged to marry and were not considered a separate order in the church. Lutheran churches developed a variety of ministries, some retaining a modified episcopal form and others adopting congregational and PRESBYTERIAN forms.

The presbyterian form of ministry, developed by JOHN CALVIN, is used in most Presbyterian and Reformed churches. Ministers are teaching elders and share with lay elders and collegial regional bodies (presbyteries) the governance of the church. Congregational church government, adopted by BAPTISTS, the United Church of Christ in the United States, and various others, accepted much of the Reformed theology but emphasized the authority of the congregation rather than any central or regional authority. Although historical METHODISM rejected episcopacy, in the United States a modified form was developed, retaining the office of bishop and strengthening congregational influence. Pentecostal and evangelical groups consider charismatic gifts more important than ORDINATION or any office as such. Some churches (*e.g.*, the SOCIETY OF FRIENDS) do not have an ordained ministry.

MINOS \\'mī-nəs, -,näs\\, mythical ruler of Crete; he was the son of ZEUS and EUROPA. Minos obtained the Cretan throne by the aid of the god POSEIDON, and from Knossos (or Gortyn) he gained control over the Aegean islands, colonizing many of them and ridding the sea of pirates. He married Pasiphaë, the daughter of HELIOS, who bore him, among others, Androgeos, ARIADNE, and Phaedra, and who was also the mother of the MINOTAUR. Sir Arthur Evans used his name to refer to the Bronze Age civilization of Crete, the Minoans.

Minos fought successfully against Athens and Megara to obtain redress after his son Androgeos was killed by the Athenians. In Athenian drama and legend Minos became the tyrannical exactor of the tribute of children to feed the Minotaur. Minos was killed in Sicily by the daughters of King Cocalus, who poured boiling water over him as he was taking a bath. After his death he became a judge in HADES.

Theseus grapples with the Minotaur, detail of a vase painting, 6th century BCE
By courtesy of the trustees of the British Museum

MINOTAUR \\'mi-nə-,tȯr, 'mī-\\, Greek Minotauros ("Minos' Bull"), in Greek mythology, monster of Crete that had the body of a man and the head of a bull. It was the offspring of Pasiphaë, the wife of MINOS, and a snow-white bull sent to Minos by the god POSEIDON for sacrifice. Minos, instead of sacrificing it, kept it alive; Poseidon as a punishment made Pasiphaë fall in love with it. Her child by the bull was shut up in the Labyrinth created for Minos by DAEDALUS.

According to Athenian tradition, a son of Minos, Androgeos, was killed by the Athenians; to avenge his death, Minos demanded that seven Athenian boys and seven girls should be sent every ninth year (or, according to another version, every year) to be devoured by the Minotaur. When the third time of sacrifice came, the Athenian hero THESEUS volunteered to go, and, with the help of ARIADNE, daughter of Minos and Pasiphaë, he killed the monster.

MĪRĀBAĪ \'mē-rä-'bä-ē\ (b. 1450?, Kudaki, India—d. 1547?, Dwārkā, Gujarāt), Hindu mystic and poet whose lyrical songs of devotion to the god KRISHNA are widely popular in northern India.

Mīrābāī was a Rājput princess, the only child of Ratan Singh, younger brother of the ruler of Merta. An image of Krishna given to her during childhood by a holy man began a lifetime of devotion to Krishna, whom she worshiped as her divine lover.

Legend tells that after the death of her husband (Bhoj Rāj, crown prince of Mewar) in 1521, Mīrābāī spent most of her days in her private temple dedicated to Krishna, receiving *sādhu*s (holy men) and pilgrims and composing songs of devotion. She was something of a rebel, and her religious pursuits did not fit the established pattern for a Rājput princess and widow. At least two attempts made on her life are alluded to in her poems, both foiled by miraculous means. Finally, Mīrābāī set out on a series of PILGRIMAGES, eventually settling in Dwārkā. In 1546 a delegation of BRAHMINS came to bring her back to Mewar. Reluctant, she asked permission to spend the night at the temple of Ranchorjī (Krishna) and the next morning was found to have disappeared. According to popular belief, she miraculously merged with the image of Ranchorjī.

Mīrābāī belonged to a strong tradition of BHAKTI (devotional) poets in medieval India who expressed their love of God through the analogy of human relations—a mother's love for her child, a friend for a friend, or a woman for her beloved. The immense popularity and charm of her lyrics lies in her use of everyday images and in the sweetness and directness of her emotional expression.

MIRACLE, extraordinary and astonishing happening that is attributed to the presence and action of a supernatural or divine power. Belief in miraculous happenings occurs in all cultures and is a feature of practically all religions.

Not all cultures oppose the natural world with some notion of the supernatural, yet extraordinary events, forces, and operations which conventionally are accepted as normal, though uncommon, features of the world's operations are recognized by these cultures as well. Similarly the religions of the ancient world had few formal miracles, precisely because certain kinds of divine action or cosmic operation (*e.g.,* oracles) were largely accepted as part of the normal order of things.

Ancient Indian MYTHOLOGY abounds in fantastic accounts of the doings of the gods, but the UPANISHADS and BRĀHMANAS evince an increasing indifference to miracles. Like other expressions of higher MYSTICISM, they consider the spiritual experience of religious insight and transformation as the only "miracle" worth talking about. Nevertheless Hindu popular religion sets no bounds to the miraculous powers of yogis, and India has been the classic land of wonders.

There is little room for the miraculous element in CONFUCIANISM, but TAOISM has produced a rich crop of thaumatur-

gy and magic on all levels of Chinese folk religion. Miracles are taken for granted throughout the OLD TESTAMENT: God "does wondrous things" especially in the history of his people Israel (*e.g.,* the ten plagues of Egypt). In the Greco-Roman world miracles were not uncommon; there were miraculous cures (*e.g.,* at the SANCTUARY of ASCLEPIUS in Epidaurus), moving statues of gods, RESURRECTIONS of the dead, VIRGIN BIRTHS, and the like, though Cicero in the *De divinatione* denied the possibility of miracles.

According to the earliest Buddhist accounts, the BUDDHA GOTAMA deprecated the miraculous powers that he possessed as a matter of course, being "the greatest of all yogis," as utterly devoid of spiritual significance. Nevertheless, miraculous accounts of his birth and life (and those of later Buddhist saints), as well as miracles in connection with his relics, proliferated as time went on, particularly in the MAHĀYĀNA tradition.

The Christian NEW TESTAMENT records various miracles of healing and of providing abundantly for specific human needs performed by JESUS CHRIST, and miracles form part of the career, in life as well as after death, of the Christian saints, and their occurrence continues (*e.g.,* LOURDES); duly established miracles are among the requirements for a process of CANONIZATION.

MUHAMMAD was the only great founder who renounced miracles and miraculous powers as a matter of principle—the QUR'AN was the great miracle—but subsequent HAGIOGRAPHY invested his life with miraculous details. Muslim popular religion, particularly under Sufi influence, abounds in miracles and PILGRIMAGES to the tombs of wonder-working saints.

MI'RĀJ \mi-'räj\, in Islamic tradition, ascension of the Prophet MUHAMMAD into heaven. As alluded to in the QUR'AN (17:1), a journey was made by a servant of God, in a single night, from the "sacred place of worship" (*al-masjid al-ḥarām*) to the "further place of worship" (*al-masjid al-aqṣā*). Muhammad is prepared for his meeting with God by the archangels JIBRĪL (Gabriel) and MĪKĀL one evening while he is asleep in the KA'BA, the sacred shrine of MECCA. They open up his body and purify his heart by removing all traces of error, doubt, IDOLATRY, and paganism and by filling it with wisdom and belief.

In the original version of the *mi'rāj*, the prophet is then transported by Jibrīl directly to the lowest heaven. But early in Muslim history the story of the ascension came to be associated with the story of Muhammad's night journey (ISRĀ'), which also originated in Mecca, the "sacred place of worship" and proceeded to the "further place of worship" (initially interpreted as heaven). In the period of the Umayyad caliphate (661–750), the "further place of worship" came to be read as Jerusalem, and the two versions were reconciled by regarding the *isrā'* simply as the night journey and relocating the point of Muhammad's ascension from Mecca to Jerusalem to avoid confusion.

The *isrā'* story, greatly elaborated by tradition, relates that Muhammad made the journey astride BURĀQ, a mythical winged creature, in the company of the archangel Jibrīl. Muhammad and Jibrīl enter the first heaven and proceed through all seven levels until they reach the throne of God. Along the way they meet the prophets Adam, Yaḥyā (JOHN), 'Īsā (JESUS), Yūsuf (JOSEPH), IDRĪS, Hārūn (AARON), Mūsā (MOSES), and Ibrāhīm (ABRAHAM) and visit hell and paradise. Mūsā says that Muhammad is more highly regarded by God than himself and that Muhammad's following outnumbers his own. Once Muhammad appears before God he is told to perform the *ṣalat* (ritual prayer) 50 times each day. Mūsā, however, advises Muhammad to plead for a reduction of the number as being too difficult for believers, and the obligation is eventually reduced to five prayers each day.

Parallels have been drawn between the *mi'rāj* and the manner in which a dead man's soul will progress to judgment at God's throne; and the Sufi mystics claim it describes the soul's leap into mystic knowledge. The ascension is celebrated with readings of the legend on the 27th day of Rajab, called *Laylat al-Mi'rāj* ("Night of the Ascension").

MĪR DĀMĀD \'mēr-dä-'mäd\, *original name* Muhammad Bāqir ibn al-Dāmād (d. 1631/32, near Najaf, Iraq), philosopher, teacher, and leader in the cultural renascence of Iran during the Ṣafavid dynasty.

A descendant of a well-known SHI'ITE family, Mīr Dāmād spent most of his life in Isfahan as a student and teacher. His major contribution to Islamic philosophy was his concept of time and nature. Within a major controversy as to whether the universe was created or eternal, Mīr Dāmād was the first to advance the notion of *ḥuduth-e dahrī* ("eternal origination") as an explanation of creation. He argued that, with the exception of God, all things, including the Earth and other heavenly bodies, are of both eternal and temporal origin. He influenced the revival of *al-falsafa al-yamanī* ("philosophy of Yemen"), a philosophy based on revelation and the sayings of prophets rather than the RATIONALISM of the Greeks, and he is widely recognized as the founder of the School of Isfahan, which embraced a theosophical outlook known as *ḥikmat-i ilāhī* ("divine wisdom").

Mīr Dāmād's many works on Islamic philosophy include *Taqwīm al-īmān* ("Calendar of Faith," a treatise on creation and God's knowledge). He also wrote poetry under the pseudonym of Ishrāq. As a measure of his stature, he was given the title *al-mu'allim al-thālith* (*i.e.*, "third teacher"—the first two being Aristotle and AL-FĀRĀBĪ). His work was continued by his pupil MULLĀ ṢADRĀ, who became a prominent Muslim philosopher of the 17th century.

MISHNAH \mēsh-'nä, 'mish-nə\, philosophical law code of JUDAISM, arranged by topics in a strict logical order dictated by the principles of natural history, that came to closure in the Land of Israel about 200 CE. The Mishnah comprises 62 tractates, divided by topics among 6 divisions, as follows: ZERA'IM (Agriculture); MO'ED (Appointed Times); NASHIM (Women); NEZIQIN (Damages); QODASHIM (Holy Things); and TOHOROT (Purity).

In volume, the sixth division, on purity, covers approximately a quarter of the entire document. Topics of interest to the PRIESTHOOD and the Temple, such as priestly fees, conduct of the cult on holy days, conduct of the cult on ordinary days, management and upkeep of the Temple, and the rules of cultic cleanness, predominate in the first, second, fifth, and sixth divisions. Rules governing the social order form the bulk of the third and fourth. Of these tractates, only 'Eduyyot (in Damages) is organized along other than topical lines, as a collection of sayings on diverse subjects attributed to particular authorities. The Mishnah as printed today always includes Abot (Sayings of the Sages), but that tractate reached closure about a generation later than the Mishnah.

The stress throughout the Mishnah on the priestly CASTE and the Temple cult point to the document's principal concern, which centered upon sanctification, understood as the correct arrangement of all things, each in its proper category and each called by its rightful name, just as at the creation as portrayed in the Priestly Source and just as with the cult itself as set forth in Leviticus. Further, the thousands of rules and cases (with sages' disputes thereon) that comprise the document upon close reading turn out to express in concrete language abstract principles of hierarchical classification. These define the document's method and mark it as a work of a philosophical character. Not only so, but a variety of specific, recurrent concerns—for example, the relationships of being to becoming, actual to potential, the principles of economics, and those of politics—correspond point by point to comparable ones in Greco-Roman philosophy, particularly in Aristotle's tradition. This stress on proper order and right rule and the formulation of a philosophy, politics, and economics within the principles of natural history set forth by Aristotle explains why the Mishnah makes a statement to be classified as philosophy, concerning the order of the natural world in its correspondence with the supernatural world.

The Mishnah's system focused upon the holiness of the life of Israel, the people, a holiness that had formerly centered on the Temple. The logically consequent question was, "What is the meaning of sanctity, and how shall Israel attain, or give evidence of, sanctification?" The answer to this question derived from the original creation, the end of the Temple directing attention to the beginning of the natural world that the Temple had embodied. For the meaning of sanctity the framers therefore turned to that first act of sanctification, the one in creation. Sanctification came about when, all things in array, in place, each with its proper name, God blessed and sanctified the seventh day on the eve of the first SABBATH. Therefore, to receive the blessing and to be made holy, all things in nature and society must be set in right array. Given the condition of Israel, the people, in its land during the aftermath of the catastrophic war against Rome led by BAR KOKHBA in 132–135 CE, putting things in order was no easy task. The condition of society corresponded to the critical question that obsessed the system builders.

To show how the Mishnah takes its place within the TORAH of Sinai, its authorities portrayed it as the result of a process of memorization and oral transmission from Sinai. The principal figures in the span from ancient times to their own day thus take their positions on a list of the sages in that chain of tradition: "Moses received Torah at Sinai and handed it on to JOSHUA," and the list of links in the chain ends with such well-known sages of the Mishnah as HILLEL and Shammai, founders of influential houses, or schools, of legal study such as GAMALIEL I, his son Simeon ben Gamaliel, and Yohanan ben Zakkai and his disciples and continuators, Eliezer and Joshua, and so to the framers of the Mishnah itself. The Mishnah therefore is represented as the recapitulation of ORAL TRADITIONS of Sinai, ultimately given permanent form in that document and its supplement, the TOSEFTA.

MISHNE TORAH \mēsh-'ne-tō-'rä\, extensive commentary on the TALMUD, composed in the 12th century by MOSES MAIMONIDES. In 14 volumes it deals with ethical conduct, civil laws, torts, marriage and divorce, and gifts to the poor.

Maimonides attempted to make the Mishne Torah accessible to as many readers as possible and intended it to combine religious law and philosophy in a way that would teach as well as prescribe conduct. Readers are encouraged to probe into the rationale underlying the laws. Like the

Talmud that is its base, the Mishne Torah contains instruction in secular subjects, such as physics, astronomy, dietetics, and psychology.

MISSION, in CHRISTIANITY, organized effort for the propagation of the Christian faith.

During the early years, Christianity expanded through the communities of the Jewish dispersion. PAUL, the prototype of all missionaries, undertook a series of journeys to evangelize much of Asia Minor and the chief Greek cities and was also active in Rome. Because of his work and that of other missionaries, the new religion spread rapidly along the trade routes of the Roman Empire. By about 500 CE the population of the Roman Empire was predominantly Christian.

The advance of Christianity slowed after 500 as the Roman Empire, with which it had become identified, began to disintegrate. In the 7th and 8th centuries, Arab invasions established ISLAM as the dominant religion in about half the area in which Christianity had been dominant. During this time, however, Celtic and British missionaries spread Christianity in western and northern Europe, while missionaries of the Greek church in Constantinople worked in eastern Europe and Russia. From about 950 to 1350 the conversion of Europe and Russia was completed. Missions to Islamic areas and to the Orient were begun.

The ROMAN CATHOLIC church, reformed and revitalized after the COUNCIL OF TRENT (1545–63), sent missionaries into the newly discovered and conquered territories of three Catholic empires: Spain, Portugal, and France. As a result, Christianity was established in Central and South America, in the Caribbean, and in the Philippines. JESUITS established missions in Japan, China, and India. Central direction to the whole vast enterprise was provided by the establishment at Rome in 1622 of the Congregation for the Propagation of the Faith. A radical new direction was given to the missions by the SECOND VATICAN COUNCIL (1962–65): missions were to be directed only to non-Christians; and, although the aim of conversion was not disavowed, the main approach was to be through dialogue.

The Protestant churches did not undertake foreign missions until the Protestant nations acquired colonies from the 16th to the 19th century. A great upsurge of Protestant mission activity developed in the 19th and early 20th centuries, and most denominations established official organizations for missions. Early missionary activities of the various denominations were often very competitive and even disruptive, but eventually a cooperative spirit developed that helped lead to the ecumenical movement. By the mid-20th century, as former colonies won independence, the new states sharply restricted mission activities, often forbidding such efforts as conversions and permitting only nonproselytizing educational and medical service.

Mithra slaying the bull, bas-relief, 2nd century CE; in the Städtisches Museum, Wiesbaden, Ger.
Bavaria-Verlag

MITHRA \mē-'trȧ, -'thrȧ; 'mith-rə\, *also spelled* Mithras, Sanskrit Mitra, in ancient Indo-Iranian mythology, god of light and protector of OATHS, whose cult spread from India in the east to as far west as Spain, Great Britain, and Germany. The first written mention of the Vedic MITRA dates to 1400 BCE. His worship spread to Persia and, after the defeat of the Persians by Alexander the Great, throughout the Hellenic world. In the 3rd and 4th centuries CE, the cult of Mithra, carried and supported by the soldiers of the Roman Empire, was the chief rival to early CHRISTIANITY. In 307 Diocletian consecrated a temple on the Danube River to Mithra, "Protector of the Empire."

MITHRAISM \'mith-rə-ˌi-zəm, -rā-\, worship of MITHRA, the Iranian god of the sun, justice, contract, and war in pre-Zoroastrian Iran. After the acceptance of CHRISTIANITY by the emperor CONSTANTINE in the early 4th century, Mithraism rapidly declined.

Before ZOROASTER (6th century BCE or earlier), the Iranians had a polytheistic religion, and Mithra was the most important of their gods. He was the god of contract and mutual obligation, and in some Indian Vedic texts the god MITRA (the Indo-Aryan cognate of Mithra) appears as a common noun meaning both "friend" and "contract." In short, Mithra, called the Mediator, may signify any kind of communication between people and whatever establishes good relations between them. Mithra was also the god of the sun that beholds everything, and, hence, was invoked in OATHS. The Greeks and Romans considered Mithra a sun god. He was the god of mutual obligation between the king and his warriors, and, hence, the god of war. He was also the god of justice, which was guaranteed by the king.

The most important Mithraic ceremony was the sacrifice of a bull. In an Indian text Mitra reluctantly participates in the sacrifice of a god named Soma, who often appears in the shape of a white bull or of the moon. On the Roman monuments, Mithra sacrifices the white bull, who is then transformed into the moon. In the Achaemenid period, however, Zoroastrian abhorrence of sacrifice had come to predominate, and the sacrifice of the bull is never mentioned.

The worship of Mithra in Persia disappears after Alexander the Great conquered the Persian Empire about 330 BCE, but the kings and nobles of the border region between the Greco-Roman and the Iranian world still worshiped him, as did the kings of Commagene (southeast of Turkey). From 136 CE onward, there are hundreds of dedicatory inscriptions to Mithra in the Roman Empire. Roman Mithraism seems to have been encouraged by the emperors, especially Commodus (180–192), Septimius Severus (193–211), and Caracalla (211–217). Most adherents of Mithra known from inscriptions are soldiers, officials in the service of the emperor, imperial slaves, and freedmen.

In 307 CE, in a dedication from Carnuntum (at the Danube, near Vienna), Diocletian and his colleagues dedicated an altar to Mithra, as the patron of their empire (*fautori imperii sui*). But after 312, when the Christian convert Constantine ascended the throne, the dedications to Mithra ceased, even though there was no immediate public interdiction of Mithraic ceremonies.

Mithraic mythology is not known but may be reconstructed along the following lines. The sun god sent his messenger, the raven, to Mithra and ordered him to sacrifice the bull. Mithra executed the order reluctantly; in many reliefs he is seen turning aside his face in sorrow. But at the very moment of the death of the bull, it was metamorphosed into the moon; the cloak of Mithra was transformed into the sky and stars; from the tail of the bull and from his blood sprang the first ears of grain and the grape; from the genitals of the animal ran the holy seed into a mixing bowl. Every creature on earth was shaped with an admixture of the holy seed. With the bull's death and the creation of the world, the struggle between GOOD AND EVIL began. The four elements (air, fire, earth, and water) came into being, and from them all things were created. After the sacrifice, Mithra and the sun god banqueted together. Then Mithra mounted the chariot of the sun god and drove with him across the ocean, through the air to the end of the world.

MITNAGGED \\,mēt-nä-'ged\\ (Hebrew: Opponent), *plural* Mitnaggedim \\,mēt-nä-gə-'dēm\\, member of a group of tradition-minded Jews who vigorously opposed the 18th-century Hasidic movement (*see* HASIDISM). Under the leadership of ELIJAH BEN SOLOMON, called the Vilna Gaon, the Mitnaggedim excommunicated all Hasidic groups from Orthodox Jewish communities, accusing them of espousing PANTHEISM and severely criticizing them for establishing independent SYNAGOGUES with Sephardic liturgy. The Mitnaggedim were further incensed that Hasidic religious leaders (zaddikim) were looked upon as mediators between man and God and that undue emphasis on religious emotionalism undermined the traditional authority of the RABBIS by downgrading serious study of the TORAH. The controversy subsided in the 19th century.

MITRA \\'mi-trə\\, in the pantheon of Vedic HINDUISM, one of the gods in the category of Ādityas, or sovereign principles of the universe.

Mitra represents friendship, integrity, harmony, and all else that is important in the successful maintenance of order in human existence. He is usually paired with the god VARUṆA, the guardian of the cosmic order, whose powers he complements. As spirit of the day he is sometimes attributed with solar characteristics.

MITZVAH \\mēts-'vä, 'mits-və\\ (Hebrew: "commandment"), *plural* mitzvot, any commandment, ordinance, law, or statute contained in the TORAH and, for that reason, to be observed by all practicing Jews.

The TALMUD mentions 613 mitzvahs, 248 mandatory (*mitzwot 'ase*) and 365 prohibitive (*mitzwot lo ta'ase*). Many more have been added on the authority of outstanding rabbinical leaders, such as reciting the HALLEL (specific psalms) at prescribed times, reading the Book of Esther on PURIM, and lighting candles on certain festivals. Not all mitzvahs are of equal importance; CIRCUMCISION, for instance, is a direct response to a divine command, while the wearing of a skullcap (yarmulke) in public is not. In a broader context, all good deeds are the fulfillment of mitzvahs, for such actions express God's will.

MJOLLNIR \\'myœl-nir, 'myôl-\\, *Old Norse* Mjöllnir, in GERMANIC RELIGION, the hammer of the god THOR and the symbol of his power. Thor used the hammer, forged by dwarfs, as a weapon and as an instrument to hallow people and things. Mjollnir was stolen by the giant THRYM, who asked as ransom the hand of the goddess FREYJA. When Freyja refused to go to Thrym, Thor masqueraded as her and succeeded in grabbing the hammer, which had been brought out to consecrate him as Thrym's bride. Thor then slaughtered Thrym and the other giants with the hammer.

MLECCHA \\'mlā-chə, mə-'lā-\\ (Sanskrit: "babbler"), people of foreign extraction. In ancient India, the term was used by the ARYANS to indicate the uncouth and incomprehensible speech of foreigners; it later extended to their unfamiliar behavior. As a *mleccha*, any foreigner stood completely outside the CASTE system and the ritual ambience. Thus, historically, contact with them was viewed by caste Hindus as polluting.

MNEMOSYNE \\ni-'mä-sə-,nē, -zə-\\, in GREEK RELIGION, goddess of memory. She was the daughter of OURANUS and GAEA and, according to Hesiod, the mother (by ZEUS) of the nine MUSES. After the Olympians defeated the TITANS, they asked Zeus to create divinities who were capable of celebrating their victory. Zeus then went to Pieria and slept with Mnemosyne nine consecutive nights, after which she gave birth to the Muses.

MNEVIS \\'mne-vis\\, *also called* Menuis \\'men-wis\\, in ancient EGYPTIAN RELIGION, sacred bull deity worshiped at HELIOPOLIS. As one of several sacred bulls in Egypt, he was most closely associated with the sun god Re-Atum. Although not attested until later, the cult of Mnevis probably dated to the 1st dynasty (*c.* 2925–*c.* 2775 BCE), if not earlier. The Mnevis bull was either black or piebald in color, and in sculptures and paintings he was represented with a solar disc between his horns.

MOABITE \\'mō-ə-,bīt\\, member of a West-Semitic people who lived in the highlands east of the Dead Sea (now in west-central Jordan) and flourished in the 9th century BCE. The Moabites' culture is dated from about the late 14th century BCE to 582 BCE, when, according to the Jewish historian FLAVIUS JOSEPHUS (1st century CE), they were conquered by the Babylonians. The Moabite language differed only dialectally from Hebrew, and Moabite culture and religion (centered around the god CHEMOSH) were very closely related to those of the Israelites.

In OLD TESTAMENT accounts (*e.g.*, GENESIS 19:30–38), the Moabites' ancestral founder was Moab, a son of Lot, who was a nephew of ABRAHAM. The Moabites were in conflict with the Israelites from the 13th century. King SAUL of Israel in the 11th century fought against the Moabites (1 Samuel 14:47), who later granted asylum to the family of the young rebel and future king DAVID (1 Samuel 22:3–4). David in turn fought against the Moabites and forced them to pay tribute (2 Samuel 8:2). David's great-grandmother, Ruth, was a Moabite (Ruth 4:17–22), and his son SOLOMON obtained Moabite princesses for his harem (1 Kings 11:1–8) and erected near Jerusalem a shrine dedicated to Chemosh.

King Omri of Israel (reigned *c.* 884–*c.* 872 BCE), who is mentioned in 1 Kings 16:23–28, reconquered Moabite lands that had been lost since Solomon's death in 922 BCE. Omri's reconquest is known from the Moabite Stone, a stela that the Moabite king Mesha (fl. *c.* 870 BCE) erected about 40 years later in the city of Dibon (modern Dhiban, Jordan). The stone's text of 34 lines, written in a Canaanite alphabet similar to contemporary Hebrew, ascribes the renewed Israelite domination over Moab to the anger of Chemosh. Mesha then describes his own successful rebellion against Israel, which probably occurred during the reign of Omri's successor, AHAB. Moab was a tributary of Assyria by the late 8th century BCE, and after their conquest by the Babylonians the Moabites disappeared from history.

MODERNISM, in ROMAN CATHOLIC church history, movement in the last decade of the 19th century and first decade of the 20th that sought to reinterpret traditional Catholic teaching in the light of 19th-century philosophical, historical, and psychological theories and called for freedom of conscience. Influenced by non-Catholic biblical scholars, Modernists contended that the writers of both the Old and the New Testaments were conditioned by the times in which they lived and that there had been an evolution in the history of biblical religion. Modernism also reflected a reaction against the increasing centralization of church authority in the POPE and the papal bureaucracy.

In France the movement was closely associated with the writings of Alfred Firmin Loisy, who was dismissed in 1893 from his teaching position at the Institut Catholique in Paris for his views about the OLD TESTAMENT canon. These views, later expressed in *La Religion d'Israel* (1900; "The Religion of Israel"), and his theories on the Gospels in *Études évangéliques* (1902; "Studies in the Gospels") were both condemned by François Cardinal Richard, the archbishop of Paris. In England George Tyrrell, an Irish-born JESUIT priest, was dismissed from his teaching post and from the Jesuits for his views on PAPAL INFALLIBILITY and for a doctrine that minimized the intellectual element of revelation and thus seemed to contradict the teachings of the FIRST VATICAN COUNCIL (1869–70). In Italy and Germany the writings of Loisy and Tyrrell meshed with widespread concern with reform of church institutions.

The reaction of Rome included the suspension or EXCOMMUNICATION of certain priests and scholars who were associated with the movement, the placement of books on the INDEX OF FORBIDDEN BOOKS, the establishment in 1903 by Pope LEO XIII of the Pontifical Biblical Commission to monitor the work of SCRIPTURE scholars, and the formal condemnation in 1907 in the papal ENCYCLICAL *Pascendi Dominici Gregis* and the decree *Lamentabili Sane Exitu* of the Roman Curia's Holy Office. In order to ensure enforcement, the priest-scholar Umberto Benigni organized, through personal contacts with theologians, a nonofficial group of censors who would report to him those thought to be teaching

Moabite storm god, basalt relief, c. 1100 BCE; in the Louvre, Paris
The Bridgeman Art Library International, Ltd.

condemned doctrine. This group, known as Integralists (or *Sodalitium Pianum*, "Solidarity of Pius"), frequently employed overzealous and clandestine methods and hindered rather than helped the combating of Modernism. On June 29, 1908, Pius X publicly admitted that Modernism was a dead issue, but at the urging of Benigni on Sept. 1, 1910, he issued *Sacrorum Antistitum*, which prescribed that all teachers in seminaries and clerics before their ORDINATION take an OATH denouncing Modernism.

MODERNIZATION, term used to describe changes in a society usually attributed to industrialization, economic growth, social mobility, literacy, national unification, and popular vote. In the West, the concept is usually related to the historical development of the Industrial Revolution.

The publications of Sir Henry Maine (1822–88), Ferdinand Tönnies (1855–1936), and MAX WEBER (1864–1920) are often thought of as basic to understanding the process of modernization as a social system based on rational choice, self-interest, and the concept of individualism. Many scholars view the modernization process as synonymous with rationality (a means/end calculation), secularization, and the decline of religion. Thus, religion is often viewed as the opposite of or an obstacle to modernization, both in religious belief and practice. Critical evaluations of the term have led many scholars to challenge the evolutionary model that is built into the theory while others have challenged the ethnocentric Western assumptions of this theory. The rise of modern religious movements, for example, seems to challenge the notion that modernization inevitably leads to secularization.

MO'ED \mō-'ād\ (Hebrew: "Festival"), second of the six major divisions, or orders (SEDARIM), of the MISHNAH, which was completed early in the 3rd century CE by JUDAH HA-NASI. *Mo'ed* deals with the observance of major and minor religious holidays and consists of 12 tractates: *Shabbat* ("Sabbath"), *'Eruvin* ("Blendings"), *Pesaḥim* ("Paschal Lambs"), *Sheqalim* ("Shekels"), *Yoma* ("The Day"; *i.e.*, YOM KIPPUR), *Sukka* ("Booth"), *Betza* ("Egg"), *Rosh Hashanah* ("New Year"), *Ta'anit* ("Fast"), *Megilla* ("Scroll"), *Mo'ed qatan* ("Minor Festival"), and *Ḥagiga* ("Festival Offering"). The TALMUD YERUSHALMI has GEMARA on all 12 tractates; the Talmud BAVLI on all but *Sheqalim*.

MOGGALIPUTTATISSA \'mò-gə-lē-,pù-tə-'ti-sə\, president of the third Buddhist council (*c.* 250 BCE) and author of the *Kathāvatthu* ("Points of Controversy"). Included among the Pāli Abhidamma Piṭaka, the *Kathāvatthu* is a series of questions from a non-THERAVĀDA point of view, with their implications refuted in the answers; the long first chapter debates the existence of a soul. Moggaliputtatissa is credited with ordaining AŚOKA'S son Mahinda into the SANGHA (community of believers) and with bringing some organization to Buddhist missions sent to regions adjacent to India following the third council. He is said to have died at the age of 80 in the 26th year of Aśoka's reign.

MOGILA, PETER \mà-'gē-lə\, *Romanian* Petru Movilă, *Ukrainian* Petro Mohyla (b. Dec. 21, 1596, Moldavia [now in Romania]—d. Dec. 22, 1646, Kiev, Pol. [now in Ukraine]), Moldavian Orthodox monk, theologian, and METROPOLITAN of Kiev who was the author of the *Orthodox*

Confession of the Catholic and Apostolic Eastern Church.

Of royal Moldavian lineage, Mogila migrated to the Polish Ukraine; he was educated in JESUIT schools in Poland. He entered the famous Monastery of the Caves at Kiev in 1625 and was made its superior in 1627. In 1633 he was elected metropolitan of Kiev. As metropolitan, Mogila sought to improve the education of his clergy and laity at a time when both ROMAN CATHOLIC and PROTESTANT missionaries were very active among the Orthodox population of Poland and Ukraine. In 1633 he transformed the theological college of the Kiev monastery into a school of humanities and theology and enlisted a Western-trained faculty for it. The academy became the source of a theological revival in the entire Russian Orthodox church, and its influence was felt in Russia until the end of the 19th century. Mogila also obtained the Polish monarch's acknowledgment of the rights of the Orthodox church in Polish territory.

To bring order to Orthodox theology in its two-fronted controversy with the Roman church and with Protestant Reformers, Mogila in 1640 composed *The Orthodox Confession of Faith* of the Eastern Orthodox church. It was approved by the four Eastern PATRIARCHS and was formally approved at the SYNOD of Jerusalem in 1672. It remains one of the primary outlines of the doctrines of EASTERN ORTHODOXY.

MOKOŠ \\'mō-kŏsh, mō-'kŏsh\\, *also spelled* Mokosh, goddess of life-giving in ancient Slavic mythology. She is the only female deity mentioned in the Old Kievan pantheon of 980 CE and has survived in East Slavic folk beliefs as Mokoša, or Mokuša. A tall woman with a large head and long arms, she spins flax and wool at night and shears sheep. Her name is connected with spinning, plaiting, and moisture. Such associations suggest early European roots: the Great Goddess or Fate, the spinner of life's thread, dispenser of life's water.

MOKṢA \\'mōk-shə\\, *also spelled* moksha, *also called* mukti, *or* apavarga (Sanskrit: "release"), in HINDUISM and JAINISM, ultimate spiritual goal, designating the individual soul's release from the bonds (*bandha*) of transmigration. The soul remains trapped in a chain of successive rebirths (SAMṢĀRA) until it has reached perfection or the enlightenment that allows it release. Most schools consider *mokṣa* to be a person's highest purpose in life.

MOLCHO, SOLOMON \\'mŏl-kō\\, *original name* Diogo Pires \\'pē-rish\\ (b. *c.* 1500, Portugal—d. 1532, Mantua [Italy]), martyr who announced the MESSIAH.

Born to Marrano parents (Portuguese or Spanish Jews forced to become Christians), Pires was royal secretary in a Portuguese high court of justice when an Arabian adventurer, DAVID REUBENI, arrived in Portugal. Pires became possessed by mystic visions and was convinced that Reubeni was an augur of the Jewish messiah. Reubeni, claiming to be the brother of an Arabian Jewish king, had asked the Portuguese king to arm a Jewish army that would drive the Turks out of Palestine.

Pires circumcised himself, took the name Solomon Molcho, and approached Reubeni but was rebuffed. Molcho went to Salonika, Tur., where he joined a circle of Qabbalists. He began to preach that the messiah would arise in 1540 and published several sermons. After dwelling for a time in Palestine, he went to Rome (1529) where, preaching at the great SYNAGOGUE, he accurately predicted a flood in Rome (1530) and an earthquake in Portugal (1531).

In the meantime, Reubeni had come to Rome and joined

forces with Molcho. In 1532 they went to Regensburg, Ger., to persuade Emperor Charles V to arm the Marranos against the Turks. Charles imprisoned them and turned them over to the INQUISITION in Mantua. Given the choice of returning to CHRISTIANITY, Molcho refused and was burned at the stake. Reubeni died in prison, probably poisoned.

MOLINOS, MIGUEL DE \\mō-'lē-nōs\\ (b. June 29, 1628, Muniesa, Spain—d. Dec. 28, 1696, Rome, Papal States [Italy]), Spanish priest condemned for advocating an extreme form of QUIETISM.

Ordained in 1652, Molinos in 1663 was sent to Rome. There, in 1675, he published his *Spiritual Guide,* a small handbook teaching that Christian perfection is achieved by a mixture of contemplation and divine assistance. Molinos believed that humans must banish their individual wills so that God's will can work unhampered within them.

The *Guide* caused a sensation; but in 1685, at the height of Molinos' influence and when his friend Innocent XI was pope, Molinos was arrested by the papal police, tried, and sentenced to life imprisonment for HERESY. Some 20,000 of his letters were examined, and he and numerous witnesses were interrogated, resulting in the condemnation (1687) by Innocent of 68 propositions embodying Molinos' doctrine.

MOLOCH \\'mō-,lŏk, -,läk; 'mä-lək\\, *also spelled* Molech \\'mō-,lek, -,lek\\, Middle Eastern deity, mentioned in the OLD TESTAMENT, to whom child sacrifices were made. The name derives from combining the consonants of the Hebrew *melech* ("king") with the vowels of *boshet* ("shame"), the latter often being used in the Old Testament as a variant name for the god BAAL.

Old Testament writers state that kings AHAZ (2 Kings 16:3) and MANASSEH (2 Kings 21:6), who both reigned after SOLOMON, having been influenced by the Assyrians, worshiped Moloch at the hilled site of Topheth, outside the walls of Jerusalem. This site flourished under Manasseh's son King Amon but was destroyed during the reign of JOSIAH, the reformer. "And he defiled Topheth, which is in the valley of the sons of Hinnom, that no one might burn his son or his daughter as an offering to Moloch" (2 Kings 23:10).

The Mosaic Law expressly stated, "You shall not give any of your children to devote them by fire to Moloch, and so profane the name of your God" (Leviticus 18:21). Contemporary scholars now debate whether the Hebrews did initiate their children to Moloch by fire or whether the law is a prohibition against the possibility that they might take up this custom. Some archaeologists and biblical historians question the existence of a cult worshiping a deity of the name Moloch, believing this deity to be a creation of the Old Testament authors.

MONARCHIANISM \\mō-'när-kē-ə-,ni-zəm, mə-\\, Christian HERESY that developed during the 2nd and 3rd centuries. It opposed the doctrine of an independent, personal subsistence of the LOGOS, affirmed the sole deity of God the Father, and thus represented the extreme monotheistic view. Though it regarded Christ as Redeemer, it clung to the numerical unity of the Deity. Two types of Monarchianism developed: the Dynamic (or Adoptionist; *see* ADOPTIONISM) and the Modalistic (or Sabellian).

Dynamic Monarchianism held that Christ was merely human, miraculously conceived, but constituted the Son of God simply by the degree in which he had been filled with divine wisdom and power. This view was taught at Rome about the end of the 2nd century by Theodotus, who was excommunicated by Pope Victor, and taught somewhat later by Artemon, who was excommunicated by Pope Zephyrinus. About 260 it was again taught by Paul of Samosata. It is the belief of many modern Unitarians.

Modalistic Monarchianism maintained that the names Father and Son were only different designations of the same subject, the one God, who "with reference to the relations in which He had previously stood to the world is called the Father, but in reference to His appearance in humanity is called the Son." It was taught by Praxeas, a priest from Asia Minor, in Rome c. 206 and was opposed by TERTULLIAN in the tract *Adversus Praxean* (c. 213), an important contribution to the doctrine of the TRINITY.

MONASTICISM, institutionalized religious movement whose members attempt to practice works that are above and beyond those required of both the laity and the leadership of their religions. Generally celibate and universally ascetic, the monastic individual separates himself or herself from general society either by living as a HERMIT or anchorite (religious recluse) or by joining a society of others who profess similar intentions. Although first applied to Christian groups, the term monasticism is now used to denote similar, though not identical, practices in such religions as BUDDHISM, HINDUISM, JAINISM, and TAOISM.

Christian monasticism. The earliest Christian monastic communities were founded in the deserts of Egypt. The tradition of the Desert Fathers is best represented by the hermit ST. ANTHONY OF EGYPT (c. 250–355?), who organized his followers into primitive monastic communities early in the 4th century. These Egyptian monks and holy women led lives of extreme ASCETICISM, renouncing family ties, sexual relations, and possessions and practicing continual prayer. The goal of this way of life was the achievement of personal salvation or union with God through a constant spiritual battle with temptation. ST. BASIL THE GREAT (c. 329–379), with his sister Macrina the Younger (327–379), founded two communities on their family estate in Cappadocia, one for men and one for women. Basil espoused a less severe, though still strict, ascetic life in a community headed by an ABBESS or ABBOT, dedicated to service to society rather than complete withdrawal from it.

A Buddhist monk's head is shaved before he enters the monastery
Arthur Tress—Photo Researchers

Monasticism spread quickly throughout the Byzantine Empire in the 4th through the 7th century and was established in Kiev in 1050 and in Moscow by 1354. Organized monastic life was slower to move westward into Europe. When it did arrive in the West in the 5th century, it was adopted in a modified form by ST. AUGUSTINE of Hippo and others as a way of life for the clerics of the bishop's household and the orders of female virgins. Egyptian ascetic discipline was followed more closely by numerous individual ascetics and hermits in Gaul, where it found a focus and

leader in ST. MARTIN, bishop of Tours (c. 316–397). From his monastic complex of Marmoutier, evangelists went out in every direction. In particular, Gallic monasticism took root in Ireland, where it developed a high literary culture and colonized the western isles and the Celtic fringe of Britain.

The greatest legislator of Latin monasticism was ST. BENEDICT of Nursia (c. 480–c. 547), who composed a rule for his monks at Monte Cassino in Italy which sets forth the pre-eminence of the cenobitic form of monasticism, the authority of the abbot, moderation of ascetic practices, and the importance of the divine office (services of prayers and HYMNS) scheduled throughout the day and night. BENEDICTINE monks and nuns, as those who followed St. Benedict's rule came to be called, made three vows upon entrance into the monastery: obedience, stability within that monastery, and *conversio*, a change of habit. Traditionally understood as part of *conversio* are the vows of poverty and chastity. The rule gradually supplanted other rules.

Throughout the Middle Ages monasticism played vital roles in society: the propagation of CHRISTIANITY, the development of the authority of the Roman bishop, and the conservation and augmentation of learning. In its most prosperous years monasticism was a powerful economic and cultural force. Upon the founding of the MENDICANT orders (DOMINICANS and FRANCISCANS) and the flowering of the universities in the 13th century, traditional monasticism began to decline in cultural importance. A revival of interest in monasticism in the 19th century led to the establishment of numerous Roman Catholic, Eastern Orthodox, Anglican, and some Protestant communities, as well as ecumenical groups such as the Taizé community in France.

Eastern religions. In the Eastern religions the earliest type of monk was probably the solitary or hermit. *Śramaṇa*s (Sanskrit: "recluse") may already have existed before c. 1500 BCE in some of the earliest proto-Dravidian or pre-Aryan settlements in India. In early Hindu times (c. 600–200 BCE) there were hermits who lived in groups (ASHRAMS) although they did not lead a strictly organized communal life. In Jainism, perhaps the first religion that can properly be said to have had an organized monastic life, monasticism seems to have evolved from the communities of ashrams. MAHĀVĪRA, its reputed founder, organized his followers into groups of monks and nuns, who were fully professed, and laity, who saw to their needs and kept a less rigorous rule. Later the Jains split into two sects, and one of these, the DIGAMBARAS, disallowed nuns.

In Buddhism the ascetic community is called the SANGHA. Buddhists generally observe a moderate rule, avoiding the two extremes of self-indulgence and self-immolation. Like the Jains, the Buddhists ignore CASTE distinctions. Originally monks and laity were closely associated, a tradition which has continued in the THERAVĀDA Buddhist countries of Southeast Asia. The number of Buddhist nuns has never been large; indeed, the BUDDHA GOTAMA is said to have been very reluctant to allow women to form communities, but many joined them anyway. They lived apart from the monks and were always considered inferior to them. The ZEN Buddhist movement attempted a return to the original austerity of early monastic communities, stressing frugality of diet, simplicity of dress, and the duty of monastics to work as well as to meditate. *See also* CENOBITIC MONASTICISM; IDIORRHYTHMIC MONASTICISM.

MONGKUT \,mȯŋ-'küt\, *also called* Phrachomklao \,prä-,kȯm-'klaủ\, *posthumous name* Rama IV \'rä-mä\ (b. Oct. 18, 1804, Bangkok, Siam [now Thailand]—d. Oct. 15, 1868, Bangkok), king of Siam (1851–68) who opened his country to Western influence and initiated reforms and modern development.

Mongkut's father, King Rama II, died in 1824, and when his half brother was selected to reign as King Phranangklao (Rama III) Mongkut became a Buddhist monk. He became an accomplished scholar and ABBOT of a Bangkok monastery, which he made a center of intellectual discourse. The reformed BUDDHISM that Mongkut developed gradually grew into the Thammayut order, which to the present day is at the intellectual center of Thai Buddhism.

Mongkut succeeded to the throne when King Rama III died in 1851 and set about establishing closer relations with the West. Thai concessions staved off Western imperial pressure for another generation and brought rapid economic development, but Siam had to concede extraterritoriality and limits on its taxing and tariff policies. Mongkut's shrewd foreign policy, coupled with his tolerance and open-mindedness, proved far more effective in dealing with Western imperialists than the xenophobia and isolationism of some of his neighboring rulers. For a time the royal household employed an English governess, Anna Leonowens, whose published reminiscences made Mongkut the model for the king in a 20th-century musical comedy, *The King and I*.

In his own reign Mongkut was unable to achieve fundamental internal reforms, but he took pains to ensure the liberal education of his sons, who in the next generation would begin the MODERNIZATION of Siam.

MONK, man who separates himself from society and lives either alone (a HERMIT or anchorite) or in an organized community in order to devote himself full-time to religious life. *See* MONASTICISM.

MONO NO AWARE \'mō-nō-nō-'ä-wä-,re\ (Japanese: "sensitivity to the sadness of things"), a phrase coined in the late 18th century by MOTOORI NORINAGA. Norinaga felt the phrase summed up the essence of Japanese art and literature, expressing a touching intimation of transience.

MONOPHYSITE \mə-'nä-fə-,sīt\, in CHRISTIANITY, one who believed that JESUS CHRIST'S nature is single and "theanthropic," that is, divine and human, rather than manifesting two distinct natures, divine and human in one person, as asserted at the COUNCIL OF CHALCEDON in 451. In the development of Christian doctrine during the 4th, 5th, and 6th centuries, several divergent traditions had arisen. Chalcedon adopted a decree declaring that Christ was to be "acknowledged in two natures, without being mixed, transmuted, divided, or separated." This formulation was directed in part against the NESTORIAN doctrine that the two natures in Christ had remained separate and in part against the position of the monk Eutyches, who taught that, after

the INCARNATION, Christ had only one nature and that, therefore, the humanity of the incarnate Christ was not of the same substance as that of other men. Political and ecclesiastical rivalries as well as theology played a role in the decision of Chalcedon to depose and excommunicate the PATRIARCH of Alexandria, Dioscorus (d. 454). The church that supported Dioscorus and insisted that his teaching was consistent with the orthodox doctrine of ST. CYRIL of Alexandria was labeled Monophysite. Most modern scholars agree that Severus as well as Dioscorus probably diverged from what was defined as orthodoxy more in their emphasis upon the intimacy of the union between divine and human in Christ than in any denial that the humanity of Christ and that of humanity are consubstantial.

In modern times, those churches usually classified as Monophysite (the Armenian Apostolic, Coptic Orthodox, Ethiopian Orthodox, and Syrian Orthodox) are generally accepted by ROMAN CATHOLICISM, EASTERN ORTHODOXY, and PROTESTANTISM as essentially orthodox in their doctrine of the person of Jesus Christ; and various joint memoranda of agreement to that effect have been issued.

MONOTHEISM, belief in the existence of one god, or in the oneness of God. As such, monotheism is distinguished from POLYTHEISM, the belief in the existence of many gods, and from ATHEISM, or the belief that there is no god. Monotheism characterizes the traditions of JUDAISM, CHRISTIANITY, and ISLAM.

In the three great monotheistic religions, the essence and character of God are believed to be unique and fundamentally different from those of gods found in other religions. God is viewed as the creator of the world and of humanity. Moreover, he has not abandoned his creation but continues to lead it through his power and wisdom. God has created not only the natural world but also the ethical order to which humanity ought to conform. God is holy and is the source of the highest good. Such a monotheistic belief system results in the rejection of all other belief systems as false religions, and this rejection partly explains the exceptionally aggressive or intolerant stance of monotheistic religions throughout history.

Evidence in Hebrew SCRIPTURES indicates that the ancient Israelites practiced monolatry (*i.e.*, the worship of one god without denying the existence of other gods). However, Israel's rejection of other gods makes it more appropriate to label the developed religion of Israel as monotheistic, and thus also the hellenistic and RABBINIC JUDAISM that developed from it. Islamic monotheism is more literal and uncompromising than that of any other religion. ALLĀH is confessed as being one, eternal, unbegotten, unequaled, and beyond partnership of any kind.

The Trinitarian creed of Christianity, on the other hand, sets it apart from the two other traditions. The Christian BIBLE invokes the name of the Father, Son, and HOLY SPIRIT in triadic liturgical formulas; from this the early church, in reflecting upon the reality of God as related to Jesus, developed a theological language about the TRINITY, speaking of three Persons that are one in substance.

MONSIGNOR, *Italian* monsignore, title of honor in the ROMAN CATHOLIC church, borne by persons of ecclesiastic rank. All those who bear the title of monsignor belong to the "papal family" and are entitled to be present in the Cappella Pontificia (when the pope celebrates solemn MASS). The ecclesiastics who have a right to the title of monsignor include PATRIARCHS, archbishops, and bishops.

MONT \'mōnt\, *also spelled* Montu, Monthu \'mōn-tü\, *or* Mentu \'men-tü\, in ancient EGYPTIAN RELIGION, god of the 4th Upper Egyptian *nome* (province), whose original capital of HERMONTHIS (modern Armant) was replaced by Thebes during the 11th dynasty (2081–1939 BCE). Mont was a god of war. In addition to falcons, a bull was his sacred animal; from the 30th dynasty (380–343 BCE), this bull, the BUCHIS bull, received an elaborate cult. Mont was represented as a man with a falcon's head, wearing a crown of two plumes with a double uraeus (rearing cobra) on his forehead. He had important temple complexes at Karnak in Thebes and at Hermonthis, Al-Ṭūd, and Al-Mādamūd.

MONTANISM \'män-tə-ˌni-zəm\, *also called* Cataphrygian heresy, *or* New Prophecy, a heretical movement founded by the prophet MONTANUS that arose in the Christian church in Phrygia, Asia Minor, in the 2nd century. Subsequently it flourished for a time in the West. The chief sources for the history of the movement are EUSEBIUS' *Historia ecclesiastica* (*Ecclesiastical History*), the writings of TERTULLIAN and EPIPHANIUS, and inscriptions, particularly those in central Phrygia.

The essential principle of Montanism was that the Paraclete, the Spirit of truth, was manifesting himself to the world through Montanus and the prophets associated with him. This did not seem at first to deny the doctrines of the church or to attack the authority of the bishops. But Montanists induced a kind of ecstatic intensity and a state of passivity and then maintained that the words they spoke were the voice of the Spirit. It became clear that the claim of Montanus to have the final revelation of the HOLY SPIRIT implied that something could be added to the teaching of JESUS CHRIST and the APOSTLES and that, therefore, the church had to accept a fuller revelation.

Another important aspect of Montanism was the expectation of the SECOND COMING of Christ, which was believed to be imminent. The Montanists believed the heavenly Jerusalem was soon to descend on the earth in a plain between the two villages of Pepuza and Tymion in Phrygia. The prophets and many followers went there to await the arrival of Christ, and many Christian communities were almost abandoned.

In addition to prophetic enthusiasm, Montanism taught a legalistic moral rigorism. The time of fasting was lengthened, followers were forbidden to flee martyrdom, marriage was discouraged, and second marriages prohibited.

After the bishops of Asia Minor excommunicated the Montanists, probably *c.* 177, Montanism became a separate sect with its seat of government at Pepuza. It maintained the ordinary Christian ministry but added to it higher orders of PATRIARCHS and associates who were probably successors of the first Montanist prophets. It continued in the East until severe legislation against Montanism by EMPEROR JUSTINIAN I (reigned 527–565) essentially destroyed it, but remnants evidently survived into the 9th century.

The earliest record of any knowledge of Montanism in the West dates from 177, and 25 years later there was a group of Montanists in Rome. It was in Carthage in Africa, however, that the sect became important. There, its most illustrious convert was Tertullian, who became interested in Montanism *c.* 206 and finally left the CATHOLIC church in 212–213. He primarily supported the moral rigorism of the movement against what he considered the moral laxity of the Catholic bishops. Montanism had almost died out in the 5th and 6th centuries, although some evidence indicates that it survived into the 9th century.

MONTANUS \män-'tā-nəs\ (fl. 2nd century), founder of MONTANISM, a heretical movement of CHRISTIANITY in Asia Minor and North Africa from the 2nd to the 9th centuries.

Little is known about Montanus. Before his conversion to Christianity, he apparently was a priest of the cult of CYBELE. According to the 4th-century church historian EUSEBIUS OF CAESAREA, Montanus *c.* 172–173 began prophesying in the region of Phrygia, now in central Turkey. He became the leader of a group of *illuminati* ("the enlightened"), including the prophetesses Priscilla (or Prisca) and Maximilla. Convinced that the end of the world was at hand, Montanus laid down a rigoristic morality to purify Christians and detach them from their material desires. Official criticism of Montanus and his movement emphasized the new prophecy's unorthodox expression and neglect of the bishops' divinely appointed rule.

MOODY, DWIGHT L(YMAN) \'mü-dē\ (b. Feb. 5, 1837, East Northfield, Mass., U.S.—d. Dec. 22, 1899, Northfield, Mass.), prominent American evangelist who set the pattern for later evangelism in large cities.

Moody left his mother's farm at 17 to work in Boston and there was converted to fundamentalist evangelicalism. In 1856 he moved to Chicago, where he worked with the Young Men's Christian Association (YMCA; 1861–73), was president of the Chicago YMCA, founded the Moody Church, and worked among the poor.

In 1870 he met Ira D. Sankey, a HYMN writer, and with him became noted for contributing to the growth of the "gospel hymn." They made extended evangelical tours in Great Britain (1873–75, 1881–84). Moody deplored divisive sectarian doctrines, "higher criticism" of the BIBLE, the SOCIAL GOSPEL movement, and the theory of evolution. Instead he emphasized a literal interpretation of the Bible and looked toward the premillennial SECOND COMING.

Moody ardently supported various charities but felt that social problems could be solved only by divine regeneration. As well as conducting revivals, he directed annual Bible conferences at Northfield, Mass., where he founded a seminary for girls in 1879. In 1889 he founded the Chicago Bible Institute (now the Moody Bible Institute).

MOON, SUN MYUNG \'mün\ (b. Jan. 6, 1920, Kwangju Sangsa Ri, P'yŏngan-puk province, Korea), evangelist who in 1954 founded the Holy Spirit Association for the Unification of World Christianity, better known as the UNIFICATION CHURCH.

In his book *The Divine Principle* (1952), which is the basic SCRIPTURE of the church, Moon wrote that at the age of 16 he had a vision of JESUS CHRIST in which he was told to carry out Christ's unfinished task. Moon believed that God chose him to save mankind from SATANISM, and he regarded communists as Satan's representatives.

Moon began to preach his doctrines in Korea in 1946. Two years later he was excommunicated by the PRESBYTERIAN church, and shortly thereafter he was imprisoned by North Korean authorities. In 1950 he escaped—or was released—and fled to South Korea, where he founded what was to become the Unification Church. He built his Korean and Japanese enterprises, which included factories that produced armaments, paint, machinery, and ginseng tea, into a multimillion-dollar empire, and in the early 1970s he began full-scale missionary operations in the United States. As young disciples—popularly called Moonies—were drawn into the movement, Moon incurred widespread hostility from their parents, who believed that their children had been unfairly indoctrinated. Other controversies also mounted over the movement's fund-raising techniques, as well as over immigration issues and tax manipulation.

In 1973 Moon and his wife moved their headquarters to Tarrytown, N.Y., operating from there an international network of businesses. In 1981 the Unification Church's bid for U.S. tax-exempt status as a religious organization was denied when an appellate court ruled that the church's primary purpose was political. In 1982 Moon was convicted of tax evasion, sentenced to prison, and fined $25,000. Moon was released in 1985 and returned to Korea in 1988. The church experienced a resurgence in the 1990s, and he was active in Korea, the United States, Eastern Europe, and Russia. In the early 1990s, he undertook a 17-city tour of the United States.

MOON WORSHIP, adoration or veneration of the moon, a deity in the moon, or a personification or symbol of the moon. The cyclical process of disappearance and appearance of the moon is the basis of the widespread association of the moon with the land of the dead, the place to which souls ascend after death, and the power of rebirth.

The mythology of the moon emphasizes especially those periods when it disappears—the three days of darkness in the lunar cycle and eclipses. Both are usually interpreted as the result of battles between some monster who devours or slays the moon and who subsequently regurgitates or revives it. The interregnum is interpreted as an evil period necessitating strict TABOOS against beginning any new or creative period (*e.g.,* planting or sexual intercourse). In some areas loud noises are part of a ritual activity designed to scare off the moon's assailant.

In hunting cultures the moon is frequently regarded as male and, particularly in regard to women, is understood as a preeminently evil or dangerous figure. In agricultural traditions the moon is usually regarded as female and is the benevolent ruler of the cyclical vegetative process.

MOORISH SCIENCE TEMPLE OF AMERICA, religious sect founded by Timothy Drew in Newark, N.J., in 1913. He was believed by his followers to have been ordained Prophet Noble Drew Ali by ALLĀH. A Holy Koran, the sacred text, was created out of his study of Oriental philosophy. The prophet's central teaching was that all Africans were of Moorish, and thus Muslim, origins. He advocated a return to ISLAM as the only means of redemption from racial oppression. Many of the sect's formal practices were derived from Muslim observance, and the group was a forerunner of the Black Muslim movement. Drew died mysteriously during a period of internal strife, and the sect lost its impetus.

MORALITY AND RELIGION, doctrine or system that defines conformity to ideals of right human conduct. Moral

The Reverend Sun Myung Moon blesses 5,000 brides and grooms at a mass marriage ceremony
Bettina Cirone—Photo Researchers

principles often have religious justification, but moral judgment is frequently understood to apply to any area of human conduct; for instance, the ROMAN CATHOLIC church not only prohibits contraception for its members, but by declaring it contrary to "the natural law" the church declares contraception to be universally wrong.

Because of their intimate relation to one another, the religious and the moral have often been conflated. The problem has been intensified by many attempts to interpret religion as essentially morality or merely as an incentive for doing one's duty. Immanuel Kant argued in the *Critique of Practical Reason* (1788) that the existence of God, though not directly provable, is a necessary postulate of the moral life. To take seriously the awareness of a categorical imperative to act rightly is to commit oneself to work for an ideal state of affairs in which perfect goodness and happiness coincide. But as apportioning of happiness to virtue is beyond human power, a divinity capable of bringing it about must be assumed.

Other Christian thinkers, particularly during the 19th and early 20th centuries, have developed the theme that to accept the absolute demands of ethical obligation is to presuppose that this is a morally structured universe; and that this in turn implies a personal God whose commands are reflected in the human conscience. It cannot be proved that this is such a universe, it is said, but it is inevitably assumed in acknowledging the claims of morality.

The basic criticism of all attempts to trace ethical obligation to a transcendent divine source has been that it is possible to account for morality without going beyond the human realm. It is argued that communal life requires agreed codes of behavior, which become internalized in the process of socialization as moral laws; and the natural affection that develops among humans produces the more occasional sense of a call to heroic self-sacrifice on behalf of others. It seems, then, that the moral arguments for divine existence do not rise to the level of strict proofs.

MORAL RE-ARMAMENT: *see* OXFORD MOVEMENT.

MORAVIAN CHURCH, Protestant Christian denomination founded in the 18th century but tracing its origin to the UNITAS FRATRUM ("Unity of Brethren") of the 15th-century HUSSITE movement in Bohemia and Moravia.

During the 16th and 17th centuries the Bohemian Brethren movement survived suppression by the COUNTER-REFORMATION and proscription by the Peace of Westphalia (1648) through the efforts of loyal adherents. The development of German PIETISM in the late 17th century increased the unrest among underground Protestants in nearby Moravia and Bohemia. A group of families adhering to the tradition of the Bohemian Brethren fled Moravia in 1722 and settled on Count Nikolaus Ludwig von Zinzendorf's estate in Saxony, where they founded Herrnhut. The village attracted a stream of exiles from Bohemia and Moravia, as well as Pietists from Germany and beyond.

With the count's help Herrnhut became the mother community of what came to be called the Moravian church and the center for a network of societies on the established Pietist pattern, working for the nurture of spiritual life within the state churches, mostly Lutheran, but also including some Reformed churches. This latter phase of Moravianism in Europe came to be known as the "diaspora," and its members far outnumbered those who belonged to the Moravian church as a denomination. The first diaspora evangelists began their itinerations in 1727, and the first foreign missionaries left Herrnhut to work among African slaves in the West Indies in 1732. Within two decades MISSIONS to Greenland, Suriname, South Africa, Algiers, and among the Native Americans followed.

Herrnhut developed a unique type of community in which civic and church life were integrated into a theocratic society, a prototype for about 20 settlements in Europe and America, including those in Bethlehem, Pa., and Salem [now Winston-Salem], N.C.]. Fellowship groups, daily worship featuring both singing and instrumental music, boarding schools, and concentration on foreign missions and diaspora evangelism characterized these exclusive Moravian villages. They supported themselves and their projects by handicraft industries.

Each of the regional administrative units of the worldwide Moravian church is self-governing through its provincial synod with administration by a provincial elders' conference. All are linked by a general synod of elected representatives, meeting every 10 years, which is authoritative in all matters of doctrine and constitution common to the whole church.

The Moravian church adheres to its original principle of the BIBLE as the only rule of faith and practice, subscribing to both the Apostles' and NICENE CREEDS. Worship is liturgical and follows the traditional church year. German chorales figure prominently in the HYMNS used. Strongly Christocentric, the Moravian church places emphasis upon the sufferings of Christ during HOLY WEEK.

MORE, SIR THOMAS \\'mōr, 'mȯr\\, *also called* Saint Thomas More (b. Feb. 7, 1477, London, Eng.—d. July 6, 1535, London; canonized May 19, 1935; feast day June 22), humanist and statesman, chancellor of England (1529–32), who was beheaded for refusing to accept King Henry VIII as head of the Church of England. He is recognized as a saint by the ROMAN CATHOLIC church.

MORMON, a member of any of several denominations and sects, the largest of which is the CHURCH OF JESUS CHRIST OF LATTER-DAY SAINTS, that trace their origins to a religion founded by JOSEPH SMITH in the United States about 1830. The religion these churches practice is often referred to as Mormonism.

The Church of Jesus Christ of Latter-day Saints, the principal formal body embracing Mormonism, had more than 9,700,000 members in the late 20th century and is headquartered in Salt Lake City, Utah. The next-largest Mormon denomination, the REORGANIZED CHURCH OF JESUS CHRIST OF LATTER DAY SAINTS, is headquartered in Independence, Mo., and had a membership exceeding 250,000 in the late 20th century.

Mormons accept the BIBLE "as far as it is translated correctly." In addition they accept Smith's BOOK OF MORMON, which is largely similar in style and themes to the OLD TES-

TAMENT. Smith's other revealed scriptures were later incorporated into the *Pearl of Great Price*, together with his translation of papyri that he declared to be the *Book of Abraham* and the *Book of Moses*. *Doctrines and Covenants* is a selection of revelations to Smith and one given to BRIGHAM YOUNG.

Mormon doctrine diverges from orthodox CHRISTIANITY, particularly in affirming that God has evolved from man and that men might evolve into gods, that the persons of the TRINITY are distinct beings, and that human souls have preexisted. JUSTIFICATION is by faith and obedience to the ordinances of the church, repentance, BAPTISM by immersion, and laying on of hands for the spirit gifts (including PROPHECY, revelation, and speaking in tongues).

The Mormons believe that faithful members of the church will inherit eternal life as gods, and even those who had rejected God's law would live in glory. Additionally, they believe that the return of Christ to earth will lead to the first RESURRECTION and the MILLENNIUM, the main activity of which will be "temple work," especially baptism on behalf of the dead. After the millennium and second resurrection, the earth will become a celestial sphere and all people will be assigned to the eternal kingdoms.

Mormons eliminate most distinctions between the PRIESTHOOD and laity. At the age of 12, all worthy males become deacons in the AARONIC PRIESTHOOD; they become teachers when 14 years old and priests at the age of 16. About two years later they may enter the MELCHIZEDEK PRIESTHOOD as elders and may be called upon for 18 months of missionary work. A Mormon man may afterward become a "seventy" (a member of a larger priesthood quorum composed of 70 members) and ultimately a HIGH PRIEST in the church's First Quorum of Seventy.

Adult baptism, signifying repentance and obedience, has acquired additional importance as a ritual that may be undertaken by a proxy for the salvation of those who died without knowledge of the truth. The Mormons' interest in genealogy proceeds from their concern to save dead ancestors. Baptism for the dead, endowment, and sealing (which may also be undertaken by proxy for the dead) are secret but essential ceremonies. At endowment, the person is ritually washed, anointed with oil, and dressed in temple garments. Initiates witness a dramatic performance of the story of creation, learn secret passwords and grips, and receive a secret name. The sealing ceremony, which was of special importance in the period when Mormons practiced polygamy, seals men and women in marriage for eternity. Despite prohibitions (on alcohol, tobacco, tea, and coffee) and a vigorous work ethic, Mormonism is not ascetic; recreation, sport, and education are positive values.

In the main Mormon body, the First Presidency (church president and two councillors), the Council of the Twelve, the First Quorum of Seventy, and the presiding bishop and two councillors (who control the Aaronic priesthood) constitute the General Authorities of the church. They are "sustained in office" by the regular and now ritualized vote of confidence of the semiannual General Conference, which is open to all Mormons.

The Reorganized Church of Jesus Christ of Latter Day Saints holds firmly to the *Book of Mormon* but rejects the evolutionary conceptions of deity and the POLYTHEISM implicit in it, the new covenant of celestial marriage, baptism on behalf of the dead, polygamy, and tithing. The *Book of Abraham* is not accepted as of divine origin. The church's presidents continue to be lineal descendants of Smith, beginning with Joseph Smith (1832–1914).

MORMON, BOOK OF, work accepted as holy SCRIPTURE, in addition to the BIBLE, in the CHURCH OF JESUS CHRIST OF LATTER-DAY SAINTS and other Mormon churches. First published in 1830 in Palmyra, N.Y., Mormons hold that it is a divinely inspired work revealed to and translated by the founder of their religion, JOSEPH SMITH.

The Book of Mormon relates the history of a group of Hebrews who migrated from Jerusalem to America about 600 BCE, led by a prophet, Lehi. They eventually split into two groups. One group, the Lamanites, forgot their beliefs and were the ancestors of the American Indians. The other group, the Nephites, developed culturally and built great cities but were eventually destroyed by the Lamanites about 400 CE. Before this occurred, however, JESUS had appeared and taught the Nephites (after his ASCENSION). The history and teachings were abridged and written on golden plates by the prophet Mormon. His son, Moroni, made additions and buried the plates in the ground, where they remained about 1,400 years, until Moroni, a resurrected being or ANGEL, delivered them to Joseph Smith; subsequently Smith returned them to Moroni.

MORPHEUS \\'mȯr-fē-əs, -ˌfyüs\\, in Greco-Roman mythology, one of the sons of HYPNOS (Somnus), the god of sleep. Morpheus sends human shapes (Greek *morphai*) of all kinds to the dreamer, while his brothers Phobetor (or Icelus) and Phantasus send the forms of animals and inanimate things, respectively.

MORTUARY TEMPLE, in ancient Egypt, place of worship of a deceased king and the depository for food and objects offered to the dead monarch. In the Old and Middle Kingdoms (*c.* 2575–*c.* 2130 BCE; and 1938–*c.* 1600? BCE) the mortuary temple usually adjoined the PYRAMID and had an open, pillared court, storerooms, five elongated shrines, and a chapel containing a false door and an offering table. In the chapel, priests performed the daily funerary rites and presented the offerings to the dead king's KA (protective spirit). In the New Kingdom (1539–1075 BCE) the kings were buried in rock-cut tombs, but separate mortuary temples continued to be built nearby.

MOSES \\'mō-zəz, -zəs\\, *Hebrew* Moshe (fl. 14th–13th century BCE), Hebrew prophet, teacher, and leader who delivered his people from Egyptian slavery and founded the religious community known as ISRAEL, based on a COVENANT relationship with God. As the vehicle and interpreter of the Covenant, including the TEN COMMANDMENTS, he exerted a lasting influence on the religious life, moral concerns, and social ethics of Western civilization.

According to the biblical account in EXODUS and Numbers, Moses, a Hebrew foundling adopted and reared in the Egyptian court, somehow learned that he was a Hebrew and killed an Egyptian taskmaster who was beating a Hebrew slave. He fled to Midian (mostly in northwest Arabia),

Moses Showing the Tables of the Law to the People, *oil painting by Rembrandt, 1659*

By courtesy of Staatliche Museen Preussischer Kulturbesitz Gemaldegalerie, Berlin

where he became the shepherd and eventually the son-in-law of a MIDIANITE priest, JETHRO. While tending his flocks he saw a burning bush that remained unconsumed and heard there a call from the God—YAHWEH—of ABRAHAM, ISAAC, and JACOB to deliver his people, the Hebrews, from their bondage in Egypt. Because Moses was a stammerer, his brother AARON was to be his spokesman, but Moses would be Yahweh's representative.

Ramses II (reigned 1279–13 BCE) was probably the pharaoh of Egypt at the time. He rejected the demand of this unknown God and responded by increasing the oppression of the Hebrews. The biblical text states that Moses used plagues sent by Yahweh to bend Ramses' will. Whether the Hebrews were finally permitted to leave Egypt or simply fled is not clear; according to the biblical account, the pharaoh's forces pursued them eastward to the Sea of Reeds, a papyrus lake (not the Red Sea), which the Hebrews crossed safely but in which the Egyptians were engulfed. Moses then led the people to MOUNT SINAI (Horeb) at the southern tip of the Sinai Peninsula. Yahweh appeared to Moses there in a terrific storm, out of which came the Covenant between Yahweh and the people of Israel, including the Ten Commandments; and Moses began issuing ordinances for specific situations, instituted a system of judges and hearings of civil cases.

After leaving Mount Sinai and continuing the journey toward CANAAN Moses faced increasing resistance and frustration and once got so angry at the people that, according to tradition, Yahweh accounted it a lack of faith and denied him entrance into Canaan. As his last official act, Moses renewed the Sinai Covenant with the survivors of the wanderings and then climbed Mount Pisgah to look over the land that he would not enter. The Hebrews never saw him again, and the circumstances of his death and burial remain shrouded in mystery.

Tradition states that Moses wrote the whole PENTATEUCH, but this is untenable. Moses did formulate the Decalogue, mediate the Covenant, and begin the process of rendering and codifying interpretations of the Covenant's stipulations. In a general sense, therefore, the first five books of the Hebrew BIBLE can be described as Mosaic. Without him there would have been no Israel and no collection known as the TORAH.

MOSES DE LEÓN \\'mō-səs-thä-lä-'ōn\\, *original name* Moses ben Shem Tov (b. 1250, León [Spain]—d. 1305, Arevalo), Jewish Qabbalist and presumably the author of the SEFER HA-ZOHAR ("Book of Splendor"), the most important work of Jewish mysticism; its influence among Jews once rivaled that of the OLD TESTAMENT and the TALMUD.

Until 1290 Moses de León lived in Guadalajara (the Spanish center of adherents of the QABBALAH). He then traveled a great deal and finally settled in Ávila. On a trip to Valladolid, he met a Palestinian Qabbalist, Isaac ben Samuel of

Acre; to him Moses confided that he possessed the centuries-old, original manuscript of the *Zohar*, which was ascribed to the 2nd-century Palestinian rabbinic teacher SIMEON BEN YOḤAI. He promised to show it to Isaac, but unfortunately, Moses died before he could fulfill his promise, and Isaac subsequently heard rumors that Moses' wife had denied the existence of this manuscript, claiming rather that Moses himself was the author of the *Zohar*.

The *Zohar* is primarily a series of mystical commentaries on the PENTATEUCH, in manner much like the traditional Midrashim, or homilies based on SCRIPTURE. Against the backdrop of an imaginary Palestine, Simeon ben Yoḥai and his disciples carry on a series of dialogues. In them, it is revealed that God manifested himself in a series of 10 descending emanations, or SEFIROT (*e.g.*, "love" of God, "beauty" of God, and "kingdom" of God). In addition to the influence of NEOPLATONISM, the *Zohar* also shows evidence of the influence of JOSEPH GIKATILLA, a medieval Spanish Qabbalist thought to have been a friend of Moses de León. Gikatilla's work *Ginnat egoz* ("Nut Orchard") provides some of the *Zohar*'s key terminology.

MOSQUE, *Arabic* Masjid, *or* Jāmiʿ, any house or open area of prayer in ISLAM. The two main types of mosques include the *masjid jāmiʿ*, or "collective mosque," a large state-controlled mosque that is the center of community worship and the site of Friday prayer services, and smaller mosques operated by various groups within society.

The first mosques were modeled on the place of worship of the Prophet MUHAMMAD—the courtyard of his house at MEDINA—and were simply plots of ground marked out as sacred. Subsequently the building remained essentially an open space, generally roofed over, with a MINARET sometimes attached to it. Within, the *miḥrāb*, a semicircular niche reserved for the prayer leader (IMAM), points to the QIBLA, the direction of Mecca; the *minbar*, a seat at the top of steps placed at the right of the *miḥrāb*, is used by the preacher (*khaṭīb*) as a pulpit. Occasionally there also is a *maqṣūra*, a box or wooden screen near the *miḥrāb*, which was originally designed to shield a worshiping ruler from assassins. Mats or carpets cover the floor, where the ritual prayer (ṢALĀT) is performed by rows of worshipers, who bow and prostrate themselves under the imam's guidance. Professional chanters (QURRĀʾ) may chant the QURʾAN according to prescribed systems, but no music or singing is allowed. Statues and pictures are also proscribed.

Outside the mosque stands the minaret (*maʾdhana*), originally any elevated place but now usually a tower; it is used by the MUEZZIN ("crier") to proclaim the call to worship (ADHĀN) five times each day. A place for ABLUTION, containing running water, is usually attached to the mosque.

Since the time of the Prophet, mosques have served multiple functions—political, social, and educational, as well as religious. This multifunctionality assumed architectural expression in the great mosques of urban centers. The Ottoman Süleymaniye Mosque in Istanbul, for example, comprises a complex of prayer places, religious colleges (MADRASAS), preparatory schools, a hospital and medical school, a Sufi lodge, a hostel, public bath and fountains, kitchens, residential quarters for employees, bazaar, imperial mausoleums, and a cemetery.

MOT \\ˈmōt\\ (akin to Hebrew *met*, "death"), ancient West Semitic god of death and decay; he was the favorite son of the god EL, and the most prominent enemy of the god BAAL. Mot was the god of sterility and the master of all barren places. Traditionally, Mot and Baal (a god of springs, sky, and fertility) were perpetually engaged in a struggle in which Baal was annually vanquished and slain. Mot, however, was also annually killed by Baal's sister ANATH, who thus aided Baal's return.

MOTHER GODDESS, any of a variety of feminine deities and maternal symbols of creativity, birth, fertility, sexual union, nurturing, and the cycle of growth. There is no culture that has not employed some maternal symbolism in depicting its deities.

Mother goddesses should be distinguished from the EARTH MOTHER, with which they have often been confused. Unlike the mother goddess, the Earth Mother is a cosmogonic figure, with a role in the creation of the universe. In contrast, mother goddesses are individual, possess distinct characters, are young, are not cosmogonic, and are highly sexual. Although the male plays a relatively less important role, mother goddesses are usually part of a divine pair, and their mythology narrates the vicissitudes of the goddess and her (frequently human) consort.

The essential moments in the myth of most mother goddesses are her disappearance and reappearance and the celebration of her divine marriage. Her disappearance has cosmic implications. Sexuality and growth decline. Her reappearance, choice of a male partner, and intercourse with him restore and guarantee fertility, after which the male consort is frequently set aside or sent to the underworld to be replaced the next year.

The other major form of the mother goddess emphasizes her maternity. She is the protector and nourisher of a divine child and, by extension, of all humanity. This form occurs more frequently in iconography—a full-breasted (or many-breasted) figure holding a child—than in myth.

Motoori Norinaga, detail of a self-portrait, 1773
By courtesy of the Museum of Motoori Norinaga, Matsuzaka

MOTOORI NORINAGA \\ˌmȯ-tȯ-ˈȯ-rē-ˌnȯ-rē-ˈnä-gä\\ (b. June 21, 1730, Matsuzaka, Japan—d. Nov. 5, 1801, Matsuzaka), eminent scholar in SHINTŌ and Japanese classics.

Trained as a physician, Motoori came under the influence of the National Learning (KOKUGAKU) movement, which emphasized the importance of Japan's own literature. He applied careful philological methods to the study of the *Koji-ki*, *The Tale of Genji*, and other classical literature and stressed *mono no aware* ("sensitiveness to beauty") as the central concept of Japanese literature. Motoori's study of Japanese classics provided the theoretical foundation of the modern Shintō revival. Rejecting Buddhist and Confucian influence on the interpretation of Shintō, he instead traced Shintō to ancient Japanese myths and traditions. Motoori also reaffirmed the concept of *musubi* (the mysterious power of all creation and growth), which has become one of the main tenets of modern Shintō.

Motoori's 49-volume commentary on the *Koji-ki* (*Koji-ki-den*), completed in 1798, is incorporated in the *Moto-ori Norinaga Zenshū*, 12 vol. (1926–27; "Complete Works of Motoori Norinaga").

MO-TZU \'mō-'dzə\, *Pinyin* Mozi, *original name* Mo Ti, *Latin* Micius \'mi-shē-əs, -shəs\ (b. 470?, BCE, China—d. 391?, China), Chinese philosopher whose fundamental doctrine of universal love challenged CONFUCIANISM for several centuries and became the basis of a religious movement known as Mohism.

Born a few years after Confucius' death, Mo-tzu was raised in a period when China was divided into small, constantly warring, feudal states. He thus confronted the problem that faced all thinkers in 5th-century BCE China: how to bring political and social order out of chaos.

According to tradition, Mo-tzu was originally a follower of the teachings of CONFUCIUS until he became convinced that Confucianism laid too much emphasis on a burdensome code of rituals and too little on religious teaching. Mo-tzu was drawn to the common people and looked back to a life of primitive simplicity and straightforwardness in human relations.

The *Mo-tzu*, the principal work left by Mo-tzu and his followers, contains the essence of his political, ethical, and religious teachings. The gist of it lies in 10 major tenets: exaltation of the virtuous, identification with the superior, universal love, condemnation of offensive war, economy of expenditures, simplicity in funerals, will of heaven, on ghosts, denunciation of music as a wasteful activity, and antifatalism.

The cornerstone of Mo-tzu's system was universal love. If the world is in chaos, he said, it is owing to human selfishness and partiality, and the prescribed cure is that "partiality should be replaced by universality," for, "when everyone regards the states and cities of others as he regards his own, no one will attack the others' state or seize the others' cities." The same principle was to be applied to the welfare of the family and of the individual. The peace of the world and the happiness of humanity lie in the practice of universal love. Mo-tzu demonstrated that this principle had in it both utilitarian justification and divine sanction. He spoke of "universal love and mutual profit" in one breath, and he was convinced that this principle was both the way of humans and the way of God.

Mo-tzu's stand on religion makes him exceptional among Chinese philosophers. His call to the people was for them to return to the faith of their ancestors. The system of Motzu, with its gospel of universal love and the ascetic discipline as exemplified by his own life, soon after the master's death, was embodied in an organized church with a succession of Elder Masters and a considerable body of devotees. The religion prospered for several generations before completely disappearing.

The teachings of Mo-tzu, however, continued to be held in high respect for several centuries. Down to the early 2nd century BCE, writers referred to Confucianism and Mohism in one breath as the two leading schools of thought. But from that time, Mohism suddenly disappeared from the intellectual scene.

MOURNING, formal demonstration of grief at the death of a person. Mourning rites, which are of varying duration and rationale, usually weigh more heavily on women than on men. Mourners may deny themselves certain amusement, ornaments, or food. They may practice sexual continence or keep vigil over the body of the deceased. Changes in garb, such as the wearing of black clothing, and alterations in hairstyle may distinguish mourners, but such evidences of mourning have declined in many societies.

MU-CH'I \'mü-'chē\ (d. later half of 13th century), Chinese painter associated with the Ch'an school. Although Chinese sources ignore his religious activity and affiliation and denounce the quality of his paintings, according to Japanese sources Mu-ch'i was a disciple of the Ch'an master Wu-chun. In addition, Japanese ZEN monks who visited China during Mu-ch'i's lifetime regarded his work highly, and he soon acquired a great reputation abroad. In his painting, iconographic and realistic elements or motifs are stripped away and nature itself is made the object of focus, on par with more traditional religious figures that are being depicted. Elements from the natural world or animals are taken to be signs for ultimate reality on the same level as Buddhas or bodhisattvas. Nature is portrayed not as the mere backdrop in which divinities or other ICONS appear, but rather is the essential basis out of which they grow. Elements of the mundane or grotesque, another feature of his and other Zen paintings, are also treated as signs of true reality, a consequence of the Zen equation of the non-duality of SAṂSĀRA and NIRVANA.

MUDANG \'mü-ˌdäŋ\, in Korean shamanism, priestess who effects cures, tells fortunes, soothes spirits of the dead, and repulses evil.

The principal occasion for the performance of a *mudang* is the KUT, a trance ritual in which singing and dancing are used to invite happiness and repel evil. The *kut* usually comprises 12 *kŏri* (procedures), each of which is addressed to such specific gods or spirits as the god of childbirth, the goddesses in control of specific diseases, one's patron spirit, or the protector god of households. Before the *kut* begins, an altar is set on the floor and offerings are made. As the ritual progresses, the *mudang* goes into a trance during which the god is said to arrive, to be placated, and then to communicate a message to the client through the *mudang*.

Hereditary *mudang*, especially in former times, formed a separate religious group of low social standing and seldom married into families on a higher social level. Daughters of such figures became either *mudang* after proper training, or *kisaeng*, waitresses at Korean drinking houses. Sons usually became singers of *p'ansori*, the one-man opera of Korea, or musicians accompanying rituals.

MUDOR ŠUAN \mü-'dōr-shü-'än, -syü-'än\, ceremony of the Udmurts (Votyaks), a FINNO-UGRIC people living in the Republic of Udmurtiya in west-central Russia. The ceremony was held to consecrate a new family or clan shrine (*kuala*) and a sacred container (VORŠUD) kept on a shelf within the shrine. *Mudor* itself means "ground," thus, the ceremony was the blessing of a new site taken over by people breaking off from the ancestral lineage when it expanded past a critical point. The main ceremony of the *mudor šuan*, or *mudor* "wedding," consisted of taking ashes from the hearth of the ancestral shrine with a formula such as "I am taking the lesser and leaving the greater" and transferring them to the shrine in a new location, which would then stand in a subordinate position in relation to the greater ancestral *kuala*.

MUDRĀ \mủ-ʹdrä\ (Sanskrit: "seal," "mark," or "gesture"), in BUDDHISM and HINDUISM, a symbolic gesture of the hands and fingers used either in ceremonies and dance or in sculpture and painting. *Mudrā*s used in ceremony and dance are numerous and complex (the *hasta-mudrā*s of Hindu classical dance can express about 500 different meanings, involving the hands, fingers, wrists, elbows, and shoulders, all in movement).

In ceremonies, especially in Buddhism, a *mudrā* acts as a visual affirmation of a mystical or magical vow or utterance. A *mudrā* often accompanies the MANTRA, an uttered formula or prayer. Although pictorial *mudrā*s are used most commonly in portraying the BUDDHA, they can also appear in representations of lesser personages. The *añjali* ("reverence") *mudrā*, for example, which has the suppliant or worshiper joining his two hands before him, palm to palm, slightly cupped, in a gesture of respectful adoration, would appear only in representations of deities or persons other than the Buddha.

The hundreds of *mudrā*s of Hindu and other related Asian dances are described in technical manuals, but, in practice, performers usually limit their gestures or "phrases" (sequences of *mudrā*s) to those familiar and meaningful to their audiences. The selection may differ from region to region.

MUEZZIN \mü-ʹe-zin, myü-\, *Arabic* mu'adhdhin, in ISLAM, the official who proclaims the call to prayer (ADHĀN) on Friday for the public worship and the call to the daily prayer (ṢALĀT) five times a day, at dawn, noon, mid-afternoon, sunset, and nightfall. The muezzin stands either at the door or side of a small mosque or on the MINARET (*manāra*) of a large one. He faces each of the four directions in turn: east, west, north, and south. To each direction he cries: "Allāh is most great. I testify that there is no God but ALLĀH. I testify that MUHAMMAD is the prophet of Allāh. Come to prayer. Come to salvation. Allāh is most great. There is no God but Allāh." The Shi'ite muezzin adds, "Come to the best work," after "Come to salvation." Many mosques have installed recordings of the call to prayer, and amplifiers have displaced the muezzin.

MUFTI \ʹməf-tē, ʹmůf-\, *Arabic* muftī, an Islamic legal authority who gives a formal legal opinion (*fatwā*) in answer to an inquiry by a private individual or judge. A *fatwā* usually requires knowledge of the QUR'AN and HADITH, as well as knowledge of EXEGESIS and collected precedents, and might be a pronouncement on some problematic legal matter. Under the Ottoman Empire, the mufti of Con-

stantinople, the SHAYKH al-Islam, ranked as Islam's foremost legal authority, theoretically presiding over the whole judicial and theological hierarchy. The development of civil codes in most Islamic countries, however, has tended to restrict the authority of mufti to cases involving personal status, such as inheritance, marriage, and divorce. In Iran, however, the Shi'ite equivalent to the mufti, the *mujtahid*, has achieved political and religious predominance in the wake of the 1978–79 revolution. *See also* FIQH; IJTIHĀD; KHOMEINI, RUHOLLAH MUSAVI.

MUHAMMAD \mü-ʹk̲am-mȧd, *Angl* mō-ʹha-məd, mü-, -ʹhä-\, *in full* Abū al-Qāsim Muhammad ibn 'Abd Allāh ibn 'Abd al-Muṭṭalib ibn Hāshim, *also known as* the Messenger of God (Rasūl Allāh), *or* the Prophet (al-Nabī) (b. *c.* 570, Mecca, Arabia [Saudi Arabia]—d. June 8, 632, Medina), founder of the religion of ISLAM and of the Muslim community. Although biographical statements occur in the QUR'AN, most of what is known about his life comes from the HADITH, hagiographies (especially Ibn Isḥāq's mid-8th-century *Sīra*, later edited by Ibn Hishām), and Muslim histories (such as AL-ṬABARĪ's *Kitāb al-rusul wa'l-mulūk*, 9th–10th century). The life, teachings, and miracles of the Prophet have been the subjects of Muslim devotion and reflection for centuries.

Early life. Muhammad was born after the death of his father, 'Abd Allāh, and was placed in the care of his mother, his paternal grandfather, and, after their deaths, his paternal uncle Abū Ṭālib. During his early life in MECCA his merchant activities resulted in his marriage in about 595 to the wealthy widow Khadīja, who bore him at least two sons, who died young, and four daughters, of whom the best known was FĀTIMA, the wife of his cousin 'ALĪ. Until Khadīja's death in 619, Muhammad took no other wife.

Prophetic call and early religious activity. Mecca, inhabited by the tribe of QURAYSH, to which Muhammad's Hāshim clan belonged, was a prosperous mercantile center formed around a SANCTUARY, the KA'BA (Kaaba). The great

Muezzin calling the faithful to prayer from the minaret of the Sultan Omar Ali Saifuddin Mosque in Brunei
Paolo Koch—Photo Researchers

merchants of Mecca had obtained monopoly control of the trade into and out of the city. Most of the city's wealth was in a few hands, and as a result tribal solidarity was breaking up. About 610, as he reflected on such matters in the mountains outside Mecca, Muhammad had a vision of a majestic being (later identified with the angel GABRIEL) and heard a voice saying to him, "You are the Messenger of God." This marked the beginning of his career as prophet. From this time, at frequent intervals until his death, he received messages that he believed came directly from God or through Gabriel. About 650 they were collected and written in the Qur'an. In Muhammad's later experiences of receiving messages there was normally no vision. Most revelations were auditory, which he rendered with his voice into a "recitation" (qur'ān) of God's word.

In about 613 Muhammad began preaching publicly. The people of Mecca at the time worshiped many gods. Some regarded ALLĀH as a HIGH GOD who stood above lesser deities. The earliest passages of the Qur'an emphasize the goodness and power of God as seen in nature and in the prosperity of the Meccans and call on the latter to be grateful and to worship "the Lord of the Ka'ba." Gratitude is to be expressed in generosity and avoidance of miserliness.

The emigration from Mecca to Medina. Although Muhammad's preaching was basically religious, there was explicit in it a critique of the beliefs, conduct, and attitudes of the rich merchants of Mecca. Attempts were made to get him to soften his criticism, and commercial pressure was brought to bear on his supporters. About 619, with the deaths of Khadīja and Abū Ṭālib, Muhammad lost the protection of his clan. This meant that he could be attacked and thus could no longer propagate his religion in Mecca.

In 620 Muhammad began negotiations with clans in Yathrib (later called MEDINA, an abbreviation for Madīnat al-Nabī, "The City of the Prophet"), and with some of his followers he emigrated there, arriving on Sept. 24, 622. This is the celebrated HIJRA (Latin Hegira), which may be rendered "emigration," though the basic meaning is the severing of KINSHIP ties. It is the traditional starting point of Islamic history. The Islamic Era (AH or Anno Hegirae) begins on the first day of the Arabic year in which the Hijra took place— July 16, 622, in the Western calendar.

The Prophet in Medina. After he rejoined his followers in Medina, Muhammad set out to solidify his status. He constructed a new house for his wives and for himself that was to become the focal point of communal life and the chief mosque. As a holy man, he outlined the conditions by which he hoped to fashion a united community (umma) out of disparate and contending groups: Muslim emigrants (muhājirūn) from Mecca, Muslim helpers (anṣār) from Medina, Medinan Jews, and PAGAN Arabs. In a series of agreements, known collectively as the CONSTITUTION OF MEDINA, he formalized his role as an arbitrator of disputes and as prophet. It was during Muhammad's years at Medina that most of the Qur'an's rules concerning worship, family relations, and society were revealed.

Although Muhammad first sought to align himself and his followers with Jewish tribes of Medina and with their religion, relations between the two groups soon became increasingly strained. According to Muslim sources, Jews rejected Muhammad's claims to prophethood and seem to have joined with his opponents in alliances to defeat him.

A few emigrants from Mecca, with the approval of Muhammad, set out in normal Arab fashion on razzias (ghazawāt, "raids") in the hope of intercepting Meccan caravans passing near Medina on their way to Syria. In 624 the raids led to military conflict with Mecca. On March 15, 624, near a place called Badr, there was a battle in which at least 45 Meccans were killed, while only 14 Muslims died. To Muhammad this was a divine vindication of his prophethood, and the victory of Badr greatly strengthened him. After an indecisive battle in 625, in April 627 a great confederacy of 10,000 men moved against Medina, but the army withdrew after a two-week siege. After an abortive treaty, in 629 the Meccans formally submitted and were promised a general amnesty. Though Muhammad did not insist on their becoming Muslims, many soon did so.

Ever since the Hijra, Muhammad had been forming alliances with nomadic tribes. When he was strong enough to offer protection, he made it a condition of alliance that the tribe should become Muslim. Muhammad was soon militarily the strongest man in Arabia. He benefited from the defeat of the Persian Empire by the Byzantine (Christian) Empire (627–628), for, in the Yemen and in places on the Persian Gulf, minorities that had relied on Persian support against Byzantium now turned to Muhammad. By this time in Medina he had also repelled all serious challenges to his control; Jews had either been expelled or exterminated. Jews in settlements north of Medina capitulated to him and assumed what would later be called dhimmī (protected) status, as did Christians in other parts of Arabia.

In 632, after performing one last PILGRIMAGE to Mecca, Muhammad fell ill in Medina and died in the arms of his wife 'A'isha, the daughter of his friend Abu Bakr. Since no arrangement had been made for his succession, the Prophet's death provoked a major crisis among his followers. The dispute over the leadership of the Muslim community resulted in the most important schism in the history of Islam: the one between Sunni Muslims, led by the CALIPH, and SHI'ITE Muslims, led by the IMAM. Majoritarian religious doctrine precluded the appearance of another prophet.

Muhammad's legacy. After his death Muhammad's remains were interred in 'A'isha's quarters, next to the prayer area of his mosque. It was not long before caliphs began to expand the site and add new, more permanent architectural features. The mosque-tomb in Medina was to become the second most sacred site for Muslims, and pilgrimage there, though not a duty like the HAJJ, is considered a highly laudatory undertaking. According to one Hadith, Muhammad once proclaimed, "Whoever visits my tomb (or house) will win my intercession." In addition to being based on Muhammad's Hijra to Medina, the Islamic calendar commemorates several other events in his life. The month of RAMADĀN memorializes the revelation of the Qur'an, and the last lunar month is identified with the performance of Muhammad's final hajj. Moreover, the anniversaries of Muhammad's birth/death (MAWLID al-nabi) in the third lunar month and heavenly ascension (al-isrā' wa'l-MI'RĀJ) in the seventh lunar month became very popular religious holidays in most Muslim communities.

Muhammad's prophetic calling is a belief that Muslims are required to acknowledge in the SHAHĀDA (creed, testimony), and it constitutes one of the principle subjects of theological discourse. He is esteemed as an exemplary holy man whose words and deeds are remembered in the Hadith, which form the basis of the SUNNA, one of the roots of Islamic law (FIQH) and customary Muslim practice. Indeed, jurists regarded him as the foremost lawgiver, and philosophers saw in him the fulfillment of the ideal of Plato's philosopher-king. For Sufis (see SUFISM) Muhammad was the ascetic and visionary par excellence, the ancestral founder of their myriad orders. More recently he has been seen by some as the first unifier of the Arab peoples and the model for armed resistance against Western imperialism.

See also AHL AL-BAYT.

MUHAMMAD, ELIJAH \mō-'ha-məd, mü-\, *original name* Elijah Poole (b. Oct. 7, 1897, Sandersville, Ga., U.S.—d. Feb. 25, 1975, Chicago, Ill.), leader of the African-American separatist religious movement that is known as the NATION OF ISLAM (sometimes also called the Black Muslims).

The son of sharecroppers and former slaves, Muhammad moved to Detroit in 1923 where, around 1930, he became assistant minister to the founder of the movement, WALLACE D. FARD, at Temple No. 1. When Fard disappeared in 1934 Muhammad succeeded him as its head, proclaiming himself to be "the Prophet of God" and "Minister of ISLAM." Because of dissension within the Detroit temple, he moved to Chicago, where he established Temple No. 2. During World War II he advised followers to avoid the draft, as a result of which he was charged with violating the Selective Service Act and was jailed (1942–46).

Elijah Muhammad, 1965
Agence France Presse—Archive Photos

Muhammad's program called for the establishment of a separate nation for African-Americans and the adoption of a religion based on the worship of ALLĀH and on the belief that African-Americans are his chosen people. Muhammad became known especially for his flamboyant rhetoric directed at white people, whom he called "blue-eyed devils." In his later years, however, he moderated his tone and stressed self-help among African-Americans rather than confrontation between the races. Another group, retaining both the name and the founding principles of Elijah Muhammad's original Nation of Islam, was later established under the leadership of LOUIS FARRAKHAN.

MUHAMMAD AL-MAHDĪ AL-ḤUJJA \mü-'ḵam-mád-ùl-mä-'dē-ùl-ḵü-'jä\, *also called* Muhammad al-Muntaẓar (Arabic: "The Anticipated"), Hidden Imam, al-Qā'im ("He Who Arises"), *or* Twelfth Imam (b. *c.* 868, Sāmarrā' [now in Iraq]—disappeared 878), 12th and last IMAM, venerated by the ITHNĀ 'ASHARĪYA, or Twelvers, the main body of SHI'ITE Muslims. It is believed that Muhammad al-Mahdī al-Ḥujja has been concealed by God (a doctrine known as GHAYBA, or occultation) and that he will reappear in time as the MAHDI, or messianic deliverer. According to Shi'ite accounts he was the son of the Eleventh Imam, Hasan al-'Askarī, and a Byzantine slave. His occultation is commemorated by a cave shrine in Samarra known as Hujrat al-Ghayba ("Chamber of Occultation"), built in the 13th century. It is believed that upon his reappearance, when ISLAM is in decline and chaos prevails, he will win a decisive victory over evil and inaugurate a new messianic age. At that time, Islam will become the only religion, and the world will be filled with justice and prosperity.

MUHAMMADIYA \mù-ˌhȧ-mȧ-'dē-ə\, socioreligious organization in Indonesia, established in 1912 by proponents of purist ISLAM (*santri*) at Jogjakarta (now in Indonesia), aimed at adapting Islam to modern Indonesian life. The organization was chiefly inspired by an Egyptian reform movement, led by MUHAMMAD 'ABDUH, that had tried to bring the Muslim faith into harmony with modern rational thought. The Muhammadiya advocated the abolition of all customs deemed superstitious, mostly relics of pre-Islamic times, and the loosening of the stiff traditional bonds that tended to strangle modern cultural life. To achieve these aims, the Muhammadiya established schools along modern lines, where Western subjects (including Dutch) as well as religion were taught. It set up orphanages, hospitals, and other social services. By the 1920s the Muhammadiya was the dominant force in Indonesian Islam and the most effective organization in the country, claiming millions of members. It also promoted active participation of women in some areas of public life, but under the structures of modesty and segregation of the sexes.

The Muhammadiya was willing to cooperate with the Dutch colonial government, and its schools were qualified to receive government financial assistance. It was therefore criticized by radical Indonesian nationalists, who had adopted a noncooperation policy toward the Dutch authorities. The membership of the Muhammadiya increased steadily, however, and by 1937 there were 913 branches, although more than half of them were in the outer islands. The Muhammadiya was paralyzed by the Japanese occupation during World War II. It is still composed of several million members and must be counted as the predominant expression of reformist Islam in Indonesia.

MUḤĀSIBĪ, AL- \ùl-mù-ˌḵä-sē-'bē\ (Arabic: "He Who Examines [His Conscience]"), *in full* Abū 'Abd Allāh al-Ḥarith ibn Asad al-'Anazī al-Muḥāsibī (b. *c.* 781, Basra, Iraq—d. 857, Baghdad), eminent Sufi mystic and theologian renowned for his psychological refinement of pietistic devotion. His main work was *al-Ri'āya li-ḥūqūq Allah* ("Minding the Rights of God"), in which he acknowledges ASCETICISM to be valuable as an act of supererogation but always to be tempered by duties to God.

Al-Muḥāsibī apparently grew up in Baghdad in a prosperous home. From Basra he had brought the otherworldly spirituality of the Sufi theologian AL-ḤASAN AL-BAṢRĪ.

Muslim asceticism had developed some specific features: nightly recitals of the QUR'AN, restrictions concerning the kind and quantity of food one should eat, and a special attire consisting of woolen clothing. These habits had been adapted from the lifestyle of Christian monks. But whereas Christian monks used to live in seclusion, a Muslim ascetic felt obliged to remain an active member of his community. Thus, al-Muḥāsibī came to realize that although the practice of outward asceticism could serve to suppress the normal SINS of passion, it could also become a vehicle for vices like hypocrisy and pride. The proper instrument for tempering the inner and outer duties toward God is reason, primarily the method of *muḥāsaba*, the anticipation of the LAST JUDGMENT through constant self-examination; this tended to stifle every attempt at ecstatic exaltation.

Al-Muḥāsibī propagated his ideas in didactic conversations, which he would record immediately afterward; his books still preserve this dialogical structure. His influence on posterity was immense, especially through his pupil Junayd. During his lifetime, however, he was regarded with suspicion, and his last years were embittered by persecution. He had joined a group of theologians who, led by 'Abd Allāh ibn Kullāb (died 855), criticized the doctrines of the rationalist Mu'tazilī school dominant at that time. The Mu'tazilī, in stressing the unity of God, tended to reduce his attributes to mere nominal aspects; al-Muḥāsibī, in order to preserve their individual value, accentuated much more their independent status. And whereas the Mu'tazilī held the attribute of God's speech to be created, realized in temporal revelations like that of the Qur'an, al-Muḥāsibī believed that it was also uncreated if seen under the aspect of the eternal Word of God.

In 850–851, the CALIPH of Baghdad, al-Mutawakkil, put an end to the pro-Mu'tazilī policy of his predecessors and, two years later, prohibited rationalist theology altogether. Al-Muḥāsibī's theological position was now viewed as treasonous by his opponents, for they considered the use of any rational theological method as HERESY, regardless of the doctrine it supported. He was consequently forced to give up his public teaching and appears to have immigrated to Kūfa. Later on he was allowed to return to Baghdad. Yet the boycott persisted: when he died there in 857, only four people attended his funeral.

MUJĀHADA \mù-'ja-hà-də\ (Arabic: "striving"), in SUFISM, struggle with the carnal self; the word is related to JIHAD ("struggle"), which is often understood as "holy war." The Sufis refer to *mujāhada* as *al-jihād al-akbar* ("the greater war") in contrast to *al-jihād al-aṣghar* ("the minor war"), which is waged against unbelievers. It is one of the major duties that a Sufi must perform throughout his mystical journey toward union with God.

All acts of penance and austerity, such as prolonged fasts and abstinence from the comforts of life, have become part of the *mujāhada* practice. The purpose of *mujāhada* is to conquer the temptations of the self in order to purify one's soul and bring one's soul to a state of readiness to receive the divine light. It has been listed in Sufi treatises as a stage (*maqám*) on the way to mystical enlightenment since the 11th century.

MUKAMMAS, DAVID AL- \àl-mü-'kàm-màs\, *in full* David Abū Sulaymān ibn Marwān ar-Raqqī al-Mukammas, *also called* David ha-Bavli \hä-'bäv-lē\ (fl. 900, Raqqah, Syria), Syrian philosopher and polemicist, regarded as the father of medieval Jewish philosophy.

After converting to CHRISTIANITY, al-Mukammas became disillusioned with its doctrines and wrote two polemics faulting Christianity for the impurity of its monotheism; he also attacked ISLAM, maintaining that the style of the QUR'AN did not prove its divine origin. It is not entirely clear whether al-Mukammas returned fully to JUDAISM.

Al-Mukammas was the first Jewish thinker to introduce the methods of *kalam* (Arab religious philosophy) into Judaism and the first Jew to mention Aristotle in his writings; he cited Greek and Arab authorities, but he never quoted the BIBLE. Among the subjects presented in his *'Ishrūn maqālāt* ("Twenty Treatises") are a proof of God's existence and his creation of the world, a discussion of the reality of science, the substantial and accidental composition of the world, the utility of PROPHECY and prophets, and the signs of true prophets and prophecy. Al-Mukammas also wrote on Jewish sects.

MŪLAMADHYAMAKAKĀRIKĀ \'mü-lə-mäd-'yə-mə-kə-'kä-ri-ˌkä\ (Sanskrit: "Fundamentals of the Middle Way"), Buddhist text by NĀGĀRJUNA, the exponent of the MĀDHYAMIKA

school of MAHĀYĀNA Buddhism, that combines stringent logic and religious vision in a lucid presentation of the doctrine of ultimate "emptiness."

Nāgārjuna makes use of the classifications and analyses of the THERAVĀDA *Abhidhamma*, or scholastic, literature; he takes them to their logical extremes and thus reduces to ontological nothingness the various elements, states, and faculties dealt with in *Abhidhamma* texts. The *Mūlamadhyamakakārikā* develops the doctrine that nothing, not even the Buddha or NIRVANA, is real in itself.

MULLĀ \'mə-lə, 'mù-\ (Persian), *Arabic* mawlā \'maù-lä\, *English* mullah, a Muslim title generally denoting "lord"; it is used in the Islamic world as an honorific attached to the name of a king, SULTAN, noble, scholar, or religious leader. The term appears in the QUR'AN in reference to ALLĀH, the "Lord" or "Master," and thus came to be applied to earthly lords to whom religious sanctity was attributed.

During the era of the early Islamic conquests, however, the term was used in an opposite sense, to designate "freedmen" or "clients"—*i.e.*, non-Arab converts to ISLAM who held subordinate status vis-à-vis Arab followers of MUHAMMAD and the first CALIPHS. Originating from the conquered peoples of the Near East, these converts served in government and the military, but they also participated in revolts against caliphal authorities. They were instrumental to the 'Abbāsid revolution which brought about the demise of the Umayyad dynasty in 750. A number of leading Islamic scholars were of *mullā* heritage, such as AL-ḤASAN AL-BAṢRĪ (d. 728), ABŪ ḤANĪFAH (d. 767), and AL-BUKHARĪ (d. 870).

Subsequently, the most common application of the title *mullā* has been to religious leaders, teachers in religious schools, those versed in the canon law, leaders of prayer in the mosques (IMAMS), or reciters of the Qur'an (QURRĀ'). Normally the men called by the title have had some training in a MADRASA, or religious school. The word is often used to designate the entire class that upholds the traditional interpretation of Islam, especially in Iran. There it acquired derisive connotations in secularist circles during the 20th century.

MULLĀ ṢADRĀ \mōl-'lä-sa-'drä\, *also called* Ṣadr al-Dīn al-Shīrāzī (b. c. 1571, Shīrāz, Iran—d. 1640, Basra, Iraq), philosopher who led the Iranian cultural renaissance in the 17th century. The foremost representative of the illuminationist, or Ishrāqī, school of philosopher-mystics, he is commonly regarded as the greatest Iranian philosopher.

A scion of a notable Shīrāzī family, Mullā Ṣadrā completed his education at Iṣfahān, then the leading cultural and intellectual center of Iran, where he studied under MĪR DĀMĀD. He produced several works, the most famous of which was his *Asfār* ("Journeys") containing the bulk of his philosophy, which was influenced by a personal MYSTICISM bordering on the ascetic that he experienced during a 15-year retreat at Kahak, a village near QOM, Iran.

Expounding his theory of nature, Mullā Ṣadrā argued that the entire universe—except God and his knowledge—was originated both eternally as well as temporally. Nature, he asserted, is the substance of all things and is the cause for all movement. Thus, nature is permanent and furnishes the continuing link between the eternal and the originated.

Toward the end of his life, Mullā Ṣadrā returned to Shīrāz to teach. His teachings, however, were considered heretical by the orthodox Shi'ite theologians, who persecuted him, though his powerful family connections permitted him to continue to write. He died on a PILGRIMAGE to Arabia.

MÜLLER, (FRIEDRICH) MAX \'mŭ-lər, 'myü-\ (b. Dec. 6, 1823, Dessau, duchy of Anhalt [Germany]—d. Oct. 28, 1900, Oxford, Eng.), German Orientalist and language scholar whose works stimulated widespread interest in the study of linguistics, MYTHOLOGY, and religion.

Müller was the son of the noted German poet Wilhelm Müller. Originally a student of Sanskrit, he turned to comparative language studies, and about 1845 he began studying the AVESTA, the Zoroastrian SCRIPTURE written in Old Iranian. This led him to COMPARATIVE RELIGION and to the editing of the ṚG VEDA, which was published after he had settled at the University of Oxford (1849–75). There he was appointed deputy professor of modern languages (1850) and professor of comparative philology (1868).

Müller's exploration of mythology also led him further into comparative religion and to the publication of *The Sacred Books of the East* (1879–1904), begun in 1875. Of the 51 volumes (including indexes) of translations of major Oriental, non-Christian scriptures, all but 3 appeared under his superintendence during his lifetime. In his later years, Müller also wrote on Indian philosophy and encouraged the search for Oriental manuscripts and inscriptions.

MUMMY, body embalmed or treated for burial with preservatives after the manner of the ancient Egyptians. The process varied from age to age in Egypt, but it always involved removing the internal organs (though in a late period they were replaced, after treatment), treating the body with resin, and wrapping it in linen bandages. Among the many other peoples who practiced mummification were the people living along the Torres Strait, between Papua New Guinea and Australia, and the INCAS of South America.

MUNMYO \'mün-'myō\ (Korean: "culture shrines"), in Korean tradition, religious, educational, and cultic institutions devoted to the spirit of CONFUCIUS and his disciples. First established in Korea during the Three Kingdoms period (57 BCE–668 CE) in emulation of Han dynasty Chinese practices, these shrines became focal points for the cultural and political unification of the Korean state. In the Koryo period (918–1392), Korean scholars were added to the ranks of Chinese Confucian disciples seen in the shrines, a tradition that eventually led to the installation of the spirit tablets of 18 exemplary Korean scholars. In the modern period various Confucian groups continue to honor the ancient rituals at culture shrines throughout Korea.

MÜNTZER, THOMAS \'mŭnt-sər, 'mŭnt-\, *Müntzer also spelled* Münzer, *or* Monczer, *Latin* Thomas Monetarius (b. sometime before 1490, Stolberg, Thuringia [Germany]—d. May 27, 1525, Mühlhausen), leading German radical Reformer during the Protestant REFORMATION, and the leader of the abortive Peasants' Revolt in Thuringia in 1524–25.

Müntzer's name appears in the 1506 register of the University of Leipzig, and in 1512 he attended the University of Frankfurt an der Oder, later earning the academic ranks of master of arts and bachelor of theology. Müntzer became a specialist in Latin, Greek, and Hebrew and an accomplished scholar of ancient and humanistic literature—particularly the Old and New Testaments. He was an assistant teacher in Halle (Saale) in 1513 and a clergyman as well as a teacher in Aschersleben in 1514 and 1515.

From 1516 to 1517 Müntzer worked as a prior at Frohse monastery in Aschersleben; in 1517–18 he taught at the Braunschweig Martineum (city secondary school) until, in 1518, he was attracted to MARTIN LUTHER and his ideas of re-

form. After occasional participation in debates between Luther and the German theologian JOHANN ECK in Leipzig, he pursued intensive literary studies at the monastery of Beuditz at Weissenfels (1519–20). There, under the influence of MYSTICISM, he came to see the work inaugurated by Luther as a revolution.

In Zwickau (1520–21) Müntzer prospered as a pastor in the socially tense condition that existed between the upper classes and early miners' guilds. In this work he sided with the common people, who seemed to him to be the executors of the divine law and will on earth. He increasingly adopted the sectarian view that true authority lay in the inner light given by God, rather than in the BIBLE, a view taught by Nikolaus Storch, a leader of a radical group known as the "Zwickau prophets." In 1522 at Nordhausen, in a struggle against Luther's supporters, his theological differences with them became more pronounced. Believing that teachings came from the spirit, Müntzer placed them in opposition to the Lutheran doctrines of JUSTIFICATION by faith alone and of the exclusive authority of SCRIPTURE. The revolutionary aspect of Müntzer's theology lay in the link he made between his concept of the inevitable conquest of the anti-Christian earthly government and the thesis that the common people themselves, as the instruments of God, would have to execute this change.

Before EASTER of 1523, Müntzer found employment as pastor of a Saxon community in Allstedt, near the Mansfeld mining area. Built upon the idea of "Christian unification" and also as a self-defense organization, the Allstedt alliance originated in 1524 and remained the center of his doctrine until the fall of 1524, when he left Allstedt.

In Mühlhausen he organized the working classes into a group called the "Eternal Covenant of God." After another expulsion he went to Nürnberg, where his main political writings were published. He then went on to Hegau and Klettgau, the area where the Peasants' Revolt (an abortive revolt in 1524–25 against the nobles over rising taxes, deflation, and other grievances) was beginning, and stayed through the winter in Griessen.

His experience with the rising insurrection impelled him to go back to Mühlhausen, which became the center of the middle German revolt (after the overthrow of the governing council and the formation of what the insurgents called an "eternal council" in March 1525). Following Müntzer's dogmatic program, the common people triumphed in April–May 1525 over the religious and civil authorities. Cities and even some of the lesser nobility joined the alliance. Müntzer and his followers lent determination and consistency to the revolt. They were not, however, capable of overcoming the local and regional narrow-mindedness of the people. In the Battle of Frankenhausen, May 15, 1525, they were defeated by the superior strength of the princes.

During the rebellion, Müntzer tried to relate the battle of the peasants, tradesmen, and commoners about immediate concerns with that of the liberation of all Christendom and adapted himself to the various groups' everyday concerns. The collapse of the revolt seemed to him the judgment of God on the as yet unpurified people but not synonymous with the defeat of his idea of a new society. Müntzer was taken prisoner and tortured and on May 27, at the princes' camp at Mühlhausen, was tried and executed.

MURJI'A \'mŭr-jē-ə\, one of the earliest Islamic groups to believe in the postponement (*irjā'*) of judgment on committers of serious SINS, recognizing that God alone could decide whether or not a Muslim had lost his faith.

The Murji'a flourished during the turbulent period that began with the murder of 'UTHMĀN (third CALIPH) in 656 CE, and ended with the assassination of 'ALĪ (fourth caliph) in 661 CE and the subsequent establishment of the Umayyad dynasty (ruled until 750 CE). The Muslim community was divided into hostile factions, divided on the issue of the relationship of *islām* and *īmān*, or works and faith. The most militant were the KHĀRIJITES, who held the view that serious sinners should be ousted from the community and that JIHAD ("holy war") should be declared on them. This led the adherents of the sect to revolt against the Umayyads, whom they regarded as corrupt and unlawful rulers.

The Murji'a took the opposite stand, asserting that no one who once professed ISLAM could be declared *kāfir* (infidel), mortal sins notwithstanding. Revolt against a Muslim ruler, therefore, could not be justified under any circumstances. To the Murji'a external actions and utterances did not necessarily reflect an individual's inner beliefs. Some of their extremists, such as Jahm ibn Ṣafwān (d. 746), regarded faith as purely an inward conviction, thus allowing a Muslim outwardly to profess other religions and remain a Muslim, since only God could determine the true nature of his faith. The Murji'a remained neutral in the disputes that divided the Muslim world and called for passive resistance rather than armed revolt against unjust rulers; they regarded their tolerance of the Umayyads as based only on religious grounds and on recognition of the importance of law and order. *See also* KALĀM.

MURRAY, JOHN COURTNEY \'mər-ē\ (b. Sept. 12, 1904, New York, N.Y., U.S.—d. Aug. 16, 1967, New York City), JESUIT (Society of Jesus) theologian known for his influential thought on church-state relations.

Murray was educated at a Jesuit high school in Manhattan and entered their novitiate in 1920. After study at Boston College, where he took his M.A., he attended Woodstock College (later the Woodstock Theological Center of Georgetown University). He was ordained in 1933. After study in Rome he became a member of the faculty of Woodstock College in 1936, a position he held until his death.

In the late 1940s Murray began to grapple with the problem of how the beliefs of a pluralistic, democratic society such as that of the United States could be integrated into the teachings of the ROMAN CATHOLIC church. Murray was an outspoken opponent of censorship on the part of the Vatican, and, indeed, was opposed to any effort by the church to bring about change within states by means other than moral persuasion. Many of his writings on these topics first appeared in *Theological Studies*, a quarterly journal published by Woodstock College, of which Murray became editor in 1941. By the mid-1950s he was forbidden by the Jesuit order to write on topics pertaining to religious freedom and issues of CHURCH AND STATE without first having it approved by the head of the order in Rome.

In 1958, John F. Kennedy, a Roman Catholic, won reelection to the U.S. Senate in a landslide victory and would later enter the race for the U.S. presidency at a time when faithful Roman Catholics were expected to work toward changing the constitution of any country that did not have ROMAN CATHOLICISM as the established religion. Murray became a defender of the U.S. constitution, arguing that democracy and pluralism were not only good for the state and its citizens, but good for the church as well. The American political system, Murray argued, freed the church of the need to placate rulers of states and accorded the church and its members a new-found dignity. Murray's 1960 book on this topic, *We Hold These Truths*, laid the groundwork for many changes in the way that church-state relations were viewed, by Catholics and non-Catholics alike.

By 1965 the Catholic hierarchy had changed its mind about Murray; he was invited to serve at the SECOND VATICAN COUNCIL and is credited as the chief author of that council's *Declaration on Religious Liberty*. In 1966 he was made director of the John La Farge Institute, affiliated with the Jesuit weekly *America*. There he began holding seminars including Roman Catholic, Protestant, and Jewish theologians, aimed at stimulating ecumenical dialogue.

MURUGAN \'mùr-ù-gən\, *also spelled* Murukan, chief deity of the ancient Tamils of South India, later identified in part with the Hindu god SKANDA. He is described as joining his fierce mother, Korravai (later associated with DURGĀ), in cannibal feasts on the battlefield, a practice that may explain his association with the North Indian war god Skanda. His weapon was the trident or spear, and his banner carried the emblem of a wild fowl. The *Tirumurukārruppaṭai*, a "guide to the worship of the god Murugan," is a description of the chief shrines of the god that the worshiper is encouraged to visit; it was probably written prior to the 7th century CE. Murugan is identified with the hilly tracts of South India, the terrain associated with clandestine love in the Tamil poetic tradition.

MUSAR \'mü-,sär\, a religious movement among Orthodox Jews of Lithuania during the 19th century that emphasized personal piety as a necessary complement to intellectual studies of the TORAH and TALMUD. RABBI Israel Salanter initiated the movement as head of the YESHIVA at Vilnius. The Musar literature that Salanter and others collected and reprinted was used to foster peace of mind, humility, tolerance, thoughtful consideration of others, self-examination, and purity of mind. Yeshivas throughout the world have since made Musar readings part of their curriculum.

MUSE, Greek Mousa, *or* Moisa, in GREEK RELIGION and mythology, any of a group of sister goddesses of ancient origin, the chief center of whose cult was Mount Helicon in Boeotia, Greece. Allegedly they came from Pieria in Macedonia, but this attribution may be a misunderstanding, the real Pieria being somewhere in Greece. Very little is known of their cult, but they had a festival every four years at Thespiae, near Helicon, and a contest (*Museia*), presumably in singing and playing. They probably were originally the patron goddesses of poets (who in early times were also musicians, providing their own accompaniments), although later their range was extended to include all liberal arts and sciences—hence, their connection with such institutions as the Museum (*Mouseion*, seat of the Muses) at Alexandria, Egypt. Their father was ZEUS, and their mother was MNEMOSYNE. There were nine Muses as early as Homer's *Odyssey* (c. 700 BCE), and Homer invokes either a Muse or the Muses collectively. To begin with, they were probably one of those vague collections of deities that are characteristic of certain, probably early, strata of Greek religion.

Differentiation can be seen in Hesiod, who mentioned CLIO, EUTERPE, THALIA, MELPOMENE, TERPSICHORE, ERATO, POLYMNIA (Polyhymnia), OURANIA, and CALLIOPE, who was their chief. Although Hesiod's list became canonical in later times, it was not the only one; at both DELPHI and Sicyon there were three Muses, one of whom in the latter place bore the name Polymatheia ("Much Learning"). A common but by no means a definitive list is the following:

Calliope: Muse of heroic or epic poetry (often shown holding a writing tablet).

Clio: Muse of history (often holding a scroll).

Erato: Muse of lyric and love poetry (often playing a lyre).

Euterpe: Muse of music or flutes (often playing flutes).

Melpomene: Muse of tragedy (often holding a tragic mask).

Polymnia: Muse of sacred poetry or of the mimic art (often shown with a pensive look).

Terpsichore: Muse of dancing and choral song (often shown dancing and holding a lyre).

Thalia: Muse of comedy (often holding a comic mask).

Ourania: Muse of astronomy (often holding a globe).

The Muses are often spoken of as unmarried, but they are repeatedly referred to as the mothers of famous sons, such as ORPHEUS, Rhesus, EUMOLPUS, and others connected somehow either with poetry and song or with Thrace and its neighborhood, or both. All their myths are secondary, and hence there is no consistency in these minor tales—Terpsichore, for example, is named as the mother of several different men by various authors and Orpheus generally is called the son of Calliope but occasionally of Polymnia.

MUSHĀHADA \mù-'sha-hà-də\ (Arabic: "witnessing," or "viewing"), *also called* shuhūd ("witnesses"), in SUFISM, the vision of God obtained by the illuminated heart of the seeker of truth. Through *mushāhada*, the Sufi acquires *yaqīn* (real certainty), which cannot be achieved by the intellect or transmitted to those who do not travel the Sufi path. The Sufi has to pass various ritual stages (MAQĀM) before he can attain the state of *mushāhada*, which is eventually given to him only by the GRACE of God, bestowed upon whom he pleases. *Mushāhada*, therefore, cannot be reached through good works or MUJĀHADA (struggle with the carnal self).

Mushāhada is the goal of every Sufi who aspires to the ultimate vision of God; its opposite, *ḥijāb* (veiling of the divine face), is the most severe punishment that a Sufi can imagine. *Mushāhada* has been listed in Sufi treatises as a stage (*maqām*) on the way to mystical enlightenment since the 11th century.

MUSLIM BROTHERHOOD, *Arabic* al-Ikhwān al-Muslimūn, religio-political organization founded in 1928 at Ismāʿīlīyā, Egypt, by ḤASAN AL-BANNĀʾ. It advocated a return to the QURʾAN and the HADITH as guidelines for a healthy, modern Islamic society. The brotherhood spread rapidly throughout Egypt, the Sudan, Syria, Palestine, Lebanon, and North Africa.

After 1938 the Muslim Brotherhood began to demand purity of the Islamic world and rejected westernization, secularization, and MODERNIZATION. The brotherhood organized a terrorist arm, and when the Egyptian government seemed to weaken in the mid-1940s, the brotherhood posed a threat to the monarchy and the ruling Wafd Party. An attempt to assassinate Egyptian president Gamāl ʿAbd al-Nāṣir in Alexandria on Oct. 26, 1954, led to the Muslim Brotherhood's forcible suppression. Six of its leaders were tried and executed for treason, and many others were imprisoned.

In the 1970s the Muslim Brotherhood experienced a renewal as part of the general upsurge of religious activity in Islamic countries in the aftermath of the 1967 Arab-Israeli war and government crackdowns on leftists. An uprising by the Muslim Brotherhood in the Syrian city of Ḥamāh in February 1982 was crushed by the government of Ḥafiz al-Asad at a cost of thousands of lives. The brotherhood revived in Egypt and Jordan in the same period, and beginning in the late 1980s it emerged to compete in legislative elections in those countries.

MUSLIM CALENDAR, *also called* Islamic calendar, dating system used in the Muslim world (except Turkey, which uses the Gregorian calendar) and based on a year of 12 months, each month beginning approximately at the time of the new moon. (The Iranian Muslim calendar, however, is based on a solar year.) The months are alternately 30 and 29 days long except for the 12th, Dhu al-Hijjah, the length of which is varied in a 30-year cycle intended to keep the calendar in step with the true phases of the Moon. In 11 years of this cycle, Dhu al-Hijjah has 30 days, and in the other 19 years it has 29. Thus the year has either 354 or 355 days. No months are intercalated, so that the named months do not remain in the same seasons but retrogress through the entire solar, or seasonal, year (of about 365.25 days) every 32.5 solar years.

MUSLIM IBN AL-ḤAJJĀJ \mùs-'lēm-ˌi-bən-àl-ḵàj-'jäj\, *in full* Abū al-Ḥusayn Muslim ibn al-Ḥajjāj al-Qushayrī (b. *c.* 817, Nīshāpūr, Iran—d. 875, Naṣrābād), scholar who was one of the chief authorities on the HADITH.

Muslim traveled widely; his great work, the *Ṣaḥīḥ* ("The Genuine"), is said to have been compiled from about 300,000 traditions, which he collected in Arabia, Egypt, Syria, and Iraq; it has become one of the six canonical collections of Hadith. Muslim was careful to give a full account of the ISNĀDS (links in the chain of transmission) for each tradition and to record textual variations. The collection, organized topically, also includes a survey on early Islamic theology and a discussion of the QURʾAN.

MUSPELHEIM \'mūs-pel-ˌhām\, *Old Norse* Múspell \'mūs-pel\, in GERMANIC RELIGION, a hot, bright, glowing land in the south, guarded by Surt, the fire GIANT. In the beginning, according to one tradition, the warm air from this region melted the ice of the opposite region, NIFLHEIM, thus giving form to YMIR (Aurgelmir), the father of the destructive giants. Sparks from Muspelheim became the sun, moon, and stars. At the doom of the gods (RAGNARÖK), the sons of Muspelheim, led by Surt, will destroy the world by fire.

MUT \'mūt\, in EGYPTIAN RELIGION, a sky goddess. Mut may have originated either in the Nile River delta or in Middle Egypt. During the 18th dynasty (1539–1292 BCE),

Mut, wearing the double crown and vulture's head on her forehead, bronze statuette, c. 650–350 BCE
By courtesy of the Oriental Institute, the University of Chicago

she became the companion of the god AMON at Thebes, forming the Theban triad with him and with the youthful god KHONS, who was said to be Mut's son. The name Mut means "mother," and her role was that of an older woman among the gods. She was associated with the uraeus (rearing cobra), lionesses, and royal crowns. She was also identified with other goddesses, principally BASTET and SEKHMET.

At Thebes the principal festival of Mut was her "navigation" on the distinctive horseshoe-shaped lake, or Isheru, that surrounded her temple complex at Karnak. Mut was usually represented as a woman wearing the double crown (of Upper and Lower Egypt) worn by the king and by the god ATUM. She was also sometimes depicted with the head of a lioness.

MUT'A \'mùt-à\ (Arabic: "pleasure"), in Islamic law, a temporary marriage that is contracted often verbally, for a limited or fixed period and involves the payment of money to the female partner. Partners who engage in *mut'a* must do so freely and must predetermine the compensation and duration of the contract. The woman, therefore, has no claim for maintenance, and the two do not inherit from one another unless there is a previous agreement on these matters. Any children from a *mut'a* union go with the father. No extension of the *mut'a* is permitted, but cohabitation may be resumed if a new agreement is reached with new compensation. All Muslim legal schools agree that *mut'a* was recognized and practiced in MUHAMMAD's time. Most SUNNI Muslims, however, think the practice to have been forbidden by 'Umar I, the second CALIPH, and thus to have been abrogated. In consequence, Sunni leaders have denounced *mut'a* as simple prostitution. The Twelver SHI'ITES, in contrast, consider *mut'a* to be still valid and defend it as a guard against prostitution or license in circumstances in which regular marriage is impossible. Encouraged by religious leaders in Iran, it is typically practiced at PILGRIMAGE centers, such as QOM and MASHHAD.

MU'TAZILA \mü-'tä-zi-lə\ (Arabic: "Those Who Withdraw," or "Stand Apart"), *English* Mutazilites \-,līts\, in ISLAM, political or religious neutralists; by the 10th century the term came to refer specifically to an Islamic school of speculative theology that flourished in Basra and Baghdad.

The name first appears in early Islamic history in the dispute over 'Ali's leadership of the Muslim community after the murder of the third CALIPH, 'UTHMĀN (656). Those who would neither condemn nor sanction 'Ali or his opponents but took a middle position were termed the Mu'tazila.

The theological school is traced to WĀSIL IBN 'AŢĀ' (699–749), a student of AL-HASAN AL-BASRĪ, who by stating that a grave sinner could be classed neither as believer nor unbeliever but was in an intermediate position, withdrew (*i'tazala*, hence the name Mu'tazila) from his teacher's circle. (The same story is told of 'Amr ibn 'Ubayd [d. 762].) Maligned as free thinkers and heretics, the Mu'tazila, in the 8th century CE, were the first Muslims to use the categories and methods of Hellenistic philosophy to derive their three major and distinctive dogmatic points. (*See* KALĀM.)

First, they stressed the absolute unity or oneness (*tawhīd*) of God; thus the QUR'AN could not be the word of God (the majority view), as God has no separable parts, and so had to be created and was not coeternal with God. Under the 'Abbāsid caliph al-Ma'mūn, this doctrine of the created Qur'an was proclaimed (827) as the state dogma, and in 833, a MIHNA or tribunal was instituted to try those who disputed the doctrine (notably the theologian AHMAD IBN HANBAL);

the Mu'tazilī position was finally abandoned by the caliphate under al-Mutawakkil c. 849. The justice ('*adl*) of God is their second principle: God desires only the best for humans, but through FREE WILL they choose between GOOD AND EVIL and thus become ultimately responsible for their actions. So in the third doctrine, the threat and the promise (*al-wa'd wa al-wa'īd*), or paradise and hell, God's justice becomes a matter of logical necessity: God *must* reward the good (as promised) and *must* punish the evil (as threatened).

Among the most important Mu'tazilī theologians were Abū al-Hudhayl al-'Allāf (d. c. 841) and al-Nazzām (d. 846) in Basra and Bishr ibn al-Mu'tamir (d. 825) in Baghdad. Mu'tazilī beliefs were disavowed by the SUNNI Muslims, but the SHI'ITES accepted their premises.

MUTILATION, RITUAL, intentional modification of the living human body for religious, aesthetic, or social reasons. *See* BODY MODIFICATIONS AND MUTILATIONS.

MUWAHHIDŪN \mù-,wà-hi-'dün\ (Arabic: "Unitarians"), *also called* Wahhābīs \wà-'ha-bēz\, members of the Muslim puritan movement founded by MUHAMMAD IBN 'ABD AL-WAHHĀB in the 18th century in Najd, central Arabia, and adopted in 1744 by the Sa'ūdī family.

The political fortunes of the WAHHĀBĪS were immediately allied to those of the Sa'ūdī dynasty. By the end of the 18th century, they had brought all of Najd under their control, attacked KARBALĀ', Iraq, a holy city of the SHI'ITE branch of ISLAM, and occupied MECCA and MEDINA in western Arabia. The Ottoman SULTAN brought an end to the first Wahhābī empire in 1818 with the assistance of MUHAMMAD 'ALĪ (1769–1849) of Egypt, but the movement revived under the leadership of the Sa'ūdī Faysal I. The empire was then somewhat restored until once again destroyed at the end of the 19th century by the Rashīdīya of northern Arabia. The activities of Ibn Sa'ūd in the 20th century eventually led to the creation of the Kingdom of Saudi Arabia in 1932 and assured Wahhābī dominance on the Arabian Peninsula.

The Wahhābī call themselves al-Muwahhidūn, a name derived from their emphasis on the absolute oneness of God (*tawhid*). They deny all acts implying POLYTHEISM, such as visiting tombs and venerating saints, and advocate a return to the original teachings of Islam as incorporated in the QUR'AN and HADITH, with condemnation of all innovations (*bid'a*). Wahhābī theology and jurisprudence, based, respectively, on the teachings of IBN TAYMĪYA and on the legal school of AHMAD IBN HANBAL, stress literal belief in the Qur'an and Hadith and the establishment of a Muslim state based only on Islamic law. Their interpretation of Islam has been increasingly influential on an international level at the end of the 20th century owing to the wealth and influence of Saudi Arabia.

MYRMIDON \'mər-mə-,dän, -dən\, in Greek mythology, any of the inhabitants of Phthiotis in Thessaly.

According to some authorities, the Myrmidons later crossed over from Thessaly to Aegina. Their name was traditionally derived from one of two sources: a supposed ancestor, son of ZEUS and Eurymedusa, the daughter of King Myrmidon of Thessaly, who was seduced by Zeus in the form of an ant (Greek *myrmēx*); or the re-peopling of Aegina (after all its inhabitants had died of a plague) with ants changed into men by Zeus at the prayer of AEACUS, king of the island. As the followers of the hero ACHILLES, their name came to be applied in modern times to subordinates who carry out orders implacably.

MYSTERY
RELIGIONS

Secret cults of the Greco-Roman world that offered to individuals a way to feel RELIGIOUS EXPERIENCES not provided by the official public religions are termed mystery religions. They originated in tribal ceremonies that were performed by peoples in many parts of the world. But, whereas in these tribal communities almost every member of the clan or the village was initiated, initiation in Greece became a matter of personal choice. The mystery religions reached their peak of popularity in the first three centuries CE.

Etymologically, the word mystery is derived from the Greek verb *myein* ("to close"), referring to the lips and the eyes. Mysteries were always secret cults into which a person had to be initiated (taken in). The initiate was called *mystēs*, the introducing person *mystagōgos* (leader of the *mystēs*). The leaders of the cults included the *hierophantēs* ("revealer of holy things") and the *dadouchos* ("torchbearer"). The constitutive features of a mystery society were common meals, dances, and ceremonies, especially initiation rites. These common experiences strengthened the bonds of each cult.

HISTORY

Eleusinian. The most important SANCTUARY of DEMETER, the goddess of grain, and her daughter Kore (PERSEPHONE) was in the city of Eleusis in Attica, between Athens and Megara. Famous religious festivals—known as the Greater and the Lesser Eleusinian Mysteries—were enacted in this city. At first, the cult of Demeter was probably local and initiation was tribal rather than personal. By participating in the mysteries, a man would become a full member of the civic body. When Eleusis was annexed to the Athenian territory about 600 BCE, however, every Athenian was admitted to the Mysteries, and soon the rites were open to every Greek. Thus the ceremonies received an "international" character, under which each person had to decide for himself whether or not he wanted to be initiated. Although the doctrine of the Eleusinian rites is not clear, it is likely that the initiates expected to enjoy a special status in the afterworld after their death.

Orphic. Besides community initiations, there were ceremonies for individual persons of deeper religious longing. Such persons were called Orphics after OR-

Attis, standing against a column, 1st century CE; in the Archaeological Museum, Istanbul
Erich Lessing—Art Resource

763

PHEUS, the Greek hero with superhuman musical skills who was supposedly the author of sacred writings; these writings were called the Orphic rhapsodies, and they dealt with such subjects as purification and the afterlife. It is possible to reconstruct a common pattern for these initiations of individuals, although an Orphic "church" never existed, and the doctrines of the many small communities of individualists varied on a broad scale.

Many Orphics believed that there was a divine part in man—his soul—but it was wrapped up in the body, and man's task was to liberate the soul from the body. This could be achieved by living an Orphic life, which included abstinence from meat, wine, and sexual intercourse. After death the soul would be judged. If a man had lived a righteous life, his soul would be sent to the meadows of the blessed in ELYSIUM; but, if he had committed misdeeds, his soul would be punished in various ways. Following a period of reward or punishment, the soul would be incarnated in a new body. Only a soul that had lived a pious life three times could be liberated from the cycle. One text states that members of the Orphic community would assemble at night in a clubhouse and hold their services by the light of torches. Their rite consisted of a bloodless sacrifice and included the use of incense, prayer, and hymns.

Isis. The national religions of the peoples of the Greek Middle East also began to spread, in their Hellenized versions. A faintly exotic flavor surrounded these religions and made them particularly attractive to the Greeks and Romans. The most popular of the Middle Eastern mysteries was the cult of ISIS. It was already in vogue at Rome in the time of the emperor Augustus, at the beginning of the Christian era. The religion of Isis became widespread in Italy during the 1st and 2nd centuries CE. To a certain extent, the expansion of JUDAISM and CHRISTIANITY over the Roman world coincided with the expansion of the Egyptian cults.

Cults from Asia Minor. By 200 BCE the GREAT MOTHER OF THE GODS (Magna Mater) and her consort ATTIS were introduced into the Roman pantheon and were considered as Roman gods. Their cult seems to have been encouraged especially under Emperor Claudius about 50 CE. The mysteries symbolized, through her relationship to Attis, the relations of Mother Earth to her children and were intended to impress upon the *mystēs* the subjective certainty of having been united in a special way with the goddess. There was a strong element of hope for an afterlife in this cult. The Persian god MITHRA (Mithras), the god of light, was introduced much later, probably not before the 2nd century. The cult of Mithra was concerned with the origin of life from a sacred bull that was caught and then sacrificed by Mithra.

From Syria came the worship of several deities, of which JUPITER Heliopolitanus (the local god of Heliopolis; modern Ba'labakk, Lebanon) and JUPITER DOLICHENUS (the local god of Doliche in Commagene; modern Dülük, Turkey) were the most important. ADONIS (a god of vegetation) of Byblos (in modern Lebanon) had long been familiar to the Greeks and was often considered to be closely related to OSIRIS; the myths and rituals of the two gods were similar. Adonis' female partner was ATARGATIS (ASTARTE), whom the Greeks identified with APHRODITE.

The height of Syrian influence was in the 3rd century CE when SOL, the Syrian sun god, was on the verge of becoming the chief god of the Roman Empire. He was introduced into Rome by the emperor Elagabalus (Heliogabalus) in about 220 CE, and by about 240 CE PYTHIAN GAMES (*i.e.*, festivals of the sun god APOLLO) were instituted in many cities of the empire. The emperor Aurelian (270–275) elevated Sol to the highest rank among the gods. Sanctuaries of Sol and the gods of other planets (*septizonium*) were constructed, and 50 years later the cult of Sol had a strong influence on the emperor Constantine's understanding of Christianity.

The different mystery religions were not exclusive of one another, but they appealed to different sociological groups. Isis was worshiped by lower-middle-class people in the seaports and trading towns. The followers of the Great Mother in Italy were principally craftsmen. Mithra was the god of soldiers and of imperial officials and freedmen. There were no special societies for slaves; but they were usually admitted to the societies, and, during the time of the festival, all men were considered equal.

RITES AND FESTIVALS

A period of preparation preceded the initiation in each of the mysteries. In the Isis religion, for example, a period of 11 days of fasting, including abstinence from meat, wine, and sexual activity, was required before the ceremony. The candidates were segregated from the common folk in special apartments in the holy precinct of the community center; they were called "the chastely living ones" (*hagneuontes*).

In all the mystery religions the candidates swore an OATH of secrecy. Before initiation, confession was expected. The candidate sometimes told at length the story of the faults of his life up to the point of his BAPTISM, which was commonly a part of the initiation ceremony, and the community of devotees listened to the confession. It was believed that the rite of baptism would wash away all the candidate's misdeeds.

The baptism could be either by water or by fire, and the rites often included actions that had an exotic flavor. Sulfur torches were used during the baptism ceremony; they were dipped into water and then—contrary to the expectations of the observers—burned when drawn out of the water. In a dark room a script would suddenly become visible on a wall that had been prepared accordingly. Instructions still exist for producing a nimbus effect—the appearance of light around the head of a priest. The priest's head was shaved and prepared with a protective ointment; then a circular metal receptacle for alcohol was fixed on his head; it was set aflame in a dark room and would shine for some seconds. In the Isis mysteries, the initiation was sometimes accomplished by means of a "sacred marriage" (HIEROS GAMOS).

Seasonal festivals. The religions of Demeter and of Isis and the Great Mother had something of an ecclesiastical year. The seasonal festivals were inherited from old ceremonies that had been closely associated with the sowing and reaping of grain and with the production of wine. The dates varied greatly according to the geographic conditions and the emphasis of the seasonal rites in the country in which the mysteries had originated.

The festivals of the Isis religion were connected with the three Egyptian seasons caused by the cycle of the Nile River (inundation, sowing, and reaping). About July 19, when the whole country was almost desiccated by the heat and the drought, the high waters of the new flood miraculously arrived from Ethiopia. On that day, just before sunrise, Sirius (the Dog Star, or the star of Isis) would make its first appearance of the season on the horizon. This was the sacred New Year's Day for the Egyptians, and the festival of the Nile flood was their greatest festival. There were, in addition, the festivals of sowing and reaping. In Roman times, important Isis festivals were held on December 25, January 6, and March 5. The March festival was a spring festival that celebrated the beginning of the seafaring season. A ship was carried on a cart (*carrus navalis*) through the city. It was followed by a procession of choruses, candidates, *mystai* in bright clothes wearing masks, and priests carrying the insignia of the goddess. The ship was let into the sea, and the participants returned to the temple, where initiation ceremonies, banquets, and dances were held.

In the religion of Sol, the festivals were deter-

Isis; in the Louvre, Paris
Alinari—Art Resource

765

A relief of Mithra slaying the bull. In Mithraism the sacred bull was believed to be the first living creature from whom all other life forms sprang
Werner Forman Archive—Art Resource

mined by astronomy. The greatest festival was held on December 24–25, at the time of the winter solstice. Because from this date the length of the day began to increase, it was regarded as the day of the rebirth of the god and of the renovation of life.

THEOLOGY

One of the central subjects in mystery writings was cosmogony—the theory of the origin or creation of the world. In the Hermetic treatises, in the Chaldean Oracles, and in the little known writings of MITHRAISM, the COSMOGONY was modeled after Plato's *Timaeus,* and it always dealt with the creation of the soul and with the soul's subsequent fate.

Many of the questions that were the subject of later Christian theological discussions were already eagerly debated in the mystery religions. In a Hermetic treatise, for example, the existence of God was proved from the evident order of the world. This argument, which had first been formulated by ZOROASTER, was expressed in the form of questions: Who could have created the heavens and the stars, the sun and the moon, except God? Who could have made wind, water, fire, and earth (the elements), the seasons of the year, the crops, the animals, and man, except God?

Passionate debates were held about the question of whether man was subject to blind fate. For many Greeks and Romans, ASTROLOGY was the only sensible method of studying man's life and fortune. While the mystery religions admitted that the stars ruled the world and that the planets had evil influences, the highest god of the religion (*e.g.,* SARAPIS in the Isis Mysteries) stood far above the stars and was their master. A man who decided to become a servant of this god stepped out of the circle of determination and entered into the sphere of liberty. The god could suspend determination, because he ruled over the stars, and he could save his servant from illness and prolong his life, even against the will of fate. In the Isis Mysteries there was a theology of GRACE foreshadowing Christian doctrine.

In many of the mystery cults, there was a marked tendency toward henotheism—the worship of one god without denying the existence of other gods. Thus, Isis was the essence of all goddesses; Sarapis was the name uniting the gods ZEUS, PLUTO, DIONYSUS, ASCLEPIUS, HELIOS, and the Jewish god YHWH (YAHWEH). In the religion of Sol, an elaborate syncretistic theology was developed to show that all known gods of all nations were nothing but provisional names for the sun god.

MYSTERY RELIGIONS AND CHRISTIANITY

Christianity originated during the time of the Roman Empire, which was also the time at which the mysteries reached their height of popularity. This was by no means an accident. The parallel development was fostered by the new conditions prevailing in the Roman Empire, in which the old political units were dissolved, and the whole civilized world was ruled by one monarch. People were free to move from one country to another and became cosmopolitan. The ideas of

Greek philosophy penetrated everywhere in this society. Thus, under identical conditions, new forms of religious communities sprang from similar roots. The mystery religions and Christianity had many similar features—*e.g.*, a time of preparation before initiation and periods of fasting; baptism and banquets; vigils and early-morning ceremonies; PILGRIMAGES and new names for the initiates. The purity demanded in the worship of Sol and in the Chaldean fire rites was similar to Christian standards. In the Christian congregations of the first two centuries, the variety of rites and creeds was almost as great as in the mystery communities; few of the early Christian congregations could have been called orthodox according to later standards. The date of CHRISTMAS was purposely fixed on December 25 to push into the background the great festival of the sun god, and EPIPHANY on January 6 to supplant an Egyptian festival of the same day. The EASTER ceremonies rivaled the pre-Christian spring festivals. The religious art of the Christians continued the traditional art of the preceding generations. The Christian representations of the MADONNA and child are clearly the continuation of the representations of Isis and her son suckling her breast. The statue of the Good Shepherd carrying his lost sheep and the pastoral themes on Christian sarcophagi were also taken over from the craftsmanship of other religious traditions (*see* ART AND RELIGION).

In theology the differences between early Christians, Gnostics, and non-Christian Hermetists were slight. In the large library discovered at Naj' Ḥammādī, in upper Egypt, in 1945, HERMETIC WRITINGS were found side-by-side with Christian Gnostic texts. The doctrine of the soul taught in Gnostic communities was almost identical to that taught in the mysteries: the soul emanated from the Father, fell into the body, and had to return to its former home. The Greeks interpreted the national religions of the Greek Middle East chiefly in terms of Plato's philosophical and religious concepts. Interpretation in Platonic concepts was also the means by which the Judeo-Christian set of creeds was thoroughly assimilated to Greek ideas by the early Christian thinkers CLEMENT OF ALEXANDRIA and ORIGEN. Thus, the religions had a common conceptual framework.

The similarity of the religious vocabulary is also great. Greek life was characterized by such things as democratic institutions, seafaring, gymnasium and athletic games, theater, and philosophy. The mystery religions adopted many expressions from these domains: they spoke of the assembly (*ekklēsia*) of the *mystai*; the voyage of life; the ship, the anchor, and the port of religion; and the wreath of the initiate; life was a stage and man the actor. The Christians took over the entire terminology; but many words were strangely twisted in order to fit into the Christian world: the service of the state (*leitourgia*) became the ritual, or liturgy, of the church; the decree of the assembly and the opinions of the philosophers (*dogma*) became the fixed doctrine of Christianity; the correct opinion (*orthē doxa*) about things became orthodoxy.

There are also differences between Christianity and the mysteries. Mystery religions, as a rule, can be traced back to tribal origins, Christianity to a single person. The holy stories of the mysteries were myths, whereas the GOSPELS of the NEW TESTAMENT relate historical events. The essential features of Christianity were fixed once and for all in a book; the mystery doctrines, however, always remained in a much greater state of fluidity. The theology of the mysteries was developed to a far lesser degree than the Christian theology. The cult of rulers in the manner of the imperial mysteries was impossible in Jewish and Christian worship.

The mysteries declined quickly when the emperor CONSTANTINE raised Christianity to the status of the state religion. After a short period of toleration, the other religions were prohibited. The property of the pagan gods was confiscated and the temples destroyed, and the gold of the temple treasuries was used to mint coins. To show the beginning of a new era, the capital city of the empire was transferred to the new Christian city of Constantinople. Only remnants of the mystery doctrines, amalgamated with Platonism, were transmitted by a few philosophers and individualists to the religious thinkers of the Byzantine Empire. The mystery religions survived to exert some influence on the thinkers of the Middle Ages and the philosophers of the Italian Renaissance.

MYSTICISM, in general, a spiritual quest for hidden truth or wisdom, the goal of which is union with the divine or sacred (the transcendent realm). Forms of mysticism are found in all major world religions, by analogy in the shamanic and other ecstatic practices of nonliterate cultures, and in secular experience.

The goal of mysticism is union with the divine or sacred. The path to that union is usually developed by following four stages: purgation (of bodily desires), purification (of the will), illumination (of the mind), and unification (of one's will or being with the divine). If "the object of man's existence is to be a Man, that is, to re-establish the harmony which originally belonged between him and the divinized state before the separation took place which disturbed the equilibrium" (*The Life and Doctrine of Paracelsus*), mysticism will always be a part of the way of return to the source of being, a way of countering the experience of alienation.

Mysticism's apparent denial, or self-negation, is part of a psychological process or strategy that does not really deny the person. Indeed, many forms of mysticism satisfy the claims of rationality, ecstasy, and righteousness. There is obviously something nonmental, paradoxical, and unpredictable about the mystical phenomenon, but it is not, therefore, irrational or antirational or "religion without thought." Rather, as ZEN Buddhist masters say, it is knowledge of the most adequate kind, only it cannot be expressed in words. If there is a mystery about mystical experience, it is something it shares with life and consciousness. Mysticism, a form of living in depth, indicates that in humans there is a meeting ground of various levels of reality; we are more than one-dimensional. Despite the interaction and correspondence between levels—"What is below is like what is above; what is above is like what is below" (*Tabula Smaragdina*, "Emerald Tablet," a work on alchemy attributed to Hermes Trismegistos; *see* HERMETIC WRITINGS)—they are not to be equated or confused. At once a praxis (technique) and a gnosis (esoteric knowledge, *see* GNOSTICISM), mysticism consists of a way or discipline.

The relationship of the religion of faith to mysticism ("personal religion raised to the highest power") is ambiguous, a mixture of respect and misgivings. Though mysticism may be associated with religion, it need not be. The mystic often represents a type that the structured and hierarchical religious institution (*i.e.*, the established church) does not and cannot produce and does not know what to do with if and when one appears. As William Ralph Inge, an English theologian, commented, "institutionalism and mysticism have been uneasy bedfellows." Although mysticism has been the core of Hinduism and Buddhism, it has been little more than a minor element—and, frequently, a disturbing one—in Judaism, Christianity, and Islam. As the 15th- to 16th-century Italian political philosopher Machiavelli had noted of the 13th-century Christian monastic leaders ST. FRANCIS and ST. DOMINIC, they had saved religion but destroyed the church.

Paradigmatic pronouncements in regard to mysticism pose problems of their own. The classic Indian formula— "that thou art," *tat tvam asi* (*Chandogya Upanishad*, 6.9)—is hedged around with the profoundest ambiguity. The difficulty reappears in the thought of the medieval Christian mystic MEISTER ECKHART, who had the church raising questions for such unguarded statements as "The knower and the known are one. God and I, we are one in knowledge" and "There is no distinction between us."

Mysticism may be defined as the belief in a third kind of knowledge, the other two being sense knowledge and knowledge by inference. This same view was held by the 3rd-century-CE Greek philosopher Plotinus. But the pattern misses the other dominant quality of mystical experience—love or union through love. The medieval, theistic view of mysticism (as of religious life) was that it was "a stretching out of the soul into God through the urge of love, an experimental knowledge of God through unifying love."

Certain forms of mysticism, however, would seem to strive toward a naked encounter with the Whole or All, without and beyond symbols. Of this kind of direct apprehension of the absolute, introvertive mysticism offers examples from different times and traditions. Instead of looking out, the gaze turns inward, toward the unchanging, the undifferentiated "One without a second." The process by which this state is attained is by a blotting out or suppression of all physical sensations—indeed, of the entire empirical content of consciousness. *Cittavṛttinirodha* ("the holding or stopping of the mind stuff") was how the 2nd-century-BCE Indian mystic Patañjali described it.

Such undifferentiated unity or union between the individual and the supreme self is unacceptable to certain traditions and temperaments. The Jewish philosopher MARTIN BUBER emphasized an "I-Thou" relationship: "All real living is meeting," and one Thou cannot become It. But even his own "unforgettable experience" of union he would explain as "illusory." With a wider range, a British scholar, R.C. Zaehner, has tried to establish different kinds, or types, of mysticism: of isolation, the separation of spirit and matter, eternity from time; pantheistic, or "pan-enhenic," in which the soul is the universe—all creaturely existence is one; the theistic, in which the soul feels identified with God; and the beatific, with its hope of deification when "the perishable puts on the imperishable."

Mystical experience, which is centred in a seeking for unity, admits of wide variations but falls into recognizable types: mild and extreme, extrovertive and introvertive, and theistic and nontheistic. Another well-known typology— corresponding to the faculties of thinking, willing, and feeling—employs the Indian formula, the respective ways of knowledge (JÑANA), works (KARMA), and devotion (BHAKTI). Claims have been made on behalf of each, though many mystics have tried to accord to each its place and also to arrive at a synthesis, as in the BHAGAVAD GĪTĀ. Depending on the powers of discrimination, the intellectual or the contemplative type tries to reach the Highest, the One, or the Godhead behind God. In its approach toward the supreme identity it tends to be chary of multiplicity, "to deny the world that it may find reality." Plotinus was "ashamed of being in the body." In the 17th century, Spinoza's nondenominational concept of intellectual love of God revealed a sense of aloofness or isolation reminiscent of the ancient Hindus.

Another type of mysticism is that defined by love and devotion. A theistic attitude, or devotional mysticism, depends upon mutual attraction. In the words of a Sufi (*see* SUFISM) poet, "I sought Him for thirty years, I thought that it was I who desired Him, but no, it was He who desired me." The path of devotion includes the rituals of prayer, worship, and adoration, which—if done with sincerity, inwardness, and understanding—can bring some of the most rewarding treasures of the religious life, including ecstasy (or SAMADHI). There is a paradox and a danger here: the paradox of avoiding the loss of personality, the danger of self-indulgence.

Also, in an unpurified medium, the experiences may and do give rise to erotic feelings, a fact observed and duly warned against by the Christian CHURCH FATHERS and other leaders of other faiths as well. (Zen Buddhism, for instance, avoids both the overly personal and erotic suggestions.) Sometimes the distinction between eros (Greek: "erotic love") or KAMA (Sanskrit: "sexual love") and AGAPE (Greek: "a higher love") or prema (Sanskrit: "higher love") can be thin. In the Indian tradition the Vaiṣṇava and Tantric experiments were, in their apparently different ways, bold and honest attempts at sublimation, though some of these experiments were failures. (See VAIṢṆAVISM.)

The same fate is likely to overtake the use of pharmacological aids to visionary experience—practices that are by no means new and occur in traditions as disparate as ZOROASTRIANISM and NATIVE AMERICAN RELIGIONS. A yogic writer, Patañjali, speaks of the use of *ausadhi* (a medicinal herb) as a means to yogic experience, and the VEDAS and TANTRAS refer to wine as part of worship and the initiatory rites. The Greek Mysteries (religions of salvation) sometimes used sedatives and stimulants. Primarily meant to remove ethical, social, and mental inhibitions and to open up the subconscious no less than the subliminal, these techniques, as a rule, were frowned upon, even though those who took the help of such artificial aids had undergone prior training and discipline. (See MYSTERY RELIGION.)

All of the major religious traditions have some form of mystical thought and practice. For some traditions mysticism forms a core piece of the religion, whereas, in the major Western monotheistic traditions, mystic thought and practice has tended to be at the periphery of those traditions.

HINDUISM is often predisposed to mystical interpretation. As the highest ideal of Hindu religious practice, ascetic MOKṢA ("release") has received the most attention. At least in part, YOGA represents the rise within traditional Hinduism of a special mystical technique that was intended to make possible for the select few a high degree of mystical insight originally predicated of the many. The techniques of Yoga, including the physical discipline of HAṬHA YOGA, were combined with traditional Hindu doctrines about the absorption of the individual soul in the All. Other forms of Hindu mysticism are more personal, relating the devotee to a particular deity of the Hindu pantheon, while still others stress the passivity of faith as trust and surrender to the grace and power of KRISHNA or RĀMA.

Common to the various traditions of BUDDHISM is an emphasis upon meditation and contemplation as means of moving toward NIRVANA, but each of the Buddhist traditions sets its own distinctive interpretation on that goal. Of special interest in any discussion of Buddhist mysticism are VAJRAYĀNA and Zen. Practitioners of Vajrayāna, or Tantric Buddhism, in Tibet combine Yogic discipline with an absolutistic philosophy and highly symbolic language to cultivate mystical ECSTASY.

Sufism, a mystical form of worship in ISLAM, often expresses itself in the metaphors of intoxication and of the love between bride and bridegroom—language that is not easy to reconcile with the stress of the QUR'AN upon the sovereignty and transcendence of ALLĀH. At the same time, mysticism made the reality of the divine accessible to those who found the God of the Qur'an austere and distant.

The foundations for Jewish mysticism were laid in the visions of the biblical prophets and the apocalyptic imagery of postbiblical JUDAISM. The most characteristic and profound theme of mystical Judaism is the QABBALAH, which reached its climax in the SEFER HA-ZOHAR near the end of the 13th century. This "Book of Splendor" described the power and inner life of God and set forth the principles and commandments by means of which the true believer could regain the DEVEQUT ("adherence to God") that had been destroyed by humans' fall from pristine purity. Subsequent Jewish mysticism continued to build upon the *Sefer ha-Zohar*. The Hasidic form in particular had far-reaching effects upon the piety and practice of the common people; in the form it took in the thought of MARTIN BUBER, it shaped both Christian and secular thought as well.

The mystical aspects of CHRISTIANITY have been manifested most clearly in a recurring pattern of movements. In the religion of PAUL and JOHN, "Christ-mysticism," frequently spontaneous and unsought, is fundamental. The Desert Fathers of the 3rd and 4th centuries established an eremitic tradition of conscious preparation and practice for mystical enlightenment. AUGUSTINE'S account of the divine Light of being drew upon Neoplatonic themes and imagery that would figure strongly in the literature of subsequent mystics, perhaps culminating in Meister Eckhart (d. 1327/28?), who emphasized the reality of the ideal world, in which all things are eternally present as elements in the being of God. Mysticism flourished in the 14th century both within the church and in numerous heresies, a dichotomy that was to characterize several later periods. In general, Protestant mystics explicitly recognize that which is implied in Roman Catholic teaching: that the divine Light or Spark is a universal principle.

MYTH AND RITUAL SCHOOL, in the academic STUDY OF RELIGIONS, an analytic method that was especially important in the 1930s, particularly in the interpretation of Middle Eastern mythology. The scholars of this school, who were mainly located in Britain and the Scandinavian countries, contended that any myth functions, or at one time functioned, as the "explanation" of a ritual.

The Myth and Ritual School held that the *enuma elish*, the Babylonian creation epic, was a mythic drama re-enacted every year at the spring festival, at which time the foundation of the world is ritually renewed; the myth was, it was argued, expressing in language that which the ritual was enacting through action. The king, as the personified god, played the main role in the overall cultural pattern. The English branch of this school concentrated on anthropological and FOLKLORE studies. The Scandinavian branch (the "Uppsala School") concentrated on Semitic philological, cultural, and history-of-religions studies. It is represented in the latter part of the 20th century by Swedish historians of religion who have theorized that, for the entire ancient Middle East, certain cult patterns existed and that behind those cult patterns lay the sacred-king ideology.

Members of this school have had difficulty accounting for myths which lack a ritual context, and this method of interpretation fell out of favor in the latter half of the 20th century. The Myth-Ritual orientation, however, has persevered in some areas, and the study of sacrifice by Walter Burkert entitled *Homo Necans: The Anthropology of Ancient Greek Sacrificial Ritual and Myth* (1983) has been particularly influential. The most influential statement of the Myth and Ritual School's position is to be found in *Myth and Ritual* (1933), edited by the English biblical scholar and Orientalist Samuel Hooke; another influential work is Jane Harrison's *Themis* (1922). The most prominent critique of the theory is Joseph Fontenrose's *The Ritual Theory of Myth* (1966).

MYTHOLOGY

The body of symbolic narratives that constitute mythology are usually of unknown origin and at least partly traditional. They ostensibly relate actual events and are especially associated with RELIGIOUS BELIEF. Mythology is distinguished from symbolic behavior (cult, ritual) and symbolic places or objects (temples, ICONS). Myths are specific accounts of gods or superhuman beings involved in extraordinary events or circumstances in a time that is unspecified but which is understood as existing apart from ordinary human experience. The term mythology denotes both the study of myth and the body of myths belonging to a particular religious tradition.

While the outline of myths from a past period or from a society other than one's own can usually be seen quite clearly, to recognize the myths that are dominant in one's own time and society is always difficult. This is hardly surprising, because a myth has its authority not by proving itself but by presenting itself. In this sense the authority of a myth indeed "goes without saying," and the myth can be outlined in detail only when its authority is no longer unquestioned but has been overcome in some manner by another, more comprehensive myth.

The word *myth* derives from the Greek *mythos*, which has a range of meanings from "word," through "saying" and "story," to "fiction"; the unquestioned validity of *mythos* can be contrasted with *logos*, the word whose validity or truth can be argued and demonstrated. Because myths narrate fantastic events with no attempt at proof, it is sometimes assumed that they are simply stories with no factual basis, and the word has become a synonym for falsehood or, at best, misconception. In the STUDY OF RELIGION, however, it is important to distinguish between myths and stories that are merely untrue.

RELATION OF MYTHS TO OTHER NARRATIVE FORMS

In Western culture there are a number of literary or narrative genres that scholars have related in different ways to myths. Examples are fables, fairy tales, folktales, sagas, epics, legends, and etiologic tales (which refer to causes or explain why a thing is the way it is). Another form of tale, the PARABLE, differs from myth in its purpose and character. Even in the West, however, there is no agreed definition of any of these genres, and some scholars question whether multiplying cate-

Protected by Athena, the hero Perseus beheads the monstrous Medusa, metope from the Greek city of Selinus, Sicily, early 6th century BCE; in the Museo Nazionale, Palermo
Art Resource

gories of narrative is helpful at all, as opposed to working with a very general concept such as the traditional tale. Non-Western cultures apply classifications that are different both from the Western categories and from one another. Most, however, make a basic distinction between "true" and "fictitious" narratives, with "true" ones corresponding to what in the West would be called myths.

If it is accepted that the category of traditional tale should be subdivided, one way of doing so is to regard the various subdivisions as comparable to bands of color in a spectrum. Within this figurative spectrum, there will be similarities and analogies between myth and folktale or between myth and legend or between fairy tale and folktale. In the section that follows, it is assumed that useful distinctions can be drawn between different categories. It should, however, be remembered throughout that these classifications are far from rigid and that, in many cases, a given tale might be plausibly assigned to more than one category.

Fables. The word *fable* derives from the Latin word *fabula*, which originally meant about the same as the Greek *mythos*; like *mythos*, it came to mean a fictitious or untrue story. Myths, in contrast, are not presented as fictitious or untrue.

Fables, like some myths, feature personified animals or natural objects as characters. Unlike myths, however, fables almost always end with an explicit moral message, and this highlights the characteristic feature of fables—namely, that they are instructive tales that teach morals about human social behavior. Myths, by contrast, tend to lack this directly didactic aspect, and the sacred narratives that they embody are often hard to translate into direct prescriptions for action in everyday human terms. Another difference between fables and myths relates to a feature of the narratives that they present. The context of a typical fable will be unspecific as to time and space; *e.g.*, "A fox and a goose met at a pool." A typical myth, on the other hand, will be likely to identify by name the god or hero concerned in a given exploit and to specify details of geography and genealogy; *e.g.*, "Oedipus was the son of Laius, the king of Thebes."

Fairy tales. The term *fairy tale* is normally used to refer to stories (directed above all at an audience of children) about an individual, almost always young, who confronts strange or magical events. Like myths, fairy tales present extraordinary beings and events. Like fables, but unlike myths, fairy tales tend to be placed in a setting that is geographically and temporally vague.

Folktales. There is much disagreement among scholars as to how to define the folktale; consequently, there is disagreement about the relation between folktale and myth. Some scholars regard myths as one type of folktale, while the particular characteristic of myth is that its narratives deal with sacred events that happened "in the beginning." Others either consider folktale a subdivision of myth or regard the two categories as distinct but overlapping. Examples of folktale motifs are encounters between ordinary human beings and supernatural adversaries such as witches, GIANTS, or ogres; contests to win a bride; the "simple" person outwitting a clever foe; and attempts to overcome a wicked stepmother or jealous sisters. But these typical folktale themes occur also in stories normally classified as myths, and there must always be a strong element of arbitrariness in assigning a motif to a particular category.

Sagas and epics. The word *saga* is often used in a generalized and loose way to refer to any extended narrative re-creation of historical events. The word *saga* is Old Norse and means "what is said," and the sagas belong to a narrative type confined to a particular time and place. Epic, meanwhile, is similar to saga in that both narrative forms look back to an age of heroic endeavor, but it differs from saga in that epics are almost always composed in verse. Epics characteristically incorporate mythical events and persons, and myth is thus a prime source of the material on which epic draws.

Legends. In common usage the word *legend* usually characterizes a traditional tale thought to have a historical basis, as in the legends of King Arthur or Robin Hood. In this view, a distinction may be drawn between myth (which refers to the supernatural and the sacred) and legend (which is grounded in historical fact). But the distinction between myth and legend must be used with care: because of the assumed link between legend and historical fact, there may be a tendency to refer to narratives that correspond to one's own beliefs as legends, while exactly comparable stories from other traditions may be classified as myths.

Parables. The term *myth* is not normally applied to narratives that have as their explicit purpose the illustration of a doctrine or standard of conduct. Instead, the term parable, or illustrative tale, is used. Parables have a more subservient function than myths. They may clarify something to an individual or a group but do not take on the revelatory character of myth.

Etiologic tales. Etiologic tales are very close to myth, and some scholars regard them as merely a particular type of myth. An etiologic tale explains the origin of a custom, state of affairs, or natural feature in the human or divine world. The etiologic theme often seems to be added to a mythical narrative as an afterthought. In other words, the etiology is not the distinctive characteristic of myth.

APPROACHES TO THE STUDY OF MYTH AND MYTHOLOGY

The project of interpreting myths has a history thousands of years long. The growth of philosophy in ancient Greece promoted the allegorical interpretation of myth—*i.e.*, finding other or supposedly deeper meanings hidden below the surface of mythical texts. Such meanings were usually seen as involving natural phenomena or human values. Related to this was a tendency toward rationalism—the scrutiny of myths in such a way as to make sense of the statements contained in them without taking literally their references to gods, monsters, or the supernatural. Of special and long-lasting influence in the history of the interpretation of myth was EUHEMERISM (named after EUHEMERUS, a Greek writer who flourished about 300 BCE), according to which certain gods were originally great people venerated because of their benefactions to mankind.

The CHURCH FATHERS of early CHRISTIANITY adopted an attitude of modified Euhemerism, according to which classical mythology was to be explained in terms of mere men who had been raised to superhuman status because of their deeds. By this means, Christians were able to incorporate myths from the culturally authoritative pre-Christian past into a Christian framework while defusing their religious significance—the gods became ordinary humans.

In early 18th-century Italy, Giambattista Vico made the first clear case for the role of the human creative imagination in the formation of distinct myths at successive cultural stages, but his work had no influence in his own century. Instead, the notion that pre-Christian myths were distortions of the biblical revelation (first expressed in the Renaissance) continued to find favor. Nevertheless, Enlightenment philosophy, reports from voyages of discovery, and missionary reports (especially the Jesuits' accounts of North American Indians) contributed to scholarship and fostered greater objectivity. In the 18th

In an episode from the epic Ramāyāṇa, *Rāma and his brother Lakṣmaṇa fight Rāvaṇa, a demon with 10 heads and 20 arms, gouache on paper, Jaipur school, 19th century*
Victoria and Albert Museum, London—Art Resource

century the French scholar Bernhard Le Bovier de Fontenelle compared Greek and American Indian myths and suggested that there was a universal human predisposition toward mythology. He attributed the absurdities (as he saw them) of myths to the fact that the stories grew up among an earlier, more primitive human society.

In the late 18th century artists and intellectuals came increasingly to emphasize the role of the emotions in human life and, correspondingly, to play down the importance of reason (which had been regarded as supremely important by thinkers of the Enlightenment). Those involved in the new movement were known as Romantics. The Romantic movement had profound implications for the study of myth. Myths—both the stories from Greek and Roman antiquity and contemporary folktales—were regarded by the Romantics as repositories of experience far more vital and powerful than those obtainable from what was felt to be the artificial art and poetry of the civilization of contemporary Europe. For the German philosopher Johann Gottfried von Herder, ancient myths were the natural expressions of the concerns that would have confronted the ancients; and those concerns were the very ones that, according to Herder, still confronted the *Volk*— e.g., ordinary people—in his own day.

Since the Romantic movement, all study of myth has been comparative, although comparative attempts were made earlier. The prevalence of the comparative approach has meant that since the 19th century even the most specialized studies have made generalizations about more than one tradition or at the very least have had to take comparative works by others into account. Indeed, for there to be any philosophical inquiry into the nature and function of myth at all, there must exist a body of data about myths across a range of societies. Such data would not exist without a comparative approach.

MAX MÜLLER, a German Orientalist, was a critical figure in the modern study of mythology. In his view, the mythology of the original Indo-European peoples had consisted of allegorical stories about the workings of nature, in particular such features as the sky, the Sun, and the dawn. In the course of time, though, these original meanings had been lost (through, in Müller's notorious phrasing, a "disease of language"), so that the myths no longer told in a "rationally intelligible" way of phenomena in the natural world but instead appeared to describe the "irrational" activities of gods, heroes, NYMPHS, and others. One of the problems with this view is, of course, that it fails to account for the fact that those who tell such stories do so long after their supposed meanings had been forgotten, in the manifest belief that the stories refer, not to nature, but precisely to gods, heroes, and other beings.

Interest in myth was greatly stimulated in Germany by Friedrich von

Heracles shows the cowering Eurystheus the wild boar that he has captured on Mt. Erymanthus as one of the 12 labors imposed on him
Alinari—Art Resource

Schelling's philosophy of mythology, which argued that myth was a form of expression, characteristic of a particular stage in human development, through which humans imagine the Absolute (for Schelling an all-embracing unity in which all differences are reconciled). Scholarly interest in myth has continued throughout the 20th century. Many scholars have adopted a psychological approach because of interest aroused by the theories of SIGMUND FREUD. Subsequently, new approaches in sociology and anthropology have continued to encourage the study of myth.

One important school of thought within anthropological circles approached myth from the standpoint of FUNCTIONALISM. Functionalism is primarily associated with the anthropologists BRONISŁAW MALINOWSKI and A.R. Radcliffe-Brown. Both ask not what the origin of any given social behavior may be but how it contributes to maintaining the system of which it is a part. In this view, in all types of society, every aspect of life—every custom, belief, or idea—makes its own special contribution to the continued effective working of the whole society. Functionalism has had a wide appeal to anthropologists in Britain and the United States, especially as an interpretation of myth as integrated with other aspects of society and as supporting existing social relationships.

The structuralist study of myth has been equally important. Structuralist approaches to myth are based on the analogy of myth to language. Just as a language is composed of significant oppositions (*e.g.*, between phonemes, the constituent sounds of the language), so myths are formed out of significant oppositions between certain terms and categories. Structuralist analysis aims at uncovering what it sees as the logic of myth. It is argued that supposedly primitive thought is logically consistent but that the terms of this logic are not those with which modern Western culture is familiar. Instead they are terms related to items of the everyday world in which the "primitive" culture exists. This logic is usually based on empirical categories (*e.g.*, raw/cooked, upstream/downstream, bush/village) or empirical objects (*e.g.*, buffalo, river, gold, eagle). Some structuralists, such as the French anthropologist Claude Lévi-Strauss, have emphasized the presence of the same logical patterns in myths throughout the world.

Valhalla, in Norse mythology, the home of warriors slain in battle, stone relief, Gotland, Sweden, 9th century
Giraudon—Art Resource

NABU \\'nä-₋bü\\, *Hebrew* Nebo \\'ne-bō\\, major god in the Assyro-Babylonian pantheon. He was patron of the art of writing and a god of vegetation. Nabu's symbols were the clay tablet and the stylus, the instruments held to be proper to him who inscribed the fates assigned to humans by the gods. In the OLD TESTAMENT, the worship of Nebo is denounced by ISAIAH (46:1).

Samsuditana, the last king of the 1st dynasty of Babylon (reigned 1625–1595 BCE), introduced a statue of Nabu into ESAGILA, the temple of MARDUK, the city god of Babylon. Not until the 1st millennium BCE, however, did the relationship between Marduk and Nabu and their relative positions in theology and popular devotion become clear. Marduk, the father of Nabu, took precedence over him, at least theoretically, in Babylonia. But in popular devotion it was Nabu—who knows all and sees all—who was chief, especially during the centuries immediately preceding the fall of Babylon. He had a chapel named Ezida in his father's temple Esagila, where at the New Year feast he was installed alongside Marduk. In his own holy city, Borsippa, he was supreme.

NĀGA \\'nä-gə\\ (Sanskrit: "serpent"), in Hindu and Buddhist mythology, member of a class of semidivine beings considered to be a strong, handsome race who can assume either human or serpentine form. The *nāga*s live in an underground kingdom called Nāga-loka, or Pātāla-loka, which is filled with resplendent palaces, beautifully ornamented with precious gems. BRAHMĀ, it is said, relegated the *nāga*s to the nether regions when they became too populous on earth and commanded them to bite only the truly evil or those destined to die prematurely. They are also associated with rivers, lakes, seas, and wells and are regarded as guardians of treasure. Three notable *nāga*s are Śeṣa (or Ananta), who in the VAIṢṆAVA myth of creation supports Vishnu-Nārāyaṇa as he lies on the cosmic ocean and on whom the created world rests; Vāsuki, who was used as a churning rope to churn the cosmic MILK-OCEAN; and Takṣaka, the tribal chief of the snakes. In modern HINDUISM the birth of the serpents is celebrated on Nāga-pañcamī in the month of Śrāvaṇa (July–August).

The female *nāga*s (or *nāgī*s), according to tradition, are serpent princesses of striking beauty, and the dynasties of Manipur in northeastern India, the Pallavas in southern India, and the ruling family of Funan (ancient Indochina) traced their origin to the union of a man and a *nāgī*.

In BUDDHISM, *nāga*s are often represented as door guardians or as minor deities. The snake king Mucilinda, who sheltered the BUDDHA from rain for seven days while he was deep in meditation, is beautifully depicted in the 9th–13th century Mon-Khmer Buddhas of Thailand and Cambodia. In JAINISM, the Jain savior (TĪRTHAṄKARA PĀRŚVANĀTHA) is always shown with a canopy of snake hoods above his head.

NĀGĀRJUNA \\nä-'gär-ju̇-nə\\ (b. *c.* 150 CE—d. *c.* 250), Indian Buddhist monk-philosopher and founder of the

MĀDHYAMIKA school. He is recognized as a patriarch by several later Buddhist schools.

The earliest account of Nāgārjuna's life is in Chinese, supplied about 405 CE by a renowned Buddhist translator, KUMĀRAJĪVA. It agrees with later Chinese and Tibetan accounts that Nāgārjuna was born in South India into a BRAHMIN family. The stories of his boyhood indicate that he had an extraordinary intellectual capacity and underwent a spiritual conversion to MAHĀYĀNA BUDDHISM. According to Kumārajīva's account, Nāgārjuna mastered some Mahāyāna verses of great profundity in a short time and then propagated the truth (DHARMA) in India, successfully defeating many opponents in scholastic philosophical debates. Traditional accounts also suggest that he lived to an old age and then decided to end his life.

The fact that various texts ascribe different religious qualities to Nāgārjuna and give dates for his life that range over 500 years suggests that the references may pertain to several persons and may include some imaginary accounts. Nonetheless, some elements of Nāgārjuna's biographies are supported by historical materials. Scholarship now indicates that Nāgārjuna could have lived as early as 50 CE and as late as 280. His dates are usually given as 150–250.

Besides the verses of Mādhyamika analysis, there are a large number of Tantric and medical works attributed by Tibetan tradition to a "Nāgārjuna." There are also references in late Indian materials to a great SIDDHA, or sorcerer, by the name of Nāgārjuna, who acquired his magical power through Tantric practices. Closely allied stories tell of a powerful alchemist who, among other accomplishments, discovered the elixir of immortality. The reports of a great sorcerer, however, are generally not accepted outside the Tibetan tradition as applying to the 2nd-century philosopher.

Something of the Mādhyamika philosopher's life and attitude can be gleaned from Nāgārjuna's writings. His critical analytic verses and his didactic treatises, letters, and hymns indicate his deep concern to practice "nonattachment" in engagement with people. Through rigorous logical argumentation, as found in the *Mādhyamika Kārikā*, he criticized both Buddhist and Hindu views on existence. Most of his polemics, however, were directed toward the explanations of existence offered by the Buddhist schools of Sthaviravāda (THERAVĀDA) and SARVĀSTIVĀDA. Nāgārjuna's position is closely allied to, and probably dependent on, that found in the early Mahāyāna literature known as the *Prajñāpāramitā-sūtra*s ("Perfection of Wisdom Verses"), in which the notion of *śūnyatā* (EMPTINESS) is an important term for the wayfarer on the path to enlightenment and becomes the distinguishing term in the Mādhyamika school. Nāgārjuna's clarification of the term *śūnyatā* is regarded by Buddhists as an intellectual and spiritual achievement of the highest order.

NĀGĀRJUNAKONDA \\nä-'gär-ju̇-nə-'kōn-də\\, city and archaeological site in the Guntūr district, northeastern

Nāga *and* nāgī, *9th-century statue from Bihār Sharīf, Bihār, India; in the Indian Museum, Calcutta*
Pramod Chandra

Andhra Pradesh state, southern India, notable for its ancient Buddhist monuments (dating from the 1st to the 3rd century CE) and for an ancient university (3rd–4th century) where NĀGĀRJUNA, the founder of the MAHĀYĀNA school of BUDDHISM, once taught.

NAGUAL \nä-'gwäl\, *also spelled* nahual \nä-'wäl\, personal GUARDIAN SPIRIT believed by some Meso-American Indians to reside in an animal, in some areas the animal into which certain powerful men can transform themselves to do harm; thus, the word derives from the complex Nahuatl word *nahualli* (meaning a being who can transform into another).

The person who is to receive his nagual traditionally goes to an isolated spot and sleeps there; the animal that appears in his dreams or that confronts him when he awakens will then be his particular nagual. Many modern Meso-American Indians believe that the first creature to cross over the ashes spread before a newborn baby becomes that child's nagual. In some areas it is believed that only the most powerful leaders possess naguals.

NAḤMANIDES \näk-'mä-nə-ˌdēz\, *original name* Moses ben Nahman, *also called* Naḥamani, *or, by acronym,* Ramban \räm-'bän\ (b. *c.* 1194, Gerona, Catalonia—d. 1270, Acre, Palestine), Spanish scholar, RABBI, philosopher, poet, physician, and Qabbalist.

Naḥmanides earned his livelihood as a physician and served as rabbi at Gerona and as chief rabbi of Catalonia. As one of the leading rabbinical scholars in Spain, he was summoned by King James I of Aragon and forced to participate in a public disputation with Christians; although victorious in his arguments, he was forced to flee from Spain (1263), and he settled at Acre in Palestine. There he reorganized the Jewish settlement and began his most celebrated scholarly work, a commentary on the PENTATEUCH.

Naḥmanides' HALAKHIC works are considered classics of rabbinical literature. His commentaries on the TALMUD greatly influenced the course of subsequent Jewish rabbinical scholarship in Spain.

NAIAD \'nā-əd, 'nī-, -ˌad\ (Greek *Naias*, from *naien*, "to flow"), in Greek MYTHOLOGY, one of the NYMPHS of flowing water—springs, rivers, fountains, lakes. The Naiads were represented as beautiful, lighthearted, and beneficent. Like the other classes of nymphs, they were extremely long-lived but not immortal.

NAJAF \'nä-jáf\, *also called* an-Najaf \än-\, city, capital of al-Najaf *muḥāfaẓa* (governorate), central Iraq. One of Iraq's two holy cities (the other is KARBALĀʾ), Najaf lies on a ridge just west of the Euphrates River, about 120 miles south of Baghdad. The CALIPH Hārūn ar-Rashīd is reputed to have founded it in 791 CE ; its growth occurred mostly after the 10th century. In the city's center is the mosque containing the tomb of ʿAlī ibn Abī Ṭālib (*c.* 600–661), cousin and son-in-law of MUHAMMAD, fourth Muslim caliph, and, through a rift with other early Muslim leaders, the spiritual founder of SHIʿITE Islam; Najaf is therefore one of Shiʿism's greatest shrine cities. At the turn of the 20th century it had about 19 Shiʿite MADRASAS (religious colleges) where students from many Shiʿite communities studied with leading religious scholars. Najaf's population is predominantly Arab, but there is a sizeable Persian presence also. Najaf has long been a hotbed of Shiʿite resistance against the SUNNI rulers in Baghdad, and in the 20th century this resistance has been a source of tension between the Sunni government of Iraq and the Shiʿites in Iran. In the aftermath of the 1991 Persian Gulf War, large sections of the city were destroyed by Iraqi government forces who had mobilized to quell a widespread Shiʿite revolt. The operations of the *madrasa*s there have been severely curtailed, and the number of students and teachers had dwindled considerably as a result.

NAKAE TŌJU \'nä-kä-ˌe-'tō-jù\, *original personal name* Gen, *pseudonym* Mokken \'mȯk-ˌken\ (b. April 21, 1608, Ōmi province, Japan—d. Oct. 11, 1648, Ōmi province), NEO-CONFUCIAN scholar who established in Japan the Idealist (HSIN-HSÜEH) thought of the Chinese philosopher WANG YANG-MING.

Nakae, a retainer to his feudal lord, was originally a follower of the teachings of the Chinese Neo-Confucian CHU HSI, whose doctrines had become a part of the official ideology of the Japanese government. In 1634 he returned home to devote himself to teaching and study, eventually abandoning his adherence to the Chu Hsi school of thought and becoming a propagator of the philosophy of Wang Yangming. He subsequently attracted many distinguished disciples and became known as the sage of Ōmi province.

Both Wang and Nakae believed that the unifying principle (LI) of the universe exists in the human mind and not in the external world and that the true Way could be discovered through intuition and self-reflection, rejecting Chu Hsi's idea that it could be found through empirical investigation. Convinced that a concept can be fully understood only when acted upon, Nakae emphasized practice rather than abstract learning. This emphasis on individual action made Nakae's philosophy popular among the zealous Japanese reformers and patriots of the 19th and 20th centuries.

NĀLANDA \nä-'lən-də\, celebrated Buddhist monastic center, often spoken of as a university, southwest of Bihār city in northern Bihār state, India. The monasteries were founded in the Gupta period (5th century CE). The powerful 7th-century ruler of Kanauj (Kannauj), Harṣavardhana, is reported to have contributed to them. Nālanda continued to flourish as a center of learning under the Pāla dynasty (8th–12th century), and it became a center of religious sculpture in stone and bronze. Nālanda was probably sacked during Muslim raids in Bihār (*c.* 1200) and never recovered.

According to pilgrims' accounts, from Gupta times the monasteries of Nālanda were surrounded by a high wall. Excavations have revealed a row of 10 monasteries of the traditional Indian design—oblong brick structures with cells opening onto four sides of a courtyard, with a main entrance on one side and a shrine facing the entrance across the courtyard. In front of the monasteries stood a row of STUPAS in brick and plaster. The complex is referred to on seals discovered there as Mahāvihāra ("Great Monastery").

NĀM \'näm\ (Sanskrit: "name," specifically, "name of God"), which, as a kind of MANTRA, is to be recited or sung in certain Hindu devotional sects as the principal form of worship. According to theologians, God is identical with his name as revealed in the SCRIPTURES, which thus has great power. The repetition or recitation of God's name (*nama-japa*) is said to possess such salvific potential that its very sound, even apart from the reciter's intention, can produce results. One Hindu text says: "The utterance of the Lord's Name completely destroys all SIN, even when it is due to the Name being associated with something else or is done jocularly, as a result of involuntary sound, or in derision."

Devotees of KRISHNA recommend the repetition of the "mantra of the sixteen Names": "Hare Ram Hare Ram Ram Ram Hare Hare, Hare Krishna Hare Krishna Krishna Krishna Hare Hare." Saivites and Śāktas have produced their own versions of such mantras, and there are many versions of litanies, called *sahasranama*s, in which the thousand names of God are given. In general, repetition of the name of God serves as a form of devotional activity that is available to all, regardless of gender or CASTE.

The repetition of the divine name also plays a central role in SIKHISM. The *nām* there serves as shorthand for the total being and nature of the One God. It is through the Name and the Word (*sabad*) that God reveals himself to humans; salvation comes through hearing and knowing the Word and repeating and meditating upon the Name.

NAMBŪDIRI \nəm-'bü-drē\, *also spelled* Nampūtiri \-'pü-trē\, one of the dominant BRAHMIN castes of the southern Indian state of Kerala. Orthodox in the extreme, its members regard themselves as the true repositories of the ancient VEDIC RELIGION and of the traditional Hindu code.

The Nambūdiri caste follows a distinctive marriage alliance with the NĀYARS, an important caste group of lower ritual status. Though the eldest son of a Nambūdiri household customarily marries a Nambūdiri woman, thus observing the typical caste practice of endogamy, the younger sons marry Nāyar women and obey the matrilineal-descent system of the Nāyars. The Nambūdiris place great emphasis on their priestly status and do not normally engage in profitable professions.

There are five subdivisions within the Nambūdiri caste. The members of these different subdivisions act as priests, ritual technicians, or scholars. Some Nambūdiri men devote themselves to a very specialized style of Vedic chanting, while others practice ĀYURVEDIC medicine.

NĀMDEV \'näm-ˌthäv, -ˌdäv\ (b. 1270?, Narasi, India—d. 1350?, Pandharpur, Bahmanī), leading poet-saint of the Indian medieval period, who wrote in the Marāthī language.

The son of a tailor and thus of low CASTE, Nāmdev married and had five children. As a youth, he was a member of a gang but was overcome with remorse one day on hearing the lamentations of a woman whose husband he had killed. Following a vision of the god VISHNU, Nāmdev turned to a life of devotion and became the foremost exponent of the Vārkarī Panth (the "Pilgrims' Path"). The school is known for its expression of BHAKTI (devotion) and for its freedom from caste restrictions in a religious setting.

Nāmdev wrote a number of *abhaṅga*s (hymns). Extremely popular in Mahārāshtra and in the Punjab, some of his verses are included in the ĀDI GRANTH. Nāmdev inspired a tradition of devotional poetry that continued in Mahārāshtra for four centuries, culminating in the works of the great devotional poet TUKĀRĀM.

NĀMDHĀRĪ \näm-'där-ē\ (Punjabi: "Bearer of the [Divine] Name"), *also called* Kūkā \'kü-kä\ (from Punjabi *kūk*, "scream"), in SIKHISM, sect founded by Bālak Singh (1797–1862) and expanded by Rām Singh (1816–85) that emphasizes meditation on the divine name (Sanskrit: *nām*). Nāmdhārī worship leads to loud ecstatic cries, which gives the adherents the name Kūkās. Nāmdhārīs stress their KHĀLSĀ identity but differ from the mainstream Sikh community in their equal regard for the ĀDI GRANTH and the DASAM GRANTH and in their belief that the lineage of the living GURŪS continued after the 10th Gurū, GOBIND SINGH. The current Gurū is Jagjit Singh. The use of fire in marriage rituals and strict vegetarianism also set Nāmdhārīs apart.

NAMMĀLVĀR \ˌnəm-'mäl-ˌvär\, 8th-century-CE South Indian poet-saint, the most important and prolific of the Ālvārs, Vaiṣṇava singers and poets whose works of ecstatic love and personal experience of God, written in the Tamil vernacular, popularized the BHAKTI path.

Nammālvār was born into a low Śūdra caste and is said to have remained in a trance for the first 16 years of his life. Inspired by KRISHNA, he later composed four compilations of hymns or verses believed to contain the essence of the four VEDAS and designed to provide the message of the Vedas in simple, comprehensible terms to the masses. These hymns were compiled into the Tiruvaymoli which is sometimes known as the "Tamil Veda." Nammālvār claims in this work to be merely an instrument through which Krishna speaks about himself. Many of the hymns, however, are about the poet's longing and love for God, often phrased in highly emotional and even ecstatic language. The poet often adopts the persona of one or another of Krishna's erotic lovers. *Bhakti* here is presented as both a passive surrender to God and an active cultivation of the emotions that will lay the devotee open to God's GRACE and presence.

NĀNAK \'nä-nək\ (b. April 15, 1469, Rāi Bhoi dī Talvandī [now Nankānā Sāhib, Pak.], near Lahore, India—d. 1539, Kartārpur, Punjab), Indian spiritual teacher who was the founder of the SIKH tradition and its first GURŪ.

Nānak was born into a Punjabi Hindu family as the son of a revenue official in the Afghan administration. His CASTE affiliation was Khatrī. He probably received his early education at the village mosque as well as the HINDU temple. He married while in his teens and had two sons. In the early 1490s he moved to Sultānpur, a district headquarters, and gained employment as a storekeeper.

Sultānpur provided Nānak with a rich setting for interacting with Muslim nobles and interpreters of the ISLAMIC law. The town was between Lahore and Delhi, on the main road that Muslims traveled to and from the Middle East. Hindu pilgrims from all over India visiting the ancient temples in Kashmir and the Himalayan foothills also had to pass through Sultānpur. Toward the end of the 1490s, Nānak had a powerful spiritual experience, which resulted in his leaving his job and family and beginning a phase of travel that lasted 20 years or so.

In the early 1520s, Nānak acquired a piece of rich agricultural land and established a town named Kartārpur ("City of God"). As his followers and their families joined him, the Sikh community was founded. At Kartārpur, Nānak be-

Nānak (center), detail of a painting c. 1689; in the collection of Mahant Indresh Charan Dass, Dehra Dūn, Uttar Pradesh, India
By courtesy of Dr. M.S. Randhawa

came Gurū Nānak, their central teaching authority. He helped create the institutional structure of this nascent community, and at the time of his death he nominated AN·GAD, one of his followers, as his successor.

Gurū Nānak composed about 400 hymns, which provide a clear statement of his teachings. These teachings celebrate the unity and uniqueness of God, who is the true lord of the universe (*Sachā Pātishāh*). They explain that the world came into being as a result of the divine command (*hukam*) and that God maintains the course of human history and individual destinies by means of the twin principles of justice (*niān*) and grace (*nadar*). God's concern for his creation goes hand in hand with human responsibility. Nānak's hymns state the way human beings should live in this God-created world so as to attain liberation, which is achieved through meditating on the divine name (*nām*) and cultivating a relationship of love (*bhau*) for and fear (*bhai*) of the creator. In its mystical ascent, the human soul rises through the stages of duty (*dharam*), knowledge (*giān*), humility (*saram*), and grace (*karam*). Nonetheless, Gurū Nānak sets forth a view of spirituality that rejects ASCETICISM of any kind and instead mandates fulfillment of the mundane obligations of social life. Liberation is attained by living actively, connecting to family and community, and being guided by a strict code of ethical conduct (*achār*) that is built on the values of hard work, charity, and service to humanity.

As the Sikh community expanded, so also did the image of its founder. By the turn of the 17th century, the *Janam Sakhī* ("Life Story") literature presented a fully miraculous

Nandī, late 15th-century granite sculpture from South India
By courtesy of the Asian Art Museum of San Francisco, The Avery Brundage Collection, gift of the Atholl McBean Foundation

image of Gurū Nānak, one that has continued to serve as a source of inspiration for Sikhs.

NANDĪ \'nən-dē\, bull VAHANA (mount) of the HINDU god SHIVA. Some scholars suggest that the bull was originally the zoomorphic form of Shiva, but from the 1st century CE onward, he is identified as the god's vehicle.

Every Shiva temple has a figure of a white, humped bull reclining on a raised platform and facing the entrance door of the shrine, where Nandī acts both as guardian and as faithful devotee. Nandī occasionally is depicted in sculpture as a bull-faced dwarf figure and is known also in a wholly anthropomorphic form, called Nandikeśvara or Adhikāranandi; here he shares with Shiva such iconographic features as the third eye, crescent moon in the matted locks, and four arms, two holding a battle-ax and an antelope. The respect shown the bull in modern India is due to his association with Shiva. In sacred Hindu cities such as VARANASI, certain bulls are given the freedom to roam the streets. They are considered to belong to the lord and are branded on the flank with the trident insignia of Shiva.

NANNA \'nän-nä\, Sumerian god of the moon. *See* SIN.

NANSHE \'nän-,shä\, *also spelled* Nanšě, *or* Nazi \'nä-zē\, in Mesopotamian religion, Sumerian city goddess of Nina (modern Surghul, Iraq) in the southeastern part of the Lagash region of Mesopotamia. According to tradition, Nanshe's father, Enki (Akkadian: EA), organized the universe and placed her in charge of fish and fishing. Nanshe was also described as a divine soothsayer and dream interpreter. Although at times overshadowed by her sister Inanna (Akkadian: ISHTAR), Nanshe was, nevertheless, important in her own geographic area, and many rulers of Lagash record that they were chosen by her.

NAPHTALI \'naf-tə-,lī\, one of the 12 tribes that in biblical times constituted the people of Israel who later became the Jewish people. The tribe was named after the younger of two sons born to JACOB and Bilhah, a maidservant of Jacob's second wife, Rachel.

The tribe of Naphtali occupied a region northwest of the Sea of Galilee (Joshua 19:32–39). In 734 BCE the Naphtalites were conquered by the Assyrian king Tiglath-pileser III (2 Kings 15:29); deported into slavery and gradually assimilated by other peoples, the tribe of Naphtali lost its identity and thus became known in Jewish legend as one of the TEN LOST TRIBES OF ISRAEL.

NAQSHBANDĪYA \,näksh-bän-'dē-ə\, fraternity of SUFI mystics found in India, China, the Central Asian republics, and Malaysia. It claims a lineage extending back to Abū Bakr, the first CALIPH. Bahā' ad-Dīn (d. 1384), founder of the order at Bukhara, Turkistan, was called al-naqshband, "the painter," because of the impression of God that the repetition of his prescribed ritual prayer (DHIKR) should leave upon the heart, and so his followers became known as Naqshbandīya. The order has no mass support, for its litanies are subdued and emphasize repetition of the *dhikr* to oneself. Through the reforming zeal of Aḥmad Sirhindī (1564–1624), the Naqshbandīya were given new life in India in the 17th century and played a vital role in the reform of Muslim life in the 18th and 19th centuries.

NARASIMHA \‚nə-rə-'sim-hə, -'sin-\ (Sanskrit: "Man-Lion"), fourth of the 10 AVATARS (incarnations) of the Hindu god VISHNU. The DEMON Hiraṇyakaśipu, twin brother of the demon overthrown by Vishnu in his previous incarnation as VARĀHA (the boar), obtained a boon from BRAHMĀ that he could not be killed by man or beast, from inside or outside, or by day or by night, and that no weapon could harm him. Thus, feeling secure, he began to trouble heaven and earth. His son, Prahlāda, on the other hand, was a devotee of Vishnu. One day the demon challenged Prahlāda and, kicking a stone pillar, asked: "If your god is omnipresent, is he in this pillar also?" Vishnu emerged from the pillar in the form of a man-lion and slew the demon at dusk on the threshold of the house, disemboweling him with his claws.

Narasiṃha, 9th-century sculpture from Devangana, Rājasthān, India
Pramod Chandra

NARCISSUS \när-'si-səs\, in Greek mythology, son of the river god Cephissus and the NYMPH Leiriope; he was distinguished for his beauty. His mother was told that he would have a long life, provided he never looked upon his own features. But his rejection of the love of the nymph ECHO or of his lover Ameinias drew upon him the vengeance of the gods. He fell in love with his own reflection in the waters of a spring and pined away (or killed himself); the flower that bears his name sprang up where he died. According to another source, Narcissus, to console himself for the death of his beloved twin sister, sat gazing into the spring to recall her features.

NASHIM \nä-'shēm\ (Hebrew: "Women"), third of the six major divisions, or orders (*sedarim*), of the MISHNAH, which was given its final form early in the 3rd century CE by JUDAH HA-NASI. *Nashim* principally covers aspects of married life. Its seven tractates (treatises) are: *Yevamot* ("Levirates"; *i.e.*, husband's brothers), *Ketubbot* ("Marriage Contracts"), *Nedarim* ("Vows"), *Nazir* (a "Nazirite"; *i.e.*, a vowed ascetic), *Soṭa* ("A Woman Suspected of Adultery"), *Giṭṭin* ("Bills of Divorce"), and *Qiddushin* ("Marriages"). Both TALMUDS—the YERUSHALMI and the BAVLI—have GEMARA on each of the seven tractates.

NĀṢIR-I KHUSRAW \nà-'ser-ā-ḵòs-'rō\, *in full* Abū Muʿīn Nāṣir-i Khusraw al-Marvāzī al-Qubādiyānī (b. 1004, Qubādiyān, Merv, Khorāsān—d. *c.* 1072/77, Yumgān, Badakhshān, Central Asia), poet, theologian, and religious propagandist, one of the greatest writers in Persian literature.

Nāṣir-i Khusraw came from a family of government officials who followed the SHIʿITE sect of Islam. In 1045 he went on a pilgrimage to Mecca and continued his journey to Palestine and then to Egypt, which was ruled at that time by the Fāṭimid dynasty. The Fāṭimids headed the Ismāʿīlīs, an offshoot of Shiʿism, and their missionaries were engaged in propagating that doctrine throughout the Islamic world. Nāṣir-i Khusraw became such a missionary, though it is not certain whether he became an Ismāʿīlī before his trip to the Fāṭimid capital or after. He returned to his homeland in what is now Afghanistan, but his vigorous advocacy of the Ismāʿīlī ideology within SUNNI territory forced him to flee to Badakhshān, where he spent the rest of his days, lamenting in his poetry that he was unable to be an active missionary.

Nāṣir-i Khusraw's poetry is of a didactic and devotional character and consists mainly of long odes. His philosophical poetry includes the *Rawshana'ināme* (*Book of Lights*). Nāṣir's most celebrated prose work is the *Safarnāme* (*Diary of a Journey Through Syria and Palestine*), a diary describing his seven-year journey. He also wrote more than a dozen treatises expounding the doctrines of the Ismāʿīlīs, among them the *Jāmiʿ al-ḥikmatayn* ("Union of the Two Wisdoms"), in which he attempted to harmonize Ismāʿīlī theology and Greek philosophy. In his verse he displays great technical virtuosity, while his prose is remarkable for the richness of its philosophical vocabulary.

NAT \'nät\ (Burmese *nāt*, from Sanskrit *nātha*, protector, lord), in Myanmar (Burma), any of a group of spirits that are the objects of an extensive, probably pre-Buddhist cult; in Thailand a similar spirit is called *phi*. Most important of the *nat*s are a group collectively called the "37," made up of spirits of human beings who have died violent deaths. They are capable of protecting the believer when propitiated and of causing harm when offended or ignored.

Other types of *nat*s are nature spirits; hereditary *nat*s, whose annual tribute is an inherited obligation; and village *nat*s, who protect a community from wild animals, bandits, and illness and whose shrine is attached to a tree or pole near the entrance to the village. Most households also hang a coconut from the southeast pillar of the house in honor of Min Maha Giri, the house *nat*.

*Nat*s are appeased by offerings of food or flowers, which are given on all important occasions. Some special *nat* festivals honor the Taungbyon brothers—a prominent, rowdy pair of *nat*s said to have been executed in the 11th century—and the king of the "37," Thagya Min, associated by scholars with the Indian god INDRA (known in Myanmar as Sakka).

NAṬARĀJA \‚nə-tə-'rä-jə\ (Sanskrit: "Lord of Dance"), the Hindu god SHIVA in his form as the cosmic dancer, represented in most Śaiva (*see* ŚAIVISM) temples of South India. *See photo*, SYMBOLISM AND ICONOGRAPHY.

In the most common type of images, Shiva is shown with four arms and flying locks dancing on the figure of a dwarf, Apasmāra (a symbol of human ignorance; *apasmāra* means "forgetfulness," or "heedlessness"). The back right hand of Shiva holds the *ḍamaru* (hourglass-shaped drum); the front right hand is in the *abhaya mudrā* (the "fear-not" gesture, made by holding the palm outward with fingers pointing up); the back left hand carries AGNI (fire) in a vessel or in the palm of the hand; and the front left hand is held across the chest in the *gajahasta* (elephant-trunk) pose, with wrist limp and fingers pointed downward toward the uplifted left foot. The locks of Shiva's hair stand out in several strands interspersed with the figures of Gaṅgā (the GAṄGĀ RIVER personified as a goddess), flowers, a skull, and the crescent moon. His figure is encircled by a ring of flames, the *prabhāmaṇḍala*. This form of dance, the most common representation of Naṭarāja, is called in classic Sanskrit treatises on dance the *bhujaṃgatrāsa* ("trembling of the snake").

In the Naṭarāja sculpture Shiva is shown as the source of all movement within the cosmos, represented by the arch of flames. The purpose of the dance is to release humans from illusion, and the place where it is said to have been performed, Chidambaram (an important Śaiva center in South India), called the center of the universe, is in reality within the heart. The gestures of the dance represent Shiva's five activities (*pañcakṛtya*): creation (symbolized by the drum), protection (by the "fear-not" pose of the hand), destruction (by the fire), embodiment (by the foot planted on the ground), and release (by the foot held aloft).

NĀTHA \'nä-tə\, religious movement of India whose members strive for immortality by transforming the human body into an imperishable divine body. It combines esoteric traditions drawn from BUDDHISM, ŚAIVISM, and HAṬHA YOGA. The term is derived from the names of the nine traditional masters, all of which end in the word *nātha* ("master," "lord"). Texts do not agree on the lists of the nine. All are believed to have successfully transformed their bodies through yogic discipline into indestructible spiritual entities, and, according to popular belief, they reside as DEMIGODS in the HIMALAYAS.

The Nātha sect consists of yogis whose aim is to achieve *sahaja*, a state of neutrality transcending the duality of human existence through an awakening of the self's inherent identity with absolute reality. This is accomplished through the practice of *kāya-sādhana* ("cultivation of the body"), with great emphasis placed on control of semen, breath, and thought. Guidance of an accomplished GURU is considered essential. The Nātha yogis share with similar esoteric sects a liking for paradox and enigmatic verse.

NATHDVARA \nät-'dvär-ə\, *also spelled* Nāthdwārā, town, southern Rajasthan state, northwestern India, near Udaipur. Nathdvara receives its name as the "door" (*dvāra*) or home of KRISHNA in his form as protector (*nāth*) of Mount Govardhan—Govardhannāth, or for short, Śrī Nāth Jī. Krishna used the mountain to protect his fellow cowherders and their animals, lifting it above their heads as a shield against torrents of rain unleashed by INDRA. Nathdvara's rhythms are generated by those of the temple that houses Śrī Nāth Jī, a life-size image that was relocated from Mount Govardhan, in the Braj region, where it is said to have manifested itself in the year 1479. Śrī Nāth Jī's westward flight, which began in 1669, was caused by fears that the image might be damaged by the Muslim emperor Aurangzeb and was accomplished by the deity's custodians, descendents of the theologian VALLABHA. Nathdvara serves as the most important place of PILGRIMAGE for the Vallabha SAMPRADĀYA and is one of India's wealthiest and best-known shrines.

NĀTH YOGI \'nät-'yō-gē\, *also called* Kānphaṭa Yogi \'kän-fə-tə\, member of an order of religious ascetics in India that venerates the Hindu deity SHIVA. Nāth Yogis are distinguished by the large earrings they wear in the hollows of their ears (*kān-phaṭa*, "ear split"). They are sometimes referred to as TANTRIC (Esoteric) ascetics, because of their emphasis on the acquiring of supernatural powers in contrast to more orthodox practices of devotion and meditation. They are followers of GORAKHNĀTH (Gorakṣanātha, *c.* 11th century) and are therefore called Goraknāthīs, Nāth Panthīs, or, in the case of ascetics, Nāth Yogis. Their ideology incorporates elements of MYSTICISM, magic, and alchemy absorbed from both Śaivite and Buddhist Esoteric systems, as well as from HAṬHA YOGA.

NATIONAL COUNCIL OF THE CHURCHES OF CHRIST IN THE U.S.A., *also called* National Council of Churches, agency of Protestant, Anglican, and Eastern Orthodox denominations that was formed in 1950 in the United States by the merger of 12 national interdenominational agencies. The National Council of Churches is the largest ecumenical body in the United States, with a membership of about 40 million in the late 20th century. Its international counterpart is the WORLD COUNCIL OF CHURCHES. In the late 20th century, the council's membership was made up of 32 PROTESTANT and EASTERN ORTHODOX churches as full members, with more than 40 other church bodies, including conservative Protestants and ROMAN CATHOLICS, participating in its programs. Headquarters are in New York City.

The council has initiated a revision of the English BIBLE and the publication of religious education, evangelism, and family-life materials; promotes religious and moral values in broadcasting; and coordinates efforts against illiteracy and hunger.

NATIVE AMERICAN CHURCH, *also called* Peyotism \pä-'yō-,ti-zəm\, *or* Peyote Religion, most widespread indigenous religious movement among Native North Americans and one of the most influential forms of Pan-Indianism. The term PEYOTE derives from *peyotl*, the Nahuatl name for certain species of the cactus genus *Lophophora*. The plants contain mescaline, an alkaloid drug that has hallucinogenic effects. It was used in Mexico in pre-Columbian times as a medicine and as a means of inducing visions.

From the mid-19th century, use of peyote extended north into the Great Plains of the United States, and it probably first developed into a distinct religion about 1885 among the Kiowa and Comanche of Oklahoma. After 1891 it spread rapidly as far north as Canada and is now practiced among more than 50 tribes. Reports suggest that nearly one-fifth of the Navajo in 1951 practiced the peyote religion (despite strong tribal council opposition) as did one-third of Oklahoma Indians in 1965.

In general, peyotist doctrine consists of belief in one supreme God (the Great Spirit), who deals with men through various spirits, which include the traditional waterbird or THUNDERBIRD spirits that carry prayers to God. In many tribes peyote itself is personified as Peyote Spirit, considered to be either God's equivalent for the Indians to his JESUS CHRIST for the whites, or Jesus himself. Ritually consumed peyote enables the individual to commune with God and the spirits (including those of the departed) in contemplation and vision and so to receive from them spiritual power, guidance, reproof, and healing.

The all-night ceremony is held on Saturday evenings and led by a peyote "chief." The services include prayer, singing, sacramental eating of peyote, water rites, and contemplation; they conclude with a communion breakfast on Sunday morning. The way of life is called the Peyote Road and enjoins brotherly love, family care, self-support through steady work, and avoidance of alcohol.

NATIVE AMERICAN RELIGIONS

Religious beliefs and sacramental practices of the indigenous peoples of North and South America provide a living link to a preliterate past. Until the 1950s it was commonly assumed by the dominant European-derived culture that the religious worlds of the surviving indigenous peoples were little more than curious anachronisms, dying remnants of humankind's childhood. Native traditions lacked sacred texts and fixed doctrines or moral codes and were embedded in societies without wealth, mostly without writing, without recognizable systems of politics or justice or any of the usual indicators of civilization. Today the situation has changed dramatically. Scholars of religion, students of the ecological sciences, and individuals committed to expanding and deepening their own religious lives have turned to these traditions and have encountered a broad expanse of many distinct religious worlds that have struggled to survive and retain the capacity to inspire.

However, the histories of these worlds are also marked by loss. Five hundred years of political, economic, and religious domination have taken their toll. Scholars take notice when complex ceremonies become extinct, but often community members mourn even more the disappearance of small daily rituals and of religious vocabularies and grammars embedded in traditional languages, the erosion of sacred memories that include not only formal sacred narratives but the myriad informal strands that once composed these tightly woven ways of life. Nevertheless, despite the pervasive effects of modern society, from which there is no longer any possibility of geographic, economic, or technological isolation, there are instances of remarkable continuity with the past, as well as remarkably creative adaptation to the present and anticipation of the future.

NORTH AMERICA

First Nations people themselves often claim that their traditional ways of life do not include "religion." They find the term difficult, often impossible, to translate into their own traditional languages. This apparent incongruity arises from differences in COSMOLOGY and epistemology. Western tradition distinguishes religious thought and action as that whose ultimate authority is supernatural, which is to say, beyond, above, or outside both phenomenal nature and human reason. In

Crow Indian annual Sun Dance, Lodge Grass, Montana; the medicine man (with eagle feathers) is praying for one of the dancers
David Campbell—Photo Researchers

most indigenous worldviews there is no such antithesis. Plants and animals, clouds and mountains, both carry and embody revelation. Even where native tradition conceives of a realm or world apart from the terrestrial one and not normally visible from it, as in the case of the Iroquois Sky World or the several underworlds of Pueblo cosmologies, the boundaries between these worlds are permeable. The ontological distance between land and sky, or between land and underworld, is short and is traversed in both directions.

Instead of a duality of sacred and profane, indigenous religious traditions seem to conceive only of sacred and more sacred. Mere inert, profane matter is not defined; spirit, power, or something akin, moves in all, though not equally. For native communities, religion in its radical sense of that which binds us together is defined relationally: It is found in the relationship between living humans and other persons, powers, or entities, however these are perceived. These may include departed as well as yet-to-be-born human beings; recognizable beings in the so-called "natural world" of flora and fauna; other visible entities that are not animate by Western standards, such as mountains, springs, lakes, and clouds; and entities that are not normally visible, but are understood to inhabit and affect either this world or some other world contiguous to it—what scholars of religion might denote as "mythic beings."

Diversity and common themes. Because religions of this kind are so highly localized, it is impossible to determine exactly how many exist in Native North America now or may have existed at any given time in the past. Distinct languages in North America at the time of the first European contact are often estimated in the vicinity of 300, which linguists have variously grouped into some 30 to 50 families. There is, consequently, great diversity among these traditions. For instance, Iroquois Longhouse elders speak frequently about the Creator's "Original Instructions" to human beings, using male gender references and attributing to this divinity not only the planning and organizing of creation but qualities of goodness, wisdom, and perfection that are reminiscent of the Christian deity. By contrast, the Koyukon universe is notably decentralized. Raven, whom Koyukon narratives credit with the creation of human beings, is only one among many powerful entities in the Koyukon world. He exhibits such human weaknesses as lust and pride, is neither all-knowing nor all-good, and teaches more often by counterexample than by his wisdom (*see* TRICKSTER).

A similarly sharp contrast is seen in Navajo and Pueblo ritual. Most traditional Navajo ceremonies are enacted on behalf of individuals in response to specific needs. Most Pueblo ceremonial work is communal, both in participation and in perceived benefit, and is scheduled according to natural cycles. Still, the healing benefits of a Navajo sing naturally spread through the families of all those participating, while the communal benefits of Pueblo ceremonial work naturally redound to individuals.

Thus, there is no such thing as a generic "Native American religion." Attempts to understand these religious traditions en masse are bound to produce oversimplification and distortion. Instead, it may be useful to consider a list of broad characteristics that seem to pertain to the religious lives of many indigenous North American communities.

➤ Religious practices are localized. Place is important. Traditional knowledge includes detailed knowledge, built and maintained through generations of oral communication and memory, about visible and invisible other-than-human inhabitants of a place.

➤ Access to some kinds of knowledge is restricted. In many traditions, not only actions but words and thoughts are understood to have power in the world. Some knowledge may be considered so powerful and dangerous that a process of instruction and initiation is required for those who will use it.

➤ Participation is more important than belief. Arguments about doctrinal truth are largely absent from most Native North American religious traditions. Good-hearted participation in the ceremonial and everyday work of the community is the main requirement.

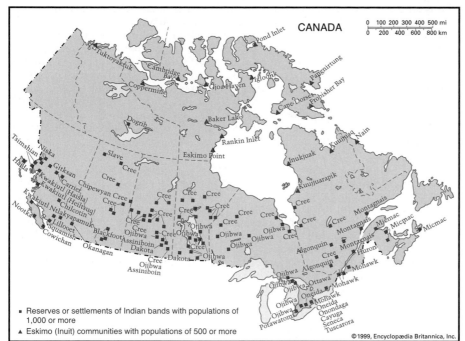

Cultural distribution of Native North Americans

➤KINSHIP obligations are central. Cooperation with and devotion to one's kin is a central part of small-scale societies. Teaching proper behavior toward others, which is defined by one's relationship to them, is an essential part of child-rearing. These cultural practices are religious as well, because one will be expected to treat the entire world, one's other-than-human relatives, one's very life, in the same way one has learned to treat one's human relatives.

➤ Generosity is a religious act as well as a social one. The value of generosity is perhaps most dramatically figured in the northern practice known in English as Giveaway, or in the Potlatch ceremony of the Northwest Coast peoples. Human beings are taught to give eagerly because in so doing they imitate the generosity of the many other-than-human entities who provide for human sustenance.

➤ A community's oral narratives constitute a record of human interaction with other-than-human beings, powers, and entities in a place. In addition to the more solemn genres, such as creation stories and migration narratives, these may include moralistic stories, family histories, instruction meant to teach traditional skills, and many kinds of jokes.

➤ Death is a transition. Attitudes and beliefs about death, and ritual responses to it, are among the more heterogeneous aspects of Native American religious life. Many Native American traditions appear to conceive of human beings as complex entities that bind together different kinds of essences, breaths, or spirits. These may undergo divergent outcomes after death. After death some of these essences may be harmful for living people to encounter without ceremonial protection.

➤ Joking, clowning, and other forms of entertainment are integral parts of many ceremonial events and settings, either formally or informally. Sometimes such performances are a means of shaming individuals into correcting troublesome behavior, but they may also be employed simply to spread happiness and lighten moods.

➤ Significant achievements and life-passages are meant to be shared by relatives and community. Various forms of coming-of-age and initiation ceremonies make up a large portion of the ritual repertoire of many American Indian traditions. These ceremonies provide structures for instruction in traditional knowledge, but more importantly they reintegrate an individual into kin, community, and cosmos when new status is attained.

Historical change. A serious misconception about Native North American religions is that they once existed in a changeless "Golden Age," before the European invasion, and that what happened later can only be described as degeneration. This view owes much to the misgivings of many 19th-century Europeans over the deep changes wrought on their own societies by the Industrial Age. Change, borrowing, and innovation are characteristic of any living religion, but indigenous communities relied on strands of oral communication to maintain both continuity and the memory of change, and Euro-American observers were ill-equipped to notice and record these sources.

At the same time, the changes that visited Native America in the wake of the European invasion were massive, unprecedented, and mostly destructive. Whole languages, and with them ceremonies, narratives, and oral libraries of accumulated knowledge about human and natural history and humor were lost. Even the most earnest and energetic efforts of younger women and men today to rejuvenate traditional ways can seem pale and pathetic to those who remember earlier days. Yet some elders reject this pessimism, citing this story: There was a community where a Snake Dance was once performed, but the ceremony became extinct. Anthropologists expressed alarm, but an elder insisted that people should not be disturbed. "If it was lost it was because we didn't need it any more," he said. "If we really need it back again, the snakes will teach it to us again. It was they who taught it to us in the first place."

Sometimes, however, disruption is so catastrophic that individuals and communities must respond with fresh, powerful visions that transplant the germ of past wisdom into entirely new seedbeds. When it succeeds, such inspiration can meld tradition and innovation in surprisingly effective ways. Two such examples are the NATIVE AMERICAN CHURCH, sometimes known as the Peyote Church, and the GHOST DANCE movement. The Native American Church, based on an ancient ritual of central Mexico but blended with Christian influences and spread in part through the medium of government-run Indian schools, is the only native religious tradition that has become truly portable, spreading from coast to coast. Although the Ghost Dance tradition ended in tragedy in 1890, it was for a time a powerful expression of both hope and despair as the Euro-American conquest of the continent neared completion. It has been revived in recent times.

A third type of response to religious disintegration can be seen in American Indian Christian congregations. In some instances conversion to CHRISTIANITY was enforced, with dire penalties for refusal. In other cases it appears to have been accepted voluntarily, out of devotion to the missionaries and their message. In yet other cases, it was probably accepted for a practical mix of reasons—often conversion meant an increased chance for physical survival, regardless of how sincere it was. Once physical survival and a degree of stability were established, many congregations of Native Christians began to recast their faith and practice to include aspects of traditional views and values. Kinship obligations, sharing of resources, and a general emphasis on community in preference to individualistic approaches to salvation, have been some of these Native Christian adaptations. In some cases traditional language and symbolism have been incorporated into Christian worship as well.

Reconstructed Tlingit longhouse with totem poles; in the Totem Bight State Park, Ketchikan, Alaska
Bob and Ira Spring

Issues and concerns. Today American Indian traditionalists still believe that the values, knowledge, narrative traditions, and the ritual worlds they were taught, however compromised by historical loss and the demands of modern life, are vital to the inner survival of their communities—their human relatives and their other-than-human relatives as well. While it is undeniable that much has already been irrevocably lost, all but the most pessimistic find much to work toward and fight for in the present. Key issues include the following:

➤ Access to, and control of, sacred sites. Many locations used for ceremonial purposes, or considered to be the home of powerful entities, have been disrupted and contaminated by recreational activities and economic exploitation. This has been especially problematic when it occurs on public lands, as in the cases of Devil's Tower in Wyoming, Mt. Shasta in California, and Mt. Graham in Arizona. In the case of Lyng *v.* Northwest Indian Cemetery Protective Association (1988), the U.S. Supreme Court ruled that the disturbance of religion need not be weighed against economic benefit in determining how public lands are to be used.

➤ The survival of traditional Native American languages. Apart from the Native American Church and Native Christian congregations, most American Indian traditionalists believe that ceremonial work and traditional knowledge are authentic and potent only when conducted in traditional languages. Yet most of these languages are eroding rapidly and among persons under 40 are nearly extinct. In ORAL TRADITION societies, it is vital that each generation identify and train individuals to memorize this knowledge and so carry it forward. Wide swaths of this knowledge can disappear with startling speed when there are no young people fluent enough to accomplish this. Some communities are trying urgently to arrest this trend; for others it is already too late.

➤ The return of sacred beings taken illegally and held as "objects" in museums. In some cases great harm is thought to have resulted from these ignorant holdings and displays, to the museums and their visitors, as well as to the native people who are the proper caretakers of these beings. It is important to understand that for indigenous traditionalists there are items, such as certain masks, that are alive, extremely powerful, and dangerous when not treated with proper ceremonial care. They are certainly not, as observers of the culture might assume, merely inanimate objects imbued with symbolic significance. The physical remains of deceased Indian persons fall into a different but related category of powerful "objects" not to be removed from their proper places and studied or displayed.

➤ The irresponsible use of traditional religious knowledge. There are two issues here: distorted or inaccurate representation of traditional knowledge, and the unsanctioned use of that knowledge, even when it is accurately represented. Scholars and New Age enthusiasts alike are accused of both these kinds of abuse. In native communities the exchange of knowledge, like any other exchange, is meant to be reciprocated. A growing number of anthropologists know this and do their best to honor it, but many still do not. The record is far worse for promoters of New Age imitations of indigenous practice, regardless of whether they have American Indian blood.

➤ The corrosive effects of modern economic life upon traditional values and practices. At the close of the 20th century, most citizens of Western nations such as Canada and the United States find that spare time, even time for weekly religious observance, has become scarce. Indigenous traditional knowledge, however, is best learned slowly. There are many young adults in First Nations communities who strongly wish to participate in traditional religious life, but the pressures of job and school make it impossible to devote enough time to learning and practicing the requisite language, natural history, traditional narratives, and ceremonial procedures.

These needs are best being met in communities with strong resolve, where internal divisions have been softened, and where elders and young people are working together. Today many American Indian youth show strong interest in traditional knowledge. Some are learning to use new technology and other skills to develop innovative means for learning and maintaining that knowledge. The results will differ from the traditions known and loved by today's elders when they were young, but Native North American religious life continues as a viable and ongoing tradition of religious thought and practice.

SOUTH AMERICA

The religious life of indigenous South American peoples is vibrant and varied. Linguists have described as many as 1,500 distinct languages and native cultures in South America. Many peoples have suffered physical and cultural extinction since the first contact with Europeans. Very few surviving communities have been uninfluenced by Christian missionaries. For centuries ROMAN CATHOLICISM was the dominant Christian influence on Native South American peoples. In the 20th century, various forms of Protestant Christianity have taken hold, especially evangelical and Pentecostal.

Nevertheless, indigenous religious ideas and practices have endured, even in communities that have long had involvement with Christian beliefs. In many of these cases Christian views have been creatively absorbed and reframed within native worldviews. In some instances, native myths have borrowed Christian features in order to offer a criticism of Christianity, putting forward Christ-like supernatural heroes who led rebellions against colonial rule and missionary zeal. A sense of the nature and variety of religious life in South America can be conveyed by examining beliefs about creation, practices associated with the calendar and with the initiation of new adults, forms of special religious authority, and prophetic movements responding to the end of the world.

Creation myths. Creation mythologies play a singularly important role in the religious life of many South American tribes. These myths describe the origin of the first world and its fate and sometimes include narratives of the creation and destruction of subsequent worlds. These narratives differ in their details: Some creations are the work of a supreme being, and some involve creation from nothing while others involve creation from a pre-existing substance.

It is important to note that many of these creation myths describe in dramatic ways the exit of the creative beings. They may be driven off, or sent into the sky in the form of stars, or move off into the forest, or take refuge in other levels of the universe, and the manner of their disappearance figures in the ritual celebrations that commemorate it. The myths of multiple world-destruction place a great question mark at the beginning of existence. Why should powerful worlds fall prey to disaster? Why should beings so perfect and powerful suffer destruction? The religious life of many South American peoples places this kind of question at the foundation of RELIGIOUS EXPERIENCE. Rather than providing resolving answers to such questions, the myths of multiple destruction install the questions themselves as fundamental.

Calendrical practices.   Scenarios of universal catastrophe and destruction mark the passage of time and can thereby lead to the institution of the calendar. The most obvious calendrical marker of time that arises from universal catastrophe and disaster is the procession of stars. South American mythologies consistently join the death of primordial beings (often later known in the form of animals) with cataclysmic destructions of the first worlds and the ascent of the stars into the heavens. For example, the Makiritare of the Orinoco River region in Venezuela tell how the stars, led by Wlaha, were forced to ascend on high when Kuamachi, the evening star, sought to avenge the death of his mother. Kuamachi and his grandfather induced Wlaha and the other stars to climb into *Dewaka* trees to gather the ripe fruit. When Kuamachi picked the fruit, it fell and broke open. Water spilled out and flooded the forest. With his powerful thought Kuamachi created a canoe in which he and his grandfather escaped. Along the way they created deadly water animals such as the anaconda, the piranha, and the caiman. One by one Kuamachi shot down the stars of heaven from the trees on which they were lodged. They fell into the water and were devoured by the animals. After they were gnawed and gored into different ragged shapes, the survivors ascended into the sky on a ladder of arrows. There the stars took their places and began shining.

Initiation.   Ceremonial initiation into adulthood is widely practiced among South American peoples, both for males and females. Many of the religious themes mentioned earlier are present in the initiation rites, for initiation is seen as a kind of new creation, the dawn of a new epoch. Initiation itself is often timed to occur in special moments of powerful change in the calendar. In this way the change in the human individual is aligned with fundamental changes in the cosmos and in society. Thus, in order for this change in the human being to be effective, it must align with the powerful and momentous changes that are occurring in the primordial world.

The Baniwa of the Northwest Amazon region of Brazil seclude girls during their initiation. The girls' bodies are covered with heron down and red paint, and each girl is hidden inside two baskets. The elders deliver dramatic speeches and whip the initiate in order to open her skin. Pepper is touched to her lips, a small hole is made in the dirt floor, and she spits into it. She is introduced to various kinds of food, over which chants are sung. The baskets are opened, the girl steps forth, and she is decorated and paraded around to the accompaniment of chants.

All of these actions commemorate events that occurred in the mythic first world. At that time a formless water serpent named Amaru was the first female being. A band of her female followers stole ritual flutes called *Kuai* from the males of that age and initiated Amaru by placing her in a basket while they blessed food for her. Insects and worms tried to penetrate the basket, and eventually a small armadillo succeeded in tunneling through the earth into the center of the women's house. The creator, Yaperikuli, led the men through this tunnel, and the resulting union of males and females marked the beginning of fertile life and the origin of species of all kinds. Thus an individual girl's initiation is brought into alignment with this cosmic fertility.

*Cultural distribution
of Native South
Americans*

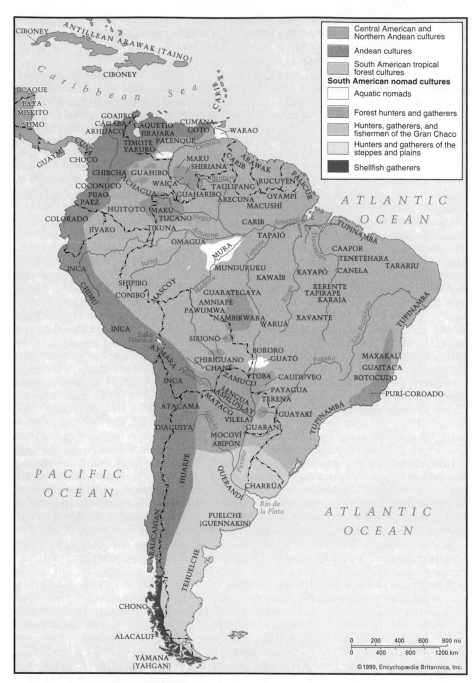

Male initiations often borrow or allude to a symbolism of female reproduction, by reference to MENSTRUATION in the symbolism or procedure of the rite or by representing the initiation as a new conception and gestation of the initiate. As the generation of new life is at the heart of initiation, the biological and the ritual here intersect in deeply meaningful ways.

Forms of religious authority. Initiations are also used to mark the ascent of individuals into positions of religious authority. Priests, diviners, and spirit mediums play special roles in religious life. The precise kinds of authority exercised by them in the community, however, varies greatly across South America.

Prominent in many parts of South America is the religious specialist in states of ECSTASY, commonly referred to by the term SHAMAN. The shaman is one who learns to control the passage of the soul out of and back into the body. As a general practitioner of the arts of the soul, however, the shaman in South America not only controls the ecstasy of his or her own soul but is devoted also to the knowledge and care of the souls of others.

The length of shamanic training varies widely from one South American culture to another. Among the Arecuna and Taulipang, Cariban groups of Venezuela and Brazil, the shamanic novitiate was reported to last from ten to twenty years. In other traditions, by contrast, knowledge might be transmitted to the novice in relatively brief but intense periods of ecstasy. The types of knowledge imparted may include the use of different forms of fire (such as ritual fires, or sparks struck from special elements, or the light contained in bright crystals), the use of musical instruments, the mastery of primordial sounds (which have the power to recreate the bodies of suffering patients, or to reorder the seasons in order to overcome drought or famine), esoteric languages, and sacred songs.

This education usually takes place under the direction of a master. That master may be a human shaman who is accomplished and practiced, or the master may be a supernatural being. Among the Makiritare of Venezuela, the sacred songs (*Ademi*) were taught to shamans at the beginning of time by *sadashe* (masters of animals and prototypes of the contemporary animal species), who cut down the tree of life, survived the subsequent flood, cleared the first garden, and celebrated the first new harvest festival. In order to preserve their power, the *Ademi* must be repeated in the exact phonetic pattern in which the *sadashe* first revealed them.

The shaman's rattle is a most sacred instrument in South America. Through its sounds, its structural features, its contents, and its connection to shamanic ecstasy, the rattle embodies the sum total of the sacred forces of the cosmos. The rattle's various parts may symbolize the structures of the world. The original of the shaman's rattle of the Warao (of the Orinoco Delta in Venezuela) was brought back to earth after the primordial mythic shaman ascended to the heavenly realm to visit the spirit of the south, from whom the rattle is a gift. The handle is the vertical path that rises into the heavenly vault. The heavenly realm is represented by the great head-gourd of the rattle that contains spirits. Joining the handle to the head represents the joining of male and female elements in the universe, an act of fertilization that gives the sounds of the instrument creative power. Safeguarding the rattle and playing it properly during ritual fulfils the destiny of the human spirit: to sustain the order of existence.

Shamanic performances are generally theatrical. The shaman's cure is miraculous, something to see. It is a deliberate exhibition of normally invisible powers and it aims to astonish spectators and compel them to admire what is real and, therefore, life-giving.

Prophetic movements and eschatology. Religious ideas and practices associated with the end of the world abound in South America (*compare* MILLENNIALISM). Eschatological movements have swept across South America since the time of European contact and, most probably, long before that. Many of the movements of resistance to colonialism have taken the form of messianic revolts led by millennial prophets and saviors. Among various Guaraní groups in Paraguay, shamans led groups on messianic PILGRIMAGES, seeking to find the Land Without Evil. The very existence of the Land Without Evil offered the Guaraní hope, security, and courage in the face of the hunger, sickness, and death that followed the Conquest. As these eschatological groups succumbed to failure, they concluded that, on their paths to paradise, they had been overtaken by *Peqó-Achy*, the weight of accumulating imperfections that blot out the light of the sun and weigh humans down so that they are incapable of ecstatic flight into the Land Without Evil.

South American propensities for eschatological thinking and behavior have recognized common ground in some of the eschatological thinking of Christianity, especially of Christian sects that emphasize this aspect of their tradition. There is no doubt that the religious life of South American Indians continues creatively to absorb and reinterpret elements in the world of contemporary experience.

NATURALISM, skeptical view of the origin and development of religion, which holds that whatever exists can be satisfactorily explained in natural terms. To explain something in natural terms is to explain it on scientific lines; naturalism is in fact a proclamation of the final competence of science. Within this view, the scientific account of a set of happenings takes precedence over any other. Scientific language is basically causal, and naturalism holds that causal explanations are fundamental.

One prominent example of the naturalistic explanation of religion is found in modern psychoanalysis. In the matter of the origins and development of religion, many have argued that there is a close connection between MYSTICISM and hallucination, between hysteria and ecstatic institutionalized inspiration as, for example, in Pentecostal churches. Religious people, according to such views, often have personality weaknesses and are psychologically disturbed. SIGMUND FREUD maintained that inner conflicts—often the result of repression, particularly in relation to sex—become expressed in peculiarities of behavior and mood, especially in the vivid imagery of dreams that erupt from the unconscious area of one's personality. By comparing the symbolism of dreams and mythology, Freud held that belief in God—in particular, the father image—merely perpetuates in fantasy what the individual must in actual fact overcome as part of his growth to maturity, thus giving RELIGIOUS BELIEF a treatment that not only made belief in God unnecessary but positively unhelpful.

Naturalism has been criticized on the grounds that one must be careful not to indulge in the genetic fallacy: no account of the origin and development of anything, of religion in particular, is necessarily a reliable analysis of what that particular phenomenon is now; a single explanation of the origin and development of a phenomenon as complex and variegated as religion is difficult to describe and maintain. Moreover, origin theories are founded on conjecture.

Compare SUPERNATURALISM; *see also* FUNCTIONALISM.

NATURAL RELIGION, attempt to establish religious truths by rational argument and without reliance upon alleged revelations; its two traditional topics are the existence of God and the immortality of the soul. In the medieval period, ST. THOMAS AQUINAS distinguished natural religion, or that kind of religious truth discoverable by unaided reason, from revealed religion, or religion resting upon divine truth, which he identified exclusively with CHRISTIANITY. Certain trends in 18th-century RATIONALISM, however, reversed the force of the argument by advocating a Christianity to be founded upon intellectual inquiry (*i.e.,* NATURAL THEOLOGY; *see also* DEISM).

Examples of occurrence of such a "natural piety" can also be found in religions other than Christianity. The spread of technology has gradually alienated many Hindus and Buddhists from their traditional beliefs, but Hindus have continued to treasure their spiritual ideology, which may well give to technological development its needed direction and wider setting. BUDDHISM in Japan, and perhaps elsewhere in the East, is still valued in the 20th century insofar as it supplies a local religious dimension to a society whose public and industrial life has been increasingly Westernized. Thus, an attitude has arisen that is sympathetic to the broad claims of religion but has been critical, if not disdainful, of theological dogma and rivalries.

NATURAL THEOLOGY, name given to discourse about God and the world that does not make reference to revelation. In natural theology are generally included the "proofs" of the existence of God, discussions about the immortality of the soul, and discussions about God's providential control of the world.

NAUS \'naùs\, *Catalan* navetas (from Greek: "ship"), Bronze Age grave found in the Balearic Isles. The *naus* was built of blocks of stone in the shape of an overturned boat.

NAVARĀTRI \,nə-və-'rä-trē\ (Sanskrit: "Nine Nights"), in HINDUISM, a nine-day festival occurring during the month of Āśvina (September–October). It usually ends with the festival of *dassera* (from Sanskrit *daśaharā,* an old epithet of the GAṄGĀ [Ganges] River, meaning "removal of the 10 sins"), celebrated on the 10th day.

Among followers of the goddess DURGĀ, DURGĀ-PŪJĀ ("Durgā Worship") is celebrated during this period. Special images of Durgā commemorating her victory over the buffalo-headed DEMON Mahiṣāsura are worshiped daily, and on the 10th day (*dassera*) the images are taken in procession to nearby rivers or reservoirs for immersion in water. In addition to family feasting and visiting, the *pūjā,* or ritual, days are also celebrated with public concerts, recitations, plays, and fairs.

In other parts of India, *dassera* is associated with the victory of the god RĀMA over the demon-king RĀVAṆA. In North India the Rām LĪLĀ ("Play of Rāma") is the highlight of the festival. On successive nights different episodes of the epic poem the RĀMĀYAṆA are dramatized; the pageant climaxes with the burning of huge effigies of the demons.

NĀYAṆĀR \'nä-yə-,när\, *also spelled* Nāyaṉmār (Tamil and Sanskrit: "Lords," "Masters"), sixty-three Tamil poetsaints of the 7th and 8th centuries CE who composed devotional hymns in honor of the Hindu god SHIVA. The images of all the poets, but especially Ñāṉacampantar, Appar, and Cuntaramūrtti (often referred to as Mūvar, or "the Three"), are worshiped in South Indian Śaiva temples as saints. The hymns of the Mūvar were collected in the 10th century by Nampiyāṇṭār Nampi as the *Tēvāram* and set to Dravidian music for incorporation into the services of South Indian temples.

NĀYAR \'nä-yər\, *also spelled* Nair, Hindu CASTE of the Indian state of Kerala that dominated high-status positions in the region's small, feudal kingdoms prior to the British conquest. During British rule, Nāyars became prominent in politics, government service, medicine, education, and law.

Unlike most Hindus, Nāyars traditionally were matrilineal. Their family unit, the members of which owned property jointly, included brothers and sisters, the latter's children, and their daughters' children. The oldest man was legal head of the group.

Between the 16th and 18th centuries, Nāyars in the central kingdoms of Calicut, Walluvanad, Palghat, and Cochin had highly unusual marriage customs. Before puberty a girl ritually married another Nāyar or a NAMBŪDIRI. The husband could visit her (but was not obliged to); in some cases ritual divorce immediately followed. After puberty a woman could receive a number of visiting husbands of her own caste or a higher one. Nāyar men might visit as many women of appropriate rank as they chose. Women were maintained by their matrilineal groups, and fathers had no rights or obligations in regard to their children.

Nāyar plural marital unions gradually died out in the 19th century. Laws passed in the 1930s enforced monogamy, permitted division of the matrilineal estate among male and female members, and gave children full rights of maintenance and inheritance from the father.

NAZARENE, CHURCH OF THE,
American Protestant church, product of several mergers stemming from the 19th-century HOLINESS MOVEMENT. The first occurred in 1907, uniting the Church of the Nazarene (organized in California in 1895) with the Association of Pentecostal Churches of America (with origins in the northeastern states from 1886 to 1896) to form the Pentecostal Church of the Nazarene. In 1908 the Holiness CHURCH OF CHRIST (with origins in the southwestern states from 1894 to 1905) joined the denomination. Later mergers brought in other groups. The term pentecostal was dropped from the name of the church in 1919.

The church government is similar to that of the Methodists, but local congregations have more autonomy. In worship there is emphasis on simplicity and revivalistic evangelism. In doctrine the church stands in the tradition of Arminian METHODISM, emphasizing God's GRACE, and regards its unique mission to be the promotion of entire sanctification, which enables a person to live a sinless life, as a work of grace subsequent to conversion.

NAZIRITE \'na-zə-ˌrīt\
(from Hebrew *nazar*, "to consecrate oneself to"), in JUDAISM, an Israelite man or woman who takes a special vow to desist from wine or strong drink and from grapes; to refrain from cutting the hair; and to avoid contracting corpse-uncleanness (Numbers 6:1–21). If the Nazirite should contract corpse-uncleanness during the spell, the days already observed are null, and the vow takes effect afresh. At the end of the specified time of the vow, he or she brings offerings of meat, oil, bread, and wine. Then the head is shaved, and the hair is put on the fire under the peace offering that the Nazirite has brought. If the Nazirite does not specify the length of the vow, it is for 30 days (Mishnah tractate Nazir 1:3). If one undertakes a Nazirite vow "like that of SAMSON," it is a vow for life. GENTILES are not subject to the Nazirite vow. Women and slaves are subject to the Nazirite vow. A master forces his slave to be subject to a Nazirite vow, but a husband does not force his wife to be subject to a Nazirite vow (Mishnah tractate Nazir 9:1). The rabbinic sages treat the Nazirite vow as they treat vows in general, as a mark of inferior character or conscience, in this case, a sign of pride.

NEBI'IM \nə-vē-'ēm\,
English The Prophets, second division of the Hebrew BIBLE, or OLD TESTAMENT, the other two being the TORAH and the KETUBIM. In the Hebrew canon the prophets are divided into (1) the Former Prophets (Joshua, Judges, Samuel, and Kings) and (2) the Latter Prophets (Isaiah, Jeremiah, Ezekiel, and the Twelve, or Minor, Prophets: Hosea, Joel, Amos, Obadiah, Jonah, Micah, Nahum, Habakkuk, Zephaniah, Haggai, Zechariah, and Malachi). This canon was fixed by a council of RABBIS at Jabneh (Jamnia), now in Israel, *c.* 100 CE.

The Protestant canon calls the Former Prophets the Historical Books and subdivides two of them into 1 and 2 Samuel and 1 and 2 Kings. The Prophets in the Protestant canon include Isaiah, Jeremiah, and Ezekiel from the Hebrew Latter Prophets. The Minor Prophets (The Twelve) are treated as 12 separate books; thus the Protestant canon has 17 prophetic books. The Roman Catholics accept the book of Baruch, including as its 6th chapter the Letter of Jeremiah, both considered apocryphal by Jews and Protestants.

NECHUNG ORACLE \'nä-jùŋ, -chùŋ\,
oracle-priest of Tibet who, until the conquest of Tibet in 1959 by the People's Republic of China, was consulted on all important occasions. The Nechung oracle was the chief medium of Pe-har, a popular folk divinity incorporated into BUDDHISM, and resided at the Nechung (Gnas-chung-lcog) monastery near Drepung ('Bras-spungs), the center of the Pe-har cult. The oracle is said to have first been appointed government adviser during the time of the fifth DALAI LAMA (1617–82). He was required to journey to Lhasa once a year, during the New Year festivities, to prophesy the year's coming events, and was consulted whenever a search was conducted for a new Dalai Lama.

NECROMANCY,
communication with the dead, usually in order to obtain insight into the future or to accomplish some task. Such activity was current in ancient times among the Assyrians, Babylonians, Egyptians, Greeks, Romans, and Etruscans.

Its practitioners were skilled magicians who used a consecrated circle in some desolate spot, often a graveyard, to protect themselves from the anger of the spirits of the dead. In the event of a premature or violent death, the corpse was thought to retain some measure of unused vitality, and so the use of parts of corpses as ingredients of charms came to be an important technique of WITCHCRAFT. Necromancy was especially popular in the European Middle Ages and Renaissance, although it came to be associated with black magic and was condemned by the Church.

NECROPOLIS \nə-'krä-pə-ləs, ne-\
(Greek: "city of the dead"), extensive and elaborate burial place of an ancient city. In the Mediterranean world, they were customarily outside the city proper and often consisted of a number of cemeteries used at different times over a period of several centuries. The locations of these cemeteries were varied. In Egypt many, such as western Thebes, were situated across the Nile River opposite the cities, but in Greece and Rome a necropolis often lined the roads leading out of town. One of the most famous necropolises was discovered in the 1940s under the central nave of St. Peter's BASILICA in Rome.

NEFERTEM \'ne-fər-ˌtem\,
also spelled Nefertum \-ˌtüm\, *or* Nefertemu \-ˌte-mü\, in ancient EGYPTIAN RELIGION, youthful god associated with the lotus flower. Nefertem was mentioned in the PYRAMID TEXTS (*c.* 2350 BCE), but he became more prominent during the New Kingdom (1539–*c.*1075 BCE) and later. As a lotus he was believed to have emerged from the primeval waters, and he was connected with the sun god because lotus flowers open in the sun. He also had a warlike aspect and could be depicted as a lion.

NEHEMIAH \ˌnē-ə-'mī-ə, ˌnē-hə-\,
also spelled Nehemias \-'mī-əs\ (fl. 5th century BCE), Jewish leader who supervised the rebuilding of Jerusalem in the mid-5th century BCE. He also instituted extensive moral and liturgical reforms.

Nehemiah was the cupbearer to the Persian King Artaxerxes I (Nehemiah 1:11b) at a time when JUDAH in Palestine had been partly repopulated by Jews released from their exile in Babylonia. The Temple at Jerusalem had been rebuilt, but the Jewish community there was dispirited and defenseless against its neighbors (Nehemiah 1:3). Nehemiah obtained permission from Artaxerxes to journey to Palestine to help rebuild its ruined structures. He was provided with an escort and with documents that guaranteed the assistance of Judah's Persian officials (Nehemiah 2:1–10). So about 444 BCE Nehemiah journeyed to Jerusalem, and in the space of 52 days the Jews under his direction succeeded in rebuilding the city's walls (Nehemiah 6:15).

Nehemiah then apparently served as governor of the district of Judea for 12 years (Nehemiah 8:9), during which he undertook various religious and economic reforms before returning to Persia. On a second visit he strengthened the observance of the SABBATH and ended the custom of Jewish men marrying foreign-born wives (Nehemiah 13:4–27). Nehemiah's reconstructive work in Palestine was subsequently continued by the religious leader EZRA.

Nehemiah's story is told in the Book of Nehemiah, part of which seems to be based upon his memoirs. The book itself, however, was compiled by a later, anonymous writer who apparently also compiled the books of Ezra and the Chronicles.

NEILAH \nə-ē-'lä, nə-'ē-lə\, *Hebrew* neʿila, *or* neʿilah, in JUDAISM, most sacred of the yearly liturgy and the last of the five YOM KIPPUR services. When the SHOFAR (ritual ram's horn) sounds at the close of the *neilah*, the SYNAGOGUE service ends and the daylong fast marking Yom Kippur is over.

In ancient times the *neilah* was prayed each day before sunset, when the gates of the Temple were closed. The *neilah* was also recited on public fast days. Modern Jews view the *neilah* as the symbolic closing of the gates of heaven when God's final judgment is passed on man.

NEITH \'nēt\, *also spelled* Neit, ancient Egyptian goddess who was the patroness of the city of Sais in the Nile River delta. Neith was worshiped as early as predynastic times (*c.* 3000 BCE), and several queens of the 1st dynasty (*c.* 2925–2775 BCE) were named after her. She also became an important goddess in the capital city of Memphis. Neith was usually depicted as a woman wearing the red crown associated with Lower Egypt, holding crossed arrows and a bow. In mythology she was the mother of the crocodile god SEBEK, and later of RE.

NEKHBET \'nek̲-ˌbet\, in EGYPTIAN RELIGION, vulture goddess who was the protector of Upper Egypt and especially its rulers.

Nekhbet was frequently portrayed as spreading her wings over the pharaoh while grasping in her claw the cartouche symbol or other emblems. She was sometimes depicted suckling the pharaoh. She also appeared as a woman, often with a vulture's head, wearing a white crown. The center of Nekhbet's cult was al-Kāb (Greek: Eileithyiaspolis), but her principal epithet made her the goddess of Hierakonpolis (or Nekhen), the ancient town on the west bank of the Nile River.

NEMEAN GAMES \'nē-mē-ən, ni-'mē-\, in ancient Greece, athletic and musical competitions held in honor of ZEUS, in

Nekhbet hovering over Menkauhor; in the Louvre, Paris
Alinari—Art Resource

July, at the great Temple of Zeus at Nemea, in Argolis. They occurred biennially, in the same years as the ISTHMIAN GAMES, *i.e.*, in the second and fourth years of each Olympiad. Their origin was attributed to such legendary figures as HERACLES and Adrastus of Argos. Winners in the competitions were awarded a wreath of fresh wild celery. After 573 BCE the games were open to all Greeks, and the Nemea became one of the great panhellenic festivals.

NEMESIS \'ne-mə-sis\, in GREEK RELIGION, probably two different divine conceptions, the first an Attic goddess and the second an abstraction of indignant disapproval, later personified. Nemesis the goddess was worshiped in Attica and was very similar to ARTEMIS. In post-Homeric mythology, she was pursued by ZEUS, who eventually turned himself into a swan and caught her in the form of a goose. Nemesis then laid an egg from which HELEN was hatched.

Nemesis the abstraction was also worshiped, at least in later times. She signified particularly the disapproval of the gods at human presumption, and her first altar was said to have been erected in Bœotia by Adrastus, leader of the SEVEN AGAINST THEBES. In Rome, especially, her cult was very popular, particularly among soldiers, by whom she was worshiped as patroness of the drill ground.

NEO-CONFUCIANISM \ˌnē-ō-kən-'fyü-shə-ˌni-zəm\, in Japan, official guiding philosophy of the Tokugawa period (1603–1867). The tradition, introduced into Japan from China by ZEN Buddhists in the medieval period, held that harmony was maintained by a relationship of justice between a benevolent superior and an obedient subordinate.

Neo-Confucianism contributed to the development of the BUSHIDŌ ("Way of the Warrior"). The emphasis of Neo-Confucianism on the study of CHINESE CLASSICS led to a renewed interest in the Japanese classics and a revival of SHINTŌ studies (as Fukko, or Reform, Shintō). Most significantly, Neo-Confucianism encouraged scholars to concern themselves with the practical side of human affairs—law, economics, and politics.

Three main traditions of Neo-Confucian studies developed in Japan. The SHUSHI-GAKU, based on the thought of the Chinese philosopher CHU HSI, became the cornerstone of education, teaching as cardinal virtues FILIAL PIETY, loyalty, obedience, and a sense of indebtedness to one's superiors. The Ōyōmeigaku centered upon the teachings of the Chinese philosopher WANG YANG-MING, who held self-knowledge to be the highest form of learning and placed great emphasis on intuitive perception of truth. The KOGAKU school attempted to revive the original thought of CONFUCIUS and MENCIUS, which it felt had been distorted by the other Japanese Neo-Confucian schools.

NEO-PAGANISM \ˌnē-ō-'pā-gə-ˌni-zəm\, any of several spiritual movements that attempt to revive the ancient polytheistic religions of Europe and the Middle East. Neo-Paganism differs from ritual magic and modern WITCHCRAFT by striving to revive authentic pantheons and rituals of ancient cultures, though often in deliberately eclectic and reconstructionist ways, and by a particularly CONTEMPLATIVE and celebrative attitude. Typically Neo-Pagans have deep environmental and ecological concerns and therefore center their rituals, holy days, and religious motifs around the changes of the seasons and the personification of nature as full of divine life.

Modern Neo-Paganism has roots in 19th-century ROMANTICISM and activities inspired by it, such as the British Order of DRUIDS. Sometimes associated with extreme nationalism, Neo-Pagan groups and sentiments were known in Europe before World War II; but contemporary Neo-Paganism is for the most part a product of the 1960s. Influenced by the works of the psychiatrist Carl Jung and the writer Robert Graves, Neo-Paganists are more interested in nature and archetypal psychology than in nationalist politics.

Neo-Paganism in the postwar decades has flourished particularly in the United States, the United Kingdom, and Scandinavia. Some of the major Neo-Pagan groups are the Church of All Worlds, the largest of the PAGAN movements, which centers on the worship of an earth-mother goddess; Feraferia, based on ancient GREEK RELIGION and also centered on goddess worship; Pagan Way, a nature religion centered on goddess worship and the seasons; the Reformed Druids of North America; the Church of the Eternal Source, which has revived ancient Egyptian religion; and the Viking Brotherhood, which celebrates Norse rites. Beginning in the late 1970s, some feminists became interested in witchcraft and Neo-Paganism as a means of celebrating feminine aspects of the divine.

NEOPLATONISM \\,nē-ō-'plā-tə-,ni-zəm\\, last school of Greek philosophy, given its definitive shape in the 3rd century CE by Plotinus. Neoplatonism had a strong influence on the development of early Christian theology. The ancient philosophers who are generally classified as Neoplatonists called themselves simple "Platonists," as did the philosophers of the Renaissance and the 17th century whose ideas derive from ancient Neoplatonism.

NEOPTOLEMUS \\,nē-äp-'tä-lə-məs\\, in Greek mythology, the son of ACHILLES and Deïdamia, daughter of King Lycomedes of Scyros; he was sometimes called Pyrrhus. In the last year of the Trojan War, ODYSSEUS brought him to Troy after the Trojan seer HELENUS had declared that the city could not be captured without the aid of a descendant of AEACUS, who had helped to build its walls; Neoptolemus was Aeacus' great-grandson. He fought bravely and took part in the capture of Troy but committed the SACRILEGE of slaying the aged king PRIAM at an altar. By ANDROMACHE, Priam's daughter-in-law, he was the father of Molossus, ancestor of the Molossian kings. He later married Hermione but shortly thereafter was murdered at DELPHI.

NEPTUNE \\'nep-,tün, -,tyün\\, *Latin* Neptunus \\nep-'tü-nùs\\, in ROMAN RELIGION, originally god of freshwater; by 399 BCE he was identified with the Greek POSEIDON and thus became a deity of the sea. His female counterpart, Salacia, was perhaps originally a goddess of springwater, subsequently equated with the Greek AMPHITRITE.

Neptune's festival (Neptunalia) took place in the heat of the summer (July 23), and its purpose was probably the propitiation of the freshwater deity. Neptune had a temple in the Circus Flaminius at Rome; one of its features was a sculptured group of marine deities headed by Poseidon and THETIS. In art Neptune appears as the Greek Poseidon, whose attributes are the trident and the dolphin.

NEREID \\'nir-ē-əd\\, in GREEK RELIGION, any of the daughters (numbering 50 or 100) of the sea god NEREUS and of Doris, daughter of OCEANUS. The Nereids were depicted as young girls, inhabiting both salt- and freshwater, and as benign toward humanity. They were popular figures in Greek literature. The best known of the Nereids were AMPHITRITE, consort of POSEIDON; THETIS, wife of PELEUS and mother of the hero ACHILLES; and Galatea, a Sicilian figure loved by the CYCLOPS POLYPHEMUS.

Nereus and the Nereids, detail of a red-figure cup; in the Louvre, Paris
Alinari—Art Resource

NEREUS \\'nir-ē-əs\\, in GREEK RELIGION, sea god called by Homer "Old Man of the Sea," noted for his wisdom, his gift of PROPHECY, and his ability to change his shape at will. He was the son of Pontus, a personification of the sea, and GAEA. The NEREIDS were his daughters by the Oceanid Doris, and he lived with them in the depths of the sea, particularly in the Aegean. APHRODITE, the goddess of love, was his pupil. HERACLES, in his quest for the golden apples of the HESPERIDES, obtained directions from Nereus by wrestling with him in his many forms. Nereus is frequently depicted in vase paintings as a dignified spectator.

NERGAL \\'ner-,gäl\\, in MESOPOTAMIAN RELIGION, secondary god of the Sumero-Akkadian pantheon. He was identified with Irra, the god of scorched earth and war, and related to or identified with MESLAMTAEA, He Who Comes Forth from Meslam. The city of Cuthah (modern Tall Ibrāhīm, in south-central Iraq) was the chief center of his cult.

The Nergal's other sphere of power was the UNDERWORLD, of which he became king. According to one text, Nergal, escorted by DEMONS, descended to the underworld where the goddess ERESHKIGAL (or Allatum) was queen. He threatened to cut off her head, but she saved herself by becoming his wife, and Nergal obtained kingship over the underworld.

NERTHUS \\'ner-thùs\\, in GERMANIC RELIGION, goddess known from a report of her given by the Roman historian Tacitus, who in his *Germania* (98 CE) refers to her as Terra Mater, or Mother Earth, and says that she was worshiped by seven tribes (among whom were the Angles, who later invaded Britannia). Her worship centered on a temple in a sacred grove on an island in the Baltic Sea. She was believed to enjoy coming among her people, riding in a chariot pulled by cows. Her presence was discerned by her priest, and while she was among them her people lived in peace, with no war or fighting and much rejoicing. When she returned to her temple, she and her chariot were washed in a sacred lake by slaves, who were then drowned in the lake.

NESTOR \'nes-tər, -,tȯr\, in Greek mythology, king of Pylos (Navarino) in Elis. All of his brothers were slain by HERACLES, but Nestor escaped. In the *Iliad* he is about 70 years old; his role is largely to incite the warriors to battle and to tell stories of his early exploits. In the *Odyssey* he entertains TELEMACHUS.

NESTORIAN \ne-'stȯr-ē-ən\, member of a Christian sect originating in Asia Minor and Syria out of the condemnation of NESTORIUS and his teachings by the COUNCILS OF EPHESUS (431 CE) and CHALCEDON (451 CE). Nestorians stressed the independence of the divine and human natures of Christ and were perceived by their opponents as suggesting that Christ was, in effect, two persons loosely united. Today they are represented by the Church of the East, or Persian Church, usually referred to in the West as the Assyrian, or Nestorian, Church. Most of its members—numbering about 170,000—live in Iraq, Syria, and Iran.

CHRISTIANITY in Persia faced intermittent persecution until the Persian Church in 424 formally proclaimed its full independence of Christian churches elsewhere, thereby freeing itself of suspicions about foreign links. Under the influence of Barsumas, the METROPOLITAN of Nisibis, the Persian Church acknowledged THEODORE OF MOPSUESTIA (d. 428/429), the chief Nestorian theological authority, as guardian of right faith, in February 486. This position was reaffirmed under the PATRIARCH Babai (497–502), and since that time the church has been Nestorian.

When supporters of Nestorius gathered at the theological school of Edessa, it was closed by imperial order in 489, and a vigorous Nestorian remnant migrated to Persia. The Persian Church's intellectual center then became the new school in Nisibis, which carried on the venerable traditions of Edessa. By the end of the 5th century there were seven metropolitan provinces in Persia and several bishoprics in Arabia and India. The church survived a period of SCHISM (*c.* 521–*c.* 537/539) and persecution (540–545) through the leadership of the patriarch Mar Aba I (reigned 540–552), a convert from ZOROASTRIANISM.

After the Arab conquest of Persia (637), the caliphate recognized the Church of the East as a MILLET, or separate religious community, and granted it legal protection. For more than three centuries the church prospered under the caliphate, but it became worldly and lost leadership in the cultural sphere. By the end of the 10th century there were 15 metropolitan provinces in the caliphate and 5 abroad, including India and China. Nestorians also spread to Egypt. In China a Nestorian community flourished from the 7th to the 10th century. In Central Asia certain Tatar tribes were almost entirely converted, Christian expansion reaching almost to Lake Baikal in eastern Siberia. Western travelers to the Mongol realm found Nestorian Christians well established there, even at the court of the Great Khan. When during the 14th century the Church of the East was virtually exterminated by the raids of the Turkic leader Timur, Nestorian communities lingered on in a few towns in Iraq but were concentrated mainly in Kurdistan.

In 1551 a number of Nestorians reunited with Rome and were called Chaldeans, the original Nestorians having been termed Assyrians. The Nestorian Church in India, part of the group known as the Christians of St. Thomas, allied itself with Rome (1599), then split, half of its membership transferring allegiance to the Syrian Jacobite (MONOPHYSITE)

patriarch of Antioch (1653). In 1898 in Urmia, Iran, a group of Nestorians, headed by a bishop, were received in the communion of the Russian Orthodox church.

NESTORIUS \ne-'stȯr-ē-əs\ (b. late 4th century CE, Germanicia, Syria Euphratensis, Asia Minor [now Maras, Turkey]—d. *c.* 451, Panopolis, Egypt), early bishop of Constantinople whose views on the nature and person of Christ led to the calling of the Council of Ephesus in 431 and to Nestorianism.

Nestorius was born of Persian parents. He studied at Antioch (now in Turkey), probably as the pupil of THEODORE OF MOPSUESTIA. He became a monk at the nearby Monastery of St. Euprepius and, after being ordained a priest, acquired a great reputation for ASCETICISM, orthodoxy, and eloquence. Owing to this reputation, Nestorius was nominated by the Eastern Roman emperor Theodosius II to become bishop of Constantinople in 428. He immediately set to work extirpating heretics of every sort, showing leniency only to Pelagians (*see* PELAGIANISM).

A crisis developed when Nestorius' domestic chaplain, Anastasius, on Nov. 22, 428, preached a sermon in which he objected to the title THEOTOKOS ("God-Bearer") as applied to MARY. Nestorius, who had already expressed doubts on the subject, supported Anastasius and began a series of addresses arguing that Mary was not Theotokos. Nestorius considered that, unless carefully qualified, the term Theotokos as applied to Mary compromised Christ's full humanity. To many people it seemed that Nestorius himself was denying the divinity of Christ and regarding him as a mere man who had been adopted by God as his son (an early HERESY, of which Nestorius was not guilty). In the resulting controversy, Nestorius' opponents found an ally in CYRIL OF ALEXANDRIA; though Cyril sincerely believed that Nestorius was undermining the purity of the faith, he also was eager to belittle the rival see of Constantinople.

In August 430 Pope Celestine I held a church council in Rome which decided that correct Christology required the use of the term Theotokos and requested Nestorius to disown his errors. When Cyril, who had been authorized to execute the sentence upon Nestorius, produced a string of provocative ANATHEMAS for him to subscribe to or face EXCOMMUNICATION, Nestorius and his allies persuaded the emperor Theodosius to convene a general church council. When the council met at Ephesus in 431, however, Nestorius' teaching was condemned and he himself was deposed from his see. Theodosius was induced to ratify these decisions, and Nestorius was exiled to his former monastery near Antioch. After 435, he was transferred to the Great Oasis (now the Oasis of Khārijah) in the Libyan Desert and was later removed to Panopolis in Upper Egypt. During his exile, he wrote the *Book of Heraclides of Damascus*, which he intended as a defense of his teaching and a history of his life. The sole treatise from his pen to have survived, it was discovered in 1895 in a Syriac translation.

Nestorius is regarded as one of the principal heretics in Christology, and the heresy traditionally linked with his name, Nestorianism, was formally condemned at the church COUNCILS OF EPHESUS (431) and CHALCEDON (451). In the orthodox view, Nestorianism denies the reality of the INCARNATION and represents Christ as a God-inspired man rather than as God-made-man. What Nestorius actually taught was a prosopic union. In Greek *prosōpon* means the external, undivided presentation, or manifestation, of an individual that can be extended by means of other things. So the Son of God used manhood for his self-manifestation, and manhood was, therefore, included in his *prosōpon*, so that he was a single object of presentation.

NEW CHURCH, *also called* Swedenborgians, church organized in the General Conference of the New Church, the General Convention of the New Jerusalem in the U.S.A., and the General Church of the New Jerusalem. Its members are followers of the theology of EMANUEL SWEDENBORG, the 18th-century Swedish scientist, philosopher, and theologian. Swedenborg did not himself found a church, but he believed that his writings would be the basis of a "New Church," which he related to the New Jerusalem mentioned in the biblical Book of Revelation.

Shortly after Swedenborg's death, a group of his followers in England decided to establish a separate church. In 1788 the first building for New Church worship was opened in Great East Cheap, London, and was rapidly followed by others. In 1789 a conference met in the London church, and, except for 1794–1806 and 1809–14, the General Conference of the New Church has met annually. Swedenborg's writings on religion were introduced into the United States in the 1780s. The General Convention of the New Jerusalem in the U.S.A. was founded in 1817 in Philadelphia. Differences of interpretation within the convention led to the formation in 1897 of a separate group, the General Church of the New Jerusalem.

Worship in the Swedenborgian churches is almost always liturgical. Preaching of the SCRIPTURES is based on Swedenborg's teaching that Scripture should be interpreted spiritually. BAPTISM and the Lord's Supper (*see* EUCHARIST) are the two SACRAMENTS of the church. To the established Christian festivals is added New Church Day (June 19).

Church government in the three New Church groups varies. The British General Conference and the U.S. General Convention annually appoint a general council, which, with a ministerial council, is the controlling authority. The General Church is episcopal. Candidates for the ministry, apart from those trained in Africa for service there, normally pass through a four-year course in one of the two U.S. colleges (in Cambridge, Mass., and Bryn Athyn, Pa.) or in Woodford Green, Essex, Eng., before being ordained.

The three groups have extensive MISSION operations, with emphasis on Africa. New Church societies, generally small, are found in many parts of the world. Australia has its own conference, closely allied to that in Britain. The New Church groups in continental Europe are nearly all assisted from the United States.

NEW FIRE CEREMONY, *also called* The Binding Up of the Years, in Aztec religion, ritual celebrated every 52 years when the 260-day ritual and 365-day civil calendars returned to the same positions relative to each other. In preparation, all sacred and domestic fires were allowed to burn out. At the climax of the ceremony, priests ignited a new sacred fire on the breast of a sacrificial victim, from which the rest of the people rekindled their hearth fires; the people then began feasting.

NEWMAN, JOHN HENRY \'nü-mən, 'nyü-\ (b. Feb. 21, 1801, London, Eng.—d. Aug. 11, 1890, Birmingham, Warwick), influential churchman and man of letters who led the OXFORD MOVEMENT in the Church of England and later became a cardinal-deacon in the ROMAN CATHOLIC church.

After pursuing his education in an evangelical home and at Trinity College, Oxford, Newman was made a fellow of Oriel College, Oxford, in 1822, vice principal of Alban Hall in 1825, and VICAR of St. Mary's, Oxford, in 1828. Under the influence of the clergyman John Keble and Richard Hurrell Froude, Newman became a convinced high churchman (one who emphasizes the Anglican church's continuation of ancient Christian tradition, particularly as regards the episcopate, PRIESTHOOD, and SACRAMENTS).

When the Oxford Movement began in 1833 Newman was its effective organizer and intellectual leader. The movement was started with the object of stressing the Catholic elements in the English religious tradition and of reforming the Church of England. Newman contributed several books, especially the *Lectures on the Prophetical Office of the Church* (1837), the classic statement of the Tractarian doctrine of authority; the *University Sermons* (1843), similarly classical for the theory of religious belief; and above all his *Parochial and Plain Sermons* (1834–42), which in their published form took the principles of the movement into the country at large.

Newman was soon contending that the Church of England represented true catholicity and that the test of this catholicity (as against Rome upon the one side and what he termed "the popular Protestants" upon the other) lay in the teaching of the ancient and undivided church of the Fathers. In 1838–39 Newman and Keble published Froude's *Remains*, in which the REFORMATION was violently denounced; in 1841 Newman released his *Tract 90*, which, in reconciling the THIRTY-NINE ARTICLES with the teaching of the ancient and undivided church, appeared to some to assert that the articles were not incompatible with the doctrines of the COUNCIL OF TRENT.

Newman resigned St. Mary's, Oxford, on Sept. 18, 1843, and preached his last Anglican sermon a week later. He applied the law of historical development to Christian society and tried to show that the early and undivided church had developed rightly into the modern Roman Catholic church and that the Protestant churches represented a break in this development, both in doctrine and in devotion. On Oct. 9, 1845, he was received into the Roman Catholic church, publishing a few weeks later his *Essay on the Development of Christian Doctrine*.

Newman went to Rome to be ordained to the priesthood and after some uncertainties founded the Oratory at Birmingham in 1848. He was suspect among the more rigorous Roman Catholic clergy because of the quasi-liberal spirit that he seemed to have brought with him from Anglicanism, and therefore his early career as a Roman Catholic priest was marked by a series of frustrations; he was helped out of this period by an unwarranted attack from Charles Kingsley upon his moral teaching. Kingsley in effect challenged him to justify the honesty of his life as an Anglican. The resulting history of his religious opinions, *Apologia pro Vita Sua* (1864; "A Defense of His Life"), was read and approved far beyond the limits of the Roman Catholic church, recaptured the almost national status that he had once held, and assured Newman's stature in the Roman Catholic church. In 1870 he expressed opposition to a definition of PAPAL INFALLIBILITY, though himself a believer in the doctrine. In 1879 Pope LEO XIII made him cardinal-deacon of St. George in Velabro.

NEW MOON, *Hebrew* Rosh Ḥodesh ("Head of the Month"), start of the Hebrew month, a Jewish festival on which fasting and mourning are not allowed. A blessing is recited on the SABBATH preceding the New Moon, and an abbreviated form of the HALLEL psalms is sung or recited on the New Moon itself.

NEW RELIGIOUS MOVEMENTS

New Religious Movement (NRM) is the generally accepted term for what is also called (often with pejorative connotations) a "cult." Depending on the scope of one's definition, NRMs can include all new religions that have arisen worldwide over the past several centuries. Others would tend to restrict the use of the term to modern religious movements that display certain characteristic traits and that are largely centered in the United States and Europe but are also sometimes found in non-Western nations such as Japan.

Some of these characteristic traits are: (1) These religions are, by definition, "new" religions; NRMs are innovative religious responses to the conditions of the modern world, despite the fact that most NRMs represent themselves, in one way or another, as rooted in ancient traditions. (2) NRMs are also usually regarded as "countercultural"; that is, they are perceived to be (by others and by themselves) alternatives to the mainstream religions of Western society, especially CHRISTIANITY in its normative forms. It is also frequently the case that NRMs are highly eclectic, pluralistic, and syncretistic; they freely combine doctrines and practices from diverse sources within their belief systems. (3) In most cases the new movement is founded by a charismatic and sometimes highly authoritarian leader who is thought to have extraordinary powers or insights. Many NRMs are tightly organized; in light of their often self-proclaimed "alternative" or "outsider" status vis-à-vis the mainstream, these groups tend to make great demands on the loyalty and commitment of their followers and sometimes come to be all-encompassing substitutes for the family and other conventional social groupings. (4) NRMs have arisen to address specific needs that many people feel they cannot satisfy through more traditional religious organizations or through modern SECULARISM. NRMs are both products of and responses to modernity, pluralism, and the scientific worldview.

THE WEST

NRMs are extremely diverse, both in their historical roots and in their doctrines and practices. The following overview organizes this diversity into categories, but many NRMs could be classified under more than one of these rubrics.

Service at the Great Cao Dai Temple at Tay Ninh, Vietnam, the seat of the sect
Paul Stepan-Vierow—Photo Researchers

Apocalyptic and millenarian movements. Some NRMs include an apocalyptic or millenarian dimension—the belief that the world as we know it is drawing to an end and that a new (and better) period is about to begin. There are apocalyptic strains in many of the world's religions, but it is Christian millenarianism in particular that has formed the backdrop for the development of many of the NRMs in the West.

Among the first new religions in the United States were the SEVENTH-DAY ADVENTISTS and the JEHOVAH'S WITNESSES, both the products of millenarian fervor set off in the mid-19th century by WILLIAM MILLER (1782–1849). Miller predicted that Christ would return to earth sometime in 1843 or 1844. When Christ failed to appear, the result was termed the "Great Disappointment." Nevertheless, many still believed in the prediction, feeling that only Miller's calculations were faulty. The Seventh-day Adventists, formed under the leadership of prophet and visionary Ellen G. White (1827–1915), and the Jehovah's Witnesses, founded by CHARLES TAZE RUSSELL (1852–1916), both continue to believe that we are living at the end of time and awaiting Christ's imminent return.

Another version of millenarianism underlies the New Age Movement that arose in the 1970s and '80s. The New Age Movement is comprised of an extremely eclectic conglomeration of beliefs and practices ranging from channeling and crystal healing to updated versions of shamanism and a variety of therapies and techniques designed to "transform" the individual into a "higher consciousness." The movement as a whole optimistically presumes that we have entered, or are on the verge of entering, a "new age" (sometimes referred to as the "Age of Aquarius") of unprecedented spiritual possibilities.

A darker side of apocalyptic expectations has resulted in mass suicides and tragic conflict with governmental agencies. In the 1970s an ordained Methodist minister named JIM JONES (1931–78) moved his congregation (called the People's Temple) from the United States to the jungles of Guyana. There he attempted to create a utopian, interracial community united by his personal CHARISMA and based on his unorthodox version of Christianity combined with communism. Jones, an increasingly authoritative and paranoid personality, warned his followers that a devastating thermonuclear war was impending. In 1978, after a group of concerned family members (led by a U.S. congressman) visited the group's commune, Jones and his followers (913 persons in all) committed what Jones called "revolutionary suicide" rather than submit to what they thought would be an attempt to compromise their community. "Death is a million times preferable to 10 more days of this life," Jones told his group, and, "If you knew what was ahead of you, you'd be glad to be stepping over tonight." Similar tragedies, fueled by apocalyptic expectations, befell David Koresh's Branch Davidians near Waco, Texas, and the Heaven's Gate group in Rancho Santa Fe, California (*see* below).

On Aug. 16–17, 1987, ceremonies, such as this gathering at Giza, Egypt, were held worldwide for the Harmonic Convergence, an attempt to harness spiritual energy for peace and enlightenment
Reuters/Aladin Abdel-nabi— Archive Photos

The influence of the East. While the religions of India have intrigued the West for millennia, it was only in the 19th century that accurate and relatively comprehensive information regarding the teachings and practices of HINDUISM and BUDDHISM began circulating in Europe and the United States. Certain Indian philosophical doctrines, especially those of monistic VEDĀNTA, began to influence Western thinkers such as Arthur Schopenhauer, Henry David Thoreau, Ralph Waldo Emerson, and Friedrich Nietzsche. Monism is a philosophical system that posits the unity of the universe. For instance, in Hindu monistic beliefs the cosmos is regarded as wholly sacred or as participating in a single divine principle (BRAHMAN, or Being itself). Esoteric groups like the Theosophical Society (*see* THEOSOPHY; BLAVATSKY, HELENA PETROVNA) and its many offshoots integrated Indian philosophical and religious concepts into a synthesis that also drew on Western MYSTICISM, NEOPLATONISM, QABBALAH, Jewish mysticism, and communication with the spirit world.

The coffin of Jim Jones among the coffins of his followers being sent home to the United States from Guyana. Jones directed 913 members of his People's Temple to commit suicide in 1978
Neal Boenzi—New York Times Co./ Archive Photos

By the end of the 19th century the first religious group to be imported from India took root in the United States. VIVEKANANDA (1863–1902) attended the 1893 World's Parliament of Religions in Chicago and shortly thereafter founded the Vedanta Society in New York. Based on the monistic philosophy of one of Hinduism's philosophical schools and on its interpretation as given in the teachings and mystical experiences of Vivekananda's teacher, Ramakrishna (1836–86), the Vedanta Society attracted the attention of many prominent members of the artistic community: the French actress Sarah Bernhardt, the American author and publisher Paul Carus, the English novelist Aldous Huxley, and the Anglo-American novelist and playwright Christopher Isherwood, among others. With centers in India and throughout the world, the Vedanta Society (also known as the Ramakrishna Mission) continues to promote a highly eclectic and tolerant form of religious unity, claiming that all world religions teach fundamentally the same truth, but nevertheless maintaining that Vedānta is uniquely capable of articulating this unified doctrine.

Some 40 years after Vivekananda's journey to the United States another teacher from India, Paramahansa Yogananda (1893–1952), founded the SELF-REALIZATION FELLOWSHIP in Los Angeles and introduced the practice and philosophy of YOGA to Americans. Drawing on traditional Hindu teachings of spiritual, mental, and physical discipline, Yogananda represented yoga in quasi-scientific terms that appealed to his audience, maintaining that other religious teachers (including JESUS and PAUL) had also preached much the same message.

While these precursors paved the way, it was not until the 1960s and '70s that NRMs based on Eastern religions became attractive to large numbers of Americans and Europeans. It was in this period that MAHARISHI MAHESH YOGI (b. 1911?) founded his Spiritual Regeneration Movement with its popularized meditation technique known as TRANSCENDENTAL MEDITATION. The Maharishi won much publicity by attracting to himself and his teachings celebrities such as the American film star Mia Farrow, the American engineer and architect Buckminster Fuller, and the English musical group the Beatles. Transcendental Meditation was also represented as a "scientific" method for obtaining both personal and social peace and harmony; it centered around the repetition of and concentration on an individualized MANTRA imparted to the initiate by the GURU.

Another group that arose in this period of cultural turmoil and change was the

International Society for Krishna Consciousness (ISKON), founded by A.C. Bhakti-vedanta (1896–1977) and popularly known as the Hare Krishna movement. Far less accommodating to American cultural and religious predilections, ISKON is fundamentally a continuation of a Hindu sect, originating in India's medieval period, that emphasizes ecstatic devotion to the god Krishna. Conversion to ISKON entails not only a shift in RELIGIOUS BELIEF and practice but an entire break with Western culture, symbolized by the adoption of Indian dress and diet and by the shaving of male followers' heads. Such radical signs of alienation from Western culture and values, together with the group's active proselytizing dimension and its internal crises and leadership struggles, engendered much controversy about the Hare Krishnas.

The Rajneesh International Foundation was another highly controversial NRM that originated in India. The group centered around the flamboyant figure of BHAGWAN SHREE RAJNEESH (1931–90), who taught a heavily revised form of Indian spirituality called Tantrism. Known to some as the "sex guru," Rajneesh urged his Western followers to overcome their repressions through a technique he dubbed "dynamic meditation," entailing shouting, screaming, and dancing—and in some cases physical violence and uninhibited (sometimes public) sex. Rajneesh thus adapted and repackaged ancient Tantric techniques for a Western audience more familiar with psychotherapy.

ISKON and other imports from the East, such as movements representing ZEN Buddhism and the various schools of TIBETAN BUDDHISM, have been introduced into the United States and Europe with little or no alterations to their traditional forms. Their appeal to Westerners may very well lie in their exotic nature and their clear-cut differences from Western religions. Many other Asian traditions, however, have been highly modified by their new contexts. Especially noteworthy is the emphasis many Eastern-based NRMs place on religious UNIVERSALISM (a response to pluralism) and on the "scientific" nature of the spiritual teachings and techniques put forward.

"Scientific" NRMs: UFO groups and Scientology. Many NRMs claim not to be religions at all but rather "scientific truth" that has not yet been acknowledged or discovered by the official scientific community. In the search for authority for new teachings certain NRMs have thus tapped into what is arguably the most powerful form of legitimizing discourse in the modern world: science. While some groups, for example, have claimed scientific authority and proof for yoga and meditation, other NRMs with few or no roots in Asian religions have developed in the West under the umbrella of scientific validity.

One such example is the variety of UFO groups, sometimes called collectively the "contact movement." Drawing on time-honored religious stories of the descent of supernatural beings from the heavens, the UFO groups have modified such notions into what has been called a "technological myth" of the arrival—whether imminent or actual and ongoing—of space aliens on Earth, bringing with them advanced knowledge and spiritual wisdom. Already by the 1950s groups such as Understanding, Inc., founded by Daniel Fry (who claimed to be a contactee), argued that UFOs carried beings who had come to Earth to promote world peace and personal development. The Amalgamated Flying Saucer Clubs of America, led by Gabriel Green, and the Aetherius Society, organized by George King, maintained that space aliens held the key to the salvation both of the planet as a whole and of every individual on Earth.

A more recent and highly publicized UFO group was Heaven's Gate, the creation of Marshall Applewhite, who preferred to call himself "Bo." Applewhite declared that he and his female partner ("Peep") were really representatives from another world, which he referred to as "the evolutionary level above human." Claiming to have come to Earth once before in the figure of Jesus, Applewhite asserted that the "kingdom of heaven" taught by Applewhite/Christ was a real, physical place inhabited by highly evolved beings. Earth was a "garden" in which human beings had been "planted" by these superior space beings; some such "plants" could hope to mature and further evolve into "members of the level above human," but only if they systematically shed all vestiges of their humani-

Vivekananda, founder of the Vedanta Society
By courtesy of the Indian High Commission Office, London

Members of the International Society for Krishna Consciousness (ISKON), popularly known as the Hare Krishna movement
Perry Ruben—Monkmeyer/Conklin

ty, including their sexuality (some members of the group had castrated themselves to further this end). Applewhite's "classroom," consisting of some 30 members, was instructed to obey absolutely the dictates of their teacher in order to be worthy of such advancement. In March 1997 Applewhite declared that the appearance of a comet signaled the arrival of a spaceship sent to gather up the "mature plants" before the impending "spading over" of the garden (*i.e.*, end of the world), and the group committed mass suicide in order to join the alien community in outer space.

UFO groups sometimes couch traditional religious themes such as APOCALYPTICISM and heavenly intervention in the language of modern technology and biological evolutionary theory. In other cases, spiritual teachings and mythology are recast in the language of modern psychology. The latter rendering is the case with SCIENTOLOGY.

Founded by science fiction writer L. Ron Hubbard (1911–86), Scientology started out under the name Dianetics, which was later changed to the Church of Scientology. Dianetics was Hubbard's term for a kind of therapy revolving around the claim that destructive imprints of past experiences, called "engrams," accumulate in one's unconscious. Hubbard devised a method—employing both discussion with an "auditor" and the use of an electrical devise called an "E-meter"—to dissipate such engrams and produce (over a long period of treatment in which one attains and passes through a variety of hierarchical levels) a state of liberation he termed "being Clear." Over time Hubbard also developed a whole COSMOLOGY, in which human beings were said to be originally divine beings, called "thetans," who had fallen into and been entrapped by material existence. The freedom of "being Clear" was equated to regaining one's status as an eternal, omniscient, omnipotent thetan.

Nature religions: Neo-Paganism and Wicca. Neo-Paganism and Wicca groups represent a different, even opposite, response to the dominance and pervasive influence of science in modern culture. Instead of integrating scientific claims into new religious options, these NRMs tend to oppose the materialism, technological excesses, and alienation from nature that science is seen to foster, offering modern people a way to return to and participate in the rhythms of the natural world. The embracing of magic and the use of SPELLS to help further one's goals in everyday life seems to fly in the face of some of the basic tenets of modern science and secular "common sense."

Some of the Neo-Pagan groups, which claim to retrieve and revitalize the pre-Christian PAGAN traditions of northern Europe, are a kind of reaction to cultural and religious pluralism and an attempt to reclaim and return to their roots, whereas others more eclectically embrace "pagan" traditions from a variety of cultures. Still other such groups, especially those that collectively go under the name Wicca, are in large part religious articulations of sentiments derived from the modern ecology movement and feminism. Wiccan NRMs, mostly but not exclusively composed of women, tend to center around the figure of a goddess and the "female principle" manifest in nature, and, like other Neo-Pagan organizations, they attempt to re-enchant and personalize the natural world that they believe science has objectified.

THE EAST

Eastern NRMs include movements that have appeared in South Asia, East Asia, and Southeast Asia since the mid-19th century. While some of these religious movements have remained small and limited in influence, others have gathered many followers under their banners and have played important roles in the socioeconomic and political development of their respective nations or regions.

While there have always been NRMs developing in Asia, there are important differences between those that developed after the 1840s and those that developed in previous centuries. Post-1850 religious movements reflect the impact of the West and of Western forms of political, economic, and cultural imperialism. From the 19th century onward the newly industrialized and expansionist West advanced into Asia for God, glory, and gold. Western nations, secure in their sense of political, military, economic, and cultural superiority and armed with either an expansionist Protestant evangelical faith or an equally expansionist Catholicism, frequently sent missionaries to act as the initial vanguard. Some areas in South and Southeast Asia—India, Vietnam (along with Laos and Cambodia), Indonesia, Malaysia, and the Philippines—were taken outright and made to fit into evolving European and American colonial networks. Even those areas that were not directly controlled by the West (such as China, Japan, and Korea) felt the influence of the West in the form of imposed unequal treaties or carefully applied military pressure. The NRMs that evolved in this new sociopolitical and cultural environment tended either to be direct reactions to Western imperialism, taking the form of reinvention of an older tradition, or to be spiritual syntheses of Western and Asian belief systems. Each of these new religions was thus designed to serve both as an answer and as an alternative to the spreading Westernization, secularization, individualism, and materialism occurring within Asian cultures.

South Asia: India. In India the 19th-century rise of the ARYA SAMAJ and the Brahmo Samaj movements, both of which were reactions to the growing British presence in India and the British challenge to Hindu traditions, paved the way for certain new religious movements. One such movement was Ramakrishna's Vedānta movement, which sought to make Vedānta philosophy and practice accessible to a Western audience. A second such movement was the Transcendental Meditation movement of Maharishi Mahesh Yogi. A third new religion, with strong ties to the 12th-century BHAKTI movement, was the Hare Krishna movement. Yet another was the cult founded by Bhagwan Shree Rajneesh, who was also known as Acharya Rajneesh and, later, as Osho. (*See* above.)

East Asia: China and Taiwan. NRMs in China evolved after the first Opium War (1839–42) and were the result of Western imperialism, difficult economic conditions in southern China owing in part to the opium trade and the war over opium, and the cultural impact created by the first generation of Anglo-American Protestant missionaries. The first and foremost of these new religions was the T'ai-p'ing T'ien-kuo (the Heavenly Kingdom of the Great Peace). A mixture of evangelical Christianity, classical quasi-Confucian methods, and various strains derived from the popular tradition, the movement was developed by its charismatic leader, HUNG HSIU-CH'ÜAN, into a religious state that controlled key provinces in southern and central China. T'ai-p'ing T'ien-kuo threatened the stability of the Ch'ing state until the movement was finally put down in 1865.

The period after the 1858 Treaty of Tientsin saw the legalization of the Western Christian missionary enterprise and the spread of many forms of Christian denominational messages throughout China. One effect of this tide of cultural and spiritual imperialism was the development of indigenous Protestant sects and denominations. One of these Christian new religions, the CHEN YESSU CHIAO-HUEI (the True Jesus Church), evolved as a result of the Pentecostal charismatic revivals that took place in the United States between 1900 and 1920 (*see* PENTECOSTALISM). A second independent church was the Ti-fang Huei (Local Church), or THE CHU-HWEI HSUO, founded by Watchman Nee.

Some of the later new religions of China evolved out of forms of sectarian and popular faith that predated the Opium War. One such major new body, which evolved out of the WHITE LOTUS millenarian tradition and the related tradition of moralistic spirit-writing (*pai-luan/fu-chi*), or shamanistic, sects, is the highly syncretistic I-kuan Tao (the Unity Sect). Another *fu-chi* sect, the Tzu-hui T'ang (Compassion Sect), began in Taiwan in 1949. Like I-kuan Tao, it has Wang Mu Niang-niang as its major deity.

The new constitution of the People's Republic of China, adopted in 1982, contains religious tolerance clauses, and both older and newer forms of religion have again begun to flourish. House churches—small evangelical and charismatic Christian bodies reminiscent of the True Jesus Church—have begun to sprout up, and the number of those who call themselves Christian has risen markedly. The *min-chien* (popular) traditions have also made a comeback, with older temples being restored and new ones being built. Much of the growth of the *min-chien* traditions is due in part to renewed contact with Taiwan and to the moral and financial support of Taiwanese followers of such mainland cults as those of Ma-tsu, the goddess of the sea; Pao-sheng Ta-ti, the god of medicine; KUAN-YIN, the popular goddess of mercy; and Kuang-kung, the martial and judicial god.

The major new religion now found in China is the faith in the semi-mystical powers of *ch'i-kung. Ch'i-kung* is the classical tradition of both spiritual and physical exercise that is often seen as the basis for the martial arts. In the 1980s and 1990s, *ch'i-kung* masters developed followings throughout China by demonstrating their powers. The movement spread to Taiwan, where *ch'i-kung* teachings were integrated into the teachings of syncretistic sects.

Taiwan's postwar experience differs from that of the mainland, and the path of development of its new religions has differed as well. Taiwan was, in turn, a Dutch colony, a Ming loyalist stronghold, a prefecture of China's Fukien province, a province of China, and a Japanese colony before Chinese Nationalists took over the island in 1945. It became the refuge for and a bastion of the Nationalist Party after 1949, and, with considerable American help and a reformed Nationalist regime, it began to develop into an economic success. Its leaders opened the nation to Christian missionaries and to independent Chinese churches, such as the True Jesus Church. The Taiwanese government also supported the mainstream traditions, such as Buddhism and TAOISM, and did little, if anything, to stifle the development of the major popular cults (many from the Fukien province) that had evolved on the island after 1600. The decades from 1949 to the end of the 20th century saw the flowering of a number of syncretistic new religions, such as the socially active, salvationistic Buddhist organization Tsi hi; charismatic Christian churches, such as the True Jesus Church and the New Testament Church; the moralistic, syncretistic sect I-kuan Tao; and a postmodern and highly eclectic millenarian sect, the CHEN TAO (the True Way).

East Asia: Japan. The traumatic political, economic, social, and cultural changes that took place in the years from 1853 to 1889—these being the final years of the Tokugawa Shogunate and the first two decades of the Meiji Restoration—led in turn to the formation of a large number of new religious entities that scholars of Japan have termed the New Religions. Such religions had their roots in SHINTŌ and Buddhism, the two dominant traditions in Japan, as well as in Tokugawa NEO-CONFUCIANISM. If one searches for the basic causes of the dynamic growth of these religions, one finds that, while the older traditions were characterized by extreme formalism and a lack of vitality, the New Religions demonstrate renewal and higher levels of enthusiasm. Like the NRMs of China, Taiwan, Korea, and Southeast Asia, they are characterized by high levels of popular participation and volunteerism, with followers running day-to-day operations and converting new adherents.

The earliest of the Japanese New Religions include TENRIKYŌ and Konkōkyō. The years between the wars saw the development of Getdatsu-kai—a sect that is a syncretistic blend of Shintō, Buddhism, and Confucianism—Ōmoto-kyō, and HITO-NO-MICHI, another Shintō-related sect. The post-war period saw further development of some of these earlier groups—Hito-no-michi, for example, became PL KYŌDAN (Perfect Liberty Church). New cults also appeared, such as TENSHŌ KŌTAI JINGŪ-KYŌ, also known as Odoru Shukyō (the Dancing Religion); Jōhrei, a Christian-based self-help movement; and the radical doomsday religion AUM SHINRIKYŌ. The latter group came to worldwide attention in 1995 when it released nerve gas on the Tokyo subway system, killing 12 people and injuring more than 5,000.

East Asia: Korea. The history of modern Korea has been one of war and division. Long influenced by both the Chinese and the Japanese, Korea became a battleground in the age of imperialism. In the late 19th century Japan entered the ranks of modern militarized and expansionist states, first taking over Taiwan in 1895 and then, in 1910, Korea. Japan ruled Korea with a strong and sometimes brutal hand until 1945. Korea was then divided into two states. In 1950 South Korea was invaded by the communist regime of North Korea. United Nations (largely U.S.) intervention saved the two-state system and allowed for a truce that redefined the borders of the two Koreas, one a communist state and the other a Westernized, quasi-military state. Only from the mid-1980s did South Korea move toward democracy, while North Korea remained a poverty-stricken, family-run dictatorship.

This painful and traumatic history created a fertile environment for the development of Korean NRMs. Meanwhile, since the mid-19th century Korea had been heavily influenced by Christian missionaries, both Catholic and Protestant. The late 19th century saw the development of TAJONG-GYO, or the Tangun Cult, a millenarian movement formulated by Na Chul. The postwar period produced not only a virtual explosion of Christian churches—by 1995 more than 25 percent of South Koreans were Christians—but the development of radical forms of Christianity and quasi-Christianity. David Yonggi Cho's Yoido Full Gospel Church in Seoul is the largest single church in the world, with a membership of over 700,000. It belongs to the ASSEMBLIES OF GOD, a major Pentecostal denomination in the United States. The major quasi-Christian new religion is Sun Myung Moon's UNIFICATION CHURCH. *See also* CH'ŎNDOGYO.

Wedding at Madison Square Garden in New York City in which the Reverend Sun Myung Moon married over 2,000 couples
David Grossman—Photo Researchers

Southeast Asia: The Philippines, Vietnam, and Indonesia. The major nations of Southeast Asia also went through periods of dramatic change in the 19th and 20th centuries, experiencing imperialistic conquest, Japanese aggression, and imperial divestiture followed by civil war and sociopolitical turmoil. One result of these dramatic and painful changes was the development of a number of major new cults and religions.

In Vietnam, for example, two major new religions evolved, helping to fuel, in some measure, the political and cultural turmoil the nation experienced. CAO DAI, a syncretistic religion that blended CONFUCIANISM, Taoism, Buddhism, and Christianity, became a military and political force with considerable power during the final years of World War II and over the course of the First Indochina War (1945–54). A second major new religion, Hoa Hoa, was founded by a Buddhist reformer, Huynh Phu So. Blending Confucianism, ANIMISM, and indigenous Vietnamese religious practices, the movement became a political and military presence that, like Cao Dai, was involved in the violent political universe of post-World War II Vietnam.

The Philippines produced its own new religions. These were the RIZALIST CULTS, named after José Rizal, a martyr in the struggle against the Spanish in the years immediately preceding the Spanish-American War. The cults were syncretistic and combined Catholic elements with pre-Spanish Malay and Filipino elements, presenting messages that were millenarian and that gave hope to the poor and oppressed.

Indonesia is the home of SUBUD, a movement founded in 1933 by a Sufi named Muhammad Subuh, also known as Bapak. It spread to the West in the 1950s. Subud is a religion in which the believers open themselves to the power of God, a state which is demonstrated by singing, dancing, shouting, laughter, and feelings of rapture and release. Thus, in form, at least, Subud parallels the charismatic Christian experience that is to be seen in worship patterns of the True Jesus Church and the New Testament Church of Taiwan.

Divine Eye at the Cao Dai Temple in Da Nang, Vietnam
Alain Evrard—Photo Researchers

CONCLUSION

NRMs, in all their diversity, represent various responses to some of the challenges of modernity: religious and cultural pluralism, the influence of science and technology, and the secularization of much of modern life. They are also attempts to find new spiritual alternatives to the mainstream religious traditions. While some NRMs have led to tragic ends for their adherents and others have faded away as quickly as they arose, many have provided religious solace to those who feel they cannot obtain it elsewhere and some show signs of enduring and becoming institutionalized. Some of these latter movements will undoubtedly become, over time, part of tomorrow's mainstream religions.

José Rizal, Filipino nationalist executed by Spanish authorities in 1896, became the object of veneration of various Rizalist cults
Culver Pictures

NEW TESTAMENT

NEW TESTAMENT, second, later, and smaller of the two major divisions of the Christian BIBLE, and the portion that is canonical (authoritative) only to CHRISTIANITY.

Christians see in the New Testament the fulfillment of the promise of the OLD TESTAMENT. It relates and interprets the new COVENANT, represented in the life and death of Jesus, between God and the followers of JESUS CHRIST. Among its 27 books are selected recollections of the life and acts and sayings of Jesus in the four GOSPELS; a historical narrative of the first years of the Christian church in the ACTS OF THE APOSTLES; EPISTLES or letters of advice, instruction, admonition, and exhortation to local groups of Christians—14 of these letters are attributed to PAUL (one of these [Hebrews] probably wrongly so) and 7 by three other authors; and an apocalyptic description of the intervention of God in history, REVELATION TO JOHN. The books are not arranged chronologically in the New Testament. The Epistles of Paul, for example, which address the immediate problems of local churches shortly after Christ's death, are considered to be the earliest texts.

The books of the New Testament were composed not in order to satisfy historical curiosity about the events they recount but to bear witness to a faith in the action of God through these events. A history of the New Testament is made difficult by the relatively short time span covered by its books when compared with the millennium and more of history described by the Old Testament. There is less historical information in the New Testament than in the Old, and many facts about the church in the 1st century therefore must be arrived at by inference from statements in one of the Gospels or Epistles.

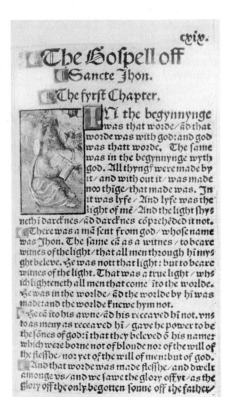

Opening page of the Gospel According to John from William Tyndale's translation of the New Testament, 1525–26
By courtesy of the Baptist College, Bristol, England

NEW THOUGHT, mind-healing movement that originated in the United States in the 19th century, based on religious and metaphysical presuppositions. The diversity of views and styles of life represented in various New Thought groups are difficult to describe because of their variety, and the same reason makes it virtually impossible to determine either membership or adherents. The influence of the various New Thought groups has been spread worldwide through lectures, journals, and books. Many adherents of New Thought consider themselves to be Christian.

Origins. The origins of New Thought may be traced to a dissatisfaction on the part of many persons with scientific EMPIRICISM and their reaction to the religious skepticism of the 17th and 18th centuries. The ROMANTICISM and idealism of the 19th century also influenced the New Thought movement, of which Phineas P. Quimby (1802–66) is usually cited as the earliest proponent. A native of Portland, Maine, Quimby practiced hypnotism and developed his concepts of mental and spiritual healing and health based on the view that illness is a matter of the mind. Quimby's influence may be seen in the writings of MARY BAKER EDDY and CHRISTIAN SCIENCE, although Mrs. Eddy retracted acknowledgment of dependence on him. Quimby's influence was readily acknowledged by others, such as the Methodist and Swedenborgian Warren F. Evans (1817–89).

Teachings and practices. There are elements of New Thought that may be traced to Platonism, particularly its Idealistic stance that the realm of ideas is more real than that of matter; to the teachings of EMANUEL SWEDENBORG, especially the view that the material realm is one of effects whose causes are spiritual and whose purpose is divine; to Hegelianism, especially Hegel's views regarding the external world, mental phenomena, and the nervous organism as the meeting ground of the body and the mind; to Orientalism, involving spiritual teachings of Eastern religions; and, particularly, to the Transcendentalism (a form of Idealism) of the 19th-century American philosopher and poet Ralph Waldo Emerson.

New Thought adherents do not accept Mary Baker Eddy's teaching or any other formulation as the final revelation. Rather, truth is viewed as a matter of continuing revelation, and no one can declare with finality what is the nature of truth. Moreover, New Thought does not oppose medical science, as Mrs. Eddy did, and it is essentially positive and optimistic about life and its outcome.

New Thought principles emphasized the immanence of God, the divine nature of humans, the immediate availability of God's power to humans, the spiritual character of the universe, and the fact that SIN, human disorders, and human disease are basically matters of incorrect thinking. Moreover, according to New Thought, humans can live in oneness with God in love, truth, peace, health, and plenty. Many New Thought groups emphasize Jesus as teacher and healer and proclaim his kingdom as being within a person. Reference to Jesus or the Christ is totally omitted in the principles, however, as revised in 1954. New Thought leaders have increasingly stressed material prosperity as one result of New Thought.

New Thought implies a kind of monism, or view of the oneness of the world, but it also has strong undertones of GNOSTICISM; that is, though New Thought is open to all, spiritual healing and strength of mind and body are available only to those who have the insights and who have been initiated into the movement at some point. There are no established patterns of worship, although the services often involve explication of New Thought ideas, testimony to healing, and prayer for the sick.

NEW YEAR FESTIVAL, any of numerous religious, social, and cultural observances worldwide celebrating the commencement of the New Year. Such festivals, which are among the oldest and most universally observed, generally include rites and ceremonies expressive of mortification, purgation, invigoration, and jubilation over life's renewal. This renewal is the essence of the New Year. It is, to varying degrees of explicitness in world cultures, a remembrance or repetition of the creation of the cosmos on the symbolic anniversary of its creation, in order that the gods, the cosmos, and the community may be strengthened.

The earliest-known record of a New Year's festival dates from about 2000 BCE in Mesopotamia, where the New Year (Akitu) commenced with the new moon nearest the spring equinox (mid-March; Babylonia) or nearest the autumn equinox (mid-September; Assyria). The year began for the Egyptians, Phoenicians, and Persians with the autumn equinox (September 21) and for the Greeks, until the 5th century BCE, with the winter solstice (December 21). By the Roman republican calendar the year began on March 1; after 153 BCE the official date was January 1, and this was confirmed by the Julian calendar (46 BCE).

In the Jewish religious calendar the year begins with the first day of the month of Tishri (September 6–October 5; ROSH HASHANAH). In early medieval times most of Europe regarded March 25 (ANNUNCIATION Day) as the beginning of the year, though for Anglo-Saxon England New Year's Day was December 25. William the Conqueror decreed that the year start on January 1, but, later, England began its year with the rest of Christendom on March 25. January 1 was restored as New Year's Day by the Gregorian calendar (1582), immediately adopted by ROMAN CATHOLIC countries. Other countries slowly followed suit: Scotland, 1660; Germany and Denmark, about 1700; England, 1752; Sweden, 1753; and Russia, 1918.

Most Eastern New Year festivals retain a distinctly religious character. In Dravidian southern India, the Tamil New Year is celebrated at winter solstice with the three-day PONGAL festival, marked by religious PILGRIMAGES and the ritual boiling of new rice. In Bangladesh the New Year is marked by the worship of the GANGA (Ganges) River.

Pre-Buddhist indigenous and Hindu influences are prominent in Southeast Asian festivals. In Thailand, Trut, or New Year (March/April), is of a mixed character. Buddhist monks exorcise ghosts from the vicinity and are presented with gifts. Oblations are made to various gods of Hindu origin. As people meet, water is playfully thrown by one on the other. Gambling, usually frowned upon, is permitted for the three-day festival.

Chinese New Year is celebrated officially for a month beginning at the second new moon after the winter solstice, in late January or early February. It is preceded by an expulsion of DEMONS and by theatrical performances. Offerings are made to gods of hearth and wealth and to ancestors. Tibetans observe the New Year in February with feasting, visiting, and a relaxation of monastic discipline.

The celebration of the New Year on January 1–3 is the most popular annual festival in Japan. In some rural districts it continues to be observed according to the lunar-solar calendar on dates varying between January 20 and February 19, and the traditions connected with the festival confirm its original connection with the coming of spring and a time of rebirth. The festival is called Ganjitsu ("Original Day"), signifying the beginning of the new year, and also Shōgatsu ("Standard Month"), referring to the belief that the good or bad fortune met with during the first few days of the new year may be taken as representative of the fortune for the entire coming year. The festival is custom-

arily celebrated with ceremonial housecleaning, feasting, and exchanging visits and gifts.

NEZIQIN \ˌne-zē-ˈkēn\ (Hebrew: "Damages"), fourth of the six major divisions, or orders (SEDARIM), of the MISHNAH, which was given its final form early in the 3rd century CE by JUDAH HA-NASI. *Neziqin* deals principally with legally adjudicated damages and financial questions. Its 10 tractates are: *Bava qamma* ("First Gate"), *Bava metzi'a* ("Middle Gate"), *Bava batra* ("Last Gate"), SANHEDRIN (the supreme executive and legislative body), *Makkot* ("Stripes"), *Shevu'ot* ("Oaths"), *'Eduyyot* ("Testimonies"), *'Avoda zara* ("Idolatry"), *Avot* ("Fathers"), and *Horayot* ("Decisions"). Both TALMUDS—the YERUSHALMI and the BAVLI—have GEMARA on all the tractates except *Avot* and *'Eduyyot*.

NGO VAN CHIEU \ˈŋō-ˈvän-jē-ˈü, *Angl* əŋ-ˈgō-\, *also called* Ngo Minh Chieu (b. 1878, Binh Tay, Vietnam—d. 1926?, Tay Ninh), founder of the Vietnamese new religious movement CAO DAI.

Ngo Van Chieu graduated from a provincial college in My Tho and entered the French colonial immigration service, where he served until 1902. In 1919, during a SÉANCE, he received a revelation calling him to a religious mission. After a period of study and meditation, he announced the formation of Cao Dai ("High Tower," a Taoist epithet for the supreme deity). Cao Dai was formally established in 1926 by Le Van Trung, a former government official, who became its leader, or "pope." Cao Dai contains elements of CONFUCIANISM, TAOISM, BUDDHISM, and ROMAN CATHOLICISM.

NICAEA, COUNCIL OF (325) \nī-ˈsē-ə\, first ecumenical council of the Christian church, meeting in ancient Nicaea (now İznik, Turkey). It was called by the emperor CONSTANTINE I, who presided over the opening session and took part in the discussions. He hoped a general council of the church would solve the problem created in the Eastern church by ARIANISM, a HERESY first proposed by ARIUS of Alexandria that posited that JESUS CHRIST is not divine but a created being. Pope Sylvester I did not attend the council but was represented by legates.

The council condemned Arius and, with reluctance on the part of some, incorporated the nonscriptural word *homoousios* ("of one substance") into a creed (the NICENE CREED) to signify the absolute equality of the Son with the Father. The emperor then exiled Arius, an act that, while manifesting a solidarity of CHURCH AND STATE, underscored the importance of secular patronage in ecclesiastical affairs.

The council failed to establish a uniform date for EASTER. But it issued decrees on many other matters, including the proper method of consecrating bishops, a condemnation of lending money at interest by clerics, and a refusal to allow bishops, priests, and deacons to move from one church to another. It also confirmed the primacy of Alexandria and Jerusalem over other sees in their respective areas.

NICAEA, COUNCIL OF (787), seventh ecumenical council of the Christian church, meeting in Nicaea (now İznik, Turkey). It attempted to resolve the ICONOCLASTIC CONTROVERSY, initiated in 726 when Emperor Leo III issued a decree against the worship of ICONS. The council declared that icons deserved reverence and veneration but not adoration. Convoked by the PATRIARCH Tarasius, it was attended by delegates of Pope Adrian I, who confirmed its decrees. Its authority was challenged in France as late as the 11th century, however, partly because certain doctrinal phrases had been incorrectly translated, though Rome's original verdict was eventually accepted.

NICENE CREED \'nī-,sēn, nī-'\, *also called* Niceno-Constantinopolitan Creed, Christian statement of faith that is the only "ecumenical" creed because, with the qualification noted below, it is accepted as authoritative by the ROMAN CATHOLIC, Eastern Orthodox, Anglican, and major Protestant churches.

The development of the Niceno-Constantinopolitan Creed has been the subject of scholarly dispute. Most likely it was issued by the COUNCIL OF CONSTANTINOPLE (381). It was probably based on a baptismal creed already in existence, but it was an independent document and not an enlargement of the Creed of Nicaea, which was promulgated at the COUNCIL OF NICAEA (325).

The so-called FILIOQUE clause (Latin *filioque,* "and from the son"), inserted after the words "the HOLY SPIRIT . . . who proceeds from the Father," was gradually introduced as part of the creed in the Western church, beginning in the 6th century. It was probably finally accepted by the PAPACY in the 11th century. It has been retained by the Roman Catholic, Anglican, and Protestant churches. The Eastern churches reject it because they consider it theological error and an unauthorized addition to a venerable document.

The Nicene Creed's principal liturgical use is in the EUCHARIST in the West and in both BAPTISM and the Eucharist in the East. A modern English version of the Western text is as follows:

◆　We believe in one God,
　　　the Father, the Almighty,
　　　maker of heaven and earth,
　　　of all that is seen and unseen.
　　We believe in one Lord, Jesus Christ,
　　　the only Son of God,
　　　eternally begotten of the Father,
　　　God from God, Light from Light,
　　　true God from true God,
　　　begotten, not made, one in Being with the
　　　　Father.
　　Through him all things were made.
　　For us men and for our salvation
　　　he came down from heaven:
　　by the power of the Holy Spirit
　　　he was born of the Virgin Mary, and
　　　　became man.
　　For our sake he was crucified under Pontius
　　　Pilate;
　　　he suffered, died, and was buried.
　　On the third day he rose again
　　　in fulfillment of the Scriptures;
　　　he ascended into heaven
　　　　and is seated on the right hand of the
　　　　Father.
　　He will come again in glory
　　　to judge the living and the dead,
　　　and his kingdom will have no end.
　　We believe in the Holy Spirit, the Lord, the
　　　giver of life,
　　who proceeds from the Father and the Son.
　　With the Father and the Son he is worshiped
　　　and glorified.
　　He has spoken through the Prophets.
　　We believe in one holy catholic and apostolic
　　　Church.

We acknowledge one baptism for the
　　forgiveness of sins.
We look for the resurrection of the dead,
　　and the life of the world to come.
　Amen. ◆

NICHIREN \'nē-chē-,ren\, *original name* Zennichi, *also called* Zenshōbō Renchō \zen-'shō-,bō-'ren-,chō\, *posthumous name* Risshō Daishi (b. March 30, 1222, Kominato, Japan—d. Nov. 14, 1282, Ikegami), militant Japanese Buddhist prophet.

Nichiren entered the Buddhist monastery of Kiyosumi-dera at the age of 11. BUDDHISM in Japan had become more and more eclectic, and the identity of the various sects was based more on institutional aspects than on doctrinal tenets. Though the monastery of Kiyosumi-dera officially belonged to the Tendai (T'ien-t'ai) sect, which was centered on the LOTUS SUTRA, the doctrine and practices were quite diverse. The young monk was dissatisfied with this situation and sought to find, through a study of all the major Buddhist schools in Japan, the authentic teaching of the BUDDHA GOTAMA.

By the year 1253 Nichiren had reached a clear conclusion: the true Buddhism was to be found in the *Lotus Sutra,* and all other Buddhist teachings were only temporary and provisional steps used by the Buddha to lead human beings to full and final truth. Moreover, the Buddha himself had decreed that this final truth was to be conveyed during the age of MAPPŌ (the then-present age of degeneration) and that a teacher would at that time appear to preach this saving message. The central focus of Nichiren's message was the sole and complete efficacy of chanting *namu Myōhō renge-kyō* ("adoration be to the Lotus of the True Law"), which is taken to be the *daimoku* ("sacred title") of the *Lotus Sutra.*

During the next three decades Nichiren presented his own message, attacked all other Buddhist schools as false, and contended that Japan could only be saved from the imminent threats of Mongol invasion and internal decadence if his version of Buddhism were adopted and all other versions were banned. Nichiren's militant stance created many enemies in the government and among the Buddhist monks. Twice during his career he was exiled by the government, and on several occasions he was subjected to attacks initiated by monastic rivals.

Nichiren's teachings came to include the claim that he was a reincarnation of the Jōgyō bodhisattva, to whom Sakyamuni (the Buddha Gotama) had entrusted the *Lotus Sutra.* In his later years he also proclaimed the central importance of the *daimandara* (Great Mandala) that had been revealed to him—a sacred design that represents the Buddha world depicted in the *Lotus Sutra.* At its center the *daimandara* has the *daimoku* of the *Lotus Sutra* surrounded by the many names of Sakyamuni.

Nichiren is perhaps the most controversial figure in the history of Japanese Buddhism. He was deeply committed to Japan and believed that its mission was to be the chosen country of Buddhism from which Buddha's salvation was to spread to the entire world. His Buddhism was typically Japanese in its concern with the salvation of society and temporal institutions, not just individuals. Many of the modern Buddhist sects now flourishing in Japan are, in various degrees, based on Nichiren's doctrines.

NICHIREN BUDDHISM \'nē-chē-,ren\, school of Japanese BUDDHISM named after its founder, the 13th-century militant prophet and saint NICHIREN. It is one of the largest schools of Japanese Buddhism; by the late 20th century the total membership of its numerous subsects was reported to be approximately 30,600,000.

Nichiren believed that the quintessence of the Buddha's teachings was contained in the LOTUS SUTRA. According to Nichiren, the other sects then existing in Japan misunderstood the truth, and he vehemently denounced them and the government that supported them.

Nichiren taught that inasmuch as all men partake of the Buddha nature (TATHĀGATA), all men are manifestations of the eternal. He devised three ways of expressing this concept, known as the *sandai-hihō* ("three great secret laws"). The first, the *honzon*, is the chief object of worship in Nichiren temples and is a ritual drawing showing the name of the *Lotus Sutra* surrounded by the names of divinities mentioned in the sutra. The second great mystery is the *daimoku*, the "title" of the sutra; Nichiren instituted the devotional practice of chanting the phrase *namu Myōhō renge-kyō* ("adoration be to the Lotus of the True Law"). The third mystery relates to the *kaidan*, or place of ORDINATION, which is sacred.

After Nichiren's death the school split into various subsects, most notably Nichiren-shū (Nichiren Sect) and Nichiren-shō-shū (True Nichiren Sect). The former, which still controls the main temple, the Kuon-ji, maintained a dominant position among Nichiren Buddhists until the years following World War II, when it was eclipsed by the Nichiren-shō-shū, whose phenomenal growth stemmed from its lay organization, the SŌKA-GAKKAI.

Nichiren-shō-shū traces its line of succession back to one of Nichiren's six disciples, Nikkō, who, according to documents held by the sect, was the prophet's chosen successor. The temple he established in 1290 at the foot of MOUNT FUJI, Daiseki-ji, is still the sect's headquarters. Nichiren-shō-shū differs from the other Nichiren sects in its elevation of the founder, Nichiren, to a rank higher even than that of the BUDDHA GOTAMA.

Among its rival Nichiren sects, Nichiren-shō-shū had only minor influence until the emergence of the Sōka-gakkai lay organization brought it into its present dominant position in Japanese politics. The sect has established branches outside Japan. In the United States the lay organization equivalent to the Sōka-gakkai is called Nichiren-shō-shū of America.

NICHOLAS, SAINT, *also called* Nicholas of Bari, Nicholas of Myra, Santa Claus (fl. 4th century, Myra, Lycia, Asia Minor [near modern Finike, Turkey]; feast day December 6), one of the most popular saints commemorated in the Eastern and Western Christian churches, and now traditionally associated with the festival of CHRISTMAS.

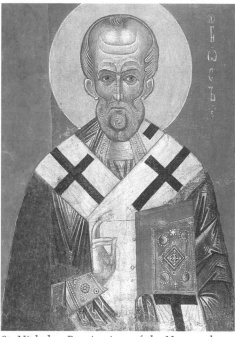

St. Nicholas, Russian icon of the Novgorod school, c. 1300; in the Hermitage, St. Petersburg
The Bridgeman Art Library

Nicholas' existence is not attested by any historical document, so nothing certain is known of his life except that he was probably bishop of Myra in the 4th century. According to tradition, he was born in the ancient Lycian seaport city of Patara, and, when young, he traveled to Palestine and Egypt. He became bishop of Myra soon after returning to Lycia. He was imprisoned during the Roman emperor Diocletian's persecution of Christians, but he was later released under the rule of Emperor CONSTANTINE the Great, and he subsequently attended the first COUNCIL OF NICAEA (325). After his death he was buried in his church at Myra, and by the 6th century his shrine there had become well known. In 1087 Italian sailors or merchants stole his alleged remains from Myra and took them to Bari, Italy; this removal greatly increased the saint's popularity in Europe, and as a result Bari became one of the most crowded of all PILGRIMAGE centers. His relics remain enshrined in the 11th-century basilica of San Nicola, Bari.

Nicholas' reputation for generosity and kindness gave rise to legends of miracles he performed for the poor and unhappy. He was reputed to have given marriage dowries of gold to three girls whom poverty would otherwise have forced into lives of prostitution, and he restored to life three children who had been chopped up by a butcher and put in a brine tub. In the Middle Ages, devotion to Nicholas extended to all parts of Europe. He became the patron saint of Russia and Greece; of charitable fraternities and guilds; of children, sailors, unmarried girls, merchants, and pawnbrokers; and of such cities as Fribourg, Switz., and Moscow. Thousands of churches throughout Europe were dedicated to him. Nicholas' traditional feast day was the occasion for the ceremonies of the Boy Bishop, a widespread European custom in which a boy was elected bishop and reigned until Holy Innocents' Day (December 28).

After the REFORMATION, Nicholas' cult disappeared in all the Protestant countries of Europe except Holland, where his legend persisted as Sinterklaas (a Dutch variant of the name Saint Nicholas). Dutch colonists took this tradition with them to New Amsterdam (now New York City) in the American colonies in the 17th century. Sinterklaas was adopted by the country's English-speaking majority under the name Santa Claus, and his legend of a kindly old man was united with old Nordic folktales of a magician who punished naughty children and rewarded good children with presents. The resulting image of Santa Claus in the United States crystallized in the 19th century, and he has ever since remained the patron of the gift-giving festival of Christmas. Under various guises Saint Nicholas was transformed into a similar benevolent, gift-giving figure in other countries. In the United Kingdom Santa Claus is known as Father Christmas.

NICHOLAS OF CUSA

NICHOLAS OF CUSA \'ni-kə-ləs . . . 'kü-sə, 'kyü- \, *German* Nikolaus von Cusa, *Latin* Nicolaus Cusanus (b. 1401, Kues, Trier—d. Aug. 11, 1464, Todi, Papal States), CARDINAL of the ROMAN CATHOLIC church, mathematician, scholar, experimental scientist, and influential philosopher who stressed the incomplete nature of man's knowledge of God and of the universe.

At the Council of Basel in 1432 Nicholas gained recognition for his opposition to the candidate put forward by Pope Eugenius IV for the archbishopric of Trier. To his colleagues at the council he dedicated *De concordantia catholica* (1433; "On Catholic Concordance"), in which he expressed support for the supremacy of the general councils of the church over the authority of the PAPACY. By 1437, however, finding the council unsuccessful in preserving church unity and enacting needed reforms, Nicholas reversed his position and became one of Eugenius' most ardent followers. Ordained a priest about 1440, Cusa was made a cardinal in Brixen (Bressanone), Italy, by Pope Nicholas V and in 1450 was elevated to bishop there. For two years Cusa served as Nicholas' legate to Germany, after which he began to serve full-time as bishop of Brixen.

A model "Renaissance man" in his disciplined and varied learning, Cusa was skilled in theology, mathematics, philosophy, science, and the arts. In *De docta ignorantia* (1440; "On Learned Ignorance") he described the learned man as one who is aware of his own ignorance. In this and other works he used ideas from geometry to demonstrate his points, as in his comparison of man's search for truth to the task of converting a square into a circle.

Among Cusa's many interests were diagnostic medicine and applied science. He emphasized knowledge through experimentation and anticipated the work of the astronomer Copernicus by discerning a movement in the universe that did not center in the Earth. He also provided the first proof that air has weight. Numerous other developments, including a map of Europe, can also be traced to Cusa. A manuscript collector who recovered a dozen lost comedies by the Roman writer Plautus, he left an extensive library that remains a center of scholarly activity in the hospital he founded and completed at his birthplace in 1458.

NIEBUHR, HELMUT RICHARD \'nē-,bùr\ (b. Sept. 3, 1894, Wright City, Mo., U.S.—d. July 5, 1962, Greenfield, Mass.), American Protestant theologian and educator who was considered a leading authority on ethics and U.S. church history. He was a foremost advocate of theological existentialism.

The younger brother of the theologian REINHOLD NIEBUHR, Helmut was educated at Elmhurst College in Illinois, Eden Theological Seminary, St. Louis, Mo., Washington University, Yale Divinity School, and Yale University, where he was one of the first students to receive a Ph.D. in religion (1924). Ordained a pastor of the Evangelical and REFORMED CHURCH in 1916, he taught at Eden Theological Seminary (1919–22; 1927–31) and also served as president of Elmhurst College (1924–27). From 1931 he taught theology and Christian ethics at Yale Divinity School.

Influenced by KARL BARTH, SØREN KIERKEGAARD, and Ernst Troeltsch, Niebuhr advocated historical criticism of RELIGIOUS BELIEFS, urging that church teachings be interpreted so as to make them meaningful in contemporary culture. His views on theological existentialism allowed for relative interpretations of revelation and values within the framework of a monotheistic faith. He argued that churches must account for the social context of their existence.

NIEBUHR, REINHOLD (b. June 21, 1892, Wright City, Mo., U.S.—d. June 1, 1971, Stockbridge, Mass.), American theologian who had extensive influence on political thought and whose criticism of the prevailing THEOLOGICAL LIBERALISM of the 1920s significantly affected the intellectual climate within American PROTESTANTISM.

Niebuhr was the son of Gustav Niebuhr, a minister of the Evangelical Synod of North America. Reinhold graduated from his denomination's Elmhurst College, Illinois (1910), and Eden Theological Seminary, St. Louis, Mo. (1913), and completed his theological education at Yale University, receiving a bachelor of divinity degree (1914) and a master of arts (1915). He was ordained to the ministry of the Evangelical Synod in 1915.

Niebuhr served as pastor of Bethel Evangelical Church in Detroit from 1915 to 1928. His experience in Detroit—and especially his exposure to the American automobile industry before labor was protected by unions and by social legislation—caused him to become a radical critic of capitalism and an advocate of socialism. Niebuhr left the pastoral ministry in 1928 to teach at Union Theological Seminary in New York City, where he served as professor of applied CHRISTIANITY (from 1930) and was a great intellectual and personal force until his retirement in 1960.

As a theologian Niebuhr is best known for his "Christian Realism," which emphasized the persistent roots of evil in human life. In his *Moral Man and Immoral Society* (1932) he stressed the egoism and the pride and hypocrisy of nations and classes. Later he saw these as ultimately the fruit of the insecurity and anxious overdefensiveness of humans in their finiteness; here he located "original SIN." His powerful polemics against liberal beliefs in assured progress and radical utopian hopes were balanced by faith in what he called "indeterminate possibilities" for humanity in history. Though he did much to encourage the revival of the theology of the REFORMATION, with its emphasis on sin and grace—so-called neo-orthodoxy—his salient theological work, *The Nature and Destiny of Man*, 2 vol. (1941–43), was planned by him as a synthesis both of the insights of the Reformation and of the Renaissance, with its hopefulness about cultural achievements.

Niebuhr's writings also include *Faith and History: A Comparison of Christian and Modern Views of History* (1949), a theological orientation; *The Self and the Dramas of History* (1955), probably his profoundest philosophical work; and *The Structure of Nations and Empires* (1959), his chief systematic discussion of international relations. Four volumes of essays, some of which are essential for understanding Niebuhr's thought and his influence on events, are *Christianity and Power Politics* (1940); *Christian Realism and Political Problems* (1953); *Pious and Secular America* (1958); and *Faith and Politics: A Commentary on Religious, Social, and Political Thought in a Technological Age*, ed. by Ronald H. Stone (1968). *Love and Justice*, ed. by D.B. Robertson (1957), is a collection of shorter writings showing Niebuhr's response to events; *Children of Light and Children of Darkness: A Vindication of Democracy and a Critique of Its Traditional Defence* (1944), is a brief but comprehensive discussion of social ethics.

NIFLHEIM \'ni-vəl-,hām\, *Old Norse* Niflheimr \-,hā-mər\, in GERMANIC RELIGION, cold, dark, misty world of the dead, ruled by the goddess HEL. In some accounts it was the last of nine worlds, a place into which evil men passed after reaching the region of death (Hel). Situated below one of the roots of the WORLD TREE, YGGDRASILL, Niflheim contained a well, Hvergelmir, from which many rivers flowed. In the Norse creation story, Niflheim was the misty region north of the void (GINNUNGAGAP) in which the world was created.

NIHON SHOKI \nē-'hȯṅ-'shȯ-kē\, *also called* Nihon-gi \-ˌgē\ (Japanese: "Chronicles of Japan"), text that, with the KOJIKI, comprises the oldest official history of Japan, covering the period from its mythical origins to 697 CE.

Written in Chinese, it reflected the influence of Chinese civilization in Japan. It was compiled in 720 by order of the imperial court. The first part deals with many Japanese myths and legends and is an important source for SHINTŌ thought. The later chapters, for the period from about the 5th century on, contain records of several of the politically powerful clans as well as of the imperial family. Among the events described are the introduction of BUDDHISM and the Taika reforms of the 7th century.

NIKĀYA \ni-'kä-yə\ (Sanskrit and Pāli: "group," "class," or "assemblage"), in BUDDHISM, any of the so-called "Eighteen Schools" of Indian sectarian Buddhism. After the second Buddhist council, at which time the MAHĀSAṄGHIKAS separated from the Sthaviravādins, a number of Buddhist "schools" or "sects" began to appear over the course of many years. Each of these schools maintained slight (or sometimes greater) differences in doctrine, and each adhered to slightly different monastic codes. This early period of Buddhist history (prior to the formation of MAHĀYĀNA Buddhism) with its proliferation of many different Buddhist sects and divisions of schools is often referred to as the period of "Nikāya Buddhism" or sectarian Buddhism. In addition, in Southeast Asian countries such as Burma and Thailand, Buddhist sects are still called *nikāya*.

A second meaning of the word *nikāya* refers not to a group or class of people, but to a group or assemblage of texts. The five major divisions of the SUTTA PIṬAKA of the Pāli canon are called *nikāya*s: *Dīgha Nikāya* (containing long *sutta*s), *Majjhima Nikāya* (containing *sutta*s of middle length), *Saṃyutta Nikāya* (containing *sutta*s organized according to content), *Aṅguttara Nikāya* (containing *sutta*s arranged according to the number of doctrinal items under discussion), and the *Khuddaka Nikāya* (containing *sutta*s not included in any of the other four *nikāya*s).

NIKE \'nī-kē, 'nē-kā\, in GREEK RELIGION, goddess of victory, daughter of the GIANT Pallas and of the River STYX. As an attribute of both ATHENA and ZEUS, Nike was represented in art as a small figure carried in the hand by those divinities. Athena Nike was always wingless; Nike alone was winged. She also appears carrying a palm branch, wreath, or HERMES staff as the messenger of victory. Nike gradually came to be recognized as a mediator of success between gods and humans.

Among artistic representations of Nike are the sculpture by Paeonius (*c.* 424 BCE) and the "Nike of Samothrace," or "Winged Victory." The latter, discovered in 1863 and now in the

Nike, sculpture from a bronze vessel, c. 490 BCE

Louvre Museum, Paris, was probably erected by Rhodians about 203 BCE to commemorate a sea battle. Excavations have shown that the sculpture was placed alighting on a flagship, which was set in the ground in such a way that it appeared to float.

NIMBĀRKA \nim-'bär-kə\, *also called* Nimbāditya, *or* Niyamānanda (fl. 12th or 13th century?, South India), Telugu-speaking BRAHMAN, yogi, philosopher, and prominent astronomer who founded one of the four main devotional sects (or SAMPRADĀYAS) of VAIṢṆAVISM, variously called the Nimbārkas, Nimandi, or Nimāvats, who worshiped KRISHNA and his consort, RĀDHĀ.

Nimbārka probably lived in the 12th or 13th century, judging from similarities between his philosophical and devotional attitudes and those of RĀMĀNUJA (traditionally dated 1017–1137). Both adhered to *viśiṣṭādvaita* (Sanskrit: "qualified non-dualism"), the belief that the creator-god and the souls he created were distinct but shared in the same substance, and both stressed devotion to Krishna as a means of liberation from the cycle of rebirth. Nimbārka also placed great emphasis on total surrender to the GURU (spiritual preceptor).

The Nimanda sect flourished in the 13th and 14th centuries in eastern India. Its philosophy held that humans were trapped in physical bodies constricted by *prakṛti* (matter) and that only by surrender to Rādhā-Krishna (not through their own efforts) could they attain liberation from rebirth; then, at death, the physical body would drop away. Thus Nimbārka stressed BHAKTI yoga, or the YOGA of devotion. Most sources concerning the sect were destroyed by Muslims during the reign of the Mughal emperor Aurangzeb (1659–1707).

NIMROD \'nim-ˌräd\, *also spelled* Nemrod, legendary figure, described in GENESIS 10:8–12 as "the first on earth to be a mighty man. He was a mighty hunter before the Lord." The beginning of his kingdom is Babel, Erech, and Akkad in the land of Shinar. Elsewhere Assyria is called the land of Nimrod (Micah 5:6), and he is said to have built Nineveh, Calah (modern Nimrūd), Rehoboth-Ir, and Resen.

NINAZU \nē-'nä-ˌzü\, in MESOPOTAMIAN RELIGION, Sumerian deity, city god of Enegir, which was located on the Euphrates River between Larsa and Ur in the southern orchard region. Ninazu was also the city god of Eshnunna (modern Tall al-Asmar in eastern Iraq). Ninazu, whose name means "water knower," was primarily an underworld deity, although the exact nature of his character or functions is not clear. In Enegir he was considered the son of ERESHKIGAL, goddess of the netherworld; according to another tradition, however, he was the son of ENLIL (Akkadian BEL) and Ninlil (BELIT). His spouse was Ningirda, a daughter of Enki (EA).

NINETY-FIVE THESES, propositions for debate concerned with the question of INDULGENCES, written (in Latin) by MARTIN LUTHER. Luther was long believed to have posted the theses on the door of the Schlosskirche (Castle Church) in Wit-

Indulgences being sold in church, woodcut from the title page of a pamphlet by Martin Luther, 1525
By courtesy of the trustees of the British Museum; photograph, John R. Freeman & Co. Ltd.

tenberg on Oct. 31, 1517, but the historicity of this event has been questioned. Evidence suggests, rather, that Luther wrote to the bishops on Oct. 31, 1517, did not receive an answer, and then circulated the theses among friends and learned acquaintances. In any case, this event came, in the 17th century, to be considered the beginning of the Protestant REFORMATION.

Ordinarily, Luther's theses would have been of interest only to theologians, but the political and religious situation of the time and the fact that the printing press had recently been invented combined to make the theses known throughout Germany within a few weeks. Thus, they became a manifesto that turned a protest about an indulgence scandal into the greatest crisis in the history of the Western Christian church.

Indulgences were the commutation for money of part of the temporal penalty due for sin—*i.e.,* the practical satisfaction that was a part of the SACRAMENT of penance. They were granted on papal authority and made available through accredited agents. Not at any time did they imply that divine forgiveness could be bought or sold or that they availed for those who were impenitent or unconfessed. But during the Middle Ages, as papal financial difficulties grew more complicated, they were resorted to very often, and abuses grew common. Further misunderstanding developed after Pope Sixtus IV extended indulgences to souls in PURGATORY. The often outrageous statements of indulgence sellers were a matter of protest among theologians.

The immediate cause of scandal in Germany in 1517 was

the issue of an indulgence that was to pay for the rebuilding of St. Peter's in Rome. But by secret agreement of which most Germans were unaware, half the proceeds of the German sales were to be diverted to meet the huge debt owed to the financial house of Fugger by the archbishop and elector Albert of Mainz, who had incurred the debt in order to pay the Pope for appointing him to high offices. The agent in Germany, the DOMINICAN Johann Tetzel, made extravagant claims for the indulgence he was selling. The sale of this indulgence was forbidden in Wittenberg by the elector Frederick III the Wise, who preferred that the faithful should make their offerings at his own great collection of relics, exhibited in the Church of All Saints. Nevertheless, Wittenberg church members went to Tetzel, and they showed the pardons received from him to Luther. Outraged at what he considered grave theological error, Luther wrote the Ninety-five Theses.

The theses were tentative opinions, about some of which Luther had not decided. In the theses the papal prerogative in this matter was not denied, though by implication papal policy was criticized. The spiritual, inward character of the Christian faith was stressed. The fact was emphasized that money was being collected from poor people and sent to the rich PAPACY in Rome, a point popular with the Germans, who had long resented the money they were forced to contribute to Rome.

Subsequently, the Archbishop of Mainz, alarmed and annoyed, forwarded the documents to Rome in December 1517, with the request that Luther be inhibited. A counter-thesis was prepared by a Dominican theologian and defended before a Dominican audience at Frankfurt in January 1518. When Luther realized the extensive interest his tentative theses had aroused, he prepared a long Latin manuscript with explanations of his Ninety-five Theses, published in the autumn of 1518.

NINGISHZIDA \nin-'gish-zē-ˌdä, ˌnin-gish-'zē-dä\, in MESOPOTAMIAN RELIGION, Sumerian deity, city god of Gishbanda, near Ur in the southern orchard region. Although Ningishzida was a power of the netherworld, where he held the office of throne bearer, he seems to have originally been a tree god, for his name apparently means "Lord Productive Tree." In particular, he probably was god of the winding tree roots, since he originally was represented in serpent shape. When pictured in human form, two serpent heads grow from his shoulders in addition to the human head, and he rides on a dragon. He was a son of NINAZU and Ningirda and was the husband of Ninazimua ("Lady Flawlessly Grown Branch").

NINHAR \'nin-ˌhär\, *also called* Ningubla \nin-'gü-blä\, in MESOPOTAMIAN RELIGION, Sumerian deity, city god of Kiabrig, near Ur in the southern herding region. Ninhar was god of the thunder and rainstorms; he was represented in the form of a roaring bull. He was the son of NANNA (Akkadian Sin) and Ningal and the husband of Ninigara ("Lady of Butter and Cream"), goddess of the dairy.

NINHURSAG \nin-'kûr-ˌsäg\, *also spelled* Ninhursaga \nin-'kûr-ˌsä-ˌgä\ (Sumerian), *Akkadian* Belit-ili, in MESOPOTAMIAN RELIGION, city goddess of ADAB and of Kish in the northern herding regions; she was the goddess of the stony, rocky ground, the *hursag.* In particular, she had the power in the foothills and desert to produce wildlife. Especially prominent among her offspring were the onagers (wild asses) of the western desert. She appears in a lament for her son, a young colt, but she also is the Mother of All Children, a mother-goddess figure. Her other names include: Dingirmakh ("Exalted Deity"), Ninmakh ("Exalted Lady"), Aruru ("Dropper," *i.e.*, the one who "loosens" the child in birth), and Nintur ("Lady Birth Giver"). Her husband is the god Shulpae, and among their children were the sons Mululil and Ashshirgi and the daughter Egime. Mululil seems to have been a dying god, like Dumuzi, whose death was lamented in yearly rites.

NINIGI \ˈnē-nē-ˌgē\, *in full* Ninigi no Mikoto, Japanese SHINTŌ deity, grandson of the sun goddess AMATERASU. Ninigi's descent to earth established the divine origin of the YAMATO clan, the imperial house of Japan.

Amaterasu delegated Ninigi to assume ownership and rule of the central land of the reed plains (Japan) and gave him three signs of his charge: a jewel (symbolizing benevolence), a mirror (purity), and Kusanagi, the "grass-mowing" sword (courage). The jewel, the mirror, and the sword are still the Japanese imperial symbols. On his descent to earth, Ninigi landed on Kyushu. ŌKUNINUSHI no Mikoto, who was already sovereign there, submitted when he was permitted to retain control of religious affairs, with Ninigi supervising political affairs. Today, Ōkuninushi remains an important folk deity, while Ninigi is no longer venerated.

NINSUN \ˈnin-ˌsùn\, in MESOPOTAMIAN RELIGION, Sumerian deity, city goddess of Kullab in the southern herding region. As Ninsun's name, "Lady Wild Cow," indicates, she was originally represented in bovine form and was considered the divine power behind, as well as the embodiment of, all the qualities the herdsman wished for in his cows: she was the "flawless cow" and a "mother of good offspring that loves the offspring." She was, however, also represented in human form and could give birth to human offspring. The Wild Bull Dumuzi (as distinct from Dumuzi the Shepherd) was traditionally her son, whom she lamented in the yearly ritual marking his death. In her role as a mother figure, her other Sumerian counterparts include NINHURSAG (Akkadian: Belit-ili) and Ninlil (BELIT). Ninsun's husband was the legendary hero Lugalbanda.

NINURTA \ni-ˈnùr-tä\, *also called* Ningirsu \nin-ˈgir-ˌsü\, in MESOPOTAMIAN RELIGION, war god and city god of Girsu (Ṭalʻah, or Telloh) in the Lagash region. Ninurta was a god of thunder and rainstorms. He was also the power in the floods and was god of the plow and of plowing. The storm bird ZU (Anzu), or Imdugud, was considered his chief enemy. One story tells how he reclaimed the Tablet of Destinies, the emblem of his power, from Zu, who had stolen it.

Ninurta was the son of ENLIL (Akkadian: BEL) and Ninlil (BELIT) and was married to BAU, in Nippur called Ninnibru, Queen of Nippur. His major festival, the Gudsisu Festival, marked in Nippur the beginning of the plowing season.

NINUS \ˈnī-nəs\, in Greek mythology, king of Assyria and the eponymous founder of the city of Nineveh, which is sometimes called Ninus. He was said to have been the son of Belos, or BEL, and to have conquered in 17 years all of western Asia with Ariaeus, king of Arabia. During the siege of Bactra he met Semiramis, the wife of one of his officers, Onnes; he then took her from Onnes and married her. The fruit of the marriage was Ninyas—*i.e.*, the Ninevite.

NIOBE \ˈnī-ō-bē\, in Greek mythology, daughter of TANTALUS and wife of King Amphion of Thebes. She is the prototype of the bereaved mother endlessly weeping for her lost children. According to Homer's *Iliad,* she had six sons and six daughters and boasted of her progenitive superiority to LETO, who had only two children, APOLLO and ARTEMIS. As punishment for her pride, Apollo killed all Niobe's sons, and Artemis killed all her daughters. The bodies lay for nine days unburied because ZEUS had turned all the Thebans to stone, but on the 10th day they were buried by the gods. Niobe went back to her Phrygian home, where she was turned into a rock on Mount Sipylus (Yamanlar Dağı, northeast of Izmir, Turkey), which continues to weep when the snow melts above it. Niobe is the subject of lost tragedies by both Aeschylus and Sophocles, and Ovid tells her story in his *Metamorphoses.*

NIRAṄKĀRĪ \ni-ˌräŋ-ˈkär-ē\ (Punjabi: "Followers of the Formless One," *i.e.*, God), religious movement within SIKHISM. Bābā Dayāl (d. 1855), the founder of the movement, emphasized that God is formless, or *niraṅkār* (hence the name Niraṅkārī). He also stressed the importance of meditation in life.

The movement expanded in northwest Punjab, Bābā Dayāl's native region, under the leadership of his successors Darbārā Singh (1855–70) and Rattā Jī (1870–1909). Its following is drawn primarily from among the urban trading communities. Unlike mainstream Sikhs, but like other groups (*e.g.*, NĀMDHĀRĪ, Radhāsoāmī) closely related to them, Niraṅkārīs accept the authority of a living GURŪ. They do not necessarily stress the Singh identity. Since 1947, the sect's headquarters has been in Chandīgarh.

NIRGUṆA \ˈnir-gù-nə\ (Sanskrit: "without qualities"), concept of primary importance in the orthodox Hindu philosophy of VEDĀNTA in the debate over whether the supreme being, BRAHMAN, is to be characterized as without qualities (*nirguṇa*) or as possessing qualities (SAGUṆA).

The *Bṛhadāraṇyaka Upaniṣad* defines Brahman as *neti-neti* ("not this! not that!"). The ADVAITA (Nondualist) school of Vedānta therefore argues that Brahman is beyond all polarity and cannot be characterized in the normal terms of human discursive thought. Thus Brahman cannot possess qualities that distinguish it from all other magnitudes, as Brahman is not a magnitude but is all. The scriptural texts that ascribe qualities to Brahman are, according to the Advaita school, merely preparatory aids to meditation. The theistic schools of Vedānta (for example, VIŚIṢṬĀDVAITA), argue that Brahman is possessed of all perfections and that SCRIPTURE denies only the imperfect qualities.

NIRVANA \nir-ˈvä-nə\ (Sanskrit: *nirvāṇa* "extinction," or "blowing out"), *Pāli* nibbāna \nib-ˈbä-nə\, in Indian religious thought, supreme goal of the meditation disciplines. In BUDDHISM it signifies the transcendent state of freedom achieved by the extinction of desire and of individual consciousness. The Buddhist analysis of the human situation is that delusions of egocentricity and their resultant desires bind man to a continuous round of rebirths and its consequent suffering (DUKKHA). It is release from these bonds that constitutes enlightenment, or the experience of nirvana. Liberation from rebirth does not imply immediate physical death; the death of an ARHAT or a buddha is usually called the *parinirvāṇa*, or complete nirvana.

In the THERAVĀDA tradition, nirvana is thought of as tranquillity and peace. In the schools of the MAHĀYĀNA tradition, nirvana is equated with *śūnyatā* (EMPTINESS), with *dharma-kāya* (the real and unchanging essence of the buddha), and with *dharma-dhātu* (ultimate reality). Also in the Mahāyāna tradition, the realization of nirvana is deferred by the BODHISATTVA, while he continues, out of compassion, to work for the salvation of others.

NISABA \nē-'sä-bä\, in MESOPOTAMIAN RELIGION, Sumerian deity, city goddess of Eresh on the Euphrates River near Erech in the farming regions; she was goddess of the grasses and seed crops. As goddess of the reeds and provider of the reed stylus used by the scribes, she became the patroness of writing and the scribal arts, particularly of accounting.

NISUS \'nī-səs\, in Greek mythology, son of King Pandion of Megara. His name was given to the Megarian port of Nisaea. Nisus had a purple lock of hair with magic power, which, if preserved, guaranteed him life and continued possession of his kingdom. When King MINOS of Crete besieged Megara, Nisus' daughter Scylla fell in love with Minos (or, in some accounts, was bribed): she betrayed her city by cutting off her father's purple lock. Nisus was killed (or killed himself) and became transformed into a sea eagle. Scylla later drowned, possibly at the hand of Minos, and was changed into a sea bird (Greek *keiris*, Latin *ciris*), possibly a heron, constantly pursued by the sea eagle Nisus.

NIX \'niks\, *also called* nixie, or nixy \'nik-sē\, in Germanic MYTHOLOGY, water being, half human, half fish, that lives in an underwater palace and mingles with humans by assuming a variety of physical forms (*e.g.*, that of a fair maiden or an old woman) or by making itself invisible. Nixes are music lovers and excellent dancers, and they have the gift of PROPHECY. Usually malevolent, a nix can easily be propitiated with gifts. In some regions, nixes are said to abduct human children and to lure people into deep water to drown. According to some sources, nixes can marry human beings and bear human children.

NJÖRD \'nyȯrd, 'nyȯrth\, *Old Norse* Njörðr \'nyȯr-thər\, in GERMANIC RELIGION, god of the sea and its riches. His aid was invoked in seafaring and in hunting, and he was considered the god of "wealth-bestowal," or prosperity. He was the father of Frey and FREYJA by his sister. Njörd's native tribe, the VANIR, gave him as a hostage to the rival tribe of AESIR, the giantess SKADI choosing him to be her husband. The marriage failed because Njörd preferred to live in Nóatún, his home by the sea, while Skadi was happier in her father's mountain dwelling place. Several traditions hold that Njörd was a divine ruler of the Swedes, and his name appears in numerous Scandinavian place-names.

NOAH, hero of the biblical Flood story in the OLD TESTAMENT book of GENESIS, the originator of vineyard cultivation, and the head of a Semitic genealogical line. A synthesis of at least three BIBLICAL SOURCE traditions, Noah is the image of the righteous man made party to a COVENANT with YAH-

WEH, the God of ISRAEL, in which protection against future catastrophe is assured.

Noah appears in Genesis 5:29 as the son of Lamech and ninth in descent from ADAM. In the story of the Deluge (Genesis 6:11–9:19), he is represented as the PATRIARCH who, because of his blameless piety, was chosen by God to perpetuate the human race after his wicked contemporaries had perished in the Flood. Noah was instructed to build an ARK, and he took into it male and female specimens of all the world's species of animals, from which the stocks might be replenished.

After Noah's survival of the Flood, he built an altar on which he offered burnt sacrifices to God, who then bound himself to a pact never again to curse the earth on man's account. God then set a rainbow in the sky as a visible

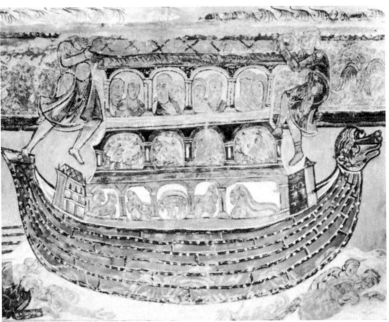

Depiction of Noah's Ark from a 12th-century fresco in the church at Saint-Savin-sur-Gartempe, France
Jean Roubier

guarantee of his promise in this covenant. God also renewed his commands given at creation but with two changes: man could now kill animals and eat meat, and the murder of a man would be punished by men.

The story has close affinities with Babylonian traditions of apocalyptic floods; tablet XI of the GILGAMESH epic introduces UTNAPISHTIM, who, like Noah, survived cosmic destruction by heeding divine instruction to build an ark. The Babylonian mythologies are the source of such features of the biblical Flood story as the building and provisioning of the ark, its flotation, and the subsidence of the waters, as well as the part played by the human protagonist.

The narrative concerning Noah in Genesis 9:20–27 belongs to a different cycle apparently unrelated to the Flood story. Three different themes may be traced: first, the passage attributes the beginnings of agriculture, and in particular the cultivation of the vine, to Noah; second, it attempts to provide, in the persons of Noah's three sons,

Shem, Ham, and Japheth, ancestors for three of the races of mankind and to account in some degree for their historic relations; and third, Noah's drunkenness and the disrespect it provokes in his son Ham (or CANAAN) result in Noah's laying of a curse on Ham and his descendants. By this censure of Ham, it offers a veiled JUSTIFICATION for the later Israelite conquest and subjugation of the Canaanites.

The symbolic figure of Noah was known in ancient Israel, before the compilation of the PENTATEUCH. Ezekiel (14:14, 20) speaks of him as a prototype of the righteous man who, alone among the Israelites, would be spared God's vengeance. In the NEW TESTAMENT, Jesus uses the story of the Flood that came on a worldly generation of men "in the days of Noah" as an example of BAPTISM, and Noah is depicted as a preacher of repentance.

NOAHIDE LAWS \\'nō-ə-ˌkīd\\, *also called* Noachian Laws \\nō-'ā-kē-ən\\, Jewish Talmudic designation for seven laws given to Adam and to NOAH before the revelation to MOSES on Mt. Sinai.

In the TALMUD (Sanh 56–60), the Noahide laws are the minium requirements of every person's moral duty. Beginning with GENESIS 2:16, the laws derive from expositions of commandments given to the ancestors of humankind, *i.e.*, Adam and Noah, and are therefore universal for all humanity. The resident alien ("Noahide") is one who keeps these laws. Some Jewish sources considered Muslims to be Noahides because of their strict monotheism; the status of Christians was less assured. There is some debate in the rabbinic literature as to whether the Noahide laws, if universally observed by non-Jews, are the penultimate step toward the final stage of humanity, or whether Noahidism together with JUDAISM will constitute the final stage. Maimonides regarded anyone who observed these laws as one "assured of a portion in the world to come" (Maim Yad Melakhim 8:10).

The first five Noahide laws are negative: prohibitions against IDOLATRY, BLASPHEMY, murder, adultery, and robbery; the sixth, positive: the command to establish courts of justice. The last (given to Noah after the flood) forbids eating flesh cut from a living animal (Genesis 9:4). There are similar lists in other Jewish literature: 1) the TOSEFTA (Av Zar 8:6) names four prohibitions in addition to the seven: drinking blood, emasculation, SORCERY, and magic; 2) Jubilees 7:20ff. records that Noah gave six commandments to his sons: observe righteousness, cover the shame of the flesh, bless the Creator, honor parents, love your neighbor, abstain from fornication, uncleanliness, and all iniquity; 3) Acts 15:20 contains four Mosaic prohibitions to be observed by GENTILE Christians: "to abstain only from things polluted by idols and from fornication and from whatever has been strangled and from blood."

NOAIDE \\nō-'ī-dē\\, in Sami religion, SHAMAN who mediated between the people that he served and the supernatural beings and forces that he either confronted or made use of for the benefit of his clients.

The shamanic practices of the Finno-Ugric peoples have been best preserved among the Khanty (Ostyak) and Mansi (Vogul), as well as the Sami. Basically they consist of the manipulation of the supernatural by a specially trained, usually naturally gifted, person in order to aid people in various troubles, of which illness was the most common. On being asked to help, the *noaide* performs a dramatic SÉANCE with a traditional sequence of steps, including divinatory procedures, falling into a trance, confrontation of

supernatural beings either to fight them or to receive aid from them, and the actual ritual treatment of the patient, in the case of illness. The *noaide*s can perform both GOOD AND EVIL and formerly were much feared owing to their powers, which they also used to political and economic advantage. In Finland the term *noita* survives mainly in the sense of an evil-working sorcerer, with another term, TIETÄJÄ, applied to the specialist in beneficial mediation with the supernatural.

The word *noaide* is related to several other terms used by the Finno-Ugric peoples for their religious specialists, including Finnish *noita*, Mansi *nait*, and Estonian *noit*, and these words' origin may be traced back to the common Finno-Ugric period before 2500 BCE.

NONCONFORMIST, *also called* Dissenter, *or* Free Churchman, any English Protestant who does not conform to the doctrines or practices of the ESTABLISHED CHURCH of England. The word Nonconformist was first used in the penal acts following the Restoration of the monarchy (1660) and the Act of Uniformity (1662) to describe the conventicles (places of worship) of the congregations that had separated from the Church of England (Separatists). Nonconformists are also called Dissenters (a word first used of the five Dissenting Brethren at the Westminster Assembly of Divines in 1643–47). Because of the movement begun in the late 19th century by which Nonconformists of different denominations joined together in the Free Church Federal Council, they are also called Free Churchmen.

The term Nonconformist is generally applied in England and Wales to all Protestants who have dissented from Anglicanism—Baptists, Congregationalists, PRESBYTERIANS, Methodists, and Unitarians—and also to independent groups such as the QUAKERS, PLYMOUTH BRETHREN, English Moravians, Churches of Christ, and the SALVATION ARMY. In Scotland, where the established church is Presbyterian, members of other churches, including Anglicans, are considered Nonconformists.

NONVIOLENCE, abstention from violence as a matter of ethical principle; such principle may or may not be based in religious conviction. Among religions that have held nonviolence to be at least an ideal are HINDUISM, BUDDHISM, and CHRISTIANITY; JAINISM, by contrast, makes it an absolute principle of behavior (*see* AHIMSĀ). In the 20th century, nonviolence was the fundamental principle and tactic of MOHANDAS GANDHI'S resistance to British rule in India (*see* SATYĀGRAHA) and also served as the basis of Martin Luther King, Jr.'s campaign against civil rights abuses in the United States.

Nonviolence may be distinguished from pacifism in that the latter term is more often used in the context of war and the state's demands that citizens support and take part in it, while nonviolence usually suggests private and social behavior. Nevertheless, one committed to nonviolence will likely also be a pacifist, and a pacifist will likely also prefer nonviolent solutions to more local problems, as well.

NORITO \\'nȯ-rē-tō\\, in Japanese SHINTŌ, words, or prayer, addressed to a deity. The concept of *koto-dama* states that there is a spiritual power that resides in words: beautiful, correct words bring about good, whereas ugly, coarse language can cause evil. Accordingly, *norito* are expressed in elegant, classical language. Prayers usually include words of praise for the deities, lists of offerings, and petitions. During the period when STATE SHINTŌ was under state control, the wording of prayers recited at public shrines was determined by the government. At present, the chief priest of a shrine pronounces the *norito* on behalf of the worshipers, and the contents and wordings of the prayer may vary.

NORN \\'nȯrn\\, in Germanic MYTHOLOGY, group of supernatural beings, usually represented as three maidens who spun or wove the fate of humans. Some sources name them Urd, Verdandi, and Skuld, perhaps meaning "past," "present," and "future." They were depicted as living by YGGDRASILL, the WORLD TREE, under Urd's well and were linked with both GOOD AND EVIL. Being frequently attendant at births, they were sometimes associated with midwifery. The name Norn appears only in Scandinavian sources, but the cult of Nornlike beings occurs in several European FOLKLORES.

NŌRŪZ \\nō-'rüz\\, *also spelled* Nō Rūz, *or* Nō-Rūz (Persian: "New Day"), NEW YEAR FESTIVAL often associated with ZOROASTRIANISM AND PARSIISM, celebrated in many countries, including Iran, Iraq, India, and Afghanistan. It usually begins on March 21 (the first day of the new year in many of these countries).

Among the PARSIS, during the Nōrūz five liturgies are performed: the Āfringān, prayers of love or praise; the Bāj, prayers honoring YAZATAS ("ones worthy of worship") or FRAVASHIS ("preexistent souls"); the Yasna, which includes the offering and ritual drinking of the sacred liquor, *haoma*; the Fravartigan, or Farokhshi, prayers commemorating the dead; and the Satum, prayers recited at funeral feasts. Parsis greet one another with the rite of *hamāzor*, in which one's right hand is passed between the palms of another.

NO-SELF: *see* ANĀTMAN.

NU, U \\'ü-'nü\\, *formerly* Thakin Nu (b. May 25, 1907, Wakema, Burma [Myanmar]—d. Feb. 14, 1995, Yangôn), Burmese independence leader, prime minister of Burma (Myanmar; 1948–58, 1960–62), and Buddhist monk.

While studying law at the University of Rangoon (Yangôn), U Nu became president of the Student Union of Rangoon and joined student political movements. His expulsion in 1936 resulted in a student strike. One of the first confrontations between young Burmese nationalists and the British colonial authorities, it gained Nu national prominence. The following year he joined the We-Burmans Association and played an important part in the struggle for independence. Jailed by the British in 1940 for sedition, he was released only after the Japanese invaded Burma.

In 1943 U Nu served as foreign minister in Ba Maw's government. Following the assassination in 1947 of Aung San, the principal nationalist leader, U Nu was asked to become head of the government and of Burma's leading political party, the Anti-Fascist People's Freedom League (AFPFL). When independence was declared in January 1948 U Nu became the first prime minister of Burma and served for 10 years, with only a brief interlude out of office in 1956–57. Although U Nu was an able and highly respected statesman, his government was plagued by communist and ethnic-minority insurrections, economic stagnation, and administrative inefficiency. In 1958 he resigned his post as prime minister and a "caretaker" government took over, headed by General Ne Win. In 1960 parliamentary government was restored, and U Nu again became prime minister after his party won elections. In March 1962, however, Ne Win staged a coup d'état, establishing a military government and putting U Nu in prison.

Following his release from prison U Nu left Burma (1969) and began organizing a resistance movement against the Ne Win government. When this movement failed he took up residence in India, but he returned to Burma in 1980 at the invitation of Ne Win and in July became a Buddhist monk in Rangoon. He made an unsuccessful bid for power after pro-democracy demonstrations toppled Ne Win's government in 1988.

NUADU \\'nü-ə-thü\\, in Celtic MYTHOLOGY, king of the TUATHA DÉ DANANN, who lost his hand in the battle of MAG TUIRED and with it his right to govern. DIAN CÉCHT replaced the hand with a hand made of silver; he later received a functional human hand from Dian Cécht's son Miach and was thereupon able to overthrow his successor, Bres. From inscriptional evidence it is clear that Nuadu was originally a god.

NÜ KUA \\'nǖ-'gwä\\, *Pinyin* Nü Gua, in Chinese MYTHOLOGY, patroness of matchmakers; as wife or sister of the legendary emperor FU HSI, she helped establish norms for marriage and regulated conduct between the sexes. She is described as having a human head and the body of a snake or fish.

Mythology credits Nü Kua with repairing the pillars of heaven and the broken corners of earth after the rebel Kung Kung had destroyed them, building a palace that became a prototype for the later walled cities of China, and taming the monstrous King of Oxen by slipping a miraculous rope through his nose. One story names Nü and Kua as the first human beings, who found themselves at the moment of creation among the Kunlun Mountains. While offering sacrifice, they prayed to know if they, as brother and sister, were meant to be man and wife. The union was sanctioned when the smoke of the sacrifice remained stationary.

NUN \\'nün\\, *also spelled* Nu \\'nü\\, ancient Egyptian god and father of RE, the sun god. Nun's name means "water," and he represented the primeval waters of CHAOS out of which Re-Atum began creation. Nun's qualities were boundlessness, darkness, and the turbulence of stormy waters. Nun, his female counterpart Naunet, and three further pairs together formed the Ogdoad (group of eight gods) of Hermopolis. Since it was believed that the primeval ocean continued to surround the ordered cosmos, the CREATION MYTH was reenacted each day as the sun god rose from the waters of chaos. Nun was also thought to continue to exist as subsoil water beneath the earth and as the source of the annual flooding of the Nile River.

NUN, woman who is a member of a monastic religious order or group. In most religious traditions of the world, the status of nuns is considerably lower than that of monks. This has been variously justified by reference to issues of ritual impurity (women being held to be impure because of MENSTRUATION) or social and theological convention (as in ROMAN CATHOLICISM, in which women are denied ORDINATION). *See* MONASTICISM; BHIKṢU.

NUSKU \\'nùs-ˌkü\\, in MESOPOTAMIAN RELIGION, Sumero-Akkadian god of light and fire. His father was Sin (Sumerian: NANNA), the moon god. Semitic texts describe Nusku as the king of the night, who illuminates the darkness and repels the DEMONS of the dark. On Babylonian boundary stones he is identified by a lamp. He is visible at the NEW MOON and thus is called its son. The last day of the month is sacred to him, so that he is a LUNAR DEITY. He figures much in incantations and rituals as the fire.

NUT \'nüt\, in EGYPTIAN RELIGION, goddess of the sky, vault of the heavens, often depicted as a woman arched over the earth god GEB. Nut swallowed the sun every evening and gave birth to it again on each morning.

Nut was also represented as a woman wearing a waterpot or pear-shaped

Bath of the Nymphs, *bas-relief by François Girardon; in the gardens of Versailles, France*
Giraudon—Art Resource

vessel on her head, this being the hieroglyph of her name. She was sometimes portrayed as a cow, for this was the form she took to carry the sun god RE on her back to the sky. On five special days preceding the New Year, Nut gave birth successively to the deities OSIRIS, HORUS, SETH, ISIS, and Nephthys. These gods, with the exception of Horus, were commonly referred to as the "children of Nut."

NYĀYA \'nyä-yə\ (Sanskrit: "Rule," or "Method"), one of the six orthodox systems (*darśanas*) of Indian philosophy, important for its analysis of logic and epistemology.

Nyāya's ultimate concern is to bring an end to human suffering, which results from ignorance of reality. Liberation is brought about through right knowledge. Nyāya is thus concerned with the means of right knowledge. The Nyāya school holds that there are four valid means of knowledge: perception (*pratyakṣa*), inference (*anumāna*), comparison (*upamāna*), and testimony (ŚABDA). Invalid knowledge involves memory, doubt, error, and hypothetical argument.

The Nyāya theory of causation defines a cause as an unconditional and invariable antecedent of an effect. Three kinds of causes are distinguished: inherent, or material cause (the substance out of which an effect is produced); noninherent cause (which helps in the production of a cause); and efficient cause (which helps the material cause produce the effect). God is not the material cause of the universe, since atoms and souls are also eternal, but is rather the efficient cause.

The Nyāya system—from Gautama (*c.* 2nd century BCE) through his important early commentator Vātsyāyana (*c.* 450 CE) until Udayanācārya (Udayana; 10th century)—became qualified as the Old Nyāya (Prācīna-Nyāya) in the 11th century when a new school of Nyāya (Navya-Nyāya, or New Nyāya) arose in Bengal. The best known philosopher of the Navya-Nyāya, and the founder of the modern school of Indian logic, was Gaṅgeśa (13th century).

NYINGMAPA: *see* RNYING-MA-PA.

NYMPH (Greek *nymphē*, "young woman," "bride," or "minor goddess"), in Greek mythology, any of a large class of female divinities, usually associated with growing things, such as trees, or with water. They were not immortal but were extremely long-lived and were on the whole kindly disposed toward human beings. They were distinguished according to the sphere of nature with which they were connected: the Oceanids were sea nymphs; the NEREIDS inhabited both saltwater and freshwater; the NAIADS presided over springs, rivers, and lakes. The Oreads (*oros*, "mountain") were nymphs of mountains and grottoes; the Napaeae (*napē*, "dell") and the Alseids (*alsos*, "grove") were nymphs of glens and groves; the Dryads or Hamadryads presided over forests and trees.

Italy had native divinities of springs and streams and water goddesses (called Lymphae) with whom the Greek nymphs tended to become identified.

NYMPHAEUM \nim-'fē-əm\, ancient Greek and Roman SANCTUARY consecrated to water NYMPHS. The *nymphaeum*, originally a natural grotto with springs and streams but later an artificial grotto or a building filled with plants and flowers, sculpture, fountains, and paintings, served as a sanctuary, a reservoir, and an assembly chamber where weddings were held. *Nymphaea* existed at Corinth, Antioch, and Constantinople (now Istanbul); the remains of about 20 have been found in Rome; and others exist as ruins in Asia Minor, Syria, and North Africa. The word *nymphaeum* was also used in ancient Rome to refer to a bordello and also to the fountain in the atrium of the Christian BASILICA. In the 16th century the *nymphaeum* became a feature of Italian gardens.

NYX \'niks\, in Greek mythology, female personification of night and a great cosmogonical figure, feared even by ZEUS.

According to one tradition, she was the daughter of CHAOS and the mother of numerous primordial powers, including Sleep and Death. Another tradition made her the daughter and successor of Phanes, a creator god; she continued to advise her own successors (OURANUS, her son by Phanes; CRONUS, youngest son of Ouranus; and Zeus) by means of her oracular gifts. Throughout antiquity she frequently caught the imagination of poets and artists but she was seldom worshiped.

OANNES \ō-'än-ˌnes\, in Mesopotamian mythology, amphibious being who taught mankind wisdom. Oannes, as described by the Babylonian priest Berosus, had the form of a fish but with the head of a man under his fish's head and under his fish's tail the feet of a man. In the daytime he came up to the seashore of the Persian Gulf and instructed humans in writing, the arts, and the sciences. Oannes was probably the emissary, or even a version, of EA, god of the freshwater deep and of wisdom.

OATH, sacred or solemn voluntary promise usually involving the penalty of divine retribution for intentional falsity and often used in legal procedures. It is not certain that the oath was always considered a religious act; such ancient peoples as the Germanic tribes, Greeks, Romans, and Scythians sometimes swore by their swords or other weapons. Even these peoples, however, were generally invoking a symbol of the power of a god as a guarantee of their trustworthiness.

The swearing of an oath before divine symbols reaches back at least to the Sumerian civilization (4th–3rd millennia BCE) of the ancient Middle East and to ancient Egypt, where one often swore by his life, or ANKH. In the Hittite Empire of the 14th–13th centuries BCE, various gods (*e.g.*, INDRA and MITHRA) were appealed to in agreements between states. Mithra was viewed as the god of the contract. Modern-day Hindus might swear an oath while holding water from the holy river Gaṅgā (Ganges), which is a positive symbol of the divine.

In JUDAISM, two kinds of oaths are forbidden: (1) a vain oath, in which one attempts to do something that is impossible to accomplish, denies self-evident facts, or attempts to negate the fulfillment of a religious precept, and (2) a false oath, in which one uses the name of God to swear falsely, thus committing a SACRILEGE. In ISLAM, the *qasam* ("oath") is primarily a pledge to God, and consequently a false oath is considered a danger to one's soul.

OCCULTISM, various theories, practices, and rituals based on an alleged or esoteric knowledge of the world of spirits and unknown forces. The wide range of beliefs and practices generally held to be occult includes alchemy, DIVINATION, magic, and WITCHCRAFT. The Western tradition of occultism is that of an ancient "secret philosophy," which has its roots in Hellenistic magic—the principal source of which is the *Corpus Hermeticum* associated with Hermes Trismegistos (*see* THOTH), thus the "Hermetic" tradition—and in Jewish MYSTICISM, associated with the QABBALAH.

OCEANIC RELIGIONS, RELIGIOUS BELIEFS and practices of the peoples of Polynesia, Melanesia, and Micronesia. Many traditional institutions have been abandoned or modified under the pressures of Christian evangelism and Western capitalist economics, but the outline of the old religions may still be discerned.

Gods. Although there was wide variation in the beliefs of the various Oceanic peoples, POLYTHEISM was widespread prior to the arrival of CHRISTIANITY. Human effort in the uncertain projects of war, agriculture, and the pursuit of prestige was thought to succeed only when complemented by support from invisible beings and forces, which were manipulated by magical formulas and elicited through prayer and sacrifice. The presence and effects of invisible ghosts and spirits were manifested in dream, revealed in DIVINATION, and inferred from human success or failure, prosperity or disaster, health or death. In such a world, religion was not a separate sphere of the transcendental but a part of everyday life; and religion and magic were not clearly distinguishable. The most sacred rituals often entailed the performance of magic, and performance of magic for personal ends might be accompanied by prayer or sacrifice.

Polynesian peoples believed that there was a host of gods of various degrees of importance, ranging from the great gods of the pantheon, such as Tangaroa, Tu, and Lono, to strictly local gods who were deified priests or chiefs of great renown. All of these gods had to be worshiped in their own way, the most important by full-time priests of highest status, those of lesser importance by part-time priests.

Spirits and ancestors. Oceanic peoples believed that the universe was peopled with spiritual beings of various types, some attached to specific localities or performing specific functions. Ancestral spirits were often contacted in dreams and in the trances of spirit mediums, as were the HIGH GODS and other nonhuman spirits. They would give people information about the causes of disease, deaths, and other misfortunes and would sometimes prescribe new medicines or new varieties of magic. In Melanesia, in fact, beliefs in gods and powerful spirits were less important in everyday life than were beliefs in ancestral ghosts and other spirit beings, who were regarded as daily participants in social life.

Mana and tapu. In Polynesia and some areas of Melanesia all things, animate and inanimate, were believed to be endowed with a greater or lesser degree with mana, or sacred supernatural power. This power could be nullified by various human actions. Polynesian chiefs had such great mana that in some islands if a commoner touched the chief's shadow the injury to the chief's mana could only be compensated by the death of the commoner. In many Polynesian cultures it is still considered to be in very poor taste to step over a person's legs, pass one's hand over a person's head, or stand with one's head higher than that of a person of high rank. These actions are believed to sap a person's mana, rendering him profane.

It was not only people who had mana, however, but buildings, stones, tools, canoes, and all things. Life was infused with a wide variety of complicated rules designed to prevent damage to the mana inherent in various things. Groves, trees, temples, or tracts of land were considered sacred and could not be entered by ordinary people because they were pervaded by the mana of a high-status person or god. Women were not permitted in canoes under normal conditions in the Marquesas because their presence defiled the canoe. In many societies, men preparing for war or for any other hazardous undertaking had to go through a period of purification—avoiding the company of women, eating certain foods only, and often going into seclusion so as to protect their powers from defilement. The penalty for major violations of these tapu (TABOO), or prohibitions, was often death. Violations of lesser tapu, such as trespassing in a sacred grove or disturbing the bones of the dead, were believed to result in supernatural punishment, manifested in some form of illness, bad luck, or debilitation.

Rites and ceremonies. In pre-Christian Micronesia, ceremonies for the high gods appear to have been principally seasonal offerings of first fruits, performed often in private by a specialist priest with a few helpers. Special appeals to the high gods were probably also made at times of community crisis, such as wars or typhoons, but HUMAN SACRIFICE apparently was not practiced.

In Polynesia, various procedures were called for to announce the birth of a child to the community, to the ancestors, and to the gods, and to care for the welfare (both physical and supernatural) of the infant and mother by application of medical and magical techniques. CIRCUMCISION was a major event in the male life cycle and was marked by elaborate rituals, which increased in importance with the status of the male. Although no such rite is reported for girls, some societies, such as the Marquesas, had ceremonies in which adolescent girls made a more or less public debut, in a sexual sense. Other milestones in Polynesian cultural life—the formal presentation of a royal heir, the completion of a tattooing operation or ear piercing in a high-status child, the formal investiture of a priest or chief—were marked with a variety of rituals and quite often included human sacrifice.

Death, the terminal milestone, was universally celebrated with extravagant behavior, increasing in extravagance in direct proportion to the status of the deceased. In many societies these ceremonies were marked by violence, with mourners mutilating themselves and others, and by human sacrifices, obtained from within the social group or without. Feasts were also common, as was orgiastic behavior. The extravagance of funeral rites was surpassed, in some societies, by ceremonies to deify a departed chief or priest. These went on for prolonged periods, involving prodigious feasting and drinking, violence, and sexuality.

Magic. Some forms of everyday magic—for gardening, fishing, attracting valuables

Initiation scene in a cult house, Papua New Guinea
Museum fur Volkerkunde, Basel, Switz. (Vb 28418–71); photograph, P. Horner

or lovers—were widely known. Other forms, for powers of fighting or theft, tended to be closely guarded, and magic for destructive ends was secretly held and generally used in clandestine fashion. In many Melanesian societies SORCERY was seen as the major cause of death or illness, and in New Guinea, accusations of sorcery are a major cause of hostility between groups and of blood feuding. Some highland peoples believe that witches—humans acting in the grip of forces or agencies beyond their conscious control—prey on the living, taking possession of them or draining their bodily substances.

See also CARGO CULT.

OCEANUS \ō-'sē-ə-nəs\, in Greek mythology, river that flowed around the earth (conceived as flat). Beyond it, to the west, were the sunless land of the Cimmerii, the country of dreams, and the entrance to the underworld. In Hesiod's *Theogony*, Oceanus was the son of OURANUS and GAEA, the husband of the TITAN Tethys, and father of 3,000 stream spirits and 3,000 ocean NYMPHS. In Homer's works he was the origin of the gods. As a common noun the word received almost the modern sense of ocean.

OCKHAM, WILLIAM OF \'ä-kəm\, *also called* William Ockham, *Ockham also spelled* Occam (b. *c.* 1285, Ockham, Surrey?, Eng.—d. 1347/49, Munich, Bavaria [now in Germany]), FRANCISCAN philosopher, theologian, and political writer. He was a late Scholastic thinker who was regarded as the founder of a form of nominalism—the school of thought that denies that universal concepts such as "father" have any reality apart from the individual things that the term signifies.

Little is known of Ockham's childhood. His early schooling in a Franciscan CONVENT concentrated on the study of logic; his interest in logic never waned, and in all his future disputes it served as his chief weapon. Ockham took the traditional course of theological studies at the University of Oxford and apparently between 1317 and 1319 lectured on the *Sentences* of PETER LOMBARD, the official textbook of theology in the universities until the 16th century. His opinions aroused strong opposition from members of the theological faculty of Oxford, however, and he left the university without a master's degree in theology; at the time the chancellor of the university was John Lutterell, who was dismissed from his post in 1322 at the demand of the teaching staff. Ockham continued his academic career, apparently in English convents.

Ockham's writings reveal two primary aspects of his intellectual and spiritual attitude. On the one hand, he referred to the primary importance of God, whose omnipotence determines the gratuitous salvation of men; God's saving action consists of giving without any obligation and is already profusely demonstrated in the creation of nature. On the other hand, he insisted on evaluations that are severely rational, on distinctions between the necessary and the incidental and differentiation between evidence and degrees of probability—an insistence that places great trust in man's natural reason and his human nature. "Ockham's razor" is the logical principle that "plurality should not be assumed without necessity"; Ockham employed it to eliminate many entities that had been devised to explain reality, especially by the Scholastic philosophers.

Ockham met Lutterell again at Avignon, France; in a treatise addressed to Pope John XXII, Lutterell denounced Ockham's teaching on the *Sentences*, extracting from it 56 propositions that he showed to be in serious error. Lutterell then became a member of a committee of six theologians that produced two critical reports on Ockham's commentary. Ockham, however, presented to the pope another copy of the *Ordinatio* in which he had made some corrections. Though it appeared that he would be condemned for his teaching, the condemnation never came.

At a convent in Avignon, Ockham met Bonagratia of Bergamo, a doctor of civil and CANON LAW who had been battling John XXII over the problem of Franciscan poverty. On Dec. 1, 1327, the Franciscan general Michael of Cesena arrived in Avignon and stayed at the same convent; he, too, had been summoned by the pope in connection with the dispute. They were at odds over the theoretical problem of whether Christ and his Apostles had renounced the right of property and the right to the use of property. Michael maintained that because Christ and his Apostles had renounced all ownership and all rights to property, the Franciscans were justified in attempting to do the same thing.

The relations between John and Michael grew steadily worse, and on May 26, 1328, Michael fled from Avignon accompanied by Bonagratia and Ockham. Ockham, who was already a witness in an appeal secretly drafted by Michael, publicly endorsed the appeal in September at Pisa, where the three Franciscans were staying under the protection of Emperor Louis IV the Bavarian, who had been excommunicated in 1324 and proclaimed by John XXII to have forfeited all rights to the empire. They followed him to Munich in 1330, and thereafter Ockham wrote fervently against the PAPACY in defense of both the strict Franciscan notion of poverty and the empire.

Instructed by his superior general in 1328 to study three papal bulls on poverty, Ockham found that they contained many errors that showed John XXII to be a heretic who had forfeited his mandate by reason of his HERESY. His status of pseudo-pope was confirmed in Ockham's view in 1330–31 by his sermons proposing that the souls of the saved did not enjoy the vision of God immediately after death but only after they were rejoined with the body at the LAST JUDGMENT, an opinion that contradicted tradition and was ultimately rejected.

For Ockham the power of the pope is limited by the freedom of Christians that is established by the gospel and the natural law. It is therefore legitimate and in keeping with the gospel to side with the empire against the papacy or to defend, as Ockham did in 1339, the right of the king of England to tax church property. From 1330 to 1338, in the heat of this dispute, Ockham wrote 15 or 16 more or less political works, some in collaboration.

Excommunicated after his flight from Avignon, Ockham

maintained the same basic position after the death of John XXII in 1334, during the reign of Benedict XII (1334–42), and after the election of Clement VI. Ockham was long thought to have died at a convent in Munich in 1349 during the Black Death, but he may have died there in 1347.

ODIN \'ō-dən\, *also called* Wodan, Woden \'wō-dən\, *or* Wotan \'vō-ˌtän\, one of the principal gods in GERMANIC RELIGION. The Roman historian Tacitus stated that the Teutons worshiped Mercury; and because *dies Mercurii* ("Mercury's day") was identified with Wednesday ("Woden's day"), there is little doubt that the god Woden (the earlier form of Odin) was meant. Though Woden was worshiped preeminently, it is not clear whether it was practiced by all the Teutonic tribes or what the nature of the god was. Later sources indicate that at the end of the pre-Christian period Odin was the principal god in Scandinavia.

From earliest times Odin was a war god, and he appeared in heroic literature as the protector of heroes; fallen warriors joined him in VALHALLA, the "Hall of the Slain." The wolf and the raven were dedicated to him. His magical horse, SLEIPNIR, had eight legs, teeth inscribed with runes, and the ability to gallop through the air and over the sea. Odin was the great magician among the gods and was associated with runes. He was also the god of poets. In outward appearance he was a tall, old man, with flowing beard and only one eye (the other he gave in exchange for wisdom).

ODYSSEUS \ō-'di-sē-əs, ō-'dis-ˌyüs\ (Greek), *Latin* Ulixes \yü-'lik-sēz\, *English* Ulysses \yü-'li-sēz\, hero of Homer's epic poem the *Odyssey* and one of the most frequently portrayed figures in Western literature. According to Homer, Odysseus was king of Ithaca, son of Laertes and Anticleia (the daughter of AUTOLYCUS of Parnassus), and father, by his wife, PENELOPE, of TELEMACHUS. (In later tradition, Odysseus was the son of SISYPHUS and fathered sons by CIRCE, CALYPSO, and others.)

Homer portrayed Odysseus as a man of shrewdness, eloquence, resourcefulness, courage, and endurance. In the *Iliad* he plays a leading part in achieving the reconciliation between AGAMEMNON and ACHILLES. His bravery and skill in fighting are demonstrated repeatedly, and his wiliness is shown most notably in the night expedition he undertakes with DIOMEDES against the Trojans.

Odysseus' wanderings and the recovery of his house and kingdom are the central theme of the *Odyssey*. After leaving Troy he first comes to the land of the LOTUS-EATERS and only with difficulty rescues some of his companions from their *lōtos*-induced lethargy; he encounters and blinds POLYPHEMUS the CYCLOPS, a son of POSEIDON, escaping from his cave by clinging to the belly of a ram; he loses 11 of his 12 ships to the cannibalistic Laistrygones and reaches the island of the enchantress Circe, where he has to rescue some of his companions whom she had turned into swine. Next he visits the Land of Dead, where he learns from the Theban seer TIRESIAS how he can expiate Poseidon's wrath. He then encounters the SIRENS, SCYLLA AND CHARYBDIS, and the Cattle of the Sun, which his companions, despite warnings, plunder for food. He alone survives the ensuing storm and reaches the idyllic island of the NYMPH Calypso.

After almost nine years, Odysseus leaves Calypso and at last arrives in Ithaca, where his wife, Penelope, and son, Telemachus, have been struggling to maintain their authority during his prolonged absence. Recognized at first only by his faithful dog and a nurse, Odysseus proves his identity by accomplishing Penelope's test of stringing and shoot-

Odysseus slaying Penelope's suitors, detail of a skyphos (cup) from Latium (now central Italy), c. *450 BCE*
By courtesy of the Staatliche Museen zu Berlin, Germany

ing with his old bow. He then, with the help of Telemachus, slays Penelope's suitors and is accepted as her long-lost husband and the king of Ithaca.

Classical Greek writers presented Odysseus sometimes as an unscrupulous politician, sometimes as a wise and honorable statesman. Philosophers usually admired his intelligence and wisdom. Some Roman writers (such as Virgil and Statius) tended to disparage him as the destroyer of Rome's supposed mother city, Troy; others (such as Horace and Ovid) admired him. The early Christian writers praised him as an example of the wise pilgrim.

OEDIPUS \'e-də-pəs, 'ē-\, in Greek mythology, king of Thebes who unwittingly killed his father and married his mother. Homer related that Oedipus' mother hanged herself when the truth of their relationship became known, though Oedipus apparently continued to rule at Thebes until his death. In the post-Homeric tradition, most familiar from Sophocles' *Oedipus Rex* and *Oedipus Coloneus,* there are notable differences in emphasis and detail.

Laius, king of Thebes, was warned by an oracle that his son would slay him. Accordingly, when his wife, Jocasta (Iocaste; in Homer, Epicaste), bore a son, he exposed the baby on Mount Cithaeron, first pinning his ankles together (hence the name Oedipus, meaning Swell-Foot). A shepherd took pity on the infant, who was adopted by King Polybus of Corinth and his wife and was brought up as their son. In early manhood Oedipus visited DELPHI and upon learning that he was fated to kill his father and marry his mother, he resolved never to return to Corinth.

Traveling toward Thebes, he encountered Laius, who provoked a quarrel in which Oedipus killed him. Continuing on his way, Oedipus found Thebes plagued by the SPHINX, who put a riddle to all passersby and destroyed those who could not answer. Oedipus solved the riddle, and the Sphinx killed herself. In reward, he received the throne of Thebes and the hand of the widowed queen, his mother, Jocasta. They had four children: Eteocles, Polyneices, ANTIGONE, and Ismene. Later, when the truth became known, Jocasta committed suicide, and Oedipus (according to another version), after blinding himself, went into exile, accompanied by Antigone and Ismene, leaving his brother-in-law Creon as regent. Oedipus died at Colonus near Ath-

ens, where he was swallowed into the earth and became a guardian hero of the land.

SIGMUND FREUD chose the term Oedipus complex to designate a son's feeling of love toward his mother and jealousy and hate toward his father, although these were not emotions that motivated Oedipus' actions or determined his character in any ancient version of the story.

OENEUS \'ēn-,yüs, 'ē-nē-əs\, in Greek mythology, king of Calydon, husband of Althaea, and father of Meleager—the leader of the Calydonian boar hunt. He was connected with HERACLES as the father of Heracles' bride Deianeira, whom he won from the river god Achelous. Oeneus may have been originally a wine god; his name is derived from the Greek word for wine. According to one story, DIONYSUS, the great god of wine, was the real father of Deianeira.

OENGHUS \'ē-nəs, 'ȯin-ḡəs\ (Irish deity): *see* MAPONOS.

OENONE \ē-'nō-nē\, in Greek mythology, fountain NYMPH of Mount Ida, the daughter of the River OENEUS, and the lover of PARIS, a son of PRIAM of Troy. Oenone and Paris had a son, Corythus, but Paris soon deserted her for HELEN. Bitterly jealous, Oenone refused to aid the wounded Paris during the Trojan War, even though she was the only one who could cure him. She at last relented but arrived at Troy too late to save him. Overcome with grief, she killed herself.

OGMA \'ōḡ-mə\, ancient Irish god portrayed as a swarthy man whose battle ardor was so great that he had to be chained and held back by other warriors until the right moment for military action occurred. Ogham script, an Irish writing system dating from the 4th century CE, seems to have been named for him, suggesting that, like his Celtic equivalent OGMIOS, he was a god of eloquence. *See also* CELTIC RELIGION.

OGMIOS \'ōḡ-mē-ōs\, in CELTIC RELIGION, god identified with the Roman Hercules (HERACLES). He was portrayed as an old man with dark skin and armed with a bow and club. He was also a god of eloquence, and in that aspect he was represented as drawing along a company of men whose ears were chained to his tongue. Ogmios' Irish equivalent was OGMA.

OGYŪ SORAI \ō-'gyü-'sȯ-,rī\ (b. March 21, 1666, Edo, Japan—d. Feb. 28, 1728, Edo), leading Japanese scholar of Chinese culture and CONFUCIANISM (Japanese: KOGAKU), who stressed the pragmatic application of Confucianism to promote social and political reforms by means of uniform, rational laws.

ŌKUNINUSHI \'ō-kṳ-nē-'nṳ-shē\, *in full* Ōkuninushi no Mikota, in the mythology of the Izumo branch of SHINTŌ in Japan, the central hero, a son-in-law of the storm god, SUSA-NOO.

Before becoming "Master of the Great Land," Ōkuninushi offered compassionate advice to the suffering white hare of Inaba (who had been stripped of his fur by a crocodile), who rewarded him by helping to arrange his marriage with Yakami, the princess of Inaba. His chief consort was Princess Suseri, the daughter of Susanoo. After escaping from Susanoo's palace in the netherworld with the storm god's most precious possessions—his sword, lute, and bow and arrows—Ōkuninushi then commenced to build the world with the help of the dwarf deity Sukunahikona. The two together formulated the arts of medicine and the means of controlling disasters caused by birds and insects. He continued to rule Izumo until the appearance of NINIGI, when he turned over political rule to him while retaining control of religious affairs. In modern Japanese folk belief, he is venerated as a god who heals and who makes marriages happy.

Ogmios, carved relief; in the Musée Granet, Aix-en-Provence, France
Jean Roubier

OLCOTT, HENRY STEEL \\'ȯl-kət\\ (b. Aug. 2, 1832, Orange, N.J., U.S.—d. Feb. 17, 1907, Adyar, Madras, India), American author, attorney, philosopher, and cofounder of the Theosophical Society, a religious movement incorporating aspects of BUDDHISM, Brahmanism, and Christian esotericism.

With HELENA PETROVNA BLAVATSKY, William Q. Judge, and others Olcott founded the Theosophical Society in 1875 and became its president. In 1878 he and Blavatsky visited India. The two settled there in 1879 and in 1882 established the permanent headquarters of the Theosophical Society of Adyar, Madras. He assisted Annie Besant in establishing the Central Hindu College at VARANASI (Benares). With her, he expounded their Theosophist ideas in appearances in India and Ceylon and contributed to the founding of three colleges and 250 schools in Ceylon.

Olcott edited the *Theosophist* (1888–1907). His *Buddhist Catechism* (1881) was translated into many languages.

OLD BELIEVER, *Russian* Starover, *or* Staroobryadets, member of a group of Russian religious dissenters who refused to accept the liturgical reforms imposed upon the Russian Orthodox church by the PATRIARCH of Moscow Nikon (1652–58). Numbering millions of faithful in the 17th century, the Old Believers split into a number of different sects, of which several survived into modern times.

Patriarch Nikon faced the difficult problem of deciding on an authoritative source for the correction of the liturgical books in use in Russia. These books, used since the conversion of Rus to CHRISTIANITY in 988, were literal translations from the Greek into Old Church Slavic made less reliable by scribal errors over the centuries. Nikon chose to follow exactly the texts and practices of the Greek church as they existed in 1652, and to this effect he ordered the printing of new liturgical books. His decree also required the adoption of Greek usages, Greek forms of clerical dress, and a change in the manner of crossing oneself: three fin-

gers were to be used instead of two. The reform, obligatory for all, was considered "necessary for salvation" and was supported by Tsar Alexis Romanov.

Opposition to the reforms was led by a group of Muscovite priests, notably the archpriest Avvakum Petrovich. Even after the deposition of Nikon (1658) a series of church councils culminating in that of 1666–67 endorsed the reforms and anathematized the dissenters. Several of them, including Avvakum, were executed.

The dissenters, sometimes called Raskol'niki ("Schismatics"), were most numerous in the inaccessible regions of northern and eastern Russia (but later also in Moscow itself) and were important in the colonization of these remote areas. Opposed to all change, they strongly resisted the Western innovations introduced by Peter the Great, whom they regarded as ANTICHRIST. Having no episcopal hierarchy, they split into two groups. One group, the Popovtsy (priestly sects), sought to attract ordained priests and were able to set up an episcopate in the 19th century. The other, the Bezpopovtsy (priestless sects), renounced priests and all SACRAMENTS, except BAPTISM. Many other sects developed out of these groups.

The Old Believers benefited from the edict of toleration (April 17, 1905), and most groups survived the Russian Revolution of 1917. Numerous branches of both the Popovtsy and the Bezpopovtsy succeeded in becoming registered and thus officially recognized by the Soviet state. Little is known, however, of the Old Believer settlements supposed to exist in Siberia, the Urals, Kazakstan, and the Altai. Some groups exist elsewhere in Asia, Brazil, and in the United States and Canada.

In 1971 the Council of the Russian Orthodox church rescinded the ANATHEMAS of the 17th century and recognized the full validity of the old rites.

OLD CATHOLIC CHURCH, any of the groups of Western Christians who believe themselves to maintain in complete loyalty the doctrine and traditions of the undivided church but who separated from the see of Rome after the FIRST VATICAN COUNCIL of 1869–70.

The steady process of centralization in the see of Rome and in the person of the POPE, which has marked the later history of the Christian church in the West, has led to recurrent opposition. Plans for the first Vatican Council and the promulgation of the doctrine of the infallibility of the pope in 1870 provoked widespread hostility, the most notable figure being the distinguished church historian J.J.I. von Döllinger.

After the council, all the bishops of the opposition one by one assented to the new dogma. Döllinger remained obdurate and in time was excommunicated by name. He himself took no part in forming separatist churches, but it was largely as a result of his advice and guidance that Old Catholic churches came into being in Germany, Switzerland,

Austria, and elsewhere. As no bishop had joined any of these groups, recourse was had to the Jansenist church in Holland, which had maintained a somewhat precarious existence in separation from Rome since the 18th century but had preserved an episcopal succession recognized by Rome as valid though irregular.

The first consecration of the new order was that of Joseph H. Reinkens, who was made bishop in Germany by a sympathetic bishop of the Jansenist Church of Holland, Bishop Heykamp of Deventer, on Aug. 11, 1873. Rather later the Polish National Catholic Church came into being in the United States and Canada.

In 1889 the Union of Utrecht was formed, and the declaration of Utrecht is the charter of Old Catholic doctrine and polity. Adherents to this union are the Old Catholic Church of The Netherlands, the Old Catholic Church of Germany, the Christian Catholic Church of Switzerland, the Old Catholic Church of Austria, and the Polish National Catholic Church. The chief authority in the Old Catholic churches is the conference of bishops. The archbishop of Utrecht exercises a kind of honorary primacy. Each DIOCESE has its SYNOD, with full participation of both clergy and laity in every aspect of the life of the church, including the election of bishops.

The Old Catholics accept the SCRIPTURES, the APOSTLES' CREED and NICENE CREED, and the dogmatic decisions of the first seven ecumenical councils. They uphold the conciliar basis of the church and accord a high place to tradition. They accept seven SACRAMENTS as of permanent obligation in the life of the church. The episcopate is accepted as a gift given by God to the church, in which all Catholic bishops share equally, having been admitted thereto by bishops who themselves stand in unbroken historical succession from the time of the APOSTLES. By adopting in all countries the use of the vernacular in public worship, the Old Catholics accepted what at the time was regarded as one of the fundamental principles of the Protestant REFORMATION (although that situation was significantly altered by the decisions of the SECOND VATICAN COUNCIL allowing a vernacular liturgy). CONFESSION to God in the presence of a priest is not obligatory, and CELIBACY of the clergy was made optional in some Old Catholic churches.

Döllinger's founding principles included a pledge to work persistently for Christian union. This was stressed at the first Bonn conference on Christian union, held in 1874, and was repeated at all the international Old Catholic congresses, held at intervals of roughly five years. In 1931, by the agreement of Bonn, full intercommunion was established between the Church of England and the Old Catholic churches; this was followed in 1946 by a similar agreement between the Polish National Catholic Church and the Protestant Episcopal Church in the United States. Most of the Anglican churches have accepted these agreements; through mutual participation in episcopal consecrations, rather more than half the Anglican episcopate in the world has the Old Catholic as well as the Anglican episcopal succession.

OLD TESTAMENT, biblical literature, canonical for Jews and Christians. Except for a few passages in Aramaic, the Old Testament was written originally in Hebrew during the period from 1200 to 100 BCE. The term Old Testament was devised by a Christian, Melito of Sardis, about 170 CE to distinguish this part of the BIBLE from the NEW TESTAMENT.

In its general framework, the Old Testament is the account of God's dealing with the Jews as his CHOSEN PEOPLE.

Its first six books narrate how the Israelites became a people and settled in the Promised Land. The following seven books describe the establishment and development of the monarchy and the messages of the prophets. The last 11 books contain poetry, theology, and some additional historical works. Throughout the Old Testament, the Jews' historical relation to God is conceived in reference to the ultimate redemption of all humanity.

The Hebrew canon recognizes three main divisions: (1) the TORAH, or Pentateuch; (2) the NEBI'IM, or Prophets; and (3) the KETUBIM, or Writings. The total number of books in the Hebrew canon is 24, the number of scrolls on which these works were written in ancient times. The Old Testament as adopted by CHRISTIANITY numbers more works because the ROMAN CATHOLIC canon, derived initially from the Greek-language SEPTUAGINT translation of the Hebrew Bible, absorbed a number of books that Jews and Protestants later determined were not canonical (*see* APOCRYPHA). Christians divided some of the original Hebrew works into two or more parts, specifically, Samuel, Kings, and Chronicles (two parts each), Ezra-Nehemiah (two separate books), and the Minor Prophets (12 separate books).

OLYMPIA \ō-'lim-pē-ə\, ancient SANCTUARY and site of the Olympic Games, located in the western Peloponnese, 10 miles inland from the Ionian Sea, near a point where the Alpheus (Alfios) and Cladeus (Kladios) rivers meet. The earliest remains date from 2000 to 1600 BCE, the sanctuary itself from around 1000. First controlled by the town of Pisa, after 570 BCE Olympia came under the jurisdiction of Elis and Sparta. The religious festival, of which the Games were a part, was held there every four years from the 8th century BCE until the end of the 4th century CE.

The sacred precinct, the ALTIS, or Sacred Grove of ZEUS, was bounded on the north by the hill of CRONUS and enclosed by a wall on the other three sides. In it were the temples, the principal altars and votive offerings, the treasuries, and administration buildings. Outside were the athletic installations and the hostels, baths, and other accommodations for visitors. In 426 the emperor Theodosius II ordered the temples destroyed; subsequent man-made and natural disasters further damaged the site.

The Temple of Zeus was the largest and most important building at Olympia and one of the largest Doric temples in Greece. Built about 460 BCE by the architect Libon of Elis, the temple was richly decorated with sculpture, much of which has survived. In the front gable the chariot race between PELOPS and Oenomaus was represented, and both parties were shown preparing for the race. In the back gable was the battle of the Lapiths and CENTAURS at the wedding of Perithous. The frieze that ran above the front and back porches had sculptured metopes with the 12 labors of HERACLES, 6 at each end. At the peak of the gable was a gilded figure of Victory and at each corner a gilded caldron, but these have not survived.

Within the temple was the great gold and ivory (chryselephantine) statue of Zeus, the work of the Athenian sculptor Phidias, the most famous of all ancient statues and counted one of the Seven Wonders of the World. It made a profound impression on all who saw it, and people generally agreed that Phidias had succeeded in creating the image of Homer's Zeus. The god was represented seated on an elaborately wrought throne. He held a figure of the goddess of victory (NIKE) in his right hand and a sceptre in his left.

The great altar of Olympian Zeus, to one side of the temple, was elliptical in shape and consisted of an elevated base approached by steps. From the base rose a large mound made of the ashes of the thighs of animal victims sacrificed to Zeus. The whole height of the altar was 22 feet.

The oldest temple at Olympia and one of the most venerable in all Greece was that of HERA, originally a joint temple of Hera and Zeus until a separate temple was built for him. The existing temple was probably built about 600 BCE, and an earlier phase, without peristyle (colonnade), may go back to the 8th century. Pausanias says that in the temple was an image of Hera seated on a throne with an image of Zeus standing beside her. Pausanias also reports the existence of a stone statue of HERMES carrying the young DIONYSUS, a work of Praxiteles that was found in the cella of the temple in 1877. Between the temples of Zeus and Hera, the Elean hero Pelops had a sanctuary in the Altis that was open to the sky and surrounded by a wall, with trees and statues within. The Metroum, or Temple of the GREAT MOTHER OF THE GODS, was a small Doric temple of the 4th century BCE just below the treasuries.

The stadium lay to the east of the Altis. In early classical times it was not cut off from the sanctuary, and one end of the track was in the area directly in front of the temple and the great ash altar of Zeus (beneath the later Echo Colonnade). About the middle of the 4th century BCE the stadium was shifted about 90 yards eastward and a little to the north.

Doric colonnade of the ruins of the Palaestra, the structure where wrestlers and boxers trained, adjacent to the sacred district at Olympia
Dan J. McCoy—Black Star

There were no stone seats in the stadium except for a box on the south side; here sat the *hellanodikai*, or chief judges, of the Games. Directly opposite the box was the altar of DEMETER Chamyne, from which the priestess of that cult was privileged to watch the Games (married women were excluded from the Olympic festival, but unmarried girls were permitted).

When the stadium embankments were excavated many votive offerings were discovered, including bronze statuettes and reliefs, several terra-cotta statues, and arms or armor that had been dedicated in the sanctuary.

The hippodrome where the horse races were held lay south of the stadium in the open valley of the Alpheus. No trace of this has been found.

OM \'ōm\, in HINDUISM and other religions chiefly of India, sacred syllable considered to be the greatest of all MANTRAS. The syllable *Om* is composed of the three sounds *a-u-m* (in Sanskrit, the vowels *a* and *u* coalesce to become *o*), which represent several important triads: the three worlds of earth, atmosphere, and heaven; the three major Hindu gods, BRAHMĀ, VISHNU, and SHIVA; and the three sacred Vedic SCRIPTURES, Ṛg, Yajus, and Sāma. *Om* is uttered at the beginning and end of Hindu prayers, chants, and meditation and is freely used in rituals of JAINISM and BUDDHISM. From the

6th century, the written symbol designating the sound is used to mark the beginning of a text or an inscription.

The syllable is discussed in a number of the UPANISHADS, and it forms the entire subject matter of one, the *Māṇḍūkya*. It is used in the practice of YOGA and is related to techniques of auditory meditation. Śaivites mark the LIṄGA, or sign of Shiva, with the syllable *Om*, whereas Vaiṣṇavas identify the three sounds as referring to a trinity composed of Vishnu, his wife LAKṢMĪ, and the worshiper.

OMEN, observed phenomenon that is interpreted as signifying good or bad fortune. In ancient times omens were numerous and varied and might be found in lightning or the flight of birds. The different kinds of bird in flight or the direction of flight in relation to the observer often had a special meaning. *See* DIVINATION.

OMETECUHTLI \ˌō-mā-'tā-ku̇t-lē\ (Nahuatl: "Two-Lord"), in Aztec religion, supreme deity in its masculine aspect, the Lord of Duality, or Lord of Life. With his consort Omecihuatl, Ometecuhtli resided in Omeyocan ("The Place of Duality"), the 13th and highest Aztec heaven, and together they constituted the dual god Ometeotl. The opposing factors in the Aztec universe included male and female, light and dark, motion and stillness, order and chaos. Ometecuhtli was the only Aztec god to whom no temple was erected, nor was any formal cult active in his name, as he was seen as remote and inaccessible in the heavens though far from unimportant.

Ometecuhtli is depicted by symbols of fertility and adorned with ears of corn. He was believed to be responsible for releasing the souls of infants from Omeyocan in preparation for human births on earth.

ŌMOTO \ō-'mò-tò\ (Japanese: "Great Fundamentals"), *also called* Ōmoto-kyō \-ˌkyō\ ("Religion of Ōmoto"), religious movement of Japan that had a large following between the two World Wars and that served as a model for numerous other sects. The teaching of Ōmoto is based on divine oracles transmitted through a peasant woman, Deguchi Nao (1836–1918), whose healing powers attracted an early following. Her first revelation in 1892 foretold the destruction of the world and the appearance of a leader who would usher in the new heaven on earth.

The doctrine was systematized and organized by her son-in-law, Deguchi Onisaburō (1871–1948), who denounced armament and war and identified himself as the leader who would establish the new order. He attracted more than 2,000,000 believers in the 1930s but aroused the hostility of the government, which twice arrested him and destroyed Ōmoto temples and buildings at the sect's headquarters in

Ayabe, near Kyōto. He was released on bail in 1942 and initiated the revival of the movement in 1946 under the name Aizen-en (Garden of Divine Love). The sect was known by several names but has reverted to its most commonly used name, Ōmoto.

Though the membership of the sect in 1978 was estimated at only 163,760 believers, other new religious movements of Japan that owe their original inspiration to Ōmoto include Seichōno-ie (Household of Growth) and Sekai Kyūsei-kyō (Religion of World Salvation), both founded by former disciples of Onisaburō. Ōmoto emphasizes the universal character of religion. It promotes the use of Esperanto and sponsors an organization called ULBA (Universal Love and Brotherhood Association).

ONEIDA COMMUNITY \ō-'nī-də\, *also called* Perfectionists, *or* Bible Communists, utopian religious community established by John Humphrey Noyes and some of his disciples in Putney, Vt., U.S., in 1841.

Noyes experienced a religious conversion when he was 20 years old. He then gave up law studies and attended Andover Theological Seminary and Yale Divinity School. His acceptance and preaching of the doctrine of perfectionism, the idea that after conversion one was free of all SIN, was considered too unorthodox, and he was denied ORDINATION. He also became convinced that the SECOND COMING of JESUS CHRIST was not an event of the future but had already occurred within a generation of Christ's ministry on earth. But it was Noyes's ideas concerning sexual union that made him notorious. He rejected monogamy and the idea that one man and one woman should become closely attached to each other. The application of his views led to the practice of complex marriage in his community, in which every woman was the wife of every man and every man was the husband of every woman. Noyes also believed that socialism without religion was impossible and that the extended family system could dissolve selfishness and demonstrate the practicality of perfectionism on earth.

In 1847, Noyes proclaimed that the Spirit of Christ had earlier returned to earth and had now entered into his group at Putney. This proclamation, together with the practice of complex marriage, aroused the hostility of the surrounding community, and the group left Putney to found a new community at Oneida, N.Y. For the next 30 years Oneida flourished. The community, which in the early years numbered about 200 persons, earned a living by farming and logging before a new member gave the community a steel trap that he had invented. Manufacture and sale of Oneida traps became the basis of a thriving group of industrial enterprises that included silverware, embroidered silks, and canned fruit.

The community was organized into 48 departments that carried on the various activities of the settlement, and these activities were supervised by 21 committees. Though marriage was complex, the Perfectionists denied the charge of free love. Sexual relations were strictly regulated, and the propagation of children was a matter of community control. Those who were to produce children were carefully chosen and paired. The central feature of the community was the custom of holding criticism sessions, or cures, a practice that Noyes had discovered at Andover. They were attended by the entire community at first and, later, as the community grew, were conducted before committees presided over by Noyes. The criticism sessions had the effect of enforcing social control and promoting community cohesion.

Hostility mounted in the surrounding communities to the Perfectionists' marriage arrangements, and in 1879 Noyes advised the group to abandon the system. As the reorganization of the community began, the entire socialist organization of property in Oneida also was questioned. Noyes and a few adherents went to Canada, where he died in 1886. The remaining members set up a joint stock company, known as Oneida Community, Ltd., which carried on the various industries, particularly the manufacture of silver plate, as a commercial enterprise.

OPET \'ō-,pet\, ancient Egyptian festival of the New Year. In the celebration of Opet, the god AMON together with MUT, his consort, and KHONS, their son, made a ritual journey from their shrines at Karnak to the temple of Luxor (called *Ipet resyt* in pharaonic Egyptian, hence the name of the festival). Scenes of the festival in the Colonnade of the Temple of Luxor carved during Tutankhamen's reign (1333–23 BCE) show white-robed priests carrying statues of Amon, Mut, and Khons in golden barks through the streets of ancient Thebes, onto river barges, and on to Luxor. Following this appearance to the populace, the statues remained in the temple of Luxor for about 24 days, during which the city remained in festival. The images were returned by the same route to their shrines in Karnak in a second public appearance that closed the festival. A direct survival of the ancient cult is seen in the present-day feast of the Muslim holy man Sheikh Yūsuf al-Haggāg, whose boat is carried about Luxor amid popular celebration. His mosque stands in the northeastern corner of the first court of the temple of Luxor, over the foundations of a Byzantine church.

Through an association with Mut, the name Opet (or Apet) was also applied to a local city goddess of Thebes, who was depicted in a manner similar to that of TAURT, the hippopotamus goddess of fertility and childbirth.

OPHITE \'ä-,fīt, 'ō-\ (Greek *Ophitēs*, from *ophis*, "serpent"), member of any of several Gnostic sects that flourished in the Roman Empire during the 2nd century CE and for several centuries thereafter. A variety of Gnostic sects, such as the Naassenes and the CAINITES, are included under the designation Ophites. These sects' beliefs differed in various ways, but central to them all was a dualistic theology that opposed a purely spiritual Supreme Being, who was both the creator and the highest good, to a chaotic and evil material world. To the Ophites, the human dilemma resulted from humans being a mixture of these conflicting spiritual and material elements. Only gnosis, the esoteric knowledge of GOOD AND EVIL, could redeem humans from the bonds of matter and make them aware of the unknown God who was the true source of all being.

The Ophites regarded the JEHOVAH of the OLD TESTAMENT as merely a DEMIURGE—a subordinate deity who had created the material world. They attached special importance to the serpent in the biblical book of GENESIS because he had enabled men to obtain the all-important knowledge of good and evil that Jehovah had withheld from them. Accordingly, the serpent was a true liberator of mankind, since he first taught humans to rebel against Jehovah and to seek knowledge of the true, unknown God. The Ophites regarded the Christ as a purely spiritual being who through his union with the man Jesus taught the saving gnosis. *See* GNOSTICISM.

OPUS DEI \'ō-pəs-'dē-,ī, -'dā-ē\ (Latin: "God's Work"), ROMAN CATHOLIC organization of laymen and priests whose members pledge to seek personal Christian perfection and strive to implement Christian ideals in their chosen occupations. It is conservative with respect to theological and disciplinary loyalty to the teaching authority of the church. There are separate organizations for men and women, which, since 1982, have been headed by a PRELATE appointed by the pope.

Opus Dei was founded in 1928 in Spain by Josemaría Escrivá de Balaguer y Albás (b. Jan. 9, 1902—d. June 26, 1975; beatified 1992), a priest with both legal and journalistic training. Opus Dei was definitively approved by the Holy See in 1950. On Nov. 28, 1982, Pope John Paul II established Opus Dei as a personal prelature with the title Prelature of the Holy Cross and Opus Dei. This new status is analogous to that of a DIOCESE.

Most of the members of Opus Dei are supernumeraries—workers who may be married or single. Certain members, called numeraries, must be unmarried and prepared to devote a large part of their time to the organization. All members serve a period of probation. The organization is assisted by cooperators, who are not members and, by permission of the Holy See, need not even be Christians.

Opus Dei has counted a number of highly educated persons of acknowledged ability among its members, and Spain's leader, Generalissimo Francisco Franco, turned to some of these individuals for help in 1956 following his decision to implement a program of economic reform. In his final years, several cabinet members belonged to Opus Dei. After the death of Franco in 1975, the influence of Opus Dei members waned as other parties and associations began to compete in the political arena.

Opus Dei founded and endowed (with government assistance) the University of Navarre, which has come to be regarded by many as the best university in Spain. The organization also operates a university in Piura, Peru, as well as conference centers and presses in other countries.

ORACLE (Latin *oraculum,* from *orare,* "to pray to," or "to supplicate"), divine communication delivered in response to a petitioner's request; also, the seat of PROPHECY itself. Oracles were a branch of DIVINATION but differed from the casual pronouncements of augurs by being associated with a definite person or place.

Oracular shrines were numerous in antiquity, and at each the god was consulted by a fixed means of divination. The method could be simple, such as the casting of lots or the rustling of tree leaves, or more sophisticated, taking the form of a direct inquiry of an inspired person who then gave the answer orally. One of the most common methods was incubation, in which the inquirer slept in a holy precinct and received an answer in a dream.

The most famous ancient oracle was that of APOLLO at DELPHI, located on the slopes of Mt. Parnassus above the Corinthian Gulf. Traditionally, the oracle first belonged to Mother Earth (GAEA) but later was either given to or stolen by Apollo. At Delphi the medium was a woman over fifty, known as the Pythia, who lived apart from her husband and dressed in a maiden's clothes. The Pythia's counsel was most in demand to forecast the outcome of projected wars or political actions.

Consultations were normally restricted to the seventh day of the Delphic month, Apollo's birthday, and were at first banned during the three winter months when Apollo was believed to be visiting the HYPERBOREANS in the north, though DIONYSUS later took Apollo's place at Delphi during that time. In the usual procedure, sponsors were necessary,

as was the provision of a *pelanos* (ritual cake) and a sacrificial beast that conformed to rigid physical standards. The Pythia and her consultants first bathed in the Castalian spring; afterward, she drank from the sacred spring Cassotis and then entered the temple. There she apparently descended into a basement cell, mounted a sacred tripod, and chewed leaves of the laurel, Apollo's sacred tree. While in her abnormal state, the Pythia would speak, intelligibly or otherwise. Her words were interpreted and written down by the priests in what was often highly ambiguous verse.

There were less frequented oracles at Thebes, Tegyra, and Ptoon in Boeotia, at Abae in Phocis, at Corope in Thessaly, and on Delos, Apollo's birthplace. In Anatolia the god's oracles at Patara, Branchidae, CLAROS, and Grynium were well known, though none rivaled Delphi.

The oracle of ZEUS at DODONA in northwestern Greece was regarded as the oldest. At Dodona the priests (later priestesses) revealed the god's will from the whispering of the leaves on a sacred oak, from a sacred spring, and from the striking of a gong. Zeus also prophesied from his altar at OLYMPIA, where priests divined from offerings, as well as from the oasis of Siwa in Libya, which was originally an oracle of the Egyptian god AMON.

Oracles delivered through incubation were believed to come from chthonian (underworld) powers. Thus invalids slept in the hall of ASCLEPIUS, the god of medicine, at Epidaurus and claimed to receive cures through dreams. At the oracle of the hero Amphiaraus at Oropus in Attica, consultants slept on skins, while visitors to the oracle of Trophonius (son of Erginus the ARGONAUT) at Levádhia slept in a hole in the ground. Incubation was also practiced at the oracle of Dionysus at Amphicleia. An oracle for consulting the dead existed beside the river Acheron in central Greece.

Oracles in the formal sense were generally confined to the classical world. The Egyptians, however, divined from the motion of images paraded through the streets, and the Hebrews from sacred objects and dreams. Babylonian temple prophetesses also interpreted dreams. In Italy the lot oracle of FORTUNA Primigenia at Praeneste was consulted even by the emperors. The goddess Albunea possessed a dream oracle at Tibur (Tivoli), and the incubation rites of the god FAUNUS resembled those of Amphiaraus.

ORACLE BONES, name given to Shang-period animal scapular bones and tortoise shells inscribed with the archaic Chinese script. These objects were ritual implements used in DIVINATION and were under the charge of a specialized group of diviners who were charged by the Shang king to prognosticate the fortunes of the state. These materials show the presence of a developed cult of ancestors and a theocratic concern for maintaining a harmonious relationship between the world of the living and the dead.

ORAL TRADITION, transmission of cultural values by word of mouth. Songs, stories, proverbs, epics and rituals are the most obvious forms used in the transmission of oral culture. Oral tradition is usually contrasted with textual tradition. The study of oral traditions as an academic discipline is quite new; *The Journal of Oral Tradition* was founded in 1986. John Miles Foley, *The Theory of Oral Composition: History and Methodology* (1988) remains the most useful overview and bibliography of the work in oral tradition.

ORDINATION, in Christian churches, a rite for the dedication and commissioning of ministers. The essential ceremony consists of the laying of hands of the ordaining minister upon the head of the one being ordained, with prayer for the gifts of the HOLY SPIRIT and of GRACE required for the carrying out of the ministry. The service also usually includes a public examination of the candidate and a sermon or charge concerning the responsibilities of the ministry.

CHRISTIANITY derived the ceremony from the Jewish custom of ordaining RABBIS by the laying on of hands (the *Semikha*). According to the Pastoral Letters (1 Timothy 4:14; 2 Timothy 1:6), ordination confers a spiritual gift of grace. The oldest ordination prayers extant are contained in the *Apostolic Tradition* of HIPPOLYTUS of Rome (*c.* 217 CE). In medieval times the Latin rites were elaborated by the addition of various prayers and of such ceremonies as the anointing of hands, clothing the ordinand with the appropriate vestments, and presenting him with the symbols pertinent to his rank; *e.g.*, the Gospels to a deacon and the CHALICE and paten with the bread and wine to a candidate for the PRIESTHOOD. The rites of ordination in the ROMAN CATHOLIC church were considerably simplified in 1968.

In churches that have retained the historic episcopate, including the Anglican church, the ordaining minister is always a bishop. In PRESBYTERIAN CHURCHES, ordination is conferred by ministers of the presbytery. In the Reformed Protestant tradition lay persons are ordained to be ruling elders and deacons by the minister joined by others so ordained previously. In Congregational churches ordination is conducted by persons chosen by the local congregation.

According to Eastern Orthodox and Roman Catholic theology, ordination (holy orders) is a SACRAMENT essential to the church, and it bestows an unrepeatable, indelible character upon the person ordained.

Orestes being purified by Apollo after his acquittal by the court of the Aeropagus, detail of a 5th-century-BCE Greek vase; in the Louvre, Paris
Alinari—Art Resource

ORESTES \ȯ-'res-tēz\, in Greek mythology, son of AGAMEMNON and his wife, Clytemnestra. According to Homer, Orestes was away when his father returned from Troy and met his death at the hands of Aegisthus, his wife's lover. On reaching manhood, Orestes avenged his father by killing Aegisthus and Clytemnestra.

In Aeschylus' *Oresteia,* Orestes killed his mother in accordance with Apollo's commands; he posed as a stranger with tidings of his own death, and, after killing her, he found his way to Athens and pleaded his case before the Areopagus. The jury divided equally, ATHENA gave her deciding vote for acquittal, and the FURIES were placated by being given the epithet Eumenides (kindly goddesses).

In Euripides' play *Iphigenia in Tauris* some of the Furies remained unappeased, and Orestes was ordered by APOLLO to go to Tauris and bring the statue of ARTEMIS back to Athens. Accompanied by his friend Pylades, they were arrested on arrival because it was the local custom to sacrifice all strangers to the goddess. The priestess in charge of the sacrifice was Orestes' sister Iphigeneia; they recognized each other and escaped together, taking the statue with them. Orestes inherited his father's kingdom, adding to it Argos and Lacedaemon. He married Hermione, daughter of HELEN and MENELAUS, and eventually died of snakebite.

ORIENTAL JEW, *Hebrew* Ben Ha-Mizraḥ \,ben-hä-mēz-'räk\ ("Son of the East"), *plural* Bene Ha-Mizraḥ, any of the approximately 1,500,000 Diaspora Jews who lived for several centuries in North Africa and the Middle East. This group is distinct from the two other major groups of Diaspora Jews—the ASHKENAZI and the SEPHARDI.

In Morocco, Algeria, Tunisia, Libya, Egypt, Yemen, Jordan, Lebanon, Iraq, and Syria, Oriental Jews speak Arabic as their native tongue. In Iran, Afghanistan, and Bukhara they speak Farsi (Persian), whereas in Kurdistan their language is a variant of ancient Aramaic. Some Oriental Jews migrated to India, other parts of Central Asia, and China. In some Oriental Jewish communities (notably those of Yemen and Iran), polygyny has been practiced. Following the establishment of the state of Israel in 1948, practically all the Yemenite, Iraqi, and Libyan Jews and major parts of the other Oriental Jewish communities migrated to Israel.

ORIGEN \'ȯr-i-jən\, *Latin in full* Oregenes Adamantius \ȯ-'ri-jə-,nēz-,a-də-'man-shē-əs\ (b. *c.* 185, probably Alexandria, Egypt—d. *c.* 254, Tyre, Phoenicia [now Ṣūr, Lebanon]), the most important theologian and biblical scholar of the early Greek church. His most massive work was the *Hexapla,* a parallel edition of six versions of the OLD TESTAMENT.

Eusebius stated that Origen's father, Leonides, was martyred in the persecution of 202, so that Origen had to provide for his mother and six younger brothers. He earned money by teaching grammar and lived a life of strenuous ASCETICISM. Eusebius added that he was a pupil of CLEMENT OF ALEXANDRIA, whom he succeeded as head of the Catechetical school under the authority of the bishop Demetrius. Eusebius also alleged that Origen, as a young man, castrated himself so as to work freely in instructing female catechumens; but this may merely have been hostile gossip.

According to Porphyry, Origen attended lectures given by Ammonius Saccas, the founder of NEOPLATONISM. A letter of Origen mentions his "teacher of philosophy," at whose lectures he met Heraclas, who was to become his junior colleague, then his rival. During this period (from *c.* 212), Origen learned Hebrew and began to compile his *Hexapla.* At Alexandria he wrote *Stromateis* (*Miscellanies*), *Peri anastaseos* (*On the Resurrection*), and *De principiis* (*On First Principles*). He also began his immense commentary on ST. JOHN, written to refute the commentary of the Gnostic follower of VALENTINUS, HERACLEON.

About 229–230 Origen went to Greece to dispute with another follower of Valentinus, Candidus. On the way he was ordained PRESBYTER at Caesarea Palestinae. The Valentinian doctrine that salvation and damnation are predestinate, independent of volition, was defended by Candidus on the ground that SATAN is beyond repentance; Origen replied that if Satan fell by will, even he can repent. Demetrius, bishop of Alexandria, was appalled by such a doctrinal view and instigated a synodical condemnation, which, however, was not accepted in Greece and Palestine. Thenceforth, Origen lived at Caesarea, where he attracted many pupils. One of his most notable students was Gregory Thaumaturgus, later bishop of Neocaesarea.

Origen's main lifework was on the text of the Greek Old Testament and on the exposition of the whole BIBLE. The *Hexapla* was a synopsis of Old Testament versions: the Hebrew and a transliteration, the SEPTUAGINT, the versions of Aquila, Symmachus, and Theodotion and, for the Psalms, two further translations (one being discovered by him in a jar in the Jordan Valley). The purpose of the *Hexapla* was to provide a secure basis for debate with RABBIS to whom the Hebrew alone was authoritative.

Origen's great apologetic work, *Contra Celsum*, written (probably in 248) at Ambrose's request, answers the *Alēthēs logos* ("The True Doctrine" or "Discourse") of the 2nd-century anti-Christian philosopher Celsus and is therefore a principal source for the PAGAN intelligentsia's view of 2nd-century CHRISTIANITY. Celsus' dismissal of Christianity as a crude and bucolic onslaught on the religious traditions and intellectual values of classical culture provoked Origen to argue that a philosophic mind has a right to think within a Christian framework and that the Christian faith is neither a prejudice of the unreasoning masses nor a crutch for social outcasts or nonconformists.

Everything in Origen's theology ultimately turns upon the goodness of God and the freedom of the creature. The transcendent God is the source of all existence and is good, just, and omnipotent. In overflowing love, God created rational and spiritual beings through the LOGOS (Word); this creative act involves a degree of self-limitation on God's part. In one sense, the cosmos is eternally necessary to God since one cannot conceive such goodness and power as inactive at any time. Yet in another sense, the cosmos is not necessary to God but is dependent on his will, to which it also owes its continued existence. Origen was aware that there is no solution of this dilemma.

Origen speculated that souls fell varying distances, some to be ANGELS, some descending into human bodies, and the most wicked becoming devils. Redemption is a grand education by Providence that restores all souls to their original blessedness, for no one, not even Satan himself, is so depraved and has so lost rationality and freedom as to be beyond redemption.

The influence of Origen's biblical EXEGESIS and ascetic ideals is hard to overestimate; his commentaries were freely plagiarized by later exegetes, both Eastern and Western, and he is a seminal mind for the beginnings of MONASTICISM. Through the writings of the monk EVAGRIUS PONTICUS (346–399), his ideas passed not only into the Greek ascetic tradition but also to John Cassian (360–435), a semi-Pelagian monk (who emphasized the worth of man's moral effort), and to the West. He was often attacked, suspected of adulterating the Gospel with pagan philosophy and his teachings were condemned by the Second COUNCIL OF CONSTANTINOPLE (553). Nevertheless, Origen's influence persisted, such as in the writings of the Byzantine monk Maximus the Confessor (*c.* 550–662) and the Irish theologian John Scotus Erigena (*c.* 810–877).

ORIGINAL SIN, in Christian doctrine, condition or state of SIN into which each human being is born; also, the origin, or cause, of this state. Traditionally, the origin has been ascribed to the sin of ADAM, who disobeyed God in eating the forbidden fruit and, in consequence, transmitted his sin and guilt by heredity to his descendants.

Although the human condition (suffering, death, and a universal tendency toward sin) is accounted for by the story of the fall of Adam in the early chapters of the book of GENESIS, the OLD TESTAMENT says nothing about the transmission of hereditary sin to the entire human race. In the GOSPELS also there are no more than allusions to the notion of the Fall of Man and universal sin. The main scriptural affirmation of the doctrine is found in the writings of ST. PAUL and particularly in Romans 5:12–19, a difficult passage in which Paul establishes a parallelism between Adam and JESUS CHRIST, stating that whereas sin and death entered the world through Adam, GRACE and eternal life have come in greater abundance through Christ.

ST. AUGUSTINE's controversy with the Pelagians (*see also* PELAGIUS) helped to fix the sinful state of humanity as a central element of orthodox Christian theology.

ORION \ȯ-'rī-ən\, in Greek mythology, GIANT and very handsome hunter who was identified as early as Homer with the constellation known by his name.

The story of Orion has many different versions. He is considered to be Boeotian by birth, born (according to a late legend) of the earth (from a buried bull hide on which three gods had urinated). Some legends have him as the son of POSEIDON. He is associated with the island of Chios, from which he is said to have driven the wild beasts. There he fell in love with Merope, daughter of the king of Chios. The king, who disapproved of Orion and continually deferred the nuptials, eventually had Orion blinded.

His vision restored by the rays of the rising sun, Orion is said to have gone to Crete to live with ARTEMIS as a hunter. Accounts of his death vary widely: some have him a victim of Artemis' jealousy, others of Apollo's jealousy over Artemis' love of Orion; still others have him killed by a scorpion. After his death he was placed among the stars.

ORPHEUS \'ȯr-fē-əs, -ˌfyüs\, ancient Greek hero endowed with superhuman musical skills. He became the patron of a religious movement based on sacred writings that were said to be his own.

Traditionally, Orpheus was the son of a MUSE and Oeagrus, a king of Thrace (other versions give APOLLO). According to some tales, Apollo gave Orpheus his first lyre. Orpheus' singing and playing were so beautiful that animals, trees, and rocks danced about him.

Orpheus was one of the ARGONAUTS, and he saved them from the music of the SIRENS by playing his own music. On his return, he married EURYDICE, who was soon killed by a snakebite. Overcome with grief, Orpheus attempted to bring Eurydice back from the land of the dead. With his singing and playing he charmed the ferryman CHARON and the dog Cerberus. His music and grief so moved HADES that Orpheus was allowed to take Eurydice back with him. Hades set one condition, however: upon leaving the land of death, both Orpheus and Eurydice were forbidden to look back. The couple climbed up toward the opening into the land of the living, and Orpheus, seeing the sun again, turned back to share his delight with Eurydice. In that moment, she disappeared.

Orpheus himself was killed by the women of Thrace.

The earliest known account, that of Aeschylus, says that they were Maenads urged by DIONYSUS to tear him to pieces in a Bacchic orgy because he preferred the worship of the rival god Apollo. His head, still singing, with his lyre, floated to Lesbos, where an ORACLE of Orpheus was established. The head prophesied until the oracle became more famous than that of Apollo at DELPHI, at which time Apollo bade the Orphic oracle stop. The dismembered limbs of Orpheus were gathered up and buried by the Muses. His lyre they placed in the heavens as a constellation.

A MYSTERY RELIGION based on the teachings and songs of Orpheus is thought to have arisen in ancient Greece, although no coherent description of such a religion can be constructed from historical evidence. By the 5th century BCE there was at least an Orphic movement, with traveling priests who offered teaching and initiation, based on a body of legend and doctrine said to have been founded by Orpheus. Orphic ESCHATOLOGY laid great stress on rewards and punishment after bodily death, the soul then being freed to achieve its true life.

ORTHODOX, true doctrine and its adherents as opposed to heterodox or heretical doctrines and their adherents. The word was first used in early 4th-century CHRISTIANITY by the Greek Fathers. Because almost every religious group believes that it holds the true faith (though not necessarily exclusively), the meaning of "orthodox" in a particular instance can be correctly determined only after examination of the context in which it appears. More conservative movements within a particular religious tradition may lay exclusive claim to orthodoxy so as to distance themselves from the reforms or institutions of competing movements.

The term *orthodox* forms part of the official titles of the Eastern Orthodox church, those in communion with it, and some of the smaller Eastern churches; because the Greek word *doxa* can mean either "teaching" or "praise," Eastern Orthodox Christianity (*Pravoslavie*, in the Slavic languages) defines itself as both "right teaching" and "right worship." Within JUDAISM, ORTHODOX JUDAISM is the mainline tradition that adheres most strictly to ancient tradition. The term is also used to distinguish true Islamic doctrine from allegedly heretical teachings, such as those of the Muʿtazilites. The term evangelical orthodoxy is commonly applied to Protestant Christianity that insists on the full or literal authority and inerrancy of the BIBLE.

ORTHODOX CHURCH: *see* EASTERN ORTHODOXY.

ORTHODOX JUDAISM, in common parlance, "traditional," or "observant," JUDAISM. More accurately, the diversity of Orthodox Judaisms requires differentiation into subdivisions, for no single organizational structure encompasses all its religious worlds. Nonetheless, all Orthodox Judaisms can be said to affirm the divine revelation of the TORAH by God to MOSES at Sinai, to concur on the dual character of the revelation (oral and written), and to accept the authority of the sages of the TALMUD as participants in the process of the revelation of the Torah at Sinai.

Orthodox Judaism was first articulated by Jews who rejected the initiatives of REFORM JUDAISM and made a self-conscious decision to remain within the way of life and world view that they had known and cherished all their lives. They framed the issues in terms of change and history. The Reformers held that Judaism could change—that it was a product of history. The Orthodox opponents denied this, insisting that Judaism derived from God's will at Sinai and was eternal and supernatural, not historical and manmade.

One critical criterion for distinguishing among communities of Orthodox belief is social. Some Judaisms of the dual Torah maintain that holy Israel should live wholly apart from GENTILES, segregating itself socially and culturally. Other Judaisms of the dual Torah—the so-called "modern" or "Western" Orthodoxy—differ by affirming social and cultural integration into Western culture, maintaining that one may both keep the law of the Torah and participate in the politics and affairs of the secular world. Integrationist and, later on, Zionist Orthodox Judaism came into being in Germany in the middle of the 19th century. In the state of Israel segregationist Orthodoxy competes with Zionist and integrationist Orthodoxy, the former in great *yeshivot,* the latter at Bar Ilan University. The former maintains its own educational system, while the latter runs the "state-religious" schools. Each Judaism has its own political party as well. In the United States and in western Europe integrationist Orthodoxy predominates.

Another point of differentiation centers on the issues of ZIONISM and the state of Israel. Some Orthodox Judaisms completely reject the legitimacy of the state of Israel as the Jewish state; some accept the state of Israel as a secular fact; and some affirm the state of Israel as a chapter in the story of the coming of the MESSIAH in time to come.

OSIRIS \ō-'sī-rəs\, *also called* Usiri, one of the most important gods of ancient EGYPTIAN RELIGION. Osiris was a local god of BUSIRIS, in Lower Egypt, and may have been a personification of Underworld fertility, or possibly he was a deified hero. By about 2400 BCE, however, Osiris clearly played a double role: he was both a god of fertility and the embodiment of the dead and resurrected king within the Egyptian concept of divine kingship. The king after his death became Osiris, god of the Underworld, and the dead king's son, the living king, was identified with HORUS, a god of the sky. The goddess ISIS was the mother of the king and was thus the mother of Horus and consort of Osiris. The god SETH was considered the murderer of Osiris and adversary of Horus.

According to the form of the myth reported by the Greek author Plutarch, Osiris was slain or drowned by Seth, who tore the corpse into 14 pieces and flung them over Egypt. Eventually, Isis and her sister Nephthys found and buried all the pieces, except the phallus, thereby giving new life to Osiris, who thenceforth remained in the Underworld as ruler and judge. Isis revived Osiris by magical means and conceived her son Horus by him. Horus later successfully fought against Seth and became the new king of Egypt.

Bronze figurine of Osiris; in the Egyptian Museum, Berlin
By courtesy of the Staatliche Museen Preussischer Kulturbesitz, Berlin; photograph, Art Resource

Osiris was not only ruler of the dead but also the power that granted all life from the Underworld, from sprouting vegetation to the annual flood of the Nile River. From about 2000 BCE onward it was believed that every man, not just the deceased kings, became associated with Osiris at death. This identification with Osiris, however, did not imply RESURRECTION, but rather the renewal of life both in the next world and through one's descendants on earth. In this universalized form Osiris' cult spread throughout Egypt, often joining with the cults of local fertility and Underworld deities.

The idea that rebirth in the next life could be gained by following Osiris was maintained through certain cult forms. In the Middle Kingdom the god's festivals consisted of processions and nocturnal rites and were celebrated at the temple of ABYDOS, where Osiris had assimilated the very ancient god of the dead, Khenty-Imentin. This name, meaning "Foremost of the Westerners," was adopted by Osiris as an epithet. Because the festivals took place in the open, public participation was permitted, and by the early 2nd millennium BCE it became fashionable to be buried on the processional road at Abydos or to erect a cenotaph there as a representative of the dead.

Osiris festivals symbolically reenacting the god's fate were celebrated annually in various towns throughout Egypt. A central feature of the festivals was the construction of the "Osiris garden," a mold in the shape of Osiris, filled with soil and various drugs. The mold was moistened with the water of the Nile and sown with grain. Later, the sprouting grain symbolized the vital strength of Osiris.

At Memphis the holy bull, APIS, was linked with Osiris, becoming Osiris-Apis, which eventually became the name of the Hellenistic god SARAPIS. Greco-Roman authors connected Osiris with the god DIONYSUS. Osiris was also identified with Soker, an ancient Memphite god of the dead.

The oldest known depiction of Osiris dates to about 2300 BCE, but representations of him are rare before the New Kingdom (1539–1075 BCE), when he was shown in an archaizing form as a MUMMY with his arms crossed on his breast, one hand holding a crook, the other a flail. On his head was the atef-crown, composed of the white crown of Upper Egypt and two ostrich feathers.

OSSIAN \ˈä-shən, ˈȯ-; ˈä-sē-ən\, *Gaelic* Oisín \ˈō-shēn\, Irish warrior-poet of the Fenian cycle of hero tales about Finn and his war band, the Fianna Éireann.

The name Ossian became known throughout Europe in 1762, when the Scottish poet James Macpherson "discovered" the poems of Oisín and published the epic *Fingal* and the following year *Temora*, supposedly translations from 3rd-century Gaelic originals. Actually, although based in part on genuine Gaelic ballads, the works were largely the invention of Macpherson. These poems won wide acclaim and were a central influence in the early Romantic movement. They infuriated Irish scholars because they mixed Fenian and Ulster legends indiscriminately and because Macpherson claimed that the Irish heroes were Caledonians and therefore a glory to Scotland's past, rather than to Ireland's.

The Ossianic controversy was finally settled in the late 19th century, when it was demonstrated that the only Gaelic originals that Macpherson had been able to produce were translations in a barbarous Gaelic of his own English compositions. The name Ossian, popularized by Macpherson, superseded Oisín, though they are often used interchangeably. The term Ossianic ballads refers to genuine late Gaelic poems that form part of the common Scots-Irish Gaelic tradition.

OTTO, RUDOLF \ˈȯ-tō, ˈä-\ (b. Sept. 25, 1869, Peine, Prussia—d. March 6, 1937, Marburg, Ger.), German theologian, philosopher, and historian of religions, who exerted wide influence through his investigation of RELIGIOUS EXPERIENCE.

Otto studied theology and philosophy at the University of Erlangen and, later, at the University of Göttingen, where he was made a *Privatdozent* ("lecturer") in 1897, teaching theology, history of religions, and history of philosophy. From 1904 to 1914 he was professor of systematic theology at Göttingen, after which he became professor of theology at the University of Breslau. In 1917 he became professor of systematic theology at the University of Marburg and for one year (1926–27) served as rector of the university. He retired from his university post in 1929. Otto was a liberal and progressive member of the Prussian Parliament from 1913 to 1918 and a member of the Constituent Chamber in 1918, and he participated widely in Christian ecumenical activities.

Rudolf Otto, 1925
Foto—Jannasch, Marburg/L.

Otto's study of the life and thought of MARTIN LUTHER prompted his concern to elucidate the distinctive character of the religious interpretation of the world, reflected in his first book, *Die Anschauung vom heiligen Geiste bei Luther* (1898; "The Perception of the Holy Spirit by Luther"). He was to expand his inquiry in his book, *Naturalistische und religiöse Weltansicht* (1904; *Naturalism and Religion*), in which he contrasted the naturalistic and the religious ways of interpreting the world and raised the question of whether their contradictions can be or should be reconciled. The sciences and the religious interpretation, he insisted, are to be heeded for what they purport to disclose concerning the world in which we live. Otto's principal concern, however, was to justify what the religious interpretation of the world conveys as a distinctive dimension of understanding beyond the discoveries of the sciences. In *Kantische-Fries'sche Religionsphilosophie* (1909; *The Philosophy of Religion Based on Kant and Fries*), a discussion of the religious thought of the German philosophers Immanuel Kant and Jacob Friedrich Fries, he sought to specify the kind of rationality that is appropriate to religious inquiry.

During 1911–12 Otto visited North Africa, Egypt, and Palestine, continued to India, China, and Japan, and returned by way of the United States. His travels turned him to an exploration of religious experience among various religions of the world. He was well equipped for such an exploration; in addition to being at home with the languages of Near Eastern religions, he had mastered Sanskrit sufficiently to translate many ancient Hindu texts into German as well as to write several volumes comparing Indian and Christian religious thought.

Initially in his studies Otto gave particular attention to the thought of the German Protestant theologian FRIEDRICH SCHLEIERMACHER. Schleiermacher perceived religion as a unique feeling or awareness, distinct from ethical and rational modes of perception, though not exclusive of them. Schleiermacher was later to speak of this feeling as one of "absolute dependence." At first impressed by this formulation, Otto later criticized it on the grounds that what Schleiermacher had pointed to was merely a close analogy with ordinary, or "natural," feelings of dependence. For "absolute dependence" Otto substituted "creature-feeling," a feeling which points to some object outside of the self. Otto called this object "the numinous" or "Wholly Other"—*i.e.*, that which utterly transcends the mundane sphere, roughly equivalent to "supernatural" and "transcendent" in traditional usage.

In *Das Heilige* (1917; *The Idea of the Holy*) Otto sought to explore this idea of the numinous (from the Latin *numen* ["divine power," or "deity"]), which he considered to be the nonrational aspect of the religious dimension, the awe-inspiring element of religious experience that, Otto contended, evades precise verbal formulation. His concern was to attend to that elemental experience of apprehending the numinous itself. In such moments of apprehension, said Otto, "we are dealing with something for which there is only one appropriate expression, *mysterium tremendum*."

Although the *mysterium*, the form of the numinous experience, is beyond conception, it can be experienced in feelings that convey the qualitative content of the numinous experience. This content presents itself under two aspects: (1) that of "daunting awfulness and majesty," and (2) "as something uniquely attractive and *fascinating*." From the former comes the sense of the uncanny, of divine wrath and judgment; from the latter, the reassuring and heightening experiences of GRACE and divine love.

Otto took all religions seriously as occasions to experience the holy yet had much respect for their distinctive characteristics. He argued for a lively exchange between representatives of the various religions, in service of which he created the Religious Collection in Marburg, including religious symbols, rituals, and apparatus from around the world.

OUIJA BOARD \'wē-jə, -jē\, in OCCULTISM, device ostensibly used for obtaining messages from the spirit world, usually employed by a medium during a SÉANCE. The name derives from the French and German words for "yes" (*oui* and *ja*). The Ouija board consists of an oblong piece of wood with letters of the alphabet inscribed along its longer edge in a wide half-moon. On top of this is placed a much smaller, heart-shaped board, or planchette, mounted on casters, which enable it to slide freely.

Each participant lightly places a finger on the planchette, which then slides about because of the resultant pressure. The letters pointed out by the apex of the board may in some instances spell out words or even sentences. In the late 19th century, when the Ouija board was a popular pastime, it was fashionable to ascribe such happenings to spirits; more recent opinion is skeptical.

OURANIA \ü-'rā-nē-ə\, *also spelled* Urania \yù-\, in GREEK RELIGION, one of the nine MUSES, patron of astronomy. In some accounts she was the mother of LINUS the musician (in other versions, his mother is the Muse CALLIOPE); the father was either HERMES or Amphimarus, son of POSEIDON. Her attributes were the globe and compass.

OURANUS \'ùr-ə-nəs, ü-'rā-\, *also spelled* Uranus \'yùr-ə-nəs, yù-'rā-\, in Greek mythology, the personification of heaven. According to Hesiod's *Theogony*, GAEA, emerging from primeval CHAOS, produced Ouranus, the Mountains, and the Sea. From Gaea's union with Ouranus were born the TITANS, the Cyclopes, and the Hecatoncheires.

Ouranus hated his offspring and hid them in Gaea's body. She appealed to them for vengeance, but CRONUS alone responded. With the *harpē* (a scythe) Cronus castrated Ouranus as he approached Gaea. From the drops of Ouranus' blood that fell on Earth were born the FURIES, the GIANTS, and the Meliai (ash-tree NYMPHS). The severed genitals floated on the sea, producing a white foam, from which sprang the goddess APHRODITE. Cronus by his action had separated Heaven and Earth. Ouranus also had other consorts: HESTIA, NYX, Hemera, and Clymene.

The story of the castration of Ouranus bears a close resemblance to the Hittite myth of Kumarbi.

OUROBOROS \ü-'rä-bə-rəs\, emblematic serpent of ancient Egypt and Greece represented with its tail in its mouth continually devouring itself and being reborn. A Gnostic and alchemical symbol, Ouroboros expresses the unity of all things, material and spiritual, which perpetually change form in an eternal cycle of destruction and re-creation.

In the 19th century, a vision of Ouroboros gave the German chemist Friedrich August Kekule von Stradonitz the idea of linked carbon atoms forming the benzene ring.

OXFORD MOVEMENT \'äks-fərd\, 19th-century movement centered at the University of Oxford that sought a renewal of ROMAN CATHOLIC thought and practice within the Church of England (*see* ANGLICAN COMMUNION) in opposition to the church's Protestant tendencies. From 1828 to 1832, laws that required members of municipal corporations and government-office holders to receive the EUCHARIST in the Church of England were repealed, and a law was passed that removed most of the restrictions formerly imposed on Roman Catholics. For a short time it seemed possible that the Church of England might be disestablished and that it might lose its endowments. Consequently, many loyal Anglicans wished to assert that the Church of England was not dependent on the state and that it gained its authority from the fact that it taught Christian truth and its bishops were able to trace their authority and office back in an unbroken line to the APOSTLES. The movement rapidly became involved in theological, pastoral, and devotional problems.

Leaders of the movement were JOHN HENRY NEWMAN (1801–90), a clergyman and subsequently a convert to Roman Catholicism and a cardinal; Richard Hurrell Froude (1803–36), a clergyman; John Keble (1792–1866), a clergyman and poet; and Edward Pusey (1800–82), a clergyman and professor at Oxford.

The ideas of the movement were published in 90 *Tracts for the Times* (1833–41), 24 of which were written by Newman, who edited the entire series. The Tractarians asserted the doctrinal authority of the Catholic church to be absolute, and by "catholic" they understood that which was faithful to the teaching of the early and undivided church. They believed the Church of England to be such a church.

The movement gradually spread its influence throughout the Church of England. Some of the results were increased use of ceremony and ritual in church worship, the establishment of Anglican monastic communities for men and for women, and better-educated clergy who were more concerned with pastoral care of their church members.

PACHACAMAC \pä-'chä-kä-,mäk\, creator deity who, along with his consort Pachamama (Mother of the Earth), was worshiped by the pre-Inca maritime population of Peru; it was also the name of a PILGRIMAGE site in the Lurín Valley (south of Lima) dedicated to the god. Pachacamac was believed to be a god of fire and a son of the sun god; he rejuvenated the world originally created by the god VIRACOCHA and taught men the crafts. Pachacamac was also believed to be invisible and thus was never represented in art. After the INCAS conquered the coast, they incorporated Pachacamac into their own pantheon.

The ruins of the shrine in the Lurín Valley include several PYRAMIDS and TEMPLES and are partially restored.

PACHACUTI INCA YUPANQUI \,pä-chä-'kü-tē-'iŋ-kə-yù-'päŋ-kē\, *also called* Pachacutec \,pä-chä-'kü-tek\ (fl. 15th century), INCA emperor (1438–71), an empire builder who, because he initiated the swift, far-ranging expansion of the Inca state, has been likened to Philip II of Macedonia. (Similarly, his son Topa Inca Yupanqui is regarded as a counterpart of Philip's son Alexander III the Great.)

Pachacuti first conquered various peoples in what is now southern Peru and then extended his power northwesterly to Quito, Ecuador. He is said to have devised the city plan adopted for his capital, Cuzco (in present southern Peru).

PACHOMIUS, SAINT \pə-'kō-mē-əs\ (b. *c.* 290, probably in Upper Egypt—d. 346; feast day May 9), founder of Christian CENOBITIC MONASTICISM, whose rule for monks is the earliest extant.

Pachomius encountered Coptic CHRISTIANITY among his cohorts in the Roman emperor Constantine's North African army and, on leaving the military about 314, withdrew alone into the wilderness at Chenoboskion, near his Theban home. Soon after, he joined the HERMIT Palemon and a colony of anchorites in the same area at Tabennisi, on the east bank of the Nile River. Pachomius built the first monastic enclosure, replacing the scattered hermits' shelters, and he drew up a common daily program providing for proportioned periods of work and prayer patterned around a cooperative economic and disciplinary regimen.

This rule was the first instance in Christian monastic history of the use of a cenobitic, or uniform communal, habit as the norm, the first departure from the individualistic, exclusively CONTEMPLATIVE practice that had previously characterized religious life. Pachomius, moreover, instituted a monarchic structure that saw the religious superior's authority over the community as symbolic of God's evoking a response from man as he strives to overcome his egoism by self-denial and CHARITY. By the time he died, Pachomius had founded 11 monasteries, numbering more than 7,000 monks and nuns.

Though none of Pachomius' manuscripts has survived, his life and bibliography have been preserved by the 5th-century historian Palladius in his *Lausiac History*. The Rule of Pachomius is extant only in the early-5th-century Latin translation of ST. JEROME.

PADMASAMBHAVA \'pəd-mə-'səm-bə-və\, *also called* Guru Rin-po-che \'rim-bō-chā\, *Tibetan* Slob-dpon \'lō-bēn\ ("Teacher"), *or* Padma-'byung-gnas \'bā-mä-'jùŋ-nä\ ("Lotus Born") (fl. 8th century), legendary Indian Buddhist mystic who introduced VAJRAYĀNA (Tantric) BUDDHISM to Tibet.

Padmasambhava's background is a matter of controversy, though Tibetan sources suggest that he was a native of Udyāna (now in Pakistan). He was supposedly invited to come to Tibet by King Khri-srong-lde-brtsan (reigned 755–797) in the 8th century CE. In Tibet Padmasambhava is credited with quelling the local DEMONS, with helping to establish Bsam-yas, the nation's first Buddhist monastery, and with writing, translating, and lecturing on a number of important texts. The Tibetan Buddhist sect RNYING-MA-PA claims to follow his teachings most closely, emphasizing Vajrayāna ritual, worship, and YOGA. Texts basic to Rnying-ma-pa teachings that were said to have been buried by Padmasambhava, began to be found about 1125. He became an important figure in a number of Tibetan rituals concerned with the establishment and maintenance of Buddhism in Tibet.

PAGAN \'pā-gən\ (from Latin: *paganus,* "villager"), term often used as a synonym for "primitive," "uncivilized," or "heathen." It has been used primarily as a derogatory term and applied to those who followed polytheistic traditions rather than a monotheistic religion such as JUDAISM or CHRISTIANITY.

PAGAN \pə-'gän\, site of the old capital city of the kingdom of Pagan (now in Myanmar) and PILGRIMAGE center containing ancient Buddhist shrines, some of which have been restored and are in current use. Ruins of other shrines and PAGODAS cover a wide area. (An earthquake on July 8, 1975, severely damaged more than half the important structures, irreparably destroying many of them.)

Pagan's importance lies primarily in its heritage. It was probably first established in 849 CE, and, from the 11th century to the end of the 13th, it was the capital of a region roughly the size of modern Myanmar. Old Pagan was a walled city that probably originally contained only royal, aristocratic, religious, and administrative buildings. (The populace is thought to have lived outside the city walls.) The city, whose moats were fed by the Irrawaddy River, was thus a sacred dynastic fortress. The earliest surviving structure in the city is probably the 10th-century Nat Hlaung Gyaung. The shrines that stand by the Sarabha Gate in the eastern wall, although they are later than the wall they adjoin, are also of early date. These are shrines of protecting NATS—the traditional spirit deities of the ethnic Burmans.

Between about 500 and 950, people of the Burman ethnic

The Ananda Temple at Pagan, restored after the 1975 earthquake
Van Bucher—Photo Researchers

group had been infiltrating a southern region occupied by other peoples who had already appropriated some aspects of Indian religion, including many forms of BUDDHISM. Under King Anawrahta (reigned 1044–77), the ethnic Burmans finally conquered the other peoples of the region, including a people called the Mon, who were previously dominant in the south. In 1056 they transported the Mon royal family, Mon scholars and monks committed to the THERAVĀDA (Pāli) form of Buddhism, and Mon craftsmen to Pagan, where the Theravāda tradition received royal support. This initiated the period of Pagan's greatest achievements in the largely overlapping areas of politics, economics, religion, architecture, and art. The enormous number of monasteries and shrines built and maintained during the next 200 years was made possible both by great wealth and by large numbers of slaves, skilled and unskilled, whose working lives were dedicated to the support of each institution. The city became one of the most important centers of Buddhist learning.

Lesser buildings are grouped around the more important pagodas and temples. Scattered around these are smaller pagodas and buildings, some of which may once have been aristocratic palaces and pavilions later adapted to monastic uses—*e.g.*, as libraries and preaching halls. All are based on Indian prototypes, modified during subsequent develop-

ment by the Mon. The principal architectural form in Pagan is the STUPA, a tall bell-shaped dome, designed originally to contain near its apex the sacred relics of the Buddha or of Buddhist saints. Another prominent structural type is the high, terraced plinth (subbase) that symbolizes a sacred mountain. Many buildings, especially those that have been left undisturbed, bear substantial remnants of external stucco and terra-cotta decorations and internal paintings and terra-cottas that recount Buddhist legends and history.

Anawrahta oversaw construction of the Shwezigon Pagoda, along with a nearby shrine filled with images of *nat*s. The Shwezigon is a huge, terraced pyramid; square below and circular above, it is crowned by a bell-shaped stupa of traditional Mon shape and adorned with stairways, gates, and decorative spires. It is much revered and famous for its huge golden umbrella finial encrusted with jewels. (It was one of the structures damaged in the earthquake of 1975.) Also revered are the late 12th-century Mahābodhi Temple, which was built as a copy of the temple at the site of the Buddha's Enlightenment at BODH GAYĀ, and the Ananda Temple just beyond the east gate, founded in 1091 during the reign of King Kyanzittha. By the time the Thatpyinnyu Temple was built (1144), Mon influence was waning, and a Burman style of architecture had evolved. Thatpyinnyu has four stories and resembles a two-staged PYRAMID. Its interior rooms are spacious halls, rather than sparsely lit openings within a mountain mass as in the earlier style. This building functioned as stupa, temple, and monastery. The Burman style was further developed in the great Sulamani Temple and culminated in the Gawdawpalin Temple (late 12th century). The latter, which was dedicated to the ancestral spirits of the dynasty, had an exterior dotted with miniature pagodas and an interior decorated with lavishly colored ornamentation.

PAGODA: *see* STUPA.

PA-HSIEN \'bä-'shyen\, *Pinyin* Baxian, *English* Eight Immortals, in TAOISM, a group of saints, each of whom earned the right to immortality and had free access to the Peach Festival of HSI-WANG-MU, Queen Mother of the West. The eight are frequently depicted as a group. In Chinese art they sometimes also stand alone or appear in smaller groups. They are often associated with symbolic objects.

PAI-YÜN KUAN \\ˌbī-ˈywen-ˈgwän, -ˈywän-\, *Pinyin* Baiyunguan (Chinese: "White Cloud Temple"), major Taoist temple in Beijing, which was traditionally the center of the Lung-men subsect of the Ch'üan-chen, or Perfect Realization, school of TAOISM. Today it is the center of the state-controlled Taoist Association and is both a religious and a tourist attraction in Beijing.

PALAMAS, SAINT GREGORY \ˌpä-lä-ˈmäs\ (b. Nov. 11/14, 1296, Constantinople [now Istanbul, Tur.]—d. 1359, Thessalonica, Byzantine Empire [now in Greece]; canonized 1368), Orthodox monk, theologian, and intellectual leader of HESYCHASM (from the Greek word *hēsychia*, or "state of quiet"), an ascetical method of mystical prayer. Though controversial in Palamas' time, Hesychast spirituality is now sanctioned by the Orthodox church as a legitimate form of prayer.

Born of a distinguished family with ties to the imperial court, Palamas became a monk in 1316 at Mount Athos, the spiritual center of Greek Orthodoxy. For 25 years he immersed himself in study and reflection on the SCRIPTURES and the writings of the CHURCH FATHERS. He was introduced to CONTEMPLATIVE prayer by a spiritual master and in turn became a master for other initiates. Raids by the Turks about 1325 forced him to flee. He was ordained a priest in 1326 and later, with 10 companions, retired to a hermitage in Macedonia. He returned to Mount Athos in 1331 to the community of St. Sabas and about 1335 was chosen a religious superior (*hēgoumenos*) of a neighboring CONVENT. Because of differences with the monks who considered his spiritual regimen too strict, he resigned after a short term and returned to St. Sabas.

Beginning in 1332 Palamas entered into a lengthy theological dispute with a series of Greek and Latin scholastic theologians and certain rationalistic humanists. His first adversary was Barlaam the Calabrian, a Greek monk who denied that any rational concepts could express mystical prayer and its divine-human communication even metaphorically. Subsequently, Barlaam composed a satirical work defaming Hesychasm. Palamas responded to this attack by composing his "Apology for the Holy Hesychasts" (1338), also called the "Triad" because of its division into three parts.

The "Apology" established the theological basis for mystical experience that involves not only the human spirit but the entire human person, body and soul. Hesychast spirituality strove to bridge the gulf between human and divine existence. Hesychast prayer aspires to attain the most intense form of God-human communion in the form of a vision of the "divine light," or "uncreated energy," analogous to the Gospel account of Christ's Transfiguration on Mount Tabor, as noted in Matthew 16:17 and Mark 8:9. The corporeal disposition for this contemplative state involves intense concentration and a methodical invocation of the name of Jesus (the Hesychastic "Jesus prayer").

After a succession of public confrontations with critics, and a politically motivated EXCOMMUNICATION in 1344, Palamas had his teaching systematized in the *Hagioritic Tome* ("The Book of Holiness"), which became the fundamental textbook for Byzantine MYSTICISM. The Hesychast controversy became part of a larger Byzantine political struggle that erupted in civil war. At its conclusion in 1347, Palamas, with support from the conservative, anti-Zealot party, was appointed bishop of Thessalonica.

In his fusion of Platonic and Aristotelian philosophy, used as a vehicle to express his own spiritual experience, Palamas set a definitive standard for Orthodox theological acumen. At the provincial COUNCIL OF CONSTANTINOPLE in 1368, nine years after his death, he was acclaimed a saint and titled "Father and Doctor of the Orthodox Church," thus placing him among the ranks of those who determined the ideological shape of the Eastern church.

PALAMEDES \ˌpa-lə-ˈmē-dēz\, in Greek mythology, son of Nauplius, king of Euboea, and a hero of the Trojan War. Before the war he exposed the trickery of Odysseus—who had feigned madness to avoid military service—by placing the infant TELEMACHUS in the path of Odysseus' plow in the field and forcing him to reveal his sanity.

During the siege of Troy, Palamedes alternated with two other Greek heroes, ODYSSEUS and DIOMEDES, in leading the army in the field, but his ability aroused their envy. In one version the other two drowned Palamedes while fishing or persuaded him to seek treasure in a well, which they thereupon filled with stones. In another AGAMEMNON, Diomedes, and Odysseus had an agent steal into his tent and conceal a letter that contained money and purported to come from King PRIAM. They then accused Palamedes of treason, and he was stoned to death.

Palamedes had a reputation for sagacity, and a number of inventions were attributed to him, including the alphabet, numbers, weights and measures, coinage, and the practice of eating at regular intervals.

PALE (from Latin: *palus*, "stake"), district separated from the surrounding country by defined boundaries or distinguished by a different administrative and legal system. It is this definition of pale from which the phrase "beyond the pale" is derived.

In imperial Russia, what came to be called the Pale of Settlement (Cherta Osedlosti) came into being as a result of the introduction of large numbers of Jews into the Russian sphere after the three partitions of Poland (1772, 1793, 1795). Russian leadership responded to the difficulty of adjusting to a population that had often been banned from the country altogether by allowing Jews to remain in their current areas of residence and by permitting their settlement in areas of the Black Sea littoral annexed from Turkey, where they could serve as colonists. In three decrees issued in 1783, 1791, and 1794, Catherine II the Great restricted the commercial rights of Jews to those areas newly annexed. In ensuing years, this area became a strictly defined pale, as legal restrictions increasingly proscribed Jewish settlement elsewhere in Russia.

By the 19th century the pale included all of Russian Poland, Lithuania, Belarus (Belorussia), most of Ukraine, the Crimean Peninsula, and Bessarabia. During the 1860s some merchants and artisans, those with higher educations, and those who had completed their military service were allowed to settle anywhere but in Finland. A period of reaction, however, arrived with the ascension of Tsar Alexander III in 1881, who promulgated the "Temporary Laws," which, among many regressive measures, prohibited further Jewish settlements outside the pale; and Christians within the pale were allowed to expel Jews from their areas. Occasionally, new areas were proscribed, such as the city and province of Moscow in 1891.

The census of 1897 indicated that most Jews remained confined to the pale; almost 5,000,000 lived within it; only about 200,000 lived elsewhere in European Russia. The pale ceased to exist during World War I, when Jews in great numbers fled to the interior to escape the invading Germans. The Provisional Government formally abolished it in April 1917.

PALESTINIAN TALMUD \täl-'müd; 'täl-,mùd, 'tal-məd \: *see* YERUSHALMI.

PALI TEXT SOCIETY, organization founded with the intention of editing and publishing the texts of the THERAVĀDA canon and its commentaries, as well as producing English translations of many of those texts for an audience of scholars and interested readers. The Pali Text Society (PTS) was established by T.W. Rhys Davids in 1881. The output of the PTS in its early decades was plentiful, issuing editions of dozens of texts by the end of the 19th century. Rhys Davids was succeeded as president by his wife, Caroline, after his death in 1922.

In 1959 I.B. Horner was elected president of the PTS. Horner had worked and produced editions for the PTS since 1942, and the era in which she was president was especially productive and prosperous. Under her leadership the society produced revised editions of older PTS editions that were in need of correction or in need of new translations, and the society also produced editions of other, formerly neglected Pāli texts. Horner died in April 1981. Also in 1981, during its centenary anniversary year, the society completed the reissuing (in eight volumes) of the first issues of the *Journal of the Pali Text Society.* The society continues to produce issues of the journal periodically as material and resources permit.

In addition to its editions and translations of Pāli primary texts, the PTS has produced introductory works for students on Pāli language and meter, and compiled a Pāli-English dictionary, as well as commencing work on other scholarly volumes, such as the *Pāli Tipiṭakaṁ Concordance,* intended to serve as an aid to researchers in their work in Theravāda Buddhist studies.

PALLADIUM \pə-'lā-dē-əm\, in GREEK RELIGION, image of the goddess Pallas (ATHENA), especially the archaic wooden statue of the goddess that was preserved in the citadel of Troy. As long as the statue was kept safe within Troy, it was believed, the city could not be conquered. It was said that ZEUS had thrown the statue down from heaven when Troy was founded, and that

ODYSSEUS and DIOMEDES carried it off from the temple of Athena there, thus making the capture of Troy by the Greeks possible. Many cities in Greece and Italy claimed to possess the genuine Trojan Palladium, but it was particularly identified with the statue in the shrine of the goddess VESTA at Rome; it had supposedly been brought to Italy by the Trojan hero AENEAS. The story of its fall from heaven perhaps signifies that the Palladium was originally a BAETYLUS, or sacred stone.

PALM SUNDAY, *also called* Passion Sunday, in the Christian tradition, first day of HOLY WEEK and the Sunday before EASTER, commemorating JESUS CHRIST's triumphal entry into Jerusalem. It is associated in the ROMAN CATHOLIC church (and others) with the blessing and PROCESSION of palms (leaves of the date palm or twigs from locally available trees). These special ceremonies were taking place toward the end of the 4th century in Jerusalem. In the West the earliest evidence of the ceremonies is found in the Bobbio Sacramentary (8th century). During the Middle Ages the ceremony for the blessing of the palms was elaborate: the procession began in one church, went to a church in which the palms were blessed, and returned to the church in which the procession had originated for the singing of the liturgy, the principal feature of which was the chanting by three deacons of the account of the Passion of Christ (Matthew 26:36–27:54). After reforms of the Roman Catholic liturgies in 1955 and 1969, the ceremonies were simplified in order to emphasize the suffering and death of Christ. The day is now called officially Passion Sunday; the liturgy begins with a blessing and procession of palms, but prime attention is given to a lengthy reading of the Passion, with parts taken by the priest, lectors, and the congregation.

In the Byzantine liturgy the EUCHARIST on Palm Sunday is followed by a procession in which the priest carries the ICON representing the events being commemorated. In the churches of the ANGLICAN COMMUNION some traditional ceremonies were revived in the 19th century, but in most Protestant churches the day is celebrated without ceremonies.

PAN \'pan\, in GREEK RELIGION, a god, more or less bestial in form. Originally an Arcadian deity, his name was common-

Pan, terra-cotta statuette from Eretria on the Greek island of Euboea, c. 300 BCE
By courtesy of the Staatliche Museen zu Berlin

The Panchen Lama at a session of the National People's Congress in Peking in 1988
Reuters—Guy Dinmore—Archive Photos

Nārāyaṇa (who came to be identified with VISHNU) and, in merger with the BHĀGAVATA sect, formed the earliest sectarian movement within HINDU-ISM. The new group was a forerunner of modern VAIṢṆAVISM.

The Pāñcarātras originated in the Himalayan region perhaps in the 3rd century BCE. The sect's name is attributed to a "five-night" sacrifice (*pañca-rātra*) performed by Nārāyaṇa by which he obtained superiority over all beings and became all beings.

The Pāñcarātra doctrine was first systematized by Śāṇḍilya (*c.* 100? CE); that the Pāñcarātra system was also known in South India is evident from 2nd-century-CE inscriptions. By the 10th century the sect had acquired sufficient popularity to influence other groups.

ly (though erroneously) supposed in antiquity to be connected with *pan* ("all"). His father was usually said to be HERMES, but, because his mother was often named PENELOPE, one or another of the characters in the *Odyssey* was sometimes called his father. A fertility deity, Pan was generally represented as a lustful figure having the horns, legs, and the ears of a goat; in later art the human parts of his form were much more emphasized. He haunted the hills, and his chief concern was with flocks and herds. Hence he can make humans, like cattle, stampede in "panic." Like a shepherd, he was a piper and he rested at noon. Pan was insignificant in literature, aside from Hellenistic bucolic literature, but he was a very common subject in ancient art.

PANATHENAEA \ˌpa-ˌna-thə-'nē-ə\, in GREEK RELIGION, annual Athenian festival of great antiquity and importance. It was eventually celebrated every fourth year, probably in deliberate rivalry to the Olympic Games. The festival consisted solely of the sacrifices and rites proper to the season (mid-August) in the cult of ATHENA. At the Great Panathenaea, representatives of all the dependencies of Athens were present, bringing sacrificial animals. After the presentation of a new embroidered robe to Athena, the sacrifice of several animals was offered. The great PROCESSION, made up of the heroes of Marathon, is the subject of the frieze of the PARTHENON. The Athenian statesman Pericles (*c.* 495–429 BCE) introduced a regular musical contest in place of the recitation of rhapsodies (portions of epic poems), which were a long-standing accompaniment of the festival.

In addition to major athletic contests, many of which were not included at OLYMPIA, several minor contests also were held between the Athenian tribes.

PĀÑCARĀTRA \ˌpän-chə-'rä-trə\, early Hindu religious movement whose members worshiped the deified sage

PAṆCHEN LAMA \'pän-chən-'lä-mə\, in Tibetan BUDDHISM, title traditionally given to head ABBOTS of the Tashilhunpo Monastery, near Zhikatse in Tibet. Paṇchen is a short form of the Sanskrit-Tibetan Paṇḍita Chen-po, or "Great Scholar," suggesting the original nature of the position.

In the 17th century the fifth DALAI LAMA declared that his tutor, Blo-bzang chos-kyi-rgyal-mtshan (1570–1662), who was the current Paṇchen Lama, would be reincarnated in a child. He thus became the first of the line of reincarnated lamas, who were each regarded as physical manifestations of the self-born Buddha, AMITĀBHA. (Sometimes the three lamas who preceded Blo-bzang chos-kyi-rgyal-mtshan as abbots are also included in the list of REINCARNATIONS.)

Disagreements between the government of the 13th Dalai Lama and the Tashilhunpo administration over tax arrears led to the Paṇchen Lama's flight to China in 1923. Bskal-bzang Tshe-brtan, a boy born of Tibetan parents in the Chinese province of Tsinghai about 1938, was recognized as his successor by the Chinese government, but without the usual exacting tests that determine the authenticity of the transmission through reincarnation. He was brought to Tibet in 1952 under military escort and enthroned as head abbot of Tashilhunpo. The Paṇchen Lama remained in Tibet in 1959 after the anti-Chinese revolt and the Dalai Lama's flight into exile. However, his refusal to denounce the Dalai Lama as a traitor brought him into disfavor with the Chinese government and resulted in his imprisonment in Beijing in 1964. He was released in the late 1970s and died in 1989.

PANDARUS \'pan-də-rəs\, in Greek mythology, son of LYCA-ON, a Lycian. In Homer's *Iliad*, Pandarus broke the truce between the Trojans and the Greeks by treacherously wounding Menelaus; he was finally slain by DIOMEDES.

PĀNDAVAS \\'pän-də-vəz\\, in the Sanskrit epic MAHĀBHĀRATA, five sons of the king Pāṇḍu who were victorious in the great war with their cousins, the Kauravas.

PANDHARPUR \\'pən-dər-ˌpūr\\, village, southern Maharashtra state, western India. Lying along the Bhīma or Candrabhāgā River, it is host to annual festivals that honor the deities Viṭhobā (or Viṭṭhal), who is associated with KRISHNA and his consort Rukmiṇī. The main temple of Viṭhobā and Rukmiṇī was built in the 12th century by the Yādavas of Devagiri. It becomes the destination for more than 100,000 pilgrims from all over Maharashtra during the summer Vārkarī festival, which culminates on the 11th day of the waxing half of the lunar month Āṣāḍh. Various CASTE and regional groups converge on Pandharpur carrying palanquins with images of the sandals of Viṭhobā's most storied devotees, some of whom thereby retrace the PILGRIMAGE to Pandharpur as they are remembered to have made it in their own lives. These BHAKTI poet-saints include JÑĀNEŚVAR, Muktābāī, NĀMDEV, and TUKĀRĀM. The PROCESSION gives religious definition to Maharasthra as a region, and the performance of the saints' songs, which accompanies it, celebrates Marathi as a language of BHAKTI.

PANDORA \\pan-'dȯr-ə\\ (Greek Pandōra, "All-gifts," or "All-giving"), in Greek mythology, the first woman. After PROMETHEUS, a trickster, had stolen fire from heaven and bestowed it upon mortals, ZEUS determined to counteract this blessing by commissioning HEPHAESTUS to fashion a woman out of earth, upon whom the gods bestowed their choicest gifts. She had or found a jar—the so-called Pandora's box—containing all manner of misery and evil. Zeus sent her to Epimetheus, who forgot the warning of his brother Prometheus and made her his wife. Pandora afterward opened the jar, from which the evils flew out over the earth. According to another version, Hope alone remained inside, the lid having been shut down before she could escape. In a later story the jar contained not evils but blessings, which would have been preserved had they not been lost through the opening of the jar out of curiosity.

PANEGYRIS \\pə-'ne-jə-ris, -'nē-\\, also spelled Panegyry \\-rē\\, Greek Panēgyris ("Gathering"), plural Panēgyreis, in GREEK RELIGION, an assembly that met on certain fixed dates for the purpose of honoring a specific god. The gatherings varied in size from the inhabitants of a single town to great national meetings, such as the Olympic Games. The meetings centered around prayers, feasts, and processions, though the amusements, games, fairs, and festive orations (panegyrics) that also occurred at the gatherings were far more popular.

PAN KU \\'pän-'gü\\, Pinyin Ban Gu, central figure in popular Chinese CREATION MYTHS. Pan Ku, the first man, is said to have come forth from a primal egg, with two horns, two tusks, and a hairy body. Some accounts credit him with the separation of heaven and earth, setting the sun, moon, stars, and planets in place, and dividing the four seas. He shaped the earth by chiselling out valleys and stacking up mountains.

Others assert that the universe derived from Pan Ku's corpse. His eyes became the sun and moon, his blood and sweat formed rivers, his hair grew into trees and plants, and

his body became soil. The human race evolved from parasites that infested Pan Ku's body.

PANTHEISM \\'pan-thē-ˌi-zəm\\, doctrine that the universe conceived of as a whole is God and, conversely, that there is no God but the combined substance, forces, and laws that are manifested in the existing universe. The cognate doctrine of panentheism asserts that God includes the universe as a part though not the whole of his being.

The adjective pantheist was coined by John Toland in his book *Socinianism Truly Stated* (1705). The noun pantheism was first used a few years later by one of Toland's opponents. K.C.F. Krause introduced the term panentheism in 1828 as a designation for his own philosophy. Both of these terms have since been applied to aspects of numerous philosophical traditions, both Eastern and Western.

There are several types of pantheism, ranging from the attribution of consciousness to nature as a whole (panpsychism) to the interpretation of the world as merely an appearance and ultimately unreal (acosmic pantheism), and from the rational Neoplatonic, or emanationistic, strain to the intuitive, mystical strain. Pantheism of one form or another is deeply rooted in the VEDAS, the UPANISHADS, and the BHAGAVAD GĪTĀ. Numerous Greek philosophers, notably Xenophanes, Heracleitus, Anaxagoras, Plato, Plotinus, and the proponents of Stoicism, contributed to the foundations of Western pantheism. Through NEOPLATONISM and Judeo-Christian MYSTICISM, the tradition was continued in the medieval and Renaissance periods by John Scotus Erigena, MEISTER ECKHART, NICHOLAS OF CUSA, Giordano Bruno, and JAKOB BÖHME.

The Jewish rationalist Benedict Spinoza (1632–77) formulated the most thoroughly pantheistic system, insisting that there could be by definition only one unlimited substance possessing an infinitude of attributes. Therefore, God and Nature are but two names for one identical reality; otherwise, God-and-world would be a greater totality than God alone. The necessity of God thus implies the necessity of the world. Pantheism has traditionally been rejected by orthodox Christian theologians because it is interpreted to obliterate the distinction between the creator and creation, to make God impersonal, to imply a purely immanent rather than transcendent deity, and to exclude human and divine freedom.

Panentheism constitutes a middle way between the denial of individual freedom and creativity that characterizes many varieties of pantheism and the remoteness of the divine that characterizes classical THEISM. Though elements of quasi-panentheism reach as far back as Plato's *Laws*, it is in 19th-century German Idealism (Johann Gottlieb Fichte, Friedrich Wilhelm Joseph von Schelling, G.W.F. Hegel) and 20th-century process philosophy (Alfred North Whitehead) that the doctrine receives systematic elaboration. Charles Hartshorne, a follower of Whitehead, provided the definitive analysis of panentheism, based upon the analogy of an organism (God) comprising individual, semiautonomous cells (all known and unknown constituents of reality).

PAO \\'baŭ\\, Pinyin bao (Chinese: "reciprocity," or "recompense"), generalized principle of Chinese social relations. It refers to the idea that each action necessarily elicits a reaction and that it is therefore necessary to establish a code of balanced interactions appropriate to particular social, natural, and cosmic circumstances. Primarily a system of debts and obligations (and coupled with the Buddhist karmic system), it is at the heart of Chinese popular morality.

PAO-CHÜAN \\'baủ-'jwän\\, *Pinyin* baojuan (Chinese: "sacred scrolls," or "precious scriptures"), revealed Chinese SCRIPTURES that are often foundational narratives for various schools of TAOISM, sects of BUDDHISM, and SECRET SOCIETIES. They are written in a vernacular idiom and constitute a widely distributed corpus of popular scripture distinct from the more orthodox Taoist and Buddhist texts, called *ching*. They also constitute the source of the genre of folk religious literature known as the SHAN-SHU, or "good books," of popular morality.

PAO-P'U-TZU, *Pinyin* Baopuzi: *see* KO HUNG.

PAPACY, system of central government of the ROMAN CATHOLIC church, the largest of the three major branches of CHRISTIANITY, presided over by the POPE, the bishop of Rome.

The papal system, which has not gone undisputed, developed over the centuries since the early church until 1870 when the FIRST VATICAN COUNCIL officially defined as a matter of faith the absolute primacy of the pope and his infallibility when pronouncing on "matters of faith and morals." According to this definition the pope exercises judicial, legislative, and executive authority over the church as the direct successor of ST. PETER, who is thought to have been the head of the apostles and the first bishop of Rome. His authority rested on the words of Jesus quoted in Matthew 16:18–19 and elsewhere that have been interpreted as giving him authority in heaven and on earth in the place of Jesus. The early history of the papacy can be told as the history of the development of this Petrine theory, and the later history as the development of the papal claim to both spiritual and temporal authority over Christian society.

There is a strong tradition, but no direct historical evidence, that St. Peter was the first leader of the church of Rome and that he was martyred there during a persecution of the Christians (*c.* 67 CE). By the end of the 1st century, however, the see of Rome seems to have been accorded a place of honor among the bishoprics claiming apostolic foundation, perhaps because of Rome's claim to the graves of both Peter and PAUL, its many MARTYRS and defense of what has triumphed as orthodoxy, and its status as the capital of the Roman Empire.

The Roman position was challenged in the middle of the 3rd century when Pope Stephen I (reigned 254–257) and St. Cyprian, bishop of Carthage, clashed over Stephen's claim to exercise doctrinal authority over the universal church. In the 4th and 5th centuries, the growing power of Constantinople as the capital of the Eastern Empire challenged that of Rome. Over Pope Leo I's objections, the COUNCIL OF CHALCEDON, called by the Eastern emperor in 451 and largely directed by him, accorded the PATRIARCH of Constantinople an equivalence in authority in the East such as Rome held in the West. This was the first decisive demonstration of the Eastern church's historic rejection of Rome's claim to hegemony based on the Petrine theory, which culminated in the SCHISM between the two churches in 1054. The East accepted the primacy of Peter, but as *primus inter pares*—that is, first among equals—and not as a monarch.

During the next centuries of increasing political chaos, popes were often forced to trade their spiritual power for imperial protection. After the demise of effective Roman or Byzantine imperial control over Italy, the Roman pope became the representative of Roman imperial glory to the new Frankish and other German kingdoms. Stephen II (reigned 752–757) and other popes, in linking the fate of the Roman primacy to the support of Charlemagne and his house, gained a powerful protector and temporal power in Italy. They did not, however, gain the freedom to exercise the spiritual power over the universal church for which they had hoped, since Charlemagne and his successors ignored the pope's claim to the right to crown the emperor and instead followed in the footsteps of their Byzantine and Roman predecessors by asserting a large measure of control over the Frankish church and the papacy itself.

During the late 9th and 10th centuries the decadence of the papal court and political conditions in Italy led to the virtual takeover of the papacy by the German emperors. By 1049 the papacy's desperate need for reform was met in the person of Pope Leo IX, a reformer whose attitudes had been shaped in the monastic reform movements of Burgundy and Lorraine. One important measure was the election decree of 1059, which vested the right of naming a new pope exclusively with the CARDINALS, thus encouraging the independence of papal elections from then on. A significant point in the so-called GREGORIAN REFORM begun by Leo, and in the history of the papacy itself, was the INVESTITURE CONTROVERSY. It was precipitated by Gregory VII in 1075 when he threatened to excommunicate any civil ruler who attempted to invest the holder of an ecclesiastical office with the secular symbols of power, a practice that emphasized the control the lay ruler had over the selection and operation of bishops and local clergy. In this assertion the papacy committed itself to a course it was unable to maintain.

Later popes actively intervened in political issues in an attempt to prove the validity of papal monarchy, rather than mere papal leadership, of Christian society. Papal monarchy reached its zenith in the pontificate of INNOCENT III, who ruled from 1198 to 1216. Thirteenth-century centralization of administrative as well as jurisdictional power in the Curia (the body of officials surrounding the pope) led to increasing financial difficulties and eventually to the practice of "selling" benefices and other church services. This and other corruptions of the papal court, as well as the "Babylonian Captivity" of the papacy at Avignon, France (1309–77), led to both the conciliar movement, an attempt by bishops to regain control over the church, and loud calls for sacramental and organizational reform.

The Renaissance popes, most of whom often seemed to be too involved in political and financial alliances to do more for the church than patronize the arts, were unable to deal with or to understand the significance of the Protestant REFORMATION of the 16th century. The papacy finally acceded to demands for reform by calling the COUNCIL OF TRENT (1545), which instituted what has been called the COUNTER-REFORMATION, or the Catholic Reformation. The theological and ecclesiastical decisions of this council largely determined the shape of the Catholic church until the second half of the 20th century.

The alignment of the papacy with conservative political forces during the 19th century resulted in the loss of liberal and modernizing influences within the church and led to the loss of the Papal States to the new Kingdom of Italy. Divested of its temporal power, the papacy increasingly turned to its spiritual or teaching authority to retain control over Catholics, proclaiming infallibility and espousing the Ultramontane position (the idea that the pope is the absolute ruler of the church).

A generally unfavorable view toward liberal ideas and modern culture was articulated in the *Syllabus of Errors* issued by POPE PIUS IX in 1864. It persisted, even though the social ENCYCLICALS of several modern popes, beginning with *Rerum Novarum* of POPE LEO XIII in 1891, strove to align the papacy with the cause of social reform. At the SECOND VATICAN COUNCIL, called by POPE JOHN XXIII in 1962, the theological and organizational changes significantly revitalized the church and opened it to new reform, ecumenical dialogue, and the increased participation of bishops, clergy, and laity. Toward the end of the 20th century, however, the papacy met with increasing controversy in regard to what were seen by many as uniquely modern moral, ethical, and political issues.

PAPAL INFALLIBILITY, in ROMAN CATHOLIC theology, the doctrine that the pope, acting as supreme teacher and under certain conditions, cannot err when he teaches in matters of faith or morals. As an element of the broader understanding of the infallibility of the church, this doctrine is based on the belief that the church has been entrusted with the teaching mission of JESUS CHRIST and that, in view of its mandate from Christ, it will remain faithful to that teaching through the assistance of the HOLY SPIRIT. As such, the doctrine is related to, but distinguishable from, the concept of indefectibility, or the doctrine that the GRACE that has been promised to the church assures its perseverance until the end of time.

The term infallibility was rarely mentioned in the early and medieval church. Critics of the doctrine have pointed to various occasions in the history of the church when popes are said to have taught heretical doctrines, the most notable case being that of Honorius I (625–638), who was condemned by the third COUNCIL OF CONSTANTINOPLE (680–681, the sixth ecumenical council).

The definition promulgated by the FIRST VATICAN COUNCIL (1869–70), which was established amid considerable controversy, states the conditions under which a pope may be said to have spoken infallibly, or *ex cathedra* ("from his chair" as supreme teacher). It is prerequisite that the pope intend to demand irrevocable assent from the entire church in some aspect of faith or morals. Despite the rarity of recourse to this claim, and despite the emphasis given to the authority of the bishops in the SECOND VATICAN COUNCIL (1962–65), the doctrine of infallibility remained a major obstacle to ecumenical endeavors in the late 20th century and was the subject of controversial discussion even among Roman Catholic theologians.

PAPYRUS COLUMN, in EGYPTIAN RELIGION, AMULET that conveyed freshness, youth, vigor, and the continuance of life to its wearer. The amulet, made of glazed pottery or stone, was shaped like a papyrus stem and bud. Its significance was perhaps derived from its ideographic value (Egyptian *wadj,* "green, fresh, vigorous"), for, just as the plant was vigorous and growing, so also would the wearer of the papyrus column possess these qualities.

PARABLE (from Greek: *parabolē,* "comparison," or "illustration"), short fictitious narrative by which moral or spiritual relations are set forth. The term originally referred to a Greek rhetorical figure, a kind of extended simile, involving the use of a literary illustration. The storytelling aspect of a parable is usually subordinated to the analogy it draws between a particular instance of human behavior and human behavior at large. The simple narratives of parables give them a mysterious, suggestive tone and make them especially useful for the teaching of moral and spiritual truths. Parables can often be fully understood only by an informed elite, who can discern the meaning within their brief, enigmatic structures.

There are parables in the OLD TESTAMENT (2 Samuel 12:1–9; 14:1–13), but the most famous parables are in the NEW TESTAMENT. Jesus uses the form to illustrate his message to his followers by telling a fictitious story that is nevertheless true-to-life. Throughout Christian history, the pious tale or parable has been a popular preaching device. The more paradoxical aspects of the parable were revived in the 19th century through SØREN KIERKEGAARD's treatises on Christian faith and practice. His use of the form influenced the enigmatic works of Franz Kafka and the writings of Albert Camus.

PARADISE, place of exceptional happiness and delight. The term paradise is often used as a synonym for the GARDEN OF EDEN before the expulsion of ADAM AND EVE. An earthly paradise is often conceived of as existing in a time when heaven and earth were very close together or actually touching, and when humans and gods had free and happy association. Many religions also include the notion of a fuller life beyond the grave, a land in which there will be an absence of suffering and a complete satisfaction of bodily desires. Accounts of a primordial earthly paradise in the higher religions range from that of a garden of life (JUDAISM, CHRISTIANITY, ISLAM) to that of a golden age of human society at the beginning of each cycle of human existence (BUDDHISM, HINDUISM). A final state of bliss is variously conceived of as a heavenly afterlife (Islam, Christianity), union with the divine (Hinduism), or an eternal condition of peace and changelessness (Buddhism).

PARAMĀRTHA \,pär-ə-'mär-tə\ (b. 499—d. 569), Indian Buddhist missionary and translator whose arrival in China in 546 was important in the development of Chinese BUDDHISM. The basic teachings of the consciousness-oriented YOGĀCĀRA school of thought became known in China primarily through the work of Paramārtha; working out of Chien-k'ang in southern China, he is credited with the translation of more than 60 Buddhist texts, most prominently the *Mahāyānasaṃgraha,* the *Viṃśatikā,* and the *Madhyāntavibhāga-śāstra.* These translations facilitated the development of the FA-HSIANG school.

PĀRAMITĀ \'pär-ə-mē-,tä\, in MAHĀYĀNA Buddhism, any of the perfections, or transcendental virtues, practiced by BODHISATTVAS ("buddhas-to-be") in advanced stages of the path toward Enlightenment. The six virtues are generosity (*dāna-pāramitā*); morality (*śīla-pāramitā*); perseverance (*kṣānti-pāramitā*); vigor (*vīrya-pāramitā*); meditation, or concentration (*dhyāna-pāramitā*); and wisdom (*prajñā-pāramitā*). Some lists expand the number of virtues to 10 by adding to the list also skill at helping others (*upāya* [*kauśalya*]-*pāramitā*s), profound resolution to attain Enlightenment (*praṇidhāna-pāramitā*), perfection of the 10 powers (*bala-pāramitā*), and practice of transcendent knowledge (*jñāna-pāramitā*).

PARAŚURĀMA \,pə-rə-shù-'rä-mə\ (Sanskrit: "Rāma with the Ax"), sixth of the 10 *avatāra*s (incarnations) of the Hindu god VISHNU. The MAHĀBHĀRATA and the PURĀṆAS record that Paraśurāma was born to the BRAHMAN sage Jamadagni in order to deliver the world from the arrogant oppression of the KṢATRIYAS (warriors and kings). He killed all the male Kṣatriyas on earth 21 successive times (each time their wives survived and gave birth to new generations) and filled five lakes with blood. Paraśurāma is the traditional founder of Malabar and is said to have bestowed land there

Paraśurāma (center) slaying Kārtavīrya, king of the Kṣatriyas, Basohli miniature painting from the early 18th century
Pramod Chandra

on members of the priestly CASTE whom he brought down from the north in order to expiate his slaughter of the Kṣatriya race.

PARENTALIA \ˌpar-ən-ˈtā-lē-ə, ˌper- \, in ROMAN RELIGION, festival held in honor of the dead. The festival, which began at noon on February 13 and culminated on February 21, was essentially a private celebration of the rites of deceased family members that was extended to incorporate the dead in general. During the days of the festival, all temples were closed and no weddings could be performed. On the last day a public ceremony, the Feralia, was held, during which offerings and gifts were placed at the graves and the anniversary of the funeral feast was celebrated.

PAREVE \ˈpär-ə-və\, also spelled parve \ˈpär-və\, or parveh (Yiddish: "neutral"), in Jewish dietary laws (KASHRUTH), those foods that may be eaten with either meat dishes or dairy products. (Meat and dairy being two general classes of food that may not, under Jewish law, be consumed at the same meal.) Fruits and vegetables are classified as pareve unless cooking or processing alters their status, while cakes and similar foods are pareve, provided they are made without dairy products.

PARILIA \pə-ˈri-lē-ə\, in ROMAN RELIGION, festival celebrated annually on April 21 in honor of the goddess Pales. The festival, basically a purification rite for herdsmen, animals, and stalls, was at first celebrated by the early KINGS OF ROME, later by the PONTIFEX maximus, or chief priest. The VESTAL VIRGINS opened the festival by distributing straw and the ashes and blood of sacrificial animals. Ritual cleaning, anointment, and adornment of herds and stalls followed, together with offerings of food. The celebrants jumped over a bonfire three times to complete the purification, and an open-air feast ended the festival.

According to later tradition, April 21 was the day on which Romulus began building the city of Rome and was thus celebrated as the *dies notalis* of the city.

PARIS \ˈpar-əs\, also called Alexandros \ˌa-lig-ˈzan-dräs, -drōs\, in Greek legend, son of PRIAM and his wife, HECUBA. A dream about his birth was interpreted as an evil portent, and so he was expelled from his family as an infant. Left for dead, he was either nursed by a bear or found by shepherds. He was raised as a shepherd, unknown to his parents. As a young man he defeated Priam's other sons in a boxing contest at a Trojan festival. After his identity was revealed, he was received home by Priam.

Paris was chosen by ZEUS to determine which of three goddesses was the most beautiful. Rejecting bribes of kingly power from HERA and military might from ATHENA, he chose APHRODITE and accepted her bribe to help him win the most beautiful woman alive. His subsequent seduction of HELEN, wife of king MENELAUS of Sparta, was the cause of the Trojan War.

Near the end of the war, Paris shot the arrow that, by Apollo's help, caused the death of the hero ACHILLES. Paris himself, soon after, received a fatal wound from an arrow shot by the archer PHILOCTETES.

The Judgment of Paris, Hermes leading Athena, Hera, and Aphrodite to Paris, detail of a 6th-century-BCE kylix (drinking bowl)
By courtesy of Staatliche Museen Antikenabteilung, Berlin

PARIS CODEX \'par-əs-'kō-ˌdeks\: *see* MAYA CODICES.

PARISH, in some Christian churches, a geographic unit served by a pastor or priest. It is a subdivision of a DIOCESE.

In the NEW TESTAMENT the Greek word *paroikia* (from Ancient Greek: *paroikos*, "neighbor, non-native resident") means "residence in a strange land." Figuratively it alludes to a Christian's earthly life—a brief sojourn away from eternal life in heaven—and hence to a community of such "sojourners." In the very early church, the parish was the entire body of Christians in a city under the bishop, who stood in the same relationship to the Christians of the entire city as does the parish priest to the parish in modern times. In the 4th century, when CHRISTIANITY in western Europe spread to the countryside, Christians in an important village were organized into a unit with their own priest under the jurisdiction of the bishop of the nearest city. The unit was called a parish. The parish system was essentially created between the 8th and 12th centuries. The COUNCIL OF TRENT (1545–63) reorganized and reformed the parish system of the ROMAN CATHOLIC church to make it more responsive to the needs of the people.

In Anglo-Saxon England the first parish churches were founded in important administrative centers. They were called minsters, and subsequently old minsters, to distinguish them from the later village churches. When the Church of England became independent of Rome during the 16th century, it retained the parish as the basic unit of the church.

PARKER, THEODORE \'pär-kər\ (b. Aug. 24, 1810, Lexington, Mass., U.S.—d. May 10, 1860, Florence, Italy), American UNITARIAN theologian, pastor, scholar, and social reformer who was active in the antislavery movement. He repudiated much traditional Christian dogma, putting in its place an intuitive knowledge of God derived from one's experience of nature and insight into one's own mind, an outlook not unlike that of Ralph Waldo Emerson.

Although Parker passed the entrance examination for Harvard College in 1830, he had no funds to attend. He was allowed, however, to take the examinations for his course of study without enrolling and was granted an honorary degree. He then attended Harvard Divinity School, from which he graduated in 1836. The next year he was ordained pastor of the Unitarian Church in West Roxbury, Mass.

By 1841 he had formulated his liberal religious views and had incorporated them in the sermon "The Transient and Permanent in Christianity." The transient, to him, was Christianity's theological and scriptural dogma, and the permanent was its moral truths. He elaborated his views in lectures published as *A Discourse of Matters Pertaining to Religion.* Opposition to his liberalism forced him to resign his pastorate. His supporters founded the 28th Congregational Society of Boston and installed him as minister.

Parker worked for prison reform, temperance, women's education, and other such causes. He made impassioned speeches against slavery, helped fugitive slaves to escape, and wrote an Abolitionist tract, *A Letter to the People of the United States Touching the Matter of Slavery* (1848). He also served on the secret committee that aided the Abolitionist John Brown.

PARSI \'pär-sē, pär-'sē\: *see* ZOROASTRIANISM AND PARSIISM.

PĀRŚVANĀTHA \'pärsh-və-'nä-tə\, *also called* Parśva, in JAINISM, 23rd TĪRTHAṄKARA, or saint, of the present age. Pārś-

vanātha was the first Tīrthaṅkara of whom there is historical evidence. He is said to have preceded MAHĀVĪRA, who died probably in 527 BCE, by about 250 years. The four vows that Pārśvanātha made binding on members of his community (not to take life, not to steal, not to lie, not to own property) became, with the addition of the explicit vow of CELIBACY introduced by Mahāvīra, the five "great vows" (*mahāvrata*s) of later Jainism. Pārśvanātha allowed monks to wear garments, while Mahāvīra gave up clothing. The followers of Pārśvanātha were eventually won over to Mahāvīra's reforms.

Pārśvanātha's mother is said to have seen a black serpent crawling by her side (Sanskrit: *pārśva*) before his birth, and in sculpture and painting he is always identified by a canopy of snake hoods shown over his head. According to accounts in the JAINA text the *Kalpa Sūtra*, Pārśvanātha once saved a family of serpents that had been trapped in a burning log. One of these snakes, later reborn as Dharaṇa, the lord of the underworld kingdom of NĀGAS (snakes), sheltered Pārśvanātha from a storm sent by an enemy DEMON.

PARTHENON \'pär-thə-ˌnän\, chief temple of the Greek goddess ATHENA on the hill of the Acropolis at Athens, Greece. It was built in the mid-5th century BCE and is generally considered to be the culmination of the development of the Doric order of Greek architecture. The name Parthenon refers to the cult of Athena Parthenos ("Athena the Virgin") that was associated with the temple.

Directed by the Athenian statesman Pericles, the Parthenon was built by the architects Ictinus and Callicrates under the supervision of the sculptor Phidias. Work at the site began in 447 BCE, and the building itself was completed by 438 BCE. The same year a great gold and ivory statue of Athena, made by Phidias for the interior, was dedicated. Work on the exterior decoration of the building continued until 432 BCE.

The Parthenon's basic structure has remained intact. A colonnade of fluted, baseless columns with square capitals stands on a three-stepped base and supports a stone roof structure; a frieze of alternating triglyphs (vertically grooved blocks) and metopes (plain blocks with relief sculpture, now partly removed); and, at the east and west ends, a low triangular pediment, also with relief sculpture (now mostly removed). The colonnade, consisting of 8 columns on the east and west and 17 on the north and south, encloses a walled interior rectangular chamber, or cella, originally divided into three aisles by two smaller Doric colonnades closed at the west end just behind the great cult statue. Behind the cella, but not originally connected with it, is a smaller, square chamber entered from the west. The east and west ends of the interior of the building are each faced by a portico of six columns.

The metopes over the outer colonnade were carved in high relief and represented, on the east, a battle between gods and giants; on the south, Greeks and centaurs; and on the west, probably Greeks and AMAZONS. Those on the north are almost all lost. The continuous, low-relief frieze around the top of the cella wall, representing the annual procession of citizens honoring Athena at the PANATHENAEA, culminated on the east end with a priest and priestess of Athena flanked by two groups of seated gods. The pediment groups, carved in the round, show, on the east, the birth of Athena and, on the west, her contest with POSEIDON for domination of the region around Athens.

The Parthenon remained essentially intact until the 5th century CE, when Phidias' colossal statue was removed and the temple was transformed into a Christian church. By the 7th century, structural alterations in the inner portion had also been made. In 1460 the Turks adopted the Parthenon as a mosque and raised a MINARET at the southwest corner. During the bombardment of the Acropolis in 1687 by Venetians fighting the Turks, a powder magazine located in the temple blew up, destroying the center of the building. In 1801–03 a large part of the sculpture that remained was removed, with Turkish permission, by the British art collector Thomas Bruce, Lord Elgin, and sold in 1816 to the British Museum in London. Other sculptures from the Parthenon are now in the Louvre Museum in Paris, in Copenhagen, and elsewhere, but many are still in Athens.

PĀRVATĪ \'pär-və-ˌtē\ (Sanskrit: "Daughter of the Mountain"), wife of the Hindu god SHIVA. Pārvatī is the benevolent aspect of the Goddess and is sometimes referred to as Umā or DEVĪ. She and Shiva had two children, the elephant-headed GAṆEŚA and the six-headed SKANDA. The Śaiva TANTRAS—texts of sects worshiping Shiva—are generally written as a discussion between Pārvatī and Shiva, during which Pārvatī assumes the role of the questioning disciple and Shiva of the preceptor. In *tantras* dedicated to the Goddess, Shiva and Pārvatī reverse these roles.

PARYUṢAṆA \pər-'yü-shə-nə\ (Sanskrit), Prākrit Pajjusaṇa, eight-day festival in JAINISM. It is celebrated by members of the ŚVETĀMBARA sect from the 13th day of the dark half of the month Bhādrapada (August–September) to the 5th day of the bright half of the month. Among DIGAMBARAS, a corresponding festival called Daśalakṣaṇa begins immediately following the Paryusaṇa.

Paryuṣaṇa closes the Jaina year. Jainas make confessions at the meetinghouse to settle existing quarrels, and many lay members temporarily live the lives of monks, an observance called *poṣadha*. The fourth day coincides with the birth anniversary of MAHĀVĪRA.

On the eighth day, Bhadra-śukla-pañcamī ("Fifth Day of the Bright Fortnight of Bhādra"), Jainas distribute alms to the poor and take out a JINA (savior) image in a PROCESSION that is headed by an ornamental pole called Indra-dhvaja ("Staff of INDRA"). The KALPA SŪTRA is read before the laity by monks, and its illustrations are shown and revered. The last day is a day of fasting, though the very pious observe a fast throughout the festival.

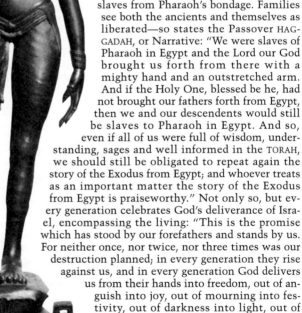

Pārvatī, bronze image from the 10th century CE
By courtesy of the Smithsonian Institution, Freer Gallery of Art, Washington, D.C.

PASCHAL LAMB, in JUDAISM, the lamb sacrificed at the first PASSOVER, on the eve of the EXODUS from Egypt. The Jews marked their doorposts with the blood of the lamb, and this sign spared them from destruction (Exodus 12).

An unblemished year-old lamb was sacrificed in the TEMPLE OF JERUSALEM on the 14th of Nisan (or a month later for those who could not visit the Temple at the prescribed time) to commemorate the eve of the Exodus, and was eaten later by the family. Modern Jews use a roasted shank bone at the SEDER meal as symbolic of the Paschal lamb. The Apostle PAUL referred to JESUS CHRIST as the Paschal lamb (1 Corinthians 5:7); hence, the Christian view of Christ as the Lamb of God who by his death freed humanity from the bonds of SIN.

PASSOVER \'pas-ˌō-vər\, *Hebrew* Pesaḥ, *or* Pesach, in JUDAISM, "the festival of our freedom." Passover commemorates God's deliverance of the Israelites from Egypt in the events described at EXODUS 1–15. Celebrated from the 15th day of Nisan, the first full moon after the vernal equinox, generally in April, the festival lasts for eight days in the diaspora, seven in the Land of Israel, with the first and final days holy days; during that time all leaven is forbidden, and in place of bread, the faithful eat MATZAH, unleavened bread.

Passover is marked in Judaism by a home banquet, or SEDER, that follows an order of song and story. With unleavened bread and sanctified wine, the holy people, ISRAEL, celebrate the liberation of slaves from Pharaoh's bondage. Families see both the ancients and themselves as liberated—so states the Passover HAGGADAH, or Narrative: "We were slaves of Pharaoh in Egypt and the Lord our God brought us forth from there with a mighty hand and an outstretched arm. And if the Holy One, blessed be he, had not brought our fathers forth from Egypt, then we and our descendents would still be slaves to Pharaoh in Egypt. And so, even if all of us were full of wisdom, understanding, sages and well informed in the TORAH, we should still be obligated to repeat again the story of the Exodus from Egypt; and whoever treats as an important matter the story of the Exodus from Egypt is praiseworthy." Not only so, but every generation celebrates God's deliverance of Israel, encompassing the living: "This is the promise which has stood by our forefathers and stands by us. For neither once, nor twice, nor three times was our destruction planned; in every generation they rise against us, and in every generation God delivers us from their hands into freedom, out of anguish into joy, out of mourning into festivity, out of darkness into light, out of bondage into redemption."

PĀŚUPATA \'pä-shù-ˌpə-tə, ˌpä-shù-'pə-\, earliest Hindu sect to worship SHIVA as the supreme deity; it spread as far as Java and Cambodia. The name refers to Paśupati, an epithet of Shiva meaning Lord of Cattle, which was extended to mean "Lord of Souls" in later Śaiva Siddhānta theology.

The Pāśupata sect is mentioned in the MAHĀBHĀRATA (c. 400 CE). Shiva himself was believed to have been its first preceptor. Shiva was said to have revealed that he would make an appearance on earth during the age of VISHNU's appearance as Vāsudeva-Krishna, when he would enter a dead body and incarnate himself as Lakulī (or Lakulīśa, *lakula* meaning "club"). Inscriptions of the 10th and 13th centuries refer to a teacher named Lakulī, who was believed by his followers to be an AVATAR of Shiva. Historians place the rise of the Pāśupatas between the 2nd century BCE and the 2nd century CE.

Pāśupata ascetic practices included the thrice-daily smearing of their bodies with ashes, meditating on the five MANTRAS sacred to Shiva, and dancing. Out of the Pāśupata doctrine developed two extreme schools, the Kālāmukhas and the Kāpālikas, as well as one moderate sect, adherents to the Śaiva Siddhānta school. The Pāśupatas and the extreme sects came to be called Atimārgika (schools of the "higher" or "outer" path) to maintain their distinction from the more acceptable followers of Śaiva Siddhānta, the development of which led into modern orthodox ŚAIVISM.

PATAÑJALI \pə-'tən-jə-lē\, *also called* Gonardīya, or Goṇikāputra (fl. 2nd century BCE or 5th century CE), author or one of the authors of the YOGA *Sutras*, a categorization of Yogic thought arranged in four volumes with the titles "Samādhi" (transcendental state induced by trance), "Practice of Yoga," "Psychic Power," and "Kaivalya" (liberation); and the *Mahābhāṣya* ("Great Commentary"), which is both a defense of the grammarian Pāṇini and a refutation of some of Pāṇini's aphorisms.

The first three volumes of the *Yoga Sutras* were apparently written in the 2nd century BCE and the *Mahābhāṣya* in the 5th century CE. The name Patañjali was used by the authors of a number of other works on such diverse subjects as medicine and music.

PATH OF PURIFICATION: *see* VISUDDHIMAGGA.

PĀTIMOKKHA \ˌpä-tē-'mȯk-kə\: *see* PRĀTIMOKṢA.

PATRIARCH, *Latin* patriarcha, *Greek* patriarchēs, title used for some OLD TESTAMENT leaders (ABRAHAM, ISAAC, JACOB, and Jacob's 12 sons) and, in some Christian churches, a title given to bishops of important sees.

The biblical appellation patriarch appeared occasionally in the 4th century to designate prominent Christian bishops. By the end of the 5th century, however, in the course of growing ecclesiastical centralization, it acquired a specific sense. After the COUNCIL OF NICAEA in 325, the church structure was patterned on the administrative divisions of the Roman Empire; thus, each civil province was headed by a METROPOLITAN, or bishop of the metropolis (the civil capital of the province), while larger administrative units, called DIOCESES, were presided over by an exarch of the diocese, a title gradually replaced by patriarch. Some patriarchs exercised authority over several dioceses: the bishop of Rome over the entire West; the bishop of Alexandria over the dioceses of Egypt, Libya, and Pentapolis; and, after the COUNCIL OF CHALCEDON (451), the bishop of Constantinople (Istanbul) over the dioceses of Pontus, Asia, and Thrace.

Controversy over the growth of major ecclesiastical centers contributed to the SCHISM between East and West. Rome maintained that only apostolic sees, those originally established by apostles, had the right to become patriarchates. The East, however, always took for granted that primacies were based on such empirical factors as the economic and political importance of cities and countries. Constantinople, the new imperial capital and the ecclesiastical center of the East, had no claims to apostolicity (although a later tradition attributed its founding to the apostle Andrew), but new jurisdictional rights were bestowed upon it at Chalcedon (451) for the explicit reason that it was "the residence of the emperor and the Senate."

Five patriarchates, collectively called the pentarchy, were the first to be recognized by the legislation of the emperor Justinian (reigned 527–565), later confirmed by the Council in Trullo (692); these five were Rome, Constantinople, Alexandria, Antioch, and Jerusalem, though, after the Muslim invasions of Egypt and Syria in 638–640, the bishops of Rome and Constantinople were alone in possessing any real power. Despite Constantinople's efforts to resist any proliferation of patriarchates, new centers emerged in the Slavic centers of Preslav (now Veliki Preslav; 932), Tŭrnovo (1234), Peć (1346), and Moscow (1589). At present there are nine patriarchates of EASTERN ORTHODOXY: Constantinople, Alexandria, Antioch, Jerusalem, Moscow, Georgia, Serbia, Romania, and Bulgaria. Except in the title, there is no difference between a patriarch and any other head of an autocephalous (independent) church.

PATRICK, SAINT \'pa-trik\ (fl. 5th century, Britain and Ireland; feast day March 17), patron saint and apostle of Ireland, credited with bringing CHRISTIANITY to Ireland and probably responsible in part for the Christianization of the Picts and Anglo-Saxons. He is known from two short works, the *Confessio*, a spiritual autobiography, and his *Epistola*, a denunciation of British mistreatment of Irish Christians.

Patrick was born in Britain of a Romanized family. At 16 he was carried off to slavery in Ireland by raiders, where, during six years spent as a herdsman, he turned with fervor to his faith. Hearing at last in a dream that the ship in which he was to escape was ready, he fled his master and found passage to Britain. There he suffered a second brief captivity before he was reunited with his family. Thereafter, he may have paid a short visit to continental Europe.

The best-known passage in the *Confessio* tells of a dream, after his return to Britain, in which one Victoricus delivered him a letter headed "The Voice of the Irish." As he read it he seemed to hear a certain company of Irish beseeching him to walk once more among them. His MISSION to the Irish was his response to this dream. On at least one occasion he was cast into chains. On another, he addressed with lyrical pathos a last farewell to his converts who had been slain or kidnapped by the soldiers of Coroticus.

The phenomenal success of Patrick's mission is not the full measure of his personality. Since his writings have come to be better understood, it is increasingly recognized that, despite their occasional incoherence, they mirror a truth and a simplicity of the rarest quality.

Before the end of the 7th century Patrick had become a legendary figure. One legend asserts that he drove the snakes of Ireland into the sea to their destruction. Another, probably the most popular, is that of the shamrock, which has him explain the concept of the Holy TRINITY, three Persons in one God, to an unbeliever by showing him the three-leaved plant with one stalk. Today Irishmen wear shamrocks, the national flower of Ireland, in their lapels on St. Patrick's Day, March 17.

PAULICIAN \pȯ-'li-shən\, member of a dualistic Christian sect that originated in Armenia in the mid-7th century. It was influenced most directly by the DUALISM of Marcionism (*see* MARCIONITE) and of MANICHAEISM, both forms of GNOSTICISM. The identity of the Paul after whom the Paulicians are called is disputed.

The fundamental doctrine of the Paulicians was that there are two principles, an evil God and a good God; the former is the creator and ruler of this world, the latter of the world to come. From this they deduced that JESUS CHRIST was not truly the son of MARY, because the good God could not have taken flesh and become man. They especially honored the Gospel According to Luke and the Letters of ST. PAUL, rejecting the OLD TESTAMENT and the Letters of ST. PETER. They rejected also the SACRAMENTS, the worship, and the hierarchy of the established church.

The founder of the Paulicians seems to have been an Armenian, Constantine, who took the additional name of Silvanus (Silas; one of St. Paul's companions). He gave a more distinctively Christian character to the Manichaeism that was prevalent in the Asian provinces of the Byzantine Empire. The sect seems to have started a widespread political and military rebellion shortly after its appearance. Between 668 and 698 Constantine III and Justinian II sent two expeditions to repress it. Constantine (Silvanus) was stoned to death, and his successor, Simeon (Titus), was burned alive.

In the early 9th century Paulicianism was revived. It expanded into Cilicia and Asia Minor under Sergius (Tychicus), who made it strong enough to survive the persecution and massacre instigated by the emperor Michael I and the empress Theodora. The number and power of the Paulicians were greatest under Karbeas and Chrysocheir, the leaders in the third quarter of the 9th century. An expedition sent by Basil I in 872 broke their military power, but they survived in Asia at least until the Crusades. After the 9th century their importance lay chiefly in Thrace, where many Paulicians had been forcibly located to serve as a frontier force against the Bulgarians.

Paulician doctrines were disseminated among the Macedonians, Bulgarians, and Greeks, especially among the peasants, and it seems that they contributed to the development of the doctrines and practices of the BOGOMILS, another neo-Manichaean sect, who first appeared in Bulgaria in the early 10th century.

PAUL THE APOSTLE, SAINT \'pȯl\, *original name* Saul of Tarsus (b. 10? CE, Tarsus in Cilicia [now in Turkey]—d. 67?,

Rome [Italy]), 1st-century Jew who, after being a bitter enemy of the Christian church, became its leading missionary and possibly its greatest theologian. His extensive travels and his vision of a universal church were responsible for the speed with which CHRISTIANITY became a world religion. Over half of THE ACTS OF THE APOSTLES deals with his career, and this, together with the letters written by him or in his name, constitutes one-third of the NEW TESTAMENT.

Paul had a strict Jewish upbringing, but he also inherited Roman citizenship and grew up with a good command of idiomatic Greek. At some stage he became an enthusiastic member of the PHARISEES, a Jewish sect that promoted purity and fidelity to the Law of MOSES. According to Acts, he received training as a RABBI in Jerusalem under GAMALIEL I. Like most rabbis he supported himself with a trade, tent making. It is clear that he never met JESUS; he became known rather as an opponent and even persecutor of the Christian movement.

Paul was converted as a result of a vision on the road to Damascus, on his way to apprehend some of the scattered Christians. His vision of Jesus risen from the dead and exalted as Lord in heaven convinced Paul that his vocation was to prepare people of every nation for God's imminent coming. Paul believed that Jesus, having died for the sins of mankind, was now reserved in heaven as God's agent for the judgment.

Three years after his conversion Paul visited Jerusalem, where he met Peter and James, Jesus' brother. This meeting established Paul as a recognized Apostle alongside the founders of the church. At some later point Paul moved to Antioch, the capital of Syria, to assist Barnabas in his successful MISSION there. The converts included a large number of GENTILES. This eventually led to a serious crisis: primitive Christianity was a closely knit fellowship of converts from JUDAISM with the common meal and the EUCHARIST at the heart of it, but Jewish purity rules made Jews reluctant to eat with Gentiles for fear of transgressing the Law. Some of the Jerusalem Christians who were converted Pharisees held the view that Gentile converts should be required to accept CIRCUMCISION and the obligations of the Law, while Paul opposed this stance.

Antioch continued to be Paul's base for further pioneer-

St. Paul preaching the Gospel, detail of a 12th-century mosaic; in the Cappella Palatina, Palermo, Sicily
Alinari—Art Resource

ing work, first to Cyprus, then to the mainland (modern Turkey). In some places the new congregations he founded may have been entirely composed of Gentiles. Shortly afterwards a deputation came from Jerusalem to Antioch to insist that the Gentile converts should be circumcised. This led Paul to visit Jerusalem, where it was determined that the Gentile mission should continue without pressure to Judaize converts. Paul's insistence on this point assured that Christianity would not be simply a Jewish sect.

After missionary visits to Galatia, Macedonia, Athens, Corinth, and Ephesus, Paul wrote his most important letters. In 1 Corinthians Paul tackles a whole array of problems. Paul's teaching on freedom from the Law had been interpreted to justify licentiousness. The question of which foods a Gentile Christian might eat was causing problems. In dealing with these matters Paul gave the account of the LAST SUPPER in its oldest known form. A section on the gifts of the HOLY SPIRIT includes his famous chapter on love (chapter 13). A long section on RESURRECTION shows that Paul still thought that Jesus' return was near and that the full experience of eternal life lay beyond this event. In his letters to the Galatians and the Romans he lays down the doctrine of JUSTIFICATION by faith.

In Jerusalem Paul was accused of bringing a Gentile into the inner courts of the Temple, beyond the barrier excluding non-Jews. He was arrested, partly to save his life from the mob, but given good treatment on account of his Roman citizenship. To avoid trial in Jerusalem Paul appealed to Caesar; he was taken to Rome for trial and arrived in the spring of 60 CE. There Paul was kept under house arrest for two years. Of the four letters said to be written during his captivity, Philippians and Philemon are generally accepted as genuine; Colossians and Ephesians are questioned. No more is known of this stage in his life, though it may be assumed that Paul was eventually convicted of the charges against him; no reliable account of his death exists.

It can be justly claimed that it was due to Paul more than anyone else that Christianity became a world religion. His surviving letters were collected for general circulation and quickly became a standard of reference for Christian teaching. In the Western (Latin) half of Christendom Paul had a profound effect upon the history of the church through the writings of St. Augustine. In arguing for the necessity of divine GRACE for salvation, Augustine built on Paul's idea of PREDESTINATION. The reformers of the 16th century were similarly indebted to him: MARTIN LUTHER seized on the doctrine of justification by faith and made the distinction between faith and works the basis of his attack on the late medieval church. JOHN CALVIN drew from Paul his concept of the church as the company of the ELECT.

PAX \\'paks, 'päks\\, in ROMAN RELIGION, personification of peace, probably recognized as a deity for the first time by the emperor Augustus. An altar of Pax Augusta (the ARA PACIS) was dedicated in 9 BCE and a great temple of Pax completed by the emperor Vespasian in 75 CE.

PEACE MISSION, predominantly African-American 20th-century religious movement in the United States, founded and led by FATHER DIVINE (1878/80–1965), who was regarded, or worshiped, by his followers as God, Dean of the Universe, and Harnesser of Atomic Energy.

According to most accounts, Father Divine was born George Baker and reared in Savannah, Ga., during the post-Reconstruction period. He received indelible impressions from his immersion in MYSTICISM and the Holiness and Pen-

tecostal movements. Father Divine set up his first "heaven" in Sayville, Long Island, N.Y., in 1919. Legal entanglements forced him to relocate in Manhattan (Harlem) and Philadelphia, Pa., but the movement continued to grow and spread through many cities of the northern and western United States.

Heaven, according to Father Divine, was symbolized by separation of sexes and union of all races in a communion composed of a multicourse feast. He also preached total racial integration, that all things and persons are to be forsaken for the Father, and that heaven is on earth. The key to Father Divine's success was the devotion of competent disciples. In the late 20th century, this cohesion diminished and the movement dwindled.

PEGASUS \\'pe-gə-səs\\, in Greek mythology, winged horse that sprang from the neck of MEDUSA as she was beheaded by the hero PERSEUS. With the help of ATHENA (or POSEIDON), another Greek hero, BELLEROPHON, captured Pegasus and rode him first in his fight with the CHIMERA and later while he was taking vengeance on Sthenoboea (Anteia), who had falsely accused him. Subsequently Bellerophon attempted to fly to heaven but was unseated and killed, the winged horse becoming the servant of ZEUS.

PEKO \\'pä-kȯ\\, in Estonian religion, agricultural deity who aided the growth of grain, especially barley. Peko was represented by a wax image that was kept buried in the grain in the granary and brought out on the night of October 1 for a ritual of agricultural increase. The worshipers were a kind of secret society, and the rites were performed like a mystery. After the feast, the men would engage in wrestling or fence jumping to determine who would be the host for Peko in the following year. The first one to get a bleeding wound would take Peko home and store him in his granary. Another rite, more public, was held at sowing time.

PELAGIANISM \\pə-'lā-jē-ə-,ni-zəm\\, *also called* Pelagian Heresy, 5th-century Christian HERESY taught by PELAGIUS and his followers that stressed the essential goodness of human nature and the freedom of the human will. Rejecting the argument that SIN exists because of human weakness, Pelagius insisted that God made human beings free to choose between GOOD AND EVIL and that sin is a voluntary act committed by a person against God's law. Celestius, a disciple of Pelagius, denied the church's doctrine of ORIGINAL SIN and the necessity of infant BAPTISM.

Pelagianism was opposed by ST. AUGUSTINE, who asserted that human beings could not attain righteousness by their own efforts and were totally dependent upon the GRACE of God. Condemned by two councils of African bishops in 416, and again at Carthage in 418, Pelagius and Celestius were excommunicated in 418; Pelagius' fate is unknown.

The controversy, however, was not over. Julian of Eclanum continued to assert the Pelagian view and engaged Augustine in literary polemic until the latter's death in 430. Julian himself was finally condemned, with the rest of the Pelagian party, at the COUNCIL OF EPHESUS in 431. Another heresy, known as SEMI-PELAGIANISM, flourished in southern Gaul until it was finally condemned at the second Council of Orange in 529.

PELAGIUS \\pə-'lā-jē-əs\\ (b. *c.* 354, probably Britain—d. after 418, possibly Palestine), monk and theologian whose heterodox theological system known as PELAGIANISM emphasized the primacy of human effort in spiritual salvation.

Coming to Rome about 380, Pelagius, though not a priest, became a highly regarded spiritual director for both clergy and laymen. Distressed by what he viewed as the spiritual sloth of many Roman Christians, he blamed Rome's moral laxity on the doctrine of divine GRACE that he heard a bishop cite from the *Confessions* of ST. AUGUSTINE, who in his prayer for continence beseeched God to grant whatever GRACE the divine will determined. Pelagius attacked this teaching on the grounds that it imperiled morality, and he soon gained a considerable following at Rome. Henceforth, his closest collaborator was a lawyer named Celestius.

After the fall of Rome to the Visigoths in 410, Pelagius and Celestius went to Africa. There they encountered the hostile criticism of Augustine, who published several denunciatory letters concerning their doctrine, particularly Pelagius' insistence on man's basically good moral nature and on man's own responsibility for voluntarily choosing Christian ASCETICISM for his spiritual advancement.

Pelagius left for Palestine *c.* 412. There, although he was accused of HERESY at the SYNOD of Jerusalem in 415, he succeeded in clearing himself and avoiding censure. In response to further attacks from Augustine and the Latin biblical scholar JEROME, Pelagius wrote *De libero arbitrio* ("On Free Will") in 416, which resulted in the condemnation of his teaching by two African councils. Pope Innocent I endorsed the condemnations and excommunicated Pelagius and Celestius. Innocent's successor, Zosimus, at first pronounced the Pelagians innocent on the basis of Pelagius' *Libellus fidei* ("Brief Statement of Faith"). However, after renewed investigation at the Council of Carthage in 418, Zosimus confirmed the council's nine canons condemning Pelagius.

PELEUS \\'pēl-ˌyüs, 'pē-lē-əs\\, in Greek mythology, king of the MYRMIDONS of Thessaly; he was most famous as the husband of THETIS, the NEREID, and as the father of ACHILLES. When Peleus and his brother Telamon were banished from their father Aeacus' kingdom of Aegina, Peleus went to Phthia to be purified by his uncle King Eurytion, whose daughter Antigone he married, receiving a third of Eurytion's kingdom. During the Calydonian boar hunt he accidentally killed Eurytion. He then went to Iolcos to be purified by King Acastus, whose wife Astydameia made advances to him. When he refused her, she told Antigone that he wanted to marry her daughter, causing Antigone to hang herself. Peleus later won Thetis by capture, and all the gods except ERIS (the goddess of discord) were invited to the wedding. The golden apple that Eris spitefully tossed amongst the wedding guests led to the "judgment of Paris" and thence to the Trojan War. Thetis, who had returned to the sea after bearing Achilles, eventually fetched Peleus to dwell with her.

PELIAS \\'pē-lē-əs\\, in Greek mythology, king of Iolcus in Thessaly who imposed on his half-nephew JASON the task of fetching the Golden Fleece. According to Homer, Pelias and Neleus were twin sons of Tyro by POSEIDON, who came to her disguised as the river god Enipeus, whom she loved. The twins were exposed at birth but were found and raised by a horse herder. Later, Pelias seized the throne and exiled Neleus.

On Jason's return with the fleece, his wife MEDEA took revenge on Pelias by persuading his daughters, except for Alcestis, to cut up and boil their father in the mistaken belief that he would thereby recover his youth.

PELOPS \\'pē-ˌläps, 'pe-\\, legendary founder of the Pelopid dynasty at Mycenae in the Greek Peloponnese, which was probably named for him. Pelops was a grandson of ZEUS. According to many accounts, his father, TANTALUS, cooked and served Pelops to the gods at a banquet. Only DEMETER, bereaved over the loss of her daughter, failed to recognize him and partook. When the body was restored by the gods, the shoulder, Demeter's portion, was missing; the goddess provided a replacement of ivory.

According to Pindar, however, POSEIDON loved Pelops and took him up to heaven. Pelops had to return to mortal life because his father had abused the favor of heaven by feeding mortals with nectar and ambrosia, of which only gods partook. Later, according to Pindar, Pelops strove for the hand of Hippodamia, daughter of King Oenomaus of Pisa in Elis. Oenomaus, who had an incestuous love for his daughter, had previously killed 13 suitors. He challenged Pelops to a chariot chase, with Hippodamia the prize of victory and death the price of defeat. Though Oenomaus' team and chariot were the gift of his father, the god ARES, Pelops' chariot was from Poseidon. Pelops won the bride and killed Oenomaus.

In other versions, Pelops bribed Oenomaus' charioteer, Myrtilus, to remove the linchpins from Oenomaus' chariot. After his victory he threw Myrtilus into the sea that afterward was called the Myrtoan. Myrtilus—or Oenomaus—was said to have uttered the curse that dogged the Pelopid house of ATREUS. Preparations for the race are depicted in the east pediment of the Temple of Zeus at OLYMPIA.

PENATES \\pə-'nā-tēz, -'nä-\\, *formally* Di Penates, household gods of the Romans and other Latin peoples. They were gods of the *penus* ("household provisions"), but by extension their protection reached the entire household. They are associated with other deities of the house, such as VESTA, and the name was sometimes used interchangeably with that of the Lares. Their number and precise identity were a puzzle even to the Romans.

The Penates were worshiped privately as protectors of the individual household and also publicly as protectors of the Roman state. Each house had a shrine with images of them that were worshiped at the family meal and on special occasions. Offerings were of portions of the regular meal or of special cakes, wine, honey, incense, and, more rarely, a blood sacrifice. The state as a whole worshiped the Penates Publici. This state cult occupied a significant role as a focal point of Roman patriotism and nationalism.

PENELOPE \\pə-'ne-lə-pē\\, in Greek mythology, daughter of Icarius of Sparta and the NYMPH Periboea and wife of the hero ODYSSEUS. In the *Odyssey*, during her husband's long absence after the Trojan War, many chieftains of Ithaca and nearby islands became her suitors. She insisted that they wait until she had woven a shroud for Laertes, father of Odysseus. Every night for three years, until one of her maids revealed the secret, she undid the work that she had woven by day in order to delay the date at which she would have to forsake her lost husband by remarrying. She was finally relieved by the arrival of Odysseus. According to later writers, after the death of Odysseus, Penelope married TELEGONUS, son of Odysseus and CIRCE. A late tradition names her the mother of the god PAN by HERMES (who came to her in the shape of a goat); another variant stated that Pan was born from the accumulated seed of all the suitors, with each of whom Penelope had coupled; this was most likely based on the mistaken translation of Pan as "all."

PENTATEUCH \'pen-tə-,tük, -,tyük\, first five books of the Jewish BIBLE (the Christian OLD TESTAMENT).

PENTECOST (from Greek: *pentekostē* [*hēmera*], "50th day"), *also called* Whitsunday, major festival in the Christian church, celebrated on the Sunday concluding the 50-day period beginning with EASTER. It commemorates the descent of the HOLY SPIRIT on the disciples, which occurred on the Jewish Pentecost, after the death, RESURRECTION, and ASCENSION of JESUS CHRIST (Acts 2), and it marks the beginning of the Christian church's MISSION to the world.

The Jewish feast was a thanksgiving for the first fruits of the wheat harvest, associated with remembrance of the Law given by God for the Hebrews to MOSES on MOUNT SINAI. The transformation of the Jewish feast to a Christian festival was thus related to the belief that the gift of the Holy Spirit to the followers of Jesus was the first fruits of a new dispensation that fulfilled and succeeded the old dispensation of the Law.

When the festival was first celebrated in the Christian church is not known, but it was mentioned in a work from the Eastern church, the *Epistola Apostolorum,* in the 2nd century. In the 3rd century it was mentioned by ORIGEN, theologian and head of the catechetical school in Alexandria, and by TERTULLIAN, a Christian writer of Carthage.

In the early church, Christians often referred to the entire 50-day period following Easter as Pentecost. BAPTISM was administered both at the beginning (Easter) and end (the day of Pentecost) of the season. Eventually, Pentecost became a more popular time for baptism than Easter in northern Europe, and in England the feast was commonly called White Sunday (Whitsunday) for the special white garments worn by the newly baptized.

PENTECOSTALISM \,pen-tə-'kòs-tə-,li-zəm\, charismatic religious movement that gave rise to a number of Protestant churches in the United States in the 19th and 20th centuries and that is characterized by the belief that all Christians should seek a postconversion RELIGIOUS EXPERIENCE called the BAPTISM with the HOLY SPIRIT. This experience corresponds to the first outpouring or descent of the Holy Spirit upon the 12 disciples of Christ assembled in Jerusalem on the day of PENTECOST, as recorded in Acts 1:12–2:4, and it is accompanied by the same sign: the gift of glosso-

lalia, or "speaking in tongues." Pentecostals also hold that a Spirit-baptized believer may receive at least one of the other supernatural gifts that were known to have been in existence in the early church—the ability to prophesy, to heal, or to interpret what is said when someone speaks in unknown tongues. Beyond these unique distinctions, Pentecostal churches reflect those patterns of faith and practice characteristic of the Fundamentalist-Holiness branches of PROTESTANTISM that also originated in 19th-century America, with their emphases on biblical literalism, conversion, and moral rigor. Despite a common belief in certain doctrines, Pentecostals have not united in a single denomination.

The roots of the modern Pentecostal movements are traceable to a number of charismatic outgrowths of the 19th-century Holiness revival that developed in various parts of the United States. Perhaps the most far-reaching of these movements originated around the turn of the 20th

The descent of the Holy Spirit at Pentecost, *pen and brush drawing by Sir Anthony van Dyck, 1620–21; in the Hermitage, St. Petersburg*
The Bridgeman Art Library

century at Bethel Bible College in Topeka, Kan. The director of the institution, Charles Fox Parham, one of many ministers who had been influenced by the Holiness movement, believed that what he saw as a complacent, prosperity-ridden, and coldly formalistic church of the era needed to be revived and that such a revival could only be achieved by another outpouring of the Holy Spirit. He therefore instructed his students, many of whom already held ministerial credentials with Methodist, Friends, or Holiness churches, to pray, fast, study the SCRIPTURES, and await an endowment of Pentecostal blessing and power that would be very much like the events recounted in Acts.

On Jan. 1, 1901, the first of Parham's many students to experience a Spirit baptism began speaking in an unknown tongue. From that time forward, most Pentecostals usually declared that glossolalia was the "initial evidence" that one had been truly Spirit-baptized. These recurrences of Pentecost also had prophetic overtones that Parham and his students interpreted as meaning that they must be living in the last days. Imbued with this sense of urgency, they set out to evangelize the American Southwest. According to Parham, by 1905 some 25,000 persons in Texas alone had embraced Pentecostalism. The embryonic charismatic movement was at first significant in only a few regions: in the states of Kansas, Missouri, Texas, Alabama, and western Florida.

The national and international expansion occurred as a consequence of what is recorded as the Azusa Street revival of 1906. The Apostolic Faith Gospel Mission of Los Angeles was led by William Seymour, a former Holiness preacher, who had been exposed to Pentecostal teaching at a Bible school in Houston, Texas. Under his guidance, from April 1906 onward, rich and poor, blacks and whites, and seekers and skeptics flocked to the Mission to receive spiritual help. Soon groups of Pentecostal believers sprang up all over the world. These congregations represented the effects of a novel revival that was known variously as the Latter Rain, Apostolic Faith, or Pentecostal movement.

From the very beginning of the Pentecostal revival, its evangelists—Mrs. Mary B. Woodworth-Etter, Charles Price, AIMEE SEMPLE MCPHERSON, and, more recently, Oral Roberts—have taught that deliverance from sickness was provided for in Christ's ATONEMENT and is, therefore, the privilege of all who have faith. This effort to minister to the physical needs of people likely has been responsible for winning many followers to Pentecostalism.

Despite the fact that many members of the historic Protestant churches embraced the teachings and practices of healing, prophesying, and speaking in tongues, they initially had no intention of withdrawing from their own churches. They wished rather to be the agents of reform and revival, helping to rid their churches of formalism, modernism, and worldliness. But the embryonic Pentecostal movement became the object of widespread opposition. Those who desired to retain their charismatic religious way of life found it increasingly difficult to do so within the institutional framework of conventional Protestantism, with the result that many withdrew from their churches to form new and distinctly Pentecostal groups.

Pentecostal denominations are widespread throughout the United States and are found in many other countries, notably Mexico, Chile, and other Latin-American countries and Sweden, Norway, Great Britain, South Africa, and Russia. Forty or more identifiable groups in America practice glossolalia; in addition, there are hundreds of obscure "storefront" congregations that cannot be included in any reliable computation. Pentecostal churches abound also in remote mountain and other rural areas, and it is mainly among these that the pronounced emotional manifestations are found. The larger bodies are organized in the Pentecostal World Conference, an international fellowship headquartered in Wales.

PERFECTION OF WISDOM SUTRAS \\'sü-trəz\\: *see* PRA-JÑĀPĀRAMITĀ.

PĒRKONS \\'par-kwȯns\\ (Latvian: "Thunder"), *Lithuanian* Perkūnas \\pᵉ er-'kü-nȧs\\, *Old Prussian* Perkunis, sky deity of BALTIC RELIGION, renowned as the guardian of law and order. The oak, as the tree most often struck by lightning, is sacred to him. Pērkons is related to the Slavic PERUN, Germanic THOR, and Greek ZEUS.

Often visualized as a bearded man holding an ax, Pērkons rides across the sky striking fire with his two-wheeled chariot and bringing rain. In the spring his lightning purifies the earth and stimulates plant growth. Pērkons also directs his thunderbolts against evil spirits and unjust men and even disciplines the gods. Lithuanian legend recounts that when Mėnuo, the moon god and husband of SAULE, goddess of the sun, committed adultery, Perkūnas punished his infidelity by cutting him to pieces.

According to ancient tradition, thunderbolts—"bullets of Pērkons," found buried in the ground as prehistoric flint or bronze implements—or any object or person struck by lightning could be used by mortals as protection against devils or as cures for toothache, fever, and fright. Probably the most popular of all Baltic gods, Perkūnas is often referred to in Lithuanian as *dievaitis*, an archaic diminutive of *dievas* ("god").

PERSEPHONE \\pər-'se-fə-nē\\, *Latin* Proserpina *or* Proserpine, in GREEK RELIGION, daughter of ZEUS, the chief god, and DEMETER, the goddess of agriculture; she was the wife of HADES, king of the Underworld. In Homer she is queen of the Underworld and there is no mention of her relationship to Demeter. Hesiod was the first to relate that she was the daughter of Demeter and was carried off by Hades. In the Homeric "Hymn to Demeter," the story is told of how Persephone was gathering flowers in the Vale of Nysa when she was seized by Hades and removed to the Underworld. Upon learning of the abduction, her mother, in her misery, became unconcerned with the harvest or the fruitfulness of the earth, so that widespread famine ensued. Zeus therefore intervened, commanding Hades to release Persephone to her mother. Because Persephone had eaten one or more pomegranate seeds in the Underworld, she could not be completely freed but had to remain one-third of the year with Hades, spending the other two-thirds with her mother. On one level the story that Persephone spent four months of each year in the Underworld accounted for the barren appearance of Greek fields in full summer (after harvest), before their revival in the autumn rains, when they are plowed and sown; other possible interpretations suggest that her descent followed the storage of seed grain in underground silos, or that the myth was a metaphor for human marriage rites.

The figure and name of Persephone may well have been of pre-Hellenic origin. Once the connection with Demeter was formed she became identified with Kore (Greek: "maiden"), a grain goddess and also daughter of Demeter. Demeter and Kore/Persephone figured in the ELEUSINIAN MYSTERIES.

PERSEUS \'pər-sē-əs, -ˌsyüs, -ˌsüs\, in Greek mythology, the slayer of MEDUSA and the rescuer of ANDROMEDA from a sea monster. Perseus was the son of ZEUS and DANAË, the daughter of Acrisius of Argos. As an infant he was cast into the sea in a chest with his mother by Acrisius, to whom it had been prophesied that he would be killed by his grandson. After Perseus had grown up on the island of Seriphus, King Polydectes of Seriphus, who desired Danaë, tricked Perseus into promising to obtain the head of Medusa, the only mortal among the GORGONS.

Aided by HERMES and ATHENA, Perseus pressed the Graiae, sisters of the Gorgons, into helping him by seizing the one eye and one tooth that the sisters shared and refusing to return them until they provided him with winged sandals (which enabled him to fly), the helmet of HADES (which conferred invisibility on its wearer), a curved sword, or sickle, with which to decapitate Medusa, and a bag in which to conceal the head. (According to another version, the Graiae merely directed him to the Stygian NYMPHS, who told him where to find the Gorgons and gave him the bag, the sandals, and the helmet; Hermes gave him the sword.) Because the gaze of Medusa turned all who looked at her to stone, Perseus guided himself by looking at her reflection in a shield given him by Athena, and he beheaded Medusa as she slept. He then returned to Seriphus and rescued his mother by turning Polydectes and his supporters to stone at the sight of Medusa's head.

A further deed attributed to Perseus was his rescue of the Ethiopian princess Andromeda when he was on his way home with Medusa's head. Andromeda's mother, Cassiopeia, had claimed to be more beautiful than the sea nymphs, or NEREIDS; so POSEIDON had punished Ethiopia by flooding it and plaguing it with a sea monster. An oracle informed Andromeda's father, King Cepheus, that the ills that had befallen his land would cease if he exposed Andromeda to the monster, which he did. Perseus, passing by, turned the sea monster to stone by showing it Medusa's head and afterward married Andromeda.

Perseus, *bronze sculpture by Benvenuto Cellini, 1545–54; in the Loggia dei Lanzi, Florence*
Alinari—Art Resource

Later Perseus gave Medusa's head to Athena, who placed it on her shield, and he gave his other accoutrements to Hermes. He accompanied his mother back to her native Argos, where he accidentally struck her father, Acrisius, dead when throwing the discus, thus fulfilling the PROPHECY that he would kill his grandfather. He consequently left Argos and founded Mycenae as his capital, becoming the ancestor of the Perseids, including HERACLES. The Perseus legend was a favorite subject in painting and sculpture, both ancient and Renaissance. The chief characters in the Perseus legend, Perseus, Cepheus, Cassiopeia, Andromeda, and the sea monster (Cetus), all figure in the night sky as constellations.

PERUN \pʸi-'rün\, thunder-god of the ancient Slavs, a fructifier, purifier, and overseer of right and order. His actions are perceived by the senses: seen in the thunderbolt, heard in the rattle of stones or the bellow of the bull or the bleat of the goat (thunder), and felt in the touch of an ax blade. The word for Thursday (Thor's day) in the Polabian language was *peründan.* Polish *piorun* and Slovak *parom* denote "thunder" or "lightning."

The "Lightning-god" and his cult among the Slavs is attested by the Byzantine historian Procopius in the 6th century. In the *Primary Russian Chronicle,* compiled c. 1111, Perun is mentioned as having been invoked in the treaties of 945 and 971, and his name is the first in the list of gods of St. Vladimir's pantheon of 980. He was worshiped in oak groves by western Slavs, who called him Prone, which name appears in Helmold's *Chronica Slavorum* (c. 1172). Porenut, Perun's son, is mentioned by the Danish historian Saxo Grammaticus in the early 13th century.

In the Christian period the worship of Perun was gradually transferred to St. Elijah (Russian Iliya), but in folk beliefs, his fructifying, life-stimulating, and purifying functions are still performed by his vehicles: the ax, the bull, the goat, the dove, and the cuckoo. Sacrifices and communal feasts on July 20 in honor of Perun or Iliya continued in Russia until modern times.

PESHAṬ \pe-'shät\ (Hebrew: "spread out"), in Jewish HERME-NEUTICS, the literal meaning of a biblical text. In the interpretation of the HALAKHAH, *peshaṭ* was preferred. Other interpretive principles, however, could be used simultaneously: *remez* (meaning "hint," in reference to allegorical interpretations), *derash* (meaning "search," in reference to biblical study according to the MIDDOT, or rules), and *sod* (meaning "secret," or mystical interpretation).

PETER LOMBARD \'pē-tər-'läm-,bärd, -bərd\, *French* Pierre Lombard, *Latin* Petrus Lombardus (b. *c.* 1100, Novara, Lombardy—d. Aug. 21/22, 1160, Paris), bishop of Paris whose *Four Books of Sentences* (*Sententiarum libri IV*) was the standard theological text of the Middle Ages.

After schooling at Bologna, he went to France to study at Reims and Paris. From 1136 to 1150 he taught theology in the school of Notre Dame, Paris, where in 1144–45 he became a staff clergyman. Lombard was present at the Council of Reims (1148) that assembled to examine the writings of the French theologian Gilbert de La Porrée. In June 1159 he was consecrated bishop of Paris, and he died the following year.

Although he wrote sermons, letters, and Scriptural commentaries, Lombard's *Four Books of Sentences* (1148–51) established his reputation and subsequent fame, earning him the title of *magister sententiarum* ("master of the sentences"). The *Sentences*, a collection of teachings of the CHURCH FATHERS and opinions of medieval masters arranged as a systematic treatise, marked the culmination of a long tradition of theological pedagogy, and until the 16th century it was the official textbook in the universities. Thousands of scholars wrote commentaries on it, including the celebrated philosopher ST. THOMAS AQUINAS.

Book I of the *Sentences* discusses God, the TRINITY, divine guidance, evil, and predestination; Book II, ANGELS, DEMONS, the Fall of man, GRACE, and SIN; Book III, the INCARNATION of JESUS CHRIST, the redemption of sins, virtues, and the TEN COMMANDMENTS; Book IV, the SACRAMENTS and the four last things—death, judgment, hell, and heaven. Of special importance to medieval theologians was Lombard's clarification of the theology of the sacraments. He asserted that there are seven sacraments and that a sacrament is not merely a "visible sign of invisible grace" (as ST. AUGUSTINE had defined it) but also the "cause of the grace it signifies." In ethical matters, he decreed that a man's actions are judged good or bad according to their cause and intention, except those acts that are evil by nature. Later theologians rejected a number of his views, but

Painting by Annibale Carracci known as Domine Quo Vadis *("Lord, Whither Goest Thou?"), in which Christ appears to Peter on the Appian Way to encourage him to return to Rome for his martyrdom*
By courtesy of the trustees of the National Gallery, London; photograph, A.C. Cooper, Ltd.

he was never regarded as unorthodox, and efforts to have his works condemned were unsuccessful. The fourth LATERAN COUNCIL (1215) approved his teaching on the Trinity.

PETER THE APOSTLE, SAINT, *original name* Simeon, *or* Simon (d. *c.* 64 CE, Rome), disciple of JESUS CHRIST, recognized in the early church as the leader of the disciples and by the ROMAN CATHOLIC church as the first of its unbroken succession of popes.

Peter probably was known originally by the Hebrew name Simeon or the Greek form of that name, Simon. There is indirect evidence (Matthew 8:14; 1 Corinthians 9:5) that Peter was the son of John and was married. His family originally came from Bethsaida (John 1:44), but during the period of Jesus' ministry he lived in Capernaum, at the northwest end of the Sea of Galilee, where he and his brother ANDREW were in partnership as fishermen with JAMES and JOHN, the sons of Zebedee (Luke 5:10). Peter was untrained in the Mosaic Law (Acts 4:13), and it is doubtful that he knew Greek.

With differing degrees of emphasis, the SYNOPTIC GOSPELS agree that Peter served as spokesman for the disciples and enjoyed a certain precedence over the others. Whenever the disciples are listed, Peter is invariably mentioned first. In what may be a grouping of Petrine material (Matthew 16:18, 19) Jesus gave to Simon the title of Cephas, or Peter (from Greek *petra*). Matthew continues that upon this rock—that is, upon Peter—the church will be built. The word church in the Gospel is to be understood as referring to the community of the faithful rather than to a definite ecclesiastical organization.

Given the information supplied by the Gospels, it is not unexpected that Peter should emerge immediately after Jesus' death as the leader of the earliest church. For approximately 15 years after the RESURRECTION, the figure of Peter dominated the community. It was Peter who first "raised his voice" and preached at PENTECOST, the day when the church came into being (Acts 1:14–39). It was Peter who served as an advocate for the Apostles before the Jewish religious court in Jerusalem (Acts 4:5–22). Peter likewise led the Twelve Apostles in extending the church "here and there among them all" (Acts 9:32), going first to the SAMARITANS (Acts 8:4–17), then venturing to the Mediterranean coast (Acts 9:36–43; 10:1–11:18), where he introduced GENTILES into the church. In accepting the Gentiles and ordering "them to be baptized in the name of Jesus Christ" (Acts 10:48) without submission to the prior rite of CIRCUMCISION,

Peter introduced an innovation that insured the opposition of the Jewish Christians and others. Soon the unchallenged leadership of Peter in Jerusalem came to an end.

The problems surrounding the residence, martyrdom, and burial of Peter are among the most complicated of all those encountered in the study of the NEW TESTAMENT and the early church. The absence of any reference in Acts or Romans to a residence of Peter in Rome gives pause but is not conclusive. It may be said that by the end of the 1st century there existed a tradition that Peter had lived in Rome. It is probable that the tradition of a 25-year episcopate of Peter in Rome is not earlier than the beginning or the middle of the 3rd century. The claims that the church of Rome was founded by Peter or that he served as its first bishop are in dispute and rest on evidence that is not earlier than the middle or late 2nd century. Words of John 21:18, 19 clearly allude to the death of Peter and are cast into the literary form of PROPHECY. The author of this chapter is aware of a tradition concerning the martyrdom of Peter when the Apostle was an old man. And there is a possible reference here to CRUCIFIXION as the manner of his death. But as to when or where the death took place there is not so much as a hint. Archaeological investigation has not solved the question of the location of the tomb of Peter.

PETTAZZONI, RAFFAELE \‚pet-täd-'dzō-nē\ (b. Feb. 3, 1883, Persiceto, Italy—d. Dec. 8, 1959, Rome), Italian historian of religions and educator, a founder and president (1950–59) of the International Association for the Study of History of Religions. His comparative works include *Dio, formazione e sviluppo del monoteismo nella storia delle religioni* (1922; "God, the Formation and Development of Monotheism in the History of Religions"), *La confessione dei peccati*, 3 vol. (1929–35; "The Confession of Sins"), *L'essere supremo nelle religioni primitive* (1957; "The Supreme Being in Primitive Religions"), and *Essays on the History of Religions* (1954).

PEYOTE \pā-'ō-tē\, *also called* mescal-button \me-'skal\, two species of the cactus genus *Lophophora*, native to North America, almost exclusively to Mexico.

Peyote, well known for its hallucinogenic effects, contains at least 28 alkaloids, the principal one of which is mescaline. Peyote figures prominently in old religious rituals of certain Native American peoples and in the ritual of the NATIVE AMERICAN CHURCH.

PHAETHON \'fā-ə-thən, -‚thän\ (Greek: "Shining," or "Radiant"), in Greek mythology, son of HELIOS and a woman or NYMPH variously identified as Clymene, Prote, or Rhode. Taunted with illegitimacy, Phaethon appealed to his father, who swore to prove his paternity by giving him whatever he wanted. Phaethon asked to be allowed to drive the chariot of the sun for a single day. Helios, bound by his OATH, had to let him make the attempt. Phaethon was unable to control the horses of the sun chariot, which came too near to the earth and began to scorch it. To prevent further damage, ZEUS killed Phaethon with a thunderbolt; he fell to the earth at the mouth of the river Eridanus.

PHALLICISM \'fa-lə-‚si-zəm\, worship of the generative principle as symbolized by the sexual organs or the act of sexual intercourse.

The most important forms of sexual rituals are those in which intercourse is believed to promote fertility, those that release a flood of creative energy by breaking bound-aries and by returning a culture to the state of primeval and powerful CHAOS, or those in which sexual intercourse symbolizes the bringing together of opposites (*e.g.*, alchemy or Tantrism, a Hindu esoteric meditation system).

In other traditions objects of adoration are representations of the sexual organs (*e.g.*, the phallus borne in Dionysian PROCESSIONS in Greece and Rome; the male LIŃGA and female YONI in India) or deities with prominent genitals (*e.g.*, PRIAPUS in Rome, PAN in Greece). In these instances, the powers of creativity that the sexual organ represents, rather than the organ itself, are worshiped.

PHARISEES \'far-ə-‚sēz\, political party in the Land of Israel in the second and first centuries BCE, later on represented by the Christian Gospels and certain rabbinic traditions also as a religious sect in the first century CE. The sect was characterized by the belief in life after death and the revelation of "traditions of the fathers," and by the practice of requiring purity not only in the Temple, where the TORAH required it, but also in eating ordinary meals at home.

The Pharisees are of special interest for two reasons. First, they are mentioned in the SYNOPTIC GOSPELS as contemporaries of Jesus, represented sometimes as hostile, sometimes as neutral, and sometimes as friendly to the early Christians represented by Jesus. Second, they are commonly supposed to stand behind the authorities who, in the second century, made up the materials that come to us in the MISHNAH, the first important document, after SCRIPTURE, of JUDAISM in its classical or normative form. Hence the Mishnah and some related writings are alleged to rest upon traditions going back to the Pharisees before 70 CE. However, these views impute to the Pharisees greater importance than they are likely to have enjoyed in their own day.

Three discrete sources refer to Pharisees: (1) the Gospels (*c.* 70–90 CE), (2) the historical writings of JOSEPHUS (*c.* 90–100 CE), and (3) the later rabbinic compositions, beginning with the Mishnah (*c.* 200–600 CE). No writings survive that were produced by the Pharisees themselves; all we do know is what later writers said about them.

These sources have little in common in the picture they give of the Pharisees. On the one hand, in Josephus' historical work the Pharisees appear as a political party which tried to gain control of the government of Jewish Palestine. On the other hand, the rabbinic traditions about the Pharisees present them as forming a rather self-centered group, concerned with its internal issues, its own laws, and its own partisan conflicts. Of the rabbinic traditions that allude to persons or groups we assume to have been Pharisees, approximately two-thirds deal with dietary laws. These laws concern (1) ritual purity for meals and (2) agricultural rules governing the fitness of food for Pharisaic consumption, with observance of SABBATHS and festivals a distant third. Pharisaic laws deal not with the governance of the country but with the party's rules for table-fellowship. The political issues are not whether one should pay taxes to Rome or how one should know the MESSIAH, but whether in the Temple the rule of Shammai or that of HILLEL should be followed in a minor festal sacrifice. Josephus' portrayal thus has little, if anything, in common with the rabbis' portrait, except the rather general allegation that the Pharisees had "traditions from the fathers," a point made also by the Synoptic Gospels.

A similar difficulty arises in terms of chronology. Josephus' Pharisees are important in the reigns of John Hyrcanus and Alexander Jannaeus but drop from the picture after Alexandra Salome. But the Synoptics' Pharisees are much like those of the rabbis; they belong to the Roman period, and their legal agenda is virtually identical, including such issues as tithing, purity laws, Sabbath-observance, and vows. The question of who the Pharisees were, and the conflicts in which they figured, is still open to debate.

PHERECYDES OF SYROS \\,fer-ə-'sī-dēz . . . 'sī-ˌräs\\ (fl. *c.* 550 BCE), Greek mythographer and cosmogonist traditionally associated with the Seven Wise Men of Greece (especially Thales). Pherecydes is credited with originating metempsychosis, a doctrine that holds the human soul to be immortal, passing into another body, either human or animal, after death. He is also known as the author of *Heptamychos*, a work, extant in fragments only, describing the origin of the world. Pherecydes was characterized by Aristotle as a theologian who mixed philosophy and myth. Tradition says that he was the teacher of Pythagoras.

PHILEMON AND BAUCIS \\fi-'lē-mən, fī- . . . 'bȯ-sis\\, in Greek mythology, pious Phrygian couple who hospitably received ZEUS and HERMES when their richer neighbors turned away the two gods, who were disguised as wayfarers. As a reward, they were saved from a flood that drowned the rest of the country; their cottage was turned into a temple, and at their own request they became priest and priestess of it. Long after, they were granted their wish to die at the same moment, being turned into trees.

PHILOCTETES \\,fi-läk-'tē-tēz\\, Greek legendary hero who played a decisive part in the final stages of the Trojan War.

He (or his father, Poeas) had been bequeathed the bow and arrows of HERACLES in return for lighting his funeral pyre; Philoctetes thus became a notable archer. En route to Troy he was incapacitated by a snakebite and was left behind. After a seer revealed that Troy could be taken only with the aid of Heracles' bow, ODYSSEUS and DIOMEDES persuaded Philoctetes to accompany them to Troy. There he was healed of his wound and killed PARIS. He returned home but later wandered as a colonist to southern Italy, where he ultimately died in battle. This story was used as the basis of Sophocles' tragedy *Philoctetes.*

PHILO JUDAEUS \\'fī-lō-jü-'dē-əs\\, *also called* Philo of Alexandria (b. 15–10 BCE, Alexandria—d. 45–50 CE, Alexandria), Greek-speaking Jewish philosopher, the most important representative of Hellenistic JUDAISM. His writings provide the clearest view of this development of Judaism in the Diaspora. As the first to attempt to synthesize revealed faith and philosophic reason, he occupies a unique position in the history of philosophy. He is also regarded by Christians as a forerunner of Christian theology.

Philo's works include scriptural essays and homilies based on specific verses or topics of the PENTATEUCH, especially GENESIS, general philosophical and religious essays, and essays on contemporary subjects (including defenses of the Jews against anti-Semitic charges). A number of works ascribed to Philo are almost certainly spurious. Most important of these is *Biblical Antiquities*, an imaginative reconstruction of Jewish history from Adam to the death of SAUL, the first king of Israel.

The key influences on Philo's philosophy were Plato, Aristotle, the Neo-Pythagoreans, the Cynics, and the Stoics. Philo's basic philosophic outlook is Platonic; his reverence for Plato is such that he never took open issue with him, as he did with the Stoics and other philosophers. To Aristotle he was indebted primarily in matters of COSMOLOGY and ethics. To the Neo-Pythagoreans he owed his views on the mystic significance of numbers and the scheme of a peculiar, self-disciplined way of life as a preparation for immortality. The Cynics, with their diatribes, influenced him in the form of his sermons. Though Philo more often employed the terminology of the Stoics than that of any other school, he was critical of their thoughts.

Philo was the first to distinguish between the knowability of God's existence and the unknowability of his essence. He was equally original in insisting on an individual Providence able to suspend the laws of nature in contrast to the prevailing Greek philosophical view of a universal Providence who is himself subject to the laws of nature. Philo saw the cosmos as a great chain of being presided over by the LOGOS, which is the mediator between God and the world, though at one point he identifies the Logos as a second God. In anticipation of Christian doctrine he called the Logos the first-begotten Son of God, the man of God, the image of God, and second to God.

In his ethical theory Philo described two virtues that are otherwise unknown in Greek philosophic literature—religious faith and humanity. Like Plato, Philo regarded the body as the prison house of the soul, and in his DUALISM of body and soul he anticipated much of Gnostic thought. But unlike the Greek philosophers who believed in limited freedom of will, Philo held that man is completely free to act against all the laws of his own nature. Perfect happiness comes, however, not through men's own efforts to achieve virtue but only through the GRACE of God.

PHILOKALIA \\,fē-lō-kä-'lē-ä, ,fi-lō-, -'kä-lē-ə, -'kä-lē-ə\\ (Greek: "Love of the Good, the Beautiful"), prose anthology of Greek Christian monastic texts that was part of a movement for spiritual renewal in Eastern MONASTICISM and Orthodox devotional life in general. Compiled by the Greek monk Nikodimos and by Makarios, the bishop of Corinth, the *Philokalia* was first published in Venice in 1782 and gathered the unpublished writings of all major Hesychasts (*see* HESYCHASM) of the Christian East, from EVAGRIUS PONTICUS to ST. GREGORY PALAMAS.

The *Philokalia* is concerned with "inner ASCETICISM," which means, above all, daily recollection of death and judgment, together with perpetual remembrance of God as omnipresent and omnipotent, and ceaseless prayer. It is through this compilation that the tradition of Gregory Palamas prescribing the "prayer of the mind," or Jesus prayer, uttered in a particular bodily position with a special way of breathing, became better known and gained new followers among Orthodox as well as Western Christians.

The *Philokalia* had great success in the Slavic countries, especially Russia, and a Church Slavonic version appeared in 1793 in St. Petersburg under the title of *Dobrotoliubie*. It was translated by the starets (spiritual leader) Paissy Velitchkovsky, who introduced a neo-Hesychast spiritual renewal to Russian and Moldavian monasticism. Whereas in Greece the *Philokalia* apparently had little influence outside certain schools of monasticism (although attempts were made to reach a wider public with new editions in 1867 and 1957), the Church Slavic version became, through the influence of the startsy, one of the favorite spiritual books of all classes of Russian laity during the 19th century. In 1877 Feofan Zatvornik (Theophanes the Recluse), the former bishop of Tambov, compiled a Russian version.

PHOCUS \\'fō-kəs\\, in Greek mythology, son of AEACUS, king of Aegina, and the NEREID Psamathe, who had assumed the likeness of a seal (Greek: *phoce*) in trying to escape Aeacus' embraces. PELEUS and Telamon, Aeacus' legitimate sons, resented Phocus' athletic prowess. At the instigation of their mother, Endeis, they plotted his death, drawing lots to decide who should destroy him. The lot fell to Telamon, who murdered Phocus, feigning an accident. Aeacus discovered the truth and banished both his sons.

PHOEBE \'fē-bē\, in Greek mythology, a TITAN, daughter of OURANUS and GAEA. By Coeus she was the mother of LETO and grandmother of APOLLO and ARTEMIS. She was also the mother of Asteria and HECATE. In later mythology she was identified with the moon.

PHOENIX \'fē-niks\, in ancient Egypt and in classical antiquity, fabulous bird associated with the worship of the sun. The Egyptian phoenix was said to be as large as an eagle, with brilliant scarlet and gold plumage and a melodious cry. Only one phoenix existed at any time, and it was very long-lived—no ancient authority gave it a life span of less than 500 years. As its end approached, the phoenix fashioned a nest of aromatic boughs and spices, set it on fire, and was consumed in the flames. From the pyre miraculously sprang a new phoenix, which, after embalming its father's ashes in an egg of myrrh, flew with the ashes to HELIOPOLIS ("City of the Sun") in Egypt, where it deposited them on the altar in the temple of the Egyptian god of the sun, RE. A variant of the story made the dying phoenix fly to Heliopolis and immolate itself in the altar fire, from which the young phoenix then rose.

The Egyptians associated the phoenix with immortality, and that symbolism had a widespread appeal in late antiquity. The phoenix was compared to undying Rome, and it appears on the coinage of the late Roman Empire as a symbol of the Eternal City. As an ALLEGORY of RESURRECTION and life after death it also appealed to emergent CHRISTIANITY.

In Islamic mythology the phoenix was identified with the ʿanqāʾ (Persian: *sīmorgh*), a huge, mysterious bird (probably a heron) that was created by God with all perfections but had thereafter become a plague and was killed.

PHOENIX \'fē-niks\, in Greek mythology, son of Amyntor, king of Thessalian Hellas. After a violent quarrel Amyntor cursed him with childlessness, and Phoenix escaped to PELEUS, who entrusted him with the upbringing of ACHILLES. Phoenix accompanied Achilles to Troy and was one of the envoys who tried to reconcile him with AGAMEMNON after the two had quarreled.

In another version, Amyntor blinded his son, whose sight was later restored by CHIRON.

PHOTIUS, SAINT \'fō-shē-əs\ (b. *c.* 820, Constantinople [now Istanbul, Tur.]—d. Feb. 6, 891?, Bordi, Armenia; canonized 10th century?; feast day February 6), PATRIARCH of Constantinople (858–867 and 877–886), defender of the au-

St. Photius, lead seal
Dumbarton Oaks—Trustees for Harvard University, Washington, D.C.

tonomous traditions of his church against Rome, and leading figure of the 9th-century Byzantine renaissance.

Photius became a distinguished teacher. A circle gathered around him for regular readings in classical and Christian literature, including medical and scientific works. On the basis of notes taken at these readings, which continued after he left the schools for the civil service, he composed his *Myriobiblon* or *Bibliotheca* (*Bibliothēkē*), a digest of Greek prose, with more than 270 articles.

He became first secretary of state, probably before 855, and in 858 he was promoted through all the ecclesiastical orders to be made patriarch of Constantinople on CHRISTMAS Day, replacing the austere Ignatius. The deposition of Ignatius offended not only the Studites and other monks, who objected to the promotion of a civil servant, but also Pope Nicholas I, who did not understand the role of laymen educated in theology and in Byzantine civilization. Photius offended him further by refusing to restore DIOCESES transferred from the Roman to the Byzantine patriarchate during the ICONOCLASTIC CONTROVERSY. The importance of these dioceses had been increased by the conversion to CHRISTIANITY of leading chiefs among the Slavonic nations (the Moravians, Croats, and Bulgarians); jurisdictionally they might belong to either the Roman or the Byzantine patriarchate.

As conflicts developed among Roman, German, and Byzantine missions, Photius wrote a circular letter to the other Eastern patriarchs complaining of theological, liturgical, and other innovations by Latin missionaries in Bulgaria. At a council in Constantinople in 867, he condemned and excommunicated Nicholas I, who had refused to recognize him as the lawful patriarch—thus bringing about the Photian Schism—and in letters to other bishops had represented him as a persistent adversary of the West.

When he protested the murder of the emperor Michael III by Basil the Macedonian, Photius was deposed and Ignatius was restored. Pope Adrian II, who had just succeeded Nicholas I at Rome, now envisioned a settlement of the differences between Rome and Constantinople. The terms proposed by his legates to a council in Constantinople in 869–870, however, were unacceptable to many Byzantine ecclesiastics. Ignatius himself in 870 consecrated bishops for Bulgaria. Without help from the friends of Photius, however, he could neither reach a satisfactory settlement between East and West nor solve the internal problems of the Byzantine Orthodox church.

Photius returned to the court before 876 as tutor to the princes of the imperial family, and at the death of Ignatius in 877 or 878 he also returned to the patriarchate. He now won support from Rome, since Pope John VIII was in need of Byzantine naval assistance against the Moors, who were harrying the Italian coastline. The pope sent legates to a new council at the church of HAGIA SOPHIA in Constantinople in 879–880. In the resulting settlement, Bulgaria was assigned to the Roman patriarchate, but the continued presence of Greek bishops secured its cultural links with the

East. Bulgaria soon became a center from which the Byzantine liturgy in the language of the Macedonian Slavs spread to other Slavonic-speaking lands.

Rome did not press its claims to Greek dioceses in Italy and Greece, and the Roman legates consented to the Byzantine demand to condemn Western additions to the NICENE CREED, without explicit mention of the contentious use of the word FILIOQUE (Latin: "and the Son"), whereby the HOLY SPIRIT was said to proceed from the Father "and the Son." This interpolation had been introduced into the Nicene Creed in Spain and had spread among the Franks, but it was not yet in use in Rome. Photius' Latin was limited, and on the *filioque* controversy his information was inadequate, though he showed more understanding of the question in his later work on *The Mystagogia of the Holy Spirit*, completed in or after his second patriarchate. In 886 Photius resigned the patriarchate on the accession to the throne of his pupil the emperor Leo VI.

Phylacteries shown on the left arm and forehead in Portrait of a Rabbi *by Marc Chagall; in the Museo d'Arte Moderno di Ca Pesaro, Venice*
The Bridgeman Art Library

PHRYGIAN RELIGIONS \'fri-jē-ən, -jən\: *see* ANATOLIA, RELIGIONS OF.

PHYLACTERY, *Hebrew* tefillin, *also spelled* tephillin, *or* tfillin, in JUDAISM, one of two small, black leather, cube-shaped cases containing TORAH texts written on parchment, which are to be worn by male Jews of 13 years and older as reminders of God and of the obligation to keep the Law during daily life (Deuteronomy 6:8, 11:18; EXODUS 13:9, 16).

According to rabbinic regulations, one of the phylacteries is worn on the left hand and arm facing the heart and the other on the forehead at the morning service (except on the SABBATH and festivals) and at the afternoon service on the Ninth of Av. They are worn in a prescribed manner so as to represent the letters *shin, daleth,* and *yod,* which together form the divine name Shaddai. The hand phylactery (*tefillin shel yad*) has one compartment with the texts written on a single parchment; the head phylactery (*tefillin shel rosh*) has four compartments, each with one text. The extracts are Exodus 13:1–10, 11–16; Deuteronomy 6:4–9, 11:13–21.

PICUS \'pī-kəs\, in Roman mythology, woodpecker sacred to the god MARS. It was widely worshiped in ancient Italy and developed into a minor god. Picus was associated particularly with the fertilization of the soil with manure. The woodpecker was also an important bird in AUGURY.

Later rationalizations made Picus an early king of Italy. Virgil made him son of SATURN, father of FAUNUS, and grandfather of LATINUS. According to Ovid, his bride, CIRCE, changed him into a woodpecker for reasons of unrequited love. As son of Saturn he later came to be identified with ZEUS. His earliest representations were as a wooden pillar mounted with the image of a woodpecker. Later he was shown as a youth with a woodpecker on his head. In zoology, *Picus* is a genus of woodpecker.

PIDYON HA-BEN \pēd-'yōn-hä-'ben, 'pid-yən-hə-'ben\ (Hebrew: "redemption of the son"), Jewish ceremony in which the father redeems his wife's firstborn son by offering to a KOHEN the equivalent of five silver shekels (ancient coins). The ceremony, which normally takes place 30 days after the child's birth, dates from OLD TESTAMENT times, when the firstborn sons of the Israelites were spared from death on the first PASSOVER (EXODUS 12). These children subsequently belonged to God in a special way and would have constituted the Jewish PRIESTHOOD had not the LEVITES been substituted in their place. *Pidyon ha-ben* thus commemorates a historical event, for the father ritually gives money to a kohen in order to keep his son. If the father is a kohen or if either parent is related to the tribe of Levi, such children already belong to God by reason of heredity, and no redemption is required. *Pidyon ha-ben* also acknowledges the general law that, in the broadest sense, all "first fruits" (including grain, animals, and fruit) rightfully belong to God.

PIETAS \'pī-ə-,tas, 'pē-ə-,täs\, in ROMAN RELIGION, personification of a respect of gods, country, and relatives, especially parents. Pietas had a temple at Rome, dedicated in 181 BCE, and was often represented on coins as a female figure carrying a palm branch and a sceptre or as a matron casting incense upon an altar, sometimes accompanied by a stork, the symbol of FILIAL PIETY.

PIETISM \'pī-ə-,ti-zəm\, influential religious reform movement that began in German LUTHERANISM in the 17th century. Emphasizing personal faith in protest against secularization in the church, Pietism spread and later expanded its emphases to include social and educational concerns.

Throughout Christian history, pietistic movements have arisen whenever religion has seemed to become divorced from experience. By the beginning of the 17th century, Lutheranism had hardened into a scholastic system, but out of the devastation wrought by the Thirty Years' War there appeared some notable signs of renewal. Interest was awakened in devotional literature and the pious mystical tradition. Influences of English PURITANISM reached the European continent through the translation of works by Richard Baxter, John Bunyan, and others. Religious exiles in the Netherlands, among them William Ames, generated a distinctive brand of Dutch Pietism that soon spread into Germany as part of the reform movement that had already begun to take shape in German Lutheran circles as "Reform Orthodoxy," which found its highest expression and widest audience in the writings of Johann Arndt (1555–1621).

The various streams of the renewal movement converged in the life and work of PHILIPP JAKOB SPENER (1635–1705), who organized the first *collegia pietatis* ("assemblies of piety"), in which lay Christians met regularly for devotional reading and spiritual exchange. The practice quickly became characteristic of the movement, and those who attended the conventicles acquired the name Pietists. In his most famous work, *Pia Desideria* (1675; *Pious Desires*), Spener assessed orthodoxy's weaknesses and advanced proposals for reform: (1) greater private and public use of the SCRIPTURES, (2) greater assumption by the laity of their priestly responsibilities as believers, (3) the importance of bearing the practical fruits of a living faith, (4) ministerial training that emphasized piety and learning rather than disputation, and (5) preaching with the aim of edification.

From Spener, the leadership of German Pietism eventually passed to August Hermann Francke (1663–1727) of the University of Halle. Francke's capable leadership made Halle a thriving institutional center of Pietism. Among the illustrious figures sent out from Halle was Henry Melchior Mühlenberg, the organizer of colonial American Lutheranism. Another Halle alumnus, Nikolaus Ludwig, count von Zinzendorf (1700–60), founded the MORAVIAN CHURCH among Pietist-influenced Moravian refugees on his estate in Saxony. In contrast to the Halle Pietists' demand for penitential remorse, Zinzendorf's followers preached belief in Christ's ATONEMENT as the only requisite for salvation.

JOHN WESLEY, the founder of METHODISM, received his inspiration among the Moravians and incorporated important Pietistic elements, such as the emphasis on saving GRACE, into his evangelical movement. Other denominations felt the influence of Pietism on pastoral theology, MISSION activity, and modes of worship. It was under the influence of Pietism that the foreign missionary enterprise, which had been neglected in Lutheranism, received a new lease on life. The zenith of Pietism had been reached by the mid-18th century, but the movement still survives, both explicitly in parts of Germany and in the Moravian church elsewhere and implicitly in evangelical PROTESTANTISM at large. The revival movements of the 19th and 20th centuries were connected directly or indirectly with Pietism, which in its turn received stimulation from them.

PILATE, PONTIUS \'pän-chəs-'pī-lət, 'pən-\ (d. after 36 CE), Roman prefect (governor) of Judaea (26–36 CE) under the emperor Tiberius; he presided at the trial of JESUS and gave the order for his CRUCIFIXION.

According to the traditional account of his life, Pilate was a Roman equestrian (knight) of the Samnite clan of the Pontii (hence his name Pontius). He was appointed prefect of Judaea through the intervention of Sejanus, a favorite of the Roman emperor Tiberius. Protected by Sejanus, he incurred the enmity of the Jews by insulting their religious sensibilities, as when he hung worship images of the Emperor throughout Jerusalem and had coins bearing PAGAN religious symbols minted. After Sejanus' fall (31 CE) the Jews may have capitalized on his vulnerability by obtaining a death sentence on Jesus (John 19:12). The SAMARITANS reported him to Vitellius, legate of Syria, after he attacked them on Mt. Gerizim in 36. He was ordered back to Rome to stand trial for cruelty and oppression, particularly on the charge that he executed men without proper trial. According to an uncertain 4th-century tradition, Pilate killed himself on orders from Emperor Caligula in 39.

The historian FLAVIUS JOSEPHUS' references to Pilate picture a strong-willed, authoritarian Roman leader who was,

nevertheless, both rational and practical and who knew how far he should go in a given case. The NEW TESTAMENT, however, suggests a weak, vacillating personality. Would the mob be just as happy if he released Jesus instead of Barabbas on the feast day (Mark 15:6 ff.)? Pilate weakly capitulates. His wife sends him word of her dream (Matthew 27:19), and Pilate abdicates his responsibility. In John's Gospel, Pilate is depicted as having accepted the Christian interpretation of the meaning of Jesus (John 19:7–11), and he rejects the Jews' reminder that Jesus has merely said that he is "the king of the Jews" (19:21). Clearly, as an index to the character and personality of Pilate, the New Testament is devastating. Eventually, in Christian tradition, Pilate and his wife became converts, and the latter is a saint in the Eastern church.

PILGRIMAGE, journey to a shrine or other sacred place undertaken to gain supernatural help, as an act of thanksgiving or penance, or for the sake of devotion.

Records indicate that Christian pilgrimages were made to Jerusalem as early as the 2nd century. The Roman liturgical calendar of the year 354 CE lists 29 local sanctuaries of the saints at which the faithful gathered annually.

The medieval Christian pilgrim began his journey with a blessing by a priest. His garb was recognizable, and on his return trip he would wear on his hat the badge of the shrine visited. Along the way he would find hospices set up specifically for pilgrims. The chief attractions for pilgrims in medieval times were the Holy Land, Santiago de Compostela in Spain, and Rome; but there were hundreds of pilgrim resorts of more local reputation, including the tombs of ST. FRANCIS (died 1226) in Assisi, Italy; of ST. MARTIN (died 397) in Tours, France; of ST. BONIFACE (died 754) in Fulda, Ger.; of THOMAS BECKET (died 1170) at Canterbury, Eng.; and of ST. PATRICK at Downpatrick, Ire.

Though many medieval centers still attract ROMAN CATHOLIC pilgrims, the more recent shrines of ST. FRANCIS XAVIER (died 1552) in Goa, India; of the SHROUD OF TURIN (1578) at Turin, Italy; of St. Anne de Beaupré (1658) in Canada; of St. Jean-Baptiste-Marie Vianney (died 1859) at Ars and of St. Thérèse de Lisieux (died 1897) at Lisieux, both in France; and the Marian centers of Our Lady of Guadalupe (1531) in Mexico, of La Salette (1846) and LOURDES (1858) in France, of Fátima (1917) in Portugal; and Medjugorje (1981 and continuing) in Bosnia and Herzegovina have grown steadily in importance. Eastern Orthodox Christians commonly make pilgrimages to celebrated monasteries to ask for spiritual and practical help from the holy men (*startsy*). The attitude of the 16th-century Protestant Reformers found expression in 1530 in the AUGSBURG CONFESSION, which portrayed pilgrimages as "childish and useless works."

Pilgrimages became an important component in the life of the Buddhist community already within the first two centuries following the BUDDHA GOTAMA's death. During these early centuries of Buddhist history there were at least four major pilgrimage centers—the place of the Buddha's birth at Lumbini, the place of his enlightenment at BODH GAYA, the Deer Park in VARANASI (Benares) where he is said to have delivered his first sermon, and the village of Kusinara, which was recognized as the place of his *parinirvāṇa* (escape from the cycle of rebirth). During this period Bodh Gaya was the most important pilgrimage center, and it has continued to hold its preeminent position up to the present day.

In addition to these four primary sites, major pilgrimage centers have emerged in every region or country where BUD-

DHISM has been established. Many local temples have their own festivals associated with a relic enshrined there or an event in the life of a sacred figure. Some of these, such as the display of the tooth relic (TEMPLE OF THE TOOTH) at Kandy, Sri Lanka, are occasions for great celebrations attracting many pilgrims. In many Buddhist countries famous mountains have become sacred sites and centers of pilgrimage. In China, for example, four such sites are especially important: O-mei, Wu t'ai, P'u-t'o, and Chiu-hua. Each is devoted to a different BODHISATTVA, whose temples and monasteries are located on the mountainside. In many Buddhist regions there are pilgrimages that include stops at a whole series of sacred places. One of the most interesting and elaborate of these is the SHIKOKU pilgrimage in Japan, which involves visits to 88 temples located along a route that extends for more than 700 miles.

Within ISLAM the HAJJ, the pilgrimage to the holy city of MECCA in Saudi Arabia, is one of the PILLARS OF ISLAM and something which every adult Muslim must do at least once in his life. 'Umrah, the "minor pilgrimage" undertaken by Muslims whenever they enter Mecca, is often performed in combination with the hajj, but pilgrims have the choice of performing the 'umrah separately. As in the hajj, the pilgrim begins the 'umrah by assuming the state of ihram (ritual purity). Following a formal declaration of intent (nīyah) to perform the 'umrah, he enters Mecca and circles the sacred shrine of the KA'BA seven times. He may then touch the Black Stone, pray at the sacred stone Maqām Ibrāhīm, drink the holy water of the Zamzam spring, and touch the Black Stone again, though these ceremonies are supererogatory. The sa'y, running seven times between the hills of aṣ-Ṣafā and al-Marwah, and the ritual shaving of the head complete the 'umrah.

PILGRIM FESTIVALS, *Hebrew* Shalosh Regalim, in JUDAISM, the three occasions—PASSOVER, SHAVUOT, and SUKKOT—on which male Israelites were required to go to Jerusalem to offer sacrifice at the TEMPLE and bring offerings of their produce from the fields. In SYNAGOGUE liturgy, special Psalms (called collectively HALLEL) are read and prayers are recited that vary with the nature of the festival. Thus, the Song of Solomon is read on Passover, the Book of Ruth on Shavuot, and Ecclesiastes on Sukkot.

PIRITHOUS \pī-'ri-thō-əs\, *also spelled* Peirithous, in Greek mythology, companion of the hero THESEUS; it was his idea to make the descent into HADES to carry off PERSEPHONE. The two were detained there until HERACLES rescued THESEUS, but Pirithous was left behind.

Pirithous belonged to the Lapiths, a northern mountain tribe, and at his marriage to Hippodamia (daughter of Butes the beemaster) the CENTAURS, who had come to the wedding as guests, in drunken fury tried to rape the bride and her attendants; this led to the battle of the Lapiths and the Centaurs, a favorite subject of Greek art.

PĪṬHĀ \'pi-tə\ (Sanskrit), "seats," or "benches," of the Goddess, usually numbered at 108 and associated with the parts of the deity's body and with the various aspects of her divine female power, or *śakti*. Many of the 108 *pīṭhās* have become important PILGRIMAGE sites for members of the Śakti sects of HINDUISM.

The origin myth for the creation of the pīṭhās is recounted in several texts, most fully in the MAHĀBHĀRATA and the *Brahma Purāṇa*. The legend concerns the Goddess SATĪ, daughter of Dakṣa and wife of SHIVA. When Dakṣa held a

great sacrifice and refused to invite Shiva and Satī, Satī took offence, came to the sacrifice uninvited, and there committed suicide. Shiva thereupon became enraged, killed Dakṣa, and destroyed the sacrifice. Carrying the body of Satī on his shoulder, he began a dance that threatened the cosmos. The gods, in order to stop Shiva's dance, caused the body of Satī to disintegrate, whereupon the parts of her body fell to earth.

The *pīṭhā*s are scattered throughout India, with a high concentration in West Bengal. Each *pīṭhā* is located on or near a body of water believed to be infused with the energy of the Goddess; here the pilgrims bathe. Many are also near trees that are identified with the Goddess as Earth Mother, and the images of the various female deities at the *pīṭhā*s are accompanied by the appropriate animal companions, or *vāhana*s. Every *pīṭhā* is also associated with a manifestation of Shiva.

The *pīṭhā*s are places where believers can interact and communicate with the manifest deity, and taken together they represent the Goddess' body on earth, as well as a symbol of the unity of all the various temples and traditions of ŚĀKTISM. *See* TĪRTHA.

PITṚ \'pi-trē, -tər\, *also spelled* Pitṛi (Sanskrit: "father"), in HINDUISM, ancestral spirits or any of the dead who have been cremated or buried in accordance with the proper rites. In the VEDAS, the "fathers" shared with the gods in the sacrifice, though they received different offerings. The "way of the fathers," characterized by observance of sacrifice, almsgiving, and traditional austerities, came to be distinguished from the "way of the gods," which was directed toward the goal of liberation from rebirth.

PITTSBURGH PLATFORM, in JUDAISM, declaration drawn up by a conference of Reform RABBIS at Pittsburgh, Pa., in 1885. The platform declared that Judaism was an evolutionary, and no longer a national, faith. While the conference recognized the value of Jewish historical identity, it dissociated this from a continuity of tradition: the TALMUD was to be considered merely as religious literature, and not as legislation; meanwhile, Jews should no longer look forward to a return to Israel. The rationalist principles of the Pittsburgh Platform remained the official philosophy of the American Reform movement until the issuance of the CO-LUMBUS PLATFORM in 1937. *See* REFORM JUDAISM.

PIUS IX \'pī-əs\, *original name* Giovanni Maria Mastai-Ferretti (b. May 13, 1792, Senigallia, Papal States—d. Feb. 7, 1878, Rome), pope whose pontificate (1846–78) was the longest in history. Notable events of his reign included the declaration of the dogma of the IMMACULATE CONCEPTION (1854) and the sessions of the FIRST VATICAN COUNCIL (1869–70), during which the doctrine of PAPAL INFALLIBILITY was authoritatively defined.

Pius IX was the fourth son of Girolamo Mastai-Ferretti, gonfalonier of Senigallia, and the countess Caterina Solazzi. He first came into prominence as archbishop of Spoleto from 1827 to 1832, a time of revolutionary disturbance. He was made bishop of the important DIOCESE of Imola in 1832 and CARDINAL in 1840.

At Pius' accession all Europe considered that the Papal States (*see* PAPACY) stood in dire need of reform, with France, Austria, Russia, and Prussia urging a more representative government. In addition, the papacy was under attack by Italian nationalists as an instrument through which Austria maintained its domination over the peninsula. On March 14, 1848, Pius was compelled to grant a constitution establishing a two-chamber parliament with full legislative and fiscal powers subject only to the pope's personal veto. Pius claimed that his program of reform was merely the one long pressed upon the papacy by European powers, but it was seen as hostile to the national cause, and the papacy was never again able to appear in Italy as anything other than a bulwark of reaction.

To prevent revolution from breaking out in Rome itself, Pius consented to the appointment of popular ministries, but none of the appointees was able to control the situation and a radical ministry was appointed. On November 24–25 he fled to Naples. In his absence a democratic republic was established. The papacy thereupon issued a formal appeal to the rulers of France, Austria, Spain, and Naples for assistance, Pius holding out against any concessions and asserting his determination to exercise his temporal power without any restrictions whatsoever. A period of military and diplomatic maneuvers on the part of France and Austria resulted in the restoration of papal rule in April 1850.

Papal government formed a barrier to Italian unification, however. On Sept. 20, 1870, Italian troops occupied Rome, and in October an overwhelming majority voted for the incorporation of Rome in the kingdom of Italy. For the rest of his days Pius regarded himself a prisoner in the Vatican. He refused any contact with the Italian government.

The doctrinal developments of Pius' pontificate sprang directly out of these political disasters. After 1850, Pius became increasingly convinced that the real danger to the church lay in the modern secular ideas that the liberal Catholics were endeavoring to incorporate into its doctrines. The ENCYCLICAL *Jamdudum Cernimus* (1861) denounced all modern political doctrines as Pius moved toward a new kind of Ultramontanism, one that would concentrate all church authority in the pope's hands.

Calls for greater freedom within the church and the right of scholars to pursue independent inquiries made it clear that the church stood in need of authoritative pronouncements about its relations with the state and with modern society, and discussion began about the possibility of calling an ecumenical council for this pur-

Pius IX
Felici

pose. But on Dec. 8, 1864, Pius issued the encyclical *Quanta Cura* with, attached to it, the famous Syllabus listing 80 of the "principal errors of our times"; the 80th article stigmatized as an error the view that "the Roman Pontiff can and should reconcile himself to and agree with progress, liberalism, and modern civilization." The Syllabus completely undermined the liberal Catholics' position and destroyed their following among intellectuals.

In the doctrine of papal infallibility itself there was nothing new. It had been employed to define, on Dec. 8, 1854, the dogma of the Immaculate Conception. Its opponents objected, however, that such a definition was inopportune, tending to widen the breach between the church and modern society, and that it would present a one-sided view of the source of authority in the church. When the first Vatican Council opened on Dec. 8, 1869, however, Pius intervened to postpone all deliberation except that upon infallibility. The decisive vote came on July 13 when 451 voted for it, 88 against it, and 62 in favor of some amendment. Thereupon the minority left Rome and the final definition was carried on July 18 by 533 votes to 2. Infallibility was confined to those occasions upon which the pope made pronouncements *ex cathedra*.

During the remainder of his reign Pius became further estranged from the Italian government and witnessed a general outbreak of anticlericalism in western Europe.

PIUS X, SAINT, *original name* Giuseppe Melchiorre Sarto (b. June 2, 1835, Riese, Venetia, Austrian Empire [now in Italy]—d. Aug. 20, 1914, Rome, Italy; canonized May 29, 1954; feast day August 21), pope from 1903 to 1914, whose staunch political and religious conservatism dominated the early 20th-century church.

Ordained in 1858, he became a PARISH priest in the Italian region of Venetia. POPE LEO XIII made him bishop of Mantua (1884) and in 1893 CARDINAL and PATRIARCH of Venice. He was elected pope on Aug. 4, 1903.

Tepid toward Leo's social reforms, Pius decided to concentrate on apostolic problems and to make the defense of ROMAN CATHOLICISM his cause. Three aspects of his policy particularly aroused bitter controversy: the repression of MODERNISM, a contemporary intellectual movement seeking to reinterpret traditional Catholic teaching in the light of 19th-century philosophical, historical, and psychological theories; his reaction against Christian Democrats; and his attitude toward separation of CHURCH AND STATE in France.

Because Modernism tended to ignore certain traditional values in order to achieve its ends, Pius placed several Modernist books on the INDEX OF FORBIDDEN BOOKS and issued (1907) the decree *Lamentabili Sane Exitu* (*On a Deplorable Outcome*) and the ENCYCLICAL *Pascendi Dominici Gregis* (*Feeding the Lord's Flocks*), rejecting Modernist teachings and suggesting remedies to extirpate it. He also urged immediate compliance with his strict censorship program. In 1910 he ordered that all teachers in seminaries and clerics before ORDINATION take an OATH denouncing Modernism and supporting Lamentabili and Pascendi.

Pius' opposition to Christian Democracy was a reaction to the trend in European countries where Christians reacted against doctrines of materialism by forming their own social movements or popular action groups independent of the church hierarchy. Accordingly, he formally condemned the Italian priest Romolo Murri's popular action movement in 1903 and the pioneering Christian Democrat Marc Sangnier's Sillon movement in France.

On Pius' accession, the separation of church and state in France was already inevitable, given growing anticlericalism in France. In 1905 the French formally separated church from state, an act condemned by Pius on Feb. 11, 1906. Most of the French bishops were willing to try the new French legislation, which safeguarded all that could still be preserved of the church's material interests, but Pius rejected the compromise.

Some of his directives, though outmoded by later social developments, mark him as one of the forerunners of Catholic Action, such as the organization of the laity for special and direct collaboration in the church's apostolic work. His eucharistic decrees eased the regulations governing daily communion, and his revival of the Gregorian plainsong and his recasting of the breviary and of the missal were important liturgical reforms. In many ways Pius X was the founder of the movement toward liturgical reforms that culminated with the SECOND VATICAN COUNCIL, and it was largely for this that he was canonized in 1954. His decision to adapt and systematize CANON LAW led to the publication of the new code in 1917, effective in 1918. His reorganization of the Curia modernized the church's central administration, including a codification of the conclave.

PIUS XII, *original name* Eugenio Maria Giuseppe Giovanni Pacelli (b. March 2, 1876, Rome, Italy—d. Oct. 9, 1958, Castel Gandolfo), Italian head of the ROMAN CATHOLIC church during World War II and the years of postwar reconstruction (reigned 1939–58).

Pacelli's family came from Tuscany and had supplied Vatican lawyers since 1819. He grew up in a home of deep piety and of devotion to the PAPACY. He was educated at Roman day schools and studied for the priesthood at the Gregorian University there. He was ordained in 1899. Passing into the Vatican Secretariat of State, he rose rapidly and in 1917 was made archbishop and sent as nuncio—a diplomat—to the Bavarian Court to negotiate a concordat (a Vatican-state agreement). He was sent (1925) to Berlin with the same aim and remained there until he was named CARDINAL, by Pius XI, and recalled to Rome at the end of 1929 to become secretary of state. As archbishop he had inherited a diplomatic technique centered on the principle of the concordat, which aims to preserve the church's privileges and freedom of action, even under regimes irreconcilable with Christian principles. After 10 years in this office, he was elected pope in the shortest conclave since 1623.

Fascism had come to power in Italy (1922) during Pacelli's absence in Germany, and his brother, a lawyer, helped to fashion the concordat with the dictator Benito Mussolini—to achieve which the Catholic Popular Party and any chance of ousting Mussolini were sacrificed. This settlement, which created the Vatican city-state (1929), satisfied Pius XI's ambition but created many problems for the Vatican, in relations both with the increasingly hostile dictatorship and with the uneasy democracy that succeeded it after the war.

Twelve years in Germany had made Pacelli fluent in German and had given him great love and respect for the Germans, but he had no illusions about Nazism, and the concordat with Hitler's Germany (1933), largely his work, was (he often said) a calculated risk, aimed at preserving a platform for Catholic life and ministry in a hostile German society. His part in the anti-Nazi ENCYCLICAL *Mit brennender Sorge* (1937; *With Burning Sorrow*), his frigid and outspoken reception of the Nazi foreign minister Joachim von Ribbentrop in Rome, and his bitter reproach of the Austrian cardinal Theodor Innitzer's weakness in face of the union of Austria and Germany in 1938, all showed his true estimate of the German tyranny. During the few months between his election and the outbreak of war, Pius XII turned his diplomatic gifts to preventing the catastrophe. Pius especially strove to keep Italy neutral and was deeply saddened when he failed.

The demands of war harmonized with Pius' austerity and immense capacity for work; they enhanced his exalted, almost dramatic, conception of his office. His efforts to humanize war and to relieve suffering, anxiety, and grief have

Pius XII, photograph by Yousuf Karsh
© Karsh from Rapho—Photo Researchers

been generally applauded. There has been less agreement about Pius' conduct and utterance in relation to the war itself. He has been charged with neglecting to raise an authoritative voice in defense of the persecuted, Christian or Jewish. Others have claimed that protests would have aggravated Nazi policy without achieving any good result. The deeper question may be asked whether the nuances and the hints of traditional diplomacy were any longer appropriate to the savagery and cynicism of a struggle for world domination and of deliberate genocide.

Though Pius refused to be drawn into a crusade against communism, he enacted severe measures against Catholics collaborating with communists (1946), and the precarious balance between Christian Democrats and the extreme left in postwar Italy led him to encourage the Catholic Action leader Luigi Gedda, whose meddling in politics embarrassed the parliamentary Christian Democratic Party. When Pius' failing health left power in the hands of a bureaucracy of cardinals, including the autocratic head of the Holy Office, Alfredo Ottaviani, clerical interference in Italian public life reached a high pitch.

In the encyclical *Divino Afflante Spiritu* (1943; "With the Help of the Divine Spirit") Pius ended the strict opposition to modern historical and biblical scholarship that had been church policy since PIUS X. In other matters his contributions were less memorable.

PLATFORM SUTRA \'sü-trə\ (Chinese: *Liu-Tsu t'an-ch'ing*), important text from the Ch'an (ZEN) school of Chinese BUDDHISM, most likely composed in the 8th century CE. It is attributed to the sixth patriarch of the Ch'an tradition, HUI-NENG (638–713), although it is most likely the work of subsequent disciples who sought to legitimate their school by devising a lineage of DHARMA masters leading back to BODHIDHARMA, the first patriarch. Hui-neng, who is portrayed in the *Platform Sutra* as an illiterate commoner, receives the robe of dharma transmission from Hung-jen, the fifth patriarch, secretly, at night, after Hui-neng had successfully defeated Shen-hsiu in a contest of writing dharma verses that revealed true understanding of the nature of enlightenment. Shen-hsiu, a learned monk of the Northern Ch'an school, is portrayed as being outdone by Hui-neng, who is able to grasp the nature of enlightenment simply by hearing the *Diamond Sutra* (a MAHĀYĀNA Perfection of Wisdom sutra) and by his intuitive grasp of its truth. The *Platform Sutra* encapsulates the debate between the Northern and Southern Ch'an schools concerning whether enlightenment was gradual, the result of prolonged study and attainment of levels of progress along the Buddhist path (the position of the Northern school), or sudden, an instantaneous grasp of the pure nature of one's mind (the position of the Southern school). The *Platform Sutra* thus represents the emergence and eventual dominance of the orthodox, Southern position wherein it is held that the mind is fundamentally pure by nature, and it advocates the twin methods of meditation and insight as the means to attain enlightenment.

PLEIADES \\'plē-ə-,dēz, 'plā-, 'plī-\\, in Greek mythology, the seven daughters of the Titan ATLAS and the Oceanid Pleione: Maia, Electra, Taygete, Celaeno, Alcyone, Sterope, and Merope.

The Pleiades eventually formed a constellation. One myth recounts that they all killed themselves out of grief over the death of their sisters, the HYADES. Another explains that after seven years of being pursued by ORION, they were turned into stars by ZEUS. Orion became a constellation, too, and continued to pursue the sisters across the sky. The faintest star of the Pleiades was thought to be either Merope, who was ashamed of loving a mortal, or Electra, grieving for Troy, her son's city.

PL KYŌDAN \\'kyō-dän\\, *in full* Perfect Liberty Kyōdan, church (Japanese: *kyōdan*) founded in Japan in 1946 by Miki Tokuchika. The movement, unique for the use of English words in its name, is based on the earlier HITO-NO-MI-CHI sect. In the late 20th century the group claimed more than 2.5 million adherents worldwide.

PL Kyōdan teaches that the goal of humanity is joyful self-expression. Forgetting God brings misfortune and suffering, but the believer may pray that his or her troubles be transferred by divine mediation to the patriarch, who is strengthened for vicarious suffering by the group's collective prayers.

Headquarters of the movement are at Habikino, near Ōsaka. PL Kyōdan operates a hospital, a golf course, and other sports facilities. Considerable missionary activity is carried on in Japan and among Japanese living abroad.

PLUTO \\'plü-tō\\: *see* PLUTUS.

PLUTUS \\'plü-təs\\, in GREEK RELIGION, a personification of wealth (Greek: *ploutos*). According to Hesiod, Plutus was born in Crete, the son of DEMETER and the Cretan IASION. In art he appears chiefly as a child with a CORNUCOPIA. Pluto, as a cognomen signifying "the wealthy," became an epithet for HADES in his milder, gentler aspect.

PLYMOUTH BRETHREN \\'pli-məth\\, community of Christians whose first congregation was established in Plymouth, Devon, Eng., in 1831. The movement originated in Ireland and England a few years earlier with groups who

met for prayer and fellowship. John Nelson Darby, a former clergyman in the Church of Ireland (Anglican), soon became the dominant personality in the movement. He founded groups of Brethren in many parts of Britain and in continental Europe, especially in French Switzerland, where he spent the greater part of the period 1838–45.

After Darby returned to England in 1845, disputes over doctrine and church government split the Brethren into two groups, one forming a closely knit federation of churches known as Exclusive Brethren, and the other, called Open Brethren, maintaining a congregational form of church government and less rigorous standards for membership. Exclusive Brethren have suffered further divisions.

Brethren recognize no order of clergy or ministers as distinct from the laity. A communion service is celebrated every Sunday. Practically all groups practice believer's BAPTISM, although some Exclusives, following Darby's practice, baptize children of members.

Brethren have been active in foreign missionary work, principally in Central Africa, India, and Latin America. Brethren are found throughout the English-speaking world and in most European countries. In the United States, which they reached in the early 1860s, there are eight groups.

POHJOLA \\'pōh-yō-,lä\\: *see* MANALA.

POLTERGEIST (from German *poltern*, "to make a racket"; *Geist*, "spirit"), disembodied spirit or supernatural force credited with certain malicious or disturbing phenomena, such as inexplicable noises, breakage of household items, or violent actions—throwing stones or setting fire to clothing and furniture. Such events are said to be sporadic, unpredictable, and often repetitive.

According to popular belief, a poltergeist's activity appears to concentrate on a particular member of a family, often an adolescent, its object being harassment or, rarely, physical harm. When strangers are present, the unusual phenomena often cease. In many instances, the activities attributed to poltergeists have been explained as natural phenomena—*e.g.*, the normal creaking of boards in an old house.

POLUDNITSA \\pə-'lüd-nʸit-sə\\, in Slavic MYTHOLOGY, female field spirit, generally seen either as a tall woman or a girl dressed in white. The *poludnitsa* customarily appears in the field at noon, when the workers are resting. Any human who disturbs her risks his health and his life.

The *poludnitsa* is related to the *polevoy*, the male field spirit, who is seldom seen and then only at noon in the fields. Some describe him as a man black as the earth, with grass instead of hair growing out of his head. Others say he dresses in white. In some areas offerings are made to the *polevoy* at night to ensure fertility.

POLYMNIA \\pä-'lim-nē-ə\\, *also called* Polymnis \\pä-'lim-nis\\, *or* Polyhymnia \\,pä-lē-'him-nē-ə\\, in GREEK RELIGION, one of the nine MUSES, patron of dancing or geometry. She was said to have been the mother of Triptolemus, the first priest of DEMETER and the inventor of agriculture, by Cheimarrhus, son of ARES, or by Celeus, king of Eleusis. In other variants, she was the mother of ORPHEUS or of EROS.

POLYPHEMUS \\,pä-li-'fē-məs\\, in Greek mythology, most famous of the Cyclopes, son of POSEIDON and the NYMPH Thoösa. Homer relates that when ODYSSEUS, sailing home from the Trojan War, was cast ashore on the coast of Sicily, he fell into the hands of Polyphemus, who trapped him with 12 of his companions in his cave and then began eating them one by one. Odysseus succeeded in making Polyphemus drunk, blinded him by plunging a burning stake into his eye while he lay asleep, and, with his six remaining friends escaped by clinging to the bellies of Polyphemus' sheep as they were let out to pasture. Later tradition tells of his love for the Sicilian NEREID Galatea.

POLYTHEISM, the belief in many gods, which has characterized the majority of religions throughout history. The many gods may be subordinate to a supreme god and object of devotion (as in some stages of HINDUISM), or subordinate to an enlightened one (as in BUDDHISM), or subordinate to one god that is dominant though not supreme (as in GREEK RELIGION). In addition to belief in many gods, polytheistic cultures generally also include belief in many other malevolent or benevolent spiritual forces or powers. *Compare* MONOTHEISM.

POLYXENA \pə-'lik-sə-nə\, in Greek mythology, daughter of PRIAM and HECUBA. After the fall of Troy, she was claimed by the ghost of ACHILLES as his share of the spoils and was therefore put to death at his tomb. In post-classical times the story was elaborated to include a love affair between Polyxena and Achilles before his death.

POMERIUM \pō-'mir-ē-əm\, in ancient Rome, sacred open space located just inside the wall surrounding the four hills—the Esquiline, the Palatine, the Quirinal, and the Capitoline—of the early city. In historic times it was marked by stones and was extended several times. In most Italian walled cities, such spaces, which ran along the complete length of the city walls, were originally left clear to facilitate the maneuvering of defenders in times of attack. The space was also invested with religious significance, being dedicated to the gods in gratitude for their protection, and building and planting upon it remained forbidden. Religiously it marked the sacred space of the city as opposed to the "outside" where different rules applied. Long after Rome expanded beyond its pomerium, the legendary date of its demarcation—April 21—was celebrated as the anniversary of the city's foundation.

POṄGAL \'pəŋ-gäl\, important Hindu festival in South India marking the beginning of the Tamil New Year. It is celebrated on the first day of the Tamil month of Tai (January–February).

The name of the festival comes from the Tamil word meaning "to boil"; rice is boiled in milk and offered first to the gods, then to the cows, and then to family members. During the festival, the anticipated greeting, "Has the rice boiled?" is answered, "It has boiled." Cows are especially venerated on the second day of Poṅgal: their horns are painted, and they are garlanded with flowers and fruit, taken in PROCESSION, and allowed to graze freely.

PONTIFEX \'pän-tə-ˌfeks\, *plural* pontifices, member of a council of priests in ancient Rome. The college, or *collegium*, of the *pontifices* was the most important Roman PRIESTHOOD, being especially charged with the administration of the *jus divinum* (*i.e.*, that part of the civil law that regulated the relations of the community with the deities recognized by the state), together with a general superintendence of the worship of gens and family.

The college existed under the monarchy, when its members were probably three in number; they probably were legal advisers of the *rex* in all matters of religion. Under the republic a *pontifex maximus*, or supreme priest, took over the king's duties as chief administrator of religious law. During the republican period the number of *pontifices* increased until by the time of Julius Caesar there were 16. Included in the *collegium* were also the *rex sacrorum*, the *flamines*, three assistant *pontifices* (*minores*), and the VESTAL VIRGINS, who were all chosen by the *pontifex maximus*. From the second Punic War onward the *pontifex maximus* was chosen by popular election, and in the last age of the republic this was true for all the members. They all held office for life.

The immense authority of the *collegium* centered in the *pontifex maximus*, the other *pontifices* forming his *consilium*, or advising body. His functions were partly sacrificial or ritualistic, but the real power lay in the administration of the *jus divinum*, the chief departments of which may briefly be described as follows: (1) the regulation of all expiatory ceremonials needed as the result of pestilence, lightning, etc.; (2) the consecration of all temples and other sacred places and objects dedicated to the gods by the state through its magistrates; (3) the regulation of the calendar both astronomically and in detailed application to the public life of the state; (4) the administration of the law relating to burials and burying places and the worship of the Manes, or dead ancestors; (5) the superintendence of all marriages by *confarreatio* (*i.e.*, originally, of all legal patrician marriages); and (6) the administration of the law of adoption and of testamentary succession. They had also the care of the state archives and of the lists of magistrates and kept records of their own decisions (*commentarii*) and the chief events (*annales*).

For the first three centuries of the republic it is probable that the *pontifex maximus* was its most powerful member. The office might be combined with a magistracy, and, though its powers were declaratory rather than executive, it may be described as quasi-magisterial. Under the later republic it was coveted chiefly for the great dignity of the position; Julius Caesar held it for the last 20 years of his life, and Augustus took it after the death of Lepidus in 12 BCE, after which it became inseparable from the office of the reigning emperor.

Pontifex was used of ROMAN CATHOLIC bishops and *pontifex maximus* of the pope by the end of the 4th century. In modern usage, both terms generally refer to the pope.

POOR CLARE \'klar\, *also called* Clarissine, *or* Clarisse, member of any order of nuns descending from the FRANCISCAN order founded at Assisi, Italy, in 1212 by ST. CLARE OF ASSISI (1194–1253), a noblewoman who took a vow of poverty and became a follower of ST. FRANCIS OF ASSISI. She and her following of nuns, often called the Second Order of St. Francis, devoted themselves to a cloistered life of prayer and penance; but, when the society spread elsewhere in Europe, some communities accepted property and revenues. The society's rule was revised a number of times until, in 1263/64, Pope Urban IV issued a rule permitting common ownership of property, greater self-governance for the order, and other concessions. The monasteries adopting this rule came to be called the Urbanist Poor Clares, or, officially, the Order of St. Clare (O.S.C.), whereas those communities who continued to observe the stricter Rule of St. Clare (as revised in 1253) became known as the Primitives, or Poor Clares (P.C.). Early in the 15th century St. Colette of Corbie

(1381–1447), in France, sought to reform the order, restoring the primitive observance in 17 monasteries during her lifetime and reasserting the strict principle of poverty; her followers came to be called the Colettine Poor Clares, or Poor Clares of St. Colette (P.C.C.), and today are located mostly in France. The Capuchin Sisters, originating in Naples in 1538, and the Alcantarines, of 1631, are also Poor Clares of the strict observance.

POPE (Latin *papa*, from Greek *pappas*, "father"), ecclesiastical title expressing affectionate respect, formerly given, especially from the 3rd to the 5th century, to any BISHOP and sometimes to PRIESTS. The title is still used in the East for the Orthodox PATRIARCH of Alexandria and for Orthodox priests, but, since about the 9th century, it has been reserved in the West for the bishop of Rome.

The official directory of the Holy See describes the office of the pope by the following titles: Bishop of Rome, VICAR OF JESUS CHRIST, Successor of the Prince of the Apostles, Supreme Pontiff of the Western Church, Patriarch of the West, PRIMATE of Italy, Archbishop and METROPOLITAN of the Province of Rome, Sovereign of the State of Vatican City. The title pope or *papa* (abbreviated PP.) is officially used only as a less solemn style.

In CATHOLIC churches, the pope is regarded as the successor of ST. PETER (the head of the APOSTLES) and thus, as bishop of Rome, has supreme power of jurisdiction over the church in matters of faith, morals, discipline, and government. The understanding of papal primacy developed as the church developed, two notable factors being the role of Rome as the imperial city until the 5th century and the religious and political role of the bishop of Rome afterward.

The teaching of the SECOND VATICAN COUNCIL (1962–65) on the role of bishops counterbalanced the emphasis on papal prerogatives while maintaining the view that the authority of the bishops as a body cannot be separated from that of the pope as its head. Although EASTERN ORTHODOXY has long been willing to give the bishop of Rome the primacy of honor accorded to patriarchs, and, although many Protestants have appreciated the moral leadership shown by some popes, the Catholic doctrine was still a major obstacle to ecumenical efforts in the 20th century. *See also* PAPACY.

POPOL VUH \\'pō-pōl-'vü, -'wük\\ (Quiché: "Council Book"), MAYA document, an invaluable source of knowledge of ancient Mayan mythology, history, and culture. Written in Quiché (a Guatemalan Mayan language) with Spanish letters by a Mayan author or authors between 1554 and 1558, it chronicles the creation of man, the actions of the gods, the origin and history of the Quiché people, and the chronology of their kings down to 1550.

The original text, now lost, was discovered and translated at the beginning of the 18th century by a Guatemalan PARISH priest of Chichicastenango, Francisco Jiménez (or Ximénez).

POPULAR RELIGON, term often used in the past to describe the RELIGIOUS BELIEFS and practices of members of a society that are unsophisticated or opposite of an elite class. Thus many books have been written on "Popular TAOISM" in contrast to "Philosophical Taoism," or "Popular HINDUISM" or BUDDHISM as opposed to the "Philosophical Hinduism" of ascetics and Buddhist monks. The use of "Popular Religion" usually indicates that a distinction is being drawn between religious classes in society relative to literacy or rationality; for instance, the mythic PURĀṆAS in Hinduism were often classified as belonging to "Popular Hinduism" in contrast to the UPANISHADS and philosophical literature of the ascetic or Brahminic elite.

POSEIDON \\pə-'sī-dən\\, in GREEK RELIGION, god of the sea and of water generally; he is to be distinguished from Pontus, the personification of the sea. Originally he was probably a god of fresh water and the underworld regions. Traditionally he was a son of CRONUS and RHEA, and was brother of ZEUS and HADES. When the three brothers deposed their father, the kingdom of the sea fell by lot to Poseidon. His weapon was the trident, but it may originally have been a long-handled fish spear.

Poseidon was also the god of earthquakes; his primary epithet was "Earth-Shaker," and many of his oldest places of worship in Greece were inland. He was also closely associated with horses. He was the father of the winged horse PEGASUS by the winged monster MEDUSA. Most scholars agree that Poseidon was brought to Greece by the earliest Hellenes, who also probably introduced horses to the country.

Although Poseidon lost a contest for sovereignty over Attica to the ATHENA, he was also worshiped there, particular-

Poseidon, marble statue from Melos, Greece, 2nd century BCE; in the National Archaeological Museum, Athens
Alinari—Art Resource

ly at Colonus, as *hippios* ("of horses"). Elsewhere he was associated with freshwater springs. Poseidon was the father of PELIAS and Neleus by Tyro, the daughter of Salmoneus, and thus became the divine ancestor of the royal families of Thessaly and Messenia. Otherwise his offspring were mostly GIANTS and savage creatures, such as ORION, ANTAEUS, and POLYPHEMUS.

The chief festival in Poseidon's honor was the Isthmia, the scene of famous athletic contests, celebrated in alternate years near the Isthmus of Corinth.

POSSESSION, in religious and folk traditions, condition characterized by unusual behavior and a personality change that is interpreted as evidence that the person is under the direct control of an external powerful spirit. Symptoms of spirit possession include violent or unusual movements, shrieking, groaning, and uttering strange speech. Occasionally a normally pious person becomes incapable of prayer, utters blasphemies, or exhibits terror or hatred of sacred persons or objects. CHRISTIANITY and some other religions allow for the possibility that some of these states have an evil transcendental cause.

In some traditions the "possessed" individual becomes ill and is regarded by his community as having committed some spiritual transgression; recovery is held to require expiation of his SIN, often by a sacrifice. In other traditions the "possessed" person is conceived as a medium for the controlling spirit and functions as an intermediary between spirits and humans. His major role is usually to diagnose and heal other spirit-afflicted individuals. In this tradition the trance behavior of the medium is often self-induced (autohypnotic); it may be stimulated by drugs, drumming, or collective hysteria. In his trance the medium appears genuinely insensible to ordinary stimuli.

POTALA PALACE \\'pō-tə-lə\\, winter palace of the DALAI LAMAS, located in Lhasa, Tibet, and built during the reign of Ngag-dbang-rgya-mtsho (1617–82). Potala exhibits a combination of Tibetan, Indian, and Chinese decorative and structural elements; its tiered, ornamented roof was of Indian inspiration, while its magnificent interior carving was inspired by Indian and Nepalese originals.

PRACTICAL LEARNING SCHOOL, *Korean* Silhak \\'shēl-'häk\\, *also spelled* Sirhak, school of thought that came into existence in the midst of the chaotic conditions of 18th-century Korea, dedicated to a practical approach to statecraft, instead of the blind and uncritical following of Confucian teachings. The SILHAK school attacked NEO-CONFUCIANISM, particularly its formalism and concern with ritual. Members of the school originated many ideas for social reform, especially for land reform and the development of farming.

The greatest contribution to the Silhak school came from Yi Ik (1681–1763) and Pak Chi-won (1737–1805). Yi's concern was largely with such matters as land reform, farming, and the abolition of class barriers and slavery. Pak advocated the development of commerce and technology.

With the introduction of Western culture in the late 19th century, the Practical Learning school contributed to the development and spread of ideas that stimulated the gradual modernization of Korea.

PRADAKṢIṆA \\prə-'dək-shi-nə\\, in HINDUISM and BUDDHISM, the rite of circumambulating in a clockwise direction an image, relic, shrine, or other sacred object. PILGRIMAGES

sometimes consist of circumambulating an entire town or the GANGĀ (Ganges) River from source to sea and back, a trip that when undertaken on foot requires several years.

Explanations of the rite vary from the delineation of an area for a particular sacred purpose to an attempt to influence the course of events and produce good fortune by imitating the auspicious journey of the sun. Circumambulating in a counterclockwise movement, called *prasavya*, is observed in funeral and in certain Tantric ceremonies.

PRAJĀPATI \\prə-'jä-pə-tē\\ (Sanskrit: "Lord of Creatures"), one of the creator figures of the Vedic period of ancient India; later he came to be identified with BRAHMĀ, who gradually surpassed him in importance.

Early Vedic literature alludes to various primal figures, such as Hiraṇyagarbha ("Golden Embryo") and VIŚVAKARMAN ("All-Accomplishing"), and the title of Prajāpati was applied to more than one such figure. Later it signified one deity, the lord of all creatures. According to myth, Prajāpati produced the universe and all its beings after preparing himself by undergoing *tapas* (ascetic practices); other stories allude to his own creation from the primal waters. His female emanation was Vāc, the personification of the sacred word, but sometimes his female partner is given as Uṣas, the dawn, who is also regarded as his daughter.

Collectively, the Prajāpatis are the "mind born" children of Brahmā. They are generally considered to number 10, though some authorities reduce them to seven and relate them to the seven great ṛṣis (ancient sages).

PRAJÑĀPĀRAMITĀ \\'prəg-,nyä-'pär-ə-mē-,tä\\ (Sanskrit: "Perfection of Wisdom"), body of sutras and their commentaries that represents the oldest of the major forms of MAHĀYĀNA Buddhism; the name also denotes the female personification of literature or of wisdom, sometimes called the Mother of All Buddhas.

The main creative period of *Prajñāpāramitā* thought extended from perhaps 100 BCE to 150 CE. In these works wisdom *(prajna)* becomes the supreme *paramita* and the primary avenue to NIRVANA. The best-known work from this period is the *Aṣṭasāhasrikā* ("8,000-Verse") *Prajñā-pāramitā*. The first Chinese translation appeared in 179 CE. Later, some 18 "portable editions" were forthcoming, the best known of which is the DIAMOND CUTTER SUTRA. Still later, schematic and scholastic commentaries were produced in the MĀDHYAMIKA ("Middle Way") monasteries of eastern India, thus introducing into the *Prajñāpāramitā* movement the same confining RATIONALISM against which it had reacted in the first place.

Of the personified *Prajñāpāramitā* the Chinese traveler FA-HSIEN described images of her in India as early as 400 CE, but all known existent images date from 800 or later. She is usually represented yellow or white in color, with one head and two arms (sometimes more), the hands in the teaching gesture *(dharmacakra-mudrā)* or holding a lotus and the sacred book. Also frequently associated with her are a ROSARY, sword (to cleave away ignorance), thunderbolt (VAJRA, symbolizing the EMPTINESS of the void), or begging bowl (renunciation of material goods being a prerequisite to the obtaining of wisdom).

See also HEART SUTRA.

PRAKṚTI AND PURUṢA \\'prə-kri-tē . . . 'pü-rü-shə\\ (from Sanskrit *prakṛti*, "source," or "principal"; *puruṣa*, "person," or "spirit"), prakṛti *also called* pradhāna, in Indian philosophy, two fundamental concepts, the first designating material nature in its germinal state, eternal and beyond perception, while the second denotes the soul or self. In the dualistic philosophies of Sāṃkhya and YOGA, *puruṣa* is opposed to *prakṛti*, as the two ontological realities. *Prakṛti*, a feminine construct, comes into contact with *puruṣa*, a male construct, and starts on a process of evolution that leads through several stages to the creation of the existing material world. *Prakṛti* is made up of three *guṇas* ("strands," or constituent cosmic factors) that characterize all nature. In the Sāṃkhya view, only *prakṛti* is active, while the self is incarcerated in it and only observes and experiences. Release (MOKṢA) consists in the self's extrication from *prakṛti* by the recognition of its total difference from it and noninvolvement in it.

Puruṣa is also, in one of the creation myths related in the VEDAS, the primal man from whose body the universe was created. He was both sacrificer and victim, and his rite was the prototype for all later Vedic and Hindu sacrifices.

PRAMĀṆA \prə-'mä-nə\ (Sanskrit: "measure"), in Indian philosophy, means by which one obtains accurate and valid knowledge (*pramā, pramiti*) about the world. The accepted number of *pramāṇas* varies, according to the philosophical system or school; the exegetical system of Mīmāṃsā accepts five, whereas VEDĀNTA as a whole proposes three.

The three principal means of knowledge are (1) perception, both direct sensory perception (*anubhava*) and such perception remembered (SMṚTI); (2) inference (*anumāna*), based on perception but able to conclude something that may not be open to perception; and (3) word (ŚABDA), most fundamentally the VEDA, the validity of which is self-authenticated. Some philosophers broaden *śabda* to include the statement of a reliable person (*āpta-vākya*). To these, two additional means of knowledge have been added: (4) analogy (*upamāna*), and (5) circumstantial implication (*arthāpatti*), which appeals to common sense.

PRĀṆA \'prä-nə\ (Sanskrit: "breath"), in Indian philosophy, the body's vital "airs" or energies. In early Hindu philosophy, *prāṇa* was thought to survive as a person's "last breath" for eternity or until a future life.

Prāṇa was at times identified with the self. It is also the first in a series of "five *prāṇas*," windlike vital forces that are supposed to assist breathing, distribution of food in the body, and digestion. In YOGA philosophy, full control of the *prāṇa* is achieved through the practice of PRĀṆĀYĀMA ("breath control"), for its therapeutic effects and so that one might meditate without respiratory distraction.

PRĀṆĀYĀMA \'prä-nä-'yä-mə\ (Sanskrit: "breath control"), in the YOGA system of Indian philosophy, fourth of the eight stages intended to lead the aspirant to SAMĀDHI, a state of perfect concentration. The immediate goal of *prāṇāyāma* is to reduce breathing to an effortless, even rhythm, thus helping to free the mind from attention to bodily functions. The practitioners of Yoga recognize four states of consciousness—waking, sleep with dreams, sleep without dreams, and a state resembling cataleptic consciousness—each of which has its own respiratory rhythm. By prolonging each respiration as long as possible in simulation of the unconscious states, the yogi learns to pass from one state to another, without loss of consciousness.

PRAPATTI \'prə-pə-,tē\, practice sometimes regarded as the central act of devotion among the Hindu BHAKTI (devotional) sects. *Prapatti* refers to the individual's complete self-surrender to the Supreme Being owing to feelings of utter helplessness and to an absolute belief in God's GRACE. *Prapatti* was analyzed by the philosopher RĀMĀNUJA into five individual components: the intention of submitting to God; the surrender of resistance; the belief in God's protection; the prayer for salvation; and the consciousness that one is helpless to attain salvation on one's own.

PRASĀDA \prə-'sä-də\ (Sanskrit: "favor, grace"), in HINDUISM, food and water offered to a deity in worship (*pūjā*). It is believed that the deity partakes of and then returns the offering, thereby consecrating it. The offering is then distributed and eaten by the worshipers. The efficacy of the *prasāda* comes from its having been touched by the deity. Food left by a GURU is considered *prasāda* by his followers, as the guru is a living god. All food, if silently offered to God with the proper prayers before eating, becomes consecrated and thus *prasāda*.

Among the Sikhs of India, the distribution of *karāh-prasād*, a sweet dish of wheat flour, sugar, and clarified butter, is customarily part of a worship service or of any special ceremony such as an initiation, wedding, or funeral. Communal eating reinforces the ideals of social equality that are an integral part of Sikh belief.

PRATIMA \'prə-ti-mə\ (Sanskrit: "image," or "likeness," of the deity), in HINDUISM, also referred to as *mūrti*, or *vigraha*. The image, or ICON, is not intended to be a representation of an earthly form but rather, through depicting the deity with multiple heads, arms, or eyes or with part animal features, is meant to point to the transcendent "otherness" of the divine. Traditionally the image serves as a vehicle through which the infinite, unmanifest god willingly takes finite and manifest form; when invoked, the deity is believed literally to be present in the icon. Worship centering around the image (*pūjā*) has been a form of Hindu religious practice for about 2,000 years.

Most Hindu images are man-made, constructed by artisans following strict guidelines, and consecrated in a ceremony. Such images can be permanent and housed in temples or homes; others are temporary and used only for the duration of a festival. Still other images are aniconic and found in nature, such as a special type of fossil known as the *śālagrāma* that is sacred to the god VISHNU. The mass printing of color reproductions in poster form has extended the availability of images to greater numbers of devotees.

PRATIMA \'prə-ti-məz\, in JAINISM, one of the 11 stages of a householder's spiritual progress. Medieval writers conceived *pratima* (literally, "statue") as a regular progressing series, a ladder leading to higher stages of spiritual development. The last two stages lead logically to renunciation of the world and assumption of the ascetic life.

PRĀTIMOKṢA \,prä-tē-'mōk-shə\ (Sanskrit: "that which is binding"), Pāli pātimokkha \,pä-tē-'mòk-kə\, Buddhist monastic code, set of 227 rules that govern the daily activities of monks and nuns. The prohibitions of the *prātimokṣa* are arranged in the Pāli canon according to the severity of the offense—from those that require immediate expulsion from the order to those that require confession only. Also given are rules for settling disputes within the monastic community. The entire *prātimokṣa* is recited during the *uposatha*, or biweekly assembly of THERAVĀDA monks.

A comparable set of 250 monastic rules is contained in the Sanskrit canon of the SARVĀSTIVĀDA ("Doctrine That All

Is Real") tradition that was widely known in northern Buddhist countries. The MAHĀYĀNA tradition in China and Japan more generally rejected those rules that were not applicable locally and substituted disciplinary codes that differed from sect to sect and sometimes even from monastery to monastery.

PRATĪTYA-SAMUTPĀDA \prə-'tēt-yə-,sə-mùt-'pä-də\ (Sanskrit: "origination by dependence"), *Pāli* paṭicca-samuppāda, chain of causation—a fundamental concept of BUDDHISM describing the causes of pain and the course of events that lead a being through rebirth, old age, and death.

Existence is seen as an interrelated flux of phenomenal events that have no permanent, independent existence of their own. These events happen in a series, one interrelating group of events producing another. The series is usually described as a chain without beginning or end that is constituted by twelve links (Sanskrit: *nidāna*s, "causes"). According to one very widespread way of interpreting the chain, the first two links are related to the past (or previous life) and explain the present, the next eight belong to the present, and the last two represent the future as determined by the past and what is happening in the present. The series consists of (1) ignorance (Sanskrit: *avidyā*; Pāli: *avijja*), which leads to (2) faulty thought constructions about reality (*saṃskāra/sankhāra*). These in turn provide the structure of (3) knowledge (*vijñāna/viññāṇa*), the object of which is (4) name and form—*i.e.*, the principle of individual identity (*nāma-rūpa*) and the sensory perception of an object—which are accomplished through (5) the six domains (*ṣaḍāyatana*)—*i.e.*, the five senses and their objects—and the mind as the coordinating organ of sense impressions. The presence of objects and senses leads to (6) contact (*sparśa/phassa*) between the two, which provides (7) sensation (*vedanā*). Because this sensation is agreeable, it gives rise to (8) thirst (*tṛṣṇā/taṇhā*) and in turn to (9) grasping (*upādāna*), as of sexual partners. This sets in motion (10) the process of becoming (*bhava*), which fructifies in (11) birth (*jāti*) of the individual and hence to (12) old age and death (*jarā-maraṇa*).

The BUDDHA GOTAMA is said to have reflected on the series just prior to his enlightenment, thus demonstrating that a correct understanding of the causes of pain and the cycle of rebirth is closely associated with emancipation from the ongoing bondage that the chain generates. The formula led to much discussion within the various schools of early Buddhism. Later it came to be pictured as the outer rim of the wheel of becoming (*bhavacakra*), frequently reproduced in Tibetan painting.

PRAYER, act of communication by humans with the sacred or holy—God, the gods, the transcendent realm, or supernatural powers. Found in all religions in all times, prayer may be a communal or personal act utilizing various forms and techniques. Prayer has been described in its sublimity as "an intimate friendship, a frequent conversation held alone with the Beloved" by ST. TERESA OF ÁVILA, a 16th-century Spanish mystic.

Prayer is a significant and universal aspect of religion that expresses the broad range of religious feelings and attitudes that command man's relations with the sacred or holy. Described by some scholars as religion's primary mode of expression, prayer is said to be to religion what rational thought is to philosophy; it is the very expression of living religion. Prayer distinguishes the phenomenon of religion from those phenomena that approach it or resemble it,

such as religious and aesthetic feelings. Of the various forms of religious literature, prayer is considered by many to be the purest in expressing the essential elements of a religion. The Islamic QUR'AN is regarded as a book of prayers, and the book of Psalms of the BIBLE is viewed as a meditation on biblical history turned into prayer. The CONFESSIONS of the great Christian thinker ST. AUGUSTINE (354–430) are, in the final analysis, a long prayer with the Creator.

Prayer expresses a desire on the part of men to enter into contact with the sacred or holy. As a part of that desire, prayer is linked to a feeling of presence (of the sacred or holy), which is neither an abstract conviction nor an instinctive intuition but rather a volitional movement conscious of realizing its higher end. Thus, prayer is described not only as meditation about God but as a step, a "going out of one's self," a PILGRIMAGE of the spirit "in the presence of God." It has, therefore, a personal and experiential character that goes beyond critical analysis.

The forms that prayer takes in the religions of the world, though varied, generally follow certain fixed patterns. These include BENEDICTIONS (blessings), litanies (alternate statements, titles of the deity or deities, or petitions and responses), ceremonial and ritualistic prayers, free prayers (in intent following no fixed form), repetition or formula prayers (*e.g.*, the repetition of the name of Jesus in Eastern Christian HESYCHASM, a quietistic monastic movement, or the repetition of the name of AMITĀBHA Buddha in Japanese BUDDHISM), HYMNS, doxologies (statements of praise or glory), and other forms.

Although the various types of prayer are connected and permit a flow from one type to another, it is possible to distinguish several, even if more on the basis of psychology than on history.

Petition. The role of the request in religion has played such a central part that it has given its name to prayer. The requests that occur most often are for preservation of or return to health, the healing of the sick, long life, material goods, prosperity, or success in one's undertakings. A request for the attainment of such goals may be tied to a magical invocation; it may also be a deviation from prayer when it takes the form of a bargain or of a request for payment due: "In payment of our praise, give to the head of the family who is imploring you glory and riches" (from the RG VEDA [Rigveda], a sacred scripture of HINDUISM). CHRISTIANITY has never condemned material requests but rather has integrated them into a single providential order while at the same time subordinating them to spiritual values. Thus, in essence though not always in practice, requests are only on the fringe of prayer.

Confession. The term confession expresses at the same time an affirmation of faith and a recognition of the state of SIN. In Mazdaism (ZOROASTRIANISM AND PARSIISM), as in ancient Christianity, the CONFESSION OF FAITH accompanies the renunciation of DEMONS. In a similar fashion, ancient and primitive men recognize that their sins unleash the anger of the gods. To counter the divine wrath, a member of the West African Ewe tribe, for example, throws a little bundle of twigs—which symbolizes the confessor's sins—into the air and he says words symbolizing the deity's response, "All your sins are forgiven you."

The admission of sin cannot be explained only by anguish or by the feeling of guilt; it is also related to what is deepest in man—*i.e.*, to what constitutes his being and his action. The awareness of sin is one of the salient features of religion, as, for example, in Hinduism: "Varuṇa is merciful even to him who has committed sin" (Ṛg Veda). Confession is viewed as the first step toward salvation in both JUDAISM and Christianity; in Buddhism, monks confess their sins publicly before the Buddha and the congregation two times every month.

Intercession. Intercessory prayers derive from and express a sense of social solidarity—with family, tribe, nation, or other structure. In the hymns of the Ṛg Veda the father implores the god AGNI (god of fire) for all of those who "owe him their lives and are his family." In the Greek play *Alcestis* by Euripides (5th century BCE), the mother, on her death, entrusts the orphans she is about to leave to HESTIA, the goddess of the home. Among the Babylonians and the Assyrians, a PRIESTHOOD was established primarily to say prayers of intercession.

Prayers of intercession to the divine are supported by mediatory minor gods or human protectors (alive or dead)—MARABOUTS (dervishes, or mystics, believed to have special powers) in ISLAM, or saints in Christianity, for example—whose mediation ensures that the prayer will be efficacious.

In biblical religion, intercession is spiritualized in view of a consciousness of the messianic (salvatory) MISSION. MOSES views himself as one with his people even when they fail in their duty: "Pardon your people," he prays, "or remove me from the Book of Life." Such solidarity finds its supreme form in the prayer of Christ on the cross—"Father, forgive them, for they know not what they do."

Praise and thanksgiving. Praise can be traced to salutations, such as in the prayer of the Khoikhoin (of South Africa) to the New Moon—"Welcome." Praise among most of the ancient peoples was expressed in the hymn, which was primarily a prayer of praise (whether ritual or personal) for the gift of the created world. Israel praises its Creator for "his handiwork," as does the Qur'an.

Praise—in addition to concerns for the created world—plays an important role in the prayer of mystics, for whom it is a form of adoration. Praise in this instance constitutes an essential element of the mystic experience and celebrates God, no longer for his works, but for himself, his greatness, and his mystery.

When the great deeds of God are the theme of praise, it becomes benediction and thanksgiving. Even when words denoting thanksgiving are not present, the substance of thanksgiving is manifest. Mealtime prayers in both ancient and modern religions give thanks for the goods of the earth and are linked to the giving of an offering.

Adoration. Adoration is generally considered the most noble form of prayer, a kind of prostration of the whole being before God. Names given to the divinity in prayers of adoration express dependency and submission, as, for example, in the prayer of the Kekchí Indians of Central America: "O God, you are my lord, you are my mother, you are my father, the lord of the mountains and the valleys." To express his adoration man often falls to the ground and prostrates himself. The feeling of submissive reverence also is expressed by body movements: raising the hands, touching or kissing a sacred object, deep bowing of the body, kneeling with the right hand on the mouth, prostration, or touching the forehead to the ground. The gesture often is accompanied by cries of fear, amazement, or joy; *e.g., has* (Hebrew), *hū* (Islam), or *svāhā* (Hindu).

Adoration takes on another meaning in the presence of the transcendental God who reveals himself to man in the religions of revelation (Judaism, Christianity, and Islam). The supreme form of adoration is generally considered to be holy silence, which expresses the most adequate attitude toward the immeasurable mystery of God: "I am in a dark sanctuary, I pray in silence; O silence full of reverence" (Gerhard Tersteegen, an 18th-century Protestant mystic).

Unitative: mystical union or ecstasy. ECSTASY is literally a departure from, a tearing away from, or a surpassing of human limitations and also a meeting with and embracing of the divine. The mystic experiences God himself in an inexpressible encounter because it is beyond the ordinary experiences of man. The mystical union may be a lucid and conscious progression of CONTEMPLATIVE prayer, or it may take a more passive form of a "seizing" by God of the one who is praying. Ecstatic prayer goes beyond the frame of ordinary prayer and becomes an experience in which words fail. It is found in the accounts of Hindu, Persian, Hellenistic, and Christian mystics. "You are me, supreme divinity, I am you," says Nimbāditya. The Sufi (mystic) of Islam JALĀL AD-DĪN AR-RŪMĪ sighs in the same words as a Christian mystic, Angela da Foligno: "I am you and you are me." Such reciprocity that is so complete that it becomes identity is the supreme expression of ecstatic prayer. It is found in all of the mystic writings, from the Orient to the West.

PRAYER BEADS: *see* ROSARY; SUBḤAH.

PRAYER WHEEL, *Tibetan* maṇi chos'khor \'mä-nē-'chœ̄-kōr\, in TIBETAN BUDDHISM, an often beautifully embossed hollow metal cylinder, mounted on a rod handle and containing a consecrated written MANTRA (sacred syllable). Each turning of the wheel by hand is equivalent in efficacy to one oral recitation of the prayer.

Variants to the hand-held prayer wheel are large cylinders that can be attached to windmills or waterwheels and thus kept in continuous motion. The mantra on a prayer flag is similarly activated by the blowing of the wind.

Tibetan prayer wheel, gilt sliver, 18th–19th century
By courtesy of the Seattle Art Museum, Washington, Eugene Fuller Memorial Collection

PRE-COLUMBIAN MESO-AMERICAN RELIGIONS

Beliefs and practices of the peoples of the part of Mexico and Central America that had developed urbanized societies before the arrival of the Spanish in the 16th century. The Meso-American system of thought was ultimately organized around a calendar in which a ritual cycle of 260 (13 × 20) days intermeshed with a "vague year" of 365 days (18 × 20 days, plus five "nameless" days), producing a 52-year Calendar Round. The Meso-American pantheon was associated with the calendar and featured an old, dual creator god; a god of royal descent and warfare; a Sun god and a Moon goddess; a rain god; a fire god; a culture hero called the FEATHERED SERPENT; and many other deities. Also characteristic was a layered system of 13 heavens and 9 underworlds, each with its presiding god. Much of the system was under the control of a PRIESTHOOD that maintained an advanced understanding of COSMOLOGY, genealogy, and astronomy.

EARLY RELIGIOUS LIFE

Early religious phenomena can be deduced only from archaeological remains. Numerous clay figurines have been found that date to the Pre-Classic period (roughly 1500 BCE to the 1st century CE); among these are terra-cotta statuettes of women that may have represented agricultural goddesses. Two-headed figurines found at Tlatilco, a site of the late Pre-Classic, may portray a supernatural being. Depictions of a fire god in the form of an old man with an incense burner on his back date from the same period.

The first elaborate pre-Columbian culture of Meso-America was that of the Olmecs, who inhabited present-day southern Mexico. The Olmecs worshiped at least ten distinct gods, several of which were depicted as "were-jaguars," hybrids between jaguars and human infants. Later evidence suggests that their deities probably included a fire god, a rain god, a corn god, and a Feathered Serpent. The Izapan civilization was focused on Izapa, a huge temple center near modern Tapachula, Chiapas, on the Pacific coast plain. A large number of carved stone stelae have been found at Izapa, and in front of most stelae is a round altar, often crudely shaped like a toad. Izapan stelae are carved in relief with narrative scenes derived from mythology and legend; among the depictions are warfare and decapitation,

Tourists climbing the Pyramid of the Magician at Uxmal, a ruined ancient Mayan city about 50 miles south of modern Mérida, Yucatán state, Mex.

ceremonies connected with a sacred tree, and meetings of what seem to be tribal elders. Many deities are shown, each of which is derived from what is perhaps an Olmec prototype.

The first monumental ceremonial center on the Mexican plateau is the PYRAMID of Cuicuilco, near Mexico City. It was doubtless a religious monument, crowned by a temple built on the terminal platform and surrounded by tombs. By the Late Formative Period (300 BCE–100 CE) the construction of temple-pyramids had become common. It was a Meso-American custom to bury the dead beneath the floors of their own houses, which were often then abandoned by the bereaved. As an elite class of noble lineages became distinguished from the mass of the people, these simple house platforms might have become transformed into more imposing structures, ending in the huge pyramids of the Late Formative and Classic, which surely had funerary functions. The deceased leader or the gods from which he claimed descent, or sometimes both, would then have been worshiped in a "house of god" on the temple summit. These pyramids became the focal point of Meso-American ceremonial life as well as the centers of settlement.

THE MAYA

The problem of the origin of the Mayan-speaking people has not been solved. It may be that they were Olmec people who had been forced out of their homeland to the west, or it could be that the earliest Maya descended to their lowland homelands from the Guatemalan highlands.

Maya chronology envisioned a 260-day sacred year (*tzolkin*) formed by the combination of the numbers 1 through 13 and 20 day names. The *tzolkin* were the most sacred means of DIVINATION, enabling the priests to detect the favorable or evil influences attached to every day. ITZAMNÁ was the supreme Maya deity, functioning as creator god and lord of fire (and therefore of the hearth). The Feathered Serpent was known to the Maya as Kukulcán.

The Maya lavished great attention on their royal dead, who almost surely were thought of as descended from the gods and partaking of their divine essence. Reliefs and pictorial pottery found in tombs deal with the underworld and the dangerous voyage of the soul through that land, which was ruled by a number of gods, including several old men often embellished with jaguar emblems. While the Classic Maya did practice HUMAN SACRIFICE, this was not on the scale of the Aztecs. The victims were captives, including defeated rulers and nobles. Self-sacrifice or self-mutilation was also common; blood drawn by jabbing spines through the ear or penis or by drawing a thorn-studded cord through the tongue was spattered on paper or otherwise collected as an offering to the gods.

By 300 BCE, if not earlier, with the appearance of major centers and pyramid and temple constructions, an elaborate worldview had evolved. Deified heavenly bodies and time periods were added to the earlier corn and rain gods. Religion became increasingly esoteric, with a complex mythology interpreted by a closely organized priesthood.

Creation. The Maya, like other Meso-American Indians, believed that several worlds had been successively created and destroyed before the present universe had come into being. People were made successively of earth (who, being mindless, were destroyed), then of wood (who, lacking souls and intelligence and being ungrateful to the gods, were punished by being drowned in a flood or devoured by DEMONS), and finally of a corn gruel (the ancestors of the Maya). The Yucatec Maya worshiped a creator deity called Hunab Ku, "One-God." Itzamná ("Iguana House"), head of the Maya pantheon worshiped by the ruling class, was his son, whose wife was Ix Chebel Yax, patroness of weaving.

Four Itzamnás, one for each direction, were represented by celestial monsters or two-headed, dragonlike iguanas. Four gods, the BACABS, sustained the sky. Each geographic direction was associated with a Bacab; a sacred ceiba, or silk cotton tree; a bird; and a color, according to the following scheme: east–red, north–white, west–black, and south–yellow. Green was the color of the center.

The main act of creation, as stated in the POPOL VUH (a Maya document) was the dawn: the world and humanity were in darkness, but the gods created the Sun and the Moon. According to other traditions, the Sun (male) was the patron of hunting and music, and the Moon (female) was the goddess of weaving and childbirth. Both the Sun and the Moon originally inhabited the Earth, but they were translated to the heavens as a result of the Moon's sexual license. Lunar light is less bright than that of the Sun because, it was said, one of her eyes was pulled out by the Sun in punishment for her infidelity.

Cosmology. The Maya believed that 13 heavens were arranged in layers above the Earth, which itself rested on the back of a huge crocodile or reptilian monster floating on the ocean. Under the Earth were nine underworlds, also arranged in layers. Thirteen gods, the Oxlahuntiku, presided over the heavens; nine gods, the Bolontiku, ruled the subterranean worlds.

Time was an all-important element of Maya cosmology. The priest-astronomers viewed time as a majestic succession of cycles without beginning or end. All the time periods were considered gods; time itself was believed to be divine.

The gods. Among the several deities represented by statues and sculptured panels of the Classic period are such gods as the young corn god, whose statue is to be seen at Copán, the Sun god shown at Palenque in the form of the solar disk engraved with anthropomorphic features, the nine gods of the night (also at Palenque), and a snake god especially prominent at Yaxchilán. Another symbol of the corn god is a foliated cross or life tree represented in two Palenque sanctuaries. The rain god (CHAC) has a mask with characteristic protruding fangs, large round eyes, and a proboscis-like nose.

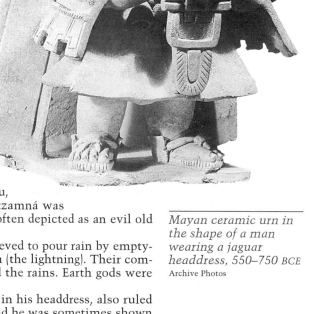

Mayan ceramic urn in the shape of a man wearing a jaguar headdress, 550–750 BCE
Archive Photos

Itzamná, lord of the heavens, ruled over the pantheon; he was closely associated with Kinich Ahau, the Sun god, and with the Moon goddess Ix Chel. Itzamná was considered an entirely benevolent god, but Ix Chel, often depicted as an evil old woman, had unfavorable aspects.

The Chacs, the rain gods of the peasants, were believed to pour rain by emptying their gourds and to hurl stone axes upon the earth (the lightning). Their companions were frogs (*uo*), whose croakings announced the rains. Earth gods were worshiped in the highlands.

The corn god, a youthful deity with an ear of corn in his headdress, also ruled over vegetation in general. His name was Ah Mun, and he was sometimes shown in combat with the death god, Ah Puch, a skeleton-like being, patron of the sixth day-sign Cimi ("Death") and lord of the ninth hell. Several other deities were associated with death—*e.g.*, Ek Chuah, a war god and god of merchants and cacao growers, and Ixtab, patron goddess of suicides.

Eschatology. The present world, the Maya believed, was doomed to end in cataclysms, as the other worlds had done previously. According to the priestly concept of time, cycles repeated themselves. Therefore, prediction was made possible by probing first into the past and then into the future: hence the calculations, bearing on many millennia, carved on temples and stelae. The priests probably believed that the present world would come to a sudden end, but a new world would be created so that the succession of cycles would remain unbroken.

Sacrifice. Sacrifices were made for many reasons, including agricultural and cosmic renewal, preparation for warfare, purification, and especially to repay the gods for divine gifts of life. Sacrifices made in return for divine favor were numerous: animals, birds, insects, fish, agricultural products, flowers, rubber, jade, and blood drawn from the tongue, ears, arms, legs, and genitals. Human sacrifice was known in Classic times, but even in the Postclassic era, when the Maya increased ritual violence, their sacrifices did not become as frequent as in central Mexico. Toltec-Maya art shows many instances of human sacrifice: removal of the heart, shooting with arrows, or beheading. At Chichén Itzá, in order to obtain rain, sacrificial victims were hurled into a deep natural well together with copper, gold, and jade offerings. Prayers for material benefits (which were usually recited in a squatting or standing position), fasting and continence (often for 260 days), and the drawing of blood from the supplicant's body often preceded important ceremonies and sacrifices.

Rites. Ritual activities, held on selected favorable days, were complex and intense. Performers submitted to preliminary fasting and sexual abstinence. Features common to most rites were: offerings of incense (*pom*), of balche (an intoxicating drink brewed from honey and a tree bark), bloodletting from ears and tongues, sacrifices of animals (human sacrifices in later times), and dances. Special ceremonies took place on New Year's Day, 0 Pop, in honor of the "Year-Bearer"; *i.e.*, the *tzolkin* sign of that day. Pottery, clothes, and other belongings were renewed. The second month, Uo, was devoted to Itzamná, Tzec (the 5th month) to the Bacabs, Xul (6th) to Kukulcán, Yax (10th) to the planet VENUS, Mac (13th) to the rain gods, and Muan (15th) to the cocoa-tree god. New idols were made during the 8th and 9th months, Mol and Ch'en, respectively.

The priesthood. Bejeweled, feather-adorned priests are often represented in Classic sculpture. The high priests of each province taught in priestly schools such subjects as cosmology, dynastic history, divination, and glyph writing. The priesthood was hereditary. *Ahkin*, "he of the Sun," was the priests' general title. Specialized functions were performed by the *nacom*s, who split open the victims' breasts; the *chac*s, who held their arms and legs; and the *chilan*s, who interpreted the sacred books and predicted the future. Some priests used hallucinatory drugs in their roles as prophets and diviners.

THE AZTEC

The Aztec, whose origin is uncertain, may have been several communities of hunters and gatherers, but they also brought agricultural skills into the Basin of Mexico in the 13th century. Their religious ideology was a synthesis of myths, symbols, and ritual practices, some of which they had brought with them and some of which they borrowed and inherited from well-established societies in central Mexico. Their religion was a combination of "blood" and "flowers," of commitments to social and military aggression, as well as to traditions of beauty and artistry in the areas of speech, sculpture, painting, dance, and philosophy. In all aspects, the priesthood lived rigorous lives, preparing the community for disciplined cultivation of agricultural fields, periodic and intense warfare, and the expression of sacred truths and beauty. Aztec religion was organized and expressed in the great ceremonial center of Tenochtitlán, the magnificent imperial capital that shocked and thrilled visitors (including the Spaniards). This capital and its various sacred precincts were organized as a microcosm of the principal myths and cosmologies, which the Aztecs combined from various competing traditions during the two hundred years of their rise and florescence.

The cult of the gods required a large professional priesthood. Spanish documents indicate that the priesthood was one of the most elaborate of Aztec institutions. Each temple and god had its attendant priestly order. Within the splendid ceremonial center in the heart of the capital, where the Great Aztec Temple—

called by the Aztecs Coatepec, or Serpent Mountain—received the most precious tributary payments and sacrificial offerings, the High Priests of TLALOC and HUITZILOPOCHTLI served as head of the entire priestly organization. Within the orders were priests in charge of ceremonies, the education of novices, ASTROLOGY, and the temple lands.

Aztec religion, though also characterized by philosophies of truth, the afterlife, and the nature of human life in relation to a divine duality, emphasized sacrifice and ascetic behavior as the necessary preconditions for approaching the supernatural. Priests were celibate and were required to live a simple, spartan life. They performed constant self-sacrifice in the form of bloodletting as penitence (by passing barbed cords through the tongue and ears). This pattern of worship reached its climax in the practice of human sacrifice, which was an institution of great cultural importance. Aztec warfare was waged for many purposes, including the extraction of tributary payments to the capital, the suppression of rebellions, territorial control, and it always included the collection of sacrificial victims.

Aztec human sacrifice, depicted in the Codex Magliabecchiano; in the Biblioteca Nazionale, Florence
Scala—Art Resource

Cosmogony and eschatology.   The Aztec believed that four worlds had existed before the present universe. Those worlds, or "suns," had been destroyed by catastrophes. Humankind had been entirely wiped out at the end of each sun. The present world was the fifth sun, and the Aztec thought of themselves as "the People of the Sun." Their divine duty was to wage cosmic war in order to provide the Sun with his *tlaxcaltiliztli* ("nourishment"). Without it the Sun would disappear from the heavens. Thus the welfare and very survival of the universe depended on the offerings of blood and hearts to the Sun, a notion that the Aztec extended to all the deities of their pantheon.

Present humanity had been created by Quetzalcóatl. The Feathered Serpent, with the help of his twin, Xólotl, the dog-headed god, had succeeded in reviving the dried bones of the old dead by sprinkling them with his own blood. The present Sun was called Nahui-Ollin, "Four-Earthquake," and was doomed to disappear in a tremendous earthquake. The skeleton-like monsters of the West, the *tzitzimime*, would then appear and kill all people. The present Sun and Moon had been created when the gods, assembled in the darkness at Teotihuacán, had built a huge fire; two of them, Nanahuatzin and Tecciztécatl, threw themselves into the flames, from which the former emerged as the Sun and the latter as the Moon. When the Sun refused to move across the sky the gods realized they must give blood and were compelled to sacrifice themselves to feed the Sun.

Cosmology.   Above the Earth, which was surrounded by the "heavenly water" (*ilhuicáatl*) of the ocean, were 13 heavens, the uppermost of which was the abode of the Supreme Couple. Under the "divine Earth," *teotlalli*, were the nine hells of Mictlan, with nine rivers that the souls of the dead had to cross. Thirteen was considered a favorable number, nine extremely unlucky.

All the heavenly bodies and constellations were divinized, such as the Great Bear (TEZCATLIPOCA), Venus (Quetzalcóatl), the stars of the North (Centzon Mimixcoa, "the 400 Cloud-Serpents"), and the stars of the South (Centzon Huitznáua, "the 400 Southerners"). The solar disk, TONATIUH, was supposed to be borne from the East to the zenith on a litter surrounded by the souls of dead warriors and from the zenith to the West among a retinue of divinized women, the Cihuateteo. When the night began on Earth, day dawned in Mictlan, the abode of the dead.

Deities. The ancient societies of central Mexico had worshiped fertility gods for many centuries when the Aztec invaded the valley. The cult of these gods remained extremely important in Aztec religion. Tlaloc, the giver of rain but also the wrathful deity of lightning, was the leader of a group of rain gods, the Tlaloques, who dwelt on mountaintops, in caves, and in waters. CHALCHIUHTLICUE ("One Who Wears a Jade Skirt") presided over fresh waters, Huixtocíhuatl over salt waters and the sea. Numerous Earth goddesses were associated with the fertility of the soil and with the fecundity of women, such as Teteoinnan ("Mother of the Gods"), COATLICUE ("One Who Wears a Snake Skirt"), Cihuacóatl ("Serpent-Woman"), and Itzpapálotl ("Obsidian-Butterfly"). Their significance was twofold: as fertility deities, they gave birth to the young gods of corn, Centéotl, and of flowers, Xochipilli; as symbols of the Earth that devoured bodies and drank blood, they appeared as warlike godheads. TLAZOLTÉOTL, a Huastec goddess, presided over carnal love and the confession of sins. XIPE TOTEC, borrowed from the Yopi people, was a god of the spring and of the renewal of vegetation, as well as the patron of goldsmiths. Human victims were killed and flayed to honor him.

Among the Aztec the concept of a supreme couple took the form of Intonan, Intota ("Our Mother, Our Father"), the Earth and the Sun. But the fire god Huehuetéotl was also associated with the Earth. In addition, OMETECUHTLI ("Lord of the Duality") and Omecihuatl ("Lady of the Duality") were held to abide in the 13th heaven: they decided on which date a human being would be born, thus determining his destiny.

Among the fertility gods are to be counted the "400 Rabbits" (Centzon Totochtin), little gods of the crops, among which are Ometochtli, the god of *octli* (a fermented drink), and Tepoztécatl, the god of drunkenness.

The Aztec brought with them the cult of their Sun and war god, Huitzilopochtli, "the Hummingbird of the Left," who was considered to be the conquering Sun of midday. According to a legend probably borrowed from the Toltec, he was born near Tula. His mother, the Earth goddess Coatlicue, had already given birth to the

Sites of Meso-American civilization

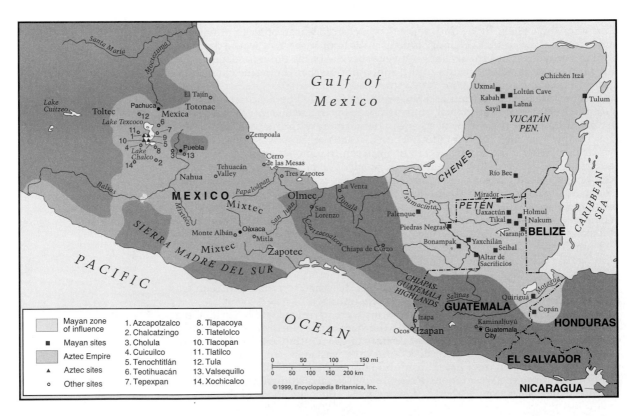

©1999, Encyclopædia Britannica, Inc.

Legend:
Mayan zone of influence
Mayan sites
Aztec Empire
Aztec sites
Other sites

1. Azcapotzalco
2. Chalcatzingo
3. Cholula
4. Cuicuilco
5. Tenochtitlán
6. Teotihuacán
7. Tepexpan
8. Tlapacoya
9. Tlatelolco
10. Tlacopan
11. Tlatilco
12. Tula
13. Valsequillo
14. Xochicalco

400 Southerners and to the Moon goddess Coyolxauhqui, whom the newborn god exterminated with his *xiuhcoatl* ("turquoise serpent"). Tezcatlipoca, god of the night sky, was the protector of the young warriors.

Quetzalcóatl, the ancient Teotihuacán deity of vegetation and fertility, had been transformed into a god of the morning star. He was also revered as a wind god and as the ancient priest-king of the Toltec golden age: the discoveries of writing, of the calendar, and of the arts were attributed to him.

Death. The beliefs of the Aztec concerning the other world and life after death also showed the same syncretic combination of various traditions. The old paradise of the rain god Tlaloc, depicted in the Teotihuacán frescoes, opened its gardens to those who died by drowning, lightning, or as a result of leprosy, dropsy, gout, or lung diseases. He was supposed to have caused their death and to have sent their souls to paradise.

Two categories of dead persons went up to the heavens as companions of the Sun: the Quauhteca ("Eagle People"), who comprised the warriors who died on the battlefield or on the sacrificial stone and the merchants who were killed while traveling; and the women who died while giving birth to their first child and thus became Cihuateteo, "Divine Women." The Cihuateteo were said to appear at night at the crossroads and strike the passersby with palsy. All other dead went to Mictlan, under the northern deserts, the abode of MICTLANTECUHTLI, the god of death. There they traveled for four years until they arrived at the ninth hell, where they disappeared altogether.

Offerings were made to the dead 80 days after the funeral, then one, two, three, and four years later, after which all links between the dead and the living were severed. But the warriors who crossed the heavens in the retinue of the Sun were thought to come back to Earth after four years as hummingbirds.

Ritual calendar. *Tonalpohualli*, an Aztec term meaning "the count of days," was the name of the ritual calendar of 260 days. It ran parallel to the solar calendar of 365 days, which was divided into 18 months of 20 days and five supplementary unlucky days. The word *tonalli* means both "day" and "destiny": the 260-day calendar was mainly used for purposes of divination. The days were named by the combination of 20 signs—natural phenomena such as the wind and the earthquake, animals such as the rabbit and the jaguar, plants such as the reed, and objects such as the flint knife and the house—with the numbers 1 to 13. Thus the calendrical round included 20 series of 13 days.

Specialized priests called *tonalpouhque* interpreted the signs and numbers on such occasions as births, marriages, departures of traders to faraway lands, and elections of rulers. Each day, and each 13-day series, was deemed lucky, unlucky, or indifferent according to the deities presiding over it. Thus Ce-Coatl ("One-Snake") was held as favorable to traders, Chicome-Xochitl ("Seven-Flower") to scribes and weavers, and Nahui-Ehécatl ("Four-Wind") to magicians. The men who were born during the Ce-Ocelotl ("One-Jaguar") series would die on the sacrificial stone, those whose birth took place on the day Ometochtli ("Two-Rabbit") would be drunkards, and so on. The *tonalpohualli* influenced every aspect of public and private life.

Olmec basalt head, c. *1100–800 BCE; these colossal figures weighing more than 15 tons were the largest sculptures found in the Western Hemisphere; in the Anthropology Museum, Veracruz, Mex.*

Werner Forman—Art Resource

PRE-COLUMBIAN SOUTH AMERICAN RELIGIONS

Comprising the beliefs and practices of the peoples of the Andean region (western South America) prior to Spanish exploration in the 16th century, these pre-Columbian religions include those of both the Inca and their precursors.

THE PRE-INCA PERIODS

In the Andean area, the threshold of a successful village agricultural economy can be placed at *c.* 2500 BCE with the cultivation of corn, beans, squash, potatoes, and other foods. Indications of a more complex sociopolitical order—large-scale constructions and densely populated centers—occurred very soon after this (*c.* 1800 BCE). Prior to this date llamas and alpacas were domesticated. In about 1000 BCE there was an invasion of highlanders into the coastal Casma Valley who brought with them their own architectural styles, ceramics, and food plants and animals. Archaeologists at one time generally agreed that their chief object of worship was a cat, probably the jaguar, but this has been questioned. Many natural bird, animal, and human forms were depicted with feline mouths and other attributes, and feline representations were widespread.

Most temples in this time seem to have been ceremonial centers without people living around them. The most elaborate temple known is that at Chavín, which contains a shaft of white granite, carved in low relief to symbolize a standing human figure with snakes representing the hair and a pair of great fangs in the upper jaw. This figure, which has variously been called El Lanzón, the Great Image, and the Smiling God, is thought to have been the chief object of worship in the original temple.

Elsewhere in the temple, one facade has a lintel bearing 14 eagles in low relief, supplied with feline jaws with prominent fangs behind their beaks. The columns supporting the lintel are entirely covered by mythical birds bristling with feline fangs and faces. These have been interpreted as attendants of the god worshiped in that part of the temple, who perhaps superseded the Smiling God and could have been the god shown on the Raimondi Stone, now in Lima. The stone shows the Staff God, a standing semihuman figure having claws, a feline face with crossed fangs, and a staff in each hand. Above his head is a towering, pillarlike

The Sun Temple in Cuzco, Peru
Francois Gohier—Photo Researchers

877

structure fringed with snakes and emerging from a double-fanged face. Unlike the Smiling God, this figure has been found in areas as far from Chavín as the northern and southern coasts of Peru. Also found was the Tello obelisk, a pillar covered with symbolic carvings, such as bands of teeth and animal heads. This is considered to be an object of worship like the Smiling God and Staff God. Other carvings found on and around the temple include jaguars, eagles, and snakes, and a number of heads of men and the Smiling God; they are thought to be decorations or the attendants of gods rather than objects of worship.

At a later period (c. 400–200 BCE) in the south highlands, depictions of a new divine figure appear: at Tiahuanaco near Lake Titicaca, temple carvings depict a figure that may represent a spear thrower carrying staves and darts and attended by three rows of smaller winged figures that appear to run inward toward him. This divinity has been termed the Doorway, or Gateway, God. Versions of the Doorway God and his attendants are found almost everywhere within the range of Tiahuanaco influence in the subsequent period.

INCA RELIGION

Religion was a complex and fundamental part of Inca life with emphasis on formality and ritual, agricultural, curing, and the devotion to the gods and HUACAS (sacred sites). A central practice was the worship of the sun, which was presided over by the priests of the last native pre-Columbian conquerors of the Andean regions of South America. Though there was an Inca state religion of the sun, the substrata RELIGIOUS BELIEFS and practices of the pre-Inca peoples exerted an influence on the Andean region prior to and after the conquest of most of South America by the Spaniards in the 16th century.

Gods. The creator god of the Inca and of pre-Inca peoples was VIRACOCHA, who was also a culture hero. Creator of earth, humans, and animals, Viracocha had a long list of titles, including Lord Instructor of the World, the Ancient One, and the Old Man of the Sky. Some have said that he also was the creator of the Tiahuanaco civilizations, of which the Inca were the cultural heirs. Viracocha went through several transmogrifications, often with grotesque or humorous effects. He made peoples, destroyed them, and re-created them of stone; once they were re-created, he dispersed humankind in four directions. As a culture hero he taught people various techniques and skills. He journeyed widely until he came to the shores of Manta (Ecuador), where he set off into the Pacific—some say in a boat made of his cloak, others that he walked on the water. This part of the myth has been seized upon by modern mythmakers, and, as Kon-Tiki, Viracocha was said to have brought Inca culture to Polynesia.

INTI, the sun god, was the ranking deity in the Inca pantheon. His warmth embraced the Andean earth and matured crops, and for this intercession he was beloved by farmers. Inti was represented with a human face on a ray-splayed disk. He was considered to be the divine ancestor of the Inca.

Apu Illapu, the rain giver, was an agricultural deity to whom commoners addressed their prayers for rain. He was often depicted as a man in the sky wearing radiant clothing and holding a war club in one hand and a sling in the other. Temples to Illapu were usually on high structures; in times of drought, PILGRIMAGES were made to them and prayers were accompanied by sacrifices—often human, if the crisis was sufficient. The people believed that Illapu's shadow was in the Milky Way, from whence he drew the water that he poured down as rain.

Mama-Quilla, wife of the sun god, was the Moon Mother and regulator of women's menstrual cycles. The waxing and waning of the moon was used to calculate monthly cycles, from which the time periods for festivals were set. Silver was considered to be tears of the moon. The stars had minor functions. The constellation Lyra, which was believed to have the appearance of a llama, was entreated for protection. The constellation Scorpio was believed to have the shape of a cat; the Pleiades were called "little mothers," and festivals were celebrated on their reappearance in the sky. Earth was called Pacha-Mama, or "Earth Mother." Mama-Cocha or "Sea Mother" was the ultimate source of all waters including the ocean, streams, rivers, and irrigation water and therefore important to all agricultural peoples. She was also important to fishing peoples living near the coast.

Temples and shrines. Temples and shrines housing cult objects were occupied by priests, their attendants, and the CHOSEN WOMEN. In general, temples were not intended to shelter the celebrants, since most ceremonies were held outside the temple proper. The ruins of the Temple of Viracocha at San Pedro Cacha (Peru), however, had a ground plan that measured 330 by 87 feet, which indicates that it was designed for use other than the storage of priestly regalia. The Sun Temple in Cuzco is the best known of the Inca temples. Built with stones, it had a circum-

Sites of Andean civilization

ference of more than 1,200 feet. Within the temple was a large image of the sun, and in another precinct, the Golden Enclosure (Corincancha), were gold models of cornstalks, llamas, and lumps of earth. Portions of the land which supported the temples, the priests, and the Chosen Women, were allotted to the sun and administered for the priests. Another temple, at Vilcashuman (which was regarded as the geographic center of the empire), is still in existence. Near Mount Aconcagua in Argentina, at the southern limit of the Inca Empire, there was a temple and oracle at which important sacrifices were performed, and on Titicaca Island, one of the largest of several islands in Lake Titicaca, there was a temple of the sun. As the Inca conquered new territories, temples were erected in the new lands. In Caranqui, Ecuador, one such temple was described by a chronicler as being filled with great vessels of gold and silver. At Latacunga (Llacta cunga) in Ecuador there was a sun temple where sacrifices were made.

Along with the shrines and temples, *huaca*s were widespread. A *huaca* could be a man-made temple, mountain, hill, or bridge, such as the great *huacachaca* across the Apurímac River near Cuzco. A *huaca* also might be a MUMMY bundle, especially if it was that of a lord-Inca. On high points of passage in the Andes, propitiatory CAIRNS (*apacheta*, "piles of stones") were made, to which passing persons would add a small stone.

The priesthood.   Priests resided at all important shrines and temples. The priests were organized into a complex hierarchy according to the prestige of the shrine in which they worked. At the top was the HIGH PRIEST who was a close relative of the king, who was the manifestation of the Sun. A chronicler suggests that a priest's title was *umu*, but in usage his title was geared to his functions as diviner of lungs, sorcerer, confessor, and curer. The title of the chief priest in Cuzco, who was of noble lineage, was *villac umu.* He held his post for life, was married, had power over all shrines and temples, and could appoint and remove priests. The temples of the official Inca cult were served by the macmaconas, a group of consecrated women under the supervision of a noble woman who guided their tasks of making chicha and textiles for the temple communities. These women were selected from a larger group known as the Chosen Women or acllyaconas. The Chosen Women were selected around the age of 10, on the basis of their physical beauty, from the conquered communities as well as from the noble families of Cuzco. The most perfect women were sacrificed to the gods. Others became attendants to temples and secondary wives to the Inca king. Still others became macmaconas.

Divination.   DIVINATION was the prerequisite to all meaningful action. It was used to diagnose illness, to predict the outcome of battles, to ferret out crimes, and to determine what sacrifice should be made to what god. Life was believed to be controlled by the all-pervading unseen powers, and oracles were considered to be the most important and direct means of access to the gods. Oracles were sacred figures who could answer questions about the future. There were four main oracles in the empire. One ora-

Pre-Inca burial site and ceremonial center near Lake Titicaca, Peru
Kenneth Murray—Photo Researchers

cle of a *huaca* close by the Apurímac River near Cuzco was described by a chronicler as a wooden beam as thick as a fat man, with a girdle of gold about it with two large golden breasts like a woman. These and other idols were blood-spattered from sacrifices. "Through this large idol," a chronicler wrote, "the DEMON of the river used to speak to them." Another well-known oracle was housed in a temple in the large adobe complex of PACHACAMAC near Lima.

Divination also was accomplished by watching the meandering of spiders and the arrangement that coca leaves took in a shallow dish. Another method of divination was to drink *ayahuasca*, a narcotic that had profound effects on the central nervous system. This was believed to enable one to communicate with the supernatural powers.

Fire was also believed to provide spiritual contact. The flames were blown to red heat through metal tubes, after which a practitioner (*yacarca*) who had narcotized himself by chewing coca leaves summoned the spirits with fiery conjuration to speak—"which they did," wrote a chronicler, by "ventriloquism." Divination by studying the lungs of a sacrificed white llama was considered to be efficacious. The lungs were inflated by blowing into the dissected trachea, and the future was foretold by priests who minutely observed the markings and patterns of the veins. On the reading of this augury, political or military action was taken.

Should rain not fall or a water conduit break without cause, it was believed that such an occurrence could arise from someone's failure to observe the required ceremonies. This was called *hocha*, a ritual error. The *ayllu*, a basic social unit identified with communally held land, was wounded by individual misdeeds. It was important that crimes be confessed and expiated by penitence so as not to call down the divine wrath.

Sacrifice. Sacrifice, human or animal, was offered on every important occasion; guinea pigs (more properly *cui*), llamas, certain foods, coca leaves, and *chicha* (an intoxicant corn beverage) were all used in sacrifices. Many sacrifices were daily occurrences for the ritual of the sun's appearance. A fire was kindled, and corn was thrown on the coals and toasted. "Eat this, Lord Sun," was the objuration of officiating priests, "so that you will know that we are your children." On the first day of every lunar month 100 pure-white llamas were driven into the Great Square, Huayaca Pata in Cuzco; they were moved about to the various images of the gods and then assigned to 30 priestly attendants, each representing a day of the month. The llamas were then sacrificed; chunks of flesh were thrown onto the fire, and the bones were powdered for ritual use. Ponchos of excellent weave or miniature vestments were burned in the offering. The Inca ruler wore his poncho only once: it was ceremoniously sacrificed in fire each day.

Humans also were sacrificed; when the need was extreme, 200 children might be immolated, such as when a new Inca ruler took power. Even a Chosen Woman from the Sun Temple might be taken out for sacrifice. Children were feasted before being sacrificed, "so that they would not enter the presence of the gods hungry and crying." It was important in HUMAN SACRIFICE that the sacrificed person be without blemish. Many victims were chosen from conquered provinces as part of regular taxation.

Festivals. The 30-day calendar was religious, and each month had its own festival. The 17th-century Andean writer Felipe Guamán Poma de Ayala, in a letter to Philip II of Spain, described two different versions of the religious calendar, one centering on state ceremonies and sacrifices performed at Cuzco, and the other describing the agricultural practices at the local level in the highlands. Quite different calendars prevailed on the irrigated coast, but surviving sources do not record them in any detail.

Pre-Columbian Peruvian sculpture of a priest
Alfa—Monkmeyer

PREDESTINATION, in CHRISTIANITY, the doctrine that God has eternally chosen those whom he intends to save. In modern usage, predestination is distinct from both determinism and fatalism and is subject to the free decision of the human moral will; but the doctrine also teaches that salvation is due entirely to the eternal decree of God. In its fundamentals, the problem of predestination is as universal as religion itself, but the emphasis of the NEW TESTAMENT on the divine plan of salvation has made the issue especially prominent in Christian theology.

The Apostle PAUL stated (Romans 8:29–30) that "those whom he [God] knew he also predestined to be conformed to the image of his Son . . . and those whom he predestined he also called; and those whom he called he also justified; and those whom he justified he also glorified." Three types of predestination doctrine, with many variations, have developed subsequently. One theory (associated with SEMI-PELAGIANISM, some forms of nominalism, and ARMINIANISM) makes foreknowledge the ground of predestination and teaches that God predestined to salvation those whose future faith and merits he foreknew. At the opposite extreme is the doctrine of double predestination, commonly identified with JOHN CALVIN but more correctly associated with the SYNOD OF DORT, and appearing also in some of the writings of ST. AUGUSTINE and MARTIN LUTHER and in the thought of the Jansenists (*see* JANSEN, CORNELIUS). According to this doctrine, God has determined from eternity whom he will save and whom he will damn, regardless of their merit or lack thereof. A third doctrine was set forth in other writings of St. Augustine and Luther, in the decrees of the second Council of Orange (529), and in the thought of ST. THOMAS AQUINAS. It ascribes the salvation of man to the unmerited GRACE of God and thus to predestination, but it attributes divine reprobation to man's SIN and guilt.

PREHISTORIC RELIGION, wide variety of beliefs and ritual practices prevalent throughout the world during the Pleistocene Ice Age and the early Holocene, or Recent, Epoch—a period of approximately 500,000 years. During this period, the climates and environments of the world fluctuated considerably, and there were no ethnological regions that conformed in any meaningful way to those of the present. There was no such thing, therefore, as a unitary "prehistoric religion," but certain widespread features of the religions that the various prehistoric cultures practiced can be identified.

Throughout the Paleolithic Period (from about 600,000–700,000 years ago to roughly 8000 BCE) humans subsisted by gathering food, as well as by hunting and fishing. The Upper Paleolithic saw the beginning of the basic techniques of drawing, modeling, sculpture, and painting, as well as the earliest manifestations of dancing, music, the use of masks, ceremonies, and the organization of society into complex patterns. From this period dates the first material evidence of fertility magic, private property, and possible social stratification. After c. 8000 BCE the Mediterranean zone became the first center of cultural modifications from hunting and food gathering to the earliest farming, followed by similar

changes in southwestern Asia about 7000 BCE and in southern Mesopotamia about 4500 BCE.

Burial customs and cults of the dead. The first known burials can be dated to the Middle Paleolithic Period. The corpses, accompanied by stone tools and parts of animals, were laid in holes in the ground, and sometimes the corpses were especially protected; these practices imply a belief in life after death in some form. The Upper Paleolithic Period saw the first adoption of practices such as secondary burials or the burning of bodies (evident from the Neolithic period). The disposition of the individual parts of the body, especially the skull, is important. Ritual deposition of skulls is confirmed for the Middle Paleolithic Period. From even earlier periods, however, individual or multiple human skulls and long bones have been found within a single burial site. Evidence for ancestor cult practices dating to the 7th century BCE was first discovered from excavations at JERICHO in Palestine, where several skulls were found to have been deposited in a separate room, some of them covered with a sculpted face.

In finds belonging to the Paleolithic Period parts of human bodies as well as the bones of animals are found scattered throughout the archaeological layers and are sometimes broken or charred. By the Neolithic Period, human remains occasionally are found in association with remains of foodstuffs in waste pits or in holes and tunnels that served as sacrificial sites. Especially where human skulls have been broken open and the hollow bones split, the inference of CANNIBALISM is unavoidable. Cannibalism was likely practiced to acquire the powers and other qualities of the victim.

Sacrifice. Sacrifices appear as early as the Middle Paleolithic Period. Pits containing animal bones have been found in the vicinity of burial sites; thus, it is likely that they represent offerings to the dead or offerings to a deity believed to control the fertility of the animals. With conspicuous frequency human victims in ceremonial remains are females and children, sometimes along with young pigs. The inclusion of servants or women in the burial sites of highly placed persons most likely reflects the social status of the deceased leader and his need for servants or consorts in the afterlife, rather than a sacrificial offering in the strict sense.

The Venus of Willendorf, a fertility symbol, 30,000–25,000 BCE; in the Naturhistorisches Museum, Vienna
Ali Meyer—The Bridgeman Art Library

Hunting rites and animal cults. In the oldest known examples of graphic art, the representations of animals play a large part; humans appear rarely, and then frequently with animal attributes or as mixed human-animal figures. This would seem to indicate a special and intimate relationship between humans and animals, a belief system often accompanied by practices such as placating and begging for forgiveness of the game killed, performing DIVINATION with animal bones, and performing mimic animal dances and fertility rites for animals. Several finds and pictures from the Upper Paleolithic Period indicate a practice in which a bear skin with attached head was draped over the body of a bear made out of clay; the bear's skull and long bones were buried separately; the bear was shot with arrows and killed by a shot or a thrust into the lungs; and the animal or a bearlike figure was surrounded by dancers.

Female fertility deities.   Small female figures, the so-called Venus statuettes, appear for the first time in the Upper Paleolithic Period (beginning 40,000 years ago). Typically they are naturalistic representations of corpulent women whose breasts and buttocks are given special prominence, an emphasis that easily conveys the idea of female fertility. Such figures may have been conceived, among other things, as mothers or rulers of the animals, goddesses of the Underworld, helpers during hunting and donators of game, and sovereigns both of the land and other regions and of natural forces, including fertility.

Shamanism.   Shamanism is a complex of practices and conceptions, typically including the use of ecstasy, the belief in GUARDIAN SPIRITS (who are often in animal form, with the function of helping and guiding the dead on their voyage to the beyond), and beliefs concerning metamorphosis (change of form) and traveling to the beyond. Pictures from the Upper Paleolithic Period indicate the existence of ecstatic practices and of beliefs in protective and helping spirits, which assume the forms of birds and other animals. Noisemaking objects (to drive away evil spirits) are often found in the material remains of the Iron Age and probably are connected with shamanism.

PRELATE, ecclesiastical dignitary of high rank. In the RO-MAN CATHOLIC church, prelates are those who exercise the public power of the church. True prelacy is defined as "pre-eminence with jurisdiction," and true, or real, prelates are distinguished as (1) greater prelates, who possess episcopal jurisdiction (such as PATRIARCHS, archbishops, and bishops), and (2) lesser prelates, who possess a quasi-episcopal or other jurisdiction (such as ABBOTS and prelates "of no diocese" and religious superiors, withdrawn from the ordinary diocesan jurisdiction). In some Protestant churches the title of prelate was retained after the REFORMATION.

PRESBYTER (from Greek *presbyteros*, "elder"), officer or minister in the early Christian church intermediate between bishop and deacon or, in modern Presbyterianism, an alternative name for elder. The word presbyter is etymologically the original form of "priest."

The history of presbyterial government in the early church is not known in detail. During the last quarter of the 1st century a threefold organization is found in the church: (1) a spiritual organization composed of apostles, prophets, and teachers; (2) an administrative organization, consisting of the bishop and the deacons; and (3) a patriarchal organization based upon the natural deference of the younger to the older members of the church, though the senior members held no official position and were not appointed for any particular work as were the bishops and deacons. In the 2nd century the patriarchal element in the organization was merged in the administrative, and the presbyters became a definite order in the ministry.

The Epistles of Ignatius suggest that by the year 115 "the three orders" as they were afterward called—bishops, presbyters, and deacons—already existed in most of the churches. The presbyters occupied an intermediate position between the bishop and the deacons. They constituted "the council of the bishop." It was their duty to maintain order, exercise discipline, and superintend the affairs of the church. At the beginning of the 3rd century, TERTULLIAN attests, they had no spiritual authority of their own with regard to the SACRAMENTS. The right to baptize and celebrate the communion (*see* EUCHARIST) was delegated to them by the bishop.

With the rise of the diocesan bishops, the position of the presbyters became more important. The charge of the individual church was entrusted to them, and gradually they took the place of the local bishops of earlier days, so that in the 5th and 6th centuries an organization was reached that approximated in general outline to the system of the priesthood, as known in modern times.

PRESBYTERIAN, form of church government developed by Swiss and Rhineland Reformers during the 16th-century Protestant REFORMATION and used with variations by REFORMED and PRESBYTERIAN CHURCHES throughout the world. JOHN CALVIN believed that the system used by him and his associates in Geneva, Strassburg, Zürich, and other places was based upon the BIBLE and the experience of the church, but he did not claim that it was the only acceptable form. Some of his successors did make such a claim.

According to Calvin's theory of church government, the church is a community or body in which Christ is head and all members are equal under him. The ministry is given to the entire church and is distributed among many officers. All who hold office do so by election of the people. The church is to be governed and directed by assemblies of officeholders, pastors, and elders chosen to provide just representation for the church as a whole.

Since the Reformation the various Reformed and Presbyterian churches have made many adaptations of the basic structure but have not departed from it in essentials. In the Presbyterian churches of British-American background, there are usually four categories of church government: the congregational level (including the session, deacons, and trustees, and administering local church matters); the presbytery (composed of all ministers and a few elders in a given area, and administering the financial, legal, and religious affairs of the member congregations, as well as ordaining and installing minsters); the SYNOD (composed of representatives of several presbyteries, acting as a court of appeal in judicial matters); and the General Assembly (an annual meeting of commissioners, ministers, and elders, elected by all the presbyteries according to their membership, that is in charge of the general concerns of the church's faith, order, property, MISSIONS, and education and functions as the final court of appeal on cases that come up from the congregational sessions, presbyteries, and synods).

PRESBYTERIAN CHURCHES, one of the major representative groups of classical Protestant CHRISTIANITY that arose in the 16th-century REFORMATION. Generally speaking, the modern Presbyterian churches trace their origins to the Calvinist churches of Britain, the Continental counterparts of which came to be known by the more inclusive designation REFORMED. The term presbyterian denotes a collegiate type of church government by pastors and lay leaders called elders, or PRESBYTERS. Strictly speaking, all Presbyterian churches are a part of the Reformed, or Calvinist, tradition, although not all Reformed churches are presbyterian in their form of government.

PRESTER JOHN \'pres-tər-'jän\, *also called* Presbyter John, *or* John the Elder, legendary Christian ruler of the East, popularized in medieval chronicles and traditions as a hoped-for ally against the Muslims. Believed to be a NESTORIAN and a king-priest reigning "in the Far East beyond Persia and Armenia," Prester John was the center of a number of legends that harked back to the writings of "John the Elder" in the NEW TESTAMENT.

The legend arose during the period of the Crusades (late 11th–13th century), when European Christians hoped to regain the Holy Land (Palestine) from the Muslims, and was first recorded by Bishop Otto of Freising, Germany, in his *Chronicon* (1145). According to this, John, a wealthy and powerful "priest and king," reputedly a lineal descendant of the MAGI who had visited the Christ child, defeated the Muslim kings of Persia in battle, stormed their capital at Ecbatana, and intended to proceed to Jerusalem but was impeded by difficulties in crossing the Tigris River. The battle referred to may have been that fought at Qatwan, Persia, in 1141, when the Mongol khan Yeh-lü Ta-shih, the founder of the Karakitai empire in Central Asia, defeated the Seljuq SULTAN Sanjar. The title of the Karakitai rulers was Gur-khan, or Kor-khan, which may have been changed phonetically in Hebrew to *Yoḥanan* or, in Syriac, to *Yuḥanan*, thus producing the Latin Johannes, or John. In 1221, Jacques de Vitry, bishop of Acre in Palestine, and Cardinal Pelagius, a Western churchman accompanying crusaders at Damietta in Egypt, reported to Rome information about a Muslim defeat by a certain King David of India, the son or grandson of Prester John. This King David probably was Genghis Khan.

A 13th-century chronicler, Alberic de Trois-Fontaines, recorded that in 1165, a letter was sent by Prester John to several European rulers, especially Manuel I Comnenus, the Byzantine emperor, and Frederick I Barbarossa, the Holy Roman emperor. A literary fiction, the letter was in Latin and was translated into various languages. The realm of Prester John, "the three Indies," is described as a land of natural riches, marvels, peace, and justice administered by a court of archbishops, priors, and kings. Preferring the simple title PRESBYTER, John declared that he intended to come to Palestine with his armies to battle with the Muslims and regain the HOLY SEPULCHRE, the burial place of Jesus. The letter notes that John is the guardian of the shrine of St. Thomas, the apostle to India, at Mylapore, India.

In response to an embassy from Prester John, Pope Alexander III sent a reply in 1177 to John. The fate of this letter is unknown. In the 13th and 14th centuries various missionaries and lay travelers, such as Giovanni da Pian del Carpini, Giovanni da Montecorvino, and Marco Polo, all searching for the kingdom of Prester John, established direct contact between the West and the Mongols. After the mid-14th century, Ethiopia became the center of the search for the kingdom of Prester John, who was identified with the negus (emperor) of that African Christian nation.

PRIAM \'prī-əm, -ˌam\, in Greek mythology, last king of Troy. He succeeded his father, LAOMEDON, as king and extended his control over the Hellespont. He married first Arisbe (a daughter of Merops the seer) and then HECUBA, by whom he had many children, including his favorites, HECTOR and PARIS. Homer described Priam as an old man, powerless but kindly, not even blaming HELEN for all his personal losses resulting from the Trojan War. In the final year of the conflict, Priam saw 13 sons die: ACHILLES killed Polydorus, Lycaon, and Hector within one day. The death of Hector, which sig-

nified the end of Troy's hopes, also broke the spirit of the king. Priam's paternal love impelled him to brave the anger of Achilles and to ransom the corpse of Hector; Achilles, respecting the old man's feelings and foreseeing his own father's sorrows, returned the corpse. When Troy fell, NEOPTOLEMUS, the son of Achilles, butchered Priam on an altar.

PRIAPUS \prī-'ā-pəs\, in GREEK RELIGION, god of animal and vegetable fertility whose cult was originally located in the Hellespontine regions, centering especially on Lampsacus. He was represented in a caricature of the human form, grotesquely misshapen, with an enormous phallus. The ass was sacrificed in his honor, probably because the ass was symbolized lecherousness and was associated with the god's sexual potency. In Greek mythology his father was Dionysus; his mother was either a local NYMPH or APHRODITE.

In Hellenistic times Priapus' worship spread throughout the ancient world. Sophisticated urban society tended to regard him with ribald amusement, but in the country he was adopted as a god of gardens, his statue serving as a combined scarecrow and guardian deity. He was also the patron of seafarers and fishermen and of others in need of good luck; his presence was thought to avert the EVIL EYE.

PRIEST (from Old English *prēost*, ultimately from Greek *presbyteros*, "elder"), in the Christian churches that have an episcopal policy, an officer or minister who is intermediate between a bishop and a deacon.

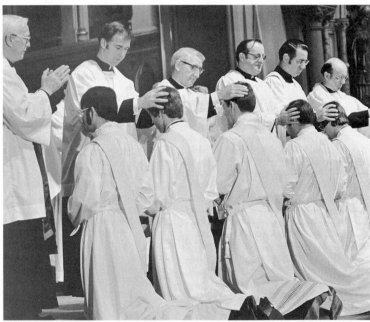

New Roman Catholic priests during their ordination services at Holy Cross Cathedral, Boston
Spencer Grant—Photo Researchers

A priesthood developed gradually in the early Christian church as first bishops and then elders, or "presbyters," began to exercise certain priestly functions, mainly in connection with celebration of the EUCHARIST. By the end of the 2nd century, the church's bishops were called priests (Latin:

sacerdos). Although the priestly office was vested primarily in the bishop, a PRESBYTER shared in his priestly functions and, in his absence, could exercise certain of them as his delegate. With the spread of CHRISTIANITY and the establishment of PARISH churches, the presbyter, or parish priest, adopted more of the bishop's functions and became the principal celebrant of the Eucharist. In this capacity, as well as by hearing CONFESSION and granting ABSOLUTION, the priest eventually assumed the role of the church's chief representative of God to the people.

During the 16th-century Protestant REFORMATION, the Reformers rejected the ROMAN CATHOLIC doctrine of the sacrifice of the MASS and the conception of the priesthood that went along with it. The priesthood of all Christians was emphasized. Consequently, ministers were substituted for priests in Protestant churches except for those of the ANGLICAN tradition.

The priesthood has been traditionally made up of men, so the Anglican churches' admission of women to the priesthood has been controversial. Women had been ordained priests in Hong Kong in 1944 and in 1971. American Episcopalians approved women as priests in 1976 after heated debate. After several other Anglican churches took a similar course, the Church of England ordained its first women candidates in 1994.

PRIESTHOOD, office of a holy person, a ritual expert learned in a special knowledge of the techniques of worship and accepted as a religious leader.

In many societies certain forms of social organization (the family, clan, etc.) have a sacral character; hence, a priestly quality often attaches to the head of the group by virtue of the sacerdotal functions that he or she is required to perform. On the other hand, most civilizations also exhibit a definite tendency toward cultic specialization, and it has been suggested that the term priest should be limited to the holder of such special office.

The full-fledged priest, as a religious functionary and cultic specialist, is distinct from the ordinary people, or "laity," who require priestly services and mediation. Specialization, in its turn, leads to social differentiation and to the establishment of a "clergy"—that is, of a priestly class, or CASTE. Obviously such specialization arises only in societies able to exempt some individuals from the common toil for subsistence and to provide for their needs in exchange for their ritual contribution to the general welfare. Where such institutionalized division of labor does not exist, as in many indigenous societies, suitably gifted or knowledgeable persons will perform priestly duties in addition to their ordinary activities.

Generally speaking, the term priest denotes religious functionaries whose activity is concerned with the right performance of the ritual acts required by the divine powers and supernatural beings recognized by the group. Because sacrifice is one of the most prominent features of the human ritual relation with gods and spirits, it has come to be associated with priesthood as one of its chief functions; the BRAHMINS, or priestly caste of HINDUISM, for example, derive from those who performed the ritual sacrifice in Vedic times. Medieval ROMAN CATHOLICISM owed much of its doctrine of the priesthood to the connection of the latter with the EUCHARIST conceived as a propitiatory sacrifice.

The ancient Inca, Maya, and Aztec (*see* PRE-COLUMBIAN MESO-AMERICAN RELIGIONS) distinguished between priests responsible for the cult of the great national gods and such ritual experts as those engaged in DIVINATION or curing. Similarly, many African societies differentiated between priests responsible for the worship of the tribal ancestors, on the one hand, and SHAMANS, on the other.

Priesthood, in its fully developed form, generally implies large societies with centralized authority, a fairly elaborate culture, and the existence of an organized cult with fixed rituals and well-formulated doctrines. However, not every highly developed religion of necessity possesses a priesthood. ISLAM is a religion without priests, religious authority being defined in other than sacerdotal terms. In JUDAISM, the decline of the priesthood in ancient times resulted in the assumption of many priestly functions by the RABBI, or teacher. The former hereditary priesthood of the KOHEN is still recognized symbolically in ORTHODOX JUDAISM.

Many indigenous societies exhibit patterns of "priesthood of all believers"—*i.e.,* of all members of the group. Thus the Pueblo Indians in the southwestern United States were organized in religious fraternities, and their highly formalized and elaborate rituals were performed by these groups and not by priestly functionaries. The principle of the priesthood of all believers was also a cardinal doctrine of the churches of the 16th-century REFORMATION, both LUTHERAN and REFORMED, and of the Protestant Free churches that arose from the Reformation churches. In its PROTESTANT form the doctrine asserts that all men have access to God through JESUS CHRIST, the high priest, and thus do not need a priestly mediator.

PRIESTLY CODE, in JUDAISM, the Holiness Code of Leviticus 17–26 and EXODUS 26–40, the rest of Leviticus and most of Numbers. The Priestly Code was produced by the Temple priests and completed when the Temple, destroyed in 586 BCE, was rebuilt c. 450 BCE. Israel was admonished to form "a kingdom of priests and a holy people," thus: "You shall be holy to me, for I the Lord am holy and have separated you from the peoples that you should be mine" (Leviticus 20:26). To the priests, what mattered in 586 was the destruction of the Temple, and what made a difference "three generations later" was the restoration of ZION and the rebuilding of the Temple. To them the cult was the key, the Temple the nexus between heaven and earth. The story of creation (GENESIS 1:1–2:3) stressed the perfection of the order of nature, culminating in the SABBATH repose with all things at rest and in place. The Priestly Code builds upon the theme of restoration to perfection through the right ordering of nature as celebrated in the Temple and its sacrificial service. That is why the Priestly Code centers upon the Temple and its procedures, the governance of the PRIESTHOOD and its emoluments, the genealogical purity of Israel, culminating in that of the priesthood, and the perfection of world order embodied in the cultic center and the rhythm of holy time set there.

PRIMATE \'prī-mət, -ˌmāt\, in CHRISTIANITY, bishop who has precedence in a province, group of provinces, or a nation.

PROCESSION, in CHRISTIANITY, organized body of people advancing in formal or ceremonial manner as an element of Christian ritual or as a less official expression of popular piety. Public processions seem to have come into vogue soon after the recognition of Christianity as the religion of the Roman Empire by CONSTANTINE in the 4th century.

Of the vast number of processions that developed during the Middle Ages, some of the more important still have a place in the ritual of the ROMAN CATHOLIC church. They include ordinary processions, held on certain yearly festivals throughout the universal church and on other days according to the customs of the local churches, and extraordinary processions, held for special occasions (e.g., to pray for divine assistance in time of storm, famine, plague, war, and other disasters). Other processions characteristic of certain localities, though not regulated so strictly by the church and considered nonliturgical, play an important part in the religious life of the people; in the United States, for example, May processions are sometimes conducted in honor of the Virgin MARY.

The Major Rogation procession (April 25), a penitential observance with the object of obtaining God's blessing on crops that have been planted, seems to have been adopted from one of the festivals in the pre-Christian calendar of Rome. The Minor Rogations, observed on the three days before the Feast of the ASCENSION, date from the 5th century. The procession on CANDLEMAS (February 2), which includes the blessing and carrying of candles, might well be another instance of the church's subrogating a procession from a prior tradition. Another procession with a long history is that celebrated on PALM SUNDAY, commemorating the triumphant entrance of Christ into Jerusalem.

Processions have been a part of the Roman Catholic eucharistic liturgy (MASS) at the entrance rite and at the offertory rite, when the bread and wine to be used in the liturgy are brought up to the altar. Although these processions were discontinued at the end of the Middle Ages, strong efforts have been made by liturgists in the 20th century to reintroduce them to promote participation by the people.

In the Protestant REFORMATION, processions associated with the eucharistic Host and those honoring the Virgin Mary and the saints were abolished. The Anglican and Lutheran traditions still retain certain processions.

In the EASTERN ORTHODOX church, two noteworthy processions connected with the celebration of the EUCHARIST are the "little entrance" before the reading of the Gospel and the "great entrance" before the eucharistic prayer, when the offerings of bread and wine are carried in a more elaborate procession. The separation of the people from the SANCTUARY by a solid wall known as the ICONOSTASIS has tended to concentrate their devotion on these processions.

PROCRUSTES \prō-'krəs-tēz\, *also called* Polypemon \,pä-li-'pē-män\, Damastes \də-'mas-tēz\, *or* Procoptas \prō-'käp-təs\, in Greek mythology, robber dwelling somewhere in Attica—in some versions, in the neighborhood of Eleusis. His father was said to be POSEIDON. Procrustes had an iron bed (or, according to some accounts, two beds) on which he compelled his victims to lie. If a victim was shorter than the bed, he stretched him by hammering or racking the body to fit. If the victim was longer than the bed, he cut off the legs to make the body fit the bed's length. In either event the victim died. Ultimately Procrustes was slain by his own method at the hands of the hero THESEUS, who as a young man went about slaying robbers and monsters that pervaded the countryside.

The "bed of Procrustes," or "Procrustean bed," has become proverbial for arbitrarily forcing someone or something to fit into an unnatural scheme or pattern.

PROETUS \prō-'ē-təs\, in Greek mythology, king of Argos, grandson of DANAUS. He quarreled with his brother Acrisius and divided the kingdom with him, Proetus taking Tiryns, which he fortified. Proetus' daughters were driven mad either because they insulted the goddess HERA or because they would not accept the new rites of DIONYSUS. They imagined

themselves cows until the seer MELAMPUS cured them on condition that he be given a third of the kingdom and his brother, Bias, another third.

PROKOPOVICH, FEOFAN \prə-kə-'pȯ-vʸich\ (b. June 18, 1681, Kiev, Ukraine, Russian Empire—d. Sept. 19, 1736, St. Petersburg), Russian Orthodox theologian and archbishop of Pskov, who by his administration, oratory, and writings directed the reformation of the Russian orthodox church (*see* EASTERN ORTHODOXY) in accordance with a LUTHERAN model and effected a political integration of CHURCH AND STATE that was to last two centuries.

After an Orthodox education, Prokopovich became a ROMAN CATHOLIC and in 1698 entered the Greek College of San Anastasio in Rome. He returned to Kiev in 1701, reverted to his Orthodox faith, and later became ABBOT of the Kiev monastery and rector of its celebrated ecclesiastical academy, where he taught theology, literature, and rhetoric. After publicizing laudatory statements on the cultural-political reform of Peter the Great, he was called to the court at St. Petersburg in 1716 and was made a counselor to the tsar on church and educational affairs. As principal theorist in the restructuring of the Russian church as a political arm of the state, Prokopovich cooperated in replacing the patriarchate with a Holy Synod, or supreme ecclesiastical council, by drawing up in 1720 the *Spiritual Regulations*, a new constitution for Orthodoxy. Appointed synodal first vice president, he was responsible for the legislative reform of the entire Russian church, subordinating it to the secular and spiritual authority of Tsar Peter, and for effecting a church-state relationship, sometimes termed a Protestantized CAESAROPAPISM, that was to continue until the Russian Revolution of 1917. Such a theory was derived by combining concepts from the 17th-century English political philosopher Thomas Hobbes with Byzantine theocratic thought.

As a theologian, Prokopovich promoted the autonomy of doctrinal theology from moral and ascetic teaching. Basing his theology mainly on liberal Protestant sources, he formed a body of doctrine markedly Lutheran in orientation, particularly in its insistence on sacred SCRIPTURE as the sole source of Christian revelation and in its account of GRACE, FREE WILL, and JUSTIFICATION. His design of the theological curriculum for St. Petersburg's ecclesiastical academy was patterned after the Lutheran faculty of Halle, Ger., and became the center for the propagation of his Orthodox reform.

Prokopovich's teachings prevailed until about 1836, when a movement toward more traditional Orthodox beliefs set in. (Indeed, during the reign of Peter's second successor, the empress Anna Ivanovna [1730–40], Prokopovich himself assumed a more conservative theological outlook.)

PROMETHEUS \prə-'mē-thē-əs, -,thyüs\, in GREEK RELIGION, one of the TITANS and a trickster. His intellectual side was emphasized by the apparent meaning of his name, Forethinker. In common belief he developed into a master craftsman, and in this connection he was associated with fire and the creation of humanity.

The Greek poet Hesiod related two principal legends concerning Prometheus. The first is that ZEUS, who had been tricked by Prometheus into accepting the bones and fat of a sacrifice instead of the meat, hid fire from humans. Prometheus, however, stole it and returned it to Earth once again. As the price of fire, and as punishment for mankind in general, Zeus created the woman PANDORA and sent her down to Epimetheus (Hindsight), who, though warned by Prometheus, married her. Pandora took the great lid off the jar she carried, and evils, hard work, and disease flew out to wander among mankind. Hope alone remained within.

Hesiod relates in his other tale that, to avenge himself on Prometheus, Zeus had him chained and sent an eagle to eat his liver, which constantly replenished itself; in *Prometheus Bound* Aeschylus made Prometheus not only the bringer of fire and civilization to humans but also their preserver, bestowing all the arts and sciences in addition to the means of survival.

An eagle pecks at the liver of the bound Prometheus; Etruscan painted vase in the Vatican Museums and Galleries, Rome
The Bridgeman Art Library

PROPHECY, divinely inspired revelation or interpretation. Although prophecy is perhaps most commonly associated with JUDAISM and CHRISTIANITY, it is found throughout the religions of the world, both ancient and modern.

In its narrower sense, the term prophet (Greek: *prophētēs*, "interpreter," "expounder [of divine will]") refers to an inspired person who believes that he has been sent by his god with a message to tell. In a broader sense, the word can refer to anybody who utters the will of a deity, often ascertained through visions, dreams, or the casting of lots; the will of the deity also may be spoken in a liturgical setting. The prophet, thus, is often associated with the PRIEST, the SHAMAN, the diviner (foreteller), and the mystic.

The nature of prophecy is twofold: either inspired (by visions or revelatory auditions) or acquired (by learning certain techniques). In many cases both aspects are present. The goal of learning certain prophetic techniques is to reach an ecstatic state in which revelations can be received. That state might be reached through the use of music, dancing, drums, violent bodily movement, and self-laceration. The ecstatic prophet is regarded as being filled with the divine spirit, and in this state the deity speaks through him. Ecstatic oracles, therefore, are generally delivered by the prophet in the first-person singular pronoun and are spoken in a short, rhythmic style.

Types of prophecy can be classified on the basis of inspiration, behavior, and office. Divinatory prophets include seers, oracles, soothsayers, and mantics, all of whom predict the future or tell the divine will in oracular statements by means of instruments, dreams, telepathy, clairvoyance, or visions received in the state of ECSTASY. Predictions and foretellings, however, may also be the result of inspiration or common sense by the intelligent observation of situations and events, albeit interpreted from a religious point of view.

The diviner, sometimes compared with the prophet, performs the priestly art of foretelling (*see* DIVINATION). His art is to augur the future on the basis of hidden knowledge discerned almost anywhere, as in the constellations (ASTROLO-GY), the flight of birds (auspices), the entrails of sacrificial animals (haruspicy), hands (chiromancy), casting lots (cleromancy), the flames of burning sacrifices (pyromancy), and other such areas of special knowledge.

The cult prophet, or priest-prophet, is of broad importance to the religious community. Under the mandate of the cult, the priest-prophet (who may be an ordinary priest) is part of the priestly staff of a SANCTUARY, and his duty is to pronounce the divine oracular word at the appropriate point in a liturgy. As such, he is an "institutional" prophet. The difference between a cult prophet and a prophet in the classical sense is that the latter has always experienced a divine call, whereas the cult prophet, pronouncing the word of the deity under cultic mandate, repeats his messages at a special moment in the ritual.

Missionary (or apostolic) prophets are those who maintain that the religious truth revealed to them is unique to themselves alone. Such prophets—*e.g.*, ZOROASTER, JESUS, and MUHAMMAD—acquire a following of disciples who accept that their teachings reveal the true religion. The result of this kind of prophetic action may lead to a new religion. The founders of many modern religious sects also should be included in this type.

Another type of prophet is of the reformative or revolutionary kind (looking to the past and the future), closely related to the restorative or purificatory type (looking to the past as the ideal). The best examples are the OLD TESTAMENT classical prophets—*e.g.*, AMOS and JEREMIAH—who were working to reform the religion of YAHWEH. In ISLAM Muhammad is included in this category. The social sympathy found among such prophets is rooted in their religious conscience. What may have been preached as religious reform, therefore, often took on the shape of social reform. This kind of prophecy is also found in India and Africa, where prophets in modern times have arisen to restore or purify the old tribal religious forms, as well as the customs and laws that had their sources in the older precolonial religious life. Many of these movements became revolutionary not only by force of logic but also by force of social and political pressure.

Though scholars may distinguish several categories of prophecy, no sharp line of demarcation differentiates the various types. Any given prophet may be both predictive and missionary, ecstatic and reformative.

PROPHET, THE, byname of Tenskwatawa \ten-'skwä-tə-ˌwä\ (b. *c.* March 1768, Old Chillicothe, Ohio [U.S.]—d. 1834, Argentine, Kan.), North American Shawnee Indian religious revivalist, who worked with his brother Tecumseh for an Indian confederacy to resist U.S. encroachment on the American Northwest.

The Prophet declared in 1805 that he had a message from the "Master of Life," and in 1806 he followed this declaration with an accurate prediction of a solar eclipse. He advocated a return to distinctively Indian ways of life, rejecting the use of alcohol and of textile clothing, the concept of individual ownership of property, and racial intermarriage. Witch-burning was also a feature of his program. In November 1811, while Tecumseh was away, he allowed the Shawnees to be drawn into military action with General William Henry Harrison; the defeat on the Tippecanoe River (November 7) discredited him and destroyed the Indian confederacy.

PROPHET DANCE, North American Plateau Indian ritual of the early 19th century, precursor of the famous GHOST DANCE movement of the 1870s and 1890s. The participants danced in order to hasten the return of the dead and the return of the world to its state before European contact.

PROPHET'S MOSQUE, courtyard of the Prophet MUHAMMAD in MEDINA, Arabian Peninsula, which was the model for later Islamic architecture. The home of Muhammad and his family was a simple structure, made of raw brick, that opened on an enclosed courtyard where people gathered to hear him. In 628 a *minbar,* or pulpit, was added so that the Prophet was raised above the crowd; besides leading prayer, Muhammad declared his new law and decided disputes from the *minbar.* In 634 Muhammad decreed that prayer be directed toward MECCA; against the wall facing Mecca, the QIBLA wall, he built a roofed shelter supported by pillars made of palm trunks. Against the opposite wall of the courtyard stood a roofed gallery to shelter his companions, the antecedent of the roofed oratories in later mosques. In 706 CALIPH al-Walīd I destroyed the original brick buildings and created a new mosque on the site. The new mosque, containing the tomb of Muhammad, is one of the three holiest places of ISLAM.

PROTESILAUS \prō-ˌte-sə-ˈlā-əs\, Greek mythological hero in the Trojan War, leader of the force from Phylace and other Thessalian cities west of the Pegasaean Gulf. Though aware that an oracle had foretold death for the first of the invading Greeks to land at Troy, he was the first ashore and the first to fall. His bride, Laodameia, was so grief-stricken that the gods granted her request that Protesilaus be allowed to return from the dead for three hours. At the expiration of the time she accompanied him to the Underworld by taking her own life.

PROTESTANT ETHIC, in sociological theory, the high value attached to hard work, thrift, and efficiency in one's worldly calling, which, especially in the Calvinist view, were deemed signs of an individual's election, or eternal salvation.

The German sociologist MAX WEBER in *The Protestant Ethic and the Spirit of Capitalism* (1904–05) held that the Protestant ethic was an important factor in the economic success of Protestant groups in the early stages of European capitalism, owing to the mandate that all sinners should work for the glorification of God. Calvinism's antipathy to the worship of the flesh, its emphasis on the religious duty to make fruitful use of the God-given resources at each individual's disposal, and its orderliness and systemization of ways of life were also regarded by Weber as economically significant aspects of the ethic.

Weber's thesis has been subject to criticism by various writers. The English historian R.H. Tawney expanded Weber's thesis in his *Religion and the Rise of Capitalism* (1926) by arguing that political and social pressures and the spirit of individualism with its ethic of self-help and frugality were more significant factors in the development of capitalism than Calvinist theology.

PROTESTANTISM, one of the three major branches of CHRISTIANITY, originating in the 16th-century REFORMATION, characterized by its doctrines of JUSTIFICATION by GRACE through faith, the priesthood of all believers, and the authority of the SCRIPTURES.

The historical origin of the word Protestant is in the second imperial Diet of Speyer (1529), which reversed by a majority vote the decision of the first Diet of Speyer (1526) to allow each prince of the Holy Roman Empire to determine the religion of his territory. The minority, consisting of 6 princes and 14 cities, issued a formal *Protestation,* the primary purpose of which was to protest that "in matters which concern God's honour and salvation and the eternal life of our souls, everyone must stand and give account before God for himself." A secondary purpose was to protest against the ban on the expansion of evangelical religion.

The supporters of the Reformation doctrines gradually came to be called Protestants both by their opponents and by themselves, since it was a convenient name to cover the many varieties of Reformed Christianity. No communion incorporated the word Protestant into its title, however, until this was done by the Protestant Episcopal Church of America. The 19th-century OXFORD MOVEMENT persuaded an increasingly large number of clergy and laity of the Church of England (*see* ANGLICAN COMMUNION) to repudiate the word Protestant as a description of their church. The term is officially used on both sides of the Atlantic Ocean by a number of societies propagating the view that the principles of the Reformation are being neglected.

The basic doctrines of Protestantism at the Reformation, in addition to those of the traditional creeds, were the supremacy of Holy Scripture in matters of faith and order, the justification by grace alone through faith alone, and the priesthood of all believers. There has been variation in sacramental doctrine among Protestants, but the limitation of the number to the two "sacraments of the Gospel," BAPTISM and Holy Communion (*see* EUCHARIST), has been almost universal. In the 18th century the Enlightenment produced liberal Protestantism, which cast doubt on some doctrines in the creeds and stressed reason, RELIGIOUS EXPERIENCE, and the principle of private judgment in a way that would have been repugnant to the original Reformers. But, through the efforts of such thinkers as SØREN KIERKEGAARD and KARL BARTH, Protestant theology and devotion have regained a deeper appreciation of the values of pre-Reformation Christianity. Though the doctrine of the verbal inerrancy of Scripture is maintained by several Protestant groups, the supremacy of the biblical revelation usually has been reasserted without it.

PROTEUS \ˈprō-tē-əs, -ˌtyüs, -ˌtüs\, in Greek mythology, prophetic old man of the sea and shepherd of the sea's flocks (*e.g.,* seals). He was subject to the sea god POSEIDON, and his dwelling place was either the island of Pharos, near the mouth of the Nile River, or the island of Carpathus, between Crete and Rhodes. He knew all things—past, present, and future—but disliked telling what he knew. Those who wished to consult him had first to surprise and bind him during his noonday slumber. Even when caught he would try to escape by assuming all sorts of shapes. But, if his captor held him fast, the god at last returned to his proper shape, gave the wished-for answer, and plunged into the sea.

PSEUDEPIGRAPHA \,sü-di-'pi-grə-fə\, in biblical literature, a work affecting biblical style and usually spuriously attributing authorship to some biblical character. Pseudepigrapha are not included in any canon. *See* APOCRYPHA.

PSILOCIN AND PSILOCYBIN \'sī-lə-sən, 'si- . . . ,sī-lə-'sī-bən, ,si-\, hallucinogenic principles contained in certain mushrooms (notably two Mexican species, *Psilocybe mexicana* and *Stropharia cubensis*). Hallucinogenic mushrooms used in religious ceremonies by the Native Americans of Mexico were considered sacred and were called "god's flesh" by the Aztecs. In the 1950s the active principles psilocin and psilocybin were isolated from the Mexican mushrooms.

PSYCHE \'sī-kē\ (Greek: "Soul"), in classical mythology, princess of outstanding beauty who aroused VENUS' jealousy and CUPID'S love. The fullest version of the tale is that told by the Latin author Apuleius in his *Metamorphoses* (*The Golden Ass*).

According to Apuleius, the jealous Venus commanded her son Cupid to inspire Psyche with love for the most despicable of men. Instead, Cupid placed Psyche in a remote palace where he could visit her secretly and, by his warning, only in total darkness. One night Psyche lit a lamp and found that the figure at her side was the god of love himself. When a drop of oil from the lamp awakened him, he reproached Psyche and fled. Wandering the earth in search of him, Psyche fell into the hands of Venus, who imposed upon her difficult tasks. Finally, touched by Psyche's repentance, Cupid rescued her, and, at his request, JUPITER made her immortal and gave her in marriage to Cupid.

The sources of the tale are a number of folk motifs; the handling by Apuleius, however, conveys an ALLEGORY of the progress of the Soul guided by Love, which adhered to Psyche in Renaissance literature and art. In Greek FOLKLORE the soul was pictured as a butterfly, which is another meaning of the word *psychē*.

Psyche, a Greek sculpture from the classical period; in the Louvre, Paris
Alinari—Art Resource

PTAH \'ptä\, in EGYPTIAN RELIGION, creator-god and maker of things, a patron of craftsmen, especially sculptors; his high priest was called "chief controller of craftsmen." The Greeks identified Ptah with HEPHAESTUS, the divine blacksmith. Ptah was originally the local deity of Memphis, capital of Egypt from the 1st dynasty onward; the political importance of Memphis caused Ptah's cult to expand over the whole of Egypt. With his companion SEKHMET and the youthful god NEFERTEM, he was one of the Memphite Triad of deities. He was represented as a man in MUMMY form, wearing a skullcap and a short, straight false beard. As a mortuary god, Ptah was often fused with Seker (or Soker) and OSIRIS to form Ptah-Seker-Osiris.

PTAHHOTEP \,ptä-'hō-tep\ (fl. 2400 BCE), vizier of ancient Egypt who attained high repute in wisdom literature. His treatise "The Maxims of Ptahhotep," probably the earliest extant large piece of Egyptian wisdom literature, was written primarily for young men of influential families who would assume higher civil offices. Ptahhotep's proverbial sayings upheld obedience to a father and a superior as the highest virtue, but they also emphasized humility, faithfulness in performing one's own duties, and the ability to keep silence when necessary.

P'U \'pü\, *Pinyin* pu (Chinese: "simple," "in primordial condition"), in TAOISM, metaphorical expression signifying the "uncarved block"—*i.e.,* the primordial condition of the mind before it has been affected by experiences. In the state of *p'u* there are no distinctions between right and wrong, black and white, beautiful and ugly. Because truth becomes relative, ideas have no value and all contradictions are resolved. Taoists desire to return to this state by abandoning conventional knowledge and by suppressing desires that bind them to the world. Individuals who achieve this state of mental unity thereby align their existence with the unity of the Absolute TAO.

PUDGALAVĀDIN \,pùd-gə-lə-'vä-din\, *also called* Vātsīputrīya \,vät-sē-'pù-trē-yə\, ancient Buddhist school in India that affirmed the existence of an enduring person (*pudgala*) distinct from both the conditioned (*saṃskṛta*) and the unconditioned (*asaṃskṛta*); the sole *asaṃskṛta* for them was NIRVANA. If consciousness exists, there must be a subject of consciousness, the *pudgala*; it is this alone that transmigrates from life to life.

The Sammatīya school, a derivation of the Pudgalavādin, had a wide diffusion, extending from India to Bengal and Champa, located in what now is central Vietnam; the Chinese pilgrim HSÜAN-TSANG described it in the 7th century as one of the four main Buddhist sects of that time. The Sammatīya believed that, although humans do not exist independently from the five SKANDHAS (components) that make up their personalities, still they are greater than the mere sums of their parts. The Sammatīya were severely criticized by other Buddhists, who considered the theory close to the rejected theory of ĀTMAN—*i.e.,* the supreme universal self.

PŪJĀ \'pü-jä\ (Sanskrit: "worship"), in HINDUISM, ceremonial worship, ranging from brief daily rites in the home to elaborate temple ritual. The components of a *pūjā* vary greatly according to the sect, community, location, time of day, needs of the worshiper, and religious text followed. Basically, in a *pūjā*, a deity, manifested in his or her image, is accorded the honor given to a royal guest. The attentions (*upacāras*) paid to the deity begin in the morning and continue all day, including ritual bathing and dressing, serving the usual three meals, and putting the deity to bed at night.

A *pūjā* may also include a circumambulation (PRADAKṢI-NA) of the image or shrine and, in an elaborate ritual, a sacrifice (*bali*) and oblation to the sacred fire (*homa*). Special ceremonies according to the festival calendar may also be observed, such as swinging the deity or playing games according to the season.

One important type of *pūjā* in Indian temple and private worship is *āratī* (Sanskrit *ārātrika*), the waving of lighted lamps before an image of a deity or a person to be honored. In performing the rite, the worshiper circles the lamp three or more times in a clockwise direction while chanting a prayer or singing a hymn. In Indian households, *āratī* is a commonly observed ritual element accorded specially honored guests. It is also a part of many domestic ceremonies.

Some *pūjā*s may be performed by the worshiper alone, while others may require the services of a ritually pure person such as a PRIEST. A *pūjā* may be performed for a specific announced purpose or simply as an act of devotion.

PUÑÑA \\'pùn-yə\\ (Pāli: "merit"), primary attribute sought by Buddhists in order to build up better KARMA (the cumulative consequences of deeds) and thus to achieve a more favorable future rebirth. The concept is particularly stressed in the THERAVĀDA tradition of Southeast Asia.

Puñña can be acquired through DANA ("giving," such as the offering of food and robes to monks or donation to a temple or monastery); *sila* (the keeping of the moral precepts); and *bhavana* (the practice of meditation). Merit can also be transferred from one being to another. This is a central feature of the MAHĀYĀNA schools, in which the ideal Buddhist is the BODHISATTVA who dedicates himself to the service of others and transfers merit from his own inexhaustible store to benefit others.

PURĀṆA \\pù-'rä-nə\\ (Sanskrit: "Ancient Lore"), any of a number of popular encyclopedic collections of Hindu religious narrative, legend, and genealogy, varying greatly as to date and origin.

Traditionally a *Purāṇa* treats five subjects: primary creation of the universe, secondary creation after periodical annihilation, genealogy of gods and saints, grand epochs, and history of the royal dynasties. *Purāṇa*s are connected in subject with the MAHĀBHĀRATA and have some relationship to the lawbooks (DHARMA ŚĀSTRAS). Other materials of religious concern were accumulated in Purāṇic texts during the period *c.* 400 CE to *c.* 1000, concerning customs, ceremonies, sacrifices, festivals, CASTE duties, donations, construction of temples and images, and places of PILGRIMAGE. *Purāṇa*s are written almost entirely in narrative couplets.

The 18 principal surviving *Purāṇa*s are often grouped loosely according to whether they exalt VISHNU, SHIVA, or BRAHMĀ, but they all deal with similar material. The main *Purāṇa*s are usually regarded as (1) the *Viṣṇu, Nāradīya, Bhāgavata, Garuḍa, Padma,* and *Vārāha,* (2) the *Matsya, Kūrma, Liṅga, Śiva, Skanda,* and *Agni* (or *Vāyu*) and (3) the *Brāhmāṇḍa, Brahmavaivarta, Mārkaṇḍeya, Bhaviṣya, Vāmana,* and *Brahma Purāṇa*s. By far the most popular is the BHĀGAVATA PURĀṆA, which in its treatment of the early life of KRISHNA has had profound influence on the RELIGIOUS BELIEFS of India. Narratives that glorify the goddess and her exploits are found primarily in the *Devī-bhāgavata-purāṇa* and in the *Devī-māhātmya,* a section of the *Mārkaṇḍeya Purāṇa.* There are also 18 "lesser," or *Upapurāṇa*s, treating similar material, and a large number of *sthala purāṇa*s, or *māhātmya*s, glorifying temples or sacred places, which are recited in the services of the temples.

PURDAH \\'pər-də\\, *also spelled* pardah, *Hindi* pardā (Persian: "screen," or "veil"), practice that was inaugurated by Muslims and later adopted by various Hindus, especially in India, which involves the seclusion of women from public observation by means of concealing clothing (including the veil) and by the use of high-walled enclosures, screens, and curtains within the home.

The practice of purdah is said to have originated in the Persian culture and to have been acquired by the Muslims during the Arab conquest of what is now Iraq in the 7th century CE. Muslim domination of northern India influenced the practice of HINDUISM, and purdah became usual among the Hindu upper classes of northern India. Purdah has largely disappeared in Hindu practice, though the seclusion and veiling of women is practiced to a greater or lesser degree in many ISLAMIC countries. *See also* HIJĀB.

PURE LAND BUDDHISM, *Chinese* (Wade-Giles romanization) Ch'ing-t'u \\'chiṇ-'tü \\, *or* (Pinyin) Qingtu, *Japanese* Jōdo \\'jō-,dò \\, devotional cult of the Buddha AMITĀBHA (Sanskrit: "Buddha of Infinite Light"), known in China as O-mi-t'o-fo and in Japan as Amida Butsu. It is one of the most popular forms of MAHĀYĀNA BUDDHISM in eastern Asia. Pure Land schools believe that rebirth in Amitābha's Western Paradise, Sukhāvatī (known as the Pure Land, or Pure Realm), is assured for all those who invoke Amitābha's name with sincere devotion (*nembutsu,* referring to the Japanese formula of invocation, *namu Amida Butsu*).

The Pure Land belief is based on three Sanskrit SCRIPTURES, the *Amitāyur-dhyāna Sūtra* ("Discourse Concerning Meditation on Amitāyus") and the "larger" and "smaller" Pure Land *sūtra*s, the *Sukhāvatī-vyūha Sūtra*s ("Description of the Western Paradise Sutras"). These texts relate the story of the monk Dharmākara, the future Amitāyus, or Amitābha, who made a series of vows that were meant to be fulfilled when he became a buddha. The most important of these, the 18th, promised rebirth in the Pure Land to all the faithful who called upon his name, who would then remain in that beautiful land until they were ready for final Enlightenment.

According to the larger Pure Land *sūtra,* in addition to calling upon Amitābha, one needs to accumulate merit and concentrate on Enlightenment. In the later, smaller Pure Land *sūtra,* however, the Blessed Land is not a reward for good works but is accessible to anyone who invokes Amitābha at the hour of death.

In China the beginnings of the Pure Land cult can be traced back to the 4th century, when the scholar Hui-yüan formed a society of monks and laymen who meditated on the name of Amitābha. T'an-luan and his successors Tao-ch'o and Shan-tao systematized and spread the doctrine in the 6th and 7th centuries and are recognized as the first patriarchs of the Pure Land school. In devotional art, new emphasis was given to the representation of Amitābha, together with AVALOKITEŚVARA and Mahāsthāmaprāpta, his attendant BODHISATTVAS. In China the Pure Land tradition prospered throughout the premodern period, and many of its beliefs and practices were accepted by members of other Buddhist sects.

The Pure Land teaching was transmitted from China to Japan by monks of the Tendai (T'ien-t'ai) school, and in the 12th–13th century the sect took on a separate and distinctively Japanese identity, mainly through the efforts of HŌNEN, who founded the Jōdo-shū (Pure Land sect). Hōnen believed that most men were, like himself, incapable of obtaining buddhahood on this earth through their own efforts (such as learning, good deeds, or meditation) but were dependent on Amida's help. Hōnen stressed the recitation of *nembutsu* as the one act necessary to gain admittance to the Pure Land.

With the passage of time the Jōdo sect split up into five branches, of which two are still in existence—the Chinzei, the larger of the two, which is often referred to simply as Jōdo, and the Seizan. The Ji, or Time, sect was another variant; its name derived from the sect's rule of reciting the hymns of Zendo (Shan-tao) six times a day.

Hōnen's disciple SHINRAN is regarded as the founder of the Jōdo Shinshū, or True Pure Land sect, which has become the largest Pure Land group. According to Shinran, faith alone is sufficient to ensure rebirth into Amida's paradise. The school is distinguished by the fact that it discourages the worship of other Buddhist deities and also by the fact that it was one of the first of many Japanese schools explicitly to sanction the practice of clerical marriage.

PURGATORY, in ROMAN CATHOLIC doctrine, state of existence or condition of the soul of a person who has died in a state of GRACE but who has not been purged, or purified, from all possible stain of unforgiven venial SINS (pardonable less-serious offenses against God), forgiven mortal sins (serious offenses against God that destroy sanctifying grace), imperfections, or evil habits. Souls in such conditions must thus be purified before entering heaven.

The doctrine of purgatory is derived from 2nd–1st-century BCE Jewish concepts that persons will be judged by God according to their deeds and that the faithful should pray that God show mercy to souls. Primarily based on 2 Maccabees 12:45, Roman Catholic teaching also derives from indirect references in the NEW TESTAMENT.

During the period of the early church, purgatory was in many circles considered a fundamental doctrine, but it was not until the councils of Lyon and Florence in the Middle Ages and the COUNCIL OF TRENT in the REFORMATION period that the teaching was authoritatively defined. The matter of the place, duration, and nature of the punishments of purgatory has not been definitively answered. Roman Catholic doctrine also holds that the souls who are in purgatory may be aided by the faithful on earth by way of prayers, almsgiving, INDULGENCES, fasting, sacrifices, and other works of piety.

The existence of purgatory has been denied by PROTESTANT churches and most EASTERN ORTHODOX churches, as well as by the independent churches of Eastern CHRISTIANITY (*e.g.*, Syrians, NESTORIANS, and MONOPHYSITES), although most Eastern Christians believe that the dead can be helped by the prayers and good deeds of the living faithful.

PURI \'pùr-ē\: *see* JAGANNĀTHA.

PURIFICATION, use of ritual techniques to protect against what are held to be unclean, sinful, or otherwise undesirable situations. In a society with a strong sense of solidarity, if one individual violates a prohibition, the whole community may feel itself menaced until the violator is purified.

Childbirth, puberty, marriage, warfare or bloodshed, and death are commonly marked by purifying rites. Contaminating factors may include foods (as the flesh of totem animals), persons (as menstruating women or persons of inferior CASTE), places, and so on. Rituals of purification may entail the use of water (as in BAPTISM), mutilation (as in CIRCUMCISION), fasting, prayer, and CONFESSION.

Illustration from the Megillat Esther, Italian, late 15th–early 16th century, showing the gallows upon which Haman and his sons were hanged
Jewish Museum, New York City—Art Resource

PURIM \'pùr-im, pù-'rēm\, *English* Feast of Lots, Jewish festival commemorating the survival of the Jews who, in the 5th century BCE, were marked for death by their Persian rulers.

The story is related in the OLD TESTAMENT Book of Esther. Haman, chief minister of King Ahasuerus, arranged for the Jews to be slaughtered because of a personal grudge he had against Mordecai, a Jew. Haman, by casting lots, selected the 13th day of the month of Adar as the date of execution. Esther, the Jewish queen of Ahasuerus and adopted daughter of Mordecai, convinced the king to have Haman hanged and to elevate Mordecai to chief minister. A royal edict allowed Jews throughout the empire to attack their enemies on Adar 13, and after their victory they declared the following day a holiday named Purim (alluding to the lots Haman had cast).

The ritual observance of Purim begins with a day of fasting, Ta'anit Esther (Fast of Esther) on Adar 13, the day preceding the actual holiday. The SYNAGOGUE service includes a reading of the Book of Esther. Jews are enjoined to exchange gifts and make donations to the poor. Many nonreligious customs have come to be associated with the festival, including Purim plays, which became popular during the 17th century, and the baking of three-cornered pastries called *hamantaschen* ("Haman's pockets").

PURITANISM, religious reform movement in the late 16th and 17th centuries that sought to "purify" the Church of England (*see* ANGLICAN COMMUNION) from remnants of Roman Catholic "popery" that the Puritans claimed had been retained after the religious settlement reached early in the reign of Queen Elizabeth I. Puritans became noted for a spirit of moral and religious earnestness that determined their whole way of life, and they sought through church reform to make their lifestyle the pattern for the whole nation.

King Henry VIII separated the Church of England from Rome in 1534, and the cause of PROTESTANTISM advanced rapidly under Edward VI (reigned 1547–53). During the reign of Queen Mary (1553–58) England returned to ROMAN CATHOLICISM, and many Protestants were martyred or forced into exile. Many of the exiles found their way to Geneva, where John Calvin's church provided a working model of a disciplined church. Elizabeth's accession was enthusiastically welcomed by these Protestants in 1558, but her settlement disappointed those who sought extensive reform, and they were unable to achieve their objectives in the Convocation, the primary governing body of the church.

Many of these Puritans—as they came to be known during a controversy over vestments in the 1560s—sought parliamentary support for an effort to institute a PRESBYTERIAN form of polity for the Church of England. Other Puritans, concerned with the long delay in reform, decided upon a "reformation without tarrying for any." These "Separatists" repudiated the state church and formed voluntary congregations based on a covenant with God and among themselves. Both groups were repressed by the establishment. Denied the opportunity to reform the ESTABLISHED CHURCH, English Puritanism turned to preaching, pamphlets, and a variety of experiments in religious expression and in social behavior and organization. Its successful growth also owed much to patrons among the nobility and in Parliament and its control of colleges and professorships at Oxford and Cambridge.

Puritan hopes were again raised when the Calvinist James VI of Scotland succeeded Elizabeth as James I of England in 1603. But in 1604 he dismissed the Puritans' grievances. Puritans remained under pressure. Some were deprived of their positions; others got by with minimal conformity; and still others fled England. The pressure for conformity increased under Charles I (1625–49) and his archbishop, William Laud. Nevertheless, the Puritan spirit continued to spread, and, when civil war broke out between Parliament and Charles in the 1640s, Puritans seized the opportunity to urge Parliament and the nation to renew its covenant with God. Parliament called together a body of clergy to advise it on the government of the church, but this body—the Westminster Assembly—was so badly divided that it failed to achieve reform of church government and discipline. Meanwhile, the New Model Army, which had defeated the royalist forces, feared that the Assembly and Parliament would reach a compromise with King Charles that would destroy their gains for Puritanism, so it seized power and turned it over to Oliver Cromwell. The religious settlement under Cromwell's Commonwealth allowed for a limited pluralism that favored the Puritans. A number of radical Puritan groups appeared, including the Levelers, the Diggers, the Fifth Monarchy Men, and the Quakers (the only one of lasting significance).

After Cromwell's death in 1658, Laud's strict episcopal pattern was reinstituted. Thus, English Puritanism entered a period known as the Great Persecution. English Puritans made a final unsuccessful attempt to secure their ideal of a comprehensive church during the Glorious Revolution, but England's religious solution was defined in 1689 by the Act of Toleration, which continued the established church as episcopal but also tolerated dissenting groups.

The Puritan ideal of realizing the Holy Commonwealth by the establishment of a covenanted community was carried to the American colony of Virginia by Thomas Dale, but the greatest opportunity came in New England. The original pattern of church organization in the Massachusetts Bay colony was a "middle way" between presbyterianism and Separatism, yet in 1648 four New England Puritan colonies jointly adopted the Cambridge Platform, establishing a congregational form of church government. Only the elect could vote and rule. When this raised problems for second-generation residents, they adopted the Half-Way Covenant, which permitted baptized, moral, and orthodox persons to share the privileges of church membership. Other variations of the Puritan experiment were established in Rhode Island by ROGER WILLIAMS, who was banished from the Massachusetts Bay colony, and in Pennsylvania by the Quaker William Penn.

Puritans believed that conversion was necessary to redeem one from one's sinful condition, that God had chosen to reveal salvation through preaching, and that the HOLY SPIRIT rather than reason was the energizing instrument of salvation. In the place of contemporary Anglican preaching and ritual, the Puritans emphasized plain preaching that drew on images from SCRIPTURE and from everyday experience. Still, because of the importance of preaching, the Puritans placed a premium on a learned ministry. The conversion experience that was characteristic of Puritans combined with the doctrine of PREDESTINATION inherited from CALVINISM to produce a sense of themselves as elect spirits chosen by God to revolutionize history.

PURITY AND IMPURITY, set of opposing conceptions found throughout the history of religions. Although variously defined, they are important for the establishment of order and structure for both the individual and society.

It is important to remember that the pure and the impure are not defined by certain natural properties. What is defined as pure and impure across religions can be quite arbitrary. For instance, in some systems animal excrement might be viewed as inherently impure, yet among Hindus, cow urine and dung are used and classified as pure (see COW, SANCTITY OF THE). The CASTE system in India involves notions of purity and impurity as well: the Brahmin ritual specialist is held to be most pure, while the ŚŪDRA, the service workers, are regarded as most impure, and the Śūdra castes themselves are distinguished from one another by varying degrees of purity and impurity.

In the various religions of the world it is commonly held that a worshiper must attain a degree of ritual purity before approaching the divinity. In ancient Greece, for example, the Homeric heroes washed their hands before praying or performing sacrifice. With time, this developed into the principle that one must be pure both externally (physically) and internally (ethically) if one is to address the divine. Similar systems in contemporary religions include ṬAHĀRA, the Muslim code on ritual cleanliness. See also TOHORAH.

PURUSHA: see PRAKṚTI AND PURUṢA.

PWYLL \'pü-əhl\, in Celtic mythology, king of Dyfed, a beautiful land containing a magic cauldron of plenty. He became a friend of Arawn, king of Annwn (the Underworld), and exchanged shapes and kingdoms with him for a year and a day, thus gaining the name Pwyll Pen Annwn ("Head of Annwn"). With the aid of the goddess RHIANNON, who loved him, Pwyll won her from his rival, Gwawl. She bore him a son, Pryderi, who was abducted by Gwawl. Pryderi was later restored to his parents and succeeded Pwyll as ruler both in Dyfed and in Annwn. In Arthurian legend, Pwyll's cauldron became the Holy Grail, and Pwyll appeared as Pelles, the keeper of the Grail.

PYANOPSIA \ˌpī-ə-'näp-sē-ə\, also spelled Pyanepsia \-'nep-\, in ancient GREEK RELIGION, festival in honor of APOLLO, held at Athens on the seventh day of the month of Pyanopsion (October). The festival's rites included two offerings, consisting of a hodgepodge of pulse (edible seeds) and a branch of olive or laurel bound with wool, around which were hung fruits of the season, pastries, and small jars of honey, oil, and wine. The offerings were carried to the temple of Apollo, where they were suspended on the gate. The doors of private houses were similarly adorned. Both offerings have been connected with the Cretan expedition of THESEUS, who vowed to make a thanks offering to Apollo if he was successful in slaying the MINOTAUR.

PYGMALION \pig-'māl-yən, -'mā-lē-ən\, in Greek mythology, king of Cyprus who fell in love with a statue of the goddess APHRODITE. Ovid, in his *Metamorphoses*, embellished the tale: Pygmalion, a sculptor, made an ivory statue representing his ideal of womanhood and then fell in love with his own creation; the goddess VENUS brought the statue to life in answer to his prayer.

The Pyramids of Giza, Egypt, from the south
Hirmer Fotoarchiv, Munchen

PYRAMID, in architecture, monumental structure constructed of or faced with stone or brick and having a rectangular base and four sloping triangular (or sometimes trapezoidal) sides meeting at an apex (or truncated to form a platform). Pyramids have been built at various times in Egypt, The Sudan, Ethiopia, western Asia, Greece, Cyprus, Italy, India, Thailand, Mexico, South America, and some islands of the Pacific Ocean.

The pyramids of ancient Egypt were funerary edifices. They were built over a period of 2,700 years, ranging from the beginning of the Old Kingdom to the close of the Ptolemaic Period; from *c.* 2686–2345 BCE the pyramid was the regular type of royal tomb. It was not, as such, an isolated structure but rather was always part of an architectural complex. The essential components were the pyramid itself, containing or surmounting the grave proper and standing within an enclosure on high desert ground; an adjacent mortuary temple; and a causeway leading down to a pavilion that was situated at the edge of the cultivation and probably connected with the Nile by a canal. About 80 royal pyramids have been found in Egypt, many of them reduced to mere mounds of debris and long ago plundered of their treasures.

The prototype of the pyramid was the *mastaba*, a form of tomb that was characterized by a flat-topped rectangular superstructure of mud brick or stone with a shaft descending to the burial chamber far below it. Djoser, the second king of the 3rd dynasty, undertook for the first time the construction of a *mastaba* entirely of stone; once the base was completed it was extended on the ground on all four sides, and its height was increased by building rectangular additions of diminishing size superimposed upon its top. This monument, which lies at Saqqarah, is known as the Step Pyramid; it is probably the earliest stone building of importance erected in Egypt.

The earliest tomb known to have been designed and executed throughout as a true pyramid is the North Stone Pyramid at Dahshur, thought by some also to have been erected by Snefru. It is about 720 feet wide at the base and 340 feet high. The greatest of the Egyptian pyramids are those of the pharaohs Khufu, Khafre, and Menkure at Giza.

Among American pyramids the best known include the Pyramid of the Sun and the Pyramid of the Moon at Teotihuacán in central Mexico, the Castillo at Chichén Itzá, and various Inca and Chimú structures in Andean settlements. American pyramids were generally built of earth and then faced with stone, and they are typically of stepped form and topped by a platform or temple structure. The Pyramid of the Sun, with base dimensions of 720 feet by 755 feet, rivals in size the Great Pyramid of Khufu at Giza.

PYRAMID TEXTS, collection of Egyptian mortuary prayers, hymns, and SPELLS intended to protect a dead king or queen and ensure life and sustenance in the hereafter. The texts, inscribed on the walls of the inner chambers of the PYRAMIDS, are found at Ṣaqqārah in several 5th- and 6th-dynasty pyramids, of which that of Unas (*c.* 2400 BCE), last king of the 5th dynasty, is the earliest known. The texts constitute the oldest surviving body of Egyptian religious and funerary writings.

PYTHIAN GAMES \'pi-thē-ən\, in ancient Greece, various athletic and musical competitions held in honor of APOLLO, chiefly those at DELPHI. The musicians' contest there dated from very early times. In 582 BCE it was made quadrennial, and athletic events including foot and chariot races were added in emulation of the Olympic Games. Open to all Greeks, the contests were held either at the Delphic shrine on Mount Parnassus or on the Crisaean plain below. The victor was awarded a laurel wreath. The games took place in August of the third year of each Olympiad (the four-year period between Olympic Games). They continued to be held until the 4th century CE.

PYTHON \'pī-,thän, -thən\, in Greek mythology, huge serpent that was killed by the god APOLLO at DELPHI either because it would not let him found his oracle, being accustomed itself to giving oracles, or because it had persecuted Apollo's mother, LETO, during her pregnancy. In the earliest account the serpent is nameless and female, but later it is male and named Python (Pytho was the old name for Delphi). Python was traditionally the child of GAEA, who according to myth, had had an oracle at Delphi long before Apollo came.

893

QABBALAH AND JEWISH MYSTI-
CISM, in JUDAISM, system that entails the attempt on the part of a believer to interact with God on a personal and highly intense level. Visions, applying special spiritual techniques to the study of SCRIPTURE, and performing Jewish ritual in a certain manner are all modes of mystical experience in which people conceive themselves as coming close to God. Jewish mysticism is often identified with Qabbalah (also spelled Kabbalah). The Hebrew word *qabbalah* means "the Act of Receiving" or "(Religious) Tradition." There is no word in Hebrew for "mysticism." Indeed, mysticism itself is a difficult word to define but may be seen for the purposes of this article as a crystallizing of the human wish to interact with the divine and the divine world (ANGELS, spirits, etc.) in a direct and immediate manner. Therefore, aspects of experiences and notions that in other religions are called mysticism are present in a number of phenomena in Judaism. There is also no Hebrew word for "ECSTASY," which in many mystical phenomena designates the highest point that a mystic can reach. Still, Jewish mysticism has a number of terms that cover the experience of mystical ecstasy—the feeling that the gap between the human and the divine has been bridged, even if only temporarily; such terms include the Hebrew word DEVEQUT. In other cases, this state of union is sometimes defined as "Holy Marriage."

The earliest phases of Jewish mystical experience can be traced back to Scripture, which contains various accounts of people who experienced visions of the divine, apparently while losing consciousness. In all likelihood these accounts describe ecstatic fits (these descriptions are made, for instance, of Abram [later ABRAHAM] in GENESIS 15 and of SAUL in 1 Samuel).

The earliest accounts of experiences that substantially depart from the kind of experiences reported in Scripture are found in what became known as APOCALYPTICISM (literature of divine revelations that are secretly received and fictitiously attributed to biblical figures). This literature was created mostly in the Hellenistic period—that is, in the days of the Second Temple (6th century BCE–1st century CE). Among the more essential features not represented in Scripture are: the descriptions of heavenly ascensions (from which the visionaries come back); vision of angels that come to earth to disclose cosmological and historical secrets; the application of semi-magical means to obtain the relevant experiences and survive; and the element of exclusive secrecy that is imposed on those who receive the apocalyptic information. Apocalypticism in its radical forms of interpretation of Scripture involved, at times, a rewriting of biblical texts. As the apocalyptic trend among the QUMRĀN people shows, the rewriting of Scripture can even involve the Law-sections of Scripture (as in the case of the Temple Scroll; *see* DEAD SEA SCROLLS). Scholars believe that the mystical aspects of Apocalypticism were inherited by Christianity; this can be seen in the writings of ST. PAUL. The Apocalypse of John (or, REVELATION

TO JOHN) clearly translates Jewish apocalyptic lore to a Christian provenance.

In the wake of Apocalypticism, further mystical aspects can be discovered among the rabbinic sages of the MISHNAH and the TALMUD. It is surprising that the sages, who are generally viewed as having been singularly engaged in the advancement of Judaism in its legalistic framework, were openly engaged in mystical experiences as well. In this context the mystical experiences were referred to as the "[Works of the] Chariot" (Hebrew: [Maʿaseh] *Merkabah*)—referring to the visions that the prophet EZEKIEL had in regard to the departure of the Divine Glory (God) from the demolished temple, and the future return of that Glory to the rebuilt temple. Another term that became current among the RABBIS and which in all likelihood indicated a mystical translation to heaven was "Pardes," that is (in Persian), "an orchard [or forest] surrounded by a fence." (There may be erotic implications with this term, but, even if this is not so, eroticism is clearly expressed in medieval Qabbalah and in subsequent developments of Jewish mysticism.) This branch of Jewish Merkabah mysticism is fully developed in the Hekhalot ("The Heavenly Palaces") literature, attributed to some of the Mishnah authorities (*e.g.*, Rabbi AKIBA BEN JOSEPH, Rabbi ISHMAEL BEN ELISHA). Among other things, these Hekhalot writings (in Hebrew) influenced Jewish liturgical poetry, including the daily prayer book. *See also* MERKABAH MYSTICISM.

Jewish mysticism took a completely new turn when *Sefer Yetsirah* ("The Book of Creation") became known, most probably in the 6th or 7th century CE. As with many books from early times, this book is known in more than one version (three of them, in this case), and in its enigmatic brevity it outlines the creation of the world through the 10 SEFIROT and the 22 letters of the Hebrew alphabet. This is done on three parallel dimensional levels: in the cosmic world (in Hebrew, ʿOlam), in the dimension of time (Shanah, literally "year"), and in the human realm (Nefesh, that is, "soul"). The book actually says very little on how the world was created; it just sets the factual process and means in a sequential and paradigmatic order. Some scholars have suggested that the book is not mystical at all. Its inclusion in the mystical literature is justified by its mentioning the term *Sefirot* for the first time. It is not exactly clear what the term means. A likely suggestion is that in *Sefer Yetsirah* it refers to the mathematical value of letters and words as employed in the divine structuring of the world. Other suggestions refer to the Greek word *Sphaira*, metaphysical circles. In any event, when the word became the key notion in the mystical doctrine of the Qabbalah, it indicated 10 spiritual principles that paradigmatically stand for the whole of the scriptural vocabulary.

The first book that employs the notion of the 10 *Sefirot* in this elaborate sense is SEFER HA-BAHIR ("The Book of Clear Light"). It first appeared in Provence, France, about the 12th century. The principle that the book sets forth is that every word in Scripture corresponds to one of these *Sefirot*. Thus, every phrase or clause in Scripture outlines a process that is inherent in the divine world. However, the more systematic writing, in this respect, is the SEFER HA-ZOHAR ("The Book of [the Divine] Splendor").

The *Zohar* is attributed to Rabbi SIMEON BEN YOHAI, a 2nd-century-CE authority on the TANNA, but in all likelihood was written by a group of mystics affiliated with MOSES DE LEÓN, who lived in Spain and was active there in the second half of the 13th century. The book is written mostly in Aramaic and runs as a mystical Midrashic commentary to almost every verse in the Hebrew PENTATEUCH. Once again, every phrase or clause in Scripture reflects in a symbolic manner the special dynamic that is believed to be inherent in the celestial manifestations of the divine powers. The names of these *Sefirot* as they are given in the *Zohar* are Keter (Crown), Hokhamah (Wisdom), Binah (Sagacity), Chesed (Grace), Gevurah (Power), Tif'eret (Glory), Netsach (Longevity), Hod (Magisterial Dignity), Yesod (Foundation), and Malkhut (Kingdom). These names may seem rather arbitrary, and the internal logic upon which they are based is never made clear in any known text.

There are several kinds of spiritual dynamic that go through this doctrine of the 10 *Sefirot*. Three of the more essential ones are: God is conceived as En Sof (The Limitless), and he is dwelling in the remote recesses of the unknown above the *Sefirot*. En Sof acts through the *Sefirot* who emanate from him and in this respect are his manifested powers. They are either his own essence or else the vessels containing the divine essence. The *Sefirot* are structurally arranged in three columns. The right one is dominated by Chesed; the left one is dominated by Gevurah and is the source of stern judgment and, hence, of evil. The middle section is dominated by the interaction between Tif'eret and Malkhut, respectively the male and female principles in the divine world. Union between the two is brought about by the predominance of the right side of the *Sefirot*, and separation by the predominance of the left side. Predominance, in this respect, is the result of what the People of ISRAEL do in the lower world. When they do good things and are obedient to the laws of God, Chesed prevails and therefore the union between Tif'eret and Malkhut, as well. However, when the opposite is the case, Gevurah prevails, and hence separation and exilic conditions. The onslaught of the mythic powers of evil—generally described as the Sitra Achra ("The Other Side," SATAN) and the Qelippot ("Shells")—are let loose and cause fatal damage to the divine powers and to the People of Israel, alike. We may define this doctrine as theurgic THEOSOPHY. That is to say, divine history is effected by processes that come into being through the acts of Israel. This is considered the apex of Jewish mysticism. It is noteworthy that such a radical form of interpreting Scripture could be suggested in the Middle Ages. There were, of course, many who did, and many who still do, define all this as the culmination of mythological APOSTASY. Nevertheless, the effect of this doctrine on all later forms of Jewish thinking and spirituality was enormous. Hardly any later books or historical events—in particular, messianic events like 17th-century Shabbetaianism (*see* SHABBETAI TZEVI) and modern HASIDISM (*e.g.*, Chabad)—were not in one way or another affected by these doctrines. Several Halakhic matters, too, are influenced by Qabbalistic ideas and notions.

The publication of the *Zohar* led to a proliferation of mystical activity. Hundreds of books were written in its wake, some of which imitate its genre, others seeking new approaches. A few key authors were Abraham ben Samuel Abulafia (1240–c. 1291), MOSES BEN JACOB CORDOVERO (1522–70) and ISAAC BEN SOLOMON LURIA (1534–72).

A Christian type of "Qabbalah" became known in Europe from the 16th century onward. In its wake Qabbalistic notions, particularly those of the 10 *Sefirot*, were blended with the philosophical ALLEGORY of the Hebrew Scripture as known in the Christian HERMENEUTICS of Scripture and Christian doctrine. All this was mainly conceived as a Platonic program, in which new philosophical and scientific ideas created the needed intellectual background.

Today, Qabbalah is often identified with a number of manifestations of popular religion and spirituality, as people seek new types of RELIGIOUS EXPERIENCE that are not identified with established forms of religiousness. There is actually a precedent for this, as, since the days of the Renaissance, Qabbalah has often housed divergent forms of religious ideas and experiences that had very little to do with the Judaic notion of the term.

QADARĪYA \,kä-də-'rē-ə\, in ISLAM, adherents of the doctrine of FREE WILL (from *qadar*, meaning "fate" or "destiny"). The name was also applied to the MU'TAZILA, the theological school that believed that humans, through their free will, can choose between GOOD AND EVIL. The Mu'tazila themselves, however, preferred to be called *ahl al-'adl* ("the people of justice").

On the question of free will and predetermination, the Qadarīya based their stand on the necessity of divine justice. They maintained that without responsibility and freedom humans cannot justly be held accountable for their actions. Their opponents disregarded the question of justice and argued that to allow humans any freedom is equal to denying God's omnipotence and his absolute creative power. Two compromise views were held by moderate theological schools, the Ash'arīya and the MĀTURĪDĪYA.

QĀDĪ \'kä-,dē\ (Arabic), *also spelled* Cadi, or Kadi, Muslim judge who renders decisions according to the SHARĪ'A. The *qāḍī* hears only religious cases such as those involving inheritance, pious bequests (*waqf*), marriage, and divorce, though theoretically his jurisdiction extends to both civil and criminal matters. Originally, the *qāḍī*'s work was restricted to nonadministrative tasks—arbitrating disputes and rendering judgments. Eventually, however, he assumed the management of pious bequests, the guardianship of property for orphans and others incapable of overseeing their own interests, and the control of marriages for women without guardians. The *qāḍī*'s decision in all such matters was final.

The *qāḍī* must be an adult Muslim male of good character, possessing sound knowledge of the Sharī'a, and a free man. In the 7th and 8th centuries the *qāḍī* was expected to be capable of deriving the specific rules of law from their sources in the QUR'AN, HADITH, and IJMĀ' (consensus of the community). This view was later modified to allow the *qāḍī* to accept as absolute the opinions of one of the four SUNNI law schools.

The second caliph, 'Umar I, was the first to appoint a *qāḍī* to eliminate the necessity of his judging every dispute that arose in the community. Thereafter it was considered a religious duty for authorities to provide for the administration of justice through the appointment of *qāḍī*s.

QĀDIRĪYA \,kä-di-'rē-ə\, in ISLAM, probably the oldest of the Sufi orders, founded by the Ḥanbalī scholar 'ABD AL-

QĀDIR AL-JĪLĀNĪ (1078–1166) in Baghdad. Al-Jīlānī had only a small circle of followers, but his sons broadened this community into an order and encouraged its spread into North Africa, Central Asia, and India. The order, which stresses philanthropy, humility, piety, and moderation, is loosely organized, allowing each regional community to develop its own ritual prayers (DHIKRS). The main body (the Qādirīya proper) maintains a moderate Sufi (see SUFISM) system and is governed by a descendant of al-Jīlānī, who serves as the keeper of his tomb in Baghdad. A smaller group in North Africa, the Jīlālīya, worships al-Jīlānī as a supernatural being and combines Islamic MYSTICISM with pre-Islamic beliefs and practices.

QALANDARĪYA \ˌkä-lȧn-dȧ-ˈrē-ə\, loosely organized group of wandering Muslim dervishes who form an "irregular" (bī-sharʿ) or ANTINOMIAN mystical order in SUFISM. The Qalandarīya seem to have arisen from the earlier MALĀMATĪYA in Central Asia and exhibited Buddhist and perhaps Hindu influences. The adherents of the order were notorious for their contempt for the norms of Muslim society and their use of drugs. They shaved their heads, faces, and eyebrows, dressed only in blankets or in hip-length hairshirts. They led a wandering, nomadic life, and regarded all acts as lawful. The movement is first mentioned in Khorāsān in the 11th century; from there it spread to India, Syria, and western Iran.

QARMATIANS \kär-ˈmä-tē-ənz\, also spelled Qarmathians \-thē-ənz\, Karmatians, or Karmathians, Arabic Qarmatī, plural Qarāmita, members of the SHIʿITE Muslim subdivision known as the Ismāʿīlis. The Qarmatians flourished in Iraq, Yemen, and especially Bahrain during the 9th to 11th centuries, taking their name from Ḥamdān Qarmaṭ, who led the sect in southern Iraq during the second half of the 9th century. The Qarmatians were notorious for an insurrection in Syria and Iraq in 903-906 and for the exploits of two Bahraini leaders, Abū Saʿīd al-Jannābī and his son, Abū Ṭāhir Sulaymān, who invaded Iraq several times and sacked MECCA in 930, carrying off the Black Stone of the KAʿBA.

QIBLA \ˈki-blə\, also spelled qiblah, direction of the sacred shrine of the KAʿBA in MECCA, toward which Muslims turn five times each day when performing the ṢALĀT (daily ritual prayer). Soon after MUHAMMAD'S emigration (HIJRA) to MEDINA in 622, he indicated Jerusalem as the qibla, probably influenced by Jewish tradition. When Jewish–Muslim relations no longer seemed promising, Muhammad changed the qibla to Mecca.

The qibla is used not only for prayer but also for burial; the dead, including slaughtered animals, are interred facing Mecca. In a mosque, the qibla is indicated by the mihrab, a niche in the mosque's interior wall facing Mecca.

QIYĀS \kē-ˈyäs\, in Islamic law, analogical reasoning as applied to the deduction of juridical principles from the QURʾAN and the SUNNA (the normative practice of the community). With the Qurʾan, the sunna, and IJMĀʿ (scholarly consensus), it constitutes the four sources of SUNNI Islamic

Dome of the Shrine of Fāṭima, Qom, Iran
Kurt Scholz—Shostal

jurisprudence (UṢŪL AL-FIQH). The SHIʿITE counterpart for qiyās is ʿaql ("reason").

The need for qiyās developed soon after the death of MUHAMMAD, when the expanding Islamic state came in contact with societies and situations beyond the scope of the Qurʾan and the sunna. Very often, qiyās was used to deduce new beliefs and practices on the basis of analogy with past practices and beliefs.

Muslim scholars consider qiyās a specific variant of the general concept of IJTIHĀD, which is original interpretation and thought. It is also related to raʾy, personal thought and opinion, a forerunner of qiyās criticized by traditional authorities as too arbitrary.

QODASHIM \ˌkō-dä-ˈshēm\ (Hebrew: "Holy Things"), fifth of the six major divisions, or orders (SEDARIM), of the MISHNAH, which was given its final form early in the 3rd century CE by JUDAH HA-NASI. Qodashim deals primarily with rites and sacrifices that took place in the TEMPLE OF JERUSALEM. The 11 tractates of Qodashim are Zevaḥim ("Animal Sacrifices"), Menaḥot ("Meal Offerings"), Ḥullin ("Profane Objects"), *Bekhorot* ("Firstborn"), *'Arakhin* ("Estimates"), *Temura* ("Exchange"), *Keretot* ("Excisions"), *Me'ila* ("Transgression"), *Tamid* ("Burned Offering"), MIDDOT ("Dimensions"), and *Qinnim* ("Birds' Nests"). GEMARA are found in the Talmud BAVLI on all but the last two of the tractates.

QOM \\'kùm\\, *also spelled* Qum, city, north-central Iran. The town lies on both banks of the Rūd-e Qom and beside a salt desert, the Dasht-e Kavīr, 92 miles south of Tehrān.

In the 8th century Qom was one of the centers of Shi'ism; in 816 Fāṭima, the sister of the IMAM 'ALĪ AL-RIḌĀ, died in the town and was buried there. In the 17th century it became a place of PILGRIMAGE (second only to MASHHAD in Iran), when the Ṣafavid rulers built a golden-domed shrine over Fāṭima's tomb. The modern city has the largest MADRASA (religious college) in the country; at this school students can specialize in Islamic law, philosophy, theology, and logic. There are some 10 kings and 400 Islamic saints interred in Qom and its surrounding area.

The modernization programs that were launched by Reza Shah in the 1920s and again in the 1960s by his son Muhammad Reza Shah were seen by leading SHI'ITE scholars and jurists in Qom as assaults on their prerogatives. Qom's *madrasa*s and bazaars consequently became a nexus for the revolutionary movement that, under the charismatic leadership of Ayatollah Ruhollah Khomeini, would topple the monarchy and replace it with an Islamic republic in 1978–79. Many of the key positions in the post-revolutionary government were occupied by teachers and students from Qom's *madrasa*s, and, at the end of the 20th century, the city continues to be Iran's foremost center for religious learning.

QUAKER, *byname* of Friend, member of a Christian group (the SOCIETY OF FRIENDS, or Friends church) that stresses the guidance of the HOLY SPIRIT and rejects outward rites and an ordained ministry. It also actively works for peace. GEORGE FOX, founder of the society in England, recorded that in 1650 "Justice Bennet of Derby first called us Quakers because we bid them tremble at the word of God."

QUESTIONS OF MILINDA \\mi-'lin-də\\, *Pāli* Milinda-pañha \\-'pən-hə\\, lively dialogue on Buddhist doctrine with questions and dilemmas posed by King Milinda—*i.e.*, Menander, Greek ruler in the late 2nd century BCE—and answered by Nāgasena, a senior monk. Composed in northern India in perhaps the 1st or 2nd century CE by an unknown author, the "Questions of Milinda" is the one noncanonical work whose authority was accepted implicitly by such commentators as BUDDHAGHOSA. The problems discussed are common themes in the Pāli canon and the doctrine is orthodox THERAVĀDA.

QUETZALCOATL \\,kät-säl-'kō-ä-təl, -kō-'ä-təl\\ (from Nahuatl: *quetzalli*, "tail feather of the quetzal bird," and *coatl*, "serpent"), the FEATHERED SERPENT, one of the major deities of the ancient PRE-COLUMBIAN MESO-AMERICAN pantheon. Representations of a feathered snake occur as early as the Teotihuacán civilization (3rd to 8th century CE) on the central plateau. At that time, Quetzalcoatl seems to have been conceived as a vegetation god also associated with time and the calendar—an earth and water deity closely associated with the rain god TLALOC.

Historical changes including the rise of other city-states and the immigration of Nahua-speaking tribes from the north, resulted in innovations in Quetzalcoatl's cult. The subsequent Toltec culture (9th through 12th centuries), centered at the city of Tula, emphasized war and HUMAN SACRIFICE linked with the worship of heavenly bodies. Quetzalcoatl became the god of the morning and evening star, and his temples were the center of ceremonial life in Tula.

In Aztec times (14th through 16th centuries) Quetzalcoatl was revered as the patron of priests, the inventor of the calendar and of books, and the protector of goldsmiths and other craftsmen; he was also identified with the planet VENUS. As the morning and evening star, Quetzalcoatl was the symbol of death and rebirth. With his companion Xolotl, a dog-headed god, he was said to have descended to the Underworld of Mictlan to gather the bones of the ancestors. He anointed those bones with his own blood, giving birth to the men who inhabit the present universe.

One important body of myths relates Quetzalcoatl to Topiltzin Quetzalcoatl, the priest-king of Tula, the capital of the Toltecs. He refused to offer human victims for sacrifice, offering instead only snakes, birds, and butterflies. But the human representative of the god of the night sky, TEZCATLIPOCA, expelled him from Tula by performing feats of magic. Quetzalcoatl wandered down to the coast and then immo-

Quetzalcoatl, limestone figure from Mexico, 900–1250 CE

By courtesy of the Brooklyn Museum, New York, Henry L. Batterman and Frank S. Benson Funds

lated himself on a pyre, emerging from this as the planet Venus. According to another version, Quetzalcoatl embarked upon a raft made of snakes and disappeared beyond the eastern horizon.

In addition to his guise as a plumed serpent, Quetzalcoatl was sometimes represented as a man with a beard; as Ehécatl, the wind god, he was shown with a mask with two protruding tubes (through which the wind blew) and a conical hat typical of the Huastec tribe of northeastern Mexico. The temple of Quetzalcoatl at Tenochtitlán, the Aztec capital, was a round building, a shape that fitted the god's power as Ehécatl.

As the god of learning, of writing, and of books, Quetzalcoatl was particularly venerated in the calmecac, religious colleges annexed to the temples, in which the future priests and the sons of the nobility were educated. Outside of Tenochtitlán, the main center of Quetzalcoatl's cult was Cholula, on the Puebla plateau.

QUIETISM, doctrine of Christian spirituality that holds that perfection consists in passivity (quiet) of the soul, in the suppression of human effort so that divine action may have full play. Quietistic elements have been discerned in several religious movements through the centuries, but the term is usually identified with the doctrine of MIGUEL DE MOLINOS, a Spanish priest who became an esteemed spiritual director in Rome during the latter half of the 17th century and whose teachings were condemned as heretical by the ROMAN CATHOLIC church.

For Molinos, the way of Christian perfection was the interior way of contemplation to which anyone with divine assistance can attain and that can last for years, even for a lifetime. To wish to act is an offense against God, who desires to do everything in man. Inactivity brings the soul back to its principle, the divine being, into which it is transformed. God, the sole reality, lives and reigns in the souls of those who have undergone this mystic death. They can will only what God wills because their own wills have been taken away. They should not be concerned about salvation, perfection, or anything else but must leave all to God. According to Quietist tenets, at least as they were interpreted by hostile critics, the devil can make himself master of the contemplative's body and force him to perform acts that seem sinful; but because the CONTEMPLATIVE does not consent, they are not SINS. Molinos' teachings were condemned by Pope Innocent XI in 1687, and he was sentenced to life in prison.

Quietism was perhaps paralleled among Protestants by some of the tenets of PIETISM and among the QUAKERS. It certainly appeared in a milder form in France, where it was propagated by JEANNE-MARIE BOUVIER DE LA MOTTE GUYON, an influential mystic.

QUIPU \'kē-pü\, *also spelled* quipo \-pō\, in PRE-COLUMBIAN MESO-AMERICAN RELIGIONS, Incan accounting apparatus consisting of a long rope, from which hung 48 secondary cords and various tertiary cords attached to the secondary ones. Knots were made in the cords to represent units, tens, and hundreds; and, in imperial accounting, the cords were colored to designate the different concerns of government—such as tribute, economic productivity, ceremonies, and matters relating to war and peace. The *quipu*s were created and maintained as historical records and were kept not only by high officials at the capital of Cuzco—judges, commanders, and important heads of extended families—but also by regional commanders and village headmen.

QUIRINUS \kwə-'rī-nəs, -'rē-\, major Roman deity ranking close to JUPITER and Mars; the *flamines* of these gods constituted the three major priests at Rome in ancient times. Both modern scholars and the Romans themselves link Quirinus with *Quirites*, a name for the citizens of Rome in republican times, though earlier usage was probably restricted to the inhabitants of the northernmost of Rome's seven hills, called after Quirinus the Quirinal (*collis Quirinalis*). The Quirinal was the traditional site of a Sabine settlement that united with the Palatine community to form the original Rome.

In spite of his importance, little is known about Quirinus. He bears a similarity to MARS, and some believe that he is only another form of that deity. By the late republic he is identified completely with Romulus. His was the name under which the immortalized Romulus was worshiped, and his festival fell on the same date that Romulus was said to have ascended to the gods, perhaps to assume the identity of Quirinus. He had a festival, the Quirinalia, on February 17; his temple on the Quirinal was one of the oldest in Rome. A cult partner, HORA, is spoken of, as are minor deities, the Virites Quirini, of whom nothing else is known. JANUS appears with the epithet Quirinus, but the relationship between the two is a matter of conjecture.

QUMRĀN \kûm-'rän\, *also spelled* Kumran, region on the northwestern shore of the Dead Sea, notable since 1947 as the site of the caves where the DEAD SEA SCROLLS were first discovered. Excavations (since 1949) at a site called Khirbet Qumrān (Arabic: "Qumrān Ruins"), less than a mile from the sea and north of the waterway Wadi Qumrān, have revealed the ruins of buildings believed by some scholars to have been occupied by a community of ESSENES, who have been posited as the owners of the Scrolls.

Excavations at Qumrān in the 1950s were led by the French archaeologist Roland de Vaux, whose workers revealed a complex of structures occupying an area about 260 by 330 feet. An extensive aqueduct system, fed by the Wadi Qumrān, traversed the site and filled as many as eight internal reservoirs (cisterns), as well as two baths. In the eastern part of the ruins stood the principal building; east and south of this are several rooms, one of which served seemingly as a scriptorium. A cemetery near Qumrān holds the remains of about 1,100 male adults; two lesser grave sites were reserved for some 100 women and children.

The Essenes separated from the rest of the Jewish community in the 2nd century BCE, when Jonathan Maccabeus and, later, Simon Maccabeus, usurped the office of HIGH PRIEST, which conferred secular as well as religious authority. Simon felt compelled to persecute the Essenes, who opposed the usurpation. Hence, they fled into the wilderness with their leader, the Teacher of Righteousness. Some scholars hold that Essenes established a monastic community at Qumrān in the mid-2nd century BCE.

Living apart, like other Essenian communities in Judaea, the members of the Qumrān community turned to apocalyptic visions of the overthrow of the wicked priests of Jerusalem and of the ultimate establishment of their own community as the true PRIESTHOOD and the true Israel. They devoted their time to study of the SCRIPTURES, manual labor, worship, and prayer. Meals were taken in common as prophetic celebrations of the messianic banquet. The BAPTISM they practiced symbolized repentance and entry into the company of the "Elect of God."

During the reign (37–4 BCE) of Herod the Great an earthquake (31 BCE) and fire caused the temporary abandonment of Qumrān, but the community resumed its life there until the center was destroyed (68 CE) by Roman legions under Vespasian. Until about 73 CE the site was garrisoned by Roman soldiers; during the Second Jewish Revolt (132–135) rebels under BAR KOKHBA were based there.

QUR'AN \kur-'än; kə-'ran, -'ran\, *also spelled* Koran (Arabic: "Recitation"), the sacred SCRIPTURE of ISLAM, regarded by Muslims as the infallible Word of God, a perfect transcription of an eternal tablet preserved in heaven and revealed to the Prophet MUHAMMAD.

The intermittent revelations to Muhammad were first memorized by followers and used in ritual prayers. Although verses were later written down during the Prophet's lifetime, according to Muslim sources they were first compiled in their present authoritative form during the reign of the third CALIPH (deputy or successor to the Prophet), 'Uthmān (d. 656).

The Qur'an consists of 114 chapters (SŪRAS) of unequal length. The earliest *sūra*s of the Meccan period are generally shorter and written in dynamic rhymed prose. The *sūra*s of the later Medinan period are longer and more prosaic in style. With the exception of the first *sūra* the FĀTIḤA ("Opening"), the *sūra*s are arranged roughly according to length, with the longer *sūra*s preceding the shorter ones. Consequently, the present arrangement is partly an inversion of the text's chronological order.

The emphases of Qur'anic teachings differ according to the periods of revelation. The early *sūra*s convey an emphatic call to moral and religious obedience in light of the coming Day of Judgment, while the late Medinan *sūra*s provide directives for the creation of a social fabric supportive of the moral life called for by God.

Absolute MONOTHEISM governs all Qur'anic ideas about God. The imperative to recognize no divinity besides God is reiterated throughout the scriptures. The God who revealed his word to Muhammad is identified with the God worshiped by both Jews and Christians, though these communities failed to hear and incorporate God's revelation to their prophets. The Qur'an emphasizes God as the absolute creator and sustainer of an ordered universe, an order that reflects his infinite power, wisdom, and authority. Although God is completely unlike his creation, He is also recognized as omnipresent. Through his revealed word, God has provided guidance for humanity, and by the standard of that guidance he will judge humanity on the Day of Reckoning. Emphasis on the stern justice of God is tempered by recurrent references to his mercy and compassion.

The Qur'an describes the human both as "God's vicegerent" within the created order as well as an "ignorant and foolhardy" creature. While humans are endowed with the greatest potential of any created beings, they alone are susceptible to evil. The Qur'an states explicitly that humanity is responsible, both individually and collectively, for its action. Though numerous passages refer to human freedom to accept or reject the Qur'anic teachings, other verses speak of God's control of history in terms more akin to PREDESTINATION. This ambiguity has given rise to a variety of Muslim interpretations of human nature and destiny. *See also* MATURIDĪYA; MUʿTAZILA; QADARĪYA.

The Qur'an demands absolute submission (*islām*) to God and his word. This submission requires the implementation of moral principles both individually and within the sociopolitical order. With the end of history, each person will face judgment, with the joys of the gardens of paradise or the punishment and terror of hell awaiting the outcome.

Although the Qur'an is the primary source of Islamic law, it does not enumerate the detailed requirements of that law. Similarly, the scriptures provide merely fragmentary directives for the basic duties of the faithful, referred to as the FIVE PILLARS OF ISLAM.

Correct interpretation of the Qur'an has been a central concern of all schools of Islamic thought. A special branch of learning, called TAFSĪR, deals exclusively with Qur'anic EXEGESIS. Commentators use *tafsīr* to study Qur'anic texts in terms of auxiliary branches of learning such as Arabic grammar, lexicography, and the Prophetic tradition. This development of exegesis, however, did not forestall doctrinal disputes; instead, various theological and legal schools used this discipline to support their respective systems of thought.

The Qur'an is regarded as immutable in both form and content, and its translation has traditionally been forbidden. Muslims throughout the world thus continue to recite its *sūra*s in Arabic, although they may not understand the language. The many translations now available are viewed as "paraphrases" to facilitate understanding of the actual scripture. *See also* BIBLE.

QURAYSH \kủ-'rīsh\, *also spelled* Kuraish, *or* Koreish, in ISLAM, ruling tribe of MECCA at the time of the birth of the Prophet MUHAMMAD. There were 10 main clans, the names of some of which gained great luster through their members' status in early Islam.

QURRĀ' \kủ-'rả\ (Arabic: "Reciters"), *singular* qāri', professional reciters of the text of the QUR'AN. In the early Islamic community MUHAMMAD's revelations had often been memorized by the COMPANIONS OF THE PROPHET, a practice derived from the pre-Islamic tradition of preserving poetry orally. It became common for Muslims to memorize the Qur'an in its entirety, even after it had been assembled in written form. Such reciters were often called upon by scholars to elucidate points of pronunciation and meaning obscured by the early Arabic script, and they helped to define the rudiments of Arabic grammar and linguistics.

The sheer number of reciters—who by the 9th century formed an established, specialized class—produced such a variety of subtly differing interpretations that in the time of the 'Abbāsid CALIPH al-Qāhir (reigned 932–934) seven *qurrā'* were declared the sole orthodox interpreters of the Qur'an and all other readings were banned. As early as the 7th century CE, in the confrontation at Ṣiffīn (657) between the fourth caliph, 'ALĪ, and Muʿāwiya, a contender for the caliphate, the *qurrā'* forced 'Alī to submit to the arbitration that cost him the caliphate. At the beginning of the 9th century, a union of *qurrā'*, with its own elected head, the SHAYKH al-qurrā', is recorded in Baghdad.

The science of reciting the Qur'an (*qirā'a*) soon produced a corresponding art of intoning the Qur'an (TAJWĪD), and this unaccompanied ritual chanting enabled large congregations of Muslims to follow the texts with relative ease. Religious figures employed in the mosques still memorize the Qur'an to aid them in interpreting the revelations to the faithful. In some Arab countries the professional duties of reciting the Qur'an at festivals and mosque services are generally reserved for blind men, who are trained in *qirā'a* from childhood as a means of supporting themselves. The art of recitation is highly esteemed in all Muslim communities; recordings by the best reciters are broadcast on radio and television, and they are available on audio cassettes and CDs.

RABBI (Hebrew: "my teacher," or "my master"), in JUDAISM, a title of respect. Used generically for great sages or teaching authorities, the title ultimately came to signify the sages of the Judaism of the dual TORAH, oral and written, which therefore is called "RABBINIC JUDAISM." A sage in that Judaism acquired the status of rabbi through a process of discipleship to a great master. That accords with the myth of divine revelation of the Torah at Sinai in two media, the oral part being passed on from master to disciple in an ongoing chain of memorization and verbatim tradition. The rabbis of rabbinic Judaism served not only as teachers of a circle of disciples but also as judges and administrators of the community of Judaism.

In modern times, especially in Western countries, rabbis became clergy and undertook tasks of preaching and conducting such rites as marriage and burial, while in Reform and Conservative SYNAGOGUES they also became principal leaders of public worship. In the United States rabbis also undertake pastoral counseling, hospital and military chaplaincies, Jewish community administration, as well as teaching in Jewish schools and YESHIVAS. Rabbis in Western countries ordinarily complete a secular education as well as a rabbinical study and ordination; those in the state of Israel study only in yeshivas. Rabbis in parts of Europe and the state of Israel are paid by the state. REFORM, RECONSTRUCTIONIST, and CONSERVATIVE JUDAISM ordain women as rabbis; no ORTHODOX JUDAISM does so.

RABBINICAL ASSEMBLY, THE, organization of Conservative RABBIS in the United States, Canada, Latin America, Europe, and Israel. It was founded in 1900 as the Alumni Association of the Jewish Theological Seminary and was reorganized in 1940 as the Rabbinical Assembly of America; in 1962 it acquired its present name and international scope. The Rabbinical Assembly recommends rabbis for appointment to Conservative congregations and promotes the goals of CONSERVATIVE JUDAISM. In 1985 the Rabbinical Assembly voted to allow the admittance of women as rabbis for the first time. Its publications include the quarterly *Conservative Judaism* and several prayer books.

RABBINIC JUDAISM, normative form of JUDAISM that developed after the fall of the TEMPLE OF JERUSALEM (70 CE). Originating in the work of the Pharisaic RABBIS, it was based on the legal and commentative literature in the TALMUD, and it set up a mode of worship and a life discipline that have been practiced by Jews through modern times.

RADCLIFFE-BROWN, A(LFRED) R(EGINALD) \'rad-,klif-'braun\ (b. Jan. 17, 1881, Birmingham, Warwick, Eng.—d. Oct. 24, 1955, London), English social anthropologist who developed a system of concepts and generalizations relating to the social structures of relatively simple societies.

Radcliffe-Brown went to the Andaman Islands (1906–08), where his fieldwork won him a fellowship at Trinity Col-

lege, Cambridge. On an expedition to Western Australia (1910–12), he concentrated on KINSHIP and family organization. He became director of education for the kingdom of Tonga (1916) and served as professor of social anthropology at the University of Cape Town (1920–25), where he founded the School of African Life and Languages. At the University of Sydney (1925–31) he developed a vigorous teaching program involving research in theoretical and applied anthropology.

His theory had its classic formulation and application in *The Social Organisation of Australian Tribes* (1931). Treating all Aboriginal Australia known at the time, the work cataloged, classified, analyzed, and synthesized a vast amount of data on kinship, marriage, language, custom, occupancy and possession of land, sexual patterns, and COSMOLOGY. He attempted to explain social phenomena as enduring systems of adaptation, fusion, and integration of elements. He held that social structures are arrangements of persons and that organizations are the arrangements of activities; thus, the life of a society may be viewed as an active system of functionally consistent, interdependent elements.

At the University of Chicago (1931–37) Radcliffe-Brown was instrumental in introducing social anthropology to American scholars. He joined the faculty of the University of Oxford from 1937–46. His later works include *Structure and Function in Primitive Society* (1952) and *Method in Social Anthropology* (1958).

RĀDHĀ \'rä-,dä\, in HINDUISM, consort of the god KRISHNA when he lived among the cowherds of Vṛndāvana. Rādhā was the wife of another *gopa* (cowherd) but was the most beloved of Krishna's consorts and his constant companion. In the BHAKTI (devotional) movement of VAIṢṆAVISM, Rādhā symbolizes the human soul and Krishna the divine.

The allegorical love of Rādhā has been given expression in the lyrical poetry of many Indian languages. Jayadeva's 12th-century Sanskrit poem, the GĪTAGOVINDA, celebrates their love in its many forms. The Bengali saint CAITANYA was said to be an incarnation of the two lovers; he was Krishna on the inside and Rādhā on the outside. Caitanya also composed many lyrics celebrating this divine love, which have not survived. The bronze images of Krishna playing the flute that are enshrined in temples are often accompanied, particularly in the northern and eastern parts of India, by images of his beloved Rādhā. She is also worshiped as Krishna's *hlādinī śakti* ("blissful energy") or as a goddess in her own right.

RADHASOAMI SATSANG \'rä-dä-'svä-mē-,sət-'səŋ-gä, -'swä-mē-, -'sət-,səŋg\, *also spelled* Rādhāsvāmī Satsaṅg \'rä-dä-'svä-mē-\, guru-focused esoteric religious sect of India that has followers among both Hindus and Sikhs, as well as a significant international following. The sect was founded in 1861 by Shiv Dayal Singh (later called Soamiji Maharaj),

Rādhā and Krishna on the terrace, Indian miniature painting, c. 1760
By courtesy of the Victoria and Albert Museum, London

the son of a Punjabi moneylender and follower of SIKHISM. He believed that human beings could perfect their highest capabilities only through repetition of the *śabd* ("sound"), or NĀM ("name"), of the Lord. The term *Radha-soami* signifies the union of the soul with God, the name of God, and the sound heard internally that emanates from God. Great emphasis is placed on the Satsang ("congregation of good people") and on the experience of the GURU externally through visual contact and internally through meditation. After the death of Shiv Dayal Singh, the sect split into several factions, now located in Agra, Delhi, and Gwalior and at Beas in the Punjab, the latter of which is far more influenced by Sikh traditions than the former. Two of its branches—at Dayalbagh in Agra and at Beas—have established Utopian communities.

RAGNARÖK \\'räg-nə-₁rœk, -₁räk\\ (Old Norse: "Doom of the Gods"), in GERMANIC RELIGION, the end of the world of gods and men. The Ragnarök is fully described only in the Icelandic poem *Völuspá* ("Sibyl's Prophecy"), probably of the late 10th century, and in the 13th-century *Prose* EDDA of Snorri Sturluson (d. 1241), which largely follows the *Völuspá*. According to those two sources, the Ragnarök will be preceded by cruel winters and moral chaos. GIANTS and DEMONS approaching from all points of the compass will attack the gods, who will meet them and face death like heroes. The sun will be darkened, the stars will vanish, and the earth will burn and then sink into the sea. Afterward, the earth will rise again, the old enemies BALDER and Hoder

will be reconciled and return from the dead, and the just will live in a hall roofed with gold.

Disjointed allusions to the Ragnarök, found in many other sources, show that conceptions of it varied. According to one poem, two human beings, Lif and Lifthrasir ("Life" and "Vitality"), will emerge from the WORLD TREE (which was not entirely destroyed) and repeople the earth.

RAHITNĀMĀ \\'rə-hit-'nä-mä\\ (Punjabi: "Manual of Conduct"), in SIKHISM, sets of guidelines that govern the behavior of Sikhs. The *Rahitnāmā*s provide systematic statements of the principles of the KHĀLSĀ and the way of life lived in accordance with these principles.

NĀNAK (1469–1539), the founder of the Sikh tradition, used the term *rahit* to designate a distinctive way of living, but it was not until the turn of the 17th century that formula statements of what Sikhs should and should not do began to appear. With the declaration of the Sikh community as the Khālsā in 1699, the earlier *rahit* expanded to include new obligations, such as keeping the hair uncut and abjuring the use of tobacco. This comprehensive *rahit* came to be recorded in texts called *Rahitnāmā*s. The earliest extant *Rahitnāmā* is attributed to Chaupa Singh (d. 1723); others followed during the 18th and 19th centuries. This literature was codified into the authoritative text *Sikh Rahit Maryādā* ("The Sikh Code of Conduct") in the mid-20th century by the Shiromanī Gurdwārā Prabandhak Committee, the most important Sikh governing body.

RAHNER, KARL \\'rä-nər\\ (b. March 5, 1904, Freiburg im Breisgau, Baden, Ger.—d. March 30, 1984, Innsbruck, Austria), German JESUIT priest who is widely considered to have been one of the foremost ROMAN CATHOLIC theologians of the 20th century. He is best known for his work in Christology and for his integration of an existential philosophy of personalism with Thomistic realism, by which human self-consciousness and self-transcendence are placed within a sphere in which the ultimate determinant is God.

Rahner was ordained in 1932. He studied at the University of Freiburg under Martin Heidegger before earning a doctorate at the University of Innsbruck. He taught at the Universities of Innsbruck, Munich, and Münster. He was an editor of *Lexikon für Theologie und Kirche*, 10 vol. (1957–68; "Lexicon for Theology and the Church"), and of *Sacramentum Mundi*, 6 vol. (1968–70; "Sacrament of the World").

Rahner's many books emphasize the continuity of modern and ancient interpretations of Roman Catholic doctrine. His works include *Geist in Welt* (1939; *Spirit in the World*), *Hörer des Wortes* (1941; *Hearers of the Word*), *Sendung und Gnade*, 3 vol. (1966; *Mission and Grace*), *Grundkurs des Glaubens* (1976; *Foundations of Christian Faith*), and *Die siebenfältige Gabe: über die Sakramente der Kirche* (1974; *Meditations on the Sacraments*).

RAIN DANCE, ceremonial dance performed in many cultures to invoke rain.

Agrarian cultures, including the Mayan civilization and that of ancient Egypt, have most commonly employed rain dances; Egyptian tomb scenes depicted rain dancers as early as 2700 BCE. Rain dances often feature dancing in a circle, the participation of young girls, decoration with green vegetation, nudity, the pouring of water, phallic rites, and whirling, meant to act as a wind charm. Thus, the South African Angoni carry tree branches, and Papuan mythology teaches that grass carried in such dances pierces the eye of the sun, causing it to weep and be covered with clouds. The Sioux Indians perform a ceremonial dance around a jug of water, while the Hopi snake dance is based on the belief that the snakes carry prayers to the Rainmakers beneath the earth. In southeastern European ceremonies, a group of girls proceed from house to house, their leader clothed in leaves and grass and whirling in their midst while housewives pour water on her.

RAJNEESH, BHAGWAN SHREE \'rəj-nēsh, räj-'nēsh\, *original name* Chandra Mohan Jain (b. Dec. 11, 1931, central India—d. Jan. 19, 1990, Pune, India), spiritual leader who preached an eclectic doctrine of Eastern MYSTICISM, individual devotion, and sexual freedom while amassing vast personal wealth.

He taught philosophy at Jabalpur University, where he received his B.A. degree (1955); he also attended the University of Saugar (M.A., 1957). He acquired the nickname Rajneesh and took the honorific Bhagwan (Hindi: "God"). After lecturing throughout India he established an ASHRAM (spiritual community) in Pune (Poona). By the early 1970s he had attracted 200,000 devotees, many from Europe and the United States.

In 1981 Rajneesh's cult purchased a dilapidated ranch in Oregon, U.S., which became the site of Rajneeshpuram, a community of several thousand disciples. Rajneesh was widely criticized by outsiders for his private security force and his ostentatious display of wealth. By 1985 many of his most trusted aides had abandoned the movement, which was under investigation for arson, attempted murder, drug smuggling, and vote fraud in the nearby town of Antelope. In 1985 Rajneesh pleaded guilty to immigration fraud and was deported from the United States. He was refused entry by 21 countries before returning to Pune, where his ashram soon grew to 15,000 members. In later years he took the Buddhist title Osho and altered his teaching of unrestricted sexual activity because of his growing concern over AIDS.

RĀKṢASA \'räk-shə-sə\ (Sanskrit: "demon"), *feminine form* rākṣasī ("demoness"), in HINDUISM, type of DEMON or goblin. *Rākṣasa*s have the power to change their shape at will and appear as animals, as monsters, or in the case of the female demons, as beautiful women. They are most powerful in the evening, particularly during the dark period of the new moon, but they are dispelled by the rising sun. They especially detest sacrifices and prayer. The best-known rākṣasa is the 10-headed RĀVAṆA, demon king of Laṅkā, who abducts SĪTĀ, Rāma's wife, in the epic *Rāmāyaṇa*. Pūtanā, a female demon, is well known for her attempt to kill the infant KRISHNA by offering him milk from her poisoned breast; Krishna, however, sucked away her life.

Some *rākṣasa*s are akin to YAKṢAS (nature spirits), while others are similar to ASURAS, the traditional opponents of the gods. The term *rākṣasa*, however, generally applies to those demons who haunt cemeteries, eat the flesh of men, and drink the milk of cows dry.

Rāma and Lakṣmaṇa attended by Hanumān in the forest, detail of a relief, Madhya Pradesh, India, 5th century CE
P. Chandra

RĀMA \'rä-mə\, one of the most widely worshiped deities of HINDUISM, the embodiment of chivalry and virtue. Although there are three Rāmas in Indian tradition (PARAŚURĀMA, BALARĀMA, and Rāmacandra), the name is most associated with Rāmacandra, the seventh incarnation (AVATAR) of VISHNU. His story is told briefly in the MAHĀBHĀRATA and at great length in the RĀMĀYAṆA ("Story of Rāma").

References to Rāma as an incarnation of Vishnu appear in the early centuries of the common era; there was apparently no widespread special worship of him before the 11th century, as would be attested by independent Rāma temples. It was not until the 14th or 15th century that sects appeared venerating him as the supreme god (see RĀMĀNANDA). Rāma's popularity is especially associated with vernacular versions of the *Rāmāyaṇa*, such as those composed by Kampaṇ in Tamil (12th century) and by TULSĪDĀS in Hindi (16th century; see RĀMCARITMĀNAS).

Rāma and KRISHNA are the two most popular recipients of adoration from the BHAKTI (devotional) cults that swept India from the 6th century onward. Rāma is conceived as a model of reason, right action, and desirable virtues, but his subordination, at crucial moments, of his duties as husband to his responsibilities as king have also made him the object of questions and criticism. In North India Rāma's name is a popular form of greeting among friends ("Rām! Rām!") and is the focus of a name-mysticism that parallels the sort found in other religious traditions. Rāma is the deity most invoked at death.

The image of Rāma in a shrine or temple is almost invariably attended by figures representing his wife SĪTĀ, his half-brother Lakṣmaṇa, and his devotee, the monkey chief HANUMĀN.

RAMAḌĀN \ˌra-mə-'dän\, in ISLAM, the month of FASTING, the ninth month of the Muslim year, in which "the QUR'AN was sent down as a guidance for the people" (Qur'an 2:185).

Islamic law prescribes abstention from food, drink, and sexual intercourse from dawn until dusk throughout the month for all rational adult Muslims. The young, the ill, travelers, soldiers, and women in menses or childbed are generally exempted; though all but the young are expected to fulfill their fasting obligation later when their condition allows. The beginning and end of Ramaḍān are announced when one trustworthy witness testifies before the authorities that the new moon has been sighted; a cloudy sky may, therefore, delay or prolong the fast. The end of the fasting period is marked by the 'ĪD al-Fiṭr, a three-day festival.

In the Qur'an, the development of the Ramaḍān fast, which is one of the FIVE PILLARS OF ISLAM, may be traced from the injunction to fast on 'ĀSHŪRĀ', the 10th of Muḥarram, probably once identical with the Jewish Day of Atonement. This injunction was abrogated by a command to fast during Ramaḍān (2:184).

RAMAKRISHNA PARAMAHAMSA \ˌra-mə-'krish-nə\, *also spelled* Rāmakṛṣṇa Paramahaṃsa, *original name* Gadādhar Chattopādhyāya (b. 1836, Kamarpukar, India—d. Aug. 16, 1886, Calcutta), founder of a school of religious thought that became the Rama Krishna order and considered by many Hindus to be not just a GURU but a saint.

Ramakrishna lived the life of a Hindu villager until late adolescence when poverty forced him and his older brother Ramkumar to move to Calcutta and seek employment. There they found work in a temple dedicated to the Hindu goddess KĀLĪ. Shortly after the move, however, Ramkumar died. Ramakrishna, now alone, turned to Kālī-Mā (Kālī the Mother) and prayed to the goddess for a vision that would not come. Traditional accounts tell a story of the young priest despairing of a vision and attempting suicide, only to find himself overwhelmed in an ocean of blissful conscious light that he interpreted as a manifestation of the Mother he had sought so desperately.

Soon after this first vision, Ramakrishna commenced on a series of SĀDHANAS, or "practices," in the various mystical traditions, including Bengali VAIṢṆAVISM, Śākta Tantrism, ADVAITA Vedānta, and even Islamic SUFISM and ROMAN CATHOLICISM. (The last practice ended with a vision of Jesus "the great yogi" who embraced the young priest and disappeared into his body, after which Ramakrishna is said to have experienced BRAHMAN.) Ramakrishna claimed to experience this same formless Brahman after each of these *sādhana*s, and later in life he became famous for his pithy PARABLES about the ultimate unity of the different religious traditions in this formless Vedantic Brahman.

This message, that all religions lead to the same Brahman, was certainly a politically and religiously powerful one, as it answered in classical Indian terms the challenges of British missionaries and colonial authorities who had battered HINDUISM for almost a century with a barrage of social, religious, and ethical criticisms. That all religions could be seen as different paths to the same divine source or, even better, that this divine source showed itself in classically Sanskritic ways (that is, in Hindu categories) was welcome and truly liberating news.

Partly because of the timeliness and attractiveness of this most basic message, and partly because of Ramakrish-na's own undeniable CHARISMA as a guru and ecstatic mystic, a small band of disciples, most of them Western-educated, started to gather around Ramakrishna in the early 1880s. It was also about this time that Calcutta newspaper and journal articles began to refer to Ramakrishna as "the Hindu saint" or as "the Paramahamsa" (a religious title of respect and honor). Much of what is known about Ramakrishna's teachings comes from a remarkable text whose diary-sources date back to the early 1880s, Mahendranath Gupta's five-volume Bengali classic *The Nectar-Speech of the Twice-Blessed Ramakrishna*, best known to English readers as *The Gospel of Sri Ramakrishna*.

After Ramakrishna's death, his disciple and successor, Narendra Nath Datta (d. 1902) became the world-traveling Swami VIVEKANANDA and helped establish the Ramakrishna Order, whose teachings, texts, and rituals divinized Ramakrishna as a new AVATAR, or "descent," of God. With its headquarters in Belur Maṭh, the Ramakrishna Order played an important role in the dissemination of Hindu ideas and practices in the West, particularly in the United States.

RAMANA MAHARSHI \'rə-mə-nə-mə-'hər-shē, -'här-; -mə-ˌhä-'ri-shē\, *original name* Venkataraman Aiyer (b. Dec. 30, 1879, Madurai, Tamil Nadu, India—d. April 14, 1950, Tiruvannāmalai), Hindu philosopher and yogi called "Great Master," "Bhagavān" (the Lord), and "the Sage of Aruṇāchala," whose views of the identity between individual souls and the world-soul BRAHMAN and of the illusory nature of phenomenal reality (MĀYĀ) roughly parallel those of Śaṃkara (*c.* 700–750 CE), a founder of the ADVAITA school of philosophy. His original contribution to yogic philosophy is the technique of *vicāra* (self-"pondering" inquiry).

Born to a middle-class, southern Indian, Brahmin family, Venkataraman read mystical and devotional literature, particularly the lives of South Indian Śaiva saints and the life of KABĪR, the medieval mystical poet. At the age of 17 he had a spiritual experience from which he derived his *vicāra* technique: he suddenly felt a great fear of death, and, lying very still, imagined his body becoming a stiff, cold corpse. Following a traditional "not this, not that" (*neti-neti*) practice, he began self-inquiry, asking "Who am I?" and answering not the body, nor the mind, nor the personality, nor the emotions, for all these will decay and die. He arrived at SAMĀDHI, a state of blissful consciousness beyond the mind. He immediately adopted the life of a HERMIT at Mount Aruṇāchala, some 120 miles southwest of Madras, which had for centuries served as a dwelling place for renunciants. In time he became celebrated for his absolute indifference to bodily needs, and his frequent preference for remaining silent attracted to him a devoted company of followers, many of whom experienced great calm and healing—both physical and psychological—in his presence.

Ramana Maharshi believed that death and evil were MĀYĀ, or illusion, which could be dissipated by the practice of *vicāra*, by which the true self and the unity of all things would be discovered. This he coupled with intense religious devotion, especially to SHIVA and Mount Aruṇāchala itself, as expressed in the HYMNS of his own composition.

RĀMĀNANDA \ˌra-mä-'nən-də\, *also called* Rāmānand, *or* Rāmadatta \ˌram-'dət\ (fl. 14th–15th century?), North Indian BRAHMIN, held by his followers (Rāmānandīs) to be fifth in succession in the lineage of the philosopher-mystic RĀMĀNUJA. According to his standard HAGIOGRAPHY, Rāmānanda left home as a youth and became a SANNYĀSĪ (ascetic) before settling in VARANASI (Banaras) to study Vedic texts, Rāmānuja's philosophy, and yogic techniques. His studies completed, he wandered about teaching and eating with his students, regardless of their CASTE, but the opposition of his upper-caste companions so angered Rāmānanda that he left the lineage to found his own sect, the Rāmānandīs. His original 12 disciples are said to have included at least one woman, members of the lowest castes (including the leatherworker Ravidās), and a Muslim (the mystic KABĪR). However, the almost complete absence of any reference to Rāmānanda in poetry attributed to them has caused some scholars to question the historical veracity of this connection, especially in light of its clear hagiographic utility as a device for anchoring the NIRGUṆA *bhakti* traditions of North India in a SAGUṆA *bhakti* tradition that had historical roots in the South and was superintended by Brahmins.

The connection between the historical Rāmānanda and the important monastic community (Rāmānandīs) that claims him as its founder has also been called into question—both by academic scholars and by a group of "radical Rāmānandīs" in the early 20th century who disputed the Brahmin tie with Rāmānuja. The history of the present Rāmānandī SAMPRADĀYA apparently does not reach back before the 17th century, but this does nothing to diminish the fact that it is the largest Vaiṣṇava monastic order in North India today, and perhaps the largest monastic order of any sectarian affiliation throughout the Indian subcontinent.

RĀMĀNUJA \rä-ˈmä-nủ-jə\, *also called* Rāmānujācārya, *or* Iḷaiya Perumāḷ (Sanskrit and Tamil: "Designations of Lakṣmaṇa") (b. *c.* 1017, Śrīperumbūdūr, India—d. 1137, Śrīraṅgam), South Indian Brahmin theologian and philosopher and probably the single most influential thinker of devotional HINDUISM. He organized temple worship, founded centers to disseminate his doctrine of devotion to VISHNU and his consort LAKṢMĪ, and provided an intellectual basis for the practice of BHAKTI (devotional worship) in three major commentaries: the *Vedārtha-saṃgraha* (on the VEDA), the *Śrī-bhāṣya* (on the *Brahma sūtras*), and the *Bhagavadgītā-bhāṣya* (on the BHAGAVAD GĪTĀ).

According to tradition, Rāmānuja was born in southern India, in what is now Tamil Nadu state. He showed early signs of theological acumen and was sent to Kanchipuram for schooling, under the teacher Yādavaprakāśa, who was a follower of the monistic system of VEDĀNTA of Śaṃkara, the famous 8th-century philosopher. Rāmānuja was soon at odds with a doctrine that offered no room for a personal god. After falling out with his teacher he had a vision of Vishnu and Lakṣmī and instituted a daily worship ritual at the place where he beheld them.

He became a temple priest at the Varadarāja temple at Kanchipuram, where he began to expound the doctrine that the goal of those who aspire to final release from transmigration is not the impersonal BRAHMAN but rather Brahman as represented in the personal god Vishnu. In Kanchipuram, as well as Śrīraṅgam, where he was to become associated with the Raṅganātha temple, he taught that the worship of a personal god and the soul's union with that deity are essential parts of the doctrines of the UPANISHADS on which the system of Vedānta is built; therefore, the teachings of the Vaiṣṇavas and BHĀGAVATAS are not heterodox. In this he continued the teachings of Yāmuna (Yāmunācārya; 10th century), his predecessor at Śrīraṅgam.

Like many Hindu thinkers, he is reported to have made an extended PILGRIMAGE, circumambulating India. In Mysore he converted numbers of Jains, as well as King Bittideva of the Hoyśala dynasty; this led to the founding in 1099 of the town Milukote (Melcote, present Karnataka state) and the dedication of a temple to Śelva Piḷḷai (Sanskrit, Sampatkumāra, the name of a form of Vishnu). He returned after 20 years to Śrīraṅgam, where he reorganized the temple worship and, reputedly, founded 74 centers to disseminate his doctrine. After a life that supposedly lasted 120 years—its length reflecting his eminence—Rāmānuja died in 1137.

Rāmānuja's chief contributions to Indian philosophy follow from his conviction that discursive thought is necessary in the human search for ultimate truth, that the phenomenal world is real and provides real knowledge, and that the exigencies of daily life are not detrimental or even contrary to the life of the spirit. His conception that this world constitutes the body of Vishnu established a metaphysic consonant with *bhakti*. Rāmānuja's explication of the necessity of religious worship as a means of salvation gave systematic meaning to the devotional outpourings of the Āḷvārs, the 7th–10th-century poet-mystics of southern India, justifying the incorporation of their verse into formal temple worship.

Rāmānuja's worldview accepts the ontological reality of three distinct orders: matter, soul, and God. He admits that there is nonduality (*advaita*), an ultimate identity of the three orders, but this nonduality for him is asserted of God, who is modified (*viśiṣṭa*) by the orders of matter and soul; hence his doctrine is known as VIŚIṢṬĀDVAITA ("modified nonduality"). Just as the body modifies the soul, has no separate existence from it, and yet is different from it, just so the orders of matter and soul constitute God's "body," modifying it, yet having no separate existence from it. The goal of the human soul, therefore, is to serve God just as the body serves the soul.

All the phenomenal world is a manifestation of the glory of God (*vibhūti*), and to detract from its reality is to detract from divine glory. Rāmānuja aimed at transforming ritual practice into divine worship and meditation into a continuous pondering of God's qualities; thus both become aspects of loving *bhakti*. Release is not merely a shedding of the bonds of transmigration but a positive quest for the contemplation of God.

RĀMATĪRTHA \ˌrä-mə-ˈtir-tə\, *also spelled* Rama Tirtha, *original name* Tirath Ram (b. 1873, Mīrāliwāla, Punjab province, India [Pakistan]—d. Oct. 17, 1906, Tehri, United Provinces of Agra and Oudh [India]), Hindu religious leader who taught what he styled "Practical VEDĀNTA," using common experiences to illustrate the divine nature of human beings. For Rāmatīrtha, any object whatever could be approached as a "mirror to God."

Educated at the Foreman Christian College and Government College, Lahore, in 1895 Tirath Ram was appointed a professor of mathematics at Foreman Christian College. A meeting with the Bengali ascetic VIVEKANANDA strengthened his inclination toward religious study and the desire to spend his life in the propagation of the system of ADVAITA Vedānta. He helped to found an Urdu journal, *Alif*, in which many of his articles on Vedānta appeared.

In 1901 Tirath Ram went into seclusion in the HIMALAYAS, but later he emerged to travel to Japan and the United States. Rāmatīrtha (the name by which he then became known) advocated a "wholesale liberation of mankind, beginning with the personal liberation of the individual." His mystical leanings were coupled with an appreciation of Western science and technology as a means of solving India's social and economic problems, and he never failed to

Rāma and Lakṣmaṇa are attacked with a nāgapāśa,
a magical noose; from the Rāmāyaṇa
Art Resource

support public education in all forms. He died by drowning
in the Gaṅgā River; whether by accident or design is still a
matter of conjecture among his followers.

RĀMĀYAṆA \rä-'mä-yə-nə\ (Sanskrit: "Story of Rāma"),
great epic poem of India, whose oldest extant form, attributed to the poet Vālmīki, was composed in Sanskrit, probably not before 300 BCE. In its present "Vulgate" form it consists of some 24,000 couplets.

Vālmīki's poem describes the royal birth of RĀMA in the
kingdom of AYODHYĀ (Oudh), his tutelage under the sage Viśvāmitra, and his success in bending Shiva's mighty bow at
the bridegroom tournament of SĪTĀ, the daughter of King
Janaka, thus winning her for his wife. After Rāma is banished from his position as the result of a family intrigue, he
retreats to the forest with his wife and his favorite half
brother, Lakṣmaṇa, to spend 14 years in exile. There RĀVA-
ṆA, the demon-king of Laṅkā, carries off Sītā, while her two
protectors are busy pursuing a golden deer sent to the forest
to mislead them. After numerous adventures Rāma and his
brother enter into alliance with Sugrīva, king of the monkeys; and with the assistance of the monkey-general HANU-
MĀN and Rāvaṇa's own brother, Vibhīṣana, they attack
Laṅkā. Rāma slays Rāvaṇa and rescues Sītā, who in a later
version undergoes an ordeal by fire to clear herself of any
suspicion of infidelity while in Rāvaṇa's domain. When

Rāma and Sītā return to Ayodhyā, however, the people
question the queen's chastity, and Rāma banishes her to
the forest. There she meets the sage Vālmīki (the reputed
author of the *Rāmāyaṇa*) and at his hermitage gives birth
to Rāma's two sons. The family is reunited when the sons
come of age, but Sītā, after again protesting her innocence,
asks to be received by the earth, who initially bore her, and
the earth swallows her up.

Exploring perennial tensions between humanity and divinity, duty (DHARMA) and devotion (BHAKTI), civilization and
wilderness, rulership and renunciation, the *Rāmāyaṇa* enjoys immense popularity in India. Its recitation is considered an act of great merit. It is even better known in India's
spoken languages than in Sanskrit, and it functions less as a
single text than as an encompassing narrative complex that
encourages constant acts of questioning, interpretation,
and reshaping. For many devotees Sītā and Hanumān are its
focus as much or more than Rāma.

Throughout North India the events of the poem are enacted in an annual pageant, the Rām LĪLĀ, which may last as
long as a month, and in South India the two epics, the *Rāmāyaṇa* and the MAHĀBHĀRATA, make up the ancient story
repertoire of the kathakali dance-drama of Kerala. The story has spread in various forms throughout Southeast Asia
(especially Cambodia, Indonesia, and Thailand), where
Rāma and Sītā are held up as exemplars with every bit the
intensity that one finds in India. Their romance—tragic in
many of its aspects—is one of the world's great love stories.

RĀMCARITMĀNAS \'rām-ˌchə-rit-'mä-nəs\ ("Sacred Lake of
the Acts of Rāma"), 16th-century version of the RĀMĀYAṆA,

written by the poet TULSĪDĀS in Avadhī, an eastern dialect of Hindi. Distinguished by its expression of love for a personal god; its exemplification of the ideal conduct of a husband and ruler (RĀMA), wife (SĪTĀ), brother (Lakṣmaṇa), and servant-devotee (HANUMĀN); and its incorporation of SHIVA and PĀRVATĪ as narrators of this Vaiṣṇava epic, the *Rāmcaritmānas* has had a remarkable influence on modern HINDUISM. It has proved even more popular than the *Bhagavad Gītā* and was sometimes perceived by British missionaries as the BIBLE of North India—the primary SCRIPTURE to be reckoned with if Christian evangelism was to succeed. It is sung, recited, and enacted in numerous contexts, both in India and abroad, and served as the basis for the most widely watched television series in India's history, the 1987–88 *Rāmāyaṇa* of Ramanand Sagar.

RĀMDĀS \'räm-'däs\ (b. 1534, Lahore, Punjab, India [now Pakistan]—d. 1581, Amritsar), fourth Sikh GURŪ (1574–81) and founder of the great Sikh center of AMRITSAR. Unlike Goindvāl, the seat of his predecessor Guru Amardās (1552–74), the location of Amritsar lay at a distance from the direct Mughal gaze, providing the Sikhs a period of 30 or so years to organize themselves into an effective unit. RĀMDĀS wrote over 400 hymns of great beauty that appear in the ĀDI GRANTH. He nominated his younger son, ARJAN (1563–1606), as his successor.

RĀMPRASĀD SEN \'räm-prə-ˌsäd-'sen\, 18th-century Śākta poet-saint of Bengal. Not much is known with certainty about his life. Legends abound, however, all of which are meant to highlight Rāmprasād's all-encompassing love for and devotion to the goddess ŚAKTI. One such tale concerns the poet's early career as a clerk for an accountant in a wealthy household in Calcutta. Rāmprasād's obsession with the Goddess precluded paying much attention to his work; every day he would sit at his desk and fill his account book with the name of the deity or with a song like this one: "Make me your accounts clerk, O Mother, I will never betray your trust. . . . Let me die at those feet of yours which dispel all misfortunes, In that position I will be safe from all dangers." According to the story, when the master of the household saw this poem he released Rāmprasād from his duties and supplied him with a stipend so that the poet could devote himself fully to service to the Goddess. Rāmprasād is said to have been later associated with the court of Raja Krishnachandra of Krishnagore and to have composed a work called *Bidyasundar*, containing both erotic and Tantric elements, under the Raja's patronage.

Rāmprasād is reputed to have composed some 100,000 songs, some of which became extremely popular among his followers, who regard them as sacred MANTRAS. The Goddess Rāmprasād portrays is sometimes beautiful, nurturing, and even erotic and at other times grotesque, dangerous, and fickle. Rāmprasād contributed to a revival of ŚĀKTISM and Tantricism in Bengal and also, in the wake of increased Western presence in India, identified the Goddess with MOSES and JESUS as well as with the Hindu deities.

RANJIT SINGH \rən-'jit-'siŋ-gə, 'rən-jit, -'siŋ\, *also spelled* Runjit Singh (b. Nov. 13, 1780, Budrukhan, or Gujrānwāla, India—d. June 27, 1839, Lahore [now in Pakistan]), founder and maharaja (1801–39) of the Sikh kingdom of the Punjab.

At the turn of the 19th century, Ranjit Singh created a large Sikh kingdom that included the Mughal provinces of Lahore, Kashmir, and parts of Multan and Kabul. A great warrior and an able administrator, he helped materialize the 18th-century Sikh dream of the KHĀLSĀ Rāj, the Kingdom of God on earth. In the process, he built a large Sikh army trained along European lines. His descendants, however, failed to keep control of his vast kingdom, which ultimately fell to the British in 1849.

Ranjit Singh believed in benevolent monarchy. There was no capital punishment in his administration. Even when there were

Ranjit Singh leading his men on horseback, Indian miniature painting, c. 1850

attempts on his life, his attackers were let go. He donated 7 percent of his revenue to charitable grants. A large number of new grants came to the Sikhs, but the existing grants to non-Sikh establishments were permitted to continue. It was during his reign that the GOLDEN TEMPLE (Darbār Sāhib) in AMRITSAR attained the features that have made it famous as a physical structure: its domes were covered with gold-plated copper, and its walls were rebuilt in marble inlaid with precious stones. Ranjit Singh's reign is often seen as a golden chapter in the history of SIKHISM.

RAPITHWIN \\'rä-pith-win, rä-'pith-\\, in ZOROASTRIANISM, personification of summer and noonday, the time of the midday meal. The NEW YEAR FESTIVAL, Noruz, is celebrated in Rapithwin's honor as a solemn and joyful celebration of new life in nature and the anticipated RESURRECTION of the body at the end of times.

RASA \\'rə-sə\\ (Sanskrit: "aesthetic flavor"), concept developed by Indian philosophers in their theoretical treatments of Hindu temple artwork. *Rasa* consists of a kind of contemplative abstraction in which the inwardness of human feelings irradiates the surrounding world of embodied forms. The theory of *rasa* is attributed to Bharata, a sage-priest who may have lived about 500 CE. It was developed by the rhetorician and philosopher ABHINAVAGUPTA (c. 1000 CE), who applied it to all varieties of theater and poetry. The principal human feelings, according to Bharata, are delight, laughter, sorrow, anger, fear, disgust, heroism, and astonishment, all of which may be recast as contemplative *rasas*: erotic, comic, pathetic, furious, terrible, odious, marvelous, and quietistic. These *rasas* comprise the components of aesthetic experience. The power to taste *rasa* is a reward for merit in some previous existence.

RASHI \\'rá-shē\\, *acronym of* Rabbi Shlomo Yitzḥaqi \\shlō-'mō-yis-'hä-kē\\ (b. 1040, Troyes, Champagne—d. July 13, 1105, Troyes), renowned medieval French commentator on the BIBLE and TALMUD. His commentary is considered a landmark in Talmudic EXEGESIS, and his work still serves among Jews as the most substantive introduction to biblical and postbiblical JUDAISM. Rashi also composed some penitential hymns (*seliḥot*), which revolve around the harsh reality of exile and the comforting belief in redemption.

Shlomo (Solomon) Yitzḥaqi (son of Isaac) studied in the schools of Worms and Mainz, the old Rhenish centers of Jewish learning, where he absorbed the methods, teachings, and traditions associated with RABBI GERSHOM BEN JUDAH (c. 960–1028/40), who was called the "Light of the Exile" because of his preeminence as the first great scholar of northern European Judaism. Rashi then left for the valley of the Seine (c. 1065), where he was the unofficial head of the small Jewish community (about 100–200 people) in Troyes.

In his Bible commentary, which was the first book printed in Hebrew (1475), Rashi seeks the literal meaning, deftly using rules of grammar and syntax and carefully analyzing both text and context, but does not hesitate to mount Midrashic explanations, utilizing ALLEGORY, PARABLE, and SYMBOLISM, upon the underlying literal interpretation. As a result, some of his successors have been critical of his searching literalism and deviation from traditional Midrashic exegesis, while others find his excessive fondness for nonliteral homilies uncongenial. The commentary had a significant influence on Christian Bible study from the 12th-century Victorines to the FRANCISCAN scholar Nicholas of Lyra (c. 1270–1349), who, in turn, was a major source of

MARTIN LUTHER'S Bible work. Its influence continues in contemporary exegesis and revised translations.

Rashi's commentary on the Talmud, sometimes referred to as *kuntros* (literally, "notebook"), seeks to explain the text in its entirety, guides the student in methodological and substantive matters, resolves linguistic difficulties, and indicates the normative conclusions of the discussion. Unlike Maimonides' commentary on the MISHNAH, which may be read independently of the underlying text, Rashi's commentary is interwoven with the underlying text.

Rashi's work was epochal, and the agreement of subsequent scholars that the basic needs of text commentary had been fulfilled stimulated the rise of a new school of writers known as *tosafists*, who composed TOSAFOT (glosses), refining, criticizing, expanding, or qualifying Rashi's interpretations and conclusions.

RASHĪD RIḌĀ, MUHAMMAD \\rà-'shēd-rē-'dä\\ (b. 1865, Syria—d. 1935, Syria), Syrian scholar who helped Muslims formulate an intellectual response to the problem of reconciling the heritage of ISLAM to the modern world.

Rashīd Riḍā was educated in Islamic religion and the Arabic language. He was profoundly influenced in his early years by the writings of MUHAMMAD 'ABDUH and JAMĀL AL-DĪN AL-AFGHĀNĪ, Muslim reformist and nationalist thinkers, and he became 'Abduh's biographer and the leading exponent and defender of his ideas. Rashīd Riḍā founded the newspaper *al-Manār* in 1898 and published it throughout his life. To a limited extent, he also participated in the political affairs of Syria and Egypt.

He was concerned with the backwardness of the Muslim countries, which he believed resulted from a neglect of the true principles of ISLAM. He believed that these principles could be found in the teachings of the Prophet MUHAMMAD and in the practices of the first generation of Muslims, before corruptions began to spread among the religious practices of the faithful (c. 655). He was convinced that positive effort to improve the material basis of the community was of the essence of Islam.

Rashīd Riḍā urged Arabs to emulate the scientific and technological progress made by the West. In the political affairs of the Muslim community, he wanted rulers to respect the authority of the men of religion and to consult with them in the formulation of governmental policies. He sanctioned the bending of Islam to fit the demands of modern times in other important respects; for example, the Prophet had forbidden the taking of interest, but Rashīd Riḍā believed that, to combat effectively the penetration of Western capitalism, Muslims had to accept the practice.

To realize a political and cultural revival, Rashīd Riḍā saw the need to unify the Muslim community. He advocated the establishment of a true CALIPH, who would be the supreme interpreter of Islam and whose prestige would enable him to guide governments in the directions demanded by an Islam adapted to the needs of modern society.

RASHĪDŪN \\,rà-shi-'dün\\ (Arabic: "Rightly Guided"), first four CALIPHS of the Islamic community, known in Muslim history as the orthodox or patriarchal caliphs: Abū Bakr (reigned 632–634), 'Umar (reigned 634–644), 'UTHMĀN (reigned 644–656), and 'ALĪ (reigned 656–661).

The 29-year rule of the Rashīdūn was Islam's first experience without the leadership of the Prophet MUHAMMAD. His example, however, in both private and public life, came to be regarded as the norm (SUNNA) for his successors, and a large and influential body of *anṣār* (COMPANIONS OF THE

907

PROPHET) kept close watch on the caliphs to ensure their strict adherence to the QUR'AN and the *sunna.* The Rashīdūn thus assumed all of Muhammad's duties except the prophetic: as IMAMS, they led the congregation in prayer at the mosque; as *khaṭībs,* they delivered the Friday sermons; and as *umarā' al-mu'minīn* ("commanders of the faithful"), they commanded the army.

The caliphate of the Rashīdūn, in which virtually all actions had religious import, began with the wars of the *ridda* ("apostasy"; 632–633), tribal uprisings in Arabia, and ended with the first Muslim civil war (*fitna*; 656–661). It effected the expansion of the Islamic state beyond Arabia into Iraq, Syria, Palestine, Egypt, Iran, and Armenia. The Rashīdūn were also responsible for the adoption of an Islamic calendar, dating from Muhammad's emigration (HIJRA) from MECCA to MEDINA (622), and the establishment of an authoritative reading of the Qur'an, which strengthened the Muslim community and encouraged religious scholarship. The controversy over 'Alī's succession split ISLAM into two divisions, the SUNNI (traditionalists) and the SHI'ITE (*shi'at 'Alī,* "party of 'Alī"), which have survived to modern times.

The religious and very traditionalist strictures on the Rashīdūn were somewhat relaxed as Muhammad's contemporaries, especially the *anṣār,* began to die off, and the conquered territories became too vast to rule along theocratic lines; thus the Umayyads, who followed the Rashīdūn as caliphs, were able to secularize the operations of the state.

RASHNU \'rash-nü, 'räsh-\, in ZOROASTRIANISM, the deity of justice, who with MITHRA, the god of truth, and SRAOSHA, the god of religious obedience, determines the fates of the souls of the dead. Rashnu is praised in a *yasht,* or hymn, of the AVESTA; the 18th day of the month is sacred to Rashnu.

The name Rashnu originally may have referred to AHURA MAZDĀ, the supreme Iranian god, and to Mithra, in their capacities as judges. Rashnu eventually took over their functions and now stands on the Bridge of the Requiter (Rashnu himself), where, assisted by Mithra and Sraosha, he weighs on his golden scales the deeds of the souls that wish to pass in order to determine their futures. The divine triad may attempt to intercede for souls and obtain forgiveness for their SINS.

RASHTRIYA SEVA SANGH \'räsh-trē-yä-'sā-vä-'səŋ-gə, -'soŋg\, *also called* Rashtriya Swayamsevak Sangh \-,svə-yəm-'sā-vək-\ ("National Volunteer Organization") *or* RSS, organization founded in 1925 by Keshav Baliram Hedgewar (1889–1940), a physician living in the Mahārāshtra region of India, as part of the movement against British rule and as a response to rioting between Hindus and Muslims.

Hedgewar was heavily influenced by the writings of the Hindu nationalist ideologue VINAYAK DAMODAR SAVARKAR and adopted much of his rhetoric concerning the need for the creation of a "Hindu nation." Hedgewar formed the RSS as a disciplined cadre consisting mostly of upper-caste Brahmins who were dedicated to independence and the protection of Hindu political, cultural, and religious interests. Upon Hedgewar's death, leadership of the group was assumed by Madhava Sadashiv Golwalkar and later by Madhhukar Dattatray Deoras.

The RSS presents itself as a cultural, not a political, organization that nevertheless advocates a Hindu nationalistic agenda under the banner of HINDUTVA, or "Hindu-ness." The group is structured hierarchically under the guidance of a national leader, while regional leaders are charged with overseeing the local branches. A major emphasis is placed on dedication and discipline, both mental and physical, as a means to restore strength, valor, and courage in Hindu youth and to foster unity among Hindus of all CASTES and classes. Paramilitary training and daily exercise and drills are part of this discipline.

The RSS has historically played a major role in the Hindu nationalist movement. On several occasions it has been banned by the Indian government, led by the Congress Party, for its alleged role in communal violence. Some of the major political leaders of India's Bharatiya Janatā Party were or still are members of the RSS.

A Rastafarian man in Jamaica wears his hair in the traditional dreadlocks
Chester Higgins, Jr.—Photo Researchers

RASTAFARIAN \,ras-tə-'fer-ē-ən, ,räs-tə-'fär-\, *also spelled* Ras Tafarian, member of a politico-religious movement among the black population of Jamaica and several other countries. Rastafarians worship Haile Selassie I, former emperor of Ethiopia, under his precoronation name, Ras (Prince) Tafari. They believe him to have been a divine being and the champion of the black race. According to the Rastafarians, blacks are the Israelites reincarnated and have been subjected to the evil and inferior white race in divine punishment for their sins; they will eventually be redeemed by repatriation to Africa, their true home and heaven on earth, and will compel the whites to serve them.

These beliefs, first enunciated in 1953, can be traced to several independent prophets and particularly to the Back to Africa movement led by Marcus Garvey in the early 20th century. The various groups that make up the Rastafarians rejected Jamaica's

European-oriented culture and Christian revivalist religion and developed their own identity while awaiting the exodus. From the early 1950s the Rastafarian movement grew in complexity. The identification with Africa remained, but repatriation received less emphasis and the Rastafarians began to lean toward either political black militancy or a MYSTICISM supported by the OLD TESTAMENT and incorporating African forms. Rastafarian lifestyle may include dietary rules (often vegetarianism), the wearing of uncombed locks and beards, and the smoking of ganja (marijuana).

RATANA CHURCH \rə-'tä-nə\, 20th-century religious awakening among the New Zealand Maori and a national political influence, especially during the period 1943–63, when its members held all four Maori parliamentary seats in the national capital.

The Ratana church was founded by Tahupotiki Wiremu Ratana, a Methodist Maori farmer who acquired a reputation as a visionary and faith healer, preaching a doctrine of moral reform under the one God of the BIBLE that drew Maori (and some whites) from all parts of New Zealand. In 1920 he established an interdenominational church at the village of Ratana Pa. Ratana's movement gave new hope and a trans-tribal unity to the Maori, who had many grievances against the New Zealand government.

The association of Ratana's movement with other Christian denominations ended in 1925. The self-proclaimed Ratana church had developed a syncretic Maori CHRISTIANITY, marked by heterodox rituals and an elaborate hierarchy of religious officials; HYMNS and prayers glorified Ratana as God's *mangai* ("mouth-piece"). Displeased by these developments, several of New Zealand's Anglican bishops denounced the new religion. Furthermore, the doctrine of FAITH HEALING discouraged the taking of medicines, a fact that alienated religious and secular authorities alike.

Combining political activism with its RELIGIOUS BELIEFS, the Ratana church began to sponsor political candidates in 1922. Although it was not until 1931 that a Ratana candidate was elected, the church eventually established a position in which it could exercise some political power.

In the 1960s the church renewed relationships with other Christian churches in New Zealand and reemphasized the original biblical principles of Ratana.

RATHAYĀTRĀ \ˌrə-tə-'yä-trä\, festival of India, observed by taking an image of a deity in a procession through the streets. This affords *darśan* (auspicious viewing) of the deity to worshipers who, because of CASTE or sectarian restrictions, are not admitted to the SANCTUARY. It also dramatizes the Hindu conviction that however much the power of an image deity may be associated with a particular, familiar place, that power has a wider orbit as well. The most famous Rathayātrā festival is that of KRISHNA worshiped as JAGANNĀTHA, which takes place at Puri in Orissa and at Shrīrāmpur in West Bengal, but many similar festivals for other deities are observed in India and Nepal. Important images may be carried on elaborately carved wooden chariots, which are often extremely large and heavy, requiring hundreds of worshipers to pull them, while village deities may travel on far simpler, lighter palanquins.

RATIONALISM, *also called* intellectualism, mode of analysis that, with respect to religion, regards religion as a more or less systematic and comprehensive attempt to explain the world or the experience of the world. Thus, rationalism views religion as primarily a cognitive, explanatory phenomenon. This view of religion was especially popular during the late 19th and early 20th century and aroused interest again at the close of the 20th century.

The classic texts on the intellectualist theory of the nature of religion can be found in the work of Sir Edward Burnett Edward Tylor (*Primitive Culture*, 1871) and SIR JAMES GEORGE FRAZER (*The Golden Bough*, 1890). For them, religion, like science, is an attempt to explain the world. Both were at pains to point out that to say religion is rational is not to claim that religion is true. Robin Horton (*Patterns of Thought in Africa and the West*, 1993) and Melford E. Spiro (*Burmese Supernaturalism*, 1967) are contemporary exponents of this approach to religion.

RAUSCHENBUSCH, WALTER \'raù-shən-ˌbùsh\ (b. Oct. 4, 1861, Rochester, N.Y., U.S.—d. July 25, 1918, Rochester), clergyman and theology professor who led the SOCIAL GOSPEL movement in the United States.

Rauschenbusch was the son of a Lutheran missionary. On June 1, 1886, he was ordained a minister of the Second German BAPTIST Church in New York City, where he became aware of social problems because of the personal distress he encountered in a depressed neighborhood and because of the mayoral campaign based on a social-welfare platform by the economist Henry George. Even more influential, however, were two young Baptist preachers, Leighton Williams and Nathaniel Schmidt. Together with Rauschenbusch they formed a Society of Jesus, which was later expanded into the Brotherhood of the Kingdom. *For the Right*, a monthly periodical "in the interests of the working people," was launched in November 1889 in an effort to reach the working classes and to aid in the formulation of a Christian socialist program. Publication ceased in March 1891 when Rauschenbusch left for a year of study in Germany and a visit to England, where he became interested in Fabian socialism. In 1897 he joined the faculty of Rochester Theological Seminary and in 1902 became professor of church history.

Upon the publication of *Christianity and the Social Crisis* (1907), Rauschenbusch gained recognition as the major spokesman of the Social Gospel movement in the United States. He believed that the KINGDOM OF GOD required social as well as individual salvation, and he demanded "a new order that would rest on the Christian principles of equal rights and democratic distribution of economic power."

RĀVAṆA \'rä-və-nə\, in HINDUISM, ferocious, fabulously wealthy demonic (*rākṣasa*) king. His abduction of SĪTĀ and eventual defeat by her husband RĀMA are the central incidents of the RĀMĀYAṆA. Rāvaṇa ruled in the kingdom of Laṅkā, believed by some to be modern Sri Lanka, from which he had expelled his brother KUBERA. The Rām LĪLĀ festival, popular particularly in northern India, is climaxed with the defeat of Rāvaṇa and the burning of huge effigies of the DEMONS on the festival day called DASSEHRA.

Rāvaṇa is described as having 10 heads and 20 arms and is vividly portrayed in painting and sculpture throughout India. Glorification of Rāvaṇa is not unknown. According to a minor tradition, the demons of VISHNU are successive REINCARNATIONS of his attendants, who take this form in order to be near him. In modern times, Tamil groups who oppose what they believe to be the political domination of southern India by the north have come to view the story of Rāma as exemplifying the ARYAN invasion of the south and consequently express their sympathies for Rāvaṇa and against Rāma.

RAVIDĀS \ˌrə-vi-ˈdäs\, *also known as* Raidas, mystic and poet-saint of the 15th or 16th centuries. Ravidās was born in VARANASI as a member of an UNTOUCHABLE leather-working CASTE and became one of the most renowned of the saints of the North Indian BHAKTI movement. His poems and songs often revolve around his low social position. While objecting to the notion that caste plays a fundamental role in an individual's relationship to God, Ravidās contrasted his own lowliness to the exalted place of the divine: God, he said, was finer than he, as silk was to a worm, and more fragrant than he, as sandalwood was to the stinking castor oil plant. In relation to God, all persons, no matter what their castes, are "untouchables," and "A family that has a true follower of the Lord is neither high caste nor low caste, lordly nor poor." Ravidās' CHARISMA and reputation were such that Brahmins were said to have bowed before him.

Some 40 of the poems attributed to Ravidās were included in the *Ādi Granth*, the Sikh SCRIPTURE, and it is generally accepted that Ravidās met NĀNAK, the founding GURŪ of the Sikh tradition. In the 19th and 20th centuries a new religious movement formed around his figure; a temple was built in his hometown where he was worshiped, his HYMNS were recited every morning and night, and his birthday was celebrated as a religious event. His egalitarian teachings made him a figure of veneration and pride among various DALIT social reform movements of the 20th century.

RE \ˈrā\, *also spelled* Ra \ˈrä\, *or* Phre, in ancient EGYPTIAN RELIGION, god of the sun and creator god. He was believed to travel across the sky in his solar bark and, during the night, to make his passage in another bark through the underworld, where, in order to be born again for the new day, he had to vanquish the evil serpent APOPIS. As the creator, he rose from the ocean of CHAOS on the primeval hill, creating himself and then engendering eight other gods.

By the 4th dynasty (*c.* 2575–*c.* 2465 BCE), Re had taken his leading position. Many syncretisms were formed between Re and other gods, producing such names as Re-Harakhty, Amon-Re, Sebek-Re, and Khnum-Re. Re's falcon-headed appearance as Re-Harakhty originated through association with HORUS. The influence of Re was spread from On (HELIOPOLIS), which was the center of his worship. From the 4th dynasty, kings held the title "Son of Re," and "Re" later became part of the throne name they adopted at accession. As the father of MA'AT, Re was the ultimate source of right and justice in the cosmos.

At Thebes, by the late 11th dynasty (*c.* 1980 BCE), Re was associated with AMON as Amon-Re, who was for more than a millennium the principal god of the pantheon and the patron of kings. The greatest development of solar religion was during the New Kingdom (1539–*c.* 1075 BCE). The revolutionary worship of the sun disk ATON during the abortive Amarna period (1353–1336 BCE) was a radical simplification of the cult of Re. During the New Kingdom, beliefs about Re were harmonized with those concerning OSIRIS, the ruler of the Underworld.

REANIMATION RITE, in EGYPTIAN RELIGION, rite to prepare the deceased for afterlife, performed on statues of the deceased, the MUMMY itself, or statues of a god located in a temple. An important element of the ceremony was the ritual opening of the mouth so the mummy might breathe and eat. The rite, which symbolized the death and regeneration concept of the OSIRIS myth (in which the dismembered god Osiris was pieced together again and infused with life), was performed on a statue in the sculptor's workshop, but on a mummy it was performed at the tomb entrance. By this rite the statue or mummy was endowed with life and power so that he might enjoy the daily funeral service conducted before his tomb. In the case of temple statues, the ceremony was included in the daily temple ritual.

RECHABITE \ˈre-kə-ˌbīt\, member of a conservative, ascetic Israelite sect that was named for Rechab, the father of Jehonadab. The Rechabites apparently were related to the KENITES (a tribe eventually absorbed into JUDAH in the 10th century BCE) according to 1 Chronicles 2:55.

The Rechabites were separatists who refused to participate in agricultural pursuits, drink wine, or engage in any practices associated with the Canaanites or the worship of their god BAAL. Believing that the seminomadic way of life was a religious obligation, they herded their flocks over much of Israel and Judah. They are best known for their connection with the slaughter of the worshipers of Baal during the revolt led by JEHU, a 9th-century-BCE king of Israel. According to later tradition, the Rechabites intermarried with the LEVITES.

RECONSTRUCTIONISM, American Jewish religious movement based on the teachings of RABBI Mordecai Kaplan. All of its institutions—the Jewish Reconstructionist Federation (founded 1954, with 100 affiliates in 1998), the Reconstructionist Rabbinical College (founded 1968), and the Reconstructionist Rabbinical Association (founded 1974)—are based in Philadelphia.

Following Kaplan's definition of JUDAISM as the evolving religious civilization of the Jewish people, Reconstructionists emphasize the formation of intensive, participatory decision-making communities in which contemporary Jews can embrace their Jewish heritage. Rabbis serve as teachers who enable communities of Jews to immerse themselves in Jewish learning and practice and thus to decide democratically the policies of their communities.

Reanimation rite, from the Egyptian Book of the Dead, *Hunefer Papyrus*
By courtesy of the trustees of the British Museum

Wearing a traditional turban, a Muslim prays in the Great Mosque in Ṣanʻāʼ, Yemen
R&S Michaud—Photo Researchers

(Opposite page) Roman Catholic cardinals
Reuters—Paolo Cocco/Archive Photos

(Above) Russian Orthodox patriarch
Reuters—Yuri Romanov/Archive Photos

(Left) Hindu sadhu, or holy man
Reuters—Sunil Malhotra/Archive Photos

Ordination ceremony for Buddhist monks
Photo Researchers

Communion service at a Lutheran seminary

Apache medicine man with an eagle-bone whistle
David Weintraub—Photo Researchers

Jain monks

Shintō priest at a shrine near Tokyo
Marcello Bertinetti—Photo Researchers

Orthodox Jewish rabbi wearing ṭallit and phylacteries
Reuters—David Gray/ Archive Photos

Girl with body paint for puberty ritual, Monrovia, Liberia
Thomas S. England—Photo Researchers

Beginning with the introduction of the first bat mitzvah (*see* BAR MITZVAH) ceremony in 1922, Reconstructionist communities have been committed to full gender equality. Women play a prominent role in the movement's leadership, and the movement's prayer books are gender neutral and include alternative, feminist God language. The initial inclusion of women has led to the inclusion of all Jews who have traditionally been excluded, including lesbian and gay Jews, and intermarried families.

While Reconstructionist theology pictures God in naturalistic terms, Reconstructionist communities are known for their spirited, fervent prayer and singing, and for their embrace of Jewish meditation and other practices that deepen one's internal, contemplative life. High percentages of Reconstructionists observe the dietary laws and other ritual practices—not because they believe that such practice is commanded by God but rather because of the meaning they find in it and the way that ritual and prayer open up the treasures of the tradition. In this regard as in all others, pluralism and respect for diversity are the norm.

Reconstructionist communities are also known for their emphasis on social action that provides Jewish contexts for addressing injustice and for adapting Jewish ethical teachings to contemporary moral dilemmas. While Reconstructionists have always been Zionists, they tend to align themselves with progressive forces who work for justice and peace in the Middle East.

RECUSANT \'re-kyə-zənt, ri-'kyü-\, English ROMAN CATHOLIC from the period about 1570 to 1791 who refused to attend services of the Church of England and thereby committed a statutory offense.

RED HEIFER, *Hebrew* para adumma, in Jewish history, unblemished, never-before-yoked animal that was slaughtered and burned to restore ritual purity to those who had become unclean through contact with the dead (Numbers 19). Certain spoils of war and captives were also purified in this way. After the blood had been sprinkled by a priest, the carcass was immolated with cedarwood, hyssop, and a scarlet thread. The ashes were carried to a clean place and mixed with water in an earthen vessel. A sprinkling of the mixture restored purity to all who had taken part in the ritual.

In SYNAGOGUES the command to sacrifice a red heifer to restore ritual purity is read on *Shabbat Para*, a special SABBATH that precedes by a few weeks the festival of PASSOVER.

REDUCTIONISM, theory that asserts that entities of a given kind are collections or combinations of entities of a simpler or more basic kind or that expressions denoting such entities are definable in terms of expressions denoting the more basic entities. Thus, the ideas that physical bodies are collections of atoms or that thoughts are combinations of sense impressions are forms of reductionism. Within religious studies, the reductionist position would be one in which RELIGIOUS BELIEFS are explained by reference to basically nonreligious sentiments, sociopsychological circumstances, and other factors.

Two very general forms of reductionism have been held by philosophers in the 20th century: (1) Logical positivists have maintained that expressions referring to existing things or to states of affairs are definable in terms of directly observable objects, or sense-data, and, hence, that any statement of fact is equivalent to some set of empirically verifiable statements. In particular, it has been held that the theoretical entities of science are definable in terms of observable physical things, so that scientific laws are equivalent to combinations of observation reports. (2) Proponents of the unity of science have held that the theoretical entities of particular sciences, such as biology or psychology, are definable in terms of those of some more basic science, such as physics; or that the laws of these sciences can be explained by those of the more basic science.

The logical positivist version of reductionism also implies the unity of science insofar as the definability of the theoretical entities of the various sciences in terms of the observable would constitute the common basis of all scientific laws. Although this version of reductionism is no longer widely accepted, primarily because of the difficulty of giving a satisfactory characterization of the distinction between theoretical and observational statements in science, the question of the reducibility of one science to another remains controversial.

REFORMATION, religious revolution that took place in the Western Christian church in the 16th century. Having far-reaching political, economic, and social effects, the Reformation became the basis for the founding of PROTESTANTISM, one of the three major branches of CHRISTIANITY.

Over the centuries, the church had become deeply involved in the political life of western Europe. The resulting intrigues and political manipulations, combined with the church's increasing power and wealth, led to such abuses as SIMONY (the sale of INDULGENCES, or spiritual privileges) and corruption of the clergy.

The Reformation of the 16th century was not unprecedented. Reformers within the medieval church such as ST. FRANCIS, Peter Waldo, JAN HUS, and JOHN WYCLIFFE addressed abuses in the life of the church in the centuries before 1517. In the 16th century, ERASMUS of Rotterdam was the chief proponent of liberal Catholic reform that attacked moral abuses and popular superstitions in the church. These movements reveal an ongoing concern for reform within the church in the years before MARTIN LUTHER is said to have posted his NINETY-FIVE THESES on the door of the Castle Church, Wittenberg, on Oct. 31, 1517, the eve of All Saints' Day—the traditional date for the beginning of the Reformation.

Luther sought to attack what he considered to be the theological root of corruption in the life of the church—the perversion of the church's doctrine of redemption and GRACE. A pastor and professor at the University of Wittenberg, he attacked the indulgence system in his Ninety-five Theses, insisting that the POPE had no authority over PURGATORY and that the doctrine of the merits of the saints had no foundation in the GOSPEL. Here lay the key to Luther's concerns for the ethical and theological reform of the church; SCRIPTURE alone is authoritative (*sola sciptura*) and JUSTIFICATION is by faith (*sola fide*), not by works. While he did not intend to break with the Catholic church, in 1521 Luther was tried before the Imperial DIET OF WORMS and was eventually excommunicated; thus, what had begun as an internal reform movement had become a fracture in western Christendom.

Other reform movements arose independently of Luther. HULDRYCH ZWINGLI built a Christian theocracy in Zürich in which CHURCH AND STATE were combined. Zwingli agreed with Luther in the centrality of the doctrine of justification by faith, but he espoused a more radical understanding of the EUCHARIST. Luther had rejected the Catholic Church's doctrine of TRANSUBSTANTIATION, according to which the bread and wine in the Eucharist became the actual body and blood of Christ. According to Luther's doctrine of the Eucharist, the body of Christ was truly present in the elements because Christ is present everywhere, but Zwingli went further to claim that the Eucharist was simply a memorial of the death of Christ and a declaration of faith by the recipients.

From the group surrounding Zwingli emerged those more radical than himself—the Radical Reformers, who insisted that the principle of scriptural authority be applied without compromise. They broke with Zwingli over the issue of infant BAPTISM, thereby receiving the nickname "ANABAPTISTS" on the grounds that they rebaptized adults who had been baptized as children. The Swiss Anabaptists sought to follow the example of JESUS found in the Gospels. They refused to swear OATHS or bear arms, taught the strict separation of church and state, and insisted on the visible church of adult believers—distinguished from the world by its disciplined, regenerated life.

Another important form of Protestantism is CALVINISM, named for JOHN CALVIN, a French lawyer who fled France after his conversion to the Protestant cause. In Basel, Calvin brought out the first edition of his *Institutes of the Christian Religion* in 1536, the first systematic theological treatise of the reform movement. Calvin agreed with Luther's teaching on justification by faith. However, he found a more positive place for law within the Christian community than did Luther. In Geneva, Calvin was able to experiment with his ideal of a disciplined community of the ELECT in a combination of church and state under Calvin's forceful leadership.

The Reformation spread to other European countries over the course of the 16th century. By mid-century, LUTHERANISM dominated northern Europe, and eastern Europe offered a seedbed for even more radical varieties of Protestantism. Spain and Italy were to be the great centers of the COUNTER-REFORMATION, and Protestantism never gained a strong foothold there.

In England the Reformation's roots were primarily political. Henry VIII, incensed by Pope Clement VII's refusal to grant him a divorce, repudiated papal authority and in 1534 established the Anglican Church with the king as the supreme head (*see* ANGLICAN COMMUNION). Henry's reorganization of the church permitted the beginning of religious reform in England, which included the preparation of a liturgy in English, THE BOOK OF COMMON PRAYER. In Scotland, JOHN KNOX, who was greatly influenced by John Calvin, led the establishment of Presbyterianism, which made possible the eventual union of Scotland with England.

REFORMED CHURCH, any of several major representative groups of classical PROTESTANTISM that arose in the 16th-century REFORMATION. Originally, all of the Reformation churches used this name (or the name Evangelical) to distinguish themselves from the "unreformed" ROMAN CATHOLIC church. After the controversy among these churches over the Lord's Supper (after 1529), the followers of Luther began to use the name Lutheran as a specific name, and the name Reformed became associated with the Calvinistic churches (and also for a time with the Church of England). Eventually the name PRESBYTERIAN, which denotes the form of church polity used by most of the Reformed churches, was adopted by the Calvinistic churches of British background. The modern Reformed churches thus trace their origins to the Continental Calvinistic churches that retained the original designation of "reformed in accordance with the word of God."

REFORM JUDAISM, religious movement that has modified or abandoned many traditional Jewish beliefs, laws, and practices in an effort to adapt JUDAISM to the changing conditions of the modern world.

The movement began in early 19th-century Germany, when the liberation of Jews from their ghettos led many to question their allegiance to such traditions as dietary laws, prayers in Hebrew, and special clothing that set them apart as Jews. Many felt that Judaism would lose Jews to other religions if it was not brought into the 19th century.

Israel Jacobson (1768–1828), a layman, established a school in Seesen, Brunswick, in 1801, where he held the first Reform services in 1809, attended by adults as well as children. Jacobson's liturgy, which was in German rather than Hebrew, omitted all references to a personal MESSIAH who would restore ISRAEL. Men and women sat together, the service featured organ and choir music, and CONFIRMATION for both boys and girls replaced the traditional boys' BAR MITZVAH ceremony. Jacobson held Reform services in Berlin in 1815; and from there Reform practices spread to Denmark, Hamburg, Leipzig, Vienna, and Prague. Although the Prussian government issued prohibitions under pressure from Orthodox leaders, the movement grew. Reform worshipers were no longer required to cover their heads or wear the prayer shawl (TALLIT). Daily public worship was abandoned; work was permitted on the Sabbath; and dietary laws (KASHRUTH) were declared obsolete.

RABBI ABRAHAM GEIGER (1810–74), one of the leading ideologists of the Reform movement, concluded that the essence of Judaism is belief in the one true God of all mankind, the practice of eternally valid ethical principles, and the communication of these truths to all nations of the world. SAMUEL HOLDHEIM (1806–60) rejected Jewish marriage and divorce laws as obsolete, arguing that such codes fell outside the ethical and doctrinal functions of Judaism and were superseded by the laws of the state.

Reform Judaism took root in the United States in 1841 when a congregation in Charleston, S.C., joined the movement. Rabbi ISAAC MAYER WISE (1819–1900), a German emigrant, issued a widely influential prayer book (1857) and established the UNION OF AMERICAN HEBREW CONGREGATIONS (1873), the Hebrew Union College (1875) for the education of Reform rabbis, and the CENTRAL CONFERENCE OF AMERICAN RABBIS (1889). Two other emigrants, David Einhorn (1809–79) and SAMUEL HIRSCH (1815–89), provided the theoretical foundations of American Reform. Hirsch was chairman of the first conference of American Reform rabbis, which met in Philadelphia in 1869. It rejected belief in bodily RESURRECTION after death and declared that Jews should no longer expect a return to Palestine. The question of ZIONISM was controversial within the Reform movement until the establishment of the state of Israel in 1948.

In 1937 a conference of Reform rabbis issued the COLUMBUS PLATFORM, supporting the use of traditional customs and ceremonies and the liturgical use of Hebrew. In the late 20th century the Central Conference of American Rabbis issued several new prayer books and continued to consider such issues as inclusion of single parents in the congregation, the position of women in the congregation and in the rabbinate, and homosexuality.

REINCARNATION, *also called* transmigration, *or* metempsychosis, belief in the rebirth of the soul in one or more successive existences, which may be human, animal, or, in some instances, vegetable. While belief in reincarnation is most characteristic of Asian religions and philosophies, it also appears in the religious and philosophical thought of indigenous religions, in some ancient Middle Eastern religions (*e.g.*, the Greek Orphic mysteries), MANICHAEISM, and some Gnostic movements, as well as in such modern religious movements as THEOSOPHY.

In indigenous religions, belief in multiple souls is common. The soul is frequently viewed as being capable of leaving the body through the mouth or nostrils and of being reborn, for example, as a bird, butterfly, or insect. The Venda of southern Africa believe that, when a person dies, the soul stays near the grave for a short time and then seeks a new resting place or another body—human, mammalian, or reptilian.

Among the ancient Greeks, Orphism held that there is a preexistent soul that survives bodily death and is later reincarnated in a human or other mammalian body, eventually receiving release from the cycle of birth and death and regaining its former pure state. Plato, in the 5th–4th century BCE, believed in an immortal soul that participates in frequent incarnations.

The Asian religions, especially HINDUISM, JAINISM, BUDDHISM, and SIKHISM (all of which arose in India) hold in common a doctrine of KARMA ("act"), the law of cause and effect, which states that what one does in this present life will have its effect in the next life. In Hinduism the process of birth and rebirth—*i.e.*, transmigration of souls—is endless until one achieves MOKSHA, or salvation, by realizing the truth that liberates—*i.e.*, that the individual soul (ĀTMAN) and the absolute soul (BRAHMAN) are one. Thus, one can escape from the wheel of birth and rebirth (SAMSĀRA).

Jainism, reflecting a belief in an absolute soul, holds that karma is affected in its density by the deeds that a person does. Thus, the burden of the old karma is added to the new karma that is acquired during the next existence until the soul frees itself by religious disciplines, especially by AHIMSĀ ("noninjury"), and rises to the place of liberated souls at the top of the universe.

Although Buddhism denies the existence of an unchanging, substantial soul, it holds to a belief in multiple existences. A complex of psycho-physical elements and states changing from moment to moment, the self, composed of the five SKANDHAS ("groups of elements")—*i.e.*, body, sensations, perceptions, impulses, and consciousness—ceases to exist at the individual's death, but the karma of the deceased conditions the birth of a new self. By becoming a monk and practicing discipline and meditation, one can stop the wheel of birth and rebirth and achieve NIRVANA, the extinction of desires and suffering.

Sikhism teaches a doctrine of reincarnation based on the Hindu view but in addition holds that, after the LAST JUDGMENT, souls—which have been reincarnated in several existences—will be absorbed in God.

REINDEER SACRIFICE, Upper Paleolithic and Mesolithic religious practice among various northern European and Asian peoples, consisting primarily of submerging a young doe in a lake or pond or burying it in the ground. The submerging or burial of these reindeer may indicate that prehistoric man believed that the god of the hunt resided underground. Other personal possessions often were thrown into the water or buried near the reindeer. On special occasions, Mesolithic hunters set up the skull and antlers of an older reindeer on a pole at the edge of the pool.

RELATIVISM, view that what is right or wrong and good or bad is not absolute but is instead variable and relative, de-

pending on the person, circumstances, or social situation. Relativism is the view that what is really right depends solely upon what the individual or the society thinks is right. Because what one thinks will vary with time and place, what is right will also vary accordingly. Relativism is, therefore, a view about the truth status of cognitive and moral principles, according to which changing and even conflicting moral principles are equally true, so that there is no objective way of justifying any principle as valid for all people and all societies.

The sociological argument for relativism proceeds from the diversity of different cultures. Ruth Benedict, an American anthropologist, suggested, for example, in *Patterns of Culture* (1934) that the differing and even conflicting moral beliefs and behavior of the North American Indian Kwakiutl, Pueblo, and Dobu cultures provided standards that were sufficient within each culture for its members to evaluate correctly their own individual actions. Thus, relativism does not deprive one of all moral guidance. However, some anthropologists, such as Clyde Kluckhohn and Ralph Linton, have pointed up certain "ethical universals," or cross-cultural similarities, in moral beliefs and practices—such as prohibitions against murder, incest, untruth, and unfair dealing—that are more impressive than the particularities of moral disagreement, which can be interpreted as arising within the more basic framework that the universals provide. Some critics point out, further, that a relativist has no grounds by which to evaluate the social criticism arising within a free or open society, that such views, in fact, appear to undercut the very idea of social reform.

A second argument for relativism holds that moral utterances are not cognitive statements, verifiable as true or false, but are, instead, emotional expressions of approval or disapproval or are merely prescriptions for action. In this view, variations and conflicts between moral utterances are relative to the varying conditions that occasion such feelings, attitudes, or prescriptions, and there is nothing more to be said. Critics of this view may observe that, even if moral utterances are not cognitive, it does not follow that they are related, as the relativist suggests, only to the changeable elements in their background; they may also be related in a special way to needs and wants that are common and essential to human nature and society everywhere and in every age. If so, these needs can provide good reasons for the justification of some moral utterances over others. The relativist will then have to reply either that human nature has no such common, enduring needs or that, if it does, they cannot be discovered and employed to ground man's moral discourse.

The basic problem with all relativist claims is that at least one assertion is not relative to some context; the claim that all truth is relative.

RELIC, in religion, strictly, the mortal remains of a saint; in the broad sense, any object that has been in contact with the saint. Among the major religions, CHRISTIANITY, almost exclusively in ROMAN CATHOLICISM, and BUDDHISM have emphasized the veneration of relics.

The basis of Christian cult veneration of relics is the conception that reverence for the relics redounds to the honor of the saint. While expectation of favors may accompany the devotion, it is not integral to it. The first Christian reference to relics speaks of handkerchiefs carried from the body of ST. PAUL to heal the sick. During the 2nd century CE, in the *Martyrdom of Polycarp*, the bones of the martyred bishop of Smyrna are described as "more valuable than precious stones." The veneration of relics continued and grew in Christianity. Generally, the expectation of miracles increased during the Middle Ages, while the flood of Oriental relics into Europe during the Crusades raised serious questions as to their authenticity and ethical procurement. ST. THOMAS AQUINAS, however, considered it natural to cherish the remains of the saintly dead and found sanction for the veneration of relics in God's working of miracles in the presence of relics.

Roman Catholic thought, defined in 1563 at the COUNCIL OF TRENT and subsequently affirmed, maintained that relic veneration was permitted and laid down rules to assure the authenticity of relics and exclude venal practices. Among the most venerated of Christian relics were the fragments of the TRUE CROSS. In EASTERN ORTHODOXY, devotion is focused on ICONS rather than upon relics, though the antimension (the cloth upon which the divine liturgy is celebrated) always contains a relic. The veneration of relics has not been widely accepted in PROTESTANTISM.

Like Christianity, ISLAM has had a cult of relics associated with its founder and with saints. In Islam, however, the use of relics has had no official sanction; indeed, Muslim theologians have frequently denounced the veneration of relics and the related practice of visiting the tombs of saints as conflicting with the Prophet Muhammad's insistence on his own purely human, nondivine nature and his stern condemnation of IDOLATRY and the worship of anyone other than God himself.

Relic worship was canonically established in Buddhism from its earliest days. Tradition (*Mahāparinibbāna Sutta*) states that the cremated remains of the BUDDHA GOTAMA (d. *c.* 483 BCE) were distributed equally among eight Indian kings in response to a demand for his relics. Commemorative mounds (STUPAS) were built over these relics, over the vessel from which the bones were distributed, and over the collective ashes of the funeral pyre. The emperor AŚOKA (3rd century BCE) is said to have redistributed some of the relics among the innumerable stupas he had erected. Such shrines became important centers of PILGRIMAGE.

According to legend, seven bones (the four canine teeth, the two collarbones, and the frontal bone) were exempted from the primary distribution, and these have been the object of widespread devotion, with a number of shrines dedicated to them throughout Asia. Most famous of these *sar-*

A relic, the cassock of St. Francis of Assisi; in the sacristy of the church of Santa Croce, Florence
Scala—Art Resource

īra ("corporeal relics") is the left canine tooth, honored at the TEMPLE OF THE TOOTH at Kandy, Sri Lanka. Other shrines reportedly have housed certain personal possessions of the Buddha, such as his staff or alms bowl. In addition, the bodily remains and personal effects of the great Buddhist saints and heroes are also venerated. In TIBETAN BUDDHISM, worship is accorded the carefully preserved bodies of the DALAI LAMAS, who are regarded as REINCARNATIONS of a heavenly being, the Bodhisattva AVALOKITEŚVARA.

RELIGION, ANTHROPOLOGY OF, STUDY OF RELIGION via the methods of anthropology.

Anthropology began with an interest in questions of origins and evolution. One early attempt was that of the English anthropologist John Lubbock (1834–1913). His book, *The Origin of Civilisation and the Primitive Condition of Man* (1870), outlined an evolutionary scheme, beginning with ATHEISM and continuing with fetishism, nature worship, TOTEMISM, shamanism, ANTHROPOMORPHISM, MONOTHEISM, and, finally, ethical monotheism. The English ethnologist SIR EDWARD BURNETT TYLOR (1832–1917) expounded, in his book *Primitive Culture* (1871), the thesis that ANIMISM is the earliest and most basic religious form. Out of this evolves fetishism, belief in DEMONS, POLYTHEISM, and, finally, monotheism, which derives from the exaltation of a great god in a polytheistic context. A somewhat similar system was advanced by Herbert Spencer (1820–1903) in his *The Principles of Sociology* (1876–96), though he stresses ANCESTOR WORSHIP rather than animism as the basic consideration.

Another important figure in the development of theories of religion was the British folklorist SIR JAMES FRAZER (1854–1941), in whose major work, *The Golden Bough* (1890), is set forth a mass of evidence to establish the thesis that humans must have begun with magic and progressed to religion and from that to science. He owes much to Tylor but places magic in a phase anterior to belief in supernatural powers that have to be propitiated—this belief being the core of religion. Because of the realization that magical rituals do not in fact work, primitive man then turns, according to Frazer, to reliance on supernatural beings that are outside his control, beings who need to be treated well and with respect if they are to cooperate with human purposes. With further scientific discoveries and theories, such as the mechanistic view of the operation of the universe, religious explanations gave way to scientific ones. Frazer's scheme is reminiscent of that of the French "father of sociology," Auguste Comte.

The German Roman Catholic priest and ethnologist Wilhelm Schmidt (1868–1954) brought anthropological expertise to bear in a series of investigations of such indigenous societies as those of the Tierra del Fuegians (South America), the Negrillos of Rwanda (Africa), and the Andaman Islanders (Indian Ocean). The results were assembled in his *Der Ursprung der Gottesidee* ("The Origin of the Idea of God"), which appeared in 12 volumes from 1912 to 1955. Not surprisingly, Schmidt and his collaborators saw in various HIGH GODS a sign of a primordial monotheistic revelation that later became overlaid with other elements. While controversial, Schmidt's approach produced grounds for rejecting the earlier rather naive theory of evolutionism. Modern scholars do not, on the whole, accept Schmidt's scheme; it is a very long jump from the premise that primitive tribes have high gods to the conclusion that the earliest humans were monotheists.

Functional and structural studies of religion. Through the course of the 20th century, anthropologists became more concerned with functional and structural accounts of religion in society and relinquished the apparently futile search for origins. Notable among these accounts was the theory of the French sociologist ÉMILE DURKHEIM (1858–1917). According to Durkheim, totemism was fundamentally significant (he wrongly supposed it to be virtually universal), and in this he shared the view of some other 19th-century savants, notably Salomon Reinach (1858–1932), Robertson Smith (1846–94), and SIGMUND FREUD (1856–1939). Because Durkheim treated the totem as symbolic of the god, he inferred that the god is a representation of the clan. This conclusion, if generalized, suggested that all the objects of religious worship symbolize social relationships and, indeed, play an important role in the continuance of the social group.

Various forms of FUNCTIONALISM in anthropology—which understood social patterns and institutions in terms of their function in the larger cultural context—proved illuminating for religion. The Polish-British anthropologist BRONISŁAW MALINOWSKI (1884–1942), for instance, emphasized in his work on the Trobriand Islanders (New Guinea) the close relationship between myth and ritual—a point also made emphatically by the "myth and ritual" school of the history of religions. Also, many anthropologists, notably Paul Radin (1883–1959), moved away from earlier categorizations of so-called primitive thought and pointed to the crucial role of creative individuals in the process of mythmaking.

A rather different approach to myths was made by the 20th-century French anthropologist Claude Lévi-Strauss, whose structuralist analysis tended to reinforce analogies between "primitive" and sophisticated thinking and also provided a new method of analyzing myths and stories. His views had wide influence, though they are by no means universally accepted by anthropologists.

Claude Lévi-Strauss
AP—Wide World Photos

Specialized studies. The impact of Western culture, including missionary CHRISTIANITY, and technology upon a wide variety of primitive and tribal societies has had profound effects and represents a specialized area of study closely related to religious anthropology. One pioneering work is *The Religions of the Oppressed* (1963) by the Italian anthropologist and historian of religion Vittorio Lanternari. Among a number of contemporary anthropologists, including the American Clifford Geertz, there is a concern with exploring more deeply and concretely the symbolism of cultures. The English social anthropologist E.E. Evans-Pritchard (1902–73), noted among other things for his work on the religion of Nuer people (of The Sudan), produced in his *Theories of Primitive Religion* (1965) a penetrating critique of many earlier anthropological stances.

RELIGION, DEFINITION OF, any attempt to formulate a description of religion that is adequate for all religions, past and present. Most introductions to the STUDY OF RELIGION stress the difficulty of defining religion and then append a list of definitions as illustrative of the problem. In fact, defining religion is not difficult at all—the list demonstrates only that there is little agreement among scholars, whose definitions reflect their particular interests. Thus, a definition of religion that specifies religion as a representation of social relations is obviously rooted in the social sciences. If one were interested in psychology, one might define religion as a symbolic representation of mental, or unconscious, reality. If one were more theologically or metaphysically minded, one might insist on defining religion as the ultimate concern, as a feeling of absolute dependence, or as a representation of the sacred. Since the first two definitions are dependent on a theory of religion, the adequacy of the sociological or psychological theory concerned will determine the adequacy of the definition. Since theological and metaphysical definitions refer to a transcendental reality, the means for checking their adequacy is lacking; we accept them on faith or as a commitment to a tradition.

Most definitions of religion are not helpful largely because they are vague or ambiguous. For instance, suppose religion to be defined as "worldview"; are all worldviews religions? If so, it would seem that just about anything can become a religion. Similarly, if religion is defined as the "ultimate concern," is concern with holding onto a job religious? If religion is defined as "the sacred," the question usually asked is "What is the sacred?"—a sure sign that the definition is not very helpful.

Other definitions of religion are too restrictive. The definition "belief in God" is a good example. Although it includes all monotheistic religions, it excludes all polytheistic religions, and those religions that do not believe in a god at all. To define religion as belief in the "supernatural" or "transcendental" reality is also too restrictive, since some cultures deny such realities. These examples demonstrate that empirical evidence is available to test the adequacy of our definition of religion.

A definition that has received reasonable acceptance among scholars is as follows: religion is a system of communal beliefs and practices relative to superhuman beings. This definition moves away from defining religion as worldview or as some kind of special experience. It emphasizes that religion is a communal system or structure related to superhuman beings. Superhuman beings are beings that can do things we cannot do. Their miraculous powers set them apart from ordinary mortals. They can be either male or female, neither, or both, and they can take the form of ancestors, gods, goddesses, or spirits. They can be malevolent or benevolent or both. What is important is the relation of these beings to specific communal beliefs and practices, the myths and rituals of particular human beings. This definition excludes Nazism, Marxism, SECULARISM, humanism, and other -isms, including nationalism and other quasi-religious movements. Except for its stress on system or structure this definition is theoretically neutral and empirically verifiable.

RELIGION, ORIGIN OF, subject within the STUDY OF RELIGIONS. The quest for the origin of religion was a popular academic enterprise at the beginning of the 20th century and is to be seen in the works of the economist and historian Karl Marx, of the sociologist ÉMILE DURKHEIM, and of the psychologist SIGMUND FREUD. This quest is directly related to the quest for the meaning of religion; that is, if we can determine the origin of religion we might be able to determine its meaning. Thus, for Freud, in the beginning was "the deed"—religion grew out of experiences surrounding certain primal actions. For Durkheim it was the appearance of the "collective conscience," as society itself was deified in symbolic, totemic form. For the anthropologist SIR EDWARD BURNETT TYLOR the origin of religion was to be found in the first human attempts to explain experience. For other scholars MYSTICISM was the origin, indeed the very essence, of religion.

Two counterarguments seek to put an end to the quest for origins. The first argues from the basis that the quest is sheer conjecture: none of these claims can ever hope to be proven. The second argues from linguistic grounds: the meaning of religion, like the meaning of language, cannot be explained by a study of its history or origin, even if we could discover them. That is, to know the meaning of English is to know something other than its history or origin. Nevertheless, in the late 20th century conjectures concerning the origin once again came to the fore in the study of religion, as they did in linguistics.

RELIGION, PHENOMENOLOGY OF \fi-,nä-mə-'nä-lə-jē\, approach to the STUDY OF RELIGION that is descriptive rather than historical or a causal explanation of its existence. Phenomenologists of religion also contrast their study of religion from normative approaches to religion such as theology, metaphysics, or PHILOSOPHY OF RELIGION. Gerardus van der Leeuw's *Phänomenologie der Religion* (1933; *Religion in Essence and Manifestation*) remains the classic text of this movement in the study of religion. Van der Leeuw describes the method as (1) entailing a suspension of one's beliefs and preconceptions about the reference of religion; (2) perceiving religion on its own terms, or essence; (3) using a comparative approach to reveal what is essential in religion; and (4) maintaining a proper understanding or empathy of religion to prevent a reduction of religion to another plane of explanation. Most phenomenologists of religion have claimed that the proper understanding of religion views the essence of religion as a manifestation of "the Sacred" or "the Holy." Rudolf Otto's *Das Heilige* (1917; *The Idea of the Holy*) is considered a classic account of this position. Mircea Eliade's *Das Heilige und das Profane* (1957; *The Sacred and the Profane*) is a good example of a contemporary statement of this approach to the study of religion.

Critics of this approach have focused on the claims of neutrality and "value-free" descriptions of religion, pointing out that the concept of "the Sacred" or "the Holy" are for the most part reinterpretations of Christian theology.

RELIGION, PHILOSOPHY OF, academic discipline which attempts to (1) analyze and describe the nature of religion in the framework of a general view of the world; (2) defend or attack various religious positions in terms of philosophy; and (3) analyze RELIGIOUS LANGUAGE. Thus, much of philosophy of religion is concerned with questions not so much of the description of religion (historically and otherwise) as with the truth of religious claims. For this reason philosophy can easily become an adjunct of theology or of antireligious positions; thus, it is often difficult to disentangle descriptive problems from those bearing on the truth of the content of what is being described. The following brief account of philosophical trends leans toward those theories that have a stronger content of, or relevance to, descriptive claims about religion.

Theories of Hume and Kant. Studies of religion in the late 17th and 18th centuries reflected the growing RATIONALISM of the epoch. The Scottish philosopher David Hume (1711–76) argued in such works as *Enquiry Concerning Human Understanding* (first published in 1748 under another title), *Natural History of Religion* (1757), and the posthumous *Dialogues Concerning Natural Religion* (1779) that there can be no true knowledge of anything beyond direct experience. These considerations dispose of all the classical arguments for the existence of God, as such arguments are not based on the requisite empirical evidence. Whatever order man discerns in the world around him, he argued, should be attributed to the universe itself and not to any postulated outside cause. Hume's distinctive contribution was methodological: the contention that the principles and presuppositions upon which the critical historian must rely, in first interpreting the remains of the past as historical evidence and in then building up from this evidence his account of what actually happened, are such as to make it impossible for him "to prove a miracle and make it a just foundation for any such system of religion."

The culmination of 18th-century rationalism was found in the works of the German philosopher Immanuel Kant (1724–1804), but it was a rationalism modified to leave room for religion, which he based essentially on ethics. He held that all men in their awareness of the categorical imperative (*i.e.*, the notion that one must act as though what one does can become the universal law for mankind) and reverence for it share in the one religion and that the preeminence of CHRISTIANITY lay in the conspicuous way in which JESUS CHRIST enshrined the moral ideal.

Theories of Schleiermacher and Hegel. Kant's system depended on drawing certain distinctions, such as that between pure and practical reason, which were open to challenge. One reaction that attempted to place religion as neither primarily to do with pure nor with practical reason was that of the German theologian and philosopher FRIEDRICH SCHLEIERMACHER (1768–1834), who, in his *On Religion: Speeches to Its Cultured Despisers*, written in 1799, attempted to carve out a territory for RELIGIOUS EXPERIENCE distinct from both science and morality. For him the central attitude in religion is "the feeling of absolute dependence." In drawing attention to the affective and experiential side of religion, Schleiermacher set in motion the modern concern to explore the subjective or inner aspect of religion. Schleiermacher's main goal was the construction of a new type of theology—the "theology of consciousness." In so doing he relegated doctrines to a secondary role, their function being to express and articulate the deliverances of religious consciousness.

Georg Wilhelm Friedrich Hegel (1770–1831) argued that

religion arises as the relation between man and the Absolute (the spiritual reality that undergirds and includes the whole universe), in which the truth is expressed symbolically, and so conveyed personally and emotionally to the individual. As the same truth is known at a higher—that is, more abstract—level in philosophy, religion is ultimately inferior to philosophy. The Hegelian account of religion was worked out in the context of the dialectical view of history, according to which opposites united in a synthesis, which in turn produced its opposite, and so on.

Empiricism and logical positivism. In the 19th century the Hegelian school was very influential, particularly in the study of early Christianity, but it attracted some radical criticism (*see also* KIERKEGAARD, SØREN). Hegelianism entered a period of rapid decline in the early part of the 20th century. The common sense and scientifically oriented philosophy of G.E. Moore (1873–1958) and Bertrand Russell (1872–1970) introduced a period of EMPIRICISM in Britain, while William James's PRAGMATISM had a similar effect in the United States. (On the continent of Europe, the increasing influence of existentialism after World War I was also hostile to the old type of metaphysics.) British empiricism was expressed very strongly in logical positivism (maintaining the exclusive value of scientific knowledge and the denial of traditional metaphysical doctrines). This stimulated the analysis of religious language, and the movement was complicated by the transformation in the thought of Ludwig Wittgenstein (1889–1951), who in his later work was very far removed from his early, rather formalistic treatment of language.

Though Wittgenstein stressed the idea of "forms of life," according to which the meaning of RELIGIOUS BELIEFS would have to be given a practical and living contextualization, little has been done to pursue the idea empirically. The analytic attempt to exhibit the nature of religious language has generally occurred in the context of questions of truth—thus some scholars have been concerned with exhibiting how it is possible to hold religious beliefs in an empiricist framework, and others with showing the meaninglessness or incoherence of belief.

Existentialist and phenomenological studies. The most influential modern existentialists have been Martin Heidegger (1889–1976) and Jean-Paul Sartre (1905–80); the former was especially important in the development of modern European theology, particularly for the use made of some of his ideas by RUDOLF BULTMANN. According to Heidegger, human existence is characterized as "care." This care is shown first in possibility: one makes things instrumental to one's concerns and so projects forward. Secondly, there is one's facticity, for a person exists as a finite entity with particular limitations. Heidegger's term for this limit on existence is *Geworfenheit* ("thrownness"), by which he means, for instance, that one does not choose to have existence, does not choose the time one finds oneself in, but is instead *thrown* into that existence or time without choice. Thirdly, humans seek to avoid the anxiety of their limitations and thus seek what Heidegger termed "inauthentic" existence. Authenticity, on the other hand, involves a kind of stoicism (positive attitude toward life and suffering) in which death is taken up as a possibility and one faces the "nothing." The structure of the world as analyzed by Heidegger is revealed, in a sense, affectively—*i.e.*, through care, anxiety, and other existential attitudes and feelings.

Sartre's thought has had less direct impact on the study of religion, partly because his account of human existence

represents an explicit alternative to traditional religious belief. Sartre's analysis begins, however, from the human desire to be God: but God is, on Sartre's analysis, a self-contradictory notion, for nothing can contain the ground of its own being. In searching for an essence humans fail to see the nature of their freedom, which is to go beyond definitions, whether laid down by God or by other human beings.

Edmund Husserl (1859–1938) has been the main exponent of phenomenology, and his program of describing experience and "bracketing" the objects of experience, in the pursuit of essences of types of experience, was in part taken up in the PHENOMENOLOGY OF RELIGION. Husserl distinguished phenomenology from psychology, in that the latter concerns facts in a spatiotemporal setting, whereas phenomenology intends to uncover timeless essences.

RELIGION, PSYCHOLOGY OF, study of religious psychology involves both the gathering and classification of data and the building and testing of various (usually rather wide-ranging) explanations. The former activity overlaps with the PHENOMENOLOGY OF RELIGION, so it is to some extent an arbitrary decision under which head one should include descriptive studies of RELIGIOUS EXPERIENCE.

Psychological studies. Notable among investigations by psychologists was *The Varieties of Religious Experience* (1902), by the American philosopher and psychologist William James (1842–1910), in which he attempted to account for experiences such as conversion through the concept of invasions from the unconscious. Because of the clarity of his style and his philosophical distinction, the work has had a lasting influence, though it is dated in a number of ways and his examples come from a relatively narrow selection of individuals, largely within the sphere of Protestant CHRISTIANITY. This points to a recurring problem in the field—that of relating individual psychology to the institutions and symbols of different cultures and traditions.

William James
By courtesy of the Harvard University News Service

More radical, but drawing from a rather larger range of examples, was the American psychologist J.H. Leuba (1868–1946). In *A Psychological Study of Religion* (1912) he attempted to account for mystical experience psychologically and physiologically, pointing to analogies with certain drug-induced experiences. Leuba argued forcibly for a naturalistic treatment of religion, which he considered to be necessary if religious psychology was to be looked at scientifically. Others, however, have argued that psychology is in principle neutral, neither confirming nor ruling out belief in the transcendent.

Psychoanalytical studies. More influential than James and Leuba and others in that tradition were the psychoanalysts. SIGMUND FREUD gave explanations of the genesis of religion in various of his writings. In *Totem and Taboo* (1918) he applied the idea of the OEDIPUS complex (involving unresolved sexual feelings of, for example, a son toward his mother and hostility toward his father) and postulated its emergence in the primordial stage of human development. This stage he conceived to be one in which there were small groups, each dominated by a father. According to Freud's reconstruction of primordial society, the father is displaced by a son (probably violently); further attempts to displace the new leader bring about a truce in which incest taboos (proscriptions against intrafamily sexual relations) are formed. The slaying of a suitable animal, symbolic of the deposed and dead father, connected TOTEMISM with taboo. His ideas were also developed in *Moses and Monotheism* (1939) and *The Future of an Illusion* (1928).

The Swiss psychoanalyst C.G. Jung (1875–1961) adopted a very different posture, one that was more sympathetic to religion and more concerned with a positive appreciation of religious symbolism. Jung considered the question of the existence of God to be unanswerable by the psychologist and adopted a kind of AGNOSTICISM. Yet he considered the spiritual realm to possess a psychological reality that cannot be explained away. Jung postulated, in addition to the personal unconscious (roughly as in Freud), the collective unconscious, which is the repository of human experience and which contains "archetypes" (*i.e.*, basic images that are universal in that they recur in independent cultures). The irruption of these images from the unconscious into the realm of consciousness he viewed as the basis of religious experience and often of artistic creativity. Religion can thus help people, who stand in need of the mysterious and symbolic, in the process of individuation—of becoming individual selves. Some of Jung's writings have been greatly influential in stimulating the investigations of other interested scholars. Thus, the Eranos circle, a group of scholars meeting around the leadership of Jung, contributed considerably to the history of religions. Associated with this circle of scholars have been MIRCEA ELIADE, the eminent Romanian-French historian of religion, and the Hungarian-Swiss historian of religion Károly Kerényi (1897–1973). This movement has been one of the main factors in the modern revival of interest in the analysis of myth.

Among other psychoanalytic interpreters of religion, the American scholar Erich Fromm (1900–80) modified Freudian theory and produced a more complex account of the functions of religion. Part of the modification is viewing the Oedipus complex as based not so much on sexuality as on the childish desire to remain attached to protecting figures. The right religion, in Fromm's estimation, can, in principle, foster an individual's highest potentialities, but religion in practice tends to relapse into being neurotic.

Other studies. Apart from Jung's work, there have been various attempts to relate psychoanalytic theory to comparative material. Thus, the English anthropologist Meyer Fortes, in his *Oedipus and Job in West African Religion* (1959), combined elements from Freud and Durkheim; and G.M. Carstairs (a British psychologist), in *The Twice-Born* (1957), investigated in depth the inhabitants of an Indian town from a psychoanalytic point of view and with special reference to their RELIGIOUS BELIEFS and practices. Among the more systematic attempts to evaluate the evidences of the various theories is *Religious Behaviour* (1958), by Michael Argyle, another British psychologist.

A certain amount of empirical work in relation to the effects of meditation and mystical experience—and also in relation to drug-induced "higher" states of consciousness—has also been carried on. Investigation of religious responses as correlated with various personality types is another area of enquiry; and developmental psychology of

religion, largely under the influence of the French psychologist Jean Piaget (1896–1980), has played a prominent part in educational theory in the teaching of religion.

RELIGION, SOCIOLOGY OF, approach to the STUDY OF RELIGION grounded in the methods and assumptions of sociology. Auguste Comte (1798–1857) is usually considered the founder of modern sociology. His general theory hinged substantially on a particular view of religion, and this view has somewhat influenced the sociology of religion since that time. In his *The Positive Philosophy of Auguste Comte* (1853) Comte expounded a naturalistic positivism and sketched out the following stages in the evolution of thought. First, there is what he called the theological stage, in which events are explained by reference to supernatural beings; next, there is the metaphysical stage, in which more abstract unseen forces are invoked; finally, in the positivistic stage, humans seek causes in a scientific and practical manner. Among the leading figures in the development of sociological theories were Herbert Spencer (1820–1903), in his work *The Principles of Sociology* (1876–96), and ÉMILE DURKHEIM (1858–1917), in his classic work *The Elementary Forms of the Religious Life* (1915).

A rather separate tradition was created by the German economic theorist Karl Marx (1818–83). A number of Marxists, notably Lenin (1870–1924) and K. Kautsky (1854–1938), have developed social interpretations of religion based on the theory of the class struggle. Whereas sociological functionalists posited the existence in a society of some religion or a substitute for it, the Marxists implied the disappearance of religion in a classless society. Thus, in their view, religion in the human primordial communist condition, at the dawn of the historical dialectic, reflects ignorance of natural causes, which are explained animistically. The formation of classes leads, through alienation, to a projection of the need for liberation from this world into the transcendental or heavenly sphere. Religion, both consciously and unconsciously, thus becomes an instrument of exploitation. Since the theory was a product of a rather early and unsophisticated stage of theorizing about religion, it did not deal particularly well with the role of religion in other cultures—which led to a considerable debate in China on the status of Chinese religion in the light of Marxism, some holding that Marx's critique did not, for example, fit BUDDHISM.

Comparative studies. One of the most influential theoreticians of the sociology of religion was the German scholar MAX WEBER (1864–1920). He observed that there is an apparent connection between PROTESTANTISM and the rise of capitalism, and in *The Protestant Ethic and the Spirit of Capitalism* (1930) he accounted for the connection in terms of Calvinism's inculcating a this-worldly asceticism—which created a rational discipline and work ethic, together with a drive to accumulate savings that could be used for further investment. Weber noted, however, that such a thesis ought to be tested; and a major contribution of his thinking was his systematic exploration of other cultural traditions from a sociological point of view. He wrote influentially about ISLAM, JUDAISM, and Indian and Chinese religions and, in so doing, elaborated a set of categories, such as types of PROPHECY, the idea of CHARISMA (spiritual power), routinization, and other categories, which became tools to deal with the comparative material; he was thus the real founder of comparative sociology.

Other sociological studies. Coordination between sociology and the history of religions is not usually very close, since the two disciplines operate as separate departments in most universities and often in different faculties. From the sociological end, Weber represents one kind of synthesis; from the history-of-religions end, the writings of the German-American scholar JOACHIM WACH were quite influential. In his book *Sociology of Religion* (1944) he attempted to exhibit the ways in which the community institutions of religion express certain attitudes and experiences. This view was in accordance with his insistence on the practical and existential side of religion, over against the intellectualist tendency to treat the correlate of the group as being a system of beliefs.

Among the more recent theorists of the sociology of religion is the influential and eclectic American scholar Peter Berger. In *The Sacred Canopy* (1967; also published as *The Social Reality of Religion*, 1969) he draws on elements from Marx, Durkheim, Weber, and others, creating a lively theoretical synthesis. One problem is raised by his method, however; despite Berger's sympathy in dealing with religious phenomena, the methodological stance adopted in this book seems to imply a reductionist position—namely, one in which religious beliefs are explained by reference to basically nonreligious sentiments, sociopsychological circumstances, and other factors. Although the study of religion cannot rule out *a priori* the thesis that religion is a projection—*e.g.*, that it rests upon an illusion—the question arises as to whether or not the methods espoused in the scientific study of religion have already secretly prejudged the issue.

On the whole, modern sociology is largely geared to dealing with Western religious institutions and practices, although there is some notable work that has been done, especially since World War II, in Asian sociology of religion. Emphasis has been placed upon the process of secularization in a number of Western sociological studies (which have had some impact on the formation of modern Christian theology), notably in *The Secular City* (1965) of the American theologian Harvey Cox. There are indications, however, that the process of secularization does not occur in the same degree or occurs in a different manner in non-Western cultures.

In general, the main question of the sociology of religion concerns the effectiveness with which it can relate to other studies of religion. This question is posed in *The Scientific Study of Religion* (1970), by the American sociologist J. Milton Yinger. A similar tendency is noted in the synthesis between the history and the sociology of religion in a new-style evolutionism propounded by another American scholar, Robert Bellah.

RELIGIONSGESCHICHTLICHE SCHULE \ˌre-li-ˈgyōns-gə-ˈshikt-li-ḵə-ˈshü-lə\ (German: "history of religions"), *also called* Religionswissenschaft \-ˈvi-sən-ˌshäft\ ("science of religion"), comparative, historical method in the STUDY OF RELIGION. The Religionsgeschichtliche Schule developed in German biblical studies during the 19th century and emphasized the degree to which biblical ideas were the product of the cultural milieu. Important in this line of development was ALBERT SCHWEITZER, in whose *Quest of the Historical Jesus* (1906) the eschatological teachings of Jesus are emphasized, together with the dissimilarity of his thought world from our own. The history of religions is generally understood to be nonnormative—that is, it attempts to delineate facts, whether historical or structural, without judging them from a Christian or other religious standpoint.

The modern history of religions came into its own from about the time of MAX MÜLLER. During the latter part of the 19th century an attempt was made to place the methodology of COMPARATIVE RELIGION and mythology on a systematic basis. During this period, various lectureships and chairs in the subject were instituted in Western Europe and the United States. The first congress of Religionswissenschaft took place in Stockholm in 1897, and a similar one in the history of religions was held at Paris in 1900. Later, the International Association for the History of Religions was formed.

A great amount of the work of scholars in the field has been devoted to exploring particular histories—piecing together, for instance, the history of GNOSTICISM or of early BUDDHISM. In principle, CHRISTIANITY is considered from the same point of view, but much significant work has also been comparative and structural. This can range from the attempt to establish rather particular comparisons, such as RUDOLF OTTO's comparison (in his MYSTICISM East and West) of the medieval German mystic Meister Eckehart and the medieval Hindu philosopher Śankara, to a systematic typology, as in *Religion in Essence and Manifestation* by Gerardus van der Leeuw.

There have been many significant scholars in the history and PHENOMENOLOGY OF RELIGION since Müller. In the 20th century, Rudolf Otto (1869–1937) made a profound impression on the scholarly world with the publication of *The Idea of the Holy* (in its German edition of 1917), which delineated a central experience and sentiment and elucidated the concept of the Holy. The German-American historian of religions JOACHIM WACH (1898–1955) established Religionswissenschaft at the University of Chicago and was thus the founder of the modern "Chicago school." Wach was concerned with emphasizing three aspects of religion—the theoretical (or mental; *i.e.*, religious ideas and images), the practical (or behavioral), and the institutional (or social); and because of his concern for the study of RELIGIOUS EXPERIENCE, he interested himself in the SOCIOLOGY OF RELIGION, attempting to indicate how religious values shaped the institutions that expressed them.

MIRCEA ELIADE (1907–1986), a Romanian scholar who immigrated to the United States after World War II, had a wide influence, partly because of his substantive studies on YOGA and on shamanism and partly because of his later writings, which attempt to synthesize data from a wide variety of cultures. The synthesis incorporates a theory of myth and history. Two important elements in the theory of Eliade are, first, that the distinction between the sacred and the profane is fundamental to religious thinking and is to be interpreted existentially (the symbols of religion are, typically, profane in literal interpretation but are of cosmic significance when viewed as signs of the sacred); and, second, that archaic religion is to be contrasted with the linear, historical view of the world. The latter essentially comes from biblical religion; the former viewpoint tends to treat time cyclically and mythically—referring to foundational events, such as the creation, the beginning of the human race, and the Fall of man, on to *illud tempus* (the sacred primordial time), which is reenacted in the repetitions of the ritual and in the retelling of the myth.

Since the days of Wach and Eliade, the history of religions has been identified primarily with the University of Chicago. Scholars who are associated with the "Chicago school" have included Joseph Kitagawa, Jonathan Z. Smith, Charles Long, Wendy Doniger, Frank Reynolds, and Lawrence Sullivan.

RELIGIOUS EXPERIENCE

Attempts to define religious experience have included such concepts as wonder at the infinity of the cosmos, the sense of awe and mystery in the presence of the holy, feelings of dependence on a divine power or an unseen order, the sense of guilt and anxiety accompanying belief in a divine judgment, and the feeling of peace that follows faith in divine forgiveness. Some thinkers also argue that the purpose of life and the destiny of the individual have a religious aspect.

Religious experience has been variously identified in the following ways: the awareness of the holy, which evokes awe and reverence; the feeling of absolute dependence that reveals man's status as a creature; the sense of being at one with the divine; the perception of an unseen order or of a quality of permanent rightness in the cosmic scheme; the direct perception of God; the encounter with a reality "wholly other"; the sense of a transforming power as a presence. Sometimes, as in the striking case of the OLD TESTAMENT prophets, the experience of God has been seen as a critical judgment on man and as the disclosure of his separation from the holy. Those who identify religion as a dimension or aspect of experience point to man's attitude toward an overarching ideal, to a total reaction to life, to an ultimate concern for the meaning of one's being, or to a quest for a power that integrates human personality. In all these cases, it is the fact that the attitudes and concerns in question are directed to an ultimate object beyond man that justifies their being called religious. All interpreters are agreed that religious experience involves what is final in value for man and concerns belief in what is ultimate in reality.

"Religious experience" was not widely used as a technical term in the academic STUDY OF RELIGION prior to the publication of *The Varieties of Religious Experience* (1902) by William James, an American psychologist and philosopher, but the interpretation of religious concepts and doctrines in terms of individual experience reaches back at least to the 16th-century Spanish mystics and to the age of the Protestant Reformers. A special emphasis on the importance of experience in religion is found in the works of such thinkers as JONATHAN EDWARDS, FRIEDRICH SCHLEIERMACHER, and RUDOLF OTTO. Basic to the experiential approach is the belief that it allows for a firsthand understanding of religion as an actual force in human

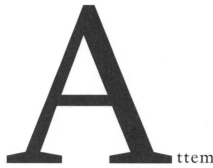

Hindu devotees in Puri, Orissa, India, offer prayers and votive candles to Jagannāth during the Rathayātrā festival
Bernard Pierre Wolff—Photo Researchers

RELIGIOUS EXPERIENCE

life, in contrast with religion taken either as church membership or as belief in authoritative doctrines. The attempt to interpret such concepts as God, faith, conversion, sin, salvation, and worship through personal experience and its expressions opened up a wealth of material for the investigation of religion by psychologists, historians, anthropologists, and sociologists as well as the more traditional examination by theologians and philosophers. A focus on religious experience is especially important for phenomenologists (who seek the basic structures of human consciousness) and existentialist philosophers.

Proponents of MYSTICISM, such as Rudolf Otto, Rufus Jones, and W.T. Stace, have maintained the validity of immediate experience of the divine, and theologians such as Emil Brunner have stressed the self-authenticating character of man's encounter with God, while naturalistically oriented psychologists, such as Freud and J.H. Leuba, have rejected such claims, explaining religion in psychological and genetic terms as a projection of human wishes and desires. Philosophers such as William James, Josiah Royce, William E. Hocking, and Wilbur M. Urban have represented an idealist tradition in interpreting religion, stressing the concepts of purpose, value, and meaning as essential for understanding the nature of God. Naturalist philosophers, of whom John Dewey was typical, have focused on the "religious" as a quality of experience and an attitude toward life that is more expressive of the human spirit than of any supernatural reality. Theologians Douglas Clyde Macintosh and Henry N. Wieman sought to build an "empirical theology" on the basis of religious experience understood as involving a direct perception of God. Unlike Macintosh, Wieman held that such a perception is sensory in character. Personalist philosophers, such as Edgar S. Brightman and Peter Bertocci, have regarded the person as the basic category for understanding all experience and have interpreted religious experience as the medium through which God is apprehended as the cosmic person. Existential thinkers, such as SØREN KIERKEGAARD, Gabriel Marcel, and PAUL TILLICH, have seen God manifested in experience in the form of a power that overcomes estrangement and enables man to fulfill himself as an integrated personality. Process philosophers, such as Alfred North Whitehead and Charles Hartshorne, have held that the idea of God emerges in religious experience but that the nature and reality of God are problems calling for logical argument and metaphysical interpretation, in which emphasis falls on the relation between God and the world being realized in a temporal process. Logical empiricists, of whom A.J. Ayer is typical, have held that religious and theological expressions are without literal significance because there is no way in which they can be either justified or falsified (refuted). On this view, religious experience is entirely emotive, lacking all cognitive value. Analytic philosophers, following the lead of Ludwig Wittgenstein, approach religious experience through the structure of RELIGIOUS LANGUAGE, attempting to discover exactly how this language functions within the community of believers who use it.

A number of controversial issues have emerged from these studies, involving not only different conceptions of the nature and structure of religious experience but also different views of the manner in which it is to be evaluated and the sort of evaluation possible from the standpoint of a given discipline. Four such issues are basic: (1) whether religious experience points to special experiences of the divine or whether any experience may be regarded as religious by virtue of becoming related to the divine; (2) the kinds of criteria that can serve to distinguish religion or the religious from both secular life and other forms of spirituality, such as morality and art; (3) whether religious experience can be understood and properly evaluated in terms of its origins and its psychological or sociological conditions or is *sui generis*, calling for interpretation in its own terms; and (4) whether religious experience has cognitive status, involving encounter with a being, beings, or a power transcending human consciousness, or is merely subjective and composed entirely of ideas that have no reference beyond themselves. The last issue, transposed in accordance with either a positivist outlook or some types of EMPIRICISM, which restrict reality to the realm of sense experience, would be resolved by the claim that the problem cannot be meaningfully discussed, since key terms, such as "God" and "power," are strictly meaningless.

Cutting across all theories of experience is the basic fact that experience demands expression in language and symbolic forms. To know what has been experienced and how it is to be understood requires the ability to identify things, persons, and events through naming, describing, and interpreting, which involve appropriate concepts and language. No experience can be the subject of analysis while it is being undergone; communication and critical inquiry require experiences to be cast into symbolic form that preserves them for further scrutiny. The uses of language—political, scientific, moral, religious, aesthetic, and others—represent many purposes through which experience is described and interpreted.

Indonesian Muslims
face Mecca for prayers
Photo Researchers

RELIGIOUS SCIENCE, movement founded in the United States by Ernest Holmes (1887–1960). Holmes and his brother Fenwicke were drawn to NEW THOUGHT teachings and to a belief in the power of the mind for healing and fulfillment of life. In 1926 Holmes's major work, *The Science of Mind,* was published, and the following year he established the Institute of Religious Science and Philosophy in Los Angeles, Calif., to teach his principles. Some of the graduates established churches based on Holmes's teachings, and in 1949 he reluctantly agreed to the establishment of a Religious Science denomination. There are now two branches: the United Church of Religious Science and the smaller Religious Science International, which prefers a less centralized polity. The two organizations have identical doctrines. The United Church publishes the magazine *Science of Mind.*

Like the New Thought tradition, Religious Science is basically monistic. The individual human mind is an expression of the Universal Mind, and the universe is its material manifestation. Man and nature are, therefore, like the God who is their true being, considered to be fundamentally good, and apparent evil stems from ignorance of the highest identity. The mind, working with creative faith and knowledge of its identity with the infinite, draws on infinite resources in what is called "affirmative prayer." When directed to a particular end, such as healing of mind or body, this employment of mind is called "spiritual mind treatment" and its results a "demonstration." Religious Science trains both ministers and practitioners, who are qualified to give spiritual mind treatments. Services are generally similar in format to those of mainstream Protestant churches, but they are conducted with an especially affirmative, optimistic tone.

REMONSTRANT, any of the Dutch Protestants who, following the views of JACOBUS ARMINIUS, presented to the States General in 1610 a "remonstrance" setting forth their points of divergence from stricter CALVINISM. The Remonstrants were expelled from the Netherlands by the Protestant SYNOD OF DORT (1618–19) but were officially recognized in 1798. The movement is still strong, and its liberal school of theology has been a powerful influence both on the Dutch state church and on other Christian denominations.

RENENUTET \,re-ne-'nü-tet\, *also called* Rannut, *Greek name* Thermuthis, in EGYPTIAN RELIGION, goddess of fertility and of the harvest, sometimes depicted in the form of a snake. In addition to her other functions, she was also counted as the protector of the king.

RENNYO \'ren-nyȯ, *Angl* 'ren-yō\, *posthumous name* Kenju Daishi, *assumed name* Shinshō-in (b. April 4, 1415, Kyōto, Japan—d. May 5, 1499, Kyōto), important figure in the development of the Japanese True Pure Land (Jōdo Shinshū) sect of BUDDHISM, which was founded in the mid-13th century by SHINRAN.

Rennyo was the eighth patriarch of the Hongan Temple in Kyōto, where his success at proselytizing provoked warrior-monks from the competing Tendai (*see* T'IEN-T'AI) sect to destroy the original temple. Rennyo's success continued, however, and he proved to be a superb leader and organizer. His writings (including a compilation of the poems and hymns of Shinran, as well as many of his own pastoral letters and sayings) have become an integral component in the subsequent True Pure Land tradition. Before his death he was able to return to the Kyōto area to oversee the building of the magnificent new Hongan Temple, which has remained a major center of True Pure Land activity. *See also* PURE LAND BUDDHISM.

REORGANIZED CHURCH OF JESUS CHRIST OF LATTER DAY SAINTS, church that claims to be the legal continuation of the church founded by JOSEPH SMITH at Fayette in Seneca County, N.Y., in 1830. World headquarters are in Independence, Mo. The church's members number about 190,000, with congregations in more than 30 countries in addition to the United States and Canada. The Reorganized Church does not accept the appellation MORMON because of the association with polygamy.

After Joseph Smith's death in 1844, the church that he founded broke into factions following various leaders. Rejecting the leadership of BRIGHAM YOUNG, who led the majority group to Utah, a number of the members, holding that the son of the founder had been designated his successor, reorganized under the original name, the Church of Jesus Christ of Latter Day Saints, at Beloit, Wis., in 1852. The word *Reorganized* was added to the title in 1869. Joseph Smith III accepted the leadership of this body in 1860 and was elected president. He was succeeded by his sons, and all of the successors were descendants of the founder until the seventh president, W. Grant McMurray, assumed the post in 1996.

The Reorganized Church rejects the doctrine of polygamy and denies that it was taught and practiced by Joseph Smith. It claims that polygamy was introduced by Brigham Young and his associates and that the revelation on polygamy, which was made public in 1852 by Young in Utah and was attributed to Smith, was not in harmony with the original tenets of the church or with the teachings and practices of Smith.

Its system of belief is based upon the teachings of the BIBLE, the BOOK OF MORMON, and the *Doctrine and Covenants,* a book of revelations received by the prophets of the Latter Day Saints and accepted by the vote of the general conference. The Reorganized church believes in the TRINITY; the doctrines of faith in God, repentance of SIN, BAPTISM by immersion, laying on of hands, and RESURRECTION of the dead; graded reward or punishment after death according to conduct in this life; the continuity of divine revelation and the open canon of scripture; the restoration of Christ's church on the NEW TESTAMENT pattern; and the doctrine of stewardship in personal and economic life. It anticipates the return of Christ and a millennial reign (*see* MILLENNIUM).

Local congregations are grouped for administrative purposes into two forms of area organizations, districts and stakes. The district organization ties the individual congregations of an area into a fellowship presided over by officers elected at district conferences. The stake organization consists of a number of congregations administered by a central authority, the stake presidency, stake bishopric, and stake high council. Business of the stake is conducted in conferences at which all members of the stake can vote.

The World Conference, which meets biennially in Independence, is the supreme legislative body of the church, and all general administrative officers, including those of the first presidency, must receive its endorsement.

The church conducts Graceland College in Lamoni, Iowa, and Park College in Kansas City, Mo. Temple School, a ministerial and leadership seminary, is in Independence.

RESHEPH \'re-,shef, 're-\ (akin to Hebrew *reshef,* "The Burner," or "The Ravager"), ancient West Semitic (Syrian) god of war, the plague, and the Underworld, the companion of ANATH.

Resheph was represented as a bearded man, brandishing an ax, holding a shield, and wearing a tall, pointed headdress with a goat's or gazelle's head on his forehead. Resheph was worshiped especially at Ras Shamra, Byblos, and Arsūf (later Apollonia, near modern Tel Aviv–Yafo). Under the title Mikal (or Mekal), he was also worshiped at Beth-shean in eastern Palestine and at Ialium in Cyprus. Resheph's associations also seem to have included well-being, plenty, and fertility.

RESPONSA \ri-'spän-sə\, *Hebrew* she'elot u-teshubot ("questions and answers"), replies made by rabbinic scholars in answer to submitted questions about Jewish law, written since the 6th century after final redaction of the TALMUD. Published *responsa* range in length from a few words to lengthy monographs and compendia and number from 250,000 to 500,000. The *responsa* frequently deal with such practical questions as rulings on which activities may or may not be done on the SABBATH.

RESURRECTION, rising from the dead of a divine or human being who still retains his own personhood, or individuality, though the body may or may not be changed. The belief in the resurrection of the body is usually associated with CHRISTIANITY, because of the doctrine of the Resurrection of Christ, but it also is associated with later JUDAISM, which provided basic ideas that were expanded in Christianity and ISLAM.

The expectation of the resurrection of the dead is found in several OLD TESTAMENT works. In the Book of Ezekiel, there is an anticipation that the righteous Israelites will rise from the dead. The Book of Daniel further developed the hope of resurrection with both the righteous and unrighteous Israelites being raised from the dead, after which will occur a judgment, with the righteous participating in an eternal messianic kingdom and the unrighteous being excluded from that kingdom. In some intertestamental literature, such as *The Syriac Apocalypse of Baruch*, there is an expectation of a universal resurrection at the advent of the MESSIAH.

The Resurrection of Christ, a central doctrine of Christianity, is based on the belief that JESUS CHRIST was raised from the dead on the third day after his CRUCIFIXION and that through his conquering of death all believers will subsequently share in his victory over "sin, death, and the Devil." The celebration of this event, called EASTER, or the Festival of the Resurrection, is the major feast day of the church.

Islam also teaches a doctrine of the resurrection. First, at Doomsday, all humans will die and then be raised from the dead. Second, each person will be judged according to the record of his life that is kept in two books, one listing the good deeds, the other the evil deeds. After the Judgment the unbelievers will be placed in hell and the faithful Muslims will go to paradise, a place of happiness and bliss.

ZOROASTRIANISM holds a belief in a final overthrow of evil, a general resurrection, a LAST JUDGMENT, and the restoration of a cleansed world to the righteous.

REUBEN \'rü-bən\, one of the 12 tribes of Israel that in biblical times constituted the people of Israel. The tribe was named for Jacob's first son born of LEAH, his first wife.

Fresco by Piero della Francesca depicting the Resurrection of Christ, c. 1463; in the Palazzo Comunale, Sansepolcro, Italy
Anderson—Alinari from Art Resource

After the EXODUS out of Egypt, the tribe of Reuben apparently settled east of the Dead Sea (Joshua 13:8–23). The 10 northern tribes formed the Kingdom of Israel under Jeroboam I that in 721 BCE fell to Assyrian conquerors (2 Kings 18:9–12). In time these tribes were assimilated to other peoples, and thus the tribe of Reuben became known as one of the legendary TEN LOST TRIBES OF ISRAEL.

REUBENI, DAVID \rü-'bā-nē\ (d. after 1532), Jewish adventurer whose grandiose plans inspired the messianic visions of the martyr SOLOMON MOLCHO (d. 1532). Reubeni claimed to be a prince descended from the tribe of REUBEN (hence his name) of a Jewish state in Arabia. He gained the favor and protection of Pope Clement VII and King John III of Portugal with his plan to lead a Jewish army against the Turks in Palestine. Eventually losing his royal support in Portugal, Reubeni and Molcho were brought before the Inquisition. Molcho was burned at the stake and Reubeni died in a Spanish prison. It is believed that he was poisoned.

REVELATION, transmission of knowledge from a god or the gods to humans. Revelation in this sense is an essential aspect of all religions, although the specific forms it takes in particular traditions vary widely. In the three great religions of the West—JUDAISM, CHRISTIANITY, and ISLAM—revelation is the basic category of religious knowledge. Man knows God and his will because God has freely revealed himself—his qualities, purpose, or instructions.

The forms of revelation can generally be portrayed as lying somewhere along a spectrum between two contrasting types. On the one hand, in religious traditions that posit a high degree of conformity between temporal and transcendent reality, the cosmos itself is viewed as the primary medium through which the transcendent is disclosed. In religions of this general type, revealed reality is usually conceived of as more or less nonpersonal. Revelation in this context may be characterized as "cosmic." A notable example of this is the inspired poetry of the ancient Indian VEDAS, which portray the natural world as a system of interconnecting powers that ultimately express the single underlying divine power, BRAHMAN. Buddhist enlightenment and many of the forms of "hierophany," or manifestations of the sacred, that characterize the archaic religions described by the religious historian MIRCEA ELIADE also constitute cosmic revelation.

On the other hand, in traditions emphasizing the discontinuity between the profane realm and the sacred, revelation occurs as historical event, signifying the transmission of divine will through a human receiver. Such revelation, in which the divine is perceived as a personal entity, is generally termed "prophetic." Oracular pronouncements and the teachings of ZOROASTER and MUHAMMAD are examples of this prophetic revelation. This type of revelation is found in Judaism, Christianity, and Islam, as well.

The Israelite faith looked back to the Pentateuch (the first five books of the OLD TESTA-

MENT) for its fundamental revelation of God. God was believed to have revealed himself to the PATRIARCHS and prophets by various means not unlike those known to the primitive religions—theophanies (visible manifestations of the divine), dreams, visions, auditions, and ecstasies—and also, more significantly, by his mighty deeds, such as his bringing the Israelites out of Egypt and enabling them to conquer the Holy Land. MOSES and the prophets were viewed as the chosen spokesmen who interpreted God's will and purposes to the nation. Their inspired words were to be accepted in loving obedience as the Word of God. Thus, all of Judaic and subsequent Christian biblical literature is regarded as, to a greater or lesser extent, revealed.

The NEW TESTAMENT took its basic notions of revelation from the contemporary forms of Judaism (1st century BCE and 1st century CE)—*i.e.*, from both normative RABBINIC JUDAISM and the esoteric doctrines current in Jewish apocalyptic circles in the Hellenistic world. Accepting the Hebrew SCRIPTURES as preparatory revelation, Christianity maintains that revelation is brought to its unsurpassable climax in the person of JESUS CHRIST, who is God's own Son (Hebrews 1:1–2), his eternal Word (John 1:1), and the perfect image of the Father (Colossians 1:15). The Christian revela-

A 13th-century Spanish manuscript illumination depicts the New Jerusalem described in Revelation to John
The Granger Collection

tion is viewed as occurring primarily in the life, teaching, death, and RESURRECTION of Jesus, all interpreted by the apostolic witnesses under the illumination of the HOLY SPIRIT. Commissioned by Jesus and empowered by the divine spirit at PENTECOST, the Apostles, as the primary heralds, hold a position in Christianity analogous to that of the prophets in ancient Israel.

Christianity has traditionally viewed God's revelation as being complete in Jesus Christ, or at least in the lifetime of the Apostles. Further development is understood to be a deeper penetration of what was already revealed, in some sense, in the 1st century. Periodically, in the course of Christian history, there have been sectarian movements that have attributed binding force to new revelations occurring in the community, such as the 2nd-century Montanists (a heretical group that believed they were of the Age of the Holy Spirit), the 16th-century ANABAPTISTS (radical Protestant sects), and the 17th-century Quakers (see SOCIETY OF FRIENDS). In the 19th century the Church of Jesus Christ of Latter-day Saints (popularly known as MORMONS) recognized, alongside the BIBLE, additional canonical scriptures (notably, the BOOK OF MORMON) containing revelations made to the founder, JOSEPH SMITH.

Islam, the third great prophetic religion of the West, has its basis in revelations received by Muhammad (c. 7th century CE). These were collected shortly after his death into the QUR'AN, which is regarded by Muslims as the final, perfect revelation—a human copy of the eternal book, dictated to the Prophet. While Islam accords prophetic status to Moses and Jesus, it looks upon the Qur'an as a correction and completion of all that went before. More than either Judaism or Christianity, Islam is a religion of the Book. Revelation is understood to be a declaration of God's will rather than his personal self-disclosure.

Such a typology is useful for indicating the degree of diversity to be found among world religions, but it can also lead to misunderstanding if applied as a norm rather than as a heuristic device. Although the Vedas, for example, were cited above as an example of cosmic revelation, the texts also contain elements of prophetic disclosure, namely a discourse that does not merely describe the cosmos but enjoins transformative action within it. Conversely, the Scriptures of the ancient Hebrews include cosmic elements, as evinced most notably in the so-called wisdom literature.

REVELATION TO JOHN, also called Book of Revelation, or Apocalypse of John, last book of the NEW TESTAMENT. It is the only book of the New Testament classified as apocalyptic literature rather than didactic or historical, indicating thereby its extensive use of visions, symbols, and ALLEGORY, especially in connection with future events. Revelation to John appears to be a collection of separate units composed by unknown authors who lived during the last quarter of the 1st century, though it purports to have been written by JOHN, "the beloved disciple" of JESUS CHRIST, at Patmos, in the Aegean Sea.

The book comprises two main parts, the first of which (chapters 2–3) contains moral admonitions (but no visions or symbolism) in individual letters addressed to the seven Christian churches of Asia Minor. In the second part (chapters 4–22:5), visions, allegories, and symbols (to a great extent unexplained) so pervade the text that exegetes necessarily differ in their interpretations. Many scholars, however, agree that Revelation deals with a contemporary crisis of faith, probably brought on by Roman persecutions.

Christians are consequently exhorted to remain steadfast in their faith and to hold firmly to the hope that God will ultimately be victorious over his (and their) enemies. Because such a view presents current problems in an eschatological context, the message of Revelation also becomes relevant to future generations of Christians who would likewise suffer persecution. The victory of God over SATAN (in this case, the perseverance of Christians in the face of Roman persecution) typifies similar victories over persecution and evil in ages still to come and God's final victory at the end of time.

An understanding of Revelation presupposes familiarity with OLD TESTAMENT language and concepts, especially those taken from the books of Daniel and Ezekiel. References to "a thousand years" (chapter 20) have led some to expect that the final victory over evil will come after the completion of some millennium.

REVEREND, ordinary English prefix of written address to the names of ministers of most CHRISTIAN denominations. In the 15th century it was used as a general term of respectful address, but it has been habitually used as a title prefixed to the names of ordained clergymen since the 17th century. In the Church of England (see ANGLICAN COMMUNION) and in most other denominations in English-speaking countries, prefects apostolic who are not in episcopal orders (e.g., deans, provosts, cathedral canons, rectors of seminaries and colleges, and priors and prioresses) are addressed as "very reverend." Bishops, ABBOTS, abbesses, and vicars-general are addressed as "right reverend," and archbishops "most reverend." See also MONSIGNOR.

REVIVALISM, generally, renewed religious fervor within a CHRISTIAN group, church, or community, but primarily a movement in some PROTESTANT churches to revitalize the spiritual ardor of their members and win new adherents. Revivalism in its modern form can be attributed to a shared emphasis within ANABAPTISM, PURITANISM, German PIETISM, and METHODISM during the 16th, 17th, and 18th centuries on personal RELIGIOUS EXPERIENCE, the priesthood of all believers, and holy living, in protest against ESTABLISHED CHURCH systems that seemed excessively sacramental, priestly, and worldly.

In England, the Puritans protested against the sacramentalism and ritualism of the Church of England (see ANGLICAN COMMUNION) in the 17th century, and many migrated to America, where they continued their fervor for experiential religion and devout living. The Puritan fervor waned toward the end of the 17th century, but the GREAT AWAKENING (c. 1720–50), America's first great revival, under the leadership of JONATHAN EDWARDS, George Whitefield, and others, revitalized religion in the North American colonies. The Great Awakening was a part of a larger religious revival that was also influential in Europe and Great Britain. In Germany and Scandinavia, LUTHERANISM was revitalized by the movement known as Pietism. The British revival led by JOHN WESLEY and others eventually resulted in the Methodist church.

Toward the end of the 18th century another revival, known as the Second Great Awakening (c. 1795–1835), began in the United States. The Second Great Awakening produced a great increase in church membership, made soul winning the primary function of the ministry, and stimulated several moral and philanthropic reforms, including temperance, the emancipation of women, and the establishment of foreign MISSIONS.

After 1835 professional revivalists traveled through the towns and cities of the United States and Great Britain, organizing annual revival meetings at the invitation of local pastors who wanted to reinvigorate their churches. In 1857–58 a "prayer meeting revival" swept American cities following a financial panic. It indirectly instigated a revival in Ulster and England in 1859–61.

The preaching tour of the American lay evangelist Dwight L. Moody through the British Isles in 1873–75 marked the beginning of a new surge of Anglo-U.S. revivalism. The interdenominationally supported revivalism of Moody and his imitators in 1875–1915 constituted, in part, a conscious cooperative effort by the Protestant churches to alleviate the unrest of urban industrial society by evangelizing the masses. It was also, in part, an unconscious effort to counter the challenge to Protestant orthodoxy brought on by the new critical methods of studying the BIBLE and by scientific ideas concerning the evolution of the human species. After an initial decline at the outset of the 20th century, a renewed interest in mass evangelism appeared in America to greet the revival "crusades" of the Southern BAPTIST evangelist BILLY GRAHAM and various regional revivalists.

ṚG VEDA \rig-'vā-də\, *also spelled* Rig Veda, collection of hymns that forms the oldest part of the Vedas of ancient India and their central core. *See* VEDA.

RHEA \'rē-ə\, in GREEK RELIGION, ancient goddess who was worshiped sporadically throughout the Greek world. She was associated with fruitfulness and had affinities with GAEA (Earth). A daughter of OURANUS (Heaven) and Gaea, she married her brother CRONUS, who, having been warned that one of his children would be fated to overthrow him, swallowed his children HESTIA, DEMETER, HERA, HADES, and POSEIDON soon after they were born. Rhea concealed the birth of ZEUS in a cave on Mount Dicte in Crete and gave Cronus a stone wrapped in swaddling clothes. This he swallowed in the belief that it was Zeus. Subsequently, Cronus was vanquished by Zeus and was forced to disgorge the swallowed children.

RHIANNON \hrē-'ä-nōn\, in CELTIC RELIGION, Welsh horse goddess. She is best known from the MABINOGION, a collection of medieval Welsh tales, in which she appears on horseback and meets King PWYLL, whom she marries. Later she was unjustly accused of killing her infant son, and in punishment she was forced to act as a horse and to carry visitors to the royal court. According to another story, she was made to wear the collars of asses about her neck in the manner of a beast.

RICCI, MATTEO \'rēt-chē\, *Chinese* (Wade-Giles romanization) Li Ma-tou \'lē-'mä-'dō\, (Pinyin) Li Madou (b. Oct. 6, 1552, Macerata, Papal States—d. May 11, 1610, China), Italian JESUIT missionary who introduced CHRISTIAN teaching to the Chinese Empire in the 16th century. By adopting the language and culture of the country, he gained entrance to the interior of China, which was normally closed to foreigners.

Early life and education. Ricci was from a noble family in Macerata, in central Italy, and, after preliminary studies at home, he entered the school that the Jesuit priests opened there in 1561. After completing his classical studies, he set out at the age of 16 for Rome to study law. There he was attracted to the life of the Jesuits, and on Aug. 15, 1571, he requested permission to join the order.

Matteo Ricci, Jesuit missionary to China; 17th-century portrait in the Gesù, Rome
The Bridgeman Art Library

Approved by the pope in 1540, the Society of Jesus (Jesuits) was already well known for its spirit of apostolic initiative. Its members were distinguishing themselves in scientific research as well as in their voyages to Asia, Africa, and the New World. Stimulated by the examples of his seniors, Ricci dedicated himself to efforts in both fields. Shortly after beginning his study of science under the noted mathematician Christopher Clavius, Ricci volunteered for mission work overseas in the Far East. In May 1577 he left Italy and set off for Portugal, and in the following year he arrived at Goa, the Portuguese outpost on the central west coast of India. Ricci carried on his studies for the PRIESTHOOD and was ordained in 1580 at Cochin, on the Malabar Coast in southwestern India. In April 1582 Ricci was ordered to proceed to China.

With its huge population, China was an area that Christian missionaries, especially the Jesuits, greatly wished to enter. When Ricci arrived, China was still closed to outsiders; but the missionary strategy of the Jesuits had undergone modification and great stress was put on the importance of learning the Chinese language and of acquiring knowledge of the culture. (This practice eventually raised the issue of whether rites honoring CONFUCIUS and family ancestors were allowable within the ROMAN CATHOLIC framework; the issue became highly politicized during the 17th–18th century in a conflict known as the CHINESE RITES CONTROVERSY.)

Mission to China. Ricci arrived at Macau, a small peninsula on the east coast of China, in August 1582, and he began at once his study of Chinese. The following year he and another Jesuit, Michele Ruggieri, were given permission to settle in Chao-ch'ing, then the capital of Kwangtung province. Ruggieri published the first Catholic CATECHISM in Chinese, and Ricci produced the first edition of his remarkable map of the world, the "Great Map of Ten Thousand Countries," which showed to the Chinese intelligentsia China's geographic relation to the rest of the world.

In 1589 Ricci moved from Chao-ch'ing to Shao-chou (Shiuhing), where he became a close friend of the Confucian scholar Ch'ü T'ai-su. It was from Ch'ü that Ricci received an introduction into the circles of the mandarins (high civil or military officials of the Chinese Empire) and of the Confucian scholars.

Feeling increasingly at home, Ricci decided to make an attempt to enter the Imperial city of Beijing. His effort in 1595, however, was not successful because a Sino-Japanese conflict in Korea had made all foreigners suspect. He had to return from Beijing to stop first at Nan-ch'ang and then Nanking. He settled at Nanking in February 1599, where he studied astronomy and geography.

Encouraged by the reception he received at Nanking, Ricci made a second attempt to reach Beijing. He entered the city in January 1601, accompanied by his Jesuit colleague, the young Spaniard Diego Pantoja. Although Ricci was not received by the emperor, he was given permission to remain in the capital. From then on, he never left Beijing, and he dedicated the rest of his life to its people, teaching them science and preaching the gospel. His efforts to attract and convert the Chinese intelligentsia brought him into contact with many outstanding personalities, among them Li Chih-tsao, Hsü Kuang-ch'i, and Yang T'ing-yün (who became known as the "Three Pillars of the Early Catholic Church" in China and who assisted the missionaries, especially in their literary efforts) and Feng Ying-ching, a scholar and civic official who was imprisoned in Beijing. During his years in Beijing, Ricci wrote several books in Chinese: "The Secure Treatise on God" (1603), "The Twenty-five Words" (1605), "The First Six Books of Euclid" (1607), and "The Ten Paradoxes" (1608).

RICE MOTHER, widely distributed and variegated figure in the MYTHOLOGY of the peoples of Indonesia. There are three main types of Rice Mother, which are found either separately or combined.

The first is that of a goddess from whose body rice was first produced. The second is that of an all-nourishing Mother Rice (*Me Posop*), who is the guardian of crops and good fortune and whose milk is rice—it is considered to be the substance that makes up the souls of all living things. The third is the last sheaf of harvested rice, which is ritually cut and dressed as a woman. This is believed to contain the concentrated soul-stuff of the field (analogous customs occur in peasant Europe, where the last sheaf is designated Wheat Mother, Barley Mother, and other grain names).

In other traditions a particular rice plant is designated as Mother Rice from the time of planting, and its vitality is believed to influence the growth of all of the other plants in the field.

RIFĀ'ĪYA \,ri-fà-'ē-ə\, fraternity of Sufi mystics, known in the West as howling dervishes, found primarily in Egypt and Syria and in Turkey until outlawed in 1925. Established in the marshlands around Basra, Iraq, by Aḥmad al-

Rifā'ī (d. 1187), the order stressed poverty, abstinence, and self-mortification. It also performed the Sufi ritual prayer (DHIKR) in a distinct manner: to the accompaniment of music, members linked arms to form a circle and threw the upper parts of their bodies back and forth until ECSTASY was achieved. Then the mystics fell on fire or a dangerous object, such as sword or snake, though such extremes probably appeared under Mongol influence during their 13th-century occupation of Iraq and have always been rejected by the majority of Muslim authorities.

The Syrian branch of the order, the Sa'dīya (or Jibāwīya), was given its form by Sa'd al-Dīn al-Jibāwī in Damascus sometime during the 14th century. Among the Sa'dīya, ecstasy was induced by physical motion—whirling around on the right heel—and the SHAYKH, or head of the order, rode on horseback over the prone bodies of the members. The order achieved its greatest popularity in the 15th century, but after that time it was superseded by the QĀDIRĪYA. *See also* SUFISM.

RIGHT-LEFT, SYMBOLISM OF, symbolic opposition found among most religions. ÉMILE DURKHEIM pointed out that the ability to classify is one of our primary social and religious abilities. The right-left opposition seems to be a near-universal category that provides the framework for various complex classifications. It is almost universally the case that the right is sacred, pure and auspicious, while the left is profane, impure and inauspicious. We generally circle sacred objects clockwise, that is from the right side. In the West people greet each other, exchange and make vows with the right hand. Male is usually associated with the right, female with the left; accordingly the image of the Hindu god SHIVA is often half male (right side) and half female (left side).

It might seem natural to think of the right-left opposition (and others of a similar nature) as being caused by natural experiences or perceptions. Robert Hertz, however, in "The Preeminence of the Right Hand" (1907), demonstrates in a convincing way that these sets of oppositions and classification systems are cultural systems and cannot be reduced to simple biology.

RIN-CHEN-BZANG-PO \'rin-chen-,säŋ-bō\ (b. 958—d. 1055), Tibetan Buddhist monk, called the "Great Translator" for his extensive translations of Indian Buddhist texts into Tibetan, thus furthering the development of BUDDHISM in that country. Sent to India in the late 10th century, Rin-chen-bzang-po eventually succeeded in bringing back to Tibet a number of Indian Buddhist monks with whom he then collaborated both in the new translation of Indian Buddhist texts and in the revision of 8th-century translations.

RINGATU \,riŋ-gə-'tü\, oldest Maori prophetic movement in New Zealand. It was founded in 1867 by the Maori guerrilla leader Te Kooti (1830–93) while he was imprisoned on the Chatham Islands. His BIBLE study produced a new religion that included traditional TABOOS and FAITH HEALING. The movement spread following Te Kooti's escape to the mainland in 1868 and his pardon in 1883.

Services are held in tribal meetinghouses on Saturdays and on the 12th day of each month, when a love feast and a communion without bread or wine is celebrated. The memorized liturgy includes thematic medleys of Bible verses, songs, chants, and prayers and ends with members raising their right hands in homage (hence Ringatu, or "Upraised Hand"). Te Kooti is celebrated as a prophet and a martyr, and Ringatu is identified with suffering Israel. The liturgy was first printed in the 1960s as *The Book of the Eight Covenants of God and Prayers of the Ringatu Church.*

RINZAI \'rēn-'zī, *Angl* 'rin-ˌzī\, *Chinese* Lin-chi \'lēn-'jē, 'lin-\, one of two major Ch'an (ZEN) Buddhist sects that developed in eastern Asia. It stresses the abrupt awakening of transcendental wisdom. Among the methods it practices are shouts (*katsu*) or blows delivered by the master to the disciple, question-and-answer sessions (*mondō*), and meditation on paradoxical statements (KOAN), all intended to accelerate a breakthrough of the normal boundaries of consciousness and to awaken insight that transcends logical distinctions.

The sect was founded in China, where it is known as Lin-chi, in the 9th century by I-hsüan, and it was transmitted to Japan in 1191 by the priest EISAI. The celebrated master HAKUIN was a major reformer of Rinzai during the 18th century.

Modern Rinzai is divided into 15 subsects. Among its great temples are the Tenryū and the Myōshin temples in Kyōto and the Kenchō and the Engaku temples in Kamakura.

RISING SUN, in EGYPTIAN RELIGION, AMULET conveying life to its wearer. It was made in the shape of a sun disk rising on the horizon and was the symbol of Harmakhis, the epithet of HORUS as god of the horizon. This amulet, often found with or on the MUMMY, provided the dead person with the assurance of RESURRECTION in the afterlife.

RISSHŌ-KŌSEI-KAI \ˌrē-'shō-ˌkō-'sā-kī\ (Japanese: "Society for Establishing Righteousness and Friendly Relations"), lay religious group in Japan based on the teachings of the NICHIREN school of BUDDHISM. The Risshō-Kōsei-kai is an offshoot of the Reiyū-kai, from which it separated in 1938. It was founded by Niwano Nikkyō and Naganuma Myōkō. It emphasizes devotion to the LOTUS SUTRA and the efficacy of chanting its name. Daily services in the Tokyo headquarters of the sect are attended by up to 10,000 people who chant in unison. This service is followed by daily *hōza*, or group counseling sessions, in which the application of faith to the problems of daily life is stressed.

RITES OF PASSAGE, any of numerous ritual events, existing in all historically known societies, that mark the passage of an individual from one social or religious status to another. Many of the most important and common rites are connected with the biological stages of life—birth, maturity, reproduction, and death; other rites celebrate changes that are wholly cultural, such as initiation into special societies or groups.

The worldwide distribution of passage rites first attracted the attention of the French anthropologist and folklorist Arnold van Gennep, who coined the term *rite de passage* in 1909. Van Gennep emphasized the structural analogies among such various rites by demonstrating that all are characterized by three phases: separation, transition, and reincorporation. Though van Gennep cautioned that these three categories are not developed to the same extent by all peoples or in every set of ceremonies, he declared them to constitute a universal pattern.

The first phase, separation, entails symbolic behavior that severs the individual from a previously fixed point in the social structure. The old status is erased in preparation for a new one. During the middle phase the ritual subject, or "passenger," stripped of all manifestations of rank or role, enters into a suspended, or liminal, state between past and future identities eluding the usual cultural categories of classification. This phase is frequently likened to death, or to being in the darkness of the womb awaiting a rebirth. Victor Turner first applied the term *communitas* to describe this middle stage of a passage rite. In the final phase the ritual subject is reincorporated in society in his new social or religious role.

Rites of passage are characteristically rich in symbolism. In the widespread ritual reenactment of death and rebirth, initiates are often ceremonially "killed" to remove them from their former life, treated as infants in the transitional period, and made to mature into their new status. Successful passage of ordeals form a regular feature of the transitional requirements, and doorways are often used to signify entry into the new domain. The new status is usually indicated by some alteration of the body (*e.g.*, CIRCUMCISION, removal of teeth, tattooing and scarification, dressing of the hair, etc.) or by the addition of special clothing and ornaments.

Most scholarly explanations of passage rites view them in terms of sociological function. Social systems require a certain amount of equilibrium in order to function smoothly. Changes in either individuals or groups threaten to disrupt this equilibrium. Thus, the primary sociological function of rites of passage may be to foster the achievement of a new state of equilibrium after such changes, to restore social order and thereby maintain the society as a system of congruent parts. As a dramatization of the individual's entry into the new order, it provides instruction to the individual and allows the community to demonstrate support of its constituents. The equally important psychological function of passage rites has received less scholarly attention. According to some interpretations, these rites serve to bridge critical stages in the life process and, by providing a predictable, communal context for individual experience, to help the individual confront certain uncontrollable aspects of the world he or she inhabits, thereby alleviating the inevitable anxiety that accompanies change.

For one treatment of rites of passage, *see* FUNCTIONALISM.

RITSCHL, ALBRECHT \'ri-chəl\ (b. March 25, 1822, Berlin—d. March 20, 1889, Göttingen, Ger.), German Lutheran theologian who synthesized the teaching of the Christian SCRIPTURES and the Protestant REFORMATION with some aspects of modern knowledge. Most of the results of Ritschl's scholarship were presented in his major work, *Die christliche Lehre von der Rechtfertigung und Versöhnung,* 3 vol. (1870–74; *The Christian Doctrine of Justification and Reconciliation*), which deals with the historical and biblical materials (vols. 1–2) and with Ritschl's own reconstruction (vol. 3).

The son and grandson of LUTHERAN clergymen, Ritschl was trained in theology and philosophy at the universities of Bonn (1839–41) and Halle (1841–43). After receiving his doctorate in 1843, Ritschl joined the ranks of the Tübingen school, a theological movement involved in reconstructing the origins of CHRISTIANITY and the early history of the church and its theology. Ritschl's youthful biblical conservatism was shaken by the Hegelianism of the Tübingen theologian Ferdinand Christian Baur. In his earliest writings he agreed with Baur that Christianity is a historical development of perfectly logical pattern rather than a dogma revealed once and for all. By the time the second edition of his first significant publication, *Die Entstehung der alt-katholischen Kirche* ("The Origin of the Old Catholic Church"), appeared in 1857, he had abandoned this position completely. Henceforth, he refused to force the results of historical research into preconceived speculative patterns. Ritschl's was a theology of revelation based on a unity of history with practical moral or value judgments. Influenced heavily by Immanuel Kant, Ritschl viewed religion as the triumph of the spirit (or moral agent) over humanity's natural origins and environment. But he rejected for use in theology what he understood to be the impersonal generalizations of metaphysics and the natural sciences. The mystical and intuitive elements of the religious life were also completely foreign to his activist outlook; the

As part of a three-month initiation ceremony that was photographed in 1953, Sepik River youths in New Guinea stand behind their spears and hold spear throwers without moving for 60 hours
Jen and Des Bartlett—Photo Researchers

goal of Christian life, he maintained, is work in and for the KINGDOM OF GOD. Against Protestant PIETISM, which emphasized the spiritual piety of the individual, Ritschl argued for the ethical development of man in the context of his community, which for Ritschl took precedence even over the church itself.

Ritschl shared with FRIEDRICH SCHLEIERMACHER the belief that for Christianity God is not known as self-existent; he is known only insofar as he conditions human trust in his self-revelation through Christ. Ritschl rejected such doctrines as ORIGINAL SIN, the miraculous birth of Christ, the TRINITY, and the INCARNATION. His attempt to apply the tenets of Kantian philosophy to Protestant Christianity was typical of an era that had little feeling for the mystery of religion and no dread of a divine judgment. His effort to maintain a theology of divine revelation without the faith in miracles underlying the older dogma was bitterly attacked by both liberal and conservative critics, but his influence on German Protestant theology in the second half of the 19th century was nevertheless immense.

Ritschl taught at the University of Bonn (1846–64) and at Göttingen from 1864 until his death.

RITUAL

Ceremonial acts prescribed by tradition or by sacerdotal decree are rituals. Just as language is a system of symbols that is based upon arbitrary rules, ritual may be viewed as a system of symbolic acts that is based upon arbitrary rules. In most explanations of ritual behavior, language becomes a necessary factor in the theory concerning the nature of ritual, and the specific form of language that is tied to explanations of ritual is the language of myth. Both myth and ritual remain fundamental to any analysis of religions. Ritual, however, can also be studied as nonverbal communication disclosing its own structure and semantics. A complete analysis of ritual would also include its relation to art, architecture, and the specific objects used in ritual such as specific forms of ritual dress.

TYPES OF RITUAL

Imitative. All rituals are dependent upon some belief system for their complete meaning. A great many rituals are patterned after myths. Such rituals can be typed as imitative rituals in that the ritual repeats the myth or an aspect of the myth. Some of the best examples of this type include rituals of the New Year, which very often repeat the story of creation. Rituals of this imitative type can be seen as a repetition of the creative act of the gods, a return to the beginning.

This type of myth has led to a theory that all rituals repeat myths or basic motifs in myths. A version of this line of thought, often called the MYTH AND RITUAL SCHOOL, is that myth is the thing said over ritual. In other words, myths are the librettos for ritual. The works of such scholars as Jane Harrison and S.H. Hooke are examples of this theory. Some rituals do repeat the story of a myth (*e.g.*, a myth of creation) and this represents an important type of ritual behavior, but the type cannot be universalized as a description of all ritual action.

Positive and negative. Rituals may also be classified as positive or negative. Most positive rituals are concerned with consecrating or renewing an object or an individual, and negative rituals are always in relation to positive ritual behavior. Avoidance is a term that better describes the negative ritual; the Polynesian word *tabu* (English, TABOO) also has become popular as a descriptive term for this kind of ritual. The word taboo has been applied to those rituals that concern some-

In a voudou ceremony in Gonaïves, Haiti, adherents enter the water in a ritual invocation of the loa *spirits*
Chester Higgins—
Photo Researchers

933

thing to be avoided or forbidden. Thus, negative rituals focus on rules of prohibition, which cover an almost infinite variety of rites and behavior. The one characteristic they all share, however, is that breaking the ritual rule results in a dramatic change in the ritual participant, usually bringing him some misfortune.

Variation in this type of ritual can be seen from within a culture as well as cross-culturally. What is prohibited for a subject, for example, may not be prohibited for a king, chief, or SHAMAN. Rituals of avoidance also depend upon the belief system of a community and the ritual status of the individuals in their relation to each other. Contact with the forbidden or transgression of the ritual rule is often offset by a ritual of purification.

Sacrificial. Another type of ritual is classified as sacrificial. One of the best descriptions of the nature and structure of sacrifice is to be found in *Sacrifice: Its Nature and Function* (1899), by the French sociologists Henri Hubert and MARCEL MAUSS, who differentiated between sacrifice and rituals of oblation, offering, and consecration. They argued that the distinctive feature of sacrificial ritual is to be found in the destruction, either partly or totally, of a victim. The victim need not be human or animal; vegetables, cakes, milk, and the like are also "victims" in this type of ritual. The total or partial destruction of the victim may take place through burning, dismembering or cutting into pieces, eating, or burying.

Hubert and Mauss have provided a very useful structure for dividing this type of ritual into subtypes. Though sacrificial rituals are very complex and diverse throughout the world, nevertheless, they can be divided into two classes: those in which the participant or participants receive the benefit of the sacrificial act and those in which an object is the direct recipient of the action. This division highlights the fact that it is not just individuals who are affected by sacrificial ritual but in many instances objects such as a house, a particular place, an action (such as a hunt or war), a family or community, or spirits or gods that become the intended recipients of the sacrifice. The variety of such rituals is very extensive, but the unity in this type of ritual is maintained in the "victim" that is sacrificed.

Life crisis. Any typology of rituals would not be complete that did not include a number of very important rites that can be found in practically all religious traditions and mark the passage from one domain, stage of life, or vocation into another. Such rituals have often been classified as RITES OF PASSAGE, and the French anthropologist Arnold van Gennep's study *Les Rites de Passage* (1909; *The Rites of Passage*) remains the classic book on the subject.

The basic characteristic of the life-crisis ritual is the transition from one mode of life to another. Rites of passage have often been described as rituals that mark a crisis in individual or communal life. They include rituals of birth, puberty (entrance into the full social life of a community), marriage, conception, and death. Many of these rituals mark a separation from an old situation or mode of life, a transition rite celebrating the new situation, and a ritual of incorporation. Rituals of passage do not always manifest these three divisions; many such rites stress only one or two of these characteristics.

One of the dominant motifs of the life-crisis ritual is the emphasis on separation, as either a death or a return to infancy or the womb. Rituals such as BAPTISM in CHRISTIANITY and the complex puberty rituals among North American Indian cultures (*see* NATIVE AMERICAN RELIGIONS) exemplify this motif of death and rebirth in rites of passage.

Rituals of crisis and passage are often classified as types of initiation. From this point of view (exemplified in the work of MIRCEA ELIADE), rituals, especially initiation rituals, are related both to the history and structure of a particular society and to an experience of the sacred that is both transhistorical and transcendent of a particular social or cultural context. Culture, from this perspective, can be viewed as a series of rituals that transform natural experiences into cultural modes of life. This transformation involves both the transmission of social structures and the disclosure of the sacred and spiritual life of man.

Initiation rituals can be classified in many ways. The patterns emphasized by Eliade all include a separation or symbolic death, followed by a rebirth. They include rites all the way from separation from the mother to the more complex and dramatic rituals of CIRCUMCISION, ordeals of suffering, or a descent into hell, all of which are symbolic of a death followed by a rebirth. Rites of withdrawal and quest, as well as rituals characteristic of shamans and religious specialists, are typically initiatory in theme and structure. Some of the most dramatic rituals of this type express a death and return to a new period of gestation and birth and often in terms that are specifically embryological. Finally, there are the actual rituals of physical death itself, a rite of passage and transition into a spiritual or immortal existence.

The various typologies of ritual that can be found in texts on religion and culture exhibit a striking contrast in the uses to which they are put in the interpretation of ritual. In general, this contrast can be described in terms of two positions: the first emphasizes the sociopsychological function of ritual; the second, although not denying the first, asserts the religious value of ritual as a specific expression of a transcendental reality.

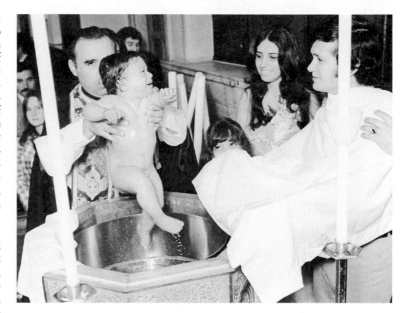

At a Greek Orthodox church, an infant becomes a member of the body of believers through the rite of baptism
Katrina Thomas—
Photo Researchers

FUNCTIONS OF RITUAL

In the study of ritual behavior, the terms SACRED (the transcendent realm) and *profane* (the realm of time, space, and cause and effect) have remained useful in distinguishing ritual behavior from other types of action. Although there is no consensus on a definition of the sacred and the profane, there is common agreement on the characteristics of these two realms by those who use the terms to describe religions, myth, and ritual.

For the French sociologist ÉMILE DURKHEIM and others who use these terms, ritual is a determined mode of action. According to Durkheim, the reference, or object, of ritual is the belief system of a society, which is constituted by a classification of everything into the two realms of the sacred and the profane. This classification is taken as a universal feature of religion. Belief systems, myths, and the like, are viewed as expressions of the nature of the sacred realm in which ritual becomes the determined conduct of the individual in a society expressing a relation to the sacred and the profane. The sacred is that aspect of a community's beliefs, myths, and sacred objects that is set apart and forbidden. The function of ritual in the community is that of providing the proper rules for action in the realm of the sacred as well as supplying a bridge for passing into the realm of the profane.

Although the distinction between the sacred and profane is taken as a universal concept, there is very nearly an infinite variation on how this dichotomy is represented—not only between various cultures but also within a culture. What is profane for one culture may be sacred to another. This may also be true, however, within a culture. The relative nature of things sacred and the proper ritual conducted in relation to the sacred as well as the profane varies according to the status of the participants. What is set apart, or holy, for a sacred king, priest, or shaman, for example, will differ from the proper ritual behavior of others in the community who are related to them, even though they share the same belief systems. The crucial feature that both sustains these relations and sets their limits is the ritual of initiation.

Three further characteristics are generally used to specify ritual action beyond that of the dichotomy of sacred and profane thought and action. The first characteristic is a feeling or emotion of respect, awe, fascination, or dread in relation to the sacred. The second characteristic of ritual involves its dependence upon a belief system that is usually expressed in the language of myth. The third characteristic is that it is symbolic in relation to its reference. Agreement on these characteristics can be found in most descriptions of the functions of ritual.

The scholarly disputes that have arisen over the functions of ritual center around the exact relation between ritual and belief or the reference of ritual action. There is little agreement, for example, on the priority of ritual or myth. In some cases, the distinction between ritual, myth, and belief systems is so blurred that ritual is taken to include myth or belief.

The function of ritual depends upon its reference. Once again, although there is common agreement about the symbolic nature of ritual, there is little agreement with respect to the reference of ritual as symbolic. Ritual is often described as a symbolic expression of actual social relations, status, or the roles of individuals in a society. Ritual is also described as referring to a transcendent, numinous (spiritual) reality and to the ultimate values of a community.

Whatever the referent, ritual as symbolic behavior presupposes that the action is nonrational. That is to say, the means–end relation of ritual to its referent is not intrinsic or necessary. Such terms as latent, unintended, or symbolic are often used to specify the nonrational function of ritual. The fundamental problem in all of this is that ritual is described from an observer's point of view. Whether the participant in ritual is basically nonrational or rational, as far as his behavior and his belief system are concerned, is largely dependent upon whether he also understands both his behavior and belief to be symbolic of social, psychological, or numinous realities. It is difficult to imagine a Buddhist, a Christian, or an Australian Aborigine agreeing that his ritual action and beliefs are nothing but symbols for social, psychological, or ultimate realities. The idea of the sacred as a transcendent reality may, however, come closest to the participant's own experience. The universal nature of the sacred-profane dichotomy, however, remains a disputed issue.

The Chinese spring ritual of praying at the graves of ancestors and leaving offerings of food and flowers is carried out at a cemetery in the United States
Katrina Thomas—
Photo Researchers

THE STUDY OF RITUAL

The origin approach. The earliest approach to the study of ritual was an attempt to explain ritual, as well as religion, by means of a theory concerned with historical origin. In most cases, this theory also assumed an evolutionary hypothesis that would explain the development of ritual behavior through history. The basic premise, or law, for this approach is the biological theory that ontogeny (development of an individual organism) recapitulates phylogeny (evolution of a related group of organisms), just as the human embryo recapitulates, at least to an extent, the stages of human evolutionary history in the womb—*e.g.*, the gill stage. The solution to explaining the apparently universal scope of ritual depended upon the success in locating the oldest cultures and cults. Scholars believed that if they could discover this origin, they would be able to explain the contemporary rituals of the human species.

There are almost as many solutions as authors in this approach. In the search for an origin of ritual, research turned from the well-known literate cultures to those that appeared to be less complex and preliterate. The use of the terms primitive religion and primitive cultures comes from this approach in seeking an answer to the meaning of ritual, myth, and religion. Various cultures and rituals were singled out, sacrifice of either humans or animals becoming one of the main topics for speculation, though the exact motivation or cause of sacrificial ritual was disputed among the leading authors of the theory. For the British biblical scholar W. Robertson Smith, sacrifice was motivated by the desire for communion between members of a primitive group and their god. The origin of ritual, therefore, was believed to be found in totemic (animal symbolic clan) cults; and TOTEMISM, for many authors, was thus believed to be the earliest stage of religion and ritual. The various stages of ritual development and evolution, however, were never agreed upon. Given this origin hypothesis, rituals of purification, gift giving, piacular (expiatory) rites, and worship were viewed as developments, or secondary stages, of the original sacrificial ritual. The Christian EUCHARIST (Holy Communion), along with contemporary banquets and table etiquette, were explained as late developments or traits that had their origin and meaning in the totemic sacrifice.

The influence of Smith's theory on the origin of ritual can be seen in the works of Durkheim, the British anthropologist Sir JAMES FRAZER, and SIGMUND FREUD, the father of psychoanalysis. Although they were not in complete agreement with Smith, sacrifice and totemism remained primary concerns in their search for the ORIGIN OF RELIGION. For Frazer, the search led to magic, a stage preceding religion. Both Smith and Frazer led Durkheim to seek the origin of ritual and religion in totemism as exemplified in Australia. Durkheim believed that in totemism scholars would find the original form of ritual and the division of experience into the sacred and the profane. Ritual behavior, they held, entails an attitude that is concerned with the sacred; and sacred acts and things, therefore, are nothing more than symbolic representations of society. In his last major work, *Moses and Monotheism* (1939), Freud also remained convinced that the origin of religion and ritual is to be found in sacrifice.

Among modern scholars, the origin-evolutionary hypothesis of ritual behavior has been rejected as quite inadequate for explaining human behavior because no one can verify any of these bold ideas; they remain creative speculations that cannot be confirmed or denied.

The functional approach. Turning from origin hypotheses, scholars next emphasized empirical data gathered by actual observation and moved toward the position that the nature of ritual is to be defined in terms of its function in a society.

Most functional explanations of ritual attempt to explain ritual behavior in relation to the needs and maintenance of a society. Ritual is thus viewed as an adaptive and adjustive response to the social and physical environment. Many leading authorities on religion and ritual have taken this approach as the most adequate way to explain rituals, including BRONISŁAW MALINOWSKI, A.R. RADCLIFFE-BROWN, E.E. EVANS-PRITCHARD, Clyde Kluckhohn, Talcott Parsons, and Edmund Leach. While FUNCTIONALISM has had some success in describing the role of ritual within its social environment, it has difficulty accounting for ritual's origins.

The history of religions approach. A third approach to the study of ritual is centered on the studies of historians of religion. Historians of religions, such as Gerardus van der Leeuw in The Netherlands, RUDOLF OTTO in Germany, JOACHIM WACH and Eliade in the United States, and E.O. James in England, have traditionally held the view that ritual behavior signifies or expresses the sacred (the realm of transcendent or ultimate reality). This approach, however, has never been represented as an explanation of ritual, and the theory cannot be confirmed unless scholars agree beforehand that such a transcendent reality exists.

RITUAL BATH, ceremony involving the use of water to immerse or anoint a subject's body. The many forms of BAPTISM, ranging from total submersion to a symbolic sprinkling, indicate how ritual baths can vary in form even while retaining the same purificatory meaning. Ritual baths may be taken while the subject is dressed or nude, in churches or other buildings, in rivers, streams, or ponds; but often the bath and the locus have mutually reinforcing symbolic meanings, as in the *tīrthayātrā*, the typical Hindu PILGRIMAGE bath in a holy river or stream, or the UPANAYANA, the Hindu rite of initiation before a young man's GURU.

To bring rain, the Zande of Central Africa poured water over a person accused of delaying or preventing rain. The Hebrew MIKVEH sought ritual purification through the use of prescribed amounts and kinds of water, and SHINTŌ followers practiced water ablution—a kind of ritual bath in microcosm—to prepare for visits to shrines. Christian footwashing (*pedilavium*), signifying humility, traditionally took place in the early church on MAUNDY THURSDAY, to the accompaniment of chanted HYMNS.

RIZALIST CULT \ri-'zä-list, -'sä-\, any of numerous religious groups in the Philippines that believe in the divinity of José Rizal, the national hero martyred by the Spanish in 1896. It is commonly believed that he is still alive and will return to deliver his followers from poverty and oppression. Rizal has been identified as God, as the second (or Filipino) Christ, and as the god of the pre-Spanish Malay religion. Rizalist cults, such as the Iglesia Sagrada ni Lahi (Holy Church of the Race) and the Banner of the Race Church (the largest group), synthesize ROMAN CATHOLIC rituals, images, and organization with traditional Filipino elements. These rural movements have some 300,000 members.

RNYING-MA-PA \'nʸiŋ-mä-bä\, *also spelled* Nyingmapa (Tibetan: "Old Order"), major Buddhist sect in Tibet; it claims to transmit the original teachings of the celebrated Indian VAJRAYĀNA (Tantric BUDDHISM) master PADMASAMBHAVA, who visited Tibet in the 8th century and helped to found the country's first monastery at Samye (c. 775). The sect makes wide use of shamanistic practices and local divinities borrowed from the indigenous, pre-Buddhist BON religion. Monks of the sect are not, as a rule, required to observe CELIBACY.

ROCK EDICTS, narrative histories and announcements carved into cliff rock, onto pillars, and in caves throughout India by King AŚOKA (reigned c. 265–238 BCE), the most powerful emperor of the Maurya dynasty. After Aśoka's slaughter of thousands of people during the conquest of Kalinga he learned of the moral teachings (DHARMA) of Buddhism—teachings based on the necessity for NONVIOLENCE and compassion—and was moved to deep remorse for his actions. He converted to BUDDHISM and as a record of his understanding of moral law had Buddhist lessons carved into stone in the hope that he could provide inspiration and guidance to the people of his extensive kingdom. The rock edicts are important sources for modern understanding of ancient Indian political and religious history, particularly with regard to the influence of Buddhist teachings on the king and, through him, on the people at large.

ROD \'rōd\, in SLAVIC RELIGION, god of fate and the creator of the world. Ceremonial meals in his honor, consisting of meatless dishes such as bread and cheese, survived into Christian times.

ROMAN CATHOLICISM, Christian church characterized by its uniform, highly developed doctrinal and organizational structure that traces its history to the APOSTLES of JESUS CHRIST in the 1st century CE. Along with EASTERN ORTHODOXY and PROTESTANTISM, it is one of the three major branches of CHRISTIANITY.

The history of the Roman church in the early period is essentially that of a small sect composed of recruits attracted from the lower classes of the empire. Its continued existence during these years can be attributed to the relatively tolerant attitude of the imperial authorities and to a steady influx of converts attracted by the CHARITY and moral tenor of the church's members. The 3rd century witnessed an upsurge in Roman alarm at the spread of the church and the opposition between traditional Roman piety and the apparent misanthropic and unpatriotic atheism of the Christians. Even in this troubled period, however, the doctrinal and governmental structures of the church were being defined: a scriptural canon emerged; the threefold ministry (bishop, priest, and deacon) established itself and displaced other forms of leadership; and the See of Rome began to exercise a universal care over other churches.

The reign of CONSTANTINE ushered in a new era in the life of the church. The EDICT OF MILAN (314) recognized the church as a legal religion, and by the end of the 4th century Christianity was the state religion of the empire. During this period, the hierarchical structure of the church was further elaborated, and the emergence of heretical elements was met with a more exact definition of Christological beliefs. The fall of the Western Empire in 476 left the pope as the only effective force for order in the West. In the ensuing centuries the PAPACY allied itself with the Frankish Carolingian dynasty and, with the assistance of a remarkably vital and active monastic community, Christianized the barbarian invaders and cemented the ties between a distinctly Roman form of Christianity and western European culture. During the Middle Ages, the church's influence in European life was all-pervasive: education, charity, and politics all came under the sway of the church.

The break (1054) with the Eastern churches marked yet another turning point in the history of Roman Catholicism. During the centuries between the reign of Pope GREGORY VII (1073–85) and the REFORMATION, the papacy articulated a doctrine of papal authority that laid claim to authority in both the spiritual and temporal realms. Both secular rulers and scholars challenged the papal position. The prestige and power of the papacy reached a low ebb during the 14th and 15th centuries when the humiliation of BONIFACE VIII (reigned 1294–1303), the AVIGNON PAPACY (1309–77), and the Western SCHISM (1378–1417) followed one another in quick succession. By the mid-15th century HERESY, CONCILIARISM, and corruption had taken their toll on the church. Moreover, the papacy seemed unable either to rule effectively or to reform itself or the church.

During the 16th century a general demand for a reform of the church swept through the Christian West as MARTIN LUTHER, JOHN CALVIN, HULDRYCH ZWINGLI, and others attacked the corruption and lack of spiritual vitality in the church. The Reformation destroyed Rome's spiritual hegemony in the West at the same time that it forced the Roman church to undertake a program of internal renewal. The COUNTER-REFORMATION reached its high point at the COUNCIL OF TRENT (1545–63). Trent's decrees, which were to govern church life for four centuries, effected some pastoral reforms but also hardened the church's traditional doctrinal stance. Moreover, in the aftermath of the council, in order to press

The pope of the Roman Catholic church depicted as ruler over the worldly powers and the laity (on his left) and the clergy and religious (on his right); detail of The Church Militant and Triumphant, *fresco by Andrea da Firenze, c. 1365; in the Spanish Chapel of the church of Santa Maria Novella, Florence*
SCALA—Art Resource

the church's program of reconquest, the papacy and its newly reorganized and more efficient ROMAN CURIA assumed more and more control over the life and government of the church. The Tridentine church was thus a centralized, authoritarian, and traditional church.

The momentum of the Counter-Reformation was lost when, in the aftermath of the wars of religion, Europe entered into a period of religious decline. During the ages of Reason and Revolution, the church suffered challenges both to its teaching authority and to its very right to exist. During the 19th century the church responded to these threats by assuming a posture of hostility to the modern world and by stressing uniformity of belief and strict obedience to authority. In the century following the FIRST VATICAN COUNCIL (1869–70), the church continued to be beset by crises. The Papal States were lost in 1870; the church's tardiness in committing itself to the cause of social justice in industrial relations led large segments of the working class-

es in Europe to turn away from it; and anticlerical regimes succeeded in reducing the political power and freedom of the church. In 1962–65, the church convened the SECOND VATICAN COUNCIL in an attempt to update its message and internal structure. In the years following the council, the church's attempts at modernization have proved divisive.

Theologically, Roman Catholicism differs from other Christian churches with regard to its understanding of the sources of revelation and the channels of GRACE. Roman Catholicism, together with Eastern Orthodoxy, asserts that both SCRIPTURE and church tradition are revelatory of the basis of Christian belief and church polity, and thus sets the number of SACRAMENTS at seven (BAPTISM, penance, EUCHARIST, marriage, holy orders, CONFIRMATION, and the anointing of the sick). Catholicism's rich sacramental life is supplemented by other devotions, chiefly paraliturgical eucharistic services and devotions to the saints. Liturgical reforms after the second Vatican Council shifted the focus from such devotional activity to the celebration of the Eucharist as the central act of worship; in it Catholics believe that the events of both the LAST SUPPER and the death of Jesus are repeated and that the Christ is truly present in the communion elements by virtue of TRANSUBSTANTIATION.

For a much fuller exposition of Christian history and theology, *see* CHRISTIANITY.

ROMAN CURIA: *see* CURIA, ROMAN.

ROMAN RELIGION

The term *Roman religion* is used in this article to describe the religious beliefs and practices of the inhabitants of the Italian peninsula from ancient times until the ascendancy of CHRISTIANITY in the 4th century CE.

The Romans, according to Cicero, excelled all other peoples in the wisdom that made them realize that everything is subordinate to the rule and direction of the gods. Their religion was based on mutual trust (*fides*) between divine and human, and its object was to secure the cooperation, benevolence, and "peace" of the gods (*pax deorum*). They believed that this divine help would allow them to master the unknown forces around them that inspired awe and anxiety (*religio*), and thus they would be able to live successfully. Consequently, they developed a body of rules, the *jus divinum* ("divine law"), ordaining what had to be done or avoided. Roman religion is singularly free of mythology (apart from what they borrowed from Greece) or CREED. Instead, Roman religion laid almost exclusive emphasis on cult acts, endowing them with all the sanctity of patriotic tradition.

EARLY ROMAN RELIGION

Early in the 1st millennium BCE, two villages at Rome were founded by Latin and Sabine shepherds and farmers from the Alban Hills and the Sabine Hills. About 620 the two communities merged. It appears that these early Romans, like many other Italians, sometimes saw divine force operating in pure function and act, such as in human activities like opening doors or giving birth to children, and in nonhuman phenomena such as the movements of the sun and seasons of the soil. They multiplied functional deities of this kind to an extraordinary degree, so that countless powers or forces were identified with one phase of life or another. Their functions were sharply defined, and in approaching them it was important to use their right names and titles. If the names and titles were unknown, it was often best to cover every contingency by admitting that the deity was "unknown" or adding the precautionary phrase, "or whatever name you want to be called" or "if it be a god or goddess."

Veneration of objects. The same sort of anxious awe was extended to certain objects that inspired a belief that they were in some way more than natural:

A Roman sacrifice, in bas-relief
Alinari—Art Resource

941

springs and woods, for instance, or stones that were believed to be of uncanny origin, or products of human action such as burial places and boundary stones. To describe the powers in these objects and functions that inspired the horror, or sacred thrill, the Romans eventually employed the word *numen*, suggestive of a god's nod, *nutus*; though so far there is no evidence that this usage was earlier than the 2nd century BCE. The Romans believed that such forces had to be propitiated and made allies, which necessitated sacrifice. The sacrifice would activate, revitalize, and nourish the divinity, whose force might otherwise run down. And so the sacrifice was accomplished by the phrase *macte esto* ("be you increased!"). Prayer was a normal accompaniment of sacrifice, and it contained varying ingredients of flattery, cajolery, justification, and sometimes attempts at coercion.

The earliest divinities.   The early Roman, like other Italians, also worshiped certain more universal gods. Chief among them was the god JUPITER. The Romans gave Jupiter his own priest (FLAMEN), and the fact that there were two other senior *flamines*, devoted to MARS and QUIRINUS, indicates that the cults of these three divinities were of very early date. Mars, whose name may or may not be Indo-European, was an important god of many Italian peoples, protecting them in war and defending their agriculture and animals against disease. Later, he was identified with the Greek god of war, ARES, and also was regarded as the father of ROMULUS AND REMUS. Mars Gradivus presided over the beginning of a war and Mars Quirinus over its end, but early Quirinus had apparently, as a separate deity, been the patron of a Quirinal village; subsequently he was believed to be the god that Romulus became when he ascended into heaven.

Two other ancient gods were JANUS and VESTA, the powers of the door and the hearth, respectively. Janus was worshiped beside the Forum in a small shrine with double doors at either end and originated either from a divine power that regulated the passage over running water or, perhaps, from sacred doorways. The gates of Janus' temple were formally closed when the state was at peace, a custom going back to the early martial ritual that required armies to march out to battle by this properly sanctified route. Vesta's circular temple recalled, perhaps, a primitive hut, and her shrine contained the eternal fire; its correspondence with the Indian *garhapatya*, "house-father's fire," suggests an origin prior to the time of the differentiation of the Indo-European–speaking peoples. The cult of Vesta, tended by her Virgins (*see* VESTAL VIRGIN) and honored by an annual festival, continued to flourish until the end of antiquity, endowed with an important role in the divine protectorship of Rome.

The Di Manes, collective powers of the dead, may mean "the good people," an anxious euphemism intended to mollify dangerous powers. As a member of the family or clan, however, the deceased would be one of the Di Parentes; reverence for ancestors was the core of Roman religious and social life. Di Indigetes was a name given collectively to these forebears, as well as to other deified powers or spirits who controlled the destiny of Rome.

The Lares originally may have been regarded as divine ancestors, but in historical times they presided over the farmland. They were worshiped wherever properties adjoined, and inside every home their statuettes were placed in the domestic shrine (*lararium*). Under state control they moved from boundaries of properties to crossroads and were worshiped as the guardian spirits of the whole community (Lares Praestites).

The Di Penates (*see* PENATES), the powers that ensured that there was enough to eat, were worshiped in every home. Like the Lares, they also came to be regarded as national protectors, the Penates Publici.

Two other deities traditionally regarded as dating to the royal period were DIANA and Fors FORTUNA. Diana, an Italian wood goddess prayed to by women who wanted children, came to be identified with the Greek ARTEMIS. Her temple on the Aventine Hill (*c.* 540 BCE) with its statue, an imitation of a Greek model from Massilia (Marseille), was based on the Temple of Artemis of Ephesus. Fors Fortuna's temple, across the Tiber River from the city, was one of the few that slaves could attend. Originally a farming deity, she came to represent luck and was identified with Tyche, the patroness of cities and goddess of fortune among the Hellenistic Greeks.

Tradition states that there were two Etruscan KINGS OF ROME, Tarquinius Priscus and Tarquinius Superbus. The Etruscan kings began and perhaps finished the most important Roman temple, devoted to the cult of the Capitoline Triad, Jupiter, JUNO, and MINERVA. Such triads, housed in temples with three chambers (*cellae*), were an Etruscan institution. But the grouping of these three Roman deities seems to depend on Greek mythology, since HERA and ATHENA, with whom Juno and Minerva were identified, were respectively the wife and daughter of ZEUS (Jupiter). In Italy, Juno (Uni in Etruscan) was sometimes the warlike goddess of a town (*e.g.*, Lanuvium [Lanuvio] in Latium), but her chief function was to supervise the life of women, and particularly their sexual life. Minerva concerned herself with craftsmen. Two gods with Etruscan names, both worshiped at open altars before they had temples in Rome, were VULCAN and SATURN, the former a fire god identified with the Greek HEPHAESTUS, and the latter an agricultural god identified with CRONUS, the father of Zeus. Saturn was worshiped in Greek fashion, with head uncovered.

The focal point of the cult of Hercules was the Great Altar (*Ara Maxima*) in the cattle market, just inside the boundaries of the original Palatine settlement. The altar may be traced to a shrine of Melkart established by traders from Phoenicia in the 7th century BCE. The name of the god was derived from the Greek HERACLES, whose worship arrived with traders via southern Italy. The Greek cult, at first private, perhaps dates from the 5th century BCE.

Diana, the huntress, bas-relief; in the Vatican Museum, Rome

Alinari—Art Resource

THE DIVINITIES OF THE REPUBLIC

An important series of temples was founded early in the 5th century BCE, including the temple of the Etruscan Saturn and a shrine dedicated to the twin horsemen, the DIOSCURI, the cult of whom spread from Greece to southern Italy and from there to Rome. In legend, the Dioscuri had helped Rome to victory in a battle against the Latins at Lake Regillus, and on anniversaries of that engagement they presided over the annual parade of knights (*equites*). From southern Italy, too, came the cult of CERES, an old Italian deity who presided over the generative powers of nature and came to be identified with DEMETER. She owed her installation in Rome to the influence of the Greek colony of Cumae, from which the Romans imported grain during a threatened famine. At this temple Ceres was associated with two other deities, Liber (a fertility god identified with DIONYSUS) and Libera (his female counterpart); this association was based on the triad at Eleusis in Greece. The Roman temple, built in the Etruscan style but with Greek ornamentation, became a rallying ground for the plebeians, a section of the community who were hard hit by the grain shortage at this time and who were pressing for their rights against the patricians.

Cumae also played a part in the introduction of APOLLO. The Sibylline oracles housed in Apollo's shrine at Cumae allegedly were brought to Rome by the last Etruscan kings. The importation of the cult (431 BCE) was prescribed by the Sibylline Books (*see* SIBYL) at a time when Rome had asked Cumae for help with grain. The Cumaean Apollo was primary prophetic, but the Roman cult was concerned principally with his gifts as a healer. Later, Augustus elevated Apollo as the patron of himself and his regime.

When APHRODITE arrived in Rome, she took on the name VENUS, possibly derived from the idea of *venus*, "blooming nature." Her significance was largely based on the myth that named her the mother of AENEAS, the ancestor of Rome. Accordingly, the 1st-century-BCE dictators Sulla and Caesar both claimed Venus as their ancestor.

A number of gods possessed accompaniments, which were often feminine— *e.g.*, Lua Saturni and Moles Martis. Sometimes spoken of as cult partners, these attachments were not the wives of the male divinites but rather expressed a special aspect of their power or will. Likewise for the divine powers worshiped as representing divine qualities: FIDES ("Faith" or "Loyalty"), for example, may at first have been an attribute of a Latin-Sabine god of OATHS, Semo Sanctus Dius Fidius, and Victoria may have come from Jupiter Victor. Some of these concepts were worshiped in a very early period, such as Ops ("Plenty," later associated with Saturn and equated with the Greek HEBE), and Juventas (who watched over the men of military age). CONCORDIA was the first of these to receive a temple (367), in celebration of the end of civil strife. SALUS (health or well-being) followed in *c.* 302 BCE, Victoria in *c.* 300 BCE, PIETAS (dutifulness to family and gods, later exalted by Virgil as the foundation of Roman religion) in 191 BCE. These divine qualities were not thought of as possessing anthropomorphic shape. They were things, objects of worship, like many other functions that were venerated. Later on, under philosophical (particularly Stoic) influences, they duly took their place as moral concepts, the Virtues and Blessings which abounded for centuries and were depicted in human form on Roman coinage as part of the imperial propaganda.

THE IMPERIAL CULT

Octavian, the adopted son of the dictator Julius Caesar and founder of the imperial regime, took for himself the name Augustus, a term indicating a claim to reverence. This act did not make him a god in his lifetime, but, combined with the insertion into certain cults of his *numen* and his GENIUS (originally the power that preserves a family through the generations), it prepared the way for his posthumous deification, just as Caesar had been deified during Augustus' reign. Both were deified by the state because they seemed to have given Rome gifts worthy of a god. It was a very old idea in Greece that, if someone saved you, you should pay him the honors you would offer to a god. Alexander the Great and his successors had demanded reverence as divine saviors, and Ptolemy II Philadelphus of Egypt introduced a cult of his own living person. Moreover, the 3rd-century-BCE mythographer EUHEMERUS had elaborated a theory that the gods themselves had once been human; the Romans applied this idea to the gods Saturn and Quirinus, the latter identified with the national founder, Romulus, risen to heaven. And so it became customary—if emperors (and empresses) were approved of in their lives—to raise them to divinity after their deaths. They were called *divi*, not *dei* like the Olympian gods, and were regarded with veneration and gratitude but not prayed to.

As the empire proceeded and successive national emergencies were faced, the cult of the *divi* remained foremost among the patriotic cults that were increasingly encouraged as unifying forces. Concentrating on the protectors of the emperor and the nation, they included the worship of Rome herself, and of the *genius* of the Roman people. The ruling emperors were more and more frequently treated as divine, and officially they were often compared with gods. As monotheistic tendencies grew, however, this custom led to the doctrine that they were the elect of the divine powers, who were defined as their companions (*comites*). As the traditional religion approached its last days, the emperors Diocletian and Maximian took the names Jovius and Herculius, respectively, after their companions and patrons Jupiter and Hercules.

THE SUN AND STARS

A complicated geocentric concept of the solar system held sway in Rome and is summed up in Cicero's *Dream of Scipio*. It formed the basis for the popular conceptions on which ASTROLOGY was based, the Sun being regarded as the center of the concentric planetary spheres encircling the Earth. From the 5th century BCE onward this solar god was identified with Apollo in his role as the supreme dispenser of agricultural wealth. Possessor of a sacred grove at Lavinium, SOL Indiges was regarded as one of the divine ancestors of Rome. During the last centuries before the Christian era, worship of the Sun spread throughout the Mediterranean world; closely associated with this cult was that of MITHRA, the Sun's ally and

Augustus of Prima Porta, marble statue, c. 20 BCE; in theVatican Museum, Rome
Alinari—Art Resource

agent who was elevated to partake of communion and the love feast as the god's companion. SUN WORSHIP was popular in the army, and particularly on the Danube. The emperor Aurelian built a magnificent temple of Sol Invictus (the "Unconquered Sun") at Rome (274 CE), and Constantine the Great declared the Sun his comrade on empire-wide coinages and devoted himself to the cult. His later adoption and practice of Christianity was probably influenced significantly by the cult of Sol Invictus.

PRIESTS

Of the various Roman priests, precedence belonged to the *rex sacrorum* ("king of the sacred rites"), who, after the expulsion of the kings, took over those religious duties and powers that had not been assumed by the Republican officers of state. Very early origins can also be attributed to some of the *flamines*, the priests of certain specific cults, and particularly to the *flamines* of Jupiter, Mars, and Quirinus. Jupiter's priest, the *flamen dialis*, was required to observe an extraordinary series of ritual prohibitions, some possibly dating to the Bronze Age.

The power of the *rex sacrorum* and his colleagues was weakened *c.* 451–450 BCE by the Law of the Twelve Tables, which extended political control over sacral law. As late as *c.* 275 BCE the religious calendar was still dated by the *rex sacrorum*, but by this time he was fading into the background. Except for the *rex sacrorum* and *flamen dialis*, almost all Roman priesthoods were held by men prominent in public life. The social distinction and political prestige carried by these part-time posts caused them to be keenly fought for.

There were four chief colleges, or boards, of priests: the *pontifices*, *augures*, *quindecimviri sacris faciundis*, and *epulones*. Originally 3, and finally 16 in number, the *pontifices* had assumed control of the religious system by the 3rd century BCE. The chief priest, the *pontifex maximus* (the head of the state clergy; *see* PONTIFEX), was an elected official. The *augures* had the task of discovering whether or not the gods approved of an action. This they performed mainly by interpreting divine signs in the movements of birds (*auspicia*). Such DIVINATION was elevated into an indispensable preliminary to state acts, though the responsibility for the decision rested with the presiding state officials, who were said to "possess the auspices." In private life too, even as late as the 1st century BCE, important courses of action were often preceded by consultation of the heavens. The Etruscan method of divining from the liver and entrails of animals (*haruspicina*) became popular in the Second Punic War, though its practitioners (who numbered 60 under the empire) never attained an official priesthood.

Of the other two major colleges, the *quindecimviri* ("Board of Fifteen," who earlier had been 10 in number) *sacris faciundis* looked after foreign rites, and the *epulones* supervised religious feasts. There were also *fetiales*, priestly officials who were concerned with various aspects of international relationships, such as treaties and declarations of war. Also six Vestal Virgins, chosen as young girls from the old patrician families, tended the shrine and fire of Vesta and lived in the House of Vestals nearby, subject to an array of ancient ritual prohibitions.

Festivals. The Roman calendar, as introduced or modified in the period of the Etruscan kings, contained 58 regular festivals. These included 45 Feriae Publicae, celebrated on the same fixed day every year, as well as the Ides of each month, which were sacred to Jupiter, and the Kalends of March, which belonged to Mars. Famous examples of Feriae Publicae were the LUPERCALIA (February 15) and Saturnalia (December 17, later extended). There were also the Feriae Conceptivae, the dates of which were fixed each year by the proper authority and which included the FERIAE LATINAE ("Latin Festival") celebrated in the Alban Hills, usually at the end of April.

Shrines and temples. *Templum* is a term derived from Etruscan divination. Initially it meant an area of the sky defined by the priest for his collection and interpretation of the OMENS. Later it came to signify a piece of ground set aside and consecrated to the gods. At first such areas did not contain sacred buildings, but there often were altars on such sites, and later shrines. In Rome, temples have been identified from *c.* 575 BCE onward, including the round shrine of Vesta and a group in a sacred area (S. Omobono), close to the Tiber River beside the cattle market (Forum Boarium). The great Etruscan temples, made of wood with terracotta ornaments, were constructed later and culminated in the temple of the Capitoline Triad. Subsequently, more solid materials, such as tuff (tufa), travertine, marble, cement, and brick, gradually came into use.

Sacrifice and burial rites.   The characteristic offering was a sacrifice accompanied by a prayer or vow. Animal sacrifices were regarded as more effective than anything else, the pig being the most common victim, with sheep and oxen added on important occasions. Best of all were the heart, liver, and kidneys. HUMAN SACRIFICE was extraneous to Roman custom, though if it was practiced among the Etruscans it may have contributed to the later institution of gladiatorial funeral games, and legend states that it was resorted to in major crises, such as the Second Punic War (216 BCE).

Ancestors were meticulously revered, but most Romans' ideas of the afterlife, unless they believed in the promises of the MYSTERY RELIGIONS, were vague. Such ideas often amounted to a cautious hope or fear that the spirit in some sense lived on, and this was sometimes combined with an anxiety that the ghosts of the dead, especially the young dead who bore the living a grudge, might return and cause harm. Graves and tombs were inviolable, protected by supernatural powers. In the earliest days of Rome both CREMATION and inhumation (burial) were practiced simultaneously, but by the 2nd century BCE the former had prevailed. Some 300 years later, however, there was a massive reversion to inhumation, probably because of the feeling that the future welfare of the soul depended on comfortable repose of the body. The designs on these tombs reflect the soul's survival as a personal entity that has won its right to paradise.

Tomb of a Roman family, beneath the Via Latina
Anderson—Art Resource

947

ROMANTICISM, attitude or intellectual orientation that characterized many works of literature, painting, music, architecture, criticism, and historiography in Western civilization from the late 18th to the mid-19th century.

Among the characteristic attitudes of Romanticism were a deepened appreciation of the beauties of nature; a general exaltation of emotion over reason and of the senses over intellect; a turning in upon the self and a heightened examination of human personality and its moods and mental potentialities; an emphasis on imagination as a gateway to transcendent experience and spiritual truth; an obsessive interest in folk culture, national and ethnic cultural origins, and the medieval era; and a predilection for the exotic, the remote, the mysterious, the weird, the occult, the monstrous, the diseased, and even the satanic.

Romanticism is visible within THEOLOGICAL LIBERALISM from the late 18th century to the end of the 19th. Marked by the discovery of the uniqueness of the individual and the consequent significance of individual experience as a distinctive source of infinite meaning, this premium on personality and on individual creativity exceeded every other value. In this vein, the German FRIEDRICH SCHLEIERMACHER seized upon the feeling of absolute dependence as being simultaneously that which "signifies God for us" and that which is distinctive in the religious response. Thus, self-consciousness in this deep religious sense becomes God-consciousness. According to Schleiermacher, the Christian is brought to this deeper vein of self-consciousness through the man Jesus, in whom the God-consciousness had been perfected. The nurture of God-consciousness in relation to JESUS CHRIST, Schleiermacher believed, led to the creation of the church as a fellowship of believers.

The Romantic movement also had profound implications for the study of myth. Myths were regarded by the Romantics as repositories of experience far more vital and powerful than those obtainable from what was felt to be the artificial art and poetry of the aristocratic civilization of contemporary Europe. This is illustrated in the work of Johann Gottfried von Herder. He believed that the more "savage"—that is, the more "alive" and "freedom-loving"—a people was, the more alive and free its songs would be. In opposition to the culture of the educated, Herder exalted the Kultur des Volkes ("culture of the people"). For Herder ancient myths were the natural expressions of the concerns that would have confronted the ancients, and those concerns were the very ones that, according to Herder, still confronted the common people.

ROMULUS AND REMUS \\'räm-yə-ləs . . . 'rē-məs\\, legendary founders of Rome. Traditionally, they were the sons of Rhea Silvia, daughter of Numitor, king of Alba Longa.

The legend of Romulus and Remus probably originated in the 4th century BCE and was set down in coherent form at the end of the 3rd century BCE. Numitor, it stated, had been deposed by his younger brother Amulius, who forced Rhea to become a VESTAL VIRGIN (and thereby vow chastity) in order to prevent her from giving birth to potential claimants to the throne. Nevertheless, Rhea bore the god MARS the twins Romulus and Remus. Amulius ordered the infants drowned in the Tiber, but the trough in which they were placed floated down the river and came to rest at the site of the future Rome, near a sacred fig tree. There a she-wolf and a woodpecker—both sacred to Mars—suckled and fed them until they were found by the herdsman Faustulus.

Reared by Faustulus and his wife, the twins became leaders of a band of youths, eventually restoring their grandfather to the throne. They subsequently founded a town on the site where they had been saved. When Romulus built a city wall, Remus jumped over it and was killed by his brother.

Romulus consolidated his power, and the city was named for him. He increased its population by offering asylum to fugitives and exiles and abducted the women of the neighboring Sabines. The women married their captors and intervened to prevent the Sabines from seizing the city. Romulus accepted the Sabine king Titus Tatius as his co-ruler. Titus Tatius' early death left Romulus sole king again, and after a long rule he mysteriously disappeared in a storm. Believing that he had been changed into a god, the Romans worshiped him as the deity QUIRINUS.

ROSARY (from Latin: *rosarium*, "rose garden"), in CHRISTIANITY, religious exercise in which prayers are recited and counted on a string of beads or a knotted cord. By extension, the beads or cord may also be called a rosary. This type of practice is widespread, occurring in Christianity, HINDUISM, BUDDHISM, and ISLAM.

In Christianity, the practice was adopted in the 3rd century by Eastern Christian monks, and various forms of the rosary were developed. In ROMAN CATHOLICISM, the rosary became a popular method of public and private prayer. The most common rosary is the rosary of the Blessed Virgin MARY, the prayers of which are recited with the aid of a chaplet, or rosary. The beads of the chaplet are arranged in five decades (sets of 10), each decade separated from the next by a larger bead. The two ends of the chaplet are joined by a small string holding a crucifix, two large beads, and three small beads.

In its most widespread form, the rosary of the Blessed Virgin requires three turns around the chaplet. It consists of the recitation of 15 decades of HAIL MARYS, each Hail Mary noted by holding a small bead. Each decade is preceded by the Lord's Prayer (a large bead), followed by the Gloria Patri (Glory Be to the Father), and accompanied by a meditation, or mystery. The 15 mysteries are events from the life, death, and glorification of Jesus and Mary; they are divided into three sets of five—the joyous, sorrowful, and glorious mysteries. The introductory and concluding prayers of the rosary vary.

The origin of the rosary of the Blessed Virgin is not certain, although it has been associated with ST. DOMINIC. The devotion probably developed gradually among the unlettered as a substitute for the recitation of the psalms or the divine office. It reached its definitive form in the 15th century through the preaching of the Dominican Alan de la Roche and his associates, who organized Rosary Confraternities at Douai in France and at Cologne. In 1520 Pope Leo X gave the rosary official approbation, and it was repeatedly commended by the Roman Catholic church. But after the 1960s, public recitation of the rosary became rare.

In EASTERN ORTHODOXY the rosary is almost exclusively a monastic devotion. The *kombologion* ("string of beads") used among the Eastern Orthodox of Greece and Turkey has 100 beads of equal size. The Russian Orthodox *vervitsa* (from the root *verv-* "string"), *chotki* (from *chet-* "count"), or *lestovka* (from *lest-* "ladder") is made of 103 beads, separated into irregular sections by 4 large beads and joined together so that the lines of beads run parallel, thus suggesting the form of a ladder. In the Romanian church, the chaplet is called *matanie* ("reverence") because the monk makes a profound bow at the beginning and end of each prayer counted on the beads. *Compare* SUBHA.

ROSENZWEIG, FRANZ \ 'rō-zən-,tsvīk \ (b. Dec. 25, 1886, Kassel, Ger.—d. Dec. 10, 1929, Frankfurt am Main), German-Jewish religious Existentialist. Rosenzweig began his academic career studying medicine but switched to modern history and philosophy at Berlin and Freiburg. While writing his doctoral dissertation (1912) and his later *Hegel und der Staat* ("Hegel and the State"), he became critical of G.F.W. Hegel's emphasis on history and his treatment of the individual's life as irrelevant to the "whole." Increasingly, Rosenzweig's thought moved toward an "existential" philosophy that emphasized the experience and concerns of the individual.

In July 1913 Franz had decided to convert to CHRISTIANITY, but in October of that year he reversed his decision after attending a YOM KIPPUR service in Berlin. He then turned his studies to an intensive reading of classical Hebrew sources. With the outbreak of World War I, Rosenzwieg joined the German armed forces, and in 1916–17 he engaged in an exchange of letters from the Balkan front with jurist and historian Eugen Rosenstock-Huessy on core theological problems in JUDAISM and Christianity, published in *Judentum und Christentum* (*Judaism Despite Christianity*, 1969). In 1918 he began composing his major work *Der Stern der Erlosung* ("The Star of Redemption") on postcards that he sent home. This work proposed a new history of culture and a new philosophical theology of Christianity and Judaism. The central point of the work is God's loving act of revelation, which awakens within humanity the consciousness of an "I". The work was highly regarded by Existentialist and younger Jewish theologians.

After the war Rosenzweig wrote *Bildung und kein Ende* (included in *On Jewish Learning* as "Towards a Renaissance of Jewish Learning"). He later organized the Freies Juedesches Lehrhaus ("Free Jewish House of Learning"), where students were encouraged to examine classical Hebrew sources. The school became a model for similar institutions elsewhere in Germany. During the 1920s he produced important essays and an annotated German version of the medieval Hebrew poetry of JUDAH HA-LEVI. He also joined with MARTIN BUBER to produce a new German translation of the Hebrew BIBLE. He died in 1929. His influence on Jewish religious thought grew remarkably in the decades after his death.

ROSH HASHANAH \,rōsh-hä-shä-'nä; ,rōsh-hə-'shȯ-nə, ,räsh-, -'shä-\ (Hebrew: "Beginning of the Year"), Hashanah *also spelled* Ha-Shanah, *also called* Day of Judgment, *or* Day of Remembrance, major Jewish observance that begins the religious New Year on Tishri 1 (September or October). Because the New Year ushers in a 10-day period of self-examination and penitence, Rosh Hashanah is also called the Day of Judgment. It is also known as the Day of Remembrance, for on this day Jews commemorate the creation of the world, and the Jewish nation recalls its responsibilities as God's chosen people. The ram's horn (SHOFAR) is blown, as prescribed in Numbers 29:1, calling the people to a spiritual awakening associated with the revelation to MOSES on MOUNT SINAI. During the SYNAGOGUE service, the shofar is sounded after the recital of each of three groups of prayers.

ROSICRUCIAN \,rō-zə-'krü-shən, ,rä-\, member of a worldwide brotherhood claiming to possess esoteric wisdom from ancient times. The name is from the order's symbol, a combination of a rose and a cross. Rosicrucianism combines elements of OCCULTISM similar to several RELIGIOUS BELIEFS and practices.

Blowing the shofar during a Rosh Hashanah celebration
Jewish Museum, New York City—Art Resource

The earliest extant document that mentions Rosicrucianism is the *Fama Fraternitatis* ("Account of the Brotherhood"), first published in 1614, which may have given the movement its initial impetus. It recounts the journeys of Christian Rosenkreuz, the reputed founder of Rosicrucianism, who was said to have been born in 1378 and lived for 106 years, though probably he was a symbolic rather than a real character. According to the *Fama*, Rosenkreuz acquired secret wisdom on trips to Egypt, Damascus, Arabia, and Morocco, which he imparted to three others after his return to Germany. The number of his disciples was later increased to eight, who went to different countries.

Rosicrucian symbol of the Golden Dawn
The Bridgeman Art Library

Paracelsus, a Swiss alchemist who died in 1541, may have been the real founder of Rosicrucianism, though some contend that Rosicrucian doctrines not only flourished in ancient Egypt but were espoused by such figures as Plato, Jesus, Philo of Alexandria, and Plotinus. There is no reliable evidence to date the order's history earlier than the 17th century.

ROY, RAM MOHUN \'rȯi\, Ram Mohun *also spelled* Rammohun, Rammohan, *or* Ram Mohan (b. May 22, 1772, Rādhānagar, Bengal, India—d. Sept. 27, 1833, Bristol, Gloucestershire, Eng.), Indian religious, social, and educational reformer who challenged traditional HINDU culture and proposed new directions for Indian society under British rule. He is sometimes called the father of modern India.

He was born in Bengal to a prosperous family of the BRAHMIN CASTE. He seems to have developed unorthodox religious ideas at an early age. As a youth he traveled widely outside Bengal and mastered several languages—Sanskrit, Persian, Arabic, and later Hebrew, Greek, and English, in addition to his native Bengali and Hindi.

In 1803 Roy composed a tract denouncing India's religious divisions and superstition, in its place advocating a monotheistic Hinduism in which reason guides the adherent to "the Absolute Originator who is the first principle of all religions." He sought a basis for his RELIGIOUS BELIEFS in the UPANISHADS and VEDAS, translating them into Bengali, Hindi, and English (violating a long-standing tradition against their vernacular translation) and writing treatises on them. The central theme of these works, for Roy, was the worship of the Supreme God, beyond human knowledge, who supports the universe. His interest in ISLAM inspired him to learn Arabic, and he learned Hebrew and Greek to read the Old and New Testaments. In 1820 he published the ethical teachings of Christ, excerpted from the four Gospels, under the title *Precepts of Jesus, the Guide to Peace and Happiness.*

In 1823, when the British imposed censorship on the Calcutta press, Roy organized a protest, arguing in favor of freedom of speech and religion as natural rights. In his newspapers, treatises, and books, Roy likewise denounced the caste system and the practice of SATĪ.

In 1826 Roy founded the Vedānta College, in order to teach his Hindu monotheistic doctrines. In August 1828 he formed the BRAHMO SAMAJ (Society of Brahman), a Hindu reformist sect that adopted Unitarian and other liberal Christian elements in its beliefs. The Brahmo Samaj played an important part, later in the century, as a Hindu reform movement. In 1829 he journeyed to England as the unofficial representative of the titular king of Delhi. He was well received in England, especially by Unitarians there and by King William IV. Roy died of a fever while in the care of Unitarian friends at Bristol, Eng., where he was buried.

Roy was a tireless social reformer, yet he revived interest in the ethical principles of the VEDĀNTA school as a counterpoise to the Western assault on Indian culture. He was the first Indian to apply to his country the fundamental ideas of the French and American revolutions.

Ram Mohun Roy
By courtesy of the Nehru Memorial Museum and Library, New Delhi

RUDRA \'rù-drə\ (Sanskrit: "Howler"), minor Vedic god associated with frightful, howling storms, and one of the names of SHIVA. In the VEDAS, Rudra is known as the divine archer, who shoots arrows of death and disease. As a healer and a source of 1,000 remedies, he has also a beneficent aspect. He is the father of the storm gods, the Rudras, and is often closely paired with AGNI (Fire), who shares his devastating power and brilliance.

RULE OF THE COMMUNITY, *also called* Manual of Discipline, one of the most important documents from the caves at QUMRĀN, produced, according to most scholars, by an ESSENE community of Jews who settled at Qumrān in the Judaean desert in the early 2nd century BCE. The major manuscript of this work was discovered in Cave I at Qumrān in 1947; fragments of other manuscripts—10 in Cave IV and 1 in Cave V—were all discovered in 1952. These fragments do not all show an identical arrangement of the contents, and it is clear that the document existed in different editions. While the Cave I manuscript has the oldest script, judging by paleographic study, it is apparently the longest, and most scholars think the latest, edition. It was also copied by two different scribes, the second of whom made additions and corrections to the text of the first scribe.

The heading to the *Rule* shows it to be intended for the Essene leader called the Maskil. The document contains an explanation of the sect's religious and moral ideals, a description of its admission ceremony, a discourse on its dualistic theology of two spirits of truth and falsehood (or light and darkness), and organizational and disciplinary statutes.

The Cave I edition also has a final HYMN or psalm praising obedience and setting forth the sacred seasons. In the same manuscript (but none of the others) are contained two other works: the *Rule of the Congregation,* or "Messianic Rule" (1QSa), with information about the composition of the congregation of Israel and its messianic feast; and a liturgical collection of BENEDICTIONS, the *Blessings* (1QSb).

Even before the publication of the Cave IV fragments, scholars (notably Jerome Murphy-O'Connor and Jean Pouilly) had detected signs that the *Manual* was composed in four stages and later edited into its present order:

(1) A Manifesto for a community of 12 men, plus 3 priests, who "shall separate from the congregation of the men of injustice and shall unite, with respect to the Law and possessions, under the authority of the sons of Zadok" (1QSV). These men were to act on behalf of the land to expiate its SIN through spiritual sacrifices.

(2) Penal legislation integrated into the founding document to deal with the problems of community life.

(3) Increasing institutionalization, incorporating more democratic processes into the selection of new members and administrating the community.

(4) An account of a covenant renewal ceremony and Instruction on the Two Spirits. A revival of the initial enthusiasm of the community and a renewed stress on study of the law and rigorous scrutiny of new recruits.

However, based on a comparison of all 12 manuscripts, Metso has suggested a different evolution:

Original edition: Community regulations, incorporating the "Manifesto" (roughly equivalent to stages 1 and 2 above).

Recension A: Addition of scriptural proof-texts and other comments strengthening community self-understanding.

Recension B: Abbreviation of original version and addition of final hymn.

Recension C: A combination of Recensions A and B (represented by 1QS).

Recension D: A revision of Recension C (second scribe of 1QS).

Although the supposed founder of this community, known as the Teacher of Righteousness, is widely thought to have been responsible for the original form of the *Rule*, he is nowhere mentioned. The purpose of the *Rule*, and the reason different editions were preserved side-by-side, remains disputed, as does its relationship to the DAMASCUS DOCUMENT and its community.

See also DEAD SEA SCROLLS.

RŪPA GOSVĀMĪ \'rü-pə-gō-'svä-mē, -'swä-\, Gosvāmī *also spelled* Gosvāmin (fl. 1500–50), scholar, poet, and author of many Sanskrit works; he was one of the most influential and remarkable of the medieval saints of India.

Rūpa Gosvāmī was the most eminent of the six *gosvāmī*s appointed as his successors by the founder of Gauḍīya VAIṢ-ṆAVISM, the Bengali saint CAITANYA. Rūpa's great achievement was to establish the theological foundation of the sect Caitanya founded, emphasizing ecstatic devotion to KRISHNA and techniques for participation in the deity's infinite bliss. One of the principal themes of Rūpa's theology is *bhakti-rasa*, the "aesthetic enjoyment of participatory devotion." He developed the philosophical underpinnings for the practice of cultivating a highly emotional love for God. This practice centers around dramatic enactments whereby the devotee enters into Krishna's divine "play" (LĪLĀ)—which for this tradition is ultimate reality. Various "roles" (*bhāva*s) are identified as paradigms for the devotee's encounters with the divine, including servitude, friendship, and erotic love, the latter being the most important and based on the roles played by RĀDHĀ and other of Krishna's lovers in the tradition's mythology.

Rūpa thus presents religious life in terms of drama, using the language of aesthetics and redirecting it toward the development and expression of devotion, or BHAKTI. It is through participation in the absolute, eternal drama of Krishna's play that salvation occurs in this sect, and Rūpa Gosvāmī was instrumental in systematizing this practice.

RUSALKA \rü-'sál-kə\, *plural* rusalki \-k^yē\, in Slavic mythology, lake-dwelling soul of a child who died unbaptized or of a virgin who was drowned. Around the Danube River, where they are called *vile*, they are beautiful, charming girls, dressed in light robes of mist, singing bewitching songs to passersby. The *rusalki* of northern Russia are ugly, unkempt, wicked, invariably naked, and always eager to ambush humans. All *rusalki* love to entice men—the *vile* to enchant them and the northern *rusalki* to torture them.

During *rusalki* week, at the beginning of the summer, the NYMPHS are supposed to emerge from the water and climb into weeping willow and birch trees until night, when they dance in rings in the moonlight. Anyone joining them must dance until he dies. After that week, grass grows thicker where they trod.

RUSSELL, CHARLES TAZE \'tāz-'rə-səl\, *byname* Pastor Russell (b. Feb. 16, 1852, Pittsburgh, Pa., U.S.—d. Oct. 31, 1916, Pampa, Texas), founder of the International Bible Students Association, forerunner of the JEHOVAH'S WITNESSES.

At the age of 20, an encounter with some ADVENTISTS introduced Russell to the idea that the BIBLE could be used to predict God's plan of salvation, especially as the plan related to the end of the world.

He formed his first Bible classes in 1872. Basing his judgment on complex biblical calculations, he preached from 1877 that Christ's "invisible return" had occurred in 1874 and that the end of the Gentile times would come in 1914, followed by war between capitalism and communism or socialism, after which God's kingdom by Christ would rule the earth. Russell (who was never ordained) dedicated his life and his fortune to preaching Christ's millennial reign. In 1879 he started a Bible journal, which later came to be called *The Watchtower*, and in 1884 he founded the Watch Tower Bible and Tract Society, and this became a flourishing business. His own books and booklets (notably seven volumes of *Studies in the Scriptures*) reached an enormous circulation.

Russell's movement survived the embarrassment caused by the apparent failure of his apocalyptic prediction, as well as the problems caused by his separation from his wife and numerous lawsuits.

RUYSBROECK, JAN VAN \'rȯis-ˌbrük\, Jan *also rendered* Johannes, Ruysbroeck *also spelled* Ruusbroec \'rūs-ˌbrük\ (b. 1293, Ruisbroek, near Brussels, Brabant [now in Belgium]—d. Dec. 2, 1381, Groenendaal, Brabant), Flemish mystic whose writings influenced JOHANN TAULER, Gerhard Groote, and others.

After 1343, Ruysbroeck founded the AUGUSTINIAN abbey at Groenendaal, where he wrote all but the first of his works, *Van den Rike der Ghelieven* (*The Kingdom of the Lovers of God*). Ruysbroeck viewed the relationship of the soul to God as similar to that between the lover and the beloved. *Die Chierheit der gheesteliker Brulocht* (1350; *The Spiritual Espousals*), considered his masterpiece, develops his view of the TRINITY and is a guide for the soul in search of God. Though his many writings were produced for his contemporary Augustinians, they spread rapidly through Latin translations and anticipated the 15th-century DEVOTIO MODERNA. Ruysbroeck was beatified in 1908; his feast is traditionally celebrated on the anniversary of his death.

RYŌBU SHINTŌ \'ryō-bü-'shēn-ˌtō, *Angl* rē-'ō-bü-'shin-tō\, *also called* Shingon Shintō \'shēŋ-ˌgȯŋ-, *Angl* 'shiŋ-ˌgän-\ (Japanese: "Dual Aspect Shintō"), in Japanese religion, syncretic school that combined SHINTŌ with the teachings of the SHINGON sect of BUDDHISM. The school developed during the late Heian (794–1185) and Kamakura (1192–1333) periods. It argued that Shintō deities (KAMI) were manifestations of Buddhist divinities and identified the sun goddess AMATERASU with the Buddha Mahāvairocana (Japanese name Dainichi Nyorai: "Great Sun Buddha"). The Shingon belief in the two realms of Dainichi was interpreted as corresponding to the two *kami* at the Ise Shrine: Amaterasu was considered the equivalent of *taizō-kai* ("womb world"), and Toyuke Ōkami, the *kami* of food, clothing, and shelter, was equated with *kongō-kai* ("diamond world"). Their shrines at Ise were identified with the two MANDALAS used to represent the dual nature of Dainichi.

Ryōbu Shintō was highly influential in the development of other syncretic schools, notably Sannō Ichijitsu Shintō.

SA'ADIA BEN JOSEPH \'sä-dē-à-ben-'jō-səf, -zəf\, *Arabic* Sa'īd ibn Yūsuf al-Fayyūmī (b. 882, Dilaz, al-Fayyūm, Egypt—d. September 942, Sura, Babylonia), Jewish exegete, philosopher, and polemicist whose influence on Jewish literary and communal activities made him one of the most important Jewish scholars of his time.

As a young man, Sa'adia left Egypt, living in Palestine and, later, Babylon. His early works include a Jewish-Arabic dictionary and a work intended to refute the Jewish heresy KARAISM. In 921 Sa'adia was appointed by the exilarch (head of Babylonian Jewry) David ben Zakkai as the GAON ("head") of the academy of Sura, which had been transferred to Baghdad. (*See also* JUDAISM: RABBINIC JUDAISM: THE GAONATE OF SA'ADIA.) Upon assuming this office, he recognized the need to systematize Talmudic law and canonize it by subject. Toward this end he produced *Kitāb al-mawārīth* ("Book on the Laws of Inheritance"); *Aḥkam al-wadī'ah* ("The Laws on Deposits"); *Kitāb ash-shahādah wa al-wathā'iq* ("Book Concerning Testimony and Documents"); *Kitāb aṭ-ṭerefot* ("Book Concerning Forbidden Meats"); and the SIDDUR, a complete arrangement of the prayers and the laws pertaining to them. In the *Siddur* he included his original religious poems.

His accomplishments intensified his sense of chosenness and made him more unyielding and less compromising. In 932, when Sa'adia refused to endorse a decision issued by the Exilarch in a litigation, the Exilarch excommunicated Sa'adia, and the latter retaliated by excommunicating the Exilarch. After three years of embittered struggle, Ben Zakkai succeeded in having the Muslim ruler al-Qāhir remove Sa'adia from office. The Gaon went into seclusion.

In the years that followed he composed his major philosophical work, *Kitāb al-amānāt wa al-i'tiqādāt.* The objective of this work was the harmonization of revelation and reason. In structure and content it displays a definite influence of Greek philosophy and of the theology of the MU'TAZILA (a great Islamic sect of speculative theology, which emphasized the doctrines of God's uniqueness and absolute justice). The introduction refutes skepticism and establishes the foundations of human knowledge. Chapter one seeks to establish *creatio ex nihilo* (creation out of nothing) in order to ascertain the existence of a Creator-God. Sa'adia then discusses God's uniqueness, justice, revelation, FREE WILL, and other doctrines accepted both by JUDAISM and by the Mu'tazila. The second part of the book deals with the essence of the soul and eschatological problems and presents guidelines for ethical living.

A reconciliation between the Gaon and the Exilarch occurred, and Sa'adia was reinstated as *gaon.* In 940 Ben Zakkai died. Sa'adia himself died in September 942.

An exact chronology for many of Sa'adia's works cannot be definitely determined. The most important of his works in philology are: *Kutub al-lughah* ("Books on Grammar") and *Tafsīr as-sab 'īn lafẓah* ("The Explanation of the Seven-

ty Hapaxlegomina"). Sa'adia's opus magnum was on EXEGESIS. He prepared an Arabic translation of the whole PENTATEUCH (published by Joseph Derenbourg) and a translation with an extensive commentary on GENESIS 1–28, EXODUS, and Leviticus. His translation and commentaries on Isaiah, Proverbs, Job, and Psalms are extant in their entirety. Fragments of his commentaries on Daniel and Canticles, Esther, and Lamentations are preserved in the GENIZAH collection (fragments of medieval texts found in an old synagogue in Cairo and transferred to various libraries).

Sa'adia's anti-Karaite works include *Kitāb ar-radd 'alā Ibn Sākawayhī* ("Refutation of Ibn Sākawayhī") and *Kitāb taḥṣīl ash-sharā'i' as-samā'īyah* ("Book Concerning the Sources of the Irrational Laws"). In the latter work the Gaon contends that matters pertaining to the irrational commandments of the Mosaic Law may never be decided by means of analogy but only by the regulations transmitted through ORAL TRADITION. Talmudic tradition is therefore indispensable. The *Maqālah fī sirāj as-sabt* ("Treatise on the Lights of Sabbath") refutes the Karaite injunction forbidding the preparation of light for the SABBATH.

SABBATH \'sa-bəth\, *Hebrew* Shabbat \shä-'bät\ (from *shavat*, "cease," or "desist"), day of holiness and rest observed by Jews from sunset on Friday to nightfall of the following day. The Sabbath marks the celebration of creation's perfection (GENESIS 2:1–3). Food for the day is to be prepared in advance (EXODUS 16:22–26; 29–30). Fire is not to be kindled on that day, thus there is no cooking (Exodus 34:2–3). Servile labor is not to be carried on during that day by the householder and his dependents (Exodus 20:5–11; 31:12–17; 34:21). The "where" matters as much as the "when" and the "how": people are supposed to stay in their place: "Let each person remain in place, let no one leave his place on the seventh day" (Exodus 16:29–30), understanding by place the private domain of the household.

In RABBINIC JUDAISM, the advent of the Sabbath transforms creation, specifically reorganizing space and time and reordering the range of permissible activity. First comes the transformation of space that takes effect at sundown at the end of the sixth day and that ends at sundown of the Sabbath day. At that time, for holy ISRAEL, the entire world is divided into public domain and private domain, and what is located in the one may not be transported into the other. What is located in the public domain may be transported only four cubits, that is, within the space occupied by a person's body. What is in private domain may be transported within the entire demarcated space of that domain. The net effect is to move nearly all permitted activity to the private domain and to close off public domain for all but the most severely limited activities.

Second comes the matter of time and how the advent of sacred time registers. Objects may be handled only if they are designated in advance of the Sabbath for the purpose for

Habdalah ceremony marking the end of the Sabbath, with wine and candle; woodcut from the Minhagim Book, Amsterdam, 1662
Jewish Museum, New York—Art Resource

which they will be utilized on the Sabbath. But if tools may be used for a purpose that is licit on the Sabbath, and if those tools are ordinarily used for that same purpose, they are deemed ready at hand and do not require reclassification; the accepted classification applies. What requires designation for Sabbath use in particular is any tool that may serve more than a single purpose, or that does not ordinarily serve the purpose for which it is wanted on the Sabbath.

The affect upon activity that the advent of the Sabbath makes concerns constructive labor. In a normal way one may not carry out entirely on his own a completed act of constructive labor, which is to say, work that produces enduring results. The advent of the Sabbath prohibits activities carried out in ordinary time in a way deemed natural: acts that are complete, consequential, and in accord with their accepted character. No prohibition impedes performing an act of labor in an other than normal way. In theory, one may go out into the fields and plough, if he does so in some odd manner. One may build an entire house, so long as it collapses promptly. The issue of activity on the Sabbath therefore is removed from the obvious context of work, conventionally defined.

To act like God on the Sabbath of Creation is what Israel is enjoined to do; thus, on the Sabbath, the Israelite rests. And, the traits of an act of labor for God in creation define the prohibited conditions of an act of labor on the Sabbath, when Israel goes home to Eden. Israel's Eden takes place in the household open to others, on the Sabbath, in acts that maintain life, share wealth, and desist from creation. On the Sabbath Israel gives up the situation of man in ordinary time and space—destructive, selfish, dissatisfied and doing. Then, on the Sabbath, and there, in the household, with each one in place, Israel enters the situation of God in that initial, that perfected and sanctified then and there of creation: the activity that consists in sustaining life and perfecting repose through acts of restraint and sufficiency.

SABBATH RIVER: *see* SAMBATION.

ŚABDA \\'shəb-də\ (Sanskrit: "sound"), in Indian philosophy, verbal testimony as a means of obtaining knowledge. In the orthodox philosophical systems (DARŚAN), *śabda* is equated with the authority of the VEDAS as the only infallible testimony. These are deemed eternal, authorless, and without contradiction. The exegetic Mimāṃsā school defines the authoritativeness as applying bindingly only to scriptural statements that exhort to purposive action and whose efficacy would not be known by any other means of knowledge. The VEDĀNTA school extends this authoritativeness to suprasensual objects, especially BRAHMAN, the ultimate reality. The school of logic, NYĀYA, accepts verbal testimony, both human and divine, as a valid means of knowledge but notes that only the divine knowledge conveyed in the Vedas is infallible.

The systems of BUDDHISM and JAINISM reject the authoritativeness of the Vedas but appeal to the authority of their own SCRIPTURES.

SABZAVĀRĪ, HĀJJĪ HĀDĪ \sab-ze-,vä-'rē\, *also spelled* Sabzevārī (b. 1797/98, Sabzavār, Iran—d. 1878, Sabzavār), Iranian teacher and philosopher who advanced the *ḥikma* (wisdom) school of Islamic philosophy. His doctrines—composed of diverse elements of esoteric spiritual knowledge, philosophy, and revelation—are an exposition and clarification of the philosophical concepts of MULLĀ ṢADRĀ. But he classified knowledge as an essence, rather than an outward quality, of the human soul.

After spending his early childhood in Sabzavār, a center for Shi'i and Sufi studies (*see* SHI'ITE *and* SUFISM), Sabzavārī was educated in MASHHAD, and in Iṣfahān, where he was first influenced by the teachings of the *ḥikmat*. On completing his studies, he returned to his native city, where he founded a MADRASA (school) that attracted students of philosophy from as far away as Arabia and India.

The fame of Sabzavārī was such that Nāṣir al-Dīn Shāh, the fourth Qājār king of Iran, visited him in 1857/78. At the request of the Shāh, he wrote the *Asrār al-ḥikma* ("The Secrets of Wisdom"), which, together with his Arabic treatise *Sharḥ manẓūma* ("A Treatise on Logic in Verse"), remains a basic text for the study of *ḥikmat* doctrines in Iran. He also wrote poetry under the name of Asrār and completed a commentary on the *Māsnavī* of JALĀL AL-DĪN AL-RŪMĪ, the great mystic poet of ISLAM. Devout and pious, Sabzavārī led the ascetic life of a mystic. Miracles were attributed to him, and he is said to have cured the sick. On his death the Shāh ordered that a mausoleum be constructed for him in Mashhad. *See also* MĪR DĀMĀD.

SACRAMENT, religious sign or symbol, especially associated with the Christian church, in which a sacred or spiritual power is believed to be transmitted through material elements viewed as channels of divine GRACE.

Among early agriculturalists and herders, the fertility of the soil, beneficence of the weather, and succession of the seasons became the focuses of sacramental practices designed to ensure their continuation, such as the rites of spring and feasts of harvest. Inasmuch as the cycle of the individual life was seen to reflect the natural order, sacramental ceremonies were conducted to promote successful passage from one status to another.

In CHRISTIANITY, the sacramental principle became the fundamental system and institution for the perpetuation of the union of God and man in the person of JESUS CHRIST through the visible organization and constitution of the church, which was viewed as the mystical body of Christ.

Children in a Roman Catholic church receive their First Communion, a ceremony that celebrates their partaking in the sacrament of the Eucharist
Mimi Forsyth—Monkmeyer

According to the NEW TESTAMENT, Jesus instituted and commanded various practices, among them BAPTISM, a common meal, the washing of feet, anointing, and the casting out of DEMONS. Some of these were continued by Christians; some were dropped; still others were adopted and attributed to the institution of Christ. Consideration of all these rites led to the development of the concept "sacrament," but both the definition and the exact number remained fluid well beyond the end of the 1st millennium of church history.

As set forth by PETER LOMBARD, codified by THOMAS AQUINAS, and promulgated by the COUNCIL OF TRENT, the sacraments were said to be seven in number (baptism, CONFIRMATION, EUCHARIST, penance, anointing or extreme unction, holy orders or ORDINATION, and matrimony) and to be efficacious signs of the grace of God instituted by Christ. Part of almost every definition of a sacrament, however, is the requirement that it have been, in some sense, "instituted by Christ." Of these seven, such institution can be incontrovertibly documented from the New Testament for only baptism and the Eucharist.

The REFORMATION accordingly questioned both the definition and the number of sacraments in scholastic theology, as well as the use of sacraments in medieval piety, liturgy, and churchmanship. Protestant biblical scholarship eventually came to recognize that even the accounts of the institution of the Eucharist by Christ are, in their present form at least, products of the recollection of the early Christian community rather than verbatim transcripts of the sayings of the historical Jesus. ROMAN CATHOLIC theology likewise surrendered the effort to find explicit historical support for each of the seven sacraments and concentrated instead on the implicit significance of the very establishment of the church: Christ instituted the sacraments in a theological sense, even though there is no way of proving that the historical Jesus instituted them.

SACRED, THE, power, being, or realm understood by religious persons to be at the core of existence and to have a transformative effect on their lives and destinies. Other terms, such as divine, transcendent, ultimate being (or reality), mystery, and perfection (or purity) have been used for this domain.

Basic characteristics. The term *sacred* comes from Latin *sacer* ("set off, restricted"). A person or thing was designated as sacred when it was unique or extraordinary. Various terms from different traditions have been recognized as correlates of *sacer:* Greek *hagios*, Hebrew *qadosh*, Polynesian *tapu* (tabu), and Arabic *ḥarām*.

Set off from the profane world, the sacred in many cultures is extraordinary, prohibited for daily use or contact, and often powerful. In ancient Rome the word *sacer* could mean that which would pollute someone or something that came into contact with it, as well as that which was restricted for divine use. Similarly, the Polynesian *tapu* designated something as not "free" for common use. It might be someone or something specially blessed because it was full of power, or it might be something accursed, as a corpse. Whatever was *tapu* had special restrictions around it, for it was full of extraordinary energy that could destroy anyone unprotected with special power himself.

Because the sacred contains notions both of a positive, creative power and a danger that requires stringent prohibitions, a common reaction is a mixture of fear and fascination. On the one hand, the sacred is the limit of human effort both in the sense of that which meets human frailty and that which prohibits human activity; on the other hand, it is the unlimited possibility that draws mankind beyond the limiting temporal-spacial structures that are constituents of human existence.

The emergence of the concept of the sacred. It was during the first quarter of the 20th century that the concept of the sacred (or holy) became dominant in the comparative STUDY OF RELIGIONS. Nathan Söderblom, an eminent Swedish churchman and historian of religions, asserted in 1913 that the central notion of religion was "holiness" and that the distinction between sacred and profane was basic to "real" religious life. In 1917 RUDOLF OTTO'S *Heilige* (*The Idea of the Holy*) appeared and exercised a great influence on the study of religion through its description of religious man's experience of the "numinous" (a mysterious, majestic presence inspiring dread and fascination), which Otto, a German historian of religions, claimed, could not be derived from anything other than an *a priori* sacred reality. In 1915 the sociologist ÉMILE DURKHEIM published *The Elementary Forms of the Religious Life*, in which sacredness referred to those things in society that were forbidden or set apart; since these sacred things were set apart by society, the sacred force, he concluded, was society itself.

Since the first quarter of the 20th century many historians of religions have accepted the notion of the sacred and of sacred events, places, people, and acts as being central in religious life if not indeed the essential reality in religious life. For example, phenomenologists of religion such as

Gerardus van der Leeuw and W. Brede Kristensen have considered the sacred (holy) as central and have organized the material in their systematic works around the (transcendent) object and (human) subject of sacred (cultic) activity, together with a consideration of the forms and symbols of the sacred. Significant contributions to the analysis and elaboration of the sacred have been made by Roger Caillois, a sociologist, and by MIRCEA ELIADE, an eminent historian of religions.

Critical problems. Phenomenologists of religion who use the concept "sacred" as a universal term for the basis of religion differ in their estimation of the nature of the sacred manifestation. Otto and Gerardus van der Leeuw hold that the sacred is a reality that transcends the apprehension of the sacred in symbols or rituals. The forms (ideograms) through which the sacred is expressed are secondary and are simply reactions to the "wholly other." Kristensen and Eliade, on the other hand, regarded the sacred reality to be available through the particular symbols or ways of apprehending the sacred.

A second problem is the continuing question of whether or not the sacred is a universal category. There is a serious question regarding the usefulness of this term in interpreting a large part of Chinese religion, the social relationships (DHARMA) in HINDUISM, the effort to achieve superconscious awareness in Hinduism (YOGA), JAINISM, BUDDHISM (ZEN), some forms of TAOISM, and some contemporary options of total commitment that, nevertheless, reject the notion of an absolute source and goal essentially different from human existence. If one takes the notion of sacred as something above (beyond, different from) the religious structure dominated by divine or transcendent activity, then this suggests that the notion of sacredness should not be limited to that structure. Thus, some scholars have found it confusing to use the notion of sacred as a universal religious quality, for it has been accepted by many religious people and by scholars of religion as referring to only one (though important) type of religious consciousness.

SACRED ARCHITECTURE, within the religious sphere, the art and the technique of building. The history of architecture is concerned more with religious buildings than with any other type because in many cultures the appeal of religion made the church or temple the most expressive, the most permanent, and the most influential building in the community. Since a wide range of considerations—theological, technological, social, political, artistic, and economic—enter into the design and construction of sacred edifices, the historical roles they have played also tend to be broad and diverse.

Throughout history, sacred architecture has been of critical social and economic importance. Within a community defined by shared beliefs, architecture may provide the house of worship, the meeting place, the pivot-point around which the entire society turns. Thus, many communities have devoted large portions of their available resources to the construction of magnificent sacred edifices. In return, however, these CATHEDRALS, STUPAS, and TEMPLES often become centers of PILGRIMAGE and tourism, and can thereby become a source of wealth and prestige for the community for centuries, or even millennia. For example, Muslims performing the HAJJ (a PILGRIMAGE to MECCA, one of the FIVE PILLARS OF ISLAM) are required to walk seven times around the KA'BA, a small shrine that houses the BLACK STONE OF MECCA. The focus of religious energies on this location, and the shrine that marks it, has ensured the importance of Mecca even as ISLAM has become a world religion.

On a social level, architecture can often provide the focal point of a community's energies. Thus the GOLDEN TEMPLE (Darbār Sāhib) of SIKHISM or the HAGIA SOPHIA in Istanbul, Turkey (formerly Constantinople), serve as the symbolic

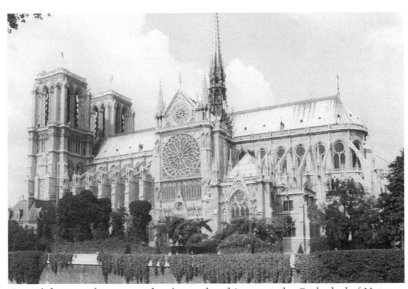

One of the most famous works of sacred architecture, the Cathedral of Notre-Dame de Paris
By courtesy of Electa, Milano

center of their respective religious communities, no matter how far-flung those communities have become. Likewise, the TEMPLE OF JERUSALEM, though destroyed by the Romans in 70 CE, still stands as the emotional center of JUDAISM for a large number of Jews throughout the world. In ancient communities it was common to conceive of the world as roughly circular, with one's country at the center of the world, one's city at the center of the country, and a temple at the center of the city.

Frequently the sacredness of a piece of architecture can be the result of something that it contains: an important sculpture, a piece of especially hallowed ground, or a RELIC of a SAINT or religious leader. Thus in Sri Lanka the TEMPLE OF THE TOOTH was built to house a tooth of the BUDDHA GOTAMA, and the medieval cathedrals of Europe were often built to house the relics of a saint. In some religions the temple was felt to be the actual residence of the god, as in ancient Egypt; in such cases entrance to the temple is usually restricted to a special priestly caste. In these ways, sacred architecture marks a point of intersection between the divine and the human, between the natural and the supernatural. The two elements—the building and that which it contains—are mutually supportive; the beauty of the edifice underscores how special the place or the object is, while the perceived holiness of the relic magnifies the sacredness of the building that houses it.

On a symbolic level, sacred architecture provides an opportunity to impose a logical scheme on physical space. Creation myths and cosmologies often describe the physical world as being laid out in a meaningful way: heaven above earth, hell beneath all, certain symbolic attributes attached to the four cardinal directions, and so on. The construction of a building allows the builders to construct a space along the same lines; on a microcosmic level they can reproduce the ideal structure of the cosmos. Thus sacred architecture often takes on the form of space—not as it is but as RELIGIOUS BELIEF dictates that it should be. Thus in medieval HINDUISM, every aspect of the design of temples was thought to be symbolic of some feature of the cosmos. Temples were laid out geometrically to mirror the structure of the universe, with its four geometric quarters and a celestial roof. The temple itself represented the mountain at the navel of the world and often somewhat resembled a mountain. Likewise, the ZIGGURATS of ancient Mesopotamia may have been intended to represent a sacred mountain at the center of the world. In this way, the construction of a temple can symbolically mirror the creation of the world itself, and the building thereby becomes a mirror and signifier of all that is important in this world.

SACRED CLOWN, ritual or ceremonial figure, in various cultures throughout the world, who represents a reversal of the normal order, especially during NEW YEAR FESTIVALS.

In certain traditions clowning is an apotropaic (designed to avert evil) ritual, a way of deflecting demonic attention from serious religious activities. In other contexts it serves as an initiatory ordeal in which the initiate must persevere through the jests and insults hurled at him.

The Koyemshi, the dancing clowns of the Pueblo Indians (see NATIVE AMERICAN RELIGIONS), punctuate the most important religious ceremonies with obscene and sacrilegious actions and serve as a sign of the presence of the powerful primordial beings and as a means of social control by their satire of the antisocial behavior of particular individuals.

SACRED COW, English-language formulation of the Hindu principle of the sanctity of all life, including animal life and especially that of the cow, which is accorded veneration. *See* COW, SANCTITY OF THE.

SACRED KINGSHIP, religio-political concept that views a ruler as an incarnation, mediator, or agent of the transcendent or supernatural powers considered to be the source of the existence of a community. It is the relation between the king and divine power that defines sacred kingship rather than a more limited definition as head of state.

Various types of sacred kingship have prevailed in different cultures, and is to be found in the ancient Middle and Far East, Hellenistic and European cultures, pre-Columbian Meso-America and South America, and in various indigenous cultures of the twentieth century. While important features may be described as common to these traditions, each individual variety can be properly understood only in its particular social, historical, and religious context.

There are three basic types of sacred kings: (1) the receptacle of divine power; (2) the divine or semidivine ruler; and

(3) the agent or mediator of the sacred. The first views the king as an ICON of the sacred realm. The ruler's power may be both malevolent and beneficial, and it is believed to be essential in all dimensions of communal life, particularly in agriculture where the ruler's influence over the weather and the land's fertility ensure the harvest necessary for survival. In this concept of sacred kingship, the ruler's power is supported by or identical to his own divine body.

Some societies, particularly those of ancient China, the Middle East, and South America, exhibited the second type of sacred kingship. There the ruler was identified with a particular god or as a god himself. However, these god-kings were usually considered to be an individual deity, while another frequent type of divine king is one regarded as the son of a god, an idea found in the cultures of Japan, Peru (among the Incas), Mesopotamia, and the larger Greco-Roman world, among others. The queen mother may then be referred to as mother of god, though the future sacred king may be adopted, rather than begotten, by the reigning monarch. Finally, a king or ruler may become deified after his death, but this transformation appears rather more akin to ANCESTOR WORSHIP than to sacred kingship in its fullest sense.

The third form of sacred kingship is that of the ruler as mediator, servant, or executive agent of a god. In this form it is the institution of kingship, more than an individual ruler, that bears the mark of the sacred. The deity remains the true lord, while the king seeks to do the will of this god in the community; the king is the link between divine and human, the spiritual and the material.

Religious duties are frequently connected with sacred kingship, and the king may often be a seer or priest as well. This priestly function is particularly important to communities who regard the king as a mediator or divine executive, and his oracles, dreams, or prophecies are believed to hold the divine commands. Another ritual function of the sacred king is as the center of a cult, which may help a king to unify his people and so consolidate his power; such cults may arise from political motivations. Ruler cults were known in ancient Egypt and were especially widespread throughout the Greco-Roman world.

Among the more important ceremonies of sacred kingship are those involving succession, legitimation, and coronation. A king may be selected on the basis of a number of criteria including birth, adoption, omens, and divination; the new king may take power before or after the death of his predecessor. A new king often legitimates his right to rule by pointing to his selection as king, by possessing such symbols of kingship as the crown and scepter, and by ascending to the throne. Frequently, the new ruler chooses a royal or throne name and declares a new era. Sacred kings also participate in the religious rites of the community, particularly in the great festivals and cultic dramas, sometimes to atone for the misdeeds of the community but more often to ensure fertility, harmony, and order in society and the cosmos.

SACRED PIPE, *also called* peace pipe, *or* calumet \'kal-yə-ˌmet, -mət\, one of the central ceremonial objects of North American Indian culture (see NATIVE AMERICAN RELIGIONS). Though smoked for relaxation, it was primarily an object of veneration and smoked on all ceremonial occasions. The pipe was revered and employed as a major means of communication between the spiritual world and man. The parts, colors, and motifs used in its decoration, and in the attached pendants of feathers or horsehair, corresponded to

Calumet, a ceremonial American Indian peace pipe
By courtesy of the Museum of the American Indian, Heye Foundation, New York

the essential parts of the universe according to this belief system. The pipe was also smoked in personal prayer, as well as at collective rituals. Its most common use was in invocations to the six directions. Among some tribes (*e.g.*, the Pawnee, Omaha, Crow) complex pipe dances were developed that presented smoke offerings to the Great Spirit.

SACRED SPACE AND TIME, set of categories many scholars use to interpret religion. ÉMILE DURKHEIM thought that the categories were essential to the DEFINITION OF RELIGION. MIRCEA ELIADE turned the categories into a fundamental ontology that defined all religions as the sacred opposite the profane. Most scholars of religion find the terms useful as methodological categories for describing religion.

Both sacred space and sacred time provide a means for describing a specific religious orientation or structure. Durkheim and Eliade agreed that all significant human acts are encompassed if not constituted by sacred space and time. Eliade argued that the great myths of creation, which tell us how the cosmos was formed "in the beginning," provide the model for sacred space and time; thus every meaningful structure is a sacred space, in that it is a microcosm of the great cosmogonic act of creation itself. By this definition, all great monuments to a particular religion are examples of sacred space, as are traditional towns and cities, houses, sacred places of PILGRIMAGE, and other forms of SACRED ARCHITECTURE.

To build, to make or produce something of significance, usually entails an act that imitates a sacred model. The primary structure of this model is usually the four cardinal points with a sacred center. Sacred places such as Jerusalem, VRINDĀBAD, VARANASI, MECCA, Beijing, and Rome mark a sacred center, the center of the cosmos in microcosmic terms. As sacred spaces they are holy places and tend to become places of pilgrimage. Most religious structures and geography emphasize a particular orientation from the center; in ISLAM, HINDUISM, and BUDDHISM it is the East that is endowed with particular significance.

Sacred time is generally cyclical: it has a beginning and an end usually marked by great cosmological time spans. The Christian BIBLE is an excellent example of such a span, beginning with creation (GENESIS) and ending with de-creation (REVELATION TO JOHN). The huge Hindu and Buddhist cosmic cycles through which all life migrates is another example of sacred time as cosmic cyclical time. Each SABBATH in JUDAISM signifies the cosmic act of creation and rest. In Hinduism each month, fortnight, and day represent either the dark or bright half of the day of BRAHMĀ, the god of creation. The ritual year of all religions begins and ends with a periodic new year ritual, and most RITES OF PASSAGE are marked by a specific time in the ritual calendar of a religion. The auspicious and inauspicious times for certain activities, rituals, and plans also are defined by sacred time: significant acts take place in sacred time.

SACRIFICE ("to make sacred"), act of offering objects to a divinity, thereby making them holy.

There are many theories about the nature of sacrifice, including the theory that sacrifice is the origin of religion—its very foundation. Henri Hubert and MARCEL MAUSS' "Essai sur la nature et le fonction du sacrifice" (1899; *Sacrifice: Its Nature and Function*, 1964), remains the classic study.

SACRILEGE, originally, the theft of something sacred; as early as the 1st century BCE, however, the Latin term for sacrilege came to mean any injury, violation, or profanation of sacred things. Legal punishment for such acts was sanctioned in the Levitical code of ancient ISRAEL, and the Israelites also had extensive rules to safeguard whatever was considered to be holy or consecrated.

In GREEK RELIGION sacrilege was closely connected with treason: a temple was regarded as the home of a protector of the state, and thievery of temple property was consequently a crime against the state. Roman cults were protected by ritual prohibitions, and there was no precise term in Roman law equivalent to sacrilege. Early Christians most frequently used sacrilege in the restricted sense of theft of sacred things; but by the mid-4th century the broader meaning had been adopted. In the Theodosian Code (published 438 CE) of the Eastern Roman Empire, the term sacrilege applied to APOSTASY (from CHRISTIANITY), HERESY, SCHISM, JUDAISM, adherence to pre-Christian religions, actions against the immunity of churches and clergy or the privileges of church courts, the desecration of SACRAMENTS, and the violation of the SABBATH. The Frankish SYNODS of the Middle Ages emphasized the crime of seizing church property. The worst sacrilege of all was to defile the Host of the EUCHARIST, an act generally punishable by torture and death.

During the Protestant REFORMATION, sacrilege was a cause of great enmity between Roman Catholics and Protestants. Contemporary Protestants generally deny the inherent sacredness of objects and give little attention to the notion of sacrilege. In ROMAN CATHOLICISM it is dealt with in the Code of CANON LAW and extends to persons as well as to objects.

SADDUCEE \'sa-jə-,sē, -dyə-\, *Hebrew* Tzedoq, *plural* Tzedoqim, member of a Jewish priestly sect that flourished for about two centuries before the destruction of the Second TEMPLE OF JERUSALEM in 70 CE. The Sadducees' name may be derived from that of Zadok, who was HIGH PRIEST in the time of kings DAVID and SOLOMON. Zadokites formed the Temple hierarchy from the time of EZEKIEL to the 2nd century BCE.

The Sadducees were the party of high priests, aristocratic families, and merchants—the wealthier elements of the population. They came under the influence of Hellenism, tended to have good relations with the Roman rulers of Palestine, and generally represented the conservative view within JUDAISM. While their rivals, the PHARISEES, claimed the authority of piety and learning, the Sadducees claimed that of birth and social and economic position.

A Hindu sadhu, or holy person
J. Allan Cash

The Sadducees and Pharisees were in constant conflict with each other, most importantly over the content and extent of God's revelation to the Jewish people. The Sadducees refused to go beyond the written TORAH and thus, unlike the Pharisees, denied the immortality of the soul, bodily resurrection after death, and the existence of angels. For the Sadducees, the Oral Law—*i.e.*, the body of post-biblical Jewish legal traditions—meant next to nothing.

Though the Sadducees were conservative in religious matters, their wealth and their willingness to compromise with the Roman rulers aroused the hatred of the common people. Their lives and political authority were so intimately bound up with Temple worship that after Roman legions destroyed the Temple, the sect ceased to exist.

SĀDHANA \'sä-də-nə\, *or* sādhanā (Sanskrit: "realization"), in TANTRIC HINDUISM and Buddhist Tantrism (VAJRAYĀNA), a spiritual exercise by which practitioners evoke a divinity, identifying and absorbing it into themselves. *Sādhana* involves the body in MUDRAS (sacred gestures), the voice in MANTRAS (sacred utterances), and the mind in the visualization of sacred designs and the figures of divinities. One collection of *sādhana*s is the *Sādhanamālā* (Sanskrit: "Garland of Realization"), composed c. 400–1000 CE, includes those designed for practical results as well as those intended to further spiritual realization.

SADHU \'sä-dü\, *Sanskrit* sādhu, *feminine* sādhvī, in India, religious ascetic or holy person. The class of sadhus includes renunciants of many types and faiths. They are sometimes designated by the term swami (Sanskrit *svāmī*, "master"), which refers especially to an ascetic who has been initiated into a specific religious order and has come to be applied particularly to monks of the Ramakrishna mission; the term, however, is SANNYĀSĪ in ŚAIVISM or VAIRĀGĪ in VAISNAVISM.

Sadhus may live together in monasteries (*maṭha*s) that usually belong to a particular order, may wander throughout the country alone or in small groups, or may isolate themselves in small huts or caves. They generally take vows of poverty and CELIBACY and depend on the CHARITY of householders for their food. Their dress and ornaments differ according to sectarian allegiances and personal tastes, but they usually wear ochre-colored (more rarely, white) robes. (*See also* SANGHA.) They shave their heads, or they allow their hair to lie matted on their shoulders or twist it in a knot on top of their heads. They usually retain only the few possessions they carry with them: a staff (*daṇḍa*), a waterpot (*kamaṇḍalu*), an alms bowl, PRAYER BEADS, and perhaps an extra cloth or a fire tong.

ṢAFĪ AL-DĪN \sȧ-'fē-ȧl-'dēn\ (b. 1253, Ardabīl, Iran—d. Sept. 12, 1334, Ardabīl), mystic and founder of the Ṣafavid order of mystics.

Ṣafī al-Dīn, a descendant of a family of provincial administrators, obtained his early education in Ardabīl. Later, in Shiraz, he was influenced by Sufi teachings (*see* SUFISM). He then traveled to the province of Gilan (the Iranian Caspian province), where he spent 25 years as a follower of Shaykh Zāhid, whose daughter Bībī Fāṭima he married. After Shaykh Zāhid's death, his other spiritual followers transferred their allegiance to Ṣafī al-Dīn, who then returned to Ardabīl, where he formed the Ṣafavid order.

The fame of Ṣafī al-Dīn increased as the new order gained recruits. The popularity of the order can be attributed in part to Ṣafī al-Dīn's policy of hospitality, especially to all who sought refuge. One of the shaykh's appellations was Khalīl-e ʿAjam (a figure noted for hospitality in Iranian FOLKLORE). The order appears to have been a SUNNI order of mystics that made concessions to the followers of ʿALĪ (the fourth CALIPH of ISLAM) without actually adhering to the doctrines of his party, that of the SHIʿITES. The claim made by Ṣafavid court historians that Safī al-Dīn was a Shiʿite and a SAYYID (descendant of ʿAlī) is false and misleading. Safī al-Dīn, himself, was a Sunni of the SHĀFIʿĪ LEGAL SCHOOL.

SAGUNA \'sə-gu̇-nə\ ("with qualities or attributes"), position within Hindu philosophy and theology that God (or the impersonal Cosmic One known as the BRAHMAN) is manifest and describable. Its conceptual opposite is NIRGUNA, the notion that God or Brahman is "without qualities" and therefore wholly indescribable.

The *saguṇa* position underwrites the Hindu practice of creating and worshiping images of the deity. For some, the *saguṇa* form of God is primarily a support for meditation: "Without a form, how can God be meditated upon? If he is without any form, where will the mind fix itself?" For others, the position allows for the notion that God willingly takes on attributes and qualities out of his love for human beings and in order to make himself accessible to them. The deity can incarnate in human or animal form (this is the doctrine of the AVATAR) or in a properly consecrated image or icon.

SAHAJIYĀ \,sə-hə-'jē-yä, ,shə-\, member of an esoteric cult of TANTRIC HINDUISM, centered in Bengal, that sought RELIGIOUS EXPERIENCE through the world of the senses, specifically human sexual love. The Sahajiyā cult developed from the 17th century onward through a meeting of the Tantric *sahaja* (Sanskrit: "easy," or "natural") system of worship (prevalent in Bengal as early as the 8th–9th centuries), with mystic explorations of the parallels between human love and divine love such as were pursued by CAITANYA and his followers in devotion to KRISHNA and RĀDHĀ.

The Sahajiyās elevated *parakīyā-rati* (the love of a man for a woman who legally belongs to another) above *svakīyā-rati* (conjugal love) as the more intense of the two, as it was felt to be without consideration for the conventions of society or for personal gain and thus was more analogous to divine love. Rādhā, Krishna's lover, is conceived as the ideal of the *parakīyā* woman.

The Sahajiyās were looked upon with disfavor by other religious groups and operated in secrecy. Because of the extreme privacy of the cult, little is known about its prevalence or its practices today. *See also* BĀUL.

SAICHŌ \'sī-ˌchō\, *posthumous name* Dengyō Daishi \'deŋ-ˌgyō-'dī-shē\ (b. 767, Ōmi province, Japan—d. 822, Mount Hiei), monk who established the Tendai sect in Japan.

A priest at the age of 13, Saichō was sent to China to study and returned with the highly eclectic teachings of Tendai (T'IEN-T'AI) BUDDHISM. Unlike other Buddhist sects then in existence in Japan, the Tendai sect taught that there could be meaning and value in the external material world and that the teachings of the BUDDHA are accessible to all, not just to a select few.

Saichō built his monastery on MOUNT HIEI. He soon became a favorite of the emperor, and his monastery became one of the most powerful centers of Buddhist learning. While the monks of the older Buddhist sects lived in the cities, Saichō required his monks to spend 12 years in seclusion under strict discipline. He foreshadowed later Japanese Buddhist trends in his reverence for the SHINTŌ deities and his emphasis on the patriotic mission of Buddhism.

SAINT, person believed to be connected in a special manner with what is viewed as sacred, such as a divinity or divinities, spiritual powers, mythical realms, and other aspects of the sacred or holy.

Throughout history and in many religions of the world, various types of religious personages have been recognized as saints both by popular acclaim and by official pronouncement, and their influence on the broad spectrum of religious believers has been of considerable significance.

In CONFUCIANISM, saintliness was a state of ethical perfection best exemplified in the lives of certain ideal "holy rulers of primal times." TAOISM posits a more mystical sainthood, characterized by a passionless acceptance of the Way (TAO) of nature. Practicers of SHINTŌ venerate a number of mythical saints but regard all members of the human community, whether good or evil, as attaining a supernatural existence after death.

In THERAVĀDA BUDDHISM, all disciples of the BUDDHA GOTAMA, specifically monks, who have attained NIRVANA are recognized as ARHATS (roughly equivalent to "saint"). MAHĀYĀNA BUDDHISM, by contrast, views all people as capable of buddhahood and, thus, of sainthood. Those who postpone their own enlightenment in order to further the spiritual progress of others are known as BODHISATTVAS and are also regarded as saints. Tantric Buddhism of Tibet enlarges the range further still with the inclusion of numerous REINCARNATIONS of past saints.

The Jains of India venerate the founder of JAINISM, MAHĀVĪRA, as the 24th in a line of saintly prophets known as TĪRTHAŃKARAS. HINDUISM, the predominant religion of India, abounds in figures regarded as SADHUS ("good ones") and AVATARS, which are incarnations of a deity in human or animal form. Some of these avatars include saints of other reli-

gions. ZOROASTRIANISM AND PARSIISM recognize numerous FRAVASHIS, or preexistent souls that are good by nature.

The term saint is applied in the Hebrew BIBLE to any Israelite as one of the CHOSEN PEOPLE of God. In the NEW TESTAMENT it was used of any member of the Christian churches. It was not until about the 6th century that the word became a title of honor specially given to the dead whose cult was publicly celebrated in the churches.

SAIVA \'sī-ˌvü\, one of the Sami regions of the dead, where the deceased, called *saivoolmak*, lead happy lives with their families and ancestors, in every way acting as they did on earth. (*See* FINNO-UGRIC RELIGION.) In Norway the *saiva* world was thought to exist in the mountains, whereas in Finland it was usually believed to be under special double-bottomed lakes connected by a small hole. The *saiva* localities were regarded as sacred and as sources of power that could be used by the SHAMAN, or NOAIDE.

ŚAIVA SIDDHĀNTA \'shī-və-si-'dän-tə\, religio-philosophical system of South India in which SHIVA is worshiped as the supreme deity. It draws primarily on the Tamil devotional hymns written by Śaiva (*see* ŚAIVISM) saints from the 5th to the 9th centuries, known in their collected form as *Tirumuṟai*.

Śaiva Siddhānta posits three universal realities: the individual soul (*paśu*), the Lord (*pati*—i.e., Shiva), and the soul's bondage (*pāśa*) within the fetters of existence. These fetters comprise ignorance, KARMA, and the delusory nature of phenomenal reality (MĀYĀ). Acts of service and good conduct (*caryā*), structured worship (*kriyā*), spiritual discipline (YOGA), and deep learning (JŃĀNA) enable the soul to be freed from bondage.

ŚAIVISM \'shī-ˌvi-zəm\, *also spelled* Shaivism, worship of the Indian god SHIVA, with VAIṢṆAVISM and ŚĀKTISM, one of the three principal forms of modern HINDUISM. Śaivism includes such diverse movements as the highly philosophic ŚAIVA SIDDHĀNTA and KASHMIR schools, the socially distinctive VĪRAŚAIVA (or Liṅgāyat), ascetic orders such as the *daśnāmī sannyāsīs* and KĀPĀLIKAS AND KĀLĀMUKHAS, and innumerable folk variants.

While scholarly speculation that the worship of Shiva predates ARYAN religion has not been conclusive, it is clear that the Vedic god RUDRA ("the Howler") had been amalgamated with the figure of Shiva ("Auspicious One") by the period of the later UPANISHADS. The *Śvetāśvatara Upanishad* treats Shiva as the paramount deity, but it is not until sometime between the 2nd century BCE and the 2nd century CE, with the rise of the PĀŚUPATA sect, that we are able to observe sectarian worship of Shiva. *See also* VĪRAŚAIVA.

ŚAKTI \'shək-tē\, in HINDUISM, "creative energy" that is inherent in and proceeds from God, also sometimes imagined as a female deity; *see* ŚĀKTISM. Śakti is the deciding factor in the salvation of the individual and in the processes of the universe because God (SHIVA) acts only through his energy, which, personified as a goddess, is his spouse. Her role is very different in the various systems: she may be considered the central figure in a philosophically established doctrine, the dynamic aspect of BRAHMAN, producing the universe through her MĀYĀ, or mysterious power of illusion; a capricious demoniac ruler of nature in its destructive aspects; a benign mother goddess; the queen of a celestial court; or even the source of all things, including Shiva himself. Iconographically she is represented by the YONI.

In TANTRIC HINDUISM, Śakti represents mental activity and the female aspect of Supreme Reality and is paired with Shiva, the representative of the male aspect. Within the human body, the blissful realization of supreme nonduality is realized by awakening Śakti, conceived of as lying coiled around the lowest chakra of the body, and drawing her upward along the spinal cord to be united with Shiva at the top of the head. *See also* TANTRA; KUṆḌALINĪ.

ŚĀKTISM \\'shək-ˌti-zəm\\, *also spelled* Shaktism ("The Worship of the Goddess Śakti"), major form of worship in HINDUISM. The millennia-old river of what is now called "Hinduism" can be divided into three broad, interflowing, overlapping currents: VAIṢṆAVISM, the worship of the god VISHNU; ŚAIVISM, the worship of the god SHIVA; and Śāktism, the worship of the Goddess as ŚAKTI ("Power"). Śāktism is thus a general term used to designate a wide variety of goddess traditions in South Asia whose general focus is the worship of the Goddess. As an academic or popular religious category, Śāktism is a reflection of the common Hindu belief that the innumerable goddesses of village and Sanskritic lore are all manifestations of a single Mahādevī, or "Great Goddess." This concept of a Great Goddess is usually held to be ancient but, historically speaking, probably dates back to the medieval period when it was used to fuse the wildly disparate local and pan-Indian traditions into an ideologically unifying theology. As a theological category, the term Śāktism is no doubt helpful, but it is imprecise, as it can refer to historically and doctrinally distinct traditions, from the mythologies of various goddesses that appear in the medieval PURĀṆAS to the two major goddess-branches, or "families" (*kula*) of Śākta Tantrism (the *Śrī-kula* and the *Kālī-kula*), to the virtually endless number of local village goddesses past and present.

Followers of Śāktism are often called Śāktas ("Empowered Ones"). Śāktas not only worship the Śakti as Goddess but also attempt to enhance, control, and transform the Goddess' power-manifestations in the *śakti*, or "energy," of the human body and the living cosmos. Specifically, the Goddess is believed to

Muslims prostrating themselves during ṣalāt *at the mosque of Mahābat Khān, Peshāwar, Pak.*
Robert Harding—Robert Harding Picture Library, London

dwell at the anal base of the human body in the form of a sleeping coiled serpent (KUṆḌALINĪ). Through complex meditations and sexual-yogic rituals, this "serpent power" can be aroused or awakened, at which time she moves up the central channel (*suṣumnā*) of the subtle body (usually superimposed upon the spinal column), piercing the various energy centers (CHAKRAS) located along the way until she enters the final chakra at the top of the head and ecstatical-ly unites there with her husband-lover SHIVA. This mythological union of the Goddess and the God is experienced psycho-physiologically as an ecstatic-mystical trance whose exploding bliss is said to overflow from the cranial region and flow down the entire body in a flood of ECSTASY and intense pleasure.

Historically, Śāktism has been popular on the geographic eripheries of South Asia, particularly in Kashmir, South India, Assam, and Bengal, although its Tantric symbols and rituals have been omnipresent within the Hindu traditions since at least the 6th century CE. More recently, various forms of traditional, philosophical, and popular Śāktism have entered the West, with traditional immigrant Indian populations, among some Indological academic communities, and with various "New Age" and feminist-oriented traditions, usually in the West under the more popular rubric of Tantrism or TANTRA.

SALAFIYAH \\ˌsà-là-'fē-ə\\, *also spelled* Salafiyya, Islamic reform movement that originated in the late 19th century and aimed at a regeneration of ISLAM by a return to the tradition of the "pious forefathers" (*al-salaf al-ṣāliḥ*). In most locations the movement was opposed to the process of secularization and Western imperialism, while in some areas (*e.g.*, Egypt) it came to be associated with Arab nationalism. *See also* ʿABDUH, MUHAMMAD; RASHĪD RIḌĀ, MUHAMMAD.

ṢALĀT \\sə-'lät\\ (Arabic), *also spelled* salah \\-'lä\\, daily ritual prayer enjoined upon all Muslims as one of the FIVE PILLARS OF ISLAM (*arkān al-Islam*). There is disagreement among Islamic scholars as to whether some passages about prayer in the QURʾAN are actually references to the ṣalāt. Within MUHAMMAD's lifetime five ritual prayers, each preceded by ABLUTION, were observed: ṣalāt al-fajr (dawn), al-ẓuhr (midday), al-ʿaṣr (afternoon), al-maghrib (sunset), and al-ʿishāʾ (evening). Under such special circumstances as illness, a journey, or war, a modification or limited postponement of these ṣalāts is allowed.

Though individual performance of ṣalāt is permissible, collective worship in the mosque has special merit. With their faces turned in the direction (QIBLA) of the shrine of the KAʿBA in MECCA, the worshipers align themselves in parallel rows behind the IMAM, or prayer leader, who directs them as they execute the *rakʿas* (physical postures coupled with Qurʾanic recitations).

On Fridays, instead of the prayer just after noon, a congregational prayer (*ṣalāt al-jumʿa*) is offered; it includes two sermons (KHUTBAS) delivered from the pulpit. Special congregational prayers are offered in the middle of the morning on the two festival days (ʿĪDS), one immediately following the month of fasting, RAMADĀN, and the other following the PILGRIMAGE, or HAJJ. Although not obligatory, individual devotional prayers, especially during the night, are emphasized and are a common practice among pious Muslims.

SALII \ʹsā-lē-ˌī\ (Latin: "Dancers"), in ancient Italy, PRIESTHOOD usually associated with the worship of MARS. Chapters of the priesthood existed in Rome and in other central Italian cities. The Salii, who were all born patricians, were usually young men with both parents living. Their resignation from the priesthood was common on the assumption of high political office, and vacancies were filled by vote of the Salii. The chief Salii festivals were held at the opening (March) and closing (October) of the summer campaigning season.

SĀLIMĪYA \ˌsà-li-ʹmē-ə\, school of Muslim theologians founded by the Muslim scholar and mystic Sahl at-Tustarī (d. 896 CE). The school was named after one of his disciples, Muhammad ibn Sālim (d. 909 CE). Even though the Sālimīya were not a Sufi group in the strict sense of the word, they utilized many Sufi terms and ideas in their doctrines.

The Sālimīya spoke of God's *tajallī* (appearance) in human form on the day of judgment for all his creatures to see. When this happens, God's light will overwhelm the scene, and salvation will be granted to everyone and everything. Upon the doctrine that God created humans after his image, they hold that *ittiḥād* (mystical union) with God can be achieved through contemplation of one's own personality until complete consciousness of it is achieved, as every human has an element of divinity that he or she must try to realize through constant contemplation.

SALMĀN AL-FĀRISĪ \sàl-ʹmán-əl-fà-rē-ʹsē\ (fl. 7th century; b. near Iṣfahān, Iran), popular figure in Muslim legend and a national hero of Iran. He was a COMPANION OF THE PROPHET.

While still a boy he converted from ZOROASTRIANISM to CHRISTIANITY and began a long religious quest. He traveled to Syria and then to central Arabia, seeking the prophet who, he was told, would revive the religion of ABRAHAM. On the way he was sold into slavery. In MEDINA he met MUHAMMAD, with whose aid he purchased his freedom. According to tradition, when the Meccans came to besiege Muhammad in Medina, it was Salmān who suggested that, instead of the usual practice of the besieged sallying out to meet their opponents, a ditch be dug across the city's approaches as a form of protection. This innovation in Arabian warfare, which led to the BATTLE OF THE DITCH in 627, was instrumental in Muhammad's successful defense.

Salmān al-Fārisī's fame is due largely to his nationality—he was a prototype of the Persians who were converted to ISLAM and who played a central role in the course of Muslim history. Salmān also has been important in Muslim religious thought. The SHIʿITE moderates gave him special respect because of his nearness to the Prophet, and the extreme Shiʿites count him as one of the divine emanations recognized by their theology.

SALUS \ʹsā-ləs\, in ROMAN RELIGION, the goddess of safety and welfare, later identified with the Greek Hygieia. Her temple on the Quirinal at Rome, dedicated in 302 BCE, was the scene of an annual sacrifice on August 5.

The *augurium salutis* was an annual ascertainment of the acceptability to the gods of prayers for the public *salus*. Because it was required to be performed on a day of peace,

the constant warfare of the late republic caused its interruption, but it was revived by the emperor Augustus. In the empire, the goddess appeared both as Salus Publica and Salus Augusti.

SALVATION, *also called* redemption, in religion, deliverance of humankind from fundamentally negative conditions, such as suffering, evil, finitude, and death; also, in some religions, the restoration or raising up of the natural world to a higher realm, or state. The notion is not present in some religions.

Divine agents of salvation are known from the ancient world, particular in the person of the DIOSCURI, who often were termed *Sotēr* ("Savior"). The doctrine is, however, perhaps most characteristic of CHRISTIANITY, in which context it signifies the action of God within history whereby humanity is delivered from SIN and death through the life, death, and RESURRECTION of JESUS CHRIST.

JUDAISM posits a collective salvation for the people of ISRAEL. In the Hebrew BIBLE, redemption is usually described as deliverance from material disasters, but in Psalms 130 it is promised that God "will redeem Israel from all his iniquities." The restoration of the holy nation and the vindication of the Jews as God's chosen people in the LAST JUDGMENT are regarded as the salvatory culmination of history.

The concept of salvation from future punishment by submission to ALLĀH appears as the ultimate aim of the faithful in ISLAM. ZOROASTRIANISM AND PARSIISM envision a universal salvation of mankind through the ultimate triumph of good over evil.

Although religions of the East tend to regard salvation or deliverance from the bondage of life and death as a matter of self-effort through practice and discipline, there have appeared in these contexts notions of intervening divine aid. In MAHĀYĀNA BUDDHISM, the figure of AMITĀBHA, or Amida, Buddha is an important example. The AVATARS of VISHNU are also a means of deliverance and restoration.

SALVATION ARMY, international Christian religious and charitable movement organized on a military pattern. The Army is established in more than 80 countries, preaching in about 112 languages in 16,000 evangelical centers and operating more than 3,000 social welfare institutions, hospitals, schools, and agencies. Its continuing concerns include a relief program in postwar Rwanda, programs for helping the homeless, rehabilitation centers, and aid to victims of disasters, to name a few. Its international headquarters are in London.

William Booth, a Methodist minister, established mission stations in London's East End to feed and house the poor and in 1878 changed the name of his organization to the Salvation Army. He and his son, William Bramwell Booth, gradually established the Army on a military pattern, with the elder Booth as general for life. It spread quickly over Britain and then expanded internationally.

In 1884 the U.S. organization sought to establish its independence of General Booth. Upon being expelled, its leaders set up the American Salvation Army, which soon declined. In 1896 Ballington Booth, another son of the general and national commander in the United States, resigned after a dispute and set up the Volunteers of America, which endured as a national organization with headquarters in New York.

The basic unit of organization within the Army is the corps, commanded by an officer of a rank ranging from lieutenant to brigadier, who is responsible to a divisional headquarters. Divisions are grouped into territories (usually a territory is a country, except in the United States, where there are four territories).

Converts who desire to become soldiers in the Army are required to sign Articles of War and volunteer their services. The officers are the equivalent of ministers of other Protestant churches. Training for each officer consists of a two-year residence at one of the schools, followed by a five-year plan of advanced studies. Women have absolute equality with men.

A Salvation Army soldier helps with the Christmas-season collection
Arvind Garg—Photo Researchers

The doctrines of the Army include the basic principles common to most evangelical denominations of PROTESTANTISM. William Booth believed that the SACRAMENTS were not necessary to the salvation of the soul. He sought to bring into his worship services an informal atmosphere that would put new converts at their ease. Joyous singing, instrumental music, clapping of hands, personal testimony, free prayer, and an open invitation to repentance characterize the services.

SAMĀ' \sä-'ma\ (Arabic: "listening"), in SUFISM, the practice of listening to music and chanting to reinforce ECSTASY and induce mystical trance. The scripturalists regarded such practices as un-Islamic, and the more puritanical among them associated the Sufis' music, song, and dancing with drinking parties and immoral activities. The Sufis countered such attitudes by pointing out that MUHAMMAD himself permitted the QUR'AN to be chanted and that the ADHĀN (call for prayer) was also chanted.

Sufis maintain that melodies and rhythms prepare the soul for a deeper comprehension of the divine realities and a better appreciation of divine music. Music, like other beautiful things, draws the Sufis closer to God, who is the source of beauty. Many Sufis have held that a true mystic does not lose himself in such forms as music but uses them only to bring himself into a spiritual realm, after which he must experience deeper meanings and realities. While Muslim conservative legalists reproved *samā'* as an innovation (BID'A), some Muslim scholars held that it was a useful innovation since it might bring souls nearer to God.

Many Sufis—*e.g.,* the MAWLAWĪYA dervishes—combined dancing with *samā'*. Often Sufis requested that after their death there should be no mourning at their funerals, insisting instead that *samā'* sessions be held to celebrate their entrance into eternal life. The Sufis warned, nevertheless, that the full appreciation of *samā'* requires strong ascetic training. An individual must be pure in heart and strong in character before indulging in *samā'*; otherwise music and song would arouse his base instincts instead of elevating his spirituality. Some Sufis reject the practice of *samā'* altogether. *See also* DHIKR.

SAMĀDHI \sə-'mä-dē\ (Sanskrit: "total self-collectedness"), in HINDUISM and BUDDHISM, the highest state of mental concentration that a person can achieve while still bound to the body. *Samādhi* is a state of profound and utterly absorp-

tive contemplation of the Absolute that is undisturbed by desire, anger, or any other ego-generated thought or emotion. According to some Hindus, the power to attain *samādhi* is a precondition of attaining release from the cycle of rebirths (SAMSĀRA). Hence the death of a person having this power is also considered to be entrance into *samādhi*, as is the site where a person believed to be so empowered was buried. The adept is buried in a seated pose, marking the meditative state, and the very practice of burial sets the *samādhin* apart from ordinary mortals, whose less pure bodies are appropriately cremated, according to the Hindu norm. Shrines honoring the *samādhi*s of well-known saints often serve as sites of PILGRIMAGE for Buddhists and Hindus.

SAMARITAN \sə-'mar-ə-tən\, member of a community of Jews, now nearly extinct, that claims to be descended from those Jews of ancient Samaria who were not deported by the Assyrian conquerors of the kingdom of Israel in 722 BCE. The Samaritans call themselves Bene-Yisrael ("Children of Israel"), or Shamerim ("Observant Ones"), for their sole norm of religious observance is the PENTATEUCH. Other Jews call them simply Shomronim (Samaritans); in the TALMUD, they are called Kutim, suggesting that they are rather descendants of Mesopotamian Cuthaeans, who settled in Samaria after the Assyrian conquest.

Jews who returned to their homeland after the BABYLONIAN EXILE would not accept the help of the Samaritans in the building of the Second TEMPLE OF JERUSALEM. Consequently, in the 4th century BCE, they built their own temple in Nābulus (Shechem), at the base of Mount Gerizim, some 25 miles north of Jerusalem. Nābulus is the residence of the HIGH PRIEST, and a SYNAGOGUE is maintained in the city of Ḥolon, just south of Tel Aviv–Yafo. All live in semi-isolation, marrying only within their own community. They pray in Hebrew but adopted Arabic as their vernacular after the Muslim conquest of 636 CE.

SĀMA VEDA \'sä-mə-'vä-də\ (Sanskrit: "Veda of Chants"), in HINDUISM, Vedic text made up of a selection of verses (drawn almost wholly from the ṚG VEDA) that are provided with musical notation and are intended as an aid to the performance of sacred songs. The hymns are sung by priests in a melodic and melismatic (one word to two or more notes) style, with a range of six or more tones. *See also* VEDA.

SAMBATION \ˌsäm-bä-'tyōn\, legendary "Sabbath River" beyond which the TEN LOST TRIBES OF ISRAEL were exiled in 721 BCE by Shalmaneser V, king of Assyria. Legends describe it as a roaring torrent (of water or of stones), the turbulence of which ceases only on the SABBATH, when Jews are not allowed to travel.

The ancient Jewish historian FLAVIUS JOSEPHUS located the river in Syria and Pliny asserted it was in Judaea, while the Spanish-Jewish scholar NAḤMANIDES identified it with the River Habor (al-Khābūr River) of the BIBLE (2 Kings 17:6). The 17th-century Jewish scholar MANASSEH BEN ISRAEL carefully studied Eldad ha-Dani's 9th-century account of his reputed discovery of the "sons of Moses" beyond the river.

From the Middle Ages to the 19th century, the river was sought in India, Africa, China, Japan, and Spain. Legends of the river produced a vast Jewish literature that eventually entered into Arabic and Christian writings. Among eastern European Jews, an unruly child was sometimes referred to as a "Sambation."

SAMHAIN \'så-vən^y, 'saůn^y\, *also spelled* Samain (Old Irish *Samain:* "first day of November," or "the festival held on that day"), in CELTIC RELIGION, one of the most important calendar festivals of the year. At Samhain, held on November 1, the world of the gods was believed to be made visible to mankind, and the gods played many tricks on mortals. Sacrifices and propitiations of every kind were thought to be vital, for without them the Celts believed they could not prevail over the perils of the season or counteract the activities of the deities. Samhain was a precursor to HALLOWEEN.

ŚAMKARA \'shən-kə-rə\, *also spelled* Sankara, *or* Shankara, (fl. late 7th–early 8th centuries; traditionally b. Kāladi, Kerala, India—d. Kedārnāth, HIMALAYAS), philosopher and theologian, the most renowned exponent of the ADVAITA VEDĀNTA school of philosophy. Works indisputably written by him include his *Brahma-sūtra-bhāṣya*, his commentaries on the *Bṛhadāraṇyaka* and *Taittirīya* UPANISHADS, and his systematic treatise *Upadeśasāhasrī*. Many scholars also accept his authorship of a commentary on the BHAGAVAD GĪTĀ and a subcommentary on Gauḍapāda's analysis of the *Māṇḍūkya Upanishad*, but the schematic works *Vivekacūḍāmaṇi* and *Ātmabodha* almost certainly have to be rejected as Śaṃkara's, although they are widely accepted as authentic by Advaitans. Śaṃkara's writings affirm his belief in an unchanging, nondual reality (BRAHMAN) distinct from the illusion of plurality and differentiation that characterizes our waking consciousness, but his "illusionism" (*māyāvāda*) is far less thoroughgoing than works like the *Vivekacūḍāmaṇi* make it appear.

It has been customary to assign Śaṃkara the birth and death dates 788–820, but the approximate dates 700–750, or slightly earlier, are more probable. According to one tradition, Śaṃkara was born into a BRAHMIN family in a village called Kāladi. After his father's death he became a SANNYĀSĪ (ascetic) against his mother's will. He studied under Govinda, a pupil of Gauḍapāda. Gauḍapāda is notable as the author of an important Vedānta work, *Māṇḍūkya-kārikā*, in which the influence of MAHĀYĀNA BUDDHISM is evident.

A tradition says that SHIVA was Śaṃkara's family deity and that he was, by birth, a Śākta, or worshiper of ŚAKTI. Although his *Dakṣiṇāmūrti-stotra* presents him as a worshiper of Shiva, other apparently authentic texts such as his commentary on the *Gītā* align him more closely with VAIṢNAVISM. Nonetheless, he is widely regarded as the founder of the *daśanāmī* order of ascetics, Śaivite in orientation (*see* ŚAIVISM).

Śaṃkara is said to have traveled all over India, holding discussions with philosophers of different creeds. His legendary debate with Maṇḍana Miśra, a philosopher of the Mīmāṃsā (Investigation) school, whose wife served as an umpire, may reflect the historical conflict between Śaṃkara, who regarded the knowledge of Brahman as the only means to final release, and followers of the Mīmāṃsā school, which emphasized the performance of ordained duty and the Vedic rituals.

Śaṃkara is said to have founded four monasteries, at Srngeri (south), Puri (east), Dvaraka (west), and Badarinath (north). Whether or not this is literally true, the foundation of these institutions was doubtless one of the most significant factors in according to Śaṃkara's teachings the leading

role they have played in the history of Indian philosophy.

More than 300 works—commentative, expository, and poetical—written in Sanskrit, are attributed to him, but few are regarded as authentic. His *Brahma Sūtra Bhāṣya*, the commentary on the *Brahma Sūtra*, is a fundamental text of the Vedānta school. The *Upadeśasāhasrī* is a good introduction to Śaṃkara's philosophy in that it is the only noncommentative work that is certainly authentic.

A vivid contrast to these, because of its clearly devotional tone, is the *Dakṣiṇāmūrti-stotra*, but there worship and philosophy merge, since the "south-facing" (*dakṣiṇāmūrti*) Shiva being praised by Śaṃkara is the Himalayan yogi who contemplates the nondual nature of (his own) reality. Śaṃkara's works reveal that he was not only versed in the orthodox Brahminical traditions but also was well acquainted with Mahāyāna Buddhism; he made full use of his knowledge of Buddhism to attack Buddhist doctrines severely and to transmute them into his own Vedāntic nondualism. Thus philosophically as well as institutionally, Śaṃkara is often credited with having laid the basis for Hindu orthodoxy in India, after centuries of challenge from the heterodox systems of JAINISM and especially Buddhism.

SĀMKHYA \'sən-ˌkyä, 'səm-\, *also spelled* Sānkhya (Sanskrit: "Enumeration," *or* "Number"), one of the six orthodox systems (DARŚANS) of Indian philosophy. Sāmkhya adopts a consistent DUALISM of the orders of matter (*prakṛti*) and soul, or self (*puruṣa*).

Although many references to the system are given in earlier texts, Sāmkhya received its classical form and expression in the *Sāmkhya Kārikās* ("Stanzas of Sāmkhya") by Īśvarakṛṣṇa (c. 3rd century CE).

In Sāmkhya there is belief in an infinite number of similar but separate *puruṣas* ("selves"), no one superior to the other. PRAKṚTI AND PURUṢA being sufficient to explain the universe, the existence of a god is not hypothesized. The *puruṣa* is ubiquitous, all-conscious, all-pervasive, motionless, unchangeable, immaterial, and without desire. *Prakṛti* is the universal and subtle (*i.e.*, unmanifest) matter, or nature, and, as such, is determined only by time and space.

When *puruṣa* impinges on *prakṛti*, the *puruṣa* becomes focused on *prakṛti*, and out of this is evolved *mahat* ("great one") *or buddhi* ("spiritual awareness"). Next to evolve is the individualized ego consciousness (*ahaṃkāra*, "I-maker"), which imposes upon the *puruṣa* the misapprehension that the ego is the basis of the *puruṣa*'s objective existence.

The *ahaṃkāra* further divides into the five gross elements (space, air, fire, water, earth), the five fine elements (sound, touch, sight, taste, smell), the five organs of perception (with which to hear, touch, see, taste, smell), the five organs of activity (with which to speak, grasp, move, procreate, evacuate), and mind, or thought (*manas*). The universe is the result of the combinations and permutations of these various principles, from which *puruṣa* remains separate. This thoroughgoing distinction between psychological and physical functions on the one hand and pure "personhood" on the other is one of Sāmkhya's enduring contributions to Indian thought. It has been matched from earliest times by disciplines associated with YOGA, whose purpose is to create in the adept a realization of the singular *puruṣa* apart from the manifoldness of *prakṛti*.

Another broadly influential idea first encountered in Sāmkhya is the parsing of matter (*prakṛti*) into three *guṇa*s ("qualities") that cross-cut the elements listed above; these are *sattva* (associated with illumination), *rajas* (energy and passion), and *tamas* (obscurity and ignorance).

SAMMATĪYA \\,səm-mə-'tē-yə\\: *see* PUDGALAVĀDIN.

SAMPO \\'säm-pȯ\\, mysterious object often referred to in the mythological songs of the Finns, most likely a cosmological pillar or some similar support holding up the vault of heaven. In a cycle of songs, referred to by scholars as the *sampo*-epic, the *sampo* is forged by the creator-smith IL-MARINEN for Louhi, the hag-goddess of the underworld, and is then stolen back by Ilmarinen and the shaman-hero VÄINÄMÖINEN. They are pursued by Louhi, and in the ensuing battle *sampo* is smashed into little pieces, which still preserve enough potency to provide for "sowing and reaping" and other forms of prosperity.

The comments of early informants reveal that the songs were part of a ritual cycle that was sung at a spring sowing ceremony to further the growth of grain. Scholars are more or less in agreement that *sampo* refers to the support holding up the firmament, a concept found in many early cosmologies. The name *sampo* may even be a cognate of words such as Sanskrit *skambha*, "pillar," and Altaic *sumbur*, the "world mountain." Because it is the mythical *axis mundi*, the axis around which the heavens revolve, all life is dependent on the *sampo*, which the Finnish songs depict as the source of all good.

SAMPRADĀYA \\,səm-prə-'dä-yə\\, in HINDUISM, school of religious thought and practice, transmitted from one teacher to another. From about the 11th century onward, several sects emerged out of VAIṢṆAVISM in South India. They include the Sanaka Sampradāya (also known as Nimbārkīs, the followers of NIMBĀRKA); the Śrī Sampradāya (or Śrī Vaiṣṇavas, following the teaching of RĀMĀNUJA); the Brahmā Sampradāya (or Madhvas, the followers of MADHVA); and the Rudra Sampradāya (or Viṣṇusvāmīs, the followers of Viṣṇusvāmī). Each school is named after a distant and perhaps mythological founder, such as Śrī (the goddess LAKṢMĪ), from whom it has been transmitted through a succession of teachers to the earthly founders of the sects. More recently established *sampradāya*s, such as those associated with CAITANYA, VALLABHA, or RĀMĀNANDA, have typically claimed philosophical lineages, rooting them in one of the four earlier *sampradāya*s, which they are then held to have fulfilled and, in effect, superseded.

SAṂSĀRA \\səm-'sär-ə, səŋ-\\ (Sanskrit: "the running around"), in Indian philosophy, the central conception of metempsychosis: the soul, finding itself awash in the "sea of *saṃsāra*," strives to find release (MOKṢA) from the bonds of its own past deeds (KARMA), which form part of the general web of which *saṃsāra* is made. BUDDHISM, which does not assume the existence of a permanent soul, accepts a semipermanent personality core that goes through the process of *saṃsāra*.

The SĀṂKHYA school of Hindu philosophy assumes the existence of two bodies, a "gross" one (*sthūla*), which is the material body, and a "subtle" one, which is immaterial. When the gross body has perished, the subtle one survives and migrates to another one; this subtle body consists of the higher psychomaterial functions of *buddhi* ("consciousness"), *ahaṃkāra* ("I-consciousness"), *manas* ("mind as coordinator of sense impressions"), and PRĀṆA ("breath"), the principle of vitality.

The range of *saṃsāra* stretches from insects (and sometimes vegetables and minerals) to the generative god BRAHMĀ. A variety of explications of the workings of the karmic process within *saṃsāra* have been proposed. According to several, the soul after death first goes to a heaven or hell until it has consumed most of its good or bad karma. Then it returns to a new womb, the remainder of its karma having determined the circumstances of its next life. The so-called JĀTAKA stories record the Buddha's previous lives and illustrate the moral and salvific potential that comes with an accurate, enlightened appraisal of the vast network of interconnections described by the idea of *saṃsāra*.

SAṂSKĀRA \\səm-'skär-ə, səŋ-\\, any of the personal sacraments traditionally observed at every stage of a Hindu's life, from the moment of conception to the final scattering of one's funeral ashes. The observance of the *saṃskāra*s is based on custom and on texts such as the *Gṛhya Sūtra*s, the epics, or the PURĀṆAS and differs considerably according to region, CASTE, or family. Most rites prescribed in the Brahminical texts are performed by the father in the home and tend to be more carefully observed in the case of male children. The most generally accepted list of 16 traditional *saṃskāra*s begins with the prenatal ceremonies of *garbhādhāna* (for conception); *puṃsavana* (to favor a male birth); and *sīmantonnayana* ("hair-parting," to ensure safe delivery). The rites of childhood begin before the severing of the cord, with the ceremony of *jātakarman* (birth); followed at a later date by *nāmakaraṇa* (name-giving); *niṣkramana* (the child's first view of the sun); *annaprāśana* (first feeding of solid food); *cūḍākaraṇa* (first TONSURE of the boy's head); and *karṇavedha* (boring of the ears for the wearing of ornaments). The educational *saṃskāra*s can commence as early as the fifth year with the *vidyārambha* (the learning of the alphabet). The UPANAYANA (initiation) confers the sacred thread on male children of the three upper social classes; the *vedārambha* signals the beginning of the student's study of the VEDAS; the *keśānta*, or *godāna* (first shaving of the beard), marks the approach of manhood; and the *samāvartana* (returning home from the house of the GURU) or *snāna* ("bathing"), the completion of his student life. The sacrament of marriage is known as *vivāha*. The final *saṃskāra* to be performed is the ANTYEṢṬI, the funeral rite.

In modern times the full *saṃskāra*s are not generally performed, and this may always have been the case beyond the observant Brahminical communities assumed in the ancient texts. At present the ceremonies most commonly observed are those of initiation, marriage, and death.

While certain of the above-mentioned *saṃskāra*s, including even tonsure and *upanayana*, have been and are increasingly observed for both sexes, there exists an additional set of Hindu life-cycle rituals that are specifically appropriate to women. These are usually not inscribed in Brahminical texts and vary significantly by region and community, commonly focusing on various aspects of childbirth. Other rites, such as vows and austerities aimed at securing a good husband, may have both life-cycle and calendrical associations. Many such rites—*e.g.*, the cleansing and blessing ceremony called *cauk* or *chatī* that is performed in middle India about a week after childbirth—cast women themselves in the role of ritual specialists and vary minimally, if at all, as to the sex of the newborn child.

SAMSON \\'sam-sən\\, *Hebrew* Shimshon, Israelite hero portrayed in an epic narrative in the OLD TESTAMENT (Judges 13–16). He was a NAZIRITE and a warrior whose incredible exploits hint at the weight of Philistine pressure on Israel during much of the early, tribal period of Israel in CANAAN (1200–1000 BCE).

In a French manuscript illumination, Samuel exhorts the Israelites to put away Baal and Ashtaroth and to serve the Lord only (1 Samuel 7), c. 1250
The Granger Collection

Before Samson's birth his parents, peasants of the tribe of DAN at Zorah, near Jerusalem, learned through a THEOPHANY that he was to be dedicated to the life of a Nazirite. Credited with remarkable exploits—*e.g.,* slaying a lion and moving the gates of Gaza—he first broke his Nazirite vow by feasting with a woman from the neighboring town of Timnah who was a Philistine, one of Israel's mortal enemies. On another occasion he repulsed the Philistines' assault on him at Gaza, where he had gone to visit a harlot. He finally fell victim to his foes through love for DELILAH, a woman of the valley of Sorek, who beguiled him into revealing the secret of his strength: his long Nazirite hair. As he slept, Delilah had his hair cut and betrayed him. He was captured, blinded, and enslaved by the Philistines, but in the end his strength was returned, whereupon he demolished the great Philistine temple of the god Dagon at Gaza, destroying his captors and himself (Judges 16:4–30).

SAMUEL \'sam-yŭ-wəl\, *Hebrew* Shmu'el (fl. *c.* 11th century BCE, Israel), religious hero in the history of Israel, represented in the OLD TESTAMENT as seer, priest, judge, prophet, and military leader. His greatest distinction was his role in the establishment of the monarchy in Israel.

Biblical accounts of his life. Information about Samuel is contained in 1 Samuel (called in the ROMAN CATHOLIC canon 1 Kings). Samuel, the son of Elkanah (of EPHRAIM) and HANNAH, was born in answer to the prayer of his previously childless mother. In gratitude she dedicated him to the service of the chief SANCTUARY of SHILOH, in the priest Eli's charge. As a boy Samuel received a divine oracle in which the fall of the house of Eli was predicted (1 Samuel 1–3). When he became an adult he inspired Israel to victory over the Philistines at Ebenezer (chapter 7). The proposal of the elders of Israel to install a king was rejected by Samuel as infidelity to God (chapter 8). By the revelation of YAHWEH, however, he anointed and installed SAUL (chapters 9–10). Saul was vindicated as king by his leadership of Israel in a

campaign against the AMMONITES (chapter 11); after this, Samuel retired from the leadership of Israel (chapter 12). He reappeared, however, to announce the oracle of Yahweh rejecting Saul as king, once for arrogating to himself the right of sacrifice (chapter 13) and a second time for failing to carry out the law of the ban against the AMALEKITES (chapter 15). By the oracle of Yahweh, Samuel secretly anointed David as king (chapter 16). After he died, his ghost was evoked by a necromancer at the request of Saul; he then announced a third time the rejection of Saul (chapter 28).

Conflicting traditions about Samuel. Samuel thus appears as a leader of all Israel; his authority is basically religious, mostly prophetic, although with some features of priestly authority. He is the spokesman of Yahweh in the election of both Saul and David. Yet he appears at first as hostile to the monarchy and then as favorable to it.

The two major divergences in 1 Samuel lie in those passages that critics call the "pro-monarchic" source (1 Samuel 9:1–10:16) and those passages called the "antimonarchic" source (1 Samuel 8 and 10:17–27). In the promonarchic account, Samuel is an obscure village seer (with distinct evidence of occult practices). The institution of the monarchy and the election of the king occur according to the will of Yahweh as revealed to Samuel. Saul is chosen king by a charismatic display of military courage and leadership: his victory over the Ammonites.

In the antimonarchic account Samuel is a figure known through "all Israel"; his authority rests on his position as judge. The institution of kingship comes from the request of the elders of Israel, and this request is treated by Samuel as rebellion against Yahweh. Samuel is clearly presented as the last of the judges; it is indicated that the system of the judges was rejected by the Israelites because of their worldliness.

Significance. There must have been some reason why Samuel was important enough to be remembered for a major role in the establishment of the monarchy, yet the conflicting features of the story surrounding him are not easily resolved. Clearly, those behind the narrative must have been torn between the protection that the royal political system offered against the Philistines and the threat they posed to religious and national traditions. This internal division in Israel is reflected in the person of Samuel, who stood with most Israelites on both sides of the question.

SAMUEL HA-NAGID \hä-'nä-gēd\, *Arabic* Ismail ibn Nagrel'a (b. 993, Córdoba, Spain—d. 1055/56, Granada), Talmudic scholar, grammarian, philologist, poet, warrior, and statesman who for two decades was the power behind the throne of the caliphate of Granada.

As a youth Samuel received a thorough education in all

branches of Jewish and Islamic knowledge (*see* JUDAISM; ISLAM). When Córdoba was sacked in 1013 by the Berbers, Samuel fled to Málaga, at that time part of the Muslim kingdom of Granada. He soon became the private secretary and political adviser to the Granadan vizier, who, at his death, commended Samuel to the CALIPH Ḥabbūs. The caliph made Samuel the new vizier, and as such he assumed direction of Granada's diplomatic and military affairs. When Ḥabbūs died in 1037, Samuel became the de facto caliph. He steered Granada through years of continuous warfare and actively participated in all major campaigns. His influence became so great that he was able to arrange for his son Joseph to succeed him as vizier.

Samuel was also *nagid* (Hebrew: "chief") of Granadan Jewry. As such, he appointed all the judges and headed the TALMUDIC academy. He is generally believed to be the author of *Mevo ha-Talmud* ("Introduction to the Talmud"), a long-lived Talmudic manual. He also wrote a concordance to the Hebrew BIBLE, encouraged learning in all fields, and became a respected figure among both Arabs and Jews.

SANATANA DHARMA \ˌsən-'tä-nə-'dər-mə, sə-'nä-tə-nə-\, in HINDUISM, term used to denote the "eternal" or absolute set of duties or religiously ordained practices incumbent upon all Hindus, regardless of class, CASTE, or sect. Different texts give different lists of the duties, but in general *sanatana dharma* consists of virtues such as honesty, refraining from injuring living beings, purity, goodwill, mercy, patience, forbearance, self-restraint, generosity, and ASCETICISM. *Sanatana dharma* is contrasted with *svadharma*, one's "own duty" or the particular duties enjoined upon an individual according to his or her class or caste and stage of life. The potential for conflict between the two types of DHARMA (*e.g.*, between the particular duties of a warrior and the general injunction to practice non-injury) is addressed in Hindu texts such as the BHAGAVAD GĪTĀ, where it is said that in such cases SVADHARMA must prevail.

The term has also more recently been used by Hindu leaders, reformers, and nationalists to refer to Hinduism as a unified world religion. *Sanatana dharma* has thus become a synonym for the "eternal" truth and teachings of Hinduism, the latter conceived of as not only transcendent of history and unchanging but also as indivisible and ultimately nonsectarian.

SĀNCHI \'sän-chē\, *also spelled* Sāñcī, historic site, west-central Madhya Pradesh state, central India, location of the best-preserved group of BUDDHIST monuments in India. Most noteworthy is the Great Stupa, which was probably begun by the emperor AŚOKA in the mid-3rd century BCE and later enlarged. The STUPA consists of a base bearing a hemispherical dome (*aṇḍa*) representing the dome of heaven enclosing the Earth; it is surmounted by a squared rail unit, or *harmikā*, the world mountain, from which rises a mast (*yaṣṭi*) to symbolize the cosmic axis. The mast bears umbrellas (*chatra*s) that represent the various heavens (*devaloka*). The stupa is enclosed by a massive stone railing pierced by four gateways on which are elaborate carvings depicting the life of the BUDDHA. Other remains include several smaller stupas, an assembly hall (*caitya*), an Aśokan pillar with inscription, and several monasteries (4th–11th century CE). Several relic baskets and more than 400 epigraphical records have also been discovered.

SAN-CHIAO \'sän-'jyaù\, *Pinyin* Sanjiao (Chinese: "Three Religions"), Chinese SYNCRETISTIC movement that became popular in Sung and Ming China. Its composite moral teachings, drawn from a mixture of CONFUCIAN ethics, the TAOIST system of merits, and the BUDDHIST concept of REINCARNATION, are represented by popular tracts, the so-called "books on goodness" (SHAN-SHU), which have been in extremely wide circulation since the 14th century. San-chiao was rejected by most Confucians and Buddhists but received wide support in Taoist circles. Many Taoist masters of those periods transmitted techniques of inner cultivation to their disciples while at the same time preaching the moralism of the "Three Religions" to outsiders.

SAN-CH'ING \'sän-'chiŋ\, *Pinyin* Sanqing (Chinese: "Three Pure Ones"), highest triad of deities in the generalized pantheon of sectarian religious TAOISM. First in evidence during the T'ang dynasty, the triad represented a ranking of three deities associated with the three highest heavens (or "pure" realms) in the Taoist COSMOLOGY. Today the deities are identified as: Yüan-shih t'ien-tsun (Original Beginning Heavenly Worthy), Ling-pao t'ien-tsun (Numinous Jewel Heavenly Worthy; also known as T'ai-shang tao-chün, or Grand Lord of the TAO), and Tao-te t'ien-tsun (Tao and Its Power Heavenly Worthy; also known as T'ai-shang Lao-chün, or Grand Lord Lao). In contemporary Taoism, these deities are often invoked during community renewal rituals that are known as *chiao*.

SANCTUARY, in religion, sacred place, set apart from the profane, ordinary world. Originally, sanctuaries were natural locations, such as groves or hills, where the divine or sacred was believed to be especially present. The concept was later extended to include man-made structures—*e.g.*, the TABERNACLE (tent) of the ancient Hebrews, the later TEMPLE OF JERUSALEM, the sacred lodge of the Algonquin and Sioux, or, especially, sacred parts of such structures. Sanctuaries were reserved for special religious functions, and a state of purity was required of participants. Special TABOOS and rules prevented the profanation of sanctuaries. It was because of this special sacred quality and the protection that it afforded that the sanctuary became a place of asylum for fugitives or criminals. In addition to the fear of shedding blood in a holy place, a dominant motive in protecting the fugitive was the fear of the evil force that would emanate from his curse, believed dangerous to gods as well as men.

Christian sanctuaries, first recognized by Roman law toward the end of the 4th century, developed through recognition of the office of bishop as intercessor. Sanctuary privileges were gradually extended to wider areas of and around churches. JUSTINIAN, however, limited the privilege to persons not guilty of serious crimes. In the Germanic kingdoms, a fugitive was usually surrendered to authorities after an OATH had been taken not to put him to death.

In English common law a person accused of a felony might take refuge in a sanctuary; once there, he had a choice between submitting to trial or confessing the crime to the coroner and swearing to leave the kingdom (abjuration of the realm) and not return without the king's permission. If he would neither submit to trial nor abjure the realm after 40 days, he was starved into submission. In continental Europe the right of sanctuary (called asylum), though much restricted in the 16th century, survived until the French Revolution.

The institution of sanctuary, whatever its origin and meaning, appears to have performed a social function. Although often abused, it prevented excessive use of capital punishment and safeguarded against uncontrolled blood

Navajo sand painting
Emil Muench—Photo Researchers

place in a study retreat led gradually to the settling of the community.

The modern *sangha* is governed by disciplinary rules *(vinaya)* that form part of the sacred canon and by the traditions of interpretation that have developed over the centuries. Generally, the monastic order is dependent on the lay community for economic support in the form of alms or large gifts of money and property, since Buddhist monks in many sects—in particular those of the THERAVĀDA tradition in Southeast Asia—are discouraged from engaging in either commerce or agriculture.

SANHEDRIN \san-'he-drən, sän-; san-'hē-\, *also spelled* Sanhedrim \-drəm\, supreme Jewish administrative body from the 1st century BCE through the 5th or 6th century CE. While the term refers to a court and seems usually to have applied to the highest court, the Sanhedrin's exact composition and powers—religious, judicial, and legislative—are reported variously in different sources. The Gospels and the historian JOSEPHUS describe the Sanhedrin primarily as a judicial council headed by the HIGH PRIEST or king and active in various locales in the promotion of Jewish political programs. But the term *Sanhedrin* becomes most prominent in the rabbinic literature, where a complete tractate of law dedicated to this topic pictures the Sanhedrin primarily as a legislative body, centered in Jerusalem and headed by the preeminent rabbinic authority of each age—the Pharisaic schools while the Temple stood and the rabbinic PATRIARCH thereafter. Here the Sanhedrin is depicted as concerned, among other matters, with religious issues.

Despite scholars' attempts to reconcile these contradictory descriptions, there is no coherent picture of the legal and judicial institutions in this period and thus the actual role of the Sanhedrin remains unclear. It is most likely that diverse groups in early Judaism—PHARISEES, SADDUCEES, and others—had their own judicial and legislative organizations, such that a variety of structures existed simultaneously. It is equally likely that forms of Temple-based administration that existed while the Temple stood gave way to new and different institutions after the destruction. Therefore, just as the confusion of the sources seems to suggest, no single conception of the Sanhedrin can accurately convey its historical diversity and development.

In the MISHNAH, the term *Sanhedrin* overlaps with the term *bet din,* that is, "house of judgment" or "court." While Mishnah-tractate Sanhedrin is concerned for the most part with judicial courts that try capital cases, it refers to a wide range of the Sanhedrin's functions. A Sanhedrin of 71 members, referred to as a Great Sanhedrin, judged tribes, false prophets, and high priests; declared war; permitted additions to the city of Jerusalem; and declared a city to be "an apostate city." This Sanhedrin is distinguished from a "small" Sanhedrin of 23 members, which

vengeance and execution without trial. The sanctuary was also the source of parliamentary immunities and the custom of diplomatic asylum in embassies.

SAND PAINTING, *also called* dry painting, type of art that exists in highly developed forms among the Navajo and Pueblo Indians of the American Southwest and in simpler forms among several Plains and California Indian tribes. Although sand painting is an art form, it is valued primarily for religious rather than aesthetic reasons. Its main function is in connection with healing ceremonies.

Sand paintings are stylized, symbolic pictures prepared by trickling small quantities of crushed, colored sandstone, charcoal, pollen, or other dry materials in white, blue, yellow, black, and red hues on a background of clean, smoothed sand. About 600 different pictures are known, consisting of various representations of deities, animals, lightning, rainbows, plants, and other symbols described in the chants that accompany various rites. In healing, the choice of the particular painting is left to the curer. Upon completion of the picture, the patient sits on the center of the painting (*i.e.,* a microcosm of the cosmos), and sand from the painting is applied to parts of his or her body. When the ritual is completed, the painting is destroyed.

SANGHA \'səŋ-gə\, Buddhist monastic order, traditionally composed of four groups: monks, nuns, laymen, and laywomen. The *sangha* is a part—together with the Buddha and the DHARMA (teaching)—of the Threefold Refuge, a basic creed of BUDDHISM.

The *sangha* is thought to have originated in the group of disciples of the BUDDHA GOTAMA. After the Buddha's death his disciples continued to live together as a community, wandering from place to place and living off the receipt of alms. At the time of the full and new moon (the *uposatha* days), followers of the Buddha would gather to reaffirm their sense of community and purpose by reciting their basic beliefs, such as the Threefold Refuge and the codes of conduct. The custom of spending the rainy season in one

judged cases involving the death penalty, as well as from courts of 3 judges, which adjudicated a variety of civil and criminal issues.

Increasingly severe constraints on Jewish powers of self-government meant that from the end of the Talmudic period, if not earlier, no supreme Jewish judicial court was convened. A notable exception occurred under Napoleon, who, in 1806–07, convened an Assembly of Notables to answer 12 questions designed to determine whether or not the Jews of France deserved French citizenship. To answer these questions, the Assembly established a Sanhedrin of 71 members, two-thirds of them RABBIS and one-third lay people. In the introduction to its response, this Sanhedrin declared that its right to speak for all French Jewry derived specifically from ancient custom and law, which vested in such a court the power to pass legislation that would promote the welfare of the people of Israel.

SAN-KUAN \ˈsän-ˈgwän\, *Pinyin* Sanguan, in Chinese mythology, the Three Officials: T'ien-kuan, official of heaven who bestows happiness; Ti-kuan, official of earth who grants remission of sins; and Shui-kuan, official of water who averts misfortune. Reflecting a Taoist principle that held heaven, earth, and water to be three transcendent powers, Chang Heng (2nd century CE) proposed that the confession of sins be written in triplicate, one to be burned for heaven, another to be buried in earth, and the third to be sunk in water.

SAN-LUN \ˈsän-ˈlùn\ ("Three Treatises," or Middle Doctrine), school of Chinese BUDDHISM derived from the Indian MĀDHYAMIKA school.

SANNYĀSĪ \ˌsən-ˈyä-sē\, *also spelled* sannyāsin \-ˈyä-sin\, *feminine* sannyāsinī (Sanskrit: "abandoning," or "throwing down"), in HINDUISM, religious ascetic, one who has renounced the world by performing his or her own funeral and abandoning all claims to social or family standing. Since the 5th century CE major texts have associated this achievement with the fourth ASHRAM, or stage, of life, but initially it was not so; and it is uncertain what proportion of SADHUS have ever actually exemplified this ideal. According to his standard biography, even the philosopher ŚAMKARA did not, although he is often regarded as the archetypal *sannyāsī*. The name *sannyāsī* also designates an ascetic who pays particular allegiance to the god SHIVA, especially one who belongs to the *daśanāmī* order said to have been established in the 8th century CE by Śaṃkara.

Among *daśanāmī sannyāsīs*, the highest stage of achievement is recognized by the title *paramahaṃsa* ("great swan"). This honorific is usually given only after a probation of at least 12 years as an ascetic and only to those who have achieved full self-knowledge. They are then regarded as free of all worldly rules and duties, including formal religious obligations, and are often expected to worship internally only. Although his own practices were both Śākta and deeply devotional, the 19th-century saint RAMAKRISHNA is sometimes regarded as the great *paramahaṃsa* of modern times, in part because his behavior transcended any fixed expectation.

*Sannyāsī*s, like other sadhus, or holy men, are not cremated but are generally buried in a seated posture of meditation. *See* SAMĀDHI.

SANTERÍA \ˌsän-tə-ˈrē-ə, ˌsan-\, religious movement that originated in Cuba and spread to neighboring islands and the United States, principally among Africans and Hispanics. It developed out of the traditions of the Yoruba people (of modern Nigeria and Benin), who, from the 16th to the 19th century, were transported to Cuba to work as slaves on the sugar plantations.

In common with other cults brought to the New World by Africans—such as the VOUDOU of Haiti or the MACUMBA of Brazil—Santería blends elements of CHRISTIANITY and West African beliefs (*see* AFRICAN RELIGIONS). It includes belief in one Supreme Being but also in saints or spirits known as orisha, in each of which is found a force of nature and a set of humanlike behavioral characteristics. Priests or advocates known as *santero*s are said to possess *ache*, the magical power of the orisha. Ritual devotions involving musical rhythms (usually drumming and dancing), offerings of food and animal sacrifice, DIVINATION with fetishes made of bones or shells, trancelike seizures, and other rites are thought to reveal the sources of day-to-day problems and point the way to their resolution. Adherents also believe that orisha can intervene on one's behalf or may even enter into one's being, becoming part of one's personality.

In Santería, elements of ROMAN CATHOLICISM are mixed with African traditions: St. Peter is Oggun, the Yoruba patron of miners and workers, while St. Barbara, the Christian patron of artillery, is the warrior orisha Chango (Shango). Such blending of beliefs enabled Africans to retain their native faith even while they appeared to have converted to Roman Catholicism.

ŚĀNTIRAKṢITA \ˌshän-tē-ˈrək-shi-tə\ (fl. 8th century), Indian BUDDHIST teacher and saint. Invited to Tibet by its king, Śāntirakṣita was forced to flee to Nepal after adherents of

Devotees of Santería, with dolls used in their rituals, gather in Havana
Reuters—Luis Galdamez—Archive Photos

the indigenous BON religion blamed him for the outbreak of an epidemic. After his return to Tibet, according to accounts, he urged the king to invite the Indian Buddhist teacher PADMASAMBHAVA to help him.

Śāntirakṣita became the first ABBOT of the monastery at Samye (Bsam-yas), teaching the doctrines associated with the YOGĀCĀRA and Tantric forms of BUDDHISM. He ordained the first seven Tibetan Buddhist monks and is credited with incorporating several elements of Bon, including its pantheon, into the lowest level of Tantric Buddhism and with instituting Buddhist rituals to take the place of Bon animal sacrifices.

SANŪSĪ, AL- \ȧl-sä-'nü-sē\, *in full* Sīdī Muhammad ibn ʿAlī al-Sanūsī al-Mujāhirī al-Ḥasanī al-Idrīsī (b. *c.* 1787, Tursh, near Mostaganem, in northern Africa—d. Sept. 7, 1859, Jaghbūb, Cyrenaica), North African ISLAMIC theologian who founded a militant mystical movement, the Sanūsīya, which helped Libya win its independence in the 20th century.

During his formative years in his native country, which was incorporated in the Ottoman Empire, al-Sanūsī observed the corruption of the Ottoman administrators. To continue his religious studies, in 1821 he went to Fès, in Morocco, which was nominally independent but actually a colony of France. Al-Sanūsī's experiences under foreign rule and his observation of the inherent weakness of the Islamic states convinced him of the need for a revitalized Islamic community.

After a PILGRIMAGE to MECCA in 1828, al-Sanūsī visited Egypt. He had initially been attracted to MYSTICISM in Morocco, and in Egypt he joined many different religious orders. In 1837, while in the Hijaz (now in Saudi Arabia), he founded his own order, which later became known as the Sanūsīya. He limited his activities to the Bedouin tribes of the area, and he made no effort to challenge tribal patterns of authority or RELIGIOUS BELIEFS. In 1841 he was expelled from the Hijaz by the Ottoman authorities, and in 1843 he moved the order to Cyrenaica, where he used the same tribal tactics as before to create a reliable instrument for challenging the existing power structure. In about 1856 the order was moved to Jaghbūb, also in Cyrenaica but away from the sphere of Egyptian and Ottoman political control and near the caravan route from North Africa to the Hijaz and equatorial Africa.

The Sanūsīya became popular among the tribes of Cyrenaica. In the 20th century it spearheaded the liberation movement against Italian colonization. Al-Sanūsī's grandson Idrīs I ruled as king of Libya from 1951 to 1969. *See also* SUFISM.

SAOSHYANT \saȯsh-'yänt, sōsh-, -'yäns\, in Zoroastrian ESCHATOLOGY, final savior of the world and quencher of its evil; the Saoshyant Astvatereta is the foremost of three saviors (the first two are Ōshētar and Ōshētarmāh) who are all posthumous sons of ZOROASTER. One will appear at the end of each of the three last millennia of the world, miraculously conceived by a virgin who swims in a lake where Zoroaster's seed was preserved. After 57 years Astvatereta, aided by 30 of the dead, will break demonic power and resurrect the bodies of the dead. Astvatereta and six helpers will then lead the work in the seven zones of the world. When all souls have been cleansed, including those of the damned, Astvatereta will prepare for them white HAOMA—the ritual drink of the Zoroastrians—which will bestow eternal perfection on their bodies.

SAPTAMĀTṚKĀ \'sǝp-tǝ-'mä-tri-ˌkä\ (Sanskrit: "Seven Mothers"), in HINDUISM, group of seven mother-goddesses, each of whom is the *śakti*, or female counterpart, of a god. They are Brahmāṇī, Māheśvarī, Kaumārī, Vaiṣṇavī, Vārāhī, Indrāṇī, and Cāmuṇḍā, or Yamī. (One text, the *Varāha-Purāṇa*, states that they number eight, including Yogeśvarī, created out of the flame from SHIVA's mouth.)

Representations of the goddesses are found in shrines throughout India, frequently flanked by Vīrabhadra (a ferocious form of Shiva) on the left and GAṆEŚA on the right. They can be identified by their weapons, ornaments, VAHANAS ("mounts"), and banner emblems, which are in each case the same as that of their corresponding male deities. Saptamātṛkā cults seem to have disappeared by the 11th century, perhaps having been absorbed by the growing worship of ŚAKTI.

SARAH \'sar-ǝ\, *also spelled* Sarai \'sar-ˌī, -ä-ˌī\, in the OLD TESTAMENT, wife of ABRAHAM and mother of ISAAC. Sarah was childless until she was 90 years old. God promised Abraham that she would be "a mother of nations" (GENESIS 17:16) and that she would conceive and bear a son. Isaac was the fulfillment of this promise. Sarah had not believed that the promise would be fulfilled; thus she embodies the themes of fear and doubt, Abraham those of faith and hope. Her doubt drives Sarah to devise her own way of realizing the promise—she gives Abraham her maidservant, HAGAR, so that Hagar might bear a child for them. When the promise is repeated, Sarah expresses her doubt in sarcastic laughter (Genesis 18:12). And when the promise is kept, Sarah, overcome by joy, still implies her doubt had been reasonable (Genesis 21:6–7). Her tomb at Hebron (Genesis 23) was a sign of Abraham's faith that God's promise of the land would also be kept.

SARAPEUM \ˌsar-ǝ-'pē-ǝm, ˌser-\, *also spelled* Serapeum, *or* Sarapieion, either of two temples of ancient Egypt, dedicated to the worship of the Greco-Egyptian god SARAPIS (Serapis). The original elaborate temple of that name was located on the west bank of the Nile near Ṣaqqārah and originated as a monument to the deceased APIS bulls, sacred animals of the god PTAH. Though the area was used as a cemetery for the bulls as early as 1400 BCE, it was Ramses II (1279–13 BCE) who designed a main gallery and subsidiary chambers (repeatedly enlarged by succeeding kings) to serve as a CATACOMB for the deceased Apis bulls who, in death, became assimilated to the god OSIRIS as Osiris-Apis. The Greeks living near Ṣaqqārah worshiped this god as Osorapis, which under the Ptolemaic dynasty became Sarapis, and the temple was thereafter called the Sarapeum.

Another important Sarapeum was built at Alexandria, the new Ptolemaic capital. Ptolemy I Soter (reigned 305–284 BCE) chose Sarapis as the official god of Egypt, ordering his architect Parmeniscus to design what became one of the largest and best known of the god's temples. There Sarapis was worshiped in a purely Greek ritual until 391 CE, when the Sarapeum was destroyed by the PATRIARCH Theophilus and his followers. In Roman times other Sarapeums were constructed throughout the empire.

SARAPIS \sǝ-'ra-pis, -'rä-\, *also spelled* Serapis, Greco-Egyptian deity of the sun first encountered at Memphis, where his cult was celebrated in association with that of the sacred Egyptian bull APIS (who was called Osorapis when deceased). He was originally a god of the underworld but he was reintroduced as a new deity with many Hellenic as-

SARASVATĪ

pects by Ptolemy I Soter (reigned 305–284 BCE), who centered the worship of the deity at Alexandria.

The SARAPEUM at Alexandria was the largest and best known of the god's temples. The cult statue there represented Sarapis as a robed and bearded figure regally enthroned, his right hand resting on Cerberus (the three-headed dog who guards the gate of the underworld), while his left held an upraised sceptre. Gradually Sarapis became revered not only as a sun god ("Zeus Sarapis") but also as a lord of healing and of fertility. His worship was established in Rome and throughout the Mediterranean, being particularly prominent in the great commercial cities. Among the Gnostics he was a symbol of the universal godhead. The destruction of the Sarapeum at Alexandria by the PATRIARCH Theophilus and his followers in 391 CE signaled the final triumph of CHRISTIANITY throughout the Roman Empire.

SARASVATĪ \\'sə-rəs-ˌvə-tē\\, Hindu goddess of learning and the arts, especially music. First appearing as the personification of the sacred river Sarasvatī and also identified with Vāc, the goddess of speech, later she is named the consort, daughter, or granddaughter of BRAHMĀ. She is regarded as the patroness of art, music, and letters and as the inventor of the Sanskrit language and the Devanāgarī script in which it is written. She is usually represented as riding on a *haṃsa* bird and holding a lute and a manuscript or book. The *haṃsa* bird is a goose notable for its pure white color and its ability to undertake very long flights to Himalayan altitudes; in modern times it has frequently come to be represented as a swan. Sarasvatī is worshiped at the advent of spring (January–February in the Hindu year), when her image is taken out in jubilant procession, but she is also invoked perennially and at examination times by students, and by artists and performers of all kinds. Sarasvatī is also popular in Jain and Buddhist mythology.

The river Sarasvatī is revered above all others in the VEDAS and is by far the one most frequently mentioned. Because it corresponds to none of the major rivers of modern South Asia, it has for centuries been regarded as subtle or mythic, depending on one's perspective, converging unseen with the GAṄGĀ (Ganges) and JAMUNĀ rivers when they flow together at Prayāg (Allahabad). The millions of pilgrims who participate in the KUMBH MELA every 12 years at this site are thus said to bathe in the *triveṇi* ("triple confluence"), as do all pilgrims to Prayāg, which is therefore sometimes called "king of TĪRTHAS."

A major debate at the end of the 20th century focused on whether the Vedic Sarasvatī corresponds to a major dry riverbed forming part of the Indus complex and containing many as yet unexcavated archaeological sites. If so, this forgotten Sarasvatī might promise to provide a major link between Vedic and Indus Valley cultures.

SARCOPHAGUS, stone COFFIN. The original term is of doubtful meaning; Pliny explains that the word denotes a coffin of limestone which had the property of dissolving the body quickly (Greek *sarx*, "flesh"; *phagein*, "to eat"). This explanation is questionable; religious and folkloristic ideas may have been involved in calling a coffin a body-eater. The word came into general use as the name for a large coffin in imperial Rome and is now used as an archaeological term.

ŚĀRIPUTRA \\ˌshär-ē-'pu̇-trə\\ (Sanskrit), *Pali* Sariputta \\ˌsär-ē-'pu̇t-tə\\, *given name* Upatissa, BRAHMIN ascetic and famous early disciple of the BUDDHA GOTAMA. Śāriputra first heard of the Buddha and his new teaching from Assaji, one of the original 60 disciples. Quickly achieving Enlightenment, he developed a reputation as a master of the Abhidharma; his disciples included ĀNANDA, the Buddha's personal attendant; Rā, the Buddha's son; and Moggallāna. The *Niddesa* ("Exposition") is attributed to him; its two parts give a philological exegesis of the last two (fourth and fifth) sections of the *Suttanipāta*. He is said to have died shortly before the Buddha, and his relics were taken to Sāvatthi.

SARPEDON \\sär-'pē-dən\\, in Greek mythology, son of ZEUS and Laodameia, the daughter of Bellerophon; he was a Lycian prince and a hero in the Trojan War. After he was killed by the Greek warrior Patroclus, a struggle took place for the possession of his body until APOLLO rescued it from the Greeks, washed it, anointed it with ambrosia, and handed it over to HYPNOS ("Sleep") and Thanatos ("Death"), by whom it was conveyed for burial to Lycia. There a SANCTUARY (Sarpedoneum) was erected in his honor.

In later tradition Sarpedon was the son of Zeus and EUROPA and the brother of King MINOS of Crete. Expelled from Crete by Minos, he and his comrades sailed for Asia Minor, where he finally became king of Lycia.

SARVĀSTIVĀDA \\sər-ˌväs-ti-'vä-də\\, important school of HĪNAYĀNA Buddhism. The Sarvāstivāda school is generally considered to be one of the 18 Hīnayāna schools that developed during the first four to five centuries following the death of the BUDDHA GOTAMA. During the 1st millennium of the Common Era the Sarvāstivādins and Sarvāstivāda offshoots exerted a strong influence in many parts of the Buddhist world, particularly in northwest India and portions of Southeast Asia.

The term Sarvāstivāda literally means the teaching that everything exists, and it was especially associated in the Sarvāstivāda tradition with the notion that the past, the present, and the future all exist. The major work that expounded Sarvāstivāda teaching was the *Mahāvibhāṣa* ("Great Elucidation"), which was written in the late 2nd century CE. The importance of this text is suggested by the fact that the Sarvāstivādins were often called the Vaibhāṣikas, a name that means followers of the (Mahā) Vibhāṣa.

SARVODAYA \sər-'vō-də-yə\ (Hindi, literally, "uplifting of all," from Sanskrit *sarva*, "all" + *udaya*, "rise, coming up"), MAHATMA GANDHI's philosophy, which advocated community sharing of all resources for the mutual benefit and enhancement of peasant life.

SA-SKYA-PA \'sä-gʸä-bä\, *also spelled* Sakyapa, Tibetan Buddhist sect named for the great Sa-skya (Sakya) monastery founded in 1073 some 50 miles north of Mount Everest. The sect follows the teachings of 'Brog-mi (992–1072), who translated into Tibetan the important Tantric work called the *Hevajra Tantra*, which remains one of the basic texts of the order (*see* TANTRA). He also transmitted the teachings of the *lam-'bras* ("way and effect"), which uses the symbolism of sexual union as a means of achieving mystical reintegration of the self.

The tutelary deity of the sect is the fierce, protective Hevajra. Abbots are permitted to marry, and succession passes from father to son or from uncle to nephew.

A major phase in the history of the Sa-skya-pa sect came in the 13th–14th century when its members, with the help of their Mongol military allies, established the first theocratic state in Tibet and maintained their control for more than a hundred years.

SATAN \'sä-tən\, in JUDAISM and CHRISTIANITY, the adversary of God.

The word *Satan* is the transliteration of a Hebrew word for "adversary." In THE BOOK OF JOB, "the adversary" comes to the heavenly court with the "sons of God." His task is to roam through the earth seeking out acts or persons to be reported adversely. Satan is cynical about disinterested human goodness and is permitted to test it under God's authority and within the limits that God sets.

In the NEW TESTAMENT the Greek transliteration *Satanas* is used, and this usually appears as *Satan* in English translations. He is spoken of as the prince of evil spirits, the inveterate enemy of God and of Christ, who takes the guise of an ANGEL of light. Through his subordinate DEMONS Satan can take possession of men's bodies, afflicting them or making them diseased. According to the Book of Revelation, when the risen Christ returns from heaven to reign on earth, Satan will be bound with a great chain for a thousand years. He is then to be released, but he will almost immediately face final defeat and thereafter be cast into eternal punishment. His name, Beelzebul, used in the Gospels mainly in reference to demoniac possession, comes from the name of the god of Ekron, Baalzebub (2 Kings 1). He is also identified with the DEVIL (*diabolos*), and this term occurs more frequently in the New Testament

The Devil, an aspect of Satan, on a French tarot card from the 19th century
The Bridgeman Art Library

XV

LE DIABLE.

than does Satan. In the Qur'an the proper name *Shaitan* ("Satan") is used.

See also LUCIFER.

SATANISM \'sā-tən-ˌi-zəm\, *also called* devil worship, worship of SATAN, or the DEVIL, personality or principle regarded by the Judeo-Christian tradition as embodying absolute evil in complete antithesis to God. This worship may be regarded as a gesture of extreme protest against Judeo-Christian spiritual hegemony. Satanic cults have been documented in Europe and the Americas as far back as the 17th century; but their earlier roots are difficult to trace, just as the number of real satanists in any period is frequently overestimated. Churchmen have readily attributed satanism to witches and to such heretics as GNOSTICS, CATHARI, and BOGOMILS, but that charge does not correspond with those groups' own understanding of their beliefs. By the same token, devil worship ascribed to non-Christian religions is usually based on polemic or misunderstanding. Modern WITCHCRAFT and NEO-PAGANISM are not to be confused with satanism, since these groups worship not Satan but pre-Christian gods. Satanism, as devotion to the Judeo-Christian source of evil, can only exist in symbiosis with that tradition, for it shares but inverts its worldview.

Satanist worship has traditionally centered on the "black mass," a corrupted rendition of the Christian EUCHARIST, and ritual magic evocations of Satan. Some recent satanist groups have supplanted those practices with rites of self-expression reminiscent of psychodrama and hyperventilation.

SATHYA SAI BABA \'sət-yə-'sä⁻ē-'bä-bä\, *originally* Sathya Narayana Raju (b. 1926, Puttaparthi, India), Indian spiritual leader. Born into a BRAHMIN family, at an early age Sathya Narayana Raju began to perform miracles, and at 14 he declared himself an incarnation of SHIRDI SAI BABA. Soon after, he took up residence in the garden of a sympathizer, where he led prayers and devotional singing until his first ashram, Prasanthi Nilayam, was completed in 1950. In 1960, Baba revealed his identity further, claiming to be an incarnation of both SHIVA and his consort ŚAKTI in one, as well as the second in a succession of three incarnations of Shiva of whom the first was Shirdi Sai Baba.

Sathya Sai Baba was revered by his many followers for his healing of the sick and his ability to read minds and foretell the future. He offered basic HINDU teachings with little concern for specific doctrines, and his devotees ranged from the ascetics in his ashrams to lay believers. Devotees also included many non-Indians, especially from Europe and the United States. While his detractors criticized his flamboyance and dismissed his dramatic miracle-working as the antics of a charlatan, his ashram sponsored the construction of a hospital, schools, and colleges, and ashram workers frequently engaged in community service. In addition to Prasanthi Nilayam, he had a large Sathya Sai Baba ashram in Whitefield, outside of Bangalore in Karnātaka, and numerous smaller centers in other Indian cities and around the world.

SATĪ \'sə-ˌtē, ˌsə-'tē\, *also spelled* suttee (Sanskrit: "good woman"), in English usage, the custom of a Hindu widow burning herself to death, either on the funeral pyre of her dead husband or soon after his death. In Indic languages, *sati* refers less to the action than to the woman herself, who thereby demonstrates her truthfulness (*sat*) and her virtue. This is sometimes said to blaze forth so intensely at the moment of her impending death that it alone is responsible for igniting the pyre. Strictly speaking, such a woman avoids the inauspicious status of widowhood, which religious law calculates as commencing with the ritual of the husband's death, not its physical occurrence. In fact, her courage, purity, and auspiciousness are held in certain parts of India (*e.g.*, Rajasthan) to generate a protective power that makes a *satī* worthy of veneration as a "*satī* mother" (*satīmātā*). Opponents of the practice of *satī* reject such notions as horrifying indices of a deeply misogynic value system and therefore prefer to use the term *satī* as meaning widow immolation.

The word *satī* can also be employed as a proper noun to designate the consort of SHIVA, who protested her father Dakṣa's failure to include Shiva among the guests at a sacrifice by throwing herself into the fire. The myth of Satī does not involve the death of her husband. Rather, he rescues her body from the flames and carries it, grief-stricken, throughout India, dismembering it as he goes. Thus the connection between the mythical Satī and the practice called *satī* is indirect. Critics of *satī* have often pointed this out, but many Hindus continue to assume it, nonetheless.

Numerous *satī* stones, memorials to women who died in this way, are found all over India, the earliest dated 510 CE. The first reference to the practice in a Sanskrit text is in the MAHĀBHĀRATA, in which some queens undergo *satī*; but it is mentioned by the 1st-century-BCE Greek author Diodorus Siculus in his account of the Punjab in the 4th century BCE. In the medieval period certain Rājputs practiced *jauhar* (probably from *jīvahar*, "taking one's life") to save women from dishonor by foes, most notably at Chitorgarh. BRAHMINS may have adopted this practice from warrior classes, modifying it over time to suit their own gender ideology of pure womanhood and producing the phenomenon the British saw as "suttee." The considerable incidence of *satī* among the Brahmins of Bengal also undoubtedly followed from the *dāyabhāga* system of law (*c.* 1100), which prevailed in Bengal and which gave inheritance to widows—an economic threat to sons, who would otherwise have been the sole heirs. *Satī* was often committed voluntarily, if one allows that such a term can be meaningful given the patriarchal context, but cases of compulsion, escape, and rescue are also known. Steps to prohibit *satī* were taken by the Mughal rulers Humāyūn and his son AKBAR, and it was abolished in British India in 1829. In spite of this, however, frequent instances of *satī* continued to occur in Indian states for more than 30 years, and, in fact, occasional instances in remote areas are still reported, as in the famous case of 18-year-old Roop Kanwar of Deorala in the Shekhāvatī region of Rajasthan in 1987. Many students of Roop Kanwar's death have concluded it was murder. *Satī* has never been at all as frequent as travelers' accounts made it seem, but its symbolic importance is great. Hence the right of *satī* temples (often founded by Shekhāvat communities), shrines,

and rituals to exist in India today is a matter of continued and heated debate.

SATNĀMĪ SECT \ˌsət-'nä-mē\, any of several groups in India that have challenged political and religious authority by rallying around an understanding of God as *satnām* ("whose name is truth").

The earliest Satnāmīs were a sect of mendicants and householders founded by Bīrbhan in Narnaul, eastern Punjab, in 1657 that defied the Mughal emperor Aurangzeb in 1672 and were crushed by his army. Remnants of this sect or group may have contributed to the formation of another known as Sadhs (*i.e.*, *sādhu*, "pure") in the early 19th century, who also designated their deity as *satnām*. A similar and roughly contemporary group gathered under the leadership of Jagjīvandās of Barabanki district, near Lucknow, that was said to have been formatively influenced by a disciple of the SUFI mystic Yārī Shāh (1668–1725). He projected an image of an overarching creator God as NIRGUṆA, devoid of sensible qualities and best worshiped through a regimen of self-discipline and by use of "the true name" alone. Yet Jagjīvandās also wrote works about Hindu deities, and the elimination of CASTE was not part of his message.

The most important Satnāmī group was founded in 1820 in the Chattisgarh region of middle India by Ghāsīdās, a CAMĀR farm servant. His Satnām Panth ("Path of the True Name") succeeded in providing a religious and social identity for large numbers of Chattisgarhi *camār*s (who formed one-sixth of the total population), defying their derogatory treatment by upper-caste Hindus and exclusion from Hindu temple worship. Ghāsīdās is remembered as having thrown images of Hindu gods onto a rubbish heap. He preached a code of ethical and dietary self-restraint and social equality. Connections with the KABĪR Panth have been historically important at certain stages, and over time Satnāmīs have negotiated their place within a wider Hindu order in complex, even contradictory ways.

SATORI \'sä-tō-ˌrē, *Angl* sə-'tōr-ē, sä-, -'tȯr-\ (Japanese), *Chinese* Wu \'wü\, in Zen BUDDHISM, the inner, intuitive experience of Enlightenment; Satori is said to be unexplainable, indescribable, and unintelligible to reason and logic. It is comparable to the experience undergone by the BUDDHA GOTAMA when he sat under the Bo tree and, as such, is the central ZEN goal. Satori constitutes a complete reordering of the individual in his relation to the universe; it usually is achieved only after a period of concentrated preparation and may occur spontaneously as a result of a chance incident, such as a sudden noise. The relative importance of the period of concentrated attention to the sudden "breaking through" is weighed differently by the two major branches of Zen: the SŌTŌ sect emphasizes quiet sitting (*zazen*), whereas the RINZAI sect devotes more attention to the various methods of bringing about an abrupt awakening. (*See also* KOAN.)

SATSAṄG \ˌsət-'səŋ-gä, 'sət-ˌsəŋg\, in SIKHISM, "the assembly of true believers," a practice that dates back to the first GURŪ of the religion, NĀNAK. While not unique to Sikhism, the convention of gathering together and singing the compositions of the Gurū was understood in peculiarly Sikh terms, at first as a sign of loyalty to the Gurū and the community that formed around him and later as a means of participating in the power of the divine Word that emanated from the hymns and songs of the Gurūs. Such gatherings take place in a *dharamsala*s or GURDWĀRĀS (Sikh places of worship), are open to men and women of all CASTES, and allow all assembled to share in the merit of the Gurū and the divine word.

SATURN \\'sa-tərn\\, *Latin* Saturnus \\sa-'tər-nəs\\, in ROMAN RELIGION, god of sowing or seed. The Romans equated him with the Greek deity CRONUS. Saturn's temple at the west end of the Roman Forum at the foot of the Clivus Capitolinus served as the state treasury (*aerarium Saturni*). Saturn's cult partner was the obscure goddess Lua, whose name is connected with *lues* ("plague," or "affliction"); but he was also associated with Ops, another obscure goddess, the cult partner of CONSUS, probably a god of the storage bin.

Saturn's great festival, the Saturnalia, became one of the most popular of Roman festivals, and its influence is still felt in the celebration of CHRISTMAS and the Western world's New Year. The Saturnalia was originally celebrated only on December 17, but it was later extended to seven days. All work and business were suspended, slaves were given a measure of freedom to say and to do what they liked, moral restrictions were eased, and presents were exchanged. The weekday Saturday (Latin: *Saturni dies*) was named for Saturn.

SATYĀGRAHA \\,sət-'yä-grə-hə, -'yä-greh\\ (Hindi: "insistence on, or zeal for, truth," from Sanskrit *satya*, "true, truth" + *āgraha*, "insistence, obstinance," or "zeal, assiduity"), concept introduced in the early 20th century by Mahātmā GANDHI to designate a determined but nonviolent resistance to evil. Gandhi's *satyāgraha* became a major tool in the Indian struggle against British imperialism and has since been adopted by protest groups in other countries.

According to this philosophy, *satyāgrahī*s—practitioners of *satyāgraha*—achieve correct insight into the real nature of a situation by seeking truth in a spirit of peace and love and undergoing a rigorous process of self-scrutiny. By refusing to submit to the wrong or to cooperate with it in any way, *satyāgrahī*s assert the overarching truth bearing on that situation, a truth that transcends the narrower interest of any one party in a struggle. To keep this truth in view, NONVIOLENCE is essential, since violence would preclude the assent of at least one combatant. Thus *satyāgraha* seeks to conquer through conversion; in the end, there is no defeat and no victory but rather a new harmony.

Satyāgraha appeals to the ancient Indian ideal of AHIṂSĀ ("not desiring to harm"), which is pursued with particular rigor by Jains; Gandhi's great friend Rajchandra Rajivbhai was Jain. In developing *ahiṃsā* into a modern concept with

broad political consequences, as *satyāgraha*, Gandhi also drew from the writings of Leo Tolstoy and Henry David Thoreau, from the BIBLE, and from the BHAGAVAD GĪTĀ. Gandhi first conceived *satyāgraha* in 1906 in response to a law discriminating against Asians that was passed by the British colonial government of the Transvaal in South Africa. In 1917 the first *satyāgraha* campaign in India was mounted in the indigo-growing district of Champaran. Over the following years, fasting and economic boycotts were employed as methods of *satyāgraha*, until the British left India in 1947.

Critics of *satyāgraha*, both in Gandhi's time and subsequently, have argued that it is unrealistic and incapable of universal success since it relies upon a high standard of ethical conduct in the opponent, the representative of "evil," and demands an unrealistically strong level of commitment from those struggling for social amelioration. Nonetheless *satyāgraha* played a significant role in the Civil Rights Movement led by Martin Luther King, Jr., in the United States and has spawned a continuing legacy in South Asia itself.

Head of the Dancing Satyr, *bronze statue from Pompeii, 2nd century* BCE; *in the Museo Archeologico Nazionale, Naples*
Bruckmann Munchen

SATYR AND SILENUS \\'sā-tər, 'sa-...sī-'lē-nəs\\, in Greek mythology, creatures of the wild, part man and part beast, who in classical times were closely associated with the god DIONYSUS. Satyrs and Sileni were at first represented as uncouth men, each with a horse's tail and ears and an erect phallus, and they later came to be represented as men having a goat's legs and tail. The relation of the two names is not certain; Silenus may have been slightly earlier, but Satyr became the dominant term by the Classical period. In the Great Dionysia festival at Athens three tragedies were followed by a Satyr play (*e.g.*, Euripides' *Cyclops*), in which the chorus was dressed to represent Satyrs. Silenus, although bibulous like the Satyrs in the Satyr plays, also appeared in legend as a dispenser of homely wisdom. In art the Satyrs and Sileni were depicted in company with NYMPHS or Maenads whom they pursued.

SAUL \\'sȯl\\, *Hebrew* Sha'ul \\shä-'ül\\ (fl. 11th century BCE, Israel), first king of Israel (c. 1021–1000 BCE). His chief contribution was to defend Israel against its many enemies, especially the Philistines.

Biblical account of his life. The account of Saul's life comes from the OLD TESTAMENT book of 1 Samuel. The son of Kish, a well-to-do member of the tribe of BENJAMIN, he was made king by the league of 12 Israelite tribes to meet the growing Philistine threat. Two literary strands are discernible in the accounts in 1 Samuel involving Saul. One of these (9:1–10:16), reflecting a favorable attitude toward the monarchy, relates how the son of Kish was initially selected by SAMUEL and how he delivered the town of Jabesh-Gilead from oppression by the AMMONITES, an act that brought him to the attention of all Israel and resulted in his acclamation as king in a public ceremony at Gilgal. A second body of tradition (1 Samuel 8; 10:17–27; 12), however, stresses Samuel's misgivings about the kingship.

Saul's reign. Saul's chief service to Israel lay in the sphere of military defense. He won significant victories over the Philistines and waged a successful campaign against the AMALEKITES in the south (1 Samuel 15). Saul's subsequent disintegration, however, was largely caused by his break with Samuel. Separate accounts attributed this to Saul's failure in religious duties—presumption in offering unauthorized sacrifice before battle and a reluctance to devote Amalek to destruction according to the principle of HOLY WAR. Samuel's rejection of Saul withdrew from the king the religious sanctions essential for popular support.

David came into Saul's court because of either his military prowess or his skill as a harpist, according to varying accounts in 1 Samuel. Jealous of David's military successes, Saul declared his intention to slay David, and only David's flight to Philistia saved him. Saul's progressive mental deterioration culminated in the slaughter of the 85 priests at Nob (1 Samuel 22).

When the Philistines mounted new attacks on the Israelite heartland, Saul gathered his forces at Mount Gilboa. On the eve of the fateful battle he sought, through a necromancer at Endor, some word of encouragement from the dead Samuel (1 Samuel 28). The oracle of Samuel's ghost, however, could foretell only the defeat of the Israelite forces and the death of Saul and of his sons.

SAULE \ˈsaů-le\, in BALTIC RELIGION and mythology, the sun goddess, who determines the well-being and regeneration of all life on earth.

According to Baltic myth, Saule rides each day through the sky on a horse-drawn chariot with copper wheels. Toward evening Saule washes the horses in the sea, sitting on top of a hill, holding the golden reins in her hand. Then she goes beyond the silver gates into her castle at the end of the sea. The red ball of the setting sun, one aspect of Saule, is portrayed in Baltic art as a ring, a falling red apple, or a crown. As the full light of the sun, she is also represented by a daisy, a wheel, or a rosette.

One myth says that Saule's daughters were courted by the moon god, MĒNESS. Another myth, found in both Lithuanian and Latvian traditions, tells that Mēness married the sun goddess, but he soon began to court the goddess of the dawn, the morning star. PĒRKONS (Lithuanian: Perkūnas), the Thunderer, cut the moon god to pieces in revenge for this slight to Saule.

Because of her association with growth and fertility, Saule was remembered in prayers by the farmers at both sunrise and sunset. The major event in her honor was the LĪGO FEAST, a midsummer festival celebrated on June 23 (now St. John's Eve). On that day, the sun, wreathed in a garland of red flowers, was said to observe the summer solstice by dancing on a silver hill while wearing silver shoes. Great fires were lit on the hills to ward off evil spirits who might threaten health and fertility. Young people, wearing wreaths of flowers, danced and sang Līgo songs and leaped over the fires.

A harmless green snake, ŽALTYS, was a special favorite of Saule's, and, because of that, it was considered to be good luck to have a *žaltys* in the house—and, conversely, bad luck to kill one.

SAUTRĀNTIKA \saů-ˈträn-ti-kə\, ancient school of HĪNAYĀNA Buddhism that emerged in India about the 2nd century BCE as an offshoot of the SARVĀSTIVĀDA. The school is so called because of its reliance on the SŪTRAS, or words of the Buddha, and because of its rejection of the authority of the *Abhidharma.*

The Sautrāntikas maintained that, although events (DHARMAS) have only momentary existence, there is a transmigrating substratum of consciousness that contains the goodness that exists in every person. The Sautrāntika sometimes is characterized as a transitional school that pointed in the direction of MAHĀYĀNA thought and eventually came to influence the YOGĀCĀRA branch of Mahāyāna philosophy.

SAVARKAR \ˌsə-vər-ˈkär\: *see* HINDUTVA.

SĀVITRĪ \ˈsä-vi-ˌtrē\, goddess in Hindu mythology, the daughter of the SOLAR DEITY Savitr and the wife of the creator god BRAHMĀ. The more common use of the term *sāvitrī* is to designate one of the most important MANTRAS in HINDUISM, taken from ṚG VEDA 3.62.10, which is also known as the *gayatri:* "We contemplate the excellent glory of the divine Savitr; may he inspire our intellect."

This mantra is employed in several ritual contexts, the most important of which is the initiation ceremony (UPANAYANA) traditionally incumbent upon boys of all the "twice-born" CASTES (*i.e.,* excluding ŚŪDRAS and UNTOUCHABLES). Depending on the class or caste of the young initiate, the verse would be recited in different meters; this was done at the instruction of the teacher or GURU after the imparting of the sacred thread, the symbol of the "second birth." The Sāvitrī verse inaugurated the period of study of the VEDA under the guidance of this teacher and was meant to inspire the boy to success in his endeavor.

Another principal ritual context in which this mantra is featured is the morning prayer, or *samdhya,* that forms a part of the daily religious practice of millions of Hindus. Some SCRIPTURES recommend that this verse be repeated several times during the course of this ceremony and that the recitation be drawn out as long as possible, for it is through this prolonged recitation that the ancestors supposedly attained long life, understanding, honor, and glory.

SAVONAROLA, GIROLAMO \ˌsa-və-nə-ˈrō-lə, *Italian,* sä-vō-nä-ˈrò-lä\ (b. Sept. 21, 1452, Ferrara, Duchy of Ferrara—d. May 23, 1498, Florence), Italian Christian preacher, reformer, and martyr. After the overthrow of the Medici in 1494, Savonarola was the sole leader of Florence, setting up a democratic republic.

Early years. Girolamo Savonarola was born at Ferrara. He was educated by his paternal grandfather, Michele, a celebrated doctor and a man of rigid moral and religious principles. Even at an early age, as he wrote in a letter to his father, Savonarola found unbearable the humanistic paganism that corrupted manners, art, poetry, and religion itself. He saw as the cause of this spreading corruption a clergy that was corrupt even in the highest levels of the church hierarchy. On April 24, 1475, he entered the DOMINICAN order at Bologna. Returning to Ferrara four years later, he taught SCRIPTURE in the Convento degli Angeli. The subject had always been, together with the works of THOMAS AQUINAS, his great passion.

Career in Florence. In 1482 Savonarola was sent to Florence to take up the post of lecturer in the convent of San Marco, where he gained a great reputation for his learning and ASCETICISM. At San Gimignano in LENT 1485 and 1486, he put forward his famous propositions: the church needed reforming; it would be scourged and then renewed. The following year (1487) he left Florence to become master of studies in the school of general studies at Bologna. Returning to Florence in 1490, Savonarola preached boldly against the abuses of the government, and popular enthusiasm for Savonarola's preaching began to grow.

Medici rule in Florence did not long survive Lorenzo and was overthrown by the invasion of Charles VIII (1494). Two years before, Savonarola had predicted the coming of Charles and his easy victory. These authenticated prophecies and the part he had played in negotiations with the king enormously increased his authority, and he found himself Florence's master. He introduced a democratic government; he wanted to found his city of God in Florence as a well-organized Christian republic that might initiate the reform of Italy and of the church.

Political intrigues. Savonarola's triumph soon aroused opposition. A Florentine party called the Arrabbiati formed an alliance with the duke of Milan and the pope, who had joined in the Holy League against the king of France and saw in Savonarola the main obstacle to Florence's joining them. It was then that the pope sent to Savonarola the brief of July 21, 1495, in which he praised Savonarola's work and called him to Rome to pronounce his prophecies from his own lips. As that pope was the corrupt Alexander VI, Savonarola saw a trap and asked to be allowed to put off his journey. On September 8 the pope sent him a second brief in which he ordered him to go to Bologna under pain of EXCOMMUNICATION, which met with another refusal. The brief was replaced by another of October 16, in which he was forbidden to preach. After a few months, as Lent 1496 drew near, Alexander VI verbally revoked the ban. Thus Savonarola was able to give his sermons on AMOS, in which he attacked the Roman Court with renewed vigor. He also appeared to refer to the pope's scandalous private life, and the latter took offense at this. A college of theologians found nothing to criticize in what the FRIAR had said, and after Lent he was able to begin further sermons.

As Savonarola's authority grew, the pope tried to win him over by offering him a cardinal's hat, which he declined. Then Alexander VI, in a brief of Nov. 7, 1496, incorporated the Congregation of San Marco, of which Savonarola was VICAR, with another in which he would have lost all his authority. If he obeyed, his reforms would be lost. If he disobeyed, he would be excommunicated. As no one came forward to put the brief into force, Savonarola went on unperturbed in ADVENT 1496 and Lent 1497 with another series of sermons.

Events in Italy now turned against Savonarola, however, and even in Florence his power was lessened by unfavorable political and economic developments. A government of Arrabbiati forced him to stop preaching and incited riots against him on Ascension Day. The Arrabbiati obtained from the Roman Court a bull of excommunication against their enemy. In effect the excommunication was full of such obvious errors of form and substance as to render it null and void, and the pope himself had to disown it. When Rome proposed an arrangement that made withdrawal of the censure dependent on Florence's entry into the League, Savonarola was finally silenced by the interdict with which the city was threatened.

Trial and execution. With public opinion turning against Savonarola, the Arrabbiati raised a mob, marched to San Marco, and took Savonarola prisoner along with two of his followers. After formal examination, torture, and a perfunctory ecclesiastical trial, he was handed over to the secular arm to be hanged and burned. Before mounting the scaffold he received the pope's ABSOLUTION and plenary INDULGENCE.

Assessment. After Savonarola's death a cult was dedicated to him, which had a long history. He was venerated as a saint, an office was said for him, and miracles he had performed were recorded. In the ACTA SANCTORUM he was included among the *praetermissi*. When the 500th anniversary of his birth came around in 1952, there was again talk of his CANONIZATION. Savonarola's greatest work is the *Triumphus crucis*, a clear exposition of Christian APOLOGETICS. His *Compendium revelationum*, an account of visions and prophecies that came true, went through many editions in several countries.

ṢAWM \'saŭm\ (Arabic: "fasting"), *also spelled* ṣiyām, in IS-LAM, any religious fast, but particularly the fast of the month of RAMAḌĀN. *See also* FIVE PILLARS OF ISLAM.

SAYYID \'sī-yid, 'sā-\ (Arabic: "master," or "lord"), Arabic title of respect, sometimes restricted, as is the title SHARĪF, to the Banū Hāshim, members of MUHAMMAD's clan—in particular, to the descendants of Muhammad's uncles al-ʿAbbās and Abū Ṭālib and of ʿAlī ibn Abī Ṭālib by Muhammad's daughter FĀṬIMA. In the Hijaz, sayyid is further restricted to the descendants of Ḥusayn, who was the younger son of ʿAlī and Fāṭima.

In Pakistan and India sayyids are numerous, being one of the four main groups of Muslims. They also constitute an influential extratribal class in Yemen, claiming descent from the Prophet through an ancestor who came south from Iraq more than a millennium ago. Many dynasties have also claimed to be sayyids in the restricted sense. *See also* ISLAMIC CASTE.

SCAPEGOAT, *Hebrew* saʿir la-ʿAzaʾzel ("goat for Azazel"), in the OLD TESTAMENT ritual of YOM KIPPUR (Leviticus 16:8–10), a goat symbolically burdened with the SINS of the Jewish people. Some scholars believe that the animal was chosen by lot to placate AZAZEL, a wilderness DEMON, then thrown over a precipice outside Jerusalem to rid the nation of its iniquities.

The use of scapegoats has a long and varied history involving many kinds of animals, as well as human beings. In ancient Greece, human scapegoats (*pharmakoi*) were used to mitigate a calamity. The Athenians chose a man and woman for the festival of THARGELIA. After being feasted, the couple was led around the town, beaten with green twigs, driven out of the city, and possibly even stoned.

During the Roman feast of LUPERCALIA, priests (Luperci) cut narrow strips of hide (thongs) from the sacrificial animals (goats and a dog), then raced around the walls of the old Palatine city, striking women (especially) as they passed with the thongs. A blow from the hide of the scapegoat was said to cure sterility.

SCARAB \'skar-əb\, *Latin* scarabaeus \ˌskar-ə-'bē-əs\, in ancient EGYPTIAN RELIGION, important symbol in the form of the dung beetle (*Scarabaeus sacer*). This beetle may be seen on sunny days forming a ball of dung and rolling it over the sand to its burrow, where the ball is consumed in the following days. The Egyptians apparently shared the widespread belief that the beetle lays its eggs in this ball of dung and saw in the life cycle of the beetle a microcosm of the daily rebirth of the sun; the ancient sun-god Khepri was conceived as a great scarab beetle rolling the sun across the heavens. The scarab became a symbol of the enduring human soul as well— hence its frequent appearance, often

Scarab commemorating the marriage of Amenhotep and Queen Tiy, 18th dynasty
By courtesy of the Oriental Institute, the University of Chicago

with wings spread, in funerary art. Quantities of dead beetles have been discovered in burials of the earliest period; the later mummification of scarabs stems from the fact that they were sacred to Khepri at HELIOPOLIS.

Scarabs of various materials, glazed steatite being most common, form an important class of Egyptian antiquities. Such objects usually have the bases inscribed or decorated with designs and are simultaneously AMULETS and seals. Though they first appeared in the late Old Kingdom (*c.* 2575–*c.* 2130 BCE), scarabs remained rare until Middle Kingdom times (1938–*c.* 1600? BCE), when they were fashioned in great numbers. Some were used simply as ornaments, while others were purely amuletic in purpose, as the large basalt "heart scarabs" of the New Kingdom (1539–1075 BCE) and later times, which were placed in the bandages of mummies and were symbolically identified with the heart of the deceased. A winged scarab might also be placed on the breast of the MUMMY, and later a number of other scarabs were placed about the body.

SCÁTHACH \ˈskä-thək\ (Gaelic: "The Shadowy One"), in Celtic mythology, female warrior, especially noted as a teacher of warriors.

Scáthach was the daughter of Árd-Greimne of Lethra. She lived on an island (thought to be the Isle of Skye) in an impregnable castle, the gate of which was guarded by her daughter Uathach. At this fortress Scáthach trained numerous Celtic heroes in the military arts. Her best-known student was CÚ CHULAINN, who stayed with her for a year. A number of other heroes of Celtic mythology also owed their prowess to the training of Scáthach.

SCHISM, in CHRISTIANITY, break in the unity of the church.

In the early church, schism was used to describe those groups that broke with the church and established rival churches. The terms HERESY and schism were originally almost synonymous, but later schism came to refer to those divisions that were caused by disagreement over something other than basic doctrine. Thus, the schismatic group was not necessarily heretical. Eventually, however, the distinctions between schism and heresy became less clear, and all disruptions in the church came to be referred to as schismatic.

The most significant medieval schism was the East-West schism that divided Christendom into Western (ROMAN CATHOLIC) and Eastern (EASTERN ORTHODOX) branches. It began in 1054, and it has never been healed, although in 1965 Pope Paul VI and the ecumenical patriarch Athenagoras I abolished the mutual EXCOMMUNICATIONS of 1054 of the pope and the patriarch of Constantinople. Another important medieval schism was the Western Schism between the rival popes of Rome and Avignon and, later, even a third pope. The greatest Christian schism in the West was that involving the Protestant REFORMATION and the division from Rome.

According to Roman Catholic CANON LAW, a schismatic is a baptized person who, though continuing to call himself a Christian, refuses submission to the pope or fellowship with members of the church. Other churches have similarly defined schism juridically in terms of separation from their own communion.

In the 20th century the ecumenical movement worked for cooperation among and reunion of churches, and the greater cooperation between Roman Catholics and Protestants after the SECOND VATICAN COUNCIL (1962–65) resulted in more flexible attitudes within the churches concerning the problems of schism.

SCHLEIERMACHER, FRIEDRICH (ERNST DANIEL) \ˈshlī-ər-ˌmä-kər\ (b. Nov. 21, 1768, Breslau, Silesia, Prussia—d. Feb. 12, 1834, Berlin), German theologian, preacher, and classical philologist. He is generally recognized as being the founder of modern Protestant theology. His major work, *Der christliche Glaube* (1821–22; 2nd ed. 1831; *The Christian Faith*), is a systematic interpretation of Christian dogmatics.

Schleiermacher's father, a Reformed (Calvinist) military CHAPLAIN, and his mother both came from families of clergymen. From 1783 to 1785 he attended a school of the Moravian Brethren (Herrnhuters; *see* MORAVIAN CHURCH), an influential Pietistic (*see* PIETISM) group, at Niesky. In this milieu, individualized study was combined with a piety based on the joy of salvation and a vividly imaginative relation with Jesus as savior. Here Schleiermacher developed his lifelong interest in the Greek and Latin classics and his distinctive sense of the religious life. Later he called himself a Herrnhuter "of a higher order." Feeling constricted by the lifeless and dogmatic narrowness of the Moravian seminary at Barby, which he attended from 1785 to 1787, he left it with his father's reluctant permission and at EASTER he matriculated at the University of Halle.

A diligent and independent student, Schleiermacher began the study of theology and Immanuel Kant's philosophy. In his epistemology (theory of knowledge) he remained a Kantian throughout his life. After two years he moved to Drossen (Ośno), and began preparing for his first theological examinations. Though he read more in ethics than in theology, he took his examinations in Reformed theology in 1790, achieving marks of "very good" or "excellent" in all fields except dogmatics, the one in which he was later to make his most original contribution.

Schleiermacher then took a position as tutor for the family of the Graf (count) zu Dohna in Schlobitten, East Prussia. Besides tutoring, he preached regularly, chiefly on ethical themes, and continued his philosophical study, particularly of the question of human freedom. After taking his second theological examinations in 1794, Schleiermacher became assistant pastor in Landsberg and then, in

1796, pastor of the Charité, a hospital and home for the aged just outside Berlin. In that city he found his way into the circle of the German Romantic writers through the creator of early ROMANTICISM, Friedrich von Schlegel, with whom he shared an apartment for a time, began a translation of Plato's works, and became acquainted with the new Berlin society.

In *Über die Religion. Reden an die Gebildeten unter ihren Verächtern* (*On Religion: Speeches to Its Cultured Despisers*), written in 1799, Schleiermacher addressed the Romantics with the message that they were not as far from religion as they thought; for religion is the "feeling and intuition of the universe" or "the sense of the Infinite in the finite," and CHRISTIANITY is one individual shaping of that feeling. This work, perennially attractive for its view of a living union of religion and culture, greatly impressed the young theologians of the time. The *Monologen* (1800; *Soliloquies*) presented a parallel to religion in the view of ethics as the intuition and action of the self in its individuality. The individuality of each human being is in this work seen as a unique "organ and symbol" of the Infinite itself.

In *Die Weihnachtsfeier* (1805; *Christmas Celebration*), which was written in the style of a Platonic dialogue, Schleiermacher adopted the DEFINITION OF RELIGION he later incorporated into *Der christliche Glaube*. Instead of speaking of religion as "feeling and intuition," he now called it simply "feeling"—namely, the immediate feeling that God lives and works in us as finite human beings.

In 1807 Napoleon's invasion of Prussia forced Schleiermacher to move to Berlin, giving lectures on his own and traveling about to encourage national resistance; he also assisted Wilhelm von Humboldt in laying plans for the new university to be founded in Berlin. He married Henriette von Willich, the widow of a close friend of his, in 1809. In that same year he became pastor of Dreifaltigkeitskirche (Trinity Church) in Berlin and, in 1810, professor of theology at the new university. This latter position he retained to the end of his life.

Schleiermacher, detail of an engraving by F. Lehmann, 19th century
By courtesy of Bildarchiv Preussischer Kulturbesitz BPK, Berlin

His activities in the years following were many and varied. He lectured on theology and philosophy; he preached in Dreifaltigkeitskirche almost every Sunday until the end of his life; he was a member (from 1800) and permanent secretary of the Berlin Academy of Sciences; he carried on an extensive correspondence; and he was active in promoting the Prussian Union, which brought Lutheran and Calvinist churches into one body. His major publications during this period were the *Kurze Darstellung des theologischen Studiums* (1811; *Brief Outline of the Study of Theology*), presenting a curriculum in which the function of theology is to shape and direct the church as a religious community, and *Der christliche Glaube*.

In 1834 there were an estimated 20,000 to 30,000 people in his long funeral procession through the streets of Berlin. He was buried in the cemetery of Dreifaltigkeitskirche.

Schleiermacher's thought continued to influence theology throughout the 19th century and the early part of the 20th. Between about 1925 and 1955 it was under severe attack by followers of the "kerygmatic" theology of the Word of God (founded by KARL BARTH and Emil Brunner) as leading away from the Gospel toward a religion based on human culture. Since then, however, there has been a renewed study and appreciation of Schleiermacher's contributions, partly because the critique was one-sided, and partly because of a new interest in 19th-century theology.

SCHMALKALDIC ARTICLES \shmäl-'kal-dik, -'käl-\, *also called* Smalcald Articles \'shmäl-,käld\, one of the CONFESSIONS OF FAITH of LUTHERANISM, written by MARTIN LUTHER in 1536. The articles were prepared as the result of a bull issued by Pope Paul III calling for a general council of the ROMAN CATHOLIC church to deal with the REFORMATION movement. John Frederick I, Lutheran elector of Saxony, wished to determine what issues could be negotiated with the Roman Catholics and what could not be compromised. He asked Luther to review earlier statements of faith by the Reformers to determine what was absolutely essential to the faith. Luther prepared the articles, and after further discussion they were sent to the elector in January 1537.

In February 1537 the PROTESTANT secular heads of state who were members of the Schmalkaldic League met with several theologians at Schmalkalden to decide how to deal with a council of the Roman Catholic church. John Frederick I presented Luther's articles to the gathering. Because of Luther's somewhat controversial doctrine of the EUCHARIST, the AUGSBURG CONFESSION and its Apology was adopted as an adequate presentation of the reformers' faith and the Schmalkaldic Articles were not officially accepted. Forty-four theologians signed them as an expression of their personal faith, however, and subsequently they were included in the BOOK OF CONCORD (1580).

The Schmalkaldic Articles are divided into three sections. The first discusses the unity of God, the TRINITY, the INCARNATION, and Christ. The second section dealt with Christ and JUSTIFICATION by faith. According to Luther, "On this article rests all that we teach and practice against the pope, the devil, and the world." This section also discusses the MASS, monastic orders, and the PAPACY. The third section dealt with such subjects as SIN, the Law, repentance, the SACRAMENTS, confession, the ministry, and a definition of the church.

SCHOLASTICISM \skə-'las-tə-,si-zəm\, philosophical systems and speculative tendencies of various medieval Christian thinkers who, working on a background of fixed religious dogma, sought to solve anew general philosophical problems—as of faith and reason, will and intellect, realism and nominalism, and the provability of the existence of God—initially under the influence of the mystical and intuitional tradition of the CHURCH FATHERS (especially AUGUSTINE) and later under that of Aristotle.

In the early Middle Ages the authority of the Church Fathers still remained important. The impact of the theologians PETER ABELARD and ANSELM OF CANTERBURY in the 11th century, however, brought logic to the forefront of scholastic philosophy and rendered reliance upon the authority of the Fathers alone inadequate.

For such medieval theologians as ALBERTUS MAGNUS and

ST. THOMAS AQUINAS, reason assumed an important role in theology, not as the antithesis of faith, but as its supplement. Thus, the scholastics made a systematic attempt to map out the field of theology as a science and in so doing developed new treatises on matters, such as the SACRAMENTS, that had previously belonged to preaching. They borrowed freely from the philosophy of Aristotle, which came to them largely via the Islamic philosophers IBN RUSHD (Averroës; 1126–98) and IBN SĪNĀ (Avicenna; 980–1037), and aimed at a synthesis of learning in which theology surmounted the hierarchy of knowledge.

The primary methods of teaching were lecture and formal debate, which consisted largely in the presentation and analysis of syllogisms. Although there was fairly general agreement as to method and aim, scholastics did not always agree among themselves on points of doctrine. Distinct schools of theology emerged, the most influential being those of the Franciscan DUNS SCOTUS, for whom a world created in God's groundless, absolute freedom could exhibit no "necessary reasons," and the Dominican St. Thomas Aquinas, for whom faith, in general, presupposed and therefore required natural reason. The Thomist position tended increasingly to prevail, and Aquinas was eventually considered the repository of sound and orthodox doctrine. His *Summa Theologiae* ("Summary of Theology") became the standard textbook of theology, and the era of the great commentaries on Aquinas began. One of the most famous was that of a 16th-century Dominican, Cardinal Tommaso de Vio, commonly known as Cajetan.

In the period following the REFORMATION, while PROTESTANT theologians stressed scriptural and patristic authority and despised the scholastics as logic-chopping obscurantists, Catholic theologians came to rely on the latter more and more heavily. The *Metaphysical Disputations* of the late-16th-century Jesuit FRANCISCO SUÁREZ, however, reveal a concern for the spirit rather than the letter of scholasticism. Rather than a commentary on Aquinas, his work is an original philosophical treatise inspired by Aquinas and others.

The first author to try to extract a philosophy (apart from theology) from Aquinas was the Dominican John of St. Thomas in the 17th century with his *Cursus Philosophicus*, and this example was much followed. Though subsequent philosophers and theologians saw themselves as heirs to the scholastic tradition, by the 18th and 19th centuries scholasticism had fallen out of touch with contemporary thought and science.

A Thomist revival was announced and stimulated by Pope Leo XIII's ENCYCLICAL *Aeterni Patris* (1879); so-called neo-scholasticism became the dominant school in the Roman Catholic universities. Subsequently, neo-scholasticism and neo-Thomism earned renewed respect on the basis of the historical scholarship of the French Christian philosopher Étienne Gilson and others, who traced the original contributions of the scholastics and their influence on subsequent philosophy.

SCHWEITZER, ALBERT \'shwīt-sər\ (b. Jan. 14, 1875, Kaysersberg, Upper Alsace, Ger. [now in France]—d. Sept. 4, 1965, Lambaréné, Gabon), Alsatian-German theologian, philosopher, organist, and MISSION doctor in equatorial Africa, who received the 1952 Nobel Peace Prize for his efforts on behalf of "the Brotherhood of Nations."

The son of a Lutheran pastor, Schweitzer studied philosophy and theology at Strasbourg, where he took the doctor's degree in philosophy in 1899. At the same time, he was also a lecturer in philosophy and a preacher at St. Nicholas' Church, and the following year he received a doctorate in theology. His book *Von Reimarus zu Wrede* (1906; *The Quest of the Historical Jesus*) established him as a world figure in theological studies. In this and other works he stressed the eschatological views (concerned with the consummation of history) of JESUS and ST. PAUL, asserting that their attitudes were formed by expectation of the imminent end of the world. During these years Schweitzer also became an accomplished musician, beginning his career as an organist in Strasbourg in 1893.

In 1905 Schweitzer announced his intention to become a mission doctor in order to devote himself to philanthropic work, and in 1913 he became a doctor of medicine. With his wife, Hélène Bresslau, who had trained as a nurse in order to assist him, he set out for Lambaréné in the Gabon province of French Equatorial Africa, where he built a hospital. Interned there briefly as an enemy alien (German), and later in France as a prisoner of war during World War I, he turned his attention increasingly to world problems and was moved to write his *Kulturphilosophie* (1923; "Philosophy of Civilization"), in which he set forth his personal philosophy of "reverence for life," an ethical principle involving all living things, which he believed essential to the survival of civilization.

Schweitzer returned to Africa in 1924. By 1963 there were 350 patients with their relatives at the hospital and 150 patients in an associated leper colony.

Schweitzer never entirely abandoned his musical or scholarly interests. He published *Die Mystik des Apostels Paulus* (1930; *The Mysticism of Paul the Apostle*), gave lectures and organ recitals throughout Europe, made recordings, edited J.S. Bach's works, and wrote a widely influential book on Bach. His address upon receiving the Nobel Peace Prize, *Das Problem des Friedens in der heutigen*

Albert Schweitzer
Yousuf Karsh from Rapho/Photo Researchers

Welt (1954; *The Problem of Peace in the World of Today*), had a worldwide circulation. Despite the occasional criticisms of Schweitzer's medical practice as being autocratic and primitive, and despite the opposition sometimes raised against his theological works, his influence continues to have a strong moral appeal.

SCIENCE AND RELIGION: *see* MAGIC, SCIENCE, AND RELIGION.

SCIENTOLOGY \ˌsī-ən-'tä-lə-jē\, *official name* Church of Scientology, religio-scientific movement developed in the United States in the 1950s by the author L. Ron Hubbard (1911–86). Its forerunner was Dianetics, a form of psychotherapy originated by Hubbard and later incorporated into Scientology. *See* NEW RELIGIOUS MOVEMENTS.

SCIROPHORIA \ˌskir-ə-'fōr-ē-ə, -'fȯr-\, *also spelled* Skirophoria, *also called* Skira, in GREEK RELIGION, annual Athenian festival held at threshing time on the 12th of Skirophorion (roughly, June/July). The priestess of ATHENA and the priests of POSEIDON and HELIOS walked from the Acropolis to a place on the road to Eleusis called Skiron. The solemnity, which was probably a companion festival to the THESMOPHORIA, may have been held in honor of the goddess Athena; more reliable traditions, however, indicate that it was in honor of DEMETER and her daughter Kore (PERSEPHONE).

SCRIPTURE, *also called* sacred scripture, the revered texts, or Holy Writ, of the world's religions. Scriptures comprise a large part of the literature of the world. They vary greatly in form, volume, age, and degree of sacredness; but their common attribute is that their words are regarded by the devout as sacred.

Most sacred scriptures were originally oral and were passed down through memorization from generation to generation until they were finally committed to writing. A few are still preserved orally, such as the hymns of the Native Americans. Many bear the unmistakable marks of their oral origin and can best be understood when recited aloud; in fact, it is still held by many Hindus and Buddhists that their scriptures lack, when read silently, the meaning and significance they have when recited aloud, for the human voice is believed to add to the recited texts dimensions of truth and power that cannot readily be grasped by the solitary reader.

The greater part of recorded scripture has either a narrative or an expository character. The types of sacred and semisacred texts are, in fact, many and of a great variety. Besides magical runes (ancient Germanic alphabet characters) and SPELLS, they include hymns, prayers, chants, myths, stories about gods and heroes, epics, fables, sacred laws, directions for the conduct of rituals, the original teachings of major religious figures, expositions of these teachings, moral anecdotes, dialogues of seers and sages, and philosophical discussions.

Types of sacred literature vary in authority and degree of sacredness. The centrally important and most holy of the sacred texts have in many instances been gathered into canons (standard works of the faith). These canons, after being determined either by general agreement or by official religious bodies, then become fixed—*i.e.*, they are limited to certain works that are alone viewed as fully authoritative and beyond all further change or alteration. The works that are not admitted to the canons (those of a semisacred

or semicanonical character) may still be quite valuable as supplementary texts.

A striking instance of making a distinction between canonical and semicanonical scriptures occurs in HINDUISM. The Hindu sacred literature contains ancient elements and every type of religious literature that has been listed, except historical details on the lives of the seers and sages who produced it. Its earliest portions, namely, the four ancient VEDAS (hymns) seem to have been provided by Indo-Aryan families in northwest India in the 2nd millennium BCE. These and the supplements to them composed after 1000 BCE, the BRĀHMAṆAS (commentaries and instruction in ritual), the ĀRAṆYAKAS (forest books of ascetics), and the UPANISHADS (philosophical treatises), are considered more sacred than any later writings. They are collectively referred to as ŚRUTI ("heard"; *i.e.*, communicated by revelation); whereas the later writings are labeled SMṚTI ("remembered"; *i.e.*, recollected and reinterpreted at some distance in time from the original revelations). The former are canonical and completed, not to be added to nor altered, but the latter are semicanonical and semisacred.

The most precisely fixed canons are those that have been defined by official religious bodies. The Jewish canon, known to Christians as the OLD TESTAMENT, was fixed by a synod of RABBIS held at Yavneh, Palestine, about 90 CE. The semisacred books that were excluded were labeled by Christians the APOCRYPHA (Greek: "hidden, secret, noncanonical"). ROMAN CATHOLICISM and EASTERN ORTHODOXY later included them in their canons. JESUS left nothing in writing, but he so inspired his followers that they preserved his sayings and biographical details about him in oral form until they were written down in the four Gospels. To these were added the letters of PAUL THE APOSTLE and others (many of them written before the Gospels), and the Book of REVELATION TO JOHN, the whole forming a sacred canon called the NEW TESTAMENT, which was ecclesiastically sanctioned by the end of the 4th century CE. There were also New Testament Apocrypha, but they did not achieve canonical status because of numerous spurious details.

Where no religious body has provided sanction or authorization, scriptures have had to stand on their own authority. Muslims believe that the QUR'AN does this easily. The Qur'an, their only sacred canon or standard of faith, authenticates itself, they believe, by its internal self-evidencing power, for it is composed of the very words of God communicated to MUHAMMAD and recited by him without addition or subtraction. This faith of Muslims in the Qur'an is somewhat similar to that of CHRISTIAN FUNDAMENTALISTS who believe that the BIBLE, as God's word, is verbally inspired from beginning to end.

There exists a large body of literature that possesses less of the aura of true scripture than the works just noted. They are interpretations about divine truth and divine commands, or stories that illustrate how persons, exalted or lowly, have acted (with or without awareness) in response to a divine stimulus. They are, in effect, supportive of true scripture. An outstanding instance is the TALMUD, which to many Jews has very nearly the authority of the Mosaic TORAH (the Law, or the Pentateuch). Indeed, in the postbiblical rabbinical writings it was generally considered a second Torah, complementing the Written Law of MOSES. Similarly, Christianity's major CREEDS have, at one time or another, been regarded as infallible statements, to depart from which would be HERESY. This is particularly true of the APOSTLES' CREED and the three "ecumenical creeds" of Nicaea (325), Constantinople (381), and Chalcedon (451).

SCYLLA AND CHARYBDIS

SCYLLA AND CHARYBDIS \'si-lə...kə-'rib-dis\, in Greek mythology, two immortal and irresistible monsters who beset the narrow waters traversed by the hero ODYSSEUS in his wanderings. Scylla was a supernatural creature, with 12 feet and 6 heads on long, snaky necks, each head having a triple row of sharklike teeth, while her loins were girt with the heads of baying dogs. From her lair in a cave she devoured whatever ventured within reach, including six of Odysseus' companions. She was sometimes said to have been originally human in appearance but transformed out of jealousy through the magic of CIRCE or AMPHITRITE into her fearful shape.

Charybdis, who lurked under a fig tree a bowshot away on the opposite shore, drank down and belched forth the waters three times a day. She was most likely the personification of a whirlpool. The shipwrecked Odysseus barely escaped her clutches by clinging to a tree until the improvised raft that she swallowed floated to the surface again after many hours.

SÉANCE (French: "session," or "sitting"), in OCCULTISM, meeting centered on a medium who seeks to communicate with spirits of the dead. A séance generally involves six or eight persons who normally form a circle and hold hands.

Believers assert that communication has been established when a disembodied voice is heard, a voice speaks through the medium, or a ghostly apparition appears. Sometimes music from an unknown source seems to fill the room; objects appear to move for unnatural reasons; or a hand, a limb, or an entire body may take shape from ectoplasm (a peculiar viscous substance said to issue from the medium's body). Other alleged means of communication include automatic writing, trance speaking, or a OUIJA BOARD or planchette. Whether some spiritualists actually possess the ability to communicate with spirits of the dead remains open to debate.

SEBEK \'se-ˌbek\, *also spelled* Sobek \'se-ˌbek\, *Greek* Suchos \'sü-ˌkōs\, in ancient EGYPTIAN RELIGION, god whose chief SANCTUARY in Fayyūm province included a sacred crocodile, Petesouchos (Hellenized form of Egyptian *pa-ti-sbk*, "the one Sebek has given"), in whom the god was believed to be incarnate.

Sebek may have been associated with fertility or death and burial before becoming a major deity and patron of kings in the Middle Kingdom (c. 1850–c. 1630 BCE). He was merged with RE, the sun god, to constitute a crocodile form of that God known as Sebek-Re. The worship of Sebek continued into Ptolemaic and Roman times in the Fayyūm, at Kawm Umbū (Kom Ombo) in Upper Egypt, and elsewhere. Cemeteries of mummified crocodiles have been found in the Fayyūm and at Kawm Umbū.

SECOND COMING, *also called* Second Advent, *or* Parousia, in CHRISTIANITY, the future return of JESUS CHRIST, when it is understood that he will set up his kingdom, judge his enemies, and reward the faithful. Early Christians believed the Advent to be imminent, and those who profess what is known as Adventism believe that the visible appearance of Jesus may occur at any moment. Such believers find evidence in the Gospels (Matthew 24, 25; Mark 13; Luke 21:5–26; John 14:25–29), in the REVELATION TO JOHN, and in other sources.

SECRET SOCIETIES, politically dissident messianic movements that have existed and developed separately from the established Taoist religion from the very beginning (2nd century CE). Their leaders were priest-shamans, similar to the modern *fa-shih* priests of folk TAOISM. Their followers were from the lower social classes, and their organization was similar to that of the syncretistic religions and of modern secret societies. Although the secret societies have had no organizational contact with the Taoist tradition for centuries, their religious beliefs, practices, and symbols contain some Taoist elements, such as initiation rites, worship of Taoist deities, mediumism, and the use of charms and AMULETS for invulnerability. These influences reached them either directly or through popular religion.

SECT SHINTŌ \'shēn-ˌtō, *Angl* 'shin-tō\, *Japanese* Kyōha Shintō \'kyō-hä-\, group of folk religious sects in Japan that were separated by a government decree in 1882 from the suprareligious national cult, State or SHRINE SHINTŌ. They were denied public support, and their denominations were called *kyōkai* ("church"), or *kyōha* ("sect"), to distinguish them from the established shrines, called JINJA, which were considered state institutions.

By 1908, 13 sects had been recognized by the government. The main groups are:

Revival Shintō: Shintō Taikyō ("Great Teaching of Shintō"); Shinrikyō ("Divine Truth Religion"); Izumo-ōyashirokyō, also called Taishakyō ("Religion of the Grand Shrine of Izumo").

Confucian sects: Shintō Shūsei-ha ("Improving and Consolidating School of Shintō"); Shintō Taisei-ha ("Great Accomplishment School of Shintō").

Mountain-worship sects: Jikkōkyō ("Practical Conduct Religion"); Fusōkyō ("Religion of Mount Fuji"); Mitakekyō, or Ontakekyō ("Religion of Mount Ontake").

Purification sects: Shinshūkyō ("Divine Learning Religion"); Misogikyō ("Purification Religion").

Utopian or faith-healing cults: Kurozumikyō ("Religion of Kurozumi," named after its founder); Konkōkyō ("Religion of Konkō," the name of the KAMI); TENRIKYŌ ("Religion of Divine Wisdom").

The sects developed many splinter sects and devotional associations, so that by the end of World War II, when they were allowed to separate themselves, they had multiplied from the original 13 to 75. Most influential of the Sect Shintō is Tenrikyō.

Sebek, bronze figurine, c. 600–300 BCE
By courtesy of the trustees of the British Museum

SECULARISM, any movement in society directed away from otherworldliness to life on earth. In the Middle Ages there was a strong tendency for religious persons to despise human affairs and to meditate on God and the afterlife. As a reaction to this medieval tendency, secularism exhibited itself in the development of Renaissance humanism, when people began to show more interest in human cultural achievements and the possibilities of their fulfillment in this world. The movement toward secularism has often been viewed as being anti-Christian and antireligious. In the latter half of the 20th century, however, some theologians (*e.g.,* MARTIN BUBER, DIETRICH BONHOEFFER, PAUL TILLICH) began advocating a more secular CHRISTIANITY. They suggested that Christianity should not be concerned only with the sacred and the otherworldly,

Articles for the Seder: a 15th-century Spanish Haggadah, wineglasses atop 19th-century German Seder plates, and a 19th-century Polish silver cup for Elijah
Jewish Museum, New York City—Art Resource

but that people should find in the world the opportunity to promote Christian values. Secularism, in most uses of the term, has either a theological or political significance. Thus, the term has no value in an objective account of either religion or politics as cultural systems.

See also DEISM; UNITARIANISM; ERASMUS, DESIDERIUS.

SEDARIM \se-dä-'rēm, sə-'där-əm\, the major orders, or divisions, of the MISHNAH.

SEDER \'sā-dər\ (Hebrew: "Order"), in JUDAISM, ritual meal that, on the first night of PASSOVER, celebrates the EXODUS from Egypt (for Jews living outside Israel, it is celebrated on both the first and second nights of Passover). The foundations of the Seder appear in the MISHNAH (in the tractate *Pesahim*), which sets out a sequence of symbolic foods and required liturgy (hence the Hebrew term *seder,* meaning "order") that focus upon three foods (unleavened bread [MATZAH], bitter herbs [maror], and the Passover offering) and recitation of some of the HALLEL psalms of praise. In Talmudic times this basic ceremony was embellished with a discussion of Israelite history leading up to and including the captivity in Egypt. Since then, liturgical poems and other homilies have been added. The Seder remains one of the most powerful ceremonies in contemporary Judaism, depicting the power of God's miraculous acts of redemption. In modern times the Seder's message and symbols have been used to respond to issues ranging from feminist concerns to economic and social injustice.

The traditional Seder liturgy, contained in a book called the HAGGADAH, begins with the blessing (KIDDUSH) over wine that introduces all festivals and continues with a statement associating unleavened bread with "the bread of affliction" consumed by the Israelites in Egypt. The head of the fami-

ly, having usually donned a KITTEL, gives this BENEDICTION over the wine, and traditionally leads the entire Seder ceremony. In all, four cups of wine (*arba' kosot*) will be poured at certain intervals. This passage continues and expresses the hope that all who participate in the Passover celebration soon will enjoy freedom in the land of Israel.

After a second cup of wine is poured comes a set of four questions, traditionally recited by the youngest child present, regarding the ways in which the nights of the Passover Seder differ from other nights: "Why does this night differ from all other nights? For on all other nights we eat either leavened or unleavened bread; why on this night only unleavened bread? On all other nights we eat all kinds of herbs; why on this night only bitter herbs? On all other nights we need not dip our herbs even once; why on this night must we dip them twice? On all other nights we eat either sitting up or reclining; why on this night do we all recline?" The answers, found in a passage that begins "We were enslaved by Pharaoh," introduce the EXODUS story, embellished by homilies focusing on the inability of the Egyptians to break the spirit of their Israelite captives, on the miracle of the 10 plagues, and on God's dividing of the Reed Sea (traditionally mislocated as the Red Sea).

Consumption of the festive Passover meal proper is introduced by explanations of the Passover sacrifice, the bitter herbs, representing the bitterness of slavery, are dipped into a mixture of crushed fruits and wine (*charoset*), signifying that freedom and spiritual progress are the reward of suffering and sacrifice—and the unleavened bread, symbolizing the haste with which the Israelites left Egypt. At this point the meal is eaten and is then followed, as are all meals in the home of observant Jews, by recitation of the grace after meals and, in the case of the Passover Seder, by the drinking of the third cup of wine.

The meal is followed by a medieval addition beginning, "Pour out your wrath," which is a compilation of Scriptural verses urging God to take vengeance upon nations that oppress the people of Israel and to bring ELIJAH the Prophet, the precursor of the MESSIAH. At this point a cup of wine (which is not drunk) is poured for Elijah, whose appearance at some future Seder will signify the imminent arrival of the Messiah.

SEFER HA-BAHIR \'se-fer-,hä-bä-'hir, 'sä-fər-\ (Hebrew: "Book of Brightness"), largely symbolic commentary on the OLD TESTAMENT, written in a mixture of Hebrew and Aramaic, the basic motif of which is the mystical significance of the shapes and sounds of the Hebrew alphabet. The influence of the *Bahir* on the development of QABBALAH was profound and lasting. Whereas Qabbalists viewed the *Bahir* as authoritative, others rejected it as heretical.

The book seems to have first appeared in Provence, France, in the latter half of the 12th century. Qabbalists themselves attributed parts to RABBI Nehunya ben Haqana (about 1st century CE) and credited many of the book's sayings to early Jewish *tannaim* (1st to 3rd century; *see* TANNA) and *amoraim* (3rd to 6th century; *see* AMORA). It seems, however, that the author of the *Bahir* merely appropriated certain mystical texts and concepts that had earlier made their way to Europe from the East.

The *Bahir* successfully introduced into Qabbalah—and through Qabbalah, into Judaism—an extensive mystical symbolism. It contains the earliest-known explanation of the 10 "divine emanations," which are said to symbolize and explain the creation and continued existence of the universe. These 10 *ma'amarot* ("sayings"), divided into 3 upper and 7 lower manifestations, became widely known in Qabbalah as SEFIROT ("numbers").

The *Bahir* also introduced into Qabbalistic speculations the concept of the transmigration of souls (*gilgul*) and the notion of a cosmic, or spiritual, tree to symbolize the flow of divine creative power. In addition, evil was said to be a principle found within God himself.

SEFER ḤASIDIM \'se-fer-,k̲ä-sē-'dēm, 'sä-fər-, -k̲ä-'sē-dəm\ (Hebrew: "Book of the Pious"), *also spelled* Sepher Ḥasidim, account of the day-to-day religious life of medieval German Jews known as Hasidim. The authentic Hasid is described in terms of ASCETICISM, humility, serenity, altruism, and strict ethical behavior. The work presents the combined teachings of the three leaders of German HASIDISM during the 12th and 13th centuries: Samuel the Hasid, Judah the Hasid of Regensburg (his son), and ELEAZAR BEN JUDAH OF WORMS.

SEFER HA-TEMUNA \'se-fer-,hä-tə-mü-'nä, 'sä-fər-\ (Hebrew: "Book of the Image"), anonymous work that first appeared in Spain in the 13th century; it imbues the letters of the Hebrew alphabet with a mystical significance and claims that there are invisible parts of the TORAH. The book advances the notion of cosmic cycles (*shemiṭṭot*), each of which provides an interpretation of the Torah according to a corresponding divine attribute. Its primary treatment is of the first three *shemiṭṭot*, governed respectively by "grace," "judgment," and "mercy." Humankind, currently living under "judgment," reads the Torah as a series of prohibitions and commandments. This relativistic interpretation of the Torah strongly influenced Shabbetaianism (*see* SHABBETAI TZEVI) by helping to shape its theory that the Torah can be fulfilled only by its seeming annulment.

SEFER HA-ZOHAR \'se-fer-hä-'zō-,här, 'sä-fər-\ (Hebrew: "Book of Splendor"), 13th-century book, mostly in Aramaic, that is the classic text of QABBALAH. Many Qabbalists invested the *Zohar* with a sanctity that is normally accorded only to the TORAH and the TALMUD.

The *Zohar* consists of several units, the largest of which—usually called the *Zohar* proper—deals with the "inner" meaning of biblical texts, especially those from the Torah, the Book of Ruth, and the Song of Solomon. Lengthy homilies are mixed with short discourses and PARABLES, all centered on SIMEON BEN YOḤAI (2nd century CE) and his disciples. Though ostensibly authored by Simeon, the major portion of the *Zohar* should be credited to MOSES DE LEÓN (1250–1305) of Spain, though earlier mystic materials may have been used or incorporated into the present text.

Because the mystery of creation is a recurrent theme in the *Zohar*, there are extensive discussions of the 10 divine emanations (SEFIROT, literally "numbers") of God the Creator, which reputedly explain the creation and continued existence of the universe. Other major topics are the PROBLEM OF EVIL and the significance of prayer and good deeds.

The greatest popular influence of the *Zohar* did not occur until after the expulsion of the Jews from Spain in 1492, when it came to be consulted as a guide for mystical speculations about the MESSIAH and ESCHATOLOGY.

SEFER TORAH \'se-fer-tō-'rä; 'sä-fər-'tō-rə, -'tȯr-ə\ (Hebrew: "Book of the Law"), *also spelled* Sepher Torah, in JUDAISM, the PENTATEUCH written in Hebrew by a qualified calligrapher (SOFER) on vellum or parchment and enshrined in the Ark of the Law (*aron ha-qodesh*) in SYNAGOGUES. The Sefer TORAH is used for public readings during services on SABBATHS, Mondays, Thursdays, and religious festivals. The SEPHARDIM often enclose the Sefer Torah in a case of wood or metal and display it to the congregation before the reading of the Law. ASHKENAZIM generally cover it with an ornate mantle of cloth and display it to the congregation only after the daily reading has been completed.

SEFER YETZIRA \'se-fer-,yet-sē-'rä, 'sä-fər-\ (Hebrew: "Book of Creation"), oldest known Hebrew text on magic and cosmology; it contends that the cosmos derived from the 22 letters of the Hebrew alphabet and from the 10 divine numbers (SEFIROT). Taken together, they were said to comprise the "32 paths of secret wisdom" by which God created the universe. The book, falsely attributed to ABRAHAM and thus sometimes called *Otiyyot de Avraham Avinu* ("Alphabet of Our Father Abraham"), appeared between the 3rd and 6th century CE, but interpolations were later added.

The *Yetzira* developed the concept of the 10 *sefirot*, which profoundly influenced subsequent JUDAISM. The first group of four represented universal elements (the spirit of God, air, water, and fire), whereas the last group represented the six spatial directions. The *sefirot* and the letters of the alphabet were likewise correlated to parts of the human body, thereby making man a microcosm of creation.

Medieval German pietistic HASIDISM associated formulas of the *Yetzira* with the GOLEM. Among the more important commentaries on the *Yetzira* were those of SA'ADIA BEN JOSEPH (882–942) and ISAAC BEN SOLOMON LURIA (1534–72).

SEFIROT \se-fē-'rȯt\ (Hebrew: "numbers"), *also spelled* sephiroth, *singular* sefira \-'rä\, *or* sephira, in the speculations of QABBALAH, the 10 emanations, or powers, by which God the creator is manifest. The *sefirot* have also been called "crowns," "attributes," "principles," and "steps."

The concept first appeared in the SEFER YETZIRA ("Book of Creation"), as the 10 ideal numbers. In the development of Qabbalistic literature, the idea was expanded and elaborated to denote the 10 stages of emanation from *En Sof* (the Infinite; the unknowable God), by which God the Creator can be discerned; the rhythm by which one *sefira* unfolds to another was believed to represent the rhythm of creation. Qabbalists used them as one of their principal subjects of mystical contemplation, despite criticism that such speculations were implicitly heretical.

The *sefirot* are *keter 'elyon* ("supreme crown"), *halhma* ("wisdom"), *bina* ("intelligence"), *ḥesed* ("love"), *gevura* ("might"), *tif'eret* ("beauty"), *netzah* ("eternity"), *hod* ("majesty"), *yesod* ("foundation"), and *malkhut* ("kingship").

SEKHMET \'sek-,met\, *also spelled* Sakhmet \'säk-\, in EGYPTIAN RELIGION, goddess of war and the destroyer of the enemies of the sun god RE. Sekhmet was associated both with disease and with healing and medicine. Like other fierce goddesses in the Egyptian pantheon, she was called the "Eye of Re." Sekhmet was the companion of the god PTAH and was worshiped principally at Memphis. She was usually depicted as a lioness or as a woman with the head of a lioness, on which was placed the solar disk and the uraeus serpent. Sekhmet was sometimes identified with other Egyptian goddesses such as HATHOR, BASTET, and MUT.

SELENE \sə-'lē-nē\ (Greek: "Moon"), *Latin* Luna \'lü-nə\, in GREEK RELIGION and ROMAN RELIGION, personification of the moon as a goddess. She was worshiped at the new and full moons. Her parents were the TITANS Hyperion and Theia; her brother was HELIOS (sometimes called her father); her sister Eos; and her husband ZEUS. She is most connected with ENDYMION, whom she loved and whom Zeus cast into eternal sleep in a cave on Mount Latmus; there, Selene visited him and became the mother of 50 daughters. In another story she was loved by PAN. By the 5th century BCE Selene was sometimes identified with ARTEMIS, or PHOEBE, "the bright one." As Luna, she had temples at Rome on the Aventine and Palatine hills.

SELF-REALIZATION FELLOWSHIP, spiritual society founded in the United States by Paramahansa Yogananda (1893–1952), a teacher of YOGA, who was one of the first Indian spiritual teachers to reside permanently in the West. The fellowship was chartered in 1935, with headquarters in Los Angeles; there are now centers worldwide, as well as several independent groups influenced by his teachings. His *Autobiography of a Yogi* (1946) became highly popular and influential.

Sekhmet, black granite statue, c. 1360 BCE
By courtesy of the Metropolitan Museum of Art, New York, gift of Henry Walters, 1915

Yogananda's teaching was based on the *Yoga Sūtra*s of PATAÑJALI (2nd century BCE). He also taught a specific method, *kriyā* yoga, which combines deep meditation with techniques to control the movement of "life energy" and withdraw energy and attention from "outer" to "inner" concerns. Self-Realization Fellowship centers emphasize classes in *kriyā* yoga and also offer Churches of All Religions, which have services that combine elements of HINDUISM and CHRISTIANITY and include meditation, lectures, and music. The Self-Realization Fellowship consists of lay members as well as those who have taken monastic vows and generally play the role of clergy.

SELKET \'sel-,ket\, *also spelled* Selqet, *or* Serqet \'ser-,ket\, in Egyptian mythology, goddess of the dead. Her symbolic animal was the scorpion. She was one of the underworld deities charged with protecting the CANOPIC JAR in which the intestines of the deceased were stored after EMBALMING.

SEMELE \'se-mə-,lē\, *also called* Thyone \'thī-ō-,nē\, in Greek mythology, daughter of CADMUS and HARMONIA and mother of DIONYSUS by ZEUS.

Semele's liaison with Zeus enraged HERA, who, disguised as an old nurse, coaxed Semele into asking Zeus to visit her in the same splendor in which he would appear before Hera. Zeus had already promised to grant Semele her every wish and thus was forced to grant a wish that would kill her: his lightning and thunder destroyed Semele. Zeus saved the unborn Dionysus from the womb. According to some versions of the story, Dionysus descended into HADES after reaching maturity and brought Semele back, and she too became an immortal or even a goddess.

SEMI-ARIANISM, 4th-century Trinitarian HERESY in CHRISTIANITY. Though it modified the extreme position of ARIANISM, it still fell short of the church's orthodox teaching that Father, Son, and HOLY SPIRIT are of the same substance.

ARIUS held that the Father, Son, and Holy Spirit were three separate essences (*ousiai*) or substances (*hypostaseis*) and that the Son and Spirit derived their divinity from the Father, were created in time, and were inferior to the Godhead. Semi-Arians, however, admitted that the Son was "like" (*homoiousios*) the Father but not of one substance (*homoousios*) with him. Both Arianism and semi-Arianism were condemned at the COUNCIL OF NICAEA (325) and the COUNCIL OF CONSTANTINOPLE (381).

SEMI-PELAGIANISM, in 17th-century theological terminology, a doctrine that flourished from about 429 to 529 in southern France. The surviving evidences of the original movement are limited, but it is clear that the fathers of semi-Pelagianism were monks who stressed the need of ascetic practices and who were respected leaders in the church. The writings of three of these monks had positive influence on the history of the movement. They were JOHN CASSIAN, who had lived in the East and who founded two monasteries in Massilia (Marseille); Vincent, a monk of the celebrated Abbey of Lèrins; and Faustus, bishop of Riez, a former monk and ABBOT at Lèrins, who at the request of Provence bishops wrote *De gratia* ("Concerning Grace"), in which semi-Pelagianism was given its final form.

Unlike the Pelagians, who denied ORIGINAL SIN and believed in perfect human FREE WILL, the semi-Pelagians believed in the universality of original SIN as a corruptive force in man. They also believed that without God's GRACE this corruptive force could not be overcome, and they therefore admitted the necessity of GRACE for Christian life and action. They also insisted on the necessity of BAPTISM, even for infants. But contrary to AUGUSTINE, they taught that the innate corruption of man was not so great that the initiative toward Christian commitment was beyond the powers of man's native will.

This commitment was called by John Cassian *initium fidei* ("beginning of faith") and by Faustus of Riez *credulitatis affectus* ("feeling of credulity"). According to this view, man by his unaided will could desire to accept the gospel of salvation, but he could not be actually converted without divine help. In later semi-Pelagianism, divine help was conceived not as an internal empowering graciously infused by God into man but as purely external preaching or the biblical communication of the Gospel, of the divine promises, and of the divine threats. The strong point for all semi-Pelagians was the justice of God: God would not be just if man were not natively empowered to make at least the first step toward salvation. If salvation depended initially and unilaterally only on God's free election of the saved, those not chosen could complain that they were doomed by the mere fact of being born.

The result of semi-Pelagianism, however, was the denial of the necessity of God's unmerited, supernatural, gracious empowering of man's will for saving action. It contradicted ST. PAUL and St. Augustine, and the latter was by papal declaration the approved Catholic doctor in the question of grace and thus beyond attack.

After Faustus' death (c. 490), semi-Pelagianism was still highly respected, but the doctrine declined in the 6th century. At the instigation of Pope Felix IV (526–530), semi-Pelagianism was condemned at the second Council of Orange (529). The condemnation was approved by Pope Boniface II, Felix's successor. From that point on, semi-Pelagianism was recognized as a HERESY in the Roman Catholic church.

SEN, KESHAB CHUNDER \ˈkä-shəb-ˈchən-der-ˈsen, -ˈchən-drə-\, Chunder *also spelled* Chandra (b. Nov. 19, 1838, Calcutta, India—d. Jan. 8, 1884, Calcutta), Hindu philosopher and social reformer who attempted to incorporate Christian theology within the framework of Hindu thought.

Although not of the BRAHMIN caste, Sen's family was prominent in Calcutta. At age 19 he joined the Brahmo Samaj (Society of BRAHMAN, also translated as Society of God), founded in 1828 by the Hindu religious and social reformer RAM MOHUN ROY. The Brahmo Samaj was intended to revitalize Hindu religion through use of ancient Hindu sources and the authority of the VEDAS. Sen was convinced, however, that only Christian doctrine could bring new life to Hindu society.

Using Christian missionary methods, Sen effected social reforms in India; he organized relief campaigns for the poor, promoted literacy by founding schools for children and adults, and issued a number of inexpensive publications to bring reading matter within the reach of all. He condemned child marriage and was instrumental in having the marriage rites of his society recognized by law in 1872.

While his contemporaries DEBENDRANATH TAGORE and RAMAKRISHNA remained thoroughly Hindu in outlook, Sen was almost a complete convert to CHRISTIANITY. The deterrent was his belief that JESUS CHRIST, however admirable, was not unique. Nevertheless, he did want his people to emulate Jesus, believing that only a vital Christianity would be the salvation of a stratified and ossified Hindu society. Sen formed a new society in 1866 called the Bhāratvarṣiya Brahmo Samaj ("Society of Brahman of India"). The Brahmo Samaj was renamed the Ādi Samaj ("Original Society") and was quickly purged of Christian teaching.

In 1870 Sen lectured widely in England. Back in India, however, he allowed his 14-year-old daughter to marry, thus repudiating his avowed opposition to child marriage. As a result, some of his followers broke away, and he organized a new society, Naba Bidhān, or Nava Vidhāna ("New Dispensation"), and continued to preach a mixture of Hindu philosophy and Christian theology. Sen revived many ancient Vedic practices and sent out 12 disciples to preach under a flag bearing a crescent, a cross, and a trident.

SEPHARDI \sə-ˈfär-dē\ (from Hebrew: *Sefarad*, Spain), *plural* Sephardim, a Jew native to or tracing descent from the Jewish communities of medieval Spain and Portugal.

The Sephardim were expelled from the Iberian Peninsula in the last decades of the 15th century; initially they fled to North Africa and other parts of the Ottoman Empire, and many of these eventually settled in France, Holland, England, Italy, and the Balkans. Salonika (Thessaloníki) in Macedonia and Amsterdam became major sites of Sephardic settlement. The transplanted Sephardim largely retained their native Judeo-Spanish language (Ladino), literature, and customs. They became noted for their cultural and intellectual achievements within the Mediterranean and northern European Jewish communities. The Sephardim differ notably from the Ashkenazim in preserving Babylonian rather than Palestinian Jewish ritual traditions. Of the estimated 700,000 Sephardic Jews in the world today, many now reside in the state of Israel. The chief rabbinate of Israel has both a Sephardic and an ASHKENAZI chief RABBI.

The designation Sephardim frequently is taken to signify all North African Jews and others who, under the influence of the "Spanish Jews," have adopted the Sephardic rite.

SEPTUAGINT \sep-ˈtü-ə-jənt, -ˈtyü-; ˈsep-ˌ\, earliest extant Greek translation of the OLD TESTAMENT from the original Hebrew, presumably made for the Jewish community in Egypt when Greek was the lingua franca throughout the region. The TORAH, OR PENTATEUCH, was translated near the middle of the 3rd century BCE and the rest of the Old Testament was translated in the 2nd century BCE.

The name Septuagint (from Latin *septuaginta*, "70") was derived from later legend that there were 72 translators, 6 from each of the 12 tribes of Israel, who worked in separate cells, translating the whole, and in the end all their versions were identical. A tradition that translators were sent to Alexandria by Eleazar, the chief priest at Jerusalem, at the request of Ptolemy II Philadelphus (285–246 BCE), first appeared in the *Letter of Aristeas*, an unreliable source.

It was in the Septuagint text that many early Christians located the prophecies they claimed were fulfilled by JESUS CHRIST. Jews considered this a misuse of Holy SCRIPTURE and stopped using the Septuagint. Its subsequent history lies within the Christian church. It was the Septuagint, not the original Hebrew, that was the main basis for the Old Latin, Coptic, Ethiopic, Armenian, Georgian, and Slavic, and part of the Arabic translations of the Old Testament. It has never ceased to be the standard version of the Old Testament in the Greek church, and from it JEROME began his translation of the VULGATE Old Testament.

In addition to all the books of the Hebrew canon, the Septuagint under Christian auspices separated the minor prophets and some other books and added the extra books known to Protestants and Jews as apocryphal and to ROMAN CATHOLICS as deuterocanonical. The Hebrew canon has three divisions: the Torah (Law), the NEBI'IM (Prophets), and the Ketubim (Writings). The Septuagint has four: law, history, poetry, and prophets, with the books of the APOCRYPHA inserted where appropriate. This division has continued in the Western church in most modern BIBLE translations, except that in Protestant versions the Apocrypha are either omitted or grouped separately.

SERAPH, *plural* seraphim, in Jewish, Christian, and Islamic literature, celestial being variously described as having two or three pairs of wings and serving as a throne guardian of God. Often called the burning ones, seraphim in the OLD TESTAMENT appear in the Temple vision of the prophet ISAIAH as six-winged creatures praising God (Isaiah 6:3). In Christian angelology the seraphim are the highest-ranking celestial beings in the hierarchy of ANGELS.

In art the four-winged cherubim are painted blue (symbolizing the sky) and the six-winged seraphim red (symbolizing fire). *Compare* CHERUB.

SERMON ON THE MOUNT, biblical collection of religious teachings and ethical sayings of Jesus of Nazareth, as found in Matthew, chapters 5–7. The sermon was addressed to disciples and a large crowd of listeners, and contains many of the most familiar Christian homilies and sayings, including the BEATITUDES and the LORD'S PRAYER. It is paralleled in the Sermon on the Plain (Luke 6:20–49).

SERVETUS, MICHAEL \sǝr-'vē-tǝs, ser-'vā- \, *Spanish* Miguel Servet (b. 1511?, Villanueva or Tudela, Spain—d. Oct. 27, 1553, Champel, Switz.), Spanish physician and theologian whose unorthodox teachings led to his condemnation as a heretic by both Protestants and ROMAN CATHOLICS and to his execution by Calvinists from Geneva.

In February 1530 Servetus attended the coronation of Emperor Charles V at Bologna. Distressed by papal ostentation and by the emperor's deference to the worldly

Michael Servetus
By courtesy of the National Library of Medicine, Bethesda, Md.

pope, he met with REFORMATION leaders John Oecolampadius, MARTIN BUCER, and Kaspar Schwenckfeld. Servetus published a work on the TRINITY in *De Trinitatis erroribus libri vii* (1531), asserting that the Word is eternal, a mode of God's self-expression, whereas the Spirit is God's motion or power within the hearts of men. The Son is the union of the eternal Word with the man Jesus.

Servetus remained outwardly a conforming Roman Catholic while pursuing his private theological studies. He soon published at Lyon his most important work, *Biblia sacra ex Santis Pagnini tra[ns]latione* (1542), notable for its theory of PROPHECY.

Servetus forwarded the manuscript of an enlarged revision of his ideas, the *Christianismi Restitutio*, to JOHN CALVIN in 1546 and expressed a desire to meet him. After their first few letters, Calvin would have nothing more to do with him and kept the manuscript. He declared that if Servetus ever came to Geneva he would not allow him to leave alive.

A rewritten version of Servetus' manuscript was secretly printed at Vienne in 1553. In discussing the relationship between the Spirit and regeneration in that book, Servetus almost incidentally made known his discovery of the pulmonary circulation of blood. In the book, Servetus argued that both God the Father and Christ his Son had been dishonored by the Constantinian promulgation of the NICENE CREED, thus obscuring the redemptive role of Christ and bringing about the fall of the church; Servetus felt he could restore the church by separating it from the state and by using only those theological formulations that could be proved from SCRIPTURE and the pre-Constantinian fathers.

When some of Servetus' letters to Calvin fell into the hands of Guillaume de Trie, a former citizen of Lyon, he exposed Servetus to the inquisitor general at Lyon. Servetus and his printers were seized. During the trial, however, Servetus escaped, and the Roman Catholic authorities had to be content with burning him in effigy. He quixotically appeared in Geneva and was arrested and tried for HERESY.

Calvin played a prominent part in the trial and pressed for execution. Despite his intense biblicism and his wholly Christocentric view of the universe, Servetus was found guilty of heresy, mainly on his views of the Trinity and BAPTISM. He was burned alive at Champel on Oct. 27, 1553. His execution produced a Protestant controversy on imposing the death penalty for heresy, drew severe criticism upon Calvin, and influenced Laelius Socinus, a founder of modern unitarian views.

SETH \'seth\, *also called* Setekh \'se-ˌtek̲\, Setesh \'se-ˌtesh\, *or* Set \'set\, ancient Egyptian god, patron of the 11th nome, or province, of Upper Egypt.

The worship of Seth originally centered at Nubt (Greek Ombos), near modern Ṭūkh, on the western bank of the Nile River. Nubt, with its vast cemetery at nearby Naqādah, was the principal predynastic center in Upper Egypt. The town lost its preeminent position with the unification of Egypt about 3050 BCE, which was carried out under kings whose capital was ABYDOS and whose royal god was HORUS. This historical event probably gave rise to the myth concerning the struggle between Horus and Seth, who became perpetual antagonists.

Seth was represented as a composite figure with a canine body, slanting eyes, square-tipped ears, tufted (in later representations, forked) tail, and a long, curved, pointed snout; various animals have been suggested as the basis for his form. Because even the ancient Egyptians rendered his figure inconsistently, it is probably a mythical composite.

Originally Seth was a sky god, lord of the desert, master of storms, disorder, and warfare—in general, a trickster. During the 2nd dynasty (c. 2775–c. 2650 BCE), King Peribsen identified himself with Seth for the first time, giving himself a Seth title instead of the traditional Horus name. His successor, Khasekhemwy, gave both Horus and Seth equal prominence in his titulary. During the rule of the Hyksos invaders (c. 1630–1521 BCE), Seth was worshiped at their capital, Avaris, in the northeastern Nile River delta, and was identified with the Canaanite storm god BAAL. During the New Kingdom (1539–c. 1075 BCE), Seth was esteemed as a martial god who could sow discord among Egypt's enemies. The Ramesside pharaohs (1292–c. 1075 BCE), originating in the northeastern delta, ranked him among the great gods of Egypt, used his name in their personal names (Seti I and II, Setnakht), and promoted the image of Seth as the protector of RE in the prow of his bark, slaying Re's enemy, APOPIS. Seth also joined AMON, Re, and PTAH as the fourth of the principal gods of the cosmos.

In myths, Seth was the brother of Osiris; he was depicted as bursting out of the womb of his mother, NUT, as being an unfaithful husband to his consort and sister, Nephthys, and murdering OSIRIS, whom he tricked into entering a chest which he then closed and hurled into the sea. After Osiris' murder, Horus was conceived miraculously by ISIS, the wife and sister of Osiris. Horus struggled with Seth. This struggle forms the theme of the Ramesside text *The Contending of Horus and Seth*, which borders on satire, and the later, much more somber version recorded by Plutarch.

After the close of the New Kingdom, as Egypt lost its empire and later its independence, and as the cult of Osiris grew in prominence, Seth was gradually ousted from the Egyptian pantheon. In the 1st millennium BCE his name and image were effaced from many monuments. He was now identified as a god of the eastern invaders of Egypt, including the Persians. No longer able to reconcile Seth with Horus, the Egyptians equated the former with evil and the DEMON Apopis, or with the Greek TYPHON. Elaborate rituals of the repeated defeat of Seth as enemy largely replaced the earlier ritual destructions of Apopis.

SEVEN AGAINST THEBES \\'thēbz\\, in Greek mythology, seven champions who were killed fighting against Thebes after the fall of OEDIPUS, the king of that city. His twin sons Eteocles and Polyneices failed to agree on which of them was to succeed to the Theban throne and decided to rule in alternate years. As Eteocles' turn came first, Polyneices withdrew to Argos, where he married Argeia, daughter of King Adrastus. When Eteocles refused to give up the throne at the end of the year, Adrastus mobilized an army, whose chieftains, in Aeschylus' tragedy about the Seven, were his brother-in-law Tydeus, Capaneus, Eteoclus, Hippomedon,

Parthenopaeus, Amphiaraus, and Polyneices. Other authors count Adrastus as one of the Seven and omit Hippomedon or Polyneices. Polyneices and Eteocles killed each other. When the sons of the dead Seven, the Epigoni, or second generation, had grown to manhood, Adrastus again attacked the city and occupied it after the Thebans had evacuated it by night.

SEVENERS \\'se-və-nərz\\: *see* ISMĀʿĪLĪS.

SEVEN SAGES OF THE BAMBOO GROVE, *also called* Seven Worthies of the Bamboo Grove, *Wade-Giles romanization* Chu-lin ch'i-hsien \\'jü-'lin-'chē-'shyen\\, *Pinyin* Zhulin Qixian, group of Chinese scholars and poets of the mid-3rd century CE who banded together to escape from the hypocrisy and danger of the official world to a life of drinking wine and writing verse in the country. Their retreat was typical of the Taoist-oriented *ch'ing-t'an* ("pure conversation") movement that advocated freedom of individual expression and hedonistic escape from the corruption of the short-lived Wei-dynasty (220–265/266 CE) court. The retirement of the Seven Sages served as a model for that of later Chinese writers living in troubled times.

Most prominent among the Seven Sages was the poet Yüan Chi (210–263 CE). Another of the group's poets was Liu Ling (225?–280? CE). Hsiang Hsiu (230?–280 CE) wrote a famous commentary, the *Chuang-tzu chu*, with KUO HSIANG, a Neo-Taoist contemporary, on the works of the early Taoist philosopher Chuang-tzu (d. c. 300 BCE). Other members of the group included the musician Yüan Hsien, the devout Taoist Shan T'ao, and Wang Jung. Host of the group at his country home in Shan-yang was the writer and amateur smith Hsi K'ang (223–262 CE), whose independent thinking and scorn for court custom led to his execution by the state.

SEVENTH-DAY ADVENTIST \\ad-'ven-tist, 'ad-,\\, member of the largest organized modern denomination of Adventism, a millennialist Christian sect founded in the United States in the 19th century. (*See also* ADVENTIST.)

SHABBETAI TZEVI \\'shä-bə-,tī-tsə-'vē\\, *also spelled* Sabbatai Zebi, *or* Zevi (b. July 23, 1626, Smyrna, Ottoman Turkey [now İzmir, Turkey]—d. 1676, Ulcinj [Dulcigno] Republic of Montenegro), false MESSIAH who developed a mass following and threatened rabbinical authority.

As a young man, Shabbetai steeped himself in the QABBALAH. His extended periods of ECSTASY and his strong personality combined to attract many disciples, and at the age of 22 he proclaimed himself the Messiah. Driven from Smyrna by the rabbinate, he journeyed to Salonika (now Thessaloníki) and then to Constantinople (now Istanbul). There he encountered an esteemed and forceful Jewish preacher and Qabbalist, Abraham ha-Yakini, who possessed a document affirming that Shabbetai was the Messiah. Shabbetai then traveled to Palestine and after that to Cairo, where he won over Raphael Halebi, the wealthy and powerful treasurer of the Turkish governor.

With a retinue of believers and assured of financial backing, Shabbetai triumphantly returned to Jerusalem. There, a 20-year-old student known as Nathan of Gaza ecstatically prophesied the imminent restoration of ISRAEL and world salvation through the bloodless victory of Shabbetai. In accordance with millenarian belief, he cited 1666 as the apocalyptic year.

Threatened with excommunication, Shabbetai returned

to Smyrna in the autumn of 1665. His movement spread to Venice, Amsterdam, Hamburg, London, and several other European and North African cities. At the beginning of 1666, Shabbetai went to Constantinople and was imprisoned on his arrival. After a few months, he was transferred to the castle at ABYDOS, which became known to his followers as Migdal Oz, the Tower of Strength. In September, he was brought before the Sultan in Adrianople and, under threat of torture, converted to ISLAM. Most of his disciples were disillusioned by his APOSTASY, while Shabbetai eventually fell out of favor and was banished.

The movement that became known as Shabbetaianism attempted to reconcile Shabbetai's claims of spiritual authority with his subsequent seeming betrayal of the Jewish faith by interpreting his apostasy as a step toward ultimate fulfillment of his messiahship and, in some cases, following their leader's example. They argued that such outward acts were irrelevant as long as one remains inwardly a Jew. Those who embraced the theory of "sacred sin" believed that the TORAH could be fulfilled only by amoral acts representing its seeming annulment (see SEFER HA-TEMUNA). Others felt they could remain faithful Shabbetaians without having to apostatize. The sect reached a peak in the 18th century with JACOB FRANK.

SHABISTARĪ, SA'D AL-DĪN MAḤMŪD AL- \ˌshä-bi-ˈstä-rē\ (b. c. 1250, Shabistar, near Tabrīz, Iran—d. c. 1320, Tabrīz), Persian mystic whose poetic work *Golshan-e rāz* (*The Mystic Rose Garden*) became a classic of SUFISM.

Apparently al-Shabistarī spent most of his life in Tabrīz. He grew up in an age of spiritual confusion, following the Mongol invasion of Iran, the sack of Baghdad, and the final fall of the 'Abbāsid caliphate (1258) to the Mongols. Tabrīz was a capital of the new Mongol empire, and al-Shabistarī's life was clearly influenced by fierce doctrinal disputes and by a struggle between CHRISTIANITY and ISLAM for the allegiance of the Mongol rulers. In order to come to terms with the distressed status of a Muslim under heathen rule, he, like many of his contemporaries, withdrew from the outer world and sought refuge in spirituality and MYSTICISM.

Al-Shabistarī's *Golshan-e rāz*, written in 1311 or possibly 1317, is a poetical expression of his retreat from the temporal world. It consists of questions and answers about mystical doctrines. The work was introduced into Europe in about 1700, where it soon became popular in translation. European readers often regarded it as the major work of Sufism, and it enjoyed a vogue among Christian followers of mystical theology.

SHĀDHILĪ, AL- \ˌash-ˈsha-thi-ˌlē\, *in full* Abū al-Ḥasan 'Alī ibn 'Abd Allāh al-Shādhilī (b. 1196/97, Ghumāra, near Ceuta, Mor.—d. 1258, Humaithrā), Sufi Muslim theologian who was the founder of the order of the SHĀDHILĪYA.

Al-Shādhilī was said to be a direct descendant of the Prophet MUHAMMAD and to have gone blind in his youth because of excessive study. In 1218/19 he traveled to Tunisia, where his ascetic Sufi teachings aroused the hostility of the traditional 'ULAMĀʾ. Al-Shādhilī was forced to go into exile in Egypt, where he was more favorably received. He died returning from a PILGRIMAGE to the Islamic holy cities of Arabia. It was while he was in Egypt that he founded the Shādhilīya order, which became one of the most popular of the mystical brotherhoods of the Middle East and North Africa and from which 15 other orders derive their origin.

Although al-Shādhilī left no writings, his biography and certain sayings and some poetry have been preserved in Taj

al-Dīn Aḥmad ibn 'Aṭā' Allāh al-Iskandarī's *Laṭā'if al-minan* (1284).

SHĀDHILĪYA \ˌsha-thi-ˈlē-ə\, *also spelled* Shāzilīya, widespread brotherhood of Sufis, founded on the teachings of Abū al-Ḥasan AL-SHĀDHILĪ (d. 1258) in Alexandria. Shādhilī teachings stress five points: fear of God, living the SUNNA (practices) of the Prophet, disdain of mankind, fatalism, and turning to God in times of happiness and distress. The order, which spread throughout North Africa and the Sudan and into Arabia, was created by disciples, as al-Shādhilī discouraged MONASTICISM and urged his followers to maintain their ordinary lives, a tradition still followed. The order has given rise to an unusually large number of suborders, notably the Jazūlīya and the DARQĀWĀ in Morocco and the 'Īsāwīya in Morocco, Algeria, and Tunisia. *See also* SUFISM.

SHADRAPA \ˈshä-drä-ˌpä\, ancient West Semitic deity. His name may possibly be translated as "Spirit of Healing." He was often represented as a youthful, beardless male, standing on a lion above mountains, wearing a long, trailing garment and a pointed headdress, and holding a small lion in one hand and, perhaps, a whip in the other. In representations from Palmyra, Shadrapa is shown with serpents and scorpions. Probably equated with ADONIS, Shadrapa was worshiped in North Africa as the tutelary deity of Leptis Magna and was equated there with Liber-Dionysus.

SHĀFI'Ī, ABŪ 'ABD ALLĀH (MUHAMMAD IBN IDRĪS) AL- \ˌash-ˈsha-fi-ˌē\ (b. 767, Arabia—d. Jan. 20, 820, al-Fusṭāṭ [now Cairo], Egypt), Muslim legal scholar who played an important role in the formation of Islamic legal thought and was the founder of the Shāfi'īya school of law.

He belonged to the tribe of the QURAYSH, the tribe of the Prophet MUHAMMAD, to whom his mother was distantly related. His father died when he was very young, and he was brought up, in poor circumstances, by his mother in MECCA. He came to spend much time among the Bedouins and from them acquired a thorough familiarity with Arabic poetry. When he was about 20 he traveled to MEDINA to study with the great legal scholar MĀLIK IBN ANAS. On Mālik's death in 795, al-Shāfi'ī went to Yemen, where he became involved in seditious activities for which he was imprisoned by the CALIPH Hārūn al-Rashīd at al-Raqqa (in Syria) in 803. He was soon freed, however, and after a period of study in Baghdad with an important jurist of the Ḥanafī school, al-Shaybānī, he went to al-Fusṭāṭ (now Cairo), where he remained until 810. Returning to Baghdad, he settled there as a teacher for several years. He returned to Egypt in 815/816 and remained there for the rest of his life. His tomb in al-Fusṭāṭ has long been a place of PILGRIMAGE.

During the course of his travels, al-Shāfi'ī studied at most of the great centers of jurisprudence and acquired a comprehensive knowledge of the different schools of legal theory. His great contribution was the creation of a new synthesis of Islamic legal thought. Primarily he dealt with the question of what the sources of Islamic law were and how these sources could be applied by the law to contemporary events. His book, the *Risāla*, earned for him the title of "father of Muslim jurisprudence."

SHĀFI'Ī LEGAL SCHOOL \ˈsha-fi-ˌē\, *also called* Madhhab Shāfi'ī, *English* Shafiites \ˈsha-fē-ˌīts\, in ISLAM, one of the four SUNNI schools of religious law, derived from the teachings of ABŪ 'ABD ALLĀH AL-SHĀFI'Ī (767–820). This legal school (*madhhab*) stabilized the bases of Islamic legal theory, admitting the validity of both divine will and human speculation. Rejecting provincial dependence on the living SUNNA (traditional community practice) as the source of precedent, the Shafiites argued for the unquestioning acceptance of HADITH as the major basis for legal and religious judgments and the use of *qiyas* (analogical reasoning) when no clear directives could be found in the QUR'AN or Hadith. IJMĀʿ (consensus of scholars) was accepted but not stressed. The Shāfiʿī school predominates in eastern Africa, parts of Arabia, and Indonesia.

SHAHĀDA \shà-ʼhà-də\ (Arabic: "testimony"), Muslim profession of faith: "There is no god but God; MUHAMMAD is the prophet of God." The *shahāda* is the first of the FIVE PILLARS OF ISLAM (*arkān al-Islam*). It must be recited by every Muslim at least once in a lifetime, aloud, correctly, and purposively, with a full understanding of its meaning and with an assent of the heart. Conversion to ISLAM involves performing this action, as does the daily call to prayer (ADHĀN), and many Sufi DHIKRS (ritual prayer or litany practiced by Sufis [*see* SUFISM] for the purpose of glorifying God and achieving spiritual perfection). SUNNIS have accused SHIʿITES of violating its monotheistic content because of their faith in the imams—a charge that they refute. Ideally the *shahāda* should be the last words uttered at the moment of death.

Shahāda also refers to the idea of martyrdom—that is, violent death while fighting "in God's path." Among the Shiʿites, ḤUSAYN IBN ʿALĪ (d. 680), is considered the MARTYR par excellence. *See also* ʿĀSHŪRĀʾ; MUSHĀHADA.

SHAIṬĀN \shā-ʼtän, shī-\ (Arabic), *also spelled* sheitan, in Islamic myth, unbelieving class of JINN ("spirits"); it is also the name of IBLĪS when he is performing demonic acts.

In the system of evil jinn outlined by the Arab writer al-Jāḥiẓ, the *shaiṭāns* are identified simply as unbelieving jinn. FOLKLORE, however, describes them as exceptionally ugly creatures, either male or female, capable of assuming human form—though their feet always remain hooves. They eat excrement and use disease as their weapon and exist on the borderline between light and darkness.

The exact nature of the *shaiṭāns*, however, is difficult to determine. Historically, among the pre-Islamic Arabs, they functioned as familiars, providing inspiration for soothsayers and poets. In the stories of SOLOMON, the *shaiṭāns* seem to be no more than particularly knowledgeable jinn. In the QUR'AN, however, they assume the role of the devil, an obvious borrowing from Judaic tradition. While they are not necessarily evil, they belong to the hordes commanded by Iblīs, who is also called in Arabic *al-Shayṭān*. He and the *shaiṭāns* whisper evil suggestions into people's ears but have no real power over them. It is said that they are as close to humans as their blood, but the *shaiṭāns* can only tempt, and their success depends on their ingenuity.

SHAKER, member of the United Society of Believers in Christ's Second Appearing, celibate millenarian sect that established communal settlements in the United States in the 18th century. Dedicated to productive labor as well as to a life of perfection, Shaker communities flourished economically and contributed a distinctive style of architecture, furniture, and handicraft to American culture before the sect's decline in the late 19th and 20th centuries.

The Shakers derived originally from a small branch of radical English Quakers (*see* SOCIETY OF FRIENDS) who had adopted the French Camisards' ritual practices of shaking, shouting, dancing, whirling, and singing in tongues. ANN LEE, an illiterate textile worker of Manchester, was converted to the "Shaking Quakers" in 1758. After experiencing persecution and imprisonment for participation in noisy worship services, "Mother Ann" had a series of revelations, after which she regarded herself—and was so regarded by her followers—as the female aspect of God's dual nature and the second INCARNATION of Christ.

In 1774 Ann Lee came to America with eight disciples, having been charged by a new revelation to establish the church in the New World. Settling in 1776 at Niskeyuna (now Watervliet), N.Y., within five years the community was enlarged by several thousand converts.

After Mother Ann's death (1784), the Shaker church came under the leadership of Elder Joseph Meacham and Eldress Lucy Wright, who together worked out the communal pattern that was to be the distinctive Shaker social organization. The first Shaker community, established at New Lebanon, N.Y., in 1787, remained the head of influence as the movement spread through New England and westward into Kentucky, Ohio, and Indiana. By 1826, 18 Shaker villages had been set up in eight states.

Although often persecuted for pacifism or for bizarre beliefs falsely attributed to them, the Shakers won admiration for their model farms and orderly, prosperous communities. Their industry and ingenuity produced numerous (usually unpatented) inventions. They were the first to package and market seeds and were once the largest producers of medicinal herbs in the United States. In exchanges with outsiders they were noted for their fair dealing. Shaker music and craftsmanship have had a lasting influence on American culture.

The Shaker impulse reached its height during the 1840s, when about 6,000 members were enrolled in the church, but by 1905 there were only 1,000 members, and by the late 20th century only a few remained.

SHAKTI \ʼshək-tē\: *see* ŚĀKTI.

SHAMAN \ʼshä-mən, ʼshā-, ʼsha-\ (from Evenki: *šamān, samān*), a religious diviner or healer. In the religious systems of Uralic, Altaic, and other indigenous peoples of northern Eurasia, and in certain analogous systems of other peoples worldwide, a person believed to have the power to heal the sick and to communicate with the world beyond.

Broadly speaking, shamanism is encountered in the societies of the Arctic, the Central Asian regions, Southeast Asia, Oceania, and among many North American aboriginal groups. A distinction should be made, however, between the religions dominated by a shamanistic ideology and techniques (as is the case with Siberian and Indonesian religions) and those in which shamanism constitutes a supplementary phenomenon (*e.g.*, African religions).

The shaman cures sicknesses, directs communal sacrifices, and escorts the souls of the dead to the other world. He is able to do all this by virtue of his techniques of ECSTASY; *i.e.*, by his power to leave his body at will during a trance-like state.

The most important function of the shaman in all cultures is healing. Since sickness is thought of as a loss of the soul, the shaman must determine first whether the soul of the sick individual has strayed from the body or has been stolen and is imprisoned in the other world. In the former case the shaman captures the soul and reintegrates it in the body of the sick person. The latter case necessitates a descent to the netherworld, and this is a complicated and dangerous enterprise. Equally stirring is the voyage of the

to the netherworld and of his ascents to heaven constitute the material of popular epic poetry among many groups.

SHAMASH \\'shä-ˌmäsh\ (Akkadian), *Sumerian* Utu \\'ü-ˌtü\, in Mesopotamian religion, god of the sun. Shamash was the son of Sin (Sumerian: NANNA), the moon god.

Shamash, as the SOLAR DEITY, exercised the power of light over darkness and evil. In this capacity he became known as the god of justice and equity and was the judge of both gods and men. (According to legend, the Babylonian king Hammurabi received his code of laws from Shamash.) At night, Shamash became judge of the Underworld.

Shamash was not only the god of justice but also governor of the whole universe; in this aspect he was pictured seated on a throne, holding in his hand the symbols of justice and righteousness, a staff and a ring. Also associated with Shamash is the notched dagger. The god is often pictured with a disk that symbolized the sun.

As the god of the sun, Shamash was the heroic conqueror of night and death who swept across the heavens on horseback or, in some representations, in a boat or chariot. He bestowed light and life. The chief centers of his cult were at Larsa in Sumer and at Sippar in Akkad. Shamash's consort was Aya, who was later absorbed by ISHTAR.

SHĀMIL \\'shä-ˌmēl\, *also spelled* Shāmyl, Schāmil, *or* Schāmyl (b. 1797?, Gimry, Dagestan [Russia]—d. March 1871, Medina?, Arabia), leader of Muslim Dagestan and Chechen mountaineers, whose fierce resistance delayed Russia's conquest of the Caucasus for 25 years.

The son of a free landlord, Shāmil acquired prestige as a learned man and in 1830 joined the Murīdīs, a Sufi brotherhood. Under the leadership of Ghāzī Muhammad, the brotherhood had become involved in a HOLY WAR against the Russians, who had formally acquired control of Dagestan from Iran in 1813. After Ghāzī Muhammad was killed by the Russians (1832) and his successor, Gamzat Bek, was assassinated by his own followers (1834), Shāmil was elected to serve as the third IMAM of Dagestan.

Establishing an independent state in Dagestan (1834), Shāmil led raids against the Russian positions in the Caucasus region. Despite the Russians' successful penetration

A Mongol shaman in a ritual gown holding a drum, c. 1909
National Museum of Finland

shaman to the other world to escort the soul of the deceased to its new abode; the shaman narrates to those present all the vicissitudes of the voyage as it goes on.

Shamanism is the mystical experience that is characteristic of indigenous religions, but the shaman is not only a mystic. He is just as much the guardian of the traditional lore of the tribe. The narrations of his adventurous descents

Shamash seated in his temple and holding his emblem, the solar disk, bas-relief, c. 870 BCE
By courtesy of the trustees of the British Museum

into Shāmil's territory and their conquests of his forts and towns, they were never able to defeat him. In 1857 the Russians determined to suppress Shāmil; sending large, well-equipped forces, their military successes resulted in the surrender of many villages and tribes to the Russians. On Aug. 25 (Sept. 6, New Style), 1859, Shāmil finally surrendered and effectively ended the resistance of the Caucasian peoples to Russian subjugation. Shāmil was taken to St. Petersburg and then was exiled to Kaluga, south of Moscow. With permission from the Russian tsar, he made a PILGRIMAGE to MECCA in 1870.

Shāmil, detail of a lithograph by V.F. Timm, 1859
Novosti Press Agency

SHANG-CH'ING TAOISM
\'shäŋ-'chiŋ-'daŭ-,i-zəm\, *Pinyin* Shangqing (Chinese: "Highest Purity," or "Supreme Clarity"), important early sectarian movement associated with the emergence of religious TAOISM during the southern Six Dynasties Period (3rd through 6th centuries CE). The origins of the sect go back to the revelations made to Yang Hsi in the 4th century, which were gathered together as an early corpus of SCRIPTURES (particularly important were the *Huang-t'ing ching*, or Scripture of the Yellow Court, and the *Ta-tung ching*, or Scripture of the Great Profundity), emphasizing spiritual fulfillment through the mental and physiological practices of inner visualization and ecstatic journeying. Eventually the famed scholar T'ao Hung-ching collated these scriptures and established a religious center on MAO SHAN (Shang-ch'ing is also known as Mao Shan Taoism). Stressing ecstatic experience and the arduous achievement of the HSIEN condition, or spiritual-physical "immortality," this tradition was especially influential during the T'ang dynasty but gradually was absorbed into the more liturgical Ling-pao tradition of Taoism.

SHANG-TI
\'shäŋ-'dē\, *Pinyin* Shangdi, *also called* Ti ("Supreme Ruler," or "Lord on High"), ancient Chinese deity, the greatest ancestor and deity who controlled victory in battle, harvest, the fate of the capital, and the weather. He had no cultic following, however, and was probably considered too distant and inscrutable to be influenced by mortals. Shang-ti was considered to be the supreme deity during the Shang dynasty (18th–12th century BCE), but during the Chou dynasty (1122–256/255 BCE) he was gradually supplanted by Heaven (T'ien).

SHAN-SHU
\'shän-'shü\, *Pinyin* shanshu (Chinese: "good books," or "morality books"), popular texts devoted to a moral accounting of actions leading to positive and negative merit. These works often combine traditional Confucian notions of FILIAL PIETY and reciprocity, Taoist ideas of selfless action (WU-WEI), and especially Buddhist ideas of karmic retribution. First appearing in the Sung dynasty, these were non-revealed works related to popular revealed stories called PAO-CHÜAN or "precious SCRIPTURES." They continue to be popular in Chinese communities.

SHAO YUNG
\'shaŭ-'yŭŋ\, *Pinyin* Shao Yong (b. 1011, Kung-ch'eng, China—d. 1077, Honan), Chinese philosopher who greatly influenced the development of the idealist school of NEO-CONFUCIANISM.

Originally a Taoist, Shao refused all offers of government office, preferring to live in a hermitage outside Honan, where he engaged in mystical speculation. He became interested in CONFUCIANISM through his study of the I-CHING ("Classic of Changes"), through which he developed his theories that numbers are the basis of all existence. To Shao, the spirit that underlies all things could be comprehended if one understood the division of the different elements into numbers. He believed the key to the world hinged on the number four; thus the universe is divided into four sections (sun, moon, stars, and zodiac), the body into four sense organs (eye, ear, nose, and mouth), and the earth into four substances (fire, water, earth, and stone). In a similar way, all ideas have four manifestations, all actions four choices, and so forth.

The importance of this system resides in its basic theory: there is an underlying unity to existence, which can be grasped by the superior man who understands its basic principles, an idea which was the basis of the idealist school of Neo-Confucianism. Moreover, Shao brought into Confucianism the Buddhist idea that history consists of series of repeating cycles (*kalpas*), which Shao called *yüan* and reduced to a duration of 129,600 years. This theory was later accepted by all branches of Neo-Confucianism and made part of the official state ideology by the 12th-century Sung scholar CHU HSI.

SHAPASH
\'shä-,päsh\ ("Light of the Gods"), in ancient Mesopotamian religion, sun goddess. In the cycle of myths recovered from UGARIT, Shapash helps ANATH in her retrieval of the dead BAAL and intervenes in the final conflict between Baal and MOT.

SHA'RĀNĪ, AL-
\al-,sha-rä-'nē\, *original name* 'Abd al-Wahhāb ibn Aḥmad (b. 1492, Cairo—d. 1565, Cairo), Egyptian scholar and mystic who founded an Islamic order of SUFISM.

Al-Sha'rānī's formal education was concerned with the *'ulūm al-wahb* ("gifted knowledge of the mystic"), as opposed to a traditional and rigorous study of Islamic sciences. He attempted to seek the middle ground between the rigid learning and legalism of the 'ULAMĀ (the religious authorities) and the mystics' PANTHEISM and pursuit of spirituality. He consistently ignored distinctions and niceties within the major schools of Islamic law, as well as the marked differences between the various Sufi orders. This approach antagonized the most traditionalist 'ulamā' and the Sufis, and he was persecuted for his beliefs and doctrines and forced to earn his living as a weaver.

Al-Sha'rānī criticized the 'ulamā' for their legal rigidity, neglect of duties, mock learning, and inability to come to terms with the social problems of Egyptian society. He believed that the distinctions between the schools of Islamic law were socially divisive and advocated instead a unified approach to the law, using the best elements of each school. He castigated many of the Sufi orders as being corrupt and believed that their practices were contrary to the SHARĪʿA—the body of Islamic legal doctrines that regulated society.

Initiated into the SHĀDHILĪYA order, Al-Shaʿrānī founded his own Sufi order known as al-Shaʿrawīya. It was housed in a well-endowed ZĀWIYA, a kind of monastery, and had attached to it a school for the training of law students; it also provided care for the needy and for travelers. Unlike most Sufi orders, it had practical aims and eschewed esoteric pursuits.

Al-Shaʿrānī was unsystematic in his thoughts. Although his MYSTICISM was not influenced by pantheism, he found it possible to defend the pantheism of the 13th-century mystic IBN AL-ʿARABĪ. The bulk of al-Shaʿrānī's writing was concerned with traditional learning. Of special interest is his ṭabaqāt, a biographical dictionary of mystics, and his autobiography, Laṭāʾif al-mīnan. Upon his death he was succeeded by his son ʿAbd al-Raḥmān as head of the order. ʿAbd al-Raḥmān was more concerned with temporal matters, however, and the order declined, though it remained popular until the 19th century.

SHARĪʿA \shȧ-ʹrē-ȧ\, fundamental religious concept of ISLAM, namely its legal and moral code, systematized during the 2nd and 3rd centuries of the Muslim era (8th–9th century CE).

The formulation of the Sharīʿa rests on four bases (uṣūl):

1. The QURʾAN.
2. The SUNNA ("the way") of the Prophet as recorded in the HADITH.
3. The IJMĀʿ, or universal agreement, which has been materially perhaps the most important factor in formulating the doctrine and practice of the Muslim community but which itself has curiously remained the least clearly formulated religious institution of Islam.

Ijmāʿ, in the premodern Islamic usage, has always had reference to the past, near or remote, and does not denote a contemporaneous agreement. In the modern Muslim usage of the term, however, ijmāʿ has come to mean a democratic institution opposed to traditional authority. Consequently, far from working as a monolithic principle of unique standardization, ijmāʿ came to operate as a principle of toleration of different traditions within Islam.

4. The fourth principle of the Sharīʿa formulation, known as qiyas, or analogical reasoning, is the genuine basis of interpretation and thought (IJTIHĀD) in Islam. It is this which makes progressive ijmāʿ possible. Its earlier form was personal thought and opinion (raʾy), which was criticized by many eminent traditional authorities as arbitrary. In Shiʿi jurisprudence this principle is known as ʿaql ("reason").

There are four sciences known as the sciences of the Sharīʿa: the prophetic Tradition (Hadith), the Qurʾanic exegesis (TAFSĪR), theology (KALĀM), and law (FIQH). The first two are the materials for theology and law. In the four schools of law, the ḤANAFĪ, the MĀLIKĪ, the SHĀFIʿĪ, and the ḤANBALĪ, which took shape early—during the first two centuries of Islam—law and theology were a unity and were not separated, although theology at that time was merely a statement of the doctrine. As a result of increased exposure to other religious systems, a cleavage occurred between the law and the doctrine, and the former, which ideally presupposed the latter as its base, came not only to be an independent discipline but to claim for itself the title of the science of the Sharīʿa par excellence and was even identified with the Sharīʿa itself. Thus fiqh, which originally meant an understanding of the entire range of the faith, came to be applied to law alone.

Sharīʿa differs fundamentally from Western law in that it is, in theory, grounded in divine revelation. Among modern Muslim countries, Saudi Arabia and Iran retain the Sharīʿa as the law of the land, secular as well as religious, but the westernized civil codes of most other Muslim countries have departed from the precepts of Sharīʿa when this was deemed unavoidable.

SHARĪʿATI, ʿALI \shȧ-ˌrē-ȧ-ʹtē\ (b. Mazīnān, Iran, 1933—d. June 19[?], 1977, England), Iranian intellectual and critic of the regime of the Shah (Mohammad Reza Shah Pahlavi, 1919–80), ʿAli Shariʿati developed a new perspective on the history and sociology of ISLAM and gave highly charged lectures in Tehran that laid the foundation for the Iranian revolution of 1979.

Shariʿati received early training in religion from his father before attending a teachers college. He later studied at the University of MASHHAD where he earned a degree in Arabic and French. He became active in politics while a student and was imprisoned for eight months. He received a Ph.D. in sociology from the Sorbonne in Paris, and while there he met Jean-Paul Sartre, French sociologists, and Iranian student dissidents. Profoundly influenced by his experience in Paris, Shariʿati returned to Iran and was jailed for six months in 1964. After his release, he taught at the University of Mashhad until his lectures and popularity were deemed threatening by the administration. He then went to Tehran where he helped establish the Husayniya-yi Irshad (a center for religious education) in 1969. In the following years Shariʿati wrote and lectured on the history and sociology of Islam and criticized the current regime, Marxism, Iranian intellectuals, and conservative religious leaders. His teachings brought him great popularity with the youth of Iran but also trouble from the clerics and government. He was imprisoned again in 1972 for 18 months and then placed under house arrest. He was released and left Iran for England in 1977. Shortly after he arrived Shariʿati died of an apparent heart attack but his supporters blame the SAVAK, the Iranian security service, for his death.

Shariʿati's teachings may be said to have laid the foundation for the Iranian revolution because of their great influence on the Iranian youth. His teachings attacked the tyranny of the Shah and his policy of Westernization and modernization that, Shariʿati believed, damaged Iranian religion and culture and left the people without their traditional social and religious moorings. Shariʿati called for a return to true, revolutionary Shiʿism. He believed that SHIʿITE Islam itself was a force for social justice and progress but also that it had been corrupted in Iran by its institutionalization by political leaders.

SHARĪF \shȧ-ʹrēf\ (Arabic: "noble," or "illustrious"), plural ashrāf \ash-ʹräf\, Arabic title of respect, restricted, after the advent of ISLAM, to members of MUHAMMAD's clan of Hāshim—in particular, to descendants of his uncles al-ʿAbbās and Abū Ṭālib and of the latter's son ʿALĪ by Muhammad's daughter FĀṬIMA. In the Hijaz (western coast of Arabia), the title of sharif is said to have been further restricted to the descendants of ḤASAN, the elder son of ʿAlī and Fāṭima. Sharīfs originally were heads of prominent families. Later they supplied the local semiautonomous rulers of MECCA and MEDINA, especially under the suzerainty of Baghdad and Cairo, while after the establishment of Ottoman rule, the Ottomans normally recognized the senior representative of the sharīfs as prince of Mecca.

SHAṬḤ \'shath\, *plural* shaṭaḥāt, in Sufi ISLAM, divinely inspired statements that Sufis utter in their mystical state of *fanāʾ* ("passing away of the self"). The Sufis claim that there are moments of ecstatic fervor when they are overwhelmed by the divine presence to such a degree that they lose touch with worldly realities. In such moments they utter statements that may seem incoherent or blasphemous if taken literally but are understood by fellow Sufis who have shared the same experiences. *Shaṭaḥāt*, Sufis warn, must be interpreted allegorically.

Muslim legalists tended to brand as HERESY all Sufi *shaṭaḥāt* that did not conform to Islamic teachings. The mystic AL-ḤALLĀJ was persecuted and finally executed for his famous cry, "I am the Truth." Since "the Truth" is one of the names of God, legalists interpreted the utterance as a blasphemous claim to divinity. Sufi defenders of al-Ḥallāj argued that in his mystical state he found himself in union with God.

Since the state of mystical trance is normally of short duration, *shaṭaḥāt* rarely exceed six or seven words. The Sufis, however, regard all their writings, and particularly their poetry, as possessing an element of *shaṭḥ*. For this reason it also must be interpreted allegorically. Among often quoted *shaṭaḥāt* are:

"For the perfect lover, prayer becomes impiety" (al-Ḥallāj, d. 922).

"Praise be to me. How great is my majesty!" (Bāyazīd al-Besṭāmī, d. 874).

"I am the proof of God." "Divine omnipotence has a secret; if it is revealed there is an end of the prophetic mission" (Ibn Sahl al-Tustarī, d. 896).

"Ritual acts are only impurities" (al-Shiblī, d. 945).

"In my robe there is only God" (Ibn Abī al-Khayr, d. 1048).

"The slave is the Lord and the Lord is the slave; how can one tell which of the two is the debtor?" (Ibn al-ʿArabi, d. 1240).

SHAṬṬĀRĪYA \ˌshä-tə-'rē-ə\, Sufi order deriving its name from either the 15th-century Indian mystic ʿAbd Allāh al-Shaṭṭār (d. 1485) or the Arabic word *shāṭir* ("breaker"), referring to one who has broken with the world. It developed in northern India but spread as far as Indonesia.

Most Muslim mystics emphasize the servantship of humans and the lordship of God, the *fanāʾ* ("dissolution") of self and the *baqāʾ* ("subsistence") of God. The Shaṭṭārīya, on the contrary, stress the self, personal deeds, personal attributes that make a person godlike, and personal union with God. They maintain that *fanāʾ* would imply two selves, one that is to be annihilated and another that is to be readied for the final stage of the vision of God; and that such duality is opposed to the *tawhīd* ("unity") on which SUFISM is based. They also reject the Sufi practice of MUJĀHADA ("struggle with the carnal self"), saying that excessive focusing on the self distracts from the knowledge of God through personal experience and ultimate union.

Its most famous member was Muhammad Ghauth of Gwalior (d. 1562) who composed accounts of his spiritual journey and of Sufi beliefs and practices. The Mughal SULTAN AKBAR built a shrine for him in Gwalior.

SHAVUOT \ˌshä-vü-'ōt; shə-'vü-ˌōt, -əs\, *in full* Ḥag Shavuot ("Festival of the Weeks"), Shavuot *also spelled* Shabuot, or

Shabouth, *also called* Pentecost (from Greek: *pentekostē*, "50th"), Jewish festival that falls 50 days—that is, a week of weeks—after the first day of PASSOVER. In the BIBLE, it is an agricultural festival called "Feast of Weeks" (EXODUS 34:22, Deuteronomy 16:10), "Feast of the Harvest" (Exodus 23:16), or "Day of First Fruits" (Numbers 28:26). The later RABBIS called it Atzeret (M. Rosh Hashanah 1:2, M. Hagigah 2:4), a term generally translated as "solemn assembly."

In SCRIPTURE, Shavuot occasioned the bringing of first fruits to the Temple-sanctuary and a declaration of God's role in freeing the Israelites from Egyptian bondage and giving them a land flowing with milk and honey (Deuteronomy 26:1–11). Rabbinic interpretation tightens the connection with the Exodus, viewing Shavuot specifically as the commemoration of God's revealing of the TORAH at Sinai, which took place seven weeks after the Exodus. It thus serves in particular to celebrate the COVENANT between ISRAEL and God that the revelation at Sinai confirmed.

In the SYNAGOGUE, Shavuot is celebrated with special worship services and, in honor of God's revelation, an all night session of Torah study (*Tikkun lel Shavuot*). A frequent subject of study is the Book of Ruth, appropriate because it depicts a MOABITE woman's determination to accept the covenant and life within the Jewish people, seen as parallel to the Israelites' own resolve to embrace the covenant. It is traditional on Shavuot to eat dairy foods.

SHAYKH \'shāk, 'shīk, 'shēk\, *also spelled* sheik, shaikh, *or* sheikh, Arabic title of respect dating from pre-Islamic antiquity. It strictly means a venerable man of more than 50 years of age. The title shaykh is especially borne by heads of religious orders, heads of colleges, chiefs of tribes, and headmen of villages and of separate quarters of towns. It is also applied to learned men, especially members of the class of ʿulamaʾ (religious scholars and jurists), and has been applied to anyone who has memorized the whole QURʾAN, however young he might be.

Shaykh al-jabal ("the mountain chief") was a popular term for the head of the Assassins and was mistranslated by the Crusaders as "the old man of the mountain." By the 11th century the title *shaykh al-islām* was given to eminent ʿulamaʾ and mystics and by the 15th century was open to any outstanding MUFTĪ (canonical lawyer). In the Ottoman Empire the use of this title was restricted by Süleyman I (1520–66) to the *muftī* of Istanbul, who, equal in rank to the grand vizier, was head of the religious institutions that controlled law, justice, religion, and education. Because of his right to issue binding *fatwā*s (Islamic legal opinions), this official came to wield great power. In 1924, under the Turkish Republic, the institution was abolished.

SHE-CHI \'shə-'jē\, *Pinyin* Sheji, term referring to the ancient Chinese spirits of the soil and harvests and the rituals associated with those spirits. China's earliest legendary emperors are said to have worshiped She (Earth), for they alone had responsibility for the entire earth and country. Later Chinese emperors worshiped the gods of the soil as a more particularized cult.

Since ordinary people had no part in this sacrifice, they gradually focused their worship on such gods as HOU-CHI to protect their land and grain. Small communities, or even single families, thus also came to have their local gods, or T'u-ti. Throughout the country small shrines or temples were constructed, each with two images. Originally meant to represent the god of soil (She) and the god of grain (Chi), these images eventually were considered man and wife.

SHEKHINAH \shə-ḵē-'nä; shə-'ḵē-nə, -'ḵē-\ (Hebrew: "Dwelling," or "Presence"), *also spelled* Shechina, *or* Schechina, in Jewish theology, the presence of God in the world. The designation was first used in the Aramaic form, *shekinta*, in the interpretive Aramaic translations of the OLD TESTAMENT known as TARGUMS, and it was frequently used in the TALMUD, MIDRASH, and other postbiblical writings. In the Targums it is used as a substitute for "God" where the ANTHROPOMORPHISM of the original Hebrew seemed likely to detract from the transcendence of God. In many passages Shekhinah is a reverential substitute for the divine name.

It is said that the Shekhinah descended on the TABERNACLE and on Solomon's Temple, though it is also said that it was one of the five things lacking in the Second Temple. The Shekhinah is sometimes conceived as a bright radiance. There is an affinity between the Shekhinah and the Christian conception of the Holy Spirit; both signify some forms of divine immanence, both are associated with PROPHECY, both may be lost because of SIN, and both are connected with the study of the TORAH. Certain medieval theologians viewed the Shekhinah as a created entity distinct from God (the divine "light," or "glory").

SHEMA \shə-'mä\ (Hebrew: "Hear"), in JUDAISM, a CONFESSION OF FAITH made up of three scriptural texts—from Deuteronomy and Numbers—which, together with appropriate prayers, forms an integral part of the evening and morning services. The name derives from the initial word of the scriptural verse "Hear, O Israel: The Lord our God, the Lord is one" (Deuteronomy 6:4). The time for recital was determined by the first two texts: "when thou liest down, and when thou risest up." The Shema texts are also chanted at other times during the Jewish liturgy. The biblical verses inculcate the duty of total devotion to the study of the TORAH. Since, however, meditation on the Torah "night and day" was a practical impossibility, the Shema became a substitute for Torah study or, more exactly, the minimum requirement for observing the precept.

Following the example of the scholar-martyr RABBI AKIBA BEN JOSEPH (2nd century CE), the Shema has been uttered by Jewish martyrs throughout the ages as their final profession of faith. Pious Jews hope to die with the words of the Shema on their lips.

The text of the Shema follows:

◆ Hear, O Israel: The Lord our God, the Lord is One. And thou shalt love the Lord thy God with all thy heart, and with all thy soul, and with all thy might. And these words, which I command thee this day, shall be upon thy heart; and thou shalt teach them diligently unto thy children, and shalt talk of them when thou sittest in thy house, and when thou walkest by the way, and when thou liest down, and when thou risest up. And thou shalt bind them for a sign upon thy hand, and they shall be for frontlets between thine eyes. And thou shalt write them upon the door-posts of thy house, and upon thy gates. (Deuteronomy 6:4–9)

And it shall come to pass, if ye shall hearken diligently unto My commandments which I command you this day, to love the Lord your God, and to serve Him with all your heart and with all your soul, that I will give the rain of your land in its season, the former rain and the latter rain, that thou mayest gather in thy corn, and thy wine, and thine oil. And I will give grass in thy fields for thy cattle, and thou shalt eat and be satisfied. Take heed to yourselves, lest your heart be deceived, and ye turn aside, and serve other gods, and worship them; and the anger of the Lord be kindled against you, and He shut up the heaven, so that there shall be no rain, and the ground shall not yield her fruit; and ye perish quickly from off the good land which the Lord giveth you. Therefore shall ye lay up these My words in your heart and in your soul; and ye shall bind them for a sign upon your hand, and they shall be for frontlets between your eyes. And ye shall teach them your children, talking of them, when thou sittest in thy house, and when thou walkest by the way, and when thou liest down, and when thou risest up. And thou shalt write them upon the door-posts of thy house, and upon thy gates; that your days may be multiplied, and the days of your children, upon the land which the Lord sware unto your fathers to give them, as the days of the heavens above the earth. (Deuteronomy 11:13–21)

And the Lord spoke unto Moses, saying: "Speak unto the children of Israel, and bid them that they make them throughout their generations fringes in the corners of their garments, and that they put with the fringe of each corner a thread of blue. And it shall be unto you for a fringe, that ye may look upon it, and remember all the commandments of the Lord, and do them; and that ye go not about after your own heart and your own eyes, after which ye use to go astray; that ye may remember and do all My commandments, and be holy unto your God. I am the Lord your God, who brought you out of the land of Egypt, to be your God: I am the Lord your God." (Numbers 15:37–41) ◆

SHEMINI ATZERET \shə-'mē-nē-ät-'ser-et\ (Hebrew: "Eighth Day of the Solemn Assembly"), Jewish religious festival on the eighth day of SUKKOT (Feast of Booths). In ancient times 70 sacrifices were offered on the first seven days of Sukkot to signify the "70 nations" constituting all humanity, while a single ram and bullock were sacrificed on the eighth day to symbolize Israel's special relationship to God. In Israel, SIMHATH TORAH is also celebrated on the eighth day of Sukkot, although in other countries it is celebrated on the ninth day.

SHEN \'shən\, *Pinyin* shen, in popular Chinese religion, beneficent spirit of the dead; the term is also applied to deified mortals and gods. *Shen* are associated with the yang (bright, active) aspect of the cosmos and with the spiritual component of the human soul. After a person's death, the soul becomes either of two spirits: the *shen*, which ascends to the spirit world, or the KUEI, a dark, passive yin spirit, which remains within the grave. The successful ascent of the *shen* depends on adequate ritual offerings from the family, without which it seeks revenge on the human world in the form of the malevolent *kuei*, or ghost.

SHENG \'shəŋ\ ("sage," or "saint"), in Chinese belief, mortal who attains extraordinary powers by self-cultivation and serves as a model for others.

SHEN NUNG \'shən-'nùŋ\, *Pinyin* Shen Nong (Chinese: "Divine Husbandman"), *formally* Yen-ti, second of China's

Shen Nung, engraving from San-ts'ai t'u-hui *(1607–09)*
By courtesy of the University of Hong Kong

mythical emperors, said to have been born in the 28th century BCE with the head of a bull and the body of a man. He was said to have invented the cart and plow, domesticated horses and oxen, and the clearing of land with fire, thereby establishing agriculture. His catalog of 365 medicinal plants became the basis of later herbological studies.

SHEWBREAD \'shō-ˌbred\, *also spelled* showbread, *also called* bread of the Presence, any of the 12 loaves of bread that stood for the 12 tribes of Israel, presented and shown in the TEMPLE OF JERUSALEM in the Presence of God. The arrangement of the bread on a table in two rows of six (Leviticus 24) was an important aspect of the presentation because some verses in the BIBLE literally speak of "the bread of the arrangement" (1 Chronicles 9:32, 23:29; NEHEMIAH 10:33). The bread was changed every SABBATH, and the priests ate that which had been displayed. Many aspects of the Christian EUCHARIST show that it was influenced by Israel's shewbread.

SHI'ITE \'shē-ˌīt\, the smaller of the two major branches of ISLAM, distinguished from the majority SUNNIS.

In early Islamic history the Shi'ites were a political faction (*shī'at 'Alī*, "party of 'ALĪ") that supported the power of 'Alī, who was a son-in-law of MUHAMMAD and the fourth CALIPH (temporal and spiritual ruler) of the Muslim community. 'Alī was killed while trying to maintain his authority as caliph, and the Shi'ites gradually developed a religious movement that asserted the legitimate authority of 'Alī's lineal descendants, the 'Alīds. This stand contrasted with that of the more pragmatic Sunni majority of Muslims, who were generally willing to accept the leadership of any caliph whose rule afforded the proper exercise of religion and the maintenance of order in the Muslim world.

Over the centuries the Shi'ite movement has deeply influenced all Sunni Islam, and its adherents numbered about 80 to 100 million in the late 20th century, or one-tenth of all Islam. Shi'ism (Arabic: Shi'a, or Shī'ī Islam) is the majority religion in Iran, Iraq, and perhaps Yemen and has adherents in Syria, Lebanon, East Africa, India, and Pakistan (*see* ITHNĀ 'ASHARĪYA).

In 656 'Alī had been raised to the caliphate with the support, among many others, of the murderers of the third caliph, 'UTHMĀN. 'Alī never quite received the allegiance of all the Muslims, however, and thus had to wage increasingly unsuccessful wars to maintain himself in power. 'Alī was murdered in 661, and Mu'āwiya, his chief opponent, became caliph. 'Alī's son, ḤUSAYN, later refused to recognize the legitimacy of Mu'āwiya's son and successor as caliph, Yāzid. The Muslims of the Shi'ite-dominated town of Kūfa in Iraq, 'Alī's former capital, invited Ḥusayn to become caliph. The Muslims in Iraq generally failed to support Ḥusayn, however, and he and his small band of followers were cut down (680) near Kūfa at the Battle of KARBALĀ', which is now a PILGRIMAGE spot for Shi'ites.

Swearing vengeance against the triumphant Umayyad government, the Kūfans soon gained support from other groups that opposed the status quo, including aristocratic Muslim families of MEDINA, Muslims protesting a too worldly interpretation of Islam, and non-Arab Muslims (*mawālī*), who were denied equality by the ruling Arabs. Over time the Shi'ites became a distinct collection of sects who were alike in their recognition of 'Alī and his descendants as the legitimate leaders of the Muslim community. The Shi'ites' conviction that the 'Alīds should be the leaders of the Islamic world was never fulfilled over the centuries. But though the 'Alids never won such power, 'Alī himself was rehabilitated as a major hero of Sunni Islam, and his descendants by FĀṬIMA, Muhammad's daughter, received the courtesy titles of "sayyids" and "sharīfs."

The largest Shi'ite subdivision is that of the ITHNĀ 'ASHARĪYA, or Twelvers, who recognize the legitimacy of a succession of twelve 'Alid claimants (beginning with 'Alī himself) who are known as IMAMS. Other, smaller Shi'ite sects include the Ismā'īlīya and ZAYDĪYA.

Despite occasional Shi'ite rulers, the Shi'ites remained almost everywhere an Islamic minority until the start of the 16th century, when the Iranian Ṣafavid dynasty made it the sole legal faith of their empire, which then embraced the Persians of Iran, the Turks of Azerbaijan, and many of the Arabs of Iraq proper. These peoples have since been overwhelmingly Ithnā 'Asharīya and have given that branch of Shi'ism a vigorous life. In the late 20th century, Shi'ite religious leadership became a major political force in Iran, where they toppled a secularist monarchy in 1978–79, and in Lebanon, where they led resistance to Israeli occupation in the south during the 1980s and '90s.

SHIKOKU \shē-'kō-kü\, island, smallest of the four main islands of Japan. It is separated from Honshu by the Inland Sea and from Kyushu by the Bungo Strait. The city of Takamatsu is the base for PILGRIMAGES to the Kotohira Shrine, 19 miles southwest, while Tokushima is famous for the annual Japanese festival with the folk dance of *awa odori* and puppet shows.

SHILOH \'shī-lō\, Canaanite town that became the central SANCTUARY site of the Israelite confederacy during the period of the judges (12th–11th century BCE). After the Israelite conquest of CANAAN, the TABERNACLE and the ARK OF THE COV-

ENANT were installed in Shiloh until the ARK was captured by the Philistines (c. 1050 BCE), and Shiloh was soon thereafter destroyed.

SHINBUTSU SHŪGŌ \'shen-,but-su-'shü-,gō\, in Japan, amalgamation of BUDDHISM with the indigenous religion SHINTŌ. Even today Japanese frequently retain in their homes both Shintō god shelves (KAMIDANA) and Buddhist altars (butsudan) and observe Shintō rites for marriage and Buddhist rites for funerals.

Before construction of the Daibutsu ("Great Buddha") at Nara in 741 CE, the proposal to build the statue was first reported to AMATERASU Ōmikami, the Shintō sun goddess, at the Ise Shrine, the chief shrine of Japan. Aid was also requested of the KAMI (god) HACHIMAN, and a branch of the (Shintō) Usa Hachiman Shrine on the island of Kyushu was built in the compound of the (Buddhist) TŌDAI TEMPLE to protect it. From that time a practice developed of building Shintō shrines in Buddhist temple compounds and temples or PAGODAS near Shintō shrines, and also of reciting Buddhist SCRIPTURES at Shintō shrines.

In the Heian period (9th–12th century), Shintō kami came to be identified as incarnations of the Buddha, and for a time Shintō priests were dominated by Buddhist ecclesiastics. During the Kamakura period (1192–1333 CE), however, Shintō attempted to emancipate itself from Buddhist domination, and the ISE SHINTŌ movement claimed that Shintō divinities were not incarnations of the Buddha but that buddhas and BODHISATTVAS were rather manifestations of Shintō kami. In 1868 the Meiji regime issued an edict ordering Buddhist priests connected with Shintō shrines either to be reordained as Shintō priests or to return to lay life. Buddhist temple lands were confiscated and Buddhist ceremonies abolished in the imperial household. Shintō was proclaimed as the national religion; later it was reinterpreted as a national cult (see STATE SHINTŌ).

SHINGON \'shen-,gòn, Angl 'shin-,gän\ (Japanese: "True Word"), Chinese Chen-yen \'zhən-'yan, -'yen\, Esoteric Buddhist sect that has maintained a considerable following in Japan since its introduction from China in the 9th century. Shingon may be considered an attempt to reach the eternal wisdom of the BUDDHA GOTAMA that was not expressed in words and, thus, is not contained in his public teaching. The sect believes that this wisdom may be developed and realized through special ritual means employing body, speech, and mind, such as the use of symbolic gestures (mudrās), mystical syllables (dhāraṇī), and mental concentration (YOGA).

The principal SCRIPTURE of the Shingon school is the MAHĀVAIROCANA SŪTRA, in which the universe is conceived to be the body of the Buddha Mahāvairocana (the "Great Illuminator"). He has two aspects, each of which has its characteristic depiction in the MANDALA, the ritual diagram often painted on the Shingon altar. Entry into the mandala is called kanjō (Sanskrit: abhiṣekha), an initiation ceremony involving sprinkling with water.

Shingon esotericism is a part of Esoteric, or Tantric, BUDDHISM, which spread in the 8th century from India to Tibet and Java, as well as to China and from there to Japan. In Japan, however, the doctrine was much modified and systematized by the great religious leader KŪKAI.

Kūkai studied the doctrine in China under a Tantric master and returned to found the Kongōbu Temple monastic center at MOUNT KOYA in 819; he later established the Tō Temple in Kyōto as the sect's headquarters.

SHINRAN \'shen-,rän\, original name Matsuwaka-Maru, also called Han'en, Shakkū, Zenshin, or Gutoku Shinran, posthumous name Kenshin Daishi (b. 1173, near Kyōto—d. Jan. 9, 1263, Kyōto), Buddhist philosopher and religious reformer whose concern for the salvation of the masses led him to establish the Jōdo Shinshū (True PURE LAND sect), the largest school of BUDDHISM in modern Japan.

Shinran entered the PRIESTHOOD when he was nine, and for 20 years he studied Buddhism on MOUNT HIEI, where an eminent monk, SAICHŌ, had established the center of the Tendai (T'IEN-T'AI) school. A long spiritual struggle in quest of salvation occupied Shinran's early years as a monk of the Tendai school, but despite the most rigorous ASCETICISM, his quest proved fruitless. During this time, at the beginning of the Kamakura period (1192–1333), the decline of the aristocratic class and its fierce struggles with the military class for political supremacy brought so much confusion and distress that the people began to accept a pessimistic view of history (known as MAPPŌ).

Shinran then came down from Mt. Hiei to continue his quest for salvation. It was at this time that he met the Buddhist saint HŌNEN, founder of the Jōdo (Pure Land) sect, who had been teaching to the masses the practice known as nembutsu—i.e., calling upon the name of the Amida Buddha (or AMITĀBHA) for salvation. Shinran abandoned ascetic practices and took refuge in this practice, also known as the Original Vow. He was allowed to copy Hōnen's main work, the Senchaku hongan nembutsu-shū ("Collection on the Choice of the Nembutsu of the Original Vow"). This was a great source of inspiration to Shinran, for copies of the document were entrusted to only a few close disciples.

In 1207 the government issued an edict against Hōnen's nembutsu movement. Hōnen was exiled to Tosa Province and Shinran to Echigo Province, and two other nembutsu teachers were beheaded. Soon after his arrival in Echigo, Shinran married Eshinni, in violation of the traditional Buddhist precept of CELIBACY for the priesthood.

Shinran moved to the Kantō region in east central Japan, where, between 1212 and 1235 or 1236, he lived an academic and missionary life. During this period he compiled the six volumes of the Kyōgyōshinshō (1224; "Teaching-Action-Faith-Attainment"). His ministry had great success. In 1256, however, after returning to Kyōto, Shinran had to disown Zenran, his oldest son, who tried to control the community with an alternative interpretation of the faith. It was, perhaps, the most tragic experience in Shinran's long life. Despite spiritual depressions and economic difficulties, he was able to compile a number of derivative works designed to make his teachings accessible to the masses. Works that are regarded as important include three volumes of Buddhist poems and hymns (wasan) that were later compiled by the patriarch RENNYO in the Sanjō wasan; Jinen hōni shō ("Treatise on the Ultimate Truth of Things"); and Yuishinshō mon'i ("Notes on 'The Essentials of Faith Alone' ").

SHINTAI \'shen-,tī\ (Japanese: "god-body"), in SHINTŌ, manifestation of the deity (KAMI), its symbol, or an object of worship in which it resides; also referred to as mitama-shiro ("the material object in which the divine soul resides"). The shintai may be a natural object in which the divinity's presence was discovered, such as a stone, mountain, or well, or an object made for him, such as a sword, comb, or mirror. The shintai is usually enclosed in cloth or in a box and kept in the main SANCTUARY of the shrine within a small room or cupboard whose doors are seldom opened.

SHINTŌ

he indigenous RELIGIOUS BELIEFS and practices of Japan are termed Shintō. The word Shintō literally means "the way of KAMI" (the "mystical," "superior," or "divine," generally sacred or divine power, specifically the various gods or deities). It came into use in order to distinguish indigenous Japanese beliefs from BUDDHISM, which had been introduced into Japan in the 6th century CE. Shintō has no founder, no official sacred SCRIPTURES in the strict sense (although the NIHON SHOKI and KOJIKI are often used as authoritative collections of mythology), and no fixed dogmas, but it has preserved its guiding beliefs throughout the ages.

HISTORICAL BACKGROUND

Little is known about the religious practices that gave expression to Shintō's immanent, monistic world view during the period before the introduction of Sino-Korean culture and the establishment of a unified nation-state (4th–7th century). Presumably, agricultural rites were celebrated seasonally, and most communal religious functions centered around objects or places considered to be especially steeped in *kami*-nature. Gradually the *kami* of some of these places were associated with local ruling clans (*uji*) and acquired the name *ujigami*. The leaders of one clan in the YAMATO region (near the present city of Nara) came to be regarded as descendants of the sun goddess AMATERASU Ōmikami. By virtue of this distinction the family was recognized as the Japanese imperial household and became the cornerstone of Japanese nationhood.

With the emergence of the unified nation-state, centered in Yamato, Shintō festivals and ceremonies (MATSURI) became inseparable from the ordinary affairs of government. These activities were called *matsuri-goto* (literally, "affairs of religious festivals"), and the term has retained its meaning of "government" in the modern Japanese language.

This ancient union was revived and reemphasized after the Meiji Restoration of 1868, when the shrines of Shintō were magnified into the primary agencies for dramatizing, celebrating, and supporting the major interests of the national life. At the end of World War II, the ideology of this so-called State Shintō (Kokka Shintō) was discredited and the religion was officially banned, but it was reorga-

A Japanese woman in traditional dress bows at the entrance of a Shintō temple
Fujihira—Monkmeyer

SHINTŌ

nized without its political associations as SHRINE SHINTŌ (JINJA Shintō), which remained closely associated with the imperial family.

Throughout its history, Shintō, as a foundation of belief and practice, has been subject to a variety of external influences. The successive inroads made by CONFUCIANISM, TAOISM, and Buddhism into Japan left distinctive marks on the indigenous religion. Despite the revived orthodoxy of State Shintō, the tendency toward assimilation and hybridization reached a peak during the Meiji period (1868–1912), when some 13 new movements, known collectively with other such movements as Sect Shintō (Kyōha Shintō), arose around various points of emphasis from ASCETICISM to FAITH HEALING to Confucian ethics. Sect Shintō underwent further fragmentation after World War II.

While especially the sectarian groups, but also State and later Shrine Shintō, took on aspects of imported religions and philosophies, the beliefs and practices of the rural population remained remarkably true to the ancient tradition. Folk Shintō (Minzoku Shintō), as it is called, has no formal organizational structure or doctrinal formulation but is centered in the veneration of small roadside images and in the agricultural rites of rural families.

Although distinctive in flavor, the three types of Shintō are integrally related: Folk Shintō exists as the substructure of Shintō faith, and a SECT SHINTŌ follower is usually a parishioner (*ujiko*) of a certain Shrine Shintō shrine at the same time.

MYTHOLOGY

Though Shintō has no official scripture, the *Kojiki* ("Records of Ancient Matters") and the *Nihon-gi*, or *Nihon shoki* ("Chronicles of Japan"), are regarded in a sense as sacred books of Shintō. They were written in 712 and 720 CE, respectively, and are compilations of the ORAL TRADITIONS of ancient Shintō. But they are also books about the history, topography, and literature of ancient Japan. It is possible to construct Shintō doctrines from them by interpreting the myths and religious practices they describe.

The core of the mythology consists of tales about Amaterasu, and tales of how her direct descendants unified the Japanese people under their authority. In the beginning, according to Japanese mythology, a certain number of *kami* simply emerged, and a pair of *kami*, IZANAGI AND IZANAMI, gave birth to the Japanese islands, as well as to the *kami* who became ancestors of the various clans. Amaterasu, the ruler of Takama no Hara; the moon god Tsukiyomi no Mikoto; and SUSANOO (Susanowo) no Mikoto, the ruler of the nether regions, were the most important among them. A descendant of Amaterasu, JIMMU, is said to have become the first emperor of Japan. Japanese mythology says that the Three Sacred Treasures (the mirror, the sword, and the jewels), which are still the most revered symbols of the imperial household, were first given by Amaterasu to her grandson. The Inner Shrine (Naikū) of the Ise-jingū is dedicated to this ancestral goddess and is the most venerated shrine in Shintō.

The Japanese classics also contain myths and legends concerning the so-called 800 myriads of *kami* (*yao-yorozu no kami*; literally, *yao* equals 800 and *yorozu* 10,000). Some of them are the tutelary deities of clans and later became the tutelary *kami* of their respective local communities. Many others are not enshrined in sanctuaries and have no direct connections with the actual Shintō faith.

CONCEPT OF THE SACRED

At the core of Shintō are beliefs in the mysterious creating and harmonizing power (*musubi*) of *kami* and in the truthful way or will (*makoto*) of *kami*. The nature of *kami* cannot be fully explained in words, because *kami* transcends the cognitive faculty of man. Devoted followers, however, are able to understand *kami* through faith and usually recognize various *kami* in polytheistic form.

Parishioners of a shrine believe in their tutelary *kami* as the source of human life and existence. Each *kami* has a divine personality and responds to truthful

Sacred places and temples of Shintō

prayers. The *kami* also reveals *makoto* to people and guides them to live in accordance with it. In traditional Japanese thought, truth manifests itself in empirical existence and undergoes transformation in infinite varieties in time and space. *Makoto* is not an abstract ideology. It can be recognized every moment in every individual thing in the encounter between man and *kami*.

In Shintō all the deities are said to cooperate with one another, and life lived in accordance with a *kami*'s will is believed to produce a mystical power that gains the protection, cooperation, and approval of all the particular *kami*.

MORAL PRECEPTS

As the basic attitude toward life, Shintō emphasizes *makoto no kokoro* ("heart of truth"), or *magokoro* ("true heart"), which is usually translated as "sincerity, pure heart, uprightness." This attitude follows from the revelation of the truthfulness of *kami* in man. It is, generally, the sincere attitude of a person in doing his best in the work he has chosen or in his relationship with others, and the ultimate source of such a life-attitude lies in man's awareness of the divine.

Although Shintō ethics do not ignore individual moral virtues such as loyalty, FILIAL PIETY, love, faithfulness, and so forth, it is generally considered more important to seek *magokoro*, which constitutes the dynamic life-attitude that brings forth these virtues. In ancient scriptures *magokoro* was interpreted as "bright and pure mind" or "bright, pure, upright, and sincere mind." Purification, both physical and spiritual, is stressed even in contemporary Shintō to produce such a state of mind. The achievement of this state of mind is necessary in order to make communion between *kami* and man possible and to enable individuals to accept the blessings of *kami*.

At a children's cemetery on south Honshu, grave decorations reflect contemporary culture. Cemeteries, even those near Shintō shrines or temples, are most commonly Buddhist, and many Japanese consider themselves followers of both traditions
Marcello Bertinetti—
Photo Researchers

RITUAL PRACTICES AND INSTITUTIONS

Shintō does not have a weekly religious service. Instead, people visit shrines at their own convenience. There are some who may go to the shrines on the 1st and 15th of each month and on the occasions of rites or festivals (*matsuri*), which take place several times a year. Devotees, however, may pay respect to the shrine every morning.

Rites of passage. Various Shintō RITES OF PASSAGE are observed in Japan. The purpose of the first visit of a newborn baby to the tutelary *kami*, which takes place between 30 and 100 days after birth, is to initiate the baby as a new adherent. The Shichi-go-san (Seven-Five-Three) festival on November 15 is the occasion for boys of five years and girls of three and seven years of age to visit the shrine to give thanks for *kami*'s protection and to pray for their healthy growth. January 15 is Adults' Day. Youth in the village used to join the local young men's association on this day. At present it is the commemoration day for those Japanese who have attained their 20th year. The Japanese usually have their wedding ceremonies in Shintō style and pronounce their wedding vows to *kami*. Shintō funeral ceremonies, however, are not popular. The majority of the Japanese are Buddhist and Shintōist at the same time and have their funerals in Buddhist style. A traditional Japanese house has two family altars: one, Shintō, for their tutelary *kami* and the goddess Amaterasu Ōmikami, and another, Buddhist, for the family ancestors. Pure Shintō families, however, will have all ceremonies and services in Shintō style. There are other Shintō *matsuri* concerning occupations or daily life, as, for example, a ceremony of purifying a building site or for setting up the framework for a new building, a firing or purifying ceremony for the boilers in a new factory, a completion ceremony for a construction work, or a launching ceremony for a new ship.

Festivals and worship. Each Shintō shrine has several major festivals each year, including the Spring Festival (Haru Matsuri, or Toshigoi-no-Matsuri; Prayer for Good Harvest Festival), Autumn Festival (Aki Matsuri, or Niiname-sai; Harvest Festival), an Annual Festival (Rei-sai), and the Divine procession (Shinkō-sai). The Divine Procession usually takes place on the day of the Annual Festival, and miniature shrines (*mikoshi*) carried on the shoulders are transported through the parish.

The rituals at a grand festival will usually include purification rites, adoration at the altar, opening and closing of the door of the inner SANCTUARY, prayer, sacred music and dance, feasting, and the offering of food and little branches of the evergreen sacred tree to which strips of white paper are tied. Since World War II it has become popular to have a brief sermon or speech before the feast.

Torii, ritual gates that mark the division between the secular and the sacred, in the Inland Sea, at the entrance to Itsuku Island
George Holton—Photo Researchers

SHIRDI SAI BABA \shir-'dē-'sän-ē-'bä-bä, 'shir-dē-\, *or* Sai Baba of Shirdi (b. 1836—d. 1918), spiritual leader dear to Hindu and Muslim devotees throughout India and in diaspora communities as far flung as the United States and the Caribbean. The name Sai Baba comes from *sai*, a Persian word used by Muslims to denote a holy person, and *baba*, Hindi for father. Though it is generally agreed that Sai Baba was born in 1836, his early years are a mystery. Most accounts mention his birth as a Hindu Brahmin and his subsequent adoption by a Sufi FAKIR, or MENDICANT. Later in life he claimed to have had a Hindu GURU. Sai Baba arrived in Shirdi, in the western Indian state of Maharashtra, about 1858 and remained there until his death in 1918.

At first denounced by the villagers of Shirdi as a madman, by the turn of the century Sai Baba had a considerable following of Hindus and Muslims, attracted by his compelling teachings and his performance of miracles, which often involved the granting of wishes and the healing of the sick. He wore a Muslim cap and for the better part of his life lived in an abandoned mosque in Shirdi, where he daily kept a fire burning, a practice reminiscent of some Sufi orders. Yet he named this mosque Dvarakamai, a decidedly Hindu name, and is said to have had substantial knowledge of the PURĀNAS, the BHAGAVAD GĪTĀ, and various branches of Hindu philosophy. Sai Baba's teachings often took the form of paradoxical PARABLES and displayed both his disdain for the rigid formalism that HINDUISM and ISLAM could fall prey to and his empathy for the poor and diseased. Shirdi is a major PILGRIMAGE site, and other spiritual figures like Upasani Baba and MEHER BABA credit the teachings of Sai Baba, while SATHYA SAI BABA (b. 1926) claims to be his incarnation.

SHIRK \'shirk\ (Arabic: "making a partner [of God]"), in ISLAM, IDOLATRY, POLYTHEISM, and the association of God with other deities.

The QUR'ĀN stresses in many verses that God does not share his powers with any partner (*sharīk*). It warns those who believe their idols will intercede for them that they and the idols will become fuel for hellfire on the Day of Judgment (21:98). Most *mushrikūn* (polytheists) in the Prophet's time were not Muslims; thus the words of the Qur'an were addressed not only to Muslims to keep them firm in their faith, but also to polytheistic Arabs.

Different grades of *shirk* have been distinguished in Islamic law. There is *shirk al-'āda* ("*shirk* of custom"), which includes all superstitions, such as the belief in OMENS. *Shirk al-'ibāda* ("*shirk* of worship") is the belief in the powers of created things—*e.g.*, revering saints, kissing holy stones, and praying at the grave of a holy man. There is *shirk al-'ilm* ("*shirk* of knowledge")—*e.g.*, to credit anyone, such as astrologers, with knowledge of the future. All these are *shirk saghīr* ("minor *shirk*") compared with polytheism.

Shiva, bronze statue, Madras, c. 900 CE
By courtesy of the Government Museum, Madras; photograph, Royal Academy of Arts, London

SHIROMAṆĪ GURDWĀRĀ PRABANDHAK COMMITTEE (SGPC) \'shir-ō-mə-nē-'gur-dwä-rä-prä-'bən-dək\ (Punjabi: Shiromaṇī Gurdwāra Prabandhak Kameṭi, "Principal Committee of Gurdwara Management"), leading Sikh institution of the 20th century; it emerged as a part of the Singh Sabhā's efforts to adjust core Sikh institutions in response to changed conditions created by British rule in the Punjab. In 1920 a meeting of the *sarbat khālsā* (Punjabi: literally, "total Sikh community," but in reality a representative gathering of the community) at the GOLDEN TEMPLE, Amritsar, resolved to create the SGPC to manage the historical GURDWĀRĀS—those associated with the 10 GURŪS—and the large land grants attached to them by Maharaja Ranjit Singh (1780–1839). In 1925 the British government legalized the SGPC with 175 members to be elected every five years by Sikh voters in the Punjab and assigned it statutory powers under the Gurdwara Reform Act.

Since its inception, the central office of the SGPC has been situated in the Golden Temple precincts, from where it has overseen the day-to-day functioning of a large number of historical *gurdwārā*s in the Punjab. The SGPC has also produced the standard text of the ĀDI GRANTH, the primary Sikh scripture; codified Sikh religious and ritual conduct, the authoritative edition of which was first published as *Sikh Rahit Maryādā* in 1950; published scholarly works on Sikh history and religion; and run several Sikh educational institutions, including an engineering and a medical college. Often called the Sikh Parliament, the SGPC has also played an extremely important role in Sikh politics by serving as the power base of the AKĀLĪ DAL party.

SHIVA \'shi-və\, *also spelled* Śiva (Sanskrit: "Auspicious One"), one of the main deities of HINDUISM, worshiped as the paramount lord by the Śaiva (*see* ŚAIVISM) sects of India and the Hindu diaspora. Shiva is both the destroyer and the restorer, the great ascetic and the symbol of sensuality, the benevolent herdsman of souls and the wrathful avenger.

Shiva's female consort is known under various manifestations as Umā, SATĪ, PĀRVATĪ, DURGĀ, KĀLĪ, and sometimes ŚAKTI. The divine couple, together with their sons—SKANDA and GAṆEŚA—dwell on Mount Kailāsa in the HIMALAYAS. Shiva's mount and animal image is the bull NANDĪ; in temples and in private shrines Shiva is worshiped in the form of the LIṄGA, his aniconic emblem that has close historical and mythic associations with the phallus but is not so perceived by many devotees.

Shiva is usually depicted with a blue neck (from holding in his throat the poison thrown up at the CHURNING OF THE MILK-OCEAN, which threatened to destroy humankind), his hair arranged in a coil of matted locks (*jatāmakuṭa*) and adorned with the crescent moon and the GAṄGĀ RIVER (he brought the Gaṅgā to Earth by allowing her to trickle through his hair, thus breaking her fall). He has three eyes, the third eye bestowing inward vision but capable of burning destruction when focused outward. He wears a garland of skulls and a serpent around his neck and carries in his two (sometimes four) hands a deerskin, a trident, a small hand drum, or a club with a skull at the end.

Shiva is variously represented as the cosmic dancer (NA-ṬARĀJA), a naked ascetic, a MENDICANT beggar, a yogi, and the androgynous union of Shiva and his consort in one body (ARDHANĀRĪŚVARA). Among his epithets are Śambhu ("Benignant"), Śaṃkara ("Beneficent"), Paśupati ("Lord of Beasts"), Maheśa ("Great Lord"), and Mahādeva ("Great God").

SHIVĀJĪ: *see* ŚIVĀJĪ.

SHOFAR \shō-'fär, 'shō-fər\, in ancient JUDAISM, musical instrument (perhaps made out of, or in the shape of, a "ram's horn," thus the name "shofar") used on important sacred occasions. In JOSHUA 6:4–20 and Judges 3:27, 6:34 the shofar is sounded in battle. Other texts recount the use of the shofar as a signaling device (1 Samuel 13:3; ISAIAH 18:3, 27:13, 58:1; JEREMIAH 51:27), as communication by watchmen (Jeremiah 6:1; EZEKIEL 33:3–6), and as a call to repent (AMOS 2:2, 3:6; HOSEA 5:8, 8:1). As an instrument of worship, the shofar signaled the Day of Atonement (Leviticus 25:9) and the coronations of kings (1 Kings 1:34–41; 2 Kings 9:13)—which custom is preserved in modern Israel at the swearing in of the president of the state. The most important modern use of the shofar in religious ceremonies takes place on ROSH HASHANAH; it is also sounded on YOM KIPPUR.

SHOGHI EFFENDI RABBĀNĪ \'shaù-ē-e-'fen-dē-räb-'bä-nē\ (b. March 1, 1897, Acre, Palestine [now 'Akko, Israel]—d. Nov. 4, 1957, London, Eng.), leader of the international BA-HĀ'Ī FAITH, who held the title of Guardian of the Cause of God from 1921 until his death.

Shoghi Effendi grew up in Acre. In 1918 he earned a B.A. from the American University in Beirut, Lebanon. His education was directed to serving as secretary and translator to his grandfather, Abd al-Bahā', then leader of the Bahā'ī faith and son of the faith's founder, BAHĀ' ULLĀH.

After further education at Balliol College, Oxford, he returned to Haifa (1921) to assume the office of the Guardian at the death of his grandfather, who had designated him as successor. His next year was spent in maintaining the organization and unifying its followers.

Within the context of his office as Guardian, Shoghi Effendi wrote extensively as chief interpreter of the Bahā'ī teachings from his home and headquarters of the religion in Haifa, Israel. His writings are collected in *The World Order of Bahā Ullāh* and other volumes published between 1930 and 1958. Additionally, as a result of his travels in Africa, the membership in the Bahā'ī faith increased considerably on that continent.

Although the office of Guardian had been envisioned as hereditary, it terminated with his death. The assistants appointed by Shoghi Effendi, known as the Hands of the Cause of God, currently serve under the Universal House of Justice, which is the supreme administrative body that assumed world leadership of the religion in 1963.

SHOU-HSING \'shō-'shiŋ\, *Pinyin* Shouxing, in Chinese mythology, one of three stellar gods known collectively as Fu-Shou-Lu. He was also called Nan-chi lao-jen ("Old Man of the South Pole"). Greatly revered as the god of longevity (*shou*), Shou-hsing has no temples, but at birthday parties for older people his statue is draped in silk robes.

SHRINE SHINTŌ \'shēn-ˌtō, *Angl* 'shin-tō\, *Japanese* Jinja Shintō \'jēn-jä-\, form of SHINTŌ that focuses on worship in public shrines, in contrast to folk and sectarian practices (*see* Kyōha Shintō). It succeeded STATE SHINTŌ when the latter was disbanded. More than 80,000 shrines, nearly all of those formerly administered by the government, have formed themselves into an Association of Shintō Shrines (Jinja Honchō). They depend on private contributions for their maintenance and for the support of their priests.

SHU \'shü\, in EGYPTIAN RELIGION, god of the air and supporter of the sky, created by ATUM. Shu and his sister and companion, Tefnut (goddess of moisture), were the first couple of the group of nine gods called the Ennead of HELIOPOLIS. Of their union were born GEB, the earth god, and NUT, the goddess of the sky. Shu was portrayed in human form with the hieroglyph of his name, an ostrich feather, on his head. He was often represented separating Geb and Nut, supporting with uplifted arms the body of Nut arched above him. In some Middle Kingdom texts Shu was given the status of a primeval creator god. Later he was frequently termed the "Son of Re" (the sun god), and he was also identified with Onuris, a warrior god, thus acquiring martial associations.

SHU-CHING \'shü-'jiŋ\ (Chinese: "Classic of History"), *Pinyin* Shujing, *also called* Shang-shu \'shäŋ-'shü\ ("Official History"), compilation of documentary records of events in China's ancient history, one of the FIVE CLASSICS (*Wu-ching*) of Chinese antiquity. Though certain chapters are forgeries, the authentic parts constitute the oldest Chinese writing of its kind.

The SHU-CHING consists of 58 chapters. Of these, 33 are considered to be authentic works of the 4th century BCE or earlier. The first five chapters relate the sayings and deeds of the emperors who reigned during China's legendary golden age. The next four are devoted to the Hsia dynasty (c. 2205–c. 1766 BCE), the historicity of which has not been definitively established. The next 17 deal with the Shang dynasty and its collapse in 1122 BCE. The final 32 chapters cover the Hsi- (Western) Chou dynasty that ruled China until 771 BCE.

SHUGEN-DŌ \shü-'gen-'dō\, Japanese religious tradition combining folk beliefs with SHINTŌ, BUDDHISM, and elements of religious TAOISM. The Shugen-dō practitioner, the *yamabushi* (literally, "one who bows down in the mountains"), engages in spiritual and physical disciplines in order to attain power against evil spirits.

Shugen-dō (meaning "way of mastering power") flourished during the Heian period (794–1185 CE) and allied itself with the esoteric schools of Buddhism, Tendai (*see* T'IEN-T'AI), and SHINGON. As a "mountain religion," Shugen-dō emphasized PILGRIMAGES and retreats to sacred mountains. The *yamabushi* served as guides for pilgrims visiting Yoshino and Kumano, sacred mountains inhabited by Shintō KAMI. The *yamabushi* helped the spread of Buddhism through northern Japan.

Many Buddhist priests belonging to esoteric traditions regularly developed their *yamabushi* techniques, and Shugen-dō practitioners often served as priests of Shintō shrines. This latter practice was discontinued by the Meiji government, which abolished the Shugen-dō in 1872. Three of the religious movements recognized by the Meiji regime under Sect Shintō—the Jikko-kyō, the Fusō-kyō, and the Ontake-kyō—are mountain cults, featuring practices similar to those of Shugen-dō.

After 1945, with the disbandment of STATE SHINTŌ, some Shugen-dō groups that had survived within Buddhism once more attempted to establish Shugen-dō organizations. However, the membership and influence of Shugen-dō groups are now greatly diminished. *See also* ASCETICISM.

SHULḤAN ʿARUKH \shul-ˈkän-ä-ˈruk\ (Hebrew: "Prepared Table"), 16th-century codification of Jewish religious law and practice that is still the standard reference work for Orthodox observance. The *Shulḥan ʿarukh*, compiled and published by JOSEPH BEN EPHRAIM KARO (1488–1575) as a compendium of his larger work *Bet Yosef* ("House of Joseph"), contains opinions of various other codifiers before his time as well as Karo's personal decisions on disputed points.

The *Shulḥan ʿarukh* is in four parts: observance of the SABBATH, festivals and the daily commandments are covered in *Oraḥ Ḥayyim*; guidelines for mourning, usury and purity (*see* TOHORAH) are discussed in *Yoreh Deʾah*; marriage and divorce are handled in *Even ha-Ezer*; and both criminal and civil legal issues are addressed in *Ḥoshen Mishpat*.

The *Shulḥan ʿarukh* was criticized by ASHKENAZI RABBIS for its overemphasis on Sephardic customs. Accordingly, Moses Isserles (c. 1525–72) wrote a commentary (called *Mappa*, "Tablecloth") on the *Shulḥan ʿarukh* that was subsequently printed with Karo's work so that both rites were represented. Thereafter, the *Shulḥan ʿarukh* became a universally accepted guide for Orthodox observance.

SHUN \ˈshun\, *Pinyin* Shun, in Chinese mythology, one of three legendary emperors, along with YAO and Yu, of the golden age of antiquity (c. 23rd century BCE), singled out by CONFUCIUS as a model of integrity and resplendent virtue.

Though Shun's father repeatedly tried to murder him, the boy's FILIAL PIETY never faltered. Because of his virtue, birds helped him weed his paddies and animals pulled his plow. The emperor Yao bypassed his own son to choose Shun as most worthy to rule and gave him his daughters, O Huang and Nü Ying (also known as Hsiang Chün and Fu-jen), in marriage. Shun offered sacrifice to the Six Honored Ones (whose identity is uncertain) and to the spirits of earth.

SHŪRĀ \ˈshur-ə\ (Arabic: "consultation"), in early Islamic history, board of electors that was constituted by the second CALIPH (head of the Muslim community), ʿUmar I (634–644), to elect his successor. Thereafter, in Muslim states, *shūrā* variously designated a council of state, or advisers to the sovereign, a parliament (in modern times), and a court of law with jurisdiction over claims made by citizens and public officials against the government. The word *shūrā* provides the title of the 42nd chapter of the QURʾAN, in which believers are exhorted to conduct their affairs "by mutual consultation." Conservative Muslim ideologues in the 20th century understand *shūrā* to be an expression of divine unity (*tawḥīd*) rather than purely human agency.

SHUSHIGAKU \ˈshü-shē-ˌgä-kù\ (Japanese: "Chu Hsi school"), most influential of the schools of NEO-CONFUCIANISM that developed in Japan during the Tokugawa period (1603–1867).

SHWE DAGON \ˈshwā-ˌdä-gün\, PAGODA in Yangôn (Rangoon), the capital of Myanmar (Burma). A great Buddhist temple complex about one mile north of the Cantonment (the city's center), the pagoda is a solid brick STUPA completely covered with gold. It rises 326 feet on a hill 168 feet above the city.

SIBYL \ˈsi-bəl\, *also called* Sibylla \si-ˈbi-lə\, prophetess in Greek legend and literature. She was always a figure of the mythical past, and her prophecies, in Greek hexameters, were handed down in writing. In the 5th and early 4th centuries BCE, she was always referred to in the singular. From the late 4th century the number of sibyls was multiplied; they were localized traditionally at all the famous oracle centers, particularly in association with APOLLO, and "sibyl" was treated as a title.

A famous collection of sibylline prophecies, the Sibylline Books, was traditionally offered for sale to Tarquinius Superbus, the last of the seven KINGS OF ROME, by the Cumaean sibyl. He refused to pay her price, so the sibyl burned six of the books before finally selling him the remaining three at the price she had originally asked for all nine. The books were thereafter kept in the temple of JUPITER on the Capitoline Hill, to be consulted only in emergencies.

Augustus and the Tiburtine Sibyl, by Antoine Caron, c. 1580; in the Louvre, Paris
Giraudon—Art Resource

SIBYLLINE ORACLES \'si-bə-,līn, -,lēn\, collection of oracular prophecies in which Jewish or Christian doctrines were allegedly confirmed by a SIBYL (legendary Greek prophetess); the prophecies were actually the work of certain Jewish and Christian writers from about 150 BCE to about 180 CE and are not to be confused with the much earlier collection known as the Sibylline Books.

In the Oracles the sibyl proved her reliability by first "predicting" events that had actually recently occurred; she then predicted future events and set forth doctrines peculiar to Hellenistic JUDAISM or CHRISTIANITY. Modern scholars have dated the various Oracles by comparing actual historical events with what was predicted in the Oracles. At the point where errors begin, the oracle-writer was predicting the future, and it is possible to assign a date from the last correct prediction.

In the Byzantine period 12 of the compositions were collected in a single manuscript containing 14 books (of which numbers 9 and 10 are lost). An incomplete text of this collection was first published in 1545.

SIDDHA \'sid-də\, in JAINISM, one who has achieved perfection. By right faith, right knowledge, and right conduct a Siddha has freed himself from the cycle of rebirths and resides in a state of perpetual bliss in the *siddha-śīlā*, at the top of the universe. The Siddha and the other ascetics constitute the *pañca-parameṣṭhin*, the five chief divinities of the Jains. Their figures are represented on a silver or brass tray called a *siddha-cakra* (saint-wheel), to which great sanctity and power are attributed. In the twice-yearly ceremony known as *oḷī*, the images are washed and anointed, and offerings of rice, sweetmeats, and fruit are made.

In BUDDHISM under the Pāla kings of India (8th–12th century CE) Tantric Buddhism (*i.e.*, VAJRAYĀNA) became the dominant sect. Adepts of this sect were called Siddhas, and they identified NIRVANA with the passions, maintaining that one could "touch the deathless element with his body." *See also* MAHĀSIDDHA.

SIDDUR \sē-'dùr, 'si-dər\ (Hebrew: "order"), *plural* siddurim \,sē-dù-'rēm\, *or* siddurs, Jewish prayer book that contains the entire liturgy used on the ordinary SABBATH and on weekdays for domestic as well as SYNAGOGUE ritual. It is distinguished from the MAHZOR, which is the prayer book used for the High Holidays. Because tradition long allowed the addition of new prayers and hymns (*piyyutim*) to voice contemporary needs and aspirations, the siddurim reflect Jewish religious history expressed in liturgy and prayers. Variations persist, but the basic elements are unchanging.

SIEGFRIED \'sig-,frēd, 'sēg-, *German* 'zēk-,frēt\, *Old Norse* Sigurd \'si-gùrd, -gərd\, figure from the heroic literature of the ancient Germanic people. He appears in both German and Old Norse literature, although the versions of his stories do not always agree. He plays a part in the story of Brunhild, in which he meets his death, but in other stories he is the leading character and triumphs. A feature common to all versions is his outstanding strength and courage. It is still disputed whether the figure of Siegfried is of mythical or historical (Merovingian) origin.

Siegfried was a boy of noble lineage who grew up without parental care. One story tells of Siegfried's fight with a dragon, and another of how he acquired a treasure from two brothers who quarreled over their inheritance. These two stories are combined into one in the Norse *Poetic* EDDA. Siegfried plays a major part in the *Nibelungenlied*, where

this old material is used but is much overlaid with more recent additions. *Das Lied vom hürnen Seyfrid*, not attested before about 1500, also retains the old material in identifiable form, although the poem's central theme is the release of a maiden from a dragon; and an *Edda* poem tells how Sigurd awakened a VALKYRIE maiden from a charmed sleep There is doubt about the antiquity of both poems.

SIFRA \si-'frä\, compilation of midrashic exegeses on the book of Leviticus produced by Jewish sages in the 2nd and 3rd centuries and closed at *c*. 300 CE. Sifra contends that the law of the MISHNAH is not the product of logic—but that it is, and can only be, the product of EXEGESIS of SCRIPTURE. The Mishnah is subordinated to Scripture and validated only through Scripture. The framers of the Mishnah effect their taxonomy through the traits of things. The authorship of Sifra insists that the only true source of classification is Scripture. In the Mishnah one seeks connection between fact and fact, sentence and sentence, by comparing and contrasting two things that are both like and not alike. But, Sifra insists, only Scripture reliably defines the governing classifications by which facts are formed into intelligible patterns.

SIFRÉ TO DEUTERONOMY \si-'frä . . . ,dü-tə-'rä-nə-mē, ,dyü-\, systematic, verse by verse commentary to the book of Deuteronomy by the sages of RABBINIC JUDAISM. Since the MISHNAH (*c*. 200 CE) and the TOSEFTA (*c*. 250 CE) are cited verbatim, a probable date for the work is *c*. 300 CE. Out of cases and examples, the sages sought generalizations and governing principles. The document's compilers took the details of cases and carefully reframed them into rules that then pertained to all cases. These rules show what details restrict the prevailing law to the conditions of the case, and what details exemplify the encompassing traits of the overall law. Four principal topics comprise the document's propositions—the first three yield systematic statements that concern the relationships between ISRAEL (the Jewish people) and God, with special reference to the COVENANT, the TORAH, and the land; Israel and the nations, with interest in Israel's history, past, present, and future, and how that cyclic time is to be recognized; and Israel on its own terms, focusing upon Israel's distinctive leadership. The fourth rubric examines prevailing modes of thought that demonstrate the inner structure of intellect—whether that be the intellect underlying *sifré* itself, the cases of SCRIPTURE, or the encompassing rules.

SIFRÉ TO NUMBERS \si-'frä\, commentary to the book of Numbers that dates to *c*. 300 CE and that provides a miscellaneous reading of most of that book. All authorities quoted in it enjoy the status of MISHNAH sages, called *tannaim* (those who repeat ORAL TRADITIONS), and so the EXEGESIS is called "tannaitic." The document cites as complete, extraneous compositions passages of the Mishnah and the TOSEFTA, *c*. 200 and 250 CE, respectively; thus the indicated date, which is at the very end of the period of the TANNA, is probable.

The word *sifré* corresponds to the Hebrew *sefarim*, meaning books. The document as a whole through its fixed and recurrent literary structures makes two complementary points: (1) reason unaided by SCRIPTURE produces uncertain propositions, and (2) reason operating within the limits of Scripture produces truth. These two principles are never articulated but are left implicit in the systematic reading of most of the book of Numbers, verse by verse.

SIKHISM

Founded in the late 15th century CE by GURŪ NĀNAK, Sikhism is the youngest and probably the least known of the world's monotheistic religious traditions. The word Sikh is derived from the Pāli *sikkha* or Sanskrit *śiṣya*, meaning "follower." Sikhs are a community of 18 million people. Though historically associated with the Punjab, a region that connects southern Asia with the Middle East, over 2 million Sikhs have left the Punjab and now live and work in North America, western Europe, and many former British colonies.

HISTORY

Nānak (1469–1539) was a Hindu by birth. While in his late twenties, he is said to have had a divine revelation that resulted in his leaving the routine domestic life behind and embarking on extensive travel. After about twenty years, he ceased traveling, acquired farmland in the lush plains of the central Punjab, and founded a town named Kartārpur (City of God). At Kartārpur, Nānak became Gurū Nānak (Nānak, the preceptor), and the daily routine of the lives of his Sikhs—followers—was constructed around his spiritual ideals.

Gurū Nānak provided the early Sikh community at Kartārpur with an institutional structure. He composed hymns of great beauty and had them recorded in a distinct script called Gurmukhī. These hymns formed the core of the Sikh sacred text, the ĀDI GRANTH ("original book"). He also created the practice of three daily prayers at Kartārpur and established the institution of community kitchen (*langar*), where (contrary to Hindu custom) all Sikhs were to eat together to signal their belief in human equality. At the time of his death in 1539, Gurū Nānak appointed one of his followers, AṄGAD, to be his successor, and by doing so he institutionalized the office of Gurū, which continued until the death of Gurū GOBIND SINGH, the tenth Sikh Gurū (1675–1708).

By the end of the 16th century the Sikhs had become powerful enough to be seen as a threat by the Mughal (Muslim) administration in both Lahore (the provincial headquarters) and Delhi. A period of tension culminated in the execution of Gurū ARJAN, the fifth Sikh Gurū (1581–1606). The Sikh community, under the leadership of his successor, Gurū HARGOBIND (1606–44), responded by formally re-

A Sikh guard at the entrance to the Golden Temple in Amritsar, the most important Sikh temple and pilgrimage site

jecting Mughal authority and declaring the Gurū to be both temporal (*mīr*) and spiritual (*pīr*) head. Sikhs were forced to leave the Punjab plains and move to the Himalayan foothills, where they remained throughout the 17th century. An attempt to revive the community in the plains during the leadership of Gurū TEGH BAHĀDUR, the ninth Sikh Gurū (1664–75), ended with his execution in Delhi.

Given this hostile political climate, the Sikh belief in God's justice took the form of Gurū Gobind Singh's declaration of the Sikh community as the KHĀLSĀ ("pure"). In the process, he gave the community a new understanding of its special relationship to God on the one hand, and its mission to participate in establishment of the *khālsā rāj* (kingdom of God) on the other. Gurū Gobind Singh introduced a ceremony of initiation in which fresh water was transformed into nectar by reciting on it the compositions of the Gurūs, the divine word as revealed to the Sikhs, while stirring it with a double-edged sword (*khandā*) symbolizing God's power and justice. Having taken the nectar, a Sikh became a Singh

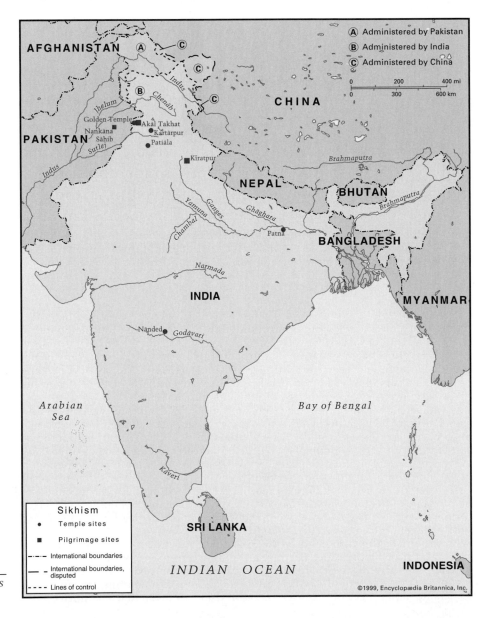

Important Sikh temples and pilgrimage sites

("lion") and followed an expanded version of the existing code of conduct (*rahit*). The new code involved the carrying of five Ks: *kes* (uncut hair), *kaṅghā* (a comb), *kirpān* (a sword), *karhā* (a steel bracelet), and *kachhā* (long shorts), as well as abstinence from tobacco.

Gurū Gobind Singh thus gave the community both a strengthened identity and a political vision. On this basis Sikhs developed a powerful myth that the land of the Punjab belongs to them, the special gift of the tenth Gurū. They waged relentless military campaigns, and finally, under the leadership of Ranjīt Singh (1780–1839) created a powerful kingdom in the region. The community's understanding of itself as the Khālsā, the special ones, did not permit any concerted effort among Sikhs to convert others to their faith, and even at the peak of their political power they remained a small minority in the Punjab. Despite their minority status, they were able to hold on to the Punjab by determination and military skill.

The death of Ranjīt Singh in 1839 ushered in a period of instability, and the

Punjab was ultimately annexed by the British in 1849. After a time of painful introspection and reflection on the fall of the *khālsā rāj*, the Sikhs began to work closely with their conquerors. The British declared the Sikhs to be a martial race and recruited them into the imperial army and the police, creating opportunities for worldwide travel.

Late in the 19th century the SINGH SABHĀ ("Society of Singhs") emerged. The leaders of this movement undertook to make

Pilgrims follow a rocky path to Hemkund in the Himalayas, where the last Sikh Gurū meditated
Photo Researchers

the Sikhs aware of what they saw as correct Sikh doctrines and practices, using the newly arrived print medium to propagate Sikh history and literature. They worked closely with the British administration, convincing them of the importance of treating the Sikhs as a distinct political community.

The idea of an independent Sikh state figured prominently in the protracted negotiations that preceded the partition of the Punjab in 1947, but the small numbers of Sikhs in relation to other residents made this an unviable proposition. In independent India, the Akālī Dal—the Sikh political party whose programs and criteria for membership have a distinctly religious character—has historically found itself in conflict with the central government of India in New Delhi. In 1966 its efforts led to the founding of the present-day state of Punjab, in which Sikhs are a majority and Punjābī is the official language. In the 1980s a movement led by Sant Jarnail Singh Bhindrānwale (1947–84) to create an independent Khālistān ("Land of the Khālsā") paralyzed the Punjab.

Although an overwhelming majority of the Sikhs still live in the Punjab, approximately 10 percent of them have settled in other parts of the world. This development has created a new situation in which issues of religious authority, sacred language, Sikh relationship with the land of the Punjab, and social practice are receiving new scrutiny in the diaspora community. The positions taken on these issues will have a lasting impact on the future shape of Sikhism, not only in the diaspora community but also, because of the sharing of Sikh leadership internationally, in the Punjab itself.

DOCTRINE

Gurū Nānak's theology is built on the foundational concept of the unity of God, the creator lord (*kartār/pātishāh/sāhib*) who governs the universe with his

Although primarily a religion of India, Sikhism has gained some adherents abroad; a convert and his son in Brooklyn, New York
Photo Researchers

command (*hukam*) centered on twin principles of justice (*niān*) and grace (*nadar*). As the creator, God is the sole legitimate object of human worship.

The universe came into being as part of the divine decision. Being the creation of God, the world and all the human beings in it are assigned a high degree of sanctity, with the humans positioned at the top of the hierarchy. Human beings, irrespective of their social and gender distinctions, have the unique opportunity to achieve liberation (*mukatī*), which is release from the cycle of birth and death and becoming one with God.

The pursuit of liberation, however, is obstructed by a core human flaw: self-centeredness (*haumai*). This can be brought under control by developing a relationship with God based on love (*bhau*) and fear (*bhai*) and by cultivation of a constant remembrance (*nām simran*) of his power. Gurū Nānak traced the movement toward liberation in five distinct realms. The first three mark the preparation: the recognition that the universe runs according to a divine plan and God alone judges man's activity (*dharam*); the realization of the vastness and complexity of the divine creation (*giān*); and the humility arising from an understanding of the humble nature of human existence in this God-created universe (*saram*). These complete the preparation for the believer to receive the divine grace (*karam*), which then leads to the ineffable realm of truth (*sach*).

Commitment to hard work (*kirat*), sharing the fruits of one's labor (*vand ke chhako*), and service to humanity (*sevā*) are the other enduring assets in pursuit of liberation. The family and community are not simply a passive backdrop for the individual's search for liberation; they are very much a part of that agenda. Gurū Nānak believed in the individual's obligation to work toward collective liberation. A successful individual is one who attains liberation for himself or herself but who in addition assists in the liberation of all others. It is not a matter of choice but a moral imperative.

The social and ethical dimensions of early Sikh doctrine evolved into a belief in the indivisibility of the spiritual and temporal. The characteristic Sikh thinking on this issue is manifest in the proximity in AMRITSAR of the GOLDEN TEMPLE (Darbār Sāhib), the most sacred religious site of the Sikhs, and the AKĀL TAKHAT, the highest temporal seat of Sikh authority. This belief paved the way for the Khālsā's declared mission of bringing divine victory on earth. The Khālsā saw itself as the army of God (*Akāl Purukh kī fauj*) in the firm belief that if peaceful means fail to bring justice, it is legitimate to wage war.

At the time of his death, Gurū Gobind Singh declared that henceforth the *Ādi Granth* would be the Gurū, elevating its position to that of *Gurū Granth Sāhib* (honorable Gurū in book form). The office of the personal Gurū was thus effectively replaced with the divine word as enshrined in the *Ādi Granth*. The text functions as the central authority in the presence of which the community (*Gurū-Panth*) gathers and attempts to reach a consensus (*gurmatā*) that is considered mandatory for all Sikhs, whether present or not.

SACRED LITERATURE

The *Ādi Granth* is the canonical SCRIPTURE of the Sikhs. It includes the hymns of the six Sikh Gurūs, of bards associated with the Sikh court, and of fifteen non-Sikh saint-poets known in the Sikh tradition as *bhagat*s ("devotees"). The text plays the central role in the Sikh devotional and ceremonial life.

The DASAM GRANTH ("the book of the tenth Gurū") comes second in the hierarchy. The orthodox Sikh view attributes its entire corpus to Gurū Gobind Singh, but many scholars argue that a large part of the text was produced by others associated with his court during the closing decades of the 17th century.

The *Janam Sākhī*s ("Life Stories"), a hagiographic genre, celebrate the life and works of Gurū Nānak. The earliest written versions of these stories can be traced to the mid-17th century. Gurū Nānak is presented as the greatest teacher and spiritual master of the age. At the beginning of the 18th century an offshoot of this genre surfaced in the form of the *Gurbilās* literature, which celebrates the heroic accomplishments of Gurū Hargobind and Gurū Gobind Singh. To these the *rahit nāmā* ("manual of conduct") literature may be added. This literature was codified into the authoritative text entitled *Sikh Rahit Maryādā* ("the Sikh code of conduct") in the mid-20th century by the SHIROMANĪ GURDWĀRĀ PRABANDHAK COMMITTEE, the most important Sikh governing body.

DEVOTIONAL AND CEREMONIAL LIFE

Each day most Sikhs recite three prayers: the *Japjī* ("meditation") and a set of other hymns in the morning, the *Rahirās* ("supplication") in the evening, and the *Sohilā* ("praise"), a thanksgiving prayer, just before going to sleep. On the first day of each month of the lunar calendar a special prayer called the *Barānmāh* ("twelve months") is recited.

Almost all Sikh families possess anthologies of sacred hymns (*gutkās*), which are used for recitation over and above the daily prayers. Families who can do so usually keep the *Ādi Granth* in their house. This requires some space, since the text is normally kept in a separate room, to be opened (*prakāsh*) in the morning and put to rest (*sukhāsan*) after sunset. The women in the family assume this responsibility. Family members often undertake the complete reading of the *Ādi Granth* over a period lasting from six months to one year. A reading of the text over a week and an unbroken reading taking 48 hours mark special occasions.

Soon after the birth of a child, the family visits the *gurdwāra*, offers supplication for his or her happy and healthy life, and takes "the command" (*hukam*) from the *Ādi Granth* (the text is opened at random and the hymn that appears on the left-hand top corner is considered to be the divine reply to the supplication). The opening letter of the hymn is used as the first in the name of the child.

Sikh marriage ceremonies are preceded by an unbroken reading of the *Ādi Granth*. The bride and groom circumambulate the *Ādi Granth* four times while a specific hymn of four stanzas is recited from its text. The ceremony concludes with a supplication seeking the divine blessings for the new couple.

At the time of death the body is cremated, and the remains are taken to Kīratpur, the town where Gurū Hargobind died, and dispersed in the river Sutlej. A reading of the *Ādi Granth* is completed on the tenth day after death, and relatives and friends offer supplication seeking the peace of the departed soul.

Other Sikh celebrations include: the birth anniversaries of Gurū Nānak and Gurū Gobind Singh; the martyrdom of Gurū Arjan and Gurū Tegh Bahādur; and the Vaisākhī, the day of the inauguration of the Khālsā by Gurū Gobind Singh.

After the religious service at a Sikh temple in the United States, a langar, *or communal meal, is served, symbolizing the equality of all before God*
Eugene Gordon—Photo Researchers

SĪLA \'sē-lə\ (Pāli), *Sanskrit* śīla \'shē-lə\, in BUDDHISM, morality, or right conduct. *Sīla* comprises three stages along the EIGHTFOLD PATH—right speech, right action, and right livelihood. Evil actions are considered to be the product of defiling passions, but their causes are rooted out only by the exercise of wisdom (*prajna*).

Buddhist morality is codified in the form of 10 precepts (*dasa-sīla*), which require abstention from (1) taking life, (2) taking what is not given, (3) committing sexual misconduct (nonchastity for the monk and sexual conduct contrary to proper social norms, such as adultery, for the layman), (4) engaging in false speech, (5) using intoxicants, (6) eating after midday, (7) participating in worldly amusements, (8) adorning the body with ornaments and using perfume, (9) sleeping on high and luxurious beds, and (10) accepting gold and silver.

Laymen are to observe the first five precepts (*pañca-sīla*) at all times. Occasionally, such as during a fast day, they may observe eight precepts (*aṣṭā-sīla*; the first nine, with the seventh and eighth combined as one). Normally the full 10 vows are observed only by monks or nuns, who also follow the detailed monastic rules (*see* PRĀTIMOKṢA) that are a further elaboration of the precepts.

SILHAK: *see* PRACTICAL LEARNING SCHOOL.

SILVANUS \sil-'vā-nəs\, in ROMAN RELIGION, god of the countryside, similar in character to FAUNUS, the god of animals, with whom he is often identified. Initially the spirit of the unreclaimed woodland fringing the settlement, he developed into a god of woodland pastures, of boundaries, and of villas, parks, and gardens. He never enjoyed a state cult or temple, but the simple ritual of his private worship at a sacred grove or tree had wide appeal. In Latin literature his character tended to merge with that of the Greek gods Silenus or PAN, and to be assimilated into the Greco-Roman mythological tradition.

SIMEON \'si-mē-ən\, one of the 12 tribes that in biblical times comprised the people of Israel. The tribe was named after the second son born to JACOB and his first wife, LEAH (GENESIS 29:33).

Following the EXODUS out of Egypt, the tribe of Simeon seems to have settled in the south of Palestine beyond the powerful tribe of JUDAH (Joshua 19:1–8). In time, part of the tribe of Simeon was apparently absorbed by Judah (Joshua 19:9), while other members possibly relocated in the north. If the tribe of Simeon is counted among the tribes that later formed the northern Kingdom of Israel, then it too was assimilated by other peoples after Israel was conquered by the Assyrians in 721 BCE (2 Kings 18:9–12). One way or another, the tribe of Simeon disappeared from history and is thus numbered among the TEN LOST TRIBES OF ISRAEL.

SIMEON BEN YOḤAI \'si-mē-ən-ˌben-yō-'k̲ī\, *also known as* bar Yohai, important rabbinic authority of the mid-2nd century CE, one of the five students of AKIBA BEN JOSEPH who, ordained by Judah ben Bava (or Baba), revived rabbinic learning after the failed BAR KOKHBA revolt (Talmud BAVLI Yebamot 62b). In the MISHNAH he is always referred to simply as Simeon. Later tradition assigns to him authorship of all anonymous statements in *Sifre* (Talmud Bavli Sanhedrin 86a). He also was claimed to be the author of the SEFER HA-ZOHAR; his name became central in Jewish mystical lore.

During the Hadrianic persecutions that followed the Bar Kokhba revolt, Simeon is said to have fiercely opposed Roman culture and rule. Talmud Bavli Shabbat 33b reports that, because of his derogatory statements against the Roman people, he was sentenced to death and forced to flee with his son to a cave, in which they hid for 13 years. Simeon is known for his homiletical remarks, as well as many legal dicta. He stated that the MESSIAH will come after all Jews correctly observe two SABBATHS (Talmud Bavli Shabbat 118b), and he emphasized the importance of rabbinic learning by asserting that a person who breaks off from study to contemplate a tree or other natural phenomenon deserves death (Mishnah Abot 3:7).

SIMHATH TORAH \sēm-'k̲ät-tō-'rä, 'sim-k̲əs-'tōr-ə\, Simhath *also spelled* Simhat, Simchas, Simchath, *or* Simchat, *Hebrew* Simḥat Torah ("Rejoicing of the Torah"), in JUDAISM, religious observance held on the last day of SUKKOT (Festival of Booths), when the yearly cycle of TORAH reading is completed and the next cycle is begun. Torah scrolls are removed from the ARK and carried through the SYNAGOGUE seven times, sometimes followed by children waving flags. The rejoicing characteristic of Simhath Torah is meant to express the joy that Jews feel in their possession and observance of the words of the Torah.

SIMON MAGUS \'sī-mən-'mā-gəs\ (Latin), *English* Simon the Magician, *or* the Sorcerer (fl. 1st century CE), magician who, according to the NEW TESTAMENT account (Acts 8:9–24), offered to purchase from the Apostles PETER and JOHN the power of transmitting the HOLY SPIRIT, thus giving rise to the term SIMONY as the buying or selling of sacred things or ecclesiastical office. Later references in early Christian writings identify him as the founder of post-Christian GNOSTICISM and as the archetypal heretic of the Christian church.

The 2nd-century theologian JUSTIN MARTYR relates that Simon visited Rome at the time of the emperor Claudius (41–54) and was there deified by followers who were fascinated with his miracle working; no archaeological verification of this claim has been found. According to legend, Simon fell to his death from the Roman Forum in an attempt to demonstrate his ability to fly. Other sources portray him as the individual responsible for the eclectic fusion of stoicism and gnosticism, known as "The Great Pronouncement."

Simon's quasi-Trinitarian teaching is contained in the early Christian writings known as the Clementine literature. In the 2nd century a Simonian sect arose that viewed Simon Magus as the first God, or Father, and he was sometimes worshiped as the incarnation of the Greek god ZEUS. His consort Helen was regarded by his followers as the earthly manifestation of ATHENA.

SIMONY \'si-mə-nē-, 'sī-\, buying or selling of something spiritual or closely connected with the spiritual. The name is taken from SIMON MAGUS (Acts 8:18), who sought to buy the power of conferring the gifts of the HOLY SPIRIT.

Simony, in the form of buying church offices, became familiar when the Christian church gained positions of wealth and influence to bestow. The first legislation on the point was the second canon of the COUNCIL OF CHALCEDON (451). From that time prohibitions and penalties were reiterated against buying or selling promotions to the episcopate, priesthood, and diaconate. Later, the offense of simony was extended to include all traffic in benefices and all pecuniary transactions on masses (apart from the authorized offering), blessed oils, and other consecrated objects.

From an occasional scandal, simony became widespread in Europe in the 9th and 10th centuries, after which Pope

GREGORY VII (1073–85) rigorously attacked the problem. It recurred in the 15th century, but after the 16th century, it gradually disappeared in its most flagrant forms with the disendowment and secularization of church property.

SIN \'sēn\ (Akkadian), *Sumerian* Nanna \'nän-nä\, in MESOPOTAMIAN RELIGION, god of the moon. Sin was the father of the sun god, SHAMASH, and, in some myths, of ISHTAR, who was seen as the planet VENUS.

NANNA, the Sumerian name for the moon god, may originally have referred only to the full moon, whereas Su-en, later contracted to Sin, designated the crescent moon. At any rate, Nanna was intimately connected with the cattle herds that were the livelihood of the people in the marshes of the lower Euphrates River, where the cult developed. (The city of Ur, of the same region, was the chief center of the worship of Nanna.) The crescent, which later was definitely Nanna's emblem, was sometimes represented by the horns of a great bull. Nanna bestowed fertility and prosperity on the cowherds, governing the rise of the waters, the growth of reeds, the increase of the herd, and therefore the quantity of dairy products produced. His consort, Ningal, was a reed goddess. Each spring, Nanna's worshipers reenacted his mythological visit to his father, ENLIL, at Nippur with a ritual journey, carrying with them the first dairy products of the year. Gradually Nanna became more human: from being depicted as a bull or boat, because of his crescent emblem, he came to be represented as a cowherd or boatman.

Sin was represented as an old man with a flowing beard—a wise god—wearing a headdress of four horns surmounted by a crescent moon. The last king of Babylon, Nabonidus (reigned *c.* 556–539 BCE), attempted to elevate Sin to a supreme position within the Babylonian pantheon.

SIN, moral evil as considered from a religious standpoint. SIN is regarded in JUDAISM, CHRISTIANITY, and ISLAM as the deliberate and purposeful violation of the will of God.

Concepts similar to sin have been present in many cultures throughout history, where they were usually equated with an individual's failure to live up to external standards of conduct or with his or her violation of prohibitions, laws, or moral codes. In the OLD TESTAMENT, sin is viewed as a defiance of God's commandments or hatred of God. The NEW TESTAMENT added the doctrine that humanity's state of collective and individual sinfulness is a condition that JESUS came into the world to heal. Redemption through Christ could enable humans to overcome sin and thus to become whole. Both Christianity and Judaism see sin as being attributable to human pride, self-centeredness, and disobedience.

Theologians have divided sin into "actual" and "original." Actual sin consists of evil acts, whether of thought, word, or deed. ORIGINAL SIN is the morally vitiated condition in which one finds oneself at birth as a member of a sinful race. In GENESIS 3, this is depicted as a consequence of the first human sin, *i.e.,* that of ADAM AND EVE; this doctrine arises from human beings having come into the world not as isolated individuals but as members of a corporate race inheriting both GOOD AND EVIL features from its past history.

Actual sin is in turn subdivided, on the basis of its gravity, into mortal and venial. A mortal sin is a deliberate turning away from God; it is a sin in a grave matter that is committed in full knowledge and with the full consent of the sinner's will, and until it is repented it cuts the sinner off from God's sanctifying GRACE. A venial sin usually involves a less important matter and is committed with less awareness of wrongdoing. While a venial sin weakens the sinner's union with God, it is not a deliberate turning from him and so does not impede all God's sanctifying grace.

Actual sin is also subdivided again into material and formal. Formal sin is both wrong in itself and known by the sinner to be wrong; it therefore involves the sinner with personal guilt. Material sin, however, consists of an act that is wrong in itself (because it is contrary to God's law and human moral nature) but which the sinner does not know to be wrong and for which he or she is therefore not personally culpable.

SINAI, MOUNT \'sī-,nī, -nē-,ī\, *also called* Mountain of Moses, *or* Mount Hareh, *Hebrew* Har Sinai, *Arabic* Jabal

The summit of Mount Sinai
W.P. Jacob, Greenwich, Conn.

Mūsā, granitic peak of the south-central Sinai Peninsula, Janūb Sīnāʾ (South Sinai) *muḥāfaẓah* (governorate), Egypt. Mount Sinai is renowned as the principal site of divine revelation in Jewish history, where God is purported to have appeared to MOSES and given him the TEN COMMANDMENTS (EXODUS 20; Deuteronomy 5). According to Jewish tradition, the entire corpus of biblical text and interpretation was revealed to Moses on Sinai. The mountain is also sacred in both the Christian and Islamic traditions. A positive identification of the biblical Mount Sinai cannot be made, but Mount Sinai itself has long been accepted as the site in the traditions of JUDAISM, CHRISTIANITY, and ISLAM.

In the early Christian era the area was frequented by HERMITS, and in 530 CE the monastery of St. Catherine was built at the northern foot of the mountain. Still inhabited by a few monks of the autonomous ORTHODOX CHURCH of Mount Sinai, it is probably the world's oldest continuously inhabited Christian monastery.

SINGH SABHĀ \\'siŋ-gə-'sə-,bä, 'siŋ-\ (Punjabi: "Society of the Singhs," *i.e.*, Sikhs who have undergone *khande kī pahul*), 19th-century movement within SIKHISM which began as a defense against the proselytizing activities of Christians and Hindus. Its chief aims were the revival of the teachings of the Sikh GURŪS, the production of religious literature in Punjabi, and a campaign against illiteracy.

After the annexation of the KHĀLSĀ Rāj by the British in 1849, Christian missionaries increased activities in central Punjab. In 1853, Dalīp Singh, the last Sikh ruler, decided to join the Christian fold, and Harnam Singh, a Sikh aristocrat from Kapurthala, followed soon thereafter. Christian missionary activity was thus quickly perceived as a threat to local religious traditions, but it did not stand alone. The lower rung of the British administration in the Punjab was comprised of English-speaking Bengalis, who were largely BRAHMO SAMAJĪS (members of a Hindu reform movement). They actively established their branches in several Punjab cities in the 1860s. Punjabi Muslims concerned with saving their heritage formed the first Anjuman-i-Islamia (an association created to improve religious, educational, and social conditions in the Muslim community) in Lahore in 1869.

In response to these developments, Sikhs initiated the Singh Sabhā movement, forming the first unit in AMRITSAR in 1873. This was followed by a branch in Lahore, and by the end of the 19th century the number of Singh Sabhās exceeded 100. The movement sought to revive Sikh doctrine in its pristine purity. Building on the early 18th-century understanding of Singh identity as the accepted Sikh ideal, Singh Sabhā leaders undertook a major effort to make Sikhs aware of what they saw as correct doctrines and practices, using the newly arrived print culture to propagate Sikh history and literature. These leaders emphasized the religious significance of learning Punjābī written in the Gurmukhī script (a script developed by the Sikhs in India for their sacred literature), while simultaneously stressing the importance of Western education. They worked closely with the British administration, convincing them of the importance of treating the Sikhs as a distinct political community. Modern scholars have stressed the broad effects of the Singh Sabhā movement in establishing clear boundaries between Sikhs and other Punjabis, creating the sort of exlusively defined community behaviors and beliefs easily recognized as "religion" by Westerners and Western-educated Indians.

SIREN \\'sī-rən\, in Greek mythology, creature half-bird and half-woman who lured sailors to destruction by the sweetness of her song. According to Homer there were two Sirens on an island in the western sea between Aeaea and the rocks of Scylla. Later the number was usually increased to three. They were variously said to be the daughters of the sea god Phorcys or of the river god Achelous.

ODYSSEUS, advised by CIRCE, escaped their lure by stopping the ears of his crew with wax; he had himself tied to the mast so that he could not steer the ship out of course. Another story relates that when the ARGONAUTS sailed that way, ORPHEUS sang so divinely that none of them listened to the Sirens. In later legend, after one or other of these failures the Sirens committed suicide.

The Sirens may have originally have developed from an imported Near Eastern image of a bird-woman. Anthropologists explain the Near Eastern image as a soul-bird—*i.e.*, a winged ghost that stole the living to share its fate. In that respect the Sirens had affinities with the Harpies.

SIRHINDĪ, SHAYKH AḤMAD \sir-'hin-dē\ (b. 1564?, Sirhind, Patiala, India—d. 1624, Sirhind), Indian mystic and theologian who was largely responsible for the reassertion and revival in India of scripturalist Sunni ISLAM as a reaction against the inclusivist religious tendencies prevalent during the reign of the Mughal emperor AKBAR.

SHAYKH Aḥmad, who through his paternal line traced his descent from the CALIPH 'Umar I (the second caliph of Islam), received a traditional Islamic education at home and later at Siālkot (now in Pakistan). He reached maturity when Akbar, the renowned Mughal emperor, attempted to unify his empire by forming a new syncretistic faith (Dīn-e-Ilāhī), which sought to combine the various mystical forms of belief and religious practices of the many communities making up his empire.

Shaykh Aḥmad joined the mystical order NAQSHBANDĪYA, the most important of the Indian Sufi orders (*see* SUFISM), in 1593–94. He spent his life preaching against the inclination of Akbar and his successor, Jahāngīr (1605–27), toward PANTHEISM and SHI'ITE Islam. Of his several written works, the most famous is *Maktūbāt*, a compilation of his letters written in Persian to his friends in India and the region north of the Oxus River. In refuting the extreme monistic position of *waḥdat al-wujūd* (the concept of divine existential unity of God and the world, and hence humans), he advanced the notion of *waḥdat ash-shuhūd* (the concept of unity of vision). According to this doctrine, there exists only a subjective experience of unity, which occurs only in the mind of the believer; it has no objective counterpart in the real world. The former position, he felt, led to pantheism, which was contrary to SUNNI tenets.

His posthumous title Mujaddid-e Alf-e Sānī ("Renovator of the Second Millennium") was a reference to the fact that he lived at the beginning of the second millennium of the Muslim calendar. His teachings were not always popular in official circles. In 1619, by the orders of the emperor Jahāngīr who was offended by his aggressive opposition to Shi'ite views, Shaykh Aḥmad was temporarily imprisoned in the fortress at Gwalior. His burial place at Sirhind is still a site of PILGRIMAGE.

SISYPHUS \\'si-sə-fəs\, in Greek mythology, cunning king of Corinth who was punished in HADES by having repeatedly to roll a huge stone up a hill only to have it roll down again as soon as he had brought it to the summit. This fate is related in the *Odyssey*. In the *Iliad* Sisyphus, living at Ephyre (later Corinth), was the son of AEOLUS and the father of GLAUCUS. In post-Homeric times he was called the father of ODYSSEUS. Sisyphus was the reputed founder of the ISTHMIAN GAMES. Later legend related that when Death came to fetch him, Sisyphus chained him up so that no one died until ARES came to aid Death, and Sisyphus had to submit. In the meantime, Sisyphus had told his wife, Merope, not to perform the usual sacrifices and to leave his body unburied. Thus, when he reached the Underworld he was permitted

The punishment of Sisyphus, *detail of a painting on a Greek amphora, late 6th century* BCE; *in the State Collections of Classical Art, Munich*
Bildarchiv Foto Marburg—Art Resource

to return to punish her for the omission. Once back at home, he continued to live to a ripe old age before dying a second time.

SĪTĀ \'sē-,tä\, *also called* Jānakī (Sanskrit: "Furrow"), in Hindu mythology, the consort of RĀMA and the embodiment of wifely devotion and self-surrender, yet also, on occasion, of defiance. Her abduction by the DEMON king RĀVA-ṆA and subsequent rescue are the central incidents in the great Hindu epic, the RĀMĀYAṆA.

Sītā sprang from a furrow when King Janaka was plowing his field. Rāma won her as his bride by bending Shiva's bow, and she accompanied Rāma when he went into exile. When carried away to Laṅkā by Rāvaṇa, she kept herself chaste throughout her long imprisonment. On her return she asserted her purity and proved it by voluntarily undergoing an ordeal by fire. Rāma, however, banished her to the forest in deference to public opinion. There she gave birth to their two children, Kuśa and Lava. After they reached maturity and were acknowledged by Rāma to be his sons, she called upon her mother, Earth, to swallow her up.

Sītā is worshiped as the incarnation of LAKṢMĪ, the consort of VISHNU. Surveys have shown her to be the single most highly revered figure in the Hindu pantheon. Symbol of the sufferings and strengths of women, she is often regarded as exemplifying even higher standards of DHARMA (duty) and BHAKTI (love) than her celebrated husband. So central is her story to the *Rāmāyaṇa* that in many performances and retellings, especially those of women, that epic could more fittingly be described as a *Sītāyaṇa*.

ŚIVĀJĪ \shi-'vä-jē\, *also spelled* Shivājī (b. Feb. 19, 1630, or April 1627, Shivner, Pune, India—d. April 3, 1680, Rājgarh), Indian king (reigned 1674–80), founder of the Marāthā kingdom of India. This kingdom's security was based on religious toleration and on the functional integration of the BRAHMINS, Marāthās, and Prabhus.

Śivājī was descended from a line of prominent nobles. India at that time was under Muslim rule: the Mughals in the north and the Muslim SULTANS of Bijāpur and Golkundā in the south. Śivājī found the Muslim oppression and religious persecution of the Hindus so intolerable that, by the time he was 16, he had already convinced himself that he was the divinely appointed instrument of the cause of Hindu freedom—a conviction that was to sustain him throughout his life.

Collecting a band of followers, he began in about 1655 to seize territory from the Muslims. His depredations grew increasingly audacious, and a series of expeditions sent to chastise him proved ineffective. Ultimately faced with an army said to number 100,000 men, Śivājī was compelled to sue for peace; he and his son were placed under house arrest, where they lived under the threat of execution. They were, however, able to escape on Aug. 17, 1666, hiding in enormous baskets of sweets that Śivājī had delivered to the poor. His followers welcomed him back as their leader, and within two years he had expanded his domain. He collected tribute from Mughal districts and plundered their rich mart; he reorganized the army and instituted reforms for the welfare of his subjects; and he began the building of a naval force for trade and defense.

In the summer of 1674 Śivājī had himself enthroned with great fanfare as an independent sovereign. The Hindu majority rallied to him as their leader. He ruled his domain for six years, through a cabinet of eight ministers. A devout Hindu who prided himself on being a protector of his religion, he also respected the beliefs and protected the places of worship of both Christians and Muslims. Many Muslims were in his service.

Śivājī's last years were shadowed by the defection of his elder son, Śambājī, to the Mughals. Śambājī was reconciled to his father only with the utmost difficulty. The strain of guarding his kingdom from its enemies in the face of bitter domestic strife and discord among his ministers hastened Śivājī's end. He died after an illness in April 1680, in the mountain stronghold of Rājgarh, which he had made his capital.

SIYYUM \sē-'yùm, 'sē-ùm\ (Hebrew: "termination"), in JU-DAISM, celebration, either when a study group completes a tractate of the TALMUD or when the writing of a TORAH scroll is completed.

The study of the Talmud is frequently arranged so that a tractate can be finished on the eve of PASSOVER (Pesaḥ). Because a special meal (se'uddat mitzva) follows a study of the final passage, the firstborn is exempt from his usual fast on that day. When a Torah scroll is near completion, males are generally allowed the privilege of writing one of the final letters on the sacred manuscript. This event is followed by a celebration.

SKADI \'skä-the̱\, *Old Norse* Skaoi, in Norse mythology (*see* GERMANIC RELIGION), giantess wife of the sea god Njörd. In order to avenge the death of her father, the giant Thiazi, Skadi attacked the rival tribe of the gods (the AESIR) in AS-GARD, home of the gods. The Aesir, wanting to appease her anger, offered her the choice of one of their number for a husband, with the stipulation that she choose a god by his knees (or feet) alone. She chose Njörd, thinking that he was Balder; their marriage failed because Njörd preferred to live by the sea, and Skadi was happier in her father's home in the mountains (Thrymheim). In some sources, Skadi was known as the goddess of snowshoes. Another tradition relates that Skadi bore sons to the god ODIN.

SKANDA \'skən-də\, *also called* Kārttikeya, Kumāra, *or* Subrahmaṇya, Hindu god of war and the first-born son of

SHIVA. The gods wished for Skanda to be born in order to destroy the DEMON Tāraka, who had been granted a boon that he could only be killed by a son of Shiva. Shiva, however, was lost in meditation and was not attracted to PĀRVATĪ until struck by an arrow from the bow of KĀMA, the god of love. After the many years of abstinence Shiva's seed was so strong that the gods feared the result, and some accounts say it was deposited into the fire (from which comes the name Skanda, in Sanskrit: "Spurt of Semen").

One tradition has it that Skanda was reared by, or was even the son of, the Kṛttikās, six wives of ṛṣis who as stars make up the Pleiades, hence the name Kārttikeya ("Son of Kṛttikās"). He developed his six faces to drink the milk of his six nurses. He is also often depicted as a six-headed child held by his mother Pārvatī and accompanied by his brother GAṆEŚA. He is called Kumāra (Sankskrit: "Youth," "Boy") because he never married and in YOGA represents the power of chastity. He has enormous strength and is sometimes shown leading the army of the gods.

In South India, where the god originated as Murukaṉ before merging with the North Indian Skanda, he has a large following under the name Subrahmaṇya ("Dear to the Brāhmaṇas"), and he is also important among Hindus residing in Southeast Asia.

SKANDHA \\'skən-də\\ (Sanskrit: "aggregates"), *Pāli* khandha \\'kən-də\\, according to Buddhist thought, the five elements that constitute an individual's mental and physical existence. The self cannot be identified with any one of the parts, nor is it the total of the parts. They are: (1) matter (*rūpa*), the manifest form of the four elements—earth, air, fire, and water; (2) sensations (*vedanā*); (3) perceptions of sense objects (Sanskrit: *saṃjñā*; Pāli: *saññā*); (4) mental formations (SAṂSKĀRAS, or *sankhāra*s); and (5) consciousness (*vijñāna*, or

Skanda, stone sculpture from the Gupta period (c. 320–540); in Bharat Kala Bhavan, Varanasi, India
By courtesy of Bharat Kala Bhavan, Banaras Hindu University

viññāṇa). All individuals are subject to constant change, as the elements of consciousness are never the same. The individual may be compared to a river, which retains an identity though the drops of water that make it up are different from one moment to the next.

SKULL CULT, veneration of human skulls, usually those of ancestors, by various prehistoric and some modern peoples. Begun as early as the Early Paleolithic Period, the practice of preserving and honoring the skull apart from the rest of the skeleton continued in different forms throughout prehistoric times. Most authorities agree that the skulls were cleaned and set up for worship after death. Prehistoric peoples also paid special attention to animal skulls. This practice is believed to have been a type of hunting magic, whereas the human skulls were honored with the reverence accorded to heroic ancestors.

SLAVIC RELIGION, beliefs and practices of the ancient Slavic peoples of eastern Europe. Slavs are usually subdivided into East Slavs (Russians, Ukrainians, and Belarusians), West Slavs (Poles, Czechs, Slovaks, and Lusatians [Sorbs]), and South Slavs (Serbs, Croats, Slovenes, Macedonians, and Bulgars).

Cosmogony. A myth known to all Slavs tells how God ordered a handful of sand to be brought up from the bottom of the sea and created the land from it. Usually it is the Devil who brings up the sand; in Slovenia it is God himself. The 12th-century German missionary Helmold of Bosau recorded his surprise in encountering among the Slavs on the Baltic a belief in a single heavenly God, who ignored the affairs of this world, having delegated the governance of it to certain spirits begotten by him (*see* DEUS OTIOSUS). This is the only instance in which the sources allude to a hierarchy of divinities.

Divine beings. The 12th- to 13th-century *Kiev Chronicle* (*Povest vremennykh let*) enumerates seven Russian pre-Christian divinities: PERUN, Volos, Khors, DAZHBOG, STRIBOG, Simargla, and Mokosh. An earlier Russian text mentions SVAROG, apparently the son of Dazhbog. Of all these figures only two, Perun and Svarog, are at all likely to have been common to all the Slavs.

Common to Slavic Eurasia is a divinity called Zcerneboch (or Chernobog), the Black God, and Tiarnoglofi, the Black Head (Mind or Brain). The Black God survives in numerous Slavic curses, and the aid of the White God is sought to obtain protection or mercy in Bulgaria, Serbia, and Pomerania. This religious DUALISM of white and black gods is common to practically all the peoples of Eurasia.

In Estonia the prophet ELIJAH is considered to be the successor to UKKO, the ancient spirit of lightning. Similarly, the prophet Elijah replaces Elwa in Georgia and Zeus in Greece. It is therefore probable that, among the Slavs also, Elijah is to be considered a successor of Perun. According to a popular Serbian tradition, God gave the lightning to Elijah when he decided to retire from governing the world. The Serbian story agrees with Helmold's description of the distribution of offices by an inactive God. Elijah is a severe and peevish saint. It is rare that his feast day passes without some ill fortune. Fires—even spontaneous combustion—are blamed on him.

A similar complex may be seen if the Slavic Perun is equated with Perkunas, the lightning deity of the Lithuanians. In Latvia, creatures with black fur or plumage were sacrificed to Perkons, as they were to the fire god Agni in ancient India. Such deities are therefore generic deities of fire, not specifically celestial and even less to be regarded as supreme. Scholarly efforts to place Perun at the center of Slavic religion and to create around him a pantheon of deities of the Greco-Roman type cannot yield appreciable results. Russian sources treat Svarog, present as Zuarasici among the Liutici of Rethra (an ancient locality in eastern Germany), as a god of the drying-house fire. But the Belarusians of Chernigov, when lighting the drying-house fire, invoke Perun and not Svarog, as if Svarog (apparently from *svar*, "litigation" or "dispute," perhaps referring to the friction between the pieces of wood used to produce ignition) were an appellation of Perun.

Places of worship. Though the idols of which the Russian chronicles speak appear to have been erected outdoors, the German chronicles provide detailed descriptions of enclosed sacred places and temples among the Baltic Slavs. Such enclosures were walled and were usually of triangular shape at the confluence of two rivers, fortified with earthwork and palisades. Religious buildings contained wooden structures including a cell for the statue of a god, also made of wood and sometimes covered in metal. These representations, all anthropomorphic, very often had supernumerary body parts—*e.g.*, seven arms or three or five heads (Trigelavus, Suantevitus, and Porenutius, respectively). The temples were in the custody of priests, who enjoyed prestige and authority even in the eyes of the chiefs and received tribute and shares of military booty. HUMAN SACRIFICES, including eviscerations, decapitations, and TREPANNING (drilling of a hole into the human skull), had a propitiatory role in securing abundance and victory. One enclosure might contain up to four temples; those at Szczecin (Stettin), in northwestern Poland, were erected in close proximity to each other. They were visited annually by the whole population of the surrounding district, who brought oxen and sheep to be butchered. The boiled meat was distributed to all the participants without regard to sex or age. Dances and plays, sometimes humorous, enlivened the festival.

Communal banquets and related practices. The custom of communal banquets has been preserved into modern times in Russia in the *bratchina* (from *brat*, "brother"), in the *mol'ba* ("entreaty" or "supplication"), and in the *kanun* (a short religious service); in the Serbian *slava* ("glorification"); and in the *sobor* ("assembly") and *kurban* ("victim" or "prey") of Bulgaria. In Russia the feasts are dedicated to the memory of a deceased person or to the patron saint of the village and in Serbia to the protecting saint from whom the rod or *pleme* ("clan") took its name. In the Serbian *seoska slava*, or "*slava* of the village," the whole community participates and consumes in common the flesh of the victims prepared in the open air. In Russia sometimes the animals (or their flesh) are first brought into the church and perfumed with incense. The social unit sought to secure for itself the favor of a powerful figure of the past, or even of more than one, representing them in several forms on the same pillar or giving to their statues supernumerary body parts that would express their superhuman powers. A hollow bronze idol, probably ancient Russian, was found at Ryazan, Russia. The idol has four faces with a fifth face on its breast. The eastern Finns and the Ugrians venerated their dead in the same way, representing them as polycephalic (multiple-headed), and also held communal banquets in their honor.

Until the 19th century there survived here and there throughout the Danubian-Balkan region the custom of reopening graves three, five, or seven years after interment, taking out the bones of the corpses, washing them, wrapping them in new linen, and reinterring them. In protohistoric times the tumuli (BURIAL MOUNDS) of the mortuaries of the Krivichi (a populous tribe of the East Slavs of the north-

west)—the so-called long kurgans—contained cinerary urns buried in the TUMULUS together and all at one time. Such a practice could occur only as the consequence of collective and simultaneous CREMATION. There must, therefore, have existed a periodic cremation season or date, in preparation for which the corpses were temporarily exhumed.

SLEIPNIR \'slāp-nir\, in Norse mythology, the god Odin's magical horse. The offspring of LOKI, disguised as a mare, and SVADILFARI, the stallion of a giant, Sleipnir had eight legs and could ride in the air.

SMĀRTA SECT \'smär-tə\, orthodox Hindu sect composed primarily of BRAHMINS characterized by their allegiance to all the gods of the Hindu pantheon and by their adherence to rules of ritual and of conduct laid down in the ancient SŪTRA texts.

The *sūtra*s followed by the Smārta sect form part of the SMṚTI, a class of sacred texts that are considered to be of human authorship. Their greatest teacher and, according to some, the founder of the sect was the 8th-century philosopher ŚAMKARA. The monastery he founded at Sringeri, in Karnataka (formerly Mysore state), continues to be the center of the sect, and the head of the monastery, the *jagadguru* ("teacher of the world"), is the spiritual authority of the Smārtas in south India and Gujarāt and one of the chief religious personages in India.

The Smārtas pay allegiance in their worship to the five gods they regard as primary—SHIVA, VISHNU, ŚAKTI, SŪRYA, and GAŅEŚA—in the *pañcāyatana pūjā* ("five-shrines worship"), though Shiva is particularly favored among them today. They are active in all branches of learning and have earned the honorary title of *śāstrī* (Sanskrit: "men of learning"), or, in Tamil, *ayyar*, which often follows their names.

SMITH, JOSEPH \'smith\ (b. Dec. 23, 1805, Sharon, Vt., U.S.—d. June 27, 1844, Carthage, Ill.), American prophet whose writings, along with the BIBLE, provide the theological foundation of the Church of Jesus Christ of Latter-day Saints and other MORMON denominations.

Smith grew up in western New York at a time of intense religious REVIVALISM. He was a literate but unschooled child, remembered by his neighbors as a diviner who dug for buried treasure. One day in the woods, at the age of 14, Joseph Smith experienced an intense spiritual revelation of God and JESUS CHRIST. In 1827 he claimed that an ANGEL had directed him to buried golden plates whose engraved surfaces contained a history of the American Indians describing them as descendants of the lost tribes of Hebrews who centuries earlier had sailed to North America by way of the Pacific. This BOOK OF MORMON he translated from "reformed Egyptian" with the aid of special stones. Published in 1830, the book was offered as scientific evidence of his divine calling. Most non-Mormon scholars, however, regard the book as a collection of local legends of Indian origin, fragments of autobiography, and current religious and political controversies (especially that connected with the Anti-Masonic movement).

Smith claimed that the church that he organized on April 6, 1830, at Fayette, N.Y., restored the ancient, primitive Christian religion. The converts whom it attracted followed him from New York to Ohio, Missouri, and Illinois, as their neighbors were suspicious of the Mormons' unorthodox cooperative society ruled by an ecclesiastical oligarchy. Non-Mormons were also hostile toward the sect's practice of polygamy. Although Smith's revelation on this subject was not made public until 1852, and it is not supported in the *Book of Mormon*, there is evidence that he may have married as many as 50 wives. Publicly, however, he acknowledged only his first, Emma Hale Smith, who bore him nine children.

Smith governed by announcing periodic revelations on widely divergent matters. He combined elements of Jewish and Christian MYSTICISM with the goal of perpetual prosperity and sought to establish Mormonism as a complete way of life.

In 1839 Smith led his followers to Commerce, Ill., which he renamed Nauvoo. The Mormon population soon reached 20,000, making it the largest city in Illinois. Smith served as the city's mayor and commanded a part of the state militia, gaining a reputation as one of the West's most illustrious citizens.

In February 1844, when he announced his candidacy for the U.S. presidency, Mormon dissenters attacked him in their opposition newspaper on grounds of polygamy and political ambition. Smith ordered their press destroyed, and threats of mob violence followed. After Smith called out the Nauvoo militia to protect the town, he was charged with treason and imprisoned, along with his brother Hyrum. A mob of armed men with blackened faces stormed the jail on June 27 and murdered them both.

In addition to the *Book of Mormon*, the Latter-day Saints also use as scriptural sources Smith's *Doctrine and Covenants* (1835) and *The Pearl of Great Price* (1842).

Joseph Smith, detail of a painting by an unknown artist; in the Heritage Hall Museum, the Auditorium, Independence, Mo.
By courtesy of the Reorganized Church of Jesus Christ of Latter-day Saints, Independence, Mo.

SMITH, WILLIAM ROBERTSON (b. Nov. 8, 1846, Keig, Aberdeenshire, Scot.—d. March 31, 1894, Cambridge, Cambridgeshire, Eng.), encyclopedist, and scholar of Semitic languages, COMPARATIVE RELIGION, and social anthropology.

Smith was ordained a minister in 1870 on his appointment as professor of Oriental languages and Old Testament Exegesis at the Free Church College of Aberdeen. The authorities of the Free Church took strong exception to his early publications on biblical subjects; in 1877 they suspended him from his teaching duties. He was formally tried, and in 1880 the assembly dropped the indictment against him. After a second attack on his opinions, he was again suspended; in 1881 he was removed from his chair.

Appointed later that year as joint editor of *Encyclopædia Britannica*, he wrote *The Old Testament in the Jewish Church* (1881) and *The Prophets of Israel* (1882) and took academic positions at the University of Cambridge in 1883. His article "Sacrifice" (1886), his book *Kinship and Marriage in Early Arabia* (1885), and his most original work, *Lectures on the Religion of the Semites* (1889), are important landmarks in the study of comparative religion. These

works had a significant influence on such scholars as ÉMILE DURKHEIM and SIGMUND FREUD.

SMOHALLA \smə-'ha-lə\, *also called* Smowhola, Smoholler, Smokeholer, Smuxale, Snohallow, *and* Somahallie (b. *c.* 1815/20, Upper Columbia River, Oregon Country [U.S.]—d. 1895), North American Indian prophet, preacher, and teacher, one of a series of such leaders who arose in response to the encroachment of white settlers. He founded the Dreamers, a religious movement that emphasized traditional Indian values (*see also* NATIVE AMERICAN RELIGIONS).

Smohalla belonged to the Wanapum, a small Sahaptian-speaking tribe in what is now eastern Washington state. He grew up to become a celebrated MEDICINE MAN and warrior. After a fight with a rival, he left his home to travel and was away for several years. When he returned, he announced that he had died and been resurrected by God. He began to preach and by 1872 had a large following.

Smohalla taught that the Indians alone were real people, the first created, and that whites, blacks, and Chinese had been created later by God to punish the Indians for leaving their ancient ways. They must live as their fathers had done and, above all, not plow land or sign papers for land, which was against nature.

If they lived as their fathers had and followed the ritual of his Dreamer cult, they would be aided by the forces of nature, as well as by hordes of Indian dead who would be resurrected. God would drive away the non-Indians. The Dreamers got their name from the emphasis Smohalla placed on dreams sent to himself and his priests by God to direct them in the right ways. The ritual emphasized drumming, ringing of bells, and ecstatic dancing, all of which combined to bring on visions and exaltation.

Smohalla's influence spread among the Plateau Indians, Chief Joseph and the Nez Percé being among his most devoted followers. For a generation the cult was the greatest barrier to the U.S. government's efforts to settle the Indians of the region and to convert them to European ways, and it persisted for several years after Smohalla's death.

SMRTI \'smri-tē, 'smər-\ (Sanskrit: "recollection"), class of Hindu sacred literature in Sanskrit that is based on human memory, as distinct from Vedic literature, which is considered to be ŚRUTI, or revealed. Formally speaking, *smrti* is said to elaborate, interpret, and codify authoritative Vedic thought, but in practice Hindus usually have a greater familiarity with *smrti* SCRIPTURES than with Vedic *śruti*. Smrti texts include the KALPA SŪTRAS (important religious manuals); the PURĀNAS (compilations of ancient myth, legends, and history); the BHAGAVAD GĪTĀ; and very importantly the RĀMĀYANA and MAHĀBHĀRATA epics. The term *smrti* has come to refer particularly to texts relating to law and social conduct, such as the MANU-SMRTI ("Tradition of Manu"). Vernacular texts, which surely constitute the great bulk of "scripture" held dear by Hindus, largely escape the *śruti/ smrti* distinction, although some (especially Tamil hymns) have been claimed as "vernacular Veda" and others have been identified as *smrti* by the Sanskrit-knowing elite on grounds that only Sanskrit is the "language of the gods." Many dispute this point of view.

SMYTH, JOHN \'smith, 'smīth\, Smyth *also spelled* Smith (d. August 1612, Amsterdam), English religious libertarian and NONCONFORMIST minister, called "the Se-baptist" (self-baptizer), who is generally considered the founder of the organized BAPTISTS of England. He also influenced the Pilgrim

Fathers who immigrated to North America in search of religious toleration in 1620.

Smyth studied at Christ's College, Cambridge, where he was a fellow during 1594–98. He was a city preacher at Lincoln from 1600 to 1602, but he renounced Anglicanism in 1606 and became minister at Gainsborough, Lincolnshire, to a group of Separatists. With John Robinson, the minister to the Pilgrims in England and later in Holland, Smyth helped organize Separatists in Nottinghamshire. In 1608 both Smyth and Robinson went with their followers to Amsterdam. Adopting Baptist principles there, Smyth baptized first himself and then others, including THOMAS HELWYS, later an influential London Baptist.

He frequently revised his convictions according to conscience, a characteristic that naturally caused divisions among his congregation. When excommunicated by that congregation, he sought in vain for a favorable reception from Dutch MENNONITES. He eventually rejected the doctrine of ORIGINAL SIN and asserted the right of every Christian to hold his own religious views. Among Smyth's works is *The Differences of the Churches of the Separation* (probably 1608 or 1609).

SNORRA EDDA \'snȯr-rə-'e-də\, *or* Younger Edda, *or* Prose Edda, work by Snorri Sturluson. *See* EDDA.

SOCIAL GOSPEL, American religious social-reform movement that was prominent from about 1870 to 1920, especially among liberal Protestant groups dedicated to the betterment of industrialized society. Especially important were the works of Charles Monroe Sheldon (*e.g., In His Steps; "What Would Jesus Do?"*; 1897) and WALTER RAUSCHENBUSCH (*e.g., Christianity and the Social Crisis*; 1907). Labor reforms—abolition of child labor, a shorter workweek, a living wage, and factory regulation—constituted the Social Gospel's most prominent concerns. During the 1930s many of these ideals were realized through the rise of organized labor and the legislation of the New Deal.

SOCIETY AND RELIGION, relation between cultural elements termed "religious" and the wider social context. It has often been stated, ever since the work of ÉMILE DURKHEIM, that religion is preeminently social. This means two things: that religion is not simply reducible to individual, subjective experiences, and that religion is not simply a representation, in symbolic form, of a particular social system. As the CASTE system illustrates, religion and society are inextricably intertwined. Accordingly, such an experience as a religious conversion must first of all be understood as a social fact, before the experience, causes, or transformations that take place in the event can be discussed. It is best, therefore, to think of religion and society in the same way we think of society and language: just as the notion of a "private language" is a contradiction in terms, there can be no such phenomenon as a "private religion." That is, we are born into performing a religion just as we are born into speaking or performing a language. Society and religion are thus two elements whose relations and structures constitute human life; it is the relations between the two elements that describe what we mean by community. *See also* RITES OF PASSAGE.

SOCINUS, FAUSTUS \'faüs-təs-sō-'sī-nəs, 'fȯ-\, *Italian* Fausto (Paolo) Socini, Sozini, *or* Sozzini (b. Dec. 5, 1539, Siena [Italy]—d. March 3, 1604, Lusławice, Pol.), Italian-born lay theologian whose anti-Trinitarian teachings led to the founding of the Socinian sect and were later influential in the development of the theology of UNITARIANISM.

Socinus had no systematic education but early began to reject orthodox ROMAN CATHOLIC religious doctrines. He was denounced by the INQUISITION in 1559 and sought refuge until 1562 in Zürich. His first published work was an interpretation of the prologue of the Gospel According to John, in which he wrote of Christ as divine by office rather than by nature. After fifteen years in Florence and Basel living in outward conformity to the Roman Catholic church, he wrote *De Jesu Christo servatore* (completed 1578, published 1594), his most important work.

Central to Socinus' teaching was the attainment of eternal life through the study of divinely revealed SCRIPTURE. He saw Christ as a real man, though without SIN, who by his suffering taught men how to bear their own sufferings. In his view, faith is more than the belief that the teaching of Christ is true; faith also results in repentance for sins and in an obedience that leads to eternal life.

From 1587 to 1598 Socinus lived in Kraków, but in the latter year an enraged mob tried to take his life, and he took refuge at the neighboring village of Lusławice, where he spent his final years. His incomplete work, *Christianae religionis institutio*, is possibly the basis for the Racovian CATECHISM (1605), which is a thorough exposition of Socinian thought.

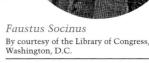

Faustus Socinus
By courtesy of the Library of Congress, Washington, D.C.

Unitarian theology, particularly the doctrines of the person and work of Christ, was greatly influenced by the introduction of Socinian writings to England in the 17th century.

SODOM AND GOMORRAH \'sä-dəm . . . gə-'mȯr-ə\, notoriously sinful cities in the biblical Book of GENESIS; sexual acts attributed to the Sodomites gave the city's name to the modern term sodomy. Sodom and Gomorrah constituted, along with the cities of Admah, Zeboiim, and Zoar (Bela), the five biblical "cities of the plain." Destroyed by "brimstone and fire" because of their wickedness (Genesis 19:24), Sodom and Gomorrah presumably were devastated by an earthquake about 1900 BCE. The cities are now possibly covered by the shallow waters south of Al-Lisān, a peninsula near the southern end of the Dead Sea in Israel.

Archaeological evidence indicates that the area was once fertile in the Middle Bronze Age (*c.* 2000–1500 BCE), with sufficient fresh water to sustain agriculture. Because of the fertile land, the biblical Lot, the nephew of the Hebrew patriarch ABRAHAM, selected the area of the cities of the Valley of Siddim (the Salt Sea, or the Dead Sea) to graze his flocks.

SOFER \sō-'fer, 'sō-fər\ (Hebrew: "scribe"), *also spelled* sopher, *plural* soferim, *or* sopherim \,sō-fe-'rēm\, any of a group of Jewish scholars who interpreted and taught biblical law and ethics from about the 5th century BCE to about 200 BCE; the first of the *soferim* was the biblical prophet EZRA. Previously the word had designated an important administrator connected with the Temple but without religious status. Ezra and his disciples initiated a tradition of rabbinic scholarship that remains to this day a fundamental feature of JUDAISM. Historically, the *soferim* are credited with initiating rabbinic studies, fixing the canon of OLD TESTAMENT scriptures, and, as copyists and editors, working to safeguard the purity of the original text.

Under foreign rule, the Jews enjoyed cultural autonomy and were allowed to govern themselves under the constitution of the Law of MOSES. The *soferim* became experts in the Law, applying the idealistic aspirations of the TORAH and ORAL TRADITION to the exigencies of daily life. With the decline of the *soferim*, their tradition of biblical scholarship was largely taken over by the PHARISEES and, in later generations, by the *tannaim*, *amoraim*, and *geonim* (see TANNA, AMORA, and GAON). The *soferim* disappeared about the 2nd century BCE, and NEW TESTAMENT references to "scribes" (often in connection with the Pharisees) are to doctors of the law, or jurists (usually called *ḥakhamim*), who gave legal advice to judges entrusted with administration of the law.

As time passed, *sofer* came to mean one who taught the BIBLE to children; it could also signify a copyist, notary, or calligrapher qualified to write Torah scrolls or other religious documents. The Talmud BAVLI (*c.* 500 CE) has a *soferim* tractate that stipulates how such work is to be performed. Modern Hebrew translates *sofer* as a "man of letters."

SŌKA-GAKKAI \\'sō-kä-'gäk-ˌkī\\ (Japanese: "Value-Creation Society"), lay religious group associated with the Japanese Buddhist sect Nichiren-shō-shū (see NICHIREN). Sōka-gakkai is the most successful of the new religious movements of the 20th century in Japan; but insofar as it draws upon the teachings of the Buddhist saint Nichiren, it belongs to a tradition dating from the 13th century.

The Sōka-gakkai follows an intensive policy of conversion (*shakubuku*, literally, "break and subdue"). Membership increased within a seven-year period (1951–57) from 3,000 to 765,000 families, and in the late 20th century the group claimed a membership of more than 6,000,000. In 1964 Sōka-gakkai established its own political party, Kōmeitō (Clean Government Party), which by the 1980s had become the third largest political party in Japan.

The association was founded in 1930 by Makiguchi Tsunesaburō under the name Sōka-kyōiku-gakkai ("Value-Creation Educational Society"). The society suffered from the government's repressive policies during World War II and for a time was disbanded. Makiguchi died in detention during this period. His chief disciple, Toda Jōsei, revived the organization in 1946, renaming it Sōka-gakkai.

In common with other Nichiren movements, Sōka-gakkai places great emphasis on the LOTUS SUTRA.

SŌKKURAM \\'sòk-'kùr-'äm\\, Buddhist artificial-cave temple on the crest of Mount T'oham, near the Pulguk Temple, Kyŏngju, South Korea. Built in the 8th century, Sŏkkuram is a domed circular structure of granite blocks. A square anteroom houses eight guardian figures in relief. On an elevated lotus pedestal a large statue of the BUDDHA GOTAMA (or AMITĀBHA, according to some) seated, about 11.5 feet high, carved out of a single block of granite, occupies the center of the main chamber. On the surrounding walls are 15 slabs in relief depicting BODHISATTVAS and 10 disciples in atten-

dance. The sculpture of this cave temple is one of the finest achievements of Buddhist art in the East.

SOL \\'säl\\, in ROMAN RELIGION, name of two distinct sun gods at Rome. The original Sol, or Sol Indiges, had a shrine on the Quirinal, an annual sacrifice on August 9, and another shrine, together with Luna, in the Circus Maximus.

After the importation of various sun cults from Syria, the Roman emperor Elagabalus (reigned 218–222 CE) built a temple to Sol Invictus on the Palatine and attempted to make his worship the principal religion at Rome. The emperor Aurelian (reigned 270–275) later reestablished the worship and erected a magnificent temple to Sol in the Campus Agrippae. The worship of Sol as special protector of the emperors and of the empire remained the chief imperial cult until the rise of CHRISTIANITY.

SOLAR DEITY, divinity conceived of as sovereign, all-seeing and usually active in terrestrial life, often identified with the supreme deity of a culture or with the ruler.

SOLOMON \\'sä-lə-mən\\, *Hebrew* Shlomo (fl. mid-10th century BCE), son and successor of DAVID and traditionally regarded as the greatest king of ISRAEL. He maintained his dominions with military strength and established Israelite colonies outside his kingdom's borders. The crowning achievement of his vast building program was the famous temple at his capital, Jerusalem (see TEMPLE OF JERUSALEM).

Nearly all that is factually known of Solomon comes from the BIBLE (especially 1 Kings 1–11 and 2 Chronicles 1–9). His father, David, was a self-made king, who founded the Judaean dynasty and carved out an empire from the border of Egypt to the Euphrates River. In addition, he made common cause with King Hiram of Tyre, forming a land and sea alliance that endured into Solomon's reign. Solomon's mother was BATHSHEBA, formerly the wife of David's Hittite general, Uriah. It was only through her efforts, in concert with the prophet Nathan, that Solomon, who was younger than several of his brothers, was anointed king while David was still alive.

Empire builder. As soon as he acceded to the throne, Solomon consolidated his position by liquidating his opponents ruthlessly, one by one. Once rid of his foes, he established his friends in the key posts of the military, governmental, and religious institutions. Solomon also strengthened his position through marital alliances. Although the astonishing harem of Solomon—700 wives and 300 concubines—recorded in 1 Kings is no doubt an exaggeration of popular tradition, the figures do indicate his position as a grand monarch. Such a ménage brought prestige as well as pleasure; in addition, the marriages were a form of diplomacy.

The passage in 2 Chronicles 8 recounts Solomon's successful military operations in Syria, where his targets included Tadmor-Palmyra, a caravan oasis city in the desert, midway between Syria and Mesopotamia. His aim was the control of a great overland trading route. To consolidate his interests in the province, he planted Israelite colonies to look after military, administrative, and commercial matters. This network of Solomon's far-flung trading posts would eventually form the nucleus of the first great JEWISH DIASPORA.

Palestine was strategically located for trade by land and sea. By land, it connects Asia and Africa, with ports on the Atlantic-Mediterranean and Red Sea–Indian Ocean waterways. The nature of Solomon's empire was predominantly commercial, and so it served him and friendly rulers to increase trade by land and sea. A celebrated episode in the reign of Solomon is the visit of the Queen of Sheba. Her southern Arabian kingdom lay along the Red Sea route into the Indian Ocean, and her terrain was rich in gold, frankincense, and myrrh. Solomon needed her products and her trade routes for maintaining his commercial network; she needed Solomon's cooperation for marketing her goods in the Mediterranean via his Palestinian ports.

Solomon's Temple. The demand for fortresses and garrison cities throughout his homeland and empire made it necessary for Solomon to embark on a vast building program; the prosperity of the nation made such a program possible. He was especially lavish with his capital, Jerusalem, where he erected a city wall, a construction called the Millo, the royal palace, and the famous Temple. Around Jerusalem, he built facilities, including shrines, for the main groups of foreigners on trading missions in Israel. Later generations, in less secure and less prosperous times, destroyed those shrines in a parochial spirit that could not accommodate itself to Solomon's ecumenical outlook.

The vigor of Solomon's building program made it oppressive. Men had to put in one month out of every three in forced labor. In theory, such labor was to be performed by the Canaanites—not by the noble Hebrew tribesmen, who were supposed to be the administrators, priests, and fighters. But Solomon's demands were such that there were not enough Canaanites to go around, so that Israelites were forced to do menial labor for the crown.

Solomon was a vigorous administrator, and he reorganized the old division of the nation into 12 tribes into 12 administrative districts, deviating, for the most part, from the tribal boundaries. The figure of 12 was retained because each district was to "support the palace" (*i.e.*, shoulder federal obligations) for one of the 12 months in the year. Each district had its royally appointed governor, and a chief ruled over the 12 governors. Another important but unpopular appointee of the king was the chief of taxation; taxes were exacted most commonly in the form of forced labor and in kind (taxes paid in a commodity, such as grain).

His legendary wisdom. Solomon also became famous as a sage. The biblical Book of Proverbs contains collections of aphorisms and other wise teachings attributed to him. He was also famed as a poet who composed 1,005 songs, and the biblical Song of Solomon is (spuriously) attributed to him in the opening verse. Post-biblical tradition attributed later works to him: the apocryphal Wisdom of Solomon and the *Odes of Solomon* and *Psalms of Solomon* are tributes to him as sage and poet, respectively.

Decline of the kingdom. During Solomon's reign, it is suspected that the increase in Israel's wealth was matched by an increase in extravagance and that the wealth was not diffused to the people. It is also considered possible that Solomon's treatment of the northern tribes showed favoritism to his own tribe of JUDAH. When his son Rehoboam succeeded him, the northern tribes wanted to know his policy concerning the burdens borne by the people. Rehoboam ill-advisedly announced a harsher course, whereupon the northern tribes seceded and formed their own Kingdom of Israel, leaving the descendants of Solomon with the southern Kingdom of Judah. Thus Solomon's empire was lost beyond recall, and even the homeland was split into two, often hostile, kingdoms.

SOLOVYOV, VLADIMIR SERGEYEVICH \sə-lə-'vyȯf\, *also spelled* Soloviev (b. Jan. 16 [Jan. 28, New Style], 1853,

Moscow, Russia—d. July 31 [Aug. 13], 1900, Uzkoye, near Moscow), Russian philosopher and mystic who, reacting to European rationalist thought, attempted a synthesis of religious philosophy, science, and ethics in the context of a universal CHRISTIANITY uniting the EASTERN ORTHODOX and ROMAN CATHOLIC churches under papal leadership.

He was the son of the historian Sergey M. Solovyov. After a basic education in languages, history, and philosophy at his Orthodox home, he took his doctorate at Moscow University in 1874 with the dissertation "The Crisis of Western Philosophy: Against the Positivists." After travels in the West, he wrote a second thesis, a critique of abstract principles, and accepted a teaching post at the University of St. Petersburg, where he delivered his celebrated lectures on "Godmanhood" (1880). This appointment was later rescinded because of Solovyov's clemency appeal for the March 1881 assassins of Tsar Alexander II. He also encountered official opposition to his writings and to his activity in promoting the union of Eastern Orthodoxy with the Roman Catholic church.

Solovyov criticized Western empiricist and idealist philosophy for attributing absolute significance to partial insights and abstract principles. Drawing on the writings of Benedict de Spinoza and G.W.F. Hegel, he regarded life as a dialectical process, involving the interaction of knowledge and reality through conflicting tensions. Assuming the ultimate unity of Absolute Being, termed God in the Judeo-Christian tradition, Solovyov proposed that the world's multiplicity, which had originated in a single creative source, was undergoing a process of reintegration with that source. Solovyov asserted, by his concept of Godmanhood, that the unique intermediary between the world and God could only be man, who alone is the vital part of nature capable of knowing and expressing the divine idea of "absolute unitotality" in the chaotic multiplicity of real experience. Consequently, the perfect revelation of God is Christ's INCARNATION in human nature.

For Solovyov, ethics became a dialectical problem of basing the morality of human acts and decisions on the extent of their contribution to the world's integration with ultimate divine unity, a theory expressed in his *The Meaning of Love* (1894).

SOMA \'sō-mə\, in ancient Indian cult worship, unidentified plant, the juice of which was a fundamental offering of the Vedic sacrifices. The stalks of the plant were pressed between stones, and the juice was filtered through sheep's wool and then mixed with water and milk. After first being offered as a LIBATION to the gods, the remainder of the *soma* was consumed by the priests and the sacrificer. It was highly valued for its exhilarating, probably hallucinogenic, effect. The personified deity Soma was the "master of plants," the healer of disease, and the bestower of riches.

The *soma* plant grows in the mountains, but its true origin is believed to be heaven, whence it was brought to earth by an eagle, and the pressing of *soma* was associated with the fertilizing rain. In the post-Vedic classical period, *soma* is identified with the moon, which wanes when *soma* is drunk by the gods but which is periodically reborn.

SOMNĀTH \sōm-'nät\, *also called* Pātan-Somnāth, *or* Somnāth-Patān, ancient ruined city, southwestern Gujarāt state, west-central India. It is the site of the temple of Śiva as Somanātha (which means "lord of the SOMA" and, by extension, "lord of the moon"). The temple was sacked by the Turkic Muslim invader Maḥmud of Ghazna in 1024–25 CE.

Reconstructed in 1169, it was destroyed again in the final Muslim invasions of the late 13th century. Subsequently rebuilt and destroyed on several occasions, it was reconstructed again beginning in 1951. According to an ancient tradition in the MAHĀBHĀRATA, Somnāth was the scene of the internecine massacre of the Yādava clan and of the subsequent death of KRISHNA. Recent excavations there have revealed a settlement dating from about 1500 BCE.

SON: *see* ZEN.

SORANUS \sȯ-'rā-nəs\, in RO-MAN RELIGION, Underworld deity worshiped on Mount Soracte in southern Etruria. As priests, the *hirpi Sorani* celebrated a rite in which they marched barefoot over burning coals. Soranus was identified with Dis, the Roman god of the underworld, and he also had a female partner, Feronia, a goddess of uncertain attributes.

SORCERY, use of power gained from the assistance or control of spirits. Sorcery is distinguished by some writers from WITCHCRAFT in that it may be practiced by anyone with the appropriate knowledge, using charms, SPELLS, potions, and the like; whereas witchcraft is considered to result from an inherent mystical power, often inherited, and to be practiced by invisible means. During the witch-hunts of the 16th and 17th centuries, courts frequently regarded witches and sorcerers alike as candidates for burning.

SOTERIA \ˌsō-te-'rē-ə\ (from Greek: "Deliverance"), in HELLENISTIC RELIGIONS, any sacrifice or series of sacrifices performed either in commemoration of or in expectation of deliverance from a crisis; also used for a large-scale commemorative festival held at planned intervals. Sixteen Soteria festivals are known; the most famous was that at DELPHI celebrating the defeat of the Celts in 279–278 BCE.

SŌTŌ \'sō-ˌtō\, *Chinese* Ts'ao-tung \'tsaù-'dùŋ\, largest of the ZEN Buddhist sects in Japan. It follows the method of quiet and meditation (*zazen*) as a means of obtaining Enlightenment. The sect was founded in China in the 9th century by Liang-chieh and Pen-chi. It was transmitted to Japan in the 13th century by DŌGEN and further popularized in the 13th–14th century by Keizan.

The headquarters of the sect are the Eihei Temple (founded in 1244 in what is now Fukui prefecture) and the Sōji

The circle has special power and significance in sorcery. The Magic Circle *by John William Waterhouse, 1886; in the Tate Gallery, London*
Tate Gallery, London—Art Resource

Temple (founded in 1321 in what is now Ishikawa prefecture and moved in 1911 to Yokohama). *Compare* RINZAI.

SOUL, immaterial aspect or essence of a human being, conjoined with the body and separable at death.

Many cultures have recognized some incorporeal principle of human life or existence corresponding to the soul, and many have attributed souls to all living things. There is evidence even among prehistoric peoples of a belief in an aspect distinct from the body and residing in it. Different religions and philosophers have developed a variety of theories as to its nature, its relationship to the body, and its origin and mortality.

Both the Egyptians and the ancient Chinese conceived of a dual soul. The Egyptian KA (breath) survived death but remained near the body, while the spiritual BA proceeded to the region of the dead. The Chinese distinguished between a lower, sensitive soul, which disappears with death, and a rational principle, the *hun,* which is the object of ANCESTOR WORSHIP. The early Hebrews apparently had a concept of the soul, related to the concept of breath, but established no distinction between the ethereal soul and the corporeal body; later Jewish writers would develop the idea of the soul further.

Ancient Greek concepts of the soul varied considerably according to the particular era and philosophical school. The Epicureans considered the soul to be made up of atoms like the rest of the body. For the Platonists, the soul was an immaterial and incorporeal substance, akin to the gods yet part of the world of change and becoming. Christian concepts of a body-soul dichotomy originated with the ancient Greeks and were introduced into Christian theology at an early date by GREGORY OF NYSSA and by AUGUSTINE. Augustine spoke of the soul as a "rider" on the body, with the soul representing the "true" person. However, although body and soul were separate, yet still, it was not possible to conceive of a soul without its body.

Just as there have been different concepts of the relation of the soul to the body, there have been numerous ideas about when the soul comes into existence and when and if it dies. Pythagoras held that the soul was of divine origin and existed before and after death. Plato and Socrates also accepted the immortality of the soul, while Aristotle considered only part of the soul, the *noûs,* or intellect, to have that quality. Epicurus believed that both body and soul ended at death. The early Christian philosophers adopted the Greek concept of the soul's immortality and thought of the soul as being created by God and infused into the body at conception.

In HINDUISM, each ĀTMAN ("breath," or "soul") is considered to have been created at the beginning of time and imprisoned in an earthly body at birth. At the death of the body, the atman passes into a new body, its position in the Chain of Being determined by KARMA, or the cumulative consequences of actions. The cycle of death and rebirth (SAMSĀRA) is eternal according to some Hindus but others say it persists only until the soul has attained karmic perfection, thus merging with the Absolute. BUDDHISM negates the concept of ātman, asserting that any sense of the individual soul or self is illusory.

SOUL LOSS, departure of the soul from the body and its failure to return, which in many cultures, especially those in Siberia, Mesoamerica, and the northwestern coast of North America, is believed to be the cause of illness. Though the soul may wander inadvertently when its owner's guard is relaxed—*e.g.*, in sleep or when sneezing or yawning—the most common cause of soul loss is its enticement and capture by an adversary through WITCHCRAFT.

When the owner is conscious of the danger, the soul may be prevented from wandering by ritual measures. In the case of witchcraft, the retrieval of the soul from an enemy's power requires complex techniques and the services of a religious specialist.

SPELL, words uttered in a set formula with magical intent. The correct recitation, often with accompanying gestures, is considered to unleash supernatural power. Some societies believe that incorrect recitation can not only nullify the magic but cause the death of the practitioner.

The language of spells is sometimes archaic and is not always understood by the reciter. In some cases meaningless but familiar terms are believed to be efficacious because of their traditional value. Much magical language, however, is clearly and directly correlated with the aim of the recital. Through analogy it represents and foreshadows the technical achievement, and metaphor and simile are freely used. An example is a Maori spell giving speed and grace to a canoe, which speaks of the swiftness of a bird on the wing and the lightness of a seagull and which uses such onomatopoeic effects as speed noises or the wailing of the sea.

In blessings and curses, which are similar types of verbal expressions, the efficacy of the recitation is also believed to be connected to the magical power of the words themselves or to the sacred power of a supernatural being. Certain gestures as well as words may be bound up with the act of blessing, as in putting one's hands on the head of the person being blessed. The curse, a wish to cause harm or misfortune, is usually directed against others, although an important form of curse, associated with oaths, contracts, and treaties, is conditionally directed against oneself, should one fail to keep one's word or tell the truth.

SPENER, PHILIPP JAKOB \ˈshpā-nər\ (b. Jan. 23, 1635, Rappoltsweiler, Upper Alsace [now Ribeauvillé, Fr.]—d. Feb. 5, 1705, Berlin, Prussia [Germany]), theologian, author, and a leading figure in German PIETISM, a movement among 17th- and 18th-century Lutherans that stressed personal improvement and upright conduct.

During his studies at Strassburg (1651–59) Spener developed an interest in reforming Lutheran orthodox theology and practice, objecting to the rigidity of ecclesiastical structures and the lack of moral discipline among the clergy. In 1666, Spener became president of the Lutheran Church at Frankfurt am Main, where he began his *collegia pietatis* ("schools of piety"), devotional gatherings intended to encourage personal spiritual growth, prayer, and BIBLE study. His correspondence with the German clergy contributed to the growth of Pietism, as did his major work, *Pia Desideria* (1675; *Pious Desires*), which outlined Pietism's basic program and earned Spener a reputation as the movement's spokesman. In 1686 he was made first court CHAPLAIN at Dresden, then the most valued position in the German Lutheran Church, but his views soon aroused opposition. Attacks upon Pietism came from the orthodox Lutherans at the University of Leipzig and from the Saxon court, whose elector, John George III, had been rebuked by Spener for drunkenness.

Spener moved to Berlin in 1691 to become provost of St. Nicholas' Church. There he gained from the Brandenburg-Prussian court the support that enabled him to carry out numerous reforms. Spener obtained positions for his disciples at the University of Halle, founded on a Pietist basis in 1694. By the time of Spener's death, Pietism was well established in Germany, and its influence reached to England and eventually to the British colonies in America.

SPENTA MAINYU \span-ˈtä-mīn-ˈyü\, in ZOROASTRIANISM, HOLY SPIRIT, created by AHURA MAZDĀ to oppose the Destructive Spirit, Angra Mainyu. Spenta Mainyu is an aspect of Ahura Mazdā himself. According to Zoroastrian belief, Spenta Mainyu protects and maintains the sky, water, earth, plants, and children yet to be born.

SPHAGIA \ˈsfä-jē-ə, ˈsfa-gē-ə\, in ancient GREEK RELIGION, term for the propitiatory sacrifice made to the CHTHONIC (Underworld) deities and forces (including the winds and the spirits of the dead). The *sphagia* was not eaten by the worshipers, as in the cults of the Olympian gods; instead the victim was cut to pieces and burned, buried, or cast into a river.

SPHINX, mythological creature with a lion's body and human head, an important image in Egyptian and Greek art and legend. It was once thought that the word *sphinx* was derived by Greek grammarians from the verb *sphingein* ("to bind," or "to squeeze"). Such an origin is unlikely, however, and leaves unexplained the early variants Sphix and Phix, the latter of which is the oldest known form, found in Hesiod's *Theogony*. Herodotus, who visited Egypt in the 5th century BCE, applied the word *androsphinx*, "male-headed sphinx," to statues he saw at Sais in the Nile Delta. It has been hypothesized that the Greek application of *sphinx* to lion-bodied Egyptian figures—and perhaps even the form of the Greek word—was influenced by an Egyptian epithet that may be phoneticized as *shep-ankh*, "living image," applied to representations of gods, or of pharaohs viewed as "living images" of gods such as Re.

In myth the winged sphinx of Boeotian Thebes was said to have terrorized the people by demanding the answer to a riddle taught her by the Muses—what is it that has one voice and yet becomes four-footed and two-footed and three-footed?—and devouring a man each time the riddle was answered incorrectly. Eventually OEDIPUS gave the proper answer: man, who crawls on all fours in infancy, walks on two feet when grown, and leans on a staff in old age; the sphinx thereupon killed herself. From this tale ap-

The Great Sphinx at Giza, Egypt, 4th dynasty
E. Streichan—Shostal Assoc.

and the wings developed a beautiful curving form unknown in Asia. Sphinxes decorated vases, ivories, and metal works and in the late Archaic period occurred as ornaments on temples; their appearance on temples suggests a protective function. By the 5th century clear illustrations of the encounter between Oedipus and the sphinx appeared on vase paintings, usually with the sphinx perched on a column. Other monuments of classical age showed Oedipus in armed combat with the sphinx and suggested an earlier stage of the legend in which the contest was physical instead of mental.

parently grew the legend that the sphinx was omniscient, and even today the wisdom of the sphinx is proverbial.

The earliest and most famous example in art is the colossal recumbent Sphinx at Giza, Egypt, dating from the reign of King Khafre (4th king of 4th dynasty, c. 2575–c. 2465 BCE). This is known to be a portrait statue of the king, and the sphinx continued as a royal portrait type through most of Egyptian history. (Arabs, however, know the Sphinx of Giza by the name of Abū al-Hawl, or "Father of Terror.") The sphinx did not occur in Mesopotamia until about 1500 BCE, when it was clearly imported from the Levant. In appearance the Asian sphinx differed from its Egyptian model most noticeably in the addition of wings to the leonine body, a feature that continued through its subsequent history in Asia and the Greek world. Another innovation was the female sphinx, which first began to appear in the 15th century BCE. On seals, ivories, and metalwork they were portrayed sitting on their haunches, often with one paw raised, and were frequently paired with a lion, a GRIFFIN (part eagle and part lion), or another sphinx.

About 1600 BCE the sphinx first appeared in the Greek world. Objects from Crete at the end of the middle Minoan period and from the shaft graves at Mycenae throughout the late Helladic age showed the sphinx characteristically winged. Although derived from the Asian sphinx, the Greek examples customarily wore a flat cap with a flame-like projection on top.

After 1200 BCE the depiction of sphinxes disappeared from Greek art for about 400 years, though they continued in Asia in forms and poses similar to those of the Bronze Age. By the end of the 8th century, the sphinx reappeared in Greek art and was common down to the end of the 6th century. The later Greek sphinx was almost always female and usually wore a long-tiered wig; the body became graceful,

SPIRITUAL, in North American white and black folk music, an English-language folk HYMN.

White spirituals include both revival and camp-meeting songs and a smaller number of other hymns. They derived variously, notably from the "lining out" of psalms, dating from at least the mid-17th century. Where congregations could not read, a leader intoned (lined out) the psalm text, one line at a time, alternating with the congregation's singing of each just-given line to a familiar melody. The tune, sung slowly, was ornamented with passing notes, turns, and other graces, each singer producing his own improvised embellishment at the pitch level he found comfortable.

A second source was the singing of hymns (as opposed to psalms only), reintroduced by such 18th-century religious dissenters as John and CHARLES WESLEY, the founders of METHODISM. Hymn verses were composed and set to borrowed melodies, often secular folk tunes. Many of these evangelical hymns passed into ORAL TRADITION.

In the late 18th century and up to the mid-19th, there were several waves of religious REVIVALISM. The resulting camp meetings and revivals were marked by spontaneous mass singing. It is not completely known how the camp-meeting songs and revival spirituals were sung; but it is thought that they were sung unharmonized, the tune typically begun by the high male voices, the women and basses joining in an octave (or other comfortable interval) above or below. A call-and-response pattern (as in lining out) may have at times been used.

The texts had verses and refrains that wandered from song to song; these and a common stock of folk-melody fragments allowed new songs to be improvised upon inspiration. The songs were passed on orally, though many were eventually written down in folk hymnbooks using special shape-note notation.

A 19th-century offshoot of the spiritual was the gospel song. Influenced by "correct" European music, it had composed melodies and texts, was sung with instrumental accompaniment, and (unlike the folk hymns) was written to be harmonized.

The black spirituals developed mostly from white rural folk hymnody. The borrowing of melodies with pentatonic (five-note) and major scales is especially prominent. In voice quality, vocal effects, and type of rhythmic accompaniment, black spirituals differ markedly from white ones. Black spirituals were sung not only in worship but also as work songs; the text imagery often reflects concrete tasks.

Musically, it is believed that a complex intermingling of African and white folk-music elements occurred and that complementary traits of African music and white American folksong reinforced each other. For example, the call-and-response pattern occurs in both, as do certain scales and the variable intonation of certain notes. Most authorities see clear African influence in vocal style and in the complex polyrhythmic clapped accompaniments. African tradition also included polyphonic and choral singing. The ring shout (a religious dance usually accompanied by the singing of spirituals and clapped rhythms) is also of African ancestry.

After the Civil War the black spirituals were "discovered" by Northerners and either developed toward harmonized versions, often sung by trained choirs, or, conversely, preserved in the older traditional style, especially in rural areas and certain sects.

Like the white gospel song, the modern black gospel song is a descendant of the spiritual and is instrumentally accompanied. Black GOSPEL MUSIC is closely related to secular black music (as is the spiritual to the work song and blues) and often includes jazz rhythms and instruments alongside traditional clapped accompaniment and often dance. Though gospel songs are usually composed, the melodies are taken for improvisational bases in church services, as popular tunes are improvised upon in jazz.

SPIRITUAL ASSEMBLY, in the BAHĀ'Ī FAITH, any of numerous administrative units that conduct an extensive work of missions, publication, education, and general philanthropy. Spiritual assemblies consist of nine members elected or designated annually on the local, national, and world levels during the holy days (April 21, April 29, May 2) commemorating the declaration of the founder's mission. Since they are said to be invested with their authority by God himself, the members of the spiritual assemblies have absolute jurisdiction over their electorates and are not answerable to them for their decisions and actions. Financial support comes from voluntary contributions from the community.

A local spiritual assembly exists in any community of nine or more Bahā'ī members. In the mid-1980s there were some 33,000 local assemblies. National spiritual assemblies—numbering 148 by the mid-1980s—appear when there are enough local assemblies in a country to elect a 19-member convention, which in turn will elect the nine members of the national group from among all Bahā'īs in the country. World leadership of the faith was held by SHOGHI EFFENDI RABBĀNĪ as Guardian of the Cause of God until his death in 1957; since 1963, this leadership has been assumed by the highest order of spiritual assembly, the Universal House of Justice, a body elected by the national spiritual assemblies and possessing the sole right to institute new laws or abrogate the old laws laid down in Bahā'ī sacred SCRIPTURES.

SPIRITUALISM, belief, or practices based upon the belief, that departed souls hold intercourse with mortals, usually through a medium by means of physical phenomena or during abnormal mental states, such as trances.

Within the terms of spiritualism, "spirit" is the essential part of the human. After the death of the body the spirit lives on. The "spirit world" is the world of disembodied spirits, while a "medium" is a person on earth who is sensitive to vibrations from the spirit world and is able to convey messages from that world and to produce other spiritualist phenomena. A "control" is a disembodied spirit who gives messages to a medium who in turn gives them to men and women on Earth.

The attempt to communicate with discarnate spirits seems to be one of the forms that religion may take in human societies and to be widely distributed in space and time. Practices very like those of a modern spiritualistic seance have been reported in various parts of the world, as, for example, Haiti and among Native North Americans, and there is no reason for supposing that these are of recent origin. The record of an ancient materialization seance is preserved in the OLD TESTAMENT account of Saul's visit to the witch of Endor, in the course of which a materialization appeared that was regarded by the king as the prophet Samuel (1 Samuel 28:7–19).

ŚRĀDDHA \'shrä-də, 'srä-\, in HINDUISM, ceremony performed in honor of a dead ancestor. The rite is both a social and a religious responsibility enjoined on all male Hindus (with the exception of some SANNYĀSĪS, or ascetics).

The rite is performed for the deceased father, grandfather, and great-grandfather and also for the mother, grandmother, and great-grandmother. It is intended to nourish, protect, and support the spirits of the dead in their pilgrimage from the lower to higher realms, preceding their REINCARNATION and reappearance on Earth. The rites are performed between the 11th and 31st days after death, depending on CASTE traditions, and at regular intervals thereafter. During a *śrāddha* ceremony, rice balls (*piṇḍa*s) are offered to the deceased, which constitute a "body" for the dead person in the *preta* (or ghostly) world. The first annual death anniversary is observed by a *śrāddha* ceremony that enables the deceased (*preta*) to be admitted into the assembly of forefathers (PITṚ).

SRAOSHA \sraŭ-'shä, -'sha\, in ZOROASTRIANISM, divine being who is the messenger of AHURA MAZDĀ, the embodiment of the divine word, and the mediator between human and divine. His name, related to the Avestan word for "hearing," signifies man's obedient hearkening to Ahura Mazdā's word and also signifies Ahura Mazdā's omnipresent listening. Zoroastrians believe that no ritual is valid without his presence, and he is very prominent in their liturgy. He has, in addition, a protective role. Three times each night Ahura Mazdā sends Sraosha to combat the DEMONS that harass men. His strongest weapon is prayer. In the end of time, he will be the agent of the final extermination of evil. Sraosha also leads the righteous soul through the ordeal of judgment three days after its body's death.

ŚRAUTA SŪTRA \'shraŭ-tə-'sü-trə\, any of a number of Hindu ritual manuals used by priests engaged in the performance of the Vedic sacrifices requiring three fires and the services of many specialized priests. The manuals are called *śrauta* (from Sanskrit ŚRUTI, "revelation") because they are based on the Vedic literature considered to be *śru-*

ti, or revealed. The *Śrauta* SUTRAS, together with the *Gṛhya Sūtra*s (dealing with domestic ceremonies) and the DHARMA SUTRAS (dealing with rules of conduct), make up the KALPA SŪTRAS. Each *Śrauta Sūtra* guides the priests of its own Vedic school in the performance of specialized functions.

SRAVANA BELGOLA \\'shrə-və-nə-,be-lə-'gō-lə\\, Indian town, 56 miles from Mysore, which contains notable examples of Mauryan architecture (from the Mauryan Empire, which dated from about 1500 BCE to 1200 CE). In addition to notable architecture, the town also has a giant stone figure, believed to be 1,000 years old, of Bāhubali (Gommateśvara), the Jain saint.

SRI PADA \\,shrē-'pä-də, ,srē-\\, *also called* Adam's Peak, mountain in southwestern Sri Lanka, 7,360 feet high and 11 miles northeast of Ratnapura. Its conical summit terminates in an oblong platform about 74 by 24 feet, on which there is a large hollow resembling the print of a human foot, 5 feet 4 inches by 2 feet 6 inches. The depression is venerated alike by Buddhists, Muslims, and Hindus, who regard it as the footprint of the BUDDHA, ADAM, and SHIVA, respectively. Many pilgrims of all faiths visit the peak every year. Heavy chains on the mountain's southwestern face, said to have been placed there by Alexander the Great, mark the route to the summit.

SRIRANGAM \\,srē-'raŋ-gəm\\, city, east-central Tamil Nādu state, southeastern India. Lying on an island at the division of the Cauvery and Coleroon rivers near the city of Tiruchchirāppali, Srirangam is one of the most frequently visited PILGRIMAGE centers in southern India. Its main Raṅganātha temple, though primarily Vaiṣṇavite, is also holy to Śaivites (*see* VAIṢṆAIVISM and ŚAIVISM).

The temple is composed of seven rectangular enclosures, one within the other, the outermost having a perimeter more than 2 miles in length. A remarkable feature of the temple is the Hall of a Thousand Pillars with its colonnade of rearing horses. The temple and 1,000-pillared hall were constructed in the Vijayanagar period (1336–1565) on the site of an older temple.

SRI VAIṢṆAVA \\,shrē-'vīsh-nə-və\\, member of a sect of Vaiṣṇavite Hindus, most numerous in South India, who follow the teachings of the philosopher RĀMĀNUJA. "Śrī" refers to Vishnu's consort, also called LAKṢMĪ, to whom VISHNU first taught the doctrine. She functions both independently, as auspiciousness (Śrī) itself, and as a maternal, loving mediator between Vishnu's somewhat formal authoritative personality and the needs of devotees.

The sect reached its peak of creativity in the late 10th or 11th century, when the devotional hymns of the ĀḶVĀRS were introduced into the temple service by Nāthamuni. He is called the first *ācārya* ("teacher") of the sect and founded a Sanskrit-Tamil school at Śrīraṅgam (Tamil Nadu state), which continues to be a great Vaiṣṇava center. Rāmānuja (11th/12th century), in an exposition of the VEDĀNTA SŪTRAS called *Śrībhāṣya* ("Beautiful Commentary"), gave the sect a philosophical doctrine to fit its views.

Toward the end of the late 14th century, the Śrī Vaiṣṇavas split into their present two subsects, the Vaṭakalai (or school of northern learning), which relied more on the Sanskrit SCRIPTURES, and the Teṅkalai (or school of southern learning), which stressed the Tamil hymns of the Āḷvārs.

The Śrī Vaiṣṇavas worship only Vishnu and his consorts and attendants and do not acknowledge Krishna's mistress RĀDHĀ. Brahmin members strictly observe CASTE regulations in such matters as diet and interdining. Śrī Vaiṣṇava Brahmins are given to scholarly pursuits and have earned for themselves the honorary title of *ācārya*, or, in Tamil, *ayyangar*, often spelled *iyengar*.

ŚRUTI \\'shrú-tē\\ (Sanskrit: "learning by hearing"), classically the most revered body of sacred literature in HINDUISM, all of it existing in Sanskrit (or Vedic, its archaic form). *Śruti* works are considered divine revelation, heard and transmitted by earthly sages, as contrasted to SMṚTI, or that which is remembered. Though *śruti* is considered to be the more authoritative, in practice the *smṛti* texts are more influential in modern Hinduism and have probably been so for millennia. The revealed texts encompass the four VEDAS—Ṛg, Yajur, Sāma, and Atharva—and the BRĀHMAṆAS (ritual treatises), the *Āraṇyaka*s ("Books of the Forest"), and the UPANISHADS.

SSU-MA CH'ENG-CHEN \\'sə-'mä-'chəŋ-'jən\\, *Pinyin* Sima Chengzhen (b. 647—d. 735), sixth patriarch of the Shangch'ing school of TAOISM, who had many associations with famous poets such as Li Po and Wang Wei during the T'ang period. Called to court during the reign of Emperor Juitsung (reigned 710–712), Ssu-ma recommended a government that followed the principles of WU-WEI, or "non-action." He was also influential with Emperor Hsüan-tsung (reigned 712–756) and was known as an accomplished calligrapher. He is especially famous for blending Taoist, Confucian, and Buddhist methods of mental cultivation. Generally he recommended religious methods that emphasized "inner alchemy" over the external practices and drugs of "outer alchemy."

STATE SHINTŌ \\'shēn-,tō, *Angl* 'shin-tō\\, *Japanese* Kokka Shintō \\'kók-kä-\\, nationalistic official religion of Japan from the Meiji Restoration in 1868 through World War II. It focused on ceremonies of the imperial household and public SHINTŌ shrines.

State Shintō was founded on the ancient precedent of *saisei itchi*, the unity of religion and government. Traditionally, the prosperity of the nation was believed to be assured by harmony between human politics and the will of the gods. But Shintō came to be dominated by BUDDHISM and NEO-CONFUCIANISM, and the emperor was overshadowed by military rulers. Various efforts to restore Shintō and the emperor came to naught in the medieval period.

Finally, during the Meiji period (1868–1912) the government set about to institutionalize Shintō. It assumed control of the Shintō shrines, established a Department of Shintō (later the Shintō Ministry), and adopted restrictive policies against the other religions, including sect movements within Shintō. Though the 1889 constitution included a nominal guarantee of religious freedom, obeisance at Shintō shrines was considered the patriotic duty of all Japanese. The administration of the country's more than 100,000 Shintō shrines was carried on by the government, Shintō moral teaching (*shūshin*) was made compulsory in the schools, and the divine status of the emperor was fostered by the political authorities.

State Shintō was abolished in 1945 by a decree of the Allied occupation forces that forbade government subsidy and support to Shintō shrines and repudiated the emperor's divinity. The ban was continued in the postwar constitution. Most of the shrines previously administered by the government reorganized themselves as SHRINE SHINTŌ.

STEINER, RUDOLF \'shtī-nər, *Angl* 'stī-\ (b. Feb. 27, 1861, Kraljević, Austria—d. March 30, 1925, Dornach, Switz.), Austrian-born scientist, editor, and founder of ANTHROPOSOPHY, a movement based on the notion that there is a spiritual world comprehensible to pure thought but accessible only to the highest faculties of mental knowledge.

Attracted in his youth to the works of Goethe, Steiner edited that poet's scientific works and from 1889 to 1896 worked on the standard edition of his complete works at Weimar. Coming gradually to believe in spiritual perception independent of the senses, he called the result of his research "anthroposophy," relating it to "knowledge produced by the higher self in man." In 1912 he founded the Anthroposophical Society.

Steiner believed that humans once participated more fully in spiritual processes of the world through a dreamlike consciousness but had since become restricted by their attachment to material things. The renewed perception of spiritual things required training the human consciousness to rise above attention to matter. The ability to achieve this goal by an exercise of the intellect is theoretically innate in everyone.

In 1913 at Dornach, near Basel, Switz., Steiner built his first Goetheanum, which he characterized as a "school of spiritual science." The Waldorf School movement, derived from his experiments with the Goetheanum, by 1969 was responsible for some 80 schools attended by more than 25,000 children in Europe and the United States. Other projects that have grown out of Steiner's work include schools for disabled children; a therapeutic clinical center at Arlesheim, Switz.; scientific and mathematical research centers; and schools of drama, speech, painting, and sculpture.

STIGMATA, *singular* stigma, in Christian MYSTICISM, bodily marks, scars, or pains corresponding to those of the crucified JESUS CHRIST—that is, on the hands or feet, near the heart, and sometimes on the head (from the crown of thorns) or shoulders and back (from carrying the Cross and scourging). They are often presumed to accompany religious ECSTASY.

While in his cell on Mount Alverno in 1224, pondering on the sufferings of Christ, ST. FRANCIS OF ASSISI was purportedly visited by a SERAPH who produced upon his body the five wounds of Christ. Pope Alexander IV and others attested that they had seen these marks both before and after Francis' death. In the next century the same alleged wonder occurred to the DOMINICAN sister, ST. CATHERINE OF SIENA, who received her first stigma at the age of 23. From the

St. Francis of Assisi receiving the stigmata, the five wounds of Christ, from a seraph
Rosenwald Collection, National Gallery of Art—Culver

14th to the 20th century, more than 330 persons were identified as having been stigmatized; 60 were declared saints or the blessed in the ROMAN CATHOLIC church.

STONEHENGE \'stōn-,henj, ,stōn-'henj\, circular setting of large standing stones surrounded by a circular earthwork, built in prehistoric times beginning about 3100 BCE and located about eight miles north of Salisbury, Wiltshire, Eng.

The monument consists of a number of structural elements, mostly circular in plan. On the outside is a circular ditch, with a bank immediately within it, all interrupted by an entrance gap on the northeast, leading to the Avenue. At the center of the circle is a stone setting consisting of a horseshoe of tall uprights of sarsen (Tertiary sandstone) encircled by a ring of tall sarsen uprights, all originally capped by horizontal sarsen lintels. Within the sarsen stone circle were also configurations of smaller and lighter bluestones (igneous rock of diabase, rhyolite, and volcanic ash), but most of these bluestones have disappeared. Additional stones include the so-called Altar Stone, the Slaughter Stone, two Station stones, and the Heel Stone, the last standing on the Avenue outside the entrance. Small circular ditches enclose two flat areas on the inner edge of the bank, known as the North and South Barrows, with empty stone holes at their centers.

Archaeological excavations since 1950 suggest three main periods of building. In Stonehenge I, about 3100 BCE, the native Neolithic people, using deer antlers for picks, excavated a roughly circular ditch about 320 feet in diameter; the ditch was about 20 feet wide and 4.5 to 7 feet deep, and the excavated chalky rubble was used to build the high bank within the circular ditch. They also erected two parallel entry stones on the northeast of the circle (one of which, the Slaughter Stone, still survives). Just inside the circular bank they dug—and seemingly almost immediately refilled—a circle of 56 shallow holes, named the Aubrey Holes (after their discoverer, the 17th-century antiquarian John Aubrey). The Station stones also probably belong to this period, but the evidence is inconclusive. Stonehenge I was used for about 500 years and then reverted to scrubland.

During Stonehenge II, about 2100 BCE, the complex was radically remodeled. About 80 bluestone pillars, imported 240 miles from the Preseli Mountains in southwestern Wales and weighing up to 4 tons each, were erected in the center of the site to form what was to be two concentric circles, though the circles were never completed. The entranceway of this earliest setting of bluestones was aligned approximately with the sunrise at the summer solstice, the alignment being continued by a newly built and widened approach, called the Avenue, together with a pair of Heel stones. The double circle of bluestones was dismantled in the following period.

The initial phase of Stonehenge III, starting about 2000 BCE, saw the erection of the linteled circle and horseshoe of large sarsen stones whose remains can still be seen today. The sarsen stones were transported from the Marlborough Downs 20 miles north and were erected in a circle of 30 uprights capped by a continuous ring of stone lintels. Within this ring was erected a horseshoe formation of five trilithons (three stones, two of them upright and the third forming a lintel), each of which consisted of a pair of large stone uprights supporting a stone lintel. The sarsen stones are of exceptional size, up to 30 feet long and 50 tons in weight. Their visible surfaces were laboriously dressed smooth by pounding with stone hammers; the same technique was used to form the mortise-and-tenon joints by which the lintels are held on their uprights, and it was used to form the tongue-and-groove joints by which the lintels of the circle fit together. The lintels are not rectangular; they were curved to produce all together a circle. The pillars are tapered upward.

In the second phase of Stonehenge III, which probably followed within a century, about 20 bluestones from Stonehenge II were dressed and erected in an approximate oval setting within the sarsen horseshoe. Sometime later, about 1550 BCE, two concentric rings of holes (the Y and Z Holes, today not visible) were dug outside the sarsen circle. The holes in both circles were left open to silt up over the suc-

ceeding centuries. The oval setting in the center was also removed.

The final phase of building in Stonehenge III probably followed almost immediately. Within the sarsen horseshoe the builders set a horseshoe of dressed bluestones set close together, alternately a pillar followed by an obelisk followed by a pillar and so on. The remaining unshaped 60-odd bluestones were set as a circle of pillars within the sarsen circle (but outside the sarsen horseshoe). The largest bluestone of all, traditionally misnamed the Altar Stone, probably stood as a tall pillar on the axial line.

About 1100 BCE the Avenue was extended from Stonehenge eastward and then southeastward to the River Avon, a distance of about 9,120 feet. This suggests that Stonehenge was still in use at the time.

Why Stonehenge was built is unknown, though it probably was constructed as a place of worship of some kind. Speculations that the builders were DRUIDS or sun worshipers, or that Stonehenge was a complicated computer for predicting eclipses, have been severely criticized.

STRANG, JAMES JESSE \\'straŋ\\, *also called* Jesse James Strang (b. March 21, 1813, Scipio, N.Y., U.S.—d. July 9, 1856, Voree, Wis.), American churchman, dissident of the Church of Jesus Christ of Latter-day Saints (MORMONS), whose futile attempt to succeed JOSEPH SMITH as its leader led him to found the Strangite sect.

Admitted to the bar in 1836 after teaching for a brief period, Strang also served as postmaster for five years at Ellington, N.Y., and owned and edited a weekly paper. In 1843 he followed his wife's family to Burlington, Wis. He met Joseph Smith the next year in Nauvoo, Ill., where the Mormons had established a large settlement. Despite an earlier philosophical skepticism, Strang became a Mormon convert and was ordained an elder by Smith. After Smith's as-

Aerial view of Stonehenge, near Salisbury, Wiltshire
Aerofilms Ltd.

sassination in June 1844, Strang exhibited a letter, purportedly written by Smith, that named Strang his successor. He also claimed to have had a vision appointing him "seer, revelator, and prophet" of the Mormon Church. However, the Twelve Apostles denounced Strang as an impostor and forger and expelled him from the church. Strang and a group of his own followers then organized a new sect in Voree, Wis. There in 1845 he allegedly translated (with the aid of magic spectacles given him by an ANGEL) *The Book of the Law of the Lord* from golden plates from the ARK OF THE COVENANT. Strang then established a secret society that swore allegiance to him and operated under puritanical rules.

Dissension prompted Strang to relocate the colony in 1847 to Beaver Island, in northern Lake Michigan. In 1850 Strang received another revelation in the "plates of Laban." It sanctioned polygyny, and he was married to four wives at one time. He also claimed that it sanctioned his coronation, and in July he became King James I. The Strangites endured considerable persecution, but Strang was able to preserve the sect and to gain acquittal in the several lawsuits brought against him.

Twice elected to the legislature in Michigan (1852, 1854), Strang had more than 5,000 followers when he was shot on June 16, 1856, by two former Strangites. More than 2,000 Strangites were driven from their homes and the sect was all but extinguished.

STRAUSS, DAVID FRIEDRICH \'shtraüs\ (b. Jan. 27, 1808, Ludwigsburg, Württemberg [Germany]—d. Feb. 8, 1874, Ludwigsburg), controversial German-Protestant philosopher, theologian, and biographer whose use of dialectical philosophy, emphasizing social evolution through the inner struggle of opposing forces, broke new ground in biblical interpretation by explaining the NEW TESTAMENT accounts of Christ mythologically.

Influenced during his studies at the universities of Tübingen and Berlin (1825–31) by the doctrine of G.W.F. Hegel, Strauss proposed a developmental theory of formative CHRISTIANITY in which the interaction of inherent, conflicting forces and interpretations led to a higher religious synthesis. Such an analysis inspired his first major work, *Das Leben Jesu kritisch bearbeitet*, 2 vol. (1835–36; *The Life of Jesus Critically Examined*), which was translated into English by the British Victorian novelist George Eliot. In it Strauss denied the historical value of the Gospels and rejected their supernatural claims, describing them as "historical myth," or the unintentionally created, legendary embodiment by 2nd-century writers of the primitive Christian community's popular hopes.

The ensuing furor among German Protestants prompted Strauss to mitigate his attack by commenting that such criticism did not essentially destroy Christianity, because all religions were based on ideas, not facts. This apology, however, did not avert his exclusion from further university teaching at Tübingen or at the University of Zürich, where previously he had been offered a professorship.

In retirement from academic theological circles for more than 20 years, he resided in Ludwigsburg and Darmstadt, where he produced several biographies of political and intellectual figures and held political office as provincial legislator. His religious odyssey closed with the publication of *Der alte und der neue Glaube* (1872; *The Old Faith and the New*), in which he ventured to replace Christianity with scientific materialism, a personalized form of Darwinism. Criticized for an inadequate understanding of the biblical and theological texts he criticized, Strauss nevertheless not

only influenced 20th-century liberal and eschatological schools of biblical thought but also challenged subsequent scholars with the search for the "historical Jesus."

STRIBOG \strē-'bōg\, one of seven Russian pre-Christian deities, the others being PERUN, Volos, Khors, DAZHBOG, Simargla, and Mokosh. The deities are mentioned in the *Kiev Chronicle* (*Povest vremennykh let*)—a 12th- to 13th-century account of events and life in the Kievan state.

STRUCTURALISM, theory and critical method applied in such disciplines as anthropology, sociology, linguistics, and literary studies. Modern versions of structuralism in the cultural sciences trace their origin to the linguistic work of Ferdinand de Saussure (1857–1913) and the theories of the anthropologist Claude Lévi-Strauss (b. 1908).

The first principle of structuralism is that the true object of study is not immediately given. Thus, appeal to sensations, experience, or intuitive insights is of no use in the discovery of the object of study since such things are always external to the structure or system. As Lévi-Strauss once said, sensations, emotions, and intuitions cannot be the foundation of an explanation but rather are that which must be explained. Accordingly, structuralism rejects such notions as the sui generis nature of religion, or the converse idea, that religion is the mere satisfaction of bodily needs.

The second principle asserts that understanding cultural phenomena requires a kind of analysis, revealing the relations which constitute a particular system, whether ritual, myth, or RELIGIOUS BELIEF. This principle rejects the contention that the significance of a myth or ritual or religious symbol is to be found in an analysis of the elements of the myth or ritual. A symbol or an element in a myth—a goddess for example—has significance only in the relations that constitute this element in the system. Elements, symbols, and signs in themselves are held to be meaningless and arbitrary.

A third principle states that system and practice must be distinguished. Saussure made this distinction in linguistics when he separated language from speech, asserting that the proper object of linguistics is language. Speech is the practice, the actual speech acts of a language, which exists as an abstraction. A similar distinction may be made between religion as a system or structure and the practice or performance of religion or religious acts. From a structuralist point of view one cannot arrive at language, or the meaning of religion, by an examination of speech or religious acts.

Lévi-Strauss insisted upon the importance of these principles for the establishment of a new anthropology and the study of myth, KINSHIP, and TOTEMISM. He was fully aware of the Saussurian axiom that knowledge of the history of a symbol would not yield its structure, syntax, or semantics. Lévi-Strauss held, for example, that totemism, which was once viewed as the ORIGIN OF RELIGION, never in fact existed as an institution but can be understood as an element in a wider system of classifications.

Work done in religion from a structuralist perspective includes the work of Louis Dumont who has shown that the notion of CASTE may be explained as a relation between the contraries pure–impure, which are ritual categories. Stanley Tambiah has demonstrated that the rituals of THERAVĀDA BUDDHISM are more adequately explained as elements within a larger system constituted by the set of relations that might be indicated as householder/renouncer. Jean-Pierre Vernant has used structuralist principles for explicating the myths of classical Greece.

STUDY OF RELIGION

The study of religion is an attempt to understand the nature and various aspects of religion through the use of established intellectual disciplines. Broadly speaking, it comprehends two aspects: gathering information and systematically interpreting it.

The first aspect involves the psychological and historical study of religious life, whereas the second involves the attempt to understand the structure, nature, and dynamics of RELIGIOUS EXPERIENCE.

An acceptable DEFINITION OF RELIGION is difficult to attain. Attempts have been made to find an essential ingredient in all religions (*e.g.*, the numinous, or spiritual, experience; the contrast between the sacred and the profane; belief in gods or in God) so that an "essence" of religion might be described. But it has become evident that, because of the rich variety of religions, it is always possible to find counterexamples—an element suggested as essential is found in some religions to be peripheral. A more promising method might be to list elements that are typical of religions, though they may not be universal.

The fact that the possibility of finding an essence of religion is disputed means that there is likewise a problem in speaking too generally of the study of religion or of religions themselves. In practice, a religion is a particular system or set of systems in which doctrines, myths, rituals, sentiments, institutions, and other similar elements are interconnected. In order to understand a given belief as it occurs in such a system, it is necessary to look at its particular context—that is, at the other beliefs held in the system, at rituals, and at the other elements. Every religion has its unique properties, and attempts to make comparisons between religions may obscure these unique aspects. Most students of religion agree, however, that valid comparisons are possible, though they are difficult to make. Indeed, since comparison also includes contrast, one may be able to illuminate the very uniqueness of a religion through such comparison.

In modern times there is an emphasis on neutral description—*i.e.*, description of RELIGIOUS BELIEFS and practices that does not reflect any judgment of whether they are valuable or harmful, true or false. To some extent this emphasis arises as a reaction against committed accounts of religion, which were long the norm and still exist. Conflict sometimes arises because the committed point of view is like-

Orthodox Jewish men study under the direction of a rabbi
Doug Goodman—Monkmeyer

ly to begin with a conservative stance—*e.g.,* to accept at face value a scriptural account of events—whereas the secular historian may be more skeptical, especially of records of miraculous events.

There are, however, questions about how possible or even desirable the qualities of neutrality and objectivity are in the study of religion. It may be asked, for example, whether we can understand a faith without holding it. One of the challenges to the student of religion is the problem of evoking its inner, individual side, which is not observable in any straightforward way.

The scholar is concerned also with communal responses. The adherent of a faith is no doubt authoritative as to his own experience, but he is not necessarily so in regard to the communal significance of the rites and institutions in which he participates. Thus, the effort to understand the inner side of a religion involves a dialectic between observation of and dialogical (interpersonal) relationship with the adherents of the faith. Consequently, the study of religion has strong similarities to, and indeed overlaps with, anthropology.

The study of religion can be broadly divided between descriptive and historical inquiries and normative inquiries. The latter primarily concern the truth of religious claims, the acceptability of religious values, and other such aspects; the former are primarily concerned with its history, structure, and similar observable elements. The distinction is not an absolute one, for descriptions of religion may sometimes be shaped by theories that imply something about the truth or other normative aspects of some or all religions. Conversely, theological claims may imply something about the history of a religion.

The study of religion may thus be characterized as being concerned with human religious behavior in relation to its object (the transcendent God or gods or whatever is regarded as sacred or holy) and as a study that attempts to be faithful to both the outer and inner facts. Its present-day concern is predominantly descriptive and explanatory and hence embraces such disciplines as history, sociology, anthropology, psychology, and archaeology.

HISTORY OF THE STUDY OF RELIGION

Some qualities that characterize the modern study of religion have their roots in classical Greek thought. The rise of speculative philosophy in ancient Greece led to a critical and somewhat rationalistic treatment of religion and the gods. The 4th-century-BCE philosopher Plato was strongly critical of the older poets' (*e.g.,* Homer's) accounts of the gods and substituted a form of belief in a single creator, the DEMIURGE, or supreme craftsman. This line of thought was developed by Aristotle in his conception of a supreme intelligence that is the unmoved mover.

Criticism of the ancient tradition was reinforced by the reports of travelers who carried Greek culture into other cultures. The historian Herodotus (5th century BCE) attempted to solve the problem of the plurality of cults by identifying foreign deities with Greek deities (*e.g.,* the Egyptian AMON with ZEUS). Among the later Greek thinkers, EUHEMERUS (*c.* 330–*c.* 260 BCE) gave his name to the doctrine called EUHEMERISM, which held that the gods are divinized men.

In the early Roman Empire, Euhemerism became fashionable among the Christian CHURCH FATHERS as an account of paganism. Christianity's own contribution to theories of the genesis of POLYTHEISM was through the doctrine of the fall of man, by which the truth of MONOTHEISM was believed to have become overlaid by demonic cults of false gods. In this view there

Young pupils studying in a Buddhist monastery
S.E. Hedin—Ostman Agency

is the germ of an evolutionary account of religion.

During the Middle Ages, ISLAMIC theology had an impact on Western CHRISTIANITY through the promotion of the values of reason and revelation. The reports of European travelers brought Westerners some knowledge of Asian religions, which opened the way toward a more informed consideration of other religions. With the Renaissance and the Protestant REFORMATION there arose a new respect for the Greek and Roman classics, which lessened the force of antipagan Christian polemics. A new tendency developed among some PROTESTANT authors to compare the Roman church to pre-Christian Rome, which brought the idea of a comparative study of religion into focus; meanwhile the popularity of compilations of mythological and other material gave Europe a vivid sense of the richness and variety of human customs and histories.

Attempts at a developmental account of religion were undertaken in the late 17th and 18th centuries. The Italian philosopher Giambattista Vico (1668–1774) suggested that GREEK RELI-

Muslim students in India learning the Qur'an
Mimi Forsyth—Monkmeyer

GION passed through various stages: the divinization of nature, then of those powers that man had come at least partly to control (such as fire and crops), then of institutions (such as marriage); the final step was the process of humanizing the gods, as in the works of Homer. For English philosopher David Hume (1711–76), original polytheism was the result of a naive ANTHROPOMORPHISM (conceiving the divine in human form) in the assignment of causes to natural events. The intensification of propitiatory and other forms of worship, he believed, led ultimately to the exaltation of one infinite divine Being (*see also* RELIGION, PHILOSOPHY OF).

In the meantime, the beginning of Oriental studies, ethnology, and anthropology were making available more data about religion. The French scholar Charles de Brosses (1709–77) attempted to explain Greek polytheism partly through the fetishism (belief in the magical powers of certain objects) found in West Africa. This foreshadowed later endeavors in the comparative study of religion. The French abbé Bergier (1718–90) explained early religions by means of a belief in spirits arising from a variety of psychological causes, which thus was a precursor of ANIMISM (a belief in souls in persons or certain natural objects).

The French social philosopher Auguste Comte (1798–1857), from a positivistic and materialistic point of view, devised an evolutionary scheme in which there are three stages of human history: the theological, in which the supernatural is important; the metaphysical, in which the explanatory concepts become more abstract; and the positivistic—*i.e.*, the empirical. A rather different positivism was expressed by the English philosopher Herbert Spencer (1820–1903), in which religion has a place beside science in attempting to refer to the unknown and unknowable Absolute. Attempts to produce evolutionary accounts of religion were much encouraged in the latter part of the 19th century by the success of the new theory of biological evolution, and they left a marked effect on the history of both religion and anthropology. These movements were supplemented by the progress of scientific history, archaeology, anthropology, and other sciences, which increased comparative knowledge of civilizations and cultures.

STUPA \\'stü-pə\\, Buddhist commemorative monument usually housing sacred relics associated with the Buddha, a royal personage, or a saint; it is an architectural symbol of the Buddha's *parinirvāṇa,* or final death and release from the cycle of death and rebirth. The hemispherical form of the stupa appears to have derived from pre-Buddhist BURIAL MOUNDS in India. The classic form is most characteristically seen in the series of stupas at SĀNCHI, India, especially in

Stupa III and its single gateway, one of several stupas at Sānchi, Madhya Pradesh state, India
Holle Bildarchiv

the Great Stupa (3rd–1st centuries BCE). The monument, which is believed to contain a relic of the BUDDHA GOTAMA, consists of a circular base supporting a massive solid dome (the *aṇḍa,* "egg," or *garbha,* "womb") at the summit of which projects an umbrella (*chatra*). The whole of the Great Stupa is encircled by a railing and four gateways, which are richly decorated with relief sculpture depicting JĀTAKAS (stories of events in the Buddha's previous lives), events in the Buddha's "historical" life, and popular mythological figures.

In South and Southeast Asia later reliquary stupas display many variations. For example, bell-shaped stupas are common in Sri Lanka, pyramidal and conical designs are prominent in mainland Southeast Asia, and a great terraced stupa was built at BOROBUḌUR in Java, Indonesia. However, most of the South and Southeast Asian edifices of this type retain the basic form of the Great Stupa.

In other parts of the Buddhist world—particularly in China, Korea, and Japan—the change in form has been more dramatic. In these areas—where the term PAGODA usually replaces the term *stupa*—the edifice has become a tall tower consisting of the repetition of a basic story unit ascending in regularly diminishing proportions.

Whatever the form of the stupa or pagoda, the basic symbolic identification between the central object enclosed in the edifice (usually a relic but sometimes a bit of sacred text), the person or teaching being honored, and the building itself is retained. Worship consists in walking around the monument in the direction taken by the path of the Sun (*pradakṣiṇā*). Miniature stupas and pagodas are used by Buddhists throughout Asia as votive offerings. Stupas were also built by Jains to commemorate their saints.

STYLITE \\'stī-ˌlīt\\, Christian ascetic who lived standing on top of a column (Greek: *stylos*) or pillar. The first to do this was St. Simeon Stylites (the Elder), who took up residence atop a column in Syria in 423 CE.

The stylite was permanently exposed to the elements, though he might have a little roof above his head. He stood night and day in his restricted area, usually with a rail around him, and was dependent for his sustenance on what his disciples brought him by ladder. He spent most of his time in prayer but also did pastoral work among those who gathered around his column. A stylite might continue this practice briefly or for a long period.

STYX \\'stiks\\, in Greek mythology, one of the rivers of the Underworld. The word is a derivative of a Greek verb and noun base *styg-* that denotes both abhorrence and repulsion (hence *stygein,* "to regard with loathing") and extreme cold (*Styx* was the name of an icy spring in Arcadia). In the epics of Homer, the gods swore by the water of the Styx as their most binding oath; if a god perjured himself, he was rendered insensible for a year and then banished from the divine society for nine years. Hesiod personified Styx as the daughter of OCEANUS and the mother of Emulation, Victory, Power, and Might. The ancients believed that its water was poisonous and would dissolve any vessel containing it except one made of the hoof of a horse or an ass. There is a legend that Alexander the Great was poisoned by Styx water.

SUÁREZ, FRANCISCO \\'swä-res, -reth, *Angl* -rez\\, *byname* Doctor Eximius (b. Jan. 5, 1548, Granada, Spain—d. Sept. 25, 1617, Lisbon), Spanish theologian and philosopher, a founder of international law, often considered the most prominent Scholastic philosopher (*see* SCHOLASTICISM) after THOMAS AQUINAS, and the major theologian of the ROMAN CATHOLIC order the Society of Jesus (JESUITS).

Suárez began the study of law in Salamanca in 1561 but left to join the Jesuits in 1564. From 1571 he taught philosophy, in 1580 becoming a theology instructor at the Jesuit college in Rome and later at Alcalá. In 1593 King Philip II of Spain appointed him to teach, and he eventually served as a professor at Coimbra (1597–1616), after obtaining his doctorate from Évora (1597).

His principal study in philosophy is the *Disputationes Metaphysicae* (1597), which was used for more than a century as a textbook at most European universities, Catholic and Protestant alike. In this work, which treats especially the problems of human will and the concept of general versus particular phenomena, Suárez drew upon Aristotle and Aquinas, although he took into consideration the criticisms of other Scholastic philosophers such as Duns Scotus.

Suárez also wrote apologetic works on the nature of the Christian state. Among them were *De Virtute et Statu Religionis* (1608–09) and *Defensio Fidei Catholicae* (1613), opposing Anglican theologians who defended the divine right of kings. At the time this theory was being advanced in England by James I, who subsequently burned Suárez' *Defensio* on the steps of St. Paul's Cathedral in London.

Suárez expounded his political theory and philosophy of law in *De Legibus* (1612; "On Laws") as well as in the *Defensio*. Having refuted the divine-right theory of kingly rule, he declared that the people themselves are the original holders of political authority; the state is the result of a social contract to which the people consent. Arguing for the natural rights of the human individual to life, liberty, and property, he rejected the Aristotelian notion of slavery as the natural condition of certain men. He criticized most of the practices of Spanish colonization in the Indies in his *De Bello et de Indis* ("On War and the Indies"). The islands of the Indies he viewed as sovereign states legally equal to Spain as members of a worldwide community of nations.

SUBHA \\'sùb-hə\\, string of Muslim PRAYER BEADS whose units (100, 25, or 33) represent the names of God. As the beads (made of wood, bone, or precious stones) are touched one by one, Muslims may recite any of numerous formulas, the most common being "Glory to ALLĀH." But because prayer may also be recited in the secret of one's heart, a person can multiply his praises of God by merely moving the beads through his fingers. Sufi orders make use of the *subha* in reciting their litanies.

SUBUD \\'sü-büd\\, religious movement based on spontaneous and ecstatic exercises, founded by an Indonesian, Muhammad Subuh, called Bapak. A student of SUFISM as a youth, Bapak had a powerful mystical experience in 1925, and in 1933 he claimed that the mission to found the Subud movement had been revealed to him. The movement was restricted to Indonesia until the 1950s, when it spread to Europe and America.

The central feature of Subud is the *latihan*, its only group spiritual activity, which is usually held for an hour twice a week. During the *latihan*, undergone by men and women in separate rooms, members allow the power of God to express itself through unrestrained spontaneous activity. The *latihan* includes unprogrammed singing, dancing, shouting, and laughter. Subud has little doctrinal teaching, except for the belief in divine power and higher centers of consciousness implied by the *latihan*.

SUCCUBUS \\'sə-kyə-bəs\\, female form of an INCUBUS.

SUCELLUS \\sü-'ke-ləs\\, powerful and widely worshiped Celtic god; his iconographic symbols were usually his mallet and LIBATION saucer. His Irish equivalent seems to have been the DAGDA. Sucellus was possibly one of the Gaulish gods who were equated by Julius Caesar with the Roman god DIS PATER, from whom all the Gauls believed themselves to be descended.

SŪDRA \\'sü-drə, 'shü-\\, fourth and lowest of the traditional VARṆAS, or social classes, of Hindu India, traditionally artisans and laborers. The term does not appear in the earliest Vedic literature. In its first application it probably included all conquered peoples of the Indus civilization as they were assimilated as menials to the tripartite society of the BRAHMINS (priests and teachers), KṢATRIYAS (nobles and warriors), and VAIŚYAS (merchants). Sūdras are not permitted to perform the UPANAYANA initiatory rite, which introduces members of the three upper classes to the study of the VEDAS and gives them their status as DVIJA ("twice-born").

The Sūdra *varṇa* includes a wide spectrum of endogamous status groups with dominant, landowning groups at one end of the scale and near-untouchables at the other. These variations derive from the belief that certain behavior patterns and occupations are polluting, a concept that gave rise to a distinction between "clean" and "unclean"

Śūdra groups. Many CASTES claiming Kṣatriya and Vaiśya status gradually emerged from the Śūdra class.

SUFISM \\'sü-ˌfi-zəm\\, mystic Islamic belief and practice that seeks to find divine love and knowledge through direct personal experience of God. Sufism consists of a variety of mystical paths that are designed to ascertain divine and human nature and to facilitate the experience of divine love and wisdom in the world.

The Arabic term *ṣūfī* ("mystic") derives from *ṣuf*, "wool," probably in reference to the woolen garments worn by early Islamic ascetics. Sufism as an organized movement arose, in part, as a reaction against the worldliness of the early Umayyad period (661–750 CE). Yearning for a personal union with God, the mystics found the externalities of the law, divorced from a personal theology, very unsatisfactory and increasingly asserted a way (*tarīqa*, "path") and a goal (*ḥaqīqa*, "reality") alternative to those of the SHARĪʿA, or traditional law. Sufism similarly opposed its intuitionism (*maʿrifa*, "interior knowledge") to the rational deductions of formal theology (*ʿilm al-kalām*).

The mainstream of the Sufis strove to remain within the bounds of the belief and practice of the majority and declared that the observance of the Sharīʿa was indispensable; indeed, from the early period they had attempted to develop a scheme of partly antithetical and partly complementary categories (*e.g.*, annihilation and restoration; intoxication and sobriety) to achieve a synthesis of the external and the internal. But the opposition of these two aspects continued to be emphasized. During the late 12th and early 13th centuries, under the influence of speculative MYSTICISM, IBN AL-ʿARABĪ produced a system that created a complete chasm between the law and Sufism. In societies, such as Islamic India, that had a strong pre-Islamic heritage of mysticism, this chasm became much wider. Sufism developed into DERVISH orders, which emphasized emotionalism and hypnotic and ecstatic states and which remained influential until very recent times.

The flowering of Sufi literature, especially mystical love poetry, represents a golden age among the Arabic, Persian, Turkish, and Urdu languages. And it was largely through the efforts of Sufi missionaries that ISLAM was extended into India, Central Asia, Turkey, and sub-Saharan Africa. Numerous Sufi orders and suborders exist, each characterized by variations in certain basic practices. A primary spiritual technique of Sufism is DHIKR, the recitation of the name of God or of certain Qurʾanic phrases. Through discipline and the gift of grace, the "wayfarer" seeks to loosen the bonds of his lower self until they are severed altogether, enabling the soul to experience the true reality (ḤAQĪQA) toward which it naturally aspires.

See also AHMADIYAH; BEKTASHĪ; CHISTIYA; MAWLAWIYA; NAQSHBANDIYA; QADIRIYA; RIFAʿIYA; SHADHILIYA; SHATTARIYA; TIJANIYA.

SUHRAWARDĪ, AL- \\al-sùh-ˌrȧ-wȧr-'dē\\, *in full* Shihāb al-Dīn Yaḥyā ibn Ḥabash ibn Amīrak al-Suhrawardī (b. *c.* 1155, Suhraward, near Zanjān, Iran—d. 1191, Ḥalab, Syria), theologian and philosopher who was a leading figure of the illuminationist school of Islamic philosophy, which attempted to create a synthesis between philosophy and MYSTICISM.

After studying at Iṣfahān, a leading center of Islamic scholarship, al-Suhrawardī traveled through Iran, Anatolia, and Syria. Influenced by mystical teachings, he spent much time in meditation and retreat. His teachings, particularly the pantheistic overtones of his mystical doctrines, aroused the opposition of established 'ULAMĀ', who had him put to death. The appellation al-Maqtūl ("the Killed") meant that he was not to be considered a *shahīd* ("martyr").

The more than 50 separate works that were attributed to al-Suhrawardī fall into two categories: doctrinal and philosophical accounts containing commentaries on the works of Aristotle and Plato, as well as his own contribution to the illuminationist school; and shorter treatises, generally written in Persian and of an esoteric nature, meant to illustrate the paths and journeys of a mystic before he could achieve *ma'rifa* (esoteric knowledge).

In his best-known work, *Ḥikmat al-ishrāq* ("The Wisdom of Illumination"), he said that essences are creations of the intellect, having no objective reality or existence. Concentrating on the concepts of being and non-being, he held that existence is a single continuum that culminates in a pure light that he called God. Other stages of being along this continuum are a mixture of light and dark.

Al-Suhrawardī also founded a mystical order known as the Ishrāqīya. The Nūrbakhshīya order of dervishes (itinerant holy men) also traces its origins to him.

SUHRAWARDĪYA \ˌsüh-rä-wär-'dē-ə\, Sufi Muslim order noted for the severity of its spiritual discipline, founded in Baghdad by Abū Najīb al-Suhrawardī and developed by his nephew 'Umar al-Suhrawardī. The order's ritual prayers (DHIKR) are based upon thousands of repetitions of seven names of God, identified with seven "subtle spirits" (*laṭā'if sab'a*) which in turn correspond to seven lights.

The main order became concentrated in Afghanistan and the Indian subcontinent, while other branches moved westward. The Khalwatīya, also strictly disciplined, was founded in Iran by 'Umar al-Khalwatī, then spread into Turkey and Egypt in many branches. The Ṣafawīya, organized by ṢAFĪ AL-DĪN, at Ardabīl, Iran, gave rise to the Iranian Ṣafavid dynasty (1502–1736) and several Turkish branches active against the Ottomans early in the 16th century. The Algerian Raḥmānīya grew out of the Khalwatīya in the second half of the 18th century.

SUKHĀVATĪ VYŪHA SŪTRAS \sü-'kä-və-tē-'vyü-hə-'sü-trəz\, MAHĀYĀNA Buddhist texts that describe Sukhāvatī (Sanskrit: "Pure Land"), the Western Paradise of the Buddha AMITĀBHA. According to followers of the PURE LAND sects, rebirth in Sukhāvatī is ensured by invoking the name of Amitābha, particularly at the moment of death. Sukhāvatī is expressively described in the *sutra*s as being a joyous and beautiful world where Amitābha sits on a lotus in the midst of a terraced pond, attended by the BODHISATTVAS AVALOKITEŚVARA and Mahāsthāmaprāpta. The newly dead enter into lotus buds, which unfold when the occupants have become entirely purified. They remain in this land until their final enlightenment.

SUKKOT \sü-'kōt, 'su-kəs\ (Hebrew: "huts," or "booths"), *also spelled* Sukkoth, *also called* Feast of Tabernacles, *or* Feast of Booths, *singular* Sukka \sü-'kä, 'su-kə\, in JUDAISM, a festival that begins on the 15th day of Tishri (in September or October), five days after YOM KIPPUR. It is one of the three PILGRIM FESTIVALS of the OLD TESTAMENT.

The BIBLE refers to *ḥag ha-asif* ("Feast of the Ingathering," EXODUS 23:16) at the harvest's end, and to *ḥag ha-sukkot* ("Feast of Booths," Leviticus 23:34), recalling the days when the Israelites lived in huts (*sukkot*) during their years of wandering after the Exodus from Egypt. The festival is characterized by the building of huts made of branches and by the gathering of four species of plants, with prayers of thanksgiving for the fruitfulness of the land. A sevenfold circuit of the SYNAGOGUE is made with the four plants on the seventh day of the festival, called by the special name Hoshana Rabba ("Great Hosanna").

SULTAN \'səl-tən, sul-'tän\, *Arabic* sulṭān, originally, according to the QUR'AN, moral or spiritual authority; the term later came to denote political or governmental power and from the 11th century was used as a title by Muslim sovereigns. Maḥmūd of Ghazna (reigned 998–1030 CE) was the first Muslim ruler to be called sultan by his contemporaries, and under the Seljuqs of Anatolia and Iran it became a regular title. Thereafter it was frequently conferred on sovereigns by the CALIPH and came to be used throughout the Islamic world.

SUN DANCE, most spectacular and important religious ceremony of the Plains Indians of 19th-century North America, ordinarily held by each tribe once a year in early summer in order to give thanks to the creator and ask for the rejuvenation of the cosmos (*see* NATIVE AMERICAN RELIGIONS).

The ceremony was most highly developed among the Arapaho, Cheyenne, and Oglala Sioux (and may have originated with these tribes). By the end of the 19th century, it had spread with local variations to include most of the tribes from the Plains Ojibwa in Saskatchewan south to the Kiowa in Texas. The development of total tribal participa-

Sukkot festival, engraving after a drawing by Bernard Picart, 1722
The Bettmann Archive

tion, widespread cooperative effort, direction by tribal and religious leaders, and elaboration beyond the immediate Sun Dance indicate the meaning of this ceremony in terms of tribal aspirations (secular and religious) and in the reinforcement of social control.

In the most elaborate versions a great camp circle was formed, preliminary instruction was given to the pledger and his associates, necessary supplies were gathered, and a dance lodge was erected with a central pole to symbolize the sun; usually parts of sacred animals such as the eagle and buffalo were placed on the pole. Preliminary dances and the erection of an altar were followed by the Sun Dance itself. This continued intermittently for several days and nights; during this time those dancers who were fulfilling a vow or seeking power neither ate nor drank. Among some tribes self-torture and mutilation ended the rite.

In an effort to curb such practices, the United States government outlawed the Sun Dance in 1904. Among a number of tribes benign forms of the ceremony continued, usually as part of Fourth of July celebrations. There were a few tribes, however, that attempted to revive the Sun Dance in its original form and meaning.

SUNDAY, in CHRISTIANITY, the Lord's Day, the weekly memorial of JESUS CHRIST'S RESURRECTION. The practice of Christians gathering for worship on Sunday dates to apostolic times. It replaced Saturday, observed as SABBATH by Jews, and became the Christian "Sabbath." Before the end of the 1st century CE, the author of Revelation gave the first day its name of the "Lord's Day" (Revelation 1:10). ST. JUSTIN MARTYR (c. 100–c. 165) described the style of worship on this day: The Gospel or the OLD TESTAMENT was read, the presiding minister preached a sermon, and the group prayed together and celebrated the Lord's Supper.

The emperor Constantine (d. 337) introduced the first civil legislation concerning Sunday in 321, when he decreed that all work should cease on Sunday, except that farmers could work if necessary. This law, aimed at providing time for worship, was followed later and in subsequent centuries by further restrictions on Sunday activities.

SUNNA \'sû-nə, 'sə-\, *also spelled* sunnah (Arabic: "prescribed way," or "habitual practice"), in ISLAM, body of traditional social and legal custom and practice. In pre-Islamic Arabia, sunna referred to ancestral, normative practices of the tribe or community. The early Muslims did not immediately concur on what constituted their sunna. Some looked to the people of MEDINA, others followed the behavior of the Companions of MUHAMMAD, whereas the provincial legal schools attempted to equate sunna with an ideal system—based partly on what was traditional and partly on precedents that they themselves had developed. These varying sources, which created differing community practices, were finally reconciled late in the 8th century by the legal scholar AL-SHĀFI'Ī (767–820), who accorded the sunna of the Prophet Muhammad, as preserved in eyewitness records of his words, actions, and approbations, and known as the HADITH, normative and legal status second only to that of the QUR'AN.

The authoritativeness of the sunna was further strengthened when Muslim scholars, in response to the wholesale fabrication of hadiths by supporters of various doctrinal, legal, and political positions, developed 'ilm al-ḥadīth, the science of attesting the authenticity of individual traditions. The sunna was then used in TAFSĪR, Qur'anic EXEGESIS, to supplement the meaning of the text, and in FIQH, Islamic

jurisprudence, as the basis of legal decisions not discussed in the Qur'an.

SUNNI \'sûn-nē, 'sû-nē\, the larger of the two major branches of ISLAM. Sunni Muslims regard theirs as the mainstream and traditionalist branch of Islam, as distinguished from the minority branch, the SHI'ITES.

Sunnis recognize the first four CALIPHS as Muhammad's rightful successors, whereas the Shi'ites believe that Muslim leadership properly belonged to Muhammad's son-in-law, 'ALĪ, and his descendants alone. In contrast to the Shi'ites, the Sunnis have long conceived of the theocratic state built by MUHAMMAD as an earthly, temporal dominion and have thus regarded the leadership of Islam as being determined not by divine order or inspiration but by the prevailing political realities of the Muslim world. This led historically to Sunni acceptance of the leadership of the foremost families of Mecca and to the acceptance of unexceptional and even foreign caliphs, so long as their rule afforded the proper exercise of religion and the maintenance of order. The Sunnis accordingly held that the caliph must be a member of Muhammad's tribe, the QURAYSH, but devised a theory of election that was flexible enough to permit that allegiance be given to the caliph, whatever his origins. The distinctions between the Sunnis and other Islamic groups regarding the holding of spiritual and political authority remained firm even after the end of the caliphate itself in the 13th century.

Sunni orthodoxy is marked by an emphasis on the views and customs of the majority of the community. The institution of consensus evolved by the Sunnis allowed them to incorporate various customs and usages that arose through ordinary historical development but that nevertheless had no roots in the QUR'AN.

In the 20th century the Sunnis constituted the majority of Muslims in all nations except Iran, Iraq, Bahrain, and perhaps Yemen. They numbered nearly one billion in the late 20th century. *See also* CALIPH; FIQH; FIVE PILLARS OF ISLAM; KALĀM.

SUN WORSHIP, veneration of the sun or a representation of the sun as a deity.

Elaborate sun worship is relatively rare. Though almost every culture uses solar motifs, only a relatively few cultures (Egyptian, Indo-European, and Pre-Columbian) developed solar religions. Most of these groups had in common a strong ideology of SACRED KINGSHIP with a well-developed urban civilization; important exceptions to the urban setting for solar worship include the various Plains Indian communities of North America. In all of them, a prominent image is the sun as the ruler of both the upper and the lower worlds that he majestically visits on his daily round.

In ancient Egypt the sun god RE was the dominant figure among the high gods and retained this position from early in that civilization's history. When the pharaoh Ikhnaton reformed EGYPTIAN RELIGION, he took up the cult of the ancient deity Re-Horakhte under the name of ATON, an older designation of the sun's disk. Under Akhenaton, the sun's qualities as creator and nourisher of the Earth and its inhabitants are glorified.

The sun god occupied a central position in both Sumerian and Akkadian religion, and was one of the most popular deities among the Indo-European peoples as a symbol of divine power to them. The Indo-European character of sun worship is seen in the conception of the SOLAR DEITY, drawn in his carriage, common to many Indo-European peoples, and recurring in Indo-Iranian, Greco-Roman, and Scandinavian mythology.

During the later periods of Roman history, sun worship gained in importance and ultimately led to what has been called a "solar MONOTHEISM." Nearly all the gods of the period were possessed of solar qualities, and both JESUS CHRIST and MITHRA acquired the traits of solar deities; the date of December 25 as CHRISTMAS once belonged to the feast of SOL Invictus (Unconquered Sun).

An impressive example of the solar cult is the SUN DANCE of the Plains Indians of North America which is still carried out in several communities. In the Pre-Columbian civilizations of Mexico and Peru, sun worship was a prominent feature. In Aztec religion extensive HUMAN SACRIFICE was demanded by the sun gods Toniatruh and HUITZ-ILOPOCHTLI. In both Mexican and Peruvian ancient religion, the Sun occupied an important place in myth and ritual. The ruler in Peru was an incarnation of the sun god, INTI. In Japan the sun goddess, AMATERASU, who played an important role in ancient mythology and was considered to be the supreme ruler of the world, was the tutelary deity of the imperial clan, and to this day the sun symbol represents the Japanese state.

SUPERNATURALISM, term opposite in meaning to "naturalism" or "nature." *See also* OCCULTISM.

SUPERSTITION, term used to imply that religion or certain religions are irrational. It is a pejorative which usually implies an evolution of rationality from the "primitive" to a "civilized," or "modern" mode of thought. Thus, religion, when viewed as superstition, is viewed as a less rational stage of human cognitive development.

Egyptian sun worship—the royal family offers a sacrifice to the sun god Aton, 1350 BCE; in the Egyptian Museum, Cairo
Erich Lessing—Art Resource

SUPPLICATIO \,sü-plē-'kä-tē-ō\, in ROMAN RELIGION, rite or series of rites celebrated either as a thanksgiving to the gods for a great victory or as an act of humility after a national calamity. During those times the public was given general access to some or all of the gods; the statues or sacred emblems of the gods often were placed on platforms or couches. Originally a *supplicatio* lasted from one to five days, but in later times it was extended to 10, 20, or even 50 days. On one occasion an expiatory *supplicatio* was celebrated in association with a LECTISTERNIUM, in which images of pairs of gods were exhibited on couches before tables spread with food, but the *supplicatio* was originally a Roman custom and not, as with the *lectisternium*, imported from Greece.

SŪRA \'sü-rə\ (Arabic), *also spelled* surah, chapter in the QUR'AN. Each of the 114 *sūra*s, which vary in length from several pages to several words, encompasses one or more revelations received by MUHAMMAD from ALLĀH (God). In the traditional Muslim classification, the word Madanīya ("of Medina") or Makkīyah ("of Mecca") appears at the beginning of each *sūra*, indicating to some Muslim scholars that the *sūra* was revealed to Muhammad in the period of his life when he was preaching in one or the other of these cities. In some cases an intermixture of verses is similarly designated; modern critical scholarship, however, does not accept the validity of these divisions. Except for the first *sūra*, the FĀTIḤA (Arabic: "the opening"), the *sūra*s are mostly arranged in descending order of length and are numbered serially. They are further identified by a name, usually derived from an unusual image appearing in the text but not necessarily indicative of the general content (for example: Cow, Spider, Blood Clot). About one-fourth of the *sūra*s are also preceded by the *fawātiḥ*; these are detached letters, the function and meaning of which have not yet been satisfactorily determined.

Every *sūra* but the ninth opens with the *basmala* formula ("in the name of God, the Compassionate, the Merciful") and is followed by numbered verses (*āyas*) written in prose, much of which is of a highly intense quality and is often rhymed. All the *sūra*s—except the *fātiḥa*, which is a short devotional prayer, and the last two *sūra*s—are in the form of an address from God, either speaking himself in the first person or speaking through the imperative form *qūl*, "say!," and ordering that the words that follow be proclaimed. The subject matter of the revelations is varied, ranging from stories of previous prophets (ABRAHAM, MOSES, JESUS) to ESCHATOLOGY. The general tone is deeply moralistic and theocentric, reverberating with a demand for obedience to a transcendent but compassionate God.

In pious circles the Qur'an is often divided into 30 equal sections known as *juz'* (Persian and Urdu *sipāra*, or *pāra*). These break up the *sūra*s arbitrarily, without regard to content, into 30 parts in order to facilitate the systematic reading of the entire Qur'an in 30 days, or one lunar month.

SŪRDĀS \sür-'däs\ (fl. 16th century, probably in Braj, India; traditionally b. 1483—d. 1563), North Indian devotional poet known for lyrics addressed especially to KRISHNA that are usually considered to be the finest expressions of Brajbhasa, one of Hindi's two principal literary dialects. Owing to a biographical tradition preserved in the VALLABHA SAMPRADĀYA, Sūrdās (or Sūr, for short) is usually regarded as having taken his inspiration from the teachings of Vallabha, whom he is supposed to have met in 1510. Sūr is said to have become foremost among the poets the Sampradāya designates as its AṢṬACHĀP ("eight seals"), following the convention that each poet affixes his oral signature (*chāp*, or "seal") at the conclusion of each composition. Yet a number of factors render this connection historically doubtful: the awkward logic of the story of the meeting of the poet and philosopher, and the absence from early Sūrdās poems of any mention of Vallabha and of any clear debt to major themes in his theology. More likely, Sūrdās was an independent poet, as is suggested by his continuing appeal to members of all sectarian communities and well beyond. He probably became blind in the course of later life (the Vallabhite story makes him blind from birth), and to this day blind singers in North India refer to themselves as Sūrdās.

Poems attributed to Sūrdās have been composed and collected gradually, swelling a corpus of about 400 poems that must have been in circulation in the 16th century to editions of some 5,000 in the 20th century. A 19th-century manuscript boasts twice that number. The size of this cumulative tradition, in which later poets evidently composed in Sūr's name, justifies a title that had already been assigned to the corpus by 1640: *Sūrsāgar* ("Sūr's Ocean"). The *Sūrsāgar*'s modern reputation focuses on descriptions of Krishna as a lovable child, usually drawn from the perspective of one of the cowherding women (*gopīs*) of Braj. In its 16th-century form, however, the *Sūrsāgar* gravitates much more to descriptions of Krishna and RĀDHĀ as beautiful, youthful lovers; the pining (*viraha*) of Rādhā and the *gopīs* for Krishna when he is absent—and sometimes vice versa; and a set of poems in which the *gopīs* lambast Krishna's messenger Ūdho (Sanskrit: Uddhava) for trying to satisfy them with his spiritual presence once he has finally left their midst. They will have nothing less than the real, physical thing. In addition, poems of Sūr's own personal BHAKTI are prominent, whether as celebration or longing, and episodes from the RĀMĀYAṆA and MAHĀBHĀRATA also appear.

SURPLICE, white outer vestment worn by clergymen, ACOLYTES, choristers, or other participants in ROMAN CATHOLIC and in ANGLICAN, LUTHERAN, and other Protestant religious services. It is a loose garment, usually with full sleeves.

SŪRYA \\'sür-yə\\, in HINDUISM, the sun and the sun god. Although in the Vedic period several other deities also possessed solar characteristics, most of these were merged into a single god in later Hinduism. Sūrya was once ranked along with VISHNU, SHIVA, ŚAKTI, and GAṆEŚA, and many temples dedicated to him are found throughout India. These five deities are worshiped by a very important group of BRAHMINS, the Smārtas, and Sūrya is worshiped as the supreme deity by only a small following, the Saura sect, though he is invoked by most Hindus, and the *Gāyatrī-mantra*, uttered daily at dawn by orthodox Hindus, is addressed to the sun.

Sūrya is the mythological father of MANU (progenitor of the human race), YAMA (lord of death), the Aśvins (twin physicians to the gods), Karṇa (a great warrior of the MAHĀBHĀRATA), and Sugrīva (king of monkeys). The PURĀṆAS record that the weapons of the gods were forged from pieces

Sūrya, stone image from Deo-Barunarak, Bihār, India, 9th century CE
Pramod Chandra

trimmed from Sūrya, whose full emanation was too bright to bear. His wife Uṣas—in some accounts, his mother or mistress—is the personification of dawn.

SUSANOO \\sü-ˌsä-nō-'ō\\, *in full* Susanoo no Mikoto, *also spelled* Susanowo (Japanese: "Impetuous Male"), in Japanese mythology, the storm god, younger brother of the sun goddess AMATERASU. He was born as his father Izanagi washed his nose.

Susanoo, driven out of heaven because of his outrageous behavior, descended into the land of Izumo in western Japan and killed an eight-headed dragon that had been terrorizing the countryside. From the dragon's tail he recovered the marvelous sword Kusanagi that he presented to his sister and that later came to form part of the Imperial Treasures of Japan. Susanoo married the girl he had rescued from the dragon; the most famous of their offspring was ŌKUNINUSHI, the "Master of the Great Land" (Izumo).

SUSO, HEINRICH \\'sü-sō\\, *also spelled* Seuse, *also called* Henry Suso, *original name* Heinrich von Berg (b. March 21, 1295?, probably Constance, Swabia—d. Jan. 25, 1366, Ulm), one of the chief German mystics and leaders of the Friends of God (Gottesfreunde), a circle of devout ascetic Rhinelanders who opposed contemporary evils and aimed for a close association with God.

Of noble birth, Suso joined the DOMINICAN order in Constance. Between *c.* 1322 and *c.* 1325 he was in Cologne for theological studies under MEISTER ECKHART, considered to be one of the greatest German speculative mystics. Suso returned *c.* 1326 to teach at Constance, where he wrote his first work, *Little Book of Truth*, in defense of Eckhart, who had been tried for his controversial works (1327). Suso's masterpiece is considered to be his *Little Book of Eternal Wisdom* (*c.* 1328), which became the most popular religious treatise for a hundred years. Although containing mystical topics and theological reflections, *Eternal Wisdom* is a practical work written in simple language.

In 1327/30 Suso was removed from his professorship for his doctrine and for his defense of Eckhart, who was condemned by the pope in 1329. He became a preacher in Switzerland and the upper Rhine. He was prior of the Friends of God in Constance (1343–44), then exiled to Diessenhofen, Switz., by the German king Louis IV the Bavarian. He was beatified by Pope Gregory XVI in 1831, and his traditional feast day is March 15.

SŪTRA \'sü-trə\ (Sanskrit: "thread"), *Pāli* sutta, in HINDU-ISM, a brief, aphoristic composition; in BUDDHISM, a more extended exposition, the basic form of the SCRIPTURES of both the THERAVĀDA and MAHĀYĀNA traditions. The early Indian philosophers did not work with written texts and later often disdained the use of them; thus, there was a need for very brief explanatory works that could be committed to memory. The earliest *sutras* were expositions of ritual procedures, but their use spread. The *sutras* of the Sanskrit grammarian Pāṇini (5th–6th century BCE) became in many respects a model for later compositions. Nearly all the Indian philosophical systems had their own *sutras*, most of which were preserved in writing in the early centuries CE.

In the Buddhist *sutras* a particular point of doctrine is propounded and deliberated. The most important collection of the Theravāda *sutras* is to be found in the SUTTA PIṬAKA section of the Pāli canon, which contains the discourses attributed to the BUDDHA GOTAMA. In Mahāyāna Buddhism *sutra* is applied to expository texts.

SUTTA PIṬAKA \'sút-tə-'pi-tə-kə\ (Pāli: "Basket of Discourse"), *Sanskrit* Sūtra Piṭaka, extensive collection of texts that contain—usually in a sermonic or poetic mode—the basic teachings of the THERAVĀDA school of BUDDHISM. For the most part the contents of the Sutta Piṭaka are attributed to the Gotama Buddha himself. In the few instances where this is not the case they are attributed to his closest disciples and most accomplished early followers.

The schools whose works were written in Sanskrit divided this body of literature into four collections, called *Āgama*s. Roughly comparable collections, called *Nikāya*s, comprise the Pāli Sutta Piṭaka of the Theravāda school, but with a fifth group, the *Khuddaka Nikāya*, added. The four *Nikāya*s that correlate with the four *Āgama*s are:

1. *Dīgha Nikāya* ("Long Collection"; Sanskrit *Dīrghāgama*), which includes basic teachings, legends, and moral rules. The first *sutta*, the *Brahmajāla* ("Divine Net") *Sutta*, deals with fundamental Buddhist doctrines and with rival philosophies and reveals much about everyday life and religious practices of the period. The famous *Mahāparinibbāṇa Sutta* ("Discourse on the Great Final Extinction"—*i.e.*, the Buddha's release from the round of rebirths), one of the oldest texts in the canon, narrates the activities and teachings of the Buddha's last year and describes his death and the events that followed immediately thereafter.

2. *Majjhima Nikāya* ("Medium [Length] Collection"; Sanskrit *Madhyamāgama*), covers nearly all aspects of Buddhism. Included are texts dealing with monastic life, the excesses of ASCETICISM, the evils of caste, Buddha's debates with the Jains, and meditation, together with basic doctrinal and ethical teachings and many legends and stories.

3. *Saṃyutta Nikāya* ("Cluster Collection"; Sanskrit *Saṃyuktāgama*), *sutta*s arranged more or less by subject matter into clusters. The best known *sutta* is the *Dhammacakkappavattana-sutta* ("Discourse on the Turning of the Wheel of the Law"), which contains the Buddha's first sermon.

4. *Aṅguttara Nikāya* ("Item-more Collection"; Sanskrit *Ekottarikāgama*), a numerical arrangement, for mnemonic purposes, of 9,557 terse *sutta*s. The first *nipāta* ("group") in the collection contains *sutta*s dealing with single things, such as the mind or the Buddha; the *sutta*s in the second *nipāta* speak of pairs (two kinds of SIN); in the third there are triplets (three praiseworthy acts); and so on up to 11. The *Khuddaka Nikāya*—to which there is no Sanskrit parallel that is considered to be an *Āgama*—includes 15

*sutta*s. Among these are a number of famous and probably quite early *sutta*s, such as the DHAMMAPADA and the *Suttanipāta*.

SUTTEE: *see* SATĪ.

SUZUKI DAISETSU TEITARŌ \su-'zü-kē-'dī-,set-su-'tā-tä-rō\ (b. Oct. 28, 1870, Kanazawa, Japan—d. July 12, 1966, Kamakura), Japanese Buddhist scholar and thinker who, during the first half of the 20th century, was the chief interpreter of the ZEN school of BUDDHISM to the West.

Suzuki studied at the University of Tokyo. He became a disciple of Sōen, a noted Zen master of the day, and believed that under Sōen's guidance he had attained the experience of SATORI (sudden enlightenment), which remained of fundamental importance throughout his life. During 1897–1909 Suzuki lived in the United States and collaborated with Paul Carus as a magazine editor. He attracted interest with his translation *The Discourse on the Awakening of Faith in the Mahayana* (1900) and the publication of *Outline of Mahayana Buddhism* (1907). The latter half of his life he spent teaching, writing, and lecturing both in Japan and abroad, mostly in the United States, and he contributed substantially to interest in Buddhism in Western countries.

SVADILFARI \'svä-thil-,fär-ē\, in Norse mythology, horse belonging to a giant who offered to build a great wall around ASGARD (the kingdom of the gods) to keep invaders away. The gods stipulated that, if the builder completed the wall in one winter's time, his reward would be the goddess FREYJA and possession of the sun and the moon. Svadilfari gave his owner such assistance that the wall was almost completed a few days before the end of winter. The gods, however, were able to cheat the giant with the aid of LOKI, who changed himself into a mare and attracted Svadilfari away from his work. From their union Loki bore Odin's magical horse, SLEIPNIR.

SVANTOVIT \,svän-tō-'vēt\, *or* Svantevit, Slavic war god. His citadel-temple at ARKONA was destroyed in the 12th century by invading Christian Danes.

SVAROG \svä-'rōg\, *also called* Zuarasici, Slavic deity, divine smith and instigator of monogamous marriage. The root *svar* means "quarrel" or "dispute." Svarog was considered the father of DAZHBOG.

SVAROZHICH \svä-'rō-zhēch\, *also spelled* Svarozic, Svaroshigh, *or* Svaroziczu, in SLAVIC RELIGION, god of the sun, of fire, and of the hearth. He was worshiped in a temple at Radegast (now in eastern Germany). In myth he may have been the son of SVAROG and the brother of DAZHBOG, or he may have been identical to the latter.

ŚVETĀMBARA \swä-'täm-bə-rə, shwä-\ (Sanskrit: "White-robed," *or* "White-clad"), one of two principal sects of JAIN-ISM, concentrated chiefly in Gujarāt and western Rājasthān states but found throughout northern and central India. The monks and nuns of the Śvetāmbara sect wear simple white garments, in contrast to the practice of the DIGAMBARA sect, which does not admit women into the ascetic order and whose monks are always nude.

Though the date of the schism is given by the Śvetāmbara sect as 83 CE, the earliest image of a TĪRTHAṄKARA (Jain savior) wearing a lower garment has been ascribed to the late 5th or 6th century.

SWĀMĪNĀRĀYAṆ \'swä-mē-nä-'rä-yən\, *also spelled* Swāmīnārāyaṇa, Hindu reform sect with a large popular following in Gujarāt state. The sect was founded in Ahmedabad about 1804 by Swāmī Nārāyaṇa, who emphasized the observance of traditional Hindu law, particularly in matters of CASTE, diet, and ritual. The sect worships KRISHNA and also the five major gods of orthodox HINDUISM, and it employs the VALLABHA MANTRA.

SWASTIKA, equilateral cross with arms bent at right angles, all in the same rotary direction, usually clockwise. The swastika is a symbol widely distributed throughout the ancient and modern world. The word is derived from Sanskrit *svastika*, "symbol promoting good fortune" (ultimately from the noun *svasti*, "well-being"). It was a favorite symbol on ancient Mesopotamian coinage. In Scandinavia the left-hand swastika was the sign for Thor's hammer. The swastika also appeared in early Christian and Byzantine art, and it occurred in South and Central America (among the MAYA) and in North America (principally among the Navajo).

In India the swastika continues to be the most widely used auspicious symbol of Hindus, Jains, and Buddhists. Among the Jains it is the emblem of their seventh TIRTHANKARA (saint). Both Hindus and Jains use the swastika to mark the opening pages of their account books, thresholds, doors, and offerings. The right-hand swastika, which moves in a clockwise direction, is considered a solar symbol and imitates in the rotation of its arms the course taken daily by the Sun. The left-hand swastika (more correctly called the *sauvastika*), more often stands for night, the goddess KĀLĪ, and magical practices.

In the Buddhist tradition the swastika symbolizes the feet, or the footprints, of the Buddha. It is often placed at the beginning and end of inscriptions, and modern Tibetan Buddhists use it as a clothing decoration.

In Nazi Germany the swastika (German: *Hakenkreuz*) became the national symbol. In 1910 the poet and nationalist Guido von List had suggested the swastika as a symbol for all anti-Semitic organizations; and when the National Socialist Party was formed in 1919–20, it adopted it. This use of the swastika ended in World War II with the German surrender in May 1945, though the swastika is still favored by neo-Nazi groups.

SWEDENBORG, EMANUEL \'swē-dən-,bȯrg\, *original name* Emanuel Swedberg, *or* Svedberg (b. Jan. 29, 1688, Stockholm, Swed.—d. March 29, 1772, London, Eng.), Swedish scientist, Christian mystic, philosopher, and theologian who wrote voluminously in interpreting the SCRIPTURES as the immediate word of God. Soon after his death, followers created Swedenborgian societies dedicated to the study of his thought. These societies formed the nucleus of the Church of the New Jerusalem, or NEW CHURCH, also called the Swedenborgians.

Swedenborg was born at Stockholm. His father was a prominent member of the Swedish clergy. After graduating from the University of Uppsala in 1709, Swedenborg began to publish that country's first scientific journal, called *Daedalus Hyperboreus*, in 1715. Several years of anatomical research were concluded by a painful religious crisis from which there survives his *Journal of Dreams* (1743–44). On April 7, 1744, he had his first vision of Christ, which gave him a temporary rest from the temptations of his own pride and the evil spirits he believed to be around him. A definite call to abandon worldly learning occurred in April

1745, Swedenborg told his friends in his later years. The call apparently came in the form of a waking vision of the Lord. Swedenborg thereafter left his remaining works in the natural sciences unfinished.

For the remainder of his long career, Swedenborg interpreted the BIBLE and related what he had seen and heard in the world of spirits and ANGELS. From 1749 to 1771 he wrote some 30 volumes, the major part anonymously. Among these were *Arcana Coelestia*, 8 vol. (1749–56; *Heavenly Arcana*) and *Apocalypsis Explicata*, 4 vol. (1785–89; *Apocalypse Explained*), which contain his commentaries on the internal spiritual meaning of GENESIS and EXODUS and on the Book of Revelation, respectively. *De Coelo et ejus Mirabilibus et de Inferno* (1758; *On Heaven and Its Wonders and on Hell*) is perhaps his best-known theological work. He gave a summary of his theological thinking in his last work, the *Vera Christiana Religio* (1771; *True Christian Religion*).

Swedenborg maintained that the infinite, indivisible power and life within all creation is God. The Father, the Son, and the HOLY SPIRIT represent a TRINITY of essential qualities in God; love, wisdom, and activity. This divine trinity is reproduced in human beings in the form of the trinity of soul, body, and mind. Swedenborg asserted that all created things are forms and effects of specific aspects of that love and wisdom and thus "correspond," on the material plane, to spiritual realities. This true order of creation, however, has been disturbed by man's diversion of his love from God to his own ego, thus bringing evil into the world.

In order to redeem and save mankind, the divine being of God had to come into the world in the form of a human being—*i.e.*, JESUS CHRIST. During the course of his life on earth, Jesus resisted every possible temptation and lived to their divine fullness the truths of the Word of God; in so doing he laid aside all the human qualities he had received from MARY, and his nature was revealed as the divine embodiment of the divine soul. Redemption, for Swedenborg, consisted in mankind being re-created in God's image through the vehicle of Christ's glorification.

Swedenborg died in London in 1772, where he was buried in the Swedish Church. At the request of the Swedish government, his body was removed to Uppsala Cathedral in 1908. The first Swedenborgian societies appeared in the 1780s, and the first independent congregation, the origin of the various Church of the New Jerusalem organizations, was founded in London by the end of that decade. Swedenborg's influence was by no means restricted to his immediate disciples. His visions and religious ideas inspired such writers as August Strindberg, Ralph Waldo Emerson, and W.B. Yeats. His theological writings have been translated into many languages.

Emanuel Swedenborg, oil painting by Per Krafft the Elder; in Gripsholm Castle, Sweden

By courtesy of Svenska Portrattarkivet, Stockholm

SYMBOLISM
AND
ICONOGRAPHY

Artistic forms and gestures, often complex, have long been used to convey religious concepts and in the visual, auditory, and kinetic representation of religious ideas and events. The importance of symbolical expression and of the pictorial presentation of religious facts and ideas has been confirmed, and the understanding of them widened and deepened, by the comparative study of the religions of the world. Systems of symbols and pictures that are constituted in a certain ordered and determined relationship to the form, content, and intention of presentation are believed to be among the most important means of knowing and expressing religious facts. The symbolic aspect of religion has been considered by some scholars of psychology and mythology to be the main characteristic of religious expression.

Nevertheless, there is little agreement among scholars as to how symbols should be interpreted. Some scholars have approached symbolism as if it were a code: match a given symbol with a given meaning, and the interpretation of all the world's symbols inexorably develops. However, as Sigmund Freud pointed out in *The Interpretation of Dreams* (1899), symbols are so deeply involved in the particular aspects of a given situation—language, cultural context, even individual experience and psychology—that any universalist approach is likely to miss the mark. STRUCTURALISM, meanwhile, insists that symbols acquire meaning only through the relations they bear to other symbols within the same cultural and linguistic context. Thus they cannot be interpreted except as a member of that set of symbols. Some scholars have asserted, on the same grounds, that symbols cannot be interpreted at all, or that they are not useful in the STUDY OF RELIGION.

THE NATURE OF RELIGIOUS SYMBOLS AND SYMBOLIZATION

The word *symbol* comes from the Greek *symbolon*, which means contract, token, insignia, and a means of identification. Parties to a contract, allies, guests, and hosts could identify each other with the help of the parts of the *symbolon*. In its original meaning the symbol represented and communicated a coherent greater whole by means of a part. The part, as a sort of certificate, guaranteed the presence of the whole and, as a concise meaningful formula, indicated the larger con-

Levels of symbolism: The Hindu god Shiva, represented by a statuette that shows him in his role as Naṭarāja, the Lord of Dance. The ring of fire, the drum held in one hand, and the small figure at his feet are among the symbols embedded in the work
Giraudon—Art Resource

Buddhist pilgrims in Japan have their albums stamped at the temples they visit. The hats, shoes, bells, and staffs they collect are symbolic of their journey and are left at the final temple
Arthur Tress—Photo Researchers

text. The idea of a symbol is based, therefore, on the principle of complementation. The symbolic object, picture, sign, word, or gesture requires the association of certain conscious ideas in order to fully express what is meant by it. To this extent it has both an esoteric and an exoteric, or a veiling and a revealing, function. The discovery of its meaning would thus presuppose a certain amount of active cooperation. As a rule, it is based on the convention of a group that agrees upon its meaning.

Concepts of symbolization. In examining the historical development and present use of the concepts of symbolization, a variety of categories and relationships must necessarily be differentiated. Religious symbols are used to convey concepts concerned with the relationship between humans and "the sacred" and also their social and material world. Other nonreligious types of symbols have been important in the modern world, especially those dealing with our relationship to and conceptualization of the material world. This type of secularized symbol functions in a manner similar to that of the religious symbol by associating a particular meaning with a particular sign. The rationalization of symbols and symbolical complexes as well as the rationalization of myth have been in evidence at least since the Renaissance.

The concept of the religious symbol embraces an abundantly wide variety of types and meanings. ALLEGORY, personifications, figures, analogies, metaphors, PARABLES, pictures (or, more exactly, pictorial representations of ideas), signs, emblems as individually conceived, artificial symbols with an added verbal meaning, and attributes as a mark used to distinguish certain persons all are formal, historical, literary, and artificial categories of the symbolical. The symbol (religious and other) is intended primarily for the circle of the initiated and involves the acknowledgment of the experience that it expresses. The meaning of the symbol is not, however, kept hidden; to some extent, the symbol even has a revelatory character (*i.e.*, it goes beyond the obvious meaning for those who contemplate its depths). It indicates the need for communication and yet conceals the details and innermost aspects of its contents.

Varieties and meanings associated with the term symbol. Different forms and levels of the experience of and relationship to reality (both sacred and profane) are linked with the concepts of symbol, sign, and picture. The function of the symbol is to represent a reality or a truth and to reveal them either instantaneously or gradually. The relationship of the symbol to a reality is conceived of as somewhat direct and intimate and also as somewhat indirect and distant. The symbol is sometimes identified with the reality that it represents and sometimes regarded as a pure transparency of it. As a "sign" or "picture" the representation of the experience of and relationship to reality has either a denotative or a truly representative meaning. For instance, the doctrines of the nature of the presence of JESUS CHRIST in the sacrament of the EUCHARIST in the teachings of EASTERN ORTHODOXY, ROMAN CATHOLICISM, and the leaders of the Protestant REFORMATION demonstrate the various and extensive levels of symbolical understandings. These levels range all the way from the concept of physical identity in the TRANSUBSTANTIATION theory of Roman Catholicism (in which the substance of breadness and wineness is believed to be changed into the body and blood of Christ, though the apparent properties of the elements remain the same) through Luther's Real Presence theory (in which Christ is viewed as present, though the question of how is not answered because the question of why he is present is considered more important), and Huldrych Zwingli's sign (symbolic or memorial) theory, to the concept of mere allusion. The concept of the symbol permits all these interpretations.

Furthermore, a symbol in its intermediary function has aspects of epistemology (theory of knowing) and ontology (theory of being). As a means of knowledge, it operates in a characteristically dialectical process of veiling and revealing truths. It fulfills an interpretative function in the process of effectively apprehending and comprehending RELIGIOUS EXPERIENCE. In doing so, the word, or symbol—with its meaning, contextual use, relationship to other types of religious expression, and interpretative connection with the various forms of sign, picture, gesture, and sound—plays an important part in the process of symbolical perception and reflection. Although the symbol is an abbreviation, as a means of communication it brings about—through its connection with the object of reli-

The bodhisattva Avalokiteśvara, whose infinite compassion and mercy are symbolized by the 11 heads and 8 arms by which he senses man's needs everywhere in the universe
Rijksmuseum voor Volkenkunde, Leiden, The Netherlands

1045

The Aztec god Xipe Totec, the Flayed Lord, dressed in the skin of a sacrificial victim; the statue represents an actual ritual, which in turn represented the germination of the maize (corn) seed
Werner Forman—Art Resource

gion—not only an interpretative knowledge of the world and a conferral or comparison of meaning to life but also a means of access to the sacred reality. It may even promise a fusion, or union of some sort, with the divine.

The symbolic process. To trace the origin, development, and differentiation of a symbol is a complicated process. Almost every symbol and picture in religion is at first either directly or indirectly connected with the sense impressions and objects of the environment. Many are derived from the objects of nature, and others are artificially constructed in a process of intuitive perception, emotional experience, or rational reflection. In most cases, the constructions are again related to objects in the world of sense perception. A tendency toward simplification, abbreviation into signs, and abstraction from sense objects is quite evident, as well as a tendency to concentrate several processes into a single symbol. On the other hand, there is a tendency to accumulate, combine, multiply, and differentiate symbolical statements for the same thought or circumstance. Here, the same idea may be symbolically expressed in various manners; *e.g.*, by means of representing persons, objects, animals, and signs, all side by side.

The foundations of the symbolization process lie in the areas of the conscious and the unconscious, of experience and thought, and of sense perception, intuition, and imagination. From these arises the structure of religious symbolism. Sensation and physiological and psychological processes participate in the formation of the symbol structure. Extraordinary experiences and conditions, visions, ECSTASY, and states of delirium must also be taken into consideration. The symbol itself, however, is intended as an objective concentration of experiences of the transcendent world and not as a subjective construction of a personally creative process. The process of rational conceptualization and structuralization also plays a part in the origin and development of many symbols. There is a correlation between sense perception, imagination, and the work of the intellect.

ICONS AND SYSTEMS OF ICONOGRAPHY

Throughout the history of their development, religious ICONOGRAPHY and symbolism have been closely interrelated. Many religious symbols can be understood as conceptual abbreviations, simplifications, abstractions, and stylizations of pictures or of pictorial impressions of the world of sense objects that are manifested in iconographic representations. In conceiving, describing, and communicating the experience of reality, the realistic picture and the nonrepresentational sign both have as their primary function the expression of this experience in religious terms. These pictures may also include other types of symbolic representation, such as words, tones, gestures, rituals, and architecture (*see* SACRED ARCHITECTURE).

Icons may portray the ritual means of attaining salvation or explain moral relationships and duties. They may borrow from myths and other religious narrative material to depict the historical past and the present, as well as the future and the afterlife. Or they may represent religious doctrine and the theological treatment of dogmatic themes, as well as other RELIGIOUS BELIEFS, religious experiences, and conceptions of a more individualistic nature.

Painted or sculptured tableaus of historical or mythical events originally belonged in a ritual setting. These tableaus also may occasionally be found on the interiors and sometimes the exteriors of houses and on cemetery monuments. They are made for the purpose of serving private devotion and a personal confession of faith. In the form of a framed picture, Oriental roll picture, print, or book illustration, such an iconographic tableau contains religious information, and it thereby serves both to mediate and to stimulate contemplation and devotion.

It is generally the case that the religions of JUDAISM, ISLAM, and ancient SHINTŌ have rejected any representation of the divine (*see* ANICONISM).

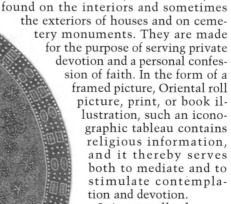

(Above) A raven totem—perhaps representing a guardian spirit—tops a pole that once formed the corner of an Alaskan Indian tribal house
Alaska Department of Economic Development

(Left) Mosaic incorporating iconic symbols (the cross, the starry sky) and words and letters symbolic of Christian ideas
Scala—Art Resource

SYMEON THE NEW THEOLOGIAN, SAINT

SYMEON THE NEW THEOLOGIAN, SAINT \'si-mē-ən\, *also spelled* Simeon (b. *c.* 949, Paphlagonia, in Asia Minor—d. March 12, 1022, Chrysopolis, near Constantinople [now Istanbul, Turkey]), Byzantine monk and mystic, called the New Theologian to mark his difference from two key figures in Greek Christian esteem both surnamed "the Theologian," ST. JOHN THE EVANGELIST and the 4th-century theologian ST. GREGORY OF NAZIANZUS. Through his spiritual experiences and writings Symeon prepared the way for the MYSTICISM of HESYCHASM, a 14th-century Eastern movement in CONTEMPLATIVE prayer. (*See also* GREGORY PALAMAS.)

Symeon's writings consist mainly of *catecheses* (Greek: "doctrinal and moral instructions"); sermons preached to his monks at St. Mamas; a series of short rules, *capita* (Latin: "chapters"); and the *Hymns of the Divine Loves*, describing his spiritual experiences. Symeon's mystical theology is a distinct phase of an evolutionary process in Greek spirituality that began in the late 2nd century. Its central theme is the conviction that, by applying the classical methods of mental prayer, one experiences a contemplative "vision of light," a symbolic term denoting the intuitional illumination that the mystic realizes in his encounter with the Divine Unknown. Symeon emphasized that such experience is attainable by all who earnestly immerse themselves in the life of prayer and is essential to interpreting sacred SCRIPTURES.

SYNAGOGUE, in JUDAISM, community house of worship that serves as a place not only for liturgical services but also for assembly and study. Its traditional functions are reflected in three Hebrew synonyms for synagogue: *bet ha-tefilla* ("house of prayer"), *bet ha-kneset* ("house of assembly"), and *bet ha-midrash* ("house of study"). The Greek word *synagōgē*, literally, "bringing together, assembly" (hence English *synagogue*), was first regularly applied to a house of worship by Jewish writers (and in the NEW TESTAMENT) in the 1st century CE. The Medieval Latin word *schola*, in the sense "assemblage, corporate body," was used to refer to the synagogue and is most likely continued in the Yiddish word *shul*—a merger of a corresponding Judeo-Romance word with the Middle High German word *schuole* ("school"). In modern times, the word "temple" is common among some Reform and Conservative congregations.

The oldest dated evidence of a synagogue is from the 3rd century BCE, but synagogues doubtless have an older history. Some scholars feel that the destruction of Solomon's Temple in 586 BCE gave rise to synagogues after private homes were temporarily used for public worship and religious instructions.

Other scholars trace the origin of synagogues to the Jewish custom of having representatives of communities outside Jerusalem pray together during the two-week period when priestly representatives of their community attended ritual sacrifices in the TEMPLE OF JERUSALEM.

Whatever their origin, synagogues flourished side by side with the ancient Temple cult and existed long before Jewish sacrifice and the established PRIESTHOOD were terminated with the destruction and plundering of the Second Temple by Titus in 70 CE. Thereafter, synagogues took on an even greater importance as the unchallenged focal point of Jewish religious life.

Literature of the 1st century refers to numerous synagogues not only in Palestine but also in Rome, Greece, Egypt, Babylonia, and Asia Minor. By the middle of that century, all sizable Jewish communities had a synagogue where regular morning, afternoon, and evening services

Synagogue, Spanish manuscript on vellum, c. 1350
The British Library/The Bridgeman Art Library

were held, with special liturgies on the SABBATH and on religious festivals.

Modern synagogues carry on the same basic functions associated with ancient synagogues but have added social, recreational, and philanthropic programs as the times demand. They are essentially democratic institutions established by a community of Jews who seek God through prayer and sacred studies. Since the liturgy has no sacrifice, no priesthood is required for public worship. Because each synagogue is autonomous, its erection, its maintenance, and its RABBI and officials reflect the desires of the local community.

A typical synagogue contains an ARK (where the scrolls of the Law are kept), an "eternal light" burning before the Ark, two candelabra, pews, and a raised platform (*bimah*), from which scriptural passages are read and from which, often, services are conducted. The segregation of men and women, still observed in Orthodox synagogues, has been abandoned by Reform and Conservative congregations. A RITUAL BATH (*mikveh*) is sometimes located on the premises.

SYNCRETISM, RELIGIOUS \'siŋ-krə-,ti-zəm\, fusion of diverse RELIGIOUS BELIEFS and practices. Instances of religious syncretism—as, for example, GNOSTICISM, which is a religious dualistic system that incorporated elements from the Oriental MYSTERY RELIGIONS, JUDAISM, CHRISTIANITY, and Greek religious philosophical concepts—were particularly prevalent during the Hellenistic period (*c.* 300 BCE–*c.* 300 CE). The fusion of cultures that was effected by the conquest of Alexander the Great (4th century BCE), his successors, and the Roman Empire tended to bring together a variety of religious and philosophical views that resulted in a strong tendency toward religious syncretism. Orthodox Christianity, although influenced by other religions, generally looked negatively upon these syncretistic movements.

Syncretistic movements in the Orient, such as MAN-ICHAEISM (a dualistic religion founded by the 3rd-century-CE Iranian prophet MANI, who combined elements of Christianity, Zoroastrianism, and BUDDHISM) and SIKHISM (a religion founded by the 15th–16th-century Indian reformer GURŪ NĀNAK, who combined elements of ISLAM and HINDU-ISM), also met with resistance from the prevailing religions of their respective areas.

See also CAO DAI; MACUMBA; SANTERIA; VOUDOU; CH'ŎN-DOGYO.

SYNOD (from Greek *synodos*, "assembly"), in the Christian church, a local or provincial assembly of bishops and other church officials meeting to resolve questions of discipline or administration.

A solemn mass at St. Peter's Basilica opening a month-long synod of bishops in Rome, November 1997
Reuters—Max Rossi—Archive Photos

The earliest synods can be traced to meetings held by bishops from various regions in the middle of the 2nd century. A synod of bishops from the worldwide ROMAN CATHO-LIC church meets in Rome at regular but infrequent intervals for the purpose of discussing matters of vital church interest, in an advisory capacity to the pope. In some Protestant churches, the term synod has come to signify an organizational unit.

The actions taken by individual synods sometimes have had lasting significance. In the SYNOD OF DORT (1618–19), the Dutch REFORMED CHURCH dealt with ARMINIANISM and sponsored reforms aimed at personal religious renewal.

SYNOPTIC GOSPELS \si-'näp-tik\, the Gospels of Matthew, Mark, and Luke in the NEW TESTAMENT. They have been called the Synoptic Gospels since the 1780s because, as distinguished from the Gospel of John, they are so similar in structure, content, and wording that they can easily be set side by side to provide a synoptic (presenting the same or common view) comparison of their content. The striking similarities between the first three Gospels prompt questions regarding the actual literary relationship that exists between them. This question, called the Synoptic problem, has been elaborately studied in modern times.

ṬABARĪ, AL-

ṬABARĪ, AL- \át-'tä-bə-ˌrē\, *in full* Abū JaʿFar Muhammad ibn Jarīr al-Ṭabarī (b. 839, Āmol, Ṭabaristān [Iran]—d. 923, Baghdad, Iraq), Muslim scholar, author of enormous compendiums of early Islamic history and Qurʾanic EXEGESIS, who made a distinct contribution to the consolidation of SUNNI thought during the 9th century. His major works were the *Qurʾan Commentary* and the *History of Prophets and Kings*.

Life. The young al-Ṭabarī demonstrated a precocious intellect and journeyed from his native town to study in the major centers of learning in Iraq, Syria, and Egypt. Over the course of many years he collected oral and written material from numerous scholars and libraries for his later work. Al-Ṭabarī enjoyed sufficient financial independence to enable him to devote the latter part of his life to teaching and writing in Baghdad, the capital of the ʿAbbāsid caliphate, where he died in 923. The times in which he lived were marked by political disorder, social crisis, and philosophical-theological controversy. Discontent, of diverse cause and circumstance, brought open rebellion to the very heart of the caliph's empire, and, like all movements of socioeconomic origin in medieval ISLAM, sought legitimacy in religious expression directed against official Sunni orthodoxy.

Likewise retreating from the ultraorthodox Sunni faction, al-Ṭabarī established his own school of jurisprudence, which did not long survive his own death. He nevertheless made a distinct contribution to the consolidation of Sunni thought during the 9th century through his reorganization of material for historical and Qurʾanic studies, condensing the vast wealth of exegetical and historical erudition of the preceding generations of Muslim scholars (many of whose works are not extant in their original form).

Major works. His labor began with the *Qurʾan Commentary*, in which his method was to follow the QURʾAN text word by word, juxtaposing all of the juridical, lexicographical, and historical explanations transmitted in reports from the Prophet MUHAMMAD, his companions, and their followers. To each report (HADITH) was affixed a chain of "transmitters" (ISNĀD) purporting to go back to the original informant. Divergent reports were seldom reconciled, the scholar's only critical tool being his judgment as to the soundness of the *isnād* and not of the content of the Hadith. Thus plurality of interpretation was admitted on principle. This was followed by the *History of Prophets and Kings*, which began with the Creation, followed by accounts regarding the patriarchs, prophets, and rulers of antiquity. The history of the Sāsānian kings came next. For the period of the Prophet's life, al-Ṭabarī drew upon the extensive research of 8th-century Medinan scholars whose perspective of Muslim history evolved as a theocentric (god-centered) universal history of PROPHECY culminating in the career of Muhammad.

The sources for al-Ṭabarī's *History*, covering the years from the Prophet's death to the fall of the Umayyad dynasty (661–750), were short monographs, each treating a major event or the circumstances attending the death of an important person. Al-Ṭabarī supplemented this material with historical reports embodied in works on genealogy, poetry, and tribal affairs. Further details of the early ʿAbbāsid period were available to him in a few histories of the CALIPHS that unfortunately have come down only in the fragments preserved by al-Ṭabarī. From the beginning of the Muslim era (dated from 622, the date of the HIJRA—the Prophet Muhammad's migration from MECCA to MEDINA), the *History* is arranged as a set of annals according to the years after the Hijra, terminating in the year 915. It grew so popular that the Sāmānid prince Manṣūr ibn Nūḥ had it translated into Persian (c. 963).

Views of history. Al-Ṭabarī saw no relevance in searching for the nature and causes of events, for any ultimate explanation lay beyond history itself and was known to God alone. Prophetic tradition, like the Qurʾan, provided positive commands and injunctions from God. History pointed to the consequences of heeding or ignoring him. For al-Ṭabarī, therefore, history was the divine will teaching by example. *See also* TAFSĪR.

TABERNACLE

TABERNACLE, *Hebrew* Mishkan ("Dwelling"), in Jewish history, portable SANCTUARY constructed by MOSES as a place of worship for the Hebrew tribes during the period of wandering that preceded their arrival in the Promised Land. The Tabernacle no longer served a purpose after the erection of Solomon's TEMPLE IN JERUSALEM in 950 BCE.

The entire Tabernacle complex consisted of a large court surrounding a comparatively small building that was the Tabernacle proper. The court, enclosed by linen hangings, had the shape of two adjacent squares. In the eastern square stood the altar of sacrifice for burnt offerings; nearby stood a basin holding water used by the priests for ritual ABLUTIONS. The western square was occupied by the ARK of the Law, situated in the inner sanctuary of the Tabernacle.

The Tabernacle was constructed of tapestry curtains decorated with cherubim. The interior was divided into two rooms. The outer room, or "holy place," contained the table on which the bread of the Presence (SHEWBREAD) was placed, the altar of incense, and the seven-branched candelabrum (MENORAH). The inner room, or HOLY OF HOLIES, was thought to be the actual dwelling place of the God of Israel, who sat invisibly enthroned above a solid slab of gold that rested on the ARK OF THE COVENANT and had a CHERUB at each end. This Ark was a gold-covered wooden box containing the tablets of the TEN COMMANDMENTS.

TABOO

TABOO, *Tongan* tabu, *Maori* tapu, prohibition of an action or the use of an object based on ritualistic distinctions as being either sacred and consecrated or dangerous, unclean, and accursed. The term is of Polynesian origin and was first noted by Captain James Cook during his visit to Tonga in 1771; he introduced the term into the English language. Taboos were most highly developed in the Polynesian societ-

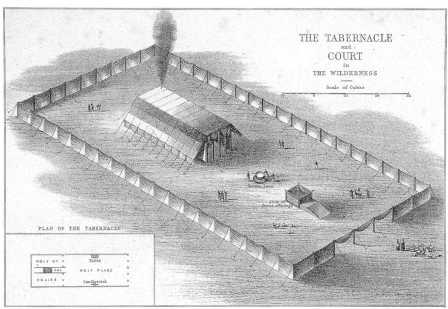

THE TABERNACLE
and
COURT
in
THE WILDERNESS
Scale of Cubits

PLAN OF THE TABERNACLE

HOLY OF   Table
ARK   HOLY PLACE
HOLIES   Candlestick

The Tabernacle and Court in the Wilderness, *lithograph*
Private collection—The Bridgeman Art Library

TAFSĪR \tăf-'sēr\ (Arabic: "explanation"), science of explanation of the QUR'AN or of Qur'anic commentary. So long as MUHAMMAD was alive, no other authority for interpretations of the Qur'anic revelations was recognized by Muslims. Upon his death, however, commentaries were needed because the text, when it achieved written form, lacked historical sequence in the arrangement of materials, suffered from ambiguity of both text and meaning, showed a variety of differing readings, was recorded in a defective script, and even contained apparent contradictions. Many Muslims in the early period sought to explain the Qur'an on the basis of pure personal speculation, known as *tafsīr bi'l-ra'y*, and such interpretation, though generally disapproved, has persisted down to the present time. Others explained or embellished Qur'anic passages using stories drawn from Christian—and especially from Jewish—sources (*Isrā'īlīyāt*). To counter the arbitrariness of such interpretation, in the fourth Islamic century (10th century CE) there emerged the religious science called *'ilm al-tafsīr*, a systematic EXEGESIS of the Qur'anic text, which proceeds verse by verse, and sometimes word by word. Over time this science developed several methods and forms of its own.

The Hungarian scholar Ignáz Goldziher traced the development of *tafsīr* through several stages. In the first, or primitive, stage, Muslims were concerned principally to establish the proper text of the Qur'an. The second stage, known as traditional *tafsīr*, featured explanations of Qur'anic passages based upon explanations attributed either to the Prophet himself or to his Companions. It relied, therefore, upon HADITH. As Muslims sought to establish their identity as a religious community and to define their doctrinal stance, there arose a dogmatic type of *tafsīr*. The Qur'an was interpreted by various sectarian groups to establish their own peculiar doctrinal positions; notable among them were the MU'TAZILA, so-called rationalists, who insisted that interpretation (*ta'wīl*) of the Qur'an must conform with reason. SUFIS and SHI'ITES with esoteric inclinations also practiced *ta'wīl*, departing sharply from a purely external analysis. A British scholar, John Wansbrough, classified *tafsīr* literature according to its form and function. He distinguished five types, which he held to have appeared in roughly chronological order: attempts to supply a narrative context for passages, efforts to explain the implications for conduct of various passages, concern with details of the text, concern with matters of rhetoric, and allegorical interpretation.

The monumental commentary compiled by the historian AL-ṬABARĪ (839–923) assembled all the traditional scholarship that had been produced until his time. It remains the

ies of the South Pacific, but such ritual prohibitions have been present in virtually all cultures.

Taboos could include prohibitions on certain activities, dietary restrictions, prohibitions on talking to or touching certain people, prohibitions on walking or traveling in certain areas, and various taboos that function during important life events such as birth, marriage, and death. The two primary classes of taboos are those in which notions of sacredness or holiness are apparent and those in which notions of uncleanliness are the motivating factor.

Generally, the prohibition that is inherent in a taboo includes the idea that a breach or defiance of the taboo will automatically be followed by some kind of trouble to the offender, such as lack of success in hunting or fishing, sickness, or the death of a relative. A person meets with an accident or has no success in a given pursuit, and, in seeking a reason for this turn of events, he or others infer that he has in some manner committed a breach of taboo.

Taboos as manifested in various cultures have stimulated an extensive scholarly literature that seeks to compare, analyze, and explain them. The most important researchers or theorists on the topic have included WILLIAM ROBERTSON SMITH, Wilhelm Wundt, and SIGMUND FREUD in his book *Totem and Taboo* (1913). Freud provided one of the most persuasive and ingenious explanations for the apparently irrational nature of taboos, positing that they were generated by ambivalent social attitudes and in effect represent forbidden actions for which there nevertheless exists a strong unconscious inclination. Freud directly applied this viewpoint to the most widespread of all taboos, the incest taboo, which prohibits sexual relations between close blood relatives. There is no generally accepted explanation of taboos, but there is broad agreement that the taboos current in any society tend to relate to objects and actions that are significant to the social order and that belong to the general system of social control.

most basic of all *tafsīr*s. Subsequent commentaries of note include those by al-Zamakhsharī (1075–1143), AL-RĀZĪ (1149–1209), al-Bayḍāwī (d. 1280), and al-Suyūṭī (1445–1505). Commentaries continue to be compiled at the present time; Muslim modernists, for example, have used them as a vehicle for their reformist ideas. *See also* EXEGESIS; SCRIPTURE.

TAGORE, DEBENDRANATH \'tä-,gȯr, *Angl* tə-'gȯr\, Debendranath *also spelled* Devendranath, *Bengali* Debendranāth Ṭhākur \də-'ben-drə-,nät-'tä-,kür\ (b. May 15, 1817, Calcutta, India—d. Jan. 19, 1905, Calcutta), Hindu philosopher and religious reformer, active in the BRAHMO SAMAJ.

Born into a wealthy landowning family, Tagore was educated in Sanskrit, Persian, English, and Western philosophy. He became a close friend of his fellow reformer KESHAB CHUNDER SEN. Tagore spoke out vehemently against SATĪ, a practice that was especially prevalent in Bengal. Together, Tagore and Sen attempted to raise the Indian literacy rate and to bring education within the reach of all. While Sen drifted toward CHRISTIANITY, Tagore remained a more conservative Hindu. This philosophical break between the two men eventually resulted in a SCHISM within the Brahmo Samaj in 1866.

Tagore, in his zeal to erase Hindu IDOLATRY as well as divisive and undemocratic practices, finally rejected the whole of the VEDAS, claiming that no set of writings could furnish complete and satisfying guidelines to human activity. Failing to find a middle path between radical RATIONALISM and fanatical BRAHMIN conservatism, Tagore retired from public life, although he continued to instruct a small band of followers. In 1863 he founded Śāntiniketan ("Abode of Peace"), a retreat in rural Bengal later made famous by his son RABINDRANATH TAGORE, whose educational center there became an international university. Until his death Tagore bore the title Maharishi ("Great Sage").

One of Tagore's books was translated into English, *Vedantic Doctrines Vindicated* (1845). His *Brahmo-Dharma* (1854; "The Religion of God"), a commentary in Bengali on the Sanskrit SCRIPTURES, is considered to be a masterpiece.

TAGORE, RABINDRANATH, *Bengali* Rabīndranāth Ṭhākur \rə-'bēn-drə-,nät-'tä-,kür\ (b. May 7, 1861, Calcutta, India—d. Aug. 7, 1941, Calcutta), Bengali poet, short-story writer, song composer, playwright, essayist, and painter who was awarded the Nobel Prize for Literature in 1913. Tagore introduced new prose and verse forms and the use of colloquial language into Bengali literature, thereby freeing it from traditional models based on classical Sanskrit. He was highly influential in introducing Indian culture to the West and vice versa and is generally regarded as the outstanding creative artist of modern India.

The son of the religious reformer DEBENDRANATH TAGORE, he early began to write verses and studied for a time in England. Returning to India, he published several books of poetry in

Rabindranath Tagore
EB Inc.

the 1880s and completed *Mānasī* (1890), a collection that contains some of his best-known poems, including many in verse forms new to Bengali, as well as some social and political satire that was critical of his fellow Bengalis.

In 1891 Tagore went to East Bengal (now in Bangladesh) to manage his family's estates at Shilaidah and Shazadpur for 10 years. His sympathy for the poverty and backwardness of the village folk there became the keynote of much of his later writing. During these years he published several poetry collections, notably *Sonār Tarī* (1894; *The Golden Boat*), and plays, notably *Chitrāṅgadā* (1892; *Chitra*). His more than 2,000 songs remain extremely popular among all classes of Bengali society.

In 1901 Tagore founded an experimental school in rural West Bengal at Śantiniketan ("Abode of Peace"), where he sought to blend the best in the Indian and Western traditions. He settled there permanently; the school became Viśva-Bhāratī University in 1921. His later poetry was introduced to the West in *Gitanjali, Song Offerings* (1912), containing Tagore's English prose translations of religious poems from several of his Bengali verse collections. Hailed by W.B. Yeats and André Gide, it won him the Nobel Prize in 1913. He was awarded knighthood in 1915, but he repudiated it in 1919 as a protest against the AMRITSAR Massacre.

Tagore's novels include *Gora* (1910) and *Ghare-Baire* (1916; *The Home and the World*). In the late 1920s Tagore took up painting and produced works that won him a place among India's foremost contemporary artists.

ṬAHĀRA \tà-'hàr-ə\ (Arabic: "purity"), system of ritual purity in ISLAM. This system is based on two premises: the first is that humans lapse from a state appropriate to ritual activity as a result of certain bodily acts, such as defecation, sexual intercourse, or MENSTRUATION. Second, there are certain substances, such as pork or blood, that are either unclean by nature or have the effect of defiling a space, person, or object, rendering it unfit for ritual use. In both cases, the unfitness of the thing or person can be remedied by the ritual application of water or of a simulacrum (sand, clean rock, etc.).

All things and places are presumed to be ritually acceptable or neutral unless Scripture—either QUR'AN or HADITH—indicates otherwise. Items that are always defiling are called *naja*s and include swine, blood, dog saliva, and wine. All *naja*s should be avoided when possible, and if clothing or dishes come in contact with these items they should be washed with water until there is no smell, sight, or other evidence of the proscribed item. Pork or carrion should never be eaten and neither should carrion eaters such as vultures or dogs; products such as feces or hides from these animals should also be avoided.

There are two ritually disabling states into which humans fall—affected (*muḥdath*) and precluded (*junub*). Acts that are "affects" are called *ḥadath*, and these include defecation, urination, breaking wind, touching a person of the opposite sex (with desire, for most schools of Islamic jurisprudence), or touching one's own genitals. For most jurists, unconsciousness or sleeping in a prone position make it probable that one has at least broken wind and so is affected. Likewise, violent laughter, coughing, or anger, according to many jurists, ought to occasion ritual purification, if they do not actually require it. Until the affected person undoes this state, he or she cannot perform ritual worship (ṢALĀT), circumambulate the KAʿBA, or handle the Qurʾan.

The ritual purification for being affected is called ABLUTION (*wuḍūʾ*). It consists of (1) intending to perform the *wu-*

ḍūʾ, (2) washing the hands three times, (3) rinsing out the mouth and snuffing water into the nostrils three times, and (4) washing the face from the hairline to the neck, the chin, and the openings of the nostrils. (5) The beard (if there is one) is then combed with wet fingers, and (6) the hands are washed up to the wrists three times. (7) The head—from the forehead to the nape of the neck, including the ears—is then rubbed with both hands, and (8) the feet, particularly the tops and including the ankles, are rubbed. Finally, (9) the Muslim says, "I bear witness that there is no God but God, the unique, who has no partner. I bear witness that MUHAMMAD is his servant and his Messenger."

The other state of impurity, which is sometimes called the major impurity, is referred to in ritual texts as preclusion (janābah). It arises from sexual intercourse, seminal emission, menstruation, and childbirth. A person in a state of preclusion is ritually disabled like the affected person, but in addition he or she may not recite the Qurʾan, perform ritual recollections (DHIKR) of God, or fast for RAMAḌĀN. This disability is reversed by—according to most schools—adding the pouring of water over the entire body to the rituals of ablution. This LUSTRATION (ghusl) is the reason why bathhouses are found throughout Islamdom, since every act of sexual intercourse, every menstruation, and every childbirth requires lustration before the Muslim can resume his or her ritual life. Only women are ritually disabled in this major way by acts they cannot control, and only women cannot immediately lustrate themselves into a state of ritual capability.

Unlike in many other ritual communities, however, in SUNNI law a ritually disabled person does not, by touch, conversation, or other contact, have the power to disable another person ritually. Shiʿism differs from Sunni law precisely on this issue of the contamination through ritually disabled persons and impure substances. For Imami SHIʿITES, women who are menstruating can render a man in need of ablution by contact with her. Indeed, according to some legists, the very sweat of a menstruating woman, passing through her clothing, can ritually disable a man. Also, prayer in an area contaminated by an impure substance or person is invalid. In addition, Christians, Jews, and other non-Muslims have been seen in much of Shiʿite legal theory as ritually contaminating. According to some, food cooked by non-Muslims cannot be eaten, water being drunk by non-Muslims and the cup that contains it are ritually impure, and (as one of the distinctive features of Shiʿite law) Christians and Jews cannot be acceptable butchers, as they may be for Sunnis.

The penalties for transgressions of the rules of purity are generally mild. Muslims who have intercourse when the woman is menstruating must make a small donation to charity. Impure foods eaten inadvertently require no penance. Prayer or other rituals deliberately offered in a state of ritual impurity are simply invalid, causing one to suffer the double fault of disobeying God and failing validly to perform one's ritual obligations.

One of the most striking features of the Islamic legal (FIQH) literature on purity (as on most things) is the nearly complete absence of any justification for ritual rules. Why God ordained washing in a certain way as a precondition of prayer or excluded menstruating women from ritual was not explained by the legists. The arbitrariness of these rules—from a human point of view—was recognized in legal and theological discourse. The Sufi tradition, by contrast, did not shy from venturing such explanations, and works like Abū Ṭālib al-Makkī's Qut al-qulub and AL-GHA-

ZĀLĪ's Iḥyāʾ ʿulum al-dīn are filled with explanations of the reasons or symbolism behind the rituals of purity. In SUFISM, they were particularly prone to see in the rituals of ablution and lustration figures of moral or spiritual purity. The cleansing of the body and the cleansing of the heart were conflated by Sufi legists, so that these rituals took on a deeper significance and acquired many layers of meaning.

In modern times the justification of ritual as obedience has seemed embarrassing to apologists, and from the 19th century both liberals and Islamists have labored to find the real point of these rituals. Most have assimilated ritual purity to "cleanliness" or "hygiene" and have seen in the rules for ablution a wise anticipation by God and his Prophet of the insights of modern scientists such as Louis Pasteur and Joseph Lister.

TA-HSÜEH \ˈdä-ˈshwe\, *Pinyin* Daxue (Chinese: "Great Learning"), text generally attributed to CONFUCIUS and TSENG-TZU. For centuries the text existed only as a chapter of the LI-CHI ("Collection of Rituals"). When CHU HSI, a 12th-century philosopher, published it separately as one of the "FOUR BOOKS" (*Ssu-shu*), it gained lasting renown.

Ta-hsüeh states that world peace is impossible unless a ruler first regulates his own country. But no ruler can do this without first setting his own household in order, which in turn is impossible before he has oriented his personal life by rectifying his heart and acquiring sincerity. These virtues are the natural consequence of expanded wisdom that results from investigating all things. It thus views good government and world peace as inseparably bound up with a ruler's personal virtue.

In his preface, Chu Hsi explained that the treatise is a means to personal development. Each individual, he says, must cultivate benevolence (JEN), righteousness (*i*), propriety (LI), and wisdom (*chih*), but virtue will not be acquired in equal measure by all. T'ien (Heaven), therefore, will see to it that the most virtuous man will rule.

ṬAHṬĀWĪ, RIFĀʿA RĀFIʿ AL- \täḵ-ˈtä-wē\ (b. 1801, Ṭaḥṭā, Egypt—d. 1873, Egypt), teacher and scholar who was one of the first Egyptians to grapple with the question of adjusting to the West and to provide answers to this question in Islamic terms.

In 1826 al-Ṭahṭāwī went to Paris as a religious teacher to a group of Egyptian students there. After five years he returned to Egypt, and in 1836 he became head of the new School of Languages in Cairo. In 1841 he was placed in charge of a translation bureau, which dealt with books on history, geography, and military science. Under the Khedive ʿAbbās I, who ascended the throne in 1848, Western influences were suspect, and al-Ṭahṭāwī was sent to Khartoum, where he taught school. On the succession of Saʿīd (1854), al-Ṭahṭāwī returned to Cairo, where he continued his own scholarly work.

Al-Ṭahṭāwī saw the social order as being established by God and the ruler as God's representative. He believed that the only limitations on the ruler's authority were the dictates of his own conscience. Although the people had no rights, the ruler should rule with justice and should strive to foster their material well-being. The people in turn should conscientiously fulfill their duties as citizens, and the state should educate them to that end. Al-Ṭahṭāwī's modernism lay in his conception of the material progress that could be possible within the framework of a harmoniously functioning government and society, achieved with the aid of Western technology.

TAHUANTINSUYU \tä-ˌwän-tēn-ˈsü-yü\, *also spelled* Tawantinsuyu (Quechua: "Realm of the Four Parts"), territories spread over parts of Ecuador, Peru, Bolivia, Chile, and Argentina that, by the 1500s, were all part of a single Inca state. *See also* PRE-COLUMBIAN MESO-AMERICAN RELIGIONS.

T'AI, MOUNT \ˈtī\, *Chinese* (Wade-Giles) T'ai Shan \ˈtī-ˈshän\, *also called* Yu-huang Shan \ˈyǖ-ˈhwäŋ-\, (Pinyin) Tai Shan, *or* Yuhuang Shan, principal peak of the T'ai Shan (mountain range); it lies to the north of the city of T'ai-an in Shantung Province, China. Since Ch'in times (221–206 BCE) it has also been known as Tung-yüeh (Eastern Peak), one of the five holy peaks of China, and has usually ranked as the first among them. Its name was changed from Mount T'ai to Mount Yu-huang by the Chinese Communists.

Historically an object of continuous veneration in the cult of the official state religion, Mount T'ai was also the site of the most awesome of all the state rituals of the traditional Chinese empire, the sacrifices called Feng and Shan, which symbolized the absolute establishment of a dynasty's fortunes. They were carried out at rare intervals—by the Former Han dynasty (206 BCE–8 CE) in 110, 106, 102, and 98 BCE; by the Later Han dynasty (23–220 CE) in 56 CE; and by emperors of the T'ang dynasty (618–907) in 666 and again in 725. These sacrifices announced to heaven and earth alike the accomplishment of dynastic success. Mount T'ai was also a deity in its own right, to which prayers were offered in spring for a good harvest and in autumn to give thanks for a completed harvest. Because Mount T'ai was the chief regional deity of eastern China, prayers were also offered to it in case of floods or earthquakes.

The mountain also became associated with a wide range of beliefs connected with TAOISM. It was considered the center of the Yang principle, the source of life, and from the Later Han period onward it was believed that the spirit of Mount T'ai commanded the fates of all humans and that after death their souls returned to Mount T'ai for judgment. In Ming times (1368–1644) the center of the popular cult was transferred from the god to his daughter, T'ai Shan Niang-niang (The Lady of Mount T'ai)—also called Pi-hsia Yüan-chün (The Goddess of the Variegated Clouds)—whose cult began to grow from about 1000 and who became a northern Taoist equivalent to the Buddhist KUAN-YIN (Goddess of Mercy), whose cult was powerful in central and southern China.

The slopes of Mount T'ai have remained covered with temples and shrines dedicated to the complex pantheon of minor deities with whom it is associated. In former times vast numbers of pilgrims visited it annually, and a great festival was held in the third month of the Chinese year.

T'AI-CHI \ˈtī-ˈjē\, *Pinyin* Taiji (Chinese: "Great Ultimate"), in Chinese philosophy, the eternal source and cause of all reality. The concept is first mentioned in the I-CHING, where T'ai-chi is the source and union of the two primary aspects of the cosmos, yang (active) and yin (passive). The Neo-Confucian philosophers of the Sung dynasty (960–1279 CE) associated T'ai-chi with LI ("principle"), the supreme rational principle of the universe. *Li* engenders *ch'i* ("vital matter"), which is transformed through the yang and yin modes of development into the Five Elements (wood, earth, fire, metal, and water), which form the basic constituents of the physical universe.

T'AI-CHI CH'UAN \ˈtī-ˈjē-ˈchwän\, *Pinyin* Taijichuan (Chinese: from *T'ai-chi*, "Great Ultimate" plus *ch'uan*, "fist,"

"boxing"), ancient and distinctive Chinese form of exercise or attack and defense. As exercise, T'ai-chi ch'uan is designed to provide relaxation in the process of body-conditioning exercise and is drawn from the principles of T'ai-chi, notably including the harmonizing of the yin and yang. It employs flowing, rhythmic, deliberate movements, with carefully prescribed stances and positions. As a mode of attack and defense, T'ai-chi ch'uan resembles kung fu and is properly considered a martial art. It may be used with or without weapons.

Freehand exercise to promote health was practiced in China as early as the 3rd century, and, by the 5th century, monks at the Buddhist monastery of Shao-lin were performing exercises emulating the five creatures: bear, bird, deer, monkey, and tiger. The snake was added later, and, by the early Ming dynasty (1368), the yin and yang principles had been added to harmonize the whole.

There have been many schools of T'ai-chi ch'uan, and two, the Wu and the Yang, survive. Depending on school and master, the number of prescribed exercise forms varies from 24 to 108 or more. The forms all start from one of three stances, weight forward, weight on rear foot, and horse riding, or oblique.

T'AIGO WANGSA \ˈta-ˈgō-ˈwäŋ-ˌsä\ (b. 1301, Korea—d. 1382, Korea), Buddhist monk, founder of the T'aigo sect of Korean BUDDHISM. T'aigo entered into Buddhism at the age of 13 and at 25 passed the national Buddhist service examination. He built a temple north of Seoul in the mountain T'aigoam (whence his name was derived). In 1346 he went to China and received further training under the guidance of Shih-wu, the 18th patriarch in the Lin-chi branch of the Ch'an (ZEN) sect in China. In an attempt to reform Korean Buddhism, T'aigo adopted the *Regulations of the Ch'an Sect* and in 1356 he established a new Buddhist administration office called Wonyung-bu. Though he became head of the office, his reform did not take, and the T'aigo sect remained relatively small.

T'AI HSÜ \ˈtī-ˈshǖ\, *Pinyin* Taixu, *original name* (Wade-Giles romanization) Lü P'ei-Lin (b. Jan. 8, 1890, Haining, Chekiang province, China—d. March 17, 1947, Shanghai), Chinese Buddhist monk and philosopher.

T'ai Hsü received his early training in BUDDHISM in the T'ien-tung Monastery near Ningpo. In 1912 he helped organize the Association for the Advancement of Buddhism with headquarters in Nanking. During 1918 he made an extended tour of Formosa (later Taiwan) and Japan, and in 1921 he began the publication of the influential journal *Hai-ch'ao-yin* ("The Voice of the Sea Tide"). T'ai Hsü was heavily influenced by Sun Yat-sen and by the revolution of 1911. He sought to reform the education of monks and promoted social welfare activities. In his attempts to form national and international Buddhist organizations he traveled to Japan again in 1925, to Europe and the United States in 1928–29, and to South and Southeast Asia in 1939 and 1941. T'ai Hsü attempted to harmonize Buddhism with modern scientific and philosophical thought. He also tried to synthesize the teachings of the rival schools of HUA-YEN and T'IEN-T'AI to bring them into harmony with Wei-shih (Ideation Only) philosophy.

TÁIN BÓ CÚAILGNE \ˈtänʸ-ˈbō-ˈkü-əlʸ-nʸə, -ˈkü-lʸē\ (Irish Gaelic), *English* The Cattle Raid of Cooley, old Irish epic-like tale, the longest of the ULSTER CYCLE of hero tales dealing with the conflict between Ulster and Connaught over possession of the brown bull of Cooley. The tale was composed in prose with verse passages in the 7th and 8th centuries, probably by an author who was acquainted with epics such as the Latin Aeneid. It is partially preserved in *The Book of the Dun Cow* (*c.* 1100) and is also found in *The Book of Leinster* (*c.* 1160) and *The Yellow Book of Lecan* (late 14th century).

MEDB (Maeve), the warrior-queen of Connaught, disputes with her husband, Ailill, over their respective wealth. Because possession of the white-horned bull guarantees Ailill's superiority, Medb resolves to secure the even more famous brown bull of Cooley from the Ulstermen. Although Medb is warned by a prophetess of impending doom, the Connaught army proceeds to Ulster. The Ulster warriors are temporarily disabled by a curse, but CÚ CHULAINN, the youthful Ulster champion, is exempt from the curse and singlehandedly holds off the Connaughtmen. The climax of the fighting is a three-day combat between Cú Chulainn and FER DÍAD, his friend and foster brother, who has been bribed to fight him by Medb. Cú Chulainn is victorious, and, nearly dead from wounds and exhaustion, he is joined by the Ulster army, which routs the enemy. The brown bull, however, has been captured by Connaught and defeats Ailill's white-horned bull, after which peace is made.

TAIPING REBELLION \\'tī-'piŋ\\, *Pinyin* Taiping (1850–64), radical political and religious upheaval in China during the 19th century. It ravaged 17 provinces, took an estimated 20 million lives, and irrevocably altered the Ch'ing (Qing) dynasty (1644–1911/12).

The rebellion began under the leadership of Hung Hsiuch'üan (1814–64), who, influenced by Christian teachings, had a series of visions and believed himself to be the son of God, the younger brother of JESUS CHRIST, sent to reform China. A friend of Hung's, Feng Yün-shan, utilized Hung's ideas to organize a new religious group, the God Worshipers' Society (Pai Shang-ti hui), which he formed among the impoverished peasants of Kwangsi. In 1847 Hung joined Feng and the God Worshipers, and three years later he led them in rebellion. On Jan. 1, 1851, he proclaimed his new dynasty, the T'ai-p'ing t'ien-kuo (Heavenly Kingdom of Great Peace), and assumed the title of T'ien-wang, or Heavenly King.

Their slogan—to share property in common—attracted many famine-stricken peasants, workers, and miners, as did their propaganda against the foreign Manchu rulers of China. Their ranks swelled to more than one million soldiers, organized into separate men's and women's divisions. Sweeping north through the Yangtze River Valley, they reached Nanking. After capturing the city on March 10, 1853, they renamed it T'ien-ching (Heavenly Capital) and dispatched a northern expedition to capture the Manchu capital at Beijing. This failed, but another expedition into the Upper Yangtze Valley scored many victories.

Meanwhile, the Taiping ministers and generals began a prolonged struggle for power among themselves, in which thousands were killed and the rebel forces divided. In 1860 an attempt by the Taipings to regain their strength by taking Shanghai was stopped by a Western-trained army commanded by the American adventurer Frederick Townsend Ward and later by the British officer "Chinese" Gordon. The gentry, who usually rallied to support a successful rebellion, had been alienated by the radical anti-Confucianism of the Taipings and moved in opposition. Nanking fell in July 1864, and Hung committed suicide. Sporadic Taiping resistance continued in other parts of the country until 1868. After the capture of Nanking, almost 100,000 of the Taiping followers preferred death to capture.

Taiping CHRISTIANITY emphasized a wrathful God who demanded worship and obedience. Prostitution, foot binding, and slavery were prohibited, as well as opium smoking, adultery, gambling, and use of tobacco and wine. The Chinese language was simplified, and equality between men and women was decreed. All property was to be held in common, and equal distribution of the land was planned. Some Western-educated Taiping leaders proposed the development of industry and the building of a Taiping democracy. The Ch'ing dynasty was so weakened by the rebellion that it never again was able to establish an effective hold over the country.

TAJONG-GYO \\'tä-'jōŋ-'gyō\\, *also called* Tan'Gun \\'tän-'gün\\, *or* Tangun Cult, modern Korean millenarian movement that originated in the late 19th century. Tajong-gyo was formulated by Na Chul. It worships the Lord, the Light, or the Progenitor of the Heaven. The triune deity consists of Great Wisdom, Power, and Virtue, which are parallel to the mind, body, and breath of humanity. The union and harmony of the heavenly trinity with the trinity of humanity, adherents believe, will renew humanity and reform society. The trichotomy of man, his universe, and its pursuit of ultimate harmony in terms of YIN-YANG theory was derived mainly from NEO-CONFUCIANISM.

TAJWĪD \\täj-'wēd\\, in ISLAM, sophisticated and artistic form of the recitation of the Qur'an. *See* QURRĀ'.

TALBĪYA \\täl-'bē-ə\\, in ISLAM, the formulaic pronouncement *labbayka allāhumma labbayka* ("at your service, O Lord, at your service"), recited especially during the HAJJ and 'UMRA when pilgrims perform the *ṭawāf*—i.e., walk around the sacred shrine of the KA'BA in MECCA. The question whether the *talbīya* is obligatory or merely a commendable tradition has been much discussed, but no consensus has emerged. All Islamic branches and legal schools thus continue to use the *talbīya* during PILGRIMAGES and on other religious occasions. There are several longer versions of *talbīya* that have been attributed to certain prominent Muslims, particularly to MUHAMMAD and the Companions, and some have even been attributed to such pious figures from the past as ADAM and NOAH.

ṬALLIT \\tä-'lēt, 'tä-lis\\, prayer shawl worn by male Jews during the daily morning service (*shaḥarit*) and by the leader of the service during the afternoon service (*minḥa*). On YOM KIPPUR, males wear it for all five services and on TISHA BE-AV only during the afternoon service.

The rectangular wool or silk shawl has black or blue stripes with fringes (*tzitzit*) affixed to the four corners as prescribed (Numbers 15:38). Two fringes fall in front, two behind. Often an embroidered collar is added, inscribed with the blessing to be recited when the *ṭallit* is put on. A pious Jew is often buried in his *ṭallit* after one of the fringes has been removed.

TALMUD \\täl-'müd; 'täl-ˌmüd, 'tal-məd\\ (Hebrew: "Study," or "Learning"), sustained, systematic amplification and analysis of passages of the MISHNAH and other collections of Jewish oral law, including the TOSEFTA. Two Talmuds exist, produced in two locations by two different groups of scholars: the Palestinian Talmud (YERUSHALMI), *c.* 400 CE, and the Babylonian Talmud (BAVLI), *c.* 600 CE. The former treats the

Children in Jerusalem study the Talmud
Joel Fishman—Photo Researchers

first four divisions of the Mishnah; the latter, the second through the fifth; each is independent of the other, the two meeting only at parts of the Mishnah and sharing, further, some sayings attributed to authorities after the Mishnah, although reading these sayings in different ways.

In form the two Talmuds are identical. Both consist of commentaries to some of the same passages of the Mishnah. Both are laid out in the same way, that is, as ad hoc analyses of phrases (or even whole paragraphs) of the Mishnah. The two Talmuds defined Mishnahic commentary in a distinctive way, through their active program of supplying not merely information but guidance on the meaning of the Mishnah. That program was fully realized, however, only in the second of the Talmuds, the Bavli.

The two are further comparable in that they organize their materials in the same way and take up pretty much the same topical agenda, selecting in common some divisions of the Mishnah and ignoring others, agreeing in particular to treat the matters of everyday practice, as distinct from theory. The two Talmuds also share certain definitive traits. One of these is the harmonization of one Mishnah rule or principle with another. Further, both propose to uncover the scriptural foundation of these rules. Both Talmuds, therefore, undertake the sustained demonstration of the theology of the TORAH: its perfection, on the one side, its unity (oral and written), on the other.

Both Talmuds' framers deal with Mishnah tractates of their own chosing, and neither group of authors provide a Talmud to the entirety of the Mishnah. What the Mishnah therefore contributed to the Talmuds was not received in a spirit of humble acceptance by the sages who produced the two Talmuds. Important choices were made about what to treat, hence what to ignore. This discrete reading of sentences or, at most, paragraphs, denying all context, avoiding all larger generalizations except for those transcending the specific lines of tractates facilitated the revision of the whole into a quite different pattern—thus, the Talmud represents a re-presentation of the Torah, and one of considerable originality indeed.

The writers of the Mishnah created a coherent document, with a topical program formed in accord with the logical order dictated by the characteristics of a given topic, and with a set of highly distinctive formal traits as well. But these are obscured when the document is taken apart into bits and pieces and reconstituted. The re-definition of the Torah accomplished by the Talmuds therefore represented a vast revision of the initial writing down of the oral component of the Torah—a point at which the HERMENEUTICS shaded over into a profoundly theological activity.

For the Mishnah as read by the Talmuds is a composite of discrete and essentially autonomous rules, a set of atoms, not an integrated molecule, so to speak. In the process, the most striking formal traits of the Mishnah are obliterated. More importantly, the Mishnah as a whole and complete statement of a single viewpoint no longer exists. Its propositions are reduced to details. But what is offered instead? The answer is, a statement that, on occasion, recasts details in generalizations encompassing a wide variety of other details across the gaps between one tractate and another. This immensely creative and imaginative approach to the Mishnah vastly expands the range of discourse. At the same time, however, it denies to the Mishnah both its own mode of speech and its distinctive and coherent message. So the two Talmuds formulate their own hermeneutics, to convey their theological system: (1) defining the Torah and (2) demonstrating its perfection and comprehensive character: unity, harmony, lineal origin from Sinai.

TALMUD TORAH \täl-'müd-tō-'rä; 'täl-ˌmud-'tō-rə, 'tal-məd-, -'tȯr-ə\ (Hebrew: "Study of the Torah"), in JUDAISM, religious study of the TORAH in quest of the God who makes himself known in that work. TALMUD Torah focuses upon learning God's message for today through inquiry into the books of the Hebrew SCRIPTURES of ancient Israel (the OLD TESTAMENT of CHRISTIANITY) or those that record the originally oral Torah of Sinai, the MISHNAH, MIDRASH compilations, and Talmuds. More broadly, Talmud Torah may refer to any act of learning under rabbinic auspices, the teaching of Torah being regarded as a sacred action. The term applies also to educational institutions of Judaism, particularly schools for children, so that one may say, "I go to the Talmud Torah to study Torah."

In Judaism, Talmud Torah not only enlightens but also empowers. It stands for more than acquiring information; it represents an encounter, through study of the Torah, with God, whose meeting with humanity is recorded therein. Talmud Torah outweighs all of the other religious obligations of Judaism put together—hence, Mishnah-tractate Peah 1:1: "These are things, the benefits of which a person enjoys in this world, while the principal remains for him in the world-to-come: (1) deeds done in honor of father and mother, (2) performance of righteous deeds, and (3) doing acts that bring about peace between one person and another. But (4) study of Torah is equal to all of them put together."

TAM, JACOB BEN MEIR \'tän, *Angl* 'tam\ (b. 1100, Ramerupt, France—d. June 9, 1171, Troyes), outstanding Talmudic authority of his time and one of the most eminent of the French *tosafists* (commentators on the Talmud; *see* TOSAFOT).

Tam, a grandson of RASHI, was attacked by a band of crusaders in 1147, who wounded his head five times as revenge for the five wounds that the Jews allegedly inflicted on Christ. Saved by a passing knight, he fled to neighboring Troyes. There he became a leading participant in the rabbinical synods that about 1160 began to develop rules to govern the relations between Christians and Jews. The key ordinances of Rabbenu ("Our Teacher") Tam provided that (1) disputes between Jews were to be resolved by the Jewish authorities; (2) the law of Rabbenu Gershom (*c.* 960—*c.* 1028/40) abrogating polygamy was essentially reinforced; and (3) no Jew could lightly challenge the legality of a Jewish deed of divorce.

Tam's major legal work is *Sefer ha-yashar* ("Book of the Righteous"). It contains explanations of 30 tractates of the TALMUD, as well as RESPONSA. Some of his religious poetry was later incorporated into the Hebrew prayer book.

TAMA \'tä-,mä\, *formally* mitama \'mē-tä-mä\, in Japanese religions, a soul or semidivine spirit. Several *mitama* are recognized; among them are the *ara-mitama* (with the power of ruling), the *kushi-mitama* (with the power of transforming), the *nigi-mitama* (with the power of unifying, or harmonizing), and the *saki-mitama* (with the power of blessing). Some SHINTŌ shrines pay homage to a particular *mitama* of a deity or KAMI.

TAMMUZ \'tä-,müz\, *Akkadian* Dumuzi \'dü-mü-zē\, in MESOPOTAMIAN RELIGION, god of fertility embodying the powers for new life in nature in the spring. The name Tammuz seems to have been derived from the Akkadian form Tammuzi, based on early Sumerian Damu-zid, The Flawless Young. The later standard Sumerian form, Dumu-zid, in turn became Dumuzi in Akkadian. The earliest known mention of Tammuz is in texts dating to the early part of the Early Dynastic III period (*c.* 2600–*c.* 2334 BCE), but his cult probably was much older. Although the cult is attested for most of the major cities of Sumer in the 3rd and 2nd millennia BCE, it centered in the cities around the central grasslands area, for example, at Bad-tibira (modern Madīnah) where Tammuz was the city god.

As shown by his most common epithet Sipad (Shepherd), Tammuz was essentially a pastoral deity. His father Enki is rarely mentioned, and his mother, the goddess Duttur, was a personification of the ewe. His own name, Dumu-zid, and

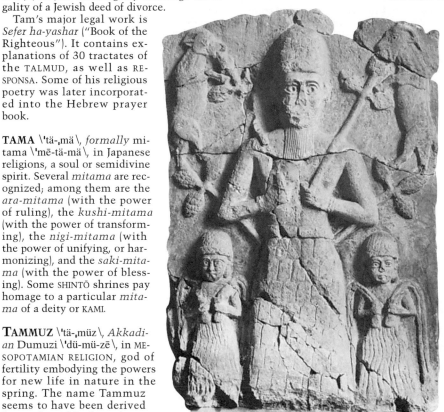

Tammuz, alabaster relief from Ashur, c. 1500 BCE; in the Staatliche Museen zu Berlin
Foto Marburg—Art Resource

two variant designations for him, Ama-ga (Mother Milk) and U-lu-lu (Multiplier of Pasture), suggest that he actually was the power for everything that a shepherd might wish for: grass to come up in the desert, healthy lambs to be born, and milk to be plentiful in the mother animals.

When the cult of Tammuz spread to Assyria in the 2nd and 1st millennia BCE, the character of the god seems to have changed from that of a pastoral to that of an agricultural deity. The texts suggest that, in Assyria (and later among the Sabaeans of Haran), Tammuz was viewed as the power in the grain, dying when the grain was milled.

The cult of Tammuz centered around two yearly festivals, one celebrating his marriage to the goddess INANNA, the other lamenting his death at the hands of DEMONS from the netherworld. During the 3rd dynasty of Ur (*c.* 2112–*c.* 2004 BCE) in the city of UMMA (modern Tell Jokha), the marriage of the god was dramatically celebrated in February–March, Umma's Month of the Festival of Tammuz. During the Isin–Larsa period (*c.* 2004–*c.* 1792 BCE), the texts relate that in the marriage rite the king actually took on the identity of the god and thus, by consummating the marriage with a priestess incarnating the goddess, fertilized all of nature for the year.

The celebrations in March–April that marked the death of the god also seem to have been dramatically performed. Many of the laments for the occasion have as a setting a procession out into the desert to the fold of the slain god. In Assyria, however, in the 7th century BCE, the ritual took place in June–July. In the major cities of the realm, a couch was set up for the god upon which he lay in state. His body appears to have been symbolized by an assemblage of vegetable matter, honey, and a variety of other foods.

Among the texts dealing with the god is "Dumuzi's Dream," a myth telling how Tammuz had a dream presaging his death and how the dream came true in spite of all his efforts to escape. A closely similar tale forms the second half of the Sumerian myth "The Descent of Inanna," in which Inanna (Akkadian ISHTAR) sends Tammuz as her substitute to the netherworld. His sister, Geshtinanna, eventually finds him, and the myth ends with Inanna decreeing that Tammuz and his sister may alternate in the netherworld, each spending half of the year among the living.

Eventually a variety of originally independent gods seem to have become identified with Tammuz. Tammuz of the cattle herders, whose main distinction from Tammuz the

Shepherd was that his mother was the goddess NINSUN, Lady Wild Cow, and that he himself was imagined as a cattle herder, may have been an original aspect of the god. The agricultural form of Tammuz in the north, where he was identified with the grain, may also have been an originally independent development of the god from his role as the power in the vegetation of spring. A clear fusion, though very early, was the merger of Tammuz in Uruk with Amaushumgalana, the One Great Source of the Date Clusters, *i.e.*, the power of fertility in the date palm.

A later important fusion was the merger of Tammuz and DAMU, a fertility god who probably represented the power in the sap to rise in trees and plants in spring. The relation of still other figures to Tammuz, such as DUMUZI-ABZU—a goddess who appears to have been the power in the waters underground (the Abzu) to bring new life to vegetation—is not entirely clear.

TAMMUZ, FAST OF \tä-'müz, 'tä-,müz\, minor Jewish observance (on Tammuz 17) that inaugurates THREE WEEKS of mourning that culminate in the 24-hour fast of TISHA BE-AV, probably originally adapted from foreign rites. The fast is commonly associated with the various misfortunes of the Jewish people at the hands of the Babylonians and Romans, such as the conquest of Jerusalem by Babylon in 586 BCE and the capture of Jerusalem by the Romans in 70 CE.

TAMOANCHÁN \,tä-mō-än-'chän\, in Aztec mythology, the verdant paradise of the west, birthplace of XOCHIQUETZAL, the goddess of beauty. *See* PRE-COLUMBIAN MESO-AMERICAN RELIGIONS.

TANGUN \'tän-'gün\, mythological first king of the Koreans, the grandson of Hwanin, the creator, and the son of Hwanung, who fathered his child by breathing on a woman. Tangun reportedly became king in 2333 BCE.

According to one account, Hwanung left heaven to rule earth from atop Mt. T'aebaek (Daebaik). When a bear and a tiger asked to become human beings, he ordered them into a cave for 100 days where they were to eat only mugwort and garlic and to avoid the sunlight. The tiger grew impatient and left the cave, but the bear remained and after three weeks was transformed into a beautiful woman; she became the mother of Tangun.

BUDDHISM and TAOISM clothed themselves with a Korean mantle by crediting Tangun with starting a national religion of Heavenly Teaching and with originating the Korean maxim *Hongik-ingan* ("Love humanity"). An altar on Kanghwa Island, which is said to have been built by Tangun himself, is periodically refurbished. Tangun's birthday ("Opening of Heaven Day") on the 3rd day of the 10th month is a holiday for schoolchildren.

TANIT \'tä-nit\, *also spelled* Tinith, Tinnit, *or* Tint, chief goddess of Carthage, equivalent of ASTARTE. Although she seems to have had some connection with the heavens, she was also a MOTHER GODDESS, and fertility symbols often accompany representations of her. She was probably the consort of BAAL Hammon (or AMON), the chief god of Carthage, and was often given the attribute "face of Baal." Although Tanit did not appear at Carthage before the 5th century BCE, she soon eclipsed the more established cult of Baal Hammon and, in the Carthaginian area at least, was frequently listed before him on the monuments. In the worship of Tanit and Baal Hammon, children, probably firstborn, were sacrificed. Ample evidence of the practice has been found

west of Carthage in the precinct of Tanit, where a *tofet* (a SANCTUARY for HUMAN SACRIFICE) was discovered. Tanit was also worshiped on Malta and Sardinia and in Spain.

TANNA \tä-'nä, 'tä-nä\, *plural* tannaim \,tä-nä-'ēm\ (Aramaic: "teacher"), memorizer of ORAL TRADITION, generally in the 1st and 2nd centuries CE, ordinarily in the land of Israel; the oral traditions memorized and handed on by *tanna* authorities were held to originate in the revelation by God to MOSES of the TORAH at MOUNT SINAI and handed on in a chain of tradition from then to their inclusion in the law codes, the MISHNAH (*c.* 200 CE) and the TOSEFTA (*c.* 300 CE). *Tannaite* sayings also reached formulation in a fixed-word composition called a BARAITA (plural Baraitot), which are marked *tny*—meaning external to the Mishnah—a process that continued into the 5th century CE and yields sayings in both the Talmud YERUSHALMI and the Talmud BAVLI.

The *tannaim* were succeeded by other scholars, called *amoraim* ("interpreters," or "reciters"). The *amoraim*, located in both Palestine and Babylonia, commented on teachings of the Mishnah and the Tosefta and also wrote extensive analysis of the law, their work all together being called "Gemara" or simply "TALMUD." The *tannaim* opinions occur in the Mishnah, Tosefta, and Baraita corpus, the *amoraim* in the Gemara—*i.e.*, the commentary on that corpus. The differentiation is by groupings in temporal relationship, 1st and 2nd centuries as against 3rd and 4th centuries. The Yerushalmi and Bavli Talmuds, based on the differences in the dates of their compilation, have the same Mishnaic content but significantly different GEMARA. *See also* AMORA.

TANTALUS \'tan-tə-ləs\, in Greek mythology, son of ZEUS or Tmolus (a ruler of Lydia) and PLUTO (daughter of CRONUS and RHEA) and the father of NIOBE and PELOPS. He was the king of Sipylus in Lydia (or of Phrygia) and was the intimate friend of the gods, to whose table he was admitted. In punishment for a crime (various ancient sources identified the crime as (1) abuse of divine favor by revealing to humans divine secrets he had learned in heaven, (2) the theft of nectar and ambrosia, food of the gods, which he turned over to humans, or (3) the murder of his son Pelops, whom he cooked and served to the gods in order to test their powers of observation) Tantalus was condemned to stand up to his neck in water, which flowed away from him when he tried to drink it; over his head hung fruits that the wind wafted away whenever he tried to grasp them. The modern term "tantalizing" derives from this myth.

TANTRA \'tən-trə\ (Sanskrit: "loom"), any of numerous texts dealing with the esoteric practices of some Indian sects. In the orthodox classification of Hindu religious literature *tantra*s are, theoretically, considered to treat of theology, YOGA, construction of temples and images, and religious practices; in reality, they tend to deal with such aspects of popular HINDUISM as SPELLS, rituals, and symbols. They are distinguished along Hindu sectarian lines between the Śaiva *Āgama*s, the Vaiṣṇava Saṃhitās, and the Śākta *tantra*s.

Lists of the Śākta *tantra*s differ considerably from one another but suggest that the earliest manuscripts date from about the 7th century. They emphasize the goddess ŚAKTI as the female personification of the creative power or energy of the god. This view taken to its extreme holds that SHIVA without his Śakti is like a corpse. The *tantra*s also stress the efficacy of YANTRAS, MANDALAS, and MANTRAS. Among the major Śākta *tantra*s (*see* ŚAKTISM) are the *Kulārṇava*, which treats of "left-hand" practices, such as ritual copulation; the *Kulacūḍāmaṇi*, which discusses ritual; and the *Śaradātilaka*, which deals almost exclusively with magic.

The Buddhist *tantra*s are traced to the 7th century or earlier, the *Guhyasamāja* being one of the first and most important. They were accepted and utilized by Esoteric Buddhists associated with the Indian-Tibetan VAJRAYĀNA tradition, the Chen-yen tradition in China, and the SHINGON tradition in Japan. The Buddhist *tantra*s include some very sophisticated texts that combine profound philosophical orientations, rich symbolic content, and guidance for complex rituals, including "left hand" rituals. Some of these Buddhist rituals were designed to facilitate rapid progress toward the attainment of the highest religious goals, including the attainment of buddhahood itself. Many other rituals prescribed within the very large corpus of Buddhist *tantra*s were designed to generate and employ sacred power for quite mundane purposes.

Jain *tantra*s were also produced. However, Tantric elements did not become as important in JAINISM as they did in Hinduism and BUDDHISM.

TANTRIC HINDUISM \'tən-trik, 'tan-\, system of esoteric practices used for both the attainment of spiritual experiences and the fulfillment of worldly desires. TANTRA designates a particular group of post-Vedic Sanskrit treatises, heterogeneous in content, that deals with worship of gods and goddesses, rites and rituals, magic, and secret practices aiming at the purification of the body and the control of physiological and psychological processes by which the body and the mind may be made perfect media for the realization of the highest truth. Tantrism also plays a significant part in BUDDHISM (*see* VAJRAYĀNA) and, to a limited degree, in JAINISM. It is practiced in India, Nepal, and Bhutan and especially among Tibetan Buddhists.

Tantric HINDUISM is mostly concerned with practical methods and lays little stress on religious theories, which it accepts from the main philosophical schools of Hinduism. Theologically it holds that the nondual Supreme Reality has two aspects, SHIVA (male) and ŚAKTI (female), the one representing pure consciousness and transcendent passivity, the other representing mental activity. The human body is believed to be a microcosm of the universe. The spinal cord represents MOUNT MERU; and the three main nerve connections (*iḍā*, *piṅgalā*, and *suṣumṇā*) running along the left, the right, and the middle of the spine represent the three sacred rivers GAṄGĀ (Ganges), JAMUNĀ, and SARASVATĪ; the breathing process represents the course of time. Śakti, the female force, also called KUṆḌALINĪ, lying coiled and dormant in serpent form in the lowest psychic center, or CHAKRA ("wheel"), of the body, has to be awakened and made to move upward through the five (in some systems, six) higher chakras along the spinal cord, so as to be united with Shiva, the male force, at the *sahasrāra padma* chakra, the "thousand-petaled lotus" at the top of the head. This union brings about the transcendently blissful realization of supreme nonduality.

Tantrics sometimes use, as a yogic practice, disciplined forms of sexual intercourse aimed at channeling the semen of the male adept along the path of ascending bodily chakras until he senses that his ordinary mental processes have been suspended and that he and his partner are recapitulating the primordial union of Shiva and PĀRVATĪ. Tantric texts disagree as to whether physical ejaculation aids this process or should be restrained.

T'AN-YAO \'tän-'yaú\ (fl. 450 CE), monk and head of the Buddhist church in China. He instituted the earliest five temples at the YÜN-KANG CAVES.

TAO \'daú\, *Pinyin* dao (Chinese: "road," or "way"), in Chinese philosophy, fundamental concept signifying "the correct way," or "heaven's way." In the Confucian tradition, tao signifies a morally correct path of human conduct and is thus limited to behavior. In TAOISM (the name of which derives from tao), the concept takes on a metaphysical sense transcending the human realm. The TAO-TE CHING opens with these words: "The tao that can be spoken about is not the Absolute Tao." The Absolute Tao thus defies verbal definition, but language can make suggestions that may lead to an intuitive or mystical understanding of this fundamental reality.

One aspect of the tao, however, can be perceived, namely, the visible process of nature by which all things change. From an observation of the visible manifestation of the Absolute Tao, it is possible to intuit the existence of an ultimate substratum that is the source of all things. Awareness of this process then leads toward an understanding of the Absolute Tao.

TAO-AN \'daú-'än\, *Pinyin* Dao'an (b. 312—d. 385), pioneer Chinese Buddhist monk who facilitated the assimilation of BUDDHISM in China through his work in translating Buddhist SCRIPTURES into Chinese. Tao-an's work influenced Kumarājīva, the greatest translator of the Buddhist scriptures. In addition to his translations and commentaries on the scriptures, he is also known for developing a disciplinary code for Chinese monastic communities.

TAO-CH'O \'daú-'chwò\, *Pinyin* Daochuo (562–645), Chinese Buddhist monk and advocate of the PURE LAND doctrine. His predecessor T'an-luan had preached that invocation of the name AMITĀBHA would allow even evil persons to gain access to the Western Paradise; Tao-ch'o argued that in this degenerate age people must take the "easy path" to salvation of complete trust in Amitābha, for they no longer possessed the capacity to follow the more difficult path of the saints.

T'AO HUNG-CHING \'taú-'hùŋ-'jiŋ\, *Pinyin* Tao Hongjing (b. 451, Mo-ling, China—d. 536, Hua-yang), Chinese poet, calligrapher, physician, naturalist, and the most eminent Taoist of his time.

A precocious child, T'ao was tutor to the imperial court while still a youth. In 492 he retired to MAO SHAN, a chain of hills southeast of Nanking, where he established a mountain retreat and devoted himself to the study of Shang-ch'ing TAOISM. T'ao was adviser and friend to the emperor Wu-ti, and his retreat survived the proscription of all other Taoist sects in 504.

His major work was the editing and annotation of the religious writings of Yang Hsi, Hsü Mi, and Hsü Hui, composed at Mao Shan in the 4th century. T'ao produced two compendiums of the literature, the *Chen-kao* ("Declarations of the Perfected") and the *Teng-chen yin-chüeh* ("Secret Instructions for Ascent to Perfection"). In the course of his research into proper eating and living practices, he produced the *T'u ching yen-i pen-ts'ao*, one of the major pharmacological works of China. T'ao also effected a working synthesis of the private and individual practices of the Mao Shan literature with the 4th-century public rites of the LING-PAO liturgies.

TAOISM

An indigenous religio-philosophical tradition that has shaped Chinese life for more than 2,000 years, Taoism includes the ideas and attitudes peculiar to the Lao-tzu (or TAO-TE CHING; "Classic of the Way of Power"), the CHUANG-TZU, the LIEH-TZU, the *Huai-nan Tzu*, and related writings; the Taoist religion and the collected writings known as the *Tao Tsang*, which is concerned with the ritual meditational practices of the TAO; and those who identify themselves as Taoists.

Taoist thought permeates Chinese culture, while in Chinese religion the Taoist tradition—often serving as a link between the Confucian tradition and folk tradition—has generally been more popular and spontaneous than the official (Confucian) state cult and less diffuse and shapeless than folk religion. Taoist philosophy and religion have also found their way into all Asian cultures influenced by China, especially those of Vietnam, Japan, and Korea. In recent decades an acculturated Western-style Taoism has started to emerge in North America and Europe.

Both Western Sinologists and Chinese scholars themselves have distinguished—since Han times (206 BCE–220 CE)—between a Taoist philosophy of the great mystics and their commentators (*Tao-chia*) and a later Taoist religion (*Tao-chiao*). This theory, no longer considered valid, was based on the view that the "ancient Taoism" of the mystics antedated the "later Neo-Taoist superstitions" that were misinterpretations of the mystics' metaphorical images. The mystics, however, should be viewed against the background of the religious practices existing in their own times. Their ecstasies, for example, were closely related to the trances and spirit journeys of the early magicians and SHAMANS. Not only are the authors of the *Tao-te ching*, the *Chuang-tzu* (book of "Master Chuang"), and the *Lieh-tzu* (book of "Master Lieh") not the actual and central founders of an earlier "pure" Taoism later degraded into superstitious practices, but they can even be considered somewhat on the margin of older Taoist traditions. Therefore, because there has been a nearly continuous mutual influence between Taoists of different social classes—philosophers, ascetics, alchemists, and the priests of popular cults—the distinction between philosophical and religious Taoism in this article is made simply for the sake of descriptive convenience.

There is also a tendency among scholars today to draw a less rigid line between

Spiral coils of incense hang in the Man Mo Temple, the oldest Taoist temple in Hong Kong
Rick Browne—Photo Researchers

what is called Taoist and what is called Confucian. The two traditions share many of the same ideas about man, society, the ruler, heaven, and the universe—ideas that were not created by either school but that stem from a tradition prior to either CONFUCIUS or LAO-TZU. In the case of BUDDHISM, meanwhile, competition with Taoism for influence among the people resulted in mutual borrowings, numerous superficial similarities, and essentially Chinese developments inside Buddhism, such as the Ch'an (Japanese: ZEN) sect. In folk religion, since Sung times (960–1279), Taoist and Buddhist elements have coexisted without clear distinctions in the minds of the worshipers.

GENERAL CHARACTERISTICS

The great sages and their associated texts. Behind all forms of Taoism stands the figure of Lao-tzu, traditionally regarded as the author of the classic text known as the *Lao-tzu*, or the *Tao-te ching*. Modern scholars, however, regard the *Tao-te ching* as a compilation that reached its final form only about three centuries later, in the 3rd century BCE. The work was meant as a handbook for the ruler. He should be a sage whose actions pass so unnoticed that his very existence remains unknown. The sacred aura surrounding kingship was rationalized and expressed as "inaction" or "nonintrusive action" (WU-WEI), demanding of the sovereign no more than right cosmological orientation at the center of an obedient universe. Survivals of archaic notions concerning the compelling effect of renunciation—which the Confucians sanctified as ritual "deference" (*jang*)—are echoed in the recommendation to "hold to the role of the female," with an eye to the ultimate mastery that comes of passivity.

It is more particularly in the function attributed to the Tao, or Way, that this little tract stands apart. The term Tao was employed by all schools of thought. The universe has its Tao; there is a Tao of the sovereign, his royal mode of being; while the Tao of man comprises continuity through procreation. Each of the schools, too, had its own Tao, its way or doctrine. But in the *Tao-te ching* the ultimate unity of the universal Tao itself is being proposed as a *social* ideal. It is this idealistic peculiarity that seems to justify later historians and bibliographers in their assignment of the term Taoist to the *Tao-te ching* and its successors.

Knowledge of the sage Chuang-tzu is even more scanty than that of Lao-tzu, but the *Chuang-tzu* is valuable as a monument of Chinese literature and because

Scribes copying the Tao-te ching *and presenting it to the emperor*
Erich Lessing—Art Resource

it contains considerable documentary material describing numerous speculative trends and spiritual practices of the Warring States period (475–221 BCE). Whereas the *Tao-te ching* is addressed to the sage-king, the *Chuang-tzu* is the earliest surviving Chinese text to present a philosophy for private life, a wisdom for the individual. Its PARABLES demonstrate the relativity of all values and the sliding scales of size, utility, beauty, and perfection. Life and death are equated, and the dying are seen to welcome their approaching transformation as a fusion with the Tao. Its concluding chapter is a systematic account of the preeminent thinkers of the time, and the note of mock despair on which it closes typifies the *Chuang-tzu*'s position regarding the more formal, strait-laced ideologies that it parodies.

Among the strange figures that people the pages of *Chuang-tzu* are a very special class of spiritualized beings who dine on air, are immune to the effects of the elements, and possess the power of flight. Their effortless existence is the ultimate in autonomy, the natural spontaneity that

Pa-hsien, the Eight Immortals of Taoism
Giraudon—Art Resource

Chuang-tzu ceaselessly applauds. These striking portraits may have been intended to be allegorical, but whatever their original meaning, these Immortals (HSIEN), as they came to be called, were construed as practical objectives by later generations. By a variety of practices, men attempted to attain their qualities in their own persons, and in time *Chuang-tzu*'s unfettered paragons of liberty were to see themselves classified according to kind and degree in a hierarchy of the heavenly hosts.

Basic concepts of philosophical Taoism. Certain concepts of ancient agrarian religion have dominated Chinese thought without interruption from before the formation of the philosophic schools until the first radical break with tradition and the overthrow of dynastic rule at the beginning of the 20th century, and they are thus not specifically Taoist. The most important of these concepts are the solidarity of nature and man (that is, the interaction between the universe and human society); the cyclical character of time and the universal rhythm and the law of return; and the worship of ancestors, the cult of heaven, and the divine nature of the sovereign.

What Lao-tzu calls the "permanent Tao" in reality is nameless. The act of bestowing a name (*ming*) in ancient Chinese thought implied an evaluation assigning an object its place in a hierarchical universe. The Tao is outside these categories: "It is something formlessly fashioned, that existed before Heaven and Earth." Tao is the "imperceptible, indiscernible," about which nothing can be predicated but that latently contains the forms, entities, and forces of all particular phenomena. Not-Being (WU) and Tao are not identical; *wu* and Being (*yu*) are two aspects of the permanent Tao. Nor does *wu* mean Nothingness but rather the absence of perceptible qualities; in Lao-tzu's view it is superior to Being. It is the Void, or chaos (that is, empty incipience), that harbors in itself all potentialities and without which even Being lacks its efficacy.

When EMPTINESS is realized in the mind of the Taoist who has freed himself from all obstructing notions and distracting passions, it allows the Tao to act through him without obstacle. An essential characteristic that governs the Tao is spontaneity (TZU-JAN), the unconditioned. The Tao, in turn, governs the universe. This is the way of the saint who does not intervene but possesses the total power of spontaneous realization that is at work in the universe.

The conception of the universe common to all Chinese philosophy can be called magical or even alchemical. The universe is viewed as a hierarchically organized mechanism in which every part reproduces the whole. Man is a microcosm (small universe) corresponding rigorously to this macrocosm (large universe); his body reproduces the plan of the cosmos. Between man and universe there exists a system of correspondences and participations. The five organs of the body and its orifices and the dispositions, features, and passions of man correspond to the five directions, the five holy mountains, the sections of the sky, the seasons, and the elements (WU-HSING), which in China are not material but more like five fundamental phases of any process in space-time. Whoever understands man thus understands the structure of the universe.

Fishing in a Mountain Stream, *an 11th-century ink drawing by Hsü Tao-ning, suggests the Taoist ideal of man in harmony with the universal order*
By courtesy of the Nelson Gallery-Atkins Museum, Kansas City, Missouri (Nelson Fund)

One concept of the natural order is the law of the Tao. The law of the Tao refers to the continuous reversion of everything to its starting point. Anything that develops extreme qualities will invariably revert to the opposite qualities. All being issues from the Tao and ineluctably returns to it; undifferentiated unity becomes multiplicity in the movement of the Tao. Life and death are contained in this eternal transformation from Not-Being into Being and back to Not-Being, but the underlying primordial unity is never lost.

For society, any reform means a type of return to the ideals established in the remote past; civilization is considered a degradation of the natural order, and the ideal is the return to an original purity. For the individual, wisdom is the state of conforming to the rhythm of the universe. The Taoist mystic creates a void inside himself that permits him to return to nature's origin.

Another Taoist belief concerning the universe is that all parts of the universe are attuned in a rhythmic pulsation. Nothing is static; all beings are subjected to periodical mutations and transformations that represent the Chinese view of creation. Instead of being opposed to a static ideal, change itself is systematized and made intelligible, as in the theory of the five phases (*wu-hsing*) and in the 64 hexagrams of the I-CHING, which are basic recurrent constellations in the general flux. An unchanging unity (the permanent Tao) was seen as underlying the kaleidoscopic plurality.

The imperceptible Tao shapes the universe continuously out of primordial chaos (HUN-TUN); the perpetual transformation of the universe by the alternations of yin and yang, or complementary energies (seen as night and day or as winter and summer), is nothing but the external aspect of the same Tao.

Concepts of man and society. The power acquired by the Taoist is TE, the efficacy of the Tao in the realm of Being, which is translated as "virtue." The virtue of Taoism is a latent power that never lays claim to its achievements; it is the "mysterious power" (*hsüan-te*) of Tao present in the heart of the sage—"the man of superior virtue never acts (*wu-wei*), and yet there is nothing he leaves undone."

Wu-wei is not an ideal of absolute inaction nor a mere "not-overdoing." It is an action so well in accordance with things that its author leaves no trace of himself in his work. There is no true achievement without *wu-wei* because every deliberate intervention in the natural course of things will sooner or later turn into the opposite of what was intended and will result in failure.

Any willful human intervention is believed to be able to ruin the harmony of the natural transformation process. The spontaneous rhythm of the primitive agrarian community and its unself-conscious symbiosis with nature's cycles is thus the Taoist ideal of society. Chuang-tzu liked to oppose the heaven-made and the man-made—that is, nature and society. He wanted man to renounce all artificial "cunning contrivances" that facilitate his work but lead to "cunning hearts" and agitated souls in which the Tao will not dwell.

Characteristic of Chuang-tzu are his ideas of knowledge and language developed under the stimulus of his friend and opponent, the philosopher Hui Shih. Because, in the Taoist view, all beings and everything are fundamentally one, opposing opinions can arise only when people lose sight of the Whole and regard their partial truths as absolute. Thus, Chuang-tzu's holy man fully recognizes the relativity of notions like GOOD AND EVIL and true and false. He is neutral and open to the extent that he offers no active resistance to any would-be opponent, whether it be a person or an idea. The mystic does not speak because declaring unity, by creating the duality of the speaker and the affirmation, destroys it.

Mystic realization also does away with the distinction between the self and the world. This idea also governs Chuang-tzu's attitude toward death. Life and death are but one of the pairs of cyclical phases, such as day and night or summer and winter. Death is natural, and men ought neither to fear nor to desire it. Chuang-tzu's attitude thus is one of serene acceptance.

The Confucian saint (SHENG) is viewed as a ruler of antiquity or a great sage who taught men how to return to the rites of antiquity. The Taoist sainthood, however, is internal (*nei-sheng*), although it can become manifest in an external royalty (*wai-wang*) that brings the world back to the Way by means of quietism: variously called "nonintervention" (*wu-wei*), "inner cultivation" (*nei-yeh*), or "art of the heart and mind" (*hsin-shu*).

Whereas worldly ambitions, riches, and (especially) discursive knowledge scatter the person and drain his energies, the saint "embraces Unity" or "holds fast to the One" (*pao-i*); that is, he aspires to union with the Tao in a primordial undivided state underlying consciousness. "Embracing Unity" also means that he maintains the balance of yin and yang within himself and the union of his spiritual (*hun*) and vegetative (*p'o*) souls, the dispersion of which spells death; Taoists usually believed there were three *hun* and seven *p'o*. The spiritual soul tends to wander (in dreams), and any passion or desire can result in loss of soul. To retain and harmonize one's soul is important for physical life as well as for the unification of the whole human entity. Cleansed of every distraction, the saint creates inside himself a void that in reality is plenitude. Empty of all impurity, he is full of the original energy (*yüan-ch'i*), which is the principle of life that in the ordinary person decays from the moment of birth on.

Because vital energy and spirituality are not clearly distinguished, old age in itself becomes a proof of sainthood. The aged Taoist sage became a saint because he had been able to cultivate himself throughout a long existence; his longevity in itself was the proof of his saintliness and union with the Tao. Externally he had a healthy, flourishing appearance and inside he contained an ever-flowing source of energy that manifested itself in radiance and in a powerful, beneficial influence on his surroundings, which is the charismatic efficacy (*te*) of the Tao.

Physical immortality was a Taoist goal probably long before and alongside the unfolding of Taoist MYSTICISM. The adept of immortality had a choice among many methods that were all intended to restore the pure energies possessed at birth by every infant. Through these methods, the adept became an immortal (*hsien*) who lived 1,000 years in this world if he so chose and, once satiated with life, transformed his body into pure yang energy and ascended to heaven.

Mythology. Much ancient Chinese mythology has been preserved by the Taoists, who drew on it naturally to illustrate their views. A chaos (*hun-tun*) myth is recorded as a metaphor for the undifferentiated primal unity; the mythical emperors (HUANG-TI and others) are extolled for wise Taoist rule or blamed for introducing harmful civilization. Dreams of mythical paradises and journeys on clouds and flying dragons are metaphors for the wanderings of the soul, the attainment of the Tao, and the identity of dream and reality.

Taoists have transformed and adapted some ancient myths to their beliefs. Thus, the Queen Mother of the West (HSI-WANG-MU), who was a mountain spirit, pestilence goddess, and tigress, became under Taoism a high deity.

Early eclectic contributions. Yin and yang, which literally mean the "dark side" and "sunny side" of a hill, are primary concepts of Taoism. Yin and yang are two complementary, interdependent principles or phases alternating in space and time; they are emblems evoking the harmonious interplay of all pairs of opposites in the universe.

First conceived by musicians, astronomers, or diviners and then propagated by a school that came to be named after them, yin and yang became the common stock of all Chinese philosophy. The Taoist treatise HUAI-NAN-TZU (book of "Master Huai-nan") describes how the one "Primordial Breath" (*yüan-ch'i*) split into the light ethereal yang breath, which formed heaven, and the heavier, cruder yin breath, which formed earth. The diversifications and interactions of yin and yang produced the Ten Thousand Beings.

Yin and yang are often referred to as two "breaths" (*ch'i*). *Ch'i* means air, breath, or vapor—originally the vapor arising from cooking cereals. It also came to mean a cosmic energy. The Primordial Breath is a name of the chaos (state of Unity) in which the original life force is not yet diversified into the phases that the concepts yin and yang describe.

Every person has a portion of this primordial life force allotted to him at birth, and his task is not to dissipate it through the activity of the senses but to strengthen, control, and increase it in order to live out a full span of life.

Another important set of notions associated with the same school of YIN-YANG are the "five agents," or "phases" (*wu-hsing*), or "powers" (*wu-te*): water, fire, wood, metal, and earth. They are also "breaths" (*i.e.,* active energies), the idea of which enabled the philosophers to construct a coherent system of correspondences and participations linking all phenomena of the macrocosm to those of the microcosm. Associated with spatial directions, seasons of the year, colors, musical notes, animals, and other aspects of nature, they also correspond, in the human body, to the five inner organs. The Taoist techniques of longevity are grounded in these correspondences. The idea behind such techniques was that of nourishing the inner organs with the essences corresponding to their respective phases and during the season dominated by the latter.

HISTORY

Taoism in the Ch'in and Han periods (221 BCE–220 CE). *Esoteric traditions of eastern China.* The textual remains of Taoism during the Warring States period were all presumably produced in connection with official patronage; similarly, developments in Taoist thought and practice during the early Imperial age principally have to be studied from the vantage point of the court. At the Imperial court, representatives of different local traditions met as competitors for official favor, and the court consequently served as the principal meeting place for the exchange of ideas. The historians who recorded the progress of these various intellectual and religious currents were themselves court officials and often were active participants in the movements they describe. The emperors, anxious to consolidate and expand their power, were a natural focus for wonder-workers and specialists in esoteric arts (known as the *fang-shih*).

A series of such wonder-workers from the eastern seaboard visited the courts of the Ch'in and early Han. They told of islands in the ocean, peopled by immortal beings—which the *Chuang-tzu* had described—and so convincing were their accounts that sizable expeditions were fitted out and sent in search of them. The easterners brought the cults of their own region to the capital, recommending and supervising the worship of astral divinities who would assure the emperor's health and longevity. One of their number, LI SHAO-CHÜN, bestowed on the Han emperor Wu-ti counsels that are a résumé of the spiritual preoccupations of the time. The emperor was to perform sacrifices to the furnace (*tsao*), which would enable him to summon spiritual beings. They in turn would permit him to change cinnabar powder (mercuric sulfide) into gold, from which vessels were to be made, out of which he would eat and drink. This would increase his span of life and permit him to behold the immortals (*hsien*) who dwell on the Isles of P'eng-lai, in the midst of the sea. Here, for the first time, alchemy joins the complex of activities that were supposed to contribute to the prolongation of life.

The Huang–Lao tradition.   Also originating in the eastern coastal region (Shantung), alongside these same thaumaturgic (wonder-working) tendencies, was the learned tradition of the HUANG-LAO masters, devotees of the legendary "Yellow Emperor" (Huang-ti) and Lao-tzu. The information on the life of Lao-tzu transmitted by Ssu-ma Ch'ien is probably directly from their teaching. They venerated Lao-tzu as a sage whose instructions, contained in his book, describe the perfect art of government. The Yellow Emperor, with whose reign Ssu-ma Ch'ien's universal history opens, was depicted as a ruler of the Golden Age who achieved his success by applying his teachers' precepts to government. The Yellow Emperor also was the patron of technology; and the classic works of many arcane arts, including alchemy, medicine, sexual techniques, cooking, and dietetics, were all under his aegis. Unlike Lao-tzu, the Yellow Emperor is always the disciple, the unremitting seeker of knowledge, and the Huang–Lao masters' ideal of the perfect ruler.

Lao-tzu, revered as the founder of Taoism, detail from a fresco Lord of the Southern Dipper
The Granger Collection

From the court of the king of Ch'i (in present-day Shantung province), where they were already expounding the *Lao-tzu* in the 3rd century BCE, the teachings of the Huang–Lao masters soon spread throughout learned and official circles in the capital. Many early Han statesmen became their disciples and, following their teachings, attempted to practice government by inaction (*wu-wei*); among them there were also scholars who cultivated esoteric arts. Although their doctrine lost its direct political relevance during the reign of the emperor Wu-ti (reigned 141/140–87/86 BCE), their ensemble of teachings concerning both ideal government and practices for prolonging life nonetheless continued to evoke considerable interest and is perhaps the earliest truly Taoist movement for which there is clear historical evidence.

Revolutionary messianism.   Among the less welcome visitors at the Han court had been a certain Kan Chung-k'o. At the end of the 1st century BCE he presented to the emperor a "Classic of the Great Peace" (*T'ai-p'ing ching*) that he claimed had been revealed to him by a spirit who had come to him with the order to renew the Han dynasty. His temerity cost him his life, but the prophetic note of dynastic renewal became stronger during the interregnum of Wang Mang (9–23 CE); and other works—bearing the same title—continued to appear. At this time, promoters of a primitivistic and utopian T'ai-p'ing (Great Peace) ideology continued to support the Imperial Liu (Han) family, claiming that they would be restored to power through the aid of the Li clan. A century and a half later, however, as the power of the Eastern Han dynasty (25–220 CE) declined, the populace no longer hoped for a renewal of Han rule.

The great Yellow Turban Rebellion broke out in the east in 184 CE. Its leader, Chang Chüeh, declared that the "blue heaven" was to be replaced by a "yellow heaven"; and his followers wore YELLOW TURBANS in token of this expectation. Worshiping a "Huang-lao chün," the movement gained a vast number of adherents throughout eastern China. Though they were eventually defeated by the Imperial forces, the tendency towards messianic revolt continued to manifest itself at frequent intervals. A great many charismatic leaders came from the Li family, and certain of them claimed to be the god Lao-tzu returned to earth; a sage of western China, Li Hung, who had actually lived during the 1st century BCE, became the favorite recurrent figure of later would-be messiahs. Such revolutionary religious movements, which included Taoist ideological elements, remained a persistent feature of medieval Chinese history. The last recorded Li Hung was executed in 1112. These sporadic popular manifestations of revolutionary messianism, though, did not represent the activities of the formal Taoist organization and must be distinguished from the organized religious Taoism that also appeared at the end of the Later Han period.

The development of Taoist religion, 2nd–6th century. *The emergence of a "Taocracy."* The protagonist of the *Classic of the Great Peace* is a celestial master. When another important religious movement began in China's far west about the same time as the group in the northeast arose, in the second half of the 2nd century CE, the same title was given to its founder, CHANG TAO-LING. It is with this Way of the Celestial Masters (T'ien-shih tao) that the history of organized religious Taoism may be said to begin, in that the movement soon spread to all of China and has persisted with an unbroken continuity from that time down to the present day.

In 142 CE, in the mountains of the province of Szechwan, Chang is said to have received a revelation from T'ai-shang Lao-chün (Lord Lao the Most High). The deified Lao-tzu bestowed on Chang his "orthodox and sole doctrine of the authority of the covenant" (*cheng-i meng-wei fa*), meant as a definitive replacement for the religious practices of the people, which are described as having lapsed into demonism and degeneracy.

The new dispensation at first was probably intended as a substitute for the effete rule of the Han central administration. Chang is said in time to have ascended on high and to have received the title of *t'ien-shih*, and by the latter part of the 2nd century, under the leadership of his descendants, the T'ien-shih tao constituted an independent religio-political organization with authority throughout the region, a "Taocracy" (rule of Tao) in which temporal and spiritual powers converged. For ceremonial and administrative purposes, the realm was divided into 24 (later 28 and 36) units, or parishes (*chih*). Here the role of the *chi-chiu* ("libationer") seems to have been the cure of disease. Illness was believed to be a sentence pronounced by the SAN-KUAN (Three Officials), judges and custodians of the dead. Using the rising flame and smoke of the incense burner, the libationer submitted petitions (*chang*) to the appropriate bureau of the three Taoist heavens (*san-t'ien*).

The officiant came to dispose of a large selection of bureaucratic stock drafts—memorials, plaints, and appeals—all of which were modeled on secular administrative usage. Also effective were written talismans (*fu*); drawn by the libationer, these would be burned, and the ashes, mixed with water, were swallowed by the demons' victim. The libationer also functioned as a moral preceptor, instructing the faithful in the sect's own highly allegorical interpretation of the *Lao-tzu*, which they considered to be the revealed work of Lord Lao the Most High. Their fundamental concern with right actions and good works as being most in the spirit of the Tao and consequently ensuring immunity from disease is also shown by their construction of way stations in which provisions and shelter were placed for the convenience and use of travelers, as well as in the numerous injunctions to charity and forbearance recorded in the written codes of the movement.

Both the nuclear communities and the "Taocratic" realm as a whole were bound together by a ritual cycle, of which only fragmentary indications remain. Among the most important ceremonial occasions were the communal feasts (*ch'u*) offered at certain specific times throughout the year (during the 1st, 7th, and 10th months) as well as on other important occasions, such as initiation into the hierarchy, advancement in rank or function, or the consecration of an oratory. These feasts were of varying degrees of elaborateness, depending on the circumstances. The common essential element, however, was the sharing of certain

Taoist priest
Foto Marburg—Art Resource

foods, in prescribed quantities, among masters and disciples. This was envisaged as a communion with the Tao, at once attesting the close compact with the celestial powers enjoyed by the members of the parish and reinforcing their own sense of cohesion as a group.

Much more notorious was the rite known as the Union of Breaths (Hoch'i), a communal sexual ritual said to have been celebrated at each new moon. Several cryptic manuals of instruction for the priest in charge of these proceedings are preserved in the canon, and they depict scenarios of a highly stylized erotic choreography of cosmic significance. Like the communal feasts, these rites might be interpreted as a concentrated and idealized adaptation of older, more diffuse agrarian religious customs. This suggests a pattern of the integration of local practices that has remained characteristic of Taoism throughout its history.

In 215 CE the celestial master Chang Lu, grandson of Chang Taoling, submitted to the authority of the Han general Ts'ao Ts'ao, who six years later founded the Wei dynasty in the north. This resulted in official recognition of the sect by the dynasty; the celestial masters in turn expressed their spiritual approbation of the Wei's mandate to replace the Han. Under these conditions a formal definition of the relations of organized Taoism to the secular powers developed. In contrast to the popular messianic movements, Lao-tzu's manifestation to Chang Tao-ling was considered to be definitive; the god was not incarnate in them but rather designated Chang and his successors as his representatives on earth. Under a worthy dynasty, which governed by

virtue of the Tao, the role of the celestial masters was that of acting as intermediaries for celestial confirmation and support. Only when a responsible ruler was lacking were the celestial masters to take over the temporal guidance of the people and hold the supreme power in trust for a new incumbent. Abetted by this flexible ideology of compromise, the sect made constant progress at the courts of the Wei and Western Chin dynasties until, by the end of the 3rd century, it counted among its adherents many of the most powerful families in North China.

Interpretative commentaries continued to be written on the classics of speculative Taoism in which the aid of the most diverse philosophies was called upon, not excluding Buddhism. Like the work of the 3rd- and 4th-century scholiasts, these represent the ideas of a tiny minority, the members of the scholar-official class. Though excursions into ever more refined scholasticism continued to be a diversion for them, the real creative vitality of Taoism was to be found elsewhere.

The Southern tradition.   The political partition of China into three parts following the collapse of the Han dynasty in 220 CE, the so-called period of the Three Kingdoms, had its spiritual counterpart in certain well-defined regional religious differences. Against the independent dynasties in the north and west stood the empire of Wu, south of the Yangtze River.

A region exposed comparatively late to Chinese influence, this southeastern area had long been famous for its aboriginal sorcerers and dancing mediums. In the course of Chinese colonization, separate learned spiritual traditions developed alongside the ecstatic practices of the populace.

To the court of the emperors of Wu came savants and wonder-workers representing a variety of traditions that were to acquire lasting influence. Among these personages was Ko Hsüan (3rd century CE), who was said to have been initiated into an ancient alchemical tradition. His great-nephew KO HUNG in the next century became one of the most celebrated writers on the various technical means for attaining immortality.

In 317 Lo-yang, capital of the Western Chin dynasty, fell to the Hsiung-nu. This event set off a considerable emigration to the unsubdued region south of the Yangtze River. The Imperial household was followed in its flight by numerous high-ranking dependents and their spiritual ministers. During this period the Way of the Celestial Masters, established at the court of Lo-yang since the early 3rd century, apparently first penetrated in force to the Southeast. While the secular, military menace remained in the North, and factional struggles raged among the emigrants, the Way of the Celestial Masters waged unremitting war against the indigenous sects and cults of DEMONS of the Southeast. Many of the old, established families, settled in the region since the end of the Han dynasty, turned away from local traditions to become members of the Taoist faith of their new political superiors.

The most brilliant synthesis of the Way of the Celestial Masters with the indigenous traditions of the Southeast occurred in the 4th century CE in a family closely related to Ko Hung (*see also* MAO SHAN). Within this movement many spiritual traditions (especially popular messianism) were adapted to provide an encompassing framework and temporal cogency. Buddhist concepts were integrated into a Taoist system, while Buddhist notions of predestination and REINCARNATION were subtly blended with native Chinese beliefs. Among the more learned traditions, alchemy received particular attention, being adopted for the first time into the context of organized religious Taoism.

Another member of the Ko family was responsible for the second great Taoist scriptural tradition. Ko Ch'ao-fu began composing the *Ling-pao ching* ("Classic of the Sacred Jewel") about 397 CE. He claimed that they had been first revealed to his own ancestor, the famous Ko Hsüan, early in the 3rd century. In these works the Tao is personified in a series of "celestial worthies" (*t'ien-tsun*), its primordial and uncreated manifestations. These in turn were worshiped by means of a group of liturgies, which, during the 5th century, became supreme in Taoist practice, completely absorbing the older, simpler rites of the Way of the Celestial Masters. As each celestial worthy represented a different aspect of the Tao, so each ceremony of worship had a particular purpose, which it attempted to realize by distinct means. The rites as a whole were called *chai* ("retreat"), from the preliminary abstinence obligatory on all participants. They lasted a day and a night or for a fixed period of three, five, or seven days; the number of persons taking part was also specified, centering on a sacerdotal unit of six officiants. One's own salvation was inseparable from that of his ancestors; the Huang-lu chai (Retreat of the Yellow Register) was directed toward the salvation of the dead. Chin-lu chai (Retreat of the Golden Register), on the other hand, was intended to promote auspicious influences on the living. The T'u-t'an chai (Mud and Soot Retreat, or Retreat of Misery) was a ceremony of collective contrition, with the purpose of fending off disease, the punishment of SIN, by prior confession; in Chinese civil law, confession resulted in an automatic reduction or suspension of sentence. These and other rituals were accomplished for the most part in the open, within a specially delimited sacred area, or altar (*t'an*), the outdoor complement of the oratory. The chanted liturgy, innumerable lamps, and clouds of billowing incense combined to produce in the participants a cathartic experience that assured these ceremonies a central place in all subsequent Taoist practices.

Though Taoism never became the exclusive state religion in the South, its most eminent representatives founded powerful organizations that received considerable official support. LU HSIU-CHING in the 5th century epitomized the Ling-pao tradition, the liturgies of which he codified. His establishment at the great Buddho-Taoist center, Lu Shan (in Kiangsi Province), carried out ceremonies and provided auspicious portents in favor of the Liu-Sung dynasty (420–479), in whose rulers Taoists complacently agreed to recognize the fulfillment of the old messianic prophesies and the legitimate continuation of the Han dynasty. Lu was frequently invited to the capital (present-day Nanking), where the Ch'ung-hsü kuan (Abbey) was founded for him and served as the focal point of the Ling-pao movement.

Like Lu, who was a member of the old aristocracy of Wu, T'ao Hung-ching of the 5th and 6th centuries enjoyed even greater renown as the most eminent Taoist master of his time. He spent years in searching out the manuscript legacy of Yang Hsi and the Hsüs, and in 492 he retired to Mao Shan, where he edited and annotated the revealed texts and attempted to re-create their practices in their original setting. T'ao's fame as a poet, calligrapher, and natural philosopher has persisted throughout Chinese history; he is perhaps best known as the founder of critical pharmacology. T'ao was an intimate friend of the great Liang emperor

Wu-ti (of the 6th century), and his Mao Shan establishment was able to survive the proscription of all other Taoist sects in 504. Though whole Taoist families lived under T'ao's spiritual rule at Mao Shan, he himself stressed the need for CELIBACY and full-time commitment to the work of the Tao. In his state-sponsored Ch'u-yang kuan, T'ao appears to have effected a working synthesis of the public rites of the Ling-pao liturgies with the private and individual practices enjoined in the Mao Shan revelations. This dual practice was to remain a feature of all subsequent Taoist sects. T'ao's primary interest, however, was in the SCRIPTURES of the perfected of Shang-ch'ing; and this is reflected in the revelations vouchsafed by these same spiritual agents to a 19-year-old disciple of T'ao's, Chou Tzu-liang, in 515–516. These revelations show a pronounced Buddhist influence, and T'ao was himself reputed to be a master of Buddhist as well as Taoist doctrine. His writings evidence a complete familiarity with Buddhist literature, and it is reported that both Buddhist monks and Taoist priests officiated at his burial rites.

State Taoism in the North. Under the foreign rulers of North China, independent developments likewise were in progress. In 415 K'ou Ch'ien-chih received a revelation from Lao-chün himself. According to this new dispensation, K'ou was designated celestial master and ordered to undertake a total reformation of Taoism. Not only were all popular messianic movements claiming to represent Lao-chün unsparingly condemned, but K'ou's mission was particularly aimed at the elimination of abuses from the Way of the Celestial Masters itself. Sexual rites and the taxes contributed to the support of the PRIESTHOOD were the principal targets of the god's denunciations; "What have such matters to do with the pure Tao?" he irately demanded. The proposed reform was far more radical than that foreseen in the Mao Shan revelations of the Southeast, and K'ou was given concrete temporal power of a sort that the Hsüs had not envisaged. Political and economic factors favored the acceptance of his message at court; Emperor T'ai Wu-ti (5th century) of the Northern Wei dynasty put K'ou in charge of religious affairs within his dominions and proclaimed Taoism the official religion of the empire. The emperor considered himself the terrestrial deputy of the deified Lao-tzu, as is indicated by the name of one of the periods of his reign: T'ai-p'ing chen-chün (Perfect Lord of the Great Peace). The dominant position of Taoism under the Northern Wei, however, apparently did not long survive K'ou Ch'ien-chih's death in 448.

Taoism under the T'ang, Sung, and later dynasties. China's reunification under the T'ang dynasty (618–907) marked the beginning of Taoism's most spectacular success. The dynasty's founder, Li Yüan, claimed to be descended from the Lao-tzu; as his power increased, even the influential Mao Shan Taoists came to accept him as the long-deferred fulfillment of messianic prophecy. This notion was built into the dynasty's state ideology, and the emperor was commonly referred to as the "sage" (sheng). Prospective candidates for the civil service were examined in either the Ling-pao "Classic of Salvation" (Tu-jen ching) or the Mao Shan "Classic of the Yellow Court" (Huang-t'ing ching). Under a series of celebrated patriarchs, the Mao Shan organization dominated the religious life of the age. One of the greatest of the line, Ssu-ma Ch'eng-chen, initiated innumerable government officials and eminent men of letters and served as spiritual master to emperors. When Ssu-ma Ch'eng-chen pointed out that the sacred peaks of the Imperial cult were in reality under the superintendence of the perfected of Shang-ch'ing, officially sponsored shrines were erected to them there; and their propitiation was incorporated into the traditional rites.

The Sung (960–1279) and Yüan (1206–1368) periods witnessed a great religious effervescence, stimulated in part, under the Sung, by the menace of foreign invasion and, during the Yüan, by Tantric (esoteric, or occult) Buddhism, which was in vogue among the new Mongol rulers of China. The Way of the Celestial Masters, previously eclipsed by Mao Shan, was revitalized by Chang Chi-hsien, the 30th celestial master, and the movement came to be called the Way of Orthodox Unity (CHENG-I TAO).

After the retreat of the Sung government south of the Yangtze River (1126), a number of new Taoist sects were founded in the occupied North and soon at-

An ornate Taoist temple in the Castle Peak section of Hong Kong
Pertti Nikkila—Photo Researchers

tained impressive dimensions. Among them were the T'ai-i (Supreme Unity) sect (founded *c.* 1140), the Chen-ta tao (Perfect and Great Tao) sect (founded in 1142), and the Ch'üan-chen (Perfect Realization) sect (founded in 1163). In the South, Mao Shan continued to prosper, while the Ko-tsao sect flourished at the mountain of that name, in Kiangsi province. This was said to be the spot where the 3rd-century immortal, Ko Hsüan, had ascended to heaven; the sect looked to him as its founder and transmitted the Ling-pao scriptures, which Ko Hsüan was first to receive.

During these dynasties, with such prestigious examples as Ch'an (ZEN) Buddhism (emphasizing intuitive meditation) and NEO-CONFUCIANISM (emphasizing knowledge and reason) before them, Taoists did not long delay in constructing interesting syntheses of their own and other beliefs. CONFUCIANISM now joined Buddhism as a fertile source of inspiration. The revelations of Hsü Sun, supposed to have lived in the 4th century CE, to Ho Chen-kung in 1131 inspired the "Pure and Luminous Way of Loyalty and Filial Obedience" (Ching-ming chung-hsiao tao). This sect preached the Confucian cardinal virtues as being essential for salvation, and consequently it won a considerable following in conservative intellectual and official circles.

Another highly popular syncretistic movement of Taoist origin was that of the Three Religions (SAN-CHIAO), so called from its blending of Taoist, Buddhist, and Confucian elements. Its composite moral teachings are represented by popular tracts, the so-called "books on goodness" (SHAN-SHU), which have been in extremely wide circulation since the Ming dynasty (1368–1644).

INFLUENCE

Taoism, Confucianism, and Buddhism.   Confucianism is concerned with human society and the social responsibilities of its members; Taoism emphasizes nature and what is natural and spontaneous in humans. The two traditions, one "within society" and the other "beyond society," balance and complement each other. This classic definition is generally correct concerning orthodox Han Confucianism; it neglects some aspects of Confucian thought, such as the speculations on the *I-ching,* that are considered to be among the Confucian Classics and the prophetic occult (*ch'an-wei*) commentaries to the classics. As far as Taoism is concerned, this definition neglects the social thought of the Taoist philosophers and the political aspects of Taoist religion. Chinese Buddhism has been viewed not as a Sinified Indian religion but as flowers on the tree of Chinese religions that blossomed under Indian stimulus and that basically maintained its Chinese character.

The first mention of Buddhism in China (65 CE) occurs in a Taoist context, at the court of a member of the Imperial family known for his devotion to the doctrines of Huang-Lao. The Indian religion was at first regarded as a foreign variety of Taoism; the particular Buddhist texts chosen to be translated during the Han period reveal the Taoist preoccupation of the earliest converts with rules of conduct and techniques of meditation. Early translators employed Taoist expressions as equivalents for Buddhist technical terms. Thus, the Buddha, in achieving enlightenment (BODHI), was described as having "obtained the Tao"; the Buddhist saints (ARHAT) become perfected immortals (CHEN-JEN); and "nonaction" (*wu-wei*) was used to render NIRVANA (the Buddhist state of bliss). A joint sacrifice to Lao-tzu and the Buddha was performed by the Han emperor in 166 CE. During this period occurred the first reference to the notion that Lao-tzu, after vanishing into the west, became the Buddha. This theory enjoyed a long and varied history. It claimed that Buddhism was a debased form of Taoism, designed by Lao-tzu as a curb on the violent natures and vicious habits of the "western barbarians," and as such was entirely unsuitable for Chinese consumption. Although there is no evidence that the earliest Taoist organization, literature, or ceremonies were in any way indebted to Buddhism, by the 4th century there was a distinct Buddhist influence upon the literary form of Taoist scriptures and the philosophical expression of the most eminent Taoist masters.

The process of interaction, however, was a mutual one, Taoism participating in the widening of thought because of the influence of a foreign religion and Buddhism undergoing a partial "Taoicization" as part of its adaptation to Chinese conditions. The Buddhist contribution is particularly noticeable in the developing conceptions of the afterlife; Buddhist ideas of PURGATORY had a most striking effect not only on Taoism but especially on Chinese popular religion. On a more profound level the ultimate synthesis of Taoism and Buddhism was realized in the Ch'an (Zen) tradition (from the 7th century on), into which the paradoxes of the ancient Taoist mystics were integrated. Likewise, the goal of illumination in a single lifetime, rather than at the end of an indefinite succession of future existences, was analogous to the religious Taoist's objective of immortality as the culmination of his present life.

As early as the T'ang dynasty, there are traces of the syncretism of the "Three Religions" (San-chiao), which became a popular movement in Sung and Ming China. A mixture of Confucian ethics, the Taoist system of merits, and the Buddhist concept of reincarnation produced such "books on goodness" (*shan-shu*) as the *Kan ying p'ien* ("Tract on Actions and Retributions"). The school of the "Three Religions" was rejected by most Confucians and Buddhists but received wide support in Taoist circles. Many Taoist masters of those periods transmitted *nei-tan* and other techniques of inner cultivation to their disciples while at the same time preaching the moralism of the "Three Religions" to outsiders.

Taoism in modern times.   The principal refuge of Taoism in the 20th century is Taiwan. Its establishment on the island was doubtless contemporary with the great emigration from the opposite mainland province of Fukien in the 17th and 18th centuries. The religion, however, has received new impetus since the 63rd celestial master, Chang En-pu, took refuge there in 1949. On Taiwan, Taoism may still be observed in its traditional setting, distinct from the manifestations of popular religion that surround it. Hereditary Taoist priests (Taiwanese *sai-kong*) called "blackheads" (*wu-t'ou*), after their headgear, are clearly set off from the exorcists (*fa-shih*) or "redheads" (*hung-t'ou*) of the ecstatic cults. Their lengthy rites are still held, now known under the term *chiao* ("offering"), rather than the medieval *chai* ("retreat"). The liturgy chanted, in expanded Sung form, still embodies elements that can be traced back to Chang Tao-ling's sect. The religion has enjoyed a renaissance since the 1960s, with great activity being carried on in temple building and restoration.

Sticks of incense burning before the entrance to the Wong Tai Sin temple
Porterfield/Chickering—Photo Researchers

TAO-TE CHING \\'daù-'də-'jiŋ\\, *Pinyin* Daodejing (Chinese: "Classic of the Way of Power"), classic of Chinese philosophical literature. The name was first used during the Han dynasty (206 BCE–220 CE); it had previously been called LAO-TZU in the belief that it was written by Lao-tzu, the reputed founder of TAOISM. The problem of authorship is, however, still unresolved. Scholars date the *Tao-te ching*'s composition to between the 6th and 3rd century BCE.

The *Tao-te ching* presented a way of life intended to restore harmony and tranquillity to a kingdom racked by widespread disorder. It was critical of the unbridled wantonness of self-seeking rulers and was disdainful of social activism based on the type of abstract moralism and mechanical propriety characteristic of Confucian ethics. The TAO ("Way") of the *Tao-te ching* consists in essence of "nonaction" (WU-WEI), understood as no unnatural action, rather than complete passivity. It implies spontaneity, non-interference, letting things take their natural course. Chaos ceases, quarrels end, and self-righteous feuding disappears because the Tao is allowed to flow unchallenged and unchallenging. By instilling in the populace the principle of Tao, the ruler precludes all cause for complaint and presides over a kingdom of great tranquillity.

Over 350 commentaries on the *Tao-te ching* have been preserved in Chinese and about 250 in Japanese. Since 1900 more than 80 translations have appeared in English.

TAO-TSANG \\'daù-'dzäŋ\\, *Pinyin* Daozang, *also called* Taoist Canon \\'daù-ist\\ (Chinese: "Canon of the Way"), collection of Taoist writings. The original canon, printed by the Taoist emperors of the Sung dynasty (960–1279 CE), comprised almost 5,000 volumes, but many of these were destroyed by imperial decree during the Yüan dynasty (1279–1368). The present *Tao-tsang*, numbering well over 1,000 volumes, includes philosophical writings and works on Taoist meditation, alchemy, and divine revelation.

TAPAS \\'tə-pəs\\ (Sanskrit: "heat," or "ardor"), in HINDUISM, ascetic practice voluntarily carried out to achieve spiritual power or purification. In the VEDAS, *tapas* refers to the "inner heat" created by the practice of physical austerities. Mythologically, *tapas* was the means by which PRAJĀPATI brought the world into existence. In later Hinduism the practice of *tapas* was especially associated with yogic discipline as a way of purifying the body in preparation for the more exacting spiritual exercises leading to liberation (MOKṢA). Among the austerities are fasting, holding difficult or painful bodily postures, and breath control.

In JAINISM, such ASCETICISM is one of the central means of breaking the cycle of rebirths by preventing new KARMA from forming and getting rid of the old. The Jains distinguish between external *tapas*, such as fasting, meditating, and living in seclusion, and internal *tapas*, such as contemplation, CONFESSION, and repentance of SINS.

In early BUDDHISM the monastic life of chastity and poverty was regarded as the only path to Enlightenment. However, the Buddha renounced both extreme self-mortification and self-indulgence in his advocation of the MIDDLE WAY.

TAPIO \\'tä-pē-ˌò\\, *also called* Metsähine \\'met-sa-ˌhē-nä\\, *or* Hiisi \\'hē-sē\\, Finnish god of the forest and ruler of animals. As the personified forest, he was sometimes depicted as being the size of a fir tree, like a human being in the front, but like a gnarled old tree from behind. Sometimes Tapio was an especially beautiful woman who enticed hunters or woodcutters staying in the woods overnight; but she, too,

turned out to be a rotting stump upon closer scrutiny. Hunters made offerings to Tapio and made sure they did not break any prohibitions in the forest, such as making excessive noise or shooting unusual birds that might be the forest spirit in disguise.

TAQĪYA \\tə-'kē-yə\\ (Arabic: "self-protection"), in ISLAM, practice of concealing one's belief and foregoing ordinary religious duties when under threat of death or injury to oneself or one's fellow Muslims.

The QUR'AN allows Muslims to profess friendship with the unbelievers (3:28) and even outwardly to deny their faith (16:106), if doing so would save them from imminent danger, on the condition that their hearts contradict their tongues. MUHAMMAD himself was regarded to have set the first example for the application of *taqīya* when he chose to migrate to MEDINA rather than face his enemies in MECCA.

Some rules have been laid down as to when a Muslim may or may not use *taqīya*. Consideration of community rather than private welfare is stressed in most cases. The threat of flogging or temporary imprisonment and other discomforts that remain within tolerable limits do not justify the use of *taqīya*. A person without responsibilities toward women or children may not use it under any circumstances short of direct and express threat to life.

The Shiʿites made *taqīya* a fundamental tenet because of their suffering from persecution and political defeats throughout their history. The ʿIbāḍīya called for prudent fear and avoidance of foolish and unnecessary martyrdom and regarded *taqīya* as a basic religious requirement. Ultimately, it is left to the conscience of each individual to judge, when the situation arises, whether *taqīya* is absolutely necessary and whether his private interests or those of the religion and the community are being served.

TAQLĪD \\ta-'klēd\\ (Arabic: "entrustment of authority," or "copy," "imitation"), in Islamic law, unquestioning acceptance of the legal decisions of another without knowing the basis of those decisions. Of the four SUNNI legal schools, the SHĀFIʿĪ, the MĀLIKĪ, and the ḤANAFĪ all embrace *taqlīd*, while the ḤANBALĪ reject it. SHIʿITE Muslims hold to an affirmative but quite different understanding of the institution.

Those Sunnis who affirm *taqlīd* believe that the legal scholars of the early period were uniquely qualified to derive authoritative legal opinions, binding upon the whole Muslim community, from the QUR'AN and the SUNNA of the Prophet. In the early period, a series of great legal scholars exercised independent interpretation (IJTIHĀD) of the sources, carrying out their efforts through the use of such legal tools as analogical reasoning (QIYĀS). In the third Islamic century (9th century CE) and subsequent centuries, with the emergence of legal schools formed around some of the most significant scholars, it came to be widely believed that all important questions of law had been dealt with and that the right of independent interpretation had been withdrawn for future generations. Henceforward, all were to accept the decisions of the early authorities—*i.e.*, to exercise *taqlīd* toward them. This doctrine is usually expressed as "the closing of the gates of *ijtihād*" (*bāb al-ijtihād*).

By contrast, Ḥanbalī scholars and others who follow the teachings of the school (*e.g.*, the modern sect of the Wahhābīs) insist on the necessity of returning directly to the sources to make independent judgments of their meaning. In the 19th and 20th centuries, Muslim modernists engaged in bitter polemics against *taqlīd*, which they held encourages stagnation of the law and Muslim backwardness.

In its use among Twelver Shi'ites following the Uṣulī ("rationalist") legal school, *taqlīd* refers to the necessity for a layman to accept and follow the opinions of a living expert in Islamic law (*mujtahid*). Every individual who does not himself have the qualifications to interpret the sources of the law must choose a member of the religious class (the 'ULAMĀ') whom he accepts as his *marja'-i taqlīd* ("source of authority") and whose teachings he observes. When his chosen *mujtahid* dies, he must select another, because to follow a dead guide is forbidden. Shi'ites following the Akhbārī ("traditionalist") legal school, however, must adhere to the authoritative legal instructions of the IMAMS. They can also follow those of a dead jurist. In both senses *taqlīd* is compulsory for Shi'ites. *See also* FĪQH.

TĀRĀ \'tä-rä\, *Tibetan* Sgrol-ma \'dœl-mä\, Buddhist savior-goddess with numerous forms, widely popular in Nepal, Tibet, and Mongolia. She is the feminine counterpart of the Bodhisattva AVALOKITEŚVARA. According to popular belief, she came into existence from a tear of Avalokiteśvara, which fell to the ground and formed a lake. From its waters rose a lotus, which, on opening, revealed the goddess. Like Avalokiteśvara, she is a compassionate deity who helps human beings "cross to the other shore." She is the protectress of navigation and earthly travel, as well as of spiritual travel along the path to Enlightenment.

In Tibet she is believed to be incarnate in every pious woman, and the two wives—a Chinese princess and a Nepali princess—of the first Buddhist king of Tibet, Srong-brtsan-sgam-po, were identified with the two major forms of Tārā. The White Tārā (Sanskrit: Sitatārā; Tibetan: Sgroldkar) was incarnated as the Chinese princess. She symbolizes purity and is often represented standing at the right hand of her consort, Avalokiteśvara, or seated with legs crossed, holding a full-blown lotus. She is generally shown with a third eye.

White Tārā, gilt copper repoussé statue from Nepal, 18th century
By courtesy of the Asian Art Museum of San Francisco, The Avery Brundage Collection; photograph, Martin Grayson

The Green Tārā (Sanskrit: Śyāmatārā; Tibetan: Sgrol-ljang) was believed to be incarnated as the Nepali princess. She is considered by some to be the original Tārā and consort of Avalokiteśvara. She is generally shown seated on a lotus throne with her right leg hanging down, wearing the ornaments of a bodhisattva and holding in her hands the closed blue lotus (*utpala*).

The white and green Tārās, with their contrasting symbols of the full-blown and closed lotus, are said to symbolize between them the unending compassion of the deity who labors both day and night to relieve suffering.

TARANIS \'tär-ə-nis\ (probably akin to Old Irish *torann*, "thunder," and Welsh *taran*, "peal of thunder"), powerful Celtic deity that was one of three mentioned by the Roman poet Lucan in the 1st century CE; the other two were ESUS ("Lord") and TEUTATES ("God of the People"). According to later commentators, Taranis' sacrificial victims, either human or animal, were placed in great wickerwork images, which were then burned. Taranis was symbolically represented by the wheel and the lightning flash.

TARGUM \'tär-gəm\ (Aramaic: "Translation," or "Interpretation"), any of several translations of the Hebrew BIBLE or portions of it into the Aramaic language.

The earliest Targums date from the time after the BABYLONIAN EXILE when Aramaic had superseded Hebrew as the spoken language of the Jews in Palestine; Aramaic was firmly established in Palestine by the 1st century CE, although Hebrew still remained the learned and sacred language. Thus the Targums were designed to meet the needs of unlearned Jews to whom the Hebrew of the OLD TESTAMENT was unintelligible.

The status and influence of the Targums became assured after the Second Temple was destroyed in 70 CE, when SYNAGOGUES replaced the Temple as houses of worship. For it was in the synagogue that it became customary for a *meturgeman*, or professional interpreter (hence

Taranis, detail from the interior of the Gundestrup Caldron, silver bowl, c. 1st century BCE
By courtesy of the Nationalmuseet, Copenhagen

the name Targum) to read aloud from the Old Testament and to translate these readings into Aramaic. Since his object was to give an intelligible rendering of the biblical text, the Targums eventually took on the character of paraphrase and commentary. A *meturgeman* would generally expand and explain what was obscure, adjust the incidents of the past to the ideas of later times, emphasize the moral lessons to be learned from the biblical narratives, and adapt the rules and regulations of the SCRIPTURES to the conditions and requirements of the current age.

Throughout the Talmudic period of the early centuries of the common era, the tradition of oral translation and exposition was recognized as authoritative. The official recognition of a written Targum, and therefore the final fixing of its text, belongs to the 5th century CE. The best-known, most literal, and possibly the earliest Targum is that of Onkelos on the PENTATEUCH, which appeared in its final revision in the 3rd century CE. Others include the Targum of Pseudo-Jonathan, the SAMARITAN Targum, and the Targum of Jonathan ben Uzziel.

TARHUN \ˈtär-ˌkün\, *also spelled* Taru \ˈtär-ˌü\, Tarhu \-ˌkü\, Tarhunt \-ˌkünt\, Tarhunna \tär-ˈkün-nä\, *or* Tarhuis \ˈtär-ˌkwēsh\, ancient Anatolian weather god whose name comes from the root *tarh-*, "to conquer." His name appears in Hittite and Assyrian records (*c.* 1400–612 BCE) and later as an element in Hellenistic personal names, primarily from Cilicia. The weather god was one of the supreme deities of the Hittite pantheon, was regarded as the embodiment of the state in action, and played a prominent part in mythology. He was the consort of ARINNITTI, the Hittite sun goddess and principal deity.

In art Tarhun's symbol was a three-pronged thunderbolt, which he usually carried in one hand while brandishing a club, ax, or other weapon with the other. He is rarely identified by name, and it is often uncertain whether Tarhun or the Hurrian TESHUB was intended. His sacred animal was the bull, and in art Tarhun may be depicted standing on it. JUPITER DOLICHENUS, the god on the bull worshiped by the Roman legions, was a development of Tarhun.

ṬARĪQA \tä-ˈrē-kə\ (Arabic: "way," "manner," *or* "means"), Muslim spiritual path toward direct knowledge (*maʿrifa*) of God or reality (*ḥaqq*). In the 9th and 10th centuries *ṭarīqa* meant the spiritual path of individual Sufi mystics. After the 12th century, as communities of followers gathered around SHAYKHS (or *pīrs*, "teachers"), *ṭarīqa* came to designate the shaykh's entire ritual system, which was followed by the community or mystic order. Eventually *ṭarīqa* came to mean the order itself.

Each mystic order claimed a chain of spiritual descent (*silsila*) from the Prophet MUHAMMAD, established procedures for initiation of members (*murīd*, IKHWĀN, *darwīsh*, *fakīr*), and prescribed disciplines. By following the path of a known "friend of God," or Sufi saint, under the guidance of his shaykh, the Sufi might himself achieve the mystical state (*ḥāl*) of the friends of God. Though sober teach-

ers inveighed against excesses, the search for spiritual EC-STASY sometimes led to such practices as drug taking and wild acrobatics, activities that earned for some of the orders the names whirling, howling, and dancing dervishes. DERVISH orders frequently established monasteries (*ribāt*, *khanka*, ZĀWIYA, *tekke*) in which not only members but also laity were invited to stay.

First established in the 12th century, the orders numbered in the hundreds by the end of the 20th century, with a membership in the millions. The greatest expansion of Sufi *ṭarīqa*s has been in the central Islamic countries, where they played a vital role in the religious life of the Muslim community. Orders also exist in most countries with Muslim populations. Despite efforts to eradicate Sufi orders in Turkey and Saudi Arabia, they still provide Muslims and non-Muslims focal points for spirituality.

TAROT \ˈtar-ō, ta-ˈrō\, any of a set of cards used in fortune-telling and in certain card games. Tarot cards approximating their present form first appeared in Italy and France in the late 14th century.

Early tarot decks were of several types, each varying in the number of cards. The standard modern tarot deck is based on the Venetian or Piedmontese tarot. It consists of 78 cards divided into two groups: the Major Arcana, which has 22 cards (also known as trumps), and the Minor Arcana, which has 56 cards. The cards of the Major Arcana have pictures representing various forces, characters, virtues, and vices. The 22 cards are numbered from I through XXI, with the Fool being unnumbered. The tarots of the Major Arcana are, in order: I Juggler, or Magician; II Papess, or Female Pope; III Empress; IV Emperor; V Pope; VI Lovers; VII Chariot; VIII Justice; IX Hermit; X Wheel of Fortune; XI Strength, or Fortitude; XII Hanged Man; XIII Death; XIV Temperance; XV Devil; XVI Lightning-Struck Tower; XVII Star; XVIII Moon; XIX Sun; XX Last Judgment; XXI World, or Universe; and the Fool.

The 56 cards of the Minor Arcana are divided into four suits of 14 cards each. The suits, comparable to those of modern playing cards, are as follows: wands, batons, or rods (clubs); cups (hearts); swords (spades); and coins, pentacles,

Tarot cards of the Major Arcana: Hanged Man, Death, and Moon
Mary Evans Picture Library

or disks (diamonds). Each suit has four court cards (usually named king, queen, knight, and page) and 10 numbered cards. In ascending order, the value progression in each suit is ace to 10, then page (knave, or jack), knight, queen, and king—though the ace is sometimes assigned a high value, as in modern playing cards. The standard deck of modern playing cards was derived from that of the Minor Arcana (with the elimination of the knight).

Originally used for games, from the 18th century the cards began to take on esoteric associations, as certain European writers connected them to diverse traditions of MYSTICISM, DIVINATION, alchemy, and ritual magic. For fortune-telling, each tarot card is ascribed a meaning. The cards of the Major Arcana refer to spiritual matters and important trends in the questioner's life. In the Minor Arcana wands deal mainly with business matters and career ambitions, cups with love, swords with conflict, and coins with money and material comfort. The tarot deck is shuffled by the questioner, and then the fortune-teller lays out a few of the cards in a special pattern called a "spread." The meaning of any card is modified according to whether or not it is upside down, its position in the spread, and the meaning of adjacent cards.

TARPEIA \tär-'pē-ə\, in Roman mythology, daughter of the commander of the Capitol in Rome during the Sabine War. She offered to betray the citadel if the Sabines would give her what they wore on their left arms, *i.e.*, their bracelets; instead they threw their shields on her and crushed her to death. The story may have been an attempt to account for the Tarpeian Rock, a cliff on the Capitoline Hill over which murderers and traitors were thrown.

TASHBĪH \tàsh-'bē, -'bē-hə\ (Arabic: "assimilating"), in ISLAM, ANTHROPOMORPHISM, comparing God to created things. Both *tashbīh* and its opposite, *taʿṭīl* (divesting God of all attributes), are regarded as SINS in Islamic theology. The difficulty in dealing with the nature of God in Islam arises from the seemingly contradictory views contained in the QURʾAN. On the one hand God is described as unique and not similar to anything that the mind can imagine; on the other hand he is referred to in the language of anthropomorphism—as having eyes, ears, hands, and face, and sitting on his throne and talking and listening.

Some Muslim theologians argued that the Qurʾan used such human concepts and idioms because there are no other means of delivering God's message and urged that they be interpreted allegorically rather than literally. AL-ASHʿARĪ, a 10th-century Muslim theologian, asserted that the hands, eyes, and face of God and his sitting and talking must be recognized literally without asking how.

In the literature of the Sufis, God is spoken of in the language and style of ordinary love poetry, which the Sufis interpret allegorically. This is done on the grounds that humans are created after God's own image. When IBN AL-ʿARABĪ (Muslim mystic of the 12th century) published his collection of poems *Tarjumān al-ashwāq* ("The Interpreter of Desires"), the Muslim orthodox rejected his claim of alluding to divine realities and accused him of actually celebrating the charms of his mistress. He wrote a lengthy interpretation of the poetic text to avoid the accusation of *tashbīh*.

Both *tashbīh* and *taʿṭīl* were avoided by many theologians who spoke rather of *tanzīh* (keeping God pure) and of *tathbīt* (confirming God's attributes). The major reason for the fear of *tashbīh* is that it can easily lead to paganism and IDOLATRY, while *taʿṭīl* leads to ATHEISM.

TATHĀGATA \tə-'tä-gə-tə\ (Sanskrit and Pāli), one of the titles of a buddha and the one most frequently employed by the BUDDHA GOTAMA when referring to himself. The exact meaning is uncertain; Buddhist commentaries present many explanations. The most generally adopted interpretation is "one who has thus (*tathā*) gone (*gata*)" or "one who has thus (*tathā*) arrived (*āgata*)," implying that the historical Buddha was only one of many who have in the past and will in the future experience enlightenment and teach others how to achieve it.

In later MAHĀYĀNA Buddhism, Tathāgata came to convey the essential BUDDHA NATURE hidden in everyone. Tathāgata is the "thusness" that makes enlightenment possible. Having Tathāgata within, one yearns for enlightenment. As the true state of all that exists, Tathāgata is synonymous with ultimate reality, otherwise indefinable.

TATIAN \'tā-shən\, *Greek* Tatianos (b. *c.* 120 CE, Syria—d. April 173), Syrian compiler of the *Diatessaron* (Greek: "From Four," or "Out of Four"), a version of the four Gospels arranged in a single continuous narrative that, in its Syriac form, was an important resource for the Syrian church for centuries. Its Greek and Latin versions influenced the Gospel text. Tatian also founded, or at least was closely associated with, the heretical sect of the Encratites, a community integrating a severe ASCETICISM with elements of Stoic philosophy.

Tatian, a pupil of JUSTIN MARTYR, converted to Christianity—rejecting the classical literary and moral values of the Greeks as corrupt and repudiating their intellectualism. He embraced a synthesis of Judeo-Christian MONOTHEISM with the Stoic concept of an intermediary LOGOS (Greek: "word"), creating the rational and purposeful cohesion of the universe; the personal dimension was provided by belief in the fallen soul's ultimate return to the cosmic pneuma (Greek: "spirit") whence it came.

After Justin's martyrdom Tatian broke with the Roman church, returned to Syria about 172, and became associated with a school of the Encratites. During this period Tatian produced the two works that still survive, the *Diatessaron* and a discourse to the Greeks. The latter, a virulent polemic against Hellenistic (Greek) learning, negatively compared Greek polytheistic theology with the Christian concept of a unique deity whose sublimity transcended the foibles of Greek idols. Tatian submitted that the Judeo-Christian tradition furnished Greek moral philosophy with everything it contained of value, while the former exhibited a selflessness that was absent from the latter.

TA-TS'ANG CHING \'dä-'tsäŋ-'jiŋ\ (Chinese: "Great Storehouse Scripture"), *Japanese* Daizō-kyō \dī-'zō-,kyō\, total body of Buddhist literature deemed canonical in China and Japan and comprising more than 2,000 works in the standard Chinese edition and more than 3,000 in the latest Japanese edition. The canon began with translations of Sanskrit texts in the 1st century, and these translations continued to be made until the 8th or 9th century. Many of the Sanskrit works have perished and are known only from the translations.

The *Ta-ts'ang ching* includes the THERAVĀDA canonical works, particularly their SARVĀSTIVĀDA versions. All the great and minor MAHĀYĀNA *sūtras* are there, often in multiple translations. Also included are many late Tantric treatises, many ecclesiastical histories and hagiographic works by Chinese authors, and religious poetry composed during the Yüan and Ming dynasties (13th–17th century).

TAT TVAM ASI \\'tət-'twəm-'ə-sē, -'tvəm-\\ (Sanskrit: "that you are"), in Hindu philosophy, expression of the relationship between the individual and the absolute, frequently repeated in the sixth chapter of the *Chāndogya* UPANISHAD (*c.* 600 BCE), as the teacher Uddālaka Āruṇi instructs his son in the nature of supreme reality. The phrase was given its most literal interpretation by the 8th–9th-century thinker ŚAṂKARA of the ADVAITA (Nondualist) school, for whose doctrine the statement was fundamental.

TATTVASAMGRAHA TANTRA \\'tə-tvə-'səŋ-grə-hə-'tən-trə, 'tə-twə-\\ (Sanskrit: "Symposium of Truth [of All the Buddhas] Tantra"), TANTRA of Chen-yen BUDDHISM.

During the 7th, 8th, and 9th centuries the VAJRAYĀNA forms of Esoteric Buddhism that were developing in India spread to Southeast Asia and to East Asia. In East Asia Esoteric Buddhism became established in the Chen-yen ("True Word") school in China and in the Tendai (*see* T'IEN-T'AI) and SHINGON schools in Japan. According to the Chen-yen tradition, developed and systematized forms of the Esoteric tradition were first brought from India to China by three missionary monks: Shubhakarasimha, VAJRABODHI, and AMOGHAVAJRA. Shubhakarasimha arrived in China from the famous Indian center of learning at Nalanda in 716, and he translated into Chinese the *Mahavairocana Sūtra* and a closely related ritual compendium known as the *Susiddhikara*. Vajrabodhi and his disciple Amoghavajra arrived in 720 and produced two abridged translations of the *Sarvatathagatatattvasamgraha*, also known as the *Tattvasamgraha*. The *Tattvasamgraha* and the *Mahavairocana Sūtra* became the two basic Chen-yen texts. A fully developed "Five Buddha" complex found its primary expression in the *Tattvasamgraha*, in which Shakyamuni, as VAIROCANA, appears as the central Buddha.

TAULER, JOHANN \\'taù-lər\\ (b. *c.* 1300, Strassburg, Bishopric of Strassburg [now Strasbourg, France]—d. June 16, 1361, Strassburg), DOMINICAN, who, with MEISTER ECKHART and HEINRICH SUSO, was one of the chief Rhineland mystics. He was greatly influenced by Eckhart, though Tauler's teaching, based on ST. THOMAS AQUINAS, stresses practical rather than speculative mystical theology. References to the Friends of God (Gottesfreunde) appear in his sermons, alluding to a circle of like-minded, devout Rhinelanders. Tauler's sermons, written in Middle High German, were valued highly by MARTIN LUTHER.

TAUROBOLIUM \\,tòr-ə-'bō-lē-əm\\, bull sacrifice practiced from about 160 CE in the Mediterranean cult of the GREAT MOTHER OF THE GODS, Cybele. Celebrated primarily among the Romans, the ceremony enjoyed much popularity. The nature and purpose seem to have changed in the 2nd–3rd century. At the beginning the ceremony apparently resembled similar sacrifices performed in the cults of other deities, such as MITHRA. By about 300, however, it had changed drastically. The person dedicating the sacrifice lay in a pit with a perforated board placed over the pit's opening. A bull was slaughtered above him, and the person in the pit bathed in the blood streaming down. Thus the ceremony, perhaps influenced by CHRISTIANITY, gradually took on the elements of moral purification and seems to have been reserved for the higher initiates.

TAWERET \\'taùrt\\, *also called* Taurt, *or* Thoueris, goddess of ancient Egypt, protector of fertility and childbirth, associated also with the nursing of infants. She was depicted as having the head of a hippopotamus (sometimes with the breasts of a woman), the tail of a crocodile, and the claws of a lion. Her image often appeared in household shrines and on AMULETS.

Taweret was connected in particular with the goddess HATHOR. She was also strongly associated with the inundation of the Nile and received particular worship at Jabal al-Silsila, where rituals were performed for the inundation.

TAWḤĪD \\taù-'hēd\\ (Arabic), *also spelled* tauhid ("making one," "asserting oneness"), in ISLAM, the oneness of God, in the sense that he is one and there is no god but he, as stated in the SHAHĀDA ("witness") formula: "There is no god but God; MUHAMMAD is the prophet of God." *Tawḥīd* declares of God that he is a unity, not composed, not made up of parts, but simple and uncompounded. The doctrine of the unity of God and the issues that it raises, such as the question of the relation between the essence and the attributes of God, reappear throughout most of Islamic history. In the terminology of Sufi mystics, however, *tawḥīd* has a pantheistic sense: all essences are divine, and there is no absolute existence besides that of God. To the majority of Muslim scholars, the science of *tawḥīd* is the systematic theology through which a better knowledge of God may be reached; to the Sufis, however, knowledge of God can be achieved only through RELIGIOUS EXPERIENCE and through direct vision. *See also* ALLĀH; KALĀM; MONOTHEISM; SUFISM; IBN ʿABD AL-WAHHAB, MUHAMMAD.

TE \\'də\\, *Pinyin* de (Chinese: "virtue," or "power"), in Chinese TAOISM, potentiality of the mysterious TAO, or Way, the undefinable, transcendent reality that produces all things. In contrast, CONFUCIANISM views *te* as the virtue of internal goodness and proper behavior toward others.

As the activity of Tao, *te* occurs in all things and is a manifestation of the invisible Tao. In the TAO-TE CHING, *te* is described as the unconscious functioning of the physical self. Whoever is attuned to this inner process will live in harmony with the irresistible forces of nature. Personal *te* flourishes when one abandons ambition and the spirit of contention for a life of "naturalness" (TZU-JAN), which allows for awareness of the underlying principle of unity within the universe and encourages others in the community to adopt a similar way of life.

TEGH BAHĀDUR \\'tāg-'bə-hä-dər, -bə-'hä-dùr\\ (b. 1621, Amritsar, Punjab, India—d. Nov. 11, 1675, Delhi), ninth Sikh GURŪ (1664–75). His name literally means "brave swordsman," a title believed to have been given to him by his father Gurū HARGOBIND (Guru from 1606 to 1644) after seeing him participate in the skirmishes with the Mughals.

At the time of his father's death, Tegh Bahadur was not considered for Guruship. He left Kiratpur, the central Sikh seat, living first in Bābā Bakālā, his mother's native place, and then traveling extensively. When he did become Gurū, he established a new and thriving seat at Anandpur ("city of ecstasy"). His hymns, which were among the last to be included in the ĀDI GRANTH, sing of the need for courage to resist tyranny. His visit to the Mālwā region toward the end of his Gurūship attracted large crowds, which put him at loggerheads with the Mughal administration. He was arrested and executed in Delhi in 1675, becoming the second martyr-Gurū (after Gurū ARJAN).

TEILHARD DE CHARDIN, PIERRE \\tā-,yàr-də-shàr-'deⁿ\\ (b. May 1, 1881, Sarcenat, France—d. April 10, 1955, New

York, N.Y., U.S.), French JESUIT, philosopher, and paleontologist known for his theory that man is evolving, mentally and socially, toward a final spiritual unity.

When he was 18, Teilhard joined the Jesuit novitiate at Aix-en-Provence, France. At 24 he began a three-year professorship at the Jesuit college in Cairo. Although ordained a priest in 1911, Teilhard chose to be a stretcher bearer rather than a CHAPLAIN in World War I; his courage on the battle lines earned him a military medal and the Legion of Honor. In 1923, after teaching at the Catholic Institute of Paris, he made the first of his paleontological and geologic missions to China, where he was involved in the discovery (1929) of Peking man's skull. Teilhard enlarged the field of knowledge on Asia's sedimentary deposits and stratigraphic correlations and on the dates of its fossils.

Teilhard returned to France in 1946. Frustrated in his desire to teach at the Collège de France and publish philosophy (all his major works were published posthumously), he moved to the United States, spending the last years of his life at the Wenner-Gren Foundation, New York City, for which he made two paleontological and archaeological expeditions to South Africa.

Teilhard wrote his two major philosophical works, *Le Milieu divin* (1957; *The Divine Milieu*) and *Le Phénomène humain* (1955; *The Phenomenon of Man*), in the 1920s and '30s, but their publication was forbidden by the Jesuit order during his lifetime. He aimed at a metaphysic of evolution, holding that it was a process converging toward a final unity that he called the Omega point. He attempted to show that what is of permanent value in traditional philosophical thought can be maintained and even integrated with a modern scientific outlook if one accepts that the tendencies of material things are directed, either wholly or in part, beyond the things themselves toward the production of higher, more complex, more perfectly unified beings. A parallel process, the socialization of mankind, would follow an evolutionary development towards a convergence in a single human society.

Teilhard saw the process of organic evolution as a sequence of progressive syntheses whose ultimate convergence point is that of God. When humanity and the material world have reached their final state of evolution and exhausted all potential for further development, a new convergence between them and the supernatural order would be initiated by the Parousia, or SECOND COMING of Christ. Teilhard asserted that the work of Christ is primarily to lead the material world to this cosmic redemption, while the conquest of evil is only secondary to his purpose.

TELAKHON, *English* Fruit of Wisdom, one of the oldest Buddhist-influenced prophet movements among the Karen hill peoples of Myanmar (Burma). In their mythology, the restoration of their lost Golden Book by their white younger brothers heralds the MILLENNIUM. Ywa, a withdrawn HIGH GOD (*see* DEUS OTIOSUS) whose offer of the book to their ancestors was ignored, would then return to deliver the Karen from oppression by the Burmans or the British. The movement was founded in the mid-19th century by Con Yu. It banned traditional animal sacrifice, practiced a strict ethic, and maintained Karen culture. In 1962–65 the movement's seventh successive head, the Phu Chaik ("Elder of the Faith"), was presented with vernacular BIBLES by American missionaries. Expectations rose on both sides, and membership (mostly in eastern Myanmar) increased to 10,000, but the Bible was rejected as not revealing the mysteries of Western knowledge. Renewed opposition to the Burmese

led to armed clashes and the removal and death of the Phu Chaik in 1967. A similar movement, the Leke (founded 1860), is still in existence but others have become Christian churches or have declined.

TELEGONUS \tə-'le-gə-nəs\, in Greek mythology, son of ODYSSEUS by CIRCE. According to one story, Telegonus went to Ithaca in search of his father, whom he killed unwittingly. His spear had been tipped with the point of a stingray, thus fulfilling the PROPHECY in the *Odyssey* that death would come to Odysseus "from the sea." Telegonus then married PENELOPE, Odysseus' widow.

Nestor and Telemachus depicted on a red-figured bowl from southern Italy; 4th century BCE
Erich Lessing—Art Resource

TELEMACHUS \tə-'le-gə-nəs\, in Greek mythology, son of ODYSSEUS and PENELOPE. When Telemachus reached manhood, he visited Pylos and Sparta in search of his wandering father. On his return, he found that Odysseus had reached home before him. Then father and son slew Penelope's suitors. According to later tradition, Telemachus married CIRCE (or CALYPSO) after Odysseus' death.

TELLUS \'te-ləs\ (Latin: "ground, earth"), *also called* Terra Mater \'ter-ə-'mā-tər, -'mä-\, Roman earth goddess. Probably of great antiquity, she was concerned with the productivity of the earth and was later identified with CYBELE. Her temple on the Esquiline Hill dated from about 268 BCE. She was honored in the Fordicidia and Sementivae festivals, both of which centered on fertility and good crops.

TEMPLAR \'tem-plər\, *also called* Knight Templar, member of Poor Knights of Christ and of the Temple of Solomon, a religious military order of knighthood established at the time of the Crusades. It was founded during the early years of the kingdom of Jerusalem, when the Crusaders controlled only a few strongholds in the Holy Land, and pilgrims to the holy places were often endangered by groups of Muslim warriors. Pitying the plight of such pilgrims, eight or nine French knights, led by Hugues de Payens, vowed in late 1119 or early 1120 to devote themselves to their protection and to form a religious community for that purpose. Baldwin II, king of Jerusalem, gave them quarters in a wing of the royal palace in the area of the former Jewish Temple, and from this they derived their name.

The Templars were divided into four classes: knights, sergeants, CHAPLAINS, and servants. Only the knights wore the Templars' distinctive regalia, a white surcoat marked with a red cross. Each individual Templar took vows of poverty and chastity.

The Templars performed courageous service in the Holy Land, and their numbers increased rapidly, partly because of the propagandistic writing of ST. BERNARD OF CLAIRVAUX, who also wrote their rule of life. They soon became vital in the defense of the Christian Crusader states of the Holy Land, and they garrisoned every town of any size there. At their height the Templars numbered about 20,000 knights.

The Templars also acquired considerable wealth. By the mid-12th century they owned properties scattered throughout western Europe, the Mediterranean, and the Holy Land, and their military strength enabled them to safely collect, store, and transport bullion to and from Europe and the Holy Land. Their network of treasure storehouses and their efficient transport organization caused them to be used as bankers both by kings and by pilgrims to the Holy Land. Thus, the order grew to wield great financial power.

By 1304 rumors (probably false) of irreligious practices and blasphemies committed by the Templars during their secret rites of initiation had begun to circulate. At this juncture, King Philip IV of France had every Templar in France arrested on Oct. 13, 1307, and sequestered all the Templars' property in France. Philip accused the Templars of HERESY and immorality and had many of them tortured in order to secure false confessions to these charges. Pope Clement V, himself a Frenchman, came under strong pressure from Philip, and in response the pope ordered the arrest of the Templars in every country in November 1307. Philip eventually succeeded in his efforts to have the pope suppress the order (March 22, 1312), and the Templars' property throughout Europe was transferred to the rival Hospitaler order or confiscated by the state. Many Templars were either executed or imprisoned, and in 1314 the last grand master of the order, Jacques de Molay, was burned at the stake.

The question of the guilt of the Templars has been a matter of fierce controversy for centuries, but modern opinion inclines to the idea that the Templars were victims of a highly unjust and opportunistic persecution.

TEMPLE, edifice constructed for ritual activity. The English word is borrowed from the Latin *templum*, which first denoted the ritual space (in the sky or on the ground) delimited by a Roman augur, and later the shrine built within such a space. Depending on the religious tradition,

Temple of Athena Nike, on the Acropolis, Athens, c. 425 BCE
A.F. Kersting

the terms "church," "synagogue," and "mosque" may have equivalent meaning.

Because of ritual requirements, temple architecture varies widely between one religion and another. The ZIGGURATS of the Mesopotamian culture were elaborately designed and decorated, and their "stair-step" style ascended to a point where a god or gods could dwell and where only special priests were allowed. Ancient Egypt had temples to gods, but because the primary concern of its religion was the afterlife of souls, its pyramidal tombs became its primary shrines and most familiar architectural heritage.

In the ancient GREEK RELIGION the gods were the most important focus, and Classical Greek temple architecture created structures that emphasized that focus. An inner, windowless room housed an image of a god, and an altar stood outside the temple. Most Greek temples were built of marble or other stone, richly carved and polychromed, and were on a hill or stepped platform. The design and decoration of Greek temples had a profound effect on architecture of later eras in the West, beginning with the Roman.

During the 3rd and 2nd centuries BCE, temples of the ROMAN RELIGION began to evince Greek influence, using the Greek decorative style but placing the altar within the temple and eventually creating entire forums, or meeting places, of which the temple was the center. In Roman temples, the columns soon became engaged rather than freestanding, and circular as well as rectangular temples were built. Byzantine and Western church architecture developed from these bases in the Hellenistic styles.

Muslim temples are usually domed structures decorated with colored tiles on the outside and covering a large central SANCTUARY and arcaded courtyards within. The ASCETICISM and rich symbolism of JAINISM is reflected in that religion's beautifully decorated monastery-like structures in India, both above the ground in simple cloisters and below the ground in caves. Hindu temples, which vary regionally in style, usually consist of a towering shrine symbolizing the cosmic MOUNT MERU and a columned hall surrounded by an elaborate wall marking the four cardinal points of the cosmos. Buddhist temples range from half-buried sanctuaries with richly carved entrances to single, carved towers or statues. The Chinese (and later, Japanese) version of the Buddhist temple tends to be a one-story building of richly carved, painted, or tiled timber constructed around an atrium used for worship. By contrast, the SHINTŌ temples of Japan are simple and rustic in design.

In the Americas, Incan and Mayan temples were constructed of stone and were often highly carved. In general, they were stair-stepped PYRAMIDS, with the shrine at the top. Chichén Itzá, the ruins of which remain in the Yucatán Peninsula, has excellent examples of this type of pre-Columbian temple architecture.

Temple of the Tooth, Kandy, Sri Lanka
Hubertus Kanus—Photo Researchers, Inc.

TEMPLE OF THE TOOTH, *also known as* Dalada Maliga-wa \'dä-lə-də-ˌmə-lē-'gä-wə\, Buddhist temple in Kandy, central Sri Lanka (Ceylon). Here a sacred relic, supposed to be the BUDDHA GOTAMA'S left canine tooth, is preserved. This relic is the center of the well-known annual Esala Perahera, a torchlight procession of dancers, dignitaries, and richly decorated elephants.

TEN COMMANDMENTS, *also called* Decalogue (Greek: *deka logoi,* "10 utterances"), list of religious precepts that, according to various passages in EXODUS (20:2–17) and Deuteronomy (5:6–21), were divinely revealed to MOSES on MOUNT SINAI and were engraved on two tablets of stone. The rendering in Exodus (Revised Standard Version) appears as follows:

◆ I am the Lord your God, who brought you out of the land of Egypt, out of the house of bondage.
You shall have no other gods before me.
You shall not make for yourself a graven image, or any likeness of anything that is in heaven above, or that is in the earth beneath, or that is in the water under the earth; you shall not bow down to them or serve them; for I the Lord your God am a jealous God, visiting the iniquity of the fathers upon the children to the third and the fourth generation of those who hate me, but showing steadfast love to thousands of those who love me and keep my commandments.
You shall not take the name of the Lord your God in vain; for the Lord will not hold him guiltless who takes his name in vain.

Remember the sabbath day, to keep it holy. Six days you shall labor, and do all your work; but the seventh day is a sabbath to the Lord your God; in it you shall not do any work, you, or your son, or your daughter, your manservant, or your maidservant, or your cattle, or the sojourner who is within your gates; for in six days the Lord made heaven and earth, the sea, and all that is in them, and rested the seventh day; therefore the Lord blessed the sabbath day and hallowed it.
Honor your father and your mother, that your days may be long in the land which the Lord your God gives you.
You shall not kill.
You shall not commit adultery.
You shall not steal.
You shall not bear false witness against your neighbor.
You shall not covet your neighbor's wife, or his manservant, or his maidservant, or his ox, or his ass, or anything that is your neighbor's. ◆

Some scholars propose a date for the Ten Commandments between the 16th and 13th centuries BCE because Exodus and Deuteronomy connect the Commandments with Moses and the Sinai COVENANT between YAHWEH and IS-RAEL. For those who regard the Ten Commandments as an epitome of prophetic teachings, the date would be some time after AMOS and HOSEA (after 750 BCE). If the Ten Commandments are simply a summary of the legal and priestly traditions of Israel, they belong to an even later period.

The Ten Commandments had no particular importance in Christian tradition until the 13th century, when they were incorporated into a manual of instruction for those coming to confess their SINS. With the rise of Protestant churches, new manuals of instruction in the faith were made available and the Ten Commandments were incorporated into CATECHISMS as a fundamental part of religious training, especially of the young.

TEN DAYS OF PENITENCE: *see* ASERET YEME TESHUVA.

TENGU \'teŋ-ˌgủ\, in Japanese FOLKLORE, mischievous supernatural being, sometimes the reincarnated spirit of one who was proud and arrogant in life. *Tengu* live in trees in mountainous areas. A group of *tengu* is headed by a chief, who is dressed in red robes and carries a feather fan. He is served by a group of retainers called *koppa tengu* ("leaflet" *tengu*), who act as his messengers. In popular art they are shown as smaller winged creatures with long red noses or beaklike mouths.

TEN LOST TRIBES OF ISRAEL, ten of the original 12 Hebrew tribes, which, under the leadership of JOSHUA, took possession of CANAAN after the death of MOSES. They were named ASHER, DAN, EPHRAIM, GAD, ISSACHAR, MANASSEH, NAPH-TALI, REUBEN, SIMEON, and ZEBULUN—all sons or grandsons of JACOB (GENESIS 29:31–30:24; 41:50–52). In 930 BCE the 10 tribes formed the independent Kingdom of Israel in the north and the 2 other tribes, JUDAH and BENJAMIN, set up the Kingdom of Judah in the south (1 Kings 12:20–21). Following the conquest of the northern kingdom by the Assyrians in 721 BCE, the 10 tribes were gradually assimilated by other peoples and thus disappeared from history. Peoples who at various times were said to be descendants of the lost tribes include the NESTORIANS, the MORMONS, the Afghans, the FALASHAS of Ethiopia, the American Indians, and the Japanese. Among the immigrants to the state of Israel were a few who likewise claimed to be remnants of the Ten Lost Tribes. *See also* SAMBATIAN.

TENRIKYŌ \\'ten-rē-ˌkyō\\ (Japanese: "Religion of Divine Wisdom"), largest of the modern SHINTŌ sects in Japan.

Tenrikyō originated with Nakayama Miki (1798–1887), a peasant from Yamato Province (modern Nara Prefecture), who claimed she became possessed by a god called Tenri Ō no Mikoto ("Lord of Divine Wisdom") when she was 40 years old. She developed a worship characterized by ecstatic dancing and shamanistic practices, and a doctrine (based on the oracles transmitted through her) emphasizing CHARITY and the healing of disease through mental acts of faith. The sect became popular, though it often met with persecution from state authorities. Her writings and her deeds were considered divine models, and she was widely venerated during her lifetime and since. She was succeeded by Master Iburi (d. 1907); since his death, the leader of the sect has always been a member of the Nakayama family.

Tenrikyō was first considered a branch of the Yoshida sect of Shintō. In 1880 it changed its affiliation to BUDDHISM and from 1908 has been recognized as one of the 13 groups that compose KYŌHA SHINTŌ. Tenrikyō was one of the most powerful religious movements in Japan immediately before World War II and has retained a large following. In the late 20th century its membership was about 2,500,000.

The goal of Tenrikyō is a happy life free from disease and suffering. The center of religious activity is the *jiba,* a sacred recess in the SANCTUARY of the main temple in Tenri city (Nara Prefecture). The world is said to have been created here, and from the *jiba* salvation will finally be extended to the entire world. Every member of Tenrikyō is expected to carry on missionary work. More than 200 churches have been established worldwide; they serve mainly Japanese living abroad.

TENSHŌ KŌTAI JINGŪ-KYŌ \\'ten-ˌshō-'kō-ˌtī-'jēŋ-gü-ˌkyō\\ (Japanese: "Religion of the Shrine of the Heavenly Goddess"), *also called* Odoru Shūkyō ("Dancing Religion"), a new religious movement of Japan that emerged in the post-

A flight of tengu *rescuing Tametomo from the attack of a giant fish, 19th-century woodblock print by Utagawa Kuniyoshi*
By courtesy of the Victoria and Albert Museum, London

World War II period. It was founded by Kitamura Sayo (1900–67), of Yamaguchi Prefecture, whose charismatic preaching took the form of rhythmic singing and dancing. She had a revelation in 1945 that she was possessed by a SHINTŌ deity, Tenshō-Kōtaijin (another name for the Shintō sun goddess AMATERASU Ōmikami). She traveled widely and won followers in Europe and the Americas. Her eccentric behavior and forthright condemnation of organized institutions of religion and government won her an enthusiastic following, estimated at about 300,000 shortly after her death.

TEREFAH \\tə-rä-'fä, tə-'rä-fə\\ (from Hebrew: *ṭaraf,* "to tear"), *also spelled* terefa, tref \\'trāf\\, *or* trefa \\'trä-fə\\, any food, food product, or utensil that, according to Jewish dietary laws (KASHRUTH), is not ritually clean or is not prepared according to law and is thus unfit for Jewish use. The broad connotation of *terefah* derives from a more specific prohibition against the eating of meat that has been "torn" by a wild animal (*e.g.,* EXODUS 22:31).

Food may be *terefah* for several reasons. Shellfish, pork, malformed and sick animals, and those which have been improperly slaughtered are forbidden.

TERESA, MOTHER \\tə-'rē-sə, -'rä-zə\\, *original name* Agnes Gonxha Bojaxhiu (b. Aug. 27, 1910, Üsküp, Kosovo Vilayet, Ottoman Empire [now Skopje, Republic of Macedonia]—d. Sept. 5, 1997, Calcutta, India), founder of the Order of the Missionaries of Charity—a ROMAN CATHOLIC congregation of women dedicated to the poor, particularly to the destitute of India. She founded her order in 1948. It received canonical sanction in 1950 and became a pontifical congregation in 1965. In recognition of her work, she was honored on Jan. 6, 1971, by Pope Paul, who awarded her the first POPE JOHN XXIII Peace Prize. In 1979 she was recipient of the Nobel Peace Prize.

TERESA OF ÁVILA, SAINT \\tā-'rä-sä . . . 'ä-ˌbē-lä, *Angl* tə-'rē-sə . . . 'ä-vē-lə\\, *original name* Teresa de Cepeda y Ahumada (b. March 28, 1515, Ávila, Spain—d. Oct. 4, 1582, Alba de Tormes; canonized 1622; feast day October 15), Spanish nun, one of the great mystics and religious women of the ROMAN CATHOLIC church, and author of spiritual classics. She was the originator of the CARMELITE Reform, which restored and emphasized the austerity and CONTEMPLATIVE character of primitive Carmelite life. St. Teresa was elevated to Doctor of the Church in 1970 by Pope Paul VI, the first woman to be so honored.

Teresa entered the Carmelite CONVENT of the Incarnation at Ávila, probably in 1535. Within two years her health collapsed, and she was an invalid for three years, during which time she developed a love for mental prayer. After her recovery, however, she stopped praying. She continued for 15 years in a state divided between a worldly and a divine spirit, until, in 1555, she underwent a religious awakening.

In 1558 Teresa initiated her reform, which required utter withdrawal so that the nuns could meditate on divine law and lead a prayerful life of penance. In 1562 she opened the first convent of the Carmelite Reform. It met with hostility, but she staunchly insisted on poverty. In 1567, she met a Carmelite priest, Juan de Yepes (later ST. JOHN OF THE CROSS, the poet and mystic), and a year later Juan opened the first monastery of the Primitive Rule at Duruelo, Spain.

Despite frail health and great difficulties, she spent the rest of her life establishing and nurturing 16 more convents throughout Spain. In 1575, while she was at the Seville convent, a jurisdictional dispute erupted between the FRIARS of the restored Primitive Rule, known as the Discalced (or "Unshod") Carmelites, and the observants of the Mitigated Rule, the Calced (or "Shod") Carmelites. The Carmelite general, to whom she had been misrepresented, ordered her to retire to a convent in Castile and to cease founding additional convents; Juan was subsequently imprisoned at Toledo in 1577. Ultimately, in 1579, the Discalced Carmelites were given independent jurisdiction, confirmed in 1580 by Pope Gregory XIII. Teresa, broken in health, was then directed to resume the reform. In journeys that covered hundreds of miles, she made exhausting MISSIONS and was fatally stricken en route to Ávila from Burgos.

Teresa's ascetic doctrine has been accepted as the classical exposition of the contemplative life, and her spiritual writings are among the most widely read. Her *Life of the Mother Teresa of Jesus* (1611) is autobiographical; the *Book of the Foundations* (1610) describes the establishment of her convents. Her writings on the progress of the Christian soul toward God are recognized masterpieces: *The Way of Perfection* (1583), *The Interior Castle* (1588), *Spiritual Relations, Exclamations of the Soul to God* (1588), and *Conceptions on the Love of God*.

TEREUS \'tir-ē-əs, 'tir-yüs\, in Greek mythology, king of Thrace who married Procne, daughter of Pandion, king of Athens. Later Tereus seduced her sister Philomela, pretending that Procne was dead. In order to hide his guilt, he cut out Philomela's tongue. But she revealed the crime to her sister by working the details in embroidery. Procne sought revenge by serving up her son Itys for Tereus' supper. When Tereus pursued the two sisters with an axe, the gods took pity and changed them all into birds, Tereus into a hoopoe (or hawk), Procne into a nightingale (or swallow), and Philomela into a swallow (or nightingale).

TERMINUS \'tər-mə-nəs\ (Latin: "Boundary Marker"), originally, in ROMAN RELIGION, boundary stone or post fixed in the ground during a ceremony of sacrifice and anointment. From this sacred object evolved the god Terminus. On February 23 (the end of the old Roman year) the festival called the Terminalia was held. The owners of adjacent lands assembled at the common boundary stone, and each garlanded his own side of the stone. Offerings of cakes, grain, honey, and wine were made, and a lamb or pig was sacrificed.

TERPSICHORE \,tərp-'si-kə-,rē\, in GREEK RELIGION, one of the nine MUSES, patron of lyric poetry and dancing (in some versions, flute playing). In some accounts she was the mother of the half-bird, half-woman SIRENS, whose father was the sea god Achelous or the river god Phorcys.

TERTULLIAN \tər-'təl-yən\, *Latin in full* Quintus Septimus Florens Tertullianus (b. *c.* 155/160, Carthage [now in Tunisia]—d. after 220, Carthage), early Christian theologian, polemicist, and moralist who, as the initiator of ecclesiastical Latin, was instrumental in shaping the vocabulary and thought of Western CHRISTIANITY.

Life. Tertullian was born in Carthage, which at that time was second only to Rome as a cultural and educational center in the West. He received an exceptional education in grammar, rhetoric, literature, philosophy, and law. After completing his education in Carthage, he went to Rome to study further and became interested in the Christian movement, but not until he returned to Carthage toward the end of the 2nd century was he converted to the Christian faith. He left no account of his conversion experience, but in his early works, *Ad martyras* ("To the Martyrs"), *Ad nationes* ("To the Nations"), and *Apologeticum* ("Defense"), he indicated that he was impressed by the courage and determination of Christian MARTYRS, their moral rigor, and their uncompromising MONOTHEISM. By the end of the 2nd century the church in Carthage had become large, firmly established, and well organized and was rapidly becoming a powerful force in North Africa. Tertullian emerged as a leading member of the African church, using his talents as a teacher in instructing the unbaptized seekers and the faithful and as a literary defender (APOLOGIST) of Christian beliefs and practices. It is not clear whether Tertullian was ordained a priest.

Literary activities. During the next 20 to 25 years Tertullian devoted himself almost entirely to literary pursuits. Developing an original Latin style, the fiery and tempestuous Tertullian became a lively and pungent propagandist though not the most profound writer in Christian antiquity. Like his contemporaries, Tertullian wrote works in defense of the faith (*e.g., Apologeticum*) and treatises on theological problems against specific opponents: *Adversus Marcionem* ("Against Marcion," an Anatolian heretic who believed that the world was created by the evil god of the Jews), *Adversus Hermogenem* ("Against Hermogenes," a Carthaginian painter who claimed that God created the world out of preexisting matter), *Adversus Valentinianos* ("Against Valentinus," an Alexandrian Gnostic), and *De resurrectione carnis* ("Concerning the resurrection of the Flesh"). He also wrote the first Christian book on BAPTISM, *De Baptismo*; a book on the Christian doctrine of man, *De anima* ("Concerning the Soul"); essays on prayer and devotion, *De oratione* ("Concerning Prayer"); and a treatise directed against all HERESY, *De praescriptione haereticorum* ("Concerning the Prescription of Heretics"). In addition, he addressed himself to a whole range of moral and practical problems: on what is appropriate dress for women and on the wearing of cosmetics in *De cultu feminarum* ("Concerning the Dress of Women"); on service in the military in *De corona* ("Concerning the Crown"—a military decoration); on whether one should flee under persecution in *De fuga in persecutione* ("Concerning Flight in Persecution"); on marriage and remarriage in *De exhortatione castitatis* ("Concerning the Exhortation to Chastity") and *De monogamia* ("Concerning Monogamy"); on the arts, theater, and civic festivals in *De spectaculis* ("Concerning Spectacles");

and on repentance after baptism in *De poenitentia* ("Concerning Repentance").

Tertullian as a Montanist. Sometime before 210 Tertullian left the Orthodox church to join a new prophetic sectarian movement known as MONTANISM, which had spread from Asia Minor to Africa. His own dissatisfaction with the laxity of contemporary Christians was congenial with the Montanist message of the imminent end of the world combined with a stringent and demanding moralism. Montanism stood in judgment on any compromise with the ways of the world, but even this was not rigorous enough for Tertullian. He eventually broke with the Montanists to found his own sect, a group that existed until the 5th century in Africa. According to tradition, he lived to be an old man. His last writings date from approximately 220, but the date of his death is unknown.

In antiquity most Christians never forgave Tertullian for his APOSTASY to Montanism. Later Christian writers mention him only infrequently, and then mostly unfavorably. In the 19th and 20th centuries Tertullian was widely read and studied and was considered one of the formative figures in the development of Christian life and thought in the West.

TESHUB \\'te-,shủb\\, Hurrian weather god, assimilated by the Hittites to their own weather god, TARHUN. One myth about Teshub relates that he achieved supremacy in the pantheon after the gods Alalu, ANU, and Kumarbi had successively been deposed and banished to the netherworld. Another myth, the "Song of Ullikummi," describes the struggle between Teshub and a stone monster that grew out of the sea. Teshub's consort was HEBAT (Queen of Heaven), and they had a son, Sharruma. At the rock SANCTUARY of Yazılıkaya near the ancient Hittite capital, the leading god is named Teshub and is represented treading on the bowed necks of two mountain gods. In other representations he is shown as a standing figure carrying a *lituus* (a long crook) or driving a chariot drawn by bulls. He reappears in the Kingdom of Urartu as Tesheba, one of the chief gods, and in Urartian art he is depicted standing on a bull.

TETRAGRAMMATON \\,te-trə-'gra-mə-,tän\\, the four Hebrew letters, YHWH, in the name of God. *See* YAHWEH.

TEUTATES \\'tā-ü-,tä-tēz, ,tä-ü-'tä-\\, *also spelled* Toutates \\'tō-,tä-tēz, ,tō-'tä-\\, important Celtic deity, one of three mentioned by the Roman poet Lucan in the 1st century CE, the other two being ESUS ("Lord") and TARANIS ("Thunderer"). The initial element of the name, *teut-*, meant "tribe" or "people" (akin to Old Irish *tuath*," tribe, people, petty kingdom," and Welsh *tud*, "people, country"), and originally *teutates* may have been a descriptive term referring to any tutelary deity of a tribe rather than the proper name of a particular god. According to later commentators, victims

sacrificed to Teutates were killed by being plunged headfirst into a vat filled with an unspecified liquid, which may have been ale. Teutates was identified with both the Roman MERCURY and MARS. He is also known from dedications in Britain, where his name was written Toutates. The Irish Tuathal Techtmar, one of the legendary conquerors of Ireland, has a name that comes from an earlier form, Teutovalos ("Ruler of the People"); he was probably another manifestation of the god Teutates.

TEZCATLIPOCA \\,tä-skät-lē-'pō-kə\\, *or* Tezcatlepoca (Nahuatl, probably from the word *tezcatl*, "obsidian mirror" coupled with *i(h)poca*, "it gives off smoke or exhalations"), deity that was the omnipotent, omnipresent protean god of the Aztec pantheon. Tezcatlipoca's cult was brought to central Mexico by the Toltecs about the end of the 10th century CE. Numerous myths relate how Tezcatlipoca expelled the priest-king QUETZALCOATL, the FEATHERED SERPENT, from his capital at TOLLAN (present-day Tula). Taking the form of a wizard, he caused the death of many Toltecs and corrupted the virtuous Quetzalcoatl, thus putting an end to the Toltec golden age. Under his influence HUMAN SACRIFICE was reintroduced into central Mexico. Tezcatlipoca's NAGUAL, or animal disguise, was the jaguar, the spotted skin of which was compared to the starry sky. A creator god, Tezcatlipoca ruled over Ocelotonatiuh ("Jaguar Sun"), the first of the four worlds that were created and destroyed before the present universe.

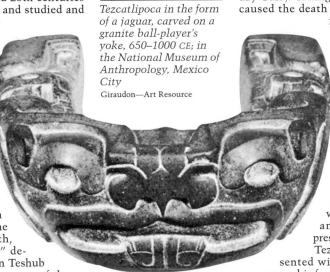

Tezcatlipoca in the form of a jaguar, carved on a granite ball-player's yoke, 650–1000 CE; in the National Museum of Anthropology, Mexico City

Giraudon—Art Resource

Tezcatlipoca was often represented with a stripe of black paint across his face and an obsidian mirror in place of one of his feet or on his chest, a mirror that granted him omniscience. The post-Classic (after 900) Quiché MAYA people of Guatemala revered him as a lightning god under the name Hurakan ("One Foot").

In Aztec times (14th–16th century CE), Tezcatlipoca's manifold attributes and functions brought him to the summit of the divine hierarchy, along with HUITZILOPOCHTLI, TLALOC, and Quetzalcoatl. He presided over the *telpochcalli* ("young men's houses"), which were district schools in which the sons of the common people received education and military training.

The main rite of Tezcatlipoca's cult took place during the fifth ritual month, Toxcatl. Every year at that time, the priest selected a young and supremely handsome war prisoner. For one year he lived in luxury with four women as his companions and received proper instruction in the Aztec arts of music and speech. On the appointed feast day, he climbed the steps of a small temple while breaking flutes that he had played. At the top he was sacrificed by the removal of his heart and was beheaded.

THALIA \\thə-'lī-ə, 'thā-lē-ə\\, in GREEK RELIGION, one of the nine MUSES, patron of comedy; also, according to the Greek poet Hesiod, a GRACE. She is the mother of the Corybantes, the father being APOLLO. In her hands she carried the comic mask and the shepherd's staff.

THAMYRIS \'tha-mə-ris\, *also spelled* Thamyras, in Greek mythology, Thracian poet who loved the beautiful youth HYACINTHUS. Thamyris' attentions, however, were rivaled by those of the god APOLLO, who jealously reported to the MUSES the boast by Thamyris that he could surpass them in song. The Muses immediately blinded Thamyris and robbed him of his voice and his talent.

THARGELIA \thär-'gē-lē-ə, -'jē-\, in GREEK RELIGION, one of the chief festivals of APOLLO at Athens, celebrated on the sixth and seventh days of Thargelion (April–May). The Thargelia was a first-fruits festival. According to scholars in antiquity, the name was derived from a noun *thargēlos*, understood as either the bread made from the first fruits or an earthenware vessel in which the grain was prepared.

On the first day of the festival one or two men acting as SCAPEGOATS were first led around the city, then thrown to the ground and whipped on the genitalia seven times. Finally they were driven across the border. Late and unreliable sources state that they were occasionally sacrificed. On the second day of the festival a thanks offering, a PROCESSION, and the official registration of adopted persons took place.

THEISM \'thē-ͺi-zəm\, the view that all limited, or finite, things, though fully real in their own right, are dependent in some way upon, yet distinct from, one supreme or ultimate being, of which one may also speak in personal terms. This being is regarded as beyond human comprehension, perfect, and self-sustained but also peculiarly involved in the world and its events.

Theists characteristically seek support for their contentions in rational argument and appeals to experience. In the history of Western thought, this has given rise to several types of arguments for the existence of God. The four primary types are the cosmological, teleological, ontological, and moral arguments. Frequently these arguments are propounded in combination.

Cosmological arguments begin with a recognition of particular features of the world, or of the fact of its existence, and then infer God as the ultimate cause. The world is seen as dependent upon some being beyond it for its intelligibility and existence. The classic statement of the cosmological argument was given by THOMAS AQUINAS in his *Summa Theologica* (Part I, Question ii, art. 3).

The teleological argument proceeds from an observation of the functional order of the universe whereby things in the world function toward ends or goals. One version of this argument is, strictly speaking, a form of cosmological argument since it depends upon a notion of final causality, holding that purposeful actions must be ultimately designed or directed by an intelligent purposive being. This argument received its clearest expression in David Hume's critical analysis of the argument from design, in which the universe is seen as an orderly machine.

The ontological argument attempts to show that the concept of God implies the necessity of God's existence. The classic statement of this argument is found in Anselm of Canterbury's *Proslogion*, which defines God as "that greater than which nothing can be conceived." One form of this argument is based on the claim that existence is a perfection among others and that, since God embraces all perfec-

tions, God must exist. Another form of ontological argument asserts that God can only be conceived as a necessary being and therefore cannot be conceived as nonexistent or merely possible.

The moral argument, which rests upon the experience of obligation or moral duty, was developed by Immanuel Kant, who argued that, in order for morality to be rationally justified and hold an influence over human actions, it must be assumed that obedience to obligation will coincide with happiness. Thus, a God must be postulated as the being who rewards worthiness and enables moral life to be rationally understood.

Theism commonly views God as somehow caringly related to the world. This has generally been expressed in some analogy of God to a personal being. Theism has also tended to affirm both the immanence and the transcendence of this ultimate being. Other attributes of God, such as infinity, eternity, omniscience, and omnipotence, are treated by theists in accordance with analogies drawn from human experience. A major problem is to understand how finite and imperfect characteristics can be understood as existing perfectly in God. Another central issue is that of reconciling the claims that God is both omnipotent and perfect with the existence of evil in the world.

It is generally agreed that no theistic argument proves the existence of God in any strict sense. All depend upon certain disputable presuppositions. Such "proofs" are generally seen as means of examining the logical correlates of belief or disbelief. Theists have encountered criticism from those who deny the ability of reason beyond ordinary experience, those who reject the role of reason in favor of revelation alone, and those who accept the rational method but reject the theistic conclusions.

THEMIS \'thē-mis\ (Greek: "Customary Law," or "Sanctioned Practice"), in GREEK RELIGION, personification of justice, goddess of wisdom and good counsel, and the interpreter of the gods' will. According to some sources, she was the daughter of OURANUS and GAEA, although at times she was apparently identified with Gaea. She was Zeus's second consort and by him the mother of the Horae, the Moirai, and, in some traditions, the HESPERIDES. Themis was a giver of oracles, and one legend relates that she once owned the oracle at DELPHI but later gave it to APOLLO.

The cult of Themis was widespread in Greece. She was often represented as a woman of sober appearance carrying a pair of scales.

THEODICY \thē-'ä-də-sē\ (from Greek *theos*, "god," and *dikē*, "justice"), justification of God, concerned with reconciling the goodness and justice of God with the observable facts of evil and suffering in the world.

A theological system that posits a creator who is infinitely good is confronted with the problem of explaining the existence of evil in the world. Most theodicies aim at solving this problem. Within polytheistic systems the solution is usually a simple one: evil can be understood simply as the outcome of a conflict of wills, one god set against another. Such an approach is evident also in the various dualist systems, in which the power of evil is held to be separate from and opposed to the power of good (*see* MANICHAEISM; GNOSTICISM; and ZOROASTRIANISM).

Strict MONOTHEISM, by contrast, must account for evil without positing the existence of a power separate from God, and different thinkers have adopted a variety of strategies in dealing with this problem. In some religions the creator is believed to have fashioned a primal paradise that was subsequently spoiled by human disobedience or sin; such an approach is evident in the GARDEN OF EDEN story in GENESIS. In other systems, the creator fashioned the world but then withdrew from it (*see* DEUS OTIOSUS); evil can then be explained as the result of a process of decay or degeneration. Most generally, the creator is credited with what is good in the world, while humans are held accountable for evil; the Indian notion of karma—in which human suffering is understood as the direct consequence of misdeeds performed in a previous incarnation—is one such approach, and indeed the sociologist MAX WEBER deemed it the most rational solution to the problem.

THEODORE OF MOPSUESTIA \ˈthē-ə-ˌdōr . . . ˌmäp-sû-ˈes-chē-ə\ (b. *c.* 350, Antioch, Syria—d. 428/429, Mopsuestia, Cilicia [now part of Turkey]), Syrian theologian, considered the greatest biblical interpreter of his time and the spiritual head of the exegetical School of Antioch.

Theodore studied with his friend JOHN CHRYSOSTOM, who in 369 influenced him to become an ascetic. Entering a monastery near Antioch, he lived and studied there until 378. Ordained in 381, he became bishop of Mopsuestia about 392. He engaged in the theological controversies then plaguing the Eastern church and wrote commentaries on the LORD'S PRAYER, the NICENE CREED, the SACRAMENTS, and most of the biblical books, as well as on theological and practical problems, such as the HOLY SPIRIT, the INCARNATION, PRIESTHOOD, exegetical method, theological controversies, and MONASTICISM. Theodore's works became normative through their translation into Syriac at Edessa (modern Urfa, Turkey).

Instead of the allegorical interpretation employed by the rival exegetical SCHOOL OF ALEXANDRIA, Egypt, Theodore used scientific, critical, philological, and historical methods that anticipated modern scholarship. By considering the historical circumstances in which the biblical books were written, he anticipated the modern view that many of the Psalms belong to the 2nd century BCE and rejected as uncanonical such books as Chronicles, Esdras, and the Catholic Letters. He composed a treatise on ALLEGORY and history, no longer extant, in which he criticized ORIGEN, considered the most influential theologian of the early Greek church, for ignoring the literal sense of SCRIPTURE. Elsewhere, Theodore said that those who interpreted Scripture allegorically "turn everything backwards, since they make no distinction in divine Scripture between what the text says and dreams."

Theologically, Theodore insisted that Christ's person has two natures: divine and human. Basing this Christological issue on a psychological analysis of personality, he believed that the human and divine natures were joined in some kind of union, as between body and soul.

Theodore had a strong impact on the NESTORIAN church, which identified itself with patriarch NESTORIUS of Constantinople, whom the Council of Ephesus (431) had con-

demned. Adhering to the School of Antioch, the Nestorian church regarded Theodore as the main authority in all matters of faith. The second COUNCIL OF CONSTANTINOPLE (553) condemned Theodore's views and writings, but a Persian council in 484 had acknowledged him as the guardian of right faith. The Church of the East (also known as the Persian, or Nestorian Church) accepted Theodore's theology and is considered Nestorian.

THEODORE STUDITES, SAINT \stü-ˈdī-ˌtēz, styü-\, *also called* Theodore of Studios, *or* Stoudion (b. 759, Constantinople [now Istanbul, Turkey]—d. Nov. 11, 826, Prinkipo, island in the Sea of Marmara; feast day November 11), ABBOT and leading opponent of ICONOCLASM.

Under the influence of his uncle, Abbot Plato of Symbola, later a saint, Theodore became a monk and, later, abbot of a monastery near Mount Olympus in Bithynia (northwestern Turkey). For opposing as adulterous the second marriage of the Byzantine emperor Constantine VI to his mistress Theodote in 795, Theodore was exiled to Thessalonica, Greece. After Constantine's overthrow in 797,

Theodore Studites and the patriarch Nicephorus argue in favor of the veneration of religious images with Emperor Leo V, while iconoclasts rub out an image of Christ; manuscript psalter from the monastery of Studios, Constantinople, 1066
Laurie Platt Winfrey, Inc.

Theodore was recalled by the empress Irene. Thereafter, his religious community moved to the monastery of Studios in Constantinople. In 806 he clashed with the emperor Nicephorus I (who asserted authority over the Eastern church) about the appointment of PATRIARCH Nicephorus of Constantinople. Theodore was condemned by a council and exiled a second time (809–811).

When iconoclasm (the doctrine opposing the veneration of religious images) was revived by the emperor Leo V, Theodore led the opposition and was again exiled (816–820). Recalled by the emperor Michael II, who nevertheless favored the iconoclastic party, Theodore was not allowed to resume his abbacy. With his monks he spent the rest of his life near Constantinople. He had fought for church independence from imperial power; because the patriarchs of Constantinople often had to compromise with the Byzantine emperors, he opposed the patriarchs too.

Most of his works—which include homilies, three polemical treatises against the Iconoclasts, and nearly 600 letters—are in J.-P. Migne, *Patrologia Graeca* ("Greek Fathers"), vol. 99 (1903).

THEODOTUS THE GNOSTIC \thē-'ä-də-təs . . . 'näs-tik\ (fl. 2nd century CE), a principal formulator of an eastern brand of GNOSTICISM.

From the scant data available, Theodotus is known to have taught Gnostic doctrines in Asia Minor *c.* 160–170, elaborating on the principles of the early-2nd-century Gnostic VALENTINUS. Theodotus' teachings survive in *Excerpta ex Theodoto* ("Extracts from Theodotus"), actually a scrapbook that the 2nd–3rd-century Christian philosophical theologian CLEMENT OF ALEXANDRIA appended to his *Stromata* ("Miscellanies"). Certain passages integrate the comments of Clement; thus, the unsystematic arrangement of the material causes problems of interpretation.

Essentially, the Gnosticism of Theodotus affirmed that the world is the product of a process of emanations, or radiations, from an ultimate principle of unconditioned being or eternal ideas. Intermediate beings in this hierarchy of perfection include God the creator of matter and Christ the redeemer, who united himself to the man Jesus at his BAPTISM to bring men *gnōsis* ("knowledge"). Salvation, he concluded, is reserved for believers infused with *pneuma* ("spirit").

Theodotus further developed the role of inferior spiritual beings, or ANGELS, and their relation to Christ. He mentions anointing and a EUCHARIST of bread and water as two means of release from the domination of the evil power.

THEOLOGY, speaking or writing about the gods or God. Originating in classical Greek thought concerning the gods of Olympus (with authors such as Homer and Hesiod), theology became an important discipline in the development of JUDAISM, CHRISTIANITY, and ISLAM. The themes of theology are God, humans, the world, salvation, and ESCHATOLOGY.

While the term theology as it originated in the works of Plato and other Greek philosophers denoted the teaching of mythological beliefs, the discipline received its most distinctive content and methodology within Christianity. Largely because of its resultant reflection of the particular concerns and categories of one tradition, theology as a neutral tool applicable to religions in general is a problematic concept. To apply such a framework indiscriminately to other religions can result in forced analogies and false conclusions. In certain Eastern traditions, BUDDHISM, for example, in which no concept of "god" in the Western sense obtains, the enterprise of theology is not applicable.

Even though the extent varies from religion to religion, theology claims in some degree a normative element—arising out of the authority of a divine teacher, personal revelation, or some other kind of spiritual encounter that elicits commitment. It is the precedent of authority that most clearly distinguishes theology from philosophy, the tenets of which are generally based on timeless evidence apprehensible by autonomous reason. Nevertheless, theology does employ reason in addressing many of the same concerns as philosophy.

THEOPHANY \thē-'ä-fə-nē\, manifestation of deity in sensible form. The term has been applied generally to the appearance of the gods in ancient Greece, the Middle East, and particularly in biblical materials. In the OLD TESTAMENT, God is depicted as appearing in human form, in natural cataclysms, in a burning bush, a cloud, or a gentle breeze—forms often associated with the divine "name" or "glory"

(originally a visible HALO accompanying the divine appearance). The extension of the term theophany to such NEW TESTAMENT events as the BAPTISM and TRANSFIGURATION of Jesus (also called epiphanies) has been questioned as inappropriate because in Orthodox Christian doctrine Christ himself in his whole life and work and death is the manifestation of God.

THEOSOPHY \thē-'ä-sə-fē\, religious philosophy with mystical concerns that has been of catalytic significance in religious thought in the 19th and 20th centuries. The term *theosophy* is derived from the Greek *theos*, "god," and *sophia*, "wisdom," and is generally translated as "divine wisdom." All theosophical speculation has as its foundation the mystical premise that God must be experienced directly in order to be known at all.

In modern times theosophy has been widely identified with the doctrines promoted by religious mystic Helena Blavatsky through the Theosophical Society. The term may also be used in a more general sense to refer to a certain strain of mystical thought found in such thinkers as the ancient Greek philosophers Pythagoras and Plato, the Gnostic teachers SIMON MAGUS and VALENTINUS, the Neoplatonist philosophers Plotinus and Proclus, the medieval northern European mystics MEISTER ECKHART and NICHOLAS OF CUSA, the Renaissance speculative mystics Paracelsus and Giordano Bruno, the German philosophical mystic JAKOB BÖHME, and the German Romantic philosopher Friedrich Schelling. But the richest and most profound source of theosophical views has been Hindu thought, where they may be traced from the earliest scriptural VEDAS through the UPANISHADS and the BHAGAVAD GĪTĀ to modern times. Elements of theosophy may also be found in the other Asian religions, especially in Islamic SUFISM, BUDDHISM, and TAOISM.

Theosophical speculation places an emphasis on mystical experience: a deeper spiritual reality exists, and direct contact may be established with that reality through intuition, meditation, revelation, or some other state transcending normal human consciousness. A distinction between an inner, or esoteric, teaching and an outer, or exoteric, teaching is commonly accepted, and much attention is devoted to deciphering the meaning concealed in sacred texts. Modern theosophists claim that all WORLD RELIGIONS, including CHRISTIANITY, contain such an inner teaching. Most theosophical speculation reveals a fascination with supernatural or other extraordinary occurrences and with the achievement of higher psychic and spiritual powers. It is held that knowledge of the divine wisdom gives access to the mysteries of nature and to humankind's deeper being. Despite a recognition of basic distinctions between the exoteric and the esoteric, between the phenomenal world and a higher spiritual reality, and between the human and the divine, which suggests DUALISM, most theosophically inclined writers have affirmed an underlying unity (monism) that subsumes all differentiation.

Since the 19th century theosophy has been identified with the Theosophical Society founded in 1875 in New York City by HELENA PETROVNA BLAVATSKY and HENRY STEEL OLCOTT. The Theosophical Society affirms the following objectives: (1) to form a nucleus of the universal fellowship of humanity, without distinction of race, creed, sex, CASTE, or color; (2) to encourage the study of COMPARATIVE RELIGION, philosophy, and science; and (3) to investigate unexplained laws of nature and the powers latent in human beings. The society insists that it is not offering a new system of thought but merely underscoring certain universal concepts of God, nature, and humanity that may be found in the teachings of all the great religions. One of the society's most controversial claims concerns the existence of a brotherhood of Great Masters, or Adepts, who, it is asserted, have perfected themselves and are directing the spiritual evolution of humanity.

The Theosophical Society almost expired in the United States in the years following Blavatsky and Olcott's removal to India. During the 1880s and '90s it was revived by William Q. Judge (1851–96), an Irish-born American mystic, who succeeded in making the American section the most active unit in the international movement. The American wing, however, was to be repeatedly disrupted by schisms in later years. Following Blavatsky's death in 1891, tensions rapidly escalated between Judge and Olcott, culminating in the secession of the American movement from Indian control in 1895. After Judge's death in 1896, Katherine Tingley (1847–1929) succeeded to the headship of the American section; at her instigation the American headquarters was transferred to Point Loma in California, and the focus of the movement's work was recast along more practical lines. In 1950–51 the headquarters was moved to Pasadena, Calif. A new schism developed, with still a third group claiming to represent theosophy in America. Such sectarianism has declined in recent years.

Though Judge came to dominate the American work after 1891, Olcott maintained an uneasy control over the international movement. Upon his death in 1907, he was succeeded as president in India by the charismatic Englishwoman Annie Besant (1847–1933), whose leadership gave Indians a sense of pride that they were exporting ideas of importance to the West. In 1911 she proclaimed Jiddu Krishnamurti (1895–1986), an obscure Indian youth, as the vehicle of a coming World Teacher, an act that led to much controversy. Krishnamurti subsequently renounced any claims to being a World Teacher and began a career of writing and teaching. Beginning in the 1920s he spent much time in the United States and Europe, where his books have enjoyed considerable popularity.

The influence of the Theosophical Society has been significant, despite its small following. The movement has been a catalytic force in the 20th-century Asian revival of Buddhism and HINDUISM and a pioneering agency in the promotion of greater Western acquaintance with Eastern thought. In the United States it has influenced a whole series of religious movements, including the I AM MOVEMENT, the ROSICRUCIANS, the Liberal Catholic Church, Psychiana, UNITY, and sections of the NEW THOUGHT movement.

THEOTOKOS \ˌthä-ō-ˈtō-ˌkōs, thē-ˈä-tə-ˌkäs\ (Greek: "One Who Has Given Birth to God"), in EASTERN ORTHODOXY, the designation of the Virgin MARY as mother of God. The NESTORIANS, who stressed the independence of the divine and human natures in Christ, opposed its use, on the ground that it compromised the human nature of Christ. The Council of Ephesus (431) anathematized all who denied that Christ was truly divine, and asserted that Mary was truly the mother of God. The COUNCIL OF CHALCEDON (451) used the term in formulating the definition of the hypostatic union (of Christ's human and divine natures).

THERA \ˈter-ə\ (Pāli: "Elders"), *Sanskrit* Sthavirās \stə-ˈvir-əz\, senior monks of the first Buddhist SANGHA. Adherents of the THERAVĀDA school of BUDDHISM accept as authoritative the Pāli canon of ancient Indian Buddhism and trace their lineage back to the Theras.

THERAGĀTHĀ/THERĪGĀTHĀ \ˌter-ə-ˈgä-tä . . . ˌter-ē-ˈgä-tä\ (Sanskrit: "Hymns of the Elders/Senior Nuns"), Buddhist lyrics, included in the *Suttanipāta* (one of the earliest books of the Pāli canon, appearing in the late *Khuddaka Nikāya* ["Short Collection"] of the *Sutta Pitaka*). In the works 264 monks speak of their inner experiences and of nature, and some 100 nuns tell of their daily lives. The songs of the monks are said to have been composed when their authors experienced the bliss of enlightenment. Within the collection about 30 different meters can be distinguished, attesting to the prosodic variety of Buddhist lyrics.

THERAPEUTAE \ˌther-ə-ˈpyü-tē\ (Greek: "Worshipers"), *singular* Therapeutes, Jewish sect of ascetics closely resembling the ESSENES, believed to have settled on the shores of Lake Mareotis in the vicinity of Alexandria, Egypt, during the 1st century CE. The only original account of this community is given in *De vita contemplativa* (*On the Contemplative Life*), attributed to Philo of Alexandria.

The origin and fate of the Therapeutae are unknown. They shared with the Essenes a dualistic view of body and soul, but differed from them in that "wisdom," according to Philo, was their main objective. For six days a week members of the community, both men and women, lived apart from one another, praying at dawn and at evening, the interval between being spent entirely on spiritual exercise. On the SABBATH they met in the common SANCTUARY, where they listened to a discourse by the member most skilled in their doctrines and then ate a common meal of bread and water. They read SCRIPTURE, which they interpreted allegorically on the pattern of books composed by the founders of their sect. Philo refers to the composition of "new psalms" to God in a variety of meters and melodies. The sect revered the number 7 and its square, but the most sacred of numbers was 50. Thus, on the eve of the 50th day they observed an all-night festival, with a discourse, hymn singing, and a meal, followed by a sacred vigil.

THERAVĀDA \ˌter-ə-ˈvä-də\ (Pāli: "Way of the Elders"), major form of BUDDHISM prevalent in Sri Lanka, Myanmar (Burma), Thailand, Cambodia, and Laos.

Theravāda, like most other Buddhist schools, claims to adhere most closely to the original doctrines and practices taught by the BUDDHA GOTAMA. Theravādins accept as authoritative the Pāli canon that has its roots in ancient Indian Buddhism, and they trace their sectarian lineage back to the Elders (Sanskrit: Sthaviras; Pāli: THERAS), who followed in the tradition of the senior monks of the first Buddhist SANGHA. To what extent this Theravāda view is historically accurate is difficult to determine. It is nevertheless clear that Theravāda-like traditions that used Pāli as their sacred language did develop before the 1st century CE in parts of India, in parts of mainland southeast Asia, and—most especially—in Sri Lanka. In the early centuries of the 1st millennium CE the Theravāda traditions emerged as the dominant form of Buddhism not only in Sri Lanka but also in Myanmar, Thailand, Cambodia, and Laos. In all these areas the relationship between the Theravādins and royal authority has been very close.

Throughout their history the Theravādins have been a relatively conservative school. Like all the (now defunct) HĪNAYĀNA schools with which they are usually grouped, the Theravādins have focused their attention on the Buddha Gotama and, to a lesser extent, on Metteyya (MAITREYA), the Buddha of the future. At the level of doctrine the Theravādins have maintained a clear ontological distinction between SAMSĀRA (the realm of suffering) and NIRVANA (release). Their religious goal is to attain the state of an ARAHANT, or fully perfected saint.

In the so-called Theravāda countries there are many Buddhist traditions and contemporary trends that are usually associated with MAHĀYĀNA and even Esoteric (Tantric) orientations. However, the authoritative character of the mainstream Theravāda heritage remains largely intact.

THERESA OF LISIEUX, SAINT \tə-'rē-sə . . . lē-'zyœ̄\, *also called* Saint Theresa of the Child Jesus, *or* The Little Flower, *original name* Marie-Françoise-

Thérèse Martin (b. Jan. 2, 1873, Alençon, France—d. Sept. 30, 1897, Lisieux; canonized May 17, 1925; feast day October 1), CARMELITE nun whose service to her order, although outwardly unremarkable, was later recognized for its spiritual accomplishments.

Theresa moved with her family to Lisieux in 1877 and was raised by older sisters and an aunt. In the deeply religious atmosphere of her home, her piety developed early and intensively. She entered the Carmelite CONVENT there at the age of 15. Though suffering

Saint Theresa
BBC Hulton Picture Library

from depression, feelings of guilt, and religious doubts, she kept the rule to perfection and maintained a smiling, pleasant, and unselfish manner. Before her death from tuberculosis she acknowledged that because of her difficult nature every day had been a struggle. Her burial site at Lisieux became a place of PILGRIMAGE, and a BASILICA bearing her name was built there (1929–54).

The story of Theresa's spiritual development was related in a collection of her epistolary essays, published in 1898 under the title *Histoire d'une âme* ("Story of a Soul"). Her popularity is largely a result of this work. St. Theresa defined her doctrine of the Little Way as "the way of spiritual childhood, the way of trust and absolute surrender."

THESEUM \thi-'sē-əm\, temple in Athens dedicated to HEPHAESTUS and ATHENA as patrons of the arts and crafts. Slightly older than the PARTHENON (*i.e.*, c. 450–440 BCE), it has been known as the Theseum since the Middle Ages, apparently because some of its sculptures represent the exploits of THESEUS. The Theseum is a Doric peripteral (*i.e.*, surrounded by a single row of columns) temple, with 13 columns at the sides and 6 at the ends.

The east pedimental sculpture dealt with the APOTHEOSIS of HERACLES. The frontal metopes represent the labors of Heracles, the lateral the exploits of Theseus. As in the Parthenon there is a sculptured frieze above the exterior of the cella walls, though this extends only over the east and west fronts and the east ends of the sides. The eastern frieze represents a battle scene with seated deities on either hand, the western one a *kentauromachia* (battle of CENTAURS). The outstanding preservation of the temple is owing to its conversion into a Christian church in the Middle Ages.

THESEUS \'thē-sē-əs, 'thēs-,yüs\, great hero of Attic legend, son of Aegeus, king of Athens, and AETHRA, daughter of Pittheus, king of Troezen (in Argolis), or of the sea god, POSEIDON, and Aethra. When Theseus reached manhood, Aethra sent him to Athens. While on the journey he killed Sinis, called the Pine Bender because he killed his victims by tearing them apart between two pine trees. Next Theseus dispatched Phaea the Crommyonian sow (or boar). Then from a cliff he flung Sciron, who had kicked his guests into the sea while they were washing his feet. Later he slew PROCRUSTES, who fitted all comers to his iron bed by hacking or racking them to the right length.

On his arrival in Athens, Theseus found his father married to MEDEA, who recognized Theseus before his father did and tried to persuade Aegeus to poison him. Aegeus, however, finally recognized Theseus and declared him heir to the throne. Theseus successfully attacked the fire-breathing bull of Marathon, after which he killed the Cretan MINOTAUR, half man and half bull, shut up in the legendary Cretan Labyrinth. Theseus had promised Aegeus that if he returned successful from Crete, he would hoist a white sail in place of the black sail with which the fatal ship bearing the sacrificial victims to the Minotaur always put to sea. But he forgot his promise; and when Aegeus saw the black sail, he flung himself from the Acropolis and died.

Theseus then united the various Attic communities into a single state and extended the territory of Attica to the Isthmus of Corinth. Alone or with the Greek hero HERACLES he captured the AMAZON princess ANTIOPE (or Hippolyte). As a result the Amazons attacked Athens, and Hippolyte fell fighting on the side of Theseus. By her he had a son, HIPPOLYTUS. Theseus is also said to have taken part in the Argonautic expedition and the Calydonian boar hunt.

Theseus and his friend PIRITHOUS cooperated to carry off HELEN, then still a child. Theseus later descended to the lower world with Pirithous to help his friend carry off PERSEPHONE, Queen of the Dead. But they were caught and confined in HADES until Heracles came and released Theseus.

When Theseus returned to Athens, he faced an uprising led by a descendant of ERECHTHEUS. Failing to quell the outbreak, Theseus sent his children to Euboea, and after solemnly cursing the Athenians he sailed away to the island of Scyros. Lycomedes, king of Scyros, killed Theseus by casting him into the sea from the top of a cliff. Later, according to the command of the Delphic oracle, the Athenians fetched the bones of Theseus from Scyros and laid them in Attic earth.

Theseus' chief festival, called Theseia, was on the eighth of the month Pyanopsion (October), but the eighth day of every month was also sacred to him.

Theseus slaying the Minotaur, Greek amphora; in the Gregorian Etruscan Museum, Rome
Alinari—Art Resource

THESMOPHORIA \,thez-mə-'fōr-ē-ə, -'fȯr-\, in GREEK RELIGION, festival held in honor of DEMETER Thesmophoros and celebrated by women in many parts of the Greek world. The name Thesmophoria is perhaps the primary one, from which the epithet of the goddess was derived; it means "the carrying of things laid down."

The celebrants were free women who seem to have been married. They observed chastity for several days and abstained from certain foods. The festival lasted three days, although in Attica it was lengthened to five. At least a great part of the Thesmophoria was carried out by torchlight and was accompanied by ceremonial coarse abuse among the women, a common ritual occurrence.

At some time in the festival pigs were thrown into an underground chamber. They were left there until the parts of them not eaten by snakes had had time to rot. The remains were then brought up by women who had observed chastity for three days. These women also carried, or some of the celebrants did, certain ritual objects, including pinecones and figures made of dough, in the shapes of serpents and men. The remains of the pigs were laid on an altar and if taken and mixed with seed were believed to ensure a good crop. Apparently the figures, like the pigs, were also thrown into the chasms. There was the day of fasting, with the women sitting upon the ground. The third day, *kalligeneia*, was "the fair birth" and may have indicated the happy issue of all the fertility of the ground.

THETIS \'thē-tis\, in Greek mythology, NEREID loved by ZEUS and POSEIDON. When THEMIS, however, revealed that Thetis was destined to bear a son who would be mightier than his father, the two gods gave her to PELEUS. Thetis, unwilling to wed a mortal, resisted Peleus' advances by changing herself into various shapes. But, assisted by the wise CENTAUR CHIRON, Peleus finally captured her.

All the gods brought gifts to their wedding. The child of their union was the warrior ACHILLES, but, according to some authorities, Thetis bore seven children, all of whom perished either when she attempted to render them immortal by fire or when she destroyed them as the tokens of an unwilling alliance. She had a SANCTUARY at Sparta.

THIRTEEN ARTICLES OF FAITH, *also called* Thirteen Principles, MOSES MAIMONIDES' summary of the basic tenets of JUDAISM. They first appeared in his commentary on the *Mishnah Kitāb al-Sirāj*. Maimonides' statement, although presented by him as a form of dogma, was a personal concept and has been much debated and revised. The numerous versions of the Articles of Faith include the hymn *Yigdal*, which was written about 1300 and has been adopted into most prayer services.

The contents of the Articles are as follows: (1) God's existence is perfect and the cause of all else that exists; (2) God's unity is unparalleled; (3) God has no corporeal nature; (4) God is eternal; (5) God should be worshiped exclusively; (6) God communicates through prophecy; (7) MOSES is the greatest of all prophets; (8) Moses received the entire TORAH; (9) Moses' law is eternally complete and immutable; (10) God is omniscient; (11) God punishes sinners and rewards those who keep Torah; (12) the MESSIAH is coming; and (13) the dead will rise.

THIRTY-NINE ARTICLES, the doctrinal statements of the Church of England. With THE BOOK OF COMMON PRAYER, they present the liturgy and doctrine of that church. The Thirty-nine Articles developed from the Forty-two Articles, written in 1553. These had been partly derived from the Thirteen Articles of 1538, designed as the basis of an agreement between Henry VIII and the German Lutheran princes, which had been influenced by the Lutheran AUGSBURG CONFESSION (1530).

The Forty-two Articles were eliminated when Mary I restored ROMAN CATHOLICISM (1553). In 1563 the Canterbury Convocation drastically revised the Forty-two Articles. A final revision by Convocation in 1571 produced the Thirty-nine Articles, which were approved by Elizabeth I and imposed on the clergy. They deal briefly with the doctrines accepted by Roman Catholics and Protestants alike and more fully with points of controversy. They are often studiously ambiguous, however, because the Elizabethan government wished to make the national church as inclusive of different viewpoints as possible. Assent to them was, into the 19th century, required for a university degree in Britain.

The status of the Thirty-nine Articles varies in the several churches of the ANGLICAN COMMUNION. Since 1865, Church of England clergy have had to declare only that the doctrine in the Articles is "agreeable to the Word of God," while, in the Protestant Episcopal Church in the United States, neither clergy nor laity is required formally to subscribe to them.

THOMAS, SAINT \'tä-məs\ (b. probably Galilee—d. traditionally 53 CE, Madras, India; Western feast day December 21, feast day in Roman and Syrian CATHOLIC churches July 3, in the Greek church October 6), one of the Twelve APOSTLES. His name in Aramaic (Te'oma) and Greek (Didymos) means "twin." He is called Judas Thomas (*i.e.*, Judas the Twin) by the Syrians.

According to John 20:19–29 Thomas was not among those disciples to whom the risen Christ first appeared, and, when they told the incredulous Thomas, he requested physical proof of the RESURRECTION (hence the phrase "doubting Thomas"). Thomas' subsequent history is uncertain. According to the 4th-century *Ecclesiastical History* of EUSEBIUS OF CAESAREA, he evangelized Parthia (modern Khorasan). Later Christian tradition says he extended his apostolate into India, where he is recognized as the founder of the Church of the Syrian Malabar Christians, or Christians of St. Thomas. In the apocryphal *Acts of Thomas*, originally composed in Syriac, his martyrdom is cited under the king of Mylapore at Madras, where are to be found St. Thomas Mount and San Thomè Cathedral, his traditional burial place. His relics, however, supposedly were taken to the West and finally enshrined at Ortona, Italy. Other works accredited to Thomas are the gnostic *Gospel of Thomas*, *The Book of Thomas the Athlete*, and *Evangelium Joannis de obitu Mariae* ("The Message of John Concerning the Death of Mary").

THOMAS À KEMPIS \'tä-məs-ä-'kem-pis\, *original name* Thomas Hemerken (b. 1379/80, Kempen, near Düsseldorf, the Rhineland [now in Germany]—d. Aug. 8, 1471, Agnietenberg, near Zwolle, Bishopric of Utrecht [now in The Netherlands]), Christian theologian, the probable author of *De Imitatione Christi* (IMITATION OF CHRIST), a devotional book that, with the exception of the BIBLE, has been considered the most influential work in Christian literature.

About 1392 Thomas went to Deventer, Neth., headquarters of the learned BRETHREN OF THE COMMON LIFE, a community devoted to education and the care of the poor, where he studied under the theologian Florentius Radewyns, the founder of the Congregation of Windesheim. Thomas joined the Windesheim congregation at Agnietenberg monastery, where he remained for over 70 years. He took his vows in 1408, was ordained in 1413, and devoted his life to copying manuscripts and to directing novices.

Although the authorship is in dispute, he probably wrote the *Imitation*. Simple in language and style, it emphasizes the spiritual rather than the materialistic life, affirms the rewards of being Christ-centered, and supports Communion as a means to strengthen faith. His writings offer what is possibly the best representation of the DEVOTIO MODERNA, a religious movement that made religion intelligible and practicable for the "modern" attitude arising in the Netherlands at the end of the 14th century. Thomas stresses ASCETICISM rather than MYSTICISM, as well as moderate, not extreme, austerity. A critical edition of his *Opera Omnia* (17 vol., 1902–22; "Complete Works") was published by M.J. Pohl.

THOMAS AQUINAS, SAINT \ə-ˈkwī-nəs\, *also called* Aquinas, *Italian* San Tommaso d'Aquino, *byname* Doctor Angelicus (b. 1224/25, Roccasecca, near Aquino, Terra di Lavoro, Kingdom of Sicily—d. March 7, 1274, Fossanova, near Terracina, Latium, Papal States; canonized July 18, 1323; feast day January 28, formerly March 7), Christian philosopher, theologian, and poet who developed his own conclusions from Aristotelian premises and systematized Latin theology. He is recognized by the ROMAN CATHOLIC church as its foremost Western philosopher and theologian.

Thomas was born in 1224 or 1225 at Roccasecca, Italy, and was offered as a prospective monk at the monastery of Monte Cassino near his home when he was still a young boy. In 1239 Thomas was forced to return to his family when the emperor expelled the monks in a conflict with the pope. He was then sent to the University of Naples, where he first encountered the scientific and philosophical works that were being translated from the Greek and the Arabic. In this setting Thomas decided to join the DOMINICANS. In 1256 he began teaching theology in one of the two Dominican schools incorporated in the University of Paris, and in 1259 Thomas was appointed theological adviser and lecturer to the papal Curia. From 1265 to 1267 he taught at the CONVENT of Santa Sabina in Rome until, in November 1268, he was sent to Paris, where he became involved in a doctrinal polemic concerning faith and reason.

IBN RUSHD (Averroës), the great Spanish Arabic commentator on Aristotle, had asserted that two truths—one of faith, the other of reason—can, in the final analysis, be contradictory, and his EXEGESIS and rational style of thought was attracting disciples in the faculty of arts at the University of Paris. Aquinas protested against the counter-orthodoxy of this trend. His own debt to Aristotle meant, how-

Apotheosis of St. Thomas Aquinas, *altarpiece by Francesco Traini, 1363; in Santa Caterina, Pisa, Italy*

Alinari—Art Resource

ever, that in 1270 Thomas was discredited along with the Averroists for his sanction of the autonomy of reason under faith. This dispute had called into question the very method of theology. According to Aquinas, reason is capable of operating within faith and yet according to its own laws. While the philosopher relies solely on reason, the theologian accepts authority and faith as his starting point and then proceeds to conclusions using reason. Thomas was the first to present theology systematically in this way, and in doing so he raised a storm of opposition. Even today this opposition endures.

In 1266 Thomas composed a treatise—*De regimine principum* ("On the Government of Princes")—that described experimental and rational attempts at government. In the face of this movement, theologians of a traditional bent firmly resisted any form of a determinist philosophy which, they believed, would atrophy liberty, dissolve personal responsibility, destroy faith in Providence, and deny the notion of a gratuitous act of creation. Imbued with Augustine's doctrines, they asserted the necessity and power of GRACE for a nature torn asunder by SIN. The optimism of the new theology concerning the religious value of nature scandalized them.

Contrary to their suspicions, Thomas taught a continuous creation in which the dependence of the created on the creative wisdom guarantees the reality of the order of nature. God, without surrendering his sovereignty, conforms his government over the universe to the laws of a creative Providence that wills each being to act according to its proper nature. This autonomy finds its highest realization in the rational creature: humans are self-moving in their intellectual, volitional, and physical existence. "To take something away from the perfection of the creature is to abstract from the perfection of the creative power itself." This metaphysical axiom, which is also a mystical principle, is the key to St. Thomas' spirituality.

In 1273, BONAVENTURE, a Franciscan friar and a colleague of Thomas' at Paris, leveled a critique at the Aristotelian ideas of philosophy as distinct from theology, a physical nature that has determined laws, a soul that is bound up with the body, and the denial of the Platonic-Augustinian theory of knowledge based upon exemplary Ideas or Forms. The disagreement was profound. Certainly, all Christian philosophers taught the distinction between matter and spirit. Some viewed the material world merely as a stage on which the history of spiritual persons is acted out and their salvation or damnation determined. In this history, the human plays a brief role only to escape as quickly as possible into the realm of pure spirit. Thomas, on the contrary, situated the human ontologically at the juncture of two universes. Within the human condition there is both a distinction between spirit and nature and an intrinsic homogeneity of the two. For Aristotle, form is that which makes a thing to be what it is; form and matter are the two intrinsic causes that constitute every material thing. For Thomas, then, the body is the matter and the soul is the form of man. The objection was raised that he was not sufficiently safeguarding the transcendence of the spirit.

Thomas Aquinas died on March 7, 1274, at the CISTERCIAN abbey of Fossanova. In 1277 the masters of Paris condemned a series of 219 propositions, of which 12 were theses of Thomas, and produced for several centuries a resistance to the cosmic and anthropological realism of Aquinas. Nonetheless, he was canonized a saint in 1323, officially named doctor of the church in 1567, and proclaimed the protagonist of orthodoxy during the modernist crisis at the end of the 19th century.

THOMISM \'tō-,mi-zəm\, philosophical and theological system developed by THOMAS AQUINAS in the 13th century, by his later commentators, and by modern revivalists of the system, known as neo-Thomists.

Medieval Thomism. Although making respectful use of Aristotle and the Platonists, and AUGUSTINE and the CHURCH FATHERS, Aquinas' originality was shown in treating existence as the supreme act or perfection of being in God as well as in created things, in reserving the creative act to God alone, and in distinguishing between God and creatures by a real composition of existence and essence as principles in all created beings. Also characteristic was his teaching that the human soul is a unique subsistent form, substantially united with matter to constitute human nature. Aquinas held that both man and lower creatures have a natural tendency or love toward God, that supernatural GRACE perfects and elevates our natural abilities, and that blessedness consists formally in knowing God Himself, a knowledge accompanied by our full love of God.

This body of Thomistic doctrines was critically explained and developed during subsequent centuries. The later 13th century was crowded with treatises attacking and defending basic positions of St. Thomas, especially on the unicity of of the human substantial form and the distinction of essence and existence. Encouragement toward consulting Aquinas' own writings came with the adoption of his doctrine by the DOMINICAN Order (1278, 1279, 1286), his CANONIZATION by Pope John XXII (1323), and the special place accorded to his works at the COUNCIL OF TRENT. The Dominican Jean Capréolus (c. 1380–1444), called the Prince of the Thomists, was the first to make a direct study of the texts of St. Thomas. Another major Dominican commentator was Tomaso de Vio, Cardinal Cajetan, who made elaborate expositions of St. Thomas' *Summa theologiae* and *De ente et essentia* (*On Being and Essence*). Cajetan moved beyond Aquinas to propose the influential division of kinds of analogy into inequality, attribution, and proportionality, and that the human soul's immortality can be supported only by probable reasons.

After the mid-16th century, the Thomistic commentators became involved in intricate theological controversies on grace and premotion. Highly systematized presenta-

tions of opposing views were introduced into the commentaries on the *Summa theologiae* made by the Spanish Dominican theologian Domingo Bañez and the Spanish JESUIT authors Francis Toletus and Gabriel Vázquez. But the new Renaissance tendency to give separate treatment to philosophical and theological issues, as well as the pressures of seminary education, undermined the usefulness of the commentary form of approach to St. Thomas. A new trend is present in the Dominican John of St. Thomas (1589–1644), who issued a separate *Cursus Philosophicus* ("Course in Philosophy") and then a *Cursus Theologicus* ("Course in Theology") in Thomistic thought. Using the framework of logic, philosophy of nature, and metaphysics, John assembled the philosophical teachings of St. Thomas under these systematic headings and reformulated the material for theology students. There were original features in his logic, including the distinction between formal and objective concepts and the stress on intentional signs.

Modern Thomism. In most Catholic seminaries and universities of the early 19th century more attention was paid to Descartes, Locke, and Wolff than to Aquinas. The modern revival of authentic Thomism began at this time in Italy. Vincent Buzzetti (1777–1824) and the Jesuit teacher Serafino Sordi (1793–1865) were instrumental in urging a direct study of the text of Aristotle and Aquinas. The revolutions of 1848 had a decisive influence upon both the Holy See and the Society of Jesus toward finding sound principles on God, man, and society in the works of St. Thomas. In editions of their philosophy manuals appearing after 1850, this renewal of Thomistic thought was advocated by three influential Jesuit writers in Italy and Germany: Luigi Taparelli d'Azeglio, Matteo Liberatore, and Joseph Kleutgen. Their own positions in epistemology, metaphysics, and social theory remained eclectic, but they did give impetus to the work of studying St. Thomas and the other Scholastics in the light of modern intellectual and social issues. Decisive support for this movement came with Pope Leo XIII's ENCYCLICAL *Aeterni Patris* (1879). It noted the importance of sound doctrine for meeting today's problems and called especially for a recovery of the wisdom of St. Thomas. St. Thomas was declared the universal patron of Catholic schools, and a canon (1366, par. 2) in the new *Code of Canon Law* (1917) required philosophy and theology teachers to adhere to the method, doctrine, and principles of St. Thomas.

Thomists of the 20th century concentrated on a historical investigation of St. Thomas' doctrine in its medieval context and a rethinking of that doctrine in reference to contemporary problems. After World War II, Thomists faced three major tasks: to develop an adequate philosophy of science, to take account of phenomenological and psychiatric findings, and to evaluate the ontologies of existentialism and NATURALISM.

THOR \'thòr\, deity common to all the early Germanic peoples, foe to the race of GIANTS but benevolent toward mankind. He was generally secondary to the god ODIN, who in some traditions was his father; but in

Thor holding his hammer, bronze statuette from northern Iceland, c. 1000 CE
By courtesy of the National Museum of Iceland, Reykjavik

Iceland, and perhaps among all northern peoples except the royal families, he was apparently worshiped more than any other god. There is evidence that a corresponding deity named Thunor, or Thonar, was worshiped in England and continental Europe, but little is known about him.

Thor's name was the Germanic word for thunder, and it was the thunderbolt that was represented by his hammer, the attribute most commonly associated with him. The hammer, MJOLLNIR, had many marvelous qualities, including that of returning to the thrower like a boomerang; it is frequently carved on runic stones and funerary stelae.

Among Thor's chief enemies was the world serpent JÖR-MUNGAND (Jörmungandr), symbol of evil. According to tradition, Thor failed to smash the skull of Jörmungand, and the two are destined to kill each other in the RAGNARÖK (the end of the world of gods and men).

THOTH \'tōth, 'thōth, 'tōt\ (Greek), *Egyptian* Djhuty \jə-'hü-tē\, Egyptian god of the moon, reckoning, learning, and writing. He was held to be the inventor of writing, the creator of languages, the scribe, interpreter, and adviser of the gods, and the representative of the sun god, RE. His responsibility for writing was shared with the goddess Seshat. The cult of Thoth was centered in the town of Khmunu (Hermopolis; modern al-Ashmūnayn) in Upper Egypt.

In the myth of OSIRIS, Thoth protected ISIS during her pregnancy and healed the eye of her son HORUS, which had been wounded by Osiris' adversary SETH. He weighed the hearts of the deceased at their judgment and reported the result to Osiris and his fellow judges. Thoth's sacred animals were the ibis and the baboon; millions of mummified bodies of these animals have been found in cemeteries near Hermopolis and Memphis. Thoth was usually represented in human form with an ibis's head. The Greeks identified Thoth with their god Hermes; a collection of religious texts is attributed to "Hermes Trismegistos," which should thus be understood as "Thoth, the thrice great."

Thoth, represented in human form with an ibis's head, detail from the Greenfield Papyrus, c. 950 BCE
Copyright British Museum

THREAD CROSS, *Tibetan* mdos \'dœ\, object made usually of two sticks bound together in the shape of a cross, with colored threads wound around their ends to resemble a cobweb, used in Tibetan magical rituals to entrap evil spirits. They are probably pre-Buddhist, or BON, in origin but now are used by Buddhist priests. Those used in purification ceremonies at the New Year or for persons suffering from illness or misfortune are broken up and burned.

THREE WEEKS, *Hebrew* Bein Hametzarim ("Between the Straits"), in JUDAISM, period of mourning running from the 17th day of TAMMUZ, the fourth month of the Jewish religious year, to the 9th day of Av (TISHA BE-AV), the fifth month (variously, about June to August). The observance commemorates the days between the first breaching of the walls of Jerusalem in 586 BCE by Babylonian troops to the subsequent destruction of the First TEMPLE OF JERUSALEM. Marriages and haircuts are forbidden. During the nine days of Av meat and wine are forbidden except on the SABBATH, the blessing of the NEW MOON is omitted, and prophecies of doom from JEREMIAH and ISAIAH are read in the SYNAGOGUE on the three Sabbaths that fall within this period. The period ends with a 24-hour fast.

THREE WORLDS ACCORDING TO KING RUANG \rü-'äŋ, -'əŋ\ (Thai: "Traiphumikatha"), 14th-century COSMOLOGY that is the oldest known full-length text written in Thai. *See* BUDDHISM.

THRYM \'thrœm, 'thrim\, in Germanic mythology, GIANT who stole MJOLLNIR, the hammer of the god THOR. Thrym asked as ransom for the hand of the goddess FREYJA in marriage, and she refused. Thor, dressed as a woman, attended the wedding in her place, recovered his hammer, and slaughtered Thrym and the other giants in attendance.

THUNDERBIRD \'thən-dər-,bərd\, in Native North American mythology, powerful spirit in the form of a bird which watered the earth and caused vegetation to grow. Lightning flashed from its beak, and thunder was the beating of its wings. It was often portrayed with an extra head on its abdomen and was frequently accompanied by lesser bird spirits, usually in the form of eagles or falcons.

Although it is best known in North America, evidence of similar figures has been found throughout Africa, Asia, and Europe.

THUNDERER, in BALTIC RELIGION, sky deity usually known as Perkūnas (Lithuanian) or PĒRKONS (Latvian).

THYRSUS \'thər-səs\, in GREEK RELIGION, staff carried by DIONYSUS and his votaries (Bacchae, Maenads). In Greek art after 530 BCE the Bacchae were usually depicted as holding the thyrsus, a staff shown as a stalk of giant fennel (*narthēx*) segmented like bamboo, sometimes with ivy leaves inserted in the hollow end. Bacchae were depicted and described using them as weapons. Some scholars believe they were fertility symbols.

TIAMAT \'tē-ä-,mät\, in MESOPOTAMIAN RELIGION, primal goddess, a personification of salt water and mother of the gods. When conflict between her husband Apsu and the other gods resulted in Apsu's death, Tiamat made war upon the other divinities, backed by an army of DEMONS she had created. Her battle with, and defeat at the hands of, the god MARDUK forms the substance of the Babylonian creation epic known as the *enuma elish*. From her body Marduk fashioned the heavens and the earth. *See* KINGU.

TIARA \tē-'ar-ə, -'är-\, in ROMAN CATHOLICISM, triple crown worn by the pope or carried in front of him, used during nonliturgical functions such as PROCESSIONS. Beehive-shaped, it is about 15 inches high and is made of silver cloth and ornamented with three diadems, as well as with two streamers, known as lappets, hanging from the back. The tiara probably developed from the Phrygian cap, or *frigium*, a conical cap worn in the Greco-Roman world. In the 10th century the tiara was pictured on papal coins, and by the 14th century it was ornamented with three crowns.

TIBETAN BUDDHISM, distinctive form of BUDDHISM that evolved from the 7th century CE in Tibet. It is based mainly on MĀDHYAMIKA and YOGĀCĀRA philosophies and utilizes the symbolic ritual practices of VAJRAYĀNA (Esoteric Buddhism). Tibetan Buddhism also incorporates the monastic disciplines of early THERAVĀDA Buddhism and the shamanistic features of the indigenous Tibetan religion, BON. Characteristic of Tibetan Buddhism is the large segment of the population actively engaged in religious pursuits (up until the Chinese Communist takeover in 1959, an estimated one-quarter of the inhabitants were members of religious orders); its system of "reincarnating lamas"; the merger of the spiritual and temporal authority in the office and person of the DALAI LAMA; and the vast number of divine beings (each with its own family, consort, and pacific and terrifying aspects), which are considered symbolic representations of the psyche by some Tibetans.

Buddhism was transmitted into Tibet mainly during the 7th to 10th centuries by such teachers as the 8th-century Tantric master PADMASAMBHAVA and the MAHĀYĀNA teacher ŚĀNTIRAKṢITA. In 1042 the reformer and teacher ATĪŚA came to Tibet, and within a century the major sects of Tibetan Buddhism had emerged. The DGE-LUGS-PA, the order of the Dalai and the PANCHEN LAMAS, has been the politically predominant Tibetan sect from the 17th century until 1959.

Tibetans succeeded in translating all available Buddhist literature in India and Tibet; many texts lost in the country of their origin are known only from their Tibetan translations. The Tibetan canon is divided into the *Bka'-'gyur*, consisting of the supposedly canonical texts, and the *Bstan-'gyur*, consisting of commentaries by Indian masters.

In the second half of the 20th century Tibetan Buddhism spread to the West, particularly after the subjugation of Tibet to Chinese Communist rule sent many refugees, including highly regarded "reincarnated LAMAS," or *tulku*s, out of their homeland.

TIELE, CORNELIS PETRUS \'tē-lə\ (b. Dec. 16, 1830, Leiden, Neth.—d. Jan. 11, 1902, Leiden), Dutch theologian and scholar, who had great influence on the comparative STUDY OF RELIGION.

Educated at the seminary of the Remonstrant Brotherhood (*see* ARMINIANISM *and* REMONSTRANT), Tiele served as pastor at Moordrecht and Rotterdam, then as professor at the Remonstrant Seminary. In 1877 he was appointed at the University of Leiden as professor of the history of religions. Among Tiele's numerous works are *Outlines of the History of Religion to the Spread of the Universal Religions* (1877) and his Gifford Lectures, published as *Elements of the Science of Religion*, 2 vol. (1897–99).

T'IEN \'tyen\, *Pinyin* Tian (Chinese, literally, "Sky" or "Heaven"), in indigenous Chinese religion, the supreme power reigning over lesser gods and humans. The term T'ien may refer to a deity, to impersonal nature, or to both.

The first mention of T'ien seems to have occurred early in the Chou dynasty (1111–255 BCE). As a god, T'ien is sometimes perceived to be an impersonal power in contrast to SHANG-TI ("Supreme Ruler"), but the two are closely identified and the terms frequently used synonymously. Both T'ien and Shang-ti had influence over the fertility of the clan and its crops; sacrifices were offered to these powers solely by the king and, later, by the emperor.

Chinese rulers were traditionally referred to as Son of Heaven (*t'ien-tzu*), and their authority was believed to emanate from heaven. Beginning in the Chou dynasty, sovereignty was explained by the concept of the T'IEN-MING (Mandate of Heaven), a grant of authority that depended on the ruler's virtue. Since his virtue was believed to be reflected in the harmony of the empire, social and political unrest were traditionally considered signs that the mandate had been revoked and would soon be transferred to a succeeding dynasty.

In later years T'ien was often likened to impersonal nature or to fate. Scholars generally agreed that T'ien was the source of moral law, but for centuries they debated whether T'ien responded to human pleas and rewarded and punished human actions or whether events merely followed the order and principles established by T'ien.

T'IEN-MING \'tyen-'miŋ\, *Pinyin* Tianming (Chinese: "Mandate of Heaven"), in Confucian thought, the notion that heaven (T'ien) conferred directly upon an emperor, the Son of Heaven, the right to rule. The doctrine had its beginnings in the early Chou dynasty (c. 1122–221 BCE).

The continuation of the mandate was believed to be conditioned by the personal behavior of the ruler, who was expected to possess *i* ("righteousness") and JEN ("benevolence"); hence, some Confucianists taught that a tyrannical ruler not only lost his right to rule but also should be removed by revolution, if necessary.

T'IEN-SHIH TAO \'tyen-'shə-'daù, -'shər-\, *Pinyin* Tianshidao (Chinese: "Way of the Celestial Masters"), *also called* Five Pecks of Rice, *Chinese* (Wade-Giles romanization) Wu-tou-mi \'wü-'dō-'mē\, *Pinyin* Wudoumi, great Taoist-inspired popular movement that occurred near the end of China's Han dynasty (206 BCE–220 CE) and greatly weakened the government. The T'ien-shih tao became a prototype of the religiously inspired popular rebellions that were to erupt periodically throughout China for the next 2,000 years. It was founded by CHANG TAO-LING in 142 CE, who is said to have received a revelation from T'ai-shang Lao-chün (Lord Lao the Most High—*i.e.*, the deified LAO-TZU), who bestowed on him his "orthodox and sole doctrine of the authority of the covenant" (*cheng-i meng-wei fa*).

Chang was succeeded as *t'ien-shih* ("celestial master") by his son Chang Heng, who was in turn succeeded by his son Chang Lu. Taking advantage of discontent among the impoverished peasantry of central China, Chang Lu formed an army and set up an independent theocratic state. He was joined by another Taoist leader, Chang Hsiu (no relation), and together they extended the rebellion until it covered all of present-day Szechwan province. For ceremonial and administrative purposes, the realm was divided into 24 (later 28 and 36) units, or parishes (*chih*). The focal point of each was the oratory, or "chamber of purity" (*ching-shih*), which served as the center for communication with the powers on high. Here the *chi-chiu* ("libationer"), the priestly functionary, officiated. Each household contributed a tax of five pecks of rice to the administration, whence came the other common name of the movement, the Way of the Five Pecks of Rice (*Wu-tou-mi tao*).

The ritual activities of the libationer seem principally to have been directed toward the cure of disease by prescribed ceremonial means. Believed to be a punishment for evil deeds, whether committed by the sufferer himself or by an ancestor, illness was in fact a sentence pronounced by the SAN-KUAN (Three Officials), judges and custodians of he dead. The sentence was carried out by the spectral hordes of the Six Heavens (Liu-t'ien), a posthumous dwelling place of all unhallowed mortals. Using the rising flame and smoke of the incense burner in the center of the oratory to transmit the message borne by spirits exteriorized from within his own body, the libationer submitted petitions (*chang*) to the appropriate bureau of the three Taoist heavens (San-t'ien). The Taoist canon contains long lists of the "officials and generals" (*kuan chiang*), each specializing in a different sort of complaint, who would respectively pronounce on the appeal and marshal the celestial forces against the offending DEMONS.

Also effective were written talismans (*fu*); drawn by the libationer, these would be burned, and the ashes, mixed with water, were swallowed by the demons' victim. The libationer also functioned as a moral preceptor, instructing the faithful in the sect's own highly allegorical interpretation of the *Lao-tzu*, which they considered to be the revealed work of Lord Lao the Most High.

Chang Lu eventually came into conflict with Chang Hsiu and killed him. In 215 CE Chang Lu surrendered to the Han general Ts'ao Ts'ao, who rewarded him with high rank and a princely fief. Despite his surrender, it is with the T'ien-shih tao that the history of organized religious TAOISM may be said to begin, in that there has been an unbroken continuity from that time down to the present day.

T'IEN-T'AI \'tyen-'tī\, *Japanese* Tendai \'ten-,dī\, *Korean* Ch'ŏnt'ae \'chən-'te\, rationalist school of Buddhist thought that takes its name from the mountain in southeastern China where its founder and greatest exponent, CHIH-I, lived and taught in the 6th century. The chief SCRIPTURE of the school is the LOTUS SUTRA, and the school is thus also known as the Fa-hua (Japanese: Hokke), or Lotus, school.

The basic philosophical doctrine is summarized as the triple truth, or *chikuan* ("perfected comprehension"): (1) all things (DHARMAS) lack reality; (2) they, nevertheless, have a temporary existence; (3) they are simultaneously unreal and temporarily existing—being the middle, or absolute, truth, which includes and yet surpasses the others. Because existence is ever-changing, the phenomenal world is regarded as identical with the world as it really is.

The doctrine of the triple truth was first taught by Hui-wen (550–577); but Chih-i, the third patriarch, is regarded as the founder of the school. Chih-i organized the whole of the Buddhist canon according to the supposition that all the doctrines were present in the mind of the BUDDHA GOTAMA at the time of his enlightenment but were unfolded gradually according to the mental capacities of his hearers. The *Lotus Sutra* was considered the supreme doctrine.

In 804 SAICHŌ, a Japanese monk, was sent to China expressly to study the T'ien-t'ai tradition. The inclusiveness of the T'ien-t'ai school, which arranged all Buddhist learning into one grand hierarchical scheme, was attractive to Saichō. On his return to Japan he attempted to incorporate ZEN meditation, *vinaya* discipline, and esoteric cults into T'ien-t'ai. The Tendai school, as it is called in Japanese, also encouraged an amalgamation of SHINTŌ and BUDDHISM

in the Ichijitsu ("One Truth"), or Sannō Ichijitsu Shintō. Saichō's efforts to establish a Tendai ritual of ORDINATION in keeping with MAHĀYĀNA teachings and independent from the *kaidan* ("ordination center") at Nara bore results only after his death but was an important step in the Mahāyāna development in Japan.

After the death of Saichō, rivalry broke out between two factions of the school, which separated in the 9th century into the Sammon and the Jimon sects, headed by the two monks ENNIN and Enchin. A third branch, the Shinsei, emphasizes devotion to the Buddha Amida.

TIETÄJÄ \'tye-ta-ya\, principal religious specialist of the Baltic Finns, functioning in the tradition of the Finno-Ugric SHAMAN.

As a shamanic specialist, the *tietäjä*'s main task was to act as the community's first line of defense against hostile supernatural forces, whether they originated in the other-world or with sorcerers and other evil-minded people. The term *tietäjä* literally means "knower," implying that as the specialist he knew more than ordinary humans about the nature of the supernatural world and of techniques for dealing with it. He could be called on to aid in almost any problem that was either not adequately understood or not amenable to correction by ordinary means. He was consulted mostly in matters of illness, but he also served as priest, diviner, judge, name giver, spokesman, and entertainer. The overall status of the *tietäjä* was higher in the agricultural society than that of the shaman in the hunting and fishing milieu because of his additional social influence and political power accruing from his multiple roles.

TIJĀNĪYA \,tē-jä-'nē-ə\, especially exclusivist and proselytizing order of Sufi mystics widespread in northern and western Africa and the Sudan. Founded by Aḥmad at-Tijānī (1737–1815), formerly of the Khalwatī order, about 1781 in Fez, Morocco, it places great emphasis on good intentions and actions rather than on elaborate or extreme ritual. Unlike the QĀDIRĪYA and Sanūsīya orders, the Tijānīya did not conduct resistance activities against European colonization in north Africa during the 19th and 20th centuries. Under the leadership of al-Hajj 'UMAR TAL (d. 1864) of west Africa, however, they engaged in an expansionist JIHAD against unbelievers and Europeans until contained by the French and overcome by local enemies. *See also* SUFISM; ṬARĪQA.

TILAK \'ti-lək\, *Sanskrit* tilaka, in HINDUISM, mark generally made on the forehead, either as an ornament or to indicate one's sectarian affiliation. The marks are made by hand or with a metal stamp, using ash from a sacrificial fire, sandalwood paste, turmeric, cow dung, clay, charcoal, or red lead. Among some sects the mark is made on 2, 5, 12, or 32 parts of the body as well as on the forehead. Among Śaivas (*see* ŚAIVISM), the tilak is usually three horizontal parallel lines across the forehead, with or without a red dot. Sometimes a crescent moon or trident denotes a Śaiva. Among Vaiṣṇavas (*see* VAIṢṆAVISM), the tilak generally involves a pattern of two or more vertical lines resembling the letter *U* and representing the footprint of VISHNU, with or without a central line or dot.

TILLICH, PAUL (JOHANNES) \'ti-lik̲, *Angl* -lik\ (b. Aug. 20, 1886, Starzeddel, Brandenburg, Ger.—d. Oct. 22, 1965, Chicago, Ill., U.S.), German-born American theologian and philosopher whose discussions of God and faith illuminated and bound together the realms of traditional CHRISTIAN-

ITY and modern culture. Some of his books, notably *The Courage to Be* (1952) and *Dynamics of Faith* (1957), reached a large public audience. The three-volume *Systematic Theology* (1951–63) was the culmination of his rigorous examination of faith.

The son of a theologically conservative father, Tillich was, however, taught the classical ideals of free thought and reason in German secondary schools. Indeed, the question of how to enjoy the freedom to explore life without sacrificing the essentials of a meaningful tradition was to appear as a major theme in Tillich's theological work: the relation of heteronomy to autonomy and their possible synthesis in theonomy. Heteronomy (alien rule) is the cultural and spiritual condition when traditional norms and values become rigid, external demands threatening to destroy individual freedom. Autonomy (self-rule) is the inevitable and justified revolt against such oppression, which nevertheless entails the temptation to reject all norms and values. Theonomy (divine rule) envisions a situation in which norms and values express the convictions and commitments of free individuals in a free society. These three conditions Tillich saw as the basic dynamisms of both personal and social life. His decisive encounter with the problem came during his theological studies at the University of Halle (1905–12), where he was forced to match the doctrinal position of the Lutheran Church, based on the established confessional documents, against the THEOLOGICAL LIBERALISM and scientific EMPIRICISM that dominated the academic scene in Germany at that time.

Ordained a Lutheran clergyman, Tillich served as a military CHAPLAIN during World War I. The war was a shattering experience to him as evidence of the bankruptcy of 19th-century humanism and the inadequacy of autonomy as sole guide. The chaotic situation in Germany after the armistice convinced him that Western civilization was nearing the end of an era. Tillich consequently joined the Religious-Socialist movement, whose members believed that the impending cultural breakdown was an opportunity for creative social reconstruction.

In most of Tillich's writings from this period, he was using the insight he had gained at Halle as a norm in analyses of religion and culture, the meaning of history, and contemporary social problems. *Das System der Wissenschaften nach Gegenständen und Methoden* (1923; "The System of the Sciences According to Their Subjects and Methods") was his first attempt to render a systematic account of man's spiritual endeavors from this point of view. As early as 1925 he was also at work on what was to become his major opus, *Systematic Theology*, 3 vol. (1951–63).

Tillich's passionate concern for freedom made him an early critic of Hitler and the Nazi movement, and in retaliation he was barred from German universities in 1933—the first non-Jewish academician "to be so honored," as he wryly put it. He joined the faculty at Union Theological Seminary in New York, and he emerged as an "apostle to the skeptics" during the years following World War II. At Union Seminary (1933–55), Harvard University (1955–62), and the University of Chicago (1962–65), he engaged in searching dialogue concerning the meaning of human existence. His public lectures and books reached large audiences; in such works as *The Courage to Be* and *Dynamics of Faith*, he argued that the deepest human concern drives us into confrontation with a reality that transcends our own finite existence. In these books Tillich shows a profound grasp of the problems brought to light by modern psychoanalysis and existentialist philosophy.

Systematic Theology is in five parts: questions about the powers and limits of human reason prepare one for answers given in revelation; questions about the nature of being lead to answers revealing God as the ground of being; questions about the meaning of existence are answered by the New Being made manifest in JESUS CHRIST; questions about the ambiguities of human experience point to answers revealing the presence of the HOLY SPIRIT in the life process; and questions about human destiny and the meaning of history find their answers in the vision of the KINGDOM OF GOD. Modern "Christian atheists" who cite Tillich in support of their "God is dead" claim overlook the fact that for Tillich the disappearance of an inadequate concept of God was the beginning of a grander vision of God.

In his last years Tillich expressed some doubts about the viability of any systematic account of man's spiritual quest. But he never abandoned the insight that all of man's cultural and spiritual life could be illuminated by the "Protestant principle" of JUSTIFICATION by faith; he was still working out its implications at his death in 1965. Tillich believed himself to be a "boundary man," standing between an old heritage imbued with a sense of the sacred and the new secular orientation of MODERNISM. He asserted that his vocation was to mediate between the concerns voiced by faith and the imperatives of a questioning reason, thus helping to heal the ruptures threatening to destroy Western civilization in the 20th century.

TINIA \'ti-nē-ə\, *also called* Tin, *or* Tina, principal Etruscan deity, god of the thunderbolt, sky, and storm. Tinia together with his wife Uni and Menerva (or Menrva, Roman MINERVA) formed the supreme triad of the Etruscan pantheon (*see* ETRUSCAN RELIGION).

TIPIṬAKA: *see* TRIPIṬAKA.

TIRESIAS \tī-'rē-sē-əs, -zē-\, in Greek mythology, a blind Theban seer. In the *Odyssey* he retained his prophetic gifts even in the Underworld, where the hero ODYSSEUS was sent by CIRCE to consult him. At Thebes he played an active part in the tragic events concerning Laius, the king of Thebes, and his son OEDIPUS. Later legend told that he lived for seven (or nine) generations, dying after the expedition of the SEVEN AGAINST THEBES, and that he had once been turned into a woman as the result of killing the female of two coupling snakes; on killing the male he regained his own sex. His blindness was variously explained. One theory was that it was a punishment for revealing the secrets of the gods, which he had learned from his mother, the NYMPH Chariclo. Another theory was that he had enraged HERA, who had contended to her husband, ZEUS, that women had less pleasure in sex than men, by telling her that sex gave women 10 times more pleasure than it gave men. Hera thereupon struck him blind, but Zeus gave him the gift of PROPHECY. A third explanation was that Tiresias was blinded by ATHENA because he had watched her undressing to bathe.

TIRMIDHĪ, AL- \al-'tir-mi-‚thē\, *in full* Abū ʿĪsā Muhammad ibn ʿĪsā ibn Sawra ibn Shaddād al-Tirmidhī (d. *c.* 892), Arab scholar and author of one of the six canonical collections of spoken traditions (HADITH) attributed to the Prophet MUHAMMAD.

Al-Tirmidhī journeyed to Khorāsān, to Iraq, and to the Hejaz in search of material for his collection and studied with such renowned scholars of Hadith as AHMAD IBN HANBAL, AL-BUKHĀRĪ, and Abū Dāʿūd al-Sijistānī.

His canonical collection *al-Jāmi' al-ṣaḥīḥ* ("The Sound Collection") includes every spoken tradition that had ever been used to support a legal decision, as well as material relating to theological questions, to religious practice, and to popular belief and custom. Of special interest are his critical remarks on the links in the chains of transmission (ISNĀDS).

In the *Kitāb al-shamā'il* ("Book of Good Qualities"), al-Tirmidhī presented those Hadiths specifically commenting on the character and life of Muhammad.

TĪRTHA \'tir-tə\, in HINDUISM, a holy river, mountain, or other place made sacred through association with a deity or saint. Honored as the seven holiest Hindu cities are Kāśī (modern VARANASI, Uttar Pradesh), the center of SHIVA worship; AYODHYA (Oudh, in Uttar Pradesh), birthplace of RĀMA; Mathura (in Uttar Pradesh), scene of KRISHNA'S nativity; Dvaraka (in Gujarāt state), where the adult Krishna ruled as king; Kanchipuram (Tamil Nadu state), where the temple to the Goddess is built in the shape of a YANTRA; Hardwar (in Uttar Pradesh), the spot where the GAṄGĀ (Ganges) River is said to have come to Earth; and Ujjain (Madhya Pradesh), site of a famous Shiva LIṄGA.

The *śakti-pīṭhā*s, or spots that mark where pieces of the body of Shiva's wife SATĪ fell to earth, are particularly sacred to the devotees of the Goddess ŚAKTI. The four great abodes of the gods, located at the four corners of India—Badrīnātha in the north, Dwārkā in the west, Rāmeswaram in the south, and Puri in the east—attract large numbers of pilgrims yearly. Hindus undertake PILGRIMAGE (called the *tīrthayātrā*) as an act of devotion, to carry out a vow, to appease a deity, or to seek prosperity. Upon reaching a *tīrtha* Hindus usually bathe (*snāna*), circumambulate the temple or holy place (*pradakṣiṇā*), make an offering, carry out a rite such as the ŚRĀDDHA ceremony that is performed in honor of dead ancestors, have their names recorded by priests, and listen to expositions of music and religious discourses.

TĪRTHAṄKARA \tir-'təṅ-kə-rə\ (Sanskrit: "Ford-Maker"), *also called* Jina \'ji-nə\ ("Victor"), in JAINISM, a savior who has succeeded in crossing over life's stream of rebirths and has made a path for others to follow. MAHĀVĪRA (6th century BCE) was the last Tīrthaṅkara to appear. His predecessor, PĀRŚVANĀTHA, lived about 250 years earlier. According to Jain belief, each cosmic age produces its own group of 24 Tīrthaṅkaras, the first of whom—if it is an age of descending purity—are GIANTS, but they decrease in stature and appear after shorter intervals of time as the age proceeds.

The names of the 24 Tīrthaṅkaras are attributed to dreams by their mothers before their births or to some other circumstance surrounding their entry into the world. The word -NĀTHA, "lord," may be added as an honorific to their names. The first of the 24 Tīrthaṅkaras is Ṛṣab-

hanātha, also known as Ādinātha, or the "First Lord." The last two Tīrthaṅkaras, Pārśvanātha and Vardhamāna, known later as Mahāvīra, "Great Hero," are the two for whom there is historical evidence. Malli, the 19th Tīrthaṅkara, is believed by the ŚVETĀMBARA sect to have been a woman, while the DIGAMBARAS maintain that Malli was male. Jain believers pay homage to images of the 24 Tīrthaṅkaras as representatives of great beings in the hope that they may be filled with a sense of renunciation and the highest virtues and thus encouraged along the path toward their final liberation.

TIRUPATI \'tir-ü-,pə-tē\, city, southeastern Andhra Pradesh state, southern India. Tirupati is known as the abode of the Hindu god Veṅkateśvara, Lord of Seven Hills, a form of VISHNU, and familiarly called Bālājī. About six miles northwest of Tirupati rises the sacred hill of Tirumala, attaining a height of 2,500 feet. It was considered so holy that before 1870 non-Hindus were not permitted to ascend it. At the hill's summit is the main temple dedicated to Veṅkateśvara. This temple, nestled among sacred waterfalls and reservoirs, is a fine example of Dravidian art and is one of the wealthiest, most important PILGRIMAGE centers in India, attracting visitors from all parts of India and abroad, many of whom perform a characteristic rite of TONSURE to express their devotion to Śrī Veṅkateśvara. Tradition associates the founding of the temple atop Tirumala with the 11th-century theologian RĀMĀNUJA, and the ŚRĪ VAIṢṆAVA sectarian association there remains strong. The Tirupati-Tirumala temple complex supports Sri Venkateswara University, founded in 1954, and has in more recent years become active in providing funds to build Hindu temples outside of India.

TIRUPPAN \'tir-ù-pən\, *also called* Tiruppanalvar, one of the "later" or "minor" South Indian poet-saint devotees of VISHNU known as the Ālvārs. Very little is known about either the work or the life of Tiruppan. His name means "the saint who was a bard," and legend has it that Tiruppan was indeed a member of this group, which, by the 9th or 10th centuries, had become an "untouchable" CASTE.

A Tamil poem attributed to Tiruppan (the *Amalan ati piran*) in which the author reflects on his emotional response upon seeing a statue of Vishnu reclining in the temple of Srirangam received great attention among later

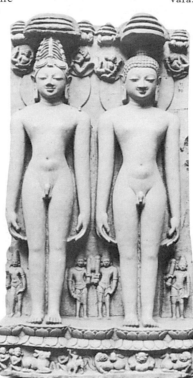

Ṛṣabhanātha and Mahāvīra, the first and last Tīrthaṅkaras, stone sculpture from Orissa, India
By courtesy of the trustees of the British Museum

poets and theologians in the ŚRĪ VAIṢṆAVA tradition and apparently influenced some of the Sanskrit literature of that sect. The later tradition also elaborated the life story of the poet-saint. Born of low caste parents (or adopted by UNTOUCHABLES in another variant), Tiruppan was wholly dedicated to Vishnu and continually sang his praises. The principal event in the legend, however, depicts Tiruppan being barred from the temple by a Brahmin because of his low caste. Vishnu himself intervenes and commands the haughty Brahmin to carry the poet-saint into the temple on his shoulders. Such a tale perhaps reflects a real struggle that occurred between the Tamil hymnists and popular saints, on the one hand, and the Brahmin temple establishment on the other.

TISCHENDORF, KONSTANTIN VON \fȯn-'ti-shən-ˌdȯrf\, *in full* Lobegott Friedrich Konstantin von Tischendorf (b. Jan. 18, 1815, Lengefeld, Saxony [Germany]—d. Dec. 7, 1874, Leipzig), German biblical critic who made extensive and invaluable contributions to biblical textual criticism, famous for his discovery of the *Codex Sinaiticus*, a celebrated manuscript of the BIBLE.

In 1844 Tischendorf went as a student to the Middle East. While working in the library of the Monastery of St. Catherine in the Sinai Peninsula, he discovered, among some old parchments, leaves of what were among the oldest biblical manuscripts that he had ever seen. He took 43 of these leaves back with him to Leipzig, and in 1846 he published a facsimile edition. In 1859 Tischendorf returned to the monastery and procured for the tsar Alexander II what is now known as the *Codex Sinaiticus* for a sum that has been estimated at about $7,000. In 1933 the codex was purchased from the Soviet government by the British Museum. These manuscripts date probably from the latter half of the 4th century, were probably written in Egypt, and include most of the OLD TESTAMENT and the entire NEW TESTAMENT, as well as the *Letter of Barnabas* and part of the *Shepherd of Hermas*.

In numerous writings, Tischendorf presented the results of his work. His eighth edition of the Greek New Testament is considered to be of most value to contemporary textual critics.

TISHA BE-AV \tē-'shä-bə-'äv; 'ti-shə-ˌbȯv, -ˌbäv\, *English* Ninth of Av, in JUDAISM, traditional day of mourning for the destruction of the First and Second Temples (*see* TEMPLE OF JERUSALEM). According to the TALMUD and tradition, also occurring on Av 9 were the decree that the Jews would wander 40 years in the wilderness, the end of the second Jewish revolt against Rome in 135 CE, the establishment in 136 of a PAGAN temple in Jerusalem, and the expulsion of the Jews from Spain in 1492. A 24-hour fast is observed. The liturgy includes the reading of the Lamentations of Jeremiah, plus the recital of dirges (*qinot*) and certain passages from the OLD TESTAMENT. If Tisha be-Av falls on the SABBATH, the observance is postponed one day. Tisha be-Av marks the end of a period of mourning called the THREE WEEKS.

TISHTRYA \'tish-trē-ə\, ancient Iranian god identified with the star Sirius. Tishtrya's principal myth involves a battle with a demonic star named APAUSHA ("Nonprosperity") over rainfall and water. In a combat that was reenacted in a yearly equestrian ritual, Tishtrya and Apausha, assuming the forms of a white stallion and a horse of horrible description, respectively, battle along the shores of the Varu-Karta sea. Initially Apausha is victorious, but after receiving worship Tishtrya conquers him, driving him away "along a path the length of a race course." At this point Tishtrya causes the cosmic sea to surge and boil, and then another star, Satavaisa (Fomalhaut), rises with the cloud-forming mists that are blown by the wind in the form of "rain and clouds and hail to the dwelling and the settlements (and) to the seven continents." As one of the stars "who contains the seeds of waters" (*i.e.*, who cause rain), Tishtrya was also

intimately connected with agriculture. He battled and defeated the shooting stars, identified as witches, especially one called "Bad Crop" (Duzhyarya). In ZOROASTRIANISM, Tishtrya was at some point, probably in late Achaemenian times, identified with the western Iranian astral deity, Tiri (MERCURY in Sasanian astronomy).

TITAN \'tī-tən\, in Greek mythology, any of the children of OURANUS (Heaven) and GAEA (Earth) and their descendants. According to Hesiod's *Theogony*, there were 12 original Titans: the brothers OCEANUS, Coeus, Crius, Hyperion, Iapetus, and CRONUS and the sisters Thea, RHEA, THEMIS, MNEMOSYNE, PHOEBE, and Tethys. At the instigation of Gaea the Titans rebelled against their father, who had shut them up inside her body. Cronus deposed Ouranus by castrating him, and himself became king. But one of Cronus' sons, ZEUS, rebelled against his father, and a struggle then ensued between them in which most of the Titans sided with Cronus. Zeus and his brothers and sisters finally defeated the Titans after 10 years of fierce battles (the Titanomachia). The Titans were then imprisoned by Zeus in a cavity beneath Tartarus.

TITHE (from Old English *teogotha*, "10th"), custom dating back to OLD TESTAMENT times and adopted by the Christian church whereby lay people contributed a 10th of their income for religious purposes, often under ecclesiastical or legal obligation. The money (or its equivalent in crops, farm stock, etc.) was used to support the clergy, maintain churches, and assist the poor. Tithing was also a prime source of subsidy for the construction of many magnificent cathedrals in Europe.

Tithing became obligatory as CHRISTIANITY spread across Europe. It was enjoined by ecclesiastical law from the 6th century and enforced by secular law from the 8th century. In the 14th century Pope GREGORY VII, in an effort to control abuses, outlawed lay ownership of tithes.

Although MARTIN LUTHER approved in general of paying tithes to the temporal sovereign, following the Protestant REFORMATION opposition to the obligation grew. Tithes were repealed in France during the Revolution (1789), without compensation to tithe holders. Other countries abolished certain kinds of tithes and indemnified the holders. The late 19th century saw an end to tithes in Italy, Ireland, and Scotland, and in England by 1936. New methods of taxation were developed in those countries that provided financial support of the church out of government funds. Remnants of the tithing system do exist, however, in certain Protestant European countries. In Germany, for example, citizens must pay a church tax unless they formally renounce membership in a church.

The EASTERN ORTHODOX churches never accepted the idea of tithes, and Orthodox church members have never paid them, nor was tithe ever a legal requirement in the United States. Members of certain churches, however, including the Latter-day Saints and SEVENTH-DAY ADVENTISTS, are required to tithe, and some Christians in other churches do so voluntarily.

TITHONUS \tī-'thō-nəs, ti-\, in Greek mythology, son of LAOMEDON, king of Troy, and of Strymo, daughter of the river Scamander. EOS (Aurora) fell in love with Tithonus and took him to Ethiopia, where she bore Emathion and MEMNON. When Eos requested that ZEUS grant him eternal life the god consented to her request. However, Eos forgot to ask also for eternal youth, and as a result her husband grew astonishingly old. Eos shut him away in a room, but eventually the gods took pity on him, and he was transformed into a cicada.

TI-TS'ANG \\'dē-'tsäŋ\\: *see* KṢITIGARBHA.

TJURUNGA \\tyù-'rəŋ-gə, chù-\\, *also spelled* churinga \\chù-'riŋ-gə\\, in AUSTRALIAN ABORIGINAL RELIGION, ritual object that is a representation or manifestation of a mythical being of the Dream Time. An Aranda word, *tjurunga* traditionally referred to sacred things, such as rites, objects, BULL-ROARERS, paintings, and songs. The term is generally applied to flat, oval, worked stones, normally incised with sacred designs, and to wooden boards ranging in length from about 2 inches to 10 feet or so and bearing intricate patterns of mythological significance. Most *tjurunga* were used in men's rituals; some small objects figured in women's rituals and still smaller objects in men's love magic.

At initiation, boys are introduced to the rituals and *tjurunga* of their local descent group and to those of others. Later they receive their own *tjurunga* object and the knowledge that goes with it (or them). At death, the *tjurunga* is sometimes buried with the corpse, or the dead person's spirit might seek the place where its *tjurunga* "body" (that is, the mythic being itself) rested.

Tjurunga represent in essence the personalities of members of the local descent groups connected with them. They are a symbol of communication between humans and the mythological time called THE DREAMING, between humans and the mythic beings, and between the material aspects of ordinary living and the human spiritual heritage.

TLACHTLI \\'tläch-tlē\\, ball court used for the ritual BALL GAME played throughout PRE-COLUMBIAN MESO-AMERICA on a variety of courts. The word *tlachtli* is the Classical Nahuatl word for both the game and the court in which it was played. Possibly originating among the Olmecs (La Venta culture, *c.* 800–*c.* 400 BCE) or earlier, the game spread to subsequent cultures, among them those of Monte Albán and El Tajín; the Maya (as *pok-ta-pok*); and the Toltec, Mixtec, and Aztec. There are various myths, especially those in the *Popul Vuh*, that mention the ball game, sometimes as a contest between day and night deities. It is still played in isolated regions.

The court was shaped like a capital I with serifs and oriented north-south or east-west. Players used elbows, knees, and hips to knock a rubber ball into the opponent's end of the court; in post-Classic times (after *c.* 900 CE), the object was to hit the ball through one of two vertical stone rings (placed on each side of the court). A sacrificial cult was part of ball court ritual.

TLALOC \\'tlä-lōk\\ (Nahuatl, probably from *tlāl-*, "earth," and *-oc* "[he] lies," hence literally, "He Who Lies on the Earth" or "He Who Rests on the Land"), Aztec rain god. Representations of a rain god wearing a peculiar mask, with large round eyes, a labial band, and long fangs, date at least to the Teotihuacán culture of the highlands (3rd to 8th century CE). His characteristic features were strikingly similar to those of the Maya rain god CHAC of the same period.

Tlaloc had been one of the main deities of the agricultural communities of central Mexico, when the northern tribes invaded and brought with them the astral cults of the sun (HUITZILOPOCHTLI) and the starry night sky (TEZCATLIPOCA). Aztec syncretism placed both Huitzilipochtli and Tlaloc at the head of the pantheon. The rain god's HIGH PRIEST, the Quetzalcóatl Tlaloc Tlamacazqui ("Feathered Serpent, Priest of Tlaloc") ruled with a title and rank equal to that of the sun god's high priest.

In the Aztec divinatory calendars, Tlaloc was the eighth ruler of the days and the ninth lord of the nights. Five months of the 18-month ritual year were dedicated to water deities and rain cults. Children were sacrificed to Tlaloc on the first month, Atlcaualo ("Water Absent"), and on the third, Tozoztontli ("The Small Vigil"). During the sixth month, Etzalqualiztli ("The Eating of Etzalli"), the rain priests ceremonially bathed in the lake; they imitated the cries of waterfowls and used magic "fog rattles" (*ayauhchicauaztli*) in order to obtain rain. The 13th month, Tepeilhuitl ("The Festival of the Mountains"), was dedicated to the mountain Tlaloque; small idols made of amaranth paste were ritually killed and eaten. A similar rite was held on the 16th month, Atemoztli ("Descent of the Water").

Tlaloc was not only highly revered, but he was also greatly feared. He could send out the rain, cause devastating storms, or provoke drought and hunger. Certain illnesses, such as dropsy, leprosy, and rheumatism, were said to be caused by Tlaloc and his fellow deities. Although the dead were generally cremated, those who had died from one of the special illnesses or who had drowned or who had been struck by lightning were buried. Tlaloc bestowed on them an eternal and blissful life in his paradise, Tlalocan.

Associated with Tlaloc was his companion CHALCHIUHTLICUE ("She Having a Skirt of Precious Green Stone"), also called Matlalcueye ("She Having a Green Skirt"), the goddess of freshwater lakes and streams. See PRE-COLUMBIAN MESO-AMERICAN RELIGIONS.

Tlaloc, detail of a reconstructed wall painting from Tepantitla, Teotihuacán culture, 3rd to 8th century
Hamlyn Group Picture Library

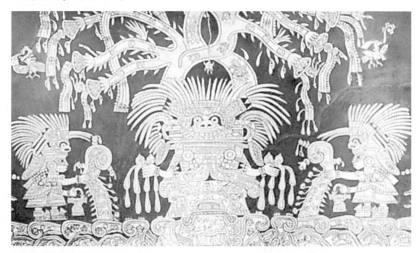

TLAZOLTÉOTL \,tlä-sōl-'tä-ō-təl\ (Nahuatl: "Filth Deity"), *also called* Ixcuina, *or* Tlaelquani, Aztec goddess who represented sexual desire and misbehavior; she was probably introduced from the lowlands of Huaxteca. Tlazoltéotl was an important and complex earth goddess who became patronness of adulterers and promiscuous women. She was known in four guises, associated with different stages of life. As a young woman, she was a carefree temptress. In her second form she was the destructive goddess of gambling and uncertainty. In her middle age she was the great goddess able to absorb human wrongdoing, and, in her final manifestation, she was a destructive and terrifying hag preying upon youths. Tlazoltéotl was thought to provoke sexual activity, but she could also forgive wrongdoers and removed corruption from the world by eating sexual filth. She was portrayed in an elaborate headdress of unspun cotton and carried a broom which was a symbol of filth and its removal.

TŌDAI TEMPLE \'tō-,dī\, *Japanese* Tōdai-ji \,tō-'dī-jē\ ("Great Eastern Temple"), monumental Japanese temple complex and center of the Kegon sect of Japanese BUDDHISM (*see* HUA-YEN), located in Nara. The main buildings were constructed between 745 and 752 CE under the emperor Shōmu and marked the adoption of Buddhism as a state religion. The temple was the largest and most powerful monastery in Japan during the Nara period (710–784). The original building was destroyed in 1180, and the present Daibutsu Hall, with its colossal bronze Buddha, dates from the early 18th century. It is the largest wooden building in the world. The 53-foot "Great Sun Buddha," or Roshana, was installed in 752 CE. The huge Shōsō House survives; it is the main repository for the temple's treasures, including 600 personal objects belonging to the emperor Shōmu and more than 9,000 works of fine and decorative art.

T'OEGYE: *see* YI HWANG.

TOHORAH \,tō-hō-'rä\, in JUDAISM, the system of ritual purity practiced by ISRAEL. Purity (*tohorah*) and uncleanness (*tum'ah*) carry forward Pentateuchal commandments that Israel—whether eating, procreating, or worshiping God in the Temple—must avoid sources of contamination, the principal one of which is the corpse (Numbers 19). There are other prohibitions in addition to avoiding the presence of death. Leviticus 11 presents the catalog of foods that are clean or unclean; Israelites may eat of the former, but not the latter. Leviticus 12 goes over the uncleanness that results from childbirth; Leviticus 13–14 deal with a skin ailment (once identified with leprosy), that scripture deems analogous to the condition of the corpse; and Leviticus 15 covers the uncleanness of a woman in her menstrual period (a Niddah), a woman whose uncleanness is brought about by other excretions, and the uncleanness of a man brought about by analogous excretions. Leviticus also outlines lesser forms of uncleanness; *e.g.*, that which results from seminal fluid.

All Israel was to follow the prohibitions on unclean food, and those forbidding sexual relations during a woman's menstrual period or when either partner was affected by the uncleanness of the sexual organs. In addition, Leviticus outlines several injunctions that apply only to the Temple priests and their families. Thus, when the priestly CASTE ate their rations of the crops set aside for them and their portion of the animal meat sacrificed at the altar, they were to do so in a condition of cultic cleanness. They accordingly immersed themselves in ritually "fit" immersion pools of water before eating. When ordinary people came to the Temple, they too observed the rules of cultic cleanness, and therefore the priestly prohibitions applied to all Israelites during the times of participation in the Temple cult. That consideration could affect many at the time of the PILGRIM FESTIVALS, *i.e.*, PASSOVER, SHAVUOT, and SUKKOT. (It should be noted that before 70 CE some sects—the PHARISEES, the ESSENES, and those people represented by the law codes found in the DEAD SEA SCROLLS, for example—kept the rules of cultic purity in eating food even when at home. This practice, however, was not widespread.)

With the destruction of the second Temple and the de-emphasis in the importance of animal sacrifice and therefore also of the priestly caste, certain purificatory rituals could no longer be performed. One such instance is the the ceremony of the RED HEIFER (Numbers 19.) This ceremony was meant to purify Israel of corpse uncleanness, and in its abeyance all Israel bears this impurity. But, even though after 70 CE, in the absence of the Temple, attaining cultic cleanness no longer pertained, uncleanness rules governing food and sexual relations continued to apply. An important distinction must be made, however, that in matters of public worship it was only in the Temple, not the SYNAGOGUE, that considerations of cleanness applied; thus, no one would refrain from attending or participating in synagogue worship by reason of having contracted uncleanness. In present day Judaism, rather, the biblical regulations regarding cultic purity are observed primarily in the case of menstrual uncleanness, which governs when sexual intercourse may take place, and the cleanness of hands, which always are ritually washed prior to meals. Through this latter ritual, observant Jews understand themselves to consume all food as though it were in the sanctified status of a Temple offering, so that their home table can be imagined as the Temple altar itself, a locus of the divine presence.

The MISHNAH greatly amplified the Pentateuchal definition of what is affected by uncleanness, how uncleanness is transmitted, and the way in which uncleanness is removed. The Mishnah's Division of Purities treats the interplay of persons, food, and liquids. Dry inanimate objects or food are not susceptible to uncleanness (Leviticus 11:34, 37). What is wet is susceptible. So liquids activate the system. What is unclean, moreover, emerges from uncleanness through the operation of liquids, specifically, through immersion in fit water that is of requisite volume and in natural condition. Liquids thus also deactivate the system. Therefore, water in its natural condition, not affected by human intervention, is what concludes the process by removing uncleanness. (*See* MIKVAH.)

The uncleanness of persons, furthermore, is also signified by body liquids (or flux) in most cases. (Additionally, the uncleanness that comes from contact with a corpse is conceived to be a kind of effluent, a viscous gas, but is thought to flow like a liquid; Mishnah tractate *Ohalot*.) Utensils for their part only receive uncleanness when they form receptacles that are able to contain liquid (Mishnah Tractate Kelim). So the invisible flow of fluidlike substances or powers transmits uncleanness and the visible fluid of fit water purifies.

Some of these prohibitions may have been borrowed by Israel from other cultures, and they no doubt had a multiplicity of meanings. In Judaism as it has evolved, however, what is unclean has come to be perceived as abnormal and disruptive of the economy of nature, and what is clean is normal and constitutive of the economy and the wholeness of nature. What is unclean is restored to a condition of cleanness through the activity of nature alone (*e.g.*, naturally flowing water that has collected in sufficient volume to afford immersion). Procreation and sustenance of life define what is at stake in the condition of cleanness, en route to the state of sanctification, as in the hierarchical statement by RABBI Phineas ben Yair in the Mishnah tractate *Sotah* 9:15: Rabbi Yair says, "Heedfulness leads to cleanliness, cleanliness leads to cleanness, cleanness leads to abstinence, abstinence leads to holiness, holiness leads to modesty, modesty leads to the fear of SIN, the fear of sin leads to piety, piety leads to the Holy Spirit, the Holy Spirit leads to the RESURRECTION of the dead, and the resurrection of the dead comes through ELIJAH, blessed be his memory, AMEN."

ṬOHOROT \,tō-hō-'rōt\ (Hebrew: "Purifications"), last of the six major divisions, or orders (SEDARIM), of the MISHNAH. *Ṭohorot* consists of 12 tractates that deal with ritual impurity and rites of purification: *Kelim* ("Vessels"), *Ohalot* ("Tents"), *Negaʿim* ("Plagues"), *Para* ("Cow"), *Ṭohorot* ("Purifications"), *Miqwaʾot* ("Ritual Baths"), *Nidda* ("A Menstruous Woman"), *Makhshirin* ("Predisposers"), *Zavim* ("Those with Unclean Discharges"), *Ṭevul yom* ("Daytime Bathers"), *Yadayim* ("Hands"), and ʿUqtzin ("Stalks"). The Talmuds YERUSHALMI and BAVLI both have GEMARA on *Nidda* but on none of the other tractates.

TOLLAN \'tōl-län\, *also called* Tula \'tü-lä\, ancient capital of the Toltecs in Mexico; it was primarily important from about 900 CE to about 1200. Although its exact location is not certain, an archaeological site near the contemporary town of Tula in Hidalgo state has been the persistent choice of historians. Some scholars, however, believe it more likely to be the site of Teotihuacán near Mexico City.

The archaeological remains near contemporary Tula are concentrated in two clusters at opposite ends of a low ridge. The original urban area covered at least three square miles and the town probably had a population in the tens of thousands. The major civic center consists of a large plaza bordered on one side by a five-stepped temple PYRAMID, which was probably dedicated to the god Quetzalcóatl. The sides of the five terraces were covered with painted and sculptured friezes of marching felines and canines, birds of prey devouring human hearts, and human faces extending from the jaws of serpents. A stairway on the south side led to a highly ornamented temple at the summit.

Stone columns at the main temple pyramid, Tollan
George Holton—Photo Researchers, Inc.

Other structures include a palace complex, two other temple pyramids, and two courts for the ceremonial BALL GAME. Separated from the main temple pyramid by a narrow alley are the partial remains of what may have been the palace of the ruler of Tollan, the excavated portions of which consist of three great halls. In general, the art and architecture of Tollan show a striking similarity to that of Tenochtitlán, the Aztec capital, and the artistic themes indicate a close approximation in religious ideology and behavior. Many scholars believe that the Aztecs' concept of themselves as warrior-priests of the sun god was directly borrowed from the people of Tollan.

TOMB, in the strictest sense, home or house for the dead; the term is applied loosely to all kinds of graves, funerary monuments, and memorials. In many cultures the dead were buried in their own houses, and the tomb form may have developed out of this practice, as a reproduction in permanent materials of primeval house types. Thus prehistoric tomb BARROWS were usually built around a round hut in which the body was placed. Later, brick and stone tombs appeared, often of great size, but still preserving primitive house forms.

In many cultures and civilizations the tomb was superseded by, or coexisted with, monuments or memorials to the dead; sometimes, as in ancient Greece, the bodies were burned and the ashes put in funerary urns. In medieval Christian thought, the tomb was considered an earthly prototype and symbol of a heavenly home. This concept appeared in the Roman CATACOMBS, the walls of which were decorated with scenes of the resurrected in paradise. The church building itself sometimes functioned as a tomb (*e.g.*, HAGIA SOPHIA in Istanbul was the tomb of the emperor Justinian). Since the Renaissance, the idea of the tomb as a home has died out, except as a faint reminiscence in the mausoleums sometimes erected above graves or serving as burial vaults in modern cemeteries. *See also* DOLMEN; SARCOPHAGUS.

TOMINAGA NAKAMOTO \,tō-mē-'nä-gä-nä-'kä-,mō-tō\ (b. 1715—d. 1746), Japanese Neo-Confucian scholar who is famous for his theory of the development of CONFUCIANISM, BUDDHISM, and SHINTŌ. His was a critical and historical approach to these traditions that anticipated the introduction of Western methods of interpretation in the 19th century.

TONALPOHUALLI \,tō-näl-pō-'wäl-lē\ (Nahuatl: "Count of Days"), 260-day sacred almanac of many ancient Meso-American cultures, including the Maya, Zapotec, and Aztec, which set the date for rituals and was a means of DIVINATION. It is a cycle of days resulting when the numbers 1 to 13 are juxtaposed with 20 day names: 1 Alligator, 2 Wind . . . 13 Reed, 1 Jaguar, etc. Each combination of name and number occurs once in 260 (20 × 13) days. The cycle is still observed by the Mixe (Oaxaca) and the Maya, among others.

TONATIUH \tō-'nä-tē-ü\ (Nahuatl: "the Sun"), in Meso-American religion, Nahua sun deity of the fifth and final era (the Fifth Sun). In most myths of the Nahua peoples, including those of the Aztecs, there were four eras that preceded the era of Tonatiuh, each of which ended by cataclys-

Tonatiuh, detail of an Aztec relief
Henri Stierlin

mic destruction. Tonatiuh was associated with the eagle (at sunrise and sunset) and, in Aztec versions, with the deity HUITZILOPOCHTLI.

Tonatiuh was constantly threatened by the immense effort of making his journey across the sky each day. The worship of Tonatiuh, whose sustenance required human blood and hearts, involved militaristic cults and frequent HUMAN SACRIFICE to ensure perpetuation of the world.

Tonatiuh is best known as he is depicted in the center of the Aztec calendar, with his eagle's claw hands clutching human hearts.

TONGUES, SPEAKING IN, *also called* glossolalia (from Greek *glōssa,* "tongue," and *lalia,* "talk, chatter"), utterances approximating words and speech, usually produced during states of intense religious excitement. According to religious interpretations of the phenomenon, the speaker is possessed by a supernatural spirit, is in conversation with divine beings, or is the channel of a divine proclamation. Glossolalia occurred in some of the ancient GREEK RELIGIONS and in various primitive religions. There are references to ecstatic speech in the OLD TESTAMENT (1 Samuel 10:5–13, 19:18–24; 2 Samuel 6:13–17; 1 Kings 20:35–37), and in CHRISTIANITY it has occurred periodically since the beginning of the church.

Glossolalia first occurred among the followers of Jesus at PENTECOST when "they were all filled with the HOLY SPIRIT and began to speak in other tongues, as the Spirit gave them utterance" (Acts 2:4). The apostle PAUL referred to it as a spiritual gift (1 Corinthians 12–14) and claimed that he possessed exceptional ability in that gift (1 Corinthians 14:18). The account in Acts (4:31, 8:14–17, 10:44–48, 11:15–17, 19:1–7) indicates that in the beginning of the Christian church the phenomenon reappeared wherever conversion and commitment to Christianity occurred.

The greatest emphasis upon the gift in the early church was made by followers of the 2nd-century prophet MONTANUS. His EXCOMMUNICATION in about 177 and the later decline of the sect probably contributed to a climate of opinion unfavorable to speaking in tongues, and the practice declined.

During later church history, glossolalia occurred in various groups. In modern times, it occurred during various Protestant revivals in the United States in the early 20th century. These revivals resulted in the establishment of many Pentecostal churches, which in the late 20th century had more than 8,000,000 members. During the 20th century speaking in tongues also occurred occasionally in some of the older Christian churches as part of the charismatic movement.

TONSURE, in various religions, ceremony of initiation in which hair is clipped from the head as part of the ritual marking one's entrance into a new stage of religious development or activity.

Tonsure has been used in both the ROMAN CATHOLIC and the EASTERN ORTHODOX churches on occasions of solemn personal dedication to God. Until it was abolished by Pope Paul VI (effective in 1973), tonsure was the ceremony by which a man was initiated into the clerical state and became eligible for ORDINATION to the PRIESTHOOD. Early Christian ascetics may have imitated similar religious practices among the ancient Greeks and Semites.

In BUDDHISM tonsure is performed as a part of the ceremony of ordination as a novice (*pravrajyā* ceremony) and as a monk (*upasaṃpadā* ceremony). Thereafter, the monk keeps his head and face clean-shaven. Jain monks also cut their hair as a sign of renouncing the worldly life—traditionally, by plucking out the hairs one by one (*see* JAINISM). Both Jain and Buddhist customs are theoretically in imitation of their teachers MAHĀVĪRA and the BUDDHA GOTAMA, who cut off their hair upon embarking on the spiritual life.

In HINDUISM the first tonsure undergone by a young boy (the ceremony of *cūḍākaraṇa*) is one of the *saṃskāras,* or personal SACRAMENTS, that mark the boy's transition from an infant to a child. It is usually performed when the boy is about two years old. The Hindu tonsure leaves a tuft of hair (the *cūḍa*) at the crown of the head. Tonsure formerly marked other Hindu RITES OF PASSAGE, such as the putting on of the sacred thread or the change of ritual status incurred by the death of the father (customs now largely observed only symbolically). Full tonsure is performed as part of the initiation rite into most Hindu ascetic orders.

TORAH \tō-'rä, 'tō-rə, 'tor-ə\, with the Prophets (Nebi'im) and the Writings (Ketubim), one of the three parts of the Hebrew SCRIPTURES. The Torah is composed of the books of GENESIS, EXODUS, Leviticus, Numbers, and Deuteronomy and has a written and an oral part. Both parts are held to represent God's statement of his will and plan for the world, but while the former is read as a verbatim record of God's word of his will, the latter, as written down in the sayings of the great sages, is not represented as a verbatim record, since much that is deemed part of the Torah is assigned to named sages, upward to MOSES himself. In the theology of JUDAISM, ISRAEL meets God in the Torah, and it is through study of the Torah with the sage that the encounter takes place.

Jewish tradition states that the nations of the world were offered the Torah but declined; only Israel accepted. The main points of insistence of the whole of Israel's life and history come to full symbolic expression in that single word: Torah. Torah stood for salvation and accounted for Israel's this-worldly condition and the hope, for individual and nation alike, of life in the world-to-come.

TORII \tō-'rē-ē, *Angl* 'tōr-ē-,ē, 'tōr-ē, 'tor-\ (Japanese: "bird perch"), symbolic gateway marking the entrance to the sacred precincts of a SHINTŌ shrine in Japan. The *torii* characteristically consists of two cylindrical vertical posts topped by a crosswise rectangular beam extending beyond the posts on either side and a second crosswise beam a short distance below. The *torii*, often painted bright red, demarcates the boundary between sacred space of the shrine and ordinary space. *Torii* also identify other sacred places, such as a mountain or rock.

TOSAFOT \,tō-sä-'fōt\ (Hebrew: "additions"), *also spelled* tosaphoth, critical remarks and notes on passages of the TALMUD that were written by Jewish scholars in Germany, Italy, and especially France during the 12th to 14th centuries. *Tosafot* may have been meant to be commentaries on the MISHNAH and the GEMARA or supplements to systematic commentary by RASHI on the BAVLI.

The first *tosafists* (*ba'ale ha-tosafot*) were Meir ben Samuel and Judah ben Nathan, two of Rashi's sons-in-law who lived in northern France. The most highly regarded *tosafist*, however, was Rabbenu Tam (JACOB BEN MEIR TAM), Rashi's grandson. All editions of the Bavli (since its first printing in Venice, 1520–23) carry Rashi's commentaries on the inside margin of the page, with the *tosafot* located on the outside margin. This arrangement, however, is not followed in some modern editions in translation.

TOSEFTA \,tō-sef-'tä, tō-'sef-tə\ (Aramaic: "Supplement," or "Addition"), supplements to the MISHNAH, *c.* 300 CE. As a compilation of laws assigned to the names of authorities called *tannaim* (repeaters of legal traditions) who occur also in the Mishnah, the Tosefta generally depends upon and follows the topical program and organization of the Mishnah. Approximately a third of its statements cite and gloss a passage of the Mishnah; a sixth is completely independent of the law of the Mishnah on a topic treated by the Mishnah; and about half respond to and amplify rules of the Mishnah and can be fully understood only in the context of the Mishnah's laws.

The Tosefta arranges its materials in this order: (1) Mishnah-citation and gloss; (2) secondary amplification of the Mishnah's laws; (3) free-standing rules of its own. Some passages of the Tosefta generalize upon cases put forth in the Mishnah, with a more comprehensive picture of matters. Others recast the law of the Mishnah, reframing issues under debate in the Mishnah in secondary and more refined terms than those of the Mishnah. In some cases, the premises of the rule of the Tosefta are logically prior to those of the Mishnah. It follows, in those instances, that the formulation of the Mishnah's law or problem builds upon that of the Tosefta's counterpart. Seen whole, the Tosefta serves as the Mishnah's first commentary, but with the proviso that it contains some passages autonomous of the Mishnah and others logically antecedent to the Mishnah's counterparts.

TOTEMISM \'tō-tə-,mi-zəm\, complex of ideas and practices based on the belief in KINSHIP or a mystical relationship between humans and natural objects, such as animals and plants. The term totem derives from the Ojibwa (Algonquian Indian) word *ototeman*, signifying a brother–sister blood relationship. Totemism refers to a wide variety of relationships, including the reverential and genealogical, between social groups or individual persons and animals or other natural objects, the so-called totems.

In its strictest sense, totemism is restricted to the association of a group of persons with the totem object. A society may be said to exhibit totemism if it is divided into an identifiable and apparently fixed number of clans, each of which has a specific relationship to an animate or inanimate species (totem); if a member of such a clan ordinarily cannot change his membership; and if people living in the same locality belong to different totemic clans. A totem may be a feared, emulated, or dangerous hunted animal; an edible plant; or any staple food. Very commonly connected with origin legends and with instituted morality, the totem is generally associated with strict rules of avoidance or ritualized contact. Membership in the totemic group is in some sense inherited and lifelong, regulating relationships of the child to his or her blood kin, and designating families that provide acceptable partners for procreation. Totem, ritual prohibitions, and exogamy (marriage outside the group) are in these societies inextricably intertwined.

John Ferguson McLennan wrote the first significant theoretical treatment of totemism in his study "The Worship of Animals and Plants" (1869). Totemism attracted wide attention during the flowering of sociology and cultural anthropology in the first decades of the 20th century. The most incisive critique, one that denied the reality of totemism, was supplied by the French ethnologist Claude Lévi-Strauss in *Totemism* (1963). Later, in *The Savage Mind* (1966), Lévi-Strauss compared the idea of totemism with his "science of the concrete."

TOTEM POLE, carved and painted log, mounted vertically, constructed by the Native Americans of the northwest coast of the United States and Canada. There are seven principal kinds of totem pole: memorial, or heraldic, poles, erected when a house changes hands to commemorate the past owner and to identify the present one; grave markers (tombstones); house posts, which support the roof; portal poles, which have a hole through which a person enters the house; welcoming poles, placed at the edge of a body of water to identify the owner of the waterfront; mortuary poles, in which the remains of the deceased are placed; and ridicule poles, on which an important individual who had failed in some way had his likeness carved upside down.

The carving on totem poles separates and emphasizes the flat, painted surfaces of the symbolic animals and spirits depicted on them. Each pole generally has from one (as with a grave marker) to many (as with a family legend) animal images on it.

The significance of the real or mythological animal carved on a totem pole is its identification with the lineage of the head of the household, as the animal is displayed as a type of family crest. More widely known, but in fact far less common, are the elaborately carved tall totem poles that

Totem pole from Kitwancool Creek, British Columbia, Can.
W.E. Ferguson—Shostal

relate an entire family legend in the form of a pictograph. Each animal or spirit carved on the pole has meaning, and when combined on the pole in sequence, each figure is an important symbol constituent of a story or myth.

TRADITION, patterns of belief and practice, usually identified with the mythic actions of superhuman beings, that have been inherited, transmitted, or established from generation to generation. Tradition is usually set in opposition to modernity and SECULARISM, while the secular world is often held to be clearly in opposition to the religious world, as monks (the religious) are opposed to the laity (the secular or worldly.) The term "traditional" is also used in place of "primitive" when speaking of religions that do not share a written history.

TRANSCENDENTAL MEDITATION (TM), movement founded by the MAHARISHI MAHESH YOGI that was popular in the West during the 1960s. TM is based more on the practice of specific techniques of meditation than on a set of religious or philosophical beliefs. As a monk in India in the 1940s and '50s the Maharishi developed a form of meditation that could be easily practiced by people in the modern world. In 1958 he began teaching it in India, and in 1959 he made his first tour of the West.

Transcendental Meditation uses one of a variety of Sanskrit MANTRAS, each of which is a short word or phrase that, repeated in the mind, helps the user still the activity of thought and find a deeper level of consciousness. Through this process it is claimed that the practitioner finds deep relaxation, which leads to enhanced inner joy, vitality, and creativity. The perspective behind TM, based on VEDĀNTA philosophy, is called the Science of Creative Intelligence.

TRANSFIGURATION, FEAST OF THE, in CHRISTIANITY, commemoration of the occasion upon which JESUS CHRIST took three of his disciples, PETER, JAMES, and JOHN, up on Mount Tabor, where MOSES and ELIJAH appeared and Jesus was transfigured, his face and clothes becoming white and shining as light (Mark 9:2–13; Matthew 17:1–13; Luke 9:28–36). The festival celebrates the revelation of the eternal glory of the Second Person of the TRINITY, which was normally veiled during his life on earth.

It is not known when the festival was first celebrated, but it was kept in Jerusalem as early as the 7th century and in most parts of the Byzantine Empire by the 9th century. It was gradually introduced into the Western church, and its observance was fixed as August 6.

TRANSUBSTANTIATION, in CHRISTIANITY, change by which the substance (though not the appearance) of the bread and wine in the EUCHARIST becomes Christ's Real Presence—that is, his body and blood. In ROMAN CATHOLICISM and some other Christian churches the doctrine—which was first called transubstantiation in the 12th century—aims at safeguarding the literal truth of Christ's Presence while emphasizing the fact that there is no change in the empirical appearances of the bread and wine.

The doctrine of transubstantiation was incorporated into the documents of the fourth LATERAN COUNCIL (1215) and of the COUNCIL OF TRENT (1545–63). In the mid-20th century some Roman Catholic theologians shifted the emphasis from a change of substance to a change of meaning and coined the terms transsignification and transfinalization to be used in preference to transubstantiation. In his ENCYCLICAL *Mysterium fidei* in 1965, however, Pope Paul VI called for a retention of the dogma of transubstantiation together with the terminology in which it has been expressed.

TRAPPIST, member of the Order of the Reformed Cistercians of the Strict Observance (O.C.S.O.), a branch of the Roman Catholic CISTERCIANS, founded by the converted courtier Armand de Rancé (1626–1700), who had governed the Cistercian abbey of La Trappe in France, which he transformed (1662) into a community practicing extreme austerity of diet, penitential exercises, and absolute silence. He became its regular ABBOT in 1664 and remained so for more than 30 years.

In 1792 the monks were ejected from La Trappe, and a number of them, led by Dom Augustine de Lestrange, settled at Fribourg, Switz., where they made several foundations before their expulsion in 1798. A period in Russia and Germany was followed in 1814 by a return to La Trappe; they were the first religious order to revive after the French Revolution. By the late 20th century there were abbeys worldwide. The three existing congregations of Trappists were united by Pope LEO XIII as the independent Reformed Cistercians of the Strict Observance.

TRENT, COUNCIL OF \'trent\, 19th ecumenical council of the ROMAN CATHOLIC church (1545–63), highly important for its sweeping decrees on self-reform and for its dogmatic definitions that clarified virtually every doctrine contested by the Protestants. Despite internal strife, external dangers, and two lengthy interruptions, the council played a vital role in revitalizing the Roman Catholic church in many parts of Europe.

Though Germany demanded a general council following the EXCOMMUNICATION of the German REFORMATION leader MARTIN LUTHER, Pope Clement VII held back for fear of renewed attacks on his supremacy. France, too, preferred inaction, afraid of increasing German power. Clement's successor, Paul III, however, was convinced that Christian unity and effective church reform could come only through a council. After his first attempts were frustrated, he convoked a council at Trent (northern Italy), which opened on Dec. 13, 1545.

Period I (1545–47): Initially the council laid the groundwork for future declarations: the Niceno-Constantinopolitan Creed was accepted as the basis of Catholic faith; the canon of OLD TESTAMENT and NEW TESTAMENT books was definitely fixed; tradition was accepted as a source of faith; the Latin VULGATE was declared adequate for doctrinal proofs; the number of SACRAMENTS was fixed at seven; and the nature and consequences of ORIGINAL SIN were defined. After months of intense debate, the council ruled against Luther's doctrine of JUSTIFICATION by faith alone: man, the council said, was inwardly justified by cooperating with divine GRACE that God bestows gratuitously. By enjoining on bishops an obligation to reside in their respective sees, the church effectively abolished plurality of bishoprics. Political problems forced the council's transfer to Bologna and finally interrupted its work altogether.

Period II (1551–52): Before military events forced a second adjournment of the council, the delegates finished an important decree on the EUCHARIST that defined the Real Presence of Christ in opposition to the interpretation of HULDRYCH ZWINGLI, the Swiss Reformation leader, and the doctrine of TRANSUBSTANTIATION as opposed to that of Luther. The sacrament of penance was extensively defined, extreme unction (anointing of the sick) explained, and decrees issued on episcopal jurisdiction and clerical discipline.

Period III (1562–63): Pope Paul IV (1555–59) was opposed to the council, but it was reinstated by Pius IV (1559–65). The council defined that Christ is entirely present in both the consecrated bread and the consecrated wine in the Eucharist but left to the pope the practical decision of whether or not the CHALICE should be granted to the laity. It defined the MASS as a true sacrifice; issued doctrinal statements on holy orders, matrimony, PURGATORY, INDULGENCES, and the veneration of saints, images, and relics; and enacted reform decrees on clerical morals and the establishment of seminaries.

By the end of the 16th century, many of the abuses that had motivated the Protestant Reformation had disappeared, and Roman Catholicism had reclaimed many of its followers in Europe. The council, however, failed to heal the SCHISM that had sundered the Western Christian church.

TREPANNING, *also spelled* trephining, practice of making a hole, one to two inches across, in the skull of a human, perhaps as a primitive method of providing disease with a means of escape. Trepanned skulls of prehistoric date have been found in Britain, France, and other parts of Europe and in Peru. Many of them show evidence of healing and, presumably, of the patient's survival. The practice still exists among people in parts of Algeria and in Melanesia, though it is fast becoming extinct in those places. Some New Age religionists, however, were practicing trepanning in the late 1990s.

TRICKSTER TALE, in ORAL TRADITIONS worldwide, anecdote of deceit and violence perpetrated by an animal-human with special powers. Usually grouped in cycles, these tales feature a trickster-hero who within a single society may be regarded as creator god and innocent fool, evil destroyer and childlike prankster.

Trickster stories may be told in a variety of situations ranging from pure amusement and entertainment to serious, sacred occasions. A single tale may be told or the narrative may be a complex series of interrelated incidents. The characteristic trickster tale is in the form of a picaresque adventure: the trickster was "going along"; he encountered a situation to which he responded by knavery or stupidity; he met a violent or ludicrous end; and then the next incident is told. Frequently, he is accompanied by an animal companion who either serves as a stooge or tricks the trickster.

Coyote, the trickster of Native American tales from California, the Southwest, and the plateau region, is perhaps the most widely known. In the Pacific Northwest the trickster is the Raven, Mink, or Blue Jay—each of whom is also viewed as a transformer figure, responsible for bringing the ordered world out of CHAOS, and a cultural hero, credited with transmitting the skills of survival, such as fire making, from the gods to humans. Wisakedjak, anglicized to Whiskey Jack, is a cultural hero trickster of the Eastern Woodlands. Another is Nanabozho (the Hare), who in the Southeast is called Rabbit and who became identified with the African Hare trickster as Brer Rabbit. South American tricksters include Fox of the Chaco people, who is always bested, and the Twins of the Amazon region, one of whom plays tricks that end badly and are then repaired by the other, a cultural hero.

In East, Central, and southern Africa and the western Sudan, the trickster is the Hare. In West Africa the Spider (Ghana, Liberia, and Sierra Leone) or the Tortoise (the Igbo and Yoruba people of Nigeria) is the trickster. Many African tribes also have tales about human tricksters (*e.g.,* the stories of Yo in Benin). In most African cycles the trickster is smaller in stature and strength than his opponents but much more clever and always well in control of the situation. He is ruthless, greedy, and a glutton and often outwits his opponent through a calculating suaveness combined with sheer lack of scruples. Although in an occasional cycle the trickster is an admirable figure, in most cases any good that results from his actions is inadvertent. In other African tales, particularly those of the spider Anansi, the trickster often appears as a rival of the sky god who steals the Sun or tricks him in one way or another. In this function he shows some similarity to the Yoruba trickster god Eshu, who constantly opposes the other gods and thwarts their intentions.

TRIKAYA \tri-'kä-yə\ (Sanskrit: "three bodies"), in MAHĀYĀNA Buddhism, concept of the three bodies, or modes of being, of the buddha: the *dharmakaya* (body of essence), the unmanifested mode, and the supreme state of absolute knowledge; the *sambhogakaya* (body of enjoyment), the heavenly mode; and the *nirmanakaya* (body of transformation), the earthly mode, the buddha as he appeared on earth or manifested himself in an earthly BODHISATTVA, an earthly king, a painting, or a natural object, such as a lotus. The concept applies not only to the BUDDHA GOTAMA but to all other buddhas as well.

TRIMŪRTI \tri-'mùr-tē\ (Sanskrit: "three forms"), in HINDUISM, triad of the three great gods, BRAHMĀ, VISHNU, and SHIVA. Scholars consider the *trimūrti* doctrine an attempt to reconcile different monotheistic approaches with one another and with the philosophic doctrine of ultimate reality (BRAHMAN). The doctrine was given classical expression in Kālidāsa's poem *Kumārasambhava* (c. 4th–5th century CE). In *trimūrti* symbolism, the three gods are collapsed into a single form with three faces. Each god is in charge of one aspect of creation, with Brahmā as creator, Vishnu as preserver, and Shiva as destroyer.

TRINITY, in Christian doctrine, the unity of Father, Son, and HOLY SPIRIT as three persons in one Godhead.

Neither the word Trinity nor the explicit doctrine appears in the NEW TESTAMENT, nor did JESUS and his followers intend to contradict the SHEMA in the OLD TESTAMENT: "Hear, O Israel: The Lord our God is one Lord" (Deuteronomy 6:4). The earliest Christians, however, had to cope with the implications of the coming of Jesus Christ and of the presumed presence and power of God among them—*i.e.,* the Holy Spirit, whose coming was connected with the celebration of the PENTECOST. The Father, Son, and Holy Spirit were associated in such New Testament passages as Matthew 28:19 and 2 Corinthians 13:14, and thus it established the basis for the doctrine of the Trinity.

The doctrine developed gradually over several centuries and through many controversies. The COUNCIL OF NICAEA in 325 stated the crucial formula for that doctrine in its CONFESSION that the Son is "of the same substance [*homoousios*] as the Father," even though it said very little about the Holy Spirit. Over the succeeding half century, ATHANASIUS both defended and refined the Nicene formula, and, by the end of the 4th century, under the leadership of BASIL of Caesarea, GREGORY OF NYSSA, and GREGORY OF NAZIANZUS (the Cappadocian Fathers), the doctrine of the Trinity had taken substantially the form it has maintained ever since. *See also* INCARNATION.

TRIPIṬAKA \tri-'pi-tə-kə\ (Sanskrit: "Triple Basket"), *Pāli* Tipiṭaka \ti-\, total canon of the southern schools of BUDDHISM, pejoratively dubbed HĪNAYĀNA ("Lesser Vehicle") by the self-styled MAHĀYĀNA ("Great Vehicle") schools. The collections that constitute this southern canon were nearly all compiled in South Asia within 500 years of the time of the Buddha (between about 500 BCE and the beginning of the Common Era). They appeared in two languages—in Pāli within the THERAVĀDA school and in Sanskrit among the SARVĀSTIVĀDA, MAHĀSAṄGHIKA, and other schools that did not survive the demise of Buddhism in India. The collection

The trimūrti, *depicted as a three-headed bust of Shiva, Vishnu, and Brahmā; in a cave on Elephanta Island, near Bombay, India*
Harrison Forman

that has been best preserved is the Pāli version that remains authoritative for contemporary Theravadins.

Each school's canonical collection differed. There was more agreement on the first two sections, the VINAYA PIṬAKA and the SUTTA PIṬAKA than on the third, the ABHIDHAMMA PIṬAKA. The first of the three, which is also the earliest and smallest, provides for the regulation of monastic life. The second and largest contains the sermons and doctrinal and ethical discourses attributed to the BUDDHA GOTAMA or, in a few cases, to his disciples. The *Abhidhamma Piṭaka*, which was absent in some schools and had quite different contents in its different versions, is basically a schematization of doctrinal material from the *suttas*. In the northern schools of Buddhism, particularly those of eastern Asia, the term Tripiṭaka was sometimes used to refer to collections of texts that were considered to be "canonical" or authoritative. The Tripiṭaka in this extended sense contained a great variety of texts that included, as a small component, translations of segments of the early Hīnayāna texts.

TRIRATNA \trē-'rət-nə\ (Sanskrit: "three jewels"), *Pāli* ti-ra-tana, the three components of the Buddhist and Jain creeds. In BUDDHISM the *triratna* comprises the BUDDHA, the DHARMA (doctrine, or law), and the SANGHA (the monastic order, or community of believers). From the time of the Buddha, initiation into the order has consisted of the formal recognition of the trinity in the words "I go to the Buddha for refuge, I go to the Doctrine for refuge, I go to the Order for refuge." In JAINISM the three jewels (also referred to as *ratnatraya*) are understood as *samyagdarśana* ("right faith"), *samyagjñāna* ("right knowledge"), and *samyakcāritra* ("right conduct"). One of the three cannot exist exclusive of the others, and all are required for spiritual liberation. The *triratna* is symbolized frequently in art as a trident.

TRITON \'trī-tən\, in Greek mythology, DEMIGOD of the sea; he was the son of POSEIDON and AMPHITRITE. According to Hesiod, Triton dwelt with his parents in a golden palace in the depths of the sea. Some traditions stated that there were many Tritons. He was represented as human down to his waist, with the tail of a fish. Triton's special attribute was a twisted seashell, on which he blew to calm or raise the waves.

TROELTSCH, ERNST \'trœlch\ (b. Feb. 17, 1865, Haunstetten, near Augsburg, Bavaria—d. Feb. 1, 1923, Berlin), German scholar of considerable influence on younger theologians of his time for his insistence that the church reexamine its claims to absolute truth.

Troeltsch's father, a medical practitioner, early instilled in his son a passion for scientific observation and led him to see problems of history and civilization within a framework of the development of the sciences. Troeltsch decided to study theology because, according to an autobiographical sketch, this seemed to him at that time the only study in which his historical, philosophical, and social interests could meet in the investigation of a worthwhile subject matter. He studied Lutheran theology at the universities of Erlangen, Göttingen, and Berlin, becoming in turn *Privatdocent* (lecturer) at Göttingen, extraordinary (associate) professor at Bonn (1892), and ordinary (full) professor in the chair of theology at Heidelberg (1894).

During 21 years at Heidelberg he published, besides his *Grundprobleme der Ethik* (1902; *Fundamental Problems of Ethics*), a large number of articles on various subjects thematically linked with the development of the Christian churches. Many of these were later integrated into his best-known work, *Die Soziallehren der christlichen Kirchen und Gruppen* (1912; *The Social Teaching of the Christian Churches*), which spanned the disciplines of theology, social history and theory, PHILOSOPHY OF RELIGION, and philosophy of history. In that work he explored the relationships between and within social and cultural groups in the context of the social ethics of the Christian churches, denominations, and sects. In 1915, realizing that his strength lay more in the philosophy of religion than in orthodox theology, he moved to a chair of philosophy at Berlin, a post he held until his death in 1923.

Influence of his thought. Troeltsch was both fascinated and troubled by "historicism" (historical relativism): the view that whatever is valued, pursued, conceived, or achieved at any given time or place is only understandable in the context of the conditions of that time or place. Although the view seemed inescapable, he surmised that it applied inadequately to the norms that govern human conduct. If consistently applied, the historicist view would make any present understanding of past ages impossible. The historically changing dogmas of the church had to be

Triton abducting a nymph; in the Vatican Museum, Rome
Alinari—Art Resource

reconciled with the absolute aspects of revealed truth interpreted anew by every generation. Despite this, many theologians (including PAUL TILLICH) have seen in Troeltsch only a critic of the certainties of CHRISTIANITY.

Within PROTESTANTISM, Troeltsch made important contributions to the study of the origins of LUTHERANISM and CALVINISM and their differing social ethics and social impact. Here he was in close sympathy concerning the nature of PROTESTANT ETHICS with his friend the German sociologist and economist MAX WEBER (1864–1920). Troeltsch was familiar with the Marxist approach to sociology and found its perspective on the socioeconomic substructure of civilization exciting, yet he rejected Marxism in favor of a more flexible conception of the interaction of cultural, social, and economic factors.

After his death, a course of five undelivered lectures was published under a title that puts his work in perspective: *Der Historismus und seine Überwindung* ("Overcoming Historical Relativism"), a more revealing title than that of the English edition (*Christian Thought: Its History and Application*). Three volumes of Troeltsch's collected works appeared toward the end of his life, a fourth being published after his death (*Gesammelte Schriften*, 4 vol., 1922–25).

TROILUS \\'trȯi-ləs, 'trō-ə-ləs\\, in Greek mythology, son of PRIAM and HECUBA. In the *Iliad*, Troilus was killed before the action of Greece's war with Troy began. In medieval literature he was portrayed as an innocent young lover betrayed by a girl (Briseida or Cressida) who abandoned him for the Greek hero DIOMEDES. The 14th century saw two important treatments of the Troilus and Cressida theme: Giovanni Boccaccio's poem *Il filostrato* and Geoffrey Chaucer's *Troilus and Criseyde* (based mainly on Boccaccio). Their story was also the subject of Shakespeare's play *Troilus and Cressida*.

TROJAN HORSE, huge, hollow wooden horse constructed by the Greeks to gain entrance into Troy during the Trojan War. The horse was built by Epeius. The Greeks, pretending to desert the war, sailed to the nearby island of Tenedos, leaving behind Sinon, who persuaded the Trojans that the horse was an offering to ATHENA that would make Troy impregnable. Despite the warnings of Laocoon and CASSANDRA, the horse was taken inside the walls. That night warriors emerged from it and opened the city's gates to the returned Greek army. The story is mentioned in the *Odyssey*, and it is told at length in the *Aeneid*.

TRUE CROSS, Christian relic, reputedly the wood of the cross on which JESUS CHRIST was crucified. Legend relates that the True Cross was found by ST. HELENA, mother of Constantine the Great, during her PILGRIMAGE to the Holy Land about 326.

The earliest historical reference to veneration of the True Cross occurs in the mid-4th century. By the 8th century the accounts were enriched by legendary details describing the history of the wood of the cross before it was used for the CRUCIFIXION.

Veneration of the True Cross gave rise to the sale of its fragments, which were sought as relics. JOHN CALVIN pointed out that all the extant fragments, if put together, would fill a large ship, an objection regarded as invalid by some RO-MAN CATHOLIC theologians who claimed that the blood of Christ gave to the True Cross a kind of material indestructibility, so that it could be divided indefinitely without being diminished. Such beliefs resulted in the multiplication of relics of the True Cross wherever CHRISTIANITY expanded in the medieval world, and fragments were deposited in most of the great cities and in a great many abbeys. Reliquaries designed to hold the fragments likewise multiplied, and some precious objects of this kind survive.

TS'AI-SHEN \'tsī-'shən\, *Pinyin* Caishen, Chinese god (or gods) of wealth. During the two-week New Year celebration, incense is burned in Ts'ai-shen's temple (especially on the fifth day of the first lunar month), and sometimes friends exchange the traditional New Year greeting "May you become rich" ("*Kung-hsi fa-ts'ai*").

The Ming dynasty novel *Feng-shen yen-i* relates that when a HERMIT, Chao Kung-ming, employed magic to support the collapsing Shang dynasty (12th century BCE), Chiang Tzu-ya, a supporter of the subsequent Chou-dynasty clan, made a straw effigy of Chao and, after 20 days of incantations, shot an arrow made of peach-tree wood through the heart of the image, killing Chao. Later, during a visit to the temple of Yüan Shih, Chiang was rebuked for causing the death of a virtuous man. He carried the corpse, as ordered, into the temple, apologized, extolled Chao's virtues, canonized Chao as Ts'ai-shen, god of wealth, and proclaimed him president of the Ministry of Wealth.

Another account identifies Ts'ai-shen as Pi Kan, put to death by order of Chou Hsin, last Shang emperor, for criticizing the emperor's dissolute life. Chou Hsin is said to have exclaimed that he now had a chance to verify the rumor that every sage has seven openings in his heart.

TSAO-CHÜN \'dzaù-'jūen\, *Pinyin* Zaojun, in Chinese mythology, the Furnace Prince who by alchemy produced gold dinnerware that conferred immortality on the diner. The Han dynasty emperor Wu-ti offered the first sacrifice to Tsao-chün in 133 BCE. At that time, Tsao-chün's chief duty was to watch over the furnace that produced gold.

The Han emperor Hsüan-ti (reigned 74–48/49 BCE) is said to have seen Tsao-chün in human form: he called himself Ch'an Tzu-fang, wore yellow garments, and had unkempt hair. About the 7th century (the similarity of names caused Tsao-chün to be identified with Tsao-shen, god of the kitchen (or hearth), who in turn was later confused with Ho-shen, the god of fire.

TSENG-TZU \'dzəŋ-'dzə\, *Pinyin* Zengzi, *also called* Tseng Ts'an \-'tsän\ (b. 505 BCE—d. c. 436 BCE), Chinese philosopher, disciple of CONFUCIUS, believed to be the author of the TA-HSÜEH ("Great Learning"), which extols the virtues *chung* ("loyalty") and SHU ("reciprocity").

Tseng-tzu was highly influential in reaffirming the Confucian emphasis on HSIAO ("filial piety"). He enumerated the three degrees of FILIAL PIETY: honoring father and mother, not disgracing them, and being able to support them.

TSONG-KHA-PA \'dzōŋ-gä-bä\ (b. 1357—d. 1419), Tibetan LAMA who founded a new Tibetan Buddhist sect known as the DGE-LUGS-PA, literally "Model of Virtue" but more commonly referred to as the Yellow Hat sect to distinguish it from the older Red Hat sect. Hoping to restore monastic discipline Tsong-kha-pa enforced CELIBACY, required the

wearing of yellow robes, and insisted on adherence to a rigorous routine. The sect eventually gained considerable influence in Mongolia; with Mongol aid Tsong-kha-pa's successors were eventually (1642) installed as the rulers of Tibet with the title DALAI LAMA.

TSO-WANG \'dzwò-'wäŋ\, *Pinyin* zuowang (Chinese: "sitting and forgetting"), term for a Taoist meditation technique first seen in the ancient text known as the CHUANG-TZU. It is a method that recommends the practice of stilling the body and mind ("sitting") and the progressive "forgetting" of selfish attachments and the distractions of desire. Eventually combined with Buddhist meditational techniques and theory, *tso-wang* was one of the most important methods of spiritual and mental cultivation leading to an enlightened "return" to the primordial TAO.

TUATHA DÉ DANANN \'tü-ə-thə-'d^yā-'dà-nən\ (Middle Irish: "People of the Goddess Danu"), in Celtic mythology, race inhabiting Ireland before the arrival of the MILESIANS (the ancestors of the modern Irish). They were said to have been skilled in magic, and the earliest reference to them relates that, after they were banished from heaven because of their knowledge, they descended on Ireland in a cloud of mist. They disappeared into the hills when overcome by the Milesians. The *Leabhar Gabhála* (*Book of Invasions*), a fictitious history of Ireland from the earliest times, treats them as actual people, and they were so regarded by native historians up to the 17th century. There can be no doubt that this "race" represents the Celtic pantheon, as several main characters, notably LUGUS and NUADU, are found in Continental British place-names or inscriptions. In popular legend they have become associated with the numerous fairies still supposed to inhabit the Irish landscape.

ṬU BI-SHEVAṬ \'tü-bi-shə-'vät, -'shvät\ (Hebrew: "Fifteenth of Shevaṭ"), minor Jewish festival of the new year of trees, or arbor day, occuring on Shevaṭ 15 (January or early February). Thereafter, the fruit of a tree is considered, for tithing, to belong to a new year. Certain penitential prayers are omitted from the liturgy, and fasting is not allowed. Among ASHKENAZI Jews, fruits—traditionally, 15 different kinds—are eaten and often accompanied by the recital of Psalms. Among Sephardic Jews, Ṭu bi-Shevaṭ is a significant festival, a "feast of fruits" accompanied by songs called *complas*. In modern Israel, the day has become popular in symbolizing the reclaiming of land from the desert for agriculture. Schoolchildren plant trees and sing songs.

TUKĀRĀM \'tù-kä-'räm\ (b. 1598? or 1608?, Dehu, near Pune, India—d. 1649), Marathi poet who is often considered the most powerful voice in the language. His *abhaṅgas*—"unbroken" outpourings—are among the most famous Indian poems.

The son of a shopkeeper, Tukārām was orphaned in childhood. Failing in business and family life, he renounced the world and became an itinerant ascetic. Tukārām is thought to have written over 4,000 *abhaṅgas*, most of which were addressed to the god Viṭhobā of PANDHARPUR.

TU KUANG-T'ING \'dü-'gwäŋ-'tiŋ\, *Pinyin* Du Guangting (b. 850—d. 933), Taoist scholar of the T'ang period who contributed to the development of Taoist liturgical ritual and the blending of the T'ien-shih and Ling-pao SCRIPTURES. His ideas on Taoist ritual were especially influential in the articulation of the common Taoist "fasting," or *chia*, rites and of the liturgies, or *chiao*, of communal renewal. He also wrote a famous commentary on the TAO-TE CHING and several important hagiographical accounts of Taoist immortals and adepts.

TULSĪDĀS \'túl-sē-'däs, túl-ˌsē-'däs\ (b. 1532?, 1543?, India—d. 1623, Varanasi), Indian poet whose principal work, the RĀMCARITMĀNAS ("Sacred Lake of the Acts of Rāma"), is often regarded as the greatest achievement of medieval Hindi literature and has exercised an abiding influence on the Hindu culture of northern India.

The *Rāmcaritmānas* expresses par excellence the religious sentiment of BHAKTI to the god RĀMA, especially as mediated through the devotion of his brother Lakṣmaṇa, his monkey devotee HANUMĀN, and his wife SĪTĀ. In all these cases, the sentiment is reciprocal—the strength of Rāma's own devotion being one of his defining traits. Another resource for *bhakti* is the sheer power of Rāma's name (*rām* NĀM). Tulsīdās's eclectic approach to doctrinal questions allowed him to rally wide support for the worship of Rāma in northern India, and the success of the *Rāmcaritmānas* has been a prime factor in elevating the worship of Rāma to a place of dominance in the religious sensibility of many regions of north and central India.

Little is known about Tulsīdās' life. Seven locales claim to be his birthplace. He apparently lived most of his adult life at Varanasi, which helps to account for the prominent role played by Shiva—that city's principal deity—in the *Rāmcaritmānas*'s frame story. The *Rāmcaritmānas* was written between 1574 and 1576 or 1577. The poem, written in Avadhi, an Eastern Hindi dialect, consists of seven cantos of unequal lengths. Although the ultimate source of the central narrative is the Vālmīki RĀMĀYAṆA, Tulsīdās' immediate source was the *Adhyātma Rāmāyaṇa*, a late medieval recasting of the epic that had already sought to harmonize the ADVAITA system and the Rāma cult. The influence of the BHĀGAVATA-PURĀṆA, the chief SCRIPTURE of the KRISHNA cult, is also discernible, with that of a number of minor sources.

Eleven other works are attributed with some certainty to Tulsīdās. These include *Kṛṣṇagītāvalī*, a series of 61 songs in honor of Krishna; *Vinayapatrikā*, a series of 279 verse passages addressed to Hindu sacred places and deities (chiefly Rāma and Sītā); and *Kavitāvalī*, telling incidents from the story of Rāma.

TUMULUS \'tü-myə-ləs, 'tyü-, 'tə-\, prehistoric grave form in continental Europe. *See* BURIAL MOUND.

TUNG CHUNG-SHU \'dùŋ-'jùŋ-'shü\, *Pinyin* Dong Zhongshu (b. *c.* 179 BCE, Kuang-ch'uan, China—d. *c.* 104 BCE, China), scholar instrumental in establishing CONFUCIANISM as the state cult of China and as the basis of official political philosophy—a position it was to hold for 2,000 years. As a philosopher, Tung merged the Confucianist and YIN-YANG schools of thought.

As a chief minister to the emperor Wu (*c.* 140–87 BCE) of the Han dynasty, Tung was chiefly responsible for the dismissal of all non-Confucian scholars from government. His proposal that Confucianism become the unifying ideology of the Han empire was put into effect, as were his proposals to set up an imperial college (*t'ai-hsüeh*) for training promising students and to require nobles and governors to recommend annually persons of talent and good moral character for official appointment. Out of these institutional means developed the civil-service examinations that became the basis of recruitment into the bureaucracy.

As a philosopher, Tung made the theory of the interaction between heaven (*t'ien*) and humanity his central theme. The emperor is heaven's ambassador on earth, and natural catastrophes are heaven's way of warning the emperor to examine his personal conduct and correct his mistakes. Yang (light, positive, male) and yin (dark, negative, female) are the two fundamental forces of the universe and as such should be kept in harmony. The ruler has the duty to preserve that harmony. He may reform institutions when necessary but may never alter or destroy the basic moral principles of heaven. Confucian scholars are to interpret the portents and thus exercise a check on the policies of the ruler.

Tung's *Ch'un-ch'iu fan-lu* ("Luxuriant Dew of the Spring and Autumn Annals"), an interpretation of the classic "Spring and Autumn Annals" (*Ch'un-ch'iu*), is one of the most important philosophical works of the Han period.

TUN-HUANG \'dùn-'hwäŋ\, *Pinyin* Dunhuang, city in western Kansu *sheng* (province), China. Situated in an oasis in the Kansu-Sinkiang desert, Tun-huang is at the far-western limit of traditional Chinese settlement along the Silk Road across Central Asia. It was the first trading town reached by foreign merchants entering Chinese-administered territory from the west.

Tun-huang was one of the chief places of entry for Buddhist monks and missionaries from the kingdoms of Central Asia, and these Buddhists founded the first of Tun-huang's caves—known as the Cave of the Thousand Buddhas (Ch'ien-fo Tung)—in 366 CE. From this period onward the town became a major Buddhist center and place of PILGRIMAGE, until the fall of the Western Hsia dynasty in the early 13th century. There were numbers of monastic communities (many of them non-Chinese) that played a predominant role in local society and to which successive governors were generous patrons. In one of the cave temples a rich collection of about 60,000 paper manuscripts, printed documents, and fragments dating from the 5th to the 11th century was walled up about 1015. This collection included not only Buddhist but also Taoist, Zoroastrian, and Nestorian scriptures, as well as vast numbers of secular texts.

TUONELA \'tü-ò-nä-ˌlä, 'twò-\: *see* MANALA.

TURIN, SHROUD OF \tü-'rēn, *Angl* 'túr-in, 'tyúr-; tù-'rin, tyü-\, *Italian* Santa Sindone, length of linen that for centuries was purported to be the burial garment of JESUS CHRIST; it has been preserved since 1578 in the royal chapel of the Cathedral of San Giovanni Battista in Turin, Italy. Measuring 14 feet 3 inches long and 3 feet 7 inches wide, it seems to portray images of the back and front of a gaunt, 5-foot 7-inch man—as if a body had been laid lengthwise along one half of the shroud while the other half had been doubled over the head to cover the whole front of the body from face to feet. The images contain markings that allegedly correspond to the STIGMATA of Jesus, as well as various stains of what is presumed to be blood.

The shroud first emerged in 1354 in the hands of Geoffroi de Charnay, seigneur de Lirey. In 1389, when it went on exhibition, it was denounced as false by the local bishop of Troyes, who declared it "cunningly painted, the truth being attested by the artist who painted it." The Avignon ANTI-POPE Clement VII (reigned 1378–94) sanctioned its use as an object of devotion provided that it were exhibited as a "representation" of the true shroud, but subsequent popes accepted its authenticity. The shroud was damaged by fire and water in 1532. It was moved to the new Savoyard capital of Turin in 1578.

Scholarly analyses have been applied to the shroud since the late 19th century. It was early noticed (1898) that the images on the shroud seem to have the character of photographic negative. Beginning in the 1970s, tests were made to determine whether the images were the result of pigments, scorches, or other agents; none proved conclusive. In 1988 three laboratories concluded by carbon-14 dating that the cloth of the shroud had been made sometime between 1260 and 1390 CE. The ROMAN CATHOLIC church accepted the results and announced that the Shroud of Turin was not authentic, but encouraged Christians to continue venerating the shroud as an inspiring pictorial image of Christ. More recently, however, a vigorous campaign has been launched by those who wish to vindicate its authenticity.

The Shroud of Turin
Gianni Tortoli—Science Source

TURNUS \'tər-nəs\, in Roman legend, king of the Rutuli (an ancient Italic tribe on the coast of Latium), and the accepted suitor of Lavinia, daughter of LATINUS, king of the Latins. After Latinus betrothed Lavinia instead to the hero AENEAS, Turnus, joined by the Rutuli and the Latins, made war against Aeneas and the Trojans. Though Turnus was protected by the goddess JUNO, Aeneas finally succeeded in killing him.

ṬŪSĪ, NAṢĪR AL-DĪN AL- \'tü-sē\ (b. Feb. 18, 1201, Ṭūs, Khorāsān—d. June 26, 1274, Baghdad), outstanding Persian philosopher, scientist, and mathematician.

Al-Ṭūsī became astrologer to the Ismāʿīlī governor Naṣīr al-Dīn ʿAbd al-Raḥīm, and later, pretending to be an ISMĀʿĪLĪ, lived and studied at the castle of Alamut, headquarters of the Ismāʿīlī terrorist sect, the Assassins. In 1256 he betrayed the defenses of the fortress to the invading Mongols, whose army he joined; Hülegü Khan took him along as a confidential adviser when he attacked and destroyed Baghdad in 1258. Al-Ṭūsī used his office as head of the ministry of religious bequests to build a fine observatory at Marāgheh. A man of exceptionally wide erudition, he wrote many books in Arabic and Persian. He improved upon earlier Arabic translations of Euclid, Ptolemy, Autolycus, Theodosius, Apollonius, and others and made original contributions to mathematics and astronomy, including an accurate table of planetary movements. His *Tajrīd al-ʿaqāʾid* is a highly esteemed treatise on SHĪʿITE dogmatics. His most famous and popular work is *The Nasirean Ethics*, a treatise on ethics in the Greek tradition resting upon the 11th-century *Tahdhīb al-akhlāq* of Ibn Miskawayh, which he drafted while a prisoner of the Assassins and later revised for his Mongol master. Al-Ṭūsī was a Twelver Shiʿite but is credited with a number of distinctively Ismāʿīlī dissertations, notably the *Tasavvurat*.

T'U-TI \'tü-'dē\, *Pinyin* Tudi (Chinese: "Earth or Place God"), in Chinese popular religions, type of god whose deification and functions are determined by local residents. The chief characteristic of a T'u-ti is his limitation to a single place—*e.g.*, a bridge, a street, a temple, a public building, a private home, or a field. T'u-ti is often identified with the god of riches and is always subservient to the Ch'eng-huang, the spiritual magistrate of the city.

In most cases, these gods originated as historical persons who in life came to the assistance of their respective communities in times of need. It is supposed that deifying such persons and offering sacrifices to them will move them to show similar solicitude after death. If misfortunes visit a locality, the T'u-ti is judged to have lost interest and a new patron is chosen.

TWELVE, THE, *also called* The Twelve Prophets, *or* The Minor Prophets, book of the Hebrew BIBLE that contains the books of 12 minor prophets—Hosea, Joel, AMOS, Obadiah, Jonah, Micah, Nahum, Habakkuk, ZEPHANIAH, Haggai, Zechariah, and Malachi—consolidated into the last of eight books in the second division of the Hebrew Bible, known as NEBIʾIM, or the Prophets.

TWELVE TRIBES OF ISRAEL, in the OLD TESTAMENT, the Hebrew people who took possession of the Promised Land under the leadership of JOSHUA. Because the tribes were named after sons or grandsons of JACOB (whose name was changed to Israel by God, GENESIS 32:28; 35:10), the Hebrew people became known as Israelites.

Ten of the tribes (REUBEN, SIMEON, JUDAH, ISSACHAR, ZEBULUN, GAD, ASHER, BENJAMIN, DAN, and NAPHTALI) were named after sons of Jacob by his first wife, Leah; by Zilpah, Leah's maidservant; by Rachel (his second wife); and by Bilhah, the maidservant of Rachel (Genesis 29:31–30:24; 35:16–18). Two tribes—MANASSEH and EPHRAIM—were named after sons of Joseph—Joseph being a son of Rachel and Jacob (Genesis 41:50–52). The 10 tribes that settled in northern Palestine became known as the TEN LOST TRIBES OF ISRAEL.

TYAGARAJA \'tyə-gə-'rä-jə\ (b. 1767, Tamil Nādu, India—d. 1847), Indian composer renowned in southern India for his Telugu *kīrtana*s (devotional songs) and ragas. These songs were mostly in praise of RĀMA. Tyagaraja is regarded as an exponent of *gāna-mārga*—*i.e.*, salvation through devotional music.

TYCHĒ \'tī-kē\, in GREEK RELIGION, goddess of chance, and a capricious dispenser of good and ill fortune. Hesiod called her the daughter of the Titan OCEANUS and Tethys; other writers attributed her fatherhood to ZEUS. She was also associated with the more beneficent Agathos Daimon, a good spirit, protective of individuals and families, and with NEMESIS, who represented punishment of overprosperous man and so was believed to act as a moderating influence. Among her monuments was a temple at Argos, where the legendary PALAMEDES is said to have dedicated to her the first set of dice, which he is supposed to have invented.

TYLOR, SIR EDWARD BURNETT \'tī-lər\ (b. Oct. 2, 1832, London, Eng.—d. Jan. 2, 1917, Wellington, Somerset), English anthropologist regarded as the founder of cultural anthropology. His most important work, *Primitive Culture* (1871), influenced by Darwin's theory of biological evolution, developed the theory of an evolutionary, progressive relationship between "primitive" and modern cultures.

Tylor was the son of a prosperous QUAKER brass founder. He attended a Quaker school until he was 16, when, barred by his faith from entering a university, he became a clerk in the family business. In 1855 he traveled to America and in 1856 to Cuba, where he met the archaeologist and ethnologist Henry Christy. Christy was on his way to Mexico to study remnants of the ancient Toltec culture in the Valley of Mexico, and he persuaded Tylor to accompany him. The expedition lasted for six months, and after its conclusion Tylor returned to England. His experiences were published in his first book, *Anahuac; or, Mexico and the Mexicans Ancient and Modern* (1861). Although mainly a travelogue, *Anahuac* contains elements that characterize Tylor's later work: a firm grasp on factual data, a sense of cultural differences, and a curious combination of empirical methods with occasional hints of the superiority of a 19th-century Englishman in judging other cultures.

After *Anahuac*, Tylor published three major works. *Researches into the Early History of Mankind and the Development of Civilization* (1865) elaborated the thesis that cultures past and present, civilized and "primitive," must be studied as parts of a single history of human thought. Tylor's fame, however, is based chiefly upon the publication of *Primitive Culture*. In it he again traced a progressive development from a "savage" to a civilized state and pictured primitive man as an early philosopher applying his reason to explain events in the human and natural world that were beyond his control, even though his scientific ignorance produced erroneous explanations. Tylor identified the earliest form of RELIGIOUS BELIEF as "animism," a belief in spiritual beings, arrived at by primitive attempts to explain the difference between the living body and the corpse and the separation of soul and body in dreams.

Primitive Culture also elaborated upon a theme that became a central concept in his work: the relation of the life of primitive to that of modern populations. Thus, "culture," he argued, should be studied not only in the artistic and spiritual achievements of civilizations but in human technological and moral accomplishments made at all stages of development. Tylor noted how customs and beliefs from a distant past seemed to have lived on into the modern world, and he became well-known for his examination of such "survivals," a concept that he introduced. His evolutionary view of human development was endorsed by most of his colleagues and, of course, by Charles Darwin, who had established biological evolution as the key to human development. Tylor's evolutionary theory was rejected by most scholars as both ethnocentric and purely conjectural by the close of the 20th century.

TYNDALE, WILLIAM \'tin-dəl\ (b. c. 1490–94, near Gloucestershire, Eng.—d. Oct. 6, 1536, Vilvoorde, near Brussels, Brabant), English biblical translator, humanist, and Protestant martyr.

Tyndale was an instructor at the University of Cambridge, where, in 1521, he became convinced that the BIBLE alone should determine the practices and doctrines of the church and that every believer should be able to read the Bible in his own language. After church authorities in England prevented him from translating the Bible there, he went to Germany in 1524. His NEW TESTAMENT translation, strongly influenced by that of MARTIN LUTHER, was completed in 1525 and printed at Cologne and, when ROMAN CATHOLIC authorities suppressed it, at Worms. Tyndale was working on an OLD TESTAMENT translation when he was captured in Antwerp; he was executed at Vilvoorde in 1536.

At the time of his death, several thousand copies of his New Testament had been printed; however, only one intact copy remains today at London's British Library. The first vernacular English text of any part of the Bible to be so published, Tyndale's version became the basis for most subsequent English translations, beginning with the KING JAMES VERSION of 1611.

TYPHON \'tī-,fän\, *also spelled* Typhaon \tī-'fā-,än\, in Greek mythology, youngest son of GAEA (Earth) and Tartarus. He was a grisly monster with a hundred dragons' heads who was conquered and cast into the underworld by ZEUS, but continued as the source of destructive winds. In other accounts, he was confined in the land of the Arimi in Cilicia or under Mount Etna or in other volcanic regions, where he was the cause of eruptions. Among his children by his wife, ECHIDNA, were the hell-hound Cerberus, the multi-headed HYDRA, and the CHIMERA.

TYR \'tir, 'tēr, 'tür\, *Old Norse* Týr, *Old English* Tiw \'tē-ü\, *or* Tiu, one of the oldest gods of the Germanic peoples. He was apparently the god of the formalities of war, especially treaties. In the most famous myth about him, as a guarantee of good faith, he placed his hand between the jaws of the monstrous wolf FENRIR while the gods, pretending sport but intending a trap, bound the wolf; when Fenrir realized he had been tricked he bit off Tyr's hand (hence Tyr's identification as the one-handed god).

TZU-JAN \'dzə-'rän\, *Pinyin* ziran (Chinese: "self-so," "naturalness"), in TAOISM, an ideal state of human existence that results from living in complete harmony with the forces of nature. As everything in the world has its natural state, Taoists strive to attain a state of complete spontaneity in order to become what nature intended them to be. As a consequence, life becomes exceedingly simple; and such things as life and death, good health and illness are accepted as part of the irresistible cycle of nature, which ceaselessly makes and unmakes the world. This process is best achieved by first observing the ever-changing world and then "fatalistically" abstaining from struggle against powers beyond one's control.

TZU-SSU \'dzə-sə\, *Pinyin* Zisi, *also called* K'ung Chi \'kùŋ-'jē\ (b. 483—d. 402 BCE), Chinese philosopher, grandson of CONFUCIUS, native of the state of Lu (present Shantung province), and traditional author of the *Doctrine of the Mean*. This classic reaffirms Confucius' interpretation of the mean as the state of equilibrium (CHUNG-YUNG) of the exemplary man and broadens the concept through discussion of the "timely mean" (*shih-chung*) that is relative and varies according to situation.

UCHIMURA KANZŌ

UCHIMURA KANZŌ \ü-ʹchē-mü-rä-ʹkän-ˌzō\ (b. May 2, 1861, Edo [now Tokyo], Japan—d. March 28, 1930, Tokyo), Japanese religious thinker and critic, an important formative influence on many writers and intellectual leaders of modern Japan.

Uchimura came from a samurai (warrior) family and studied at the Sapporo Agricultural School, where he was baptized in 1871. Refusing foreign missionary help, in 1882 he founded his own independent Japanese Christian Church. He continued his studies in the United States (1884–88) and returned to Japan to teach in Tokyo. There he became the center of controversy in 1891 when he questioned the divinity of the emperor by refusing to bow when presented with the Imperial Rescript on Education. Among his writings are *Kirisuto-shinto no nagusame* (1893; "Consolations of a Christian"), *Kyuanroku* (1893; "Seeking Peace of Mind"), and *Yo wa ikanishite Kirisuto-shinto to narishi ya* (1895; "How I Became a Christian"). Uchimura's interpretation of CHRISTIANITY emphasized the central importance of the BIBLE and the individual conscience and denied the need for a church or SACRAMENTS, a tradition still known in Japan by the word he coined for it, *mukyōkai* ("nonchurch movement").

UDĀSĪS \ü-ʹdä-sē\ (Punjabi: "Detached Ones"), monastic followers of Srīchand (1494–1612?), the elder son of GURŪ NĀNAK (1469–1539). The authoritative text of the Udāsī movement is the *Mātrā* ("Discipline"), a hymn comprised of 78 verses and attributed to Srīchand. The *Mātrā* emphasizes the need for spiritual elevation, to be attained by living an ascetic life of CELIBACY and detachment from the world. The UDĀSĪS wear matted hair and have the ICON of Srīchand as the central object of worship in their temples.

After Nānak's death, Srīchand established a *dehrā* ("center") in his father's name, and his movement started from there. By the middle of the 18th century, Udāsīs had 25 centers in the Punjab, and their number grew to over 100 with the coming of Sikh political dominance in the area.

The relationship between Sikhs and Udāsīs is historically complex. Many Udāsī beliefs, devotional practices, and modes of living are in clear opposition to mainstream Sikh doctrine, reflecting ascetic and iconic dispositions that are generally identified as Hindu. Indeed, Srīchand remained in fierce competition with Nānak's nominated successors. Yet the fact that he was Nānak's son meant that he enjoyed a degree of respect in the eyes of Nānak's successors and their followers. Moreover, while many Sikhs, especially Jats, harbored a marked distaste for celibacy and all it represents, others accepted the complementary relationship between householders and ascetics that characterizes many Indian religious traditions. Thus it was not unseemly that Udāsīs took custody of some GURDWĀRĀS (Sikh places of worship) during the period of Sikh persecution by the Mughal state in the 18th century or that, as part of his liberal policy toward religious establishments, Maharaja Ranjīt

Singh (1780–1839) gave revenue-free land grants to the Udāsī centers. With the turn of the 20th century, however, lines of religious definition became increasingly firm in the Punjab, and the Udāsīs came to view themselves as an ascetic group within the larger Hindu—not Sikh—fold. Today their largest center is in Haridwār.

UGARIT \yü-ʹgär-it, ʹyü-gə-rit\, ancient city lying in a large artificial mound called Ras Shamra, six miles north of Al-Lādhiqīyah (Latakia) on the Mediterranean coast of northern Syria. Its ruins, about half a mile from the shore, were first uncovered by the plow of a peasant at Al-Baydā Bay. Excavations were begun in 1929.

Ugarit's history. The most prosperous and the best-documented age in Ugarit's history, dated from about 1450 to about 1200 BCE, produced great royal palaces and temples and shrines, with a high priests' library and other libraries on the acropolis. Some of the family vaults built under the stone houses show strong Mycenaean influence. Mycenaean and Cypriot pottery in great amounts has also been found.

After the discovery of the temple library, which revealed a hitherto unknown cuneiform alphabetic script as well as an entirely new mythological and religious literature, several other palatial as well as private libraries were found, along with archives dealing with all aspects of the city's politica, social, economic, and cultural life. Scribes used four languages: Ugaritic, Akkadian, Sumerian, and Hurrian. Seven different scripts were used in this period: Egyptian and Hittite hieroglyphic and Cypro-Minoan, Sumerian, Akkadian, Hurrian, and Ugaritic cuneiform. These show clearly the cosmopolitan character of the city.

Soon after 1200 BCE Ugarit came to an end. Its fall coincided with the invasion of the Northern and Sea Peoples and certainly with earthquakes and famines. In the Iron Age and during the 6th–4th century BCE, there were small settlements on the site (Leukos Limen).

Ras Shamra religious and mythological texts. Most of what is known about Canaanite religion is derived from the tablets discovered at Ras Shamra. The principal god was EL, but the jurisdiction over rainfall and fertility was delegated to BAAL, or HADAD. Other important deities included RESHEPH, lord of plague and the nether world; KOTHAR, the divine craftsman; ASHERAH, consort of El; and ASTARTE, goddess of fertility. Many of these texts, including the "Legend of Keret," the "Aghat Epic" (or "Legend of Danel"), the "Myth of Baal-Aliyan," and the "Death of Baal," reveal an Old Canaanite mythology. A tablet names the Ugaritic pantheon with Babylonian equivalents; El, Asherah of the Sea, and Baal were the main deities. By similarities of theme and character, it is now evident that the patriarchal stories in the OLD TESTAMENT were not merely transmitted orally but were based on written documents of Canaanite origin, the discovery of which at Ugarit has led to a new appraisal of the Old Testament.

ŬISANG \'ə̄-ē-'säŋ\ (b. 625, Korea—d. 702, Korea), Buddhist monk and founder of the Hwaŏm (Chinese: HUA-YEN) sect of Korean BUDDHISM. He devoted himself to the propagation of the teaching of the *Avataṃsaka Sūtra.*

Ŭisang became a monk about 650, and at age 37 he went to China, where he studied under the direction of Chih-yen, the 2nd patriarch of the Chinese Hua-yen (Garland) sect. While in China he wrote his major work, *An Explanatory Diagram on the Garland World System,* which is still read widely in the Buddhist circles of East Asia. On returning home in 671, he built the Pusŏk Temple as the center of the Hwaŏm sect.

UJIGAMI \'ü-jē-ˌgä-mē\, in SHINTŌ, tutelary deity of a village or geographic area. Originally the term referred to the ancestral deity (KAMI) of a family or clan (*uji*), blood KINSHIP forming the basis of the spiritual relationship. The extent of the *ujigami*'s protection was later enlarged to cover those who lived with the clan or near it and since has extended over the parish into which one is born. *Ujiko* are those who live or were born within the geographic boundaries of the tutelary deity and who help manage the shrine affairs.

UKEMOCHI NO KAMI \ù-'ke-ˌmò-chē-nō-'kä-mē\ (Japanese: "Goddess Who Possesses Food"), in SHINTŌ mythology, the goddess of food. She is also sometimes identified as Wakaukanome ("Young Woman with Food") and is associated with Toyuke (Toyouke) Ōkami, the god of food, clothing, and housing, who is enshrined in the Outer Shrine of the GRAND SHRINE OF ISE.

According to the legend recounted in the NIHON SHOKI ("Chronicles of Japan"), the moon god, Tsukiyomi, was dispatched to earth by his sister, the sun goddess AMATERASU, to visit Ukemochi no Kami. (According to the KOJIKI, "Records of Ancient Matters," it was another brother, the storm god SUSANOO, who was sent on the mission.) The food goddess welcomed him by facing the land and disgorging from her mouth boiled rice, turning toward the sea and spewing out all kinds of fishes, and turning toward the land and disgorging game. She presented these foods to him at a banquet, but he was displeased at being offered the goddess's vomit and drew his sword and killed her. When he returned to heaven and informed his sister of what he had done, she became angry and said, "Henceforth I shall not meet you face to face," which is said to explain why the sun and the moon are never seen together.

Another messenger sent to the food goddess by Amaterasu found various stuffs produced from her dead body. From her head came the ox and the horse; from her forehead, millet; from her eyebrows, silkworms; from her eyes, panic grass (a cereal); from her belly, rice; and from her genitals, wheat and beans. Amaterasu had the food grains sown for humanity's future use and, placing the silkworms in her

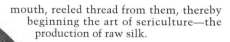

Golden bowl from Ugarit, 14th century BCE; in the National Museum, Aleppo, Syria
Hirmer Fotoarchiv, Munchen

mouth, reeled thread from them, thereby beginning the art of sericulture—the production of raw silk.

UKKO \'ük-kò\, in Finnish folk religion, god of thunder, one of the most important deities. The name Ukko is derived from *ukkonen*, "thunder," but it also means "old man" and is used as a term of respect. Ukko had his abode at the center of the sky; hence he was often called Jumala, "Heaven God." He controlled rainfall, and sacrifices were directed toward him at the beginning of the planting season and in times of drought.

'ULAMĀ' \ˌü-lə-'mä, 'ü-lə-ˌmä\ (Arabic), *also spelled* ulema, the learned of ISLAM, those who possess the quality of *'ilm*, "learning," in its widest sense. From the *'ulamā'*, who are versed theoretically and practically in the Muslim sciences, come the religious teachers of the community—theologians (*mutakallimun*), canon lawyers (MUFTIS), judges (*qadis*), professors—and high state religious officials. They receive their education in Islamic colleges (MADRASAS). In a narrower sense, *'ulamā'* may refer to a council of learned men holding government appointments in a Muslim state.

Historically, the *'ulamā'* have been a powerful class, and in early Islam it was their consensus (IJMĀ') on theological and juridical problems that determined the communal practices of future generations. Although there is no PRIESTHOOD in Islam, and every believer may perform priestly functions such as leading the liturgical prayer, the *'ulamā'* have played an important political and clerical role.

In modern times the *'ulamā'* have lost ground to the Western-educated classes; although they have been abolished in Turkey, their hold on conservatives in the rest of the Muslim world remains firm. As a result of the 1978–79 revolution in Iran, SHI'ITE *'ulamā'* became dominant in that country's religious and political affairs and inspired opposition movements in the Persian Gulf region and Lebanon. Some Sunni *'ulamā'* have given support to Islamic opposition movements in countries such as Syria and Egypt.

ULL \'ùl\, *Old Norse* Ullr \'ù-lər\, in Norse mythology, god of snowshoes, hunting, the bow, and the shield, commonly called upon for aid in individual combat. He resided at Ydalir (Yew Dales).

Ull must have been a very prominent deity in the Norse pantheon at one time because, according to one tradition, the god ODIN was replaced by Ull during one of his long journeys. In addition, Ull's name appears as part of many Swedish and Norwegian place-names.

ULSTER CYCLE \'əl-stər\, *Irish Gaelic* Ulaid Cycle \'ü-ləth\ᵞ\, in ancient Irish Gaelic literature, a group of legends and tales dealing with the heroic age of the Ulaids, a people of northeast Ireland from whom the modern name Ulster derives. The stories, set in the 1st century BCE, were recorded from ORAL TRADITION between the 8th and 11th century and are preserved in the 12th-century manuscripts *The Book of the Dun Cow* (*c.* 1100) and *The Book of Leinster* (*c.* 1160) and also in later compilations, such as *The Yellow Book of Lecan* (14th century). Mythological elements are freely intermingled with legendary elements that have an air of authenticity. Events center on the reign of the semi-historical King Conor (CONCHOBAR MAC NESSA) at EMAIN MACHA (near modern Armagh) and his Knights of the Red Branch (*i.e.*, the palace building in which the heads and arms of vanquished enemies were stored). A rival court at Connaught is ruled by King Ailill and Queen MEDB. The chief hero of the Red Branch is the Achilles-like CÚ CHULAINN, born of a mortal mother, Dechtire, the sister of King Conor, and a divine father, the god Lug of the Long Arm.

Most of the stories are short prose narratives, using verse for description and for scenes of heightened emotion. They fall into types such as destructions, cattle raids, or elopements. The longest tale and the closest approach to an epic is TÁIN BÓ CÚAILGNE (The Cattle Raid of Cooley), dealing with a conflict between the men of Ulster and of Connaught. One tale portrays the familiar father-son duel, in which Cú Chulainn unknowingly kills his own son, who has come to seek him. Another tale, BRICRIU'S FEAST, contains a beheading game that is the source for Sir Gawayne and the Grene Knight. The tale having the most profound influence on later Irish literature is The Fate of the Sons of Usnech, the tragic love story of DEIRDRE and Noíse, which was retold in dramatic form in the 20th century by John Millington Synge and William Butler Yeats.

'UMAR TAL \,ù-mȧr-'tȧl\, *in full* al-Ḥājj 'Umar ibn Sa'īd Tal, *also spelled* el-Hadj Omar ibn Sa'īd Tal (b. *c.* 1797, Halvar, Fouta-Toro [now in Senegal]—d. Feb. 12, 1864, near Hamdalahi, Tukulor empire [now in Mali]), West African Tukulor leader who, after launching a JIHAD (holy war) in 1854, established a Muslim realm, the Tukulor empire, between the upper Sénégal and Niger rivers (in what is now upper Guinea, eastern Senegal, and western and central Mali). The empire survived until the 1890s under his son, Aḥmadu Seku.

'Umar Tal was born in the upper valley of the Sénégal River, in the land of the Tukulor people. His father was an educated Muslim who instructed students in the QUR'AN, and 'Umar, a mystic, perfected his studies with North African scholars who initiated him into the Tijānī brotherhood. At the age of 23, 'Umar set out on a pilgrimage to MECCA and was received with honor in the countries through which he traveled. Muhammad Bello, emir of Sokoto in Nigeria, offered him his daughter Maryam in marriage. Enriched by this princely alliance, 'Umar had become an important personage when he reached Mecca about 1827. He visited the tomb of the Prophet in MEDINA, returned to Mecca, and then settled for a while in Cairo. In Mecca he was designated CALIPH for black Africa by the head of the Tijānī brotherhood.

'Umar returned to the interior of Africa in 1833. Trained for political leadership by his father-in-law, with whom he spent several years, and his position strengthened by the title of caliph, he now decided to convert the Africans to ISLAM. Upon the death of Bello, he departed for his native country, hoping to conquer the Fouta region with the assistance of the French, in exchange for a trade treaty, an agreement the French declined because of 'Umar's growing strength. In northeastern Guinea, where he established himself, he wrote down his teachings in a book called

Kitāb rimāḥ ḥizb al-raḥīm ("Book of the Spears of the Party of God"). Deriving his inspiration from SUFISM he defined the Tijānī "way" as the best one for saving one's soul and for approaching God. He recommended meditation, self-denial, and blind obedience to the SHAYKH. He gained many followers in Guinea, but, when in 1845 he went to preach in his own country, he met with little success.

In March 1854 'Umar issued an order for a jihad to sweep away the PAGANS and bring back the Muslims who had strayed from the fold. In 1855 he defeated the Bambaras of Mali and forcibly converted them, yet these conversions proved to be ineffectual. To defend his authority 'Umar had 300 hostages executed, but revolt broke out again as soon as his armies were removed.

'Umar was to spend the next 10 years trying to contain his empire. When 'Umar attacked the Fulani people of the Masina, who were Muslims, followers of the Qādirī brotherhood, his mission turned into a fratricidal war. 'Umar, recognizing the danger to his divine mission, proposed a duel with Aḥmadu III, the leader of the Fulani army, but the latter refused. 'Umar won the battle, and Aḥmadu was captured and beheaded.

In 1863, attacked by the Tuaregs, the Moors, and the Fulani, 'Umar's army was destroyed. He withdrew to the city of Hamdalahi, where he was besieged. He escaped and took refuge in a cave but was killed when the cave was blown up with gunpowder.

Al-Ḥājj 'Umar Tal's empire lasted 50 years, from 1848 to 1897, when it was annexed by the French. Few of the Mali people still remember it, except the descendants of the Tijānī initiates or the Fulani and Bambaras, who suffered his cruelties. The mosque of Dinguiraye in Guinea is all that remains of 'Umar's empire.

'UMRA \'ùm-rə\, "minor PILGRIMAGE" undertaken by Muslims in MECCA at anytime of the year. It is also meritorious, though optional, for Muslims residing in Mecca. As in the HAJJ, the pilgrim begins the *'umra* by assuming the state of *iḥrām* (ritual purity). Following a formal declaration of intent (*nīya*) to perform the *'umra*, he enters Mecca and circles the sacred shrine of the KA'BA seven times. He may then touch the Black Stone, pray at the sacred stone Maqām Ibrāhīm, drink the holy water of the Zamzam spring, and touch the Black Stone again, though these ceremonies are supererogatory. The *sa'y*, running seven times between the hills of aṣ-Ṣafā and al-Marwah, and the ritual shaving of the head complete the *'umra*.

Pilgrims have the choice of performing the *'umra* separately or in combination with the hajj. In its present form, the *'umra* dates from Muhammad's lifetime and is a composite of several pre-Islamic ceremonies that were reinterpreted in monotheistic terms and supplemented by Muslim prayers.

UNDERWORLD, place of departed souls. *See also* HADES.

UNIATE CHURCH \'yü-nē-,at, -ət\: *see* EASTERN RITE CHURCH.

UNIFICATION CHURCH, *byname of* Holy Spirit Association for the Unification of World Christianity, religious movement that was founded in South Korea in 1954 by SUN MYUNG MOON. The movement shifted its base to New York City in 1971. Its network of missionary, cultural, and economic enterprises extends to more than 100 countries and is said to involve more than 200,000 believers. Only about

10,000, with considerable turnover, are members of the highly visible American branch.

The movement, influenced by YIN-YANG motifs and Korean shamanism, seeks to establish divine rule on earth through the restoration of the family based on the union of the Lord and Lady of the Second Advent (believed to be Moon and his wife, Hak Ja Han). According to Unification doctrine, God's efforts to reestablish rightful order reached a provisional climax in JESUS, who, by exemplifying individual oneness with God, inaugurated the kingdom spiritually but was prevented by his CRUCIFIXION from restoring divine rule through procreative marriage. The completion of Christ's thwarted work is believed to be approaching its final stages in the mission conferred by the ascended Jesus on Moon.

Unification stresses communal and devotional discipline as well as unreserved commitment to such practical work as fund-raising, business operations, and educational, missionary, and humanitarian activity. Controversy has mounted with regard to the movement's recruitment practices (which have been said to include protein starvation and brainwashing), appeals for money, business policies, and conformity to tax and immigration laws.

UNITARIANISM, religious movement that stresses the free use of reason in religion, holds generally that God exists only in one person, and denies the divinity of JESUS CHRIST.

Theological foundations for the view of God as a unity and for the humanity of Jesus are found in 2nd- and 3rd-century MONARCHIANISM and in the teachings of ARIUS (c. 250–c. 336) and his followers (Arians)—both groups of early Christians whose doctrines were later declared heretical by the church. In the 16th-century Protestant REFORMATION, certain liberal, radical, and rationalist reformers revived the Platonic emphasis on reason and the unity of God. Chief among these was FAUSTUS SOCINUS, whose theology stressed the complete humanity of Jesus, a view still held by most Unitarians and Universalists. Another important early figure was Ferenc Dávid, who was convicted as a heretic for teaching that prayers could not be addressed to Jesus (since Jesus was merely human). He died in prison in 1579. The church that Dávid founded in Transylvania is the world's oldest extant Unitarian body.

Joseph Priestley, a founder of the English Unitarians, portrait in chalk by Ellen Sharples, c. 1795
By courtesy of the National Portrait Gallery, London

The mainstream of British Unitarianism and American Unitarianism grew out of Calvinist PURITANISM. Calvin's doctrine of providence, coupled with an increasingly scientific view of the universe, led to an increased emphasis on reason and morals among the more liberal Calvinist clergy. Joseph Priestley, an English scientist and dissenting minister, was among those who began preaching "Unitarian CHRISTIANITY," emphasizing Jesus' humanity, God's omnipotence, and the rational faculty of man. The English Unitarians became a force in Parliament, the professions, and social reform. The name "Free Christian" was adopted by some groups who opposed the name "Unitarian" as sectarian and divisive. The movement fared somewhat less well in Scotland and Ireland.

American Unitarianism developed out of New England Congregationalist churches that rejected the 18th-century revival movement. The Transcendentalist movement of the 19th century injected Unitarianism with a new interest in the intuitive and emotional aspects of religion. When Unitarianism spread into the Middle West, its religious fundamentals changed to human aspiration and scientific truth, rather than Christianity and the BIBLE.

Both British and American Unitarian groups formed national associations in 1825. In 1961 American Unitarians merged with the national organization of Universalist churches, with whom they shared a history of liberal idealism. In polity, most Unitarians and Universalists are congregational. Forms of worship, based on Protestant tradition, vary widely from group to group.

UNITAS FRATRUM \'ü-nē-ˌtäs-'frä-ˌtrům, 'yü-ni-ˌtas-'frä-trəm\ (Latin: "Unity of Brethren"), Protestant religious group inspired by HUSSITE spiritual ideals in Bohemia in the mid-15th century. They followed a simple life of NONVIOLENCE, using the BIBLE as their sole rule of faith. They denied TRANSUBSTANTIATION but received the EUCHARIST and deemed religious HYMNS of great importance. In 1501 they printed the first Protestant hymnbook, and in 1579–93 they published a Czech translation of the Bible (the Kralice, or Kralitz, Bible), the outstanding quality of which made it a landmark in Czech literature. About the mid-16th century, Unitas emigrants moved into Poland and survived there for some two centuries. By the 17th century the Unitas Fratrum constituted more than half of the Protestants in Bohemia and Moravia.

The Unitas Fratrum joined the Czech estates in their fight with the Holy Roman emperor Ferdinand I (Thirty Years' War), and in 1627 an imperial edict outlawed all Protestants in Bohemia. The Unitas was destroyed, with all its churches, its Bible, and its hymnbooks, and its members were forcibly "catholicized" or exiled. Remnants of the group eventually found refuge in Saxony and under the name of Herrnhuters had great religious influence through their missionary activities. Both the MORAVIAN CHURCH and the Evangelical Czech Brethren Church trace their origin to the Unitas Fratrum.

UNITED HOUSE OF PRAYER FOR ALL PEOPLE, Pentecostal Holiness church founded by Bishop Charles Emmanuel ("Sweet Daddy") Grace (1881/84?–1960).

After leaving a job as a cook on a Southern railway, he began to preach, assuming the name "Grace" and proclaiming himself "Bishop." He established a house of worship in 1926 in Charlotte, N.C., and later moved to Newark, N.J. He claimed to be an emissary of God with authority to grant or withhold salvation. The death of Grace led to temporary difficulties for the group over tax litigation and the succession to Grace's leadership.

The church is headquartered in Washington, D.C., and has a reported active membership of 25,000.

UNITED SYNAGOGUE OF AMERICA (USA), central federation of some 835 Conservative Jewish congregations located in the United States and Canada. It was organized in 1913 by Solomon Schechter, a Talmudic scholar and spokesman for the Conservative movement. The United Synagogue has administrative divisions for youth activities, Jewish education, adult studies, music, social action, dietary laws, and congregational standards. The USA is affiliated with the National Federation of Jewish Men's Clubs, THE RABBINICAL ASSEMBLY, and the Women's League for Conservative Judaism.

UNITY SCHOOL OF CHRISTIANITY, *also called* Unity, religious movement founded in Kansas City, Mo., in 1889 by Charles Fillmore (1854–1948) and his wife, Myrtle (1845–1931). Mrs. Fillmore believed that spiritual healing had cured her of tuberculosis. As a result, the Fillmores began studying spiritual healing. They were deeply influenced by Emma Curtis Hopkins, a former follower of MARY BAKER EDDY. Unity, however, is closer to NEW THOUGHT, which in general emphasizes the primacy of mind and spiritual healing. Until 1922 it was a member of the International New Thought Alliance.

Unity developed gradually as the Fillmores attempted to share their insights concerning religion and spiritual healing. They began publishing magazines, books, and pamphlets and started the service known as Silent Unity, which, through prayer and counseling, helps people by telephone and by mail. After World War I, the Fillmores began developing Unity Village, 15 miles from Kansas City and eventually covering 1,400 acres, and by 1949 all departments of Unity were there. After Charles Fillmore's death, Unity was led by the Fillmores' sons and grandchildren.

Unity emphasizes spiritual healing, prosperity, and practical CHRISTIANITY. Unlike some New Thought groups, it stresses its agreements with traditional Christianity. Illnesses are considered unnatural and curable by spiritual means. The practice of medicine, however, is not rejected. There is no definite creed, although a statement written by Charles Fillmore, the *Unity Statement of Faith,* is available in a pamphlet. Unity is tolerant of the beliefs and practices of others.

It has been reported that as many as 2,500,000 requests for aid are received by Silent Unity each year. All are answered by mail or by telephone free of charge, but many persons who make requests give a contribution. Unity also conducts classes for interested individuals and a course of study for those who wish to become Unity ministers and teachers in the approximately 300 Unity centers, which are located in many states in the United States and abroad. Unity ministers must complete a course of study and be approved by the Unity School of Christianity. The Unity movement is thought to reach some 6,000,000 persons, most of whom, however, are not members.

UNIVERSALISM, belief in the salvation of all souls. Although Universalism has appeared at various times in Christian history, most notably in the works of ORIGEN of Alexandria in the 3rd century, as an organized movement it had its beginnings in the United States in the middle of the 18th century. Building on Enlightenment thought, the Universalists believed it impossible that a loving God would ELECT only a portion of mankind to salvation and doom the rest to eternal punishment. They insisted that punishment in the afterlife was for a limited period during which the soul was purified and prepared for eternity in the presence of God.

The forerunner of Universalism in the United States was George De Benneville (1703–93), who in 1741 migrated from Europe to Pennsylvania, where he preached and practiced medicine. The early Universalist movement was given its greatest impetus by the preaching of John Murray (1741–1815), who moved from England to colonial America in 1770. He propagated the doctrine throughout most of the colonies, often against much opposition from orthodox Christians who believed that Universalism would lead to immorality. Near the close of the 18th century Hosea Ballou introduced a Unitarian conception of God and reinterpreted the death of Jesus: it was not a vicarious ATONEMENT for the SINS of mankind but rather a demonstration of God's infinite and unchangeable love for his children. Ballou also stressed the use of reason in religion.

From the 19th century, Universalists felt a close kinship with Unitarians, since the two groups shared many views and practices. Various attempts to unite the national bodies of the two denominations, the Universalist Church of America and the American Unitarian Association, culminated in the formation of the Unitarian Universalist Association in 1960 and formal merger in 1961. Each Universalist church is free to choose its own form of worship. Simple, nonliturgical services are most common, with great emphasis put on the sermon.

From the beginning, Universalists have differed widely in matters of belief. Liberalism, freedom of individual interpretation, tolerance of diversity, agreement on methods of approaching theological and church issues, and belief in the inherent dignity of man have been the strongest elements keeping the movement together. Universalists generally stress the use of reason in religion and modification of belief in the light of the discoveries of science. Thus, the miraculous elements of traditional CHRISTIANITY are rejected as incompatible with modern knowledge. Jesus is considered a great teacher and worthy of imitation, but he is not held to be divine. A broader conception of Universalism began to emerge in the 20th century. Although stressing their ties to the Christian tradition, Universalists were exploring the universal elements of religion and seeking closer relationships with non-Christian religions.

UNTOUCHABLE, *also called* Harijan \hə-'ri-jən\, *or* DALIT \'də-lit\, in traditional Hindu society, any member of a wide range of Hindu groups outside the traditional four-tiered class structure and, more generally, any person outside the CASTE system.

Many different hereditary castes have been traditionally subsumed under the title of untouchable, each of which subscribes to the social rule of endogamy (marriage exclusively within the caste community) that governs the caste system in general.

Traditionally, the groups characterized as untouchable were those whose occupations and habits of life involved polluting activities, of which the most important were (1) taking life for a living (for example, fishermen), (2) killing or disposing of cattle or working with their hides, (3) pursuing activities that brought the participant into contact with emissions of the human body (for instance, sweepers and washermen), (4) handling corpses, and (5) eating the flesh of cattle or of domestic pigs and chickens, a category into which many of the indigenous tribes of India fell. Because of the pollution associated with these jobs and the castes responsible for them, the untouchables have been disadvantaged and discriminated against for many centuries; they have been prohibited from entering upper-caste temples and from drawing water from the wells used by those above them in the caste hierarchy or sharing the same food. Indeed, the very sight of an untouchable was thought to defile those of higher caste. Religious texts going back thousands of years have been used to legitimate the oppression of the untouchable, in part by arguing that untouchability is a just punishment for evil deeds committed in a former life. These factors led many untouchables to seek some de-

Untouchables wait outside a temple for donations of food
Porterfield/Chickering—Photo Researchers

gree of emancipation through conversion to CHRISTIANITY, ISLAM, or BUDDHISM.

The use of the term "untouchable" and the social disadvantages associated with it were declared illegal in the constitutions adopted by the Constituent Assembly of India in 1949 and that of Pakistan in 1953. In much of India, especially the villages, prejudice and discrimination against those so labeled continues. Owing in part to the emergence of Dalit leaders like BHIMRAO RAMJI AMBEDKAR, however, laws have been passed outlawing the most grievous abuses, and legislation now provides formerly untouchable groups with specific educational and vocational privileges and special representation in the Indian parliament, and penalties for preventing anyone from enjoying a wide variety of religious, occupational, and social rights on the grounds that he is an untouchable.

UPĀDHI \ù-'pä-dē\ (Sanskrit: "imposition"), in Indian philosophy, the concept of adventitious limiting conditions. In logic, *upādhi* operates as follows: a syllogism requires a ground (*hetu*) to prove the proposition; *e.g.*, that there is fire on the mountain is proved by the presence of smoke. But this ground needs a qualification: there can be fire without smoke. An *upādhi* is recognized for the *hetu*. Since smoke is produced by fire in living wood, the *hetu* must be

refined thus: smoke is present wherever there is fire in living wood.

In BHEDĀBHEDA philosophy, the concept of *upādhi* is used to account for the relationship between BRAHMAN, the supreme being, and its product, the evolved world: Brahman and world are nondifferent in their essence but are different inasmuch as limiting conditions such as time and space, adventitious to this essence, are imposed on them.

UPANAYANA \,ü-pə-'nə-yə-nə\, Hindu ritual of initiation, restricted to the three upper VARNAS, or social classes; it marks the male child's entrance into the life of a student (*brahmacārī*) and his acceptance as a full member of his religious community. The ceremony is performed between the ages of 5 and 24.

After a RITUAL BATH the boy is dressed as an ascetic and brought before his GURU, who invests him with a deerskin to use as an upper garment, a staff, and the sacred thread (*upavīta*, or *yajñopavīta*). The thread, consisting of a loop made of three symbolically knotted and twisted strands of cotton cord, is normally worn over the left shoulder and diagonally across the chest to the right hip. It identifies the wearer as DVIJA, or "twice-born," the second birth understood as having taken place with the imparting by the guru to the student of the "Gāyatrī" MANTRA, a sacred verse of the ṚG VEDA. The initiation ceremony concludes with the student's kindling of the sacrificial fire and his begging for alms, symbolic of his dependence on others during his *brahmacārī* period. The actual observance of *upanayana* is increasingly confined to more orthodox Hindus, particularly those of the BRAHMIN caste. Although the DHARMA ŚĀSTRA claims that marriage is a woman's *upanayana*, there are also such RITES OF PASSAGE for girls, but from oral, non-Sanskrit sources.

A corresponding rite among PARSIS is called *nowzād* (Persian: "new birth"); it invests both six-year-old boys and girls with a thread worn around the waist. Some scholars suggest that this indicates a common and ancient Indo-Iranian origin of the two ceremonies.

UPANISHAD \ü-'pə-ni-,shəd, -'pä-ni-,shäd\, Sanskrit Upaniṣad ("Connection"), any of the speculative texts of the VEDAS that contain elaborations in prose and verse.

The Upanishads, of which approximately 108 are known, record the views of a succession of Hindu teachers and sages who were active as early as 1000 BCE and who flourished about 600 BCE. The texts form the basis of much of later Indian philosophy. They represent the final stage in the tradition of the Vedas, so the teaching based on them is known as the VEDĀNTA (Sanskrit: "Conclusion of the Veda"). The older Upanishads may be part of the BRĀHMAṆAS (commentaries) of their respective Vedas but are distinguished from them both by increased philosophical and mystical questioning and by their diminished concern with Vedic deities and sacrificial rites.

The special philosophical concern of the Upanishads is with the nature of reality. There is a development toward the concept of a single supreme being, and knowledge is directed toward reunion with it. Some of the Upanishads equate ĀTMAN (the self) with BRAHMAN (ultimate reality). The nature of morality and of eternal life are discussed, as are such themes as the transmigration of souls and causality in creation.

UPĀSAKA \ü-'pä-sə-kə\, *feminine* upāsikā (Sanskrit: "servant"), lay devotee of the BUDDHA GOTAMA. The term correctly refers to any Buddhist who is not a member of a monastic order, but its modern usage in Southeast Asia more often connotes the particularly pious person who visits the local monastery on the weekly holy days and who undertakes special vows.

Since its beginnings in India, BUDDHISM has accepted both men and women of any race, social class, or CASTE. All that is required of believers is the simple affirmation of the TRI-RATNA ("Threefold Refuge"), composed of the Buddha, the DHARMA (teachings), and the SANGHA (community of believers). The Buddhist layperson is expected to observe the five precepts (not to kill, steal, commit sexual misconduct, lie, or take intoxicants) and to support the monastic community by giving alms.

The THERAVĀDA Buddhist tradition distinguishes between the religious paths of the layperson and the monk; achievement of NIRVANA (spiritual emancipation) is normally considered possible only if a devotee renounces worldly life and joins a monastic order. The MAHĀYĀNA tradition of Tibet and East Asia, however, recognizes several celebrated spiritual masters who at the same time have been married householders.

UPASAMPADA \ˌü-pə-'sam-pə-ˌdä\, Buddhist rite of higher ORDINATION, by which a novice becomes a monk, or BHIKṢU. The ceremony as observed in the THERAVĀDA tradition is basically the same as in ancient BUDDHISM. Ordination is not necessarily permanent and, in some countries, may be repeated in a monk's lifetime. A candidate for ordination must be at least 20 years old, have the permission of his parents, be exempt from military service, be free from debt and from contagious disease, and have received at least some elementary instruction in Buddhism.

The ceremony may be performed on any day determined to be auspicious, except during VASSA (*varsa*), the rainy season retreat. It takes place within the SANCTUARY in the presence of monks already ordained. The *pabbajja*, or ceremony of lower ordination to the rank of novice, is repeated even if the candidate has undergone it previously. He dons the garments of a monk and repeats the TRIRATNA ("Threefold Refuge") of the Buddha, the DHARMA (teaching), and the SANGHA (community of believers) and the 10 precepts (basic rules of ethical conduct for a monk); the candidate then stands before the assembly in the company of his sponsoring tutors and is questioned on his fitness to be received into the order. The assembly is questioned three times, and, if there is no objection to his ordination, the candidate is accepted into the PRIESTHOOD. Female novices are ordained nuns (Pāli: *bhikṣuṇīs*) in a similar rite.

UPPSALA \'üp-ˌsä-ˌlä\, city and capital of the *län* (county) of Uppsala, east-central Sweden. It lies 40 miles north-north-west of Stockholm. Originally known as Östra Aros, it was founded as a trading post at the head of navigation on the Fyris River at a point a few miles from Gamla (Old) Uppsala, which was the political and religious center of the ancient kingdom of Svea. Adam of Bremen described the pre-Christian temple there: the building was of wood covered in gold and reputedly contained statues of THOR, Wodan (ODIN), and Fricco (FREY). By the 13th century the new Uppsala had become a royal residence and an important commercial center.

Although it later relinquished its political primacy to Stockholm, Uppsala has remained a religious center as the seat of the archbishop of Sweden. The Gothic cathedral, the largest such structure in Sweden, dominates the city. Work began on this edifice in the late 13th century but progressed slowly, and not until 1435 was the church consecrated. The cathedral was ravaged by fire several times but was finally restored in the late 19th century.

'UQQĀL \ü-'käl\ (Arabic: "the wise"), *singular* 'āqil \'ä-kil\, in the DRUZE religion, elite of initiates who alone know Druze doctrine (*ḥikma*, literally "wisdom"), participate fully in the Druze religious services, and have access to Druze SCRIPTURE. The religious system of the Druzes is kept secret from the rest of their numbers, who are known as *juhhāl* ("the ignorant"), as well as from the outside world. Any Druze man or woman deemed worthy after serious scrutiny is eligible for admission into the *'uqqāl*.

Once initiated, the *'uqqāl* adopt distinctive dress and white turbans and must pursue lives of religious piety, sobriety, and virtue. They abstain from alcohol and tobacco and attend secret Thursday-evening services at the *khilwa*, a house of worship usually located outside the village. The *'uqqāl* are further bound by the seven Druze principles of conduct: utter honesty under all circumstances but specifically avoidance of theft, murder, and adultery; Druze solidarity; renunciation of other religions; avoidance of unbelievers; belief in the oneness of God; acceptance of God's acts; and submission to God's will.

The *'uqqāl* may deepen their knowledge of Druze doctrine in progressive stages until some finally become "the generous," *ajāwīd*. Any rise in the hierarchy brings with it greater obligations to live a blameless life. The more learned or devout among the *'uqqāl* are distinguished as SHAYKHS and after special schooling devote themselves to the study and copying of the religious texts; they often retire completely to the *khilwa*s.

The *'uqqāl* bear responsibility for the *juhhāl*, who in their ignorance are denied the possibility of spiritual growth. The *juhhāl*, whose lives are not so restricted morally and sensually as those of the *'uqqāl*, are aware of the doctrine of the unity of God and possess detailed mythologies of creation and *tanāsukh*, transmigration of souls, in which Druze souls are always reborn as Druze souls.

The *juhhāl* generally live by the principle of TAQĪYA, or dissimulation of faith, and when living among Muslims or Christians they may superficially adopt their practices.

URANIA: *see* OURANIA.

URANUS: *see* OURANUS.

URARTIAN RELIGIONS \ü-'rär-tē-ən\: *see* ANATOLIAN RELIGIONS.

USHABTI FIGURE \ü-'shäb-tē, -'shab-\, any of the small statuettes made of wood, stone, or faience that are often found in large numbers in ancient Egyptian tombs. The figures range in height from four to nine inches and often hold hoes in their arms. Their purpose was to act as a magical substitute for the deceased owner when the gods requested him to undertake menial tasks in the afterlife. The word *ushabti* is sometimes translated "answerer," on the assumption that it is a derivative of *usheb* ("to answer [for]"); however, this etymology is not easily reconcilable with *shawabti*, the earlier form of the word, the origin of which is unclear. During the New Kingdom (1539–1075 BCE) the figures were made to resemble the tomb owner by being fashioned in the form of a MUMMY bearing the owner's name.

UṢŪL AL-FIQH \ù-ˌsül-àl-'fik\: *see* FIQH.

'UTHMĀN IBN 'AFFĀN \ùth-'màn-ˌi-bən-af-'fàn\ (d. June 17, 656, Medina, Arabian Peninsula), third CALIPH to rule after the death of MUHAMMAD. He centralized the administration of the caliphate and established an official version of the QUR'AN. His death marked the beginning of open religious and political conflicts within the Islamic community.

'Uthmān was born into the rich and powerful Umayyad clan of MECCA, and he became a wealthy merchant. When Muhammad began preaching in Mecca *c.* 615, he soon aroused the hostility of the Umayyads, but about five years later 'Uthmān accepted Muhammad and thus became the first convert of high social and economic standing. Muhammad valued this contact with the Meccan aristocracy, and he allowed 'Uthmān to marry one of his daughters. 'Uthmān's role in the first years of Islamic history was essentially passive.

'Umar, the second caliph, died in 644, and 'Uthmān was elected successor by a council named by 'Umar before his death, apparently selected as a compromise when the more powerful candidates canceled each other out. He also represented the Umayyad clan, which had suffered a partial eclipse during the Prophet's lifetime but was now reasserting itself. As caliph 'Uthmān promulgated an official version of the Qur'an, which had existed in various versions. He continued the conquests that had steadily increased the size of the Islamic empire, but the victories now came at a greater cost and brought less booty in return. 'Uthmān tried to create a cohesive central authority to replace the loose tribal alliance that had emerged under Muhammad. He established a system of landed fiefs and distributed many of the provincial governorships to members of his family. Thus much of the treasure received by the central government went to 'Uthmān's family and to other provincial governors rather than to the army. As a result of his

Ushabti figure, 26th dynasty
By courtesy of the Fitzwilliam Museum, Cambridge, Eng.

policies, 'Uthmān was opposed by the army, and he was often dominated by his relatives.

By 650 rebellions had broken out in the provinces of Egypt and Iraq. In 655 a group of Egyptians marched upon MEDINA, the seat of caliphal authority. 'Uthmān, however, was conciliatory, and the rebels headed back to Egypt. Shortly thereafter, however, another group of rebels besieged 'Uthmān in his home, and, after several days of desultory fighting, he was killed. *See also* COMPANIONS OF THE PROPHET.

UTNAPISHTIM \ˌüt-nä-'pish-tim\, in the Babylonian GILGAMESH epic, survivor of a mythological flood whom Gilgamesh consults about the secret of immortality. Utnapishtim was the only man to escape death, since, having preserved human and animal life in the great boat he built, he and his wife were deified by the god ENLIL. Utnapishtim directed Gilgamesh to a plant that would renew his youth, but the hero failed to return with it to his home city. *See* NOAH; ZIUSUDRA.

UTRAQUIST \'yü-trə-kwist, 'ü-\, *also called* Calixtin, *or* Calixtine \kə-'liks-tin\, any of the spiritual descendants of JAN HUS who believed that the laity, like the clergy, should receive the EUCHARIST under the forms of both bread and wine (Latin *utraque*, "each of two"; *calix*, "chalice"). The Utraquists were moderates, maintaining amicable relations with the ROMAN CATHOLIC church, and the Council of Basel in 1433 declared them to be true Christians. When, however, the Utraquists developed into an independent church, Rome withheld approval, even though Roman bishops officiated at Utraquist ORDINATIONS to the PRIESTHOOD. The Utraquists, together with all other Protestant sects, were outlawed in Bohemia after the Battle of White Mountain in 1620.

UZZIAH \ə-'zī-ə\, *also spelled* Ozias \ō-'zī-əs\, *also called* Azariah \ˌa-zə-'rī-ə\, *or* Azarias \-'rī-əs\, in the OLD TESTAMENT (2 Kings 14:21–22; 15:2–3; 2 Chronicles 26), son and successor of Amaziah, and king of JUDAH for 52 years (*c.* 791–739 BCE). Assyrian records indicate that he reigned for 42 years (*c.* 783–742).

Uzziah's reign marked the height of Judah's power. He fought successfully against other nations, exacted tribute from the AMMONITES, and expanded Judah westward with settlements in Philistia. Jerusalem's walls were reconstructed, towers were added, and engines of war were mounted at strategic points. A large army was also maintained. According to the biblical record, Uzziah's strength caused him to become proud: he attempted to burn incense in the Temple, an act restricted to priests. When the priests attempted to send him from the Temple, the king became angry and was immediately stricken with leprosy. His son Jotham ruled for his father until Uzziah died.

VAHANA \\'və-hə-nə\\ (Sanskrit: "mount," or "vehicle"), in Hindu mythology, the creature that serves as the vehicle and as the sign of a particular deity. The *vahana* accompanies, pulls the chariot of, or serves as the seat or mount of his god. The *vahana* is used on banners and emblems to identify the god or the cult affiliation of the devotee.

Some scholars understand the concept as a way of incorporating local theriomorphic (animal form) deities into the classical pantheon of Hindu deities. Others suggest the mythological pattern might have been borrowed from Mesopotamian art and mythology. The *vahana*s of the major gods, such as SHIVA's bull Nandi and VISHNU's bird GARUDA, have a considerable mythology of their own.

The *vahana*s of other gods include the hamsa (goose or swan) of BRAHMA, the rat of GANEŚA, the peacock of SKANDA, the elephant Airavata of INDRA, the parrot of KĀMA, the owl of LAKṢMĪ, the lion of PĀRVATĪ, and the man of KUBERA.

VAILALA MADNESS \\vī-'lä-lə\\, CARGO CULT of the Papua area (now Papua New Guinea) that began in 1919. This movement was based on the revelations of local prophets that the ancestors were withholding European material goods from indigenous peoples. Cult doctrines included the iconoclastic destruction of old ceremonial objects and the moral, social, and logistical preparation for the arrival of vast quantities of Western "cargo," expected to be delivered by ship or plane. Cargo cults such as the Vailala Madness were widespread in New Guinea, the Bismarcks, and parts of the Solomons and New Hebrides, and some of the movements were highly political and explicitly anticolonial in character.

VÄINÄMÖINEN \\'va-ē-na-,mœ-ē-nen, *Angl* 'vā-nə-,mȯi-nən\\, in Finnish mythology, seer and culture hero credited with the invention of the kantele, a harplike instrument. He played a prominent role in the KALEVALA.

VAIRĀGĪ \\vī-'rä-gē\\, in HINDUISM, a religious ascetic who principally worships a form of VISHNU. *Vairāgī*s generally wear white robes, in contrast to the ochre-colored robes worn by Śaiva ascetics (*see* ŚAIVISM), while their TILAK is never made of ash and is always vertical in design. Most reside in monastic communities called *sthānas* ("spots" or "places"); but the militant *nagna* ("naked") *vairāgī*s form their own groups, called *akhāṛā*s. In the past, battles between groups of naked ascetics belonging to different sects centered mainly on bathing and processional rights during PILGRIMAGE assemblies, such as the KUMBH MELA.

VAIROCANA \\vī-'rō-chə-nə\\ (Sanskrit: "Illuminator"), *also called* Mahāvairocana \\mə-'hä-vī-'rō-chə-nə\\ ("Great Illuminator"), recognized by many MAHĀYĀNA and Esoteric Buddhists (that is, Tantric, *see* VAJRAYĀNA) as the supreme buddha who is the cosmic counterpart of Śākyamuni in his teaching mode. Some traditions view Vairocana and Ma-

hāvairocana as separate, but others conflate them into one deity.

Vairocana is a great celestial buddha with a Vedic background. In the Mahāyāna/Esoteric tradition (particularly in Tibet) he is given special prominence in the set of five DHYĀNI or self-born buddhas. In some contexts he is regarded as the progenitor of the other four; in some cases Mahāvairocana becomes the buddha who transcends the set of five in which Vairocana is included. Vairocana is given a special role in the *Avataṃsaka Sūtra* (and in the HUA-YEN/Kegon school) where he is recognized as the solar buddha who is both the ultimate reality of the cosmos and the one who pervades all of its component parts.

In the Esoteric tradition there are two texts—the *Mahāvairocana Sūtra* and *Tattvasaṃgraha*—in which Mahāvairocana is installed as the supreme buddha and associated with highly sophisticated forms of Esoteric ritual. These texts played a significant role in TIBETAN BUDDHISM, but in East Asia they became the most authoritative texts for the Ch'en-yen school in China and the much more important SHINGON sect in Japan. In the Shingon school Mahāvairocana is known as Dainichi Nyorai ("Great Sun Buddha") or Roshana. He is frequently represented in Japanese painting and sculpture. As the supreme buddha, his characteristic gesture is the MUDRĀ of the six elements, in which the index finger of the left hand is clasped by the five fingers of the right, symbolizing the uniting of the five elements of the material world (earth, water, fire, air, and ether) with the spiritual world (consciousness).

VAIŚEṢIKA \\vī-'shā-shi-kə\\ (Sanskrit: "Distinction," or "Characteristic"), one of the six orthodox systems (DARŚANS) of Indian philosophy, significant for its NATURALISM. The Sanskrit philosopher Kaṇāda Kāśyapa (2nd–3rd century CE?) expounded its theories and is credited with founding the school. Important later commentaries were written by Praśastapāda, Udayana, and Śrīdhara. The VAIŚEṢIKA school fused entirely with the NYĀYA school by the 11th century. Thereafter the combined school was referred to as Nyāya-Vaiśeṣika.

The Vaiśeṣika school attempts to identify, inventory, and classify the entities and their relations that present themselves to human perceptions. It lists six categories of being (*padārtha*s), to which was later added a seventh. These are:

(1) *Dravya*, the substratum that exists independently of all other categories, and the material cause of all compound things produced from it. *Dravya*s are nine in number: earth, water, fire, air, ether, time, space, spirit, and mind.

(2) *Guṇa*, or quality, which in turn is subdivided into 24 individual species.

(3) KARMA, or action. Both *guṇa* and karma inhere within *dravya* and cannot exist independently of it.

(4) *Sāmānya*, or genus, which denotes characteristic similarities that allow for two or more objects to be classed together.

(5) *Viśeṣa*, or specific difference, which singles out an individual of that class, and for which this school of philosophy is named.

(6) *Samavāya*, or inherence, which indicates things inseparably connected.

To these six was later added *abhāva*, nonexistence or absence. Four absences are recognized: previous absence, as of a new product; later absence, as of a destroyed object; total absence, as of color in the wind; and reciprocal absence, as of a jar and a cloth, neither of which is the other.

The Vaiśeṣika system holds that the smallest, indivisible, indestructible part of the world is an atom (*aṇu*). All physical things are a combination of the atoms of earth, water, fire, and air. Inactive and motionless in themselves, the atoms are put into motion by God's will and through the unseen forces of moral merit and demerit.

VAIṢṆAVA-SAHAJIYĀ \\'vīsh-nə-və-ˌsə-hə-'jē-yä, -ˌshə- \\: *see* SAHAJIYĀ.

VAIṢṆAVISM \\'vīsh-nə-ˌvi-zəm\\, *also called* Vishnuism \\'vish-nü-ˌi-zəm\\, *or* Viṣṇuism, worship of the god VISHNU and of his INCARNATIONS, principally as RĀMA and as KRISHNA. It is one of the major forms of modern HINDUISM—with ŚAIVISM and ŚĀKTISM.

A major characteristic of Vaiṣṇavism is the emphasis on BHAKTI, or religious devotion. The ultimate goal of the devotee is to escape from the cycle of birth and death to enjoy the presence of Vishnu. This cannot be achieved without the grace of God. For his part, the devotee must cultivate the auxiliary disciplines of KARMA and JÑĀNA.

Sectarian Vaiṣṇavism began in the cult of Vāsudeva-Krishna, who may have been a Yādava tribal leader (*c.* 7th–6th century BCE). The VĀSUDEVA cult coalesced with others worshiping the deified sage Nārāyaṇa so that by about the 2nd century CE Vāsudeva, Krishna, and Nārāyaṇa appeared in the BHAGAVAD GĪTĀ as interchangeable names of Lord Vishnu. The cult of the pastoral Krishna was soon added.

The philosophical schools of Vaiṣṇavism differ in their interpretation of the relationship between individual souls and God. The doctrines of the most important schools are (1) VIŚIṢṬĀDVAITA ("qualified monism"), associated with the name of RĀMĀNUJA (11th century) and continued by the ŚRĪ VAIṢṆAVA sect, prominent in South India; (2) DVAITA ("dualism"), the principal exponent of which was MADHVA (13th century), who taught that although the soul is dependent on God the two are separate entities; (3) *dvaitādvaita* ("dualistic monism"), taught by NIMBĀRKA (12th century), according to which the world of souls and matter is both different and not different from God; (4) *śuddhādvaita* ("pure monism") of VALLABHA, which explains the world without the doctrine of MĀYĀ (illusion); (5) *acintya-bhedābheda* ("inconceivable duality and nonduality"), the doctrine of CAITANYA, in which the relation between the world of souls and matter and God is not to be grasped by thought but is both different and nondifferent.

In addition to these philosophical schools, each of which has its own sectarian following, Vaiṣṇavism also includes a number of popular expressions of devotionalism, which were furthered in the late medieval period by the vernacular writings of RĀMĀNANDA and his disciples and by Vaiṣṇava poets such as TULSĪDĀS in the Hindi area, MĪRĀBĀĪ in Gujarāt, and NĀMDEV and TUKĀRĀM in the Marāthā country.

VAIŚYA \\'vīsh-yə\\, *also spelled* Vaishya, third highest in ritual status of the four VARṆAS, or social classes, of Hindu India, traditionally described as commoners. Legend states that the *varṇa*s sprang from Prajapati—in order of status, the BRAHMIN (white) from his head, the KṢATRIYA (red) from his arms, the VAIŚYA (yellow) from his thighs, and the ŚŪDRA (black) from his feet. Vaiśyas were commoners who engaged in productive labor, agricultural and pastoral tasks, and trading. Early SCRIPTURES show that Vaiśyas could and occasionally did rise even to the rank of Brahmin, as in the case of the two sons of Nābhāgariṣṭa, mentioned in the sacred work *Harivaṃśa*.

Like the two higher classes, Vaiśyas are DVIJA, or "twiceborn," achieving their spiritual rebirth when they assume the sacred wool thread at the UPANAYANA ceremony. Vaiśyas, along with Kṣatriyas, are credited in history with favoring the rise of the reformist religious beliefs of BUDDHISM and JAINISM. In modern times, the Vaiśya class has become a stepping-stone used by Indians to raise their status in the system through modified behavior and via the adoption of more prestigious CASTE names.

VAJRA \\'vəj-rə\\, *Tibetan* Rdo-Rje \\'dōr-jā\\, five-pronged ritual object extensively employed in Tibetan Buddhism. *Vajra*, in Sanskrit, has both the meanings of "thunderbolt" and "diamond." Like the thunderbolt, the *vajra* cleaves through ignorance. The thunderbolt was originally the symbol of the Hindu god INDRA (who became the Buddhist Śakra) and was employed by the Tantric master PADMASAMBHAVA to conquer the non-Buddhist deities of Tibet. Like the diamond, the *vajra* destroys but is itself indestructible and is thus likened to *śūnya* (that is, the all-inclusive void).

In ritual use the *vajra* is frequently employed in conjunction with the bell (Sanskrit *ghaṇṭā*; Tibetan *dril bu*). The various gestures (MUDRĀS), when correctly executed, are believed to have considerable metaphysical power; the *vajra* (symbolizing the male principle, fitness of action) is held in the right hand and the bell (symbolizing the female principle, intelligence) in the left hand, the interaction of the two ultimately leading to enlightenment. In art the *vajra* is an attribute of many divinities, such as the celestial Buddha AKṢOBHYA and his manifestation as VAJRAPĀṆI (In Whose Hand Is the *Vajra*). The *vajra* is the symbol of the VAJRAYĀNA school of BUDDHISM. The *viśva-vajra* is a double *vajra*.

Vajra
By courtesy of the Newark Museum, New Jersey

VAJRABODHI \\ˌvəj-rə-'bō-dē\\, Indian Buddhist monk who helped transmit BUDDHISM to China. Vajrabodhi and his disciple AMOGHAVAJRA arrived in China in 720, where they produced two abridged translations of the *Sarvatathagatatattvasamgraha* ("Symposium of Truth of All the Buddhas"), also known as the *Tattvasamgraha*. This work and the *Mahāvairocana Sūtra* became the two basic Chen-yen texts.

VAJRAPĀṆI \ˌvəj-rə-ˈpä-nē\ (Sanskrit: "Thunderbolt-Bearer"), in Buddhist mythology, one of the great celestial BODHISATTVAS of the MAHĀYĀNA and Esoteric (VAJRAYĀNA) traditions. Vajrapāṇi first appears as one of the two attendants of the BUDDHA GOTAMA, probably as a replacement for INDRA who seems to have played this role at an earlier date. Later, in the Esoteric, or Tantric, tradition, he emerged as the bodhisattva who headed one of the three major Buddha "families" that were recognized. His "family" consisted of fierce deities he was able to control through the use of his VAJRA (thunderbolt).

VAJRAYĀNA \ˌvəj-rə-ˈyä-nə\ (Sanskrit: "Vehicle of the Diamond" [or "Thunderbolt"]), a form of Esoteric (Tantric) BUDDHISM that emerged in India in the 1st millennium CE. This form of Esoteric Buddhism developed rapidly in India and subsequently spread to Tibet, where it has remained the dominant tradition in TIBETAN BUDDHISM.

Vajrayāna Buddhists extended MAHĀYĀNA Buddhology by recognizing new buddhas, BODHISATTVAS, and related figures, including many who exhibited a fierceness not previously associated with members of the Buddhist pantheon, as well as a significant number who were feminine. Vajrayāna teachers also extended Mahāyāna doctrine by placing a special emphasis on the notion that Enlightenment arises from the realization that seemingly opposite principles are in truth one. The passive concepts *śūnyatā* ("voidness") and *prajñā* ("wisdom"), for example, must be resolved with the active *karuṇā* ("compassion") and *upāya* ("means"). This fundamental polarity in the world, and its resolution, as well, are often expressed through symbols of sexuality.

The most crucial Vajrayāna innovations occurred at the level of practice. The distinctive genre of Vajrayāna texts (the TANTRAS), and the ORAL TRADITIONS associated with them, focus very strongly on matters of ritual practice and correlated meditative techniques. These practices and techniques involved use of MANTRAS (sacred sounds, syllables, or phrases), the widespread deployment of visual or iconographic symbols (including sacred MANDALAS depicting various configurations of the Buddhic cosmos) and—in some relatively rare cases—yogically-disciplined sexual activities. The Vajrayānists believed that these practices and techniques could lead, even in this life, to the attainment of Buddhahood itself.

VÄKI \ˈva-kē\, supernatural power believed by the Baltic Finns to reside in various natural sites, objects, and animals. *Väki* was often conceived of as an impersonal power, but it also referred to the agents of the power, diffuse spiritual entities that frequent natural sites or man-made places, such as cemeteries or other religious locales. People with special gifts were able to see the individual entities that constituted what was generally conceived as a vague impersonal power.

Vajrapāṇi, bronze statuette from Nepal, 19th century
By courtesy of the Rijksmuseum voor Volkenkunde, Leiden, The Netherlands

VALENTINE, SAINT \ˈva-lən-ˌtīn\ (d. 3rd century, Rome; feast day February 14), name of two legendary martyrs whose lives seem to be historically based. One was a Roman priest and physician who suffered martyrdom during the persecution of Christians by the emperor Claudius II Gothicus and was buried on the Via Flaminia. Pope St. Julius I reportedly built a BASILICA over his grave. The other, bishop of Terni, Italy, was martyred, apparently also in Rome, and his relics were later taken to Terni. St. Valentine's Day as a lovers' festival dates at least from the 14th century.

VALENTINUS \ˌva-lən-ˈtī-nəs\ (fl. 2nd century CE), Egyptian religious philosopher, founder of a Roman and Alexandrian GNOSTIC school. Valentinian communities, founded by his disciples, provided the major challenge to 2nd- and 3rd-century Christian theology.

Valentinus studied philosophy at Alexandria, was said to have been educated by Theodas, a pupil of ST. PAUL, and was baptized a Christian. According to documentary fragments of 2nd- and 3rd-century theologians, Valentinus moved to Rome about 136 and for some 25 years expounded his synthesis of Christian and Near Eastern Gnostic teaching. Aspiring to be bishop of Rome, he left the Christian community when he was passed over for that office around 140 CE.

On abandoning Rome about 160 for Cyprus, and possibly Alexandria, Valentinus continued to develop his system of religious philosophy. He is the reputed author of the *Gospel of Truth*, which achieved a fusion of Christian Pauline theology with Gnostic principles. The Valentinian system developed into Eastern and Western forms, although the earlier structure was similar to Pauline mystical theology, with its emphasis on the instrumentality of Christ's death and RESURRECTION in effecting salvation. Valentinian doctrine had a notable influence on the later rise of anthropocentric modes of Christian spirituality, leaving traces in every era of the church down to the present, culminating in the emergence of a Western prototype, PELAGIANISM.

VALHALLA \val-ˈha-lə, väl-ˈhä-\, *Old Norse* Valhöll \ˈväl-ˌhœl\, in GERMANIC RELIGION, hall of slain warriors, who live blissfully under the leadership of the god ODIN. Valhalla is depicted as a splendid palace, roofed with shields, where the warriors feast on the flesh of a boar slaughtered daily and made whole again each evening. They drink mead that flows from the udders of a goat, and their sport is to fight one another every day, with the slain being revived in the evening. Thus they will live until the RAGNARÖK, when they will march out the 540 doors of the palace to fight at the side of Odin against the GIANTS.

VALKYRIE \val-ˈkir-ē, -ˈkī-rē; ˈval-kə-rē\, *also spelled* Walkyrie \väl-ˈkir-ē, -ˈkī-rē; ˈväl-kə-rē\, *Old Norse* Valkyrja ("Chooser of the Slain"), in GERMANIC RELIGION, any of a group of maidens who were sent by the god ODIN to the battlefields to choose the slain who were worthy of a place in VALHALLA. They rode to the battlefield on horses, wearing helmets and shields; in some accounts, they flew through the air and sea. Some Valkyries had the power to cause the death of the warriors they did not favor; others guarded the lives and ships of those dear to them. They were associated with fairness, brightness, and gold, as well as bloodshed.

VALLABHA \'vəl-ləb, -lə-bə\, *also called* Vallabhācārya \'vəl-lə-ˌbä-'chär-yə\ (b. 1479?, Caudānagar, near Raichur, Madhya Pradesh, India—d. 1531, Banaras), Hindu philosopher and founder of the important and influential devotional sect, the Vallabha SAMPRADĀYA, also known as the *puṣṭimārga* ("the way of flourishing"). Vallabha's sect propagated the doctrine of BHAKTI (devotion) to KRISHNA.

Born to a Telegu Brahmin family, Vallabha initiated his first disciple in 1494 at Gokul, across the JAMUNĀ River from Mathura, upon receiving a revelation of Krishna. Nearby Govardhan, the sacred mountain of Braj, became the center of his activities; Krishna's manifestation in an image as lord of the mountain (Govardhannāthjī) is said to have coincided exactly with Vallabha's own birth. With funding from a wealthy merchant, Vallabha constructed a new temple to Govardhannāthjī (Śrī Nāthjī for short), which housed the life-size image until it fled the advances of the Mughal emperor Aurangzeb in 1669. Śrī Nāthjī eventually was resettled in NATHDVARA, near Udaipur, western Rajasthan, which is the present headquarters of the sect. A strong basis in the merchant communities of north and west India continues to serve as its backbone; lineal descendents of Vallabha are the GURUS in its several *baiṭhak*s or *gaddī*s ("seats").

Vallabha's theological system is called śuddhādvaita ("pure nondualism"), and is notable for its thoroughgoing ("pure") affirmation of the phenomenal world, which it regards as an emanation and expression—although in veiled form—of Krishna himself. Hence God is never to be worshiped by renunciation or self-deprivation, but by regarding every aspect of this world, including one's physical substance, as Krishna's gracious gift. The community's ritual life bears this out, with punctilious attention to regular offerings of music, decoration, and cuisine and a proscribing of anything unjoyful, which would show ingratitude for the Lord's bounty. It finds ritual expression not just in the eschewing of any monastic order as part of the sect but in the insistence that

Vāmana, stone relief from Bādāmi Cave II, Karnataka state, India
By courtesy of the Archaeological Survey of India, New Delhi

each Vallabhite temple is a *havelī*, a part of the home of one of Vallabha's descendents and therefore a feature of his family life. As initiates, all members of the *sampradāya* belong to that family. Similarly, home worship is the community's main ritual focus.

Vallabha was married and had two sons, though surprisingly he became a SANNYĀSĪ (ascetic) shortly before his death. His son Viṭṭhala succeeded him as head of the sect and was probably its organizational genius, even more so than his father.

VĀMANA \'vä-mə-nə\, fifth of the 10 AVATARS of the Hindu god VISHNU. He made his appearance when the DEMON king Bali ruled the entire universe and the gods had lost their power. One day the dwarf Vāmana visited the court of Bali and begged of him as much land as he could step over in three paces. The king laughingly granted the request. Vāmana with one step covered the whole earth, and with the second step the midworld between earth and heaven. As there was nowhere left to go, the demon king lowered his head and suggested Vāmana place his foot on it for the promised third step. Vāmana was pleased, and with the pressure of his foot sent Bali down below to rule the netherworld.

VAMSA \'vəm-sə\, particular class of Buddhist literature that in many ways resembles conventional Western histories. The word *vaṃsa* means "lineage," or "family," but when it is used to refer to a particular class of narratives it can be translated as "chronicle," or "history." These texts, which may be ecclesiastically oriented, dynastically oriented, or both at the same time, usually either relate the lineage of a particular individual, king, or family or describe in concrete terms the history of a particular object, region, place, or thing.

Three of the most famous *vaṃsa*s in the South Asian context are the *Buddhavaṃsa*, *Dipavaṃsa*, and *Mahāvaṃsa*. The *Buddhavaṃsa* provides an account of the lineage of 24 buddhas who preceded the historical Buddha, Gotama. The *Dipavaṃsa* primarily chronicles the history of the island of Ceylon (Sri Lanka) from the time of the BUDDHA GOTAMA until the end of the reign of Mahāsena (4th century CE). The *Mahāvaṃsa*, attributed to Mahānāma, is also a history of Ceylon, but it is composed in a more refined and polished style, and it includes more details than the *Dipavaṃsa*.

Some *vaṃsa*s are devoted to chronicling particular objects or places of note in Buddhist history. The *Dā-*

thāvaṃsa, for example, tells the history of the Buddha's tooth relic until it reached Ceylon in the 9th century CE. The *Thūpavaṃsa*, dating from the 13th century, purports to be an account of the history and construction of the great STUPA in Ceylon during the reign of King Duṭṭagāmaṇi in the 1st century BCE. The *Sāsanavaṃsa*, compiled in the 19th century, is a Burmese text of ecclesiastical orientation that charts the history of central India up to the time of the third Buddhist council and then provides an account of the missionary activities of monks in other countries. The *Sangītivaṃsa*, an 18th-century text from Thailand, combines many of these themes, since it gives an account of the Buddha lineage; presents a history of BUDDHISM in India, Sri Lanka, and, especially, Thailand; and provides an account of the decline of the Buddhist age.

VANIR \\'vä-nir\\, in GERMANIC RELIGION, race of gods responsible for wealth, fertility, and commerce and subordinate to the warlike AESIR. As reparation for the torture of their goddess Gullveig, the Vanir demanded from the Aesir monetary satisfaction or equal status. Declaring war instead, the Aesir suffered numerous defeats before granting equality. The Vanir sent their gods NJÖRD and FREY to live with the Aesir and received Hoenir and MIMIR in exchange. The birth of the poet-god KVASIR resulted from the peace ritual in which the two races mingled their saliva in the same vessel. Only three Vanir are known, namely Njörd, the god of the wealth of the sea, and his children Frey and FREYJA.

Varāha, stone sculpture from Jhālrapātan, Rājasthān, India, c. 10th century CE; in Jhālawār Archaeology Museum, India
Pramod Chandra

VARĀHA \\və-'rä-hə\\, third of the 10 AVATARS of the Hindu god VISHNU. When the DEMON Hiraṇyākṣa dragged the earth to the bottom of the sea, Vishnu took the form of Varāha, a boar, in order to rescue it. Varāha and Hiraṇyākṣa fought for a thousand years. Varāha slew the demon and raised the earth out of the water with his tusks. The myth reflects an earlier creation legend of PRAJĀPATI, who assumed the shape of a boar to lift the earth up out of the primeval waters.

VARANASI (VĀRĀNASĪ) \\vä-'rä-nə-sē, ,vär-ä-'nə-sē\\, *also called* Banaras, Benares \\bə-'när-əs\\, *or* Kāśī \\'kä-shē\\, city, southeastern Uttar Pradesh state, northern India. It is located on the left bank of the GAṄGĀ RIVER (Ganges River) and is one of the seven sacred cities of the Hindus.

Varanasi is one of the oldest continuously inhabited cities in the world, and was already an important center of re-

The widow's ghāṭ on the Gaṅgā river, at Varanasi, India
J. Allan Cash—Rapho/Photo Researchers

ligious learning when the BUDDHA GOTAMA (6th century BCE) came there to preach his first sermon at nearby Sarnath. The city remained a center of religious, educational, and artistic activities as attested by the celebrated Chinese traveler HSÜAN-TSANG, who visited it in about 635 CE. Many of Varanasi's temples were destroyed—sometimes more than once—during the period of Muslim domination that began with the establishment of the Delhi Sultanate in 1206, with the result that no major religious structure survives intact from a period before the rule of the Mughal emperor Aurangzeb in the 17th century. By the same token, however, Varanasi's significant Muslim presence has contributed greatly to its religious landscape. In the late 17th century, with the dissolution of the Mughal empire, Varanasi became the seat of an independent Hindu kingdom. It lasted until British annexation in 1794, when a new period of interreligious ferment—this time with Christian missionaries—began.

Many of the foci of religious life in modern-day Varanasi, including the temples of Viśvanāth ("Lord of the World," *i.e.*, SHIVA) and the goddess Annapūrṇā, which are at the heart of the city, date to the period of 18th century reconstruction, financed especially by MARĀṬHĀ commercial interests. Others, such as the Tulsī Mānas temple that honors the 16th–17th-century saint TULSĪDĀS and his RĀMCARITMĀNAS, are- 20th-century creations. At Sarnath, a few miles north of Varanasi, there are ruins of ancient Buddhist monasteries, as well as temples built by the MAHABODHI SOCIETY, headquartered in Sri Lanka, and by Japanese, Burmese, and Tibetan Buddhists. Varanasi has perhaps the finest river frontage in India, with miles of *ghāt*s, or steps, for religious bathing; an array of shrines, temples, and palaces rises tier on tier from the water's edge. The sacred city is bounded by a circumambulatory road known as Pañcakośī; many Hindus hope to walk this road and to visit the city once in a lifetime. Some also hope to die there in old age, for it is said that to die in Varanasi is to gain instant access to liberation (MOKṢA). This follows from the city's reputation as being the living emblem (LIṄGA) of Shiva, connecting this plane of existence with the beyond, and from its position on the Gaṅgā, which is believed to have eternally purifying powers. Similarly, unlike any other city, Varanasi positions its most important CREMATION ground, Manikarnikā Ghāṭ, at the very center of its riverfront rather than exiling it to the periphery of urban settlement. More than one million pilgrims visit Varanasi each year.

VARṆA \ˈvər-nə, ˈvär-\, any one of the four traditional social classes of Hindu India. Although the literal meaning of the word (Sanskrit: "color") suggests that class distinctions were originally based on differences in degree of skin pigmentation, and though this might have been true between the fairer-skinned ARYANS and the darker indigenous populations of ancient India, the notion of "color" may be regarded as a device of classification.

The ṚG VEDA hymn 10.90 declares that the BRAHMIN, the KṢATRIYA, the VAIŚYA, and the ŚŪDRA issued forth at creation from the mouth, arms, thighs, and feet of the primeval person (*puruṣa*), respectively. The Śūdras, surely representing the indigenous non-Aryan population, live in servitude to the other three, who are "twice-born" (DVIJA) after undergoing the ceremony of spiritual rebirth (UPANAYANA) that initiates them into manhood. The Vaiśyas, in turn, contrast as commoners with the governing classes—*i.e.*, the secular Kṣatriyas and the sacerdotal Brahmins. Brahmins and Kṣatriyas themselves contrast in that the former are their priests, while the latter have actual political dominion.

Within their system of the four classes (*cāturvarṇya*), the traditional lawgivers specified a different set of obligations for each: the task of the Brahmin is to study and advise, the Kṣatriya to protect, the Vaiśya to cultivate, and the Śūdra to serve. History shows, however, that the four-class system was more a social model than a reality. A move to accommodate still others not so distinguished led to the rather unofficial construction of yet a fifth class, the *pañcama* (Sanskrit: "fifth"), which include the "untouchable" (*aspṛṣṭa*) classes and others, such as tribal groups, who are outside the system and, consequently, *avarṇa* ("classless").

In modern times, individual CASTES have sought to raise their social rank by identifying with a particular *varṇa* and demanding its privileges of rank and honor.

VARUṆA \ˈvə-rū-nə\, in the Vedic phase of HINDUISM, the god-sovereign, the personification of divine authority. He is the ruler of the sky realm and the upholder of cosmic and moral law (*ṛta*), a duty shared with the group of gods known as the Ādityas, of whom he was the chief. He is often jointly invoked with MITRA, who represents the more juridical side of their sovereignty, or the alliance between humans, while Varuṇa represents the relationship between human and divine. In later Hinduism, Varuṇa plays a lesser role. He is guardian of the west and is particularly associated with oceans and waters. Thus he is often attended by the river goddesses GAṄGĀ and JAMUNĀ.

VASSA \ˈvə-sə\ (Pāli: "rains"), the Buddhist monastic retreat observed primarily in communities in Southeast Asia

during the three-month monsoon period each year. The tradition that monks—who ordinarily would be MENDICANT wanderers—gather in monasteries during the rainy season for a time of study and religious discourse may derive from the ancient custom among South Asian ascetics of retreating to a forest grove, usually near a village, during the monsoon when travel was difficult. Residing in their retreat during the rains, they continued to pursue their meditative quest and begged alms from local townspeople. The practice was well known in India by the time of the BUDDHA GOTAMA (6th century BCE), who after his enlightenment is said to have spent the rainy season in a sheltered spot in the forest near VARANASI.

The Buddha's followers assumed the same practice and after his death continued to gather during the monsoon to recite the rules of Buddhist discipline and to reaffirm their commitment to the Buddha's vision of DHARMA. As the monastic community (SANGHA) became wealthier, more permanent meditation and study centers, or VIHARAS, were constructed. With the ascendency of the powerful Mauryan king AŚOKA (3rd century BCE), who admired and followed the Buddha's teachings, these *vihara*s flourished throughout northeast India. The *vihara*s are the institutional precursors of both the great Buddhist monastic centers, or MAHĀVIHĀRAS, of South and Southeast Asia and of the custom of the annual religious retreat still practiced in THERAVĀDA Buddhist countries today. The *vassa* has been largely forgotten by MAHĀYĀNA Buddhists, especially those in China and Japan.

In Thailand, where all Buddhist males customarily spend some time in a monastery, *vassa* is a favored period for temporarily experiencing the life of a monk. Seniority as a monk is commonly measured by the number of *vassa* seasons spent in a monastery.

VASUBANDHU \ˈvə-sü-ˈbən-dü\ (fl. 4th/5th century CE), Indian Buddhist philosopher and logician, younger brother of the philosopher ASAṄGA. His conversion from the SARVĀSTIVĀDA to the MAHĀYĀNA Buddhist tradition is attributed to Asaṅga. Vasubandhu refined classical Indian syllogistic logic and wrote several *śāstra*s ("treatises") holding that all seemingly external objects are only mental representations. He is also reputed to be the author of the *Abhidharmakośa*, a systematization of Sarvāstivāda doctrine written before his conversion.

VĀSUDEVA \ˈvä-sü-ˈdā-və\, in HINDUISM, the patronymic of KRISHNA, who, according to one tradition, was a son of Vāsudeva. The worshipers of Vāsudeva, or Krishna, formed one of the earliest theistic devotional movements within Hinduism. When they merged with other groups, namely the BHĀGAVATA, they represented the beginnings of modern VAIṢṆAVISM. Even though in the earliest parts of the MAHĀBHĀRATA the divinity of Krishna appears to be still open to doubt, by the time of the writing of the *Bhagavad Gītā* (1st–2nd century CE), Vāsudeva-Krishna was clearly identified with the god VISHNU.

VATICAN COUNCIL, FIRST \ˈva-ti-kən\, 20th ecumenical council of the ROMAN CATHOLIC church (1869–70), convoked by POPE PIUS IX. The council, which was never formally dissolved, promulgated two doctrinal constitutions: *Dei Filius*, a greatly shortened version of the schema on Roman Catholic faith, which deals with faith, reason, and their interrelations; and *Pastor Aeternus*, which deals with the authority of the POPE.

The statement on the pope's authority was approved only after long and heated debate both preceding and during the council. The decree states that the true successor of ST. PETER has full and supreme power of jurisdiction over the whole church; that he has the right of free communication with the pastors of the whole church and with their flocks; and that his primacy includes the supreme teaching power to which JESUS CHRIST added the prerogative of infallibility, whereby the pope is preserved free from error when he teaches definitively that a doctrine concerning faith or morals is to be believed by the whole church. The original schema had not included a statement of PAPAL INFALLIBILITY, but the majority of the council fathers, urged on by Pius IX, overrode vociferous opposition from those who argued that a formal definition was inopportune and gave their approval to the dogmatic definition.

VATICAN COUNCIL, SECOND, 21st ecumenical council of the ROMAN CATHOLIC church (1962–65), announced by POPE JOHN XXIII on Jan. 25, 1959. In opening the council on Oct. 11, 1962, the pope advised the council fathers to try to meet the pastoral needs of the church. Invited to the council sessions, but without the right to vote, were a number of observers from the major Christian churches and communities separated from Rome and a number of Catholics called auditors.

Preliminary work had been done by members of the Curia (the papal bureaucracy) on preparatory commissions; once the council had been opened, however, council fathers from diverse parts of the world were added to the commissions. The revised decrees that grew out of the council discussions and the work of the enlarged commissions tended to have a more progressive viewpoint. The work of the council continued under Pope John's successor, Paul VI, and sessions were convened each autumn until the work of the council was completed on Dec. 8, 1965. Sixteen documents were enacted by the council fathers.

The "Dogmatic Constitution on the Church" reflects the attempt of the council fathers to utilize biblical terms rather than juridical categories to describe the church. The treatment of the hierarchical structure of the church counterbalances somewhat the monarchical emphasis of the first Vatican Council's teaching on the PAPACY by giving weight to the role of the bishops. The teaching of the constitution on the nature of the laity (those not in holy orders) was intended to provide the basis for the call of lay people to holiness and to share in the missionary vocation of the church.

The "Dogmatic Constitution on Divine Revelation" attempts to relate the role of SCRIPTURE and tradition (the postbiblical teaching of the church) to their common origin in the Word of God that has been committed to the church. The document affirms the value of Scripture for the salvation of men while maintaining an open attitude toward the scholarly study of the BIBLE.

The "Constitution on the Sacred Liturgy" establishes the principle of greater participation by the laity in the celebration of MASS and authorizes significant changes in the texts, forms, and language used in the celebration of mass and the administration of the SACRAMENTS.

The "Pastoral Constitution on the Church in the World of Today" acknowledges the profound changes humanity is experiencing and attempts to relate the church's concept of itself and of revelation to the needs of modern culture.

The council also promulgated decrees (documents on practical questions) on the pastoral duties of bishops, ECU-MENISM, the Eastern-rite churches, the ministry and life of priests, the education for the PRIESTHOOD, the religious life, the missionary activity of the church, the apostolate of the laity, and the media of social communication. Furthermore, declarations (documents on particular issues) on religious freedom, the church's attitude toward non-Christian religions, and on Christian education were produced. These documents reflected the renewal in various areas of church life begun decades before Pope John—biblical, ecumenical, liturgical, lay apostolate.

VĀTSĪPUTRĪYA: *see* PUDGALAVĀDIN.

VAYU \'vä-yü\, ancient Iranian wind-god, likely related to the Hindu god Vāyu; he was also connected with battle as an AVATAR of the war-god Vrthraghna. Also connected with fate, he was believed to have a beneficient and a baleful aspect. As part of an ancient pantheon Vayu appears to have been eclipsed following Zoroaster's reforms but re-emerged in the later AVESTA (*see* ZOROASTRIANISM AND PARSIISM).

VEDA \'vā-də\, sacred hymn or verse composed in archaic Sanskrit and current among the Indo–European-speaking peoples who entered India from the Iranian regions. No definite date can be ascribed to the composition of the Vedas, but the period of about 1500–1200 BCE would be acceptable to most scholars. The hymns formed a liturgical body that in part grew up around the cult of the SOMA ritual and the sacrifice. They extolled the hereditary deities, who for the most part personified various natural and cosmic phenomena, such as fire (AGNI), sun (SŪRYA and Savitṛ), dawn (Uṣas), storms (the RUDRAS), war and rain (INDRA), honor (MITRA), divine authority (VARUṆA), and creation (Indra, with some aid of VISHNU). Hymns were composed to these deities, and many were recited or chanted during rituals. The whole of the literature seems to have been preserved orally.

The foremost collection, or Saṃhitā, of such hymns, from which the *hotṛ* (chief priest) drew the material for his recitations, is the ṚG VEDA. Sacred formulas known as MANTRAS were recited by the priest responsible for the sacrificial fire and the carrying out of the ceremony; these mantras and verses in time were drawn in Saṃhitās known collectively as Yajurveda. A third group of priests, headed by the *udgātṛ* ("chanter"), performed melodic recitations linked to verses that, although drawn almost entirely from the Ṛg Veda, came to be arranged as a separate Saṃhitā, the SĀMA VEDA ("Veda of the Chants"). To these three Vedas—Ṛg, Yajur, and Sāma, known as the *trayī-vidyā* ("threefold knowledge")—is added a fourth, the ATHARVA VEDA, a collection of hymns, magic SPELLS, medical cures and prescriptions, and incantations that represents religion at the popular level and remains partly outside the Vedic sacrifice.

The entire corpus of Vedic literature—the Saṃhitās and the expositions that came to be attached to them, the BRĀHMAṆAS, the ĀRAṆYAKAS, and the UPANISHADS—was considered ŚRUTI, the product of divine revelation.

VEDĀNTA \vā-'dän-tə\, one of the six orthodox systems (DARŚANS) of Indian philosophy and the one that forms the basis of most modern schools of HINDUISM. The term means the "conclusion" (*anta*) of the Vedas; it applies to the UPANISHADS and to the school that arose out of the "study" (*mīmāṃsā*) of the Upanishads. Thus Vedānta is also referred to as Vedānta-Mīmāṃsā ("Reflection on Vedānta"), Uttara-Mīmāṃsā ("Reflection on the Latter Part of the Vedas"), and Brahma-Mīmāṃsā ("Reflection on Brahman").

The three fundamental Vedāntic texts are: the Upanishads; the *Brahma* SŪTRAS (also called *Vedānta Sūtras*), which are very brief, even one-word interpretations of the doctrine of the Upanishads; and the BHAGAVAD GĪTĀ, which, because of its immense popularity, was drawn upon for support of the doctrines found in the Upanishads.

Several schools of Vedānta developed, differentiated by their conceptions of the nature of the relationship and the degree of identity between the individual self (ĀTMAN) and the absolute (BRAHMAN). These range from the nondualism (ADVAITA) of the 8th-century philosopher ŚAṂKARA to the THEISM (VIŚIṢṬĀDVAITA) of the 11th–12th-century thinker RĀMĀNUJA and the DUALISM (DVAITA) of the 13th-century thinker MADHVA.

The Vedāntic schools do, however, hold in common a number of beliefs: transmigration of the self (SAṂSĀRA) and the desirability of release from the cycle of rebirths; the authority of the VEDA on the means of release; that Brahman is both the material (*upādāna*) and the instrumental (*nimitta*) cause of the world; and that the self (*ātman*) is the agent of its own acts (KARMA) and therefore the recipient of the fruits, or consequences, of action (*phala*).

VEDĀNTADEŚIKA \vā-'dän-tə-'dā-shi-kə\, *also called* Veṅkaṭanātha (b. 1268, Tuppule, near Kāñchipuram, Vijayanagar, India—d. 1370, Śrīrangam), leading theologian of the VIŚIṢṬĀDVAITA school of philosophy and founder of the Vaṭakalai, a subset of the Śrīvaiṣṇavas, a religious movement of South India.

Vedāntadeśika was born into a distinguished Śrī Vaiṣṇava family that followed the teachings of RĀMĀNUJA. He married and had a family but lived on alms in order to devote himself fully to his philosophic and literary efforts. He was a prolific writer in Sanskrit, Prākrit, and Tamil; his more than 100 works include commentaries on Vaiṣṇava scriptures; *Nyāya-pariśuddhi*, a comprehensive work on Viśiṣṭādvaita logic; *Yādavābhyudaya*, a poetic work on the life of Krishna; *Saṃkalpa-sūryodaya*, an allegorical drama; and devotional hymns.

According to Vedāntadeśika's interpretation of PRAPATTI (surrender to the GRACE of God), some effort is required on the part of the worshiper to secure God's grace, just as the baby monkey must cling to its mother (the *markaṭa-nyāya*, or "monkey logic"). This view—together with ritual and linguistic differences—became the basis for the split between the two subsects, the Vaṭakalai and the Teṅkalai, who held that God's grace is unconditional and that the human soul is as unassertive as a kitten carried by its mother.

VED-AVA \'vä-dä-vä\, among the Mordvins of Russia, spirit believed to rule the waters and their bounty; she is known as Vete-ema among the Estonians and Veen emo among the Finns. Fishermen sacrificed to Ved-ava as a personification of their concerns, giving her the first of their catch and observing numerous prohibitions while fishing; she was also responsible for promoting fertility. In appearance Ved-ava resembled a mermaid: she had long hair that she combed while seated on a stone, large breasts, and a fishlike lower body. She could often be seen or heard playing music to entice people, but seeing Ved-ava generally boded misfortune, most often drowning. Ved-ava has also been thought of as the spirit of a drowned person or, at other times, simply as a personification of the water itself.

VEDIC CHANT \'vä-dik\, Hindu religious chant, the expression of hymns from the VEDAS. The practice dates back

at least 3,000 years and is probably the world's oldest continuous vocal tradition. The earliest collection, or Saṃhitā, of Vedic texts is the ṚG VEDA, containing 1,028 hymns. These are chanted in syllabic style—a type of heightened speech with one syllable to a tone. Three levels of pitch are employed: a basic reciting tone is embellished by neighboring tones above and below, which are used to emphasize grammatical accents in the texts. The Ṛg Veda hymns are the basis for a later collection, the Sāmaveda ("Veda of the Chants"), the hymns of which are sung in a style that is more florid, melodic, and melismatic (one word to two or more notes) rather than syllabic, and the range of tones is extended to six or more.

VEDIC RELIGION, *also called* Vedism \'vā-,di-zəm\, the religion of the ancient Indo-European-speaking peoples who entered India about 1500 BCE from the region of present-day Iran; it takes its name from the collections of sacred texts known as the VEDAS. The Vedas provide at present our only textual resource for understanding the religious life of ancient India. Though it is impossible to say when Vedism eventually gave way to "classical" HINDUISM with its characteristic pantheon (*e.g.*, VISHNU, SHIVA, DURGĀ) and practices (*e.g.*, PŪJĀ), a decrease in literary activity among the Vedic schools from the 5th century BCE onward can be observed, and about this time texts of a specifically Hindu character began to appear.

Vedic texts. The only extant Vedic materials are the Vedas, composed and compiled from about the 15th to the 5th century BCE. The language of the Vedas is an archaic Sanskrit. The oldest and most important texts are the four collections (Saṃhitā) that we call the Veda, or Vedas. The ṚG VEDA, or "Veda of Verses," the earliest of these, is composed of about 1,000 hymns mostly arranged to serve the needs of priestly families. The YAJUR VEDA, or "Veda of Sacrificial Formulas," contains prose formulas and verses applicable to various cultic rites. The SĀMA VEDA, or "Veda of Chants" is made up of a selection of verses (drawn almost wholly from the Ṛg Veda) and musical notation intended as an aid to the performance of sacred songs. Finally, the ATHARVA VEDA is less sophisticated and more heterogeneous in character, containing prayers and SPELLS for health and social well-being, some specifically addressing the needs of rulers.

To each Veda is attached a body of prose writings of later date called BRĀHMAṆAS (*c.* 800–600 BCE), which are intended to explain the ceremonial applications of the texts. Further appendices, the *Āraṇyaka*s (*c.* 600 BCE) and the UPANISHADS (*c.* 700–500 BCE), respectively expound the symbolism of the more difficult rites and speculate on the nature of the universe and the human relation to it.

When Vedic religion gradually developed into Hinduism between the 6th and 2nd centuries BCE, these texts were exalted as the most sacred literature of Hinduism. They are known as ŚRUTI, or the divinely revealed section of Hindu literature, in contrast to religious literature known as SMṚTI, texts based on human memory.

Mythology and ritual. The complex Vedic ceremonies, for which the hymns of the Ṛg Veda were composed, centered on the ritual sacrifice of animals and with the pressing and drinking of a sacred intoxicating liquor called SOMA. The basic Vedic rite was performed by offering these edibles to a sacred fire, and this fire, which was itself deified as AGNI, carried the oblations to the gods of the Vedic pantheon. The god of highest rank was INDRA, a warlike god who conquered innumerable human and DEMON enemies and vanquished the sun. Along with VARUṆA, the upholder of the cosmic and moral laws, Vedism had many other lesser deities, among whom were gods, DEMIGODS, and demons.

The rites of Vedic sacrifice were relatively simple in the early period, when the Ṛg Veda was composed. Every sacrifice was performed on behalf of an individual, the *yajamāna* ("sacrificer"), who bore the expenses. The altar (*vedi*) was a quadrangle marked out by hollowing or slightly raising the ground. The *agnyādheya* ("installation of the fire") was a necessary preliminary to all the large public rituals and was preceded by the patron's fast. Domestic (*gṛhya*) rites were observed by the householder himself or with the help of a single priest and were performed over the domestic hearth fire. Some occurred daily or monthly, and others accompanied a particular event, such as the SAMSKĀRAS. The grand rites (*śrauta*, or *vaitānika*) performed in public, lasted several days or months and required the services of many priests. Most characteristic of the public ceremonies was the *soma* sacrifice, which ensured the prosperity and well-being of both humans and gods. Animal sacrifice—the killing of a ram—existed either independently or as an integral part of the sacrifice of *soma*. The celebrated AŚVAMEDHA, or "horse-sacrifice," was an elaborate variant of the *soma* sacrifice.

Development and decline. Over the centuries, the Vedic rites grew so complex and were governed by so many rules that only highly trained Brahmins and priests could carry them out correctly. In reaction against this trend (as well as the growing power of the Brahmins), Vedic thought in its late period became more speculative and philosophical in approach. In the *Āraṇyaka*s, Vedic ritual is interpreted in a symbolic rather than a literal manner, and the Upanishads question the very assumptions on which Vedism rested. From this emerged the idea of BRAHMAN, an emcompassing cosmic principle in which each individual entity participates by virtue of its self (*ātman*). The equation of ĀTMAN (the self) with Brahman (ultimate reality) became the principal basis of Hindu metaphysics. The spread in the 8th to 5th centuries BCE of the related concepts of REINCARNATION, KARMA, and the attainment of release from this cycle by meditation rather than sacrifice marked the end of the Vedic period and the appearance of Hinduism.

The legacy of Vedic worship is apparent in several aspects of modern Hinduism. The Hindu rite of initiation (UPANAYANA) is a direct survival of Vedic tradition, while sacrifices performed according to Vedic rites continue to be performed occasionally. The idea of there being a pure Vedic period or strand in India's religious life—as distinguished from a broader, more vulgar range of subsequent or ancillary Hindu practice and belief—became a potent force in India in the 19th century (*see* ĀRYA SAMĀJ).

VEJOVIS \'wā-ˌyō-wis, 'vā-ˌyō-vis \, *also spelled* Vediovis, *or* Vedivs, in ROMAN RELIGION, a god worshiped at Rome between the two summits of the Capitoline Hill (the Arx and the Capitol) and on Tiber Island (both temples date from just after 200 BCE) and at Bovillae, 12 miles southeast of Rome. His name may be connected with that of JUPITER (Jovis): he may be a "little Jupiter" or a "sinister Jupiter" or "the opposite of Jupiter" (*i.e.*, a CHTHONIC, or Underworld, god). The last seems most likely, since his offering was a she-goat *humano ritu*; the term *humano ritu* has been defined both as on behalf of the dead and as a substitute for a HUMAN SACRIFICE.

VELNS \'valns \ (Latvian), *Lithuanian* Velnias \'vᵛel-nᵛäs \, in ancient SLAVIC RELIGIONS, the devil, who has a well-defined role, such as few other peoples have documented so well. Besides the usual outer features, several characteristics are especially emphasized. Velns, for instance, is a stupid devil. In addition, the Balts are the only colonialized people in Europe who have preserved a large amount of FOLKLORE that in different variations portrays the devil as a German landlord. Another evil being is the Latvian Vilkacis, Lithuanian Vilkatas, who corresponds to the werewolf in the traditions of other peoples. The belief that the dead do not leave this world completely is the basis for both good and evil spirits. As good spirits the dead return to the living as invisible beings (Latvian *velis*, Lithuanian *vele*), but as evil ones they return as persecutors and misleaders (Latvian *vadatajs*, Lithuanian *vaidilas*).

VENUS \'vē-nəs \, ancient Italian goddess associated with cultivated fields and gardens and later identified with the Greek goddess APHRODITE.

Venus had no worship in Rome in early times, as the scholar Marcus Terentius Varro (116–27 BCE) shows, attesting that he could find no mention of her name in the old records. This is corroborated by the absence of any festival for her in the oldest Roman calendar and by her lack of a FLAMEN (special priest). Her cult among the Latins, however, seems to be very old, for she had apparently at least two ancient temples, one at Lavinium, the other at Ardea, at which festivals of the Latin cities were held. How she came to be identified with so important a deity as Aphrodite remains a puzzle. The name *Venus* is grammatically a femine form of what most likely was originally a neuter abstract noun stem (**venes-*), meaning "charm, qualities exciting desire," and earlier "desire, wish." This root—as exemplified by the derivatives *venerari*, "to solicit the good will of (a deity) by propitiatory acts, worship," and *venenum*, "magic herb or potion"—seems to have linked the notions "desire" and "propitiatory magic to fulfill one's desire."

That Venus' identification with Aphrodite took place fairly early is certain. A contributory reason for it is perhaps the date (August 19) of the foundation of one of her Roman temples. August 19 is the Vinalia Rustica, a festival of Jupiter; hence, he and Venus came to be associated, and this facilitated their equation, as father and daughter, with the Greek deities Zeus and Aphrodite. She was, therefore, also a daughter of Dione, was the wife of Vulcan, and was the mother of Cupid. Like Aphrodite, she was famous in myth and legend for her romantic intrigues and affairs with both gods and mortals, and she became associated with many aspects, both positive and negative, of femininity. As Venus Verticordia, she was charged with the protection of chastity in women and girls. But the most important cause of the identification was the reception into Rome of the famous cult of Venus Erycina—*i.e.*, of Aphrodite of Eryx (Erice) in Sicily. This reception took place during and shortly after the Second Punic War. A temple was dedicated to Venus Erycina on the Capitol in 215 BCE and a second outside the Colline gate in 181 BCE. The latter developed in a way reminiscent of the temple at Eryx with its harlots, becoming the place of worship of Roman courtesans, hence the title of *dies meretricum* ("prostitutes' day") attached to April 23, the day of its foundation.

The *gens Iulia*, the clan of Julius Caesar and Augustus, claimed descent from Iulus, the son of AENEAS; Aeneas was the alleged founder of the temple of Eryx and, in some legends, of the city of Rome also. From the time of Homer onward, he was made the son of Aphrodite, so that his descent gave the Iulii divine origin. Julius Caesar dedicated a

The Birth of Venus, *oil on canvas by Sandro Botticelli, c. 1485; in the Uffizi, Florence*
Anderson—Alinari/Art Resource

temple (46 BCE) to Venus Genetrix, and as Genetrix ("Begetting Mother") she was best known until the death of Nero in 68 CE. But despite the extinction of the Julio-Claudian line, she remained popular, even with the emperors; Hadrian completed a temple of Venus at Rome in 135 CE.

As a native Italian deity, Venus had no myths of her own. She therefore took over those of Aphrodite and, through her, became identified with various foreign goddesses. The most noteworthy result of this development is perhaps the acquisition by the planet Venus of that name. The planet was at first the star of the Babylonian goddess Ishtar and thence of Aphrodite. Because of her association with love and with feminine beauty, the goddess Venus has been a favorite subject in art since ancient times; notable representations include the statue known as the *Venus de Milo* (c. 150 BCE) and the painting *The Birth of Venus*.

VENUS, in astronomy, second major planet from the sun. Named for the Roman goddess of love and beauty, it is, after the moon, the most brilliant natural object in the nighttime sky. Venus comes closer to the Earth than any other planet.

Venus is probably the celestial figure that has received the most extensive elaboration in the mythologies of the world. Before the Romans identified the planet with their goddess, the Mesopotamian civilizations personified the star as the goddess Inanna-Ishtar, viewed as a being sometimes female and at other times hermaphroditic. African cultures also have been significantly impressed by this planet, as can be seen in the figure of a Zulu heavenly goddess who determines the agricultural work of the women but even more as the evening and morning star, who are the wives of the moon. In the royal culture of Mwene Monomotapa (Rhodesia) and its influences in Buganda and southern Congo, the king is related to the moon, and his wedding with the Venus women is a type of HIEROS GAMOS (sacred marriage). In large areas of Africa the concept of "Venus wives of the moon" is preserved, although the moon is usually considered as the wife (or sister) of the sun.

the starry heaven. Because the deity is associated with the pillar supporting the heavens, he is also responsible for the continued maintenance of life. Veralden-radien is believed to support all growth. The goddess of childbirth, MADDERAK-KA, receives the souls of unborn children from him, while he takes the souls of the departed down to *yabme-aimo,* the Sami realm of the dead. He was also the object of a phallic cult; each autumn a bull reindeer was traditionally sacrificed to him, then its genitalia were tied around his statue and the blood smeared over the statue.

The worship of Veralden-radien has many Scandinavian features; he is often mentioned in connection with the Swedish deity FREY, and the Saxon world-supporting pillar Irminsul, which may have influenced some of the mythological concepts of the Sami.

VERETHRAGHNA \\,vər-ə-'thräg-nə, 'vər-ə-,thräg-\\, *also called* Bahrān, in ZOROASTRIANISM, spirit of victory. Together with MITHRA, Verethraghna shares martial characteristics that relate him to the Vedic war-god INDRA. In Zoroastrian texts, Verethraghna appears as an agent of Mithra and RASH-NU, the god of justice, and as the means of vengeance for Mithra in his capacity as god of war.

Verethraghna was an especially popular deity in Sāsānian Iran, where five kings bore his name. The 14th *yasht,* or hymn, of the AVESTA is dedicated to Verethraghna, and the 20th day of the month is named for him.

VESSANTARA \\ve-'sən-tə-rə\\, *also called* Viśvāntara \\vish-'vän-tə-rə\\, *or* Phra Wes \\'prä-'wes\\, in Buddhist mythology, a previous INCARNATION of the BUDDHA GOTAMA. A crown prince, Vessantara was famous for his vast generosity, and, to the despair of his more practical-minded father, he accepted banishment to the forest, where he attained the ultimate self-abnegation by giving away his children and his wife and in some accounts even his own eyes. These and all the rest were restored to him miraculously, and, responding to the demands of his countrymen, he returned home to become the best of kings. This tradition underscores the char-

This concept was most likely prevalent at a time when the moon-king ideology was widespread in the eastern half of Africa from the Nile to South Africa.

The ancient Mayan civilization of the Americas had a highly developed astronomical tradition, in which the planet Venus figures prominently. The DRESDEN CODEX contains very precise Venusian and lunar tables and a method of predicting solar eclipses. The duration of the solar year had been calculated with amazing accuracy, as well as the synodical revolution of Venus.

VERALDEN-RADIEN \\'ve-ä-,räl-dän-'rä-dē-en\\, *also called* Veralden-Olmai \\-'ōl-,mī\\ (Sami: "Ruler of the World"), the deity believed by the Sami (Lapps) to be closest to

acteristic Buddhist combination of the ideals of universal kingship and universal religious preeminence.

An integral part of the harvest celebrations in many Buddhist countries is the sacred performance of an episode in the life of a buddha or a BODHISATTVA. In Thailand, the recitation of the story of Phra Wes constitutes one of the most important festival events of the agricultural calendar.

VESTA \\'ves-tə\\, in ROMAN RELIGION, goddess of the hearth, identified with the Greek HESTIA. Her worship was observed in every household along with that of the PENATES and the Lares (see LAR), and her image was sometimes encountered in the household shrine.

The state worship of Vesta was much more elaborate. Her SANCTUARY was traditionally a circular building, in imitation of the early Italian round hut and symbolic of the public hearth. The Temple of Vesta in the Roman Forum was of great antiquity and underwent many restorations and rebuildings in both republican and imperial times. There burned the perpetual fire of the public hearth attended by the VESTAL VIRGINS. This fire was officially extinguished and renewed annually on March 1 (originally the Roman new year), and its extinction at any other time, either accidentally or not, was regarded as a portent of disaster to Rome. The temple's innermost sanctuary was not open to the public; once a year, however, on the Vestalia (June 7–15), it was opened to matrons who visited it barefoot. The days of the festival were unlucky. On the final day occurred the ceremonial sweeping out of the building, and the period of ill OMEN did not end until the sweepings were officially disposed of by placing them in a particular spot along the Clivus Capitolinus or by throwing them into the Tiber.

Vesta was represented as a fully draped woman. As goddess of the hearth fire, Vesta was the patron deity of bakers, hence her connection with the donkey, usually used for turning the millstone, and her association with Fornax, the spirit of the baker's oven. She is also found allied with the primitive fire deities CACUS AND CACA.

VESTAL VIRGIN \\'ves-təl\\, in ROMAN RELIGION, any of the six priestesses, representing the daughters of the royal house, who tended the state cult of the goddess VESTA. Chosen between the ages of 6 and 10 by the PONTIFEX *maximus* ("chief priest"), they served for 30 years, during which time they had to remain virgins. Afterward they could marry, but few did, as it was considered unlucky. Those chosen as Vestal Virgins had to be of the required age, be of freeborn and respectable parents (though later the daughters of freedmen were eligible), have both parents alive, and be free from physical and mental defects. The Vestal Virgins' duties included tending the perpetual fire in the Temple of Vesta, fetching water from a sacred spring, preparing ritual food, caring for objects in the temple's inner SANCTUARY, and officiating at the public worship of Vesta (the Vestalia,

Vesta (seated) with Vestal Virgins, classical relief sculpture
By courtesy of the Palermo Museum, Italy

June 7–15). Failure to attend to their duties was punished by a beating; violation of the vow of chastity, by burial alive. The Vestal Virgins enjoyed many honors and privileges, including emancipation from their fathers' rule.

VICAR (from Latin *vicarius,* "substitute"), an official acting in some special way for a superior, primarily an ecclesiastical title in the Christian church. In the Roman Empire as reorganized by Emperor Diocletian (reigned 284–305), the *vicarius* was an important official, and the title remained in use for secular officials in the Middle Ages. In the ROMAN CATHOLIC church, "vicar of Christ" became the special designation of the popes starting in the 8th century, replacing the older title of "vicar of ST. PETER."

In the early church, the name vicar, or legate, was used for the representative of the pope to the Eastern councils. Beginning in the 4th century, vicar of the apostolic see or vicar apostolic came to mean a residential bishop with certain rights of surveillance over neighboring bishops. By the 13th century a vicar was an emissary sent from Rome to govern a DIOCESE that was without a bishop or in special difficulties. The Roman Catholic church in England was governed by vicars apostolic from 1685 until 1850 when POPE PIUS IX reestablished the English hierarchy. In modern times vicars apostolic are generally titular bishops appointed to rule territories not yet organized into dioceses.

In the Church of England, a vicar is the priest of a PARISH the revenues of which belong to another, while he himself receives a stipend.

VIHARA \\vi-'här-ə\\, early type of Buddhist monastery consisting of an open court surrounded by open cells accessible through an entrance porch. The *vihara*s in India were originally constructed to shelter the monks during the rainy season. They took on a sacred character when small STUPAS (housing sacred relics) and images of the Buddha were installed in the central court.

Examples exist still in western India, where the *vihara*s were often excavated into the rock cliffs. This tradition of rock-cut structures spread along the trade routes of Central Asia (as at Bāmiān), leaving many splendid monuments rich in sculpture and painting.

As the communities of monks grew, great monastic establishments (*mahāvihāras,* "great viharas") developed. Renowned centers of learning, or universities, grew up at Nālanda, in present-day Bihar state, during the 5th to 12th centuries and at Nāgārjunakoṇḍa, Andhra Pradesh, in the 3rd–4th century.

VILNA GAON \\'vil-nə-gä-'ōn\\: *see* ELIJAH BEN SOLOMON.

VIMALAKĪRTI SŪTRA \\,vi-mə-lə-'kir-tē-'sü-trə\\, *also called* Vimalakīrtinirdeśa Sūtra, MAHĀYĀNA Buddhist SŪTRA. It dates from no later than the 3rd century CE, based on its earliest Chinese translations, and most likely from the 1st or 2nd centuries CE.

In the *sūtra* the layman and householder Vimalakīrti, who is also, significantly, a model BODHISATTVA, instructs deities, learned Buddhist ARAHANTS, and lay people in all matters concerning the nature of enlightenment and Buddhist truth. He does so while lying sick in bed, although this is just a ruse designed to draw an audience of visitors who have come to wish him well and inquire about his health. As crowds of well-wishers come to see him, Vimalakīrti employs his superior understanding of "skill in means" (*upāya*) to teach them about the nature of "emptiness" (*śūnyatā*), the Mahāyāna Buddhist doctrine that culminates in the counter-intuitive claim that NIRVANA and SAMSĀRA, at an ultimate level, are not different.

Throughout the *sūtra* several famous Hinayāna Buddhist *arahants* are ridiculed for what Mahāyāna practitioners perceived as their selfish pursuit of nirvana, for their incomplete understanding of the nature of enlightenment, or for their pursuit of wisdom without compassion in aiding others. Vimalakīrti, by contrast, explains how a bodhisattva is able to live in the world, engaging it fully, even to the point of partaking in its pleasures, passions, and defilements, without being attached to them, constrained by them, or corrupted by them. The *sūtra* reaches its peak dramatic moment when Vimalakīrti asks his audience of bodhisattvas to describe the nature of non-duality. After each of them has responded verbally to his question, using technical, philosophical language, Vimalakīrti, prompted by his chief MAÑJUŚRĪ to supply his own answer, responds with silence, indicating that true understanding of non-duality is ineffable.

VINAYA PIṬAKA \ˈvi-nə-yə-ˈpi-tə-kə\ (Pāli and Sanskrit: "Basket of Discipline"), the oldest and smallest of the three sections of the Buddhist canonical TRIPIṬAKA and the one that regulates monastic life. It varies less from school to school than does either the *Sutta* (discourses of the BUDDHA GOTAMA and his disciples) or *Abhidhamma* (scholastic) sections of the canon, and the rules themselves are basically the same even for MAHĀYĀNA schools. Three works compose the Pāli *Vinaya*:

1. *Sutta Vibhaṅga* ("Classification of the Suttas"; corresponds to *Vinaya Vibhaṅga* in Sanskrit), an exposition of the monastic rules (PĀTIMOKKHA) and the disciplinary actions prescribed for each offense, arranged according to severity. Each rule is accompanied by the story of the incident that first prompted the Buddha's ruling and an early word-for-word commentary on the rules. In some instances there is also a later discussion of exceptions.

2. *Khandhaka* ("Divisions"; Sanskrit *Vinaya Vastu*, "Vinaya Subjects"), a series dealing with such matters as admission to the order; monastic ceremonies; rules governing food, clothing, lodging, and the like. As in the *Sutta Vibhaṅga*, an account is given of the occasion when each regulation was formulated by the Buddha. The arrangement is chronological and provides a picture of the evolving life of the early monastic community.

3. *Parivāra* ("Appendix"), a classified digest of the rules in the other *Vinaya* texts, apparently confined to the THERAVĀDA school. *Compare* ABHIDHAMMA PIṬAKA; SUTTA PIṬAKA.

VIOLENCE AND RELIGION, two realms that seem to be intricately related. Most religions share a history of bloody conflicts and holy wars, myths and epics that are filled with horrendous battles, and important symbols of violence such as the executioner's cross in CHRISTIANITY. Sacrifice, or ritual killing, is central to many religions.

Although there is no agreed upon explanation concerning the relation between violence and religion there are several theories that do attempt to explain it. SIGMUND FREUD in *Totem and Taboo* (1913) asserted that "In the beginning was the deed," this deed being the killing of the senior male (father) by the younger males (sons) in order to obtain females for themselves. This act of killing, Freud argued, is the origin of civilization, and religion was the consequence of the younger males' guilt which led to the institution of prohibitions, laws, and a projected almighty father as constraints against such violence. Rene Girard has extended Freud's thesis in *Violence and the Sacred* (1972) by arguing that the release of violent impulses is based on the displacement of mimetic desire, the urge to imitate the father.

Walter Burkert, in *Homo Necans* (1983), believes that the vast corpus of violent myths and the history of bloody sacrifices are best explained as a means of confronting the reality of death; ritual violence thus contributes to social solidarity and group survival and acts as a constraint on violence outside of the sacred sphere. Maurice Bloch, meanwhile, has argued that religion and politics are two sides of the same coin—power. Thus, sacrifice can be seen, on the one hand, as the ritual formalization of, and thus a constraint on, violence as a religious/political act. On the other hand, however, it can also become the ritualization of power/violence. Religious violence then becomes political power at work through covert means. The basic problem with all of these explanations is they assume the satisfaction of certain needs, and thus are subject to the difficulties that afflict many functionalist theories of religion. *See also* FUNCTIONALISM.

VIPASSANA \vi-ˈpä-sə-nə\, in THERAVĀDA Buddhism, method of insight meditation. Vipassana requires concentration (produced by exercises such as concentrating on one's breathing), which lead to one-pointedness of mind. This one-pointedness of mind is then used to attain direct insight into the saving truth that all reality is without self and impermanent and is filled with suffering, even exalted states of consciousness. This insight, from the Buddhist perspective, gives direct access to progress along the path and to the actual attainment of NIRVANA itself.

VIRACOCHA \ˌbē-rä-ˈkō-chä\, *also spelled* Huiracocha \ˌwē-rä-\, *or* Wiraqoca, creator deity originally worshiped by the pre-Inca inhabitants of Peru and later assimilated into the Inca pantheon (*see* PRE-COLUMBIAN SOUTH AMERICAN RELIGIONS). A god of rain, he was believed to have created the sun and moon on the waters and foam of Lake Titicaca. After forming the rest of the heavens and the earth, Viracocha traditionally wandered through the world teaching men the arts of civilization. At Manta (Ecuador) he walked westward across the waves of the Pacific Ocean, promising to return one day.

The cult of Viracocha was extremely ancient, but he probably entered the Inca pantheon at a relatively late date. The Incas believed that Viracocha was a remote being who left the daily working of the world to the surveillance of the other deities that he had created. He was actively worshiped by the nobility, who urgently called upon him in times of crisis.

VĪRAŚAIVA \ˌvē-rə-ˈshī-və\, *also called* Liṅgāyat \liṅ-ˈgä-yət\, member of a Hindu sect with a wide following in

South India that worships SHIVA as the only deity. The followers take their name ("LINGA-wearers") from the small representations of a *linga* worn on a cord around the neck, in place of the sacred thread worn by most orthodox upper CASTE Hindu men.

The sect is generally regarded as having been founded by BASAVA in the 12th century, but he may have furthered an already existing creed. Philosophically, their qualified spiritual monism and their conception of BHAKTI ("devotion") as an intuitive and loving knowledge of God show the influence of the 11th- and 12th-century thinker RĀMĀNUJA.

The Vīraśaiva's earlier overthrow of caste distinctions has been modified in modern times, but the sect continues to be strongly anti-Brahminical and opposed to worship of any image other than the *linga*. In their rejection of the authority of the VEDAS, the doctrine of transmigration of souls, child marriage, and ill treatment of widows, they anticipated the social-reform movements of the 19th century.

VIRGIN BIRTH, fundamental doctrine of orthodox CHRISTIANITY, based on the infancy narratives in the GOSPELS of MATTHEW and LUKE, that JESUS CHRIST had no natural father but was conceived by MARY through the power of the HOLY SPIRIT. It was universally accepted in the Christian church by the 2nd century, was enshrined in the APOSTLES' CREED, and was not seriously challenged until the 19th century. It remains a basic article of belief in ROMAN CATHOLICISM, EASTERN ORTHODOXY, and most Protestant churches. ISLAM also accepts the Virgin Birth of Jesus.

A corollary of this doctrine is that of Mary's perpetual virginity, in the birth of the child (*i.e.*, freedom from the pain of childbirth) and throughout her life. This doctrine, found in the writings of the CHURCH FATHERS and accepted by the COUNCIL OF CHALCEDON (451), is part of the teaching of the Orthodox and Roman Catholic churches and is also maintained by some Anglican and Lutheran theologians.

VISHNU \'vish-nü \, *Sanskrit* Viṣṇu ("All-Pervading"), one of the principal Hindu deities, worshiped as the protector and preserver of the world and restorer of DHARMA (moral order). Vishnu, like SHIVA, is a syncretic personality who combines many lesser cult figures and local heroes. He is known chiefly through his AVATARS (incarnations), particularly RĀMA and KRISHNA.

Vishnu was not a major deity in the Vedic period. A few hymns of the ṚG VEDA associate him with the sun and relate the legend of his three strides across the universe (*see* VĀMANA). Legends of other avatars are found in the early literature and by the time of the MAHĀBHĀRATA they begin to be identified with Vishnu. In theory, Vishnu manifests a portion of himself anytime he is needed to fight evil, and his appearances are innumerable; but in practice, 10 are most commonly recognized.

Temple images of Vishnu often depict him in the company of his consorts LAKṢMĪ (also called Śrī) and Bhūmidevī (Earth) or reclining on the coils of the serpent Śeṣa, asleep on the cosmic ocean during the period between the periodic annihilation and renewal of the world. Vishnu holds in his four (sometimes two) hands the *śaṅkha* (conch), *cakra* (discus), *gadā* (club), or *padma* (lotus). On his chest is the curl of hair known as the *śrīvatsa* mark, a sign of his immortality, and around his neck he wears the auspicious jewel Kaustubha. Vishnu is usually depicted as dark complexioned, a distinguishing feature also of his incarnations.

Vishnu's mount is the vulturelike bird GARUḌA; his heavenly abode is called Vaikuṇṭha. Among the 1,000 names of Vishnu (repeated as an act of devotion by his worshipers) are VĀSUDEVA, Nārāyaṇa, and Hari.

VISHVA HINDU PARISHAD \'vish-və-'hin-dü-'pə-ri-,shəd \ ("All-Hindu Council"), *commonly known as* VHP, organization founded in Bombay in 1964 as a religious and cultural group with several objectives: to unify and raise consciousness among the Hindus in India; to protect and spread Hindu ethical and spiritual values; to establish contacts with the Hindu diaspora around the world; and to work for CASTE reform and the amelioration of the condition of the lower castes. The VHP is organizationally structured into two levels, a central body of secular and spiritual leaders and "advisory committees" at the state level composed of representatives of the various participating religious communities.

The VHP maintains close ties with the Rashtriya Swayamsevak Sangh, or RSS, and shares much of the same ideology of Hindu nationalism and Hindu cultural pride. It is distinctive from the RSS and other similar organizations by virtue of the central place it gives to Hindu religious leaders from a variety of sects and its emphasis on articulating ideas and practices to which Hindus, in India and elsewhere, of all stripes can ascribe. Like other such groups, it rejects the notion of the secular state and what it perceives to be the "pampering" of religious minorities in India. The VHP also claims to combat Hindu "weakness," stemming from external threats and internal divisions and has developed rituals and doctrines designed to unify and thereby strengthen the Hindu

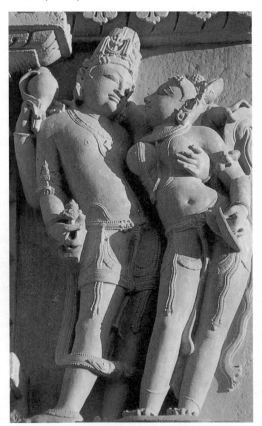

Vishnu with his consort Lakṣmī, from the temple dedicated to Pārśvanātha at Khajrāho, Madhya Pradesh, India, c. 950–970 CE
© Anthony Cassidy

community in India and abroad (inclusive of Jains, Buddhists, and Sikhs who are also regarded as part of this "Hindu community"). As an important organization in the Hindu nationalist movement, the VHP is also controversial among secularists and the minority religious communities in India.

VISION QUEST, among the Native American hunters of the eastern woodlands and the Great Plains, an essential part of a youth's initiation into adulthood. The boy (or rarely, the girl) was sent out from the camp after a period of instruction and purification on a solitary vigil involving fasting and prayer in order to gain some sign of the presence and nature of his GUARDIAN SPIRIT.

In some traditions the youth would watch for an animal who behaved in a significant way; in others he discovered an object (usually a stone), which resembled some animal. In the predominant form, he had a dream in which his guardian appeared (usually in animal form), instructed him, took him on a visionary journey, and taught him songs. Upon receiving these signs and visions he returned to his home, indicated his success, and sought out a religious specialist for help in interpreting his visions.

The techniques of the vision quest underlie every visionary experience of the Native American, from those of the ordinary man to the visions of the great prophets and SHAMANS. Among some South American Indians, the vision quest, like the guardian spirit, is confined exclusively to the shamans (a category that can include numerous individuals within a group). *See also* NATIVE AMERICAN RELIGIONS.

VIŚIṢṬĀDVAITA \vi-'shish-täd-'vī-tə\ (Sanskrit: "Qualified Nondualism"), one of the principal schools of VEDĀNTA. This school grew out of the Vaiṣṇava devotional movement prominent in South India from the 7th century on. One of the early Brahmins who began to guide the movement was Nāthamuni (10th century), head priest of the temple at Śrīraṅgam (in modern Tamil Nadu state). He was succeeded by Yāmuna (11th century), who wrote some philosophic treatises but no commentaries.

The most towering figure is his successor, RĀMĀNUJA (c. 1050–1137). Rāmānuja was the first of the Vedānta thinkers who made the identification of a personal God with the BRAHMAN of the UPANISHADS and the *Vedānta* SŪTRAS the cornerstone of his system. For him the relation between the infinite and the finite is like that between the soul and the body. Soul and matter are totally dependent on God for their existence, as is the body on the soul.

God has two modes of being, as cause and as product. As cause, he is in his essence qualified only by his perfections; as product, he has as his body souls and the phenomenal world. For Rāmānuja, release is the joy of the contemplation of God. This joy is attained by a life of exclusive devotion (BHAKTI) to God. God will return his GRACE, which will assist the devotee in gaining release.

Viśiṣṭādvaita flourished after Rāmānuja, but a schism developed over the importance of God's grace. For the Sanskrit-using school, the Vaṭakalai ("the Northern Branch"), God's grace in gaining release is important, but man himself should make his best efforts. This school is represented by the thinker Veṅkaṭanātha, who was known by the honorific name of VEDĀNTADEŚIKA ("Teacher of Vedānta"). The Tamil-using school, the Teṅkalai ("the Southern Branch"), holds that God's grace alone is necessary.

The influence of Viśiṣṭādvaita spread far to the north, where it played a role in the devotional renaissance of VAIṢṆAVISM, particularly under the Bengali devotee CAITANYA (1485–1533). In southern India the philosophy itself is still an important intellectual influence.

VISUDDHIMAGGA \vi-ˌsù-dē-'mə-gə\ (Pāli "Path to Purification"), encyclopedic and masterful summary and exposition of Buddhist teaching of the MAHĀVIHĀRA branch of the THERAVĀDA school. It was written during the reign of the Sri Lankan king Mahānāma in the 5th century CE by the great Buddhist commentator BUDDHAGHOSA. Along with two other notable counterparts, Dhammapāla and Buddhadatta, Buddhagosa wrote new commentaries on Theravāda doctrine in Pāli, based on older Sinhalese commentaries that dated from the early centuries CE. The *Visuddhimagga* is perhaps the most famous of Buddhagosa's considerable literary output. It organizes its material broadly under three headings: SĪLA (morals), SAMĀDHI (meditation), and *paññā* (wisdom), but it also comments on and explains a wide range of details of Buddhist doctrine through the use of narrative and by means of direct quotation from and explanation of the canonical texts of the TIPIṬAKA, presenting Theravāda doctrines as a systematic whole. In addition, the *Visuddhimagga* contains a detailed description of Buddhist meditative techniques and can be regarded as a general reference work on Theravāda doctrine.

VIŚVAKARMAN \'vish-və-'kər-mən, -'kär-\ (Sanskrit: "All Accomplishing"), in HINDUISM, the architect of the gods. Viśvakarman is the divine carpenter and master craftsman who fashioned the weapons of the gods and built their cities, their chariots, and the mythical city, Laṅkā. He revealed the sciences of architecture and mechanics to men and is the patron deity of workmen, artisans, and artists.

VITAL, ḤAYYIM BEN JOSEPH \vē-'täl\ (b. 1543, Safed, Palestine [now Ẕefat, Israel]—d. May 6, 1620, Damascus [now in Syria]), one of Judaism's outstanding Qabbalists.

In Safed, in about 1570, Vital became the disciple of ISAAC BEN SOLOMON LURIA, the leading Qabbalist of his time, and after Luria's death (1572) Vital professed to be the sole interpreter of the Lurian school. He became the leader of Palestinian Jewish Qabbalism and served as RABBI and head of a YESHIVA in Jerusalem (1577–85). His major work was the *'Etz ḥayyim* ("Tree of Life"), an exposition of Lurian Qabbalah, which also appeared in altered editions by rivals that he repudiated. His son Samuel published accounts of Vital's dreams and visions posthumously under the title *Shivḥe R. Ḥayyim Vital.* (*See* QABBALAH.)

VIVEKANANDA \'vē-vā-kə-'nən-də\, *also spelled* Vivekānanda, *original name* Narendranath Datta (b. Jan. 12, 1863, Calcutta, India—d. July 4, 1902, Calcutta), Hindu spiritual leader and reformer who attempted to combine Indian spirituality with Western material progress.

Born into an upper-middle-class Kāyastha family in Bengal, he was educated at a Western-style university where he was exposed to Western philosophy, CHRISTIANITY, and science. He subsequently joined the BRAHMO SAMAJ (Society of Brahman), dedicated to eliminating child marriage and illiteracy and determined to spread education among women and the lower CASTES, and became the most notable disciple of RAMAKRISHNA. Always stressing the universal and humanistic side of the VEDA (by which he meant principally the UPANISHADS) as well as belief in service rather than dogma, Vivekananda attempted to infuse vigor into Hindu thought. He was an activating force behind the VEDĀNTA movement in the United States and England, which traces its intellectual lineage to the 8th-century philosopher ŚAMKARA, attempts to integrate all religious systems into its own, and owes its particular energy to the vision and example of Ramakrishna, Vivekananda's teacher and GURU. In 1893 Vivekananda appeared in Chicago as a spokesman for HINDUISM at the World's Parliament of Religions. Thereafter he lectured throughout the United States and England, making converts to the Vedānta movement and establishing a network of Vedānta Societies.

On his return to India with a small group of Western disciples in 1897, Vivekananda founded the Ramakrishna mission at the monastery of Belur Maṭh on the GAṄGĀ RIVER near Calcutta. Self-perfection and service were his ideals, and the order continues to stress them.

VODYANOY \və-dʸə-'nȯi\, in Slavic mythology, the water spirit, essentially an evil and vindictive spirit. Anyone bathing after sunset, on a holy day, or without having first made the sign of the cross risks being drowned by the *vodyanoy*. He can assume many different forms. The *vodyanoy* lives alone in his particular body of water and is known to favor rivers with strong currents and swamps.

VOHU MANAH \vō-'hü-ma-'näh, -'na\ (Avestan: "Good Mind"), in ZOROASTRIANISM, one of the six *amesha spenta*s ("beneficent immortals") created by AHURA MAZDĀ to assist him in furthering good and destroying evil. Because the prophet Zoroaster was, in a vision, conducted into the presence of Ahura Mazdā by Vohu Manah, any individual who seeks to know Ahura Mazdā must approach him through this immortal.

Since Vohu Manah is the closest of the AMESHA SPENTAS to Ahura Mazdā, the second month of the Zoroastrian calendar is dedicated to him. His sacred animal is the cow.

VOLADORES, JUEGO DE LOS \'hwā-ḡō-thā-lōs-,bō-lä-'thō-räs\ (Spanish: "game of the fliers"), ritual dance of Mexico, possibly originating among the pre-Columbian Totonac and Huastec Indians. Four or six men (the *voladores*, or "flyers") dance on a platform atop a pole 60 to 90 feet high; at the end of the dance, they circle downward around the pole as the ropes that fasten them to it unwind. The number of dancers preserves the pre-Christian ritual orientation to the four points of the compass plus the zenith and the nadir.

Juego de los voladores *performed by Totonac Indians at Tajín, Mexico*
By courtesy of the Mexican Museum of Tourism

VORŠUD \vȯr-'shüd\, among the Finno-Ugric Udmurt (Votyak) people, family spirit, literally "luck protector"; the term also designates a birchbark container kept in the family shrine, or *kuala*, as a receptacle for offerings and possibly as an image of the protector. The *voršud* was believed to watch over the welfare and prosperity of the family members worshiping at the *kuala*. The *voršud* case was kept on a shelf on the back wall of the *kuala* resting on a bed of twigs, which were renewed for ceremonies. The original *voršud* case was handed down from father to eldest son, but lesser *voršud* could also be made as the family expanded. The new *voršud* had to be made in the old *kuala*, left there for a while, and then transferred with some ashes from the hearth to dedicate the new shrine.

VOUDOU \'vü-,dü\, *also spelled* voodoo, *French* vaudou \vō-'dü\, national folk religion of Haiti. Voudou is a mixture of ROMAN CATHOLIC ritual elements, which date from the period of French colonization, and theological and magical elements taken from AFRICAN RELIGIONS, which were brought to Haiti by slaves formerly belonging to the Yoruba, Fon, Kongo, and other peoples of Africa. The term *voudou* is derived from the word *vodun*, which denotes a god, or spirit, in the language of the Fon people of Benin (formerly Dahomey).

Although voudouists profess belief in a distant supreme God, the effective divinities are a large number of spirits called the *loa*, which can be variously identified as local or African gods, deified ancestors, or Catholic saints. The *loa* are believed to demand ritual service, which thereby attaches them to individuals or families. In voudou ritual services, a number of devotees congregate at a temple, usually a meeting place, where a priest or priestess leads them in ceremonies involving song, drumming, dance, prayer, food preparation, and the ritual sacrifice of animals. The voudou priest, or *houngan*, and the priestess, or *mambo*, also act as counselors, healers, and expert protectors against SORCERY or WITCHCRAFT.

The *loa* are thought by devotees to act as helpers, protectors, and guides to people. The *loa* communicate with an individual during the cult services by possessing him during a trance state in which the devotee may eat and drink, perform stylized dances, give supernaturally inspired advice to people, perform medical cures, or display special physical feats; these acts exhibit the incarnate presence of the *loa* within the entranced devotee. Many urban Haitians believe in two sharply contrasting sets of *loa*s, a set of wise and benevolent ones called Rada *loa*s, and a harsher, more malevolent group of spirits called Petro *loa*s. Petro spirits are called up by more agitated or violent rituals than those which evoke Rada spirits.

A peculiar, and much sensationalized, aspect of voudou is the zombi. A zombi is regarded as being either a dead person's disembodied soul that is used for magical purposes, or an actual corpse that has been raised from the grave by magical means and is then used to perform agricultural labor in the fields as a sort of will-less automaton. In actual practice, certain voudou priests do appear to create "zombis" by administering a particular poison to the skin of a victim, who then enters a state of profound physical paralysis for a number of hours.

For decades the Roman Catholic church in Haiti denounced voudou and even advocated the persecution of its devotees, but because voudou has remained the chief religion of at least 80 percent of the people in Haiti, the Catholic church by the late 20th century seemed resigned to coexisting with it.

VOW, sacred voluntary promise to dedicate oneself or members of one's family or community to a special obligation that goes beyond usual requirements.

In the ancient Middle East, individuals often made vows to a deity to perform certain acts or to live in a certain way in return for a divine favor. HANNAH, the mother of the OLD TESTAMENT judge Samuel, for example, vowed that if YAHWEH, the God of Israel, would grant her a son she would devote him to the service of the Lord. Persons dedicated to the service of Yahweh might be released from their vows, however, by paying a certain amount of money.

Ancient ROMAN RELIGION encouraged vows to a deity in the name of the state, thereby putting the vow-giver in debt to the gods until the vows were fulfilled. During wars, vows were made to MARS, the god of war, to sacrifice a large number of animals in exchange for support in battle.

Among the Vikings, vows to the gods, often considered a type of prayer, were viewed as sacrosanct, and those who broke vows were cast out of their community.

Vows are very common in HINDUISM, BUDDHISM, and JAINISM. Buddhist monks vow to practice 10 precepts, which include NONVIOLENCE, chastity, and honesty. Buddhist laymen and laywomen also take on some of the vows of monks and nuns at some time or times during their lives. MAHĀYĀNA Buddhists sometimes adopt the vow of the BODHISATTVA, which is very strict. Jain monks follow the five vows, or *vrata*s of MAHĀVĪRA—renunciation of killing, lying, taking what is not given, sexual pleasures, and all attachments.

In JUDAISM, vows (Hebrew *nedarim*) may be positive or negative. A positive *neder* is a voluntary pledge to consecrate something to God or to do something in God's honor that is not required by law. A negative *neder* (Hebrew *issar*) is a voluntary pledge to abstain from or deprive oneself of a legitimate pleasure. ROMAN CATHOLIC religious orders in general take three vows—poverty, chastity, and obedience—and in some cases an added vow of stability, *i.e.*, to remain in a monastery. In PROTESTANTISM, vows are made during certain rites (*e.g.*, CONFIRMATION, ORDINATION, and marriage ceremonies).

VRINDĀBAD \\'vrin-dä-bəd\\, *also called* Vrndavana, *or* Brindaban, North Indian town about 80 miles south of Delhi on the west bank of the Yamuna River. It is the sacred center of the Hindu deity KRISHNA and those who worship him. It is especially important to the sect known as the Gaudīya Vaisnavas and is a major pilgrimage site.

It was in Vrindābad and its surrounding forests that the key events of Krishna's mythological life took place, and as such it functions as a kind of heavenly world in which a religious drama unfolds apart from and transcendent of the normal confines of ordinary human society. It was here that Krishna was born, lived his precocious childhood, and grew into the attractive and intoxicating youth who would lure young maidens into the forest to participate in his divine play and circle dance. For the devotees of Krishna, these events and the mythological participants in them are paradigms for the ideal religious setting and salvific imaginative relationships the devotee forms with the deity.

As a historical locale, Vrindābad was the site where the founder of the Gaudīya Vaisnavas (*see* VAISNAVISM), the Bengali poet-saint CAITANYA, sent a group of theologians to reside. These theologians became known as the Six Gosvamins of Vrindābad and were responsible for systematizing the beliefs and practices of the group.

VULCAN \\'vəl-kən\\, in ROMAN RELIGION, god of fire, particularly in its destructive aspects as volcanoes or conflagrations. He was associated with the Greek god HEPHAESTUS. His worship was very ancient, and at Rome he had his own priest (FLAMEN). His chief festival, the Volcanalia, was held on August 23 and was marked by a rite in which the heads of Roman families threw small fish into the fire. Vulcan was invoked to avert fires, as his epithets Quietus and Mulciber ("[Fire] Allayer") suggest. His temples were located outside the city.

VULGATE (from Latin *editio vulgata*, "common version"), Latin BIBLE used by the ROMAN CATHOLIC church, primarily translated by ST. JEROME. In 382 Pope Damasus commissioned Jerome, the leading biblical scholar of his day, to produce an acceptable Latin version of the Bible from the various translations then being used. His revised Latin translation of the GOSPELS appeared about 383. Using the SEPTUAGINT Greek version of the OLD TESTAMENT, he produced new Latin translations of the Psalms (the so-called Gallican Psalter), THE BOOK OF JOB, and some other books. Later, he decided that the Septuagint was unsatisfactory and began translating the entire Old Testament from the original Hebrew versions, completing it about 405.

Jerome's translation was not immediately accepted, but from the mid-6th century a complete Bible with all the separate books bound in a single cover was commonly used. It usually contained Jerome's Old Testament translation from the Hebrew, except for the Psalms; his Gallican Psalter; his translation of the books of Tobias (Tobit) and Judith (apocryphal in the Jewish and Protestant canons); and his revision of the Gospels. The remainder of the NEW TESTAMENT was taken from older Latin versions, which may have been slightly revised by Jerome. Certain other books found in the Septuagint—the APOCRYPHA for Protestants and Jews; the DEUTEROCANONICAL BOOKS for Roman Catholics—were included from older versions.

In 1546 the COUNCIL OF TRENT decreed that the Vulgate was the exclusive Latin authority for the Bible, but it required also that it be printed with the fewest possible faults. The so-called Clementine Vulgate, issued by Pope Clement VIII in 1592, became the authoritative biblical text of the Roman Catholic church. From it the Confraternity Version was translated in 1941.

WACH, JOACHIM \'väk\ (b. Jan. 25, 1898, Chemnitz, Ger.—d. Aug. 27, 1955, Orselina, Switz.), Protestant theologian and a prominent scholar in the STUDY OF RELIGION.

As a professor of the history of religion at the University of Leipzig (1929–35) and the University of Chicago (1945–55), Wach contributed significantly to the field of study that became known as the SOCIOLOGY OF RELIGION. He is credited with introducing into American scholarship the phenomenological method of analyzing RELIGIOUS BELIEFS and practices. He established the discipline known as the comparative study of religion (*Religionswissenschaft*) at the University of Chicago and is considered the founder of the Chicago School, which stressed methodology in the study of religion.

Wach conceived *Religionswissenschaft* as a comparative, phenomenological, and psychological approach to religion, including the theoretical (or mental), the practical (or behavioral), and the institutional (social) aspects of religion. Among Wach's writings in English are *Sociology of Religion* (1944), *Types of Religious Experience—Christian and Non-Christian* (1951), and *The Comparative Study of Religions* (1958). His publication *Das Verstehen*, 3 vols. (1926–33), remains a classic.

WAHHĀBĪS: *see* MUWAḤḤIDŪN.

WAKAN \wä-'kän\ (Dakota and Lakota *wakhą*, "sacred, consecrated," or cognates in other Siouan languages), *also called* wakonda, *or* wakanda \wä-'kän-də\, among various Native American groups, spiritual power belonging to some natural objects, people, horses, and celestial and terrestrial phenomena. Wakan has no essential characteristics in itself; rather, it is a kind of holiness or wonderfulness inherent in some objects. Wakan, and the wakan beings who bestow it, may be conceived of as weak or strong powers; the weak powers can be ignored, but the strong ones must be placated. Poisonous plants and reptiles can contain wakan, as can intoxicating drinks. *Compare* MANA.

WAKE, watch or vigil held over the body of a dead person before burial and sometimes accompanied by festivity; also, in England, a vigil kept in commemoration of the dedication of the PARISH church. The latter type of wake consisted of an all-night service of prayer and meditation in the church. These services, officially termed Vigiliae by the church, appear to have existed from the earliest days of Anglo-Saxon CHRISTIANITY.

Side by side with these church wakes there existed the custom of "holding a wake over" a corpse. The custom appears to predate Christianity in England. The Anglo-Saxons called the custom lich-wake, or like-wake (from Old English *lic*, a corpse). With the introduction of Christianity, the offering of prayer was added to the vigil. As a rule, the corpse, with a plate of salt on its breast, was placed under the table, on which was liquor for the watchers. These private wakes soon tended to become drinking orgies. With

the REFORMATION and the consequent disuse of prayers for the dead, the custom of waking became obsolete in England but survived in Ireland. Many countries and peoples have a custom equivalent to waking, which is, however, distinct from funeral feasts.

WALDENSES \wȯl-'den-ˌsēz\, *also spelled* Valdenses, *French* Vaudois, *Italian* Valdesi, members of a Christian movement that originated in 12th-century France. Waldenses sought to follow the example of JESUS CHRIST by living in poverty and simplicity. The name has been applied to members of a modern church (centered on the Franco-Italian border) that formed when remnants of the earlier movement became Swiss Protestant Reformers.

Early ROMAN CATHOLIC and Waldensian sources are few and unreliable, and little is known with certainty about the reputed founder, Valdes (also called Peter Waldo, or Valdo). As a layman, Valdes preached in Lyon (1170–76), but ecclesiastical authorities were disturbed by his lack of theological training and by his use of a non-Latin version of the BIBLE. Valdes attended the third LATERAN COUNCIL (1179) in Rome and was confirmed in his vow of poverty by Pope Alexander III. Probably during this council Valdes made his *Profession of Faith* (which still survives); it is a statement of orthodox beliefs such as accused heretics were required to sign. Valdes did not receive the ecclesiastical recognition that he sought. Undeterred, he and his followers (Pauperes: "Poor") continued to preach; the archbishop of Lyon condemned him, and Pope Lucius III placed the Waldenses under ban with his bull *Ad Abolendam* (1184), issued during the SYNOD of Verona.

Thereafter, the Waldenses departed from the teaching of the Roman Catholic church by rejecting prayers for the dead, veneration of the saints, the notion of PURGATORY, and the authority of secular courts. Their views were based on a simplified biblicism, moral rigor, and criticism of abuses in the church. Their movement spread throughout Europe, and Rome responded with EXCOMMUNICATION, active persecution, and execution. By the end of the 13th century the sect was virtually eliminated in some areas, and for safety the survivors abandoned their distinctive dress. By the end of the 15th century they were confined mostly to the French and Italian valleys of the Cottian Alps.

A second period in their history began when the French reformer Guillaume Farel introduced REFORMATION theology to the Waldensian ministers (*barbes*) in 1526. At a conference at Cianforan in 1532 most Waldenses accepted secular law courts and CELIBACY for their *barbes* and agreed to accept only two SACRAMENTS (BAPTISM and Holy Communion) and the doctrine of PREDESTINATION as presented by the Protestants in attendance. By adapting themselves to Genevan forms of worship and church organization, they became in effect a Swiss Protestant church. Persecution continued, however, until they received full civil rights in 1848.

During the second half of the 19th century, Waldensian emigrants arrived in Uruguay and later moved from there to the United States. There, strengthened by arrivals from France and Switzerland, they established small communities in Missouri, Texas, and Utah and, most importantly, around Valdese, in Burke county, N.C.

WALĪ ALLĀH, SHAH \wä-'lē-ä-'lä\, *also spelled* Waliu'llah, *full name* Shah Walī Allāh al-Dihlāwī (b. 1702/03, Delhi [India]—d. 1762, Delhi), Indian theologian who first attempted to reassess Islamic theology in light of modern changes.

Walī Allāh received a traditional Islamic education from his father and is said to have memorized the QUR'AN at the age of seven. In 1732 he made a PILGRIMAGE to MECCA, and he then remained in the Hijaz (now in Saudi Arabia) to study religion with eminent theologians. He reached adulthood at a time of disillusionment following the death in 1707 of Aurangzeb, the last of the great Mughal emperors of India. Because large areas of the empire had been lost to Hindu and Sikh rulers of the Deccan and the Punjab, Indian Muslims had to accept the rule of non-Muslims.

Walī Allāh believed that the Muslim polity could be restored to its former splendor by a policy of religious reform that would harmonize the religious ideals of ISLAM with the changing social and economic conditions of India. According to him, religious ideas were universal and eternal, but their application could meet different circumstances. The main tool of his policy was the doctrine of *tatbīq*, whereby the principles of Islam were reconstructed and reapplied in accordance with the Qur'an and the HADITH. He thereby allowed the practice of IJTIHĀD (independent thinking by jurists in matters relating to Islamic law), which hitherto had been curtailed. As a corollary, he reinterpreted the concept of *taqdīr* (determinism) and condemned its popularization, *qismat* (absolute predetermination). Walī Allāh held that humans could achieve their full potential by their own exertion in a universe that was determined by God. Theologically, he opposed the veneration of saints or anything that compromised strict MONOTHEISM. He was jurisprudentially eclectic, holding that a Muslim could follow any of the four schools of Islamic law on any point of dogma or ritual.

The best known of Walī Allāh's writings was *Asrār al-dīn* ("The Secrets of Belief"). His annotated Persian translation of the Qur'an is still popular in India and Pakistan.

The wandering Jew, illustration by Gustave Doré, 1856
By courtesy of the British Museum; photograph, J.R. Freeman & Co. Ltd.

His synthesis of theology, philosophy, and MYSTICISM with Ḥanafī jurisprudence reinvigorated Islam so effectively that it became the prevailing understanding of religion among 'ULAMĀ' in India until well into the 20th century.

WANDERING JEW, in Christian legend, character doomed to live until the end of the world because he taunted JESUS on his way to the CRUCIFIXION. A reference in John 18:20–22 to an officer who struck Jesus at his arraignment before Annas is sometimes cited as the basis for the legend. The medieval English chronicler Roger of Wendover states that there was in Armenia a man formerly called Cartaphilus who claimed he had been Pontius Pilate's doorkeeper and had struck Jesus on his way to Calvary, urging him to go faster. Jesus replied, "I go, and you will wait till I return." Cartaphilus was later baptized Joseph and lived piously among Christian clergy, hoping in the end to be saved. An Italian variant of the story named the culprit as Giovanni Buttadeo ("Strike God").

The legend was revived in 1602 in a German pamphlet, "Kurze Beschreibung und Erzählung von einem Juden mit Namen Ahasverus" ("A Brief Description and Narration Regarding a Jew Named Ahasuerus"). The popularity of the pamphlet may have been the result of the anti-Jewish feeling aroused by belief that the ANTICHRIST would appear in 1600 and be aided by the Jews. Appearances of the wandering Jew were reported in various European cities. As late as 1868 he was reputedly seen in Salt Lake City, Utah.

The wandering Jew has been the subject of many works of literary and visual art. One of the best-known treatments is Eugène Sue's Romantic novel *Le Juif errant*, 10 vol. (1844–45; *The Wandering Jew*). Gustave Doré produced a series of 12 wood engravings on the theme in 1856.

WANG CHE \'wäŋ-'jə\, *Pinyin* Wang Zhe, *also called* Wang Ch'ung-yang \'chüŋ-'yäŋ\ (b. 1112—d. 1170), founder of the Ch'üan-chen (Perfect Realization) sect of TAOISM, in 1163. After receiving secret teachings, Wang established a monastery in Shantung to propagate the Way of Perfect Realization as a synthesis of CONFUCIANISM, Taoism, and Ch'an (ZEN) BUDDHISM. Wang's new sect flourished with the imperial patronage.

WANG CH'UNG \'wäŋ-'chüŋ\, *Pinyin* Wang Chong (b. 27 CE, K'uei-chi, China—d. 100?, K'uei-chi), one of the most original and independent Chinese thinkers of the Han period (206 BCE–220 CE). A rationalistic naturalist, Wang helped pave the way for the critical spirit of the next philosophical period and prepared China for the advent of Neo-Taoism.

Wang opposed contemporary CONFUCIANISM, declaring that natural things occur spontaneously and rejecting the notion that human actions influence the workings of the natural universe (*e.g.*, a bad king will produce bad weather). A rationalist, he insisted that any theory must be supported by concrete evidence and experimental proof. He stated that humans, though noble and intelligent, have no exceptional position in the universe.

Wang has never been greatly popular in China, though in the 20th century the prevailing critical spirit, scientific method, and revolt against the past have attracted new attention to his ideas. His outstanding work is the trenchant and critical *Lun-heng* ("Disquisitions").

WANG YANG-MING \'wäŋ-'yäŋ-'miŋ\, *Pinyin* Wang Yangming, *canonized as* Wen-ch'eng \'wən-'chəŋ\, *Japanese* Ōyō-mei \,ō-'yō-,mä\ (b. 1472, Yu-yao, Chekiang province, China—d. 1529, Nan-an, Kiangsi), Chinese scholar-official whose idealistic interpretation of NEO-CONFUCIANISM influenced philosophical thinking in East Asia for centuries. Though his government career was rather unstable, his suppression of rebellions brought a century of peace to his region. His philosophical doctrines, emphasizing understanding of the world from within the mind, were in direct conflict with the RATIONALISM espoused by CHU HSI, a highly esteemed Neo-Confucianist of the 12th century, and Wang's "false teaching" was for a time proscribed.

Wang was the son of a high government official. Having failed in the metropolitan civil service examinations in 1493 and 1495, he shifted his interest to military arts and Taoist studies, focusing on techniques for immortality. In 1499, however, Wang passed the "advanced scholar" (*chin-shih*) examination and held several government positions. In 1504 he returned to Peking (Beijing), supervised provincial examinations in Shantung, and then became a secretary in the Ministry of War. In 1505 he began to lecture on Confucism.

A critical event occurred in 1506, when Wang was banished to remote Kweichow as head of a dispatch station. The hardship and solitude brought him to the sudden conviction that to investigate the principles of things is not to seek for them in actual objects, as the rationalistic Chu Hsi had taught, but in one's own mind. Thus he brought Idealist (HSIN-HSÜEH) Neo-Confucianism—as first taught by a 12th-century philosopher, Lu Hsiang-shan—its highest expression. A year later he pronounced another epoch-making theory: that knowledge and action are one. One knows FILIAL PIETY, he argued, only when one acts upon it, and correct action requires correct knowledge.

As a magistrate in Kiangsi in 1510, he carried out many reforms. An imperial audience followed and then a series of appointments of increasing rank, and by 1516 he was named governor of southern Kiangsi and adjacent areas. Bandits and rebels had controlled Kiangsi for decades. In four military campaigns in 1517–18, Wang eliminated them. He carried out reconstruction, tax reform, joint registration, establishment of schools, and the "community compact" to improve community morals and solidarity. In 1519 he suppressed a rebellion led by Chu Ch'en-hao, prince of Ning. Though accused by his enemies of collaboration with the prince, Wang was exonerated and made governor of Kiangsi.

In 1521 the new emperor appointed him war minister and awarded him the title of earl of Hsin-chien. His father died in 1522, however, and after mourning him he stayed home for more than five years and discussed doctrines with followers, who now numbered in the hundreds. These conversations and those earlier constitute his main work, *Ch'uan-hsi lu* (*Instructions for Practical Living*). In 1521 he had enunciated his doctrine of complete realization of the innate knowledge of the good. In June 1527 Wang was called to suppress a rebellion in Kwangsi. He succeeded in six months. He became very ill and died on his way back in Nan-an, Kiangsi, in 1529.

Because a powerful minister hated him, his earldom and other hereditary privileges were revoked. Some who protested were dismissed or banished; his teachings were severely proscribed. Thirty-eight years later (1567), a new emperor honored him with the title of marquis of Hsin-chien and the posthumous title of Wen-ch'eng (Completion of Culture). Beginning in 1584 he was offered sacrifice in the Confucian temple, the highest honor. Wang's philosophy spread all over China for 150 years and greatly influenced Japanese thought during that time. He is regarded as one of the greatest Chinese thinkers in the past 2,000 years.

WAR OF THE SONS OF LIGHT AGAINST THE SONS OF DARKNESS, THE, *Hebrew* Megillat Milḥamat B'ne, *or* Beb'ne Ḥoshekh, one of the most important DEAD SEA SCROLLS intended to guide the Sons of Light, a sect whom most scholars believe to have been the Essenes, at the end of time in their war with the enemies of Israel, the Sons of Darkness.

The *War Rule*, discovered in Cave I of QUMRĀN in 1947, is a manual for military organization and strategy, including detailed specifications for battle gear and signals. It is also a theological discourse that develops the doctrine of the spirits of truth and perversity mentioned in the sect's *Rule of the Community*. The scroll portrays an apocalyptic 40-year "holy war": the ELECT of Israel will be joined by an angelic host, while the devil and the evil ANGELS will fight alongside other nations of the earth. The victory of the forces of light would signal the final destruction of evil, after which the God of Israel would rule eternally in justice.

Most scholars identify the enemy "Kittim" of the scroll as Romans, who invaded and occupied Judaea in 63 BCE. If this is so, the major sections of the scroll (probably a composite work) were written after that date but before 68 CE, when the Qumrān community was disbanded because of the Jewish revolt of 66–70 CE.

WĀṢIL IBN 'AṬĀ' \'wä-shēl-,i-bən-ä-'tä\, *in full* Wāṣil Ibn 'Aṭā' al-Ghazzāl, *also called* Abū Ḥudhayfa (b. c. 700, Arabia—d. 748, Arabia), Muslim theologian considered the founder of the MU'TAZILA school of theology.

Wāṣil studied under the celebrated ascetic Ḥasan al-Baṣrī in Basra, Iraq, and met other influential religious figures there. In Wāṣil's time discussions began that led to the development of Islamic speculative theology. At first theological controversies among Muslims were closely tied to political events, the principal issue being the legitimacy of the rule of the Umayyad house, which seized power after the death of the fourth CALIPH, 'ALĪ.

Wāṣil's doctrinal formulations gave the Mu'tazila faction coherence as a religious sect. At the same time, both Wāṣil and the Mu'tazila became involved in a revolutionary movement led by the 'Abbāsids that was to result in the overthrow of the Umayyads. Wāṣil gathered around himself many devoted believers and ascetics, whom he often sent out as emissaries to spread his doctrines in distant provinces. *See also* KALĀM.

WATER, RELIGIOUS ASPECTS OF, derive from the nature of water as one of the most plentiful and essential of compounds, vital to life, and participating in virtually every process that occurs in plants and animals. Many of the qualities of water make it appear to be animated; on this basis it is psychologically understandable that water (*e.g.*, rain, sea, lakes, and rivers) might become a natural phenomenon worthy of worship. Water is always in motion, changes color, reflects the world, "speaks" with murmuring and roaring, brings new life to dried-out vegetation, refreshes humans and animals, and heals. Because it cleanses it is also most suitable for purification. Water also demonstrates destructive forces (seaquakes, floods, and storms). The most important mythical-religious facts symbolized by water are the following: the primal matter; the instrument of the purification and expiation; a vivifying force; a fructifying force; and a revealing and judging instrument.

The conception of a primal body of water from which everything is derived is especially prevalent among peoples living close to coasts or in river areas—*e.g.*, the Egyptian Nu (the primordial ocean), the Mesopotamian Apsu (the primeval watery abyss), and TIAMAT (the primeval chaos dragon). The earth may be taken from or emerge from the primeval water; heavenly beings appear on the emerged earth; and birds lay an egg that is later divided into two halves (heaven and earth) on the chaotic sea.

Water is viewed as an instrument for purification and expiation, especially in arid areas. Cultic acts, in such areas, generally take place only after LUSTRATIONS, sprinkling, or immersion in water. The same view holds true for entry into new communities or into life (*e.g.*, BAPTISM). Myths of a great flood are widespread over Eurasia and America. This flood, which destroys with a few exceptions a disobedient original population, is an expiation by the water, after which a new type of world is created.

Water is viewed as vivifying, like the heaven-sent rainwater that moistens the earth. Water is also equated with the flowing life forces of the body (*e.g.*, blood, sweat, and semen). The African Ashanti designate their patrilinear groups as *ntoro*, which means water, river, and semen, and the Wogeo of Papua call their patrilinear clans Dan (*i.e.*, both water and semen). The myth of the Kasuar ancestress of the But of Papua related how Kasuar's blood became sea (and salt).

Wherever early archaic culture spread the myth of the world parents heaven and earth, there also was a belief that heaven fructifies the earth with heaven's seed. The springs, pools, and rivers on the earth, therefore, bring fertility. Rites in which water serves as a substitute for semen or the fertility of men are numerous. Battles of gods and heroes with mythical beings, beasts, and monsters that hold back the fructifying water are widespread in mythology. The liberation of water during the mythical battle is equivalent to the end of the dry season or a drought.

Water also serves as an instrument that reveals and judges. Reflections in the water led to a whole series of oracles originating from an alleged prophetic or divinatory power of water. The custom of water DIVINATION is found in ancient Europe, North Africa, the Near East (*e.g.*, Babylonian fortune telling by means of cups), eastern and northern Asia (where the use of metal mirrors by the SHAMANS often replaces the water), and in Southeast Asia and Polynesia.

Water is also used as a judging element: in ordeals believed to demonstrate the judgment of the gods, water ordeals (*e.g.*, immersion in water), as well as the more frequent fire ordeals, appear. Here also the purifying character of the water plays a role.

WEBB, CLEMENT CHARLES JULIAN \\'web\\ (b. June 25, 1865, London, Eng.—d. Oct. 5, 1954, Pitchcott, Buckinghamshire), English scholar and philosopher who contributed to the study of the societal aspects of religion.

A fellow and tutor in philosophy at Magdalen College, Oxford, from 1889 to 1922, Webb served as the first Oriel Professor of the Philosophy of the Christian Religion at Oriel College, Oxford, from 1920 to 1930. Cautious of extreme claims, Webb criticized the theories of the pioneer sociologists ÉMILE DURKHEIM and Lucien Lévy-Bruhl, who had treated religion as only a social phenomenon, in his *Group Theories of Religion and the Individual* (1916). Two of his works—*God and Personality* (1918) and *Divine Personality and Human Life* (1920)—discussed the relationship between divine personality and human social, political, scientific, and religious activities.

WEBER, MAX \\'vā-bər\\ (b. April 21, 1864, Erfurt, Prussia [Germany]—d. June 14, 1920, Munich, Ger.), German sociologist and political economist best known for his thesis of the "Protestant Ethic," relating PROTESTANTISM to capitalism, and for his ideas on bureaucracy. Through his insistence on the need for objectivity in scholarship and his analysis of human action in terms of motivation, Weber profoundly influenced sociological theory.

Weber enrolled at the University of Heidelberg in 1882, interrupting his studies after two years to fulfill his year of military service at Strassburg (Strasbourg). During this time he became very close to the family of his mother's sister, Ida Baumgarten, and her husband, the historian Hermann Baumgarten, whose influence on Weber's intellectual development was profound. After his release from the military, Weber finished his studies at the University of Berlin while living at home. In 1893 he received a temporary position in jurisprudence at the University of Berlin and married Marianne Schnitger, a second cousin.

Weber's great capacity for disciplined intellectual effort, together with his unquestionable brilliance, brought the reward of meteoric professional advance. Only a year after his appointment at Berlin, he became a full professor in political economy at Freiburg, and then, in 1896, at Heidelberg. His work in this period focused on the agrarian history of ancient Rome, the evolution of medieval trading societies, the agrarian problems of the German east, the German stock exchange, and the social basis of the decline of Latin antiquity.

After a lengthy bout with a nervous condition, Weber was able to resume scholarly work in 1903, though he did not teach again until after World War I. He had resigned his professorship at Heidelberg at the height of

Max Weber, 1918
Leif Geiges

his illness, but came into an inheritance in 1907 that made him independent.

Die protestantische Ethik und der Geist des Kapitalismus (1904–05; *The Protestant Ethic and the Spirit of Capitalism*, 1930), his best-known and most controversial work, Weber noted the statistical correlation in Germany between interest and success in capitalist ventures and Protestant background. He attributed the relationship to certain accidental psychological consequences of the notions of PREDESTINATION and the calling in Puritan theology, notions that were deduced with the greatest logical severity by Calvin and his followers.

In Calvin's formulation, the doctrine of predestination invested God with such omnipotence and omniscience that sinful humanity could know neither why nor to whom God had extended the GRACE of salvation. The psychological insecurity that this doctrine imposed on Calvin's followers was too great, and they began to look for loopholes that would indicate the direction of divine will. The consequence was an ethic of unceasing commitment to one's worldly calling and ascetic abstinence from any enjoyment of the profit reaped from such labors. The practical result of such beliefs and practices was the most rapid possible accumulation of capital.

Weber's political sociology is concerned with the distinction between charismatic, traditional, and legal forms of authority. CHARISMA refers to the gift of spiritual inspiration underlying the power of religious PROPHECY and political leadership. Throughout his life Weber believed that life was essentially a flux, a non-rational flow which human beings "rationalized" through various world-views. Human history he saw as a struggle between emotion (the nonrational) and calculating reason (rational), between the charismatic leader and the technocrat. Thus the history of religions was a history of the rationalization and demystification of the world through RELIGIOUS BELIEFS and practices beginning with myths and rituals and ending with impersonal bureaucratic organizations. Further tracing the relation between religion and RATIONALISM, in his work on the SOCIOLOGY OF RELIGION Weber claimed that the doctrine of KARMA in India was the most rational solution to the THEODICY problem since it removed the mystery of evil by placing it solely in the actions and responsibilities of each individual.

Weber's most powerful impact on his contemporaries came in the last years of his life, when, from 1916 to 1918, he argued against Germany's annexationist war goals and in favor of a strengthened parliament. He stood for sobriety in politics and scholarship against the apocalyptic mood in the months following Germany's defeat. His last achievements were assisting in the drafting of the new constitution and in the founding of the German Democratic Party.

WEN-TI \\'wən-'dē\\, *Pinyin* Wendi, *also called* Wen Ch'ang \\-'chän\\, or Wen-ch'ang-ti-chün \\-'jūen\\, *Pinyin* Wen Chang, or Wenchangdijun, Chinese god of literature, charged by the JADE EMPEROR (Yü-huang) with keeping a log of men of letters and a register of their titles and honors so that he can mete out rewards and punishments to each according to his merit.

WEN-TI is said to have had 17 REINCARNATIONS, during the ninth of which he appeared on earth as Chang Ya. He is said to have lived during T'ang dynasty times (618–907 CE) or during the 3rd or 4th century or earlier. His brilliant writing led to his canonization during the T'ang dynasty and to his appointment as lord of literature in the 13th century. Because Chang is said to have lived at Tzu-t'ung in Szech-

wan province, in that region he is worshiped as Tzu-t'ung Shen (Spirit of Tzu-t'ung). He has two assistants, K'uei Hsing, the god of examinations, with whom he is sometimes confused, and Chu I (Red Coat).

WESAK \\'wā-ˌsäk\\, *also spelled* Vesak, *Sanskrit* Vaiśākha, *Pāli* Vesākha, most important of the THERAVĀDA Buddhist festivals, commemorating the birth, Enlightenment, and death of the BUDDHA GOTAMA. The event is observed on the full-moon day of the lunar month Vesākha, which falls in April or May. The day is observed as a public holiday in many Southeast Asian countries. It is marked by devotional services and deeds intended to be meritorious, such as the presentation of food or alms to monks or the release of captive birds in memory of the Buddha's compassion.

WESLEY, CHARLES \\'wes-lē, *commonly* 'wez-\\ (b. Dec. 18, 1707, Epworth, Lincolnshire, Eng.—d. March 29, 1788, London), English clergyman, poet, and HYMN writer, who, with his elder brother John, started the Methodist movement in the Church of England.

After attending Westminster School, Wesley was elected to Christ Church, Oxford, in 1726. He underwent a spiritual awakening during the winter of 1728–29 and initiated, with his brother and two other undergraduates, the Holy Club. In 1735, in order to aid his brother John in a MISSION to Georgia (in North America), he accepted holy orders.

Charles was subject to extremes of emotion, and his spiritual despair and physical exhaustion in Georgia led him to return to England after only a few months. With the help of the Moravians, like his brother John, he found spiritual peace. On Whitsunday, May 21, 1738, he found himself "at peace with God." He became an eloquent preacher for the Methodist cause and translated the Gospel into hymns, which became important means of evangelism.

Personal and professional disagreements between Charles and his brother after 1749 caused an estrangement between the two, and Charles withdrew from active leadership of the Methodist societies. His work as an evangelist and hymn writer for METHODISM, however, had already made its permanent mark. He published more than 4,500 hymns and left some 3,000 in manuscript. Among Wesley's best-known hymns are "Love divine, all loves excelling"; "Hark, the herald angels sing"; "Christ the Lord is ris'n today"; "Soldiers of Christ, arise"; "Rejoice, the Lord is king"; and "Jesu, lover of my soul."

WESLEY, JOHN (b. June 17, 1703, Epworth, Lincolnshire, Eng.—d. March 2, 1791, London), Anglican clergyman, evangelist, and founder, with his brother Charles, of the Methodist movement in the Church of England.

John Wesley was the second son of Samuel, a former NONCONFORMIST (dissenter from the Church of England) and rector at Epworth, and Susanna Wesley. Graduating in 1724 from Christ Church, Oxford, he was made a deacon in 1725 and the following year was elected a fellow of Lincoln College. After assisting his father at Epworth and Wroot, he was ordained a priest on Sept. 22, 1728.

Recalled to Oxford in October 1729 to fulfill the residential requirements of his fellowship, John joined his brother Charles, Robert Kirkham, and William Morgan in a religious study group that was derisively called the "Methodists" because of their emphasis on methodical study and devotion. Taking over the leadership of the group from Charles, John helped the group to grow in numbers. The Methodists, also called the Holy Club, were known for their frequent communion services and for fasting two days a week. After 1730, the group became socially active, visiting Oxford prisoners, teaching them to read, paying their debts, and attempting to find employment for them. The Methodists extended their activities to workhouses and the poor; distributing food, clothes, medicine, and books; and also to running a school. When the Wesleys left the Holy Club in 1735, the group disintegrated.

Following his father's death in April 1735, John was persuaded by an Oxford friend, John Burton, and Col. James Oglethorpe, governor of the colony of Georgia in North America, to oversee the spiritual lives of the colonists and to preach to the Indians as an agent for the Society for the Propagation of the Gospel. Accompanied by Charles, who was ordained for this MISSION, John was introduced to some Moravian emigrants who appeared to him to possess the spiritual peace for which he had been searching. The mission to the Indians proved abortive, nor did Wesley succeed with most of his flock, who were antagonized by his stiff high churchmanship.

Back in London, John met a Moravian, Peter Böhler, who convinced him that what he needed was simply faith, and he also discovered MARTIN LUTHER'S commentary on the Letter of Paul to the Galatians, which emphasized the scriptural doctrine of JUSTIFICATION by GRACE through faith alone. On May 24, 1738, in Aldersgate Street, London, during a meeting composed largely of Moravians under the auspices of the Church of England, Wesley's intellectual conviction was transformed into a personal experience when Luther's preface to the commentary to the Letter of Paul to the Romans was read.

From this point onward, at the age of 35, Wesley viewed his mission as one of preaching salvation by faith. Rejected by the Church of England, he went to religious societies, trying to inject new spiritual vigor into them by introducing "bands"—*i.e.*, small groups within each society that were confined to members of the same sex and marital status who were prepared to share intimate secrets with each other and to receive mutual rebukes. For such groups Wesley drew up *Rules of the Band Societies* in December 1738.

For a year he worked through existing church societies, but resistance to his methods increased. In 1739, Wesley gathered converts into societies for continuing fellowship and spiritual growth. Soon other such groups were formed in London, Bristol, and elsewhere. To avoid unworthy members, Wesley published, in 1743, *Rules for the Methodist Societies*. To promote new societies he became an itinerant preacher. Because most ordained clergymen did not favor his approach, Wesley was compelled to seek the services of laymen, who also became itinerant preachers and helped administer the Methodist societies.

Many of Wesley's preachers had gone to the American colonies, but after the American Revolution most returned to England. Because the bishop of London would not ordain some of his preachers to serve in the United States, Wesley took it upon himself, in 1784, to do so. He also declared his independence from the Church of England.

WESTMINSTER ABBEY \'west-min-stər\, church, originally a BENEDICTINE monastery, refounded as the Collegiate

Westminster Abbey, London
A.F. Kersting

Church of St. Peter in Westminster (today one of the boroughs constituting Greater London) by Queen Elizabeth I in 1560. Legend relates that Sebert, the first Christian king of the East Saxons, founded a church on a small Thames island, then known as Thorney but later called the west minster, or monastery, and that this church was miraculously consecrated by ST. PETER.

St. Edward the Confessor (reigned 1042–66) built a new church on the site, which was consecrated in 1065. It was of considerable size, cruciform in plan, and with a central and two western towers. In 1245 Henry III pulled down Edward's church (except the nave) and replaced it with the present abbey church in the pointed Gothic style of the period. The rebuilding of the Norman-style nave was begun by 1376 and continued intermittently until Tudor times. The chapel of Henry VII (begun *c.* 1503), in Perpendicular Gothic style, replaced an earlier Lady chapel and is famed for its exquisite fan vaulting. The western towers were the last addition to the building. They are usually attributed to Sir Christopher Wren, but they were actually built by Nicholas Hawksmoor and John James and completed in 1745. The choir stalls in the body of the church date from 1848, and the high altar and reredos were remodeled by Sir George Gilbert Scott in 1867. Scott and J.L. Pearson also restored the north transept front (1880–90).

Since William the Conqueror, every British sovereign has been crowned in the abbey except Edward V and Edward VIII, neither of whom was crowned. Many kings and queens are buried near the shrine of Edward the Confessor or in Henry VII's chapel. The last sovereign to be buried in the abbey was George II (died 1760).

The abbey is also crowded with the tombs and memorials of British subjects. Part of the south transept is well known as Poets' Corner, while the north transept has memorials to British statesmen. The grave of the "Unknown Warrior," whose remains were brought from Flanders in 1920, is in the center of the nave near the west door.

WESTMINSTER CONFESSION, CONFESSION OF FAITH of English-speaking PRESBYTERIANS. It was produced by the Westminster Assembly, which was called together in 1643 during the English Civil War, and was completed in 1646 and approved by Parliament after some revisions in June 1648. When the English monarchy was restored in 1660, the episcopal form of church government was reinstated, and the Presbyterian confession lost its official status in England. It was adopted by the Church of Scotland in 1647, by various American and English Presbyterian bodies, and by some Congregationalists and BAPTISTS.

Patterned after the Irish Articles of Religion (1615), the Reformed tradition of the European continent, and the creedal heritage of the early Christian church, the confession was a theological consensus of international CALVINISM. Stating that the sole doctrinal authority is SCRIPTURE, it restates the doctrines of the TRINITY and of JESUS CHRIST from the creeds of the early church and gives Reformed views of the SACRAMENTS, the ministry, and the two COVENANTS of works and GRACE. It states that the doctrine of the eternal decree (PREDESTINATION) is that "some men and ANGELS are predestinated unto everlasting life, and others foreordained to everlasting death," and yet "neither is God the author of SIN, nor is violence offered to the will of creatures."

WHITE LOTUS, or Pai-lien chiao \'bī-'lyen-'jyaù\, Chinese Buddhist millenarian movement founded by Mao Tzu-yüan in the 12th century. An offshoot of PURE LAND BUDDHISM, the White Lotus Society was a loose association of laymen and monks devoted to restraint of the passions and rebirth into the Pure Land, via recitation of the name AMITĀBHA, dietary restrictions, and other means. It appealed in particular to women and to the poor, and the Society became most prominent through its role in the White Lotus Rebellion (1786–1804), a large-scale uprising in central China that contributed to the decline of the Ch'ing dynasty. The movement was banned in 1322.

WILAYAH \wi-'lī-ə\ (Arabic: "divine friendship," "sainthood"), in ISLAM, a special friendship with God that is available to all believers. More specifically, wilayah describes the relationship Muslim saints have with God. The saints, generally Sufis, are those who have been specially chosen by God as friends of ALLĀH. They are selected by God as leaders of his kingdom and have been granted miraculous powers. The saints were often objects of special devotion in their lifetimes and in death their tombs were centers which devotees visited to receive blessings. The Sufis themselves discussed wilayah extensively and developed a hierarchy of the friends of Allāh culminating in the quṭb, the "pole" or "axis" who was the spiritual center of the community and who was responsible for its well-being. (See SUFISM.)

WILLIAMS, ROGER \'wil-yəmz\ (b. 1603?, London—d. Jan. 27/March 15, 1683, Providence, R.I.), English colonist in New England, founder of the colony of Rhode Island and pioneer of religious liberty. The son of a merchant tailor, he was educated at Cambridge. In 1630 he left his post as CHAPLAIN, which had brought him into contact with such politically active Puritans as Oliver Cromwell and Thomas Hooker, to pursue his NONCONFORMIST religious ideals in New England.

Arriving in Boston in 1631, Williams refused to associate himself with the Anglican Puritans and in the following year moved to the separatist Plymouth Colony. Invited by the church at Salem to become pastor in 1634, Williams was banished from Massachusetts Bay by the civil authorities in part for his view that magistrates had no right to interfere in matters of religion. Consequently, in January 1636 Williams set out for Narragansett Bay, and in the spring, on land purchased from the Narragansett Indians, he founded the town of Providence and the colony of Rhode Island. Providence became a haven for ANABAPTISTS, QUAKERS, and others whose beliefs were denied public expression. Williams was briefly an Anabaptist but in 1639 declared himself a Seeker. He remained a steadfast believer in Calvinist theology. Williams went to England in 1643 to obtain a charter for Rhode Island and again in 1651–54 to have it confirmed. He was the first president of Rhode Island under its charter.

Williams was a vigorous controversialist and a prolific writer. His greatest work was *The Bloudy Tenent of Persecution* (1644).

WISE, ISAAC MAYER \'wīz\ (b. March 29, 1819, Steingrub, Bohemia [now Kamenný Dvůr, Czech Rep.]—d. March 26, 1900, Cincinnati, Ohio, U.S.), RABBI and organizer of American Reform Jewish institutions.

After serving as a rabbi for two years in Radnice, Bohemia, Wise immigrated in 1846 to Albany, N.Y., where he was a rabbi for eight years. In 1854 Wise accepted the pulpit of Bene Yeshurun in Cincinnati, a post he retained for the rest of his life.

Wise propagandized tirelessly for centralized Reform institutions in his English-language weekly, the *American Israelite*; in his German-language paper, *Die Deborah*; and in many rabbinical conferences. The fruits of his efforts were the Union of American Hebrew Congregations—its educational arm, the Hebrew Union College (now Hebrew Union College–Jewish Institute of Religion), was the first permanent American rabbinical college—and the CENTRAL CONFERENCE OF AMERICAN RABBIS. Wise served as president of both institutions until his death.

Wise tried to compile a standard Reform prayer book and in 1857 published the *Minhag America* ("American Usage"), which was superseded in 1894 by the Union Prayer Book. A believer in the universal mission of JUDAISM, he was a firm opponent of the establishment of a Jewish state in Palestine. Although Wise failed in his efforts to unite American Jews of all persuasions, he did bring about great unanimity among Reform Jews. In addition, he succeeded in adapting REFORM JUDAISM to American life.

WISE, STEPHEN SAMUEL (b. March 17, 1874, Budapest, Hung., Austria-Hungary—d. April 19, 1949, New York, N.Y., U.S.), Reform RABBI and leader of the Zionist movement in the United States.

Wise earned his Ph.D. at Columbia University in 1901 and received his rabbinical training from private teachers. After serving as rabbi to congregations in New York City and Portland, Ore., he founded the influential Free SYNAGOGUE (1907) in New York City, which he led until his death. Wise subsequently became a noted civic reformer.

Wise was one of the first Jewish leaders in the United States to become active in the Zionist movement (*see* ZIONISM). He attended the Second Zionist Congress in Basel, Switz., in 1898, and that same year he helped found the Zionist Organization of America (ZOA), of which he served as president in 1936–38. He also helped found and led the permanent American Jewish Congress and the World Jewish Congress (1936). As a prominent member of the Democratic Party, Wise influenced the U.S. government toward approval of the Balfour Declaration, supporting the establishment of a Jewish homeland in Palestine. He was a leader in the struggle to marshal American public opinion against Adolf Hitler in the 1930s.

In 1922 Wise founded the Jewish Institute of Religion in New York City, a seminary that was especially designed to train liberal rabbis for the New York area; this school merged with Hebrew Union College in 1950.

WITCHCRAFT, term that functions in three very different and discrete spheres of meaning that are often confused one with the other. The first refers to the accusations made by the Christian church of "diabolical" witchcraft supposedly practiced by some people of the late medieval and early modern periods of Europe and the colonial period in America. The second usage is as a comparative category in anthropology and religious studies; here it refers to a phenomenon involving SORCERY and magic found in various historical periods and cultures. The third and most recent use of the term is as a label of self-identification for the practice of certain types of Neo-Pagans in the 20th century.

History. The first and oldest meaning of witchcraft refers to the exercise of supernatural power by persons supposedly in league with the devil and thus is a type of SATANISM. Individuals named as witches were identified with those the Christian church regarded as heretics, and both types of enemies of the orthodox were persecuted in waves beginning in the late Middle Ages.

The church accused suspected witches of having made a pact with devil, from whom their malevolent powers derived and with whom they would meet in secret, nocturnal gatherings called sabbats. The mostly female witches supposedly were able to fly to these meetings, where they desecrated Christian symbols, indulged in sacrificial infanticide and CANNIBALISM, and participated in sexual orgies with Satan. These and other lurid details of the witchcraft cult were codified in manuals produced during the INQUISITION, the most infamous of which is the MALLEUS MALEFICARUM ("The Hammer of Witches") first published in the 15th century. Suspected witches were tortured until they admit-

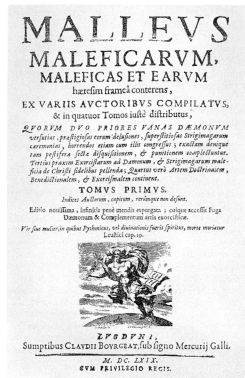

French edition, published in Lyon in 1669, of Malleus Maleficarum (c. 1486), the standard treatise on witchcraft and demonology
The Granger Collection

ted such practices, thereby confirming the existence of the witchcraft cult in the eyes of church officials. Between 1450 and 1700 it has been estimated that at least 100,000 people—predominantly women—were executed as witches, and perhaps overall millions suffered through what has been called one of the longest and most bizarre delusions in Western history.

There is, nonetheless, no historical evidence of any such organized witchcraft religion, let alone one with tentacles as wide-ranging as the church believed. The most important function of the witchcraft craze was scapegoating and the promotion of social cohesion at the expense of an enemy. Various kinds of otherwise unexplained personal and social misfortunes could be blamed on individuals who were, in one way or another, marginal to the group or outright outcasts and pariahs. There was certainly a strong misogynist streak present as well, and women who were elderly, poor, or single were often accused. The authors of the *Malleus maleficarum* wrote that "all witchcraft comes from carnal lust, which is in women insatiable" and that women are "intellectually like children" and also subject to the devil's temptations. The last major outbreak of witch-hunting occurred in Salem, Mass., at the end of the 17th century.

In contrast to this hostility, many societies distinguish between "good" magic or witchcraft and "bad." The Azande of Sudan, for example, traditionally regarded witchcraft that involved oracles, DIVINATION, and AMULETS as benevolent, whereas sorcery aimed at nefariously and illicitly harming or even killing those one hated or resented was regarded as antisocial and malevolent. The roles witchcraft is seen to play in traditional societies are various, depending on whether it is the magical practitioner or the anthropologist who is evaluating the practice. The practitioners may see witchcraft as serving to heal sicknesses or foretell the future. Ethnologists tend to explain witchcraft as reducing social tensions and hostilities; reinforcing order, justice, and solidarity; or providing the weak with power and society with SCAPEGOATS. Indeed, one of the most important functions of witchcraft may be explanatory, for attributing all kinds of events, conditions, and misfortunes to the workings of witches provides those living in premodern society with a sense of understanding, or provides lived experience with a socially meaningful explanatory context. Witchcraft as identified in the second usage is found not only in certain tribal societies, but also in ancient Greece, Rome, China, India, and other civilizations.

Modern developments. Witchcraft has come to take on quite a different meaning in recent decades as it has been adopted as a label of self-identification (also called Wicca, from the Old English root of the term) among a segment of the so-called Neo-Pagan movement. A diverse and only minimally affiliated conglomeration of various groups, the Neo-Pagans consist not only of those calling themselves witches but also those practicing revived or reinvented forms of ancient EGYPTIAN RELIGION or GREEK RELIGION, Druidism, pre-Christian European folk religion, ceremonial magic, or any number of other traditions that worship the powers of nature or deities closely connected to the natural world (see NEW RELIGIOUS MOVEMENTS).

Some practitioners of Wicca claim an unbroken tradition stretching back in time for millennia. In 1921 Egyptologist and folklorist Margaret Murray published an influential work entitled *The Witch-cult in Western Europe* in which she argued that witchcraft was the ancient religion of pre-Christian Europe. This religion was comparable to other "fertility cults" around the world and was forced underground by the Christian church. While virtually no historians today accept this thesis, it has provided some Wiccans with a myth of antiquity for their new religion.

In fact, however, modern witchcraft arguably has much more recent origins. In 1939 an Englishman, Gerald B. Gardner, was, according to his own account, initiated into a COVEN of witches who practiced an ancient and hereditary form of the religion, although it is not certain such a group ever existed. In any event, Gardner and his partner Doreen Valiente went public after the last Witchcraft Act was repealed in Britain in 1951 and created the first modern cult of witchcraft out of beliefs and rituals eclectically borrowed from FOLKLORE and mythology, Masonic rites, the works of the occultist Aleister Crowley, Rosicrucianism, and Eastern MYSTICISM. Gardner's theology centered around a "Horned God" of fertility, sometimes identified with PAN, and a great Earth Goddess figure who gradually took on more and more importance. Gardner is also credited with the invention of the term *Wicca*; the three major branches of British Wicca, and their American extensions, all can be traced back to him.

In the United States during the 1960s and '70s another form of modern witchcraft arose and has now spread to Europe and elsewhere: feminist or "Dianic" Wicca. This type of witchcraft revolves around the Goddess conceived of as the supreme being and usually worshiped more or less exclusively. The majority of such groups exclude men, and Dianic Wicca has sometimes been called the spiritual arm of the feminist movement (see also WOMEN AND RELIGION).

Taken together, the members and practitioners of all forms of modern witchcraft are numbered at about 100,000, and Wicca has been called one of the fastest growing of the new religious movements of Western Europe and North America.

Most, if not all, modern witches share certain broadly conceived beliefs. Most would subscribe to the theological importance of the feminine principle, or Goddess, and the need to balance what many regard as the overly male (and often patriarchal) view of divinity in mainstream religions of the West. All modern witchcraft traditions share a deep respect for nature and tend to be both pantheisitic and polytheistic. All witches practice some form of ritual magic, almost always considered "good," or constructive. Virtually all practitioners of modern witchcraft subscribe to what has been dubbed the "Wiccan Rede" or ethical code: "An' it harm none, do what thou wilt."

While there are many "solitary" witches, who practice their craft alone, witches are also organized into covens of as few as three and as many as several dozen. Covens meet at regular times, most frequently on the nights of the new and full moons and at the eight high festivals of the Neo-Pagan calendar: Yule (winter solstice), Imbolg (CANDLEMAS, February 2), the vernal equinox, BELTANE (May Day, May 1), Midsummer (summer solstice), Lammas (August 1), the autumnal equinox, and SAMHAIN (HALLOWEEN). The rituals usually include the casting of a circle, which sacralizes the place of meeting, the invoking of the gods and goddesses, the practice of ceremonial magic, and a sharing of food and drink as well as stories and songs. While some few traditions have occasions that call for the so-called "Great Rite," which involves ritual sex, most forms of Wicca do not include this in their ritual repetoire.

There has been a tendency toward increased institutionalization among Wiccan groups. Legally recognized religious organizations, churches, and seminaries have arisen and antidefamation leagues have been formed. Representatives from Wiccan groups have joined in ecumenical initiatives and are especially active in environmental issues.

WITCH DOCTOR, healer or benevolent worker of magic in a nonliterate society. The term originated in England in the 18th century and is generally considered to be pejorative and anthropologically inaccurate. *See also* MEDICINE MAN; SHAMAN.

WITCHES' SABBATH, nocturnal gathering of witches, a colorful and intriguing part of the lore surrounding witchcraft in Christian European tradition. The concept dates only from *c.* 1400 CE, when the INQUISITION began investigating witchcraft seriously. It was believed that the sabbath, or sabbat might be held on any day of the week, though Saturday was considered rare as being sacred to the Virgin MARY.

Reports of attendance at sabbaths varied; one confessed witch reported a gathering of 10,000. Witches reputedly traveled to the sabbath by smearing themselves with special ointment that enabled them to fly through the air, or they rode on a goat, ram, or dog supplied by the devil. Favorite locations included the Brocken, in the Harz Mountains, Germany; the Bald Mountain, near Kiev, Russia; the Blocula, Sweden; and the Département du Puy-de-Dôme, Auvergne, France. Typical dates included the two traditional DRUID festivals, the eve of May Day (April 30) and All Hallows Eve (October 31), and the seasonal festivals of winter (February 2), spring (June 23), summer (August 1), and fall (December 21). Occurrences at the sabbath were represented by inquisitors as including obeisance to the devil by kissing him under his tail, dancing, feasting, and indiscriminate intercourse.

WOMEN AND RELIGION, study of women's roles within religious life, particularly in societies in which religion is regulated and controlled by men. In the early days of the history of religions the dominant approach to the study of women and religion began from the hypothesis that matriarchy and goddess-oriented religions preceded the patriarchal cultures of historical times. This approach began with Johann Jakob Bachofen's *Das Mutterrecht* (1861; "Mother Right"), and was further developed by Friedrich Engels in *The Origin of the Family, Private Property and the State* (1884), and revived by Elizabeth Gould Davis in *The First Sex* (1971).

The belief that in prehistoric times all, or most, religions were centered around a single, supreme Goddess has inspired many writers, including Jessie Weston (*From Ritual to Romance*, 1920), Carl Gustav Jung (*Four Archetypes*, 1969), Erich Neumann (*The Great Mother*, 1955), Robert Graves (*The White Goddess*, 1948), Adrienne Rich (*Of Woman Born*, 1976), and Mary Daly (*Beyond God the Father*, 1973, and *Gyn/ecology*, 1978).

One of the most influential books about the primeval Goddess was Marija Gimbutas' *The Gods and Goddesses of Old Europe, 7000 to 3500 BC: Myths, Legends and Cult Images* (1974). Gimbutas' archaeological research was both solid and original, but as her interpretations became increasingly ideological they were appropriated by the Goddess-worshiping wing of the women's movement known as feminist spirituality, or the "Goddess-feminists," whose characteristic style of interpretation too often trivialized and exaggerated Gimbutas' ideas. The reduction of all goddesses to one, a tendency that for a time was dominant, too easily led to the reduction of all aspects of women to what Mary Lefkowitz calls a "genital identity." In recent years several excellent collections of essays combated this trend by emphasizing the striking differences between goddesses in different cultures.

Women intersect with religion at two primary points: in the divine sphere as divinities and in the human sphere as members of a society. A common characteristic of Goddess-feminist interpretation has been to subsume the two by claiming that a Goddess-oriented religion can develop only within a culture in which women play an important and valued role. By contrast, what we know about cults of goddesses from historic texts and the evidence of contemporary society indicates that women may be treated quite poorly where goddesses are worshiped. For instance, the feminist historian of JUDAISM Tikva Frymer-Kensky argues that, although polytheistic systems did give females a certain separate status, they subordinated women, marginalized them, and limited them to roles of fertility, sexuality, nurturance, and wisdom. In contrast, she argues, women were actually regarded as more equal partners under patriarchal Judaism, despite their subordinate social position. As a rule, the more powerful, and hence dangerous, goddesses are perceived to be, the more intrinsically powerful, and hence dangerous, human women are perceived to be.

While Christian and Jewish scholars long revered their female saints and leaders (*e.g.*, JOAN OF ARC, Judith), Hindus, Buddhists, and Muslims also revered their own great women. The history of religions, however, tended to neglect non-Western woman religious leaders. Only in the last decades of the 20th century did scholars begin to take seriously the construction of human women within the texts and the lives of actual women, as storytellers and ritualists, for example, in living religions. This period saw the early stirrings of studies of women who founded, transformed, or maintained religious movements in their own right.

Wŏnhyo Daisa

Wŏnhyo Daisa \'wən-'hyō-'ta-ˌsä, -'da-ˌsä\, *also called* Wŏnhyo (b. 617, Korea—d. 686, Korea), Buddhist priest who is considered the greatest of the ancient Korean religious teachers and one of the Ten Sages of the Ancient Korean Kingdom.

A renowned theoretician, Wŏnhyo was the first to systematize Korean BUDDHISM, bringing the various Buddhist doctrines into a unity that was sensible to both the philosophers and the common people. Wŏnhyo's realization of the need to practice a life that maintained harmony between the ideal and the real is illustrated by an anecdote that tells how he, as a priest, assumed to be practicing ASCETICISM,

one night slept with a beautiful princess. Rather than chastise himself the next morning, he merely admitted that true spirituality was obtained not by pursuing unreal ends but by admitting the limitations of one's person.

His works exerted a profound influence on the history of Korean Buddhism. Most famous are "A Commentary on the Awakening of Faith in the Mahāyāna," "A Commentary on the Avataṃsaka Sūtra," "A Study on the Diamond Samādhi Sūtra," and "The Meaning of Two Desires."

WORKER-PRIEST

WORKER-PRIEST, in the ROMAN CATHOLIC church, member of a movement, especially in France and Belgium after World War II, seeking to reach the working classes, who had become alienated from the church. The worker-priests took construction and factory jobs, sharing the living conditions and social and economic problems of their coworkers. The movement was supported by Cardinal Emmanuel Suhard of Paris. Some worker-priests became politically active, joining in demonstrations on such matters as housing, racial discrimination, and peace. The movement was ordered discontinued by PIUS XII in 1954 and by John XXIII in 1959. In 1965 Paul VI approved it in modified form.

WORLD COUNCIL OF CHURCHES

WORLD COUNCIL OF CHURCHES (WCC), ecumenical organization founded in 1948 in Amsterdam. The WCC works for the unity and renewal of the Christian denominations and offers them a forum in which to work together in the spirit of tolerance and mutual understanding.

The WCC originated in the ecumenical movement after World War I. The Life and Work Movement had concentrated on the practical activities of the churches, and the Faith and Order Movement had focused on the beliefs and organization of the churches and the problems involved in reunion. Before long, the two movements began to work toward establishing a single organization. A conference of church leaders met in 1938 in Utrecht, Neth., to prepare a constitution; but World War II intervened, and the first assembly of the WCC was not held until 1948. In 1961 the International Missionary Council united with the WCC.

The WCC's members include most Protestant and Eastern Orthodox bodies but not the ROMAN CATHOLIC church or the Southern BAPTISTS of the United States. The controlling body of the WCC is the assembly, which meets at intervals of approximately six years at various locations. The assembly appoints a central committee that in turn chooses from its membership an executive committee of 26 members, which, along with specialized committees and 6 copresidents, carries on the work between assemblies. The headquarters of the council is in Geneva, Switz.

The work of the WCC is divided into three main areas: church relations, ecumenical study and promotion, and interchurch aid and service to refugees. Under these divisions are a number of groups and commissions, such as faith and order, the commission on the life and work of the laity in the church and on the cooperation of men and women in church and society.

WORLD FELLOWSHIP OF BUDDHISTS, THE

WORLD FELLOWSHIP OF BUDDHISTS, THE, ecumenical organization that promotes the growth, strength, and unity of the world Buddhist community. The World Fellowship of Buddhists (WFB) was founded in May 1950 in Colombo, Sri Lanka, by G.P. Malalasekera (1899–1973), a noted Buddhist scholar. Its headquarters have been in Bangkok, Thai., for the past 30 years, although it was previously located in Sri Lanka and Myanmar (Burma), respectively, for eight years at each location.

The organization's aims and objectives are to promote the study and practice of BUDDHISM, in part by establishing regional branches of the WFB and founding DHARMA centers worldwide. The WFB holds biannual conferences devoted to discussing contemporary issues of importance for the maintenance and advancement of Buddhism worldwide, and it is involved in the development and maintenance of institutions for educational, social, economic, cultural, and humanitarian efforts. It also coordinates and promotes the exchange of MISSIONS and students of Buddhism between countries. Although the WFB has an apolitical aim in its charter, it nonetheless has also supported environmental and anti-nuclear causes.

WORLD RELIGIONS, classification made popular in the 19th century that referred to an exclusive set of religions that crossed national boundaries. At first only three religions met the requirement: BUDDHISM, CHRISTIANITY, and ISLAM. Later the set of religions was increased to seven: Buddhism, Christianity, CONFUCIANISM/TAOISM, HINDUISM, Islam, JUDAISM, and SHINTŌ. For most scholars of religion the typology is no longer useful.

WORLD TREE, *also called* cosmic tree, center of the world, a widespread motif in many myths and folktales among various peoples, especially in Asia, Australia, Meso-America, and North America. There are three main forms.

In the vertical tradition, the tree extends between earth, heaven, and underworld. It is the vital connection between the world of the gods and the human world. Oracles and judgments or other prophetic activities are performed at its base.

In the horizontal form, the tree is planted at the center of the world and is protected by supernatural guardians. It is the source of terrestrial fertility and life. Human life is descended from it; its fruit confers everlasting life; and if it were cut down, all fecundity would cease.

In some cultures, cosmic trees grow at the four quarters of the universe and, together with the tree at the axis, coordinate the emanation and collection of supernatural forces on a daily basis.

Wovoka, charcoal drawing by James Mooney from a photograph, 1891
Laurie Platt Winfrey, Inc.

WORMS, CONCORDAT OF \kən-'kȯr-ˌdat . . . 'wȯrmz, *German* 'vȯrms\, compromise arranged in 1122 between Pope Calixtus II (1119–24) and the Holy Roman emperor Henry V (reigned 1106–25) settling the INVESTITURE CONTROVERSY, a struggle between the empire and the PAPACY over the control of church offices. The concordat marked the end of the first phase of the conflict between Emperor Henry IV (1056–1106) and POPE GREGORY VII (1073–85) and made a clear distinction between the spiritual side of a prelate's office and his position as a landed magnate and vassal of the crown. BISHOPS and ABBOTS were to be chosen by the clergy, but the emperor was authorized to decide contested elections. The man chosen was first to be invested with the powers, privileges, and lands pertaining to his office as vassal, for which he did homage to the emperor, and then with the ecclesiastical powers and lands, which he acquired from his ecclesiastical superior, who represented the authority of the church.

WORMS, DIET OF (1521), meeting of the Diet (assembly) of the Holy Roman Empire held at Worms, Ger., in 1521, that was made famous by the appearance before it of MARTIN LUTHER to defend his beliefs.

Pope Leo X had condemned 41 propositions of Luther's in June 1520 and excommunicated him on Jan. 21, 1521, but it was several months later before the condemnation was received in Germany. Frederick III, elector of Saxony, refused to take any action against Luther but agreed with the Holy Roman Emperor, Charles V, that Luther would appear for a hearing at the Diet under the emperor's safe-conduct.

On April 17–18, 1521, Luther went before the Diet. He admitted that the books displayed before the court were his, but he refused to repudiate his works unless convinced of error by SCRIPTURE or by reason. Otherwise, he stated, his conscience was bound by the Word of God. Disorder broke out at Luther's refusal to recant, and the emperor dismissed the Diet for the day.

A hero to the Germans but a heretic to others, Luther soon left Worms but spent the next nine months in hiding. In May the Diet passed the Edict of Worms, which declared that Luther was an outlaw and a heretic who should be captured and turned over to the emperor and whose writings were forbidden. The edict, never enforced, nevertheless inhibited Luther's travels throughout his lifetime and made him dependent on his prince for protection.

WOVOKA \wō-'vō-kə\, *also called* Jack Wilson (b. 1858?, Utah Territory [U.S.]—d. October 1932, Walker River Indian Reservation, Nev.), Native American religious leader who founded the second messianic GHOST DANCE cult, which peaked about 1890.

His father, Tävibo, had been an assistant to Wodziwob, the Paiute leader of the first Ghost Dance movement of the 1870s. By 1888, he had acquired a reputation as a MEDICINE MAN. In 1889 Wovoka claimed that God had informed him that in two years the ancestors of his people would rise from the dead, buffalo again would fill the Plains, and the white man would vanish. To bring this about, Indians must remain peaceful and profess their faith in the RESURRECTION of the dead by taking part in a ritual dance, the so-called Ghost Dance. The practice quickly spread to other tribes, notably the Sioux. Wovoka was revered as a new MESSIAH.

The ensuing religious fervor frightened white settlers, and the hostility between the two cultures culminated in the massacre by U.S. troops of about 200 Sioux men, women, and children at Wounded Knee, S.D., on Dec. 29, 1890. After this tragic incident the movement went into decline.

WU \'wü\, *Pinyin* wu, *English* "Not-Being," fundamental Taoist philosophical concept. In the thought of LAO-TZU interpreted by Wang Pi, Not-Being (*wu*) and Being (*yu*), the Nameless (*wu-ming*) and the Named (*yu-ming*), are interdependent and "grow out of one another." *Wu* and *yu* are two aspects of the permanent TAO: "In its mode of being Unseen, we will see its mysteries; in the mode of the Seen, we will see its boundaries." Not-Being does not mean Nothingness but rather the absence of perceptible qualities; in Lao-tzu's view it is superior to Being. It is the Void (that is, empty incipience) that holds all potentialities and without which even Being lacks its efficacy. According to the scholar Ho Yen, *wu* is beyond name and form, hence absolute and complete and capable of accomplishing anything.

WU-CHING, *Pinyin* Wujing: *see* FIVE CLASSICS.

WU-HSING \'wü-'shiŋ\, *Pinyin* wuxing (Chinese: "five elements"), in ancient Chinese COSMOLOGY, the five basic dynamic components of the physical universe: earth, wood, metal, fire, and water. These elements were believed to destroy and succeed one another in an immutable cycle and were correlated with the cardinal directions, seasons, colors, musical tones, and bodily organs.

The WU-HSING cycle served as a broad explanatory principle in Chinese history, philosophy, and medicine; it was first linked to dynastic history by the sage-alchemist Tsou Yen (3rd century BCE). The Neo-Confucian philosophers of the Sung dynasty (960–1279 CE) extended the *wu-hsing* to encompass the Five Virtues (benevolence, righteousness, reverence, wisdom, and sincerity).

WU-WEI \'wü-'wā\, *Pinyin* wuwei (Chinese: "nonaction"), in TAOISM, the principle of yielding to others as the most effective response to the problems of human existence. *Wuwei* is nonaggressive behavior that compels others to desist voluntarily from violence or overly aggressive conduct. Ideally, Taoists do not argue or debate. They rely on proper timing to set forth what they believe to be true, and they speak out against unseemly conduct only when their words are likely to be heeded. Taoists view laws and controls as undesirable repressions of human nature. For them a society with the fewest controls governs itself best. *Wu-wei* is thus regarded as the secret to human happiness, for through "nonaction" all things can be accomplished.

WYCLIFFE, JOHN \'wi-klif, 'wī-\ (b. *c.* 1330, Yorkshire, Eng.—d. Dec. 31, 1384, Lutterworth, Leicestershire), English theologian, church reformer, and promoter of the first complete translation of the BIBLE into English. He was one of the forerunners of the Protestant REFORMATION.

Wycliffe received his formal education at the University of Oxford. He became a bachelor of divinity about 1369 and a doctor of divinity in 1372. On April 7, 1374, Edward III appointed Wycliffe to the rectory of Lutterworth. He received a royal commission to the deputation sent to discuss with the papal representatives at Brugge the outstanding differences between England and Rome, such as papal taxes and appointments to church posts. He complemented this activity with his political treatises on divine and civil do-

minion (*De dominio divino libri tres* and *Tractatus de civili dominio*), in which he argued men exercised "dominion" (possession and authority) straight from God. The righteous alone could properly have dominion, even if they were not free to assert it. Therefore, as the church was in SIN, it should give up its possessions and return to evangelical poverty. Such disendowment was to be carried out by the state, and particularly by the king.

Wycliffe preached in London in support of moderate disendowment, but his political connections displeased his ecclesiastical superiors, and he was summoned to appear before them in February 1377. The proceedings broke up in disorder, and Wycliffe retired uncondemned. That year saw Wycliffe at the height of his popularity and influence. Parliament and the king consulted him as to whether it was lawful to keep back treasure of the kingdom from Rome, and Wycliffe replied that it was. In May Pope Gregory XI issued five bulls against him, denouncing his theories and calling for his arrest. The call went unanswered.

He began a systematic attack on the beliefs and practices of the church. Theologically, this was facilitated by a strong predestinarianism that led him to believe in the "invisible" church of the ELECT, rather than in the "visible" church of Rome—that is, in the organized, institutional church. But his chief target was the doctrine of transubstantiation—that the substance of the bread and wine used in the EUCHARIST is changed into the body and blood of JESUS CHRIST. As a Realist philosopher—believing that universal concepts have a real existence—he attacked it because, in the annihilation of the substance of bread and wine, the cessation of being was involved. He then proceeded on a broader front and condemned the doctrine as idolatrous and unscriptural. He sought to replace it with a doctrine of remanence (remaining)—"This is very bread after the consecration"—combined with an assertion of the Real Presence in a noncorporeal form.

Meanwhile, he pressed his attack ecclesiastically. The pope, the CARDINALS, the clergy in remunerative secular employment, the monks, and the FRIARS were all castigated in language that was bitter even for 14th-century religious controversy. His attack on the church was not simply born of anger. It carried the marks of moral earnestness and a genuine desire for reform.

From August 1380 until the summer of 1381, Wycliffe was busy with his plans for a translation of the Bible and an order of Poor Preachers who would take his message to the people. The Bible had become necessary to his theories to replace the discredited authority of the church and to make the law of God available to everyone who could read. This, allied to a belief in the effectiveness of preaching, led to the formation of the Lollards, though the precise extent to which Wycliffe was involved in their creation is uncertain.

In 1381 the discontent of the working classes erupted in the Peasants' Revolt. Wycliffe's social teaching was not a significant cause of the uprising because it was known only to the learned. The archbishop of Canterbury, Simon of Sudbury, was murdered in the revolt, and his successor, William Courtenay (1347–96), moved against Wycliffe. Many of his works were condemned at the SYNOD held at Blackfriars, London, in May 1382; and at Oxford his followers capitulated, and his writings were banned. He continued to write prolifically until his death in December 1384.

Most of Wycliffe's post-Reformation, Protestant biographers see him as the first Reformer. There has now been a reaction to this view, which some modern scholars have attacked as the delusion of uncritical admirers.

XAVIER, SAINT FRANCIS

XAVIER, SAINT FRANCIS \'zā-vē-ər, 'za-\, *Spanish* San Francisco Javier (b. April 7, 1506, Xavier Castle, near Sangüesa, Navarre [Spain]—d. Dec. 3, 1552, Sancian Island, China; canonized March 12, 1622; feast day December 3), the greatest ROMAN CATHOLIC missionary of modern times, who was instrumental in the establishment of CHRISTIANITY in India, the Malay Archipelago, and Japan. In Paris in 1534 he pronounced vows as one of the first seven members of the Society of Jesus, or JESUITS, under the leadership of ST. IGNATIUS OF LOYOLA.

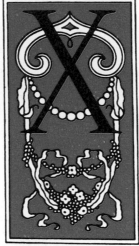

Xavier was born in Navarre (now in northern Spain), at the family castle of Xavier, where Basque was the native language. He was the third son of the president of the council of the king of Navarre, most of whose kingdom was soon to fall to Castile (1512). In 1525 Xavier journeyed to the University of Paris, the theological center of Europe, to begin his studies.

In 1529, Ignatius Loyola, another Basque student, was assigned to room with Xavier; Ignatius had undergone a conversion and gathered together a group who shared his ideals. Gradually, Ignatius won over the initially recalcitrant Xavier, and Xavier was among the band of seven who, in a chapel on Montmartre in Paris, on Aug. 15, 1534, vowed lives of poverty and CELIBACY and promised to devote themselves to the salvation of believers and unbelievers alike. Xavier then performed the *Spiritual Exercises,* a series of meditations lasting about 30 days that had been devised by Ignatius. They implanted in Xavier the motivation that carried him for the rest of his life and prepared the way for his recurrent mystical experiences.

Xavier was ordained a priest in Venice on June 24, 1537. The seven, along with fresh recruits, had become widely popular as a result of their preaching and care of the sick throughout central Italy. King John III of Portugal sought their services to minister to the Christians and to evangelize the peoples in his new Asian dominions. On March 15, 1540, Xavier left Rome for the Indies, traveling first to Lisbon, Portugal. In the following fall, Pope Paul III formally recognized the followers of Ignatius as a religious order, the Society of Jesus.

Beginning in 1542, Xavier spent almost three years on the southeastern coast of India among the pearl fishers, the Paravas. Using a small CATECHISM he had translated into Tamil with the help of interpreters, Xavier traveled from village to village instructing converts and confirming them in their faith. Shortly afterward the Macuans on the southwestern coast indicated their desire for BAPTISM, and, after brief instruction, in the last months of 1544 Xavier baptized 10,000 of them. He anticipated that the schools he planned and Portuguese pressure would keep them constant in their faith.

In the fall of 1545 Xavier moved on to the Malay Archipelago, where he founded MISSIONS among the Malays and in the Spice Islands (Moluccas). In 1548 he returned to India, where more Jesuits had since arrived to join him. In Goa

the College of Holy Faith, founded several years previously, was turned over to the Jesuits, and Francis began to develop it into a center for the education of native priests and catechists for the DIOCESE of Goa, which stretched from the Cape of Good Hope, at the southern tip of Africa, to China.

On Aug. 15, 1549, a Portuguese ship bearing Xavier and several companions entered the Japanese port of Kagoshima. Xavier's first letter from Japan, which was to be printed more than 30 times before the end of the century, revealed his enthusiasm for the Japanese, "the best people yet discovered." He grew conscious of the need to adapt his methods. His poverty that had impressed the Paravas and Malays often repelled the Japanese, so he abandoned it for studied display. In late 1551, having received no mail since his arrival in Japan, Xavier decided to visit India, leaving to the care of his companions about 2,000 Christians in five communities.

Back in India, administrative affairs awaited him as the superior of the newly erected Jesuit Province of the Indies. On Dec. 3, 1552, Xavier died of fever on the island of Sancian (now Shang-ch'uan TAO, off the Chinese coast) as he attempted to secure entrance to the country, then closed to foreigners.

A modern estimate puts the figure of those baptized by Xavier at about 30,000. He is justly credited for his idea that the missionary must adapt to the customs and language of the people he evangelizes, and for his advocation of an educated native clergy—initiatives not always followed by his successors. The areas he evangelized in India have remained Roman Catholic to the present day. Even before his death Francis Xavier was considered a saint, and he has been formally venerated as such by the Roman Catholic church since 1622. In 1927 he was named patron of all missions.

XIPE TOTEC \'shē-pä-'tō-tek, 'hē-pä-\ (Nahuatl: "Our Lord the Flayed One"), in PRE-COLUMBIAN MESO-AMERICAN RELIGION, god of spring (the beginning of the rainy season) and new vegetation and the patron of precious metals.

Described as *anavatl itec* ("Lord of the Coastland"), Xipe Totec was originally a deity of the Zapotec and Yopi Indians in the present states of Oaxaca and Guerrero. Among the Zapotecs he was considered a vegetation god and was associated with the FEATHERED SERPENT (Quetzalcóatl). As a symbol of the new vegetation, his statues and stone masks always show him wearing a flayed skin—the "new skin" that covered the earth in the spring.

Representations of Xipe Totec first appeared at Xolalpan, near Teotihuacán, and at Texcoco, during the post-Classic Toltec phase (9th–12th century CE). The Aztecs officially adopted his cult under the reign of Axayacatl (1469–81). During the second ritual month of the Aztec year, Tlacaxipehualiztli ("Flaying of Men"), the priests killed human victims, flayed the bodies, and put on the skins, which were dyed yellow and designated *teocuitlaquemitl* ("golden

Xipe Totec, pottery figure from Monte Albán, Zapotec culture, 8th–11th century CE
Hamlyn Group Picture Library

clothes"). A hymn sung in honor of Xipe Totec called him Yoalli Tlauana ("Night Drinker") because he carried "waters of jade on his back" and because beneficent rains fell during the night.

XIUHTECUHTLI \,shē-ü-'tä-kùt-lē\ (Nahuatl: "Turquoise [Year] Lord"), *also called* Huehueteotl \,wä-wä-'tä-ō-təl\ ("Old God"), Aztec god of fire and creator of all life. "Old God" is a reflection of his age in the Aztec pantheon. With Chantico, his feminine counterpart, he was believed to be a representation of the divine creator, OME-TECUHTLI.

One of the important duties of an Aztec priest was the maintenance of the perpetually burning sacred fire. The two festivals of Xiuhtecuhtli coincide with the two extremes in the climatological cycle, the heat of August and the cold of January. Xiuhtecuhtli was also the center of a ceremonial fire transfer, first from temple to temple, and then from temples to homes, which occurred once every 52 years at the end of a complete cycle in the calendar of the Aztecs.

The god of fire appears in various guises, one of which represents him as a toothless old man with a stooped back, carrying an enormous brazier on his head. His insignia was the Xiuhcóatl, or serpent of fire, characterized by a nose of horn, decorated with seven stars.

XOCHICALCO \,sō-chē-'käl-kō\, city known for its impressive ruins and FEATHERED SERPENT pyramid, located near Cuernavaca, in Morelos state, Mexico.

Main temple pyramid at Xochicalco, near Cuernavaca, Mex.
Lawrence Cherney—FPG

Xochicalco was built primarily during the 8th and 9th centuries CE and became an important trading and religious center. It was apparently turned into a defensive stronghold before the Spanish conquest (*c.* 1520).

Excavations have revealed two separate building complexes, one centering on the La Malinche temple PYRAMID and ball court, the other built around the main temple pyramid, the principal monument at Xochicalco. Built on a four-sided base, the main pyramid is famous for its lower facing of perfectly fitted and intricately carved images. The reliefs, which show a strong Mayan influence, portray plumed serpents, priests with elaborate headdresses, squatting warriors, calendar glyphs, and fire symbols.

XOCHIQUETZAL \,sō-chē-kät-'säl, ,shō-, -'kät-säl\ (Nahuatl: "Flower Quetzal Feather"), Aztec goddess of beauty, sexual love, and household arts. She is associated with flowers and plants and came from TAMOANCHÁN, the terrestrial paradise.

Her consort was Piltzintecuhtli, "Prince Lord," who, weeping, loses her and searches for her. She is identified by two bunches of quetzal feathers on her headdress.

Xochiquetzal, illustration from the Codex Fejérváry-Mayer
By courtesy of the Liverpool City Museum

YAHRZEIT \\'yär-ˌtsīt, 'yȯr-\\ (Yiddish *yort-sayt*, from *yor*, "year," and *tsayt*, "time," "occasion"), *also spelled* yortzeit, *or* jahrzeit, in JUDAISM, anniversary of the death of a parent or close relative, commonly observed by burning a candle for an entire day. *Yahrzeit* apparently developed from an early Jewish custom of fasting on the anniversaries of the deaths of certain important leaders.

During the last centuries of the Second Temple period (*c.* 520 BCE–70 CE), Jews vowed never to partake of meat or wine on the anniversaries of their parents' deaths. As observed today, *yahrzeit* probably began in Germany about the 14th century and gradually spread to other regions. On the anniversary, a male (or female, in Reform and Conservative congregations) usually recites the KADDISH (hymn of praise) in the SYNAGOGUE at all three services, and males may be called up (*aliyah*) for the public reading of the TORAH. If the anniversary falls on a day on which the Torah is not read, the calling up takes place before the anniversary, as near as possible to the actual date of death. On the SABBATH that precedes the anniversary, Sephardic Jews recite the HAFṬARAH (a passage from the prophets).

More scholarly or pious Jews may mark the anniversary by studying portions of the MISHNAH, choosing sections from the sixth division (laws of purity) that begin with letters from the name of the deceased. While some Jews observe a strict fast on *yahrzeit*, others abstain only from meat and drink.

YAHWEH \\'yä-ˌwā, -ˌvā\\, God of the Israelites, his name revealed to MOSES as four Hebrew consonants (YHWH) called the TETRAGRAMMATON. As JUDAISM became a world religion through its proselytizing in the Greco-Roman world, the more common noun ELOHIM, meaning "god," tended to replace Yahweh to demonstrate the universal sovereignty of Israel's God over all others. At the same time, the divine name was increasingly regarded as too sacred to be uttered; it was thus replaced in the SYNAGOGUE ritual by the Hebrew word Adonai ("My Lord").

The meaning of Yahweh has been variously interpreted. Many scholars believe that the most proper meaning may be "He Brings Into Existence Whatever Exists" (Yahweh-Asher-Yahweh). In 1 Samuel, God is known by the name Yahweh Teva-'ot, or "He Brings the Hosts Into Existence," the hosts possibly referring to the heavenly court or to Israel. The name of Moses' mother was Jochebed (Yokheved), a word based on Yahweh. Thus, the tribe of Levi, to which Moses belonged, probably knew the name, which originally may have been (in its short form Yo, Yah, or Yahu) a religious invocation of no precise meaning. *See also* JEHOVAH.

YAHWIST SOURCE \\'yä-wist, -vist\\, *abbreviated as* J (labeled J after the German transliteration of YHWH), an early source that provides a strand of the Pentateuchal narrative. The basis for identifying a strand of the PENTATEUCH as the writing of the Yawhist—the Yahwist strands being specifically, GENESIS 2–11, 12–16, 18–22, 24–34, 38, and 49; EXODUS

1–24, 32, and 34; Numbers 11–12, 14, and 20–25; and Judges 1—is not only the use of the name YAHWEH for God. The identification is also based upon the use of Yahweh in association with other indications. For example, in the Yahwist source, the name given to Moses's father is Reuel, the mountain is always named as Sinai, and the Palestinians are referred to as Canaanites. In the source known as E in which God is called ELOHIM, Moses's father-in-law is JETHRO, the mountain is called Horeb, and the Palestinians are called Amorites.

One can see examples of these different sources when comparing similar biblical stories. For example, the creation-myth of Genesis 1:1 has God/Elohim create the world, then Genesis 2:5–25 has God/Yahweh make the world; these two creation myths differ from each other on both substantive and stylistic issues. There are other places in which the biblical narrative covers the same ground two or more times, *e.g.*, in Genesis there are three stories in which a PATRIARCH fools a foreign king about the status of the patriarch's wife, claiming her instead to be his sister. This event is reported between ABRAHAM and Pharaoh over SARAH (12:10–20), with Abraham and Abimelekh over Sarah (20:2–18), and with ISAAC and Abimelekh over Rebekah (26:1–11). Moreover, there are two flood stories: in the first only certain animals (*e.g.*, seven pairs of clean animals, seven pairs of birds) are brought onto the Ark (Genesis 7:2–4); while in the second story all the animals living are brought in pairs to the ark (Genesis 7:11).

These and other indications have persuaded biblical scholars that there are four strands interwoven in the Pentateuch: the Yawhist, Elohist, DEUTERONOMIST, and PRIESTLY, hence J, E, D, and P. The Yahwist's account, written in the time of DAVID and SOLOMON around 950 BCE, asks these questions about the Jewish empire: for what purpose was this empire created? For how long will it exist? Why was the gift of the empire granted to the Jews? J is a firm and final statement. At this point in history, the Jews looked backward in an account for the period of greatness at hand. The Yahwist's account, produced at the height of the glory of the Davidic monarchy, told the story of the federation of the tribes of Israel, now a single kingdom under Solomon—with a focus on ZION and Jerusalem, the metropolis of the federation.

YAḤYĀ ṢOBḤ-E AZAL, MĪRZĀ \\'yäh-yä-'sȯb-he-a-'zal\\ (b. 1831, Tehran—d. April 29, 1912, Famagusta, Cyprus), half brother of BAHĀ' ULLĀH (the founder of the BAHĀ'Ī FAITH) and leader of his own Bābist movement in the mid-19th century Ottoman Empire.

Yaḥyā was the designated successor of Sayyid Alī Muhammad, a SHI'ITE sectarian leader known as THE BĀB. The Bāb was executed in 1850, and by the next year his followers regarded Yaḥyā Mīrzā as the Bāb, in spite of his youth. To avoid persecution by Shi'ite authorities, he fled in 1853 to Baghdad, where he remained for a decade with his followers, called AZALĪS or Bābīs. In 1866, in Edirne, a schism erupted between Yaḥyā and Bahā' Ullāh, who now claimed to be divine. The Ottoman authorities exiled both, sending Yaḥyā to Cyprus in 1868. When Cyprus came under British rule in 1878 he became a pensioner of the crown.

Although reviled by the followers of Bahā' Ullāh, some, particularly in Iran, still regard Yaḥyā as the true spiritual leader. *See also* BĀBISM.

YAJÑA \'yəg-nə, -nyə\ (Sanskrit: "sacrifice," "offering"), in HINDUISM, worship based on rites prescribed in the VEDAS, in contrast to PŪJĀ, which may include image worship and devotional practices that are non-Vedic in origin.

Correct performance of the *yajña* and recitation of the MANTRAS is considered essential; and the performer and the objects employed must all be in a high state of purity. Such requirements are the domain of the Brahmins, who are still required to officiate at all important public *yajña*s. Many orthodox Hindus continue to perform the *mahāyajñas*, the five daily domestic offerings.

YĀJÑAVALKYA \'yäg-nə-'vəl-kyə\, sage and teacher who figures prominently in the earliest of the Hindu philosophical and mystical texts known as the UPANISHADS, the *Bṛhadāraṇyaka Upanishad*. The teachings attributed to Yājñavalkya include many that are representative of the break with earlier Vedic ritualism and are distinctive to the new worldview of the Upanishads.

These include the first appearance in Sanskrit literature of the doctrine of KARMA and rebirth, which contends that the individual's future destiny is determined in accordance with one's past "knowledge and action": "According as one acts, according as one behaves, so does he become. The doer of good becomes good, the doer of evil becomes evil." Yājñavalkya also analyzes the nature and process of karma and identifies desire as the ultimate cause of all action and the source of continued rebirth.

Yājñavalkya is said to have taught that the true self, or ĀTMAN, is distinct from the individual ego and therefore not subject to karma and rebirth; the *ātman* is eternal, unchanging, and identified with the monistic principle underlying the universe, the BRAHMAN. Release from rebirth and the attainment of bliss comes from knowledge of this identity between the true self and the Cosmic One and is procured by "the man who does not desire, who is without desire, whose desire is satisfied, whose desire is the self."

Yājñavalkya is also reputed to be the author of one of the principal texts of DHARMA or religious duty, the *Yājñavalkya Smriti*, although it is unlikely that this is the same Yājñavalkya.

YAJUR VEDA \'yə-jùr-'vā-də\, collection of short formulas that forms part of the VEDAS of ancient India. There are two

Yakṣa, *stone figure from Vidiṣa, Madhya Pradesh, India, c. 1st century* BCE; *in the Vidiṣa Museum*
Pramod Chandra

recensions of the YAJUR VEDA. The Kṛṣṇa, or "Black" Yajur Veda, is a mixture of prose and verse and is composed of three distinct books. The Śukla, or "White" Yajur Veda, is composed of a single book in verse.

YAKṢA \'yək-shə\, *Sanskrit feminine singular* yakṣī, *or* yakṣinī, in Indian religions, a class of generally benevolent nature spirits who are the custodians of treasures that are hidden in the earth and in the roots of trees. Principal among the YAKṢAS is KUBERA, who rules in the mythical Himalayan kingdom called Alakā.

*Yakṣa*s were often given homage as tutelary deities of a city, district, lake, or well. In art, sculptures of *yakṣa*s were among the earliest of deities, apparently preceding images of the BODHISATTVAS and of the deities of later HINDUISM, whose representation they influenced. They were also the prototypes for the attendants of later Hindu, Buddhist, and Jain art.

YAMA \'yə-mə\, in the mythology of India, the lord of death. The VEDAS describe him as the first man who died. The son of the sun god Sūrya, Yama presides over the resting place of the dead, which is located in the south under the earth. In the Vedas Yama was king of the departed ancestors, but in later mythology he became known as the just judge who weighs the good and evil deeds of the dead and determines their retribution.

YAMATO \yä-'mä-tō\, geographic and cultural center of the ancient Japanese state in the Nara region. It is a term that refers to the unique religious, social, and political culture of the early imperial, or *tennō*, tradition.

YAMATO TAKERU \yä-'mä-tō-tä-'ke-rü\, *in full* Yamato Takeru no Mikoto (Japanese: "Prince Brave of Yamato"), Japanese folk hero who may have lived in the 2nd century CE. His tomb at Ise is the Mausoleum of the White Plover.

The son of the legendary 12th emperor Keikō, Yamato Takeru was supposedly responsible for expanding the territory of the Yamato court. His story appears in the chronicles KOJIKI (completed in 712) and NIHON SHOKI ("Japanese Chronicles"; completed in 720). In the stories, he subdued two uncouth Kumaso warriors by cleverly disguising himself as a woman and killing them while they were drunk. With the miraculous sword Kusanagi, he cut away the burning grass of a fire set by the Ainu tribesmen and escaped. His adventures ended on the plains of Tagi, where he was stricken with illness, changed into a white plover, and disappeared.

YAMAZAKI ANSAI \'yä-mä-,zä-kē-'än-,sī\ (b. Jan. 24, 1619, Kyōto, Japan—d. Oct. 16, 1682, Kyōto), propagator in Japan of the philosophy of the Chinese Neo-Confucian philosopher CHU HSI (1130–1200). Ansai reduced NEO-CONFUCIANISM to a simple moral code, which he then blended with SHINTŌ doctrines. This amalgamation became known as Suika Shintō.

A Buddhist monk early in life, Ansai began to study CON-FUCIANISM and gradually turned against BUDDHISM. By the time he was 29, he had become a Confucian teacher, gathering thousands of students, among whom were some of the greatest scholars of the day.

From the complex philosophic system of Chu Hsi, Ansai extracted the simple formula "Devotion within, righteousness without." By the former he meant the Neo-Confucian emphasis on sincerity and seriousness. As Ansai grew older, he came to equate Chinese speculations on the universe with Shintō creation legends and identified elements of the Neo-Confucian metaphysical principles with the Shintō gods. The Supreme Ultimate (T'ai Chi) of the Neo-Confucianists became identified with the first two divinities in the Shintō religious chronicles. His amalgamation of Confucian morality with the Shintō tradition of the divine origin of the imperial line was one philosophical root of the later extreme Japanese nationalism and emperor worship.

YAMIM NORA'IM \yä-'mēm-ˌnō-rä-'ēm\ (Hebrew: "days of awe"), *English* High Holy Days, in JUDAISM, the holy days of ROSH HASHANAH (on Tishri 1 and 2) and YOM KIPPUR (on Tishri 10), in September or October. *Yamim nora'im* is sometimes used to designate the first 10 days of the religious year: the three High Holy Days, and also the days between.

YAMM \'yäm\, *also spelled* Yam (akin to Hebrew *yam*, "sea"), ancient West Semitic deity who ruled the oceans, rivers, lakes, and underground springs. Tablets at UGARIT say that at the beginning of time Yamm was awarded the divine kingship by EL, the head of the pantheon. One day, Yamm's messengers requested that the gods surrender BAAL to be a bond servant to Yamm. El agreed, but Baal instead engaged Yamm in battle. After a furious fight, in which the craftsman KOTHAR supplied Baal with special weapons, Yamm was slain and the kingship given to Baal. According to some scholars, Yamm was the same deity as Lotan (Hebrew: Leviathan), represented as a dragon or serpent.

YANG-HSING \'yäŋ-'shiŋ\, *Pinyin* yangxing (Chinese: "nourishing life," or "nourishing nature"), term often associated with TAOISM that refers to various physiological and mental methods for self-cultivation and the attainment of longevity or immortality. One's "nature," or "life," is made up of the three principles of *ching* (organic/spermatic vitality), *ch'i* (aerial/respiratory vitality), and SHEN (spiritual/ mental vitality).

YANTRA \'yən-trə\ (Sanskrit: "instrument"), in TANTRIC HINDUISM and VAJRAYĀNA BUDDHISM, a linear diagram used as a support for meditation. In its more elaborate and pictorial form it is called a MANDALA. Yantras range from those traced on the ground or on paper and disposed of after the rite, to those etched in stone and metal, such as are found in temples. When used along with yogic practices, the component parts of the yantra diagram take the believer along the different steps leading to Enlightenment.

One characteristic yantra in the ritual worship of the goddess ŚAKTI is the *śrīyantra*. It is composed of nine triangles: five pointing downward, to represent the YONI, or vulva, and four pointing upward, to represent the LIṄGA, or phallus. The dynamic interplay is understood to be an expression of all the cosmic manifestations, beginning and ending with union at the center, visualized as a dot (*bindu*).

YAO \'yaù\, *formally* (Wade-Giles romanization) T'ang Ti Yao, in Chinese mythology, along with SHUN and YU THE GREAT, one of the three legendary emperors (*c.* 24th century BCE) of the golden age of antiquity, exalted by CONFUCIUS as a model of virtue, righteousness, and unselfish devotion.

Two remarkable events marked Yao's reign: a rampaging flood was controlled by Ta Yü; and Hou I, the Lord Archer, saved the world from destruction by shooting down 9 of the 10 suns burning up the earth. After 70 years of Yao's rule, the sun and moon were as resplendent as jewels, the five planets shone like strung pearls, phoenixes nested in the palace courtyards, crystal springs flowed from the hills, pearl grass covered the countryside, rice crops were plentiful, two unicorns (OMENS of prosperity) appeared in the capital at P'ing-yang, and the wondrous calendar bean made its appearance, producing one pod each day for half a month before the 15 pods withered one by one on successive days.

Yao had special temples dedicated in his honor. He is said to have offered sacrifices and to have practiced DIVINATION. In choosing a successor, Yao bypassed his own less worthy son in favor of Shun and served as counselor to him.

YARIKH \'yär-ēk\, *also spelled* Yareah, ancient West Semitic moon god whose marriage to the moon goddess Nikkal (Sumerian: Ningal, "Queen") was the subject of a poem from ancient UGARIT. Fertility was believed to be the principal result of the marriage.

YAZATA \yä-'zä-tə\, in ZOROASTRIANISM, member of an order of ANGELS created by AHURA MAZDĀ to help him maintain the flow of world order and quell the forces of AHRIMAN and his DEMONS. *Yazata*s gather the light of the sun and pour it on the earth. They teach humans to dispel demons and free themselves of the future torments of hell. Persons who remember the *yazata*s through ritual offerings receive their favor and prosper. Zoroaster prayed to them to grant him strength for his mission. The principal *yazata*s mostly are ancient Iranian deities reduced to auxiliary status: Ātar (Fire), MITHRA, ANĀHITI, RASHNU (The Righteous), SRAOSHA, and VERETHRAGHNA.

YAZĪDĪ \'yä-zi-dē\, *also spelled* Yezīdī, Azīdī, Zedī, *or* Izdī, religious movement, found primarily in the districts of Mosul, Iraq; Diyarbakır, Turkey; Aleppo, Syria; Armenia and the Caucasus region; and in parts of Iran. The Yazīdī religion is a syncretic combination of Zoroastrian, Manichaean, Jewish, Nestorian Christian, and Islamic elements. The Yazīdīs themselves are thought to be descended from supporters of the Umayyad CALIPH Yazid I. They believe that they were created separately from the rest of mankind, and they have kept themselves strictly segregated from the people among whom they live. Although scattered and probably numbering fewer than 100,000, they have a well-organized society, with a chief SHAYKH as the supreme religious head and an emir, or prince, as the secular head.

The chief divine figure of the Yazīdīs is Malak Ṭā'ūs ("Peacock Angel"), who is worshiped in the form of a peacock. He rules the universe with six other ANGELS, but all seven are subordinate to the supreme God, who has had no direct interest in the universe since he created it. The seven angels are worshiped by the Yazīdī in the form of seven bronze or iron peacock figures called *sanjaq*.

Yazīdīs deny the existence of evil and thus also reject SIN, the devil, and hell. The breaking of divine laws is expiated by way of the transmigration of souls, which allows for the progressive purification of the spirit. Yazīdīs relate that, when the devil repented of his sin of pride before God, he was pardoned and replaced in his previous position as chief of the angels; this myth has earned the Yazīdīs an undeserved reputation as devil worshipers. Shaykh ʿAdī, the chief Yazīdī saint, was a 12th-century Muslim mystic whom the Yazīdīs believe to have achieved divinity.

The Yazīdī religious center and object of the annual PILGRIMAGE is the tomb of Shaykh ʿAdī, located at a former Christian monastery in the town of al-Shaykh ʿAdī, north of Mosul. Two short books written in Arabic, *Kitāb al-jilwa* ("Book of Revelation") and *Maṣḥaf rash* ("Black Writing"), form the sacred SCRIPTURES of the Yazīdīs, and an Arabic hymn in praise of Shaykh ʿAdī is held in great esteem.

YELLOW TURBANS, Chinese Taoist movement whose members' uprising (184–c. 204 CE) contributed to the fall of the Han dynasty (220 CE). Led by Chang Chüeh, a Taoist faith healer who gained many adherents during a pestilence, the rebellion was directed against the eunuchs who dominated the emperor. The rebels wore yellow headdresses to signify their association with the "earth" element, which they believed would succeed the red "fire" element that represented Han rule. Chang Chüeh was killed in 184 CE, but the rebellion continued for the next two decades.

YERUSHALMI, THE \,yer-ü-'shäl-mē\, *also called* the Talmud Yerushalmi, the Palestinian Talmud, *or* the Talmud of the Land of Israel, commentary from about 400 CE on the MISHNAH (c. 200 CE) that comments on only the first four divisions of the Mishnah—that is, ZERAʿIM, MOʿED, NASHIM, and NEZIQIN. It is broken up into brief discussions on the meanings of the phrases of the Mishnah. Indeed, perhaps 90 percent of the Yerushalmi addresses the meaning of the Mishnah. Thus, the traits of the Mishnah defined the problems confronting those authors responsible for the Mishnah's redaction and formulation and those disciples who followed them. The disciples set the pattern of treating the Mishnah as TORAH, proposing both to receive and realize its revelation.

The Yerushalmi speaks about the Mishnah in essentially a single voice, about fundamentally few things. Its mode of speech as much as of thought is uniform throughout. The same sorts of questions phrased in the same rhetoric—a moving, or dialectical, argument composed of questions and answers—are used for every passage of the Mishnah. The Yerushalmi chooses from a limited selection of conventional forms of speech, and it repeatedly asks a few basic questions in reading any given passage of the Mishnah.

The consistent message of the Yerushalmi was derived from a collective of sages who were located in the Land of Israel in Galilee, Caesarea, Tiberias, and Beth Shearim. The document seems, in the main, to intend to provide notes, an abbreviated script that anyone may use to reconstruct and reenact formal discussions of problems: in

Yggdrasill, line engraving from Finn Magnusen's Eddalæren, Copenhagen, 1824
The Granger Collection

a situation like this, one says that. Curt and often arcane, these notes can be translated only with immense bodies of inserted explanation. We must assume the sages took for granted that, out of the signs of speech, it would be possible for anyone to reconstruct speech, doing so in accurate and fully conventional ways.

The framers of the Yerushalmi had in hand a tripartite corpus of inherited materials awaiting their composition into a final, closed document. First, they took up materials, in various states and stages of completion, pertinent to the Mishnah or to the principles of laws that the Mishnah had brought to articulation. Second, they had in hand received materials, again in various conditions, pertinent to the SCRIPTURE, both as the Scripture related to the Mishnah and as it laid forth its own narratives. And, third, they occasionally pursued their own theoretical problems, formulated out of the principles implicit in the Mishnah's law.

The TALMUD Yerushalmi did not compete successfully with the Talmud BAVLI, which became authoritative. The law of JUDAISM, therefore, emerged from ancient times in the form given to it in Babylonia. While circumstances may explain the priority of the latter (for example, superior means of communication with Jews throughout the world gave the Babylonian authorities greater influence), the quality of intellect in the Babylonian Talmud explains much as well. It is simply a better-conceived and more effectively executed document, spelled out with great clarity and argued with enormous force. Hence, over time, study of the Talmud Yerushalmi diminished. In modern times, however, interest in the Yerushalmi revived—important commentaries were written and philological studies were undertaken. Thus, the Talmud of the Land of Israel gained a prominence that it had not had for centuries.

YESHIVA \yə-'shē-və\, *also spelled* yeshivah, *or* yeshibah, *plural* yeshivas, yeshivot \yə-,shē-'vōt\, yeshivoth, *or* yeshibot (Hebrew: "sitting"), academy of higher Talmudic study. In traditional JUDAISM, it is the setting for the training and ORDINATION of RABBIS, contrasted with the heder and TALMUD TORAH, where children and young adults are educated. The yeshiva has its origins in the bet MIDRASH ("house of study") of the Talmudic period, the rabbinic center for study and prayer that was distinct from and, according to some authorities, holier than, the communal SYNAGOGUE.

In the post-Talmudic period, the word *yeshiva* (and its Aramaic equivalent, *metivta*) increasingly was applied specifically to academies of higher rabbinic learning and ordination. The yeshiva also became distinguished from the bet midrash, which remained open to all men who wished to study.

YGGDRASILL \'ig-drə-,sil\, *also called* Mimameidr \'mē-mə-,mā-thər\, in Norse mythology, the WORLD TREE, a giant ash supporting the universe. One of its roots extended into

NIFLHEIM, the Underworld; another into JÖTUNHEIM, land of the giants; and the third into ASGARD, home of the gods. At its base were three wells: Urdarbrunnr (Well of Fate), from which the tree was watered by the NORNS (the Fates); Hvergelmir (Roaring Kettle), in which dwelt Nidhogg, the monster that gnawed at the tree's roots; and Mímisbrunnr (Mimir's Well), source of wisdom, for the waters of which ODIN sacrificed an eye. According to some sources the world tree, though badly shaken, was to be the source of new life after RAGNARÖK.

YHWH, in Hebrew, the name of God as revealed to MOSES. Because of its four letters, it is also known as the Tetragrammaton. *See* YAHWEH.

YI CHEHYON \ˈē-ˈche-ˈhyən\ (b. 1287—d. 1367), Korean poet, minister, and important Neo-Confucian scholar. He traveled in Yüan dynasty China, where he studied with several Chinese Neo-Confucians and successfully participated in the Chinese examination system, which focused on the Confucian canon of texts. Upon his return to Korea he stressed the pragmatic implications of Neo-Confucian thought and became a leading critic of BUDDHISM and other religious traditions he considered economically wasteful. He was honored as an exemplary Confucian scholar and supporter of the state system, and his spirit tablet was included among the 18 Korean tablets honored in the MUN-MYO, or Confucian "cultural shrines."

YI-GI DEBATES \ˈē-ˈgē\, series of religious and philosophical arguments about the essential (*yi*; Chinese LI: "principle") or existential/material (*gi*, or *ki*; Chinese CH'I: "matter-energy") nature of reality conducted by two groups of Korean Neo-Confucians in the 16th and 17th centuries. They paralleled similar arguments in Chinese Neo-Confucian thought and, as in China, often had political implications. The difference between the two positions came down to a distinction between an essentialist, idealist, and conservative perspective favoring a priori and absolutist values and an empiricist, pragmatic, and liberal perspective favoring the adaptive relativity of all mental constructs.

YI HWANG \ˈē-ˈhwäŋ\, *or* T'oegye \ˈtō-ˈgye\ (b. 1501—d. 1570), single most important Korean Confucian, who helped shape the character of Yi CONFUCIANISM through his creative interpretation of Chu Hsi's teaching. Critically aware of the philosophical turn engineered by WANG YANG-MING, Yi Hwang transmitted the CHU HSI legacy as a response to the advocates of the learning of the mind. His Discourse on the Ten Sagely Diagrams, an aid for educating the king, offered a depiction of all the major concepts in Sung learning. His exchange of letters with Ki Taesung (1527–72) in the famous FOUR-SEVEN DEBATE, which discussed the relationship between MENCIUS' four basic human feelings—commiseration, shame, modesty, and right and wrong—and seven emotions, such as anger and joy, raised the level of Confucian dialogue to a new height of intellectual sophistication.

YIMA \ya-ˈmä, ˈyē-mə\, in ancient Iranian religion, the first man, the progenitor of the human race, and son of the sun.

According to one legend, Yima declined God's (AHURA MAZDĀ'S) offer to make him the vehicle of the religion and was instead given the task of establishing man's life on earth. He became king in a golden age which ended, says one tale, when Ahura Mazdā told Yima of a terrible winter

to come. He was instructed to build an excellent domain under the earth, lit by its own light, and take in it the best individuals from each species to preserve their seed. There they should dwell through the winter's destruction, then emerge and repopulate the earth.

Zoroastrian tradition dislodged Yima as the first man, replacing him with GAYŌMART. In later Persian literature Yima, under the name Jamshīd, is the subject of many tales.

YIN-YANG \ˈyin-ˈyäŋ, -ˈyaŋ\, *Pinyin* yinyang, *Japanese* in-yō, in East Asian thought, the two complementary forces, or principles, that make up all aspects and phenomena of life. Yin is conceived of as earth, female, dark, passive, and absorbing; it is present in even numbers, valleys, and streams and is represented by the tiger, the color orange, and a broken line. Yang is conceived of as heaven, male, light, active, and penetrating; it is present in odd numbers and mountains and is represented by the dragon, the color azure, and an unbroken line. They both proceed from the Supreme Ultimate (T'ai-chi). In harmony, the two are depicted as the light and dark halves of a circle.

The origins of the yin-yang idea are obscure but ancient. In the 3rd century BCE in China, it formed the basis of an entire school of COSMOLOGY (the Yin-Yang school), whose main representative was Tsou Yen. The concept of yin-yang is associated in Chinese thought with the idea of the five agents, phases, or elements (WU-HSING)—metal, wood, water, fire, and earth—both of these ideas lending substance to the belief in a cyclical theory of becoming and dissolution and an interdependence between the world of nature and human events. The concept entered Japan in early times as *in-yō*. *In-yō* notions permeated every level of Japanese society and are still evident in the belief in lucky and unlucky days and directions and in consideration of the ZODIAC signs when arranging marriages.

YI SAEK \ˈē-ˈsak\ (b. 1328—d. 1396), Korean literary figure and Neo-Confucian scholar. Patronized by kings during the Koryo period (918–1392), he promoted an educational system based on the Confucian texts and was responsible for establishing a Confucian tradition of public mourning. While favoring CONFUCIANISM in public matters, he was sympathetic to Ch'an (Son, *see* ZEN) Buddhist SCRIPTURES and practices. Toward the end of his life he was the revered head of the Confucian National Academy. He is remembered as one of the "Three Hermit Scholars" who were loyal to Confucian principles and were exiled by Yi Song-gye, the military leader who overthrew the Koryo regime.

YI YULGOK \ˈē-ˈyül-ˈgōk\, *also known as* Yi Yi (b. 1536—d. 1584), Korean ministerial official and great Neo-Confucian scholar. Never a supporter of the orthodox CHU HSI school of NEO-CONFUCIANISM in Korea, Yi Yulgok had eclectic interests in Ch'an BUDDHISM, TAOISM, and Wang Yang-ming's school of mind. His famous philosophical work on "The Way of Heaven" emphasized the practical priority of matter-energy (*ki*; Chinese CH'I) in relation to abstract principle (*yi*; Chinese LI). He also wrote important works on the moral theme of "sincerity" in the act of knowing. In this way, he influenced the emergence of the Korean school of Practical Learning and greatly contributed to the overall Neo-Confucian transformation of Korean society.

YMIR \ˈi-mir\, *also called* Aurgelmir \ˈaür-gəl-ˌmir\, in Norse mythology, the first being, a GIANT who was created from the drops of water that formed when the ice of NIFL-

HEIM met the heat of MUSPELHEIM. Ymir was the father of all the giants. A cow, Audumla, nourished him with her milk. She was herself nourished by licking salty, rime-covered stones. She licked the stones into the shape of a man; this was Buri, who became the grandfather of the great god ODIN and his brothers. These gods later killed Ymir, and the flow of his blood drowned all but one frost giant. The three gods put Ymir's body in the void, GINNUNGAGAP, and fashioned the earth from his flesh, the seas from his blood, mountains from his bones, stones from his teeth, the sky from his skull, and clouds from his brain. Four dwarfs held up his skull. His eyelashes (or eyebrows) became the fence surrounding MIDGARD, or Middle Earth, the home of mankind.

YOGA \\'yō-gə\\ (Sanskrit: "Yoking," or "Discipline"), one of the six orthodox systems (*darśana*s) of Indian philosophy. Its influence has been widespread among many other schools of Indian thought. Its basic text is the *Yoga sūtra*s by PATAÑJALI (*c.* 200 BCE?).

The practical aspects of Yoga play a more important part than does its intellectual content, which is largely based on the philosophy of SĀṂKHYA. Yoga holds with Sāṃkhya that the achievement of spiritual liberation occurs when the self (*puruṣa*) is freed from the bondages of matter (*prakṛti*) that have resulted because of ignorance and illusion. The Sāṃkhya view of the evolution of the world through stages leads Yoga to an attempt to reverse this order, so that a person can undertake a regimen of "dephenomenalization" until the self reenters its original state of purity and consciousness. Once the aspirant has learned to control and suppress obscuring mental activities and has succeeded in ending attachments to material objects, he or she is able to enter SAMĀDHI, a state of deep concentration accompanied by a sense of blissful, ecstatic union with ultimate reality.

Generally the Yoga process is described in eight stages (*aṣṭāṅga-yoga*, "eight-membered Yoga"). The first two stages are ethical preparations. They are YAMA ("restraint"), which denotes abstinence from injury (AHIṂSĀ), falsehood, stealing, lust, and avarice; and *niyama* ("observance"), which denotes cleanliness of body, contentment, austerity, study, and devotion to God.

The next two stages are physical preparations. ĀSANA ("seat"), a series of exercises in physical posture, is intended to condition the aspirant's body and make it supple, flexible, and healthy. *Prāṇāyāma* ("breath control") is a series of exercises intended to stabilize the rhythm of breathing in order to encourage complete respiratory relaxation.

The fifth stage, *pratyāhāra* ("withdrawal"), involves control of the senses, or the ability to withdraw the attention of the senses from outward objects to the mind.

The first five stages are called external aids to Yoga; the remaining three are purely mental or internal aids. *Dhāraṇā* ("holding on") is the ability to hold and confine awareness of externals to one object for a long period of time. *Dhyāna* ("concentrated meditation") is the uninterrupted contemplation of the object, beyond any memory of ego. *Samādhi* ("self-collectedness") is the final stage. In this stage the meditator understands the underlying character of awareness itself, and that it obliterates the distinction between the meditator and the object.

YOGĀCĀRA \\'yō-gä-'chär-ə\\ (Sanskrit: "Practice of Yoga [Union]"), *also called* Vijñānavāda ("Doctrine of Consciousness"), important idealistic school of MAHĀYĀNA Buddhism. Yogācāra attacked both the realism of THERAVĀDA Buddhism and the provisional practical realism of the MĀDHYAMIKA school. The name is derived from the title of an important 4th- or 5th-century text, the *Yogācārabhūmi-śāstra* ("Science of the Stages of Yoga Practice").

The other name of the school, Vijñānavāda, is more descriptive of its philosophical position, which is that the reality a human being perceives does not exist. Only the consciousness that one has of the momentary interconnected events (DHARMAS) that make up the cosmic flux can be said to exist. Consciousness, however, also clearly discerns in these so-called unreal events consistent patterns of continuity and regularity; in order to explain this order in which only chaos really could prevail, the school developed the tenet of the *ālaya-vijñāna*, or "storage consciousness." Sense perceptions are ordered as coherent and regular by a store of consciousness. Sense impressions produce certain configurations (SAMSKĀRAS) in this unconscious that "perfume" later impressions so that they appear consistent and regular. Each being possesses this storage consciousness, which thus becomes a kind of collective consciousness that orders human perceptions of the world, though this world does not exist. This doctrine was attacked by the adherents of the Mādhyamika school, who pointed out the obvious logical difficulties of such a tenet.

Yogācāra emerged in India about the 2nd century CE but had its period of greatest productivity in the 4th century, during the time of ASAṄGA and Vasubandha. Following them, the school divided into two branches, the Āgamānusariṇo Vijñānavādinaḥ ("School of the Scriptural Tradition") and the Nyāyānusariṇo Vijñānavādinaḥ ("School of the Logical Tradition").

The teachings of the Yogācāra school were introduced into China by the 7th-century monk-traveler HSÜAN-TSANG and formed the basis of the FA-HSIANG school founded by Hsüan-tsang's pupil K'uei-chi. Because of its idealistic content it is also called Wei-shih.

Transmitted to Japan, as Hossō, sometime after 654, the Yogācāra school split into two branches, the Northern and the Southern. In modern times the school retained the important temples of Horyū, Yakushi, and Kōfuku, all located in or near Nara and all treasure-houses of religious art.

YOM KIPPUR \\,yōm-kē-'pùr, ,yòm-, ,yäm-, -'ki-pər\\ *Hebrew* Yom Ha-Kippurim, *English* Day of Atonement, Jewish holiday, observed on the 10th day of the lunar month of Tishri (in the course of September and October). Yom Kippur concludes the "10 days of repentance" that begin with ROSH HASHANAH on the first day of Tishri. The purpose of Yom Kippur is to effect individual and collective purification by the practice of forgiveness of the SINS of others and by sincere repentance for one's own sins against God.

Before the destruction of the Temple in Jerusalem, the HIGH PRIEST performed a sacrificial ceremony in the Temple, successively confessing his own sins, the sins of priests, and the sins of all Israel. Clothed in white linen, he then entered the HOLY OF HOLIES to sprinkle the blood of the sacrifice and to offer incense. The ceremony concluded when a goat (the SCAPEGOAT), symbolically carrying the sins of Israel, was driven to its death in the wilderness.

Today, Yom Kippur is marked by abstention from food, drink, and sexual relations. Among extremely Orthodox Jews the wearing of leather shoes and anointing oneself with oil are forbidden. The eve of Yom Kippur and the entire day is spent in prayer and meditation. The eve of Yom Kippur includes the recitation of the KOL NIDRE, a declaration annulling all vows made during the course of the year (obligations toward others are excluded). Friends also ask

Yom Kippur at the Western Wall, Jerusalem; the blowing of the shofar
Reuters/Corbis—Bettmann

and accept forgiveness from one another for past offenses on this evening. God is believed to forgive the sins of those who sincerely repent and show their repentance by improved behavior and performance of good deeds.

The services on Yom Kippur itself last continuously from morning to evening and include readings from the TORAH and the reciting of penitential prayers. Yiskur, which are memorial prayers for the recently deceased, may also be recited by members of the congregation. The services end with closing prayers and the blowing of the SHOFAR.

YONI \\'yō-nē\ (Sanskrit: "abode," "source," "womb," "vagina"), in HINDUISM, aniconic representation of the female sexual organ and the symbol of the goddess ŚAKTI, feminine generative power and, as a goddess, consort of SHIVA. The *yoni* is often associated in the ICONOGRAPHY of ŚAIVISM together with the phallic LIṄGA, Shiva's symbol. The *liṅga* is depicted in sculpture and paintings as resting in the *yoni* as a cylinder in a spouted dish. The two symbols together represent the eternal process of creation and regeneration.

YOUNG, BRIGHAM \\'bri-gəm-'yəŋ\ (b. June 1, 1801, Whitingham, Vt., U.S.—d. Aug. 29, 1877, Salt Lake City, Utah), American religious leader, second president of the MORMON church, and colonizer who significantly influenced the development of the American West.

A carpenter, joiner, painter, and glazier, Young was baptized into the CHURCH OF JESUS CHRIST OF LATTER-DAY SAINTS in 1832. In the spring of 1834 he joined in the march to Missouri to help dispossessed Mormons regain their lands. He was named third of the Quorum of the Twelve Apostles in 1835. In 1838, when the Mormons were driven out of Missouri, Young, who had become senior member of the Quorum, directed the move to Nauvoo, Ill. In 1839 he went to England, where he established a mission.

When JOSEPH SMITH was murdered (June 1844), Young returned to Nauvoo and took command of the church. In the face of mob pressure, he led the Mormons westward out of Illinois in 1846. He got no farther than the Missouri River that summer, but in 1847, after selecting the site of Salt Lake City as a gathering place for the Mormons, Young returned to Winter Quarters (Florence, Neb.) and in December 1847 became president of the church. He returned to

Utah with the Mormon emigration of 1848 and remained there for the rest of his life.

In 1849 the Mormons established the provisional state of Deseret, with Young as governor. The next year this area became the territory of Utah, again with Young as governor. Friction between the Mormons and the federal judiciary led President James Buchanan to replace him in 1857, at which time an army was sent to establish the primacy of federal rule in Utah. He never again held political office, but as president of the Mormon church he effectively ruled the people of Utah until his death.

An eminently practical man, Young made few doctrinal contributions. He was an iron-fisted administrator who stabilized Mormon society and gave it a cohesion made possible, in part, by its comparative isolation. Young encouraged education and the theater, always stressed self-sufficiency, and became a notably wealthy man. Having accepted the doctrine of plural marriage, he took more than 20 wives and fathered 47 children.

YOUNG MEN'S CHRISTIAN ASSOCIATION (YMCA), nonsectarian, nonpolitical Christian lay movement that aims to develop high standards of Christian character through group activities and citizenship training. It originated in London in 1844, when 12 young men, led by George Williams, an employee in a drapery house, formed a club for the "improvement of the spiritual condition of young men in the drapery and other trades." Similar clubs spread rapidly in the United Kingdom and reached Australia in 1850 and North America in 1851, where the organization eventually reached its greatest development. At the centennial of the World Alliance of YMCAs in 1955, a series of conferences held in Paris was attended by 8,000 delegates representing more than 4,000,000 members in 76 countries and territories.

The YMCA programs include sports and physical education, camping, counseling, formal and informal education, public affairs, and citizenship activities. In addition to other activities, the YMCA sponsors hotels, residence halls, and cafeterias. In the United States it operates several degree-granting institutions as well as many other schools at all levels, including night classes for adults.

YMCA services to the armed forces began, in the United States, with the Civil War, and it continued giving service through all wars thereafter. By the Geneva Convention of 1929, it was charged with promoting educational and recreational facilities in many prisoner of war camps.

YOUNG WOMEN'S CHRISTIAN ASSOCIATION (YWCA), nonsectarian Christian organization that aims "to advance the physical, social, intellectual, moral, and spiritual interests of young women." The YWCA and the Young Men's Christian Association (YMCA) are completely independent organizations.

The first YWCA was established in England in 1855, when two groups met to aid women: one group formed a Prayer Union to pray for women, and the other founded Christian homes for young women. The two groups merged in 1877 and took the name Young Women's Christian Association. In 1884 the organization adopted a constitution.

In the United States 35 women met in New York City and formed the first Ladies' Christian Association to provide for the "temporal, moral, and religious welfare of young women who are dependent on their own exertions for support." In 1866, in Boston, another group formed an organization with similar aims and wrote the constitution for the Young Women's Christian Association. By 1900 hundreds of YWCAs were in existence in the United States; the national organization was formed in 1906. Local YWCA organizations are affiliated with their national associations, which in turn are members of the World YWCA, organized in London in 1894, with headquarters in Geneva. By the end of the 20th century YWCA programs reached more than 25 million women in more than 100 countries. The focus of their programs had broadened to include shelter, child care, employment training, racial justice, physical fitness, youth development, leadership training, and world relations.

YUGA \'yu̇-gə\, in Hindu COSMOLOGY, an age or eon. Each *yuga* is progressively shorter than the preceding one, corresponding to a decline in the moral and physical state of humanity. Four such *yuga*s (called Kṛta, Tretā, Dvāpara, and Kali or Satya after throws of an Indian game of dice) make up a *mahāyuga* ("great yuga"), and 2,000 *mahāyuga*s make up the basic cosmic cycle, the *kalpa*. The first *yuga* (Kṛta) was an age of perfection, lasting 1,728,000 years. The fourth and most degenerate *yuga* (Kali) began in 3102 BCE and will last 432,000 years. At the close of the Kali *yuga*, the world will be destroyed by fire and flood, to be re-created as the cycle resumes. In a partially competing vision of time, Vishnu's 10th and final AVATAR, KALKĪ, is described as bringing the present cosmic cycle to a close by destroying the evil forces that rule the Kali *yuga* and ushering in an immediate return to the idyllic Kṛta *yuga*.

YÜN-KANG CAVES \'yʊ̇en-'gäŋ\, *Pinyin* Yungang, series of magnificent Chinese Buddhist cave temples, created in the 5th century CE (Six Dynasties period). They are located about 10 miles west of Ta-t'ung (Datong), near the northern border of Shansi province (and the Great Wall).

The caves are among the earliest remaining examples of the first major flowering of Buddhist art in China. A low ridge of soft sandstone was excavated to form about 20 major cave temples and many smaller niches and caves, stretching for over half a mile from east to west. Some of the caves served merely as cell-like enclosures for colossal figures of the Buddha (up to about 45 feet tall), while others contained chapels.

The earliest five temples were instituted by a leader of the Buddhist SANGHA, a monk named T'an-yao, about 460; their construction was among the first acts of propitiation

Interior of Cave VI, Yün-kang, Shansi province, China, second half of the 5th century CE
Seiichi Mizuno

sponsored by the foreign T'o-pa, or Northern Wei, rulers (386–535) for their persecution of BUDDHISM during the period 446–452. The Buddha images in each cave were equated with the first five emperors of the Northern Wei, thus emphasizing the political and economic role that the court imposed upon Buddhism.

The remaining temples were constructed in the succeeding decades until 494, when the Northern Wei court was moved to the city of Lo-yang (Honan province) and a new series of cave temples was instituted at the site of Lung-men (*see* LUNG-MEN CAVES).

The predominant sculptural style of the innumerable images is a synthesis of various foreign influences—including Persian, Byzantine, and Greek—with elements ultimately derived from the Buddhist art of India. Late in the period of major work at the site, a new "Chinese style" appeared, based on indigenous styles and forms; Yün-kang, however, is considered as the type site for the first style, and the later caves at Lung-men the type site for the second style.

YUNUS EMRE \yü-'nüs-em-'re\ (b. *c.* 1238, Turkey—d. *c.* 1320, Turkey), poet and mystic who exercised a powerful influence on Turkish literature.

He is known to have been a Sufi who sat for 40 years at the feet of his master, Tapduk Emre. Yunus Emre was well versed in mystical philosophy, especially that of the 13th-century poet and mystic JALĀL AL-DĪN AL-RŪMĪ. Like Rūmī, Yunus Emre became a leading representative of MYSTICISM in Anatolia but on a more popular level; he was venerated as a saint after his death.

His poems are devoted mainly to the themes of divine love and human destiny. He wrote in a straightforward, almost austere style and mainly in the traditional syllabic meter of Anatolian folk poetry. His verse had a decisive influence on later Turkish mystics and inspired the poets of the renaissance of Turkish national poetry after 1910.

YÜ THE GREAT \'yǖ\, *Chinese* Ta Yü \'dä-'yǖ\, *Pinyin* Da Yu, in Chinese mythology, Tamer of the Flood, one of China's savior-heroes and reputed founder of China's oldest dynasty, the Hsia. One legend recounts Yü's extraordinary birth: a man called Kun was given charge of controlling a great deluge. To dam the water, he stole a piece of magic soil from heaven. Angered by the theft, the Lord on High ordered his execution. After three years, Kun's miraculously preserved body was slit open and a son brought forth. This was Yü who, after years of strenuous labor, provided outlets to the sea through dredging, with the aid of dragons, thus making the world suitable for human habitation.

YÜ TI, *Pinyin* Yudi: *see* JADE EMPEROR.

ZADDIK \'tsä-dik, tsä-'dēk\ (Hebrew: "righteous man"), *also spelled* tzaddiq, tsaddik, *or* zaddik, *plural* zaddikim, tzaddiqim, tsaddikim, *or* zaddikim, one who embodies the religious ideals of JUDAISM. The TALMUD asserts that the continued existence of the world is due to the merits of 36 individuals, each of whom is *gamur tzaddiq* ("completely righteous"). While recognizing that zaddikim have special privileges, the Talmud also notes their special obligations. They are at least partially responsible for the SINS of their generation.

In HASIDISM, the religious leader (zaddik) was viewed as a mediator between human and divine. Because the zaddik's life was expected to be a living expression of the TORAH, his behavior was even more important than his doctrine. In early Hasidism, the zaddik traveled widely and often engaged in such secular matters as idle talk and the consumption of wine. The Hasidic formula for such conduct was "descent on behalf of ascent" (*'aliyya tzrikha yerida*)—a calculated risk to strengthen the spiritual life of the Jewish community. Toward the end of the 18th century the zaddikim ceased to travel. Thereafter, they were available at home for those who sought advice and instructions. This change gave rise to "practical zaddikism," a development that included, among other things, the writing of a *quittel* ("prayer note") to guarantee the success of petitions made by visitors who offered money for the service. Such developments contributed to the gradual deterioration of an institution that had earlier been a vital spiritual force within Jewish communities.

ZAGREUS \'zā-grē-əs, 'za-\, in Orphic myth, divine child who was the son of ZEUS (as a snake) and his daughter PERSEPHONE. Zeus intended to make Zagreus his heir and bestow on him unlimited power, but HERA out of jealousy urged the TITANS to attack the child. The Titans tore Zagreus to pieces and consumed him except for his heart. ATHENA saved the child's heart and brought it to Zeus, who swallowed it. Zeus blasted the Titans into soot with his thunderbolts and from these remains arose mortals, who were partly wicked and partly divine. Zeus then begot a son in the body of SEMELE, and this child, made from the heart of Zagreus, was called DIONYSUS.

ZĀHIRĪYA \,zä-hi-'rē-ə\ (Arabic: "Literalists"), followers of an Islamic legal school that insisted on strict adherence to the literal text (*zāhir*) of the QUR'AN and HADITH as the only source of Muslim law. Founded in Iraq by Dāwūd Khalaf in the 9th century, it spread to Iran, North Africa, and Muslim Spain, where the philosopher IBN HAZM was its chief exponent. Although it was strongly attacked by most SUNNI theologians, the Zāhirī school nevertheless survived for about 500 years in various forms and seems finally to have merged with the HANBALĪ LEGAL SCHOOL.

ZAKĀT \zà-'kat, zə-'kät\ (Arabic: "alms," "charity"), obligatory tax required of Muslims, one of the FIVE PILLARS OF IS-

LAM. The *zakāt* is levied on five categories of property—food grains; fruit; camels, cattle, sheep, and goats; gold and silver; and movable goods—and is payable each year. The tax levy required by religious law varies with the category. Recipients of the *zakāt* include the poor and needy, the collectors themselves, and "those whose hearts it is necessary to conciliate"—*e.g.*, discordant tribesmen, debtors, volunteers in JIHAD (HOLY WAR), and pilgrims.

Under the caliphates, the collection and expenditure of *zakāt* was a function of the state. In the modern Muslim world it has been left up to the individual, except in such countries as Saudi Arabia, where the Sharī'ah (Islamic law) is strictly maintained. Among Twelver SHI'ITES, it is collected and disbursed by the 'ULAMĀ', who act as representatives for the Hidden IMAM.

The QUR'AN and Hadith also stress *sadaqa*, or voluntary almsgiving, which, like *zakāt*, is intended for the needy. Twelver Shi'ites, moreover, require payment of an additional one-fifth tax, the KHUMS, to the Hidden Imam and his deputies. It is intended to be spent for the benefit of orphans, the poor, travelers, and, of course, the imams.

ŽALTYS \zhȧl-'tᵞēs\, in ancient BALTIC RELIGION, a snake highly respected as a symbol of fertility and wealth. To ensure the prosperity of family and field, a *žaltys* was kept in a special corner of the house, and the entire household gathered at specified times to recite prayers to it.

On special occasions the snake was asked to the table to share the family meal from their plates; should he refuse, misfortune was imminent. To encounter a snake accidentally was also considered auspicious and portended a marriage or a birth. Paralysis or great misfortune awaited anyone who dared kill a *žaltys*, the "sentinel of the gods" and a favorite of SAULE, the goddess of the sun.

ZAMAKHSHARĪ, ABU AL-QĀSIM MAHMŪD IBN 'UMAR AL- \zȧ-,mȧk-shȧ-'rē\ (b. March 8, 1075, Khwārezm [now in Turkmenistan and Uzbekistan]—d. June 14, 1144, al-Jurjānīya, Khwārezm), Persian-born Arabic scholar whose chief work is his commentary on the QUR'AN.

As a theologian, he was one of the Mu'tazilite school. His commentary on the Qur'an, *Al-Kashshāf 'an Haqā'iq at-tanzīl* ("Discoverer of the Truths of Revelation"), was completed in 1134 (published at Calcutta in 1856 in 2 vol.) and, in spite of its Mu'tazilite bias, was widely read, especially in the East; in the western portions of the Islamic world, his dogmatic point of view was offensive to the Mālikī school. Of Zamakhsharī's grammatical works, *Al-Mufassal fī 'ilm al-Arabīya* ("Detailed Treatise on Arabic Linguistics," written 1119–21, published 1859) is celebrated for its concise but exhaustive exposition. He was also the author of a collection of old proverbs, three collections of apothegms composed by himself, moral discourses, and poems. *See also* MU'TAZILA; TAFSĪR.

ZĀWIYA \za̲-'wē-ə\ (Arabic), *Persian* Khānqāh \k̲an̲-'gáh, k̲a-nā-\, *Turkish* Tekke \tek-'ke\, in the Muslim world, a monastic complex, usually the center or a settlement of a Sufi brotherhood. In some Arabic countries the term *zāwiya* is also used for any small, private oratory not paid for by community funds. (*See* SUFISM.)

The first North African *zāwiya*, dating from about the 13th century, was akin to a hermitage (*rābiṭa*), housing an ascetic holy man and his disciples. Linked to the Sufi movement that was making its way westward across North Africa, the *zāwiya* seems to have proliferated rapidly. Eventually it became an extensive center of religious and paramilitary power. The essential structure of the medieval *zāwiya* has survived intact into the 20th century. It may include an area reserved for prayer, a shrine, a religious school, and residential quarters for students, guests, pilgrims, and travelers.

By the mid-19th century the Sānusīya, a religious brotherhood of Cyrenaica (modern Libya), had established a network of *zāwiya*s in areas remote from central authority and had attained political, as well as religious, control of the province. After World War I, the Italians wiped out most of the *zāwiya*s in that country.

ZAYDĪYA \zī-'dē-ə\, *also spelled* Zaidiya, *or* Zaidīs, *English* Zaydis \'zī-dēz\, subdivision of SHI'ITE Muslims owing allegiance to Zayd ibn 'Alī (d. 740), grandson of ḤUSAYN IBN 'ALĪ. Zaydīs participated in a number of anti-caliphal revolts in the 8th and 9th centuries and succeeded in establishing control in northern Iran until the 11th century. They are credited with fostering the conversion of peoples in this region to ISLAM. Early in the 10th century the Zaydīya became dominant in Yemen, and thereafter Zaydī IMAMS were the spiritual rulers of that area. From the departure of the Turks in 1917 until 1962, they were also the temporal rulers of Yemen.

Zaydī doctrine on imams differs markedly from that of Twelver Shi'ites. Imams acquire position by their own abilities, rather than by designation by their father, and they do not possess any miraculous qualities. Indeed, anyone descended from 'ALĪ and FĀṬIMA can become an imam. Zaydīs recognize the legitimacy of the first two CALIPHS, Abū Bakr and 'Umar. In theology Zaydīs follow the Mu'tazilites, and in law they are so close to the SUNNIS that they are sometimes called "the fifth school" (after the ḤANAFĪ, MĀLIKĪ, SHĀFI'Ī, and ḤANBALĪ schools).

ZEALOT, member of a Jewish sect noted for its uncompromising opposition to Rome. A census of Galilee ordered by Rome in 6 CE spurred the Zealots to rally the populace to noncompliance on the grounds that agreement was an implicit acknowledgment of the right of non-Jews to rule their nation. Extremists among the Zealots, known as Sicarii (Latin: "assassins" or "murderers"), frequented public places to assassinate persons friendly to Rome. In the first revolt against Rome (66–70 CE) the Zealots played a leading role, and at Masada in 73 they committed suicide rather than surrender the fortress.

ZEBULUN \'ze-byə-lən\, one of the 12 tribes of ISRAEL that in biblical times constituted the people of Israel. The tribe was named for the sixth son born of JACOB and his first wife, LEAH. After the Israelites took possession of the Promised Land, the tribe of Zebulun settled northeast of the Plain of Jezreel. After the northern Kingdom of Israel was conquered by the Assyrians in 721 BCE, Zebulun and the other northern tribes dispersed; thus Zebulun became known as one of the legendary TEN LOST TRIBES OF ISRAEL.

ZEMES MĀTE \'ze-mes-'mä-te\ (Latvian), *Lithuanian* Žemyna \zh^ye-'m^yē-nȧ g̣\, in BALTIC RELIGION, the female aspect of nature and the source of all life—human, animal, and plant. Interacting with DIEVS (the sky), Zemes māte stimulates and protects the power of life. LIBATIONS of beer were offered to her at the opening of every festival, and bread, ale, and herbs were buried in the ground or thrown into rivers and lakes or tied to trees in her honor. The birth of a child was also celebrated with an offering to her. The various functions of Zemes māte were eventually assumed by demigoddesses of forests, fields, stones, animals, water, and, in the Christian era, by the Blessed Virgin MARY.

The male counterpart of Zemes māte is Zemnieks (Latvian), known as Žemininkas, or Žemėpatis, among the Lithuanians. Žemėpatis, the brother of Žemyna, functioned as master of the earth and guardian of farms.

ZEN \'zen\, *Chinese* Ch'an \'chän\, *Korean* Son \'sən\ (from Sanskrit *dhyāna*, "meditation"), important school of BUDDHISM in Japan that claims to transmit the spirit or essence of Buddhism—experience of the Enlightenment (BODHI) achieved by the BUDDHA GOTAMA. The school arose in the 6th century in China as Ch'an, but Zen did not fully develop in Japan until the 12th century.

Zen teaches that the potential to achieve enlightenment is inherent in everyone but lies dormant because of ignorance. It is best awakened not by the study of SCRIPTURES, the practice of good deeds, rites and ceremonies, or worship of images but by a sudden breaking through of the boundaries of common, everyday, logical thought. The differing sects have various methods for achieving this enlightenment. The RINZAI sect emphasizes sudden shock and meditation on the paradoxical statements called KOAN. The SŌTŌ sect prefers the method of sitting in meditation (*zazen*). A third sect, the Ōbaku, employs the methods of Rinzai and the continual invocation *nembutsu*, the continual invocation of Amida (the Japanese name for the Buddha AMITĀBHA), with the devotional formula *namu Amida Butsu* (Japanese: "homage to Amida Buddha").

During the 16th-century period of political unrest, Zen priests not only contributed their talents as diplomats and administrators but also preserved the cultural life; it was under their inspiration that art, literature, the tea cult, and the nō theatre, for example, developed and prospered.

In modern Japan, Zen sects and subsects claim some 9,600,000 adherents. Considerable interest in various aspects of Zen thought developed also in the West in the latter half of the 20th century, and a number of Zen groups have been formed in North America and Europe.

ZEPHANIAH \,ze-fə-'nī-ə\, *also spelled* Sophonias \,sä-fə-'nī-əs, ,sō-\ (fl. 7th century BCE), Israelite prophet who proclaimed the approaching divine judgment. The prophet's activity probably occurred during the early part of the reign of JOSIAH, king of JUDAH (reigned c. 640–609 BCE), for his criticism of the worship of certain gods in Jerusalem (BAAL, Milcom, and the host of the heavens) would have been meaningless after Josiah's reform, which took place about 623/622 BCE.

ZERA'IM \ze-rä-'ēm\ (Hebrew: "Seeds"), first of the six major divisions, or orders (SEDARIM), of the MISHNAH. *Zera'im* contains 11 tractates, the first of which (*Berakhot*, "Blessings") deals with public worship and private prayer. The other 10 all deal with laws regarding agriculture and are called: *Pe'a* ("Corner"), *Demai* ("Dubiously Tithed Produce"), *Kilayim* ("Mixed Kinds"), *Shevi'it* ("Seventh Year"), *Terumot* ("Heave Offerings"), *Ma'aserot* ("Tithes"), *Ma'aser sheni* ("Second Tithe"), *Ḥalla* ("Dough Offering"), *'Orla* ("Uncircumcision"—applied to restricted fruit), and *Bikkurim* ("Firstfruits"). The Talmud YERUSHALMI has GEMARA on all 11 tractates of *Zera'im*, but the Talmud BAVLI has Gemara only on *Berakhot*.

ZERUBBABEL \zə-'rə-bə-bəl\, *also spelled* Zorobabel \zȯ-'rä-bə-bəl\ (fl. 6th century BCE), governor of Judaea under whom the rebuilding of the Jewish TEMPLE OF JERUSALEM took place (Ezra 3ff.). Zerubbabel is thought to have been a Babylonian Jew who returned to Jerusalem and became governor of Judaea under the Persians (Ezra 2:2). As a descendant of the House of David, Zerubbabel rekindled Jewish messianic hopes (Haggai 2:20–23; Sirach 49:11).

ZEUS \'züs\, in ancient GREEK RELIGION, chief deity of the pantheon, a sky and weather god. Zeus was regarded as the sender of thunder and lightning, rain, and winds, and his traditional weapon was the thunderbolt. He was called the father (i.e., the ruler and protector) of both gods and men. His name, from the earlier unattested *Diēus*, is an elaboration of an Indo-European root that denoted day and the clear daytime sky as well as a deity of the heavens; the invocatory formula *Zeus patēr*, "Father Zeus," has exact counterparts in the Sanskrit *Dyauṣ pitā* and the Latin *Iuppiter.* No other Greek deity has such a clear Indo-European ancestry.

Hesiod's *Theogony* states that CRONUS, king of the TITANS, upon learning that one of his children was fated to dethrone him, swallowed his children as soon as they were born. But RHEA, his wife, saved the infant Zeus by substituting a stone wrapped in swaddling clothes for Cronus to swallow and hiding Zeus in a cave on Crete. There he was nursed by the NYMPH (or female goat) AMALTHAEA and guarded by the Curetes (young warriors), who clashed their weapons to disguise the baby's cries. After Zeus grew to manhood he led a revolt against the Titans and succeeded in dethroning Cronus, after which he divided dominion over the world with his brothers POSEIDON and HADES.

As ruler of heaven Zeus led the gods to victory against the GIANTS and successfully crushed several revolts against him by his fellow gods. From his exalted position atop Mount Olympus, Zeus was thought to omnisciently observe the affairs of men, seeing everything, governing all, and rewarding good conduct and punishing evil. Besides dispensing justice, Zeus was the protector of cities, the home, property, strangers, guests, and suppliants.

Zeus hurling a thunderbolt, bronze statuette from Dodona, Greece, early 5th century BCE
By courtesy of the Staatliche Museen zu Berlin, Antikenabteilung

Zeus was well known for his amorousness—a source of perpetual discord with his wife, HERA—and he had many love affairs with both mortal and immortal women. Notable among his offspring were the twins APOLLO and ARTEMIS, by the Titaness Leto; HELEN and the DIOSCURI, by LEDA of Sparta; PERSEPHONE, by the goddess Demeter; ATHENA, born from his head after he had swallowed her mother Metis; DIONYSUS, by Semele; HEPHAESTUS, HEBE, ARES, and EILEITHYIA, by Hera; and many others.

Zeus's very universality tended to reduce his importance compared to that of powerful local divinities like Athena and Hera. Although statues of Zeus Herkeios (Guardian of the House) and altars of Zeus Xenios (Hospitable) graced the forecourts of houses, and though his mountaintop shrines were visited by pilgrims, Zeus did not have a temple at Athens until the late 6th century BCE, and even his temple at OLYMPIA postdated that of Hera.

In art Zeus was represented as a bearded, dignified, and mature man of stalwart build; his most prominent symbols were the thunderbolt and the eagle.

ZIGGURAT \'zi-gə-ˌrat\ (Akkadian *ziqqurratu*), pyramidal, stepped temple tower that is an architectural and religious structure characteristic of the major cities of Mesopotamia (now in Iraq) from about 2200 until 500 BCE. The ziggurat was always built with a core of mud brick and an exterior covered with baked brick. It had no internal chambers and was usually square or rectangular, averaging either 170 feet square or 125 × 170 feet at the base. Approximately 25 ziggurats are known, being equally divided in number among Sumer, Babylonia, and Assyria.

No ziggurat is preserved to its original height. Ascent was by an exterior triple stairway or by a spiral ramp, but for almost half of the known ziggurats, no means of ascent has been discovered. The sloping sides and terraces were often landscaped with trees and shrubs. The best-preserved ziggurat is at Ur (modern Tall al-Muqayyar). The largest, at Choghā Zanbīl in Elam, is 335 feet square and 80 feet high and stands at less than half its estimated original height. The legendary TOWER OF BABEL has been associated with the ziggurat of the great temple of MARDUK in Babylon.

ZION \'zī-ən\, in the OLD TESTAMENT, easternmost of the two hills of ancient Jerusalem. It was the site of the Jebusite city captured by DAVID, king of ISRAEL and JUDAH, in the 10th century BCE (2 Samuel 5:6–9) and established by him as his royal capital. Some scholars believe that the name also belonged to the "stronghold of Zion" taken by David (2 Samuel 5:7), which may have been the fortress of the city. The Jewish historian JOSEPHUS identified Zion with the western hill of Jerusalem; this incorrect identification of the site was retained until the late 19th or early 20th century, when the site of Zion was identified as the eastern hill (modern Ophel). The site was not included in the walls of Jerusalem's 16th-century fortifications. (The Old City Wall, erected 1538–40 by the Ottoman SULTAN Süleyman the Magnificent, was built largely on the foundations of earlier walls going back chiefly to the period of the Crusades but in some places dating to Byzantine, Herodian, and even Hasmonean times.)

The etymology and meaning of the name are obscure. It appears to be a pre-Israelite Canaanite name of the hill upon which Jerusalem was built; the name "mountain of Zion" is common. In biblical usage, however, "Mount Zion" often means the city rather than the hill itself. In the Old Testament, "Zion" is overwhelmingly a poetic and prophetic designation and is infrequently used in ordinary prose. Mount Zion is the place where YAHWEH, the God of Israel, dwells (ISAIAH 8:18; Psalms 74:2), the place where He is king (Isaiah 24:23) and where He has installed his king, David (Psalms 2:6). It is thus the seat of the action of Yahweh in history. After Jerusalem was destroyed by the Babylonians in 586 BCE, the Israelites could not forget Zion (Psalms 137), and, in the PROPHECY after the BABYLONIAN EXILE, Zion is the scene of Yahweh's messianic salvation. It is to Zion that the exiles will be restored (JEREMIAH 3:14), and there they will find Yahweh (Jeremiah 31). Bearing all these connotations, Zion came to mean the Jewish homeland, symbolic of JUDAISM or Jewish national aspirations (whence the name ZIONISM for the 19th–20th-century movement to establish a Jewish national center or state in Palestine).

ZIONISM \ˈzī-ə-ˌni-zəm\, Jewish nationalist movement whose goal has been the creation and support of a Jewish national state in Palestine, the ancient homeland of the Jews (Hebrew: Eretz Yisra'el, "the Land of Israel"). Though Zionism originated in eastern and central Europe in the latter part of the 19th century, it is in many ways a continuation of the ancient nationalist attachment of the Jews and of JUDAISM to the historical region of Palestine, where one of the hills of ancient Jerusalem was called ZION.

In the 16th and 17th centuries a number of "messiahs" tried to persuade Jews to return to Palestine. The Haskalah ("Enlightenment") movement of the late 18th century,

however, urged Jews to assimilate into Western secular culture, and by the early 19th century interest in a return of the Jews to Palestine was kept alive mostly by Christian millenarians. Despite the Haskalah, eastern European Jews tended not to assimilate and in reaction to tsarist pogroms formed the Hovevei Ziyyon ("Lovers of Zion") to promote the settlement of Jewish farmers and artisans in Palestine.

THEODOR HERZL, an Austrian journalist, convened the first Zionist Congress (1897) at Basel, Switz., which drew up the Basel program of the movement; this stated that "Zionism strives to create for the Jewish people a home in Palestine secured by public law." Prior to World War I Zionism represented only a minority of Jews, mostly from Russia but led by Austrians and Germans. It developed propaganda through orators and pamphlets, created its own newspapers, and gave an impetus to what was called a "Jewish renaissance" in letters and arts. The development of Modern Hebrew largely took place during this period.

The failure of the Russian Revolution of 1905 and the wave of pogroms and repressions that followed caused growing numbers of Russian Jewish youth to immigrate to Palestine as pioneer settlers. By 1914 there were about 90,000 Jews in Palestine. Upon the outbreak of World War I political Zionism reasserted itself, and its leadership passed to Russian Jews living in England. Chaim Weizmann and Nahum Sokolow were instrumental in obtaining the Balfour Declaration from Great Britain (Nov. 2, 1917), which promised British support for the creation of a Jewish national home in Palestine.

In the following years the Zionists built up the Jewish urban and rural settlements in Palestine, perfecting autonomous organizations and solidifying Jewish cultural life and Hebrew education. In March 1925 the Jewish population in Palestine was officially estimated at 108,000, and it had risen to about 238,000 by 1933. The Arab population feared Palestine eventually would become a Jewish state and bitterly resisted Zionism and the British policy supporting it. Several Arab revolts, especially in 1929 and 1936–39, caused the British to devise schemes to reconcile the Arab and Zionist demands. As tensions grew among Arabs and Zionists, Britain submitted the Palestine problem to the United Nations, which on Nov. 29, 1947, proposed partition of the country into separate Arab and Jewish states and the internationalization of Jerusalem. The creation of the State of Israel on May 14, 1948, brought about the Arab-Israeli war of 1948–49, in the course of which Israel obtained

Ziggurat of Choghā Zanbīl, near Sūsa, Iran
Robert Harding Picture Library—Sybil Sassoon

more land than had been provided by the UN resolution, and drove out 800,000 Arabs who became displaced persons known as Palestinians.

During the next two decades Zionist organizations in many countries continued to raise financial support for Israel and to encourage Jews to immigrate there. Most Jews, however, reject the view propagated by many very Orthodox Jews in Israel that the Jews outside Israel are living in "exile" and can live a full life only in Israel. *See also* JUDAISM: TWENTIETH-CENTURY JUDAISMS BEYOND THE RABBINIC FRAMEWORK: ZIONISM.

ZIONIST CHURCH, any of several prophet-healing groups in southern Africa; they correspond to the independent churches called Aladura in Nigeria, "spiritual" in Ghana, and "prophet-healing" in most other parts of Africa.

The use of the term ZION derives from the Christian Catholic Apostolic Church in Zion, founded in Chicago in 1896 and having missionaries in South Africa by 1904. That church emphasized divine healing, BAPTISM by threefold immersion, and the imminent SECOND COMING of Christ. Its African members encountered U.S. missionaries of the Apostolic Faith pentecostal church in 1908 and learned that the Zion Church lacked the second Baptism of the Spirit (recognition of extra powers or character); they therefore founded their own pentecostal Zion Apostolic Church. The vast range of independent churches that stem from the original Zion Apostolic Church use in their names the words Zion (or Jerusalem), Apostolic, Pentecostal, Faith, or Holy Spirit to represent their biblical charter, as for example the Christian Catholic Apostolic Holy Spirit Church in Zion of South Africa. These are known in general as Zionists or Spirit Churches. The churches were introduced into Rhodesia (Zimbabwe) in the 1920s by migrant workers returning from South Africa; schisms and new foundations followed.

Zionist churches include the following features: (1) origination from a mandate received by a prophet in a dream, vision, or death-resurrection experience; (2) a chieflike head, often called a bishop, who is succeeded by his son and who is occasionally regarded as a MESSIAH. Women also figure as founders and leaders; (3) security received by the church's possession of its own holy place, such as a New Jerusalem, Zion, or Moriah City, as headquarters; organization of farms and other economic activities; (4) healing, through CONFESSION, repeated baptisms, purification rites and EXORCISMS, especially at "Bethesda pools" and "Jordan rivers"; (5) revelation and power from the Holy Spirit through prophetic utterances and pentecostal phenomena; (6) ritualistic and Africanized worship, with special garments and innovative festivals, characterized by singing, dancing, clapping, and drumming; (7) a legalistic and Sabbatarian ethic, which includes TABOOS against certain foods, beer, and tobacco and which does not admit Western medicines but tolerates polygamy; and (8) repudiation of traditional magic, medicines, DIVINATION, and ancestor cults; the Christian replacements for these traditional practices, however, are sometimes similarly used and interpreted.

ZIUSUDRA \,zē-ü-'sü-drä\, in MESOPOTAMIAN RELIGION, rough counterpart to the biblical NOAH as survivor of a god-sent flood. When the gods had decided to destroy humanity with a flood, the god Enki (Akkadian EA), who did not agree with the decree, revealed it to Ziusudra, a man well known for his humility and obedience. Ziusudra did as Enki commanded him and built a huge boat, in which he successful-

ly rode out the flood. Afterward, he prostrated himself before the gods An (ANU) and ENLIL (BEL), and, as a reward for living a godly life, Ziusudra was given immortality. *See* UT-NAPISHTIM.

ZIYĀRA \zē-'yár-ə\ (Arabic: "visit"), in ISLAM, a visit to the tomb of the Prophet MUHAMMAD in the mosque at MEDINA, Saudi Arabia; also a visit to the tomb of a saint or a holy person. The legitimacy of these latter visits has been questioned by Muslim religious authorities, particularly by the Wahhābīya, who consider *ziyāra* to be a BID'A ("innovation") that should be condemned by all true believers and maintain that such veneration of saints is a form of POLYTHEISM, for God alone can grant salvation to a troubled person. However, according to a popular HADITH, Muhammad promised his intercession to whoever visited his tomb.

Despite objections from some quarters, Muslims in great numbers continue to make such visits in hope of obtaining cures or the blessings of the saint, especially on that saints feast day (known as MAWLID or, in India and Pakistan, 'urs). Millions include a visit to the Prophet's mosque in Medina with the performance of the HAJJ or 'UMRA in MECCA (about 250 miles to the south). Since most Muslims are unable to perform the required *hajj*, visiting regional shrines is popularly regarded to be a suitable alternative. Women, whose access to mosques is limited, are among the most common patrons of saint shrines, where they gather to engage in social as well as devotional activities. Visitors bring votive offerings with them, or slaughter animals as sacrifices to be fed to the poor. They often circumambulate the shrine, as is also done by pilgrims in Mecca.

Aside from the Prophet's mosque, among the most popular shrines are those of Aḥmad al-Badawī, Sayyida Zaynab, and ḤUSAYN in Egypt; 'ABD AL-QĀDIR AL-JĪLĀNĪ in Tunisia; Moulay Idrīs in Morocco; Aḥmadou Bamba in Senegal; al-Nabī Mūsā (MOSES) in Palestine; JALĀL AL-DĪN AL-RŪMĪ in Turkey; Bahā' al-Dīn Naqshbānd in Uzbekistan; and Mu'īn al-Dīn Chistī in India. Shrines most favored in SHI'ITE *ziyāra*s include those of the IMAMS and their relatives in KARBALĀ', NAJAF, and Sāmarrā' in Iraq and in MASHHAD and QOM in Iran. Almost every Muslim community in North Africa, the Middle East, and Asia has its own saint, whose tomb is visited by the local inhabitants and by pilgrims from afar. During the 20th century some *ziyāra* sites were imbued with nationalist sentiments.

ZODIAC, in astronomy and ASTROLOGY, belt around the heavens extending 9° on either side of the ecliptic, the plane of the earth's orbit and of the sun's apparent annual path. Because most of the constellations through which the ecliptic passes represent animals, the ancient Greeks called its zone *zodiakos kyklos*, "circle of animals," or *ta zodia*, "the little animals." The 12 constellations of the zodiac include Aries (Ram), Taurus (Bull), Gemini (Twins), Cancer (Crab), Leo (Lion), Virgo (Virgin), Libra (Balance), Scorpius (Scorpion), Sagittarius (Archer), Capricornus (Goat), Aquarius (Water Bearer), and Pisces (Fish). In Chinese astrology the zodiac comprises a 12-year cycle with an animal attribute for each: Rat, Ox, Tiger, Rabbit, Dragon, Snake, Horse, Sheep, Monkey, Rooster, Dog, and Boar.

ZOROASTER \'zōr-ə-,was-tər, 'zòr-\, *Old Iranian* Zarathushtra, *or* Zarathustra \za-ra-,tōsh-'trä; ,zar-ə-'thüsh-trə, -'thüs-\ (b. *c.* 628 BCE, probably Rhages, Iran—d. *c.* 551, site unknown), Iranian religious reformer and founder of ZOROASTRIANISM, or Parsiism, as it is known in India.

The dates of Zoroaster's life cannot be ascertained with any degree of certainty. His birthdate may have been 628 BCE. Zoroaster was born into a modestly situated family of knights, the Spitama, probably at Rhages (now Rayy, a suburb of Tehrān), a town in Media. The area in which he lived was not yet urban, its economy being based on animal husbandry and pastoral occupations. Nomads, who frequently raided those engaged in such occupations, were viewed by Zoroaster as aggressive violators of order, and he called them followers of the Lie.

Zoroaster probably was a priest. Having received a vision from AHURA MAZDĀ, the Wise Lord, who appointed him to preach the truth, Zoroaster apparently was opposed in his teachings by the civil and religious authorities in the area in which he preached. Confident in the truth revealed to him, Zoroaster apparently did not try to overthrow belief in the polytheistic Iranian religion, but he did place Ahura Mazdā at the center of a kingdom of justice that promised immortality and bliss.

Zoroaster's teachings centered on Ahura Mazdā, who is the highest god and alone is worthy of worship. According to the *Gāthās*, hymns thought to be the words of Zoroaster, he is the creator of heaven and earth. He is the source of the alternation of light and darkness, the sovereign lawgiver, and the very center of nature, as well as the originator of the moral order and judge of the entire world. He is surrounded by six or seven entities, which the later AVESTA calls AMESHA SPENTAS, "beneficent immortals." In the words of the *Gāthās*, Ahura Mazdā is the father of SPENTA MAINYU (Bounteous Spirit), of Asha Vahishta (Justice, Truth), of VOHU MANAH (Righteous Thinking), and of Armaiti (Spenta Armaiti, Devotion). The other three beings (entities) of this group are said to personify qualities attributed to Ahura Mazdā: they are Khshathra Vairya (Desirable Dominion), Haurvatāt (Wholeness), and Ameretāt (Immortality). The good qualities represented by these beings are also to be earned and possessed by Ahura Mazdā's followers.

The Wise Lord, though supreme, has an opponent, AHRIMAN, who embodies the principle of evil, and whose followers, having freely chosen him, also are evil. In the beginning there was a meeting of the two spirits, who were free to choose "life or not life." This choice gave birth to a good and an evil principle. Corresponding to the former is a Kingdom of Justice and Truth; to the latter, the Kingdom of the Lie (Druj), populated by the *daevas*, the evil spirits (originally old Indo-Iranian gods).

The Wise Lord, together with the *amesha spentas*, will at last vanquish the spirit of evil: this message, implying the end of the cosmic and ethical dualism, seems to constitute Zoroaster's main religious reform. His monotheistic solution resolves the old strict dualism. After his death, however, the dualist principle was strengthened by bringing Ahura Mazdā, by then called Ohrmazd, down to the level of his opponent, Ahriman.

The *Gāthās* are permeated by eschatological thinking. The earthly state is connected with a state beyond, in which the Wise Lord will reward the good act, speech, and thought and punish the bad. After death, the soul of man must pass over the Bridge of the Requiter (Činvat). After judgment is passed by Ahura Mazdā, the good enter the kingdom of everlasting joy and light, and the bad are consigned to the regions of horror and darkness. During an end phase for the visible world, "the last turn of creation," Ahriman will be destroyed and the world will be wonderfully renewed and be inhabited by the good, who will live in paradisiacal joy.

Zoroaster forbade all sacrifices in honor of Ahriman or of his adherents, the *daevas*, who from pre-Zoroastrian times had degenerated into hostile deities. In his reform, he did not abolish all animal sacrifice but simply the orgiastic and intoxicating rites that accompanied it. The HAOMA sacrifice, too, was to be thought of as a symbolic offering; it may have consisted of unfermented drink or an intoxicating beverage or plant. Zoroaster retained the ancient cult of fire. This cult and its various rites were later extended and given a definite order by the priestly class of the MAGI. Its center, the eternal flame in the Temple of Fire, was linked with the priestly service and with the *haoma* sacrifice.

After converting a king called Vishtāspa to such teachings, Zoroaster remained at the royal court. Other officials were converted, and a daughter of Zoroaster apparently married Jāmāsp, a minister of the king. According to tradition, Zoroaster died about 551 BCE. After his death, many legends arose about him—for example, that nature rejoiced at his birth. He was viewed as a model for priests, warriors, and agriculturalists, as well as a skilled craftsman and healer. The Greeks regarded him as a philosopher, mathematician, astrologer, or magician. Jews and Christians regarded him as an astrologer, magician, prophet, or arch heretic. Not until the 18th century did a more scholarly assessment of Zoroaster's career and influence emerge.

The Tower of Silence near Yazd, Iran, used by Zoroastrians to dispose of their dead by laying the bodies out to be stripped of flesh by eagles and vultures; prayers are said facing the light, so fires are built in the small fire tower at the left
Ray Ellis—Photo Researchers

ZOROASTRIANISM AND PARSIISM \‚zōr-ə-'was-trē-ə-‚ni-zəm, ‚zȯr-. . . 'pär-sē-‚i-zəm\, ancient pre-Islamic religion of Iran that survives there in isolated areas and more prosperously in India, where the descendents of Zoroastrian Iranian (Persian) immigrants are known as Parsis, or Parsees. Founded by the Iranian prophet and reformer ZOROASTER in the 6th century BCE, this religion, containing both monotheistic and dualistic features, influenced the other major Western religions—JUDAISM, CHRISTIANITY, and ISLAM.

In the tradition into which Zoroaster was born and educated, society tended to be divided into three classes: chiefs and priests, warriors, and husbandmen and cattle breeders. This class structure is reflected in the religion, with particular gods or *daevas* ("heavenly ones") associated with each of the three classes. The *ahuras* ("lords"), which included MITRA and VARUNA, seem to have been connected only with the first class. Zoroaster rejected the cults of all the gods except one *ahura*, AHURA MAZDĀ, the "Wise Lord." At the beginning of creation, Zoroaster taught, the twin sons of Ahura Mazdā entered into an eternal rivalry. One, SPENTA MAINYU (Bounteous Spirit), chose good, thus acquiring the attributes of truth, justice, and life. The other, Angra Mainyu (Destructive Spirit), chose evil and its attendant forces of destruction, injustice, and death. According to Zoroaster the world was soon to be consumed in a mighty conflagration from which only the followers of the good would rise to share in a new creation. Until this came to pass, the souls of those who died would cross the Bridge of the Requiter from whence the good would be led to wait in heaven, the wicked in hell.

Later Zoroastrian COSMOLOGY conceives the history of the world as a drama divided into four periods of 3,000 years each. In Infinite Time there existed Ormazd, who dwelt in the light, and AHRIMAN, who dwelt below him in the darkness. At the end of the first 3,000 years Ahriman crossed the Void that separated them and attacked Ormazd, who, perceiving that their struggle would last forever unless realized in finite terms, made a pact with Ahriman limiting the duration of their struggle. Ormazd then recited the Ahuna Vairya, the most sacred prayer of the Zoroastrians, which is believed to contain the germ of their whole religion. Ahriman, aghast, fell back into the abyss where he lay for another 3,000 years. During this time Ormazd brought about, first, the spiritual creation including the "beneficent immortals," then a corresponding material creation—sky, water, earth, plants, the Primeval Ox, and Primeval Man (GAYŌMART). Next, to the FRAVASHIS (preexistent souls) of men Ormazd offered a choice between staying forever in their embryonic state and becoming incarnate in the physical world in order to secure his triumph over Ahriman; they chose birth and combat. Meanwhile Ahriman generated six DEMONS and an opposing material creation.

At the end of the second period of 3,000 years Ahriman, instigated by Primeval Woman, the Whore, burst through the sky. He killed Gayōmart, from whose body mankind and the metals were generated, and the Ox, from which arose animals and plants. In the third period Ahriman triumphed in the material world but was unable to escape from it; trapped by Ormazd, he was doomed to generate his own destruction. The beginning of the last period witnesses the birth of Zoroaster. The end of each of its millennia is to be marked by the coming of a new savior, successor and posthumous son of Zoroaster. The third and last savior, SAOSHYANT, will bring about the final judgment, dispense the drink of immortality, and usher in the new world.

The literature of Zoroastrianism falls into two distinct parts: the AVESTA, the original scriptural work, composed in a form of the ancient Iranian language called Avestan; and the much later texts written in Pahlavi, a dialect of Middle Persian, or in Persian.

After Zoroaster's death his religion slowly spread southward, through what is now Afghanistan, and westward into the territory of the Medes and Persians. As it did so, worship of the ancient gods and goddesses again entered the tradition. This development, which seems to have taken place in Achaemenid times (559–330 BCE), is reflected in the later part of the Avesta. For about four centuries after Alexander's conquest (330 BCE), it seems, Iran was more or less hellenized and the indigenous religion neglected; a revival did not come about until toward the end of the Arsacid, or Parthian, Empire (247 BCE–224 CE).

With the advent of a new and decidedly national Persian dynasty, the Sāsānian, in 224 CE, Zoroastrianism became the official religion. Its hierarchy possessed considerable political power, and other religions (Christianity, MANICHAEISM, and BUDDHISM) were persecuted. The Avesta was compiled, edited, and provided with a translation and commentary in the vernacular, Pahlavi. The dualistic, or Mazdean, doctrine, which had gradually replaced the monotheistic system of the *Gāthās* during the Achaemenid period, became finally accepted as orthodox.

Under Muslim rule the bulk of the population was persuaded or forced to embrace Islam, but Zoroastrianism was tolerated to a certain extent. Between the 8th and 10th centuries, however, religious persecution and forced conversion to Islam led some of the remaining Zoroastrians to leave Iran and settle in India, most of them eventually in the region of Bombay. By the 19th century these Zoroastrians, called Parsis, were distinguished for their wealth, education, and beneficence. In the 19th century the Parsis renewed contact with the only remaining Zoroastrians in Iran, the GABARS. These two groups and their immigrants to other countries are today the only surviving practitioners of Zoroastrianism.

ZU \ˈzü\, *also called* Imdugud, in MESOPOTAMIAN RELIGION, bird god who steals the prophetic tables of fate that confer supreme power. Zu was slain and the tables recovered. Zu is identified with Anzu.

ZUHD \ˈzü-həd\ (Arabic: "renunciation," or "abstinence"), in ISLAM, ASCETICISM. Even though a Muslim is permitted to enjoy fully whatever unforbidden pleasure God bestows on him, Islam nevertheless praises those who shun luxury in favor of a simple and pious life. The QURʾAN holds in great esteem those "servants of God who pass the night prostrating themselves in the worship of their Lord" (25:63–65). There are students of Islam, however, who maintain that *zuhd* was influenced directly by the Christian HERMITS, with whom early Muslims had some familiarity. Some scholars also point to the pre-Islamic Arab ḤANĪFS, who practiced the ascetic life and who may have had considerable influence on the Prophet MUHAMMAD.

Zuhd developed in Islam as a result of the Muslim conquests, which brought with them material wealth and widespread indulgence in luxurious living. The growth of the Islamic state had also brought with it bitter political disputes that pitted Muslim against Muslim in fierce struggles for power. The resulting bloodshed spurred devout Muslims to seek peace of mind in abstinence from all that distracts from the worship of God.

The terms *zuhd* and *zāhid* ("ascetic") were not used by pre-Islamic Arabs or by early Muslims to describe the elaborate and systematic ascetic doctrines that became characteristic of later periods, from the 8th century on. Among the earliest *zāhid*s was AL-ḤASAN AL-BAṢRĪ (d. 728), whose sayings remained for a long time the chief guide of the ascetics. But it was not until after his death that *zuhd* became a significant and forceful movement in the religious and political life of the Muslim community. Many scholars have referred to Ibrāhīm ibn Adham and to his student and disciple Shaqīq al-Balkhī (d. 810) as the real founders of *zuhd,* as it became known in later periods. Ibn Adham stressed poverty and self-denial; indeed, he abandoned the wealth of his father and became a poor wanderer.

Because of the close ties among these pietists, the *zāhid*s are often regarded as being identical with the early Sufis, whose name, "wool-wearers," points to the ascetic practice of wearing hair shirts. Later Sufis, however, dismiss the *zāhid*s as men who worship God not out of love but for fear of hell or expectation of paradise. *See also* ASCETICISM; SUFISM.

Zᴜʀᴠᴀɴɪsᴍ \'zər-və-,ni-zəm\, *also spelled* Zervanism, modified form of ZOROASTRIANISM that appeared in Persia during the Sāsānian period (3rd–7th century CE). It was opposed to orthodox Zoroastrianism, which by that time had become dualistic in doctrine. According to Zurvanism, time alone—limitless, eternal, and uncreated—is the source of all things.

Zurvān, god of time and fate, remotely influences human destinies, appearing under two aspects: Limitless Time (*i.e.,* eternal lord; Zurvān Akarana) and Time of Long Dominion (*i.e.,* lord of the existing world; Zurvān Dareghō-Chvadhāta). His worship was bound up with speculations about ASTROLOGY and the world-year.

In later writings Zurvān is seen as the father of Ormazd and AHRIMAN (*see* AHURA MAZDĀ), perhaps a result of contact between Zoroastrianism and Greco-Babylonian astrological speculations. (Zurvanism appears to have had its stronghold in western Persia, bordering Babylonia.) Some scholars seek an origin for Zurvanism outside Zoroastrianism, in the worship of an ancient Median or pre-Iranian god. It was in Zurvanite form that Zoroastrianism influenced MITHRAISM (in which Zurvān was an important deity) and MANICHAEISM.

Zᴡɪɴɢʟɪ, Hᴜʟᴅʀʏᴄʜ \'zwiŋ-lē, -glē, *German* 'tsviŋ-lē\, Huldrych *also spelled* Ulrich (b. Jan. 1, 1484, Wildhaus in the Toggenburg, Sankt Gallen, Switz.—d. Oct. 11, 1531, near Kappel), first important reformer in the Swiss Protestant REFORMATION and the only major reformer of the 16th century whose movement did not evolve into a church.

Zwingli was the son of a free peasant who was a village magistrate. Ordained to the PRIESTHOOD, he became a pastor in 1506. In 1518, despite much opposition, he was appointed people's priest at the Grossmünster (Great Minster) at Zürich. He commenced a series of expositions of the NEW TESTAMENT enlivened by topical application. Serious illness in 1519, followed by his brother's death in 1520, deepened the spiritual and theological elements in his thinking and teaching. That same year he delivered a series of sermons that helped to initiate the Swiss Reformation (1522).

In 1523 Zwingli published his *67 Artikel.* His main contentions were adopted by most priests in the district and, in consequence, the CELIBACY of clergy came to be flouted and liturgical reform was begun, as was a plan for the reconstitution of the Grossmünster as both a grammar school and a theological seminary to train Reformed pastors. Successive steps taken during 1524 and 1525 included the removal of images from the church, the suppression of organs, the dissolution of religious houses, the replacement of the MASS by a simple Communion service, the reform of the baptismal office, the introduction of prophesyings or BIBLE readings, the reorganization of the ministry, and the preparation of a native Bible (the *Zürcher Bibel* appeared in 1529).

From the city of Zürich the movement spread to neighboring cantons, including important centers like Basel and Bern. In 1528 Zwingli took part in a disputation at Bern, putting forth the theses (1) that the church is born of the Word of God and has Christ alone as its head; (2) that its laws are binding only insofar as they agree with the Scripture; (3) that Christ alone is man's righteousness; (4) that the Holy SCRIPTURE does not teach Christ's corporeal presence in the bread and wine at the Lord's Supper; (5) that the mass is a gross affront to the sacrifice and death of Christ; (6) that there is no biblical foundation for the mediation or intercession of the dead, for PURGATORY, or for images and pictures; and (7) that marriage is lawful to all.

Huldrych Zwingli, detail of an oil portrait by Hans Asper, 1531
By courtesy of the Kunstmuseum Winterthur, Switz.; photograph, Schweizerisches Institut fur Kunstwissenschaft

From 1525 Zwingli's work was hampered by disagreements, particularly with the ANABAPTISTS who desired the abolition of TITHES, a severance of the state connection, the creation of a pure or gathered church of true believers (those who have experienced a conversion according to the moral beliefs and precepts of the New Testament), and the consequent ending of infant BAPTISM. Meanwhile, his thinking and practice in relation to the mass had led to a sharp disagreement with MARTIN LUTHER. Luther taught the real presence of Christ's body and blood not in place of, but in, with, and under the bread and wine. Zwingli, on the other hand, did not maintain a "real" presence but simply the divine presence of Christ or his presence to the believer by the power of the HOLY SPIRIT, as signified by the elements. Luther and his supporters refused to see in the Swiss movement a true work of evangelical reformation. The Colloquy of Marburg (1529) was arranged with a view to reconciliation; Luther, Zwingli, and MARTIN BUCER all participated. Cordial agreement was reached on most issues, but the critical gulf remained in relation to the sacramental presence. In the Second War of Kappel (1531), Zwingli accompanied the Zürich forces as CHAPLAIN and was killed in the battle.

Zwingli's rejection of the SACRAMENTS as means of obtaining GRACE and as forms of intervention between the soul and God underlay the deepened conception of other Reformation leaders such as Heinrich Bullinger, Pietro Martire Vermigli, and JOHN CALVIN. Obvious defects of disjointedness and intellectualism mark his writings. Behind them, however, lay an open, warm, and friendly disposition, and they embody a bold attempt to rethink all Christian doctrine in consistently biblical terms.

BIBLIOGRAPHY

ANCIENT RELIGIONS

Anatolian

• O.R. Gurney, *Some Aspects of Hittite Religion* (1977)
• Seton Lloyd, *Early Highland Peoples of Anatolia* (1967)
• J.G. Macqueen, *The Hittites and Their Contemporaries in Asia Minor*, rev. and enlarged ed. (1986)

Arabian

• Adel Allouche, "Arabian Religions," in Mircea Eliade (ed.), *The Encyclopedia of Religion*, vol. 1 (1987), pp. 363–367
• Hishām ibn al-Kalbi, *The Book of Idols*, trans. and ed. by Nabih Amin Faris (1952)
• Gordon Darnell Newby, *A History of the Jews of Arabia: From Ancient Times to Their Eclipse Under Islam* (1988)
• W. Robertson Smith, *Lectures on the Religion of the Semites*, new ed., rev. (1894, reprinted as *The Religion of the Semites*, 1972)
• Javier Teixidor, *The Pagan God: Popular Religion in the Greco-Roman Near East* (1977)
• J. Spencer Trimingham, *Christianity Among the Arabs in Pre-Islamic Times* (1979)

Baltic

• Haralds Biezais, "Baltic Religion," in Mircea Eliade (ed.), *The Encyclopedia of Religion*, vol. 2 (1987), pp. 49–55
• Marija Gimbutas, *The Balts* (1963), pp. 179–204

Celtic

• Miranda Green, *The Gods of the Celts* (1986, reissued 1997)
• Ronald Hutton, *The Pagan Religions of the Ancient British Isles: Their Nature and Legacy* (1991)
• Proinsias Mac Cana, *Celtic Mythology*, new rev. ed. (1983)
• Marie-Louise Sjoestedt, *Gods and Heroes of the Celts* (1949, reissued 1994; originally published in French, 1940)

Chinese

• Sarah Allan, *The Shape of the Turtle: Myth, Art, and Cosmos in Early China* (1991)
• Anne Birrell, *Chinese Mythology: An Introduction* (1993)
• K.C. Chang, *Art, Myth, and Ritual: The Path to Political Authority in Ancient China* (1983)
• A.C. Graham, *Disputers of the Tao: Philosophical Argument in Ancient China* (1989)
• Michael Loewe, *Divination, Mythology, and Monarchy in Han China* (1994)
• Michael Loewe, *Ways to Paradise: The Chinese Quest for Immortality* (1979)
• Henri Maspero, *China in Antiquity* (1978; originally published in French, new ed., 1955)
• Donald J. Munro, *The Concept of Man in Early China* (1969)
• Mu-chou Poo, *In Search of Personal Welfare: A View of Ancient Chinese Religion* (1998)
• Benjamin I. Schwartz, *The World of Thought in Ancient China* (1985)

Egyptian

• Rosalie David (A. Rosalie David), *The Ancient Egyptians: Beliefs and Practices*, rev. and expanded ed. (1998)
• Henri Frankfort, *Ancient Egyptian Religion* (1948, reissued 1961)
• George Hart, *A Dictionary of Egyptian Gods and Goddesses* (1986)
• Erik Hornung, *Conceptions of God in Ancient Egypt: The One and the Many* (1982, reissued 1996; originally published in German, 1971)
• Veronica Ions, *Egyptian Mythology*, new rev. ed. (1982, reissued 1990)
• Anthony S. Mercatante, *Who's Who in Egyptian Mythology*, 2nd ed., edited and rev. by Robert Steven Bianchi (1995)
• Siegfried Morenz, *Egyptian Religion* (1973, reissued 1992; originally published in German, 1960)
• Serge Sauneron, *The Priests of Ancient Egypt* (1960, reissued 1980; originally published in French, 1957)
• Byron E. Shafer (ed.), *Religion in Ancient Egypt: Gods, Myths, and Personal Practice* (1991)
• Pascal Vernus and Erich Lessing, *The Gods of Ancient Egypt* (1998; originally published in French, 1998)

Etruscan

• Larissa Bonfante (ed.), *Etruscan Life and Afterlife: A Handbook of Etruscan Studies* (1986)
• Georges Dumézil, "The Religion of the Etruscans," in his *Archaic Roman Religion*, vol. 2 (1970, reissued 1996; originally published in French, 1966), pp. 625–696
• Michael Grant, *The Etruscans* (1980, reissued 1997)
• Massimo Pallottino, *The Etruscans*, rev. and enlarged ed. edited by David Ridgway (1975;
originally published in Italian, 6th ed. rev. and enlarged, 1973)

Finno-Ugric

• Louis Herbert Gray et al. (eds.), *The Mythology of All Races*, vol. 4, *Finno-Ugric, Siberian*, by Uno Holmberg (1927, reissued 1964)
• Lauri Honko, "Finno-Ugric Religions: An Overview," in Mircea Eliade (ed.), *The Encyclopedia of Religion*, vol. 5 (1987), pp. 330–335
• Rafael Karsten, *The Religion of the Samek: Ancient Beliefs and Cults of the Scandinavian and Finnish Lapps* (1955)
• Ivar Paulson, *The Old Estonian Folk Religion* (1971; originally published in Swedish, 1966)

Germanic

• H.R. Ellis Davidson, *Gods and Myths of Northern Europe* (1964, reissued 1990)
• H.R. Ellis Davidson, *The Lost Beliefs of Northern Europe* (1993)
• H.R. Ellis Davidson, *Pagan Scandinavia* (1967)
• Jacob Grimm, *Teutonic Mythology*, trans. by James Steven Stallybrass, 4 vol. (1883–88, reprinted 1976; originally published in German, 4th ed., 3 vol., 1875–78)
• Gabriel Turville-Petre, *Myth and Religion of the North: The Religion of Ancient Scandinavia* (1964, reprinted 1975)

Greek

• Walter Burkert, *Greek Religion* (1985; originally published in German, 1977)
• Walter Burkert, *Homo Necans: The Anthropology of Ancient Greek Sacrificial Ritual and Myth* (1983; originally published in German, 1972)
• P.E. Easterling and J.V. Muir (eds.), *Greek Religion and Society* (1985)
• Robert Garland, *Introducing New Gods: The Politics of Athenian Religion* (1992)
• W.K.C. Guthrie, *The Greeks and Their Gods* (1950, reprinted 1985)
• Jane Ellen Harrison, *Prolegomena to the Study of Greek Religion*, 3rd ed. (1922, reprinted 1992)
• Jane Ellen Harrison, *Themis: A Study of the Social Origins of Greek Religion*, 2nd ed., rev. (1927, reissued 1989)
• Martin P. Nilsson, *Greek Popular Religion* (1940, reissued as *Greek Folk Religion*, 1972)

- Martin P. Nilsson, *A History of Greek Religion*, 2nd ed. (1949, reprinted 1980)
- Martin P. Nilsson, *The Minoan-Mycenaean Religion and Its Survival in Greek Religion*, 2nd rev. ed. (1950, reprinted 1971)
- Jean-Pierre Vernant, *Myth and Society in Ancient Greece* (1979, reissued 1990; originally published in French, 1974)
- Jean-Pierre Vernant, *Myth and Thought Among the Greeks* (1983; originally published in French, 1965)
- Louise Bruit Zaidman and Pauline Schmitt Pantel, *Religion in the Ancient Greek City* (1992; originally published in French, 1989)

Hellenistic

- Frederick C. Grant (ed.), *Hellenistic Religions: The Age of Syncretism* (1953)
- Luther H. Martin, *Hellenistic Religions: An Introduction* (1987)
- Arthur Darby Nock, *Essays on Religion and the Ancient World*, compiled and ed. by Zeph Stewart, 2 vol. (1972, reprinted 1986)
- M. Rostovtzeff, *The Social & Economic History of the Hellenistic World*, 3 vol. (1941, reissued 1986)
- Arnold Toynbee (ed.), *The Crucible of Christianity: Judaism, Hellenism, and the Historical Background to the Christian Faith* (1969)

Indo-European

- Georges Dumézil, *Gods of the Ancient Northmen*, trans. from French (1973)
- Marija Gimbutas, *The Goddesses and Gods of Old Europe, 6500–3500 BC: Myths and Cult Images*, new and updated ed. (1982)
- Bruce Lincoln, *Death, War, and Sacrifice: Studies in Ideology and Practice* (1991)
- Bruce Lincoln, *Myth, Cosmos, and Society: Indo-European Themes of Creation and Destruction* (1986)
- Edgar C. Polomé (ed.), *The Indo-Europeans in the Fourth and Third Millennia* (1982)
- Jaan Puhvel (ed.), *Myth and Law Among the Indo-Europeans: Studies in Indo-European Comparative Mythology* (1970)

Iranian

- Émile Benveniste, *The Persian Religion According to the Chief Greek Texts* (1929)

- E.S. Drower, *The Mandaeans of Iraq and Iran* (1937, reissued 1962)
- John R. Hinnells, *Persian Mythology*, new rev. ed. (1985, reissued 1997)
- John R. Hinnells (ed.), *Mithraic Studies*, 2 vol. (1975)
- William W. Malandra (trans. and ed.), *An Introduction to Ancient Iranian Religion* (1983)
- M.J. Vermaseren, *Mithras, the Secret God* (1963; originally published in Dutch, 1959)
- Geo Widengren, *Mani and Manichaeism* (1965; originally published in German, 1961)

Mesopotamian

- Jeremy Black, Anthony Green, and Tessa Rickards, *Gods, Demons, and Symbols of Ancient Mesopotamia: An Illustrated Dictionary* (1992)
- C.J. Gadd, *Ideas of Divine Rule in the Ancient Near East* (1948, reissued 1980)
- S.H. Hooke, *Babylonian and Assyrian Religion* (1953, reissued 1975)
- Thorkild Jacobsen, *Toward the Image of Tammuz and Other Essays on Mesopotamian History and Culture*, ed. by William L. Moran (1970)
- Thorkild Jacobsen, *The Treasures of Darkness: A History of Mesopotamian Religion* (1976)
- A. Leo Oppenheim, *Ancient Mesopotamia: Portrait of a Dead Civilization*, rev. ed., completed by Erica Reiner (1977)

Mystery Religions

- Walter Burkert, *Ancient Mystery Cults* (1987)
- Lewis Richard Farnell, *The Cults of the Greek States*, 5 vol. (1896–1909, reissued 1977)
- John Ferguson, *An Illustrated Encyclopaedia of Mysticism and the Mystery Religions* (1976, reissued as *Encyclopedia of Mysticism and Mystery Religions*, 1982)
- Joscelyn Godwin, *Mystery Religions in the Ancient World* (1981)
- W.K.C. Guthrie, *Orpheus and Greek Religion: A Study of the Orphic Movement*, 2nd ed. rev. (1952, reissued 1993)
- Harold R. Willoughby, *Pagan Regeneration: A Study of Mystery Initiations in the Graeco-Roman World* (1929, reprinted 1974)

Near Eastern

- Fred Gladstone Bratton, *Myths and Legends of the An-*

cient Near East (1970, reprinted 1993)
- André Caquot and Maurice Sznycer, *Ugaritic Religion* (1980)
- Godfrey R. Driver, *Canaanite Myths and Legends*, 2nd ed. edited by J.C.L. Gibson (1978)
- Henri Frankfort et al., *The Intellectual Adventure of Ancient Man* (1946, reissued 1977; also published as *Before Philosophy*, 1946, reissued 1974)
- Cyrus H. Gordon, *The Ancient Near East*, 3rd ed., rev. (1965)
- John Gray, *Near Eastern Mythology*, new rev. ed. (1983)
- Gwendolyn Leick, *A Dictionary of Ancient Near Eastern Mythology* (1991)
- Patrick D. Miller, Jr., Paul D. Hanson, and S. Dean McBride (eds.), *Ancient Israelite Religion* (1987)
- Sabatino Moscati, *The Face of the Ancient Orient: A Panorama of Ancient Near Eastern Civilizations in Pre-Classical Times* (1960; originally published in Italian, 1955)
- Helmer Ringgren, *Religions of the Ancient Near East* (1973; originally published in Swedish, 1967)
- D.J. Wiseman (ed.), *Peoples of Old Testament Times* (1973)

Pre-Columbian Meso-American

- Richard E.W. Adams, *Prehistoric Mesoamerica*, rev. ed. (1991)
- Alfredo López Austin, *The Human Body and Ideology: Concepts of the Ancient Nahuas*, 2 vol. (1988; originally published in Spanish, 1980)
- Davíd Carrasco, *Religions of Mesoamerica: Cosmovision and Ceremonial Centers* (1990)
- Michael D. Coe, *The Maya*, 6th ed., fully rev. and expanded (1999)
- Norman Hammond, *Ancient Maya Civilization*, updated ed. (1988)
- Leonardo López Luján, *The Offerings of the Templo Mayor of Tenochtitlan* (1994; originally published in Spanish, 1993)
- Mary Miller and Karl Taube, *The Gods and Symbols of Ancient Mexico and the Maya: An Illustrated Dictionary of Mesoamerican Religion* (1993)
- Eduardo Matos Moctezuma, *Life and Death in the Templo Mayor* (1995; originally published in Spanish, 1986)
- William T. Sanders and Barbara J. Price, *Mesoamerica: The Evolution of a Civilization* (1968)

- Jacques Soustelle, *The Daily Life of the Aztecs: On the Eve of the Spanish Conquest* (1961, reissued 1970; originally published in French, 1955)
- J. Eric S. Thompson, *Maya History and Religion* (1970, reissued 1990)
- J. Eric S. Thompson, *Mexico Before Cortez: An Account of the Daily Life, Religion, and Ritual of the Aztecs and Kindred Peoples* (1933, reissued 1940)
- J. Eric S. Thompson, *The Rise and Fall of Maya Civilization*, 2nd ed. enl. (1966, reissued 1987)

Pre-Columbian South American

- Wendell C. Bennett and Junius B. Bird, *Andean Culture History*, 2nd and rev. ed. (1960)
- Geoffrey W. Conrad and Arthur A. Demarest, *Religion and Empire: The Dynamics of Aztec and Inca Expansionism* (1984)
- Richard W. Keatinge (ed.), *Peruvian Prehistory: An Overview of Pre-Inca and Inca Society* (1988)
- Walter Krickeberg et al., *Pre-Columbian American Religions* (1968; originally published in German, 1961)
- Luis G. Lumbreras, *The People and Cultures of Ancient Peru* (1974; originally published in Spanish, 1969)
- Gary Urton, *At the Crossroads of the Earth and the Sky: An Andean Cosmology* (1981)

Roman

- Lesley Adkins and Roy A. Adkins, *Dictionary of Roman Religion* (1996)
- Mary Beard, John North, and Simon Price, *Religions of Rome*, vol. 1, *History* (1998)
- Georges Dumézil, *Archaic Roman Religion*, 2 vol. (1970, reissued 1996; originally published in French, 1966)
- John Ferguson, *The Religions of the Roman Empire* (1970, reissued 1985)
- W. Warde Fowler, *The Religious Experience of the Roman People, from the Earliest Times to the Age of Augustus* (1911, reprinted 1971)
- Michael Grant, *Roman Myths* (1971, reissued 1984)
- J.H.W.G. Liebeschuetz, *Continuity and Change in Roman Religion* (1979)
- Ramsay MacMullen, *Paganism in the Roman Empire* (1981)
- A.D. Nock, *Conversion: The Old and the New in Religion*

from *Alexander the Great to Augustine of Hippo* (1933, reprinted 1998)
• R.M. Ogilvie, *The Romans and Their Gods in the Age of Augustus* (1969, reissued 1986)
• Robert E.A. Palmer, *Roman Religion and Roman Empire* (1974)
• H.J. Rose, *Ancient Roman Religion* (1948, reprinted in *Ancient Greek and Roman Religion*, 2 vol. in 1, 1995)
• H.H. Scullard, *Festivals and Ceremonies of the Roman Republic* (1981)
• Robert Turcan, *The Cults of the Roman Empire* (1996; originally published in French, 1989)
• Alan Wardman, *Religion and Statecraft Among the Romans* (1982)

Slavic
• Marija Gimbutas, "Slavic Religion," in Mircea Eliade (ed.), *The Encyclopedia of Religion*, vol. 13 (1987), pp. 353–361
• W.R.S. Ralston, *The Songs of the Russian People, as Illustrative of Slavonic Mythology and Russian Social Life*, 2nd ed. (1872, reprinted 1970)
• Myroslava T. Znayenko, *The Gods of the Ancient Slavs: Tatishchev and the Beginnings of Slavic Mythology* (1980)

ART AND ARCHITECTURE
• Albert C. Moore, *Iconography of Religions: An Introduction* (1977)
• Helene E. Roberts (ed.), *Encyclopedia of Comparative Iconography*, 2 vol. (1998)
• Lawrence E. Sullivan (ed.), *Enchanting Powers: Music in the World's Religions* (1997)

African
• Henry John Drewal and Margaret Thompson Drewal, *Gẹlẹdẹ: Art and Female Power Among the Yoruba* (1983, reissued 1990)
• Rosalind I.J. Hackett, *Art and Religion in Africa* (1996)
• Henry Pernet, *Ritual Masks: Deceptions and Revelations* (1992; originally published in French, 1988)
• Robert Farris Thompson, *African Art in Motion* (1974)
• Denis Williams, *Icon and Image: A Study of Sacred and Secular Forms of African Classical Art* (1974)

Australian Aboriginal
• Ronald M. Berndt (ed.), *Australian Aboriginal Art* (1964)

• Albert C. Moore, *Arts in the Religions of the Pacific: Symbols of Life* (1995)

Buddhism
• Francisca Cho Bantly, *Embracing Illusion: Truth and Fiction in The Dream of the Nine Clouds* (1996)
• Robert L. Brown, *The Dvāravatī Wheels of the Law and the Indianization of South East Asia* (1996)
• Anna Libera Dallapiccola and Stephanie Zingel-Avé Lallemant (eds.), *The Stūpa: Its Religious, Historical, and Architectural Significance* (1979)
• Luis O. Gómez and Hiram W. Woodward, Jr. (eds.), *Barabuḍur: History and Significance of a Buddhist Monument* (1981)
• John Clifford Holt, *The Religious World of Kīrti Śrī: Buddhism, Art, and Politics in Late Medieval Sri Lanka* (1996)
• William R. LaFleur, *The Karma of Words: Buddhism and the Literary Arts in Medieval Japan* (1986)
• Denise Patry Leidy and Robert A.F. Thurman, *Mandala: The Architecture of Enlightenment* (1997)
• Victor H. Mair, *Painting and Performance: Chinese Picture Recitation and Its Indian Genesis* (1988)
• Geri H. Malandra, *Unfolding a Maṇḍala: The Buddhist Cave Temples at Ellora* (1993)
• David Snellgrove (ed.), *The Image of the Buddha* (1978)
• Susan C. Tyler, *The Cult of Kasuga Seen Through Its Art* (1992)
• Sheila L. Weiner, *Ajaṇṭā: Its Place in Buddhist Art* (1977)

Celtic
• Miranda Green, *Symbol and Image in Celtic Religious Art* (1989)
• Françoise Henry, *Irish Art in the Early Christian Period*, rev. ed. (1965; originally published in French, 1963)

Christianity
• Henry Adams, *Mont-Saint-Michel and Chartres* (1904, reissued 1986)
• G.W. Ferguson, *Signs & Symbols in Christian Art* (1955, reissued 1981)
• André Grabar, *Christian Iconography* (1968, reissued 1980)
• Edwin Liemohn, *The Chorale Through Four Hundred Years of Musical Development as a Congregational Hymn* (1953)

• Eric Newton and William Neil, *2000 Years of Christian Art* (1966)
• Konrad Onasch and Annemarie Schnieper, *Icons: The Fascination and the Reality* (1995; originally published in German, 1995)
• Erwin Panofsky, *Gothic Architecture and Scholasticism* (1951, reissued 1985)
• Gertrud Schiller, *Iconography of Christian Art*, vol. 1–2 (1971–73; originally published in German, 1969–70)
• Edward N. West, *Outward Signs: The Language of Christian Symbolism* (1989)

Egyptian
• Manfred Lurker, *The Gods and Symbols of Ancient Egypt*, trans. from German, rev. and enlarged by Peter A. Clayton (1980, reissued as *An Illustrated Dictionary of the Gods and Symbols of Ancient Egypt*, 1994)
• Byron E. Shafer (ed.), *Temples of Ancient Egypt* (1997)

Greek
• A.W. Lawrence, *Greek Architecture*, 5th ed. rev. by R.A. Tomlinson (1996)
• Vincent Scully, *The Earth, the Temple, and the Gods: Greek Sacred Architecture*, rev. ed. (1979)
• R.A. Tomlinson, *Greek Sanctuaries* (1976)

Hinduism
• Richard H. Davis, *Lives of Indian Images* (1997)
• Vidya Dehejia, *Indian Art* (1997)
• Susan L. Huntington and John C. Huntington, *The Art of Ancient India: Buddhist, Hindu, Jain* (1985)
• Michael W. Meister and M.A. Dhaky (eds.), *Encyclopaedia of Indian Temple Architecture* (1983–)
• Partha Mitter, *Much Maligned Monsters: A History of European Reactions to Indian Art* (1977, reissued 1992)

Islam
• Sheila S. Blair and Jonathan M. Bloom, *The Art and Architecture of Islam, 1250–1800*, corrected ed. (1995)
• Peter J. Chelkowski (ed.), *Ta'ziyeh: Ritual and Drama in Iran* (1979)
• Richard Ettinghausen and Oleg Grabar, *The Art and Architecture of Islam, 650–1250* (1987, reissued 1994)

• Oleg Grabar, *The Formation of Islamic Art*, rev. and enlarged ed. (1987)
• Raymond Lifchez (ed.), *The Dervish Lodge: Architecture, Art, and Sufism in Ottoman Turkey* (1992)
• Regula Burckhardt Qureshi, *Sufi Music of India and Pakistan: Sound, Context, and Meaning in Qawwali* (1986, reissued 1995)
• Annemarie Schimmel, *Calligraphy and Islamic Culture* (1984)
• Fadlou Shehadi, *Philosophies of Music in Medieval Islam* (1995)
• Amnon Shiloah, *Music in the World of Islam: A Socio-Cultural History* (1995)
• M.J.L. Young, J.D. Latham, and R.B. Serjeant (eds.), *Religion, Learning, and Science in the 'Abbasid Period* (1990)

Jainism
• B.C. Bhattacharya, *The Jaina Iconography*, 2nd rev. ed. (1974)
• Moti Chandra, *Jain Miniature Paintings from Western India* (1949)
• A. Ghosh (ed.), *Jaina Art and Architecture*, 3 vol. (1974–75)
• Jyotindra Jain and Eberhard Fischer, *Jaina Iconography*, 2 vol. (1978)
• Pratapaditya Pal, *The Peaceful Liberators: Jain Art from India* (1994)

Judaism
• Marilyn Joyce Segal Chiat, *Handbook of Synagogue Architecture* (1982)
• Erwin R. Goodenough, *Jewish Symbols in the Greco-Roman Period*, abridged ed., edited by Jacob Neusner (1988)
• Joseph Gutmann (compiler), *Beauty in Holiness: Studies in Jewish Customs and Ceremonial Art* (1970)
• Joseph Gutmann (compiler), *The Synagogue: Studies in Origins, Archaeology, and Architecture* (1975)
• Carol Herselle Krinsky, *Synagogues of Europe: Architecture, History, Meaning* (1985, reissued 1996)
• Lee I. Levine, *Ancient Synagogues Revealed* (1981)
• Amnon Shiloah, *Jewish Musical Traditions* (1992)
• Eric Werner, *The Sacred Bridge: The Interdependence of Liturgy and Music in Synagogue and Church During the First Millennium*, vol. 1 (1959, reprinted 1979), and vol. 2 (1984)

Native North American

• Akwe:kon Press and National Museum of the American Indian, *Native American Expressive Culture* (1994)
• Margaret Archuleta and Rennard Strickland (eds.), *Shared Visions: Native American Painters and Sculptors in the Twentieth Century*, 2nd ed. (1993)
• William N. Fenton, *The False Faces of the Iroquois* (1987)
• Audrey Hawthorne, *Kwakiutl Art* (1979, reissued 1988)
• Peter Nabokov and Robert Easton, *Native American Architecture* (1989)
• Henry Pernet, *Ritual Masks: Deceptions and Revelations* (1992; originally published in French, 1988)
• Vincent Scully, *Pueblo: Mountain, Village, Dance*, 2nd ed. (1989)
• Brian Swann (ed.), *Coming to Light: Contemporary Translations of the Native Literatures of North America* (1994)
• Gary Witherspoon, *Language and Art in the Navajo Universe* (1977)

Native South American

• Luis Eduardo Luna and Pablo Amaringo, *Ayahuasca Visions: The Religious Iconography of a Peruvian Shaman* (1991)
• Gerardo Reichel-Dolmatoff, *Beyond the Milky Way: Hallucinatory Imagery of the Tukano Indians* (1978)

Oceanic

• Albert C. Moore, *Arts in the Religions of the Pacific: Symbols of Life* (1995)
• Carl Schmitz, *Oceanic Art: Myth, Man, and Image in the South Seas* (1969)

Pre-Columbian Meso-American

• Johanna Broda, Davíd Carrasco, and Eduardo Matos Moctezuma, *The Great Temple of Tenochtitlan: Center and Periphery in the Aztec World* (1988)
• Davíd Carrasco (ed.), *To Change Place: Aztec Ceremonial Landscapes* (1991)
• Lindsay Jones, *Twin City Tales: A Hermeneutical Reassessment of Tula and Chichén Itzá* (1995)
• George Kubler, *The Art and Architecture of Ancient America: The Mexican, Maya, and Andean Peoples*, 3rd ed. (1984, reissued 1993)
• H.B. Nicholson (ed.), *Origins of Religious Art & Iconography in Preclassic Mesoamerica* (1976)
• Linda Schele and David Freidel, *A Forest of Kings: The Untold Story of the Ancient Maya* (1990)
• Linda Schele, Mary Ellen Miller, and Justin Kerr, *The Blood of Kings: Dynasty and Ritual in Maya Art* (1986)
• Richard F. Townsend (ed.), *The Ancient Americas: Art from Sacred Landscapes* (1992)

Pre-Columbian South American

• Christopher B. Donnan (ed.), *Early Ceremonial Architecture in the Andes* (1985)
• Christopher B. Donnan (ed.), *Moche Art of Peru: Pre-Columbian Symbolic Communication*, rev. ed. (1978)
• Graziano Gasparini and Luise Margolies, *Inca Architecture* (1980; originally published in Spanish, 1977)
• George Kubler, *The Art and Architecture of Ancient America: The Mexican, Maya, and Andean Peoples*, 3rd ed. (1984, reissued 1993)
• Sabine MacCormack, *Religion in the Andes: Vision and Imagination in Early Colonial Peru* (1991)
• Richard F. Townsend (ed.), *The Ancient Americas: Art from Sacred Landscapes* (1992)
• R. Tom Zuidema, *Inca Civilization in Cuzco* (1990; originally published in French, 1985)

Prehistoric

• Paul G. Bahn, *The Cambridge Illustrated History of Prehistoric Art* (1998)
• Jean Clottes and David Lewis-Williams, *The Shamans of Prehistory: Trance and Magic in the Painted Caves* (1998; originally published in French, 1996)
• John E. Pfeiffer, *The Creative Explosion: An Inquiry into the Origins of Art and Religion* (1982)
• Colin Renfrew (ed.), *The Megalithic Monuments of Western Europe* (1983)
• Noel W. Smith, *An Analysis of Ice Age Art: Its Psychology and Belief System* (1992)
• Elizabeth Shee Twohig, *The Megalithic Art of Western Europe* (1981)

Roman

• Axel Boëthius, *Etruscan and Early Roman Architecture*, 2nd integrated ed., rev. by Roger Ling and Tom Rasmussen (1978)

Shintō

• Christopher Dresser, *Japan: Its Architecture, Art, and Art Manufactures* (1882, reprinted as *Traditional Arts and Crafts of Japan*, 1994)
• Christine Guth, *Shinzō: Hachiman Imagery and Its Development* (1985)
• Christine Guth (trans. and adapter), *The Arts of Shinto*, trans. from Japanese (1973)
• Loraine Kuck, *The World of the Japanese Garden: From Chinese Origins to Modern Landscape Art* (1968, reprinted 1980)
• Brian Moeran, *Folk Art Potters of Japan: Beyond an Anthropology of Aesthetics* (1997)
• Günter Nitschke, *From Shinto to Ando: Studies in Architectural Anthropology in Japan* (1993)
• Robert Treat Paine and Alexander Soper, *The Art and Architecture of Japan*, 3rd ed. (1981)
• Kenzō Tange and Noboru Kawazoe, *Ise: Prototype of Japanese Architecture* (1965; originally published in Japanese, 1962)
• Susan C. Tyler, *The Cult of Kasuga Seen Through Its Art* (1992)
• Yasutada Watanabe, *Shinto Art: Ise and Izumo Shrines* (1974; originally published in Japanese, 1964)
• Soetsu Yanagi, *The Unknown Craftsman: A Japanese Insight into Beauty*, adapted by Bernard Leach, rev. ed. (1989)

BAHA'I

• Hugh C. Adamson, *Historical Dictionary of the Bahá'í Faith* (1998)
• H.M. Balyuzi, *Bahá'u'lláh, the King of Glory* (1980)
• A. Bausani, "Bahā'īs," in *The Encyclopaedia of Islam*, new ed., vol. 1 (1960), pp. 915–918
• Juan R.I. Cole, *Modernity and the Millennium: The Genesis of the Baha'i Faith in the Nineteenth-Century Middle East* (1998)
• Juan R.I. Cole et al., "Bahai Faith or Bahaism," in *Encyclopædia Iranica*, vol. 3 (1989), pp. 438–475
• Roger Cooper et al., *The Baha'is of Iran*, rev. and updated ed. (1985)
• Denis MacEoin, *Rituals in Babism and Baha'ism* (1994)
• Moojan Momen (ed.), *The Bábí and Bahá'í Religions, 1844–1944: Some Contemporary Western Accounts* (1981)
• Moojan Momen (ed.), *Studies in Bábí and Bahá'í History* (1982–)
• Peter Smith, *The Babi and Baha'i Religions: From Messianic Shi'ism to a World Religion* (1987)
• Robert H. Stockman, *The Bahá'í Faith in America* (1985–)
• Will C. van den Hoonaard, *The Origins of the Bahá'í Community of Canada, 1898–1948* (1996)

BUDDHISM

• Heinz Bechert and Richard Gombrich (eds.), *The World of Buddhism: Buddhist Monks and Nuns in Society and Culture* (1984, reissued 1995)
• Robert E. Buswell and Robert M. Gimello (eds.), *Paths to Liberation: The Mārga and Its Transformations in Buddhist Thought* (1992)
• José Ignacio Cabezón (ed.), *Buddhism, Sexuality, and Gender* (1992)
• Heinrich Dumoulin, *Understanding Buddhism: Key Themes*, trans. from German and adapted by Joseph O'Leary (1994)
• Rita M. Gross, *Buddhism After Patriarchy: A Feminist History, Analysis, and Reconstruction of Buddhism* (1993)
• Joseph M. Kitagawa and Mark D. Cummings (eds.), *Buddhism and Asian History* (1989)
• William R. LaFleur, *Buddhism: A Cultural Perspective* (1988)
• Donald S. Lopez, Jr. (ed.), *Buddhism in Practice* (1995)
• Donald S. Lopez, Jr. (ed.), *Buddhist Hermeneutics* (1988, reissued 1992)
• Donald S. Lopez, Jr. (ed.), *Curators of the Buddha: The Study of Buddhism Under Colonialism* (1995)
• Richard H. Robinson et al., *The Buddhist Religion: A Historical Introduction*, 4th ed. (1996)
• Alan Sponberg and Helen Hardacre (eds.), *Maitreya: The Future Buddha* (1988)
• John S. Strong (compiler), *The Experience of Buddhism: Sources and Interpretations* (1995)

Major figures and movements

• Philip C. Almond, *The British Discovery of Buddhism* (1988)
• Galen Amstutz, *Interpreting Amida: History and Orientalism in the Study of Pure Land Buddhism* (1997)

BIBLIOGRAPHY

- Carl Bielefeldt, *Dōgen's Manuals of Zen Meditation* (1988)
- George D. Bond, *The Word of the Buddha: The Tipiṭaka and Its Interpretation in Theravada Buddhism* (1982)
- José Ignacio Cabezón, *Buddhism and Language: A Study of Indo-Tibetan Scholasticism* (1994)
- Kenneth K.S. Ch'ên, *Buddhism in China: A Historical Survey* (1964, reissued 1972)
- Steven Collins, *Nirvana and Other Buddhist Felicities: Utopias of the Pali Imaginaire* (1998)
- Steven Collins, *Selfless Persons: Imagery and Thought in Theravāda Buddhism* (1982, reissued 1990)
- James C. Dobbins, *Jōdo Shinshū: Shin Buddhism in Medieval Japan* (1989)
- Georges B.J. Dreyfus, *Recognizing Reality: Dharmakīrti's Philosophy and Its Tibetan Interpretations* (1997)
- Malcolm David Eckel, *To See the Buddha: A Philosopher's Quest for the Meaning of Emptiness* (1992)
- Bernard Faure, *The Rhetoric of Immediacy: A Cultural Critique of Chan/Zen Buddhism* (1991)
- Bernard Faure, *Visions of Power: Imagining Medieval Japanese Buddhism*, trans. from French (1996)
- Rick Fields, *How the Swans Came to the Lake: A Narrative History of Buddhism in America*, 3rd ed., rev. and updated (1992)
- Rebecca Redwood French, *The Golden Yoke: The Legal Cosmology of Buddhist Tibet* (1995)
- David N. Gellner, *Monk, Householder, and Tantric Priest: Newar Buddhism and Its Heirarchy of Ritual* (1992)
- Jacques Gernet, *Buddhism in Chinese Society: An Economic History from the Fifth to the Tenth Centuries* (1995; originally published in French, 1956)
- R.M.L. Gethin, *The Buddhist Path to Awakening: A Study of the Bodhi-Pakkhiyā Dhammā* (1992)
- Melvyn C. Goldstein and Matthew T. Kapstein (eds.), *Buddhism in Contemporary Tibet: Religious Revival and Cultural Identity* (1998)
- Richard F. Gombrich, *Theravāda Buddhism: A Social History from Ancient Benares to Modern Colombo* (1988, reissued 1995)

- Peter N. Gregory, *Tsung-mi and the Sinification of Buddhism* (1991)
- Paul J. Griffiths, *On Being Buddha: The Classical Doctrine of Buddhahood* (1994)
- Paul J. Griffiths, *On Being Mindless: Buddhist Meditation and the Mind-Body Problem* (1986)
- Paul Groner, *Saichō: The Establishment of the Japanese Tendai School* (1984)
- Janet Gyatso (ed.), *In the Mirror of Memory: Reflections on Mindfulness and Remembrance in Indian and Tibetan Buddhism* (1992)
- John Clifford Holt, *Buddha in the Crown: Avalokiteśvara in the Buddhist Traditions of Sri Lanka* (1991)
- T.P. Kasulis, *Zen Action/Zen Person* (1981)
- James Edward Ketelaar, *Of Heretics and Martyrs in Meiji Japan: Buddhism and Its Persecution* (1990)
- Anne Carolyn Klein, *Meeting the Great Bliss Queen: Buddhists, Feminists, and the Art of the Self* (1995)
- William R. LaFleur, *Liquid Life: Abortion and Buddhism in Japan* (1992)
- Donald S. Lopez, Jr., *Prisoners of Shangri-La: Tibetan Buddhism and the West* (1998)
- John J. Makransky, *Buddhahood Embodied: Sources of Controversy in India and Tibet* (1997)
- John R. McRae, *The Northern School and the Formation of Early Ch'an Buddhism* (1986)
- E. Michael Mendelson, *Sangha and State in Burma: A Study of Monastic Sectarianism and Leadership* (1975)
- Jan Nattier, *Once Upon a Future Time: Studies in a Buddhist Prophecy of Decline* (1991)
- Sherry B. Ortner, *Sherpas Through Their Rituals* (1978)
- Charles D. Orzech, *Politics and Transcendent Wisdom: The Scripture for Humane Kings in the Creation of Chinese Buddhism* (1998)
- Reginald A. Ray, *Buddhist Saints in India: A Study in Buddhist Values and Orientations* (1994)
- Paula Richman, *Women, Branch Stories, and Religious Rhetoric in a Tamil Buddhist Text* (1988)
- Juliane Schober (ed.), *Sacred Biography in the Buddhist Traditions of South and Southeast Asia* (1997)
- Russell F. Sizemore and Donald K. Swearer (eds.), *Eth-*

ics, Wealth, and Salvation: A Study of Buddhist Social Ethics (1990)
- Melford E. Spiro, *Buddhism and Society: A Great Tradition and Its Burmese Vicissitudes*, 2nd, expanded ed. (1982)
- Fredrick J. Streng, *Emptiness: A Study in Religious Meaning* (1967)
- John S. Strong, *The Legend and Cult of Upagupta: Sanskrit Buddhism in North Indian and Southeast Asia* (1992)
- Donald K. Swearer, *Wat Haripuñjaya: A Study of the Royal Temple of the Buddha's Relic, Lamphun, Thailand* (1976)
- Stanley Jeyaraja Tambiah, *Buddhism and the Spirit Cults in North-East Thailand* (1970)
- Stanley Jeyaraja Tambiah, *The Buddhist Saints of the Forest and the Cult of Amulets: A Study in Charisma, Hagiography, Sectarianism, and Millennial Buddhism* (1984)
- Stephen F. Teiser, *The Ghost Festival in Medieval China* (1988, reissued 1996)
- Kevin Trainor, *Relics, Ritual, and Representation in Buddhism: Rematerializing the Sri Lankan Theravāda Tradition* (1997)
- Andrew P. Tuck, *Comparative Philosophy and the Philosophy of Scholarship: On the Western Interpretation of Nāgārjuna* (1990)
- Holmes Welch, *The Practice of Chinese Buddhism, 1900–1950* (1967)
- Paul Williams, *Mahāyāna Buddhism: The Doctrinal Foundations* (1989)
- E. Zürcher, *The Buddhist Conquest of China: The Spread and Adaptation of Buddhism in Early Medieval China*, 2 vol. (1959, reprinted 1972)

CHRISTIANITY
- Geoffrey Barraclough (ed.), *The Christian World: A Social and Cultural History* (1981)
- David B. Barrett (ed.), *World Christian Encyclopedia: A Comparative Study of Churches and Religions in the Modern World, AD 1900–2000* (1982)
- Louis Bouyer, Jean Leclercq, and François Vandenbroucke, *History of Christian Spirituality*, 3 vol. (1960–68, reissued 1982; originally published in French, 1960–65)
- Henry Chadwick and G.R. Evans (eds.), *Atlas of the Christian Church* (1987)

- Owen Chadwick (ed.), *The Pelican History of the Church*, 6 vol. (1961–70)
- F.L. Cross (ed.), *The Oxford Dictionary of the Christian Church*, 3rd ed. edited by E.A. Livingstone (1997)
- Erwin Fahlbusch et al. (eds.), *The Encyclopedia of Christianity* (1999–)
- Everett Ferguson, Michael P. McHugh, and Frederick W. Norris (eds.), *Encyclopedia of Early Christianity*, 2nd ed., 2 vol. (1997)
- Adolf von Harnack, *History of Dogma*, 7 vol. (1894–96, reissued 7 vol. in 4, 1961; originally published in German, 3rd ed., 3 vol., 1894–97)
- Adolf von Harnack, *What Is Christianity?* (1901, reissued 1986; originally published in German, 1900)
- James Hastings, John A. Selbie, and Louis H. Gray (eds.), *Encyclopaedia of Religion and Ethics*, 13 vol. (1908–26, reissued 1979–81)
- Kenneth Scott Latourette, *Christianity in a Revolutionary Age: A History of Christianity in the Nineteenth and Twentieth Centuries*, 5 vol. (1958–62, reissued 1973)
- Kenneth Scott Latourette, *A History of the Expansion of Christianity*, 7 vol. (1934–45, reissued 1971)
- Horace K. Mann, *The Lives of the Popes in the Early Middle Ages*, 18 vol. in 19 (1902–32, reissued 1979)
- Stephen C. Neill, Gerald H. Anderson, and John Goodwin (eds.), *Concise Dictionary of the Christian World Mission* (1970)
- Ludwig Pastor, *The History of the Popes, from the Close of the Middle Ages*, trans. from German, 40 vol. (1891–1953, reprinted 1969)
- Jaroslav Pelikan, *The Christian Tradition: A History of the Development of Doctrine*, 5 vol. (1971–89)
- Johannes Quasten, *Patrology*, 4 vol. (1950–86)
- Ruth Rouse, Stephen C. Neill, and Harold E. Fey (eds.), *A History of the Ecumenical Movement*, vol. 1, 4th ed. (1993), and vol. 2, 3rd ed. (1993)
- Steven Runciman, *A History of the Crusades*, 3 vol. (1951–54, reissued 1988)
- William Smith and Henry Wace (eds.), *A Dictionary of Christian Biography, Literature, Sects, and Doctrines*, 4 vol. (1877–87, reprinted 1984), also available in a 1-volume rev. and abridged ed., *A Dictionary of Christian Biography and Lit-*

erature to the End of the Sixth Century A.D., ed. by Henry Wace and William C. Piercy (1911, reprinted 1994)
• Tomáš Špidlík, The Spirituality of the Christian East (1986; originally published in French, 1978)
• Ernst Troeltsch, The Social Teaching of the Christian Churches, 2 vol. (1931, reissued 1992; originally published in German, 1912)
• R.E.O. White, Christian Ethics: The Historical Development (1981, reissued 1994)
• George Hunston Williams, The Radical Reformation, 3rd ed. (1992)

Major figures and movements

• Donald Attwater, The Christian Churches of the East, 2 vol. (1947–48, reissued 1961)
• Roland H. Bainton, Here I Stand: A Life of Martin Luther (1950, reissued 1995)
• Donald G. Bloesch, The Future of Evangelical Christianity (1983)
• Günther Bornkamm, Jesus of Nazareth (1960, reissued 1995; originally published in German, 1956)
• John Bossy, Christianity in the West, 1400–1700 (1985)
• Peter Brown, The Cult of the Saints: Its Rise and Function in Latin Christianity (1981)
• Raymond E. Brown et al. (eds.), Mary in the New Testament: A Collaborative Assessment by Protestant and Roman Catholic Scholars (1978)
• Robert McAfee Brown, Liberation Theology: An Introductory Guide (1993)
• Louis Châtellier, The Europe of the Devout: The Catholic Reformation and the Formation of a New Society (1989; originally published in French, 1987)
• Marcia L. Colish, Medieval Foundations of the Western Intellectual Tradition, 400–1400 (1997)
• A.G. Dickens, The Counter Reformation (1968, reissued 1979)
• A.G. Dickens, The English Reformation, 2nd ed. (1989)
• Jay P. Dolan, The American Catholic Experience: A History from Colonial Times to the Present (1985, reissued 1992)
• Paula Fredricksen, From Jesus to Christ: The Origins of the New Testament Images of Jesus (1988)
• B.A. Gerrish, Reformers in Profile (1967)

• Adrian Hastings (ed.), Modern Catholicism: Vatican II and After (1991)
• J.M. Hussey, The Orthodox Church in the Byzantine Empire (1986)
• Charles H. Lippy and Peter W. Williams (eds.), Encyclopedia of the American Religious Experience: Studies of Traditions and Movements, 3 vol. (1988)
• Nicholas Lossky et al. (eds.), Dictionary of the Ecumenical Movement (1991)
• Henri Marrou, St. Augustine and His Influence Through the Ages (1957; originally published in French, 1956)
• Alister E. McGrath, Iustitia Dei: A History of the Christian Doctrine of Justification, 2nd ed. (1998)
• John Meyendorff, The Orthodox Church: Its Past and Its Role in the World Today, 4th rev. ed. (1996; originally published in French, 1960)
• New Catholic Encyclopedia, 15 vol. (1967–79, reissued 1981), and 4 supplements (1974–96)
• Francis Oakley, The Western Church in the Later Middle Ages (1979, reissued 1985)
• Steven Ozment, The Age of Reform (1250–1550) (1980)
• Jaroslav Pelikan, Jesus Through the Centuries: His Place in the History of Culture (1985)
• Jaroslav Pelikan, Mary Through the Centuries: Her Place in the History of Culture (1996)
• Methodios Phouyas (Methodios G. Phougias), Orthodoxy, Roman Catholicism, and Anglicanism (1972, reprinted 1984)
• Arthur Carl Piepkorn, Profiles in Belief: The Religious Bodies of the United States and Canada, 4 vol. in 3 (1977–79)
• Michele Ranchetti, The Catholic Modernists: A Study of the Religious Reform Movement, 1864–1907 (1969; originally published in Italian, 1963)
• Daniel G. Reid et al. (eds.), Dictionary of Christianity in America (1990)
• W. Stanford Reid (ed.), John Calvin: His Influence in the Western World (1982)
• Edward Schillebeeckx, Jesus: An Experiment in Christology (1979; originally published in Dutch, 1974)
• Albert Schweitzer, The Quest of the Historical Jesus (1910, reissued 1998; originally published in German, 1906)
• Kallistos Ware (Timothy Ware), The Orthodox Church, new ed. (1993)

• Marina Warner, Alone of All Her Sex: The Myth and Cult of the Virgin Mary (1976, reissued 1985)
• Claude Welch, Protestant Thought in the Nineteenth Century, 2 vol. (1972–85)
• Garry Wills, Saint Augustine (1999)

CONFUCIANISM

• John H. Berthrong, Transformations of the Confucian Way (1998)
• Chung-ying Cheng, New Dimensions of Confucian and Neo-Confucian Philosophy (1991)
• Julia Ching, Confucianism and Christianity: A Comparative Study (1977)
• H.G. Creel, Confucius: The Man and the Myth (1949, reissued 1975; also published as Confucius and the Chinese Way, 1949, reissued 1960)
• Wm. Theodore de Bary, The Trouble with Confucianism (1991)
• Wm. Theodore de Bary et al., The Unfolding of Neo-Confucianism (1975)
• Irene Eber (ed.), Confucianism: The Dynamics of Tradition (1986)
• Herbert Fingarette, Confucius—the Secular as Sacred (1972, reissued 1998)
• David L. Hall and Roger T. Ames, Thinking Through Confucius (1987)
• Phillip J. Ivanhoe, Confucian Moral Self Cultivation (1993)
• Lionel M. Jensen, Manufacturing Confucianism: Chinese Traditions & Universal Civilization (1997)
• D. Howard Smith, Confucius (1973)
• Rodney L. Taylor, The Religious Dimensions of Confucianism (1990)
• Tu Wei-ming (Wei-ming Tu), Centrality and Commonality: An Essay on Confucian Religiousness (1989)
• Tu Wei-ming (Wei-ming Tu), Confucian Thought: Selfhood as Creative Transformation (1985)

Major figures and movements

• Guy S. Alitto, The Last Confucian: Liang Shu-ming and the Chinese Dilemma of Modernity, 2nd ed. (1986)
• John H. Berthrong, All Under Heaven: Transforming Paradigms in Confucian-Christian Dialogue (1994)
• Hok-lam Chan (trans. and ed.), Li Chih, 1527–1602, in Contemporary Chinese Histori-

ography: New Light on His Life and Works (1980)
• Wing-tsit Chan, Chu Hsi: Life and Thought (1987)
• Hao Chang, Liang Ch'i-ch'ao and Intellectual Transition in China, 1890–1907 (1971)
• Kai-wing Chow, The Rise of Confucian Ritualism in Late Imperial China: Ethics, Classics, and Lineage Discourse (1994)
• A.S. Cua, Ethical Argumentation: A Study in Hsün Tzu's Moral Epistemology (1985)
• Daniel K. Gardner, Chu Hsi and the Ta-hsueh: Neo-Confucian Reflection on the Confucian Canon (1986)
• Jerome B. Grieder, Hu Shih and the Chinese Renaissance: Liberalism in the Chinese Revolution, 1917–1937 (1970)
• Charles Hartman, Han Yü and the T'ang Search for Unity (1986)
• Kung-chuan Hsiao, A Modern China and a New World: K'ang Yu-wei, Reformer and Utopian, 1858–1927 (1975)
• Hsün-tzu, Xunzi: A Translation and Study of the Complete Works, 3 vol., ed. and trans. by John Knoblock (1988–94)
• Siu-chi Huang, Lu Hsiang-shan: A Twelfth-Century Chinese Idealist Philosopher (1944, reprinted 1978)
• Philip J. Ivanhoe, Ethics in the Confucian Tradition: The Thought of Mencius and Wang Yang-ming (1990)
• Joseph R. Levenson, Confucian China and Its Modern Fate, 3 vol. (1958–64)
• Thomas A. Metzger, Escape from Predicament: Neo-Confucianism and China's Evolving Political Culture (1977)
• Heiner Roetz, Confucian Ethics of the Axial Age: A Reconstruction Under the Aspect of the Breakthrough Toward Postconventional Thinking (1993)
• Laurence A. Schneider, Ku Chieh-kang and China's New History: Nationalism and the Quest for Alternative Traditions (1971)
• Hoyt Cleveland Tillman, Confucian Discourse and Chu Hsi's Ascendancy (1992)
• Hoyt Cleveland Tillman, Utilitarian Confucianism: Ch'en Liang's Challenge to Chu Hsi (1982)
• Tu Wei-ming (Wei-ming Tu), Milan Hejtmanek, and Alan Wachman (eds.), The Confucian World Observed: A Contemporary Discussion of Confucian Humanism in East Asia (1992)

BIBLIOGRAPHY

- Thomas A. Wilson, *Genealogy of the Way: The Construction and Uses of the Confucian Tradition in Late Imperial China* (1995)

HINDUISM

- Agehananda Bharati, *The Tantric Tradition* (1965, reprinted 1977)
- Lawrence A. Babb, *The Divine Hierarchy: Popular Hinduism in Central India* (1975)
- Lawrence A. Babb and Susan S. Wadley (eds.), *Media and the Transformation of Religion in South Asia* (1995)
- Hans Bakker, *Ayodhyā*, 3 vol. in 1 (1986)
- A.L. Basham, *The Wonder That Was India: A Survey of the History and Culture of the Indian Sub-Continent Before the Coming of the Muslims*, 3rd rev. ed. (1967, reissued 1996)
- Madeleine Biardeau, *Hinduism: The Anthropology of a Civilization* (1989, reissued 1994; originally published in French, 1981)
- Sitansu S. Chakravarti, *Hinduism: A Way of Life* (1991)
- Vasudha Dalmia and Heinrich von Stietencron (eds.), *Representing Hinduism: The Construction of Religious Traditions and National Identity* (1995)
- Louis Dumont, *Homo Hierarchicus: The Caste System and Its Implications*, rev. ed. (1980; originally published in French, 1966)
- Diana L. Eck, *Banāras, City of Light* (1982)
- Diana L. Eck, *Darśan: Seeing the Divine Image in India*, 3rd ed. (1998)
- A.W. Entwistle, *Braj: Centre of Krishna Pilgrimage* (1987)
- Anne Feldhaus, *Water and Womanhood: Religious Meanings of Rivers in Maharashtra* (1995)
- Gavin Flood, *An Introduction to Hinduism* (1996)
- C.J. Fuller, *The Camphor Flame: Popular Hinduism and Society in India* (1992)
- Ann Grodzins Gold, *Fruitful Journeys: The Ways of the Rajasthani Pilgrims* (1988)
- Wilhelm Halbfass, *India and Europe: An Essay in Understanding* (1988; originally published in German, 1981)
- Ronald Inden, *Imagining India* (1990)
- Klaus K. Klostermaier, *A Survey of Hinduism*, 2nd ed. (1994)
- Kim Knott, *Hinduism* (1998)

- Julius Lipner, *Hindus: Their Religious Beliefs and Practices* (1994)
- Donald S. Lopez, Jr. (ed.), *Religions of India in Practice* (1995)
- Raj Bali Pandey, *Hindu Samskāras*, 2nd rev. ed. (1969, reissued 1987)
- Jonathan P. Parry, *Death in Banaras* (1994)
- David Dean Shulman, *Tamil Temple Myths: Sacrifice and Divine Marriage in the South Indian Śaiva Tradition* (1980)
- Jean Varenne, *Yoga and the Hindu Tradition* (1976; originally published in French, 1973)
- Steven Vertovec, *Hindu Trinidad* (1992)
- R.C. Zaehner, *Hinduism*, 2nd ed. (1966, reissued 1985)

Major deities, figures, and movements

- John Braisted Carman, *The Theology of Rāmānuja* (1974)
- Paul B. Courtright, *Gaṇeśa* (1985)
- Sushil Kumar De, *Early History of the Vaisnava Faith and Movement in Bengal*, 2nd ed. (1961)
- Wendy Doniger, *Asceticism and Eroticism in the Mythology of Śiva* (1973, reprinted as *Śiva, the Erotic Ascetic*, 1981)
- Saurabh Dube, *Untouchable Pasts: Religion, Identity, and Power Among a Central Indian Community, 1780–1950* (1998)
- Kathleen M. Erndl, *Victory to the Mother: The Hindu Goddesses of Northwest India in Myth, Ritual, and Symbol* (1993)
- David L. Haberman, *Acting as a Way of Salvation: A Study of the Rāgānugā Bhakti Sādhana* (1988)
- Friedheim Hardy, *Viraha-Bhakti: The Early History of Kṛṣṇa Devotion in South India* (1983)
- John Stratton Hawley, *Krishna, the Butter Thief* (1983)
- John Stratton Hawley and Donna M. Wulff (eds.), *Devī: Goddesses of India* (1996)
- Alf Hiltebeitel, *The Cult of Draupadī* (1988–)
- Mark Juergensmeyer, *Religion as Social Vision: The Movement Against Untouchability in 20th-Century Punjab* (1982)
- David Kinsley, *Hindu Goddesses* (1986, reissued 1997)
- Jeffrey J. Kripal, *Kali's Child: The Mystical and the Erotic in the Life and Teachings of Ramakrishna*, 2nd ed. (1998)

- David N. Lorenzen (ed.), *Bhakti Religion in North India* (1995)
- William R. Pinch, *Peasants and Monks in British India* (1996)
- Paula Richman (compiler), *Extraordinary Child: Poems from a South Indian Devotional Genre* (1997)
- William S. Sax, *Mountain Goddess: Gender and Politics in a Himalayan Pilgrimage* (1991)
- Karine Schomer and W.H. McLeod (eds.), *The Sants: Studies in a Devotional Tradition of India* (1987)
- Charlotte Vaudeville, *A Weaver Named Kabir* (1993)
- Peter van der Veer, *Religious Nationalism: Hindus and Muslims in India* (1994)
- David Gordon White, *The Alchemical Body: Siddha Traditions in Medieval India* (1996)

INDIGENOUS RELIGIONS

- Sam D. Gill, *Beyond the Primitive: The Religions of Nonliterate Peoples* (1982)

African

- Margaret Thompson Drewal, *Yoruba Ritual: Performers, Play, Agency* (1992)
- E.E. Evans-Pritchard, *Nuer Religion* (1956, reissued 1974)
- Marcel Griaule, *Conversations with Ogotemmêli: An Introduction to Dogon Religious Ideas* (1965, reissued 1980; originally published in French, 1948)
- Rosalind I.J. Hackett, *Art and Religion in Africa* (1996)
- E. Bolaji Idowu, *African Traditional Religion: A Definition* (1973)
- Michael Jackson, *Paths Toward a Clearing: Radical Empiricism and Ethnographic Inquiry* (1989)
- Jacob K. Olupona (ed.), *African Traditional Religions in Contemporary Society* (1991)
- Philip M. Peek (ed.), *African Divination Systems: Ways of Knowing* (1991)
- Robert D. Pelton, *The Trickster in West Africa: A Study of Mythic Irony and Sacred Delight* (1980)
- Benjamin C. Ray, *African Religions: Symbol, Ritual, and Community* (1976)
- Rosalind Shaw, "The Invention of 'African Traditional Religion'," *Religion*, 20(4):339–353 (October 1990)
- Victor Turner, *Revelation and Divination in Ndembu Ritual* (1975)

- Victor Turner, *The Ritual Process: Structure and Anti-Structure* (1969, reissued 1995)

Australian Aboriginal

- Ronald M. Berndt, *Australian Aboriginal Religion*, 4 vol. (1974)
- Alan W. Black and Peter E. Glasner (eds.), *Practice and Belief: Studies in the Sociology of Australian Religion* (1983)
- Max Charlesworth et al. (eds.), *Religion in Aboriginal Australia: An Anthology* (1984)
- Mircea Eliade, *Australian Religions: An Introduction* (1973)
- Erich Kolig, *The Silent Revolution: The Effects of Modernization on Australian Aboriginal Religion* (1981)
- W.E.H. Stanner, *On Aboriginal Religion* (1966, reissued 1989)
- Tony Swain, *A Place for Strangers: Towards a History of Australian Aboriginal Being* (1993)

Native Meso-American

- Ralph L. Beals, *The Comparative Ethnology of Northern Mexico Before 1750* (1932, reprinted 1973)
- Davíd Carrasco, *Religions of Mesoamerica: Cosmovision and Ceremonial Centers* (1990)
- Macduff Everton, *The Modern Maya: A Culture in Transition*, ed. by Ulrich Keller and Charles Demangate (1991)
- David Freidel, Linda Schele, and Joy Parker, *Maya Cosmos: Three Thousand Years on the Shaman's Path* (1993)
- Gary H. Gossen and Miguel León-Portilla (eds.), *South and Meso-American Native Spirituality: From the Cult of the Feathered Serpent to the Theology of Liberation* (1993)
- Carl Lumholtz, *Symbolism of the Huichol Indians* (1900, reprinted as *A Nation of Shamans*, 1989)
- Walter F. Morris, Jr., and Jeffrey J. Foxx, *Living Maya* (1987)
- Victor Sanchez, *Toltecs of the New Millennium*, trans. by Robert Nelson (1996; originally published in Spanish, 1994)
- Alan R. Sandstrom, *Corn Is Our Blood: Culture and Ethnic Identity in a Contemporary Aztec Indian Village* (1991)

Native North American

- Keith H. Basso, *Wisdom Sits in Places: Landscape and Language Among the Western Apache* (1996)
- Peggy V. Beck, Anna Lee Walters, and Nia Francisco, *The*

Sacred: Ways of Knowledge, Sources of Life, redesigned ed. (1990)
• Denise Lardner Carmody and John Tully Carmody, *Native American Religions* (1993)
• D.M. Dooling and Paul Jordan-Smith (eds.), *I Become Part of It: Sacred Dimensions in Native American Life* (1989)
• Sam D. Gill, *Native American Religions* (1982)
• Sam D. Gill, *Native American Religious Action: A Performance Approach to Religion* (1987)
• Sam D. Gill, *Native American Traditions: Sources and Interpretations* (1983)
• Arlene Hirschfelder and Paulette Molin, *The Encyclopedia of Native American Religions* (1992)
• Åke Hultkrantz, *Belief and Worship in Native North America*, ed. by Christopher Vecsey (1981)
• Åke Hultkrantz, *Religions of the American Indians* (1979; originally published in Swedish, 1967)
• Lee Irwin, *The Dream Seekers: Native American Visionary Traditions of the Great Plains* (1994)
• Richard K. Nelson, *Make Prayers to the Raven: A Koyukon View of the Northern Forest* (1983)
• Alfonso Ortiz, *The Tewa World: Space, Time, Being and Becoming in a Pueblo Society* (1969)
• William K. Powers, *Yuwipi: Vision and Experience in Oglala Ritual* (1982)
• Dennis Tedlock and Barbara Tedlock (eds.), *Teachings from the American Earth: Indian Religion and Philosophy* (1975, reprinted 1992)
• Christopher Vecsey (ed.), *Religion in Native North America* (1990)
• Ray A. Williamson and Claire R. Farrer (eds.), *Earth & Sky: Visions of the Cosmos in Native American Folklore* (1992)
• Leland C. Wyman, *Blessingway* (1970)

Native South American

• John Bierhorst, *The Mythology of South America* (1988)
• Gary H. Gossen and Miguel Léon-Portilla (eds.), *South and Meso-American Native Spirituality: From the Cult of the Feathered Serpent to the Theology of Liberation* (1993)
• Gerardo Reichel-Dolmatoff, *Yuruparí: Studies of an Amazonian Foundation Myth* (1996)

• Lawrence E. Sullivan, *Icanchu's Drum: An Orientation to Meaning in South American Religions* (1988)
• Johannes Wilbert, *Mystic Endowment: Religious Ethnography of the Warao Indians* (1993)
• Johannes Wilbert and Karin Simoneau (eds.), *Folk Literature of South American Indians*, 24 vol. (1970–92)

Oceanic

• Robert D. Craig, *Dictionary of Polynesian Mythology* (1989)
• Gilbert Herdt and Michele Stephen (eds.), *The Religious Imagination in New Guinea* (1989)
• Antony Hooper and Judith Huntsman (eds.), *Transformations of Polynesian Culture* (1985)
• P. Lawrence and M.J. Meggitt (eds.), *Gods, Ghosts, and Men in Melanesia: Some Religions of Australian New Guinea and the New Hebrides* (1965)
• Roslyn Poignant, *Oceanic and Australian Mythology*, new rev. ed. (1985)
• Tony Swain and Garry Trompf, *The Religions of Oceania* (1995)
• Garry Trompf, *Melanesian Religion* (1991)
• Andrew P. Vayda (ed.), *Peoples and Cultures of the Pacific: An Anthropological Reader* (1968)
• Peter Worsley, *The Trumpet Shall Sound: A Study of "Cargo" Cults in Melanesia*, 2nd augmented ed. (1968, reissued 1986)

Shamanism

• Marjorie Mandelstam Balzer (ed.), *Shamanic Worlds: Rituals and Lore of Siberia and Central Asia* (1997)
• Carmen Blacker, *The Catalpa Bow: A Study of Shamanistic Practices in Japan*, 2nd ed. (1986, reissued 1992)
• David L. Browman and Ronald A. Schwarz (eds.), *Spirits, Shamans, and Stars: Perspectives from South America* (1979)
• V. Diószegi and M. Hoppál (eds.), *Shamanism in Siberia* (1978)
• Mircea Eliade, *Shamanism: Archaic Techniques of Ecstasy*, rev. and enlarged ed. (1964, reissued 1989; originally published in French, 1951)
• Richard W.L. Guisso and Chai-shin Yu (eds.), *Shamanism: The Spirit World of Korea* (1988)
• M. Hoppál (ed.), *Shamanism in Eurasia*, 2 vol. (1984)

• Halla Pai Huhm, *Kut: Korean Shamanist Rituals* (1980)

ISLAM

• Aziz Ahmad, *An Intellectual History of Islam in India* (1969)
• Leila Ahmed, *Women and Gender in Islam: Historical Roots of a Modern Debate* (1992)
• Donna Lee Bowen and Evelyn A. Early (eds.), *Everyday Life in the Muslim Middle East* (1993)
• Juan Eduardo Campo, *The Other Sides of Paradise: Explorations into the Religious Meanings of Domestic Space in Islam* (1991)
• Frederick Mathewson Denny, *An Introduction to Islam*, 2nd ed. (1994)
• *Encyclopædia Iranica* (1982–)
• *The Encyclopaedia of Islam*, new ed. (1960–)
• Gerhard Endress, *An Introduction to Islam* (1988, reissued 1994; originally published in German, 1982)
• John L. Esposito, *Islam: The Straight Path*, 3rd ed. (1998)
• Ismaʿīl R. al Fārūqī and Lois Lamyāʾ al Fārūqī, *Cultural Atlas of Islam* (1986)
• Yvonne Yazbeck Haddad and Jane Idleman Smith (eds.), *Muslim Communitites in North America* (1994)
• Wael B. Hallaq, *A History of Islamic Legal Theories: An Introduction to Sunnī Uṣūl al-Fiqh* (1997)
• Marshall G.S. Hodgson, *The Venture of Islam: Conscience and History in a World Civilization*, 3 vol. (1974)
• Albert Hourani, *A History of the Arab Peoples* (1991)
• R. Stephen Humphreys, *Islamic History: A Framework for Inquiry*, rev. ed. (1991)
• Salma Khadra Jayyusi (ed.), *The Legacy of Muslim Spain*, 2nd ed. (1994)
• Ira M. Lapidus, *A History of Islamic Societies* (1988)
• Bernard Lewis, *The Jews of Islam* (1984)
• Bernard Lewis, *The Political Language of Islam* (1988)
• George Makdisi, *The Rise of Colleges: Institutions of Learning in Islam and the West* (1981)
• Richard C. Martin, *Islamic Studies: A History of Religions Approach*, 2nd ed. (1996)
• Michael G. Morony, *Iraq After the Muslim Conquest* (1984)
• Azim A. Nanji (ed.), *The Muslim Almanac: A Reference Work on the History, Faith, Culture, and Peoples of Islam* (1996)

• Seyyed Hossein Nasr and Oliver Leaman (eds.), *History of Islamic Philosophy*, 2 vol. (1996)
• Jørgen S. Nielsen, *Muslims in Western Europe*, 2nd ed. (1995)
• *The Oxford Encyclopedia of the Modern Islamic World*, 4 vol. (1995)
• Joseph Schacht and C.E. Bosworth (eds.), *The Legacy of Islam*, 2nd ed. (1974)
• Jane Idleman Smith and Yvonne Yazbeck Haddad, *The Islamic Understanding of Death and Resurrection* (1981)
• Steven M. Wasserstrom, *Between Muslim and Jew: The Problem of Symbiosis under Early Islam* (1995)

Major figures and movements

• Azīz Aḥmad, *Islamic Modernism in India and Pakistan, 1857–1964* (1967)
• Said Amir Arjomand, *The Turban for the Crown: The Islamic Revolution in Iran* (1988)
• Farhad Daftary, *The Ismāʿīlīs: Their History and Doctrines* (1990)
• Ross E. Dunn, *The Adventures of Ibn Battuta, a Muslim Traveler of the 14th Century* (1986)
• John L. Esposito, *The Islamic Threat: Myth or Reality?*, 2nd ed. (1995)
• Albert Hourani, *Arabic Thought in the Liberal Age, 1798–1939* (1962, reissued 1983)
• Bernard Lewis, *The Emergence of Modern Turkey*, 2nd ed. (1968, reprinted 1979)
• Muhsin Mahdi, *Ibn Khaldūn's Philosophy of History: A Study in the Philosophic Foundation of the Science of Culture* (1957, reissued 1971)
• Clifton E. Marsh, *From Black Muslims to Muslims: The Resurrection, Transformation, and Change of the Lost-Found Nation of Islam in America, 1930–1995*, 2nd ed. (1996)
• Richard P. Mitchell, *The Society of the Muslim Brothers* (1969)
• Moojan Momen, *An Introduction to Shiʿi Islam: The History and Doctrines of Twelver Shiʿism* (1985)
• Roy Mottahedeh, *The Mantle of the Prophet: Religion and Politics in Iran* (1985)
• Yitzhak Nakash, *The Shiʿis of Iraq* (1994)
• Seyyed Hossein Nasr, *Three Muslim Sages: Avicenna, Suhrawardī, Ibn ʿArabī* (1964, reissued 1976)
• Seyyed Vali Reza Nasr, *The Vanguard of the Islamic Revo-*

lution : The Jama'at-i Islami of Pakistan (1994)
• James L. Peacock, Muslim Puritans: Reformist Psychology in Southeast Asian Islam (1978)
• F.E. Peters, Muhammad and the Origins of Islam (1994)
• Rudolph Peters, Islam and Colonialism: The Doctrine of Jihad in Modern History (1979)
• Abdulaziz Abdulhussein Sachedina, Islamic Messianism: The Idea of the Mahdī in Twelver Shī'ism (1981)
• Edward W. Said, Covering Islam: How the Media and the Experts Determine How We See the Rest of the World, rev. ed. (1997)
• Annemarie Schimmel, And Muhammad Is His Messenger: The Veneration of the Prophet in Islamic Piety (1985; originally published in German, 1981)
• Haim Shaked, The Life of the Sudanese Mahdi (1978)
• D.A. Spellberg, Politics, Gender, and the Islamic Past: The Legacy of 'A'isha bint Abi Bakr (1994)
• John Obert Voll, Islam, Continuity, and Change in the Modern World, 2nd ed. (1994)
• W. Montgomery Watt, The Faith and Practice of al-Ghazālī (1953, reprinted 1982)
• W. Montgomery Watt, Muhammad: Prophet and Statesman (1961, reissued 1978)

JAINISM

• Lawrence A. Babb, Absent Lord: Ascetics and Kings in a Jain Ritual Culture (1996)
• Marcus Banks, Organizing Jainism in India and England (1992)
• Narendra Nath Bhattacharyya, Jain Philosophy: Historical Outline (1976)
• Johann George Buhler (Georg Bühler), On the Indian Sect of the Jainas, 2nd ed., trans. from German (1963)
• Collette Caillat and Ravi Kumar, The Jain Cosmology (1981)
• Michael Carrithers and Caroline Humphrey, The Assembly of Listeners: Jains in Society (1990)
• John E. Cort (ed.), Open Boundaries: Jain Communities and Culture in Indian History (1998)
• Paul Dundas, The Jains (1992)
• Kendall W. Folkert, Scripture and Community: Collected Essays on the Jains, ed. by John E. Cort (1993)
• Caroline Humphery and James Laidlaw, The Archetypal Actions of Ritual: A Theory of

Ritual Illustrated by the Jain Rite of Worship (1994)
• Jagmanderlal Jaini, Outlines of Jainism (1916, reissued 1982)
• Padmanabh S. Jaini, The Jaina Path of Purification (1979)
• James Laidlaw, Riches and Renunciation: Religion, Economy, and Society among the Jains (1995)
• Satkari Mookerjee, The Jaina Philosophy of Non-Absolutism: A Critical Study of Anekāntavāda, 2nd ed. (1978)
• Vilas Adinath Sangave, Jaina Community: A Social Survey, 2nd rev. ed. (1980)
• Nathmal Tatia, Studies in Jaina Philosophy (1951)

Major figures and movements

• K.C. Lalwani, Sramana Bhagavan Mahavira: Life & Doctrine (1975)
• Bimala Churn Law, Mahavira: His Life and Teachings (1937)
• Amulyachandra Sen, Schools and Sects in Jaina Literature (1931)

JUDAISM

• Salo Wittmayer Baron, A Social and Religious History of the Jews (1952–   )
• H.H. Ben-Sasson (ed.), A History of the Jewish People (1976; originally published in Hebrew, 3 vol., 1969)
• Encyclopaedia Judaica, 16 vol. (1972), and a supplement (1982)
• Louis Finkelstein (ed.), The Jews, 4th ed., 3 vol. (1970)
• Louis Jacobs, The Book of Jewish Belief (1984)
• Elie Kedourie (ed.), The Jewish World: History and Culture of the Jewish People (1979, reissued 1986)
• Jacob Neusner, Self-Fulfilling Prophecy: Exile and Return in the History of Judaism (1987)
• Jacob Neusner, The Way of Torah: An Introduction to Judaism, 6th ed. (1997)
• Cecil Roth, A History of the Jews: From Earliest Times Through the Six Day War, rev. ed. (1961, reissued 1970)
• Robert M. Seltzer, Jewish People, Jewish Thought: The Jewish Experience in History (1980)
• D.J. Silver and B. Martin, A History of Judaism, 2 vol. (1974)
• Milton Steinberg, Basic Judaism (1947, reissued 1987)
• R.J. Zwi Werblowsky and Geoffrey Wigoder (eds.), The Encyclopedia of the Jewish Religion, new rev. ed. (1986)

• Herman Wouk, This Is My God (1959, reissued 1992)

Major figures and movements

• Eliyahu Ashtor, The Jews of Moslem Spain, 3 vol. (1973–84, reissued 3 vol. in 2, 1992; originally published in Hebrew, 2 vol., 1960–66)
• Yitzhak Baer, A History of the Jews in Christian Spain, 2 vol. (1961–66, reissued 1992; originally published in Hebrew, 2nd ed., 1959)
• Eliezer Berkovits, Major Themes in Modern Philosophies of Judaism (1975)
• Joseph L. Blau, Judaism in America: From Curiosity to Third Faith (1976)
• Joseph L. Blau, Modern Varieties of Judaism (1966)
• David R. Blumenthal (ed.), Approaches to Judaism in Medieval Times, 3 vol. (1984–88)
• Eugene B. Borowitz, Reform Judaism Today, 3 vol. (1977–78, reissued 3 vol. in 1, 1983)
• Zachary Braiterman, (God) After Auschwitz: Tradition and Change in Post-Holocaust Jewish Thought (1998)
• Martin Buber, Hasidism and Modern Man, trans. from German (1958, reprinted 1988)
• Martin Buber, The Origin and Meaning of Hasidism, trans. from German (1960, reissued 1988)
• Reuven P. Bulka (ed.), Dimensions of Orthodox Judaism (1983)
• Simon Dubnow, Nationalism and History: Essays on Old and New Judaism (1958, reissued 1970)
• Louis Ginzberg, Students, Scholars, and Saints (1928, reprinted 1985)
• Heinrich Graetz, The Structure of Jewish History and Other Essays, trans. from German (1975)
• Ben Halpern, The Idea of the Jewish State, 2nd ed. (1969)
• Arthur Hertzberg (ed.), The Zionist Idea: A Historical Analysis and Reader (1959, reissued 1997)
• Irving Howe and Kenneth Libo, World of Our Fathers (1976, reissued 1994; also published as The Immigrant Jews of New York, 1881 to the Present, 1976)
• Isaac Husik, A History of Mediaeval Jewish Philosophy (1916, reissued 1974)
• Max Kadushin, Worship and Ethics: A Study in Rabbinic Judaism (1963, reprinted 1978)
• Israel Kane, In Quest of the Truth: A Survey of Medieval Jewish Thought (1985)

• Jacob Katz, Exclusiveness and Tolerance: Studies in Jewish-Gentile Relations in Medieval and Modern Times (1961, reprinted 1980)
• Steven T. Katz, The Holocaust in Historical Context (1994–   )
• Steven T. Katz, Post-Holocaust Dialogues: Critical Studies in Modern Jewish Thought (1983)
• William E. Kaufman, Contemporary Jewish Philosophies (1976, reissued 1992)
• Robert A. Kraft and George W.E. Nickelsburg, Early Judaism and Its Modern Interpreters (1986)
• Nora Levin, While Messiah Tarried: Jewish Socialist Movements, 1871–1917 (1977; also published as Jewish Socialist Movements, 1871–1917, 1978)
• Michael A. Meyer, Response to Modernity: A History of the Reform Movement in Judaism (1988, reissued 1995)
• Jacob Neusner, Judaism in the Beginning of Christianity (1984)
• Marc Lee Raphael, Profiles in American Judaism: The Reform, Conservative, Orthodox, and Reconstructionist Traditions in Historical Perspective (1984)
• Simon Rawidowicz, Studies in Jewish Thought (1974)
• David G. Roskies, Against the Apocalypse: Responses to Catastrophe in Modern Jewish Culture (1984)
• Nathan Rotenstreich, Jewish Philosophy in Modern Times: From Mendelssohn to Rosenzweig (1968)
• Anthony J. Saldarini, Pharisees, Scribes, and Sadducees in Palestinian Society: A Sociological Approach (1988)
• E.P. Sanders, Jesus and Judaism (1985)
• Solomon Schechter, Some Aspects of Rabbinic Theology (1909, reprinted as Aspects of Rabbinic Theology, 1998)
• Lawrence H. Schiffman, From Text to Tradition: A History of Second Temple and Rabbinic Judaism (1991)
• Hershel Shanks, The Mystery and Meaning of the Dead Sea Scrolls (1998)
• Marcel Simon, Jewish Sects at the Time of Jesus (1967, reissued 1980; originally published in French, 1960)
• Marshall Sklare, Conservative Judaism: An American Religious Movement, new augmented ed. (1972, reprinted 1985)

• Geza Vermes, *Jesus and the World of Judaism* (1983)
• Geza Vermes, *The Dead Sea Scrolls: Qumran in Perspective*, rev. 3rd ed. (1994)
• Bernard Weinryb, *The Jews of Poland: A Social and Economic History of the Jewish Community in Poland from 1100–1800* (1973, reissued 1982)
• Mark Zborowski and Elizabeth Herzog, *Life Is with People: The Jewish Little-Town of Eastern Europe* (1962, reissued as *Life Is with People: The Culture of the Shtetl*, 1995)

MILLENNIALISM

• Michael Adas, *Prophets of Rebellion: Millenarian Protest Movements Against the European Colonial Order* (1979, reissued 1987)
• Michael Barkun, *Disaster and the Millennium* (1974, reprinted 1986)
• Suliman Bashear, "Muslim Apocalypses and the Hour: A Case Study in Traditional Reinterpretation," *Israel Oriental Studies*, 13:75–99 (1993)
• Ruth H. Bloch, *Visionary Republic: Millennial Themes in American Thought, 1756–1800* (1985)
• Norman Cohn, *Cosmos, Chaos, and the World to Come: The Ancient Roots of Apocalyptic Faith* (1993)
• Norman Cohn, *The Pursuit of the Millennium: Revolutionary Millenarians and Mystical Anarchists of the Middle Ages*, rev. and expanded ed. (1970, reissued 1993)
• John J. Collins, *The Apocalyptic Imagination: An Introduction to Jewish Apocalyptic Literature*, 2nd ed. (1998)
• John J. Collins, Bernard McGinn, and Stephen J. Stein, *The Encyclopedia of Apocalypticism*, 3 vol. (1998)
• David Cook, "Moral Apocalyptic in Islam," *Studia Islamica*, 86:37–69 (1997)
• Stephen L. Cook, *Prophecy & Apocalypticism: The Postexilic Social Setting* (1995)
• Mal Couch (ed.), *Dictionary of Premillennial Theology* (1996)
• Richard K. Emmerson and Bernard McGinn (eds.), *The Apocalypse in the Middle Ages* (1992)
• John G. Gager, *Kingdom and Community: The Social World of Early Christianity* (1975)
• Andrew Colin Gow, *The Red Jews: Antisemitism in an Apocalyptic Age, 1200–1600* (1995)

• Weston La Barre, *The Ghost Dance: Origins of Religion* (1970, reissued 1990)
• Vittorio Lanternari, *The Religions of the Oppressed: A Study of Modern Messianic Cults* (1963; originally published in Italian, 1960)
• Bernard McGinn, *Antichrist: Two Thousand years of the Human Fascination with Evil* (1994)
• Bernard McGinn, *Visions of the End: Apocalyptic Traditions in the Middle Ages* (1979, reissued 1998)
• Arthur P. Mendel, *Vision and Violence* (1992)
• Susan Naquin, *Millenarian Rebellion in China: The Eight Trigrams Uprising of 1813* (1976)
• Stephen D. O'Leary, *Arguing the Apocalypse: A Theory of Millennial Rhetoric* (1994)
• Aviezer Ravitsky, *Messianism, Zionism, and Jewish Religious Radicalism* (1996; originally published in Hebrew, 1993)
• Hillel Schwartz, *Century's End: An Orientation Manual Toward the Year 2000*, rev. and abridged ed. (1996)
• Jonathan D. Spence, *God's Chinese Son: The Taiping Heavenly Kingdom of Hong Xiuquan* (1996)
• Michael J. St. Clair, *Millenarian Movements in Historical Context* (1992)
• Damian Thompson, *The End of Time: Faith and Fear in the Shadow of the Millennium* (1996)
• Werner Verbeke, Daniel Verhelst, and Andries Welkenhuysen (eds.), *The Use and Abuse of Eschatology in the Middle Ages* (1988)
• Ann Williams (ed.), *Prophecy and Millenarianism* (1980)
• Daniel Wojcik, *The End of the World as We Know It: Faith, Fatalism, and Apocalypse in America* (1997)

MONASTICISM

Buddhism

• Tessa J. Bartholomeusz, *Women Under the Bō Tree: Buddhist Nuns in Sri Lanka* (1994)
• Robert E. Buswell, Jr., *The Zen Monastic Experience: Buddhist Practice in Contemporary Korea* (1992)
• Martin Collcutt, *Five Mountains: The Rinzai Zen Monastic Institution in Medieval Japan* (1981)
• Ilana Friedrich-Silber, *Virtuosity, Charisma, and Social Order: A Comparative Sociological Study of Monasticism in Theravada Buddhism and Medieval Catholicism* (1995)
• R.A.L.H. Gunawardana, *Robe and Plough: Monasticism and Economic Interest in Early Medieval Sri Lanka* (1979)
• Hanna Havnevik, *Tibetan Buddhist Nuns: History, Cultural Norms, and Social Reality* (1989)
• Patrick G. Henry and Donald K. Swearer, *For the Sake of the World: The Spirit of Buddhist and Christian Monasticism* (1989)
• John Clifford Holt, *Discipline: The Canonical Buddhism of the Vinayapiṭaka* (1981)
• John Kieschnick, *The Eminent Monk: Buddhist Ideals in Medieval Chinese Hagiography* (1997)
• Charles S. Prebish (ed.), *Buddhist Monastic Discipline* (1975, reissued 1996)
• Gregory Schopen, *Bones, Stones, and Buddhist Monks: Collected Papers on the Archaeology, Epigraphy, and Texts of Monastic Buddhism in India* (1997)
• Mohan Wijayaratna, *Buddhist Monastic Life: According to the Texts of the Theravāda Tradition* (1990; originally published in French, 1983)

Christianity

• Cuthbert Butler, *Benedictine Monachism*, 2nd ed. (1924, reissued 1962)
• Susanna Elm, *Virgins of God: The Making of Asceticism in Late Antiquity* (1994)
• David Knowles, *Christian Monasticism* (1969, reissued 1977)
• David Knowles, *From Pachomius to Ignatius: A Study in the Constitutional History of the Religious Orders* (1966)
• C.H. Lawrence, *Medieval Monasticism: Forms of Religious Life in Western Europe in the Middle Ages*, 2nd ed. (1989)
• Jo Ann Kay McNamara, *Sisters in Arms: Catholic Nuns Through Two Millennia* (1996)
• Walter Nigg, *Warriors of God: The Great Religious Orders and Their Founders* (1959, reissued 1972; originally published in German, 1953)
• John W. O'Malley, *The First Jesuits* (1993)

Hinduism

• Johannes Bronkhorst, *The Two Sources of Indian Asceticism* (1993)
• Austin B. Creel and Vasudha Narayanan (eds.), *Monastic Life* in the Christian and Hindu Traditions (1990)
• Mircea Eliade, *Yoga: Immortality and Freedom*, 2nd ed. (1969; originally published in French, 1954)
• G.S. Ghurye, *Indian Sadhus*, 2nd ed. (1964)
• Robert Lewis Gross, *The Sādhus of India: A Study of Hindu Asceticism* (1992)
• T.N. Madan, *Non-Renunciation: Themes and Interpretations of Hindu Culture* (1987, reissued 1996)
• David M. Miller and Dorothy C. Wertz, *Hindu Monastic Life*, rev. ed. (1996)
• Patrick Olivelle (trans. and ed.), *Saṃnyāsa Upaniṣads: Hindu Scriptures on Asceticism and Renunciation* (1992)
• William R. Pinch, *Peasants and Monks in British India* (1996)
• Wendy Sinclair-Brull, *Female Ascetics: Hierarchy and Purity in an Indian Religious Movement* (1997)

MYSTICISM

• Donald H. Bishop (ed.), *Mysticism and the Mystical Experience: East and West* (1995)
• Bruno Borchert, *Mysticism: Its History and Challenge* (1994; originally published in Dutch, 1989)
• Denise Lardner Carmody and John Tully Carmody, *Mysticism: Holiness East and West* (1996)
• John Ferguson, *Encyclopedia of Mysticism and Mystery Religions* (1982)
• Geoffrey Parrinder, *Mysticism in the World's Religions* (1976, reissued 1995)
• Ben-Ami Scharfstein, *Mystical Experience* (1973)
• Sidney Spencer, *Mysticism in World Religion* (1963, reissued 1971)

Christianity

• David Knowles, *The English Mystical Tradition* (1961)
• Vladimir Lossky, *The Mystical Theology of the Eastern Church* (1957, reissued 1976; originally published in French, 1944)
• Bernard McGinn, *The Presence of God: A History of Western Christian Mysticism*, 4 vol. (1991–)
• Evelyn Underhill, *Mysticism* (1911, reissued 1993)

Islam

• Vincent J. Cornell, *Realm of the Saint: Power and Authority in Moroccan Sufism* (1998)

• Carl W. Ernst, *The Shambhala Guide to Sufism* (1997)
• Gershom Scholem, *Major Trends in Jewish Mysticism*, 3rd rev. ed. (1954, reissued 1995)
• Valerie J. Hoffman, *Sufism, Mystics, and Saints in Modern Egypt* (1995)
• Louis Massignon, *The Passion of al-Hallāj: Mystic and Martyr of Islam*, 4 vol. (1982; originally published in French, 2 vol., 1922), also available in a one-volume abridged ed. with the same title, trans. and ed. by Herbert Mason (1994)
• Seyyed Hossein Nasr (ed.), *Islamic Spirituality*, 2 vol. (1987–91)
• Annemarie Schimmel, *Mystical Dimensions of Islam* (1975)
• Annemarie Schimmel, *The Triumphal Sun: A Study of the works of Jalāloddin Rum*, rev. ed. (1980, reissued 1993)
• J. Spencer Trimingham, *The Sufi Orders in Islam* (1971, reissued 1998)
• Mark R. Woodward, *Islam in Java: Normative Piety and Mysticism in the Sultanate of Yogyakarta* (1989)

Judaism
• J. Abelson, *Jewish Mysticism: An Introduction to the Kabbalah*, 3rd ed. (1981)
• D.R. Blumenthal, *Understanding Jewish Mysticism*, 2 vol. (1978–82)
• Ben Zion Bokser, *The Jewish Mystical Tradition* (1981)
• Lawrence Fine (trans.), *Safed Spirituality: Rules of Mystical Piety, Beginning of Wisdom* (1984)
• Arthur Green (ed.), *Jewish Spirituality: From the Bible Through the Middle Ages* (1986)
• Louis Jacobs (ed.), *Jewish Mystical Testimonies* (1977, reissued as *The Jewish Mystics*, 1990)
• Ronald C. Kiener (trans.), *The Early Kabbalah*, ed. by Joseph Dan (1986)
• Lawrence Kushner, *God Was in This Place and I, I Did Not Know* (1991)
• Daniel Chanan Matt (trans.), *Zohar: The Book of Enlightenment* (1983)

MYTH AND MYTHOLOGY
• Yves Bonnefoy (compiler), *Mythologies*, ed. by Wendy Doniger, trans. from French, 2 vol. (1991)
• Marcel Detienne, *The Creation of Mythology* (1986; originally published in French, 1981)
• Alan Dundes (ed.), *Sacred Narrative: Readings in the Theory of Myth* (1984)

• G.S. Kirk, *Myth: Its Meaning and Functions in Ancient and Other Cultures* (1970)
• William A. Lessa and Evon Z. Vogt (eds.), *Reader in Comparative Religion: An Anthropological Approach*, 4th ed. (1979)
• Pierre Maranda (compiler), *Mythology: Selected Readings* (1972)
• John Middleton (ed.), *Myth and Cosmos: Readings in Mythology and Symbolism* (1967, reprinted 1986)
• Henry A. Murray (ed.), *Myth and Mythmaking* (1960)
• Thomas A. Sebeok, *Myth: A Symposium* (1955, reissued 1974)

NEW RELIGIOUS MOVEMENTS
• Margot Adler, *Drawing Down the Moon: Witches, Druids, Goddess-Worshippers, and Other Pagans in America Today*, rev. and expanded ed. (1986, reissued 1997)
• Leonard E. Barrett, *The Rastafarians: Sounds of Cultural Dissonance*, 20th anniversary ed. (1997)
• Roger Bastide, *The African Religions of Brazil: Toward a Sociology of the Interpenetration of Civilizations* (1978; originally published in French, 1960)
• Mary Farrell Bednarowski, *New Religions and the Theological Imagination in America* (1989)
• George Brandon, *Santeria from Africa to the New World: The Dead Sell Memories* (1993)
• Robert S. Ellwood and Harry B. Partin, *Religious and Spiritual Groups in Modern America*, 2nd ed. (1988)
• Migene Gonzáles-Wippler, *Santería: The Religion*, 2nd ed. (1994)
• Stephen Gottschalk, *The Emergence of Christian Science in American Religious Life* (1973)
• Michel S. Laguerre, *Voodoo Heritage* (1980)
• H. Neill McFarland, *The Rush Hour of the Gods: A Study of New Religious Movements in Japan* (1967)
• Alfred Métraux, *Voodoo in Haiti* (1959, reissued 1972; originally published in French, 1958)
• Kiyomi Morioka, *Religion in Changing Japanese Society* (1975)
• Joseph M. Murphy, *Santeria* (1988, reissued 1993)
• Clark B. Offner and Henry van Straelen, *Modern Japanese Religions* (1963)

• Joseph Owens, *Dread: The Rastafarians of Jamaica* (1976, reissued 1982)
• Robert Peel, *Christian Science: Its Encounter with American Culture* (1958, reissued 1965)
• John A. Saliba, *Understanding New Religious Movements* (1996)
• George Eaton Simpson, *Black Religions in the New World* (1978)
• Harry Thomsen, *The New Religions of Japan* (1963, reprinted 1978)
• Garry Trompf (ed.), *Cargo Cults and Millenarian Movements: Transoceanic Comparisons of New Religious Movements* (1990)
• Harold W. Turner, *Religious Innovation in Africa: Collected Essays on New Religious Movements* (1979)

PREHISTORIC RELIGIONS
• Aubrey Burl, *Rites of the Gods* (1981)
• D. Bruce Dickson, *The Dawn of Belief: Religion in the Upper Paleolithic of Southwestern Europe* (1990)
• Marija Gimbutas, *The Civilization of the Goddess* (1991)
• E.O. James, *Prehistoric Religion: A Study in Prehistoric Archaeology* (1957, reissued 1963)
• Adolf E. Jensen, *Myth and Cult Among Primitive Peoples* (1963; originally published in German, 1951)
• Johannes Maringer, *The Gods of Prehistoric Man*, trans. from German (1960)
• John E. Pfeiffer, *The Creative Explosion: An Inquiry into the Origins of Art and Religion* (1982)
• Chester G. Starr, *Early Man: Prehistory and the Civilizations of the Ancient Near East* (1973)

RITUAL STUDIES
• Catherine Bell, *Ritual Theory, Ritual Practice* (1992)
• Maurice Bloch, *Ritual, History, and Power* (1989)
• Mary Douglas, *Purity and Danger: An Analysis of Concepts of Pollution and Taboo* (1966, reissued 1996)
• Caroline Humphrey and James Laidlaw, *The Archetypal Actions of Ritual: A Theory of Ritual Illustrated by the Jain Rite of Worship* (1994)
• Jonathan Z. Smith, *To Take Place: Toward Theory in Ritual* (1987)
• Victor Turner, *The Ritual Process: Structure and Anti-Structure* (1969, reissued 1995)

SACRED WRITINGS
• Harold Coward, *Sacred Word and Sacred Text: Scripture in World Religions* (1988)

Buddhism
• Robert E. Buswell (ed.), *Chinese Buddhist Apocrypha* (1990)
• Janet Gyatso, *Apparitions of the Self: The Secret Autobiographies of a Tibetan Visionary* (1998)
• Oskar von Hinüber, *A Handbook of Pāli Literature* (1996)
• Donald S. Lopez, Jr., *Elaborations on Emptiness: Uses of the Heart Sūtra* (1996)
• Donald S. Lopez, Jr., *The Heart Sūtra Explained: Indian and Tibetan Commentaries* (1988)
• Isshū Miura and Ruth Fuller Sasaki, *Zen Dust: The History of the Koan and Koan Study in Rinzai (Lin-chi) Zen* (1966)
• K.R. Norman, *Pāli Literature: Including the Canonical Literature in Prakrit and Sanskrit of All the Hīnayāna Schools of Buddhism* (1983)
• John S. Strong, *The Legend of King Aśoka: A Study and Translation of the Aśokāvadāna* (1983)
• George J. Tanabe, Jr., and Willa Jane Tanabe (eds.), *The Lotus Sutra in Japanese Culture* (1989)
• Stephen F. Teiser, *The Scripture on the Ten Kings and the Making of Purgatory in Medieval Chinese Buddhism* (1994)
• Charles Willemen, Bart Dessein, and Collett Cox, *Sarvāstivāda Buddhist Scholasticism* (1998)
• Liz Wilson, *Charming Cadavers: Horrific Figurations of the Feminine in Indian Buddhist Hagiographic Literature* (1996)

Christianity
• *Black's New Testament Commentaries* (1957–)
• G. Johannes Botterweck and Helmer Ringgren (eds.), *Theological Dictionary of the Old Testament* (1974– ; originally published in German, 1973–)
• David Noel Freedman (ed.), *The Anchor Bible Dictionary*, 6 vol. (1992)
• James Hastings et al. (eds.), *A Dictionary of the Bible*, 5 vol. (1898–1904, reprinted 1988)
• Gerhard Kittel, *Theological Dictionary of the New Testament*, 10 vol. (1964–76; originally published in German, 9 vol., 1932–72)

Confucianism

• Li Fu Chen, *The Confucian Way: A New and Systematic Study of the "Four Books,"* trans. from Chinese (1972, reissued 1987)
• Chu Hsi (Hsi Chu) and Lü Tsu-ch'en (Tsu-ch'en Lü) (compilers), *Reflections on Things at Hand: The Neo-Confucian Anthology*, trans. by Wing-tsit Chan (1967)
• Confucius, *The Analects (Lun yü)*, trans. by D.C. Lau (1979, reissued with the Chinese text, 1992)
• Confucius, *The Analects of Confucius*, trans. by Arthur Waley (1938, reissued 1989)
• Confucius, *The Analects of Confucius*, trans. by Chichung Huang (1997)
• Confucius, *The Analects of Confucius*, trans. by Simon Leys (1997)
• Confucius, *The Original Analects: Sayings of Confucius and His Successors*, trans. by E. Bruce Brooks and A. Taeko Brooks (1998)
• John B. Henderson, *Scripture, Canon, and Commentary: A Comparison of Confucian and Western Exegesis* (1991)
• E.R. Hughes (trans.), *The Great Learning & The Mean-in-Action* (1942, reissued 1979)
• James Legge (trans.), *The Chinese Classics*, 5 vol. (1861–72, reissued 5 vol. in 4, 1985)
• Sarah A. Queen, *From Chronicle to Canon: The Hermeneutics of the Spring and Autumn, According to Tung Chung-shu* (1996)
• Edward L. Shaughnessy, *I Ching=The Classic of Changes* (1997)
• Wang Yang-ming (Yang-Ming Wang), *Instructions for Practical Living, and Other Neo-Confucian Writings*, trans. by Wing-tsit Chan (1963)
• Burton Watson (trans.), *Basic Writings of Mo Tzu, Hsün Tzu, and Han Fei Tzu* (1964)

Hinduism

• J.A.B. van Buitenen (trans. and ed.), *The Mahābhārata* (1973–)
• Thomas B. Coburn (trans.), *Encountering the Goddess: A Translation of the Devī-māhātmya and a Study of Its Interpretation* (1991)
• Robert Goldman (trans.), *The Rāmāyaṇa of Vālmīki*, annotated by Robert Goldman and Sally J. Sutherland (1984–)
• Dominic Goodall (ed. and trans.), *Hindu Scriptures* (1996)

• John Stratton Hawley and Shrivatsa Goswami, *At Play with Krishna: Pilgrimage Dramas from Brindavan* (1981)
• John Stratton Hawley and Mark Juergensmeyer (trans.), *Songs of the Saints of India* (1988)
• Linda Hess and Shukdev Singh (trans.), *The Bījak of Kabir* (1983)
• Philip Lutgendorf, *The Life of a Text: Performing the Rāmcaritmānas of Tulsidas* (1991)
• Barbara Stoler Miller (trans.), *The Bhagavad-Gita* (1986, reissued 1991)
• Barbara Stoler Miller (ed. and trans.), *Love Song of the Dark Lord: Jayadeva's Gitagovinda* (1977, reissued 1997)
• Barbara Stoler Miller (trans. and ed.), *Yoga: Discipline of Freedom: The Yoga Sutra Attributed to Patanjali* (1995)
• Wendy Doniger O'Flaherty (ed. and trans.), *The Rig Veda* (1981)
• Wendy Doniger O'Flaherty (trans.), *Hindu Myths* (1975)
• Patrick Olivelle (trans.), *Upaniṣads* (1996)
• Indira Viswanathan Peterson (trans.), *Poems to Śiva: The Hymns of the Tamil Saints* (1989)
• A.K. Ramanujan (trans.), *Speaking of Śiva* (1973)
• A.K. Ramanujan, Velcheru Narayana Rao, and David Dean Shulman (eds. and trans.), *When God Is a Customer: Telugu Courtesan Songs* (1994)
• Paula Richman (ed.), *Many Rāmāyaṇas: The Diversity of a Narrative Tradition in South Asia* (1991)

Islam

• A.F.L. Beeston et al. (eds.), *Arabic Literature to the End of the Umayyad Period* (1983)
• Richard Bell, *Bell's Introduction to the Qur'ān*, new ed. rev. and enlarged by W. Montgomery Watt (1970)
• John Burton, *An Introduction to the Ḥadīth* (1994)
• Helmut Gätje, *The Qur'ān and Its Exegesis* (1976; originally published in German, 1971)
• William A. Graham, *Divine Word and Prophetic Word in Early Islam* (1977)
• Jane Dammen McAuliffe, *Qur'ānic Christians: An Analysis of Classical and Modern Exegesis* (1991)
• Kristina Nelson, *The Art of Reciting the Qur'an* (1985)
• Fazlur Rahman, *Major Themes of the Qur'ān*, 2nd ed. (1989, reissued 1994)

• Andrew Rippin (ed.), *Approaches to the History of the Interpretation of the Qur'ān* (1988)
• Muhammad Zubayr Siddiqi, *Ḥadīth Literature: Its Origin, Development, and Special Features*, rev. ed. by Abdal Hakim Murad (1993)
• A.T. Welch, "Kur'ān," in *The Encyclopaedia of Islam*, new ed., vol. 5 (1986), parts 1–8, pp. 400–429

Jainism

• Hermann Jacobi (trans.), *Gaina Sûtras*, 2 vol. (1884–95, reissued as *Jaina Sutras*, 1973)
• Padmanabh S. Jaini, *Gender and Salvation: Jaina Debates on the Spiritual Liberation of Women* (1991)
• Hiralal Rasikdas Kapadia, *A History of the Canonical Literature of the Jainas* (1941)
• R. Williams, *Jaina Yoga* (1963, reprinted 1983)

Judaism

• Michael Fishbane, *The Garments of Torah: Essays in Biblical Hermeneutics* (1989)
• Susan A. Handelman, *The Slayers of Moses: The Emergence of Rabbinic Interpretation in Modern Literary Theory* (1982)
• Geoffrey H. Hartman and Sanford Budick, *Midrash and Literature* (1986)
• David Kraemer, *The Mind of the Talmud: An Intellectual History of the Bavli* (1990)
• C.G. Montefiore and H. Loewe (compilers and eds.), *A Rabbinic Anthology* (1938, reprinted 1970)
• Jacob Neusner, *The Bavli: An Introduction* (1992)
• Jacob Neusner, *Invitation to Midrash: The Workings of Rabbinic Bible Interpretation* (1989, reissued 1998)
• Jacob Neusner, *Invitation to the Talmud*, rev. and expanded ed. (1984, reissued 1998)
• Jacob Neusner, *Judaism: The Evidence of the Mishnah*, 2nd ed., augmented (1988)
• Jacob Neusner, *The Midrash: An Introduction* (1990)
• George W.E. Nickelsburg, *Jewish Literature Between the Bible and the Mishnah: A Historical and Literary Introduction* (1981)
• Jakob J. Petuchowski, *Our Masters Taught: Rabbinic Stories and Sayings* (1982; originally published in German, 1979)
• Gary G. Porton, *Understanding Rabbinic Midrash: Texts and Commentary* (1985)

• H.L. Strack and G. Stemberger, *Introduction to the Talmud and Midrash*, trans. from German (1992)

Sikhism

• Surindar Singh Kohli, *A Critical Study of Ādi Granth*, 2nd ed. (1976)
• W.H. McLeod, *Early Sikh Tradition: A Study of the Janamsākhīs* (1980)
• Gurinder Singh Mann, *The Goindval Pothis: The Earliest Extant Source of the Sikh Canon* (1996)
• Nikky-Guninder Kaur Singh (trans.), *The Name of My Beloved: Verses of the Sikh Gurus* (1995)

Taoism

• Steven R. Bokenkamp and Peter Nickerson, *Early Daoist Scriptures* (1997)
• Ellen M. Chen, *The Tao Te Ching: A New Translation with Commentary* (1989)
• Chuang-tzu, *The Complete Works of Chuang Tzu*, trans. by Burton Watson (1968)
• Hung Ko, *Alchemy, Medicine, Religion in the China of A.D. 320: The Nei P'ien of Ko Hung (Pao-p'u tzu)* (1966, reissued 1981)
• Livia Kohn, *The Taoist Experience: An Anthology* (1993)
• Lao-tzu, *Lao-tzu: Te-Tao Ching: A New Translation Based on the Recently Discovered Ma-wang-tui Texts*, trans. by Robert G. Henricks (1989)
• Lao-tzu, *The Tao of the Tao Te Ching: A Translation and Commentary*, trans. by Michael LaFargue (1992)
• Lieh-tzu, *The Book of Lieh-tzu*, trans. by A.C. Graham (1960, reissued 1990)
• Michael R. Saso, *The Gold Pavilion: Taoist Ways to Peace, Healing, and Long Life* (1995)
• Eva Wong (trans.), *Seven Taoist Masters: A Folk Novel of China* (1990)

SHINTŌ

• H. Byron Earhart, *Japanese Religion: Unity and Diversity*, 3rd ed. (1982)
• Daniel C. Holtom, *The National Faith of Japan: A Study in Modern Shintō* (1938, reissued 1995)
• Joseph M. Kitagawa, *On Understanding Japanese Religion* (1987)
• Joseph M. Kitagawa, *Religion in Japanese History* (1966, reissued 1990)
• John K. Nelson, *A Year in the Life of a Shinto Shrine* (1996)

BIBLIOGRAPHY

- Sokyo Ono (Motonori Ono), *The Kami Way: An Introduction to Shrine Shinto* (1960, reissued as *Shinto: The Kami Way*, 1976)
- Donald L. Philippi (trans.), *Kojiki* (1968)
- Donald L. Philippi (trans.), *Norito: A New Translation of the Ancient Japanese Ritual Prayers* (1959, reissued 1990)
- Stuart D.B. Picken, *Essentials of Shinto: An Analytical Guide to Principal Teachings* (1994)
- Stuart D.B. Picken, *Shinto, Japan's Spiritual Roots* (1980)
- Ian Reader, *The Simple Guide to Shinto* (1998)
- H. Paul Varley, *Japanese Culture*, 3rd ed. (1984)

Major figures and movements

- Wilhelmus H.M. Creemers, *Shrine Shinto After World War II* (1968)
- Robert S. Ellwood, *The Feast of Kingship: Accession Ceremonies in Ancient Japan* (1973)
- Helen Hardacre, *Kurozumikyō and the New Religions of Japan* (1986)
- Daniel C. Holtom, *Modern Japan and Shinto Nationalism: A Study of Present-Day Trends in Japanese Religions*, rev. ed. (1947, reissued 1963)
- Shigeru Matsumoto, *Motoori Norinaga, 1730–1801* (1970)
- Tsunetsugu Muraoka, *Studies in Shinto Thought*, trans. from Japanese (1964, reprinted 1988)
- Herbert Plutschow and P.G. O'Neill, *Matsuri: The Festivals of Japan* (1996)
- Jūbutso Saka, *The Ise Daijingū Sankeiki; or, Diary of a Pilgrim to Ise*, trans. by A.L. Sadler (1940)

SIKHISM

- Avtar Singh, *Ethics of the Sikhs* (1970, reissued 1983)
- N. Gerald Barrier and Verne A. Dusenbery (eds.), *The Sikh Diaspora: Migration and the Experience Beyond Punjab* (1989)
- W. Owen Cole and Piara Singh Sambhi, *The Sikhs: Their Religious Beliefs and Practices*, 2nd rev. ed. (1995)
- J.S. Grewal, *The Sikhs of the Punjab*, rev. ed. (1998)
- Harbans Singh, *The Heritage of the Sikhs*, 2nd rev. and updated ed. (1994)
- John Stratton Hawley and Gurinder Singh Mann (eds.), *Studying the Sikhs: Issues for North America* (1993)
- Mark Juergensmeyer and N. Gerald Barrier (eds.), *Sikh Studies: Comparative Perspectives on a Changing Tradition* (1979)

- Madanjit Kaur, *The Golden Temple: Past and Present* (1983)
- Khushwant Singh, *A History of the Sikhs*, 2 vol. (1963–66, reissued 1984)
- W.H. McLeod, *Sikhism* (1997)
- Joseph T. O'Connell et al. (eds.), *Sikh History and Religion in the Twentieth Century* (1988)
- Nikky-Guninder Kaur Singh, *The Feminine Principle in the Sikh Vision of the Transcendent* (1993)

Major figures and movements

- Fauja Singh, *Guru Amar Das: Life and Teachings* (1979)
- Fauja Singh, *Kuka Movement: An Important Phase in Punjab's Role in India's Struggle for Freedom* (1965)
- J.S. Grewal, *Guru Nanak in History* (1969)
- J.S. Grewal and S.S. Bal, *Guru Gobind Singh: A Biographical Study* (1967)
- Harbans Singh, *Guru Gobind Singh* (1966)
- W.H. McLeod, *Gurū Nānak and the Sikh Religion* (1968, reissued 1996)
- W.H. McLeod, *Who Is a Sikh? The Problem of Sikh Identity* (1989)
- Harjot Oberoi, *The Construction of Religious Boundaries: Culture, Identity, and Diversity in the Sikh Tradition* (1994)
- Gurbachan Singh Talib, *Guru Tegh Bahadur: Background and the Supreme Sacrifice* (1976)
- John C.B. Webster, *The Nirankari Singhs* (1979)

STUDY OF RELIGION

- E. Thomas Lawson and Robert N. McCauley, *Rethinking Religion: Connecting Cognition and Culture* (1990)
- Hans H. Penner, *Impasse and Resolution: A Critique of the Study of Religion* (1989)
- Eric J. Sharpe, *Comparative Religion: A History*, 2nd ed. (1986)
- Jonathan Z. Smith, *Imagining Religion* (1982)
- Dan Sperber, *Rethinking Symbolism* (1975; originally published in French, 1974)
- Jacques Waardenburg, *Classical Approaches to the Study of Religion*, vol. 1, *Introduction and Anthology* (1973)

Anthropology

- Talal Asad, *Genealogies of Religion* (1993)
- Michael Banton (ed.), *Anthropological Approaches to the Study of Religion* (1966)

- E.E. Evans-Pritchard, *Theories of Primitive Religion* (1965, reprinted 1985)
- Clifford Geertz, *The Interpretation of Cultures* (1973, reissued 1993)
- Claude Lévi-Strauss, *Totemism* (1963; originally published in French, 1962)
- Bronislaw Malinowski, *Magic, Science, and Religion, and Other Essays* (1948, reprinted 1992)
- Roy A. Rappaport, *Ecology, Meaning, and Religion* (1979)

Gender and religion

- Caroline Walker Bynum, Steven Harrell, and Paula Richman (eds.), *Gender and Religion: On the Complexity of Symbols* (1986)
- Gilbert Herdt (ed.), *Third Sex, Third Gender: Beyond Sexual Dimorphism in Culture and History* (1994)
- Ursula King (ed.), *Religion and Gender* (1995)
- Ursula King, "Religion and Gender," in Ursula King (ed.), *Turning Points in Religious Studies* (1990), pp. 275–286
- Wendy Doniger O'Flaherty, *Women, Androgynes, and Other Mythical Beasts* (1982)

History of religions

- Mircea Eliade, *Patterns in Comparative Religion* (1958, reissued 1996; originally published in French, 1949)
- William James, *The Varieties of Religious Experience* (1902, reissued 1997)
- Jonathan Z. Smith, *Map Is Not Territory: Studies in the History of Religions* (1978, reissued 1993)
- Wilfred Cantwell Smith, *The Meaning and End of Religion* (1963, reprinted 1991)
- Joachim Wach, *The Comparative Study of Religions* (1958, reissued 1969)

Phenomenology

- C.J. Bleeker, *The Sacred Bridge: Researches into the Nature and Structure of Religion* (1963)
- Mircea Eliade, *The Quest: History and Meaning in Religion* (1969, reissued 1984)
- Åke Hultkrantz, "The Phenomenology of Religion," *Temenos*, 6:68–88 (1970)
- W. Brede Kristensen, *The Meaning of Religion* (1960, reissued 1971)
- G. van der Leeuw, *Religion in Essence and Manifestation* (1938, reprinted 1986; originally published in German, 1933)

Philosophy

- Nancy K. Frankenberry and Hans H. Penner (eds.), *Language, Truth, and Religious Belief: Studies in Twentieth-Century Theory and Method in Religion* (1999)
- Terry F. Godlove, Jr., *Religion, Interpretation, and Diversity of Belief* (1989, reissued 1997)
- J.L. Goodall, *An Introduction to the Philosophy of Religion* (1966)
- J. Samuel Preuss, *Explaining Religion: Criticism and Theory from Bodin to Freud* (1987, reissued 1996)
- Wayne Proudfoot, *Religious Experience* (1985)
- John Skorupski, *Symbol and Theory: A Philosophical Study of Theories of Religion in Social Anthropology* (1976, reprinted 1983)

Psychology

- L.B. Brown (ed.), *Psychology and Religion: Selected Readings* (1973)
- Sigmund Freud, *The Future of an Illusion*, trans. and ed. by James Strachey (1961, reissued 1989; originally published in German, 1927)
- Sigmund Freud, *Totem and Taboo: Resemblances Between the Psychic Lives of Savages and Neurotics* (1918, reissued 1998; originally published in German, 1913)
- William James, *The Varieties of Religious Experience* (1902, reissued 1997)
- Carl G. Jung et al., *Man and His Symbols* (1964, reissued 1990)

Sociology

- Pierre Bourdieu, *Outline of a Theory of Practice* (1977, reissued 1995; originally published in French, 1972)
- Émile Durkheim, *The Elementary Forms of the Religious Life*, trans. by Karen E. Fields (1995; originally published in French, 1912)
- Anthony Giddens, *Capitalism and Modern Social Theory: An Analysis of the Writings of Marx, Durkheim, and Weber* (1971)
- Guy E. Swanson, *The Birth of the Gods: The Origin of Primitive Beliefs* (1960, reissued 1974)
- Max Weber, *The Sociology of Religion* (1963, reissued 1993; originally published in German, 1922)
- Bryan Wilson, *Religion in Sociological Perspective* (1982)

Women and religion

• Cynthia Eller, *Living in the Lap of the Goddess: The Feminist Spirituality Movement in America* (1993)
• Marija Gimbutas, *The Language of the Goddess: Unearthing the Hidden Symbols of Western Civilization* (1989)
• Karen L. King (ed.), *Women and Goddess Traditions: In Antiquity and Today* (1997)
• Ursula King (ed.), *Women in the World's Religions, Past and Present* (1987)
• David Kinsley, *The Goddess' Mirror: Visions of the Divine from East and West* (1989)
• James J. Preston (ed.), *Mother Worship: Theme and Variation* (1982)
• Arvind Sharma (ed.), *Religion and Women* (1994)
• Arvind Sharma (ed.), *Women in World Religions* (1987)

TAOISM

• John Blofeld, *Taoism: The Road to Immortality* (1978)
• Chang Chung-yuan (Chung-yuan Chang), *Creativity and Taoism: A Study of Chinese Philosophy, Art & Poetry* (1963, reissued 1975)
• N.J. Girardot, *Myth and Meaning in Early Taoism: The Theme of Chaos (Hun-tun)* (1983)
• Benjamin Hoff, *The Tao of Pooh* (1982)
• Max Kaltenmark, *Lao Tzu and Taoism* (1969; originally published in French, 1965)
• Livia Kohn, *Early Chinese Mysticism: Philosophy and Soteriology in the Taoist Tradition* (1991)
• John Lagerwey, *Taoist Ritual in Chinese Society and History* (1987)
• Henri Maspero, *Taoism and Chinese Religion* (1981; originally published in French, 1971)
• Isabelle Robinet, *Taoism: Growth of a Religion*, trans. by Phyllis Brooks (1997; originally published in French, 1991)
• Michael R. Saso, *Taoism and the Rite of Cosmic Renewal*, 2nd ed. (1990)
• Kristofer Schipper, *The Taoist Body* (1993; originally published in French, 1982)
• Raymond M. Smullyan, *The Tao Is Silent* (1977, reissued 1992)
• Holmes Welch, *Taoism: The Parting of the Way*, rev. ed. (1965)
• Eva Wong, *The Shambhala Guide to Taoism* (1997)

Major movements and figures

• Roger T. Ames, *The Art of Rulership: A Study in Ancient Chinese Political Thought* (1983, reissued 1994)
• T.H. Barrett, *Taoism Under the T'ang: Religion & Empire During the Golden Age of Chinese History* (1996)
• Judith A. Berling, *The Syncretic Religion of Lin Chao-en* (1980)
• Suzanne E. Cahill, *Transcendence & Divine Passion: The Queen Mother of the West in Medieval China* (1993)
• Alan K.L. Chan, *Two Visions of the Way: A Study of the Wang Pi and the Ho-shang Kung Commentaries on the Lao-Tzu* (1991)
• K'ang Chi, *Philosophy and Argumentation in Third-Century China: The Essays of Hsi K'ang*, trans. by Robert G. Henricks (1983)
• Thomas Cleary (trans. and ed.), *Immortal Sisters: Secrets of Taoist Women* (1989)
• Kenneth Dean, *Taoist Ritual and Popular Cults of Southeast China* (1993)
• Deng Ming-Dao (Ming-Dao Deng), *Chronicles of Tao: The Secret Life of a Taoist Master* (1993)
• Kenneth J. DeWoskin, *Doctors, Diviners, and Magicians of Ancient China: Biographies of Fang-shih* (1983)
• Kwok Man Ho and Joanne O'Brien (trans. and eds.), *The Eight Immortals of Taoism: Legends and Fables of Popular Taoism* (1990)
• Jane Huang and Michael Wurmbrand (trans.), *The Primordial Breath: An Ancient Chinese Way of Prolonging Life Through Breath Control* (1987–   )
• Livia Kohn and Yoshinobu Sakade (eds.), *Taoist Meditation and Longevity Techniques* (1989)
• Charles Le Blanc, *Huai-Nan Tzu: Philosophical Synthesis in Early Han Thought* (1985)
• Laszlo Legaza, *Tao Magic* (1975, reissued 1987)
• Joseph Needham et al., *Science and Civilisation in China*, vol. 5, *Chemistry and Chemical Technology*, parts 2 (1974), 3 (1976), and 5 (1983)
• Isabelle Robinet, *Taoist Meditation: The Mao-shan Tradition of Great Purity* (1993; originally published in French, 1979)
• Jay Sailey, *The Master Who Embraces Simplicity: A Study of the Philosopher Ko Hung, A.D. 283–343* (1978)

• Michael R. Saso, *The Teachings of Taoist Master Chuang* (1978)
• Edward H. Schafer, *Mirages on the Sea of Time: The Taoist Poetry of Ts'ao T'ang* (1985)
• Nathan Sivin, *Chinese Alchemy: Preliminary Studies* (1968)

ZOROASTRIANISM AND PARSIISM

• Janet Kestenberg Amighi, *The Zoroastrians of Iran: Conversion, Assimilation, or Persistence* (1990)
• Mary Boyce, *A Persian Stronghold of Zoroastrianism* (1977, reprinted 1989)
• Mary Boyce, *Zoroastrianism: Its Antiquity and Constant Vigour* (1992)
• Mary Boyce, *Zoroastrians: Their Religious Beliefs and Practices* (1979, reissued 1986)
• Mary Boyce and Frantz Grenet, *A History of Zoroastrianism* (1975–   )
• Jamsheed K. Choksy, *Purity and Pollution in Zoroastrianism: Triumph Over Evil* (1989)
• Ernst Herzfeld, *Zoroaster and His World*, 2 vol. (1947, reprinted 1974)
• John R. Hinnells, *Zoroastrians in Britain* (1996)
• Eckehard Kulke, *The Parsees in India: A Minority as Agent of Social Change* (1974)
• S.A. Nigosian, *The Zoroastrian Faith: Tradition and Modern Research* (1993)
• Cyrus R. Pangborn, *Zoroastrianism: A Beleaguered Faith* (1982)
• Jer D. Randeria, *The Parsi Mind: A Zoroastrian Asset to Culture* (1993)
• R.C. Zaehner, *The Dawn and Twilight of Zoroastrianism* (1961)